Badger

STATE ANIMAL

Muskellunge

STATE FISH

Sugar Maple

STATE TREE

Wood Violet

STATE FLOWER

State of Wisconsin

2015 - 2016

Blue Book

Compiled by the
Wisconsin Legislative Reference Bureau

*Published Biennially
In Odd-Numbered Years*

The following LRB staff members produced the
2015-2016 Wisconsin Blue Book:

Julie Pohlman, editor
Lynn Lemanski, lead publications editor and co-editor

Jason Anderson, legislative analyst
Lauren Jackson, legislative analyst
Michael J. Keane, senior legislative analyst
Jenni Le, legislative analyst
Kristina Martinez, reference and instruction librarian
Ciara O'Neill, legislative analyst
Robert A. Paolino, senior legislative analyst
Daniel F. Ritsche, senior legislative analyst

Sold and Distributed By:
Document Sales Unit
Department of Administration
4622 University Avenue
Madison, WI 53705-2156
Telephone: (608) 266-3358
DOADocumentSalesInformation@wisconsin.gov

Front cover photograph by Jay Salvo, Legislative Photographer
Back cover images provided by Greg Anderson, Legislative
Photographer

The full text of the Conscription Act was included in the 1864 edition, as well as a separate accounting of the military votes for governor.

This edition of the *Blue Book* also demonstrates the changes that have occurred since the prior edition, albeit on a much smaller scale. Federal agencies have made a number of changes in terms of what information they collect and report on, altering a number of annual statistical tables. Wisconsin's cash receipts from farm marketings are now only available at a category level; the United States Department of Agriculture no longer reports at the individual crop level. The United States Census Bureau has also ceased to report per capita federal expenditures by state. A list of famous citizens of Wisconsin will no longer be published; the number of citizens with significant achievements surpasses what can be compiled in a few, succinct pages. Noteworthy additions in the book occurred with the constitution, reflecting two constitutional amendments in 2014 and 2015, and with the addition of new statistical tables. A table on University of Wisconsin System budgeted faculty positions by institution, as well as a table of county-level data regarding nonirrigated cropland cash rents have been added to provide further perspective on education and agricultural industries in the state.

The *2015-2016 Wisconsin Blue Book* continues to serve as the single, most comprehensive resource of information on the government and citizens of the state of Wisconsin. Research staff at the Legislative Reference Bureau have compiled, verified, and updated content from every branch of the government, state agency, and elected officials. I would like to acknowledge and thank the research staff, not only for their contributions, but for their commitment to providing a detailed and valued almanac of the state. I would also like to thank feature article authors Michael Telzrow, Russell Horton, and Kevin Hampton from the Wisconsin Veterans Museum for writing a concise overview of the Civil War from the perspective of this state and its citizens, and providing an engaging collection of accompanying images from their collection. Wisconsin has undergone significant change and growth since this momentous war ended 150 years ago and the *Blue Book* provides a fitting platform to contextualize the story within the state's background. From constitution, to feature article, branch and agency descriptions, to statistical tables, the *Blue Book* provides a way to map the development of the state since 1848.

Julie Pohlman
Blue Book Editor
July 2015

TABLE OF CONTENTS

State symbols . . . . Front and back endpapers
Governor's letter. iii
Introduction iv
BIOGRAPHIES. 1
Alphabetical index to biographies. 2
   Constitutional executive officers 4
   Supreme court justices. 8
   Wisconsin members of the 114th Congress 11
   Congressional district map 17
   State senate officers 18
   State assembly officers 19
   Members of the state senate and assembly; district maps. 20
   Chief clerks and sergeants at arms of the state legislature 86
   Legislative district maps. 87
FEATURE ARTICLE: Wisconsin in the Civil War 99
   Index to special articles in prior blue books. 170
   Capitol Visitor's Guide 171
WISCONSIN CONSTITUTION 173
   History of constitutional amendments. 218
   Statewide referenda elections 225
FRAMEWORK OF WISCONSIN STATE GOVERNMENT. 227
   Location of state agencies in the Madison area; map 228
   The framework of Wisconsin government .230
   Organization chart of Wisconsin state government 234
LEGISLATIVE BRANCH. 237
   Officers of the 2015 legislature 238
   A profile of the legislative branch 239
   The Wisconsin legislature 240
   Session schedule, 2015-2016 244
   News media correspondents accredited to the 2015 legislature. 247
   How a bill becomes a law 250
   Legislative service. 255
   Executive vetoes, 1931-2013 sessions. 257
   Political composition of the Wisconsin legislature, 1885-2015. 258
   Wisconsin statutes, session laws, administrative code 259
   Committees of the 2015 legislature 260
   Personal data on Wisconsin legislators 2005-2015 sessions 264
   Joint legislative committees 265
   Administrative rules, joint committee for review of 265
   Building commission, state of Wisconsin. .267
   Criminal penalties, joint review committee on 268
   Employment relations, joint committee on .268
   Finance, joint committee on. 270
   Information policy and technology, joint committee on. 271
   Legislative audit committee, joint. 272
   Legislative council, joint 272
   Legislative organization, joint committee on 279
   Retirement systems, joint survey committee on. 280

State supported programs study and advisory committee, joint legislative 280
Tax exemptions, joint survey committee on. 281
Transportation projects commission. 282
Uniform state laws, commission on 283
Legislative service agencies 284
Legislative audit bureau 284
Legislative fiscal bureau. 287
Legislative reference bureau. 287
Legislative technology services bureau 288
Summary of significant 2013 legislation 291

EXECUTIVE BRANCH 305
Constitutional executive state officers. 306
A profile of the executive branch 307
Office of the governor 316
Governor's appointments to miscellaneous committees and organizations. 320
Governor's special committees 321
State officers appointed by the governor as required by statute. 331
Office of the lieutenant governor 348
Administration, department of. 349
Agriculture, trade and consumer protection, department of. 371
Children and families, department of 379
Corrections, department of 385
Educational communications board 394
Employee trust funds, department of 397
Financial institutions, department of 399
Government accountability board 405
Health services, department of 407
Higher educational aids board 416
Historical society of Wisconsin, state 418
Insurance, office of the commissioner of 423
Investment board, state of Wisconsin 426
Justice, department of 428
Military affairs, department of. 433
Natural resources, department of 441
Public defender, office of the state 454
Public instruction, department of 456
Public service commission 465
Revenue, department of 469
Safety and professional services, department of 473
Secretary of state, office of the 484
State treasurer, office of the 485
Technical college system 485
Tourism, department of 489
Transportation, department of 496
University of Wisconsin system 502
Veterans affairs, department of 518
Workforce development, department of 522
State authorities 531

Aerospace, Economic development corporation, Fox River navigational system,
Lower Fox River remediation, University of Wisconsin hospitals and clinics,
Health and educational facilities, Housing and economic development 531
Nonprofit corporations. 539
Bradley center sports and entertainment corporation, Wisconsin artistic
endowment foundation 539
Regional agencies. 540
Regional planning commissions. 540
Madison cultural arts district board 544
Professional football stadium district 544
Southeast Wisconsin professional baseball park district 544
Wisconsin center district. 545
Interstate agencies and compacts 546
JUDICIAL BRANCH 557
Justices of the Wisconsin supreme court 558
A profile of the judicial branch 559
Supreme court 563
Court of appeals 565
Circuit courts 567
Municipal courts 574
Statewide judicial agencies 575
Director of state courts 575
State law library 575
Office of lawyer regulation 576
Board of bar examiners 579
Judicial conduct advisory committee 580
Judicial conference 580
Judicial education committee 581
Planning and policy advisory committee 581
Judicial commission 582
Judicial council 583
State bar of Wisconsin 584
**Summary of significant decisions of the supreme court and
court of appeals of Wisconsin, June 2013 – June 2015** 586
STATISTICAL INFORMATION ON WISCONSIN .597
Agriculture 598
Number, size, and value of farms, Wisconsin 599
Cash receipts and income 601
Wisconsin's rank among the states 602
Number and acreage of farms 603
Agricultural land sales, by county 605
Nonirrigated cropland cash rents 606
Farm income, assets 607
Associations, statewide, of Wisconsin 608
Commerce and industry 623
Energy, petroleum, and gasoline consumption .624
Motor vehicle fuel tax, Wisconsin. 625
Value added by manufacturing 626
Wisconsin exports 627
Basic data on Wisconsin corporations 628
Financial institutions in Wisconsin 629

Conservation and recreation 631
Fish and game 632
State parks, forests, and trails: location, features, size, attendance 633
Natural resources department, funding sources, expenditures 637
Conservation and recreation land acquisitions .639
Education 641
Higher education enrollments 642
University of Wisconsin System budget faculty positions 643
Diplomas and earned degrees, by state 647
School districts 648
Enrollment, completion rates 648
Public school teacher salaries 652
Educational costs 654
Home-based enrollments 657
State document depository libraries 658
Public library systems 659
Employment and income 660
Employment in Wisconsin 661
Wisconsin business establishments, by number of employees 663
Employees in nonagricultural establishments, by state 664
Unemployment insurance benefits, by state 666
Earned income, by industry 668
Personal income 670
Geography and climate 671
Wisconsin's lakes and land area 671
High points in Wisconsin 673
Wisconsin temperature, precipitation 674
History 675
Significant events in Wisconsin history 676
Historic sites and historical markers 688
Wisconsin vote in presidential elections, 1848-2012 696
Vote for governor, general elections, 1848-2014 699
Wisconsin constitutional officers, 1848-2015 703
Justices of the Wisconsin supreme court, 1836-2015 707
Legislative officers, 1848-2015 709
Wisconsin legislative sessions, 1848-2013 715
Members of the U.S. Congress from Wisconsin, 1848-2015 720
Local and state government 725
State and local government employment and payrolls 725
State and local government employees, number and earnings 727
Local units of government by state and type 728
Wisconsin counties, basic data and officers 729
Wisconsin municipalities 735
Military and veterans affairs 761
Wisconsin's military service 762
Veterans' benefits, 1943-2014 762
Wisconsin national guard units 764
Wisconsin veterans homes membership, 1888-2014 766
Federal expenditures for veterans 767
News media 768
Wisconsin newspapers, periodicals 768
Broadcasting stations in Wisconsin: television, radio 779

Population and vital statistics 782
Wisconsin population statistics 783
Wisconsin vital statistics: births, deaths, marriages, divorces. 792
Postal ZIP codes 796
Social services. 803
Public welfare expenditures 804
Medical assistance in Wisconsin 807
Prison and mental institution population and correctional expenditures 809
State and local finance 812
State government revenues, expenditures 813
Per capita state and local revenue, expenditures .822
Federal tax collections, by state 824
Distribution of federal funds, by state. 825
Federal aids to Wisconsin 826
State and local public debt. 827
Property tax assessments, rates and levies. 829
Transportation 832
Wisconsin airports, usage and type 832
Railroad mileage, usage and revenue, 1920-2013. .833
Highway and road mileage 834
Motor vehicles. 835
Transit systems 839
Harbor commerce 840
WISCONSIN POLITICAL PARTIES 841
Political party organization in Wisconsin. 842
Party officers and platforms: Constitution, Democratic, Green,
Libertarian, Republican 845
ELECTIONS IN WISCONSIN 869
Elections in Wisconsin 870
Constitutional amendments 877
Supreme court justice 879
Court of appeals judges 880
Circuit court judges 882
Members of 114th Congress, vote by district 885
State senators, vote by county and district 891
Representatives to the assembly, vote by county and district 897
State officers, vote by county 912
Governor and lieutenant governor, vote by ward .921
WISCONSIN STATE SYMBOLS 949
ALPHABETICAL INDEX. 955

Biographies

Biographies and photos: Wisconsin constitutional executive officers, Supreme Court justices, members of the U.S. Congress from Wisconsin, and legislators (also includes congressional and legislative district maps)

Battle Flags from the Civil War

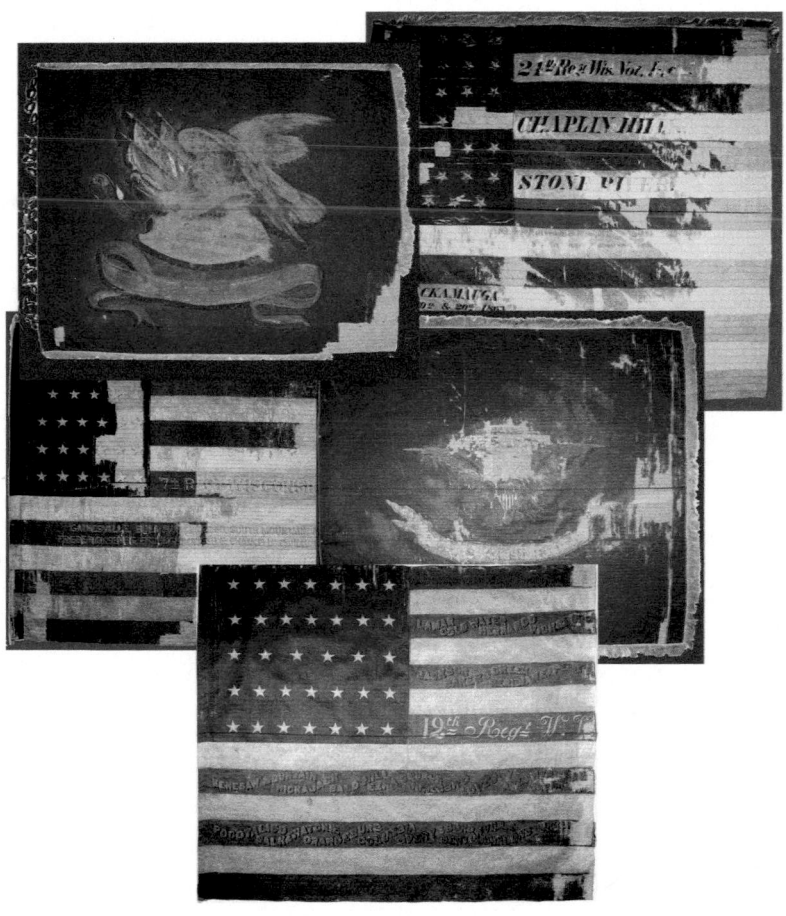

(Wisconsin Veterans Museum)

ALPHABETICAL INDEX TO BIOGRAPHIES

Page

Abrahamson, Shirley S. 8
Adamczyk, Matt 6
Allen, Scott 85
August, Tyler. 41

Baldwin, Tammy 11
Ballweg, Joan 47
Barca, Peter W 63
Barnes, Mandela 27
Berceau, Terese 71
Bernier, Kathy 65
Bewley, Janet. 68
Billings, Jill 83
Born, Mark L. 45
Bowen, David 27
Bradley, Ann Walsh 8
Brandtjen, Janel 35
Brooks, Ed 53
Brooks, Robert. 59
Brostoff, Jonathan 33

Carpenter, Tim. 24
Considine, Dave 73
Cowles, Robert L. 22
Craig, David 75
Crooks, N. Patrick 10
Czaja, Mary J. 43

Danou, Chris. 81
Darling, Alberta 34
Doyle, Steve 83
Duffy, Sean P. 16

Edming, James W.. 77
Erpenbach, Jon B. 72
Evers, Tony 6

Farrow, Paul 84
Fitzgerald, Scott L.. 44

Gableman, Michael J. 10
Gannon, Bob 59
Genrich, Eric. 79
Goyke, Evan 31
Grothman, Glenn. 15
Gudex, Rick 54

Hansen, Dave 78
Harris Dodd, Nikiya 30
Harsdorf, Sheila E.. 38

Heaton, Dave. 77
Hebl, Gary Alan 51
Hesselbein, Dianne 73
Hintz, Gordon 55
Horlacher, Cody J.. 41
Hutton, Rob 29

Jacque, André 21
Jagler, John. 45
Jarchow, Adam. 39
Johnson, La Tonya 31
Johnson, Ron. 12
Jorgensen, Andy 49

Kahl, Robb 51
Kapenga, Chris. 85
Katsma, Terry 37
Kerkman, Samantha 61
Kessler, Frederick P.. 27
Kind, Ron 14
Kitchens, Joel C.. 21
Kleefisch, Joel 45
Kleefisch, Rebecca. 4
Knodl, Dan. 35
Knudson, Dean. 39
Kolste, Debra 49
Kooyenga, Dale 29
Kremer, Jesse 59
Krug, Scott S. 67
Kuglitsch, Michael. 75
Kulp, Bob 65

La Follette, Douglas J.. 6
Larson, Chris. 32
Larson, Tom 65
Lasee, Frank 20
Lassa, Julie M.. 66
Lazich, Mary A. 74
LeMahieu, Devin 36
Loudenbeck, Amy 41

Macco, John J.. 79
Marklein, Howard 52
Mason, Cory 63
Meyers, Beth. 69
Miller, Mark 50
Milroy, Nick 69
Moore, Gwendolynne S.. 14
Moulton, Terry 64
Murphy, Dave 57
Mursau, Jeffrey L.. 43

Murtha, John 39

Nass, Stephen L.. 40
Nerison, Lee 83
Neylon, Adam 85
Novak, Todd 53
Nygren, John. 79

Ohnstad, Tod 63
Olsen, Luther S. 46
Ott, Alvin R. 21
Ott, Jim. 35

Petersen, Kevin David. 47
Petrowski, Jerry 76
Petryk, Warren 81
Pocan, Mark 13
Pope, Sondy 73
Prosser, David T., Jr. 10

Quinn, Romaine Robert 69

Ribble, Reid J.. 16
Riemer, Daniel 25
Ringhand, Janis 48
Ripp, Keith. 47
Risser, Fred 70
Rodriguez, Jessie. 33
Roggensack, Patience Drake. 8
Rohrkaste, Mike 57
Roth, Roger 56
Ryan, Paul 13

Sanfelippo, Joe 29
Sargent, Melissa 51
Schimel, Brad 6
Schraa, Michael 55
Sensenbrenner, F. James, Jr. 15

Shankland, Katrina. 67
Shilling, Jennifer. 82
Sinicki, Christine. 33
Skowronski, Ken. 75
Spiros, John 77
Spreitzer, Mark. 49
Steffen, David 23
Steineke, Jim. 23
Stroebel, Duey 58
Stuck, Amanda. 57
Subeck, Lisa 71
Swearingen, Rob. 43

Tauchen, Gary. 23
Taylor, Chris 71
Taylor, Lena C.. 26
Thiesfeldt, Jeremy 55
Tiffany, Tom 42
Tittl, Paul. 37
Tranel, Travis 53

Vander Meer, Nancy Lynn 67
Vinehout, Kathleen 80
Vorpagel, Tyler. 37
Vos, Robin J.. 61
Vukmir, Leah. 28

Wachs, Dana 81
Walker, Scott. 4
Wanggaard, Van H. 60
Weatherston, Thomas 61
Wirch, Robert W. 62

Young, Leon D. 31

Zamarripa, JoCasta 25
Zepnick, Josh 25
Ziegler, Annette K.. 10

GOVERNOR

Scott Walker (Rep.): Born Colorado Springs, CO, November 2, 1967; married; 2 children. Graduate Delavan-Darien H.S. 1986; attended Marquette U. 1986-90. Former salesman, IBM Corporation; financial developer, American Red Cross. State representative 1993-2002; Milwaukee County Executive 2002-10.

Elected to Assembly in June 1993 special election; reelected 1994-2000; resigned 5/9/2002.

Elected governor 2010; reelected 2014.

Telephone: Office: (608) 266-1212; Fax: (608) 267-8983.

E-mail: governor@wisconsin.gov

Mailing address: Office: P.O. Box 7863, Madison 53707-7863.

LIEUTENANT GOVERNOR

Rebecca Kleefisch (Rep.): Born Pontiac, MI, August 7, 1975; married; 2 children. Graduate Anthony Wayne H.S. (Whitehouse, OH) 1993; B.A. journalism UW-Madison 1997. Former news reporter, media and marketing consultant. Member: National Lieutenant Governors Association; National Rifle Association, Aerospace States Association (manufacturing chair), Executive Committee of Republican Lieutenant Governors Association.

Elected lieutenant governor 2010; reelected 2014.

Telephone: Office: (608) 266-3516; Fax: (608) 267-3571.

E-mail: ltgov@wisconsin.gov

Mailing address: Office: P.O. Box 2043, Madison 53701-2043.

**Governor
SCOTT WALKER**

SECRETARY OF STATE

Douglas J. La Follette (Dem.): Single. B.S. in chemistry Marietta College 1963; M.S. in chemistry Stanford U. 1964; Ph.D. in organic chemistry Columbia U. 1967. Former director of training and development with an energy marketing company; assistant professor, UW-Parkside; public affairs director, Union of Concerned Scientists; owner and operator of a small business; research associate, UW-Madison. Member: Amer. Solar Energy Society; Audubon Society; Friends of the Earth; Phi Beta Kappa. Former member: Council of Economic Priorities; Amer. Federation of Teachers; Federation of American Scientists; Lake Michigan Federation; Southeastern Wis. Coalition for Clean Air; Clean Wisconsin (formerly Wis. Environmental Decade, founder).

Elected secretary of state 1974 and 1982; reelected since 1986. Member: State Board of Commissioners of Public Lands.

Elected to Senate 1972.

Telephone: Office: (608) 266-8888 press 3; Fax: (608) 266-3159.

Mailing address: Office: 30 West Mifflin Street, 10th Floor, P.O. Box 7848, Madison 53707-7848.

STATE TREASURER

Matt Adamczyk (Rep.): Born Milwaukee, June 9, 1978; single. Graduate Pius XI H.S. 1996; B.A. UW-Madison 2000. Small business manager. Former educator; legislative aide. Member: Republican Party of Milwaukee County; National Rifle Association; Americans for Prosperity.

Elected state treasurer 2014. Member: State Board of Commissioners of Public Lands; Wisconsin Insurance Security Fund.

Telephone: Office: (608) 266-1714.

Mailing address: Office: Room B38 West, State Capitol, Madison 53701.

ATTORNEY GENERAL

Brad D. Schimel (Rep.): Born West Allis, February 18, 1965; married; 2 children. Graduate Mukwonago H.S. 1983; B.A. political science, UW-Waukesha, UW-Milwaukee 1987; J.D. UW-Madison 1990. Attorney. Waukesha County Assistant District Attorney (1990-2007); Waukesha County District Attorney (2007-15). Former member: Addiction Resource Council (treasurer); Interfaith Senior Programs (president); Potowatomi Boy Scout Council (advisory board); Rotary International; Safe Babies, Healthy Families (president); UW-Waukesha Foundation (vice-president); Waukesha Food Pantry (board director).

Elected attorney general 2014. Member: State Board of Commissioners of Public Lands.

Telephone: Office: (608) 266-1221; Fax: (608) 267-2779.

Mailing address: Office: Room 114 East, State Capitol, P.O. Box 7857, Madison 53707-7857.

STATE SUPERINTENDENT OF PUBLIC INSTRUCTION

Tony Evers (nonpartisan office): Born Plymouth, November 5, 1951; married; 3 children, 6 grandchildren. Graduate Plymouth H.S. 1969; B.S. UW-Madison 1973; M.S. UW-Madison 1976; Ph.D. UW-Madison 1986. Former teacher, technology coordinator, principal, Tomah; superintendent of schools, Oakfield, Verona; CESA 6 administrator, Oshkosh; deputy state superintendent of public instruction. Member: Council of Chief State School Officers (Board of Directors). Former member: Wis. Association of CESA Administrators; Wis. Association of School District Administrators.

Elected state superintendent 2009; reelected 2013. Member: UW Board of Regents; Wisconsin Technical College System Bd.

Telephone: Office: (608) 266-1771.

E-mail: dpistatesuperintendent@dpi.wi.gov

Mailing address: Office: 125 South Webster Street, P.O. Box 7841, Madison 53707-7841.

**Lieutenant Governor
KLEEFISCH**

**Secretary of State
La FOLLETTE**

**State Treasurer
ADAMCZYK**

**Attorney General
SCHIMEL**

**State Superintendent of
Public Instruction
EVERS**

SUPREME COURT JUSTICES

Mailing address: Supreme Court, P.O. Box 1688, Madison 53701-1688. Telephone: (608) 266-1298.

CHIEF JUSTICE

Patience Drake Roggensack: Born Joliet, IL, July 7; married; 3 children. Graduate Lockport Township H.S.; B.A. Drake University; J.D. UW-Madison Law School (*cum laude*). Former practicing attorney. Participation: Commissioner, Uniform Laws Commission; Fellow, American Bar Foundation; Wisconsin Judicial Council; Supreme Court Rules Procedure Committee; Supreme Court Finance Committee; Committee for Public Trust and Confidence in the Courts; American Bar Association; State Bar Association of Wisconsin; Western District of Wisconsin Bar Association (past pres.); Dane County Bar Association, served on Personnel Review Board (supreme court delegate); 2005 Judicial Conference (co-chair); 2005 Statewide Bench Bar Conference (co-chair). Board service on: YMCA; YWCA; Wisconsin Center for Academically Talented Youth; Olbrich Botanical Society; International Women's Forum (past president); A Fund For Women; Friends of the Arboretum.

Court of Appeals Judge, District IV (1996-2003). Served on Judicial Conference (legislative liaison); Publication Committee for the Court of Appeals; State Court/Tribal Court Planning Committee (co-chair); Personnel Review Board (appeals court delegate).

Elected to Supreme Court 2003; reelected 2013; elected chief justice May 1, 2015.

JUSTICES

(In Order of Seniority)

Shirley S. Abrahamson: Born New York City, December 17, 1933; married; 1 child. Graduate Hunter College H.S. 1950; B.A. N.Y.U. 1953; J.D. Indiana U. Law Sch. 1956; S.J.D. UW Law Sch. 1962; D.L. (honorary) Willamette U. 1978, Ripon College 1981, Beloit College 1982, Capital U. 1983, John Marshall Law Sch. 1984, Northeastern U. 1985, Indiana U. 1986, Northland College 1988, Hamline U. 1988, Notre Dame U. 1993, Suffolk U. 1994, DePaul U. 1996, Lawrence U. 1998, Marian College 1998, Roger Williams U. School of Law 2007. Member: American Philosophical Society (elected 1998); American Academy of Arts and Sciences (fellow 1997). Recipient: ABA *John Marshall Award* 2010; Wisconsin Counties Association *Friend of County Government Award* 2007; American Judicature Society *Dwight D. Opperman Award* 2004 and *Herbert Harley Award* 1999; ABA Commission on Women in the Profession *Margaret Brent Women Lawyers of Achievement Award* 1995; UW-Madison *Distinguished Alumni Award* 1994. Featured in *Great American Judges: An Encyclopedia* 2003.

Appointed to Supreme Court August 1976 to fill vacancy created by death of Chief Justice Horace W. Wilkie; elected to full term 1979; reelected 1989, 1999, and 2009. Became chief justice August 1, 1996, upon the retirement of Chief Justice Roland B. Day, served as chief justice until 2015.

Ann Walsh Bradley: Born Richland Center, July 5, 1950; married; 4 children. Graduate Richland Center H.S.; B.A. Webster College (St. Louis, MO) 1972; J.D. UW-Madison (Knapp Scholar) 1976. Former high school teacher, practicing attorney, and Marathon Co. circuit court judge. Member: Elected member of the American Law Institute; Bd. of Directors, International Judicial Academy; North American Director, International Assn. of Women Judges; Bd. of Directors, National Assn. of Women Judges; state coordinator for iCivics; Wisconsin Bench Bar Committee; UW Law School Board of Visitors; Amer. Judicature Soc.; American Bar Assn.; State Bar of Wis.; Federal-State Judicial Council; Rotary International; lecturer for the ABA's Asian Law Initiative. Former member: National Conference on Uniform State Laws; Wis. Judicial College (associate dean and faculty); Wis. Rhodes Scholarship Com. (chp.); Wis. Judicial Council; Wis. Equal Justice Task Force; Wis. Jud. Conference (chp. and legis. com.); Civil Law Com. (exec. com.); Task Force on Children and Families; Wis. State Public Defender Board (bd. of dir.); Com. on the Admin. of Courts. Recipient: American Judicature Society's *Herbert Harley Award; Business and Professional Woman of the Year; Business Woman of the Year Athena Award.*

Elected to Supreme Court 1995; reelected 2005, and 2015.

Justice
ABRAHAMSON

Justice
BRADLEY

Justice
CROOKS

Chief Justice
ROGGENSACK

Justice
PROSSER

Justice
ZIEGLER

Justice
GABLEMAN

N. Patrick Crooks: Born Green Bay, May 16, 1938; married; 6 children. Graduate Green Bay Premontre H.S. 1956; B.A. (*magna cum laude*) St. Norbert Coll. 1960; J.D. U. of Notre Dame Law Sch. 1963; Army Judge Advocate General's School at U. of VA 1963-64; Natl. Jud. Coll. at U. of Nevada-Reno May 1984; Inst. of Jud. Admin. at N.Y.U. Law Sch. 1996. Former practicing attorney (1966-77); business law instructor, UW-Green Bay (1970-72); faculty, Wis. Jud. Coll.; attorney, Military Affairs Div., Army Judge Advocate General Office, Pentagon (1964-66); legal intern, Internal Security Div., U.S. Dept. of Justice (1962). Vietnam Era vet.; served in Army (capt.) 1963-66. Member: Federal-State Judicial Council; Amer. Bar Assn. and law school evaluator in its judicial division; Fellow of the American Bar Foundation; State Bar of Wis. and its Media and Law Relations Com.; Dane Co. Bar Assn.; Brown Co. Bar Assn. (pres. 1977); Assn. for Women Lawyers of Brown Co.; Notre Dame Law Assn. (bd. of dir.); Wis. Law Foundation (exec. com.). Former member: Wis. Judicial Council (1998-2002); Juvenile Justice Study Task Force (1994-95); United Way of Brown Co. (pres. 1976-78); East Central Criminal Justice Planning Coun. (1973-85); Brown Co. Legal Aid (chp. 1971-73); Fed. Bar Assn. (1964-65). Participant, Fifth Sir Richard May Seminar on International Law and International Courts, The Hague (2009). Recipient: Notre Dame *Academy Distinguished Alumnus of the Year Award* 2002; Amer. Bd. of Trial Advocates *Trial Judge of the Year* 1994; St. Norbert Coll. *Alma Mater Award* 1992 and *Distinguished Achievement Award in Social Science* 1977; U. of Notre Dame *Award of the Year* 1978; Army Judge Advocate General *Commendation Medal* 1966. Author of works in *Notre Dame Lawyer* 1961-63; *Judges Bench Book-Juvenile*. Brown Co. Ct. judge 1977-78; Brown Co. Circuit Ct. judge 1978-96.

Elected to Supreme Court 1996; reelected 2006.

David T. Prosser, Jr.: Born Chicago, IL, December 24, 1942; single. Graduate Appleton H.S.; B.A. DePauw Univ. 1965; J.D. UW-Madison Law School 1968. Former practicing attorney; admin. asst. to U.S. Congressman Harold V. Froehlich 1973-74; attorney-advisor, U.S. Dept. of Justice 1969-72; lecturer, Indiana U.-Indianapolis Law School 1968-69. Member: Friends of the Fox. Former member: National Conference of Commissioners on Uniform State Laws 1983-96, 2005-07, 2012-present. Outagamie Co. District Attorney 1977-78. Commissioner, Wis. Tax Appeals Comn. 1997-98. Supreme Court Planning and Policy Advisory Committee's Court Financing Subcommittee 2002-04; Judicial Council of Wis. 2002-06; Citation of Unpublished Opinions Committee (2009); Rules Procedures Committee (2010-11).

Elected to Wisconsin Assembly 1978 and served nine terms through 1996. Speaker of the Assembly 1995-96; Minority Leader 1989-94.

Appointed to Supreme Court September 1998 to fill vacancy created by resignation of Justice Janine P. Geske; elected to full term 2001; reelected 2011.

Annette K. Ziegler: Born Grand Rapids, MI, March 6, 1964; married with children. Graduate Forest Hills Central H.S.; B.A. in Business Administration and Psychology Hope College (Holland, MI) 1986; J.D. Marquette University Law School 1989. Former practicing attorney (civil litigation) 1989-1995; Pro bono Special Asst. D.A. Milwaukee County 1992, 1996; Asst. U.S. Atty. Eastern Dist. of Wis. 1995-1997; Washington County Circuit Court Judge 1997-2007; Ct. of Appeals Dist. II (Judicial Exchange Program 1999); Deputy Chief Judge – Third Judicial District; Judicial faculty at various seminars. Member: State Bar of Wis.; American Bar Assn.; American Law Institute (elected member); American Bar Foundation (fellow); International Women's Forum; Washington County Bar Assn.; Milwaukee County Bar Assn.; Eastern Dist. of Wis. Bar Assn.; Governor's Juvenile Justice Commission; Wisconsin Judicial Council, State Bar of Wisconsin Bench and Bar Committee; Boys & Girls Club of Washington County (trustee bd. pres.); Marquette U. Law Sch. Advisory Bd.; Rotary Club West Bend-Noon. Former member: Criminal Benchbook Com.; Criminal Jury Instruction Com.; Legal Assn. for Women; James E. Doyle American Inn of Court.

Elected to Supreme Court 2007.

Michael J. Gableman: Born West Allis, September 18, 1966. Raised in Waukesha County. Graduate New Berlin West H.S. 1984; B.A. in History/Education Ripon College 1988; J.D. Hamline U. Law School 1993. Former teacher of American History, Milwaukee Public School system, George Washington High School, 1988-89. Former law clerk, Minnesota District Court and Wisconsin Circuit Court; former practicing attorney; Deputy corporation counsel, Forest County 1997-99; Assistant District Attorney, Langlade County 1996-99; Assistant District Attorney, Marathon County 1998-99; District Attorney, Ashland County, appointed 1999, elected 2002; Administrative Law Judge, Department of Workforce Development 2002; Burnett County Circuit Court Judge, appointed 2002, elected 2003. Established inmate community service program, juvenile community service program, drug and alcohol court, restorative justice program (six year chair) in Burnett County. Former Professor of Law at Hamline University Law School (criminal procedure and professional responsibility). Member: State Bar of Wis.; Grantsburg Rotary International; Siren Fraternal Order of Moose. Past member: Ashland County Republican Party (chairman); Ashland Knights of Columbus (Grand Knight); Ashland Masons; Milwaukee Teachers Assoc.; Burnett County Drug and Alcohol Court (founding and first presiding judge); Siren Rotary International; Siren Fraternal Order of Moose.

Elected to Supreme Court 2008.

WISCONSIN MEMBERS OF THE 114th CONGRESS
2015-2016
MEMBERS OF THE U.S. SENATE

U.S. Senator
BALDWIN

Tammy Baldwin (Dem.)

Born Madison, February 11, 1962. Graduate Madison West H.S.; A.B. in mathematics and government, Smith College (MA) 1984; J.D. UW-Madison 1989. Former practicing attorney, 1989-92. Madison City Council 1986; Dane Co. Board 1986-94.

State legislative service: Elected to Assembly, 78th District, 1992-96 (served until January 4, 1999).

Elected to U.S. House of Representatives 1998; reelected 2000-2010. Elected to U.S. Senate 2012. Committee assignments: **114th Congress** — Appropriations Committee and its Subcommittees on Agriculture, Rural Development, Food and Drug Administration, and Related Agencies, on Labor, Health and Human Services, Education, and Related Agencies, on Commerce, Justice, Science, and Related Agencies, on Military Construction, Veterans Affairs, and Related Agencies, on Homeland Security; Budget Committee (since the 113th Congress); Health, Education, Labor, and Pensions Committee (since the 113th Congress) and its Subcommittees on Primary Health and Retirement Security, on Employment and Workplace Safety; Homeland Security and Governmental Affairs Committee (since the 113th Congress) and its Subcommittees on Financial and Contracting Oversight, on the Efficiency and Effectiveness of Federal Programs and the Federal Workforce, and Permanent Subcommittee on Investigations. **113th Congress** — Energy and Natural Resources Committee and its Subcommittees on Energy, on National Parks, on Public Lands, Forests, and Mining; Special Committee on Aging.

Telephones: Washington office: (202) 224-5653; District offices: Eau Claire: (715) 832-8424; La Crosse: (608) 796-0045; Madison: (608) 264-5338; Milwaukee: (414) 297-4451 or (800) 247-5645; Wausau: (608) 796-0045.

Internet address: http://www.baldwin.senate.gov/

Voting address: Madison 53703.

Mailing addresses: Washington office: 717 Hart Senate Office Building, Washington, D.C. 20510; District offices: 402 Graham Street, Suite 206, Eau Claire 54701; 1039 West Mason, Suite 119, Green Bay 54303; 205 5th Avenue South, Room 216, La Crosse 54601; 30 West Mifflin Street, Suite 700, Madison 53703; 310 West Wisconsin Avenue, Suite 950, Milwaukee 53203; 2100 Stewart Avenue, Suite 250B, Wausau 54401.

U.S. Senator
JOHNSON

Ron Johnson (Rep.)

Born Mankato, MN, April 8, 1955; 3 children. Graduate Edina H.S. 1973; B.S.B. U. of Minnesota 1977. Former CEO Pacur LLC. Former member: Partners in Education Council, Oshkosh Chamber of Commerce (business co-chair); Oshkosh Opera House Foundation (treas.); Lourdes Foundation (bd. pres.); Diocese of Green Bay Finance Council; Oshkosh Chamber of Commerce Board of Directors (chairman-elect); Oshkosh Area Community Foundation Investment Council.

Elected to U.S. Senate 2010. Committee assignments: **114th Congress** — Budget Committee (since 112th Congress); Commerce, Science and Transportation Committee (since 112th Congress) and its Subcommittees, on Communications, Technology, Innovation and the Internet, on Oceans, Atmosphere, Fisheries, and Coast Guard, on Surface Transportation and Merchant Marine Infrastructure, Safety, and Security; Foreign Relations Committee (since 113th Congress) and its Subcommittees on European and Regional Security Cooperation (chair), on East Asian, the Pacific, and International Cybersecurity Policy, on Near East, South Asia, Central Asia, and Counterterrorism, on State Department and USAID Management, International Operations, and Bilateral International Development; Homeland Security and Governmental Affairs Committee (chair; mbr. since 112th Congress) and its Subcommittees on Federal Spending Oversight and Emergency Management, on Regulatory Affairs and Federal Management, and Permanent Subcommittee on Investigations.

Telephones: Washington office: (202) 224-5323; District offices: Milwaukee: (414) 276-7282; Oshkosh: (920) 230-7250.

Internet address: http://www.ronjohnson.senate.gov

Voting address: Oshkosh 54901.

Mailing addresses: Washington office: 328 Hart Senate Office Building, Washington, D.C. 20510; District offices: 517 East Wisconsin Avenue, Suite 408, Milwaukee 53202; 219 Washington Avenue, Suite 100, Oshkosh 54901.

U.S. Representative
RYAN

U.S. Representative
POCAN

MEMBERS OF THE U.S. HOUSE OF REPRESENTATIVES

Paul Ryan (Rep.), 1st Congressional District

Born Janesville, 1970; married; 3 children. Graduate Janesville Craig H.S.; B.A. in economics and political science Miami U. of Ohio 1992. Former aide to U.S. Senator Robert Kasten and employed at family construction business. Member: Janesville Bowmen, Inc.; St. John Vianney's Parish.

Elected to U.S. House of Representatives 1998; reelected since 2000. Committee assignments: **114th Congress** — Ways and Means Committee (chp., mbr. since 107th Congress) and on Assignment of Members to the Joint Committee on Taxation. **109th Congress** — Joint Economic Committee (also 108th and 106th Congresses). **106th Congress** — Banking Committee; Government Reform Committee.

Telephones: Washington office: (202) 225-3031; District offices: Janesville: (608) 752-4050; Kenosha: (262) 654-1901; Racine: (262) 637-0510; Toll free: (888) 909-7926.

Internet address: http://paulryan.house.gov

Voting address: Janesville 53545.

Mailing addresses: Washington office: 1233 Longworth House Office Building, Washington, D.C. 20515; District offices: 20 South Main Street, Suite 10, Janesville 53545; 5455 Sheridan Road, Suite 125, Kenosha 53140; 216 6th Street, Racine 53403.

1st Congressional District: Kenosha, Milwaukee (part), Racine, Rock (part), Walworth (part), and Waukesha (part) Counties. (For detailed description, see Section 3.11, Wisconsin Statutes.)

Mark Pocan (Dem.), 2nd Congressional District

Born Kenosha, August 14, 1964; married. Graduate Mary D. Bradford H.S. (Kenosha); B.A. UW-Madison 1986. Small businessperson.

State legislative service: Elected to Assembly, 78th District, 1998-2010 (served until January 3, 2013).

Elected to U.S. House of Representatives 2012; reelected 2014. Committee assignments: **114th Congress** — Budget Committee; Education and the Workforce Committee. **113th Congress** — Oversight and Government Reform Committee.

Telephones: Washington office: (202) 225-2906; District offices: Beloit: (608) 365-8001; Madison: (608) 258-9800.

Internet address: http://pocan.house.gov/

Voting address: Town of Vermont, 53515

Mailing addresses: Washington office: 313 Cannon House Office Building, Washington, D.C. 20515; District offices: 100 State Street, 3rd floor, Beloit 53511; 10 East Doty Street, Suite 405, Madison 53703.

2nd Congressional District: Dane, Green, Iowa, Lafayette, Richland (part), Rock (part), Sauk Counties. (For detailed description, see Section 3.12, Wisconsin Statutes.)

| U.S. Representative | U.S. Representative |
| KIND | MOORE |

Ron Kind (Dem.), 3rd Congressional District

Born La Crosse, March 16, 1963; married; 2 children. Graduate Logan H.S.; B.A. Harvard U. 1985; M.A. London School of Economics (England); J.D. U. of Minnesota Law School 1990. Attorney. Former La Crosse County assistant district attorney and State of Wisconsin special prosecutor. Member: U.S. Supreme Court Bar; State Bar of Wis. and La Crosse Co. Bar Assn.; Assn. of State Prosecutors; Democratic Party; Wis. Harvard Club (bd. of dir.); Boys and Girls Club of La Crosse (bd. of dir.); Coulee Council on Alcohol and Other Drug Abuse (bd. of dir.); Moose Club; Optimist Club.

Elected to U.S. House of Representatives 1996; reelected since 1998. Committee assignments: **114th Congress** — Ways and Means Committee (since 110th Congress) and its Subcommittees on Health, on Trade. **111th Congress** — Natural Resources Committee (since 105th Congress) and its Subcommittees on Insular Affairs, Oceans and Wildlife, on National Parks, Forests and Public Lands. Congressional memberships: New Democrat Coalition (chair); Upper Mississippi River Task Force (founder and co-chair); Congressional Wildlife Refuge Caucus (founder); Rural Health Care Coalition; Congressional Sportsmen's Caucus (former co-chair); Human Rights Caucus; Native American Caucus (vice chair); Renewable Energy and Energy Efficiency Caucus (vice chair); National Parks Caucus (co-chair); Congressional Caucus of the EU (co-chair); Congressional Organic Caucus (co-chair); Congressional Fitness Caucus (co-chair). House Leadership: Regional Whip.

Telephones: Washington office: (202) 225-5506; District offices: Eau Claire: (715) 831-9214; La Crosse: (608) 782-2558; Toll free: (888) 442-8040; TTY: (888) 880-9180.

Internet address: http://kind.house.gov/

Voting address: La Crosse 54603.

Mailing addresses: Washington office: 1502 Longworth House Office Building, Washington, D.C. 20515-4906; District offices: 131 S. Barstow Street, Suite 301, Eau Claire 54701; 205 5th Avenue South, Suite 400, La Crosse 54601.

3rd Congressional District: Adams, Buffalo, Chippewa (part), Crawford, Dunn, Eau Claire, Grant, Jackson (part), Juneau (part), La Crosse, Monroe (part), Pepin, Pierce, Portage, Richland (part), Trempealeau, Vernon, and Wood (part) Counties. (For detailed description, see Section 3.13, Wisconsin Statutes.)

Gwendolynne S. Moore (Dem.), 4th Congressional District

Born Racine, April 18, 1951; 3 children. Graduate North Division H.S. (Milwaukee); B.A. in political science, Marquette U. 1978; certification in credit union management, Milwaukee Area Technical College 1983. Former housing officer with Wisconsin Housing and Economic Development Authority; development specialist Milwaukee City Development; program and planning analyst with Wisconsin Departments of Employment Relations and Health and Social Services. Member: National Black Caucus of State Legislators; National Conference of State Legislatures' Host Committee, Milwaukee 1995; National Black Caucus of State Legislators – Host Committee (chair) 1997; Wisconsin Legislative Black and Hispanic Caucus (chair since 1997).

State legislative service: Elected to Assembly 1988 and 1990; elected to Senate 1992, 1996, and 2000. Senate President Pro Tempore 1997, 1995 (eff. 7/15/96).

Elected to U.S. House of Representatives 2004; reelected since 2006. Committee assignments: **114th Congress** — Budget Committee (since 110th Congress); Financial Services Committee (since 109th Congress) and its Subcommittees on Monetary Policy and Trade Subcommittee (ranking member), on Housing and Insurance. **110th Congress** — Small Business Committee and its Subcommittees on Contracting and Technology, on Regulations, Healthcare and Trade, on Rural and Urban Entrepreneurship.

Telephones: Washington office: (202) 225-4572; District office: Milwaukee: (414) 297-1140.

Internet address: http://gwenmoore.house.gov

Voting address: 4043 North 19th Place, Milwaukee 53209.

Mailing addresses: Washington office: 2245 Rayburn House Office Building, Washington, D.C. 20515; District office: 316 North Milwaukee Street, Suite 406, Milwaukee 53202-5818.

4th Congressional District: Milwaukee County (part) consisting of the Villages of Bayside (part), Brown Deer, Fox Point, Shorewood, West Milwaukee, and Whitefish Bay; the Cities of Cudahy, Glendale, Milwaukee (part), St. Francis, and South Milwaukee; Waukesha County (part). (For detailed description, see Section 3.14, Wisconsin Statutes.)

U.S. Representative
SENSENBRENNER

U.S. Representative
GROTHMAN

F. James Sensenbrenner, Jr. (Rep.), 5th Congressional District

Born Chicago, June 14, 1943; married; 2 children. Graduate Milwaukee Country Day School 1961; A.B. Stanford U. 1965; J.D. UW-Madison Law School 1968. Attorney. Former assistant to State Senate Majority Leader Jerris Leonard and to U.S. Congressman Arthur Younger. Member: State Bar of Wis.; Riveredge Nature Center; American Philatelic Society; Waukesha Co. Republican Party. Former member: Whitefish Bay Jaycees; Shorewood Men's Club.

State legislative service: Elected to Assembly 1968-74; elected to Senate in April 1975 special election and reelected 1976. Assistant Minority Leader 1977.

Elected to U.S. House of Representatives 1978; reelected since 1980. Committee assignments: **114th Congress** — Judiciary Committee (chp. 107th-109th Congress, mbr. since 97th Congress) and its Subcommittees on Crime, Terrorism, and Homeland Security (chp.), on Courts, Intellectual Property, and the Internet; Science, Space, and Technology Committee (chp. 105th-106th Congress, mbr. since 97th Congress) and its Subcommittees on Environment, on Oversight. **106th Congress** — Science Committee (chp., also mbr. since 97th Congress). **103rd Congress** — House Select Committee on Narcotics Abuse and Control (since 100th Congress). **96th Congress** — Standards of Official Conduct Committee.

Telephones: Washington office: (202) 225-5101; District office: (262) 784-1111; Toll free: (800) 242-1119.

Internet address: http://sensenbrenner.house.gov

. Voting address: N76 W14726 North Point Drive, P.O. Box 186, Menomonee Falls 53052-0186.

Mailing addresses: Washington office: 2449 Rayburn House Office Building, Washington, D.C. 20515-4905; District office: 120 Bishops Way, Room 154, Brookfield 53005-6294.

5th Congressional District: Dodge (part), Jefferson, Milwaukee (part), Walworth (part), Washington, Waukesha (part) Counties. (For detailed description, see Section 3.15, Wisconsin Statutes.)

Glenn Grothman (Rep.), 6th Congressional District

Born Milwaukee, July 3, 1955. Graduate Homestead H.S. (Mequon); B.B.A.; J.D. UW-Madison. Former practicing attorney. Member: Kiwanis-West Bend Early Risers; Washington Co. Bar Assn.; Loyal Order of the Moose-West Bend; UW-Madison Alumni Assn. of Washington Co.; Kettle Moraine Symphony (bd. member). Recipient: Milwaukee Co. Rep. Party *Assembly Tax Cutter of the Year* 2002; Ind. Bus. Assn. *Legislator of the Year* 2000; Wis. Counties Assn. *Outstanding Legislator Award* 1997-98; Wis. Right to Life *Pro-Life Hero Award* 1996, *Sanctity of Life Award* 2004; Pro-Life Wis. *Legislator of the Year* 2010, 1995; Wis. Grocers Assn. *Friend of Grocers Award* 1997-2014; Wis. Farm Bureau *Friend of Agriculture Award* 1995-2007; Wis. Dairy Business Assn. *Milk Bottle Award* 2006, 2004; Wis. Curves for Women *Legislator of the Year Award* 2003; Wis. Builders Assn. *Friend of Housing Award* 2001-2014, *Legislator of the Year* 2005; Apartment Assoc. *Legislator of the Year* 2000; Nat'l Fed. of Independent Businesses *Guardian of Small Business Award* 1999-2000, 2005-06; WMC *Working for Wisconsin Award* 1998-2006, *Exemplar Award* for work on manufacturing tax credit 2012; Wis. Guild of Midwives *Legislator of the Year* 2006; Eagle Forum *Leadership Award* 2007; Wis. Bear Hunters Assn. *Hero Award* 2010; *Friends of Wis. Craft Brewers Award* 2012; Milw. Metropolitan Assn. of Commerce *Champion of Commerce* Award 2012; Associated Builders and Contractors of Wisconsin *Building WI Award* 2014.

State legislative service: Elected to Assembly in December 1993 special election; reelected 1994-2002; elected to Senate 2004; reelected 2008-2012. Assistant Majority Leader 2013, 2011; Assistant Minority Leader 2009; Minority Caucus Chairperson 2007; Majority Caucus Vice Chairperson 2003, 2001, 1999.

Elected to U.S. House of Representatives 2014. Committee assignments: **114th Congress** — Budget Committee; Education and the Workforce Committee and its Subcommittees on Early Childhood, Elementary and Secondary Education, on Health, Employment, Labor and Pensions; Oversight and Government Reform Committee and its Subcommittees on Government Operations, on Transportation and Public Assets (vice chair); Joint House and Senate Economic Committee.

Telephone: Washington office: (202) 225-2476; District office: Fond du Lac: (920) 907-0624.

Internet address: https://grothman.house.gov

Voting address: N5154 Highway U, Glenbeulah 53023.

Mailing address: Washington office: 501 Cannon House Office Building, Washington D.C. 20515; District office: 1020 South Main Street, Suite B, Fond du Lac 54935.,

6th Congressional District: Columbia, Dodge (part), Fond du Lac, Green Lake, Manitowoc, Marquette, Milwaukee (part), Ozaukee, Sheboygan, Waushara, Winnebago (part) Counties. (For detailed description, see Section 3.16, Wisconsin Statutes.)

U.S. Representative
DUFFY

U.S. Representative
RIBBLE

Sean P. Duffy (Rep.), 7th Congressional District

Born October 3, 1971; married; 7 children. Graduate Hayward H.S.; B.A. in business marketing St. Mary's (Winona, MN) 1994; J.D. William Mitchell College of Law 1999. Attorney. Former special prosecutor and district attorney, Ashland County.

Elected to U.S. House of Representatives 2010; reelected since 2012. Committee assignments: **114th Congress** — Financial Services Committee (also 113th Congress) and its Subcommittee on Oversight and Investigations (chair). **113th Congress** — Budget Committee; Joint Economic Committee.

Telephones: Washington office: (202) 225-3365; District offices: Hudson: (715) 808-8160; Superior: (715) 392-3984; Wausau: (715) 298-9344.

Voting address: 5805 Pine Terrace, Weston 54476.

Mailing addresses: Washington office: 1208 Longworth House Office Building, Washington, D.C. 20515; District offices: 502 2nd Street, Suite 202, Hudson 54016; 823 Belknap Street, Suite 225, Superior 54880; 208 Grand Avenue, Wausau 54403.

7th Congressional District: Ashland, Barron, Bayfield, Burnett, Chippewa (part), Clark, Douglas, Florence, Forest, Iron, Jackson (part), Juneau (part), Langlade, Lincoln, Marathon, Monroe (part), Oneida, Polk, Price, Rusk, St. Croix, Sawyer, Taylor, Vilas, Washburn, and Wood (part) Counties. (For detailed description, see Section 3.17, Wisconsin Statutes.)

Reid J. Ribble (Rep.), 8th Congressional District

Born Neenah, April 5, 1956; married; 2 children. Graduate Appleton East H.S. 1974; attended Grand Rapids School of Bible and Music 1975. Former president, Ribble Group, Inc., Reid Ribble Properties LLC, Reel Loud Records. Member: YMCA of the Fox Valley (fmr. bd. mbr.); National Roofing Contractors Assn. (fmr. pres.); Brown County Home Builders Assn.; Fox Valley Chamber of Commerce; National Association of Home Builders; United States Chamber of Commerce; Wisconsin Roofing Contractors Assn.

Elected to U.S. House of Representatives 2010; reelected since 2012. Committee assignments: **114th Congress** — Foreign Affairs Committee and its Subcommittees on Europe, Eurasia, and Emerging Threats (vice chp.), on Terrorism, Nonproliferation, and Trade; Transportation and Infrastructure Committee (since 113th Congress) and its Subcommittees on Aviation, on Highways and Transit (vice chp. 113th), on Water Resources and Environment. **113th Congress** — Agriculture Committee (mbr. since 112th Congress) and its Subcommittees on Conservation, Energy and Forestry, on Livestock, Rural Development, and Credit; Budget Committee (since 112th Congress).

Telephones: Washington office: (202) 225-5665; District offices: Appleton: (920) 380-0061; Green Bay: (920) 471-1950.

Voting address: Sherwood 54169.

Mailing addresses: Washington office: 1513 Longworth House Office Building, Washington, D.C. 20515; District offices: 333 West College Avenue, Appleton 54911; 550 North Military Avenue, Suite 4B, Green Bay 54303.

8th Congressional District: Brown, Calumet, Door, Kewaunee, Marinette, Menominee, Oconto, Outagamie, Shawano, Waupaca, Winnebago (part) Counties. (For detailed description, see Section 3.18, Wisconsin Statutes.)

CONGRESSIONAL DISTRICTS
Enacted by 2011 Wisconsin Act 44

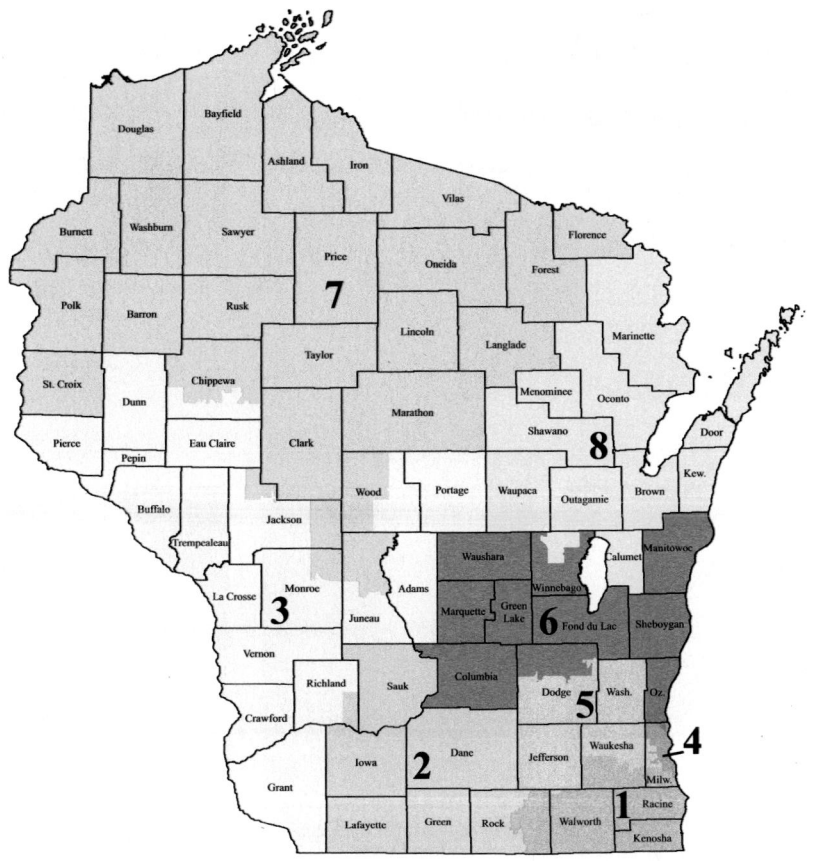

2010 POPULATION OF CONGRESSIONAL DISTRICTS

District	Population*	Deviation from Equal Population		Minority Population	
		Number	Percent	Hispanic	Other
Cong. Dist. 1	710,874	+1	+0.00	63,235	61,428
Cong. Dist. 2	710,874	+1	+0.00	41,423	71,683
Cong. Dist. 3	710,873	0	0.00	14,983	33,270
Cong. Dist. 4	710,873	0	0.00	110,488	285,413
Cong. Dist. 5	710,873	0	0.00	35,606	38,816
Cong. Dist. 6	710,873	0	0.00	27,087	36,154
Cong. Dist. 7	710,873	0	0.00	12,537	37,728
Cong. Dist. 8	710,873	0	0.00	30,697	48,027
TOTAL	5,686,986			336,056	612,519

*Wisconsin's 8 congressional districts were established by 2011 Wisconsin Act 44, based on the 2010 U.S. Census of Population. The ideal size of each district is 710,873.

Source: U.S. Department of Commerce, Census Bureau, P.L. 94-171 Redistricting File, March 2011.

18

**President
LAZICH**

**President Pro Tempore
GUDEX**

**Majority Leader
FITZGERALD**

**Assistant Majority Leader
VACANT**

**Minority Leader
SHILLING**

**Assistant Minority Leader
HANSEN**

**Chief Clerk
RENK**

**Sergeant at Arms
BLAZEL**

2015 STATE ASSEMBLY OFFICERS

Speaker
VOS

Speaker Pro Tempore
AUGUST

Majority Leader
STEINEKE

Assistant Majority Leader
KNODL

Minority Leader
BARCA

Assistant Minority Leader
SHANKLAND

Chief Clerk
FULLER

Sergeant at Arms
TONNON BYERS

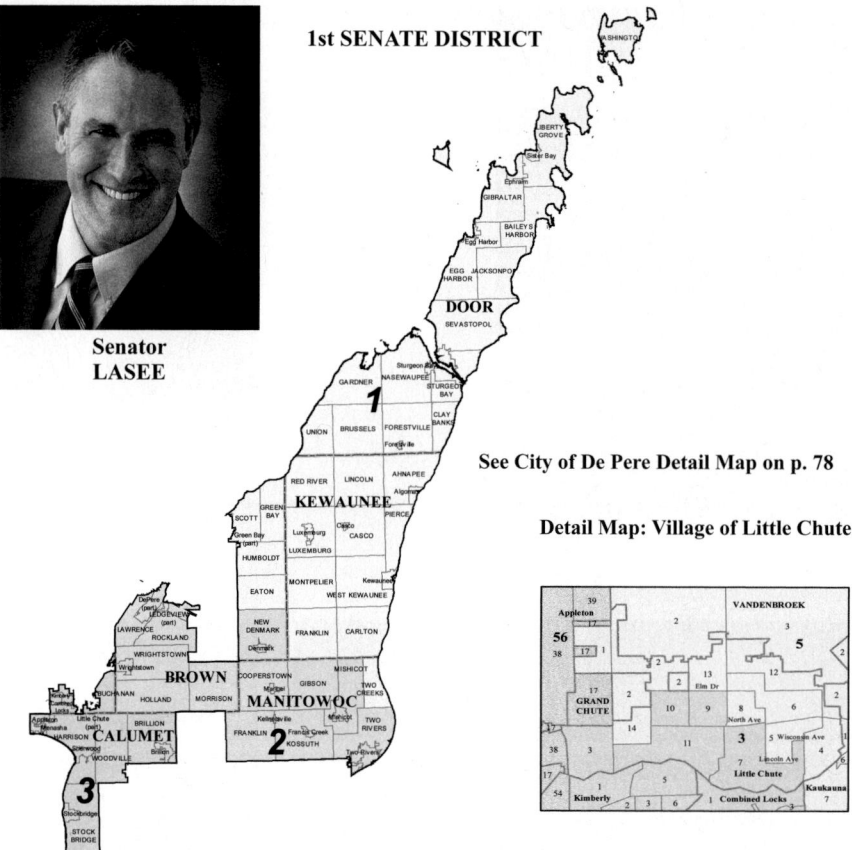

1st SENATE DISTRICT

Senator
LASEE

See City of De Pere Detail Map on p. 78

Detail Map: Village of Little Chute

Frank Lasee (Rep.), 1st Senate District

Born Oceanside, CA, December 11, 1961; married; 7 children. B.A. UW-Green Bay 1986. Full-time legislator. Former manufacturing computer hardware and software salesman, business long-distance salesman. Former real estate salesman. Former member: Optimists; Rotary; Telecommunications Specialists of Wisconsin. Town of Ledgeview chairman 1993-97.

Elected to Assembly 1994-2006; elected to Senate 2010; reelected 2014. Majority Caucus Chairperson 2013. Biennial committee assignments: **2015** — Insurance, Housing and Trade (chp.); Jt. Survey Com. on Retirement Systems (co-chp.); Judiciary and Public Safety; Natural Resources and Energy; Jt. Com. for Review of Administrative Rules. **2013** — Insurance and Housing (chp., also 2011); Jt. Survey Com. on Tax Exemptions (co-chp.); Financial Institutions and Rural Issues (vice chp., also 2011); Elections and Urban Affairs; Government Operations, Public Works, and Telecommunications. **2011** —State and Federal Relations and Information Technology (vice chp.); Transportation and Elections.

Telephone: Office: (608) 266-3512.

E-mail: Sen.Lasee@legis.wisconsin.gov

Voting address: Town of Ledgeview 54115.

Mailing address: Office: Room 316 South, State Capitol, P.O. Box 7882, Madison 53707-7882.

Representative KITCHENS   **Representative JACQUE**   **Representative A. OTT**

Joel C. Kitchens (Rep.), 1st Assembly District

Born Washington, DC, September 20, 1957; married; 3 children. Graduate Ballard H.S. (Louisville, Ky.) 1975; B.S. Ohio St. U. 1979; D.V.M. Ohio St. U. 1983. Large animal veterinarian. Member: Sturgeon Bay Moravian Church; Wis. Veterinary Medicine Assn.; American Veterinary Medicine Assn. Sturgeon Bay Bd. of Education, 2000-14.

Elected to Assembly 2014. Biennial committee assignments: **2015** — Education (vice chp.); Agriculture; Environment and Forestry; Financial Institutions; Tourism; Workforce Development.

Telephone: Office: (608) 266-5350; (888) 482-0001 (toll free); District: (920) 743-7990.

E-mail: Rep.Kitchens@legis.wisconsin.gov

Voting address: 1117 Cove Road, Sturgeon Bay 54235.

Mailing address: Office: Room 10 West, State Capitol, P.O. Box 8952, Madison 53708.

André Jacque (Rep.), 2nd Assembly District

Born Beaver Dam, October 13, 1980; married; 4 children. Graduate Green Bay Southwest 1999; B.S. UW-Madison 2003; graduate certificate from UW-Madison La Follette Inst. of Public Affairs. Full-time legislator. Former transit planning coordinator, communications dir., grant-writing consultant. Member: Wis. Council on Domestic Abuse; Wis. Small Business Environmental Council; Green Bay Area Crimestoppers (bd. mbr.); Golden House Domestic Abuse Shelter Community Leadership Council; Brown Co. Taxpayers Assn; Knights of Columbus. Former member: Brown Co. Teen Leadership (bd. mbr.); Brown Co. United Way (marketing and communications com.); Higher Educ. Aids Bd. 2001-03. Recipient: Wis. Coalition Against Domestic Violence *Legislative Champion Award*; Wis. Counties Assn. *Outstanding Legislator Award;* Pro-Life Wis. *Legislator of the Year*; NFIB *Guardian of Small Business Award*; American Wis. Coalition of Virtual Schools Families *Shining Star of Education Reform;* Dairy Business Assn. *Legislative Excellence Award;* Phillips Foundation *Distinguished Young Conservative Leader of the Year*; Green Bay Area Chamber of Commerce *Legislator of the Year*; Mothers Against Drunk Driving (MADD) *Legislator of the Year*; Wis. Towns Assn. *Friend of Towns*; Wis. Professional Police Assn. *Law Enforcement Honor Roll*; U.S. Chamber of Commerce Inst. for Legal Reform *State Legislative Achievement Award.*

Elected to Assembly 2010; reelected since 2012. Biennial committee assignments: **2015** — Interstate Affairs (chp.); Labor (chp.); Jt. Review Com. on Criminal Penalties (co-chp., also 2013); Energy and Utilities (also 2013); Ways and Means. **2013** — Public Safety and Homeland Security (chp.); Jt. Legis. State Supported Programs Study and Adv. Com. (co-chp.); Judiciary (vice chp.); Criminal Justice; Jobs, Economy and Mining; Urban and Local Affairs (also 2011). **2011** — Criminal Justice and Corrections (vice chp.); Judiciary and Ethics.

Telephone: Office: (608) 266-9870; (888) 534-0002 (toll free); District: (920) 819-8066.

E-mail: Rep.Jacque@legis.wisconsin.gov

Voting address: 1615 Lost Dauphin Road, De Pere 54115.

Mailing address: Office: Room 212 North, State Capitol, P.O. Box 8952, Madison 53708.

Al Ott (Alvin R. Ott) (Rep.), 3rd Assembly District

Born Green Bay, June 19, 1949; married; 4 children, 8 grandchildren. Graduate Brillion H.S.; UW-Madison Farm and Industry Short Course 1968; 1st Class of Participants in WI Rural Leadership Program 1984. Former agri-business salesman, owner/operator of independent agri-business, tenant dairy farmer, and cash crop farmer. Member: Republican Party of Wis.; Calumet Co. Agricultural Assn.; Calumet Co. Farm Progress 1993 Exec. Com. (chm.). Calumet Co. Board 1973-92 (vice chp.), chp. of its Ag/Extension Educ. Com. and vice chp. of its Land Conservation and Planning/ Zoning Coms.; Wis. Land Conservation Bd. 1984-88 (secy.).

Elected to Assembly since 1986. Biennial committee assignments: **2015** — Natural Resources and Sporting Heritage (chp., also 2013); Agriculture (since 1995, also 1989, 1987, chp. 1995-2007); Interstate Affairs; Tourism (also 2013); Transportation (since 2003). **2013** — Consumer Protection. **2011** — Rural Economic Development and Rural Affairs (chp.). **2009** — Public Safety. **2007** — Rural Economic Development (vice chp.); Forestry. **2005** — Natural Resources (mbr. since 1995); Rural Development (mbr. since 2003). **2001** — Energy and Utilities; Environment.

Telephone: Office: (608) 266-5831; (888) 534-0003 (toll free); District: (920) 989-1240.

E-mail: Rep.Ott@legis.wisconsin.gov

Voting address: (Town of Brillion) W2168 Campground Road, Forest Junction 54123-0112.

Mailing address: Office: Room 323 North, State Capitol, P.O. Box 8953, Madison 53708; District: P.O. Box 112, Forest Junction 54123-0112.

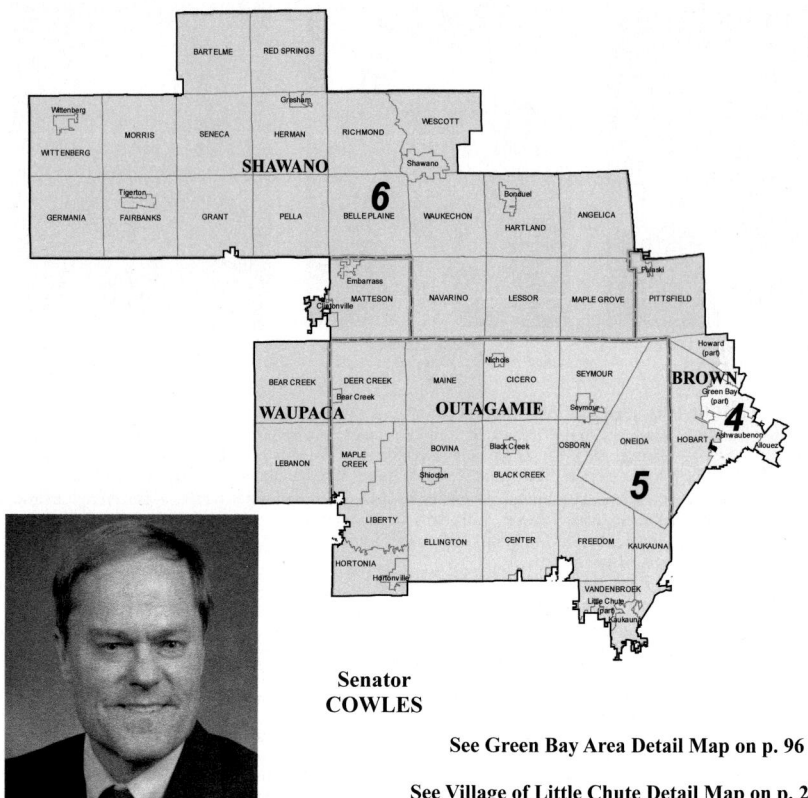

Senator
COWLES

See Green Bay Area Detail Map on p. 96

See Village of Little Chute Detail Map on p. 20

2nd SENATE DISTRICT

Robert L. Cowles (Rep.), 2nd Senate District

Born Green Bay, July 31, 1950. B.S. UW-Green Bay 1975; graduate work UW-Green Bay. Full-time legislator. Former director of an alternative energy division for a communications construction company. Member: Allouez Kiwanis; Salvation Army Volunteer.

Elected to Assembly 1982-86 (resigned 4/21/87); elected to Senate in April 1987 special election; reelected since 1988. Biennial Senate committee assignments: **2015** — Natural Resources and Energy (chp.); Jt. Legis. Audit Com. (co-chp. since 2011, mbr. since 2003, also 1993); Jt. Com. on Information Policy and Technology (vice chp. since 2011, mbr. 2009); Transportation and Veterans Affairs; Transportation Projects Comn. (also 2013). **2013** — Energy, Consumer Protection, and Governmental Reform (chp.); State and Federal Relations (vice chp.); Transportation, Public Safety, and Veterans and Military Affairs. **2011** — Energy, Biotechnology, and Consumer Protection (chp.); Workforce Development, Small Business and Tourism. **2009** — Commerce, Utilities, Energy, and Rail; Joint Com. for Review of Administrative Rules (also 2001, 1987 to 4/20/93). **2007** — Commerce, Utilities and Rail; Public Health, Senior Issues, Long-Term Care and Privacy. **2005** — Energy, Utilities and Information Technology (chp.); Jt. Com. on Finance (also 1993-99). **2003** — Energy and Utilities (chp.); Higher Education and Tourism; Building Comn. **2001** — Environmental Resources; Health, Utilities, Veterans and Military Affairs. **1999** — Jt. Survey Com. on Tax Exemptions; Joint Legislative Council (also 1997). **1997** — Environmental Education Bd. (since 1991). **1995** — Environment and Energy (chp. since 4/20/93). **1993** — Urban Affairs, Financial Institutions and Environmental Resources (mbr. and vice chp. to 4/20/93); Judiciary and Consumer Affairs (mbr. to 4/20/93); Legis. Coun. Com. on State Fire Programs (co-chp.). **1991** — Urban Affairs, Environmental Resources and Elections; Legis. Coun. Com. on Energy Resources; Gov.'s Council on Recycling. **1989** — Educational Financing, Higher Education and Tourism; Science, Technology, Communications and Energy; Legis. Coun. Com. on Nonpoint Source Pollution; Low-Level Radioactive Waste Council. **1987** — Economic Development, Financial Institutions and Fiscal Policies; Housing, Government Operations and Cultural Affairs. Assembly committee assignments: **1987** — Jt. Com. for Review of Administrative Rules (since 1983); Trade, Industry and Small Business. **1985** — Jt. Com. on Debt Management; Energy; Legis. Coun. Com. on Environmental Resource Management. **1983** — Energy and Utilities; Economic Development (eff. 10/25/83); Family and Economic Assistance; Revenue.

Telephone: Office: (608) 266-0484; (800) 334-1465 (toll free); District: (920) 448-5092; Fax: (920) 448-5093.

E-mail: Sen.Cowles@legis.wisconsin.gov

Voting address: 300 West St. Joseph Street, Green Bay 54301.

Mailing address: Office: Room 118 South, State Capitol, P.O. Box 7882, Madison 53707-7882.

| Representative | Representative | Representative |
| STEFFEN | STEINEKE | TAUCHEN |

David Steffen (Rep.), 4th Assembly District

Born October 12, 1971; married; 1 child. Graduate Ashwaubenon H.S. 1990; B.A. political science UW-Madison 1995. Small business owner. Former external affairs director and government affairs representative. Member: Howard Small Business Partnership (founder, vice chp.); Howard Go Green Save Green Initiative (founder, chp.); Ashwaubenon Business Assn. (pres.); Prevent Blindness – Northeastern Wis. (pres.); Team Lambeau (ex. dir.); Green Bay Area Chamber of Commerce State and Federal Issues Com. (chp.). Village of Howard Bd. of Trustees 2007-15; Brown Co. Bd. of Supervisors 2012-15.

Elected to Assembly 2014. Biennial committee assignments: **2015** — Energy and Utilities (vice chp.); Insurance; Jobs and the Economy; Urban and Local Affairs; Ways and Means.

Telephone: Office: (608) 266-5840; District: (920) 662-1492; E-mail: Rep.Steffen@legis.wisconsin.gov

Voting address: 1320 Sunray Lane, Howard 54313.

Mailing address: Office: Room 21 North, State Capitol, P.O. Box 8953, Madison 53708.

Jim Steineke (Rep.), 5th Assembly District

Born Milwaukee, November 23, 1970; married, 3 children. Graduate Wauwatosa West H.S. 1989; attended UW-Milwaukee and UW-Oshkosh. Realtor, salesman. Member: Realtors Assn. of Northeast Wis.; Wis. Realtors Assn. Town supervisor, Town of Vandenbroeck 2005-07; town chp. 2007-11. Outagamie Co. supervisor 2006-11.

Elected to Assembly 2010; reelected since 2012. Majority Leader 2015; Assistant Majority Leader 2013. Biennial committee assignments: **2015** — Rules (chp., mbr. 2013); Assembly Organization (vice chp., mbr. 2013); Jt. Com. on Employment Relations; Jt. Com. on Legislative Organization (also 2013); Jt. Legislative Council. **2013** — Natural Resources and Sporting Heritage. **2011** — Rural Economic Development (vice chp.); Housing; Natural Resources.

Telephone: Office: (608) 266-2401; (888) 534-0005 (toll free).

E-mail: Rep.Steineke@legis.wisconsin.gov

Voting address: Kaukauna 54130.

Mailing address: Office: Room 115 West, State Capitol, P.O. Box 8953, Madison 53708.

Gary Tauchen (Rep.), 6th Assembly District

Born Rice Lake, November 23, 1953; single. Graduate Bonduel H.S. 1971; attended UW-Madison 1971-72; B.S. in Animal Science, UW-River Falls 1976. Dairy farmer. Member: Wis. Farm Bureau; Badger AgVest, LLC (dir.); Professional Dairy Producers of Wis. (fmr. dir.); Dairy Business Assn.; Wis. Livestock Identification Consortium (fmr. dir.); Brown, Shawano, Outagamie, Waupaca Co. Republican Party; Shawano Area Chamber of Commerce; Shawano Co. Dairy Promotions (fmr. dir.); Cooperative Resources International (fmr. vice chm.); AgSource Cooperative Services (fmr. chm.); National Dairy Herd Improvement Assn. (fmr. dir.); UW Center for Dairy Profitability (fmr. chm.); Shawano Rotary.

Elected to Assembly 2006; reelected since 2008. Minority Caucus Sergeant at Arms 2009. Biennial committee assignments: **2015** — Small Business Development (chp., also 2013); Agriculture (vice chp. 2013, mbr. since 2007); Jobs and the Economy; Public Benefit Reform; State Affairs and Government Operations; Tourism. **2013** — Rural Affairs (chp., vice chp. 2007); Constitution and Ethics; International Trade and Commerce; State and Local Finance. **2011** — Elections and Campaign Reform (chp.); Energy and Utilities; Rural Economic Development and Rural Affairs. **2009** — Renewable Energy and Rural Affairs; Workforce Development. **2007** — Biofuels and Sustainable Energy; State Affairs.

Telephone: Office: (608) 266-3097; (888) 529-0006 (toll free); District: (715) 758-6181.

E-mail: Rep.Tauchen@legis.wisconsin.gov

Voting address: Bonduel 54107.

Mailing address: Office: Room 13 West, State Capitol, P.O. Box 8953, Madison 53708.

3rd SENATE DISTRICT

See Milwaukee County Detail Map on pp. 92 & 93

**Senator
CARPENTER**

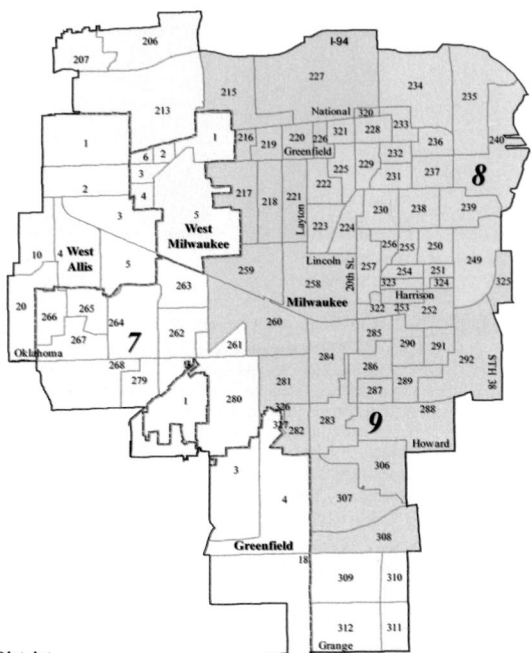

Tim Carpenter (Dem.), 3rd Senate District

Born Milwaukee. Graduate Pulaski H.S.; B.A. UW-Milwaukee; M.A. UW-Madison La Follette Institute. Member: Sierra Club; Jackson Park Neighborhood Assn.; Story Hill Neighborhood Assn.; Milw. VA Soldiers Home Advisory Council; Citizens Utility Board; Milwaukee LGBT Community Center; Wisconsin Humane Society. Recipient: Wisconsin Professional Police Assn. 2014 *Law Enforcement Honor Roll*; Wisconsin Public Health Association's *Champion of Public Health* 2008; Coalition of Wisconsin Aging Groups *Russ Feingold Award for Service to Seniors* 2007; Shepherd Express *Best State Legislator* 2008; Wisconsin League of Conservation Voters *Conservation Champion* 2014, 2008; Shepherd Express *Legislator of the Year* 2003; Wis. Professional Fire Fighters *Legislator of the Year* 2002; Environmental Decade *Clean 16 Awards*.

Elected to Assembly 1984-2000; elected to Senate 2002; reelected since 2006. President Pro Tempore 2011 (eff. 7/17/12), 2007; Speaker Pro Tempore 1993. Biennial Senate committee assignments: **2015** — Health and Human Services (also 2013); Transportation and Veterans Affairs; Jt. Com. on Information Policy and Technology (also 2013); Jt. Survey Com. on Tax Exemptions (also 2011); Coun. On Alcohol and Other Drug Abuse (also 2013, 2003-07; State Fair Park Bd. (also 2013); Transportation Projects Comn. (also 2013). **2013** — State and Federal Relations (also 2005); Transportation, Public Safety, and Veterans and Military Affairs. **2011** — Health; Insurance and Housing; Public Health, Human Services, and Revenue; Leg. Council Study Com. on Strategic Job Creation. **2009** — Public Health, Senior Issues, Long-Term Care and Job Creation (chp.); Health, Health Insurance, Privacy, Property Tax Relief, and Revenue (vice chp.); Veterans and Military Affairs, Biotechnology and Financial Institutions (also 2007); Jt. Survey Com. on Retirement Systems. **2007** — Public Health, Senior Issues, Long-Term Care and Privacy (chp.); Small Business, Emergency Preparedness, Workforce Development, Technical Colleges and Consumer Protection (vice chp.); Health and Human Services (Health, Human Services, Insurance and Job Creation eff. 11/6/07); Jt. Legislative Council. **2005** — Health, Children, Families, Aging and Long-Term Care (also 2003); Labor and Election Process Reform. **2003** — Jt. Com. for Review of Administrative Rules (through 5/23/03); Administrative Rules (through 5/23/03); Judiciary, Corrections and Privacy; Council on Migrant Labor. Assembly committee assignments: **2001** — Aging and Long-Term Care (also 1997, 1995); Health (chp. 1991, mbr. since 1987); Public Health (also 1999); State and Local Finance. **1999** — Census and Redistricting; Urban and Local Affairs (also 1985). **1997** — Managed Care. **1995** — Legis. Coun. Com. to Review the Election Process. **1993** — Financial Institutions and Housing; Insurance, Securities and Corporate Policy; Joint Legislative Council and co-chp. of its Com. on Communication of Governmental Proceedings; Rules. **1991** — Elections and Constitutional Law (chp. 1989); Financial Institutions and Insurance (mbr. 1989, 1987, vice chp. 1985); Judiciary; Labor (since 1985); Public Health and Regulation; Special Com. on Reapportionment (vice chp.); Special Com. on Reform of Health Insurance; Legis. Coun. Com. on Campaign Financing. **1989** — Select Com. on the Census (co-chp.); Environmental Resources and Utilities; Legis. Coun. Coms. on Prenatal Care, on Privacy and Information Technology. **1987** — Elections (vice chp., also 1985); Housing and Securities; Legis. Coun. Com. on Solid Waste Management. **1985** — Economic Development; Transportation.

Telephone: Office: (608) 266-8535; (800) 249-8173 (toll free); Fax: (608) 282-3543.

E-mail: Sen.Carpenter@legis.wisconsin.gov

Voting address: Milwaukee 53215.

Mailing address: Office: Room 109 South, State Capitol, P.O. Box 7882, Madison 53707-7882.

| **Representative** | **Representative** | **Representative** |
| RIEMER | ZAMARRIPA | ZEPNICK |

Daniel Riemer (Dem.), 7th Assembly District

Born Milwaukee, December 10, 1986; single. Graduate Rufus King H.S. (Milwaukee) 2005; B.A. U. of Chicago 2009; J.D. U. of Wisconsin Law School 2013. Full-time legislator. Member: Wis. State Bar Assn.; World Economic Forum: Global Shapers, Milwaukee Hub.

Elected to Assembly 2012; reelected 2014. Biennial committee assignments: **2015** — Health (also 2013); Mental Health Reform; Veterans and Military Affairs; Ways and Means (ranking min. mbr., mbr. 2013); Workforce Development; Leg. Council Study Com. on the Review of Criminal Penalties. **2013** — International Trade and Commerce; Transportation; State Fair Park Bd.

Telephone: Office: (608) 266-1733; District: (414) 617-9141; E-mail: Rep.Riemer@legis.wisconsin.gov

Voting address: 3721 West Oklahoma Avenue, #7, Milwaukee 53215.

Mailing address: Office: Room 122 North, State Capitol, P.O. Box 8953, Madison 53708.

JoCasta Zamarripa (Dem.), 8th Assembly District

Born Milwaukee, March 8, 1976. Graduate St. Joan Antida H.S. (Milwaukee) 1994; BFA UW-Milwaukee 2005. Full-time legislator. Former nonprofit professional. Member: Wisconsin Minority Health Leadership Council.

Elected to Assembly 2010; reelected since 2012. Minority Caucus Vice Chairperson 2015, 2013. Biennial committee assignments: **2015** — Campaigns and Elections (also 2013); Criminal Justice and Public Safety; Health; Jobs and the Economy; Rules; State Affairs and Government Operations. **2013** — Corrections; Jobs, Economy and Mining; Public Safety and Homeland Security; Rules; State Affairs; Gov.'s Council on Migrant Labor. **2011** — Homeland Security and State Affairs; Public Health and Public Safety; Ways and Means.

Telephone: Office: (608) 267-7669; (888) 534-0008 (toll free); District: (414) 384-2786.

E-mail: Rep.Zamarripa@legis.wisconsin.gov; Internet address: www.legis.wisconsin.gov/assembly/zamarripa

Voting address: Milwaukee 53204.

Mailing address: Office: Room 112 North, State Capitol, P.O. Box 8953, Madison 53708.

Josh Zepnick (Dem.), 9th Assembly District

Born Milwaukee, March 21, 1968; married. Graduate Rufus King H.S. (Milwaukee); B.A. UW-Madison 1990; M.A. Univ. of Minnesota 1998. Full-time legislator. Former project consultant, Milwaukee Jobs Initiative, Milwaukee Community Service Corps, and Urban Economic Development Association of Wisconsin; research associate, Center for Democracy and Citizenship; aide to State Senator Bob Jauch and Congressman David R. Obey. Member: Jackson Park Neighborhood Assn.; Jackson Park Business Assn.; South Side Business Club. Former member: UFCW Local 1444.

Elected to Assembly since 2002. Minority Caucus Sergeant at Arms 2015, 2013, 2011. Biennial committee assignments: **2015** — Energy and Utilities (since 2005, vice chp. 2009); Financial Institutions (since 2003); Interstate Affairs; Ways and Means (also 2009). **2013** — State and Federal Relations; State and Local Finance. **2011** — Tourism, Recreation and State Properties; Leg. Coun. Spec. Com. on Local Service Consolidation (chp.). **2009** — Jt. Com. for Review of Administrative Rules (co-chp.); Workforce Development (also 2007, 2003). **2007** — Gov.'s Council on Workforce Investment (also 2005). **2005** — Government Operations and Spending Limitations (also 2003); Southeast Wisconsin Freeways; State-Federal Relations; Jt. Select Com. on Road to the Future. **2003** — Transportation.

Telephone: Office: (608) 266-1707; (888) 534-0009 (toll free).

E-mail: Rep.Zepnick@legis.wisconsin.gov

Voting address: Milwaukee 53221.

Mailing address: Office: Room 7 North, State Capitol, P.O. Box 8953, Madison 53708.

4th SENATE DISTRICT

**Senator
TAYLOR**

See Milwaukee County Detail Map on pp. 92 & 93

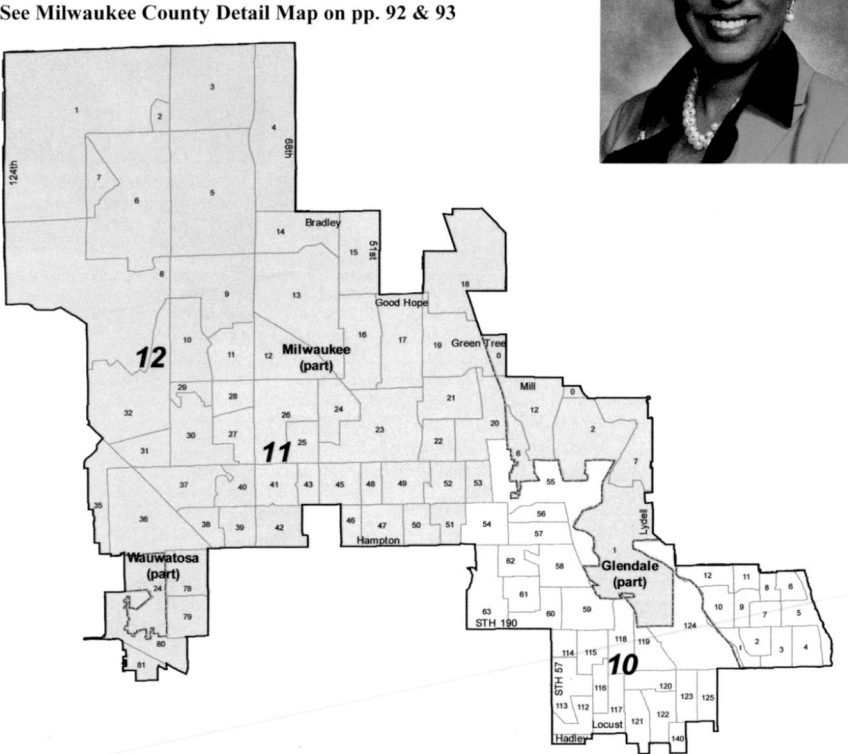

Lena C. Taylor (Dem.), 4th Senate District

Born Milwaukee, July 25, 1966; 1 child. Graduate Rufus King H.S. (Milwaukee) 1984; B.A. in English UW-Milwaukee 1990; J.D. SIU-Carbondale 1993. Attorney. Member: Democratic Party of Wisconsin (former 1st vice chr.); Milwaukee Boy Scouts (advisory bd.); NAACP; Urban League of Milwaukee; Girl Scouts of Milwaukee Area; Unity Caucus; Black and Latino Caucus; Milwaukee Community Justice Council; Governor's Task Force on Minority Unemployment (co-chp.); Women's Action For New Directions (Ed. Fund bd. mbr.); NCSL Women's Legislative Network Bd.; Alpha Kappa Alpha (central region connection com.); Cancer Center Comm. Advisory Bd.; Natl. Organization of Black Elected Legislative Women (ambassador). Milw. Metropolitan Sewerage Dist. Commissioner 2010-14.

Elected to Assembly in April 2003 special election; elected to Senate 2004; reelected since 2008. Biennial Senate committee assignments: **2015** — Agriculture, Small Business and Tourism (also 2013); Judiciary and Public Safety; Jt. Com. on Finance (also 2005-2011, co-chp., 2011, eff. 7/24/12); Jt. Legislative Council (also 2011); Jt. Review Com. on Criminal Penalties (since 2007, co-chp. 2009). **2013** — Economic Development and Local Government; Elections and Urban Affairs. **2011** — Economic Development, Veterans and Military Affairs; Health, Revenue, Tax Fairness and Insurance; Judiciary and Government Operations (vice chp.); Jt. Legis. Audit Com; Jt. Com. on Employment Relations; Jt. Com. for Review of Admin. Rules; Wis. Center Dist. Bd.; Claims Bd. **2009** — Judiciary, Corrections, Insurance, Campaign Finance Reform, and Housing (chp.); Judicial Council (also 2007); Wisconsin Housing and Economic Development Authority (since 2005). **2007** — Judiciary and Corrections (chp., Judiciary, Corrections and Housing eff. 11/6/07); Health, Human Services, Insurance and Job Creation (eff. 11/6/07); Jt. Survey Com. on Retirement Systems; Sentencing Commission. **2005** — Judiciary, Corrections and Privacy. Assembly committee assignments: **2003** — Criminal Justice; Economic Development; Financial Institutions; Tourism; Urban and Local Affairs.

Telephone: Office: (608) 266-5810; District: (414) 342-7176.
E-mail: Sen.Taylor@legis.wisconsin.gov
Internet address: www.senatortaylor.com
Facebook: facebook.com/SenLenaTaylor
Twitter: @sentaylor
Voting address: Ward 59, City of Milwaukee.
Mailing address: Office: Room 19 South, State Capitol, P.O. Box 7882, Madison 53707-7882.

| **Representative** | **Representative** | **Representative** |
| BOWEN | BARNES | KESSLER |

David Bowen (Dem.), 10th Assembly District

Born Milwaukee, January 28, 1987; single. Graduate Bradley Tech H.S. 2005; B.A. UW-Milwaukee. Full-time legislator. Former program director. Member: Milw. Co. Juvenile Detention Alternative Initiative Advisory Com.; Beyond the Bell Milwaukee (steering com.); Black Youth Project-100; Democratic Party of Wisconsin. Former member: American Legacy Foundation Activism Fellow. Milwaukee Co. Bd. of Supervisors 2012-14.

Elected to Assembly 2014. Biennial committee assignments: **2015** — Corrections; Small Business Development; Transportation; Workforce Development.

Telephone: Office: (608) 266-7671.

Voting address: 4080 North 21st Street #3, Milwaukee 53209.

Mailing address: Office: Room 3 North, State Capitol, P.O. Box 8952, Madison 53708.

Mandela Barnes (Dem.), 11th Assembly District

Born Milwaukee, December 1, 1986; single. Graduate John Marshall H.S. (Milwaukee) 2003; attended Alabama A&M U. 2003-08. Full-time legislator. Former community organizer; lead organizer and Exec. Dir. of MICAH (Milwaukee Inner City Congregations Allied for Hope). Member: ACLU of Wisconsin; NAACP Milwaukee Branch; Kappa Alpha Psi Fraternity, Inc.; Democratic Party of Wisconsin; Citizen Action of Wisconsin (bd. mbr.); Milwaukee Secure Detention Facility (advisory bd. mbr.); New Leaders Council (advisory bd. mbr.); Milwaukee Urban League; Fuel Milwaukee. Recipient: Democratic Party of Milwaukee *Elected Official of the Year* 2015; NEWaukee Young Professional *Bubbler Award* 2014. Chair, Black and Latino Caucus, Wis. Legislature.

Elected to Assembly 2012; reelected 2014. Biennial committee assignments: **2015** — Corrections; Education; Jobs and the Economy; Small Business Development. **2013** — State and Federal Relations; Urban and Local Affairs; Urban Education; Ways and Means; Workforce Development.

Telephone: Office: (608) 266-3756; (888) 534-0011 (toll free).

E-mail: Rep.Barnes@legis.wisconsin.gov

Voting address: Milwaukee 53223.

Mailing address: Office: Room 5 North, State Capitol, P.O. Box 8952, Madison 53708.

Frederick P. Kessler (Dem.), 12th Assembly District

Born Milwaukee, January 11, 1940; married; 2 children. Graduate Milw. Luth. H.S. and Capitol Page School 1957; B.A. U. of Wisconsin-Madison 1962; L.L.B. U. of Wisconsin 1966. Labor arbitrator. Member: Goethe House (vice pres., former pres.); Milwaukee Chap. ACLU (bd. mbr., former pres.); World Affairs Council of Milw. (bd. mbr.); Wis. Bar Assn.; Labor/Employment Relations Assn. (advisory com. mbr.); Democratic Party; DANK (German-American National Congress), Milwaukee chap. (former vice pres.); Milwaukee Donauschwaben; Amnesty International Group 107 (former chairman); Milw. Turners; NAACP. Former member: City of Milwaukee Harbor Comn. Recipient: Wisconsin ACLU *Eunice Edgar Lifetime Service Award* 2008; State Bar of Wis. *Scales of Justice Award* 2010; German Immersion Foundation *Lifetime Achievement Award* 2013. Presidential Elector for President Barack Obama 2012. County court judge (Milw. Co.) 1972-78; Circuit court judge (Milw. Co.) 1978-81, 1986-88. On January 11, 1961, his 21st birthday, he became the youngest person, up to that time, ever to serve in the legislature.

Elected to Assembly 1960, 1964-70; reelected since 2004. Biennial committee assignments: **2015** — Agriculture; Campaigns and Elections (also 2013, 2005); Constitution and Ethics; Criminal Justice and Public Safety. **2013** — Criminal Justice (vice chp. 2009, mbr. 2007); Public Safety and Homeland Security. **2011** — Criminal Justice and Corrections; Election and Campaign Reform (also 2009). **2009** — State Affairs and Homeland Security (chp.); Corrections and the Courts; Judiciary and Ethics (also 2007). **2007** — Elections and Constitutional Law. **2005** — Criminal Justice and Homeland Security; Judiciary (also 1965-71). **1971** — Elections (chp., mbr. 1969, 1965); Rules. **1961** — Education.

Telephone: Office: (608) 266-5813; (888) 534-0012 (toll free); District: (414) 368-3015.

E-mail: Rep.Kessler@legis.wisconsin.gov

Voting address: 9312 West Clovernook Street, Milwaukee 53224.

Mailing address: Office: Room 111 North, State Capitol, P.O. Box 8952, Madison 53708.

5th SENATE DISTRICT

Senator
VUKMIR

See Milwaukee County Detail Map on pp. 92 & 93

See Waukesha County Detail Map on pp. 94 & 95

Leah Vukmir (Rep.), 5th Senate District

Born Milwaukee, April 26, 1958; 2 children. Graduate Brookfield East H.S. 1976; B.S. in nursing Marquette U. 1980; M.S. in nursing UW-Madison 1983. Registered nurse; nationally certified pediatric nurse practitioner for 20 years; research fellow, Wisconsin Policy Research Institute; Past Pres. and Co-founder of Parents Raising Educational Standards in Schools (PRESS). Member: Republican Party of Milwaukee Co., Republican Party of Waukesha Co., Wauwatosa Republican Club; West Allis Speedskating Club (former ASU Speedskating Referee). Former member: Standards and Assessments Subcommittee of Gov. Thompson's Task Force on Education and Learning; English/Language Arts Task Force of Gov. Thompson's Council on Model Academic Standards; American Legislative Exchange Council (first vice chp.). Nationally recognized authority and speaker on education issues and educational standards. Recipient: Center for Education Reform's *Unsung Hero Award* 1998; Brookfield East High School *Alumni Achievement Award* 2002; American Legislative Exchange Council Legislator of the Year 2009; Right Women Iron Lady Award 2014.

Elected to Assembly 2002-08; elected to Senate 2010; reelected 2014. Biennial Senate committee assignments: **2015** — Health and Human Services (chp., also 2013); Judiciary and Public Safety (vice chp.); Education (since 2011, vice chp. 2011). **2013** — Jt. Com. for Review of Admin. Rules (co-chp., also 2011); Judiciary and Labor (vice chp.). **2011** — Health (chp.); Public Health, Human Services, and Revenue. Assembly committee assignments: **2009** — Education (also 2007); Education Reform (chp. 2005, 2003, eff. 8/17/04, vice chp. 2003); Health and Health Care Reform (chp. 2007); Public Health (vice chp. 2007). **2007** — Criminal Justice (also 2003). **2005** — Health (vice chp., mbr. 2003); Children and Families (since 2003); Criminal Justice and Homeland Security; Medicaid Reform. **2003** — Economic Development.

Telephone: Office: (608) 266-2512.
E-mail: Sen.Vukmir@legis.wisconsin.gov
Voting address: Wauwatosa 53226.
Mailing address: Office: Room 131 South, State Capitol, P.O. Box 7882, Madison 53707-7882.

| **Representative** | **Representative** | **Representative** |
| HUTTON | KOOYENGA | SANFELIPPO |

Rob Hutton (Rep.), 13th Assembly District

Born Milwaukee, April 7, 1967; married; 4 children. Graduate Brookfield East H.S. 1985; B.A. history UW-Whitewater 1990. 20 years executive experience in trucking industry. Waukesha County Supervisor 2005-12.

Elected to Assembly 2012; reelected 2014. Biennial committee assignments: **2015** — Corrections (chp.); Urban and Local Affairs (vice chp., also 2013); Constitution and Ethics; Education; Small Business Development (also 2013); Wis. Economic Development Corp. Bd. **2013** — Government Operations and State Licensing; Urban Education.

Telephone: Office: (608) 267-9836; (888) 534-0013 (toll free); District: (414) 380-9665.

E-mail: Rep.Hutton@legis.wisconsin.gov

Voting address: Brookfield 53045.

Mailing address: Office: Room 220 North, State Capitol, P.O. Box 8952, Madison 53708.

Dale Kooyenga (Rep.), 14th Assembly District

Born Oak Lawn, IL, February 12, 1979; married; 4 children. Graduate Chicago Christian H.S. 1997; A.A. Moraine Valley Comm. College 2000; B.A. Lakeland College 2000; M.B.A. Marquette U. 2007. Certified public accountant. Member U.S. Army Reserve, 2005-present. Iraq War veteran. Member: American Legion; American Institute of Certified Public Accountants; Wis. Institute of Certified Public Accountants, LISC.

Elected to Assembly 2010; reelected since 2012. Biennial committee assignments: **2015** — Jt. Com. on Finance (also 2013); UW Hosp. and Clinics Auth. Bd. **2013** — Government Operations and State Licensing. **2011** — Financial Institutions (vice chp.); Consumer Protection and Personal Privacy; Homeland Security and State Affairs.

Telephone: Office: (608) 266-9180; District: (414) 678-1586

E-mail: Rep.Kooyenga@legis.wisconsin.gov

Voting address: Brookfield 53005.

Mailing address: Office: Room 324 East, State Capitol, P.O. Box 8952, Madison 53708.

Joe Sanfelippo (Rep.), 15th Assembly District

Born Milwaukee February 26, 1964; married; 3 children. Graduate Thomas More H.S. 1982; attended Marquette U. 1982-84. Small businessman; currently operates a small Christmas tree farm. Owned and operated a landscaping business for 20 years. Member: Mary Queen of Heaven Catholic Church, West Allis and St. John the Evangelist Parish, Greenfield. Milwaukee County Bd. of Supervisors 2008-12.

Elected to Assembly 2012; reelected 2014. Biennial committee assignments: **2015** — Health (chp., mbr. 2013); Campaigns and Elections; Financial Institutions; Mental Health Reform; Transportation (also 2013). **2013** — Housing and Real Estate (vice chp.); Jobs, Economy and Mining; Urban Education; Speaker's Task Force on Mental Health.

Telephone: Office: (608) 266-0620; (888) 534-0015 (toll free).

E-mail: Rep.Sanfelippo@legis.wisconsin.gov

Voting address: 20770 West Coffee Road, New Berlin 53146.

Mailing address: Room 306 North, State Capitol, P.O. Box 8953, Madison 53708.

6th SENATE DISTRICT

See Milwaukee County Detail Map on pp. 92 & 93

**Senator
HARRIS DODD**

Nikiya Harris Dodd (Dem.), 6th Senate District

Born Milwaukee, February 22, 1975; married; 1 child. Graduate Washington H.S. 1994; B.S. education and community studies UW-Milwaukee 2001; M.S. administrative leadership UW-Milwaukee 2007. Full-time legislator. Former nonprofit fundraising professional, precollege coordinator, preschool teacher. Member: African American Chamber of Commerce – Milwaukee; Nia Imani Family (bd. mbr.). Former member: Kids Matter, Inc. (bd. mbr.); Milw. Urban League Young Professionals; Assn. of Fundraising Professionals. Milwaukee County Bd. of Supervisors 2010-12.

Elected to Senate 2012. Minority Caucus Sergeant at Arms 2013. Biennial committee assignments: **2015** — Education Reform and Government Operations; Insurance, Housing and Trade; Jt. Com. for Review of Administrative Rules (also 2013); WHEDA Bd. **2013** — Education; Government Operations, Public Works and Telecommunications; Judiciary and Labor; Law Revision.

Telephone: Office: (608) 266-2500.

E-mail: Sen.HarrisDodd@legis.wisconsin.gov

Voting address: Milwaukee 53222.

Mailing address: Office: Room 3 South, State Capitol, P.O. Box 7882, Madison 53707-7882.

| Representative | Representative | Representative |
| YOUNG | JOHNSON | GOYKE |

Leon D. Young (Dem.), 16th Assembly District

Born Los Angeles, July 4, 1967; single. Graduate Rufus King H.S.; attended UW-Milwaukee. Full-time legislator. Former police aide and police officer. Member: Democratic Party; Harambee Ombudsman Project; Milwaukee Police Association; League of Martin; House of Peace (Love Committee); NAACP; Urban League; Social Development Commission Minority Male Forum on Corrections; National Black Caucus of State Legislators' Task Force on African American Males; 100 Black Men; Milwaukee Metropolitan Fair Housing; Boy Scouts of America (Urban Emphasis Com.); Martin Luther King Community Center (Revitalization Com.).

Elected to Assembly since 1992. Biennial committee assignments: **2015** — Consumer Protection; Housing and Real Estate (also 2013); Insurance (since 2011); Interstate Affairs; Urban and Local Affairs (also 1993). **2013** — State and Federal Relations (co-chp.); Financial Institutions (also 2011). **2011** — Housing (since 2005, chp. 2009); Tourism, Recreation and State Properties (also 2007). **2009** — State Affairs and Homeland Security (vice chp.); Education Reform. **2007** — State Affairs (since 1993, vice chp. 1993). **2005** — Highway Safety (since 1999); Tourism (also 2003 eff. 2/14/03). **2003** — Criminal Justice (since 1999); Ways and Means (eff. 5/13/03). **2001** — Council on Alcohol and Other Drug Abuse (also 1999). **1999** — Transportation. **1997** — Government Operations; Highways and Transportation (also 1995). **1995** — Urban Education (also 1993). **1993** — Children and Human Services; Small Business and Economic Development; Speaker's Task Force on African American Males; Legis. Coun. Com. on Educational Communications Technology.

Telephone: Office: (608) 266-3786; (888) 534-0016 (toll free); District: (414) 374-7414.

E-mail: Rep.Young@legis.wisconsin.gov

Voting address: 2224 North 17th Street, Milwaukee 53205.

Mailing address: Office: Room 11 North, State Capitol, P.O. Box 8953, Madison 53708.

La Tonya Johnson (Dem.), 17th Assembly District

Born Somerville, Tenn., June 22, 1972; 1 child. Graduate Bay View H.S. 1990; B.S. criminal justice Tennessee State U. 1997; attended UW-Milwaukee 1990-92. Full-time legislator. Former family child care provider/owner 2002-12; insurance agent 2000-02; financial employment planner 1997-2000. Member: AFSCME Wisconsin Child Care Providers Together Local 502 (pres.) AFSCME District Council 48 (vice pres.); African American Chamber of Commerce; Emerge Wisconsin Class 2012; CBTU-Coalition of Black Trade Unionists; Milwaukee Legislative Caucus (chp.).

Elected to Assembly 2012; reelected 2014. Biennial committee assignments: **2015** — Children and Families (also 2013); Criminal Justice and Public Safety; Family Law; Financial Institutions. **2013** — Consumer Protection; Criminal Justice; Urban Education.

Telephone: Office: (608) 266-5580; (888) 534-0017 (toll free); District: (414) 871-8306.

E-mail: Rep.Johnson@legis.wisconsin.gov

Voting address: Milwaukee 53210.

Mailing address: Office: Room 320 West, State Capitol, P.O. Box 8952, Madison 53708.

Evan Goyke (Dem.), 18th Assembly District

Born Neenah, November 24, 1982; single. Graduate Edgewood H.S. (Madison) 2001; B.A. political science St. John's U. (Minnesota) 2005; J.D. Marquette U. Law School 2009. Attorney. Former state public defender. Member: St. Michael's/St. Rose of Lima Catholic Church; American Federation of Teachers Local 4822; ACLU; NAACP; State Bar of Wisconsin; Milwaukee Young Lawyers Assn. (fmr. bd. mbr.); Historic Concordia Neighborhood Assn.; Eagle Scout, Boy Scouts of America; Progressive Community Health Center (bd. mbr.)

Elected to Assembly 2012; reelected 2014. Biennial committee assignments: **2015** — Agriculture (also 2013); Constitution and Ethics; Criminal Justice and Public Safety; Judiciary (also 2013); Public Benefit Reform; Veterans and Military Affairs. **2013** — Criminal Justice; Veterans; Jt. Review Com. on Criminal Penalties; Comn. on Uniform State Laws.

Telephone: Office: (608) 266-0645; (888) 534-0018 (toll free).

E-mail: Rep.Goyke@legis.wisconsin.gov

Voting address: Milwaukee 53208.

Mailing address: Office: Room 303 West, State Capitol, P.O. Box 8952, Madison 53708.

7th SENATE DISTRICT

**Senator
LARSON**

**See Milwaukee County Detail Map on
pp. 92 & 93**

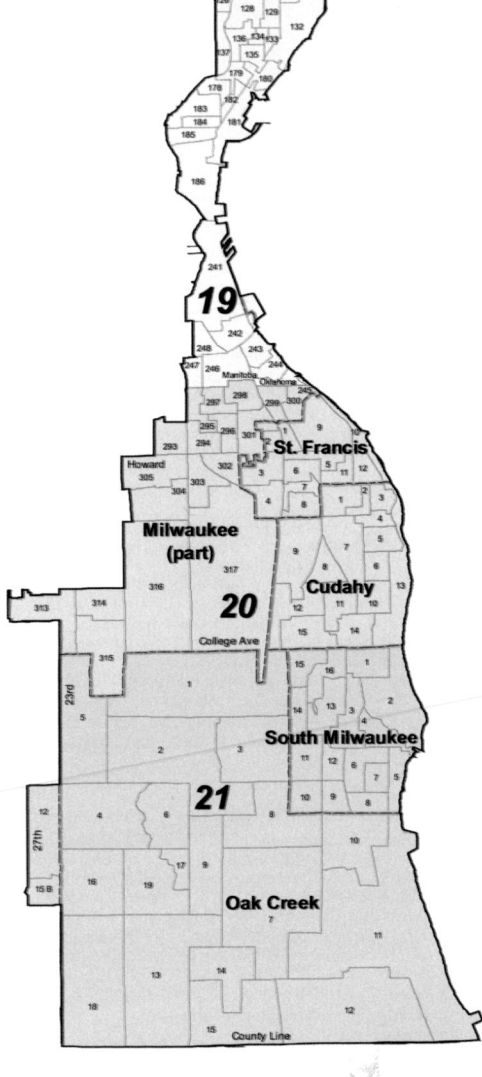

Chris Larson (Dem.), 7th Senate District

Born Milwaukee County, November 12, 1980; married; 2 children. Graduate Thomas More H.S. 1999; degree in finance, UW-Milwaukee 2007. Full-time legislator. Former business manager. Member: Coalition to Save the Hoan Bridge (co-founder); League of Conservation Voters; Airport Area Economic Development Group; Bay View Neighborhood Assn.; Planned Parenthood Advocates of Wis.; Sierra Club; Humboldt Park Watch; South Side Business Club of Milw.; Bay View Historical Soc.; Arbor Day Foundation; Tri-Wisconsin; Badgerland Striders; Young Elected Officials; Bay View Lions Club; Lake Park Friends; MPTV Friends. Former member: WISPIRG (campus intern). Milwaukee Co. Bd. supervisor 2008-10.

Elected to Senate in 2010; reelected 2014. Minority Leader 2013. Biennial committee assignments: **2015** — Education (also 2011); Labor and Government Reform; Workforce Development, Public Works and Military Affairs. **2013** — Senate Organization; Jt. Com. on Employment Relations; Jt. Com. on Legislative Organization. **2011** — Jt. Com. on Review of Admin. Rules (co-chp., eff. 7/24/12); Education and Corrections; Environment, Natural Resources and Tourism; Insurance and Housing; Natural Resources and Environment; Jt. Com. on Audit (eff. 7/24/12); Jt. Com. on Finance (eff. 7/24/12); Jt. Com. on Information Policy and Technology; Gov.'s Comn. on Waste, Fraud and Abuse; Spec. Task Force on UW Restructuring and Operational Flexibilities.

Telephone: Office: (608) 266-7505; (800) 361-5487 (toll free).

E-mail: Sen.Larson@legis.wisconsin.gov

Voting address: 3261 South Herman Street, Milwaukee 53207.

Mailing address: Office: Room 5 South, State Capitol, P.O. Box 7882, Madison 53707-7882.

Representative
BROSTOFF

Representative
SINICKI

Representative
RODRIGUEZ

Jonathan Brostoff (Dem.), 19th Assembly District

Born September 25, 1983; married. B.A. political science UW-Milwaukee 2011. Full-time legislator. Former district director for Sen. Larson, backup shift supervisor – Pathfinders; program director, SDC Family Support Center; public ally, Americorps; volunteer, Street Beat, Big Brothers, Big Sisters, Casa Maria. Member: Democratic Party of Milwaukee Co. (bd. mbr.); Bay View Neighborhood Assn.; Historic Water Tower Neighborhood Assn.; Planned Parenthood; Urban Ecology Center. Former member: ACLU-Wisconsin (bd. mbr.); Tikkun Ha-Ir (bd. mbr.).

Elected to Assembly 2014. Biennial committee assignments: **2015** — Aging and Long Term Care; Financial Institutions; Mental Health Reform; State Affairs and Government Operations; Ways and Means.

Telephone: Office: (608) 266-0650; (888) 534-0019 (toll free).

E-mail: Rep.Brostoff@legis.wisconsin.gov.

Voting address: 920 East Pleasant Street #2, Milwaukee 53212.

Mailing address: Office: Room 3 North, State Capitol, P.O. Box 8952, Madison 53708.

Christine Sinicki (Dem.), 20th Assembly District

Born Milwaukee, March 28, 1960; married; 2 children. Graduate Bay View H.S. Former small business manager. Member: Delegate-U.S. Pres. Electoral College, 2000; Amer. Coun. of Young Political Leaders, Delegate to Israel and Palestine, 2001; Milw. Com. on Domestic Violence and Sexual Assault; Wis. Civil Air Patrol, Major; Milw. City Coun. Parents and Teachers Assn.; Bay View Historical Soc.; Bay View Neighborhood Assn.; Fellow, Bowhay Institute, La Follette School, UW-Madison 2001; Flemming Fellow, Center for Policy Alternatives 2003. Awards: Wis. Environmental Decade *Clean 16 2000;* Wis. Ob/Gyn Physicians' *Legislator of the Year* 2000; Wis. Coalition Against Domestic Violence *DV Diva* 2003; Wis. Dept. of Veterans Affairs *Certificates of Commendation* 2006, 2005; Wis. League of Conservation Voters *Conservation Champion* 2014, 2011, 2009, 2007; Wis. Women's Alliance *Legislation Award* 2009-10; Professional Firefighters of Wis. *Legislator of the Year* 2010; Wis. Grocers Assn. *Friend of Grocers* 2010; Cudahy Veterans' *Service Award* 2010; AMVETS *State Legislative Advocacy Award* 2011. Assembly Democratic Task Force on Working Families (chp.) 2003. State Assembly Milw. Caucus (chp. 2005, 2003). Dept. of Workforce Development State Minimum Wage Council (gov. appointee) 2005. Milw. School Board 1991-98.

Elected to Assembly since 1998. Minority Caucus Secretary 2001. Biennial committee assignments: **2015** — Consumer Protection; Education (also 2011, 2009, 2001); Labor (chp. 2009, mbr. 2013, 2005, 2003); State Affairs and Government Operations; Veterans and Military Affairs (also 2007-2011, 2003). **2013** — Government Operations and State Licensing; Urban Education; Veterans.

Telephone: Office: (608) 266-8588; (888) 534-0020 (toll free); District: (414) 481-7667.

E-mail: Rep.Sinicki@legis.wisconsin.gov

Voting address: Milwaukee 53207.

Mailing address: Office: Room 114 North, State Capitol, P.O. Box 8953, Madison 53708.

Jessie Rodriguez (Rep.), 21st Assembly District

Born Puerto el Triunfo, El Salvador, July 5, 1977; married. Graduate Alexander Hamilton H.S. (Milwaukee) 1996; B.A. Marquette U. 2002. Full-time legislator. Former analyst for a supermarket company; outreach coordinator for Hispanics for School Choice.

Elected to Assembly in November 2013 special election; reelected 2014. Majority Caucus Secretary 2015. Biennial committee assignments: **2015** — Children and Families (chp.); Colleges and Universities; Criminal Justice and Public Safety; Education (also 2013); Mental Health Reform. **2013** — Criminal Justice; Health; Jobs and the Economy; Joint Legislative Council.

Telephone: Office: (608) 266-0610; (888) 534-0021 (toll free).

E-mail: Rep.Rodriguez@legis.wisconsin.gov

Voting address: 9312 South 33rd Street, Franklin 53132.

Mailing address: Office: Room 204 North, State Capitol, P.O. Box 8953, Madison 53708.

8th SENATE DISTRICT

See Waukesha County Detail Map on pp. 94 & 95

See Milwaukee County Detail Map on pp. 92 & 93

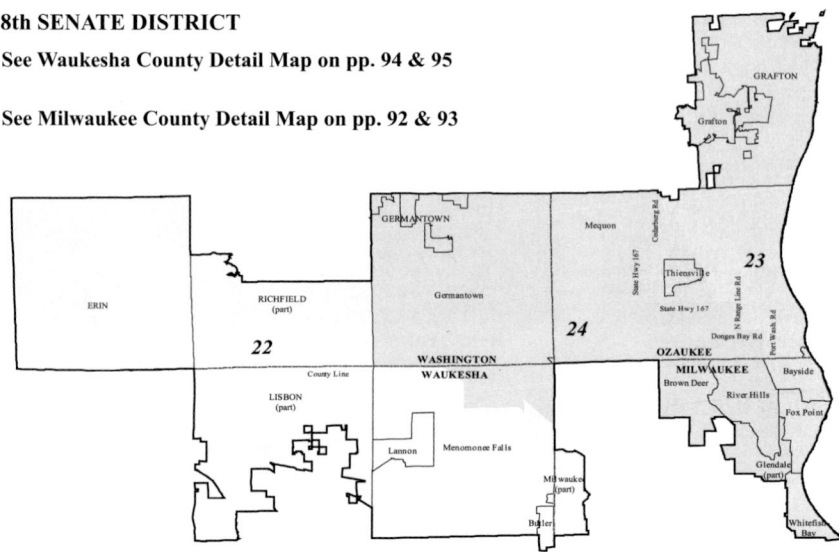

Senator
DARLING

Alberta Darling (Rep.), 8th Senate District

Born Hammond, IN, April 28; married; 2 children, 3 grandchildren. Graduate UW-Madison 1966; grad. work UW-Milwaukee 1972-74. Former teacher and marketing director. Member: North Shore Rotary; College Savings Program Bd. (EdVest); Junior League of Milwaukee (former pres.); Tempo Professional Women's Organization; Blood Center of Wis. Bd. Former member: Next Door Foundation; Public Policy Forum; Wis. Strategic Planning Council for Economic Development; Greater Milwaukee Com.; Goals for Greater Milwaukee 2000 Project (exec. com.); United Way Bd. (chp., allocations com.); Future Milwaukee (pres.); Milwaukee Forum; Children's Service Soc. of Wis. (bd. of dir.); American Red Cross of Wis. (exec. com., bd. of dir.); League of Women Voters; Today's Girls/Tomorrow's Women/Boys Girls Club (founder); NCSL Education Com. (chp.); YMCA (bd. mbr.). Recipient: *Shining Star of Education Reform* 2011; Hispanic Chamber of Commerce *Government Advocates Award;* Greater Milwaukee Committee *Leadership Award* 2011; Leukemia and Lymphoma Society *Legislative Leadership Award* 2011, Friend of Housing *Legislator of the Year* 2012, 2006-2011, 2002, Wisconsin Manufacturers and Commerce *Working for Wisconsin* 2012, 2002; American Conservative Union Foundation *Defender of Liberty Award* 2012; *Friend of Grocers* 2014; 2011 Coalition of Wisconsin Aging Groups *Tommy G. Thompson Award for Service;* Wis. Stem Cell Now *Courage Award;* Right Wis. Iron Lady Award 2013; Wis. *Charter Champion* Award 2014; 2006 Inductee into the National MS Hall of Fame; Wisconsin Manufacturers and Commerce *100% Pro-Business Legislator* 2006; Wis. Builders Assn. *Friend of Housing* 2008; Amer. Cancer Soc. *Legislative Champion* 2014, 2006; Fair Air Coalition *Friend of Education;* Metropolitan Milwaukee Assn. of Commerce *Champion of Commerce;* Wis. Head Start Directors Assn. *Award of Excellence;* National Assn. of Community Leadership *Leadership Award;* United Way *Gwen Jackson Leadership Award;* St. Francis Children's Center *Children Service Award.*

Elected to Assembly in May 1990 special election; reelected November 1990; elected to Senate 1992; reelected since 1996. Biennial committee assignments: **2015** — Jt. Com. on Finance (co-chp. since 2011, also 2003, mbr. since 1999, eff. 2/7/00); Economic Development and Commerce; Education (since 2011, also 2005, 2001, 1999, 1997, 1993); Jt. Legis. Audit (since 2011, also 2003); Jt. Com. on Employment Relations (since 2011, also 2003); Jt. Legislative Council (since 2001). **2013** — Workforce Development, Forestry, Mining and Revenue (vice chp.); Milwaukee Child Welfare Partnership Council (since 1995); Wis. Center District Board of Dir. (also 2011, 2005, 2003); UW Hospitals and Clinics Authority Bd. (also 2003). **2011** — Economic Development, Veterans and Military Affairs. **2009** — Economic Development; Health, Health Insurance, Privacy, Property Tax Relief, and Revenue. **2007** — Economic Development, Job Creation, Family Prosperity and Housing. **2005** — Health, Children, Families, Aging and Long-Term Care. **1999** — Jt. Com. for Review of Administrative Rules (since 1993); Jt. Com. on Information Policy (also 1995); Judiciary and Consumer Affairs; Child Abuse and Neglect Prevention Bd. (since 1993). **1997** — Education and Financial Institutions (chp., eff. 4/21/98, also 1995); Business, Economic Development and Urban Affairs (eff. 4/21/98, also 1995); Judiciary (eff. 4/21/98, also 1995); Labor, Transportation and Financial Institutions; Education Comn. of the States (eff. 4/30/98, also 1995).

Telephone: Office: (608) 266-5830; E-mail: Sen.Darling@legis.wisconsin.gov
Voting address: River Hills 53217.
Mailing address: Office: Room 317 East, State Capitol, P.O. Box 7882, Madison 53707-7882.

| Representative | Representative | Representative |
| BRANDTJEN | J. OTT | KNODL |

Janel Brandtjen (Rep.), 22nd Assembly District

Born Milwaukee, March 1966; married; 2 children. Graduate Marshall H.S.; B.B.A. Finance and Marketing, UW-Milwaukee 1988. Business owner. Member: Republican Party of Waukesha Co.; Republican Party of Washington Co.; Republican Women of Waukesha Co.; Washington Co. Republican Women; National Rifle Association; Immanuel Lutheran Church; Menomonee Falls Chamber of Commerce. Waukesha Co. Supervisor 2008-present.

Elected to Assembly 2014. Biennial committee assignments: **2015** — Corrections (vice chp.); Children and Families; Public Benefits Reform; State Affairs and Government Operations; Workforce Development.

Telephone: Office: (608) 267-2367; (888) 534-0022 (toll free); District: (262) 455-8311.

E-mail: Rep.Brandtjen@legis.wisconsin.gov

Voting address: N52 W16632 Oak Ridge Trail, Menomonee Falls 53051.

Mailing address: Office: P.O. Box 8952, Madison 53708-8952.

Jim Ott (Rep.), 23rd Assembly District

Born Milwaukee, June 5, 1947; married; 2 sons, 1 grandchild. Graduate Milwaukee Washington H.S. 1965; B.S. UW-Milwaukee 1970; M.S. UW-Milwaukee 1975; J.D. Marquette U. 2000. Full-time legislator. Former broadcast meteorologist and instructor at UW-Parkside. Served in U.S. Army 1970-73; Vietnam veteran. Member: State Bar of Wisconsin; American Meteorological Society; Mequon/Thiensville Noon Rotary; Mequon/Thiensville Chamber of Commerce; American Legion; Ozaukee County Republican Party; North Shore Branch Milwaukee Co. Republican Party; Lumen Christi Catholic Church (past parish council pres.). Recipient: National Weather Service *Public Service Award* 2006; Archbishops Vatican II *Service Award* 1999; Vietnam Campaign Medal and Meritorious Unit Citation; Emerging Political Leaders Program; BILLD Leadership Fellow.

Elected to Assembly 2006; reelected since 2008. Biennial committee assignments: **2015** — Judiciary (chp., also 2013); Criminal Justice and Public Safety; Veterans and Military Affairs; Jt. Com. for Review of Admin. Rules (co-chp. 2011); Judicial Council (since 2013); Law Revision Com. (co-chp. 2013, also 2011); Leg. Coun. Study Com. on Transfer of Structured Settlement Payments (chp.). **2013** — Criminal Justice; Urban and Local Affairs; Veterans. **2011** — Judiciary and Ethics (chp.); Natural Resources (through 5/23/11, also 2009, vice chp. 2007). **2009** — Education Reform (also 2007); Fish and Wildlife. **2007** — Elections and Constitutional Law; Workforce Development.

Telephone: Office: (608) 266-0486; (888) 534-0023 (toll free).

E-mail: Rep.OttJ@legis.wisconsin.gov

Voting address: Mequon 53092.

Mailing address: Office: Room 317 North, State Capitol, P.O. Box 8953, Madison 53708-8953.

Dan Knodl (Rep.), 24th Assembly District

Born Milwaukee, December 14, 1958; 4 children. Graduate Menomonee Falls East H.S. 1977; attended UW-Madison. Resort owner. Member: Washington Co. Convention and Visitors Bureau; Ozaukee/Washington Land Trust; Pike Lake Sportsmans Club. Pike Lake Protection District 2000-present (secy.). Washington County Board 2006-08.

Elected to Assembly 2008; reelected since 2010. Assistant Majority Leader 2015, 2011. Biennial committee assignments: **2015** — Labor (chp. 2013, mbr. 2009); Assembly Organization (also 2011); Rules (also 2011); Jt. Com. on Legislative Organization (also 2011); Jt. Legislative Council. **2013** — Jobs, Economy and Mining (vice chp.); Government Operations and State Licensing; State Affairs; Urban Education; Workforce Development. **2011** — Aging and Long-Term Care (chp.); Jt. Survey Com. on Tax Exemptions (co-chp.); Colleges and Universities; Ways and Means (also 2009). **2009** — State Affairs and Homeland Security.

Telephone: Office: (608) 266-3796; (888) 529-0024 (toll free); District: (262) 502-0118.

Voting address: N101 W14475 Ridgefield Court, Germantown 53022.

Mailing address: Office: Room 218 North, State Capitol, P.O. Box 8952, Madison 53708.

9th SENATE DISTRICT

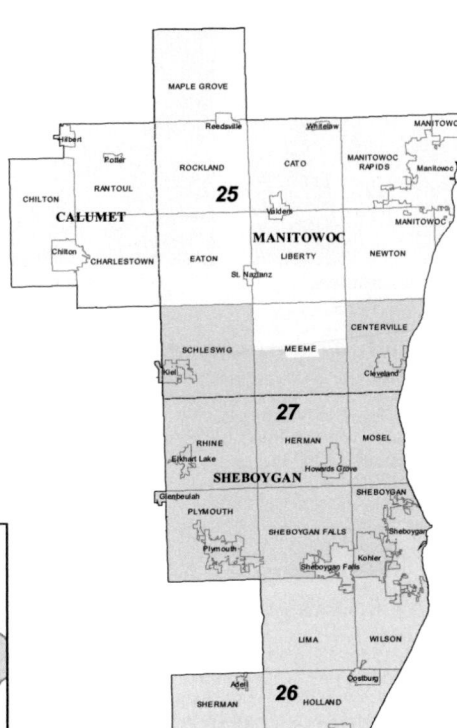

Senator
LEMAHIEU

Detail Map: City of Sheboygan

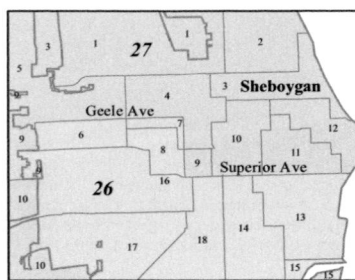

Devin LeMahieu (Rep.), 9th Senate District

Born Sheboygan, August 8, 1972; single. Graduate Sheboygan Co. Christian H.S. 1991; B.A. business administration and political science, Dordt College (Sioux Center, Iowa) 1995. Publisher/owner, Lakeshore Weekly. Member: Oostburg Kiwanis Club (fmr. pres.); Oostburg Chamber of Commerce; Sheboygan Co. Chamber of Commerce; Oostburg Civic Pride Com.; Bethel OPC (deacon); NRA (life mbr.). Sheboygan Co. Bd. Supervisor 2006-present, Human Resources Com. 2006-present (chm., 2010-14), Finance Com. 2012-present, Exec. Com. 2010-12.

Elected to Senate 2014. Biennial committee assignments: 2015 — Elections and Local Government (chp.); Jt. Survey Com. on Tax Exemptions (co-chp.); Agriculture, Small Business and Tourism; Health and Human Services; Jt. Com. for Review of Administrative Rules.

Telephone: Office: (608) 266-2056; (888) 295-8750 (toll free); District: (920) 254-3044.

E-mail: Sen.LeMahieu@legis.wisconsin.gov

Voting address: 21 South 8th Street, Oostburg 53070.

Mailing address: Office: Room 15 South, State Capitol, P.O. Box 7882, Madison 53707-7882.

| Representative | Representative | Representative |
| TITTL | KATSMA | VORPAGEL |

Paul Tittl (Rep.), 25th Assembly District

Born Delavan, November 23, 1961; married; 2 children, 3 grandchildren. Graduate Lincoln High (Manitowoc) 1980. Owner, Vacuum and Sewing Center. Member: National Rifle Association; Eagles Manitowoc; Manitowoc Co. Home Builders Association. Former member: Economic Development Corp.; Wastewater Treatment Facility Bd.; Manitowoc Crime Prevention Com.; Community Development Authority; Safety Traffic and Parking Commission; Wisconsin Utility Tax Assn. 2009-13; WCA Taxation and Finance Steering Com. 2010-13; WCA Judicial and Public Safety Steering Com. 2010-13. Manitowoc City Council 2004-08 (pres. 2006-07); Manitowoc Co. Bd. of Supervisors 2006-13 (chm. 2010-12).

Elected to Assembly 2012; reelected 2014. Biennial committee assignments: **2015** — Mental Health Reform (chp.); Insurance (vice chp.) Health; Jobs and the Economy; Natural Resources and Sporting Heritage; Veterans and Military Affairs. **2013** — Consumer Protection (vice chp.); Family Law; Small Business Development; State and Federal Relations; Veterans.

Telephone: Office: (608) 266-0315; (888) 529-0025 (toll free); District: (920) 682-6203 (home).

E-mail: Rep.Tittl@legis.wisconsin.gov

Voting address: Manitowoc 54220.

Mailing address: Office: Room 219 North, State Capitol, P.O. Box 8953, Madison 53708.

Terry Katsma (Rep.), 26th Assembly District

Born Sheboygan, April 23, 1958; married; 3 children. Graduate Sheboygan Co. Christian H.S. 1976; B.A. business administration Dordt College (Sioux Center, Iowa) 1980; M.B.A. Marquette U. 1985. Full-time legislator. Former community bank president and CEO. Member: Trinity Christian College Bd. of Trustees (Palos Heights, Ill. – treas.); Oostburg State Bank Bd. of Dir. (fmr. pres. and CEO); Oostburg Chamber of Commerce (fmr. pres.-elect); Oostburg Kiwanis Club (fmr. pres.); Oostburg Christian Reformed Church (elder, fmr. deacon); Workbound, Inc. (fmr. pres.); YMCA of Sheboygan Co. Bd. of Managers. Former member: Dordt College Bd. of Trustees (vice chp.); Sheboygan Co. Christian H.S. (bd. pres.); Oostburg Christian School Bd. (secy.); Oostburg Community Education Foundation.

Elected to Assembly 2014. Biennial committee assignments: **2015** — Financial Institutions (vice chp.); Consumer Protection; Housing and Real Estate; Ways and Means; Workforce Development.

Telephone: Office: (608) 266-0656; (888) 529-0026 (toll free); District: (920) 564-3184.

E-mail: Rep.Katsma@legis.wisconsin.gov

Voting address: 705 Erie Avenue, Oostburg 53070.

Mailing address: Office: Room 18 North, State Capitol, P.O. Box 8952, Madison 53708.

Tyler Vorpagel (Rep.), 27th Assembly District

Born Plymouth, March 24, 1985; married. Graduate Plymouth H.S. 2003; B.A. political science, B.S. public administration UW-Green Bay 2007. Full-time legislator. Former district director, Congressman Tom Petri. Member: Plymouth Rotary; B.P.O. Elks; National Assn. of Parliamentarians; Republican Party of Sheboygan Co. (fmr. mbr. exec. com.); 6th Dist. Republican Party (vice chair); RPW Executive Com. Former member: Exchange Club (pres.).

Elected to Assembly 2014. Biennial committee assignments: **2015** — Campaigns and Elections (vice chp.); Children and Families; Public Benefit Reform; State Affairs and Government Operations; Transportation.

Telephone: Office: (608) 266-8530; (888) 529-0027.

E-mail: Rep.Vorpagel@legis.wisconsin.gov

Voting address: Plymouth 53073.

Mailing address: Office: 18 West, State Capitol, P.O. Box 8953, Madison 53708.

10th SENATE DISTRICT

Senator
HARSDORF

Detail Map: Town of Richmond

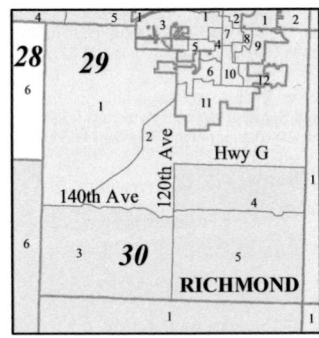

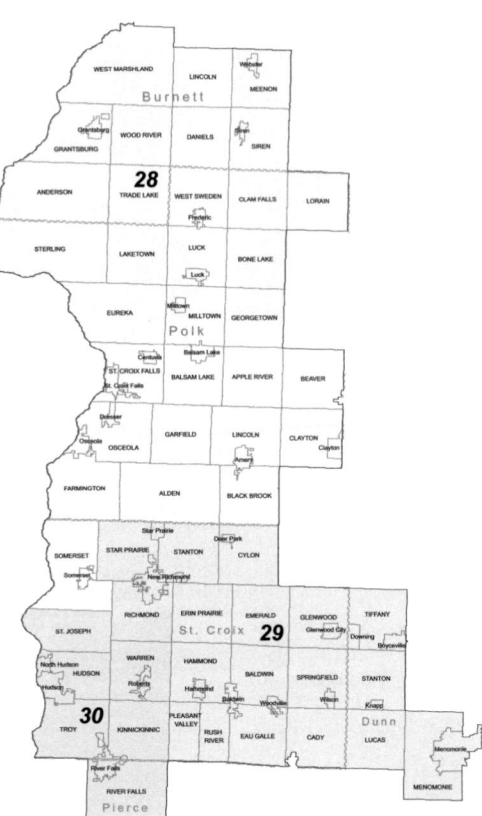

Sheila E. Harsdorf (Rep.), 10th Senate District

Born St. Paul, MN, July 25, 1956; 1 son. Graduate River Falls H.S.; B.S. in animal science, U. of Minnesota 1978; Wis. Rural Leadership Program, grad. of 1st class (1986). Member: Pierce Co. Republican Party; Pierce Co. Farm Bureau (former dir. and treas.); Luther Memorial Church. Former member: Wis. State FFA Sponsors Bd. (chp.); Wis. Conservation Corps Bd. (secy.); Kinnickinnic River Land Trust Bd.; Pierce Co. Dairy Promotion Com. (past chm.); Wis. State ASCS Com.; Adv. Council on Small Business, Agriculture, Labor for Federal Reserve Bank of Minneapolis.

Elected to Assembly 1988-96; elected to Senate 2000; reelected since 2004. Majority Caucus Chairperson 2015; Majority Caucus Vice Chairperson 2013, 2011; Minority Caucus Vice Chairperson 2009; Majority Caucus Sergeant at Arms 2005. Biennial Senate committee assignments: **2015** — Universities and Technical Colleges (chp., also 2013); Jt. Com. on Information Policy and Technology (co-chp. since 2011, mbr. 2001); Education Reform and Government Operations (vice chp.); Agriculture, Small Business and Tourism (also 2013); Jt. Com. on Finance (since 2011, also 2003); Midwestern Higher Education Compact (chp. 2014, vice chp., 2011, mbr. 2003-07). **2013** — Energy, Consumer Protection and Government Reform. **2011** — State and Federal Relations and Information Technology (chp.); Agriculture, Forestry, and Higher Education (vice chp.). **2009** — Agriculture and Higher Education (also 2007); Commerce, Utilities, Energy, and Rail; Jt. Legislative Council (also 2007, 2003); Mississippi River Parkway Commission (since 2001); World Dairy Center Authority (since 2003). **2007** — Commerce, Utilities and Rail. **2005** — Higher Education and Tourism (chp., also 2003); Jt. Survey Com. on Tax Exemptions (co-chp., mbr. 2003); Education (also 2001); Housing and Financial Institutions. **2003** — Law Revision Com. (also 2001). **2001** — 2001-2003 Biennial Budget; Labor and Agriculture; Environmental Education Bd.; Ad. Bd. for Midwest Center for Agricultural Research, Education, and Disease and Injury Prevention; Jt. Legis. Council Special Com. on the Public Health System's Response to Terrorism and Public Health Emergencies. Assembly committee assignments: **1997** — Jt. Com. on Finance (also 1995). **1993** — Agriculture, Forestry and Rural Affairs; Colleges and Universities (ranking minority mbr. since 1991); Natural Resources (since 1989); Veterans and Military Affairs (eff. 4/26/93); Educational Communications Bd. (since 1989). **1991** — Agriculture, Aquaculture and Forestry; State Affairs (also 1989). **1989** — Agriculture and its Subcom. on Aquaculture.

Telephone: Office: (608) 266-7745; (800) 862-1092 (toll free); Fax: (608) 267-0369.

E-mail: Sen.Harsdorf@legis.wisconsin.gov

Voting address: Town of River Falls 54022.

Mailing address: Office: Room 122 South, P.O. Box 7882, Madison 53707-7882.

Representative	Representative	Representative
JARCHOW	**MURTHA**	**KNUDSON**

Adam Jarchow (Rep.), 28th Assembly District

Born St. Paul, Minn., November 10, 1978; married; 2 children. Graduate Clear Lake H.S. 1997; B.S. finance U. of South Florida 2001; J.D. U. of Florida 2004. Attorney. Member: Polk Co. Economic Development Corporation (secy.); National Rifle Assn.; Polk Co. Sportsmen's Club; Wis. Bear Hunters Assn.; Apple River Fire Dept.

Elected to Assembly 2014. Biennial committee assignments: **2015** — Tourism (vice chp.); Energy and Utilities; Financial Institutions.

Telephone: Office: (608) 267-2365; (888) 529-0028 (toll free).

E-mail: Rep.Jarchow@legis.wisconsin.gov

Voting address: 971 Apple River Court, Balsam Lake 54810.

Mailing address: Office: Room 19 North, State Capitol, P.O. Box 8952, Madison 53708.

John Murtha (Rep.), 29th Assembly District

Born Baldwin, August 8, 1951; married; 4 children. Graduate St. Croix Central H.S. (Hammond) 1969; Chippewa Valley Tech. (Eau Claire) wood tech. 1970. Self employed. Member: NRA; AOPA. Town of Eau Galle Board (St. Croix Co.) supervisor 1999-2003, chairman 2003-09.

Elected to Assembly 2006; reelected since 2008. Majority Caucus Chairperson 2015; Majority Caucus Vice Chairperson 2013, 2011. Biennial committee assignments: **2015** — Housing and Real Estate (chp. 2013); Assembly Organization; Rules (since 2011); Jt. Legislative Council. **2013** — Agriculture (since 2007); International Trade and Commerce; Public Safety and Homeland Security; Rural Affairs. **2011** — Housing (chp., mbr. 2009); Forestry; Rural Economic Development and Rural Affairs. **2009** — Rural Economic Development (also 2007). **2007** — Small Business (vice chp.); Labor and Industry.

Telephone: Office: (608) 266-7683; (888) 529-0029 (toll free).

E-mail: Rep.Murtha@legis.wisconsin.gov

Voting address: Baldwin 54002.

Mailing address: Office: Room 309 North, State Capitol, P.O. Box 8953, Madison 53708.

Dean Knudson (Rep.), 30th Assembly District

Born Mayville, ND, April 29, 1961; married; 2 children. Graduate May-Port H.S. (Mayville, ND) 1979; attended Mayville St. College, North Dakota St. U.; D.V.M. Iowa St. U. 1986. Veterinarian. Member: Hudson Daybreak Rotary (fmr. pres.); Trinity Lutheran Church; Hudson Area Chamber of Commerce (fmr. pres.); Am. Veterinary Medical Assn.; Wisconsin Veterinary Medical Assn.; Minnesota Veterinary Medical Assn.; Republican Party of Wis.; Republican Party of St. Croix Co. (fmr. chm.); Republican Party of Pierce Co.; Iowa St. U. Alumni Assn.; Omega Tau Sigma. Mayor of Hudson 2008-10; Alderperson, Hudson 1996-2002; Hudson Library Bd. 1996-2002; Hudson Plan Commission 2008-10; St. Croix Business Park Bd. since 2010.

Elected to Assembly 2010; reelected since 2012. Biennial committee assignments: **2015** — Education (also 2011); Jt. Com. on Finance (also 2013); Jt. Com. for Review of Admin. Rules. **2013** — Colleges and Universities (vice chp. 2011). **2011** — Urban and Local Affairs.

Telephone: Office: (608) 266-1526; (888) 529-0030 (toll free); District: (715) 690-9225.

E-mail: Rep.Knudson@legis.wisconsin.gov

Voting address: 1753 Laurel Avenue, Hudson 54016.

Mailing address: Office: Room 304 East, State Capitol, P.O. Box 8952, Madison 53708.

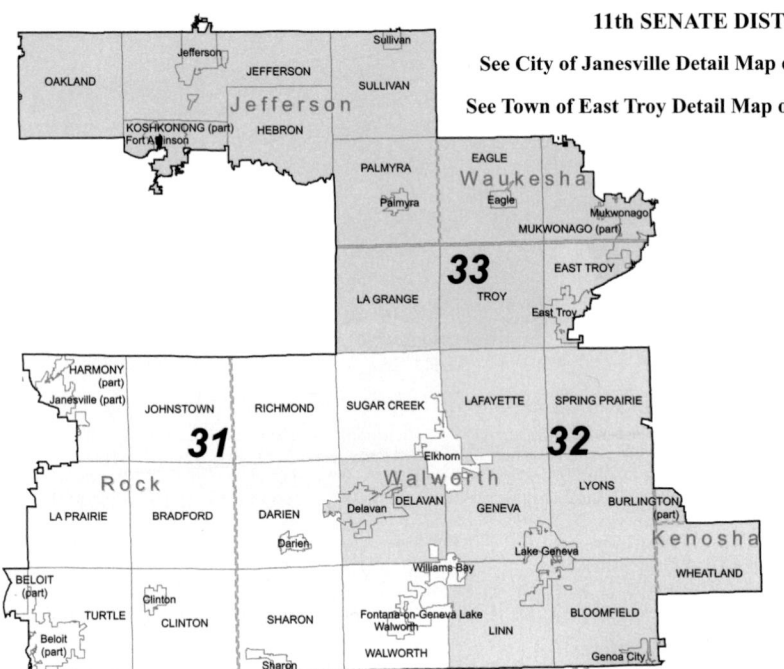

11th SENATE DISTRICT

See City of Janesville Detail Map on p. 48

See Town of East Troy Detail Map on p. 74

See Waukesha County Detail
Map on pp. 94 & 95

Senator
NASS

Stephen L. Nass (Rep.), 11th Senate District

Born Whitewater, October 7, 1952. Graduate Whitewater H.S.; B.S. UW-Whitewater 1978; M.S. Ed. in school business management UW-Whitewater 1990. Former payroll benefits analyst and information analyst/negotiator. Member of Wis. Air National Guard (retired, 33 years of service), served in Middle East in Operations Desert Shield and Desert Storm. Member: American Legion; Veterans of Foreign Wars; Mukwonago Business Breakfast Club; Jefferson Co. Agribusiness Club. Whitewater City Council 1977-81; UW-Whitewater Bd. of Visitors 1979-89.

Elected to Assembly 1990-2012; elected to Senate 2014. Biennial Senate committee assignments: **2015** — Labor and Government Reform (chp.); Jt. Com. for Review of Admin. Rules (co-chp.); Universities and Technical Colleges (vice chp.); Education; Education Reform and Government Operations. Assembly committee assignments: **2013** — Colleges and Universities (chp., also 2011, 2007, mbr. since 2003); Education (vice chp. 1995-2001, mbr. since 1991); Government Operations and State Licensing; Housing and Real Estate; Labor; State and Local Finance. **2011** — Ways and Means (vice chp., also 2005, mbr. 2009, 2003); Labor and Workforce Development (also 2001). **2009** — Labor (chp. 2005, 2003). **2007** — Education Reform (vice chp., also 2003, chp. 2001, mbr. since 1999); Labor and Industry. **2005** — Property Rights and Land Management (vice chp.). **2001** — Personal Privacy; Education Commission of the States (also 1999). **1999** — Government Operations; Labor and Employment (vice chp. 1997, mbr. 1995); Jt. Com. on Audit. **1997** — Mandates (chp.); Criminal Justice and Corrections; Rural Affairs; Legis. Coun. Com. on Services for Visually Handicapped Students.

Telephone: Office: (608) 266-2635; (800) 578-1457 (toll free); District: (262) 495-3424.

E-mail: Sen.Nass@legis.wisconsin.gov

Voting address: N 8330 Jackson Road, Whitewater 53190.

Mailing address: Office: Room 10 South, State Capitol, P.O. Box 7882, Madison 53707-7882.

| **Representative** | **Representative** | **Representative** |
| **LOUDENBECK** | **AUGUST** | **HORLACHER** |

Amy Loudenbeck (Rep.), 31st Assembly District

Born Midland, MI, September 29, 1969; married. Graduate Hinsdale Central H.S. (Hinsdale, IL) 1987; B.A. political science, international relations UW-Madison 1991; studied abroad in Kingston, Jamaica. Former chamber of commerce executive, compliance manager, environmental/engineering services project manager. Member: Wisconsin Family Impact Seminar (adv. bd. mbr.); Clinton Community Historical Soc.; Wis. DNR Green Tier Advisory Bd.; Friends of Clinton Public Library. Former member: Town of Linn Fire Dept. Town of Clinton supervisor 2010-12.

Elected to Assembly 2010; reelected since 2012. Biennial committee assignments: **2015** — Jt. Com. on Finance; Jt. Com. on Information Policy and Technology; State Capitol and Executive Residence Bd. (since 2011); Wis. Housing and Economic Development Authority (also 2013). **2013** — Workforce Development (chp.); Children and Families (vice chp.); Environment and Forestry; International Trade and Commerce; State and Federal Relations; Jt. Legis. Council. **2011** — Tourism, Recreation and State Properties (vice chp.); Jobs, Economy and Small Business; Public Health and Public Safety.

 Telephone: Office: (608) 266-9967.
 E-mail: Rep.Loudenbeck@legis.wisconsin.gov
 Voting address: 10737 South State Road 140, Clinton 53525.
 Mailing address: Office: Room 306 East, State Capitol, P.O. Box 8952, Madison 53708.

Tyler August (Rep.), 32nd Assembly District

Born Wisconsin, January 26, 1983; single. Graduate Big Foot H.S. 2001; attended UW-Eau Claire and UW-Madison; completed 2012 Emerging Leader Program at Univ. of Virginia Darden School of Business. Full-time legislator. Former chief of staff to Rep. Thomas Lothian. Member: Republican Party of Wis. (fmr. bd. mbr.); Republican Party of 1st Congressional Dist. (fmr. chm.); Republican Party of Walworth Co. (fmr. chm, vice-chm.); National Rifle Association. Recipient: American Conservative Union *Defender of Liberty* 2012; GOPAC *Emerging Leader* 2012.

Elected to Assembly 2010; reelected since 2012. Speaker Pro Tempore 2015. Biennial committee assignments: **2015** — Jt. Survey Com. on Tax Exemptions (co-chp., also 2013); Insurance (also 2011); Rules; Jt. Legislative Council. **2013** — Government Operations and State Licensing (chp.); Labor (vice chp.); Health; Judiciary; State Affairs; Jt. Com. for Review of Admin. Rules. **2011** — Consumer Protection and Personal Privacy (vice chp.); Homeland Security and State Affairs.

 Telephone: Office: (608) 266-1190.
 E-mail: Rep.August@legis.wisconsin.gov
 Voting address: 110 Hank Jay Drive, Unit B, Lake Geneva 53147.
 Mailing address: Office: Room 119 West, State Capitol, P.O. Box 8952, Madison 53708.

Cody J. Horlacher (Rep.), 33rd Assembly District

Born Burlington, April 10, 1987; single. Graduate East Troy H.S. 2006; B.A. marketing UW-Whitewater 2010; J.D. Marquette U. Law School 2014. Special prosecutor, Walworth Co.; former assistant district attorney, Walworth Co. Member: Carroll U. President's Advisory Council; Wis. State Bar. Former member: Walworth Co. Republican Party (secy., vice chair, chairman); Federalist Society.

Elected to Assembly 2014. Biennial committee assignments: **2015** — Judiciary (vice chp.); Campaigns and Elections; Constitution and Ethics; Criminal Justice and Public Safety; Education; Interstate Affairs.

 Telephone: Office: (608) 266-5715; (888) 529-0033 (toll free).
 E-mail: Rep.Horlacher@legis.wisconsin.gov
 Voting address: 1254 Bear Pass #7, Mukwonago 53149.
 Mailing address: Office: Room 17 North, State Capitol, P.O. Box 8952, Madison 53708.

12th SENATE DISTRICT

Senator
TIFFANY

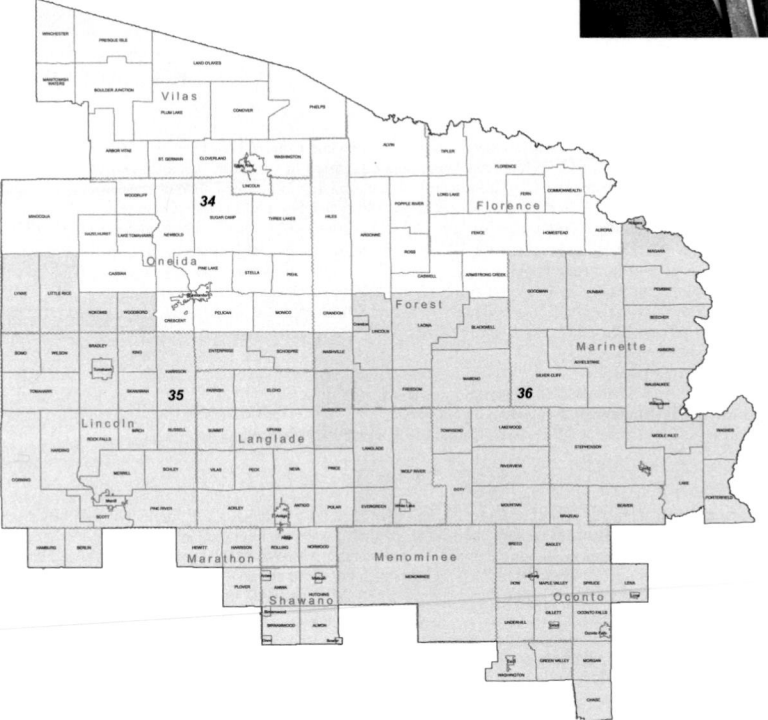

Tom Tiffany (Rep.), 12th Senate District

Born Wabasha, MN, December 30, 1957; married; 3 children. Graduate Elmwood H.S. 1976; B.S. Agricultural Economics UW-River Falls 1980. Dam tender, Wis. Valley Improvement Co. Member: National Rifle Association; Ruffed Grouse Society. Town supervisor 2009-13.

Elected to Assembly 2010; elected to Senate 2012. Biennial Senate committee assignments: **2015** — Sporting Heritage, Mining and Forestry (chp.); Agriculture, Small Business, and Tourism (vice chp., also 2013); Revenue, Financial Institutions and Rural Issues; Jt. Com. on Finance; Jt. Survey Com. on Tax Exemptions (also 2013). **2013** — Workforce Development, Forestry, Mining, and Revenue (chp.); Natural Resources; Jt. Com. for Review of Administrative Rules. Assembly committee assignments: **2011** — Forestry (vice chp.); Natural Resources; Tourism, Recreation and State Properties.

Telephone: Office: (608) 266-2509.

E-mail: Sen.Tiffany@legis.wisconsin.gov

Voting address: Town of Little Rice, Oneida County.

Mailing address: Office: Room 409 South, State Capitol, P.O. Box 7882, Madison 53708-7882.

Representative	Representative	Representative
SWEARINGEN	CZAJA	MURSAU

Rob Swearingen (Rep.), 34th Assembly District

Born Oneida Co., July 23, 1963; married; 2 children. Graduate Rhinelander H.S. 1981. Restaurant owner/operator. Member: Tavern League of Wisconsin (former pres., zone vice pres., district director); American Beverage Licensees (former member, bd. of dir.); Oneida Co. Tavern League (former pres., vice pres.); Rhinelander Chamber of Commerce; Oneida County Republican Party.

Elected to Assembly 2012; reelected 2014. Biennial committee assignments: **2015** — State Affairs and Government Operations (chp.); Environment and Forestry; Small Business Development (also 2013); Tourism (also 2013); Transportation; Jt. Survey Com. on Tax Exemptions (also 2013); Wis. Building Commission. **2013** — Speaker's Task Force on Rural Schools (chp.); State Affairs (vice chp.); Housing and Real Estate; Natural Resources and Sporting Heritage; Public Safety and Homeland Security.

Telephone: Office: (608) 266-7141; (888) 534-0034 (toll free); District: (715) 369-5493.

E-mail: Rep.Swearingen@legis.wisconsin.gov

Voting address: 4485 Oakview Lane, Rhinelander 54501.

Mailing address: Office: Room 123 West, State Capitol, P.O. Box 8953, Madison 53708.

Mary J. Czaja (Rep.), 35th Assembly District

Born Tomahawk, September 25, 1963; 4 children. Graduate Tomahawk H.S. 1981; B.S. in finance and economics UW-River Falls 1986. Insurance agency owner. Member: Tomahawk Main St. Inc. (fmr. pres.); Tomahawk Regional Chamber of Commerce; Tomahawk Child Care (fmr. pres.); National Alliance for Insurance Education and Research (bd. mbr.); NRA (lifetime mbr.). Former member: Professional Insurance Agents of Wis. (secy., treas., vice pres., pres., national dir.).

Elected to Assembly 2012; reelected 2014. Biennial committee assignments: **2015** — Environment and Forestry (also 2013); Jt. Com. on Finance. **2013** — Aging and Long Term Care (vice chp.); Insurance; Small Business Development; Tourism.

Telephone: Office: (608) 266-7694; (888) 534-0035 (toll free).

E-mail: Rep.Czaja@legis.wisconsin.gov

Voting address: Irma 54442.

Mailing address: Office: Room 321 East, State Capitol, P.O. Box 8952, Madison 53708; District: P.O. Box 321, Tomahawk 54487.

Jeffrey L. Mursau (Rep.), 36th Assembly District

Born Oconto Falls, June 12, 1954; married; 4 sons, 9 grandchildren. Graduate Coleman H.S. 1972; attended UW-Oshkosh. Small business owner; electrical contractor. Member: Crivitz Ski Cats waterski team (advisor, former pres.); Crivitz Lions Club; Crivitz, WI – Crivitz, Germany Sister City Organization (fmr. dir.); Wings over Wisconsin; St. Mary's Catholic Church; 4th Degree Knights of Columbus; Friends of Gov. Thompson State Park; Master Loggers Certifying Bd. Recipient: Crivitz Business Association *Citizen of the Year* 1994. Crivitz Village President 1991-2004.

Elected to Assembly since 2004. Biennial committee assignments: **2015** — Environment and Forestry (chp., also 2013); Mining and Rural Development (vice chp.); Family Law; Natural Resources and Sporting Heritage (also 2013); Tourism (vice chp. 2005). **2013** — Agriculture (also 2011, 2007); Rural Affairs; State and Federal Relations; Spec. Com. on State-Tribal Relations (chp., also 2011, 2007, vice chp. 2009); Gov. Council on Forestry; Wis. Environmental Education Bd. **2011** — Forestry (chp., vice chp. 2007, mbr. since 2005); Natural Resources (chp., mbr. since 2005). **2009** — Workforce Development. **2007** — Rural Economic Development (chp.); Consumer Protection and Personal Privacy. **2005** — Rural Development; Small Business.

Telephone: Office: (608) 266-3780; (888) 534-0036 (toll free).

Voting address: 4 Oak Street, Crivitz 54114.

Mailing address: Office: Room 113 West, State Capitol, P.O. Box 8953, Madison 53708.

13th SENATE DISTRICT

See City of Hartford Detail Map on p. 58

See Village of DeForest Detail Map on p. 46

See Waukesha County Detail Map on pp. 94 & 95

Senator
FITZGERALD

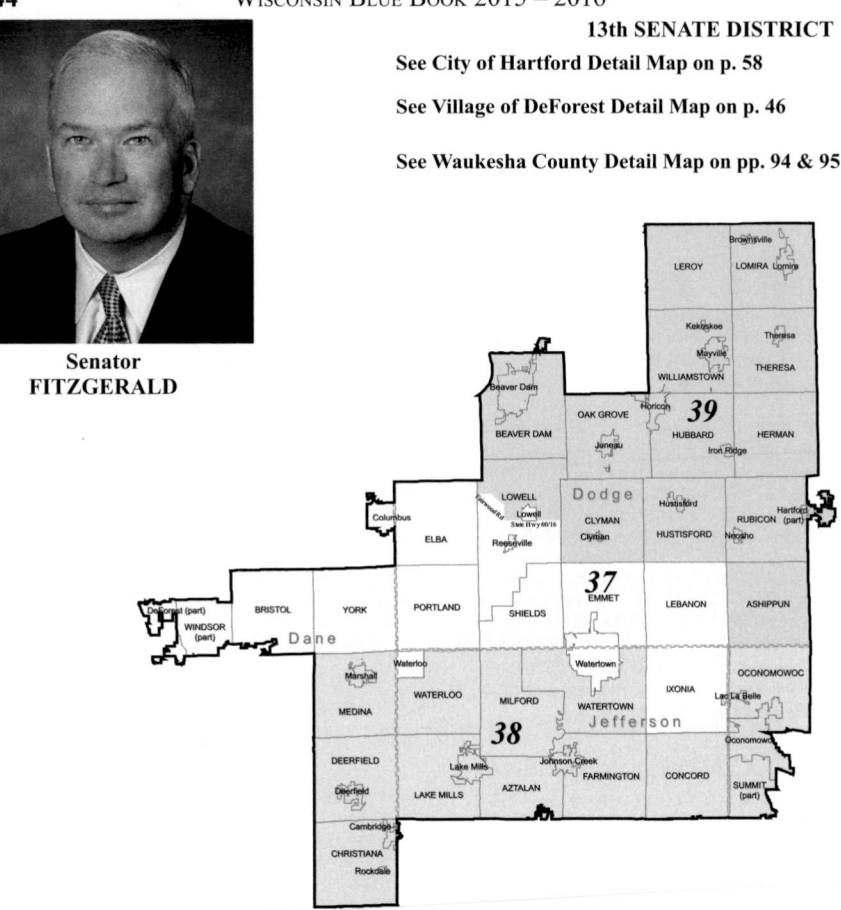

Scott L. Fitzgerald (Rep.), 13th Senate District

Born Chicago, IL, November 16, 1963; married; 3 children. Graduate Hustisford H.S. 1981; B.S. in journalism UW-Oshkosh 1985; U.S. Army Armor Officer Basic Course 1985; U.S. Army Command and General Staff College. Former associate newspaper publisher; U.S. Army Reserve Lt. Colonel (ret.). Member: Dodge Co. Republican Party (chm. 1992-94); Juneau Lions Club; Reserve Officers Assn.; Knights of Columbus.

Elected to Senate 1994; reelected since 1998. Majority Leader 2015, 2013, 2011 (through 7/24/12); Minority Leader 2011 (eff. 7/24/12), 2009, 2007; Majority Leader 9/17/04 to 11/10/04. Biennial committee assignments: **2015** — Senate Org. (chp. since 2011, mbr. since 2007); Jt. Com. on Employment Relations (since 2007); Jt. Com. on Legis. Org. (since 2007); Jt. Legislative Council (since 2005). **2005** — Jt. Com. on Finance (co-chp., mbr. since 2003); Jt. Legis. Audit. **2003** — Jt. Com. for Review of Criminal Penalties (co-chp.); Education, Ethics and Elections; Homeland Security, Veterans and Military Affairs and Government Reform; Judiciary, Corrections and Privacy; Claims Bd. (eff. 12/5/03). **2001** — Health, Utilities, Veterans and Military Affairs; Judiciary, Consumer Affairs, and Campaign Finance Reform; Privacy, Electronic Commerce and Financial Institutions (also 1999); Wis. Housing and Economic Development Authority. **1999** — Economic Development, Housing and Government Operations (member to 2/24/99, also 1997); Rural Economic Development Bd. (also 1997). **1997** — State Government Operations and Corrections (chp., eff. 4/21/98); Education (eff. 1/7/98); Health, Human Services, Aging, Corrections, Veterans and Military Affairs (1/15/97 to 4/20/98); Government Effectiveness (eff. 4/21/98, also 1995); Human Resources, Labor, Tourism, Veterans and Military Affairs (eff. 4/21/98); Jt. Com. on Information Policy (eff. 4/21/98, also 1995); Legis. Coun. Coms. on Local Government Spending (vice chp.), on the School Calendar. **1995** — Business, Economic Development and Urban Affairs (member to 6/96); Agriculture, Transportation, Utilities and Financial Institutions; Legis. Coun. Coms. on Americans with Disabilities Act (co-chp.), on Recodification of Fish and Game Laws.

Telephone: Office: (608) 266-5660.

E-mail: Sen.Fitzgerald@legis.wisconsin.gov

Voting address: Juneau 53039.

Mailing address: Office: Room 211 South, State Capitol, P.O. Box 7882, Madison 53707-7882.

Representative
JAGLER

Representative
KLEEFISCH

Representative
BORN

John Jagler (Rep.), 37th Assembly District

Born Louisville, KY, November 4, 1969; married; 3 children. Graduate Oak Creek H.S. 1987; graduate Trans-American School of Broadcasting (Madison) 1989; attended UW-Parkside 1987-88. Owner, communications consulting company. Former radio morning show host, news anchor; communications director, assembly speaker Jeff Fitzgerald. Member: Down Syndrome Association of Wisconsin; Wisconsin Upside Down; Honorable Order of Kentucky Colonels; Watertown Elks Club. Former member: RTNDA – Radio TV News Directors Assn.; Milwaukee Press Club.

Elected to Assembly 2012; reelected 2014. Biennial committee assignments: **2015** — Housing and Real Estate (chp., mbr. 2013); Mental Health Reform (vice chp.); Constitution and Ethics (also 2013); Education (vice chp. 2013); Insurance (also 2013); Rules; State Affairs and Government Operations. **2013** — Consumer Protection; Urban Education.

Telephone: Office: (608) 266-9650; (888) 534-0037 (toll free).

E-mail: Rep.Jagler@legis.wisconsin.gov

Voting address: Watertown 53094.

Mailing address: Office: Room 316 North, State Capitol, P.O. Box 8952, Madison 53708.

Joel Kleefisch (Rep.), 38th Assembly District

Born Waukesha, June 8, 1971; married; 2 children. Graduate Waukesha North H.S. 1989; B.A. Pepperdine U. 1993. Former investigative television news reporter for WISN-TV; legislative policy advisor and constituent director. Member: Watertown Elks Club; Watertown Moose Club; Stone Bank Lions Club; Ducks Unlimited; National Wild Turkey Federation; National Rifle Assn.; Wings Over Wisconsin; Lakewatch Volunteer Organization (founder).

Elected to Assembly since 2004. Minority Caucus Vice Chairperson 2009. Biennial committee assignments: **2015** — Criminal Justice and Public Safety (chp.); Corrections (also 2013); Family Law; Natural Resources and Sporting Heritage (vice chp. 2013); State Affairs and Government Operations; Tourism (also 2013). **2013** — Criminal Justice (chp., also 2007, mbr. 2009); Labor; State Affairs (vice chp. 2007, mbr. 2005). **2011** — Jt. Review Com. on Criminal Penalties (co-chp.); Natural Resources; Jt. Com. on Finance. **2009** — Consumer Protection; Rules; State Affairs and Homeland Security. **2007** — Children and Family Law; Colleges and Universities. **2005** — Financial Institutions; Judiciary; State-Federal Relations.

Telephone: Office: (608) 266-8551; (888) 534-0038 (toll free).

E-mail: Rep.Kleefisch@legis.wisconsin.gov

Voting address: Oconomowoc 53066.

Mailing address: Office: Room 216 North, State Capitol, P.O. Box 8952, Madison 53708; District: P.O. Box 273, Okauchee 53069.

Mark L. Born (Rep.), 39th Assembly District

Born Beaver Dam, April 14, 1976; married; 1 child. Graduate Beaver Dam H.S. 1994; B.A. political science and history, Gustavus Adolphus College (St. Peter, MN) 1998. Full-time legislator. Former corrections supervisor, Dodge Co. Sheriff Dept. Member: Downtown Beaver Dam, Inc.; Friends of Horicon Marsh; Beaver Dam Area Arts Assn.; Dodge Co. Historical Society (vice pres.); Leadership Beaver Dam Steering Com.; Beaver Dam Lake Improvement Assn. (fmr. vice pres.); Republican Party of Dodge Co. (fmr. chm.); Beaver Dam Elks Lodge 1540; St. John's Lutheran Church, Beaver Dam. Beaver Dam Fire and Police Commission 1993-95; Beaver Dam City Council 1995-99.

Elected to Assembly 2012; reelected 2014. Biennial committee assignments: **2015** — Public Benefit Reform (chp.); Criminal Justice and Public Safety; Financial Institutions (also 2013); Insurance (also 2013); Natural Resources and Sporting Heritage (also 2013); Rules; Tourism (also 2013); Building Commission. **2013** — State and Local Finance (vice chp.); Workforce Development.

Telephone: Office: (608) 266-2540; District: (920) 887-2202.

E-mail: Rep.Born@legis.wisconsin.gov

Voting address: 121 Franklin Street, Beaver Dam 53916.

Mailing address: Office: Room 312 North, State Capitol, P.O. Box 8952, Madison 53708.

14th SENATE DISTRICT

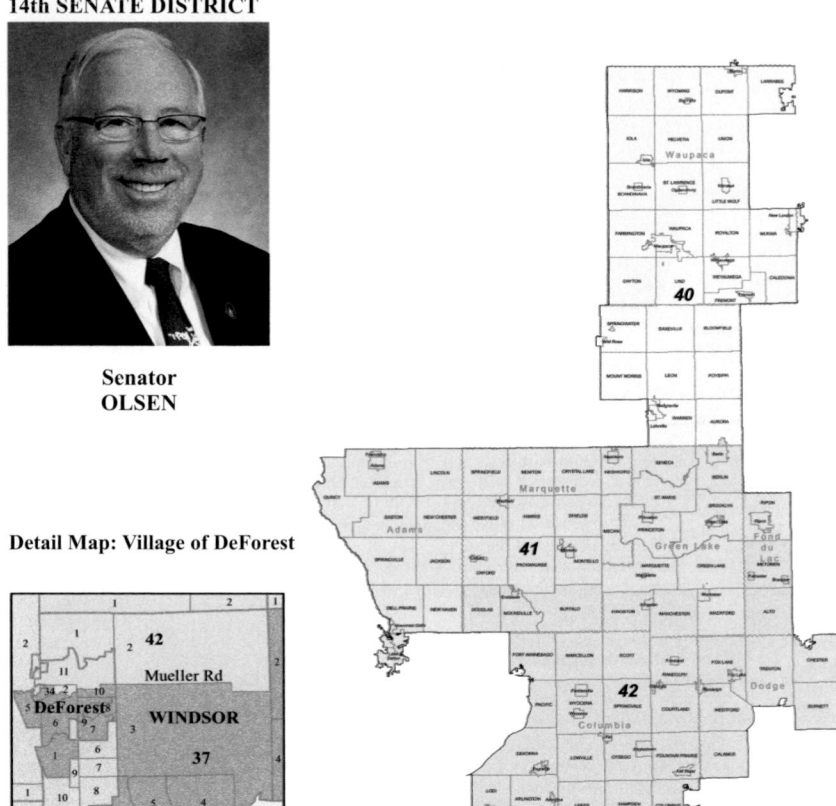

**Senator
OLSEN**

Detail Map: Village of DeForest

Luther S. Olsen (Rep.), 14th Senate District

Born Berlin, February 26, 1951; married. Graduate Berlin H.S. 1969; B.S. UW-Madison 1973; Wis. Rural Leadership Program Group IV 1990-92. Partner in farm supply dealerships. Member: Green Lake Co. Republican Party; Waushara Co. Republican Party; Education Commission of the States (bd. of dir.); NCSL Education Committee Co-Chair 2012-14. Former member: Waushara Co. Fair Bd. (dir.); Family Health/La Clinica director (1995-99); Berlin Area School Board 1976-97 (pres. 1986-95).

Elected to Assembly 1994-2002; elected to Senate 2004; reelected since 2008. Biennial Senate committee assignments: **2015** — Education (chp. since 2011, also 2005, mbr. 2009, 2007); Jt. Com. on Finance (vice chp. since 2011, mbr. since 2005); Insurance, Housing, and Trade (vice chp.); Natural Resources and Energy; Educ. Communications Bd. (since 2005); State Capitol and Executive Residence Bd. (since 2009); University of Wisconsin Hospitals and Clinics Authority Bd. (exec. bd., also 2013, mbr. since 2011, also 2007, 2005). **2013** — Insurance and Housing (also 2011). **2011** — Leg. Coun. Spec. Coms. on Health Care Access (chp.), on Review of Spousal Maintenance Awards in Divorce. **2009** — Environment. **2007** — Jt. Survey Com. on Retirement Systems; Child Abuse and Neglect Prevention Bd. (also 2005). **2005** — Agriculture and Insurance; Legis. Coun. Spec. Com. on School Aid Formula (chp.). Assembly committee assignments: **2003** — Education (chp. since 1997, mbr. 1995); Education Reform (since 1999, vice chp. 2001); Health (since 1997); Housing; Rural Affairs; Workforce Development. **2001** — Ways and Means; Migrant Labor Council (since 1995). **1999** — Tourism and Recreation; Legis. Coun. Coms. on Dental Care Access, on Navigable Waters Recodification. **1997** — Colleges and Universities; State-Federal Relations; Gov.'s Council on Model Academic Standards; Legis. Coun. Coms. on Services for Visually Handicapped Students (chp.), on Children at Risk Program, on the School Calendar. **1995** — Government Operations (vice chp.); Jt. Com. for Review of Administrative Rules; Agriculture; Mandates; State Supported Programs Study and Adv. Com.; Legis. Coun. Coms. on Public Libraries, on Public School Open Enrollment, on the School Aid Formula.

Telephone: Office: (608) 266-0751; (800) 991-5541 (toll free).

E-mail: Sen.Olsen@legis.wisconsin.gov

Voting address: Ripon 54971.

Mailing address: Room 313 South, State Capitol, P.O. Box 7882, Madison 53707-7882.

| Representative | Representative | Representative |
| PETERSEN | BALLWEG | RIPP |

Kevin David Petersen (Rep.), 40th Assembly District

Born Waupaca, December 14, 1964; married; 2 children. Graduate Waupaca H.S. 1983; B.S.M.E. U. of New Mexico 1989. Co-owner family-run electronics corporation. Served in U.S. Navy sub service 1983-94, Persian Gulf War veteran. Member U.S. Naval Reserve 1994-2008. Member: Waupaca Co. Republican Party; Waushara Co. Republican Party; VFW Post 1037 (life member); Amvets Post 1887 (life member); American Legion Post 161; United States Submarine Veterans, Inc.; Waupaca Area Chamber of Commerce; New London Chamber of Commerce; National Rifle Association. Town of Dayton Supervisor 2001-07.

Elected to Assembly 2006; reelected since 2008. Biennial committee assignments: **2015** — Insurance (chp. since 2011); Jt. Com. on Information Policy and Technology (co-chp., mbr. 2013); Energy and Utilities (vice chp. 2007, mbr. since 2009); Financial Institutions; Health (since 2011); Ways and Means (also 2011). **2013** — Jobs, Economy and Mining; State and Federal Relations. **2011** — Jt. Com. on Audit. **2009** — Aging and Long-Term Care (also 2007); Veterans and Military Affairs (also 2007). **2007** — Homeland Security and State Preparedness.

Telephone: Office: (608) 266-3794; (888) 947-0040 (toll free).

E-mail: Rep.Petersen@legis.wisconsin.gov

Voting address: Waupaca 54981.

Mailing address: Office: Room 105 West, State Capitol, P.O. Box 8953, Madison 53708.

Joan Ballweg (Rep.), 41st Assembly District

Born Milwaukee, March 16, 1952; married; 3 children, 1 grandson. Graduate Nathan Hale H.S. (West Allis) 1970; attended UW-Waukesha; B.A. Elementary Education UW-Stevens Point 1974. Co-owner of farm equipment business. Former 1st grade teacher. Member: Markesan Chamber of Commerce (former treas.); Waupun Chamber of Commerce; Green Lake County Farm Bureau; Waupun Memorial Hospital (bd. of dir., fmr. chp.); Agnesian HealthCare Enterprises, LLC management com. (fmr. secy.); volunteer, Markesan District Schools; Markesan PTA (fmr. pres.); Markesan AFS Chapter (hosting coordinator, pres., fmr. host family, liaison). Former member: FEMA V Regional Advisory Council. Recipient: Markesan District Education Assn. *Friend of Education Award* 1990. Markesan City Council 1987-91; Mayor of Markesan 1991-97.

Elected to Assembly since 2004. Majority Caucus Chairperson 2013, 2011. Biennial committee assignments: **2015** — Jt. Com. for Review of Admin. Rules (co-chp.); Jt. Legis. Council (co-chp. since 2011); Colleges and Universities (vice chp. 2007, 2005, mbr. since 2009); Financial Institutions; Mental Health Reform; Rules (since 2011); Tourism (also 2013); Leg. Coun. Steering Com. Symposia Series on Supporting Healthy Early Brain Development (chp.). **2013** — Assembly Org. (also 2011); Leg. Coun. Spec. Com. on 911 Communications (chp.). **2011** — Labor and Workforce Development (chp.); Homeland Security and State Affairs; Leg. Coun. Spec. Coms. on Review of Higher Education Financial Aid Programs (chp.), on Review of Emergency Detention and Admission of Minors Under Chapter 51. **2009** — Renewable Energy and Rural Affairs; State Affairs and Homeland Security; Leg. Coun. Spec. Com. on Emergency Management and Continuity of Government (vice chp.). **2007** — Homeland Security and State Preparedness (chp.); Insurance (also 2005); Public Health; Small Business (also 2005); Leg. Coun. Spec. Com. on Disaster Preparedness Planning (chp.). **2005** — Family Law; Rural Affairs and Renewable Energy.

Telephone: Office: (608) 266-8077; (888) 534-0041 (toll free); District: (920) 398-3708.

E-mail: Rep.Ballweg@legis.wisconsin.gov

Voting address: 170 West Summit Street, Markesan 53946.

Mailing address: Office: Room 210 North, State Capitol, P.O. Box 8952, Madison 53708.

Keith Ripp (Rep.), 42nd Assembly District

Born Madison, November 13, 1961; married; 3 children. Graduate Lodi H.S. 1980; UW-Madison farm and industry short course 1981. Farmer and small business owner. Member: Wis. Soybean Marketing Bd. (fmr. pres., vice pres.); Badger Agvest LLC (fmr. pres. and co-founder); Wis. Corn Growers Assn. (fmr. pres., vice pres.); Wis. Farm Bureau; Lodi FFA Alumni (fmr. pres., co-founder); Columbia and Dane Co. Republican Party; Yellow Thunder Snowmobile Club; Ducks Unlimited. Town of Dane Supervisor 2006-08.

Elected to Assembly 2008; reelected since 2010. Biennial committee assignments: **2015** — Transportation (chp., also 2013, mbr. since 2009); Agriculture (since 2011); Natural Resources and Sporting Heritage; State Affairs and Government Operations; Workforce Development. **2013** — Rural Affairs; Small Business Development; State Affairs; Ways and Means. **2011** — Consumer Protection and Personal Privacy (chp.); Rural Economic Development and Rural Affairs; State Fair Park Bd. **2009** — Criminal Justice; Renewable Energy and Rural Affairs.

Telephone: Office: (608) 266-3404.

Voting address: Lodi 53555.

Mailing address: Office: Room 223 North, State Capitol, P.O. Box 8953, Madison 53708.

15th SENATE DISTRICT

Detail Map: City of Janesville

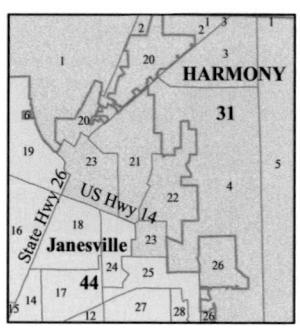

**Senator
RINGHAND**

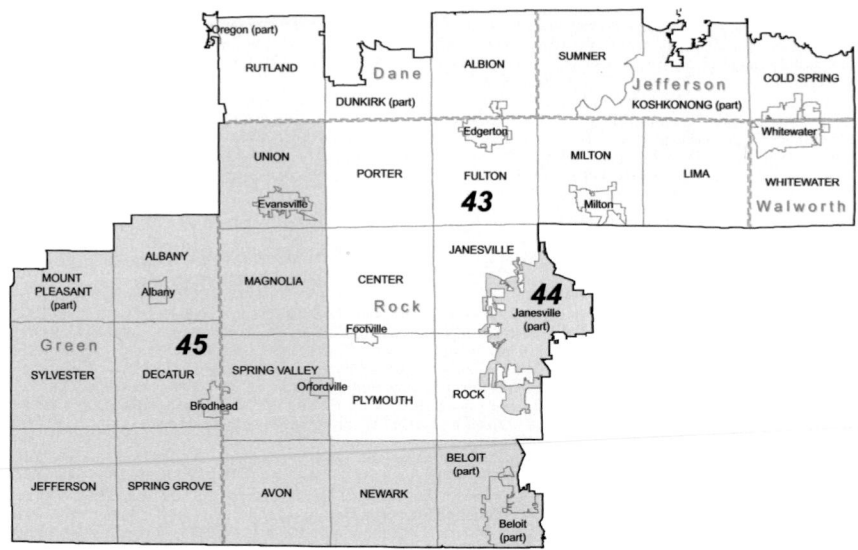

Janis Ringhand (Dem.), 15th Senate District

Born Madison, February 13, 1950; married; 2 children, 5 grandchildren, 1 great-grandchild. Graduate Evansville H.S. 1968; Associate Degree Madison Area Tech. Coll. 1985. Full-time legislator. Former accountant for small businesses, executive director of nonprofit. Member: Rock Co. Literacy Connection; Evansville Chamber of Commerce; VFW Auxiliary Post 6905 (pres.); Evansville Energy Independence Team. Former member: Stoughton Hospital Bd. (chp.); Creekside Place, Inc. (bd. of dir.); Evansville Community Partnership (secy.). Evansville City Council 1998-2002, 2008-10. Mayor of Evansville 2002-06.

Elected to Assembly 2010-12; elected to Senate 2014. Minority Caucus Secretary 2013. Biennial Senate committee assignments: **2015** — Economic Development and Commerce; Revenue, Financial Institutions and Rural Issues; Building Commission. Assembly committee assignments: **2013** — Government Operations and State Licensing; Small Business Development; Urban and Local Affairs (also 2011); Veterans; Workforce Development. **2011** — Rural Economic Development and Rural Affairs; Veterans and Military Affairs.

Telephone: Office: (608) 266-2253; District: (608) 882-5879.

E-mail: Sen.Ringhand@legis.wisconsin.gov

Voting address: 412 Fowler Circle, Evansville 53536.

Mailing address: Office: Room 22 South, State Capitol, P.O. Box 7882, Madison 53707-7882.

Representative	Representative	Representative
JORGENSEN	KOLSTE	SPREITZER

Andy Jorgensen (Dem.), 43rd Assembly District

Born Berlin, September 10, 1967; married; 3 children. Graduate Omro H.S. 1986; Brown Institute (MN) 1987. Former morning radio personality, assembly line operator, UAW shop steward, General Motors Janesville, worked on family dairy farm. Bd. member: Respite Care Assn. of Wis.; Jefferson Co. Local Emergency Planning Council. Member: Rock Co. Farm Bureau; Trinity Lutheran Church, Fort Atkinson.

Elected to Assembly 2006; reelected since 2008. Minority Caucus Chairperson 2015, 2013. Biennial committee assignments: **2015** — Agriculture (since 2007); Assembly Organization (also 2013); Colleges and Universities; Public Benefit Reform; Rules (also 2013); Small Business Development (also 2013). **2013** — International Trade and Commerce; Rural Affairs (also 2007). **2011** — Rural Economic Development and Rural Affairs; Transportation; Jt. Legis. Audit (vice chp. 2009). **2009** — Renewable Energy and Rural Affairs (chp.); Rural Economic Development (vice chp.); Labor. **2007** — Biofuels and Sustainable Energy; Consumer Protection and Personal Privacy.

Telephone: Office: (608) 266-3790; (888) 534-0043 (toll free).

E-mail: Rep.Jorgensen@legis.wisconsin.gov

Voting address: 10 Division Street, Milton 53563.

Mailing address: Office: Room 113 North, State Capitol, P.O. Box 8952, Madison 53708.

Debra Kolste (Dem.), 44th Assembly District

Born O'Neill, NE, June 20, 1953; married; 3 children. Graduate Kimball Co. H.S. (Kimball, NE) 1971; B.S. medical technology U. of Nebraska 1975. Full-time legislator. Former medical technologist. Volunteer, Health Net of Rock Co. Member: League of Women Voters; Friends of Rotary Gardens. Former member: Mercy Health Systems Volunteers (pres.); Rock Futbol Soccer League (founding bd. mbr.); PTO Bd.; PTA Bd. Janesville School Board 2000-09.

Elected to Assembly 2012; reelected 2014. Biennial committee assignments: **2015** — Health (also 2013); Public Benefit Reform; Transportation (also 2013); Workforce Development (also 2013). **2013** — Small Business Development.

Telephone: Office: (608) 266-7503; (888) 947-0044 (toll free); District: (608) 921-0200.

E-mail: Rep.Kolste@legis.wisconsin.gov

Voting address: Janesville 53546.

Mailing address: Office: Room 8 North, State Capitol, P.O. Box 8952, Madison 53708.

Mark Spreitzer (Dem.), 45th Assembly District

Born Evanston, Ill., December 16, 1986; single. Graduate Northside College Preparatory H.S. (Chicago, Ill.) 2005; B.A. political science Beloit College 2009. Full-time legislator. Former assistant director of alumni and parent relations and annual support, Beloit College. Member: United Church of Beloit (deacon's bd.); Welty Environmental Center; Wis. League of Conservation Voters; Fair Wisconsin; Democratic Party of Rock Co.; Greater Beloit Chamber of Commerce Rising Professionals; Youth2Youth 4 Change Coalition. Former member: Community Action, Inc. of Rock and Walworth Cos. (bd. mbr.); Lifecourse Initiative for Healthy Families. City of Beloit Appointment Review Com. (chp.). Beloit City Council 2011-15, president 2014-15.

Elected to Assembly 2014. Biennial committee assignments: **2015** — Jobs and the Economy; Mining and Rural Development; Natural Resources and Sporting Heritage; Public Benefit Reform; Workforce Development.

Telephone: Office: (608) 266-1192; (888) 534-0080.

E-mail: Rep.Spreitzer@legis.wisconsin.gov

Voting address: 1718 Henderson Avenue, Beloit 53511.

Mailing address: Office: Room 420 North, State Capitol, P.O. Box 8953, Madison 53708.

16th SENATE DISTRICT

**Senator
MILLER**

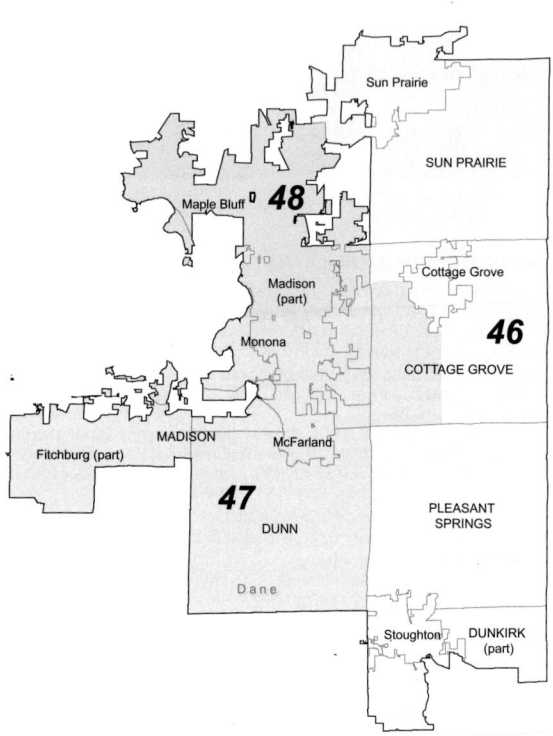

See Madison Area Detail Map on pp. 90 & 91

Mark Miller (Dem.), 16th Senate District

Born Boston, MA, February 1, 1943. Graduate Middleton H.S.; B.S. UW-Madison; Bowhay Institute for Legislative Leadership Development (BUILLD) 1999; Flemming Fellows Leadership Institute 2002. Former military pilot; Wis. Air National Guard 1966-95 (ret. Lt. Colonel); former real estate property manager. Dane County Bd. of Health 1998-2004; Bd. of Health for Madison and Dane Co. 2004-07. Dane Co. Board of Supervisors 1996-2000.

Elected to Assembly 1998-2002; elected to Senate 2004; reelected since 2008. Minority Leader 2011 (through 7/17/12); Majority Leader 2011 (eff. 7/17/12); Majority Caucus Chairperson 2007. Biennial Senate committee assignments: **2015** — Elections and Local Government; Natural Resources and Energy; Jt. Com. for Review of Administrative Rules (also 2005); Jt. Legislative Council (since 2005); Midwest Interstate Passenger Rail Comn. (also 2013). **2013** — Elections and Urban Affairs; Energy, Consumer Protection, and Government Reform; Natural Resources. **2011** — Senate Org.; Jt. Com. on Employment Relations; Jt. Com. on Legislative Organization. **2009** — Environment (chp.); Jt. Com. on Finance (co-chp. since 11/5/07, mbr. 2007). **2007** — Environment and Natural Resources (chp.). **2005** — Agriculture and Insurance; Campaign Finance Reform and Ethics; Child Abuse and Neglect Prevention Bd. (also 2003). Assembly committee assignments: **2003** — Children and Families (since 1999); Health (since 1999); Natural Resources (also 2001); Veterans and Military Affairs; Environmental Education Bd. (also 2001). **2001** — Environment. **1999** — Campaigns and Elections; Consumer Affairs; Public Health; Law Revision Com.

Telephone: Office: (608) 266-9170; District: (608) 221-2701.

E-mail: Sen.Miller@legis.wisconsin.gov

Voting address: Monona 53716.

Mailing address: Office: Room 7 South, State Capitol, P.O. Box 7882, Madison 53707-7882.

Representative   **Representative**   **Representative**
HEBL   **KAHL**   **SARGENT**

Gary Alan Hebl (Dem.), 46th Assembly District

Born Madison, May 15, 1951; married; 3 children, 1 grandson. Graduate Sun Prairie H.S. 1969; B.A. Political Science UW-Madison 1973; Gonzaga U. Law School 1976. Bowhay Institute 2008. Attorney and owner of a title insurance company. Sacred Hearts 8th grade basketball coach, 1980-99. Member: Wis. League of Conservation Voters; Dane Co. Bar Assn.; Wis. Bar Assn.; Sun Prairie Optimist Club (fmr. pres.); Sun Prairie Chamber of Commerce (fmr. pres.); U.W. Flying Club (bd. of dir.); AOPA; EAA Young Eagles Program; KC (4th deg. mbr.); Sun Prairie Cable Access Bd.; YMCA (fmr. pres.); Sun Prairie Public Library Bd. (fmr. pres.); Sacred Heart Parish Council (fmr. trustee); Sun Prairie Quarterback Club (fmr. pres.). Recipient: State Bar of Wis. *Scales of Justice Award* 2009-10; Wis. Dietetic Assn. *Nutrition Champion Award* 2010; Pharmacy Society of Wis. *Legislator of the Year* 2010, 2009; Sun Prairie *Star* poll *Best Attorney in Sun Prairie* 2008-14; *James J. Reininger Award* for lifetime achievement 2008; Wis. Assn. of PEG Channels *Friend of Access Award* 2010, 2007; Wis. League of Conservation Voters *Conservation Champion* 2013-14, 2011-12, 2009-10, 2005-06; Sun Prairie Exchange Club *Book of Golden Deeds Award* 2003; Chamber of Commerce *Judith Krivsky Business Person of the Year Award* 2002; Sun Prairie Business and Education Partnership *Outstanding Small Business of the Year* 2001; Sun Prairie H.S. Wall of Success, 2015.

Elected to Assembly since 2004. Biennial committee assignments: **2015** — Environment and Forestry; Family Law (also 2013); Judiciary (also 2013); Rules; Jt. Com. for Review of Administrative Rules (since 2009). **2013** — Natural Resources and Sporting Heritage; Tourism. **2011** — Consumer Protection and Personal Privacy; Criminal Justice and Corrections (eff. 5/11/11); Judiciary and Ethics (ranking mbr., chp. 2009); Tourism, Recreation and State Properties (eff. 2/7/12); Leg. Coun. Spec. Com. on Judicial Discipline and Recusal (co-chp.). **2009** — Ways and Means (chp. eff. 9/18/09, vice chp., mbr. since 2005); Insurance; Natural Resources (since 2005). **2007** — Housing; Small Business (also 2005). **2005** — Property Rights and Land Management.

Telephone: Office: (608) 266-7678.
E-mail: Rep.Hebl@legis.wisconsin.gov
Voting address: Sun Prairie 53590.
Mailing address: Office: Room 120 North, State Capitol, P.O. Box 8952, Madison 53708.

Robb Kahl (Dem.), 47th Assembly District

Born Menomonee Falls, January 5, 1972; married; 4 children. Graduate L.P. Goodrich H.S. (Fond du Lac) 1990; B.A. *cum laude* Ripon College 1994; J.D. *cum laude* U. of Wisconsin Law School 1997; attended Syracuse College of Law 1994-95. Attorney, small business owner. Member: State Bar of Wis.; Democratic Party of Wis.; Monona Chamber of Commerce; Fitchburg Chamber of Commerce; McFarland Chamber of Commerce; Monona Grove Businessmen's Assn.; International Union of Operating Engineers; Ripon College Bd. of Trustees. Law clerk, Wis. court of appeals 1997-98; Wis. Transportation Finance and Policy Commission 2011-13; Monona Community Development Authority (chair) 2011-13; Monona City Council 2001-03; Mayor of Monona 2003-11.

Elected to Assembly 2012; reelected 2014. Biennial committee assignments: **2015** — Children and Families (also 2013 eff. 5/10/13); Energy and Utilities (also 2013); Insurance (also 2013); State Affairs and Government Operations; Transportation; Leg. Council Steering Com. Symposia Series on Personal Property Tax. **2013** — Aging and Long Term Care; State Affairs; Jt. Com. for Review of Administrative Rules.

Telephone: Office: (608) 266-8570; District: (608) 224-0342.
Voting address: Monona 53716.
Mailing address: Office: Room 322 West, State Capitol, P.O. Box 8952, Madison 53708.

Melissa Sargent (Dem.), 48th Assembly District

Born Madison, March 28, 1969; married; 4 sons. Graduate Madison East H.S. 1987; B.A. UW-Madison 1991. Graduate Bowhay Inst. for Legislative Development; Emerging Leader program, U. of Virginia, 2014. Small business owner. Member: Women in Government (state dir.); WiLL/WAND (state dir.); Emerge Wis. (bd. of dir.); Dane Co. Democratic Party; Wis. League of Conservation Voters; Sierra Club; Democratic Party; Wis. Business Alliance; Emerge Wis.; NARAL Pro-Choice Wis.; Make Room for Youth; Friends of Cherokee Marsh. Former member: Midwest Shiba Inu Dog Rescue (pres.); Gompers PTO (pres.). Recipient: National Federation of Women Legislators *Woman of Excellence*; Arc Dane Co. *Elected Official of the Year* 2014; Citizen Action *Activist Achievement Award* 2014; *Eleanor Roosevelt Award* nominee 2013; Wis. League of Conservation Voters *Conservation Champion* 2014. Dane Co. Bd. of Supervisors 2010-14.

Elected to Assembly 2012; reelected 2014. Biennial committee assignments: **2015** — Aging and Long Term Care (also 2013); Energy and Utilities; Financial Institutions (also 2013); Mental Health Reform; Small Business Development (also 2013); Jt. Legis. Audit Com. (also 2013). **2013** — International Trade and Commerce.

Telephone: Office: (608) 266-0960.
E-mail: Rep.Sargent@legis.wisconsin.gov
Voting address: 1638 Mayfield Lane, Madison 53704.
Mailing address: Office: Room 321 West, State Capitol, P.O. Box 8953, Madison 53708.

17th SENATE DISTRICT

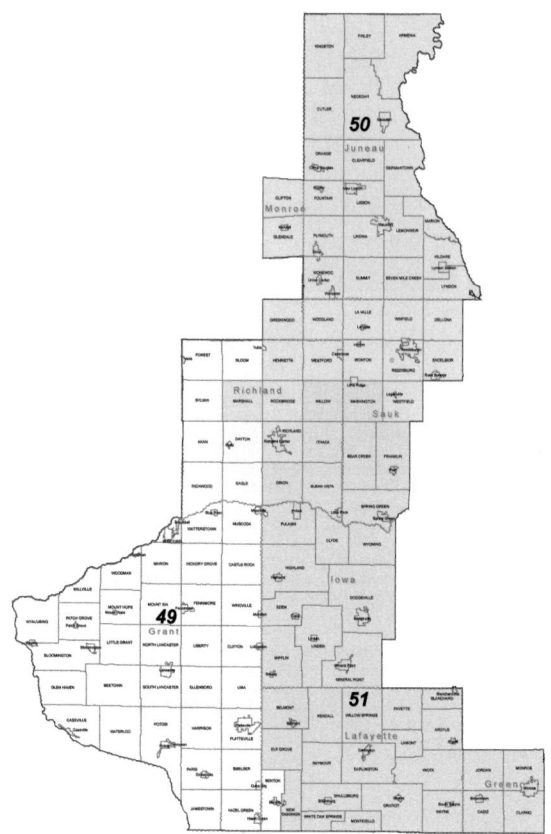

Senator
MARKLEIN

Howard Marklein (Rep.), 17th Senate District

Born Madison, October 3, 1954; married; 2 children, 3 stepchildren, 3 grandchildren. Graduate River Valley H.S. (Spring Green) 1972; B.A. UW-Whitewater 1976. Certified public accountant; certified fraud examiner. Member: St. John's Catholic Church, Spring Green (fin. com. mbr.); Taliesin Preservation Inc. Bd. of Trustees (treas.); UW-Whitewater Natl. Alumni Assn. (pres.). Former member: UW-Whitewater Foundation (bd. of dir. pres.); Fort Health Care Bd. of Dir. (chp., treas.); Fort Atkinson Rotary Club (pres.); Fort Atkinson Chamber of Commerce (pres.); Whitewater Chamber of Commerce (pres.); Dodgeville Chamber of Commerce (vice pres.). Recipient: WMC *Working for Wisconsin Award* 2014, 2012; MMAC *Champion of Commerce Award* 2014, 2012; Wisconsin Pork Association *Distinguished Service Award* 2013; Wisconsin Newspaper Association *Badger Award* 2013; Wisconsin Aquaculture Association *Legislator of the Year* 2013; Dairy Business Association *Legislative Excellence Award* 2012.

Elected to Assembly 2010, 2012; elected to Senate 2014. Biennial Senate committee assignments: **2015** — Revenue, Financial Institutions and Rural Issues (chp.); Transportation and Veterans Affairs (vice chp.); Labor and Government Reform; Jt. Com. on Finance; Jt. Survey Com. on Retirement Systems; Council on Highway Safety; Governor's Small Business Regulatory Review Bd. (chp.); Transportation Projects Comn.; WHEDA Bd. Assembly committee assignments: **2013** — Ways and Means (chp.); Agriculture (also 2011); Education (vice chp. 2011); Financial Institutions (also 2011); Rural Affairs; Jt. Legis. Audit Com.; Small Business Regulatory Review Bd. (chp.). **2011** — UW Hospitals and Clinics Authority.

Telephone: Office: (608) 266-0703; District: (608) 588-5632.

E-mail: Sen.Marklein@legis.wisconsin.gov

Voting address: S11665 Soeldner Road, Spring Green 53588.

Mailing address: Office: Room 8 South, State Capitol, P.O. Box 7882, Madison 53707-7882.

**Representative
TRANEL**

**Representative
E. BROOKS**

**Representative
NOVAK**

Travis Tranel (Rep.), 49th Assembly District

Born Dubuque, IA, September 12, 1985; married; 4 children. Graduate Wahlert Catholic H.S. (Dubuque, IA) 2004; B.A. Loras College (Dubuque, IA) 2007. Dairy farmer, small business owner. Member: St. Joseph Sinsinawa Parish Council 2010-12 (pres., 2011-12); Wis. Farm Bureau; Knights of Columbus; National Rifle Association; Ducks Unlimited; Platteville Regional Chamber of Commerce; Grant Co. Republican Party. Recipient: DBA *Legislative Excellence Award* 2014, 2012; WMC *Working for Wisconsin Award* 2014, 2012; MMAC *Champion of Commerce Award* 2014, 2012; WAFP *Friends of Family Medicine* 2014.

Elected to Assembly 2010; reelected since 2012. Biennial committee assignments: **2015** — Tourism (chp.); Agriculture (also 2013, vice chp. 2011); Colleges and Universities; Energy and Utilities; Insurance (since 2011); Small Business Development. **2013** — State and Federal Relations (chp.); Campaigns and Elections; Family Law. **2011** — Financial Institutions.

Telephone: Office: (608) 266-1170; (888) 872-0049 (toll free).

E-mail: Rep.Tranel@legis.wisconsin.gov

Voting address: Cuba City 53807.

Mailing address: Office: Room 308 North, State Capitol, P.O. Box 8953, Madison 53708.

Ed Brooks (Rep.), 50th Assembly District

Born Baraboo, July 1, 1942; married; 3 children, 5 grandchildren. Graduate Webb H.S. (Reedsburg) 1960; B.S. agricultural economics UW-Madison 1965. Farmer. Former co. sup. f/USDA, FmHA, loan officer f/PCA Madison. Served in U.S. Army Reserve 1965-71. Member: Wis. Fed. of Co-ops (fmr. chairman); Wis. Farm Bureau; American Legion Post 350. Former member: C.A.L.S. B.O.V.; Endeavor 4-H Club (leader); St. John Lutheran Church (past pres. church council). Recipient: Dairy Business Assn. *Legislative Excellence Award* 2014; American Conservative Union *Defender of Liberty* 2013-14; Wis. Electric Cooperative's *Enlightened Legislator of the Year Award* 2014; Wis. Academy of Family Physicians *Friend of Family Medicine* 2013-14; Wis. Counties Assn. *Outstanding Legislator Award* 2013-14; *Friend of Cooperatives* 2012; Associated Builders and Contractors *Building Wisconsin Award* 2014; Wis. Town Assn. *Friend of Wisconsin Towns* 2014, 2011; WMC *Working for Wisconsin Award* 2013-14, 2011-12; *Friend of Education* 1998; *Friend of Extension*. Town supervisor 1979-1985; town chairman 1985-present.

Elected to Assembly 2008; reelected since 2010. Biennial committee assignments: **2015** — Urban and Local Affairs (chp. since 2011); Agriculture (since 2009); Corrections (also 2013); Interstate Affairs; Mining and Rural Development. **2013** — Public Safety and Homeland Security (vice chp.); Veterans. **2011** — Criminal Justice and Corrections. **2009** — Corrections and the Courts; Criminal Justice.

Telephone: Office: (608) 266-8531; (877) 947-0050 (toll free); District: (608) 524-2406.

E-mail: Rep.Brooks@legis.wisconsin.gov

Voting address: Reedsburg 53959.

Mailing address: Office: Room 20 North, State Capitol, P.O. Box 8952, Madison 53708.

Todd Novak (Rep.), 51st Assembly District

Born April 23, 1965; 2 children. Graduate Iowa-Grant H.S. 1983; attended Southwest Technical College 1983-85. Former government/associate newspaper editor 1990-2014. Member: Wis. League of Municipalities; NRA; Wis. Farm Bureau. Former member: Iowa Co. Humane Soc. (founding mbr., treas.); Wis. Newspaper Assn.; National Newspaper Assn. Southwest Regional Planning Comn. 2012-present. Mayor of Dodgeville 2012-present.

Elected to Assembly 2014. Biennial committee assignments: **2015** — Agriculture (vice chp.); Criminal Justice and Public Safety; Mental Health Reform; Mining and Rural Development; Urban and Local Affairs; Ways and Means.

Telephone: Office: (608) 266-7502; (888) 534-0051 (toll free); District: (608) 574-0100.

E-mail: Rep.Novak@legis.wisconsin.gov

Voting address: 202 West Division Street, Dodgeville 53533.

Mailing address: Office: Room 304 North, State Capitol, P.O. Box 8953, Madison 53708.

18th SENATE DISTRICT

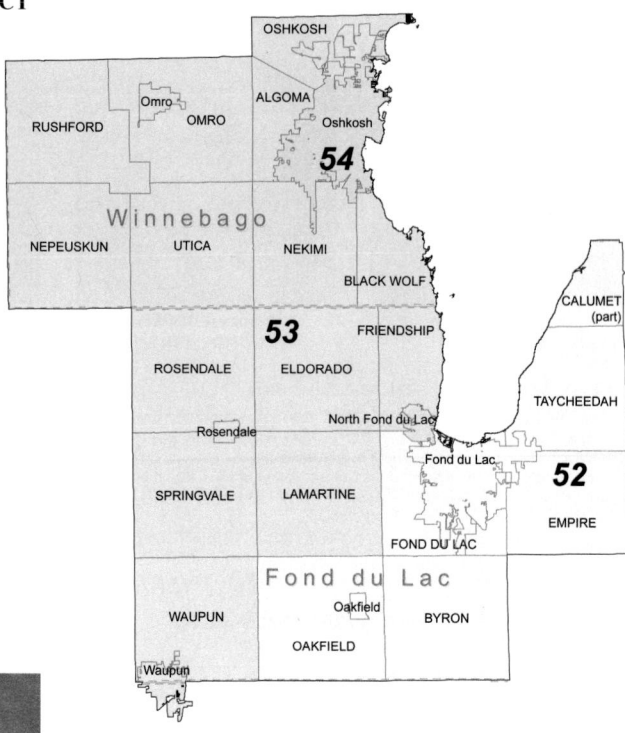

**Senator
GUDEX**

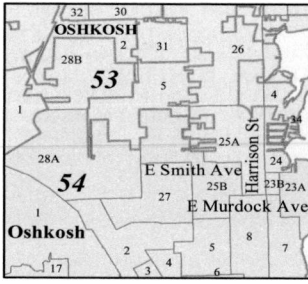

Detail Map: Oshkosh Area

Rick Gudex (Rep.), 18th Senate District

Born Fond du Lac, July 23, 1968; married; 2 children. Graduate St. Mary Springs H.S. (Fond du Lac) 1986. Full-time legislator. Former production manager. Member: Knights of Columbus Council 664; Elks Club BPOE #57; Wis. Small Business Development Center Adv. Bd.; Fond du Lac Co. Farm Bureau; Fond du Lac Co. Republican Party; Winnebago Co. Republican Party. Mayor of Mayville 1998-2000. Fond du Lac City Council 2009-12.

Elected to Senate 2012. President Pro Tempore 2015. Biennial committee assignments: **2015** — Economic Development and Commerce (chp.); Workforce Development, Public Works and Military Affairs (vice chp.); Universities and Technical Colleges (also 2013); Jt. Legislative Council; Wis. Economic Development Corp. Bd. **2013** — Economic Development and Local Government (chp.); Government Operations, Public Works, and Telecommunications (vice chp.); Education; Jt. Com. on Information Policy and Technology.

Telephone: Office: (608) 266-5300; (888) 736-8720 (toll free).

E-mail: Sen.Gudex@legis.wisconsin.gov

Voting address: Fond du Lac 54935.

Mailing address: Office: Room 415 South, State Capitol, P.O. Box 7882, Madison 53707-7882

| Representative | Representative | Representative |
| THIESFELDT | SCHRAA | HINTZ |

Jeremy Thiesfeldt (Rep.), 52nd Assembly District

Born Fond du Lac, November 22, 1966; married; 4 children. Graduate Kettle Moraine Lutheran H.S. (Jackson) 1985; B.S. Elementary education Dr. Martin Luther College 1989, attended U. of Minnesota 1992. Full-time legislator. Former teacher. Member: Fond du Lac Noon Rotary; Fond du Lac County Rep. Party; Redeemer Lutheran Church, Thrivent Financial; National Rifle Association; Fond du Lac Assn. of Commerce; Leadership Fond du Lac; Young Professionals of Fond du Lac; Wis. Farm Bureau. Former member: Camp Croix; Minnesota District Lutheran Teachers' Conf.; Wisconsin Lutheran State Teachers' Conf.; Wisconsin Area Lutheran Educators' Conf. Fond du Lac city council 2005-10.

Elected to Assembly 2010; reelected since 2012. Biennial committee assignments: **2015** — Education (chp., mbr. since 2011); Campaigns and Elections (also 2013); Family Law; Judiciary; Transportation (vice chp. 2013). **2013** — Consumer Protection (chp.); Select Com. on Common Core Standards (chp.); Urban Education (vice chp.); Corrections; Council on Highway Safety. **2011** — Urban and Local Affairs (vice chp.); Children and Families; Criminal Justice and Corrections (eff. 5/23/11).

Telephone: Office: (608) 266-3156; (888) 529-0052 (toll free); District: (920) 933-2086.

E-mail: Rep.Thiesfeldt@legis.wisconsin.gov

Voting address: 604 Sunset Lane, Fond du Lac 54935.

Mailing address: Office: Room 16 West, State Capitol, P.O. Box 8953, Madison 53708.

Michael Schraa (Rep.), 53rd Assembly District

Born Fort Carson, CO, April 17, 1961; married; 3 children. Graduate Oshkosh North H.S. 1979; attended UW-Oshkosh 1980-82. Restaurant owner. Former stock broker/investment advisor. Member: Winnebago Co. Republican Party (ex. bd.); Fond du Lac Co. Republican Party; Southwest Rotary (Oshkosh); Oshkosh Chamber of Commerce; Portico Church (Oshkosh); Wis. Ind. Business; NRA. Former member: Fond du Lac Co. Farm Bureau; NFIB; Oshkosh Jaycees; Big Brothers/Big Sisters; Exchange Club.

Elected to Assembly 2012; reelected 2014. Biennial committee assignments: **2015** — Public Benefit Reform; Jt. Com. on Finance. **2013** — Corrections (vice chp.); Agriculture; Children and Families; Colleges and Universities; Rural Affairs; Small Business Development.

Telephone: Office: (608) 267-7990; District: (920) 267-0217.

Voting address: Oshkosh 54904.

Mailing address: Office: Room 320 East, State Capitol, P.O. Box 8953, Madison 53708; District: P.O. Box 2253, Oshkosh 43903-2253.

Gordon Hintz (Dem.), 54th Assembly District

Born Oshkosh, November 29, 1973; married. Graduate Oshkosh North H.S. 1992; B.A. Hamline U. (St. Paul, Minn.) 1996; M.P.A. UW-Madison 2001. Municipal consultant. Former legislative staff assistant, U.S. Representative Jay Johnson, U.S. Senator Herb Kohl; management and budget analyst, City of Long Beach, CA; instructor, political science dept., UW-Oshkosh. Member: Oshkosh Rotary Club; First Congregational Church; Oshkosh Chamber of Commerce; Winnebago Co. Safe Streets Committee; Winnebago Co. Democratic Party.

Elected to Assembly 2006; reelected since 2008. Biennial committee assignments: **2015** — Jt. Com. on Finance; Building Comn. (since 2011). **2013** — Financial Institutions (ranking min. mbr., mbr. 2011); Urban and Local Affairs (ranking min. mbr., mbr. 2009, 2007); Jobs, Economy and Mining; State and Local Finance; State Capitol and Executive Residence Bd. **2011** — Education; Labor and Workforce Development (eff. 4/26/11). **2009** — Colleges and Universities (since 2007); Consumer Protection (chp.); Workforce Development (vice chp.); Jobs, the Economy, and Small Business. **2007** — Aging and Long-Term Care; Judiciary and Ethics.

Telephone: Office: (608) 266-2254; (888) 534-0054 (toll free); District: (920) 232-0805.

E-mail: Rep.Hintz@legis.wisconsin.gov

Voting address: 1209 Waugoo Avenue, Oshkosh 54901.

Mailing address: Office: Room 109 North, State Capitol, P.O. Box 8952, Madison 53708.

Senator
ROTH

See Fox Cities Detail Map on p. 98

Detail Map: Grand Chute

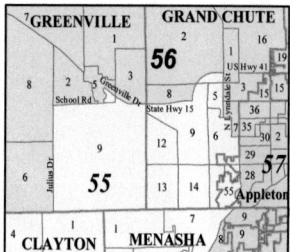

19th SENATE DISTRICT

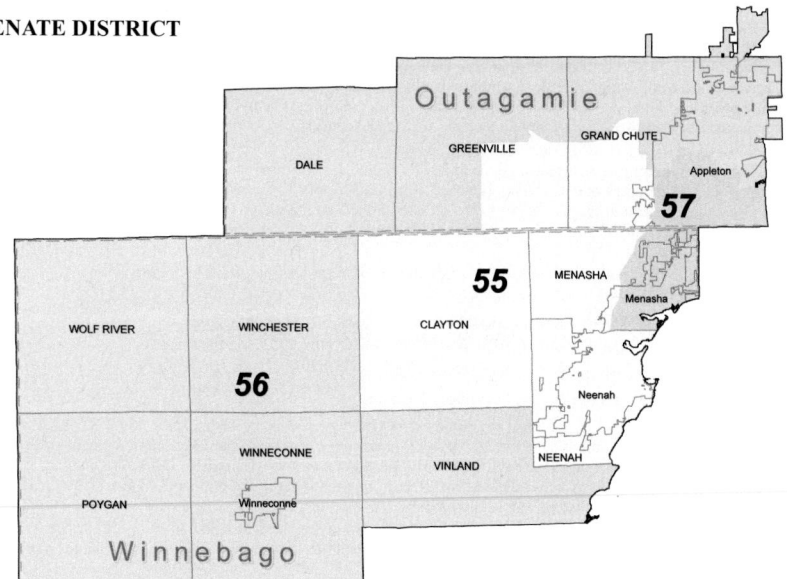

Roger Roth (Rep.), 19th Senate District

Born Appleton, February 5, 1978; married; 2 children. Graduate St. Mary Central H.S. (Menasha) 1996; B.S. history UW-Oshkosh 2001. Self-employed home builder. Member Wis. Air National Guard since 2003; Iraq War veteran. Member: Valley Homebuilders Assn.; American Legion; AMVETS; VFW.

Elected to Assembly 2006-08; elected to Senate 2014. Biennial Senate committee assignments: **2015** — Workforce Development, Public Works and Military Affairs (chp.); Sporting Heritage, Mining and Forestry (vice chp.); Insurance, Housing, and Trade; Jt. Com. on Information Policy and Technology. Assembly committee assignments: **2009** — Elections and Campaign Finance Reform; Housing (vice chp. 2007); Insurance; Jt. Leg. Coun. Spec. Com. on High-Risk Juvenile Offenders; Law Revision. **2007** — Financial Institutions; Jobs and the Economy; Workforce Development; State Capitol and Executive Residence Bd.

Telephone: Office: (608) 266-0718.

Voting address: 1910 West Charles Street, Appleton 54914.

Mailing address: Office: Room 306 South, State Capitol, P.O. Box 7882, Madison 53707-7882.

| **Representative** | **Representative** | **Representative** |
| ROHRKASTE | MURPHY | STUCK |

Mike Rohrkaste (Rep.), 55th Assembly District

Born Dayton, Ohio, September 24, 1958; married; 2 children. Graduate Chaminade-Julienne H.S. (Dayton, Ohio) 1976; B.S. Michigan St. U. 1980; Masters in labor and industrial relations Michigan St. U. 1982. Full-time legislator. Former chief human resources officer, vice president of human resources; over 30 years' business/human resources experience. Member: YMCA of Fox Cities (bd. mbr.); Samaritans Counseling Center Fox Valley (bd. mbr.); Neenah Club; Fox Cities Morning Rotary (chair, vocational com.). Former member: Fox Valley Christian Academy (bd. mbr.); Calvary Bible Church.

Elected to Assembly 2014. Biennial committee assignments: **2015** — Health (vice chp.); Interstate Affairs; Colleges and Universities; Jobs and the Economy; Mental Health Reform.

Telephone: Office: (608) 266-5719; (888) 534-0055 (toll free); District: (920) 284-9507.

E-mail: Rep.Rohrkaste@legis.wisconsin.gov

Voting address: 1417 Mahler Boulevard, Neenah 54956.

Mailing address: Office: Room 208 North, State Capitol, P.O. Box 8953, Madison 53708.

Dave Murphy (Rep.), 56th Assembly District

Born Appleton, November 26, 1954; married; 2 children. Graduate Hortonville H.S. 1972; attended UW-Fox Valley 1972-74; Wis. School of Real Estate 1975. Full-time legislator. Former owner, fitness center and agri-business; real estate broker. Member: Fox Valley Lutheran Homes (delegate); Greenville Lions Club; Zion Lutheran Church Council. Former member: Paper Valley Soccer Club (vice-pres.).

Elected to Assembly 2012; reelected 2014. Biennial committee assignments: **2015** — Colleges and Universities (chp., vice chp. 2013); Jt. Survey Com. on Retirement Systems (co-chp.); Education; Financial Institutions; Housing and Real Estate (also 2013); Workforce Development. **2013** — Constitution and Ethics; Insurance; Urban and Local Affairs.

Telephone: Office: (608) 266-7500; District: (920) 378-1424.

Voting address: Greenville 54942.

Mailing address: Office: Room 318 North, State Capitol, P.O. Box 8953, Madison 53708.

Amanda Stuck (Dem.), 57th Assembly District

Born Appleton, December 16, 1982; married; 2 children. Graduate Appleton North H.S. 2001; B.A. political science UW-Oshkosh 2007; Masters of public administration UW-Oshkosh 2012. Full-time legislator. Former housing specialist, Appleton Housing Authority; legislative aide, Cong. Steve Kagan; rural mail carrier.

Elected to Assembly 2014. Biennial committee assignments: **2015** — Energy and Utilities; Environment and Forestry; Housing and Real Estate; Jobs and the Economy.

Telephone: Office: (608) 266-3070; (888) 534-0057 (toll free).

E-mail: Rep.Stuck@legis.wisconsin.gov

Voting address: 1404 North Harriman, Appleton 54911.

Mailing address: Office: Room 4 West, State Capitol, P.O. Box 8953, Madison 53708.

20th SENATE DISTRICT

Detail Map: City of Hartford

Detail Map: Town of Trenton

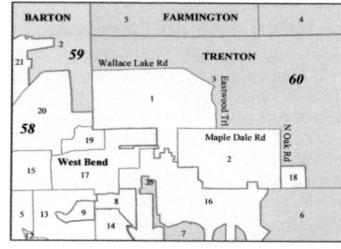

Senator
STROEBEL

Duey Stroebel (Rep.), 20th Senate District

Born Cedarburg, September 1, 1959; married; 8 children. Graduate Cedarburg H.S. 1978; B.B.A. UW-Madison 1984; M.S. UW-Madison 1987. Real estate. Member: Ozaukee Board of Realtors; Cedarburg Chamber of Commerce; Greater Cedarburg Foundation (fmr. pres.); Concordia University President's Council. Former member: City of Cedarburg Downtown Ad Hoc Committee; Ozaukee Bank and Cornerstone Bank (bd. of dir.). Town of Cedarburg Parks Commission 2001-04; Town of Cedarburg Planning Commission 2003-05; Cedarburg School Board 2007-12.

Elected to Assembly in May 2011 special election; reelected 2012; elected to Senate in April 2015 special election. Biennial Senate committee assignments: **2015** — Government Operations and Consumer Protection (chp.); Revenue, Financial Institutions and Rural Issues (vice chp.); Workforce Development, Public Works and Military Affairs. Assembly committee assignments: **2013** — State and Local Finance (chp.); Jt. Survey Com. on Retirement Systems (cochp.); Colleges and Universities; Environment and Forestry; Financial Institutions (also 2011); Insurance (also 2011). **2011** — Natural Resources.

Telephone: Office: (608) 266-7513; (800) 662-1227 (toll free); District: (262) 822-1520.

E-mail: Sen.Stroebel@legis.wisconsin.gov

Voting address: 2428 Covered Bridge Road, Saukville 53080.

Mailing address: Office: Room 18 South, State Capitol, P.O. Box 7882, Madison 53707-7882.

Representative	Representative	Representative
GANNON	**KREMER**	**R. BROOKS**

Bob Gannon (Rep.), 58th Assembly District

Born Mequon, January 6, 1959; married; 2 children. Graduate West Bend East H.S. 1977; attended various colleges and vocational courses. Owner, independent insurance agency, hotel and investment property. Member: West Bend Sunrise Rotary (fmr. pres.); Family Promise of Washington Co. (fmr. pres.); West Bend Economic Development (fmr. vice pres.); Still Waters United Methodist; Independent Insurance Agents of Wis.; Professional Insurance Agents of Wis.; NRA; West Bend Chamber of Commerce (fmr. pres.). Former member: West Bend Jaycees (pres.); Washington Co. Youth Hockey Assn. (pres.).

Elected to Assembly 2014. Biennial committee assignments: **2015** — Children and Families (vice chp.); Corrections; Insurance; Small Business Development; State Affairs and Government Operations.

Telephone: Office: (608) 264-8486.

E-mail: Rep.Gannon@legis.wisconsin.gov

Voting address: 4833 Cedar Hills Drive, Slinger 53086.

Mailing address: Office: Room 12 West, State Capitol, P.O. Box 8952, Madison 53708.

Jesse Kremer (Rep.), 59th Assembly District

Born Moline, Ill., February 28, 1977; married; 3 children. Graduate Kettle Moraine Lutheran H.S. 1995; A.S. Fox Valley Tech. Coll. 1997; Certificate, firefighter and police recruit academy, Waukesha Co. Tech Coll. 1999; Certificate, EMT-Basic, Milwaukee Area Tech Coll. 1999. Pilot, small business owner, firefighter/EMT. Former emergency services dispatcher, flight instructor, airline captain, charter pilot. Served in Army National Guard, U.S. and Army Reserves 2002-10; Iraq War veteran. Member: Kewaskum Volunteer Fire Dept.; American Legion Fohl-Martin Post 483; National Rifle Association.

Elected to Assembly 2014. Biennial committee assignments: **2015** — Criminal Justice and Public Safety (vice chp.); Constitution and Ethics; Health; Mining and Rural Development; Public Benefit Reform.

Telephone: (608) 266-9175; District: (262) 297-9572.

E-mail: Rep.Kremer@legis.wisconsin.gov

Web site: www.RepKremer.com

Voting address: 119 Hillcrest Road, Kewaskum 53040.

Mailing address: Office: Room 17 West, State Capitol, P.O. Box 8952, Madison 53708.

Robert Brooks (Rep.), 60th Assembly District

Born Rockford, Ill., July 13, 1965; married; 2 children. Graduate Orfordville Parkview H.S. 1983; attended UW-La Crosse 1983-86. Real estate broker since 1990, restaurant/tavern owner. Former member: Stars and Stripes Honor Flight (bd. of dir.); Wis. County Mutual (bd. of dir.); Wis. Board of Realtors; Ozaukee Co. Tavern League (bd. of dir.). Southeastern Wis. Regional Planning Comn. Ozaukee Co. Board 2000-14.

Elected to Assembly 2014. Biennial committee assignments: **2015** — Colleges and Universities (vice chp.); Aging and Long Term Care; Children and Families; Education; Environment and Forestry; Housing and Real Estate.

Telephone: Office: (608) 267-2369; (888) 534-0060 (toll free) District: (262) 268-7880.

E-mail: Rep.Rob.Brooks@legis.wisconsin.gov

Voting address: 204 East Dekora Street, Saukville 53080.

Mailing address: Office: Room 107 West, State Capitol, P.O. Box 8952, Madison 53708.

21st SENATE DISTRICT

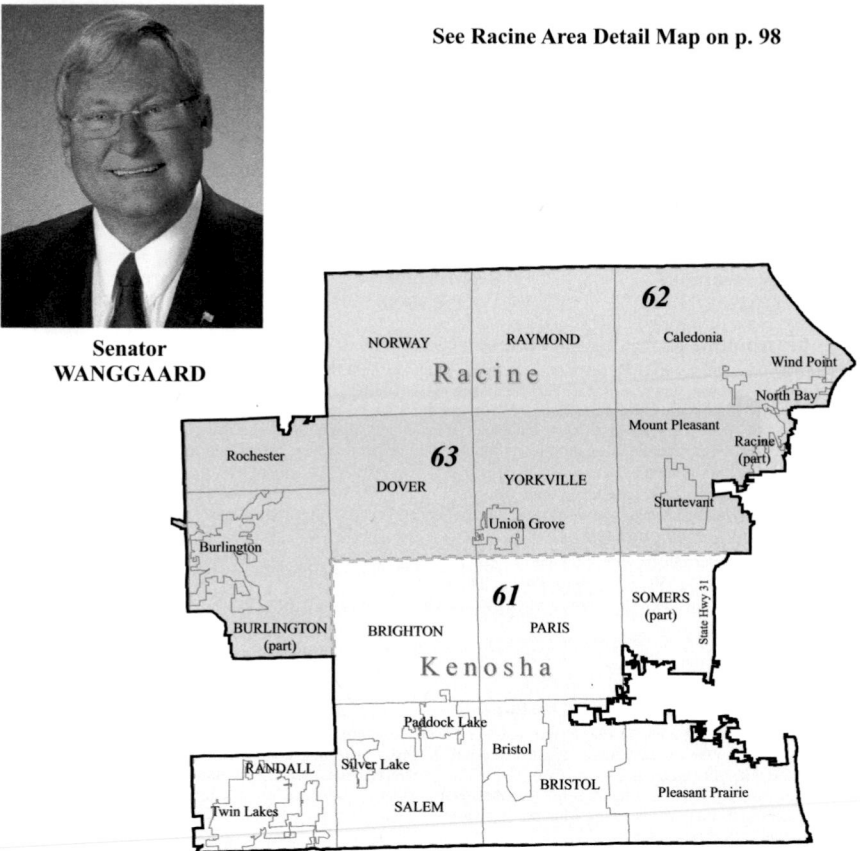

See Racine Area Detail Map on p. 98

**Senator
WANGGAARD**

Van H. Wanggaard (Rep.), 21st Senate District

Born Ft. Leavenworth, Kan., April 1952; married; 2 children, 2 grandchildren. Graduate Racine Lutheran H.S. 1970; Racine Police Academy; Wis. State Patrol Academy Accident Investigation; Northwestern U. Traffic Institute – Reconstruction; U.S. Coast Guard Natl. SAR School; attended John F. Kennedy U. Cal.; UW-Extension; UW-Parkside; Green Bay Tech. Coll.; Milw. Area Tech. Coll.; Fox Valley Tech. Coll. Full-time legislator. Retired traffic investigator, Racine Police Dept.; adjunct instructor, Gateway Tech. Coll. and Northwestern Traffic Institute; police liaison and security, Racine Unified School Dist. Member: Racine Zoological Soc. (bd. of dir.); National Rifle Assn. (life mbr.); Racine County Line Rifle Club (bd. of dir.); Racine Police Credit Union (fmr. pres., vice pres.); Former member: Racine Jaycees; Racine Police Explorers (adv.); Traffic Accident Consultants, Inc. (bd. of dir.); Assn. of SWAT Personnel; Racine Innovative Youth Service (bd.); Hostage Negotiation Team, RAPD; Racine Junior Deputy Sheriffs Assn.; Racine Alateen (adv.); Nat'l Assn. for Search and Rescue (psar. Chp.). Racine Police and Fire Commission 2003-13 (chp., vice chp., secy.). Racine County Bd. 2002-11.

Elected to Senate 2010; reelected 2014. Majority Caucus Vice Chairperson 2015. Biennial committee assignments: **2015** — Judiciary and Public Safety (chp.); Jt. Review Com. on Criminal Penalties (co-chp.); Labor and Government Reform; Elections and Local Government; Jt. Legislative Council. **2011** — Labor, Public Safety and Urban Affairs (chp.); Economic Development, Veterans and Military Affairs; Insurance and Housing; Natural Resources and Environment; Jt. Survey Com. on Retirement Systems.

Telephone: Office: (608) 266-1832; (866) 615-7510 (toll free).

E-mail: Sen.Wanggaard@legis.wisconsin.gov

Voting address: Racine 53405.

Mailing address: Office: Room 319 South, State Capitol, P.O. Box 7882, Madison 53707-7882.

| Representative | Representative | Representative |
| KERKMAN | WEATHERSTON | VOS |

Samantha Kerkman (Rep.), 61st Assembly District

Born Burlington, March 6, 1974; 2 children. Graduate Wilmot H.S.; B.A. UW-Whitewater 1996. Member: Kenosha Area Business Alliance; Twin Lakes Chamber and Area Business Assn.; Twin Lakes American Legion Auxiliary Post 544; VFW Auxiliary, Bloomfield Center Post 5830; St. Alphonsus Catholic Church. Former member: Burlington Area Chamber of Commerce; Powers Lake Sportsmen Club.

Elected to Assembly since 2000. Majority Caucus Sergeant at Arms 2015, 2013, 2011. Biennial committee assignments: **2015** — Jt. Legis. Audit Com. (co-chp. since 2011, mbr. since 2001); Children and Families (also 2013); Interstate Affairs; Judiciary (also 2013, 2001-05); Ways and Means (vice chp. 2013, chp. 2011, 2007, mbr. since 2001). **2011** — Financial Institutions (also 2003, 2001); Judiciary and Ethics (since 2007). **2007** — Homeland Security and State Preparedness (vice chp.); Consumer Protection and Personal Privacy; Jobs and the Economy. **2005** — Budget Review (chp., also 2003); State-Federal Relations (vice chp.); Southeast Wisconsin Freeways. **2001** — Urban and Local Affairs (vice chp.); Government Operations.

Telephone: Office: (608) 266-2530; (888) 529-0061 (toll free); District: (262) 279-1037.
E-mail: Rep.Kerkman@legis.wisconsin.gov
Internet: www.legis.state.wi.us/assembly/asm61/news/default.htm
Voting address: Town of Salem.
Mailing address: Office: Room 315 North, State Capitol, P.O. Box 8952, Madison 53708; District: P.O. Box 156, Powers Lake 53159.

Thomas Weatherston (Rep.), 62nd Assembly District

Born Buffalo, NY, February 15, 1950; married; 1 child. Graduate Williamsville Central H.S. 1968; A.A.S. construction management, Erie Community College 1975; B.S. industrial engineering State University College of NY at Buffalo 1977. Full-time legislator. Former director of facilities management at Modine Manufacturing Company, and adjunct instructor at Gateway Technical College. Vietnam veteran, served in U.S. Air Force 1968-72. Member: Vietnam Veterans of America Chapter 767; Veterans of Foreign Wars Post 10301. Former member: Kiwanis; Racine Area Veterans Inc. (pres.); St. Catherine H.S. (bd. mbr.); Salvation Army (advisory bd.). Caledonia Utility District Commission 2011-13. Caledonia Village Trustee 2010-13.

Elected to Assembly 2012; reelected 2014. Biennial committee assignments: **2015** — Aging and Long Term Care (chp.); Workforce Development (vice chp., mbr. 2013); Energy and Utilities; Financial Institutions; Transportation; Veterans and Military Affairs. **2013** — Veterans (vice chp.); Colleges and Universities; Consumer Protection; State and Local Finance.

Telephone: Office: (608) 266-0731; (888) 534-0062 (toll free); District: (262) 989-3424.
E-mail: Rep.Weatherston@legis.wisconsin.gov
Voting address: Racine 53402.
Mailing address: Office: Room 307 North, State Capitol, P.O. Box 8953, Madison 53708.

Robin J. Vos (Rep.), 63rd Assembly District

Born Burlington, July 5, 1968. Graduate Burlington H.S. 1986; UW-Whitewater 1991. Owner of several small businesses. Former congressional district director; former legislative assistant. Member: Rotary Club (past pres.); Racine/Kenosha Farm Bureau; Knights of Columbus; Racine Co. Rep. Party; Racine Area Manufacturers and Commerce; Union Grove Chamber of Commerce; Burlington Chamber of Commerce. UW Board of Regents 1989-91. Racine Co. Board 1994-2004 (former chp. of Finance and Personnel Com.).

Elected to Assembly since 2004. Speaker of the Assembly 2015, 2013. Biennial committee assignments: **2015** — Assembly Organization (chp., also 2013); Jt. Com. on Legis. Organization (co-chp., also 2013); Jt. Com. on Employment Relations (co-chp. 2013, mbr. 2011); Rules (vice chp., also 2013); Jt. Legislative Council (since 2009). **2011** — Jt. Com. on Finance (co-chp., mbr. since 2007); Jt. Com. on Audit. **2009** — Insurance. **2007** — Elections and Constitutional Law (vice chp. eff. 1/3/08); Jobs and the Economy (eff. 1/17/08).

Telephone: Office: (608) 266-3387; (888) 534-0063 (toll free); Fax: (608) 282-3663; District: (262) 514-2597.
Internet: SpeakerVos.com
E-mail: Rep.Vos@legis.wisconsin.gov
Voting address: 960 Rock Ridge Road, Burlington 53105.
Mailing address: Office: Room 211 West, State Capitol, P.O. Box 8953, Madison 53708.

22nd SENATE DISTRICT

Detail Map: City of Kenosha

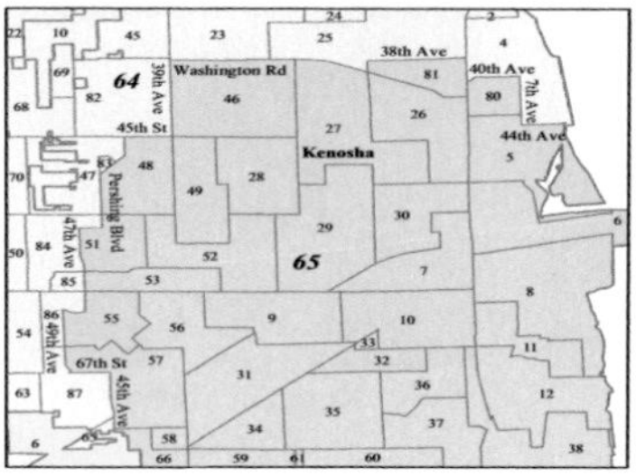

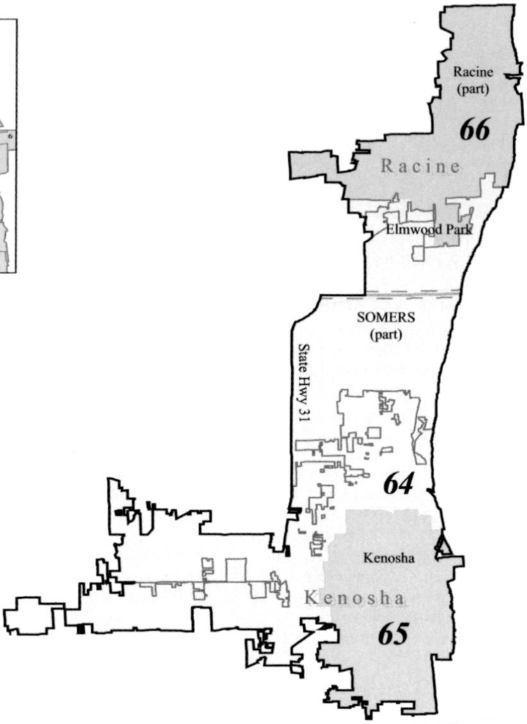

**Senator
WIRCH**

Robert W. Wirch (Dem.), 22nd Senate District

Born Kenosha, November 16, 1943; married; 2 children. Graduate Mary D. Bradford H.S.; B.A. UW-Parkside 1970. Full-time legislator. Former factory worker and liaison to JTPA programs. Served in Army Reserve 1965-71. Member: Danish Brotherhood; Kenosha Sport Fishing and Conservation Assn.; Democratic. Party of Wis. Former member: Kenosha Boys and Girls Club (bd. of dir.). Kenosha County supervisor 1986-94 (served on Health and Human Services Com., Welfare Bd., and Developmental Disabilities Bd.).

Elected to Assembly 1992; reelected 1994; elected to Senate since 1996. Minority Caucus Chairperson 2003. Biennial committee assignments: **2015** — Labor and Government Reform; Natural Resources and Energy; Sporting Heritage, Mining and Forestry. **2013** — Government Operations, Public Works, and Telecommunications; Natural Resources; Jt. Com. on Finance (also 2001). **2011** — Energy, Biotechnology, and Consumer Protection; Labor, Public Safety, and Urban Affairs; Natural Resources and Environment. **2009** — Small Business, Emergency Preparedness, Technical Colleges, and Consumer Protection (chp.); Jt. Survey Com. on Retirement Systems (co-chp., also 2007, 2001, 1999, mbr. since 1997); Commerce, Utilities, Energy and Rail; Environment; Labor, Elections and Urban Affairs (vice chp. 2007); Jt. Legislative Council. **2007** — Small Business, Emergency Preparedness, Workforce Development, Technical Colleges and Consumer Protection (chp.); Commerce, Utilities and Rail; Environment and Natural Resources. **2005** — Energy, Utilities and Information Technology; Natural Resources and Transportation; Veterans, Homeland Security, Military Affairs, Small Business and Government Reform; Retirement Research Com. (since 1997). **2003** — Energy and Utilities; Environment and Natural Resources; Homeland Security, Veterans and Military Affairs and Government Reform. **2001** — Environmental Resources; Human Services and Aging (also 1999); Judiciary, Consumer Affairs, and Campaign Finance Reform. **1999** — Economic Development, Housing and Government Operations (chp.); Agriculture, Environmental Resources and Campaign Finance Reform; State of Wis. Building Comn.; Law Revision Com.; Transportation Projects Comn. **1997** — Jt. Legis. Audit (co-chp., eff. 1/15/97 to 4/20/98); Jt. Com. for Review of Administrative Rules (eff. 1/15/97 to 1/5/98, also 1995); Agriculture and Environmental Resources (eff. 1/15/97 to 4/20/98); Health, Family Services and Aging (eff. 4/21/98); Health, Human Services, Aging, Corrections, Veterans and Military Affairs (eff. 1/15/97 to 1/7/98); Judiciary, Campaign Finance Reform and Consumer Affairs (chp., eff. 1/5/98); Council on Workforce Excellence.

Telephone: Office: (608) 267-8979; District: (262) 694-7379; Office Hotline: (888) 769-4724.

E-mail: Sen.Wirch@legis.wisconsin.gov

Voting address: Somers 53144.

Mailing address: Office: Room 127 South, State Capitol, P.O. Box 7882, Madison 53707-7882.

| **Representative** | **Representative** | **Representative** |
| BARCA | OHNSTAD | MASON |

Peter W. Barca (Dem.), 64th Assembly District

Born Kenosha, August 7, 1955; married; 2 children. Graduate Mary D. Bradford H.S. 1973; B.S. UW-Milwaukee 1977; attended Harvard U.; M.A. UW-Madison 1983. Past president, Aurora Assoc. International. Former CEO, Northpointe Resources; National Ombudsman and Midwest Regional Administrator, U.S. Small Bus. Admin. Member: Foundation Bd. of Dir., UW-Parkside; Internatl. Society for ISCTR (co-founder, secy./treas.); WISITALIA (past pres.). Former member: Com. to Found the Boys and Girls Club of Kenosha (chp.); Lake County Partnership on Econ. Dev. (exec. com.) and Econ. Dev. Com. on Small Business (chp.); Small Business Forum of DNC (nat'l co-chair); Kenosha Family and Aging Ser. (bd. mbr.); Kenosha Incubator Assn. (chm.); Partnership for a Stronger Economy.

Elected to Assembly 1984-1992 (resigned 6/8/93 upon election to U.S. Congress); reelected since 2008. Minority Leader 2015, 2013, 2011; Majority Caucus Chairperson 2009, 1993, 1991. Biennial committee assignments: **2015** — Assembly Organization (since 2009, also 1993, 1991); Rules (since 2009, also 1993, 1991); Jt. Com. on Employment Relations (since 2011); Jt. Com. on Information Policy and Technology (also 2013); Jt. Legislative Council (since 2011); Jt. Com. on Legislative Organization (since 2011); Wisconsin Economic Development Corporation Bd. (since 2011). **2009** — Jt. Legis. Audit Com. (co-chp.); Financial Institutions; Jobs, the Economy and Small Business.

Telephone: Office: (608) 266-5504; (888) 534-0064 (toll free).

E-mail: Rep.Barca@legis.wisconsin.gov

Voting address: Kenosha 53144.

Mailing address: Office: Room 201 West, State Capitol, P.O. Box 8952, Madison 53708.

Tod Ohnstad (Dem.), 65th Assembly District

Born Eau Claire, May 21, 1952; married. Graduate Altoona Public H.S. 1970; attended UW-Parkside. Former member: UAW Local 72 (chm. of trustees, shop committeeman, bargaining committee, executive bd.). City of Kenosha Alderman 2008-14.

Elected to Assembly 2012; reelected 2014. Biennial committee assignments: **2015** — Jobs and the Economy; Labor (also 2013); State Affairs and Government Operations; Tourism (also 2013); Ways and Means. **2013** — Insurance; Jobs, Economy and Mining.

Telephone: Office: (608) 266-0455; (888) 534-0065 (toll free); District: (262) 764-1950.

E-mail: Rep.Ohnstad@legis.wisconsin.gov

Voting address: Kenosha 53140.

Mailing address: Office: Room 128 North, State Capitol, P.O. Box 8953, Madison 53708.

Cory Mason (Dem.), 66th Assembly District

Born Racine, January 25, 1973; married; 2 daughters, 1 son. Graduate Case H.S. (Racine); B.A. in philosophy UW-Madison. Full-time legislator. Member: River Alliance of Wis. (fmr. bd. mbr.); UW Center for Tobacco Research and Intervention (fmr. bd. mbr.); League of Conservation Voters; Racine Heritage Museum; Root River Council; Wild Root Co-op; I-94 Labor Development Com. (fmr. co-chp.). Former member: Wis. Coastal Management Bd.; Racine Rotary West. Redevelopment Authority of Racine 2005-11 (commissioner).

Elected to Assembly 2006; reelected since 2008. Biennial committee assignments: **2015** — Environment and Forestry (ranking min. mbr.); Labor; Tourism; Jt. Legis. Council (ranking min. mbr., mbr. 2013); Jt. Survey Com. on Retirement Systems (ranking min. mbr.). **2013** — Jt. Com. on Finance (ranking min. mbr. also 2013 eff. 1/12/12, mbr. 2009). **2011** — Jobs, Economy and Small Business; Natural Resources (ranking min. mbr., mbr. since 2007); Tourism, Recreation and State Properties; Legis. Coun. Spec. Com. on Infant Mortality. **2009** — Jt. Com. on Information Policy and Technology; Spec. Com. on Clean Energy Jobs; UW Hospitals and Clinics Authority Board; Groundwater Work Group. **2007** — Education; Jobs and the Economy.

Telephone: Office: (608) 266-0634; (888) 534-0066 (toll free).

Voting address: 1948 Michigan Boulevard, Racine 53402.

Mailing address: Office: Room 6 North, State Capitol, P.O. Box 8953, Madison 53708.

23rd SENATE DISTRICT

See Eau Claire Area Detail Map on p. 97

Detail Map: City of Marshfield

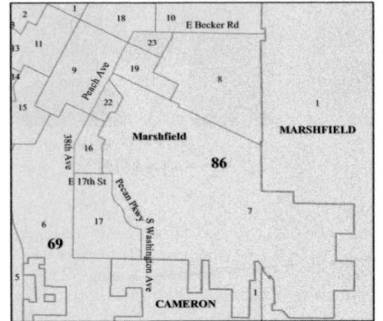

**Senator
MOULTON**

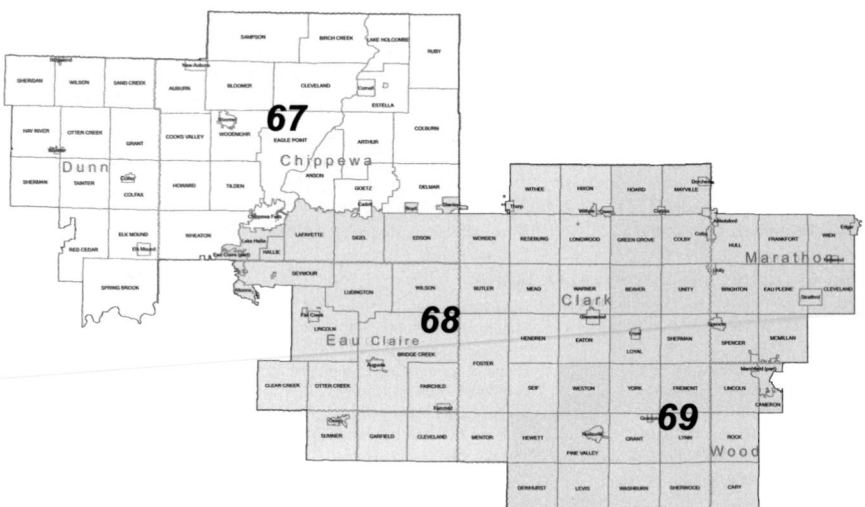

Terry Moulton (Rep.), 23rd Senate District

Born Whitefish, MT, July 19, 1946; married; 2 children, 8 grandchildren. Graduate Chippewa Falls H.S. 1964; attended UW-Eau Claire. Owner of archery and tackle shop and fishing tackle manufacturer. Former hospital accountant and business manager. Member: Chippewa Falls and Eau Claire Chambers of Commerce; Archery Range and Retailers Organization; Muskies, Inc.; Chippewa Bowhunters; Chippewa Rod and Gun; Eau Claire Archers; Eau Claire Rod and Gun Club.

Elected to Assembly 2004, 2006; elected to Senate 2010; reelected 2014. Biennial committee assignments: **2015** — Agriculture, Small Business, and Tourism (chp., also 2013); Health and Human Services (vice chp., also 2013); Sporting Heritage, Mining and Forestry; Jt. Legis. Council; Agricultural Education and Workforce Development Council; State of Wis. Building Comn. (also 2013); Council on Tourism (since 2011). **2013** — Natural Resources (vice chp.); Small Business Regulatory Review Bd. (also 2011). **2011** — Workforce Development, Small Business, and Tourism (chp.); Natural Resources and Environment (vice chp.); Agriculture, Forestry, and Higher Education; Health.

Telephone: Office: (608) 266-7511; (888) 437-9436 (toll free).

E-mail: Sen.Moulton@legis.wisconsin.gov

Voting address: Chippewa Falls 54729.

Mailing address: Office: Room 310 South, State Capitol, P.O. Box 7882, Madison 53707-7882.

Representative
LARSON

Representative
BERNIER

Representative
KULP

Tom Larson (Rep.), 67th Assembly District

Born Eau Claire, February 11, 1948; married; 3 children. Graduate Colfax H.S. 1966; attended Chippewa Valley Tech. Coll. Full-time legislator. Master electrician, licensed designer. Member: NFIB; Chippewa Valley Home Builders; ABC of Wisconsin; Colfax Kiwanis; Int'l. Assn. of Electrical Inspectors; Menomonie Chamber of Commerce; Colfax Sportsman Club; NRA; Chippewa Falls Chamber of Commerce.

Elected to Assembly 2010; reelected since 2012. Biennial committee assignments: **2015** — Family Law (chp., also 2013); Energy and Utilities (vice chp. 2013, mbr. 2011); Judiciary (also 2013); Mining and Rural Development; Small Business Development (also 2013); Transportation (also 2013). **2013** — Jobs, Economy and Mining. **2011** — Judiciary and Ethics (vice chp.); Rural Economic Development and Rural Affairs.

Telephone: Office: (608) 266-1194; (888) 534-0067 (toll free); District: (715) 962-3030.

E-mail: Rep.Larson@legis.wisconsin.gov

Voting address: Colfax 54730.

Mailing address: Office: Room 214 North, State Capitol, P.O. Box 8952, Madison 53708.

Kathy Bernier (Rep.), 68th Assembly District

Born Eau Claire, April 29, 1956; 3 children, 6 grandchildren. Graduate Chippewa Falls Senior H.S. 1974; B.A. UW-Eau Claire; certificate in public management essentials, UW-Green Bay 2005. Member: American Legislative Exchange Council; Chippewa Falls Chamber of Commerce; Lake Hallie Optimists Club; Wis. Women in Government; National Foundation for Women Legislators (state chp.). Former member: Wis. County Clerks Assn. (legis. chair, fmr. treas.); Wis. County Constitutional Officers; Chippewa County Humane Assn.; Kiwanis Noon Club; National Conference of State Legislatures, Elections and Redistricting Com. (vice chp). Village of Lake Hallie trustee 2007-present. Chippewa County Clerk 1999-2011.

Elected to Assembly 2010; reelected since 2012. Biennial committee assignments: **2015** — Campaigns and Elections (chp., also 2013); Family Law (vice chp.); Aging and Long-Term Care (since 2011); Agriculture; Mining and Rural Development; Workforce Development (also 2013). **2013** — Rural Affairs (vice chp.); Public Safety and Homeland Security. **2011** — Election and Campaign Reform (vice chp.); Tourism, Recreation and State Properties.

Telephone: Office: (608) 266-9172; (888) 534-0068 (toll free).

E-mail: Rep.Bernier@legis.wisconsin.gov

Voting address: 10923 40th Avenue, Chippewa Falls 54729.

Mailing address: Office: Room 314 North, State Capitol, P.O. Box 8952, Madison 53708.

Bob Kulp (Rep.), 69th Assembly District

Born Elkhart, IN, March 21, 1966; married; 7 children. Roofing and insulation contractor. Member: Small Business Administration Regulatory Fairness Bd.; National Roofing Contractors Assn. (vice pres.); Construction Specifications Institute – Wausau Chapter (past pres.); Wausau Area Builders Assn. (fmr. mbr., governmental com.); Noon Rotary Club of Marshfield.

Elected to Assembly in November 2013 special election; reelected 2014. Biennial committee assignments: **2015** — Mining and Rural Development (chp.); Jobs and the Economy; Labor (also 2013); State Affairs and Government Operations; Workforce Development (also 2013). **2013** — Judiciary; Transportation; Ways and Means.

Telephone: Office: (608) 267-0280; (888) 534-0069 (toll free); District: (715) 687-3287.

E-mail: Rep.Kulp@legis.wisconsin.gov

Voting address: C4098 Pauline Lane, Stratford 54484.

Mailing address: Office: Room 15 West, State Capitol, P.O. Box 8952, Madison 53708.

24th SENATE DISTRICT

Detail Map: Town of Grant

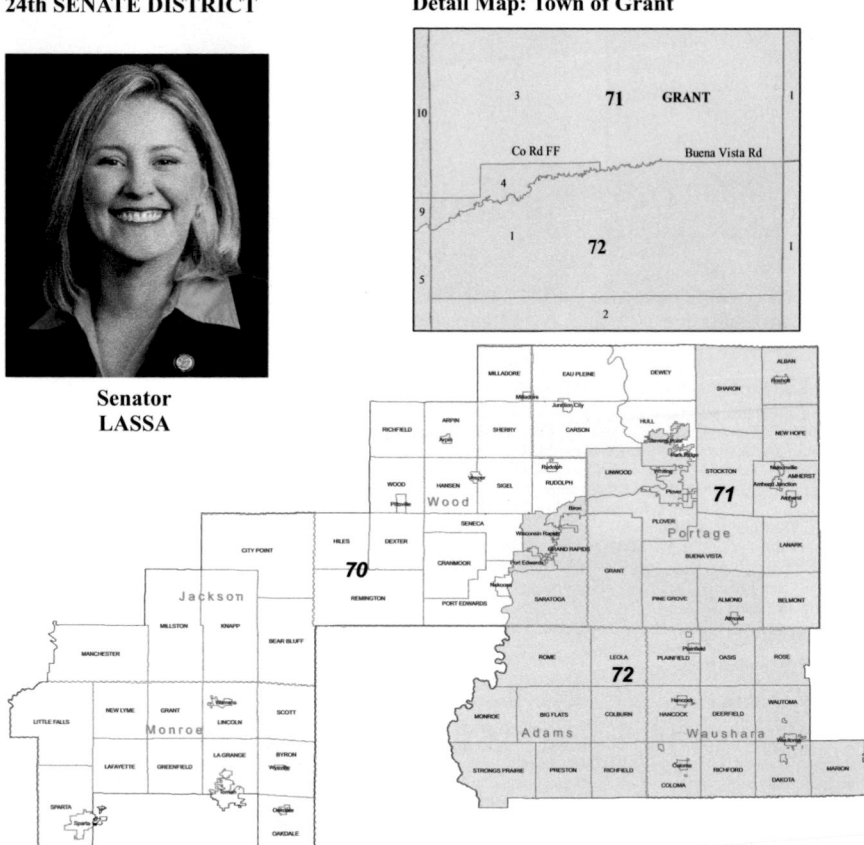

**Senator
LASSA**

Julie M. Lassa (Dem.), 24th Senate District

Born Stevens Point; married; 3 children. Graduate Stevens Point Area Senior H.S.; B.S. in political science and public administration UW-Stevens Point 1993; UW-Madison La Follette Institute of Public Affairs graduate work. Former legislative aide and executive director, Plover Area Business Assn. Member: Heart of Wisconsin Business and Economic Alliance; Adams County Chamber of Commerce; Sparta Area Chamber of Commerce; Greater Tomah Area Chamber of Commerce; Black River Area Chamber of Commerce; Waushara Area Chamber of Commerce; Portage Co. Democratic Party (former chp.); Portage Co. Business Council; Small Business Environmental Council; Gov.'s Council on Workforce Investment; Small Business Development Center Adv. Bd.; UW Population Health Inst. Adv. Bd.; NCSL Early Learning Fellows Program. Former member: Oral Health Coalition Steering Com. Dewey Town Board 1993-94.

Elected to Assembly 1998-2002 (resigned eff. 5/9/03); elected to Senate in April 2003 special election; reelected since 2004. Minority Caucus Chairperson 2015, 2013, 2011; Minority Caucus Secretary 1999. Biennial Senate committee assignments: **2015** — Economic Development and Commerce (ranking min. mbr.); Revenue, Financial Institutions and Rural Affairs (ranking min. mbr.); Workforce Development, Public Works and Military Affairs; Wisconsin Economic Development Corporation Bd. (also 2013); Child Abuse and Neglect Prevention Bd. (since 2007, also 2003, 2001). **2013** — Agriculture, Small Business, and Tourism; Economic Development and Local Government; Financial Institutions and Rural Affairs. **2011** — Economic Development, Veterans and Military Affairs; Financial Institutions and Rural Issues; Jt. Legislative Audit (also 2007, 2005). **2009** — Economic Development (chp.); Children and Families and Workforce Development; Health, Health Insurance, Privacy, Property Tax Relief, and Revenue; Jt. Com. on Finance. **2007** — Economic Development, Job Creation, Family Prosperity and Housing (chp.); Agriculture and Higher Education (vice chp.); Campaign Finance Reform, Rural Issues and Information Technology. **2005** — Housing and Financial Institutions; Job Creation, Economic Development and Consumer Affairs (ranking min. mbr.). **2003** — Agriculture, Financial Institutions and Insurance; Jt. Com. for Review of Administrative Rules. Assembly committee assignments: **2003** — Agriculture (since 1999); Budget Review (ranking min. mbr.); Economic Development (ranking minority mbr., 2001); Financial Institutions; Rural Affairs. **2001** — Colleges and Universities (also 1999); Labor and Workforce Development. **1999** — Small Business and Economic Development; Transportation; World Dairy Center Authority.

Telephone: Office: (608) 266-3123; (800) 925-7491 (toll free); District: (715) 342-3806.

E-mail: Sen.Lassa@legis.wisconsin.gov

Voting address: Stevens Point 54482.

Mailing address: Office: Room 20 South, State Capitol, P.O. Box 7882, Madison 53707-7882.

Representative **VANDER MEER**	Representative **SHANKLAND**	Representative **KRUG**

Nancy Lynn Vander Meer (Rep.), 70th Assembly District

Born Evergreen Park, Ill., December 15, 1958; married. Graduate Evergreen Park Community H.S. 1976; B.S. psychology UW-La Crosse 1988. Automobile dealer, small business owner, family dairy farmer. Member: Farm Bureau; Gloria Dei Lutheran Church (former council pres.); Tomah Chamber of Commerce (former bd. of dir. mbr.); Tomah Memorial Hospital Bd. (former officer); American Business Women's Assn. (former mbr., pres.); NRA; American Legion Auxiliary.

Elected to Assembly 2014. Biennial committee assignments: **2015** — Veterans and Military Affairs (vice chp.); Agriculture; Consumer Protection; Mental Health Reform; Mining and Rural Development; Small Business Development.

Telephone: Office: (608) 266-8366; (888) 534-0070 (toll free); District: (608) 372-2139.

E-mail: Rep.VanderMeer@legis.wisconsin.gov

Voting address: 18940 Eden Avenue, Tomah 54660.

Mailing address: Office: Room 11 West, State Capitol, P.O. Box 8953, Madison 53708.

Katrina Shankland (Dem.), 71st Assembly District

Born Wausau, August 4, 1987; single. Graduate Wittenberg-Birnamwood H.S. 2005; B.A. political science UW-Madison 2009; attended UW-Marathon Co. 2004-05, Marquette U. 2005-06. Full-time legislator. Former nonprofit professional. Member: National Caucus of Environmental Legislators; Young Elected Officials Network; Council of State Governments Henry Toll Fellow, 2013; Midwest Renewable Energy Assn.; Clean Wisconsin; Portage Co. Business Council; Central Rivers Farmshed; Portage Co. Democratic Party.

Elected to Assembly 2012; reelected 2014. Assistant Minority Leader 2015. Biennial committee assignments: **2015** — Natural Resources and Sporting Heritage (also 2013); Rules; Workforce Development (also 2013); Jt. Com. for Review of Admin. Rules; Jt. Com. on Legislative Organization; Jt. Legis. Council; Gov.'s Council on Domestic Abuse (also 2013). **2013** — Constitution and Ethics; Energy and Utilities; State Affairs (eff. 4/29/13).

Telephone: Office: (608) 267-9649; (888) 534-0071 (toll free).

E-mail: Rep.Shankland@legis.wisconsin.gov

Voting address: 5782 Sandpiper Drive., Stevens Point 54482.

Mailing address: Office: Room 119 North, State Capitol, P.O. Box 8953, Madison 53708.

Scott S. Krug (Rep.), 72nd Assembly District

Born Wisconsin Rapids, September 16, 1975; married; 6 children. Graduate Lincoln H.S. 1993; attended UW-Stevens Point; A.D. Mid-State Tech. Coll. 1999; B.A.S. psychology UW-Green Bay 2008. Employment and training specialist. Former Wood Co. drug court coordinator; jail discharge planner; Juneau Co. sheriff's deputy. Member: Heart of Wisconsin Chamber of Commerce; Wisconsin Rapids Rotary. Recipient: Wis. Industrial Energy Group *Legislator of the Year Award* 2014; Dairy Business Association *Legislative Excellence Award* 2014, 2012; Wis. Paper Council *Legislator of the Year* 2014; Child Support Enforcement Assn. *Legislator of the Year* 2014; League of Conservation Voters *Honor Roll* 2014; Wis. Troopers Assn. *Legislator of the Year* 2014; Wis. Counties Assn. *Outstanding Legislator* 2014; WMC *Working for Wisconsin Award* 2014, 2012; 3rd Congressional District *State Legislator of the Year* 2012.

Elected to Assembly 2010; reelected since 2012. Biennial committee assignments: **2015** — Consumer Protection (chp.); Environment and Forestry (vice chp., also 2013); Mining and Rural Development; Public Benefit Reform. **2013** — Children and Families (chp, vice chp. 2011); Corrections; Rural Affairs. **2011** — Criminal Justice and Corrections; Rural Economic Development and Rural Affairs.

Telephone: Office: (608) 266-0215; (888) 529-0072 (toll free); District: (715) 459-2267.

E-mail: Rep.Krug@legis.wisconsin.gov

Voting address: (Town of Rome) Nekoosa 54457.

Mailing address: Office: Room 207 North, State Capitol, P.O. Box 8952, Madison 53708.

25th SENATE DISTRICT

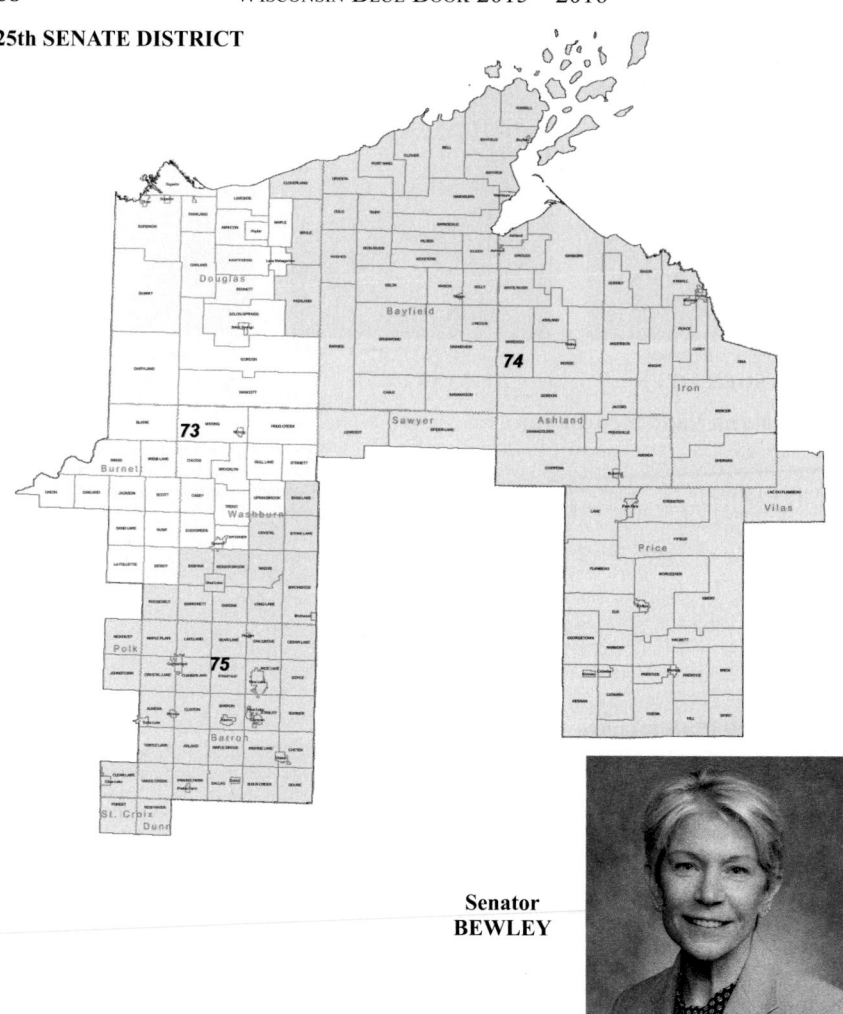

Senator
BEWLEY

Janet Bewley (Dem.), **25th Senate District**

Born Painesville, OH, November 10, 1951; married; 5 children. Graduate James Ford Rhodes H.S. (Cleveland, OH) 1969; B.A. Case Western Reserve U. 1973; M. Ed. U. of Maine 1977. Full-time legislator. Former Community Relations Officer, WHEDA; former Dean of Students Northland College, former exec. dir., Mary H. Rice Foundation. One of the original cast members at Lake Superior Big Top Chautauqua and current member of the Rittenhouse Chamber Singers. Ashland City Council 2007-09.

Elected to Assembly 2010-12; elected to Senate 2014. Biennial Senate committee assignments: **2015** — Education; Insurance, Housing and Trade; Universities and Technical Colleges; Jt. Legis. Audit; Spec. Com. on State-Tribal Relations; Council on Alcohol and Other Drug Abuse; Council on Tourism. Assembly committee assignments: **2013** — Colleges and Universities; Housing and Real Estate; Public Safety and Homeland Security; Rural Affairs; Transportation Projects Comn.; Leg. Coun. Spec. Com. on State-Tribal Relations (also 2011). **2011** — Forestry; Homeland Security and State Affairs; Housing; Transportation.

Telephone: Office: (608) 266-3510; (800) 469-6562 (toll free); District: (715) 746-4100.
E-mail: Sen.Bewley@legis.wisconsin.gov
Voting address: 60995 Pike River Road, Mason 54856.
Mailing address: Office: Room 126 South, State Capitol, P.O. Box 7882, Madison 53707-7882.

| Representative | Representative | Representative |
| MILROY | MEYERS | QUINN |

Nick Milroy (Dem.), 73rd Assembly District

Born Duluth, MN, April 15, 1974; married; 3 children. Graduate Superior Senior H.S. 1992; B.S. UW-Superior 1998; attended UW-Eau Claire 1999-2000. Full-time legislator. Former fisheries biologist. Served in U.S. Navy 1992-94, U.S. Naval Reserve 1994-2000; deployed to Persian Gulf during Operation Southern Watch. Member: Exec. Bd. of the Great Lakes Caucus of the Council of State Governments; Wisconsin Chapter of the Congressional Sportsmen's Foundation (co-chp.); Natl. Conf. of Environmental Legislators; Douglas Co. Democratic Party (former secy.). Former member: Lake Superior Bi-national Forum; St. Louis River Watershed TMDL Partnership (bd. of dir.); Am. Fisheries Soc.; Duluth-Superior Metropolitan Interstate Council (policy bd. mbr.); Head of the Lakes Fair (bd. of dir.). Superior City Council 2005-09.

Elected to Assembly 2008; reelected since 2010. Biennial committee assignments: **2015** — Environment and Forestry (also 2013); Mining and Rural Development; Natural Resources and Sporting Heritage (also 2013); Veterans and Military Affairs (also 2011, 2009); Leg. Council. Com. on State-Tribal Relations; Wis. Council on Military and State Relations; Wis. Sporting Heritage Council. **2013** — Rural Affairs; Veterans; Leg. Council Spec. Com. on State-Tribal Relations (also 2011). **2011** — Forestry (also 2009); Natural Resources (also 2009). **2009** — Fish and Wildlife (vice chp.).

Telephone: Office: (608) 266-0640; (888) 534-0073 (toll free); District: (715) 392-8690.

E-mail: Rep.Milroy@legis.wisconsin.gov

Voting address: 4543 South Sam Anderson Road, South Range 54874.

Mailing address: Office: Room 126 North, State Capitol, P.O. Box 8953, Madison 53708.

Beth Meyers (Dem.), 74th Assembly District

Born Ashland, May 29, 1959; married; 2 children. Graduate Bayfield H.S. 1977; B.S. Northland College 1989. Full-time legislator. Former executive director, CORE Community Resources. Bayfield Co. Bd. of Supervisors 2010-present.

Elected to Assembly 2014. Minority Caucus Secretary 2015. Biennial committee assignments: **2015** — Aging and Long-Term Care; Tourism; Transportation; Gov.'s Council on Highway Safety.

Telephone: Office: (608) 266-7690; (888) 534-0074 (toll free); District: (715) 779-5014.

E-mail: Rep.Meyers@legis.wisconsin.gov

Voting address: 36505 Aiken Road, Bayfield 54814.

Mailing address: Office: Room 409 North, State Capitol, P.O. Box 8953, Madison 53708.

Romaine Robert Quinn (Rep.), 75th Assembly District

Born Rice Lake, July 30, 1990. Graduate Rice Lake H.S. 2009; interdisciplinary degree (B.A.), political science with emphasis on public leadership, UW Green Bay 2014; attended UW-Barron Co. and UW-Eau Claire. Full-time legislator. Former salesman and waiter. Rice Lake City Council 2009-10; Mayor of Rice Lake 2010-12.

Elected to Assembly 2014. Biennial committee assignments: **2015** — Aging and Long-Term Care (vice chp.); Natural Resources and Sporting Heritage (vice chp.); Colleges and Universities; Education; Mining and Rural Development; Urban and Local Affairs.

Telephone: Office: (608) 266-2519; (888) 534-0075 (toll free); District: (715) 651-9578.

E-mail: Rep.Quinn@legis.wisconsin.gov

Voting address: 15 West John Street, Rice Lake 54868.

Mailing address: Office: Room 7 West, State Capitol, P.O. Box 8953, Madison 53708.

26th SENATE DISTRICT

See Madison Area Detail Map on pp. 90 & 91

Senator
RISSER

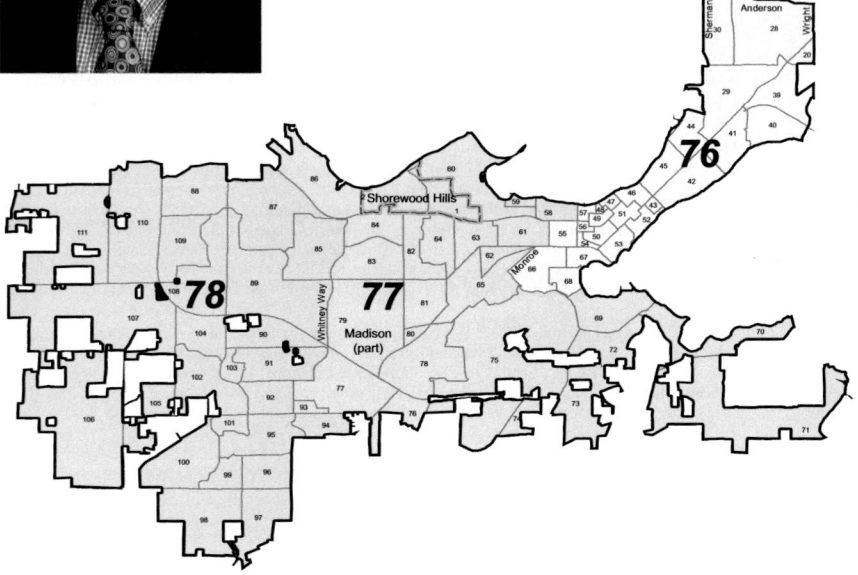

Fred Risser (Dem.), 26th Senate District

Born Madison, May 5, 1927; married; 3 children. Attended Carleton College (MN), UW-Madison; B.A. U. of Oregon 1950; LL.B. U. of Oregon 1952. Attorney. World War II veteran; Navy. Member: State Bar of Wis. and Oregon and Dane Co. Bar Assns.; NCSL (past mbr. Natl. Exec. Com.); CSG (past mbr. Natl. Exec. Com., Midwestern Conf. chp. 1993, 1982). Presidential Elector 2012, 2008, 1964.

Elected to Assembly 1956-60; elected to Senate in 1962 special election; reelected since 1964. Longest serving legislator in Wisconsin history and longest serving state legislator in U.S. President of the Senate 2011 (eff. 7/17/12), 2009, 2007, 2001, 1999, 1997 (eff. 1/15/97 to 4/20/98), 1995 (eff. 7/9/96), also 1979 to 4/20/93; Co-Majority Leader 2001 (eff. 10/22/02); Assistant Minority Leader 1995 (eff. 1/5/95 to 7/12/96), 1993 (eff. 4/20/93, also 1965); Sen. Pres. Pro Tempore 1977, 1975; Minority Ldr. 1967-73. Biennial committee assignments: **2015** — Education; Elections and Local Government; Judiciary and Public Safety; Joint Legislative Council (co-chp. 2011 eff. 7/17/12, also 2007, 2001, 1999, 1997, chp. 1987, 1983, 1971, mbr. since 1967); Comn. on Uniform State Laws (since 2005); State Historical Society Bd. of Curators (since 1983); State Capitol and Executive Residence Bd. (chp. since 2003, co-chp. 1989 to 4/20/98, mbr. since 1983). **2013** — Judiciary and Labor; State and Federal Relations; State of Wis. Building Comn. (vice chp. 2009, 2007, 2001, 1999, 1971 to 5/19/93, mbr. since 1969). **2011** — Judiciary, Utilities, Commerce, and Government Operations; Senate Organization (chp. 1987 to 4/20/98, also chp. 1977-1981, mbr. 2011 eff. 7/17/12, 2009, 2007, 1967-2003); Jt. Com. on Legislative Organization (co-chp. eff. 7/17/12, also 2009, 2007, 2001, 1999, 1997, eff. 1/15/97 to 4/20/98, also 1977 to 4/20/93, mbr. 1967-2003); Jt. Com. for Review of Admin. Rules (also 2009); Jt. Com. on Employment Relations (co-chp. eff. 7/17/12, also 2009, 2007, 2001, 1999, 1997, eff. 1/6/97 to 4/20/98, also 1995, eff. 7/9/96, also 1979 to 4/20/93, mbr. 1973-2009); Jt. Com. on Information Policy and Technology. **2009** — Ethics Reform and Government Operations (chp., also 2007). **2007** — Wis. Environmental Education Bd. (also 2005). For committee activities prior to 2007, see previous editions of the *Wisconsin Blue Book.*

Telephone: Office: (608) 266-1627.

E-mail: Sen.Risser@legis.wisconsin.gov

Voting address: Madison 53703.

Mailing address: Office: Room 130 South, State Capitol, P.O. Box 7882, Madison 53707-7882.

| Representative | Representative | Representative |
| TAYLOR | BERCEAU | SUBECK |

Chris Taylor (Dem.), 76th Assembly District

Born January 13, 1968, Los Angeles, CA; married; 2 children. Graduate Birmingham H.S. (Van Nuys, CA) 1986; B.A. U. of Pennsylvania 1990; J.D. U. of Wisconsin Law School 1995. Full-time legislator. Former public policy director, Planned Parenthood of Wisconsin and practicing attorney. Member: State Bar of Wisconsin; Wisconsin League of Conservation Voters; Planned Parenthood Advocates of Wisconsin; Planned Parenthood Federation; Sierra Club; Democratic Party of Wisconsin. Former member: Public Interest Law Bd. (legislative subcom. chair).

Elected to Assembly in August 2011 special election; reelected since 2012. Biennial committee assignments: **2015** — Jt. Com. on Finance; Jt. Legis. Council. **2013** — Children and Families; Family Law; Health (also 2011); Labor; Jt. Legis. Council Law Revision Com. (also 2011); Steering Com. for Symposia Series on State Income Tax. **2011** — Labor and Workforce Development; Ways and Means.

Telephone: Office: (608) 266-5342.

E-mail: Rep.Taylor@legis.wisconsin.gov

Voting address: Madison 53704.

Mailing address: Office: Room 306 West, State Capitol, P.O. Box 8953, Madison 53708.

Terese Berceau (Dem.), 77th Assembly District

Born Green Bay, August 23, 1950. B.S. UW-Madison 1973; graduate studies in Urban and Regional planning UW-Madison. Staff, UW-Madison Robert M. La Follette School; staff, Wis. Counties Assn.; real estate sales; substitute teacher. Member: Dane Co. Dem. Party; Planned Parenthood Advocates of Wisconsin; League of Conservation Voters. Former member: Monona Terrace Community and Convention Center Bd.; Greater Madison Convention and Visitors Bureau Bd.; Gov.'s Coun. on Domestic Abuse. Recipient: Wis. Coalition Against Domestic Violence *Legislative Champion Award* 2010; Wis. Women's Network *Stateswoman of the Year* 2006; Wis. League of Conservation Voters Award 2002-2010; Wis. Council of the Blind *Legislator of the Year* 2005; Wis. Coalition Against Sexual Assault *Voices of Courage Award* 2005; Wis. Alliance of Cities *Urban Families Recognition* 2004; Domestic Abuse Intervention Services *Certificate of Recognition* 2004; Wis. Coalition Against Domestic Violence *"DV Diva" Award* 2003; Domestic Abuse Intervention Service *Public Service Award* 2002; National Alliance for the Mentally Ill – Dane County *Community Action Citizen Award* 2003. City of Madison Community Development Authority (chp. 1989-92); Dane Co. Bd. of Supervisors 1992-2000.

Elected to Assembly since 1998. Biennial committee assignments: **2015** — Campaigns and Elections (also 2013); Colleges and Universities (also 2013); Insurance (also 2013); Jt. Legis. Audit; Jt. Legis. Coun. Steering Com. for Symposia Series on Supporting Early Healthy Brain Development. **2013** — State and Local Finance; Jt. Survey Com. on Retirement Systems; Jt. Legislative Council.

Telephone: Office: (608) 266-3784; District: (608) 225-8193.

E-mail: Rep.Berceau@legis.wisconsin.gov

Web site: http://www.terese.org

Voting address: Madison 53711.

Mailing address: Office: Room 104 North, State Capitol, P.O. Box 8952, Madison 53708.

Lisa Subeck (Dem.), 78th Assembly District

Born Chicago, Ill., June 17, 1971; single. Graduate Rich Central H.S. 1989; B.A. UW-Madison 1993. Full-time legislator. Former early childhood education/Head Start program manager; technical college instructor; nonprofit executive director. Former member: Am. Federation of Teachers. City of Madison Common Council 2011-15.

Elected to Assembly 2014. Biennial committee assignments: **2015** — Children and Families; Family Law; Health; Public Benefit Reform; Urban and Local Affairs.

Telephone: Office: (608) 266-7521.

E-mail: Rep.Subeck@legis.wisconsin.gov

Voting address: 818 South Gammon Road #4, Madison 53719.

Mailing address: Office: Room 418 North, State Capitol, P.O. Box 8953, Madison 53708.

27th SENATE DISTRICT   See Madison Area Detail Map on pp. 90 & 91

Senator
ERPENBACH

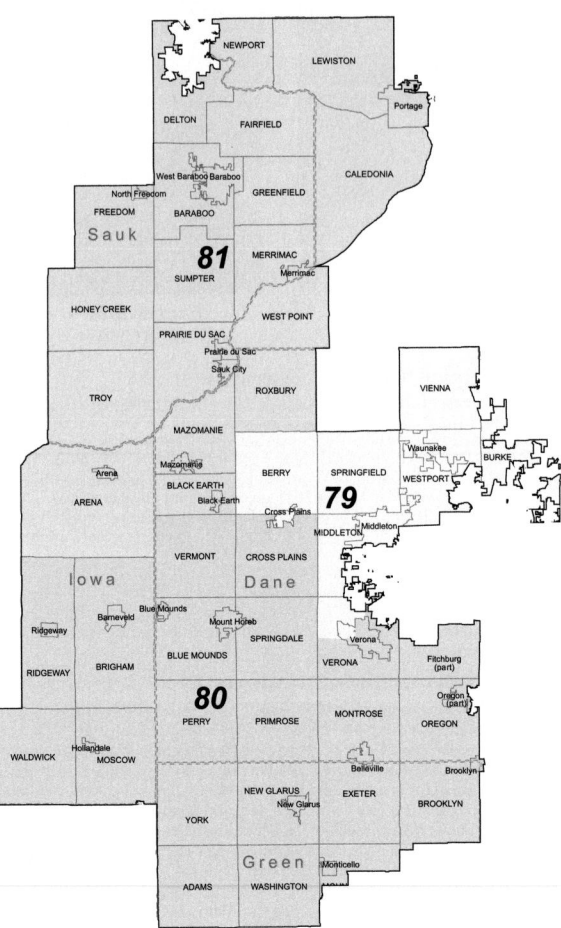

Jon B. Erpenbach (Dem.), 27th Senate District

Born Middleton, January 28, 1961; 2 children. Graduate Middleton H.S.; attended UW-Oshkosh 1979-81. Former communications director, legislative aide, radio personality, short order cook, meat packer, truck driver, and City of Middleton recreation instructor.

Elected to Senate 1998; reelected since 2002. Minority Leader 2003 session. Biennial committee assignments: **2015** — Agriculture, Small Business and Tourism; Health and Human Services (also 2013, chp. 2007); Jt. Com. on Finance; Jt. Survey Committee on Retirement Systems (also 1999). **2013** — Insurance and Housing; Universities and Technical Colleges. **2011** — Health; Judiciary, Utilities, Commerce, and Government Operations; Transportation and Elections; Jt. Legis. Coun. (also 2003, 1999). **2009** — Health, Health Insurance, Privacy, Property Tax Relief, and Revenue (chp.); Jt. Survey Com. on Tax Exemptions (co-chp., also 2007); Commerce, Utilities, Energy, and Rail; Education (vice chp. 2007, mbr. 2005, 2001, 1999); Judiciary, Corrections, Insurance, Campaign Finance Reform, and Housing. **2007** — Campaign Finance Reform, Rural Issues and Information Technology (vice chp.); Transportation, Tourism and Insurance. **2005** — Agriculture and Insurance; Health, Children, Families, Aging and Long-Term Care. **2003** — Jt. Com. on Employment Relations; Jt. Com. on Legislative Organization; Senate Organization; Jt. Legis. Coun. Spec. Com. on Review of Open Records Law (co-chp. since 2001). **2001** — Privacy, Electronic Commerce and Financial Institutions (chp., also 1999); 2001-03 Biennial Budget; Health, Utilities, Veterans and Military Affairs (also 1999); Jt. Com. on Information Policy and Technology; Law Revision Committee (also 1999); Legis. Coun. Com. on Condominium Law Review (co-chp. since 1999). **1999** — Jt. Committee on Information Policy; Lambeau Field; Census Education Bd.; Governor's Blue Ribbon Task Force on Passenger Rail.

Telephone: Office: (608) 266-6670; District: (888) 549-0027 (toll free).

E-mail: Sen.Erpenbach@legis.wisconsin.gov

Voting address: 7777 S. Elmwood Avenue, #204, Middleton 53562.

Mailing address: Office: Room 104 South, State Capitol, P.O. Box 7882, Madison 53707-7882.

| Representative | Representative | Representative |
| HESSELBEIN | POPE | CONSIDINE |

Dianne Hesselbein (Dem.), 79th Assembly District

Born Madison, March 10, 1971; married; 3 children. Graduate La Follette H.S. (Madison) 1989; B.S. UW-Oshkosh 1993; M.A. Edgewood College 1996. Full-time legislator. Member: Dane Co. Democratic Party; Friends of Pheasant Branch; Clean WI; Middleton Action Team; VFW Ladies Auxiliary Council. Former member: Parent Teacher Organization (pres.); Boy Scouts of America (cubmaster); Girl Scout troop leader. Middleton-Cross Plains Area School District Bd. 2005-08. Dane Co. Bd. 2008-14.

Elected to Assembly 2012; reelected 2014. Biennial committee assignments: **2015** — Colleges and Universities (also 2013); Natural Resources and Sporting Heritage (also 2013); Veterans and Military Affairs; Jt. Survey Com. on Tax Exemptions. **2013** — Education; Tourism; Veterans.

Telephone: Office: (608) 266-5340; (888) 534-0079 (toll free).

E-mail: Rep.Hesselbein@legis.wisconsin.gov

Voting address: Middleton 53562.

Mailing address: Office: Room 9 North, State Capitol, P.O. Box 8952, Madison 53708.

Sondy Pope (Dem.), 80th Assembly District

Born Madison, April 27, 1950; married. Graduate River Valley H.S.; attended Madison Area Technical College and Edgewood College. Former Associate Director of the Foundation for Madison's Public Schools. Member: Natl. Caucus of Environmental Legislators; Honorary Life Member, Wis. Congress of Parents and Teachers; Midwestern Higher Education Compact Commission; Fellow, Bowhay Institute, La Follette School, UW-Madison; Fellow, Flemming Institute, Center for Policy Alternatives; Oakhill Correctional Institute Advisory Bd.

Elected to Assembly since 2002. Biennial committee assignments: **2015** — Consumer Protection (also 2013, 2009); Corrections; Education (chp. 2009, mbr. since 2003); Rules (also 2013); Leg. Council Study Committee on the Student Achievement Guarantee in Education (SAGE). **2013** — Urban Education; Select Com. on Common Core Standards; Speaker's Task Force on Rural Schools; Jt. Legis. Council Spec. Com. on Improving Educational Opportunities in High School. **2011** — Children and Families (also 2009); Housing; Jt. Leg. Council Spec. Com. on Infant Mortality; Educator Effectiveness Coordinating Council; Read to Lead Development Council; School and District Accountability Team. **2009** — Corrections and the Courts (since 2005); State Affairs and Homeland Security; Leg. Coun. Spec. Com. on School Safety; Agricultural Education and Workforce Dev. Council; State Superintendent's Entrepreneurship Task Force (co-chp.). **2007** — Aging and Long-Term Care (since 2003); Education Reform. **2005** — Medicaid Reform. **2003** — Rural Affairs; Small Business.

Telephone: Office: (608) 266-3520; (888) 534-0080 (toll free).

E-mail: Rep.Pope@legis.wisconsin.gov

Voting address: 9262 Moen Road, Cross Plains 53528.

Mailing address: Office: Room 118 North, State Capitol, P.O. Box 8953, Madison 53708.

Dave Considine (Dem.), 81st Assembly District

Born Janesville, March 29, 1953; married; 5 children. Graduate Mukwonago Union H.S. 1970; B.S. education UW-Whitewater 1974; certificate in EBD UW-Madison 1990; M.A. education Viterbo U. 2005; certificates – instructor certificate, autism spectrum, and enhanced verbal skills, Crisis Prevention Institute (Milwaukee) 2008, 2010, 2013. Full-time legislator. Former dairy goat farmer, special education teacher. Member: St. John's Episcopal Church (worship leader); Columbia Co. Democratic Party; Pheasants Forever; Ducks Unlimited. Former member: Baraboo Education Assn. (pres.); American Dairy Goat Assn. (judge); Wisconsin Dairy Goat Assn. (pres.); Crisis Prevention Institute (instructor).

Elected to Assembly 2014. Biennial committee assignments: **2015** — Agriculture; Education; Environment and Forestry; Mental Health Reform; Mining and Rural Development.

Telephone: Office: (608) 266-7746; (888) 534-0081 (toll free); District: (608) 356-9693.

Voting address: N6194 Breezy Hill Road, Baraboo 53913.

Mailing address: Room 412 North, State Capitol, P.O. Box 8952, Madison 53708.

28th SENATE DISTRICT

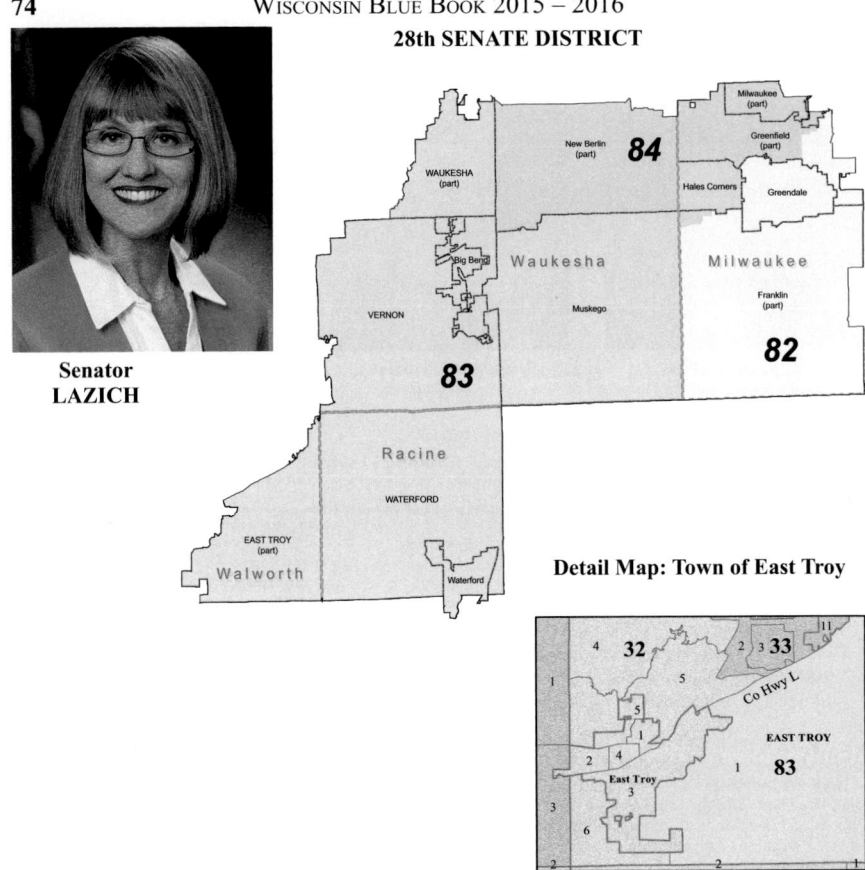

**Senator
LAZICH**

Detail Map: Town of East Troy

See Milwaukee Area Detail Map on pp. 92 & 93
See Waukesha County Area Detail Map on pp. 94 & 95

Mary A. Lazich (Rep.), 28th Senate District

Born Loyal, October 3, 1952; married; 3 children. B.A. UW-Milwaukee, *summa cum laude*. Former county board supervisor and city council member. Member: Waukesha Co. Republican Party; Waukesha Co. Republican Women's Club; New Berlin Lioness; New Berlin Historical Society; Boy Scout Advisory Com., Potawatomi Area Council. Waukesha Co. Board supervisor 1990-93, and mbr. of its Legislative, Intergovernmental and Education Com., Health and Human Services Com., Transportation Com., and Community Development Block Grant Bd.; New Berlin City Council 1986-92 (former president, chm. of Finance Com., chm. of Board of Public Works, mbr. of Planning Commission and Crime Prevention Com.).

Elected to Assembly 1992-96 (resigned eff. 4/20/98); elected to Senate in April 1998 special election; reelected since 2000. President of the Senate 2015; Majority Caucus Chairperson 2003. Biennial Senate committee assignments: **2015** — Jt. Com. on Legislative Organization (co-chp.); Jt. Legis. Council. (co-chp., also 2011); Jt. Legis. Audit (since 2009, 2001, 1999, co-chp. 1997 eff. 4/21/98); Jt. Com. on Employment Relations. **2013** — Elections and Urban Affairs (chp.); Health and Human Services (also 2007); Jt. Com. on Finance (also 2005, 2003). **2011** — Transportation and Elections (chp.); Public Health, Human Services, and Revenue (vice chp.); Labor, Public Safety, and Urban Affairs. **2009** — Health, Health Insurance, Privacy, Property Tax Relief, and Revenue; Small Business, Emergency Preparedness, Technical Colleges, and Consumer Protection. **2007** — Education (also 2001, 1999); Judiciary and Corrections; Sentencing Comn. **2005** — Labor and Election Process Reform; Women's Council (also 1999, 1997). **2003** — Jt. Com. on Administrative Rules; Energy and Utilities; Law Revision Com. (co-chp.). **2001** — Health, Utilities, Veterans and Military Affairs; Jt. Com. on Information Policy and Technology. **1999** — Council on Highway Safety. **1997** — Education and Financial Institutions; Government Effectiveness; State Government Operations and Corrections; Forward Wisconsin, Inc. Assembly committee assignments: **1997** — Jt. Legis. Audit (co-chp., also 1995); Working Families (vice chp.); Financial Institutions; Health (since 1993); Labor and Employment (also 1995). **1995** — Insurance, Securities and Corporate Policy; Urban Education (also 1993); Welfare Reform; Legis. Coun. Com. on Health Care Information. **1993** — Excise and Fees; Judiciary; Transportation; Legis. Coun. Com. on Child Care Economics.

Telephone: Office: (608) 266-5400; (800) 334-1442 (toll free); District: (414) 425-9452.

E-mail: Sen.Lazich@legis.wisconsin.gov

Voting address: New Berlin 53151.

Mailing address: Office: Room 219 South, State Capitol, P.O. Box 7882, Madison 53707-7882.

Representative	Representative	Representative
SKOWRONSKI	**CRAIG**	**KUGLITSCH**

Ken Skowronski (Rep.), 82nd Assembly District

Born Milwaukee, May 31, 1938; widowed; 2 children. Graduate Boys Tech H.S. 1958. Journeyman carpenter, MATC (Milwaukee) 1961; NARI certified remodeler. General contractor; radio host, monthly talk show; 4H construction skills instructor; seminar speaker, Wis. Burglar and Fire Alarm Assn. and WPR. Wis. Air National Guard 1956-62. Member: Milwaukee/NARI Foundation (trustee; fmr. pres.); Franklin Noon Lions Club (trustee, fmr. pres.); Polish Heritage Alliance (bd. mbr.); Knights of Columbus (fmr. deputy grand knight); National Rifle Assn. (endowment life mbr.); Ducks Unlimited (life mbr.); Rocky Mountain Elk Foundation (life mbr.); South Suburban Chamber of Commerce (fmr. bd. mbr.); Milwaukee/NARI Chapter (fmr. pres.); NARI National Foundation/NRF (fmr. pres.). Former member: Franklin Lions Club (pres.); NKBA Wis./Upper Michigan Chapter (treas.); City of Franklin Plan Commission; City of Franklin Economic Dev. Commission (chm.); City of Franklin Community Development Authority; City of Franklin 50th Anniversary Com. (chm.). Recipient: City of Franklin *Distinguished Service Award* 1983; Lions Intl. *Melvin Jones Fellowship Award* 1995; Remodeling Magazine *Big 50 Industry Impact Award* 1992; National Brand Names Foundation *First Place Remodelers Award* 1972; Milwaukee/NARI Chapter *Hank Fenderbosh Award* 1995, *Harold Hammerman Award* (nominee) 1994-95, *Lifetime Achievement Award* 2002, 1997. Alderman, City of Franklin 2005-14.

Elected to Assembly in December 2013 special election; reelected 2014. Biennial committee assignments: **2015** — Veterans and Military Affairs (chp.); Health; Natural Resources and Sporting Heritage (also 2013); Small Business Development; Urban and Local Affairs (also 2013). **2013** — Veterans.

Telephone: Office: (608) 266-8590; (888) 534-0082 (toll free); District: (414) 425-2034.

E-mail: Rep.Skowronski@legis.wisconsin.gov

Voting address: 8642 South 116th Street, Franklin 53132.

Mailing address: Office: Room 209 North, State Capitol, P.O. Box 8953, Madison 53708.

David Craig (Rep.), 83rd Assembly District

Born Waukesha, March 16, 1979; married; 5 children. Graduate Wisconsin Lutheran H.S. 1997; attended UW-Waukesha; B.A. UW-Milwaukee 2002. Realtor. Former aide to Congressman Paul Ryan. Village of Big Bend trustee 2008-10.

Elected to Assembly in May 2011 special election; reelected since 2012. Biennial committee assignments: **2015** — Financial Institutions (chp., also 2013, mbr. 2011); State Affairs and Government Operations (vice chp.); Campaigns and Elections (also 2013); Family Law (also 2013); Insurance (since 2011); Public Benefit Reform. **2013** — Government Operations and State Licensing; Judiciary. **2011** — Judiciary and Ethics.

Telephone: Office: (608) 266-3363; (888) 534-0083 (toll free).

E-mail: Rep.Craig@legis.wisconsin.gov

Voting address: P.O. Box 323, Big Bend 53103.

Mailing address: Office: Room 127 West, State Capitol, P.O. Box 8952, Madison 53708.

Michael Kuglitsch (Rep.), 84th Assembly District

Born Milwaukee, February 3, 1960; married; 4 children. Graduate New Berlin West H.S. 1978; B.A. Business UW-Whitewater 1983. Business consultant. Former member: Wisconsin Restaurant Assn. (pres.); Wisconsin Bowling Centers Assn. (pres.); New Berlin Chamber of Commerce (pres.).

Elected to Assembly 2010; reelected since 2012. Biennial committee assignments: **2015** — Energy and Utilities (chp.); Jobs and the Economy; Labor (also 2013); Workforce Development (also 2013); Rules; Jt. Survey Com. on Retirement Systems. **2013** — State Affairs (chp.); International Trade and Commerce (vice chp.); Jobs, Economy and Mining. **2011** — Homeland Security and State Affairs (vice chp.); Jobs, Economy and Small Business; Labor and Workforce Development.

Telephone: Office: (608) 267-5158.

E-mail: Rep.Kuglitsch@legis.wisconsin.gov

Voting address: New Berlin 53146.

Mailing address: Office: Room 129 West, State Capitol, P.O. Box 8952, Madison 53708.

29th SENATE DISTRICT

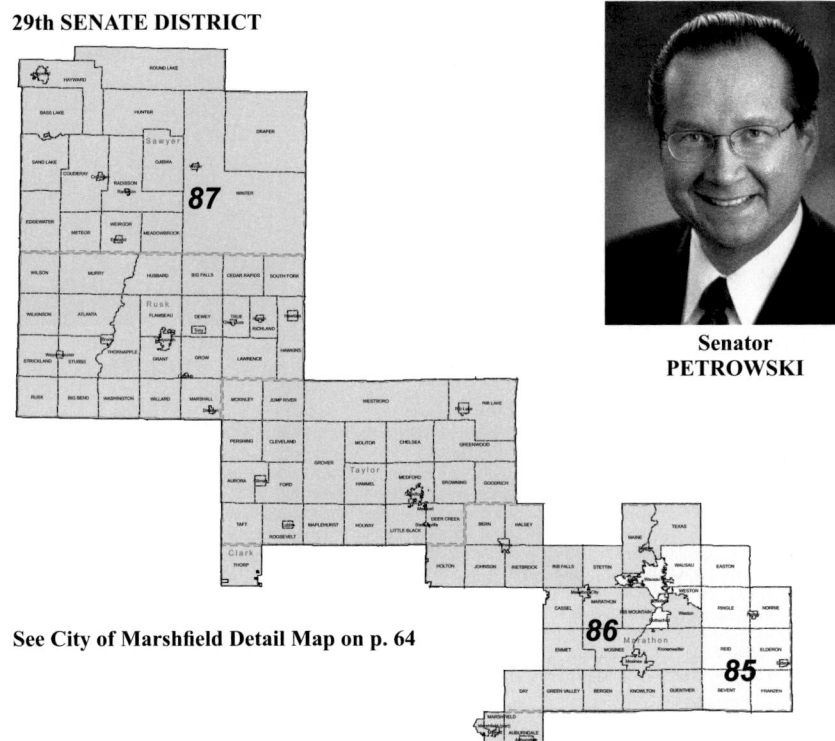

**Senator
PETROWSKI**

See City of Marshfield Detail Map on p. 64

Jerry Petrowski (Rep.), **29th Senate District**

Born Wausau, June 16, 1950; married; 4 children, 3 grandchildren. Graduate Newman H.S. (Wausau); attended UW-Marathon County and Northcentral Tech. College. Former ginseng, dairy, and beef farmer. Served in Army Reserve 1968-74. Member: 7th Cong. District, Marathon, Wood, Taylor, Rusk, Sawyer, Price, Lincoln, Portage, and Shawano Co. Republican Parties; Farm Bureau; Natl. Rifle Assn.; Friends of Rib Mountain; Wausau Elks; Marathon Lions. Former member: Wis. Rifle and Pistol Assn.; Internatl. Brotherhood of Electrical Workers Local #1791; Childcare Connection Bd.; DOT Law Enforcement Adv. Coun.; Marathon Co Hunger Coalition. Recipient: American Heart Assn. *Legislator of the Year Award* 2014; End Domestic Abuse Wis. *Legislative Leader Award* 2014; Wis. VFW *Legislator of the Year Award* 2014; Wis. Amer. Legion *Legislator of the Year Award* 2014; Wis. Vietnam Veterans *Legislator of the Year Award* 2002; Wis. Dept. of Veterans Affairs *Certificate of Commendation* 2005; Wis. Towns Assn. *Friend of Wis. Towns Award* 2014, 2011; Wis. Counties Assn. *Outstanding Legislator Award* 2014; Wis. Urban and Rural Transit Assn. *Legislative Statesman of the Year* 2014; Wis. Prof. Police Assn. *Legislator of the Year Award* 2014; Wis. Troopers Assn. *Legislator of the Year Award* 2014, 2003; Center for Driver's License Recovery and Employability *Legislative Champion Award* 2014; State Bar of Wis. *Scales of Justice Award* 2014; Wis. Dental Assn. Champion Award 2013 & *Award of Honor (Mission of Mercy)* 2011; Wis. Academy of Family Physicians *Friend of Family Medicine Award* 2014; Amer. Academy of Pediatrics *Childhood Legislative Advocate of the Year* 2005; Wis. Council on Physical Disabilities *Appreciation Award* 2014; Wis. Electric Cooperatives Assn. *Enlightened Legislator of the Year Award* 2013; Wis. Farm Bureau *Friend of Agriculture Award* 2006, 2004; Wis. Dairy Business Assn. Award 2014, 2012, 2010, 2008; Wis. Grocers Assn. *Friend of the Grocers Award* 2014, 2012, 2008, 2006; WMC *Working for Wisconsin Award* 2014, 2012, 2002, 2000; MMAC *Champion of Commerce Award* 2014; Wis. Builders Assn. *Friend of Housing Award* 2013, 2006; Associated Builders and Contractors of Wis. *Building Wisconsin Award* 2014; State Farm Insurance *Golden Car Seat Award* 2007; Chiropractic Society of Wis. *Legislator of the Year Award* 2014; Allied Health Chiropractic Centers *Commitment and Dedication to the Chiropractic Profession Award* 2004; 3M *Award of Appreciation* 2001; Wis. Paper Council *Champion of Paper Award* 2007; UWSP Paper Science Foundation *Friends of the Foundation Award* 2005; The Amer. Conservative Union *Defender of Liberty Award* 2013; Wis. Ginseng Board *Assistance to the Wis. Ginseng Industry Award* 2005; Wis. Bear Hunters Assn. *Hero Award* 2014, 2012.

Elected to Assembly 1998-2010; elected to Senate in June 2012 special election; reelected 2014. Majority Caucus Sergeant at Arms 2003-2007. Biennial Senate committee assignments: **2015** — Transportation and Veterans Affairs (chp.); Economic Development and Commerce (vice chp.); Agriculture, Small Business, and Tourism (also 2013); Jt. Leg. Council (also 2013); Building Comn.; State Councils on: Military and State Relations; Highway Safety; Transportation Projects Commission. **2013** — Transportation, Public Safety, and Veterans and Military Affairs (chp.); Economic Development and Local Government (vice chp.); Financial Institutions and Rural Issues; State Council on Interstate Compact on Educational Opportunity for Military Children. Assembly committee assignments: **2011** — Transportation (chp., also 2007, vice chp. 2001-05, mbr. 2009, 1999); Public Health and Public Safety; Rural Economic Development and Rural Affairs; Veterans and Military Affairs (since 2007, also 1999-2003). **2009** — Renewable Energy and Rural Affairs. **2007** — Rural Affairs (since 1999); Gov.'s Council on Highway Safety (since 2003).

Telephone: Office: (608) 266-2502. E-mail: Sen.Petrowski@legis.wisconsin.gov

Voting address: Marathon 54448.

Mailing address: Office: Room 123 South, State Capitol, P.O. Box 7882, Madison 53707-7882.

| **Representative** | **Representative** | **Representative** |
| HEATON | SPIROS | EDMING |

Dave Heaton (Rep.), 85th Assembly District

Born Chicago, Ill.; married; 3 children. Graduate Marmion Military Academy (Aurora, Ill.) 1990; B.A. Northern Illinois U. 1995; J.D. DePaul U. College of Law 1998. Reinsurance consultant. Attorney, former prosecutor. Served in Air National Guard 1990-96. Member: American Bar Assn.; Illinois Bar; Wis. Farm Bureau Federation; National Conf. of State Legislatures; National Rifle Assn.; Rib Mountain Bowmen; St. Michael's Parish (Wausau); St. Mary's Oratory (Wausau). Former member: Universal Telephone Assistance Corp. (secy. and treas.); Junior Achievement (instructor).

Elected to Assembly 2014. Biennial committee assignments: **2015** — Consumer Protection (vice chp.); Children and Families; Judiciary; Veterans and Military Affairs.

Telephone: Office: (608) 266-0654; (888) 534-0085 (toll free).

E-mail: Rep.Heaton@legis.wisconsin.gov

Voting address: Town of Wausau.

Mailing address: Office: Room 9 West, State Capitol, P.O. Box 8952, Madison 53708.

John Spiros (Rep.), 86th Assembly District

Born Akron, Ohio, July 28, 1961; married; 5 children, 2 grandchildren. Graduate Marietta H.S. (Marietta, Ohio) 1979; A.A.S. criminal justice MTCC (Omaha, NE) 1985. Vice president, safety and claims management for a transport company. Served in U.S. Air Force 1979-85. Member: Trucking Industry Defense Assn. (bd. mbr.); Wis. Farm Bureau; Marshfield Elks Club. Former member: Marshfield Rotary Club. City of Marshfield Alderman 2005-13.

Elected to Assembly 2012; reelected 2014. Biennial committee assignments: **2015** — Ways and Means (chp., mbr. 2013); Labor (vice chp.); Transportation (vice chp.); Criminal Justice and Public Safety. **2013** — Criminal Justice (vice chp.); Children and Families.

Telephone: Office: (608) 266-1182; (888) 534-0086 (toll free).

E-mail: Rep.Spiros@legis.wisconsin.gov

Voting address: Marshfield 54449.

Mailing address: Office: Room 15 North, State Capitol, P.O. Box 8953, Madison 53708.

James W. Edming (Rep.), 87th Assembly District

Born Ladysmith, November 22, 1945; married; 3 sons, 2 granddaughters, 1 great granddaughter. Graduate Flambeau H.S. (Tony) 1964; teacher's certificate Taylor Co. Teacher's Coll. 1967; attended UW-Superior, UW-Eau Claire, UW-Menomonie, UW-Barron Co. Convenience store owner, metal stamping co. owner, farmer. Former frozen pizza manufacturer. Member: 3rd degree Master Mason; 32nd degree Scottish Rite; Shriner; NRA (gun instructor); Model T Ford Club. Rusk Co. Hospital Bd. 1980-82, 2010-present. Rusk Co. Bd. of Supervisors 1976-87.

Elected to Assembly 2014. Biennial committee assignments: **2015** — Small Business Development (vice chp.); Environment and Forestry; Health; Natural Resources and Sporting Heritage; Veterans and Military Affairs.

Telephone: Office: (608) 266-7506; (888) 534-0087 (toll free); District: (715) 475-9292.

E-mail: Rep.Edming@legis.wisconsin.gov

Voting address: N4998 Edming Road, Glen Flora 54526.

Mailing address: Office: Room 109 West, State Capitol, P.O. Box 8952, Madison 53708.

30th SENATE DISTRICT

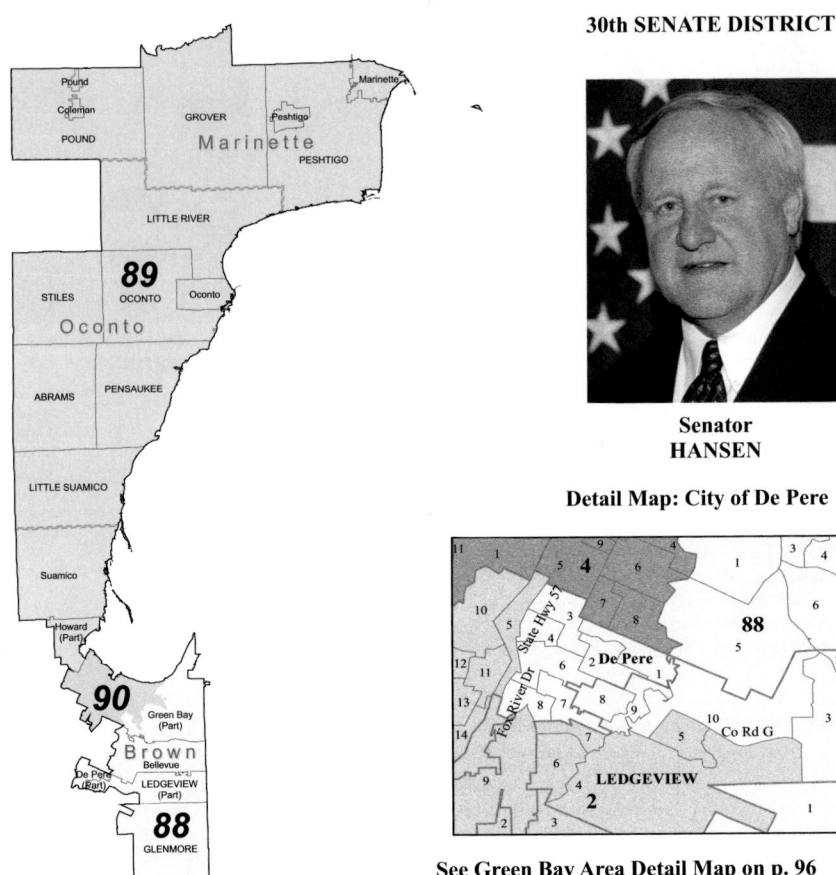

Senator
HANSEN

Detail Map: City of De Pere

See Green Bay Area Detail Map on p. 96

Dave Hansen (Dem.), 30th Senate District

Born Green Bay, December 18, 1947; married; 3 children, 11 grandchildren. Graduate Green Bay West H.S.; B.S. UW-Green Bay 1971. Full-time legislator. Former teacher. Former truck driver for Green Bay Department of Public Works. Former Teamster's Union steward. Former member: Brown Co. Human Services Bd. (chp.); N.E.W. Zoo Advisory Bd.; Brown Co. Education and Recreation Com. (chp.); Great Lakes Compact Commission. Brown Co. Bd. Supervisor 1996-2002.

Elected to Senate 2000; reelected since 2004. Assistant Minority Leader 2015, 2013, 2011, 2005, 2003; Majority Leader 2009 (eff. 12/15/10); Assistant Majority Leader 2011 (eff. 7/24/12); 2009, 2007. Biennial committee assignments: **2015** — Agriculture, Small Business and Tourism (also 2013); Transportation and Veterans Affairs; Universities and Technical Colleges; Senate Organization (since 2003); Jt. Com. on Legislative Organization (since 2003); Transportation Projects Commission (also 2011, 2009, 2001). **2013** — Energy, Consumer Protection and Government Reform; Transportation, Public Safety, and Veterans and Military Affairs; Jt. Survey Com. on Retirement Systems (co-chp. 2011, eff. 7/24/12). **2011** — Transportation, Infrastructure, Financial Institutions and Retirement Security (chp.); Job Creation, Energy & Utilities, and Rural Affairs (vice chp.); Agriculture, Forestry, and Higher Education; Energy, Biotechnology, and Consumer Protection; State and Federal Relations and Information Technology; Jt. Com. on Finance (eff. 7/24/12, 2009, vice co-chp. 2007). **2009** — Education (since 2005); Transportation, Tourism, Forestry, and Natural Resources; Jt. Leg. Coun. Spec. Com. on State-Tribal Relations; Claims Bd.; Women's Council. **2007** — Commerce, Utilities and Rail; Transportation, Tourism and Insurance. **2005** — Agriculture and Insurance; Labor and Election Process Reform. **2003** — Jt. Legis. Audit (through 5/23/03); Agriculture, Financial Institutions and Insurance; Education, Ethics and Elections; Labor, Small Business Development and Consumer Affairs. **2001** — Labor and Agriculture (chp.); Jt. Com. for Review of Administrative Rules; Environmental Resources; Human Services and Aging; Universities, Housing, and Government Operations; Law Revision Committee; Unemployment Insurance Advisory Council (*ex officio* member).

Telephone: Office: (608) 266-5670; (866) 221-9395 (toll free); District: (920) 391-2000.

E-mail: Sen.Hansen@legis.wisconsin.gov

Voting address: 3489 Blackwolf Run, Green Bay 54311.

Mailing address: Office: Room 106 South, State Capitol, P.O. Box 7882, Madison 53707-7882.

| Representative | Representative | Representative |
| MACCO | NYGREN | GENRICH |

John J. Macco (Rep.), 88th Assembly District

Born Green Bay, September 23, 1958; married; 2 children. Graduate Green Bay Southwest H.S. 1976; attended NWTC and UW-Green Bay. Branch manager, financial advisor. Founder of floor covering center and financial group. Member: National Rifle Association; Experimental Aircraft Association. Former board member: American Cancer Society of Wood County; Old Main Street Marshfield; Old Main Street De Pere; Old Main Street Green Bay; U.S. Ski Patrol; Aircraft Owners and Pilots Association. Former Deacon and Church Elder at Central Church, Green Bay.

Elected to Assembly 2014. Biennial committee assignments: **2015** — Ways and Means (vice chp.); Jt. Legis. Audit (vice chp.); Colleges and Universities; Jobs and the Economy; Transportation.

Telephone: Office: (608) 266-0485; (888) 534-0088 (toll free); District: (920) 884-3377.

E-mail: Rep.Macco@legis.wisconsin.gov

Voting address: 1874 Old Valley Road, De Pere 54115.

Mailing address: Office: Room 22 West, State Capitol, P.O. Box 8953, Madison 53708.

John Nygren (Rep.), 89th Assembly District

Born Marinette, February 27, 1964; married; 3 children. Graduate Marinette H.S. 1982; attended UW-Marinette. Insurance and financial representative. Former restaurant owner and operator. Member: Jaycees (lifetime mbr., fmr. chapter, state, U.S. pres.); Marinette Kiwanis (fmr. pres.); Marinette Co. GOP (fmr. chm.). City of Marinette Recreation and Planning Bd. 2003-06.

Elected to Assembly 2006; reelected since 2008. Biennial committee assignments: **2015** — Jt. Com. on Finance (co-chp., also 2013, mbr. 2011); Corrections; Jt. Com. on Audit (also 2013); Jt. Com. on Employment Relations (also 2013); Jt. Legis. Council (also 2013). **2011** — Insurance (also 2009, vice chp. 2007). **2009** — Education (also 2007); Health and Health Care Reform (also 2007). **2007** — Jobs and the Economy.

Telephone: Office: (608) 266-2343; (888) 534-0089 (toll free).

E-mail: Rep.Nygren@legis.wisconsin.gov

Voting address: Marinette 54143.

Mailing address: Office: Room 309 East, State Capitol, P.O. Box 8953, Madison 53708.

Eric Genrich (Dem.), 90th Assembly District

Born Green Bay, October 8, 1979; married; 2 children. Graduate Notre Dame Academy 1998; B.A. UW-Madison 2002; MLIS UW-Milwaukee 2010. Full-time legislator. Former librarian and legislative aide. Member: Neighbor-Works Green Bay; Emerging Leaders Soc. of the Brown Co. United Way; Brown Co. Historical Soc.; Democratic Party of Brown County; AFSCME Local 1901B; Current Young Professionals Network; Wisconsin Literacy.

Elected to Assembly 2012; reelected 2014. Biennial committee assignments: **2015** — Education; Energy and Utilities; Financial Institutions (also 2013); Housing and Real Estate (also 2013); Urban and Local Affairs; Jt. Com. on Information Policy and Technology (also 2013). **2013** — Ways and Means.

Telephone: Office: (608) 266-0616; (888) 534-0090 (toll free); District: (920) 593-8528.

E-mail: Rep.Genrich@legis.wisconsin.gov

Voting address: 1089 Division Street, Green Bay 54303.

Mailing address: Office: Room 304 West, State Capitol, P.O. Box 8952, Madison 53708.

31st SENATE DISTRICT

Senator
VINEHOUT

See Eau Claire Area Detail Map on p. 97

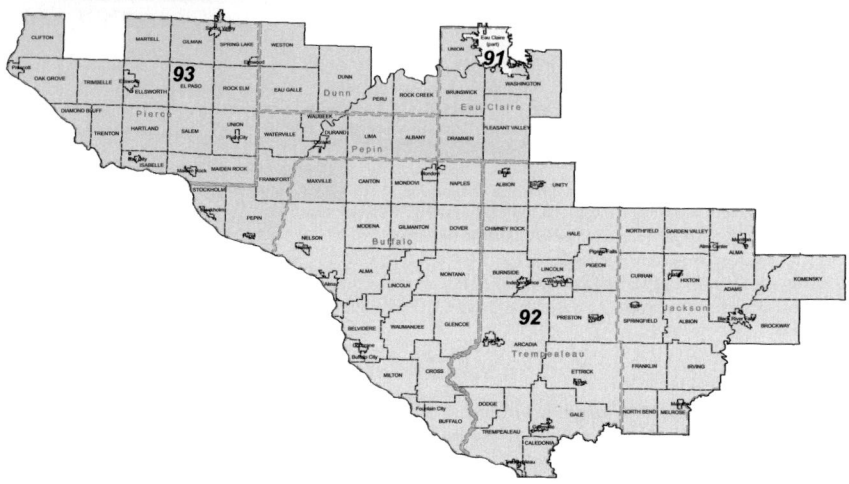

Kathleen Vinehout (Dem.), 31st Senate District

Born June 16, 1958; married; 1 child. B.S. with honors in education Southern Illinois U. 1980; M.P.H. St. Louis U. 1982; Ph.D. St. Louis U. 1987; A.D. in agriculture. Organic farmer. Former dairy farmer, university professor, health care manager. Member: Wis. Farmers Union; Wis. Farm Bureau Federation (fmr. bd. mbr., Buffalo Co.); Alma Chamber of Commerce; Democratic Party of Buffalo Co. (fmr. chp.); Andrew Blackfoot American Legion Auxiliary Post 129. Former member: Buffalo Co. Agricultural Fair Assn. (bd. mbr.); American Federation of Teachers (treas., Local 4100). Recipient: Sierra Club *Environmental Champion* 2014; Wis. Public Health Assn. *Friend of Public Health* 2014; Wis. Farmers Union *Friend of Farmers Union Award* 2013; Wis. Congress of Parents and Teachers *Joan Dykstra Friends of Children Award* 2012; Wis. Aquaculture Assn. *Friend of Wisconsin Aquaculture* 2011; La Crosse Area Development Council *Triangle of Achievement;* AFSCME Council 40 *Protector of Quality Services Award* 2010; School Administrators Alliance *Legislator of the Year* 2010; Wis. Academy of Family Physicians *Friend of Family Medicine;* Wis. Grocers Assn. *Friend of Grocers* 2010; Wis. Crop Production Assn. *Outstanding Service to Agriculture Award;* Wis. Assn. of County Homes 2010 *Outstanding Legislative Service Award;* Wis. Troopers Assn. *Legislator of the Year* 2010; Wis. League of Conservation Voters *Conservation Champion* 2014, 2010, 2008; Wis. Assn. of PEG Channels *Friend of Access* 2008; Wis. Assn. of FFA *Honorary State FFA Degree* 2008; Pharmacy Soc. of Wis. *Legislator of the Year* 2008; Wis. Federation of Cooperatives *Friend of Cooperatives* 2008. Mississippi River Regional Planning Commission 2004-2011.

Elected to Senate 2006; reelected since 2010. Minority Caucus Vice Chairperson 2015, 2013, 2011; Majority Caucus Vice Chairperson 2009. Biennial committee assignments: **2015** — Agriculture, Small Business and Tourism (also 2013); Education Reform and Government Operations; Sporting Heritage, Mining and Forestry; Jt. Legislative Audit Com. (co-chp. 2011 eff. 7/24/12, also 2009, mbr. since 2009); Jt. Com. on Information Policy and Technology (also 2013); Mississippi River Parkway Comn. (since 2011). **2013** — Education (also 2011); Jt. Com. for Review of Admin. Rules. **2011** — Agriculture, Forestry, and Higher Education; Financial Institutions and Rural Issues. **2009** — Agriculture and Higher Education (chp., also 2007); Children, Families and Workforce Development; Economic Development; Public Health, Senior Issues, Long-Term Care, and Job Creation. **2007** — Health and Human Services (vice chp.); Economic Development, Job Creation, Family Prosperity and Housing; Judiciary and Corrections.

Telephone: Office: (608) 266-8546; (877) 763-6636 (toll free).

E-mail: Sen.Vinehout@legis.wisconsin.gov

Voting address: Alma 54610.

Mailing address: Office: Room 108 South, State Capitol, P.O. Box 7882, Madison 53707-7882.

Representative   Representative   Representative
WACHS   **DANOU**   **PETRYK**

Dana Wachs (Dem.), 91st Assembly District

Born Eau Claire, August 25, 1957; married; 3 children. Graduate Memorial H.S. (Eau Claire) 1975; attended UW-Eau Claire 1975-76; B.S. Marquette U. 1981; J.D. Valparaiso U. 1985. Attorney. (Martindale-Hubbell AV Rated). Member: American Bar Assn.; Wis. State Bar; Eau Claire County Bar Assn; Wis. Assn. of Justice; Rotary; Chippewa Valley Jazz Orchestra (bd. mbr.); Wis. Farmers Union; Muskies, Inc. Eau Claire City Council 2009-12 — Eau Claire City County Bd. of Health, Eau Claire Transit Comn., Eau Claire Affirmative Action Com., Eau Claire Parks and Waterways Com., L.E. Phillips Memorial Library (bd. mbr.), Eau Claire Economic Policy Adv. Com.

Elected to Assembly 2012; reelected 2014. Biennial committee assignments: **2015** — Colleges and Universities (also 2013); Constitution and Ethics (also 2013); Judiciary (also 2013); Jt. Legis. Council Study Com. on Transfer of Structured Settlement Payments (vice chp.). **2013** — Criminal Justice (eff. 1/15/14); Workforce Development; Law Revision.

Telephone: Office: (608) 266-7461; (888) 534-0091 (toll free); District (715) 552-1439.

E-mail: Rep.Wachs@legis.wisconsin.gov

Voting address: Eau Claire 54701.

Mailing address: Office: Room 302 North, State Capitol, P.O. Box 8953, Madison 53708.

Chris Danou (Dem.), 92nd Assembly District

Born Bloomington, IL, 1967; married; 2 children. Graduate Columbus H.S. (Marshfield) 1985; A.A. UW-Marshfield/Wood Co. 1987; B.A. with distinction UW-Madison 1989; M.A. international affairs The American U. (Washington, D.C.) 1991; M.S. natural resources UW-Stevens Point 1997. Full-time legislator. Former police officer, City of Onalaska. Member: Wis. Farm Bureau Fed.; Ducks Unlimited; National Farmers Union; Pheasants Forever; Trout Unlimited; The Nature Conservancy. Former member: Onalaska Professional Police Assn. (pres.); Wis. Professional Police Assn; Wis. Crime Victims Council. Recipient: Wisconsin Professional Police Association *Legislator of the Year* 2009-10; *Friend of Grocers* 2012, 2010. UW-Stevens Point College of Natural Resources Advisory Committee.

Elected to Assembly 2008; reelected since 2010. Biennial committee assignments: **2015** — Agriculture (since 2009); Insurance (also 2013); Mining and Rural Development; Natural Resources and Sporting Heritage (also 2013); Transportation (also 2013). **2013** — Environment and Forestry; Speaker's Task Force on Mental Health; Speaker's Task Force on Rural Schools; Wis. Environmental Education Bd. **2011** — Homeland Security and State Affairs; Natural Resources (vice chp. 2009); Rural Economic Development and Rural Affairs. **2009** — Fish and Wildlife; Renewable Energy and Rural Affairs.

Telephone: Office: (608) 266-7015; (888) 534-0091 (toll free); District: (608) 534-5016.

E-mail: Rep.Danou@legis.wisconsin.gov

Voting address: Trempealeau 54661.

Mailing address: Office: Room 107 North, State Capitol, P.O. Box 8952, Madison 53708.

Warren Petryk (Rep.), 93rd Assembly District

Born Eau Claire, January 24, 1955; single. Graduate Boyceville H.S. 1973; attended UW-Stout; B.A. *with highest honors* UW-Eau Claire 1978. Eagle Scout, November 1969. Worked in community relations for United Cerebral Palsy of West Central Wis.; co-founder of musical entertainment group "The Memories". Member: Eau Claire, Menomonie, Ellsworth, and Prescott Chambers of Commerce; National Rifle Association; Eau Claire Rod and Gun Club; Eau Galle-Rush River, Ellsworth, Durand, Rock Falls, and Arkansaw Sportsmen's Clubs; Wis. Farm Bureau; Cleghorn Lions Club; Chippewa Valley Council of Boy Scouts of America (bd. dir.). Recipient: Wis. Veterans of Foreign Wars *Legislator of the Year* 2013; Wis. AMVETS *Veteran's Advocate of the Year* 2014. Governor's Council on Workforce Investment.

Elected to Assembly 2010; reelected since 2012. Biennial committee assignments: **2015** — Workforce Development (chp., vice chp. 2013); Aging and Long-Term Care (also 2013, vice chp. 2011); Colleges and Universities; Energy and Utilities; Insurance; Veterans and Military Affairs (also 2011); Jt. Com. on Information Policy and Technology (vice chp., mbr. 2013); Leg. Coun. Special Study Com. on Problem-Solving Courts, Alternatives and Diversions. **2013** — Veterans (chp.); Jobs, Economy and Mining; Natural Resources and Sporting Heritage; Speaker's Task Force on Rural Schools. **2011** — Jobs, Economy and Small Business.

Telephone: Office: (608) 266-0660; (888) 534-0093 (toll free).

E-mail: Rep.Petryk@legis.wisconsin.gov

Voting address: Eleva 54738.

Mailing address: Office: Room 103 West, State Capitol, P.O. Box 8953, Madison 53708.

32nd SENATE DISTRICT

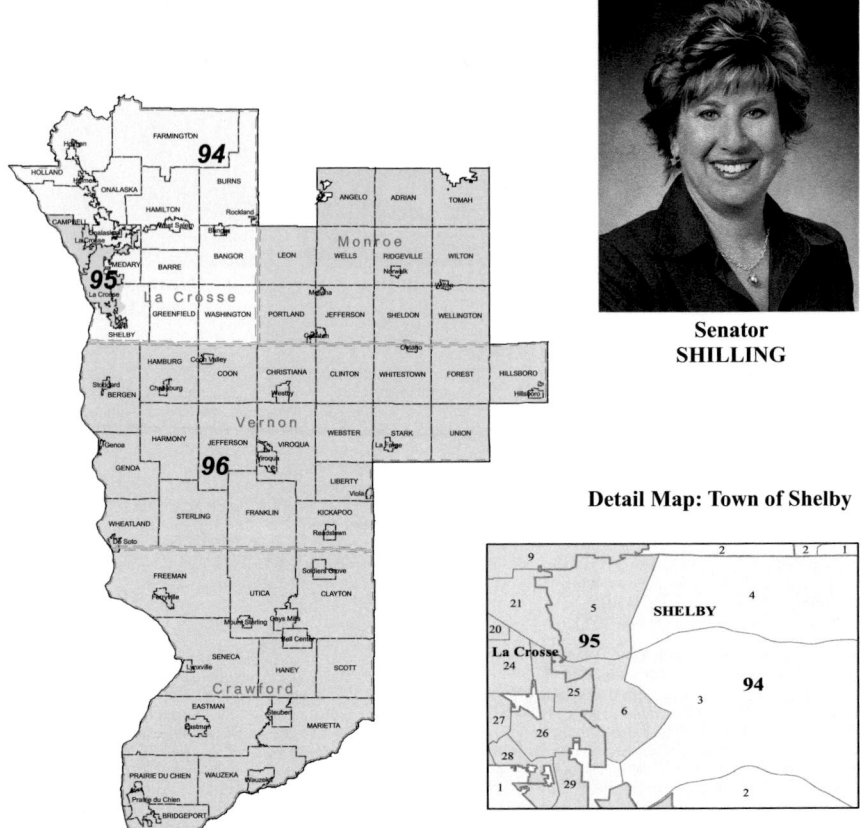

Senator
SHILLING

Detail Map: Town of Shelby

Jennifer Shilling (Dem.), 32nd Senate District

Born Oshkosh, July 4; married; 2 children. Graduate Buffalo Grove, IL H.S.; B.A. in political science and public administration, UW-La Crosse 1992. Former congressional aide and legislative aide. Member: UW-La Crosse Alumni Assn. (fmr. pres.); La Crosse Co. League of Women Voters; La Crosse Co. Democratic Party (former chp.); UW-La Crosse Chancellor's Community Council; Viterbo University Bd. of Advisors; La Crosse Area Chamber of Commerce; La Crosse County Local Emergency Planning Com.; La Crosse Area Habitat for Humanity Women Build; Vernon Women's Alliance; Viroqua Chamber Main Street; Riverfront La Crosse Community Advisory Bd. La Crosse Co. Bd. 1990-92.

Elected to Assembly 2000-10; elected to Senate in special election August 2011; reelected 2012. Minority Leader 2015; Minority Caucus Sergeant at Arms 2005. Biennial Senate committee assignments: **2015** — Senate Organization; Jt. Com. on Employment Relations; Jt. Com. on Legis. Organization; Jt. Legis. Council. **2013** — Government Operations, Public Works, and Telecommunications; Universities and Technical Colleges; Jt. Com. on Finance (also 2011). Assembly committee assignments: **2011** — Jt. Com. on Finance (also 2009). **2009** — Health and Health Care Reform (also 2007); Rules. **2007** — Colleges and Universities (since 2003); Workforce Development; State of Wisconsin Building Commission (also 2005). **2005** — Financial Institutions (since 2001); Health (since 2001); Highway Safety (also 2003). **2003** — Insurance (also 2001). **2001** — Personal Privacy; Legis. Adv. Com. to the Minn.-Wis. Boundary Area Comn.

Telephone: Office: (608) 266-5490; (800) 385-3385 (toll free).

E-mail: Sen.Shilling@legis.wisconsin.gov

Voting address: La Crosse 54601.

Mailing address: Office: Room 206 South, State Capitol, P.O. Box 7882, Madison 53707-7882.

| Representative | Representative | Representative |
| DOYLE | BILLINGS | NERISON |

Steve Doyle (Dem.), 94th Assembly District

Born La Crosse, May 21, 1958; married; 2 children. Graduate Aquinas H.S. 1976; B.A. UW-La Crosse 1980; J.D. U. of Wisconsin Law School 1986. Attorney. Former instructor, UW-La Crosse. Former member: Family Resource Center (bd. mbr.); Family and Childrens Center (bd. mbr.); Coulee Region Humane Society (bd. mbr., pres.). La Crosse Co. Bd. 1986-present (chairperson 2002-11).

Elected to Assembly in May 2011 special election; reelected since 2012. Biennial committee assignments: **2015** — Financial Institutions; Insurance (since 2011); Small Business Development; Tourism (also 2013); Jt. Review Com. on Criminal Penalties. **2013** — Corrections; Transportation (also 2011). **2011** — Rural Economic Development and Rural Affairs; Tourism, Recreation and State Properties.

Telephone: Office: (608) 266-0631; (888) 534-0094 (toll free); District: (608) 783-1204; (608) 784-7299.

E-mail: Rep.Doyle@legis.wisconsin.gov

Voting address: N5525 Hauser Road, Onalaska 54650.

Mailing address: Office: Room 124 North, State Capitol, P.O. Box 8952, Madison 53708.

Jill Billings (Dem.), 95th Assembly District

Born Rochester, MN, January 19, 1962; 2 children. Graduate Stewartville H.S. 1980; B.A. Augsburg College, Minneapolis, MN 1989. Council of State Governments: BILLD Fellow 2012, Toll Fellow 2014. Full-time legislator. Former teacher of English and Citizenship to Hmong adults. Member: Women in Government; Children's Trust Fund; Viterbo University Board of Advisors; UW-La Crosse Chancellor's Community Council; La Crosse County League of Women Voters; La Crosse County Democratic Party. Former member: Wisconsin Counties Association County Ambassador Program; La Crosse Area Family Policy Board; Stepping Stones Children's Advocacy Center; La Crosse County Economic Development Fund; La Crosse Community Foundation Granting Advisory Board. La Crosse County Board 2004-12.

Elected to the Assembly in November 2011 special election; reelected since 2012. Biennial committee assignments: **2015** — Interstate Affairs (vice chp.); Children and Families (also 2013); Colleges and Universities (also 2013); Mining and Rural Development; Tourism (also 2013); Council on Tourism (also 2013); Leg. Council. Spec. Com. on SAGE Program. **2013** — Constitution and Ethics (co-chp.); Workforce Development; Legis. Coun. Spec. Com. on Permanency for Young Children in the Child Welfare System. **2011** — Public Health and Safety; Consumer Protection and Personal Privacy.

Telephone: Office: (608) 266-5780; (888) 534-0095 (toll free).

Voting address: La Crosse 54601.

Mailing address: Office: Room 307 West, State Capitol, P.O. Box 8952, Madison 53708.

Lee Nerison (Rep.), 96th Assembly District

Born La Crosse, July 31, 1952; married; 3 children, 3 grandchildren. Graduate Viroqua H.S. 1970; UW-Madison Farm and Industry Short Course 1971. Farmer. Former dairy farmer. Member: Coon Valley Lions. Former member: Vernon Co-op Oil and Gas (bd. mbr., secretary); Viroqua FFA Alumni (reporter); Westby FFA Alumni; Church Council (vice pres., treasurer). Vernon Co. Board 1998-2006 (chairperson 2002-06).

Elected to Assembly since 2004. Majority Caucus Vice Chairperson 2015. Biennial committee assignments: **2015** — Agriculture (chp. since 2011, vice chp. 2007, 2005, mbr. 2009); Aging and Long-Term Care (also 2013); Consumer Protection (also 2013); Natural Resources and Sporting Heritage (also 2013); Veterans and Military Affairs (also 2011). **2013** — Veterans. **2011** — Natural Resources (since 2007). **2009** — Public Safety; Rural Economic Development. **2007** — Rural Affairs (chp.); Energy and Utilities (also 2005); Public Health. **2005** — Rural Affairs and Renewable Energy; Tourism.

Telephone: Office: (608) 266-3534; District: (608) 634-4562.

Voting address: Westby 54667.

Mailing address: Office: Room 310 North, State Capitol, P.O. Box 8953, Madison 53708.

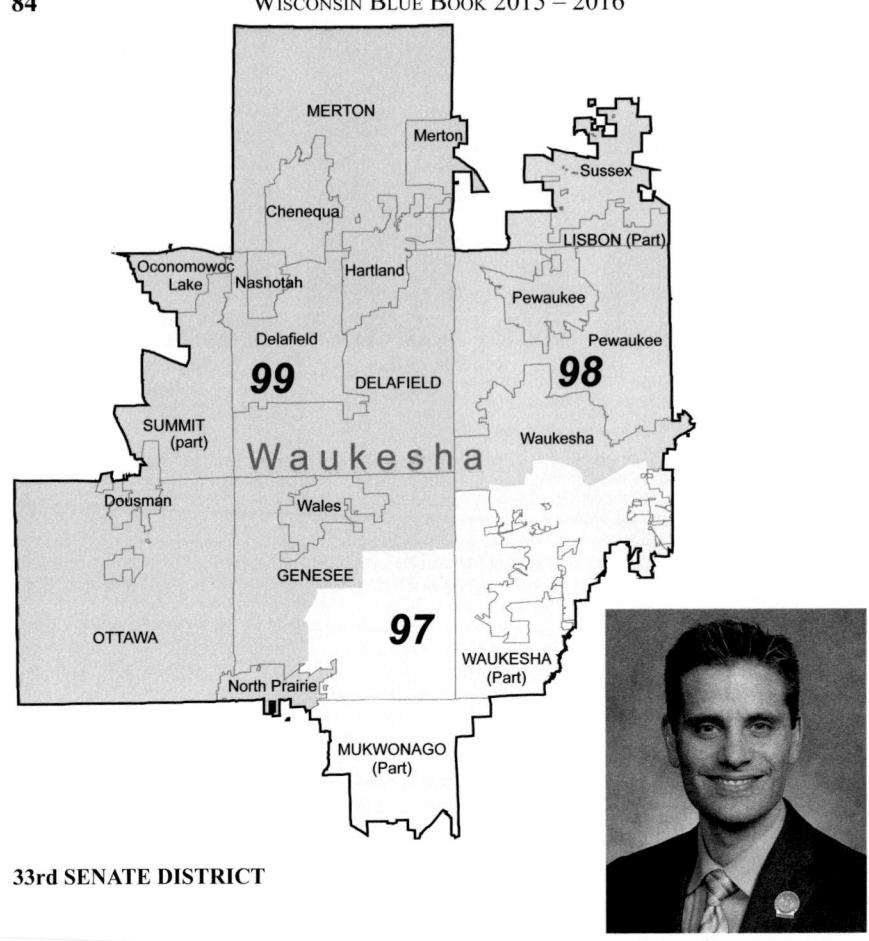

33rd SENATE DISTRICT

See Waukesha County Detail Map on pp. 94 & 95

See Waukesha Area Detail Map on p. 97

Senator
KAPENGA

Chris Kapenga (Rep.), 33rd Senate District

Born Zeeland, MI, February 19, 1972; married; 2 children. Graduate Holland Christian (Holland, MI) 1990. B.S. in accountancy, Calvin College (Grand Rapids, MI) 1994. Business owner. Certified public accountant. Member: Assembly of State Legislatures (co-pres.); NFIB; Elmbrook Church Financial Counseling (dir.). Former member: WSCA School Bd. (vice chm., treas., secy.); WICPA; MMAC; Institute of Management Accountants (bd. mbr.).

Elected to Assembly 2010; reelected 2012-2014; elected to Senate in July 2015 special election. Biennial Assembly committee assignments: **2015** — Constitution and Ethics (chp., also 2013); Public Benefit Reform (vice chp.); Financial Institutions (vice chp. 2013); Health (also 2013); Labor (also 2013). **2013** — Jobs, Economy and Mining. **2011** — Labor and Workforce Development (vice chp.); Insurance; Jobs, Economy and Small Business; Ways and Means.

Telephone: Office: (608) 266-9174.

Voting address: Delafield 53018.

Mailing address: Office: State Capitol, P.O. Box 7882, Madison 53707-7882.

Representative	Representative	VACANT
ALLEN	NEYLON	

Scott Allen (Rep.), 97th Assembly District

Born Racine, December 18, 1965; married; 2 children. Graduate Kettle Moraine H.S. 1984; attended UW-Oshkosh, UW-Waukesha; B.A. UW-Milwaukee 1989; Master of Public Administration and Master of Planning U. of Southern California 1992. Realtor and sales coach. Former sales director, home builder, and risk management analyst. Served in U.S. Army Reserve 1984-90. Member: Greater Milwaukee Assoc. of Realtors (fmr. bd. mbr.); Wis. Realtors Assn.; National Assn. of Realtors; Republican Party of Waukesha Co.; Spring Creek Church. Former member: Waukesha Civic Theatre (pres.). Waukesha Co. Community Development Block Grant Bd. 2010-14. Alderman, City of Waukesha 1998-2001.

Elected to Assembly 2014. Biennial committee assignments: **2015** — Housing and Real Estate (vice chp.); Environment and Forestry; Jobs and the Economy; Small Business Development; Veterans and Military Affairs.

Telephone: Office: (608) 266-8580; (888) 534-0097 (toll free); District: (262) 442-8695.

Voting address: Waukesha 53189.

Mailing address: Office: Room 8 West, State Capitol, P.O. Box 8952, Madison 53708.

Adam Neylon (Rep.), 98th Assembly District

Born Elgin, IL, December 30, 1984; married. Graduate H.D. Jacobs H.S. 2003; B.A. Carroll U. 2008. Small business owner. Former legislative staffer for U.S. Rep. Jim Sensenbrenner and Republican leadership in the Wis. Assembly. Member: Presidents Advisory Council at Carroll U.; Waukesha Co. Business Alliance; Republican Party of Waukesha Co. (fmr. youth chm.); National Rifle Association.

Elected to Assembly in April 2013 special election; reelected 2014. Biennial committee assignments: **2015** — Jobs and the Economy (chp.); Children and Families (also 2013); Consumer Protection; Energy and Utilities (also 2013); Public Benefit Reform. **2013** — Government Operations and State Licensing; State Affairs; State Supported Programs Study and Advisory Com.

Telephone: Office: (608) 266-5120.

E-mail: Rep.Neylon@legis.wisconsin.gov

Voting address: Pewaukee 53072.

Mailing address: Office: Room 125 West, State Capitol, P.O. Box 8953, Madison 53708.

99th Assembly District – Vacant

Jeffrey Renk: Senate Chief Clerk

Born Wauwatosa, January 31, 1960; married; 1 child. Graduate Wauwatosa West H.S. 1978; attended UW-Milwaukee 1978-80; B.S. political science UW-Madison 1984. Former Senate assistant chief clerk 2004-12; computer programmer, Legislative Technology Services Bureau 1998-2004; Assembly chief clerk staff 1988-98; Assembly messenger 1983-88. Member: American Society of Legislative Clerks and Secretaries. Former member: National Association of Legislative Information Technology.

Elected Senate Chief Clerk 2013; reelected 2015.

Telephone: Office: (608) 266-2517.

Voting address: Fitchburg 53719.

Mailing address: Office: Room B20 Southeast, State Capitol, P.O. Box 7882, Madison 53707-7882.

Edward (Ted) A. Blazel: Senate Sergeant at Arms

Born Quincy, IL, June 14, 1972; married; 2 children. Graduate Quincy Senior H.S. 1990; B.A. St. Norbert College (De Pere) 1994; M.A. Marquette U. (Milwaukee) 1998. Member: National Legislative Service and Security Assn.; Madison Area Youth Soccer Assn. (bd. mbr.).

Elected Senate Sergeant at Arms 2003; reelected since 2005.

Telephone: Office: (608) 266-1801.

Voting address: Madison 53714.

Mailing address: Office: Room B35 South, State Capitol, P.O. Box 7882, Madison 53707-7882.

Patrick E. Fuller: Assembly Chief Clerk

Born Toledo, Ohio, February 24, 1954; married; 1 child. Graduate St. Francis de Sales H.S. (Toledo) 1972; B.E. U. of Toledo 1980; M.B.A. Touro University International (Los Alamitos, CA) 2001. Former director Wisconsin Troops to Teachers Program, Wis. Dept. of Veterans Affairs 1998-2000. Vietnam Era and Operation Desert Storm veteran. Served in U.S. Marine Corps 1972-86; U.S. Army 1986-97. Member: NRA; Second Marine Division Assn.; Veterans of Foreign Wars; Disabled Veterans of America; American Legion; Force Recon Association; 75th Ranger Regiment Association.

Elected Assembly Chief Clerk 2003; reelected since 2005.

Telephone: Office: (608) 266-5811;

E-mail address: Patrick.Fuller@legis.wisconsin.gov

Voting address: 214 Grove Street, Ridgeway 53582.

Mailing address: Office: Suite 401, 17 West Main Street, Risser Justice Center, Madison 53708-8952.

Anne Tonnon Byers: Assembly Sergeant at Arms

Born Green Bay, December 14, 1968; married; 2 children. Graduate Green Bay East H.S. 1987; attended UW-Green Bay; B.S. UW-Madison 1991; UW Certified Public Management Program 2001. Former Assistant Assembly Sergeant at Arms 1998-2010; Office Manager for Assembly Sergeant 1993-98. Member: Boy Scout Troop 53.

Elected Assembly Sergeant at Arms 2011; reelected since 2013.

Telephone: Office: (608) 266-1503.

E-mail address: anne.tonnonbyers@legis.wisconsin.gov

Voting address: Village of McFarland.

Mailing address: Office: Room 411 West, State Capitol, P.O. Box 8952, Madison 53708-8952.

SENATE DISTRICTS

Enacted by 2011 Wisconsin Act 43

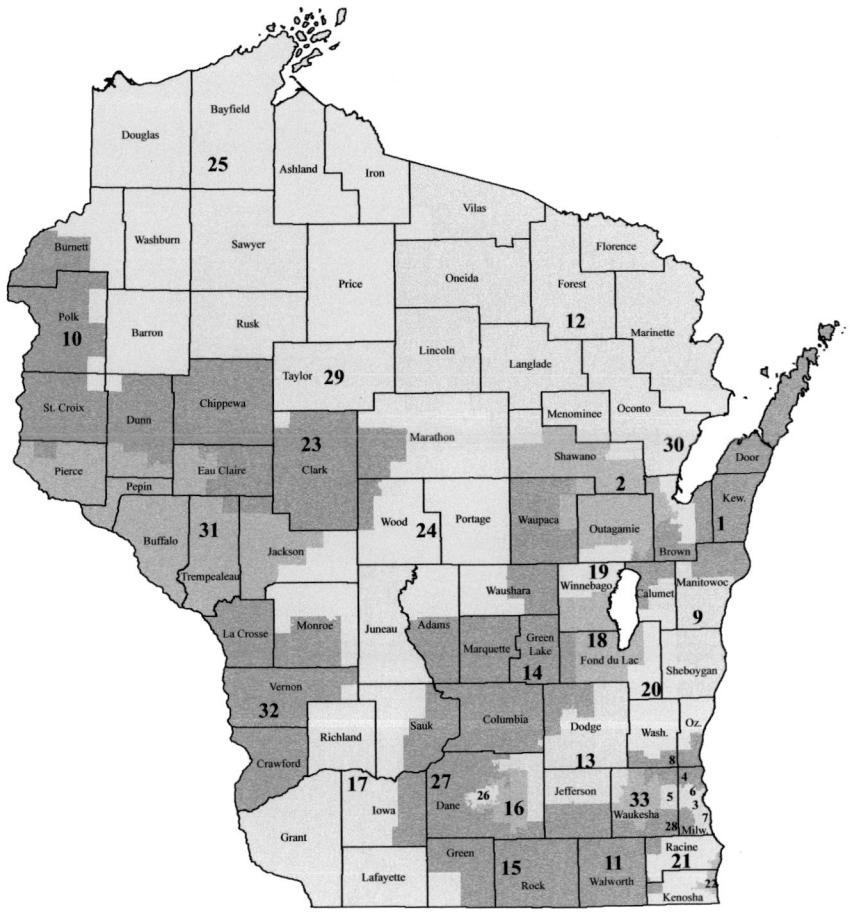

ASSEMBLY DISTRICTS

Enacted by 2011 Wisconsin Act 43

(As modified by the U.S. District Court for the Eastern
District of Wisconsin in *Baldus vs. Members of the Wisconsin
Government Accountability Board*, Case No. 11-CV-562)

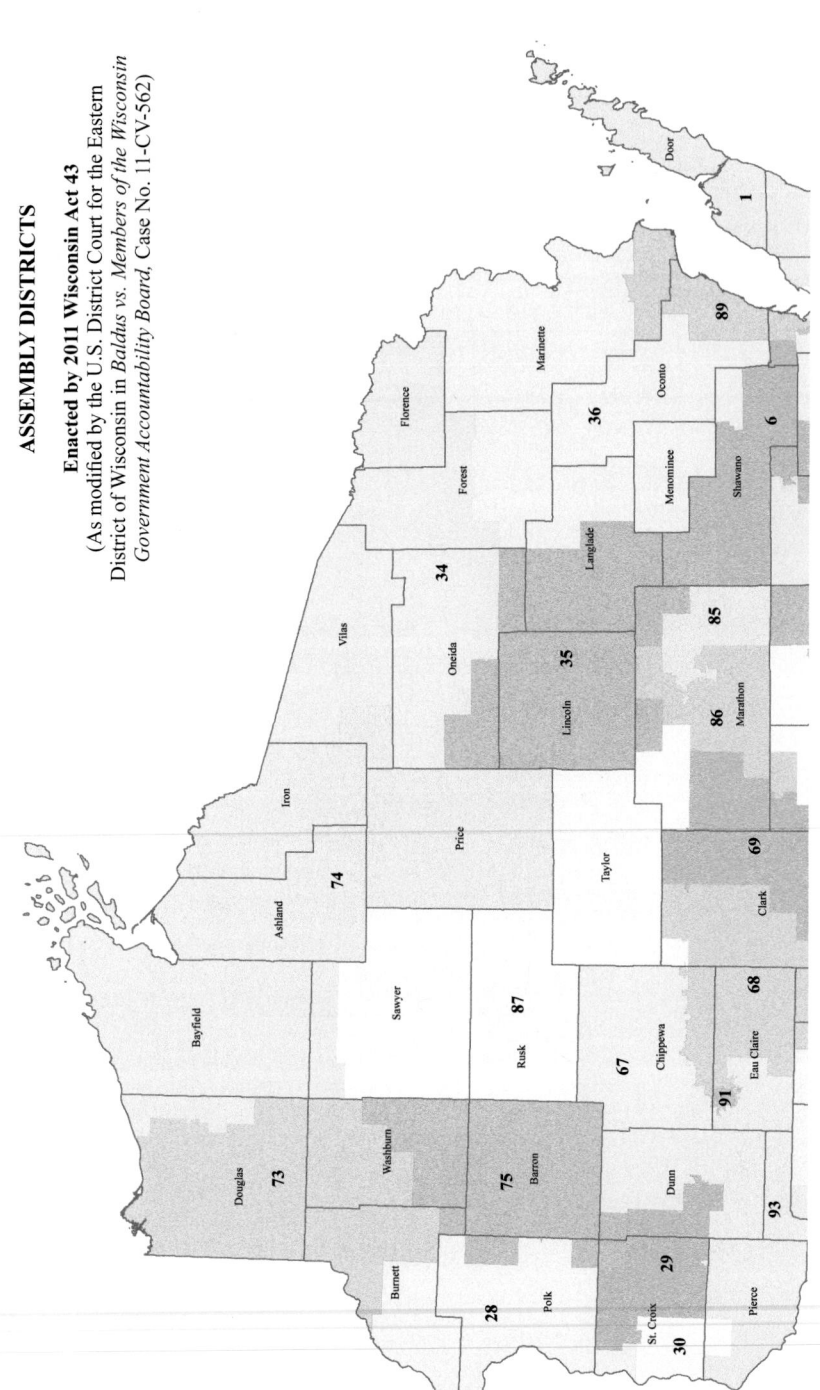

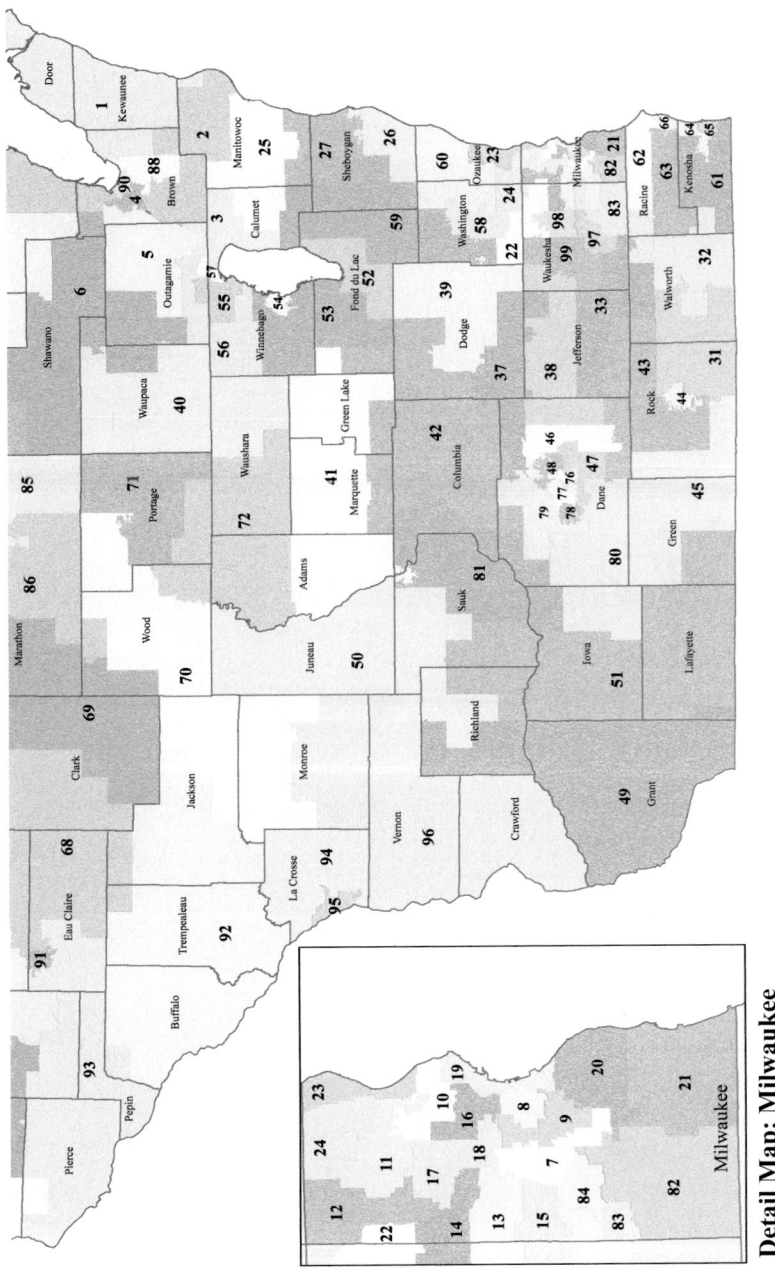

Detail Map: Milwaukee

Detail Map: Madison Area

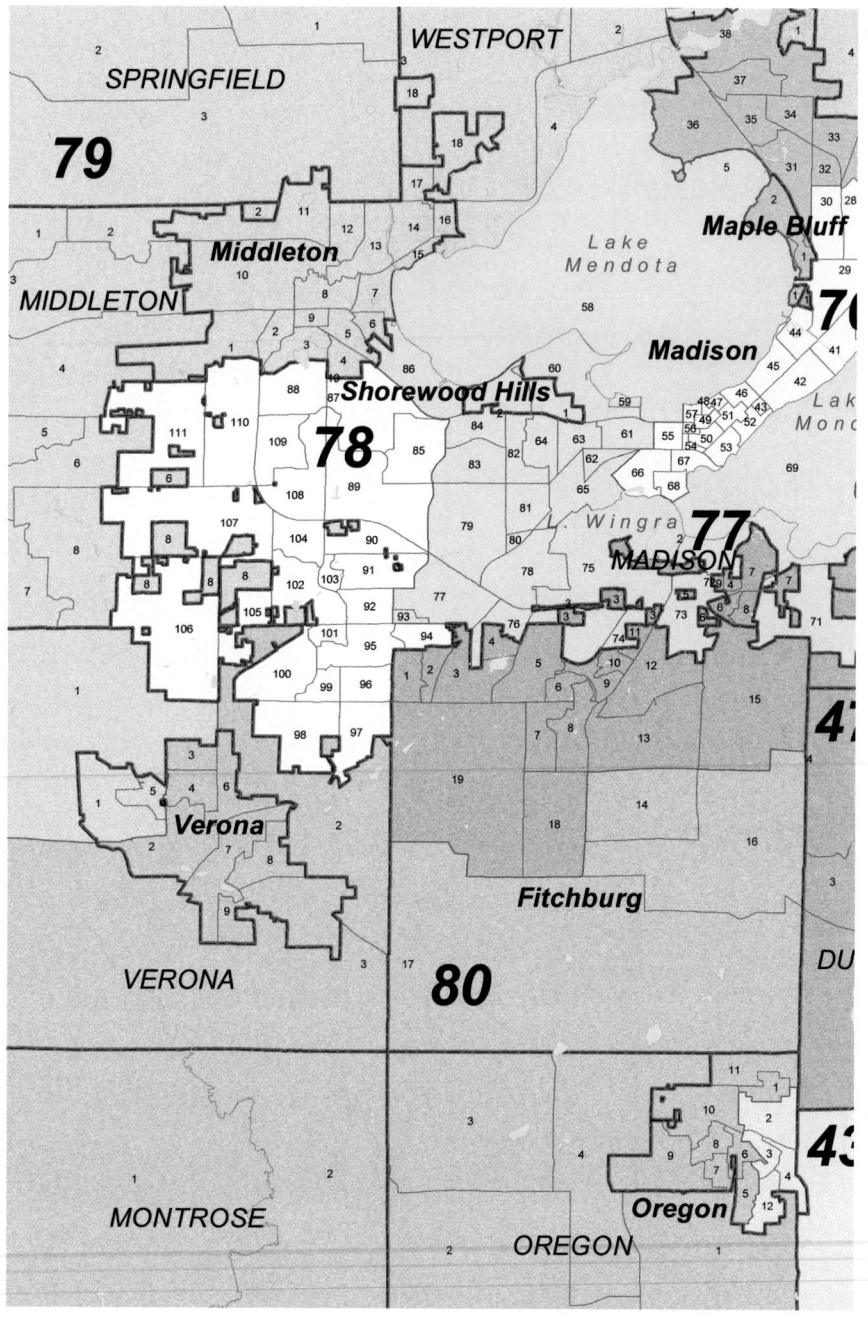

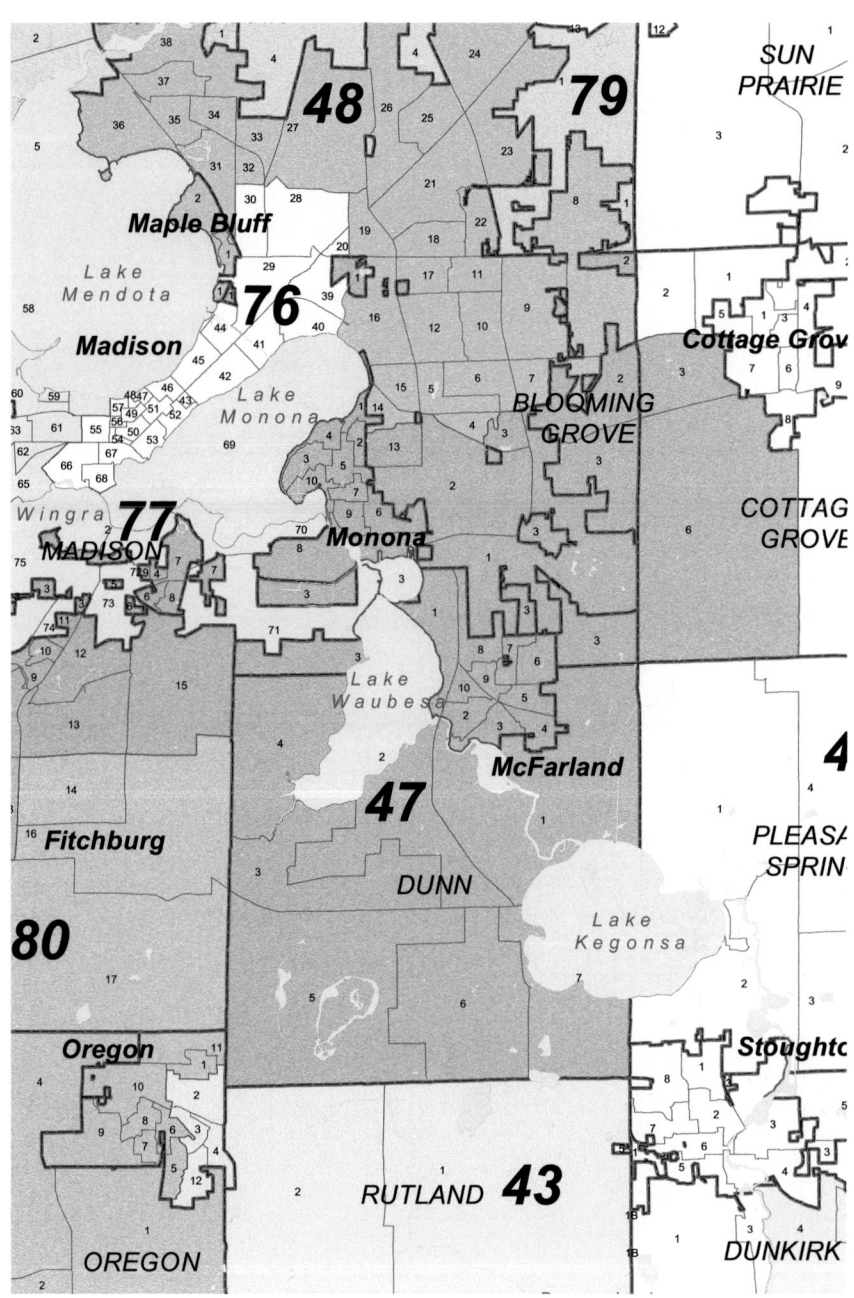

Detail Map: Milwaukee County (North)

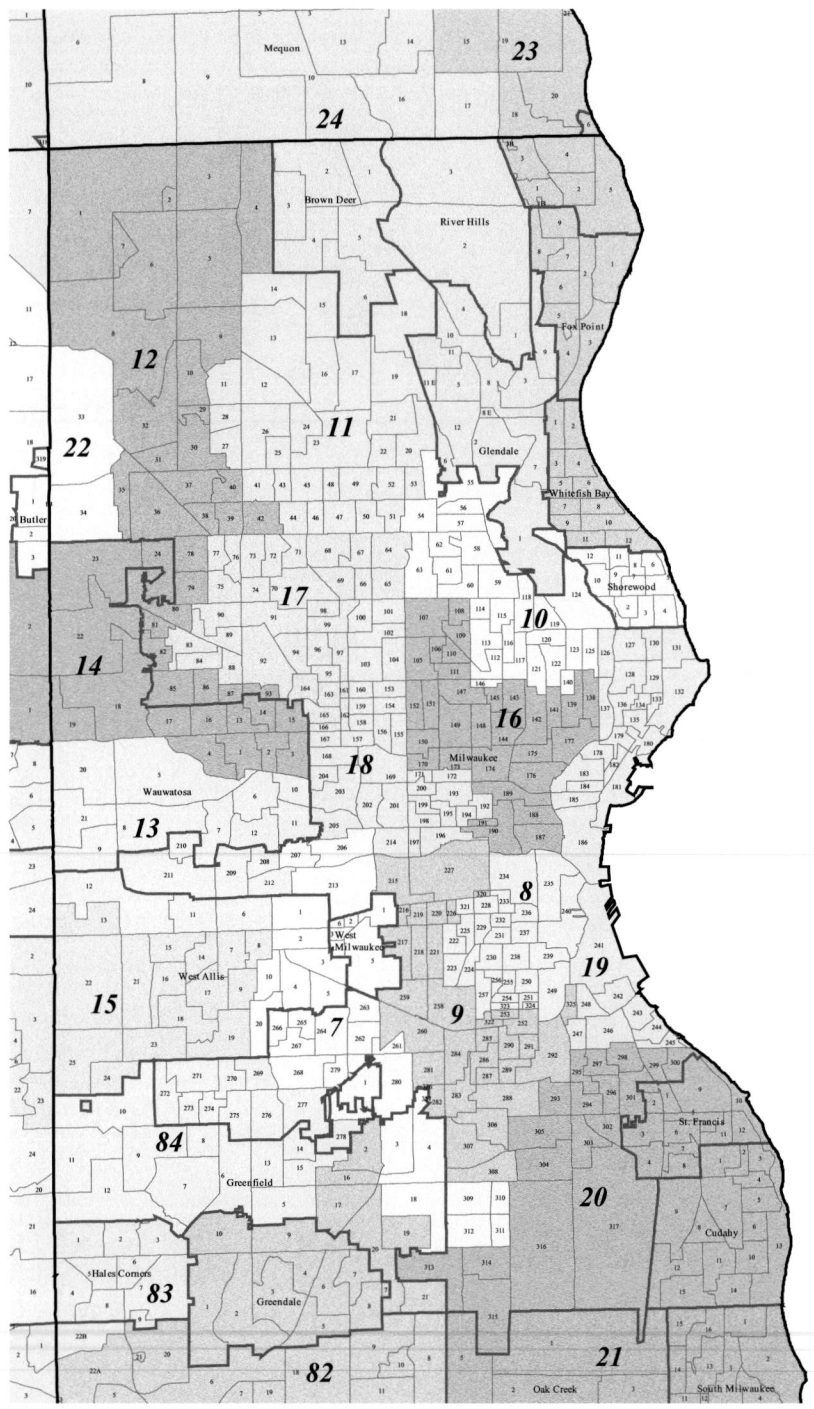

Detail Map: Milwaukee County (South)

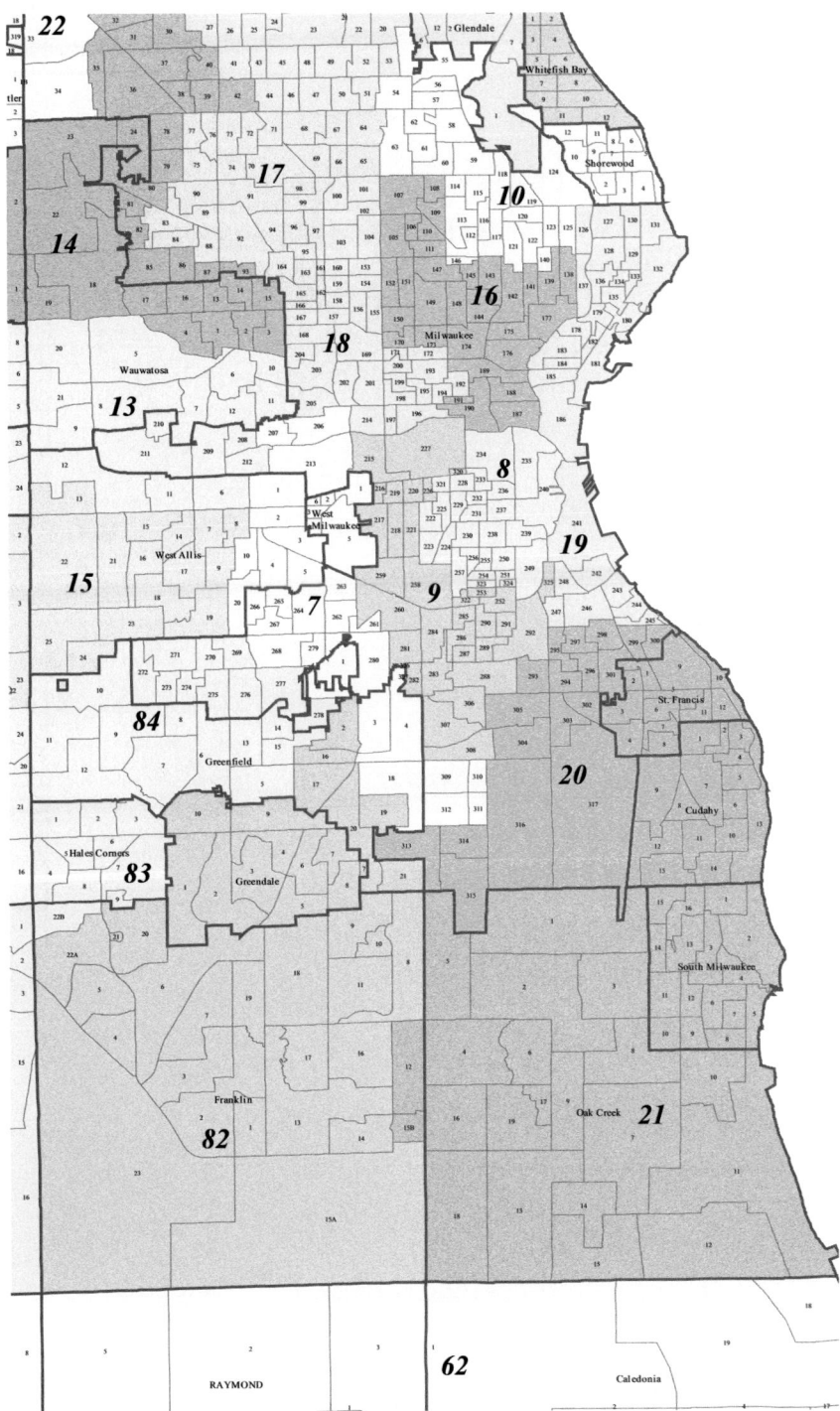

Detail Map: Waukesha County (West)

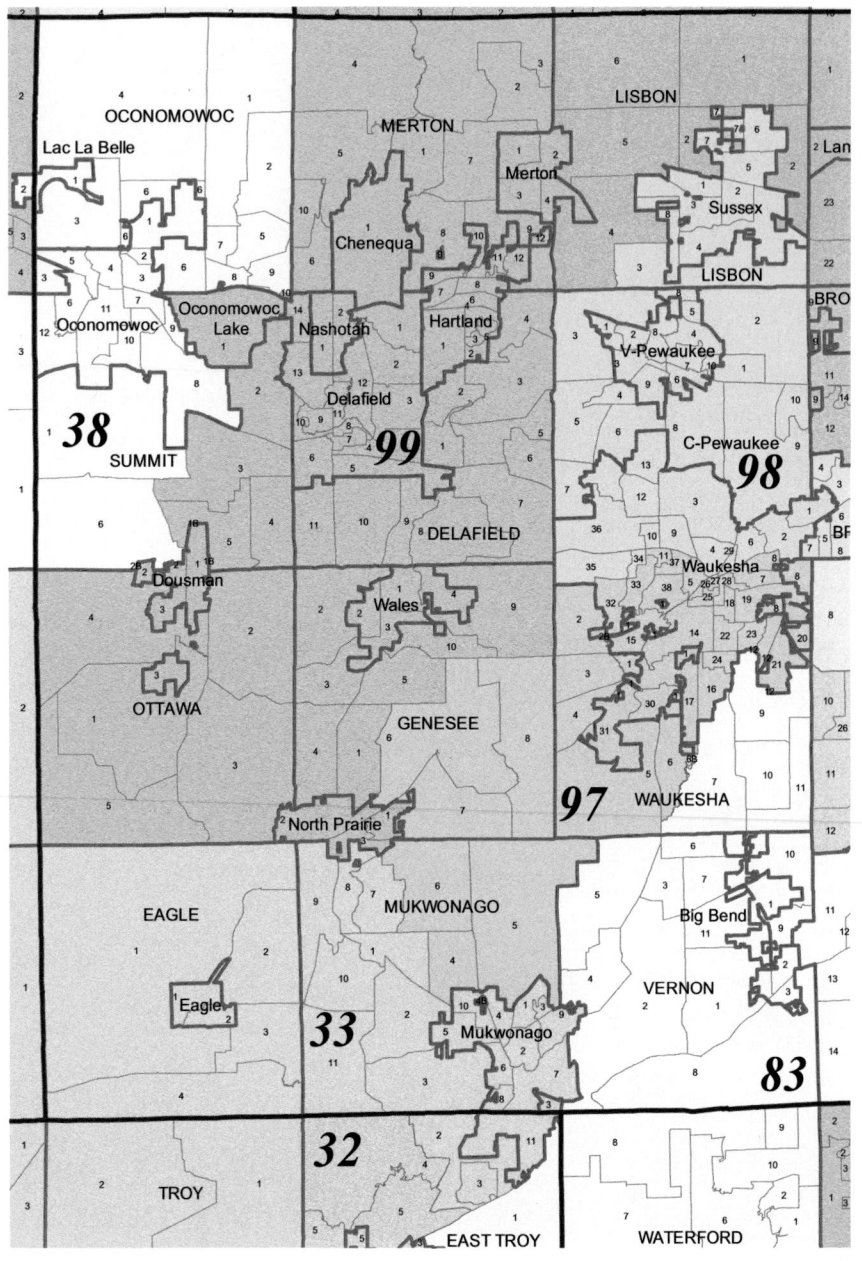

Detail Map: Waukesha County (East)

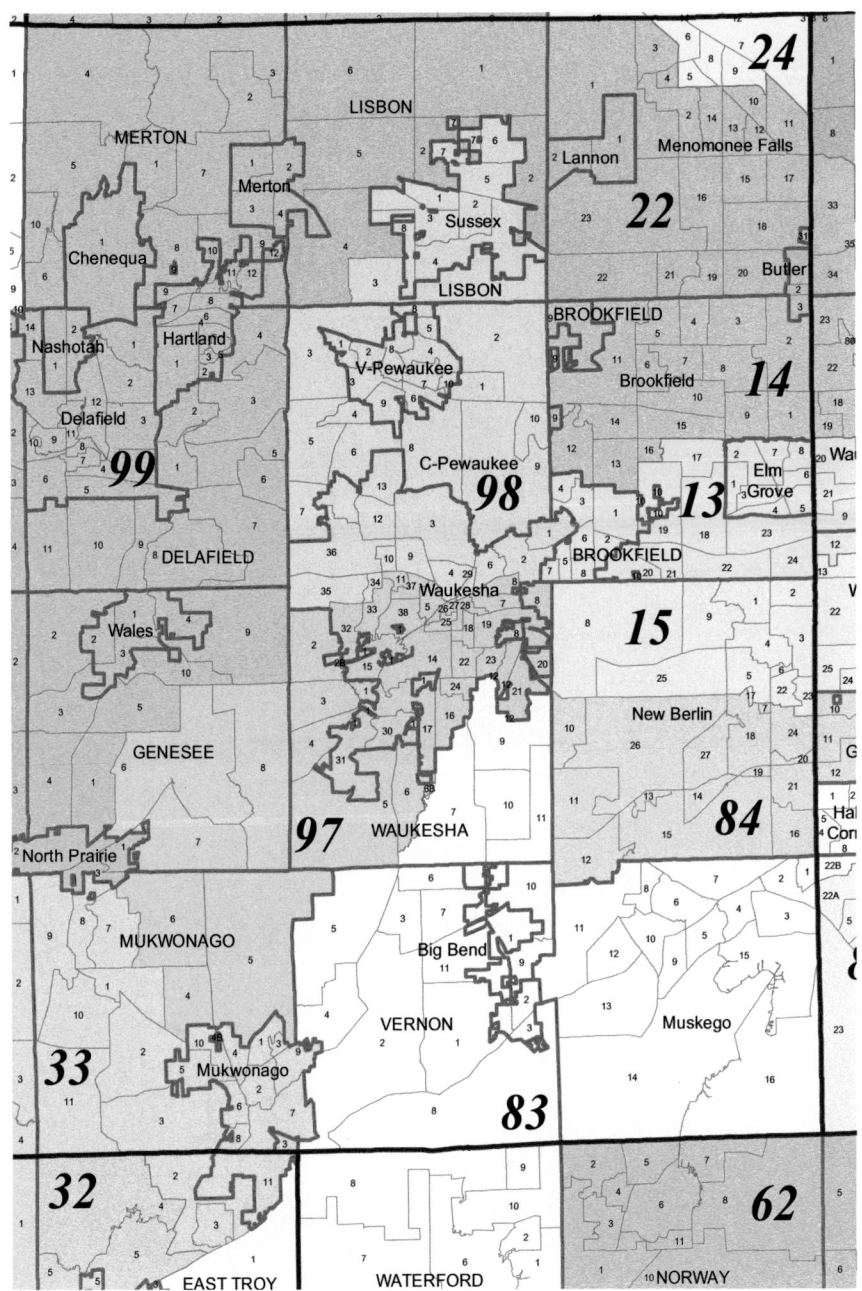

Detail Map: Green Bay Area

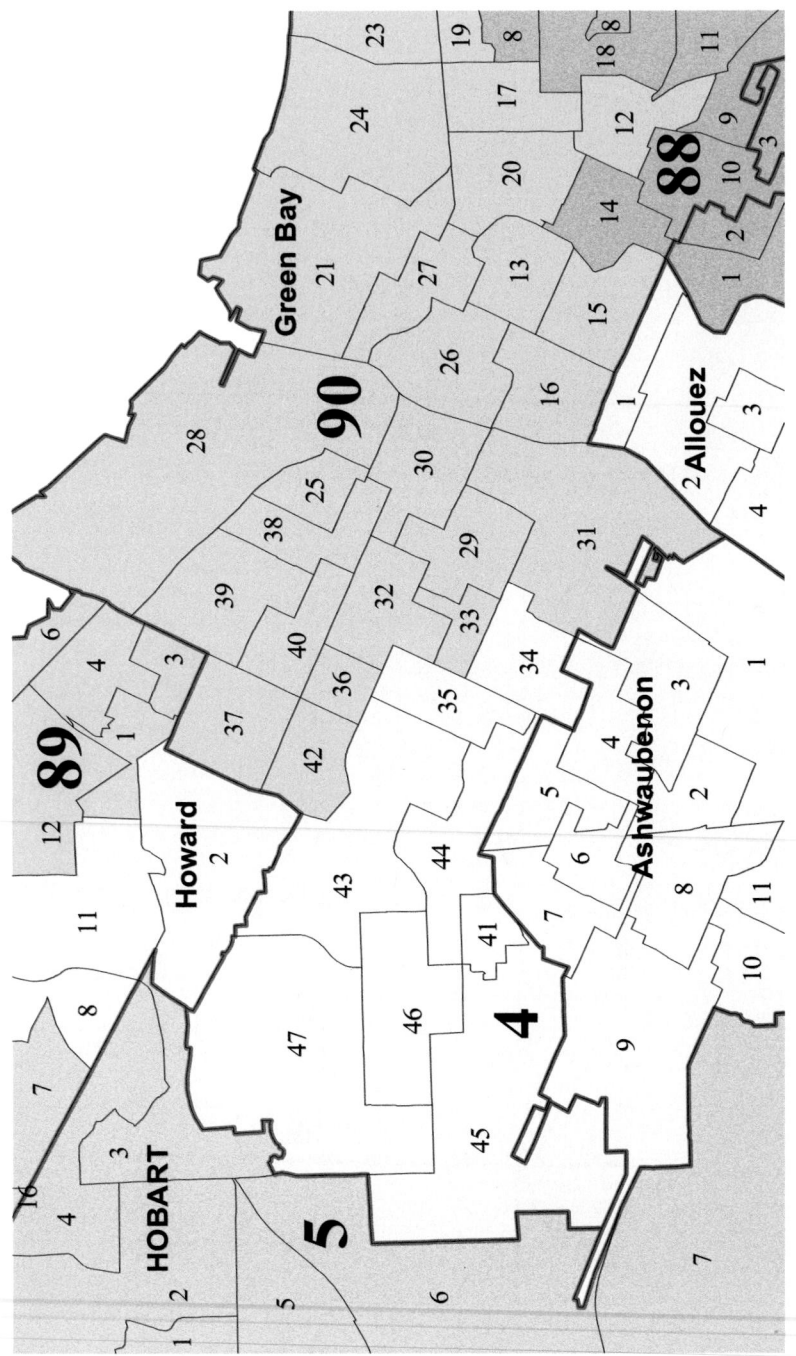

Detail Map: Eau Claire Area

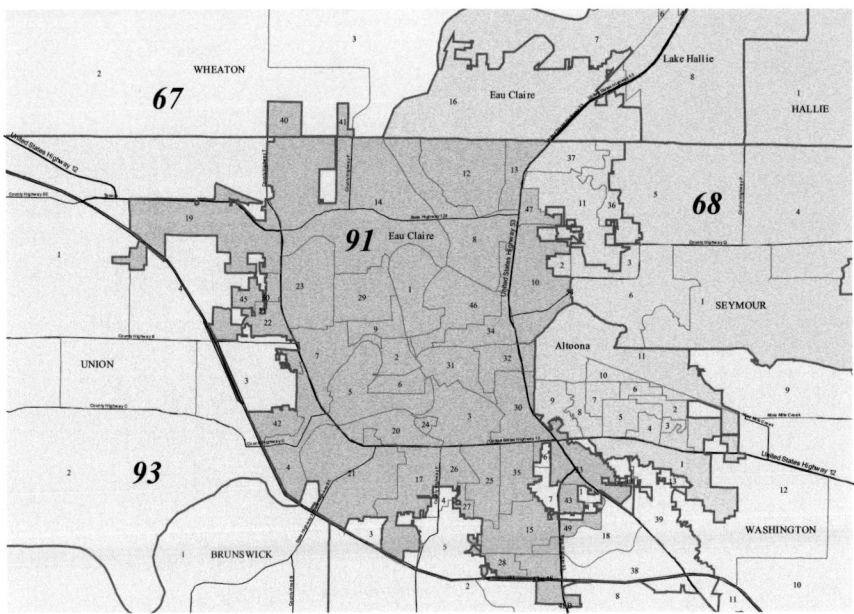

Detail Map: Waukesha Area

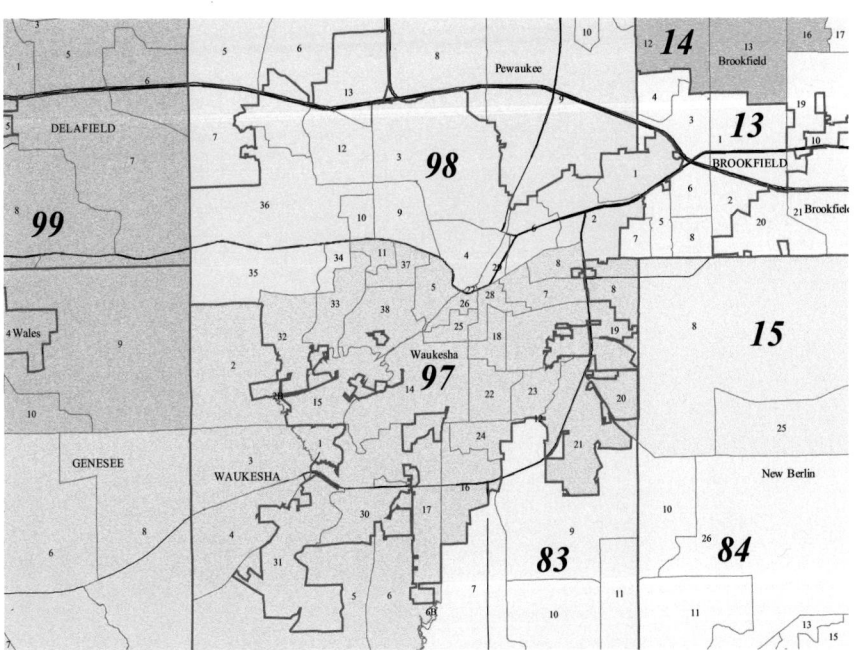

Detail Map: Racine Area

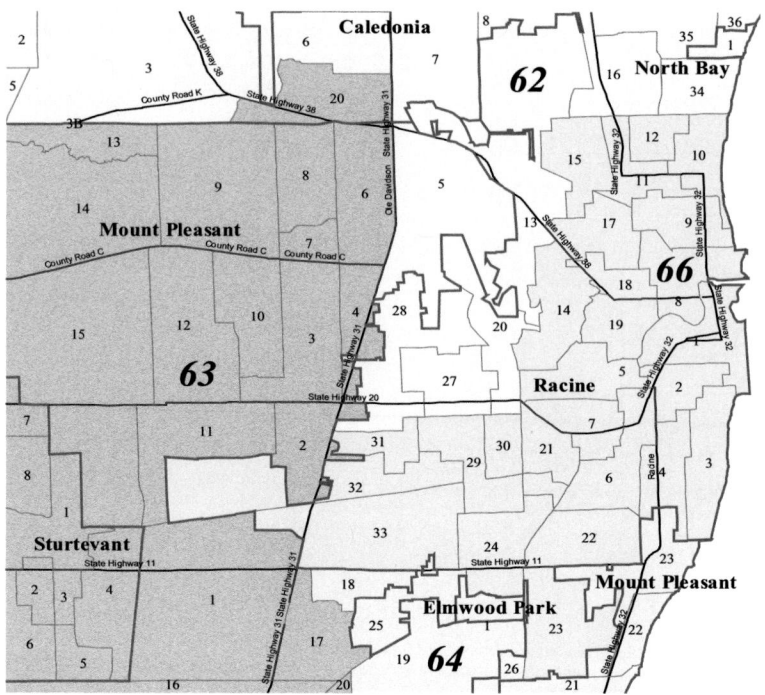

Detail Map: Fox Cities

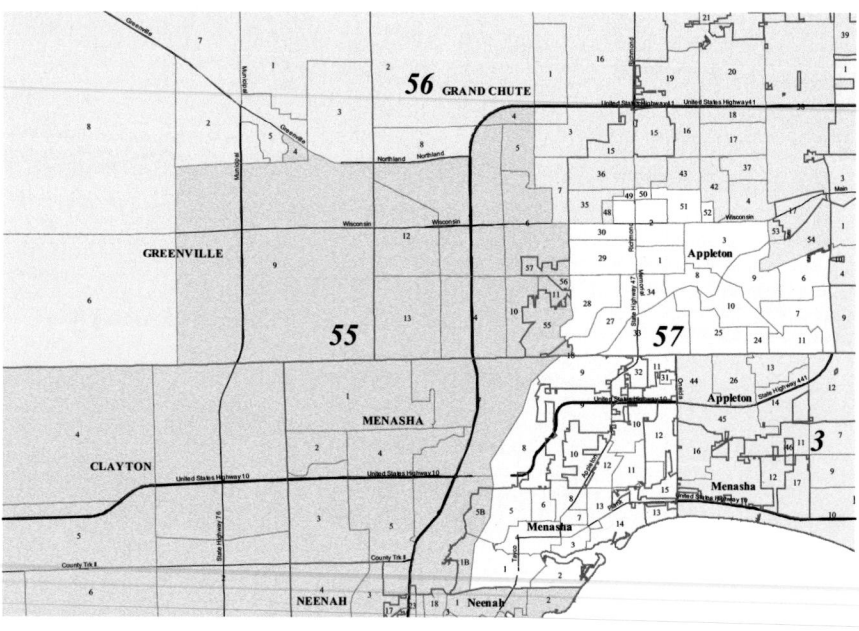

Feature
Article

Wisconsin in the Civil War

The Color Guard of the 2nd Wisconsin Infantry, July 1862. (Wisconsin Veterans Museum)

Wisconsin in the Civil War

By Michael Telzrow, Russell Horton, Kevin Hampton, Wisconsin Veterans Museum/Wisconsin Department of Veterans Affairs

Graphic Design by Lynn Lemanski
Wisconsin Legislative Reference Bureau

Table of Contents

The Eve of the War 101
A Call to Arms 104
Ethnic Regiments 113
Arming the Troops 116
Training and Deployment 116
Combat – On Wisconsin! 121
The Eastern Theater 123
Waiting for the Storm 124
Baptism of Fire in the East 131
The Birth of the Iron Brigade 132
Perryville 134
At the Crossroads 136
Gettysburg 139
Mascots 142
Arming African Americans 144
The End of Parole 145
The Tedium of Duty 148
The Beginning of the End 152
Making Georgia Howl! 155
The Siege of Petersburg 157
Epilogue 158
The Cost of War 159
Wisconsin Women in the Civil War 160
Lincoln: The Last Casualty 162
The Rise of the Grand Army of the Republic 162
Wisconsin's Civil War Legacy 164
The Wisconsin Veterans Museum 166

Wisconsin in the Civil War

The Eve of the War

Wisconsin's Civil War story began before Lincoln's proclamation of war against the Confederacy in April 1861. The war followed a long road to war that began years before the bombardment of Fort Sumter. Southern reliance on large-scale plantation agriculture, dependent upon slave labor, contrasted with the North's growing industrial capabilities and small-scale farm economy. A bitterly divisive sectional controversy emerged from the question of whether slavery ought to be expanded into the new United States territories west of the Mississippi. In Wisconsin, tensions caused by the slavery issue led to a political realignment. During this period of realignment, a fresh wave of new European immigrants, mostly Germans and Norwegians, flocked to the state in increasing numbers. Traditionally aligned with the Democratic Party, these immigrants and others began to seek a new party that embraced free-soil and antislavery ideals. Many native-born Yankees, former residents of the northeastern states, also felt drawn to the antislavery movement.

On the national political scene, the passage of the controversial Kansas-Nebraska Act set the stage for the establishment of a new antislavery political party. Written by Senator Stephen A. Douglas of Illinois, the Kansas-Nebraska Act as initially drafted mirrored the concept of popular sovereignty as established in the Compromise of 1850 that called for, among other things, the addition of new territories in the southwest to be organized without restrictions on slavery. In other words, the inhabitants of newly organized territories would be granted discretion over the issue of slavery. Douglas hoped to carry this concept forward in the Kansas-Nebraska Act, but Southern legislators protested and argued for a revision that would nullify the heart of the Missouri Compromise of 1820, earlier legislation that restricted slavery to territories and states below latitude 36° 30'. Douglas ultimately conceded to the Southerners, and after five months of bitter debate the Kansas-Nebraska Act passed on May 30, 1854, angering free-soil advocates in the North who opposed the expansion of slavery into new territories. As a direct result of the controversial legislation, the Whig Party was essentially torn apart. Coalitions of Free Soilers and antislavery Whigs began to meet in midwestern states like Wisconsin and Michigan and later in other Northern states, to forge a new party made up of both free-soil advocates, some Northern Whig Party members, nativists, and staunch abolitionists. The new political coalition went by many different names at first, but it was in Ripon, Wisconsin, at an anti-Nebraska rally on February 28, 1854, where it received the name "Republican." Several other state organizations, including Michigan, adopted the name and by 1855 it was nationally known as the Republican Party. With the Whig Party dead, some former Northern Whigs, like Abraham Lincoln, joined the Republican Party.

In Wisconsin, the arrest of a fugitive slave named Joshua Glover near Racine set off a constitutional crisis that illustrated the state's commitment to the antislavery movement. Abolitionist forces led by the editor of the *Milwaukee Free*

Democrat, Sherman Booth, urged residents to demonstrate against the seizure of Glover. In response, several thousand people assembled at Milwaukee's court-house in protest. Undeterred by the legality of the seizure under the authority of the Fugitive Slave Act of 1850, the restless crowd broke Glover out of jail and spirited him away to Waukesha. Booth was subsequently arrested and the federal government brought him to trial. The Wisconsin Supreme Court intervened and took the bold step of ruling the Fugitive Slave Act unconstitutional – the only state high court to do so. In 1859, the court's ruling was unanimously overturned by the United States Supreme Court, but by then the state's political battle lines had been clearly drawn.

Alexander W. Randall was the governor of Wisconsin at the beginning of the Civil War. (Wisconsin Veterans Museum)

Lincoln's election in 1860 caused 11 slave-holding states to secede from the Union. South Carolina was first in December 1860, followed quickly by Mississippi, Florida, and Alabama in January 1861. Tennessee was the last Southern state to secede in June 1861, but by that time South Carolina had already fired upon Fort Sumter and the war was on. Few were surprised that it had come to this. The slavery question had dogged the nation for decades, and the election of a Republican pro-Union, antislavery president finally moved the Southern states to secede. Wisconsin Governor Alexander W. Randall, a staunch Republican, recognized that the situation was growing ever more tenuous as early as January 1861, and he asserted the attitude of his administration in an annual message in which he likened Southern secession to treason, while characterizing it as a threat to the "hopes of civilization and Christianity...." In the same message he advised the residents of the state to expect to be asked to "respond to a call...for men and means to maintain the integrity of the Union." Randall doubtless sensed that a contribution of men and material would far exceed the state's current capacity to provide a request for military support from the president.

Following the fall of Fort Sumter, President Lincoln asked for 75,000 volunteers for three months' service to put down the rebellion. The new president broke down his request to the state level, asking for a specific number of troops from each state still in the Union. Wisconsin's quota came to one regiment composed of 10 companies, each company numbering 95 men and three officers. A typical regiment was generally considered to have up to 1,000 men, although they rarely numbered that in the field. Not to be outdone by his Northern counterparts, Governor Randall moved quickly to commit the Badger State to answer Lincoln's call for troops to support the Union cause, issuing a proclamation on April 16,

Glossary

Brigade. Typically consisted of four to six regiments commanded by a brigadier general but sometimes by a senior colonel.

Company. Usually numbered between 50 and 100 men commanded by a Captain. Companies were assigned alphabetical designations from A to K, with the letter J being omitted.

Corps. Typically contained two to four divisions. Each corps was designated by a Roman numeral, i.e., I, II, IV, etc.

Division. The second-largest unit in the field army numbering approximately 12,000 at full strength. In actuality, attrition reduced those numbers by 40 to 50 percent by 1863. Union divisions were usually commanded by brigadiers or major generals. Confederate divisions were often numerically superior to Union divisions.

Muster. A gathering of troops for any number of purposes, e.g., recruitment, inspection. To "muster in" refers to the initial gathering of troops as a formal recruited body. To "muster out" refers to the final act of disbanding an organized body of troops.

Militia. In its broadest sense refers to the entire able-bodied manpower of a state on paper. In the 19th century this largely imaginary category was often referred to as the "enrolled militia." The term "volunteer militia" refers to companies of men who actually provided for their own uniforms, drilled frequently, or at least on occasion, and endeavored to become a disciplined military entity. The volunteer militia were sometimes provided arms by the state through the federal government.

Regiment. Typically consisted of 10 companies and at full strength numbered nearly 1,000 men. Attrition almost always reduced that number and regiments rarely maintained full strength.

1861, exhorting all Wisconsin residents to support the war effort. He wrote, "All good citizens, everywhere, must join in making common cause against a common enemy."

A relatively new addition to the Union, Wisconsin had achieved statehood only 12 years before Randall's proclamation. During its first year as an organized territory in 1836, Wisconsin claimed a population of 11,683 non-Indian residents. It was a sparsely populated frontier society attached by communities along Lake Michigan and in some southern portions of the state. Anchored by the state's oldest and most populous cities, Green Bay and Milwaukee, respectively, Wisconsin was poised on the precipice of a wave of immigration. Ushered in by German political and social discontent and an exodus from New York and the New England states, Wisconsin's population soared between 1846 and 1860. Immigrants from below the border, attracted to the lead mines of the southwestern portion of the state, joined the Germans and the Yankees. Others followed, including the Dutch, the Irish, and those from Scandinavian countries. Wisconsin claimed a population of 775,881 on the eve of the war. Of that number, 407,449 were male of which a third were foreign-born – half of that number from German states, many

Governor Randall's April 16, 1861, proclamation calling upon residents to support the war. (Wisconsin Veterans Museum)

in the wake of the failed revolutions of 1848. These were the men that Randall would call upon to uphold the Union and strike at the heart of the Confederacy: farmers, machinists, craftsman, and professionals, foreign-born and native, all united under one cause.

A Call to Arms

In 1860, America's peacetime army numbered about 16,000 soldiers, most of them scattered among 79 isolated posts that stretched over 2,000 frontier miles west of the Mississippi River. There was no national plan for rapid mobilization, and without a well-organized general staff, any coordination would have to start from scratch. The Navy was similarly unprepared for war. Only 12 of its 42 ships were available for combat duty. To make matters worse, 313 regular United States Army officers resigned and offered their services to the Confederacy. Out of necessity, the U.S. government turned to the individual states for support. It was perhaps wishful thinking to expect an aging and obsolete militia system to provide the necessary manpower, but that is precisely what happened.

As was customary of the period, Wisconsin employed the time-honored militia model that provided for the "common defense" of communities in the years before the rise of a standing army in the United States. Once a defensive necessity, the mandatory militia system had largely outlived its role as a frontier bulwark against hostile native populations and foreign incursions. Local volunteer militia companies, where they still existed, were mere vestigial remnants of the old system that formerly required the participation of all able-bodied males between the ages of 16 and 45. Although some volunteer units were well-trained and properly equipped, most functioned more effectively as the guardians of 19th century ideals of masculinity and civic duty rather than as battle-ready military units. American men maintained a link to their forefathers through the external practices of martial rituals such as public military drills and evening military balls. For many, the image of the citizen soldier standing shoulder-to-shoulder at Concord or New Orleans symbolized the cherished ideals of an independent America. Militia service also served to further the assimilation of recent immigrants who were looking for an entry into American culture.

John C. Starkweather, Captain of the Milwaukee Light Guard, later Colonel of the 1st Wisconsin Voluntary Infantry Regiment. (Wisconsin Veterans Museum)

Despite the shortcomings of the volunteer militia system, Wisconsin did make an effort to maintain an enrolled militia and volunteer militia force. By 1859, there were about 55 independent companies throughout the state; the enrolled system consisting of every able-bodied male had fallen into inactivity in most areas with the exception of Milwaukee. As befitting the state's largest city, Milwaukee boasted the highest number of independent militia units, many of which were organized among the professional ranks of the city or along ethnic lines, principally German. Independent companies, or volunteer militia, were men who supplied uniforms at their own expense, drilled on their own time, and endeavored to be a disciplined military body. The Milwaukee Light Guard, organized in 1855, was the most prominent unit. Its captain, John C. Starkweather, was later made colonel of the 1st Wisconsin Volunteer Infantry Regiment at the outbreak of the war.

Milwaukee companies functioned as a battalion. The rest of the state militia companies were organized as independent companies. At the time of Governor Randall's annual address of 1861, total militia strength stood at just 1,993 men scattered among the 55 companies. Randall's anticipation of President Lincoln's call for troops drove him to urge the legislature to prepare for war by passing laws that would enable Wisconsin to better organize its volunteer militias. On April 13, 1861, the legislature passed a series of bills that authorized the organization of one regiment of infantry. By the time President Lincoln's request for troops was received on April 15, 1861, Wisconsin was well on its way to answering the call.

As expected, the Wisconsin volunteer militias provided some of the earliest troops for service to the state, although taken as a whole militia units failed to provide the majority of troops requested. Of the 55 companies of independent militia, eight joined in the first volunteer regiment, but less than half of the 55 were willing to serve in the time of crisis. Still, within the first 12 months of the war, Wisconsin provided more than the federal government's requested quota.

Governor Randall, faced with the unenviable task of turning away volunteers, selected 10 companies to form the 1st Wisconsin Volunteer Infantry Regiment. The first company accepted, the Madison Guard, was joined by another Madison company (the Governor's Guard), four Milwaukee companies (the Light Guard, Union Rifles, Black Yagers, and Riflemen), the Beloit City Guard, the Fond du Lac Badgers, the Horicon Guards, and the Park City Greys from Kenosha. The methods the state used to solicit service, the ways that men entered the state's forces, and the feelings the men had about joining the military changed considerably throughout the war.

Against the wishes of Washington, Randall approved raising additional regiments from the hundreds of remaining eager volunteers. Ten days after the fall of Fort Sumter, Wisconsin had formed another full regiment with several more organizing. By the end of 1861, when the War Department ordered Wisconsin to stop raising troops, more than 14,000 Wisconsin volunteers had been organized into 13 infantry regiments, one cavalry regiment, and a company of sharpshooters. Early in the war, then, the State had no need to solicit military service from its residents beyond Randall's initial call.

From the perspective of the volunteers, desire to preserve the Union, to punish the secessionists, and to experience adventure led to their intense spirit. The community-based militia companies added the benefit of joining and serving alongside friends and often relatives. Wisconsin's first 13 infantry regiments were composed of companies that reflected the close-knit nature of the groups. They carried names like the Lemonweir Minute Men, the Grant County Patriots, the Neenah Rifles, and the West Bend Union Guards. While the units lost those colorful names when they were assigned a letter and became a company in a Wisconsin infantry regiment, the men maintained their community pride and ties.

These themes are exemplified in the story of Alexander Wilson. Born in Pennsylvania in 1840, the youngest of seven children, Wilson moved west prior to the Civil War and settled in Dalton, Green Lake County, Wisconsin. Soon after Governor Randall's call to arms, Wilson joined the local militia company, which had begun training along with a group from a nearby town. In a July 6, 1861, letter to a cousin, Wilson wrote, "We have got up a company here for the purpose of training in order to be ready if we are needed in the present emergencies." He added, "The name of our company is the Plow Boy Guard. We are in the town of Dalton and the other company is in the town of Green Lake called the Green Lake Tigers."

More than two months later, Wilson officially joined the war effort. On October 5, he wrote from Camp Fremont in Ripon, "On the 30 of September I signed the roll making of myself a member of the first regiment of Wisconsin Cavalry." Indeed, Wilson had become part of Company E, 1st Wisconsin Cavalry Regiment. He made his reason for stepping up very clear: "I have made up my mind that the Secessionists are going too far and I want to get amongst them." He later added, "There will be some rip and cut when we get among the traitors." Wilson mustered into federal service on October 31, 1861, at Camp Harvey in Kenosha. He died of disease on January 9, 1864, in Tennessee.

The spirit of adventure that came with war drew its share of underage soldiers as well. Most of the youngest soldiers from Wisconsin enlisted with their fathers and served as drummer boys or aides. However, many 16- and 17-year-olds wanted to fight and volunteered as infantrymen. Some lied about their age, others received the permission of their parents or hoped that the patriotic fever sweeping the state would enable them to enlist without special permission.

A young Charles O. Hansen attempted to enlist in the 17th Wisconsin Infantry. (Wisconsin Veterans Museum)

Charles O. Hansen displayed remarkable tenacity in his effort to join the Union forces. Born in Norway around 1845, Hansen's family immigrated to the United States prior to the Civil War and settled in Green County, Wisconsin, where the patriarch Rasmus found work as a cabinetmaker. In February 1862, a 16-year-old Hansen volunteered for service and enlisted into Company H, 17th Wisconsin Infantry Regiment. According to muster records, he stood five feet seven and had auburn hair and blue eyes that must have shone with his anticipation to take part in the war. However, he did not remain a member of the company long – he most likely joined against the wishes of his family, and they successfully negotiated his release from service due to his age.

Undeterred, Hansen waited until July 1863, when he was 18 and, while in Oberlin, Ohio, enlisted in Company C, 86th Ohio Infantry Regiment, a six-month unit. After completing his term of service defending the State of Ohio against a feared Confederate invasion, Hansen returned to Wisconsin and, as a 19-year-old, enlisted into Company B, 18th Wisconsin Infantry Regiment, eventually joining the regiment in the Carolinas at the end of the war. Although unable to enlist early in the war, Hansen maintained the spirit of volunteerism that characterized the beginning of the conflict and served honorably with two different units.

Wisconsin was able to meet President Lincoln's first calls for troops with hundreds of volunteers to spare, but subsequent calls proved more difficult to meet. The spirit of excitement, adventure, and volunteerism among the residents dampened in 1862 as it became clear that the war would not be brief and bloodless. The federal government came to realize it needed more – many more – men to continue to execute the war in the face of rising casualties. This led to several changes that greatly affected the way Wisconsin men joined the military during the Civil War.

Governor Edward Saloman, Wisconsin's eighth governor. (Wisconsin Veterans Museum)

Wisconsin still received a quota of men to raise for each call from Washington, but starting in 1862 the threat of a draft loomed over states unable to meet their mark. Broken down to the county level, these calls revealed areas of the state that contained large pockets of antiwar sentiment. To avoid a draft, which was incredibly unpopular with the public and seemed likely to cause civil unrest, both federal and state governments took steps to encourage volunteer enlistments. The federal government began offering one month's pay in advance upon enlistment. Governor Edward Salomon, Wisconsin's third wartime governor, further encouraged the counties in danger of not meeting their quotas to offer an additional $50 enlistment bonus. These measures proved effective, and by September 1862, Wisconsin had raised 14 additional regiments, exceeding its quota of 12,000 men from President Lincoln's call in July.

While George Haw, a 26-year-old pharmacist from Boscobel, considered joining the war effort in the summer of 1862, his future wife, Annie Henry, wrote him a letter advising him of his options and telling her his preference. "No doubt it would be better for you to enlist than to be drafted. But if you should be drafted, could you not get a substitute? This is all that consoles me in regard to my brother. You may think me selfish, and I do not know but I am in this case, yet I am willing to sacrifice everything, only the life of you and my brother." Two days after receiving Annie's letter, Haw accepted a commission as 1st Lieutenant in Company B, 33rd Wisconsin Infantry Regiment. He served almost two years before resigning his commission due to medical issues.

As the war progressed, President Lincoln made additional calls. In August 1862, he asked Wisconsin for another 12,000 men and stipulated that they be raised within two weeks. Rather than asking for a three-year enlistment, however, President Lincoln wanted only a nine-month commitment, a concession made to encourage volunteers. Governor Salomon succeeded in extending the deadline, but by the end of October it became clear that several counties wouldn't meet their quotas. In November 1862, Governor Salomon ordered a draft to commence in those counties.

The fears of government officials came to pass when riots broke out in Brown, Ozaukee, and Washington Counties. The 28th Wisconsin Infantry Regiment, still training at Camp Washburn in Milwaukee, was sent to Port Washington in Ozaukee County to restore order, arrest the instigators of the riot, and round up the drafted men who failed to report for duty. The 30th Wisconsin Infantry Regiment, stationed at Camp Randall in Madison, dispatched a company to Green Bay and several more to West Bend in Washington County to perform the same function.

Benjamin Briggs, a 24-year-old farmer from New Richmond, St. Croix County, who stood five feet ten and had blue eyes and black hair, volunteered for service in Company A, 30th Wisconsin Infantry on August 11, 1862. He was among the detail sent to Green Bay to enforce the draft, and he described it in a letter to a friend written in November 1862. "We came here to put down a riot and get the drafted men. We got one hundred of them and had them here two weeks. We sent them to Milwaukee yesterday. Our boys, the most of them are hunting up the rest. They started after them this morning." Briggs served out the entire war with the 30th Wisconsin, mustering out in September 1865.

Recruiting officers in Madison take a break from their work. (Wisconsin Veterans Museum)

The year 1863 began with a new set of laws governing the draft: the Enrollment Act was passed by Congress in March. This legislation provided Wisconsin men with several interesting choices. They could voluntarily enlist to help their county meet its quota, and likely benefit from some sort of enlistment bonus. They could also test their luck and take a chance that their names wouldn't be selected in the draft. If they were drafted, they forfeited any enlistment bonus. However, even if they were drafted, they retained options. In 1863, a drafted man could pay $300 to essentially "buy" his way out of service. He also could furnish a substitute to serve in his stead; substitutes were generally paid a fee to offer this service.

Some men felt obligated to enlist both for a bonus and to support their families through a steady soldier's pay they could send home. This plan was not always reliable because pay was delayed at times, as Jackson Hicks, a 21-year-old married farmer from Walworth County who served in Company I, 28th Wisconsin Infantry Regiment, touched upon in a letter to his brother Fred in January 1863: "You know that men that enlisted in the last call are men that have families…and those families the most of them depend on government money for subsistence, and by the government not paying the soldiers, their families have to suffer for the want of clothes and provisions." Hicks endured the delayed pay, serving with the 28th Wisconsin until the end of the war. He mustered out in August 1865.

The first call for troops under the Enrollment Act came in July 1863. The federal government offered a $302 bounty to volunteers in hopes of boosting enlistment and avoiding a draft, yet to no avail in some counties. Over 30 percent of those drafted in Wisconsin hired a substitute or paid to avoid service. Many Wisconsin men struggled with this choice as is revealed in a letter written by Achsah Reynolds, a Beloit woman, to her brother: "But I almost forgot to tell you that Beloit is free from another draft. I have had the blues for the last few weeks expecting Asa would enlist, for he said that he would wait till the last day and if our quota was not full he should enlist for he would not be drafted. But I do not

Envelope proclaiming Wisconsin's support of the Union. (Wisconsin Veterans Museum)

think that six months will pass before another call is made, but we are clear for this time."

As the war continued, the federal government continued to make more calls for soldiers. Wisconsin met its quota for an early 1864 call for men but failed to meet its mark in the fall of that year. Many counties began offering sizeable bonuses, in addition to the federal bounty, to men who would help them meet their quotas, regardless of where they really lived. This led to some men leaving their home counties to enlist in another county offering a larger bonus. Desperate for men, the federal government began denying the ability to pay $300 to avoid service, which caused the price of substitutes to skyrocket.

Another tactic used to attract volunteers was reducing the term of enlistment. While the state's very first unit, the 1st Wisconsin Infantry Regiment, signed on for three months' service, most men thereafter committed to three years' service. This changed beginning with the 37th and 38th Wisconsin Infantry Regiments recruited in early 1864. The men in those two regiments were a mix of one-, two-, and three-year enlistments. The next three regiments from Wisconsin signed on for only 100 days of service, and the remainder of Wisconsin's 53 infantry regiments signed on for one year of service.

In addition to men enlisting for the first time, soldiers coming to the end of their terms of service could choose to muster out and return home, or reenlist for another term. Many men, tired of war and eager to see their families again, help with the farm or business, and return to a normal life, mustered out. Others, though they may have struggled with the decision, reenlisted. In a February 1865 letter to his wife, Frances, Charles Goodrich described his thought process and reservations about reenlisting. A 33-year-old farmer from Oakland, Wisconsin, Goodrich enlisted as a private in Company I, 1st Wisconsin Cavalry Regiment in 1861 but earned a promotion to sergeant major of the regiment in 1864. His reasoning, although it relates to reenlisting, is similar to that of many men who debated enlisting:

> My talk about returning to the service is not just to try your feelings. Dear Frankie, I am not so cruel. God knows that there is no man living who prizes home and its comforts higher than I do, or who loves his wife, his child and relations better. It would be impossible for me to express the joy I should feel if this war were ended! But the war is not ended, and I am continually asking myself questions like the following: Can I stay at home while my comrades are fighting in the field? Can I give up a struggle which I determined in the commencement to see through? If I stay at home, what kind of men will be my associates? Who stay at home, such times as these when the country needs the services of every true patriot? Could I hold up my head and look a soldier in the face?

The rest of his letter expressed concern that his wife was struggling to manage the farm and care for their young son without him. He fervently hoped that the war would end before he was forced to make a decision to reenlist. His hope was not fulfilled. Though by March 1865, a Union victory must have seemed certain enough that Goodrich decided to forego reenlistment and return home. He mustered out on March 8, 1865, roughly one month before Robert E. Lee's surrender, and returned to his family and farm as a proud veteran.

While Wisconsin is generally credited with approximately 91,000 Civil War veterans, the figure includes reenlistments and counts some men twice. Roughly 80,000 individual Wisconsin men served in the Civil War. By the time the war ended in 1865, Wisconsin had supplied 53 regiments of infantry, four cavalry units, and 13 artillery batteries, along with a company of U.S. sharpshooters.

Ethnic Regiments

The spirit of volunteerism in Wisconsin early in the war led many men to join the Union Army alongside their neighbors who were of the same ethnic background. This contributed to the formation of ethnic regiments and companies, as well as strong ethnic concentrations within companies.

Germans

Almost one million Germans immigrated to the United States between 1845 and 1855. Thousands of those immigrants came to Wisconsin, many settling in Milwaukee or buying farmland in the southeastern part of the state. While Germans were scattered among every Wisconsin regiment individually or in small groups, they also could be found in several large concentrations. For example, Company D, 1st Wisconsin Infantry Regiment, was known as the Black Yagers (an Anglicization of the German word jaeger, meaning "hunter") and Company C, 5th Wisconsin Infantry Regiment, carried the name Milwaukee German Turners.

Charles Wickesberg served in the 26th Wisconsin Infantry, one of two predominately German regiments from Wisconsin. (Wisconsin Veterans Museum)

In the fall of 1861, prominent German leaders around the state set out to raise an entire regiment of German immigrants and succeeded. The 9th Wisconsin Infantry Regiment, sometimes referred to as the 1st German Regiment, consisted almost entirely of German immigrants or the children of German immigrants. They began training at Camp Holton in Milwaukee, but soon renamed it Camp Sigel in honor of prominent German-American General Franz Sigel. Commanded by Colonel Frederick Salomon, the brother of future Governor Edward Salomon, the 9th Wisconsin deployed to Kansas in January 1862 and spent the remainder of the war fighting skirmishes in Missouri and Arkansas.

Wisconsin produced a second full German regiment – the 26th Wisconsin Infantry – soon thereafter. General Franz Sigel had asked Governor Salomon to raise another German regiment and as a result, the 26th Wisconsin was also known as the Sigel Regiment. They formed in the fall of 1862, and trained, appropriately, at Camp Sigel in Milwaukee. Deployed to the eastern theater, the Siegel Regiment saw their first action at Chancellorsville and were routed badly, gaining an unfair reputation for retreating too quickly. The men took the slight very seriously and spent the rest of the war trying to redeem their name. Charles Wickesberg, who immigrated to Sheboygan County with his family in 1848, served in Company H and wrote letters in German home to his family that described his displeasure with newspaper accounts of the 26th Wisconsin's lack of fortitude. The regiment went on to see heavy fighting at Gettysburg, at Lookout Mountain, and on Sherman's March to the Sea, displaying bravery and resilience at every turn.

Norwegians

With companies named St. Olaf's Rifles, the Norway Bear Hunters, Odin's Rifles, and the Scandinavian Mountaineers, it is clear why the 15th Wisconsin Infantry Regiment was known as the Scandinavian Regiment. Recruited from among the Norwegians, the Danes, and the Swedes living in the state, it is believed to have been the only all-Scandinavian regiment in the Union Army. The 15th Wisconsin trained during the spring of 1862 at Camp Randall under Colonel Hans Heg, a prominent Norwegian immigrant who had recently been elected state prison commissioner. Heg had personally recruited the men of the 15th with an appeal to their patriotic duty: "Scandinavians! Let us understand the situation, our duty and our responsibility. Shall the future ask, where were the Scandinavians when the Fatherland was saved?"

The men of the 15th passed through Chicago on their way to the western theater and received a special flag from a local Norwegian organization that combined traditional American and Norwegian symbols and carried the motto *For Gud Og Vort Land* (For God and Our Country). They went on to participate in the battles of Perryville, Stone's River, Chickamauga, and Missionary Ridge, as well as the Atlanta Campaign. A statue of Heg, who was killed at Chickamauga, which was erected outside the northeast entrance of the Wisconsin capitol, immortalizes the service of the 15th.

Irish

Wisconsin's Irish population was less than half that of the state's German population. Like the Germans, Irish immigrants enlisted in Wisconsin units individually or in small groups from the start of the war. In late 1861, John Doran, a prominent Irish lawyer in Milwaukee, received a commission from Governor Randall and began recruiting an Irish regiment in Wisconsin. Due to several factors, including a smaller population from which to draw, he was unable to fill a full regiment with Wisconsin Irish. For example, Company G was filled with soldiers of French descent, and Company K had a large number of Oneida and Menominee among its ranks. However, the 17th Wisconsin Infantry Regiment did contain a large number of Irish with companies named the Mulligan Guard, the Corcoran Guards, and the Peep O'Day Boys, and they became known as the Irish Regiment. Company B carried a green flag covered in various Irish symbols and sayings.

This company guidon was presented to Company B, 17th Wisconsin Infantry by the people of Kenosha. The colors, symbols, and words reflect the Irish heritage of the unit. (Wisconsin Veterans Museum)

Mustered into service on March 15, 1862, the men were toasted by Governor Randall at a St. Patrick's Day dinner at the capitol two days later. After training at Camp Randall, the 17th Wisconsin deployed to the western theater, taking part in the Siege of Corinth in May 1862 and the Battle of Corinth in October 1862. At the latter engagement, Wisconsin's Irish Regiment made a daring bayonet charge to repel the advancing Confederate forces. The men, shouting a Gaelic battle cry *Faugh a ballagh* (Clear the way), succeeded in pushing back the attack and allowed other Union forces to regroup. The 17th Wisconsin went on to take part in the Vicksburg Campaign, Sherman's March to the Sea, and the Carolina Campaign and marched in the Grand Review in Washington, DC before returning to Wisconsin.

A company from Oconto, named the Oconto Irish Guards, arrived at Camp Randall too late to join the 17th Wisconsin. They became the 11th Battery, Wisconsin Light Artillery, and through chance were attached to an Irish infantry regiment from Illinois that was stationed at Camp Douglas in Chicago. There, though they remained predominantly Wisconsin soldiers, they were rebranded Battery L, 1st Illinois Light Artillery. Deployed to the eastern theater, they spent the majority of their service in West Virginia and at Harper's Ferry.

Native Americans

At the time of the Civil War, an estimated 9,000 Native Americans were living in Wisconsin. They comprised seven nations, or tribes, including the

Menominee, Oneida, Stockbridge-Munsee, Brothertown, Ho Chunk, Ojibwe, and Potawatomi. Within a month of his 1861 call for troops, Governor Randall received a letter offering 200 Menominee men for service. Because the federal government considered Native Americans, along with African Americans, to be "colored troops," Randall declined the offer. In spite of this, dozens of Wisconsin Native Americans managed to join the Union armies, individually or in small groups. In 1863, as the number of white volunteers dropped and states began instituting drafts to meet their quotas of soldiers, the federal government lifted its ban on "colored troops," which allowed Wisconsin to begin recruiting among Native Americans. Hundreds enlisted, with two notable concentrations forming.

Company K, 37th Wisconsin Infantry Regiment, had the largest number of Native Americans in a single company, with more than 40 Menominee among its ranks. Men like James Ahshetahyash, Jerome Kahtotah, and Jacob Pequach-nahrien saw heavy fighting in the siege of Petersburg and participated in the infamous Battle of the Crater. Numerous Archiquets, Danforths, Doxators, Hills, and Powlas can be found among 50 Oneida in Companies F and G, 14th Wisconsin Infantry Regiment. They took part in the Atlanta Campaign before seeing additional action in Tennessee, Arkansas, and Alabama. All told, an estimated 500-600 Wisconsin Native Americans served in the Civil War – an impressive number for an ethnic group of men who were largely noncitizens and therefore not subject to the draft.

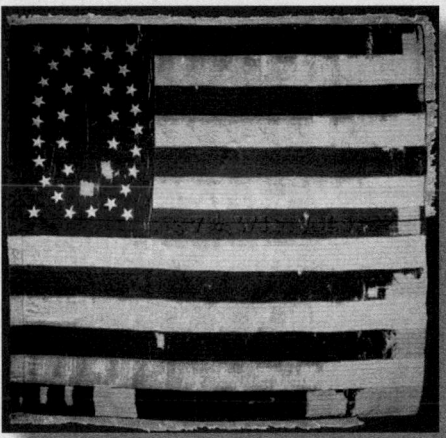

The Menominee soldiers in Co. K, 37th Wisconsin Infantry followed this national flag into the Crater at Petersburg, Virginia, on July 30, 1864. They suffered heavy casualties, and the many holes and tears on the flag attest to the intensity of the Confederate fire they faced. (Wisconsin Veterans Museum)

African Americans

While records credit most of Company F, 29th U.S. Colored Troops to Wisconsin, in reality a majority of the men had never set foot in the Badger State. Wisconsin recruiters, seeking substitutes to help meet quotas, offered attractive bounties to African Americans from Illinois and Missouri and succeeded in raising a company of men. Nevertheless, there were actual Wisconsin residents within the 29th U.S. Colored Troops, including Alfred Carroll, a 20-year-old paper hanger born in Milwaukee, and Alfred Weaver, an escaped slave from North Carolina who was working as a carpenter in Vernon County when the war began. These men took part in the Petersburg Campaign, including the Battle of the Crater, as well as the Appomattox Campaign.

Arming the Troops

The State supplied soldiers with weapons and accoutrements from the federal government, but the respective militia members privately selected and purchased uniforms. As far as uniforms were concerned, there was

very little uniformity across militia units; they were free to choose uniform styles as they saw fit, and this resulted in an array of colors and styles. The Milwaukee Light Guard, the state's most active militia unit, wore a dress uniform consisting of a double-breasted coatee, faced and piped in white, and topped with a bearskin hat. Others, like the Racine Zouave Cadets, made an attempt to copy the Algerian-inspired French military uniforms that were the sartorial rage among many eastern United States militia units. Only after the state quartermaster issued uniforms to the first volunteers at the outset of the war was uniformity achieved. Gray was the traditional color of state militias in the United States, and so it was natural that Wisconsin's quartermaster initially selected that color for the state-issued uniforms. In the summer of 1861, the state provided gray frock coats

Wisconsin's first state-issued uniforms were grey, the traditional color for militias. (Wisconsin Veterans Museum)

or short gray jackets to the first eight infantry regiments. This proved disastrous for the 2nd Wisconsin Volunteer Infantry at the First Battle of Bull Run, when it was mistaken for a Confederate unit and fired upon by the 79th New York Infantry Regiment. On September 2, 1861, the problem was addressed when Governor Randall received a letter from U.S. Army Headquarters, ordering Wisconsin soldiers be outfitted in dark blue wool uniforms. Still, the transition from gray to blue for the first eight regiments was not complete until the end of 1861, when the 8th infantry regiment was the last to receive its initial issue of blue uniforms.

Wisconsin did not maintain an extensive armory system as nearly all of the arms were in the hands of volunteer militia companies, and in any case the numbers of small arms were low. The state-issued arms were a mixture of U.S. rifled muskets, flintlock conversions, nonrifled smoothbore muskets, and an array of poor quality foreign imports. Only when the state units became federalized did the quality of arms improve.

Training and Deployment

While recruiting soldiers was not an issue for Wisconsin early in the war, transforming the eager volunteers into soldiers and transporting them to the various theaters of combat proved challenging at times. The farmers, carpenters, and other laborers who joined the military were used to making their own hours and answering to themselves. They had to learn to obey an officer's orders instantly, including when to rise, when to eat, and when to go to sleep, and to become familiar with the terminology and tactics of mid-19th century warfare. This task was made much more difficult by the fact that very few officers had any experience in these matters. Numerous accounts tell of officers staying awake late at night to pour over manuals and prepare for the next day's drills.

While Camp Randall in Madison is the most well-known Civil War training camp in the state, Wisconsin boasted a dozen other camps in several cities. Some of these sites trained a single regiment before closing, while others trained thousands of men. Some were named after prominent national figures, others after local governors or officers. Some held the same name throughout the war while others changed names when a new regiment arrived. Regardless of location or name, these camps served as the forges that produced Wisconsin's 80,000 men of iron during the Civil War.

Old Camp Randall, Madison, Wisconsin. Watercolor by John Gaddis. (Wisconsin Veterans Museum)

Training camps located throughout the state included the following: Camp Barstow (Janesville), Camp Bragg (Oshkosh), Fort Crawford (Prairie du Chien), Camp Fremont (Ripon), Camp Hamilton (Fond du Lac), Camp Harvey (Kenosha), Camp Holton (Milwaukee), Camp Randall (Madison), Camp Reno (Milwaukee), Camp Salomon (La Crosse), Camps Scott and Sigel (Milwaukee), Camp Tredway (Janesville), Camp Trowbridge (Milwaukee), Camp Utley (Racine), Camp Washburn (Milwaukee), and Camp Wood (Fond du Lac).

The first 10 companies accepted by Randall after his initial call for troops trained at Camp Scott in Milwaukee, located in the vicinity of the Marquette University campus. An anonymous Wisconsin soldier, writing home in May 1861, described the camp as follows: "Our company has 13 tents, six on each side of Fairchild street, with the captain's tent at the head of the street. The mess room, which has been built for our accommodation, is 56 x 90 feet, with kitchen attached. Mssrs. Rice and Andrews, of the Newhall House, furnish us with meals, at 39 cents per man a day. The building will accommodate half of the regiment at a time. We are allowed to form ourselves into squads of six, and each squad has a tent, spade, pickaxe, hatchet, mess pans, etc. The tents are numbered, and the names of the squad put on; so you will have no difficulty finding us."

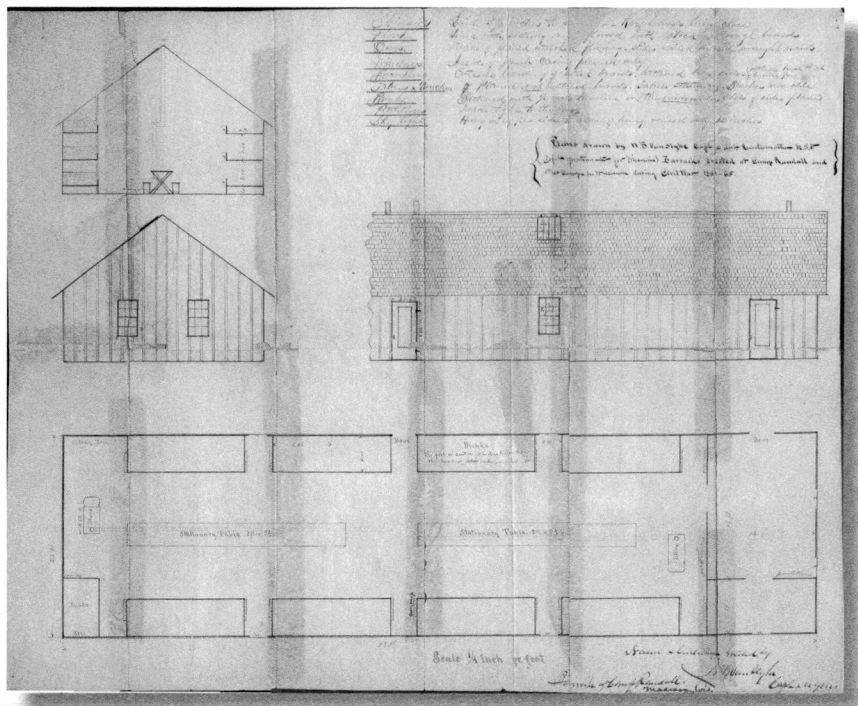

Blueprints of barracks used at Camp Randall reveal details of training soldiers' living conditions. (Wisconsin Veterans Museum)

The men found that camp life was not without its dangers. While most accounts point to George Drake of Company A as the first Wisconsin soldier to die in the Civil War at the Battle of Falling Waters on July 2, 1861, the distinction actually belongs to John H. Munroe. A 27-year-old farmer from Wauwatosa who enlisted with Company C, Munroe drowned while bathing in a river on June 3, 1861, while the regiment was still training at Camp Scott. Many more men would die from accidents and illness while still training in their home state over the next four years.

At times, the first duty of the new soldiers was to physically prepare the camp. William Noble, a 25-year-old Manitowoc resident who served in Company K, 21st Wisconsin Infantry Regiment, wrote in his diary about his company's arrival in Oshkosh to begin training. The men arrived on August 27, 1862, and rested at the camp grounds. The next day, they were examined by a doctor – 17 men were "thrown out" – and those remaining began digging outhouse vaults and clearing the grounds. On August 29, the men drilled in the morning, after which Noble, a carpenter by trade, and six others were detailed to begin building 16-by-56 foot barracks. They finished roofing them on August 30 and 31, and the rest of the regiment arrived on September 1 to the newly created Camp Bragg. Noble and his fellow soldiers did not get to enjoy the fruits of their labor for long – 10 days later they boarded trains for Cincinnati and service in Kentucky, Tennessee, and ultimately Sherman's March to the Sea. Noble, who transferred to the Veterans Reserve Corps in February 1864, mustered out of service on June 29, 1865.

James Sullivan, an 18-year-old farmer from Wonewoc who served in Company K, 6th Wisconsin Infantry Regiment, described a typical day of training at Camp Randall:

Daylight reveille and roll call; and immediately one hour's company drill; then 15 minutes for preparation, then fall in and march to breakfast; 'sick call' 'fatigue call' which meant clean up the company quarters and street. 'Guard mount' which of course took only those detailed; then two and a half hour's company and squad drill; dinner. At one o'clock fall in and have three hours' battalion drill; supper; dress parade. Tattoo and roll call at 9 o'clock, taps 15 minutes later.

Union troops organized in Wisconsin. Plaque located at Camp Randall, Madison. *(Sarah Girkin)*

Most of the drilling that Sullivan referenced consisted of teaching the men to march in a line and perform various maneuvers while marching in a line. Wounded at South Mountain and Gettysburg, Sullivan saw the war to its conclusion, mustering out in July 1865.

Residents of nearby towns often visited camps to see the men drilling. Chauncey Cook, a 21-year-old farmer from Gilmantown who was training at Camp Salomon with the 25th Wisconsin Infantry Regiment, wrote in a September 1862 letter to his family, "to see a thousand soldiers on regimental drill or parade is what visitors call a splendid sight. Hundreds of people in La Crosse come out to see us every evening. There was about five hundred visitors here last night to see us on dress parade." Cook survived the war, and he mustered out in May 1865.

When not drilling or sleeping, soldiers found various activities to fill their time. Alexander Wilson of the 1st Wisconsin Cavalry Regiment listed his extracurricular activities at Camp Fremont in Ripon in a letter to his cousin: "boxing, wrestling, running footraces, jumping, playing ball, reading, and talking, and sometimes running around the town." The men also took advantage of passes into town when possible to frequent local businesses, attend church services, or visit family and friends.

Training and deployment were inextricably linked, though the experiences of Wisconsin soldiers in these areas varied greatly. Ideally, soldiers received a full basic training before deploying. At times, however, men were needed on the battlefield and deployment interrupted training, which would resume upon arriving on location. On rare occasions, very little training occurred before a regiment deployed, with the expectation that the men would receive sufficient drill in the field.

Deployments in the first year of the war were full of pomp and circumstance. Departing soldiers were treated to speeches, parades, and cheering throngs, often at each stop on the way to their destination. James Northup, a 23-year-old farmer from Lodi, described the reception received by the 2nd Wisconsin Infantry Regiment on their way from Wisconsin to Pennsylvania in a June 1861 letter: "Such crowds of people I never saw before. All along the line from Madison to Chicago we were greeted with cheers and waving of handkerchiefs by the people, which is proof that the good wishes of all are with us in maintaining the government." He went on to write about a "grand reception" the men received in Cleveland, complete with refreshments served by "some of the fairest Ladies you ever saw," and how crowds gathered at every train station in Ohio to cheer on the men. Northup was wounded and taken prisoner during the Battle of the Wilderness, but survived to be mustered out in September 1864.

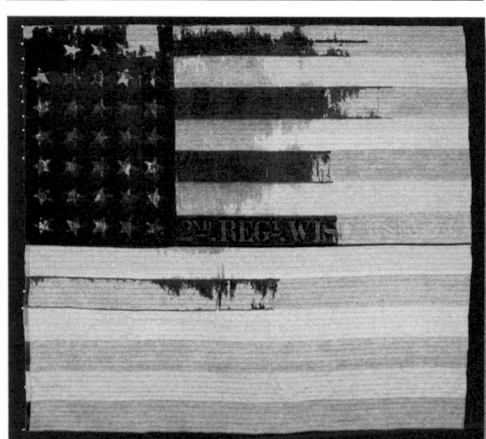

2nd Wisconsin Infantry national colors sewn by Mrs. R.C. Powers and presented to the men within hours of their deployment. (Wisconsin Veterans Museum)

Early in the war, the presentation of the colors, or flags, to a regiment often occurred before deployment and could involve speeches and crowds. The 2nd

Wisconsin Infantry Regiment contracted with a Madison woman, Mrs. R. C. Powers, to make their national colors. For just under $40, Powers cut and sewed together the silk flag and gilded on the stars and the regiment's name on both sides of the flag in roughly three weeks. However, she completed her work within hours of the 2nd Wisconsin's deployment, not leaving enough time for a formal presentation before the men boarded their trains.

Deployment did not always proceed safely or smoothly. The 3rd Wisconsin Cavalry, which trained at Camp Barstow in Janesville over the winter of 1861-62, boarded trains to deploy to St. Louis on March 26. As the train neared Chicago, the axle on one of the cars broke, causing four cars to derail. Twelve members of the 3rd Wisconsin Cavalry were killed in the accident and 20 more were wounded. The 17th Wisconsin Infantry trained at Camp Randall and received orders to deploy to St. Louis in March 1862. Because there had been a delay in paying the men, many refused to board the trains and some even took to the street, armed, to show their displeasure. Their insubordination went so far that Governor Louis P. Harvey called for Union troops from Chicago to help restore order and get all of the men on the train.

As the months and years passed, the pomp and circumstance of deployment lessened and men were moved to the front as quickly and efficiently as possible. Deployment took Wisconsin's Civil War soldiers to forts, camps, and stations all around the country, not always for battle. Regardless of their duties upon arrival, the training they received, both in state and in the field, went a long way toward preparing them for what lay ahead.

Unidentified duo from the 17th Wisconsin. *(Wisconsin Veterans Museum)*

Combat – On Wisconsin!

Union General William T. Sherman was said to have once remarked that one Wisconsin regiment was "equal to an ordinary brigade." Sherman was well acquainted with Wisconsin troops. At the brigade level, he commanded Badgers in both eastern and western theater engagements. Whether it was simply martial hyperbole, his sentiments certainly spoke to the tenacity and skill that came to define the fighting spirit of Wisconsin's military forces. Wisconsin troops took part in almost every major engagement, and hundreds of smaller engagements, and fought with distinction in every Southern state except Florida. From west of the Mississippi to the east coast, the "Badger Boys" engaged the Confederates in hundreds of battles and skirmishes. Like most soldiers, they never thought that they were making history. By the end of the war in 1865,

Wisconsin's Union soldiers crushed secession, ended slavery, and ushered in a new national concept of equality.

The first days of the war were marked by uncertainty as the untested troops, many of them 90-day volunteers, left their training sites for the theaters of battle. Most expected a short war. Any thoughts of a prolonged conflict were dismissed, replaced by a brand of bravado uninformed by past experience. Their fantasies of a swift victory evaporated quickly after their first encounter with the enemy. For the men of the 1st Wisconsin Infantry Regiment, their baptism of fire began at Falling Waters, Virginia, where they engaged a small Confederate force under the overall command of General Joseph E. Johnston. The July 2 battle was a short affair, lasting only 45 minutes, but when it was over Union troops held the field and Wisconsin had suffered its first battlefield casualties of the war. George Drake, of Company A, was killed on the battlefield, and William M. Graham of Company B, later died of wounds received in battle. Many more would follow.

A skirmish on July 18, 1861, just days before the first major battle of the war, took the life of Myron Gardner, Company B, 2nd Wisconsin Infantry Regiment. His company, known as the La Crosse Light Guards, was attached to a brigade commanded by Colonel William T. Sherman, under the divisional command of Brigadier General Daniel Tyler. In the days before the First Battle of Bull Run, Tyler had been ordered by Union Commanding General Irvin McDowell to locate the Confederate forces but to avoid bringing on a general engagement. Tyler's division subsequently encountered elements of General James Longstreet's brigade along the Bull Run at Blackburn's Ford. Although ordered to avoid a general engagement, Tyler faced the guns of the 3rd Company of the Washington Artillery, the venerable militia unit of New Orleans, Louisiana, with a pedigree dating back to 1838. A lively artillery duel ensued and Tyler ordered the men of the 1st Massachusetts forward. After driving back a few Confederate skirmishers, they encountered Colonel Longstreet's Virginians and the artillery duel quickly escalated into a spirited skirmish. Wisconsin troops were ordered into the line of battle, and after quickly arriving at the scene, the men of Company B found themselves opposite the Confederate battery. While the men of the 2nd Wisconsin stood in formation, a shot from one of the Washington Artillery's six-pound rifled cannons struck a tree, glanced off the ground, and took off Myron Gardner's right leg just above the knee. Gardner did not survive the horrific wound. The projectile

This flag was presented to the 1st Wisconsin Infantry as a gift from the 4th Indiana Battery for having saved the battery at the Battle of Perryville. (Wisconsin Veterans Museum)

that killed him was sent to Wisconsin and is now part of the permanent collection of the Wisconsin Veterans Museum in Madison.

The actions at Falling Waters and Blackburn's Ford were but a preview of the horrors of war that were to grip the country for the next four years. Wisconsin troops would see action in almost all of the major battles and play a decisive role in several.

The Eastern Theater

After their baptism of fire at the battle of Blackburn's Ford, the 2nd Wisconsin, along with the rest of the Brigade under the command of Colonel Sherman, prepared for a larger engagement as the army concentrated along the banks of Bull Run. On Sunday, July 21, 1861, Sherman's Brigade advanced into the fray at the First Battle of Bull Run. Brigaded with the 13th, 69th, and 79th New York Infantry Regiments, the 2nd Wisconsin was the only Wisconsin unit to take part in this first major infantry battle of the war. Still wearing their state-issued gray uniforms, the 2nd Wisconsin advanced up Henry House Hill and engaged the Confederate forces commanded by Colonel Thomas J. Jackson. Ordered to move forward alone, without the support of the other regiments on the flanks, the Wisconsin men crested the hill and advanced. After exchanging fire with Jackson's forces and realizing the untenable nature of their exposed position, the men of the 2nd Wisconsin began falling back. As they did so, the men of the 79th New York, who had remained at the bottom of the hill, fired into the ranks of the 2nd Wisconsin, confusing them for the enemy because of their gray uniforms.

In an official report of the action of July 21, 1861, Col. William T. Sherman wrote:

This regiment ascended to the brow of the hill steadily, received the severe fire of the enemy, returned it with spirit, and advanced delivering its fire. This regiment is uniformed in gray cloth, almost identical with that of the great bulk of the secession army, and when the regiment fell into confusion and retreated toward the road there was a universal cry that they were being fired on by our men. The regiment rallied again, passed the brow of the hill a second time, but was again repulsed in disorder.

Though the regiment rallied and advanced a second time, the battle was lost by the end of the day and the retreat of the Union army turned into a rout. During the retreat, the 2nd Wisconsin became disorganized with small groups of soldiers making their own way back toward Washington. At one point, the regiment's national colors nearly fell into the hands of the enemy but were saved by Private Robert S. Stephenson, two regimental band members, and a handful of others who rallied to the colors. For this act, Stephenson was promoted to the color guard and would remain in that honored position until the early fall of 1862.

After the First Battle of Bull Run, the army reorganized on the outskirts of Washington. In the shadow of the humiliating defeat, the 2nd Wisconsin, along with the rest of the army, entered a period of renovation. New units arrived to bolster the ranks, including the 6th and 7th Wisconsin Infantry Regiments. The

2nd joined the 6th and 7th Wisconsin to form a brigade under the command of General Rufus King of Milwaukee. General King had hoped to have the 5th Wisconsin in his command and thus have an entirely Wisconsin brigade, but he was sent the 19th Indiana instead. Though the Indiana men were no Wisconsinites, they were western men. In fact General King's brigade was the only brigade in the entire army made completely of volunteers from western states. This was a unique identity in the Army of the Potomac, which was comprised of mostly troops from eastern states like New York or Pennsylvania. The western composition of the brigade would not be the only thing that made this particular unit unique: their physical appearance would mold that identity as well.

As the fall of 1861 progressed, it became clear that the Wisconsin men were in desperate need of new uniforms. In the early weeks of October, they finally exchanged their gray frock coats for the more suitable blue uniform of the Union army. "We have a full blue suit, a fine black hat nicely trimmed with bugle and plate and ostrich feathers," wrote one excited soldier from the 2nd Wisconsin, "and you can only distinguish our boys from the regulars by their [our] good looks!"

Waiting for the Storm

That winter and early spring were spent drilling in camp and enduring the monotony of winter quarters. Finally, in the spring of 1862, the armies were on the move again. General King's western brigade was sent to occupy the town of Fredericksburg while the main force of the Army of the Potomac, including the 5th Wisconsin, moved farther south to threaten Richmond during the Peninsula Campaign.

In May, General King was promoted to command of the division and General John Gibbon took command of the brigade. General Gibbon recognized the unique nature of the western brigade in the eastern theater. He instilled an esprit de corps through a strict regimen of drilling and reinforced its unique identity by requiring all the regiments of the brigade to wear the tall black 1858 army hats that the 2nd Wisconsin had been issued the previous October. General Gibbon also introduced the practice of wearing white canvas leggings. With this new uniform, the brigade soon became known as the "Black Hat Brigade."

In the summer of 1862, the 3rd Wisconsin engaged in the Shenandoah Valley and the 5th Wisconsin engaged in the Peninsula Campaign; the 2nd, 6th, and 7th Wisconsin still had not seen any combat together. Having spent most of its service up to that point in camps outside of Washington and Fredericksburg, the Black Hat Brigade had suffered casualties only because of illness and disease, a result of the doldrums of garrison duty. August 1862 brought a change in the daily routine: the war crept closer, and the men of General Gibbon's brigade were put in motion to join the main body of the army.

Shiloh

While Wisconsin's regiments in Virginia fought hard but labored under the indecisive leadership of Army of the Potomac Commander, General George B. McClellan, the western theater regiments fared slightly better in the first two years of the war. Ulysses S. Grant's stunning successes at Forts Henry and Donelson on the Tennessee and Cumberland Rivers, respectively, ensured that Nashville would fall, and with it came control of a critical rail and transport center. On February 23, 1862, Confederate forces evacuated Nashville and retreated to Corinth, a small but important rail junction in northern Mississippi. It was there that Confederate General Albert Johnston's command linked up with General P. G. T. Beauregard. Hoping to catch General Grant's men sleeping, General Johnston proposed a daring surprise attack upon Union forces camped about 18 miles away near Pittsburg Landing on the Tennessee River. At this location, General Grant patiently waited for General Don Carlos Buell's five divisions of the Army of the Ohio to arrive from Savannah, Tennessee. General Johnston's goal was to turn the Union Army's left flank, thereby cutting them off from a base of supplies and an escape route on the Tennessee River. Among those Union forces near Shiloh Church were two inexperienced Wisconsin regiments – the 16th and 18th Infantry Regiments.

It took General Johnston's green troops three days to cover the trek between Corinth and the Union position in front of Pittsburg Landing. The advantage of surprise seemed to have been lost. The Confederates carelessly engaged Union cavalry pickets near Sherman's division, and made quite a racket getting into position. Unbelievably, neither Grant nor Sherman believed that an attack was imminent. During the early hours of the morning of April 6, 1862, Sherman's division, along with the divisions of Prentiss, McLernand and Hurlbut, were just rising and preparing breakfast when the main body of Confederates emerged from the heavily wooded terrain and met reconnaissance elements of Colonel Everett Peabody's 25th Missouri regiment. The sound of sustained firing prompted the order to "beat the long roll' and assemble for battle, but for many the order came too late. More than 40,000 Confederates easily pushed aside Peabody's pickets and drove back the Union divisions of Generals

Thomas Reynolds, 16th Wisconsin Infantry, was among the first to engage Confederate troops at Shiloh. (Wisconsin Veterans Museum)

Prentiss, Sherman, W. H. L. Wallace, Hurlbut and McLernand. Among the first Union units engaged were the 16th and 18th Wisconsin Infantry regiments, of the 6th Division, commanded by Brigadier General Benjamin M. Prentiss. Their respective positions were far out in front of the main Union body when the attack began.

For the men of the 16th Wisconsin, it was their first fight but they displayed a steadiness under fire that belied their inexperience. They fought stubbornly for three hours, giving ground grudgingly until they were forced to leave their position in the line of battle, and to fall back on their camp. Both sides suffered appalling casualties. The colonel of the 16th Wisconsin, Benjamin Allen, had two horses shot from underneath him during the grueling action. Lieutenant Colonel Cassius Fairchild, brother of Lucius Fairchild, colonel of the 2nd Wisconsin Infantry Regiment and future Wisconsin governor, received a wound to his hip that would eventually lead to his death in 1868. The 16th Wisconsin was relieved at about 11:00 a.m. and replenished its ammunition, reformed ranks, and went back into the line of battle.

Levi Annis, 14th Wisconsin Infantry, saw action on the second day of Shiloh. (Wisconsin Veterans Museum)

By mid-afternoon, Brigadier General Prentiss had rallied enough troops from the scattered Union forces to a position in the center of the Union line along a road that became known as the Hornet's Nest. Among the beleaguered troops were men separated from their regiments. The Confederates repeatedly fired at close range. The perfect storm of lead tore holes in the Union ranks, but Prentiss's men held on at a terrific cost. While directing attacks on Prentiss's position, Confederate General Johnston was mortally wounded by a rifle shot that severed an artery in his right leg. Overall command then fell to Beauregard who launched multiple assaults upon the Hornet's Nest. Had he concentrated on the Union left flank instead of investing all of his energy on the Hornet's Nest, he may have carried the day. Only after the Confederates brought up more than 50 cannons and poured volley after volley at close range into Union lines, did more than 2,000 Union soldiers surrender, including some Wisconsin troops.

Prentiss's men, however, had purchased time for Grant. The first brigade of General Buell's Army of the Ohio had arrived late in the afternoon to reinforce Grant at Pittsburg Landing. On April 7, at 6:00 a.m., Buell's forces launched an attack upon Beauregard's tired forces. Among Buell's attacking regiments were the men of the 14th Wisconsin under the command of Colonel David E. Wood. Organized in November 1861, the 14th Wisconsin had just recently arrived in St. Louis before moving up the Tennessee River. Beauregard immediately counterattacked, but the Confederates were driven back with heavy losses. Another Confederate counterattack halted the Union advance but by then it was clear that the Union had the numerical advantage, and Beauregard ordered a withdrawal to Corinth. The next day, Union troops under the command of Generals Sherman and Wood pursued the retreating Confederates, unsuccessfully engaging General Nathan B. Forrest's men at Fallen Timbers. The weary Union troops disengaged and returned to Pittsburg Landing.

While generally considered a near miss for the Union, the battle did much to contribute to the reputation of General Ulysses S. Grant. Beauregard had been sent reeling back to Corinth, and Grant's troops held the field. Although Grant had allowed his army to be surprised on April 6, his handling of the affair, once it commenced, resulted in a tactical victory for the North, something that had been lacking in the eastern theater. Undeterred by calls for his resignation, President Lincoln refused to withdraw his support for Grant, remarking, "I can't spare this man. He fights."

Despite their inexperience, Wisconsin troops had per-

Unidentified 18th Wisconsin Infantry soldier. (Wisconsin Veterans Museum)

formed admirably under fire. The 16th and 18th Regiments were badly used up after the first day and were not actively engaged during Grant's assaults of April 7. The 16th had lost a number of its company grade officers to wounds or death, and although it was moved into line on April 7, it saw no real action. The 18th Regiment had lost at least 174 men, who were missing from the fight at the Hornet's Nest, and they were in no position to render effective service on the following day. A few weeks after the battle, Elijah Forsyth of Company C, 18th Wisconsin Infantry Regiment, wrote a letter to his brother, in which he gave some indication of the devastation: "I was in the fight both days our. Reg[iment] was all cut to pieces the first day. Counting what was taken prisoners & killed

& what is sick out of 960 men we have 76 men able for duty." Replenished by recruits, the 18th Wisconsin would serve for the duration of the war.

The 14th Wisconsin Infantry, although arriving too late to take part in the action on the first day of the battle, played a role in Grant's counterassault of April 7. The 14th Wisconsin arrived at Pittsburg landing just after 11:00 p.m. on April 6, and camped for the night, having missed the initial Confederate attack. The next morning it moved into position opposite a Confederate artillery emplacement located on a bit of elevated ground with deep ravines to its front. After being driven back from their position by a determined Confederate infantry charge, the raw recruits of the 14th rallied and were ordered to take the Confederate battery. Crossing a clear field, the resolute Badgers charged up the hill and overran the rebels. During the melee, Lieutenant George Staley of the 14th Wisconsin dis-

The shell that killed Myron Gardner, Company B, 2nd Wisconsin Infantry, at Blackburn's Ford. *(Wisconsin Veterans Museum)*

abled one of the Confederate cannon tubes of William L. Harper's Mississippi Battery by driving a priming wire into the vent and snapping it off. Possession of the gun was brief as Confederate infantry positioned to the rear of the battery moved forward to pour "a storm of lead" upon the 14th. Under galling fire, the 14th fell back to within 330 yards of their original position. The Badgers, however, were not to be denied. It took two more assaults upon the position, but in the end the men of the 14th drove the Confederates from the field. Staley's cannon, a New Orleans-made six-pounder, was recovered and, despite a false claim of ownership from an Ohio regiment, it was sent to Madison as a war trophy.

Shiloh was a bloody affair and a harbinger of things to come for the nation and Wisconsin. The losses were tremendous and exceeded those of all previous American wars. It would be the bloodiest day up until the Battle of Antietam just five months later. Union losses totaled more than 13,000 soldiers. The Confederates lost over 10,000 including their most promising general officer, Albert Sidney Johnston. Colonel Woods's 14th Wisconsin reported 25 killed in action, or died from wounds, with 79 wounded or missing. The two Wisconsin regiments engaged on the first day suffered even greater casualties. The 18th lost 24 killed in action or died from wounds, with another 82 wounded, and 174 taken prisoner in the Hornet's Nest, along with more than 2,000 others from the division of General Prentiss. The 16th suffered the highest casualties of all the Wisconsin units engaged, with 77 killed in action and 149 listed as wounded.

To say Shiloh was a bloody battle would be an understatement. Writing home to his wife and children on April 13, 1862, Calvin Morley of Company C, 18th Regiment, wrote of the carnage:

I suppose you get the account of the battle, and I will not attempt a description of it. It is an awful sight to see the ground covered with dead and dying – mangled in all shapes – some with an arm off, some with severed heads and others with both legs cut off! In one place I saw five rebels killed with a cannon ball. I saw many of them with broken limbs, left to linger out a few days of pain and die for want of medical aid. Our heavy Belgian balls smash the bones so that amputation is the only remedy.

Morley's account is an accurate description of a Civil War battlefield after a major engagement. It would be repeated many times over during the next three years.

When news of the battle reached Madison, the residents of the city were shocked at the level of casualties suffered by Wisconsin troops. Recognizing the need for assistance, Governor Harvey moved to assemble supplies and aid for the wounded Wisconsin soldiers scattered among a number of hospitals. Almost immediately the residents of Wisconsin responded to the governor's call. By April 10, a party consisting of Harvey, Surgeon General Wolcott with eight assistants, and Milwaukee's General E. H. Broadhead left Madison bound for the south. After picking up supplies in Chicago, including over 150 cars of supplies from Madison, Milwaukee, Beloit, Janesville, and Clinton, Harvey and his contingent made their way to Mound City, Illinois, their first stop, where they encountered about 30 Wisconsin soldiers in hospital.

There the party rendered comfort and aid to the wounded and repeated these actions at hospitals

For the Soldiers!

Gov. HARVEY has just telegraphed the Chamber of Commerce to prepare

BOXES OF SUPPLIES,

TO BE

FORWARDED TO OUR SOLDIERS

On the Tennessee, engaged in the late Battle

Please send to the Chamber of Commerce Rooms this Afternoon and Evening.

Bed Ticks, Pillow Ticks, Pillow Cases, Bandages, Lint, Sheets, Shirts, &c., and any Delicacies suitable for the sick.

Dr. E. B. WOLCOTT, Surgeon General of the State, will leave to-morrow morning, and will take charge of all Donations.

A record of Donations will be kept.

W. B. HIBBARD,   E. D. CHAPIN,
ALEX. MITCHELL,   E. SANDERSON,
G. W. ALLEN,   O. E. BRITT,
L. H. KELLOGG,   E. KAHN,
E. H. GOODRICH,   J. RYAN,
C. F. ILSLEY,   J. P. SEAMAN,
R. P. ELMORE,   R. P. FITZGERALD
E. SALOMON,   *Committee.*

Milwaukee, April 9, 1862.

Governor Louis Harvey drowned while delivering supplies to Wisconsin's wounded at Shiloh. (Wisconsin Veterans Museum)

and depots between Paducah, Kentucky, and Savannah, Tennessee. At Savannah, where they encountered over 200 Wisconsin soldiers, Harvey and his comrades were overcome by the sufferings of the men but did their best to provide aid. Nearing the completion of their mission on April 19, Harvey and his contingent found themselves at Pittsburg Landing aboard the steamer *Dunleith*, awaiting the arrival of steamer *Minnehaha* for transport downriver. Sometime after 10:00 p.m., the *Minnehaha* came alongside the *Dunleith*, making contact with her and causing Governor Harvey to lose his footing and fall into the river. Despite attempts

Louis P. Harvey, Wisconsin's seventh governor, drowned at Pittsburg Landing. (Wisconsin Veterans Museum)

to save him, his body was swept down the river. His death by drowning shocked the state. Wisconsin's beloved governor had given his life in service of others, and the loss of Harvey on top of the casualties at Shiloh was almost too much to bear.

Lieutenant Governor Salomon assumed the duties of governor and immediately issued a proclamation calling for 30 days of mourning. Harvey's body was recovered on April 27, more than 60 miles downstream from Pittsburg Landing. Through a rather tortuous turn of events, which included disinterment from a temporary grave, the body of the 41 year-old governor arrived in Madison aboard a train car of the Chicago & Northwestern Railway. After the appropriate state honors, Governor Harvey was laid to rest at Madison's Forest Hill Cemetery.

Union efforts in the western theater for the remainder of 1862 were a mixed bag of remarkable successes, indecisive tactical engagements, and missed opportunities. Victories at Pea Ridge and Prairie Grove, Arkansas, cleared the Confederates out of Missouri. A combined navy-army effort under the command of Union General John Pope and Admiral Hull Foote compelled the Confederate garrison at Island No. 10 to capitulate, thereby opening a way down the Mississippi River. At the same time, Admiral David G. Farragut had achieved a stunning naval victory at New Orleans, delivering the city to the Union on April 27, 1862. Farragut wasted no time in sending seven ships up the Mississippi to take Baton Rouge, Louisiana's capital city. Natchez fell without resistance, and Memphis surrendered in June 1862 after a brief naval battle. The Confederates still controlled a portion of the Mississippi from Port Hudson to Vicksburg, but the Union effectively controlled the rest of the river.

Despite these successes, the Union Army in the west, as a whole, failed to follow Grant's earlier accomplishments and its naval victories on the Mississippi. Following the Battle of Shiloh, General Henry W. Halleck removed Grant from command and assigned him to a wing commander position. Rumors of alcoholism plagued Grant's reputation, and many attributed his failure to anticipate the Confederate attack at Shiloh to drinking. It was not true, but Halleck found it a convenient, if not public, reason to remove Grant. Halleck subsequently took field command of his enormous army, but mismanaged the whole affair. Instead of concentrating his forces after capturing Corinth, he dispersed them. In June 1862, a combined Union naval and land force failed to take Vicksburg, adding to a string of failures.

Baptism of Fire in the East

While Wisconsin troops in the west waited for the next great offensive, their eastern brethren were on the cusp of a major campaign which would provide plenty of chances to prove their combat effectiveness. On the evening of August 28, 1862, as the Wisconsin men of Gibbon's Black Hat Brigade marched along the Virginia road from Gainesville to Centreville, they neared the battlefield of Bull Run, where the 2nd Wisconsin had seen combat for the first time more than a year earlier. As the troops moved along the pike, they were suddenly fired upon by a battery of Confederate artillery.

General John Gibbon, commander of the Black Hat Brigade. *(Wisconsin Veterans Museum)*

Assuming the battery to be a small horse artillery unit meant only to harass the troops on the move, Gibbon ordered forward the 2nd Wisconsin to capture the battery. As the 2nd Wisconsin crested the ridge the battery was stationed on, they witnessed an entire Confederate division emerge from the woods and advance on their position. Confederate General Thomas "Stonewall" Jackson's entire corps had been lying in wait as the Union army marched past. It was not until this moment, when Jackson observed a lone Union brigade marching along the pike fairly separated from the other brigades of its division, that he ordered an attack. As the realization of the size of the force in front of them set in, Gibbon ordered his other regiments forward to aid the 2nd Wisconsin. Meeting stiffer resistance than initially anticipated, Jackson ordered more of his troops forward as well. With the casualties mounting, and neither side willing to budge, only the vanishing daylight brought the toe-to-toe battle to an end. The casualties were staggering. Of the roughly 1,800 men in Gibbon's command who engaged, nearly 800 were killed or wounded by the end of the two-hour fight. Colonel Edgar O'Connor of the 2nd Wisconsin had been killed in action, and Lieutenant Colonel Lucius Fairchild took over command. The other three regimental commanders in Gibbon's brigade were wounded and taken out of action. The Battle of Gainesville, the contemporary name known today more commonly as the Battle of Brawner's Farm, cost the brigade dearly. No longer were they untested "green" soldiers unscathed by battle. These men had stood their ground against the veterans of Stonewall Jackson and held their own for over two hours. They had proved their worth in battle and were willing to do it again. Philander Wright of Company C, 2nd Wisconsin, was wounded in the battle and wrote home of how he had changed from the innocent youth who volunteered to fight almost a year and a half earlier and that he was even more resolved to continue the fight:

But I have changed. Lie upon the battlefield bleeding – see your faithful line grow thinner and thinner & your best friends weltering in their own blood – see them, unharmed cowards straggle to the rear – and the few firm brave ones in front, outnumbered & over-powered – beaten & forced back – all for the want of help that might & should be had – then lie on the field a prisoner and think not of home, but tax your soul to conjure a Curse on Cowards!!!!

Sergeant Philander B. Wright, Color Sergeant, Company C, 2nd Wisconsin Volunteer Infantry Regiment, wore this hat as he led the charge of the Iron Brigade on the morning of July 1, 1863 outside the town of Gettysburg, PA. (Wisconsin Veterans Museum)

The Birth of the Iron Brigade

In the late summer and early fall of 1862, General John Gibbon's Black Hat Brigade of western men earned the more famous moniker, "The Iron Brigade of the West," over the course of three weeks. The brigade's first true baptism of fire on the evening of August 28 at the Battle of Gainesville progressed to a rearguard action on August 30 at the Second Battle of Bull Run. The evening of September 14 saw a determined assault at the Battle of South Mountain. The brigade's trials culminated at dawn on September 17, in a bloody cornfield, at the Battle of Antietam. The brigade paid for their distinguished nom de guerre at a heavy price.

Gibbon's newly christened Iron Brigade was tasked with the Army of the Potomac's initial assault against General Robert E. Lee's Army of Northern Virginia along the banks of Antietam Creek in Maryland. Considered, to this day, to be the bloodiest day in American history, the Battle of Antietam cost nearly 25,000 casualties in a single day. That morning, Gibbon's brigade was ordered forward, with the 2nd and 6th Wisconsin advancing through a cornfield. As they emerged from the corn, the Confederates greeted them with a hail of gunfire. Major Rufus R. Dawes of the 6th Wisconsin described the chaotic scene: "As we appeared at the edge of the corn a long line of men in butternut and gray rose up from the ground. Simultaneously, the hostile battle lines opened a tremendous fire upon each other. Men I cannot say fell; they were knocked out of the ranks by dozens."

With the momentum of the attack, the Badgers pushed the Confederate line into a retreat before fresh reinforcements emerged and counterattacked. With no other option but to fall back, the Wisconsin men retreated through the corn and rallied on the other side to repulse the Confederate advance. In the confusion, Major Dawes rallied his men with the symbol of their home state. "At the bottom of the hill," he later wrote, "I took the blue color of the state of Wisconsin, and waving it, called a rally of Wisconsin men. Two hundred men gathered around

The regimental officers of the 2nd Wisconsin, Iron Brigade, July 1862. (Wisconsin Veterans Museum)

the flag of the Badger state." The remnants of the brigade rallied, but their casualties were high and they effectively retired from the fight.

The "Bloody Cornfield" changed hands six times over the course of the day. Color Bearer Robert Stephenson, who had been in a field hospital bed that morning, upon hearing the first shots of the battle, sprang from his bed and pushed on to find his regiment. The 2nd Wisconsin was under heavy fire in the cornfield when he reported to his captain, reputedly saying, "Captain, I am with you to the last," and took the colors, carrying them until he was shot down. After the battle was over, his comrades found his bullet-pierced body lying in a line with the other members of the color guard – all of them killed.

The Iron Brigade had again played an important role in a major battle, but the cost had decimated the ranks of the regiments. An article published in the *Cincinnati Daily Commercial* on September 22, 1862, describes the terrible price the men from Wisconsin paid that day:

> The last terrible battle has reduced this brigade to a mere skeleton; there being scarcely enough members to form half a regiment, the 2nd Wisconsin, which but a few weeks since, numbered over nine hundred men, can now muster but fifty-nine. This brigade has done some of the hardest and best fighting in the service. It has been justly termed the Iron Brigade of the West.

After those destructive weeks in autumn 1862, the ranks were so depleted that Gibbon requested another regiment be added to the brigade. General McClellan, the commanding general of the Army of the Potomac, recognized the brigade's unique identity and promised the next western regiment that became available.

Perryville

Colonel Benjamin Sweet commanded the 21st Wisconsin at Perryville and was wounded during the fighting. *(Wisconsin Veterans Museum)*

Meanwhile in the west, Beauregard's failure at Shiloh and his decision to evacuate Corinth, led Confederate President Jefferson Davis to replace him with Braxton Bragg, a former corps commander and despised martinet, who promptly divided his army into three parts. Leaving 36,000 troops to defend the Mississippi River, Bragg took 30,000 troops with him and linked up with General Edmund Kirby Smith in an effort to thwart Union General Buell's attempt to take Chattanooga. He beat Buell to Chattanooga and went on the offensive with control of Kentucky as his goal. General Smith's command enjoyed early success, capturing Union troops at Richmond, Kentucky. Bragg attempted to draw Buell away from East Tennessee by invading Kentucky with his remaining force. Frankfort, Kentucky, fell to Smith, but the Confederates could not hold the territory, and Buell seemed reluctant to engage Bragg. Even with additional reinforcements, Buell seemed content to merely shadow Bragg's left flank. With the threat of removal hanging over his head, Buell finally moved to fight Bragg.

Sending two divisions to Frankfort in an effort to confuse Smith and Bragg, Buell moved his main force toward Perryville to confront Bragg's main body of forces. On October 7, 1862, the two forces met. Here the 1st and 21st Wisconsin Infantry Regiments participated as a part of Colonel Starkweather's 28th Brigade, of General Alexander M. McCook's First Corps. The 10th, 15th and 24th were with the brigades of Colonels Harris, Carlin, and Greusel, respectively.

The 1st and 21st regiments of Starkweather's brigade formed on the extreme left of the Union line which would become the hottest section of the battlefield. Starkweather ordered his troops to face the enemy's right flank, placing them on a ridge about 300 yards behind Brigadier General William R. Terrill's untested troops. On the crest of this ridge, he placed his two batteries made up of 12 guns – six each from Indiana and Kentucky.

The Confederates wasted no time in assaulting Terrill's position, sending his green troops of the 123rd Illinois and 125th Ohio regiments reeling back toward Starkweather's position. They simply could not contend with the brigades of Brigadier Generals Daniel S. Donelson and William S. Maney. To make matters worse, the 21st Wisconsin had been placed in an exposed position, unsupported and alone in a cornfield situated in a ravine between the two hills. There they lay on the ground while terrified soldiers of Terrill's brigade ran over them in disorganized retreat. Starkweather's brigade, including the 1st Wisconsin, began to fire into the Confederates from a position behind the cornfield. Caught in a deadly crossfire between friend and foe, members of the 21st began to drop. John H. Otto of the 21st, and a Prussian military veteran, later wrote of the terrible incident, "I saw some of our men fall forward and backward. Now was the moment to fix bayonet and charge. But no order of any kind was given. Then the right of the regiment gave way and ran back."

As the Confederates slammed into the cornfield, the men of the 21st Wisconsin fired two volleys into the advancing rebels, momentarily stopping the advance. It was all for naught, as the Confederates soon unleashed an unmerciful volley of their own at close range. The men broke and ran for the safety of Starkweather's hill. There they found the 1st Wisconsin holding the hill and providing support for the brigade's battery consisting of Indiana and Kentucky units. Remnants of the 21st including companies B and C, stood fast at the guns as well, and awaited the inevitable Confederate assault. John Otto was one of the 21st that remained to fight on the hill; he managed to help man the guns after the artillerymen were killed. Describing the scene in his memoirs, Otto wrote, "when we came to the battery we found it silent and deserted. Most of the artillery men being dead, or wounded."

The 1st Tennessee Regiment pressed the beleaguered Union troops in vicious hand-to-hand fighting. Aided by a Confederate battery that shelled Starkweather's men from the northern end of the battlefield, the Tennesseans eventually forced the Union troops to retire from the ridge. Outnumbered and battered, the men of Starkweather's brigade succeeded in saving six of the twelve cannons as they reformed about 100 yards to the west of their original position; the 1st Wisconsin took refuge behind a stone wall.

Although battered under the onslaught of Brigadier General Maney's 3rd Brigade, the Wisconsin regiments finally held a position of strength, perpendicular to the Benton Road. Despite suffering heavy casualties, the 1st and what was left of the 21st Wisconsin regiments awaited Maney's attack. The fighting continued unabated, with the Confederates assaulting the position four times. But Starkweather's Brigade and what was left of Terrill's held firm.

After five hours of intense fighting, the Confederate advance began to lose steam. Alexander Stewart's brigade to the left of Maney's ran out of ammunition and retired from the field, exposing Maney's left flank. Sensing the opportunity to outflank Maney's brigade, the Union troops moved forward and the 1st Wisconsin counterattacked. The Badgers poured a perfect storm of lead into the

Confederates and forced the Tennesseans to retire to Starkweather's original position. As night began to fall, the battle ended. Starkweather's stubborn defense of the Union left flank saved the day. Had his troops failed to stop Maney's brigade, it would certainly have spelled doom for the Union forces, as the Confederates would have certainly slipped between McCook's 1st Corps and the rest of Buell's Union army. Like Shiloh, the cost in human lives was staggering. Of the nearly 10,000 Union and Confederate soldiers engaged in that section of the battlefield, more than one in every five had been shot.

While the 1st and 21st Wisconsin regiments were engaged on the Union left flank, the 10th Wisconsin found itself to the center right of Starkweather's brigade. Here they stood against the troops of Colonel Thomas M. Jones's Mississippi brigade. Situated atop a hill, the men of the 10th had a clear field of fire over the doomed Mississippians.

> "We layed still…and watched our battery throw death into the rebels," wrote Private Frank Phelps of the 10th. "We could see awful gaps in their ranks and then they would close up and march over their comrades, never stopping until they got within 30 rods of us and just as they got on the top of a knowl the colonel called out for us to up and at them and we poured in a deadly fire into them.

Four times the Mississippians charged from the ravine, and four times they were repelled. But the Confederates continued to press. This time it was the fresh brigade of Brigadier General John Calvin Brown, consisting of the 1st and 3rd Florida regiments and the 41st Mississippi. Simultaneous attacks by two other Confederate brigades eventually drove the Union troops, including the 10th Wisconsin, back to a ridge line at the Russell House. There the battered Union line held until nightfall forced an end to the fighting. The 10th Wisconsin recorded that 48 men were killed or died of wounds, and 97 were wounded.

On October 13, Starkweather summed up the battle in a brief report sent to Governor Edward Salomon:

> I am making up my official reports, and will send you a copy when finished. The battle was terrible. Our enemy were defeated. We now occupy the position occupied by them, and will undoubtedly move on. Our wounded need attention and assistance. We buried the dead last night on the battle field. They first fought some men that they met at Falling Waters. All glory to Wisconsin troops. All honor to the veteran 1st and 21st.

Confederate General Polk refused to press any advantage he had at Perryville, and Bragg slipped away in the night to join forces with Smith. Outnumbered and low on ammunition and supplies, Bragg elected to withdraw from Kentucky, thus ending the Confederate high-water mark in the western theater. By the end of 1862, the Union had little to show for its efforts except a series of tactically indecisive battles managed by a revolving door of ineffective commanders.

At the Crossroads

As the Civil War entered its midpoint, the North found itself at a crossroads. A tactical stalemate at Antietam in 1862 had allowed President Lincoln to issue his preliminary Emancipation Proclamation, but a decisive blow to the South had eluded the North. The year closed out with a strategic victory at Stones River, Tennessee, but a disastrous defeat at Fredericksburg, and Grant's fizzled offensive at Vicksburg, dampened Northern spirits. Major Dawes of the 6th Wisconsin Infantry summed up the prevailing sentiment perfectly just days after the Union disaster at Fredericksburg in a letter home: "This army seems to be overburdened with second rate men in high positions, from General Burnside down. This winter is, indeed, the Valley Forge of the war."

The fortunes of war changed dramatically in the summer of 1863. For months Ulysses S. Grant and his Union soldiers had labored fruitlessly to capture the largest strategic Confederate river fortress on the Mississippi River. Vicksburg had remained in Confederate hands despite Grant's attempts to take the Southern stronghold in December 1862. Impenetrable terrain and precise maneuvering by the Confederates, particularly their cavalry under the command of Forrest, kept Grant from succeeding. Port Hudson to the south of Vicksburg also remained in Confederate hands, effectively giving the rebels control of the Mississippi between the two cities. The importance of Vicksburg was seen as critical to the defense of the Confederacy. Its rail lines linked supplies from the west and it was described by Confederate President Jefferson Davis as "the nail head that held the two halves [of the Confederacy] together."

Undeterred by failure, Grant launched a new campaign in late April 1863. Landing at Bruinsburg downriver from Vicksburg, Grant's forces moved through

Confederate cannon captured by the 14th Wisconsin on the second day of the Battle of Shiloh. (Wisconsin Veterans Museum)

Port Gibson, decisively defeated Confederate forces at Raymond, Mississippi, Champion's Hill, and Big Black Bridge, and engaged Vicksburg from the east. Confederate General John C. Pemberton had ignored Confederate Joseph E. Johnston's directive to move northward to link up with his army, and now he was trapped in Vicksburg, held captive by Grant's reinforced army of 45,000, and cut off from the Mississippi by Union gunboats.

Sensing victory within his grasp, Grant ordered frontal assaults on the Confederate lines on May 19 and May 22. More than eight miles long and anchored by nine forts, the Confederate lines were some of the strongest fortifications of the war. The Confederates cut deep ravines into the land in front of the fortifications, making a frontal assault extremely difficult. Furthermore, the Confederates had cleared much of the land, removing cover from fire that might have concealed Union forces as they amassed for an attack. The 11th Wisconsin Regiment took part in the ill-fated assault of May 22 in which 38 were killed and 69 were wounded. The 14th and 8th Wisconsin also participated in the May 22 assault on the northern end of the Confederate defenses. There the 8th Wisconsin went into battle with "Old Abe," their bald eagle mascot, held aloft with the flags of their color guard. In file formation, the 8th Wisconsin moved down the aptly named Graveyard Road to assault Stockade Redan. Before they reached the Confederate defenses, they were to assemble in a ravine to form a line of battle. They never got the chance as they were subjected to a hail of Confederate fire that led to complete disorder. The attack faltered quickly, and soon the ravine filled with the dead and wounded from the 11th Missouri and 47th Illinois. Captain William B. Britton of the 8th Wisconsin described the slaughter to the *Janesville Gazette*: "So many men were killed and wounded that the road was up so as to prevent some parts of the brigade from getting through." The fire was so fierce and unrelenting that the color guard could not move beyond the ravine. "Everyone seemed to be seeking a place of safety," wrote Lieutenant John Woodnorth of Company C, years after the war. Any thought of charging across the open field to take Stockade Redan was dismissed. In Woodnorth's words, "They simply stood and took the enemy's fire." Old Abe survived the battle unscathed, shielded from a frontal assault by taking refuge in the ravine. The 14th Wisconsin lost 107 men killed, wounded, or missing.

Both attacks failed miserably, and, wishing to avoid further loss of life, Grant settled in for an extended siege. For 47 days, the Union troops bombarded the city, and Union engineers extended their siege lines, growing closer to Confederate lines in anticipation of Vicksburg's capitulation. Writing to his wife in Lodi, from the camp of the 23rd Wisconsin, Robert Steele of Company H described the scene on May 28: "We are still before the forts, the skirmishers popping away, the cannons thundering away almost deafening us sometimes the smoke so thick it almost chokes us." While Steele endured the uncertainty of existence in the siege trenches, the inhabitants of Vicksburg suffered from want of food and safe shelter. It was only a matter of time before Pemberton would capitulate.

On June 25, Union engineers exploded a mine under the Confederate line but the ensuing Union assault failed to capitalize on the gap. Another mine was planned for July 6, but before it could be detonated, Pemberton surrendered his beleaguered garrison to Grant. Five days later Port Hudson fell to Union forces, essentially severing the Confederacy in two and giving the Union complete control of the Mississippi. Grant's success at Vicksburg was matched by a dramatic change of fortune in the eastern theater.

Gettysburg

The summer of 1863 proved to be the turning point of the Civil War. While Grant was in the process of capturing Vicksburg, General George Meade was poised to turn back Robert E. Lee's grand offensive in a small Pennsylvania town called Gettysburg. They could not have known it at the time, but the men of the Iron Brigade would soon take part in perhaps the most important battle of the war. John Hunt, an English

John Hunt, 7th Wisconsin, had to stop this letter to his wife when he received orders to march to Gettysburg. (Wisconsin Veterans Museum)

immigrant and member of Company D, 7th Wisconsin, captured the moment in a letter to his wife just before the Iron Brigade went into action on the first day at Gettysburg:

> July 1st 1863
>
> Dear Mary,
>
> I snatch a moment which I can spare to write to you to say that I am in good health & spirits. We have been marching very steady since we started from Guilford Station Va at the rate of from 5 to 25 mi a day & it has rained most of the time. I was sick with diarhae when we started. We marched about 25 mi first day which used me up & I had to get a doctor's pass to the Ambulances for 3 days running. We have traveled through Maryland & now lie in Pa just over the state line, so we have had some chance to get milk, Bread, butter, etc & I now feel fit to travel with any of them. (Orders to March right off so I must stop

On the morning of July 1, 1863, the men of the Iron Brigade found themselves marching north into Pennsylvania in pursuit of Robert E. Lee's Army of Northern Virginia. Having marched at an early hour, the men could hear the sounds of battle coming from a few miles ahead at Gettysburg. The men were rushed forward and sent directly into action.

The brigade's arrival was fortuitous as the Union cavalry line north-west of town was threatened with collapse from overwhelming Confederate forces flanking it. Immediately, the 2nd Wisconsin was sent forward into a wooded lot on McPherson's Ridge. The urgency of the situation was such that Colonel Lucius Fairchild gave the order to load on the run as they charged unsupported into the woods, directly into Confederate General James Archer's brigade.

As the regiment entered the wood and discovered the enemy in their front, they were received by a terrific volley that cut down almost 100 of the 300 men in the regiment. Shortly after the initial volley, the Iron Brigade's corps commander, Major General John Reynolds, commander of all the Union forces on the field, was killed while personally leading the 2nd Wisconsin into battle; Colonel Fairchild was hit in the left arm which would later have to be amputated; and Color Sergeant Philander Wright, bearing the national colors, stepped to the front of the regiment to lead the 2nd Wisconsin forward. As the advance continued, two bullets passed through the crown of Wright's hat, barely missing the top of his head. A few steps further, a third bullet pierced the flagstaff and passed through his side. Despite his wounds, he continued the charge, deeper into the woods. Wright described the scene after the war:

> I looked for the guards – not one was there – all shot. I guess, 'sure not a man would lag at such a time!' I know I wondered where one might be. I might have known each had been halted leaving me alone.

Advancing only a few more steps, Wright finally halted when a bullet slammed into his left thigh and another into his arm, knocking him to the ground. The other regiments of the brigade arrived to support the 2nd Wisconsin, and together they drove the enemy back. Soon Archer's Brigade broke and fled, with the Badgers, Hoosiers, and Wolverines catching many in their flight, including General Archer, the first Confederate general officer to be captured in General Lee's Army of Northern Virginia since Lee took command in 1861. The morning engagement lasted less than an hour. The brigade took up defensive positions in the woods and awaited the Confederate counterattack.

While the 2nd and 7th Wisconsin, 19th Indiana, and 24th Michigan drove Archer's brigade from the field, the 6th Wisconsin had been detached and moved toward an old railroad cut to help secure the other end of the line. Reaching a fence about 100 yards from

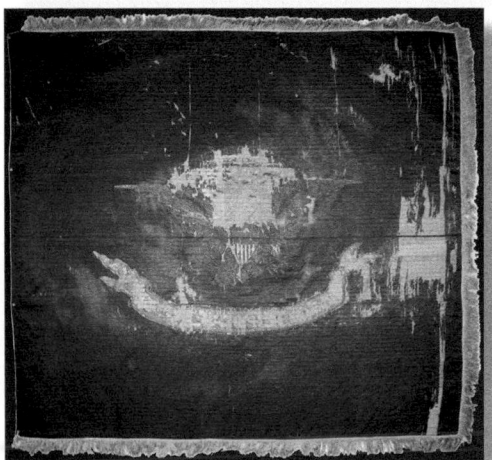

This 6th Regiment Wisconsin flag was used by Rufus Dawes to rally Wisconsin soldiers at the battle of Antietam. (Wisconsin Veterans Museum)

the advancing Confederate line, the regiment opened fire and checked the Confederate advance, who took refuge in the railroad cut. Seeing the situation before him, Lieutenant Colonel Rufus Dawes ordered the 6th Wisconsin, as well as two supporting regiments, to charge the Confederates trapped in the railroad cut. During the ensuing charge, the Confederate's regimental colors were captured by Corporal Asbury Waller, of Company I. Corporal Waller rushed into the midst of the Confederate forces and took the flag from the color bearer's hands. Though severely wounded, Waller kept possession of the flag while continuing to fire as the charge advanced. When Union forces reached the cut, the Confederates surrendered. Though the charge lasted only a few minutes and spanned only 100 yards at most, the 6th Wisconsin lost 160 to death or injury.

Late in the afternoon on July 1, Confederate forces attacked in overwhelming numbers. Completely outnumbered, the Iron Brigade held out for nearly two hours, suffering severely. With the threat of being completely surrounded, the western men finally gave ground after receiving orders to do so. Acting as the rear guard, the men of the 2nd and 7th Wisconsin turned and fired every 50 yards until they reached a defensive barricade which they held as long as they had ammunition. Finally, after the other Union regiments had fled, retreating through the town of Gettysburg, the Iron Brigade, the last Union force still on the field, began their retreat toward the higher ground on the other side of town.

It wasn't until the survivors rallied on Culp's Hill that the remnants of the Iron Brigade realized the price they had paid for their heroic actions. In the 2nd Wisconsin alone, of the 302 men who marched to Gettysburg that morning, only 69 answered roll call that night. The brigade remained on Culp's Hill for the remainder of the battle. Of the 1,885 men that went into battle, 1,153 were casualties by the end.

Gettysburg depleted the ranks of the Iron Brigade even more so than the three weeks of battles in autumn 1862 that earned them their heroic reputation. The brigade would never be the same. Nonwestern units were added to the ranks in order to bring them up to fighting strength. The Iron Brigade's original unique identity – an identity that the Wisconsin soldiers had cherished since the opening days of the war – was lost as a consequence of their heavy casualties.

The 2nd, 6th, and 7th Wisconsin went on to serve in all the maneuvers of the Army of the Potomac during the fall and winter of 1863. With the spring of 1864 came a new commander and a new strategy. General Grant was made overall commander of the Union Forces and ushered in a new style of war that had not been seen before in the eastern theater.

In May 1864, Grant began his Overland Campaign in Virginia, and what remained of the Iron Brigade went with him. At the Battle of the Wilderness on May 5, 1864, the two great armies met again. This time it was in a thickly forested tract of land in central Virginia. The bloody battle ended in a stalemate, but instead of retreating and reforming as all other Union commanders had done before when faced with a tactical setback, Grant disengaged and headed further south toward Richmond. Grant continued this strategy of battle and maneuver for weeks, resulting in nearly 40 continuous days of fighting and culminated with the siege of Petersburg, a major supply center for the Confederate capital of Richmond. At this time, the 2nd Wisconsin's enlistment ended and the regiment was pulled off the line with the majority returning home to Wisconsin.

Mascots

The men of Wisconsin were not the only ones to march off to war. A number of animal mascots also served in the ranks. While Old Abe the war eagle is the most well-known Civil War mascot from Wisconsin, possibly in the nation, many other animals kept Wisconsin soldiers company while they trained and prepared for deployment. Some even deployed with their regiments and would later see battle. They ranged in size from a rooster to a black bear, and while some of their names and fates have been lost to time, they remain an interesting side note to Wisconsin Civil War history.

Old Abe at Vicksburg with the 8th Wisconsin Infantry, 1863. (Wisconsin Veterans Museum)

A militia company called the Eau Claire Badgers purchased a young bald eaglet on their way to train at Camp Randall and named him Old Abe after President Lincoln. Following the purchase, they changed their company's name to the Eau Claire Eagles and, upon arriving in Madison, their mascot began his rise to fame by capturing the attention and affection of other soldiers, civilians, and the local press. The men built a shield-shaped perch for the eagle with a post that an "eagle bearer" could hold. They used a leather tether around his leg to keep him from flying away.

The Eau Claire Eagles became Company C, 8th Wisconsin Infantry Regiment, and Old Abe became the mascot for the entire unit, which would eventually become known as the Eagle Regiment. They deployed to the western theater and, while passing through St. Louis, some Southern sympathizers taunted Old Abe with calls of "wild goose," "Yankee crow," and "Yankee buzzard." He accompanied the 8th Wisconsin into battle on many occasions, several times breaking free of his tether and becoming the target of Confederate sharpshooters. His presence provided a morale boost for the men of the 8th Wisconsin and Union forces in general, and Confederate General Sterling Price reportedly offered a bounty on the eagle's head. While he lost several feathers to close calls on the battlefield, Old Abe was never seriously wounded.

The men of the 8th Wisconsin decided that Old Abe would not reenlist at the end of his first three-year term, so he returned to Madison and was presented to the State, which provided a caretaker and two-room "apartment" for the famous eagle. Old Abe spent his post-war years attending veterans' events and fundraisers around the country. In 1881, Old Abe grew gravely ill after inhaling smoke from a small fire in the capitol basement. He died March 26, 1881, and his preserved remains were put on display in the capitol. Unfortunately, Old Abe was completely lost when his remains were destroyed in the 1904 capitol fire. His memory lives on as statues and images of him, as well as the 101st Airborne Division's "screaming eagle" insignia that was modeled after Old Abe.

Another eagle, though less famous than Old Abe, served as a mascot for the 49th Wisconsin Infantry Regiment, organized in early 1865. The 49th acquired a wild golden eagle during its eight months of service and, after changing his name from Timothy to Phil Sheridan, eventually settled on Andy Johnson. After the war, Andy Johnson lived in the capitol with Old Abe, though his manner was much more untamed. Throughout the years, Andy Johnson and Old Abe engaged in several vicious fights, which ended when Old Abe wounded his counterpart mortally. Andy Johnson died in 1874. His remains were also preserved and displayed in the capitol but lost to fire in 1904.

Harlan Squires, a 16-year-old from Delton, enlisted with his father, Stephen, into Company E, 12th Wisconsin Infantry Regiment, in November 1861. Among the things he took to Camp Randall for training was his pet black bear, named Bruin. The men of Company E, and of the 12th Wisconsin as a whole, embraced Bruin as their mascot, built him living quarters and a 12-foot-high post to climb while they trained, and reportedly wrestled with him for fun. When the regiment deployed, they traveled through Chicago and, while marching between railroad depots, Bruin "marched" at the head of the regiment to great fanfare.

The 12th Wisconsin stopped in Weston, Missouri, and then Fort Leavenworth, Kansas, before hearing that they would be sent on an 800-mile expedition to the New Mexico Territory. Fearing that the journey and climate might prove too much for Bruin, they sold him to a local resident for $17. The men were shaken by this loss, and Corporal Hosea Rood wrote that they hoped that "Bruin would pass into more practical pursuits than his comrades were destined to follow, and become as good a citizen bear as he had been a soldier bear." There is no record of Bruin's fate after leaving the service of the 12th Wisconsin.

Calamity, a black and yellow dog, served as the mascot of the 28th Wisconsin Infantry Regiment. In addition to boosting morale and providing companionship, Calamity accompanied men foraging for food. Members of the regiment reported that when they were prohibited from shooting wildlife for fear of alerting the enemy to their presence, Calamity could catch a hog by the ear and hold it until the men could dispatch it by hand. He was remembered at a 1907 reunion of the 28th Wisconsin Infantry, where surviving veterans recalled that he returned to Wisconsin with the unit after the war and lived out his life in Eau Claire.

Other mascots about which less is known include a rooster, a badger, and a raccoon. The 30th Wisconsin Infantry Regiment kept a rooster during its service in the western theater. The men of the 30th so admired their pet rooster that they had a photograph of the rooster taken while in camp near St. Joseph, Missouri in 1864. The 26th Wisconsin Infantry Regiment, as befitted a unit from the Badger State, reportedly kept a live badger as a mascot. There is also evidence that, in addition to Bruin the bear, the 12th Wisconsin also kept a raccoon as a mascot. Regardless of their size, these mascots provided comfort, companionship, and diversion for soldiers caught up in a horrible Civil War.

Arming African Americans

President Abraham Lincoln. *(Wisconsin Veterans Museum)*

As the Union Army moved southward, it attracted runaway slaves and those that had been freed or dislocated by occupying forces. By 1862, thousands were serving the Union as laborers, cooks, and servants. Pejoratively nicknamed "contrabands" by their liberators, fugitive slaves labored for the Union Army and provided important information about the Confederates and their movements. In 1862, Rev. A. C. Berry, chaplain of the 4th Wisconsin Cavalry, wrote glowingly of the help that fugitive slaves were providing his unit as it moved through the South. "They are always ready to give information, always to be relied on; the only real friends of the Union; and they were always ready to venture life and everything else to serve the Union cause, without fee or compensation, save the hope that something might turn up to give them freedom."

Wisconsin soldiers unfamiliar with the true nature of slavery were often shocked by the application of the "peculiar institution." Jackson Thompson, of the 7th Wisconsin Light Artillery Battery, observed slavery first-hand while serving in Tennessee. Writing home to his future wife Sarah Throne, Thompson noted that even women were not spared the hard life of a field hand:

> What shall I say to you that is interesting Sarah? I guess I will have to tell you a little sight I saw the other day. I was on a cotton plantation where there was fifty acres all planted of cotton. There was seventy-five Negros and wenches to work in the field. They worked the wenches in the field just as much as the men.

Some Badgers, like Albert Foster of the 5th Wisconsin Infantry, understood that victory could only be accomplished by the complete destruction of slavery. "The war will last as long as Slavery lasts," he opined. "There will be no War without Slavery, and no Peace with it. God will never permit this war to end until that end is accomplished."

Lincoln's final Emancipation Proclamation of January 1, 1863, opened the door for Black men to serve in the Union Army. When given the chance, more than 180,000 men of color served in the ranks of the Blue. Free Black men had long served in the ranks of the Navy, but the idea of arming them was a revolutionary action for the United States. While some northern soldiers chafed at the idea of arming former slaves and freedmen, or questioned their fighting ability, Jackson Thompson adopted a somewhat more pragmatic and commonly held view. Writing home to Sarah he seemed unperturbed by the notion of arming former slaves. "There is some talk of arming them and putting them into the field to fight," he wrote. "I think there is the place for them. They will stop a ball just as well as any of us."

As the war dragged on, Wisconsin soldiers became more convinced of the righteousness of their cause as it related to slavery. By 1864, the war had become more than an effort to simply preserve the Union as it previously existed, half free and half slave. "There is one thing about this war that I am taking a great notion to, late days, and that is the emancipation of Slavery," wrote Wesley Riley, 2nd Lieutenant, of the 37th Wisconsin. "I am happy to see how they [are] freeing those poor fellows who have been serving those low minded southerners, I am sure have used them with brutality. But now I think that the back bone of slavery is broken, and mostly all the other principal bones, when it is no more, then can we boast of a truly free country."

The End of Parole

Every man we hold, when released on parole or otherwise, becomes an active soldier against us.—Lt. General Ullyses S. Grant

Union casualties were comparitively easy to replace either through the draft or through the recruitment of new volunteers. With a population 40 percent smaller than the North, Southern troop strength was more difficult to maintain. By the winter of 1863, it was clear that the complex parole system that had governed the exchange of prisoners since 1862 was merely prolonging the war. The Confederacy also refused to exchange Black soldiers – a proposition that was unacceptable to the North. On April 17, 1864, General Grant ordered that prisoner exchanges cease. The parole system remained suspended until February 1865, when both sides agreed to exchange sick prisoners at a rate of nearly 1,000 per day.

The Confederacy maintained a number of prison camps, but none were as well-known as Richmond's Libby Prison and Georgia's Andersonville. Once a ship chandlery, Libby Prison housed more than 1,000 Union prisoners, mostly officers, on its second and third floors. Open, barred windows subjected the prisoners to the elements and extremes in temperatures. Overcrowding and frequent food shortages caused high mortality rates.

Andersonville, also known as Camp Sumter, held more than 44,000 prisoners during its 14-month existence. Nearly 13,000 died there. Surrounded by a pine log stockade, prisoners were discouraged from escaping by a post-and-rail fence known as the "deadline." Guards posted in sentry boxes above and along the stockade walls were instructed to shoot any prisoners attempting to cross or reach over the line. A single, slow-moving creek divided the compound and served as both a sewer and water supply for the prisoners.

Corporal James Skeels, captured at the Battle of Varnell's Station. (Wisconsin Veterans Museum)

At its peak in August 1864, the camp held more than 33,000 prisoners in an area designed to hold no more than 10,000. Deteriorating Southern economic conditions and a scarcity of supplies contributed to the highest prison mortality rates of the war. When the war ended, the prison's commandant, Captain Henry Wirz, was charged with "murder, in violation of the laws of war." He was tried, found guilty, and hanged on November 10, 1865.

Nearly 4,000 Wisconsin soldiers were held prisoner during the Civil War. Most of them were paroled or exchanged prior to April 1863, but many Badgers captured in the last two years of the war suffered for extended periods in Southern prisons as a result of the suspension of the parole system. Some, like James Walker Skeels and Frank Ingersoll, never came home.

Skeels, a native of New York and resident of Rosendale, enlisted in Company B, 1st Wisconsin Cavalry, in September 1861. His unit saw minor action in Missouri and Arkansas before being transferred into the Army of the Cumberland. His unit took part in the Chattanooga Campaign in September 1863, playing an important role in the Battle of Chickamauga. Skeels was promoted to corporal in March 1864, but two months later he was captured at the Battle of Varnell's Station in Georgia, and held at the Confederate prison in Florence, South Carolina, for nine months. Paroled in February 1865, he was admitted to the Union hospital at Wilmington, North Carolina, in March but he was never heard from again. Twenty-five years after the war, the pain of losing an only son still haunted Martin Skeels, James's father. In an inquiry to former General Starkweather, Martin Skeels wrote, "My son was all the help I had until he enlisted and when I lost him I lost all and have not a child in the world."

A Waupun resident, Frank J. Ingersoll was 21 years old when he enlisted in Company K, 10th Wisconsin Infantry Regiment, on September 7, 1861. Listing his occupation as "artist," Ingersoll kept two diaries throughout his service. The 10th Wisconsin trained at Camp Holton in Milwaukee and spent the first year of the war performing guard duty and destroying railroads in Tennessee and Kentucky. They saw their first major action on October 8, 1862, at Perryville. Their involvement in the Battle of Stones River on December 31, 1862, was limited, but Ingersoll described a near miss in his diary entry for that day: "Fighting today. Got a ball through my coat tail and damaged this book as you see."

Ingersoll's luck ran out on September 20, 1863, when he was captured at Chickamauga, Georgia, where the 10th Wisconsin was left exposed and almost captured in its entirety. Initially held at Libby Prison, Ingersoll and his comrades tried to keep themselves in good spirits while waiting for exchange. Any hope of parole was dealt a blow when Ingersoll learned in October 1863 that the U.S. authorities would no longer exchange prisoners. A dejected Ingersoll wrote in his diary, "This afternoon the whole story of Exchange is again exploded. The papers state that our Government desires no exchange during the remainder of the war. No mention is made of paroling." Still, Ingersoll held onto the barest of hopes that something might be done. In November, he plaintively wrote, "There seems to be no prospect of any exchange taking place very soon, and we hear nothing of any parole. Something may be done however before we think of it. We must hope so." But by the end of November, Ingersoll had completely given up hope. "There is all sorts of talk of paroles and exchanges," he wrote, "but we place no confidence in anything we hear."

Frank Ingersoll, captured at Chickamauga and held in Libby, Danville, and Andersonville prisons. (Wisconsin Veterans Museum)

Ingersoll moved from Libby to Danville before spending almost five months at the infamous Andersonville Prison, which he described in a poem as, "A pen of monstrous size. Such human suffering as we saw, Ne'er greeted mortal eyes." With his hope and health failing, Ingersoll took to recording the deaths of his comrades. His final destination was the Confederate prison in Florence, South Carolina, in October 1864. There, his diary entries became increasingly unfocused as he battled illness and malnutrition. Ingersoll's diary entries came to include poetry mixed with proverbs, detailed cooking recipes, lists of dead fellow prisoners, and the price of food as his health continued to deteriorate. His last entry expressed the wish that should he die a prisoner of war, his diary be sent to his father back home in Wisconsin. Ingersoll died on February 15, 1865, mere weeks before many of the Union soldiers at Florence were finally paroled as a dying Confederacy lost the will and resources to continue to hold prisoners. His regiment, unaware of his fate, listed him as a prisoner of war when it mustered out in October 1865. The last entry in Ingersoll's diary, penned by his comrade Joseph Kolhamer, also of the 10th, simply read "The owner of this Book/Died near Florence SC/Federal Prisoner of War."

Confederate Rest, Forest Hill Cemetery, Madison, Wisconsin. (Sarah Girkin)

The Tedium of Duty

Not every Wisconsin soldier fought in epic battles like Shiloh, Antietam, Vicksburg, and Gettysburg. In fact, not every Wisconsin soldier fought in battles at all. Men from the Badger State were sent all over the country to perform a wide array of duties, ranging from guarding vital depots to protecting citizens from threats both real and perceived. Some served on the frontier in places like the Dakota Territory, Colorado, and the Texas border. Others remained in Wisconsin, performing various duties around the state. Still others rarely stayed in one place long, instead spending much of their service moving by foot, rail, and boat to different parts of the country.

There were several Wisconsin regiments that were stationed in their home state after training. The 28th Wisconsin Infantry Regiment remained in the state in November and December 1862 to quell the draft riots in Ozaukee County. The 19th Wisconsin Infantry Regiment, which organized in Racine, was called to Camp Randall in Madison for a special duty. A group of over 1,000 Confederate prisoners had been sent there in April 1862, and the 19th Wisconsin was charged with guarding them. More than 100 of the prisoners died of disease, and one was shot by Clarence Wicks, a teenage farmer from Crawford County in Company E. Wicks, who later served with Company F, 36th Wisconsin Infantry Regiment, would himself die of wounds received in Virginia in July 1864.

The 30th Wisconsin Infantry Regiment had a similar detail, though they remained in the state longer. In November 1862, Company A helped enforce the draft in Green Bay, two companies remained at Camp Randall to guard draft resisters arrested by the 28th Wisconsin in Ozaukee County, and the remainder of the regiment traveled to Milwaukee and Washington Counties to assist with the draft there. Over the course of the next 16 months, various companies of the 30th Wisconsin helped enforce the draft in many areas of the state, including on the shores of Lake Superior and in Lafayette, Dodge, and Ozaukee Counties. During the summer of 1863, a company even traveled to Juneau County in response to an anticipated attack by hostile Native Americans that never materialized.

In the spring of 1864, a number of draftees were assigned to duty at Camp Randall. They were called the Permanent Party, or Permanent Guard, and although, for administrative purposes, they were assigned to regiments in the field, they remained in Madison for the duration of their service. Later that year, a larger number of drafted men and substitutes were assigned to the 22nd Wisconsin Infantry Regiment, though in reality they joined the Permanent Party at Camp Randall.

Remains of an original Camp Randall guard house. (Sarah Girkin)

The draftees were mustered out of service in May 1865, while the substitutes were mustered out the following month.

The pervasive fear of Native American attacks, particularly following the Dakota War of 1862 in Minnesota, led three Wisconsin regiments to duty in western Minnesota and the Dakota Territory. The 25th Wisconsin Infantry, which trained at Camp Salomon in La Crosse, was the first to deploy to the West in September 1862. They remained in Minnesota through December, then returned to Wisconsin for deployment to the South. John Wildermuth, an 18-year-old farmer from Willow, Wisconsin, who served in Company B, wrote to his parents in November 1862 about the improbability of any action in Minnesota: "Indians are scarce. Soldiers are plenty, cavalry, infantry and artillery." Later he added, "We expect to go home in the spring. There is no show for a fight with the Indians." The 30th Wisconsin proceeded even farther west in 1864, going into the Dakota Territory as part of an expedition connected to the fear of further attacks by Native Americans. The 30th remained there until the late fall of 1864. Finally, the 50th

Wisconsin Infantry Regiment deployed to Fort Rice in the Dakota Territory in the spring of 1865 and remained there until June 1866, well after the war ended.

Being so near to Washington, DC, many Wisconsin troops spent time in, or at the very least passed through, Arlington, Virginia. And they were very aware of whose land they tread upon. The Iron Brigade camped at Arlington over the winter of 1861-62, and numerous letters and diaries attest to their knowledge that they were on land, until very recently, owned by Confederate General Robert E. Lee. Isaac Tucker, a 40-year-old doctor from Baraboo who served as a fifer in Company H, 6th Wisconsin Infantry Regiment of the Iron Brigade, made note of an interesting order pertaining to Arlington in a diary entry dated February 2, 1862: "[An] order issued that we cut no more wood on General Lee's Land." In May 1864, Charles Forsyth, a 29-year-old farmer from Clinton, wrote in a letter to his sister, "we are now camped on General Lee's old plantation. It is a very pretty situation."

The two Wisconsin units that were stationed farthest from their home state were likely the 48th Wisconsin Infantry and the 9th Battery Wisconsin Light Artillery. The 48th Wisconsin, organized at Camp Washburn in Milwaukee, deployed to Kansas in the spring of 1865. They remained there through August when, instead of being mustered out, they were ordered to provide escort for trains and mail heading into portions of Iowa, Kansas, and Colorado, areas considered in danger of attack by Native Americans. The 9th Light Artillery trained at Camp Utley in Racine, reached Kansas in March 1862, and immediately prepared to go farther west. Arriving in Denver in June, the battery split, with a section stationed in New Mexico and one in Colorado. The men remained there through April 1864, when they returned to Kansas for further duty.

The 12th Wisconsin Infantry trained at Camp Randall and deployed to Leavenworth, Kansas, in January 1862. Given orders to accompany an expedition into New Mexico, they began marching west. The expedition was cancelled later in the spring, but the 12th Wisconsin continued marching. From Leavenworth to Fort Scott to Lawrence to Fort Riley and back to Leavenworth. A member of Company K wrote in a March 1862 letter from Fort Scott, "We left Leavenworth City on the first of March, and shall probably reach Lawrence about the first of April; thus spending one whole month for nothing besides marching and countermarching, hauling rations, &c., which has cost the Government thousands of dollars for worse than nothing."

The 12th Wisconsin eventually left Kansas by steamer, and went on to participate in the Vicksburg and Atlanta Campaigns, Sherman's March to the Sea, and the Carolina Campaign. During their service, they marched just under 4,000 miles, rode as passengers for 2,500 miles by train, and travelled over 3,000 miles by steamer for a total of 9,500 miles traversed. For this reason, they were often referred to as the "Marching Twelfth."

In the midst of fighting the Civil War, the federal government became concerned when France took control of Mexico. There was some fear that the French would take advantage of a war-weakened United States to consolidate its hold in the Western Hemisphere, a clear violation of the Monroe Doctrine. As the Civil War wound down and came to an end in April 1865, General Ulysses S. Grant sent a significant number of Union forces to Texas to secure the border and,

Color Guard of the 12th Wisconsin Infantry

The 12th Wisconsin Infantry was known as the "Marching 12th", traveling over 9,500 miles. (Wisconsin Veterans Museum)

allegedly, to provide aid to Mexican revolutionaries fighting against French rule. Many Wisconsin units spent time in Texas in 1865.

Three Wisconsin infantry regiments and two cavalry regiments took a turn in Texas immediately following the end of the war, none seeing any significant action. The 13th Wisconsin arrived at Calhoun County, Texas, in July 1865, and suffered immensely from illness. A contemporary history stated that "many died here who had gone through the whole war without being sick." The 27th Wisconsin spent almost two months in Clarksville, Texas, beginning in June 1865. They were joined there for a short time by the 35th Wisconsin, who moved on from Clarksville to Brownsville, where they stayed through March 1866. The 2nd Wisconsin Cavalry Regiment marched over 300 miles from Alexandria, Louisiana, to Hampstead, Texas, in August 1865; they remained there until the end of October before returning to Wisconsin. The 4th Wisconsin Cavalry, originally mustered into service as an infantry regiment, arrived at San Antonio in July 1865 and patrolled various portions of the Rio Grande River through May 1866. Jerry Flint, a 21-year-old farmer from River Falls, who served as a 1st Lieutenant in Company G, wrote his brother in November 1865, "Since I wrote you last we have been marching across the wild uninhabited prairies of Texas....The boys are allowed to cross the [Rio Grande River] at any time and many avail themselves of the opportunity to see Mexico."

The Beginning of the End

While Grant laid siege to Vicksburg during the summer of 1863, Union forces under the command of Major General William Rosecrans repeatedly outmaneuvered Bragg's Confederates during the summer of 1863. By September, Rosecrans had cornered Bragg in Chattanooga – a critical rail junction in southeastern Tennessee. Through speed and clever deception, Rosecrans forced Bragg's army of 45,000 out of Chattanooga on September 9. Tennessee was now firmly in Union control, but Bragg would soon turn the tables on Rosecrans.

Rosecrans was determined to cut off Bragg's retreat. Splitting his army, he sent his three army corps through three different mountain gaps. This would have been a daring maneuver in any situation, but Rosecrans believed, incorrectly, that he had Bragg on the run. Bragg, however, was in fact concentrating his troops, which included new arrival of two divisions from Johnston in Mississippi and two divisions from Longstreet in Virginia

On September 18, two of Bragg's commanders, General Bushrod Johnson and General Nathen B. Forrest, attempted to move their forces across the Chickamauga Creek at Reed's and Alexander's bridges, with the objective of turning Rosecrans's left flank at Lee and Gordon's Mills. At Reed's bridge, the Confederates under Johnson ran into Colonel Robert Minty's 1st Cavalry Brigade of George Crook's 2nd Cavalry Division. Minty was forced to retreat, but he gave ground slowly, refusing to leave the field until after four in the afternoon. At Alexander's Bridge, the Confederates of William Walker's reserve corps encountered the mounted infantry of John T. Wilder's 1st Brigade of Joseph Reynold's 4th Division armed with Spencer repeating rifles. Wilder's men devastated the attacking Confederates, forcing them to divert downstream to find an uncontested crossing. Bragg's plan to turn the Union left flank had been thwarted, gaining time for Rosecrans to move reinforcements into position.

The Battle of Chickamauga began at dawn on September 19. The fighting was vicious and neither side prevailed. On September 20, the Confederates received a lucky break that would turn the tide of the battle from stalemate to victory for the Confederate forces. Through a series of miscommunications, compounded by poor visibility because of smoke and wooded terrain, Rosecrans ordered Thomas J. Wood's 1st Division of the 21st Corps out of the center of his line to close a supposed gap to his left. In actuality, there was no gap. Just as Wood's division moved from its position, Longstreet's Confederates struck, driving a wedge in the center. Union General Jefferson C. Davis's division to the south of the hole in the Union line was crushed by an overwhelming Confederate onslaught. Among Davis's division were the men of Colonel Hans Heg's brigade and the men of the 15th Wisconsin.

Heg's brigade had been ordered to fill the gap left by Wood's division, but he had little time to move into position before the Confederates attacked. Heg's men repulsed two Confederate charges but could not hold back a Confederate force five times the size of their own division. Heg's regiment broke ranks and ran for the safety of the rear; many were captured by the Confederates. Although the death casualties for the 15th Wisconsin were not particularly high, the cost was great because Colonel Heg was among the 11 killed in action.

While disaster struck the center right of the Union line, Union troops to the north had successfully repelled several Confederate assaults throughout the morning. There the shattered remnants of the Union's right flank would coalesce with George Thomas's corps, whose units had formed a strong line of defense in the shape of a horseshoe on higher ground. Among the units making a last stand at Chickamauga were the 1st and 21st Wisconsin Infantry Regiments.

The Badgers and Thomas's corps held the line throughout the day, but after repulsing multiple Confederate assaults they were critically low on ammunition. Sensing disaster, Thomas ordered a general retreat to Rossville. The 1st and 21st Wisconsin regiments were among Absalom Baird's 1st Division of the 14th Corps and the last to leave their section of the Union line, having not received the order to retreat. As the Confederates moved closer, the 1st and 21st found themselves alone, their flanks completely unprotected. John Otto, the veteran of Perryville, described in his post-war memoir the chaotic scene in which the 21st tried to extricate itself from the situation:

Colonel Hans Heg, killed in battle at Chickamauga. (Wisconsin Veterans Museum)

> Looking in that direction I saw over the brush, the rebel flags advancing not twenty rods away....I shouted to Captain Weisbrod whose Comp. was next to mine [on] the left: "There they come! We must get out [of] here! Company 'D' right oblike! Double quick, March!" Weisbrod ordered his Comp. the same. But Colonel Hobart who usually walked with the head down looking at the ground said: "Boys follow me"! But mine and Weisbrods Comp. were already making good time; others followed and for good half a mile we made the fastest time we ever had made in the army....All thus who followed Col. Hobart...were taken prisoners by the Johnnies and were sent to rebel prison pens where two thirds of them starved to death.

Harrison Hobart, taken prisoner at Chickamauga, was sent to Libby Prison where he and three other officers executed an escape. (Wisconsin Veterans Museum)

Hobart was taken prisoner and sent to Richmond's Libby Prison, where he and three other officers, including Lieutenant Colonel Theodore S. West of the 24th developed a plan to tunnel their way out. Working at night, and over the course of two months, Hobart's small band of fellow miners successfully dug a tunnel that led underneath an adjacent road, emerging in an old shed. When the time came to make their bid for freedom, Hobart's band informed their fellow prisoners, but warned them not to enter the tunnel more than two at a time. He and West emerged on the other side of the street and simply walked through the city. Aided by African Americans, Hobart traveled 70 miles in three weeks before making it to Union lines. In recognition of Hobart's exploit, the men of the 21st commissioned a presentation sword from the firm of Tiffany & Company and gave it to Hobart in commemoration of his daring escape. Inscribed with a reference to the Greek hero Aristomenes's legendary escape from Caeadas, the sword is now housed in the Wisconsin Veterans Museum.

Arthur McArthur, recipient of the Medal of Honor, led an assault on Missionary Ridge. (Wisconsin Veterans Museum)

The 1st and 21st suffered greatly for their steadfast actions in September 1863, but in the end they could claim with just pride the distinction of having made the last stand at Chickamauga. For his heroic defense, Major General George Thomas was thereafter known as "The Rock of Chickamauga."

Rosecrans now retired to Chattanooga where Bragg would keep him bottled up until mid-October when Grant replaced him with Major General Thomas. Grant quickly reinforced Chattanooga with Sherman's four divisions, established a new supply line, and prepared for a major offensive operation. On November 25, Union forces assaulted Bragg's position on Missionary Ridge. It was here that a young adjutant named Arthur MacArthur from the 24th Wisconsin Voluntary Infantry Division earned the Medal of Honor. Leading an assault at the crest of Missionary Ridge, MacArthur seized the regimental colors from an exhausted color bearer named John Booth, and led the regiment to the crest of the ridge, driving the Confederates from their position in a general retreat. In later years, MacArthur was credited with coining the battle cry, "On, Wisconsin!" In actuality he cried, "24th Wisconsin!"

The victory at Chattanooga, combined with earlier Union victories at Vicksburg and Gettysburg, essentially broke the Confederacy. Almost two more years of hard fighting lay ahead, but the Southern fate had been sealed by the string of decisive Union victories. After the battle, both armies settled into winter quarters. On March 3, 1864, President Lincoln appointed Grant lieutenant general in command of all Union forces. He moved to the eastern theater where he would oversee the final campaigns of the war. The "Victor of Vicksburg" relentlessly committed Union forces to battle – often at a high human cost. In the coming months, Northern resolve, coupled with industrial and manpower advantages, would simply overpower an increasingly diminished Southern rebellion.

Making Georgia Howl!

My aim, then, was to whip the rebels, to humble their pride, to follow them to their inmost recesses, and to make them fear and dread us.—William T. Sherman

From the spring of 1864 until the end of the war, Grant managed a costly but devastating campaign of continuous engagement designed to deprive the South of resources. In the western theater, Grant ordered General William T. Sherman to relentlessly move against Confederate Generals Joseph Johnston and John B. Hood in Georgia, urging the Union general "to get into the interior of the enemy's country as far as you can, inflicting all the damage you can upon their war resources."

Sherman's forces, numbering 100,000 men, began their campaign in northern Georgia. What followed was a scenario in which Sherman's three separate "armies," under Generals McPherson, Scofield, and Thomas, pursued the Confederate Army, now under the command of Joseph Johnston, through the hills and mountains of northern Georgia, with Atlanta as their target. Along the way, there were a series of battles at places such as Resaca, Dallas, and New Hope Church. Sharp action

General William T. Sherman led a relentless campaign through Georgia that included many Wisconsin soldiers. *(Wisconsin Veterans Museum)*

followed by a Confederate retreat in the direction of Atlanta characterized the heavy, continuous fighting. Wisconsin troops remained constantly engaged during the summer of 1864. At Marietta, Major Frederick C. Winkler of the 26th Wisconsin recorded a close call in which his hat was pierced by a Confederate bullet. "The bullets flew around and over us thick and fast," he wrote to his wife in Milwaukee. "As soon as I can get another I will send you my hat, to show the narrowness of my escape from a fatal bullet." Winkler's bullet-pierced hat can be found in the Wisconsin Veterans Museum.

By June 27, the Union forces found themselves at the foot of Kennesaw Mountain, within 25 miles of Atlanta. Wishing to protect his supply line to Atlanta, Joseph Johnston set up formidable defenses at the mountain. What followed was a familiar scenario during the Atlanta Campaign. Johnston had done his best to avoid an all-out battle, but Sherman was determined to break through Johnston's lines at Kennesaw. A failed attempt that resulted in 3,000 casualties did not stop Sherman. He simply outflanked Johnston again, and before long Sherman's men were on Atlanta's doorstep. Sherman was relentless and more bloody battles followed, but on September 2, 1864, the city fell to Sherman's men, opening the way to the sea.

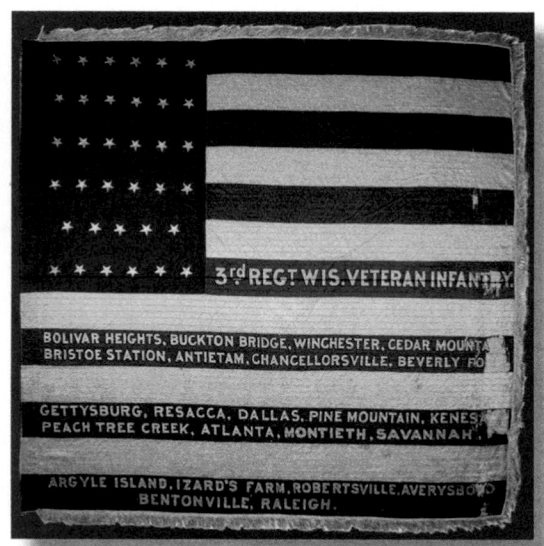

3rd Wisconsin Infantry National colors. (Wisconsin Veterans Museum)

After capturing Atlanta, Sherman's "bummers" (a nickname applied to his men on account of their ability to live off the land) cut a 250-mile swath through the heart of Georgia to Savannah, effectively breaking the back of the Confederacy. In Virginia, Grant sent General Phil Sheridan to destroy Southern resources in the Shenandoah Valley, while his Army of the Potomac kept Lee bottled up at Petersburg in a nine-month siege.

William F. Goodhue, of Company C, 3rd Wisconsin Infantry, was one of the thousands of Wisconsin soldiers who participated in Sherman's momentous march through the heart of the Confederacy. In November 1864, he described Sherman's Army as an irresistible, unstoppable force:

> Sherman has chosen the wisest plan, severed his communications himself and is going south and east. He could not have chosen a better time, for there is plenty for an army to live on anywhere in the South and it will be a good thing for a Veterans army to march through the South and live on its products; there can be no obstructions in our road; Hood cannot reach us, Grant has enough for Lee to do; the Rebs may scrape together a force of thirty, perhaps forty thousand men and these will have to be entrenched in some city on or near the seaboard.

Before leaving Atlanta, Sherman's bummers torched the city. Goodhue recorded the scene: "As we left Atlanta dense clouds of black smoke hung like a pall above it; the city was on fire, it might have resembled the burning of Moscow, all but the weather." While Atlanta burned, Goodhue noted that "the brigade band played a lively air, we marched with quick and lively steps – took our last view of Atlanta... the burial place of so many of our brave men and comrades."

By December 20, 1864, Sherman's men were before Savannah, the oldest city in Georgia and a key Southern port. Living off the land, Sherman's men were in fine shape and eager to take the city. "The army is in excellent condition; I never felt better in my life," opined Goodhue. We will have Savannah before long, are now erecting batteries." The batteries were not needed and Savannah was spared destruction. On December 21, the city surrendered to Union forces.

The Siege of Petersburg

William Goodhue was a member of Company C, 3rd Wisconsin Infantry and witnessed the burning of Atlanta. (Wisconsin Veterans Museum)

n order to sustain Grant's grueling campaign, additional troops were needed. Among those new troops assigned to the Army of the Potomac were a number of fresh Wisconsin regiments. In order to end the Siege of Petersburg, a mine was dug under the Confederate trenches and then detonated with explosives, creating a massive crater. During the resulting Battle of the Crater on July 30, 1864, Union forces were ordered to surge into the hole in the Confederate line. Lieutenant Solon Pierce of the 38th Wisconsin witnessed the explosion:

> Clods of earth weighing near a ton, and cannon, and human forms, and gun-carriages, and small arms, were all distinctly seen shooting upward in that fountain of horror, and fell again in shapeless and pulverized atoms. The explosion fully accomplished what was intended. It demolished the six-gun battery and its garrison of one regiment of South Carolina troops, and acted as the wedge which opened the way to the assault.

The 37th Wisconsin was among the units ordered to attack what was left of the Confederate works. The crater was deep and difficult to traverse, and instead of creating a passage for the Union forces to exploit, it created a bottle neck into which the Union troops rushed. For the men of the 37th Wisconsin, it was a killing ground. Of the 250 men of the 37th Wisconsin who went in, 155 were killed or wounded. Grant called the event "the saddest affair I have witnessed in this war." After failing to breach the Confederate line, Grant's men settled in for a prolonged siege. Numerous battles were fought in the late summer and fall of 1864 as both sides continued to maneuver in hopes of breaking the stalemate.

While Grant kept Lee in check at Petersburg, Sherman continued his march through the Carolinas, destroying Columbia, South Carolina, along the way. By the spring of 1865, Grant finally achieved what had eluded his predecessors – the near annihilation of Robert E. Lee's forces. After routing the Confederates at Five Forks on April 1, 1865, Grant ordered an assault along the lines at Petersburg, and the city fell on April 2. On Palm Sunday, April 9, 1865, the battered remnant of Lee's Army of Northern Virginia surrendered to Grant at Appomattox Court House. Seventeen days later, Sherman accepted Johnston's surrender near Durham, North Carolina. Wisconsin troops of the 4th Cavalry under the command of Henry Harnden assisted in the capture of Confederate President Jefferson Davis at Irwinville, Georgia, closing the chapter on the Civil War.

Epilogue

In celebration of their triumph over the Southern forces, Union veterans, 200,000 strong, marched through Washington on May 23 and 24, 1865. The 25-mile-long column took two days to pass by the presidential reviewing stand and a multitude of grateful citizens. Charles O. Hansen of the 18th Wisconsin Infantry Regiment recorded in a letter to his brother George his experience marching in the Grand Review:

> I borrowed a gun for the occasion, as I was bound to be able to say in after life that I participated in the greatest review ever held in this country. We started at six or seven in the morning, and crossed the river on the Long Bridge, down Maryland Avenue about a mile beyond the Capitol, then marched around two or three blocks to the foot of Pennsylvania Avenue, when we formed our company front and marched in solid phalanx up that thoroughfare amid thousands of people, and for more than a mile we went at quick time, at shouldered arms, bayonets fixed, and when we passed the reviewing stands where were the President, Secretary of War, Gen. Grant and about twenty-five Major Generals, with any number of Brigadier Generals, our arms were so tired we could scarcely hold our guns. Yet it was doubtless a nice thing to look at.

Demobilization of the massive army was completed with remarkable swiftness, and, by June 1866, more than one million men had been mustered out of service. The war was over, and thousands of Union veterans now looked forward to a transition back to civilian life.

A victorious Union did not impose harsh sanctions upon the defeated Confederate nation after the April 1865 surrender. There were no mass trials, executions, or confiscations of property. Instead, the national concepts of federalism and liberty were reinforced. Gone was the antebellum institution of slavery and its archaic socioeconomic culture that prevented the flourishing of free-labor capitalism in the South. Gone too was a pre-war decentralized government, now replaced with a more centralized, expanded Union version that ushered in the personal income tax to pay for the war and the Thirteenth Amendment to the U.S. Constitution outlawing slavery.

Regional differences remained, and a resistant South would later impose Jim Crow laws for more than a century in an attempt to maintain its cherished, pre-war social conventions; but the abolition of slavery ultimately ushered in a dynamic new nation that would surpass all others in agricultural and industrial pursuits by the end of the nineteenth century.

The Cost of War

Americans on both sides of the conflict went into the war certain that they were right – each side sure that opponents would cede victory sooner rather than later. But after four years of total war, our nation's bloodiest conflict claimed the lives of more than 620,000 Americans. Nearly 300,000 wounded Union soldiers survived the war, as did approximately 475,000 Confederates. Many of the survivors suffered permanent wounds: about 30,000 Union troops and roughly 25,000 Confederates underwent amputations.

General Ulysses S. Grant. (Wisconsin Veterans Museum)

The human cost was nearly eclipsed by the wreckage of the national infrastructure. This was particularly true in the South where the damage to agriculture, industry, railroads, commerce, and education numbered in the billions of dollars. Cities like Richmond, Atlanta, and Columbia lay in ruins. It would take decades for the South to recover.

About 50 percent of Wisconsin's adult male population participated in the war, over 80,000 men. More than 12,000 died; two-thirds of them perished from disease. Another 15,000 were discharged because of disabilities caused by diseases or wounds. One Wisconsin soldier in every three became a casualty and one in seven did not survive the war.

Wisconsin Women in the Civil War

When Wisconsin's soldiers marched off to war they left behind wives and families to fend for themselves. The majority of women lived in rural communities that owed their survival to agricultural pursuits. In the absence of adult men, women found themselves suddenly in charge of everything from planting and harvesting to household financial management. Close communal ties mitigated some of the hardships but neighbors could only provide limited assistance. In some cases, the male relatives and young children provided support, but for many it was the woman of the house that assumed the primary responsibility of ensuring the day-to-day welfare of the family.

Cordelia Harvey, widow of Governor Harvey, is depicted in the Governor's Conference Room mural by Hugo Ballin holding an order by President Lincoln for the establishment of three miliary hospitals in Wisconsin. (Sarah Girkin)

While most Wisconsin women busied themselves with keeping the wolf from the door, many were involved in efforts to supply the troops with necessities not otherwise provided by the state or federal governments. Soldiers' Aid societies and charitable organizations sprung up in communities big and small throughout Wisconsin. Their goals were to support the troops in the field and to provide assistance for returning soldiers, many of whom were left with life altering injuries.

Among the most prominent of these women was Cordelia Harvey, the wife of former Governor Louis Harvey who drowned in the Tennessee River in 1862. After her husband's death, Governor Edward Salamon appointed her Sanitary Agent for Wisconsin. Immediately, Harvey made it her mission to visit wounded and sick Wisconsin soldiers convalescing in hospitals along the lower Mississippi River. She was appalled by the conditions and was moved to organize the shipment of supplies and personnel to improve the care afforded to Wisconsin's soldiers. Convinced that the men would recover faster in a Northern clime, Harvey petitioned President Lincoln to establish a home for veterans in Madison. Lincoln initially balked at Harvey's request, concerned that convalescing troops returning home might desert. Harvey continued to press and was ultimately rewarded by Lincoln's authorization to establish a hospital in Madison. The hospital was constructed on the west bank of Lake Monona and incorporated the home of former Governor Farwell with its distinctive octagonal architecture. At the end of the war in 1865, the hospital was converted into a home for war orphans until it closed in 1875.

Other women looked to relieve the burdens of discharged soldiers with a more permanent solution. Milwaukee's West Side Aid Society, under the umbrella of the Wisconsin Soldiers' Aid Society, led the effort to establish one of the first soldiers' homes in the nation. By late 1863, the Society had identified the pressing need to provide housing for furloughed or discharged soldiers and in the spring of 1864, the Society severed its relationship with the Wisconsin Soldiers' Aid Society and reorganized as the Soldiers' Home at Milwaukee. Led by Lydia Ely Hewitt and Fanny Burling Buttrick, a monumental effort was launched to establish a permanent soldiers' home in Milwaukee.

Support for the project gained state-wide attention, largely through the endeavors of the various aid societies run by women. Funds in support of the project came from dances, solicitations and public events. Even small rural communities like Rubicon in Dodge County joined in the effort. In a letter to her lover stationed in a Wisconsin artillery unit, Sarah Throne wrote, "There is agoing (sic) to be a dance here the 14th of this month [June 1865] for the benefit of the Soldier's Home which is to be built in Milwaukee. Oh how I wish you could be here to attend it, for they are expecting to have a good time". Proceeds from the Soldier's Home Fair held on June 28, 1865 allowed the Society to purchase land at the present day location of 27th Street and Wisconsin Avenue. They enlisted the services of an architect but ultimately turned the project and its assets over to the federal government. The first building was constructed in 1867, additional buildings followed and the campus was noted for its tranquil natural environment. Nearly 150 years later it stands as one of three remaining original post-Civil War soldiers' homes in the country.

Governor Farwell's mansion housed Harvey Hospital. It stood at the corner of Spaight and Brearly Streets in Madison. (Wisconsin Veterans Museum)

Wisconsin's women played a major role in supporting the troops both in the field and when they returned home. They ensured the continued operation of farms and businesses and left a legacy of their service at the Milwaukee Veterans Administration Soldiers Home.

Lincoln: The Last Casualty

On April 14, 1865, the nation suffered another catastrophic loss just five days after Lee's surrender, when pro-Confederate actor, John Wilkes Booth, shot President Lincoln. Lincoln died the next day. The assassination came during a performance at Ford's Theater in Washington, DC. Present in the audience was Spencer Bronson, an Iron Brigade veteran from Columbia County. Like the majority of soldiers, 70 percent of whom voted for Lincoln in 1864, Bronson was shocked and saddened by the assassination. One day after the shooting, Bronson wrote to his sister describing the event:

> The rejoicing of our victories has been turned into mourning[.] President Lincoln has been struck down in the midst of his usefulness, the pride of his age, the benefactor of his race, the liberator of a nation & friend of suffering humanity everywhere has been murdered by a demon in human form & all because he was chief magistrate of this nation. I was present & saw this scene enacted & such an act that has no parallel since the days of Roman greatness when Caesar was struck down in the Roman senate by an idle mob.

Iron Brigade veteran Spencer Bronson was present at Ford's Theater when Lincoln was assassinated. (Wisconsin Veterans Museum)

Bronson went on to describe the mood of the city in the aftermath of the shooting: "The city is mad with excitement at the act. Three men has been shot dead by soldiers for saying they were glad the President was dead."

The president's death ensured that his vision of peace without penalty would face a challenge from some Republicans who felt less charitably towards the South than Lincoln did. The bitterness that characterized the Reconstruction Era (1865-77) endured long after the assassination of President Lincoln.

The Rise of the Grand Army of the Republic

When Union veterans returned home from active duty, many of them found few opportunities and little, if any, compensation for service-related injuries. Joining veteran's organizations provided the clout to achieve their desired political aims. On April 1, 1866, the first Grand Army of the Republic (G.A.R.) Post was established in Springfield, Illinois. The mission of the new organization was to promote fraternal sentiment among Union veterans, to provide aid to disabled and needy veterans, and to support orphans and widows. By 1867, most Northern states and some Southern states had G.A.R. Posts.

The large number of Civil War Veterans offered a strong base of voters for soldier-politicians to court after the war, and the G.A.R used its close association with the Republican Party to achieve political gains. G.A.R. politicians, like their counterparts in the United Confederate Veterans, promoted wartime experiences and "waved the bloody shirt," a reference to the blood of fallen soldiers, to earn support for their political platforms. In Wisconsin, Lucius Fairchild, who lost an arm at Gettysburg, became the state's first Civil War veteran governor, largely due to support from G.A.R. members. Fairchild, a charter member of the first Wisconsin G.A.R. post, served for three terms during the intensely political period of the Reconstruction Era. In January 1886, he was elected Wisconsin department commander of the G.A.R. and, at the 20th National Encampment at San Francisco in August that year, was elected commander-in-chief.

Colonel Lucius Fairchild, 2nd Wisconsin Volunteer Infantry, was wearing these articles during the morning of July 1, 1863, at Gettysburg when he received a severe wound that required amputation of his left arm. In order to perform the procedure, the surgeon was forced to cut the vest to facilitate removal from Fairchild's shoulder. The handkerchief is still stained with his blood from that morning. (Wisconsin Veterans Museum)

Politician-soldiers such as Fairchild and Jeremiah Rusk, capitalized on the memories of Civil War animosities to gain and hold political support. Each served three-year terms in the governor's office, and each "waved the bloody shirt" when they felt it was politically necessary. Fairchild, in particular, often reminded audiences that "every rebel, every Copperhead, every draft sneak, every dirty traitor voted with the Democrats, as did every member of the Ku Klux Klan." The "bloody shirt" invective reached its peak in the 1870s, but it was periodically revived throughout the last quarter of the nineteenth century.

Maximum membership in the G.A.R. reached 427,981 members the same year that President and ex-Civil War General Benjamin Harrison signed into law the Pension Act of 1890, providing support for all Union veterans. Supported by the Republican Party, the G.A.R dominated the affairs of the Union veterans' community until its decline in the twentieth century.

Wisconsin's Civil War Legacy

Grand Army of the Republic members lobbied strongly on behalf of veterans and their families, and they began to turn their attention to providing lasting support through the establishment of soldiers' homes. Soldiers' homes were an expanding social focus after the Civil War to assist soldiers in the transition back to civilian life. In the Midwest, Chicago was identified as a preferred site for a veterans home. However, Milwaukee native Lydia

Governor Jeremiah Rusk, a Civil War veteran, attended numerous veteran reunions with a special "guard" composed of Wisconsin veterans who lost a limb during the Civil War. (Wisconsin Veterans Museum)

Hewitt proposed a plan to construct a soldiers' home in Milwaukee and founded the Wisconsin Soldiers' Home Association. The association raised funds, and in its first year, 1865, cared for 4,842 soldiers. It also sponsored the 1865 Soldiers' Home Fair which raised $110,000 to care for veterans and construct a permanent facility. In 1867, the association's funds were turned over to the National Asylum for Disabled Soldiers. Thus, the Wisconsin Soldiers' Home Association became the United States National Soldiers' Home.

The National Home in Milwaukee admitted only veterans, raising concerns among G.A.R. members. Veterans, particularly Dr. Frederick Marden, worried about separating spouses in their "twilight years" and conceived of a facility that admitted veterans, wives, widows, and mothers. Marden developed and promoted the "cottage plan," which allowed veterans and their wives who did not require much care to live together and receive minimal health care.

The idea for such a soldiers' home was proposed at the 1884 G.A.R. Department of Wisconsin Encampment by Henry Fischer, department commander. Work began immediately after approval by the encampment. A committee of five was appointed to look into the feasibility of forming a veterans' home to be maintained by the G.A.R. that would provide for soldiers, wives, and mothers. The committee consisted of Dr. Marden, Albert O. Wright, Benjamin F. Bryant, James Cumberledge, and Joseph H. Marston, all of whom were later appointed to the first Board of Incorporators.

Committee members reported favorably to the G.A.R., and the Grand Army Home for Veterans, the first state home of its kind, was established. The eventual location was selected from the several cities (including Waupaca, Sheboygan, Watertown, Evansville, Berlin, and New Kilbourn) that volunteered their communities. The Incorporators visited each location, and Waupaca was chosen after several votes and long discussions. The Grand Army Home for Veterans is located on what was formerly the Greenwood Park Hotel, three-and-a-half miles from Waupaca on the eastern shore of Rainbow Lake. When the G.A.R. took the land, it consisted of 78 acres, which included a central building, six cottages, and a farmhouse. Originally, the land was a gift from the City of Waupaca. In 1890, the property was conveyed to the state.

Incorporated on March 10, 1887, the Grand Army Home (the name was changed to the Wisconsin Veterans Home in the 1970s) opened to residents on October 1, 1887, while the facility was still undergoing repairs. On August 29, 1888, more than 60,000 attended the official dedication.

Fundraising provided for the purchase of much of the home's furniture. The Woman's Relief Corps, a women's auxiliary to the G.A.R., began fundraising and donated the money for several cottages. Funds were raised through the War Relic exhibition, held from September 7 to October 22, 1888, in Milwaukee with all proceeds benefiting the home. Grand Army of the Republic posts throughout the state independently raised money and donated.

Although the home was controlled by the G.A.R., lobbying began almost immediately for government support. In 1887, the state legislature passed a bill by which the state treasurer paid $3 for each veteran living at the home. As time passed, however, lobbying became more frequent and aimed to address the long-term needs of the institution. By 1890, the growth of the home had already exceeded the expectations of the Incorporators and the available space. As a result, the board asked the legislature for $50,000 for permanent expansion and, in return, the Wisconsin G.A.R. turned over the home's property deed to the state.

The G.A.R. retained control and management and invoked a clause that the land would always be used to house dependent Union soldiers, sailors, and marines, along with their wives and widows. Several different organizations have had control of the Wisconsin Veterans Home. Original control by a board of trustees was changed to a board of managers in 1917. In 1929, control was given to the adjutant general of Wisconsin. In 1945, control was transferred to the Wisconsin Department of Veterans Affairs.

Today, the home is the state's largest nursing care facility, with 950 employees providing assistance to more than 700 veterans (capacity is 721). Additionally, about 450 volunteers contribute nearly 70,000 hours of service annually by visiting members and organizing activities. Policies have been updated to allow Wisconsin veterans admittance if they served on active duty for at least two years or the full period of their service obligation or served on active duty for at least 90 days, one day of which must be within a wartime period. Spouses of eligible veterans, and parents of those who died while on active duty, may also reside at the home.

FAIRCHILD HALL, WISCONSIN VETERANS' HOME, WAUPACA, WIS.

Fairchild Hall at the Wisconsin Veterans Home at King, formerly known as the Grand Army Home. (Wisconsin Veterans Museum)

The Wisconsin Veterans Museum

When state legislators passed Chapter 125, Laws of 1901, few would have guessed the significance of that enactment. The law mandated that state officials establish a memorial hall dedicated to commemorating Wisconsin's role in the Civil War and "any subsequent war." The law obligated the state to provide space in the state capitol and money for purchasing display equipment to exhibit war relics and to acquire additional artifacts. The state's collection of cherished Civil War battle flags would also be displayed in the memorial facility, and an area was set aside for a meeting room for Civil War veterans who belonged to the G.A.R. The space was designated the G.A.R. Memorial Hall.

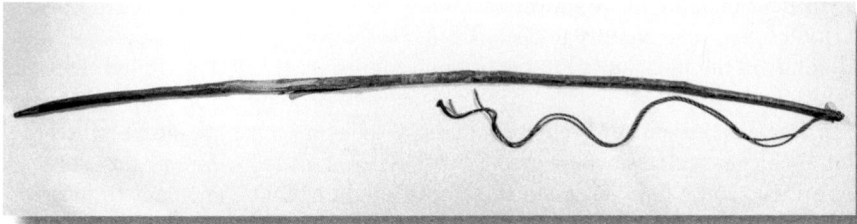

Sergeant Onesime Rondeau mounted the National Colors of the 7th Wisconsin Volunteer Infantry to this sapling after the first day of the Battle of Gettysburg. As the regiment retired through the town of Gettysburg that afternoon, Sergeant Daniel McDermott, holding the National Colors as a rallying point for his comrades, was hit by canister rounds, wounding McDermott and shattering the flag staff. His comrades placed him on a caisson and he retired through the town still waving the tattered remains of the National Colors and the shattered staff. That night the remaining members of the regiment cut this sapling from their new positions on Culp's Hill and mounted the National Colors to it. (Wisconsin Veterans Museum)

A destructive fire gutted the capitol in 1904, consuming many of the Civil War relics and historical materials in the G.A.R. Memorial Hall. Legislators authorized the establishment of another memorial space with Chapter 47, Laws of 1909. When the new capitol was completed, the G.A.R. Memorial Hall was dedicated. The Civil War battle flags, which had all been saved from the fire, were installed in the new room on the fourth floor of the Capital along with exhibits of artifacts.

In 1945, legislators assigned control of the G.A.R. Memorial Hall to the newly created Wisconsin Department of Veterans Affairs, directing the agency to "catalog, restore, conserve, preserve, safeguard, procure additions to the collections, and to display such collections as to make it instructive and attractive to visitors to the State Capitol." In 1955, an attempt to reappropriate the G.A.R. Memorial Hall space for government use and transfer display functions and collections to the Wisconsin Historical Society failed. Two years later, a new law further cemented the Department of Veterans Affairs' tenure on the capitol space by prohibiting alterations of established veterans' memorials.

The American Alliance of Museums (AAM) accredited the museum in 1974, one of the first Wisconsin museums to be awarded that distinction. Attendance figures during the 1970s averaged 80,000 visitors per year, the highest attendance of any Madison museum at that time. Since then, the museum has enjoyed an unbroken record of accreditation. Only about 11 percent of all museums in the United States enjoy AAM accreditation.

The issue of space within the capitol remained an impediment for the museum. In 1979, a well-developed modernization plan was rejected by the legislature.

Another attempt began to have the G.A.R. Museum move out of the capitol and was ultimately successful.

Governor Tommy Thompson approved the acquisition of space adjacent to the capitol in late 1989 and construction began in July 1990, after state legislative review and approval by the City of Madison. The building shell was completed in December. Work began on the museum interior and exhibit fixtures in 1991. Twelve thousand square feet were set aside for exhibits, ranging from the Civil War to the Persian Gulf. Its award-winning exhibits prompted the prestigious *Journal of American History* to describe the Wisconsin Veterans Museum as "in all likelihood the most stunning history museum of its size in the United States today."

The veterans museum collections contain Wisconsin's most important military cultural objects, including more than 2,000 Civil War artifacts. Among these artifacts are 200 battle flags issued to Wisconsin's fighting units. The flags form the core of the museum's collection and represent stories of courage and honor from every major Civil War battle. Among the collection are the flags of Wisconsin's Iron Brigade regiments and the flag of the 24th Wisconsin that was carried to the top of Missionary Ridge by Medal of Honor recipient Arthur MacArthur. Personal artifacts include Colonel Lucius Fairchild's uniform vest, stained by the blood of the wound he received at Gettysburg, and the only extant Iron Brigade black hat known to be worn during that pivotal battle. The collections of the veterans museum have expanded significantly in the past decade. Total collections have

G.A.R. Memorial Hall 1903. (Wisconsin Veterans Museum)

grown by at least 30 percent, including 6,000 objects transferred from the State Historical Society and more than 26,000 three-dimensional objects transferred from the Wisconsin National Guard. The archives, manuscripts and iconographic/photographic collections display more than 1,700 Civil War photographs and more than 1,200 letters and diaries. The veterans museum archives also house more than 5,000 books and periodicals related to military and veterans' history, as well as over 2,000 oral history interviews.

The roots of the Wisconsin Veterans Museum are deeply linked to the desire of Wisconsin's Civil War veterans to preserve the legacy of their accomplishments and the memory of their comrades. After the Civil War, the memory of those who made the ultimate sacrifice lived on in the minds of the survivors of that terrible event. They represented all walks of life and came from every corner of the state, and it was their service to the State of Wisconsin that secured the preservation of the Union and the abolition of slavery, bringing our nation closer to its cherished ideals of justice and freedom for all. In December 1881, during a stay in Washington, DC, Rufus Dawes, of the 6th Wisconsin Regiment, reflected upon his comrades who were buried at Arlington Cemetery in a letter to his wife:

December 18, 1881

My Dear Wife: I have to-day worshipped at the shrine of the dead. I went over to the Arlington Cemetery…My friends and comrades, poor fellows, who followed my enthusiastic leadership in those days, and followed it to the death which I by a merciful Providence escaped, lie here, twenty-four of them, on the very spot where our winter camp of 1861-1862 was located. I found every grave and stood beside it with uncovered head. I looked over nearly the full 16,000 headboards to find the twenty-four, but they all died alike and I was determined to find all. Poor little Fenton who put his head above the works at Cold Harbor and got a bullet through his temples, and lived three days with his brains out, came to me in memory as fresh as one of my own boys of to-day, and Levi Pearson, one of the three brothers of company 'A,' who died for their country in the Sixth regiment, and Richard Gray, Paul Mulleter, Dennis Kelly, Christ Bundy, all young men, who fell at my side and under my command. For what they died, I fight a little longer. Over their graves I get inspiration to stand for all they won in establishing our government upon freedom, equality, justice, liberty and protection to the humblest.

Special Articles in Prior Blue Books 1970 to 2013

For 1919 to 1933 *Blue Books*: see 1954 *Blue Book*, pp. 177-182.
For 1935 to 1962 *Blue Books*: see 1964 *Blue Book*, pp. 227-232.
For 1964 to 1968 *Blue Books:* see 2007-2008 *Blue Book,* pp. 192-193.

Commerce and Culture

The Indians of Wisconsin, by William H. Hodge, 1975 *Blue Book,* pp. 95-192.

Wisconsin Business and Industry, by James J. Brzycki, Paul E. Hassett, Joyce Munz Hach, Kenneth S. Kinney, and Robert H. Milbourne, 1987-1988 *Blue Book,* pp. 99-165.

Wisconsin Writers, by John O. [Jack] Stark, 1977 *Blue Book,* pp. 95-185.

Wisconsin's People: A Portrait of Wisconsin's Population on the Threshold of the 21st Century, by Paul R. Voss, Daniel L. Veroff, and David D. Long, 2003-2004 *Blue Book,* pp. 99-174.

Education

Education for Employment: 70 Years of Vocational, Technical and Adult Education in Wisconsin, by Kathleen A. Paris, 1981-1982 *Blue Book,* pp. 95-212.

The Wisconsin Idea: The University's Service to the State, by Jack Stark, 1995-1996 *Blue Book,* pp. 99-179.

The Wisconsin Idea for the 21st Century, by Alan B. Knox and Joe Corry, 1995-1996 *Blue Book,* pp. 180-192.

Environment

Exploring Wisconsin's Waterways, by Margaret Beattie Bogue, 1989-1990 *Blue Book,* pp. 99-297.

Protecting Wisconsin's Environment, by Selma Parker, 1973 *Blue Book,* pp. 97-161.

Wisconsin's Troubled Waters, by Selma Parker, 1973 *Blue Book,* pp. 102-136.

Government

The Budget - State Fiscal Policy Document, by Dale Cattanach and Terry A. Rhodes, 1970 *Blue Book,* pp. 261-272.

The Changing World of Wisconsin Local Government, by Susan C. Paddock, 1997-1998 *Blue Book,* pp. 99-172.

Equal Representation: A Study of Legislative and Congressional Apportionment in Wisconsin, by H. Rupert Theobald, 1970 *Blue Book,* pp. 70-260.

The Legislative Process in Wisconsin, by Richard L. Roe, Pamela J. Kahler, Robin N. Kite, and Robert P. Nelson, 1993-1994 *Blue Book,* pp. 99-194.

Local Government in Wisconsin, by James R. Donoghue, 1979-1980 *Blue Book,* pp. 95-218.

Rules and Rulings: Parliamentary Procedure from the Wisconsin Perspective, by H. Rupert Theobald, 1985-1986 *Blue Book,* pp. 99-215.

The Wisconsin Court System: Demystifying the Judicial Branch, by Robin Ryan and Amanda Todd, 2005-2006 *Blue Book,* pp. 99-184.

History

Capitals and Capitols in Early Wisconsin, by Stanley H. Cravens, 1983-1984 *Blue Book,* pp. 99-167.

A History of the Property Tax and Property Tax Relief in Wisconsin, by Jack Stark, 1991-1992 *Blue Book,* pp. 99-165.

Progressivism Triumphant: The 1911 Wisconsin Legislature, by John D. Buenker, 2011-2012 *Blue Book,* pp.99-169.

Restoring the Vision: The First Century of Wisconsin's Capitol, by Michael J. Keane, 2001-2002 *Blue Book,* pp. 99-188.

Ten Events That Shaped Wisconsin's History, by Norman K. Risjord, 1999-2000 *Blue Book,* pp. 99-146.

Those Who Served: Wisconsin Legislators 1848-2007, by Michael J. Keane, 2007-2008 *Blue Book,* p. 99-191.

Wisconsin at 150 Years, by Michael J. Keane and Daniel F. Ritsche, 1997-1998 *Blue Book,* color supplement.

Wisconsin at the Frontiers of Astronomy: A History of Innovation and Exploration, by Peter Susalla and James Lattis, 2009-2010 *Blue Book,* pp. 99-189.

Wisconsin Celebrates 150 Years of Statehood: A Photographic Review, 1999-2000 *Blue Book,* color supplement.

The Wisconsin Historical Society: Collecting, Preserving, and Sharing Stories Since 1846, by John Zimm, Michael Edmonds, Helmut Knies, and Michael Stevens, 2013-2014 *Blue Book,* pp. 99-171.

Capitol Visitor's Guide

Hours:
Building open daily 8 a.m. - 6 p.m.
The Capitol closes at 4 p.m. weekends and holidays.

Information Desk
Located in the rotunda, ground floor.

Tours
Daily Monday - Saturday at 9, 10, and 11 a.m., 1, 2, and 3 p.m.; Sundays at 1, 2, and 3 p.m. A 4 p.m. tour is offered weekdays between Memorial Day and Labor Day. Tours start at the Information Desk in the rotunda and last 45 to 50 minutes. Reservations are required for groups of 10 or more. Call (608) 266-0382 7:30 a.m. - 4:30 p.m. Monday - Friday, or visit the Web site at http://tours.wisconsin.gov/pub/Reservations.

Observation Deck
6th Floor, accessible from 4th floor via NW or W stairways. Open daily from Memorial Day to Labor Day. There is a small museum devoted to the Capitol at the entrance to the observation deck.

Souvenirs
Available at the Information Desk, include books, postcards, miniatures, and tour videos.

Capitol Police
Room B2 North.

Handicapped Entrances
At Martin Luther King Jr. Blvd. (automated), East Washington Avenue, Wisconsin Avenue, and West Washington Avenue.

Parking
3 handicapped spaces at East Washington entrance.
Limited parking (meters) on the Capitol Square.
Several public ramps are located within two blocks of the Capitol.

Senate Chamber
South wing, 2nd floor; visitors gallery, 3rd floor.

Assembly Chamber
West wing, 2nd floor; visitors gallery, 3rd floor.

Supreme Court Hearing Room
East wing, 2nd floor.

Governor's Office & Conference Room
East wing, 1st floor.

Lieutenant Governor's Office
East wing, ground floor.

Attorney General's Office
East wing, 1st floor.

Legislative Offices
To find a specific office, check one of the Capitol Directories located in the rotunda and on the ground floor of each wing.

Hearings
Information about the time and location of public hearings is posted at the entrance to each legislative chamber.

Hearing Rooms
North Hearing Room, North wing, 2nd floor.

Grand Army of the Republic Hall, Room 417 North.
Joint Committee on Finance, Room 412 East.
Senate Hearing Room, Room 411 South.
Additional hearing rooms are located on the 2nd and 3rd floors.

Capitol Facts & Figures
Construction Chronology
West wing: 1906 – 1909

East wing: 1908 – 1910

Central portion: 1910 – 1913

South wing: 1909 – 1913

North wing: 1914 – 1917

First meeting of legislature in building: 1909

Dedication: July 8, 1965

Renovation: 1990 – 2001

Statistics
Height of each wing: 61 feet

Height of observation deck: 92 feet

Height of dome mural: 184 feet, 3 inches

Height of dome (to top of statue): 284 feet, 9 inches

Length of building from N to S & E to W:
483 feet, 9 inches

Floor space: 448,297 square feet

Volume: 8,369,665 cubic feet

Original cost: $7,203,826.35

(including grounds, furnishings, and
power plant)

Wisconsin Constitution

Wisconsin Constitution: text as amended through April 2015 and votes on constitutional amendments and statewide referenda submitted to the people

Colonel Hans Heg Memorial, Chickamauga, Tennessee

(Steve Miller)

WISCONSIN CONSTITUTION
As amended through April 2015 *

TABLE OF CONTENTS

ARTICLE I.
DECLARATION OF RIGHTS

Section

1. Equality; inherent rights.
2. Slavery prohibited.
3. Free speech; libel.
4. Right to assemble and petition.
5. Trial by jury; verdict in civil cases.
6. Excessive bail; cruel punishments.
7. Rights of accused.
8. Prosecutions; double jeopardy; self-incrimination; bail; habeas corpus.
9. Remedy for wrongs.
9m. Victims of crime.
10. Treason.
11. Searches and seizures.
12. Attainder; ex post facto; contracts.
13. Private property for public use.
14. Feudal tenures; leases; alienation.
15. Equal property rights for aliens and citizens.
16. Imprisonment for debt.
17. Exemption of property of debtors.
18. Freedom of worship; liberty of conscience; state religion; public funds.
19. Religious tests prohibited.
20. Military subordinate to civil power.
21. Rights of suitors.
22. Maintenance of free government.
23. Transportation of school children.
24. Use of school buildings.
25. Right to keep and bear arms.
26. Right to fish, hunt, trap, and take game.

ARTICLE II.
BOUNDARIES

Section

1. State boundary.
2. Enabling act accepted.

ARTICLE III.
SUFFRAGE

Section

1. Electors.
2. Implementation.
3. Secret ballot.
4. [Repealed]
5. [Repealed]
6. [Repealed]

ARTICLE IV.
LEGISLATIVE

Section

1. Legislative power.
2. Legislature, how constituted.
3. Apportionment.
4. Representatives to the assembly, how chosen.
5. Senators, how chosen.
6. Qualifications of legislators.

7. Organization of legislature; quorum; compulsory attendance.
8. Rules; contempts; expulsion.
9. Officers.
10. Journals; open doors; adjournments.
11. Meeting of legislature.
12. Ineligibility of legislators to office.
13. Ineligibility of federal officers.
14. Filling vacancies.
15. Exemption from arrest and civil process.
16. Privilege in debate.
17. Enactment of laws.
18. Title of private bills.
19. Origin of bills.
20. Yeas and nays.
21. [Repealed]
22. Powers of county boards.
23. Town and county government.
23a. Chief executive officer to approve or veto resolutions or ordinances; proceedings on veto.
24. Gambling.
25. Stationery and printing.
26. Extra compensation; salary change.
27. Suits against state.
28. Oath of office.
29. Militia.
30. Elections by legislature.
31. Special and private laws prohibited.
32. General laws on enumerated subjects.
33. Auditing of state accounts.
34. Continuity of civil government.

ARTICLE V.
EXECUTIVE

Section

1. Governor; lieutenant governor; term
1m. [Repealed]
1n. [Repealed]
2. Eligibility.
3. Election.
4. Powers and duties.
5. [Repealed]
6. Pardoning power.
7. Lieutenant governor, when governor.
8. Secretary of state, when governor.
9. [Repealed]
10. Governor to approve or veto bills; proceedings on veto.

ARTICLE VI.
ADMINISTRATIVE

Section

1. Election of secretary of state, treasurer and attorney general; term.
1m. [Repealed]
1n. [Repealed]
1p. [Repealed]
2. Secretary of state; duties, compensation.
3. Treasurer and attorney general; duties, compensation.
4. County officers; election, terms, removal; vacancies.

ARTICLE VII.
JUDICIARY

Section

1. Impeachment; trial.
2. Court system.
3. Supreme court: jurisdiction.
4. Supreme court: election, chief justice, court system administration.
5. Court of appeals.
6. Circuit court: boundaries.
7. Circuit court: election.
8. Circuit court: jurisdiction.
9. Judicial elections; vacancies.
10. Judges: eligibility to office.
11. Disciplinary proceedings.
12. Clerks of circuit and supreme courts.
13. Justice and judges: removal by address.
14. Municipal court.
15. [Repealed]
16. [Repealed]
17. [Repealed]
18. [Repealed]
19. [Repealed]
20. [Repealed]
21. [Repealed]
22. [Repealed]
23. [Repealed]
24. Justices and judges: eligibility for office; retirement.

ARTICLE VIII.
FINANCE

Section

1. Rule of taxation uniform; income, privilege and occupation taxes.
2. Appropriations; limitation.
3. Credit of state.
4. Contracting state debts.
5. Annual tax levy to equal expenses.
6. Public debt for extraordinary expense; taxation.
7. Public debt for public defense; bonding for public purposes.
8. Vote on fiscal bills; quorum.
9. Evidences of public debt.
10. Internal improvements.
11. Transportation fund.

ARTICLE IX.
EMINENT DOMAIN AND
PROPERTY OF THE STATE

Section

1. Jurisdiction on rivers and lakes; navigable waters.
2. Territorial property.
3. Ultimate property in land; escheats.

ARTICLE X.
EDUCATION

Section

1. Superintendent of public instruction.
2. School fund created; income applied.

3. District schools; tuition; sectarian instruction; released time.
4. Annual school tax.
5. Income of school fund.
6. State university; support.
7. Commissioners of public lands.
8. Sale of public lands.

ARTICLE XI.
CORPORATIONS

Section

1. Corporations; how formed.
2. Property taken by municipality.
3. Municipal home rule; debt limit; tax to pay debt.
3a. Acquisition of lands by state and subdivisions; sale of excess.
4. General banking law.
5. [Repealed]

ARTICLE XII.
AMENDMENTS

Section

1. Constitutional amendments.
2. Constitutional conventions.

ARTICLE XIII.
MISCELLANEOUS PROVISIONS

Section

1. Political year; elections.
2. [Repealed]
3. Eligibility to office.
4. Great seal.
5. [Repealed]
6. Legislative officers.
7. Division of counties.
8. Removal of county seats.
9. Election or appointment of statutory officers.
10. Vacancies in office.
11. Passes, franks and privileges.
12. Recall of elective officers.
13. Marriage.

ARTICLE XIV.
SCHEDULE

Section

1. Effect of change from territory to state.
2. Territorial laws continued.
3. [Repealed]
4. [Repealed]
5. [Repealed]
6. [Repealed]
7. [Repealed]
8. [Repealed]
9. [Repealed]
10. [Repealed]
11. [Repealed]
12. [Repealed]
13. Common law continued in force.
14. [Repealed]
15. [Repealed]
16. Implementing revised structure of judicial branch.

WISCONSIN CONSTITUTION

As amended through April 2015 *

Preamble

We, the people of Wisconsin, grateful to Almighty God for our freedom, in order to secure its blessings, form a more perfect government, insure domestic tranquility and promote the general welfare, do establish this constitution.

ARTICLE I.

DECLARATION OF RIGHTS

Equality; inherent rights. SECTION 1. [*As amended April 1986*] All people are born equally free and independent, and have certain inherent rights; among these are life, liberty and the pursuit of happiness; to secure these rights, governments are instituted, deriving their just powers from the consent of the governed. [*1983 AJR-9; 1985 AJR-9*]

Equality; inherent rights. SECTION 1. [*As amended November 1982*] All people are born equally free and independent, and have certain inherent rights; among these are life, liberty and the pursuit of happiness; to serve these rights, governments are instituted, deriving their just powers from the consent of the governed. [*1979 AJR-76; 1981 AJR-35; submit: May '82 Spec.Sess. AJR-1*]

Equality; inherent rights. SECTION 1. [*Original form*] All men are born equally free and independent, and have certain inherent rights; among these are life, liberty and the pursuit of happiness; to secure these rights, governments are instituted among men, deriving their just powers from the consent of the governed.

Slavery prohibited. SECTION 2. There shall be neither slavery, nor involuntary servitude in this state, otherwise than for the punishment of crime, whereof the party shall have been duly convicted.

Free speech; libel. SECTION 3. Every person may freely speak, write and publish his sentiments on all subjects, being responsible for the abuse of that right, and no laws shall be passed to restrain or abridge the liberty of speech or of the press. In all criminal prosecutions or indictments for libel, the truth may be given in evidence, and if it shall appear to the jury that the matter charged as libelous be true, and was published with good motives and for justifiable ends, the party shall be acquitted; and the jury shall have the right to determine the law and the fact.

Right to assemble and petition. SECTION 4. The right of the people peaceably to assemble, to consult for the common good, and to petition the government, or any department thereof, shall never be abridged.

Trial by jury; verdict in civil cases. SECTION 5. [*As amended November 1922*] The right of trial by jury shall remain inviolate, and shall extend to all cases at law without regard to the amount in controversy; but a jury trial may be waived by the parties in all cases in the manner prescribed by law. Provided, however, that the legislature may, from time to time, by statute provide that a valid verdict, in civil cases, may be based on the votes of a specified number of the jury, not less than five-sixths thereof. [*1919 AJR-26; 1921 AJR-14; 1921 c. 504*]

Trial by jury. SECTION 5. [*Original form*] The right of trial by jury shall remain inviolate; and shall extend to all cases at law, without regard to the amount in controversy;

but a jury trial may be waived by the parties in all cases, in the manner prescribed by law.

Excessive bail; cruel punishments. SECTION 6. Excessive bail shall not be required, nor shall excessive fines be imposed, nor cruel and unusual punishments inflicted.

---

* Current provisions of the constitution are printed the full width of the page, and previous wordings (if any) follow each active provision in double-column format. Any section not indicated as having been amended and not followed by two-column text still exists as ratified by the people of Wisconsin when they adopted the Wisconsin Constitution on March 13, 1848.

Rights of accused. SECTION 7. In all criminal prosecutions the accused shall enjoy the right to be heard by himself and counsel; to demand the nature and cause of the accusation against him; to meet the witnesses face to face; to have compulsory process to compel the attendance of witnesses in his behalf; and in prosecutions by indictment, or information, to a speedy public trial by an impartial jury of the county or district wherein the offense shall have been committed; which county or district shall have been previously ascertained by law.

Prosecutions; double jeopardy; self-incrimination; bail; habeas corpus. SECTION 8. [*As amended per certification of the Board of State Canvassers dated April 7, 1982*] (1) No person may be held to answer for a criminal offense without due process of law, and no person for the same offense may be put twice in jeopardy of punishment, nor may be compelled in any criminal case to be a witness against himself or herself.

(2) All persons, before conviction, shall be eligible for release under reasonable conditions designed to assure their appearance in court, protect members of the community from serious bodily harm or prevent the intimidation of witnesses. Monetary conditions of release may be imposed at or after the initial appearance only upon a finding that there is a reasonable basis to believe that the conditions are necessary to assure appearance in court. The legislature may authorize, by law, courts to revoke a person's release for a violation of a condition of release.

(3) The legislature may by law authorize, but may not require, circuit courts to deny release for a period not to exceed 10 days prior to the hearing required under this subsection to a person who is accused of committing a murder punishable by life imprisonment or a sexual assault punishable by a maximum imprisonment of 20 years, or who is accused of committing or attempting to commit a felony involving serious bodily harm to another or the threat of serious bodily harm to another and who has a previous conviction for committing or attempting to commit a felony involving serious bodily harm to another or the threat of serious bodily harm to another. The legislature may authorize by law, but may not require, circuit courts to continue to deny release to those accused persons for an additional period not to exceed 60 days following the hearing required under this subsection, if there is a requirement that there be a finding by the court based on clear and convincing evidence presented at a hearing that the accused committed the felony and a requirement that there be a finding by the court that available conditions of release will not adequately protect members of the community from serious bodily harm or prevent intimidation of witnesses. Any law enacted under this subsection shall be specific, limited and reasonable. In determining the 10-day and 60-day periods, the court shall omit any period of time found by the court to result from a delay caused by the defendant or a continuance granted which was initiated by the defendant.

(4) The privilege of the writ of habeas corpus shall not be suspended unless, in cases of rebellion or invasion, the public safety requires it. [*June 1980 Spec.Sess. AJR-9; 1981 AJR-5*]

Prosecutions; second jeopardy; self-incrimination; bail; habeas corpus. SECTION 8. [*As amended November 1870*] No person shall be held to answer for a criminal offense without due process of law, and no person for the same offense shall be put twice in jeopardy of punishment, nor shall be compelled in any criminal case to be a witness against himself. All persons shall, before conviction, be bailable by sufficient sureties, except for capital offenses when the proof is evident or the presumption great; and the privilege of the writ of habeas corpus shall not be suspended unless when, in cases of rebellion or invasion, the public safety may require it. [*1869 AJR-6; 1870 SJR-3; 1870 c. 118*]

Criminal procedure. SECTION 8. [*Original form*] No person shall be held to answer for a criminal offense, unless on the presentment, or indictment of a grand jury, except in cases of impeachment, or in cases cognizable by justices of the peace, or arising in the army or navy, or in the militia when in actual service in time of war, or public danger; and no person for the same offence shall be put twice in jeopardy of punishment, nor shall be compelled in any criminal case to be a witness against himself; all persons shall, before conviction, be bailable by sufficient sureties except for capital offences when the proof is evident, or the presumption great; and the privilege of the writ of habeas corpus shall not be suspended unless when, in cases of rebellion, or invasion, the public safety may require.

Remedy for wrongs. SECTION 9. Every person is entitled to a certain remedy in the laws for all injuries, or wrongs which he may receive in his person, property, or character; he ought to obtain justice freely, and without being obliged to purchase it, completely and without denial, promptly and without delay, conformably to the laws.

Victims of crime. SECTION 9m. [*As created April 1993*] This state shall treat crime victims, as defined by law, with fairness, dignity and respect for their privacy. This state shall ensure that crime victims have all of the following privileges and protections as provided by law: timely disposition of the case; the opportunity to attend court proceedings unless the trial court finds sequestration is necessary to a fair trial for the defendant; reasonable protection from the accused throughout the criminal justice process; notification of court proceedings; the opportunity to confer with the prosecution; the opportunity to make a statement to the court at disposition; restitution; compensation; and information about the outcome of the case and the release of the accused. The legislature shall provide remedies for the violation of this section. Nothing in this section, or in any statute enacted pursuant to this section, shall limit any right of the accused which may be provided by law. [*1991 SJR-41; 1993 SJR-3*]

Treason. SECTION 10. Treason against the state shall consist only in levying war against the same, or in adhering to its enemies, giving them aid and comfort. No person shall be convicted of treason unless on the testimony of two witnesses to the same overt act, or on confession in open court.

Searches and seizures. SECTION 11. The right of the people to be secure in their persons, houses, papers, and effects against unreasonable searches and seizures shall not be violated; and no warrant shall issue but upon probable cause, supported by oath or affirmation, and particularly describing the place to be searched and the persons or things to be seized.

Attainder; ex post facto; contracts. SECTION 12. No bill of attainder, ex post facto law, nor any law impairing the obligation of contracts, shall ever be passed, and no conviction shall work corruption of blood or forfeiture of estate.

Private property for public use. SECTION 13. The property of no person shall be taken for public use without just compensation therefor.

Feudal tenures; leases; alienation. SECTION 14. All lands within the state are declared to be allodial, and feudal tenures are prohibited. Leases and grants of agricultural land for a longer term than fifteen years in which rent or service of any kind shall be reserved, and all fines and like restraints upon alienation reserved in any grant of land, hereafter made, are declared to be void.

Equal property rights for aliens and citizens. SECTION 15. No distinction shall ever be made by law between resident aliens and citizens, in reference to the possession, enjoyment or descent of property.

Imprisonment for debt. SECTION 16. No person shall be imprisoned for debt arising out of or founded on a contract, expressed or implied.

Exemption of property of debtors. SECTION 17. The privilege of the debtor to enjoy the necessary comforts of life shall be recognized by wholesome laws, exempting a reasonable amount of property from seizure or sale for the payment of any debt or liability hereafter contracted.

Freedom of worship; liberty of conscience; state religion; public funds. SECTION 18. [*As amended November 1982*] The right of every person to worship Almighty God according to the dictates of conscience shall never be infringed; nor shall any person be compelled to attend, erect or support any place of worship, or to maintain any ministry, without consent; nor shall any control of, or interference with, the rights of conscience be permitted, or any preference be given by law to any religious establishments or modes of worship; nor shall any money be drawn from the treasury for the benefit of religious societies, or religious or theological seminaries. [*1979 AJR-76; 1981 AJR-35; submit: May '82 Spec.Sess. AJR-1*]

Freedom of worship; liberty of conscience; state religion; public funds. SECTION 18. [*Original form*] The right of every man to worship Almighty God according to the dictates of his own conscience shall never be infringed; nor shall any man be compelled to attend, erect or support any place of worship, or to maintain any ministry, against his consent; nor shall any control of, or interference with, the rights of conscience be permitted, or any preference be given by law to any religious establishments or modes of worship; nor shall any money be drawn from the treasury for the benefit of religious societies, or religious or theological seminaries.

Religious tests prohibited. SECTION 19. No religious tests shall ever be required as a qualification for any office of public trust under the state, and no person shall be rendered incompetent to give evidence in any court of law or equity in consequence of his opinions on the subject of religion.

Military subordinate to civil power. SECTION 20. The military shall be in strict subordination to the civil power.

Rights of suitors. SECTION 21. [*As amended April 1977*] (1) Writs of error shall never be prohibited, and shall be issued by such courts as the legislature designates by law.

(2) In any court of this state, any suitor may prosecute or defend his suit either in his own proper person or by an attorney of the suitor's choice. [*1975 AJR-11; 1977 SJR-9*]

Writs of error. SECTION 21. [*Original form*] Writs of error shall never be prohibited by law.

Maintenance of free government. SECTION 22. The blessings of a free government can only be maintained by a firm adherence to justice, moderation, temperance, frugality and virtue, and by frequent recurrence to fundamental principles.

Transportation of school children. SECTION 23. [*As created April 1967*] Nothing in this constitution shall prohibit the legislature from providing for the safety and welfare of children by providing for the transportation of children to and from any parochial or private school or institution of learning. [*1965 AJR-70; 1967 AJR-7*]

Use of school buildings. SECTION 24. [*As created April 1972*] Nothing in this constitution shall prohibit the legislature from authorizing, by law, the use of public school buildings by civic, religious or charitable organizations during nonschool hours upon payment by the organization to the school district of reasonable compensation for such use. [*1969 AJR-74; 1971 AJR-10*]

Right to keep and bear arms. SECTION 25. [*As created November 1998*] The people have the right to keep and bear arms for security, defense, hunting, recreation or any other lawful purpose. [*1995 AJR-53; 1997 AJR-11*]

Right to fish, hunt, trap, and take game. SECTION 26. [*As created April 2003*] The people have the right to fish, hunt, trap, and take game subject only to reasonable restrictions as prescribed by law. [*2001 SJR-2; 2003 AJR-1*]

ARTICLE II.
BOUNDARIES

State boundary. SECTION 1. It is hereby ordained and declared that the state of Wisconsin doth consent and accept of the boundaries prescribed in the act of congress entitled "An act to enable the people of Wisconsin territory to form a constitution and state government, and for the admission of such state into the Union," approved August sixth, one thousand eight hundred and forty-six, to wit: Beginning at the northeast corner of the state of Illinois - that is to say, at a point in the center of Lake Michigan where the line of forty-two degrees and thirty minutes of north latitude crosses the same; thence running with the boundary line of the state of Michigan, through Lake Michigan, Green Bay, to the mouth of the Menominee river; thence up the channel of the said river to the Brule river; thence up said last-mentioned river to Lake Brule; thence along the southern shore of Lake Brule in a direct line to the center of the channel between Middle and South Islands, in the Lake of the Desert; thence in a direct line to the head waters of the Montreal river, as marked upon the survey made by Captain Cram; thence down the main channel of the Montreal river to the middle of Lake Superior; thence through the center of Lake Superior to the mouth of the St. Louis river; thence up the main channel of said river to the first rapids in the same, above the Indian village, according to Nicollet's map; thence due south to the main branch of the river St. Croix; thence down the main channel of said river to the Mississippi; thence down the center of the main channel of that river to the northwest corner of the state of Illinois; thence due east with the northern boundary of the state of Illinois to the place of beginning, as established by "An act to enable the people of the Illinois territory to form a constitution and state government, and for the admission of such state into the Union on an equal footing with the original states," approved April 18th, 1818.

Alternate boundary. [*An additional paragraph, adopted by the convention as part of Art. II, sec. 1, was rejected by the act which admitted Wisconsin into the Union (9 U.S. Stat. Ch. L, pp. 233-235)*]: Provided, however, that the following alteration of the foresaid boundary be, and hereby is proposed to the congress of the United States as the preference of the state of Wisconsin, and if the same shall be assented and agreed to by the congress of the United States, then the same shall be and forever remain obligatory on the state of Wisconsin, viz.: Leaving the aforesaid boundary line at the foot of the rapids of the St. Louis river; thence in a direct line, bearing south-westerly, to the mouth of the Iskodewabo, or Rum river, where the same empties into the Mississippi river, thence down the main channel of said Mississippi river as prescribed in the aforesaid boundary.

Enabling act accepted. SECTION 2. [*As amended April 1951*] The propositions contained in the act of congress are hereby accepted, ratified and confirmed, and shall remain irrevocable without the consent of the United States; and it is hereby ordained that this state shall never interfere with the primary disposal of the soil within the same by the United States, nor with any regulations congress may find necessary for securing the title in such soil to bona fide purchasers thereof; and in no case shall nonresident proprietors be taxed higher than residents. Provided, that nothing in this constitution, or in the act of congress aforesaid, shall in any manner prejudice or affect the right of the state of Wisconsin to 500,000 acres of land granted to said state, and to be hereafter selected and located by and under the act of congress entitled "An act to appropriate the proceeds of the sales of the public lands, and grant pre-emption rights," approved September fourth, one thousand eight hundred and forty-one. [*1949 AJR-64; 1951 AJR-7*]

Enabling act accepted. SECTION 2. [*Original form*] The propositions contained in the act of congress are hereby accepted, ratified and confirmed, and shall remain irrevocable without the consent of the United States; and it is hereby ordained that this state shall never interfere with the primary disposal of the soil within the same by the United States, nor with any regulations congress may find necessary for securing the title in such soil to bona fide purchasers thereof; and no tax shall be imposed on land the property of the United States; and in no case shall

nonresident proprietors be taxed higher than residents. Provided, that nothing in this constitution, or in the act of congress aforesaid, shall in any manner prejudice or affect the right of the state of Wisconsin to five hundred thousand acres of land granted to said state, and to be hereafter selected and located by and under the act of congress entitled "An act to appropriate the proceeds of the sales of the public lands, and grant pre-emption rights," approved September fourth, one thousand eight hundred and forty-one.

ARTICLE III.
SUFFRAGE

Electors. SECTION 1. [*As created April 1986*] Every United States citizen age 18 or older who is a resident of an election district in this state is a qualified elector of that district. [*1983 AJR-33; 1985 AJR-3*]

Implementation. SECTION 2. [*As created April 1986*] Laws may be enacted:

(1) Defining residency.

(2) Providing for registration of electors.

(3) Providing for absentee voting.

(4) Excluding from the right of suffrage persons:

(a) Convicted of a felony, unless restored to civil rights.

(b) Adjudged by a court to be incompetent or partially incompetent, unless the judgment specifies that the person is capable of understanding the objective of the elective process or the judgment is set aside.

(5) Subject to ratification by the people at a general election, extending the right of suffrage to additional classes. [*1983 AJR-33; 1985 AJR-3*]

Secret ballot. SECTION 3. [*As created April 1986*] All votes shall be by secret ballot. [*1983 AJR-33; 1985 AJR-3*]

Revision of Article III. The original 6 sections of Article III of the constitution were repealed in April 1986 when the wording of the article was reorganized into the 3 new sections shown above.

Electors. SECTION 1. [*As amended November 1934*] Every person, of the age of twenty-one years or upwards, belonging to either of the following classes, who shall have resided in the state for one year next preceding any election, and in the election district where he offers to vote such time as may be prescribed by the legislature, not exceeding thirty days, shall be deemed a qualified elector at such election: (1) Citizens of the United States.

(2) Persons of Indian blood, who have once been declared by law of congress to be citizens of the United States, any subsequent law of congress to the contrary notwithstanding.

(3) The legislature may at any time extend, by law, the right of suffrage to persons not herein enumerated; but no such law shall be in force until the same shall have been submitted to a vote of the people at a general election, and approved by a majority of all the votes cast on that question at such election; and provided further, that the legislature may provide for the registration of electors, and prescribe proper rules and regulations therefor. [*1931 AJR-52; 1933 SJR-74*]

Termination of voting by resident aliens. [*Subdivision 2* (of the text adopted in 1882), *as amended November

1908*] 2. Persons of foreign birth who, prior to the first day of December, A.D. 1908, shall have declared their intentions to become citizens conformable to the laws of the United States on the subject of naturalization, provided that the rights hereby granted to such persons shall cease on the first day of December, A.D. 1912. [*1905 AJR-16; 1907 AJR-47; 1907 c. 661*]

Qualifications of electors. SECTION 1. [*As amended November 1882*] Every male person of the age of twenty-one years or upwards, belonging to either of the following classes, who shall have resided in the state for one year next preceding any election, and in the election district where he offers to vote such time as may be prescribed by the legislature not exceeding thirty days shall be deemed a qualified elector at such election. 1. Citizens of the United States. 2. Persons of foreign birth who shall have declared their intention to become citizens, conformably to the laws of the United States on the subject of naturalization. 3. Persons of Indian blood who have once been declared by law of congress to be citizens of the United States, any subsequent law of congress to the contrary notwithstanding. 4. Civilized persons of Indian descent not members of any tribe; provided that the legislature may at any time extend, by law, the right of suffrage to persons not herein enumerated, but no such law shall be in force until the same shall have been submitted to a vote of the people at a general election, and approved by a majority of all the votes cast at such election; and provided further, that in incorporated cities and villages, the legislature may provide for the registration of electors and prescribe proper rules and regulations therefor. [*1881 AJR-26; 1882 SJR-18; 1882 c. 272*]

Equal suffrage to colored persons. In *Gillespie v. Palmer*, 20 Wis. (1866) 544, the Wisconsin Supreme Court ruled that Chapter 137, Laws of 1849, extending *equal suffrage to colored persons,* was approved by the voters on November 6, 1849.

Qualifications of electors. SECTION 1. [*Original form*] Every male person of the age of twenty-one years or upwards belonging to either of the following classes, who shall have resided in the state for one year next preceding any election, shall be deemed a qualified elector at such election:

[*First.*] White citizens of the United States.

[*Second.*] White persons of foreign birth who shall have declared their intention to become citizens, conformably to the laws of the United States on the subject of naturalization.

[*Third.*] Persons of Indian blood who have once been declared by law of congress to be citizens of the United States, any subsequent law of congress to the contrary notwithstanding.

[*Fourth.*] Civilized persons of Indian descent, not members of any tribe. Provided, that the legislature may at any time extend, by law, the right of suffrage to persons not herein enumerated, but no such law shall be in force until the same shall have been submitted to a vote of the people at a general election, and approved by a majority of all the votes cast at such election.

Who not electors. SECTION 2. [*Original form*] No person under guardianship, non compos mentis or insane shall be qualified to vote at any election; nor shall any person convicted of treason or felony be qualified to vote at any election unless restored to civil rights.

Votes to be by ballot. SECTION 3. [*Original form*] All votes shall be given by ballot except for such township officers as may by law be directed or allowed to be otherwise chosen.

SECTION 4. [*Repealed. 1983 JR-30; 1985 JR-14; vote April 1986*]

Residence saved. SECTION 4. [*Original form*] No person shall be deemed to have lost his residence in this state by

reason of his absence on business of the United States or of this state.

SECTION 5. [*Repealed. 1983 JR-30; 1985 JR-14; vote April 1986*]

Military stationing does not confer residence. SECTION 5. [*Original form*] No soldier, seaman or marine in the army or navy of the United States shall be deemed a resident of

this state in consequence of being stationed within the same.

SECTION 6. [*Repealed. 1983 JR-30; 1985 JR-14; vote April 1986*]

Exclusion from suffrage. SECTION 6. [*Original form*] Laws may be passed excluding from the right of suffrage all persons who have been or may be convicted of bribery or larceny, or of any infamous crime, and depriving every

person who shall make or become directly or indirectly interested in any bet or wager depending upon the result of any election from the right to vote at such election.

ARTICLE IV.
LEGISLATIVE

Legislative power. SECTION 1. The legislative power shall be vested in a senate and assembly.

Legislature, how constituted. SECTION 2. The number of the members of the assembly shall never be less than fifty-four nor more than one hundred. The senate shall consist of a number not more than one-third nor less than one-fourth of the number of the members of the assembly.

Apportionment. SECTION 3. [*As amended November 1982*] At its first session after each enumeration made by the authority of the United States, the legislature shall apportion and district anew the members of the senate and assembly, according to the number of inhabitants. [*1979 AJR-76; 1981 AJR-35; submit: May '82 Spec.Sess. AJR-1*]

Apportionment. SECTION 3. [*As amended November 1962*] At their first session after each enumeration made by the authority of the United States, the legislature shall apportion and district anew the members of the senate and assembly, according to the number of inhabitants, excluding soldiers, and officers of the United States army and navy. [*1959 SJR-12; 1961 SJR-11*]

Senate district area factor. SECTIONS 3, 4 AND 5. [*Approved by voters April 1953*] An amendment to Art. IV, secs. 3, 4, 5, relating to senate apportionment based on area and population, was approved by 1951 SJR-50 and 1953 AJR-7. However, the Supreme Court held the amendment not validly submitted to the voters in *State ex rel. Thomson v. Zimmerman*, 264 W. 644, 60 NW (2d) 416.

Apportionment. SECTION 3. [*As amended November 1910*] At their first session after each enumeration made

by the authority of the United States, the legislature shall apportion and district anew the members of the senate and assembly, according to the number of inhabitants, excluding Indians not taxed, soldiers, and officers of the United States army and navy. [*1907 SJR-18; 1909 SJR-35; 1909 c. 478*]

Census and apportionment. SECTION 3. [*Original form*] The legislature shall provide by law for an enumeration of the inhabitants of the state in the year one thousand eight hundred and fifty-five, and at the end of every ten years thereafter; and at their first session after such enumeration, and also after each enumeration made by the authority of the United States, the legislature shall apportion and district anew the members of the senate and assembly, according to the number of inhabitants, excluding Indians not taxed, and soldiers and officers of the United States army and navy.

Representatives to the assembly, how chosen. SECTION 4. [*As amended November 1982*] The members of the assembly shall be chosen biennially, by single districts, on the Tuesday succeeding the first Monday of November in even-numbered years, by the qualified electors of the several districts, such districts to be bounded by county, precinct, town or ward lines, to consist of contiguous territory and be in as compact form as practicable. [*1979 AJR-76; 1981 AJR-35; submit: May '82 Spec.Sess. AJR-1*]

Representatives to the assembly, how chosen. SECTION 4. [*As amended November 1881*] The members of the assembly shall be chosen biennially, by single districts, on the Tuesday succeeding the first Monday of November after the adoption of this amendment, by the qualified electors of the several districts, such districts to be bounded by county, precinct, town or ward lines, to consist of contiguous territory and be in as compact form as practicable. [*1880*

SJR-9; 1881 AJR-7; 1881 c. 262]

Assemblymen, how chosen. SECTION 4. [*Original form*] The members of the assembly shall be chosen annually by single districts, on the Tuesday succeeding the first Monday of November, by the qualified electors of the several districts. Such districts to be bounded by county, precinct, town, or ward lines, to consist of contiguous territory, and be in as compact form as practicable.

Senators, how chosen. SECTION 5. [*As amended November 1982*] The senators shall be elected by single districts of convenient contiguous territory, at the same time and in the same manner as members of the assembly are required to be chosen; and no assembly district shall be divided in the formation of a senate district. The senate districts shall be numbered in the regular series, and the senators shall be chosen alternately from the odd and even-numbered districts for the term of 4 years. [*1979 AJR-76; 1981 AJR-35; submit: May'82 Spec.Sess. AJR-1*]

Senators, how chosen. SECTION 5. [*As amended November 1881*] The senators shall be elected by single districts of convenient contiguous territory, at the same time and in the same manner as members of the assembly are required to be chosen, and no assembly district shall be divided in the formation of a senate district. The senate districts shall be numbered in the regular series, and the senators shall be chosen alternately from the odd and even-numbered districts. The senators elected or holding over at the time of the adoption of this amendment shall continue in office till their successors are duly elected and qualified; and after the adoption of this amendment all senators shall be chosen for the term of four years. [*1880 SJR-9; 1881*

AJR-7; 1881 c. 262]

Senators, how chosen. SECTION 5. [*Original form*] The senators shall be chosen by single districts of convenient contiguous territory, at the same time and in the same manner as members of the assembly are required to be chosen, and no assembly district shall be divided in the formation of a senate district. The senate districts shall be numbered in regular series, and the senators chosen by the odd-numbered districts shall go out of office at the expiration of the first year, and the senators chosen by the even-numbered districts shall go out of office at the expiration of the second year, and thereafter the senators shall be chosen for the term of two years.

Qualifications of legislators. SECTION 6. No person shall be eligible to the legislature who shall not have resided one year within the state, and be a qualified elector in the district which he may be chosen to represent.

Organization of legislature; quorum; compulsory attendance. SECTION 7. Each house shall be the judge of the elections, returns and qualifications of its own members; and a majority of each shall constitute a quorum to do business, but a smaller number may adjourn from day to day, and may compel the attendance of absent members in such manner and under such penalties as each house may provide.

Rules; contempts; expulsion. SECTION 8. Each house may determine the rules of its own proceedings, punish for contempt and disorderly behavior, and with the concurrence of two-thirds of all the members elected, expel a member; but no member shall be expelled a second time for the same cause.

Officers. SECTION 9. [*As amended November 2014*] (1) Each house shall choose its presiding officers from its own members.

(2) The legislature shall provide by law for the establishment of a department of transportation and a transportation fund. [*2011 SJR-23; 2013 AJR-2*]

Officers. SECTION 9. [*As amended April 1979*] Each house shall choose its presiding officers from its own members. [*1977 SJR-51; 1979 SJR-1*]

Officers. SECTION 9. [*Original form*] Each house shall choose its own officers, and the senate shall choose a temporary president when the lieutenant governor shall not attend as president, or shall act as governor.

Journals; open doors; adjournments. SECTION 10. Each house shall keep a journal of its proceedings and publish the same, except such parts as require secrecy. The doors of each house shall be kept open except when the public welfare shall require secrecy. Neither house shall, without consent of the other, adjourn for more than three days.

Meeting of legislature. SECTION 11. [*As amended April 1968*] The legislature shall meet at the seat of government at such time as shall be provided by law, unless convened by the governor in special session, and when so convened no business shall be transacted except as shall be necessary to accomplish the special purposes for which it was convened. [*1965 AJR-5; 1967 AJR-15*]

Meeting of legislature. SECTION 11. [*As amended November 1881*] The legislature shall meet at the seat of government at such time as shall be provided by law, once in two years, and no oftener, unless convened by the governor, in special session, and when so convened no business shall be transacted except as shall be necessary to accomplish the special purposes for which it was convened.

[*1880 SJR-9; 1881 AJR-7; 1881 c. 262*]

Place and time of meeting. SECTION 11. [*Original form*] The legislature shall meet at the seat of government, at such time as shall be provided by law, once in each year and not oftener, unless convened by the governor.

Ineligibility of legislators to office. SECTION 12. No member of the legislature shall, during the term for which he was elected, be appointed or elected to any civil office in the state, which shall have been created, or the emoluments of which shall have been increased, during the term for which he was elected.

Ineligibility of federal officers. SECTION 13. [*As amended April 1966*] No person being a member of congress, or holding any military or civil office under the United States, shall be eligible to a seat in the legislature; and if any person shall, after his election as a member of the legislature, be elected to congress, or be appointed to any office, civil or military, under the government of the United States, his acceptance thereof shall vacate his seat. This restriction shall not prohibit a legislator from accepting short periods of active duty as a member of the reserve or from serving in the armed forces during any emergency declared by the executive. [*1963 SJR-24; 1965 SJR-15*]

Ineligibility of federal officers. SECTION 13. [*Original form*] No person being a member of congress, or holding any military or civil office under the United States, shall be eligible to a seat in the legislature; and if any person shall, after his election as a member of the legislature, be elected to congress, or be appointed to any office, civil or military, under the government of the United States, his acceptance thereof shall vacate his seat.

Filling vacancies. SECTION 14. The governor shall issue writs of election to fill such vacancies as may occur in either house of the legislature.

Exemption from arrest and civil process. SECTION 15. Members of the legislature shall in all cases, except treason, felony and breach of the peace, be privileged from arrest; nor shall they be subject to any civil process, during the session of the legislature, nor for fifteen days next before the commencement and after the termination of each session.

Privilege in debate. SECTION 16. No member of the legislature shall be liable in any civil action, or criminal prosecution whatever, for words spoken in debate.

Enactment of laws. SECTION 17. [*As amended April 1977*] (1) The style of all laws of the state shall be "The people of the state of Wisconsin, represented in senate and assembly, do enact as follows:".

(2) No law shall be enacted except by bill. No law shall be in force until published.

(3) The legislature shall provide by law for the speedy publication of all laws. [*1975 AJR-11; 1977 SJR-9*]

Style of laws; bills. SECTION 17. [*Original form*] The style of the laws of the state shall be "The people of the state of Wisconsin, represented in senate and assembly, do enact as follows:" and no law shall be enacted except by bill.

Title of private bills. SECTION 18. No private or local bill which may be passed by the legislature shall embrace more than one subject, and that shall be expressed in the title.

Origin of bills. SECTION 19. Any bill may originate in either house of the legislature, and a bill passed by one house may be amended by the other.

Yeas and nays. SECTION 20. The yeas and nays of the members of either house on any question shall, at the request of one-sixth of those present, be entered on the journal.

SECTION 21. [*Repealed. 1927 SJR-61; 1929 SJR-7; vote April 1929*]

Compensation of members. SECTION 21. [*As amended November 1881*] Each member of the legislature shall receive for his services, for and during a regular session, the sum of five hundred dollars, and ten cents for every mile he shall travel in going to and returning from the place of meeting of the legislature on the most usual route. In case of an extra session of the legislature, no additional compensation shall be allowed to any member thereof, either directly or indirectly, except for mileage to be computed at the same rate as for a regular session. No stationery, newspapers, postage or other perquisite except the salary and mileage above provided, shall be received from the state by any member of the legislature for his services, or in any other manner as such member. [*1880 SJR-9; 1881 AJR-7; 1881 c. 262*]

Compensation of members. SECTION 21. [*As amended November 1867*] Each member of the legislature shall receive for his services three hundred and fifty dollars per annum and ten cents for every mile he shall travel in going to and returning from the place of the meeting of the legislature on the most usual route. In case of an extra session of the legislature no additional compensation shall be allowed to any member thereof either directly or indirectly. [*1865 SJR-26; 1866 SJR-16; 1867 c. 25*]

Compensation of members. SECTION 21. [*Original form*] Each member of the legislature shall receive for his services two dollars and fifty cents for each day's attendance during the session, and ten cents for every mile he shall travel in going to and returning from the place of the meeting of the legislature, on the most usual route.

Powers of county boards. SECTION 22. The legislature may confer upon the boards of supervisors of the several counties of the state such powers of a local, legislative and administrative character as they shall from time to time prescribe.

Town and county government. SECTION 23. [*As amended April 1972*] The legislature shall establish but one system of town government, which shall be as nearly uniform as practicable; but the legislature may provide for the election at large once in every 4 years of a chief executive officer in any county with such powers of an administrative character as they may from time to time prescribe in accordance with this section and shall establish one or more systems of county government. [*1969 SJR-58; 1971 SJR-4*]

Uniform town and county government. SECTION 23. [*As amended April 1969*] The legislature shall establish but one system of town and county government, which shall be as nearly uniform as practicable, except that the requirement of uniformity shall not apply to the administrative means of exercising powers of a local legislative character conferred by section 22 upon the boards of supervisors of the several counties; but the legislature may provide for the election at large once in every 4 years of a chief executive officer in any county with such powers of an administrative character as they may from time to time prescribe in accordance with this section. [*1967 AJR-18; 1969 SJR-8*]

Uniform town and county government. SECTION

23. [*As amended November 1962*] The legislature shall establish but one system of town and county government, which shall be as nearly uniform as practicable; but the legislature may provide for the election at large once in every four years of a chief executive officer in any county having a population of five hundred thousand or more with such powers of an administrative character as they may from time to time prescribe in accordance with this section. [*1959 AJR-121; 1961 AJR-61*]

Uniform town and county government. SECTION 23. [*Original form*] The legislature shall establish but one system of town and county government, which shall be as nearly uniform as practicable.

Chief executive officer to approve or veto resolutions or ordinances; proceedings on veto. SECTION 23a. [*As amended April 1969*] Every resolution or ordinance passed by the county board in any county shall, before it becomes effective, be presented to the chief executive officer. If he approves, he shall sign it; if not, he shall return it with his objections, which objections shall be entered at large upon the journal and the board shall proceed to reconsider the matter. Appropriations may be approved in whole or in part by the chief executive officer and the part approved shall become law, and the part objected to shall be returned in the same manner as provided for in other resolutions or ordinances. If, after such reconsideration, two-thirds of the members-elect of the county board agree to pass the resolution or ordinance or the part of the resolution or ordinance objected to, it shall become effective on the date prescribed but not earlier than the date of passage following reconsideration. In all such cases, the votes of the members of the county board shall be determined by ayes and noes and the names of the members voting for or against the resolution or ordinance or the part thereof objected to shall be entered on the journal. If any resolution or ordinance is not returned by the chief executive officer to the county board at its first meeting occurring not less than 6 days, Sundays excepted, after it has been presented to him, it shall become effective unless the county board has recessed or adjourned for a period in excess of 60 days, in which case it shall not be effective without his approval. [*1967 AJR-18; 1969 SJR-8*]

Chief executive officer to approve or veto resolutions or ordinances; proceedings on veto. SECTION 23a. [*Created November 1962*] Every resolution or ordinance passed by the county board in any county having a population of five hundred thousand or more shall, before it becomes effective, be presented to the chief executive officer. If he approves, he shall sign it; if not, he shall return it with his objections, which objections shall be entered at large upon the journal and the board shall proceed to reconsider the matter. Appropriations may be approved in whole or in part by the chief executive officer and the part approved shall become law, and the part objected to shall be returned in the same manner as provided for in other resolutions or ordinances. If, after such reconsideration, two-thirds of the members-elect of the county board agree to pass

the resolution or ordinance or the part of the resolution or ordinance objected to, it shall become effective on the date prescribed but not earlier than the date of passage following reconsideration. In all such cases, the votes of the members of the county board shall be determined by ayes and nays and the names of the members voting for or against the resolution or ordinance or the part thereof objected to shall be entered on the journal. If any resolution or ordinance is not returned by the chief executive officer to the county board at its first meeting occurring not less than six days, Sundays excepted, after it has been presented to him, it shall become effective unless the county board has recessed or adjourned for a period in excess of sixty days, in which case it shall not be effective without his approval. [*1959 AJR-121; 1961 AJR-61*]

Gambling. SECTION 24. [*As amended April 1993*] (1) Except as provided in this section, the legislature may not authorize gambling in any form.

(2) Except as otherwise provided by law, the following activities do not constitute consideration as an element of gambling:

(a) To listen to or watch a television or radio program.

(b) To fill out a coupon or entry blank, whether or not proof of purchase is required.

(c) To visit a mercantile establishment or other place without being required to make a purchase or pay an admittance fee.

(3) [*As amended April 1999*] The legislature may authorize the following bingo games licensed by the state, but all profits shall accrue to the licensed organization and no salaries,

fees or profits may be paid to any other organization or person: bingo games operated by religious, charitable, service, fraternal or veterans' organizations or those to which contributions are deductible for federal or state income tax purposes. All moneys received by the state that are attributable to bingo games shall be used for property tax relief for residents of this state as provided by law. The distribution of moneys that are attributable to bingo games may not vary based on the income or age of the person provided the property tax relief. The distribution of moneys that are attributable to bingo games shall not be subject to the uniformity requirement of section 1 of article VIII. In this subsection, the distribution of all moneys attributable to bingo games shall include any earnings on the moneys received by the state that are attributable to bingo games, but shall not include any moneys used for the regulation of, and enforcement of law relating to, bingo games. [*1997 AJR-80; 1999 AJR-2*]

(3) The legislature may authorize the following bingo games licensed by the state, but all profits shall accrue to the licensed organization and no salaries, fees or profits may be paid to any other organization or person: bingo games operated by religious, charitable, service, fraternal or veterans' organizations or those to which contributions are deductible for federal or state income tax purposes.

(4) The legislature may authorize the following raffle games licensed by the state, but all profits shall accrue to the licensed local organization and no salaries, fees or profits may be paid to any other organization or person: raffle games operated by local religious, charitable, service, fraternal or veterans' organizations or those to which contributions are deductible for federal or state income tax purposes. The legislature shall limit the number of raffles conducted by any such organization.

(5) [*As amended April 1999*] This section shall not prohibit pari-mutuel on-track betting as provided by law. The state may not own or operate any facility or enterprise for pari-mutuel betting, or lease any state-owned land to any other owner or operator for such purposes. All moneys received by the state that are attributable to pari-mutuel on-track betting shall be used for property tax relief for residents of this state as provided by law. The distribution of moneys that are attributable to pari-mutuel on-track betting may not vary based on the income or age of the person provided the property tax relief. The distribution of moneys that are attributable to pari-mutuel on-track betting shall not be subject to the uniformity requirement of section 1 of article VIII. In this subsection, the distribution of all moneys attributable to pari-mutuel on-track betting shall include any earnings on the moneys received by the state that are attributable to pari-mutuel on-track betting, but shall not include any moneys used for the regulation of, and enforcement of law relating to, pari-mutuel on-track betting. [*1997 AJR-80; 1999 AJR-2*]

(5) This section shall not prohibit pari-mutuel on-track betting as provided by law. The state may not own or operate any facility or enterprise for pari-mutuel betting, or lease any state-owned land to any other owner or operator for such purposes.

(6) (a) [*As amended April 1999*] The legislature may authorize the creation of a lottery to be operated by the state as provided by law. The expenditure of public funds or of revenues derived from lottery operations to engage in promotional advertising of the Wisconsin state lottery is prohibited. Any advertising of the state lottery shall indicate the odds of a specific lottery ticket to be selected as the winning ticket for each prize amount offered. The net proceeds of the state lottery shall be deposited in the treasury of the state, to be used for property tax relief for residents of this state as provided by law. The distribution of the net proceeds of the state lottery may not vary based on the income or age of the person provided the property tax relief. The distribution of the net proceeds of the state lottery shall not be subject to the uniformity requirement of section 1 of article VIII. In this paragraph, the distribution of the net proceeds of the state lottery shall include any earnings on the net proceeds of the state lottery. [*1997 AJR-80; 1999 AJR-2*]

(6) (a) The legislature may authorize the creation of a lottery to be operated by the state as provided by law. The expenditure of public funds or of revenues derived from lottery operations to engage in promotional advertising of the Wisconsin state lottery is prohibited. Any advertising of the state lottery shall indicate the odds of a specific lottery ticket to be selected as the winning ticket for each prize amount offered. The net proceeds of the state lottery shall be deposited in the treasury of the state, to be used for property tax relief as provided by law.

(b) The lottery authorized under par. (a) shall be an enterprise that entitles the player, by purchasing a ticket, to participate in a game of chance if: 1) the winning tickets are randomly predetermined and the player reveals preprinted numbers or symbols from which it can be immediately determined whether the ticket is a winning ticket entitling the player to win a prize as prescribed in the features and procedures for the game, including an opportunity to win a prize in a secondary or subsequent chance drawing or game; or 2) the ticket is evidence of the numbers or symbols selected by the player or, at the player's option, selected by a computer, and the player becomes entitled to a prize as prescribed in the features and procedures for the game, including an opportunity to win a prize in a secondary or subsequent chance drawing or game if some or all of the player's symbols or numbers are selected in a chance drawing or game, if the player's ticket is randomly selected by the computer at the time of purchase or if the ticket is selected in a chance drawing.

(c) Notwithstanding the authorization of a state lottery under par. (a), the following games, or games simulating any of the following games, may not be conducted by the state as a lottery: 1) any game in which winners are selected based on the results of a race or sporting event; 2) any banking card game, including blackjack, baccarat or chemin de fer; 3) poker; 4) roulette; 5) craps or any other game that involves rolling dice; 6) keno; 7) bingo 21, bingo jack, bingolet or bingo craps; 8) any game of chance that is placed on a slot machine or any mechanical, electromechanical or electronic device that is generally available to be played at a gambling casino; 9) any game or device that is commonly known as a video game of chance or a video gaming machine or that is commonly considered to be a video gambling machine, unless such machine is a video device operated by the state in a game authorized under par. (a) to permit the sale of tickets through retail outlets under contract with the state and the device does not determine or indicate whether the player has won a prize, other than by verifying that the player's ticket or some or all of the player's symbols or numbers on the player's ticket have been selected in a chance drawing, or by verifying that the player's ticket has been randomly selected by a central system computer at the time of purchase; 10) any game that is similar to a game listed in this paragraph; or 11) any other game that is commonly considered to be a form of gambling and is not, or is not substantially similar to, a game conducted by the state under par. (a).   No game conducted by the state under par. (a) may permit a player of the game to purchase a ticket, or to otherwise participate in the game, from a residence by using a computer, telephone or other form of electronic, telecommunication, video or technological aid. [*(1), (2)(intro.) amended; (6) (b), (c) created; June 1992 AJR-1; 1993 SJR-2*]

Lotteries and divorces. SECTION 24. [*As amended April 1987*] (1) Except as provided in this section, the legislature shall never authorize any lottery or grant any divorce.

(2) Except as otherwise provided by law, the following activities do not constitute consideration as an element of a lottery:

(a) To listen to or watch a television or radio program.

(b) To fill out a coupon or entry blank, whether or not proof of purchase is required.

(c) To visit a mercantile establishment or other place without being required to make a purchase or pay an admittance fee.

(3) The legislature may authorize the following bingo games licensed by the state, but all profits shall accrue to the licensed organization and no salaries, fees or profits may be paid to any other organization or person: bingo games operated by religious, charitable, service, fraternal or veterans' organizations or those to which contributions are deductible for federal or state income tax purposes.

(4) The legislature may authorize the following raffle games licensed by the state, but all profits shall accrue to the licensed local organization and no salaries, fees or profits may be paid to any other organization or person: raffle games operated by local religious, charitable, service, fraternal or veterans' organizations or those to which contributions are deductible for federal or state income tax purposes. The legislature shall limit the number of raffles conducted by any such organization.

(5) This section shall not prohibit pari-mutuel on-track betting as provided by law. The state may not own or operate any facility or enterprise for pari-mutuel betting, or lease any state-owned land to any other owner or operator for such purposes.

(6) The legislature may authorize the creation of a lottery to be operated by the state as provided by law. The expenditure of public funds or of revenues derived from lottery operations to engage in promotional advertising of the Wisconsin state lottery is prohibited. Any advertising of the state lottery shall indicate the odds of a specific lottery ticket to be selected as the winning ticket for each prize amount offered. The net proceeds of the state lottery shall be deposited in the treasury of the state, to be used for property tax relief as provided by law. [*Pari-mutuel: 1985 AJR-45; 1987 AJR-2. State lottery: 1985 SJR-1; 1987 AJR-3.*]

Lotteries and divorces. SECTION 24. [*As amended April 1977*] The legislature shall never authorize any lottery or grant any divorce. (1) The legislature may authorize bingo games licensed by the state, and operated by religious, charitable, service, fraternal or veterans' organizations or those to which contributions are deductible for federal or state income tax purposes. All profits must inure to the licensed organization and no salaries, fees or profits shall be paid to any other organization or person. (2) The legislature may authorize raffle games licensed by the state, and operated by local religious, charitable, service, fraternal or veterans' organizations or those to which contributions are deductible for federal or state income tax purposes. The legislature shall limit the number of raffles conducted by any such organization. All profits must inure to the licensed local organization and no salaries, fees or profits shall be paid to any other organization or person. (3) Except as the legislature may provide otherwise, the following activities do not constitute consideration as an element of a lottery: (a) To listen to or watch a television or radio program. (b) To fill out a coupon or entry blank, whether or not proof of purchase is required. (c) To visit a mercantile establishment or other place without being required to make a purchase or pay an admittance fee. [*1975 AJR-43; 1977 AJR-10*]

Lotteries and divorces. SECTION 24. [*As amended April 1973*] The legislature shall never authorize any lottery, or grant any divorce, but may authorize bingo games licensed by the state, and operated by religious, charitable, service, fraternal or veterans' organizations or those to which contributions are deductible for federal or state income tax purposes. All profits must inure to the licensed organization and no salaries, fees or profits shall be paid to any other organization or person. Except as the legislature may provide otherwise, to listen to or watch a television or radio program, to fill out a coupon or entry blank, whether or not proof of purchase is required, or to visit a mercantile establishment or other place without being required to make a purchase or pay an admittance fee does not constitute consideration as an element of a lottery. [*1971 SJR-13; 1973 AJR-6*]

Lotteries and divorces. SECTION 24. [*As amended April 1965*] The legislature shall never authorize any lottery, or grant any divorce. Except as the legislature may provide otherwise, to listen to or watch a television or radio

program, to fill out a coupon or entry blank, whether or not proof of purchase is required, or to visit a mercantile establishment or other place without being required to make a purchase or pay an admittance fee does not constitute consideration as an element of a lottery. [*1963 SJR-42; 1965 SJR-13*]

Lotteries and divorces. SECTION 24. [*Original form*] The legislature shall never authorize any lottery, or grant any divorce.

Stationery and printing. SECTION 25. The legislature shall provide by law that all stationery required for the use of the state, and all printing authorized and required by them to be done for their use, or for the state, shall be let by contract to the lowest bidder, but the legislature may establish a maximum price; no member of the legislature or other state officer shall be interested, either directly or indirectly, in any such contract.

Extra compensation; salary change. SECTION 26. [*As amended April 1992*] (1) The legislature may not grant any extra compensation to a public officer, agent, servant or contractor after the services have been rendered or the contract has been entered into.

(2) Except as provided in this subsection, the compensation of a public officer may not be increased or diminished during the term of office:

(a) When any increase or decrease in the compensation of justices of the supreme court or judges of any court of record becomes effective as to any such justice or judge, it shall be effective from such date as to every such justice or judge.

(b) Any increase in the compensation of members of the legislature shall take effect, for all senators and representatives to the assembly, after the next general election beginning with the new assembly term.

(3) Subsection (1) shall not apply to increased benefits for persons who have been or shall be granted benefits of any kind under a retirement system when such increased benefits are provided by a legislative act passed on a call of ayes and noes by a three-fourths vote of all the members elected to both houses of the legislature and such act provides for sufficient state funds to cover the costs of the increased benefits. [*1989 AJR-47; 1991 AJR-16*]

Extra compensation; salary change. SECTION 26. [*As amended April 1977*] The legislature shall never grant any extra compensation to any public officer, agent, servant or contractor, after the services shall have been rendered or the contract entered into; nor shall the compensation of any public officer be increased or diminished during his term of office except that when any increase or decrease provided by the legislature in the compensation of the justices of the supreme court or judges of any court of record shall become effective as to any such justice or judge, it shall be effective from such date as to each of such justices or judges. This section shall not apply to increased benefits for persons who have been or shall be granted benefits of any kind under a retirement system when such increased benefits are provided by a legislative act passed on a call of ayes and noes by a three-fourths vote of all the members elected to both houses of the legislature, which act shall provide for sufficient state funds to cover the costs of the increased benefits. [*1975 AJR-11; 1977 SJR-9*]

Extra compensation; salary change. SECTION 26. [*As amended April 1974*] The legislature shall never grant any extra compensation to any public officer, agent, servant or contractor, after the services shall have been rendered or the contract entered into; nor shall the compensation of any public officer be increased or diminished during his term of office except that when any increase or decrease provided by the legislature in the compensation of the justices of the supreme court, or judges of the circuit court shall become effective as to any such justice or judge, it shall become effective from such date as to each of such justices or judges. This section shall not apply to increased benefits for persons who have been or shall be granted benefits of any kind under a retirement system when such increased benefits are provided by a legislative act passed on a call of ayes and nays by a three-fourths vote of all the members elected to both houses of the legislature, which act shall provide for sufficient state funds to cover the costs of the increased benefits. [*1971 SJR-3; 1973 SJR-15*]

Extra compensation; salary change. SECTION 26. [*As amended April 1967*] The legislature shall never grant any extra compensation to any public officer, agent, servant or contractor, after the services shall have been rendered or the contract entered into; nor shall the compensation of any public officer be increased or diminished during his term of office except that when any increase or decrease provided by the legislature in the compensation of the justices of the supreme court, or judges of the circuit court shall become effective as to any such justice or judge, it shall be effective from such date as to each of such justices or judges. This section shall not apply to increased benefits for teachers under a teachers' retirement system when such increased benefits are provided by a legislative act passed on a call of yeas and nays by a three-fourths vote of all the members elected to both houses of the legislature. [*1965 AJR-162; 1967 AJR-17*]

Extra compensation; salary change. SECTION 26. [*As amended April 1956*] The legislature shall never grant any extra compensation to any public officer, agent, servant or contractor, after the services shall have been rendered or the contract entered into; nor shall the compensation of any public officer be increased or diminished during his term of office. This section shall not apply to increased benefits for teachers under a teachers' retirement system when such increased benefits are provided by a legislative act passed on a call of yeas and nays by a three-fourths vote of all the members elected to both houses of the legislature. [*1953 SJR-21; 1955 SJR-8*]

Extra compensation; salary change. SECTION 26. [*Original form*] The legislature shall never grant any extra compensation to any public officer, agent, servant or contractor after the services shall have been rendered or the contract entered into; nor shall the compensation of any public officer be increased or diminished during his term of office.

Suits against state. Section 27. The legislature shall direct by law in what manner and in what courts suits may be brought against the state.

Oath of office. Section 28. Members of the legislature, and all officers, executive and judicial, except such inferior officers as may be by law exempted, shall before they enter upon the duties of their respective offices, take and subscribe an oath or affirmation to support the constitution of the United States and the constitution of the state of Wisconsin, and faithfully to discharge the duties of their respective offices to the best of their ability.

Militia. Section 29. The legislature shall determine what persons shall constitute the militia of the state, and may provide for organizing and disciplining the same in such manner as shall be prescribed by law.

Elections by legislature. Section 30. [*As amended November 1982*] All elections made by the legislature shall be by roll call vote entered in the journals. [*1979 AJR-76; 1981 AJR-35; submit: May'82 Spec.Sess. AJR-1*]

Elections by legislature. Section 30. [*Original form*] In all elections to be made by the legislature the members thereof shall vote viva voce, and their votes shall be entered on the journal.

Special and private laws prohibited. Section 31. [*As amended April 1993*] The legislature is prohibited from enacting any special or private laws in the following cases:

(1) For changing the names of persons, constituting one person the heir at law of another or granting any divorce.

(2) For laying out, opening or altering highways, except in cases of state roads extending into more than one county, and military roads to aid in the construction of which lands may be granted by congress.

(3) For authorizing persons to keep ferries across streams at points wholly within this state.

(4) For authorizing the sale or mortgage of real or personal property of minors or others under disability.

(5) For locating or changing any county seat.

(6) For assessment or collection of taxes or for extending the time for the collection thereof.

(7) For granting corporate powers or privileges, except to cities.

(8) For authorizing the apportionment of any part of the school fund.

(9) For incorporating any city, town or village, or to amend the charter thereof. [*(1) amended; June 1992 AJR-1; 1993 SJR-2*]

Special and private laws prohibited. Section 31. [*As amended November 1892*] The legislature is prohibited from enacting any special or private laws in the following cases:

1st. For changing the name of persons or constituting one person the heir at law of another.

2d. For laying out, opening or altering highways, except in cases of state roads extending into more than one county, and military roads to aid in the construction of which lands may be granted by congress.

3d. For authorizing persons to keep ferries across streams at points wholly within this state.

4th. For authorizing the sale or mortgage of real or personal property of minors or others under disability.

5th. For locating or changing any county seat.

6th. For assessment or collection of taxes or for extending the time for the collection thereof.

7th. For granting corporate powers or privileges, except to cities.

8th. For authorizing the apportionment of any part of the school fund.

9th. For incorporating any city, town or village, or to amend the charter thereof. [*1889 SJR-13; 1891 SJR-13; 1891 c. 362*]

Special or private laws. Section 31. [*Created November 1871*] The legislature is prohibited from enacting any special or private laws in the following cases:

1st. For changing the name of persons or constituting one person the heir at law of another.

2d. For laying out, opening or altering highways, except in cases of state roads extending into more than one county, and military roads to aid in the construction of which lands may be granted by congress.

3d. For authorizing persons to keep ferries across streams at points wholly within this state.

4th. For authorizing the sale or mortgage of real or personal property of minors or others under disability.

5th. For locating or changing any county seat.

6th. For assessment or collection of taxes or for extending the time for the collection thereof.

7th. For granting corporate powers or privileges, except to cities.

8th. For authorizing the apportionment of any part of the school fund.

9th. For incorporating any town or village or to amend the charter thereof. [*1870 SJR-14; 1871 AJR-29; 1871 c. 122*]

General laws on enumerated subjects. Section 32. [*As amended April 1993*] The legislature may provide by general law for the treatment of any subject for which lawmaking is prohibited by section 31 of this article. Subject to reasonable classifications, such laws shall be uniform in their operation throughout the state. [*June 1992 AJR-1; 1993 SJR-2*]

General laws on enumerated subjects. SECTION 32. [*Created November 1871*] The legislature shall provide general laws for the transaction of any business that may be prohibited by section thirty-one of this article, and all such laws shall be uniform in their operation throughout the state. [*1870 SJR-14; 1871 AJR-29; 1871 c. 122*]

Auditing of state accounts. SECTION 33. [*Created November 1946*] The legislature shall provide for the auditing of state accounts and may establish such offices and prescribe such duties for the same as it shall deem necessary. [*1943 SJR-35; 1945 SJR-24*]

Continuity of civil government. SECTION 34. [*Created April 1961*] The legislature, in order to ensure continuity of state and local governmental operations in periods of emergency resulting from enemy action in the form of an attack, shall (1) forthwith provide for prompt and temporary succession to the powers and duties of public offices, of whatever nature and whether filled by election or appointment, the incumbents of which may become unavailable for carrying on the powers and duties of such offices, and (2) adopt such other measures as may be necessary and proper for attaining the objectives of this section. [*1959 AJR-48; 1961 SJR-1*]

ARTICLE V.

EXECUTIVE

Governor; lieutenant governor; term. SECTION 1. [*As amended April 1979*] The executive power shall be vested in a governor who shall hold office for 4 years; a lieutenant governor shall be elected at the same time and for the same term. [*1977 SJR-51; 1979 SJR-1*]

Governor; lieutenant governor; term. SECTION 1. [*Original form*] The executive power shall be vested in a governor, who shall hold his office for two years; a lieutenant governor shall be elected at the same time, and for the same term.

SECTION 1m. [*Repealed. 1977 SJR-51; 1979 SJR-1; vote April 1979*]

Governor; 4-year term. SECTION 1m. [*Created April 1967*] Notwithstanding section 1, beginning with the general election in 1970 and every four years thereafter, there shall be elected a governor to hold office for a term of four years. [*1965 AJR-4; 1967 AJR-9 and SJR-12*]

SECTION 1n. [*Repealed. 1977 SJR-51; 1979 SJR-1; vote April 1979*]

Lieutenant governor; 4-year term. SECTION 1n. [*Created April 1967*] Notwithstanding section 1, beginning with the general election in 1970 and every four years thereafter, there shall be elected a lieutenant governor to hold office for a term of four years. [*1965 AJR-4; 1967 AJR-9 and SJR-12*]

Eligibility. SECTION 2. No person except a citizen of the United States and a qualified elector of the state shall be eligible to the office of governor or lieutenant governor.

Election. SECTION 3. [*As amended April 1967*] The governor and lieutenant governor shall be elected by the qualified electors of the state at the times and places of choosing members of the legislature. They shall be chosen jointly, by the casting by each voter of a single vote applicable to both offices beginning with the general election in 1970. The persons respectively having the highest number of votes cast jointly for them for governor and lieutenant governor shall be elected; but in case two or more slates shall have an equal and the highest number of votes for governor and lieutenant governor, the two houses of the legislature, at its next annual session shall forthwith, by joint ballot, choose one of the slates so having an equal and the highest number of votes for governor and lieutenant governor. The returns of election for governor and lieutenant governor shall be made in such manner as shall be provided by law. [*1965 AJR-3; 1967 AJR-8 and SJR-11*]

Election. SECTION 3. [*Original form*] The governor and lieutenant governor shall be elected by the qualified electors of the state at the times and places of choosing members of the legislature. The persons respectively having the highest number of votes for governor and lieutenant governor shall be elected; but in case two or more shall have an equal and the highest number of votes for governor, or lieutenant governor, the two houses of the legislature, at its next annual session shall forthwith, by joint ballot, choose one of the persons so having an equal and the highest number of votes for governor, or lieutenant governor. The returns of election for governor and lieutenant governor shall be made in such manner as shall be provided by law.

Powers and duties. SECTION 4. The governor shall be commander in chief of the military and naval forces of the state. He shall have power to convene the legislature on extraordinary occasions, and in case of invasion, or danger from the prevalence of contagious disease at the seat of government, he may convene them at any other suitable place within the state. He shall communicate to the legislature, at every session, the condition of the state, and recommend such matters to them for their consideration as he may deem expedient. He shall transact all necessary business with the officers of the government, civil and military. He shall expedite all such measures as may be resolved upon by the legislature, and shall take care that the laws be faithfully executed.

SECTION 5. [*Repealed. 1929 SJR-81; 1931 SJR-6; vote November 1932*]

Compensation of governor. SECTION 5. [*As amended November 1926*] The governor shall receive, during his continuance in office, an annual compensation of not less than five thousand dollars, to be fixed by law, which shall be in full for all traveling or other expenses incident to his duties. The compensation prescribed for governor immediately prior to the adoption of this amendment shall continue in force until changed by the legislature in a manner consistent with the other provisions of this constitution. [*1923 AJR-88; 1925 AJR-50; 1925 c. 413*]

Compensation of governor. SECTION 5. [*As amended November 1869*] The governor shall receive during his continuance in office, an annual compensation of five thousand dollars which shall be in full for all traveling or other expenses incident to his duties. [*1868 AJR-13; 1869 SJR-6; 1869 c. 186*]

Compensation of governor. SECTION 5. [*Original form*] The governor shall receive during his continuance in office, an annual compensation of one thousand two hundred and fifty dollars.

Pardoning power. SECTION 6. The governor shall have power to grant reprieves, commutations and pardons, after conviction, for all offenses, except treason and cases of impeachment, upon such conditions and with such restrictions and limitations as he may think proper, subject to such regulations as may be provided by law relative to the manner of applying for pardons. Upon conviction for treason he shall have the power to suspend the execution of the sentence until the case shall be reported to the legislature at its next meeting, when the legislature shall either pardon, or commute the sentence, direct the execution of the sentence, or grant a further reprieve. He shall annually communicate to the legislature each case of reprieve, commutation or pardon granted, stating the name of the convict, the crime of which he was convicted, the sentence and its date, and the date of the commutation, pardon or reprieve, with his reasons for granting the same.

Lieutenant governor, when governor. SECTION 7. [*As amended April 1979*] (1) Upon the governor's death, resignation or removal from office, the lieutenant governor shall become governor for the balance of the unexpired term.

(2) If the governor is absent from this state, impeached, or from mental or physical disease, becomes incapable of performing the duties of the office, the lieutenant governor shall serve as acting governor for the balance of the unexpired term or until the governor returns, the disability ceases or the impeachment is vacated. But when the governor, with the consent of the legislature, shall be out of this state in time of war at the head of the state's military force, the governor shall continue as commander in chief of the military force. [*1977 SJR-51; 1979 SJR-1*]

Lieutenant governor, when governor. SECTION 7. [*Original form*] In case of the impeachment of the governor, or his removal from office, death, inability from mental or physical disease, resignation, or absence from the state, the powers and duties of the office shall devolve upon the lieutenant governor for the residue of the term or until the governor, absent or impeached, shall have returned, or the disability shall cease. But when the governor shall, with the consent of the legislature, be out of the state in time of war, at the head of the military force thereof, he shall continue commander in chief of the military force of the state.

Secretary of state, when governor. SECTION 8. [*As amended April 1979*] (1) If there is a vacancy in the office of lieutenant governor and the governor dies, resigns or is removed from office, the secretary of state shall become governor for the balance of the unexpired term.

(2) If there is a vacancy in the office of lieutenant governor and the governor is absent from this state, impeached, or from mental or physical disease becomes incapable of performing the duties of the office, the secretary of state shall serve as acting governor for the balance of the unexpired term or until the governor returns, the disability ceases or the impeachment is vacated. [*1977 SJR-51; 1979 SJR-1*]

Lieutenant governor president of senate; when secretary of state to be governor. SECTION 8. [*Original form*] The lieutenant governor shall be president of the senate, but shall have only a casting vote therein. If, during a vacancy in the office of the governor, the lieutenant governor shall be impeached, displaced, resign, die, or from mental or physical disease become incapable of performing the duties of his office, or be absent from the state, the secretary of state shall act as governor until the vacancy shall be filled or the disability shall cease.

SECTION 9. [*Repealed. 1929 SJR-82; 1931 SJR-7; vote November 1932*]

Compensation of lieutenant governor. SECTION 9. [*As amended November 1869*] The lieutenant governor shall receive during his continuance in office an annual compensation of one thousand dollars. [*1868 AJR-13; 1869 SJR-6; 1869 c. 186*]

Compensation of lieutenant governor. SECTION 9. [*Original form*] The lieutenant governor shall receive double the per diem allowance of members of the senate, for every day's attendance as president of the senate, and the same mileage as shall be allowed to members of the legislature.

Governor to approve or veto bills; proceedings on veto. SECTION 10. [*As amended April 1990; April 2008*] (1) (a) Every bill which shall have passed the legislature shall, before it becomes a law, be presented to the governor.

(b) If the governor approves and signs the bill, the bill shall become law. Appropriation bills may be approved in whole or in part by the governor, and the part approved shall become law.

(c) In approving an appropriation bill in part, the governor may not create a new word by rejecting individual letters in the words of the enrolled bill, and may not create a new sentence by combining parts of 2 or more sentences of the enrolled bill. [*2005 SJR-33; 2007 SJR-5*]

Governor to approve or veto bills; proceedings on veto. SECTION 10. [*As amended April 1990*] (c) In approving an appropriation bill in part, the governor may not create a new word by rejecting individual letters in the words of the enrolled bill.

(2) (a) If the governor rejects the bill, the governor shall return the bill, together with the objections in writing, to the house in which the bill originated. The house of origin shall enter the objections at large upon the journal and proceed to reconsider the bill. If, after such reconsideration, two-thirds of the members present agree to pass the bill notwithstanding the objections of the governor, it shall be sent, together with the objections, to the other house, by which it shall likewise be reconsidered, and if approved by two-thirds of the members present it shall become law.

(b) The rejected part of an appropriation bill, together with the governor's objections in writing, shall be returned to the house in which the bill originated. The house of origin shall enter the objections at large upon the journal and proceed to reconsider the rejected part of the appropriation bill. If, after such reconsideration, two-thirds of the members present agree to approve the rejected part notwithstanding the objections of the governor, it shall be sent, together with the objections, to the other house, by which it shall likewise be reconsidered, and if approved by two-thirds of the members present the rejected part shall become law.

(c) In all such cases the votes of both houses shall be determined by ayes and noes, and the names of the members voting for or against passage of the bill or the rejected part of the bill notwithstanding the objections of the governor shall be entered on the journal of each house respectively.

(3) Any bill not returned by the governor within 6 days (Sundays excepted) after it shall have been presented to the governor shall be law unless the legislature, by final adjournment, prevents the bill's return, in which case it shall not be law. [*1987 AJR-71; 1989 SJR-11*]

Governor to approve or veto bills; proceedings on veto. SECTION 10. [*As amended November 1930*] Every bill which shall have passed the legislature shall, before it becomes a law, be presented to the governor; if he approve, he shall sign it, but if not, he shall return it, with his objections, to that house in which it shall have originated, who shall enter the objections at large upon the journal and proceed to reconsider it. Appropriation bills may be approved in whole or in part by the governor, and the part approved shall become law, and the part objected to shall be returned in the same manner as provided for other bills. If, after such reconsideration, two-thirds of the members present shall agree to pass the bill, or the part of the bill objected to, it shall be sent, together with the objections, to the other house, by which it shall likewise be reconsidered, and if approved by two-thirds of the members present it shall become law. But in all such cases the votes of both houses shall be determined by yeas and nays, and the names of the members voting for or against the bill or the part of the bill objected to, shall be entered on the journal of each house respectively. If any bill shall not be returned by the governor within six days (Sundays excepted) after it shall have been presented to him, the same shall be a law unless the legislature shall, by their adjournment, prevent its return, in which case it shall not be a law. [*1927 SJR-35; 1929 SJR-40*]

Approval of bills. SECTION 10. [*As amended November 1908*] Every bill which shall have passed the legislature shall, before it becomes a law, be presented to the governor; if he approve, he shall sign it, but if not, he shall return it, with his objections, to that house in which it shall have originated, who shall enter the objections at large upon the journal and proceed to reconsider it. If, after such reconsideration, two-thirds of the members present shall agree to pass the bill, it shall be sent, together with the objections to the other house, by which it shall likewise be reconsidered, and if approved by two-thirds of the members present it shall become a law. But in all such cases the votes of both houses shall be determined by yeas and nays, and the names of the members voting for or against the bill shall be entered on the journal of each house respectively. If any bill shall not be returned by the governor within six days (Sundays excepted) after it shall have been presented to him, the same shall be a law unless the legislature shall, by their adjournment, prevent its return, in which case it shall not be a law. [*1905 AJR-45; 1907 AJR-46; 1907 c. 661*]

Approval of bills. SECTION 10. [*Original form*] Every bill which shall have passed the legislature shall, before it becomes a law, be presented to the governor; if he approve, he shall sign it, but if not, he shall return it, with his objections, to that house in which it shall have originated, who shall enter the objections at large upon the journal, and proceed to reconsider it. If, after such reconsideration two-thirds of the members present shall agree to pass the bill, it shall be sent, together with the objections, to the other house, by which it shall likewise be reconsidered, and if approved by two-thirds of the members present, it shall become a law. But in all such cases the votes of both houses shall be determined by yeas and nays, and the names of the members voting for or against the bill, shall be entered on the journal of each house respectively. If any bill shall not be returned by the governor within three days (Sundays excepted) after it shall have been presented to him, the same shall be a law, unless the legislature shall, by their adjournment, prevent its return, in which case it shall not be a law.

ARTICLE VI.

ADMINISTRATIVE

Election of secretary of state, treasurer and attorney general; term. SECTION 1. *[As amended April 1979]* The qualified electors of this state, at the times and places of choosing the members of the legislature, shall in 1970 and every 4 years thereafter elect a secretary of state, treasurer and attorney general who shall hold their offices for 4 years. *[1977 SJR-51; 1979 SJR-1]*

Election of secretary of state, treasurer and attorney- general; term. SECTION 1. *[Original form]* There shall be chosen by the qualified electors of the state, at the times and places of choosing the members of the legislature, a secretary of state, treasurer and attorney-general, who shall severally hold their offices for the term of two years.

SECTION 1m. *[Repealed. 1977 SJR-51; 1979 SJR-1; vote April 1979]*

Secretary of state; 4-year term. SECTION 1m. *[Created April 1967]* Notwithstanding section 1, beginning with the general election in 1970 and every four years thereafter, there shall be chosen a secretary of state to hold office for a term of four years. *[1965 AJR-4; 1967 AJR-9 and SJR-12]*

SECTION 1n. *[Repealed. 1977 SJR-51; 1979 SJR-1; vote April 1979]*

Treasurer; 4-year term. SECTION 1n. *[Created April 1967]* Notwithstanding section 1, beginning with the general election in 1970 and every four years thereafter, there shall be chosen a treasurer to hold office for a term of four years. *[1965 AJR-4; 1967 AJR-9 and SJR-12]*

SECTION 1p. *[Repealed. 1977 SJR-51; 1979 SJR-1; vote April 1979]*

Attorney general; 4-year term. SECTION 1p. *[Created April 1967]* Notwithstanding section 1, beginning with the general election in 1970 and every four years thereafter, there shall be chosen an attorney general to hold office for a term of four years. *[1965 AJR-4; 1967 AJR-9 and SJR-12]*

Secretary of state; duties, compensation. SECTION 2. *[As amended November 1946]* The secretary of state shall keep a fair record of the official acts of the legislature and executive department of the state, and shall, when required, lay the same and all matters relative thereto before either branch of the legislature. He shall perform such other duties as shall be assigned him by law. He shall receive as a compensation for his services yearly such sum as shall be provided by law, and shall keep his office at the seat of government. *[1943 SJR-35; 1945 SJR-24]*

Secretary of state. SECTION 2. *[Original form]* The secretary of state shall keep a fair record of the official acts of the legislature and executive department of the state, and shall, when required, lay the same and all matters relative thereto, before either branch of the legislature. He shall be ex officio auditor, and shall perform such other duties as shall be assigned him by law. He shall receive as a compensation for his services yearly, such sum as shall be provided by law, and shall keep his office at the seat of government.

Treasurer and attorney general; duties, compensation. SECTION 3. The powers, duties and compensation of the treasurer and attorney general shall be prescribed by law.

County officers; election, terms, removal; vacancies. SECTION 4. *[As amended April 2005]* (1) (a) Except as provided in pars. (b) and (c) and sub. (2), coroners, registers of deeds, district attorneys, and all other elected county officers, except judicial officers, sheriffs, and chief executive officers, shall be chosen by the electors of the respective counties once in every 2 years.

(b) Beginning with the first general election at which the governor is elected which occurs after the ratification of this paragraph, sheriffs shall be chosen by the electors of the respective counties, or by the electors of all of the respective counties comprising each combination of counties combined by the legislature for that purpose, for the term of 4 years and coroners in counties in which there is a coroner shall be chosen by the electors of the respective counties, or by the electors of all of the respective counties comprising each combination of counties combined by the legislature for that purpose, for the term of 4 years.

(c) Beginning with the first general election at which the president is elected which occurs after the ratification of this paragraph, district attorneys, registers of deeds, county clerks, and treasurers shall be chosen by the electors of the respective counties, or by the electors of all of the respective counties comprising each combination of counties combined by the legislature for that purpose, for the term of 4 years and surveyors in counties in which the office of surveyor is filled by election shall be chosen by the electors of the respective counties, or by the electors of all of the respective counties comprising each combination of counties combined by the legislature for that purpose, for the term of 4 years.

(2) The offices of coroner and surveyor in counties having a population of 500,000 or more are abolished. Counties not having a population of 500,000 shall have the option of retaining the elective office of coroner or instituting a medical examiner system. Two or more counties may institute a joint medical examiner system.

(3) (a) Sheriffs may not hold any other partisan office.

(b) Sheriffs may be required by law to renew their security from time to time, and in default of giving such new security their office shall be deemed vacant.

(4) The governor may remove any elected county officer mentioned in this section except a county clerk, treasurer, or surveyor, giving to the officer a copy of the charges and an opportunity of being heard.

(5) All vacancies in the offices of coroner, register of deeds or district attorney shall be filled by appointment. The person appointed to fill a vacancy shall hold office only for the unexpired portion of the term to which appointed and until a successor shall be elected and qualified.

(6) When a vacancy occurs in the office of sheriff, the vacancy shall be filled by appointment of the governor, and the person appointed shall serve until his or her successor is elected and qualified. [*2003 AJR-10; 2005 SJR-2*]

County officers; election, terms, removal; vacancies. SECTION 4. [*As amended November 1998*] (1) Except as provided in sub. (2), coroners, registers of deeds, district attorneys, and all other elected county officers except judicial officers, sheriffs and chief executive officers, shall be chosen by the electors of the respective counties once in every 2 years.

(2) The offices of coroner and surveyor in counties having a population of 500,000 or more are abolished. Counties not having a population of 500,000 shall have the option of retaining the elective office of coroner or instituting a medical examiner system. Two or more counties may institute a joint medical examiner system.

(3) (a) Sheriffs may not hold any other partisan office.

(b) Sheriffs may be required by law to renew their security from time to time, and in default of giving such new security their office shall be deemed vacant.

(c) Beginning with the first general election at which the governor is elected which occurs after the ratification of this paragraph, sheriffs shall be chosen by the electors of the respective counties once in every 4 years.

(4) The governor may remove any elected county officer mentioned in this section, giving to the officer a copy of the charges and an opportunity of being heard.

(5) All vacancies in the offices of coroner, register of deeds or district attorney shall be filled by appointment. The person appointed to fill a vacancy shall hold office only for the unexpired portion of the term to which appointed and until a successor shall be elected and qualified.

(6) When a vacancy occurs in the office of sheriff, the vacancy shall be filled by appointment of the governor, and the person appointed shall serve until his or her successor is elected and qualified. [*1995 AJR-37; 1997 SJR-43*]

County officers; election, terms, removal; vacancies. SECTION 4. [*As amended April 1982*] (1) Sheriffs, coroners, registers of deeds, district attorneys, and all other elected county officers except judicial officers and chief executive officers, shall be chosen by the electors of the respective counties once in every 2 years.

(2) The offices of coroner and surveyor in counties having a population of 500,000 or more are abolished. Counties not having a population of 500,000 shall have the option of retaining the elective office of coroner or instituting a medical examiner system. Two or more counties may institute a joint medical examiner system.

(3) Sheriffs shall hold no other office. Sheriffs may be required by law to renew their security from time to time, and in default of giving such new security their office shall be deemed vacant.

(4) The governor may remove any elected county officer mentioned in this section, giving to the officer a copy of the charges and an opportunity of being heard.

(5) All vacancies in the offices of sheriff, coroner, register of deeds or district attorney shall be filled by appointment. The person appointed to fill a vacancy shall hold office only for the unexpired portion of the term to which appointed and until a successor shall be elected and qualified. [*1979 AJR-99; 1981 AJR-7*]

County officers; election, terms, removal; vacancies. SECTION 4. [*As amended April 1972*] Sheriffs, coroners, register of deeds, district attorneys, and all other county officers except judicial officers and chief executive officers, shall be chosen by the electors of the respective counties once in every two years. The offices of coroner and surveyor in counties having a population of 500,000 or more are abolished. Counties not having a population of 500,000 shall have the option of retaining the elective office of coroner or instituting a medical examiner system. Two or more counties may institute a joint medical examiner system. Sheriffs shall hold no other office; they may be required by law to renew their security from time to time, and in default of giving such new security their office shall be deemed vacant, but the county shall never be made responsible for the acts of the sheriff. The governor may remove any officer in this section mentioned, giving to such a copy of the charges against him and an opportunity of being heard in his defense. All vacancies shall be filled by appointment, and the person appointed to fill a vacancy shall hold only for the unexpired portion of the term to which he shall be appointed and until his successor shall be elected and qualified. [*1969 SJR-63; 1971 SJR-38*]

County officers; election, terms, removal; vacancies. SECTION 4. [*As amended April 1967*] Sheriffs, coroners, registers of deeds, district attorneys, and all other county officers except judicial officers and chief executive officers, shall be chosen by the electors of the respective counties once in every two years. The offices of coroner and surveyor in counties having a population of 500,000 or more are abolished at the conclusion of the terms of office during which this amendment is adopted. Sheriffs shall hold no other office; they may be required by law to renew their security from time to time, and in default of giving such new security their office shall be deemed vacant, but the county shall never be made responsible for the acts of the sheriff. The governor may remove any officer in this section mentioned, giving to such a copy of the charges against him and an opportunity of being heard in his defense. All vacancies shall be filled by appointment, and the person appointed to fill a vacancy shall hold only for the unexpired portion of the term to which he shall be appointed and until his successor shall be elected and qualified. [*1965 AJR-72; 1967 SJR-7*]

County officers; election, terms, removal; vacancies. SECTION 4. [*As amended April 1965*] Sheriffs, coroners, register of deeds, district attorneys, and all other county officers except judicial officers and chief executive officers, shall be chosen by the electors of the respective counties once in every two years. The offices of coroner and surveyor in counties having a population of 500,000 or more are abolished at the conclusion of the terms of office during which this amendment is adopted. Sheriffs shallhold no other office, and shall not serve more than two terms or parts thereof in succession; they may be required by law to renew their security from time to time, and in default of giving such new security their office shall be deemed vacant, but the county shall never be made responsible for the acts of the sheriff. The governor may remove any officer in this section mentioned, giving to such a copy of the charges against him and an opportunity of being heard in his defense. All vacancies shall be filled by appointment, and the person appointed to fill a vacancy shall hold only for the unexpired portion of the term to which he shall be appointed and until his successor shall be elected and qualified. [*1963 AJR-14; 1965 SJR-17*]

County officers; election, terms, removal; vacancies. SECTION 4. [*As amended November 1962*] Sheriffs, coroners, registers of deeds, district attorneys, and all other county officers except judicial officers and chief executive officers, shall be chosen by the electors of the respective counties once in every two years. Sheriffs shall hold no other office, and shall not serve more than two terms or parts thereof in succession; they may be required by law to renew their security from time to time, and in default of giving such new security their office shall be deemed vacant, but the county shall never be made responsible for the acts of the sheriff. The governor may remove any officer in this section mentioned, giving to such a copy of the charges against him and an opportunity of being heard in his defense. All vacancies shall be filled by appointment, and the person appointed to fill a vacancy shall hold only for the unexpired portion of the term to which he shall be appointed and until his successor shall be elected and qualified. [*1959 AJR-121; 1961 AJR-61*]

County officers; election, terms, removal; vacancies. SECTION 4. [*As amended April 1929*] Sheriffs, coroners, registers of deeds, district attorneys, and all other county officers except judicial officers, shall be chosen by the electors of the respective counties once in every two years. Sheriffs shall hold no other office, and shall not serve more than two terms or parts thereof in succession; they may be

required by law to renew their security from time to time, and in default of giving such new security their office shall be deemed vacant, but the county shall never be made responsible for the acts of the sheriff. The governor may remove any officer in this section mentioned, giving to such a copy of the charges against him and an opportunity of being heard in his defense. All vacancies shall be filled by appointment, and the person appointed to fill a vacancy shall hold only for the unexpired portion of the term to which he shall be appointed and qualified. [*1927 AJR-8; 1929 AJR-8*]

County officers. SECTION 4. [*As amended November 1882*] Sheriffs, coroners, registers of deeds, district attorneys, and all other county officers, except judicial officers shall be chosen by the electors of the respective counties, once in every two years. Sheriffs shall hold no other office and be ineligible for two years next succeeding the termination of their offices; they may be required by law to renew their security from time to time, and in default of giving such new security their office shall be deemed vacant, but the county shall never be made responsible for the acts of the sheriff. The governor may remove any officer in this section mentioned, giving to such a copy of the charges against him and an opportunity of being heard in his defense. All vacancies shall be filled by appointment and the person appointed to fill a vacancy shall hold only for the unexpired portion of the term to which he shall be appointed, and until his successor shall be elected and qualified. [*1881 AJR-16; 1882 SJR-20; 1882 c. 290*]

County officers. SECTION 4. [*Original form*] Sheriffs, coroners, registers of deeds and district attorneys shall be chosen by the electors of the respective counties, once in every two years, and as often as vacancies shall happen; sheriffs shall hold no other office, and be ineligible for two years next succeeding the termination of their offices. They may be required by law, to renew their security from time to time; and in default of giving such new security, their offices shall be deemed vacant. But the county shall never be made responsible for the acts of the sheriff. The governor may remove any officer in this section mentioned, giving to such officer a copy of the charges against him, and an opportunity of being heard in his defence.

Article VII.
Judiciary

Impeachment; trial. SECTION 1. [*As amended November 1932*] The court for the trial of impeachments shall be composed of the senate. The assembly shall have the power of impeaching all civil officers of this state for corrupt conduct in office, or for crimes and misdemeanors; but a majority of all the members elected shall concur in an impeachment. On the trial of an impeachment against the governor, the lieutenant governor shall not act as a member of the court. No judicial officer shall exercise his office, after he shall have been impeached, until his acquittal. Before the trial of an impeachment the members of the court shall take an oath or affirmation truly and impartially to try the impeachment according to evidence; and no person shall be convicted without the concurrence of two-thirds of the members present. Judgment in cases of impeachment shall not extend further than to removal from office, or removal from office and disqualification to hold any office of honor, profit or trust under the state; but the party impeached shall be liable to indictment, trial and punishment according to law. [*1929 SJR-103; 1931 SJR-8*]

Impeachments. SECTION 1. [*Original form*] The court for the trial of impeachments shall be composed of the senate. The house of representatives shall have the power of impeaching all civil officers of this state, for corrupt conduct in office, or for crimes and misdemeanors; but a majority of all the members elected shall concur in an impeachment. On the trial of an impeachment against the governor, the lieutenant governor shall not act as a member of the court. No judicial officer shall exercise his office, after he shall have been impeached, until his acquittal. Before the trial of an impeachment, the members of the court shall take an oath or affirmation, truly and impartially to try the impeachment according to evidence; and no person shall be convicted without the concurrence of two-thirds of the members present. Judgment in cases of impeachment shall not extend further than to removal from office, or removal from office and disqualification to hold any office of honor, profit or trust under the state; but the party impeached shall be liable to indictment, trial and punishment according to law.

Court system. SECTION 2. [*As amended April 1977*] The judicial power of this state shall be vested in a unified court system consisting of one supreme court, a court of appeals, a circuit court, such trial courts of general uniform statewide jurisdiction as the legislature may create by law, and a municipal court if authorized by the legislature under section 14. [*1975 AJR-11; 1977 SJR-9*]

Judicial power, where vested. SECTION 2. [*As amended April 1966*] The judicial power of this state, both as to matters of law and equity, shall be vested in a supreme court, circuit courts, and courts of probate. The legislature may also vest such jurisdiction as shall be deemed necessary in municipal courts, and may authorize the establishment of inferior courts in the several counties, cities, villages or towns, with limited civil and criminal jurisdiction. Provided, that the jurisdiction which may be vested in municipal courts shall not exceed in their respective municipalities that of circuit courts in their respective circuits as prescribed in this constitution; and that the legislature shall provide as well for the election of judges of the municipal courts as of the judges of inferior courts, by the qualified electors of the respective jurisdictions. The term of office of the judges of the said municipal and inferior courts shall not be longer than that of the judges of the circuit courts. [*1963 SJR-32; 1965 SJR-26*]

Judicial power, where vested. SECTION 2. [*Original form*] The judicial power of this state, both as to matters of law and equity, shall be vested in a supreme court, circuit courts, courts of probate, and in justices of the peace. The legislature may also vest such jurisdiction as shall be deemed necessary in municipal courts, and shall have power to establish inferior courts in the several counties, with limited civil and criminal jurisdiction. Provided, that the jurisdiction which may be vested in municipal courts shall not exceed in their respective municipalities that of circuit courts in their respective circuits as prescribed in this constitution; and that the legislature shall provide as well for the election of judges of the municipal courts as of the judges of inferior courts, by the qualified electors of the respective jurisdictions. The term of office of the judges of the said municipal and inferior courts shall not be longer than that of the judges of the circuit courts.

Supreme court: jurisdiction. SECTION 3. [*As amended April 1977*] (1) The supreme court shall have superintending and administrative authority over all courts.

(2) The supreme court has appellate jurisdiction over all courts and may hear original actions and proceedings. The supreme court may issue all writs necessary in aid of its jurisdiction.

(3) The supreme court may review judgments and orders of the court of appeals, may remove cases from the court of appeals and may accept cases on certification by the court of appeals. [*1975 AJR-11; 1977 SJR-9*]

Supreme court, jurisdiction. SECTION 3. [*Original form*] The supreme court, except in cases otherwise provided in this constitution, shall have appellate jurisdiction only, which shall be coextensive with the state; but in no case removed to the supreme court shall a trial by jury be allowed. The supreme court shall have a general superintending control over all inferior courts; it shall have power to issue writs of habeas corpus, mandamus, injunction, quo warranto, certiorari, and other original and remedial writs, and to hear and determine the same.

Supreme court: election, chief justice, court system administration. SECTION 4. [*As amended April 1977; April 2015*] (1) The supreme court shall have 7 members who shall be known as justices of the supreme court. Justices shall be elected for 10-year terms of office commencing with the August 1 next succeeding the election. Only one justice may be elected in any year. Any 4 justices shall constitute a quorum for the conduct of the court's business.

(2) The chief justice of the supreme court shall be elected for a term of 2 years by a majority of the justices then serving on the court. The justice so designated as chief justice may, irrevocably, decline to serve as chief justice or resign as chief justice but continue to serve as a justice of the supreme court. [*2013 SJR 57; 2015 SJR-2*]

(3) The chief justice of the supreme court shall be the administrative head of the judicial system and shall exercise this administrative authority pursuant to procedures adopted by the supreme court. The chief justice may assign any judge of a court of record to aid in the proper disposition of judicial business in any court of record except the supreme court. [*1975 AJR-11; 1977 SJR-9*]

Supreme court: election, chief justice, court system administration. SECTION 4. [*As amended April 1977*] (2) The justice having been longest a continuous member of said court, or in case 2 or more such justices shall have served for the same length of time, the justice whose term first expires, shall be the chief justice. The justice so designated as chief justice may, irrevocably, decline to serve as chief justice or resign as chief justice but continue to serve as a justice of the supreme court.

Supreme court justices; term; election; quorum. SECTION 1 [4]. [*As amended April 1903*] The chief justice and associate justices of the supreme court shall be severally known as the justices of said court, with the same terms of office of ten years respectively as now provided. The supreme court shall consist of seven justices, any four of whom shall be a quorum, to be elected as now provided, not more than one each year. The justice having been longest a continuous member of said court, or in case two or more such senior justices shall have served for the same length of time, then the one whose commission first expires

shall be ex officio, the chief justice. [*1901 AJR-33; 1903 AJR-5; 1903 c. 10*]

Supreme court, how constituted. SECTION 1 [4]. [*As amended April 1889*] The chief justice and associate justices of the supreme court shall be severally known as justices of said court with the same terms of office, respectively, as now provided. The supreme court shall consist of five justices (any three of whom shall be a quorum), to be elected as now provided. The justice having been longest a continuous member of the court (or in case two or more of such senior justices having served for the same length of time, then the one whose commission first expires), shall be ex officio the chief justice. [*1887 SJR-19; 1889 AJR-7; 1889 c. 22*]

Supreme court, how constituted. SECTION 4. [*As amended November 1877*] The supreme court shall consist of one chief justice and four associate justices, to be elected by the qualified electors of the state. The legislature shall at its first session after the adoption of this amendment provide by law for the election of two associate justices of said court to hold their offices respectively for terms ending two and four years respectively after the end of the term of the justice of the said court, then last to expire. And thereafter the chief justice and associate justices of the said court shall be elected and hold their offices respectively for the term of ten years. [*1876 SJR-16; 1877 SJR-2; 1877 c. 48*]

Supreme court, how constituted. SECTION 4. [*Original form*] For the term of five years, and thereafter until the legislature shall otherwise provide, the judges of the several circuit courts, shall be judges of the supreme court, four of whom shall constitute a quorum, and the concurrence of a majority of the judges present shall be necessary to a decision. The legislature shall have power, if they should think it expedient and necessary to provide by law, for the organization of a separate supreme court, with the

jurisdiction and powers prescribed in this constitution, to consist of one chief justice, and two associate justices, to be elected by the qualified electors of the state, at such time and in such manner as the legislature may provide. The separate supreme court when so organized, shall not be changed or discontinued by the legislature; the judges thereof shall be so classified that but one of them shall go out of office at the same time; and their term of office shall be the same as is provided for the judges of the circuit court. And whenever the legislature may consider it necessary to establish a separate supreme court, they shall have power to reduce the number of circuit court judges to four, and subdivide the judicial circuits, but no such subdivision or reduction shall take effect until after the expiration of the term of some one of said judges, or till a vacancy occur by some other means.

SECTION 5. [*Repealed. 1975 AJR-11; 1977 SJR-9; vote April 1977*]

Judicial circuits. SECTION 5. [*Original form*] The state shall be divided into five judicial circuits, to be composed as follows: The first circuit shall comprise the counties of Racine, Walworth, Rock and Green; the second circuit, the counties of Milwaukee, Waukesha, Jefferson and Dane; the third circuit, the counties of Washington, Dodge, Columbia, Marquette, Sauk and Portage; the fourth circuit, the counties of Brown, Manitowoc, Sheboygan, Fond

du Lac, Winnebago and Calumet; and the fifth circuit shall comprise the counties of Iowa, LaFayette, Grant, Crawford and St. Croix; and the county of Richland shall be attached to Iowa, the county of Chippewa to the county of Crawford, and the county of La Pointe to the county of St. Croix, for judicial purposes, until otherwise provided by the legislature.

Court of appeals. SECTION 5. [*Created April 1977*] (1) The legislature shall by law combine the judicial circuits of the state into one or more districts for the court of appeals and shall designate in each district the locations where the appeals court shall sit for the convenience of litigants.

(2) For each district of the appeals court there shall be chosen by the qualified electors of the district one or more appeals judges as prescribed by law, who shall sit as prescribed by law. Appeals judges shall be elected for 6-year terms and shall reside in the district from which elected. No alteration of district or circuit boundaries shall have the effect of removing an appeals judge from office during the judge's term. In case of an increase in the number of appeals judges, the first judge or judges shall be elected for full terms unless the legislature prescribes a shorter initial term for staggering of terms.

(3) The appeals court shall have such appellate jurisdiction in the district, including jurisdiction to review administrative proceedings, as the legislature may provide by law, but shall have no original jurisdiction other than by prerogative writ. The appeals court may issue all writs necessary in aid of its jurisdiction and shall have supervisory authority over all actions and proceedings in the courts in the district. [*1975 AJR-11; 1977 SJR-9*]

Circuit court: boundaries. SECTION 6. [*As amended April 1977*] The legislature shall prescribe by law the number of judicial circuits, making them as compact and convenient as practicable, and bounding them by county lines. No alteration of circuit boundaries shall have the effect of removing a circuit judge from office during the judge's term. In case of an increase of circuits, the first judge or judges shall be elected. [*1975 AJR-11; 1977 SJR-9*]

Alteration of circuits. SECTION 6. [*Original form*] The legislature may alter the limits or increase the number of circuits, making them as compact and convenient as practicable, and bounding them by county lines; but no such alteration or increase shall have the effect to remove

a judge from office. In case of an increase of circuits, the judge or judges shall be elected as provided in this constitution and receive a salary of not less than that herein provided for judges of the circuit court.

Circuit court: election. SECTION 7. [*As amended April 1977*] For each circuit there shall be chosen by the qualified electors thereof one or more circuit judges as prescribed by law. Circuit judges shall be elected for 6-year terms and shall reside in the circuit from which elected. [*1975 AJR-11; 1977 SJR-9*]

Circuit judges; election, eligibility, term, salary. SECTION 7. [*As amended November 1924*] For each circuit there shall be chosen by the qualified electors thereof one circuit judge, except that in any circuit in which there is a county that had a population in excess of eighty-five thousand, according to the last state or United States census, the legislature may, from time to time, authorize additional circuit judges to be chosen. Every circuit judge shall reside in the circuit from which he is elected, and shall hold his office for such term and receive such compensation as the legislature shall prescribe. [*1921 SJR-24; 1923 SJR-

27; 1923 c. 408*]

Circuit judges, election. SECTION 7. [*As amended April 1897*] For each circuit there shall be chosen by the qualified electors thereof, one circuit judge, except that in any circuit composed of one county only, which county shall contain a population, according to the last state or United States census, of one hundred thousand inhabitants or over, the legislature may from time to time authorize additional circuit judges to be chosen. Every circuit judge shall reside in the circuit from which he is elected and shall hold his office for such term and receive such compensation as the legislature shall prescribe. [*1895 SJR-9; 1897 SJR-10; 1897 c. 69*]

Circuit judges, election. SECTION 7. [*Original form*] For each circuit there shall be a judge chosen by the qualified electors therein, who shall hold his office as is provided in this constitution, and until his successor shall be chosen and qualified; and after he shall have been elected, he shall reside in the circuit for which he was elected. One of said

judges shall be designated as chief justice in such manner as the legislature shall provide. And the legislature shall at its first session provide by law as well for the election of, as for classifying the judges of the circuit court to be elected under this constitution, in such manner that one of said judges shall go out of office in two years, one in three years, one in four years, one in five years and one in six years, and thereafter the judge elected to fill the office shall hold the same for six years.

Circuit court: jurisdiction. SECTION 8. [*As amended April 1977*] Except as otherwise provided by law, the circuit court shall have original jurisdiction in all matters civil and criminal within this state and such appellate jurisdiction in the circuit as the legislature may prescribe by law. The circuit court may issue all writs necessary in aid of its jurisdiction. [*1975 AJR-11;1977 SJR-9*]

Circuit court, jurisdiction. SECTION 8. [*Original form*] The circuit courts shall have original jurisdiction in all matters civil and criminal within this state, not excepted in this constitution, and not hereafter prohibited by law; and appellate jurisdiction from all inferior courts and tribunals, and a supervisory control over the same. They shall also

have the power to issue writs of habeas corpus, mandamus, injunction, quo warranto, certiorari, and all other writs necessary to carry into effect their orders, judgments and decrees, and give them a general control over inferior courts and jurisdictions.

Judicial elections, vacancies. SECTION 9. [*As amended April 1977*] When a vacancy occurs in the office of justice of the supreme court or judge of any court of record, the vacancy shall be filled by appointment by the governor, which shall continue until a successor is elected and qualified. There shall be no election for a justice or judge at the partisan general election for state or county officers, nor within 30 days either before or after such election. [*1975 AJR-11; 1977 SJR-9*]

Vacancies; judicial elections. SECTION 9. [*As amended April 1953*] When a vacancy shall happen in the office of judge of the supreme or circuit courts, such vacancy shall be filled by an appointment of the governor, which shall continue until a successor is elected and qualified; and a supreme court justice when so elected shall hold his office for a term of 10 years and a circuit judge when so elected shall hold his office for such term as the legislature prescribes for circuit judges elected under section seven of this article. There shall be no election for a judge or judges at any general election for state or county officers, nor

within 30 days either before or after such election. [*1951 SJR-3; 1953 SJR-5*]

Vacancies; judicial elections. SECTION 9. [*Original form*] When a vacancy shall happen in the office of judge of the supreme or circuit courts, such vacancy shall be filled by an appointment of the governor, which shall continue until a successor is elected and qualified; and when elected such successor shall hold his office the residue of the unexpired term. There shall be no election for a judge or judges at any general election for state or county officers, nor within thirty days either before or after such election.

Judges: eligibility to office. SECTION 10. [*As amended April 1977*] (1) No justice of the supreme court or judge of any court of record shall hold any other office of public trust, except a judicial office, during the term for which elected. No person shall be eligible to the office of judge who shall not, at the time of election or appointment, be a qualified elector within the jurisdiction for which chosen.

(2) Justices of the supreme court and judges of the courts of record shall receive such compensation as the legislature may authorize by law, but may not receive fees of office. [*1975 AJR-11; 1977 SJR-9*]

Compensation and qualifications of judges. SECTION 10. [*As amended November 1912*] Each of the judges of the supreme and circuit courts shall receive a salary, payable at such time as the legislature shall fix, of not less than one thousand five hundred dollars annually; they shall receive no fees of office, or other compensation than their salary; they shall hold no office of public trust, except a judicial office, during the term for which they are respectively elected, and all votes for either of them for any office, except a judicial office, given by the legislature or the people, shall be void. No person shall be eligible to the office of judge who shall not, at the time of his election, be a citizen of the United States and have attained the age of twenty-five years, and be a qualified elector within the jurisdiction for which he may be chosen. [*1909 AJR-36;*

1911 AJR-26; 1911 c. 665]

Compensation and qualifications of judges. SECTION 10. [*Original form*] Each of the judges of the supreme and circuit courts shall receive a salary, payable quarterly, of not less than one thousand five hundred dollars annually; they shall receive no fees of office, or other compensation than their salaries; they shall hold no office of public trust, except a judicial office, during the term for which they are respectively elected, and all votes for either of them for any office, except a judicial office, given by the legislature or the people, shall be void. No person shall be eligible to the office of judge, who shall not, at the time of his election, be a citizen of the United States, and have attained the age of twenty-five years, and be a qualified elector within the jurisdiction for which he may be chosen.

SECTION 11. [*Repealed. 1975 AJR-11; 1977 SJR-9; vote April 1977*]

Terms of courts; change of judges. SECTION 11. [*Original form*] The supreme court shall hold at least one term annually, at the seat of government of the state, at such time as shall be provided by law. And the legislature may provide for holding other terms and at other places when they may deem it necessary. A circuit court shall be held at

least twice in each year in each county of this state rganized for judicial purposes. The judges of the circuit court may hold courts for each other, and shall do so when required by law.

Disciplinary proceedings. Section 11. [*Created April 1977*] Each justice or judge shall be subject to reprimand, censure, suspension, removal for cause or for disability, by the supreme court pursuant to procedures established by the legislature by law. No justice or judge removed for cause shall be eligible for reappointment or temporary service. This section is alternative to, and cumulative with, the methods of removal provided in sections 1 and 13 of this article and section 12 of article XIII. [*1975 AJR-11; 1977 SJR-9*]

Clerks of circuit and supreme courts. Section 12. [*As amended April 2005*] (1) There shall be a clerk of circuit court chosen in each county organized for judicial purposes by the qualified electors thereof, who, except as provided in sub. (2), shall hold office for two years, subject to removal as provided by law.

(2) Beginning with the first general election at which the governor is elected which occurs after the ratification of this subsection, a clerk of circuit court shall be chosen by the electors of each county, for the term of 4 years, subject to removal as provided by law.

(3) In case of a vacancy, the judge of the circuit court may appoint a clerk until the vacancy is filled by an election.

(4) The clerk of circuit court shall give such security as the legislature requires by law.

(5) The supreme court shall appoint its own clerk, and may appoint a clerk of circuit court to be the clerk of the supreme court. [*2003 AJR-10; 2005 SJR-2*]

Clerks of circuit and supreme courts. Section 12. [*As amended November 1882*] There shall be a clerk of the circuit court chosen in each county organized for judicial purposes by the qualified electors thereof, who shall hold his office for two years, subject to removal as shall be provided by law; in case of a vacancy, the judge of the circuit court shall have power to appoint a clerk until the vacancy shall be filled by an election; the clerk thus elected or appointed shall give such security as the legislature may require. The supreme court shall appoint its own clerk, and a clerk of the circuit court may be appointed a clerk of the supreme court. [*1881 AJR-16; 1882 SJR-20; 1882 c. 290*]

Clerks of courts. Section 12. [*Original form*] There shall be a clerk of the circuit court chosen in each county organized for judicial purposes, by the qualified electors thereof, who shall hold his office for two years, subject to removal, as shall be provided by law. In case of a vacancy, the judge of the circuit court shall have the power to appoint a clerk until the vacancy shall be filled by an election. The clerk thus elected or appointed shall give such security as the legislature may require; and when elected shall hold his office for a full term. The supreme court shall appoint its own clerk, and the clerk of a circuit court may be appointed clerk of the supreme court.

Justices and judges: removal by address. Section 13. [*As amended April 1977*] Any justice or judge may be removed from office by address of both houses of the legislature, if two-thirds of all the members elected to each house concur therein, but no removal shall be made by virtue of this section unless the justice or judge complained of is served with a copy of the charges, as the ground of address, and has had an opportunity of being heard. On the question of removal, the ayes and noes shall be entered on the journals. [*1975 AJR-11; 1977 SJR-9*]

Removal of judges. Section 13. [*As amended April 1974*] Any judge of the supreme, circuit, county or municipal court may be removed from office by address of both houses of the legislature, if two-thirds of all the members elected to each house concur therein, but no removal shall be made by virtue of this section unless the judge complained of shall have been served with a copy of the charges against him, as the ground of address, and shall have had an opportunity of being heard in his defense. On the question of removal, the ayes and noes shall be entered on the journals. [*1971 AJR-31; 1973 AJR-55*]

Removal of judges. Section 13. [*Original form*] Any judge of the supreme or circuit court may be removed from office by address of both houses of the legislature, if two-thirds of all the members elected to each house concur therein, but no removal shall be made by virtue of this section unless the judge complained of shall have been served with a copy of the charges against him, as the ground of address, and shall have had an opportunity of being heard in his defense. On the question of removal, the ayes and noes shall be entered on the journals.

Municipal court. Section 14. [*As amended April 1977*] The legislature by law may authorize each city, village and town to establish a municipal court. All municipal courts shall have uniform jurisdiction limited to actions and proceedings arising under ordinances of the municipality in which established. Judges of municipal courts may receive such compensation as provided by the municipality in which established, but may not receive fees of office. [*1975 AJR-11; 1977 SJR-9*]

Judges of probate. Section 14. [*Original form*] There shall be chosen in each county, by the qualified electors thereof, a judge of probate, who shall hold his office for two years and until his successor shall be elected and qualified, and whose jurisdiction, powers and duties

shall be prescribed by law. Provided, however, that the legislature shall have power to abolish the office of judge of probate in any county, and to confer probate powers upon such inferior courts as may be established in said county.

Section 15. [*Repealed. 1963 SJR-32; 1965 SJR-26; vote April 1966*]

Justices of the peace. Section 15. [*As amended April 1945*] The electors of the several towns at their annual town meeting, and the electors of cities and villages at their charter elections except in cities of the first class, shall, in

such manner as the legislature may direct, elect justices of the peace, whose term of office shall be for 2 years and until their successors in office shall be elected and qualified. In case of an election to fill a vacancy occurring before the expiration of a full term, the justice elected shall hold for the residue of the unexpired term. Their number and classification shall be regulated by law. And the tenure of 2 years shall in no wise interfere with the classification in the first instance. The justices thus elected shall have such civil and criminal jurisdiction as shall be prescribed by law. [1943 SJR-9; 1945 SJR-6]

Justices of the peace. SECTION 15. [*Original form*] The electors of the several towns, at their annual town meeting, and the electors of cities and villages, at their charter elections, shall in such manner as the legislature may direct, elect justices of the peace, whose term of office shall be for two years, and until their successors in office shall be elected and qualified. In case of an election to fill a vacancy, occurring before the expiration of a full term, the justice elected shall hold for the residue of the unexpired term. Their number and classification shall be regulated by law. And the tenure of two years shall in no wise interfere with the classification in the first instance. The justices, thus elected, shall have such civil and criminal jurisdiction as shall be prescribed by law.

SECTION 16. [*Repealed. 1975 AJR-11; 1977 SJR-9; vote April 1977*]

Tribunals of conciliation. SECTION 16. [*Original form*] The legislature shall pass laws for the regulation of tribunals of conciliation, defining their powers and duties. Such tribunals may be established in and for any township, and shall have power to render judgment to be obligatory on the parties when they shall voluntarily submit their matter in difference to arbitration, and agree to abide the judgment or assent thereto in writing.

SECTION 17. [*Repealed. 1975 AJR-11; 1977 SJR-9; vote April 1977*]

Style of writs; indictments. SECTION 17. [*Original form*] The style of all writs and process shall be, "The state of Wisconsin;" all criminal prosecutions shall be carried on in the name and by the authority of the same, and all indictments shall conclude against the peace and dignity of the state.

SECTION 18. [*Repealed. 1975 AJR-11; 1977 SJR-9; vote April 1977*]

Suit tax. SECTION 18. [*Original form*] The legislature shall impose a tax on all civil suits commenced or prosecuted in the municipal, inferior or circuit courts, which shall constitute a fund to be applied toward the payment of the salary of judges.

SECTION 19. [*Repealed. 1975 AJR-11; 1977 SJR-9; vote April 1977*]

Testimony in equity suits; master in chancery. SECTION 19. [*Original form*] The testimony in causes in equity shall be taken in like manner as in cases at law, and the office of master in chancery is hereby prohibited.

SECTION 20. [*Repealed. 1975 AJR-11; 1977 SJR-9; vote April 1977*] See Art. 1, sec. 21.

Rights of suitors. SECTION 20. [*Original form*] Any suitor, in any court of this state, shall have the right to prosecute or defend his suit either in his own proper person, or by an attorney or agent of his choice.

SECTION 21. [*Repealed. 1975 AJR-11; 1977 SJR-9; vote April 1977*] See Art. IV, sec. 17.

Publication of laws and decisions. SECTION 21. [*Original form*] The legislature shall provide by law for the speedy publication of all statute laws, and of such judicial decisions, made within the state, as may be deemed expedient. And no general law shall be in force until published.

SECTION 22. [*Repealed. 1975 AJR-11; 1977 SJR-9; vote April 1977*]

Commissioners to revise code of practice. SECTION 22. [*Original form*] The legislature, at its first session after the adoption of this constitution, shall provide for the appointment of three commissioners, whose duty it shall be to inquire into, revise and simplify the rules of practice, pleadings, forms and proceedings, and arrange a system adapted to the courts of record of this state, and report the same to the legislature, subject to their modification and adoption; and such commission shall terminate upon the rendering of the report, unless otherwise provided by law.

SECTION 23. [*Repealed. 1975 AJR-11; 1977 SJR-9; vote April 1977*]

Court commissioners. SECTION 23. [*Original form*] The legislature may provide for the appointment of one or more persons in each organized county, and may vest in such persons such judicial powers as shall be prescribed by law. Provided, that said power shall not exceed that of a judge of a circuit court at chambers.

Justices and judges: eligibility for office; retirement. SECTION 24. [*As amended April 1977*]

(1) To be eligible for the office of supreme court justice or judge of any court of record, a person must be an attorney licensed to practice law in this state and have been so licensed for 5 years immediately prior to election or appointment.

(2) Unless assigned temporary service under subsection (3), no person may serve as a supreme court justice or judge of a court of record beyond the July 31 following the date on which such person attains that age, of not less than 70 years, which the legislature shall prescribe by law.

(3) A person who has served as a supreme court justice or judge of a court of record may, as provided by law, serve as a judge of any court of record except the supreme court on a temporary basis if assigned by the chief justice of the supreme court. [*1975 AJR-11; 1977 SJR-9*]

Retirement and eligibility for office of justices and circuit judges. SECTION 24. [*As amended April 1968*] No person seventy years of age or over may take office as a supreme court justice or circuit judge. No person may take or hold such office unless he is licensed to practice law in this state and has been so licensed for five years immediately prior to his election or appointment. No supreme court justice or circuit judge may serve beyond the July 31 following the date on which he attains the age of seventy. A person who has served eight or more years as a supreme court justice or circuit judge may serve temporarily, on appointment by the chief justice of the supreme court or by any associate justice designated by the supreme court, as a judge of a circuit court, under such general laws as the legislature may enact. [*1965 SJR-36; 1967 SJR-96*]

Retirement and eligibility for office of justices and circuit judges. SECTION 24. [*Created April 1955*] No person seventy years of age or over may take office as a supreme court justice or circuit judge. No person may take or hold such office unless he is licensed to practice law in this state and has been so licensed for five years immediately prior to his election or appointment. No supreme court justice or circuit judge may serve beyond the end of the month in which he attains the age of seventy, but any such justice or judge may complete the term in which he is serving or to which he has been elected when this section takes effect. Any person retired under the provisions of this section may,

at the request of the chief justice of the supreme court, serve temporarily as a circuit judge and shall be compensated as the legislature provides. This section shall take effect on July first following the referendum at which it is approved. [*1953 SJR-6; 1955 SJR-10*]

Article VIII.

Finance

Rule of taxation uniform; income, privilege and occupation taxes. Section 1. [*As amended April 1974*] The rule of taxation shall be uniform but the legislature may empower cities, villages or towns to collect and return taxes on real estate located therein by optional methods. Taxes shall be levied upon such property with such classifications as to forests and minerals including or separate or severed from the land, as the legislature shall prescribe. Taxation of agricultural land and undeveloped land, both as defined by law, need not be uniform with the taxation of each other nor with the taxation of other real property. Taxation of merchants' stock-in-trade, manufacturers' materials and finished products, and livestock need not be uniform with the taxation of real property and other personal property, but the taxation of all such merchants' stock-in-trade, manufacturers' materials and finished products and livestock shall be uniform, except that the legislature may provide that the value thereof shall be determined on an average basis. Taxes may also be imposed on incomes, privileges and occupations, which taxes may be graduated and progressive, and reasonable exemptions may be provided. [*1971 AJR-2; 1973 AJR-1*]

Rule of taxation uniform; income, privilege and occupation taxes. Section 1. [*As amended April 1961*] The rule of taxation shall be uniform but the legislature may empower cities, villages or towns to collect and return taxes on real estate located therein by optional methods. Taxes shall be levied upon such property with such classifications as to forests and minerals including or separate or severed from the land, as the legislature shall prescribe. Taxation of merchants' stock-in-trade, manufacturers' materials and finished products, and livestock need not be uniform with the taxation of real property and other personal property, but the taxation of all such merchants' stock-in-trade, manufacturers' materials and finished products and livestock shall be uniform, except that the legislature may provide that the value thereof shall be determined on an average basis. Taxes may also be imposed on incomes; privileges and occupations, which taxes may be graduated and progressive, and reasonable exemptions may be provided. [*1959 AJR-120; 1961 SJR-34*]

Rule of taxation uniform; income, privilege and occupation taxes. Section 1. [*As amended April 1941*]. The rule of taxation shall be uniform but the legislature may empower cities, villages or towns to collect and return taxes on real estate located therein by optional methods. Taxes shall be levied upon such property with such classifications

as to forests and minerals including or separate or severed from the land, as the legislature shall prescribe. Taxes may also be imposed on incomes, privileges and occupations, which taxes may be graduated and progressive, and reasonable exemptions may be provided. [*1939 AJR-37; 1941 AJR-15*]

Rules of taxation; income taxes. Section 1. [*As amended April 1927*] The rule of taxation shall be uniform, and taxes shall be levied upon such property with such classifications as to forests and minerals, including or separate or severed from the land, as the legislature shall prescribe. Taxes may also be imposed on incomes, privileges and occupations, which taxes may be graduated and progressive, and reasonable exemptions may be provided. [*1925 AJR-51; 1927 AJR-3*]

Uniform rule of taxation; income tax. Section 1. [*As amended November 1908*] The rule of taxation shall be uniform, and taxes shall be levied upon such property as the legislature shall prescribe. Taxes may also be imposed on incomes, privileges and occupations, which taxes may be graduated and progressive, and reasonable exemptions may be provided. [*1905 AJR-12; 1907 SJR-19; 1907 c. 661*]

Uniform rule of taxation. Section 1. [*Original form*] The rule of taxation shall be uniform, and taxes shall be levied upon such property as the legislature shall prescribe.

Appropriations; limitation. Section 2. [*As amended November 1877*] No money shall be paid out of the treasury except in pursuance of an appropriation by law. No appropriation shall be made for the payment of any claim against the state except claims of the United States and judgments, unless filed within six years after the claim accrued. [*1876 SJR-14; 1877 SJR-5; 1877 c. 158*]

Appropriations. Section 2. [*Original form*] No money shall be paid out of the treasury, except in pursuance of an

appropriation by law.

Credit of state. Section 3. [*As amended April 1975*] Except as provided in s. 7 (2) (a), the credit of the state shall never be given, or loaned, in aid of any individual, association or corporation. [*1973 AJR-145; 1975 AJR-1*]

Credit of state. Section 3. [*Original form*] The credit of the state shall never be given, or loaned, in aid of any

individual, association or corporation.

Contracting state debts. Section 4. The state shall never contract any public debt except in the cases and manner herein provided.

Annual tax levy to equal expenses. Section 5. The legislature shall provide for an annual tax sufficient to defray the estimated expenses of the state for each year; and whenever the expenses of any year shall exceed the income, the legislature shall provide for levying a tax for the ensuing year, sufficient, with other sources of income, to pay the deficiency as well as the estimated expenses of such ensuing year.

Public debt for extraordinary expense; taxation. SECTION 6. For the purpose of defraying extraordinary expenditures the state may contract public debts (but such debts shall never in the aggregate exceed one hundred thousand dollars). Every such debt shall be authorized by law, for some purpose or purposes to be distinctly specified therein; and the vote of a majority of all the members elected to each house, to be taken by yeas and nays, shall be necessary to the passage of such law; and every such law shall provide for levying an annual tax sufficient to pay the annual interest of such debt and the principal within five years from the passage of such law, and shall specially appropriate the proceeds of such taxes to the payment of such principal and interest; and such appropriation shall not be repealed, nor the taxes be postponed or diminished, until the principal and interest of such debt shall have been wholly paid.

Public debt for public defense; bonding for public purposes. SECTION 7. [*As amended April 1992*] (1) The legislature may also borrow money to repel invasion, suppress insurrection, or defend the state in time of war; but the money thus raised shall be applied exclusively to the object for which the loan was authorized, or to the repayment of the debt thereby created.

(2) Any other provision of this constitution to the contrary notwithstanding:

(a) The state may contract public debt and pledges to the payment thereof its full faith, credit and taxing power:

1. To acquire, construct, develop, extend, enlarge or improve land, waters, property, highways, railways, buildings, equipment or facilities for public purposes.

2. To make funds available for veterans' housing loans.

(b) The aggregate public debt contracted by the state in any calendar year pursuant to paragraph (a) shall not exceed an amount equal to the lesser of:

1. Three-fourths of one per centum of the aggregate value of all taxable property in the state; or

2. Five per centum of the aggregate value of all taxable property in the state less the sum of: a. the aggregate public debt of the state contracted pursuant to this section outstanding as of January 1 of such calendar year after subtracting therefrom the amount of sinking funds on hand on January 1 of such calendar year which are applicable exclusively to repayment of such outstanding public debt and, b. the outstanding indebtedness as of January 1 of such calendar year of any entity of the type described in paragraph (d) to the extent that such indebtedness is supported by or payable from payments out of the treasury of the state.

(c) The state may contract public debt, without limit, to fund or refund the whole or any part of any public debt contracted pursuant to paragraph (a), including any premium payable with respect thereto and any interest to accrue thereon, or to fund or refund the whole or any part of any indebtedness incurred prior to January 1, 1972, by any entity of the type described in paragraph (d), including any premium payable with respect thereto and any interest to accrue thereon.

(d) No money shall be paid out of the treasury, with respect to any lease, sublease or other agreement entered into after January 1, 1971, to the Wisconsin State Agencies Building Corporation, Wisconsin State Colleges Building Corporation, Wisconsin State Public Building Corporation, Wisconsin University Building Corporation or any similar entity existing or operating for similar purposes pursuant to which such nonprofit corporation or such other entity undertakes to finance or provide a facility for use or occupancy by the state or an agency, department or instrumentality thereof.

(e) The legislature shall prescribe all matters relating to the contracting of public debt pursuant to paragraph (a), including: the public purposes for which public debt may be contracted; by vote of a majority of the members elected to each of the 2 houses of the legislature, the amount of public debt which may be contracted for any class of such purposes; the public debt or other indebtedness which may be funded or refunded; the kinds of notes, bonds or other evidence of public debt which may be issued by the state; and the manner in which the aggregate value of all taxable property in the state shall be determined.

(f) The full faith, credit and taxing power of the state are pledged to the payment of all public debt created on behalf of the state pursuant to this section and the legislature shall provide by appropriation for the payment of the interest upon and instalments of principal of all such public debt as the same falls due, but, in any event, suit may be brought against the state to compel such payment.

(g) At any time after January 1, 1972, by vote of a majority of the members elected to each of the 2 houses of the legislature, the legislature may declare that an emergency exists and submit to the people a proposal to authorize the state to contract a specific amount of public debt for a purpose specified in such proposal, without regard to the limit provided in paragraph (b). Any such authorization shall be effective if approved by a majority of the electors voting thereon. Public debt contracted pursuant to such authorization shall thereafter be deemed to have been contracted pursuant to paragraph (a), but neither such public debt nor any public debt contracted to fund or refund such public debt shall be considered in computing the debt limit provided in paragraph (b). Not more than one such authorization shall be thus made in any 2-year period. [*1989 SJR-76; 1991 SJR-30*]

Public debt for public defense; bonding for public purposes. SECTION 7. [*As amended April 1975*] (1) The legislature may also borrow money to repel invasion, suppress insurrection, or defend the state in time of war; but the money thus raised shall be applied exclusively to the object for which the loan was authorized, or to the repayment of the debt thereby created.

(2) Any other provision of this constitution to the contrary notwithstanding:

(a) The state may contract public debt and pledges to the payment thereof its full faith, credit and taxing power:

1. To acquire, construct, develop, extend, enlarge or improve land, waters, property, highways, buildings, equipment or facilities for public purposes.

2. To make funds available for veterans' housing loans.

(b) The aggregate public debt contracted by the state in any calendar year pursuant to paragraph (a) shall not exceed an amount equal to the lesser of:

1. Three-fourths of one per centum of the aggregate value of all taxable property in the state; or

2. Five per centum of the aggregate value of all taxable property in the state less the sum of: a. the aggregate public debt of the state contracted pursuant to this section outstanding as of January 1 of such calendar year after subtracting therefrom the amount of sinking funds on hand on January 1 of such calendar year which are applicable exclusively to repayment of such outstanding public debt and, b. the outstanding indebtedness as of January 1 of such calendar year of any entity of the type described in paragraph (d) to the extent that such indebtedness is supported by or payable from payments out of the treasury of the state.

(c) The state may contract public debt, without limit, to fund or refund the whole or any part of any public debt contracted pursuant to paragraph (a), including any premium payable with respect thereto and any interest to accrue thereon, or to fund or refund the whole or any part of any indebtedness incurred prior to January 1, 1972, by any entity of the type described in paragraph (d), including any premium payable with respect thereto and any interest to accrue thereon.

(d) No money shall be paid out of the treasury, with respect to any lease, sublease or other agreement entered into after January 1, 1971, to the Wisconsin State Agencies Building Corporation, Wisconsin State Colleges Building Corporation, Wisconsin State Public Building Corporation, Wisconsin University Building Corporation or any similar entity existing or operating for similar purposes pursuant to which such nonprofit corporation or such other entity undertakes to finance or provide a facility for use or occupancy by the state or an agency, department or instrumentality thereof.

(e) The legislature shall prescribe all matters relating to the contracting of public debt pursuant to paragraph (a), including: the public purposes for which public debt may be contracted; by vote of a majority of the members elected

to each of the 2 houses of the legislature, the amount of public debt which may be contracted for any class of such purposes; the public debt or other indebtedness which may be funded or refunded; the kinds of notes, bonds or other evidence of public debt which may be issued by the state; and the manner in which the aggregate value of all taxable property in the state shall be determined.

(f) The full faith, credit and taxing power of the state are pledged to the payment of all public debt created on behalf of the state pursuant to this section and the legislature shall provide by appropriation for the payment of the interest upon and instalments of principal of all such public debt as the same falls due, but, in any event, suit may be brought against the state to compel such payment.

(g) At any time after January 1, 1972, by vote of a majority of the members elected to each of the 2 houses of the legislature, the legislature may declare that an emergency exists and submit to the people a proposal to authorize the state to contract a specific amount of public debt for a purpose specified in such proposal, without regard to the limit provided in paragraph (b). Any such authorization shall be effective if approved by a majority of the electors voting thereon. Public debt contracted pursuant to such authorization shall thereafter be deemed to have been contracted pursuant to paragraph (a), but neither such public debt nor any public debt contracted to fund or refund such public debt shall be considered in computing the debt limit provided in paragraph (b). Not more than one such authorization shall be thus made in any 2-year period. [*1973 AJR-145; 1975 AJR-1*]

Public debt for public defense; bonding for public purposes. SECTION 7. [*As amended April 1969*] (1) The legislature may also borrow money to repel invasion, suppress insurrection, or defend the state in time of war; but the money thus raised shall be applied exclusively to the object for which the loan was authorized, or to the repayment of the debt thereby created.

(2) Any other provision of this constitution to the contrary notwithstanding:

(a) The state may contract public debt and pledges to the payment thereof its full faith, credit and taxing power to acquire, construct, develop, extend, enlarge or improve land, waters, property, highways, buildings, equipment or facilities for public purposes.

(b) The aggregate public debt contracted by the state in any calendar year pursuant to paragraph (a) shall not exceed an amount equal to the lesser of:

1. Three-fourths of one per centum of the aggregate value of all taxable property in the state; or

2. Five per centum of the aggregate value of all taxable property in the state less the sum of: a. the aggregate public debt of the state contracted pursuant to this section outstanding as of January 1 of such calendar year after subtracting therefrom the amount of sinking funds on hand on January 1 of such calendar year which are applicable exclusively to repayment of such outstanding public debt and, b. the outstanding indebtedness as of January

l of such calendar year of any entity of the type described in paragraph (d) to the extent that such indebtedness is supported by or payable from payments out of the treasury of the state.

(c) The state may contract public debt, without limit, to fund or refund the whole or any part of any public debt contracted pursuant to paragraph (a), including any premium payable with respect thereto and any interest to accrue thereon, or to fund or refund the whole or any part of any indebtedness incurred prior to January 1, 1972, by any entity of the type described in paragraph (d), including any premium payable with respect thereto and any interest to accrue thereon.

(d) No money shall be paid out of the treasury, with respect to any lease, sublease or other agreement entered into after January 1, 1971, to the Wisconsin State Agencies Building Corporation, Wisconsin State Colleges Building Corporation, Wisconsin State Public Building Corporation, Wisconsin University Building Corporation or any similar entity existing or operating for similar purposes pursuant to which such nonprofit corporation or such other entity undertakes to finance or provide a facility for use or occupancy by the state or an agency, department or instrumentality thereof.

(e) The legislature shall prescribe all matters relating to the contracting of public debt pursuant to paragraph (a), including: the public purposes for which public debt may be contracted; by vote of a majority of the members elected to each of the 2 houses of the legislature, the amount of public debt which may be contracted for any class of such purposes; the public debt or other indebtedness which may be funded or refunded; the kinds of notes, bonds or other evidence of public debt which may be issued by the state; and the manner in which the aggregate value of all taxable property in the state shall be determined.

(f) The full faith, credit and taxing power of the state are pledged to the payment of all public debt created on behalf of the state pursuant to this section and the legislature shall provide by appropriation for the payment of the interest upon and instalments of principal of all such public debt as the same falls due, but, in any event, suit may be brought against the state to compel such payment.

(g) At any time after January 1, 1972, by vote of a majority of the members elected to each of the 2 houses of the legislature, the legislature may declare that an emergency exists and submit to the people a proposal to authorize the state to contract a specific amount of public debt for a purpose specified in such proposal, without regard to the limit provided in paragraph (b). Any such authorization shall be effective if approved by a majority of the electors voting thereon. Public debt contracted pursuant to such authorization shall thereafter be deemed to have been contracted pursuant to paragraph (a), but neither such public debt nor any public debt contracted to fund or refund such public debt shall be considered in computing the debt limit provided in paragraph (b). Not more than one such authorization shall be thus made in any 2-year period. [*1967 AJR-1; 1969 AJR-1*]

Public debt for public defense. SECTION 7. [*Original form*] The legislature may also borrow money to repel invasion, suppress insurrection, or defend the state in time of war; but the money thus raised shall be applied exclusively to the object for which the loan was authorized, or to the repayment of the debt thereby created.

Vote on fiscal bills; quorum. SECTION 8. On the passage in either house of the legislature of any law which imposes, continues or renews a tax, or creates a debt or charge, or makes, continues or renews an appropriation of public or trust money, or releases, discharges or commutes a claim or demand of the state, the question shall be taken by yeas and nays, which shall be duly entered on the journal; and three-fifths of all the members elected to such house shall in all such cases be required to constitute a quorum therein.

Evidences of public debt. SECTION 9. No scrip, certificate, or other evidence of state debt, whatsoever, shall be issued, except for such debts as are authorized by the sixth and seventh sections of this article.

Internal improvements. SECTION 10. [*As amended April 1992*] Except as further provided in this section, the state may never contract any debt for works of internal improvement, or be a party in carrying on such works.

(1) Whenever grants of land or other property shall have been made to the state, especially dedicated by the grant to particular works of internal improvement, the state may carry on such particular works and shall devote thereto the avails of such grants, and may pledge or appropriate the revenues derived from such works in aid of their completion.

(2) The state may appropriate money in the treasury or to be thereafter raised by taxation for:

(a) The construction or improvement of public highways.

(b) The development, improvement and construction of airports or other aeronautical projects.

(c) The acquisition, improvement or construction of veterans' housing.

(d) The improvement of port facilities.

(e) The acquisition, development, improvement or construction of railways and other railroad facilities.

(3) The state may appropriate moneys for the purpose of acquiring, preserving and developing the forests of the state. Of the moneys appropriated under the authority of this subsection in any one year an amount not to exceed two-tenths of one mill of the taxable property of the state as determined by the last preceding state assessment may be raised by a tax on property. [*1989 SJR-76; 1991 SJR-30*]

Internal improvements. SECTION 10. [*As amended April 1968*] The state shall never contract any debt for works of internal improvement, or be a party in carrying on such works; but whenever grants of land or other property shall have been made to the state, especially dedicated by the grant to particular works of internal improvement, the state may carry on such particular works and shall devote thereto the avails of such grants, and may pledge or appropriate the revenues derived from such works in aid of their completion. Provided, that the state may appropriate money in the treasury or to be thereafter raised by taxation for the construction or improvement of public highways or the development, improvement and construction of airports or other aeronautical projects or the acquisition, improvement or construction of veterans' housing or the improvement of port facilities. Provided, that the state may appropriate moneys for the purpose of acquiring, preserving and developing the forests of the state; but of the moneys appropriated under the authority of this section in any one year an amount not to exceed two-tenths of one mill of the taxable property of the state as determined by the last preceding state assessment may be raised by a tax on property. [*1965 SJR-28; 1967 SJR-18*]

Internal improvements. SECTION 10. [*As amended April 1960*] The state shall never contract any debt for works of internal improvement, or be a party in carrying on such works; but whenever grants of land or other property shall have been made to the state, especially dedicated by the grant to particular works of internal improvement, the state may carry on such particular works and shall devote thereto the avails of such grants, and may pledge or appropriate the revenues derived from such works in aid of their completion. Provided, that the state may appropriate money in the treasury or to be thereafter raised by taxation for the construction or improvement of public highways or the development, improvement and construction of airports or other aeronautical projects or the acquisition, improvement or construction of veterans' housing or the improvement of port facilities. Provided, that the state may appropriate moneys for the purpose of acquiring, preserving and developing the forests of the state; but there shall not be appropriated under the authority of this section in any one year an amount to exceed two-tenths of one mill of the taxable property of the state as determined by the last preceding state assessment. [*1957 SJR-39; 1959 SJR-20*]

Internal improvements. SECTION 10. [*As amended April 1949*] The state shall never contract any debt for works of internal improvement, or be a party in carrying on such works; but whenever grants of land or other property shall have been made to the state, especially dedicated by the grant to particular works of internal improvement, the state may carry on such particular works and shall devote thereto the avails of such grants, and may pledge or appropriate the revenues derived from such works in aid of their completion. Provided, that the state may appropriate money in the treasury or to be thereafter raised by taxation for the construction or improvement of public highways or the development, improvement and construction of airports or other aeronautical projects or the acquisition, improvement or construction of veterans' housing. Provided, that the state may appropriate moneys for the purpose of acquiring, preserving and developing the forests of the state; but there shall not be appropriated under the authority of this section in any one year an amount to exceed two-tenths of one mill of the taxable property of the state as determined by the last preceding state assessment. [*1948 Spec.Sess. SJR-2; 1949 SJR-5*]

Internal improvements. SECTION 10. [*As amended April 1945*] The state shall never contract any debt for

works of internal improvement, or be a party in carrying on such works; but whenever grants of land or other property shall have been made to the state, especially dedicated by the grant to particular works of internal improvement, the state may carry on such particular works, and shall devote thereto the avails of such grants, and may pledge or appropriate the revenues derived from such works in aid of their completion. Provided, that the state may appropriate money in the treasury or to be thereafter raised by taxation for the construction or improvement of public highways or the development, improvement and construction of airports or other aeronautical projects. Provided, that the state may appropriate moneys for the purpose of acquiring, preserving and developing the forests of the state; but there shall not be appropriated under the authority of this section in any one year an amount to exceed two-tenths of one mill of the taxable property of the state as determined by the last preceding state assessment. [*1943 SJR-16; 1945 SJR-7*]

Internal improvements. SECTION 10. [*As amended November 1924*] The state shall never contract any debt for works of internal improvement, or be a party in carrying on such works; but whenever grants of land or other property shall have been made to the state, especially dedicated by the grant to particular works of internal improvement, the state may carry on such particular works, and shall devote thereto the avails of such grants, and may pledge or appropriate the revenues derived from such works in aid of their completion. Provided, that the state may appropriate money in the treasury or to be thereafter raised by taxation for the construction or improvement of public highways. Provided, that the state may appropriate moneys for the purpose of acquiring, preserving and developing the forests of the state; but there shall not be appropriated under the authority of this section in any one year an amount to exceed two-tenths of one mill of the taxable property of the state as determined by the last preceding state assessment. [*1921 SJR-30; 1923 AJR-70; 1923 c. 289*]

Water power and forests. SECTION 10. [*Approved by voters November 1910*] An amendment to Art. VIII, sec. 10, authorizing a state property tax of two-tenths of one mill to finance appropriations for acquisition and development of water power and forests was approved by 1907 SJR-43. There was no "second consideration" resolution but 1909 SB\553 enacted the proposal into law as Chap. 514, Laws of 1909. The procedure was declared invalid by the Supreme Court in *State ex rel. Owen v. Donald*, 160 W 21, 151 NW 331.

Public highways. [*As amended November 1908, a new sentence was added at the end of the section*] Provided, that the state may appropriate money in the treasury or to be thereafter raised by taxation for the construction or improvement of public highways. [*1905 SJR-14; 1907 SJR-22; 1907 c. 238*]

Internal improvements. SECTION 10. [*Original form*] The state shall never contract any debt for works of internal improvement, or be a party in carrying on such works, but whenever grants of land or other property shall have been made to the state, especially dedicated by the grant to particular works of internal improvements, the state may carry on such particular works, and shall devote thereto the avails of such grants, and may pledge or appropriate the revenues derived from such works in aid of their completion.

Transportation fund. SECTION 11 [*Created November 2014*] All funds collected by the state from any taxes or fees levied or imposed for the licensing of motor vehicle operators, for the titling, licensing, or registration of motor vehicles, for motor vehicle fuel, or for the use of roadways, highways, or bridges, and from taxes and fees levied or imposed for aircraft, airline property, or aviation fuel or for railroads or railroad property shall be deposited only into the transportation fund or with a trustee for the benefit of the department of transportation or the holders of transportation-related revenue bonds, except for collections from taxes or fees in existence on December 31, 2010, that were not being deposited in the transportation fund on that date. None of the funds collected or received by the state from any source and deposited into the transportation fund shall be lapsed, further transferred, or appropriated to any program that is not directly administered by the department of transportation in furtherance of the department's responsibility for the planning, promotion, and protection of all transportation systems in the state except for programs for which there was an appropriation from the transportation fund on December 31, 2010. In this section, the term "motor vehicle" does not include any all-terrain vehicles, snowmobiles, or watercraft. [*2011 SJR-23; 2013 AJR-2*]

ARTICLE IX.
EMINENT DOMAIN AND PROPERTY OF THE STATE

Jurisdiction on rivers and lakes; navigable waters. SECTION 1. The state shall have concurrent jurisdiction on all rivers and lakes bordering on this state so far as such rivers or lakes shall form a common boundary to the state and any other state or territory now or hereafter to be formed, and bounded by the same; and the river Mississippi and the navigable waters leading into the Mississippi and St. Lawrence, and the carrying places between the same, shall be common highways and forever free, as well to the inhabitants of the state as to the citizens of the United States, without any tax, impost or duty therefor.

Territorial property. SECTION 2. The title to all lands and other property which have accrued to the territory of Wisconsin by grant, gift, purchase, forfeiture, escheat or otherwise shall vest in the state of Wisconsin.

Ultimate property in lands; escheats. SECTION 3. The people of the state, in their right of sovereignty, are declared to possess the ultimate property, in and to all lands within the jurisdiction of the state; and all lands the title to which shall fail from a defect of heirs shall revert or escheat to the people.

ARTICLE X.
EDUCATION

Superintendent of public instruction. SECTION 1. [*As amended November 1982*] The supervision of public instruction shall be vested in a state superintendent and such other officers as the legislature shall direct; and their qualifications, powers, duties and compensation shall be prescribed by law. The state superintendent shall be chosen by the qualified electors of the state at the same time and in the same manner as members of the supreme court, and shall hold office for 4 years from the succeeding first Monday in July. The term of office, time and manner of electing or appointing all other officers of supervision of public instruction shall be fixed by law. [*1979 AJR-76; 1981 AJR-35; submit: May'82 Spec.Sess. AJR-1*]

Superintendent of public instruction. SECTION 1. [*As amended November 1902*] The supervision of public instruction shall be vested in a state superintendent and such other officers as the legislature shall direct; and their qualifications, powers, duties and compensation shall be prescribed by law. The state superintendent shall be chosen by the qualified electors of the state at the same time and in the same manner as members of the supreme court, and shall hold his office for four years from the succeeding first Monday in July. The state superintendent chosen at the general election in November, 1902, shall hold and continue in his office until the first Monday in July, 1905, and his successor shall be chosen at the time of the judicial election in April, 1905. The term of office, time and manner of electing or appointing all other officers of supervision of public instruction shall be fixed by law. [*1899 SJR-21; 1901 SJR-24; 1901 c. 258*]

Superintendent of public instruction. SECTION 1. [*Original form*] The supervision of public instruction shall be vested in a state superintendent, and such other officers as the legislature shall direct. The state superintendent shall be chosen by the qualified electors of the state, in such manner as the legislature shall provide; his powers, duties and compensation shall be prescribed by law. Provided, that his compensation shall not exceed the sum of twelve hundred dollars annually.

School fund created; income applied. SECTION 2. [*As amended November 1982*] The proceeds of all lands that have been or hereafter may be granted by the United States to this state for educational purposes (except the lands heretofore granted for the purposes of a university) and all moneys and the clear proceeds of all property that may accrue to the state by forfeiture or escheat; and the clear proceeds of all fines collected in the several counties for any breach of the penal laws, and all moneys arising from any grant to the state where the purposes of such grant are not specified, and the 500,000 acres of land to which the state is entitled by the provisions of an act of congress, entitled "An act to appropriate the proceeds of the sales of the public lands and to grant pre-emption rights," approved September 4, 1841; and also the 5 percent of the net proceeds of the public lands to which the state shall become entitled on admission into the union (if congress shall consent to such appropriation of the 2 grants last mentioned) shall be set apart as a separate fund to be called "the school fund," the interest of which and all other revenues derived from the school lands shall be exclusively applied to the following objects, to wit:

(1) To the support and maintenance of common schools, in each school district, and the purchase of suitable libraries and apparatus therefor.

(2) The residue shall be appropriated to the support and maintenance of academies and normal schools, and suitable libraries and apparatus therefor. [*1979 AJR-76; 1981 AJR-35; submit: May '82 Spec.Sess. AJR-1*]

School fund created; income applied. SECTION 2. [*Original form*] The proceeds of all lands that have been or hereafter may be granted by the United States to this state for educational purposes (except the lands heretofore granted for the purpose of a university) and all moneys and the clear proceeds of all property that may accrue to the state by forfeiture or escheat, and all moneys which may be paid as an equivalent for exemption from military duty; and the clear proceeds of all fines collected in the several counties for any breach of the penal laws, and all moneys arising from any grant to the state where the purposes of such grant are not specified, and the five hundred thousand acres of land to which the state is entitled by the provisions of an act of congress, entitled "An act to appropriate the proceeds of the sales of the public lands and to grant pre-

emption rights," approved the fourth day of September, one thousand eight hundred and forty-one; and also the five per centum of the net proceeds of the public lands to which the state shall become entitled on her admission into the union (if congress shall consent to such appropriation of the two grants last mentioned) shall be set apart as a separate fund to be called "the school fund," the interest of which and all other revenues derived from the school lands shall be exclusively applied to the following objects, to wit:

1. To the support and maintenance of common schools, in each school district, and the purchase of suitable libraries and apparatus therefor.

2. The residue shall be appropriated to the support and maintenance of academies and normal schools, and suitable libraries and apparatus therefor.

District schools; tuition; sectarian instruction; released time. SECTION 3. [*As amended April 1972*] The legislature shall provide by law for the establishment of district schools, which shall be as nearly uniform as practicable; and such schools shall be free and without charge for tuition to all children between the ages of 4 and 20 years; and no sectarian instruction shall be allowed therein; but the legislature by law may, for the purpose of religious instruction outside the district schools, authorize the release of students during regular school hours. [*1969 AJR-41; 1971 AJR-17*]

District schools; tuition; sectarian instruction. SECTION 3. [*Original form*] The legislature shall provide by law for the establishment of district schools, which shall be as nearly uniform as practicable; and such schools

shall be free and without charge for tuition to all children between the ages of four and twenty years; and no sectarian instruction shall be allowed therein.

Annual school tax. SECTION 4. Each town and city shall be required to raise by tax, annually, for the support of common schools therein, a sum not less than one-half the amount received by such town or city respectively for school purposes from the income of the school fund.

Income of school fund. SECTION 5. Provision shall be made by law for the distribution of the income of the school fund among the several towns and cities of the state for the support of common schools therein, in some just proportion to the number of children and youth resident therein between the ages of four and twenty years, and no appropriation shall be made from the school fund to any city or town for the year in which said city or town shall fail to raise such tax; nor to any school district for the year in which a school shall not be maintained at least three months.

State university; support. SECTION 6. Provision shall be made by law for the establishment of a state university at or near the seat of state government, and for connecting with the same, from time to time, such colleges in different parts of the state as the interests of education may require. The proceeds of all lands that have been or may hereafter be granted by the United States to the state for the support of a university shall be and remain a perpetual fund to be called "the university fund," the interest of which shall be appropriated to the support of the state university, and no sectarian instruction shall be allowed in such university.

Commissioners of public lands. SECTION 7. The secretary of state, treasurer and attorney general, shall constitute a board of commissioners for the sale of the school and university lands and for the investment of the funds arising therefrom. Any two of said commissioners shall be a quorum for the transaction of all business pertaining to the duties of their office.

Sale of public lands. SECTION 8. Provision shall be made by law for the sale of all school and university lands after they shall have been appraised; and when any portion of such lands shall be sold and the purchase money shall not be paid at the time of the sale, the commissioners shall take security by mortgage upon the lands sold for the sum remaining unpaid, with seven per cent interest thereon, payable annually at the office of the treasurer. The commissioners shall be authorized to execute a good and sufficient conveyance to all purchasers of such lands, and to discharge any mortgages taken as security, when the sum due thereon shall have been paid. The commissioners shall have power to withhold from sale any portion of such lands when they shall deem it expedient, and shall invest all moneys arising from the sale of such lands, as well as all other university and school funds, in such manner as the legislature shall provide, and shall give such security for the faithful performance of their duties as may be required by law.

ARTICLE XI.
CORPORATIONS

Corporations; how formed. SECTION 1. [*As amended April 1981*] Corporations without banking powers or privileges may be formed under general laws, but shall not be created by special act, except for municipal purposes. All general laws or special acts enacted under the provisions of this section may be altered or repealed by the legislature at any time after their passage. [*1979 AJR-53; 1981 AJR-13*]

Corporations; how formed. SECTION 1. [*Original form*] Corporations without banking powers or privileges may be formed under general laws, but shall not be created by special act, except for municipal purposes, and in cases where, in the judgment of the legislature, the objects of the corporation cannot be attained under general laws. All general laws or special acts enacted under the provisions of this section may be altered or repealed by the legislature at any time after their passage.

Property taken by municipality. SECTION 2. [*As amended April 1961*] No municipal corporation shall take private property for public use, against the consent of the owner, without the necessity thereof being first established in the manner prescribed by the legislature. [*1959 AJR-22; 1961 SJR-8*]

Property taken by municipality. SECTION 2. [*Original form*] No municipal corporation shall take private property for public use, against the consent of the owner, without the necessity thereof being first established by the verdict of a jury.

Municipal home rule; debt limit; tax to pay debt. SECTION 3. [*As amended April 1981*] (1) Cities and villages organized pursuant to state law may determine their local affairs and government, subject only to this constitution and to such enactments of the legislature of statewide concern as with uniformity shall affect every city or every village. The method of such determination shall be prescribed by the legislature.

(2) No county, city, town, village, school district, sewerage district or other municipal corporation may become indebted in an amount that exceeds an allowable percentage of the taxable property located therein equalized for state purposes as provided by the legislature. In all cases the allowable percentage shall be 5 percent except as specified in pars. (a) and (b):

(a) For any city authorized to issue bonds for school purposes, an additional 10 percent shall be permitted for school purposes only, and in such cases the territory attached to the city for school purposes shall be included in the total taxable property supporting the bonds issued for school purposes.

(b) For any school district which offers no less than grades one to 12 and which at the time of incurring such debt is eligible for the highest level of school aids, 10 percent shall be permitted.

(3) Any county, city, town, village, school district, sewerage district or other municipal corporation incurring any indebtedness under sub. (2) shall, before or at the time of doing so, provide for the collection of a direct annual tax sufficient to pay the interest on such debt as it falls due, and also to pay and discharge the principal thereof within 20 years from the time of contracting the same.

(4) When indebtedness under sub. (2) is incurred in the acquisition of lands by cities, or by counties or sewerage districts having a population of 150,000 or over, for public, municipal purposes, or for the permanent improvement thereof, or to purchase, acquire, construct, extend, add to or improve a sewage collection or treatment system which services all or a part of such city or county, the city, county or sewerage district incurring the indebtedness shall, before or at the time of so doing, provide for the collection of a direct annual tax sufficient to pay the interest on such debt as it falls due, and also to pay and discharge the principal thereof within a period not exceeding 50 years from the time of contracting the same.

(5) An indebtedness created for the purpose of purchasing, acquiring, leasing, constructing, extending, adding to, improving, conducting, controlling, operating or managing a public utility

of a town, village, city or special district, and secured solely by the property or income of such public utility, and whereby no municipal liability is created, shall not be considered an indebtedness of such town, village, city or special district, and shall not be included in arriving at the debt limitation under sub. (2). [*1979 SJR-28; 1981 SJR-5*]

Municipal home rule; debt limit; tax to pay debt.

SECTION 3. [*As amended April 1966*] Cities and villages organized pursuant to state law are hereby empowered, to determine their local affairs and government, subject only to this constitution and to such enactments of the legislature of state-wide concern as shall with uniformity affect every city or every village. The method of such determination shall be prescribed by the legislature. No county, city, town, village, school district or other municipal corporation may become indebted in an amount that exceeds an allowable percentage of the taxable property located therein equalized for state purposes as provided by the legislature. In all cases the allowable percentage shall be five per centum except as follows: (a) For any city authorized to issue bonds for school purposes, an additional ten per centum shall be permitted for school purposes only, and in such cases the territory attached to the city for school purposes shall be included in the total taxable property supporting the bonds issued for school purposes. (b) For any school district which offers no less than grades one to twelve and which at the time of incurring such debt is eligible for the highest level of school aids, ten per centum shall be permitted. Any county, city, town, village, school district, or other municipal corporation incurring any indebtedness as aforesaid, shall before or at the time of doing so, provide for the collection of a direct annual tax sufficient to pay the interest on such debt as it falls due, and also to pay and discharge the principal thereof within twenty years from the time of contracting the same; except that when such indebtedness is incurred in the acquisition of lands by cities, or by counties having a population of one hundred fifty thousand or over, for public, municipal purposes, or for the permanent improvement thereof, the city or county incurring the same shall, before or at the time of so doing, provide for the collection of a direct annual tax sufficient to pay the interest on such debt as it falls due, and also to pay and discharge the principal thereof within a period not exceeding fifty years from the time of contracting the same. An indebtedness created for the purpose of purchasing, acquiring, leasing, constructing, extending, adding to, improving, conducting, controlling, operating or managing a public utility of a town, village, city or special district, and secured solely by the property or income of such public utility, and whereby no municipal liability is created, shall not be considered an indebtedness of such town, village, city or special district, and shall not be included in arriving at such debt limitation. [*1963 SJR-59; 1965 AJR-10*]

Municipal home rule; debt limit; tax to pay debt.

SECTION 3. [*As amended April 1963*] Cities and villages organized pursuant to state law are hereby empowered, to determine their local affairs and government, subject only to this constitution and to such enactments of the legislature of state-wide concern as shall with uniformity affect every city or every village. The method of such determination shall be prescribed by the legislature. No county, city, town, village, school district or other municipal corporation may become indebted in an amount that exceeds an allowable percentage of the taxable property located therein equalized for state purposes as provided by the legislature. In all cases the allowable percentage shall be five per centum except as follows: (a) For any city authorized to issue bonds for school purposes, an additional ten per centum shall be permitted for school purposes only, and in such cases the territory attached to the city for school purposes shall be included in the total taxable property supporting the bonds issued for school purposes. (b) For any school district which offers no less than grades one to twelve and which at the time of incurring such debt is eligible for the highest level of school aids, ten per centum shall be permitted. Any county, city, town, village, school district, or other municipal corporation incurring any indebtedness as aforesaid, shall before or at the time of doing so, provide for the collection of a direct annual tax sufficient to pay the interest on such debt as it falls due, and also to pay and discharge the principal thereof within twenty years

from the time of contracting the same; except that when such indebtedness is incurred in the acquisition of lands by cities, or by counties having a population of one hundred fifty thousand or over, for public, municipal purposes, or for the permanent improvement thereof, the city or county incurring the same shall, before or at the time of so doing, provide for the collection of a direct annual tax sufficient to pay the interest on such debt as it falls due, and also to pay and discharge the principal thereof within a period not exceeding fifty years from the time of contracting the same. An indebtedness created for the purpose of purchasing, acquiring, leasing, constructing, extending, adding to, improving, conducting, controlling, operating or managing a public utility of a town, village or city, and secured solely by the property or income of such public utility, and whereby no municipal liability is created, shall not be considered an indebtedness of such town, village or city, and shall not be included in arriving at such five or eight per centum debt limitation. [*1961 AJR-92; 1963 AJR-19*]

Municipal home rule; debt limit; tax to pay debt.

SECTION 3. [*As amended April 1961*] Cities and villages organized pursuant to state law are hereby empowered, to determine their local affairs and government, subject only to this constitution and to such enactments of the legislature of state-wide concern as shall with uniformity affect every city or every village. The method of such determination shall be prescribed by the legislature. No county, city, town, village, school district, or other municipal corporation shall be allowed to become indebted in any manner or for any purpose to any amount, including existing indebtedness, in the aggregate exceeding five per centum on the value of the taxable property therein, to be ascertained, other than for school districts and counties having a population of 500,000 or over, by the last assessment for state and county taxes previous to the incurring of such indebtedness and for school districts and counties having a population of 500,000 or over by the value of such property as equalized for state purposes; except that for any city which is authorized to issue bonds for school purposes the total indebtedness of such city shall not exceed in the aggregate eight per centum of the value of such property as equalized for state purposes and except that for any school district offering no less than grades one to twelve and which is at the time of incurring such debt eligible for the highest level of school aids, the total indebtedness of such school district shall not exceed ten per centum of the value of such property as equalized for state purposes; the manner and method of determining such equalization for state purposes to be provided by the legislature. Any county, city, town, village, school district, or other municipal corporation incurring any indebtedness as aforesaid, shall, before or at the time of doing so, provide for the collection of a direct annual tax sufficient to pay the interest on such debt as it falls due, and also to pay and discharge the principal thereof within twenty years from the time of contracting the same; except that when such indebtedness is incurred in the acquisition of lands by cities, or by counties having a population of one hundred fifty thousand or over, for public, municipal purposes, or for the permanent improvement thereof, the city or county incurring the same shall, before or at the time of so doing, provide for the collection of a direct annual tax sufficient to pay the interest on such debt as it falls due, and also to pay and discharge the principal thereof within twenty years from the time of contracting the same; except that when such indebtedness is incurred in the acquisition of lands by cities, or by counties having a population of one hundred fifty thousand or over, for public, municipal purposes, or for the permanent improvement thereof, the city or county incurring the same shall, before or at the time of so doing, provide for the collection of a direct annual tax sufficient to pay the interest on such debt as it falls due, and also to pay and discharge the principal thereof within a period not exceeding fifty years from the time of contracting the same. An indebtedness created for the purpose of purchasing, acquiring, leasing, constructing, extending, adding to, improving, conducting, controlling, operating or managing a public utility of a town, village or city, and secured solely by the property or income of such public utility, and whereby no municipal liability is created, shall not be considered an indebtedness of such town, village or city, and shall not be included in arriving at such five or eight per centum debt limitation. [*1959 SJR-6; 1961 AJR-1*]

Municipal home rule; debt limit; tax to pay debt.

SECTION 3. [*As amended November 1960*] Cities and villages

organized pursuant to state law are hereby empowered, to determine their local affairs and government, subject only to this constitution and to such enactments of the legislature of state-wide concern as shall with uniformity affect every city or every village. The method of such determination shall be prescribed by the legislature. No county, city, town, village, school district, or other municipal corporation shall be allowed to become indebted in any manner or for any purpose to any amount, including existing indebtedness, in the aggregate exceeding five per centum on the value of the taxable property therein, to be ascertained, other than for school districts and counties having a population of 500,000 or over, by the last assessment for state and county taxes previous to the incurring of such indebtedness and for school districts and counties having a population of 500,000 or over by the value of such property as equalized for state purposes; except that for any city which is authorized to issue bonds for school purposes the total indebtedness of such city shall not exceed in the aggregate eight per centum of the value of such property as equalized for state purposes; the manner and method of determining such equalization for state purposes to be provided by the legislature. Any county, city, town, village, school district, or other municipal corporation incurring any indebtedness as aforesaid, shall, before or at the time of doing so, provide for the collection of a direct annual tax sufficient to pay the interest on such debt as it falls due, and also to pay and discharge the principal thereof within twenty years from the time of contracting the same; except that when such indebtedness is incurred in the acquisition of lands by cities, or by counties having a population of one hundred fifty thousand or over, for public, municipal purposes, or for the permanent improvement thereof, the city or county incurring the same shall, before or at the time of so doing, provide for the collection of a direct annual tax sufficient to pay the interest on such debt as it falls due, and also to pay and discharge the principal thereof within a period not exceeding fifty years from the time of contracting the same. Providing, that an indebtedness created for the purpose of purchasing, acquiring, leasing, constructing, extending, adding to, improving, conducting, controlling, operating or managing a public utility of a town, village or city, and secured solely by the property or income of such public utility, and whereby no municipal liability is created, shall not be considered an indebtedness of such town, village or city, and shall not be included in arriving at such five or eight per centum debt limitation. [*1957 SJR-47; 1959 SJR-53*]

Municipal home rule; debt limit; tax to pay debt.
SECTION 3. [*As amended April 1955*] Cities and villages organized pursuant to state law are hereby empowered, to determine their local affairs and government, subject only to this constitution and to such enactments of the legislature of state-wide concern as shall with uniformity affect every city or every village. The method of such determination shall be prescribed by the legislature. No county, city, town, village, school district, or other municipal corporation shall be allowed to become indebted in any manner or for any purpose to any amount, including existing indebtedness, in the aggregate exceeding five per centum on the value of the taxable property therein, to be ascertained, other than for school district, by the last assessment for state and county taxes previous to the incurring of such indebtedness and for school districts by the value of such property as equalized for state purposes; except that for any city which is authorized to issue bonds for school purposes the total indebtedness of such city shall not exceed in the aggregate eight per centum of the value of such property as equalized for state purposes; the manner and method of determining such equalization for state purposes to be provided by the legislature. Any county, city, town, village, school district, or other municipal corporation incurring any indebtedness as aforesaid, shall, before or at the time of doing so, provide for the collection of a direct annual tax sufficient to pay the interest on such debt as it falls due, and also to pay and discharge the principal thereof within twenty years from the time of contracting the same; except that when such indebtedness is incurred in the acquisition of lands by cities, or by counties having a population of one hundred fifty thousand or over, for public, municipal purposes, or for the permanent improvement thereof, the city or county

incurring the same shall, before or at the time of so doing, provide for the collection of a direct annual tax sufficient to pay the interest on such debt as it falls due, and also to pay and discharge the principal thereof within a period not exceeding fifty years from the time of contracting the same. Providing, that an indebtedness created for the purpose of purchasing, acquiring, leasing, constructing, extending, adding to, improving, conducting, con- trolling, operating or managing a public utility of a town, village or city, and secured solely by the property or income of such public utility, and whereby no municipal liability is created, shall not be considered an indebtedness of such town, village or city, and shall not be included in arriving at such five or eight per centum debt limitation. [*1953 SJR-17; 1955 AJR-18*]

Municipal home rule; debt limit; tax to pay debt.
SECTION 3. [*As amended April 1951*] Cities and villages organized pursuant to state law are hereby empowered, to determine their local affairs and government, subject only to this constitution and to such enactments of the legislature of state-wide concern as shall with uniformity affect every city or every village. The method of such determination shall be prescribed by the legislature. No county, city, town, village, school district, or other municipal corporation shall be allowed to become indebted in any manner or for any purpose to any amount, including existing indebtedness, in the aggregate exceeding 5 per centum on the value of the taxable property therein, to be ascertained by the last assessment for state and county taxes previous to the incurring of such indebtedness; except that for any city which is authorized to issue bonds for school purposes the total indebtedness of such city shall not exceed in the aggregate 8 per centum of the value of such property. Any county, city, town, village, school district, or other municipal corporation incurring any indebtedness as aforesaid, shall, before or at the time of doing so, provide for the collection of a direct annual tax sufficient to pay the interest on such debt as it falls due, and also to pay and discharge the principal thereof within 20 years from the time of contracting the same; except that when such indebtedness is incurred in the acquisition of lands by cities, or by counties having a population of 150,000 or over, for public, municipal purposes, or for the permanent improvement thereof, the city or county incurring the same shall, before or at the time of so doing, provide for the collection of a direct annual tax sufficient to pay the interest on such debt as it falls due, and also to pay and discharge the principal thereof within a period not exceeding 50 years from the time of contracting the same. Providing, that an indebtedness created for the purpose of purchasing, acquiring, leasing, constructing, extending, adding to, improving, conducting, controlling, operating or managing a public utility of a town, village or city, and secured solely by the property or income of such public utility, and whereby no municipal liability is created, shall not be considered an indebtedness of such town, village or city, and shall not be included in arriving at such 5 or 8 per centum debt limitation. [*1949 SJR-11; 1951 SJR-9*]

Municipal home rule; debt limit; tax to pay debt.
SECTION 3. [*As amended November 1932*] Cities and villages organized pursuant to state law are hereby empowered, to determine their local affairs and government, subject only to this constitution and to such enactments of the legislature of state-wide concern as shall with uniformity affect every city or every village. The method of such determination shall be prescribed by the legislature. No county, city, town, village, school district, or other municipal corporation shall be allowed to become indebted in any manner or for any purpose to any amount, including existing indebtedness, in the aggregate exceeding five per centum on the value of the taxable property therein, to be ascertained by the last assessment for state and county taxes previous to the incurring of such indebtedness. Any county, city, town, village, school district, or other municipal corporation incurring any indebtedness as aforesaid, shall, before or at the time of doing so, provide for the collection of a direct annual tax sufficient to pay the interest on such debt as it falls due, and also to pay and discharge the principal thereof within twenty years from the time of contracting the same; except that when such indebtedness is incurred in the acquisition of lands by

cities, or by counties having a population of one hundred fifty thousand or over, for public, municipal purposes, or for the permanent improvement thereof, the city or county incurring the same shall, before or at the time of so doing, provide for the collection of a direct annual tax sufficient to pay the interest on such debt as it falls due, and also to pay and discharge the principal thereof within a period not exceeding fifty years from the time of contracting the same. Providing, that an indebtedness created for the purpose of purchasing, acquiring, leasing, constructing, extending, adding to, improving, conducting, controlling, operating or managing a public utility of a town, village or city, and secured solely by the property or income of such public utility, and whereby no municipal liability is created, shall not be considered an indebtedness of such town, village or city, and shall not be included in arriving at such five per centum debt limitation. [*1929 AJR-61; 1931 AJR-14*]

Municipal home rule; debt limit; tax to pay debt. SECTION 3. [*As amended November 1924*] Cities and villages organized pursuant to state law are hereby empowered, to determine their local affairs and government, subject only to this constitution and to such enactments of the legislature of state-wide concern as shall with uniformity affect every city or every village. The method of such determination shall be prescribed by the legislature. No county, city, town, village, school district, or other municipal corporation shall be allowed to become indebted in any manner or for any purpose to any amount, including existing indebtedness, in the aggregate exceeding five per centum on the value of the taxable property therein, to be ascertained by the last assessment for state and county taxes previous to the incurring of such indebtedness. Any county, city, town, village, school district, or other municipal corporation incurring any indebtedness as aforesaid, shall, before or at the time of doing so, provide for the collection of a direct annual tax sufficient to pay the interest on such debt as it falls due, and also to pay and discharge the principal thereof within twenty years from the time of contracting the same; except that when such indebtedness is incurred in the acquisition of lands by cities, or by counties having a population of one hundred fifty thousand or over, for public, municipal purposes, or for the permanent improvement thereof, the city or county incurring the same shall, before or at the time of so doing, provide for the collection of a direct annual tax sufficient to pay the interest on such debt as it falls due, and also to pay and discharge the principal thereof within a period not exceeding fifty years from the time of contracting the same. [*1921 SJR-5; 1923 SJR-18; 1923 c. 203*]

Organization of cities and villages. SECTION 3. [*As amended November 1912*] It shall be the duty of the legislature, and they are hereby empowered to provide for the organization of cities and incorporated villages, and

to restrict their power of taxation, assessment, borrowing money, contracting debts, and loaning their credit, so as to prevent abuses in assessments and taxation, and in contracting debts by such municipal corporations. No county, city, town, village, school district, or other municipal corporation shall be allowed to become indebted in any manner or for any purpose to any amount, including existing indebtedness, in the aggregate exceeding five per centum on the value of the taxable property therein, to be ascertained by the last assessment for state and county taxes previous to the incurring of such indebtedness. Any county, city, town, village, school district, or other municipal corporation incurring any indebtedness as aforesaid, shall, before or at the time of doing so, provide for the collection of a direct annual tax sufficient to pay the interest on such debt as it falls due, and also to pay and discharge the principal thereof within twenty years from the time of contracting the same; except that when such indebtedness is incurred in the acquisition of lands by cities, or by counties having a population of one hundred fifty thousand or over, for public, municipal purposes, or for the permanent improvement thereof, the city or county incurring the same shall, before or at the time of so doing, provide for the collection of a direct annual tax sufficient to pay the interest on such debt as it falls due, and also to pay and discharge the principal thereof within a period not exceeding fifty years from the time of contracting the same. [*1909 SJR-32; 1911 SJR-26; 1911 c. 665*]

Municipal debt limit. [*An amendment approved by the voters in November 1874 added two new paragraphs at the end of the section*] No county, city, town, village, school district, or other municipal corporation shall be allowed to become indebted in any manner or for any purpose to any amount including existing indebtedness, in the aggregate exceeding five per centum on the value of the taxable property therein to be ascertained by the last assessment for state and county taxes previous to the incurring of such indebtedness. Any county, city, town, village, school district or other municipal corporation incurring any indebtedness as aforesaid, shall before or at the time of doing so provide for the collection of a direct annual tax sufficient to pay the interest on said debt as it falls due, and also to pay and discharge the principal thereof within twenty years from the time of contracting the same. [*1872 AJR-17; 1873 SJR-6; 1874 c. 3*]

Organization of cities and villages. SECTION 3. [*Original form*] It shall be the duty of the legislature, and they are hereby empowered, to provide for the organization of cities and incorporated villages, and to restrict their power of taxation, assessment, borrowing money, contracting debts and loaning their credit, so as to prevent abuses in assessments and taxation, and in contracting debts by such municipal corporations.

Acquisition of lands by state and subdivisions; sale of excess. SECTION 3a. [*As amended April 3, 1956*] The state or any of its counties, cities, towns or villages may acquire by gift, dedication, purchase, or condemnation lands for establishing, laying out, widening, enlarging, extending, and maintaining memorial grounds, streets, highways, squares, parkways, boulevards, parks, playgrounds, sites for public buildings, and reservations in and about and along and leading to any or all of the same; and after the establishment, layout, and completion of such improvements, may convey any such real estate thus acquired and not necessary for such improvements, with reservations concerning the future use and occupation of such real estate, so as to protect such public works and improvements, and their environs, and to preserve the view, appearance, light, air, and usefulness of such public works. If the governing body of a county, city, town or village elects to accept a gift or dedication of land made on condition that the land be devoted to a special purpose and the condition subsequently becomes impossible or impracticable, such governing body may by resolution or ordinance enacted by a two-thirds vote of its members elect either to grant the land back to the donor or dedicator or his heirs or accept from the donor or dedicator or his heirs a grant relieving the county, city, town or village of the condition; however, if the donor or dedicator or his heirs are unknown or cannot be found, such resolution or ordinance may provide for the commencement of proceedings in the manner and in the courts as the legislature shall designate for the purpose of relieving the county, city, town or village from the condition of the gift or dedication. [*1953 SJR-29; 1955 SJR-9*]

Acquisition of lands by state and cities; sale of excess. SECTION 3a. [*Created November 1912*] The state or any of its cities may acquire by gift, purchase, or condemnation lands for establishing, laying out, widening, enlarging, extending, and maintaining memorial grounds, streets, squares, parkways, boulevards, parks, playgrounds, sites for public buildings, and reservations in and about and along and leading to any or all of the same; and

after the establishment, layout, and completion of such improvements, may convey any such real estate thus acquired and not necessary for such improvements, with reservations concerning the future use and occupation of such real estate, so as to protect such public works and improvements, and their environs, and to preserve the view, appearance, light, air, and usefulness of such public works. [*1909 SJR-63; 1911 SJR-25; 1911 c. 665*]

General banking law. SECTION 4. [*As amended April 1981*] The legislature may enact a general banking law for the creation of banks, and for the regulation and supervision of the banking business. [*1979 AJR-53; 1981 AJR-13*]

General banking law. SECTION 4. [*Created November 1902. This section was adopted to replace original sections 4 and 5 of this article*] The legislature shall have power to enact a general banking law for the creation of banks, and for the regulation and supervision of the banking business, provided that the vote of two-thirds of all the members elected to each house, to be taken by yeas and nays, be in favor of the passage of such law. [*P1899 AJR-16; 1901 SJR-25; 1901 c. 73*]

Legislature prohibited from incorporating banks. SECTION 4. [*Original form, repealed November 1902. 1899 AJR-16; 1901 SJR-25; 1901 c. 73*] The legislature shall not have power to create, authorize or incorporate, by any general, or special law, any bank, or banking power or privilege, or any institution or corporation having any banking power or privilege whatever, except as provided in this article.

SECTION 5. [*Repealed. 1899 JR-13; 1901 JR-2; 1901 c.73; vote November 1902*]

Referendum on banking laws. SECTION 5. [*Original form, repealed November 1902. 1899 AJR-16; 1901 SJR-25; 1901 c. 73*] The legislature may submit to the voters, at any general election, the question of "bank," or "no bank," and if at any such election a number of votes equal to a majority of all the votes cast at such election on that subject shall be in favor of banks, then the legislature shall have power to grant bank charters, or to pass a general banking

law, with such restrictions and under such regulations as they may deem expedient and proper for the security of the bill holders. Provided, that no such grant or law shall have any force or effect until the same shall have been submitted to a vote of the electors of the state, at some general election, and been approved by a majority of the votes cast on that subject at such election.

ARTICLE XII
AMENDMENTS

Constitutional amendments. SECTION 1. Any amendment or amendments to this constitution may be proposed in either house of the legislature, and if the same shall be agreed to by a majority of the members elected to each of the two houses, such proposed amendment or amendments shall be entered on their journals, with the yeas and nays taken thereon, and referred to the legislature to be chosen at the next general election, and shall be published for three months previous to the time of holding such election; and if, in the legislature so next chosen, such proposed amendment or amendments shall be agreed to by a majority of all the members elected to each house, then it shall be the duty of the legislature to submit such proposed amendment or amendments to the people in such manner and at such time as the legislature shall prescribe; and if the people shall approve and ratify such amendment or amendments by a majority of the electors voting thereon, such amendment or amendments shall become part of the constitution; provided, that if more than one amendment be submitted, they shall be submitted in such manner that the people may vote for or against such amendments separately.

Constitutional conventions. SECTION 2. If at any time a majority of the senate and assembly shall deem it necessary to call a convention to revise or change this constitution, they shall recommend to the electors to vote for or against a convention at the next election for members of the legislature. And if it shall appear that a majority of the electors voting thereon have voted for a convention, the legislature shall, at its next session, provide for calling such convention.

ARTICLE XIII.
MISCELLANEOUS PROVISIONS

Political year; elections. SECTION 1. [*As amended April 1986*] The political year for this state shall commence on the first Monday of January in each year, and the general election shall be held on the Tuesday next succeeding the first Monday of November in even-numbered years. [*1983 AJR-33; 1985 AJR-3*]

Political year; elections. SECTION 1. [*As amended November 1882*] The political year for the state of Wisconsin shall commence on the first Monday in January in each year, and the general election shall be

holden on the Tuesday next succeeding the first Monday in November. The first general election for all state and county officers, except judicial officers, after the adoption of this amendment, shall be holden in the year A.D. 1884, and thereafter the general election shall be held biennially. All state, county or other officers elected at the general election in the year 1881, and whose term of office would otherwise expire on the first Monday of January in the year 1884, shall hold and continue in such offices respectively until the first Monday in January in the year 1885. [*1881*

AJR-16; 1882 SJR-20; 1882 c. 290]

Political year; general election. Section 1. [*Original form*] The political year for the state of Wisconsin shall commence on the first Monday in January in each year, and the general election shall be holden on the Tuesday succeeding the first Monday in November in each year.

Section 2. [*Repealed. 1973 SJR-6; 1975 SJR-4; vote April 1975*]

Dueling. Section 2. [*Original form*] Any inhabitant of this state who may hereafter be engaged, either directly or indirectly, in a duel, either as principal or accessory, shall forever be disqualified as an elector, and from holding any office under the constitution and laws of this state, and may be punished in such other manner as shall be prescribed by law.

Eligibility to office. Section 3. [*As amended November 1996*] (1) No member of congress and no person holding any office of profit or trust under the United States except postmaster, or under any foreign power, shall be eligible to any office of trust, profit or honor in this state.

(2) No person convicted of a felony, in any court within the United States, no person convicted in federal court of a crime designated, at the time of commission, under federal law as a misdemeanor involving a violation of public trust and no person convicted, in a court of a state, of a crime designated, at the time of commission, under the law of the state as a misdemeanor involving a violation of public trust shall be eligible to any office of trust, profit or honor in this state unless pardoned of the conviction.

(3) No person may seek to have placed on any ballot for a state or local elective office in this state the name of a person convicted of a felony, in any court within the United States, the name of a person convicted in federal court of a crime designated, at the time of commission, under federal law as a misdemeanor involving a violation of public trust or the name of a person convicted, in a court of a state, of a crime designated, at the time of commission, under the law of the state as a misdemeanor involving a violation of public trust, unless the person named for the ballot has been pardoned of the conviction. [*1993 AJR-3; 1995 AJR-16*]

Eligibility to office. Section 3. [*Original form*] No member of congress, nor any person holding any office of profit or trust under the United States (postmasters excepted) or under any foreign power; no person convicted of any infamous crime in any court within the United States; and no person being a defaulter to the United States or to this state, or to any county or town therein, or to any state or territory within the United States, shall be eligible to any office of trust, profit or honor in this state.

Great seal. Section 4. It shall be the duty of the legislature to provide a great seal for the state, which shall be kept by the secretary of state, and all official acts of the governor, his approbation of the laws excepted, shall be thereby authenticated.

Section 5. [*Repealed. 1983 AJR-33; 1985 SJR-3; vote April 1986*]

Residents on Indian lands, where to vote. Section 5. [*Original form*] All persons residing upon Indian lands, within any county of the state, and qualified to exercise the right of suffrage under the constitution, shall be entitled to vote at the polls which may be held nearest their residence, for state, United States or county officers. Provided, that no person shall vote for county officers out of the county in which he resides.

Legislative officers. Section 6. The elective officers of the legislature, other than the presiding officers, shall be a chief clerk and a sergeant at arms, to be elected by each house.

Division of counties. Section 7. No county with an area of nine hundred square miles or less shall be divided or have any part stricken therefrom, without submitting the question to a vote of the people of the county, nor unless a majority of all the legal voters of the county voting on the question shall vote for the same.

Removal of county seats. Section 8. No county seat shall be removed until the point to which it is proposed to be removed shall be fixed by law, and a majority of the voters of the county voting on the question shall have voted in favor of its removal to such point.

Election or appointment of statutory officers. Section 9. All county officers whose election or appointment is not provided for by this constitution shall be elected by the electors of the respective counties, or appointed by the boards of supervisors, or other county authorities, as the legislature shall direct. All city, town and village officers whose election or appointment is not provided for by this constitution shall be elected by the electors of such cities, towns and villages, or of some division thereof, or appointed by such authorities thereof as the legislature shall designate for that purpose. All other officers whose election or appointment is not provided for by this constitution, and all officers whose offices may hereafter be created by law, shall be elected by the people or appointed, as the legislature may direct.

Vacancies in office. SECTION 10. [*As amended April 1979*] (1) The legislature may declare the cases in which any office shall be deemed vacant, and also the manner of filling the vacancy, where no provision is made for that purpose in this constitution.

(2) Whenever there is a vacancy in the office of lieutenant governor, the governor shall nominate a successor to serve for the balance of the unexpired term, who shall take office after confirmation by the senate and by the assembly. [*1977 SJR-51; 1979 SJR-1*]

Vacancies in office. SECTION 10. [*Original form*] The legislature may declare the cases in which any office shall be deemed vacant, and also the manner of filling the vacancy, where no provision is made for that purpose in this constitution.

Passes, franks and privileges. SECTION 11. [*As amended November 1936*] No person, association, copartnership, or corporation, shall promise, offer or give, for any purpose, to any political committee, or any member or employe thereof, to any candidate for, or incumbent of any office or position under the constitution or laws, or under any ordinance of any town or municipality, of this state, or to any person at the request or for the advantage of all or any of them, any free pass or frank, or any privilege withheld from any person, for the traveling accommodation or transportation of any person or property, or the transmission of any message or communication.

No political committee, and no member or employe thereof, no candidate for and no incumbent of any office or position under the constitution or laws, or under any ordinance of any town or municipality of this state, shall ask for, or accept, from any person, association, copartnership, or corporation, or use, in any manner, or for any purpose, any free pass or frank, or any privilege withheld from any person, for the traveling accommodation or transportation of any person or property, or the transmission of any message or communication.

Any violation of any of the above provisions shall be bribery and punished as provided by law, and if any officer or any member of the legislature be guilty thereof, his office shall become vacant.

No person within the purview of this act shall be privileged from testifying in relation to anything therein prohibited; and no person having so testified shall be liable to any prosecution or punishment for any offense concerning which he was required to give his testimony or produce any documentary evidence.

Notaries public and regular employes of a railroad or other public utilities who are candidates for or hold public offices for which the annual compensation is not more than three hundred dollars to whom no passes or privileges are extended beyond those which are extended to other regular employes of such corporations are excepted from the provisions of this section. [*1933 AJR-50; 1935 AJR-67*]

Free passes forbidden. SECTION 11. [*Created November 1902*] No person, association, co-partnership, or corporation, shall promise, offer or give, for any purpose, to any political committee, or any member or employee thereof, to any candidate for, or incumbent of any office or position under the constitution or laws, or under any ordinance of any town or municipality, of this state, or to any person at the request or for the advantage of all or any of them, any free pass or frank, or any privilege withheld from any person, for the traveling accommodation or transportation of any person or property, or the transmission of any message or communication.

No political committee, and no member or employee thereof, no candidate for and no incumbent of any office or position under the constitution or laws, or under any ordinance of any town or municipality of this state, shall ask for, or accept, from any person, association, co-partnership, or corporation, or use, in any manner, or for any purpose,

any free pass or frank, or any privilege withheld from any person, for the traveling accommodation or transportation of any person or property, or the transmission of any message or communication.

Any violation of any of the above provisions shall be bribery and punished as provided by law, and if any officer or any member of the legislature be guilty thereof, his office shall become vacant.

No person within the purview of this act shall be privileged from testifying in relation to anything therein prohibited; and no person having so testified shall be liable to any prosecution or punishment for any offense concerning which he was required to give his testimony or produce any documentary evidence.

The railroad commissioner and his deputy in the discharge of duty are excepted from the provisions of this amendment. [*1899 SJR-12; 1901 AJR-8; 1901 c. 437*]

Recall of elective officers. SECTION 12. [*As amended April 1981*] The qualified electors of the state, of any congressional, judicial or legislative district or of any county may petition for the recall of any incumbent elective officer after the first year of the term for which the incumbent was elected, by filing a petition with the filing officer with whom the nomination petition to the office in the primary is filed, demanding the recall of the incumbent.

(1) The recall petition shall be signed by electors equaling at least twenty-five percent of the vote cast for the office of governor at the last preceding election, in the state, county or district which the incumbent represents.

(2) The filing officer with whom the recall petition is filed shall call a recall election for the Tuesday of the 6th week after the date of filing the petition or, if that Tuesday is a legal holiday, on the first day after that Tuesday which is not a legal holiday.

(3) The incumbent shall continue to perform the duties of the office until the recall election results are officially declared.

(4) Unless the incumbent declines within 10 days after the filing of the petition, the incumbent shall without filing be deemed to have filed for the recall election. Other candidates may file for the office in the manner provided by law for special elections. For the purpose of conducting elections under this section:

(a) When more than 2 persons compete for a nonpartisan office, a recall primary shall be held. The 2 persons receiving the highest number of votes in the recall primary shall be the 2 candidates in the recall election, except that if any candidate receives a majority of the total number of votes cast in the recall primary, that candidate shall assume the office for the remainder of the term and a recall election shall not be held.

(b) For any partisan office, a recall primary shall be held for each political party which is by law entitled to a separate ballot and from which more than one candidate competes for the party's nomination in the recall election. The person receiving the highest number of votes in the recall primary for each political party shall be that party's candidate in the recall election. Independent candidates and candidates representing political parties not entitled by law to a separate ballot shall be shown on the ballot for the recall election only.

(c) When a recall primary is required, the date specified under sub. (2) shall be the date of the recall primary and the recall election shall be held on the Tuesday of the 4th week after the recall primary or, if that Tuesday is a legal holiday, on the first day after that Tuesday which is not a legal holiday.

(5) The person who receives the highest number of votes in the recall election shall be elected for the remainder of the term.

(6) After one such petition and recall election, no further recall petition shall be filed against the same officer during the term for which he was elected.

(7) This section shall be self-executing and mandatory. Laws may be enacted to facilitate its operation but no law shall be enacted to hamper, restrict or impair the right of recall. [*1979 SJR-5; 1981 SJR-2*]

Recall of elective officers. SECTION 12. [*Created November 1926*] The qualified electors of the state or of any county or of any congressional, judicial or legislative district may petition for the recall of any elective officer after the first year of the term for which he was elected, by filing a petition with the officer with whom the petition for nomination to such office in the primary election is filed, demanding the recall of such officer. Such petition shall be signed by electors equal in number to at least twenty-five per cent of the vote cast for the office of governor at the last preceding election, in the state, county or district from which such officer is to be recalled. The officer with whom such petition is filed shall call a special election to be held not less than forty nor more than forty-five days from the filing of such petition. The officer against whom such petition has been filed shall continue to perform the duties of his office until the result of such special election shall have been officially declared. Other candidates for such office may be nominated in the manner as is provided by law in primary elections. The candidate who shall receive the highest number of votes shall be deemed elected for the remainder of the term. The name of the candidate against whom the recall petition is filed shall go on the ticket unless he resigns within ten days after the filing of the petition. After one such petition and special election, no further recall petition shall be filed against the same officer during the term for which he was elected. This article shall be self-executing and all of its provisions shall be treated as mandatory. Laws may be enacted to facilitate its operation, but no law shall be enacted to hamper, restrict or impair the right of recall. [*1923 SJR-39; 1925 SJR-12; 1925 c. 270*]

Marriage. SECTION 13. [*Created November 2006*] Only a marriage between one man and one woman shall be valid or recognized as a marriage in this state. A legal status identical or substantially similar to that of marriage for unmarried individuals shall not be valid or recognized in this state. [*2003 AJR-66; 2005 SJR-53*]

Article XIV.
Schedule

Effect of change from territory to state. Section 1. That no inconvenience may arise by reason of a change from a territorial to a permanent state government, it is declared that all rights, actions, prosecutions, judgments, claims and contracts, as well of individuals as of bodies corporate, shall continue as if no such change had taken place; and all process which may be issued under the authority of the territory of Wisconsin previous to its admission into the union of the United States shall be as valid as if issued in the name of the state.

Territorial laws continued. Section 2. All laws now in force in the territory of Wisconsin which are not repugnant to this constitution shall remain in force until they expire by their own limitation or be altered or repealed by the legislature.

Section 3. [*Repealed. 1979 AJR-76; 1981 AJR-35; submit: May '82 Spec.Sess. AJR-1; vote November 1982*]

Territorial fines accrue to state. Section 3. [*Original form*] All fines, penalties, or forfeitures accruing to the territory of Wisconsin shall enure to the use of the state.

Section 4. [*Repealed. 1979 AJR-76; 1981 AJR-35; submit: May '82 Spec.Sess. AJR-1; vote November 1982*]

Rights of action and prosecution saved. Section 4. [*Original form*] All recognizances heretofore taken, or which may be taken before the change from territorial to a permanent state government, shall remain valid, and shall pass to and may be prosecuted in the name of the state; and all bonds executed to the governor of the territory, or to any other officer or court in his or their official capacity, shall pass to the governor or state authority and their successors in office, for the uses therein respectively expressed, and may be sued for and recovered accordingly; and all the estate, or property, real, personal or mixed, and all judgments, bonds, specialties, choses in action and claims or debts of whatsoever description of the territory of Wisconsin, shall enure to and vest in the state of Wisconsin, and may be sued for and recovered in the same manner and to the same extent by the state of Wisconsin as the same could have been by the territory of Wisconsin. All criminal prosecutions and penal actions which may have arisen, or which may arise before the change from a territorial to a state government, and which shall then be pending, shall be prosecuted to judgment and execution in the name of the state. All offenses committed against the laws of the territory of Wisconsin before the change from a territorial to a state government, and which shall not be prosecuted before such change, may be prosecuted in the name and by the authority of the state of Wisconsin with like effect as though such change had not taken place; and all penalties incurred shall remain the same as if this constitution had not been adopted. All actions at law and suits in equity which may be pending in any of the courts of the territory of Wisconsin at the time of the change from a territorial to a state government may be continued and transferred to any court of the state which shall have jurisdiction of the subject matter thereof.

Section 5. [*Repealed. 1979 AJR-76; 1981 AJR-35; submit: May '82 Spec.Sess. AJR-1; vote November 1982*]

Existing officers hold over. Section 5. [*Original form*] All officers, civil and military, now holding their offices under the authority of the United States or of the territory of Wisconsin shall continue to hold and exercise their respective offices until they shall be superseded by the authority of the state.

Section 6. [*Repealed. 1979 AJR-76; 1981 AJR-35; submit: May '82 Spec.Sess. AJR-1; vote November 1982*]

Seat of government. Section 6. [*Original form*] The first session of the legislature of the state of Wisconsin shall commence on the first Monday in June next, and shall be held at the village of Madison, which shall be and remain the seat of government until otherwise provided by law.

Section 7. [*Repealed. 1979 AJR-76; 1981 AJR-35; submit: May '82 Spec.Sess. AJR-1; vote November 1982*]

Local officers hold over. Section 7. [*Original form*] All county, precinct, and township officers shall continue to hold their respective offices, unless removed by the competent authority, until the legislature shall, in conformity with the provisions of this constitution, provide for the holding of elections to fill such offices respectively.

Section 8. [*Repealed. 1979 AJR-76; 1981 AJR-35; submit: May '82 Spec.Sess. AJR-1; vote November 1982*]

Copy of constitution for president. Section 8. [*Original form*] The president of this convention shall, immediately after its adjournment, cause a fair copy of this constitution, together with a copy of the act of the legislature of this territory, entitled "An act in relation to the formation of a state government in Wisconsin, and to change the time of holding the annual session of the legislature," approved October 27, 1847, providing for the calling of this convention, and also a copy of so much of the last census of this territory as exhibits the number of its inhabitants, to be forwarded to the president of the United States to be laid before the congress of the United States at its present session.

Section 9. [*Repealed. 1979 AJR-76; 1981 AJR-35; submit: May '82 Spec.Sess. AJR-1; vote November 1982*]

Ratification of constitution; election of officers. Section 9. [*Original form*] This constitution shall be submitted at an election to be held on the second Monday in March next, for ratification or rejection, to all white male persons of the age of twenty-one years or upwards, who shall then be residents of this territory and citizens of the United States, or shall have declared their intention to become such in conformity with the laws of congress on the subject of naturalization; and all persons having such qualifications shall be entitled to vote for or against the adoption of this constitution, and for all officers first elected under it. And if the constitution be ratified by the said electors it shall become the constitution of the state of Wisconsin. On such of the ballots as are for the constitution shall be written or printed the word "yes," and on such as are against the constitution the word "no." The election shall be conducted in the manner now prescribed by law, and the returns made by the clerks of the boards of supervisors or county commissioners (as the case may

be) to the governor of the territory at any time before the tenth day of April next. And in the event of the ratification of this constitution by a majority of all the votes given, it shall be the duty of the governor of this territory to make proclamation of the same, and to transmit a digest of the returns to the senate and assembly of the state on the first day of their session. An election shall be held for governor, lieutenant governor, treasurer, attorney-general, members of the state legislature, and members of congress, on the second Monday of May next; and no other for further notice of such election shall be required.

SECTION 10. [*Repealed. 1979 AJR-76; 1981 AJR-35; submit: May '82 Spec.Sess. AJR-1; vote November 1982*]

Congressional apportionment. SECTION 10. [*Original form*] Two members of congress shall also be elected on the second Monday of May next; and until otherwise provided by law, the counties of Milwaukee, Waukesha, Jefferson, Racine, Walworth, Rock and Green, shall constitute the first congressional district, and elect one member; and the

counties of Washington, Sheboygan, Manitowoc, Calumet, Brown, Winnebago, Fond du Lac, Marquette, Sauk, Portage, Columbia, Dodge, Dane, Iowa, LaFayette, Grant, Richland, Crawford, Chippewa, St. Croix and La Pointe, shall constitute the second congressional district, and shall elect one member.

SECTION 11. [*Repealed. 1979 AJR-76; 1981 AJR-35; submit: May '82 Spec.Sess. AJR-1; vote November 1982*]

First elections. SECTION 11. [*Original form*] The several elections provided for in this article shall be conducted according to the existing laws of the territory; provided, that no elector shall be entitled to vote except in the town, ward or precinct where he resides. The returns of election for senators and members of assembly shall be transmitted to the clerk of the board of supervisors or county commissioners, as the case may be; and the votes shall be canvassed and certificates of election issued as now provided by law. In the first senatorial district the returns of the election for senator shall be made to the proper officer in the county of Brown; in the second senatorial district to the proper officer in the county of Columbia; in the third senatorial district to the proper officer in the county of Crawford; in the fourth senatorial district to the

proper officer in the county of Fond du Lac; and in the fifth senatorial district to the proper officer in the county of Iowa. The returns of election for state officers and members of congress shall be certified and transmitted to the speaker of the assembly, at the seat of government, in the same manner as the vote for delegate to congress are required to be certified and returned by the laws of the territory of Wisconsin, to the secretary of said territory, and in such time that they may be received on the first Monday in June next; and as soon as the legislature shall be organized the speaker of the assembly and the president of the senate shall, in the presence of both houses, examine the returns and declare who are duly elected to fill the several offices hereinbefore mentioned, and give to each of the persons elected a certificate of his election.

SECTION 12. [*Repealed. 1979 AJR-76; 1981 AJR-35; submit: May '82 Spec.Sess. AJR-1; vote November 1982*]

Legislative apportionment. SECTION 12. [*Original form*] Until there shall be a new apportionment, the senators and members of the assembly shall be apportioned among the several districts, as hereinafter mentioned,

and each district shall be entitled to elect one senator or member of the assembly, as the case may be. [*Enumeration of districts omitted as obsolete: see R.S. 1849 pp. 40-43; R.S. 1858 pp. 49-53*]

Common law continued in force. SECTION 13. Such parts of the common law as are now in force in the territory of Wisconsin, not inconsistent with this constitution, shall be and continue part of the law of this state until altered or suspended by the legislature.

SECTION 14. [*Repealed. 1979 AJR-76; 1981 AJR-35; submit: May '82 Spec.Sess. AJR-1; vote November 1982*]

Officers, when to enter on duties. SECTION 14. [*Original form*] The senators first elected in the even-numbered senate districts, the governor, lieutenant governor and other state officers first elected under this constitution, shall enter upon the duties of their respective offices on the first Monday of June next, and shall continue in office

for one year from the first Monday of January next; the senators first elected in the odd-numbered senate districts, and the members of the assembly first elected, shall enter upon their duties respectively on the first Monday of June next, and shall continue in office until the first Monday in January next.

SECTION 15. [*Repealed. 1979 AJR-76; 1981 AJR-35; submit: May '82 Spec.Sess. AJR-1; vote November 1982*]

Oath of office. SECTION 15. [*Original form*] The oath of office may be administered by any judge or justice of the

peace until the legislature shall otherwise direct.

Implementing revised structure of judicial branch. SECTION 16. [*As affected November 1982*] (1), (2), (3) and (5) [*Repealed*]

(4) [*Amended*] The terms of office of justices of the supreme court serving on August 1, 1978, shall expire on the July 31 next preceding the first Monday in January on which such terms would otherwise have expired, but such advancement of the date of term expiration shall not impair any retirement rights vested in any such justice if the term had expired on the first Monday in January. [*1979 AJR-76; 1981 AJR-35; submit: May '82 Spec.Sess. AJR-1*]

Implementing revised structure of judicial branch. SECTION 16. [*Created April 1977*] (1) The 1975/1977 amendment relating to a revised structure of the judicial

branch shall take effect on August 1 of the year following the year of ratification by the voters.

(2) All county courts and the branches thereof in

existence on the effective date of this amendment shall, as trial courts of general uniform statewide jurisdiction, continue after such effective date with the same jurisdiction, powers and duties conferred by law upon such courts and the branches and judges thereof until the legislature by law alters or abolishes such county courts and their jurisdiction, powers and duties.

(3) Subject to the jurisdiction established in section 14 of article VII, municipal courts and municipal court judges shall continue after the effective date of this amendment with the same jurisdiction, powers and duties as conferred upon such courts and judges as of the effective date until the legislature acts under sections 2 and 14 of article VII to alter or abolish such municipal courts and their jurisdiction, powers and duties.

(4) The terms of office of justices of the supreme court serving on the effective date shall expire on the July 31 next preceding the first Monday in January on which such terms would otherwise have expired, but such advancement of the date of term expiration shall not impair any retirement rights vested in any such justice if the term had expired on the first Monday in January.

(5) Prior to the effective date of this amendment the legislature shall by law establish one or more appeals court districts, provide for the election of appeals judges in such districts, and determine the jurisdiction of the court of appeals under section 21 of article I and section 5 of article VII as affected by this amendment, so that the court of appeals shall become operative on the effective date. [*1975 AJR-11; 1977 SJR-9*]

Note: Attached resolutions and signatures appear at the end of the constitution as printed in the *Revised Statutes* of 1849 and 1858.

HISTORY OF CONSTITUTIONAL AMENDMENTS
April 2015

Art.	Sec.	Subject	First Approval	Second Approval	Submission to People	Date of Election	For	Against	Total Vote for Governor
IV	4	Assemblymen, 2-year terms	Ch.95 1853	Ch.89 1854	Ch.89 1854	Nov. 1854	6,549	11,580	—[1]
IV	5	Senators, 4-year terms	" "	" "	" "	"	6,348	11,885	"
IV	11	Biennial legislative sessions	" "	" "	" "	"	6,752	11,589	"
V	5	Governor's salary, changed from $1,250 to $2,500 a year	SJR 35 1861	SJR 15 1862	Ch.202 1862	Nov. 1862	14,519	32,612	142,522
IV	21	*Change legislators' pay to $350 a year	SJR 26 1865	SJR 16 1866	Ch.25 1867	Nov. 1867	58,363	24,418	130,781
V	4	*Change governor's salary from $1,250 to $5,000 a year	AJR 13 1868	SJR 6 1869	Ch.186 1869	Nov. 1869	47,353	41,764	146,953[2]
V	9	*Change lieutenant governor's salary to $1,000 a year	AJR 6 1869	" "	" "	"	"	"	147,274
I	8	*Grand jury system modified	SJR 14 1870	SJR 3 1870	Ch.118 1870	Nov. 1870	48,894	18,606	"
IV	31,32	*Private and local laws, prohibited on 9 subjects	SJR 12 1871	AJR 29 1871	Ch.122 1871	Nov. 1871	54,087	3,675	"
VII	4	Supreme court, 1 chief and 4 associate justices	AJR 17 1872	AJR 16 1872	Ch.111 1872	Nov. 1872	16,272	29,755	178,122
XI	3	*Indebtedness of municipalities limited to 5%	SJR 16 1876	SJR 6 1873	Ch.37 1874	Nov. 1874	66,061	1,509	"
VII	4	*Supreme court, 1 chief and 4 associate justices	SJR 14 1876	SJR 2 1877	Ch.48 1877	Nov. 1877	79,140	16,763	171,856
VIII	2	*Claims against state, 6-year limit	SJR 9 1880	SJR 5 1877	Ch.158 1877	"	33,046	3,371	"
IV	4,5,11	Biennial sessions; assemblymen 2-year, senators 4-year terms	SJR 9 1880	AJR 7 1881	Ch.262 1881	Nov. 1881	53,532	13,936	"
IV	21	*Change legislators' pay to $500 a year	none[3] 1881	none[3]		"	36,223	5,347	"
III	1	*Voting residence 30 days; in municipalities voter registration	AJR 26 1881	SJR 18 1882	Ch.272 1882	Nov. 1882	60,091	8,089	"
VI	4	*County officers except judicial, vacancies filled by appointment	AJR 16 1881	SJR 20 1882	Ch.290 1882	"	"	"	"
VII	12	*Clerk of court, full term election	"	"	"	"	"	"	"
XIII	1	*Political year; biennial elections	"	"	"	"			"
X	1	State superintendent, qualifications and pay fixed by legislature	AJR 16 1885	AJR 2 1887	Ch.357 1887	Nov. 1888			354,714
VII	4	*Supreme court, composed of 5 justices of supreme court	SJR 19 1887	AJR 7 1889	Ch.22 1889	Apr. 1889	12,967	18,342	211,111[4]
XI	31	*Cities incorporated by general law	SJR 13 1889	SJR 13 1891	Ch.362 1891	Nov. 1892	125,759	14,712	371,559
X	1	State superintendent, pay fixed by law	AJR 15 1893	SJR 7 1895	Ch.177 1895	Nov. 1896	15,718	9,015	444,110
VIII	7	*Circuit judges, additional in populous counties	SJR 9 1895	SJR 10 1897	Ch.69 1897	Apr. 1897	38,752	56,506	119,572[4]
X	1	State superintendent, nonpartisan 4-year term, pay fixed by law	SJR 21 1899	SJR 24 1901	Ch.258 1901	Nov. 1902	45,823	41,513	365,676
XI	4	*General banking law authorized	AJR 16 1899	SJR 25 1901	Ch.73 1901	"	71,550	57,411	"
XI	5	*Banking law referenda requirement repealed	SJR 12 1899	AJR 8 1901	Ch.437 1901	"	64,836	44,620	"
XIII	11	*Free passes prohibited	AJR 33 1899	AJR 5 1901	Ch.10 1903	Apr. 1903	67,781	40,697	114,468[4]
VII	4	*Supreme court, 7 justices, 10-year terms	AJR 16 1901	AJR 47 1907	Ch.661 1907	Nov. 1908	51,377	39,857	449,656
III	1	*Suffrage for full citizens only	AJR 45 1905	AJR 46 1905	"	"	85,838	36,733	"
V	10	*Governor's approval of bills in 6 days	AJR 12 1905	SJR 19 1907	"	"	85,958	27,270	"
VIII	1	*Income tax	SJR 14 1905	SJR 22 1907	Ch.238 1907	"	85,696	37,729	"
VIII	10	*Highways, appropriations for	SJR 18 1905	SJR 35 1909	Ch.478 1909	"	116,421	46,739	"
IV	3	*Apportionment after each federal census	SJR 30 1907	SJR 55 1909	Ch.508 1909	Nov. 1910	54,932	52,634	319,522
IV	21	Change legislators' pay to $1,000 a year	AJR 8 1907	AJR 33 1909	Ch.514 1909	"	44,153	76,278	"
VIII	10	Water power and forests, appropriations for[5]	SJR 43 1907	Ch.514 1909	Ch.514 1909	"	62,468[5]	45,924[5]	"
VII	10	*Judges' salaries, time of payment	AJR 36 1909	AJR 26 1911	Ch.665 1911	Nov. 1912	44,855	34,865	393,849

Art.	Sec.	Subject	First Approval	Second Approval	Submission to People	Date of Election	Vote For	Against	Total Vote for Governor
XI	3	*City or county debt for lands, discharge within 50 years	SJR 32 JR 44 1909	SJR 26 JR 42 1911	" "	" "	46,369	34,975	"
XI	3a	*Public parks, playgrounds, etc.	SJR 63 JR 38 1909	SJR 25 JR 48 1911	" "	" "	48,424	33,931	"
IV	1	Initiative and referendum	AJR 36 JR 74 1911	AJR 4 JR 22 1913	Ch.770 1913	Nov. 1914	84,934	148,536	325,430
IV	21	Change legislators' pay to $600 a year, 2 cents a mile for additional round trips	AJR 78 JR 66 1911	AJR 8 JR 24 1913	" "	" "	68,907	157,202	"
VII	6,7	Judicial circuits, decreased number, additional judges	AJR 134 JR 67 1911	AJR 11 JR 26 1913	" "	" "	63,311	154,827	"
VIII	new	State annuity insurance	SJR 72 JR 65 1911	AJR 38 JR 35 1913	Ch.770 1913	Nov. 1914	59,909	170,338	325,430
VIII	new	State insurance	AJR 119 JR 56 1911	AJR 9 JR 12 1913	" "	" "	58,490	165,966	"
XI	new	Home rule of cities and villages	SJR 31 JR 73 1911	SJR 19 JR 21 1913	" "	" "	86,020	141,472	"
XI	new	Municipal power of condemnation	AJR 104 JR 37 1911	AJR 10 JR 25 1913	" "	" "	61,122	154,945	"
XII	1	Constitutional amendments, submission after 3/5 approval by one legislature	SJR 57 JR 71 1911	SJR 22 JR 17 1913	" "	" "	71,734	160,761	"
XII	new	Constitution amended upon petition	AJR 36 JR 74 1911	AJR 4 JR 22 1913	" "	" "	68,435	150,215	"
XIII	new	Recall of civil officers	SJR 9 JR 41 1911	SJR 18 JR 15 1913	" "	" "	81,628	144,386	"
IV	21	Legislators' pay fixed by law	AJR 16 JR 23 1917	AJR 13 JR 37 1919	Ch.480 1919	Apr. 1920	126,243	132,258	"
VII	6,7	Judicial circuits, decreased number, additional judges	AJR 74 JR 20 1917	SJR 100 JR 92 1919	Ch.604 1919	" "	113,786	116,436	
I	5	*Jury verdict, 5/6 in civil cases	AJR 26 JR 58 1919	AJR 14 JR 17 1921	Ch.504 1921	Nov. 1922	171,433	156,820	481,828
VI	4	Sheriffs, no limit on successive terms	AJR 22 JR 38 1919	AJR 39 JR 36 1921	Ch.437 1921	" "	161,832	207,594	"
XI	new	Municipal indebtedness for public utilities	AJR 21 JR 54 1919	AJR 16 JR 37 1921	Ch.566 1921	" "	105,234	219,639	"
IV	21	Change legislators' pay to $750 a year	SJR 8 JR 28 1921	SJR 5 JR 18 1923	Ch.241 1923	Apr. 1924	189,635	250,236	344,137[4]
VII	7	*Circuit judges, additional in populous counties	SJR 24 JR 24 1921	SJR 27 JR 64 1923	Ch.408 1923	Nov. 1924	240,207	226,562	796,432
VIII	10	*Forestry, appropriations for	SJR 30 JR 29 1921	AJR 70 JR 57 1923	Ch.289 1923	" "	336,360	173,563	"
XI	3	*Home rule for cities and villages	SJR 5 JR 39 1921	SJR 18 JR 34 1923	Ch.203 1923	" "	299,792	190,165	"
V	5	*Governor's salary fixed by law	AJR 88 JR 79 1923	AJR 50 JR 52 1925	Ch.413 1925	Nov. 1926	202,156	188,302	552,912
XIII	12	*Recall of elective officials	SJR 39 JR 39 1923	SJR 12 JR 16 1925	Ch.270 1925	" "	205,868	201,125	"

Note: JR 41 of 1925, which became Joint Rule 16 of the Wisconsin Legislature, established a new procedure to incorporate the "submission to the people" clause into the proposal at second approval.

HISTORY OF CONSTITUTIONAL AMENDMENTS
April 2015—Continued

Art.	Sec.	Subject	First Approval			Second Approval			Date of Election	For	Against	Total Vote for Governor
IV	21	Change legislators' pay to $1,000 for session	AJR 16	JR 33	1925	AJR 2	JR 12	1927	Apr. 1927	151,786	199,260	308,885[4]
VIII	1	*Severance tax: forests, minerals	AJR 51	JR 61	1925	AJR 3	JR 13	1927	"	179,217	141,888	"
IV	21	*Legislators' salary repealed; to be fixed by law	SJR 61	JR 57	1927	SJR 7	JR 6	1929	Apr. 1929	237,250	212,846	397,912[2]
VI	4	*Sheriffs succeeding themselves for 2 terms	AJR 8	JR 24	1927	AJR 8	JR 13	1929	"	259,881	210,964	"
VI	10	*Item veto on appropriation bills	SJR 35	JR 37	1927	SJR 40	JR 43	1929	Nov. 1930	252,655	153,703	606,825
V	5	*Governor's salary provision repealed; fixed by law	SJR 81	JR 69	1929	SJR 6	JR 52	1931	Nov. 1932	452,605	275,175	1,124,502
V	9	*Lieutenant governor's salary repealed; fixed by law	SJR 82	JR 70	1929	SJR 7	JR 53	1931	"	427,768	267,120	"
VII	1	*Wording of section corrected	SJR 103	JR 72	1929	SJR 8	JR 58	1931	"	436,113	221,563	"
XI	3	*Municipal indebtedness for public utilities	AJR 61	JR 74	1929	AJR 14	JR 71	1931	"	401,194	279,631	"
III	1	*Women's suffrage	AJR 52	JR 91	1931	SJR 74	JR 76	1933	Nov. 1934	411,088	166,745	953,797
XIII	11	*Free passes, permitted as specified	AJR 50	JR 63	1933	AJR 67	JR 98	1935	Nov. 1936	365,971	361,799	1,237,095
VIII	1	*Installment payment of real estate taxes	AJR 37	JR 88	1939	AJR 15	JR 18	1941	Apr. 1941	330,971	134,808	547,213[2]
VII	15	*Justice of peace, abolish office in first class cities	SJR 9	JR 27	1943	SJR 6	JR 2	1945	Apr. 1945	160,965	113,408	381,192[4]
VIII	10	*Aeronautical program	SJR 16	JR 37	1943	SJR 7	JR 3	1945	"	187,111	101,169	"
VI	4	Sheriffs, no limit on successive terms	AJR 6	JR 36	1943	AJR 10	JR 47	1945	Apr. 1946	121,144	170,131	306,354[4]
IV	33	*Auditing of state accounts	SJR 35	JR 60	1943	SJR 24	JR 73	1945	Nov. 1946	480,938	308,072	1,040,444
IV	2	*Auditing (part of same proposal)	"	"		"	"		"			"
X	3	Public transportation of school children to any school	SJR 48	JR 73	1943	SJR 19	JR 78	1945	"	437,817	545,475	"
XI	2	Repeal; relating to exercise of eminent domain by municipalities	SJR 30	JR 89	1945	SJR 15	JR 48	1947	Nov. 1948	210,086	807,318	1,266,139
II	2	Prohibition on taxing federal lands repealed	AJR 26	JR 33	1947	SJR 6	JR 2	1949	Apr. 1949	245,412	297,237	633,606[4]
VIII	10	*Allow internal improvement debt for veterans' housing	SJR 2	JR 1	SS'48[6]	SJR 5	JR 1	1949	"	311,576	290,736	"
II	2	*Prohibition on taxing federal lands repealed	AJR 64	JR 11	1949	AJR 7	JR 7	1951	Apr. 1951	305,612	186,284	515,822[4]
IV	3	*City debt limit 8% for combined city and school purposes	SJR 11	JR 12	1949	SJR 9	JR 6	1951	Apr. 1951	313,739	191,897	515,822[4]
IV	3,4,5	Apportionment based on area and population[7]	SJR 50	JR 59	1951	AJR 7	JR 9	1953	Apr. 1953	433,043[7]	406,133[7]	735,860[4]
VII	9	*Judicial elections to full terms	SJR 3	JR 41	1951	SJR 5	JR 12	1953	"	386,972	345,094	"
VII	24	*Judges; qualifications, retirement	SJR 6	JR 46	1953	SJR 10	JR 14	1955	Apr. 1955	380,214	177,929	520,554[4]
XI	3	*School debt limit, equalized value	SJR 17	JR 47	1953	AJR 18	JR 12	1955	"	320,376	228,641	"
IV	26	*Teachers' retirement benefits	SJR 21	JR 41	1953	SJR 8	JR 17	1955	Apr. 1956	365,560	255,284	740,411[4]
VI	4	Sheriffs, no limit on successive terms	AJR 13	JR 23	1953	AJR 22	JR 53	1955	"	269,722	328,603	"
XI	3a	*Municipal acquisition of land for public purposes	SJR 29	JR 35	1953	SJR 9	JR 36	1955	"	376,692	193,544	"
XIII	11	Free passes, not for public use	AJR 12	JR 61	1953	AJR 47	JR 54	1955	"	188,715	380,207	"
VIII	10	*Port development	AJR 39	JR 58	1957	SJR 20	JR 15	1959	Apr. 1960	472,177	451,045	1,182,160[8]
XI	3	*Debt limit in populous counties, 5% of equalized valuation	SJR 47	JR 59	1957	SJR 53	JR 32	1959	Nov. 1960	686,104	529,467	1,728,009

Art.	Sec.	Subject	First Approval			Second Approval			Date of Election	For	Against	Total Vote for Governor
IV	26	Salary increases during term for various public officers	SJR 21	JR 29	1959	SJR 6	JR 11	1961	Apr. 1961	297,066	307,575	765,807[4]
IV	34	*Continuity of civil government	AJR 48	JR 50	1959	SJR 1	JR 10	1961	"	498,869	132,728	"
VI	4	Sheriffs, no limit on successive terms	AJR 31	JR 48	1959	AJR 7	JR 9	1961	"	283,495	388,238	"
VIII	1	*Personal property classified for tax purposes	AJR 120	JR 77	1959	SJR 34	JR 13	1961	"	381,881	220,434	"
XI	2	*Municipal eminent domain, abolished jury verdict of necessity	AJR 22	JR 47	1959	SJR 8	JR 12	1961	"	348,406	259,566	"
XI	3	*Debt limit 10% of equalized valuation for integrated aid school district	SJR 6	JR 35	1959	AJR 1	JR 8	1961	"	409,963	224,783	"
IV	3	*"Indians not taxed" exclusion removed from apportionment formula	SJR 12	JR 30	1959	SJR 11	JR 32	1961	Nov. 1962	631,296	259,577	1,265,900
IV	23	*County executive: 4-year term	AJR 121	JR 68	1959	AJR 61	JR 64	1961	"	527,075	331,393	"
IV	4	*County executive: 2-year terms	"	"	"	"	"	"	"	524,240	319,378	"
IV	23a	*County executive veto power	"	"	"	"	"	"	"	232,851	277,014	"
IV	3	Time for apportionment of seats in the state legislature	AJR 162	JR 96	1961	AJR 23	JR 9	1963	Apr. 1963	216,205	335,774	635,510[4]
IV	26	Salary increases during term for justices and judges	SJR 76	JR 68	1961	SJR 4	JR 7	1963	"	285,296	231,702	"
XI	3	*Equalized value debt limit	AJR 92	JR 71	1961	AJR 19	JR 8	1963	"	440,978	536,724	"
VIII	10	Maximum state appropriation for forestry increased	AJR 133	JR 90	1961	AJR 73	JR 32	1963	Apr. 1964	336,994	572,276	1,046,801[4]
XI	3	Property valuation for debt limit adjusted	AJR 134	JR 91	1961	AJR 74	JR 33	1963	"	317,676	582,045	"
XII	1	Constitutional amendments, submission of related items in a single proposition	SJR 15	JR 30	1961	SJR 1	JR1	SS'63[6]	"	380,059	215,169	"
VI	4	*Coroner and surveyor abolished in counties of 500,000	AJR 14	JR 30	1963	SJR 17	JR 5	1965	Apr. 1965	454,390	194,327	738,831[4]
IV	24	*Lotteries, definition revised	SJR 42	JR 35	1963	SJR 13	JR 2	1965	"	362,935	189,641	"
IV	13	*Legislators on active duty in armed forces	SJR 24	JR 34	1963	SJR 15	JR 14	1965	Apr. 1966	321,434	216,341	564,132[4]
VII	2	*Establishment of inferior courts	SJR 32	JR 48	1963	SJR 26	JR 50	1965	"	307,502	199,919	"
VII	15	*Justices of the peace abolished	"	"	"	SJR 11	JR 51	1965	"	"	"	"
XI	3	*Special district public utility debt limit	SJR 59	JR 44	1963	AJR 10	JR 58	1965	"	"	"	"
I	23	*Transportation of children to private schools	AJR 70	JR 46	1965	AJR 7	JR 13	1967	Apr. 1967	494,236	377,107	856,650[4]
IV	26	*Judicial salary increased during term	AJR 162	JR 96	1965	AJR 17	JR 17	1967	"	489,989	328,292	"
V	1m,1n	*4-year term for governor and lieutenant governor	AJR 4	JR 80	1965	SJR 12	JR 10	1967	"	534,368	310,478	"
V	3	*Joint election of governor and lieutenant governor	AJR 3	JR 45	1965	SJR 11	JR 11	1967	"	507,339	312,267	"
VI	1m	*4-year term for secretary of state	AJR 4	JR 80	1965	AJR 8	JR 14	1967	"	520,326	311,974	"
VI	1n	*4-year term for state treasurer	"	"	"	SJR 12	JR 10	1967	"	514,280	314,873	"
VI	1p	*4-year term for attorney general	"	"	"	"	"	"	"	515,962	311,603	"
VI	4	*Sheriffs, no limit on successive terms	AJR 72	JR 61	1965	SJR 7	JR 12	1967	Apr. 1967	508,242	324,544	856,650[4]
IV	11	*Legislative sessions, more than one permitted in biennium	AJR 5	JR 57	1965	AJR 15	JR 48	1967	Apr. 1968	670,757	267,997	884,996[4]
VII	24	*Uniform retirement date for justices and circuit judges	SJR 36	JR 101	1965	SJR 96	JR 56	1967	"	734,046	215,455	"
VII	24	*Temporary appointment of justices and circuit judges	SJR 28	JR 43	1965	SJR 18	JR 25	1967	"	678,249	245,807	"
VIII	10	*Forestry appropriation from sources other than property tax	AJR 18	JR 49	1967	SJR 8	JR 2	1969	Apr. 1969	652,705	286,512	706,324[2]
IV	23	*Uniform county government modified	"	"	"	"	"	"	"	326,445	321,851	"
IV	23a	*County executive to have veto power	"	"	"	"	"	"	"	"	"	"
VIII	7	*State public debt for specified purposes allowed	AJR 1	JR 58	1967	AJR 1	JR 3	1969	"	411,062	258,366	"

HISTORY OF CONSTITUTIONAL AMENDMENTS
April 2015–Continued

Art.	Sec.	Subject	First Approval			Second Approval			Date of Election	Vote For	Vote Against	Total Vote for Governor
I	24	*Private use of school buildings	AJR 74	JR 38	1969	AJR 10	JR 27	1971	Apr. 1972	871,707	298,016	—
IV	23	*County government systems authorized	SJR 58	JR 32	1969	SJR 4	JR 13	1971	"	571,285	515,255	"
VI	4	*Coroner/medical examiner option	SJR 63	JR 33	1969	SJR 38	JR 21	1971	"	795,497	323,930	"
X	3	*Released time for religious instruction	AJR 41	JR 37	1969	AJR 17	JR 28	1971	"	595,075	585,511	"
I	25	Equality of the sexes	AJR 140	JR 44	1971	AJR 21	JR 5	1973	Apr. 1973	447,240	391,499	1,008,553[2]
IV	24	*Charitable bingo authorized	SJR 13	JR 31	1971	AJR 6	JR 3	1973	"	645,544	520,936	"
IV	26	*Increased benefits for retired public employes	SJR 3	JR 12	1971	SJR 15	JR 15	1973	Apr. 1974	396,051	315,545	758,587[4]
VII	13	*Removal of judges by 2/3 vote of legislature for cause	AJR 31	JR 30	1971	SJR 25	JR 25	1973	"	493,496	193,867	"
VIII	1	*Taxation of agricultural lands	AJR 1	JR 39	1971	AJR 55	JR 29	1973	"	353,377	340,518	"
VIII	3,7	*Public debt for veterans' housing	AJR 145	JR 38	1973	AJR 1	JR 3	1975	Apr. 1975	385,915	300,232	699,043[4]
VIII	7,10	Internal improvements for transportation facilities[9]	AJR 133	JR 37	1973	AJR 2	JR 2	1975	"	342,396[9]	341,291[9]	"
XI	3	Exclusion of certain debt from municipal debt limit	SJR 44	JR 32	1973	SJR 55	JR 133	1975	"	310,434	337,925	"
XIII	2	*Dueling: repeal of disenfranchisement	SJR 6	JR 10	1973	SJR 4	JR 4	1975	"	395,616	282,726	"
XI	3	Municipal indebtedness increased up to 10% of equalized valuation	SJR 58	JR 35	1973	AJR 6	JR 6	1975	Apr. 1976	328,097	715,420	1,168,606[4]
VIII	7(2)(a),10	Internal improvements for transportation facilities[9]	AJR 133	JR 37	1973	AJR 2	JR 2	1975	Nov. 1976[9]	722,658	935,152	1,332,220[8]
IV	24	*Charitable raffle games authorized	AJR 43	JR 19	1975	AJR 10	JR 6	1977	Apr. 1977	483,518	300,473	775,490[4]
VII	2	*Unified court system [also changed I-21; IV-17 and 26; VII-3 to 11, 14, 16 to 23; XIV-16(1) to (4)]	AJR 11	JR 13	1975	SJR 9	JR 7	1977	"	490,437	215,939	"
VII	5	*Court of appeals created [also changed I-21(1); VII-2 and 3(3); XIV-16(5)]	"	"	"	"	"	"	"	455,350	229,316	"
VII	11,13	*Court system disciplinary proceedings	"	"	"	"	"	"	"	565,087	151,418	"
VII	24	*Retirement age for justices and judges set by law	"	"	"	"	"	"	"	506,207	244,170	"
IV	23	Town government uniformity	AJR 22	JR 15	1975	AJR 20	JR 18	1977	Apr. 1978	179,011	383,395	"
V	7,8	*Gubernatorial succession	SJR 51	JR 32	1977	SJR 1	JR 3	1979	Apr. 1979	538,959	187,440	840,166[4]
XIII	10	*Lieutenant governor vacancy	"	"	"	"	"	"	"	540,186	181,497	"
IV	9	*Senate presiding officer [also changed 5-8]	"	"	"	"	"	"	"	372,734	327,008	"
V	1	*4-year constitutional officer terms (improved wording) [also changed V-1m and 1n; VI-1, 1m, 1n and 1p]	"	"	"	"	"	"	"	533,620	164,768	"
I	8	*Right to bail[10]	AJR 9	JR 76	SS'80[6]	AJR 5	JR 8	1981	Apr. 1981	505,092[10]	185,405[10]	"
XI	1,4	*Obsolete corporation and banking provisions	AJR 53	JR 21	1979	AJR 13	JR 9	1981	"	418,997	186,898	"
XI	3	*Indebtedness period for sewage collection or treatment systems	SJR 28	JR 43	1979	SJR 5	JR 7	1981	"	386,792	250,866	"
XIII	12	*Primaries in recall elections	SJR 5	JR 41	1979	SJR 2	JR 6	1981	"	366,635	259,820	"
VI	4	*Counties responsible for acts of sheriff	AJR 99	JR 30	1979	AJR 7	JR 15	1981	Apr. 1982	316,156	219,752	"
I	1,18	*Gender-neutral wording (also changed X-1 and 2)	AJR 76	JR 36	1979	AJR 35	JR 29	1981	Nov. 1982	771,267	479,053	1,580,344

Art.	Sec.	Subject	First Approval			Second Approval			Date of Election	Vote For	Vote Against	Total Vote for Governor
IV	3	*Military personnel treatment in redistricting	"	"	"	"	"	"	"	834,188	321,331	"
IV	4,5	*Obsolete 1881 amendment reference	AJR 76	JR 36	1979	AJR 35	JR 29	1981	Nov. 1982	919,349	238,884	1,580,340
IV	30	*Elections by legislature	"	"	"	"	"	"	"	977,438	193,679	"
X	1	*Obsolete reference to election and term of superintendent of public instruction	AJR 76	JR 36	1979	AJR 35	JR 29	1981	Nov. 1982	934,236	215,961	"
X	2	*Obsolete reference to military draft exemption purchase; school fund	"	"	"	"	"	"	"	887,488	295,693	"
XIV	3	*Obsolete transition from territory to statehood (also changed XIV-4 to 12; XIV-14, 15)	"	"	"	"	"	"	"	926,875	223,213	"
XIV	16(1)	*Obsolete transitional provisions of 1977 court reorganization [also changed XIV-16(2), (3), (5)]	"	"	"	"	"	"	"	882,091	237,698	"
XIV	16(4)	*Terms on supreme court effective date provision	"	"	"	"	"	"	"	960,540	190,366	"
I	1	*Rewording to parallel Declaration of Independence	AJR 9	JR 40	1983	AJR 9	JR 21	1985	Apr. 1986	419,699	65,418	461,118[4]
III	1-6	*Revision of suffrage defined by general law	AJR 33	JR 30	1983	AJR 3	JR 14	1985	"	401,911	83,183	"
XIII	1	*Modernizing constitutional text	"	"	"	"	"	"	"	404,273	82,512	"
XIII	5	*Obsolete suffrage right on Indian land	"	"	"	"	"	"	"	381,339	102,090	"
IV	24(5)	*Permitting pari-mutuel on-track betting	AJR 45	JR 36	1985	AJR 2	JR 3	1987	Apr. 1987	580,089	529,729	837,747[4]
IV	24(6)	*Authorizing the creation of a state lottery	SJR 1	JR 35	1985	AJR 3	JR 4	1987	Apr. 1987	739,181	391,942	"
VIII	1	Authorizing income tax credits or refunds for property or sales taxes	AJR 117	JR 74	1987	SJR 9	JR 2	1989	Apr. 1989	405,765	406,863	882,784[4]
V	10	*Redefining the partial veto power of the governor	SJR 71	JR 76	1987	SJR 11	JR 39	1989	Apr. 1990	387,068	252,481	685,878[4]
VIII	10	Providing housing for persons of low or moderate income	AJR 101	JR 55	1989	AJR 7	JR 2	1991	Apr. 1991	295,823	402,921	[1]
VIII	7(2)(a)1	*Railways and other railroad facilities (also created VIII-10)	SJR76	JR 52	1989	SJR 30	JR 9	1991	Apr.1992	650,592	457,690	"
IV	26	*Legislative and judiciary compensation, effective date	AJR 47	JR54	1989	AJR 16	JR 13	1991	"	736,832	348,645	"
VIII	1	Residential property tax reduction	AJR 81	JR76	1989	SJR 12	JR 14	1991	Nov. 1992	675,876	1,536,975	2,531,114[8]
I	9m	*Crime victims	SJR 41	JR 17	1991	SJR 3	JR 2	1993	Apr. 1993	861,405	163,087	1,075,386[2]
IV	24	*Gambling, limiting "lottery"; divorce under general law (also amended IV-31,32)	AJR 1	JR 27	SS'92[6]	SJR 2	JR 3	1993	"	623,987	435,180	"
I	3	Removal of unnecessary references to masculine gender (also amended I-3, 7, 9, 19, 21(2); IV-6, 12, 13, 23a; V-4, 6; VI-2; VII-1, 12; XI-3a; XIII-4, 11, 12(6))	AJR 121	JR 21	1993	AJR 12	JR 3	1995	Apr. 1995	412,032	498,801	939,676[4]
IV	24(6)(a)	Authorizing sports lottery dedicated to athletic facilities	SJR 49	JR 27	1993	SJR 3	JR 2	1995	Apr. 1995	348,818	618,377	"
VII	10(1)	Removal of restriction on judges holding nonjudicial public office after resignation during the judicial term	AJR 81	JR 20	1993	AJR 15	JR 4	1995	Apr. 1995	390,744	503,239	"
XIII	3	*Eligibility to seek or hold public office if convicted of a felony or a misdemeanor involving violation of a public trust	AJR 3	JR 19	1993	AJR 16	JR 28	1995	Nov. 1996	1,292,934	543,516	2,196,169[8]
I	25	*Guaranteeing the right to keep and bear arms	AJR 53	JR 27	1995	AJR 11	JR 21	1997	Nov. 1998	1,205,873	425,052	1,756,014

HISTORY OF CONSTITUTIONAL AMENDMENTS
April 2015–Continued

Art.	Sec.	Subject	First Approval			Second Approval			Date of Election	Vote For	Vote Against	Total Vote for Governor
VI	4(1)(3) (5)(6)	*4-year term for sheriff; sheriffs permitted to hold nonpartisan office; allowed legislature to provide for election to fill vacancy during term	AJR 37	JR 23	1995	SJR 43	JR 18	1997	Nov. 1998	1,161,942	412,508	"
IV	24(3) (5)(6)	*Distributing state lottery, bingo and pari-mutuel proceeds for property tax	AJR 80	JR 19	1997	AJR 2	JR 2	1999	Apr. 1999	648,903	105,976	758,965[4]
I	(26)	*Right to fish, hunt, trap, and take game	SJR 2	JR 16	2001	AJR 1	JR 8	2003	Apr. 2003	668,459	146,182	800,785[4]
VI	4(1)(3) (4)	*4-year term for county clerks, treasurers, clerks of circuit court, district attorneys, coroners, elected surveyors, and registers of deeds (also amended VII-12)	AJR 10	JR 12	2003	SJR 2	JR 2	2005	Apr. 2005	534,742	177,037	552,790[4]
XIII	13	*Marriage between one man and one woman	AJR 66	JR 29	2003	SJR 53	JR 30	2005	Nov. 2006	1,264,310	862,924	2,161,700
V	10(1)(c)	*Gubernatorial partial veto power	SJR 33	JR 46	2005	SJR 5	JR 26	2007	Apr. 2008	575,582	239,613	830,450[4]
IV	9(2)	*Department of transportation and transportation fund (also created VIII-11)	SJR 23	JR 4	2011	AJR 2	JR 1	2013	Nov. 2014	1,733,101	434,806	2,410,314
VIII	1	*Election of Chief Justice of the supreme court	SJR 57	JR 16	2013	SJR 2	JR 2	2015	Apr. 2015	433,533	384,503	813,200[4]

*Ratified.

[1]No election for statewide office. [2]Total vote for State Superintendent. [3]No number assigned to joint resolution. [4]Total vote for Justice of Supreme Court. [5]Ratified but declared invalid by Supreme Court in State ex rel. Owen v. Donald, 160 Wis. 21 (1915). [6]Special session: July 1948, December 1964, June 1980, and August 1992. [7]Ratified but declared invalid by Supreme Court in State ex rel. Thomson v. Zimmerman, 264 Wis. 644 (1953). [8]Total vote for presidential delegate election. [9]Recount resulted in rejection (342,132 to 342,309). However, the Dane County Circuit Court ruled the recount invalid due to election irregularities and required that the referendum be resubmitted to the electorate. Resubmitted to the electorate November 1976 by the 1975 Wisconsin Legislature through Ch. 224, s.145r, Laws of 1975. [10]As a result of a Dane County Circuit Court injunction, vote totals were certified April 7, 1982, by the Board of State Canvassers.

Sources: Official records of the Government Accountability Board; Laws of Wisconsin, 2013 and previous volumes.

SUMMARY – CHANGING THE WISCONSIN CONSTITUTION

To amend the Wisconsin Constitution, it is necessary for two consecutive Wisconsin Legislatures to adopt an identical amendment (known as "first consideration" and "second consideration") and for a majority of the electorate to ratify the amendment at a subsequent election. See Art. XII, Sec. 1.

Since the adoption of the Wisconsin Constitution in 1848, the electorate has voted 145 out of 196 times to amend a total of 128 sections of the constitution (excluding the same vote for more than one item but including a vote that was later resubmitted by the legislature and two votes that were declared invalid by the courts). The Wisconsin Legislature adopted 158 acts or joint resolutions to submit these changes to the electorate.

STATEWIDE REFERENDA ELECTIONS OTHER THAN CONSTITUTIONAL AMENDMENTS

Question	Law Submitting	Date of Election	Vote For	Vote Against
Territorial				
*Formation of a state government[2]	Territorial Laws 1846, page 5 (Jan.31)	Apr. 1846	12,334	2,487
*Ratification of first constitution	Art. XIX, Sec. 9 of 1846 Constitution	Apr. 1847	14,119	20,231
*Extend suffrage to colored persons[1]	Supl. resolution to 1846 Constitution	Apr. 1847	7,664	14,615
*Ratification of second constitution	Art. XIV, Sec. 9 of 1848 Constitution	Mar. 1848	16,799	6,384
State				
*Extend suffrage to colored persons[2]	Ch.137 1849	Nov. 1849	5,265	4,075
*State banks; advisory referendum	Ch.143 1851	Nov. 1851	31,289	9,126
*General banking law	Ch.479 1852	Nov. 1852	32,826	8,711
*Liquor prohibition; advisory referendum	Ch.101 1853	Nov. 1853	27,519	24,109
Extend suffrage to colored persons.	Ch.44 1857	Nov. 1857	28,235	41,345
*Amend general banking law; redemption of bank notes	Ch.98 1858	Nov. 1858	27,267	2,837
*Amend general banking law; circulation of bank notes	Ch.242 1861	Nov. 1861	57,646	2,515
*Amend general banking law; interest rate 7% per year	Ch.203 1862	Nov. 1862	46,269	7,794
Extend suffrage to colored persons[2]	Ch.414 1865	Nov. 1865	46,588	55,591
*Amend general banking law; taxing shareholders	Ch.102 1866	Nov. 1866	49,714	19,151
*Abolish office of bank comptroller.	JR12 1867	Nov. 1868	15,499	1,948
*Incorporation of savings banks and savings societies	Ch.28 1868	Nov. 1876	4,029	3,069
*Women's suffrage upon school matters	Ch.384 1876	Nov. 1886	43,581	38,998
Revise 1897 banking law; banking department under commission	Ch.211 1885	Nov. 1898	86,872	92,607
*Primary election law	Ch.303 1897	Nov. 1904	130,366	80,102
Pocket ballots and coupon voting systems	Ch.451 1903	Apr. 1906	45,958	111,139
Women's suffrage	Ch.522 1905	Nov. 1912	135,545	227,024
*Soldiers' bonus financed by 3-mill property tax and income tax.	Ch.227 1911	Sept. 1919	165,762	57,324
*Wisconsin prohibition enforcement act	Ch.667 1919	Nov. 1920	419,309	199,876
*U.S. prohibition act (Volstead Act); memorializing Congress to amend	Ch.556 1919	Nov. 1926	349,443	177,603
*Repeal of Wisconsin prohibition enforcement act; advisory referendum	JR47 1925 SJR42	"	350,337	196,402
*Modification of Wisconsin prohibition enforcement act; advisory referendum	SJR14 1929	Apr. 1929	321,688	200,545
County distribution of auto licenses; advisory referendum	SJR26 1931	Apr. 1931	183,716	368,674
*Sunday blue law repeal; advisory referendum	AJR116 1931	Apr. 1932	396,436	271,786
*Old-age pensions; advisory referendum	AJR42 SS'33	Apr. 1934	531,915	154,729
*Teacher tenure law repeal; advisory referendum	AJR67 1939	Apr. 1940	403,782	372,524
Property tax levy for high school aid; 2 mills of assessed valuation.	Ch.525 1943	Apr. 1944	131,004	410,315
Daylight saving time; advisory referendum	JR4 1947	Apr. 1947	313,091	379,740
3% retail sales tax for veterans bonus; advisory referendum	JR62 1947 SJR24	Nov. 1948	258,497	825,990
4-year term for constitutional officers; advisory referendum	JR13 1951 SJR58	Apr. 1951	210,821	328,613
Apportionment of legislature by area and population; advisory referendum	Ch.728 1951 SJR11	Nov. 1952	689,615	753,092
*New residents entitled to vote for president and vice president	Ch.76 1953	Nov. 1954	550,056	414,680

STATEWIDE REFERENDA ELECTIONS OTHER THAN CONSTITUTIONAL AMENDMENTS-Continued

Question		Law Submitting		Date of Election	Vote For	Vote Against
Statewide educational television tax-supported; advisory referendum	AJR74	JR66	1953	Nov. 1954	308,385	697,262
*Daylight saving time		Ch.6	1957	Apr. 1957	578,661	480,656
*Ex-residents entitled to vote for president and vice president		Ch.512	1961	Nov. 1962	627,279	229,375
Gasoline tax increase for highway construction; advisory referendum	AJR3	JR3	SS'63	Apr. 1964	150,769	889,364
*New residents entitled to vote after 6 months		Chs.88,89	1965	Nov. 1966	582,389	256,246
State control and funding of vocational education; advisory referendum	AJR12	JR4	1969	Apr. 1969	292,560	409,789
*Recreational lands bonding; advisory referendum	AJR17	JR5	1969	Apr. 1969	361,630	322,882
*Water pollution abatement bonding; advisory referendum	"	"	"	"	446,763	246,968
*New residents entitled to vote after 10 days		Ch.85	1975	Nov. 1976	1,017,887	660,875
*Presidential voting revised		Ch.394	1977	Nov. 1978	782,181	424,386
*Overseas voting revised		"	"	"	658,289	524,029
*Public inland lake protection and rehabilitation districts		Ch.299	1979	Nov. 1980	1,210,452	355,024
*Nuclear weapons moratorium and reduction; advisory referendum	AJR99	JR38	1981	Sept. 1982	641,514	205,018
*Nuclear waste site locating; advisory referendum	AJR5	JR5	1983	Apr. 1983	78,327	628,414
*Gambling casinos on excursion vessels; advisory referendum		WisAct 321	1991	Apr. 1993	465,432	604,289
*Gambling casino restrictions; advisory referendum		"	"	"	646,827	416,722
*Video poker and other forms of video gambling allowed; advisory referendum		"	"	"	358,045	702,864
*Pari-mutuel on-track betting continuation; advisory referendum		"	"	"	548,580	507,403
*State-operated lottery continuation; advisory referendum		"	"	"	773,306	287,585
*Extended suffrage in federal elections to adult children of U.S. citizens living abroad		WisAct 182	1999	Nov. 2000	1,293,458	792,975
*Death penalty; advisory referendum	SJR5	JR58	2005	Nov. 2006	1,166,571	934,508

*Ratified.

[1] For text of resolution, see Wisconsin State Historical Society, Constitutional Series, Volume II, *The Convention of 1846*, edited by Milo M. Quaife, p. 755.

[2] In *Gillespie v. Palmer*, 20 Wis. 544 (1866), the Wisconsin Supreme Court ruled that Chapter 137, Laws of 1849, extending suffrage to colored persons, was ratified November 6, 1849.

Sources: Official records of the Government Accountability Board; *Laws of Wisconsin*, 2011 and previous volumes.

SUMMARY – STATEWIDE REFERENDA ELECTIONS

Statewide referendum questions are submitted to the electorate by the Wisconsin Legislature: 1) to ratify a law extending the right of suffrage (as required by the state constitution); 2) to ratify a law that has been passed contingent on voter approval; or 3) to seek voter opinion through an advisory referendum. Since 1848, the Wisconsin Legislature has presented 53 referendum questions to the Wisconsin electorate through the passage of acts or joint resolutions; 39 were ratified. During territorial times, the territorial legislature sent 4 questions to the electorate. Two of these passed: one to ratify the state constitution and one to allow the formation of a state government.

Framework of Government

4

The framework of Wisconsin government: an overall view of Wisconsin government, a chart of its organization, and a map of state agencies

Civil War Cannon at Camp Randall

(Sarah Girkin)

LOCATION OF STATE AGENCIES IN MADISON
June 1, 2015

State Agency	Street Address	Map Locator Number
Administration, Department of	101 E. Wilson St.	13
Agriculture, Trade and Consumer Protection, Department of	2811 Agriculture Dr.	—
Attorney General, Office of the	State Capitol, Rm. 114 East	1
Children and Families, Department of	201 E. Washington Ave., 2nd Floor	9
Corrections, Department of	3099 E. Washington Ave.	—
Educational Approval Board	201 W. Washington Ave., 3rd Floor	16
Educational Communications Board	3319 W. Beltline Hwy.	—
Emergency Management, Wisconsin	2400 Wright St.	—
Employee Trust Funds, Department of	801 W. Badger Rd.	—
Employment Relations Commission	4868 High Crossing Blvd.	—
Financial Institutions, Department of	201 W. Washington Ave., Suite 500	16
Government Accountability Board	212 E. Washington Ave., 3rd Floor	17
Governor, Office of the	State Capitol, Rm. 115 East	1
Health Services, Department of	1 W. Wilson St.	14
Higher Educational Aids Board	131 W. Wilson St., Suite 902	15
Housing and Economic Development Authority	201 W. Washington Ave., Suite 700	16
Insurance, Commissioner of	125 S. Webster St.	11
Investment Board	121 E. Wilson St.	12
Justice, Department of	17 W. Main St.	5
Legislative Audit Bureau	22 E. Mifflin St., Suite 500	2
Legislative Council	1 E. Main St., Suite 401	4
Legislative Fiscal Bureau	1 E. Main St., Suite 301	4
Legislative Reference Bureau	1 E. Main St., Suite 200	4
Legislative Technology Services Bureau	17 W. Main St., Suite 200	5
Lieutenant Governor, Office of the	State Capitol, Rm. 19 East	1
Military Affairs, Department of	2400 Wright St.	—
Natural Resources, Department of	101 S. Webster St.	10
Public Instruction, Department of	125 S. Webster St.	11
Public Service Commission	610 N. Whitney Way	—
Railroads, Office of the Commissioner	610 N. Whitney Way, Rm. 110	—
Revenue, Department of	2135 Rimrock Rd.	—
Safety and Professional Services, Department of	1400 E. Washington Ave., Rm. 112	—
Secretary of State, Office of the	30 W. Mifflin St., 10th Floor	8
State Courts, Director of	State Capitol, Rm. 16 East	1
State Employment Relations, Office of	101 E. Wilson St., 4th Floor	13
State Law Library	120 Martin Luther King, Jr. Blvd.	5
State Historical Society Museum	30 N. Carroll St.	7
State Historical Society of Wisconsin	816 State St.	—
State Public Defender, Office of the	315 N. Henry St., 2nd Floor	6
State Treasurer, Office of the	State Capitol, Rm. B41 West	1
Supreme Court	State Capitol, Rm. 16 East	1
Technical College System	4622 University Ave.	—
Tourism, Department of	201 W. Washington Ave.	16
Transportation, Department of	4802 Sheboygan Ave.	—
University of Wisconsin System	1220 Linden Dr.	—
Veterans Affairs, Department of	201 W. Washington Ave.	16
Wisconsin Economic Development Corporation	201 W. Washington Ave.	16
Wisconsin Veterans Museum	30 W. Mifflin St.	8
Workforce Development, Department of	201 E. Washington Ave.	9

Source: Agency Directory, at: http://www.wisconsin.gov/pages/AllAgencies.aspx [June 2015].

CENTRAL MADISON LOCATOR MAP

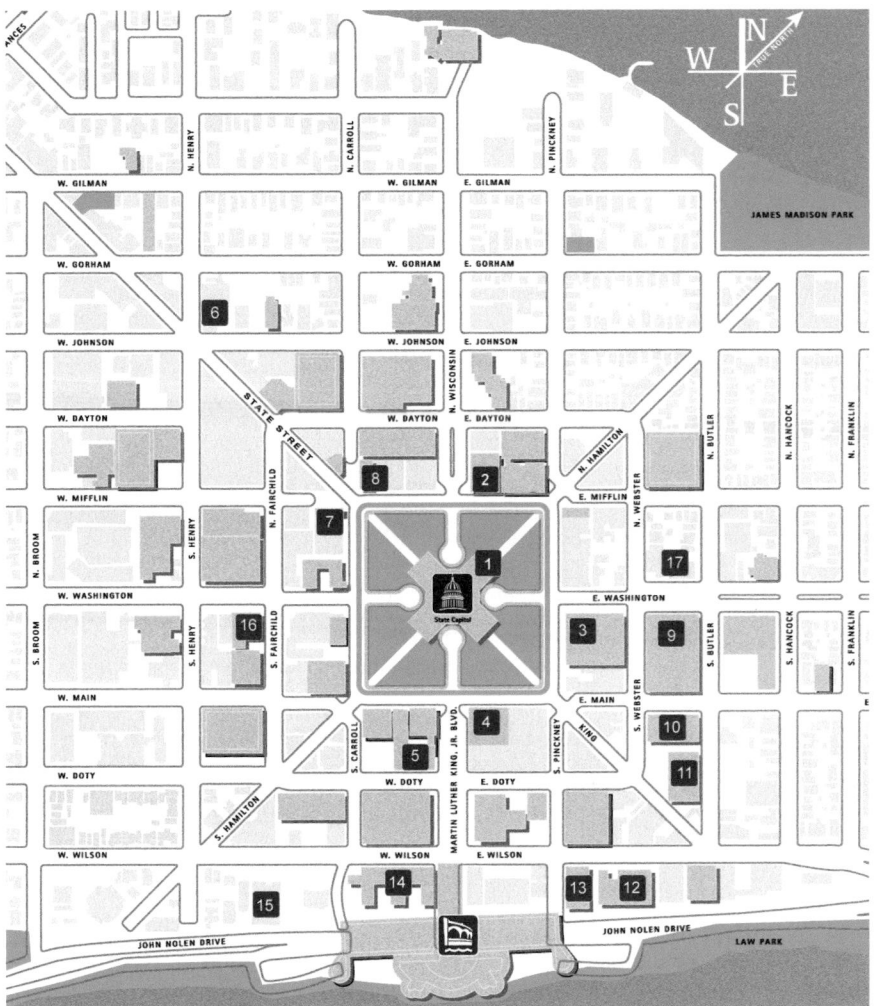

Base map: City of Madison, Planning Division.

THE FRAMEWORK OF WISCONSIN GOVERNMENT

Government at a Glance

Wisconsin state government is divided into three branches: legislative, executive, and judicial. The legislative branch includes the Wisconsin Legislature, which is composed of the senate and the assembly, and the service agencies and staff that assist the legislators. The executive branch, headed by the governor, includes five other elected constitutional officers, as well as 17 departments and 10 independent agencies created by statute. The judicial branch consists of the Wisconsin Supreme Court, the Court of Appeals, circuit courts, and municipal courts, as well as the staff and advisory groups that assist the courts. Each of the three branches is described in detail in its respective section of the *Blue Book.*

Local units of government in Wisconsin include 72 counties, 190 cities, 407 villages, 1,255 towns, and several hundred special districts.

Origins of the 30th State

Wisconsin's original residents were Native American hunters who arrived here about 14,000 years ago. The area's first farmers appear to have been the Hopewell people who raised corn, squash, and pumpkins about 2,000 years ago. They also were hunters and fishers, and their trade routes stretched to the Atlantic Coast and the Gulf of Mexico. Later arrivals included the Chippewa, Ho-Chunk (Winnebago), Mahican/Munsee, Menominee, Oneida, Potawatomi, and Sioux.

From Wilderness to Statehood. The first Europeans to reach Wisconsin were French explorers, fur trappers, and missionaries. Wisconsin was included in the French sphere of influence from the 1630s until the signing of the 1763 Treaty of Paris, which concluded the French and Indian War and ceded the land encompassing Wisconsin to Great Britain. At the end of the Revolutionary War, 20 years later, the British ceded the vast, unsettled territory west of the Appalachian Mountains to the new United States of America. (Actual British control of the area did not end, however, until 1814 at the conclusion of the War of 1812.)

As a U.S. territory, Wisconsin was initially governed by the Northwest Ordinance of 1787, and then sequentially by the laws of the Indiana Territory, the Illinois Territory, the Michigan Territory and, finally in 1836, the Wisconsin Territory.

On August 6, 1846, the Congress of the United States authorized the people living in what was then called the Territory of Wisconsin "to form a constitution and State government, for the purpose of being admitted into the Union". Based on this enabling act, the people of the territory called a constitutional convention in Madison to draft a fundamental law for governing the new state. The first proposal for a constitution was drafted in 1846 and submitted to the people on April 6, 1847, but the voters rejected it on a 20,231-to-14,119 vote because of several controversial provisions involving banking, voting rights, property rights of married women, and homesteading.

On March 13, 1848, a second convention submitted its draft, which was ratified by a vote of 16,799 to 6,384. The constitution then adopted remains in force to this day, although it has been amended on numerous occasions.

On May 29, 1848, Wisconsin became the 30th state admitted to the Union.

State Powers and Prohibitions. The enabling act passed by the U.S. Congress in 1846 declared that the Territory of Wisconsin was authorized to form a constitution and state government "on an equal footing with the original States in all respects whatsoever". From the moment of its birth, like the original states, the State of Wisconsin, its people, its lawmaking bodies, its administrative machinery, and its courts were subject to the U.S. Constitution.

In ratifying the U.S. Constitution, the 13 original states specifically delegated a number of powers to the U.S. Congress. Wisconsin agreed to this delegation when joining the Union. Congress is given the authority to regulate interstate and foreign commerce, maintain armed forces, declare war, coin money, establish a postal system, and grant patents and copyrights. Congress also has power to "make all laws which shall be necessary and proper" for carrying out its responsibilities.

The Tenth Amendment to the U.S. Constitution specifies: "The powers not delegated to the United States by the constitution, nor prohibited by it to the States, are reserved to the States, respectively, or to the people." Although the powers delegated to the federal government and the powers reserved to the states might appear to be neatly delineated, government responsibilities and activities have not been that clear-cut. In fact, many powers are exercised concurrently by the federal government and the states. Through judicial interpretation and laws enacted in response to changing societal needs, the powers exercised by Congress have been greatly expanded to include many activities once considered reserved to the states, as well as new authority not even imagined by the drafters, such as regulation of television and radio or development of a space exploration program. Likewise, the states have broadened their functions as society and technology have evolved.

The Many Sources of State Law

On April 20, 1836, the U.S. Congress passed the Organic Law establishing the Wisconsin Territory, as of July 3, 1836. It prescribed that the existing laws of the Territory of Michigan, to which Wisconsin had belonged, were to be "extended over the said territory . . . subject, nevertheless, to be altered, modified or repealed, by the governor and legislative assembly".

The Wisconsin Constitution continued the laws of the Territory of Wisconsin, by providing in Section 2 of Article XIV: "All laws now in force in the territory of Wisconsin which are not repugnant to this constitution shall remain in force until they expire by their own limitation or be altered or repealed by the legislature."

In addition to the provisions of the U.S. and Wisconsin Constitutions, the citizens of this state are governed by the wide-ranging laws contained in the six volumes of the Wisconsin Statutes. Even this body of law is not detailed enough. The Wisconsin Legislature has found that some areas are so technically complex that implementation of legislative policy must be left to certain state agencies with the power to issue administrative rules that have the effect of state law.

Notwithstanding the detailed wording of statutory law and administrative rules, there will still be specific provisions that are subject to various interpretations. In these cases, formal law is further defined by courts or administrative commissions authorized to interpret state law.

Making State Government Work

According to the general division of state government powers, the legislative branch enacts the laws; the executive branch carries them out (or *executes* them); and the judicial branch interprets them. This very simple description of state government tells only part of the story. Actually, all three branches play a part in establishing public policy, determining the meaning of the law, and ensuring that the laws are faithfully administered.

When most people think of "the law", they tend to regard it as something restrictive – a rule prohibiting certain actions. Although this may be one outcome, the real reason for the existence of law in a democratic system is to give the greatest benefit to the greatest number of people while protecting the individual rights prescribed by the federal and state constitutions. The only manner in which this can be achieved is by establishing a specific set of rules that attempt to prescribe for all citizens the limits of their rights and obligations.

Developing Public Policy. Policy cannot become law without legislative action. Each member of the legislature may introduce bills proposing new laws, joint resolutions proposing constitutional amendments, or simple and joint resolutions dealing with other matters, and each may offer amendments to proposals introduced by other members.

The governor also plays a major role in the development of formal public policy. The Wisconsin Constitution requires the governor to "communicate to the legislature, at every session, the condition of the state, and recommend such matters . . . for their consideration as he may deem expedient." This is done in the State of the State message, the budget message, and in special messages focusing on particular matters. In cases where a specific problem needs immediate legislative attention, the governor may call the legislature into a special session focusing on the matter. Before a bill becomes law, it must be passed by the legislature and signed by the governor. If the governor vetoes the bill instead of signing it, it can only become law if it is approved a second time by a two-thirds vote in each house of the legislature. In the case of appropriation bills that authorize spending, such as a budget, the governor can use the "partial veto" and veto only parts of the bill rather than the whole proposal. The veto power gives the governor a great deal of control over the content of any new law.

Once a new proposal is enacted, the governor, as the chief executive officer of the state, takes an active part in implementing the policy through oversight of the agencies involved in day-today administration of the law. According to the constitution, the governor "shall expedite all such measures as may be resolved upon by the legislature, and shall take care that the laws be faithfully executed."

The judicial branch also has an official role to play in the development of public policy. Although courts are not involved in the enactment of new laws, they do resolve conflicts about existing law – that is, they interpret the law. A court decision may occasionally result in an interpretation of a law that has quite a different effect from what the legislature originally intended. The legislature can redraft and clarify that law if it disagrees with the interpretation.

The opinions and concerns voiced by citizens of Wisconsin constitute the major source of ideas for new legislation. New policy proposals often result from everyday situations citizens encounter in their own communities. If they think that greater property tax relief is needed or that health insurance is unaffordable or that the business climate could be improved, they may determine "there ought to be a law". An individual may decide to write a letter to the editor of a newspaper, contact a legislator, or tell the governor about it. An association to which the person belongs may hire a spokesperson, called a "lobbyist", to recommend legislation or appear at legislative hearings.

State agencies are another primary source of public policy ideas. While administering current programs, departments are in a natural position to see how policies are working and whether they need to be changed, expanded, or abolished. Department heads have opportunities to discuss their insights with the governor, especially during development of the biennial budget, and they may be invited to contribute expert testimony at legislative hearings.

Increasing Services. In 1848, when Wisconsin became a state, government services were relatively simple. In his annual report of 1849, the secretary of state reported payments to only 14 people within the state's executive branch, and that included the constitutional officers. In 2014, state employment totaled 70,357 full-time equivalent positions.

This growth is primarily the result of the increasing size and complexity of today's society. At one time, many Wisconsin residents had little opportunity for formal schooling; in 2014, the University of Wisconsin System enrolled 180,979 students and public elementary and secondary enrollments totaled 870,652. In 2013, the Technical College System served 326,544 students. Once, the wooden Watertown Plank Road constituted an unequaled technological advancement over the muddy wagon trails of the day; by 2015, Wisconsin had 115,212 miles of highways and streets, more than 79% of them paved. In 2015, the state had 94 publicly owned airports. In 1915, the average U.S. life expectancy at birth was 54.5 years; by 2013, it had reached 78.8 years (76.4 for males and 81.2 for females). As Wisconsin's population increases in numbers and lives longer, the state faces many challenges, including improving education, renovating mature industries, developing the economy, protecting the environment, and improving transportation and health care.

Local Units of Government

In order to carry out its numerous responsibilities, every state has created subordinate units of local government. In most cases, these are legal, rather than constitutional, creations. This means the legislature may abolish them, change them, or give them increased or decreased powers and duties, as it chooses. In Wisconsin, the local units of government consist of counties, cities, villages, towns, and school districts. Special districts may be formed to handle regional concerns. Within the limits of statutory law, each unit has the power to tax and to make legally binding rules governing its own affairs.

Counties. Wisconsin has 72 counties. Together, they cover the entire territory of the state. The government offices for each county are located in a municipality within the county designated as the "county seat". The governing body of the county is the board of supervisors. The number of supervisors may vary from county to county, but within a particular county each supervisor must represent, as nearly as practicable, an equal number of inhabitants. County supervisors are elected in the spring nonpartisan elections for 2-year terms. (Milwaukee County Board Supervisors are elected to 2-year terms beginning in 2016. Current supervisors serve 4-year terms.) Other county officials, all of whom are elected in the fall partisan elections for 4-year terms, include the sheriff, the district attorney, clerk, treasurer, coroner, register of deeds, and clerk of circuit courts. As permitted by law, counties may employ a registered land surveyor in lieu of electing a surveyor, and the majority do. An appointed county medical examiner system may be substituted for an elected coroner. (Milwaukee County must appoint a medical examiner and a registered land surveyor.)

Since January 1, 1987, counties have been required to have a central administrative officer. Counties with a population of 500,000 or more (currently only Milwaukee County) must elect a "county executive", who is chosen for a 4-year term in the spring nonpartisan elections. Counties with a population of less than 500,000 may choose to have a "county administrator" appointed by the county board. If the county has neither an executive nor an administrator, the board must designate an elected or appointed official to serve as "administrative coordinator" for the county. The county board chairperson often is chosen for this post. There are 11 counties with elected executives; 25 have appointed administrators; and 32 have an appointed administrative coordinator.

Cities and Villages. Wisconsin's 190 cities and 407 villages are incorporated under general law. Based on a constitutional amendment ratified in 1924, they have "home rule" powers to determine their local affairs. In general, minimum population for incorporation as a village is 150 residents for an isolated village and 2,500 for a metropolitan village located in a more densely populated area. For cities, the minimums are 1,000 and 5,000, respectively, but an existing village that exceeds 1,000 population may opt for city status. Depending on population, a city qualifies to be in one of four classes. However, an increase or decrease in population does not automatically move a city to a different classification. In order to move from one class to another, a city whose population makes it eligible to be in a different class may initiate the action by making the required changes in governmental structure and by the mayor publishing a proclamation to that effect. For example, Milwaukee currently is the only "first class" city. Although Madison meets the population requirements to change from "second class" to "first class", it has not chosen to do so.

Wisconsin cities currently use two forms of executive organization. The vast majority elect a mayor and a city common council, but 10 operate under a council-manager system, in which the elected council selects the manager to serve as chief executive. In those cities with the mayor-council form of government, 76 have also appointed full- or part-time city administrators. City alderpersons are elected for 2-year terms in the spring nonpartisan elections, except in Milwaukee, where alderpersons serve 4-year terms.

In most villages, executive power is vested in the village president, who presides over the village board of trustees and votes as an *ex officio* trustee, but 9 villages use a village manager form of government with the manager chosen by the elected board. An additional 77 have created full- or part-time village administrators. Village trustees are elected for 2-year terms in the spring nonpartisan elections.

Towns. Town governments govern those areas of Wisconsin that are not included inside the corporate boundaries of either a city or a village. Wisconsin has 1,255 towns, including the entire County of Menominee, which is designated as a town. Towns have only those powers granted by the Wisconsin Statutes. In addition to their traditional responsibility for local road maintenance, town governments carry out a variety of functions and, in some instances, even undertake urban-type services. The town board is usually composed of 3 supervisors, but if a board is authorized to exercise village powers or if the town population is 2,500 or more it may have up to 5 members. (Menominee County has 7 town board members, who also serve as the county board of supervisors.) Town supervisors are elected for 2-year terms in the spring nonpartisan election. They perform a number of administrative functions, and the town board chairperson has certain executive powers and duties. A town board may also create the position of town administrator.

Supervisors are expected to carry out the policies set at the annual town meeting. The annual meeting is held on the third Tuesday of April (or another date set by the electors), and during the meeting all qualified voters of the town are entitled to discuss and vote on matters specified by state law.

School Districts. There are 424 school districts in Wisconsin. These are special units of government organized to carry out a single function, the operation of the public schools. Each district is run by an elected school board, which appoints the district administrators.

WISCONSIN STATE GOVE
July

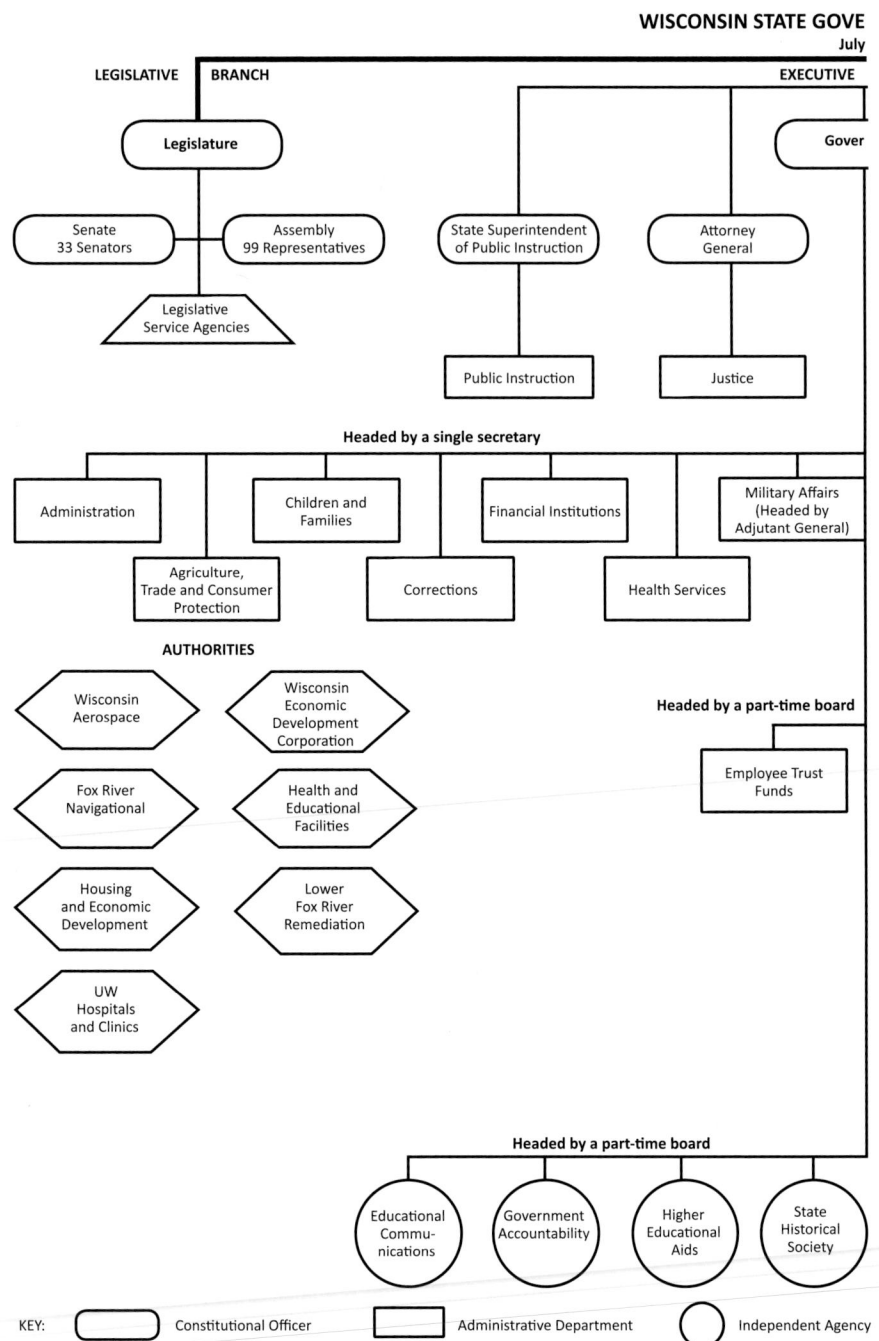

LEGISLATIVE BRANCH

EXECUTIVE

Legislature

Gover

Senate
33 Senators

Assembly
99 Representatives

State Superintendent
of Public Instruction

Attorney
General

Legislative
Service Agencies

Public Instruction

Justice

Headed by a single secretary

Administration

Children and
Families

Financial Institutions

Military Affairs
(Headed by
Adjutant General)

Agriculture,
Trade and Consumer
Protection

Corrections

Health Services

AUTHORITIES

Wisconsin
Aerospace

Wisconsin
Economic
Development
Corporation

Headed by a part-time board

Fox River
Navigational

Health and
Educational
Facilities

Employee Trust
Funds

Housing
and Economic
Development

Lower
Fox River
Remediation

UW
Hospitals
and Clinics

Headed by a part-time board

Educational
Commu-
nications

Government
Accountability

Higher
Educational
Aids

State
Historical
Society

KEY: Constitutional Officer   Administrative Department   Independent Agency

RNMENT ORGANIZATION
2015

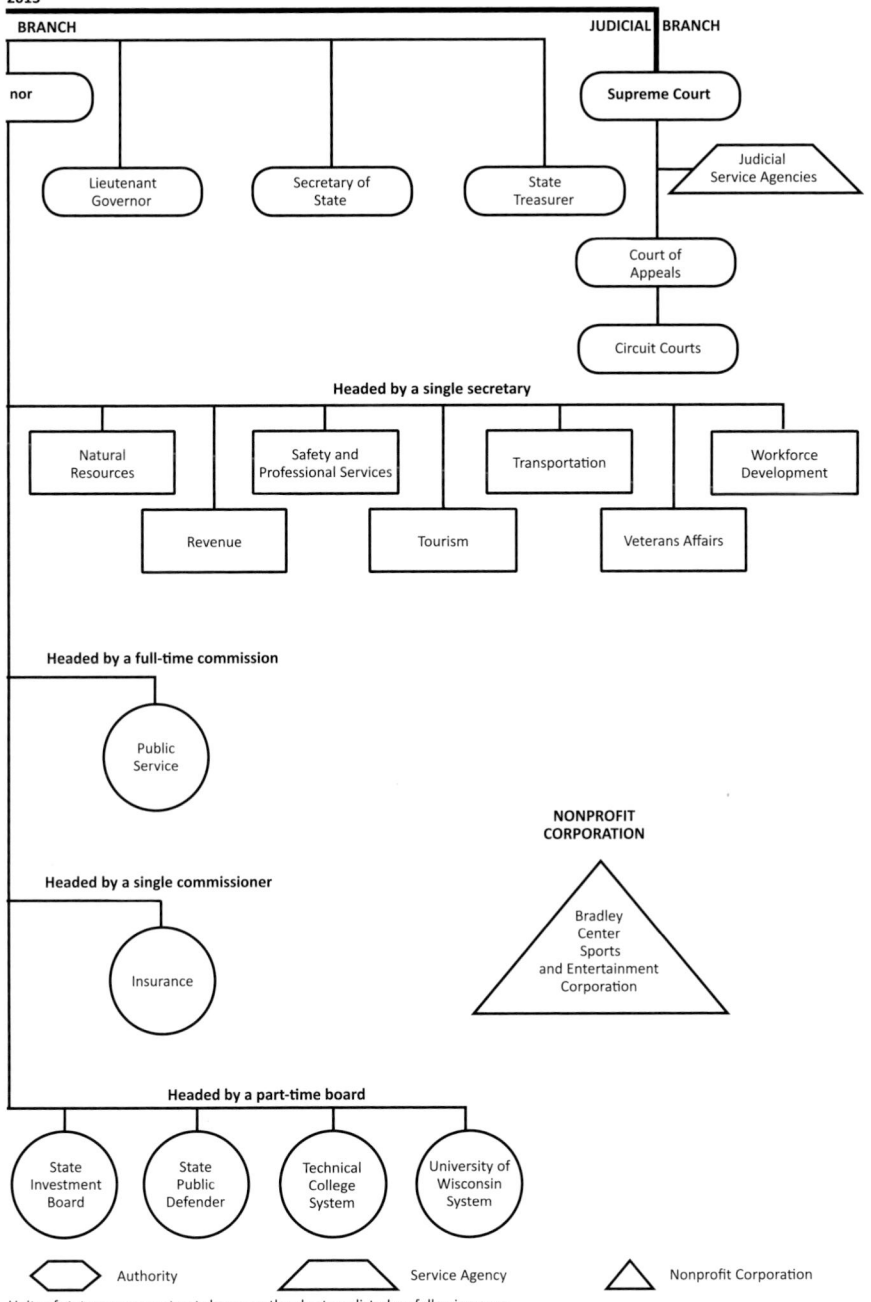

BRANCH   JUDICIAL BRANCH

nor

Supreme Court

Judicial
Service Agencies

Lieutenant
Governor

Secretary of
State

State
Treasurer

Court of
Appeals

Circuit Courts

Headed by a single secretary

Natural
Resources

Safety and
Professional Services

Transportation

Workforce
Development

Revenue

Tourism

Veterans Affairs

Headed by a full-time commission

Public
Service

**NONPROFIT
CORPORATION**

Headed by a single commissioner

Insurance

Bradley
Center
Sports
and Entertainment
Corporation

Headed by a part-time board

State
Investment
Board

State
Public
Defender

Technical
College
System

University of
Wisconsin
System

Authority   Service Agency   Nonprofit Corporation

Units of state government not shown on the chart are listed on following page.

Units of State Government Not Shown on Organization Chart

The following units of state government are independent entities, which are attached to the agencies indicated for administrative purposes under Section 15.03 of the statutes.

Boards

Board on Aging and Long-Term Care (DOA)

Building Inspector Review Board (DSPS)

Burial Sites Preservation Board (State Historical Society)

Child Abuse and Neglect Prevention Board (DCF)

Claims Board (DOA)

College Savings Program Board (DOA)

Crime Victims Rights Board (DOJ)

Depository Selection Board (DOA)

Disability Board (Governor)

Educational Approval Board (Technical College System)

Emergency Medical Services Board (DHS)

Environmental Education Board (UW)

Historic Preservation Review Board (State Historical Society)

Incorporation Review Board (DOA)

Information Technology Management Board (DOA)

Interstate Adult Offender Supervision Board (DOC)

State Board for Interstate Juvenile Supervision (DOC)

Investment and Local Impact Fund Board (DOR)

Kickapoo Reserve Management Board (Tourism)

Lake Michigan Commercial Fishing Board (DNR)

Lake Superior Commercial Fishing Board (DNR)

Land and Water Conservation Board (DATCP)

Law Enforcement Standards Board (DOJ)

Livestock Facility Siting Review Board (DATCP)

Lower Wisconsin State Riverway Board (Tourism)

National and Community Service Board (DOA)

Board for People with Developmental Disabilities (DOA)

Prison Industries Board (DOC)

Public Records Board (DOA)

Small Business Regulatory Review Board (DOA)

State Capitol and Executive Residence Board (DOA)

State Fair Park Board (Tourism)

State Use Board (DOA)

Veterinary Diagnostic Laboratory Board (UW)

Volunteer Fire Fighter and Emergency Medical Technician Service Award Board (DOA)

Waste Facility Siting Board (DOA)

Commissions

Employment Relations Commission (DWD)

Labor and Industry Review Commission (DWD)

Tax Appeals Commission (DOA)

Wisconsin Waterways Commission (DNR)

Councils

Bioenergy Council (DATCP)

Electronic Recording Council (DOA)

Groundwater Coordinating Council (DNR)

Interoperability Council (DOA)

Invasive Species Council (DNR)

Milwaukee Child Welfare Partnership Council (DCF)

Council on Offender Reentry (DOC)

Council on Physical Disabilities (DHS)

Council on Recycling (DNR)

Council on Utility Public Benefits (DOA)

Women's Council (DOA)

Divisions

Division of Hearings and Appeals (DOA)

Division of Trust Lands and Investments (DOA)

Offices

Office of Business Development (DOA)

Office of Credit Unions (DFI)

Office of the Commissioner of Railroads (PSC)

Office of State Employment Relations (DOA)

Legislative Branch

5

The legislative branch: profile of the legislative branch, description of the legislative process, summary of 2013-2014 legislation, and description of legislative committees and service agencies

Assembly Chamber

(Sarah Girkin)

OFFICERS OF THE 2015 LEGISLATURE

SENATE

President . . . . Senator Mary A. Lazich

President pro tempore . . . . Senator Rick Gudex

Chief clerk . . . . Honorable Jeffrey Renk

Sergeant at arms . . . . Honorable Edward A. Blazel

	Majority Party Officers	**Minority Party Officers**
Leader	Senator Scott L. Fitzgerald	Senator Jennifer Shilling
Assistant leader	vacant	Senator Dave Hansen
Caucus chairperson . .	Senator Sheila E. Harsdorf	Senator Julie M. Lassa
Caucus vice chairperson	Senator Van H. Wanggaard	Senator Kathleen Vinehout

Chief Clerk: Mailing Address: P.O. Box 7882, Madison 53707-7882; Location: B20 South East, State Capitol; Telephone: (608) 266-2517.

Sergeant at Arms: Mailing Address: P.O. Box 7882, Madison 53707-7882; Location: B35 South, State Capitol; Telephone: (608) 266-1801.

ASSEMBLY

Speaker. . . . . Representative Robin J. Vos

Speaker pro tempore . . . . Representative Tyler August

Chief clerk . . . . Honorable Patrick E. Fuller

Sergeant at arms . . . . Honorable Anne Tonnon Byers

	Majority Party Officers	**Minority Party Officers**
Leader	Representative Jim Steineke	Representative Peter W. Barca
Assistant leader	Representative Dan Knodl	Representative Katrina Shankland
Caucus chairperson . .	Representative John Murtha	Representative Andy Jorgensen
Caucus vice chairperson	Representative Lee Nerison	Representative JoCasta Zamarripa
Caucus secretary	Representative Jessie Rodriguez	Representative Beth Meyers
Caucus sergeant at arms	Representative Samantha Kerkman	Representative Josh Zepnick

Chief Clerk: Mailing Address: P.O. Box 8952, Madison 53708-8952; Location: 17 West Main Street, Suite 401; Telephone: (608) 266-1501.

Sergeant at Arms: Mailing Address: P.O. Box 8952, Madison 53708-8952; Location: 411 West, State Capitol; Telephone: (608) 266-1503.

LEGISLATIVE HOTLINE: Monday-Friday, 8:15 a.m.-4:45 p.m.; Telephone: Madison Area: 266-9960; Outside Madison Area: (800) 362-9472.

LEGISLATIVE INTERNET ADDRESS: http://www.legis.wisconsin.gov

LEGISLATIVE BRANCH

A PROFILE OF THE LEGISLATIVE BRANCH

The legislative branch consists of the bicameral Wisconsin Legislature, made up of the senate with 33 members and the assembly with 99 members, together with the service agencies created by the legislature and the staff employed by each house. The legislature's main responsibility is to make policy by enacting state laws. Its service agencies assist it by performing fiscal analysis, research, bill drafting, auditing, statute editing, and information technology functions.

A new legislature is sworn into office in January of each odd-numbered year, and it meets in continuous biennial session until its successor is sworn in. The 2015 Legislature is the 102nd Wisconsin Legislature. It convened on January 5, 2015, and will continue until January 3, 2017.

U.S. and Wisconsin Constitutions Grant Broad Legislative Powers. The power to determine the state's policies and programs lies primarily in the legislative branch of state government. According to the Wisconsin Constitution: "The legislative power shall be vested in a senate and assembly." This power is quite extensive, but certain limitations are imposed by both the U.S. Constitution and the Wisconsin Constitution. In addition, the legislature's power is restricted by the governor's authority to veto legislation, but a veto may be overridden by a two-thirds vote in both houses of the legislature.

All actions taken by the legislature must conform with the U.S. Constitution. For example, the U.S. Congress has exclusive powers to regulate foreign affairs and coin money, and states are denied the power to make treaties with foreign countries. In addition, state legislation may not abridge the rights guaranteed in the U.S. Bill of Rights. Powers that are not granted exclusively to the U.S. Congress or denied the states are considered to be reserved for the individual states.

In addition to the boundaries set by the U.S. Constitution, the legislature's authority is also limited by the state constitution. For instance, the Wisconsin Constitution requires the legislature to establish as uniform a system of town government as practicable, prevents it from enacting private or special laws on certain subjects, and prohibits laws that would infringe on the rights of Wisconsin citizens, as protected by the Declaration of Rights of the Wisconsin Constitution.

Biennial Sessions: 4-Year Senate Terms; 2-Year Assembly Terms. Originally, members of the assembly served for one year, while senators served for 2 years. An 1881 constitutional amendment doubled the respective terms to the current 2 and 4 years and converted the legislature from annual to biennial sessions.

Since its adoption on March 13, 1848, the Wisconsin Constitution has provided that the membership of the assembly shall be not less than 54 nor more than 100, and the membership of the senate shall consist of not more than one-third nor less than one-fourth of the number of assembly members. The first legislature had 85 members – 19 senators and 66 assemblymen. (Assembly members were renamed "representatives to the assembly" in 1969.) The number increased several times until the legislature became a 133-member body in 1862, with the constitutionally permitted maximums of 33 in the senate and 100 in the assembly. Over a century later, membership dropped to 132 in the 1973 Legislature, when the number of representatives was reduced to 99 so that each of the 33 senate districts would encompass 3 assembly districts. This is the current number and structure.

THE WISCONSIN LEGISLATURE

Number of Positions 2015 Legislature: Senate: 33 members, 202 employees (including senators); Assembly: 99 members, 317 employees (including representatives).

Total Budget 2013-15: $149,991,100 (including service agencies).

Constitutional Reference: Article IV.

Statutory Reference: Chapter 13, Subchapter I.

Election of Legislators. All members of the legislature are elected from single-member districts. At the general election on the first Tuesday after the first Monday in November of even-numbered years, the voters of Wisconsin elect all members of the assembly and approximately one-half of the senators. These legislators-elect assume office in January of the following odd-numbered year when they convene to open the new legislative session at the state capitol, together with the "holdover" senators who still have 2 years remaining of their 4-year terms. When a midterm vacancy occurs in any legislative office, it is filled through a special election called by the governor.

The 33 senators are elected for 4-year terms from districts numbered 1 through 33. The 16 senators representing even-numbered districts are elected in the years in which a presidential election occurs. The 17 senators who represent odd-numbered districts are elected in the years in which a gubernatorial election is held.

Since statehood in 1848, the Wisconsin Constitution has required the legislature, after each U.S. decennial census, to redraw the districts for both houses "according to the number of inhabitants". Thus, Wisconsin was following this practice long before the U.S. Supreme Court decided in 1962 that all states must redistrict according to the "one person, one vote" principle.

Under the campaign finance reporting law enacted by the 1973 Legislature, candidates for the legislature, as well as for other public offices, are required to make full, detailed disclosure of their campaign contributions and expenditures. Candidates must make this disclosure to the Elections Division of the Government Accountability Board. Limits are placed on the amounts of contributions received from individuals and various committees. State law also requires legislators and candidates for legislative office to file a statement of their economic interests with the Ethics and Accountability Division of the Government Accountability Board.

Political Parties in the Legislative Process. Partisan political organizations play an important role in the Wisconsin legislative process. Since 1949, all legislators, with rare exceptions, have been affiliated with either the Democratic Party or the Republican Party. The strongest representation of other parties was between 1911 and 1937, when there were one or more Socialists in the legislature, and between 1933 and 1947, when the Progressives maintained an independent party. In 1937, the Progressive Party had a plurality in both houses.

Party organization in the legislature is based on the party group called the "caucus". In each house, all members of a particular political party form that party's caucus. Thus, there are four caucuses related to the party divisions in the two houses. The primary purpose of a caucus is to help party members maintain a unified position on critical issues. Party leaders, however, do not expect to secure party uniformity on every measure under consideration.

Caucus meetings may be held at regular intervals or whenever convened by party leaders, and occasionally the senate and assembly caucuses of the same party meet in joint caucus. A caucus meeting is scheduled shortly after the general election and before the opening of the session to select candidates for the various leadership positions in each house. Although each party caucus nominates a slate of officers, the positions are usually won by the nominees of the majority party when a vote is taken in the full house.

Legislative Officers and Leadership. The Wisconsin Constitution originally required the lieutenant governor to serve as president of the senate. As a result of an April 1979 constitutional amendment, the senate now selects its own president from among its members. When the president of the senate is absent or unable to preside, the president pro tempore, elected from the membership, may preside as substitute president.

The presiding officer of the assembly is the speaker, who is elected by majority vote of the assembly membership. The speaker supervises all other officers of the chamber and appoints

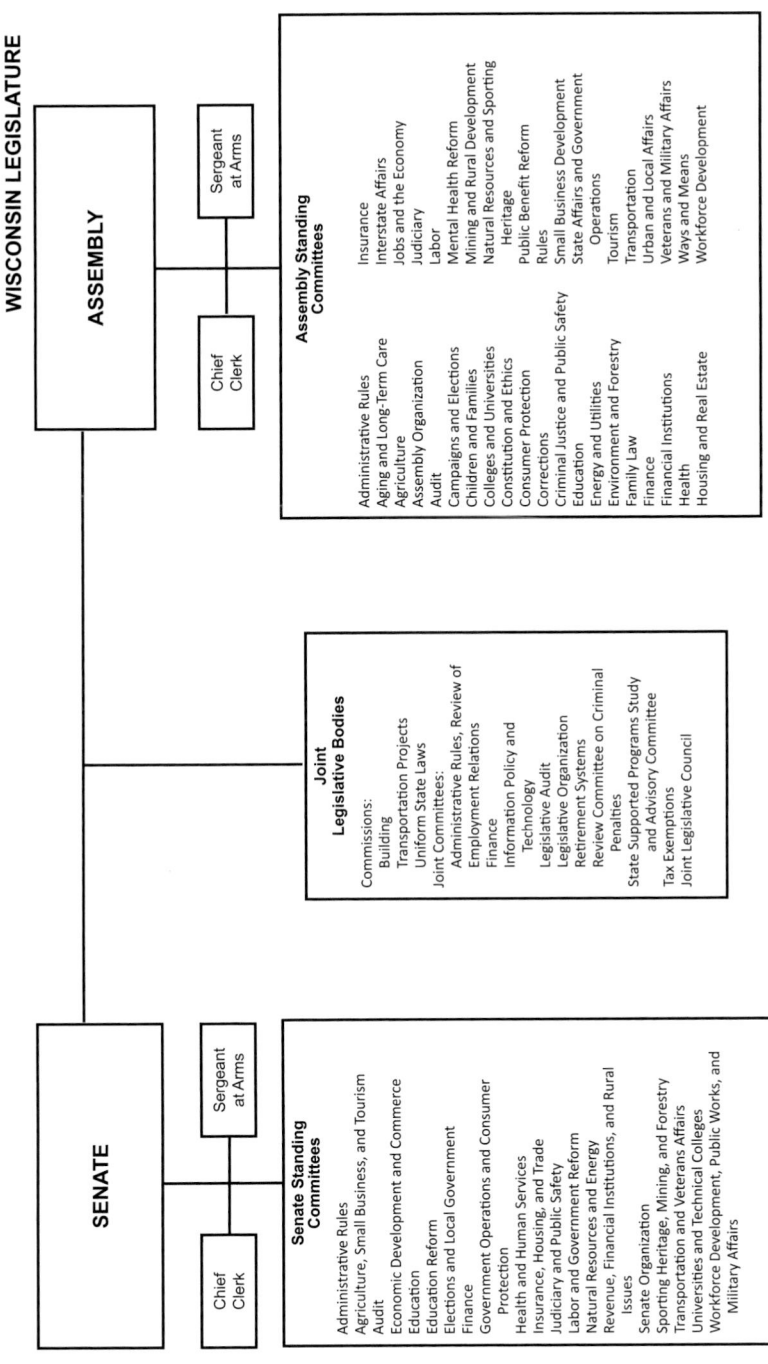

WISCONSIN LEGISLATURE

LEGISLATURE

ASSEMBLY

Chief Clerk

Sergeant at Arms

Assembly Standing Committees

Administrative Rules
Aging and Long-Term Care
Agriculture
Assembly Organization
Audit
Campaigns and Elections
Children and Families
Colleges and Universities
Constitution and Ethics
Consumer Protection
Corrections
Criminal Justice and Public Safety
Education
Energy and Utilities
Environment and Forestry
Family Law
Finance
Financial Institutions
Health
Housing and Real Estate
Insurance
Interstate Affairs
Jobs and the Economy
Judiciary
Labor
Mental Health Reform
Mining and Rural Development
Natural Resources and Sporting Heritage
Public Benefit Reform
Rules
Small Business Development
State Affairs and Government Operations
Tourism
Transportation
Urban and Local Affairs
Veterans and Military Affairs
Ways and Means
Workforce Development

Joint Legislative Bodies

Commissions:
Building
Transportation Projects
Uniform State Laws
Joint Committees:
Administrative Rules, Review of
Employment Relations
Finance
Information Policy and Technology
Legislative Audit
Legislative Organization
Retirement Systems
Review Committee on Criminal Penalties
State Supported Programs Study and Advisory Committee
Tax Exemptions
Joint Legislative Council

SENATE

Chief Clerk

Sergeant at Arms

Senate Standing Committees

Administrative Rules
Agriculture, Small Business, and Tourism
Audit
Economic Development and Commerce
Education
Education Reform
Elections and Local Government
Finance
Government Operations and Consumer Protection
Health and Human Services
Insurance, Housing, and Trade
Judiciary and Public Safety
Labor and Government Reform
Natural Resources and Energy
Revenue, Financial Institutions, and Rural Issues
Senate Organization
Sporting Heritage, Mining, and Forestry
Transportation and Veterans Affairs
Universities and Technical Colleges
Workforce Development, Public Works, and Military Affairs

Senate Majority Leader Scott Fitzgerald is responsible for shepherding his party's agenda through the Senate. President Mary Lazich presides impartially over debate. Chief Clerk Jeff Renk (right) is the chief administrative officer of the Senate. (Jay Salvo, Legislative Photographer)

committees. When the speaker is absent or unable to preside, the speaker pro tempore, who is also elected from the membership, may substitute.

Each party in each house elects floor leaders, respectively known as the majority leader and assistant majority leader and the minority leader and assistant minority leader. To varying degrees, these party officers play powerful roles in directing and coordinating legislative activities.

Each house has a chief clerk and a sergeant at arms, who are elected by, but are not themselves members of, the legislature. The chief clerk serves as the clerk of the house when it is in session and supervises the preparation of legislative records. In conjunction with the presiding officers, the chief clerks supervise personnel and administrative functions for their respective houses. The sergeants at arms maintain order in and about the chambers and supervise the messengers.

Legislative Compensation. When the 2015 Legislature convened on January 5, 2015, all members were eligible for a salary of $50,950 per year. The process for setting legislative salaries requires the Director of the Office of State Employment Relations to submit proposed changes as part of the state compensation plan to the legislature's Joint Committee on Employment Relations. If the committee approves the plan, the new salary goes into effect for all legislators at the next inauguration. The committee also sets the salaries of the chief clerks and the sergeants at arms of the two houses within a range established under civil service procedures.

Members of the legislature, the chief clerks, and the sergeants at arms are entitled to a per diem allowance for living expenses for each day spent in Madison on legislative business. For senators, the maximum per diem is $88 per day; for representatives, it is $138 per day if staying overnight and $69 per day if not staying overnight. Per diem may not be claimed in the assembly for more than 153 days in a year. All members are reimbursed for one weekly round trip from the capital to their homes. They also are reimbursed for expenses incurred while serving as legislative members of a state or interstate agency or when specifically authorized to attend meetings of such agencies as nonmembers. The speaker of the assembly also receives a stipend, currently $25 per month.

Legislative Sessions. Members of each new legislature convene in the state capitol at 2 p.m. on the first Monday in January of each odd-numbered year to take the oath of office, select officers, and organize for business. The initial meeting occurs on January 3 if the first Monday falls on January 1 or 2. The previous legislature usually holds its adjournment meeting on the same day, just prior to the convening of the new legislature. Thus, there is almost no interim between the two.

Originally, the constitution required the legislature to meet once during each annual session. An 1881 amendment restricted the body to one meeting in the 2 years comprising the biennial session. As a result, the legislature scheduled its meetings in a continuing biennial session with periodic recesses. It would meet in regular session from January to June of the odd-numbered year and then recess after completing the major portion of its work. It then might reconvene from time to time in the remainder of the year, as needed. When a legislature had completed its work for the biennium, it adjourned *sine die,* meaning it did not set a date to reconvene. At that point, the session was over even though only a portion of its 2-year term had elapsed, and the legislature could not return unless called into special session by the governor.

In 1968, the state constitution was amended to permit the legislature to determine its own meeting schedule for the biennium. Beginning with the 1971 Legislature, annual sessions were formally initiated by law with the requirement that regular sessions begin in January of each year. Early in each biennium, the Joint Committee on Legislative Organization develops a work schedule for the 2-year period and submits it to the legislature in the form of a joint resolution. The 2015-2016 session schedule, for example, is structured around 16 floorperiods, with periods of committee work interspersed throughout the biennium.

Meetings of the respective houses of the legislature are held in the senate and assembly chambers in the state capitol. Usually, the legislature meets Tuesday to Thursday of each week. Toward the end of many floorperiods, however, the houses may meet continuously during the day Tuesday to Friday and hold evening sessions. Unless otherwise ordered, daily sessions begin at 10 a.m. for the senate and 9 a.m. for the assembly (10 a.m. on the first legislative day of the week). Daily sessions usually extend beyond noon, especially later in the legislative session. If business permits, afternoons may be devoted to committee hearings or a combination of hearings and late-afternoon sessions.

The word "session" has several meanings. The "legislative session" usually refers to the 2-year period that comprises a particular legislature. If the legislature is "not in session", that may mean it is in an interim period between floorperiods. Saying that either the senate or assembly is "not in session", however, may mean that the house has adjourned for the day or that it has recessed until a later hour of the same day.

Extraordinary and Special Sessions. Beginning in 1962, the legislature adopted procedures that would permit it to reassemble through a petition signed by a majority of the members of each house. An amendment to the 1977 Joint Rules codified this procedure by allowing the legislature to call itself into an "extraordinary session". The legislature may convene in extraordinary session or extend a floorperiod at the direction of the majority of the members of the organization committee in each house, by passage of a joint resolution, or by a joint petition signed by the majority of members of each house.

In addition, the governor has the authority to call a "special session", in which the legislature can act only upon matters specifically mentioned in the governor's call. As of the adjournment of the 2013 Legislature, there had been 93 special sessions since Wisconsin became a state in 1848. It is possible for a regular session and a special session to be scheduled at different times during a week or even on the same day. Because special sessions may occur at any time during the legislative biennium, enactments resulting from a special session are now numbered within the regular sequence of biennial laws.

Session Records. Each house of the legislature keeps a record of its actions known as the daily journal. This record differs from the federal *Congressional Record* in that it does not provide a transcript or abbreviated account of speeches made on the floor. It is, instead, an outline record of the business before the house, including procedural actions taken on all measures considered on that particular day, roll call votes, communications received from the governor or the other house, special committee reports, and miscellaneous items.

2015-2016 SESSION SCHEDULE

January 5, 2015	2015 Inauguration
January 7, 2015	Floorperiod
January 13, 2015	Floorperiod
January 20 to 29, 2015	Floorperiod
February 3 and 4, 2015	Floorperiod
February 10 to 12, 2015	Floorperiod
February 24 to March 5, 2015	Floorperiod
March 12, 2015	Deadline for sending bills to governor
March 17 to 19, 2015	Floorperiod
April 14 to 23, 2015	Floorperiod
May 5 to 14, 2015	Floorperiod
June 9 to 30, 2015 (or until passage of the budget)	Floorperiod
August 6, 2015	Deadline for sending nonbudget bills to governor
August 6, 2015 (or later)	Deadline for sending budget bill to governor*
September 15 to 24, 2015	Floorperiod
October 20 to November 5, 2015	Floorperiod
December 10, 2015	Deadline for sending bills to governor
January 12 to 21, 2016	Floorperiod
February 9 to 18, 2016	Floorperiod
March 8 to 17, 2016	Floorperiod
April 5 to 7, 2016	Last general-business floorperiod
April 21, 2016	Deadline for sending bills to governor
April 26 to 28, 2016	Limited-business floorperiod
May 5, 2016	Deadline for sending bills to governor
May 17 and 18, 2016	Veto review floorperiod
April 8, 2016, to January 3, 2017	Interim committee work
June 1, 2016	Deadline for sending bills to governor
January 3, 2017	2017 Inauguration

Any floorperiod may be convened earlier or extended beyond its scheduled dates by majority action of the membership or the organization committees of the two houses. The Committee on Senate Organization may schedule sessions outside floorperiods for senate action on gubernatorial nominations, but the assembly does not have to hold skeleton sessions during these appointment reviews. The legislature may call itself into extraordinary session or the governor may call a special session during a floorperiod or on any intervening day.

*Deadline for budget bill will depend on bill's passage.
Source: 2015 Senate Joint Resolution 1.

The *Bulletin of the Proceedings of the Wisconsin Legislature* is issued periodically during the legislative session as needed. Each issue contains a cumulative record of actions taken on bills, joint resolutions, and resolutions by both houses, listed by bill or resolution number. It includes a subject and author index to legislation; a subject index to the legislative journals; a subject index to new laws and enrolled bills and joint resolutions; a numeric listing of statute sections affected by these laws; changes made to statutory court rules by supreme court orders; and the complete text of constitutional amendments ratified since the most recent publication of the *Wisconsin Statutes*. Another part indexes and reports action on administrative rule changes.

Each week during the session, the chief clerks jointly issue a *Weekly Schedule of Committee Activities,* listing the business scheduled by the various committees for the coming week, together with the time and place of each hearing and advanced notices on hearings deemed to be of special interest. Each house also issues a daily calendar indicating the business to be taken up on the floor that day.

Complete texts of bills, amendments, and resolutions; bill histories; a subject index to legislation; hearing notices and calendars; and other information on the legislature are available on the Internet at http://docs.legis.wisconsin.gov. Reference copies of all these legislative documents are available at the Legislative Reference Bureau, and numerous libraries throughout the state also receive them. Individuals and organizations may subscribe to receive printed versions of legislative documents. (See the table on legislative service in this section for fees and details.)

Standing Committees. To a large extent, the legislature does its work in committees. In the 2015 Legislature, the senate has 20 standing committees and the assembly 38, and there are 10 joint standing committees, composed of members from both houses. Joint standing committees are created in the statutes and membership is determined by law. Regular standing committees are created under the rules of their respective houses.

The standing committees in the individual houses consist of legislators only and operate throughout the biennium. Each committee is concerned with one or more broad subject areas related to government functions. It may hold public hearings on measures introduced in the legislature, conduct studies and investigations, and generally review matters within its area of concern. Legislative committees may also appoint subcommittees or study groups.

Senate rules require that each senator serve on at least one standing committee, and the Committee on Senate Organization sets the number of members on each committee. Usually the 2 major political parties are represented on the committees in proportion to their membership in the senate. The chairperson of the organization committee, who is also the majority leader, makes the appointments to committees. Committee nominations for individual members of the minority party are proposed by that party. An exception to the general method of appointment is the Committee on Senate Organization. It is an *ex officio* committee, consisting of members in leadership positions: the president, the majority and minority leaders, and the assistant leaders.

In the assembly, the speaker determines the number of members of each committee and the division of membership between the majority and minority parties. Under assembly rules, the speaker appoints majority party committee members directly and minority party committee members upon nomination by the assembly minority leader. Customarily, every member serves on at least one committee, although the rules are silent on the distribution of committee assignments. The speaker may appoint himself or herself to one or more standing committees and is a nonvoting member of all others. By rule, the Committee on Assembly Organization is composed of the speaker, the speaker pro tempore, the majority and minority leaders, the assistant leaders, and the caucus chairpersons. The Committee on Rules includes all members of the organization committee plus four majority and three minority party members appointed by the speaker.

Temporary Special Committees. In addition to the standing committees, special committees may be appointed during a legislative session to study specific problems or conduct designated investigations and report to the legislature before the conclusion of the session.

Members of the legislature often join the general public in advocating legislation before a legislative committee. Senator Luther Olsen of Ripon testified in April 2015. (Jay Salvo, Legislative Photographer)

Prior to 1947, the legislature created interim committees to investigate particular subjects. They functioned between legislative sessions and reported their findings and recommendations to the next legislature. Since 1947, almost all interim studies have been referred to the Joint Legislative Council, which coordinates a program of study and investigation after deciding which topics it will consider. The council usually appoints separate committees to study specific matters, and these committees include nonlegislative members.

Employees of the Legislature. Each house of the legislature provides staff services, which are managed by the respective chief clerk and sergeant at arms under the supervision of the Committee on Senate Organization or the speaker of the assembly. Although senate and assembly employees are not part of the classified service, they are paid in accordance with the compensation and classification plan established for employees in the classified service and within pay ranges approved by the Joint Committee on Legislative Organization.

The legislature is assisted by 5 service agencies responsible for financial and program audits, fiscal information and analysis, bill drafting, research services, statutory revision, legal counsel and policy assistance, and computer and telecommunications services.

An important part of the legislative process plays out outside the legislative chambers, in the field of public opinion. Here Senator Leah Vukmir and Representatives Rob Hutton and André Jacque address members of the press. (Jay Salvo, Legislative Photographer)

NEWS MEDIA CORRESPONDENTS
COVERING THE 2015 LEGISLATURE
January 5, 2015

Organization	Correspondents	Telephone
Newspaper and Wire Services		
Associated Press	Scott Bauer, Todd Richmond	255-3679
Capital Times	Jessica Opoien	252-6429
Isthmus	Judith Davidoff	251-5627
Milwaukee Journal Sentinel	Patrick Marley, Jason Stein	258-2262/258-2274
Wheeler News Service	Thom Gerretsen	(715) 389-2373
Wheeler Reports	Gwyn Guenther, Trevor Guenther	287-0130
Wisconsin Catholic Newspapers	John Huebscher	257-0004
Wisconsin State Journal	Matt Defour, Dee Hall, Mary Spicuzza	252-6144/252-6132/ 252-6122
Radio and Television		
WIBA-AM and FM (Madison)	Robin Colbert	271-6397
WISC-TV (Madison)	Jessica Arp, Colin Benedict	(608) 332-9453/277-5246
WKOW-TV (Madison)	Kristine Barbaresi, Tony Galli, Jennifer Kliese, Greg Neumann, Joseph Radske	273-2727
WMTV-TV (Madison)	Kate Pabich	274-1500
WOLX-FM (Madison)	Kitty Dunn	826-0077
Wisconsin Public Radio	Gilman Halsted, Shawn Johnson, Michael Leland, Shamane Mills, Noah Ovshinsky	263-4358/263-7985
Wisconsin Public Television	Kathy Bissen, Frederica Freyberg, Andy Moore, Zac Schultz, Christine Sloan-Miller, Andy Soth, Joel Waldinger	263-2121/263-8496/ 265-6646/263-5628/ 263-6023/263-7124/ 263-4599/ 890-2840
Wisconsin Radio Network	Andrew Beckett, Bob Hague, Jackie Johnson	251-3900
Internet News Service		
Wispolitics.com	J.R. Ross, Mike Schramm, Chris Thompson	441-8418

Source: Assembly Sergeant at Arms.

THE LEGISLATURE ON THE INTERNET

Legislative Information

The Wisconsin Legislature's Internet home page at **http://legis.wisconsin.gov** provides extensive information regarding the legislature and the legislative process. Follow the links under Legislative Activity to access basic information on current legislative activity. **Law and Legislation** allows users to access legislative documents by bill or act number for the current or recent sessions as well as the current statutes and Administrative Code. The **Spotlight** link provides a weekly update on recent actions in the legislature. In addition, the **legislative service agencies** have individual home pages on which many of their publications are available.

Archives enables users to search for specific acts, bills, or statutes from 1995 to date. It also offers access to a variety of other legislative documents and indexes, which can also be searched by word.

The legislature's home page links through the 2 houses of the legislature to individual legislator's home pages, which include e-mail addresses, district maps, committee assignments, and biographical information. Some legislators also provide personally designed pages to communicate with their constituents.

Live Video and Audio – WisconsinEye

WisconsinEye, a private, nonprofit public affairs network, began offering exclusive live video and audio of legislative floor sessions and certain other legislative activities in May 2007. Links to live video and audio, as well as archives of past activity, are available at **http://wiseye.org**.

Legislative Notification Service

This service allows citizens to track legislation by creating a profile of items of interest. Profiles may include specific proposals identified by author, committee, or subject matter and may specify activity occurring at various stages of the legislative process. After a profile is filed on the Internet site **http://notify.legis.state.wisconsin.gov**, users will receive daily or weekly e-mails of relevant activities.

Jennifer Shilling of La Crosse was elected Senate Minority Leader by her colleagues for the 2015 session. (Jay Salvo, Legislative Photographer)

2010 POPULATION OF LEGISLATIVE DISTRICTS
As Created by 2011 Wisconsin Act 43[1]
2010 State Population – 5,686,986

District	2010 Population	Deviation from Ideal[2] Total	Deviation from Ideal[2] Percent	District	2010 Population	Deviation from Ideal[2] Total	Deviation from Ideal[2] Percent
SD-1	172,313	−20	−0.01%	SD-18	171,722	−611	−0.35%
AD-1	57,220	−224	−0.39	AD-52	57,232	−212	−0.37
AD-2	57,649	205	0.36	AD-53	57,240	−204	−0.36
AD-3	57,444	0	0.00	AD-54	57,250	−194	−0.34
SD-2	172,461	128	0.07	SD-19	172,576	243	0.14
AD-4	57,486	42	0.07	AD-55	57,493	49	0.08
AD-5	57,470	26	0.04	AD-56	57,582	138	0.24
AD-6	57,505	61	0.11	AD-57	57,501	57	0.10
SD-3	171,977	−356	−0.21	SD-20	172,003	−330	−0.19
AD-7	57,498	54	0.09	AD-58	57,227	−217	−0.38
AD-8[1]	57,196	−248	−0.43	AD-59	57,391	−53	−0.09
AD-9[1]	57,283	−161	−0.28	AD-60	57,385	−59	−0.10
SD-4	172,425	92	0.05	SD-21	172,324	−9	−0.01
AD-10	57,428	−16	−0.03	AD-61	57,614	170	0.30
AD-11	57,503	59	0.10	AD-62	57,345	−99	−0.17
AD-12	57,494	50	0.09	AD-63	57,365	−79	−0.14
SD-5	172,421	88	0.05	SD-22	172,270	−63	−0.04
AD-13	57,452	8	0.01	AD-64	57,270	−174	−0.30
AD-14	57,597	153	0.27	AD-65	57,455	11	0.02
AD-15	57,372	−72	−0.13	AD-66	57,545	101	0.18
SD-6	172,292	−41	−0.02	SD-23	172,149	−184	−0.11
AD-16	57,458	14	0.02	AD-67	57,239	−205	−0.36
AD-17	57,354	−90	−0.16	AD-68	57,261	−183	−0.32
AD-18	57,480	36	0.06	AD-69	57,649	205	0.36
SD-7	172,423	90	0.05	SD-24	172,520	187	0.11
AD-19	57,546	102	0.18	AD-70	57,552	108	0.19
AD-20	57,428	−16	−0.03	AD-71	57,519	75	0.13
AD-21	57,449	5	0.01	AD-72	57,449	5	0.01
SD-8	172,356	23	0.01	SD-25	172,409	76	0.04
AD-22	57,495	51	0.09	AD-73	57,453	9	0.02
AD-23	57,579	135	0.23	AD-74	57,494	50	0.09
AD-24	57,282	−162	−0.28	AD-75	57,462	18	0.03
SD-9	172,439	106	0.06	SD-26	172,596	263	0.15
AD-25	57,322	−122	−0.21	AD-76	57,617	173	0.30
AD-26	57,581	137	0.24	AD-77	57,433	−11	−0.02
AD-27	57,536	92	0.16	AD-78	57,546	102	0.18
SD-10	172,245	−88	−0.05	SD-27	172,449	116	0.07
AD-28	57,467	23	0.04	AD-79	57,461	17	0.03
AD-29	57,537	93	0.16	AD-80	57,585	141	0.24
AD-30	57,241	−203	−0.35	AD-81	57,403	−41	−0.07
SD-11	172,329	−4	−0.00	SD-28	172,218	−115	−0.07
AD-31	57,240	−204	−0.36	AD-82	57,430	−14	−0.02
AD-32	57,524	80	0.14	AD-83	57,423	−21	−0.04
AD-33	57,565	121	0.21	AD-84	57,365	−79	−0.14
SD-12	172,381	48	0.03	SD-29	172,292	−41	−0.02
AD-34	57,387	−57	−0.10	AD-85	57,480	36	0.06
AD-35	57,562	118	0.20	AD-86	57,454	10	0.02
AD-36	57,432	−12	−0.02	AD-87	57,358	−86	−0.15
SD-13	172,387	54	0.03	SD-30	172,798	465	0.27
AD-37	57,507	63	0.11	AD-88	57,556	112	0.19
AD-38	57,493	49	0.08	AD-89	57,634	190	0.33
AD-39	57,387	−57	−0.10	AD-90	57,608	164	0.28
SD-14	171,988	−345	−0.20	SD-31	172,338	5	0.00
AD-40	57,366	−78	−0.14	AD-91	57,359	−85	−0.15
AD-41	57,337	−107	−0.19	AD-92	57,431	−13	−0.02
AD-42	57,285	−159	−0.28	AD-93	57,548	104	0.18
SD-15	172,496	163	0.09	SD-32	172,122	−211	−0.12
AD-43	57,443	−1	−0.00	AD-94	57,266	−178	−0.31
AD-44	57,395	−49	−0.09	AD-95	57,372	−72	−0.13
AD-45	57,658	214	0.37	AD-96	57,484	40	0.07
SD-16	172,429	96	0.06	SD-33	172,288	−45	−0.03
AD-46	57,458	14	0.02	AD-97	57,279	−165	−0.29
AD-47	57,465	21	0.04	AD-98	57,513	69	0.12
AD-48	57,506	62	0.11	AD-99	57,496	52	0.09
SD-17	172,550	217	0.13				
AD-49	57,346	−98	−0.17				
AD-50	57,624	180	0.31				
AD-51	57,580	136	0.24				

[1]This table reflects modifications made to Assembly Districts 8 and 9 by the U.S. District Court for the Eastern District of Wisconsin in its decision in *Baldus vs. Members of the Wisconsin Government Accountability Board*, Case No. 11-CV-562, April 11, 2012.

[2]Ideal Senate District: 172,333. Ideal Assembly District: 57,444.

Sources: U.S. Census Bureau, 2010 Census Redistricting Data (Public Law 94-171) Summary File, March 2011; *Appendix to: 2011 Wisconsin Act 43*. Assembly Districts 8 and 9 population and deviations calculated by the Wisconsin Legislative Reference Bureau.

HOW A BILL BECOMES A LAW

The legislature decides policy by passing bills. A bill must pass both houses of the legislature and be signed by the governor before it becomes law. Other proposals introduced in the legislature also support the body's policy-making function. Joint resolutions, which must pass both houses, may propose constitutional amendments, develop a session schedule, or modify the rules that govern both houses. They do not require the governor's signature. Simple resolutions, which are adopted by only one house, may organize the house at the beginning of the session, propose changes to house rules, or ask the attorney general for a legal opinion on a bill.

Introducing a Bill. A bill that proposes to change existing law will usually amend, create, repeal, renumber, renumber and amend, or repeal and recreate one or more sections of the *Wisconsin Statutes.* After the Legislative Reference Bureau (LRB) drafts a bill, it is ready for introduction in one of the legislative houses. Each measure must go through regular procedures and be passed by the house of origin before it can go to the other house, where the process is repeated.

No one but individual legislators or legislative committees may introduce a bill. However, the statutes direct the Joint Committee on Finance to introduce the governor's executive budget bill without change. The legislator who introduces a bill is its "author"; others in the house of origin who support the bill may sign on as "coauthors". The measure may also list "cosponsors" from the second house.

When passing laws, legislators act as the representatives of the people. Therefore, the constitution requires that every bill introduced in the legislature begin with the words: "The people of the state of Wisconsin, represented in senate and assembly, do enact as follows:".

Fiscal Estimates and Bill Analyses. Fiscal estimates put a price tag on legislation. In 1953, Wisconsin pioneered fiscal estimates, often called "fiscal notes", and many other states have copied this important legislative tool. Every measure that increases or decreases state or general local government revenues or expenditures must be accompanied by a reliable estimate of its

Occasionally, standing committees of the Senate and Assembly hold joint hearings. Representative Kathy Bernier, chairperson of the Assembly Committee on Campaigns and Elections, and Senator Devin LeMahieu, the chairperson of the Senate Committee on Elections and Local Government, held such a hearing in March 2015, on campaign finance. (Jay Salvo, Legislative Photographer)

short-range and long-range fiscal effects. Agencies that would ultimately administer the proposed program or be affected by the measure, should it be enacted, prepare most fiscal notes. In the highly technical area of public retirement systems, the Joint Survey Committee on Retirement Systems prepares fiscal estimates with the assistance of Legislative Council staff. In these cases, the note must evaluate not only the fiscal effect of a proposal but also its legality under state and federal laws and its desirability as a matter of public policy.

Since 1967, the LRB has prepared an analysis of each bill introduced in the legislature. The analysis is printed in the bill immediately following the title. Analyses are not updated to reflect amendments approved during the legislative process, so they usually describe only the content of the bill at introduction.

Introduction, First Reading, and Referral to Committee. A bill is introduced when the chief clerk of the author's house assigns it a number and records the introduction for the house journal. Traditionally, the "first reading" took place when the clerk read that part of the proposal's title known as the "relating clause" – the clause that briefly describes the subject matter of the bill, e.g., "relating to the powers and duties of state traffic patrol officers and motor vehicle inspectors" when the house was meeting. In recent times, the clerk usually distributes a report showing the numbers and relating clauses of proposals offered for introduction which takes the place of an actual reading. After first reading, the presiding officer usually refers the proposal to the appropriate standing committee for review. Generally, bills that appropriate money, provide for revenue, or relate to taxation are referred to the Joint Committee on Finance before they can be enacted into law.

Committee Hearings. All committee proceedings are open to the general public. Neither assembly nor senate rules require a chairperson to schedule a hearing. If a hearing is held, anyone may speak to the committee to support or oppose a measure or merely to present information to the committee without taking a position. Persons may also register for or against a proposal or submit written comments or petitions without making an oral presentation.

Committees do not keep verbatim transcripts of their hearings, but they do maintain appearance records listing persons who testify or register at the hearing, together with any printed information those parties submit relative to bills and resolutions before the committee. Records for the current legislative session are filed in the office of the committee chairperson. Copies of appearance records for prior sessions, beginning with the 1951 session, are filed in the LRB. Records from 1997 to the present are available on the legislature's Internet site.

The chairperson of a committee decides whether or not to take action on a particular proposal. If the decision is to act, the chairperson will call an "executive session" of the committee. In the session, committee members discuss the bill and may ask questions of persons in attendance, but no further public testimony is taken. At the close of the executive session, the committee decides whether to recommend passage of the bill as originally introduced, passage with amendments, or rejection. If the result is a tie vote, the committee can report the bill without recommendation. A committee's decision is contained in a brief report to the house. (Bills that receive a negative recommendation are almost never reported to the floor.)

The following is an example of a committee report to the assembly from the *Senate Journal,* January 16, 2015:

The committee on **Judiciary and Public Safety** reports and recommends:

Senate Joint Resolution 2

Relating to: election of chief justice (second consideration).

Adoption:

Ayes: 3 – Senators Wanggaard, Vukmir and Lasee.

Noes: 2 – Senators Risser and L. Taylor.

Van Wanggaard

Chairperson

Committee chairpersons determine the scheduling of committee hearings. A committee is allowed a reasonable period to consider matters referred to it. A majority of the members of the assembly may withdraw a bill not reported by an assembly committee 21 days after the date of referral by motion or petition. In the senate, a majority may vote to withdraw a bill from a committee at any time but not during the 7 days preceding any scheduled committee hearing nor the 7 days following the date on which the hearing was held. In both houses, when an attempt is unsuccessful, all subsequent motions to withdraw the same proposal require at least a two-thirds vote of the members. In practice, bills are very rarely withdrawn from committees without a committee report.

Scheduling Debate. Both the senate and assembly make use of a daily calendar to schedule proposals for consideration. In the 2015 Legislature, all proposals reported by senate standing committees are referred to the Committee on Senate Organization; in the assembly, they are referred to the Committee on Rules. These committees schedule business for floor debate.

Parliamentary Procedure. The rules of parliamentary procedure, which are guides for each house, facilitate the legislative process and are printed in pamphlets, titled "Senate Rules" and "Assembly Rules". Each house may create new rules and amend or repeal its current rules by passage of a simple resolution. "Joint Rules" deal with the relations between the houses and with administrative proceedings common to both. Changes in joint rules require the passage of a joint resolution.

Parliamentary procedure may seem unduly cumbersome to the onlooker, but it helps the houses operate in an organized fashion. The process is designed to protect the minority in its right to be heard and to promote careful deliberation and orderly consideration of all legislation. For particularly difficult procedural questions, the presiding officer of each house has access to such standard sources as *Mason's Manual of Legislative Procedure, Jefferson's Manual,* and *Rulings of the Chair.*

Second Reading. Once a bill is scheduled for house action, the clerk gives it a second reading by title. The purpose of a second reading is to consider amendments. An amendment may be a "simple" amendment, which makes changes within the bill, or a "substitute amendment", which completely replaces the original bill. Members may offer, debate, and vote upon amendments at any time prior to a vote to "engross" the measure and read it a third time. Engrossment of a bill incorporates all adopted amendments and all approved technical corrections into a proposal in its house of origin. The rules of both houses require a formal delay after the proposal is engrossed, which gives legislators time to reconsider the issues raised by the bill. In many cases, however, the rules are suspended by unanimous consent or a two-thirds vote so that second and third readings can occur on the same legislative day.

Third Reading. The purpose of the third reading is to make a final decision on a proposal itself. After a third reading, the proposal is put to the house for a vote with the following questions: "This bill having been read 3 separate times, the question is, 'Shall the bill pass?'" (for the senate) or "Shall the bill be passed?" (for the assembly). Members can debate the bill's contents at this point, but it is not subject to amendment. When all members finish speaking they vote. A bill may pass on a voice vote, unless a roll call vote is required by the state constitution, by law or legislative rule, or by request of a prescribed number of members.

Action in the Second House. If the bill passes, it is "messaged" to the other house, where it goes through substantially the same procedure as in the first house. In the second house, however, the bill may be referred directly to the daily calendar without referral to a standing committee. When the second house concurs in the bill, whether with or without additional amendments, the measure is messaged back to the house of origin.

If the second house amends the bill before concurring, the house of origin must vote upon those amendments. If the original house rejects amendments or further amends the bill, the resulting proposal may be sent back to the second house. The bill may pass repeatedly between the two houses, or the legislature may create a conference committee, made up of members representing both houses to iron out the differences between the 2 versions. The compromise version, drawn up by the conference committee, cannot be amended in either house when it is brought to a vote. When both houses have agreed on identical wording of a bill, the LRB enrolls it in its final form, incorporating any amendments and corrections approved by both houses, and the measure is forwarded for the governor's signature.

Representative Tyler August is the Speaker Pro Tempore and typically presides over Assembly floor sessions. *(Jay Salvo, Legislative Photographer)*

On average about 1,600 bills were introduced in each of the past 10 legislatures, but only about 20 percent of those passed. Bills fail for many reasons: the house of origin may vote to "indefinitely postpone" or "table" a bill and then never take it up again; the second house may vote to "nonconcur" or may concur but with amendments unacceptable to the house of origin; or the proposal may "die in committee" and never be reported back to the house. An unsuccessful proposal does not carry over to the following legislature. A member must reintroduce it as a new bill.

Action of the Governor. The governor has 6 days (excluding Sundays) in which to act on the bill by 1) signing it, in which case it becomes law; 2) vetoing it in whole or, if an appropriation bill, in part; or 3) failing to sign it within 6 days, in which case it becomes law without the governor's signature. Partial veto of words or numbers within a bill is permitted in the case of bills that contain an appropriation. If the governor signs the bill but vetoes part of it, the portion not vetoed becomes law.

Bills are not sent to the office of the governor immediately following passage but are presented when the governor calls for them. The legislative session schedule, however, provides deadlines after each floorperiod when all bills not yet called for must be sent to the governor. It also provides a specific floorperiod for final legislative review of the governor's vetoes.

If the governor vetoes a bill, in whole or part, the vetoed parts must be returned to the house of origin with the governor's written objections. A vetoed bill or part of a bill can become law despite the governor's objections, but it requires a two-thirds vote in each house to override the veto. If either house fails to muster the sufficient number of votes, the governor's veto is sustained, and the vetoed bill or portion dies.

Session Laws. Each new law is numbered as a Wisconsin Act, based on the year of the legislative session and its order of enactment, e.g., 2015 Wisconsin Act 1. The date of enactment is the date the governor approves the act, the date it becomes a law without the governor's signature, or the date the legislature votes to override the governor's veto. The following day is the new law's official date of publication. On or before that date, copies of the act must be available to the public electronically. The secretary of state must publish the act's number, title, and original bill number within 10 working days after the date of enactment in the newspaper designated as the official state paper for publication of legal notices (currently the *Wisconsin State Journal*). The notice contains the date of enactment and date of publication and states the act is available for public distribution. The act takes effect the day after its official publication date, unless another effective date is specified in the law itself.

Ultimately, the LRB compiles all the laws enacted during the biennium into bound volumes, called the *Laws of Wisconsin.* The LRB incorporates any portions of these laws that make changes in the statutes into the edition of the *Wisconsin Statutes* dated for that legislative biennium. Thus, the edition identified as the *2013-2014 Wisconsin Statutes* includes all statutory changes resulting from laws enacted by the 2013 Legislature.

The Budget Bill. The budget bill is the longest and most complex bill of the session. Because Wisconsin's budget covers a 2-year period from July 1 of one odd-numbered year to June 30 of the next, its development involves a chain of events stretching over almost a year. In the fall of every even-numbered year, state agencies must submit funding requests to the Department of Administration. Their funding requests include estimates of the cost of existing services over the next 2 years and may propose changes they hope are made in their programs. The Department of Administration's state budget office then compiles the data for review by the governor or governor-elect. While developing the budget, the governor may hold a hearing on any department's budget request to get additional input.

State law requires the governor to deliver the budget message to the new legislature on or before the last Tuesday in January, although the legislature may extend the deadline at the governor's request. The state budget report and the biennial executive budget bill or bills accompany the message.

In the legislature, the Joint Committee on Finance holds hearings on the departmental requests and the governor's program initiatives. When these are completed, the committee reports the budget bill to the house of the legislature in which it was introduced. The committee's report takes the form of a substitute amendment. The bill then follows the normal legislative procedure through both houses of the legislature and is submitted for the governor's approval. The

Representatives Chris Taylor of Madison and Mary Czaja of Irma, members of the Joint Committee on Finance, focus on a particular aspect of state finance. (Jay Salvo, Legislative Photographer)

governor may sign the budget bill; veto it in its entirety, which would be unlikely; or use partial vetoes, as is usually the case. To meet the state's budgetary cycle, the new budget law should be effective by July 1 of the odd-numbered year, but there sometimes is a delay of several days, or even weeks or months, during which state agencies continue to operate at their levels of appropriation from the preceding budget.

Further Reading. The preceding section has provided a brief description of how a bill becomes a law in Wisconsin. In practice, legislative procedure is more complex than explained here. The feature article in the *1993-1994 Wisconsin Blue Book* contains a more detailed description and uses a case study approach to further illustrate the legislative process. It may be accessed via the *Wisconsin Blue Book* link on the Legislative Reference Bureau's Internet site: http://legis.wisconsin.gov/lrb/pubs/bluebook.htm.

2015-2016 LEGISLATIVE SERVICE

The complete 2015-2016 Legislative Service consists of 6 parts, which may be ordered by subscription from the Document Sales office:

Bills, resolutions, and amendments (complete text of each as introduced).

Acts are the laws enacted in bill form by the legislature and signed by the governor or passed over the governor's veto. The acts are distributed separately as "slip laws".

Journals are a daily record of the business conducted in each house, but they are not verbatim accounts. The service provides preliminary editions of the journals (published on the morning after the legislative day on yellow paper for senate journals and green paper for assembly journals) and the final corrected editions (printed on white paper and distributed two or three weeks later).

The **Bulletin of Proceedings** contains a numerical listing of all bills and other measures introduced in each house of the legislature and a cumulative record of actions taken on each. It includes a subject index to all measures introduced and to all acts, a list of proposals introduced by each legislator, and a numerical listing of statutory sections affected by acts and enrolled bills. It is issued as needed during the biennial session.

The **Weekly Schedule of Committee Activities** lists the time and place of legislative committee hearings for the coming week and advanced notices for hearings on issues of special interest.

Administrative Rules lists the administrative rules submitted by executive branch agencies by clearinghouse rule number. It includes a subject index, a list of agency contacts, and a cumulative record of actions taken on each proposal.

To obtain all or part of the legislative service, contact Document Sales, Wisconsin Department of Administration, 4622 University Avenue, Madison 53705-2156 or call (608) 266-3358, or (800) 362-7253 for an order form. E-mail Document Sales at docsales@doa.state.wi.us. Any part may be ordered separately. Prepayment is required on all orders. Faxed orders are accepted at (608) 261-8150 when paying with a credit card. Subscribers receive their documents through the mail. All subscriptions to the 2015-2016 Legislative Service will expire on December 31, 2016.

SERVICE	Interdepartmental Delivery*	United Parcel Service (UPS) and U.S. Postal Service*
Complete service, including daily calendars . . .	$500	$845
Bills, resolutions, and amendments	160	335
Acts (slip laws)	20	85
Journals	55	145
Bulletin of Proceedings	200	350
Weekly Schedule of Committee Activities . . .	15	85
Administrative Rules	65	95

*All sales are subject to the 5% state sales tax, 0.5% county sales tax, and 0.5% or 0.1% stadium tax, where applicable.

Senator Lena Taylor of Milwaukee offered her views of a proposed constitutional amendment on January 20, 2015. (Jay Salvo, Legislative Photographer)

EXECUTIVE VETOES, 1931 – 2013 SESSIONS

Session	Bills Vetoed in Entirety			Bills Partially Vetoed			Partial Vetoes Contained in Biennial Budget Bills	
	Number Vetoed	Vetoes Sustained	Vetoes Overridden	Number Partially Vetoed	All Partial Vetoes Sustained	One or More Partial Vetoes Overridden	Number of Partial Vetoes[1]	Vetoes Overridden
1931	58	58	—	2	2	—	12	0
1933	15	15	—	1	1	—	12	0
1935	27	27	—	4	4	—	0	0
1937	10	10	—	1	1	—	0	0
1939	22[2]	22	—	4	4	—	1	0
1941	17	17	—	1	1	—	1	0
1943	39	19	20	1	—	1	0	0
1945	30	25	5	2	1	1	1	0
1947	10	9	1	1	1	—	2	0
1949	17	15	2	2	1	1	0	0
1951	18	18	—	2	2	—	0	0
1953	31	28	3	4[3]	4	—	2	0
1955	38	38	—	—	—	—	0	0
1957	35	34	1	3	3	—	2	0
1959	36	32	4	1	1	—	0	0
1961	70	68	2	3	3	—	2	0
1963	72	68	4	1	1	—	0	0
1965	24	23	1	4	4	—	1	0
1967	18	18	—	5	5	—	0	0
1969	34	33	1	11	11	—	27	0
1971	32	29	3	8	8	—	12	0
1973	13	13	—	18	15	3	38	2
1975	37	31	6	22	18	4	42	5
1977	21	17	4	16	13	3	67	21
1979	19	16	3	9	7	2	45	1
1981	11	9	2	11	10	1	121[4]	0
1983	3	3	—	11	10	1	70	6
1985	7	7	—	7	6	1	78	2
1987	38	38	—	20	20	—	290	0
1989	35	35	—	28	28	—	203	0
1991	33	33	—	13	13	—	457	0
1993	8	8	—	24	24	—	78	0
1995	4	4	—	21	21	—	112	0
1997	3	3	—	8	8	—	152	0
1999	5	5	—	9	9	—	255	0
2001	—	—	—	3	3	—	315	0
2003	54	54	—	10	10	—	131	0
2005	47	47	—	2	2	—	139	0
2007	1	1	—	4	4	—	33	0
2009	6	6	—	5	5	—	81	0
2011	—	—	—	3	3	—	50	0
2013	1	1	—	4	4	—	57	0

Note: The legislature is not required to act on vetoes. Any veto not acted upon is counted as sustained, including pocket vetoes. "Vetoes sustained" includes the following pocket vetoes: 1931 (20); 1937 (5); 1941 (12); 1943 (4); 1951 (14); 1955 (10); 1957 (1); 1973 (1). A "pocket veto" resulted if the governor took no action on a bill after the legislature had adjourned *sine die*. (*Sine die*, from the Latin for "without a day", means the legislature adjourns without setting a date to reconvene.) With this type of adjournment, the legislature concluded all its business for the biennium, and there was no opportunity for it to sustain or override the veto (see Article V, Section 10, *Wisconsin Constitution*). Under current legislative session schedules, in which the legislature usually adjourns on the final day of its existence, just hours before the newly elected legislature is seated, the pocket veto is unlikely.

[1]The number of individual veto statements in the governor's veto message.

[2]Attorney general ruled veto of 1939 SB-43 was void and it became law (see Vol. 28, *Opinions of the Attorney General*, p. 423).

[3]1953 AB-141, partially vetoed in two separate sections by separate veto messages, is counted as one.

[4]Attorney general ruled several vetoes "ineffective" because the governor failed to express his objections (see Vol. 70, *Opinions of the Attorney General*, p. 189).

Source: Compiled by Wisconsin Legislative Reference Bureau from the *Bulletin of the Proceedings of the Wisconsin Legislature* and the Assembly and Senate *Journals*.

POLITICAL COMPOSITION OF THE
WISCONSIN LEGISLATURE
1885 – 2015

Legislative Session[1]	Senate							Assembly						
	D	R	P	S	SD	M[4]	Vacant	D	R	P	S	SD	M[5]	Vacant
1885	13	20	—	—	—	—	—	39	61	—	—	—	—	—
1887	6	25	—	—	—	2	—	30	57	—	—	—	13	—
1889	6	24	—	—	—	3	—	29	71	—	—	—	—	—
1891	19	14	—	—	—	—	—	66	33	—	—	—	1	—
1893	26	7	—	—	—	—	—	56	44	—	—	—	—	—
1895	13	20	—	—	—	—	—	19	81	—	—	—	—	—
1897	4	29	—	—	—	—	—	8	91	—	—	—	1	—
1899	2	31	—	—	—	—	—	19	81	—	—	—	—	—
1901	2	31	—	—	—	—	—	18	82	—	—	—	—	—
1903	3	30	—	—	—	—	—	25	75	—	—	—	—	—
1905	4	28	—	—	1	—	—	11	85	—	—	4	—	—
1907	5	27	—	—	1	—	—	19	76	—	—	5	—	—
1909	4	28	—	—	1	—	—	17	80	—	—	3	—	—
1911	4	27	—	—	2	—	—	29	59	—	—	12	—	—
1913	9	23	—	—	1	—	—	37	57	—	—	6	—	—
1915	11	21	—	—	1	—	—	29	63	—	—	8	—	—
1917	6	24	—	3	—	—	—	14	79	—	7	—	—	—
1919	2	27	—	4	—	—	—	5	79	—	16	—	—	—
1921	2	27	—	4	—	—	—	2	92	—	6	—	—	—
1923	—	30	—	3	—	—	—	1	89	—	10	—	—	—
1925	—	30	—	3	—	—	—	1	92	—	7	—	—	—
1927	—	31	—	2	—	—	—	3	89	—	8	—	—	—
1929	—	31	—	2	—	—	—	6	90	—	3	—	1	—
1931	1	30	—	2	—	—	—	2	89	—	9	—	—	—
1933	9	23	—	1	—	—	—	59	13	24	3	—	1	—
1935	13	6	14	—	—	—	—	35	17	45	3	—	—	—
1937	9	8	16	—	—	—	—	31	21	46	2	—	—	—
1939	6	16	11	—	—	—	—	15	53	32	—	—	—	—
1941	3	24	6	—	—	—	—	15	60	25	—	—	—	—
1943	4	23	6	—	—	—	—	14	73	13	—	—	—	—
1945	6	22	5	—	—	—	—	19	75	6	—	—	—	—
1947	5	27	1	—	—	—	—	11	88	—	—	—	—	1
1949	3	27	—	—	—	—	3	26	74	—	—	—	—	—
1951	7	26	—	—	—	—	—	24	75	—	—	—	—	1
1953	7	26	—	—	—	—	—	25	75	—	—	—	—	—
1955	8	24	—	—	—	—	1	36	64	—	—	—	—	—
1957	10	23	—	—	—	—	—	33	67	—	—	—	—	—
1959	12	20	—	—	—	—	1	55	45	—	—	—	—	—
1961	13	20	—	—	—	—	—	45	55	—	—	—	—	—
1963	11	22	—	—	—	—	—	46	53	—	—	—	—	1
1965	12	20	—	—	—	—	1	52	48	—	—	—	—	—
1967	12	21	—	—	—	—	—	47	53	—	—	—	—	—
1969	10	23	—	—	—	—	—	48	52	—	—	—	—	—
1971	12	20	—	—	—	—	1	67	33	—	—	—	—	—
1973	15	18	—	—	—	—	—	62	37	—	—	—	—	—
1975	18	13	—	—	—	—	2	63	36	—	—	—	—	—
1977	23	10	—	—	—	—	—	66	33	—	—	—	—	—
1979	21	10	—	—	—	—	2	60	39	—	—	—	—	—
1981	19	14	—	—	—	—	—	59	39	—	—	—	—	1
1983	17	14	—	—	—	—	2	59	40	—	—	—	—	—
1985	19	14	—	—	—	—	—	52	47	—	—	—	—	—
1987	19	11	—	—	—	—	3	54	45	—	—	—	—	—
1989	20	13	—	—	—	—	—	56	43	—	—	—	—	—
1991	19	14	—	—	—	—	—	58	41	—	—	—	—	—
1993[2]	15	15	—	—	—	—	3	52	47	—	—	—	—	—
1995[2]	16	17	—	—	—	—	—	48	51	—	—	—	—	—
1997[2]	17	16	—	—	—	—	—	47	52	—	—	—	—	—
1999	17	16	—	—	—	—	—	44	55	—	—	—	—	—
2001	18	15	—	—	—	—	—	43	56	—	—	—	—	—
2003	15	18	—	—	—	—	—	41	58	—	—	—	—	—
2005	14	19	—	—	—	—	—	39	60	—	—	—	—	—
2007	18	15	—	—	—	—	—	47	52	—	—	—	—	—
2009	18	15	—	—	—	—	—	52	46	—	—	—	1	—
2011[3]	14	19	—	—	—	—	—	38	60	—	—	—	1	—
2013	15	18	—	—	—	—	—	39	59	—	—	—	—	1
2015	14	18	—	—	—	—	1	36	63	—	—	—	—	—

Note: The number of assembly districts was reduced from 100 to 99 beginning in 1973.

Key: Democrat (D); Progressive (P); Republican (R); Socialist (S); Social Democrat (SD); Miscellaneous (M).

[1]Political composition at inauguration.

[2]In the 1993, 1995, and 1997 Legislatures, majority control of the senate shifted during the session. On 4/20/93, vacancies were filled resulting in a total of 16 Democrats and 17 Republicans; on 6/16/96, there were 17 Democrats and 16 Republicans; and on 4/19/98, there were 16 Democrats and 17 Republicans.

[3]A series of recall elections during the session resulted in a switch in majority control of the senate, with 17 Democrats and 16 Republicans as of 7/16/12.

[4]Miscellaneous = one Independent and one People's (1887); one Independent and 2 Union Labor (1889).

[5]Miscellaneous = 3 Independent, 4 Independent Democrat, and 6 People's (1887); one Union Labor (1891); one Fusion (1897); one Independent (1929, 2009, 2011); one Independent Republican (1933).

Sources: Pre-1943 data is taken from the Secretary of State, *Officers of Wisconsin: U.S., State, Judicial, Congressional, Legislative and County Officers*, 1943 and earlier editions, and the *Wisconsin Blue Book*, various editions. Later data compiled from Wisconsin Legislative Reference Bureau sources.

STATUTES, SESSION LAWS, AND ADMINISTRATIVE CODE

Printed Materials

The printed state documents listed below are available from Document Sales, 4622 University Avenue, Madison 53705-2156; telephone (608) 266-3358; Fax: (608) 261-8150.

Prices listed do not reflect 5% state sales tax and, where applicable, 0.5% county sales tax and/or 0.5% or 0.1% stadium tax. Taxes must be included with payment. Prepayment is required for all orders. Make check or money order payable to Wisconsin Department of Administration. For MasterCard or Visa orders, call (800) 362-7253.

Wisconsin Statutes 2013-14:

> Hardcover 6-volume set – $94.25 (picked up); $101 (shipped)

> Softcover 6-volume set – $61.50 (picked up); $67.50 (shipped)

2013 Laws of Wisconsin: Hardcover 2-volume set – $44.15 (picked up); $48.85 (shipped)

Wisconsin Administrative Code: Individual codes can be ordered from Document Sales, (608) 266-3358.

Machine-Readable Data

WisLaw, the computer-searchable CD-ROM, contains the Wisconsin Statutes and Annotations, plus the Wisconsin and U.S. Constitutions, Supreme Court Rules, Wisconsin Acts, recent Opinions of the Attorney General, the Administrative Code, executive orders, and town law forms.

WisLaw is continuously updated and is available only by annual subscription. (The number of CD updates released in any 12-month period may vary.) The CD will only be delivered upon receipt of a signed end-user license, subscription form, and full payment. Subscription forms and *WisLaw* end-user licenses are available at Document Sales (see address above) or through the Legislative Reference Bureau home page, at: **http:// legis.wisconsin.gov/rsb/order.htm**

Sources: Wisconsin Department of Administration, *Document Sales Catalog,* and Legislative Reference Bureau.

For the third consecutive session, the Wisconsin Assembly welcomed a large freshman class. Representative David Bowen of Milwaukee is one of 25 members serving a first term. (Jay Salvo, Legislative Photographer)

STANDING COMMITTEES
OF THE 2015 WISCONSIN LEGISLATURE

All standing committees of the 2015 Wisconsin Legislature are described in this section. The standing committees of the senate are created by the Committee on Senate Organization while standing committees of the assembly are enumerated in Assembly Rule 9. In the case of each standing committee listed below, the names of committee officers are followed by those of the majority party and minority party, separated by a semicolon. An * indicates the ranking minority member.

SENATE STANDING COMMITTEES

Administrative Rules — NASS, *chairperson;* LASEE, LEMAHIEU; MILLER*, HARRIS DODD.

Agriculture, Small Business, and Tourism — MOULTON, *chairperson;* TIFFANY, *vice chairperson;* HARSDORF, PETROWSKI, LEMAHIEU; VINEHOUT*, ERPENBACH, HANSEN, L. TAYLOR.

Audit — COWLES, *chairperson;* DARLING, LAZICH; VINEHOUT*, BEWLEY.

Economic Development and Commerce — GUDEX, *chairperson;* PETROWSKI, *vice chairperson;* DARLING; LASSA*, RINGHAND.

Education — OLSEN, *chairperson;* DARLING, *vice chairperson;* VUKMIR, NASS; C. LARSON*, RISSER, BEWLEY.

Education Reform — FARROW, *chairperson;* HARSDORF, *vice chairperson;* NASS; HARRIS DODD*, VINEHOUT.

Elections and Local Government — LEMAHIEU, *chairperson;* FARROW, *vice chairperson;* WANGGAARD; RISSER*, MILLER.

Finance — DARLING, *chairperson;* OLSEN, *vice chairperson;* HARSDORF, VUKMIR, TIFFANY, MARKLEIN; L. TAYLOR*, ERPENBACH.

Senator Dave Hansen has served as Assistant Leader of the Democratic caucus since 2003. (Jay Salvo, Legislative Photographer)

Government Operations and Consumer Protection — STROEBEL, *chairperson;* LEMAHIEU, *vice chairperson;* FARROW; HARRIS DODD*, WIRCH.

Health and Human Services — VUKMIR, *chairperson;* MOULTON, *vice chairperson;* LEMAHIEU; CARPENTER*, ERPENBACH.

Insurance, Housing, and Trade — LASEE, *chairperson;* OLSEN, *vice chairperson;* ROTH; BEWLEY*, HARRIS DODD.

Judiciary and Public Safety — WANGGAARD, *chairperson;* VUKMIR, *vice chairperson;* LASEE; RISSER*, L. TAYLOR.

Labor and Government Reform — NASS, *chairperson;* WANGGAARD, *vice chairperson;* MARKLEIN; WIRCH*, C. LARSON.

Natural Resources and Energy — COWLES, *chairperson;* LASEE, *vice chairperson;* OLSEN; MILLER*, WIRCH.

Revenue, Financial Institutions, and Rural Issues — MARKLEIN, *chairperson;* FARROW (through 4/22/15), STROEBEL (from 4/22/15), *vice chairperson;* TIFFANY; LASSA*, RINGHAND.

Senate Organization — FITZGERALD, *chairperson;* LAZICH, FARROW; SHILLING*, HANSEN.

Sporting Heritage, Mining, and Forestry — TIFFANY, *chairperson;* ROTH, *vice chairperson;* MOULTON; WIRCH*, VINEHOUT.

Transportation and Veterans Affairs — PETROWSKI, *chairperson;* MARKLEIN, *vice chairperson;* COWLES; CARPENTER*, HANSEN.

Universities and Technical Colleges — HARSDORF, *chairperson;* NASS, *vice chairperson;* GUDEX; HANSEN*, BEWLEY.

Workforce Development, Public Works, and Military Affairs — ROTH, *chairperson;* GUDEX, *vice chairperson;* FARROW (through 4/22/15), STROEBEL (from 4/22/15); C. LARSON*, LASSA.

ASSEMBLY STANDING COMMITTEES

Administrative Rules — BALLWEG, *chairperson;* KNUDSON, *vice chairperson;* J. OTT; HEBL*, SHANKLAND.

Aging and Long-Term Care — WEATHERSTON, *chairperson;* QUINN, *vice chairperson;* PETRYK, NERISON, BERNIER, R. BROOKS; SARGENT*, MEYERS, BROSTOFF.

Agriculture — NERISON, *chairperson;* NOVAK, *vice chairperson;* TAUCHEN, A. OTT, BERNIER, RIPP, TRANEL, E. BROOKS, KITCHENS, VANDERMEER; DANOU*, JORGENSEN, GOYKE, KESSLER, CONSIDINE.

Assembly Organization — VOS, *chairperson;* STEINEKE, *vice chairperson;* KNODL, AUGUST, MURTHA; BARCA*, SHANKLAND, JORGENSEN.

Audit — KERKMAN, *chairperson;* MACCO, *vice chairperson;* NYGREN; SARGENT*, BERCEAU.

Campaigns and Elections — BERNIER, *chairperson;* VORPAGEL, *vice chairperson;* THIESFELDT, HORLACHER, CRAIG, SANFELIPPO; BERCEAU*, ZAMARRIPA, KESSLER.

Children and Families — RODRIGUEZ, *chairperson;* GANNON, *vice chairperson;* R. BROOKS, VORPAGEL, KERKMAN, BRANDTJEN, HEATON, NEYLON; JOHNSON*, BILLINGS, KAHL, SUBECK.

Colleges and Universities — MURPHY, *chairperson;* R. BROOKS, *vice chairperson;* ROHRKASTE, QUINN, RODRIGUEZ, PETRYK, BALLWEG, KRUG, TRANEL, MACCO; WACHS*, BERCEAU, BILLINGS, HESSELBEIN, JORGENSEN.

Constitution and Ethics — KAPENGA, *chairperson,* HUTTON, *vice chairperson;* JAGLER, KREMER, HORLACHER, JARCHOW; KESSLER*, WACHS, GOYKE.

Consumer Protection — KRUG, *chairperson;* HEATON, *vice chairperson;* KATSMA, NEYLON, NERISON, VANDERMEER; SINICKI*, POPE, YOUNG.

Corrections — HUTTON, *chairperson;* BRANDTJEN, *vice chairperson;* GANNON, E. BROOKS, NYGREN, KLEEFISCH; BARNES*, POPE, BOWEN.

Criminal Justice and Public Safety — KLEEFISCH, *chairperson;* KREMER, *vice chairperson;* SPIROS, J. OTT, RODRIGUEZ, HORLACHER, NOVAK, BORN; GOYKE*, KESSLER, ZAMARRIPA, JOHNSON.

Education — THIESFELDT, *chairperson;* KITCHENS, *vice chairperson;* JAGLER, KNUDSON, RODRIGUEZ, R. BROOKS, HORLACHER, MURPHY, QUINN, HUTTON; POPE*, SINICKI, GENRICH, BARNES, CONSIDINE.

Energy and Utilities — KUGLITSCH, *chairperson;* STEFFEN, *vice chairperson;* T. LARSON, JACQUE, PETERSEN, WEATHERSTON, TRANEL, JARCHOW, PETRYK, NEYLON; ZEPNICK*, KAHL, SARGENT, GENRICH, STUCK.

Environment and Forestry — MURSAU, *chairperson;* KRUG, *vice chairperson;* CZAJA, KITCHENS, SWEARINGEN, EDMING, R. BROOKS, ALLEN; MASON*, MILROY, HEBL, STUCK, CONSIDINE.

Family Law — T. LARSON, *chairperson;* BERNIER, *vice chairperson;* THIESFELDT, CRAIG, MURSAU, KLEEFISCH; HEBL*, JOHNSON, SUBECK.

Finance — NYGREN, *chairperson;* KOOYENGA, *vice chairperson;* KNUDSON, LOUDENBECK, SCHRAA, CZAJA; C. TAYLOR*, HINTZ.

Financial Institutions — CRAIG, *chairperson;* KATSMA, *vice chairperson;* KAPENGA, JARCHOW, SANFELIPPO, BORN, BALLWEG, WEATHERSTON, MURPHY, PETERSEN, KITCHENS; DOYLE*, ZEPNICK, GENRICH, SARGENT, JOHNSON, BROSTOFF.

Health — SANFELIPPO, *chairperson;* ROHRKASTE, *vice chairperson;* EDMING, SKOWRONSKI, KREMER, TITTL, KAPENGA, PETERSEN; KOLSTE*, ZAMARRIPA, RIEMER, SUBECK.

Housing and Real Estate — JAGLER, *chairperson;* ALLEN, *vice chairperson;* R. BROOKS, KATSMA, MURPHY, MURTHA; YOUNG*, GENRICH, STUCK.

Insurance — PETERSEN, *chairperson;* TITTL, *vice chairperson;* GANNON, STEFFEN, JAGLER, PETRYK, CRAIG, TRANEL, BORN, AUGUST; DOYLE*, DANOU, BERCEAU, KAHL, YOUNG.

Interstate Affairs — JACQUE, *chairperson;* BILLINGS, *vice chairperson;* ROHRKASTE, E. BROOKS, KERKMAN, A. OTT, HORLACHER; YOUNG*, ZEPNICK.

Jobs and the Economy — NEYLON, *chairperson;* KRUG, *vice chairperson;* TAUCHEN, ALLEN, KULP, TITTL, KUGLITSCH, MACCO, ROHRKASTE, STEFFEN; OHNSTAD*, ZAMARRIPA, BARNES, SPREITZER, STUCK.

Judiciary — J. OTT, *chairperson;* HORLACHER, *vice chairperson;* THIESFELDT, HEATON, T. LARSON, KERKMAN; WACHS*, HEBL, GOYKE.

Labor — JACQUE, *chairperson;* SPIROS, *vice chairperson;* KNODL, KAPENGA, KULP, KUGLITSCH; SINICKI*, MASON, OHNSTAD.

Mental Health Reform — TITTL, *chairperson;* JAGLER, *vice chairperson;* BALLWEG, NOVAK, SANFELIPPO, ROHRKASTE, VANDERMEER, RODRIGUEZ; RIEMER*, SARGENT, BROSTOFF, CONSIDINE.

Mining and Rural Development — KULP, *chairperson;* MURSAU, *vice chairperson;* BERNIER, NOVAK, QUINN, VANDERMEER, E. BROOKS, KRUG, T. LARSON, KREMER; MILROY*, DANOU, BILLINGS, CONSIDINE, SPREITZER.

Natural Resources and Sporting Heritage — A. OTT, *chairperson;* QUINN, *vice chairperson;* KLEEFISCH, MURSAU, NERISON, RIPP, BORN, TITTL, SKOWRONSKI, EDMING; MILROY*, DANOU, HESSELBEIN, SHANKLAND, SPREITZER.

Public Benefit Reform — BORN, *chairperson;* KAPENGA, *vice chairperson;* BRANDTJEN, VORPAGEL, SCHRAA, KREMER, CRAIG, NEYLON, KRUG, TAUCHEN; JORGENSEN*, GOYKE, KOLSTE, SPREITZER, SUBECK.

Rules — STEINEKE, *chairperson;* VOS, *vice chairperson;* AUGUST, KNODL, MURTHA, BALLWEG, KUGLITSCH, JAGLER, BORN; BARCA*, SHANKLAND, JORGENSEN, ZAMARRIPA, POPE, HEBL.

Small Business Development — TAUCHEN, *chairperson;* EDMING, *vice chairperson;* TRANEL, HUTTON, ALLEN, SWEARINGEN, T. LARSON, GANNON, VANDERMEER, SKOWRONSKI; JORGENSEN*, SARGENT, DOYLE, BARNES, BOWEN.

State Affairs and Government Operations — SWEARINGEN, *chairperson;* CRAIG, *vice chairperson;* JAGLER, BRANDTJEN, KLEEFISCH, GANNON, RIPP, KULP, TAUCHEN, VORPAGEL; ZAMARRIPA*, SINICKI, KAHL, OHNSTAD, BROSTOFF.

Tourism — TRANEL, *chairperson;* JARCHOW, *vice chairperson;* MURSAU, TAUCHEN, KLEEFISCH, KITCHENS, BORN, A. OTT, SWEARINGEN, BALLWEG; BILLINGS*, DOYLE, OHNSTAD, MASON, MEYERS.

Transportation — RIPP, *chairperson;* SPIROS, *vice chairperson;* THIESFELDT, WEATHERSTON, A. OTT, SANFELIPPO, VORPAGEL, T. LARSON, SWEARINGEN, MACCO; KAHL*, DANOU, KOLSTE, BOWEN, MEYERS.

Urban and Local Affairs — E. BROOKS, *chairperson;* HUTTON, *vice chairperson;* NOVAK, QUINN, STEFFEN, SKOWRONSKI; GENRICH*, YOUNG, SUBECK.

Veterans and Military Affairs — SKOWRONSKI, *chairperson;* VANDERMEER, *vice chairperson;* WEATHERSTON, PETRYK, ALLEN, EDMING, NERISON, HEATON, J. OTT, TITTL; HESSELBEIN*, MILROY, SINICKI, GOYKE, RIEMER.

Ways and Means — SPIROS, *chairperson;* MACCO, *vice chairperson;* KERKMAN, NOVAK, STEFFEN, JACQUE, KATSMA, PETERSEN; RIEMER*, ZEPNICK, OHNSTAD, BROSTOFF.

Workforce Development — PETRYK, *chairperson;* WEATHERSTON, *vice chairperson;* MURPHY, RIPP, KUGLITSCH, KATSMA, KULP, BERNIER, BRANDTJEN, KITCHENS; SHANKLAND*, KOLSTE, RIEMER, SPREITZER, BOWEN.

Representative Joel Kleefisch raises a point during a meeting of the Committee on State Affairs and Government Operations. *(Jay Salvo, Legislative Photographer)*

PERSONAL DATA ON WISCONSIN LEGISLATORS
2005 – 2015 Sessions

	2005 Sen.	2005 Rep.	2007 Sen.	2007 Rep.	2009 Sen.	2009 Rep.*	2011 Sen.	2011 Rep.*	2013 Sen.	2013 Rep.	2015 Sen.	2015 Rep.
Party affiliation												
Democrat	14	39	18	47	18	52	14	38	15	39	14	36
Republican	19	60	15	52	15	46	19	60	18	60	19	63
Number with previous legislative service												
In senate	28	0	29	0	31	0	26	0	30	0	27	0
In assembly	23	81	23	82	23	86	23	69	25	74	24	74
Highest number of prior sessions in same house	21	17	22	18	23	19	24	14	25	13	26	14
Occupations												
Full-time legislator	11	39	12	38	11	39	11	32	12	35	11	34
Attorney	2	11	3	11	3	12	3	8	3	7	2	7
Farmer	3	9	3	5	3	5	2	6	2	4	1	6
Other	17	40	15	45	16	43	16	53	16	53	19	52
Education												
High school only	4	9	2	7	1	7	0	4	1	5	1	4
Beyond high school	29	90	31	92	32	92	33	95	32	94	32	95
Bachelor's or associate degree	26	70	28	69	29	69	29	73	28	72	28	69
Advanced degree	8	34	10	37	11	35	10	27	9	27	9	24
Number with experience on local governing body												
County board	4	18	4	17	4	15	6	16	7	18	9	19
Municipal board	10	28	12	25	12	30	9	29	11	30	9	29
Age												
Oldest	77	77	79	79	81	80	83	72	85	72	87	76
Youngest	34	28	36	28	38	29	30	25	32	25	34	24
Average	52	50	54	50	55	50	56	49	57	49	57	48
Veterans	4	13	2	16	2	16	2	13	2	10	3	7
Marital status												
Single	10	25	8	25	9	24	7	18	9	22	10	23
Married	23	70	25	69	24	71	26	79	24	75	23	75
Widowed	0	4	0	5	0	4	0	2	0	1	0	1
Number of women	8	26	8	22	7	22	8	23	9	24	11	22

*Includes one Independent.

Sen. – Senators; Rep. – Representatives.

Note: Most data are recorded as of the date on which the legislature first convened; ages are determined as of January 1.

Sources: *Wisconsin Blue Book*, various issues, and data collected by the Wisconsin Legislative Reference Bureau, January 2015.

Representative Samantha Kerkman and Senator Robert Cowles serve as cochairpersons of the Joint Legislative Audit Committee for a second term. *(Jay Salvo, Legislative Photographer)*

JOINT LEGISLATIVE COMMITTEES AND COMMISSIONS

Joint committees and commissions are created by statute and include members from both houses. Three joint committees include nonlegislative members. Names of committee officers are followed by those of the majority and minority party, separated by a semicolon. The ranking minority member is indicated by an *. Commissions also include gubernatorial appointees and, in 2 cases, the governor. All telephone numbers that do not include an area code are Madison numbers, area code 608.

JOINT COMMITTEE FOR REVIEW OF ADMINISTRATIVE RULES

Members: SENATOR NASS, REPRESENTATIVE BALLWEG, *cochairpersons;* SENATORS LASEE, LEMAHIEU; MILLER*, HARRIS DODD; REPRESENTATIVES KNUDSON, J. OTT; HEBL*, SHANKLAND.

Mailing Addresses: Senator Nass, Room 10 South, State Capitol, P.O. Box 7882, Madison 53707-7882; Representative Ballweg, Room 210 North, State Capitol, P.O. Box 8952, Madison 53708-8952.

Telephones: Senator Nass, 266-2635; Representative Ballweg, 266-8077.

E-mail: sen.nass@legis.wisconsin.gov; rep.ballweg@legis.wisconsin.gov

Statutory References: Sections 13.56, 227.19, 227.24, 227.26, 227.40 (5), and 806.04 (11).

Agency Responsibility: The Joint Committee for Review of Administrative Rules must review proposed rules and may object to the promulgation of rules as part of the legislative oversight of the rule-making process. It also may suspend rules that have been promulgated; suspend or extend the effective period of emergency rules; and order an agency to put unwritten policies in rule form.

Following standing committee review, a proposed rule must be referred to the joint committee. The committee must meet to review proposed rules that receive standing committee objections, and may meet to review any rule received without objection. The joint committee has 30 days to review the rule, but that period may be extended for an additional 30 days. The joint committee may uphold or reverse the standing committee's action or may, on its own accord, object to a proposed rule or portion of a rule. If it objects or concurs with a standing committee's objection, it introduces bills concurrently in both houses to prevent promulgation of the rule. If either bill is enacted, the agency may not adopt the rule unless specifically authorized to do so by subsequent legislative action. If the joint committee disagrees with a standing committee's objection, it may overrule the standing committee and allow the agency to adopt the rule. The joint committee may also request the agency to modify a proposed rule.

The joint committee may suspend a rule after holding a public hearing, but suspension must be based on one or more of the following reasons: absence of statutory authority; an emergency related to public health or welfare; failure to comply with legislative intent; conflict with existing state law; a change in circumstances since passage of the law that authorized the rule; a rule that is arbitrary or capricious or imposes undue hardship; or a rule affecting construction of a dwelling that would increase the cost of construction by more than $1,000. Within 30 days following the suspension, the committee must introduce bills concurrently in both houses to repeal the suspended rule. If either bill is enacted, the rule is repealed and the agency may not promulgate it again unless authorized by the legislature. If both bills fail to pass, the rule remains in effect and may not be suspended again except for rules increasing the cost of construction of a dwelling by more than $1,000; these are suspended until specific legislation authorizing them is enacted.

The joint committee receives notice of any action in a circuit court for declaratory judgments about the validity of a rule and may intervene in the action with the consent of the Joint Committee on Legislative Organization.

Organization: The joint committee consists of 5 senators and 5 representatives, and the membership from each house must include representatives of both the majority and minority parties.

Minority Leader Peter Barca and Assistant Minority Leader Katrina Shankland make their case to Speaker Robin Vos on March 5, 2015. (Jay Salvo, Legislative Photographer)

History: The Joint Committee for Review of Administrative Rules was one of the first of its kind in the country, and it has served as a model widely copied by other states. Chapter 221, Laws of 1955, revised administrative rules procedures and created the committee with "advisory powers only". It could investigate complaints about rules and recommend changes to rule-making agencies but could not directly affect the rule-making process. Chapter 659, Laws of 1965, granted the committee authority to suspend a rule based on testimony at a public hearing. With enactment of Chapter 34, Laws of 1979, the joint committee acquired the power to review proposed rules based on the objections of a legislative standing committee. Further modifications occurred when 1985 Wisconsin Act 182 authorized the joint committee to extend its 30-day review period and allowed it to negotiate with agencies to modify existing rules. 2011 Wisconsin Act 21 modified the legislative review of proposed rules to require referral of all proposed rules to the joint committee.

State of Wisconsin
BUILDING COMMISSION

Members: GOVERNOR WALKER, *chairperson;* SENATOR MOULTON, *vice chairperson;* SENATORS PETROWSKI; RINGHAND; REPRESENTATIVES SWEARINGEN, BORN; KAHL; BOB BRANDHERM (citizen member appointed by governor). Nonvoting advisory members from Department of Administration: SCOTT A. NEITZEL (departmental secretary), vacancy (chief engineer), vacancy (chief architect).

Secretary: SUMMER R. STRAND, *administrator,* Division of Facilities Development, Department of Administration.

Mailing Address: P.O. Box 7866, Madison 53707-7866.

Location: 101 East Wilson Street, 7th Floor, Madison.

Telephone: 266-1855.

Fax: 267-2710.

Statutory Reference: Section 13.48.

Agency Responsibility: The State of Wisconsin Building Commission coordinates the state building program which includes construction of new buildings; the remodeling, renovation, and maintenance of existing facilities; necessary lands; and required capital equipment. The commission determines the projects to be incorporated into the long-range program and recommends a biennial building program to the legislature, including the amount to be appropriated in the biennial budget. The state building program for 2013-15 was $1,458,014,300. The commission oversees all state construction, except highway development. In addition, the commission may authorize expenditures from the State Building Trust Fund for construction, remodeling, maintenance, and planning of future development. The commission is the only state body that can authorize the contracting of state debt. All transactions for the sale of instruments that result in a state debt liability must be approved by official resolution of the commission.

Organization: The 8-member commission includes 6 legislators. Both the majority and minority parties in each house must be represented, and one legislator from each house must also be a member of the State Supported Programs Study and Advisory Committee. The governor serves as chairperson; one citizen member serves at the pleasure of the governor. In addition, three officials from the Department of Administration – the secretary, the head of the engineering function, and the ranking architect – serve as nonvoting, advisory members.

History: The State of Wisconsin Building Commission was created by Chapter 563, Laws of 1949, to establish a long-range public building program. Another 1949 law (Chapter 604) gave the commission authority to organize the quasi-public Wisconsin State Public Building Corporation. This legal device, familiarly known as a "dummy building corporation", was used to finance public buildings to house state agencies because the Wisconsin Constitution prevented direct borrowing by the state for such projects. The quasi-public corporation was first used in 1925, when the University Building Corporation was developed to permit construction of revenue-producing facilities on the Madison campus, including dormitories and athletic buildings.

The State Agencies Building Corporation, a similar entity, was formed in 1958 (Chapter 593, Laws of 1957) to finance nonrevenue-producing buildings, such as classroom facilities, and Chapter 267, Laws of 1961, extended the corporation's authority to the financing of public welfare buildings.

In 1969, voters amended the constitution, and the legislature passed Chapter 259, which provided for direct state borrowing and ended the use of the various building corporations. The law enlarged the powers of the commission to finance capital facilities for all state agencies.

A separate State Bond Board, including 4 members of the Building Commission, was established by Chapter 259 to supervise the contracting of state debt. Chapter 90, Laws of 1973, abolished the bond board and returned its duties and responsibilities to the Building Commission.

Joint Review Committee on
CRIMINAL PENALTIES

Members: SENATORS WANGGAARD, TAYLOR; REPRESENTATIVES JACQUE, DOYLE; BRAD SCHIMEL (attorney general); EDWARD F. WALL (secretary of corrections); KELLI S. THOMPSON (state public defender); JAMES T. BAYORGEON, DAVID G. DEININGER (reserve judges appointed by supreme court); BRADLEY GEHRING, MAURY STRAUB (public members appointed by governor).

Mailing Address: Senator Wanggaard, Room 319 South, State Capitol, P.O. Box 7882, Madison 53707-7882; Representative Jacque, Room 212 North, State Capitol, P.O. Box 8952, Madison 53708-8952.

Telephones: Senator Wanggaard, 266-1832; Representative Jacque, 266-9870.

E-mail: sen.wanggaard@legis.wisconsin.gov; rep.jacque@legis.wisconsin.gov

Statutory Reference: Section 13.525.

Agency Responsibility: The Joint Review Committee on Criminal Penalties, created by 2001 Wisconsin Act 109, reviews any bill that creates a new crime or revises a penalty for an existing crime when requested to do so by a chairperson of a standing committee in the house of origin to which the bill was referred. The presiding officer in the house of origin may also request a report from the joint committee if the bill is not referred to a standing committee.

Committee reports on bills submitted for its review concern the costs or savings to public agencies; the consistency of proposed penalties with existing penalties; whether alternative language is needed to conform the proposed penalties to existing penalties; and whether any acts prohibited by the bill are already prohibited under existing law.

Once a report is requested for a bill, a standing committee may not vote on the bill and the house of origin may not pass the bill before the joint committee submits its report or before the 30th day after the request is made, whichever is earlier.

Organization: Legislative members include one majority and one minority party member from each house; the members from the majority parties serve as cochairpersons. The attorney general, secretary of corrections, and state public defender serve *ex officio*. The supreme court appoints one reserve judge residing somewhere within judicial administrative districts one through 5, and another from districts 6 through 10. Public members appointed by the governor must include an individual with law enforcement experience and one who is an elected county official.

Joint Committee on
EMPLOYMENT RELATIONS

Members: SENATOR LAZICH (senate president), REPRESENTATIVE VOS (assembly speaker), SENATORS FITZGERALD (majority leader), SHILLING (minority leader); REPRESENTATIVES STEINEKE (majority

Senator Mark Miller and Senator Janet Bewley share a lighter moment during Senate floor debate.
(Greg Anderson, Legislative Photographer)

leader), BARCA (minority leader); SENATOR DARLING, REPRESENTATIVE NYGREN (joint finance committee cochairpersons).

Mailing Address: Legislative Council Staff, P.O. Box 2536, Madison 53701-2536.

Location: 1 East Main Street, Suite 401, Madison.

Telephone: 266-1304.

Statutory References: Sections 13.111, 20.923 (4), and 230.12; Chapter 111, Subchapter V.

Agency Responsibility: The Joint Committee on Employment Relations approves all changes to the collective bargaining agreements that cover state employees represented by unions, and the compensation plans for nonrepresented state employees. These plans and agreements include pay adjustments; fringe benefits; performance awards; pay equity adjustments; and other items related to wages, hours, and conditions of employment. The committee also approves the assignment of unclassified positions to the executive salary group ranges.

In the case of unionized employees, the Office of State Employment Relations or, for University of Wisconsin bargaining units, the Board of Regents or the UW-Madison, submits tentative agreements negotiated between it and certified labor organizations to the committee. If the committee disapproves an agreement, it is returned to the bargaining parties for renegotiation.

When the committee approves an agreement for unionized employees, it introduces those portions requiring legislative approval in bill form and recommends passage without change. If the legislature fails to pass the bill, the agreement is returned to the bargaining parties for renegotiation.

The Office of State Employment Relations also submits the compensation plans for nonrepresented employees to the committee. One plan covers all nonrepresented classified employees and certain officials outside the classified service, including legislators, justices of the supreme court, court of appeals judges, circuit court judges, constitutional officers, district attorneys, heads of executive agencies, division administrators, and others designated by law. The faculty and academic staff of the UW System are covered by a separate compensation plan, which is based on recommendations made by the UW Board of Regents.

After public hearings on the nonrepresented employee plans, the committee may modify the office's recommendations, but the committee's modifications may be disapproved by the governor. The committee may set aside the governor's disapproval by a vote of 6 committee members.

Organization: The committee, which was established by Chapter 270, Laws of 1971, is a permanent joint legislative committee comprised of 8 members: the presiding officers of each house; the majority and minority leaders of each house; and the cochairpersons of the Joint Committee on Finance. It is assisted in its work by the Legislative Council Staff and the Legislative Fiscal Bureau.

Joint Committee on
FINANCE

Members: SENATOR DARLING, REPRESENTATIVE NYGREN, *cochairpersons;* SENATORS OLSEN, HARSDORF, VUKMIR, TIFFANY, MARKLEIN; L. TAYLOR*, ERPENBACH; REPRESENTATIVES KOOYENGA, KNUDSON, LOUDENBECK, SCHRAA, CZAJA; C. TAYLOR*, HINTZ.

Mailing Addresses: Senator Darling, Room 317 East, State Capitol, P.O. Box 7882, Madison 53707-7882; Representative Nygren, Room 309 East, State Capitol, P.O. Box 8953, Madison 53708-8953.

Telephones: Senator Darling, 266-5830; Representative Nygren, 266-2343.

E-mail: sen.darling@legis.wisconsin.gov; rep.nygren@legis.wisconsin.gov

Statutory References: Sections 13.09-13.11, 16.47, 16.505, 16.515, and 20.865 (4).

The role of the Joint Committee on Finance is central to Wisconsin's budget process. Assembly cochairperson John Nygren confers with Senator Jon Erpenbach during deliberations on the 2015 budget bill. (Jay Salvo, Legislative Photographer)

Agency Responsibility: The Joint Committee on Finance examines all legislation that deals with state income and spending. It also gives final approval to a wide variety of state payments and assessments. Any bill introduced in the legislature that appropriates money, provides for revenue, or relates to taxation must be referred to the joint committee.

The joint committee introduces the biennial budget as recommended by the governor. After holding a series of public hearings and executive sessions, it submits its own version of the budget as a substitute amendment to the governor's budget bill for consideration by the legislature.

At regularly scheduled quarterly meetings, the joint committee considers agency requests to adjust their budgets. It may approve a request for emergency funds if it finds that the legislature has authorized the activities for which the appropriation is sought. It may also transfer funds between existing appropriations and change the number of positions authorized to an agency in the budget process.

When required, the joint committee introduces legislation to pay claims against the state, resolve shortages in funds, and restore capital reserve funds of the Wisconsin Housing and Economic Development Authority to the required level. As an emergency measure, it may reduce certain state agency appropriations when there is a decrease in state revenues.

Organization: The committee is a joint standing committee composed of the 8 senators on the Senate Finance Committee and the 8 representatives on the Assembly Finance Committee. It includes members of the majority and minority party in each house. Cochairpersons of the joint committee are appointed in the same manner as are standing committees of their respective houses.

History: The use of a joint standing committee to consider appropriation bills dates back to 1857 when the legislature created the Joint Committee on Claims. In 1911 (Chapter 6), the Joint Committee on Finance replaced the claims committee and was given the responsibility to consider all bills related to revenue and taxation. Chapter 609, Laws of 1915, authorized the governor, secretary of state, and state treasurer to approve emergency appropriations when the legislature was not in session to permit departments with insufficient funds to carry out their normal duties. Chapter 97, Laws of 1929, transferred this function to a new Emergency Board, which consisted of the governor and the cochairpersons of the joint finance committee. The power to approve supplemental appropriations, transfer funds between appropriations, and handle other interim fiscal matters was given to a joint legislative committee called the Board on Government Operations (BOGO) by Chapter 228, Laws of 1959. BOGO's functions were transferred to the Joint Committee on Finance by Chapter 39, Laws of 1975.

Joint Committee on
INFORMATION POLICY AND TECHNOLOGY

Members: SENATOR HARSDORF, REPRESENTATIVE PETERSEN, *cochairpersons;* SENATORS COWLES, ROTH; CARPENTER, VINEHOUT; REPRESENTATIVES PETRYK, LOUDENBECK; BARCA, GENRICH.

Statutory Reference: Section 13.58.

Agency Responsibility: The Joint Committee on Information Policy and Technology reviews information management practices of state and local units of government to ensure economic and efficient service, maintain data security and integrity, and protect the privacy of individuals who are subjects of the databases. It studies the effects of proposals by the state to expand existing information technology or implement new technologies. With concurrence of the Joint Committee on Finance, it may direct the Department of Administration to report on any information technology system project that could cost $1 million or more in the current or succeeding biennium. The committee may direct the Department of Administration to prepare reports or conduct studies and may make recommendations to the governor, the legislature, state agencies, or local governments based on this information. The University of Wisconsin Board of Regents is required to submit a report to the committee twice annually, detailing each information technology project in the University of Wisconsin System costing more than $1 million or deemed "high-risk" by the board. The committee may make recommendations on the identified projects to the governor and the legislature. The committee is composed of 3 majority and 2 minority party members from each house of the legislature. It was created by 1991 Wisconsin Act 317 and its membership was revised by 1999 Wisconsin Act 29.

Joint
LEGISLATIVE AUDIT COMMITTEE

Members: SENATOR COWLES, REPRESENTATIVE KERKMAN, *cochairpersons;* SENATOR DARLING, REPRESENTATIVE NYGREN (joint finance committee cochairpersons); SENATORS LAZICH; VINEHOUT*, BEWLEY; REPRESENTATIVES MACCO; SARGENT*, BERCEAU.

Mailing Addresses: Senator Cowles, Room 118 South, State Capitol, P.O. Box 7882, Madison 53707-7882; Representative Kerkman, Room 315 North, State Capitol, P.O. Box 8952, Madison 53708-8952.

Telephones: Senator Cowles, 266-0484; Representative Kerkman, 266-2530.

E-mail: sen.cowles@legis.wisconsin.gov; rep.kerkman@legis.wisconsin.gov

Statutory Reference: Section 13.53.

Agency Responsibility: The Joint Legislative Audit Committee, which was created by Chapter 224, Laws of 1975, advises the Legislative Audit Bureau, subject to general supervision of the Joint Committee on Legislative Organization. Its members include the cochairpersons of the Joint Committee on Finance, plus 2 majority and 2 minority party members from each house of the legislature. The committee evaluates candidates for the office of state auditor and makes recommendations to the Joint Committee on Legislative Organization, which selects the auditor.

The committee may direct the state auditor to undertake specific audits and review requests for special audits from individual legislators or standing committees, but no legislator or standing committee may interfere with the auditor in the conduct of an audit.

The committee reviews each report of the Legislative Audit Bureau and then confers with the state auditor, other legislative committees, and the audited agencies on the report's findings. It may propose corrective action and direct that followup reports be submitted to it.

The committee may hold hearings on audit reports, ask the Joint Committee on Legislative Organization to investigate any matter within the scope of the audit, and request investigation of any matter relative to the fiscal and performance responsibilities of a state agency. If an audit report cites financial deficiencies, the head of the agency must report to the Joint Legislative Audit Committee on remedial actions taken. Should the agency head fail to report, the committee may refer the matter to the Joint Committee on Legislative Organization and the appropriate standing committees.

When the committee determines that legislative action is needed, it may refer the necessary information to the legislature or a standing committee. It can also request information from a committee on action taken or seek advice of a standing committee on program portions of an audit. The committee may introduce legislation to address issues covered in audit reports.

JOINT LEGISLATIVE COUNCIL

Members: SENATOR LAZICH (senate president), REPRESENTATIVE BALLWEG (designated by assembly speaker), *cochairpersons;* SENATORS GUDEX (president pro tempore), FITZGERALD (majority leader), SHILLING (minority leader), DARLING (cochairperson, Joint Committee on Finance), L. TAYLOR (ranking minority member, Joint Committee on Finance), MOULTON, PETROWSKI, WANGGAARD, RISSER, MILLER; REPRESENTATIVES VOS (assembly speaker), AUGUST (speaker pro tempore), STEINEKE (majority leader), BARCA (minority leader), NYGREN (cochairperson, Joint Committee on Finance), C. TAYLOR (ranking minority member, Joint Committee on Finance), MURTHA, KNODL, MASON, SHANKLAND. (Members designated by title serve *ex officio.*)

Director of Legislative Council Staff: TERRY C. ANDERSON, terry.anderson@legis.wisconsin.gov

Representative Jessie Rodriguez presides over a session of the Committee on Children and Families. The chairperson is flanked by the committee clerk and a member of the Joint Legislative Council Staff. (Jay Salvo, Legislative Photographer)

Deputy Director: JESSICA KARLS-RUPLINGER, jessica.karls-ruplinger@legis.wisconsin.gov

Legislative Council Rules Clearinghouse: SCOTT GROSZ, *director,*
scott.grosz@legis.wisconsin.gov; MARGIT KELLEY, *assistant director,*
margit.kelley@legis.wisconsin.gov

Mailing Address: P.O. Box 2536, Madison 53701-2536.

Location: 1 East Main Street, Suite 401, Madison.

Telephone: 266-1304.

Fax: 266-3830.

Internet Address: http://www.lc.legis.wisconsin.gov

Publications: General Report of the Joint Legislative Council to the Legislature; State Agency Staff Members With Responsibilities Related to the Legislature; Wisconsin Legislator Briefing Book; Directory of Joint Legislative Council Committees; Comparative Retirement Study; rules clearinghouse reports; staff briefs; information memoranda on substantive issues considered by council committees; staff memoranda; amendment and act memoranda.

Number of Employees: 34.17.

Total Budget 2013-15: $8,005,300.

Statutory References: Sections 13.81-13.83, 13.91, and 227.15.

Agency Responsibility: The Joint Legislative Council creates special committees made up of legislators and interested citizens to study various problems of state and local government. Study topics are selected from requests presented to the council by law, joint resolution, and individual legislators. After research, expert testimony, and public hearings, the study committees draft proposals and submit them to the council, which must approve those drafts it wants introduced in the legislature as council bills.

The council is assisted in its work by the Legislative Council staff, a bureau created in Section 13.91, Wisconsin Statutes. The staff provides legal and research assistance to all of the legislature's substantive standing committees and joint statutory committees (except the Joint Committee on Finance) and assists individual legislators on request. The staff operates the rules clearinghouse to review proposed administrative rules and assists standing committees in their oversight of rulemaking. The staff also assists the legislature in identifying and responding to issues relating to the Wisconsin Retirement System.

By law, the Legislative Council staff must be "strictly nonpartisan" and must observe the confidential nature of the research and drafting requests received by it. The law requires that state agencies and local governmental units cooperate fully with the council staff in its carrying out of its statutory duties.

Organization: The council consists of 22 legislators. The majority of them serve *ex officio,* and the remainder are appointed as are members of standing committees. The president of the senate and the speaker of the assembly serve as cochairpersons of the council, but each may designate another member to assume that office or decline to serve on the council. The council operates two permanent statutory committees and various special committees appointed to study selected subjects. The Legislative Council staff director is appointed from outside the classified service by the Joint Committee on Legislative Organization, and the director makes staff appointments from outside the service.

History: Chapter 444, Laws of 1947, created the council to conduct interim studies on subjects affecting the general welfare of the state. The first council was organized later that year with 12 members. In 1967, the council began to appoint staff members to provide legal counsel and technical assistance to legislative standing committees. The 1979 executive budget (Chapter 34) assigned the administrative rules clearinghouse function to the council. 1993 Wisconsin Act 52 made a number of reorganizational changes. The act renamed the council the Joint Legislative Council and designated the president of the senate and the speaker of the assembly (or their designees) cochairpersons. Under Act 52, the council was directed to reorganize at the beginning of the biennial session, instead of May 1 of the odd-numbered year, and its support agency was officially named the Legislative Council Staff. 2005 Wisconsin Act 316 transferred

Senator Sheila Harsdorf of River Falls addresses the Senate. (Jay Salvo, Legislative Photographer)

the functions of the retirement research director to the council staff, making the staff responsible for supporting the Joint Survey Committee on Retirement Systems and the legislature regarding legislation involving the Wisconsin Retirement System.

PERMANENT STATUTORY COMMITTEES

Special Committee on State-Tribal Relations

Members: REPRESENTATIVE MURSAU, *chairperson;* SENATOR VINEHOUT, *vice chairperson;* SENATOR BEWLEY; REPRESENTATIVE MILROY; RUSSELL BARBER (Lac Courte Oreilles Band of Lake Superior Chippewa Indians of Wisconsin), DEE ANN ALLEN (Lac du Flambeau Band of Lake Superior Chippewa Indians), BRYAN BAINBRIDGE (Red Cliff Band of Lake Superior Chippewa Indians), AIMEE AWONOHOPAY (St. Croix Chippewa Indians of Wisconsin), CHRIS MCGESHICK (Sokaogon Chippewa Community), JON GREENDEER (Ho-Chunk Nation), GARY BESAW (Menominee Indian Tribe of Wisconsin), MELINDA DANFORTH (Oneida Tribe of Indians of Wisconsin), HAROLD G. FRANK (Forest County Potawatomi Community), WALLACE A. MILLER (Stockbridge-Munsee Community).

The Special Committee on State-Tribal Relations is appointed by the Joint Legislative Council each biennium to study issues related to American Indians and the Indian tribes and bands in this state and develop specific recommendations and legislative proposals relating to such issues. Legislative membership includes not fewer than 6 nor more than 12 members with at least one member of the majority and the minority party from each house. The council appoints no fewer than 6 and no more than 11 members from names submitted by federally recognized Wisconsin Indian tribes or bands or the Great Lakes Inter-Tribal Council. The council may not appoint more than one member recommended by any one tribe or band or the Great Lakes Inter-Tribal Council. The committee has its origins in the Menominee Indians Committee, created in 1955 to study the governmental status of the Menominee Indian Tribe at that time. Chapter 39, Laws of 1975, replaced that committee with the more broadly focused Native American Study Committee. Its name was changed to the American Indian Study Committee in 1982. 1999 Wisconsin Act 60 gave it its current name and revised the membership. The committee's composition and duties are prescribed in Section 13.83 (3) of the statutes.

Technical Advisory Committee

Members: LOA PORTER (Department of Children and Families), GAIL NAHWAHQUAW (Department of Health Services), TOM BELLAVIA (Department of Justice), QUINN WILLIAMS (Department of Natural Resources), DAVID O'CONNOR (Department of Public Instruction), THOMAS D. OURADA (Department of Revenue), KELLY JACKSON (Department of Transportation), TRISTAN COOK (Department of Workforce Development).

Under Section 13.83 (3) (f), Wisconsin Statutes, as created by Chapter 39, Laws of 1975, the Technical Advisory Committee, consisting of representatives of 8 major executive agencies, assists the Special Committee on State-Tribal Relations.

Law Revision Committee

Members: vacancy.

The Law Revision Committee is appointed each biennium by the Joint Legislative Council. The membership of the committee is not specified, but it must include majority and minority party representation from each house. The committee reviews minor nonsubstantive remedial changes to the statutes as proposed by state agencies and reviews attorney general's opinions and court decisions declaring a Wisconsin statute unconstitutional, ambiguous, or otherwise in need of revision. It considers proposals by the Legislative Reference Bureau to correct statutory language and session laws that conflict or need revision, and it may submit recommendations for major law revision projects to the Joint Legislative Council. It serves as the repository for interstate compacts and agreements and makes recommendations to the legislature regarding revision of such agreements. The committee was created by Chapter 204, Laws of 1979, as a combination of the Judiciary Committee, which had its origins in a 1951 mandate to prepare a criminal code, and the Remedial Legislation Committee, created in 1959. Its composition and duties are prescribed in Section 13.83 (1) of the statutes.

SPECIAL COMMITTEES REPORTING IN 2015

Study Committee on Adoption Disruption and Dissolution

Members: REPRESENTATIVE KLEEFISCH, *chairperson;* REPRESENTATIVE JOHNSON, *vice chairperson;* SENATOR HARRIS DODD; REPRESENTATIVES JACQUE, KESSLER, TITTL; SAM BENEDICT, ORIANA CAREY, JILL LIST, MARY OSGOOD, RAY PRZYBELSKI, THERESA ROETTER, MARK SANDERS, JACLYN SKALNIK, HEATHER YAEGER.

The study committee shall study the extent of adoption disruption and dissolution in Wisconsin and the efforts in Wisconsin to prevent it. The committee shall consider legislative options such as preventing disruptions and dissolutions and meeting the needs of adoptive children and parents if this occurs. The committee shall also consider options for tracking the number of and reasons for such adoption issues.

Study Committee on Problem-Solving Courts, Alternatives, and Diversions

Members: REPRESENTATIVE BIES, *chairperson;* REPRESENTATIVE GOYKE, *vice chairperson;* SENATOR WIRCH; REPRESENTATIVES KOOYENGA, PETRYK, TAYLOR; CAROL CARLSON, TROY CROSS, TONY GIBART, MATTHEW JOSKI, JANE KLEKAMP, ELLIOTT LEVINE, JOANN STEPHENS, KELLI THOMPSON, MARY TRIGGIANO, MICHAEL WAUPOOSE.

The study committee is directed to review the more than 50 courts currently in operation in Wisconsin that utilize nontraditional adjudication methods, the effect they have on recidivism, and the net fiscal impact of these courts. The committee shall examine courts, such as veterans courts, drug and alcohol courts, mental health courts, and drunk driving courts, in Wisconsin and nationally and consider: a) effectiveness of existing problem-solving courts in Wisconsin in reducing recidivism, the costs to administer these courts, and the savings realized; b) best practices of existing problem-solving courts, both in Wisconsin and elsewhere, and potential

JOINT LEGISLATIVE COUNCIL

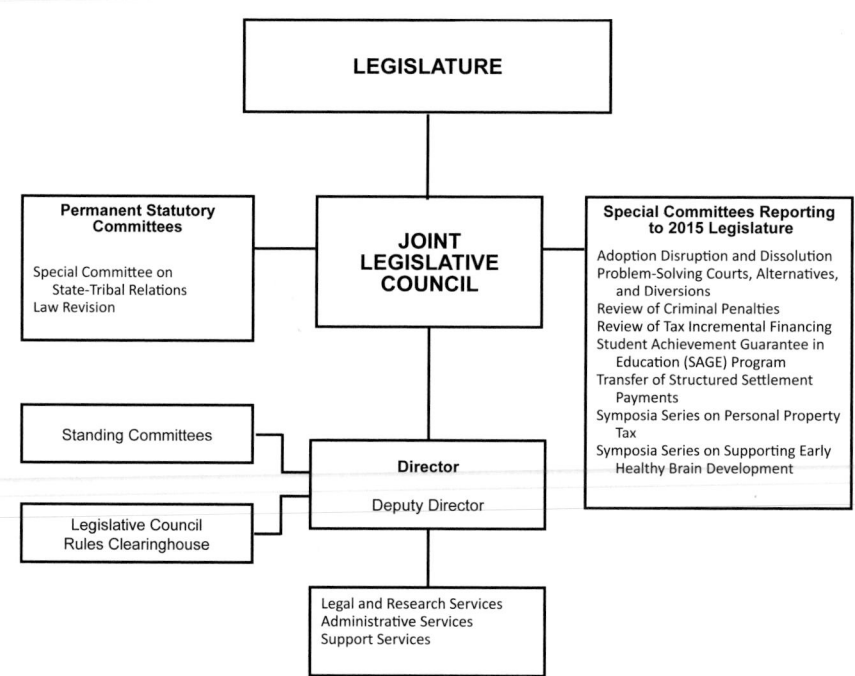

Representative Sondy Pope speaks to Representative Jim Steineke, Majority Leader for the 2015 session. (Greg Anderson, Legislative Photographer)

implementation of these practices at the state level; c) efforts to establish problem-solving courts that serve multiple counties, impediments to these efforts, and potential changes to improve regionalization of such courts; and d) appropriate role and structure of state-level training and coordination.

Study Commitee on the Review of Criminal Penalties

Members: REPRESENTATIVE HUTTON, *chairperson;* SENATOR RISSER, *vice chairperson;* REPRESENTATIVES BARNES, NEYLON, RIEMER, SPIROS; EDWARD BAILEY, KEITH BELZER, ADAM GEROL, SCOTT HORNE, JILL KAROFSKY, BEN KEMPINEN, DAVID REDDY, MICHAEL TOBIN, DONALD ZUIDMULDER.

The study committee is directed to review the penalties for misdemeanor and low-level felony offenses. The committee shall: determine whether current misdemeanor or low-level felony penalties are appropriate; whether any crimes should be classified; and whether any offenses are outdated or should be decriminalized.

Study Committee on Review of Tax Incremental Financing

Members: SENATOR GUDEX, *chairperson;* REPRESENTATIVE LOUDENBECK, *vice chairperson;* SENATOR JAUCH; REPRESENTATIVES KUGLITSCH, OHNSTAD, ZEPNICK; JENNIFER ANDREWS, MICHAEL HARRIGAN, EILEEN KELLEY, JOHN KOVARI, RICHARD LINCOLN, DAVID RASMUSSEN, BRIAN RUECHEL, JASON SERCK, MIKE SLAVISH, PETER THILLMAN, THOMAS WILSON, HAL WORTMAN.

The study committee is directed to study and review the intent behind tax incremental financing (TIF) laws and how TIF laws are utilized by cities, villages, towns, and counties. The committee shall also evaluate current TIF laws and recommend legislation that could improve their effectiveness and study how they impact a local governmental unit's finances and property taxes, economic and community development, and job growth.

Study Committee on the Student Achievement Guarantee in Education (SAGE) Program

Members: SENATOR OLSEN, *chairperson;* REPRESENTATIVE CZAJA, *vice chairperson;* SENATOR HANSEN; REPRESENTATIVES BILLINGS, POPE, THIESFELDT; JOHN GAIER, BETH GRAUE, N. DAVID KIPP, RANDY NELSON, MIGUEL SANCHEZ, ANNE SMITH, ROBERT WAY, ANGELA WIEMER.

The study committee is directed to study the SAGE program; whether there are alternatives to current class size limitations that would allow schools to achieve the aims of SAGE; and whether the Department of Public Instruction should be authorized to waive the class size limitations in a school that implements alternative interventions, or to otherwise provide funds and assistance for alternatives to class size limitations.

Study Committee on Transfer of Structured Settlement Payments

Members: REPRESENTATIVE J. OTT, *chairperson;* REPRESENTATIVE WACHS, *vice chairperson;* SENATOR TAYLOR; REPRESENTATIVE SCHRAA; BRUCE BACHHUBER, MICHAEL FITZPATRICK, CATHERINE LA FLEUR, BENJAMIN MALSCH, ELIZABETH NEVITT, GERALD PTACEK.

The study committee shall be directed to do the following: a) review the current method by which structured settlement payments are transferred in Wisconsin; b) examine statutes regulating the practice in other states and under federal law; and c) recommend a statute for adoption in Wisconsin that governs transfers of structured settlement payments. The committee shall consider items such as standards for disclosure of information to structured settlement recipients by entities seeking to purchase future settlement payments, the ability of parents and guardians to enter into structured settlements on behalf of minor children, and guidelines for use by judges in approving the transfer of structured settlement agreements.

Steering Committee Symposia Series on Personal Property Tax

Members: SENATOR STROEBEL, *chairperson;* SENATOR TIFFANY, *vice chairperson;* SENATORS CARPENTER, HARSDORF, SHILLING; REPRESENTATIVES BARNES, KAHL, KULP, SANFELIPPO.

The Speaker serves as the assembly's preeminent constitutional officer in a body with 99 diverse constituencies. The Assembly has elected Robin J. Vos to that role for the second consecutive session.
(Jay Salvo, Legislative Photographer)

The steering committee is directed to conduct information symposia and develop recommendations regarding the state's personal property tax. The steering committee shall study the fiscal effect of the personal property tax and personal property tax exemptions, the constitutional concerns that may arise in the context of personal property tax reform, and the administrative and compliance costs associated with personal property taxation; and shall develop recommendations, in the form of a committee report, for personal property tax reform.

Steering Committee for Symposia Series on Supporting Early Healthy Brain Development

Members: REPRESENTATIVE BALLWEG, *chairperson;* SENATOR DARLING, *vice chairperson;* SENATORS LASSA, MILLER, OLSEN; REPRESENTATIVES BERCEAU, BORN, GENRICH, RODRIGUEZ, WRIGHT.

The steering committee is directed to conduct information symposia regarding: a) research on the impact of early brain development on lifetime physical and mental health, educational achievement, and economic security and the factors that hinder or promote healthy early brain development; b) policy initiatives implemented in other states that are intended to positively influence early brain development; and c) relevant programs and initiatives currently in place in Wisconsin. The steering committee shall also develop policy recommendations designed to improve the early brain development of Wisconsin's infants and young children.

Joint Committee on
LEGISLATIVE ORGANIZATION

Members: SENATOR LAZICH (senate president), REPRESENTATIVE VOS (assembly speaker), *cochairpersons;* SENATORS FITZGERALD (majority leader), SHILLING (minority leader), FARROW (assistant majority leader), HANSEN (assistant minority leader); REPRESENTATIVES STEINEKE (majority leader), BARCA (minority leader), KNODL (assistant majority leader), SHANKLAND (assistant minority leader).

Mailing Address: Legislative Council Staff, P.O. Box 2536, Madison 53701-2536.

Location: 1 East Main Street, Suite 401, Madison.

Telephone: 266-1304.

Statutory References: Sections 13.80 and 13.90.

Agency Responsibility: The Joint Committee on Legislative Organization is the policy-making body for the legislative service bureaus: the Legislative Audit Bureau, the Legislative Fiscal Bureau, the Legislative Reference Bureau, and the Legislative Technology Services Bureau. In this capacity, it assigns tasks to each bureau, approves bureau budgets, and sets the salary of bureau heads. The joint committee selects the four bureau heads, but it acts on the recommendation of the Joint Legislative Audit Committee when appointing the state auditor. The joint committee also selects the director of the Legislative Council Staff.

The committee may inquire into misconduct by members and employees of the legislature. It oversees a variety of operations, including the work schedule for the legislative session, computer use, space allocation for legislative offices and legislative service agencies, parking on the State Capitol Park grounds, and sale and distribution of legislative documents. The joint committee recommends which newspaper should serve as the official state newspaper for publication of state legal notices. It advises the Government Accountability Board on its operations and, upon recommendation of the Joint Legislative Audit Committee, may investigate any problems the Legislative Audit Bureau finds during its audits. The committee may employ outside consultants to study ways to improve legislative staff services and organization.

Organization: The 10-member joint committee is a permanent body, consisting of the presiding officers and party leadership of both houses. The committee has established a Subcommittee on Legislative Services to advise it on matters pertaining to the legislative institution, including the review of computer technology purchases. The Legislative Council Staff provides staff assistance to the committee.

History: The joint committee was created by Chapter 149, Laws of 1963, as part of a legislative reorganization proposed by the Committee on Legislative Organization and Procedure under the authority of Chapter 686, Laws of 1961. The 1963 law also transferred the Legislative Reference Bureau and the Statutory Revision Bureau to the legislative branch and placed them under the supervision of the joint committee. The three other service agencies were placed under the committee's authority by later legislation: the Legislative Audit Bureau in Chapter 659, Laws of 1965; the Legislative Fiscal Bureau in Chapter 215, Laws of 1971; and the Legislative Technology Services Bureau in 1997 Wisconsin Act 27. 2007 Wisconsin Act 20 eliminated the Revisor of Statutes Bureau and transferred its duties to the Legislative Reference Bureau.

In 1966, the joint committee was empowered to investigate misconduct by legislators and legislative staff. Actions by subsequent legislatures expanded the joint committee's supervision of legislative operations to include legislative office space, legislative computer operations, and publication of notices and documents.

Joint Survey Committee on
RETIREMENT SYSTEMS

Members: SENATOR LASEE, REPRESENTATIVE MURPHY, *cochairpersons;* SENATORS MARKLEIN; ERPENBACH; REPRESENTATIVES KUGLITSCH; MASON; CHARLOTTE GIBSON (assistant attorney general appointed by attorney general), *secretary;* ROBERT J. CONLIN (secretary of employee trust funds), TED NICKEL (insurance commissioner); TIM PEDERSON (public member appointed by governor).

Mailing Address: Legislative Council Staff, P.O. Box 2536, Madison 53701-2536.

Telephone: 266-1304.

Statutory Reference: Section 13.50.

Agency Responsibility: The Joint Survey Committee on Retirement Systems makes recommendations on legislation that affects retirement and pension plans for public officers and employees, and its recommendations must be attached as an appendix to each retirement bill. Neither house of the legislature may consider such a bill until the joint survey committee submits a written report that describes the proposal's purpose, probable costs, actuarial effect, and desirability as a matter of public policy.

Organization: The 10-member joint survey committee includes majority and minority party representation from each legislative house. An experienced actuary from the Office of the Commissioner of Insurance may be designated to serve in the commissioner's place on the committee. The public member cannot be a participant in any public retirement system in the state and is expected to "represent the interests of the taxpayers". Appointed members serve 4-year terms unless they lose the status upon which the appointment was based. The joint survey committee is assisted by the Joint Legislative Council staff in the performance of its duties, but may contract for actuarial assistance outside the classified service.

Joint Legislative
STATE SUPPORTED PROGRAMS
STUDY AND ADVISORY COMMITTEE

Members: vacancy.

Statutory Reference: Section 13.47.

Agency Responsibility: Members of the Joint Legislative State Supported Programs Study and Advisory Committee visit and inspect the state capitol and all institutions and office buildings owned or leased by the state. They are granted free and full access to all parts of the buildings, the surrounding grounds, and all persons associated with the buildings. The committee may also examine any institution, program, or organization that receives direct or indirect state financial support.

Inauguration Day is usually marked by some ceremony. Justice Annette Ziegler addressed the Senate before administering the oath of office to the senators from odd-numbered districts on January 5, 2015. (Greg Anderson, Legislative Photographer)

Organization: The committee consists of 5 senators and 6 representatives. Members appointed from each house must represent the two major political parties, and one legislator from each house must also be a member of the State of Wisconsin Building Commission. Assistance to the committee is provided by the Legislative Council Staff.

History: The use of a legislative committee to visit and supervise the use of state institutions and property dates back to 1881. The current joint committee was created by Chapter 266, Laws of 1973. It replaced the Committee to Visit State Properties, which had combined the functions of the Committee to Visit State Institutions, created in 1947 to inspect state property and state institutions, and the Committee on Physical Plant Maintenance, created in 1957 to manage the state capitol and the single state office building then in existence.

Joint Survey Committee on
TAX EXEMPTIONS

Members: SENATOR LeMAHIEU, REPRESENTATIVE AUGUST, *cochairpersons;* SENATORS TIFFANY, CARPENTER*; REPRESENTATIVES SWEARINGEN, HESSELBEIN*; RICHARD G. CHANDLER (secretary of revenue); PAUL CONNELL (Department of Justice representative appointed by attorney general); KIMBERLY SHAUL (public member appointed by governor).

Mailing Address: Legislative Council Staff, P.O. Box 2536, Madison 53701-2536.

Telephone: 266-1304.

Statutory Reference: Section 13.52.

Agency Responsibility: The Joint Survey Committee on Tax Exemptions, created by Chapter 153, Laws of 1963, considers all legislation related to the exemption of persons or property from state or local taxes. It is assisted by the Legislative Council Staff.

Any legislative proposal that affects tax exemptions must be referred to the committee immediately upon introduction. Budget bills containing tax exemptions are referred simultaneously to the joint survey committee and the Joint Committee on Finance. The joint survey committee must report within 60 days on the tax exemptions contained within a budget bill. Neither house of the legislature may consider tax exemption proposals until the joint survey committee has issued its report, attached as an appendix to the bill, describing the proposal's legality, desirability as public policy, and fiscal effect. In the course of its review, the committee is authorized to conduct investigations, hold hearings, and subpoena witnesses.

Organization: The 9-member committee includes representation from each house of the legislature with 2 members from the majority party and one from the minority party. The public member must be familiar with the tax problems of local government. Members' terms expire on January 15 of odd-numbered years.

TRANSPORTATION PROJECTS COMMISSION

Members: GOVERNOR WALKER, *chairperson;* SENATORS COWLES, MARKLEIN, PETROWSKI; CARPENTER, HANSEN; REPRESENTATIVES RIPP, SPIROS, 3 vacancies; JEAN M. JACOBSON, BARBARA FLEISNER LAMUE, MICHAEL RYAN (citizen members appointed by governor). Nonvoting member: MARK GOTTLIEB (secretary of transportation).

Commission Secretary: KRIS SOMMERS, kristen.sommers@dot.wi.gov

Mailing Address: P.O. Box 7913, Madison 53707-7913.

Location: Hill Farms State Transportation Building, 4802 Sheboygan Avenue, Room 901, Madison.

Telephone: 266-3341.

Fax: 267-0294.

Representative Dan Knodl, Assembly Assistant Majority Leader, confers with his colleague Chris Kapenga during a session of the Assembly Committee on Labor. (Jay Salvo, Legislative Photographer)

Statutory Reference: Section 13.489.

Agency Responsibility: The Transportation Projects Commission, created by 1983 Wisconsin Act 27, includes representation from each house of the legislature with 3 members from the majority party and 2 from the minority party. The commission reviews Department of Transportation recommendations for major highway projects. The department must report its recommendations to the commission by September 15 of each even-numbered year, and the commission, in turn, reports its recommendations to the governor or governor-elect, the legislature, and the Joint Committee on Finance before December 15 of each even-numbered year. The department must also provide the commission with a status report on major transportation projects every 6 months. The commission also approves the preparation of environmental impact or assessment statements for potential major highway projects.

Commission on
UNIFORM STATE LAWS

Members: JOANNE HUELSMAN, *chairperson;* AARON GARY (designated by chief, Legislative Reference Bureau), *secretary;* SENATOR RISSER; REPRESENTATIVE RIEMER, JUSTICE DAVID PROSSER, JR.; MARGIT KELLEY (designated by director, Legislative Council Staff); JOHN MACY, JUSTICE PATIENCE ROGGENSACK (public members appointed by governor).

Mailing Address: 1 East Main Street, Suite 200, Madison 53701-2037.

Telephone: 261-6926.

Fax: 264-6948.

Statutory Reference: Section 13.55.

Agency Responsibility: The Commission on Uniform State Laws advises the legislature on uniform laws and model laws. It examines subjects on which interstate uniformity is desirable and the best methods for achieving it, cooperates with the national Uniform Law Commission, in preparing uniform acts, and prepares bills adapting the uniform acts to Wisconsin. The commission reports biennially to the Law Revision Committee of the Joint Legislative Council.

Organization: The commission consists of 8 members, including 2 public members appointed by the governor for 4-year terms. Legislative members serve 2-year terms, must represent the 2 major political parties, and must be state bar association members. A legislative seat may be filled by a former legislator if no current legislator meets the criteria, or if no eligible legislator is willing or able to accept the appointment. In addition to the members prescribed by law, the commission may include a number of life-members.

History: The commission was originally created by Chapter 83, Laws of 1893, which authorized the governor to appoint 3 members to serve as the Commissioners for the Promotion of Uniformity of Legislation in the United States. In 1931, Chapter 67 designated the Revisor of Statutes as the sole Wisconsin commissioner. Chapter 173, Laws of 1941, added the chief of the Legislative Reference Library as a commissioner. The commission was created in its present form by Chapter 312, Laws of 1957, and its membership was expanded to include 2 members of the State Bar appointed by the governor. Chapter 135, Laws of 1959, added the director (then called the executive secretary) of the Legislative Council Staff as a member. Chapter 294, Laws of 1979, added 4 legislative members and deleted the requirement that public members appointed by the governor be members of the State Bar. 2003 Wisconsin Act 2 added a requirement that legislative members must be state bar association members. 2007 Wisconsin Act 20 eliminated the Revisor of Statutes, reducing the total membership to 8.

LEGISLATIVE SERVICE AGENCIES

LEGISLATIVE AUDIT BUREAU

State Auditor: JOE CHRISMAN, joe.chrisman@

Special Assistant to the State Auditor: ANNE SAPPENFIELD, anne.sappenfield@

Deputy State Auditor for Financial Audit: BRYAN NAAB, bryan.naab@

Deputy State Auditor for Program Evaluation: PAUL STUIBER, paul.stuiber@

Audit Directors: SHERRY HAAKENSON, sherry.haakenson@; CAROLYN STITTLEBURG, carolyn.stittleburg@; DEAN SWENSON, dean.swenson@

Mailing Address: 22 East Mifflin Street, Suite 500, Madison 53703-2512.

Telephones: 266-2818; Fraud, waste, and mismanagement hotline: (877) FRAUD-17.

Fax: 267-0410.

Internet Address: http://www.legis.wisconsin.gov/lab

E-mail Address: leg.audit.info@legis.wisconsin.gov

Address e-mail by combining the user ID and the state extender: userid@**legis.wisconsin.gov**

Publications: Audit reports of individual state agencies and programs; biennial reports.

Number of Employees: 86.80.

Total Budget 2013-15: $16,574,400.

Statutory Reference: Section 13.94.

   Agency Responsibility: The Legislative Audit Bureau is responsible for conducting financial and program audits to assist the legislature in its oversight function. The bureau performs financial audits to determine whether agencies have conducted and reported their financial

LEGISLATIVE SERVICE AGENCIES

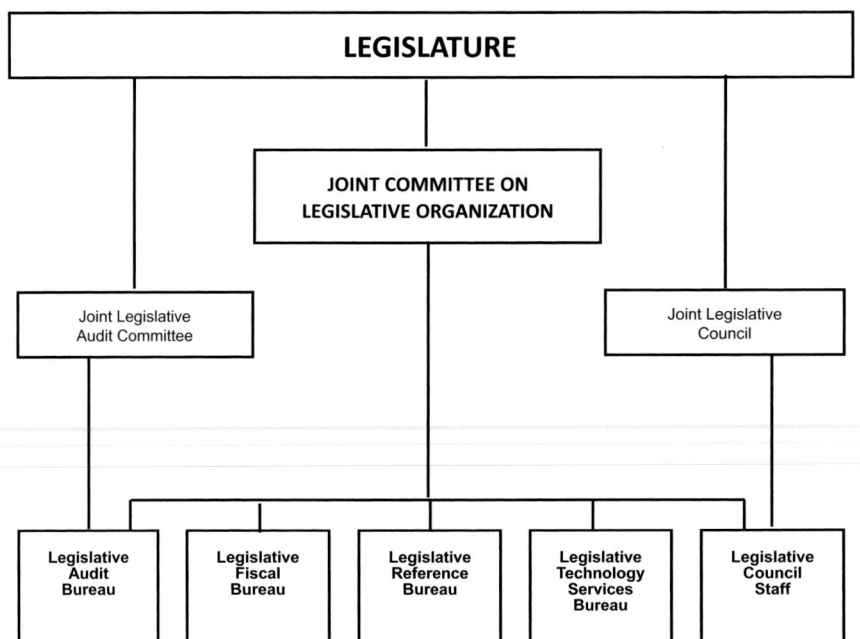

Representative Peter W. Barca of Kenosha is serving his third consecutive session as Assembly Minority Leader. (Jay Salvo, Legislative Photographer)

transactions legally and properly. It undertakes program audits to analyze whether agencies have managed their programs efficiently and effectively and have carried out the policies prescribed by law.

The bureau's authority extends to executive, legislative, and judicial agencies; authorities created by the legislature; special districts; and certain service providers that receive state funds. The bureau may audit any county, city, village, town, or school district at the request of the Joint Legislative Audit Committee.

The bureau provides an annual audit opinion on the state's comprehensive financial statements by the Department of Administration and prepares audits and reports on the financial transactions and records of state agencies at the state auditor's discretion or at the direction of the Joint Legislative Audit Committee. The bureau maintains a toll-free number (1-877-FRAUD-17) to receive reports of fraud, waste, and mismanagement in state government.

Typically, the bureau's program audits are conducted at the request of the Joint Legislative Audit Committee, initiated by the State Auditor, or required by legislation. The reports are reviewed by the Joint Legislative Audit Committee, which may hold hearings on them and may introduce legislation in response to audit recommendations.

Organization: The director of the bureau is the State Auditor, who is appointed by the Joint Committee on Legislative Organization upon the recommendation of the Joint Legislative Audit Committee. Both the State Auditor and the bureau's staff are appointed from outside the classified service and are strictly nonpartisan.

History: The bureau was created as a legislative service agency under the jurisdiction of the Joint Committee on Legislative Organization by Chapter 659, Laws of 1965. It replaced the Department of State Audit, which was created by Chapter 9, Laws of 1947, as an executive agency. This followed a 1946 constitutional amendment that removed auditing powers from the secretary of state and authorized the legislature to provide for state audits by law.

Statutory Advisory Council

Municipal Best Practices Reviews Advisory Council: STEVE O'MALLEY, ADAM PAYNE (representing the Wisconsin Counties Association); MARK ROHLOFF (representing the League of Wisconsin Municipalities); RICHARD NAWROCKI (representing the Wisconsin Towns Association). (All are appointed by the State Auditor.)

The 4-member Municipal Best Practices Reviews Advisory Council advises the State Auditor on the selection of county and municipal service delivery practices to be reviewed by the State Auditor. The State Auditor is required to conduct periodic reviews of procedures and practices used by local governments in the delivery of governmental services; identify variations in costs and effectiveness of such services between counties and municipalities; and recommend practices to save money or provide more effective service delivery. Council members are chosen from candidates submitted by the organizations represented. The council was created by 1999 Wisconsin Act 9 in Section 13.94 (8), Wisconsin Statutes, and succeeds the council created by 1995 Wisconsin Act 27.

LEGISLATIVE COUNCIL STAFF

See Joint Legislative Council pp. 272-275

Representatives Melissa Sargent, Samantha Kerkman, and Amanda Stuck wore red to a February floor session in recognition of "Go Red Heart Association" Day. (Greg Anderson, Legislative Photographer)

LEGISLATIVE FISCAL BUREAU

Director: ROBERT WM. LANG.

Assistant Director: DAVID LOPPNOW.

Program Supervisors: FRED AMMERMAN, JERE BAUER, DARYL HINZ, CHARLES MORGAN, ROB REINHARDT.

Administrative Assistant: VICKI HOLTEN.

Mailing Address: 1 East Main Street, Suite 301, Madison 53703.

Telephone: 266-3847.

Fax: 267-6873.

Internet Address: www.legis.wisconsin.gov/lfb

E-mail Address: fiscal.bureau@legis.wisconsin.gov

Publications: Biennial budget and budget adjustment: summaries of state agency budget requests; cumulative and comparative summaries of the governor's proposals, Joint Committee on Finance provisions and legislative amendments, and separate summaries of legislative amendments when necessary; summary of governor's partial vetoes. Informational reports on various state programs, budget issue papers, and revenue estimates. (Reports and papers available on the Internet or upon request.)

Number of Employees: 35.00.

Total Budget 2013-15: $7,901,600.

Statutory Reference: Section 13.95.

Agency Responsibility: The Legislative Fiscal Bureau develops fiscal information for the legislature, and its services must be impartial and nonpartisan. One of the bureau's principal duties is to staff the Joint Committee on Finance and assist its members. As part of this responsibility, the bureau studies the state budget and its long-range implications, reviews state revenues and expenditures, suggests alternatives to the committee and the legislature, and prepares a report detailing earmarks in the budget bill. In addition, the bureau provides information on all other bills before the joint committee and analyzes agency requests for new positions and appropriation supplements outside of the budget process.

The bureau provides fiscal information to any legislative committee or legislator upon request. On its own initiative, or at legislative direction, the bureau may conduct studies of any financial issue affecting the state. To aid the bureau in performing its duties, the director or designated employees are granted access, with or without notice, to all state departments and to any records maintained by the agencies relating to their expenditures, revenues, operations, and structure.

Organization: The Joint Committee on Legislative Organization is the policy-making body for the Legislative Fiscal Bureau, and it selects the bureau's director. The director is assisted by program supervisors responsible for broadly defined subject areas of government budgeting and fiscal operations. The director and all bureau staff are chosen outside the classified service.

History: The bureau was created by Chapter 154, Laws of 1969. It evolved from the legislative improvement study that was initiated by Chapter 686, Laws of 1961, using a Ford Foundation grant and state funding. Through the improvement program, the legislature developed its own fiscal staff, known as the Legislative Budget Staff, under the supervision of the Legislative Programs Study Committee. In February 1968, the study committee renamed the budget staff the Legislative Fiscal Bureau and specified its functions. Chapter 215, Laws of 1971, transferred responsibility for the bureau's supervision to the Joint Committee on Legislative Organization.

LEGISLATIVE REFERENCE BUREAU

Chief and General Counsel: RICHARD A. CHAMPAGNE.

Deputy Chief and Chief Operating Officer: CATHLENE M. HANAMAN.

Legal Services Manager: JOE KREYE.

Library Manager: JULIE POHLMAN.

Administrative Services Manager: WENDY L. JACKSON.

Mailing Address: P.O. Box 2037, Madison 53701-2037.

Location: 1 East Main Street, Suite 200, Madison.

Telephones: Legal: 266-3561; Research: 266-0341; Library: 266-7040.

Fax: Legal: 264-6948; Research and Library: 266-5648.

Internet Address: www.legis.wisconsin.gov/lrb

Publications: Wisconsin Statutes and Annotations; Laws of Wisconsin; Wisconsin Administrative Code and Register; *Wisconsin Blue Book;* various sections of the *Bulletin of the Proceedings of the Wisconsin Legislature;* informational and research reports.

Number of Employees: 60.00.

Total Budget 2013-15: $12,514,800.

Statutory Reference: Section 13.92.

Agency Responsibility: The Legislative Reference Bureau provides nonpartisan, confidential bill drafting and other legal services to the Wisconsin Legislature. The bureau employs a staff of attorneys and editors who serve the legislature and its members and who draft and prepare all legislation, including the executive budget bill, for introduction in the legislature. Bureau attorneys also draft legislation at the request of state agencies. The bureau publishes all laws enacted during each biennial legislative session and incorporates the laws into the Wisconsin Statutes. The bureau prints the Wisconsin Statutes and Annotations every two years and updates continuously the Wisconsin Statutes on its Internet site. The bureau publishes and updates the Wisconsin Administrative Code and the Wisconsin Administrative Register.

The Legislative Reference Bureau employs research analysts and librarians who provide information and research services to the legislature and the public. The bureau publishes the *Wisconsin Blue Book* and many informational and research reports. The bureau responds to inquiries from the public, elected officers, and legislative staff on current law and pending legislation and the operations of the legislature and state government. The bureau operates a legislative library that contains an extensive collection of materials pertaining to Wisconsin. The library staff prepare the Index to the *Bulletin of the Proceedings of the Wisconsin Legislature.* The bureau maintains for public inspection the drafting records of all legislation introduced in the Wisconsin Legislature, beginning with the 1927 session.

Organization: The Joint Committee on Legislative Organization is the policy-making body for the Legislative Reference Bureau, and it selects the bureau chief. The chief employs all bureau staff. The chief and the bureau staff serve outside the classified service.

History: The creation of the Legislative Reference Bureau, originally the Legislative Reference Library, by Chapter 168, Laws of 1901, was the first organized effort in the United States to provide a state legislature with professional staff assistance. Initially under the governance of the Free Library Commission, the bureau soon began providing bill drafting services to the legislature, a task officially assigned by Chapter 508, Laws of 1907. The bureau acquired the duty of editing the *Wisconsin Blue Book* in 1929 (Chapter 194). In 1963, the legislature renamed the agency the Legislative Reference Bureau and placed it under the direction of the Joint Committee on Legislative Organization. In 2008, the legislature transferred statutory revision duties to the bureau.

LEGISLATIVE TECHNOLOGY SERVICES BUREAU

Director: JEFF YLVISAKER.

Business Manager: ERIN ESSER.

Enterprise Operations Manager: MATT HARNED.

Geographic Information Systems Manager: TONY VAN DER WIELEN.

Software Development Manager: DOUG DEMUTH.

Senator Tim Carpenter, one of the longest serving state legislators, engages in floor debate. (Jay Salvo, Legislative Photographer)

Technical Support Manager: NATE ROHAN.

Mailing Address: 17 West Main Street, Suite 200, Madison 53703.

Telephone: 264-8582.

Internet Address: http://www.legis.wisconsin.gov/ltsb

Number of Employees: 43.00.

Total Budget 2013-15: $8,466,100.

Statutory Reference: Section 13.96.

Agency Responsibility: The Legislative Technology Services Bureau (LTSB) provides confidential, nonpartisan information technology services and support to the Wisconsin Legislature. LTSB creates, maintains, and enhances specialized software used for bill drafting, floor session activity, committee activity, managing constituent interactions, production of the *Wisconsin Statutes* and *Administrative Code,* and publication of the *Wisconsin Blue Book.* It supports the publication of legislative documents including bills and amendments, house journals, daily calendars, and the Bulletin of the Proceedings. The bureau also maintains network infrastructure, data center operations, electronic communications, desktops, laptops, printers, and other technology devices. It keeps an inventory of computer hardware and software assets and manages technology replacement schedules. It supports the redistricting project following each decennial U.S. Census and provides mapping services throughout the decade. LTSB also supports the legislature during floor sessions, delivers audio and video services, manages the technology for the Wisconsin Legislature's Internet Web sites, and offers training services for legislators and staff in the use of information technology.

Organization: The director is appointed by the Joint Committee on Legislative Organization, and has overall management responsibilities for the bureau. The director appoints bureau staff; both the director and the staff serve outside the classified service.

History: The bureau was statutorily created by 1997 Wisconsin Act 27 as the Integrated Legislative Information Staff and was renamed by 1997 Wisconsin Act 237.

A member's maiden speech is always a notable event in the Wisconsin Assembly. Representative Adam Jarchow of Balsam Lake addressed the body for the first time on January 22, 2015. (Jay Salvo, Legislative Photographer)

SUMMARY OF SIGNIFICANT LEGISLATION ENACTED BY THE 2013 LEGISLATURE

This section highlights significant legislation enacted by the 2013 Wisconsin Legislature in the biennial session that began January 7, 2011, and concluded January 5, 2013. The legislation is categorized by subject matter and in cases when an act affects more than one area of state law, such as 2013 Wisconsin Act 20 (the budget act), significant provisions are separately described under multiple subject headings. The section concludes with a summary of major proposals that failed to be enacted or adopted.

The following table summarizes activity in recent legislative sessions:

	Legislative Session				
	2005-06	2007-08	2009-10	2011-12	2013-14
Bills Introduced	1,971	1,581	1,723	1,400	1,641
Assembly Bills.	1,232	988	997	786	935
Senate Bills	739	593	726	614	706
Acts	491	242	406	286	380
Percentage of Bills Enacted . . .	24.9%	15.3%	23.6%	20.4%	23.2%
Bills Totally Vetoed	47	1	5	0	1
Bills Partially Vetoed	2	4	6	3	4

SIGNIFICANT 2013-2014 LEGISLATION

Administrative Law

Act 125 (*AB-595*) exempts an administrative rule that is repealed or modified by an act of the legislature from statutory rule-making procedures.

Act 172 (*AB-568*) clarifies the effective dates of administrative rules and the notice requirements that apply to certain administrative rules.

Beverages

Act 65 (*AB-61*) allows an alcohol beverages retailer to bring a civil action, for $1,000 plus costs, against an underage person or his or her parent for an underage violation on the retailer's premises. The act also allows an underage person to be on the retailer's premises, and to order, possess, or consume alcohol beverages, if he or she is assisting law enforcement in investigating and enforcing underage violations.

Act 106 (*AB-169*) creates an exception to the alcohol beverages laws that allows beer consumption on a commercial quadricycle, unless an ordinance negates the exception. A commercial quadricycle is a four-wheeled vehicle with at least 12 passenger seats that is powered by pedaling passengers. The act also imposes certain operating restrictions on commercial quadricycles.

Act 268 (*SB-250*) allows a fair association holding a temporary retail license to conduct a beer or wine judging or tasting event, involving servings of no more than one ounce, without a licensed bartender present to supervise.

Buildings and Safety

Act 270 (*SB-617*) makes the following changes to the laws relating to the construction and alteration of public buildings and buildings that are places of employment:

- With specified exemptions, prohibits a municipality from enacting an ordinance that establishes building standards unless the ordinance strictly conforms to construction standards in the Department of Safety and Professional Services (DSPS) rules.
- Creates a building code council that reviews and makes recommendations for rules relating to construction and alteration of such buildings.

Business and Consumer Law

Act 41 (*AB-181*) requires the Department of Administration (DOA) to establish and administer a venture capital investment program. The secretary of administration must establish a committee consisting of members from the Investment Board and the Capital Finance Office in DOA. The committee must select an investment manager, who, subject to certain restrictions, must invest the following amounts in at least four different venture capital funds: $25,000,000 contributed by DOA; at least $300,000 of the investment manager's own moneys; and at least $5,000,000 that the investment manager raises from nonstate sources. Each of the venture capital funds must invest those moneys in Wisconsin businesses and, among other requirements, must at least match its investment with moneys the venture capital fund has raised from other sources. The investment manager must ensure that, on average, a venture capital fund invests at least $2 from other funding sources for every $1 invested as required under the program. The investment manager must pay to the state its proceeds from investments of the moneys DOA contributed. If the investment manager pays the state $25,000,000 in proceeds, then the investment manager must pay to the state 90 percent of its future proceeds from such investments.

Act 232 (*AB-368*) allows a person to obtain a rifle or shotgun from any state, instead of from a contiguous state as allowed under former law.

Act 234 (*SB-155*) makes changes to the Department of Agriculture, Trade and Consumer Protection's (DATCP) regulation of telephone solicitors, including prohibiting certain solicitations to residences with Wisconsin telephone numbers that are included in the national do-not-call list. Former law prohibited solicitations to residences with telephone numbers on DATCP's state do-not-call list, which the act eliminates.

Children

Act 314 (*AB-581*) relating to the unauthorized placement of children does the following:

- Prohibits advertising related to the adoption or other permanent physical placement of a child by any computerized communication system, including electronic mail, an Internet site, or a social media account. Former law prohibited adoption advertising only by means of print media, radio, or television.
- Eliminates an exception to the prohibition on adoption advertising that allowed a parent to advertise for the adoption of his or her own child.
- Allows a parent who has legal custody of a child to delegate for longer than one year the parent's powers regarding the care and custody of the child to a relative or, if approved by the juvenile court, a nonrelative. Former law allowed such a delegation only for up to one year.
- Prohibits the permanent interstate placement of a child with a nonrelative, unless that placement is authorized by law or approved by a court.

Constitutional Amendments

Enrolled Joint Resolution 1 (*AJR-2*) proposed by the 2013 legislature on second consideration, requires the legislature to create a department of transportation and a transportation fund. All state funds from transportation-related revenues will be placed in the fund and used only for planning, promotion, and protection of the state's transportation systems. The amendment was ratified by the voters at the November 2014 general election.

Enrolled Joint Resolution 16 (*SJR-57*) proposed by the 2013 legislature on first consideration, would require the supreme court to elect a chief justice for a term of two years. Currently, the justice with the longest continuous service is automatically chief justice. To become part of the constitution, the amendment must be concurred in by the 2015 legislature and ratified by the voters.

Crime

Act 79 (*SB-40*) allows a law enforcement officer to search the person, residence, or property of a person who is on parole, extended supervision, or probation for a felony or certain misdemeanors if the officer has reasonable suspicion that the person is committing, is about to commit, or has committed a crime or a violation of a condition of his or her release or probation.

Act 254 (*AB-274*) eliminates immunity for family members from being charged with the crime of harboring or aiding a felon and increases the penalty for that crime based on the seriousness of the felon's crime.

Act 317 (*AB-556*) allows for a visual strip search of a person who is arrested or otherwise lawfully detained in a jail or prison if the person will be held for at least 12 hours and will be housed with another person.

Act 323 (*SB-160*) requires each law enforcement agency to have a policy that requires a law enforcement officer who has reasonable grounds to believe that a person is committing domestic abuse to provide to the victim information regarding shelters, services, and his or her legal rights, and a statement of how to file a petition for an injunction. The act also requires that, in the annual report regarding domestic abuse arrests that each district attorney must submit to the Department of Justice (DOJ), the district attorney include the number of responses that law enforcement made that involved a domestic abuse incident that did not result in an arrest.

Act 348 (*AB-409*) requires each law enforcement agency to have a written policy regarding the investigation of deaths that involve a law enforcement officer that the agency employs. The policy must require at least two investigators from other agencies to investigate the death, and the investigators must provide a complete report to the district attorney.

Act 362 (*AB-620*) makes the following changes to human trafficking laws:

- Eliminates the element that the victim has not consented to be trafficked.
- Creates a process for a victim of human trafficking to request a court to vacate a conviction, adjudication, or finding of not guilty by reason of mental disease or defect for the crime of prostitution if the person committed the crime as a result of being a victim of trafficking.
- Allows, in a prosecution alleging human trafficking or certain other offenses, evidence of other crimes, wrongs, or acts to be admitted.

Act 375 (*AB-536*) generally prohibits law enforcement from identifying or tracking the location of a wireless or mobile device without a warrant.

Accompanied by his two children, Duey Stroebel took the oath of office in April 2015, to fill a vacancy in the 20th Senate District. The oath was administered by Court of Appeals Judge Mark Gundrum, a former member of the Wisconsin Assembly. (Jay Salvo, Legislative Photographer)

Education

Higher Education

Act 56 (*AB-201*) gives University of Wisconsin (UW) and Wisconsin Technical College System (WTCS) students who are veterans or members of the U.S. armed forces priority in registering for courses.

Act 60 (*SB-334*) creates a technical excellence higher education scholarship program, administered by the Higher Educational Aids Board (HEAB), to award scholarships, based on proficiency in technical subjects, to selected high school seniors who enroll in technical colleges.

Act 128 (*AB-454*) creates a grant program, administered by HEAB, to provide tax-exempt financial assistance to primary care physicians and psychiatrists who practice in underserved areas in this state.

Act 145 (*January 2014 Special Session SB-1*) provides property tax relief aid to WTCS districts, distributed annually to each district on the basis of its equalized value as compared to the equalized value of all districts. The act eliminates the current limit on a district's tax levy and imposes, instead, a revenue limit. With certain exceptions, the act provides that a district's revenue (consisting of the sum of its tax levy and the amount of property tax relief aid it receives) may not exceed its revenue in the previous school year increased by the district's valuation factor, which is the percentage change in the district's equalized value due to new construction, less improvements removed.

Act 208 (*SB-223*) generally prohibits an institution of higher education, technical college, or proprietary school from requesting or requiring a current or prospective student to grant access to his or her personal social media account.

Act 289 (*AB-729*) allows the Board of Regents to accept research contracts involving government security classifications or similar restrictions if the research furthers national security interests. Also, the chancellors must consult with faculty to establish conditions for accepting the contracts and conducting the research at their institutions.

High turnover in recent years has resulted in an Assembly with only 15 of 99 members who have at least 10 years of legislative experience. Representative Joan Ballweg, in her 6th term, offers an experienced voice. (Jay Salvo, Legislative Photographer)

Senator Fred Risser, the longest-serving state legislator in United States history, lends his voice to the Senate debate in 2015. (Greg Anderson, Legislative Photographer)

Primary and Secondary Education

Act 20 (*AB-40*) makes the following changes to parental choice programs (PCPs):

- Creates an expanded, statewide PCP under which pupils who reside in a school district other than the Milwaukee Public School District or the Racine Unified School District may attend a private school participating in a PCP with financial assistance from the state. The program is substantially similar to the Racine Parental Choice Program (RPCP) under preexisting law with several exceptions. Only 500 pupils may participate in the 2013-14 school year and only 1,000 pupils in every school year thereafter. If the pupil cap is reached in the 2013-14 school year, the 25 schools that received the most applications may participate. These 25 private schools receive priority to participate in subsequent school years, with any additional pupils assigned to those schools that received the most applications. There is no pupil cap and no restriction on the number of schools that may participate in the RPCP. Only pupils with a family income that does not exceed 1.85 times the federal poverty level may participate in the expanded program; under the RPCP, the family income threshold for pupil participation is three times the federal poverty level.
- Allows a private school participating in the Milwaukee Parental Choice Program (MPCP) or the RPCP to give preference in accepting certain pupils rather than selecting the pupils randomly as under preexisting law.
- Allows a private school participating in a PCP to submit to the Department of Public Instruction (DPI) a letter indicating that the municipality where the school is located does not issue certificates of occupancy.
- Modifies current law to require DPI to include a portion of the fair market value of a participating private school's buildings as facilities costs when determining the private school's costs of educational programming. These educational

Floor debate is the one point in the legislative process when a legislator can try to persuade all her colleagues at once. Representative Amy Loudenbeck addressed the Assembly in February 2015.
(Jay Salvo, Legislative Photographer)

programming costs are used to determine the payment by the state to the private school for each pupil attending the school under a PCP.

- Allows a private school participating in a PCP to accumulate a portion of its annual educational programming costs in a reserve account and requires DPI to include that portion in determining the private school's costs of educational programming.
- Requires a private school participating in a PCP to maintain an approved accreditation and annually notify DPI of its accreditation status. The act authorizes DPI to bar from a PCP a private school that has failed to maintain accreditation.
- Requires DPI, when releasing certain information related to pupils participating in a PCP, to release all of the data at the same time.
- Allows a person who has obtained a degree higher than a high school diploma in lieu of a high school diploma to be employed as a teacher's aide in a private school participating in a PCP.
- Increases the per pupil payment amount for pupils in PCPs and sets a higher amount for grades 9 to 12 than for grades kindergarten to 8.

Act 20 also requires DPI annually to publish a school and school district accountability report on a school's performance or a school district's improvement. Subject to certain deadlines, the report must include independent charter schools and private schools participating in a PCP.

Act 20 additionally requires the state superintendent to adopt exams to measure pupil knowledge and concepts in grades 9 and 11, in addition to grades 4, 8, and 10 as under former law.

Act 20 prohibited DPI from adopting any additional common core standard until the Joint Legislative Council had studied the standard, the Legislative Fiscal Bureau had reviewed the fiscal impacts, and the findings of the study had been presented to the public. The act required DPI to adopt new academic standards by July 1, 2014.

Act 63 (*SB-51*) increases the number of mathematics credits and science credits a pupil must complete in order to obtain a high school diploma from two credits in each subject to three credits.

Act 115 (*AB-297*) makes various changes to the process by which a school district resident may object to a school district's use of a race-based nickname, logo, mascot, or team name, including requiring a petition to include a minimum amount of signatures that is equal to 10 percent of the school district's membership; reversing the burden of proof for demonstrating that a race-based nickname, logo, mascot, or team name promotes discrimination, pupil harassment, or stereotyping; and transferring hearings on such objections from DPI to the Division of Hearings and Appeals. The act also prohibits the enforcement of any order issued under former law to terminate a school board's use of a race-based nickname, logo, mascot, or team name.

Act 208 (*SB-223*) generally prohibits a public, charter, or private school or a private educational testing service from requesting or requiring a current or prospective student to grant access to his or her personal social media account.

Elections

Act 146 (*SB-324*) modifies the procedure for receiving absentee ballot applications made in person so that applications may not be received on a legal holiday and may otherwise be received only from Monday to Friday between the hours of 8 a.m. and 7 p.m. each day. The act also provides that the municipal clerk must witness the certificate for any in-person absentee ballot cast.

Act 153 (*SB-655*) makes various changes to the campaign finance and lobbying laws, including eliminating the limit on expenditures made to solicit contributions, allowing a registrant to file reports electronically, increasing registration thresholds, and extending the time during which a lobbyist may make a campaign contribution. The act also specifies types of Internet activity that are subject to and excluded from disclosure requirements and contribution limitations. In addition, the act allows certain individuals and organizations to redirect certain campaign contributions made to the individual or organization but unclaimed for two years if the individual or organization has attempted to contact the contributor or has received authorization from the surviving spouse or estate of the contributor. Contributions may be redirected to the administrative fund of the individual or organization or to a committee associated with the individual or organization. The individual or organization must identify the associated committee on its registration statement and report any redirected contribution.

Act 159 (*AB-396*) requires the municipal clerk or board of election commissioners of each municipality to send two special voting deputies to each community-based residential facility, adult family home, and residential care apartment complex located in the municipality if the facility, home, or complex has at least five registered electors as occupants. Under former law, the decision to send deputies to those facilities, homes, or complexes was discretionary. The act requires the deputies to conduct absentee voting in person for those occupants who wish to vote.

Act 160 (*AB-420*) provides that a signature on a nomination paper is not valid unless the signer legibly prints his or her name next to his or her signature.

Act 177 (*AB-202*) requires the chief inspector at a polling place and the municipal clerk at a location where absentee voting takes place to designate areas for members of the public to observe electors participating in the voting process.

Employment

Unemployment Insurance

Act 11 (*AB-15*) allows employers to establish work-share programs pursuant to a federal law and provides certain federal funding for the programs and unemployment insurance (UI) benefits paid under the programs. Under a work-share program, employees in a work unit have their hours reduced in lieu of layoffs, receive partial UI benefits based upon the amount of the reduction, and are exempt from the UI law's work-search requirements.

Act 20 (*AB-40*) makes the following changes to the UI law:
- Changes UI benefit suspension and requalification requirements for claimants who are discharged for serious misconduct, and creates less stringent requirements for claimants who are discharged for certain absenteeism or

tardiness. The act codifies court interpretations of the term "misconduct"; identifies specific acts, including certain absenteeism or tardiness, that constitute misconduct; and creates requalification requirements for claimants who are discharged for substantial fault that are less stringent than for discharge for misconduct.

- Eliminates provisions that allowed an individual who voluntarily terminated his or her employment to receive UI benefits without satisfying statutory requalification requirements. The act also modifies those requalification requirements for certain individuals.

- Modifies work-search requirements to increase the number of actions that most claimants must take to maintain UI benefit eligibility, and to allow the Department of Workforce Development (DWD) to require, as a condition of eligibility, that claimants provide certain employment-related information and job application materials, participate in reemployment service programs, and work with DWD to find suitable reemployment.

- Changes UI contribution (tax) rates for employers to require employers with an unfavorable layoff experience to pay higher contribution rates on their payrolls.

- Appropriates up to $30,000,000 from state general tax revenues to pay interest due to the federal government during the 2013-15 fiscal biennium on federal loans to maintain the solvency of this state's unemployment reserve fund, thereby eliminating the liability of employers to cover the cost of this interest.

Other Employment

Act 20 (*AB-40*) makes the following changes to the laws relating to public employment and fringe benefits for public employees:

- Increases from 30 to 75 days the break-in-service requirement for participants in the Wisconsin Retirement System (WRS) who return to covered employment after retirement.

- Provides that a WRS annuitant who returns to covered employment or contracts with a covered employer for employment services must terminate his or her annuity if the annuitant is expected to work at least two-thirds time. The act also creates a process for suspending an annuity for an annuitant who returns to covered employment.

- Requires the Group Insurance Board (GIB), beginning on January 1, 2015, to allow state employees to receive health care coverage through a high-deductible plan and a health savings account.

- Prohibits the state from paying for state employee health insurance premiums more than 88 percent of the average premium costs of plans offered in each tier. There are currently three tiers of health insurance plans, which are based on premium costs. Under former law, the state could not pay more than 88 percent of the average premium costs of plans offered in the lowest-cost tier.

Act 123 (*SB-224*) makes various changes relating to the state civil service system. The act provides that:

- The administrator of the Division of Merit Recruitment and Selection in the Office of State Employment Relations may waive a residency requirement for a limited term appointment. Former law allowed the administrator to do so only if the employee's permanent work site was located outside this state.

- A state employee who has not obtained permanent status in class in a supervisory or management position may be required to serve a probationary period if he or she is appointed to another such position.

- Annual, termination, and accumulated sabbatical leave, as well as paid holiday leave, are subject to the state compensation plan. Under former law, for represented employees, such leave was established in collective bargaining agreements.

- Career executive employees and other management employees receive all continuous service leave if they terminate those positions and are subsequently reemployed in similar positions, regardless of the duration of their leaves of absence.

- Permanent classified state employees who take leave without pay for military training are credited, upon reemployment, for annual leave, sick leave, and legal holidays as if they had remained continuously employed by the state.

Act 208 (*SB-223*) generally prohibits an employer from requesting or requiring a current or prospective employee to grant access to his or her personal social media account.

Environment

Act 1 (*SB-1*) establishes laws that apply to iron mining, which differ procedurally and substantively from laws that formerly applied to all mining for metallic minerals and that continue to apply to mining for other metallic minerals, such as copper and zinc.

The act generally requires the Department of Natural Resources (DNR) to approve or deny the application for an iron mining permit, and any other permit needed to conduct the mining, within 14 months after the applicant files the application, unless the applicant specifies a longer deadline in the application. Under the act, before DNR acts on an application for an iron mining permit, it must hold a public informational hearing, but not a contested case hearing, on the application. If an aggrieved person requests a contested case hearing after DNR acts on a permit application, the act requires the hearing examiner to issue a final decision within five months after DNR acts.

The act establishes regulations related to all of the following that are different for activities related to iron mining than for other regulated activities: effects on wetlands, effects on navigable waters, effects on groundwater quality, withdrawals of groundwater and surface water, and disposal of waste. Under the act, iron mining is not subject to the mining moratorium law that prohibits DNR from issuing a permit to mine in a sulfide ore body that has the potential to produce acid drainage unless the applicant demonstrates that a mine that operated in such an ore body has been closed for at least 10 years without producing acid drainage. Also under the act, a person is no longer required to obtain a permit for prospecting for iron ore.

Act 378 (*SB-547*) provides a statewide variance to limits on the amount of phosphorus

Representative Andy Jorgensen of Milton presents an argument on the Assembly floor. (Jay Salvo, Legislative Photographer)

Speaker Vos confers with Representatives Jeremy Thiesfeldt and Mary Czaja on the Assembly floor. *(Jay Salvo, Legislative Photographer)*

---

discharged into a stream or lake with high levels of phosphorus. Under the act, businesses and municipalities whose wastewater treatment systems would need new treatment equipment and processes to comply with the limits may receive the variance if DOA determines that compliance would cause widespread adverse social and economic impacts and the federal Environmental Protection Agency approves the variance. A recipient of the variance must comply with specified requirements for reducing phosphorus pollution.

Health and Social Services

Act 37 (*SB-206*) makes various changes to abortion laws, including:

- Except in a medical emergency and except where the pregnancy is the result of a sexual assault, requiring that, among other things, before a person may perform or induce an abortion, the physician who is to perform or induce the abortion or any physician requested by the pregnant woman must perform, or arrange for a qualified person to perform, an ultrasound on the pregnant woman using whatever transducer the woman chooses. The act prohibits a person from requiring a pregnant woman to view the ultrasound images or to visualize any fetal heartbeat and prohibits any person from being subjected to a penalty if the pregnant woman declines to view the ultrasound images or to visualize any fetal heartbeat.
- Prohibiting a physician from performing an abortion unless the physician has admitting privileges in a hospital within 30 miles of the location where the abortion is to be performed.

Act 200 (*AB-446*) adopts a number of provisions regarding drugs known as opioid antagonists, including: 1) allowing trained certified first responders to administer opioid antagonists; 2) requiring that the Department of Health Services (DHS) permit all trained emergency medical technicians to administer opioid antagonists to individuals believed to be undergoing opioid-related drug overdoses; and 3) allowing law enforcement agencies and fire departments to obtain supplies of opioid antagonists and to be trained to administer them.

Mental Health

Act 129 (*AB-455*) requires DHS to contract with a peer-run organization to establish peer-run respite centers for individuals experiencing mental health conditions or substance abuse.

Act 130 (*AB-458*) requires DHS, in providing Medical Assistance (MA) benefits, to allow in-home therapy for a severely emotionally disturbed child without a showing of a failure to succeed in outpatient therapy and to allow qualifying families to participate in in-home therapy even if a child is enrolled in a day treatment program. The act also allows mental health services provided through telehealth to be reimbursed by the MA program if the provider of the service through telehealth satisfies certain criteria.

Act 131 (*AB-459*) requires DHS to create five regional centers for individual placement and support for employment of individuals experiencing mental illness. The act requires DHS to award grants to counties or trial unit program or employment sites that are implementing individual placement and support services or regional centers for certain activities. The act also requires DHS and the regional centers to provide work incentive benefits counseling for individuals who are not receiving vocational rehabilitation services from DWD.

Act 132 (*AB-460*) requires DHS to award grants to counties or regions comprised of multiple counties to establish certified crisis programs that create mental health mobile crisis teams in rural areas.

Justice

Act 20 (*AB-40*) requires, beginning on April 1, 2015, that law enforcement agencies must collect a biological specimen from each individual who is arrested for allegedly committing a felony and from each juvenile who is taken into custody for allegedly committing a violation that would be a felony if committed by an adult. Law enforcement agencies must submit the biological specimens to the State Crime Laboratories at DOJ for DNA analysis and inclusion in the DNA data bank for individuals 1) who are arrested or taken into custody under a warrant; 2) for whom a court finds probable cause that the individual committed the offense; or 3) who fail to appear at an initial appearance, preliminary examination, or delinquency proceeding. If a law enforcement agency is not required to submit a biological specimen within a year of collecting it, the law enforcement agency must destroy the specimen. Also beginning on April 1, 2015, the act requires that when an individual who is charged with a felony, or with a juvenile offense that would be a felony if committed by an adult, makes his or her initial appearance before a court, the individual must submit a biological specimen for DNA analysis and inclusion in the DNA data bank if a specimen was not previously submitted. Also beginning on April 1, 2015, the act requires the following individuals to submit a biological specimen to DOJ for DNA analysis and inclusion in the DNA data bank:

- A juvenile who is adjudicated delinquent, or found not responsible by reason of mental disease or defect, for a violation that would be a felony if committed by an adult or for certain sex offenses or endangering safety by use of a dangerous weapon.
- An individual who has been found not guilty by reason of mental disease or defect of a felony or of certain sex offenses or endangering safety by use of a dangerous weapon.
- An individual who is sentenced or placed on probation for any felony or misdemeanor conviction. Finally, the act provides a process by which individuals may seek expungement of their DNA profile from the DNA data bank.

Local Law

Act 14 (*AB-85*) changes the compensation structure for a Milwaukee County supervisor, reduces the term length of a Milwaukee County supervisor, affects the right of an annuitant under the Milwaukee County Employee's Retirement System to be rehired by Milwaukee County, limits the authority of Milwaukee County to enter into certain intergovernmental agreements, removes and clarifies some authority of the Milwaukee County Board of Supervisors, and increases and clarifies the authority of the Milwaukee County executive.

Act 274 (*SB-517*) does the following:

- Provides that, in certain cases, if a residential tenant has unpaid municipal utility charges, the municipality has a lien on the tenant's assets, which the municipality may transfer to the tenant's landlord.

- Allows a landlord to request that a municipal utility disconnect electric service to a residential unit if the tenant has unpaid municipal utility charges.
- Changes various requirements regarding utility service by a municipality to certain residential tenants.

Natural Resources

Act 61 (*AB-194*) makes various changes to the law regulating hunting, including:

- Eliminating the age and disability requirements under former law that allowed a person to hunt with a crossbow under certain other hunting licenses.
- Establishing new resident and nonresident crossbow hunting licenses.
- Providing that, if DNR establishes an open season for hunting certain animals, including deer, with a bow and arrow, DNR must establish an open season for hunting that animal with a crossbow.
- Requiring DNR to specify by rule the open seasons during which certain deer hunting permits are valid and the types of weapons that may be used under those permits.
- Specifying that, if DNR requires a person who kills an animal to register the animal with DNR, DNR must record the type of weapon used to kill the animal.

Real Estate

Act 208 (*SB-223*) generally prohibits a landlord from requesting or requiring a current or prospective tenant to grant access to his or her personal social media account.

Taxation

Act 20 (*AB-40*) changes laws related to taxation as follows:

- Reduces the marginal tax rates for individuals in all tax brackets and reduces the number of brackets from five to four.
- Creates an individual income tax deduction for private elementary and high school tuition.
- Creates an individual income tax exemption for income received by an active duty U.S. armed forces member whose death results from service in a combat zone.
- Removes individual income tax check-offs that do not generate at least $75,000 in a year from state income tax forms.
- Eliminates the estate tax for deaths occurring after December 31, 2012.

Transportation

Act 20 (*AB-40*) changes local assistance programs by:

- Creating a transportation alternatives program to replace the Department of Transportation's (DOT) programs for bicycle and pedestrian facilities, transportation enhancement activities, safe routes to school, and traffic marking enhancements. Under the new program, DOT must award grants to local governments and other entities for transportation alternatives activities, including planning and construction of pedestrian and bicycle lanes and trails, as well as other safe routes for children and other nondrivers.
- Allowing DOT to pay counties and municipalities aids for damage caused by any disaster, not just floods as under former law, to highways or bridges not on the state trunk highway system. The act defines "disaster" to include sudden highway failure and damage caused by a response to a disaster event.

Act 31 (*SB-62*) specifies that a person may provide proof of motor vehicle liability insurance in electronic format, including on a cellular telephone.

Senator Paul Farrow (left) speaks to Senator Scott Fitzgerald, who was again elected Majority Leader by his colleagues for the 2015 session. (Jay Salvo, Legislative Photographer)

Act 101 (*AB-200*) makes changes to the laws governing repair, replacement, and refund under a motor vehicle warranty, commonly referred to as the lemon law, including: 1) extending the time for a manufacturer to provide a comparable new motor vehicle to a consumer who elects to receive one and, under certain circumstances, allowing the manufacturer to provide a refund instead of a comparable new motor vehicle; 2) specifying circumstances under which a vehicle's nonconformity has been subject to a reasonable attempt to repair; 3) requiring a consumer to use DOT forms and suspending certain deadlines if the consumer submits incomplete forms; 4) requiring that any civil action for damages be commenced within 36 months after vehicle delivery; and 5) eliminating a prevailing consumer's right to recover double damages.

Act 188 (*AB-244*) creates special vehicle registration plates displaying "In God We Trust," which DOT may issue upon receiving contributions to cover the estimated production costs. An additional payment for these plates funds the care of residents of Wisconsin veterans homes.

Act 350 (*AB-124*) makes changes to the inattentive driving law, including creating a form of inattentive driving under which a driver generally may not operate, or be in a position to directly observe, an activated electronic device providing visual entertainment.

Act 377 (*SB-509*) makes numerous changes relating to the operation of agricultural vehicles on highways, including: 1) modifying the definition of implement of husbandry (IOH) and recognizing a new type of vehicle called an agricultural commercial motor vehicle (AgCMV); 2) increasing, until January 1, 2020, the statutory weight limits for IOHs and AgCMVs operated without a permit; 3) creating certain weight limit exceptions for IOHs and AgCMVs until January 1, 2020; 4) creating a "no fee" permit system until January 1, 2020, that allows IOHs and AgCMVs to exceed the new statutory weight limits; 5) modifying statutory size limits for IOHs and AgCMVs; 6) creating lighting and marking requirements for wide IOHs; 7) allowing a wide IOH to be operated outside its lane and over the center line of a roadway; 8) exempting AgCMVs from vehicle registration; and 9) requiring farm equipment dealers to disclose vehicle weight when selling equipment operated on a highway.

MAJOR PROPOSALS THAT FAILED ENACTMENT OR ADOPTION

Business and Consumer Law

Assembly Bill 96 and *Senate Bill 97* would have prohibited certain unsolicited prerecorded telephone messages, including political robocalls.

Education

Assembly Bill 379 would have established a school and school district accountability system and provided sanctions for public, charter, and PCP schools that performed poorly.

Senate Bill 619 would have established a model academic standards board to develop standards in mathematics, English, science, and social studies.

Employment

Assembly Bill 667 and *Senate Bill 508* would have allowed employees to voluntarily work without one day of rest in seven.

Assembly Bill 711 and *Senate Bill 550* would have made various changes relating to worker's compensation, including establishing a maximum fee schedule for health services provided to an injured employee.

Assembly Bill 750 and *Senate Bill 626* would have preempted local living wage ordinances for employees whose work is funded by state or federal funds.

Environment

Assembly Bill 476 and *Senate Bill 349* would have reduced the authority of local governments to regulate nonmetallic mining, water quality, and air quality.

Local Law

Assembly Bill 816 and *Senate Bill 632* would have reduced local control over the ability to zone and otherwise regulate nonmetallic mining operations.

Representative Dale Kooyenga listens to testimony before the Joint Committee on Finance. (Jay Salvo, Legislative Photographer)

Executive Branch

6

The executive branch: profile of the executive branch and descriptions of constitutional offices, departments, independent agencies, state authorities, regional agencies, and interstate agencies and compacts

Colonel Joseph Bailey of Red River is represented in this Hugo Ballin mural in the Governor's Conference Room

(Sarah Girkin)

ELECTIVE CONSTITUTIONAL EXECUTIVE STATE OFFICERS

Office	Officer/Party	Residence[1]	Term Expires	Annual Salary[2]
Governor.	Scott Walker (Republican)	Wauwatosa	January 7, 2019	$147,328
Lieutenant Governor.	Rebecca Kleefisch (Republican)	Oconomowoc	January 7, 2019	77,795
Secretary of State	Douglas J. La Follette (Democrat)	Madison	January 7, 2019	69,936
State Treasurer	Matt Adamczyk (Republican)	Wauwatosa	January 7, 2019	69,936
Attorney General.	Brad Schimel (Republican)	Waukesha	January 7, 2019	142,966
Superintendent of Public Instruction	Tony Evers (nonpartisan office)	Madison	July 3, 2017	120,111

[1]Residence when originally elected.

[2]Annual salary as established for term of office by the Wisconsin Legislature.

Sources: 2013-14 Wisconsin Statutes; Wisconsin Legislative Reference Bureau, Wisconsin Brief 14-15, *Wisconsin State Officers,* November 2014, and Wisconsin Brief 14-14, *Salaries of State Elected Officials,* January 2015.

The Capitol in the summer. (Greg Anderson, Legislative Photographer)

EXECUTIVE BRANCH

A PROFILE OF THE EXECUTIVE BRANCH

Structure of the Executive Branch

The structure of Wisconsin state government is based on a separation of powers among the legislative, executive, and judicial branches. The legislative branch sets broad policy and establishes the general structures and regulations for carrying them out. The executive branch administers the programs and policies, while the judicial branch is responsible for adjudicating any conflicts that may arise from the interpretation or application of the laws.

Constitutional Officers. The executive branch includes the state's six constitutional officers – the governor, lieutenant governor, secretary of state, state treasurer, attorney general, and state superintendent of public instruction. Originally, the term of office for all constitutional officers was two years, but since the 1970 elections, their terms have been four years. All, except the state superintendent, are elected on partisan ballots in the fall elections of the even-numbered years at the midpoint between presidential elections. Though originally a partisan officer, the superintendent is now elected on a nonpartisan ballot in the April election.

The governor, as head of the executive branch, is constitutionally required to "take care that the laws be faithfully executed". In Article V of the state constitution, as ratified in 1848, the people of Wisconsin provided for the election of a governor and a lieutenant governor who would become "acting governor" in the event of a vacancy in the governor's office. Originally, the lieutenant governor was also the presiding officer of the senate. (By subsequent amendments, the lieutenant governor was relieved of senate duties and now assumes the full title of "governor" if the office is vacated.)

In Article VI, the constitution provided for three additional elected officers to assist in administering the laws of the new state. The first session of the legislature in 1848 authorized the secretary of state to keep official records, including enrolled laws and various state papers, and to act as state auditor by examining the treasurer's books and preparing budget projections for the legislature. The state treasurer was given responsibility for receiving all money and tax collections and paying out only those amounts authorized by the legislature for the operation of state government. The attorney general was to provide legal advice to the legislature and other constitutional officers and represent the state in legal matters tried in the courts of this state, other states, and the federal government.

The sixth officer, created by Article X of the constitution, was the state superintendent of public instruction. The first legislature gave the superintendent very specific duties, including the mandate to travel throughout the state inspecting common schools and advocating good public schools. The superintendent was to recommend texts, take a census of school age children, collect statistics on existing schools, and determine the apportionment of school aids.

The simplicity of administering state government in the early years is illustrated by the fact that total expenditures for 1848 government operations were only $13,472, which included the expenses of the legislature and circuit courts. As prescribed by the constitution and state law, the salaries of all six constitutional officers totaled $5,050 that year. (The lieutenant governor did not receive a salary, but he was also given a double legislative per diem.) The state's annual budget totaled $34.8 billion in fiscal year 2014-15, and many of the duties first assigned to the constitutional officers are now carried out by specialized state agencies.

1967 Reorganization. Over a century later, the Wisconsin Committee on the Reorganization of the Executive Branch, in its report to the 1967 Legislature, concluded that state government could no longer be neatly divided into precise legislative, executive, and judicial domains. In many instances the subjects of legislation had become so technically complex that the legislature found it necessary to grant rule-making authority to the administrative agencies. The courts had also encountered a staggering load of technical detail and had come to depend on administrative agencies to use their quasi-judicial powers to assist the judicial branch.

Although the Wisconsin Constitution delegated ultimate responsibility for state administration to the governor, the proliferation of agencies over the years had made it increasingly difficult for one official to exercise effective executive control. The committee identified 85 state agencies within the executive branch of Wisconsin state government, many of which had no direct relationship to the governor. Chapter 75, Laws of 1967, attempted to integrate agencies by function and make them responsive to the elected chief executive, by drastically reducing the number of executive agencies from 85 to 32. Like everything else, however, state government does not remain static. Since the 1967 reorganization, the legislature has created new state agencies, while abolishing or consolidating others. In addition, there have been numerous changes to the duties and responsibilities of the various agencies. The following sections describe the current organization of the executive branch.

Departments. The term "department" is used to designate a principal administrative agency within the executive branch. Within a department, the major subunit is the division, which is headed by an administrator. Each division, in turn, is divided into bureaus, headed by directors. Bureaus may include sections, headed by chiefs, and smaller units, headed by supervisors. There currently are 17 departments in the executive branch.

Wisconsin Administrative Departments

Administration	Natural Resources
Agriculture, Trade and Consumer Protection	Public Instruction
Children and Families	Revenue
Corrections	Safety and Professional Services
Employee Trust Funds	Tourism
Financial Institutions	Transportation
Health Services	Veterans Affairs
Justice	Workforce Development
Military Affairs	

In the majority of cases, the departments are headed by a secretary appointed by the governor with the advice and consent of the senate. Only the Department of Employee Trust Funds and the Department of Veterans Affairs are headed by boards that select the secretary. When administrators are personally chosen by and serve at the pleasure of the governor, they usually work in close cooperation with the chief executive.

Debate about whether the governor should directly appoint department heads continues. Public administration theory has long held that a governor can be the chief executive only if he or she has the authority to hold department heads directly accountable. On the other hand, the original purpose of a board was to insulate a department from politics, thereby enabling its head and staff to develop expertise and a sense of professionalism.

Independent Agencies. In addition to constitutional offices and administrative departments, there are 10 units of the executive branch that have been specifically designated as independent agencies.

Independent Executive Agencies

Educational Communications Board	State Investment Board
Government Accountability Board	State Public Defender Board
Higher Educational Aids Board	Public Service Commission
State Historical Society of Wisconsin	Technical College System
Office of the Commissioner of Insurance	University of Wisconsin System

Although the independent agencies are usually headed by part-time boards or multiple commissioners, the governor appoints most of these officials, with advice and consent of the senate, which serves to strengthen executive control of these units.

Authorities. In some instances, the legislature has decided to create corporate public bodies, known as "authorities", to handle specific functions. Although they are agencies of the state, the authorities operate outside the regular government structure and are intended to be financially self-sufficient. Currently, there are 7 authorities provided for by Wisconsin law – the Wisconsin Aerospace Authority (WAA), the Wisconsin Economic Development Corporation, the Fox River Navigational System Authority, the Lower Fox River Remediation Authority, the Wisconsin Health and Educational Facilities Authority (WHEFA), the Wisconsin Housing and Economic Development Authority (WHEDA), and the University of Wisconsin Hospitals and Clinics Authority. WAA, the Lower Fox River Remediation Authority, WHEDA, WHEFA, and UW Hospitals and Clinics Authority are authorized to issue bonds to finance their respective activities. Most authority members are appointed by the governor with advice and consent of the senate, but some are chosen from the legislature or serve as *ex officio* members.

Nonprofit Corporation. In 1985, the legislature created the Bradley Center Sports and Entertainment Corporation, a public, nonprofit corporation, which operates the Bradley Center in Milwaukee, the home of the Milwaukee Bucks, the Milwaukee Admirals hockey team, and the Marquette University basketball team. The corporation is headed by a board of directors appointed by the governor.

Special Districts. The legislature may create special districts that serve "a statewide public purpose." These districts oversee the management of facilities for exposition centers, sports teams, and the cultural arts. Members of the governing boards are appointed by public officials. Currently, the Wisconsin Center, Miller Park, and Lambeau Field operate as special districts.

Boards, Councils, and Committees. Many departments and agencies have subordinate part-time boards, councils, and committees that carry out specific tasks or act in an advisory capacity. Boards may function as policy-making units, and some are granted policy-making or quasi-judicial powers. Examining boards set the standards of professional competence and conduct for the professions they supervise, and they are authorized to examine new practitioners, grant licenses, and investigate complaints of alleged unprofessional conduct. Councils function on a continuing basis to study and recommend solutions for problems arising in a specified functional area of state government. Committees usually are short-term bodies, appointed to study a specific problem and to recommend solutions or policy alternatives.

Boards are always created by statute. Councils are usually created by statute, but committees, because of their temporary nature, are created by session law rather than being written into the statutes. In addition, agency heads may create and appoint their own councils or committees as needed. The *Blue Book* describes only those units created by statute.

Attached Units. Under the 1967 reorganization, certain boards, commissions, and councils were attached to departments or independent agencies for administrative purposes only. These units are sometimes referred to as "15.03 units" because of the statutory section number that defines them. The larger agencies are expected to provide various services, such as budgeting and program coordination, but the 15.03 units exercise their statutory powers independently of the department or agency to which they are attached.

Government Employment

Classified Service. An important feature of Wisconsin state government employment is the merit system. Wisconsin's civil service, which is called "classified service", is designed to ensure that the most qualified person is hired for the job, based on test results and experience, rather than political affiliation. In 1905, Wisconsin was one of the first states to adopt such a system, and the Wisconsin classified service was considered one of the strongest because it encompassed the major portion of state personnel.

Since the 1967 reorganization of the executive branch, the trend has been to make top agency positions, including deputy secretaries, assistant deputy secretaries, and division administrators, unclassified appointments. Despite this change at the top levels, most state employees, with the principal exception of legislative staff and the University of Wisconsin faculty and academic appointments, are hired and promoted through the classified service on the basis of merit.

Salaries. Positions in the classified service are categorized so that those involving similar duties, responsibilities, and qualifications are paid on the same basis. The Office of State Employment Relations (OSER) is directed to apply the principle of equal pay for equivalent skills and responsibilities when assigning a classification to a pay range.

Each biennium, OSER establishes the compensation plan of classifications and related salary ranges for classified employees subject to modification by the Joint Committee on Employment Relations. The governor may veto the committee's actions, although the vote of six committee members can override a veto. Some provisions of the compensation plan, as approved by the committee, may require changes in existing law, in which case they must be presented in bill form to the legislature for enactment.

Number of State Employees. The increasing size and complexity of state government is reflected in the number of employees. To illustrate this, a total of 1,924 people worked for Wisconsin state government in 1906. By contrast, according to the Legislative Fiscal Bureau, 70,357 full-time equivalent employee positions were authorized for fiscal year 2014-15.

Housing State Government

The first capitol in Madison was built during the Wisconsin Territory days at a cost of more than $60,000. Construction began in 1837 but was not completed until 1845. The building, which served as the first state capitol, was demolished in 1863 to make way for a larger second capitol, which was completed in 1866. When the second state capitol was extensively damaged by fire in 1904, construction of the current capitol began. The present capitol, which was completed in 1917 for $7,203,826.35, also underwent an extensive restoration and renovation that was completed in 2001, costing more than $140 million.

Today, the agencies of state government in Madison are housed in the capitol and various state-owned office buildings, with additional space leased from private landlords. There are also state office buildings in Eau Claire, Green Bay, La Crosse, Milwaukee, Waukesha, and Wisconsin Rapids, plus district offices maintained throughout the state for the field units of many of the operating departments.

Besides its office buildings, the state owns or maintains a variety of educational, correctional, and mental health institutions across Wisconsin. The University of Wisconsin System operates 13 degree-granting institutions and 13 two-year colleges that feature freshman-sophomore instruction.

The state's adult corrections program, under the direction of the Department of Corrections, currently operates 5 maximum security prisons, 11 medium security prisons, 2 minimum security institutions, a prison for women, and 16 correctional centers. The department's juvenile corrections program operates Lincoln Hills School for male juveniles and Copper Lake School for Girls, both at Irma, and the Grow Academy.

Through the Department of Health Services, the state operates 4 mental health institutions at Madison, Mauston, and Winnebago, and 3 centers for the developmentally disabled at Madison, Chippewa Falls, and Union Grove. The department also operates the Mendota Juvenile Treatment Center, a secure juvenile correctional facility in an inpatient mental hospital setting.

The Department of Public Instruction maintains a school that offers special training for blind and visually impaired students at Janesville and a similar school for the deaf and hard-of-hearing at Delavan. The Wisconsin Veterans Homes at Chippewa Falls in Chippewa County, King in Waupaca County, and Union Grove in Racine County are operated by the state to serve eligible Wisconsin veterans and qualifying spouses.

Functions of the Executive Branch

Governor and Lieutenant Governor. The governor, as Wisconsin's chief executive officer, represents all the people of the state. Because of this, the Office of the Governor is the focal point for receiving suggestions and complaints about state affairs. Administratively, the governor exercises authority through the power of appointment, consultation with department heads, and execution of the executive budget after its enactment by the legislature. The governor plays a key role in the legislative process through drafting the initial version of the biennial budget, which is submitted to the legislature in the form of a bill. Other opportunities to influence legislative action arise in the chief executive's state of the state message and special messages to the legislature about topics of concern. The governor also shapes the legislative process through the power to veto bills, call special sessions of the legislature, and appoint committees or task forces to study state problems and make recommendations for changes in the law.

Based on a 1979 amendment, the constitution provides that if the incumbent governor dies, resigns, or is removed from office, the lieutenant governor becomes governor for the unexpired term. The lieutenant governor serves temporarily as "acting governor" when the governor is impeached, incapacitated, or absent from the state.

Commerce. While the U.S. Constitution specifically delegates to Congress the regulation of interstate commerce, each state regulates intrastate commerce within its borders. The definitions of interstate and intrastate commerce overlap at times, and over the years the U.S. Supreme Court has greatly broadened the meaning of the "commerce clause" in the federal constitution. Despite this broad interpretation, the states continue to exercise considerable authority over commerce.

Commerce involves goods, services, and commercial documents, as well as transportation and communication, so the state's involvement in regulating commerce is broad. The state's primary objective is to protect the public as consumers and as participants in financial transactions. Wisconsin state government is also interested in maintaining a stable, orderly market for carrying out commercial activities and for promoting the state's economic development.

One aspect of consumer protection is the inspection of farm products and the conditions under which they are produced. The state inspects cattle for infectious diseases, conducts research in animal and plant diseases, regulates the use of pesticides, grades fruits and vegetables for marketing, and sets standards for processed food. Explicit standards are set by law or in the administrative rules promulgated by the Department of Agriculture, Trade and Consumer Protection. The department is concerned not only with the conditions of growing and processing food but also with fair trade practices in its sale.

Students from Saint Bruno and Saint Paul elementary schools in the Kettle Moraine area brought a banner to the State Capitol on the birthday of the state, May 29, 1848. (Jay Salvo, Legislative Photographer)

Another important aspect of consumer protection is the licensing of various trades and professions. Individuals working in certain professions must achieve state-mandated levels of training and proficiency before they can offer their services to the public. Examples include professions affecting public health, such as doctors and nurses, or public safety, such as architects and engineers. The Department of Safety and Professional Services assists a variety of examining boards associated with various trades and professions and directly regulates certain types of professional activity. In the interests of public safety and welfare, the state enforces laws that regulate public and private buildings. The Department of Safety and Professional Services enforces dwelling codes, reviews construction plans for new buildings, inspects subsystems that serve buildings, and performs training and consulting services for the building industry.

The state protects consumers by maintaining an orderly market in which the public can conduct business. State activities include specifying methods of fair competition, regulating rates for public utilities, setting standards for the operation of financial institutions, regulating gambling, and regulating the sale of securities and insurance. The Department of Financial Institutions regulates banks, savings institutions, credit unions, and the sale of securities. It also registers trademarks, corporations, and other organizations and files Uniform Commercial Code documents. The Office of the Commissioner of Insurance regulates the sale of insurance. The Public Service Commission regulates public utility rates and services. The Gaming Division in the Department of Administration regulates charitable gambling and oversees gaming compacts between Indian tribes and the state. The Department of Revenue administers the Wisconsin Lottery.

The state is concerned with promoting economic development. The Wisconsin Economic Development Corporation develops and implements programs to provide business support and expertise and financial assistance to companies that are investing and creating jobs in Wisconsin and to promote new business start-ups and business growth and expansion in the state. The Department of Tourism promotes travel to Wisconsin's scenic, historic, artistic, educational, and recreational sites. It stimulates the development of private commercial tourist facilities and encourages local tourist-related businesses.

Education. Wisconsin officially recognized the importance of education within a democratic society at statehood in 1848 when it provided for the establishment of local schools in the state constitution and required that education be free to all children. The constitution further directed the legislature to establish a state university at Madison and colleges throughout the state as needed.

Wisconsin's public educational institutions now enroll an estimated one million students each year. In fall 2014, there were 870,652 pupils in the public elementary (606,869) and secondary (263,783) schools and 180,979 students enrolled in the University of Wisconsin System. The Technical College System enrolled 122,656 students in its associate degree programs for the 2013-14 school year and 203,888 in its other programs.

Wisconsin relies on 424 local school districts to administer its elementary and secondary programs. Twelve cooperative educational service agencies (CESAs) furnish support activities to the local districts on a regional basis, and the Department of Public Instruction, headed by the State Superintendent of Public Instruction, a nonpartisan constitutional officer, provides supervision and consultation for the districts.

In 1970, the state was divided into 16 vocational, technical, and adult education districts. These districts, renamed technical college districts, are each supervised by a district board that has taxing power. At the state level, the Technical College System Board supervises the districts.

At the collegiate level, all state-financed institutions of higher education are integrated into a single University of Wisconsin System. The system's 13 degree-granting institutions provide courses of baccalaureate study and offer programs leading to doctoral degrees. The 13 UW Colleges provide 2-year courses of college-level study. State funding also supports Wisconsin residents enrolled at the Medical College of Wisconsin, Inc.

Three other state agencies perform educational functions. The Higher Educational Aids Board administers federal and state student financial assistance programs. The Educational Communications Board operates the state's networks for educational radio and educational television. The State Historical Society of Wisconsin maintains the state historical library, museum, and various historic sites.

Environmental Resources and Transportation. From a wilderness inhabited by 305,391 people in 1850, the state has evolved into a complex society with a population of 5,686,986 in April 2010, according to the U.S. decennial census. According to the Wisconsin Department of Administration's Demographic Services Center, the estimated state population as of January 1, 2014, was 5,732,981. Most of Wisconsin is not densely populated, and the state has a comparatively large amount of open space. However, population growth, higher levels of consumption, and industrial development have increased environmental pollution.

Once pioneers could come to a wilderness, cut the forests, clear the land, and hunt and fish with little thought of damage to the soil, streams, or wildlife. Now these resources must be protected from destruction, depletion, or extinction. The Department of Natural Resources administers numerous programs that control water quality, air pollution, and solid waste disposal. Under state regulations, municipalities and industries cannot dump untreated sewage or industrial wastes into surface waters; smokestacks and automobiles must meet air pollution limits; farmers are encouraged to preserve soil and groundwater quality; and solid waste disposal facilities must meet construction and operation standards. The department regulates hunting and fishing to protect fish and wildlife resources and manages other programs designed to conserve and restore endangered and threatened species. It also promotes recreational and educational opportunities through state parks, forests, trails, and natural areas.

The Department of Transportation administers a variety of programs related to environmental resources. The highways that crisscross the state have a major impact on land use and people's lifestyles. Urban freeways and interstate highways greatly affect the use and development of surrounding land. They determine where people live, work, and play. When state government plans the location and financing of highways and roads, it must carefully consider both short- and long-range consequences.

The state's highway system consists of approximately 11,800 miles of interstate highways, state highways, county trunk highways, town roads, city and village streets, and park and forest roads. The state is concerned not only with building and maintaining adequate roads to meet demands, but also with providing for the safety of travelers using those roads. In 2015, nearly 5.5 million vehicles were registered in Wisconsin, and more than 4.5 million residents were licensed to drive. With 498 traffic fatalities in 2014, traffic safety is a constant concern.

The department must ensure that licensed drivers know the laws, are physically fit to drive, and have the required driving skills. It keeps track of drivers' records and can suspend the licenses of those who prove hazardous to themselves or others. It oversees highway construction and maintenance, highway patrol, and enforcement of driver and vehicle standards. The department is also involved in developing aviation and airports in Wisconsin and with promoting mass transit and passenger rail transportation.

Human Relations and Resources. Besides protecting the environment, the state must also protect its citizens directly. Population growth that affects the quality of land, water, and air resources has an increasingly complex effect on people themselves and their relationships to each other and their government. The inhabitants of a state are its prime resource, and government must ensure their general welfare. Records of birth, marriage, divorce, and death are collected and used to identify trends and potential problems.

In the state's early days, public health was primarily concerned with preventing the spread of communicable diseases. Today, the work of the Department of Health Services includes protection from biological terrorist attacks, disease prevention and detection, health education programs, and maintenance of institutions for the care and treatment of the mentally handicapped or mentally ill. The department is also responsible for a broad range of social services for the aged, the handicapped, and children.

A wide range of work-related issues are subject to state regulation. Minimum wages and maximum hours are set by law. If a worker is injured on the job, state worker's compensation may be available; unemployment compensation helps many workers faced with loss of a job. If a worker is seeking a job, the state (in partnership with the federal government) provides a job service to help the individual find work or to acquire the skills necessary for employment. If a worker suspects job discrimination because of age, race, creed, color, handicap, marital status, sex, national origin, ancestry, sexual orientation, or arrest or conviction record, the state may investigate the matter. The Department of Workforce Development is responsible for protecting and assisting workers and provides employment and assistance to rehabilitate the disabled. The Department of Children and Families provides training and other services to help welfare recipients join the labor market under the state's Wisconsin Works (W-2) program. The Employment Relations Commission mediates or arbitrates labor disputes between workers and their employers.

The Department of Veterans Affairs has grant and loan programs to help eligible veterans acquire a home, business, or education, and it provides personal and medical care for eligible elderly veterans and their spouses at the Wisconsin Veterans Homes at Chippewa Falls, King, and Union Grove.

The state also protects its citizens from society's lawless elements by maintaining stability and order. Law enforcement is largely a local matter, but the Department of Corrections is responsible for segregating convicted adult and juvenile offenders in its penal institutions and rehabilitating them for eventual return to society. The Office of the State Public Defender represents indigents in trial and postconviction legal proceedings. The Department of Justice furnishes legal services to state agencies and technical assistance and training to local law enforcement agencies. It also enforces state laws against gambling, arson, child pornography, and narcotic drugs.

The state maintains an armed military force, the Wisconsin National Guard, to protect the populace in times of state or national emergency, whether natural or human caused, and to supplement the federal armed forces in time of war. These activities come under the jurisdiction of the Department of Military Affairs.

General Executive Functions. The services described so far are direct services to the public. In order for the state to perform these functions, it must also perform certain "staff" functions. The state requires general departments that oversee the hiring of agency personnel and provide space, equipment, salaries, and a retirement system for them. It must levy and collect taxes to support its activities, manage these state funds, and ensure that they are spent according to law. It also evaluates agency operations to assure that the various departments are performing their assigned tasks and preparing for future needs.

Some agencies are designed to perform staff functions almost exclusively. The Department of Administration, for example, is called the state's "housekeeping" department. Its duties include state budgeting, preauditing, engineering and facilities management, state planning, and data processing. The Office of State Employment Relations operates the state's classified service system. The Department of Revenue collects taxes levied by state law, distributes part of that revenue to local units of government, and calculates the equalized value of the property that has been assessed by local government.

The Department of Employee Trust Funds manages the state's retirement systems and the employee insurance programs that cover state and local government workers. At any one time, the state must have large sums of money in its employee trust funds to meet its obligations. The Investment Board invests these funds in stocks, bonds, and real estate in order to earn the maximum amount of interest possible until the funds are needed. The Department of Administration processes the receipt and disbursement of these and other state moneys.

The Office of the Secretary of State handles general executive duties, such as keeping various state records and affixing the state seal on certain records. The Government Accountability Board oversees the state's election processes, monitors campaign expenditures, keeps election records, administers a code of ethics for state public officials, and regulates lobbyists and their employers.

This introduction illustrates how state government both benefits and regulates dozens of aspects of life in Wisconsin. The following sections describe in detail the agencies that make up the executive branch of state government and the numerous services they perform each day.

Total Budget, under each agency's entry, reflects the dollars budgeted during the 2013-14 legislative session for the 2013-15 fiscal biennium (July 1, 2013 to June 30, 2015). These figures are based on the final published appropriation schedule under Chapter 20, Wisconsin Statutes, and do not include statutorily-directed funding modifications or supplemental funding adjustments.

Number of Employees are the number of full-time equivalent positions authorized in the agency's 2014-15 "adjusted base", which is the set of figures each agency uses to begin budgeting for the next biennium.

Budget and employee data provided by the Legislative Fiscal Bureau. Telephone numbers listed without an area code are Madison numbers in area code 608.

Governor Walker participates in groundbreaking for Saint Gobain Portage Expansion, May 28, 2015. *(Office of the Governor)*

OFFICE OF THE GOVERNOR

Governor: SCOTT WALKER.

Chief of Staff: ERIC SCHUTT.

Deputy Chief of Staff: RICH ZIPPERER.

Chief Legal Counsel: BRIAN HAGEDORN.

Policy Director: WAYLON HURLBURT.

Deputy Chief of Staff, Communications: JOCELYN WEBSTER.

Press Secretary: LAUREL PATRICK.

Senior Director of Legislative and Local Affairs: CINDY POLZIN.

Senior Policy Advisors: JON HOELTER, PATRICK HUGHES, EILEEN SCHOENFELDT.

Budget Director: MICHAEL HEIFETZ.

Director of Gubernatorial Appointments: ELIZABETH HIZMI.

Constituent Services Director: ALAN COLVIN.

Proclamations Director: BOB NENNO.

Senior Advisor: MATT MORONEY.

Executive Assistant to Governor: DOROTHY MOORE.

Senior Director of External Operations: JENNIFER GRINDER.

Director of Federal Relations, Office of Wisconsin Governor Scott Walker, Washington D.C.: WENDY RIEMANN, (202) 624-5870; 444 North Capitol Street NW, Suite 613, Washington, D.C. 20001.

Mailing Address: P.O. Box 7863, Madison 53707-7863.

Location: 115 East, State Capitol, Madison.

Telephone: 266-1212.

Office E-mail: govgeneral@wisconsin.gov

Fax: General: 267-8983.

Internet Address: www.wisgov.state.wi.us

Number of Employees: 37.25.

Total Budget 2013-15: $7,482,600.

Constitutional Reference: Article V.

Statutory Reference: Chapter 14, Subchapter I.

Agency Responsibility: As the state's chief executive, the governor represents all the people and is responsible for safeguarding the public interest. The constitution sets certain limits on the governor's powers, but the increased size and complexity of state government have given the governor's office many more responsibilities than it originally had.

The governor gives policy direction to the state and plays an important role in the legislative process. Through the biennial budget, developed and administered in conjunction with the Department of Administration and various agency heads, the governor ultimately reviews and directs the activities of all administrative agencies. Major policy changes are highlighted in the governor's annual state of the state message and other special messages to the legislature.

The governor has other specialized powers related to the legislative process. The chief executive may call a special legislative session to deal with specific legislation, may veto an entire bill, or may veto parts of appropriation bills. In the case of either whole or partial vetoes, a two-thirds vote of the members present in each house of the legislature is required to override the governor's action.

Although various administrators direct the day-to-day operations of state agencies, the governor is considered the head of the executive branch. For the most part, the individuals, commissions, or part-time boards that head the major administrative departments are appointed by, and serve at the pleasure of the governor, although many of these appointments require senate confirmation.

As the state's chief administrative officer, the governor must approve federal aid expenditures; state land purchases; highway and airport construction; land or building leases for state use; and numerous state contracts, including compacts negotiated with Indian gaming authorities. The governor may request the attorney general to protect the public interest in various legal actions.

The statutes authorize the governor to create special advisory committees or task forces to conduct studies and make recommendations. These committees frequently attract experienced citizens from many fields, who donate their time and expertise as a public service. The governor also appoints over 1,000 persons to various councils and boards, which are created by law to advise and serve state government, and personally serves on selected bodies, such as the State of Wisconsin Building Commission.

If a vacancy occurs in the state senate or assembly, state law directs the governor to call a special election. Vacancies in elective county offices and judicial positions can be filled by gubernatorial appointment for the unexpired terms or until a successor is elected. The governor may dismiss sheriffs, district attorneys, coroners, or registers of deeds for proven malfeasance.

The governor serves as commander in chief of the Wisconsin National Guard when it is called into state service during emergencies, such as natural disasters and civil disturbances. (When National Guard units perform national service, they are under command of the U.S. President.)

The chief executive has sole power to extradite a person charged with a criminal offense and to exercise executive clemency by granting a pardon, reprieve, or sentence commutation to a convicted criminal offender.

History: Before Wisconsin entered the Union, the U.S. President appointed the territorial governor, but the state constitution, adopted in 1848, gave executive powers to an elected governor. Debate during the constitutional conventions revealed reluctance to change the duties traditionally performed by the chief executive. Questions regarding the post of governor concentrated instead on the amount of salary, length of term, location of residence and, above all, veto power. An effort to divest the governor of veto power failed, as did attempts to vest pardoning power in the legislature and to deny the governor power to remove county officials from office for cause.

There have been several constitutional amendments adopted over the years affecting the authority of the governor. A 1967 amendment lengthened the governor's term from 2 to 4 years, effective 1971. A constitutional amendment, ratified in 1930, empowered the governor to approve appropriation bills in part, thereby creating the partial veto. Another amendment, ratified in 1990, restricted the partial veto power by forbidding the governor to create new words by striking individual letters within words. An amendment ratified in 2008 further restricted the partial veto power by forbidding the governor from creating a new sentence by combining parts of two or more sentences.

Statutory Councils

State Council on Alcohol and Other Drug Abuse: CRAIG HARPER (designated to represent governor), SENATORS BEWLEY, LEMAHIEU; REPRESENTATIVES 2 vacancies; TINA VIRGIL (attorney general designee), STEVE FERNAN (superintendent of public instruction designee), TOM ENGELS (secretary of health services designee), ROGER FRINGS (commissioner of insurance designee), EDWARD WALL (secretary of corrections), BUD COXHEAD (secretary of transportation designee), CHARLOTTE RASMUSSEN (chairperson of Pharmacy Examining Board designee), DOUG ENGLEBERT (Controlled Substances Board representative), REBECCA WIGG-NINHAM (Governor's Commission on Law Enforcement and Crime representative), MICHAEL WAUPOOSE (service provider representative), SUE SHEMANSKI (nominated by Wisconsin County Human Service Association, Inc.); NORMAN BRIGGS, SANDY HARDIE, JOYCE O'DONNELL, MARY RASMUSSEN, DUNCAN SHROUT, SCOTT STOKES (public members). (All except *ex officio* members, or their designees, and legislative members are appointed by governor.)

The State Council on Alcohol and Other Drug Abuse recommends, coordinates, and reviews the efforts of state agencies to control and prevent alcohol and drug abuse. It evaluates program effectiveness, recommends improved programming, issues reports to educate people about the dangers of drug abuse, and allocates responsibility for various alcohol and drug abuse programs among state agencies. The council also recommends legislation, cooperates with federal agencies, and receives federal funds.

The 22-member council includes 6 members with a professional, research, or personal interest in alcohol and other drug abuse problems, appointed for 4-year terms, and one of them must be a consumer representing the public. It was created by Chapter 384, Laws of 1969, as the Drug Abuse Control Commission. Chapter 219, Laws of 1971, changed its name to the Council on Drug Abuse and placed the council in the executive office. It was renamed the Council on Alcohol and Other Drug Abuse by Chapter 370, Laws of 1975, and the State Council on Alcohol and Other Drug Abuse by Chapter 221, Laws of 1979. Its composition and duties are prescribed in Sections 14.017 (2) and 14.24 of the statutes.

Council on Military and State Relations: MICHAEL HINMAN (representative of the department of military affairs); LINDA FOURNIER, RICH HARVEY (representatives of Fort McCoy, Monroe County); SENATOR PETROWSKI (appointed by senate majority leader); SENATOR MILLER (appointed by senate minority leader); REPRESENTATIVE PETRYK (appointed by assembly speaker); REPRESENTATIVE MILROY (appointed by assembly minority leader); JOHN A. SCOCOS (representative of the governor).

The 7-member Council on Military and State Relations assists the governor by working with the state's military installations, commands and communities, state agencies, and economic development professionals to develop and implement strategies designed to enhance those installations. It advises and assists the governor on issues related to the location of military installations and assists and cooperates with state agencies to determine how those agencies can better serve military communities and families. It also assists the efforts of military families and their support groups regarding quality-of-life issues for service members and their families. The council was created by 2005 Wisconsin Act 26 and its composition and duties are prescribed in Section 14.017 (4) of the statutes.

Read to Lead Development Council: JON HOELTER (designated by governor), *chairperson;* BARB NOVAK (designated by state superintendent of public instruction), *vice chairperson;* SENATOR OLSEN (chair of senate education committee); SENATOR LARSON (ranking minority member of senate education committee); REPRESENTATIVE THIESFELDT (chair of assembly education committee); REPRESENTATIVE POPE (ranking minority member of assembly education committee); DONNA HEJTMANEK, DEAN KAMINSKI (elementary and secondary education teachers or principals); JILL RILEY (preschool teacher); JEANNIE FENCEROY, GINA GIALAMAS, STEVEN R. SORENSON (philanthropic community representatives); JEFF ROEPSCH, ELIZABETH THARP, vacancy (business community representatives); KATHY CHAMPEAU (Wisconsin State Reading Association representative); STEVE DYKSTRA (Wisconsin Reading Coalition representative); PAMELA HEYDE (International Dyslexia Association representative); MICHELE ERIKSON (Wisconsin Literacy, Inc., representative); ANN HARDGINSKI (Wisconsin Library Association representative); RACHEL LANDER (research community representative); JANIS M. SERAK (representative of organization serving children with disabilities). (All except legislative members appointed by the governor.)

The 22-member Read to Lead Development Council makes recommendations to the governor and state superintendent of public instruction regarding recipients of literacy and early childhood development grants. It annually submits a report on its operation to the appropriate standing committees of the legislature. All except *ex officio* and legislative members are appointed by the governor to 3-year terms. The council was created by 2011 Wisconsin Act 166 and its composition and duties are prescribed in Sections 14.017 (5) and 14.20 (1m) of the statutes.

Standards Development Council: Inactive.

The 7-member Standards Development Council, created by 1997 Wisconsin Act 27, was directed to submit to the governor, by November 14, 1997, recommendations relating to pupil academic standards in mathematics, science, reading and writing, geography, and history. The act provided that if the governor approved the standards, he or she was authorized to issue them as an executive order. The council is directed to periodically review the standards and recommend changes to the governor. The composition and duties of the council are prescribed in Sections 14.017 (3) and 14.23 of the statutes.

INDEPENDENT UNIT ATTACHED FOR BUDGETING, PROGRAM COORDINATION, AND RELATED MANAGEMENT FUNCTIONS BY SECTION 15.03 OF THE STATUTES

DISABILITY BOARD

Disability Board: GOVERNOR SCOTT WALKER, the Chief Justice of the Supreme Court, SENATOR LAZICH (senate president), SENATOR SHILLING (senate minority leader), REPRESENTATIVE VOS (assembly speaker), REPRESENTATIVE BARCA (assembly minority leader), ROBERT GOLDEN (dean, UW Medical School).

Statutory References: Sections 14.015 (1) and 17.025.

Agency Responsibility: The Disability Board is authorized by law to determine when a temporary disability exists in any of the constitutional offices because the incumbent is incapacitated due to illness or injury, and it may fill a temporary vacancy. The board, which was created by Chapter 422, Laws of 1969, originally had similar powers for supreme court justices and circuit court judges, but these were repealed by Chapter 449, Laws of 1977, and Chapter 332, Laws of 1975, respectively.

Governor Walker greets troops at the return of 32nd Military Engagement Team on January 22, 2015, at Joint Force Headquarters in Madison. (Office of the Governor)

GOVERNOR'S APPOINTMENTS TO MISCELLANEOUS COMMITTEES AND ORGANIZATIONS

Wisconsin Humanities Council

Members: Gubernatorial appointee: MARY C. KNAPP. (The governor appoints 6 members to the council. Other members are elected by the council.)

Executive Director: DENA WORTZEL.

Address: 222 South Bedford Street, Suite F, Madison 53703-3688.

Telephone: (608) 262-0706.

Fax: (608) 263-7970.

E-mail Address: contact@wisconsinhumanities.org

Internet Address: www.wisconsinhumanities.org

Publications: Grant guidelines and a periodic newsletter.

The Wisconsin Humanities Council, an independent, nonprofit organization, was established in 1972 under the provisions of federal Public Law 89-209. Members of the council include civic leaders; representatives of business, government, labor, professional, cultural, and educational institutions; and scholars and teachers in the humanities. The council receives annual funding from the National Endowment for the Humanities, the State of Wisconsin, and other sources. It creates, and through its grant program, supports programming that uses history, culture, and discussion to strengthen community life for everyone in Wisconsin. Any nonprofit organization or institution may apply to the council for project support. In planning and presenting public programs, applicant organizations must ordinarily involve scholars with graduate degrees in the humanities.

The Medical College of Wisconsin, Inc.

Board of Trustees: Gubernatorial appointees: ELIZABETH BRENNER, CURT S. CULVER, CORY L. NETTLES, GREG WESLEY. (The governor appoints two members of the board of trustees with senate consent.)

President: JOHN RAYMOND, SR.

Mailing Address: 8701 Watertown Plank Road, P.O. Box 26509, Milwaukee 53226-0509.

Telephone: (414) 456-8225.

Fax: (414) 456-6560.

State Appropriation 2013-15: $18,664,700.

Publications: *Alumni News,* annual reports, directory of physician consultants, *Facts, Medical College of Wisconsin News, World.*

Statutory Reference: Sections 13.106, 39.15, and 39.155.

The Medical College of Wisconsin, Inc., is a private nonprofit educational corporation located in Milwaukee. The college receives a specified sum under the "medical student tuition assistance" program for each Wisconsin resident it enrolls. The Higher Educational Aids Board determines whether applicants qualify as state residents. The college also receives state funds for its family medicine residency program.

The governor appoints two board of trustees members for 6-year terms. The college is required to fulfill certain reporting requirements, and the Legislative Audit Bureau conducts postaudits of expenditures made under state appropriations.

In September 1967, Marquette University terminated its sponsorship of the college, then known as the Marquette School of Medicine, Inc. To increase the supply of physicians in Wisconsin, the legislature enacted Chapter 3, Laws of 1969, which appropriated funds to the school provided Wisconsin residents received first preference for admission. The legislature made a token appropriation to test the law's constitutionality, and the Wisconsin Supreme Court ruled the law constitutional in *State ex rel. Warren v. Rueter,* 44 Wis. 2d 201 (1969). Chapter 185, Laws of 1969, fully funded state support for the college. In 1970, the college's name was changed to The Medical College of Wisconsin, Inc.

In the 2013-15 biennial budget, the legislature approved $7,384,300 in general obligation bonding for the development of two new community-based medical schools in northeast and central Wisconsin. The programs are designed to help alleviate physician shortages within medically underserved areas of the state, especially within primary care medicine, where the shortages to care are most acute. MCW-Green Bay welcomed its inaugural class on July 1, 2015, and MCW-Central Wisconsin is expected to open in mid-2016.

GOVERNOR'S SPECIAL COMMITTEES
June 30, 2015

The committees described in this section include those Governor Scott Walker created or continued. Most of the committees were created under Section 14.019, Wisconsin Statutes, which provides that "the governor may, by executive order, create nonstatutory committees in such number and with such membership as desired, to conduct such studies and to advise the governor in such matters as directed." Committee members serve at the pleasure of the governor.

Unless terminated sooner, a special committee expires automatically on the fourth Monday of January of the year in which a new gubernatorial term begins. The governor may, however, provide for its continued existence by executive order. In that event, existing members continue to serve unless they resign or until the governor replaces them.

The law also provides that the governor may designate an employee of the Office of the Governor or of the Department of Administration to coordinate the activities of nonstatutory committees. In some cases, the governor has ordered other state agencies to staff and financially support committees.

When a new gubernatorial term begins, each committee is required to submit a final report to the governor or governor-elect prior to the new term. Copies of each final report and any other report a special committee prepared must be submitted to the Reference and Loan Library in the Department of Public Instruction for distribution under Section 35.83 (3), Wisconsin Statutes.

Section 20.505 (1) (ka), Wisconsin Statutes, provides for the expenses of special committees created by executive order. In addition, certain committees receive specific state appropriations, and some receive federal funds because they are established in response to federal program requirements.

The special committees are listed in alphabetical order by the key word in each committee name.

Council on Autism

Members: NISSAN BAR-LEV, WENDY COOMER, VIVIAN HAZELL, ROSALIA HELMS, LIESL JORDAN, ROBERTA MAYO, MILANA MILLAN, PAULA PETIT, PAUL RUETEMAN, GLEN SALLOWS, PAM STOIKA, MICHAEL WILLIAMS.

Contact person: JULIE BRYDA, julie.bryda@dhs.wisconsin.gov

Aligned to: Department of Health Services, 1 West Wilson Street, Madison 53703.

Governor Jim Doyle created the council in Executive Order 94, April 5, 2005, to meet quarterly and advise the Department of Health Services on strategies for implementing statewide supports and services for children with autism. It was recreated by Governor Walker in Executive Order 150, January 26, 2015. Of the maximum 15 members appointed by the governor to the council, at least a majority must be parents of children with autism or autism spectrum disorders. The remaining members may be providers of services to children with autism, local government officials, persons who are knowledgeable of autism issues, or simply members of the general public.

Bicycle Coordinating Council

Members: DAVID SPIEGELBERG (designated by secretary of tourism); BRIGIT BROWN (designated by secretary of natural resources); JILL MROTEK GLENZINSKI (designated by secretary of transportation); RANDY THIEL (designated by state superintendent of public instruction); JON

MORGAN (designated by secretary of health services); LARRY CORSI (designated by director, Department of Transportation, Bureau of Transportation Safety); SENATOR OLSEN (appointed by senate majority leader), SENATOR SHILLING (appointed by senate minority leader); REPRESENTATIVE RIPP (appointed by assembly speaker), REPRESENTATIVE GENRICH (appointed by assembly minority leader); CHRISTOPHER S. FORTUNE, KEVIN HARDMAN, CRAIG A. HEYWOOD, KRYSTYNA KORNILOWICZ, BRENDA MAXWELL (public members).

Contact person: JILL MROTEK GLENZINSKI, jill.mrotekglenzinski@dot.wi.gov

Aligned to: Department of Transportation, 4802 Sheboygan Avenue, P.O. Box 7999, Madison 53707.

Governor Tommy G. Thompson created the council in Executive Order 122, June 24, 1991, and Governor Walker most recently recreated it in Executive Order 150, January 26, 2015. A similar council was originally created by Governor Patrick J. Lucey in June 1977 under Executive Order 43, and it has been recreated several times since. The council consists of not more than 17 members. The council considers all matters relating to: efforts of state agencies to encourage the use of the bicycle as an alternative means of transportation; promoting bicycle safety and education; promoting safe bicycling to school; promoting bicycling as a recreational and tourist activity; and disseminating information on state and federal funding for bicycle programs. The council also reviews the bicycle programs of state agencies, issues reports to the governor and the legislature, and makes recommendations concerning pertinent legislation.

Wisconsin Coastal Management Council

Members: LARRY MACDONALD, *chairperson;* vacancy, *vice chairperson;* SENATOR WIRCH; REPRESENTATIVE WEATHERSTON; JAMES P. HURLEY (UW System representative), ED EBERLE (designated by secretary of administration), STEPHEN GALARNEAU (designated by secretary of natural resources), SHERI WALZ (designated by secretary of transportation); ERVIN SOULIER (tribal government representative); SHARON COOK (City of Milwaukee representative); ROBERT D. BROWNE, JOHN DICKERT, PATRICIA HOEFT, KENNETH L. LEINBACH, WILLIAM SCHUSTER.

Contact person: MIKE FRIIS.

Aligned to: Department of Administration, 101 East Wilson Street, 9th Floor, P.O. Box 8944, Madison 53708-8944.

Internet Address: http://coastal.wisconsin.gov

Acting Governor Martin J. Schreiber established the council in Executive Order 49, October 7, 1977. It has been recreated or revised several times, and was continued most recently by Governor Walker in Executive Order 150, January 26, 2015. It succeeded the Coastal Coordinating and Advisory Council appointed by Governor Patrick J. Lucey in 1974. The 1977 council was created to comply with provisions of the federal Coastal Zone Management Act of 1972 and to implement Wisconsin's official Coastal Management Program, which received federal approval on May 22, 1978. The council advises the governor on issues pertaining to the Great Lakes coasts and assists in providing policy direction for Wisconsin's coastal management efforts. Members represent the legislature, state agencies, units of local government, tribal governments, and citizens. To provide opportunities for full participation in the program, the governor encouraged the council to establish citizens' committees to advise the council on key issues affecting the coasts. The council endorsed "Wisconsin Coastal Management Program: Needs Assessment and Multi-Year Strategy, 2011-2015" in February 2011. Annually since 2002, the program has produced the *Wisconsin Great Lakes Chronicle.* Archived copies are available from the Wisconsin Coastal Management Program's Web site.

Criminal Justice Coordinating Council

Members: EDWARD F. WALL (secretary of corrections), BRAD SCHIMEL (attorney general), *cochairpersons;* KELLI THOMPSON (State Public Defender); MATTHEW JOSKI (county sheriff); vacancy (chief of police); DAVID O'LEARY (district attorney); J. DENIS MORAN (director of state courts); REGGIE NEWSON (secretary of workforce development); ELOISE ANDERSON (secretary of children and families); KITTY RHOADES (secretary of health services); JEFF KREMERS (chair of chief judges of circuit courts); MARK ABELES-ALLISON (county administrator); TIANA GLENNA (county criminal justice coordinating council representative); JANE JENNINGS (crime victims representative); MARK CLEMENTS, MALLORY O'BRIEN (public members); PATTI JO SEVERSON (mental health and criminal justice representative); RICH VAN BOXTEL (tribal representative).

Aligned to: Department of Justice, 1 South Pinckney Street, Suite 615, P.O. Box 7857, Madison 53703.

The statewide council was created by Governor Walker in Executive Order 65 on April 9, 2012, and was most recently recreated by Governor Walker on January 26, 2015, in Executive Order 150. It is tasked with developing criminal justice policy recommendations to strengthen public safety and the justice system; investigate effective and innovative criminal justice-related programs employed at the county level, encourage the development of county or multi-county criminal justice coordinating councils; provide recommendations on the collection and synthesis of real-time criminal justice data, and with the aid of all executive branch agencies, develop and make recommendations to implement a reporting system to track key criminal justice indicators on a monthly basis; promote the evaluation of new and current criminal justice policies; and provide strategic planning and guidance for the management of federal grants.

The council must submit an annual report to the governor, the chief justice, and the chief clerk of each house. It meets on a quarterly basis.

Governor's Committee for People With Disabilities

Members: NANCY LEIPZIG, *chairperson;* JEFF FOX (Council on Physical Disabilities), *vice chairperson;* vacancy (Council on Mental Health); RAMSEY LEE (Board for People with Developmental Disabilities); ALEX H. SLAPPEY (Council for the Deaf and Hard of Hearing); vacancy (Council on Blindness); vacancy (State Council on Alcohol and Other Drug Abuse); THOMAS FELL, JOHN HARTMAN, DANIEL LAATSCH, DAVID MORSTAD, JOHN W. OLSON, SANDRA POPP, MAUREEN RYAN, PATRICIA WILLIAMS (at-large members). Nonvoting *ex officio* member: LT. GOVERNOR KLEEFISCH.

Contact person: DAN JOHNSON, dan.johnson@dhs.wisconsin.gov

Aligned to: Department of Health Services, 1 West Wilson Street, Madison 53703.

The Wisconsin Governor's Committee for People with Disabilities in its present form was established in March of 1976 by Governor Patrick J. Lucey, and has been reauthorized through executive order by every governor since that time. It was most recently recreated by Governor Walker in Executive Order 150 on January 26, 2015. The original executive order provided initial guidance for the committee to advise the governor's office on a broad range of issues affecting people with disabilities. The committee's mission, "to enhance the health and general well-being of disabled citizens in Wisconsin", was created out of a realization that state government lacked a process of systematically communicating the needs of people with disabilities to responsible state and local officials. In an effort to enhance the value of the committee, the executive order was rewritten in 2004 to support a focus on issues, policies, and programs that will encourage involvement in the workforce.

The committee consists of the Lieutenant Governor as a nonvoting, *ex officio* member, and not more than 20 members, appointed by the governor to serve at his pleasure. The committee as a whole includes Wisconsin residents with disabilities and individuals that have demonstrated interest in the concerns of all disability groups. All serve as unpaid volunteers. Six of the committee members represent specific disability constituencies: 1) Council on Blindness; 2) Wisconsin Council for the Deaf and Hard of Hearing; 3) Wisconsin Board for People with Developmental Disabilities; 4) Wisconsin Council on Mental Health; 5) State Council on Alcohol and Other Drug Abuse; and 6) Council on Physical Disabilities.

The committee meets quarterly, usually in March, June, September, and December. In addition to the Executive Committee, the Governor's Committee also has two subcommittees: the Business Leadership Network Subcommittee and the Youth Leadership Forum Subcommittee.

Early Childhood Advisory Council

Members: ELOISE ANDERSON (secretary of children and families), TONY EVERS (state superintendent of public instruction), *cochairpersons;* THERESE AHLERS, BEVERLY ANDERSON, NANCY ARMBRUST, JOHN ASHLEY, FREDI BOVE, SHEILA BRIGGS, RAY CROSS, LINDA DAVIS, DAVE EDIE, MORNA FOY, DELORES GOKEE-RINDAL, MICHELLE JENSEN GOODWIN, JILL HOITING, PETER

KELLY, KIA LABRACKE, LUPE MARTINEZ, JENNIE MAUER, JUDY NORMAN-NUNNERY, GAIL PROPSOM, KITTY RHOADES (secretary of health services), CAROLYN STANFORD TAYLOR, JON STELLMACHER, ANN TERRELL, EDWARD F. WALL (secretary of corrections), ROLF WEGENKE, RISSA WOJCIK.

Contact person: BRIDGET CULLEN, bridget.cullen@wisconsin.gov

Aligned to: Department of Children and Families, 201 East Washington Avenue, Second Floor, Madison 53708.

Internet Address: dcf.wi.gov/ecac

Governor Jim Doyle created the council in Executive Order 269 on October 30, 2008, in accordance with Federal Public Law 110-134. It was most recently recreated by Governor Walker in Executive Order 150, on January 26, 2015. The council makes recommendations to the governor regarding development of a comprehensive statewide early childhood system. Responsibilities of the council include the following: conducting needs assessments; identifying barriers to collaboration between federal and state programs; developing recommendations for increasing participation of children in early childhood services; developing recommendations for a unified data collection system; supporting professional development; assessing the capacity of higher education to support the development of early childhood professionals; and making recommendations to improve early learning standards.

Early Intervention Interagency Coordinating Council

Members: CINDY FLAUGER, *chairperson;* LAURICE LINCOLN, *vice chairperson;* vacancy (state legislator); JULIE WALSH (designated by commissioner of insurance), LINDA HUFFER (Department of Health Services, Division of Long-Term Care designee), SHARON FLEISCHFRESSER (Department of Health Services, Division of Public Health designee), LAURA SATERFIELD (State Office of Child Care designee), JILL HAGLUND (Department of Public Instruction designee); LINDA TUCHMAN (Personnel Prep); WILLIAM BARREAU, TONI DAKINS, VICTORIA DEER, THERESA VINCENT.

Contact person: JACQUELINE MOSS, jacqueline.moss@dhs.wisconsin.gov

Aligned to: Department of Health Services, 1 West Wilson Street, Madison 53703.

Governor Tommy G. Thompson first established the council in Executive Order 17, June 26, 1987, and recreated it in Executive Order 334, May 21, 1998. Governor Walker most recently recreated it in Executive Order 150, January 26, 2015. Often called the "Birth to Three" Council, it was created to comply with the federal Individuals With Disabilities Education Act of 1986 and recreated to comply with the federal Individuals With Disabilities Education Act of 1997. The council advises and assists the Department of Health Services in the development and administration of early intervention services for infants and toddlers with developmental delays and their families. It consists of at least 15 members and is directed by the governor to include at least 4 parents of infants, toddlers, or children aged 12 or younger with disabilities; at least 4 private or public providers of early intervention services; at least one state legislator; at least one member involved in personnel training; at least one representative of a Head Start agency or program; and other members representing state agencies that provide services or payment for early intervention services to infants and toddlers and their families. Members, other than those serving *ex officio,* serve 3-year terms. Administrative and support services are provided to the council by the Department of Health Services. The council issues an annual report for each federal fiscal year.

Governor's Council on Financial Literacy

Members: RAY ALLEN, MATTHEW BANASZYNSKI, WENDY BAUMANN, JENNIFER BLOCK, LORI BURGESS, SARAH CAMPBELL, J. MICHAEL COLLINS, TONY EVERS, TIMOTHY GREINERT, JESSE HARNESS, KRISTINE HACKBARTH HORN, JAIMES JOHNSON, AMY KERWIN, KENNETH KING, LLOYD LEVIN, HOWARD MARKLEIN, MARY ANN MCCOSHEN, JOE MEDINA, TED NICKEL, M. SCOTT NIEDERJOHN, LUTHER OLSEN, PABLO SANCHEZ, CATHY SCHINDLER, DENNIS TOMORSKY, WILLIAM WILCOX.

Contact person: TERESA WALKER, teresa.walker@wisconsin.gov

Aligned to: Department of Health Services, 1 West Wilson Street, Madison 53703.

Governor Jim Doyle created the council in Executive Order 92, March 30, 2005, to work with existing state agencies, private entities, and nonprofit associations in improving the financial literacy of Wisconsin citizens. It was recreated by Governor Walker in Executive Order 24, April 6, 2011. Governor Walker most recently recreated the council on January 26, 2015, in Executive Order 150. The council is directed to collaborate with the Office of the Commissioner of Insurance, implement research and policy initiatives, and serve as sounding board for the Office of the Governor and the Office of Financial Literacy in the Department of Financial Institutions to provide guidance and develop strategies to improve financial literacy among Wisconsin's citizens. The council will also promote the statewide financial literacy awareness and education campaign entitled Money Smart Week Wisconsin. The council consists of 25 members or less, with a chairperson, and two vice chairpersons selected from within the group. The Secretary of the Department of Financial Institutions is required to submit an annual progress report on the council.

Historical Records Advisory Board

Members: MENZI L. BEHRND-KLODT, CLAYBORN BENSON, ANITA T. DOERING, MARIA ESCALANTE, JANE M. PEDERSON, RICK PIFER, JANE SCHETTER, MICHELLE SWEETSER, KENNETH J. WIRTH.

Coordinator: MATTHEW BLESSING, matt.blessing@wisconsinhistory.org

Aligned to: State Historical Society of Wisconsin, 816 State Street, Madison 53706.

Governor Patrick J. Lucey created the advisory board on April 4, 1977. It was most recently continued by Governor Walker in Executive Order 150, January 26, 2015. That action enables the state to participate in the grants program of the National Historical Publications and Records Commission, which coordinates the preservation of historic records in the United States and approves federal grants to qualified Wisconsin institutions and to the state advisory board. The board promotes the availability and use of historical records as keys to improved understanding of our cultural heritage. Members serve staggered 3-year terms.

Homeland Security Council

Members: MAJOR GENERAL DONALD P. DUNBAR, *chairperson;* HENRY ANDERSON, SUSAN BUROKER, DAVID CAGIGAL, WILLIAM ENGFER, DAVID ERWIN, STEPHEN FITZGERALD, EDWARD FLYNN, BRADLEY LIGGETT, DAVID MAHONEY, DAVE MATTHEWS, ELLEN NOWAK, STEVEN RIFFEL, BRIAN SATULA, BRUCE SLAGOSKI, EDWARD WALL.

Contact person: RANDI MILSAP, randi.milsap@wisconsin.gov

Address: 2400 Wright Street, P.O. Box 14587, Madison 53708.

Internet Address: http://homelandsecurity.wi.gov

Governor Jim Doyle created the council in Executive Order 7, March 18, 2003, to advise the governor and to coordinate the efforts of state and local agencies regarding the prevention of, and response to, potential threats to the homeland security of the state. It was recreated by Governor Walker in Executive Order 101 on May 3, 2013. Governor Walker most recently recreated the council on January 26, 2015, in Executive Order 150. The council's 16 members are appointed by and serve at the pleasure of the governor. The council works with federal, state, and local agencies, nonprofit organizations, and private industry to prevent and respond to any threat of terrorism, promote personal preparedness, and make recommendations to the governor on additional steps to further enhance Wisconsin's homeland security.

Independent Living Council of Wisconsin

Members: DELORIS NASH (director of a center for independent living); TAMARA JANDROWSKI (independent living program representative); STEPHEN J. WEST (representative of the directors of Native American Vocational Rehabilitation programs); BENJAMIN BARRETT, CYNTHIA BENTLEY, MARYJANE GRANDE, CHRIS HENDRICKSON, RON JANSEN, THEODORE PYKE, THONGNGI XIONG. Nonvoting members: KATHLEEN ENDERS (representing Department of Workforce Development, Division of Vocational Rehabilitation), KEVIN COUGHLIN (representing Department of Health Services), KATHERINE PATTERSON (representing Department of Transportation), DIANE MCGINNIS-CASEY (representing Department of Administration, Division of Housing).

Contact person: MIKE BACHHUBER, director@ilcw.org

Aligned to: Department of Administration, 3810 Milwaukee Street, Madison 53714.

Internet Address: http://www.il-wisconsin.net

Governor Tommy G. Thompson created the council in Executive Order 212, January 10, 1994, to comply with the 1992 amendments to the federal Rehabilitation Act of 1973. In 2004, Governor Jim Doyle issued Executive Order 65, which outlines the current membership and established the council as a nonprofit entity. Governor Walker most recently recreated the council in Executive Order 150, January 26, 2015. In coordination with the Division of Vocational Rehabilitation, the council has the responsibility to develop and submit the state plan for independent living services for people with disabilities to state and federal agencies; monitor, review, and evaluate the state plan; and related purposes.

The council currently consists of 14 voting members and 4 *ex officio* members representing the Department of Workforce Development, the Department of Health Services, the Department of Transportation, and the Department of Administration's Division of Housing. The majority of members must be persons with disabilities who do not work for a center for independent living or the State of Wisconsin. At least one member must be a director of a center for independent living chosen by centers for independent living, and at least one must be a representative of the directors of Native American vocational rehabilitation programs. Voting members of the council serve staggered 3-year terms and may serve no more than two consecutive terms.

Governor's Information Technology Executive Steering Committee

Members: JOHN HOGAN (department of administration representative), *chairperson;* RON HUNT (department of children and families representative); SCOTT LEGWOLD (department of corrections representative); JONATHAN BARRY (department of workforce development representative); TOM ENGELS (department of health services representative); MICHAEL BRUHN (department of natural resources representative); JACK JABLONSKI (department of revenue representative); SANDY CHALMERS (department of agriculture, trade and consumer protection representative); PAUL HAMMER (department of transportation representative); DAVID CAGIGAL (State Chief Information Officer).

Contact person: VICKY HALVERSON, vicky.halverson@wisconsin.gov

Aligned to: Department of Administration, 101 East Wilson Street, P.O. Box 7864, Madison 53707.

The committee was created by Governor Walker's Executive Order 99 on April 26, 2013, and was most recently recreated in Executive Order 150 on January 26, 2015. It is a governance body responsible for the effective and efficient application of information technology (IT) assets across the state for the delivery of services to the constituents of the state. Specifically its purpose is to establish enterprise IT and IT procurement strategies, policies direction, and standards for state agencies.

The members consist of senior executive business leaders from the departments of Administration, Children and Families, Corrections, Workforce Development, Health Services, Natural Resources, Revenue, Agriculture, Trade and Consumer Protection, Transportation, and the State Chief Information Officer, or the designees of any. All cabinet-level agencies are directed to consult and align their IT efforts with the committee. The Department of Administration's Division of Enterprise Technology provides staff support to the committee.

Governor's Judicial Selection Advisory Committee

Members: MICHAEL BRENNAN, *chairperson;* WILLIAM CURRAN, DONALD DAUGHERTY, STEVEN GIBBS, KATHERINE LONGLEY, LON ROBERTS.

Contact person: BRIAN HAGEDORN, brian.hagedorn@wisconsin.gov

Aligned to: Office of the Governor, Room 115 East, State Capitol, P.O. Box 7863, Madison 53707-7863.

Governor Anthony Earl established the Governor's Advisory Council on Judicial Selection in Executive Order 1, January 6, 1983. Governor Walker recreated and restructured it as an advisory committee in Executive Order 29, May 11, 2011. The committee was most recently recreated by Governor Walker on January 26, 2015, in Executive Order 150. The committee makes recommendations to the governor on filling vacancies in the state court system. The committee consists of any number of individuals as determined by the governor. Members serve for 12-month renewable terms at the pleasure of the governor. The governor designates the chairperson, who has discretion to determine the method by which applicants are considered and recommended. The chairperson also has the authority to appoint temporary members.

Governor's Juvenile Justice Commission

Members: CARL ASHLEY, JONATHAN CLOUD, THEODORE ENGELBART, JOSE FLORES, TIERNEY GILL, STEVEN GLAMM, EDDIE JACKSON, TASHA JENKINS, JESSICA JIMENEZ, KATHLEEN MALONE, JAMES MOESER, JANET PROCTOR, MINDY TEMPELIS, PAUL WESTERHAUS, ANNETTE ZIEGLER.

Aligned to: Department of Justice, 1 South Pinckney Street, Suite 615, P.O. Box 7857, Madison 53702-3220.

Governor Tommy G. Thompson created the commission as the Juvenile Justice Advisory Group in Executive Order 55, January 30, 1989, repealed and recreated it as the Governor's Juvenile Justice Commission in Executive Order 110, February 6, 1991. Governor Walker continued it in Executive Order 8, January 25, 2011. The commission was most recently recreated by Governor Walker in Executive Order 150 on January 26, 2015.

The commission awards funds received by the state under the federal Juvenile Justice and Delinquency Prevention Act, the Juvenile Accountability Block Grant, and other state and federal programs. It also advises the governor and the legislature on juvenile justice issues. The Office of Justice Assistance provides staff and pays the expenses of the commission.

Governor's Council on Physical Fitness and Health

Members: KENNETH BERG, AMY DELONG, LEROY DEPAS, ELIZABETH FARAH, CARL HEIGL, JILL HOITING, SUSAN KUNFERMAN, SHANYN LANCASTER, LINDA LEE, KIMBERLY LIEDL (designated by governor), ERIN LORANG, KAREN MCKEOWN (designated by secretary of health services).

Address: Department of Health Services, 1 West Wilson Street, Madison 53703.

Telephones: 267-7828.

Governor Anthony Earl established the council in Executive Order 10, April 19, 1983, and Governor Walker recreated it in Executive Order 73, June 18, 2012. The council was most recently recreated by Governor Walker in Executive Order 150 on January 26, 2015. The council is directed to develop policy recommendations to improve the status of children's health, physical fitness and nutritional intake, as well as educate the public and media on the importance of those goals. It is also to encourage stakeholder and community leaders to assist in preventing obesity in all state residents throughout their lives.

The Department of Health Services provides staff support to the council, which consists of no less than nine members and no more than 15. Members include the governor, the secretary of health services or the designees of both, and citizen members appointed and serving at the pleasure of the governor.

State Rehabilitation Council

Members: LINDA VEGOE (client assistance programs), *chairperson;* JAMES DOBRINSKA (business, industry and labor representative), *vice chairperson;* MATTHEW ZELLMER (parent training and information center); ALVIN HILL (community rehabilitation program service provider); CHRIS HENDRICKSON (Statewide Independent Living Council); JULIE FERCHOFF (vocational rehabilitation counselor); vacancy (business, industry and labor representative); CAYTE ANDERSON, ROBERT BUETTNER, STEPHANIE DRUM, JODI HANNA, BARBARA KLUG-SIEJA, GAIL KOLVENBACH, JOHN LUI, BETH SWEDEEN (disability advocacy groups); PATRICIA LERCH (Native American vocational rehabilitation); WENDI DAWSON (Department of Public Instruction). Nonvoting member: MICHAEL GRECO (administrator, Division of Vocational Rehabilitation).

Contact person: KRISTIN ROLLING, kristin.rolling@dwd.wi.gov

Aligned to: Department of Workforce Development, Division of Vocational Rehabilitation, 201 East Washington Avenue, P.O. Box 7852, Madison 53707-7852.

Governor Tommy G. Thompson created the council in Executive Order 363, January 30, 1999, to advise the Department of Workforce Development on the statewide vocational rehabilitation plan for disabled individuals required under 29 U.S. Code Section 720, *et seq.* Governor

Walker most recently continued the council in Executive Order 150, January 26, 2015. The council is similar to one established in Executive Order 196, July 1, 1993, as the State Rehabilitation Advisory Council. Council members serve 3-year terms. A majority must be individuals with disabilities not employed by the Department of Workforce Development, Division of Vocational Rehabilitation Services. The administrator of that division is a nonvoting *ex officio* member of the council.

Wisconsin Technology Committee

Members: Wisconsin Technology Council chair, vice chair, president, secretary and treasurer.

Contact person: TOM STILL, *president.*

Aligned to: Wisconsin Technology Council, 455 Science Drive, Suite 240, Madison 53711.

The committee was originally created by Governor Walker in Executive Order 51, November 4, 2011. It was most recently recreated by Governor Walker in Executive Order 150 on January 26, 2015. It is an advisory committee consisting of the members of the Wisconsin Technology Council, which was created by state legislation as a nonprofit corporation, but removed from the statutes with the repeal of the Department of Commerce. Creation of the committee allows the council to coordinate with state government. The council assists the state in promoting the creation, development, and retention of science- and technology-based businesses by developing programs that stimulate innovation and entrepreneurial activity. It also provides policy guidance to lawmakers. It provides an annual report to the appropriate standing committee of each house of the legislature.

The five members of the committee include the chair, vice chair, president, secretary, and treasurer of the Wisconsin Technology Council.

One of the duties of the chief executive is to present a budget to the Legislature. Here Governor Walker delivers his budget message to the 2015 Wisconsin Legislature. (Greg Anderson, Legislative Photographer)

Telecommunications Relay Service Council

Members: THOMAS E. HARBISON, *chairperson;* RONALD E. BYINGTON, MARGARET CALTEAUX, JILL COLLINS, CHERI FRENCH, JAMES JERMAIN, KAREN E. JORGENSEN, TOM MEITNER, HELEN RIZZI, vacancy.

Contact person: JACK R. CASSELL, jack.cassell@wisconsin.gov

Aligned to: Department of Administration, Division of Enterprise Technology, 101 East Wilson Street, 8th Floor, P.O. Box 7844, Madison 53707-7844.

Governor Tommy G. Thompson created the council in Executive Order 95, June 19, 1990, recreated it in Executive Order 131, October 2, 1991, and Governor Walker continued it most recently in Executive Order 150, January 26, 2015. The council was directed to advise the Bureau of Telecommunications Management in the Department of Administration on the feasibility or desirability of: establishing requirements and procedures for a telecommunications relay service; requiring the service to be available 24 hours a day, 7 days a week; requiring users to pay rates that are no greater than rates for functionally equivalent voice telecommunications service; prohibiting relay service operators from refusing or limiting the length of calls; prohibiting relay service operators from disclosing the contents of calls, keeping records of their contents beyond the duration of the calls, and intentionally altering the content of a call; requiring relay service operators to take training on the problems faced by hearing-impaired and speech-impaired persons using the service; and authorizing the establishment by contract of a statewide telecommunications relay service. The council consists of not more than 11 members, 4 of whom must use a telecommunications relay service. These must include one speech-impaired person, one hearing-impaired person, one speech- and hearing-impaired person, and one person not having a speech or hearing impairment. Five of the members must include one representative each from the Wisconsin Association of the Deaf, Wisconsin Telecommunications, Inc., Wisconsin State Telephone Association, a local exchange telecommunications utility, and an interexchange telecommunications utility doing business in this state.

Council on Veterans Employment

Members: SCOTT NEITZEL (secretary of administration), REGGIE NEWSON (secretary of workforce development), JOHN SCOCOS (secretary of veterans affairs), RAY CROSS (UW System president), GREG GRACZ (director of office of state employment relations).

Governor Scott Walker created the council in Executive Order 137 on June 13, 2014. The council was most recently recreated by Governor Walker on January 26, 2015, in Executive Order 150. The council was created for the purpose of advising the governor to establish a coordinated effort to increase veterans' employment. In particular, the council focuses on increasing the number of veterans employed by state government through an expansion in recruitment and training. The council shall consist of the Department of Administration secretary, the Department of Workforce Development secretary, the Department of Veterans Affairs secretary, the University of Wisconsin System president, and the OSER director, or their designees.

Governor's Council on Workforce Investment

Members: DANIEL ARIENS, KURT BAUER, RAY CROSS, CEDRIC ELLIS, TONY EVERS, PAUL FARROW, ANDREW FIENE, MORNA FOY, REED HALL, GRAILING JONES, STEVE KLESSIG, JANICE LEMMINGER, STEVE LOEHR, TERRY MCGOWAN, DAN MELLA, MICHELLE METTNER, REGGIE NEWSON, A. KENT OLSON, ALAN PETELINSEK, VERNON PETERSON, WARREN PETRYK, DAWN PRATT, MARK REIHL, JANIS RINGHAND, LOLA ROEH, ROGER ROTH, KATHI SEIFERT, KATRINA SHANKLAND, DAN STEININGER, TOM STILL, TROY STRECKENBACH, VICTORIA STROBEL, S. MARK TYLER, ROLF WEGENKE.

Contact person: TRISTAN COOK, tristan.cook@dwd.wisconsin.gov

Aligned to: Department of Workforce Development, P.O. Box 7946, Madison 53707-7946.

Governor Tommy G. Thompson created the council in Executive Order 385, November 17, 1999. The council was reconstituted by Governor Scott Walker in Executive Order 152 in March 2015, due to significant changes to the publicly-funded workforce development system with the passage of the Workforce Innovation and Opportunity Act in 2014. The council consists of members appointed in accordance with federal statute and additional members designated by the governor. As specified by law, the majority of members are from the private sector.

The governor directed the council to carry out all duties and functions prescribed in 29 U.S.C. §3111: recommending strategies that align workforce development resources to support economic development; identifying and implementing best practices that will strengthen the Wisconsin Job Center system; promoting programs to increase the number of skilled workers; and providing resources to all Wisconsin workers seeking work, including persons with disabilities and youth. The governor further directed all cabinet agencies, and encouraged all other state agencies, to collaborate with the council to develop a strong, skilled workforce.

Governor Walker and Tourism Secretary Stephanie Klett promote tourism at the Milwaukee County Zoo May 1, 2015. (Office of the Governor).

STATE OFFICERS APPOINTED BY THE GOVERNOR
AS REQUIRED BY STATUTE
June 30, 2015

Officers[1]	Name	Home Address[2]	Term Expires[3]	Salary or Per Diem[4]
*Accounting Examining Board Secs. 15.08, 15.405 (1)	John Scheid[5]	Milwaukee	July 1, 2015	$25 per day
	Todd Craft[5]	Hartland	July 1, 2016	$25 per day
	Joseph Braunger	Madison	July 1, 2017	$25 per day
	Gerald Denor.	Menomonee Falls	July 1, 2017	$25 per day
	Glenn Michaelsen	Jackson	July 1, 2017	$25 per day
	Christine Anderson[5]	Lake Mills	July 1, 2018	$25 per day
	Kathleen LaBrake	Wausau	July 1, 2018	$25 per day
Adjutant General Sec. 15.31	Major Gen Donald P. Dunbar		Sept. 1, 2012	Group 4
*Administration, Dept. of, Secy. Secs. 15.05 (1) (af), 15.10	Scott Neitzel	Verona	Pleasure of Gov.	Group 8
Adult Offender Supervision Board, Interstate Sec. 15.145 (3)	Tamara Grigsby	Milwaukee	May 1, 2011	None
	Michael Bohren	Delafield	May 1, 2017	None
	Stephanie R. Hove	Oconomowoc	May 1, 2019	None
	David Rabe.	Madison	May 1, 2019	None
Adult Offender Supervision Board, Interstate Compact Administrator Sec. 304.16 (2)(d)	Tracy Hudrlik	Madison	May 1, 2017	None
*Aerospace Authority, Wis. Sec. 114.61	Thomas Crabb	Middleton	June 30, 2010	None
	Judith Schieble.	Sheboygan	June 30, 2010	None
	Thomas Mullooly	Wauwatosa	June 30, 2011	None
	Edward Wagner	Marshfield	June 30, 2011	None
	Mark Hanna	Sheboygan	June 30, 2012	None
	Mark Lee.	Middleton	June 30, 2012	None
Affirmative Action, Council on Secs. 15.09 (1)(a), 15.105 (29)(d)	David Dunham.	Madison	July 1, 2011	None
	Eileen Hocker	Madison	July 1, 2011	None
	Sandra Ryan	Madison	July 1, 2011	None
	Ronald Shaheed	Milwaukee	July 1, 2011	None
	Nancy Vue	Madison	July 1, 2011	None
	Thresessa Childs	Milwaukee	July 1, 2012	None
	Janice Hughes	Fitchburg	July 1, 2012	None
	John Magerus	Racine	July 1, 2012	None
	James Parker	La Crosse	July 1, 2012	None
	Yolanda Santos Adams.	Kenosha	July 1, 2012	None
	Lakshmi Bharadwaj	Milwaukee	July 1, 2013	None
*Aging and Long-Term Care, Board on Secs. 15.07 (1)(b) 9, 15.105 (10)	Terry Lynch	Racine	May 1, 2016	None
	Eva Arnold.	Beloit	May 1, 2017	None
	Barbara Bechtel	Brown Deer	May 1, 2017	None
	Tanya Meyer.	Gleason	May 1, 2017	None
	Michael Brooks[5]	Oshkosh	May 1, 2018	None
	James Surprise.	Wautoma	May 1, 2018	None
	Dale B. Taylor[5].	Eau Claire	May 1, 2020	None
*Agriculture, Trade and Consumer Protection, Board of Secs. 15.07 (1)(a), 15.07 (5)(d), 15.13	John Koepke	Oconomowoc	May 1, 2015	Not exc. $35 per day nor $1,000 per yr.
	Andre Diercks	Coloma	May 1, 2017	Not exc. $35 per day nor $1,000 per yr.
	Miranda Leis.	Cashton	May 1, 2017	Not exc. $35 per day nor $1,000 per yr.
	Mark Schleitwiler	Green Bay	May 1, 2017	Not exc. $35 per day nor $1,000 per yr.
	Dennis Badtke	Rosendale	May 1, 2019	Not exc. $35 per day nor $1,000 per yr.
	Nicole Hansen	Necedah	May 1, 2019	Not exc. $35 per day nor $1,000 per yr.
	Dean Strauss	Sheboygan Falls	May 1, 2019	Not exc. $35 per day nor $1,000 per yr.
	Paul Palmby	Janesville	May 1, 2021	Not exc. $35 per day nor $1,000 per yr.
	Douglas Wolf	Lancaster	May 1, 2021	Not exc. $35 per day nor $1,000 per yr.
*Agriculture, Trade and Consumer Protection, Dept. of, Secy. Secs. 15.05 (1)(d), 15.07 (1)	Ben Brancel	Madison	Pleas. of Gov.	Group 6
Alcohol and Other Drug Abuse, State Council on Secs. 14.017 (2), 15.09	Craig Harper	Whitefish Bay	Pleas. of Gov.	None
	Mark C. Seidl	Algoma	Pleas. of Gov.	None
	Michael Waupoose.	Madison	Pleas. of Gov.	None
	Rebecca Wigg-Ninham	Green Bay	Pleas. of Gov.	None
	Joyce O'Donnell	West Allis	July 1, 2017	None
	Mary Rasmussen.	Boyceville	July 1, 2017	None
	Scott A. Stokes.	Clintonville	July 1, 2017	None
	Norman Briggs.	Baraboo	July 1, 2019	None
	Sandy Hardie.	Eden	July 1, 2019	None
	Duncan M. Shrout	Milwaukee	July 1, 2019	None

Officers[1]	Name	Home Address[2]	Term Expires[3]	Salary or Per Diem[4]
*Architects, Landscape Architects, Professional Engineers, Designers and Professional Land Surveyors, Board of Secs. 15.08, 15.405 (2)	Steven Nielsen	Luck	July 1, 2009	$25 per day
	Scott Berg	Appleton	July 1, 2011	$25 per day
	Matthew Janiak	Mondovi	July 1, 2011	$25 per day
	Ruth Johnson	Madison	July 1, 2011	$25 per day
	Gary Kohlenberg	Oconomowoc	July 1, 2012	$25 per day
	Nancy Ragland	Madison	July 1, 2012	$25 per day
	Daniel Fedderly	Boyceville	July 1, 2013	$25 per day
	Thomas Gasperetti	Milwaukee	July 1, 2013	$25 per day
	Charles Kopplin	Milwaukee	July 1, 2013	$25 per day
	Rosheen Styczinski	Milwaukee	July 1, 2013	$25 per day
	Steven Tweed	Monona	July 1, 2013	$25 per day
	Bruce Bowden[5]	Dodgeville	July 1, 2014	$25 per day
	Mark Cook	Cambridge	July 1, 2014	$25 per day
	Michael Eberle	Middleton	July 1, 2014	$25 per day
	Steven Hook	Milwaukee	July 1, 2014	$25 per day
	James Mickowski	Stoughton	July 1, 2014	$25 per day
	Andrew Albright	Sun Prairie	July 1, 2015	$25 per day
	Matthew Fernholz[5]	Brookfield	July 1, 2015	$25 per day
	Andrew Gersich	Madison	July 1, 2015	$25 per day
	Kristine Cotharn[5]	Fitchburg	July 1, 2017	$25 per day
	Joseph Eberle	Pewaukee	July 1, 2017	$25 per day
	Steven Wagner	Burlington	July 1, 2017	$25 per day
	Mark Mayer[5]	Menasha	July 1, 2018	$25 per day
	5 vacancies			
*Artistic Endowment Foundation Chap. 247	Inactive			
Arts Board Sec. 15.445 (1)	Barbara Munson	Mosinee	May 1, 2011	None
	Susan Friebert	Milwaukee	May 1, 2012	None
	John Hendricks	Sparta	May 1, 2012	None
	Sharon Stewart	Washburn	May 1, 2013	None
	LaMoine MacLaughlin	Clayton	May 1, 2015	None
	Robert Wagner	Mequon	May 1, 2015	None
	Bruce Bernberg	Racine	May 1, 2016	None
	Ron Madich	La Pointe	May 1, 2016	None
	Kevin Miller	Fond du Lac	May 1, 2016	None
	Matthew Wallock	Madison	May 1, 2016	None
	Ann Brunner	Kewaunee	May 1, 2017	None
	Mary Gielow	Mequon	May 1, 2017	None
	Brian Kelsey	Fish Creek	May 1, 2017	None
	Frederick Schwertfeger	Wauwatosa	May 1, 2017	None
	Heather McDonell	Madison	May 1, 2018	None
*Athletic Trainers Affiliated Credentialing Board Sec. 15.406 (4)	Ryan Berry	Appleton	July 1, 2013	$25 per day
	Carolynn Leaman	Milwaukee	July 1, 2014	$25 per day
	James Nesbit	Phillips	July 1, 2014	$25 per day
	Kurt Fielding	Green Bay	July 1, 2015	$25 per day
	Shanyn C. Lancaster	Milwaukee	July 1, 2016	$25 per day
	Gregory Vergamini	Superior	July 1, 2016	$25 per day
*Auctioneer Board Sec. 15.405 (3)	Timothy Sweeney	Green Lake	May 1, 2012	$25 per day
	Ronald Polacek	Prairie du Sac	May 1, 2013	$25 per day
	Leonard Yoap	Peshtigo	May 1, 2014	$25 per day
	James Wenzler	Oak Creek	May 1, 2015	$25 per day
	Heather Berlinski	Oconomowoc	May 1, 2016	$25 per day
	Randy Stockwell	Dorchester	May 1, 2016	$25 per day
	Jerry Thiel	Chilton	May 1, 2018	$25 per day
*Banking Review Board Secs. 15.07 (1)(b) 1, 15.185 (1), 15.555 (1)	Thomas Spitz	Sun Prairie	May 1, 2016	$25 per day, not exc. $1,500 per yr.
	Douglas Farmer	La Crosse	May 1, 2017	$25 per day, not exc. $1,500 per yr.
	Robert C. Gorsuch	Fitchburg	May 1, 2018	$25 per day, not exc. $1,500 per yr.
	Debra R. Lins[5]	Prairie du Sac	May 1, 2019	$25 per day, not exc. $1,500 per yr.
	Thomas J. Pamperin[5]	Marion	May 1, 2020	$25 per day, not exc. $1,500 per yr.
*Bradley Center Sports and Entertainment Corporation, Bd. of Directors of the Sec. 232.03	Rolen L. Womack	Brown Deer	July 1, 2013	None
	Ted Kellner	Milwaukee	July 1, 2016	None
	Gary Sweeney	Milwaukee	July 1, 2016	None
	Ricardo Diaz	Milwaukee	July 1, 2017	None
	Patrick Lawton[5]	Oconomowoc	July 1, 2018	None
	Matthew Parlow[5]	Milwaukee	July 1, 2018	None
	Andrew Petzold	Mequon	July 1, 2018	None
	Michael Grebe	Milwaukee	July 1, 2020	None
	Jeffrey A. Joerres[5]	Milwaukee	July 1, 2010	None
	Sarah Zimmerman[5]	Milwaukee	July 1, 2020	None
Building Code Council, Commercial Sec. 15.407 (18)	Hunter Bohne	Avoca	July 1, 2015	None
	Michael F. Mamayek	Milwaukee	July 1, 2015	None
	Samuel Lawrence	Madison	July 1, 2016	None
	Corey Rockweiler	Rock Springs	July 1, 2016	None
	Peter Scheuerman	Plymouth	July 1, 2016	None
	Kevin Bierce	Waukesha	July 1, 2017	None
	David Enigl	Egg Harbor	July 1, 2017	None
	Steve Klessig	Brillion	July 1, 2017	None
	Irina Ragozin	Mequon	July 1, 2017	None
	Steven Howard	Waukesha	July 1, 2018	None

Officers[1]	Name	Home Address[2]	Term Expires[3]	Salary or Per Diem[4]
Building Commission Sec. 13.48 (2)	Robert Brandherm	Verona	Pleas. of Gov.	None
Building Inspector Review Board Sec. 15.405 (1m)	Martin Rifken	Madison	May 1, 2013	None
	James Micech	Jackson	May 1, 2015	None
Burial Sites Preservation Board Secs. 15.07 (5)(o), 15.705 (1)	Corina Williams	Oneida	July 1, 2010	$25 per day
	Robert Powless	Odanah	July 1, 2012	$25 per day
	Kathryn Eagan-Bruhy	Minocqua	July 1, 2013	$25 per day
	David Grignon	Keshena	July 1, 2014	$25 per day
	Cynthia Stiles	Rhinelander	July 1, 2014	$25 per day
	Jennifer Haas	Shorewood	July 1, 2015	$25 per day
*Cemetery Board Sec. 15.405 (3m)	Kathleen Cantu	Madison	July 1, 2012	$25 per day
	Cecelia Timmons	Madison	July 1, 2012	$25 per day
	Ed Greenfield	Green Bay	July 1, 2014	$25 per day
	Francis Groh	Appleton	July 1, 2016	$25 per day
	Clyde Rupnow	Watertown	July 1, 2016	$25 per day
	Patricia Grathen[5]	La Crosse	July 1, 2018	$25 per day
Child Abuse and Neglect Prevention Board Sec. 15.205 (4)	James Leonhart	Madison	May 1, 2011	None
	Barbara Knox	Cross Plains	May 1, 2013	None
	Jennifer Noyes	Madison	May 1, 2015	None
	Teri Zywicki	Milwaukee	May 1, 2015	None
	Kari Christenson	Onalaska	May 1, 2016	None
	Bernice C. Day	Madison	May 1, 2017	None
	Jeffrey Lamont	Wausau	May 1, 2017	None
	Sandra J. McCormick	La Crosse	May 1, 2017	None
	Jesus Mireles	Waukesha	May 1, 2017	None
	Notesong Thompson	Fitchburg	May 1, 2017	None
	Kimberly Simac	Eagle River	May 1, 2018	None
	Jon Hoelter	Madison	Pleas. of Gov.	None
*Children and Families, Dept. of, Secy. Secs. 15.20	Eloise Anderson	Madison	Pleas. of Gov.	Group 6
*Chiropractic Examining Board Secs. 15.08, 15.405 (5)	Michael McMahon[5]	Eau Claire	July 1, 2013	$25 per day
	Jodi Griffith	Cumberland	July 1, 2015	$25 per day
	Kelly Brown	Waukesha	July 1, 2016	$25 per day
	John Church[5]	Janesville	July 1, 2017	$25 per day
	Jeffrey Mackey	Middleton	July 1, 2017	$25 per day
	Patricia Schumacher	Marshfield	July 1, 2019	$25 per day
	vacancy			
*Circus World Museum Foundation Secs. 44.16 (2)	David Hoffman[5]	Black River Falls	Pleas. of Gov.	None
Claims Board Secs. 15.07 (2)(e), 15.105 (2)	Brian Hagedorn	Madison	Pleas. of Gov.	None
*College Savings Program Board 15.07 (1)(b), 15.105 (25m), 16.641	Patrick Sheehy	Mequon	May 1, 2013	None
	Robert Kieckhefer	Mequon	May 1, 2015	None
	William Oemichen	Madison	May 1, 2015	None
	John Wheeler[5]	Middleton	May 1, 2015	None
	Alberta Darling[5]	River Hills	May 1, 2017	None
	Kimberly Shaul	Cottage Grove	May 1, 2017	None
Controlled Substances Board Sec. 15.405 (5g)	Gunnar Larson	Milwaukee	May 1, 2016	None
	Alan Bloom	Fox Point	May 1, 2017	None
Conveyance Safety Code Council Sec. 15.407 (14)(a)	Jesse Kaysen	Madison	July 1, 2009	None
	Kenneth Smith	Madison	July 1, 2013	None
	Michael Dauck	Mazomanie	July 1, 2014	None
	Kelvin Nord	Slinger	July 1, 2014	None
	Adam Smith	Madison	July 1, 2014	None
	Brian Hornung	Middleton	July 1, 2015	None
	William Grubbs, Jr.	Brookfield	July 1, 2016	None
	Paul S. Rosenberg	Mequon	July 1, 2016	None
*Corrections, Dept. of, Secy. Secs. 15.05 (1)(a), 15.14	Edward F. Wall	Madison	Pleas. of Gov.	Group 6
*Cosmetology Examining Board Sec. 15.405 (17)	Kristin Allison	Monroe	July 1, 2016	None
	Vicky McNally	Edgerton	July 1, 2016	None
	Dianna Wachter	Madison	July 1, 2016	None
	Lori A. Paul[5]	Marinette	July 1, 2018	None
	Gail Sengbusch	Springbrook	July 1, 2018	None
	Denise Trokan[5]	Pewaukee	July 1, 2019	None
*Credit Union Review Board Secs. 15.07 (1)(b) 3, 15.07 (5)(s), 15.185 (7)(b)	Brian Prunty	Antigo	May 1, 2015	$25 per day, not exc. $1,500 per yr.
	J. David Christenson	Wausau	May 1, 2016	$25 per day, not exc. $1,500 per yr.
	Colleen Woggon	Kendall	May 1, 2017	$25 per day, not exc $1,500 per yr.
	Lisa M. Greco	Brookfield	May 1, 2018	$25 per day, not exc $1,500 per yr.
	Danny Wollin[5]	Green Bay	May 1, 2019	$25 per day, not exc. $1,500 per yr.
*Credit Unions, Office of, Director Sec. 15.185 (7)(a)	Suzanne T. Cowan	Oregon	Pleas. of Gov.	Group 3

Officers[1]	Name	Home Address[2]	Term Expires[3]	Salary or Per Diem[4]
Crematory Authority Council Sec. 15.407 (8)	Paul Haubrich	Bayside	July 1, 2008	None
	Kelly Coleman-Kohorn	Germantown	July 1, 2010	None
	Gary Langendorf	Racine	July 1, 2011	None
	Linda Reid	Whitewater	July 1, 2011	None
	Scott Brainard	Wausau	July 1, 2012	None
	Adam Casper	West Salem	July 1, 2012	None
	William Cress	Stoughton	July 1, 2013	None
Crime Victims Rights Bd. Sec. 15.255 (2)	Rebecca St. John	Madison	May 1, 2019	None
Criminal Penalties, Joint Review Committee on Sec. 13.525 (1)	Bradley Gehring	Appleton	Pleas. of Gov.	None
	Maury Straub	Port Washington	Pleas. of Gov.	None
Deaf and Hard of Hearing, Council for the Secs. 15.09 (1)(a), 15.197 (8)	Deborah A. Herczog	Stoddard	July 1, 2015	None
	Steven Smart	Waukesha	July 1, 2015	None
	Gary Ebben	Waukesha	July 1, 2017	None
	Nicole Everson	Eau Claire	July 1, 2017	None
	Tracy Haas	Watertown	July 1, 2017	None
	Karl Nollenberger	Oshkosh	July 1, 2017	None
	Justin Vollmar	Delavan	July 1, 2017	None
	Denise A. Johnson	Milwaukee	July 1, 2019	None
*Deferred Compensation Board Secs. 15.07 (1)(b) 14, 15.07 (5)(f), 15.165 (4)	Michael Gracz	Oregon	July 1, 2015	None
	Edward D. Main	Madison	July 1, 2015	None
	John F. Nelson	Middleton	July 1, 2017	None
	Arthur Zimmerman	Madison	July 1, 2017	None
	Gail Hanson	Oconomowoc	July 1, 2018	None
*Dentistry Examining Board Secs. 15.08, 15.405 (6)	William Anderson[5]	South Range	July 1, 2016	$25 per day
	Debra Beres[5]	Waukesha	July 1, 2016	$25 per day
	Leonardo Huck	Thiensville	July 1, 2017	$25 per day
	Timothy McConville	Verona	July 1, 2017	$25 per day
	Wendy Pietz	Milwaukee	July 1, 2017	$25 per day
	Mark Braden[5]	Lake Geneva	July 1, 2018	$25 per day
	Eileen Donohoo[5]	Milwaukee	July 1, 2018	$25 per day
	Lyndsay N. Knoell	Mount Pleasant	July 1, 2018	$25 per day
	Carrie Stempski[5]	Green Bay	July 1, 2018	$25 per day
	Beth Welter[5]	Prairie du Chien	July 1, 2018	$25 per day
	vacancy			
Developmental Disabilities, Bd. for People with Secs. 15.09 (1)(a), 15.105 (8)	Debra Glover	Milwaukee	July 1, 2007	$50 per day
	Susan Kay Nutter	La Crosse	July 1, 2007	$50 per day
	Roxanne M. Price	La Crosse	July 1, 2007	$50 per day
	Cindy Zellner-Ehlers	Sturgeon Bay	July 1, 2007	$50 per day
	Gerald Born	Madison	July 1, 2010	$50 per day
	Jackie Wenkman	Jefferson	July 1, 2010	$50 per day
	Joan Burns	Madison	July 1, 2011	$50 per day
	Kevin Fech	Cudahy	July 1, 2011	$50 per day
	Jonathan Donnelly	Madison	July 1, 2012	$50 per day
	Katherine Maloney Perhach	Whitefish Bay	July 1, 2012	$50 per day
	Andrew Gerbitz	Oconomowoc	July 1, 2014	$50 per day
	Robert Kuhr	Menasha	July 1, 2016	$50 per day
	David Pinno	New London	July 1, 2016	$50 per day
	L. Lynn Stansberry-Brusnahan	Shorewood	July 1, 2016	$50 per day
	Elsa Diaz Bautista	Milwaukee	July 1, 2017	$50 per day
	Pam Malin	De Pere	July 1, 2017	$50 per day
	Camille Nicklaus	Rothschild	July 1, 2017	$50 per day
	Judith Quigley	Elm Grove	July 1, 2017	$50 per day
	Sheila Thornton	Tomah	July 1, 2017	$50 per day
	Ramsey A. Lee	Hudson	July 1, 2018	$50 per day
	Patrick Young	Germantown	July 1, 2018	$50 per day
	Nathaniel Lentz	Reedsburg	July 1, 2019	$50 per day
*Dietitians Affiliated Credentialing Board Sec. 15.406 (2)	Scott Krueger	Shawano	July 1, 2015	$25 per day
	Gail Underbakke	Madison	July 1, 2015	$25 per day
	David Joe[5]	Madison	July 1, 2018	$25 per day
	Tara LaRowe	Madison	July 1, 2018	$25 per day
*Domestic Abuse, Council on Secs. 15.09 (1)(a), 15.207 (16)	Mariana Rodriguez	Milwaukee	July 1, 2011	None
	Gene Redhail	Oneida	July 1, 2012	None
	Maureen Funk	La Crosse	July 1, 2016	None
	Kara Schurman	Lac du Flambeau	July 1, 2016	None
	Shirley Armstrong	Stone Lake	July 1, 2016	None
	L. Kevin Hamberger	Franklin	July 1, 2017	None
	Jill Karofsky	Madison	July 1, 2017	None
	Patricia Ninmann[5]	Juneau	July 1, 2017	None
	Renee J. Schulz-Stangl	Marshfield	July 1, 2017	None
	Susan Sippel	Manitowoc	July 1, 2017	None
	Lena C. Taylor	Milwaukee	July 1, 2018	None
Dry Cleaner Environmental Response Council Sec. 15.347 (2)	Brett Donaldson	Neenah	July 1, 2015	None
	Jeanne Tarvin	Slinger	July 1, 2015	None
	Jim Fitzgerald	Mequon	July 1, 2016	None
	Richard W. Klinke	Cottage Grove	July 1, 2016	None
	Kevin D. Braden	Butler	July 1, 2017	None
	Thomas McKay	Thiensville	July 1, 2017	None

Officers[1]	Name	Home Address[2]	Term Expires[3]	Salary or Per Diem[4]
Dwelling Code Council, Uniform Secs. 15.09 (1)(a), 15.407 (10)	Thomas Doleschy	Muskego	July 1, 2010	None
	Michael Mueller	Greendale	July 1, 2010	None
	Jeffrey Bechard	Eau Claire	July 1, 2011	None
	Robert Jakel	Kaukauna	July 1, 2011	None
	Steven Levine	Madison	July 1, 2012	None
	Frank Opatik	Wausau	July 1, 2012	None
	David Dolan-Wallace	Green Bay	July 1, 2014	None
	Amy Bliss	Madison	July 1, 2015	None
	Michael A. Coello	New Berlin	July 1, 2015	None
	Jesse Jerabek	Casco	July 1, 2015	None
	Peter Krabbe	Seymour	July 1, 2015	None
	Brian Wert	Hudson	July 1, 2015	None
	Abe Degnan	DeForest	July 1, 2016	None
	Steven Gryboski	Green Bay	July 1, 2016	None
	Mike Marthaler	Eau Claire	July 1, 2016	None
	W. Scott Satula	New Berlin	July 1, 2016	None
	Mary L. Schroeder	Brookfield	July 1, 2016	None
*Economic Development Corp. Authority, Wis. Sec. 238.02 (1)	Daniel Ariens	Green Bay	Pleas. of Gov.	None
	Raymond Drager	Colfax	Pleas. of Gov.	None
	Nancy Hernandez	Milwaukee	Pleas. of Gov.	None
	Corey Hoze	Milwaukee	Pleas. of Gov.	None
	Lisa Mauer	Wauwatosa	Pleas. of Gov.	None
	Paul Radspinner	Madison	Pleas. of Gov.	None
*Economic Development Corp. Authority, Wis. Chief Exec. Officer Sec. 238.02 (3)	Reed Hall	Madison	Pleas. of Gov.	—[6]
Education Commission of the States Sec. 39.76	Jessica Doyle	Madison	Pleas. of Gov.	None
	Tony Evers	Madison	Pleas. of Gov.	None
	Tracie Happel	Onalaska	Pleas. of Gov.	None
	Bette Lang	Beloit	Pleas. of Gov.	None
	Demond Means	Mequon	Pleas. of Gov.	None
	John Reinemann	Middleton	Pleas. of Gov.	None
Educational Approval Board Sec. 15.945 (1)	Christy L. Brown	Bayside	Pleas. of Gov.	$25 per day
	Robert Hein	Janesville	Pleas. of Gov.	$25 per day
	Donald Madelung	Windsor	Pleas. of Gov.	$25 per day
	Jo Oyama-Miller	Monona	Pleas. of Gov.	$25 per day
	William Roden	Grafton	Pleas. of Gov.	$25 per day
	Katie Thiry	Prescott	Pleas. of Gov.	$25 per day
	Monica Williams	Appleton	Pleas. of Gov.	$25 per day
*Educational Communications Board Secs. 15.07 (1)(a) 5, 15.57	Diane Everson	Edgerton	May 1, 2013	None
	Karen Schroeder[5]	Birchwood	May 1, 2015	None
	Rolf Wegenke[5]	Sun Prairie	May 1, 2015	None
	Richard Lepping	Madison	May 1, 2017	None
	Eileen Littig	Green Bay	Pleas. of Gov.	None
Electronic Recording Council Sec. 15.107 (6)	Marcia Drouin-Howe	Monona	July 1, 2013	None
	John Wilcox	Eau Claire	July 1, 2013	None
	Lisa Petersen	Juneau	July 1, 2015	None
	Staci M. Hoffman	Jefferson	July 1, 2016	None
	Sharon Martin	West Bend	July 1, 2016	None
	Tyson Fettes	Burlington	July 1, 2018	None
	Jodi Helgeson	Friendship	July 1, 2018	None
*Emergency Management Div., Administrator of Sec. 15.313 (1)	Brian Satula	Oak Creek	Pleas. of Gov.	Group 1
Emergency Medical Services Board Sec. 15.195 (8)	Steven Bane	West Allis	May 1, 2015	None
	Mario Colella	Milwaukee	May 1, 2015	None
	Les Luder	Superior	May 1, 2015	None
	James Austad	Oshkosh	May 1, 2016	None
	Carrie Meier	Waunakee	May 1, 2016	None
	Steven Zils	Mequon	May 1, 2016	None
	Melinda R. Allen	Muskego	May 1, 2017	None
	Jerry R. Biggart	Milwaukee	May 1, 2017	None
	Mark C. Fredrickson	Hilbert	May 1, 2017	None
	Craig Nelson	Baldwin	May 1, 2017	None
	Gregory Neal West	Hartland	May 1, 2017	None
*Employee Trust Funds Board Secs. 15.07 (1)(a) 3, 15.07 (5)(f), 15.16 (1) (c)	Victor Shier	Kewaskum	May 1, 2017	None
Employment Relations, Office of, Dir. Sec. 15.105 (29)	Gregory L. Gracz	Madison	Pleas. of Gov.	Group 6
*Employment Relations Comn. Secs. 15.06 (1), 15.225 (2)	Rodney Pasch	Fond du Lac	March 1, 2017	Group 5
	James Daley	Oconomowoc	March 1, 2019	Group 5
	James Scott	Dousman	March 1, 2021	Group 5
Federal-State Relations Office, Director Sec. 16.548 (1)	Jen Jinks	Washington, D.C.	Pleas. of Gov.	Group 3
*Financial Institutions, Dept. of Secy. of Secs. 15.05 (1)(a), 15.18	Ray Allen	Madison	Pleas. of Gov.	Group 6

Officers[1]	Name	Home Address[2]	Term Expires[3]	Salary or Per Diem[4]
Forestry, Council on Sec. 15.347 (19)	R. Bruce Allison	Verona	Pleas. of Gov.	None
	Michael Bolton	Plover	Pleas. of Gov.	None
	Dennis G. Brown	Rhinelander	Pleas. of Gov.	None
	Troy Brown	Antigo	Pleas. of Gov.	None
	Randy Champeau	Rosholt	Pleas. of Gov.	None
	Matt Dallman	Tomahawk	Pleas. of Gov.	None
	Paul J. DeLong	Madison	Pleas. of Gov.	None
	Donald Friske	Merrill	Pleas. of Gov.	None
	James Heerey	New Auburn	Pleas. of Gov.	None
	Jeanne Higgins	Chequamegon	Pleas. of Gov.	None
	Thomas Hittle	Rhinelander	Pleas. of Gov.	None
	James Hoppe	Rhinelander	Pleas. of Gov.	None
	William J. Horvath	Stevens Point	Pleas. of Gov.	None
	Mary Hubler	Rice Lake	Pleas. of Gov.	None
	James Kerkman	Bangor	Pleas. of Gov.	None
	Kimberly Quast	Fond du Lac	Pleas. of Gov.	None
	Mark Rickenbach	Madison	Pleas. of Gov.	None
	Robert Rogers	Custer	Pleas. of Gov.	None
	Henry Schienebeck	Butternut	Pleas. of Gov.	None
	Jane Severt	Merrill	Pleas. of Gov.	None
	Jeffrey C. Stier	Madison	Pleas. of Gov.	None
	Paul Strong	Hazelhurst	Pleas. of Gov.	None
	Tom Tiffany	Hazelhurst	Pleas. of Gov.	None
	Kathleen Vinehout	Alma	Pleas. of Gov.	None
	Virgil Waugh	Milton	Pleas. of Gov.	None
	Richard Wedepohl	Madison	Pleas. of Gov.	None
*Fox River Navigational System Authority Sec. 237.02	Kathryn Curren	Suamico	July 1, 2016	None
	John Vette	Oshkosh	July 1, 2016	None
	H. Bruce Enke	Green Bay	July 1, 2017	None
	Jeffery Feldt	Kaukauna	July 1, 2017	None
	William Raaths	Menasha	July 1, 2018	None
	S. Timothy Rose	Appleton	July 1, 2018	None
*Funeral Directors Examining Board Secs. 15.08, 15.405 (16)	Kristen Piehl	Kenosha	July 1, 2014	$25 per day
	Thomas Bradley	Antigo	July 1, 2015	$25 per day
	Eric Lengell	Milwaukee	July 1, 2016	$25 per day
	Marla Michaelis	Jefferson	July 1, 2017	$25 per day
	Dean Stensberg	Middleton	July 1, 2017	$25 per day
	Marc A. Eernisse	Port Washington	July 1, 2018	$25 per day
*Geologists, Hydrologists and Soil Scientists, Examining Board of Professional Secs. 15.08, 15.405 (2m)	Patricia Trochlell	Blue Mounds	July 1, 2009	$25 per day
	Ruth Johnson	Madison	July 1, 2010	$25 per day
	John Hahn	Elm Grove	July 1, 2011	$25 per day
	Brenda Halminiak	Rhinelander	July 1, 2012	$25 per day
	Randall Hunt	Cross Plains	July 1, 2012	$25 per day
	Frederick Madison	Lodi	July 1, 2012	$25 per day
	Kenneth Bradbury	Madison	July 1, 2013	$25 per day
	William Mode	Neenah	July 1, 2013	$25 per day
	Richard Beilfuss	Baraboo	July 1, 2014	$25 per day
	James Robertson	Madison	July 1, 2014	$25 per day
	Stephanie Williams	Middleton	July 1, 2017	$25 per day
*Government Accountability Board Secs. 15.07 (1)(a) 2, 15.60	Thomas Barland	Eau Claire	May 1, 2015	None
	Harold Froehlich[5]	Appleton	May 1, 2016	None
	Timothy Vocke[5]	Rhinelander	May 1, 2017	None
	Gerald Nichol[5]	Madison	May 1, 2018	None
	Elsa Lamelas[5]	Shorewood	May 1, 2019	None
	John Franke[5]	Milwaukee	May 1, 2020	None
Great Lakes Comn. Sec. 14.78 (1)	Dean Haen	Green Bay	July 1, 2016	None
	Lynn Dufrane	Marinette	July 1, 2017	None
	Ken Johnson	Madison	Pleas. of Gov.	None
*Great Lakes Protection Fund Sec. 14.84	Richard Meeusen	Pewaukee	Jan. 9, 2015	None
	Kevin L. Shafer	Fox Point	Jan. 12, 2016	None
Groundwater Coordinating Council Secs. 15.09, 15.347 (13)	Stephen Diercks	Coloma	July 1, 2017	None
Group Insurance Board Secs. 15.07 (1)(b), 15.07 (5)(f), 15.165 (2)	Terri Carlson	Edgerton	May 1, 2017	$25 per day
	Herschel Day	Altoona	May 1, 2017	$25 per day
	Michael Farrell	Bristol	May 1, 2017	$25 per day
	Charles Grapentine	Madison	May 1, 2017	$25 per day
	Theodore Neitzke IV	Port Washington	May 1, 2017	$25 per day
	Nancy L. Thompson	Waterloo	May 1, 2017	$25 per day
	Jon Litscher	Beaver Dam	Pleas. of Gov.	None
*Health and Educational Facilities Authority, Wis. Sec. 231.02 (1)	Richard Canter	Milwaukee	June 30, 2015	None
	James Oppermann[5]	Brookfield	June 30, 2016	None
	Kevin Flaherty	Milwaukee	June 30, 2017	None
	Tim Size	Madison	June 30, 2018	None
	James Dietsche	De Pere	June 30, 2019	None
	Robert Van Meeteren[5]	Reedsburg	June 30, 2020	None
	Paul Mathews	Milwaukee	June 30, 2021	None
Health Care Liability Insurance Plan/Injured Patients and Families Compensation Fund Bd. of Governors Sec. 619.04 (3), 655.27 (2)	Dennis Conta	Milwaukee	May 1, 2010	None
	Christopher Flatter	Rothschild	May 1, 2015	None
	Susan Engler	Milwaukee	May 1, 2016	None
	Gregory Banaszynski	Fort Atkinson	May 1, 2017	None
	Carla Borda	Hubertus	May 1, 2018	None

Officers[1]	Name	Home Address[2]	Term Expires[3]	Salary or Per Diem[4]
*Health Services, Dept. of, Secy. Secs. 15.05 (1)(a), 15.19	Kitty Rhoades	Madison	Pleas. of Gov.	Group 9
*Hearing and Speech Examining Board Secs. 15.08, 15.405 (6m)	Melanie Blechl	Neenah	July 1, 2012	$25 per day
	Steven Klapperich	St. Cloud	July 1, 2015	$25 per day
	Mary Polenske	Sun Prairie	July 1, 2015	$25 per day
	Thomas Sather[5]	Eau Claire	July 1, 2015	$25 per day
	Doreen Jensen	Oshkosh	July 1, 2016	$25 per day
	Samuel P.. Gubbels[5]	Madison	July 1, 2017	$25 per day
	Barbara Johnson	De Pere	July 1, 2017	$25 per day
	Thomas Krier	Allenton	July 1, 2017	$25 per day
	Scott Larson	Onalaska	July 1, 2017	$25 per day
	Patricia Willis[5]	Waukesha	July 1, 2018	$25 per day
Higher Educational Aids Board Secs. 15.07 (1)(a) 1, 15.67 (1)	Steven DiSalvo	Fond du Lac	May 1, 2014	None
	Mary Jo Green	Nekoosa	May 1, 2015	None
	Darcy Paulson	Madison	May 1, 2015	None
	Timothy Rindahl	Arcadia	May 1, 2015	None
	Stephen D. Willett	Phillips	May 1, 2015	None
	Nathaniel Helm-Quest	Shiocton	May 1, 2016	None
	Steven Midthun	Greendale	May 1, 2016	None
	Kathleen Sahlhoff	Elk Mound	May 1, 2016	None
	Margaret A. Farrow	Pewaukee	May 1, 2017	None
	Benjamin Zellmer	Elm Grove	May 1, 2017	None
Higher Educational Aids Board, Exec. Secy. Sec. 39.29	John Reinemann	Madison	Pleas. of Gov.	Group 3
Highway Safety, Council on Secs. 15.09 (1)(a), 15.467 (3)	LaVerne Hermann	Waterloo	July 1, 2014	None
	John Corbin	Madison	July 1, 2015	None
	Stephen Fitzgerald	Madison	July 1, 2015	None
	Richard G. Van Boxtel	Oneida	July 1, 2015	None
	John Mesich	Waukesha	July 1, 2016	None
	Jeff Plale	South Milwaukee	July 1, 2016	None
	Gerald Powalisz	Manitowoc	July 1, 2016	None
	Steven Fernan	Milton	July 1, 2017	None
	Patrick Hughes	Milwaukee	July 1, 2018	None
	Kurt Schultz	Spring Green	July 1, 2018	None
Historic Preservation Review Board Sec. 15.705 (2)	Kelly Jackson	Lac du Flambeau	July 1, 2013	None
	Carol Johnson	Black Earth	July 1, 2015	None
	Neil Prendergast	Stevens Point	July 1, 2015	None
	Sissel Schroeder	Madison	July 1, 2015	None
	Anne Biebel	Cross Plains	July 1, 2016	None
	Bruce Block	Milwaukee	July 1, 2016	None
	Robert Gough	Eau Claire	July 1, 2016	None
	Kubet Luchterhand	Ellison Bay	July 1, 2016	None
	Carlen Hatala	Milwaukee	July 1, 2017	None
	Daniel J. Joyce	Kenosha	July 1, 2017	None
	Valentine Schute, Jr.	La Crosse	July 1, 2017	None
	Daniel J. Stephans	Madison	July 1, 2017	None
	Donna Zimmerman	Amherst Junction	July 1, 2017	None
	David V. Mollenhoff	Madison	July 1, 2018	None
	Paul Wolter	Baraboo	July 1, 2018	None
Historical Society Endowment Fund Council Secs. 15.09 (1)(a), 15.707 (3)	Inactive			
*Housing and Economic Development Authority, Wis. Sec. 234.02 (1)	Sue Shore	Wausau	Jan. 1, 2016	None
	McArthur Weddle	Milwaukee	Jan. 1, 2016	None
	Perry Armstrong	Madison	Jan. 1, 2018	None
	Bradley Guse	Arpin	Jan. 1, 2018	None
	Mark Hogan	Wauwatosa	Jan. 1, 2019	None
	John Horning	Pewaukee	Jan. 1, 2019	None
*Housing and Economic Development Authority, Wis., Executive Director Sec. 234.02 (3)	Wyman Winston	Madison	Jan. 3, 2015	Group 6
Information Technology Management Board Sec. 15.105 (28)	Carla Cross	Milwaukee	May 1, 2011	None
	Gina Frank	Madison	May 1, 2013	None
	Sean Dilweg	Madison	Pleas. of Gov.	None
	Lorrie Heinemann	Madison	Pleas. of Gov.	None
*Insurance, Commissioner of Secs. 15.06 (1)(b), (3)(a) 1, 15.06 (3)(b), 15.73	Ted Nickel	Madison	Pleas. of Gov.	Group 5
Interoperability Council Sec. 15.107 (18)	Melinda Allen	Juda	May 1, 2009	None
	Richard Van Boxtel	Oneida	May 1, 2012	None
	Steven Hansen	Racine	May 1, 2013	None
	Lynn Schubert	Burlington	May 1, 2013	None
	Jon Freund	Sun Prairie	May 1, 2015	None
	Matthew Joski	Kewaunee	May 1, 2015	None
	James Koleas	Milwaukee	May 1, 2015	None
	William Stolte	Grafton	May 1, 2015	None
	Bradley Wentlandt	Greenfield	May 1, 2017	None

Officers[1]	Name	Home Address[2]	Term Expires[3]	Salary or Per Diem[4]
Invasive Species Council Sec. 15.347 (18)	Charles Henriksen	Green Bay	July 1, 2012	None
	James Kerkman	Bangor	July 1, 2012	None
	Patricia Morton	Whitewater	July 1, 2014	None
	James Reinartz.	Saukville	July 1, 2015	None
	Thomas Bressner.	Madison	July 1, 2017	None
	Gregory Long	New Berlin	July 1, 2017	None
	Paul Schumacher.	Sturgeon Bay	July 1, 2017	None
	Kenneth F. Raffa	Madison	July 1, 2018	None
Investment and Local Impact Fund Board Sec. 15.435	Edward Brandis	Upson	May 1, 2015	None
	Kelly Klein.	Hurley	May 1, 2015	None
	David Pajula	Montreal	May 1, 2015	None
	Robert Walesewicz.	Hurley	May 1, 2016	None
	Rick Hermus	Crandon	May 1, 2016	None
	Leslie Kolesar	Saxon	May 1, 2018	None
	Emmer Schields, Jr.	Washburn	May 1, 2018	None
	Richard G. Chandler	Madison	Pleas. of Gov.	None
	Reed Hall	Madison	Pleas. of Gov.	None
	2 vacancies			
*Investment Board, State of Wis. Secs. 15.07 (1)(a) 4, 15.07 (2)(a), 15.07 (5)(a), 15.76	Thomas Boldt	Appleton	May 1, 2015	$50 per day
	Bruce Colburn	Milwaukee	May 1, 2015	$50 per day
	William H. Levit, Jr.	Milwaukee	May 1, 2015	$50 per day
	Norman Cummings	Brookfield	May 1, 2017	$50 per day
	Lon Roberts	Wausau	May 1, 2017	$50 per day
	David Stein[5]	Madison	May 1, 2017	
*Judicial Commission Sec. 757.83	Saied Assef.	Green Bay	Aug. 1, 2014	$25 per day
	Mark Barrette	Beaver Dam	Aug. 1, 2014	$25 per day
	Eileen Burnett	De Pere	Aug. 1, 2014	$25 per day
	William Cullinan.	New Berlin	Aug. 1, 2014	$25 per day
	Lynn Leazer	Verona	Aug. 1, 2015	$25 per day
Judicial Council Secs. 15.09 (1)(a), 758.13 (1)	Benjamin Pliskie	Brookfield	July 1, 2016	None
	Dennis Myers	Germantown	July 1, 2018	None
	Brad Schimel.	Waukesha	Pleas. of Gov.	None
*Kickapoo Reserve Management Board Secs. 15.07 (1)(b) 20, 15.07 (5)(y), 15.445 (2)	Senn Brown	Madison	May 1, 2012	$25 per day
	Tracy Littlejohn	La Crosse	May 1, 2012	$25 per day
	Adlai Mann	Black River Falls	May 1, 2013	$25 per day
	Paul Hayes	Westby	May 1, 2015	$25 per day
	Brandon Hysel	La Farge	May 1, 2015	$25 per day
	Susan C. Cushing	La Farge	May 1, 2016	$25 per day
	Dave M. Maxwell	Westby	May 1, 2016	$25 per day
	Alan Szepi	Norwalk	May 1, 2017	$25 per day
	Ronald M. Johnson	La Farge	May 1, 2017	$25 per day
	William L. Quackenbush . . .	Black River Falls	May 1, 2017	$25 per day
	Richard T. Wallin	Viroqua	May 1, 2017	$25 per day
*Labor and Industry Review Commission Secs. 15.06 (1)(a), 15.225 (1)	Laurie McCallum	Lodi	March 1, 2017	Group 5
	Clarence Jordahl	Middleton	March 1, 2019	Group 5
	David B. Falstad	Oconomowoc	March 1, 2021	Group 5
Labor and Management Council Secs. 15.09 (1)(a), 15.227 (17)	Inactive			
Laboratory of Hygiene Bd. Sec. 15.915 (2)	Barry Irmen	Edgerton	May 1, 2013	None
	Michael Ricker.	De Pere	May 1, 2013	None
	Ruth Etzel	Menomonee Falls	May 1, 2015	None
	James Morrison	Middleton	May 1, 2015	None
	Robert Corliss	Oregon	May 1, 2016	None
	Carrie Lewis	Milwaukee	May 1, 2016	None
	Jeffery Kindrai	Lancaster	May 1, 2017	None
Lake Michigan Commercial Fishing Board Sec. 15.345 (3)	Charles W. Henriksen	Baileys Harbor	Pleas. of Gov.	None
	Richard R. Johnson	Ellison Bay	Pleas. of Gov.	None
	Michael Le Clair	Two Rivers	Pleas. of Gov.	None
	Mark Maricque	Green Bay	Pleas. of Gov.	None
	Dan Pawlitzke	Two Rivers	Pleas. of Gov.	None
	Neil A. Schwarz	Sheboygan	Pleas. of Gov.	None
	Dean Swaer	Oconto	Pleas. of Gov.	None
Lake States Wood Utilization Consortium Sec. 26.37 (1)	Inactive			
Lake Superior Commercial Fishing Board Sec. 15.345 (2)	Jeff Bodin	Bayfield	Pleas. of Gov.	None
	Bill Damberg	Bayfield	Pleas. of Gov.	None
	Maurine Halvorson	Bayfield	Pleas. of Gov.	None
	Craig Hoopman	Bayfield	Pleas. of Gov.	None
	vacancy			
*Land and Water Conservation Bd. Secs. 15.07 (1)(b) 10, 15.07 (1)(cm), 15.07 (5)(h), 15.135 (4)(am)	Dennis Caneff	Madison	May 1, 2014	$25 per day
	Eric Birschbach[5]	Verona	May 1, 2015	$25 per day
	Mark Cupp.	Muscoda	May 1, 2016	$25 per day
	Lynn Harrison[5]	Elk Mound	May 1, 2019	$25 per day
	vacancy			

Officers[1]	Name	Home Address[2]	Term Expires[3]	Salary or Per Diem[4]
Law Enforcement Standards Board Sec. 15.255 (1)	Gary Cuskey	Spooner	May 1, 2014	None
	James Arts	Green Bay	May 1, 2015	None
	Jon Koch	Brussels	May 1, 2015	None
	Jean Galasinski	Trempealeau	May 1, 2016	None
	Laura Messner-Washer	Elkhorn	May 1, 2016	None
	Christopher Domagalski	Sheboygan	May 1, 2017	None
	Kim Gaffney	Oxford	May 1, 2017	None
	Jennifer Harper	Richland Center	May 1, 2017	None
	Anna Ruzinski	Richfield	May 1, 2018	None
	Michael Steffes	Rhinelander	May 1, 2018	None
	Joseph Collins	Two Rivers	May 1, 2019	None
	Nathan Henriksen	DeForest	May 1, 2019	None
Library and Network Development, Council on Secs. 15.09 (1)(a), 15.377 (6)	Michael Bahr	Germantown	July 1, 2013	None
	Ewa Barczyk	Milwaukee	July 1, 2013	None
	Bob Koechley	Fitchburg	July 1, 2013	None
	Kristi Williams	Cottage Grove	July 1, 2013	None
	Cara Cavin	Verona	July 1, 2014	None
	Patrick Wilkinson	Oshkosh	July 1, 2014	None
	Nita Burke	Darlington	July 1, 2015	None
	Kathy Pletcher	Denmark	July 1, 2015	None
	Emily Rogers	De Pere	July 1, 2015	None
	Therese Boyle	Burlington	July 1, 2016	None
	Laurie Freund	Waukesha	July 1, 2016	None
	James D. Trojanowski	Ashland	July 1, 2016	None
	Terrence Berres	Franklin	July 1, 2017	None
	Joshua Cowles	Fond du Lac	July 1, 2017	None
	Miriam Erickson	Fish Creek	July 1, 2017	None
	Thomas C. Kamenick	Saukville	July 1, 2018	None
	Douglas H. Lay	Suamico	July 1, 2018	None
	Bryan McCormick	Janesville	July 1, 2018	None
	Joan Robb	Green Bay	July 1, 2018	None
*Lower Fox River Remediation Authority Secs. 279.02	Gregory B. Conway	De Pere	June 30, 2011	None
	Patrick Schillinger	De Pere	June 30, 2011	None
	Robert Cowles	Green Bay	June 30, 2013	None
	Dave Hansen	Green Bay	June 30, 2013	None
	David Stegeman	Mequon	June 30, 2016	None
	James Wall	Green Bay	June 30, 2016	None
	vacancy			
Lower Wisconsin State Riverway Board Secs. 15.07 (1)(b) 15, 15.07 (5)(w), 15.445 (3)	Frederick Madison	Lodi	May 1, 2013	$25 per day
	George Arimond	La Crosse	May 1, 2014	$25 per day
	Ritchie Brown	Black River Falls	May 1, 2015	$25 per day
	Melody Moore	Mazomanie	May 1, 2015	$25 per day
	Gerald Dorscheid	Arena	May 1, 2016	$25 per day
	David O. Martin	Muscoda	May 1, 2016	$25 per day
	Don Greenwood	Spring Green	May 1, 2017	$25 per day
	Robert J. Leys	Prairie du Chien	May 1, 2017	$25 per day
	Robert Cary	Blue River	May 1, 2018	$25 per day
Madison Cultural Arts District Board Secs. 71.05 (1)(c) 6, 229.842	Carol Toussaint	Madison	July 1, 2014	None
	Diane Kay Ballweg	Madison	July 1, 2016	None
	Sheryl Theo	Madison	July 1, 2017	None
	Susan Hamblin	Madison	Pleas. of Gov.	None
Managed Forest Land Board Sec. 15.345 (6)	Eugene Roark	Madison	May 1, 2009	None
	Kevin Koth	Tomahawk	May 1, 2011	None
	Elroy Zemke	Rothschild	May 1, 2011	None
	Neil Paulson	Drummond	May 1, 2013	None
*Marriage and Family Therapy, Professional Counseling, and Social Work, Examining Board of Secs. 15.08 (1), 15.405 (7c)	Nancy Clark	Seymour	July 1, 2011	$25 per day
	Arlie Albrecht	Green Bay	July 1, 2012	$25 per day
	Darryl Wood	La Crosse	July 1, 2012	$25 per day
	Alice Hanson-Drew[5]	Shorewood	July 1, 2013	$25 per day
	Nick Smiar	Eau Claire	July 1, 2014	$25 per day
	Gregory Winkler	Janesville	July 1, 2015	$25 per day
	Elizabeth Krueger[5]	Waukesha	July 1, 2016	$25 per day
	Charles V. Lindsey	Sun Prairie	July 1, 2016	$25 per day
	Jennifer Anderson-Meger	La Crosse	July 1, 2017	$25 per day
	Peter Fabian	Madison	July 1, 2018	$25 per day
	Allison Gordon[5]	Waukesha	July 1, 2018	$25 per day
	Linda Pellmann[5]	Oconomowoc	July 1, 2018	$25 per day
*Massage Therapy and Bodywork Therapy Affiliated Credentialing Board Sec. 15.406 (6)	Carie Martin	Eau Claire	July 1, 2011	None
	Amy Connell	Madison	July 1, 2012	None
	Lillian Pounds	Milwaukee	July 1, 2012	None
	Xiping Zhou	Madison	July 1, 2012	None
	June Motzer	Hudson	July 1, 2013	None
	Barbara Yetter	Manitowoc	July 1, 2014	None
	Darlene Campo	La Crosse	July 1, 2018	None
	Elizabeth Krizenesky[5]	Neenah	July 1, 2018	None
	Carole Ostendorf[5]	West Allis	July 1, 2018	None
	Sharon Pollock	Hudson	July 1, 2018	None
	Mark Richardson	Cross Plains	July 1, 2018	None
	vacancy			

Officers[1]	Name	Home Address[2]	Term Expires[3]	Salary or Per Diem[4]
*Medical College of Wis., Inc., Board of Trustees of the Sec. 39.15	Linda Mellowes	Milwaukee	May 1, 2009	None
	Sheldon Lubar	Milwaukee	May 1, 2011	None
	Chris Abele	Milwaukee	May 1, 2012	None
	Cory Nettles	Milwaukee	May 1, 2013	None
	Edward Zore	Milwaukee	May 1, 2014	None
	Elizabeth Brenner	Waukesha	May 1, 2015	None
	Gregory Wesley	Milwaukee	May 1, 2015	None
	Curt S. Culver	Milwaukee	May 1, 2016	None
	3 vacancies			
Medical Education Review Committee Sec. 39.16	Inactive (7 members)			
*Medical Examining Board Secs. 15.08, 15.405 (7)	Suresh Misra	Mequon	July 1, 2015	$25 per day
	James Barr	Chetek	July 1, 2016	$25 per day
	Greg Collins[5]	De Pere	July 1, 2016	$25 per day
	Sridhar Vasudevan[5]	Belgium	July 1, 2016	$25 per day
	Timothy Westlake[5]	Hartland	July 1, 2016	$25 per day
	Russell Yale[5]	Fox Point	July 1, 2016	$25 per day
	Michael Phillips	Oconomowoc	July 1, 2017	$25 per day
	Timothy Swan	Marshfield	July 1, 2017	$25 per day
	Carolyn Ogland Vukich	Madison	July 1, 2017	$25 per day
	Mary Jo Capodice	Sheboygan	July 1, 2018	$25 per day
	Kenneth Simons	Mequon	July 1, 2018	$25 per day
	Robert Zondag[5]	Milwaukee	July 1, 2018	$25 per day
	Rodney Erickson[5]	Tomah	July 1, 2019	$25 per day
Mental Health, Council on Secs. 15.09 (1)(a), 15.197 (1)	Jackie Baldwin	St. Germain	July 1, 2012	None
	Jennifer Lowenberg	Verona	July 1, 2013	None
	Mishelle O'Shasky	Wisconsin Rapids	July 1, 2013	None
	Don Pirozzoli	Belleville	July 1, 2013	None
	Judith Wilcox	Madison	July 1, 2013	None
	Kathleen Enders	Waukesha	July 1, 2015	None
	Richard Immler		July 1, 2015	None
	David Stepien	Madison	July 1, 2015	None
	Masood Wasiullah	River Hills	July 1, 2015	None
	Donna Wrenn	Madison	July 1, 2015	None
	Julie-Anne Braun	Waterford	July 1, 2016	None
	Kathryn Bush	Madison	July 1, 2016	None
	Shel Gross	Madison	July 1, 2016	None
	Charlotte Matteson	New Berlin	July 1, 2016	None
	Walter D. Nencka	Hubertus	July 1, 2016	None
	Jodell L. Pelishek	Rice Lake	July 1, 2016	None
	Charles Szafir III	Milwaukee	July 1, 2016	None
	Matthew Strittmater	La Crosse	July 1, 2016	None
	Ann Catherine Veierstahler	Milwaukee	July 1, 2016	None
	Patrick Cork	Edgerton	July 1, 2017	None
	Edward F. Wall	Madison	July 1, 2017	None
	Joseph Worzella	Fall Creek	July 1, 2017	None
	Tracey Hassinger	Milwaukee	July 1, 2018	None
	Carol Keen	Greendale	July 1, 2018	None
*Merit Recruitment and Selection Administrator, Division of (OSER) Sec. 15.105 (29)(b)	Lynda Hanold[5]	Deerfield	March 26, 2019	Group 3
*Midwest Interstate Low-Level Radioactive Waste Comn., Wis. Commissioner Sec. 14.81 (1)	Stanley York	Middleton	Pleas. of Gov.	None
Midwest Interstate Passenger Rail Commission Sec. 14.86 (1)	Craig Anderson	Waukesha	Jan. 5, 2015	None
	Mark Gottlieb	Madison	Jan. 5, 2015	None
Midwestern Higher Educ. Comn. Sec. 14.90 (1)	Margaret A. Farrow	Pewaukee	July 1, 2016	None
	Rolf Wegenke	Sun Prairie	July 1, 2018	None
	Don Madelung	Madison	Pleas. of Gov.	None
Migrant Labor, Council on Secs. 15.09 (1)(a), 15.227 (8)	Enrique Figueroa	Milwaukee	July 1, 2012	None
	James Kern	Mondovi	July 1, 2012	None
	Teresa Tellez-Giron	Madison	July 1, 2013	None
	Steve Ziobro	Waterloo	July 1, 2013	None
	Kevin Magee	Madison	July 1, 2014	None
	Lupe Martinez	Milwaukee	July 1, 2015	None
	Richard W. Okray	Plover	July 1, 2015	None
	Liliana Parodi	Clinton	July 1, 2016	None
	Guadalupe Rendon	Racine	July 1, 2016	None
	John Bauknecht	Cross Plains	July 1, 2017	None
	Erica A. Kunze	Star Prairie	July 1, 2017	None
Military and State Relations, Council on Sec. 14.017 (4)	Jamie Aulik	Manitowoc	Pleas. of Gov.	None
	Linda Fournier	Sparta	Pleas. of Gov.	None
	Larry Olson	Madison	Pleas. of Gov.	None

Officers[1]	Name	Home Address[2]	Term Expires[3]	Salary or Per Diem[4]
Milwaukee Child Welfare Partnership Council Secs. 15.09 (1)(a), 15.207 (24)	Marshall Murray	Wauwatosa	July 1, 2013	None
	Linda Davis	Thiensville	July 1, 2015	None
	Kimberly Kampschroer	Milwaukee	July 1, 2015	None
	Earnestine Willis	Milwaukee	July 1, 2015	None
	Christine Holmes	Fox Point	July 1, 2016	None
	Tony Shields	Whitefish Bay	July 1, 2016	None
	Mary Triggiano	Wauwatosa	July 1, 2016	None
	B. Thomas Wanta	Milwaukee	July 1, 2016	None
	Colleen M. Ellingson	Milwaukee	July 1, 2017	None
	Susan Gadacz	Franklin	July 1, 2017	None
	Mallory O'Brien	Shorewood	July 1, 2017	None
	Sara Purtell Scullen	Wauwatosa	July 1, 2017	None
	Deanna Alexander	Milwaukee	July 1, 2018	None
	Willie Johnson, Jr.	Milwaukee	July 1, 2018	None
	Steve F. Taylor	Milwaukee	July 1, 2018	None
Milwaukee River Revitalization Council Secs. 15.09 (1)(a), 15.347 (15)	Richard Flood	Cedarburg	July 1, 2008	None
	Jon Richards	Milwaukee	July 1, 2009	None
	Cheryl Brickman	Mequon	July 1, 2010	None
	Raymond Krueger	Milwaukee	July 1, 2010	None
	Christine Nuernberg	Mequon	July 1, 2010	None
	Nancy Frank	Elkhorn	July 1, 2011	None
	Ronald Stadler	Cedarburg	July 1, 2011	None
	Caroline Icks Torinus	West Bend	July 1, 2011	None
	Dan Small	Belgium	July 1, 2012	None
	Christopher Svoboda	Milwaukee	July 1, 2012	None
	vacancy			
Mississippi River Parkway Commission Sec. 14.85 (1)(a)	Frank Fiorenza	Potosi	Feb. 1, 2012	None
	Maynard Cox	De Soto	Feb. 1, 2016	None
	Dennis Donath	Prescott	Feb. 1, 2016	None
	Jean Galasinski	Trempealeau	Feb. 1, 2016	None
	Joachim Kostrau	Bagley	Feb. 1, 2016	None
	Alan Lorenz	La Crosse	Feb. 1, 2016	None
	Robert Miller	Alma	Feb. 1, 2016	None
	Sherry Quamme	Ferryville	Feb. 1, 2016	None
	David Smith	Pepin	Feb. 1, 2016	None
Multifamily Dwelling Code Council Secs. 15.09 (1)(a), 15.407 (12)	Korinne Schneider	Milwaukee	July 1, 2007	None
	Michael Morey	Madison	July 1, 2008	None
	Kraig Biefeld	Ixonia	July 1, 2011	None
	Edward Gray	Kenosha	July 1, 2011	None
	Jeffery Brohmer	La Crosse	July 1, 2012	None
	Beth Gonnering	Kenosha	July 1, 2012	None
	David Nitz	Berlin	July 1, 2012	None
	Mark Scott	Pewaukee	July 1, 2012	None
	James Klett	Milwaukee	July 1, 2013	None
	Kevin Wipperfurth	McFarland	July 1, 2013	None
	Scott Burkart	Eau Claire	July 1, 2014	None
	Peter Scheuerman	Plymouth	July 1, 2014	None
	3 vacancies			
National and Community Service Board Sec. 15.105 (24)	Larry Kleinsteiber	Madison	May 1, 2008	None
	Maia Pearson	Madison	May 1, 2010	None
	Martha Kerner	Madison	May 1, 2012	None
	Thi Le	Madison	May 1, 2013	None
	Sondra LeGrand	La Crosse	May 1, 2013	None
	Scott Fromader	Madison	May 1, 2014	None
	Sue Grady	Madison	May 1, 2014	None
	Mark Mueller	Lake Mills	May 1, 2014	None
	Bob Guenther	Sheboygan	May 1, 2015	None
	Margaret Moore	Whitefish Bay	May 1, 2015	None
	Donald P. Dunbar	Madison	May 1, 2016	None
	Anthony F. Hallman	Three Lakes	May 1, 2016	None
	Kate Jaeger	Milwaukee	May 1, 2016	None
	Christine Beatty	Madison	May 1, 2017	None
	Lisa Delmore	Wisconsin Dells	May 1, 2017	None
	Robert Griffith	Kenosha	May 1, 2017	None
	Kathleen Groat	Appleton	May 1, 2017	None
	James M. Langdon	Madison	May 1, 2017	None
	Amy McDowell	Madison	May 1, 2017	None
	John Scocos	Madison	May 1, 2017	None
	Paula Horning	Pewaukee	May 1, 2018	None
	Angela Kringle	Shawano	May 1, 2018	None
	India McCanse	Milwaukee	Pleas. of Gov.	None
*Natural Resources, Dept. of, Secy. Sec. 15.05 (1)(c)	Cathy Stepp	Madison	Pleas. of Gov.	Group 7
*Natural Resources Board Secs. 15.07 (1)(a), 15.34	William Bruins	Waupun	May 1, 2017	None
	Terry Hilgenberg	Shawano	May 1, 2017	None
	Gregory Kazmierski	Mukwonago	May 1, 2017	None
	Preston D. Cole	Milwaukee	May 1, 2019	None
	Gary Zimmer	Laona	May 1, 2019	None
	Julie Anderson	Oak Creek	May 1, 2021	None
	Frederick Prehn[5]	Wausau	May 1, 2021	None

Officers[1]	Name	Home Address[2]	Term Expires[3]	Salary or Per Diem[4]
Nonmotorized Recreation and Transportation Trails Council Sec. 15.347 (20)	Rod Bartlow	Slinger	Pleas. of Gov.	None
	William Hauda	Dodgeville	Pleas. of Gov.	None
	Dana Johnson	Waukesha	Pleas. of Gov.	None
	Anne Murphy	Poynette	Pleas. of Gov.	None
	Joel Patenaude	Middleton	Pleas. of Gov.	None
	Debbie Peterson	Balsam Lake	Pleas. of Gov.	None
	David Phillips	Madison	Pleas. of Gov.	None
	Geoffrey Snudden	Green Bay	Pleas. of Gov.	None
	Blake Theisen	Madison	Pleas. of Gov.	None
	Ned Zuelsdorff	Madison	Pleas. of Gov.	None
*Nursing, Board of Secs. 15.01 (7), 15.08, 15.405 (7g)	Maria Joseph	Madison	July 1, 2013	$25 per day
	Julie Ellis	New Berlin	July 1, 2015	$25 per day
	Jeffrey Miller[5]	Cedarburg	July 1, 2016	$25 per day
	Luann Skarlupka	De Pere	July 1, 2017	$25 per day
	Peter Kallio[5]	Muskego	July 1, 2018	$25 per day
	Sheryl Krause	Cottage Grove	July 1, 2018	$25 per day
	Cheryl Streeter	Van Dyne	July 1, 2018	$25 per day
	Paul Abegglen	Waukesha	July 1, 2019	$25 per day
	Lillian Nolan	Fond du Lac	July 1, 2019	$25 per day
*Nursing Home Administrator Examining Board Secs. 15.08, 15.405 (7m)	Susan Kinast-Porter	Monroe	July 1, 2009	$25 per day
	Kenneth Arneson	Oshkosh	July 1, 2010	$25 per day
	Loreli Dickinson	Oconto	July 1, 2011	$25 per day
	Stefanie Carton[5]	Milwaukee	July 1, 2015	$25 per day
	Lori Koeppel	Birnamwood	July 1, 2015	$25 per day
	Patrick Shaughnessy[5]	Greendale	July 1, 2015	$25 per day
	Charles Hawkins[5]	Marinette	July 1, 2017	$25 per day
	Kate Bertram	Wauwatosa	July 1, 2018	$25 per day
	Timothy Conroy	Madison	July 1, 2018	$25 per day
*Occupational Therapists Affiliated Credentialing Board Sec. 15.406 (5)	David Cooper	Slinger	July 1, 2011	$25 per day
	Dorothy Olson	Appleton	July 1, 2011	$25 per day
	Brian Holmquist	Madison	July 1, 2013	$25 per day
	Corliss Rice	Milwaukee	July 1, 2013	$25 per day
	Laura O'Brien	Cottage Grove	July 1, 2015	$25 per day
	Gaye Meyer	Stoughton	July 1, 2018	$25 per day
	Amy Summers	Cleveland	July 1, 2018	$25 per day
Off-Road Vehicle Council Sec. 15.347 (9)	Adam Harden	Sheboygan	March 1, 2015	None
	Rob McConnell	Reedsburg	March 1, 2015	None
	Bryan T. Much	Oconomowoc	March 1, 2016	None
	Ernest Pulvermacher	Princeton	March 1, 2016	None
	William E. Schumann	Manitowish Waters	March 1, 2016	None
	David Traczyk	Hurley	March 1, 2017	None
	James Wisneski	Mountain	March 1, 2017	None
Offender Reentry, Council on Sec. 15.145 (5)	Melinda Danforth	Oneida	July 1, 2011	None
	Jerry Hancock	Madison	July 1, 2011	None
	Janine Geske	Milwaukee	July 1, 2012	None
	Chuck Brendel	Sheboygan	July 1, 2014	None
	John Chisholm	Milwaukee	July 1, 2014	None
	Robert Pedersen	Menasha	July 1, 2014	None
	Michael Tobin	Madison	July 1, 2014	None
	Arline Hillestad	Stevens Point	July 1, 2015	None
	Mark Podoll	Berlin	July 1, 2015	None
	Jason Witt	Onalaska	July 1, 2015	None
*Optometry Examining Bd. Secs. 15.08, 15.405 (8)	Swaminat Balachandran	Verona	July 1, 2010	$25 per day
	Ann Meier Carli	Green Bay	July 1, 2014	$25 per day
	Brian Hammes	Fond du Lac	July 1, 2015	$25 per day
	Mark Jinkins[5]	Sturgeon Bay	July 1, 2016	$25 per day
	Robert Schulz	Appleton	July 1, 2016	$25 per day
	Victor Connors	Lodi	July 1, 2017	$25 per day
	Richard L. Foss	La Crosse	July 1, 2017	$25 per day
*Parole Commission, Chairperson Secs. 15.145 (1), 17.07 (3m)	Dean Stensberg	Middleton	March 1, 2017	Group 2
Perfusionists Examining Council Sec. 15.407 (2m)	David Cobb	Madison	July 1, 2010	$25 per day
*Pharmacy Examining Board Secs. 15.08, 15.405 (9)	Suzette Renwick	La Crosse	July 1, 2012	$25 per day
	Franklin LaDien[5]	Menomonee Falls	July 1, 2016	$25 per day
	Kristi Sullivan	Fitchburg	July 1, 2016	$25 per day
	Philip Trapskin	Fitchburg	July 1, 2017	$25 per day
	Cathy Winters	Wausau	July 1, 2017	$25 per day
	Terry K. Maves	Appleton	July 1, 2018	$25 per day
	Thaddeus Schumacher	Fitchburg	July 1, 2019	$25 per day
	vacancy			
Physical Disabilities, Council on Secs. 15.09 (1)(a), 15.197 (4)	Sandra Stokes	Green Bay	July 1, 2010	None
	Jeffrey Fox	Gordon	July 1, 2011	None
	Jon Baltmanis	Waupaca	July 1, 2012	None
	Lewis Tyler	Brookfield	July 1, 2013	None
	Charles Vandenplas	Clintonville	July 1, 2013	None
	John Meissner	Little Chute	July 1, 2015	None
	Joey Torkelson	Delavan	July 1, 2015	None
	Karen E. Secor	Montreal	July 1, 2016	None
	Joanne Zimmerman	Bayside	July 1, 2016	None
	Noah Hershkowitz	Madison	July 1, 2016	None
	Benjamin Barrettt	Trego	July 1, 2016	None
	Michael Kindschi	Cottage Grove	July 1, 2017	None
	Roberto Escamilla II	Cudahy	July 1, 2018	None
	Jon Hoelter	Madison	Pleas. of Gov.	None

Officers[1]	Name	Home Address[2]	Term Expires[3]	Salary or Per Diem[4]
*Physical Therapy Examining Board Sec. 15.405 (7r)	Shari Berry	Tomah	July 1, 2016	$25 per day
	Lori Dominiczak	Brown Deer	July 1, 2017	$25 per day
	Thomas Murphy	De Pere	July 1, 2017	$25 per day
	Sarah Olson	Readstown	July 1, 2017	$25 per day
	John Greany[5]	La Crosse	July 1, 2019	$25 per day
Physician Assistants, Council on Secs. 15.08, 15.407 (2)	Mary Pangman Schmitt[5]	Waterford	July 1, 2008	None
*Podiatry Affiliated Credentialing Board Secs. 15.406 (3)	Gary Brown	Kenosha	July 1, 2014	$25 per day
	Jeffery Giesking[5]	Menomonie	July 1, 2016	$25 per day
	Thomas Komp[5]	Suamico	July 1, 2017	$25 per day
	William W. Weis[5]	Franklin	July 1, 2019	$25 per day
*Prison Industries Board Secs. 15.07 (1)(b) 12, 15.145 (2)	Lyle Balistreri	Wauwatosa	May 1, 2008	None
	James Langdon	DeForest	May 1, 2011	None
	Jose Carrillo	Janesville	May 1, 2014	None
	Tracey Isensee	Black River Falls	May 1, 2014	None
	Helen McCain	Madison	May 1, 2015	None
	Bill Smith	Madison	May 1, 2015	None
	Edward F. Wall	Windsor	May 1, 2015	None
	Bernie Spiegel[5]	Oregon	May 1, 2016	None
	James Jackson[5]	Waukesha	May 1, 2019	None
*Psychology Examining Board Secs. 15.08, 15.405 (10m)	Teresa Rose	Hazelhurst	July 1, 2012	$25 per day
	Marcus P. Desmonde	Colfax	July 1, 2017	$25 per day
	Rebecca Anderson[5]	Waukesha	July 1, 2018	$25 per day
	David Thompson	Burlington	July 1, 2018	$25 per day
	Daniel Schroeder[5]	Hartland	July 1, 2019	$25 per day
	vacancy			
*Public Defender Board Secs. 15.07 (1)(a), 15.78	Joe Morales	Racine	May 1, 2012	None
	James Brennan	Milwaukee	May 1, 2013	None
	Ellen Thorn	Sparta	May 1, 2013	None
	David Coon	Brookfield	May 1, 2015	None
	Mai N. Xiong	Kronenwetter	May 1, 2015	None
	Regina Dunkin	Beloit	May 1, 2016	None
	Daniel M. Berkos	Mauston	May 1, 2017	None
	John J. Hogan	Rhinelander	May 1, 2017	None
	Michael Maxwell	Hartland	May 1, 2017	None
Public Health Council Sec. 15.197 (13)	A. Charles Post	Milwaukee	July 1, 2011	None
	Mark Villalpando	Sturtevant	July 1, 2011	None
	Amy Bremel	Fish Creek	July 1, 2013	None
	Corazon Loteyro	Mercer	July 1, 2013	None
	Gretchen Sampson	Balsam Lake	July 1, 2013	None
	James Sanders	Milwaukee	July 1, 2013	None
	Tina Mason	Menomonee Falls	July 1, 2014	None
	Jason Shrader	Chili	July 1, 2014	None
	Bridget Clementi	Waukesha	July 1, 2015	None
	Dale Hippensteel	Sheboygan	July 1, 2015	None
	Robert Leischow	Marshfield	July 1, 2015	None
	Stephanie Schultz	Green Bay	July 1, 2015	None
	Joan Theurer	Wausau	July 1, 2015	None
	Thai Vue	Onalaska	July 1, 2015	None
	William Keeton	Oconomowoc	July 1, 2016	None
	Sandra Mahkorn	Milwaukee	July 1, 2016	None
	Darlene Weis	Pewaukee	July 1, 2016	None
	Terry Brandenburg	West Allis	July 1, 2017	None
	Mary Dorn	De Pere	July 1, 2017	None
	Gary D. Gilmore	La Crosse	July 1, 2017	None
	Alan Schwartzstein	Oregon	July 1, 2017	None
	Michael Wallace	Fort Atkinson	July 1, 2017	None
	Eric Krawczyk	Green Bay	July 1, 2018	None
Public Records Board Sec. 15.105 (4)	Carl Buesing	Sheboygan	Pleas. of Gov.	None
	Carol Hemersbach	Greenwood	Pleas. of Gov.	None
	Scott Kowalski	Madison	Pleas. of Gov.	None
	Sandra Rudd	Pardeeville	Pleas. of Gov.	None
	Peter Sorce	Germantown	Pleas. of Gov.	None
*Public Service Commission Secs. 15.06 (1), 15.79	Phil Montgomery	Green Bay	March 1, 2017	Group 5
	Ellen Nowak[5]	Mequon	March 1, 2019	Group 5
	Michael Huebsch	West Salem	March 1, 2021	Group 5
*Radiography Examining Bd. Sec. 15.405 (7e)	James Lemerond	Cleveland	May 1, 2014	None
	Gregg Bogost	Madison	May 1, 2015	None
	Tracy Marshall	Muskego	May 1, 2016	None
	Susan Sanson[5]	Greenfield	May 1, 2016	None
	Donald Borst[5]	Little Suamico	July 1, 2017	None
	2 vacancies			
*Railroads, Commissioner of Secs. 15.06 (1)(ar), 15.795 (1)	Jeff Plale	South Milwaukee	March 1, 2017	Group 5
*Real Estate Appraisers Board Secs. 15.07 (1)(b) 17, 15.07 (1)(cm), 15.07 (5)(x), 15.405 (10r)	Henry F. Simon	Middleton	May 1, 2009	$25 per day
	Marla Britton	Westby	May 1, 2011	$25 per day
	Jose Perez	Milwaukee	May 1, 2011	$25 per day
	Scott Brunner	Wauwatosa	May 1, 2016	$25 per day
	Carl Clementi	Hartland	May 1, 2016	$25 per day
	Thomas Kneesel	Pleasant Prairie	May 1, 2018	$25 per day
	Lawrence Nicholson	Delafield	May 1, 2018	$25 per day

Officers[1]	Name	Home Address[2]	Term Expires[3]	Salary or Per Diem[4]
Real Estate Curriculum and Examinations, Council on Secs. 15.09 (1)(a), 15.407 (5)	Lawrence Sager	Madison	July 1, 2004	None
	Paul G. Hoffman	Waukesha	July 1, 2006	None
	Peter Sveum	Stoughton	July 1, 2006	None
	Barbara McGill	Waukesha	July 1, 2010	None
	Casey Clickner	Franklin	July 1, 2015	None
	Kathryne Kuhl	Madison	July 1, 2015	None
	Robert Larson	Wales	July 1, 2015	None
	Robert Blakely	Beloit	July 1, 2016	None
	Kathy Zimmermann	Lake Mills	July 1, 2016	None
*Real Estate Examining Board Sec. 15.405 (11m)	Dennis Pierce	Kenosha	July 1, 2013	$25 per day
	Stephen Beers[5]	Fontana	July 1, 2014	$25 per day
	Marie Hetzer	Sun Prairie	July 1, 2016	$25 per day
	Kitty Jedwabny[5]	Keshena	July 1, 2017	$25 per day
	Randal Savaglio	Racine	July 1, 2017	$25 per day
	Brian McGrath[5]	New Berlin	July 1, 2018	$25 per day
	Michael J. Mulleady	Minocqua	July 1, 2018	$25 per day
Recycling, Council on Secs. 15.09 (1)(b), 15.347 (17)	James Birmingham	Greendale	Jan. 5, 2015	None
	Neil Peters-Michaud	Middleton	Jan. 5, 2015	None
	Gary Harter	La Crosse	Jan. 5, 2019	None
	George Hayducsko	Elk Mound	Jan. 5, 2019	None
	Joseph Liebau	Glendale	Jan. 5, 2019	None
	Heidi Woelfel	Hubertus	Jan. 5, 2019	None
	Jeff Zillich	Stevens Point	Jan. 5, 2019	None
Respiratory Care Practitioners Examining Council Secs. 15.08, 15.407 (1m)	vacancy			
Retirement Board, Wis. Secs. 15.07 (1)(a), 15.165 (3)(b)	John David	Watertown	May 1, 2008	$25 per day
	Wayne E. Koessl	Kenosha	May 1, 2009	$25 per day
	Herbert Stinski	Milton	May 1, 2012	$25 per day
	Jamie Aulik	Manitowoc	May 1, 2013	$25 per day
	Mary Von Ruden	Sparta	May 1, 2013	$25 per day
	Steven Wilding	Oak Creek	May 1, 2016	$25 per day
	2 vacancies			
Retirement Systems, Jt. Survey Com. on Sec. 13.50 (1)(c)	Tim Pederson	Hartland	Feb. 14, 2015	None
*Revenue, Dept. of, Secy. Secs. 15.05 (1)(a), 15.43	Rick Chandler	Madison	Pleas. of Gov.	Group 7
*Rural Health Development Council Sec. 15.917 (1)	Erica Hoven	Westby	July 1, 2009	None
	Linda L. McFarlin	Friendship	July 1, 2009	None
	Byron Crouse	Madison	July 1, 2012	None
	Tim Size	Sauk City	July 1, 2013	None
	Charlie Walker	Chippewa Falls	July 1, 2014	None
	Jeremy Normington-Slay	Friendship	July 1, 2015	None
	Syed Ahmed	Brookfield	July 1, 2016	None
	James O'Keefe	Mauston	July 1, 2016	None
	Blane Christman	Chippewa Falls	July 1, 2017	None
	Jacalyn Szehner	Plover	July 1, 2018	None
	3 vacancies			
*Safety and Professional Services, Dept. of, Secy. Secs. 15.05 (1)(a), 15.40	Dave Ross	Madison	Pleas. of Gov.	Group 4
*Savings Institutions Review Board Sec. 15.185 (3)	Paul Adamski	Stevens Point	May 1, 2017	$10 per day
	Charles Schmalz	Appleton	May 1, 2017	$10 per day
	George Gary	Milwaukee	May 1, 2019	$10 per day
	Robert W. Holmes[5]	Tomah	May 1, 2019	$10 per day
	James Olson	Appleton	May 1, 2019	$10 per day
*Sign Language Interpreter Council Sec. 15.407 (9)(a)	Debra Gorra Barash	Bayside	July 1, 2014	None
	Carlos Jaramillo	Madison	July 1, 2014	None
	Joel Mankowski	Greenfield	July 1, 2014	None
	Faye Jordan Peters	Appleton	July 1, 2014	None
	Joseph Riggio	Madison	July 1, 2014	None
	Steven Smart	Waukesha	July 1, 2014	None
	Christopher Woodfill	Delavan	July 1, 2014	None
Small Business Environmental Council Secs. 15.09 (1)(a), 15.347 (8)	Amy Litscher	Lake Mills	July 1, 2014	None
	Sharon Klinger-Kingsley	Fort Atkinson	July 1, 2015	None
	John Tripoli	Milwaukee	July 1, 2016	None
Small Business Regulatory Review Board Sec. 15.105 (33)	James Ring	Madison	May 1, 2014	None
	Kimberly Vele	Bowler	May 1, 2014	None
	Thomas Wulf	Sturgeon Bay	May 1, 2014	None
	Steven Davis	Oshkosh	May 1, 2015	None
	Erich Korth	Neenah	May 1, 2015	None
	Guy Wood	New Auburn	May 1, 2015	None

Officers[1]	Name	Home Address[2]	Term Expires[3]	Salary or Per Diem[4]
*Snowmobile Recreational Council Secs. 15.09 (1)(a), 15.347 (7)	Thomas Chwala[5]	Lake Mills	July 1, 2015	None
	Beverly A. Dittmar	Eagle River	July 1, 2016	None
	Gary Hilgendorf	Tomahawk	July 1, 2016	None
	Mathias Harter	La Crosse	July 1, 2016	None
	Michael Holden	Sheboygan Falls	July 1, 2016	None
	Steve Moran	Tomahawk	July 1, 2016	None
	Daniel Timmerman	Kieler	July 1, 2016	None
	Samuel J. Landes[5]	Dane	July 1, 2017	None
	Robert B. Lang[5]	Cable	July 1, 2017	None
	Andrew F. Malecki, Jr.[5]	Green Bay	July 1, 2017	None
	David Newman[5]	Unity	July 1, 2017	None
	Michelle Voight	Spooner	July 1, 2017	None
	Larry D. Erickson[5]	Hurley	July 1, 2018	None
	Dale Mayo[5]	Conover	July 1, 2018	None
	Lee Van Zeeland[5]	Appleton	July 1, 2018	None
*Southeast Wis. Professional Baseball Park Dist. Board Sec. 229.66 (2)	Erik Johnson[5]	Madison	July 1, 2015	None
	Tracey Klein	Brookfield	July 1, 2015	None
	Kristine O'Meara[5]	West Bend	July 1, 2015	None
	Don Smiley	Milwaukee	July 1, 2015	None
	William L. McReynolds[5]	Racine	July 1, 2017	None
	Jim Ott[5]	Mequon	July 1, 2019	None
Sporting Heritage Council Sec. 15.347 (21)	William Torhorst	Oregon	May 1, 2016	None
State Capitol and Executive Residence Board Sec. 15.105 (5)	Jay Fernholz	Holmen	May 1, 2015	None
	Arlan Kay	Madison	May 1, 2015	None
	Kathryn Neitzel	Verona	May 1, 2017	None
	Marijo Reed	Oconomowoc	May 1, 2017	None
	Lauren McManus Brown	Fitchburg	May 1, 2019	None
	Ronald L. Siggelkow	Madison	May 1, 2019	None
State Employees Suggestion Board Sec. 15.105 (29)(c) 1.	Danielle Johnson	Madison	May 1, 2015	None
	Paul Ruby	Sun Prairie	May 1, 2017	None
	vacancy			
*State Fair Park Board Secs. 15.07 (1)(b) 15m, 15.07 (5)(j), 15.445 (4)	Jim Sullivan	Wauwatosa	Jan. 1, 2012	None
	Leah Vukmir	Wauwatosa	Jan. 1, 2013	None
	Keith Ripp	Lodi	Jan. 1, 2013	None
	Mary Maas	Tomah	May 1, 2016	$10 per day, not exc. $600 per year
	Sue Rupnow[5]	Wausau	May 1, 2017	$10 per day, not exc. $600 per year
	Susan Crane[5]	Burlington	May 1, 2018	$10 per day, not exc. $600 per year
	Dan Devine[5]	West Allis	May 1, 2019	$10 per day, not exc. $600 per year
	James Villa	West Allis	May 1, 2019	$10 per day, not exc. $600 per year
	Aldo Madrigrano[5]	Sussex	May 1, 2020	$10 per day, not exc. $600 per year
	John Jingling[5]	Mequon	May 1, 2020	$10 per day, not exc. $600 per year
*State Historical Society of Wisconsin Board of Curators Sec. 15.70	William Van Sant[5]	Bayfield	July 1, 2015	None
	George Jacobs, Jr.	Madison	July 1, 2016	None
	Keene Winters	Wausau	July 1, 2017	None
	Dave Anderson	Malone	Pleas. of Gov.	None
State Trails Council Secs. 15.09 (1)(a), 15.347 (16)	Thomas Huber	Madison	July 1, 2007	None
	Jim Joque	Mosinee	July 1, 2011	None
	Bryan Much	Oconomowoc	July 1, 2013	None
	Robbie Webber	Madison	July 1, 2013	None
	Ken Carpenter	Fort Atkinson	July 1, 2015	None
	Randy Harden	Sheboygan	July 1, 2015	None
	Doug Johnson	DeForest	July 1, 2015	None
	Phillip Johnsrud	Iola	July 1, 2015	None
	LuAna Schneider	DeForest	July 1, 2015	None
	Michael McFadzen	Plymouth	July 1, 2017	None
	Kendal Neitzke	Waukesha	July 1, 2017	None
	John Siegert	Racine	July 1, 2017	None
	James White	Waukesha	July 1, 2017	None
State Use Board Secs. 15.07 (1)(b), 15.105 (22)	Michael Casey	Bloomington	May 1, 2011	None
	Nickolas George, Jr.	Madison	May 1, 2011	None
	Bill Smith	Madison	May 1, 2011	None
	Jean Zweifel	Albany	May 1, 2011	None
	Tim Casper	Madison	May 1, 2013	None
	Marie Danforth	Madison	May 1, 2013	None
	David Dumke	Brule	May 1, 2013	None
	Enid Glenn	Madison	May 1, 2017	None
	Helen McCain	Madison	May 1, 2017	None
*Tax Appeals Commission Secs. 15.01 (2), 15.06 (1)(a), 15.06 (3)(a) 2, 15.105 (1)	Roger LeGrand	La Crosse	March 1, 2015	Group 4
	Lorna Hemp Boll	Madison	March 1, 2017	Group 4
	David Wilmoth[5]	Greendale	March 1, 2019	Group 4
Tax Exemptions, Jt. Survey Com. on Sec. 13.52 (1) (d)	Kimberly Shaul	Cottage Grove	Jan. 15, 2013	None

Officers[1]	Name	Home Address[2]	Term Expires[3]	Salary or Per Diem[4]
Teachers Retirement Board Secs. 15.07 (5)(f), 15.165 (3)(a)	Sandra Claflin-Chalton	Menomonie	May 1, 2012	$25 per day
	Susan Harrison	Menomonie	May 1, 2014	$25 per day
	Gary Epping	Waunakee	May 1, 2018	$25 per day
	Craig Hubbell	Madison	May 1, 2018	None
*Technical College System Board Secs. 15.07 (1)(a), 15.07 (5)(e), 15.94	Andrew Petersen	Verona	May 1, 2015	$100 per year
	Susan Schaumburg[5]	Madison	May 1, 2015	$100 per year
	Philip Baranowski	Green Lake	May 1, 2017	$100 per year
	John Schwantes	Elkhart Lake	May 1, 2017	$100 per year
	Stephen Willett	Phillips	May 1, 2017	$100 per year
	W. Kent Lorenz	Oconomowoc	May 1, 2019	$100 per year
	Terrance McGowan[5]	Oxford	May 1, 2019	$100 per year
	Stephen Mark Tyler[5]	Woodville	May 1, 2019	$100 per year
	Becky Levzow	Rio	May 1, 2021	$100 per year
	vacancy			
Tourism, Council on Secs. 15.09 (1)(a), 15.447 (1)	Deborah Archer	Cross Plains	July 1, 2015	None
	James Bolen	Cable	July 1, 2015	None
	Kathy Kopp	Platteville	July 1, 2015	None
	Paul Upchurch	Milwaukee	July 1, 2015	None
	Stacey Watson	Milwaukee	July 1, 2015	None
	Cindy L. Burzinski	Eagle River	July 1, 2016	None
	Allyson Gommer	Eau Claire	July 1, 2016	None
	Brian Kelsey	Fish Creek	July 1, 2016	None
	Scott Krause	Green Lake	July 1, 2016	None
	Lola L. Roeh	Elkhart Lake	July 1, 2016	None
	Paul Cunningham	Fond du Lac	July 1, 2017	None
	Stanton Peter Helland, Jr.	Wisconsin Dells	July 1, 2017	None
	Joe Klimczak	Blue Mounds	July 1, 2017	None
	Ernest Stevens III	Green Bay	July 1, 2017	None
*Tourism, Dept. of, Secy. Secs. 15.05 (1)(a), 15.44	Stephanie Klett	Madison	Pleas. of Gov.	Group 6
*Transportation, Dept. of, Secy. Secs. 15.05 (1)(a), 15.46	Mark Gottlieb	Madison	Pleas. of Gov.	Group 7
Transportation Projects Commission Sec. 13.489 (1)	Barbara Fleisner	Mosinee	Pleas. of Gov.	None
	Jean M. Jacobson	Wind Lake	Pleas. of Gov.	None
	Michael Ryan	Waunakee	Pleas. of Gov.	None
Uniform State Laws, Commission on Sec. 13.55 (1)	Patience Roggensack	Madison	May 1, 2015	None
	John Macy	Waukesha	May 1, 2017	None
*Univ. of Wis. Hospitals and Clinics Authority Sec. 233.02	Carol L. Booth	Madison	Pleas. of Gov.	None
	Richard W. Choudoir	Columbus	Pleas. of Gov.	None
	Lisa Reardon	Nashotah	July 1, 2015	None
	Humberto Vidaillet	Marshfield	July 1, 2015	None
	John Litscher	Fitchburg	July 1, 2016	None
	Pablo Sanchez[5]	Madison	July 1, 2017	None
	Andrew Hitt	Madison	July 1, 2019	None
	David Ward	Waupaca	July 1, 2019	None
*Univ. of Wis. System, Bd. of Regents of the Secs. 15.07 (1)(a), 15.91	Nicolas Harsy[5]	Madison	May 1, 2016	None
	Chuck Pruitt	Milwaukee	May 1, 2016	None
	Jose Vasquez	Milwaukee	May 1, 2016	None
	Mark Bradley	Wausau	May 1, 2017	None
	James A. Langnes III	Whitewater	May 1, 2017	None
	Ed Manydeeds	Eau Claire	May 1, 2017	None
	Tim Higgins	Appleton	May 1, 2018	None
	Gerald Whitburn	Wausau	May 1, 2018	None
	John Behling	Eau Claire	May 1, 2019	None
	Regina Millner	Madison	May 1, 2019	None
	Margaret Farrow	Pewaukee	May 1, 2020	None
	Janice Mueller	Madison	May 1, 2020	None
	Jose Delgado[5]	Brookfield	May 1, 2021	None
	Eve M. Hall[5]	New Berlin	May 1, 2021	None
	Michael M. Grebe	Mequon	May 1, 2022	None
	Andrew Petersen	Verona	May 1, 2022	None
Utility Public Benefits Council on Sec. 15.107 (17)	James Boullion	Madison	July 1, 2011	None
	Janis Ringhand	Evansville	July 1, 2013	None
*Veterans Affairs, Board of Secs. 15.07 (1)(a), 15.49	John Townsend	Fond du Lac	May 1, 2013	None
	Alan Richards	Grafton	May 1, 2013	None
	Marvin Freedman	Middleton	May 1, 2015	None
	Peter Moran	Superior	May 1, 2015	None
	Daniel Bohlin	Stitzer	May 1, 2017	None
	Cathy Gorst	Marshfield	May 1, 2017	None
	Kevin Nicholson	Wauwatosa	May 1, 2017	None
	Leigh Neville-Neil	Green Bay	May 1, 2017	None
	John Gaedke[5]	Merrimac	May 1, 2019	None
	Carl Krueger[5]	Cudahy	May 1, 2019	None
	Larry Kutschma	Lake Geneva	May 1, 2019	None
*Veterans Affairs, Dept. of, Secy. Sec. 15.05 (1m), 15.49	John Scocos	Madison	Pleas. of Gov.	Group 6

Officers[1]	Name	Home Address[2]	Term Expires[3]	Salary or Per Diem[4]
Veterinary Diagnostic Laboratory Board Sec. 15.915 (1)	Alissa Grenawalt.	Beloit	May 1, 2015	None
	Steven Van Lannen.	Suamico	May 1, 2015	None
	James Meronek	Prairie du Sac	May 1, 2016	None
	Ray Pawlisch.	Brodhead	May 1, 2016	None
	Sandra Larson	Evansville	May 1, 2017	None
	Sheryl Shaw	Middleton	Pleas. of Gov.	None
*Veterinary Examining Bd. Secs. 15.08, 15.405 (12)	Brenda Nemec	Pewaukee	July 1, 2014	$25 per day
	Philip Johnson	Winneconne	July 1, 2015	$25 per day
	Bruce Berth	Coleman	July 1, 2015	$25 per day
	Neil Wiseley[5].	Mayville	July 1, 2016	$25 per day
	Robert Forbes	Stevens Point	July 1, 2017	$25 per day
	Diane Dommer Martin.	Cedar Grove	July 1, 2017	$25 per day
	Lisa Weisensel Nesson[5]	Sun Prairie	July 1, 2018	$25 per day
	Sheldon Schall	Waunakee	July 1, 2018	$25 per day
Volunteer Fire Fighter and Emergency Medical Technician Service Award Board Sec. 15.105 (26)	Robert H. Seitz.	Monticello	May 1, 2005	None
	Kristen Halverson	Monona	May 1, 2009	None
	Allen Schraeder	Ripon	May 1, 2012	None
	Melinda Allen	Monroe	May 1, 2013	None
	John Scherer	Middleton	May 1, 2013	None
	Kenneth A. Bartz.	Dodgeville	May 1, 2015	None
	vacancy			
*Waste Facility Siting Board Secs. 15.07 (1)(b) 11, 15.07 (5)(t), 15.105 (12)	James Schuerman	Wisconsin Rapids	May 1, 2013	$35 per day
	Jeanette DeKeyser	Neenah	May 1, 2015	$35 per day
	Dale R. Shaver.	Waukesha	May 1, 2017	$35 per day
*Waterways Commission, Wis. Secs. 15.01 (2), 15.06 (1)(ag), 15.06 (3)(a) 3, 15.345 (1)	Roger Walsh	Wauwatosa	March 1, 2013	None
	Maureen Kinney	La Crosse	March 1, 2014	None
	James Rooney	Racine	March 1, 2014	None
	Lee Van Zeeland[5]	Appleton	March 1, 2020	None
	vacancy			
Wisconsin Center District Board of Directors Sec. 229.42 (4)(e)	James Kaminski	Greenfield	May 1, 2015	None
	Joseph Bartolotta.	Elm Grove	May 1, 2016	None
	Stephen H. Marcus.	River Hills	May 1, 2016	None
Wisconsin Compensation Rating Bureau Sec. 626.31 (1)(b)	Daniel Burazin	Waterford	Pleas. of Gov.	None
	Chris Reader	Sun Prairie	Pleas. of Gov.	None
Women's Council Secs. 15.09 (1)(a), 15.107 (11)	Jane Clark	Madison	July 1, 2011	None
	Nicole Bowman-Farrell	Shawano	July 1, 2012	None
	Mary Jo Baas.	Brookfield	July 1, 2014	None
	Jessie Nicholson	Milwaukee	July 1, 2014	None
	Patricia Cadorin	Hartland	July 1, 2015	None
	Karen Katz	Wausau	July 1, 2015	None
	Michelle Mettner.	Madison	July 1, 2015	None
	Katherine Mnuk	Oregon	July 1, 2015	None
*Workforce Development, Dept. of, Secy. Secs. 15.05 (1)(a), 15.22	Reggie J. Newson	Madison	Pleas. of Gov.	Group 6

*Nominated by the governor and appointed with the advice and consent of the senate. Senate confirmation is required for secretaries of departments, members of commissions and commissioners, governing boards, examining boards, and other boards as designated by statute.

[1]List includes *only* appointments made by the governor. Additional members frequently serve *ex officio* or are appointed by other means. The governor also appoints members of intrastate regional agencies and nonstatutory committees and makes temporary appointments under statute Chapter 17 to elected state and county offices when vacancies occur. For complete membership list of unit, including officers, see full description elsewhere in the *Blue Book*. Section numbers under each entry refer to statute sections authorizing appointment by the governor. Statute Section 21.18 provides for the governor's military staff.

[2]Home address is the municipality from which the officer was appointed to a full-time office or the current address of part-time officials.

[3]Terms are specified by the following statute sections or as otherwise provided by law: Sec. 15.05 (1) - secretaries; Sec. 15.06 (1) - commissioners; Sec. 15.07 (1) - governing boards and attached boards; Sec. 15.08 (1) - examining boards and councils; Sec. 15.09 (1) - councils.

[4]Members of boards and councils are reimbursed for actual and necessary expenses incurred in performing their duties. In addition, examining board members receive $25 per day for days worked, and members of certain other boards under statute Section 15.07 (5) receive a per diem as noted in the table. Statute Section 20.923 places state officials in one of 10 executive salary groups (ESG) for which salary ranges have been established. Group salary ranges for the period June 30, 2015 through June 24, 2017, are: Group 1: $60,382-$99,632; Group 2: $65,208-$107,598; Group 3: $70,429-$116,210; Group 4: $76,066-$125,528; Group 5: $82,139-$135,533; Group 6: $88,712-$146,390; Group 7: $95,826-$158,122; Group 8: $103,480-$170,747; Group 9: $111,758-$184,413; Group 10: $120,702-$199,160.

[5]Nominated by governor but not yet confirmed by senate.

[6]Compensation set by Economic Development Corporation Board.

Source: Appointment lists maintained by governor's office and received by the Legislative Reference Bureau on or before June 30, 2015.

Lieutenant Governor Rebecca Kleefisch congratulates the City of La Crosse on its designation as one of Wisconsin's outstanding "Main Street Communities." WEDC's Wisconsin Main Street Program is designed to promote the historic and economic redevelopment of traditional business districts in cities and towns across Wisconsin. (Office of the Lieutenant Governor)

OFFICE OF THE LIEUTENANT GOVERNOR

Lieutenant Governor: REBECCA KLEEFISCH.

Chief of Staff and Legal Counsel: DANIEL SUHR.

Policy Advisor: ROBERT SCHLAEGER.

Communications Manager: TIERNEY GILL.

Mailing Address: P.O. Box 2043, Madison 53702-2043.

Location: Room 19 East, State Capitol, Madison.

Telephone: 266-3516.

Fax: 267-3571.

Agency E-mail Address: ltgov@wisconsin.gov

Internet Address: www.ltgov.wisconsin.gov

Number of Employees: 4.00.

Total Budget 2013-15: $633,200.

Constitutional References: Article V, Sections 1, 2, 3, 7, and 8; Article XIII, Section 10.

Statutory Reference: Chapter 14, Subchapter II.

Agency Responsibility: The lieutenant governor is the state's second-ranking executive officer, a position comparable to that of the Vice President of the United States. If the incumbent governor dies, resigns, or is removed from office, the lieutenant governor becomes governor for the balance of the unexpired term. (Prior to a constitutional amendment in April 1979, the lieutenant governor was considered only "acting governor" in those circumstances.) The lieutenant governor serves as acting governor when the governor is temporarily unable to perform the duties of the office due to impeachment, incapacitation, or absence from the state. If the lieutenant governor becomes governor, he or she must nominate a new lieutenant governor and the successor must be confirmed by the senate and the assembly.

The governor may designate the lieutenant governor to represent the governor's office on any statutory board, commission, or committee on which the governor is entitled to membership. Under such designation, the lieutenant governor has all the authority and responsibility granted by law to the governor. The governor may also designate the lieutenant governor to represent the chief executive's office on any nonstatutory committee or intergovernmental body created to maintain relationships with federal, state, and local governments or regional agencies. The lieutenant governor participates in national organizations of lieutenant governors and may be asked by the governor to coordinate specific state services and programs.

Organization: From 1848 until 1970, the lieutenant governor was elected for a 2-year term on a separate ballot in the November general election of even-numbered years. Since 1970, following amendment of the Wisconsin Constitution, voters have elected the governor and lieutenant governor on a joint ballot to a 4-year term. Candidates are nominated independently in the partisan August primary, but voters cast a combined ballot for the two offices in the November election.

History: The Territory of Wisconsin had no lieutenant governor, but the secretary of the territory was authorized to act as governor in the event of the governor's death or absence. The Wisconsin Constitution of 1848 provided for the post of lieutenant governor after considerable debate. Some delegates to the convention argued that the president of the senate, chosen from the membership of that body, should succeed the governor, with the secretary of state second in line of succession. The convention delegates who objected to a person's becoming governor without being elected on a statewide basis prevailed, however, and the post of lieutenant governor was included in the constitution.

Originally, the lieutenant governor was also the president of the senate and could cast a deciding vote in case of a tie. In 1979, the voters ratified a constitutional amendment enabling the senate to choose its own presiding officer from among its members, beginning in 1981.

Department of ADMINISTRATION

Address e-mail by combining the user ID and the state extender: userid@**wisconsin.gov**
All telephone numbers are 608 area code unless otherwise indicated.

Secretary of Administration: SCOTT NEITZEL, 266-1741, scott.neitzel@

Deputy Secretary: CATE ZEUSKE, 266-1741, cate.zeuske@

Assistant Deputy Secretary: JOHN HOGAN, 266-1741, john.hogan@

Chief Legal Counsel: GREGORY MURRAY, 267-0202, gregory.murray@

Communications Director: CULLEN WERWIE, 261-1710, cullen.werwie@

Mailing Address: P.O. Box 7864, Madison 53707-7864.

Location: State Administration Building, 101 East Wilson Street, Madison.

Telephone: (608) 266-1741.

Fax: (608) 267-3842.

Internet Address: www.doa.wi.gov

Number of Employees: 939.58.

Total Budget 2013-15: $1,870,318,600.

Statutory References: Sections 15.10 and 15.103; Chapter 16.

Administrative Services, Division of: JAMES LANGDON, *administrator,* 267-1001, james.langdon@; Fax: 264-9500; P.O. Box 7869, Madison 53707-7869.

> *Continuity of Government Program:* EUGENE ESSEX, *director,* 266-8566, eugene.essex@
>
> *Financial Management, Bureau of:* COLLEEN HOLTAN, *director,* 266-1359, colleen.holtan@
>
> *Personnel, Bureau of:* LINDA BARTH, *director,* 266-5847, lindas1.barth@
>
> *State Prosecutors Office:* PHILIP WERNER, *director,* 267-2700, phil.werner@

Capitol Police, Division of: DAVID ERWIN, *police chief and administrator,* 266-7546, david.erwin@; Fax: 267-9343; B2N State Capitol, Madison 53702.

Energy Services, Division of: KEVIN VESPERMAN, *administrator,* 261-6357, kevin.vesperman@; SUSAN S. BROWN, *deputy administrator,* 266-2035, susan.brown@; Fax: 267-6931; P.O. Box 7868, Madison 53707-7868.

> *Home Energy Plus, Bureau of:* BARB KLUG SIEJA, *director,* 267-0227, barbara.klugsieja@
>
> *State Energy Office:* DAVID J. JENKINS, *program manager,* 264-7651, davidj.jenkins@

Enterprise Operations, Division of: HELEN MCCAIN, *administrator,* 267-9634, helen.mccain@; Fax: 267-0600; P.O. Box 7867, Madison 53707-7867.

> *Enterprise Fleet, Bureau of:* JOHN MARX, *director,* 267-7693, john.marx@
>
> *Procurement, Bureau of:* RICK HUGHES, *director,* 266-1558, rick.hughes@
>
> *State Risk Management, Bureau of:* JASON GATES, *director,* 266-2421, jason.gates@; Fax: 264-8250.

Enterprise Technology, Division of: DAVID CAGIGAL, *administrator and state chief information officer,* 261-8406, david.cagigal@; HERB THOMPSON, *deputy administrator,* 261-7750, herb.thompson@; Fax: 266-2164; P.O. Box 7844, Madison 53707-7844.

> *Business Application Support, Bureau of:* KATHY SKIERA, *director,* 261-9570, kathy.skiera@
>
> *Business Services, Bureau of:* JAMES SYLLA, *director,* 264-6186, james.sylla@
>
> *District Attorneys Information Technology, Bureau of:* LAURA RADKE, *director,* 261-6614, laura.radke@
>
> *Infrastructure Support, Bureau of:* JIM SCHMOLESKY, *director,* 224-3777, jim.schmolesky@
>
> *Publishing and Distribution, Bureau of:* TIMOTHY SMITH, *director,* 266-5800, timothy.smith@
>
> *Security, Office of:* BILL NASH, *director,* 224-3779, bill.nash@
>
> *Technical Architecture and Project Management, Office of:* DAVE MEYER, *director,* 261-6628, davidj.meyer@

Executive Budget and Finance, Division of: MICHAEL HEIFETZ, *administrator,* 266-1035, michael.heifetz@; KIRSTEN GRINDE, *deputy administrator,* 266-1353, kirsten.grinde@; Fax: 267-0372; P.O. Box 7864, Madison 53707-7864.

> *Capital Finance Office:* DAVID ERDMAN, *deputy director,* 267-0374, david.erdman@
>
> *State Budget Office:*
>
>> *Agriculture, Environment and Justice:* CAITLIN MORGAN FREDERICK, *team leader,* 266-2081, caitlin.frederick@
>>
>> *Education and Workforce Development:* SARA HYNEK, *team leader,* 266-1037, sara.hynek@
>>
>> *General Government, Children and Families:* JENNIFER KRAUS, *team leader,* 266-5878, jennifer.kraus@
>>
>> *Health Services and Insurance:* JANA STEINMETZ, *team leader,* 266-3420, jana.steinmetz@
>>
>> *Information Technology, Operations and Federal Funds:* SCOTT THORNTON, *team leader,* 266-5051, scott.thornton@

DEPARTMENT OF ADMINISTRATION

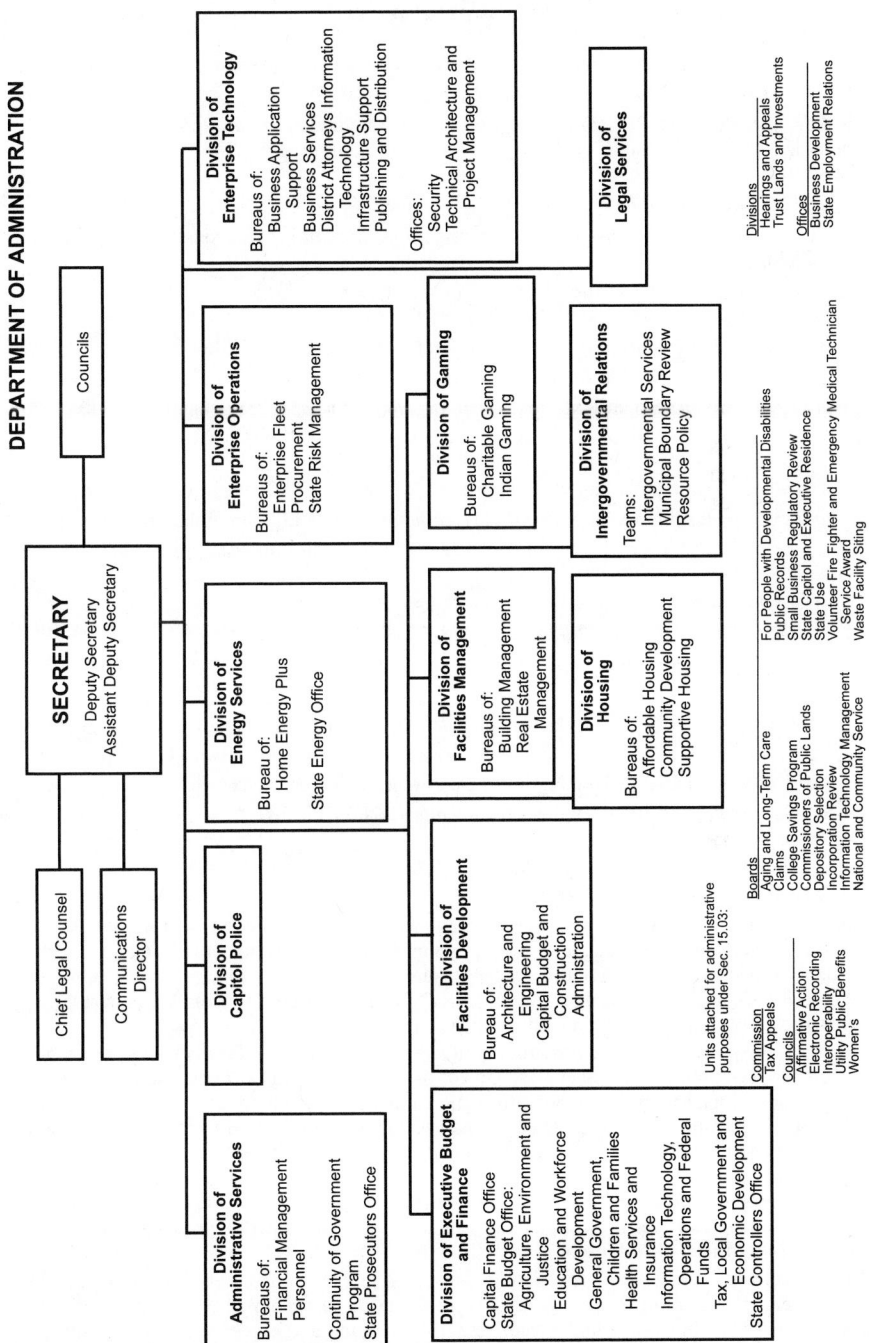

SECRETARY
Deputy Secretary
Assistant Deputy Secretary

Councils

Chief Legal Counsel

Communications
Director

Division of Administrative Services

Bureaus of:
Financial Management
Personnel
Continuity of Government
Program
State Prosecutors Office

Division of Capitol Police

Division of Executive Budget and Finance

Capital Finance Office
State Budget Office:
Agriculture, Environment and
Justice
Education and Workforce
Development
General Government,
Children and Families
Health Services and
Insurance
Information Technology,
Operations and Federal
Funds
Tax, Local Government and
Economic Development
State Controllers Office

Division of Facilities Development

Bureau of:
Architecture and
Engineering
Capital Budget and
Construction
Administration

Division of Energy Services

Bureau of:
Home Energy Plus
State Energy Office

Division of Facilities Management

Bureaus of:
Building Management
Real Estate
Management

Division of Housing

Bureaus of:
Affordable Housing
Community Development
Supportive Housing

Division of Enterprise Operations

Bureaus of:
Enterprise Fleet
Procurement
State Risk Management

Division of Gaming

Bureaus of:
Charitable Gaming
Indian Gaming

Division of Intergovernmental Relations

Teams:
Intergovernmental Services
Municipal Boundary Review
Resource Policy

Division of Enterprise Technology

Bureaus of:
Business Application
Support
Business Services
District Attorneys Information
Technology
Infrastructure Support
Publishing and Distribution

Offices:
Security
Technical Architecture and
Project Management

Division of Legal Services

Divisions
Hearings and Appeals
Trust Lands and Investments

Offices
Business Development
State Employment Relations

Units attached for administrative
purposes under Sec. 15.03:

Commission
Tax Appeals

Councils
Affirmative Action
Electronic Recording
Interoperability
Utility Public Benefits
Women's

Boards
Aging and Long-Term Care
Claims
College Savings Program
Commissioners of Public Lands
Depository Selection
Incorporation Review
Information Technology Management
National and Community Service

For People with Developmental Disabilities
Public Records
Small Business Regulatory Review
State Capitol and Executive Residence
State Use
Volunteer Fire Fighter and Emergency Medical Technician
Service Award
Waste Facility Siting

ADMINISTRATION

Tax, Local Government and Economic Development: PAUL ZIEGLER, *team leader,* 266-1040, paul.ziegler@

State Controller's Office: JEFF ANDERSON, *deputy state controller,* 266-8158, jeff.anderson@; P.O. Box 7932, Madison 53707-7932.

Facilities Development, Division of: SUMMER R. STRAND, *administrator,* 266-1031, summer.strand@; NAOMI R. DE MERS, *advisor to the administrator,* 266-2646, naomi.demers@

    Architecture and Engineering, Bureau of: vacancy.

    Capital Budget and Construction Administration, Bureau of: ROBINSON J. BINAU, *director,* 267-6927, rj.binau@

Facilities Management, Division of: CINDY TORSTVEIT, *administrator,* 264-9503, cindy.torstveit@; vacancy, *advisor to the administrator.*

    Building Management, Bureau of: KEITH BECK, *director,* 266-2645, keith.beck@

    Real Estate Management, Bureau of: MARCEL MAUL, *director,* 261-7072, marcel.maul@

Gaming, Division of: STEVE KNUDSON, *administrator,* 270-2555, steve.knudson@; Fax: 270-2564; 3319 West Beltline Highway, First Floor, P.O. Box 8979, Madison 53708-8979; Internet Address: www.doa.state.wi.us/gaming

    Charitable Gaming, Bureau of: JOSEPH GASTEL, *director,* 270-2546, joseph.gastel@

    Indian Gaming, Bureau of: JOHN DILLETT, *director,* 270-2533, john.dillett@

Housing, Division of: LISA MARKS, *administrator,* 267-0770, lisa.marks@; Fax: 266-5381; P.O. Box 7970, Madison 53707-7970.

    Affordable Housing, Bureau of: THEOLA CARTER, *director,* 264-6152, theola.carter@

    Community Development, Bureau of: vacancy, *director,* 261-7538.

    Supportive Housing, Bureau of: THEOLA CARTER, *acting director,* 267-2713, theola.carter@

Intergovernmental Relations, Division of: ED EBERLE, *administrator,* 267-1824, ed.eberle@; Fax: 267-6917; P.O. Box 8944, Madison 53707-8944.

    Intergovernmental Services Team: DAWN VICK, *team leader,* 266-7043, dawn.vick@

    Municipal Boundary Review Team: RENEE POWERS, *team leader,* 266-3200, renee.powers@

    Resource Policy Team: MIKE FRIIS, *team leader,* 267-7982, mike.friis@

Legal Services, Division of: GREGORY MURRAY, *chief legal counsel and administrator,* 267-0202, gregory.murray@; WILLIAM RAMSEY, *deputy chief legal counsel,* 261-5043, william.ramsey@; P.O. Box 7864, Madison 53707-7864.

Publications: Agency Budget Requests and Revenue Estimates; Annual Fiscal Report; Biennial Report; Budget in Brief; Budget Message; Capital Budget Recommendations; Comprehensive Annual Financial Report; Continuing Disclosure Annual Report; Decisions of Tax Appeals Commission; Executive Budget; Summary of Tax Exemption Devices; Wisconsin Energy Statistics; Wisconsin Population Estimates.

Agency Responsibility: The Department of Administration (DOA) provides a wide range of support services to other state agencies. One of the chief duties of the department is to provide the governor with fiscal management information and the policy alternatives required for preparation of Wisconsin's biennial budget. It analyzes administrative and fiscal issues facing the state and recommends solutions. The department also coordinates telecommunications, energy, and land use planning and community development. It regulates racing, charitable gaming, and Indian gaming. It is responsible for managing the state's buildings and leased office space, as well as statewide facilities project planning and analysis. The department maintains a federal-state relations office in Washington, D.C.

Organization: The department is administered by a secretary appointed by the governor with the advice and consent of the senate. The secretary must be appointed "on the basis of recognized interest, administrative and executive ability, training and experience in and knowledge of problems and needs in the field of administration." The secretary appoints the department's division administrators from outside the classified service.

Unit Functions: The *Division of Administrative Services* provides numerous services to the department and agencies attached for administrative support, including financial management, human resources, business recovery, records management, lean government and management planning. The division prepares and administers the departmental budget, advises the secretary on policies and procedures, and performs internal audits. It administers compensation for all district attorneys and their staff attorneys, and oversees payments to special prosecutors appointed on behalf of district attorney offices.

The *Division of Capitol Police* uses officers working in Madison and Milwaukee to provide a wide range of investigative, security, and related public safety services to state agencies, employees, and others. It protects state facilities; conducts criminal investigations; and provides protective services to the governor and visiting dignitaries.

The *Division of Energy Services* administers a federal and state funded low-income household energy assistance program involving bill payment and weatherization. In coordination with local government, community action agencies, and other nonprofit entities, the division distributes more than $130 million in annual energy assistance to approximately 215,000 low-income households, and approximately $60 million annually to fund weatherization measures to approximately 5,000 households throughout Wisconsin.

The State Energy Office is federally funded and administers federal funds received from the U.S. Department of Energy under the State Energy Program Strategic Plan and various federal laws. It develops policy options for consideration by the governor and state agencies, coordinates activities with other state agencies, identifies federal funding opportunities and facilitates applications for funding by state and local governments and private entities, annually publishes energy statistics, maintains an energy assurance plan, and performs duties necessary to maintain federal designation and funding.

The *Division of Enterprise Operations* manages state procurement policies and contracts, auto and air fleet transportation, and risk management. The division creates and administers statewide contracts, supports DOA and consolidated agency purchasing, municipal cooperative purchasing, work center contracting, federal and state surplus property disposition, and minority business contracting. It oversees fleet policies, central fleet and air services operations, records management, interdepartmental mail, and state agency document sales and distribution. It also manages the state's self-funded risk management programs for liability, property, and worker's compensation, and assists agencies in controlling and reducing risk management losses.

The *Division of Enterprise Technology* manages the state's information technology (IT) assets and uses technology to improve government efficiency and service delivery. It provides computer services to state agencies and operates the statewide voice data and video telecommunications network. In consultation with business and IT managers from state agencies and local governments, the division develops strategies, policies, and standards for cross-agency and multijurisdictional use of IT resources. The division provides centralized security training, research, and print and mail services to other state agencies and provides statewide computer systems for district attorneys.

The *Division of Executive Budget and Finance* provides fiscal and policy analysis to the governor for development of executive budget proposals and assists agencies in the technical preparation of budget requests. It reviews legislation and coordinates the fiscal estimates that accompany all expenditure bills. It also advises the State of Wisconsin Building Commission and the governor on the issuance of state debt and administers finances for the clean water revolving loan fund program. The division provides program and management evaluation and maintains the management information system for authorized state employee positions. It establishes accounting policies and procedures, maintains the state's central payroll and accounting systems, monitors agency internal control procedures, produces the state's annual fiscal and financial reports, and administers the state's Section 529 College Savings programs and the local government investment pool.

The *Division of Facilities Development* develops and administers the state building program under the direction of the State of Wisconsin Building Commission. Its functions include: project planning and analysis; architectural and engineering selection and design oversight; construction contract bidding and administration; construction project management; and statewide field supervision of construction projects. The division also oversees: centralized functions of the state-owned heating plants; the energy conservation bonding program; and all transactions requiring State Building Commission approval.

The *Division of Facilities Management* operates and maintains 30 major buildings in 7 cities throughout the state including the State Capitol, the Executive Residence, and state office buildings in Madison. The division is responsible for building management, tenant improvements, building service contracts, space planning and occupancy, parking administration, all state leasing and real estate transactions, and property acquisition and disposition.

The *Division of Gaming* regulates bingo, raffles, and Class III Indian gaming pursuant to state/tribal gaming compacts. The division licenses and regulates bingo games and raffles conducted by nonprofit, charitable, religious, fraternal, and service organizations. It conducts tribal gaming compliance reviews and payment audits and certifies vendors to conduct gaming business in accordance with state/tribal compacts and federal law.

The *Division of Housing* develops housing policy and offers a broad range of program assistance and funds to address homelessness and support affordable housing, public infrastructure, and economic development opportunities. The division partners with local governments and service providers, nonprofit agencies, housing authorities, developers, and housing organizations throughout the state to improve housing conditions for low- to moderate-income Wisconsin residents. It distributes over $30 million annually.

The *Division of Intergovernmental Relations* provides a variety of services to the public and state, local, and tribal governments. It advises the governor and state agencies on state, local, and tribal relationships and coordinates the state's efforts to influence federal legislation. It manages the Wisconsin Coastal Management Program, provides the state population estimates and projections, in addition to demographic research.

The Department of Administration is responsible for the care and maintenance of the State Capitol. As part of that responsibility, it offers regular tours of the building to the general public. (Greg Anderson, Legislative Photographer)

The division administers the Comprehensive Planning and Land Information Grants. Working with the Incorporation Review Board, the division reviews and issues determinations on petitions to incorporate towns into villages or cities. It oversees the Municipal Boundary Review Program and the Plat Review Program, and administers the municipal service payment program which reimburses local governments for providing police, fire, and solid waste services to state facilities.

The *Division of Legal Services,* created in Section 15.103 (1g) by 2009 Wisconsin Act 28, provides legal services to state agencies and to the Department of Administration. It provides legal assistance and advice on issues such as procurement, contracting, construction, budget development, and other common activities with the goal of bringing about greater agencywide consistency on such matters. The division is available to support and consult with agencies on contract development, negotiation, and other areas of legal expertise.

History: The legislature created the Department of Administration in Chapter 228, Laws of 1959, and authorized it to provide centralized staff services to the governor, to assume common administrative functions for other executive agencies, and to coordinate the state's business affairs. Chapter 228 also abolished the Bureaus of Engineering, Personnel, and Purchases; the Department of Budget and Accounts; and the Division of Departmental Research in the Office of the Governor. Their functions and personnel were transferred to the new department.

Since its creation, the department has assumed additional duties. State comprehensive planning responsibilities and population estimation were added in 1967 and 1972, respectively. 1976 Executive Order 36 moved the Office of Emergency Energy Assistance from the Office of the Governor to the department's State Planning Office and broadened its responsibilities to include energy policy planning and program management. The 1989 executive budget created the Division of Housing (subsequently repealed in 2003) and gave the department responsibility for grant and loan programs for low- and moderate-income housing. The 1991 executive budget created the Division of Information Technology Services (now the Division of Enterprise Technology) to consolidate and manage the state's computer and telecommunications resources.

Other functions assigned to the department have included the Coastal Management Program (1981), low-income weatherization assistance (1991), low-income energy assistance (1995), a college tuition prepayment program (1995) (transferred to the Office of the State Treasurer by 1999 Wisconsin Act 9), municipal boundary and plat review (1997), and the Wisconsin Fresh Start Program (1998).

Over the years, legislation has transferred various functions out of the department. Chapter 645, Laws of 1961, created a separate Personnel Board to review departmental decisions. Chapter 196, Laws of 1977, transferred the administration of civil service, collective bargaining, and classification and compensation to the newly created Department of Employment Relations. The Division of Emergency Government, which became part of the department in 1979, was moved to the Department of Military Affairs by 1989 Wisconsin Act 31. Regulation of mobile home dealers and mobile parks was transferred to the Department of Commerce by 1999 Wisconsin Act 9. With the repeal of the Division of Housing, 2003 Wisconsin Act 33 transferred grant and loan programs for low- and moderate-income housing to the Department of Commerce. Housing programs were transferred from the Department of Commerce back to DOA by 2011 Wisconsin Act 32.

Gaming Regulation. 1997 Wisconsin Act 27 repealed the Wisconsin Gaming Board and created the Division of Gaming in the department to monitor gaming on Indian lands and regulate pari-mutuel wagering, racing, and charitable gaming.

Originally, the Wisconsin Constitution stated: "The legislature shall never authorize any lottery." This provision was interpreted as prohibiting all forms of gambling. Following a 1973 constitutional amendment to allow charitable bingo, the legislature enacted Chapter 156, Laws of 1973, to permit bingo games and create the Bingo Control Board in the Department of Regulation and Licensing. Charitable raffles were permitted by a 1977 constitutional amendment, and the legislature assigned their regulation to the Bingo Control Board in Chapter 426, Laws of 1977.

Pari-mutuel on-track wagering and the state lottery were permitted by constitutional amendments in 1987. The legislature created the Racing Board to regulate the sport in 1987 Wisconsin Act 354. The Wisconsin Lottery, originally operated by the Lottery Board, was created by 1987 Wisconsin Act 119.

The Wisconsin Gaming Commission, created by 1991 Wisconsin Act 269, replaced the Lottery Board and the Racing Board and also assumed responsibility for Indian gaming, charitable gaming (bingo and raffles), and crane games. The Wisconsin Gaming Board, created by 1995 Wisconsin Act 27, replaced the Gaming Commission. (That act also transferred responsibility for management of the Wisconsin Lottery to the Department of Revenue.) 1997 Wisconsin Act 27 transferred gaming duties, except for lottery regulation, to the Department of Administration. 2011 Wisconsin Act 32 eliminated the Office of Energy Independence and transferred to DOA from the Office of the State Treasurer responsibility for the state's Section 529 College Savings programs and the local government investment pool.

Statutory Councils

Acid Deposition Research Council: Inactive.

The 7-member Acid Deposition Research Council makes recommendations on types and levels of funding for acid deposition research and reviews "acid rain" research. The council was created by 1985 Wisconsin Act 296, and its composition and duties are prescribed in Sections 15.107 (5) and 16.02 of the statutes.

Certification Standards Review Council: PAUL HARRIS (commercial laboratory representative), *chairperson;* PATRICK GORSKI (appointed by UW-Madison chancellor to represent Laboratory of Hygiene), *vice chairperson;* KURT BIRKETT (small municipal wastewater plant representative), *secretary;* JENNIFER PETH (industrial laboratory representative); SHARON MERTENS (large municipal wastewater plant representative); vacancy (public water utility representative); vacancy (solid and hazardous waste disposal facility representative); PAUL JUNIO (demonstrated interest in laboratory certification); vacancy (livestock farmer). (Unless otherwise designated, all are appointed by secretary of administration.)

The 9-member Certification Standards Review Council reviews the Department of Natural Resources laboratory certification and registration program and makes recommendations to the department about its programs for testing water, wastewater, waste material, soil, and hazardous waste. The council's members serve 3-year terms, and no member may serve more than two consecutive terms. The council was created by 1983 Wisconsin Act 410, and its composition and duties are prescribed in Sections 15.107 (12) and 299.11 (3) of the statutes.

Small Business, Veteran-Owned Business and Minority Business Opportunities, Council on: MOHAMMED HASHIM, *chairperson;* AGGO AKYEA, CRAIG A. ANDERSON, DAVID W. ARAGON, NORMAN BARRIENTOS, WILLIAM BECKETT, TINA CHANG, WILLIAM JOHNSON, JR., BRIAN MITCHELL, ALLEN R. SCHRAEDER, 3 vacancies. (All are appointed by secretary of administration.) Nonvoting secretary: HELEN MCCAIN (Department of Administration designee).

The 13-member Council on Small Business, Veteran-Owned Business and Minority Business Opportunities advises the department on the participation of its constituent groups in state purchasing. Its members are appointed for 3-year terms and may not serve more than two consecutive full terms. The law prescribes minimum membership numbers for the types of businesses represented on the council: racial minority-owned (2); owned by handicapped person (1); nonprofit for rehabilitation of disabled (1); and veteran-owned (2). At least one member must represent the Department of Safety and Professional Services and one must be a consumer member. The council was created by Chapter 419, Laws of 1977, and its name and membership were amended by 1991 Wisconsin Act 170 to include veteran-owned business. Its composition and duties are prescribed in Sections 15.107 (2) and 16.755 of the statutes.

INDEPENDENT UNITS ATTACHED FOR BUDGETING, PROGRAM COORDINATION, AND RELATED MANAGEMENT FUNCTIONS BY SECTION 15.03 OF THE STATUTES

BOARD ON AGING AND LONG-TERM CARE

Members: EVA ARNOLD, BARBARA BECHTEL, TERRY LYNCH, TANYA L. MEYER, JAMES SURPRISE, DALE TAYLOR, vacancy (appointed by governor with senate consent).

Executive Director: HEATHER A. BRUEMMER, (608) 246-7014,
  heather.bruemmer@wisconsin.gov

Mailing Address: 1402 Pankratz Street, Suite 111, Madison 53704.

Telephones: (608) 246-7013; Ombudsman Program: (800) 815-0015; Medigap Helpline: (800) 242-1060.

Fax: (608) 246-7001.

E-mail Address: boaltc@wisconsin.gov

Publications: Biennial Report.

Number of Employees: 37.00.

Total Budget 2013-15: $5,663,600.

Statutory References: Sections 15.07 (1)(b) 9., 15.105 (10), and 16.009.

  Agency Responsibility: The 7-member Board on Aging and Long-Term Care reports biennially to the governor and the legislature on long-term care for the aged and disabled; state involvement in long-term care; program recommendations; and actions taken by state agencies to carry out the board's recommendations. The board monitors the development and implementation of federal, state, and local laws and regulations related to long-term care facilities. The board's ombudsman service investigates complaints from persons receiving long-term care concerning improper treatment or noncompliance with federal or state law and serves as mediator or advocate to resolve disputes between patients and institutions.

  The board operates the Medigap Helpline, which provides information and counseling on various types of insurance, including health, hospital indemnity, cancer, nursing home, and long-term care and nursing home policies designed to supplement Medicare. Helpline informa-

The raising of the U.S. and Wisconsin flags over the West Wing of the State Capitol indicates that the Assembly is in session. (Greg Anderson, Legislative Photographer)

tion also covers group insurance continuation and conversion rights, and health maintenance organization plans for Medicare beneficiaries.

The board members, who serve staggered 5-year terms, must have demonstrated a continuing interest in the problems of providing long-term care for the aged and disabled. At least four must be public members with no interest in or affiliation with any nursing home. The board appoints the executive director from the classified service.

The board was created by Chapter 20, Laws of 1981, which merged the Board on Aging and the Governor's Ombudsman Program for the Aging and Disabled, as the result of a legislative study. Predecessor agencies included the State Commission on Aging, created by Chapter 581, Laws of 1961, followed in 1967 (Chapters 75 and 327) by the Council on Aging in the Department of Health and Social Services, which was subsequently renamed the Board on Aging in Chapter 332, Laws of 1971.

OFFICE OF BUSINESS DEVELOPMENT

Director: NANCY MISTELE, 267-7873, nancy.mistele@; JOE KNILANS, *deputy director,* 267-7394, joe.knilans@

Mailing Address: P.O. Box 7864, Madison 53707.

Fax: (608) 267-3842.

Statutory References: Sections 15.105 (32) and 16.28.

Agency Responsibility: The Office of Business Development provides administrative support to the Small Business Regulatory Review Board to review, reduce, or remove burdens that unnecessary laws and rules place on small business in Wisconsin, and performs other functions determined by the secretary of administration. The office is under the direction and supervision of a director appointed by and serving at the pleasure of the governor. The deputy director is also appointed by the governor to serve at his or her pleasure. The office was created by 2011 Wisconsin Act 32.

CLAIMS BOARD

Members: COREY FINKELMEYER (Department of Justice representative designated by attorney general), *chairperson;* GREG MURRAY (Department of Administration representative designated by secretary of administration), *secretary;* SENATOR OLSEN (designated by chairperson, Senate Committee on Finance), REPRESENTATIVE CZAJA (designated by chairperson, Assembly Committee on Finance); BRIAN HAGEDORN (representative of the Office of the Governor designated by governor).

Secretary: GREG MURRAY.

Mailing Address: P.O. Box 7864, Madison 53707-7864.

Location: State Administration Building, 101 East Wilson Street, 10th Floor, Madison.

Telephone: (608) 264-9595.

E-mail Address: patricia.reardon@wisconsin.gov

Internet Address: www.claimsboard.wi.gov

Number of Employees: 0.00.

Total Budget 2013-15: $288,400.

Statutory References: Sections 15.07 (2)(e), 15.105 (2), and 16.007.

Agency Responsibility: The 5-member Claims Board investigates and pays, denies, or makes recommendations on all money claims against the state of $10 or more, when such claims are referred to it by the Department of Administration. The findings and recommendations of the board are reported to the legislature and no claim may be considered by the legislature until the board has made its recommendation.

Originally, the statutory procedure for making claims against the state was to file the claim with the Director of Budget and Accounts or to have a legislator introduce it as a bill. The legislature created the Claims Commission in Chapter 669, Laws of 1955, to handle these matters.

Under the 1967 executive branch reorganization, the commission was renamed the Claims Board, and it absorbed the Commission for the Relief of Innocent Persons and the Judgment Debtor Relief Commission.

COLLEGE SAVINGS PROGRAM BOARD

Administrator: JAMES DIULIO, 264-7899, james.diulio@wisconsin.gov

Mailing Address: P.O. Box 7864, Madison 53707-7871.

Telephone: 264-7899.

Fax: 266-7645.

Internet Address: www.529.wi.gov

Statutory References: Sections 15.07 (1)(b) 2., 15.105 (25m), and 16.641.

Agency Responsibility: The 11-member College Savings Program Board was created by 1999 Wisconsin Act 44 and its members serve 4-year terms. The board consists of the secretary of administration or designee, the president of the University of Wisconsin System Board of Regents or designee, the president of the Wisconsin Association of Independent Colleges and Universities or designee, the chairperson of the State of Wisconsin Investment Board or designee, the president of the Technical College Board or designee, and six other members appointed by the governor with senate consent. It administers the EdVest and Tomorrow's Scholar college savings program that provides for tax-sheltered investment accounts held in a trust fund to cover future higher education expenses. Originally attached to the Office of the State Treasurer, it was attached to the Department of Administration by 2011 Wisconsin Act 32.

DEPOSITORY SELECTION BOARD

Members: MATT ADAMCZYK (state treasurer), SCOTT NEITZEL (secretary of administration), RICHARD G. CHANDLER (secretary of revenue).

Statutory References: Sections 15.105 (3) and 34.045.

Agency Responsibility: The 3-member Depository Selection Board, as created by Chapter 418, Laws of 1977, establishes procedures to be used by state agencies in the selection of depositories for public funds and in contracting for their banking services. The board's *ex officio* members may designate others to serve in their place. The secretary of revenue replaced the executive director of the investment board as a member as a result of 2001 Wisconsin Act 16.

ELECTRONIC RECORDING COUNCIL

Members: STACI HOFFMAN (register of deeds), *chairperson;* LISA PETERSEN (representing an association of title insurance); TYSON FETTES, JODI HELGESON, SHARON MARTIN (registers of deeds); MARCIA DROUIIN-HOWE (representing an association of bankers); JOHN F. WILCOX (representing attorneys who practice real property law). (All members are appointed by governor).

Agency Responsibility: The 7-member Electronic Recording Council recommends standards regarding the electronic recording of real estate documents for adoption by rules promulgated by the Department of Administration. The council was created by 2005 Wisconsin Act 421, and its composition and duties are prescribed in Sections 15.107 (6) and 706.25 (4) of the statutes.

DIVISION OF HEARINGS AND APPEALS

Administrator: BRIAN HAYES, 266-8007, brian.hayes@wisconsin.gov

Mailing Address: 5005 University Avenue, Suite 201, Madison 53705-5400.

Telephone: (608) 266-7709.

Fax: Madison: (608) 264-9885; Milwaukee: (414) 227-3818.

E-mail Address: dhamail@wisconsin.gov

Internet Address: http://dha.state.wi.us

Number of Employees: 51.95.

Total Budget 2013-15: $11,775,500.

Statutory References: Sections 15.103 (1), 50.04 (4)(e), 227.43, 301.035, and 949.11.

Agency Responsibility: The Division of Hearings and Appeals conducts quasi-judicial hearings for several state agencies. It must decide contested administrative proceedings for the Department of Natural Resources, cases arising under the Department of Justice's Crime Victim Compensation Program, and appeals related to actions of the Departments of Health Services, Children and Families, Safety and Professional Services, and Agriculture, Trade and Consumer Protection. It also hears appeals from the Department of Transportation, including those related to motor vehicle dealer licenses, highway signs, motor carrier regulation, and disputes arising between motor vehicle dealers and manufacturers. The division conducts hearings for the Department of Corrections regarding probation, parole, and extended supervision revocation and juvenile aftercare supervision. It also handles contested cases for the Department of Public Instruction, the Department of Employee Trust Funds, and the Low-Income Home Energy Assistance Program of the Department of Administration. Other agencies may contract with the division for hearing services.

The secretary of administration appoints the division's administrator from the classified service. By law, the division operates independently of the department except for certain budgeting and management functions. 1983 Wisconsin Act 27 created the division by combining the Division of Natural Resources Hearings and the Division of Nursing Home Forfeiture Appeals, both originating with the 1977 Legislature. In 1986, the division received jurisdiction over crime victim compensation hearings and cases involving protection of human burial sites. With the creation of the Department of Corrections in 1990, the legislature transferred a portion of the Office of Administrative Hearings from the Departments of Health and Social Services to the division, making the division responsible for parole, probation, and juvenile aftercare revocation. When the Office of the Commissioner of Transportation was abolished in 1993, the legislature transferred many Department of Transportation hearing functions to the division. Contested administrative hearings for the Department of Health Services and the Department of Children and Families were transferred to the division by 1995 Wisconsin Act 370.

INCORPORATION REVIEW BOARD

Members: ED EBERLE (designated by secretary of administration), *chairperson;* TERRENCE J. McMAHON, LONNIE MULLER (appointed by Wisconsin Towns Association); PAUL FISK (appointed by League of Wisconsin Municipalities); RICH EGGELSTON (appointed by Wisconsin Alliance of Cities).

Contact person: ERICH SCHMIDTKE, Planning Analyst, Division of Intergovernmental Relations.

Mailing Address: 101 East Wilson Street, 9th Floor, Madison 53702.

Telephone: (608) 264-6102.

E-mail Address: wimunicipalboundaryreview@wi.gov

Internet Address: http://doa.wi.gov/municipalboundaryreview

Statutory References: Sections 15.07 (2)(m), 15.105 (23), 16.53 (4), 66.0203, and 66.0207.

The 5-member Incorporation Review Board reviews petitions to incorporate territory as a city or village to determine whether the petition meets certain public interest statutory standards. These standards may include characteristics of the proposed municipality's territory, that part of the territory beyond its most densely populated core, its ability to provide services and generate revenue, and its impact on neighboring jurisdictions. The board is also charged with prescribing and collecting an incorporation review fee. The board must present its findings to the Division of Intergovernmental Relations within 180 days after receipt of referral from a circuit court unless the court sets a different time limit or all parties agree to a stay to allow time for an alternative dispute resolution of any disagreements. Any board member who owns property in, or resides in the town that is the subject of the incorporation petition, or a contiguous city or village, must be replaced for purposes of reviewing that petition. Members serve at the pleasure of the appointing authority and, with the exception of the DOA representative, serve only in an advisory capacity. The board was created by 2003 Wisconsin Act 171.

INFORMATION TECHNOLOGY MANAGEMENT BOARD

Members: Inactive.

Agency Responsibility: The Information Technology Management Board advises the Department of Administration on strategic information technology plans submitted by state agencies, the management of the state's information technology assets, and progress made on agency projects. The board may review the department's decisions on appeal from other state agencies. The board's membership includes the governor, the cochairpersons of the legislature's Joint Committee on Information Policy and Technology or their designees, a member of the minority party from the senate and the assembly, the secretary of administration or designee, 2 heads of departments or independent agencies appointed by the governor, and 2 other members appointed by the governor to 4-year terms. The board was created by 2001 Wisconsin Act 16 and attached to the Department of Administration by 2003 Wisconsin Act 33. Its composition and duties are prescribed in Sections 15.105 (28) and 16.978 of the statutes.

INTEROPERABILITY COUNCIL

Members: MATTHEW JOSKI (sheriff), *chairperson;* BRAD SCHIMEL (attorney general); DONALD DUNBAR (adjutant general); CATHY STEPP (secretary of natural resources); MARK GOTTLIEB (secretary of transportation); DAVID CAGIGAL (department of administration information technology representative); BRADLEY WENTLANDT (chief of police); STEVE HANSEN (fire chief); MINDY ALLEN (emergency medical services director); vacancy (local government elected official); WILLIAM STOLTE (local government emergency management director); RICHARD VANBOXTEL (American Indian tribe or band representative); LYNN SCHUBERT (hospital representative); vacancy (local health department representative); vacancy (person with experience or expertise in interoperable communications).

Agency Responsibility: The 15-member Interoperability Council develops strategies and recommends standards and guidelines for achieving statewide communications interoperability for Wisconsin's public safety community. The council advises the Department of Justice and the Department of Military Affairs on the allocation of homeland security grants and other funding available for the Wisconsin Interoperability Initiative. The council uses a shared governance approach with four subcommittees to develop policy and procedure recommendations: Wisconsin Interoperable System for Communications (WISCOM); Nationwide Public Safety Broadband Network (NPSBN); Land Mobile Radio (LRM); and 911 Subcommittee. Members are appointed by the governor and represent key state and local stakeholders. Through these groups, the council encourages widespread support for achieving statewide interoperability by identifying and addressing the concerns, perspectives, and any unique circumstances of the jurisdictions and organizations that will benefit most from interoperability. The council receives staff support from the Department of Justice as prescribed under Section 165.25 (17) of the statutes. Its composition and duties are prescribed in Sections 15.107 (18) and 16.9645 of the statutes.

NATIONAL AND COMMUNITY SERVICE BOARD

Members: KATHY GROAT (local government representative), *chairperson;* LISA DELMORE (private, nonprofit representative), *vice chairperson;* ANTHONY HALLMAN (youth education, training and development representative); CHRISTINE BEATTY (older adult volunteer representative); SCOTT JONES (superintendent of public instruction designee); JAMES LANGDON (secretary of administration designee); ROBERT GUENTHER (organized labor representative); PAULA HORNING (business representative); KATE JAEGER (national service program representative); vacancy (national service program youth representative); ANGELA AHLGRIM, ROBERT GRIFFITH, MARGARET MOORE, 4 vacancies (public members). Nonvoting members: INDIA MCCANSE (Corporation for National and Community Service); JOHN SCOCOS (Department of Veterans Affairs), AMY MCDOWELL (Department of Health Services), MICHAEL HINMAN (Department of Military Affairs), SCOTT FROMADER (Department of Workforce Development). (All except *ex officio* members are appointed by governor.)

Executive Director: THOMAS H. DEVINE.

Mailing Address: 1 West Wilson Street, Room B274, Madison 53703.

Telephones: (608) 261-6716; (800) 620-8307 (toll free).

Internet Address: www.servewisconsin.org

Number of Employees: 5.00.

Total Budget 2013-15: $8,479,200.

Statutory References: Sections 15.105 (24) and 16.22.

Agency Responsibility: The National and Community Service Board, created by 1993 Wisconsin Act 437, in accordance with the federal National and Community Trust Act of 1993, oversees the planning and implementation of community service programs in Wisconsin that meet previously unmet human, public safety, educational, environmental, and homeland security needs. The board is authorized to receive and distribute funds from governmental and private sources, and it acts as an intermediary between the Corporation for National and Community Service (CNCS) and local agencies providing funding for AmeriCorps State programs.

The board oversees 25 AmeriCorps programs consisting of 1,200 AmeriCorps members serving in over 300 placement sites statewide. After completing a successful year of service, AmeriCorps members in Wisconsin are eligible for Federal Education Awards that can be used to pay tuition or pay back student loans.

The board's voting members, who must number at least 16, are appointed to serve 3-year terms. No more than 4 of them may be state officers and employees, and no more than 9 may be members from the same political party. To the extent practicable, membership should be diverse in terms of race, national origin, age, sex, and disability. Nonvoting members appointed by the governor must include the state representative of the CNCS and may include representatives of state agencies providing community social services.

BOARD FOR PEOPLE WITH DEVELOPMENTAL DISABILITIES

Members: KEVIN FECH, *chairperson;* MEREDITH DRESSEL (designated by secretary of workforce development); BETH WROBLESKI (designated by secretary of health services); SUZAN VAN BEAVER (designated by state superintendent of public instruction); WILLIAM MACLEAN (designated by UW Waisman Center Director); BARBARA BECKERT (designated by Disability Rights Wisconsin); ALIZA CLAIRE BIBLE, LYNN CARUS, ELSA DIAZ-BUATISTA, WENDY GAHN-ACKLEY, DEBRA GLOVER, ROBERT KUHR, RAMSEY LEE, NATHANIEL LENTZ, PAM MALIN, CAMILLE NICKLAUS, DAVID PINNO, JUDITH QUIGLEY, LYNN STANSBERRY-BRUSNAHAN, CAROLE STUEBE, SHEILA THORNTON, PATRICK YOUNG, CINDY ZELLNER-EHLERS (all appointed by governor).

Executive Director: BETH SWEDEEN.

Mailing Address and Location: 101 East Wilson Street, Room 219, Madison 53703-2796.

Telephones: 266-7826; (888) 332-1677 (toll free); TTY: 266-6660.

Fax: 267-3906.

E-mail Address: bpddhelp@wi-bpdd.org

Internet Address: www.wi-bpdd.org

Number of Employees: 6.75.

Total Budget 2013-15: $2,809,800.

Statutory References: Sections 15.09 (1)(a), 15.105 (8), and 51.437 (14r).

Agency Responsibility: The board, formerly the Council on Developmental Disabilities, advises the Department of Administration, other state agencies, the legislature, and the governor on matters related to developmental disabilities. The statutes do not specify the exact number of board members, but all who serve are appointed to staggered 4-year terms, must be state residents, represent all geographic areas of the state, and the state's diversity with respect to race and ethnicity. The public members appointed by the governor must include representatives of public and private nonprofit agencies that provide direct services at the local level to persons with developmental disabilities. At least 60% of the board's members must be persons who have developmental disabilities or are the parents, relatives, or guardians of such individuals, but these members may not be associated with public or private agencies that receive federal funding. The members appointed by agency heads represent the relevant agencies of the state that administer federal funds related to individuals with disabilities. The Council on Developmental Disabilities was created within the Department of Health and Family Services by Chapter 322,

Laws of 1971, and made an independent unit by Chapter 29, Laws of 1977. 2007 Wisconsin Act 20 renamed it the Board for People with Developmental Disabilities, renumbered it from s. 15.197 (11n), and attached it to the Department of Administration under s. 15.03.

_____

BOARD OF COMMISSIONERS OF PUBLIC LANDS

Commissioners: DOUGLAS J. LA FOLLETTE (secretary of state), MATT ADAMCZYK (state treasurer), BRAD SCHIMEL (attorney general). (All serve as *ex officio* members.)

DIVISION OF TRUST LANDS AND INVESTMENTS

Executive Secretary: TIA NELSON, 266-8369, tia.nelson@wisconsin.gov; TOM GERMAN, *deputy secretary,* 267-2233, tom.german@wisconsin.gov

Mailing Address: P.O. Box 8943, Madison 53708-8943.

Location: 101 East Wilson Street, 2nd Floor, Madison.

Telephone: (608) 266-1370.

Fax: (608) 267-2787.

Internet Address: http://bcpl.wisconsin.gov

Email Address: bcplinfo@wisconsin.gov

District Office: JOHN SCHWARZMANN, *administrator,* john.schwarzmann@bcpl.wisconsin.gov, P.O. Box 277, 7271 Main Street, Lake Tomahawk 54539-0277, (715) 277-3366; Fax: (715) 277-3363.

Publications: Biennial Report; Common School Fund/Normal School Fund Brochure; Trust Assets and Programs Fact Sheet; State Trust Fund Loan Program Brochure.

Number of Employees: 9.50.

Total Budget 2013-15: $3,099,400.

Constitutional Reference: Article X, Sections 2, 5, 6, 7, and 8.

Statutory References: Section 15.103 (4) and Chapter 24.

Agency Responsibility and History: The Board of Commissioners of Public Lands and its Division of Trust Lands and Investments manage the state's remaining trust lands, manage trust funds primarily for the benefit of public education, and maintain the state's original 19th century land survey and land sales records.

The board was created in 1848 by Article X of the Wisconsin Constitution to manage and sell lands that were granted to the state by the federal government for the purposes of supporting public education and developing the state's infrastructure. Nearly all of the approximately 3.6 million acres from federal land grants that were placed into trust for the benefit of public education have been sold. The agency still holds title to about 77,000 acres of trust lands. Of those remaining lands, almost 71,000 acres are Normal School Trust Lands and nearly 6,100 acres are Common School Trust Lands. The School Trust Lands are managed for timber production, natural area preservation, and public use.

The constitution established "a board of commissioners for the sale of school and university lands and for the investment of funds arising therefrom" consisting of the Secretary of State, State Treasurer, and Attorney General. The Revised Statutes of 1849 created the Board of Commissioners of the School and University Lands. In 1878, the board was renamed the Board of Commissioners of Public Lands. Chapter 75, Laws of 1967, created the Division of Trust Lands and Investments, under the supervision of the board, to serve as the board's operating agency. The board appoints an executive secretary outside the classified service to administer the division. The division was originally attached to the Department of Natural Resources. Since then, the legislature has successively attached the division to the Department of Justice (Chapter 34, Laws of 1979), the Department of Administration (1993 Wisconsin Act 16), the Office of the State Treasurer (1995 Wisconsin Act 27), and again to the Department of Administration (1997 Wisconsin Act 27).

The agency manages four "trust funds", the largest of which is the Common School Fund. The principal of this fund continues to grow through the collection of fees, fines, and forfeitures that accrue to the state. Most of the trust fund assets are invested in loans to Wisconsin munici-palities and school districts through the State Trust Fund Loan Program. The loans finance a wide variety of public purpose projects statewide while providing the trust funds with a reason-able rate of return at low risk. Over the last five years, Wisconsin citizens have benefited from $695.8 million in trust fund loans used to support community, public safety, economic devel-opment, and school projects. Trust assets that are not invested in trust fund loans are invested in state and municipal bonds and the State Investment Fund. The agency is self-funded and distributes more than 96 cents of every investment dollar earned to its beneficiaries as directed by Article X of the state constitution.

The net earnings of the Common School Fund are distributed annually by the Department of Public Instruction to all Wisconsin public school districts. During the 2014 and 2015 fis-cal years, a total of $65.7 million in earnings were distributed from the Common School Fund to support public school libraries throughout Wisconsin. The other small trust funds are used to support the University of Wisconsin and the state's general fund. 2005 Wisconsin Act 352 enables the board to use the proceeds of the state of trust lands to purchase other property to improve timberland management, prevent forest fragmentation, or increase public access to ex-isting land holdings. Over the last five years, the agency has increased lands managed for timber by 25% and increased public access by 28%.

PUBLIC RECORDS BOARD

Members: MATTHEW BLESSING (representing the director, state historical society), *chairperson;* SANDRA BROADY-RUDD (governor's designee), *vice chairperson;* CARL BUESING (local government representative), *secretary;* vacancy (attorney general or designee); BRYAN NAAB (representing the state auditor); MELISSA SCHMIDT (representing the director of the legislative council staff); vacancy (small business representative); PETER SORCE (other member). (Representatives are appointed by the respective officers or the governor.)

Executive Secretary: GEORGIA THOMPSON, georgia.thompson@wi.gov

Mailing Address: 4622 University Avenue, Door 10A, Madison 53702.

Telephone: (608) 266-2770.

Fax: (608) 266-5050.

Internet Address: http://publicrecordsboard.wi.gov

Publications: General Schedules for Records Common to State Agencies and Local Units of Government; miscellaneous training and records materials.

Statutory References: Sections 15.105 (4) and 16.61.

Agency Responsibility: The 8-member Public Records Board is responsible for the preserva-tion of important state records, the cost-effective management of records by state agencies, and the orderly disposition of state records that have become obsolete. State agencies must have written approval from the board to dispose of records they generate or receive.

1991 Wisconsin Acts 39 and 269 directed the board to create a registry of those record series that contain personally identifiable information and made it the repository for general informa-tion about state computer matching programs.

Originally created by Chapter 316, Laws of 1947, as the Committee on Public Records and placed under the State Historical Society, the agency was transferred to the governor's office by Chapter 547, Laws of 1957. The committee was renamed the Public Records Board and at-tached to the Department of Administration by Chapter 75, Laws of 1967. Chapter 350, Laws of 1981, changed the board's name to the Public Records and Forms Board and added forms management to its duties. In 1995, Wisconsin Act 27 designated the board's current name and removed its forms management duties.

SMALL BUSINESS REGULATORY REVIEW BOARD

Members: SENATOR MARKLEIN (senate small business committee chairperson), REPRESENTATIVE NEYLON (assembly small business committee chairperson); STEVE DAVIS, ERICH KORTH, JIM RING, MINOO SEIFODDINI, GUY WOOD, THOMAS WULF, vacancy (appointed by governor).

Statutory References: Sections 15.105 (33), and 227.30.

State Capitol and Executive Residence Board members meeting at the Executive Residence in April 2015. *(Greg Anderson, Legislative Photographer)*

Agency Responsibility: The 9-member Small Business Regulatory Review Board may determine that a newly filed emergency rule would have a significant fiscal impact on small businesses, defined as ones that employ 25 or fewer full-time employees or have gross annual sales of less than $5 million. The board may further determine whether the issuing agency has complied with statutory provisions that seek to reduce the impact of rules on small businesses and whether the data used to propose a rule is accurate. If the board finds an agency has not complied with the law, it may request compliance from that agency, and, in addition, suggest changes to the proposed rule. The board may also review state agency rules and guidelines to determine whether they place an unnecessary burden on small businesses. If the board determines a rule or guideline does place an undue burden on small businesses, it submits a report and recommendations to the Joint Committee for Review of Administrative Rules.

The 7 members the governor appoints represent small business and serve 3-year terms. The senate majority leader and assembly speaker each appoint one chairperson from standing committees concerned with small business. The board was created by 2003 Wisconsin Act 145 and its membership was revised by 2007 Wisconsin Act 20 and 2011 Wisconsin Acts 32 and 46.

STATE CAPITOL AND EXECUTIVE RESIDENCE BOARD

Members: SENATOR RISSER, *chairperson;* CINDY TORSTVEIT (designated by secretary of administration); JIM DRAEGER (designated by director, state historical society); vacancy (engineer employed by the Department of Administration and appointed by secretary); SENATORS OLSEN, ROTH; REPRESENTATIVES BORN, HESSELBEIN, HINTZ, LOUDENBECK; ARLAN K. KAY, RON SIGGLEKOW (architects); JOHN J. FERNHOLZ (landscape architect); DEBRA ALTON, LAUREL BROWN (interior designers); MARIJO REED (citizen member or architect, landscape architect, or interior designer). (All except *ex officio* members and their designees are appointed by governor.)

Statutory References: Sections 15.105 (5) and 16.83.

Agency Responsibility: The 16-member State Capitol and Executive Residence Board (SCERB), created by Chapters 183 and 217, Laws of 1967, includes 7 citizen members with specified expertise, appointed by the governor to serve staggered 6-year terms. The purpose of the board is to ensure the architectural and decorative integrity of the buildings, decorative furniture, furnishings, and grounds of the capitol and executive residence and direct the continuing and consistent maintenance of the properties. No renovations, repairs (except of an emergency nature), installation of fixtures, decorative items, or furnishings for the ground and buildings of the capitol or executive residence may be performed by or become the property of the state by purchase wholly or in part from state funds, or by gift, loan or otherwise, until approved by the board as to design, structure, composition, and appropriateness.

History: Increasing awareness of and concern for preserving and protecting the special nature of the people's buildings led to creation of a mechanism for ensuring that the public interest and appropriate standards be carefully considered when altering or redecorating historic facilities. Building upon the *State Capitol Restoration Guidelines* prepared in 1980 by the Department of Administration's Division of State Facilities, the Legislature's Joint Committee on Legislative Organization in 1987 approved the Capitol Master Plan, which envisioned a full-scale renovation of the Capitol, balancing the integrity of the building with the need to maintain it as a modern, functioning seat of government. After approval of the plan by SCERB and the State of Wisconsin Building Commission, renovation of the Capitol, whose construction had been completed in 1917, commenced in 1990 and concluded in 2001. The project included extensive updating and improvements to the plumbing, electrical, and heating and cooling systems, and largely restored office spaces to their original décor. The board is also responsible for overseeing the upkeep of the Classical Revival home on the shores of Lake Mendota in the Village of Maple Bluff that has served as the official residence of the governor's family for over 50 years.

Office of State
EMPLOYMENT RELATIONS

Director: GREGORY L. GRACZ.

Deputy Director: DANIELLE CARNE, 266-0047, danielle.carne@

Chief Legal Counsel: DANIELLE CARNE, *acting,* 266-0047, danielle.carne@

Affirmative Action, Division of: JEANETTE JOHNSON, *administrator,* 266-3017.

Compensation and Labor Relations, Division of: KATHY KOPP, *administrator,* 266-1860.

    Compensation, Bureau of: vacancy, *director,* 266-1729.

    Labor Relations, Bureau of: vacancy.

Merit Recruitment and Selection, Division of: DANIELLE CARNE, *acting administrator,* 266-0047, danielle.carne@

    Agency Services, Bureau of: LINDA BRENNAN, *director,* 267-0408, linda.brennan@

    Outreach Services, Bureau of: JIM UNDERHILL, *director,* 267-2155, jim.underhill@

State Employee Suggestion Program: 267-2155, e-mail: wiemployeesuggestionprogram@; Internet address: http://suggest.wi.gov

Address e-mail by combining the user ID and the state extender: userid@**wisconsin.gov**

Mailing Address: P.O. Box 7855, Madison 53707-7855.

Location: 101 East Wilson Street, 4th Floor, Madison.

Telephone: State job information: (608) 266-1731.

Fax: (608) 267-1020.

Internet Address: http://oser.state.wi.us

Publications: Council on Affirmative Action Report; Wisc.Jobs Bulletin; Veterans Employment Report; W-2 Hiring Report; Workforce Planning and Fact Book; Written Hiring Reasons Report.

Number of Employees: 49.95.

Total Budget 2013-15: $11,984,700.

Statutory References: Sections 15.105 (29); Chapter 111, Subchapter V, and Chapter 230.

Agency Responsibility: The Office of State Employment Relations is responsible for personnel and employment relations policies and programs for state government employees. The office administers the state's classified service, which is designed to staff state governmental agencies with employees chosen on the basis of merit. It evaluates job categories, determines employee performance and training needs, and assists managers in their supervisory duties. The office sets standards for and ensures compliance with affirmative action plans and provides training on human resource programs to supervisors, managers, human resource staff, and other state employees. It represents the executive branch in its role as an employer under the state's employment relations statutes.

A director, appointed by the governor, administers the office. The director appoints the administrators of the Division of Affirmative Action and the Division of Compensation and Labor Relations from outside the classified service. The governor appoints the administrator of the Division of Merit Recruitment and Selection to a 5-year term, with the advice and consent of the senate, based on a competitive examination. The governor may appoint the administrator for subsequent 5-year terms with the senate's consent.

Unit Functions: The *Division of Affirmative Action* administers the state's equal employment opportunity/affirmative action (EEO/AA) program and reports annually to the governor and legislature about the affirmative action accomplishments of state agencies. It develops state EEO/AA policies, procedures and programs; establishes state standards for agencies, the University of Wisconsin System, and legislative service agencies; approves and monitors agency EEO/AA plans, analyzes state workforce data for use in developing EEO/AA reports and recommendations. It monitors the effect of personnel transactions, hiring processes and employment conditions at state agencies to ensure that AA group members are not adversely affected, provides information and technical assistance to agencies to assist in the development of innovative personnel programs to increase the effectiveness of state EEO/AA efforts, assists in compliance investigations, helps state agencies in the recruitment for hard-to-fill positions, provides EEO/AA and diversity training to supervisors and managers, and provides support staff to the Council on Affirmative Action.

The *Division of Compensation and Labor Relations* administers the state's compensation plan and leave statutes and policies. It also assists in state agency compliance with the federal and state family and medical leave acts. The division represents the state as the employer in negotiating wages, benefits, and working conditions with the certified labor unions that represent state employees, and those contracts must then be ratified by the legislature. The division serves the state in arbitration proceedings and conducts labor relations training programs for state management representatives. It assigns nonrepresented classifications to pay ranges and assigns certain represented classifications to pay ranges as part of the collective bargaining process. It also assists in state agency compliance with protective occupation determinations and the federal Fair Labor Standards Act.

The *Division of Merit Recruitment and Selection,* created in Section 15.105 (29)(b) in 2003 Wisconsin Act 33, administers the state's civil service system by coordinating the recruiting, testing, evaluating, and hiring of applicants. It conducts and coordinates training for state managers and human resources staff. The division assists agencies in workforce planning and administers layoffs, transfers, and reinstatements of nonrepresented classified employees. It allocates positions to classifications and administers the state's performance evaluation program. The division operates Wisconsin Personnel Partners, which provides personnel services to local government units, and the Wisconsin Certification Examination Services, which provides licensure examination services to agencies on a fee basis. The division also oversees the administration of employee assistance programs in all state agencies, under which state employees and their families may receive assistance with personal or work-related problems.

History: An office that administers state employment procedures dates back to the creation of a State Civil Service Commission in Chapter 363, Laws of 1905. The law declared that appointments to and promotions in the civil service would be made only according to merit. Chapter 456, Laws of 1929, reconstituted the commission as the Personnel Board within the newly created Bureau of Personnel. This structure continued for 30 years until the legislature placed the board and bureau in the new Department of Administration, created in Chapter 228, Laws of 1959.

In 1972, Governor Patrick Lucey issued an executive order creating an affirmative action unit in the Bureau of Personnel. The order also directed the head of every state agency to encourage women and minorities to apply for promotions and to designate an affirmative action officer responsible for developing an affirmative action plan.

Chapter 196, Laws of 1977, created the Department of Employment Relations and transferred to it from the Department of Administration the organizational units and functions of the Employee Relations Division, including affirmative action, personnel, collective bargaining, and human resources services.

The legislature reorganized personnel functions in 1983 Wisconsin Act 27 by assigning classification and compensation responsibility to the secretary and recruitment and examination responsibility to a statutorily created Division of Merit Recruitment and Selection. The same law created the Personnel Board as an independent agency to review civil service rules and investigate and report on their impact. 1989 Wisconsin Act 31 abolished the Personnel Board and transferred its functions to the department. The 2003-05 biennial budget, Act 33, abolished the department and created the Office of State Employment Relations attached to the Department of Administration.

Statutory Council and Board

Affirmative Action, Council on: CHRISTOPHER ZENCHENKO (appointed by senate president), *chairperson;* JAMES PARKER (appointed by governor), *vice chairperson;* ROGER L. PULLIAM (appointed by assembly speaker); vacancy (appointed by senate minority leader), vacancy (appointed by assembly minority leader); YOLANDA SANTOS ADAMS, LAKSHMI BHARADWAJ, JANICE K. HUGHES, JOHN MAGERUS, SANDRA RYAN, RONALD SHAHEED, NANCY VUE, 3 vacancies (appointed by governor).

Contact person: vacancy, *administrator,* Division of Affirmative Action and Workforce Planning, 266-3017.

The 15-member Council on Affirmative Action advises the director of state employment relations, evaluates affirmative action programs throughout the classified service, seeks compliance with state and federal regulations, and recommends improvements in the state's affirmative action efforts. The council must report annually to the legislature and governor. It may recommend legislation, consult with agency personnel and other interested groups, and conduct hearings. Council members serve 3-year terms. A majority of them must be public members, and a majority must represent minority persons, women, and people with disabilities. The council was created by Chapter 196, Laws of 1977, in the Department of Employment Relations and is located in the Office of State Employment Relations (2003 Wisconsin Act 33). Its composition and duties are prescribed in Sections 15.105 (29)(d) and 230.46 of the statutes.

State Employees Suggestion Board: DANIELLE JOHNSON, *chairperson;* PAUL RUBY, vacancy (all appointed by governor).

Internet Address: http://suggest.wi.gov

The 3-member State Employees Suggestion Board administers an awards program to encourage unusual and meritorious suggestions and accomplishments by state employees that promote economy and efficiency in government services. Board members are appointed for 4-year terms, and at least one of them must be a state officer or employee. The board was created by Chapter 278, Laws of 1953, as the Wisconsin State Employees Merit Award Board and renamed in 1987 Wisconsin Act 142. It has been successively located in the Bureau of Personnel, the Department of Administration, the Department of Employment Relations (1989 Wisconsin Act 31), and the Office of State Employment Relations (2003 Wisconsin Act 33). Its composition and duties are prescribed in Sections 15.105 (29)(c) and 230.48 of the statutes.

STATE USE BOARD

Members: JEAN ZWEIFEL (work center representative), *chairperson;* MICHAEL CASEY, vacancy (public members); vacancy (mental health services representative, Department of Health Services); ENID GLENN (vocational rehabilitation representative, Department of Workforce

Development); NICKOLAS C. GEORGE, JR. (private business representative); HELEN MCCAIN (Department of Administration representative); BILL G. SMITH (small business representative). (All are appointed by governor.)

Mailing Address: Bureau of Procurement, Division of Enterprise Operations, P.O. Box 7867, Madison 53707-7867.

Telephone: (608) 266-5462.

Fax: (608) 267-0600.

Number of Employees: 1.50.

Total Budget 2013-15: $257,600.

Statutory References: Sections 15.105 (22) and 16.752.

Agency Responsibility: The 8-member State Use Board was created by 1989 Wisconsin Act 345. Its members, who serve 4-year terms, oversee state purchases from work centers certified by the board. To be certified, centers must meet certain conditions: 1) the work center must make a product or provide a service the state needs; 2) it must offer these goods or services at a fair market price; and 3) it must employ individuals with severe disabilities for at least 75% of the direct labor used in providing the goods or services.

TAX APPEALS COMMISSION

Commissioners: LORNA HEMP BOLL, DAVID W. WILMOTH, vacancy (appointed by governor with senate consent).

Legal Assistant: NANCY BATZ, 266-9754, nancy.batz@wisconsin.gov

Mailing Address: 5005 University Avenue, Suite 110, Madison 53705.

Telephone: (608) 266-1391.

Fax: (608) 261-7060.

Number of Employees: 5.00.

Total Budget 2013-15: $1,076,400.

Statutory References: Sections 15.01 (2), 15.06 (1), 15.105 (1), and 73.01.

Publications: Decisions are at: www.wisbar.org/taxappeals.

Agency Responsibility: The 3-member Tax Appeals Commission hears and decides appeals of persons and entities of assessments and determinations of the Department of Revenue involving all major state-imposed taxes, including individual and corporate income taxes, homestead and farmland preservation tax credits, real estate transfer fees, and sales and use taxes, as well as appeals of state assessments of manufacturing property. The commission also hears and decides disputes between persons or entities and the Department of Transportation regarding certain motor vehicle taxes and fees. Cases involving the reasonableness of municipally imposed fees also fall under the jurisdiction of this commission. The commission's decisions may be appealed to circuit court.

Commissioners serve staggered 6-year terms and must be experienced in tax matters. The chairperson, who is designated by the governor to serve a 2-year term, must not serve on or under any committee of a political party. Employees of the commission are appointed by the chairperson from the classified service.

The Tax Appeals Commission was created as the Board of Tax Appeals by Chapter 412, Laws of 1939. Before 1939, individuals took appeals of income and property taxes to the local county board of review with appeal permitted to the state Tax Commission. Corporations took their appeals to the Commissioner of Taxation with appeal to the circuit court. The board was renamed the Tax Appeals Commission by Chapter 75, Laws of 1967.

COUNCIL ON UTILITY PUBLIC BENEFITS

Members: Inactive

The 11-member Council on Utility Public Benefits advises the Department of Administration on issues related to energy efficiency, conservation programs, and energy assistance to low-income households, including weatherization, payment of energy bills, and early identification and prevention of energy crises. Services are provided through community action agencies, nonprofit corporations, or local governments. Grants are also awarded to nonprofit corporations for energy conservation and efficiency services, renewable resources in the least competitive sectors of the energy conservation market, and programs that promote environmental protection, electric system reliability, or rural economic development. The council was created by 1999 Wisconsin Act 9, and its composition and duties are prescribed in Sections 15.107 (17) and 16.957 of the statutes.

VOLUNTEER FIRE FIGHTER AND EMERGENCY MEDICAL TECHNICIAN SERVICE AWARD BOARD

Members: ED EBERLE (secretary of administration designee), *chairperson;* vacancy (fire chiefs statewide organization representative); KENNETH A. BARTZ (volunteer fire fighters statewide organization representative), MELINDA R. ALLEN (volunteer emergency medical service technician), ALLEN R. SCHRAEDER, 2 vacancies (representatives of municipalities using volunteer fire fighters), JOHN SCHERER (individual experienced in financial planning). (All but *ex officio* members are appointed by governor.)

Contact person: DAWN VICK, 266-7043, dawn.vick@wisconsin.gov

Mailing Address: 101 East Wilson Street, 6th Floor, Madison 53703.

Telephone: (608) 266-7043.

Number of Employees: 0.00.

Total Budget 2013-15: $4,060,500.

Statutory References: Sections 15.105 (26) and 16.25.

The Service Award Program operates under the direction of an 8-member Volunteer Fire Fighter and Emergency Medical Technician Service Award Board appointed by the governor. It establishes by rule a tax-deferred benefit program for volunteer fire fighters, emergency medical technicians, and first responders based on their length of service to a community. The program is designed to assist municipalities in retaining volunteers. The board contracts with qualified organizations to provide investment plans and administrative services to municipalities that choose to participate in the service awards program, and the communities make payments directly to the plan providers. In appointing the board members, who serve 3-year terms, the governor must seek representatives from different regions of the state and from municipalities of different sizes. Representatives of the fire chiefs and volunteer fire fighters organizations must be volunteer fire fighters themselves. The board was created by 1999 Wisconsin Act 105.

WASTE FACILITY SITING BOARD

Members: All positions are currently vacant, and appointments would be made as necessary to resolve a case put before the board for resolution: secretary of transportation or designee; secretary of agriculture, trade and consumer protection or designee; secretary of safety and professional services or designee; two town officials; county official. (Town and county officials are appointed by governor with senate consent.)

Acting Executive Director: BRIAN HAYES.

Mailing Address: 5005 University Avenue, Suite 201, Madison 53705-5400.

E-mail Address: dhamail@wisconsin.gov

Internet Address: http://dha.state.wi.us

Telephone: (608) 261-6564.

Number of Employees: 0.00.

Total Budget 2013-15: $91,000.

Statutory References: Sections 15.07 (1)(b) 11., 15.105 (12), 289.33, and 289.64.

Agency Responsibility: The 6-member Waste Facility Siting Board supervises a mandated negotiation-arbitration procedure between applicants for new or expanded solid or hazardous waste facility licenses and local committees composed of representatives from the municipalities affected by proposed facilities. It is authorized to make final awards in arbitration hearings and can enforce legal deadlines and other obligations of applicants and local committees during the process.

When making appointments of town and county officials, the governor must consider timely recommendations of the Wisconsin Towns Association and the Wisconsin Counties Association. The board appoints an executive director who is authorized to request assistance from any state agency in helping the board fulfill its duties. The board is funded by a fee on each ton of waste disposed of in a licensed solid or hazardous waste facility. The board was created by Chapter 374, Laws of 1981.

WOMEN'S COUNCIL

Members: MARY JO BAAS (public member appointed by governor), *chairperson;* SENATORS HANSEN, SHILLING (appointed by senate majority leader); REPRESENTATIVES 2 vacancies (appointed by assembly speaker); MICHELLE METTNER (designated by governor); SARAH BRIGANTI, HEATHER SMITH (public members appointed by senate president); HEIDI GREEN, KIM NICKEL (public members appointed by assembly speaker); RENEE BOLDT, NICOLE BOWMAN-FARRELL, PATTY CADORIN, KAREN KATZ, JESSIE NICHOLSON (public members appointed by governor).

Executive Director: CHRISTINE LIDBURY.

Mailing Address: 101 East Wilson Street, 8th Floor, Madison 53702.

Telephone: (608) 266-2219.

Fax: (608) 267-0626.

E-mail Address: womenscouncil@wisconsin.gov

Internet Address: http://womenscouncil.wi.gov

Publications: Numerous publications related to the council's mission.

Number of Employees: 1.00.

Total Budget 2013-15: $280,800.

Statutory References: Sections 15.107 (11) and 16.01.

Agency Responsibility: The 15-member Women's Council is charged with identifying barriers that prevent women in Wisconsin from participating fully and equally in all aspects of life. The council promotes public and private sector initiatives that empower women through educational opportunity; provides a clearinghouse for information relating to women's issues; works in cooperation with related groups and organizations; and promotes opportunities for partnerships with various organizations to address issues affecting Wisconsin women. The council advises state agencies about the impact upon women of current and emerging state policies, laws, and rules; recommends changes to the public and private sectors and initiates legislation to further women's economic and social equality and improve this state's tax base and economy; and disseminates information on the status of women in this state.

The governor or governor's designee serves a 4-year term on the council; all other members serve 2-year terms. The governor appoints 6 public members, one of whom the governor designates as chairperson. The Women's Council was created by 1983 Wisconsin Act 27. It was preceded by a nonstatutory commission, the Governor's Commission on the Status of Women, which was created in 1964 and abolished in 1979.

Department of
AGRICULTURE, TRADE AND CONSUMER PROTECTION

> Address e-mail by combining the user ID and the state extender: userid@**wisconsin.gov**
> All telephone numbers are 608 area code unless otherwise indicated.

Board of Agriculture, Trade and Consumer Protection: ANDREW DIERCKS, *chairperson;* DENNIS BADTKE, MICHAEL DUMMER, NICOLE HANSEN, JOHN KOEPKE, MIRANDA LEIS, DOUGLAS WOLF (agricultural representatives); MARK SCHLEITWILER, DEAN STRAUSS (consumer representatives) (appointed by governor with senate consent).

Secretary of Agriculture, Trade and Consumer Protection: BEN BRANCEL, 224-5015.

Deputy Secretary: JEFF LYON, 224-5035.

Assistant Deputy Secretary: SANDRA CHALMERS, 224-5001.

Wisconsin Agricultural Statistics Service: GREG BUSSLER, *state agricultural statistician,* 224-4838, greg.bussler@nass.usda.gov

Legal Counsel, Office of: vacancy, *chief counsel,* 224-5022.

Mailing Address: P.O. Box 8911, Madison 53708-8911.

Location: 2811 Agriculture Drive, Madison.

Telephones: Consumer Protection Hotline: (800) 422-7128; Farm and Rural Services Hotline: (800) 942-2474; Wisconsin Telemarketing No-Call List sign-up: (866) 966-2255.

Fax: Office of the Secretary: 224-5034; Division of Agricultural Development: 224-5110; Division of Agricultural Resource Management: 224-4656; Division of Animal Health: 224-4871; Division of Food Safety: 224-4710; Division of Management Services: 224-4737; Division of Trade and Consumer Protection: 224-4963.

Internet Address: www.datcp.wi.gov

Departmental E-mail Address: datcp_web@wisconsin.gov

Agricultural Development, Division of: DANIEL SMITH, *administrator,* 224-5142, daniel.smith@

    Agricultural Business and Sector Development Bureau: DANIEL SMITH, *interim director.*

    Agricultural Market Development Bureau: JEN PINO-GALLAGHER, *director,* 224-5125, jen.pinogallagher@

    Farm and Rural Services Bureau: KATHY SCHMITT, *director,* 224-5048, kathy.schmitt@

    County Fair Coordinator: ROBERT WILLIAMS, 224-5131, robert.williams@

Agricultural Resource Management, Division of: JOHN PETTY, *administrator,* 224-4567, john.petty@

    Agrichemical Management, Bureau of: LORI BOWMAN, *director,* 224-4550, lori.bowman@

    Land and Water Resources, Bureau of: KEITH FOYE, *director,* 224-4603, keith.foye@

    Plant Industry, Bureau of: BRIAN KUHN, *director and assistant division administrator,* 224-4590, brian.kuhn@

Animal Health, Division of: PAUL MCGRAW, *state veterinarian, administrator,* 224-4884, paul.mcgraw@

    Animal Disease Control, Bureau of: DARLENE KONKLE, *director,* 224-4902, darlene.konkle@

    Field Services, Bureau of: MELISSA MACE, *director,* 224-4883, melissa.mace@

    State Humane Officer: YVONNE M. BELLAY, 224-4888, yvonne.bellay@

Food Safety, Division of: STEVEN C. INGHAM, *administrator,* 224-4701, steven.ingham@

    Food Safety and Inspection, Bureau of: PETER HAASE, *director,* 224-4711, peter.haase@

    Meat Safety and Inspection, Bureau of: CINDY KLUG, *director,* 224-4729, cindy.klug@

Management Services, Division of: MICHELLE WACHTER, *administrator,* 224-4743, michelle.wachter@

    Finance, Bureau of: JASON GHERKE, *director,* 224-4748, jason.gherke@

    Human Resources, Bureau of: ALISON SCHERER, *director,* 224-4761, alison.scherer@

    Information Technology Services, Bureau of: KAREN ARRIOLA, *director,* 224-4770, karen.arriola@

    Laboratory Services, Bureau of: STEVEN M. SOBEK, *director,* 267-3500, steve.sobek@

Trade and Consumer Protection, Division of: FRANK FRASSETTO, *administrator,* 224-4929, frank.frassetto@

    Business Trade Practices, Bureau of: JEREMY S. MCPHERSON, *director,* 224-4922, jeremy.mcpherson@

    Consumer Protection, Bureau of: MICHELLE REINEN, *director and assistant division administrator,* 224-4965, michelle.reinen@

DEPARTMENT OF AGRICULTURE, TRADE AND CONSUMER PROTECTION

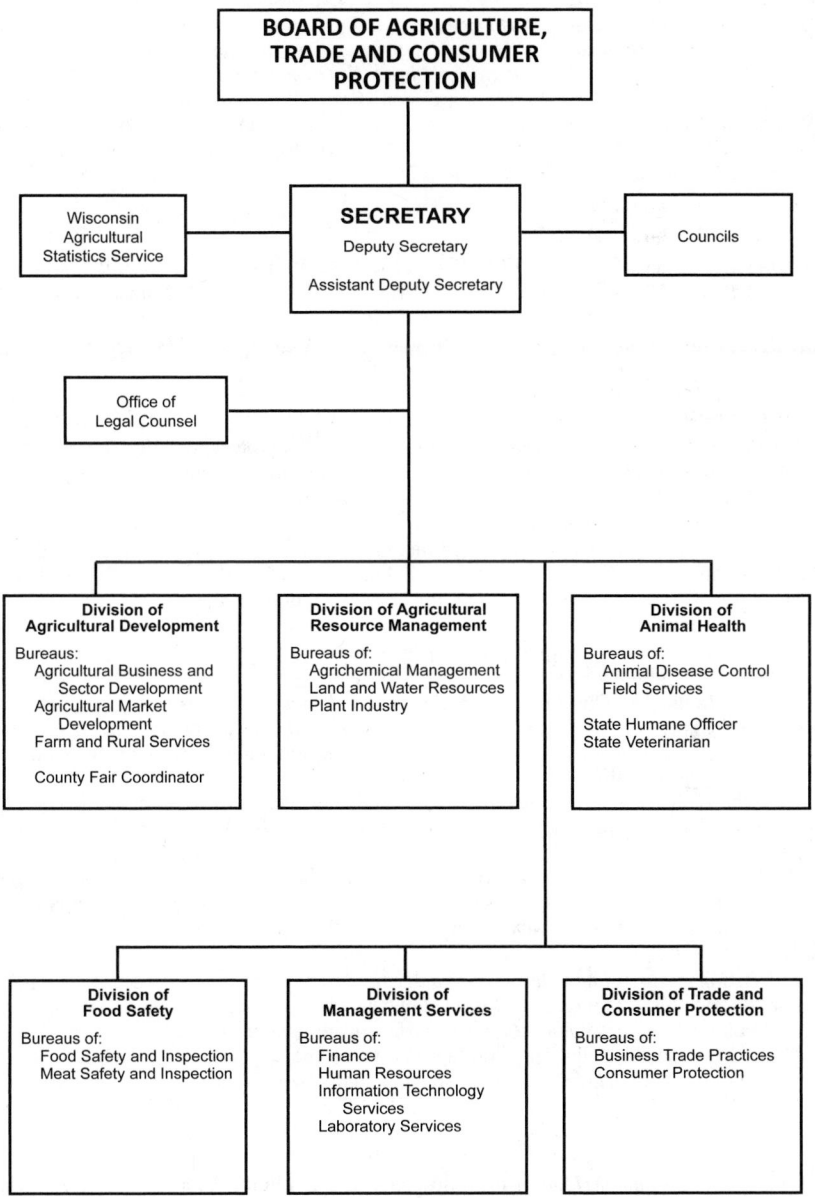

BOARD OF AGRICULTURE, TRADE AND CONSUMER PROTECTION

Wisconsin Agricultural Statistics Service

SECRETARY
Deputy Secretary
Assistant Deputy Secretary

Councils

Office of Legal Counsel

Division of Agricultural Development

Bureaus:
Agricultural Business and Sector Development
Agricultural Market Development
Farm and Rural Services

County Fair Coordinator

Division of Agricultural Resource Management

Bureaus of:
Agrichemical Management
Land and Water Resources
Plant Industry

Division of Animal Health

Bureaus of:
Animal Disease Control
Field Services

State Humane Officer
State Veterinarian

Division of Food Safety

Bureaus of:
Food Safety and Inspection
Meat Safety and Inspection

Division of Management Services

Bureaus of:
Finance
Human Resources
Information Technology Services
Laboratory Services

Division of Trade and Consumer Protection

Bureaus of:
Business Trade Practices
Consumer Protection

Units attached for administrative purposes under Sec. 15.03:   Bioenergy Council
Land and Water Conservation Board
Livestock Facility Siting Review Board

Publications: Agricultural Land Sales; *Chloroacetanilide Herbicide Metabolites in Wisconsin Groundwater; Complaint Guide for the Wisconsin Consumer;* Farm Transfers in Wisconsin – A Guide for Farmers; *Groundwater Protection: An Evaluation of Wisconsin's Atrazine Rule; Groundwater Quality – Agricultural Chemicals in Wisconsin Groundwater April 2008;* Guide to Wisconsin Cheese Factory Outlets and Tours; *Landlord and Tenants: The Wisconsin Way; Livestock Guidance: Local Planning for Livestock Operations in Wisconsin; Planning for Agriculture in Wisconsin: A Guide for Communities; Preventing Senior Citizen Rip-offs;* Wisconsin Agricultural Statistics; Wisconsin Dairy Plant Directory; Wisconsin Nursery Directory; Wisconsin Pest Bulletin; *The Wisconsin Senior Guide.* http://datcp.wi.gov/uploads/Consumer/pdf/SeniorGuide170.pdf.

Number of Employees: 623.89.

Total Budget 2013-15: $193,262,300.

Statutory References: Sections 15.13, 15.135, and 15.137; Chapters 88, 91-100, 127, and 136.

Agency Responsibility: The Department of Agriculture, Trade and Consumer Protection regulates agriculture, trade, and commercial activity in Wisconsin for the protection of the state's citizens. It enforces the state's primary consumer protection laws, including those relating to deceptive advertising, unfair business practices, and consumer product safety. The department oversees enforcement of Wisconsin's animal health and disease control laws and conducts a variety of programs to conserve and protect the state's vital land, water, and plant resources.

The department administers financial security programs to protect agricultural producers, facilitates the marketing of Wisconsin agricultural products in interstate and international markets, and promotes agricultural development and diversification.

Organization: The 9 members of the Board of Agriculture, Trade and Consumer Protection serve staggered 6-year terms. Of the board members, 2 must be consumer representatives and 7 must have an agricultural background. Appointments to the board must be made "without regard to party affiliation, residence or interest in any special organized group". The board directs and supervises the department, which is administered by a secretary appointed by the governor with the advice and consent of the senate. The secretary appoints the division administrators from outside the classified service.

Unit Functions: The *Division of Agricultural Development* provides services to assist producers, agribusinesses, and organizations to develop local, state, national, and international markets for Wisconsin agricultural products and to foster agricultural development and diversification in the state. It also provides counseling and mediation services to farmers, administers a rural electric power service program with the Public Service Commission, and oversees the operation of producer-elected marketing boards that assess fees within their respective groups for promotion, research, and education related to their commodities. The division also administers Agricultural Development and Diversification grants, a federal-state market news program, the "Something Special from Wisconsin" and Alice in Dairyland marketing programs, as well as the state aid programs for county and district fairs, the Livestock Breeders Association, and World Dairy Expo.

The *Division of Agricultural Resource Management* administers programs designed to protect the state's agricultural resources, as well as public health and the environment. It works to prevent agricultural practices that contaminate surface water and groundwater and jointly administers a nonpoint source pollution control program with the Department of Natural Resources. It directs programs related to farmland preservation and soil and land conservation, agricultural chemical cleanup, drainage districts, and agricultural impact statements. It regulates the sale and use of pesticides, animal feed, fertilizers, seed, and soil and plant additives and conducts programs to prevent and control plant pests, such as the gypsy moth.

The *Division of Animal Health* works closely with agricultural producers and veterinarians to diagnose, prevent, and control serious domestic animal diseases that threaten public health and the food chain. It licenses and inspects animal dealers and markets, regulates the import and export of animals across state lines, acts to prevent the spread of animal diseases, and assists in the enforcement of state humane laws. Through the Premises Identification Program, it registers persons who keep livestock and assigns an identification code to each place at which livestock are kept to facilitate animal disease control. It also regulates emerging industries, such as aquaculture and farm-raised deer.

The *Division of Food Safety* protects the state's food supply. From production through processing, packaging, distribution, and retail sale, the division works to ensure safe and wholesome food and to prevent fraud and misbranding in food sales. It licenses and inspects dairy plants, food and beverage processing establishments, meat slaughter and processing facilities, food warehouses, grocery stores, and other food establishments. The division inspects all dairy farms; inspects and samples food products; oversees food grading; and regulates the advertising, packaging, and labeling of food products.

The *Division of Management Services* provides administrative services to the department, including budget and accounting; facilities and fleet management; shipping, mailing, and printing; human resource management; and information technology services. The division also operates a general laboratory that provides analytical support to departmental inspection and sampling programs.

The *Division of Trade and Consumer Protection* enforces a wide range of consumer protection laws and handles nearly 200,000 consumer complaints and inquiries annually. It promulgates and enforces rules pertaining to deceptive advertising, consumer fraud, consumer product safety, landlord-tenant practices, home improvement, telecommunications, telemarketing, motor vehicle repair, fair packaging and labeling, weights and measures, and many other aspects of marketing. To promote fair and open competition in the marketplace, the division investigates and regulates unfair and anticompetitive business practices. It monitors the financial condition and business practices of dairy plants, grain warehouses, food processing plants, and public storage warehouses in order to protect agricultural producers and depositors. It also administers the state's Telemarketing No-Call List.

History: The present form of the Department of Agriculture, Trade and Consumer Protection is largely the result of the consolidation of several related agencies in 1929, but the department traces its lineage and responsibilities back to pre-statehood days.

From its beginnings, Wisconsin has been concerned with agriculture; food quality, safety, and labeling; plant and animal health; unfair business and trade practices; and consumer protection, and has taken steps to protect the public. The 1839 territorial legislature provided for the inspection of certain food and other products and established a program to regulate weights and measures. County inspectors were responsible for certifying the grade, wholesomeness, quantity, and proper packaging of food and distilled spirits, with county treasurers charged with enforcing the weights and measures standards. The 1867 Legislature, in Chapter 176, authorized the governor to appoint a treasury agent to enforce the laws relating to itinerant sales by "hawkers and peddlers". The 1889 Legislature, in Chapter 452, created the Office of the Dairy and Food Commissioner to enforce food safety, food labeling, and weights and measures laws. Other legislation over the years created various related functions such as the State Veterinarian, the State Board of Agriculture, the Inspector of Apiaries, the State Orchard and Nursery Inspector, the State Supervisor of Illuminating Oils, and the State Humane Agent.

The Department of Agriculture was created by Chapter 413, Laws of 1915, which combined the functions of several prior entities including the Board of Agriculture, Livestock Sanitary Board, State Veterinarian, Inspector of Apiaries, and Orchard and Nursery Inspector. Under the control and supervision of a Commissioner of Agriculture appointed by the governor with senate consent, the department had the responsibility to promote the interests of agriculture, dairying, horticulture, manufactures, and the domestic arts. It collected and published farm crop, livestock, and other statistics relating to state resources and regulated the practice of veterinary medicine. Through its own informational publications and paid advertisements in print media both inside the country and in foreign lands, it also sought to further the "development and enrichment" of the state by attracting "desirable immigrants" and "capital seeking profitable investment". These efforts were intended to promote the advantages and opportunities offered by the state "to the farmer, the merchant, the manufacturer, the home seeker, and the summer visitor".

The Division of Markets was created within the Department of Agriculture by Chapter 670, Laws of 1919. The duty of the division was to promote, in the interest of the producer, distributor, and consuming public, the economical and efficient distribution of farm products. Responsibilities included devising systems for marketing, grading, standardization, and storage of farm products; preventing deceptive practices; maintaining a market news service for collecting and reporting information on the supply, demand, prices, and commercial movement of farm products; and designing copyrighted trademarks, labels, and brands for Wisconsin farm products. A separate Department of Markets was created by Chapter 571, Laws of 1921, under the direction of a commissioner of markets appointed by the governor with senate consent. The department retained most of the duties of the former division, but was allowed to give assistance to cooperative associations and was specifically charged with regulating unfair methods of competition in business and unfair trade practices.

The modern department had its inception when Chapter 479, Laws of 1929, created the Department of Agriculture and Markets by consolidation of the Department of Agriculture, the Department of Markets, the Dairy and Food Commissioner, the State Treasury Agent, the State Supervisor of Inspectors of Illuminating Oils, and the State Humane Agent. The department, which was under the control of three commissioners appointed by the governor with senate consent, assumed all duties performed by the component agencies. The department was reorganized and renamed the Department of Agriculture by Chapter 85, Laws of 1939, but its basic mission and authority was not changed. The department was overseen by a 7-member State Board of Agriculture, whose members, appointed by the governor with senate consent, in turn appointed the department's director. All members of the board were required to be persons experienced in farming.

The department's name was changed to the current Department of Agriculture, Trade and Consumer Protection by Chapter 29, Laws of 1977. This law also specified that one of the 7 board members must be a consumer representative.

1995 Wisconsin Act 27 directed the governor, rather than the board, to appoint the department secretary with senate consent, and expanded the board's membership to 8, including 2 consumer representatives. The board continues to set policy for the agency. Act 27 also consolidated the administration of most consumer protection activities within the department by transferring some staff and functions from the Department of Justice. However, the Department of Justice cooperates in the enforcement of consumer protection laws by providing legal services such as civil litigation. 1997 Wisconsin Act 95 added a ninth board member to represent agriculture.

In recent decades, the legislature has expanded the department's responsibilities related to land and water resources, including the areas of soil conservation, drainage districts, groundwater protection, nonpoint source pollution abatement, pesticides, animal disease control, and agricultural chemical storage and cleanup. It has allowed the department to create marketing boards for agricultural commodities, to promote agricultural development and diversification, and promote the state's agricultural products in interstate and international markets. The department also conducts programs for protecting producers against catastrophic financial defaults, farmland preservation, and farm mediation.

Statutory Councils

Agricultural Education and Workforce Development Council: KATHY SCHMITT (secretary of agriculture, trade and consumer protection designee); SHARON WENDT (state superintendent of public instruction designee); MIKE GRECO (secretary of workforce development designee); CATE RAHMLOW (chief executive officer of the Wisconsin Economic Development Corporation designee); JD SMITH (secretary of natural resources designee); JOHN SHUTSKE (president of the University of Wisconsin System designee); TAYLOR WEICHMAN (director of the technical college system designee); DAVID WILLIAMS (chancellor of the University of Wisconsin-Extension designee); MICHAEL COMPTON (member chosen jointly by deans of specified UW System colleges and UW-Madison School of Veterinary Medicine); LORI WEYERS (technical college system director appointed by director of the technical college system); DAVID SHONKWEILER (technical college dean with authority over agricultural programs appointed by director of technical college system); SENATOR OLSEN (chairperson of a senate standing committee concerned with education); REPRESENTATIVE THIESFELDT (chairperson of an assembly standing committee concerned with education); SENATOR MOULTON (chairperson of a senate standing committee concerned with agriculture); Representative Nerison (chairperson of an assembly standing committee concerned with agriculture); Paul Larson (Wisconsin Association of Agricultural Educators representative); Karen Gefvert, Becky Levzow (general agriculture representatives); Terri Dallas, Paul Diettman (agribusiness representatives); Cheryl Todea (representative environmental stewardship); Earl Gustafson (representative of businesses related to natural resources); Liz Henry (representative of businesses related to plant agriculture); Richard Miller (representative of landscaping, golf course, greenhouse, floral, and related businesses); Laura Bahn-Wornell (representative of food product and food processing businesses); Andrea Brossard Martin (representative of businesses related to animal agriculture); Dan Wegner (representative of businesses related to renewable energy); Bob Meyer (representative of agricultural communication interests); Al Herrman (representative of businesses providing engineering, mechanical, electronic, and power services relating to agriculture); vacancy (board of agriculture, trade and consumer protection representative); Dave Kruse (teacher of science, vocational technology, business, math, or a similar field, appointed by superintendent of public instruction); vacancy (school guidance counselor, appointed by superintendent of public instruction); Bill Herr (school board member, appointed by superintendent of public instruction); vacancy (school district administrator, appointed by superintendent of public instruction) (all except *ex officio* members, legislators, and those appointed by the superintendent of public instruction are appointed by the secretary of agriculture, trade and consumer protection).

The mission of the 34-member Agricultural Education and Workforce Development Council is to recommend policies and other changes to improve the efficiency of the development and provision of agricultural education across educational systems and to support employment in industries related to agriculture, food, and natural resources by seeking to increase the hiring and retention of well-qualified employees and promote the coordination of educational systems to develop, train, and retrain employees for current and future careers. It also advises state agencies on matters relating to integrating agricultural education and workforce development systems. All except *ex officio* members and legislators are appointed for staggered 3-year terms and may not serve more than 2 consecutive terms. The council was created by 2007 Wisconsin Act 223 and its composition and duties are prescribed in Sections 15.137 (2) and 93.33 of the statutes.

Agricultural Producer Security Council: Craig Myrhe (Farmer's Educational and Cooperative Union of America, Wisconsin Division, representative), Nicholas George (Midwest Food Processor's Association, Inc., representative), Don Hamm (National Farmer's Organization, Inc., representative), vacancy (Wisconsin Agri-Service Association, Inc., representative), John Umhoefer (Wisconsin Cheese Makers Association representative), Jim Zimmerman (representative of both the Wisconsin Corn Growers Association, Inc., and the Wisconsin Soybean Association, Inc.), Louise Hemstead (Wisconsin Dairy Products Association, Inc., representative), Dave Daniels (Wisconsin Farm Bureau Federation representative), John Manske (Wisconsin Federation of Cooperatives representative), Jeremie Pavelski (Wisconsin Potato and Vegetable Growers Association, Inc., representative) (appointed by the secretary of agriculture, trade and consumer protection).

The 10-member Agricultural Producer Security Council advises the Department of Agriculture, Trade and Consumer Protection (DATCP) on the administration and enforcement of agricultural producer security programs. All members are appointed by the secretary of DATCP for 3-year terms. The council was created by 2001 Wisconsin Act 16 and its composition and duties are prescribed in Sections 15.137 (1) and 126.90 of the statutes.

Farm to School Council.

The Farm to School Council advises the Department of Agriculture, Trade and Consumer Protection regarding the promotion and administration of farm to school programs. The secretary of DATCP appoints an employee of the department and appoints an unspecified number of farmers, experts in child care, school food service personnel, and other persons with interests in agriculture, nutrition, and education. The secretary of health services appoints an employee of the department of health services and the superintendent of public instruction appoints an employee of the department of public instruction. The council was created by 2009 Wisconsin Act 293 and its composition and duties are prescribed in Sections 15.137 (3) and 93.49 of the statutes.

Fertilizer Research Council: Voting members: Bruce Andersen, Brian Madigan, Andy Walsh (industry representatives nominated by fertilizer industry); Jason Henschler, Alan Jewell, Tom Novak (crop producing farmer representatives); Joe Baeten (water quality expert appointed by secretary of natural resources). (All except the water quality expert are appointed jointly by secretary of agriculture, trade and consumer protection and dean of UW-Madison College of Agricultural and Life Sciences.) Nonvoting members: Ben Brancel (secretary of agriculture, trade and consumer protection), Cathy Stepp (secretary of natural resources), Bill Bland, Geoff Siemering (UW-Madison College of Agricultural and Life Sciences).

Mailing Address: P.O. Box 8911, Madison 53708-8911.

Telephone: 224-4614.

The Fertilizer Research Council meets annually to review and recommend projects involving research on soil management, soil fertility, plant nutrition, and for research on surface and groundwater problems related to fertilizer use. The secretary of agriculture, trade and consumer protection grants final approval for project funding. These research projects are granted to the UW System and are financed through funds generated from the sale of fertilizer and soil or plant additives in Wisconsin. The council's voting members are appointed for 3-year terms and may not serve more than 2 consecutive terms. The council was created by Chapter 418, Laws of 1977, and its composition and duties are prescribed in Sections 15.137 (5) and 94.64 (8m) of the statutes.

Independent Units Attached for Budgeting, Program Coordination, and Related Management Functions by Section 15.03 of the Statutes

BIOENERGY COUNCIL

Members: Michael Allen, Dan Bahr, Tim Clay, Jamie Derr, Mike Engel, Deborah Erwin, Dick Gorder, Jeff Landin, T.J. Morice, Pam Porter, Gary Radloff, Keith Reopelle, Bob Sather, Michael Troge, Tom Unke, 2 vacancies. (All members are appointed by the secretary of agriculture, trade and consumer protection.)

Statutory References: Sections 15.137 (6) and 93.47.

Agency Responsibility: The Bioenergy Council is responsible for identifying voluntary best management practices for sustainable biomass and biofuels production.

The number of members of the council is not specified, and all are appointed by the secretary of agriculture, trade and consumer protection to serve at the pleasure of the secretary. The council was created by 2009 Wisconsin Act 401.

LAND AND WATER CONSERVATION BOARD

Members: Caitlin Frederick (secretary of administration designee), Mary Anne Lowndes (secretary of natural resources designee), John Petty (secretary of agriculture, trade and consumer protection designee); Dale Hood, George Mika, Dave Solin (county land conservation committee members); Erik Birschbach (public member); Robin Leary (resident of city of 50,000 or more); Mark E. Cupp (representing governmental unit involved in river management); Lynn Harrison (farmer); vacancy (representing charitable natural resources organization). (All except *ex officio* members or designees are appointed by governor with senate consent.)

Advisory Members: Jimmy Bramblett (U.S. Department of Agriculture, Natural Resources Conservation Service); Susan Butler, Brad Pfaff (U.S. Department of Agriculture, Farm Service Agency); Francisco Arriaga (designated by dean of the UW-Madison College of Agricultural and Life Sciences); Ken Genskow (appointed by director of UW-Extension); Kurt Calkins, Jim VandenBrook (designated by staff of county land conservation committees).

Statutory References: Sections 15.135 (4), 91.06, and 92.04.

Agency Responsibility: The 11-member Land and Water Conservation Board advises the secretary and department regarding soil and water conservation, animal waste management, and farmland preservation. As part of its farmland preservation duties, the board certifies agricultural preservation plans and zoning. It reviews and makes recommendations to the department on county land and water resource plans, local livestock regulations, agricultural shoreland management ordinances, and funding allocations to county land conservation committees. The board also advises the UW System annually about needed research and education programs related to soil and water conservation. In addition, it assists the Department of Natural Resources with issues related to runoff from agriculture and other rural sources of pollution.

The board's 3 county land conservation committee members are chosen by the Wisconsin Land and Water Conservation Association, Inc., to serve 2-year terms. The 4 members who must fulfill statutorily defined categories serve staggered 4-year terms. The undesignated member serves a 2-year term. In addition, the board must invite the appointment of advisory members from agencies or organizations specified by statute.

The board was originally created as the Land Conservation Board by Chapter 346, Laws of 1981, which also abolished the Agricultural Lands Preservation Board and transferred its functions to the new board. Chapter 346 also transferred administration of the state's soil and water conservation program from the UW System to the department but continued the university's responsibility for soil and water conservation research and educational programs. 1993 Wisconsin Act 16 changed the name of the board to the Land and Water Conservation Board.

LIVESTOCK FACILITY SITING REVIEW BOARD

Members: LEE ENGELBRECHT (representing towns); ANDY JOHNSON (representing counties); BOB SELK (representing environmental interests); RAY DIEDERICH (representing livestock farming interests); FRAN BYERLY, JEROME GASKA, BOB TOPEL (public members). (All nominated by the secretary of agriculture, trade and consumer protection and appointed with senate consent.)

Telephone: 224-4500.

The 7-member Livestock Facility Siting Review Board may review certain decisions made by political subdivisions relating to the siting or expansion of livestock facilities, such as feedlots. An aggrieved person may challenge the decision of a city, village, town, or county government approving or disapproving the siting or expansion of a livestock facility by requesting the board to review the decision. If the board determines that a challenge is valid, it shall reverse the decision of the governmental body. The decision of the board is binding on the political subdivision, but either party may appeal the board's decision in circuit court. All members are appointed for 5-year terms. The four members representing specific interests are selected from lists of names submitted by the Wisconsin Towns Association, Wisconsin Counties Association, environmental organizations, and statewide agricultural organizations, respectively. The board was created by 2003 Wisconsin Act 235 and its composition and duties are prescribed in Sections 15.135 (1) and 93.90 of the statutes.

––––––––––––

Department of
CHILDREN AND FAMILIES

Address e-mail by combining the user ID and the state extender: userid**@wisconsin.gov**
All telephone numbers are 608 area code unless otherwise indicated.

Secretary of Children and Families: ELOISE ANDERSON, 266-8684.

Deputy Secretary: RON HUNT, 266-8684, ron.hunt@

Assistant Deputy Secretary: SARA BUSCHMAN, 266-8684, sara.buschman@

Communications Director: JOE SCIALFA, 266-8684, joe.scialfa@

Legislative Liaison: KIMBERLY LIEDL, 266-8684, kimberly.liedl@

Chief Legal Counsel: RANDALL KEYS, 266-8684, randall.keys@

Tribal Liaison: vacancy.

Inspector General, Office of the: vacancy.

Mailing Address: P.O. Box 8916, Madison 53708-8916.

Location: 201 East Washington Avenue, Second Floor, Madison.

Telephone: 267-3905.

Fax: 261-6972.

Internet Address: www.dcf.wisconsin.gov

Department E-mail Address: dcfweb@wisconsin.gov

Number of Employees: 803.11.

Total Budget 2013-15: $2,290,979,300.

Statutory References: Section 15.20; Chapter 46.

Early Care and Education, Division of: Judy Norman-Nunnery, *administrator,* 261-4359, judy.normannunnery@; Jill Chase, *deputy administrator,* 261-4359, jill.chase@

    Early Care Regulation, Bureau of: Mark Andrews, *director,* 267-7933, marke.andrews@

    Early Learning and Policy, Bureau of: Katherine McGurk, *director,* 266-7001, kathy.mcgurk@

    Operation and Planning, Bureau of: David Timmerman, *director,* 261-8670, david.timmerman@

    Program Integrity, Bureau of: Tiffany Wilson, *director,* 266-1489, tiffany.wilson@

    Milwaukee Early Care Administration: Holly Davis, *director,* (414) 289-5830, holly.davis@

Family and Economic Security, Division of: Kris Randal, *administrator,* 266-8719, kris.randal@; Janice Peters, *deputy administrator,* 266-8719, janice.peters@

    Child Support, Bureau of: Jacqueline Scharping, *director,* 267-4337, jacqueline.scharping@

    Working Families, Bureau of: Margaret McMahon, *director,* 535-3625, margaret.mcmahon@

Management Services, Division of: Robert Nikolay, *administrator,* 264-7729, robert.nikolay@; Sandra Breitborde, *deputy administrator,* 264-7729, sandra.breitborde@

    Budget and Policy, Bureau of: Kim Swissdorf, *director,* 264-7729, kimm.swissdorf@

    Finance, Bureau of: Hope Koprowski, *director,* 266-3059, hope.koprowski@

    Human Resources, Bureau of: Kim Rahal, *director,* 266-9936, kimm.rahal@

    Information Technology Services, Bureau of: Steve McDowell, *director,* 264-9831, steve.mcdowell@

    Performance Management, Bureau of: Rebecca Schwei, *director,* 267-9328, rebecca.schwei@

    Regional Operations, Bureau of: John Tuohy, *director,* 261-8084, john.tuohy@

Safety and Permanence, Division of: Fredi-Ellen Bove, *administrator,* 535-3307, frediellen.bove@; John Elliott, *deputy administrator,* 535-3307, john.elliott@

    Milwaukee Child Welfare, Bureau of: vacancy, *director.*

    Permanence and Out-of-Home Care, Bureau of: Ron Hermes, *director,* 535-3307, ron.hermes@

    Safety and Well Being, Bureau of: Michelle Rawlings, *director,* 266-8843, michelle.rawlings@

    Youth Services, Office of: Wendy Henderson, *director,* 261-8709, wendy.henderson@

Agency Responsibility: The Department of Children and Families provides or oversees county provision of various services to assist children, youth, and families, including services for children in need of protection or services for their families, adoption and foster care services, licensing of facilities that care for children, background investigations of child caregivers, and child abuse and neglect investigations. It administers the Wisconsin Works (W-2) program, including the child care subsidy program, child support enforcement and paternity establishment, and programs related to the Temporary Assistance to Needy Families (TANF) income support

DEPARTMENT OF CHILDREN AND FAMILIES

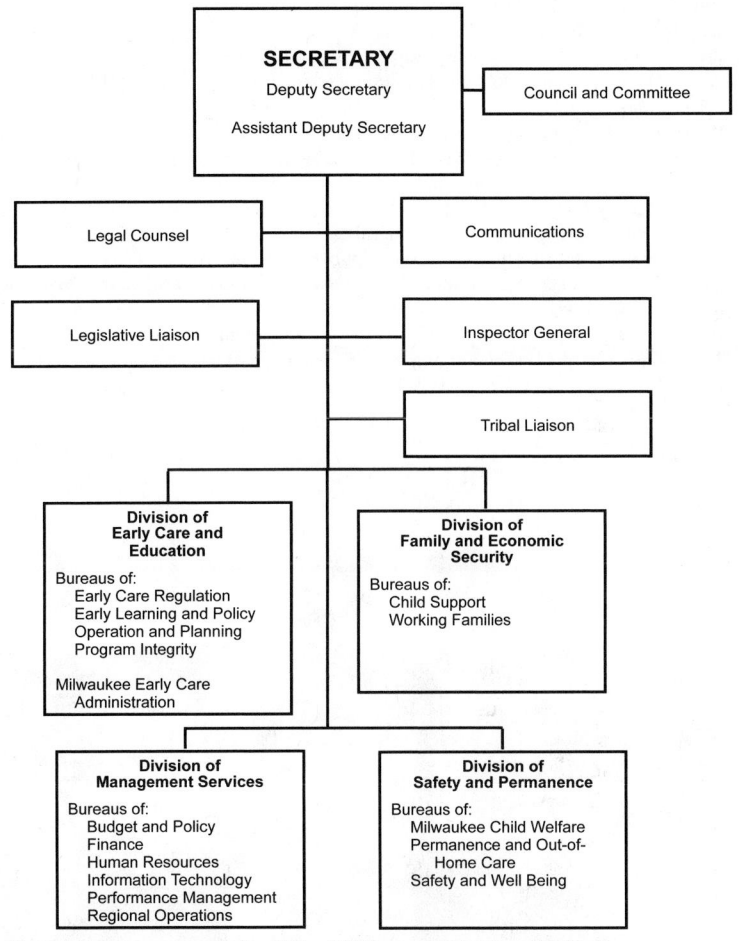

Units attached for administrative purposes under Sec. 15.03:   Child Abuse and Neglect Prevention Board
Milwaukee Child Welfare Partnership Council

program. The department works to ensure families have access to high quality and affordable early care and education and also administers the licensing and regulation of day care centers.

Organization: The department is administered by a secretary who is appointed by the governor with the advice and consent of the senate. The secretary appoints the division administrators from outside the classified service.

Unit Functions: The *Division of Early Care and Education* is responsible for the child care licensing and quality improvement programs, administering the Wisconsin Shares and YoungStar programs, managing the Milwaukee Early Care Administration, and ensuring program integrity.

The *Division of Family and Economic Security* is responsible for the W-2, Transform Milwaukee Jobs, Transitional Jobs, child support, and refugee services programs.

The *Division of Management Services* oversees the department's budget and performance management functions as well as its administrative support services, including financial, purchasing and contract administration; information systems and technology; human resources, employment relations, affirmative action and civil rights compliance; facilities management; continuity of operations; and regional operations.

The *Division of Safety and Permanence* directly administers child welfare services in Milwaukee County, supervises county-administered child welfare services in the balance of the state, and manages related programs including prevention services and the Special Needs Adoption program.

History: By the time the federal government entered the field of public welfare during the Great Depression of the 1930s, Wisconsin had already pioneered a number of programs, including aid to children and pensions for the elderly (enacted in 1931). The Wisconsin Children's Code, enacted by Chapter 439, Laws of 1929, was one of the most comprehensive in the nation. The state's initial response to federal funding was to establish separate departments to administer social security funds and other public welfare programs. After several attempts at reorganization and a series of studies, the legislature established the State Department of Public Welfare in Chapter 435, Laws of 1939, to provide unified administration of all existing welfare functions. Public health and care for the aged were delegated to separate agencies.

The executive branch reorganization act of 1967 created the Department of Health and Social Services. The Board of Health and Social Services, appointed by the governor, directed the new

First Lady Tonette Walker and Secretary Eloise Anderson honor former foster youth Desalina Smith at the Foster Youth Graduation Celebration held at the Governor's Residence. Also pictured are Wendy Henderson, Director of the DCF Office of Youth Services and commencement speaker Greta Munns. (Department of Children and Families)

department and appointed the departmental secretary to administer the agency, whose responsibilities included public welfare. In Chapter 39, Laws of 1975, the legislature abolished the board and replaced it with a secretary appointed by the governor with the advice and consent of the senate. That same law called for a reorganization of the department, which was completed by July 1977. The Department of Health and Social Services was renamed the Department of Health and Family Services (DHFS), effective July 1, 1996.

The decades of the 1960s and 1970s saw an expansion of public welfare and health services at both the federal and state levels. Especially notable were programs for medical care for the needy and aged (Medical Assistance and Medicare), drug treatment programs, food stamps, and Aid to Families with Dependent Children Program (AFDC). DHFS was assigned additional duties during the 1980s in the areas of child support, child abuse and neglect, and welfare reform.

1995 Wisconsin Act 27 revised AFDC and transferred it and other income support programs including Medical Assistance eligibility and food stamps to the Department of Workforce Development (DWD). (Wisconsin Works, known as W-2, replaced AFDC in 1995 Wisconsin Act 289.) Existing welfare reform programs, including Job Opportunities and Basic Skills (JOBS), Learnfare, Parental Responsibility, and Work-Not-Welfare, were also transferred to DWD, along with child and spousal support, the Children First Program, Older American Community Service Employment, refugee assistance programs, and vocational rehabilitation functions. Health care facilities plan review was transferred from the Department of Industry, Labor and Human Relations to DHFS by 1995 Wisconsin Act 27. Act 27 also transferred laboratory certification to the Department of Agriculture, Trade and Consumer Protection and low-income energy assistance to the Department of Administration.

As a result of 1995 Wisconsin Act 303, DHFS assumed responsibility for direct administration and operation of Milwaukee County child welfare services. 2001 Wisconsin Act 16 transferred the Medical Assistance Eligibility Program and the Food Stamp Program to DHFS from the Department of Workforce Development.

2007 Wisconsin Act 20 created the Department of Children and Families (DCF), beginning July 1, 2008. It also changed the name of DHFS to the Department of Health Services and split the responsibilities of DHFS between the two departments. Act 20 transferred from DHFS to DCF the duty to provide or oversee county supervision of various services to assist children and families, including services for children in need of protection or services and their families, adoption services, licensing of facilities that provide care for children, child caregiver background investigations, and child abuse and neglect investigations. The act also transferred from DWD to DCF administration of Wisconsin Works, including the child care subsidy program, child support enforcement and paternity establishment, and programs related to temporary assistance for needy families (TANF).

Statutory Council and Committee

Domestic Abuse, Council on: REPRESENTATIVE JACQUE (designated by assembly speaker), REPRESENTATIVE SHANKLAND (designated by assembly minority leader), PATRICIA NINMANN (designated by senate majority leader), SENATOR TAYLOR (designated by senate minority leader); SHIRLEY ARMSTRONG, MAUREEN FUNK, L. KEVIN HAMBERGER, JILL KAROFSKY, MARIANA RODRIGUEZ, RENEE SCHULZ-STANGL, KARA SCHURMAN, SUSAN SIPPEL, vacancy (members not designated by legislative leadership are nominated and appointed by governor with senate consent.)

The 13-member Council on Domestic Abuse makes recommendations to the secretary on domestic abuse, reviews grant applications, advises the department and legislature on domestic abuse policy, and, in conjunction with the Judicial Conference, develops forms for filing petitions for domestic abuse restraining orders and injunctions. Members are appointed for staggered 3-year terms. Members designated by legislative leadership do not have to be legislators. The council was created by Chapter 111, Laws of 1979, and it was transferred from the Department of Health and Family Services to the Department of Children and Families by 2007 Wisconsin Act 20. Its composition and duties are prescribed in Sections 15.207 (16) and 49.165 (3) of the statutes.

Rate Regulation Advisory Committee: Tongenell Campbell (VIC Living Center); Mark Elliott (Northwest Passage); Maria McDermott (Children's Hospital of Wisconsin Community Services); Linda Hall (Wisconsin Association of Family and Children Agencies); Ron Hauser (Lutheran Social Services of Wisconsin and Upper Michigan, Inc.); Ron Hermes (Department of Children and Families); Kelsey Hill (Department of Corrections); Jeff Pease (Lad Lake); Bruce Kamradt (Milwaukee WrapAround); James Kania (Department of Children and Families, Bureau of Milwaukee Child Welfare); Rachel Karow (Family Works); Teresa Kovach (Portage County Department of Human Services); Brent Ruehlow (Jefferson County Human Services); Patricia Lancour (Fond du Lac County Department of Social Services); Kelli Kamholz (Positive Alternatives); Jennifer Vote (Marquette County Department of Health and Human Services); Cheri Salava (Rock County Human Services); John Solberg (Rawhide, Inc.); Dave Nagy (Genesee Lake School); Ruth Wiseman (Chileda); Dawn Woodward (Columbia County Human Services); Janet Wimmer (Dodge County Department of Human Services); Shane Schumacher (Lafayette county Human Services) (appointed by secretary of children and families).

The secretary of children and families appoints members to a committee to advise the department regarding rates for child placing agencies, residential care centers and group homes. Committee membership includes purchasers; county departments of social services or human services; the Bureau of Milwaukee Child Welfare; tribes; consumers; and a statewide association of private, incorporated family and children's social services agencies representing all groups of providers that are affected by the rate regulation process. The committee was created by 2009 Wisconsin Act 335. Its composition and duties are prescribed in Section 49.343 (5) of the statutes.

Independent Units Attached for Budgeting, Program Coordination, and Related Management Functions by Section 15.03 of the Statutes

CHILD ABUSE AND NEGLECT PREVENTION BOARD

Members: Teri Zywicki (public member), *chairperson;* Jennifer Noyes (public member), *vice chairperson;* Jon Hoelter (designated by governor), Jill Karofsky (designated by attorney general), Laura Riske (designated by secretary of health services), Sheila Briggs (designated by state superintendent of public instruction), Deidre Morgan (designated by secretary of corrections), Sara Buschman (designated by secretary of children and families); Representative Ballweg (representative to the assembly appointed by speaker), Representative Billings (representative to the assembly appointed by assembly minority leader), vacancy (senator appointed by president of senate), Senator Lassa (senator appointed by senate minority leader); Kari Christenson, Bernice Day, Jeffrey Lamont, Sandra McCormick, Jesus Mireles, Kimberly Simac, Notesong Thompson, vacancy (public members appointed by governor).

Executive Director: Michelle Jensen Goodwin, michelle.jensengoodwin@wisconsin.gov

Mailing Address: 110 East Main Street, Suite 810, Madison 53703-3316.

Telephone: 266-6871.

Fax: 266-3792.

Internet Address: wichildrentrustfund.org

Publications: Adverse Childhood Experiences (ACEs) in Wisconsin; Child Sexual Abuse Prevention: Tips for Parents; Positive Parenting: Tips on Discipline; Shaken Baby Syndrome Prevention materials.

Number of Employees: 6.00.

Total Budget 2013-15: $6,005,700.

Statutory References: Sections 15.205 (4) and 48.982.

Agency Responsibility: The 20-member Child Abuse and Neglect Prevention Board administers the Children's Trust Fund. The board recommends policies to the legislature, governor, and state agencies to protect children and support prevention activities. The board supports, funds, and evaluates evidence-informed and innovative strategies that are effective in helping Wisconsin communities prevent child maltreatment through culturally competent, family-centered, coordinated approaches to the delivery of support services that strengthen families. The board also implements consumer education and social marketing campaigns and provides education on prevention and positive parenting through printed materials and informational seminars. Funding is derived through charges on duplicate birth certificates, federal funds, and private contributions. In 2001, the board created a nonprofit corporation, the Celebrate Children Foundation with funds from the sale of the Celebrate Children special license plates.

The board's 10 public members serve staggered 3-year terms. The board appoints the executive director and staff from the classified service. It was created by 1983 Wisconsin Act 27, and it was transferred from the Department of Health and Family Services to the Department of Children and Families by 2007 Wisconsin Act 20.

MILWAUKEE CHILD WELFARE PARTNERSHIP COUNCIL

Members: LINDA DAVIS (public member), *chairperson;* DEANNA ALEXANDER, WILLIE JOHNSON, JR., STEVE TAYLOR (Milwaukee County board members nominated by Milwaukee County Executive), REPRESENTATIVE RODRIGUEZ (representative to the assembly appointed by assembly speaker), REPRESENTATIVE JOHNSON (representative to the assembly appointed by assembly minority leader), SENATOR DARLING (senator appointed by senate president), SENATOR HARRIS DODD (senator appointed by senate minority leader); COLLEEN ELLINGSON, SUSAN GADACZ, CHRISTINE HOLMES, KIM KAMPSCHROER, MALLORY O'BRIEN, TONY SHIELDS, B. THOMAS WANTA, 2 vacancies (public members); JOHN CHISHOLM (Milwaukee County district attorney or designee); MARY TRIGGIANO (presiding judge of the children's division of the Milwaukee County circuit court). (All but legislators are appointed by governor.)

Contact Person: BECKY PRUDHOMME.

Mailing Address: 635 North 26th Street, Milwaukee 53233.

Telephone: (414) 343-5741.

Statutory References: Sections 15.207 (24) and 46.562.

Agency Responsibility: The 19-member Milwaukee Child Welfare Partnership Council makes recommendations to the Department of Children and Families and the legislature regarding policies and plans to improve the child welfare system in Milwaukee County, including a neighborhood-based system for delivery of services. It may also recommend funding priorities and identify innovative public and private funding opportunities. The 15 nonlegislative members are appointed to 3-year terms, and the governor designates one of the public members as chairperson. At least 6 public members must be residents of Milwaukee County. The council was created by 1995 Wisconsin Act 303, and it was transferred from the Department of Health and Family Services to the Department of Children and Families by 2007 Wisconsin Act 20.

Department of
CORRECTIONS

Address e-mail by combining the user ID and the state extender: userid**@wisconsin.gov**
All telephone numbers are 608 area code unless otherwise indicated.

Secretary of Corrections: EDWARD WALL, 240-5055, edward.wall@

Deputy Secretary: DEIRDRE MORGAN, 240-5055, deirdre.morgan@

Assistant Deputy Secretary: SCOTT LEGWOLD, 240-5055, scott.legwold@

Office of Legal Counsel: JULIO BARRON, *chief,* 240-5049, julio.barron@

Director of Public Affairs: JOY STAAB, 240-5060, joy.staab@

Legislative Liaison: DONALD FRISKE, 240-5056, donald.friske@

Research and Policy Unit: TONY STREVELER, *director,* 240-5801, anthony.streveler@

Detention Facilities, Office of: Kristi Dietz, *director,* 240-5052, kristi.dietz@; Milwaukee: (414) 227-5199.

Victim Services and Programs, Office of: Stephanie Hove, *director,* 240-5888, stephanie.hove@

Prison Rape Elimination Act Director: Christine Preston, 240-5113, christine.preston@

Reentry Director: Silvia Jackson, 240-5015, silvia.jackson@

Special Operations, Office of: Steve Wierenga, *director,* 250-5055, steve.wierenga@

Mailing Address: P.O. Box 7925, Madison 53707-7925.

Location: 3099 East Washington Avenue, Madison 53704.

Telephone: 240-5000.

Fax: 240-3300.

Internet Address: www.doc.wi.gov

Number of Employees: 10,211.02.

Total Budget 2013-15: $2,548,523,500.

Statutory References: Section 15.14; Chapter 301.

Adult Institutions, Division of: Cathy Jess, *administrator,* 240-5104, cathy.jess@; John Paquin, *assistant administrator,* john.paquin@; Jim Schwochert, *assistant administrator,* james.schwochert@; vacancy, *security chief,* 240-5105; 3099 East Washington Avenue, Madison 53704; Division Fax: 240-3310.

> *Correctional Enterprises, Bureau of:* Doug Percy, *director,* 240-5201, douglas.percy@; Fax: 240-3320.
>
> *Health Services, Bureau of:* James Greer, *director,* 240-5122, james.greer@; Fax: 240-3311.
>
> *Offender Classification and Movement, Bureau of:* Mark Heise, *director,* 240-5800, mark.heise@; Fax: 240-3350.
>
> *Program Service, Bureau of:* vacancy, *director,* 240-5160; Fax: 240-3310.
>
> *Planning and Operations Unit:* Tim Lemonds, *director,* 240-5180, tim.lemonds@; Fax: 240-3310.

PRISONS

Maximum Security:

> *Columbia Correctional Institution:* Michael Dittmann, *warden,* P.O. Box 950, Portage 53901-0950, (608) 742-9100; Fax: (608) 742-9111.
>
> *Dodge Correctional Institution:* Marc Clements, *warden,* P.O. Box 661, Waupun 53963-0661, (920) 324-5577; Fax: (920) 324-6297.
>
> *Green Bay Correctional Institution:* Brian Foster, *warden,* P.O. Box 19033, Green Bay 54307-9033, (920) 432-4877; Fax: (920) 448-6545.
>
> *Waupun Correctional Institution:* William Pollard, *warden,* P.O. Box 351, Waupun 53963-0351, (920) 324-5571; Fax: (920) 324-7250.
>
> *Wisconsin Secure Program Facility:* Gary Boughton, *warden,* P.O. Box 1000, Boscobel 53805-0900, (608) 375-5656; Fax: (608) 375-5434.

Medium Security:

> *Fox Lake Correctional Institution:* Randy Hepp, *warden,* P.O. Box 147, Fox Lake 53933-0147, (920) 928-3151; Fax: (920) 928-6981.
>
> *Jackson Correctional Institution:* Lizzie Tegels, *warden,* P.O. Box 232, Black River Falls 54615-0232, (715) 284-4550; Fax: (715) 284-7335.
>
> *Kettle Moraine Correctional Institution:* Robert Humphreys, *warden,* P.O. Box 31, Plymouth 53073-0031, (920) 526-3244; Fax: (920) 526-9320.
>
> *Milwaukee Secure Detention Facility:* Floyd Mitchell, *warden,* 1015 North 10th Street, P.O. Box 05740, Milwaukee 53205-0740, (414) 212-3535; Fax: (414) 212-6811.

New Lisbon Correctional Institution: TIMOTHY DOUMA, *warden,* P.O. Box 2000, New Lisbon 53950-2000, (608) 562-6400; Fax: (608) 562-6410.

Oshkosh Correctional Institution: JUDY SMITH, *warden,* P.O. Box 3530, Oshkosh 54903-3530, (920) 231-4010; Fax: (920) 236-2615/2626.

Prairie du Chien Correctional Facility: TIM HAINES, *warden,* P.O. Box 6000, Prairie du Chien 53821, (608) 326-7828; Fax: (608) 326-5960.

Racine Correctional Institution: PAUL KEMPER, *warden,* 2019 Wisconsin Street, Sturtevant 53177-1829, (262) 886-3214; Fax: (262) 886-3514.

Racine Youthful Offender Correctional Institution: PAMELA WALLACE, *warden,* P.O. Box 2200, Racine 53404-2713, (262) 638-1999; Fax: (262) 638-1777.

Redgranite Correctional Institution: MICHAEL MEISNER, *warden,* 1006 County Road EE, P.O. Box 900, Redgranite 54970-0925, (920) 566-2600; Fax: (920) 566-2610.

Stanley Correctional Institution: REED RICHARDSON, *warden,* 100 Corrections Drive, Stanley 54768-6500, (715) 644-2960; Fax: (715) 644-2966.

Minimum Security:

Chippewa Valley Correctional Treatment Facility: JEFFREY PUGH, *warden,* 2909 East Park Avenue, Chippewa Falls 54729, (715) 720-2850; Fax: (715) 720-2859.

Oakhill Correctional Institution: DAN WESTFIELD, *warden,* P.O. Box 140, Oregon 53575-0140, (608) 835-3101; Fax: (608) 835-9196.

Women:

Taycheedah Correctional Institution: DEANNE SCHAUB, *warden,* 751 County Road K, P.O. Box 1947, Fond du Lac 54936-1947, (920) 929-3800; Fax: (920) 929-2946.

CENTER SYSTEM

QUALA CHAMPAGNE, *warden, Wisconsin Correctional Center System,* 3099 East Washington Avenue, P.O. Box 7969, Madison 53707-7969, 240-5310; Fax: 240-3335.

Black River Correctional Center: MATTHEW GERBER, *superintendent,* W6898 East Staffon Road, Route #5, Black River Falls 54615-6426, (715) 333-5681; Fax: (715) 333-2708.

John C. Burke Correctional Center: MARK RICE, *superintendent,* 900 South Madison Street, P.O. Box 900, Waupun 53963-0900, (920) 324-3460; Fax: (920) 324-4575.

Felmers Chaney Correctional Center: MICHAEL COCKROFT, *superintendent,* 2825 North 30th Street, Milwaukee 53210, (414) 874-1600; Fax: (414) 874-1695.

Drug Abuse Correctional Center: JEFF JAEGER, *superintendent,* Kempster Hall/Winnebago Mental Health Institute, 1305 North Drive, P.O. Box 36, Winnebago 54985-0036, (920) 236-2700; Fax: (920) 426-5601.

Robert E. Ellsworth Correctional Center: MICHELLE J. HOFFMAN, *superintendent,* 21425-A Spring Street, Union Grove 53182-9408, (262) 878-6000; Fax: (262) 878-6015.

Flambeau Correctional Center: BRAD HOOVER, *superintendent,* N671 County Road M, Hawkins 54530-9400, (715) 585-6394; Fax: (715) 585-6563.

Gordon Correctional Center: MARIA SILAO, *superintendent,* 10401 East County Road G, Gordon 54838, (715) 376-2680; Fax: (715) 376-4361.

Kenosha Correctional Center: ANN KRUEGER, *superintendent,* 6353 14th Avenue, Kenosha 53143, (262) 653-7099; Fax: (262) 653-7241.

McNaughton Correctional Center: BRAD KOSBAB, *superintendent,* 8500 Rainbow Road, Lake Tomahawk 54539-9558, (715) 277-2484; Fax: (715) 277-2293.

Milwaukee Women's Correctional Center: PAMELA ZANK, *superintendent,* 615 West Keefe Avenue, Milwaukee 53212, (414) 267-6101; Fax: (414) 267-6130.

Oregon Correctional Center: PETER JAEGER, *superintendent,* 5140 Highway M, P.O. Box 25, Oregon 53575-0025, (608) 835-3233; Fax: (608) 835-3145.

DEPARTMENT OF CORRECTIONS

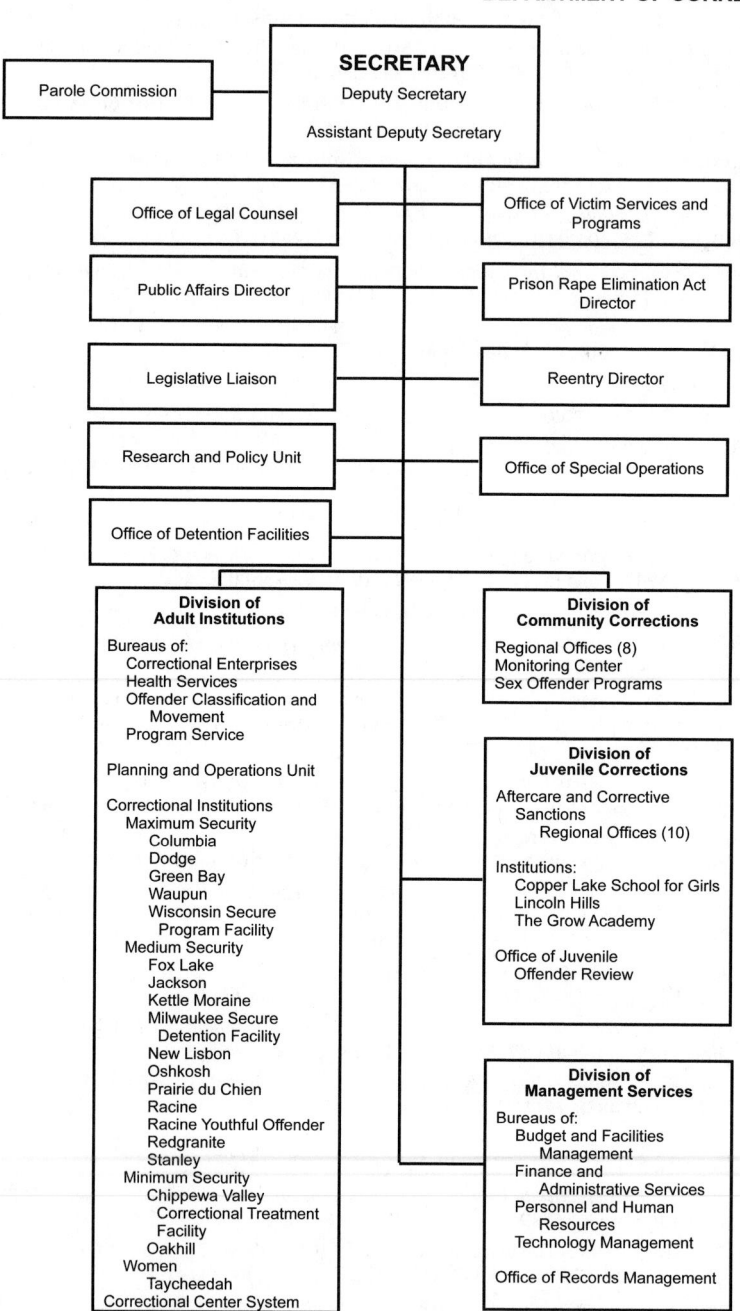

SECRETARY
Deputy Secretary
Assistant Deputy Secretary

Parole Commission

Office of Legal Counsel

Office of Victim Services and Programs

Public Affairs Director

Prison Rape Elimination Act Director

Legislative Liaison

Reentry Director

Research and Policy Unit

Office of Special Operations

Office of Detention Facilities

Division of Adult Institutions

Bureaus of:
 Correctional Enterprises
 Health Services
 Offender Classification and
  Movement
 Program Service

Planning and Operations Unit

Correctional Institutions
 Maximum Security
  Columbia
  Dodge
  Green Bay
  Waupun
  Wisconsin Secure
   Program Facility
 Medium Security
  Fox Lake
  Jackson
  Kettle Moraine
  Milwaukee Secure
   Detention Facility
  New Lisbon
  Oshkosh
  Prairie du Chien
  Racine
  Racine Youthful Offender
  Redgranite
  Stanley
 Minimum Security
  Chippewa Valley
   Correctional Treatment
   Facility
  Oakhill
 Women
  Taycheedah
Correctional Center System

Division of Community Corrections

Regional Offices (8)
Monitoring Center
Sex Offender Programs

Division of Juvenile Corrections

Aftercare and Corrective
 Sanctions
  Regional Offices (10)

Institutions:
 Copper Lake School for Girls
 Lincoln Hills
 The Grow Academy

Office of Juvenile
 Offender Review

Division of Management Services

Bureaus of:
 Budget and Facilities
  Management
 Finance and
  Administrative Services
 Personnel and Human
  Resources
 Technology Management

Office of Records Management

Units attached for administrative purposes under Sec. 15.03:
Interstate Adult Offender Supervision Board
Council on Offender Reentry

Prison Industries Board
State Board for Interstate Juvenile Supervision

Sanger B. Powers Correctional Center: PATRICK MELMAN, *superintendent,* N8375 County Line Road, Oneida 54155-9300, (920) 869-1095; Fax: (920) 869-2650.

St. Croix Correctional Center: JOANN SKALSKI, *superintendent,* 1859 North 4th Street, P.O. Box 36, New Richmond 54017-0036, (715) 246-6971; Fax: (715) 246-3680.

Marshall E. Sherrer Correctional Center: GARY MITCHELL, *superintendent,* 1318 North 14th Street, Milwaukee 53205-2596, (414) 343-5000; Fax: (414) 343-5039.

Thompson Correctional Center: WAYNE OLSON, *superintendent,* 434 State Farm Road, Deerfield 53531-9562, (608) 423-3415; Fax: (608) 423-9852.

Winnebago Correctional Center: SUSAN ROSS, *superintendent,* 4300 Sherman Road, P.O. Box 128, Winnebago 54985-0128, (920) 424-0402; Fax: (920) 424-0430.

Community Corrections, Division of: DENISE SYMDON, *administrator,* 240-5300; SHIRLEY STORANDT, *assistant administrator,* 3099 East Washington Avenue, Madison 53704; Fax: 240-3330.

Region 1: LANCE WIERSMA, *chief,* 3319 West Beltline Highway, Suite W300, Madison 53704, 261-7441; Fax: 261-7450.

Region 2: LISA YEATES, *chief,* 9531 Rayne Road, Suite 2, Sturtevant 53177-1833, (262) 884-3780; Fax: (262) 884-3799.

Region 3: NIEL THORESON, *chief,* 4160 North Port Washington Road, Milwaukee 53212, (414) 229-0600; Fax: (414) 229-0584.

Region 4: ROSE SNYDER-SPAAR, *chief,* 1360 American Drive, Neenah 54956, (920) 751-4623; Fax: (920) 751-4601.

Region 5: GENA JARR, *chief,* 770 Technology Way, Suite 500, Chippewa Falls 54729-4516, (715) 738-3001; Fax: (715) 738-3000.

Region 6: ERIC LOSEE, *chief,* 2187 North Stevens Street, Suite B, Rhinelander 54501-0497, (715) 365-2587; Fax: (715) 369-5255.

Region 7: SALLY TESS, *chief,* 141 Northwest Barstow Street, Room 126, Waukesha 53188-3756, (262) 521-5157; Fax: (262) 548-8697.

Region 8: RON KALMUS, *chief,* 427 East Tower Drive, Suite 200, Wautoma 54982-6927, (920) 787-5500; Fax: (920) 787-5589.

Monitoring Center: LUIS BIXLER, *director,* 3099 East Washington Avenue, Madison 53704, 240-5850.

Sex Offender Programs: GRACE ROBERTS, *director,* 3099 East Washington Avenue, Madison 53704, 240-5820.

Juvenile Corrections, Division of: CARI J. TAYLOR, *administrator,* 240-5900, cari.taylor@; PAUL WESTERHAUS, *assistant administrator,* 240-5902, paul.westerhaus@; 3099 East Washington Avenue, Madison 53704; Division Fax: 240-3370.

Aftercare and Corrective Sanctions:

Appleton: 2107 Spencer Street, Appleton 54914-4638, (920) 997-3870.

Eau Claire: 718 West Clairemont Avenue, Room 140, Eau Claire 54701-6143, (715) 836-6683.

Green Bay: 200 North Jefferson Street, Suite 134, Green Bay 54301, (920) 448-6548.

Madison: 2909 Landmark Place, Suite 104, Madison 53713, 288-3350.

Milwaukee: 4200 North Holton Street, Suite 120, Milwaukee 53212, (414) 229-0701.

Neenah: 1356 American Drive, Neenah 54956, (920) 729-3900.

Schofield: 1699 Schofield Avenue, Suite 120, Schofield 54476-1021, (715) 241-8890.

Sheboygan: 3422 Wilgus Avenue, Sheboygan 53081, (920) 456-6548.

Sparta: 820 Industrial Drive, Suite 6, Sparta 54656, (608) 269-1921.

Sturtevant: 9531 Rayne Road, Suite 3, Sturtevant 53177-1833, (262) 884-3748.

Institutions:

    Copper Lake School for Girls: JOHN OURADA, *superintendent,* W4380 Copper Lake Road, Irma 54442-9720, (715) 536-8386; Fax: (715) 536-8236, john.ourada@

    Lincoln Hills School: JOHN OURADA, *superintendent,* W4380 Copper Lake Road, Irma 54442-9720, (715) 536-8386; Fax: (715) 536-8236, john.ourada@

    The Grow Academy: NICOLE LAUDOLFF, *director,* 4986 County Highway M, Oregon 53575, (608) 835-5701; Fax: (608) 835-7122.

Juvenile Offender Review, Office of: SHELLEY HAGAN, *director,* 240-5918; Fax: 240-3370, shelley.hagan@

Management Services, Division of: STACEY ROLSTON, *administrator,* 240-5401, stacey.rolston@; TIM LEFAVE, *assistant administrator,* 240-5400, tim.lefave@; Division Fax: 240-3340.

    Budget and Facilities Management, Bureau of: ROLAND COUEY, *director,* 240-5405, roland.couey@

    Finance and Administrative Services, Bureau of: JERRY SALVO, *director,* 240-5412, jerry.salvo@

    Personnel and Human Resources, Bureau of: KARI BEIER, *director,* 240-5460 kari.beier@

    Records Management, Office of: BILL CLAUSIUS, *director,* 240-5407, bill.clausius@

    Technology Management, Bureau of: CURT TAYLOR, *director,* 240-5752, curt.taylor@

Agency Responsibility: The Department of Corrections administers Wisconsin's state prisons, community corrections, and juvenile corrections programs. It supervises the custody and discipline of all inmates in order to protect the public and seeks to rehabilitate offenders and reintegrate them into society. The department currently operates 19 correctional facilities and 16 correctional centers for adults, and 2 facilities for juveniles. It also supervises offenders on probation, parole, and extended supervision; monitors compliance with deferred prosecution programs; and may make recommendations for pardons or commutations of sentence when requested by the governor. The department maintains the sex offender registry for those who are required by law to register. The department also monitors sex offenders who are required by law to be on lifetime GPS.

Organization: The department is headed by a secretary who is appointed by the governor with the advice and consent of the senate. The secretary appoints the division administrators from outside the classified service.

Unit Functions: The *Office of the Secretary* ensures the overall mission of the department is achieved. Services and initiatives directly supervised by the Office of the Secretary include legal counsel, public information, reentry, and the Prison Rape Elimination Act. The reentry initiative is a crime prevention strategy designed to increase the number of offenders who live productive, law-abiding lives from admission to custody through supervision in the community.

The *Office of Detention Facilities,* in the office of the secretary, is responsible for the inspection and evaluation of all local detention facilities, including jails, houses of correction, secure juvenile detention centers, and municipal lockups. It provides technical assistance and training on various detention issues.

The *Division of Adult Institutions* supervises adult inmates in a variety of correctional settings. It assigns inmates to one of 6 security classifications, based on their records, backgrounds, and the risk they may pose to the public, correctional officers, and other inmates.

Security classifications include 2 levels each of maximum, medium, and minimum security. These levels determine how closely inmates are guarded, how restricted their movements are within the institution, and the programs in which they may participate. Although prisons are classified by the highest level of security for which the facility is built and administered, an individual facility may contain several security levels.

The prison program is designed to offer offenders opportunities to develop skills necessary to lead law-abiding lives upon release. Services include evaluation of an offender's background and needs and the provision of programs to meet those needs. Programs include academic and vocational education, alcohol and other drug abuse treatment, other clinical treatment, work, and religious observance. The division offers job training for inmates through Badger State Industries, which produces various items, including furniture, textiles and linens, license plates, and signs.

The division also administers 16 minimum security correctional centers across the state. Center staff work closely with probation and parole agents to assist the transition of inmates back into the community. Center programming includes basic education, alcohol and drug counseling, work experience, and work release.

The *Division of Community Corrections* supervises persons released on parole and extended supervision, as well as those placed on probation by the court. The supervision is community-based to strengthen family and community ties, encourage lawful behavior, and provide local treatment programs. Probation and parole agents hold offenders accountable for their behavior, provide direct services, and refer their clients to community service agencies. They also provide investigative services to the courts, the Division of Adult Institutions, and the Parole Commission to aid in sentencing, institutional programming, and parole planning. Under limited circumstances, agents supervise juveniles released to aftercare programs, persons conditionally released from mental health facilities, and sexually violent persons placed on supervised release. The division is also responsible for the sex offender registry and the electronic monitoring center.

The *Division of Juvenile Corrections,* created in Section 301.025, Wisconsin Statutes, by 1995 Wisconsin Act 27, administers programs to treat and rehabilitate delinquent youth and protect the public. It operates the state's juvenile corrections institutions and community corrections programs. Through its Juvenile Offender Review Program, the division determines whether offenders in the institutions are eligible for release, oversees the aftercare services of those who are released, and selects the participants for intensive surveillance under the Corrective Sanctions Program. The division also administers the Community Youth and Family Aids Program, which offers financial incentives to counties to divert juveniles from state institutions and into less restrictive community rehabilitation programs, and it awards grants to counties that participate in the Intensive Aftercare Program, which offers a wide range of social, educational, and employment assistance.

The *Division of Management Services* provides budgeting, research, data processing, personnel, and telecommunications services and oversees accounting, procurement, and facilities management.

History: In Chapter 288, Laws of 1851, the legislature established a commission to locate and supervise the building and administration of a state prison. The commissioners chose Waupun as the site and the facility was opened in 1852. Waupun housed both male and female offenders until 1933 when the Wisconsin Prison for Women opened in Taycheedah.

From 1853 to 1874 an elected state prison commissioner ran the prison. Beginning in 1874, the governor appointed three state prison commissioners to hire a warden and direct state prison operation. In 1881, prisons and other public welfare functions were placed under the supervision of the State Board of Supervision of Wisconsin Charitable, Reformatory and Penal Institutions, subsequently renamed the State Board of Control of the Wisconsin Reformatory, Charitable and Penal Institutions in 1891. Both adult and juvenile facilities came under the board's control.

By 1939, the Division of Corrections within the newly created Department of Public Welfare had assumed supervision of prisons, juvenile institutions, and probation and parole. Under the 1967 executive branch reorganization, the division became part of the Department of Health and Social Services. The division was reorganized as a separate Department of Corrections in 1989 Wisconsin Act 31, but responsibility for juvenile offenders remained with the Department of Health and Social Services until 1995 Wisconsin Act 27 transferred juvenile corrections and related services to the Department of Corrections.

Waupun was the state's only prison until 1898, when the Wisconsin State Reformatory for prisoners from 16 to 30 years-of-age opened at Green Bay. The age limitation was repealed in 1966 and the facility was renamed the Green Bay Correctional Institution in 1978. A separate facility for women, the Industrial Home for Women, began operations in Taycheedah in 1921. The Wisconsin Prison for Women at Taycheedah opened in 1933. Fox Lake Correctional Institution opened in 1962. Further expansion of the state prison system occurred when Kettle Moraine Boys School was converted to an adult institution in 1975, followed by the conversion of Oregon School for Girls to a minimum security prison (Oakhill) in 1977. Dodge Correctional Institution, which serves as reception and evaluation center for all adult male felons sentenced by Wisconsin courts, opened in 1978. Rapid growth of the prison population led to the opening of Columbia and Oshkosh Correctional Institutions in 1986, Racine Correctional Institution in 1991, Jackson Correctional Institution in 1996, the Wisconsin Secure Program Facility located in Boscobel, in 1999, Redgranite Correctional Institution in 2001, Stanley Correctional Institution in 2003, and New Lisbon Correctional Institution in 2004. The department opened a minimum security facility to serve the needs of inmates with alcohol and other drug abuse problems in Chippewa Falls in 2004.

While the capacity of Wisconsin prisons had grown considerably since 1986, the number of inmates confined to adult institutions grew from just over 6,000 in 1989 to more than 15,000 in 1995. As a result, 1995 Wisconsin Act 344 authorized the department to contract with other states to house Wisconsin inmates. 1997 Wisconsin Act 27 authorized housing state inmates in private prisons in other states. By the end of 2002, out-of-state prisons housed more than 3,400 Wisconsin inmates. Near the end of 2004, fewer than 300 inmates were located out-of-state, due to new institutions, an increased number of beds at existing prisons, expanded contracting with county sheriffs to house inmates in county jails, and expanded noninstitutionalization options created in 2003 Wisconsin Act 33. By 2006, all out-of-state inmates were returned to Wisconsin facilities.

Wisconsin's first juvenile institution for boys opened in 1860 at Waukesha and was replaced by Kettle Moraine at Plymouth in 1963. A second facility, Wisconsin School for Boys, which was subsequently renamed the Ethan Allen School, opened at Wales in 1959. Lincoln Hills School for Boys began operations in 1970. (It was opened to girls in 1976 and the school was renamed.) The first juvenile institution for girls was established in 1875 in Milwaukee as a private agency that received state aid. The Wisconsin School for Girls, later renamed the Oregon School for Girls, opened in 1931 and closed in 1976. Girls were then sent to Lincoln Hills. In response to concerns about overcrowding at Lincoln Hills and the need for treatment programs for girls, the legislature authorized a separate facility, which opened as Southern Oaks Girls School at Union Grove in 1994. Another juvenile facility was opened in Prairie du Chien in 1997, but it has been converted into a medium security adult prison. 2011 Wisconsin Act 32 closed the Ethan Allen School and the Southern Oaks Girls School, with the boys from Ethan Allen school transferred to Lincoln Hills and the girls from Southern Oaks transferred to a new Copper Lake Girls School located on the Lincoln Hill grounds.

Probation and parole were unknown in the early years of statehood. Criminal sentences were for definite periods of time and to be fully served. Until 1860, executive pardons were the only means for early release. Chapter 324, Laws of 1860, established early releases for good behavior, known as "good time". Calculations of good time ended with the adoption of mandatory release dates for crimes committed after May 31, 1984. Parole was first enacted in 1889, but was apparently invalidated by the Wisconsin Supreme Court. New parole provisions were enacted in 1897 for the Green Bay Reformatory and for the Waupun State Prison in Chapter 110, Laws of 1907. That law allowed the State Board of Control to parole inmates with the governor's approval, but the approval requirement was removed in 1947. The State Board of Control was also given supervisory responsibility for offenders placed on probation in 1909. Currently, the Parole Commission, created in 1989, has final authority in granting discretionary paroles. Under 1997 Wisconsin Act 283, a person who is convicted of a felony committed on or after December 31, 1999, and sentenced to prison must serve a specified time in prison followed by a specified period of extended supervision in the community. Persons given this bifurcated sentence were not eligible for parole. The Earned Release Review Commission was created by 2009 Wisconsin Act 28. It authorized the commission to consider eligible inmates to be considered for release from incarceration to extended supervision depending on the nature of the crime, the time it was committed, and other factors such as the health or age of the inmate.

Most incarcerated prisoners were able to earn "positive adjustment time" (sometimes referred to as "good time") for complying with prison regulations or performing assigned duties. 2011 Wisconsin Act 38 again renamed the body the Parole Commission and substantially repealed most early release provisions.

Statutory Commission

Parole Commission: DEAN STENSBERG (appointed by governor with senate consent), *chairperson;* EMILY DAVIDSON, DOUG DRANKIEWICZ, WILLIAM FRANCIS, DANIELLE LACOST, STEVEN LANDREMAN, 2 vacancies (appointed by chairperson from classified service).
Address: 3099 East Washington Avenue, P.O. Box 7960, Madison 53707-7960.
Telephone: 240-7280.
Fax: 240-7299.

The 8-member Parole Commission conducts regularly scheduled interviews to consider the parole of eligible inmates confined in a state correctional institution, a contracted county jail facility, or a county house of corrections or inmates transferred to mental health institutions.

The governor appoints the commission's chairperson, with senate consent, who serves at the pleasure of the governor for a 2-year term. The other members, who shall have knowledge of or experience in corrections or criminal justice, are appointed by the chairperson from the classified service.

The commission's statutory predecessor, the Parole Board, was created by Chapter 221, Laws of 1979, to advise the secretary of health and social services, and its members were appointed by the secretary. The Parole Commission was created by 1989 Wisconsin Act 107. The Earned Release Review Commission was created by 2009 Wisconsin Act 28. It authorized the commission to consider eligible inmates to be considered for release from incarceration to extended supervision depending on the nature of the crime, the time it was committed, and other factors such as the health or age of the inmate. Most incarcerated prisoners were able to earn "positive adjustment time" (some-times referred to as "good time") for complying with prison regulations or performing assigned duties. 2011 Wisconsin Act 38 again renamed the body the Parole Commission and substantially repealed most early release provisions. The commission's composition and duties are prescribed in Sections 15.145 (1), 17.07 (3m), 304.01, and 304.06 of the statutes.

INDEPENDENT UNITS ATTACHED FOR BUDGETING, PROGRAM COORDINATION, AND RELATED MANAGEMENT FUNCTIONS BY SECTION 15.03 OF THE STATUTES

INTERSTATE ADULT OFFENDER SUPERVISION BOARD

Members: TRACY HUDRLIK (compact administrator); vacancy (legislative branch representative); MICHAEL BOHREN (judicial branch representative); DAVID RABE (executive branch representative); STEPHANIE R. HOVE (victims' group representative). (All are appointed by governor).
Statutory References: Sections 15.145 (3) and 304.16 (4).
Agency Responsibility: The 5-member Interstate Adult Offender Supervision Board officially appoints the Wisconsin representative to the national commission. The board advises the department on its participation in the compact and on the operation of the compact within this state. The representatives serve 4-year terms while the compact administrator serves at the pleasure of the governor. It was created by 2001 Wisconsin Act 96.

COUNCIL ON OFFENDER REENTRY

Members: SILVIA JACKSON (reentry director), *chairperson;* SCOTT LEGWOLD (secretary of corrections designee); SCOTT JANSEN (secretary of workforce development designee); GLENN LARSON (secretary of health services designee); FREDI BOVE (secretary of children and families designee); ANN PERRY (secretary of transportation designee); PAUL CONNELL (attorney general designee); DEAN STENSBERG (chairperson of the Parole Commission or designee); CAROLYN STANFORD TAYLOR (state superintendent of public instruction designee); LISA STARK (current or former judge appointed by director of state courts); JEROME DILLARD (current or former incarcerated convict appointed by the secretary of corrections); MARK PODOLL (law enforcement officer); vacancy (representative of a crime victim's rights or crime victim services organization); vacancy (representative of a faith-based organization involved with community reintegration of offenders); JASON WITT (representative of a county department of human services); vacancy (tribal representative); vacancy (representative of a nonprofit organization involved with community reintegration that is not a faith-based organization); JOHN CHISHOLM (a district attorney); MIKE TOBIN (representative of the office of the state public defender); vacancy (an academic professional in the field of criminal justice); CHUCK BRENDEL (a representative of the Wisconsin Technical College System) (all except *ex officio* members appointed by governor).

Statutory References: Sections 15.145 (5) and 301.095.

Agency Responsibility: All except *ex officio* members, or as otherwise provided, of the 21-member Council on Offender Reentry are appointed by the governor for 3-year terms to coordinate reentry initiatives across the state, including promotion and collaboration of training opportunities, funding sources, and information sharing. The board was created by 2009 Wisconsin Act 28.

PRISON INDUSTRIES BOARD

Members: JAMES JACKSON, BILL G. SMITH, BERNIE SPIEGEL (private business and industry representatives); JOSE CARILLO, 2 vacancies (private labor organization representatives); TRACEY ISENSEE (Technical College System representative); EDWARD WALL (Department of Corrections representative); HELEN MCCAIN (Department of Administration representative). (All are appointed by governor.)

Statutory References: Sections 15.145 (2) and 303.015.

Agency Responsibility: The 9-member Prison Industries Board advises Prison Industries. It develops a plan for the manufacturing and marketing of prison industry products, the provision of prison industry services, and research and development activities. No prison industry may be established or permanently closed without board approval. The board reviews the department's budget request for Prison Industries and may make recommendations to the governor for changes. The board gives prior approval for Prison Industries purchases exceeding $250,000. Members are appointed for 4-year terms. It was created by 1983 Wisconsin Act 27.

STATE BOARD FOR INTERSTATE JUVENILE SUPERVISION

Members: SHELLEY HAGAN (administrator of Interstate Compact for Juveniles); vacancy (representative of legislative branch); T. CHRISTOPHER DEE (representative of judicial branch); MICHELLE HAVAS (representative of executive branch); TANYA NELSON (representative of victims groups) (all appointed by governor).

Statutory References: Sections 15.145 (4) and 938.999 (9).

Agency Responsibility: The 5 members of the State Board for Interstate Juvenile Supervision are appointed by the governor for 3-year terms to advise and exercise oversight and advocacy concerning the state's participation in activities of the Interstate Compact for Juveniles and may exercise any other statutorily authorized duties including the development of policy concerning the operations and procedures of the compact within the state. The board was created by 2005 Wisconsin Act 234.

EDUCATIONAL COMMUNICATIONS BOARD

Board Members: ROLF WEGENKE (private schools representative), *chairperson;* TONY EVERS (superintendent of public instruction), *vice chairperson;* SENATORS HARRIS DODD, OLSEN; REPRESENTATIVES 2 vacancies; SCOTT NEITZEL (secretary of administration), RAY CROSS (president, UW System), MORNA FOY (director, Technical College System), RICHARD LEPPING, EILEEN LITTIG (public members); KAREN SCHROEDER (public schools representative), REGINA MILLNER (appointed by UW System Board of Regents), DEAN DIETRICH (president, Wisconsin Public Radio Association), DIANE EVERSON (educational TV coverage area representative),

ELLIS BROMBERG (appointed by Technical College System Board). (Public members and representatives of public and private schools are appointed by governor.)

Executive Director: GENE PURCELL, 264-9666, gene.purcell@ecb.org

Deputy Director: MARTA BECHTOL, 264-9733, Fax: 264-9622, marta.bechtol@ecb.org

Education, Division of: vacancy, *director,* Fax: 264-9622.

Engineering Services, Division of: TERRENCE BAUN, *administrator,* 264-9746, Fax: 264-9622, terry.baun@ecb.org

Public Radio, Division of: MIKE CRANE, *director,* 821 University Avenue, Madison 53706, 265-3378, Fax: 263-9763, mike.crane@wpr.org

Public Television, Division of: vacancy, *director,* 821 University Avenue, Madison 53706, 263-1232, Fax: 263-9763.

Mailing Address: 3319 West Beltline Highway, Madison 53713-4296.

Telephone: (608) 264-9600.

Fax: (608) 264-9622.

Internet Address: www.ecb.org

Publications: Biennial report; Television Program Guide; WPR Annual Report; WPT Annual Report; teacher resources.

Number of Employees: 56.68.

Total Budget 2013-15: $39,486,500.

Statutory References: Section 15.57; Chapter 39, Subchapter I.

Agency Responsibility: The Educational Communications Board oversees the statewide public broadcasting system, its instructional telecommunications programming, and public service media for the cultural and educational needs of the state's citizens. The board plans, constructs, and operates the state's public radio and television networks, and it is the licensee for the state's 18 public radio stations and 5 public television stations. The board operates the Emergency Alert System, the Amber Alert System, National Weather Service Transmitters, a telecommunication operations center, and satellite facilities.

Operated by the Educational Communications Board's Division of Education, the Wisconsin Media Lab provides a variety of media for Wisconsin teachers and students. (Educational Communications Board)

The board shares responsibility for public broadcasting with the University of Wisconsin Board of Regents. Programming is produced through UW facilities or acquired from national, regional, state, and local sources. The board also is affiliated with public television stations licensed to Milwaukee Area Technical College, television station WSDE in Duluth, and several public radio stations.

Educational services include selection, acquisition or production, implementation, and evaluation of K-12 educational media and accompanying materials in cooperation with teachers in public and private schools, the Cooperative Educational Service Agencies, the Department of Public Instruction, the Technical College System, and the UW System.

Organization: The board includes 16 members. Those appointed by the governor, the UW Board of Regents, and the Technical College System Board serve 4-year terms. Legislative members must represent the majority and minority party in each house. The board appoints an executive director from outside the classified service. Division administrators and other agency staff are appointed by the executive director.

Unit Functions: The *Division of Education* operates the Wisconsin Media Lab which provides a wide variety of K-12 educational media for use by Wisconsin educators and students. Programming is delivered to the state online and via Public Television.

The *Division of Engineering Services* develops, operates, and maintains the statewide telecommunication systems used to receive and deliver instructional, educational, and cultural programming. It coordinates broadcasting of the Emergency Alert System, the National Weather Service, and the Amber Alert System.

The *Division of Public Radio* operates the statewide Wisconsin Public Radio service in partnership with the UW Board of Regents (through UW-Colleges and UW-Extension). Wisconsin Public Radio service includes three networks: the News and Classical Music Network; the Wisconsin Ideas Network; and an HD-2 Classical Network – all of which offer national, regional, and local programming.

The *Division of Public Television* operates the statewide Wisconsin Public Television (WPT) service in partnership with the UW Board of Regents (through UW-Colleges and UW-Extension). The service includes three broadcast channels: WPT's flagship station features programming from the Public Broadcasting System (PBS), children's educational programs, and locally produced content; The Wisconsin Channel features programming about state issues and state history, university lectures, new local programs, and performances by Wisconsin artists; and Create, an educational channel for cooking, arts and crafts, gardening, home improvement, and travel from PBS.

History: Wisconsin's history in educational broadcasting dates back to the oldest public radio station in the nation. The University of Wisconsin's research in "wireless" communication led to the beginning of scheduled radio broadcasting in 1917 on Station 9XM, which was renamed WHA-AM in 1922. Wisconsin made a commitment to statewide educational broadcasting in 1945. Chapter 570, Laws of 1945, created the State Radio Council to plan, produce, and transmit educational, cultural, and service programs over a statewide FM radio network. Over the next two decades, the council constructed and activated 10 radio transmitters. In Chapter 360, Laws of 1953, the council also assumed responsibility for research in educational television.

The 1967 executive branch reorganization renamed the council the Educational Broadcasting Board, created the Educational Broadcasting Division under its supervision, and attached the board and the division to the Coordinating Council for Higher Education. The name was changed to the Educational Communications Board in Chapter 276, Laws of 1969. With the demise of the Coordinating Council, the Educational Communications Board became an independent agency in Chapter 100, Laws of 1971. In 1971, the board began to extend educational television to the entire state, and it had constructed 5 UHF television stations by 1977. Signal translator facilities erected in the 1980s extended service to areas of the state beyond the reach of regular transmitters. Most recently, the Educational Communications Board has begun to offer HD Radio services and expanded television programming through WPT Create and WPT The Wisconsin Channel. The board has worked cooperatively with the UW Board of Regents to enhance public broadcasting service for the state's citizens.

Department of
EMPLOYEE TRUST FUNDS

Address e-mail by combining the user ID and the state extender: userid@etf.wi.gov

All telephone numbers are 608 area code unless otherwise indicated.

Employee Trust Funds Board: WAYNE E. KOESSL (Wisconsin Retirement Board member), *chairperson;* JOHN DAVID (Wisconsin Retirement Board member), *vice chairperson;* ROBERT M. NIENDORF (Teachers Retirement Board member), *secretary;* DANIELLE CARNE (designee of director, Office of State Employment Relations); WILLIAM FORD (elected by WRS annuitants); JON LITSCHER (governor's designee on Group Insurance Board); MICHAEL LANGYEL, ROBERTA RASMUS, DAVID WILTGEN (Teachers Retirement Board members); LEILANI PAUL (Technical College or educational support personnel employee); VICTOR SHIER (appointed by governor with senate confirmation); MARY VON RUDEN, vacancy (Wisconsin Retirement Board members). (Board representatives are appointed by their respective boards; the annuitant member and the technical college or public school educational support employee are elected by the constituency groups.)

Secretary of Employee Trust Funds: ROBERT CONLIN, 266-0301, bob.conlin@

Deputy Secretary: JOHN VOELKER, 266-9854, john.voelker@

Assistant Deputy Secretary: PAMELA HENNING, 267-2929, pamela.henning@

Communications Director: MARK LAMKINS, 266-3641, mark.lamkins@

Enterprise Initiatives, Office of: BOB MARTIN, *director,* 267-9036, bob.martin@

Internal Audit, Office of: YIKCHAU SZE, *director,* 261-8938, yikchau.sze@

Legal Services, Office of: DAVID NISPEL, *general counsel,* 264-6936, david.nispel@

Legislative Liaison: TARNA HUNTER, 267-0908, tarna.hunter@

Management Services, Division of: DANA PERRY, *administrator,* 264-6943, dana.perry@

Policy, Privacy and Compliance, Office of: STEVE HURLEY, *director,* 267-2847, steve.hurley@

Retirement Services, Division of: MATT STOHR, *administrator,* 266-1210, matthew.stohr@

Strategic Health Policy, Office of: LISA ELLINGER, *director,* 264-6627, lisa.ellinger@

Trust Finance, Division of: ROBERT WILLETT, *administrator,* 266-0904, bob.willett@

Mailing Address: P.O. Box 7931, Madison 53707-7931.

Location: 801 West Badger Road, Madison.

Telephones: Member services: (608) 266-3285 (Madison) or (877) 533-5020; Self-service line: (877) 383-1888; Wisconsin Relay Service 7-1-1 or (800) 947-3529 (English) or (800) 833-7813 (Spanish).

Internet Address: http://etf.wi.gov (includes e-mail inquiry form).

Publications: *Comprehensive Annual Financial Report; Employer Bulletin; WRS News;* and various employer manuals and employee brochures on the Wisconsin Retirement System, the group insurance plans, the deferred compensation program, and the employee reimbursement accounts program.

Number of Employees: 266.20.

Total Budget 2013-15: $83,421,300.

Statutory References: Sections 15.16 and Chapter 40.

Agency Responsibility: The Department of Employee Trust Funds administers various employee benefit programs, including the retirement, group insurance, disability, and deferred compensation programs and employee reimbursement and commuter benefits accounts. It serves all state employees and teachers and most municipal employees, with the notable exceptions of employees of the City and County of Milwaukee.

Organization: The 13-member Employee Trust Funds Board provides direction and supervision to the department and the Wisconsin Retirement System (WRS). Board membership includes 2 *ex officio* members and 11 members who are appointed or elected for 4-year terms to represent employers, members, employees, taxpayers, and annuitants. The member appointed by the governor to represent taxpayers must have specific professional experience and cannot be a WRS participant. The board approves all administrative rules; authorizes payment of all retirement annuities, except those for disability; and hears appeals of benefit determinations. It appoints the secretary from outside the classified service, and the secretary selects the deputy and assistant deputy from outside the service. Division and office heads are appointed from within the classified service by the secretary.

Unit Functions: The *Division of Management Services* provides support services for human resources, payroll, information technology, facility management, capital budget and inventory, records management, mail and supplies, library, and telecommunications.

The *Division of Retirement Services* develops and implements retirement policies and services for the members of the retirement system, including calculation and payment of retirement, disability, and related benefits, and the deferred compensation program.

The *Office of Strategic Health Policy* is responsible for policy development and implementation of health, life, long-term care insurance, and the employee reimbursement and commuter benefit accounts.

The *Division of Trust Finance* oversees the tax compliance retiree payroll and accounts receivable functions including retirement and health care accounting.

History: The 1891 Legislature initiated pension coverage for local government employees when it required Milwaukee to create a pension fund for retired and disabled police and fire fighters in Chapter 287. Sixteen years later, the legislature extended pension coverage to protective service employees of smaller cities through Chapter 671, Laws of 1907. The 1909 Legislature authorized a pension system for City of Milwaukee teachers in Chapter 510; and Chapter 323, Laws of 1911, created a retirement system for those school districts throughout the rest of the state that wished to enroll their teachers. With enactment of Chapter 459, Laws of 1921, Wisconsin established a mandatory, joint contributory, statewide teachers' pension system, covering virtually all teachers in public schools (outside of Milwaukee), normal schools, and the University of Wisconsin.

The legislature first provided retirement plans for general municipal employees outside of Milwaukee in Chapter 175, Laws of 1943. In the same session, a retirement system was created for general employees by Chapter 176, Laws of 1943. Local fire and police pension funds were closed to new members by Chapter 206, Laws of 1947, and these employees have since been covered with the general employees. Chapter 60, Laws of 1951, created the Public Employees Social Security Fund, making Wisconsin the first state in the nation to permit some state and local government employees to be covered by Social Security.

Chapter 211, Laws of 1959, created group life and group health insurance programs for state employees, a group life insurance program for municipal employees, and the Group Insurance Board to monitor the administration of the programs. The 1967 executive branch reorganization created the Department of Employee Trust Funds to administer the various retirement funds, and the Group Insurance Board was attached to it.

Chapter 280, Laws of 1975, initiated the merger of the existing, separate retirement funds that covered all publicly employed teachers in the state and all state and local public employees, except employees of the City of Milwaukee and Milwaukee County who have their own systems. The legislature transferred local police and fire pension funds to the overall general employee system in Chapter 182, Laws of 1977. The implementation of the merged Wisconsin Retirement System was completed, effective January 1, 1982, by Chapter 96, Laws of 1981.

Statutory Boards

Deferred Compensation Board: EDWARD D. MAIN, *chairperson;* JOHN NELSON, *vice chairperson;* GAIL HANSON, *secretary;* MICHAEL GRACZ, ARTHUR ZIMMERMAN (appointed by governor with senate consent).

The 5-member Deferred Compensation Board establishes rules for offering deferred compensation plans to state and local employees and contracts with deferred compensation plan providers. Its members are appointed for 4-year terms. The board was created by 1989 Wisconsin

Act 31, and its composition and duties are prescribed in Sections 15.165 (4) and 40.80 of the statutes.

Group Insurance Board: JON LITSCHER (designated by governor), *chairperson;* BONNIE CYGANEK (designated by attorney general), *vice chairperson;* MICHAEL FARRELL, *secretary;* DANIELLE CARNE (designated by Director of the Office of State Employment Relations); TERRI CARLSON (WRS-insured nonteacher participant); HERSCHEL DAY (WRS-insured teacher participant); CHARLES GRAPENTINE (retired WRS-insured participant); MICHAEL HEIFETZ (designated by secretary of administration); THEODORE NEITZKE (WRS-insured local government participant); DANIEL SCHWARTZER (designated by commissioner of insurance); NANCY THOMPSON (chief executive or member of local government participating in WRS). (All except *ex officio* members are appointed by governor.)

The 11-member Group Insurance Board oversees the group health, life, income continuation, and other insurance programs offered to state employees, covered local employees, and retirees. The board's 5 appointed members serve 2-year terms. The board was created by Chapter 211, Laws of 1959, and its composition and duties are prescribed in Sections 15.165 (2) and 40.03 (6) of the statutes.

Teachers Retirement Board: ROBIN STARCK (public school teacher), *chairperson;* R. THOMAS PEDERSEN (technical college teacher), *vice chairperson;* BRENT GROCHOWSKI (public school teacher), *secretary;* JON JOSLIN, PATRICK PHAIR, DAVID WILTGEN, JEFFREY ZORE (public school teachers); CRAIG HUBBELL (public school administrator appointed by governor); SANDRA CLAFLIN-CHALTON, SUSAN HARRISON (UW System teacher representatives appointed by governor); GARY EPPING (school board member appointed by governor); DENNIS MURPHY (teacher annuitant); KIM SCHROEDER (Milwaukee teacher). (Members not appointed by governor are elected by their constituent groups.)

The 13-member Teachers Retirement Board advises the Employee Trust Funds Board about retirement matters related to teachers, recommends and approves or rejects administrative rules, authorizes payment of disability annuities for teachers, and hears appeals of staff determinations of disability. Board members serve staggered 5-year terms; the 2 UW System representatives may not be from the same campus. The board was created by Chapter 204, Laws of 1953, and its composition and duties are prescribed in Sections 15.165 (3) (a) and 40.03 (7) of the statutes.

Wisconsin Retirement Board: WAYNE E. KOESSL (county or town governing body member), *chairperson;* JOHN DAVID (city or village chief executive or governing board member), *vice chairperson;* MARY VON RUDEN (participating employee of local employer other than city or village), *secretary;* JAMIE AULIK (county clerk or deputy); TED NICKEL (commissioner of insurance); HERBERT STINSKI (participating city or village finance officer); STEVEN WILDING (participating city or village employee); vacancy (not a participant or beneficiary of the WRS); vacancy (participating state employee). (All, except insurance commissioner or designee, are appointed by governor.)

The 9-member Wisconsin Retirement Board advises the Employee Trust Funds Board about retirement matters related to state and local general and protective employees and performs the same functions for these employees as the Teachers Retirement Board does for teachers. The board's appointed members serve staggered 5-year terms, and the municipal official and county board member are nominated by their respective statewide associations. The board was created by Chapter 96, Laws of 1981, and its composition and duties are prescribed in Sections 15.165 (3) (b) and 40.03 (8) of the statutes.

Department of
FINANCIAL INSTITUTIONS

Address e-mail by combining the user ID and the state extender: userid@**wisconsin.gov**
All telephone numbers are 608 area code unless otherwise indicated.

Secretary of Financial Institutions: RAY ALLEN, 267-1719, ray.allen@; Fax: 261-4334.

Deputy Secretary: vacancy.

Assistant Deputy Secretary: GEORGIA E. MAXWELL, 267-1718, georgia.maxwell@

Communications Director: GEORGE ALTHOFF, 261-4504, george.althoff@

Chief Legal Counsel: CHRISTOPHER GREEN, 266-7968, chris.green@; Fax: 261-4334.

Financial Literacy, Office of: vacancy, *director,* 261-4504.

Mailing Address: P.O. Box 8861, Madison 53708-8861.

Location: 201 West Washington Avenue, Suite 500, Madison.

Telephones: 261-9555; TDY: 266-8818.

Fax: 261-4334.

Internet Address: www.wdfi.org

Number of Employees: 141.54.

Total Budget 2013-15: $35,787,600.

Statutory Reference: Section 15.18.

Administrative Services and Technology, Division of: vacancy, *administrator,* 264-7800; P.O. Box 7876, Madison 53707-7876; Division Fax: 261-7200.

> *Budget and Fiscal Services, Bureau of:* SUSAN J. DIETZEL, *director,* 267-0399, susan.dietzel@
>
> *Information Technology, Bureau of:* vacancy, *director,* 267-1714.

Banking, Division of: vacancy, *administrator,* 266-0451; CHERYLL OLSON-COLLINS, *deputy administrator,* 267-1707, cheryll.olsoncollins@; P.O. Box 7876, Madison 53707-7876; Division Fax: 267-6889.

> *Consumer Affairs, Bureau of:* JEAN PLALE, *director,* 267-3518, jean.plale@; Consumer Act inquiries: 264-7969, (800) 452-3328 in Wisconsin; P.O. Box 8041, Madison 53708-8041.
>
> *Licensed Financial Services Bureau:* JEAN PLALE, *director,* 266-0447, jean.plale@
>
> *Mortgage Banking Bureau:* JEAN PLALE, *director,* 266-0447, jean.plale@

Corporate and Consumer Services, Division of: GEORGE PETAK, *administrator,* 266-6810, george.petak@; DAVID MANCL, *deputy administrator,* 261-9540, david.mancl@; P.O. Box 7846, Madison 53707-7846; Division Fax: 267-6813.

> *Corporations, Bureau of:* vacancy, *supervisor,* 261-7577; Corporations inquiries: 261-7577; P.O. Box 7846, Madison 53707-7846.
>
> *Uniform Commercial Code, Bureau of:* DEANNA GRAHN, *supervisor,* 267-6811, deanna.grahn@; Uniform Commercial Code, Notary Public Commissions, Registration of Marks inquiries: 261-9543; P.O. Box 7847, Madison 53707-7847.

Securities, Division of: PATRICIA STRUCK, *administrator,* 266-3432, patricia.struck@; P.O. Box 1768, Madison 53701-1768; Division Fax: 264-7979.

> *Enforcement, Bureau of:* LESLIE VAN BUSKIRK, *supervising attorney,* 261-1603, leslie.vanbuskirk@
>
> *Professional Registration and Compliance, Bureau of:* DEBORAH FABRITZ, *director,* 266-3414, deborah.fabritz@

Agency Responsibility: The Department of Financial Institutions regulates state-chartered banks, savings and loans associations, and savings banks, as well as various operations of the securities industry. It examines and files charters and other documents of businesses and organizations and registers and regulates the mortgage banking industry and other financial service providers. It oversees Uniform Commercial Code filings. It administers the Wisconsin Consumer Act and registers merchants who extend credit. It also issues notary public commissions and registers trademarks, trade names, and brands. The department is self-supporting through program revenue derived from fees and assessments paid by regulated entities and individuals.

Organization: The department is administered by a secretary, who is appointed by the governor with the advice and consent of the senate. The secretary appoints the administrators for 3 of the 4 divisions from outside the classified service and the administrator of the Division of Administrative Services and Technology from the classified service.

DEPARTMENT OF FINANCIAL INSTITUTIONS

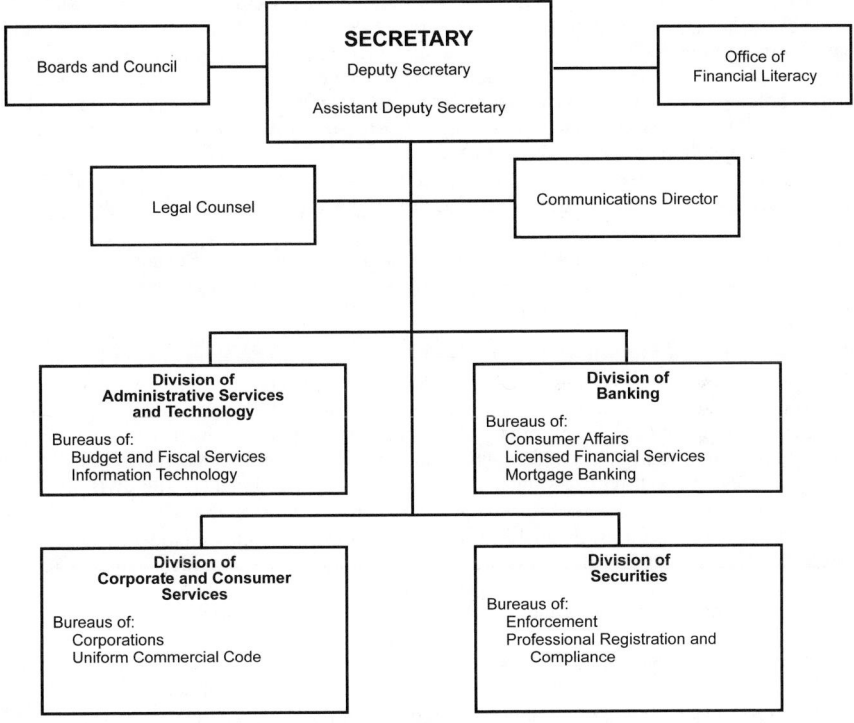

	SECRETARY Deputy Secretary Assistant Deputy Secretary	
Boards and Council		Office of Financial Literacy

Legal Counsel

Communications Director

**Division of
Administrative Services
and Technology**

Bureaus of:
  Budget and Fiscal Services
  Information Technology

**Division of
Banking**

Bureaus of:
  Consumer Affairs
  Licensed Financial Services
  Mortgage Banking

**Division of
Corporate and Consumer
Services**

Bureaus of:
  Corporations
  Uniform Commercial Code

**Division of
Securities**

Bureaus of:
  Enforcement
  Professional Registration and
  Compliance

Unit attached for administrative purposes under Sec. 15.03: Office of Credit Unions

Unit Functions: The *Office of Financial Literacy* (OFL), in the Office of the Secretary, promotes financial literacy to the public as a vital life skill and provides information to the public on matters of personal finance and investor protection. It emphasizes financial and economic literacy for Wisconsin's youth and encourages consumers to take advantage of the services offered by financial institutions.

The *Division of Administrative Services and Technology* provides support services to the department through its administration of the agency's budget, personnel, procurement, and information technology services.

The *Division of Banking,* created in Section 15.183 (1), Wisconsin Statutes, by 1995 Wisconsin Act 27, is advised by the Banking Review Board. It regulates and supervises state-chartered banks and consumer financial service industries under statutory Chapters 220 through 224. In addition to chartering and regularly examining state banks, the division licenses loan companies, mortgage bankers, mortgage brokers, loan originators, collection agencies, community currency exchanges, sales finance companies, adjustment service companies, sellers of checks, insurance premium finance companies, credit services organizations, professional employer organizations, charitable organizations, and charitable fund-raisers. It also regulates auto dealers' installment sales contracts. The division investigates applications for expanded banking powers, new financial products, and interstate bank acquisitions and mergers. It may conduct joint examinations with Federal Reserve System examiners and with the Federal Deposit Insurance Corporation.

With Banking Review Board approval, the administrator may establish uniform rules for savings programs and fiduciary operations.

The division supervises state-chartered savings and loan associations and savings banks and enforces the laws governing them under statutory Chapters 214 and 215 with the advice of the Savings Institutions Review Board. It works to resolve consumer complaints and reviews and approves applications for acquisitions, new branches and other offices, and the organization of mutual holding companies. It may rule on interstate mergers or acquisitions. It also conducts joint examinations of associations with the federal Office of Thrift Institutions and may examine savings banks with the Federal Deposit Insurance Corporation.

The division administers the Wisconsin Consumer Act, which resolves consumer complaints and advises consumers and lenders regarding their rights and responsibilities under consumer law.

The *Division of Corporate and Consumer Services* is responsible for examining and filing business records for corporations and other organizations. It examines charters, documents that affect mergers, consolidations, and dissolutions, and reviews the annual reports of various businesses, including partnerships, corporations, limited liability companies, cooperatives, and foreign corporations. It also examines and files documents under the Uniform Commercial Code, including statements of business indebtedness, consignments, terminations, and financing statements and maintains the statewide Uniform Commercial Code lien system. The division prepares certified copies of the records in its custody and responds to inquiries about corporations and other business entities and organizations for which it has records. It also issues notary public commissions and registers trademarks, trade names, and brands. The division is also responsible for the issuance of state video franchise authority certificates.

The *Division of Securities,* created in Section 15.183 (3), Wisconsin Statutes, by 1995 Wisconsin Act 27, regulates the sale of investment securities and franchises under statutory Chapters 551, 552, and 553. It examines and registers the offerings and may bar them from registration in this state. The division registers and monitors the activities of broker-dealers, securities agents, investment advisers, and investment adviser representatives. It conducts audits and inspections, and investigates complaints. When violations are detected, it initiates the appropriate administrative, injunctive, or criminal action. The division also regulates corporate takeovers.

History: The Department of Financial Institutions (DFI) was created in 1995 Wisconsin Act 27. The act reorganized formerly independent offices of the commissioners of banking, savings and loan, and securities as divisions and transferred them to the department. In addition, Act 27 transferred the responsibility for business organization filings and the Uniform Commercial Code lien information filings to the department from the Office of the Secretary of State. The same act transferred the regulation of mortgage bankers and loan originators and solicitors to the department from the Department of Regulation and Licensing. 2007 Wisconsin Act 42 replaced cable television franchises granted by municipalities with statewide video service franchises granted by DFI. 2011 Wisconsin Act 32 transferred to DFI the notary and trademark functions formerly performed by the Office of the Secretary of State. The Mortgage Loan Originator Council was repealed by 2011 Wisconsin Act 233. 2013 Wisconsin Act 20 transferred to the department, from the Department of Safety and Professional Services, the regulation of charitable organization, fund-raising counsel, professional fund-raisers, professional employer organizations, and professional employer groups.

Banking. For the first five years of statehood, no regular commercial banks existed in Wisconsin. Prior to amendment in 1902, Article XI of the Wisconsin Constitution required that any banking law must be approved in a statewide referendum. Bank regulation began when the legislature created the Office of Bank Comptroller in Chapter 479, Laws of 1852, and the voters approved the law in 1853. That law allowed any group meeting state requirements to go into the banking business. It was designed primarily to regulate the issuance of bank notes. Bank supervision was transferred to the state treasurer in 1868 and remained with that office until 1903.

The 1902 constitutional amendment gave the legislature the power to enact general banking laws without a referendum. In Chapter 234, Laws of 1903, the legislature created the State Banking Department. The department also supervised savings and loan associations until 1947 and credit unions until 1972. Under the 1967 executive branch reorganization, the department continued as an independent agency and was renamed the Office of the Commissioner of Banking. 1995 Wisconsin Act 27 reorganized the agency as the Division of Banking and transferred it to the Department of Financial Institutions.

Savings Institutions. Attempts to register and examine savings and loan associations date back to the 1850s in Wisconsin, but there are no records of any associations incorporating under these laws. In 1876, the legislature passed Chapter 384 to require that savings banks and savings societies register with the county registers of deeds and the secretary of state. Voters approved the law in November 1876. Several associations incorporated shortly afterward. Beginning with Chapter 368, Laws of 1897, building and loan associations were regulated by the bank examiner in the state treasurer's office.

In 1903, responsibility for regulating savings and loan associations was transferred to the State Banking Department. Chapter 411, Laws of 1947, moved regulation from that department to the newly created Savings and Loan Association Department. The law also created the forerunner of the current Savings Institutions Review Board. In 1967, the executive branch reorganization act renamed the department the Office of the Commissioner of Savings and Loan. In 1991 Wisconsin Act 221, the office assumed responsibility for chartering, regulating, and examining savings banks. The same law created the Savings Bank Review Board. 1995 Wisconsin Act 27 reorganized the agency as the Division of Savings and Loan and transferred it to the Department of Financial Institutions. It was renamed the Division of Savings Institutions in 1999 and repealed in 2003 Wisconsin Act 33. Its duties were transferred to the Division of Banking.

Securities. Laws enacted by states to protect the public against securities fraud are commonly referred to as "blue sky" laws. (The term "blue sky" is believed to have originated when a judge ruled that a particular stock had about the same value as a patch of blue sky.) Wisconsin's first "blue sky" law was Chapter 756, Laws of 1913. This law was revised successively in 1919, 1933, 1941, 1969, and 2007. The current Wisconsin Uniform Securities Law, effective January 1, 2009, was enacted as 2007 Wisconsin Act 196, and it is based upon the Uniform Securities Act of 2002. From 1913 until 1939, the regulation of securities came under the jurisdiction first of the Railroad Commission (and its successor the Public Service Commission) and later the State Banking Department. The Department of Securities was created by Chapter 68, Laws of 1939, to regulate the sale of stocks, bonds, and other forms of business ownership or debt. It was renamed the Office of the Commissioner of Securities by Chapter 75, Laws of 1967. 1995 Wisconsin Act 27, reorganized the agency as the Division of Securities and transferred it to the Department of Financial Institutions.

Statutory Boards

Banking Review Board: DEBRA R. LINS, *chairperson;* DOUGLAS L. FARMER, AMELIA E. MACARENO, THOMAS E. SPITZ, RALPH J. TENUTA (appointed by governor with senate consent).

The 5-member Banking Review Board advises the Division of Banking regarding the banking industry in Wisconsin and reviews the division's administrative actions. Members are appointed for staggered 5-year terms, and at least 3 of them must each have at least 5 years' banking experience. No member may act in any matter involving a bank of which the member is an officer, director, or stockholder or to which that person is indebted. The board was created by Chapter 10, Laws of Special Session 1931-32, under the State Banking Department (renamed the Office of the Commissioner of Banking in 1967), and transferred to the Department of Financial Institutions by 1995 Wisconsin Act 27. Its composition and duties are prescribed in Sections 15.185 (1) and 220.035 of the statutes.

Savings Institutions Review Board: PAUL C. ADAMSKI, *chairperson;* GEORGE E. GARY, ROBERT W. HOLMES, JAMES K. OLSON, CHARLES SCHMALZ (appointed by governor with senate consent).

The 5-member Savings Institutions Review Board advises the Division of Banking on matters impacting savings and loan associations and savings banks in Wisconsin. It reviews division orders and determinations, hears appeals on certain actions taken by the division, and may act on any matter submitted by the division. Members serve 5-year terms. At least 3 of them must each have a minimum of 5 years' experience in the savings and loan or savings bank business in this state. Chapter 441, Laws of 1974, created the board as the Savings and Loan Review Board in the Savings and Loan Association Department (renamed the Office of the Commissioner of Savings and Loan in 1967) and 1995 Wisconsin Act 27 transferred it to the Department of Financial Institutions. In 2003, Act 33 renamed the board and eliminated the Savings Bank Review Board. Its composition and duties are prescribed in Sections 15.185 (3) and 215.04 of the statutes.

Independent Unit Attached for Budgeting, Program Coordination, and Related Management Functions by Section 15.03 of the Statutes

OFFICE OF CREDIT UNIONS

Director: Kim Santos, 267-2608, kim.santos@

Mailing Address: P.O. Box 14137, Madison 53708-0137.

Location: 201 West Washington Avenue, Suite 500, Madison.

Telephone: 261-9543.

Fax: 267-0479.

Internet Address: www.wdfi.org

Publications: Quarterly Credit Union Bulletin.

Statutory References: Section 15.185 (7) (a); Chapter 186.

Agency Responsibility: The Office of Credit Unions regulates credit unions chartered to do business in Wisconsin. It charters new credit unions, examines credit union records and assets, consents to consolidation of credit unions within the state and, in cooperation with similar agencies in neighboring states, approves interstate mergers. If a credit union is not in compliance with state law, the office may remove its officers, suspend operations, or take possession of the credit union's business. The director is appointed by the governor and must have at least 3 years' experience either in the operation of a credit union or in a credit union supervisory agency or a combination of both. All personnel and budget requests by the office must be processed and forwarded without change by the department, unless the office requests or concurs in a change.

History: Regulation of credit unions began in 1913 (Chapter 733) when the legislature passed a law that required "cooperative credit associations" to obtain their charters from the State Banking Department. That law was repealed by Chapter 334, Laws of 1923, which required the department to charter and regulate "credit unions". The Office of the Commissioner of Credit Unions was created in Chapter 193, Laws of 1971, as a separate agency by removing the credit union division and its advisory board from the Office of the Commissioner of Banking and giving it expanded powers. 1995 Wisconsin Act 27 created the Office of Credit Unions and attached it to the Department of Financial Institutions under Section 15.03, Wisconsin Statutes.

Statutory Board

Credit Union Review Board: J. David Christenson, Lisa Greco, Brian Prunty, Colleen Woggon, Dan Wollin (appointed by governor with senate consent).

The 5-member Credit Union Review Board advises the Office of Credit Unions regarding credit unions in Wisconsin. It reviews rules and regulations issued by the office, acts as an appeals board for persons aggrieved by any act of the office, and may require the office to submit its actions for approval. Members serve staggered 5-year terms and each must have at least 5 years' experience in credit union operations. The board was created within the State Banking Department by Chapter 411, Laws of 1947, then transferred to the Office of the Commissioner of Credit Unions in 1971, and later made part of the Office of Credit Unions in 1995 Wisconsin Act 27. Its composition and duties are prescribed in Sections 15.185 (7) (b) and 186.015 of the statutes.

GOVERNMENT ACCOUNTABILITY BOARD

Address e-mail by combining the user ID and the state extender: userid@**wisconsin.gov**
All telephone numbers are 608 area code unless otherwise indicated.

Members: GERALD NICHOL, *chairperson;* ELSA LAMELAS, *vice chairperson;* THOMAS BARLAND, *secretary;* JOHN FRANKE, HAROLD FROELICH, TIMOTHY VOCKE. (All members are former judges appointed to staggered terms by the governor, and confirmed by two-thirds vote of the senate.)

Director and General Counsel: KEVIN J. KENNEDY, 266-8005, kevin.kennedy@

Mailing Address: P.O. Box 7984, Madison 53707-7984.

Location: 212 East Washington Avenue, Third Floor, Madison.

Telephones: General: 266-8005 or 1-800 VOTE-WIS.

Fax: 267-0500.

E-Mail Address: gab@wi.gov

Internet Address: http://gab.wi.gov

Elections Division: MICHAEL HAAS, *administrator,* 266-0136, michael.haas@

Ethics and Accountability Division: JONATHAN BECKER, *administrator,* 266-8123, jonathan.becker@

Number of Employees: 48.75.

Total Budget 2013-15: $14,007,000.

Statutory References: Chapters 5-12, Subchapter III of Chapter 13, and Subchapter III of Chapter 19.

Agency Responsibility: The Government Accountability Board (GAB) administers the state's campaign finance, elections, ethics, and lobby laws, investigates alleged violations of those laws, and brings civil actions to collect forfeitures. It may subpoena records and notify the district attorney or attorney general of any grounds for civil or criminal prosecution. The GAB issues advisory opinions to officials, local governments, and others asking about their own conduct; promulgates administrative rules; and conducts training for local election officials, campaign and lobby registrants, and state public officials.

The GAB maintains the campaign finance registration and reporting system which limits and requires full disclosure of contributions and disbursements made on behalf of every candidate for public office. The statutes specify which candidates, individuals, political parties, and groups must register and file detailed financial statements. Registration and reporting are required for nonresident committees that make contributions and for all individuals who make independent disbursements. The GAB administers the electronic filing of campaign finance reports of all registrants that receive contributions in excess of $20,000 in a campaign period for candidate committees or in excess of $20,000 in a biennium for other registrants.

The GAB administers the state elections code along with implementing the federal Help America Vote Act of 2002 that establishes certain election requirements regarding the conduct of federal elections in the state. The director and general counsel serves as the chief state election official. The GAB is responsible for the design and maintenance of the Statewide Voter Registration System (SVRS) which is required to be used by all municipalities in the state to administer federal, state, and local elections.

The GAB also has compliance review authority over local election officials' actions relating to ballot preparation, candidate nomination, voter qualifications, recall, conduct of elections, and election administration. The GAB holds information and training meetings with local election officials to promote uniform election procedures. The GAB is responsible for the training and certification of all municipal clerks and chief election inspectors in the state.

The GAB administers the Code of Ethics for State Public Officials and Wisconsin's lobbying law. The intent of the ethics code is to forbid a state official from using a public position to obtain anything of value for the personal benefit of the official, the official's family, or the official's private business. Wisconsin's lobbying law prohibits lobbyists and the organizations that employ them from furnishing anything of value to a state official or employee except in a limited number of well-defined circumstances. The GAB collects and makes available information about the financial interests of state officials, candidates, and nominees; and compiles and disseminates on its Web sites information about organizations' efforts to influence legislation and administrative rules as well as the time and money spent by those organizations in lobbying activities.

Organization: The 6 members of the board, each of whom must have formerly been elected to and served as a judge of a court of record in Wisconsin, are appointed to 6-year terms by the governor from nominations submitted by a nominating committee called the Governmental Accountability Candidate Committee. The committee consists of one court of appeals judge from each of the court of appeals districts, chosen by lot by the chief justice of the supreme court in the presence of the other justices.

Board members may not be involved in partisan political activities and may not hold another state office or position except that of reserve judge of a circuit court or court of appeals. The board appoints a legal counsel outside the classified service as agency head to perform legal and administrative functions for the board. The board includes an Elections Division and an Ethics and Accountability Division, each of which is under the direction and supervision of an administrator appointed by the board. The board designates an employee to serve as the chief election officer of the state.

History: The Government Accountability Board was created by 2007 Wisconsin Act 1. Act 1 abolished the State Ethics and Elections Boards and their functions were merged into the new agency, effective after January 10, 2008.

The Elections Board was created as an independent agency by Chapter 334, Laws of 1973, which transferred administration of the state's election laws from the secretary of state and created the campaign finance registration and reporting system.

The Ethics Board was created by Chapter 90, Laws of 1973, to administer the ethics code applicable to public officials and employees created by the act. Lobbying has been regulated in Wisconsin since 1858. The secretary of state was made responsible for the enforcement of lobbying laws by Chapter 278, Laws of 1977, and this regulation was transferred to the Ethics Board by 1989 Wisconsin Act 338.

Statutory Council

Election Administration Council: Suzette Emmer (Elections Coordinator, Milwaukee County Board of Election Commissioners); Neil Albrecht (City of Milwaukee Board of Election Commissioners); Sue Ertmer (Winnebago County Clerk); Nan Kottke (Marathon County Clerk); Marilyn K. Bhend (Johnson Town Clerk); Julee Helt (Waunakee Village Clerk); Diane Hermann-Brown (Sun Prairie City Clerk); Sue Peck (Marshall Village Clerk); Audrey Rue (Brigham Town Clerk); Kit Kerschensteiner (Managing Attorney, Disability Rights Wisconsin); Andrea Kaminski (Executive Director, League of Women Voters of Wisconsin); Sandi Wesolowski (City of Franklin Clerk); Anita Johnson (Election Administration Advocate, Citizen Action of Wisconsin, Milwaukee); Maureen Ryan (Wisconsin Coalition of Independent Living Centers); Lori Stotler (Rock County Clerk); Sandra Klister (Bristol Town Clerk); John Shaw (Community Outready/Advocacy, Board for People with Developmental Disabilities); Donna Austed (Eau Claire City Clerk); Kevin Kennedy (Government Accountability Board director and general counsel).

The Election Administration Council assists the Government Accountability Board in preparing and revising, as necessary, a state plan that meets the requirements of Public Law 107-252, the federal "Help America Vote Act of 2002", which will enable participation by the state in federal financial assistance programs authorized under that law. The members of the council are appointed by the GAB elections division administrator. The membership must include the clerk or executive director of the board of election commissioners of the two counties or municipalities having the largest population, one or more election officials of other counties or municipalities, representatives of organizations that advocate for the interests of the voting public, and other electors of Wisconsin. The council was created by 2003 Wisconsin Act 265 in the Elections Board, and was attached to the GAB by 2007 Wisconsin Act 1. The composition and duties of the council are specified in Sections 5.05 (10), 5.68 (3m), and 15.607 (1) of the statutes.

Department of
HEALTH SERVICES

Address e-mail by combining the user ID and the state extender: userid@**wisconsin.gov**
All telephone numbers are 608 area code unless otherwise indicated.

Secretary of Health Services: KITTY RHOADES, 266-9622, kitty.rhoades@

Deputy Secretary: THOMAS ENGELS, 266-9622, thomas.engels@

Assistant Deputy Secretary: LAURA RISKE, 266-9622, laura.riske@

Communications Director: STEPHANIE SMILEY, 266-9622, stephanie.smiley@

    Area Administration: WILLIAM HANNA, *director,* 261-8342, william.hanna@

    Tribal Affairs: GAIL NAHWAHQUAW, *director,* 261-9334, gail.nahwahquaw@

Legislative Advisor: ALEX IGNATOWSKI, 266-9622, alex.ignatowski@

Legal Counsel, Office of: SANDRA ROWE, *chief legal counsel,* 266-9622, sandram.rowe@

Inspector General, Office of: ALAN WHITE, *inspector general,* 266-2521, alan.white@; LORI THORNTON, *deputy inspector general,* 266-2521, lori.thornton@

Policy Initiatives and Budget, Office of: ANDREW FORSAITH, *director,* 266-7684, andrew.forsaith@

Mailing Address: P.O. Box 7850, Madison 53707-7850.

Location: Wilson Street State Human Services Building, 1 West Wilson Street, Madison.

Telephone: 266-1865.

Internet Address: http://dhs.wisconsin.gov

Publications: Annual fiscal reports; Biennial reports; Reports and informational brochures (available through divisions).

Number of Employees: 6,195.05.

Total Budget 2013-15: $20,339,075,700.

Statutory References: Section 15.19; Chapter 46.

Enterprise Services, Division of: CHERYL K. JOHNSON, *administrator,* 266-5869, cherylk.johnson@; AMY McDOWELL, *deputy administrator,* 261-8351, amy.mcdowell@

    Fiscal Services, Bureau of: ROBERT HALVERSON, *director,* 266-2019, robert.halverson@

    Human Resources, Bureau of: JENNIFER JIRSCHELE, *director,* 266-3305, jennifer.jirschele@

    Information and Technology Services, Bureau of: MATT DEDRICK, *director,* 261-8880, matt.dedrick@

    Agency Project Management, Office of: PATRICK W. COOPER, *director,* 267-2846, patrick.cooper@

    Records Management and Mail Services, Bureau of: vacancy, *director.*

    Strategic Sourcing, Bureau of: RITA PRIGIONI, *director,* 266-8472, rita.prigioni@

    Organizational and Employee Development, Office of: CHRISTINE M. MILLER, *director,* 267-3786, christinem.miller@

Health Care Access and Accountability, Division of: KEVIN MOORE, *administrator,* 266-5151, kevin.moore@; MARLIA MATTKE, *deputy administrator,* 266-9749, marlia.mattke@; P.O. Box 309, Madison 53701-0309, Fax: 266-6786.

    Benefits Management, Bureau of: RACHEL CURRANS-HENRY, *deputy director,* 267-1421, rachel.curranshenry@

    Disability Determination Bureau: SALLY FITZER, *director,* 266-0490, sally.fitzer@ssa.gov

    Enrollment Policy and Systems, Bureau of: SHAWN SMITH, *director,* 266-1935, shawn.smith@

    Fiscal Management, Bureau of: KRISTA WILLING, *director,* 266-2469, kristae.willing@

    Operational Coordination, Bureau of: TRICIA LaPLANT, *director,* 267-6847, tricia.laplant@

    Milwaukee Enrollment Services: TONYA EVANS, *director,* (414) 289-6535, tonya.evans@

Long Term Care, Division of: BRIAN SHOUP, *administrator,* 266-0554, brian.shoup@; CURTIS CUNNINGHAM, *deputy administrator,* 261-7810, curtis.cunningham@; Fax: 261-6079.

> *Aging and Disability Resources, Bureau of:* CARRIE MOLKE, *director,* 267-5267, carrie.molke@

> *Center Operations, Bureau of:* vacancy, *director.*

>> *Central Wisconsin Center for the Developmentally Disabled:* CATHERINE MURRAY, *director,* 317 Knutson Drive, Madison 53704-1197, 301-9200, Fax: 301-9438, catherine.murray@

>> *Northern Wisconsin Center for the Developmentally Disabled:* JACQUELINE NEUROHR, *director,* 2820 East Park Avenue, P.O. Box 340, Chippewa Falls 54729-0340, (715) 723-5542, Fax: (715) 723-5102, jacqueline.neurohr@

>> *Southern Wisconsin Center for the Developmentally Disabled:* JIM HENKES, *director,* 2415 Spring Street, P.O. Box 100, Union Grove 53182-0100, (262) 878-6601, Fax: (262) 878-6602, james.henkes@

> *Children's Services, Bureau of:* CAMILLE RODRIGUEZ, *director,* 266-9633, camille.rodriguez@

> *Long Term Care Financing, Bureau of:* vacancy, *director.*

> *Managed Care, Bureau of:* MARGARET KRISTAN, *director,* 261-6393, margaret.kristan@

Mental Health and Substance Abuse Services, Division of: PATRICK CORK, *administrator,* 266-2717, patrick.cork@; ROSE KLEMAN, *deputy administrator,* 266-2717, rose.kleman@

> *Client Rights Office:* ALICIA BOEHME, *supervisor,* 266-5525, alicia.boehme@

> *Prevention, Treatment and Recovery, Bureau of:* JOYCE ALLEN, *director,* 266-2717, joyce.allen@

>> *Mendota Mental Health Institute:* GREGORY VAN RYBROEK, *director,* 301 Troy Drive, Madison 53704-1599, 301-1000, Fax: 301-1390, gregory.vanrybroek@

>> *Winnebago Mental Health Institute:* THOMAS J. SPEECH, *director,* P.O. Box 9, Winnebago 54985-0009, (920) 235-4910, Fax: (920) 237-2043, thomas.speech@

>> *Sand Ridge Secure Treatment Center:* DEBORAH J. McCULLOCH, *director,* 1111 North Road, Mauston 53948, (608) 847-4438, Fax: (608) 847-1790, deborah.mcculloch@

>> *Wisconsin Resource Center:* BYRAN BARTOW, *director,* 1505 North Street, P.O. Box 16, Winnebago 54985-0016, (920) 426-4310, Fax: (920) 236-4199, byran.bartow@

Public Health, Division of: KAREN McKEOWN, *administrator,* 267-7828, karen.mckeown@; CHARLES WARZECHA, *deputy administrator,* 266-9780, charles.warzecha@; P.O. Box 2659, Madison 53701-2659, Fax: 266-6988, TTY: (888) 701-1253.

> *State Health Officer:* KAREN McKEOWN, 267-7828, karen.mckeown@

> *Communicable Diseases, Bureau of:* vacancy, *director,* 267-9363.

> *Community Health Promotion, Bureau of:* vacancy, *director,* 267-3561.

> *Environmental and Occupational Health, Bureau of:* JEFFREY PHILLIPS, *director,* 264-9880, jeffrey.phillips@

> *Health Informatics, Office of:* OSKAR ANDERSON, *director,* 267-7279, oskar.anderson@

> *Operations, Office of:* DONNA MOORE, *director,* 261-9434, donnaj.moore@

> *Policy and Practice Alignment, Office of:* TASHA JENKINS, *director,* 266-1347, tasha.jenkins@

> *Preparedness and Emergency Health Care, Office of:* JENNIFER ULLSVIK, *director,* 267-7178, jennifer.ullsvik@

Quality Assurance, Division of: OTIS WOODS, *administrator,* 267-7185, otis.woods@; SHARI BUSSE, *deputy administrator,* 266-7952, shari.busse@; Fax: 267-0352; Milwaukee office: 819 North Sixth Street, Milwaukee 53203, (414) 227-5000.

> *Caregiver Quality, Office of:* LAURIE ARKENS, *director,* 264-9876, laurie.arkens@

DEPARTMENT OF HEALTH SERVICES

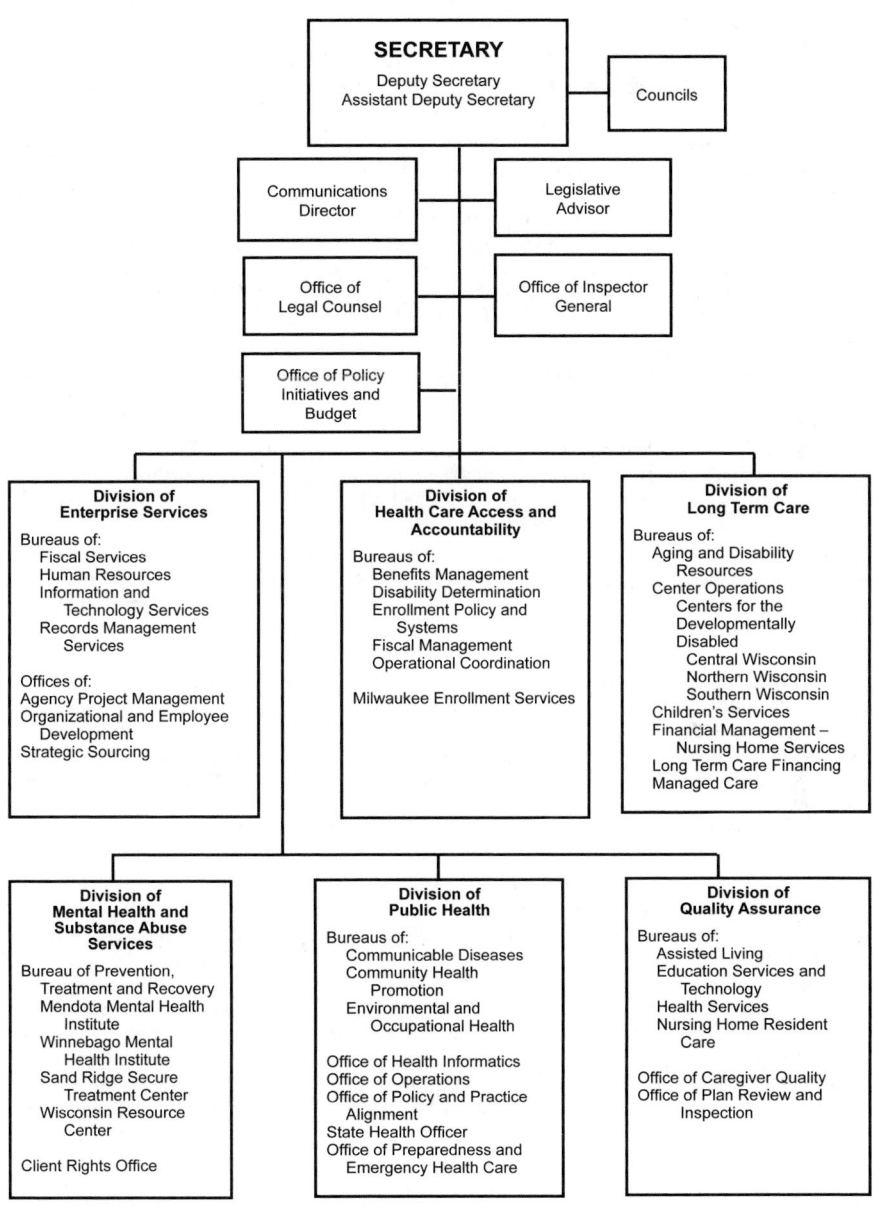

SECRETARY
Deputy Secretary
Assistant Deputy Secretary

Councils

Communications
Director

Legislative
Advisor

Office of
Legal Counsel

Office of Inspector
General

Office of Policy
Initiatives and
Budget

**Division of
Enterprise Services**

Bureaus of:
 Fiscal Services
 Human Resources
 Information and
  Technology Services
 Records Management
  Services

Offices of:
Agency Project Management
Organizational and Employee
 Development
Strategic Sourcing

**Division of
Health Care Access and
Accountability**

Bureaus of:
 Benefits Management
 Disability Determination
 Enrollment Policy and
  Systems
 Fiscal Management
 Operational Coordination

Milwaukee Enrollment Services

**Division of
Long Term Care**

Bureaus of:
 Aging and Disability
  Resources
 Center Operations
  Centers for the
  Developmentally
  Disabled
   Central Wisconsin
   Northern Wisconsin
   Southern Wisconsin
 Children's Services
 Financial Management –
  Nursing Home Services
 Long Term Care Financing
 Managed Care

**Division of
Mental Health and
Substance Abuse
Services**

Bureau of Prevention,
 Treatment and Recovery
Mendota Mental Health
 Institute
Winnebago Mental
 Health Institute
Sand Ridge Secure
 Treatment Center
Wisconsin Resource
 Center

Client Rights Office

**Division of
Public Health**

Bureaus of:
 Communicable Diseases
 Community Health
  Promotion
 Environmental and
  Occupational Health

Office of Health Informatics
Office of Operations
Office of Policy and Practice
 Alignment
State Health Officer
Office of Preparedness and
 Emergency Health Care

**Division of
Quality Assurance**

Bureaus of:
 Assisted Living
 Education Services and
  Technology
 Health Services
 Nursing Home Resident
  Care

Office of Caregiver Quality
Office of Plan Review and
 Inspection

Units attached for administrative purposes under Sec. 15.03:
 Emergency Medical Services Board
 Council on Physical Disabilities

Assisted Living, Bureau of: ALFRED JOHNSON, *director,* 266-8598, alfred.johnson@

Education Services and Technology, Bureau of: PHYLLIS VARSOS, *director,* 266-2055, phyllis.varsos@

Health Services, Bureau of: CREMEAR MIMS, *director,* (414) 227-4556, cremear.mims@

Nursing Home Resident Care, Bureau of: JUAN FLORES, *director,* 267-0351, juan.flores@

Plan Review and Inspection, Office of: vacancy, *director,* 266-9675.

Agency Responsibility: The Department of Health Services administers a wide range of services to clients in the community and at state institutions, regulates certain care providers, and supervises and consults with local public and voluntary agencies. Its responsibilities span public health; mental health and substance abuse; long-term support and care; services to people who have a disability, medical assistance, and children's services; aging programs; physical and developmental disability services; sensory disability programs; operation of care and treatment facilities; quality assurance programs; nutrition supplementation programs; medical assistance; and health care for low-income families, elderly, and disabled persons.

Organization: The department is administered by a secretary who is appointed by the governor with the advice and consent of the senate. The secretary appoints the division administrators from outside the classified service.

Unit Functions: The *Division of Enterprise Services* oversees financial management, information systems and technology, personnel and employment relations, affirmative action and civil rights compliance, purchasing and contract administration, facilities management, continuity of operations planning, project management, and other administrative services. It handles billing, collection, and related accounting for state institutions.

The *Division of Health Care Access and Accountability* provides access to health care for low-income persons, the elderly, and people with disabilities. It administers the Medical Assistance (Medicaid), BadgerCare Plus, SeniorCare, Chronic Disease Aids, General Relief, and FoodShare programs.

The *Division of Long Term Care* administers a variety of programs that provide long-term support for the elderly and people with disabilities. These programs include Family Care, Aging and Disability Resource Centers, Community Relocation Initiative, Community Integration Initiative, Pathways to Independence, and the Community Options Program. The division manages nursing home funding, nursing home policies, and reimbursement and auditing services. The division also includes the Offices for the Deaf and Hard of Hearing and the Blind or Visually Impaired as well as programs for Autism and Brain Injury. The division supports the Birth to 3 Interagency Coordinating Council and the Assistive Technology Council as required by federal law. In addition, it operates three state centers for persons with developmental disabilities: Northern Wisconsin Center (Chippewa Falls), Central Wisconsin Center (Madison), and Southern Wisconsin Center (Union Grove).

The *Division of Mental Health and Substance Abuse Services* administers programs to meet mental health and substance abuse prevention, diagnosis, early intervention, and treatment needs in community and institutional settings. The division operates Community Forensic Programs for individuals in need of competency evaluation and treatment and community-based treatment for persons found not guilty by reason of mental disease or defect when community treatment is ordered by the court. The division administers the state's institutional programs for persons whose mental health needs or developmental disabilities cannot be met in a community setting. The two mental health institutes, Mendota Mental Health Institute and Winnebago Mental Health Institute, provide treatment for persons with mental health needs which require inpatient hospitalization including medical, psychological, social, and rehabilitative services. Mendota Mental Health Institute houses a secure treatment unit to meet the mental health needs of male adolescents from the Department of Corrections' juvenile institutions. The division operates the Wisconsin Resource Center as a medium security facility for mentally ill prison inmates whose treatment needs cannot be met by the Department of Corrections. It also provides treatment at the Sand Ridge Secure Treatment Center for individuals civilly committed under the sexually violent persons law, and provides services for persons placed on supervised release. The division contracts with all counties in the state and a large number of private providers for the provision of community-based services.

The *Division of Public Health* promotes and protects public health in Wisconsin through various services and regulations. It administers programs that address environmental and occupational health, family and community health, chronic and communicable disease prevention and control, and programs relating to maternal and child health, including the Women, Infants and Children (WIC) Supplemental Food Program. It licenses emergency medical service providers and technicians and approves and supervises their training. The division is also responsible for inspecting restaurants, hotels and motels, bed and breakfast establishments, camps and campgrounds, food vendors, and swimming pools. The division performs vital recordkeeping functions including providing birth, death, marriage, and divorce certificates and the gathering, analysis, and publishing of statistical information related to the health of the state's population. The division conducts formal statutory reviews of all local health departments every five years.

The *Division of Quality Assurance* licenses and regulates over 40 different programs and facilities that provide health, long-term care, and mental health and substance abuse services including assisted living facilities, nursing homes, community-based residential facilities home health agencies, and facilities serving people with developmental disabilities. It also performs caregiver background checks and investigations.

History: The Department of Health Services combines supervision of many state and local functions that had developed separately in the 1800s. For more than two decades after statehood, Wisconsin created separate governing boards and institutions for the care of prisoners; juveniles; and blind, deaf, and mentally ill persons. By 1871, there were six such institutions. The first attempt to institute overall supervision of these services came when the legislature passed Chapter 136, Laws of 1871, creating the State Board of Charities and Reform. Its duties included examination of the operations of state institutions and their boards and investigation of practices in local asylums, jails, and schools for the blind and deaf.

In Chapter 298, Laws of 1881, the legislature abolished the separate institutional boards and combined their functions under the State Board of Supervision of Wisconsin Charitable, Reformatory and Penal Institutions. The State Board of Charities and Reform continued to operate until 1891. In that year, the two boards were combined as the State Board of Control of the Wisconsin Reformatory, Charitable and Penal Institutions in Chapter 221, Laws of 1891, thus completing the consolidation of public welfare activities.

In the early days of statehood, public health was primarily a function of local governments. In Chapter 366, Laws of 1876, the legislature established the State Board of Health to "study the vital statistics of this state, and endeavor to make intelligent and profitable use of the collected records of death and sickness among the people." The board was directed to "make sanitary investigations and inquiries respecting the causes of disease, and especially of epidemics; the causes of mortality, and the effects of localities, employments, conditions, ingesta, habits and circumstances on the health of the people." This directive defines much of the work still done in public health. Later legislation required the board to take responsibility for tuberculosis care (1905), to direct its efforts toward preventing blindness in infants (1909), and to inspect water and sewerage systems to prevent typhoid and dysentery (1919). In addition, at various times, the board licensed restaurants, health facilities, barbers, embalmers, and funeral directors.

By the time the federal government entered the field of public welfare during the Great Depression of the 1930s, Wisconsin had already pioneered a number of programs, including aid to children and pensions for the elderly (enacted in 1931). The Wisconsin Children's Code, enacted by Chapter 439, Laws of 1929, was one of the most comprehensive in the nation. The state's initial response to federal funding was to establish separate departments to administer social security funds and other public welfare programs. After several attempts at reorganization and a series of studies, the legislature established the State Department of Public Welfare in Chapter 435, Laws of 1939, to provide unified administration of all existing welfare functions. Public health and care for the aged were delegated to separate agencies.

The executive branch reorganization act of 1967 created the Department of Health and Social Services. The Board of Health and Social Services, appointed by the governor, directed the new department and appointed the departmental secretary to administer the agency. In addition to

Department of Health Services main entrance at One West Wilson Street, Madison.
(Department of Health Services)

combining public welfare, public health, and care for the aged in the reorganization act, the 1967 Legislature added the Division of Vocational Rehabilitation in Chapter 43. In Chapter 39, Laws of 1975, the legislature abolished the board and replaced it with a secretary appointed by the governor with the advice and consent of the senate. That same law called for a reorganization of the department, which was completed by July 1977. The Department of Health and Social Services was renamed the Department of Health and Family Services (DHFS), effective July 1, 1996.

The decades of the 1960s and 1970s saw an expansion of public welfare and health services at both the federal and state levels. Especially notable were programs for medical care for the needy and aged (Medical Assistance and Medicare), drug treatment programs, food stamps, Aid to Families with Dependent Children Program (AFDC), and increased regulation of hospitals and nursing homes.

While continuing to administer its established programs, the department was assigned additional duties during the 1980s in the areas of child support, child abuse and neglect, programs for the handicapped, and welfare reform. However, 1989 Wisconsin Acts 31 and 107 created a separate Department of Corrections to administer adult corrections institutions and programs, and 1995 Wisconsin Act 27 transferred responsibility for juvenile offenders to that department.

1995 Wisconsin Act 27 revised AFDC and transferred it and other income support programs including Medical Assistance eligibility and food stamps to the Department of Workforce Development (DWD). (Wisconsin Works, known as W-2, replaced AFDC in 1995 Wisconsin Act 289.) Existing welfare reform programs, including Job Opportunities and Basic Skills (JOBS), Learnfare, Parental Responsibility, and Work-Not-Welfare, were also transferred to DWD, along with child and spousal support, the Children First Program, Older American Community Service Employment, refugee assistance programs, and vocational rehabilitation functions. Health care facilities plan review was transferred from the Department of Industry, Labor and Human Relations to DHFS by 1995 Wisconsin Act 27. Act 27 also transferred laboratory certification to the Department of Agriculture, Trade and Consumer Protection and low-income energy assistance to the Department of Administration.

As a result of 1995 Wisconsin Act 303, the department assumed responsibility for direct administration and operation of Milwaukee County child welfare services. Primary responsibility for the Health Insurance Risk-Sharing Program (HIRSP) was transferred to the department from the Office of the Commissioner of Insurance by 1997 Wisconsin Act 27. 2001 Wisconsin Act 16 transferred the Medical Assistance Eligibility Program and the Food Stamp Program to DHFS from the Department of Workforce Development.

2007 Wisconsin Act 20 changed the name of the department to the Department of Health Services beginning July 1, 2008. Act 20 also created a separate Department of Children and Families and split the responsibilities of DHFS between the two departments.

The Office of Free Market Health Care, which is jointly directed by the Department of Health Services and the Office of the Commissioner of Insurance, was established by Executive Order 10 on January 27, 2011. The responsibilities of the office include developing plans that encourage competition in health care benefits and insurance plans through free-market, consumer driven approaches. The Office of Inspector General and the Office of Children's Mental Health were created by 2013 Wisconsin Act 20.

Statutory Councils and Committees

Birth Defect Prevention and Surveillance, Council on: LINDSAY ZETZSCHE (UW Medical School representative), WILLIAM RHEAD (Medical College of Wisconsin, Inc., representative), vacancy (pediatric nurse representative), MICHELLE KEMPF-WEIBEL (children and youth with special health care needs DHS program representative), CAROL NODDINGS-EICHINGER (early intervention services DHS program representative), ANN BUEDEL (Vital Records Office, health statistics research and analysis DHS representative), PHILIP GIAMPIETRO (State Medical Society representative), vacancy (Wisconsin Health and Hospital Association representative), KERRY BALDWIN JEDELE (Wisconsin Chapter, American Academy of Pediatrics representative), vacancy (Council on Developmental Disabilities representative), MIR BASIR (nonprofit organization representative), LISA B. NELSON (parent/guardian of child with a birth defect), CYNTHIA DESTEFFEN (local health department representative) (appointed by secretary of health services).

Contact Person: PEGGY HELM-QUEST, 267-2945, peggy.helmquest@

The 13-member Council on Birth Defect Prevention and Surveillance makes recommendations to the department regarding the administration of the Wisconsin Birth Defects Registry. The registry documents diagnoses and counts the number of birth defects for children up to age two. The council advises what birth defects are to be reported; the content, format, and procedures for reporting; and the contents of the aggregated reports. Members are appointed by the secretary of health services to 4-year terms. The UW Medical School and Medical College of Wisconsin, Inc., representatives must have expertise in birth defects epidemiology. Nurse representatives must specialize in pediatrics or have expertise in birth defects. The program representatives are from the appropriate subunits in the department. The nonprofit representative must be from an organization whose primary purpose is birth defect prevention and which does not promote abortion as a method of prevention. The department has added a nonstatutory council member to represent parents or guardians of children born with birth defects. The council was created by 1999 Wisconsin Act 114. Its duties and composition are prescribed in Sections 15.197 (12) and 253.12 (4) of the statutes. Additional information is available at: http://www. cbdps.state.wi.us/index.html.

Blindness, Council on: Doug Tikkanen, *chairperson;* Josephine Grove, *vice chairperson;* Jo Ann Gustavson, *secretary;* Janet Dickey (member-at-large); Bill Gallik, Troy Hergert, Roberto Torrez, Lee Young; Tom Langham (Department of Health Services council liaison) (appointed by secretary of health services).

The 9-member Council on Blindness makes recommendations to the department and other state agencies on services, activities, programs, investigations, and research that affect persons who are blind or visually impaired. Members are appointed by the secretary of health services to serve 3-year terms and are eligible to reapply to serve a second 3-year term at the conclusion of the first term. At least seven of the nine appointed members must be blind or visually impaired. The current council was created in the Department of Health and Social Services by Chapter 366, Laws of 1969. Its composition and duties are prescribed in Sections 15.197 (2) and 47.03 (9) of the statutes.

Deaf and Hard of Hearing, Council for the: Justin Vollmar (deaf member), *chairperson;* Denise Johnson (deaf member), *vice chairperson;* Nicole Everson, Karl Nollenberger (deaf members); Tracy Haas, Steven Smart, vacancy (at large members); William Mauldin, Alex Slappey (*ex officio* members) (all appointed by governor).

The 9-member Council for the Deaf and Hard of Hearing advises the department on the provision of effective services to deaf, hard-of-hearing, late-deafened, and deaf-blind people. Members are appointed by the governor for staggered 4-year terms. The council was created by Chapter 34, Laws of 1979, as the Council for the Hearing Impaired and renamed by 1995 Wisconsin Act 27. Its duties and composition are prescribed in Sections 15.09 (5) and 15.197 (8) of the statutes. Additional information is available at: http://www.dhhcouncil.state.wi.us.

Medicaid Pharmacy Prior Authorization Advisory Committee: Kevin Moore, *chairperson;* Rachel Currans-Henry, *vice chairperson;* Rosanne Barber, James Boblin, Ward Brown, Catherine Decker, Ronald Diamond, Lawrence Fleming, Kevin Izard, Steve Maike, William Raduege, Pat Towers, Alicia Walker, Michael Witkovsky (appointed by secretary of health services).

The Medicaid Pharmacy Prior Authorization Advisory Committee advises the department on issues related to prior authorization decisions concerning prescription drugs on behalf of medical assistance recipients. Section 49.45 (49) (a) of the statutes directs the secretary of health services to establish a committee, of at least 5 members, including 2 physicians, 2 pharmacists, and an advocate for recipients of medical assistance who has sufficient medical background to evaluate a prescription drug's effectiveness. Members are appointed by the secretary. Information is available at: www.forwardhealth.wi.gov/wiportal/tab/42/icscontent/provider/pac/index. htm.spage.

Mental Health, Council on: Sheldon Gross, *chairperson;* Donna Wrenn, *vice chairperson;* Mishelle O'Shasky, *second vice chairperson;* Julie-Anne Braun, Kathryn Bush, Patrick Cork, Kathleen Enders, Tracey Hassinger, Richard Immler, Carol Keen, Bonnie MacRitchie, Charlotte Matteson, David Nencka, David Stepien, Matthew Strittmater, Charles Szafir III, Masood Wasiullah, Joseph Worzella, 2 vacancies (appointed by secretary of health services).

The Council on Mental Health is composed of not less than 21 or more than 25 members nominated by the secretary of health services and the council and appointed by the governor for 3-year terms. Persons appointed shall include representatives of groups and a proportion of members as specified in 42 USC 300x-3 (c), as amended on April 2, 2008. The council advises the department, governor, and legislature on mental health programs; provides recommendations on the expenditure of federal mental health block grants; reviews the department's plans for mental health services; and serves as an advocate for the mentally ill. The council was created by 1983 Wisconsin Act 439, and its membership was amended by 2007 Wisconsin Act 20. Its composition and duties are prescribed in Sections 15.197 (1) and 51.02 of the statutes. Additional information is available at: http://www.mhc.state.wi.us.

Newborn Screening Advisory Group: Umbrella Committee: DAVID ALLEN, MEI BAKER, JEFFREY BRITTON, CHARLES BROKOPP, DAVID DIMMOCK, MICHELLE FARRELL, GARY HOFFMAN, TAMI HORZEWSKI, MURRAY KATCHER, MICHELLE KEMPF-WEIBEL, KAREN MICHALSKI, JILL PARADOWSKI, JILL RADOWICZ, GREG RICE, MICHAEL ROCK, JOHN ROUTES, J. PAUL SCOTT, TAMMY TIMMLER, AUDREY TLUCZEK, SANDRA VAN CALCAR, LUANN WEIK (appointed by secretary of health services).

The Newborn Screening Advisory Umbrella Committee advises the department regarding the statutorily required program, which generally provides that infants receive blood or other diagnostic tests for congenital and metabolic disorders. Newborn screening has been required since 1978, and is a joint effort of the Department of Health Services and the State Laboratory of Hygiene. Section 253.13 (5) of the statutes requires the department to periodically consult appropriate experts in reviewing and evaluation of the state's newborn screening programs. The number and qualifications of committee members is not specified. Members are appointed by the secretary. Information is available at: http://www.slh.wisc.edu/newborn/guide/advisory.dot.

Public Health Council: JULIE WILLEMS VAN DIJK (local health representative), *chairperson;* JOHN BARTKOWSKI, CATHERINE FREY, CORAZON LOTEYRO, DOUGLAS NELSON, THAI VUE (health care consumer representatives); MARY JO BAISCH, S. GARCIA FRANZ, JOHN MEUER, DEBORAH MILLER, CHARLES POST, AYAZ SAMADANI, JAMES SANDERS (health care provider representatives); BRIDGET CLEMENTI, GARY GILMORE, LYNN SHEETS (health professions educator representatives); BEVAN BAKER, TERRI KRAMOLIS, GRETCHEN SAMPSON (local health departments and boards representatives); FAYE DODGE (tribal representative); AMY BREMEL, MARK VILLALPANDO (public safety representatives); vacancy.

The 23-member Public Health Council advises the department, the governor, the legislature, and the public on progress made in the implementation of the department's 10-year public health plan and coordination of responses to public health emergencies. Members are nominated by the secretary of health services and appointed by the governor to serve 3-year terms and must include representatives of health care consumers, health care providers, health professions educators, local health departments and boards, federally recognized American Indian tribes or bands in this state, public safety agencies, and, if established by the secretary of health services, the Public Health Advisory Committee. 2003 Wisconsin Act 186 created the council and its composition and duties are prescribed in Sections 15.197 (13) and 250.07 (1m) of the statutes.

Trauma Advisory Council: ALEX BEUNING, GABY ISKANDER, 2 vacancies (physicians); CHERYL PAAR, vacancy (registered nurses); 2 vacancies (emergency medical service providers); MERRILEE CARLSON, vacancy (rural hospital representatives); NIRAV PATEL, vacancy (urban hospital representatives); BRENDA FELLENZ (EMS Board representative).

The 13-member Trauma Advisory Council, all appointed by the secretary of health services, advises the department on developing and implementing a statewide trauma care system. Membership must include physicians, registered nurses, prehospital emergency medical service providers, urban and rural hospital personnel, and the medical services board. They must represent "all geographical areas of the state". Physician appointees must represent urban and rural areas, and one of the prehospital emergency medical service providers must represent a municipality. The council was created by 1997 Wisconsin Act 154 and its composition and duties are prescribed in Sections 15.197 (25) and 146.56 (1) of the statutes. Additional information is available at: http://www.dhs.wisconsin.gov/trauma/councils/index.htm.

INDEPENDENT UNITS ATTACHED FOR BUDGETING, PROGRAM COORDINATION, AND RELATED MANAGEMENT FUNCTIONS BY SECTION 15.03 OF THE STATUTES

EMERGENCY MEDICAL SERVICES BOARD

Members: TROY HAASE, *chairperson;* STEVE BANE, *vice chairperson*; MINDY ALLEN, JIM AUSTAD, JERRY BIGGART, BRENDA FELLENZ, MARK FREDRICKSON, KENNETH JOHNSON, LES LUDER, GLORIA MURAWSKY, vacancy (voting members appointed by governor). *Ex officio* nonvoting members: BRIAN LITZA (designated by secretary of health services), JANET NODORFT (designated by secretary of transportation), TIMOTHY WEIR (designated by state director, Technical College System Board), MICHAEL KIM (state medical director for emergency medical services).

Mailing Address: P.O. Box 2659, Madison 53701-2659.

Telephone: 266-1568.

Statutory References: Sections 15.195 (8) and 146.55 (3).

Agency Responsibility: The 15-member Emergency Medical Services Board appoints an advisory committee of physicians to advise the department on the selection of the state medical director for emergency medical services and to review that person's performance. It also advises the director on medical issues; reviews emergency medical service statutes and rules concerning the transportation of patients; and recommends changes to the Department of Health Services and the Department of Transportation. The board includes personnel from the appropriate state agencies and related emergency services in its deliberations.

The board includes 11 voting members, appointed by the governor for 3-year terms, who must "represent the various geographical areas of the state" and various types of emergency medical service providers. The board, which was created by 1993 Wisconsin Act 16, replaced the Emergency Medical Services Assistance Board, created by 1989 Wisconsin Act 102.

COUNCIL ON PHYSICAL DISABILITIES

Members: BEN BARRET, *chairperson;* JOANNE ZIMMERMAN, *secretary;* CHRISTINE DURANCEAU, ROBERTO ESCAMILLA III, JEFF FOX, NOAH HERSKOWITZ, JOHN MEISSNER, KAREN SECOR, JOEY TORKELSON, LEWIS TYLER, CHARLES VANDENPLAS, 2 vacancies; vacancy (governor's representative) (all members are appointed by governor).

Coordinator: DAN JOHNSON.

Mailing Address: 1 West Wilson Street, Room 437, Madison 53703.

Telephones: 267-9582; TTY 267-9880.

E-mail Address: dan.johnson@

Internet Address: http://www.pdcouncil.state.wi.us

Statutory References: Sections 15.197 (4) and 46.29.

Agency Responsibility: The 14-member Council on Physical Disabilities develops and modifies the state plan for services to persons with physical disabilities. It advises the secretary of health services, recommends legislation, encourages public understanding of the needs of persons with physical disabilities, and promotes programs to prevent physical disability. The 13 appointed members are appointed by the governor to serve 3-year terms and must be state residents. At least 6 members must be persons with physical disabilities; 2 may be parents, guardians, or relatives of persons with physical disabilities; and at least one must be a service provider. The council must include equitable representation for sex, race, and urban and rural areas. The council was created by 1989 Wisconsin Act 202.

HIGHER EDUCATIONAL AIDS BOARD

Members: REGINA MILLER (UW System Board of Regents member); STEPHEN WILLETT (Technical College System Board member); KATHLEEN SAHLHOFF (UW System financial aids administrator); MARY JO GREEN (Technical College System financial aids administrator); vacancy (UW System student representative); NATHANIEL HELM-QUEST (Technical College

System student representative); vacancy (independent colleges and universities board of trustees representative); STEVE MIDTHUN (independent colleges and universities financial aid administrator); JENNIFER KAMMERUD (designated by superintendent of public instruction); BENJAMIN ZELLMER (independent colleges and universities student representative); DARCY PAULSON (public member); VERNA FOWLER (nonstatutory nonvoting representative of tribal higher educational institutions). (All members, except *ex officio* member and tribal representative, are appointed by governor.)

Executive Secretary: JOHN REINEMANN.

Mailing Address: P.O. Box 7885, Madison 53707-7885.

Location: 131 West Wilson Street, Suite 902, Madison.

Telephone: (608) 267-2206.

Fax: (608) 267-2808.

Agency E-mail Address: HEABmail@wisconsin.gov

Internet Address: http://heab.wi.gov

Publications: Biennial report; Report on Financial Aid Programs; various board reports.

Number of Employees: 11.00.

Total Budget 2013-15: $292,467,100.

Statutory References: Section 15.67; Chapter 39, Subchapter III.

Agency Responsibility: The Higher Educational Aids Board is responsible for the management and oversight of the state's student financial aid system for Wisconsin residents attending institutions of higher education. It also enters into interstate agreements and performs student loan collection services.

The board establishes policies for the state's student financial aid programs, including academic excellence scholarships, Wisconsin grants – University; Technical College; Tribal College; and Private nonprofit (formerly Wisconsin higher education grant (WHEG) and Tuition Grant (TG)), talent incentive grants, Wisconsin Covenant grant, handicapped student grants, Indian student grants, minority student grants (private sector and Technical College System), teacher education loans, minority teacher loans, nursing student loans, primary care and psychiatry shortage grants, and interstate reciprocity. It administers the contracts for medical and dental education services and approves the participants in the Medical College of Wisconsin, Inc., per capita grant program. It administers the John R. Justice loan repayment grant program which provides loan repayment assistance for local, state, and federal public defenders and local and state prosecutors.

Organization: The 11 statutory members of the board include the superintendent of public instruction or designee, 7 members who serve 3-year terms, and 3 student members who serve 2-year terms. The students must be at least 18 years old, residents of this state, enrolled at least half-time, and in good academic standing. The UW and private nonprofit institution students must be undergraduates. The governor appoints the board's executive secretary. In 2005, the board added a nonstatutory nonvoting member to represent tribal institutions of higher education.

History: The Higher Educational Aids Board originated as the State Commission for Academic Facilities. It was created by Chapter 573, Laws of 1963, to administer Title I of the Federal Higher Education Facilities Act of 1963, which funded grants for university and college building programs in Wisconsin. Chapter 264, Laws of 1965, gave the commission student financial aid responsibilities and changed its name to the State Commission for Higher Educational Aids. Chapter 313, Laws of 1967, authorized the commission to organize the Wisconsin Higher Education Corporation to administer the federal Guaranteed Student Loan Program. The corporation was given an independent board of directors as a private nonstock corporation in 1984. Chapter 276, Laws of 1969, renamed the commission the Higher Educational Aids Board. The Higher Educational Aids Board was inadvertently repealed by 1995 Wisconsin Act 27, but was continued as the Higher Educational Aids Council by Executive Order 283. The legislature recreated the board in 1997 Wisconsin Act 27.

STATE HISTORICAL SOCIETY OF WISCONSIN

For e-mail combine the user ID and the state extender: userid@**wisconsinhistory.org**
All telephone numbers are 608 area code unless otherwise indicated.

Board of Curators: CONRAD GOODKIND, *president;* BRIAN RUDE, *president-elect;* ELLEN LANGILL, *immediate past president;* DAVID ANDERSON (designated by governor); vacancy (designated by assembly speaker); SENATOR LAZICH (senate president); GEORGE JACOBS, JR., R. WILLIAM VAN SANT, KEENE WINTERS (appointed by governor with senate consent); JON ANGELI, ANGELA BARTELL, SID BREMER, NORBERT HILL, JR., JOANNE HUELSMAN, GREG HUBER, CAROL McCHESNEY JOHNSON, CHLORIS LOWE, JR., THOMAS MAXWELL, LOWELL PETERSON, JERRY PHILLIPS, WALTER RUGLAND, MICHAEL SCHMUDLACH, SAM SCINTA, THOMAS SHRINER, JR., ROBERT SMITH, JOHN THOMPSON, AHARON ZOREA; SENATOR RISSER (minority party senator), REPRESENTATIVE KESSLER (minority party representative to the assembly). *Ex officio* members: MICHAEL YOUNGMAN (Wisconsin Historical Foundation President); LAURA CRAMER (Friends of Wisconsin Historical Society President); LANE EARNS (UW President designee); ROY OSTENSO (Wisconsin Council for Local History President). (Unless otherwise indicated, curators are elected by the membership of the state historical society or serve *ex officio.*)

Board Secretary: ELLSWORTH H. BROWN.

Director: ELLSWORTH H. BROWN, 264-6440, ellsworth.brown@

Deputy Director: GREG PARKINSON, 264-6581, greg.parkinson@

   Building and Grounds: LISA HUMPHREY, *suprintendent,* 264-6431, lisa.humphrey@

   Financial Services: JAMES AMBERSON, *supervisor,* 264-6452, jamesj.amberson@

   Human Resources: KATE J. JOCHIMSEN, *director,* 264-6448, katej.jochimsen@

   Information Technology: TIMOTHY MAAHS, *director,* 261-2451, timothy.maahs@

Chief Operating Officer: WES MOSMAN BLOCK, 264-6443, wes.mosmanblock@

Special Projects: ALICIA L. GOEHRING, *director and state historian,* 264-6515, alicia.goehring@

Programs and Policy: SHANNON WENDT, *director,* 264-6456, shannon.wendt@

Historic Preservation – Public History, Division of: JIM DRAEGER, *state historic preservation officer and director of outreach,* 264-6464, jim.draeger@

   Wisconsin Historical Press: KATHRYN BORKOWSKI, *director,* 264-6461, kathy.borkowski@; JOHN H. BROIHAHN, *state archaeologist,* 264-6496, john.broihahn@

Library – Archives, Division of: MATTHEW T. BLESSING, *administrator and state archivist,* 264-6480, matt.blessing@; MICHAEL I. EDMONDS, *deputy administrator,* 264-6538, michael. edmonds@

   Collection Development: HELMUT M. KNIES, *coordinator,* 264-6478, helmut.knies@

   Collection Management Services: MAIJA S. CRAVENS, *coordinator,* 264-6522, maija.cravens@

   Preservation Services: KATIE D. MULLEN, *coordinator,* 264-6489, kathleen.mullen@

   Public Services and Reference: LISA SAYWELL, *director,* 261-2450, lisa.saywell@

   Northern Wisconsin History Center and Archives at the Northern Great Lakes Visitor Center: LINDA L. MITTLESTADT, *archivist,* (715) 685-2649; 29270 County Highway G, Ashland 54806; linda.mittlestadt@

Museums and Historic Sites, Division of: vacancy, *administrator,* 264-6434; JENNIFER KOLB, *assistant administrator,* 264-6434, jennifer.kolb@

   Black Point Estate: DAVID A. DESIMONE, *site director,* (262) 248-1888; W4270 Southland Road, Lake Geneva 53147; david.desimone@

   First Capitol: ALLEN L. SCHROEDER, *site director,* (608) 987-2122; Highway G, Belmont 53510; allen.schroeder@

   H.H. Bennett Studio: ALAN HANSON, *acting site director,* (608) 253-3523; 215 Broadway, P.O. Box 147, Wisconsin Dells 53965; alan.hanson@

Madeline Island Museum: STEVE R. COTHERMAN, *site director,* (715) 747-2415; 226 Colonel Woods Avenue, La Pointe 54850; steve.cotherman@

Old World Wisconsin: DAN FREAS, *site director,* (262) 594-6302; S103 W37890 Highway 67, P.O. Box 69, Eagle 53119; dan.freas@

Pendarvis: ALLEN L. SCHROEDER, *site director,* (608) 987-2122; 114 Shake Rag Street, Mineral Point 53565; allen.schroeder@

Reed School: ALAN HANSON, *acting site director,* (608) 253-3523; U.S. Highway 10 and N3694 Cardinal Avenue, Neillsville 54456; alan.hanson@

Stonefield: ALLEN L. SCHROEDER, *site director,* (608) 725-5210; 12195 Highway VV, Cassville 53806; allen.schroeder@

Villa Louis: SUSAN CAYA-SLUSSER, *site director,* (608) 326-2721; 521 North Villa Louis Road, P.O. Box 65, Prairie du Chien 53821; susan.cayaslusser@

Wade House: DAVID WARNER, *site director,* (920) 526-3271; W7965 State Highway 23, P.O. Box 34, Greenbush 53026; david.warner@

Wisconsin Historical Museum: MICHAEL HOLLANDER, *museum deputy director,* 264-6570, michael.hollander@

    Museum Archaeology: KELLY E. HAMILTON, *coordinator,* 264-6560, kelly.hamilton@

Wisconsin Historical Foundation: DAVID WILDER, *managing director,* david.wilder@

    Marketing and Communication: vacancy, *director,* 264-6450.

Main Information Desk: (608) 264-6400.

Mailing Address: 816 State Street, Madison 53706-1417.

Archives and Library Location: 816 State Street, Madison.

    Archives Telephone: 264-6460; Archives Fax: 264-6472; Library Telephone: 264-6534; Library Fax: 264-6520.

Museum Location: 30 North Carroll Street, Madison 53703-2707.

    Museum Information: 264-6555; Museum Tours: 264-6557; Museum Fax: 264-6575.

Internet Address: www.wisconsinhistory.org

Publications: *Columns; Wisconsin Magazine of History.* The society also publishes books, research guides, and miscellaneous brochures. Recent publications include *The Heart of Things; The Quiet Season; Polka Heartland; Seventh Generation Earth Ethics; Whispers & Shadows.*

Number of Employees: 129.04.

Total Budget 2013-15: $43,637,500.

Statutory References: Section 15.70; Chapter 44, Subchapters I and II.

    Agency Responsibility: The mission of the State Historical Society of Wisconsin, known informally as the Wisconsin Historical Society, is to help connect people to the past. The society has a statutory duty to collect and preserve historical and cultural resources related to Wisconsin and to make them available to the public. To meet these objectives, the society maintains a major history research collection in Madison and in 14 area research centers; operates 11 historic sites and museums, an office at the Northern Great Lakes Visitor Center, a field services office in Eau Claire, and statewide school services programs. It owns Circus World Museum, which is managed by the Circus World Museum Foundation. It provides public history programming such as National History Day and collaborates with other agencies such as Wisconsin Public Television to deliver history programming to the public. It provides technical services and advice to 392 affiliated local historical societies throughout the state. It conducts, publishes, and disseminates research on Wisconsin and U.S. history, and serves as the state's historic preservation office, which facilitates the preservation of historic structures and archaeological sites and administers the state and national registers of historic places. The society is also responsible for implementation of the state's Burial Sites Preservation Law.

    Organization: The society is both a state agency and a membership organization. The society's Board of Curators includes 8 statutory appointments and up to 30 members who are elected

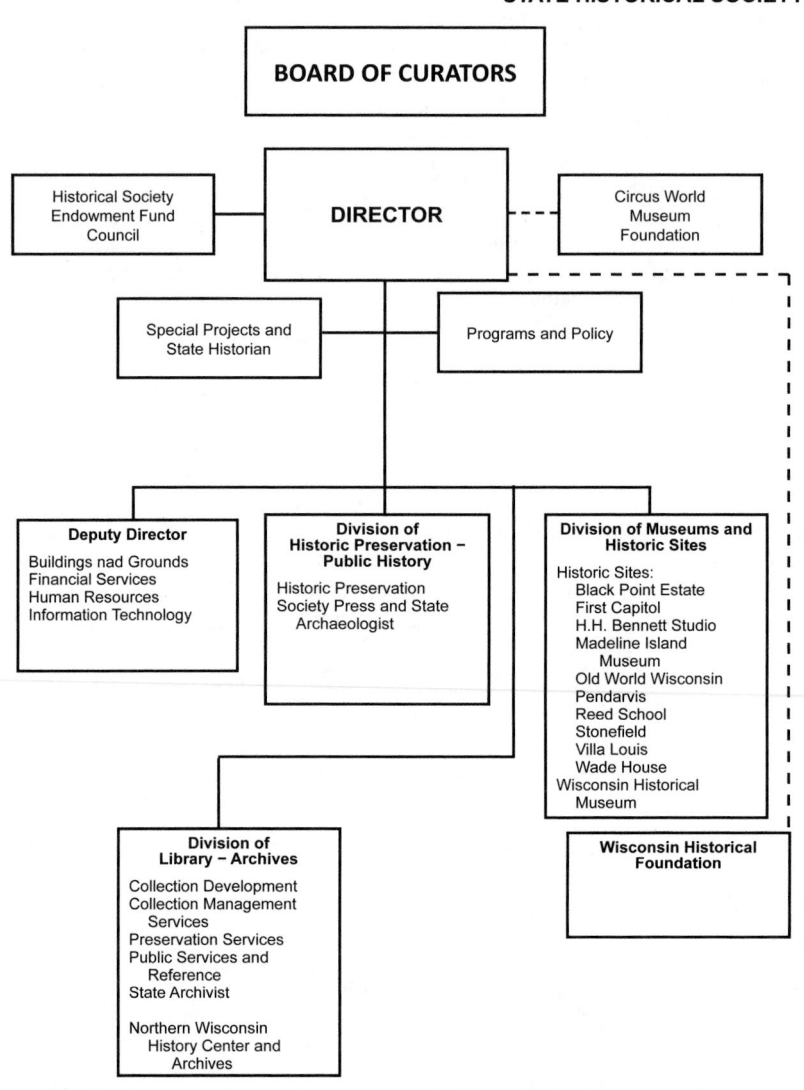

STATE HISTORICAL SOCIETY

BOARD OF CURATORS

Historical Society Endowment Fund Council

DIRECTOR

Circus World Museum Foundation

Special Projects and State Historian

Programs and Policy

Deputy Director

Buildings nad Grounds
Financial Services
Human Resources
Information Technology

Division of Historic Preservation – Public History

Historic Preservation
Society Press and State Archaeologist

Division of Museums and Historic Sites

Historic Sites:
Black Point Estate
First Capitol
H.H. Bennett Studio
Madeline Island Museum
Old World Wisconsin
Pendarvis
Reed School
Stonefield
Villa Louis
Wade House
Wisconsin Historical Museum

Division of Library – Archives

Collection Development
Collection Management Services
Preservation Services
Public Services and Reference
State Archivist

Northern Wisconsin History Center and Archives

Wisconsin Historical Foundation

Units attached for administrative purposes under Sec. 15.03:

Burial Sites Preservation Board
Historic Preservation Review Board

according to the society's constitution and bylaws. The 3 members appointed by the governor with senate consent serve staggered 3-year terms. The board selects the society's director, who serves as administrative head and as secretary to the board.

Unit Functions: The *Division of Administrative Services* provides management and program services in the areas of accounting, financial services, purchasing, human resources, payroll and benefits, as well as maintenance and repairs of the society's headquarters building and the Wisconsin Historical Museum.

The *Division of Historic Preservation – Public History* helps make the history of Wisconsin more accessible to state residents and helps preserve places of historic value. It administers Wisconsin's portion of the National Register of Historic Places in partnership with the National Park Service and manages the State Register of Historic Places. It nominates places of architectural, historic, and archaeological significance to the registers. It reviews federal, state, and local projects for their effect on historic and archaeological properties. The division certifies historic building rehabilitation projects for state and federal income tax credits, archaeological sites for property tax exemptions, and historic buildings as eligible for the state historic building code. The division administers the historical markers program, identifies and promotes underwater archaeological sites, and administers the state's burial sites preservation program. The Wisconsin Historical Society Press publishes books on Wisconsin history and culture for a general audience and the quarterly *Wisconsin Magazine of History*. The press develops educational books and curriculum guides for students and teachers to assist in the teaching of Wisconsin history (including the state history textbook for fourth graders). The division coordinates the state's National History Day program, and provides technical assistance to local historical societies affiliated with the society through the Wisconsin Council for Local History.

The *Division of Library – Archives* maintains premier collections in Wisconsin and North American history including areas such as genealogy; labor; business and industry; social action, including civil rights, antiwar movements, and reproductive rights issues; mass communications; and dramatic arts, including theater, motion pictures, and television. The library and archives serve as the North American history research collection for the UW-Madison. The library acts as a selective depository for U.S. government publications and official depository for Wisconsin state government publications. The archives program acquires, catalogs, preserves, and makes available primary source materials, including manuscripts, maps, newspapers, photographs, sound recordings, films, videos, and other records pertaining to Wisconsin history and selected fields of U.S. history. It serves as the state archives, collecting and providing access to permanent records of state and local government. The division operates a robust digitization program, having provided online access to over 90,000 photographs and 10 million pages of content over the past decade. In partnership with the University of Wisconsin System, the archives operates 14 Area Research Centers throughout Wisconsin to bring its archival holdings on regional history closer to the public. It also makes available the collections of the Wisconsin Center for Film and Theater Research, which are owned and administered by the UW-Madison.

The *Division of Museums and Historic Sites* operates 11 historic sites and museums: Black Point Estate, First Capitol, H.H. Bennett Studio, Madeline Island Museum, Old World Wisconsin, Pendarvis, Reed School, Stonefield, Villa Louis, Wade House, and the Wisconsin Historical Museum. The division collects and preserves the material culture of Wisconsin and interprets the state's history and prehistory for the public. The sites contain historic structures and visitor service buildings that reflect major themes of Wisconsin history, such as ethnic pioneer settlement, mining, farming, fur trade, exploration, transportation, rural life, and town development. The museum in Madison addresses the history of Wisconsin with exhibits covering all of these themes. The division fulfills its educational role through exhibitions, tours, school visits, and a variety of public programs conducted at the museum in Madison, the historic sites, and other venues throughout the state. The division supervises the preservation and development of artifact collections, and operates an archaeology program under a cooperative agreement with the Department of Transportation and the Department of Natural Resources.

The society owns an additional historic site in Baraboo, Circus World, which is operated by the Circus World Museum Foundation. This museum offers an extensive collection of circus memorabilia, unique circus wagons, and it operates a circus in Baraboo during the summer months.

The *Wisconsin Historical Foundation* is a 501 (c) (3) corporation and the advancement arm of the Wisconsin Historical Society. The foundation receives and administers gifts on behalf of the society and manages the society's membership program. The foundation has a separate board of directors.

History: The Wisconsin Historical Society was originally founded as a private association in 1846, two years before statehood. It was chartered by the Wisconsin Legislature in Chapter 17,

Laws of 1853, which made the society responsible for the preservation and care of all records, articles, and other materials of historic interest to the state. The society has received state funding since 1854 (Chapter 16) – longer than any other state historical society in the nation.

The legislature expanded the state's historic preservation program in Chapter 29, Laws of 1977, by making the society responsible for preservation activities associated with the designation, restoration, and repair of historic properties. Chapter 341, Laws of 1981, provided statutory support for local ordinances designed to preserve historic buildings. It set up a framework for a state historic building code with alternative standards for the preservation or restoration of historic structures. 1987 Wisconsin Act 395 strengthened the state's historic preservation laws by creating the State Register of Historic Places to protect historic and prehistoric properties. This law and 1987 Wisconsin Act 399 provided state tax credits and exemptions for owners of certain historic and archaeological properties.

1985 Wisconsin Act 29 formalized the practice of allowing the historical society to enter into a lease agreement with a nonprofit corporation, now called the Circus World Museum Foundation, for the purpose of operating the Circus World Museum.

Statutory Council

Historical Society Endowment Fund Council: Inactive.

The Historical Society Endowment Fund Council advises the state historical society regarding the raising and disbursement of funds used to support the society's historical and cultural preservation services and educational activities. The 10-member council must include representation from the Wisconsin Arts Board, the State Historical Society of Wisconsin, the Wisconsin Academy of Science, Arts and Letters, the Wisconsin Humanities Council, Wisconsin Public Radio and Wisconsin Public Television, and 4 public members, all appointed by the governor. The council was created by 1997 Wisconsin Act 27 and its composition and duties are prescribed in Section 15.707 (3) of the statutes.

INDEPENDENT UNITS ATTACHED FOR BUDGETING, PROGRAM COORDINATION, AND RELATED MANAGEMENT FUNCTIONS BY SECTION 15.03 OF THE STATUTES

BURIAL SITES PRESERVATION BOARD

Burial Sites Preservation Board: JOHN H. BROIHAHN (state archaeologist, nonvoting member); ELLSWORTH H. BROWN (state historical society director); JIM DRAEGER (state historic preservation officer, nonvoting member); KATHERINE C. EGAN-BRUHY, JENNIFER HAAS, CYNTHIA STILES (nominated by Wisconsin Archaeological Survey); DAVID J. GRIGNON, CORINA WILLIAMS, MELINDA YOUNG (nominated by the Great Lakes Inter-Tribal Council, Inc., and the Menominee Tribe). (All except *ex officio* members are appointed by governor.)

Mailing Address: 816 State Street, Madison 53706-1417.

Telephones: (608) 264-6505; (800) 342-7834 (within Wisconsin).

Statutory References: Section 15.705 (1); Chapter 157, Subchapter III.

Agency Responsibility: The Burial Sites Preservation Board was created to protect all the interests related to human burial sites and to ensure equal treatment and respect for all human burials, regardless of ethnic origin, cultural background, or religious affiliation. The board develops detailed policies to implement the burial sites preservation program; reviews decisions of the director or the administrative hearing examiner concerning applications for permits to disturb cataloged burial sites; and reviews the director's decisions regarding the disposition of human remains and burial objects removed from a burial site. This program was created by 1985 Wisconsin Act 316.

Organization: The 9-member board includes 3 members with professional qualifications in archaeology, physical anthropology, or history and 3 members of federally recognized Indian nations in Wisconsin who have a knowledge of tribal preservation planning, history, or archaeology or who serve as elders, traditional persons, or spiritual leaders of a tribe. The 6 appointed members serve 3-year terms.

HISTORIC PRESERVATION REVIEW BOARD

Historic Preservation Review Board: ANNE E. BIEBEL, BRUCE T. BLOCK, ROBERT J. GOUGH, CARLEN HATALA, KELLY S. JACKSON, DAN J. JOYCE, KUBET LUCHTERHAND, DAVID V. MOLLENHOFF, NEIL PREDERGAST, SISSEL SCHROEDER, VALENTINE J. SCHUTE, JR., DANIEL J. STEPHANS, PAUL WOLTER, DONNA ZIMMERMAN, vacancy (all appointed by governor).

Mailing Address: 816 State Street, Madison 53706-1417.

Telephone: (608) 264-6498.

Statutory References: Section 15.705 (2); Chapter 44, Subchapter II.

Agency Responsibility: The Historic Preservation Review Board approves nominations to the Wisconsin State Register of Historic Places and the National Register of Historic Places upon recommendation of the State Historic Preservation Officer. (By statute, the director of the State Historical Society serves as the state officer or designates someone to do so.) The board approves the distribution of federal grants-in-aid for preservation; advises the state historical society; and requests comments from planning departments of affected municipalities, local landmark commissions, and local historical societies regarding properties being considered for nomination to the state and national registers. The board was created by Chapter 29, Laws of 1977.

Organization: The board consists of 15 members appointed by the governor to staggered 3-year terms. At least 9 must be professionally qualified in the areas of architecture, archaeology, art history, and history. Up to 6 members may be qualified in related fields, such as landscape architecture, urban and regional planning, law, or real estate.

Office of the Commissioner of INSURANCE

Address e-mail by combining the user ID and the state extender: userid@**wisconsin.gov**
All telephone numbers are 608 area code unless otherwise indicated.

Commissioner: TED NICKEL, 267-3782, ted.nickel@

Deputy Commissioner: DAN SCHWARTZER, 267-1233, dan.schwartzer@

Public Information Officer and Legislative Liaison: J.P. WIESKE, 266-2493, jp.wieske@

Insurance Administrator for Funds and Program Management: KATE LUDLUM, 264-6232, kate.ludlum@

Legal Counsel: vacancy.

Regulation and Enforcement, Division of: vacancy, *administrator.*

Mailing Address: P.O. Box 7873, Madison 53707-7873.

Location: 125 South Webster Street, Madison 53703.

Telephones: General: 266-3585; Toll-free: (800) 236-8517.

Fax: 266-9935.

Internet Address: http://oci.wi.gov

Publications: Annual reports; *Wisconsin Insurance News;* various pamphlets and materials for consumers, insurance companies, and agents. (Contact the Office of the Commissioner of Insurance.)

Number of Employees: 153.30.

Total Budget 2013-15: $216,926,800.

Statutory References: Section 15.73; Chapter 601.

Agency Responsibility: The Office of the Commissioner of Insurance supervises the insurance industry in Wisconsin. The office is responsible for examining insurance industry financial practices and market conduct, licensing insurance agents, reviewing policy forms for compliance with state insurance statutes and regulations, investigating consumer complaints, and providing consumer information. Its goals are to ensure the financial soundness of insurers doing business in Wisconsin; secure fair treatment by insurance companies and agents of policyholders and claimants; encourage industry self-regulation; emphasize loss prevention as part of good insurance practice; and educate the public on insurance issues.

The office administers three segregated insurance funds: the State Life Insurance Fund, the Local Government Property Insurance Fund, and the Injured Patients and Families Compensation Fund. The State Life Insurance Fund offers up to $10,000 of low-cost life insurance protection to any Wisconsin resident who meets prescribed risk standards. The Local Government Property Insurance Fund provides mandatory coverage for local governments against fire loss, as well as optional coverage for certain property damage they may incur.

The agency oversees activities of the Health Care Liability Insurance Plan, which provides liability coverage for hospitals, physicians, and other health care providers in Wisconsin, and the Injured Patients and Families Compensation Fund, which provides medical malpractice coverage for qualified health care providers on claims in excess of a provider's underlying coverage.

Organization: The commissioner of insurance is appointed by the governor with the advice and consent of the senate. The commissioner cannot be a candidate for public office and there are stringent restrictions on the commissioner's political activities. The deputy commissioner is appointed from outside the classified service and the division administrators from the classified service.

Unit Functions: The *Funds and Program Management Organizational Unit* contains the Management Analysis and Planning Section, the Information Technology Section, the Local Government Property Insurance Fund, and the State Life Insurance Fund. The first two sections are responsible for providing a variety of administrative services in support of all agency programs and employees. These services include budget, finance and accounting, receivables, certain procurement tasks, training and employee development, project management, and all IT services including help desk, applications development and support, security, e-mail, and network management. The two funds operate state programs providing property insurance for local units of government in Wisconsin, and basic life insurance for Wisconsin residents, respectively.

The *Division of Regulation and Enforcement* conducts field reviews of insurer underwriting, rating, claim handling, and marketing practices. It investigates insurance agent activities, prepares enforcement proceedings, and, in conjunction with the legal unit, prosecutes offenders. It helps consumers resolve problems with insurers and agents, and carries out the agency's consumer education program. Other duties include review of premium rates and insurance policy forms and contracts filed with the office to ensure their compliance with state law; review of insurer advertising files; and licensing and testing of insurance agents.

The division also conducts field examinations of the financial condition of insurers domiciled in Wisconsin and monitors the financial condition of insurers doing business in the state. It oversees insurer rehabilitations and liquidations, and audits and collects insurer taxes and fees. It incorporates the formation of new insurers and is responsible for the licensing of nondomestic insurers that want to do business in the state. It reviews and approves, as appropriate, transactions that result in the change of control or financial structure of domestic insurers. It also administers the fire department dues program in cooperation with the Department of Safety and Professional Services, whereby dues paid by insurers who provide fire coverage are disbursed to municipalities for fire protection and the fire fighters' pension and disability funds.

The *Legal Unit* represents the office in administrative proceedings, provides legal advice to staff, represents or supervises representation of the office in litigation and insurance company receiverships, provides legal services for the Injured Patients and Families Compensation Fund, Wisconsin Health Care Liability Insurance Plan, Local Government Property Insurance Fund, the State Life Insurance Fund, and develops legislative proposals and administrative rules.

The *Legislative Relations and Communications Unit* provides advice on executive matters affecting the office's goals and initiatives including directing the office's legislative initiatives and communications activities. The unit also provides advice on technical insurance-related issues and educates underserved populations on insurance issues.

History: State regulation of insurance dates back to 1870 when Chapter 56 created a Department of Insurance in the secretary of state's office to license agents and, upon complaint, examine the books of fire and inland navigation insurance companies. In 1878 (Chapter 214), the legislature created a separate Department of Insurance, headed by a commissioner appointed by the governor, to perform these functions. From 1881 to 1911, based on Chapter 300, Laws of 1881, an elected commissioner administered the insurance department. With the enactment of Chapter 484, Laws of 1911, the insurance commissioner was again made an appointee. The 1967 executive branch reorganization act renamed the department the Office of the Commissioner of Insurance and continued it as an independent regulatory agency.

Other highlights include the development of the standard fire insurance contract in Chapter 195, Laws of 1891, and stricter regulation of the life insurance industry in 1907 to prevent fraud and misrepresentation. In 1911 and 1913, Wisconsin added coverage of local governments' property and buildings under the State Insurance Fund.

Wisconsin became the only state to establish a state life insurance fund for its residents under Chapter 577, Laws of 1911, which authorized the Department of Insurance to issue life insurance and annuity contracts. Since 1947 (Chapters 487 and 521), the office's responsibilities have included the review of all insurance policy forms and the filing of most premium rates. Wisconsin's current insurance laws are largely the result of a recodification developed between 1967 and 1979 by the Legislative Council and they have served as a basis for the model acts adopted by the National Association of Insurance Commissioners (an association of state insurance regulators).

Statutory Boards and Council

Insurance Security Fund, Board of Directors of the: TED NICKEL (insurance commissioner), BRAD SCHIMEL (attorney general), MATT ADAMCZYK (state treasurer); MARK J. BACKE, JOHN F. CLEARY, JAMES E. CRIST, DAVID G. DIERCKS, KENNETH ERLER, PETER C. FARROW, J. STANLEY HOFFERT, ALLEN OGILVIE, JANIS POTTER, SCOTT SEYMOUR, TOD J. ZACHARIAS (insurance industry representatives appointed by commissioner).

The Board of Directors of the Insurance Security Fund administers a fund that protects certain insurance policyholders and claimants from excessive delay and loss in the event of insurer liquidation. The fund consists of life, allocated annuity, health, HMO, property and casualty, and administrative accounts. The fund supports continuation of coverage under many life, annuity, and health policies. It is financed by assessments paid by most insurers in this state. The board may consist of 12 to 14 members but must include the attorney general, state treasurer, and insurance commissioner or their designees. The industry members must be chosen from representatives of insurers who are subject to the security fund law, and one member must be a representative of a service insurance corporation. The board's advice and recommendations to the commissioner are not subject to the state's open records law. The board was originally created in Chapter 144, Laws of 1969, with substantial revisions in Chapter 109, Laws of 1979, and its composition and duties are prescribed in Sections 646.12 and 646.13 of the statutes.

Injured Patients and Families Compensation Fund/Wisconsin Health Care Liability Insurance Plan, Board of Governors of the: TED NICKEL (insurance commissioner), *chairperson;* MARTY ARNOLD, DAVID MAURER, vacancy (insurance industry representatives appointed by commissioner); JOHN WALSH (named by State Bar of Wisconsin); M. ANGELA DENTICE (named by Wisconsin Association for Justice); ROBERT JAEGER, LINDA SYTH (named by Wisconsin Medical Society); RALPH TOPINKA (named by Wisconsin Hospital Association); GREGORY BANASZYNSKI, CARLA BORDA, SUSAN ENGLER, KATHRYN OSBORNE (public members appointed by governor).

The 13-member Board of Governors of the Injured Patients and Families Compensation Fund/Wisconsin Health Care Liability Insurance Plan oversees the health care liability plans for licensed physicians and nurse anesthetists, medical partnerships and corporations, cooperative sickness care associations, ambulatory surgery centers, hospitals, some nursing homes, and certain other health care providers. The board also supervises the Injured Patients and Families Compensation Fund, which pays medical malpractice claims in excess of a provider's underlying coverage. The 4 public members serve staggered 3-year terms, and at least 2 of them must not be attorneys or physicians nor be professionally affiliated with any hospital or insurance company. The insurance commissioner or the commissioner's designee, who must be an employee of the office of the commissioner, serves as chairperson. The board was created by the medical malpractice law, Chapter 37, Laws of 1975, and its composition and duties are prescribed in Sections 619.04 (3) and 655.27 of the statutes.

Injured Patients and Families Compensation Fund Peer Review Council: John Kelly, *chairperson;* Sandra Osborn, vacancy (physicians); Tom Kirschbaum, Jeff Renier (public members).

The 5-member Injured Patients and Families Compensation Fund Peer Review Council reviews, within one year of the first payment on a claim, each claim for damages arising out of medical care provided by a health care provider or provider's employee, if the claim is paid by any of the following: the Patients Compensation Fund, a mandatory health care risk-sharing plan, a private health care liability insurer, or a self-insurer. The council can recommend adjustments in fees paid to the Injured Patients and Families Compensation Fund and the Wisconsin Health Care Liability Insurance Plan or premiums paid to private insurers, if requested by the insurer. The Board of Governors of the Injured Patients and Families Compensation Fund/ Wisconsin Health Care Liability Insurance Plan appoints the council and designates its officers and the terms of the members. Not more than 3 members may be physicians. The chairperson must be a physician, who also serves as an *ex officio* nonvoting member of the Medical Examining Board. The council was created by 1985 Wisconsin Act 340, and its composition and duties are prescribed in Section 655.275 of the statutes.

State of Wisconsin
INVESTMENT BOARD

Members: Lon Roberts, *chairperson;* Thomas Boldt, *vice chairperson;* Bruce Colburn (public member), *secretary*; Bob Conlin (noneducator participant appointed by Wisconsin Retirement Board); Scott Neitzel (secretary of administration); Norman Cummings (representing Local Government Investment Pool participants); Sandra Claflin-Chalton (educator participant appointed by Teachers Retirement Board); William H. Levit, Jr., David Stein. (Except as noted, the governor appoints the members with senate consent.)

Executive Director: MICHAEL WILLIAMSON, 266-9451.

Chief Financial Officer: Cindy Klimke-Armatoski, 266-8181.

Chief Investment Officer: David Villa, 266-9734.

Chief Legal Officer: Rochelle Klaskin, 266-9904.

Chief Operating Officer: Lori Wersal, 266-2042.

Chief Human Resources Officer: Jennifer Schmeiser, 261-2404.

Internal Audit Director: Brandon Brickner, 261-6787.

Strategic Planning and Transformation Director: Elizabeth Fadell, 261-6779.

Communications Manager: Vicki Hearing, 261-2415, vicki.hearing@swib.state.wi.us

Mailing Address: P.O. Box 7842, Madison 53707-7842.

Location: 121 East Wilson Street, Madison.

Telephone: (608) 266-2381; Toll-Free Beneficiary Hotline: (800) 424-7942.

Fax: (608) 266-2436.

Internet Address: www.swib.state.wi.us

Agency E-mail Address: info@swib.state.wi.us

Publications: Annual Report; Schedule of Investments.

Number of Employees: 166.35.

Total Budget 2013-15: $70,600,000.

Statutory References: Section 15.76; Chapter 25.

Agency Responsibility: The State of Wisconsin Investment Board is responsible for investing the assets of the Wisconsin Retirement System, the State Life Insurance Fund, the Local Government Property Insurance Fund, the State Historical Society of Wisconsin Endowment Trust Fund, the Injured Patients and Families Compensation Fund, the Tuition Trust Fund, and the State Investment Fund.

For purposes of investment, the retirement system's assets are divided into two funds. The Core Retirement Investment Trust is a broadly diversified portfolio of domestic and international common stocks, corporate and government bonds, and private markets that include real estate and private debt and equity. The Variable Retirement Investment Trust is invested primarily in common stocks. On December 31, 2014, Wisconsin Retirement System trust funds constituted 93% of the $102.9 billion managed by the Investment Board.

The State Investment Fund invests the commingled cash balances of various state and local government funds in short-term investments with earnings and losses distributed on a pro rata basis to the individual component funds. The fund encompasses the cash balance of the state's general fund and about 68 separate state funds, including the Children's Trust Fund, the Lottery Fund, the Recycling Fund, the Tuition Trust Fund, and the Wisconsin Election Campaign Fund, as well as various state agency accounts. Authorized local governments may participate by depositing moneys in the Local Government Pooled-Investment Fund, which is a separate fund within the State Investment Fund.

Organization: Except for the secretary of administration, appointments to the 9-member board, which is a body corporate with power to sue and be sued, in its name, are for 6-year terms. The secretary of administration is an *ex officio* member. At least 4 of the 5 general members must have a minimum of 10 years of investment experience, and none may have a financial interest in or be employed by a dealer or broker in securities, mortgages, or real estate investments. The sixth member appointed by the governor must have 10 years of financial experience and be an employee of a government that participates in the Local Government Pooled-Investment Fund

The board appoints the executive director and the internal auditor from outside the classified service. The executive director, with the participation of the board, appoints the chief investment officer, and the managing and investment directors from outside the classified service. All other professional employees are also appointed by the executive director from outside the classified service. Board employees may not have any direct or indirect financial interest in any firm engaged in the sale or marketing of real estate or investments or give paid investment advice to others.

History: Chapter 459, Laws of 1921, created a mandatory pension system for teachers and three separate boards to invest the annuity funds of public school, normal school, and university teachers. The 1929 Legislature created the State Annuity and Investment Board and made it responsible for investing the assets of the teachers' pension funds and other state funds, except the school funds that remained under control of the Commissioners of Public Lands (Chapter 491). The board also assumed oversight and asset management of funds for the newly created state employee pension system as the result of Chapter 176, Laws of 1943.

Chapter 511, Laws of 1951, replaced the three teacher retirement boards and the Annuity and Investment Board with the State Teachers Retirement Board and the State Investment Board, which was responsible for investing the assets of all non-Milwaukee teachers. Chapter 511 also granted the State Investment Board authority to invest the assets of the nonteaching, non-Milwaukee public employees who were covered under the Wisconsin Retirement Fund. Chapter 430, Laws of 1957, brought the funds of the Milwaukee teachers under the control of the State Investment Board. Chapter 96, Laws of 1981, consolidated all public employee retirement plans, with the exception of the City and County of Milwaukee, into the Wisconsin Retirement System, and the State Investment Board has continued to invest the retirement system funds. As a result of the consolidation, the retirement system is the ninth largest public pension fund in the U.S. and the 30th largest public or private pension fund worldwide.

Chapter 449, Laws of 1925, created a State Board of Deposits to insure state funds on deposit in state banks through a deposit fund, managed by the state treasurer under the direction of the board. The board's duties were to designate the banks in which state funds could be deposited and to specify the maximum amount of state funds each could receive. Participating banks paid into the deposit fund, which was designed to reimburse any losses incurred through bank failure.

Chapter 511, Laws of 1951, authorized the State Investment Board to invest the state's operating funds and directed it to carry out the investment functions of the State Board of Deposits. Although state funds had been invested since 1911, the 1951 reorganization increased the types of investments the board could consider for the funds it managed. Previously, the state's operating funds had been placed in noninterest bearing accounts. In 1957, the legislature created the State Investment Fund, which merged all state funds except for a handful that are reported separately. The Local Government Pooled-Investment Fund, created in 1976, allows local governments to invest their idle cash at competitive rates of return and withdraw it on a two-day notice with no penalty.

The position of chief investment officer was created by 1995 Wisconsin Act 274, which also provided for an internal audit function.

Although the board has always been subject to the prudent expert fiduciary standard of responsibility, the statutes specified a legal list of authorized investments until 2007. 2007 Wisconsin Act 212 made the prudent expert fiduciary standard the prevailing standard with respect to assets of the Wisconsin Retirement System, thereby overriding the legal list and other provisions in law that previously constrained the board's investment authority.

Department of
JUSTICE

Attorney General: BRAD D. SCHIMEL, 266-1221.

Deputy Attorney General: ANDREW C. COOK, 266-1221.

Assistant Deputy Attorney General: DELANIE BREUER, 266-1221.

Communications: ANNE E. SCHWARTZ, 266-1221.

Senior Counsel: PAUL W. CONNELL, 266-1221.

Government Affairs: MIKE AUSTIN, *director,* 266-1221.

Mailing Address: P.O. Box 7857, Madison 53707-7857.

Location: Attorney General's Office, 114 East, State Capitol; Department of Justice, 17 West Main Street, Madison.

Telephones: General: 266-1221; Arson Tip Line: (800) 362-3005; Office of Crime Victim Services: (800) 446-6564; Drug Tip Helpline: (800) 622-DRUG (622-3784); Amber Alert Hotline: (866) 65AMBER (652-6237); Consumer Protection: (800) 998-0700.

Fax: 267-2779.

Internet Address: www.doj.state.wi.us

Number of Employees: 675.74.

Total Budget 2013-15: $243,664,300.

Constitutional References: Article VI, Sections 1 and 3.

Statutory References: Section 15.25; Chapter 165.

Crime Victim Services, Office of: JILL J. KAROFSKY, *executive director,* 266-0109; Fax: 267-1938.

   Crime Victim Services: KATHY ZUPAN, *director,* 264-9484.

     Program Assistance and Administration: CINDY GRADY, *director,* 264-6209.

     Victim Services: CHRISTINE NOLAN, *director,* 267-5251.

Criminal Investigation, Division of: DAVID MATTHEWS, *administrator,* 266-1671; PATRICK MITCHELL, *deputy administrator,* 266-1671; Fax: 267-2777.

   Field Operations Bureau, Eastern Region: TINA R. VIRGIL, *director,* 266-1671.

   Field Operations Bureau, Western Region: JUDY WORMET, *director,* 266-1671.

DEPARTMENT OF JUSTICE

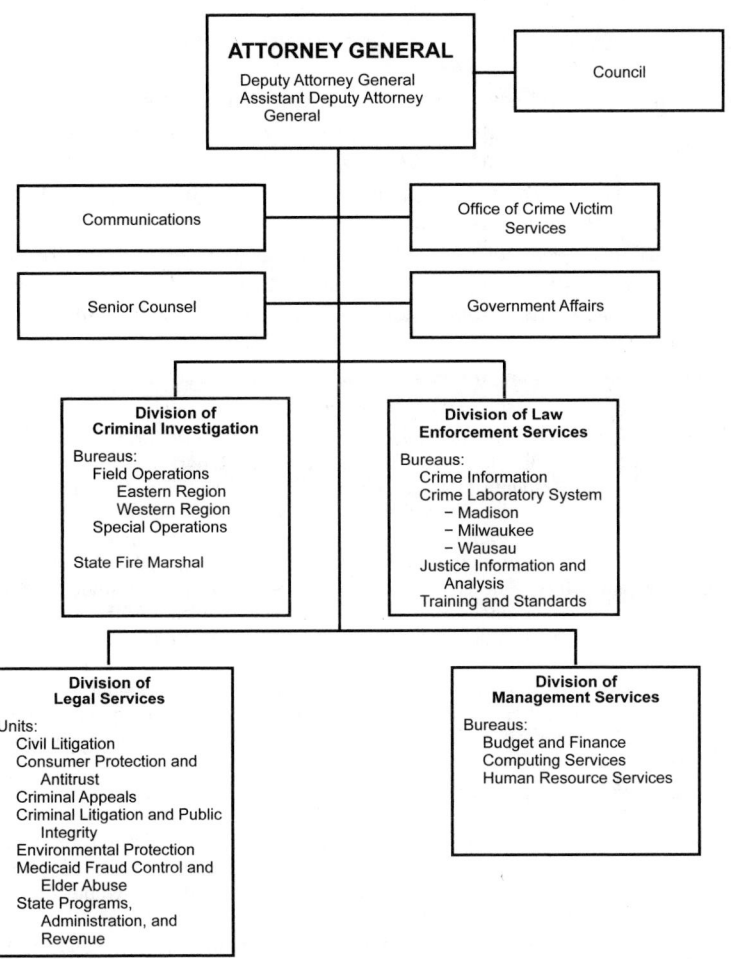

ATTORNEY GENERAL
Deputy Attorney General
Assistant Deputy Attorney
General

Council

Communications

Office of Crime Victim
Services

Senior Counsel

Government Affairs

**Division of
Criminal Investigation**

Bureaus:
  Field Operations
    Eastern Region
    Western Region
  Special Operations

State Fire Marshal

**Division of Law
Enforcement Services**

Bureaus:
  Crime Information
  Crime Laboratory System
    – Madison
    – Milwaukee
    – Wausau
  Justice Information and
    Analysis
  Training and Standards

**Division of
Legal Services**

Units:
  Civil Litigation
  Consumer Protection and
    Antitrust
  Criminal Appeals
  Criminal Litigation and Public
    Integrity
  Environmental Protection
  Medicaid Fraud Control and
    Elder Abuse
  State Programs,
    Administration, and
    Revenue

**Division of
Management Services**

Bureaus:
  Budget and Finance
  Computing Services
  Human Resource Services

Units attached for administrative purposes under Sec. 15.03:   Crime Victims Rights Board
                                                               Law Enforcement Standards Board

---

Special Operations: JENNIFFER PRICE, *director,* 266-1671.

State Fire Marshal: MATT JOY, 266-1671.

Law Enforcement Services, Division of: BRIAN R. O'KEEFE, *administrator,* 266-7052; DAVID ZIBOLSKI, *deputy administrator,* 267-2232; Fax: 266-1656.

  Crime Information Bureau: WALTER M. NEVERMAN, *director,* 264-6207.

  Crime Laboratory System: JANA CHAMPION, *director,* 267-2224.

  Locations:

  Madison: 266-2031, 4626 University Avenue, Madison 53705-2174.

  Milwaukee: (414) 382-7500, 1578 South 11th Street, Milwaukee 53204-2860.

  Wausau: (715) 845-8626, 7100 West Stewart Avenue, Wausau 54401.

Justice Information and Analysis Bureau: CONSTANCE KOSTELAC, *director.*

Training and Standards Bureau: TONY BARTHULY, *director,* 266-9606.

Legal Services, Division of: DAVID V. MEANY, *administrator,* 266-0332; KEVIN POTTER, *deputy administrator,* 266-0929; Fax: 267-2779.

> *Civil Litigation Unit:* COREY FINKELMEYER, *director,* 266-7234.
>
> *Consumer Protection and Antitrust Unit:* FRANK SULLIVAN, *director,* 267-2162.
>
> *Criminal Appeals Unit:* GREGORY WEBER, *director,* 267-2167.
>
> *Criminal Litigation and Public Integrity Unit:* ROY KORTE, *director,* 266-1447.
>
> *Environmental Protection Unit:* THOMAS DAWSON, *director,* 264-9442.
>
> *Medicaid Fraud Control and Elder Abuse Unit:* THOMAS STORM, *director,* 266-9222.
>
> *State Programs, Administration, and Revenue Unit:* CHARLOTTE GIBSON, *director,* 266-3952.

Management Services, Division of: BONNIE CYGANEK, *administrator,* 267-1300; Fax: 266-1656.

> *Budget and Finance, Bureau of:* KAREN VAN SCHOONHOVEN, *director,* 267-6714.
>
> *Computing Services, Bureau of:* IGOR STEINBERG, *director,* 266-7076.
>
> *Human Resource Services, Bureau of:* vacancy, *director,* 266-0461.

Publications: Opinions of the Attorney General; Annual Report; Criminal Investigation and Physical Evidence Handbook; Domestic Abuse Incident Report; Law Enforcement Bulletin; Safe Schools Legal Resource Manual; *When Crime Strikes: Injured Victims Can Get Help;* Wisconsin Law Enforcement Film Catalog; *Wisconsin Open Meetings Law: A Citizen's Guide; Wisconsin Open Meetings Law: A Compliance Guide; Wisconsin Public Records Law;* Wisconsin Prosecutor's Newsletter; Wisconsin Resource Directory for Crime Victims.

Agency Responsibility: The Department of Justice provides legal advice and representation, criminal investigation, and various law enforcement services for the state. It represents the state in civil cases and handles criminal cases that reach the Wisconsin Court of Appeals or the Wisconsin Supreme Court. It also represents the state in criminal cases on appeal in federal courts and participates with other states in federal cases that are important to Wisconsin. The department provides legal representation in lower courts when expressly authorized by law or requested by the governor, either house of the legislature, or a state agency head. It also represents state agencies in court reviews of their administrative decisions.

Organization: The Department of Justice is supervised by the attorney general, a constitutional officer who is elected on a partisan ballot to a 4-year term. The attorney general appoints the deputy attorney general, the executive assistant, the department's division administrators, and the executive director of the Office of Crime Victim Services. With the exception of the administrator of the Division of Criminal Investigation, which is a classified position, all of these positions serve at the pleasure of the attorney general.

Unit Functions: The *Office of Crime Victim Services* administers state and federal funding to programs that assist victims of crime. Three programs receive full or partial funding from surcharges assessed against convicted criminals: the Crime Victim Compensation Program reimburses eligible victims and their dependents for medical and other qualifying expenses; the Sexual Assault Victim Services (SAVS) Program provides grants to nonprofit organizations that offer services to sexual assault victims; and the Victim/Witness Assistance Program partially reimburses counties for their costs of providing services to crime victims and witnesses. Federal funding supports five programs: the Wisconsin Victim Resource Center, which assists victims in understanding and exercising their statutory and constitutional crime victims' rights; the Victims of Crime Act (VOCA) Program that provides grants to programs to provide direct services to innocent victims of crime; the Violence Against Women's Act (VAWA) Program that provides grants to improve criminal justice responses to domestic violence, dating violence, sexual assault, and stalking and to increase the availability of services for victims of these crimes; the Children's Justice Act, which supports improved investigation, prosecution, and judicial handling of child abuse and neglect; and the Crime Victim Compensation Program.

The *Division of Criminal Investigation,* created in Section 15.253 (2), Wisconsin Statutes, by 1991 Wisconsin Act 269, investigates crimes that are statewide in nature or importance. Special agents work closely with local officials to investigate and prosecute crimes involving homicide, arson, drug trafficking, illegal gaming, crimes against children, financial crimes, multijurisdictional crimes, computer crimes, homeland security, public integrity, and government fraud. The division provides extensive training to local, state, and federal officers.

The *Division of Law Enforcement Services* provides advanced technical services, information, and training to state and local law enforcement agencies and jails. It maintains central fingerprint identification records and computerized criminal history information, operates the Handgun Hotline, and provides criminal history background check services. The statewide telecommunications system links Wisconsin criminal justice agencies to national, state, and local crime files and databases. The crime laboratory system with locations in Madison, Milwaukee, and Wausau, analyzes forensic evidence for the Wisconsin criminal justice system and provides crime scene response in major cases.

The division administers standards and basic recruit training for statewide criminal justice professionals including law enforcement, tribal law enforcement, jail, and secure juvenile detention officers. The division maintains and enforces certification and annual recertification training standards for law enforcement, jail, and secure detention officers, instructors, and training academies. It collaborates extensively with advisory committees and criminal justice training professionals in developing and delivering law enforcement curriculum. It also promotes and provides timely and accurate training, records, reimbursements, and reference information for law enforcement, jail, and secure detention officers.

The *Division of Legal Services* provides legal representation and advice to the governor, legislature, other state officers and agencies, district attorneys, and county corporation counsels. It also provides training and education to all district attorneys and assistant district attorneys. It enforces state environmental, antitrust, employment, consumer protection, and Medicaid fraud laws. It also prosecutes economic crimes and represents the state in all felony appeals and litigation brought by prison inmates. At the request of district attorneys, the division provides special prosecutors in complex homicide, drug, and white collar and other criminal cases. It defends the state in civil lawsuits filed against the state or its officers and employees and handles matters related to public records, Indian law, and fair housing.

The *Division of Management Services* prepares the agency budget; manages agency personnel, finances, and facilities; and provides information technology services.

History: When Wisconsin became a territory in 1836, the U.S. President appointed the attorney general. In 1839, a territorial act gave the governor the power to appoint the attorney general with the consent of the Legislative Council (the upper house of the territorial legislature) to a term of 3 years. The Wisconsin Constitution, as adopted in 1848, provided for an elected attorney general with a 2-year term. A constitutional amendment ratified in 1967 increased the term to 4 years, effective in 1971.

Chapter 75, Laws of 1967, named the agency headed by the attorney general the Department of Justice and transferred to its control the State Crime Laboratory, the arson investigation program from the Commissioner of Insurance, and the criminal investigation functions of the Beverage and Cigarette Tax Division of the Department of Revenue. The 1975 Legislature returned alcohol and tobacco tax enforcement to the Department of Revenue.

The 1969 Legislature added enforcement of certain laws related to dangerous drugs, narcotics, and organized crime to the duties of the department and created the public intervenor to intervene in or initiate proceedings to protect public rights in water and other natural resources. In Chapter 189, Laws of 1979, the legislature transferred the crime victims program from the Department of Industry, Labor and Human Relations to the Department of Justice. 1995 Wisconsin Act 27 transferred the public intervenor to the Department of Natural Resources and consumer protection functions to the Department of Agriculture, Trade and Consumer Protection.

Statutory Council

Crime Victims Council: MICHELLE G. ARROWOOD, GAYLE M. PATRAW (victim services representatives); KURT D. HEUER (law enforcement representative); BRAD D. SCHIMEL (district attorney representative); SCOTT L. HORNE (judicial representative); AVE M. BIE, CHRIS H. DANOU, TOM EAGON, CHARLES S. McGEE, MARION MORGAN, MALLORY E. O'BRIEN, MICHAEL

S. ROGOWSKI, ANNA M. RUZINSKI, WILLIAM SWANSON, vacancy (citizen members). (All are appointed by attorney general.)

The 15-member Crime Victims Council provides advice and recommendations on victims' rights issues and legislation. Members are appointed for staggered 3-year terms, and the 10 citizen members must have demonstrated sensitivity and concern for crime victims. The council was created by Chapter 189, Laws of 1979, as the Crime Victims Compensation Council. It was renamed in Chapter 20, Laws of 1981, and its duties and composition are prescribed in Sections 15.09 (5) and 15.257 (2) of the statutes.

INDEPENDENT UNITS ATTACHED FOR BUDGETING, PROGRAM COORDINATION, AND RELATED MANAGEMENT FUNCTIONS BY SECTION 15.03 OF THE STATUTES

CRIME VICTIMS RIGHTS BOARD

Members: TIMOTHY GRUENKE (district attorney appointed by Wisconsin District Attorneys' Association); PAUL SUSIENKA (local law enforcement representative appointed by the attorney general); TRISHA ANDERSON (county provider of victim and witness services appointed by attorney general); CHARLES S. MCGEE (citizen member appointed by the Crime Victims Council); CARMEN PITRE (citizen member appointed by governor).

Statutory References: Sections 15.255 (2) and 950.09.

The 5-member Crime Victims Rights Board may review and investigate complaints filed by victims of crime regarding their rights. The board is an independent agency. The Department of Justice provides staff to help administer the duties of the board, but actions of the board are not subject to approval or review by the attorney general. The board may issue a private or public reprimand against a public official or agency that violates a crime victim's rights; refer a possible violation of a victim's rights by a judge to the judicial commission; seek appropriate relief on behalf of a crime victim necessary to protect that person's rights; or seek a forfeiture up to $1,000 against a public officer or agency for intentional violations. The board can also issue reports and recommendations regarding victims' rights and service provision.

Members serve 4-year terms. The 2 citizen members may not be employed in law enforcement, by a district attorney, or by a county board to provide crime victim's services. The board was created by 1997 Wisconsin Act 181.

LAW ENFORCEMENT STANDARDS BOARD

Members: JOSEPH COLLINS (law enforcement representative), *chairperson;* CHRISTOPHER DOMAGALSKI (law enforcement representative), *vice chairperson;* KIM GAFFNEY, NATHAN HENRIKSEN, ANNA RUZINSKI, MICHAEL STEFFES, LAURA WASHER (law enforcement representatives); JENNIFER HARPER (district attorney); 2 vacancies (local government representatives); JEAN GALASINSKI (public member); STEPHEN FITZGERALD (designated by secretary of transportation), BRIAN O'KEEFE (designated by attorney general), TODD SCHALLER (designated by secretary of natural resources). Nonvoting member: G.B. JONES (special agent in charge, Milwaukee FBI Office). (All except *ex officio* members are appointed by governor.)

Secretary: BRIAN O'KEEFE, *administrator,* Division of Law Enforcement Services, P.O. Box 7857, Madison 53707-7857.

Statutory References: Sections 15.255 and 165.85.

Agency Responsibility: The 15-member Law Enforcement Standards Board sets minimum employment, education, and training standards for law enforcement, tribal law enforcement, and jail and secure detention officers. It certifies persons who meet professional standards as qualified to be officers. The board consults with other government agencies regarding the development of training schools and courses, conducts research to improve law enforcement and jail administration and performance, and evaluates governmental units' compliance with standards. Its appointed members serve staggered 4-year terms. The law enforcement representatives must include at least one sheriff and one chief of police. The public member cannot be employed in law enforcement. Chapter 466, Laws of 1969, created the board.

Curriculum Advisory Committee: MIKE HARTERT, KURT HEUER, GREGORY LECK, JOHN MORRISSEY, RICHARD OLIVA, JERRY STANISZEWSKI (police chiefs); RON CRAMER, NATHAN

DRECKMAN, JOSEPH FATH, WILLIAM GREENING, MARK PODOLL, SAMUEL WOLLIN (sheriffs); GERALD VOIGHT (training director, Wisconsin State Patrol); CLARK PAGEL (training academy director, Wisconsin Technical College System) (police chiefs, sheriffs, and technical college system representative appointed by Law Enforcement Standards Board).

The 14-member Curriculum Advisory Committee advises the Law Enforcement Standards Board on the establishment of curriculum requirements for training of law enforcement, tribal law enforcement, and jail and secure detention officers. The statutes do not stipulate length of terms. Chapter 466, Laws of 1969, created the committee and its composition and duties are prescribed in Section 165.85 (3) (d) of the statutes.

Department of
MILITARY AFFAIRS

Commander in Chief: GOVERNOR SCOTT WALKER.

Adjutant General: MAJOR GENERAL DONALD P. DUNBAR, 242-3001,
donald.p.dunbar@us.army.mil

Deputy Adjutant General for Army: BRIG. GEN. MARK E. ANDERSON, 242-3010,
mark.e.anderson2.mil@mail.mil

Deputy Adjutant General for Air: BRIG. GEN. GARY L. EBBEN, 242-3020,
gary.l.ebben@ang.af.mil

Executive Assistant: MICHAEL T. HINMAN, 242-3009, michael.t.hinman.nfg@mail.mil

Mailing Address: P.O. Box 8111, Madison 53708-8111.

Location: 2400 Wright Street, Madison 53704-2572.

Telephones: General: 242-3000; Division of Emergency Management: 242-3232; 24-hour hotline for emergencies and hazardous materials spills: (800) 943-0003.

Fax: 242-3111; Division of Emergency Management: 242-3247.

Internet Address: Department of Military Affairs and Wisconsin National Guard:
http://dma.wi.gov; Wisconsin Emergency Management:
http://emergencymanagement.wi.gov; Wisconsin Homeland Security:
http://homelandsecurity.wi.gov

Number of State Employees: 456.77.

Total State Budget 2013-15: $206,406,500.

Total Federal Budget: Approximately $265 million annually.

Constitutional References: Article IV, Section 29; Article V, Section 4.

Statutory References: Sections 15.31 and 15.313; Chapters 321, 322, and 323.

Adjutant General Staff:

Assistant Adjutant General – Readiness and Training: BRIG. GEN. KENNETH KOON,
kenneth.a.koon.mil@mail.mil

Land Component Commander – BRIG. GEN. MARK MICHIE, mark.j.michie.mil@mail.mil

U.S. Property and Fiscal Office: COL. JOHN VAN DE LOOP, (608) 427-7266,
john.w.vandeloop.mil@mail.mil

Inspector General: COL. DAVID M. SEARS, 242-3086, david.m.sears6.mil@mail.mil

Director of Communications: MAJ. PAUL RICKERT, 242-3050, paul.j.rickert.mil@mail.mil

Staff Judge Advocate: COL. DAVID M. DZIOBKOWSKI, 242-3073,
david.m.dziobkowski.mil@mail.mil

Chaplain: LT. COL. DOUGLAS HEDMAN, 242-3450, douglas.v.hedman.mil@mail.mil

Legal Counsel: RANDI WIND MILSAP, 242-3072, randi.milsap@wisconsin.gov

State Budget and Finance Officer: MICHELLE GAUGER, 242-3155,
michelle.gauger@wisconsin.gov

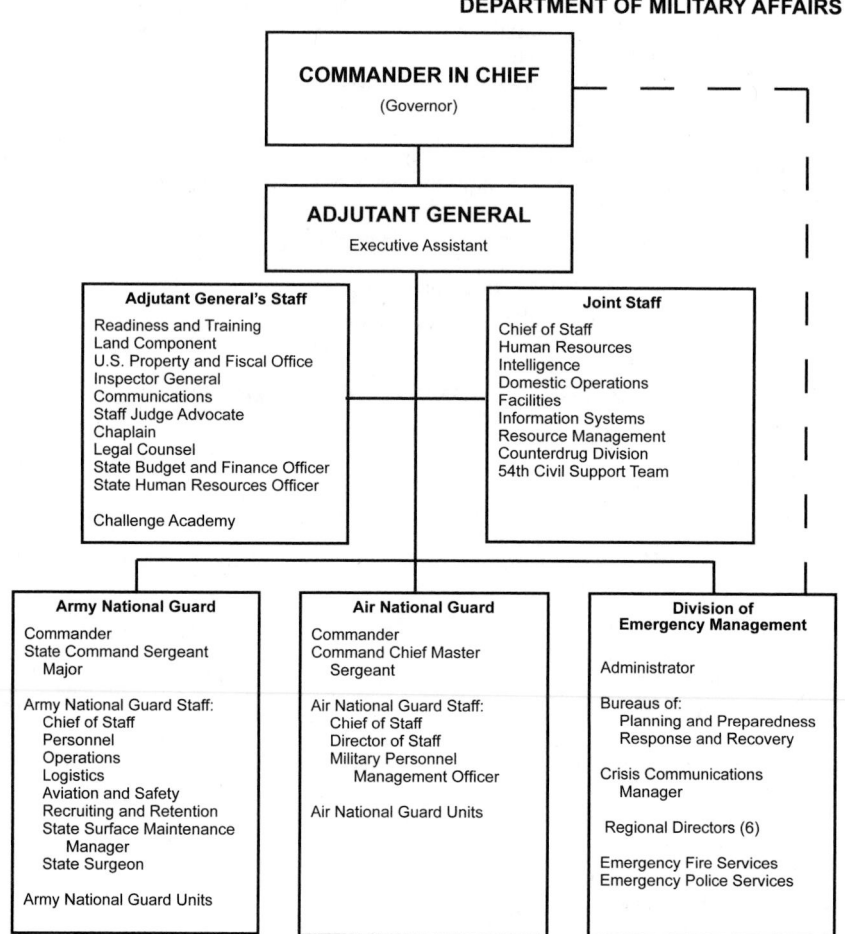

DEPARTMENT OF MILITARY AFFAIRS

State Human Resources Officer: JOANE MATHEWS, 242-3163, joane.mathews@wisconsin.gov

Wisconsin National Guard Challenge Academy (Fort McCoy): LT. COL. MIKE MURPHY, *director,* (608) 269-2105, michael.murphy@wisconsin.gov

Joint Staff:

Chief of Staff: COL. LEAH MOORE, 242-3484, leah.m.moore6.mil@mail.mil

Vice Chief, Joint Staff: MARK MICHIE, mark.j.michie.mil@mail.mil

Human Resources (J1), Director of Manpower and Personnel: LT. COL. DAVE MAY, 242-3700, david.w.may16.mil@mail.mil

Intelligence (J2), Director of Security and Intelligence: LT. COL. TIMOTHY COVINGTON, 242-3038, timothy.d.covington.mil@mail.mil

Domestic Operations (J3/5/7), Director of Domestic Operations and Strategic Plans: COL. JULIE M. GERETY, 242-3530, julie.m.gerety.mil@mail.mil

Facilities (J4), Director of Installation Management: COL. DANIEL PULVERMACHER, 242-3359, daniel.l.pulvermacher.mil@mail.mil

Information Systems (J6), Director of Information Systems: LT. COL. JEFFREY ALSTON, 242-3650, jeffrey.m.alston2.mil@mail.mil

Resource Management, Director of Property and Fiscal Operations: COL. DANIEL SAILER, (608) 427-7212, daniel.t.sailer.mil@mail.mil

Director of Counterdrug Division: LT. COL. LAURI HROVATIN, 242-3540, lauri.a.hrovatin.mil@mail.mil

Commander, 54th Civil Support Team (CST): LT. COL. ERIC LECKEL, 245-8431, eric.j.leckel.mil@mail.mil

Wisconsin Army National Guard: BRIG. GEN. MARK E. ANDERSON, *assistant adjutant general for the army,* 242-3010, mark.e.anderson2.mil@mail.mil

State Command Sergeant Major: COMMAND SGT. MAJ. BRADLEY SHIELDS, 242-3012, bradley.j.shields.mil@mail.mil

Army National Guard Staff:

Chief of Staff, Army Staff: COL. JOHN SCHROEDER, 242-3700, john.w.schroeder2.mil@mail.mil

Deputy Chief of Staff for Personnel (G1): COL. BRIAN WOLHAUPTER, 242-3444, brian.p.wolhaupter.mil@mail.mil

Deputy Chief of Staff for Operations (G3): COL. PETER ANDERSON, 242-3500, peter.k.anderson.mil@mail.mil

Deputy Chief of Staff for Logistics (G4): COL. GALEN D. WHITE, 242-3552, galen.d.white.mil@mail.mil

Deputy Chief of Staff for Aviation and Safety: COL. STEVE WATKINS, 242-3140, stephen.e.watkins.mil@mail.mil

Recruiting and Retention Command: LT. COL. ROCHELL MAIER, 242-3804, rochell.a.maier.mil@mail.mil

State Surface Maintenance Manager: LT. COL. ROBERT DIVNEY, (608) 427-7223, robert.s.divney.mil@mail.mil

State Surgeon: COL. RICK STRICKROOT, (262) 820-3093, rick.r.stickroot.mil@mail.mil

Army National Guard Units (major commands):

32nd Infantry Brigade Combat Team (Camp Douglas): COL. G. MICHAEL RAND, *commander,* george.m.rand.mil@mail.mil; LT. COL. RYAN BROWN, *administrative officer,* (608) 427-7349, ryan.c.brown.mil@mail.mil

157th Maneuver Enhancement Brigade (Milwaukee): COL. DAVID O'DONAHUE, *commander*, (414) 961-8682, david.f.odonahue.mil@mail.mil

64th Troop Command (Madison): COL. JULIE M. GERETY, *commander,* julie.m.gerety.mil@mail.mil; LT. COL. CARL MEREDITH, *administrative officer,* (608) 301-8205, carl.c.meredith2.mil@mail.mil

426th Regiment (Wisconsin Military Academy) (Fort McCoy): COL. GREGORY J. HIRSCH, *commander,* (608) 388-9990, gregory.j.hirsch.mil@mail.mil; LT. COL. ERIC BEUERMAN, *administrative officer,* (608) 388-9990, eric.g.beuerman.mil@mail.mil

Wisconsin Air National Guard: BRIG. GEN. GARY L. EBBEN, *deputy adjutant general for air,* 242-3020, gary.l.ebben@ang.af.mil

Command Chief Master Sergeant: COMMAND CHIEF MASTER SGT. GREGORY A. CULLEN, gregory.a.cullen@ang.af.mil

Air National Guard Staff:

Chief of Staff, Air Staff: BRIG. GEN. MURRAY HANSEN.

Director of Staff: COL. DAVID A. OLSON, 242-3120, david.olson@ang.af.mil

Military Personnel Management Officer: MAJ. CHRISTINA HASTINGS, 242-3122, christina.hastings@ang.af.mil

Air National Guard Units (major commands):

> *115th Fighter Wing (Madison):* COL. JEFFREY WIEGAND, *commander,* 245-4501, jeffrey.j.wiegand.mil@mail.mil

> *128th Air Refueling Wing (Milwaukee):* COL. DANIEL YENCHESKY, *commander,* (414) 944-8405, daniel.yenchesky@ang.af.mil

> *Volk Field Combat Readiness Training Center (Camp Douglas):* COL. DAVID L. ROMUALD, *commander,* (608) 427-1200, david.romuald@ang.af.mil

Emergency Management, Division of: BRIAN M. SATULA, *administrator,* 242-3210, brian.satula@wisconsin.gov

> *Planning and Preparedness, Bureau of:* GREG ENGLE, *director,* 242-3203, greg.engle@wisconsin.gov

> *Response and Recovery, Bureau of:* PATRICK O'CONNOR, *director,* 242-3204, patrick.oconnor@wisconsin.gov

> *Response Section Supervisor:* vacancy, 242-3336.

> *Crisis Communications Manager:* LORI GETTER, 242-3239, lori.getter@wisconsin.gov

> *Southwest Regional Office (Madison):* PAUL FRANCE, *director,* 242-5389, paul.france@wisconsin.gov

> *East Central Regional Office (Fond du Lac):* STEVE FENSKE, *director,* (920) 929-3730, steve.fenske@wisconsin.gov

> *Northeast Regional Office (Wausau):* MICHELLE HARTNESS, *director,* (715) 845-9517, michelle.hartness@wisconsin.gov

> *Northwest Regional Office (Spooner):* RANDY BOOKS, *director,* (715) 635-8704, randy.books@wisconsin.gov

> *Southeast Regional Office (Waukesha):* BEN SCHLIESMAN, *director,* (262) 782-1515, ben.schliesman@wisconsin.gov

> *West Central Regional Office (Eau Claire):* LISA OLSON MCDONALD, *director,* (715) 839-3825, lisa.olsonmcdonald@wisconsin.gov

> *Emergency Fire Services:* vacancy.

> *Emergency Police Services:* TODD NEHLS, *coordinator,* (608) 444-0003, todd.nehls@wisconsin.gov

> *Regional Emergency All-Climate Training (REACT) Center:* (608) 209-7860.

Publications: *@Ease Express.*

Agency Responsibility: The Department of Military Affairs (DMA) provides an armed military force through the Wisconsin National Guard, which is organized, trained, equipped, and available for deployment under official orders in state and national emergencies. The federal mission of the National Guard is to provide trained units to the U.S. Army and U.S. Air Force in time of war or national emergency. Its state mission is to assist civil authorities, protect life and property, and preserve peace, order, and public safety in times of natural or human-caused emergencies.

The *Division of Emergency Management,* also known as Wisconsin Emergency Management (WEM), is headed by a division administrator appointed by the governor with the advice and consent of the senate. It coordinates the development and implementation of the state emergency operations plan; provides assistance to local jurisdictions in the development of their programs and plans; administers private and federal disaster and emergency relief funds; administers the Wisconsin Disaster Fund; and maintains the state's 24-hour duty officer reporting and response system. The division also conducts training programs in emergency planning for businesses and state and local officials, as well as educational programs for the general public. Under Title III of the federal 1986 Superfund Amendments and Reauthorization Act and 1987 Wisconsin Act 342, the division requires public and private entities that possess hazardous substances to file reports on these substances. It establishes local emergency response committees

A HIMARS (High Mobility Artillery Rocket System) launcher belonging to the Wisconsin Army National Guard's Battery B, 1st Battalion, 121st Field Artillery, conducted a fire mission earlier this year at a military base in Afghanistan. Battery B recently completed its deployment and arrived at Fort Bliss, Texas, where it completed several days of demobilization requirements before returning to Wisconsin. (Sgt. Sean Huolihan, Wisconsin National Guard)

and oversees implementation of their plans and corresponding state plans. The division administers emergency planning performance grants that assist local emergency planning committees in complying with state and federal law. Under the Wisconsin Hazardous Material Response System, the division contracts with 26 hazardous materials teams from municipal fire departments across the state to provide a seamless, timely, uniform, and interoperable response to all types of hazardous materials incidents.

It also coordinates planning and training for off-site radiological emergencies at nuclear power plants in and near Wisconsin. The Emergency Police Services (EPS) program provides support to law enforcement in times of crisis. The program coordinates state law enforcement response to emergencies, including coordination of mutual aid for law enforcement assistance in natural disasters, prison disturbances, and other emergencies. The Emergency Fire Services Coordinator enhances fire service emergency response throughout the state and coordinates intrastate mutual aid through the Mutual Aid Box Alarm System (MABAS).

The Regional Emergency All-Climate Training (REACT) Center is located at Volk Field and is a statewide speciality training center for first responders and National Guard units.

In 2013, the State Homeland Security Grant program transferred to DMA and is managed by WEM. The program develops the Statewide Homeland Security Strategy, which includes leading efforts to identify gaps in the state's protection, set priorities for use of federal funds, and awarding grants to increase the capacity of first responders and communities to prevent, respond to, and recover from catastrophic events, including terrorist attacks.

The division administrator is appointed by the governor as the state coordinator for the U.S. Department of Defense 1033 Program. The 1033 excess property program allows transfer of excess Department of Defense supplies, vehicles, and equipment to state and local law enforcement agencies for their use in law enforcement.

A key resource within WEM is its system of 6 regional offices located throughout the state. The regional offices are co-located with the Wisconsin State Patrol regional posts in Waukesha, Fond du Lac, Eau Claire, Spooner, and Wausau, and at WEM's central office in Madison. Each office is assigned to work with a group of 8 to 14 counties. Regional directors are knowledgeable in each of the division's programs, and support both municipal and county programs in planning, training, exercising, response and recovery activities, as well as the coordination of administrative activities between the division and local governments. When disasters and emergencies strike, regional directors are the division's initial responders, serving as field liaisons for the State Emergency Operations Center.

Organization: The Wisconsin Constitution designates the governor as the commander in chief of the Wisconsin National Guard. The department is directed by the adjutant general, who is appointed by the governor for a 5-year term and may serve successive terms. The adjutant general must be an officer actively serving in the Army or Air National Guard of Wisconsin who has attained at least the rank of colonel and is fully qualified to hold the rank of major general in either the Army or Air National Guard.

In addition to state support, the Wisconsin National Guard is also funded and maintained by the federal government, and when it is called up in an active federal duty status, the president of the United States becomes its commander in chief. The federal government provides arms and ammunition, equipment and uniforms, major outdoor training facilities, pay for military and support personnel, and training and supervision. The state provides personnel; conducts training as required under the National Defense Act; and shares the cost of constructing, maintaining, and operating armories and other military facilities. The composition of Wisconsin Army and Air National Guard units is authorized by the U.S. secretary of defense through the National Guard Bureau. All officers and enlisted personnel must meet the same physical, education, and other eligibility requirements as members of the active-duty U.S. Army or U.S. Air Force.

History: Until the 20th century, the United States relied heavily on military units organized by the states to fight its wars. Known as "minutemen" in the American Revolution, state militias, which could be called up on brief notice, provided soldiers for the Revolutionary War, the Mexican War, the Civil War, and the Spanish-American War.

In 1792, the U.S. Congress passed a law that required all able-bodied men between 18 and 45 years of age to serve in local militia units, a provision that was incorporated into the territorial statutes of Wisconsin. The Wisconsin Constitution, as adopted in 1848, authorized the legislature to determine the composition, organization, and discipline of the state militia.

The 1849 Wisconsin Statutes specified the procedure for the organization of locally controlled "uniform companies". Each uniform company included 30 men who had to equip themselves with arms and uniforms.

By 1858 (Chapter 87), the legislature provided for the organization of the state militia, which ultimately replaced the uniform companies. As commander in chief of the militia, the governor appointed the adjutant general and the general officers and issued commissions to the elected officers of uniform companies. The governor could provide arms for the officers, but they were required to supply their own uniforms and horses. Not until 1873 (Chapter 202) was money appropriated from the general fund to help support militia companies. Chapter 208, Laws of 1879, changed the militia's name to the Wisconsin National Guard.

Federal supervision of and financial responsibility for the National Guard came with Congressional passage of the Dick Act in 1903. Congress passed the law in response to the lack of uniformity among state units, which became evident during the Spanish-American War and subsequent occupation of the Philippines. The act set standards for Guard units, granted federal aid, and provided for inspections by regular U.S. Army officers.

The National Defense Act of 1933 formally created the National Guard of the United States, a reserve component of the U.S. Army. The act allowed the mobilization of intact National Guard units through their simultaneous dual enlistment as state and federal military forces. This permitted Guard personnel to mobilize for federal duty directly from state status in event of a federal emergency, rather than being discharged to enlist in the federal forces, as was done in World War I. A 1990 U.S. Supreme Court case upheld the authority of the U.S. Congress to send Army National Guard units (under U.S. Army command) out of the country to train for their federal mission.

Wisconsin National Guard troops fought in the Civil War, the Spanish-American War, World War I, and World War II. Wisconsin troops from the "Iron Brigade" gained national recognition in the Civil War, and the 32nd "Red Arrow" Infantry Division won fame for its combat record in both World Wars. The Wisconsin Air National Guard became a separate service in 1947, and members of the Wisconsin Air Guard served in the Korean War. Over the past 50 years, Wisconsin units have been called to active federal service on numerous occasions. In 1961, the 32nd Division was activated during the Berlin Crisis. More than 1,400 Guard members from Wisconsin were sent to the Persian Gulf to participate in Operations Desert Shield and Desert Storm in 1990-91. Beginning in 1996, units were called to support peacekeeping efforts in the Balkans. Wisconsin Air National Guard units were deployed to enforce U.N. no-fly zones in Southwest Asia in the 1990s, and two units were called to support Operation Allied Force, the NATO air operations over Kosovo in 1999.

Within hours of the September 11, 2001, terrorist attacks on America, the Wisconsin National Guard began yet another period of extensive support to U.S. military operations. Air National Guard units in Wisconsin have provided fighter aircraft to patrol the skies over major U.S. cities and critical national infrastructure, tanker aircraft to refuel patrolling fighters and U.S. military aircraft overseas, and critical radar support to North American Aerospace Defense Command and the Federal Aviation Administration.

Wisconsin Army National Guard units began mobilizing into active federal service in December 2001. Since then, nearly every unit in the Wisconsin Army and Air National Guard has been ordered to active duty in support of operations in Afghanistan (Operation Enduring Freedom) and Iraq (Operation Iraqi Freedom and Operation New Dawn), as well as homeland defense missions in the United States (Operation Noble Eagle) and continuing operations in the Balkans. In 2009, nearly 4,000 Wisconsin Guard members deployed in support of the Global War on Terror including 3,200 members of the 32nd Infantry Brigade Combat Team who conducted the largest operational deployment of the Wisconsin National Guard since World War II. Since 2001, nearly 13,000 Wisconsin Guard members have deployed in support of the Global War on Terror.

However, while the soldiers and airmen of the state's militia continue to deploy overseas and serve in harm's way when America calls, they remain available to answer the call to service in Wisconsin and throughout the nation when a natural disaster strikes or in response to domestic emergencies. The Wisconsin National Guard has provided domestic support to the citizens of Wisconsin since the 1880s. It has assisted state and local authorities with personnel and equipment during natural disasters such as forest fires, floods, tornadoes, and snowstorms. It has also assisted local authorities in restoring order during periods of civil unrest during the late 1960s and early 1970s, as well as provided support to 25 state institutions during a state employee strike in 1977. The Wisconsin National Guard has provided assistance to other states and nations for such major catastrophic events as Hurricane Katrina and the 2010 Haiti earthquake. The most recent large-scale domestic service of the Wisconsin National Guard occurred in June 2008 when over 1,000 Wisconsin Guard members assisted state and local authorities in the response to widespread flooding across the southern part of the state.

Soldiers and Airmen from the Wisconsin National Guard work as a team to extract a patient using a special rig during a joint training exercise at the RE-ACT Center at Volk Field, Wis., on March 7, 2015. (Staff Sgt. Matthew Ard, Wisconsin National Guard)

The **Division of Emergency Management** originated as the Office of Civil Defense, which was developed to administer emergency programs in case of enemy attack and was located in the governor's office under Chapter 443, Laws of 1951. Its predecessors include the Wisconsin Council of Defense, organized by executive order of Governor Julius P. Heil in 1940, and the State Council on Civil Defense, created in the governor's office by Chapter 9, Laws of 1943. The 1943 council was abolished in 1945 and its functions transferred to the adjutant general, who was appointed director of the Office of Civil Defense by the governor, as permitted in the 1951 law.

Chapter 628, Laws of 1959, renamed the office the Bureau of Civil Defense and added responsibilities for natural and human-caused disasters. The 1967 executive branch reorganization transferred the bureau to the Department of Local Affairs and Development as the Division of Emergency Government. In Chapter 361, Laws of 1979, the division was transferred to the Department of Administration. The division became part of the Department of Military Affairs in 1989 Wisconsin Act 31 and was renamed by 1995 Wisconsin Act 247. When 1997 Wisconsin Act 27 abolished the State Emergency Response Board, the division assumed the board's responsibilities pertaining to hazardous chemical substances and spills and the contracts with regional hazardous materials response teams. Since 1997, Wisconsin Emergency Management has coordinated the state's terrorism preparedness efforts by working to deter, prevent, respond to, and recover from terrorist attacks. The Wisconsin Homeland Security Council was initially created in March 2003 (Executive Order 7) and recreated in January 2011 (Executive Order 6) to advise the governor and coordinate the efforts of state and local officials regarding the prevention of, and response to, potential threats to the homeland security of the state.

Department of
NATURAL RESOURCES

Address e-mail by combining the user ID and the state extender: userid**@wisconsin.gov**
All telephone numbers are 608 area code unless otherwise indicated.

Natural Resources Board: PRESTON COLE (southern member), *chairperson;* TERRY N. HILGENBERG (northern member), *vice chairperson;* GREGORY KAZMIERSKI (southern member), *secretary;* FREDERICK PREHN, GARY ZIMMER (northern members); JULIE ANDERSON (southern member), WILLIAM BRUINS (at-large member). (All are appointed by governor with senate consent.)

Secretary of Natural Resources: CATHY L. STEPP, 267-7556, DNRSecretary@

Deputy Secretary: KURT THIEDE, 266-5833, kurt.thiede@

Assistant Deputy Secretary: MICHAEL BRUHN, 266-5375, michael.bruhn@

Legislative and Policy Advisor: vacancy.

Legislative Liaison: TIM GARY, 266-2120, timothy.gary@

Legal Services, Bureau of: TIMOTHY A. ANDRYK, *director,* 264-9228, tim.andryk@

Communication, Office of: WILLIAM COSH, *director,* 267-2773, william.cosh@

Business Support and Sustainability, Office of: MARK AQUINO, *director,* 275-3262, mark.aquino@

    Energy, Transportation and Environmental Analysis, Bureau of: DAVID R. SIEBERT, *director,* 264-6048, david.siebert@

    Science Services, Bureau of: JOHN R. SULLIVAN, *director,* 267-9753, john.r.sullivan@

Law Enforcement, Bureau of: TODD SCHALLER, *director and chief warden,* 264-6133, todd.schaller@; KARL BROOKS, *deputy chief warden,* 266-7820, karl.brooks@

Mailing Address: P.O. Box 7921, Madison 53707-7921.

Location: State Natural Resources Building (GEF 2), 101 South Webster Street, Madison.

Telephones: Customer and General Information: (888) WDNRINFO (936-7463) or (608) 266-2621; Violation Hotline (to confidentially report suspected wildlife, recreational, and environmental violations): (800) TIP-WDNR (847-9367) or #367 by cellular phone; Hazardous Substance Spill Line: (800) 943-0003; Outdoor Report (recorded message): (608) 266-2277; Daily Air Quality: (866) 324-5924; Gypsy Moth: (800) 642-6684; Emerald Ash Borer: (800) 462-2803; Firewood: (877) 303-9663; Burning Permits (888) WIS-BURN (947-2876).

TTY: Access via relay 711.

Internet Address: dnr.wi.gov

Air, Waste, and Remediation & Redevelopment, Division of: PAT STEVENS, *administrator,* 264-9210, pat.stevens@; BART SPONSELLER, *deputy administrator,* 264-8537, bart.sponseller@

Air Management, Bureau of: BART SPONSELLER, *director,* 267-8537, bart.sponseller@

Remediation and Redevelopment, Bureau for: MARK F. GIESFELDT, *director,* 267-7562, mark.giesfeldt@

Waste and Materials Management, Bureau of: ANN COAKLEY, *director,* 261-8449, ann.coakley@

Customer and Employee Services, Division of: DIANE BROOKBANK, *administrator,* 266-2241, diane.brookbank@; MICHELE YOUNG, *deputy administrator,* 266-7566, michele.young@

   Community Financial Assistance, Bureau of: MARY ROSE TEVES, *director,* 267-7683, mary.teves@

   Customer Service and Outreach, Bureau of: vacancy, *director,* 267-7799.

   Finance, Bureau of: TIMOTHY SELL, *acting director,* 267-9601, timothy.sell@

   Human Resources, Bureau of: AMBER PASSNO, *director,* 266-6999, amber.passno@

   Management and Budget, Bureau of: JOSEPH POLASEK, *director,* 266-2794, joseph.polasek@

   Technology Services, Bureau of: DEBRA HANRAHAN, *director,* 261-2951, debra.hanrahan@

Forestry, Division of: PAUL DELONG, *administrator and State Forester,* 264-9224, paul.delong@; DARRELL E. ZASTROW, *deputy administrator,* 266-0290, darrell.zastrow@

   Forest Management, Bureau of: vacancy, *director,* 266-1727.

   Forest Protection, Bureau of: TRENT L. MARTY, *director,* 266-7978, trent.marty@

   Forestry Business Services, Bureau of: WENDY M. MCCOWN, *director,* 266-7510, wendy. mccown@

Land, Division of: SANJAY OLSON, *administrator,* 261-6453, sanjay.olson@; ERIN CRAIN, *deputy administrator,* 267-7479, erin.crain@

   Endangered Resources, Bureau of: vacancy, *director.*

   Facilities and Lands, Bureau of: STEVEN W. MILLER, *director,* 266-5782, steven.miller@

   Parks and Recreation, Bureau of: vacancy, *director,* 266-2185.

   Wildlife Management, Bureau of: THOMAS M. HAUGE, *director,* 266-2193, tom.hauge@

Water, Division of: RUSSELL A. RASMUSSEN, *administrator,* 267-7651, russell.rasmussen@

   Drinking Water and Groundwater, Bureau of: JILL D. JONAS, *director,* 267-7545, jill.jonas@

   Fisheries Management, Bureau of: vacancy, *director,* 267-0796.

   Great Lakes, Office of: STEVE GALARNEAU, *director,* 266-1956, steven.galarneau@

   Water Quality, Bureau of: SUSAN SYLVESTER, *director,* 266-1099, susan.sylvester@

   Watershed Management, Bureau of: PAM BIERSACH, *director,* 261-8447, pamela.biersach@

Field Regions:

   Northeast: JEAN ROMBACK-BARTELS, *director,* (920) 662-5114, 2984 Shawano Avenue, Green Bay 54313-6727, jean.rombackbartels@

   Northern: JOHN F. GOZDZIALSKI, *director,* (715) 635-4002, 810 West Maple Street, Spooner 54801; Co-regional office: (715) 369-8900, 107 Sutliff Avenue, Rhinelander 54501, john.gozdzialski@

   Southeast: ERIC NITSCHKE, *director,* (414) 263-8570, 2300 North Dr. Martin Luther King Jr. Drive, Milwaukee 53212, eric.nitschke@

   Southern: vacancy, *director,* (608) 275-3262, 3911 Fish Hatchery Road, Fitchburg 53711.

   West Central: DAN BAUMANN, *director,* (715) 839-3722, 1300 West Clairemont Avenue, Eau Claire 54702, dan.baumann@

Publications: *Wisconsin Natural Resources* (bimonthly magazine by subscription – call (608) 267-7410 or (800) 678-9472); parks newspapers and visitor guides; hunting, fishing, trapping, snowmobiling, ATV, and boating regulations; various brochures, fact sheets, and reports (lists available). Teachers may write to the Office of Communication for a list of publications. Individuals may subscribe to receive weekly

DEPARTMENT OF NATURAL RESOURCES

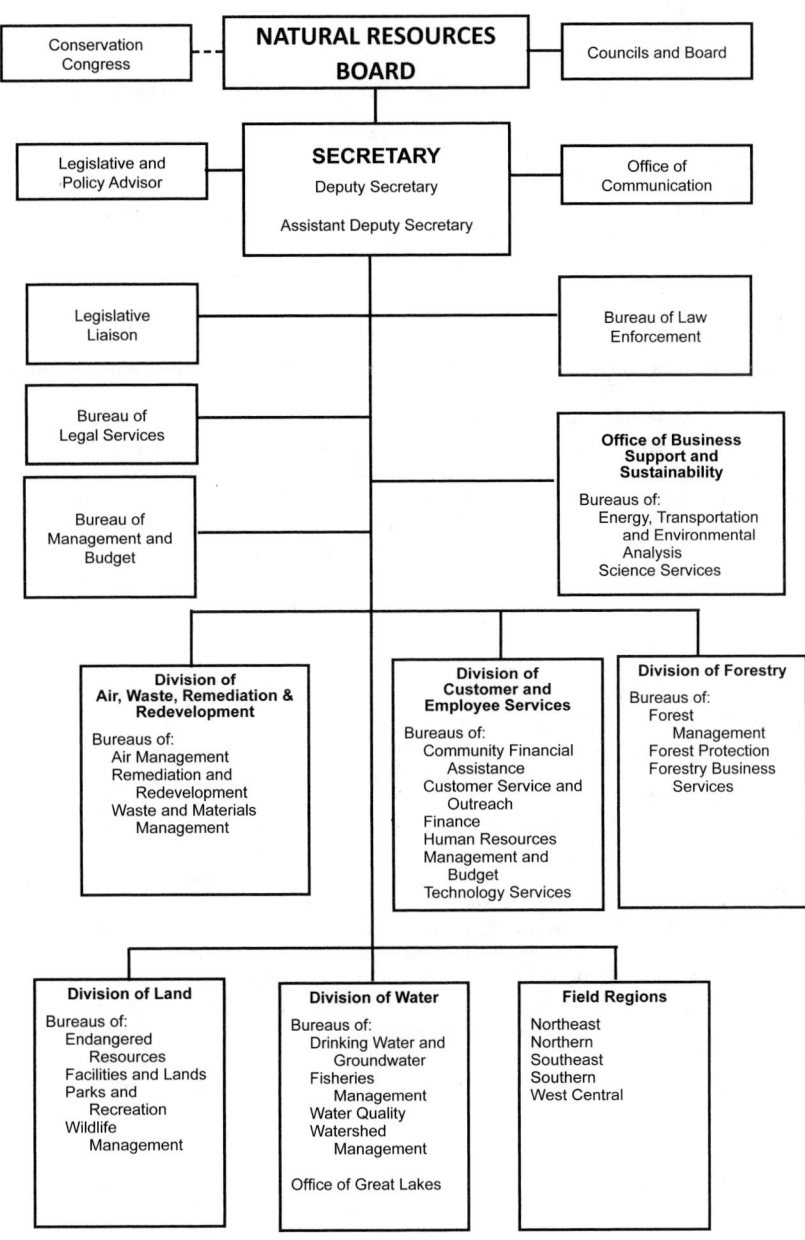

Conservation Congress

NATURAL RESOURCES BOARD

Councils and Board

Legislative and Policy Advisor

SECRETARY
Deputy Secretary
Assistant Deputy Secretary

Office of Communication

Legislative Liaison

Bureau of Law Enforcement

Bureau of Legal Services

Bureau of Management and Budget

Office of Business Support and Sustainability

Bureaus of:
Energy, Transportation and Environmental Analysis
Science Services

Division of Air, Waste, Remediation & Redevelopment

Bureaus of:
Air Management
Remediation and Redevelopment
Waste and Materials Management

Division of Customer and Employee Services

Bureaus of:
Community Financial Assistance
Customer Service and Outreach
Finance
Human Resources
Management and Budget
Technology Services

Division of Forestry

Bureaus of:
Forest Management
Forest Protection
Forestry Business Services

Division of Land

Bureaus of:
Endangered Resources
Facilities and Lands
Parks and Recreation
Wildlife Management

Division of Water

Bureaus of:
Drinking Water and Groundwater
Fisheries Management
Water Quality
Watershed Management

Office of Great Lakes

Field Regions

Northeast
Northern
Southeast
Southern
West Central

Units attached for administrative purposes under Sec. 15.03: Groundwater Coordinating Council
Invasive Species Council
Lake Michigan Commercial Fishing Board
Lake Superior Commercial Fishing Board
Council on Recycling
Wisconsin Waterways Commission

e-mail links to the DNR Weekly News, DNR Outdoor Report, and other topics at: dnr.wi.gov Search: news.

Number of Employees: 2,642.04.

Total Budget 2013-15: $1,146,017,900.

Statutory References: Sections 15.05 (1) (c), 15.34, and 15.343; Chapters 23, 26-33, 87, 88, and 160.

Agency Responsibility: The Department of Natural Resources (DNR) is responsible for implementing state and federal laws that protect and enhance Wisconsin's natural resources, including its air, land, water, forests, wildlife, fish, and plants. It coordinates the many state-administered programs that protect the environment and provides a full range of outdoor recreational opportunities for Wisconsin residents and visitors.

Organization: The 7 members of the Natural Resources Board serve staggered 6-year terms. At least 3 of them must be from the northern part of the state and at least 3 from the southern part. Effective May 1, 2017, at least one member is required to have an agricultural background, and at least 3 members must have held an annual hunting, fishing, or trapping license in at least 7 of the 10 years previous to being nominated. Board members are subject to restrictions on holding DNR permits or depending on permit holders for a significant portion of their income. The board directs and supervises the department and acts as a formal point of contact for citizens.

The department is administered by a secretary appointed by the governor with the advice and consent of the senate. The secretary appoints the department's division administrators from outside the classified service. The regional directors, who are appointed from the classified service, manage all of the agency's field operations for their respective areas and report directly to the secretary.

Unit Functions: The *Office of Business Support and Sustainability*, in the secretary's office, is made up of two bureaus that focus on proactive business support, cross-agency coordination with other state agencies, organizational effectiveness, and applied science to support agency decisions. The Bureau of Environmental Analysis and Sustainability (EAS) is responsible for coordinating the regulatory review for all energy and transportation projects statewide, coordinating Wisconsin Environmental Policy Act review and analysis activities for all permit, planning and policy actions of the agency, promoting beyond compliance companies through the flagship Green Tier program and other outreach, serving as proactive business sector specialists working with businesses and associations on environmental performance programs and new projects, and providing outreach through the Small Business Environmental Assistance program. The Bureau of Science Services provides applied scientific research and environmental analyses to inform agency policy and operational decisions on natural resource issues. The program also provides quality laboratory services (analytical chemistry and biological) through the Wisconsin State Laboratory of Hygiene and other private contract laboratories.

The *Bureau of Law Enforcement,* in the secretary's office, is responsible for enforcement of the state's conservation, hunting, fishing, environmental, and recreational safety laws. Enforcement staff promote safety and compliance with the law through enforcement and educational outreach programs, including classes in hunting, boating, snowmobile and all-terrain vehicle safety, and community involvement programs such as the Learn to Hunt Program. The bureau provides assistance in response, recovery, and mitigation of natural or human made disasters or emergency situations, such as floods, high winds, wildfires, dam outages, spills, and disruption of services.

The *Division of Air, Waste, and Remediation & Redevelopment* protects the state's air quality and general environmental health through air pollution control, cleanup and redevelopment of contaminated property, and solid and hazardous waste management in cooperation with the federal Environmental Protection Agency, international agencies, local governments, private industry, and citizens. It develops air quality implementation plans, monitors air quality, conducts inspections, operates a permit program, and initiates compliance actions in accordance with state and federal requirements. The division's waste and materials management program implements Wisconsin's waste management laws to help ensure adequate waste treatment and disposal capacity for Wisconsin citizens and businesses; efficiently regulates waste, materials, and mining facilities to minimize their impact on human health and the environment; implements waste and recycling laws to minimize waste, conserve energy, and make productive use of material resources; and ensures Wisconsin citizens and businesses have the knowledge, opportunity, and mechanisms to safely and economically minimize, reuse, recycle, manage, and dispose of the waste and materials/byproducts they generate. The division's remediation and redevelopment program is responsible for the cleanup and redevelopment of contaminated sites that fall under the following legislation: the hazardous substances spills law, the environmental repair law, the abandoned container law, the federal Superfund and Brownfields laws, the state land recycling law, and the Resource Conservation and Recovery Act. The remediation and redevelopment program also responds to emergency contamination incidents.

The *Division of Customer and Employee Services* provides a variety of customer services including the sale of hunting and fishing licenses, boat, ATV, and snowmobile registration, environmental education programs, and public information. It oversees distribution of financial aids for environmental programs that benefit local governments and nonprofit conservation organizations, such as the Clean Water Fund and the Stewardship Fund, and acts as liaison to federal and state agencies. The division also provides a variety of management services for the department, including budgetary and financial services, personnel and human resource management, computer and information technology support, affirmative action, employee assistance, training, and telecommunication services.

The *Division of Forestry,* created by 1999 Wisconsin Act 9, is responsible for the administration and implementation of programs that protect and manage the state's forest resources in a sustainable manner so as to provide economic, ecological, social, recreational, and cultural benefits. The division is involved with the management of about 17 million acres of public and private forest land and millions of urban trees in the state. All of the 1.5 million acres of DNR state land were certified by 2009 as sustainably managed by third party auditors from the Forest Stewardship Council® (FSC) and Sustainable Forestry Initiative® (SFI). More than 2.35 million acres of county forest lands, which DNR works in partnership with 29 counties to manage, were certified in 2005, as were almost 2 million acres of private lands managed under the Managed Forest Law program. By 2014, 6.5 million acres of state, county, and private forests were certified to the FSC®, SFI®, or American Tree Farm System. Foresters provide assistance to private woodlot owners; offer expertise in urban forestry; manage and monitor forest insects and diseases; operate a tree nursery; provide public education and awareness activities; and work in partnership with local governments, the timber industry, environmental groups, and recreation interests. The division administers grants and loans to county forests, urban forestry grants to communities, forest landowner grants to woodland owners, and forest fire protection grants to fire departments. The fire management program is responsible for forest fire protection on 18 million acres of forest, brush, and grassland and coordinates with local fire departments to prevent and control forest fires.

The *Division of Land* has major responsibility for protecting and conserving the state's biological diversity and providing nature-based recreational opportunities. The division administers programs related to wildlife; state lands, parks, trails, southern forests, and recreation areas; rare and endangered animal and plant species, and natural communities; and outdoor recreational resources. The division operates educational programs and helps private landowners manage their lands for the benefit of wildlife and rare resources. It manages wildlife and habitats on about 1.5 million acres of land owned or leased by the state and works with federal, county, and other local government authorities to protect and manage the resources on an additional 3.6 million acres of public lands, including national and county forests. The wildlife program manages populations such as deer, bear, furbearers, waterfowl and birds, and maintains and restores habitats such as wetlands, grasslands, and prairies. The natural heritage conservation program conserves Wisconsin's rare and declining species and natural communities through the State Natural Areas program and the species management program work that is supported primarily by funds derived from voluntary contributions designated by taxpayers on their state income tax returns and through purchase of the Endangered Resources license plate. The natural heritage conservation program also supports ecosystem management decision-making and program integration in the department through the Citizen-Based Monitoring Program, the Natural Heritage

Inventory Program, and the Aquatic and Terrestrial Resources inventory. Parks personnel manage the state's extensive parks, southern forests, recreation areas, and trails systems, including the Ice Age and North Country National Scenic Trails, which are designed for the conservation of natural resources and a wide variety of recreational activities including biking, hiking, snowmobiling, and camping. The division is also responsible for land acquisition for parks, trails, southern forests, recreation areas, wildlife areas, fishery areas, natural areas, and other state wildlife-related recreation lands, as well as property planning and the development of public use facilities on state lands. It coordinates the Stewardship Program, which provides grants for the purchase of lands for natural and recreational areas, wildlife habitats, urban green spaces, local parks, trails, and riverways.

The *Division of Water* works with many partners to protect public health and safety, and the quality and quantity of Wisconsin's groundwater, surface water, and aquatic ecosystems. The division is responsible for implementing the Clean Water Act in order to achieve the goal of fishable and swimmable waters throughout Wisconsin. Division staff works to prevent or regulate water pollution from industries, municipal sewage treatment facilities, construction sites, large farms, and urban areas. The division monitors compliance, sets water quality standards, and provides financial and technical assistance. Division programs protect drinking water and groundwater resources for both human and ecosystem health, and ensure the safety and security of the state's drinking water systems and private wells. The division strives to enhance and restore outstanding fisheries in Wisconsin's waters. It regulates sport and commercial fishing through licensing and provides fish hatchery services, fish stocking and surveying, aquatic habit improvement, angler education, and public access programs. The division helps protect the waters of the state that are held in trust for all the people of the state through the Public Trust Doctrine. Division staff oversees the placement of structures in state waters, wetland management and restoration, shoreland zoning, and floodplain management. The division helps local government units to protect lives and property through floodplain management and dam safety inspections. The division cooperates with many states and Canada to protect the water quality, quantity, and ecosystems of the Mississippi River and Great Lakes basins. The division also houses the Office of Great Lakes, which is responsible for restoring five designated Areas of Concern (AOC) in and along the Great Lakes.

The *Field Regions* enable the department to make its programs accessible to the general public. (Most DNR field staff work within county assignments.) This structure combines employees with different types of expertise into interdisciplinary teams responsible for assessing natural resource and environmental needs from a broader perspective.

History: Today, the Department of Natural Resources has dual responsibility for both traditional conservation duties and environmental protection. Its history and structure reflect more than a century of government and citizen involvement with these concerns. Wisconsin's earliest conservation legislation focused on fish, game, and forests. Chapter 253, Laws of 1874, created a Board of Fish Commissioners charged with hatching fish eggs received from the federal government and distributing the fry to Wisconsin waters. The governor was authorized in 1885 by Chapter 455 to appoint 3 fish wardens to enforce fishing regulations and collect statistics from commercial fishermen. Chapter 456, Laws of 1887, directed the governor to appoint 4 game wardens to enforce all laws protecting fish and game.

Chapter 229, Laws of 1897, established a 3-member commission to develop legislation creating a forestry department. The commission was directed to devise ways to use the state's forest resources without harming the climate or water supplies and to preserve forest resources without retarding the state's economic development. The report of this commission led to Chapter 450, Laws of 1903, which established a Department of State Forestry with a superintendent appointed by the Board of State Forest Commissioners. Chapter 495, Laws of 1907, created a State Park Board with authority to acquire and manage land for park purposes.

Chapter 406, Laws of 1915, consolidated all park and conservation functions under a 3-member Conservation Commission of Wisconsin, appointed by the governor with senate approval. From then until 1995, the management and conservation of Wisconsin's natural resources was directed by a part-time commission or board, except for the period 1923 to 1927, when a single full-time commissioner was created by Chapter 118, Laws of 1923, to head the Department of

Conservation. Since the enactment of 1995 Wisconsin Act 27, which provided that the secretary would be appointed by the governor with senate consent rather than appointed by the board, the current board's role has been an advisory one.

The 1960s saw major changes in conservation legislation. Chapter 427, Laws of 1961, created a committee charged with developing a long-range plan for acquiring and improving outdoor recreation areas. It initiated the Outdoor Recreation Act Program (ORAP) to fund land acquisitions. In 1969, Chapter 353 expanded ORAP and authorized the state to incur debt up to $56 million between 1969 and 1981 for the purpose of providing outdoor recreation opportunities. With enactment of 1989 Wisconsin Act 31, the legislature created the Stewardship Program, which authorized up to $250 million in state debt to acquire and develop land for recreational uses, wildlife habitats, fisheries, and natural areas.

Wisconsin's antipollution efforts date back to Chapter 412, Laws of 1911, when the legislature gave the State Board of Health investigative powers in water pollution cases. Prior to that, such investigations were primarily the responsibility of local government. In Chapter 264, Laws of 1927, the legislature created a committee to supervise the water pollution control activities carried out by several state agencies, including the Conservation Commission. The Department of Resource Development, which had been created by Chapter 442, Laws of 1959, assumed water pollution control duties under Chapter 614, Laws of 1965, and statewide air pollution regulation with Chapter 83, Laws of 1967.

In the 1967 executive branch reorganization, the legislature created the Department of Natural Resources by combining the Department of Conservation and the Department of Resource Development. The new department was given authority to regulate air and water quality, as well as solid waste disposal, and directed to develop an integrated program to protect air, land, and water resources.

Chapter 274, Laws of 1971, required all state agencies to report on the environmental impacts of proposed actions that could significantly affect environmental quality. Chapter 275, Laws of 1971, provided for state protection of endangered fish and wildlife, and Chapter 370, Laws of 1977, placed nongame species and endangered wild plants under state protection. A program protecting surface waters from nonpoint source pollution was created by Chapter 418, Laws of 1977, and a groundwater protection program, based on numerical standards for polluting substances, was created by 1983 Wisconsin Act 410. In Wisconsin Act 335, the 1989 Legislature made major changes in the laws governing recycling, source reduction, and disposal of solid wastes.

Statutory Board and Councils

Dry Cleaner Environmental Response Council: BRETT DONALDSON, RICHARD W. KLINKE, THOMAS MCKAY (representing dry cleaning operations); KEVIN BRADEN (wholesale distributor of dry cleaning solvent); JEANNE TARVIN (engineer, professional geologist, hydrologist, or soil scientist); JIM FITZGERALD (manufacturer or seller of dry cleaning equipment) (appointed by governor).

The 6-member Dry Cleaner Environmental Response Council advises the department on matters related to the Dry Cleaner Environmental Response Program, which is administered by DNR and provides awards to dry cleaning establishments for assistance in the investigation and cleanup of environmental contamination. Council members are appointed for staggered 3-year terms. The council, which is scheduled to sunset on June 30, 2032, was created by 1997 Wisconsin Act 27, as amended by 1997 Wisconsin Act 300 and by 2013 Wisconsin Act 69. Its composition and duties are prescribed in Sections 15.347 (2) and 292.65 (13) of the statutes.

Council on Forestry: PAUL DELONG (chief state forester); SENATORS TIFFANY, vacancy; REPRESENTATIVES MURSAU, vacancy; TOM HITTLE (forest products company which owns and manages large forest land tracts representative); RICHARD WEDEPOHL (owners of nonindustrial, private forest land representative); JANE SEVERT (counties containing county forests representative); JIM HOPPE (paper and pulp industry representative); TROY BROWN (lumber industry representative); MATT DALLMAN (nonprofit conservation organization representative); KIMBERLY QUAST (forester who provides consultation services); MARK RICKENBACH (school of forestry representative); vacancy (conservation education representative); vacancy (forestry-affiliated labor union representative); ALLISON BRUCE (urban and community forestry representative); JAMES KERKMAN (Society of American Foresters representative); HENRY SCHIENBECK (timber producer organization representative); VIRGIL WAUGH (secondary wood industry representative); PAUL STRONG (nonvoting member, Federal Department of Agriculture representative).

The 20-member Council on Forestry advises the governor, the legislature, the Department of Natural Resources, and other state agencies on topics relating to forestry in Wisconsin including: protection from fire, insects, and disease; sustainable forestry; reforestation and forestry genetics; management and protection of urban forests; increasing the public's knowledge and awareness of forestry issues; forestry research; economic development and marketing of forestry products; legislation affecting forestry; and staff and funding needs for forestry programs. The council shall submit a biennial report on the status of the state's forestry resources and industry to the governor and the appropriate standing committees of the legislature by June 1 of each odd-numbered year. All members are appointed by the governor. Lengths of terms are not specified by law. The council was created by 2001 Wisconsin Act 109. Its composition and duties are prescribed in Sections 15.347 (19) and 26.02 of the statutes.

Managed Forest Land Board.

The 5-member Managed Forest Land Board administers the program established by the Department of Natural Resources to award grants to nonprofit conservation organizations, to local governmental units, and to the department to acquire land, including conservations easements on land, to be used for hunting, fishing, hiking, sightseeing, and cross-country skiing. The department consults with the board to promulgate administrative rules establishing requirements for awarding grants. Appointed board members serve 3-year terms. The board was created by 2007 Wisconsin Act 20, and its composition and duties are prescribed in Sections 15.345 (6) and 77.895 of the statutes.

Metallic Mining Council: Inactive.

The 9-member Metallic Mining Council advises the department on matters relating to the reclamation of mined land. Its members are appointed by the secretary of natural resources for staggered 3-year terms, and they are expected to represent "a variety and balance of economic, scientific, and environmental viewpoints." The council was created by Chapter 377, Laws of 1977, and its composition and duties are prescribed in Sections 15.347 (12) and 289.08 of the statutes.

Milwaukee River Revitalization Council: Inactive.

The 13-member Milwaukee River Revitalization Council advises the legislature, governor, and department on matters related to environmental, recreational, and economic revitalization of the Milwaukee River Basin, and it assists local governments in planning and implementing projects. It is also responsible for developing and implementing a plan that encourages multiple recreational, entrepreneurial, and cultural activities along the streams of the Milwaukee River Basin. Its 11 appointed members serve 3-year terms. Each of the priority watersheds in the basin must be represented by at least one council member. The council was created by 1987 Wisconsin Act 399, and its composition and duties are prescribed in Sections 15.347 (15) and 23.18 of the statutes.

Natural Areas Preservation Council: JAMES P. BENNETT (representing University of Wisconsin System, appointed by board of regents), *chairperson;* JAMES W. PERRY (appointed by council of the Wisconsin Academy of Sciences, Arts and Letters), *vice chairperson;* ERIN E. CRAIN (representing Department of Natural Resources, appointed by the board of natural resources), *secretary;* ERIC M. ANDERSON, THOMAS L. EDDY (appointed by council of the Wisconsin Academy of Sciences, Arts and Letters); DAVID W. SAMPLE (representing Department of Natural Resources, appointed by the board of natural resources); KENNETH R. BRADBURY, SHARON L. DUNWOODY, PATRICK ROBINSON (representing University of Wisconsin System, appointed by board of regents); VICTORIA J. RYDBERG (representing the Department of Public Instruction, appointed by the state superintendent of public instruction); ELLEN CENSKY (representing Milwaukee Public Museum, appointed by MPM board of directors).

The 11-member Natural Areas Preservation Council advises the department on matters pertaining to the protection of natural areas that contain native biotic communities and habitats for rare species. It also makes recommendations about gifts or purchases for the state natural areas system. The council was created by Chapter 566, Laws of 1951, as the State Board for Preservation of Scientific Areas. It was renamed the Scientific Areas Preservation Council in Chapter 327, Laws of 1961, and given its current name in 1985 Wisconsin Act 29. One of the appointments from the Wisconsin Academy of Sciences, Arts and Letters must represent private colleges in the state. Its composition and duties are prescribed in Sections 15.347 (4) and 23.26 of the statutes.

Nonmotorized Recreation and Transportation Trails Council: ROD BARTLOW, WILLIAM HAUDA, DANA JOHNSON, ANNE MURPHY, JOEL PATENAUDE, DEBBIE PETERSON, DAVID PHILLIPS, GEOFFREY SNUDDEN, BLAKE THIESEN (appointed by governor).

The Nonmotorized Recreation and Transportation Trails Council carries out studies and advises the governor, the legislature, and the Department of Natural Resources and the Department of Transportation on matters related to nonmotorized recreation and transportation trails. The size of the council is not specified. Council members are appointed by the governor to serve at the pleasure of the governor. Membership is to represent geographic diversity and to consist of those who personally undertake nonmotorized activities or who participate in organizations that own or maintain nonmotorized trails or that promote nonmotorized trail activities. Members should be appointed to represent as many as possible of the following groups: pedestrians; persons who represent local forests or parks; persons who are interested in tourism promotion; persons who represent tribal lands; persons with physical disabilities; persons who engage in nature-based activities such as bird watching, nature study, hunting, and fishing; and persons

On June 6, 2015, National Trails Day, Wisconsin celebrated the 50th anniversary of the rails to trails program in the state. Wisconsin was the first state to convert an abandoned railroad corridor into a recreational trail – the Elroy-Sparta State Trail – in 1965. Since then, Wisconsin has developed an additional 40 state trails (36 of them rail trails) extending more than 2,000 miles. Fifty riders starting from each of the five communities along the trail joined a celebratory ride to a rededication of the trail at the historic depot and trail headquarters in Kendall. (Department of Natural Resources)

who engage in activities on water trails, horseback riding or buggy driving, long-distance hiking, snow sports, and bicycling. The council was created by 2009 Wisconsin Act 394 and its composition and duties are prescribed in Sections 15.347 (20) and 23.177 of the statutes.

Off-Road Vehicle Council: Rob McConnell, *chairperson;* Dave Traczyk, *vice chairperson;* Adam Harden, Bryan Much, Ernie Pulvermacher, Bill Schumann, Jim Wisneski (appointed by governor).

The 7-member Off-Road Vehicle Council advises the Department of Natural Resources, the Department of Transportation, the governor, and the legislature on all matters relating to all-terrain vehicle trails and routes. Council members are appointed by the governor for staggered 3-year terms ending on March 1. Each member shall be a member and represent the interests of an all-terrain vehicle or utility terrain vehicle user's group and be knowledgeable about outdoor recreation issues in Wisconsin. The council was created by 2013 Wisconsin Act 16 and its composition and duties are prescribed in Sections 15.347 (9) and 23.178 of the statutes.

Small Business Environmental Council: vacancy (appointed by senate president); Richard Klinke (appointed by assembly speaker); Shane Lauterbach (appointed by senate minority leader); Vince Ruffolo (appointed by assembly minority leader); Mark Aquino (appointed by secretary of natural resources); Andre Jacque, Amy Litscher, J.D. Tripoli (representing general public and appointed by governor).

The 8-member Small Business Environmental Council advises the Department of Natural Resources on the effectiveness of assistance programs to small businesses that enable them to comply with the federal Clean Air Act. It also advises on the fairness and effectiveness of air pollution rules promulgated by the Department of Natural Resources and the U.S. Environmental Protection Agency regarding the impact on small businesses. Members are appointed to 3-year terms. The 4 members appointed by legislative officers must own or represent owners of small business stationary air pollution sources. The 3 members appointed by the governor may not own or represent small business stationary sources. The council was created by 1991 Wisconsin Act 302, and it was transferred from the Department of Commerce to the Department of Natural Resources by 2011 Wisconsin Act 32. Its composition and duties are prescribed in Sections 15.347 (8) and 285.795 of the statutes.

Snowmobile Recreational Council: Beverly Dittmar (northern representative), *chairperson;* Larry Erickson (northern representative), *vice chairperson;* Gary Hilgendorf, Robert Lang, Andrew Malecki, Jr., Dale Mayo, Steve Moran, Dave Newman, Michelle Voight (northern representatives); Thomas Chwala, Matt Harter, Mike Holden, Samuel Landes, Dan Timmerman, Lee Van Zeeland (southern representatives). (All are appointed by governor with senate consent.)

The 15-member Snowmobile Recreational Council carries out studies and makes recommendations to the governor, the legislature, and the Department of Natural Resources and the Department of Transportation regarding all matters affecting snowmobiling. Council members are appointed for staggered 3-year terms. At least 5 must represent the northern part of the state, and at least 5 must represent the southern part. The council was created by Chapter 277, Laws of 1971, and its composition and duties are prescribed in Sections 15.347 (7) and 350.14 of the statutes.

Sporting Heritage Council: Kurt Thiede (designated by secretary of natural resources), *chairperson;* William Torhorst (appointed by governor); Senators Tiffany, Wirch; Representatives Milroy, vacancy; Ralph Fritsch (representing deer hunters); Mike Rogers (representing bear hunters); Mark LaBarbera (representing bird hunters); Benjamin Gruber (representing anglers); Scott Zimmerman (representing furbearing animal hunters and trappers); Rob Bohmann (Conservation Congress member).

The 12-member Sporting Heritage Council advises the governor, the legislature, and the natural resources board about issues relating to hunting, trapping, fishing, and other types of outdoor recreation activities, including ways improve the recruitment and retention of hunters, trappers, and anglers; to improve the management and protection of natural resources; ways to promote and implement youth outdoor recreation activities; and ways to improve access to public and private land and lakes. It is required to submit a biennial report on the status of the recruitment and retention of hunters, trappers, and anglers to the governor, the legislature, and the chairperson of the natural resources board by July 1 of each even-numbered year. Five members are appointed by the natural resources board from nominations provided by sporting organizations that have as their primary objective the promotion of hunting, fishing, or trapping, with one member each representing the interests of deer hunters, bear hunters, bird hunters, anglers, and furbearing animal hunters and trappers. Members other than the secretary of natural resources (or designee) are appointed for 3-year terms. The council was created by 2011 Wisconsin Act 168 and its composition and duties are prescribed in Sections 15.347 (21) and 29.036 of the statutes.

State Trails Council: Bryan Much, *chairperson;* John Siegert, *vice chairperson;* Luana Schneider, *secretary;* Randy Harden, Doug Johnson, Phil Johnsrud, Mike McFadzen, Ken Neitzke, Robbie Webber, James White, vacancy (appointed by governor).

The 11-member State Trails Council advises the department about the planning, acquisition, development, and management of state trails. Its members are appointed for 4-year terms. It was created by 1989 Wisconsin Act 31, and its composition and duties are prescribed in Sections 15.347 (16) and 23.175 (2) (c) of the statutes. 2011 Wisconsin Act 104 added two members and required that they be knowledgeable, and engage in, one or more of the various recreational uses of trails.

Independent Organization — Conservation Congress

Conservation Congress Executive Council: Rick Olson, Joe Weiss (District 1); Allan Brown, David Larson (District 2); Ed Choinski, Mike Riggle (District 3); Bob Ellingson, Ronn Krueger, Sr. (District 4); Kevin Smaby, Al Suchla (District 5); Stan Brownell, Scott Pitta (District 6); Dale Maas, Arlyn Splitt (District 7); Larry Bonde, Staush Gruszynski (District 8); Lee Fahrney, Mike Rogers (District 9); Jayne Meyer, Ken Risley (District 10); Robert Bohmann, Allen Shook (District 11); Jacob Janowski, Adam Kassulke (District 12).

The Conservation Congress is a 360-member publicly elected citizen advisory group, and its 24-member executive council advises the Natural Resources Board on all matters under the board's jurisdiction. The Conservation Congress is organized into 12 districts statewide. Each district elects 2 members to one-year terms on the executive council. The congress originated in 1934 and received statutory recognition in Chapter 179, Laws of 1971. Its duties are prescribed in Section 15.348 of the statutes.

Advisory Units Authorized by Section 15.04 (1)(c) of the Statutes

Fire Department Advisory Council.

The Fire Department Advisory Council (FDAC) was chartered in 1994 as an official advisory council to the state forester. The purpose of the FDAC is to strengthen partnerships between the Department of Natural Resources and the rural fire service in Wisconsin. The FDAC advises and assists the state forester on operational issues related to the department's forest fire management program to provide for an effective rural community fire protection program. In addition, the FDAC provides fundamental guidance on the Forest Fire Protection Grant administration. Membership of the FDAC includes 12 members reflecting diverse statewide geographic representation appointed by the department secretary. All levels of forest fire protection are represented (intensive, extensive, cooperative) along with representatives of the Wisconsin State Firefighter's Association and the Wisconsin Fire Chief's Association.

Urban Forestry Council.

The 28-member Urban Forestry Council is composed of at least 21 appointed, voting members, and 4 *ex officio* nonvoting members. The council advises the state forester and the Department of Natural Resources on the best ways to preserve, protect, expand, and improve Wisconsin's urban and community forest resources. The council gives awards for outstanding individuals, organizations, and communities that further urban forestry in Wisconsin. Members are appointed by the department secretary. Appointed council members serve 3-year terms. Council composition and duties are prescribed in the bylaws of the Wisconsin Urban Forestry Council.

INDEPENDENT UNITS ATTACHED FOR BUDGETING, PROGRAM COORDINATION, AND RELATED MANAGEMENT FUNCTIONS BY SECTION 15.03 OF THE STATUTES

GROUNDWATER COORDINATING COUNCIL

Groundwater Coordinating Council: RUSSELL RASMUSSEN (designated by secretary of natural resources), *chairperson;* vacancy (designated by secretary of safety and professional services), JOHN PETTY (designated by secretary of agriculture, trade and consumer protection), HENRY ANDERSON (designated by secretary of health services), DAN SCUDDER (designated by secretary of transportation), JAMES HURLEY (designated by president, UW System), JAMES ROBERTSON (state geologist), STEVE DIERCKS (representing governor).

Statutory References: Sections 15.347 (13) and 160.50.

Agency Responsibility: The 8-member Groundwater Coordinating Council advises state agencies on the coordination of nonregulatory programs related to groundwater management. Member agencies exchange information regarding groundwater monitoring, budgets for groundwater programs, data management, public information efforts, laboratory analyses, research, and state appropriations for research. The council reports annually to the legislature, governor, and agencies represented regarding the council's activities and recommendations and its assessment of the current state of groundwater resources and related management programs. Persons designated to serve on behalf of their agency heads must be agency employees with "sufficient authority to deploy agency resources and directly influence agency decision making." The governor's representative serves a 4-year term. The council was created by 1983 Wisconsin Act 410.

INVASIVE SPECIES COUNCIL

Invasive Species Council: JACK SULLIVAN (designated by secretary of natural resources); TRAVIS OLSON (designated by secretary of administration); BRIAN KUHN (designated by secretary of agriculture, trade and consumer protection); DANIELLE JOHNSON (designated by secretary of tourism); TODD MATHESON (designated by secretary of transportation); THOMAS BRESSNER, JAMES KERKMAN, GREGORY LONG, PATRICIA MORTON, KENNETH RAFFA, JAMES REINARTZ, PAUL SCHUMACHER (appointed by governor).

The 12-member Invasive Species Council conducts studies related to controlling invasive species and makes recommendations to the Department of Natural Resources regarding a system for classifying invasive species under the department's statewide invasive species control program and procedures for awarding grants to public and private agencies engaged in projects to control invasive species. All except *ex officio* members or their designees are appointed by the governor to 5-year terms to represent public and private interests affected by the presence of invasive species in the state. The council was created by 2001 Wisconsin Act 109. Its composition and duties are prescribed in Sections 15.347 (18) and 23.22 of the statutes.

LAKE MICHIGAN COMMERCIAL FISHING BOARD

Lake Michigan Commercial Fishing Board: CHARLES W. HENRIKSEN, RICHARD R. JOHNSON, MICHAEL LECLAIR, MARK MARICQUE, DEAN SWAER (licensed, active commercial fishers); NEIL A. SCHWARZ (licensed, active wholesale fish dealer); DAN PAWLITZKE (state citizen). (All are appointed by governor.)

Statutory References: Sections 15.345 (3) and 29.33 (7).

Agency Responsibility: The 7-member Lake Michigan Commercial Fishing Board was created by Chapter 418, Laws of 1977. Its members must live in counties contiguous to Lake Michigan. The 5 commercial fishers must represent fisheries in specific geographic areas. The board reviews applications for transfers of commercial fishing licenses between individuals, establishes criteria for allotting catch quotas to individual licensees, assigns catch quotas when the department establishes special harvest limits, and assists the department in establishing criteria for identifying inactive license holders.

LAKE SUPERIOR COMMERCIAL FISHING BOARD

Lake Superior Commercial Fishing Board: MAURINE HALVORSON, CRAIG HOOPMAN, vacancy (licensed, active commercial fishers); JEFF BODIN (licensed, active wholesale fish dealer); vacancy (state citizen). (All are appointed by governor.)

Statutory References: Sections 15.345 (2) and 29.33 (7).

Agency Responsibility: The 5-member Lake Superior Commercial Fishing Board was created by Chapter 418, Laws of 1977. Its members must live in counties contiguous to Lake Superior. The board reviews applications for transfers of commercial fishing licenses between individuals, establishes criteria for allotting catch quotas to individual licensees, assigns catch quotas when the department establishes special harvest limits, and assists the department in establishing criteria for identifying inactive license holders.

COUNCIL ON RECYCLING

Council on Recycling: JAMES BIRMINGHAM, GEORGE HAYDUCSKO, JR., CHARLES LARSCHEID, JOSEPH LIEBAU, JR., RICK MEYERS, NEIL PETERS-MICHAUD, WILLIAM WALTZ (appointed by governor).

Statutory References: Sections 15.347 (17) and 159.22.

Agency Responsibility: The 7 members of the Council on Recycling are appointed to 4-year terms that coincide with that of the governor. The council, which was created by 1989 Wisconsin Act 335, promotes implementation of the state's solid waste reduction, recovery, and recycling programs; helps public agencies coordinate programs and exchange information; advises state agencies about creating administrative rules and establishing priorities for market

Wisconsin is a national and international leader in sturgeon protection, restoration, and research, a reputation built since Wisconsin started regulating sturgeon harvest on the Winnebago system in 1903. Here state fisheries biologists inject an electronic microchip, called PIT tag, into fish DNR collects during spring spawning surveys on the Wolf River. The information gathered through this modern tagging technique allows DNR to more easily and accurately track individual fish and their age, key information to calculate growth, mortality and exploitation rates, and other vital information for sound management. (Department of Natural Resources)

development; and advises the DNR and the UW System about education and research related to solid waste recycling. The council also promotes a regional and interstate marketing system for recycled materials and reports to the legislature about market development and research to encourage recycling. The council advises the department about statewide public information activities and advises the governor and the legislature.

WISCONSIN WATERWAYS COMMISSION

Wisconsin Waterways Commission: James F. Rooney (Lake Michigan area), *chairperson;* Roger Walsh (inland area), *vice chairperson;* David Kedrowski (Lake Superior area), Maureen Kinney (Mississippi River area), Lee Van Zeeland (Lake Winnebago watershed). (All are appointed by governor with senate consent.)

Mailing Address: P.O. Box 7921, Madison 53707.

Location: State Natural Resources Building (GEF 2), 101 South Webster Street, Madison.

Telephone: (715) 822-8583.

Statutory References: Sections 15.345 (1) and 30.92.

Agency Responsibility: The 5-member Wisconsin Waterways Commission was created by Chapter 274, Laws of 1977. Its members serve staggered 5-year terms, and each must represent a specific geographic area and be knowledgeable about that area's recreational water use problems. The commission may have studies conducted to determine the need for recreational boating facilities; approve financial aid to local governments for development of recreational boating projects, including the acquisition of weed harvesters; and recommend administrative rules for the recreational facilities boating program.

Office of the
STATE PUBLIC DEFENDER

For e-mail combine the user ID and the state extender: userid**@opd.wi.gov**
All telephone numbers are 608 area code unless otherwise indicated.

Public Defender Board: Daniel M. Berkos, *chairperson;* Regina Dunkin (public member), *vice chairperson;* James M. Brennan, *secretary;* David Coon, John Hogan, Michael Maxwell, Ellen Thorn; Mai Neng Xiong (public member), vacancy. (Except as indicated, all are state bar members. All are appointed by governor with senate consent.)

State Public Defender: KELLI THOMPSON, 266-0087, thompsonk@

Deputy State Public Defender: Michael Tobin, 266-8259, tobinm@

Legislative Liaison: Adam Plotkin, 264-8572, plotkina@

Budget Director: Anna Oehler, 267-0311, oehlera@

Communications Director: Randy Kraft, 267-3587, kraftr@

Management Information Manager: Cindy Archer, 261-0636, archerc@

Legal Counsel: Devon Lee, 261-0633, leede@

Appellate Division: Jeremy Perri, *director,* 264-8573, perrij@

Assigned Counsel Division: Kathleen Pakes, *director,* 261-8856, pakesk@

Training Division: Gina Pruski, *director,* 266-6782, pruskig@

Trial Division: Catherine Dorl, *director,* 267-9588, dorlc@; Jennifer Bias, *deputy director and affirmative action officer,* Milwaukee: (414) 227-4028; biasj@

Mailing Address: P.O. Box 7923, Madison 53707-7923.

Location: 315 North Henry Street, 2nd Floor, Madison.

Telephone: 266-0087.

Fax: 267-0584; Assigned Counsel Division Fax: 261-0625.

Internet Address: www.wispd.org

Number of Employees: 579.85.

Total Budget 2013-15: $171,817,200.

Statutory References: Section 15.78; Chapter 977.

Agency Responsibility: The Office of the State Public Defender makes determinations of indigence and provides legal representation for persons in specified types of proceedings who are unable to afford a private attorney. The state public defender, who must be a member of the state bar, serves at the pleasure of the Public Defender Board.

Organization: The 9-member Public Defender Board appoints the state public defender, promulgates rules for determining indigence, and establishes procedures for certifying lists of private attorneys who can be assigned as counsel. Board members are appointed for staggered 3-year terms, and at least 5 of these must be members of the State Bar of Wisconsin. Members may not be or be employed by a judicial or law enforcement officer, a district attorney, a corporation counsel, or the state public defender.

Unit Functions: The *Appellate Division* uses both program staff and private attorneys to provide post-judgement legal representation to the indigent and minors in criminal, civil commitment, juvenile code, and children's code cases in the trial and appellate courts.

The *Assigned Counsel Division* oversees a variety of functions related to appointment of private attorneys to represent indigent clients in cases not handled by staff, including certification and training, logistical support, and payment of fees.

The *Trial Division* provides legal representation at the trial level to indigent persons who have been charged with adult felony crimes or misdemeanors punishable by imprisonment. It also represents minors charged with juvenile offenses, persons subject to a petition for civil commitment, and individuals involved in termination of parental rights.

History: Both the United States Constitution (Sixth and Fourteenth Amendments) and the Wisconsin Constitution (Article I, Section 7), as interpreted by the U.S. and Wisconsin Supreme Courts, guarantee the right to publicly-provided counsel for poor people charged with crimes or facing potential deprivations of liberty. In 1859, the Wisconsin Supreme Court ruled, in *Carpenter and Sprague v. the County of Dane* (9 Wis. 274), that a county is liable to pay for an attorney provided by the court in a criminal case to represent an indigent defendant who cannot otherwise afford representation.

The position of state public defender was created in 1966 by Chapter 479, Laws of 1965, under the supervision of the Wisconsin Supreme Court and funded, in part, by a private grant from the Ford Foundation. The duties of the office were originally confined to appellate defense, and its mission was to pursue post-conviction appeals for indigents before the appropriate courts, including the U.S. Supreme Court. Defense of indigents at the trial court level remained a county responsibility, dependent upon court-appointed private counsel paid by the county or privately funded public defender services.

Chapter 29, Laws of 1977, transferred the state public defender from the judicial branch to the executive branch as an independent agency under the Public Defender Board, which was authorized to appoint the defender to a 5-year renewable term with removal only for cause. (Chapter 356, Laws of 1979, later provided that the public defender serve at the pleasure of the board.) Chapter 29 also transferred the responsibility for defense of indigents at the trial level from the counties to the public defender's office, but representation by the defender's staff was limited, based on funding and statutory criteria. Client representation was, and continues to be, divided between staff attorneys and private counsel paid by the public defender.

Chapter 29, Laws of 1977, directed the public defender to determine the percentage of cases that private counsel would handle in each county. Chapter 356, Laws of 1979, established those percentages by law with the public defender staff assuming various portions of the caseloads in 47 counties and private counsel responsible for all cases in the remaining 25 counties. 1985 Wisconsin Act 29 expanded the use of public defender staff attorneys to all 72 counties and repealed the sunset provision enacted in 1979, which would have abolished the agency, effective November 15, 1985.

1995 Wisconsin Act 27 directed the public defender to enter into annual fixed fee contracts with private counsel and limited the number of trial-level cases assigned to private attorneys to one-third of all cases handled. It also eliminated public defender representation in some cases, including certain matters related to prison and jail conditions, sentence modifications, probation and parole revocations, child support, and parents of children in need of protection or services (CHIPS).

2009 Wisconsin Act 164 revised the financial criteria for public defender representation and provided for additional staff positions to provide services to 75% of the additional clients who will qualify for representation. Act 164 was designed to reduce the number of cases in which the courts appoint an attorney at county expense and to enhance consistency in appointment of attorneys statewide.

Department of
PUBLIC INSTRUCTION

Address e-mail by combining the user ID and the state extender: userid@**dpi.wi.gov**
All telephone numbers are 608 area code unless otherwise indicated.

State Superintendent: TONY EVERS, 266-1771, anthony.evers@

Deputy State Superintendent: MIKE THOMPSON, 266-1771, michael.thompson@

Chief of Staff: CHRISTINA SPECTOR, 266-1771, christina.spector@

Special Assistant: SCOTT JONES, 266-1771, scott.jones@

Legal Services, Office of: JANET JENKINS, *chief legal counsel,* 266-9353, janet.jenkins@

Education Information Services: JOHN JOHNSON, *director,* 266-1098, john.johnson@

Policy Initiatives Advisor Executive: JEFF PERTL, 267-9232, jeff.pertl@

Policy Initiatives Advisor Administrator: JENNIFER KAMMERUD, 266-7073, jennifer.kammerud@

Legislative Liaison: DEE PETTACK, 267-1063, dee.pettack@

Mailing Address: P.O. Box 7841, Madison 53707-7841.

Location: State Education Building (GEF 3), 125 South Webster Street, Madison.

Telephones: 266-3390; (800) 441-4563; TDD: 267-2427.

Fax: 267-5188.

Internet Addresses: Departmental: www.dpi.wi.gov; BadgerLink: www.badgerlink.net

Number of Employees: 647.26.

Total Budget 2013-15: $12,582,349,400.

Constitutional Reference: Article X, Section 1.

Statutory References: Section 15.37; Chapters 43 and 115-121.

Academic Excellence, Division for: SHEILA BRIGGS, *assistant superintendent,* 266-3361, sheila.briggs@; Division Fax: 267-9275.

   Career and Technical Education: SHARON WENDT, *director,* 267-9251, sharon.wendt@

   Content and Learning: REBECCA VAIL, *director,* 266-2364, rebecca.vail@

   Educator Effectiveness: KATHARINE RAINEY, *director,* 267-9551, katharine.rainey@

   Literacy and Mathematics: EMILIE AMUNDSON, *director,* 267-3726, emilie.amundson@

   Teacher Education, Professional Development, and Licensing: TAMMY HUTH, *director,* 266-0986, tammy.huth@

Finance and Management, Division for: BRIAN PAHNKE, *assistant superintendent,* 267-9124, brian.pahnke@; Division Fax: 266-3644.

   Community Nutrition: AMANDA KANE, *director,* 267-9123, amanda.kane@

   Human Resources: DENISE KOHOUT, *director,* 266-0282, denise.kohout@

   Management Services: SUE LINTON, *director,* 266-3320, suzanne.linton@

   Policy and Budget: ERIN FATH, *director,* 266-2804, erin.fath@

DEPARTMENT OF PUBLIC INSTRUCTION

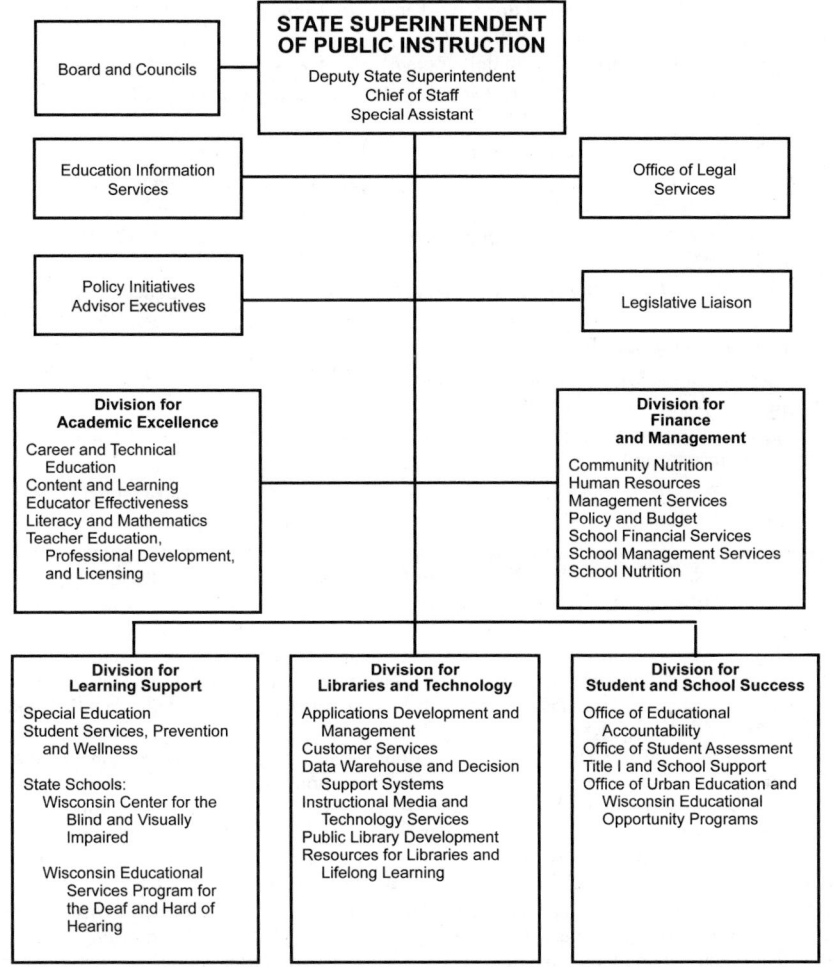

STATE SUPERINTENDENT OF PUBLIC INSTRUCTION
Deputy State Superintendent
Chief of Staff
Special Assistant

Board and Councils

Education Information Services

Office of Legal Services

Policy Initiatives Advisor Executives

Legislative Liaison

Division for Academic Excellence

Career and Technical
Education
Content and Learning
Educator Effectiveness
Literacy and Mathematics
Teacher Education,
Professional Development,
and Licensing

Division for Finance and Management

Community Nutrition
Human Resources
Management Services
Policy and Budget
School Financial Services
School Management Services
School Nutrition

Division for Learning Support

Special Education
Student Services, Prevention
and Wellness

State Schools:
Wisconsin Center for the
Blind and Visually
Impaired

Wisconsin Educational
Services Program for
the Deaf and Hard of
Hearing

Division for Libraries and Technology

Applications Development and
Management
Customer Services
Data Warehouse and Decision
Support Systems
Instructional Media and
Technology Services
Public Library Development
Resources for Libraries and
Lifelong Learning

Division for Student and School Success

Office of Educational
Accountability
Office of Student Assessment
Title I and School Support
Office of Urban Education and
Wisconsin Educational
Opportunity Programs

School Financial Services: Robert Soldner, *director,* 266-6968, robert.soldner@

School Management Services: Tricia Collins, *director,* 266-7475, tricia.collins@

School Nutrition: Jessica Sharkus, *director,* 267-9121, jessica.sharkus@

Learning Support, Division for: Carolyn Stanford Taylor, *assistant superintendent,* 266-1649, carolyn.stanford.taylor@; Division Fax: 267-3746.

Special Education: Barbara Van Haren, *director,* 266-1781, barbara.vanharen@

Student Services, Prevention and Wellness: Douglas White, *director,* 266-5198, douglas.white@

Wisconsin Center for the Blind and Visually Impaired: Peter Dally, *director,* 1700 West State Street, Janesville 53546-5399, (608) 758-6100, (800) 832-9784, Fax: (608) 758-6161, peter.dally@

Wisconsin Educational Services Program for the Deaf and Hard of Hearing: vacancy, *director,* 309 West Walworth Avenue, Delavan 53115-1099, (262) 740-2066, voice: (877) 973-3323, TTY: (877) 973-3324, Fax: (262) 728-7160.

Libraries and Technology, Division for: KURT KIEFER, *assistant superintendent,* 266-2205, kurt.kiefer@; Division Fax: 267-9207.

Division Internet Address: http://dlt.dpi.wi.gov/

Applications Development and Management: DAN RETZLAFF, *manager,* 267-2285, daniel.retzlaff@

Customer Services: JEFFERY POST, *manager,* 267-9222, jeffery.post@

Data Warehouse and Decision Support Systems: MELISSA STRAW, *manager,* 266-1089, melissa.straw@

Instructional Media and Technology Services: JEFF KNUTSEN, *director,* 266-3856, jeffrey.knutsen@

Public Library Development: JOHN DEBACHER, *director,* 267-9225, john.debacher@

Resources for Libraries and Lifelong Learning: MARTHA BERNINGER, *director,* 224-6161, martha.berninger@

Student and School Success, Division for: LYNETTE RUSSELL, *assistant superintendent,* 266-5450, lynette.russell@; Division Fax: 267-9142.

Educational Accountability, Office of: LAURA PINSONNEAULT, *director,* 267-1072, laura.pinsonneault@

Student Assessment, Office of: TROY COUILLARD, *director,* 267-1072, troy.couillard@

Title I and School Support: JONAS ZUCKERMAN, *director,* 267-9136, jonas.zuckerman@

Urban Education, Office of and *Wisconsin Educational Opportunity Programs:* CAROLYN PARKINSON, *director,* (414) 227-1847, carolyn.parkinson@

Publications: Biennial Report; Wisconsin School Directory; various curriculum, instruction, library and student services publications and research studies. Electronic publications include *DPI-ConnectED, WI Libraries for Everyone,* and various program area newsletters and Web sites, including the School District and School Performance Report and Wisconsin Information System for Education Data Dashboard (WISEdash), available on the department's Internet site.

Agency Responsibility: The Department of Public Instruction provides direction and technical assistance for public elementary and secondary education in Wisconsin. The department offers a broad range of programs and professional services to local school administrators and staff. It distributes state school aids and administers federal aids to supplement local tax resources, improves curriculum and school operations, ensures education for children with disabilities, offers professional guidance and counseling, and develops school and public library resources.

Organization: The department is headed by the State Superintendent of Public Instruction, a constitutional officer who is elected on the nonpartisan spring ballot for a term of 4 years. The state superintendent appoints a deputy state superintendent and assistant state superintendents from outside the classified service. The assistant superintendents are responsible for administering the operating divisions of the department. The superintendent also appoints the director of the Office of Educational Accountability, which was created in Section 15.374 (1), Wisconsin Statutes, by 1993 Wisconsin Act 16.

Unit Functions: The *Division for Academic Excellence (DAE)* provides leadership and professional development regarding curriculum development, academic and technical skills standards, and instructional methods and strategies, as well as professional learning and support to a variety of content area educators. The division is comprised of five teams: Career and Technical Education; Content and Learning; Educator Effectiveness; Literacy and Mathematics; and Teacher Education, Professional Development and Licensing. A service orientation and culturally responsive view guide the teams' work to provide technical assistance to educators, parents, communities, and professional organizations.

The division reviews and approves educator preparation programs and licenses teachers, pupil services personnel, administrators, and library professionals. The division monitors school district and vocational education compliance with state nondiscrimination laws and rules.

The division administers a variety of programs that provide assistance and grants to public school students and teachers on the basis of merit and need, as well as provides consultation and leadership for multicultural education. These programs include: American Indian Studies Program, American Indian Language and Culture Education, Herb Kohl Educational Foundation Award Program, Presidential Awards for Mathematics and Science Teachers, U.S. Senate Youth Program, Urban Teacher World Program, as well as international partnerships with Germany, China, Japan, Thailand, and France. DAE also directs youth options, education for employment, the career and technical student organizations, and administers the high school equivalency/general educational development (HSED/GED) program for state residents who have not completed high school.

DAE administers federal programs that provide assistance for world languages, advanced placement, and alternative education. The division administers funds for school districts under the Carl D. Perkins Career and Technical Education Act of 2006 to enhance and improve career and technical educational programs. DAE also administers part of the state and federally funded Bilingual/English as a Second Language Program.

The division provides a cradle-to-career focus for instructional leaders and educators through work done by the Office of Early Learning and by providing standards and supports through high school and the transition to postsecondary work. The division curates and creates high quality resources to assist with standards implementation. Resources and technical assistance are provided around career and technical education standards and other core academic standards. Gifted and Talented education support can also be found in the Division for Academic Excellence.

The division is leading efforts to develop and implement a statewide educator effectiveness system, where all educators will be evaluated based upon multiple measures. This complex system factors in educator practice and student performance in providing feedback to educators around their strengths and areas for improvement.

The *Division for Finance and Management* distributes state and federal school aids and grants; administers school district revenue limits; administers the Milwaukee, Racine, and Statewide Parental Choice Programs, federal charter school grant program, and the interdistrict open enrollment program; prescribes school financial accounting methods; consults with school districts on their budgets; and collects, analyzes, and publishes school finance data. Consulting services are provided to assist districts and charter schools with management and planning, school district reorganization, pupil transportation, private school relations, school board elections and duties, and finance and asset management. The division is responsible for both state and federally funded school food and nutrition services, child care food services, and elderly nutrition programs. It also provides support services to the department for financial management, human resources, budget preparation, educational policy and administrative rule development, and legislative analysis.

The *Division for Learning Support,* created in Section 15.373 (1), Wisconsin Statutes, as the Division for Handicapped Children by Chapter 327, Laws of 1967, formerly named in 1993 Wisconsin Act 335, as the Division for Learning Support: Equity and Advocacy, and most recently renamed in 2011 Wisconsin Act 158, provides technical assistance, leadership, advocacy, staff development, training, and education to help meet the diverse cultural, emotional, social, health, and educational needs of Wisconsin's youth. The mission is met through collaboration with federal, state, and local groups. The division manages state and federal resources, monitors and evaluates programs and practices, and facilitates school-district and community efforts to meet specific needs of students. The division administers programs involving school nursing, social work, psychological services, and school counseling services; alcohol, tobacco, and other drug abuse; suicide prevention; alcohol and traffic safety; school-age parents; school violence prevention; prevention of HIV and other sexually transmitted diseases; pregnancy prevention; health education; physical education and activity; coordinated school health programs; compulsory school attendance; and after-school programs.

The division offers technical assistance and financial support to help school districts provide a free appropriate public education for students with disabilities, combat educational discrimination, and train professional staff. It is responsible for special educational programs and services for students with disabilities. It must ensure that all students with disabilities are identified, evaluated, and provided appropriate education and services. It supervises all special education programs and checks their compliance with departmental standards and state and federal law. The division provides consultation for and supervision of the Pupil Nondiscrimination Program.

The division administers the Wisconsin Educational Services Program for the Deaf and Hard of Hearing (WESP-DHH) and the Wisconsin Center for the Blind and Visually Impaired (WCBVI). Each program operates a residential school for state residents who are ages 3 to 21, have a visual or hearing impairment, and need individualized instruction. Both schools provide academic and vocational education on site at no cost to families. Both programs also offer instructional and technical assistance, teaching materials, and evaluations of pupils to local school districts and other agencies.

The *Division for Libraries and Technology (DLT),* created as the Division for Library Services in Section 15.373 (2), Wisconsin Statutes, by Chapter 327, Laws of 1967, renamed as the Division for Libraries, Technology, and Community Learning in 2001 Wisconsin Act 48, and most recently renamed the Division for Libraries and Technology in 2011 Wisconsin Act 158, provides assistance for the development and improvement of public and school libraries; fosters interlibrary cooperation and resource sharing; and promotes information and instructional technology in schools and libraries. The division administers the state aid program for Wisconsin's 17 public library systems. It also administers the federal Library Services and Technology Act. The division facilitates interlibrary loan and reference services to the state's libraries and manages WISCAT (www.WISCAT.net), the interlibrary loan management system and electronic union and virtual catalog of Wisconsin library holdings. The division also acts as a state-level clearinghouse for interlibrary loan requests; administers BadgerLink (www.badgerlink.net), the statewide full-text database project that allows access to thousands of magazines, newsletters, newspapers, pamphlets, and historical documents; and, in collaboration with other Wisconsin library organizations, manages BadgerLearn, the statewide portal of training and professional development materials created by the Wisconsin library community. The division manages con-

Teacher Jeanna Raymakers confers with State Superintendent Tony Evers about her lesson plan at Bonduel High School. (Department of Public Instruction)

tracts with library organizations necessary to the provision of interlibrary loan services, library service to the blind and visually impaired, and enhancing awareness of high quality children's literature in the school and library communities. The division directs the public librarian certification program, and the summer library reading program, and provides planning and coordination for the development of libraries in schools and Wisconsin communities, as well as regional public library systems.

DLT also serves as the information technology team for the entire agency. One of the division's teams implements and supports the statewide K-12 data warehouse and dashboard system; this data warehouse system aggregates data from a variety of data collections and information systems into an easy-to-use interface for every school district across Wisconsin known as WISEdash. The division provides information and resources for and about schools through the School District Performance Report (SDPR) and other department resources. DLT also provides guidance and oversight to instructional technology efforts in all Wisconsin school districts. The DLT staff has led the development of a statewide digital learning strategic plan with the state superintendent's Digital Learning Advisory Council, creating a roadmap for all school districts. Project efforts include creation of a statewide professional learning management system and virtual professional learning community and resource portal. In addition, DLT provides guidance on development of local technology and library media program plans and utilization of the Common School Fund, and consults on school library media program staff licensure. The staff also facilitates professional learning activities associated with education technology integration within schools.

The *Division for Student and School Success* is responsible for ensuring that all children attain proficiency in meeting the Wisconsin Academic Standards. The four teams in this division, Educational Accountability, Student Assessment, Title I and School Support, and Wisconsin Educational Opportunity Programs and Urban Education, have as a major focus closing the achievement gap that exists among children of color, the economically disadvantaged, and their peers.

The Office of Educational Accountability provides data to assist district and school personnel in evaluating and making decisions related to educational planning and programming. This team provides accountability outcomes via School and District Report Cards related to state and federal legislation and gives technical assistance in evaluating results and developing approaches to using data to inform decisions ensuring students are prepared for college and careers.

The Office of Student Assessment provides statewide assessments which measure student proficiency related to the Wisconsin Academic Standards. Assessments also include screening measures in early literacy and English language proficiency. The data from these assessments are compiled into reports for district and school improvement efforts as well as meeting the expectations of state and federal reporting requirements.

The Title I and School Support Team provides a multitude of resources to districts and schools that include a number of programs under the federal Elementary and Secondary Education Act of 1965 and the No Child Left Behind Act of 2001, including programs under Title I-Part A, Even Start, Migrant Education, Neglected and Delinquent Youth, McKinney-Vento Homeless Assistance Act, the VISTA program, and the state class size reduction program Student Achievement Guarantee in Education (SAGE).

The Wisconsin Educational Opportunity Programs and Urban Education Team focuses on improving high school graduation rates, reducing dropouts and encouraging nontraditional, minority, disadvantaged, and low-income students with college potential to pursue postsecondary education. Programs to achieve team objectives include state and federal Talent Search, Talent Incentive Program, Early Identification Program, Pre-College Scholarship Program, Gear Up, and Upward Bound Program. The Urban Education program was established in 1995 to provide services to urban areas including Beloit, Kenosha, Milwaukee, and Racine to facilitate cooperative efforts to address the challenges and equity needs facing families, children, and educators in an urban setting. Programs to achieve team objectives include Special Education, Title I, and Urban Staff Development and Teacher Education Program Review.

History: The Wisconsin Constitution, as adopted in 1848, required the state legislature to provide by law for the establishment of district schools that would be free to all children between the ages of 4 and 20 years. It also created a State Superintendent of Public Instruction to supervise public education. Under the 1849 Wisconsin Statutes, the superintendent was ordered to visit schools in all the counties, recommend textbooks and courses of instruction, and distribute state money for public schools to the counties.

Originally, the superintendent was elected to a 2-year term at the partisan general election in November. With the adoption of a constitutional amendment in 1902, the superintendent was placed on the nonpartisan April ballot and given a 4-year term of office.

In the early years of statehood, the hiring of teachers was entirely a local matter. In 1861, the legislature created county superintendents of schools with the power to license teachers beginning in 1862. The state superintendent was also given licensing authority in 1868 (Chapter 169). Local districts and county superintendents continued to license teachers until 1939, when the legislature gave that power exclusively to the Department of Public Instruction.

For a number of years, state support of public education consisted of money derived principally from the sale of public lands that the federal government had granted to the state. In Chapter 287, Laws of 1885, the legislature levied a one-mill (one-tenth of a cent) state property tax to be collected by the state and distributed to counties for school support. The state's first attempt to equalize tax support for schools in property-poor districts was the Wisconsin Elementary Equalization Law of 1927 (Chapter 536). It was promoted by State Superintendent John Callahan, who also urged a 40% level of state support for local school costs – a figure not reached until after 1970. The 1995 Legislature enacted a law to ensure that state aids and school levy tax credits would cover two-thirds of local school revenues, but subsequently repealed that requirement in 2003.

Originally, Wisconsin only required tax support for elementary schools. Individual cities, such as Racine and Kenosha, funded their own high schools. The legislature enacted public support for high schools in 1875 (Chapter 323). Kindergarten originated in 1856 when Margarethe Schurz started a German-speaking program for children 2 through 5 years of age in Watertown, Wisconsin. The first public school kindergarten opened in Manitowoc in 1873 for 4- and 5-year-old children. The program continued to spread until, in 1973, the legislature required school districts to provide a 5-year-old kindergarten. In the 1990s, an increasing number of school districts offered full-day programs for 5-year-old children and kindergarten programs for 4-year-olds.

Although state law had contained some curriculum requirements as early as 1849, the legislature did not establish high school graduation requirements until 1983. In 1985, it prescribed a detailed set of standards local districts must meet to be eligible for state aid. The 1997 Legislature mandated that school boards adopt pupil academic standards in certain subjects, a series of examinations to measure pupil achievement in 4th, 8th, and 10th grades, and a high school graduation examination. The 2003 Legislature eliminated the high school graduation examination.

State concern for special education began with the establishment of the Wisconsin Institute for Education of the Blind in Janesville in 1850 and a school for the deaf in Delavan in 1852. These schools were administered by public welfare agencies until transferred to the Department of Public Instruction in 1947. The 1927 Legislature enacted laws to provide aid for special classes for "crippled children" and increased aid for districts to educate mentally handicapped children. Funding for education of all children with disabilities was enacted in 1973 to comply with federal law.

While state administration of school libraries fell under the jurisdiction of the superintendent, the Free Library Commission set standards for public libraries. In 1965, the legislature transferred this function which also now resides with the department.

Statutory Board and Councils

Alcohol and Other Drug Abuse Programs, Council on: SUSAN BAUMANN-DUREN, YOLANDA CARGILE, JEAN CHRISTIENSEN, BRIAN DEAN, BETSY GRUSZYNSKI, DELAINE MOE, BONNIE SCHEEL, JANE SCHNEIDER, MARIAN SHERIDAN.

The Council on Alcohol and Other Drug Abuse Programs advises the state superintendent about programs to prevent or reduce alcohol, tobacco, and other drug abuse by minors. The council was created by Chapter 331, Laws of 1979, and its duties are prescribed in Section 115.36 of the statutes.

The Red Feather Singers, from the Madison School District, provide music at State Superintendent Tony Evers annual state of education address in the State Capitol rotunda. (Department of Public Instruction)

Blind and Visual Impairment Education Council: NISSAN BAR-LEV (special education director), *chairperson;* KEDIBONYE CARPENTER, STEPHANIE KLAS, TONYA OLSON (parents of visually impaired children); JULIE HAPEMAN, CHERYL ORGAS, CHRIS ZENCHENKO (members of organizations affiliated with visually impaired); vacancy (licensed teacher of visually impaired); SADIQUA WHITE-HARPER (licensed teacher of orientation and mobility); vacancy (licensed general education teacher); NANCY THOMPSON (school board member); STEVE LUTZKE (school district administrator); FRED WOLLENBURG (CESA representative); vacancy (higher education representative); MARY ANN DAMM, MARY SPIDELL, vacancy (other members) (all appointed by superintendent).

The 17-member Blind and Visual Impairment Education Council advises the state superintendent on statewide activities that will benefit students who are blind or visually impaired; makes recommendations for improvements in services provided by the Wisconsin Center for the Blind and Visually Impaired; and proposes ways to improve the preparation of teachers and staff and coordination between the department and other agencies that offer services to the visually impaired. Members serve 3-year terms. At least one must be certified by the Library of Congress as a Braille transcriber. The higher education representative must either have experience as an educator of the visually impaired or an educator of teachers of the visually impaired. At least one of the three remaining members must be visually impaired. The council was created as the Council on the Blind by Chapter 276, Laws of 1969, renamed as the Council on the Education of the Blind in Chapter 292, Laws of 1971, and renamed and substantially revised by 1999 Wisconsin Act 9. Its composition and duties are prescribed in Sections 15.377 (1) and 115.37 of the statutes.

Deaf and Hard-of-Hearing Education Council: DAVID COLLINS, BETH HALL (parents of hearing impaired children); DEBRA ANKEN-DYER (teacher of hearing impaired pupils); PAULA MINIX (licensed speech-language pathologist); BRIAN ANDERSON (school district special education director); BETH LARIMER (licensed audiologist with expertise in educational audiology); AMY OTIS-WILBORN (educator of hearing impaired teachers); MARGARET JAMES (interpreter training instructor); KIP JACKSON (educational interpreter); ROBIN BARNES, ANDREW KONKEL, JOAN-NA COOKIE ROANG (other members); MICHELLE PANDIAN (itinerate teacher); KORYN KONEAZNY (regular education teacher) (all appointed by state superintendent).

The Deaf and Hard-of-Hearing Education Council advises the state superintendent on issues related to pupils who are hearing impaired. It informs the superintendent on services, programs, and research that could benefit those students. The council makes recommendations for improving services provided by the Wisconsin Educational Services Program for the Deaf and Hard of Hearing; reviews and makes recommendations on the level of quality and services available to hearing-impaired pupils; proposes ways to improve the preparation of teachers and other staff who provide services to the hearing impaired; and proposes ways to improve coordination between the department and providers of services to the hearing impaired. The council's 12 statutory members serve 3-year terms. It was created by 2001 Wisconsin Act 57, and its composition and duties are prescribed in Sections 15.377 (2) and 115.372 of the statutes.

Library and Network Development, Council on: NITA BURKE (public member), *chairperson;* BRYAN MCCORMICK (professional member), *vice chairperson;* JOSHUA COWLES (professional member), *secretary;* EWA BARCZYK, LAURIE FREUND, JOAN ROBB, EMILY ROGERS, JIM TROJANOWSKI, PATRICK WILKINSON, vacancy (professional members); TERRENCE BERRES, MARY THERESE BOYLE, CARA CAVIN, MIRIAM ERICKSON, THOMAS KAMENICK, DOUGLAS H. LAY, KATHY PLETCHER, JESS RIPP, KRISTI WILLIAMS (public members) (appointed by governor).

The 19-member Council on Library and Network Development advises the state superintendent and the administrator of the Division for Libraries and Technology on the performance of their duties regarding library service. Members serve 3-year terms. The professional members represent various types of libraries and information services. The public members must demonstrate an interest in libraries and other types of information services. The council was created by Chapter 347, Laws of 1979, and its composition and duties are prescribed in Sections 15.377 (6) and 43.07 of the statutes.

Professional Standards Council for Teachers: LINDA LUEDTKE (public school pupil services professional), *chairperson;* WENDY RIPP (public school teacher), *vice chairperson;* HEATHER STRAYER (public school pupil services professional)*;* LISA BENZ, PAULA HASE, JENNIFER NICKEL, 2 vacancies (public school teachers); MANJULA DAMMANA (public school special education teacher); MARGARET DOERING (private school teacher); BRAD PECK (public school principal); JOHN GAIER (public school district administrator); BRIAN MCALISTER (UW System educational faculty member); DEBRA DOSEMAGEN (private college education faculty member); PEGGY HILL BREUNIG, GARY WILLIAMS (public school board members); vacancy (parent of public school child); vacancy (IHE public or private faculty member); BRIANA SCHWABENBAUER (student enrolled in teacher preparatory program) (appointed by state superintendent with senate consent).

The 19-member Professional Standards Council for Teachers advises the state superintendent regarding licensing and evaluating teachers; evaluation and approval of teacher education programs; the status of teaching in Wisconsin; school board practices to develop effective teaching; peer mentoring; evaluation systems; and alternative dismissal procedures.

Members serve 3-year terms, except the student member, who serves for 2 years. Public school teachers and pupil service professionals are recommended by the largest statewide labor organization representing teachers. The private school teacher is recommended by the Wisconsin Council of Religious and Independent Schools. The public school administrator and principal are recommended by their statewide organizations. Faculty members are recommended by the UW System president and the Wisconsin Association of Independent Colleges and Universities. The council was created by 1997 Wisconsin Act 298, and its composition and duties are prescribed in Sections 15.377 (8) and 115.425 of the statutes.

School District Boundary Appeal Board: TONY EVERS (superintendent of public instruction); DAVID AMUNDSON, COLLEEN DAVIS, RICHARD ELORANTA, N. DAVID KIPP, MARY KATHLEEN MALONEY, THERESA MILES, JULIE NETT, STEVEN PATE, PATRICIA SILVER, THERESE TRAVIA, 2 vacancies (appointed by state superintendent).

The 13-member School District Boundary Appeal Board hears appeals from persons aggrieved by actions taken under Chapter 117, Wisconsin Statutes, providing for school district reorganization. The appointed members include 4 each from large, medium, and small district school boards, who are appointed for staggered 2-year terms. No two members may live within the boundaries of the same CESA. The board was created by 1983 Wisconsin Act 27, and its composition and duties are prescribed in Sections 15.375 (2) and 117.05 of the statutes.

Special Education, Council on: CARLA WITKOWSKI, *chairperson;* CAROLINE ROSSING, *vice chairperson;* JUDY BRAUN, MARGARET CARPENTER, ELSA DIAZ-BAUTISTA, JIM DIMOCK, NANCY DONAHUE, REGENA FLOYD-SAMBOU, DEBORAH FOSTER, JENNIFER GIEDD, MARLA HINTZE, SUE LARSEN, PATRICIA LUEBKE, JENNIFER MIMS-HOWELL, ANNA MOFFIT, WENDY OVERTURF, KAREN QUICK, JULIE QUIGLEY, STACEY SKONING, MARY SWIFKA, SUSANA VALDES-SHOGREN (appointed by state superintendent).

The Council on Special Education advises the state superintendent on programs for children with disabilities. It assists in developing evaluations, and reporting data to the U.S. Department of Education, developing policies, and advising the state superintendent regarding the needs of children with disabilities. The number of council members is unspecified, but the following categories must be represented: regular and special education teachers; institutions of higher education that train special education personnel; state and local education officials; administrators of programs for children with disabilities; agencies involved in financing or delivery of related services; private schools and charter schools; a vocational, community, or business organization that provides transitional services; the Department of Corrections; parents of children with disabilities; and individuals with disabilities. Council members are appointed for 3-year terms, and the majority must be individuals with disabilities or parents of children with disabilities. The council was created as the Council on Exceptional Education by Chapter 89, Laws of 1973, and renamed and revised by 1997 Wisconsin Act 164. Its composition and duties are prescribed in Section 15.377 (4) of the statutes.

PUBLIC SERVICE COMMISSION

Address e-mail by combining the user ID and the state extender: userid@**wisconsin.gov**
All telephone numbers are 608 area code unless otherwise indicated.

Commissioners: ELLEN NOWAK, 267-7899, ellen.nowak@, *chairperson;* MICHAEL HUEBSCH, 267-7898, michael.huebsch@; PHIL MONTGOMERY, 267-7897, phil.montgomery@ (appointed by governor with senate consent).

Executive Assistants: TERESA HATCHELL, 267-7898, teresa.hatchell@; ROBERT SEITZ, 267-7899, robert.seitz@; JANET WHEELER, 266-2655, janet.wheeler@

Secretary to the Commission: SANDRA PASKE, 266-1265, sandra.paske@

Administrative Law Judge, Office of: MICHAEL NEWMARK, *administrative law judge,* 261-8523, michael.newmark@

Governmental and Public Affairs, Office of: NATHAN CONRAD, *director,* 266-9600, nathan.conrad@

General Counsel: CYNTHIA SMITH, 266-1264, cynthia.smith@

Legislative Liaison: ELISE NELSON, 267-3589, elise.nelson@

Business and Communications Services, Division of: SARAH KLEIN, *administrator,* 266-3587, sarah.klein@

Natural Gas and Energy Division: JEFFREY RIPP, *administrator,* 267-9813, jeffrey.ripp@

Regional Energy Markets, Division of: JANET WHEELER, *administrator,* 266-2655, janet.wheeler@

Water, Compliance and Consumer Affairs, Division of: JEFF STONE, *administrator,* 267-7829, jeff.stone@

Mailing Address: P.O. Box 7854, Madison 53707-7854.

Location: Public Service Commission Building, 610 North Whitney Way, Madison.

Telephones: General inquiries: (888) 816-3831 (in-state only) or 266-5481; Consumer affairs (800) 225-7729; Complaints: (800) 225-7729 (in-state only) or 266-2001; Media relations: 266-9600; TTY: 267-1479.

Fax: 266-3957.

E-mail Address: pscrecs@psc.wi.gov

Internet Address: http://psc.wi.gov

Publications: Biennial report; strategic energy assessment; various statistics on electric utilities, gas utilities, and telephone companies; and guides for utility customers, including publications for consumers related to electricity, natural gas, water, and telephone services.

Number of Employees: 140.00.

Total Budget 2013-15: $47,839,200.

Statutory References: Sections 15.06 and 15.79; Chapter 196.

Agency Responsibility: The Public Service Commission (PSC) is responsible for regulating Wisconsin's public utilities and ensuring that utility services are provided to customers at prices reasonable to both ratepayers and utility owners. The commission regulates the rates and services of electric, gas distribution, heating, water, and combined water and sewer utilities. The commission has limited jurisdiction over landline telecommunications providers and services. In most instances, the commission's jurisdiction does not extend to the activities of electric cooperatives, wireless telephone providers, cable television, or Internet service.

Responsibilities of the commission include setting utility rates, determining levels for adequate and safe service, and utility bond sales and stock offerings. It confirms or rejects utility applications for major construction projects, such as power plants, transmission lines, and wind farms. In addition to ensuring utility compliance with statutes, administrative codes, and recordkeeping requirements, the commission's staff investigates and mediates thousands of consumer complaints annually. During the complaint process, commission staff reviews all pertinent information to make certain that the utility's handling of the complaint is in compliance with the applicable rules. The commission also rules on proposed mergers between utility companies.

The commission certifies various types of telecommunications providers, manages the Universal Service Fund, handles some wholesale disputes between telecommunications providers including interconnection agreement filings and disputes, and administers telephone numbering resources.

Organization: The governor appoints the 3 full-time commissioners, with senate approval, to serve staggered 6-year terms, but an individual commissioner holds office until a successor is appointed and qualified. No commissioner may have a financial interest in a railroad or public utility or water carrier or serve on or under a political party committee. By work rule, no employee or immediate family member may own stock in a utility or any entity regulated by the commission. The governor designates a chairperson who, in turn, may appoint division administrators from outside the classified service.

Unit Functions: The *Division of Business and Communications Services* has two subunits, administration services and telecommunications.

Administrative Services provides the commission's human resources and personnel management, budget development, financial management, information technology, staff development, facilities management, and intervenor financing coordination, procurement, and grants administration. Its central records management staff provides agency staff with printing, mail, and case file services.

Telecommunications is responsible for oversight of the telecommunications industry in Wisconsin and resolution of disputes involving those services that are within PSC jurisdiction. The PSC promotes competition in the state's telecommunications markets in order to ensure access to modern and affordable service throughout the state. The PSC works to resolve disputes between telecommunications service providers, administers universal service programs, administers telephone numbering resources, and advises the Federal Communications Commission on matters pertaining to Wisconsin's interests in federal telecommunications policy. The division also undertakes the PSC's efforts on broadband infrastructure mapping and planning.

The *Natural Gas and Energy Division* is responsible for all aspects of regulating electric utilities and the provision of natural gas service. PSC approval is required for utilities to change rates, build power plants, or construct major transmission lines. The division looks at need, alternatives, costs, and environmental impacts for construction cases and reviews finances, corporate structure, and affiliated interests in rate cases. It also provides the commissioners with information they need in order to make decisions regarding construction and rate cases.

The *Division of Water, Compliance and Consumer Affairs* is responsible for regulating water and sewer public utilities in Wisconsin and ensuring utility compliance with the consumer sections of the state administrative code and statutes. The division offers assistance to all of the state's utilities for compliance with the statutes, code, and record-keeping requirements and the development of consumer affairs policies. The division also coordinates consumer information and mediates resolutions to consumer complaints.

History: Public utility regulation in Wisconsin followed and was closely related to railroad regulation. Railroads were the first modern enterprise to have their rates regulated, and Wisconsin became one of the first states to pass such laws. Chapter 273, Laws of 1874, established a railroad rate structure and provided for 3 appointed railroad commissioners to supervise rail freight operations. Two years later in Chapter 57, Laws of 1876, the legislature repealed much of the 1874 law and established a single appointed commissioner of railroads. The commissioner was made an elected official in 1881 (Chapter 300).

The forerunner of today's commission dates from Chapter 362, Laws of 1905, which created and appointed a 3-member Railroad Commission to supervise rail operations, appraise railroad property, and set rates. With the enactment of Chapter 499, Laws of 1907, which extended the powers of the Railroad Commission, Wisconsin became the first state to regulate all public utilities.

Chapter 183, Laws of 1931, renamed the agency the Public Service Commission of Wisconsin and made it responsible for comprehensive motor carrier regulation in 1933 (Chapter 488). The 1967 executive branch reorganization continued the commission as an independent agency. Chapter 29, Laws of 1977, transferred the commission's railroad and motor carrier regulatory functions to the Transportation Commission (recreated in 1982 as the now defunct Office of the Commissioner of Transportation). Railroad regulation was assigned to the newly created Office of the Commissioner of Railroads by 1993 Wisconsin Act 123.

Laws passed in 1985 provided for a partial deregulation of public utility holding companies and telecommunications service. 1993 Wisconsin Act 496 significantly altered the regulation of telecommunications utilities, particularly regarding rate-setting procedures. 2011 Wisconsin Act 22 established a new regulatory framework for telecommunications utilities, which eliminated the commission's authority to regulate the prices utilities charge telecommunications customers, as well as removing the commission's authority to investigate most consumer complaints involving retail telecommunications issues.

Statutory Councils

Telecommunications Privacy Council: Inactive.

The Telecommunications Privacy Council advises the commission on guidelines designed to protect the privacy of users of telecommunications services. The number of members on the council is not specified, but all must represent telecommunications providers or consumers. The council was created by 1993 Wisconsin Act 496 and its composition and duties are prescribed in Section 196.209 of the statutes.

Universal Service Fund Council: SCOTT BOHLER, DAVID BYERS, JACK CASSELL, JAMES COSTELLO, JOHN EICH, CELESTE FLYNN, PAMELA HOLLICK, JIM JERMAIN, VANESSA JOHNSON, BOB JONES, ROBERT KELLERMAN, JASON MEYER, JEAN PAUK, KATHY SCHMITT, PAM YOUNG-HOLMES (appointed by Public Service Commission).

Universal Service Fund Director: JEFF RICHTER, Public Service Commission, P.O. Box 7854, Madison 53707-7854; Telephone: 267-9624; Fax: 266-3957; TTY: (800) 251-8345 (in-state only) or 267-1479; jeff.richter@

The Universal Service Fund Council advises the commission on the administration of the Universal Service Fund, which assists low-income customers, disabled customers, and customers in areas where telecommunications service costs are relatively high, in obtaining affordable access to basic telecommunications services. The Universal Service Fund manager acts as liaison between the commission and the council. The number of members on the council is not specified. All must represent telecommunication service providers or consumers, but the majority of members must represent consumers. The council was created by 1993 Wisconsin Act 496 and its composition and duties are prescribed in Section 196.218 (6) of the statutes.

Wind Siting Council: BILL RAKOCY, WES SLAYMAKER (representing wind energy system developers); GLEN SCHWALBACH (town representative); SCOTT GODFREY (county representative); DEB ERWIN, ANDY HESSELBACH (representing the energy industry); TYSON COOK, MICHAEL VICKERMAN (representing environmental groups); TOM MEYER, TIM ROEHL (representing realtors); JAMES AMSTADT, JARRED SEARLS (adjacent or nearby landowners not receiving compensation for hosting wind energy systems); MARY BRANDT, CARL KUEHNE (public members); vacancy (University of Wisconsin System faculty member with expertise regarding health impacts of wind energy systems) (appointed by Public Service Commission).

The 15-member Wind Siting Council advises the commission on promulgation of rules relating to restrictions a political subdivision may impose on the installation of a wind energy system including setback requirements that provide reasonable protection from any health effects. The council also surveys the peer-reviewed scientific research regarding the health impacts of wind energy systems and studies state and national regulatory developments regarding the siting of wind energy systems. The members of the council are appointed by the commission for 3-year terms. The council was created by 2009 Wisconsin Act 40 and its composition and duties are prescribed in Sections 15.797 (1) and 196.378 (4g) of the statutes.

INDEPENDENT UNIT ATTACHED FOR BUDGETING, PROGRAM COORDINATION, AND RELATED MANAGEMENT FUNCTIONS BY SECTION 15.03 OF THE STATUTES

OFFICE OF THE COMMISSIONER OF RAILROADS

Commissioner of Railroads: JEFF PLALE, 266-3182, jeff.plale@

Legal Counsel: DOUGLAS S. WOOD, 266-9536, doug.wood@

Legislative/Public Policy Analyst: HEATHER GRAVES, 266-0276, heather.graves@

Investigator: TOM CLAUDER, 266-2874, thomas.clauder@

Mailing Address: P.O. Box 7854, Madison 53707-7854.

Location: 610 North Whitney Way, Suite 110, Madison.

Telephone: 266-0276.

Fax: 261-8220.

Internet Address: http://ocr.wi.gov

Number of Employees: 6.00.

Total Budget 2013-15: $1,068,600.

Statutory References: Sections 15.06 (1) (a) and 15.795 (1); Chapters 189-192 and 195.

Agency Responsibility: The Office of the Commissioner of Railroads enforces regulations related to railway safety and determines the safety of highway crossings including the adequacy of railroad warning devices. The office also retains authority over the rates and services of intrastate water carriers. The office is funded by assessments on railroads.

The governor appoints the commissioner with senate consent to a 6-year term and the commissioner holds the office until a successor is appointed. The commissioner may not have a financial interest in railroads or water carriers and may not serve on or under any committee of a political party. The office was created by 1993 Wisconsin Act 123 as an independent regulatory agency to assume the functions relating to railroad regulation that 1993 Wisconsin Act 16 had transferred to the Public Service Commission when the Office of the Commissioner of Transportation was eliminated. The responsibility for regulating water carriers was added by 2005 Wisconsin Act 179.

Department of
REVENUE

Address e-mail by combining the user ID and the state extender: userid@**revenue.wi.gov**
All telephone numbers are 608 area code unless otherwise indicated.

Secretary of Revenue: RICHARD G. CHANDLER, 266-6466, richard.chandler@; Fax: 266-5718.

Deputy Secretary: JACK JABLONSKI, 266-6466, jack1.jablonski@

Assistant Deputy Secretary: JENNIFER WESTERN, 266-6466, jennifer.western@

General Counsel, Office of: DANA J. ERLANDSEN, *chief counsel,* 267-8970, dana.erlandsen@

Communications Director: STEPHANIE MARQUIS, 266-2300, stephanie.marquis@; Fax: 266-5718.

Legislative Advisor: NATHANIEL RISTOW, 266-6466, nathaniel.ristow@

Enterprise Services Division: JON RENEAU, *administrator,* 264-8175, jon.reneau@; Division Fax: 266-2825.

　Privacy and Records Management Officer: PAUL RIEHEMANN, 264-6863, paul.riehemann@

　Business Services Section: MARTY WRIGHT, *director,* 266-3347, martin.wright@

　Financial Management Services Bureau: LAURIE GRAMS, *director,* 266-8469, laurie.grams@

　Human Resource Services Bureau: SCOTT C. THOMPSON, *director,* 261-8979, scott.thompson@

Income, Sales and Excise Tax Division: DIANE L. HARDT, *administrator,* 266-6798, diane.hardt@; VICKI GIBBONS, *deputy administrator,* 266-3612, vicki.gibbons@; Division Fax: 261-6240.

　Audit Bureau: WENDY MILLER, *director,* 261-5154, wendy.miller@

　Compliance Bureau: CATHERINE BINK, *director,* 266-7879, catherine.bink@

　Customer Service Bureau: JULIE RENEAU, *director,* 266-1179, julie.reneau@

　　Criminal Investigations Section: JUSTIN SHEMANSKI, *chief,* 266-0286, justin.shemanski@

　　Technical Services Section: NATHANIEL WEBER, *chief,* 266-8025, nathaniel.weber@

　Tax Operations Bureau: ERIN EGAN, *director,* 261-5235, erinb.egan@

Lottery Division: MICHAEL J. EDMONDS, *administrator,* 267-4500, michael.edmonds@; JEAN ADLER, *deputy administrator,* 261-6888, jean.adler@; Division Fax: 267-4505.

　Administrative Services and Communications Bureau: vacancy, *director,* 264-6604.

　Product Development and Marketing Bureau: SAVERIO MAGLIO, *director,* 267-4817, saverio.maglio@

　Retailer Relations and Sales Bureau: COLLEEN DVORAK, *director,* 267-0976, jean.dvorak@

Research and Policy Division: JOHN KOSKINEN, *administrator and chief economist,* 267-8973, john.koskinen@; MICHAEL WAGNER, *deputy administrator,* 266-6785, michaelw.wagner@; Division Fax: 266-6240.

　Economic Team: JOHN KOSKINEN, *leader,* 267-8973, john.koskinen@

　*Income Tax Policy Team:*MICHAEL WAGNER, *leader,* 266-6785, michaelw.wagner@

　Sales and Property Tax Policy Team: ROBERT SCHMIDT, *leader,* 265-5773, robert.schmidt@

State and Local Finance Division: CLAUDE LOIS, *administrator,* 266-0939, claude.lois@; JULIE RAES, *deputy administrator,* 266-9759, julie.raes@; Division Fax: 264-6887.

　Equalization Bureau: TONYA BUCHNER, *director,* 261-5275, tonya.buchner@

　Local Government Services Bureau: VALEAH FOY, *director,* 261-5360, valeah.foy@

　Manufacturing and Utility Bureau: TIMOTHY DRASCIC, *director,* 266-3845, timothy.drascic@

DEPARTMENT OF REVENUE

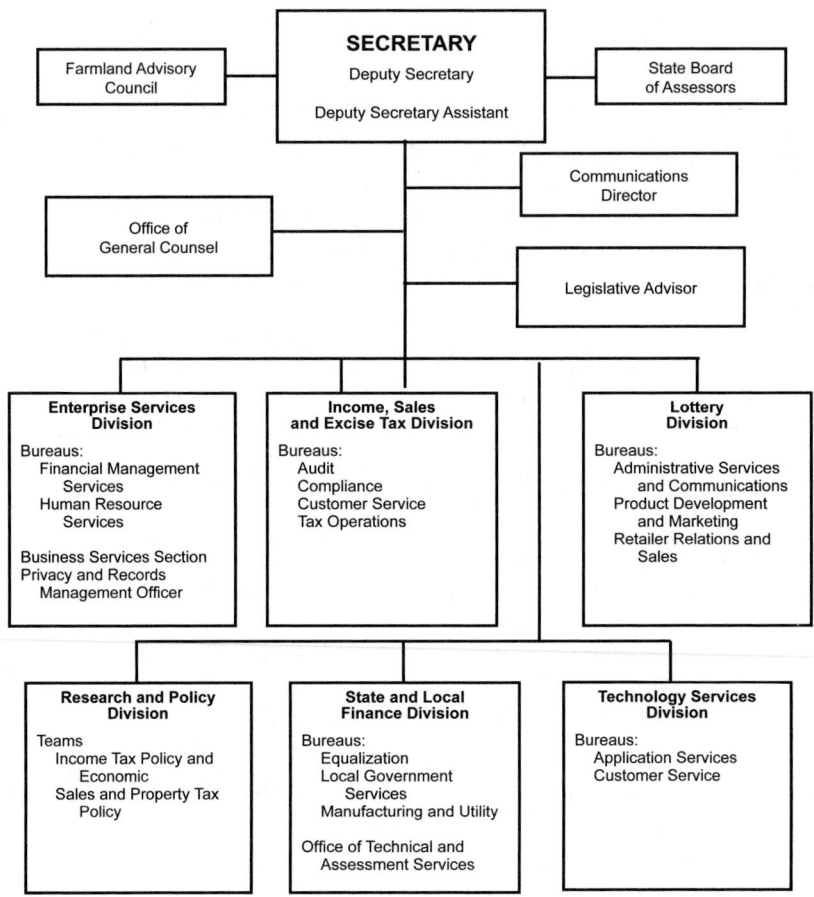

Unit attached for administrative purposes under Sec. 15.03:   Investment and Local Impact Fund Board

Office of Technical and Assessment Services: SCOTT SHIELDS, *director,* 266-8223, office telephone: 266-7750, scott.shields@

Technology Services Division: RICHARD OFFENBECHER, *administrator,* 261-2276, richard.offenbecher@; Division Fax: 266-9923.

Application Services Bureau: NEERAJ KULKARNI, *director,* 261-5183, neeraj.kulkarni@

Customer Service Bureau: PATRICK GRANT, *director,* 266-9751, patrick.grant@

Mailing Address: P.O. Box 8933, Madison 53708-8933.

Locations: 2135 Rimrock Road, Madison, and regional offices in Appleton, Eau Claire, Green Bay, Hawthorne, Milwaukee, Wausau; Bloomington, Minnesota and Chicago, Illinois.

Telephones: (608) 266-2486 – individuals; (608) 266-2776 – businesses; Telecommunications Relay Service dial "711" or visit Wisconsin Relay for more information.

Fax: (608) 267-1030.

Internet Address: www.revenue.wi.gov

Publications: *Agricultural Assessment Guide;* biennial report; *County and Municipal Revenues and Expenditures;* A Guide for Property Owners; *Quarterly Economic Outlook;* Summary of Tax Exemption Devices; *Town, Village, and City Taxes; Wisconsin Tax Bulletin;* and various brochures and publications on specific issues.

Number of Employees: 1,096.28.

Total Budget 2013-15: $368,433,700.

Statutory References: Sections 15.43 and 15.435; Chapters 70-79, 125, and 139.

Agency Responsibility: The Department of Revenue administers all major state tax laws (except the insurance premiums tax) and enforces the state's alcohol beverage and tobacco laws. It estimates state revenues, forecasts state economic activity, helps formulate tax policy, and administers the Wisconsin Lottery. It also determines equalized value of taxable property and assesses manufacturing property. It administers local financial assistance programs and assists local governments in their property assessments and financial management. The agency also oversees the Unclaimed Property program to match taxpayers with unclaimed financial assets.

Organization: The department is administered by a secretary who is appointed by the governor with the advice and consent of the senate. The secretary appoints the administrators of the Income, Sales and Excise Tax Division and the Technology Services Division from the classified service and the other division administrators from outside the classified service.

Unit Functions: The *Office of General Counsel* provides legal counsel and opinions; reviews tax legislation and administrative rules; and represents the department in all cases brought before the Tax Appeals Commission, in collections actions brought before state circuit courts and federal bankruptcy courts, and in nontax cases before administrative agencies. It is also responsible for providing a prompt and impartial review of all assessments appealed by individuals, partnerships, trusts, and corporations relating to income, franchise, sales and use, withholding, and excise taxes and the homestead tax credit.

The *Enterprise Services Division* provides departmentwide services in the areas of administration, budget and financial management, business services, printing, records management, personnel, affirmative action, equal opportunity, employee development, employment relations, and other management services.

The *Income, Sales and Excise Tax Division* administers tax laws relating to income, withholding, franchise, sales and use, local exposition, premier resort area, estate, fiduciary, liquor, beer, wine, cigarette and tobacco products, motor vehicles, alternate and aviation fuel taxes, rental vehicles, dry cleaning, and police and fire protection fees; and ambulatory surgical center assessment. The division also administers the homestead credit, earned income tax credit, and farmland preservation credit programs. The division drafts and reviews tax legislation, administrative rules, tax forms/instructions and publications; processes tax returns and payments; audits tax returns; provides taxpayer and practitioner assistance; collects delinquent taxes; and conducts criminal investigations. It also administers Wisconsin's Unclaimed Property program, including property custody and distribution, claims processing, and holder reporting.

The *Lottery Division* administers the Wisconsin Lottery. It manages the design, distribution, and sale of lottery products; conducts lottery game drawings; handles media relations; assists retailers with marketing lottery products; makes payment on winning tickets; provides product information through informational advertisements and its Web site (www.wilottery.com); and answers players' questions.

The *Research and Policy Division* provides detailed analyses of fiscal and economic policies to the departmental secretary, the governor, and other state officials. It assesses the impact of current and proposed tax laws, prepares official general fund tax collection estimates used to develop the state budget, issues quarterly forecasts of the state's economy, and develops statistical reports.

The *State and Local Finance Division* establishes the state's equalized values; assesses all manufacturing and telecommunications company property for property tax purposes; assesses and collects taxes on utilities, railroads, airlines, mining, and other special properties; and provides financial management and technical assistance to municipal and county governments. It administers the state municipal and county aid program, property tax relief for municipal services, the lottery credit program, and tax incremental financing programs. It provides property assessment administration and certifies assessment personnel.

The *Technology Services Division* administers technology services for all parts of the department, including data administration, applications development, workstation support, data collection, and technology planning.

History: The antecedents of the Department of Revenue date back at least to Chapter 130, Laws of 1868, which created a State Board of Assessors, composed of the secretary of state and the entire state senate, to perform the state's taxing functions. At that time, the property tax was the state's primary source of revenue.

Chapter 235, Laws of 1873, changed the board's composition to the secretary of state, state treasurer, and attorney general. The 1899 Legislature created the Office of Tax Commissioner (Chapter 206) to supervise the state's taxation system and made the commissioner a member and presiding officer of the State Board of Assessors.

The composition of the State Board of Assessors was changed again in Chapter 237, Laws of 1901, when the legislature replaced the constitutional officers with two assistant commissioners. The 1905 Legislature abolished the State Board of Assessors (Chapter 380) and assigned its functions to a 3-member Tax Commission, appointed by the governor with the advice and consent of the senate. This structure lasted until Chapter 412, Laws of 1939, created the Department of Taxation, headed by a single commissioner. Chapter 75, Laws of 1967, renamed the agency the Department of Revenue and the commissioner became the secretary.

Throughout the years, certain tax-related functions have been moved from one agency or level of government to another. For example, local officials originally assessed manufacturing property, but the 1973 Legislature gave the department responsibility for assessing all manufacturing property in the state.

Similarly, the 1939 Legislature made the Department of Taxation responsible for performing audits upon the request of local governmental units. After assignment to several other agencies, the legislature returned this function to the Department of Revenue in 1971. In 1983, the legislature repealed the department's mandatory municipal audit functions but left intact its discretionary oversight of municipal accounting.

The department currently is responsible for administration of the Wisconsin Lottery. The lottery was originally created by 1987 Wisconsin Act 119 and administered by the Lottery Board. It was later managed by the Wisconsin Gaming Commission. 1995 Wisconsin Act 27, which transferred the State Lottery to the Department of Revenue, also repealed the commission and created the Gaming Board. The Gaming Board was repealed in 1997 Wisconsin Act 27. The Unclaimed Property Program was transferred to the Department of Revenue from the office of the State Treasurer by 2013 Wisconsin Act 20.

Statutory Board and Council

State Board of Assessors: TIMOTHY DRASCIC, *chairperson;* KELLY COULSON, KURT KELLER, JULIE MATTHES, DANIEL STORM (Department of Revenue employees appointed by secretary).

The State Board of Assessors investigates objections to the amount, valuation, or taxability of real or personal manufacturing property, as well as objections to the penalties issued for late filing or nonfiling of required manufacturing property report forms. The number of board members is determined by the secretary, but all must be department employees. The board was created by Chapter 90, Laws of 1973, and its composition and duties are prescribed in Section 70.995 (8) of the statutes.

Farmland Advisory Council: RICHARD CHANDLER (secretary of revenue), *chairperson;* vacancy (agribusiness), AMBER KELLER (knowledgeable about agricultural lending practices), BRUCE JONES (UW System agricultural economist), TIM HANNA (mayor of a city of 40,000 or more population), JORDAN LAMB (environmental expert), vacancy (representing nonagricultural business), STEPHEN HINTZ (urban studies professor), HERB TAUCHEN (farmer) (all appointed by secretary of revenue); MELVIN RAATZ (assessor) (appointed by secretary of revenue as an advisor to council).

Agency Responsibility: The 9-member Farmland Advisory Council advises the Department of Revenue on implementing use-value assessment of agricultural land and reducing urban sprawl. It is required to report annually to the legislature on the usefulness of use-value assessment as a way to preserve farmland, discourage urban sprawl, and reduce the conversion of farmland to other uses. It also recommends changes to the shared revenue formula to compensate local governments adversely affected by use-value assessment. In carrying out its duties, it cooperates with the Wisconsin Strategic Growth Task Force of the State Interagency Land Use Council. The council was created by 1995 Wisconsin Act 27, and its composition and duties are prescribed in Section 73.03 (49) of the statutes.

INDEPENDENT BOARD ATTACHED FOR BUDGETING, PROGRAM COORDINATION, AND RELATED MANAGEMENT FUNCTIONS BY SECTION 15.03 OF THE STATUTES

INVESTMENT AND LOCAL IMPACT FUND BOARD ("Mining Board")

Investment and Local Impact Fund Board: RICHARD CHANDLER (secretary of revenue), *chairperson;* LESLIE KOLESAR (public member), *vice chairperson;* KELLY KLEIN (local official recommended by Wisconsin Counties Association), *secretary;* REED HALL (Wisconsin Economic Development Corporation CEO); EMMER SHIELDS (local official recommended by Wisconsin Counties Association); vacancy (local official recommended by League of Municipalities); DAVID PAJULA (local official recommended by Wisconsin Association of School Boards); ROBERT WALESEWICZ (public official recommended by Wisconsin Towns Association); vacancy (Native American member recommended by Great Lakes Inter-Tribal Council); EDWARD BRANDIS, RICK HERMUS (public members).

The 11-member Investment and Local Impact Fund Board administers the Investment and Local Impact Fund, created to help municipalities alleviate costs associated with social, educational, environmental, and economic impacts of metalliferous mineral mining. The board certifies to the Department of Administration the amount of the payments to be distributed to municipalities from the fund. It also provides guidance and funding to local governments throughout the development of a mining project.

In addition to the secretary of revenue and the chief executive officer of the Wisconsin Economic Development Corporation, or their designees, the board's 9 appointed members serve staggered 4-year terms. They include 3 public members; the 5 local officials recommended by: the League of Wisconsin Municipalities (1), the Wisconsin Towns Association (1), the Wisconsin Association of School Boards (1), and the Wisconsin Counties Association (2); and a Native American member is recommended by the Great Lakes Inter-Tribal Council, Inc. Certain board members must meet qualifications based on residence in or adjacent to a county or municipality with a metallic minerals ore body or mineral development. The board was created by Chapter 31, Laws of 1977, and its composition and duties are specified in Sections 15.435 (1) and 70.395 (2), Wisconsin Statutes.

Department of
SAFETY AND PROFESSIONAL SERVICES

Secretary of Safety and Professional Services: DAVE ROSS, 266-1352, dave.ross@wisconsin.gov

Deputy Secretary: JAY RISCH, 266-1352, jay.risch@wisconsin.gov

Assistant Deputy Secretary: ERIC ESSER, 266-1352, eric.esser@wisconsin.gov

General Counsel: MICHAEL BERNDT, 266-1352, michael.berndt@wisconsin.gov

Mailing Address: P.O. Box 8935, Madison 53708-8935.

Location: 1400 East Washington Avenue, Madison.

Telephones: 266-2112 (for operator, select menu option "6"); TTY: 267-2416.

Internet Address: http://dsps.wi.gov

Fax: 267-0644.

Number of Employees: 262.60.

Total Budget 2013-15: $102,105,300.

Statutory References: Sections 15.08, 15.085, 15.40, and 15.405-15.407; Chapters 101, 145, 440-462, 472, and 480.

Industry Services, Division of: JEFFREY WEIGAND, *administrator,* 267-9152, jeffrey.weigand@wisconsin.gov; Division Fax: 267-1381; Regional Fax: Green Bay: (920) 492-5604; Hayward: (715) 634-5150; La Crosse: (608) 785-9330; Stevens Point: (715) 345-5269; Waukesha: (262) 548-8614.

Legal Services and Compliance, Division of: ALOYSIUS ROHMEYER, *administrator,* 266-3445, aloysius.rohmeyer@wisconsin.gov

Management Services, Division of: ANGELA HERL, *administrator,* 261-4466, angela.herl@wisconsin.gov

Policy Development, Division of: GREG GASPER, *administrator,* 266-8419, greg.gasper@wisconsin.gov

Education and Examinations, Office of: JILL REMY, *program manager,* 266-7703, jill.remy@wisconsin.gov

Professional Credential Processing, Division of: KIRSTEN READER, *administrator,* 266-0557, kirsten.reader@wisconsin.gov

Examining Boards (Statutory Authority of Examining Boards) and Assigned Staff:

Accounting Examining Board: JOHN S. SCHEID (accountant), *chairperson;* TODD C. CRAFT (accountant), *vice chairperson;* GERALD E. DENOR (accountant), *secretary;* CHRISTINE M.

DEPARTMENT OF SAFETY AND PROFESSIONAL SERVICES

SECRETARY

Deputy Secretary

Assistant Deputy Secretary

Legislative Liaison

General Counsel

Communications Director

Division of Industry Services

Division of Legal Services and Compliance

Division of Management Services

Division of Policy Development

Office of Education and Examinations

Division of Professional Credential Processing

Examining Boards

Affiliated Credentialing Boards

Boards

Councils

ANDERSON, KATHLEEN J. LABRAKE (accountants); JOSEPH BRAUNGER*, GLENN MICHAELSEN*. *Executive Director:* BRITTANY LEWIN, 261-5406, brittany.lewin@wisconsin.gov.

Architects, Landscape Architects, Professional Engineers, Designers and Professional Land Surveyors, Examining Board of:

Examining Board Officers: ROSHEEN STYCZINSKI (landscape architect), *chairperson;* JOSEPH W. EBERLE (engineer), *vice chairperson;* LAWRENCE J. SCHNUCK (architect), *secretary.* The 5 professional sections listed below comprise the examining board for a total of 15 professional members and 10 public members. *Executive Director:* BRITTANY LEWIN, 261-5406, brittany.lewin@wisconsin.gov.

Architect Section: LAWRENCE J. SCHNUCK (architect), *chairperson;* MICHAEL P. EBERLE (architect), *vice chairperson;* MATTHEW FERNHOLZ*, *secretary;* JAMES A. GERSICH (architect); GARY KOHLENBERG*. *Executive Director:* BRITTANY LEWIN, 261-5406, brittany.lewin@wisconsin.gov.

Designer Section: STEVEN T. TWEED (designer), *chairperson;* MARK A. COOK, vacancy (designers); THOMAS J. GASPERETTI*, vacancy*. *Executive Director:* BRITTANY LEWIN, 261-5406, brittany.lewin@wisconsin.gov.

Engineer Section: JOSEPH W. EBERLE (engineer), *chairperson;* STEVEN J. HOOK*, *vice chairperson;* MARK E. MAYER (engineer), *secretary;* KRISTINE A. COTHARN (engineer); vacancy*. *Executive Director:* BRITTANY LEWIN, 261-5406, brittany.lewin@wisconsin. gov.

Landscape Architect Section: ROSHEEN M. STYCZINSKI (landscape architect), *chairperson;* MICHAEL J. KINNEY*, *vice chairperson;* ANDREW S. ALBRIGHT (landscape architect), *secretary;* vacancy (landscape architect); vacancy*. *Executive Director:* BRITTANY LEWIN, 261-5406, brittany.lewin@wisconsin.gov.

Land Surveyor Section: MATTHEW J. JANIAK (land surveyor), *chairperson;* DANIEL FEDDERLY (land surveyor), *vice chairperson;* RUTH G. JOHNSON*, *secretary;* BRUCE D. BOWDEN (land surveyor); vacancy*. *Executive Director:* BRITTANY LEWIN, 261-5406, brittany.lewin@wisconsin.gov.

Chiropractic Examining Board: PATRICIA A. SCHUMACHER (chiropractor), *chairperson;* JOHN E. CHURCH (chiropractor), *vice chairperson;* JODI GRIFFITH (chiropractor), *secretary;* JEFFREY MACKEY (chiropractor); KELLY BROWN*, vacancy*. *Executive Director:* THOMAS RYAN, 261-2378, thomas.ryan@wisconsin.gov.

Cosmetology Examining Board: VICKY L. MCNALLY (aesthetician/cosmetologist), *vice chairperson;* KRISTIN K. ALLISON (aesthetician/cosmetologist), *secretary;* LORI A. PAUL (private school of cosmetology representative); vacancy (public school of cosmetology representative); GAIL A. SENGBUSCH (electrologist); DIANNA D. WACHTER, vacancy (aestheticians/cosmetologists); 2 vacancies*. *Executive Director:* BRITTANY LEWIN, 261-5406, brittany.lewin@wisconsin.gov.

Dentistry Examining Board: LYNDSAY KNOELL (dentist), *chairperson;* MARK T. BRADEN (dentist), *vice chairperson;* DEBRA J. BERES (dental hygienist), *secretary;* LEONARDO HUCK, TIMOTHY F. MCCONVILLE, WENDY M. PIETZ, BETH R. WELTER (dentists); EILEEN DONOHOO, CARRIE G. STEMPSKI (dental hygienists); 2 vacancies*. *Executive Director:* BRITTANY LEWIN, 261-5406, brittany.lewin@wisconsin.gov.

Funeral Directors Examining Board: THOMAS J. BRADLEY (funeral director/embalmer), *chairperson;* ERIC LENGELL*, *vice chairperson;* MARLA E. MICHAELIS (funeral director/ embalmer), *secretary;* MARC A. EERNISSE, KRISTEN A. PIEHL (funeral director/embalmer); DEAN STENSBERG*. *Executive Director:* BRITTANY LEWIN, 261-5406, brittany.lewin@ wisconsin.gov.

Geologists, Hydrologists and Soil Scientists, Examining Board of Professional

Examining Board Officers: WILLIAM N. MODE (geologist), *chairperson;* BRENDA S. HALMINIAK (geologist), *vice chairperson;* RICHARD D. BEILFUSS (hydrologist), *secretary.* The 3 professional sections listed below comprise the examining board for a total of 9 professional members and 3 public members. *Executive Director:* DAN WILLIAMS, 267-7223, dan1.williams@wisconsin.gov.

Geologist Section: WILLIAM N. MODE (geologist), *chairperson;* BRENDA S. HALMINIAK (geologist), *vice chairperson;* JAMES M. ROBERTSON (geologist); STEPHANIE WILLIAMS*. *Executive Director:* DAN WILLIAMS, 267-7223, dan1.williams@wisconsin.gov.

Hydrologist Section: RANDALL J. HUNT (hydrologist), *chairperson;* KENNETH R. BRADBURY (hydrologist), *vice chairperson;* RUTH G. JOHNSON*, *secretary;* RICHARD D. BEILFUSS (hydrologist). *Executive Director:* DAN WILLIAMS, 267-7223, dan1.williams@wisconsin.gov.

Soil Scientist Section: 3 vacancies (soil scientists); vacancy*. *Executive Director:* DAN WILLIAMS, 267-7223, dan1.williams@wisconsin.gov.

Hearing and Speech Examining Board: SAMUEL P. GUBBELS (otolaryngologist), *chairperson;* THOMAS W. SATHER (speech-language pathologist), *vice chairperson;* SCOTT A. LARSON (hearing instrument specialist), *secretary;* DOREEN E. JENSEN, BARBARA J. JOHNSON (audiologists); STEVEN J. KLAPPERICH, THOMAS J. KRIER (hearing instrument specialists); PATRICIA L. WILLIS (speech-language pathologist); 2 vacancies*. *Executive Director:* BRITTANY LEWIN, 261-5406, brittany.lewin@wisconsin.gov.

Marriage and Family Therapy, Professional Counseling and Social Work Examining Board:

Examining Board Officers: LINDA G. PELLMANN (marriage and family therapist), *chairperson;* NICHOLAS P. SMIAR (social worker), *vice chairperson;* ALLISON L. GORDON (professional counselor), *secretary.* The following 3 sections comprise the examining board, for a total of 10 professional members and 3 public members. *Executive Director:* DAN WILLIAMS, 267-7223, dan1.williams@wisconsin.gov.

Marriage and Family Therapist Section: ALICE HANSON-DREW*, *chairperson;* LINDA G. PELLMANN (marriage and family therapist), *vice chairperson;* PETER FABIAN (marriage and family therapist), *secretary;* vacancy (marriage and family therapist). *Executive Director:* DAN WILLIAMS, 267-7223, dan1.williams@wisconsin.gov.

Professional Counselor Section: CHARLES V. LINDSEY (professional counselor), *chairperson;* ALLISON L. GORDON (professional counselor), *vice chairperson;* LESLIE D. MIRKIN (professional counselor), *secretary;* vacancy*. *Executive Director:* DAN WILLIAMS, 267-7223, dan1.williams@wisconsin.gov.

Social Worker Section: NICHOLAS P. SMIAR (independent social worker), *chairperson;* JENNIFER I. ANDERSON-MEGER (advanced practice social worker), *vice chairperson;* GREGORY E. WINKLER (clinical social worker), *secretary;* ELIZABETH A. KRUEGER (goverment social worker); vacancy*. *Executive Director:* DAN WILLIAMS, 267-7223, dan1.williams@wisconsin.gov.

Medical Examining Board: KENNETH B. SIMONS (physician), *chairperson;* TIMOTHY L. SWAN (physician), *vice chairperson;* MARY JO CAPODICE (physician), *secretary;* RODNEY A. ERICKSON, SURESH K. MISRA, MICHAEL J. PHILLIPS, SRIDHAR V. VASUDEVAN, CAROLYN OGLAND VUKICH, TIMOTHY W. WESTLAKE, RUSSELL S. YALE (physicians); JAMES BARR*, GREG M. COLLINS*, ROBERT ZONDAG*. *Executive Director:* THOMAS RYAN, 261-2378, thomas.ryan@wisconsin.gov (includes following boards).

Athletic Trainers Affiliated Credentialing Board: RYAN A. BERRY (athletic trainer), *chairperson;* KURT A. FIELDING (athletic trainer), *vice chairperson;* JAMES W. NESBIT (athletic trainer), *secretary;* GREGORY S. VERGAMINI (athletic trainer); vacancy (physician), vacancy*. Parent-board: Medical Examining Board. *Executive Director:* THOMAS RYAN, 261-2378, thomas.ryan@wisconsin.gov.

Dietitians Affiliated Credentialing Board: GAIL L. UNDERBAKKE (dietitian), *chairperson;* SCOTT M. KRUEGER (dietitian), *vice chairperson;* TARA L. LAROWE (dietitian); vacancy*. Parent-board: Medical Examining Board. *Executive Director:* THOMAS RYAN, 261-2378, thomas.ryan@wisconsin.gov.

Massage Therapy and Bodywork Therapy Affiliated Credentialing Board: ELIZABETH C. KRIZENESKY (massage therapist & body worker), *chairperson;* DARLENE M. CAMPO (technical college respresentative), *vice chairperson;* BARBARA YETTER (massage therapist & body worker), *secretary;* JOHN E. ANDERSON (school representative); 2 vacancies (massage therapists & body workers); vacancy*. Parent-board: Medical Examining Board. *Executive Director:* THOMAS RYAN, 261-2378, thomas.ryan@ wisconsin.gov.

Occupational Therapists Affiliated Credentialing Board: BRIAN B. HOLMQUIST (occupational therapist), *chairperson;* LAURA M. O'BRIEN (occupational therapist), *vice chairperson;* GAYE M. MEYER (occupational therapist assistant), *secretary;* AMY K. SUMMERS (occupational therapist); DOROTHY J. OLSON (occupational therapist assistant); CORLISS A. RICE*, vacancy*. Parent-board: Medical Examining Board. *Executive Director:* THOMAS RYAN, 261-2378, thomas.ryan@wisconsin.gov.

Perfusionists Examining Council: see councils.

Physician Assistants, Council on: see councils.

Podiatry Affiliated Credentialing Board: WILLIAM W. WEIS (podiatrist), *chairperson;* THOMAS R. KOMP (podiatrist), *vice chairperson;* GARY BROWN*, *secretary;* JEFFERY L. GIESKING (podiatrist). Parent-board: Medical Examining Board. *Executive Director:* THOMAS RYAN, 261-2378, thomas.ryan@wisconsin.gov.

Respiratory Care Practitioners Examining Council: see councils.

Nursing, Board of: JEFFREY G. MILLER (registered nurse), *chairperson;* SHERYL A. KRAUSE (registered nurse), *vice chairperson;* LILLIAN NOLAN*, *secretary;* PAUL L. ABEGGLEN, JULIE L. ELLIS, PETER J. KALLIO (registered nurses); MARIA JOSEPH, CHERYL A. STREETER (licensed practical nurses); LUANN SKARLUPKA*. *Executive Director:* DAN WILLIAMS, 267-7223, dan1.williams@wisconsin.gov.

Licensed Practical Nurses, Examining Council on: (Inactive), see councils.

Registered Nurses, Examining Council on: (Inactive), see councils.

Nursing Home Administrator Examining Board: KENNETH D. ARNESON (nursing home administrator), *chairperson;* TIMOTHY J. CONROY (nursing home administrator), *vice chairperson;* CHARLES D. HAWKINS (nursing home administrator), *secretary;* PATRICK M. SHAUGHNESSY (nursing home administrator); SUSAN KINAST-PORTER (physician); LORI M. KOEPPEL (registered nurse); STEFANIE CARTON*, LORELI DICKINSON*; PAUL H. PESHEK (designated by secretary of health services); vacancy (nursing home administrator). *Executive Director:* THOMAS RYAN, 261-2378, thomas.ryan@wisconsin.gov.

Optometry Examining Board: ANN MEIER CARLI (optometrist), *chairperson;* ROBERT C. SCHULZ (optometrist), *vice chairperson;* MARK A. JINKINS*, *secretary;* VICTOR J. CONNORS, RICHARD L. FOSS, BRIAN J. HAMMES (optometrists); vacancy*. *Executive Director:* BRITTANY LEWIN, 261-5406, brittany.lewin@wisconsin.gov.

Pharmacy Examining Board: THADDEUS J. SCHUMACHER (pharmacist), *chairperson;* FRANKLIN J. LADIEN (pharmacist), *vice chairperson;* PHILIP J. TRAPSKIN (pharmacist), *secretary;* TERRY K. MAVES, CATHY J. WINTERS (pharmacists); CHARLOTTE RASMUSSEN*, KRISTI SULLIVAN*. *Executive Director:* DAN WILLIAMS, 267-7223, dan1.williams@wisconsin.gov.

Pharmacist Advisory Council: (Inactive), see councils.

Physical Therapy Examining Board: LORI H. DOMINICZAK (physical therapist), *chairperson;* SHARI L. BERRY (physical therapist), *vice chairperson;* SARAH L. OLSON (physical therapist assistant), *secretary;* MICHELE A. THORMAN (physical therapist); THOMAS MURPHY*. *Executive Director:* THOMAS RYAN, 261-2378, thomas.ryan@wisconsin.gov.

Psychology Examining Board: DANIEL A. SCHROEDER (psychologist), *chairperson;* MARCUS P. DESMONDE (psychologist), *vice chairperson;* REBECCA C. ANDERSON (psychologist), *secretary;* DAVID W. THOMPSON (psychologist); 2 vacancies*. *Executive Director:* DAN WILLIAMS, 267-7223, dan1.williams@wisconsin.gov.

Radiography Examining Board: SUSAN SANSON (radiographer), *chairperson;* JAMES LEMEROND (radiographer), *vice chairperson;* KELLEY GRANT (radiographer), *secretary;*

GREGG A. BOGOST (physician-radiologist); TRACY L. MARSHALL (radiologic physicist); 2 vacancies*. *Executive Director:* THOMAS RYAN, 261-2378, thomas.ryan@wisconsin.gov.

Real Estate Examining Board: STEPHEN P. BEERS (real estate salesperson/ broker), *chairperson;* MICHAEL J. MULLEADY (real estate salesperson/ broker), *vice chairperson;* RANDAL F. SAVAGLIO (real estate sales/broker), *secretary;* MARIE H. HETZER, vacancy (real estate salesperson/brokers); BRIAN MCGRATH*, DENNIS M. PIERCE*. *Executive Director:* BRITTANY LEWIN, 261-5406, brittany.lewin@wisconsin.gov.

Veterinary Examining Board: PHILIP C. JOHNSON (veterinarian), *chairperson;* ROBERT T. FORBES (veterinarian), *vice chairperson;* NEIL A. WISELEY (veterinarian), *secretary;* DIANE C. DOMMER MARTIN, LISA M. WEISENSEL NESSON (veterinarians); BRENDA S. NEMEC (veterinarian technician); BRUCE BERTH*, SELDON SCHALL*. *Executive Director:* THOMAS RYAN, 261-2378, thomas.ryan@wisconsin.gov.

Boards (Statutory Authority of Boards) and Assigned Staff:

Auctioneer Board: TIMOTHY D. SWEENY (auctioneer), *chairperson;* JERRY L. THIEL (auctioneer), *vice chairperson;* RANDY J. STOCKWELL (auctioneer), *secretary;* LEONARD E. YOAP (auctioneer/auction company representative); HEATHER BERLINSKI*, RONALD J. POLACEK*, JAMES C. WENZLER*. *Executive Director:* BRITTANY LEWIN, 261-5406, brittany. lewin@wisconsin.gov.

Building Inspector Review Board (attached by s. 15.03): DONALD A. ESPOSITO (senate majority leader designee); DAVID R. HUEBSCH (speaker of assembly designee); GARY ROEHRIG (secretary of safety and professional services designee); MARTIN RIFKEN (representing building contractors and building developers); JAMES S. MICECH (certified building inspector). Except as indicated, all members appointed by governor with senate consent. *Policy Director:* JEFFREY GROTHMAN, 267-9794, jeffrey.grothman@wisconsin. gov.

Cemetery Board: CLYDE W. RUPNOW (licensed cemetery authority business representative), *chairperson;* FRANCIS J. GROH (licensed cemetery authority business representative), *vice chairperson;* PATRICIA A. GRATHEN (licensed cemetery authority business representative), *secretary;* WILLIAM E. GREENFIELD (licensed cemetery authority business representative); KATHLEEN M. CANTU*, vacancy*. *Executive Director:* BRITTANY LEWIN, 261-5406, brittany. lewin@wisconsin.gov.

Controlled Substances Board: DOUG ENGELBERT (designated by secretary of health services), *chairperson;* ALAN BLOOM (pharmacologist), *vice chairperson;* YVONNE M. BELLAY (designated by secretary of agriculture, trade and consumer protection), *secretary;* FRANKLIIN J. LADIEN (designated by pharmacy examining board); MARTIN G. KOCH (designated by attorney general); GUNNAR LARSON (psychiatrist). *Executive Director:* DAN WILLIAMS, 267-7223, dan1.williams@wisconsin.gov.

Real Estate Appraisers Board: LAWRENCE R. NICHOLSON (certified general appraiser), *chairperson;* CARL N. CLEMENTI (licensed appraiser), *vice chairperson;* SCOTT BRUNNER*, *secretary;* MARLA L. BRITTON (assessor); THOMAS J. KNEESEL (certified general appraiser); JOSE PEREZ*, HENRY F. SIMON*. *Executive Director:* THOMAS RYAN, 261-2378, thomas. ryan@wisconsin.gov.

Councils (Statutory Authority of Councils) and Assigned Staff:

Anesthesiologists Assistants, Council on: JAMES R. MESROBIAN (anesthesiologist), *chairperson;* MICHAEL L. BOTTCHER (anesthesiologist); ROBERT J. STUPI (anesthesiologist assistant); KENNETH B. SIMONS (Medical Examining Board designee); MARCY SALZER*. *Policy Director:* THOMAS RYAN, 261-2378, thomas.ryan@wisconsin.gov.

Automatic Fire Sprinkler System Contractors and Journeymen Council: JEFFREY GROTHMAN (department employee designated by secretary of safety and professional services), *secretary;* DAN DRIEBEL, CHRIS SCHOENBECK (licensed journeymen automatic fire sprinkler fitters); JEFF BATEMAN, GREG HINTZ (licensed automatic fire sprinkler contractors). *Policy Director:* JEFFREY GROTHMAN, 267-9794, jeffrey.grothman@wisconsin.gov.

Commercial Building Code Council: JEFFREY GROTHMAN (department employee designated by secretary of safety and professional services secretary), *secretary* (nonvoting); HUNTER BOHNE, COREY ROCKWEILER (skilled building trades representatives); DAVID ENIGL, PETER SCHEUERMAN (building inspector representatives); vacancy (fire services representative-chief); vacancy (fire services representative); STEVE KLESSIG, SAMUEL LAWRENCE (building contractors); MICHAEL F. MAMAYEK, IRINA RAGOZIN (architect, engineer, or designer). *Policy Director:* JEFFREY GROTHMAN, 267-9794, jeffrey.grothman@wisconsin.gov.

Contractor Certification Council: ABE DEGNAN, MARK A. ETRHEIM, vacancy (building contractor representatives). *Policy Director:* JEFFREY GROTHMAN, 267-9794, jeffrey. grothman@wisconsin.gov.

Conveyance Safety Code Council: JEFFREY GROTHMAN (secretary of safety and professional services designee), *secretary;* WILLIAM GRUBBS (representative of a manufacturer of elevators); vacancy (representative of an elevator servicing business); PAUL S. ROSENBERG (representative of an architectural design or elevator consulting profession); KELVIN NORD (representative of a labor organization involved in elevator installation, maintenance, and repair); ADAM SMITH (representative of a city, village, town, or county); MICHAEL DAUCK (representative of an owner or manager of a building containing an elevator); vacancy*; BRIAN HORNUNG (commercial construction building contractor involved in construction or installation of conveyances); BRIAN RAUSCH (department employee familiar with commercial building inspectors, designated by secretary of safety and professional services) (nonvoting). *Policy Director:* JEFFREY GROTHMAN, 267-9794, jeffrey.grothman@ wisconsin.gov.

Crematory Authority Council: SCOTT K. BRAINARD, WILLIAM R. CRESS, GARY A. LANGENDORF (funeral director crematory authority); ADAM J. CASPER, KELLY L. COLEMAN-KOHORN, PAUL A. HAUBRICH (cemetery crematory authority); LINDA A. REID*; JEFFREY GROTHMAN (designated by secretary of safety and professional services) (nonvoting). *Policy Director:* JEFFREY GROTHMAN, 267-9794, jeffrey.grothman@wisconsin.gov.

Dwelling Code Council, Uniform: MICHAEL COELLO (construction material supply representative), *chairperson;* MARY L. SCHROEDER (building contractor), *vice chairperson;* JEFFREY GROTHMAN (department employee designated by secretary of safety and professional services), *secretary* (nonvoting); ABE DEGNAN, STEVEN GRYBOSKI, MIKE MARTHALER (building contractors); SCOTT W. SATULA, BRIAN E. WERT (certified building inspectors employed by local government); PETER KRABBE (construction material supply representative); AMY BLISS (manufactured housing representative); JESSE JERABEK (architect, engineer, or designer). *Policy Director:* JEFFREY GROTHMAN, 267-9794, jeffrey.grothman@wisconsin.gov.

Licensed Practical Nurses, Examining Council on: (Inactive). Parent-board: Board of Nursing. *Executive Director:* DAN WILLIAMS, 267-7223, dan1.williams@wisconsin.gov.

Manufactured Housing Code Council: JEFFREY GROTHMAN (department employee designated by secretary of safety and professional services), *secretary* (nonvoting); JAY McDONALD, ROB MOBLEY (manufacturers); BART HUNTINGTON, MARK THIEDE (manufactured home dealers); ROB GULOTTA, JOHN J. SCHARLAU (owners of manufactured home communities); ANTHONY WIDOWSKI, vacancy (installers); ROSS KINZLER (industry association representative); BOB KLUWIN (suppliers of materials or services); CHUCK ONSUM*; STEVE BREITLOW (labor representative); DAN CURRAN (inspector). *Policy Director:* JEFFREY GROTHMAN, 267-9794, jeffrey.grothman@wisconsin.gov.

Multifamily Dwelling Code Council: EDWARD R. GRAY, MARK SCOTT (skilled building trades labor organization representatives); DAVID A. NITZ (municipal inspector: county with population less than 50,000); PETER SCHEUERMAN (municipal inspector: county with population over 50,000); SCOTT BURKART, vacancy (fire service workers); BETH A. GONNERING, vacancy (multifamily dwelling contractors and developers); KEVIN WIPPERFURTH, 2 vacancies (materials manufacturers and finished product suppliers); JAMES R. KLETT (architects, engineers, and designers representative); 2 vacancies*; JEFFREY GROTHMAN (department of safety and professional services employee/nonvoting secretary). *Policy Director:* JEFFREY GROTHMAN, 267-9794, jeffrey.grothman@wisconsin. gov.

Perfusionists Examining Council: SHAWN E. MERGEN (perfusionist), *chairperson;* JEFFREY P. EDWARDS (perfusionist), *vice chairperson;* GARY TSAROVSKY (perfusionist), *secretary;* DAVID F. COBB*; vacancy (physician). Parent-board: Medical Examining Board. *Executive Director:* THOMAS RYAN, 261-2378, thomas.ryan@wisconsin.gov.

Plumbers Council: TIM LAMB (department employee), *secretary;* DAVE JONES (master plumber); STEVE BRIETLOW (journeyman plumber). *Policy Director:* JEFFREY GROTHMAN, 267-9794, jeffrey.grothman@wisconsin.gov.

Pharmacist Advisory Council: (Inactive). Parent-board: Pharmacy Examining Board. *Executive Director:* DAN WILLIAMS, 267-7223, dan1.williams@wisconsin.gov.

Physician Assistants, Council on: JULIE A. DOYLE (physician assistant), *chairperson*; JODY L. WILKINS (physician assistant), *vice chairperson;* JEREMIAH L. BARRETT (educator member) *secretary;* ANNE B. HLETKO (physician assistant); MARY PANGMAN SCHMITT*. Parent-board: Medical Examining Board. *Executive Director:* THOMAS RYAN, 261-2378, thomas.ryan@wisconsin.gov.

Registered Nurses, Examining Council on: (Inactive). Parent-board: Board of Nursing. *Executive Director:* DAN WILLIAMS, 267-7223, dan1.williams@wisconsin.gov.

Respiratory Care Practitioners Examining Council: LYNN R. WALDERA (respiratory care practitioner), *chairperson;* ANN M. MEICHER (respiratory care practitioner), *vice chairperson;* WILLIAM D. ROSANDICK (respiratory care practitioner), *secretary;* vacancy (physician with a specialty in cardiothoracic surgeon or cardiovascular anesthesiologist); vacancy*. Parent-board: Medical Examining Board. *Executive Director:* THOMAS RYAN, 261-2378, thomas.ryan@wisconsin.gov.

Sign Language Interpreter Council: JOEL E. MANOKOWSKI (deaf or hard of hearing member), *chairperson;* STEVE SMART (interpreter member), *vice chairperson;* FAYE JORDAN-PETERS (deaf or hard of hearing member), *secretary;* SUZETTE GARAY, 2 vacancies (deaf or hard of hearing members); vacancy (interpreter member); CARLOS JARAMILLO (interpreter services member); JEFFREY GROTHMAN (department employee designated by secretary of safety and professional services). *Policy Director:* JEFFREY GROTHMAN, 267-9794, jeffrey. grothman@wisconsin.gov.

---

*Asterisk indicates public member. Other members represent the profession regulated, unless otherwise noted. The governor appoints all examining board and council members with the advice and consent of the senate, unless otherwise indicated.

Visit the Department of Safety and Professional Services Web site at http://dsps.wi.gov for the latest information on board memberships.

Boards and Councils Within the Department of Safety and Professional Services

Unit	Statutory Citation	Significant Session Laws Affecting	Duties Specified in Wisconsin Statutes
Accounting Examining Board	S. 15.405 (1)	1913 c. 337; 1967 c. 327; 1981 c. 356	Ch. 442
Architects, Landscape Architects, Professional Engineers, Designers and Professional Land Surveyors, Examining Board of	S. 15.405 (2)	1917 c. 644; 1931 c. 486; 1955 c. 547; 1969 c. 446; 1993 a. 463, a. 465; 1997 a. 300, 2013 a. 358	Ch. 443
Auctioneer Board	S. 15.405 (3)	1993 a. 102	Ch. 480
Automatic Fire Sprinkler System Contractors and Journeymen Council	S. 15.407 (17)	1971 c. 255; 1979 c. 221; 1995 a. 27; 2011 a. 32	S. 145.17 (2)
Building Code Council, Comercial	S. 15.407 (18)	2013 a. 270	S. 101.023
Cemetery Board	S. 15.405 (3m)	2005 a. 25	Ch. 440, Subchap.IX
Chiropractic Examining Board	S. 15.405 (5)	1925 c. 408	Ch. 446

Boards and Councils Within the Department of Safety and Professional Services – Continued

Unit	Statutory Citation	Significant Session Laws Affecting	Duties Specified in Wisconsin Statutes
Contractor Certification Council	S. 15.407 (11)	2005 a. 200; 2011 a. 32	S. 101.625
Controlled Substances Board	S. 15.405 (5g)	1969 c. 384; 1971 c. 219; 1995 a. 305	Ch. 961
Conveyance Safety Code Council	S. 15.407 (14)	2005 a. 456; 2011 a. 32	S. 101.986
Cosmetology Examining Board	S. 15.405 (17)	1939 c. 431; 1987 a. 265 2005 a. 314; 2011 a. 190; 2013 a. 124	Ch. 454, Subchap.I
Crematory Authority Council	S. 15.407 (8)	2005 a. 31	S. 15.09 (5)
Dentistry Examining Board	S. 15.405 (6)	1885 c. 129; 1997 a. 96	Ch. 447
Dwelling Code Council, Uniform	S. 15.407 (10)	1975 c. 404; 1995 a. 27; 2011 a. 32, a. 146	S. 101.62, 101.72
Funeral Directors Examining Board	S. 15.405 (16)	1905 c. 420; 1975 c. 39; 1983 a. 485	Ch. 445
Geologists, Hydrologists and Soil Scientists, Examining Board of Professional	S. 15.405 (2m)	1997 a. 300	Ch. 470
Hearing and Speech Examining Board	S. 15.405 (6m)	1969 c. 300; 1989 a. 316; 2003 a. 270	Ch. 459
Manufactured Housing Code Council	S. 15.407 (13)	2005 a. 45; 2011 a. 32	S. 101.933
Marriage and Family Therapy, Professional Counseling, and Social Work Examining Board	S. 15.405 (7c)	1991 a. 160; 2001 a. 80	Ch. 457
Medical Examining Board	S. 15.405 (7)	1897 c. 264; 1903 c. 426; 1953 c. 325; 1985 a. 340; 1993 a. 16	Ch. 448, Subchap.II
Anesthesiologist Assistants, Council on	S. 15.407 (7)	2011 a. 160	S. 448.23
Athletic Trainers Affiliated Credentialing Board	S. 15.406 (4)	1999 a. 9	Ch. 448, Subchap.VI
Dietitians Affiliated Credentialing Board	S. 15.406 (2)	1993 a. 443; 1997 a. 75	Ch. 448, Subchap.V
Massage Therapy and Bodywork Therapy Affiliated Credentialing Board	S. 15.406 (6)	2001 a. 74; 2009 a. 355	Ch. 460
Occupational Therapists Affiliated Credentialing Board	S. 15.406 (5)	1999 a. 180	Ch. 448, Subchap.VII
Perfusionists Examining Council	S. 15.407 (2m)	2001 a. 89	S. 448.40 (2)
Physician Assistants, Council on	S. 15.407 (2)	1973 c. 149; 1977 c. 418; 2011 a. 146	S. 448.20
Podiatry Affiliated Credentialing Board	S. 15.406 (3)	1997 a. 175; 2009 a. 113	Ch. 448, Subchap.IV
Respiratory Care Practitioners Examining Council	S. 15.407 (1m)	1989 a. 229	S. 15.407 (1m)
Multifamily Dwelling Code Council	S. 15.407 (12)	1991 a. 39; 1995 a. 27; 2011 a. 32	S. 101.972
Nursing, Board of	S. 15.405 (7g)	1911 c. 346; 1967 c. 327	Ch. 441, Subchap.I
Registered Nurses, Examining Council on	S. 15.407 (3)(a)	1921 c. 365	S. 441.05
Licensed Practical Nurses, Examining Council on	S. 15.407 (3)(b)	1949 c. 402	S. 441.10
Nursing Home Administrator Examining Board	S. 15.405 (7m)	1969 c. 478	Ch. 456
Optometry Examining Board	S. 15.405 (8)	1915 c. 488	Ch. 449

**Boards and Councils Within the Department of Safety and Professional Services –
Continued**

Unit	Statutory Citation	Significant Session Laws Affecting	Duties Specified in Wisconsin Statutes
Pharmacy Examining Board	S. 15.405 (9)	1882 c. 167	Ch. 450
Pharmacist Advisory Council	S. 15.407 (6)	1997 a. 68	S. 450.025
Physical Therapy Examining Board	S. 15.405 (7r)	1967 c. 327; 1993 a. 107; 2001 a. 70; 2009 a. 149	Ch. 448, Subchap.III
Plumbers Council	S. 15.407 (16)	1967 c. 327; 1979 c. 221; 1995 a. 27; 2011 a. 32	S. 145.02 (4)
Psychology Examining Board	S. 15.405 (10m)	1969 c. 290	Ch. 455
Radiography Examining Board	S. 15.405 (7e)	2009 a. 106	Ch. 462
Real Estate Appraisers Board	S. 15.405 (10r)	1989 a. 340; 1991 a. 78	Ch. 458
Real Estate Examining Board	S. 15.405 (11m)	1919 c. 656; 1981 c. 94; 2011 a. 32	Ch. 452
Real Estate Curriculum and Examinations, Council on	S. 15.407 (5)	1989 a. 341; 1989 a. 359	S. 452.06 (2)
Sign Language Interpreter Council	S. 15.407 (9)	2009 a. 360	S. 440.032
Veterinary Examining Board	S. 15.405 (12)	1961 c. 294; 1995 a. 321	Ch. 453
Attached by S. 15.03 Building Inspector Review Board	S. 15.405 (1m)	2005 a. 457; 2011 a. 32	S. 101.596

Under Section 440.042, Wisconsin Statutes, the secretary of the department of safety and professional services may appoint advisory committees to advise the department and its boards on matters relating to the regulation of credential holders.

Publications: Biennial reports; Consumer Complaints Frequently Asked Questions; Other Resources; The Impaired Professionals Procedure; Information About Your Hearing; Screening Process Brochure; Wisconsin Directory of Accredited Schools of Nursing; plus informational bulletins for credential holders and monthly disciplinary reports.

Agency Responsibility: The Department of Safety and Professional Services is responsible for ensuring the safe and competent practice of licensed professionals in Wisconsin. The department also administers and enforces laws to assure safe and sanitary conditions in public and private buildings. It provides administrative services to the state occupational regulatory authorities responsible for regulation of occupations and offers policy assistance in such areas as evaluating and establishing new professional licensing programs, creating routine procedures for legal proceedings, and adjusting policies in response to public needs. Currently, the department and regulatory authorities are responsible for regulating more than 430,000 credential holders and 200 types of credentials.

The department investigates and prosecutes complaints against credential holders and assists with drafting statutes and administrative rules. The Professional Assistance Procedure (PAP) program enforces participation agreements with credential holders who are chemically impaired, allowing them to retain their professional credentials if they comply with requirements, including treatment for chemical dependency.

The department provides direct regulation and licensing of certain occupations and activities. Numerous boards and regulatory authorities attached to the department have independent responsibility for the regulation of specific professions in the public interest. Within statutory limits, they determine the education and experience required for credentialing, develop and evaluate examinations, and establish standards for professional conduct. These standards are set by administrative rule and enforced through legal action upon complaints from the public. The regulatory authorities may reprimand a credential holder; limit, suspend, or revoke the credential of a practitioner who violates laws or board rules; and, in some cases, impose forfeitures.

Regulatory authority members must be state residents, and they cannot serve more than two consecutive terms. No member may be an officer, director, or employee of a private organization that promotes or furthers the profession or occupation regulated by that board.

Organization: The governor appoints the secretary of the department with the advice and consent of the senate. The secretary appoints a deputy secretary, an assistant deputy secretary, and the heads of various subunits from outside the classified service.

The boards and councils attached to the department consist primarily of members of the professions and occupations they regulate. In 1975, the legislature mandated that at least one public member serve on each board. In 1984, it required an additional public member on most boards. Public members are prohibited from having ties to the profession they regulate. In most cases, the governor appoints all members of the licensing and regulatory boards with the advice and consent of the senate. However, in some cases, council members are appointed by the governor without senate confirmation, by the secretary of the department, or by their related examining boards.

Unit Functions: The *Division of Industry Services* is divided into two bureaus, an administrative services section, and the Fire Prevention program.

The Bureau of Field Services performs inspections of commercial buildings, amusement rides, boilers, elevators, pressurized gas systems, and electrical systems. The bureau also performs plan reviews of elevators, boilers, and private onsite wastewater treatment systems. The bureau is also responsible for auditing third party and municipal inspection agencies.

The Bureau of Technical Services performs commercial building, plumbing, and fire suppression plan review. The bureau is also responsible for administering the Uniform Dwelling Code program, the federal HUD Manufactured Housing program, and provides consultations and training to local building officials and commercial and residential contractors.

The Administrative Services Section provides administrative support to internal and external stakeholders. It also administers the Rental Weatherization program for rental properties.

The Fire Prevention program administers the 2% Fire Dues program and provides consultation, support, and training to over 800 fire departments throughout the state.

The *Division of Legal Services and Compliance* (DLSC) is a public law office providing legal services to professional boards, regulated industries, and the department regarding the investigation, prosecution, and discipline of licensed credential holders for violations of professional standards. As part of these services, DLSC is organized into legal teams which include complaint intake personnel, consumer protection investigators, paralegals, prosecutors, and designated board counsel.

DLSC is also responsible for monitoring compliance with disciplinary orders and administering the Professional Assistance Procedure (PAP), a confidential monitoring program for impaired professionals. In addition, DLSC performs inspections of pharmacies, drug distributors and manufacturers, funeral home establishments, and barber and cosmetology establishments and schools.

The *Division of Management Services* provides administrative services to the department including budget and fiscal services, purchasing and contract administration, human resource services and employment relations, affirmative action compliance, facilities and fleet management, safety, mail, and telecommunication services. The division partners with the Department of Administration's Division of Enterprise Technology to provide information technology services to the department.

The *Division of Policy Development* provides professional and administrative support to over 60 regulatory boards, councils, and committees. This includes: preparing agendas, transcribing meeting minutes, and researching and analyzing issues related to the regulated professions and programs. The division facilitates the drafting of administrative code and implementation of new laws, rules, and policies.

The *Division of Professional Credential Processing* receives applications for licenses and permits, creates applicant records, and determines whether credential criteria have been met.

History: The 2011-13 biennial budget, 2011 Wisconsin Act 32, created the Department of Safety and Professional Services (DSPS) by combining the Department of Regulation and Licensing (DRL) and the Divisions of Safety and Buildings and Environmental and Regulatory Services from the Department of Commerce.

Chapter 75, Laws of 1967, created DRL and attached to it 14 separate examining boards that had been independent agencies. The 1967 reorganization also transferred to the department some direct licensing and registration functions not handled by boards, including those for private detectives and detective agencies, charitable organizations, and professional fund-raisers and solicitors.

DRL's responsibilities changed significantly since its creation. Initially, it performed routine housekeeping functions for the examining boards, which continued to function as independent agencies. Subsequently, a series of laws required the department to assume various substantive administrative functions previously performed by the boards and to provide direct regulation of several professions.

DSPS's Division of Industry Services traces its roots to 1911 when the Legislature created the Industrial Commission in Chapter 485 to set standards for a safe place of employment. This "safe place" statute was extended in Chapter 588, Laws of 1913, to include public buildings, defined as "any structure used in whole or in part as a place of resort, assemblage, lodging, trade, traffic, occupancy, or use by the public, or by three or more tenants." The commission adopted its first building code in 1914. Programs added over the years include plumbing, heating, ventilation, air conditioning, energy conservation, private on-site waste treatment systems, accessibility for people with disabilities, and electrical inspection and certification.

Office of the
SECRETARY OF STATE

Secretary of State: DOUGLAS La FOLLETTE, 266-8888.

Deputy Secretary of State: Susan Churchill, 266-3470.

Government Records Division: Ann Bloczynski, *administrator,* 266-1437.

Mailing Address: P.O. Box 7848, Madison 53707-7848.

Location: 30 West Mifflin Street, 10th Floor, Madison 53703.

Telephone: (608) 266-8888.

Fax: (608) 266-3159.

Internet Address: www.sos.state.wi.us

E-mail Address: statesec@wi.gov

Number of Employees: 4.0.

Total Budget 2013-15: $1,015,600.

Constitutional References: Article VI, Sections 1 and 2.

Statutory Reference: Chapter 14, Subchapter III.

Agency Responsibility: The Office of the Secretary of State performs a variety of services for state government and Wisconsin municipalities. Wisconsin's Constitution requires the secretary of state to maintain the official acts of the legislature and governor, and to keep the Great Seal of the State of Wisconsin and affix it to all official acts of the governor.

Organization: The secretary of state, a constitutional officer elected on a partisan ballot in the November general election, heads the Office of the Secretary of State.

Unit Functions: The *Government Records Division* keeps the Great Seal of the State of Wisconsin and affixes it to all official acts of the governor, coordinates the publication of state laws with the Legislative Reference Bureau, records official acts of the legislature and the governor, and files oaths of office. It also files deeds for state lands and buildings, issues authentications and apostilles (a form of international authentication of notaries public), preserves the original copies of all enrolled laws and resolutions, and files annexations, charter ordinances, and incorporation papers for villages and cities. Municipal records and deeds can be accessed via the agency Web site.

History: The 1836 congressional act that organized the Territory of Wisconsin provided for a secretary of the territory to be appointed by the President of the United States. This office was the forerunner of the post of secretary of state created by the Wisconsin Constitution. Delegates to the constitutional conventions of 1846 and 1848 determined that the secretary of state would be a constitutional officer. From the beginning of statehood until 1970, the secretary of state was elected for a 2-year term. Pursuant to a constitutional amendment ratified in 1967 and effective since the 1970 election, the term was extended to 4 years.

In the early days of statehood, the secretary of state personally performed a broad range of duties that are now delegated to other state agencies. Chapter 276, Laws of 1969, created the Office of the Secretary of State to assist the secretary.

Office of the
STATE TREASURER

State Treasurer: MATT ADAMCZYK, 266-1714, matt.adamczyk@wi.gov

Mailing Address: Room B41 West, State Capitol, Madison 53701.

Location: Room B41 West, State Capitol, Madison.

Telephone: (608) 266-1714.

Internet Address: www.statetreasury.wisconsin.gov

Number of Employees: 4.00.

Total Budget 2013-15: $1,089,600.

Constitutional References: Article VI, Sections 1 and 3; Article X, Section 7.

Statutory Reference: Chapter 14, Subchapter IV.

Agency Responsibility and Functions: The Office of the State Treasurer signs certain checks and financial instruments and participates in the promotion of the state's unclaimed property program. The state treasurer serves on the Board of Commissioners of Public Lands.

Organization: The state treasurer, a constitutional officer elected for a 4-year term by partisan ballot in the November general election, heads the Office of the State Treasurer.

History: The territorial treasurer, an office created in 1839, was appointed by the governor, but the Wisconsin Constitution, adopted in 1848, made the office an elective partisan position. From 1848 through 1968, the state treasurer was elected to a 2-year term in the November general election. Since 1970, following ratification of a constitutional amendment in April 1967, the state treasurer has been elected to a 4-year term. Chapter 276, Laws of 1969, created the Office of the State Treasurer to assist the treasurer. The state's unclaimed property program was transferred from the Office of the State Treasurer to the Department of Revenue by 2013 Wisconsin Act 20.

TECHNICAL COLLEGE SYSTEM

Address e-mail by combining the user ID and the state extender: userid@**wtcsystem.edu**
All telephone numbers are 608 area code unless otherwise indicated.

Technical College System Board: ANDREW PETERSEN (public member), *president;* JOHN SCHWANTES (public member), *vice president;* PHILIP BARANOWSKI (public member), *secretary;* REGGIE NEWSON (secretary of workforce development), TONY EVERS (superintendent of public instruction), JOSE VASQUEZ (designated by UW System Board of Regents President); TERRENCE E. McGOWAN (employee member); STEPHEN D. WILLET (employer member); BECKY LEVZOW (farmer member); SUSAN SCHAUMBURG (student member); MARY CUENE, STAN DAVIS, S. MARK TYLER (public members). (All except *ex officio* members are appointed by governor.)

President and State Director: MORNA K. FOY, 266-1770, morna.foy@

Executive Vice President: JAMES ZYLSTRA, 266-1739, james.zylstra@

Finance and Management, Office of: KELLY GALLAGHER, *associate vice president,* 266-2947, kelly.gallagher@

Information Technology, Office of: vacancy.

Provost and Vice President: KATHLEEN CULLEN, 266-9399, kathleen.cullen@

    Occupational and Academic Excellence, Office of: SANDRA SCHMIT, *associate vice president,* 267-9064, sandra.schmit@

    Student Success, Office of: WILLA PANZER, *associate vice president,* 267-9065, willa.panzer@

Strategic Advancement: CONOR SMYTH, *director,* 266-2991, conor.smyth@

Mailing Address: P.O. Box 7874, Madison 53707-7874.

Location: 4622 University Avenue, Madison.

Telephone: 266-1207.

Fax: 266-1690.

Internet Address: www.wtcsystem.edu

Publications: *Wisconsin Technical Colleges;* Technical College Facts; annual and biennial reports; annual evaluation reports of technical college offerings and services; cost allocation summaries; employer satisfaction reports; graduate follow-up reports.

Number of Employees: 58.00.

Total Budget 2013-15: $701,992,300.

Statutory References: Section 15.94; Chapter 38.

    Agency Responsibility: The Technical College System Board is the coordinating agency for the Technical College System. The board establishes statewide policies and standards for the educational programs and services provided by the 16 technical college districts that cover the state. The district boards, in turn, are responsible for the direct operation of their respective schools and programs. They are empowered to levy property taxes, provide for facilities and equipment, employ staff, and contract for services. The districts set academic and grading standards, appoint the district directors, hire instructional and other staff, and manage the district budget.

    The system board supervises district operations through reporting and audit requirements and consultation, coordination, and support services. It sets standards for building new schools and adding to current facilities. It also provides assistance to districts in meeting the needs of target groups, including services for the disadvantaged, the disabled, women, dislocated workers, the incarcerated, and minorities.

    The board administers state and federal aids. It works with the Department of Public Instruction to coordinate secondary and postsecondary vocational and technical programs. It also cooperates with the University of Wisconsin System to establish coordinated programming to make the services of the two agencies fully available to state residents. The board cooperates with the Department of Workforce Development to provide training for apprentices.

    Organization: The 13-member Technical College System Board includes 9 members appointed by the governor to serve staggered 6-year terms and a technical college student appointed for a 2-year term. The student must be 18 years of age and a state resident who is enrolled at least half-time and in good academic standing. The governor may not appoint a student member from the same technical college in any two consecutive terms. No person may serve as board president for more than two successive annual terms. A 1971 opinion of the attorney general held that a member of a technical college district board could not serve concurrently on the state board (60 *OAG* 178). The board appoints a director, called the "system president", from outside the classified service to serve at its pleasure, and the system president selects the executive assistant and division administrators from outside the classified service.

    The 16 technical college districts encompass 49 campuses. Each district is headed by a board of 9 members who serve staggered 3-year terms. For all districts except Milwaukee, district boards include 2 employers, 2 employees, a school district administrator, a state or local elected official, and 3 additional members as defined by statute. A district appointment committee, composed of county board chairpersons or school board presidents, appoints the board members, subject to approval of the state system board. Each district is administered by a director, called a "president", appointed by the district board.

For Milwaukee, 7 of the 9 board members must be residents of Milwaukee County. The board's 9 members include: 5 persons that represent employers (3 with 15 or more employees, 2 with 100 or more employees, and at least 2 manufacturers); one school district administrator; one elected official who holds a state or local office; and 2 additional members. Milwaukee board members are appointed by a committee composed of the county executive of Milwaukee County and the chairpersons of the Milwaukee, Ozaukee, and Washington County boards of supervisors.

Unit Functions: The *Policy and Government Relations Team*, which reports to the executive vice president, provides leadership for systemwide policy analysis and development, public outreach, and federal and state government relations. It is responsible for coordination of systemwide budgeting and planning; research; and labor market information.

The *Offices of Finance and Management* and *Information Technology* have oversight responsibility for operations including accounting, budgeting, procurement, payroll, human resources, facilities, and information technology. In addition, the offices provide guidance to the technical colleges in developing financial policies and standards, distribute state aid, and assist the board in determining student fees and tuition rates and approving district facility development projects. The offices are also responsible for management information and oversight of district budgets and enrollments.

The *Office of Occupational and Academic Excellence* has responsibility for program definition, approval, evaluation, and review. It focuses on programs in agriculture, office services, marketing, home economics (including family and consumer education), health occupations, trade and industry (including apprenticeship, fire service, law enforcement, safety, and technical and vocational training), general education, personnel certification, and environmental education. It also serves as a liaison to secondary schools

The *Office of Student Success* is responsible for coordination of state and federal grant programs, student financial aid, federal projects for the disabled and disadvantaged, adult and continuing education outreach, adult basic education and English language learning, and Workforce Investment Act projects. It serves as a liaison to business and industry.

History: Laws passed in 1907 permitted cities to operate trade schools for persons age 16 or older as part of the public school system (Chapter 122), and allowed them to establish technical schools or colleges, under the control of either the school board or a special board (Chapter 344). In Chapter 616, Laws of 1911, Wisconsin was the first state to establish a system of state aid and support for industrial education. The law required every community with a population of 5,000 or more to establish an industrial education board, which was authorized to levy a property tax. It created the State Board of Industrial Education and an assistant for industrial education in the office of the State Superintendent of Public Instruction.

In the Laws of 1911, Wisconsin was the first state to set up apprenticeship agreements (Chapter 347) and require employers to release 14- to 16-year-olds for part-time attendance in continuation schools for apprentices, if such schooling was available (Chapter 505). Hours in class were to count as part of the total paid work hours. The schools, established through the work of Charles McCarthy, first director of the present-day Legislative Reference Bureau, emphasized general cultural and vocational education, as well as trade skills.

Due in part to the efforts of McCarthy, the U.S. Congress passed the Smith-Hughes Act in 1917, the first federal legislation specifically designed to promote vocational education, which it modeled on Wisconsin's vocational training programs. The act offered financial aid to states to help pay teachers' and administrators' salaries and provided funds for teacher training.

Chapter 494, Laws of 1917, changed the name of the State Board of Industrial Education to the State Board of Vocational Education, authorized it to employ a state director, and designated it as the sole agency to work with the newly created federal board.

During the Great Depression, Wisconsin tightened its compulsory school attendance laws, which resulted in more 14- to 18-year-olds attending vocational school. The demand for adult education also increased, as recognized by Chapter 349, Laws of 1937, which renamed the board the State Board of Vocational and Adult Education. During that same period, the vocational school in Milwaukee began to offer college transfer courses.

Events of the 1960s transformed the Wisconsin vocational-technical system into the postsecondary system of today. Federal vocational school legislation affected business education and emphasized training for the unemployed. The federal Vocational Education Act, passed in 1963, helped the local boards build new facilities. Chapter 51, Laws of 1961, authorized the state board to offer associate degrees for 2-year technical courses. The 1965 Legislature passed Chapter 292, which required a system of vocational, technical and adult education (VTAE) districts covering the entire state by 1970 and changed the board's name to the State Board of Vocational, Technical and Adult Education. (Chapter 327, Laws of 1967, dropped "State" from the name.) College transfer programs were authorized in Madison, Milwaukee, and Rhinelander.

As a result of federal and state legislative changes in the 1960s, VTAE enrollments more than doubled to 466,000 between 1967 and 1982. The 1970s also saw significant increases in the number of associate degree programs. Other major statutory changes included the requirement that VTAE schools charge tuition and that they improve cooperation and coordination with the University of Wisconsin System.

In the past two decades, the system has increased its focus on lifelong learning; education for economic development; and services for groups that formerly had less access to education, including people in rural areas, women, and minorities. The system has placed special emphasis on assisting the unemployed, displaced homemakers, and those with literacy problems.

1993 Wisconsin Act 399 renamed the VTAE system, changing the name to the Technical College System, and designated the state board as the Technical College System Board. District VTAE schools became "technical colleges".

Since the mid-1990s, the Wisconsin Technical College System (WTCS) has experienced sustained, unprecedented enrollment growth. Six-month placement rates for WTCS graduates remained very strong, even during periods of historic economic recession. The colleges continued to develop flexible delivery options, including online offerings and career pathways that make it easy for individuals to return for training and credentials over the course of a career. In 2011, the WTCS celebrated its centennial.

INDEPENDENT BOARD ATTACHED FOR BUDGETING, PROGRAM COORDINATION, AND RELATED MANAGEMENT FUNCTIONS BY SECTION 15.03 OF THE STATUTES

EDUCATIONAL APPROVAL BOARD

Members: DON MADELUNG, *chairperson;* JO OYAMA-MILLER, *vice chairperson;* ROBERT HEIN, *secretary;* OMAR PARKS, WILLIAM RODEN (appointed by governor).

Executive Secretary: DAVID C. DIES, 267-7733.

Mailing Address: 201 West Washington Avenue, Madison 53703.

Telephone: (608) 266-1996.

Fax: (608) 264-8477.

Internet Address: http://eab.state.wi.us

E-mail: eabmail@eab.wisconsin.gov

Publications: A Guide to the EAB; School and Program Approval Guide; Wisconsin Directory of Private Postsecondary Schools.

Number of Employees: 6.50.

Total Budget 2013-15: $1,326,200.

Statutory References: Sections 15.945 (1) and 38.50.

Agency Responsibility: The Educational Approval Board (EAB) is an independent state agency responsible for protecting Wisconsin's consumers and supporting quality educational options, by regulating and evaluating for-profit postsecondary business, trade, or distance learning schools; out-of-state, nonprofit colleges and universities; and in-state, nonprofit institutions incorporated after 1991. The board currently oversees more than 250 schools serving approximately 40,000 adults in 800+ degree and nondegree programs.

The board consists of not more than 7 members who serve at the pleasure of the governor and represent state agencies and others interested in educational programs. It employs the executive secretary and other staff from the classified service. Originally formed by order of the governor in 1944, the legislature created the agency in Chapter 137, Laws of 1953, as the Governor's Educational Advisory Committee to approve and supervise schools and educational courses that trained veterans under various federal laws. A 1957 law (Chapter 438) directed the committee to certify those private vocational schools that offered adequate courses and to prevent fraud and misrepresentation. Chapter 568, Laws of 1963, gave the committee responsibility for licensing agents of private vocational schools, and Chapter 595, Laws of 1965, renamed it the Educational Approval Council. It was renamed the Educational Approval Board and administratively attached to the Department of Public Instruction by Chapter 214, Laws of 1967. The board was attached to the Board of Vocational, Technical and Adult Education by Chapter 125, Laws of 1971.

The Educational Approval Board was repealed by 1995 Wisconsin Act 27, as part of an initiative to create a state Department of Education. The Wisconsin Supreme Court ruled the measure unconstitutional and the agency's functions were continued under Executive Orders 283 and 287 which created the Educational Approval Council. The legislature recreated the board in 1997 Wisconsin Act 27 and attached it to the Higher Educational Aids Board. In 1999 Wisconsin Act 9, the board was attached to the Department of Veterans Affairs. 2001 Wisconsin Act 16 repealed statutory language which specifically made the board responsible for approving schools and courses of instruction for veterans and war orphans. The board was attached to the Wisconsin Technical College System Board (WTCSB) by 2005 Wisconsin Act 25. Under EAB's administrative attachment, budgeting, program operations, and related management functions are conducted with the help of the WTCSB. However, the EAB is treated as a distinct unit of government that exercises its powers, duties, and functions prescribed by law, including rule making, licensing and regulation, and operational planning independently of the WTCSB.

Department of
TOURISM

For e-mail combine the user ID and the state extender: userid@**travelwisconsin.com**
All telephone numbers are 608 area code unless otherwise indicated.

Secretary of Tourism: STEPHANIE KLETT, 266-2345, sklett@

Deputy Secretary: SARAH KLAVAS, 266-3750, sklavas@

Mailing Address: P.O. Box 8690, Madison 53708-8690.

Location: 201 West Washington Avenue, 2nd Floor, Madison.

Telephones: 266-2161; Personalized trip planning publications and travel information: (800) 432-8747, M-F 8:00 a.m.-4:30 p.m.

Fax: 266-3403.

Tourism Information Internet Address: www.travelwisconsin.com

Industry Internet Address: http://industry.travelwisconsin.com

Communications Bureau: LISA MARSHALL, *director,* 267-3773, lmarshall@

Marketing Bureau: SHANE BROSSARD, *director,* 266-2147, sbrossard@

Technology and Customer Services, Bureau of: JOELLYN MERZ, *director,* 261-8214, jmerz@

Number of Employees: 27.00.

Total Budget 2013-15: $30,709,400.

Statutory References: Section 15.44; Chapter 41.

Publications: *Travel Wisconsin Activity Guide; Wisconsin Travel Guide;* guides for seasonal events and recreation.

Agency Responsibility: The Department of Tourism promotes travel to Wisconsin's scenic, historic, artistic, educational, and recreational sites. Travel sectors targeted by the department include leisure, meetings and conventions, sports, group tours, and international. Through planning, research, and assistance it provides guidance to the tourism and recreation industry to aid in the development of facilities. It also assists cooperative projects between profit and nonprofit tourism ventures. The department encourages local tourism development through the Joint Effort Marketing Grant Program, the Ready, Set, Go Sports Marketing Grant Program, Meetings Mean Business Grant Program, and the Travel Information Center Grant Program.

Organization: The governor appoints the secretary, with the advice and consent of the senate, to direct the department. The secretary appoints the deputy secretary and the communications director. Bureau directors are civil servants.

Unit Functions: The secretary's office provides administrative support to the department and to its attached boards, including budget, policy planning and analysis, and accounting. The Office of the Secretary also supervises industry relations and the department's grant programs.

The *Marketing Bureau* and the *Communications Bureau* both promote and advertise Wisconsin as "the Midwest's premier travel destination for fun". The Marketing Bureau also organizes market research, publications development, graphic design, produces the annual Governor's Conference on Tourism along with special events throughout the state, and niche market development (meetings and conventions, sports groups, and international). The Communications Bureau works with the news media and travel writers worldwide to develop positive stories about Wisconsin as a travel destination.

The *Bureau of Technology and Customer Services* delivers Wisconsin travel information to visitors through various channels, including publication distribution, telephone travel assistance, and travelwisconsin.com, the official travel and tourism Web site for the State of Wisconsin. The bureau also coordinates several programs to collect local travel information from

Residents enjoy a campfire on a summer evening. *(Department of Tourism)*

destination marketing organizations around the state, and makes the details on more than 13,000 attractions, restaurants, accommodations, and events readily available to potential visitors.

History: State tourism promotion originated in the Department of Natural Resources to encourage travel to state parks and commercial recreational sites. Chapter 39, Laws of 1975, transferred tourism functions to the Department of Business Development and created the Division of Tourism as a statutory entity within the department. Chapter 361, Laws of 1979, created the Department of Development, which absorbed the division, through a merger of the Department of Business Development and the Department of Local Affairs and Development. 1995 Wisconsin Act 27 reorganized the division as the Department of Tourism, effective January 1, 1996.

Statutory Board and Council

Arts Board: KEVIN MILLER, *chairperson;* MARY GIELOW, *vice chairperson;* HEATHER A. MCDONELL, *secretary;* ANN BRUNNER, SUSAN FRIEBERT, JOHN HENDRICKS, BRIAN KELSEY, LAMOINE MACLAUGHLIN, RON MADICH, BARBARA E. MUNSON, FREDERICK C. SCHWERTFEGER, SHARON STEWART, ROBERT WAGNER, MATTHEW WALLOCK, vacancy (appointed by governor).

Executive Director: GEORGE TZOUGROS, 267-2006, george.tzougros@wisconsin.gov

Mailing Address: P.O. Box 8690, Madison 53708-8690.

Telephone: 266-0190.

E-mail Address: artsboard@wisconsin.gov

Internet Address: artsboard.wisconsin.gov

Publications: Internet only: Annual Report; Guide to Programs and Services; grant applications (all programs); Wisconsin Folks Web Site; Portal Wisconsin; Web site in collaboration with the Cultural Coalition of Wisconsin.

Number of Employees: 4.00.

Total Budget 2013-15: $3,117,000.

Statutory References: Section 15.445 (1); Chapter 44, Subchapter III.

Agency Responsibility: The legislature directs the Arts Board to study and assist artistic and cultural activities in the state, assist communities in developing their own arts programs, and plan and implement funding programs for groups or individuals engaged in the arts.

As a funding agency, the board assists arts organizations and individual artists through a variety of programs designed to provide broad public access to the arts, strengthen the state's artistic resources, and create opportunities for individuals of exceptional talent. Financial support programs for individuals and organizations include apprenticeships, artists-in-education programs, challenge grants, community activities, fellowships, opportunity grants, program assistance and support, and programs for presenters. The board also provides matching grants to local arts agencies and municipalities through the Wisconsin Regranting Program.

The board aids Wisconsin's artistic community through an information program that includes workshops, conferences, research projects, and publications. The board regularly produces and distributes materials on local, state, and national arts activities for both the arts community and the general public. It arranges for the governor's official portrait.

The 15 board members serve staggered 3-year terms and must be state residents with a concern for the arts. Each geographic quadrant of the state must be represented by at least 2 members. The board selects the executive director from outside the classified service. Chapter 90, Laws of 1973, created the board and attached it to the Department of Administration to succeed the Governor's Council on the Arts, which Governor Gaylord Nelson had established in 1963. 1995 Wisconsin Act 27 attached the board to the Department of Tourism for administrative purposes. 2011 Wisconsin Act 32 provided that the Arts Board was in the Department of Tourism.

Council on Tourism: PAUL UPCHURCH, *chairperson;* DEB ARCHER, JAMES BOLEN, CINDY BURZINSKI, PAUL CUNNINGHAM, S. PETER HELLAND, JR., BRIAN KELSEY, JOE KLIMCZAK, KATHY KOPP, SCOTT KRAUSE, LOLA ROEH, ERNIE STEVENS III, STACEY WATSON, vacancy; STEPHANIE KLETT (secretary of tourism); SENATORS BEWLEY, MOULTON; REPRESENTATIVES BILLINGS, TRANEL; GEORGE TZOUGROS (executive director, Arts Board); ELLSWORTH BROWN (director, state historical society). (All except *ex officio* members are appointed by governor.)

The 21-member Council on Tourism advises the secretary about tourism and encourages Wisconsin private companies to promote the state in their advertisements. The 14 appointed members serve 3-year terms and assist the secretary in formulating a statewide marketing plan. Nominations for public member appointments must be sought from (but are not limited to) multicounty regional associations engaged in promoting tourism; statewide associations of businesses related to tourism; area visitor and convention bureaus; arts organizations; the Great Lakes Inter-Tribal Council, Inc., and other agencies with knowledge of American Indian tourism; and persons engaged in businesses catering to tourists. Nominees must have experience in marketing and promotion strategy and must represent the different geographical areas of the state and the diversity of the tourism industry. The council was created by 1987 Wisconsin Act 1 in the Department of Development and transferred to the Department of Tourism by 1995 Wisconsin Act 27. Its composition and duties are prescribed in Sections 15.447 (1) and 41.12 of the statutes.

INDEPENDENT UNITS ATTACHED FOR BUDGETING, PROGRAM COORDINATION, AND RELATED MANAGEMENT FUNCTIONS BY SECTION 15.03 OF THE STATUTES

KICKAPOO RESERVE MANAGEMENT BOARD

Members: SUSAN C. CUSHING, BRANDON HYSEL, RONALD M. JOHNSON, ALAN SZEPI (residents of specified municipalities and school districts within watershed); PAUL HAYES, RICHARD T. WALLIN (watershed residents outside specified units); WILLIAM L. QUACKENBUSH (nonresident environmental advocate); vacancy (nonresident education representative); DAVE MAXWELL (nonresident recreation and tourism representative); TRACY LITTLEJOHN, ADLAI J. MANN (members with knowledge of watershed's cultural resources, nominated by Ho-Chunk Nation) (appointed by governor).

Executive Director: MARCY WEST, marcy.west@wisconsin.gov

Mailing Address: S 3661 State Highway 131, La Farge 54639.

Telephone: (608) 625-2960.

E-mail Address: kickapoo.reserve@wisconsin.gov

Internet Address: http://kvr.state.wi.us

Publications: Kickapoo Valley Reserve Visitors' Guide.

Number of Employees: 4.00.

Total Budget 2013-15: $1,830,800.

Statutory References: Sections 15.07 (1) (b) 20., 15.445 (2), 41.40, and 41.41.

Agency Responsibility: The 11-member Kickapoo Reserve Management Board manages 8,600 acres through a joint management agreement with the Ho-Chunk Nation. The Kickapoo Valley Reserve exists to preserve and enhance the area's environmental, scenic, and cultural features; provides facilities for the use and enjoyment of visitors; and promotes the reserve as a destination for vacationing and recreation. Subject to the approval of the governor, the board may purchase land for inclusion in the reserve and trade land in the reserve under certain conditions. The Kickapoo Valley Reserve Visitor Center offers meeting and classroom space, interactive exhibits, educational programs, and tourist information.

The board also may lease land for purposes consistent with the management of the reserve or for agricultural purposes; authorize, license, regulate, and collect and spend revenue from private concessions in the reserve; accept gifts, grants, and bequests; and cooperate with and provide matching funds to nonprofit groups organized to provide assistance to the reserve.

The board may not authorize mining in the reserve or on any land acquired by the board and may not sell land that is in the reserve. It has authority to promulgate rules about use of the waters, land, and facilities under its jurisdiction, and the Department of Tourism is responsible for enforcement of state laws and rules relating to the reserve.

The governor appoints board members for staggered 3-year terms. Four members must be residents of villages, towns, and school districts in the immediate vicinity of the reserve; 2 must be residents of the Kickapoo River watershed outside of the immediate vicinity of the reserve;

and 3 members who are not residents of the watershed are appointed by the governor to represent education, environment, and tourism issues. In addition, 2 members are nominated by the Ho-Chunk Nation who have an interest in and knowledge of the cultural resources within the watershed. Various state agencies must appoint nonmember liaisons to the board, and the board may request that any federally recognized American Indian tribe or band in this state, other than the Ho-Chunk Nation, appoint a nonmember liaison. The board appoints the executive director from outside the classified service. The board was created as the Kickapoo Valley Governing Board by 1993 Wisconsin Act 349 and attached to the Department of Administration. 1995 Wisconsin Act 27 attached the board to the Department of Tourism, and it was renamed by 1995 Wisconsin Act 216. The board's membership was revised by 2005 Wisconsin Act 396.

LOWER WISCONSIN STATE RIVERWAY BOARD

Members: DONALD GREENWOOD (Sauk County), *chairperson;* FRED MADISON (recreational user group representative), *vice chairperson;* GERALD DORSCHIED (Iowa County), *secretary;* RONALD LEYS (Crawford County), MELODY K. MOORE (Dane County), ROBERT CARY (Grant County), DAVID O. MARTIN (Richland County); GEORGE ARIMOND, RITCHIE J. BROWN (recreational user groups' representatives appointed by governor with senate consent). (County representatives are nominated by respective county boards and appointed by governor.)

Executive Director: MARK E. CUPP, 202 North Wisconsin Avenue, P.O. Box 187, Muscoda 53573-0187, mark.cupp@wisconsin.gov

Telephones: (608) 739-3188; (800) 221-3792.

Internet Address: http://lwr.state.wi.us

Publications: Summary of regulations, Strategic Plan, Biennial Report.

Number of Employees: 2.00.

Total Budget 2013-15: $417,500.

Statutory References: Section 15.445 (3); Chapter 30, Subchapter IV.

Wisconsin has over 15,000 lakes. Flyboarding is a popular activity on a lake near the Wisconsin Dells. (Department of Tourism)

Agency Responsibility: The 9-member Lower Wisconsin State Riverway Board is responsible for protecting and preserving the scenic beauty and natural character of the riverway. The board reviews permit applications for buildings, walkways, timber harvests, utility facilities, bridges, and other structures in the riverway and issues permits for activities that meet established standards.

Board members serve staggered 3-year terms. Each of the 6 county representatives must be either an elected official or a resident of a city or village that abuts the Lower Wisconsin State Riverway or of a town located at least in part in the riverway. The 3 members representing recreational user groups may not reside in any of the 6 specified counties. The board was created by 1989 Wisconsin Act 31 and attached to the Department of Natural Resources. 1995 Wisconsin Act 27 attached the board to the Department of Tourism.

STATE FAIR PARK BOARD

Members: JOHN YINGLING, *chairperson;* SUSAN CRANE (general business representative); SENATORS CARPENTER, FARROW; REPRESENTATIVES RIEMER, RIPP (legislative members recommended by party leadership and appointed by governor); MARY MAAS (general business experience); vacancy (business technology experience); DAN DEVINE (West Allis resident); SUE RUPNOW (agriculture business representative); ALDO MADRIGRANO (state resident); BEN BRANCEL (secretary of agriculture, trade and consumer protection); STEPHANIE KLETT (secretary of tourism). (All except *ex officio* members or designees are appointed by governor with senate consent.)

Chief Executive Officer: RICK FRENETTE, (414) 266-7020.

Executive Assistant: MARIAN SANTIAGO-LLOYD, (414) 266-7021.

Mailing Address: 640 South 84th Street, West Allis 53214.

Telephones: (414) 266-7000; (414) 266-7100 (ticket office); (800) 884-FAIR (recorded announcement of events).

Mirror Lake State Park near Lake Delton offers many hiking trails for park visitors to enjoy. (Department of Tourism)

E-mail Address: wsfp@wisstatefair.com

Internet Address: www.wistatefair.com

Publications: *A Brief History of the Wisconsin State Fair;* WSFP cook book; fair brochures. Daily events schedule and premium books available at www.wistatefair.com.

Number of Employees: 48.00.

Total Budget 2013-15: $45,096,600.

Statutory References: Section 15.445 (4); Chapter 42.

Agency Responsibility: The State Fair Park Board manages the State Fair Park and supervises its use for fairs, exhibits, or promotional events for agricultural, commercial, educational, and recreational purposes. It also leases or licenses the property at reasonable rates for other uses when not needed for public purposes. The board is directed to develop new facilities at State Fair Park and to provide a permanent location for an annual Wisconsin State Fair, major sports events, agricultural and industrial expositions, and other programs of civic interest.

Organization: The State Fair Park Board consists of 13 members. Legislative members, who represent the majority and minority parties, are nominated by party leadership and appointed by the governor. The 7 citizen members serve staggered 5-year terms. The departmental secretaries may designate members to serve in place of the secretaries. The board appoints the park director from outside the classified service.

History: Beginning with the first Wisconsin State Fair at Janesville in October 1851, the event has served as a showcase for Wisconsin agriculture and commerce. The State Agricultural Society, which sponsored the first fair, continued to operate it through 1897. In that year, Chapter 301 created the Wisconsin State Board of Agriculture and placed operation of the fair under its control. When the Department of Agriculture was created in 1915, the state fair became part of the new department.

In Chapter 149, Laws of 1961, the independent Wisconsin Exposition Department, headed by a 7-member board, was created to manage the fair and the park's year-round operation. Under the 1967 executive branch reorganization, the Exposition Department became the Wisconsin Exposition Council in the Department of Local Affairs and Development.

Chapter 125, Laws of 1971, created a 3-member State Fair Park Board, appointed by the governor and attached to the Department of Agriculture for administrative purposes. In 1985 Wisconsin Act 20, the legislature increased board membership to 5, specified 5-year terms of service, and required senate confirmation of the governor's nominees.

In 1990, as provided by 1989 Wisconsin Act 219, the State Fair Park Board became an independent body. 1995 Wisconsin Act 27 attached the board to the Department of Tourism, and 1999 Wisconsin Act 197 revised and increased board membership.

Over the years, the location of the state fair was debated and even its continued existence was in doubt. At various times between 1851 and 1885, Fond du Lac, Janesville, Madison, Milwaukee, and Watertown hosted the fair. Milwaukee was chosen as the state fair site from 1886 through 1891, and the fairs held there were so successful that a permanent site was purchased in what is now West Allis, a Milwaukee suburb. That site, first used for the 1892 fair, is included in the state fair's location today.

Several studies published during the 1960s recommended that the fair be moved to a larger site in the Milwaukee area. Chapter 125, Laws of 1971, decided the fair would remain at its site (partially in West Allis, partially in Milwaukee), with updated or new facilities being funded through self-amortizing state bonds. Fair operations have been self-financed since 1935. 1999 Wisconsin Act 9 provided funding for substantial construction and renovation of park facilities. 1999 Wisconsin Act 197 authorized the board to create a nonprofit corporation to raise funds and provide support and contract with that same corporation for operation and development of the park. Act 197 also authorized the park board to permit private individuals to construct facilities on fair grounds under a lease agreement with the board.

Today, State Fair Park draws more than 2 million visitors to its events and activities each year, and the Wisconsin State Fair, with attendance of more than one million, remains the state's oldest and largest annual event.

Department of
TRANSPORTATION

Address e-mail by combining the user ID and the state extender: userid@**dot.wi.gov**
All telephone numbers are 608 area code unless otherwise indicated.

Secretary of Transportation: MARK GOTTLIEB, 266-1114, mark.gottlieb@

Deputy Secretary: PAUL HAMMER, 267-9618, paul.hammer@

Assistant Deputy Secretary: TOM RHATICAN, 266-1114, tom.rhatican@

General Counsel, Office of: REBECCA J.R. ROEKER, *chief legal counsel,* 266-8928, rebecca.roeker@

Policy, Budget and Finance, Office of: CASEY NEWMAN, *director,* 267-9618, casey.newman@

Public Affairs, Office of: PEG SCHMITT, *director,* 266-5599, peg.schmitt@, Fax: 266-7186.

Mailing Address: P.O. Box 7910, Madison 53707-7910.

Location: Hill Farms State Transportation Building, 4802 Sheboygan Avenue, Madison.

Internet Address: www.dot.wisconsin.gov

Number of Employees: 3,512.04.

Total Budget 2013-15: $6,096,356,800.

Statutory References: Sections 15.46, 15.465, and 15.467; Chapters 82-86, 110, 114, 340-349, and 351.

Business Management, Division of: DENISE SOLIE, *administrator,* 266-2090, denise.solie@

  Business Services, Bureau of: PATRICIA JACKSON-WARD, *director,* 267-4479, patricia.jacksonward@; JON KRANZ, *deputy director,* 264-7700, jonathan.kranz@

  Human Resource Services, Bureau of: RANDY SARVER, *director,* 266-0507, randy.sarver@; DIANE WHITEHEAD, *deputy director,* 266-7303, diane.whitehead@

  Information Technology Services, Bureau of: ROBERT JOHNSON, *acting director,* 266-8224, bob.johnson@

Motor Vehicles, Division of: PATRICK FERNAN, *administrator,* 261-8605, patrick.fernan@; KRISTINA BOARDMAN, *deputy administrator,* 267-3348, kristina.boardman@

  Driver Services, Bureau of: ANN PERRY, *director,* 266-9890, ann.perry@

  Field Services, Bureau of: JAMES MILLER, *director,* 266-5082, james.miller@; JOE BRUNO, *deputy director,* 266-2743, josepha.bruno@

  Vehicle Services, Bureau of: MITCHELL WARREN, *director,* 267-5121, mitchell.warren@

    Vehicle Emission Testing (Southeast Wisconsin): (800) 242-7510; Milwaukee/Waukesha area: (414) 266-1080.

  Motor Vehicle Regional Managers:

    North Central Region: JILL GEOFFROY, (715) 355-4613, 5301 Rib Mountain Drive, Wausau 54401, jill.geoffroy@

    Northeast Region: DONALD GENIN, (920) 960-9092, 711 West Association Drive, Appleton 54914, donald.genin@

    Northwest Region: PATRICIA NELSON, (715) 234-3773, 735 West Avenue, Rice Lake 54868-1359, patricia.nelson@

    Southeast Region: BARNEY HALL, (262) 548-5840, 2019 Golf Road, Pewaukee 53072, barney.hall@

    Southwest Region: TRACY HOWARD, (608) 246-7540, 2001 Bartillon Drive, Madison 53704, tracy.howard@

State Patrol, Division of: STEPHEN FITZGERALD, *superintendent,* 709-0051, stephen.fitzgerald@; COLONEL BRIAN K. RAHN, 709-0052, brian.rahn@

  Division Mailing Address: Room 551, P.O. Box 7912, Madison 53707-7912.

DEPARTMENT OF TRANSPORTATION

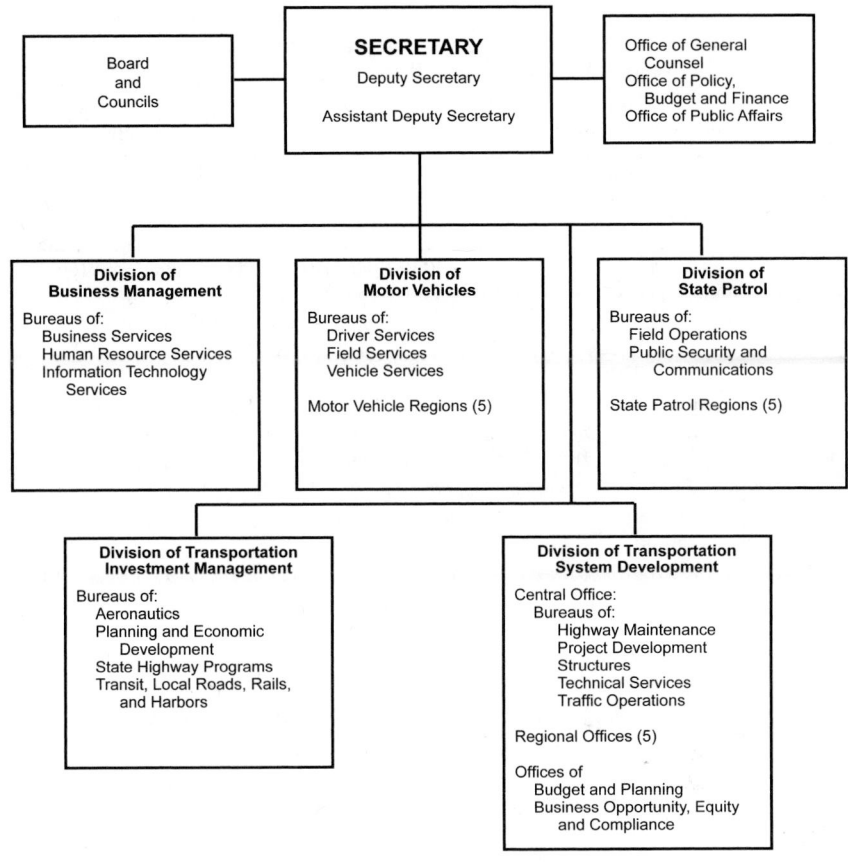

Telephones: General: (608) 266-3212; Road Condition Reports: Madison: (608) 246-7580; Milwaukee: (414) 785-7140; elsewhere in Wisconsin: (800) 762-3947.

Fax: 267-4495.

Field Operations, Bureau of: vacancy, 709-0053.

State Patrol Region Captains/Executive Officers:

North Central Region:

Wausau Post: NICHOLAS R. WANINK, *captain,* (715) 845-1143, nicholas.wanink@; STEVEN G. KRUEGER, *executive officer,* (715) 845-1143, steven.krueger@; Fax: (715) 848-9255; 2805 Martin Avenue, Wausau 54401-7172.

Northeast Region:

Fond du Lac Post: ANTHONY BURRELL, *captain,* (920) 929-3700, anthony.burrell@; vacancy, *executive officer,* (920) 929-3700; Fax: (920) 929-7666; 851 South Rolling Meadows Drive, P.O. Box 984, Fond du Lac 54936-9927.

Northwest Region:

Eau Claire Post: JEFFREY J. FRENETTE, *captain,* (715) 839-3800, jeffrey.frenette@;

Fax: (715) 839-3841; vacancy, *executive officer,* (715) 839-3800; Fax: (715) 839-3873; 5005 Highway 53 South, Eau Claire 54701-8846.

Spooner Post: Jeffrey J. Frenette, *captain,* jeffrey.frennette@; Dori L. Petznick, *executive officer,* (715) 635-2141, dori.petznick@; Fax: (715) 635-6373; W7102 Green Valley Road, Spooner 54801.

Southeast Region:

Waukesha Post: Timothy L. Carnahan, *captain,* (262) 785-4700, timothy.carnahan@; Rich Reichenberger, *executive officer,* (262) 785-4700, richard.reichenberger@; Fax: (262) 785-4722; 21115 Highway 18, Waukesha 53186-2985.

Southwest Region:

DeForest Post: Charles R. Teasdale, *captain,* (608) 846-8500, charles.teasdale@; Brad Altman, *executive officer,* (608) 846-8500, brad.altman@; Fax: (608) 846-8536; 911 West North Street, DeForest 53532-1971.

Tomah Post: Charles R. Teasdale, *captain,* charles.teasdale@; Paul D. Matl, *executive officer,* (608) 374-0513, paul.matl@; Fax: (608) 374-0599; 23928 Lester McMullin Drive, Tomah 54660-5376.

Public Security and Communications, Bureau of: Major J.D. Lind, *director,* 267-9522.

Transportation Investment Management, Division of: Aileen Switzer, *administrator,* 266-5791, aileen.switzer@; Fax: 266-0686; P.O. Box 7913, Madison 53707-7913.

Aeronautics, Bureau of: David Greene, *director,* 266-2480, david.greene@

Planning and Economic Development, Bureau of: Donald Gutkowski, *director,* 266-7575, donald.gutkowski@

State Highway Programs, Bureau of: Joseph Nestler, *director,* 266-9495, joseph.nestler@

Transit, Local Roads, Rails, and Harbors, Bureau of: Donna Brown-Martin, *director,* 266-2963, donna.brownmartin@

Transportation System Development, Division of: vacancy, *administrator,* 267-7111; Division Fax: 264-6667.

Division Mailing Address: 4802 Sheboygan Avenue, Room 451, P.O. Box 7965, Madison 53707-7965.

Division E-mail Address: dotdtsddivision-office@dot.wi.gov

Deputy Administrator – Statewide Bureaus: Rory Rhinesmith, 266-2392, rory.rhinesmith@; Fax: 264-6667.

Highway Maintenance, Bureau of: Rose Phetteplace, *director,* 267-8999, rose.phetteplace@; Fax: 267-7856.

Project Development, Bureau of: Beth Cannestra, *director,* 266-3707, beth.cannestra@; Fax: 266-8459.

Structures, Bureau of: Scot Becker, *director,* 266-5161, scot.becker@; Fax: 261-6277.

Technical Services, Bureau of: Rebecca Burkel, *director,* 516-6336, rebecca.burkel@; Fax: 267-0307.

Traffic Operations, Bureau of: Dewayne Johnson, *director,* (414) 227-2166, dewayne.johnson@; Fax: 261-6295.

Budget and Planning, Office of: Marietta Smith, *chief,* 266-2836, marietta.smith@; Fax: 264-6667.

Business Opportunity, Equity and Compliance, Office of: Aggo Akyea, *director,* 267-9527, aggo.akyea@

Deputy Administrator – Regions: Joseph Olson, 264-6677, joseph.olson@; Fax: 264-6667.

North Central Region, Rhinelander: Russ Habeck, *director,* (715) 365-3490, russ.habeck@; Fax: (715) 365-5780; 1681 Second Avenue South, Wisconsin Rapids 54495; Ken Wickham, *deputy director,* (715) 421-8300, kenneth.wickham@; Fax: (715) 423-0334; 510 North Hanson Lake Road, Rhinelander 54501-5108.

Northeast Region, Green Bay: WILL DORSEY, *director,* (920) 492-5643, will.dorsey@; Fax: (920) 492-5640; TTY: (920) 492-5673; 944 Vanderperren Way, Green Bay 54324; COLLEEN HARRIS, *deputy director,* (920) 492-5678, colleen.harris@

Northwest Region, Eau Claire: JERALD MENTZEL, *director,* (715) 392-7927, jerry.mentzel@; Fax: (715) 836-2807; 718 West Clairemont Avenue, Eau Claire 54701-5108; JESSICA FELIX, *deputy director,* (715) 392-7925, jessica.felix@; Fax: (715) 392-7863; 1701 North Fourth Street, Superior 54880-1068.

Southeast Region, Waukesha: BRETT WALLACE, *director,* (262) 548-5884, brett.wallace@; Fax: (414) 548-5662; 141 Northwest Barstow Street, Waukesha 53187-0798; SHERI SCHMIT, *deputy director,* (262) 548-5902, sheri.schmit@; Fax: (414) 548-5662; 151 Northwest Barstow Street, Waukesha 53187-0798.

Southwest Region, Madison: DAVID VIETH, *director,* (608) 246-5443, david.vieth@; Fax: (608) 246-7996; 2101 Wright Street, Madison 53704-2583; La Crosse: vacancy, *deputy director,* (608) 785-9958; Fax: (608) 785-9969; 3550 Mormon Coulee Road, La Crosse 54601-6767.

Publications: Biennial Report; Connections 2030; Five-Year Airport Improvement Program (online; updated monthly); *Rustic Roads;* Six-Year Highway Improvement Program; Traffic Safety Reporter; *Trucking Wisconsin Style;* Wisconsin Aeronautical Chart (even-numbered years); Wisconsin Airport Directory (odd-numbered years); Wisconsin Commercial Driver's Manual (online); Wisconsin Driver's Book (online); Wisconsin Highway Map; Wisconsin Motorcycle Crash Facts; Wisconsin Motorcyclists' Handbook (online); Wisconsin Motorists' Handbook (online); Wisconsin Traffic Crash Facts (annual).

Agency Responsibility: The Department of Transportation is responsible for the planning, promotion, and protection of all transportation systems in the state. Its major responsibilities involve highways, motor vehicles, motor carriers, traffic law enforcement, railroads, waterways, mass transit, and aeronautics.

There are 131 public use airports, 8 commercial airports, and about 6,000 active registered aircraft in Wisconsin. (Department of Transportation)

The department works with several federal agencies in the administration of federal transportation aids. It also cooperates with departments at the state level in travel promotion, consumer protection, environmental analysis, and transportation services for elderly and handicapped persons.

Organization: The secretary is appointed by the governor with the advice and consent of the senate and has overall management responsibility for the department. The secretary appoints the deputy secretary, assistant deputy secretary, and all division administrators from outside the classified service.

Unit Functions: The *Division of Business Management* plans and administers the department's programs for accounting and auditing, information technology, human resources, purchasing, vehicle fleet, facilities, and management services.

The *Division of Motor Vehicles* issues vehicle titles and registrations, individual identification cards, and handicapped parking permits; examines and licenses drivers, commercial driving instructors, and vehicle salespersons; certifies commercial driver examiners; licenses motor carriers, commercial driving schools, vehicle dealers, manufacturers, and distributors; and investigates consumer complaints about vehicle sales and trade practices. It keeps the records of drivers' traffic violations and demerit points. It is responsible for the vehicle emissions inspection program, and it administers reciprocal trucking agreements with other states and the Canadian provinces and provides traffic accident data to law enforcement officials, highway engineers, and traffic safety and media representatives. The division operates 5 regional offices, 81 customer service centers, and 11 travel locations to support the state's approximately 4.5 million licensed drivers and ID card holders and over 5.4 million registered vehicles.

The *Division of State Patrol* promotes highway safety by enforcing state traffic laws regarding motor vehicles and motor carriers. The State Patrol also has criminal law enforcement powers and can assist local law enforcement agencies by providing emergency police services. It oper-

There are 81 public bus and shared-ride taxi systems providing service in Wisconsin. Approximately 48% of Wisconsin transit riders are headed to work and 23% to school. (Department of Transportation)

ates the statewide mobile data communications network, which is available to local law enforcement agencies, and it makes annual inspections of Wisconsin's school buses and ambulances. The division oversees 5 regional offices and a law enforcement training academy open to all federal, state, county, local, and tribal law enforcement officers.

The *Division of Transportation Investment Management* performs statewide planning for highways, railroads, harbors, airports, and mass transit and promotes a multimodal transportation system to best serve state citizens and businesses. The division directs data collection; provides service to local governments and planning agencies; and manages state road aids, highway finance, and other transportation assistance programs. The division is responsible for uniform statewide direction in the planning, design, construction, maintenance, and operation of Wisconsin's airports, harbors, highways, and railroads. The division is involved with the state's 130 public use airports, 4,200 miles of railroad tracks, 29 commercial water ports, and harbors, and the approximately 12,000 miles of roads and streets in the State Trunk Highway (STH) system, including 743 miles of Interstate highways within the state. The division administers all state and federal funding for airport, railroad, and harbor development projects in Wisconsin.

The *Division of Transportation System Development* performs development, maintenance, and operations functions related to the STH system. The division is split into two basic areas: Statewide Bureaus and Regional Operations. It provides uniform direction in planning, design, and construction phases of project delivery as well as improving the safety and efficiency of the STH system. The division also provides leadership in the protection of public interests and resources through public and local interactions.

The six state statewide bureaus include: 1) Highway Maintenance, 2) Project Development, 3) Structures, 4) Technical Services, 5) Traffic Operations, and 6) Office of Business Opportunity, Equity and Compliance. These statewide bureaus advise the regional offices as well as other divisions regarding engineering, economic, environmental, and social standards and practices. The division also monitors the quality and efficiency of the department's various programs and assures compliance with federal and state laws and regulations. The five regions manage the operation and development of state highways and participate in the development, management, and implementation of local road and nonhighway transportation projects. They also maintain working relationships with local units of government, represent the department in local and regional planning efforts, and represent local and regional needs in departmental processes.

History: The history of the Department of Transportation mirrors the evolution of 20th century transportation. The Highway Commission was created when Chapter 337, Laws of 1911, authorized state aid for public highways. Later, Chapter 410, Laws of 1939, consolidated registration, licensing, inspection, enforcement, and highway safety promotion in the Motor Vehicle Department. The legislature established the Aeronautics Commission in Chapter 513, Laws of 1945, and directed it to cooperate with the federal government and other states to "prepare for the generally expected extensive expansion of aviation following the termination of World War II."

The Department of Transportation was created by Chapter 75, Laws of 1967, which merged the Highway Commission, the Aeronautics Commission, and the Motor Vehicle Department. Chapter 500, Laws of 1969, required three divisions within the department: aeronautics, highways, and motor vehicles. The department was strengthened by Chapter 29, Laws of 1977, which vested accountability at the departmental, instead of divisional, level and gave the secretary, rather than the governor, the authority to appoint division heads. The secretary was also allowed to reorganize the department with the governor's approval.

Statutory Board and Councils

Highway Safety, Council on: RANDALL R. THIEL (state officer), *chairperson;* RICHARD VAN BOXTEL (citizen member), *vice chairperson;* SENATORS MARKLEIN, PETROWSKI; 3 vacancies (assembly representatives); JOHN CORBIN, STEPHEN FITZGERALD, PATRICK HUGHES, JEFF PLALE (state officers); ROBERT BARTEN, LAVERNE E. HERMANN, BRIAN LUETH, KURT SCHULTZ (citizen members). (All except legislators are appointed by governor.)

The 15-member Council on Highway Safety advises the secretary about highway safety matters. The council consists of 2 senators and 3 representatives. At least one senator and at least one representative must serve on standing committees that deal with transportation matters. The other 10 members, who serve staggered 3-year terms, include 5 state officers with transportation and highway safety duties and 5 citizen members. The council was originally created in the Office of the Governor by Chapter 276, Laws of 1969, and was moved to the Department of Transportation by Chapter 34, Laws of 1979. Its composition and duties are prescribed in Sections 15.467 (3) and 85.07 (2) of the statutes.

Rustic Roads Board: MARION FLOOD, *chairperson;* DANIEL FEDDERLY, *vice chairperson;* SENATOR PETROWSKI; REPRESENTATIVE RIPP; RAYMOND DeHAHN, BARBARA LAMUE, BRUCE LINDGREN, ALAN LORENZ, CHARLES RAYALA, THOMAS SOLHEIM. (Nonlegislative members are appointed by secretary of transportation.)

The 10-member Rustic Roads Board oversees the application and selection process of locally-nominated county highways and local roads for inclusion in the Rustic Roads network. Established in 1973, the Rustic Roads Program is a partnership between local officials and state government to showcase some of Wisconsin's most picturesque and lightly-traveled roadways for the leisurely enjoyment of hikers, bikers, and motorists. The board includes the chairpersons of the senate and assembly committees with jurisdiction over transportation matters. Its 8 nonlegislative members serve staggered 4-year terms, and at least 4 of them must be nominees of the Wisconsin Counties Association. The board was created by Chapter 142, Laws of 1973, and its composition and duties are prescribed in Sections 15.465 (2) and 83.42 of the statutes.

Uniformity of Traffic Citations and Complaints, Council on

The 10-member Council on Uniformity of Traffic Citations and Complaints recommends forms used for traffic violations. The council was created by Chapter 292, Laws of 1967, as the Uniform Traffic Citation and Complaint Committee and renamed by 1985 Wisconsin Act 145. Its composition and duties are prescribed in Sections 15.467 (4) and 345.11 of the statutes.

The council meets on an as-needed basis, and members are designated when required. Members include the secretary of transportation or designee, a member of the Department of Transportation responsible for law enforcement, a member designated by the Director of State Courts, and members designated by the presidents of the following: the Wisconsin Sheriffs and Deputy Sheriffs Association, the County Traffic Patrol Association, the Chiefs of Police Association, the State Bar of Wisconsin, the Wisconsin Council of Safety, the Wisconsin District Attorneys Association, and the Judicial Conference.

UNIVERSITY OF WISCONSIN SYSTEM

Board of Regents: REGINA MILLNER, *president;* JOHN BEHLING, *vice president;* TONY EVERS (superintendent of public instruction), vacancy (president, Technical College System Board); MARK BRADLEY, JOSÉ DELGADO, MARGARET FARROW, MICHAEL M. GREBE, EVE HALL, TIM HIGGINS, EDMUND MANYDEEDS, JANICE MUELLER, DREW PETERSEN, CHARLES PRUITT, GARY ROBERTS, JOSÉ VÁSQUEZ, GERALD WHITBURN; NICOLAS HARSY, JAMES LANGNES III (students). (All except *ex officio* members are appointed by governor with senate consent.)

Executive Director and Corporate Secretary, Office of the Board of Regents: JANE RADUE, 1860 Van Hise Hall, 1220 Linden Drive, Madison 53706-1557, (608) 262-2324.

Mailing Address: Central administrative offices for the UW System and the UW Colleges are located in Madison. Individual universities and 2-year UW Colleges can be reached by contacting them directly. Administrative offices for UW-Extension are in Madison; Extension representatives are located at each county seat.

Publications: biennial and annual reports; *Fact Book; Introduction to the University of Wisconsin System;* unit bulletins, catalogs, reports, circulars; periodicals and books.

Number of Employees: 34,789.96.

Total Budget 2013-15: $11,759,875,400.

Constitutional Reference: Article X, Section 6.

Statutory References: Section 15.91; Chapter 36.

UNIVERSITY OF WISCONSIN SYSTEM

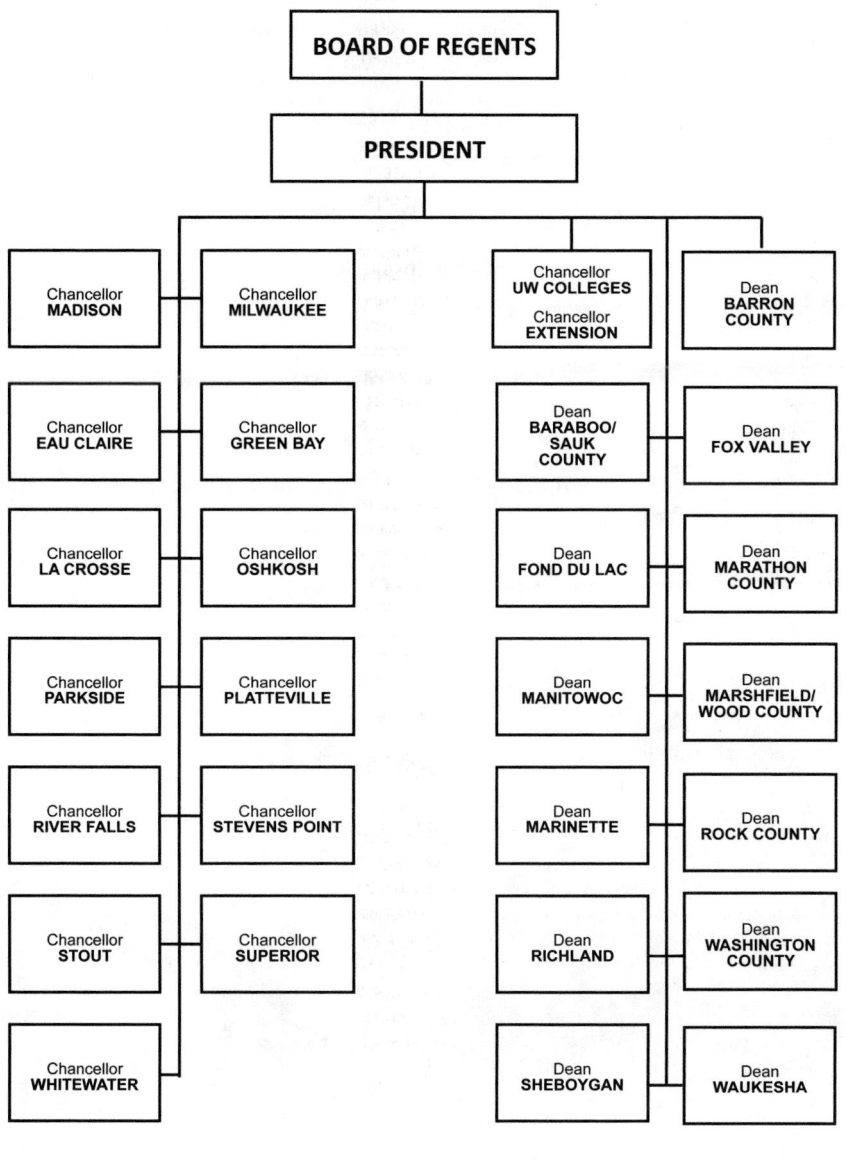

BOARD OF REGENTS

PRESIDENT

Chancellor **MADISON**

Chancellor **MILWAUKEE**

Chancellor **EAU CLAIRE**

Chancellor **GREEN BAY**

Chancellor **LA CROSSE**

Chancellor **OSHKOSH**

Chancellor **PARKSIDE**

Chancellor **PLATTEVILLE**

Chancellor **RIVER FALLS**

Chancellor **STEVENS POINT**

Chancellor **STOUT**

Chancellor **SUPERIOR**

Chancellor **WHITEWATER**

Chancellor **UW COLLEGES** Chancellor **EXTENSION**

Dean **BARRON COUNTY**

Dean **BARABOO/ SAUK COUNTY**

Dean **FOX VALLEY**

Dean **FOND DU LAC**

Dean **MARATHON COUNTY**

Dean **MANITOWOC**

Dean **MARSHFIELD/ WOOD COUNTY**

Dean **MARINETTE**

Dean **ROCK COUNTY**

Dean **RICHLAND**

Dean **WASHINGTON COUNTY**

Dean **SHEBOYGAN**

Dean **WAUKESHA**

UNIVERSITY CAMPUSES

TWO-YEAR COLLEGES

Units attached for administrative purposes under Sec. 15.03:
Environmental Education Board
Veterinary Diagnostic Laboratory Board

System Administration
1220 Linden Drive, Madison 53706-1559
General Telephone: (608) 262-2321
Internet Address: www.wisconsin.edu

President of the University of Wisconsin System: RAYMOND W. CROSS, 1720 Van Hise Hall, 1220 Linden Drive, Madison 53706-1559, (608) 262-2321.

Senior Vice President for Administration and Fiscal Affairs: DAVID L. MILLER, 1752 Van Hise Hall, 262-4048.

Interim Senior Vice President for Academic and Student Affairs: DAVID J. WARD, 1730 Van Hise Hall, 262-3826.

Vice President for Finance: vacancy, 1624 Van Hise Hall, 262-1311.

General Counsel: TOMAS STAFFORD, 1856 Van Hise Hall, 262-6497.

UW-Madison
161 Bascom Hall, 500 Lincoln Drive, Madison 53706
General Telephone: (608) 262-1234
Internet Address: www.wisc.edu

Chancellor: REBECCA BLANK, 161 Bascom Hall, 500 Lincoln Drive, Madison 53706, 262-9946.

Provost and Vice Chancellor for Academic Affairs: SARAH C. MANGELSDORF, 150 Bascom Hall, 262-1304.

Vice Chancellor for Finance and Administration: DARRELL BAZZELL, 100 Bascom Hall, 263-2467.

Barry Van Veen (right), professor of computer and electrical engineering, works with students in his ECE 330: Signals and Systems class in the Wisconsin Collaboratory for Enhanced Learning (WisCEL) on the fourth floor of Wendt Library at the University of Wisconsin-Madison on April 9, 2015. Van Veen is the recipient of a 2015 Distinguished Teaching Award. (Bryce Richter, University of Wisconsin-Madison)

Vice Chancellor for University Relations: VINCENT J. SWEENEY, JR., 92 Bascom Hall, 265-2822.

Vice Chancellor for Legal Affairs: RAYMOND P. TAFFORA, 361 Bascom Hall, 263-7400.

Vice Chancellor for Medical Affairs: ROBERT GOLDEN, 4129 Health Sciences Learning Center, 750 Highland Avenue, 263-4910.

Dean of Agricultural and Life Sciences: KATHRYN VANDENBOSCH, 140 Agricultural Hall, 262-4930.

Dean of Business: FRANCOIS ORTALO-MAGNE, 4339 Grainger Hall, 262-7867.

Dean of Education: DIANA HESS, 377 Education Building, 262-1763.

Dean of Engineering: IAN ROBERTSON, 2610 Engineering Hall, 262-3482.

Vice Chancellor for Research and Graduate Education: MARSHA R. MAILICK, 333 Bascom Hall, 262-1044.

Dean of Human Ecology: SOYEON SHIM, 141 Human Ecology Building, 262-4847.

Vice Provost and Dean, Division of International Studies: GUIDO PODESTA, 268 Bascom Hall, 262-5805.

Dean of Law: MARGARET RAYMOND, 5211 Law Building, 262-0618.

Dean of Letters and Science: JOHN KARL SCHOLZ, 105 South Hall, 263-2303.

Director of Libraries: EDWARD VAN GEMERT, 372 Memorial Library, 262-2600.

Dean of Medicine and Public Health: ROBERT GOLDEN, 4129 Health Sciences Learning Center, 750 Highland Avenue, 263-4910.

Dean of Nursing: KATHARYN MAY, BX2455 Clinical Science Center-Module K6, 263-9725.

Dean of Pharmacy: STEVEN M. SWANSON, 1126B Rennebohm Hall, 262-1414.

Dean of Veterinary Medicine: MARK D. MARKEL, 2015 Linden Drive West, 263-6716.

Dean of Students: LORI BERQUAM, 75 Bascom Hall, 263-5702.

Dean of Continuing Studies and Associate Vice Chancellor: JEFFREY S. RUSSELL, 21 North Park Street, 7th Floor, 262-5821.

Secretary of the Academic Staff: HEATHER DANIELS, 270 Bascom Hall, 263-1011.

Secretary of the Faculty: STEVEN K. SMITH, 133 Bascom Hall, 265-4562.

Director of Undergraduate Admissions and Recruitment: ADELE C. BRUMFIELD, 702 West Johnson Street, 264-0464.

Director of Campus and Visitor Relations: STEVE AMUNDSON, 329 Union South, 1308 West Dayton Street, 265-9501.

Interim Vice Provost of Enrollment Management and Registrar: STEVEN M. HAHN, Room 11601, 333 East Campus Mall, 262-2433.

Registrar: SCOTT OWCZAREK, Room 10109, 333 East Campus Mall, 262-3964.

UW-Milwaukee

P.O. Box 413, Milwaukee 53201-0413
General Telephone: (414) 229-1122
Internet Address: www.uwm.edu

Chancellor: MARK MONE, 202 Chapman Hall, P.O. Box 413, Milwaukee 53201, 229-4331.

Provost and Vice Chancellor, Academic Affairs: JOHANNES BRITZ, 215 Chapman Hall, 229-4501.

Vice Chancellor, Finance and Administrative Affairs: ROBIN VAN HARPEN, 306 Chapman Hall, 229-2629.

Vice Chancellor, Student Affairs: MICHAEL LALIBERTE, 132 Chapman Hall, 229-4038.

Vice Chancellor, University Relations and Communications: THOMAS LULJAK, 180A Chapman Hall, 229-5024.

Vice Chancellor, Global Inclusion and Engagement: JOAN PRINCE, 118 Chapman Hall, 229-3101.

Vice Chancellor, Development and Alumni Relations: Patricia Borger, 290A Hefter Conference Center, 229-3013.

Dean, Graduate School: Marija Gajdardziska-Josifovska, 251 Mitchell Hall, 229-5520.

Dean, College of Engineering and Applied Science: Brett Peters, 520 Engineering and Mathematical Sciences Building, 229-4126.

Dean, College of Letters and Science: Rodney Swain, Northwest Quadrant Building 5498, 229-5895.

Interim Dean, College of Health Sciences: Paula Rhyner, 875 Enderis Hall, 229-4878.

Dean, School of Architecture and Urban Planning: Robert C. Greenstreet, 241 Architecture and Urban Planning Building, 229-4016.

Dean, Peck School of the Arts: Scott Emmons, 291 Arts Building, 229-4258.

Dean, Lubar School of Business: Timothy Smunt, N425 Business Administration Building, 229-6256.

Interim Dean, School of Education: Barbara Daly, 595 Enderis Hall, 229-4311.

Dean, School of Information Studies: Tomas Lipinski, Northwest Quadrant Building 3598, 229-4709.

Dean, School of Nursing: Sally Lundeen, 767A Cunningham Hall, 229-4189.

Dean, School of Social Welfare: Stan Stojkovic, 1099 Enderis Hall, 229-4400.

Interim Dean, School of Continuing Education: Sammis White, 161 West Wisconsin Avenue, 53203, 227-3203.

Dean, Joseph J. Zilber School of Public Health: Magda Peck, 1240 North 10th Street, 227-4128.

Dean, School of Freshwater Sciences: David Garman, 600 East Greenfield Avenue, 53204, 382-1700.

Vice Provost, Office of Research, Academic Affairs: Mark Harris, 251 Mitchell Hall, 229-5218.

Director of Undergraduate Admissions: Brian Troyer, 125 Vogel Hall, 229-4445.

Secretary of the University: Trudy Turner, N451 Lubar Hall, 229-5989.

UW-Eau Claire
105 Garfield Avenue, P.O. Box 4004, Eau Claire 54702-4004
General Telephone: (715) 836-4636
Internet Address: www.uwec.edu

Chancellor: James C. Schmidt, 836-2327.

Provost and Vice Chancellor, Academic Affairs: Patricia A. Kleine, 836-2320.

Vice Chancellor for Student Affairs: Beth Hellwig, 836-5992.

Vice Chancellor for Administration and Finance: Martin Hanifin, 836-3279.

Dean of Students: Joseph Abhold, 836-5992.

Dean, College of Arts and Sciences: David Leaman, 836-2542.

Dean, College of Education and Human Sciences: Carmen Manning, 836-3264.

Dean, College of Business: Diane Hoadley, 836-2500.

Dean, College of Nursing and Health Sciences: Linda Young, 836-5287.

Assistant Chancellor of Facilities and University Relations: Mike Rindo, 836-3331.

President of UWEC Foundation and Executive Director of University Advancement: Kim Way, 836-5630.

Director of Admissions: Heather Kretz, 836-5188.

Registrar: Tessa Perchinsky, 836-3887.

UW-Green Bay
2420 Nicolet Drive, Green Bay 54311-7001
General Telephone: (920) 465-2000
Internet Address: www.uwgb.edu

Chancellor: GARY L. MILLER, 465-2207.
Interim Provost and Vice Chancellor for Academic Affairs: GREGORY DAVIS, 465-2254.
Interim Vice Chancellor, Business and Finance: SHERYL VAN GRUENSVEN, 465-2210.
Vice Chancellor for University Advancement: JEANNE STANGEL, 465-2074.
Interim Dean of Enrollment Services: TIMOTHY SEWALL, 465-2236.
Dean of Students: BRENDA AMENSON-HILL, 465-2159.
Dean, College of Liberal Arts and Sciences: SCOTT FURLONG, 465-2336.

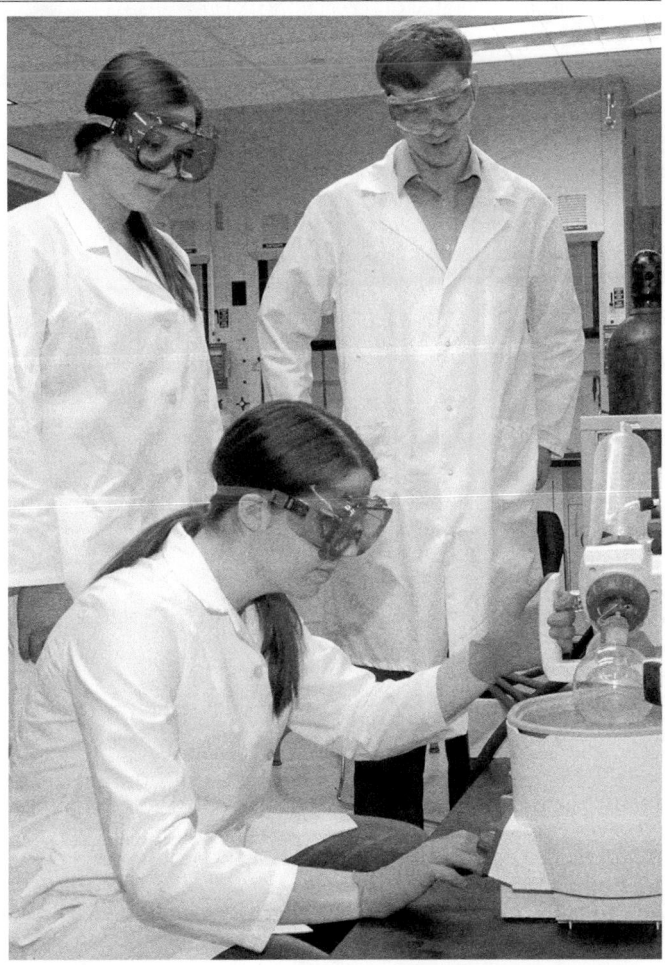

Students in a laboratory at the University of Wisconsin Green Bay. *(University of Wisconsin-Green Bay)*

Dean, College of Professional Studies: SUE JOSEPH MATTISON, 465-2050.
Director of University Communications: CHRISTOPHER SAMPSON, 465-2527.
Media Relations Coordinator: CHRISTOPHER SAMPSON, 465-2527.
Registrar: AMANDA HRUSKA, 465-2155.

UW-La Crosse
1725 State Street, La Crosse 54601-9959
General Telephone: (608) 785-8000
Internet Address: www.uwlax.edu

Chancellor: JOE GOW, 785-8004.
Interim Provost/Vice Chancellor: BETSY MORGAN, 785-8042.
Vice Chancellor, Administration and Finance: BOB HETZEL, 785-8021.
President, UW-L Foundation: WILLIAM COLCLOUGH, 785-8489.
Affirmative Action Officer: NIZAM ARAIN, 785-8541.
Associate Dean, Campus Climate and Diversity: BARBARA STEWART, 785-5092.
Interim Associate Vice Chancellor for Academic Affairs: SANDY GRUNWALD, 785-8159.
Director, Human Resources: MADELINE HOLZEM, 785-8013.
Executive Director, Facilities Planning and Management: DOUGLAS PEARSON, 785-8019.
Chief Information Officer: MOHAMED ELHINDI, 785-8662.
Vice Chancellor, Student Affairs: PAULA M. KNUDSON, 785-8062.
Vice Chancellor, University Advancement: GREG REICHERT, 785-8672.
Dean, College of Business Administration: LAURA MILNER, 785-8091.
Dean, College of Liberal Studies: JULIA JOHNSON, 785-8113.
Dean, College of Science and Health: BRUCE V. RILEY, 785-8218.
Director, Admissions: COREY SJOQUIST, 785-8939.
Registrar: CHRISTINE S. BAKKUM, 785-8577.

UW-Oshkosh
800 Algoma Boulevard, Oshkosh 54901-8617
General Telephone: (920) 424-1234
Internet Address: www.uwosh.edu

Chancellor: ANDREW J. LEAVITT, 424-0200.
Provost/Vice Chancellor: LANE EARNS, 424-0300.
Dean, College of Business: WILLIAM TALLON, 424-1424.
Dean, College of Education and Human Services: FREDERICK L. YEO, 424-3322.
Dean, College of Letters and Science: JOHN J. KOKER, 424-1210.
Dean, College of Nursing: LESLIE NEAL-BOYAN, 424-3089.
Dean, Graduate Studies: SUSAN CRAMER, 424-3095.
Assistant Vice Chancellor, Academic Support: SYLVIA CAREY BUTLER, 424-3080.
Vice Chancellor, Student Affairs: PETRA M. ROTER, 424-4000.
Assistant Vice Chancellor for Student Engagement and Success/Dean of Students: SHARON KIPETZ, 424-3100.
Vice Chancellor, Administrative Services: THOMAS G. SONNLEITNER, 424-3030.
Associate Vice Chancellor, Administrative Services: LORI WORM, 424-3033.
Vice Chancellor, Advancement: ARTHUR RATHGEN, 424-7121.
Assistant Vice Chancellor, Integrated Marketing Communications: JAMIE S. CEMAN, 424-0821.
Registrar: LISA M. DANIELSON, 424-3007.

UW-Parkside

P.O. Box 2000, Kenosha 53141-2000
General Telephone: (262) 595-2345
Internet Address: www.uwp.edu

Chancellor: DEBORAH L. FORD, 595-2211.
Interim Provost/Vice Chancellor for Academic Affairs: FRED EBEID, 595-2261.
Associate Provost: GARY WOOD, 595-2364.
Vice Chancellor, Finance and Administration: MEL KLINKNER, 595-2141.
Dean of Students: TAMMY MCGUCKIN, 595-2598.
Assistant Chancellor for University Relations and Advancement: JOHN JARACZEWSKI, 595-2591.
Associate Vice Chancellor for Institutional Effectiveness: KIMBERLY KELLEY, 595-2553.
Associate Vice Chancellor for Enrollment Management: DEANN POSSEHL, 595-2454.
Dean, College of Arts and Humanities: LESLEY WALKER, 595-2188.
Dean, College of Business, Economics and Computing: DIRK BALDWIN, 595-2243.
Dean, College of Natural and Health Science: EMMANUEL OTU, 595-2973.
Interim Dean, College of Social Sciences and Professional Studies: PEGGY JAMES, 595-2993.
Chair, Institute for Professional Educator Development: NANCY WHITAKER, 595-2341.
Interim Executive Director, Continuing Education and Community Engagement: DEBRA KARP, 595-2208.
University Diversity and Inclusion Officer: HEATHER KIND-KEPPEL, 595-2239.
Registrar: RHONDA KIMMEL, 595-2237.

UW-Platteville

1 University Plaza, Platteville 53818-3099
General Telephone: (608) 342-1491
Internet Address: www.uwplatt.edu

Chancellor: DENNIS J. SHIELDS, 342-1234.
Provost and Vice Chancellor for Academic Affairs: MITTIE DEN HERDER, 342-1261.
Vice Chancellor for Administrative Services: ROBERT G. CRAMER, 342-1226.
Chief Diversity Officer and Assistant Chancellor for Diversity and Inclusion: JENNIFER DECOSTE, 342-6152.
Assistant Chancellor for Admission and Enrollment Services: ANGELA UDELHOFEN, 342-1125.
Assistant Vice Chancellor for Student Affairs: LAURA BAYLESS, 342-1854.
Assistant Vice Chancellor for Academic Affairs: D. JOANNE WILSON, 342-1262.
Assistant Vice Chancellor for Information Technology: SUZANNE TRAXLER, 342-1421.
Senior Special Assistant to the·Chancellor: ROSE SMYRSKI, 342-7243.
Dean, College of Business, Industry, Life Science and Agriculture: WAYNE WEBER, 342-1547.
Dean, College of Engineering, Mathematics, and Science: MOLLY GRIBB, 342-1561.
Dean, College of Liberal Arts and Education: ELIZABETH THROOP, 342-1151.
Director, School of Graduate Studies: DOMINIC BARRACLOUGH, 342-1262.
Registrar: DAVID KIECKHAFER, 342-1321.

UW-River Falls

410 South Third Street, River Falls 54022-5001
General Telephone: (715) 425-3911
Internet Address: www.uwrf.edu

Chancellor: DEAN VAN GALEN, 425-3201.
Provost/Vice Chancellor for Academic Affairs: FERNANDO DELGADO, 425-3700.
Assistant Chancellor, Business and Finance: ELIZABETH FRUEH, 425-3737.
Assistant Chancellor, University Advancement: CHRIS MUELLER, 425-3545.

Dean, College of Agriculture, Food and Environmental Sciences: DALE GALLENBERG, 425-3841.

Dean, College of Arts and Sciences: BRADLEY CASKEY, 425-3777.

Dean, College of Education and Professional Studies: LARRY SOLBERG, 425-3774.

Dean, College of Business and Economics: MICHAEL FRONMUELLER, 425-3335.

Associate Vice Chancellor for Student Affairs: GREGG HEINSELMAN, 425-0720.

Interim Associate Vice Chancellor for Academic Affairs and Graduate Studies: WES CHAPIN, 425-0629.

Director of Admissions: SARAH EGERSTROM, 425-3500.

Registrar: DAN VANDE YACHT, 425-3342.

UW-Stevens Point

Room 213 Old Main, 2100 Main Street, Stevens Point 54481-3897
General Telephone: (715) 346-0123
Internet Address: www.uwsp.edu

Chancellor: BERNIE L. PATTERSON, 346-2123.

Provost/Vice Chancellor, Academic Affairs: GREGORY SUMMERS, 346-4686.

Vice Chancellor, Business Affairs: GREGORY DIEMER, 346-2641.

Vice Chancellor, Student Affairs: AL THOMPSON, JR., 346-2481.

Vice Chancellor, University Advancement: CHRISTOPHER RICHARDS, 346-3812.

Associate Vice Chancellor, Personnel, Budget, and Grants: KATIE JORE, 346-3710.

Interim Associate Vice Chancellor, Teaching, Learning and Academic Programs: TODD HUSPENI, 346-4250.

Interim Chief Information Officer, Information Technology: JIM BARRETT, 346-4093.

Interim Executive Director, University Relations and Communication: GARY WESCOTT, 346-3827.

Interim Dean, College of Fine Arts and Communication: RHONDA SPRAGUE, 346-4920.

Dean, College of Letters and Science: CHRISTOPHER CIRMO, 346-4224.

Dean, College of Natural Resources: CHRISTINE THOMAS, 346-4617.

Dean, College of Professional Studies: MARTY LOY, 346-3169.

Director, Admissions: BILL JORDAN, 346-2441.

Interim Registrar: ED LEE, 346-4301.

UW-Stout

P.O. Box 790, Menomonie 54751-0790
General Telephone: (715) 232-1122
Internet Address: www.uwstout.edu

Chancellor: BOB MEYER, 232-2441.

Provost/Vice Chancellor, Academic and Student Affairs: PATRICK GUILFOILE, 232-2421.

Vice Chancellor, Administrative and Student Life Services: PHIL LYONS, 232-1683.

Vice Chancellor, University Advancement and Marketing: MARK PARSONS, 232-1151.

Associate Vice Chancellor, Academic and Student Affairs: GLENDALI RODRIGUEZ, 232-2421.

Dean, College of Arts, Humanities and Social Sciences: MARIA ALM, 232-2596.

Dean, College of Education, Health and Human Sciences: MARY HOPKINS-BEST, 232-1088.

Dean, College of Management: ABEL ADEKOLA, 232-1234.

Dean, College of Science, Technology, Engineering and Mathematics: CHARLES BOMAR, 232-4053.

Dean of Students: JOAN THOMAS, 232-1181.

Executive Director of Enrollment Management: vacancy, 232-2639.

Registrar: SCOTT CORRELL, 232-1233.

UW-Superior

Belknap and Catlin Street, P.O. Box 2000, Superior 54880-4500
General Telephone: (715) 394-8101
Internet Address: www.uwsuper.edu

Chancellor: RENÉE WACHTER, 394-8221.
Provost: FAITH C. HENSRUD, 394-8449.
Vice Chancellor for Administration and Finance: GEORGETTE KOENIG, 394-8014.
Dean of Students: HARRY ANDERSON, 394-8241.
Vice Chancellor, University Advancement: JEANNE THOMPSON, 394-8598.
Assistant to the Chancellor for EO/AA and Diversity: vacancy, 394-8365.
Vice Chancellor for Enrollment Management: vacancy, 394-8306.
Interim Dean of Faculties: LIZ BLUE, 394-8131.
Registrar: JEFFREY KIRSCHLING, 394-8218.

UW-Whitewater

Hyer Hall, 800 West Main Street, Whitewater 53190-1790
General Telephone: (262) 472-1234
Internet Address: www.uww.edu

Chancellor: BEVERLY A. KOPPER, 472-1918.
Interim Provost/Vice Chancellor for Academic Affairs: JOHN STONE, 472-1672.
Vice Chancellor, Administrative Affairs: D. JEFF ARNOLD, 472-1922.
Vice Chancellor, Student Affairs: THOMAS R. RIOS, 472-1051.
Vice Chancellor, Advancement: JONATHAN C. ENSLIN, 472-1482.
Associate Vice Chancellor, Academic Affairs: GREG COOK, 472-1077.

In class with Tim Cleary, associate professor of sculpture, in the UW-Superior Visual Arts Department. (University of Wisconsin-Superior)

Dean, College of Arts and Communication: Mark L. McPhail, 472-1221.

Dean, College of Business and Economics: John D. Chenoweth, 472-1343.

Dean, College of Education and Professional Studies: Katharina E. Heyning, 472-1101.

Dean, College of Letters and Sciences: David J. Travis, 472-1710.

Dean, Graduate School, Continuing Education and Summer Session: John F. Stone, 472-1006.

Assistant Vice Chancellor, Enrollment and Retention: Matt Aschenbrener, 472-1512.

Registrar: Jodi M. Hare, 472-1570.

UW Colleges and UW-Extension
432 North Lake Street, Madison 53706-1498
General Telephone: (608) 262-3786

Chancellor: Cathy Sandeen, (608) 262-3786.

Assistant to the Chancellor: Barb Sandridge, (608) 262-3786.

UW Colleges
Internet Address: www.uwc.edu/

Provost/Vice Chancellor: Greg Lampe, (608) 263-1794.

Vice Chancellor, Administrative and Financial Services: Steven Wildeck, (608) 265-3040.

Associate Vice Chancellor for Administrative and Financial Services: Colleen Godfriaux, (608) 265-9807

Associate Vice Chancellor for Academic Affairs: Joseph Foy, (608) 263-7217.

Associate Vice Chancellor for Student Services and Enrollment Management: Richard Barnhouse, (608) 265-8609.

Assistant Vice Chancellor for Information Technology: Werner Gade, (608) 262-7832.

At UW-Sheboygan, more than a third of students are age 22 or older and about a fifth are students of color. (UW Colleges)

Assistant Vice Chancellor, Office of Equity, Diversity and Inclusion: CHRISTINE CURLEY, (608) 265-2406.

Assistant Vice Chancellor for Human Resources: JASON BEIER, (608) 890-1066.

Registrar: LARRY GRAVES, (608) 262-9048.

Baraboo/Sauk County: 1006 Connie Road, Baraboo 53913-1098, (608) 355-5200, www.baraboo.uwc.edu
   CEO/Dean: TRACY WHITE.

Barron County: 1800 College Drive, Rice Lake 54868-2497, (715) 234-8176, www.barron.uwc.edu
   CEO/Dean: DEAN YOHNK.

Fond du Lac: 400 University Drive, Fond du Lac 54935-2998, (920) 929-1100, www.fdl.uwc.edu
   CEO/Dean: JOHN SHORT.

Fox Valley: 1478 Midway Road, Menasha 54952-1297, (920) 832-2600, www.fox.uwc.edu
   CEO/Dean: MARTIN RUDD.

Manitowoc: 705 Viebahn Street, Manitowoc 54220-6699, (920) 683-4700, www.manitowoc.uwc.edu
   CEO/Dean: CHARLES CLARK.

Marathon County: 518 South 7th Avenue, Wausau 54401-5396, (715) 261-6100, www.uwmc.uwc.edu
   CEO/Dean: KEITH MONTGOMERY.

Marinette: 750 West Bay Shore Street, Marinette 54143-4299, (715) 735-4300, www.marinette.uwc.edu
   CEO/Dean: PAULA LANGTEAU.

Marshfield/Wood County: 2000 West 5th Street, Marshfield 54449-0150, (715) 389-6500, www.marshfield.uwc.edu
   CEO/Dean: PATRICIA STUHR.

Richland: 1200 Highway 14 West, Richland Center 53581-1399, (608) 647-6186, www.richland.uwc.edu
   CEO/Dean: PATRICK HAGEN.

Rock County: 2909 Kellogg Avenue, Janesville 53546-5699, (608) 758-6565, www.rock.uwc.edu
   CEO/Dean: CARMEN WILSON.

Sheboygan: One University Drive, Sheboygan 53081-4789, (920) 459-6600, www.sheboygan.uwc.edu
   CEO/Dean: JACKIE JOSEPH-SILVERSTEIN.

Washington County: 400 University Drive, West Bend 53095-3699, (262) 335-5200, www.washington.uwc.edu
   CEO/Dean: PAUL PRICE.

Waukesha: 1500 North University Drive, Waukesha 53188-2799, (262) 521-5200, www.waukesha.uwc.edu
   CEO/Dean: HARRY MUIR.

UW-Extension

Internet Address: www.uwex.edu

Provost/Vice Chancellor: AARON BROWER, (608) 262-6151.

Vice Chancellor, Administrative and Financial Services: STEVEN WILDECK, (608) 265-3040.

Associate Vice Chancellor for Administrative and Financial Services: MARK DORN, (608) 262-5975.

Associate Vice Chancellor: GREG HUTCHINS, (608) 263-7810.

Assistant Vice Chancellor for Information Technology: WERNER GADE, (608) 262-7832.

Assistant Vice Chancellor, Office of Equity, Diversity and Inclusion: CHRISTINE CURLEY, (608) 265-2406.

Assistant Vice Chancellor for Human Resources: JASON BEIER, (608) 890-1066.

Dean, Outreach and E-Learning Extension: DAVID SCHEJBAL, (608) 265-8692.

Dean and Director, Cooperative Extension: RICK KLEMME, (608) 263-2775.

Director, Broadcasting and Media Innovations: MALCOLM BRETT, (608) 263-9598.

Executive Director, Business and Entrepreneurship: MARK LANGE, (608) 263-7794.

Interim Secretary of the Faculty and Academic Staff: DAN HILL, (608) 262-4387.

Officers and Units Required by Statute

State Cartographer: HOWARD VEREGIN, (608) 262-6852, 384 Science Hall, 550 North Park Street, Madison 53706-1491.

State Geologist: JAMES ROBERTSON, (608) 263-7384, Geological and Natural History Survey, 3817 Mineral Point Road, Madison 53705-5100.

Agricultural Safety and Health Center: CHERYL SKJOLAAS, *interim director,* (608) 265-0568, 460 Henry Mall, Madison 53706.

Center for Environmental Education: JEREMY SOLIN, *interim director,* (715) 346-4973, 110 College of Natural Resources, 403 Learning Resources Center, Stevens Point 54481.

Geological and Natural History Survey: JAMES ROBERTSON, *state geologist,* (608) 262-1705, 3817 Mineral Point Road, Madison 53705-5100.

Area Health Education Center: NANCY SUGDEN, *director,* (608) 263-4927, Health Sciences Learning Center, 4th Floor, 750 Highland Avenue, Madison 53705.

Wisconsin State Herbarium: KENNETH CAMERON, *director,* (608) 265-9237, Department of Botany, Room 160, Birge Hall, Madison 53706-1381.

Psychiatric HealthEmotions Research Institute: NED KALIN, *director,* (608) 263-6079, 6001 Research Park Boulevard, Madison 53719.

Robert M. La Follette Institute of Public Affairs: SUSAN WEBB YACKEE, *director,* (608) 265-6017, 1225 Observatory Drive, Madison 53706.

State Soils and Plant Analysis Laboratory: ROBERT FLORENCE, *director,* (608) 262-4364, 8452 Mineral Point Road, Madison 53705.

Institute for Excellence in Urban Education: TRACEY NIX, *director,* (414) 229-6507, School of Education, P.O. Box 413, UW-Milwaukee, Milwaukee 53201.

James A. Graaskamp Center for Real Estate: MICHAEL BRENNAN, *executive director,* (608) 263-4392, 975 University Avenue, Room 5262, Grainger Hall, Madison 53706.

School of Veterinary Medicine: MARK D. MARKEL, *dean,* (608) 262-3573, 2015 Linden Drive West, Madison 53706-1102.

Agency Responsibility: The prime responsibilities of the University of Wisconsin System are teaching, public service, and research. The system provides postsecondary academic education for approximately 180,000 students, including 137,000 full-time equivalent undergraduates.

Organization: The UW System consists of 13 four-year universities, 13 two-year colleges, and statewide extension programs. UW-Madison and UW-Milwaukee offer bachelor's, master's, doctoral, and professional degrees. Eleven other universities in the UW System offer associate, bachelor's, master's, and clinical/professional doctoral degree programs: UW-Eau Claire, UW-Green Bay, UW-La Crosse, UW-Oshkosh, UW-Parkside, UW-Platteville, UW-River Falls, UW-Stevens Point, UW-Stout, UW-Superior, and UW-Whitewater.

The UW Colleges is an institution of the University of Wisconsin System comprised of 13 campuses and UW Colleges Online. UW Colleges offers an Associate of Arts and Science degree and a single Bachelor of Applied Arts and Sciences degree. By providing an affordable, accessible education, UW Colleges prepares more than 14,000 students of all ages and backgrounds for success in some 200 baccalaureate and professional programs. While UW Colleges faculty and staff are employed by the UW System, municipalities and/or counties own the campuses and buildings in which the UW Colleges are located. Visit www.uwc.edu for information.

UW-Extension serves Wisconsin families, businesses, and communities statewide through offices in all 72 Wisconsin counties and three tribal nations, continuing education services through all 26 UW System campuses, the UW Flexible Option partnership with UW System campuses, the statewide broadcasting networks of Wisconsin Public Radio and Wisconsin Public Television, and small business and entrepreneurship activities throughout the state.

The 18-member Board of Regents of the University of Wisconsin System has primary responsibility for the governance of the UW System. The board plans for the future of public higher education in Wisconsin; appoints the president of the UW System, the chancellors of the 13 universities, and the chancellor of the UW Colleges and UW-Extension; sets admission standards; reviews and approves university budgets; and establishes the regulatory framework within which the individual units operate.

Two members serve *ex officio*; all other members are appointed to the board by the governor. The student members serve staggered 2-year terms; and the other 14 citizen members serve staggered 7-year terms. At least one of the citizen members shall reside in each of the state's congressional districts.

Unit Functions: The president of the University of Wisconsin System has full executive responsibility for system operation and management. This officer carries out the duties prescribed by statute; implements the policies established by the board of regents; manages and coordinates the system's administrative offices; and exercises fiscal control through budget development, management-planning programs, and coordination and evaluation of the academic programs on all campuses.

Each chancellor serves as executive head of a particular campus or program, administers board policies under the direction of the system's president, and is accountable to the board of regents. Subject to board policy, the chancellors, in consultation with their faculties, design curricula and set degree requirements; determine academic standards and establish grading systems; define and administer institutional standards for faculty peer evaluation; screen candidates for appointment, promotion, and tenure; administer auxiliary services; and control all funds allocated to or generated by their respective programs. One chancellor administers both UW Colleges and UW-Extension.

History: Today's UW System is the product of the 1971 merger of two existing university boards – the Board of Regents of the University of Wisconsin and the Board of Regents of the State Universities – and the institutions they governed.

From earliest times, Wisconsin lawmakers recognized the need for a tax-supported university. The territorial legislature passed laws in 1836, 1838, and 1839 regarding establishment and location of a university, and Article X, Section 6, of the state constitution ratified in 1848, provided for a state university at or near the seat of state government. Chapter 20, Laws of 1848, which implemented the constitutional provision, delegated university administration to a board of regents and classes began in 1849. Critical to the university's early development was Chapter 114, Laws of 1866, which reorganized the board of regents, expanded its authority, and authorized the governor to appoint the regents. The 1866 reorganization provided for instruction in agriculture on the Madison campus and an experimental farm, thereby making the university eligible, as Wisconsin's land-grant institution, to receive the proceeds derived from sale of lands granted by the federal government to support agricultural education and research.

The State Universities originated with Chapter 82, Laws of 1857, which provided funds for a system of 2-year normal schools to train teachers and created the Board of Regents of Normal Schools. The first normal school opened at Platteville in 1866 and the ninth 50 years later at Eau Claire. In 1929, the 9 normal schools became "state teachers colleges" and were authorized to offer baccalaureate degree programs. They were renamed state colleges in 1951 and state universities in 1964. Chapter 75, Laws of 1967, renamed the governing body, designating it the Board of Regents of State Universities.

Chapter 100, Laws of 1971, mandated the merger of Wisconsin's two systems of public higher education to form the University of Wisconsin System. Chapter 335, Laws of 1973, recreated Chapter 36 of the statutes and provided a single statutory charter to govern public higher education in Wisconsin. The University of Wisconsin Colleges, which were previously called UW Centers, were renamed by 1997 Wisconsin Act 237.

Statutory Council:

Rural Health Development Council: vacancy (designated by secretary of health services); BYRON J. CROUSE (UW Medical School representative); SYED AHMED (Medical College of Wisconsin, Inc., representative); TIM SIZE (Wisconsin Health and Educational Facilities Authority representative); vacancy (private rural lender representative); JIM O'KEEFE (rural hospital representative); vacancy (physician practicing in rural area); BLANE CHRISTMAN (dentist practicing in rural area); JACALYN SZEHNER (nurse practicing in rural area); vacancy (dental hygienist practicing in rural area); vacancy (public health services representative); KATHY SCHMITT (designated by secretary of agriculture, trade and consumer protection); vacancy (designated by secretary of workforce development); CHARLIE WALKER (rural economic development representative); vacancy (public member from rural area); vacancy (rural health clinic representative); 2 vacancies. (All except *ex officio* members or their designees are appointed by governor with senate consent.)

Mailing Address: Wisconsin Office of Rural Health, UW School of Medicine and Public Health, 310 N. Midvale Boulevard, Suite 301, Madison 53705.

Telephone: 261-1883, (800) 385-0005 (toll free).

The 18-member Rural Health Development Council advises the board of regents regarding administration of the health professions loan assistance program, delivery of health care and improvement of facilities in rural areas, and coordination of state and federal programs available to assist rural health facilities. Appointed members serve 5-year terms. The council was created by 1989 Wisconsin Act 317 in the Department of Commerce and moved to the UW System under 2009 Wisconsin Act 28. Its composition and duties are prescribed in Sections 15.917 and 36.62 of the statutes.

ORGANIZATION CREATED BY STATUTE
WITHIN THE UNIVERSITY OF WISCONSIN SYSTEM

LABORATORY OF HYGIENE

Laboratory of Hygiene Board: DARRELL BAZZELL (designated by chancellor of UW-Madison), KAREN MCKEOWN (designated by secretary of health services), JACK SULLIVAN (designated by secretary of natural resources), MICHELLE WACHTER (designated by secretary of agriculture, trade and consumer protection); JEFF KINDRAI (local health department representative); ROBERT CORLISS (physician representing clinical laboratories); vacancy (representing private environmental testing laboratories); JAMES MORRISON (representing occupational health laboratories); BARRY IRMEN (medical examiner or coroner); CARRIE LEWIS, vacancy (public members). Nonvoting member: CHARLES D. BROKOPP (director, Laboratory of Hygiene). (All except *ex officio* officers or designees are appointed by governor.)

Director: CHARLES D. BROKOPP.

Medical Director: DANIEL F. KURTYCZ.

Assistant Directors: STEVE MARSHALL, DAVID WEBB.

Mailing Address: 465 Henry Mall, Madison 53706-1578; 2601 Agriculture Drive, Madison 53707-7996 (Environmental Health and Occupational Health Divisions and Proficiency Testing Program).

Telephones: Clinical Laboratories Customer service: (800) 862-1013; Administrative office: (608) 890-0288; Wisconsin Occupational Health Laboratory: (608) 224-6210, (800) 446-

0403; Proficiency Testing Program: (800) 462-5261; Environmental Health Division: (608) 224-6202, (800) 442-4618.

Internet Address: www.slh.wisc.edu

Division Fax: (608) 262-3257; Environmental Health Division Fax: (608) 224-6213.

Publications: Reference manual; annual report; research annual report, fee schedules; assorted special publications.

Number of Employees: 309.75.

Total Budget 2013-15: $68,310,600.

Statutory References: Sections 15.07 (1), 15.915 (2), and 36.25 (11).

Agency Responsibility: The Laboratory of Hygiene, headed by a director appointed by the State Laboratory of Hygiene Board upon recommendation of the chancellor of the University of Wisconsin-Madison, provides complete laboratory services for appropriate state agencies and local health departments in the areas of water quality, air quality, public health, and contagious diseases. It performs laboratory tests and consultation for physicians, health officers, local agencies, private citizens, and resource management officials to prevent and control diseases and environmental hazards. As part of the UW-Madison, the laboratory provides facilities for teaching and research in the fields of public health and environmental protection.

The laboratory operates under the direction and supervision of the Laboratory of Hygiene Board, composed of 11 members, 7 of whom are appointed by the governor to serve 3-year terms.

History: Chapter 344, Laws of 1903, created the Laboratory of Hygiene at the University of Wisconsin to examine water supplies, investigate contagious and infectious diseases, and function as the official laboratory of the State Board of Health. The executive branch reorganization act of 1967 extended the laboratory's services to the Department of Natural Resources.

INDEPENDENT UNITS ATTACHED FOR BUDGETING, PROGRAM COORDINATION, AND RELATED MANAGEMENT FUNCTIONS BY SECTION 15.03 OF THE STATUTES

ENVIRONMENTAL EDUCATION BOARD

Environmental Education Board: JIM JENSON (business and industry representative), *chairperson;* SENATOR RISSER, vacancy; REPRESENTATIVES DANOU, MURSAU; RANDY CHAMPEAU (designated by president, UW System), JANET HUTCHENS (designated by secretary of natural resources), VICTORIA RYDBERG (designated by superintendent of public instruction), CARRIE MORGAN (designated by president, Technical College System Board); BETH CARRENO (nature centers, museums, zoos representative), CONNIE LAWNICZAK (energy representative), RUTH ANN LEE (conservation and environmental organizations representative), THERESA LEHMAN (labor representative), DONALD PETERSON (forestry representative), AMY SCHIEBEL (higher education institutions faculty representative), DEBRA WEITZEL (environmental educators representative), LOREN WOLFE (agricultural representative). (Unless otherwise designated, members are appointed by president of UW System.)

Mailing Address: 110H Trainer Natural Resources Building, UW-Stevens Point, 800 Reserve Street, Stevens Point 54481.

Telephone: (715) 346-3805.

Internet Address: www.uwsp.edu/cnr/weeb

Statutory References: Sections 15.915 (6), 36.54.

Agency Responsibility: The Environmental Education Board awards matching grants to public agencies and nonprofit corporations to develop and distribute environmental education programs. The board consults with the state's educational agencies, the Department of Natural Resources, and other state agencies to identify needs and establish priorities for environmental education. Its 17 members include 9 representatives of educational institutions and nongovernmental interest groups who are appointed to serve 3-year terms. The senate and assembly members must represent the majority and the minority parties in their respective houses. The board was created by 1989 Wisconsin Act 299 and was transferred from the Department of Public Instruction to the UW System by 1997 Wisconsin Act 27.

VETERINARY DIAGNOSTIC LABORATORY BOARD

Veterinary Diagnostic Laboratory Board: SANDRA LARSON (livestock producer), *chairperson;* BEN BRANCEL (secretary of agriculture, trade and consumer protection), DARRELL BAZZELL (designated by chancellor of UW-Madison), MARK MARKEL (dean of the UW-Madison School of Veterinary Medicine), SHERRY SHAW (veterinarian employed by the federal government); ALISSA GRENAWALT (livestock producer); JAMES MERONEK, STEVE VAN LANNEN (representing animal agriculture); RAY PAWLISCH (practicing veterinarian); PHILIP BOCHSLER (laboratory director) (nonvoting member). (All except *ex officio* members are appointed by governor.)

Mailing Address: 445 Easterday Lane, Madison 53706.

Telephone: (608) 262-5432.

Fax: (847) 574-8085.

Statutory References: Sections 15.915 (1) and 36.58.

Agency Responsibility: The Veterinary Diagnostic Laboratory Board oversees the Veterinary Diagnostic Laboratory, which provides animal health testing and diagnostic services on a statewide basis for all types of animals. The board has 10 members, 6 of whom are appointed by the governor. Five of these members serve staggered 3-year terms, while one member, a veterinarian employed by the federal government, serves at the pleasure of the governor. The board prescribes policies for the laboratory's operation, develops its biennial budget, and sets fees for laboratory services. It also consults with the UW-Madison chancellor on the appointment of the laboratory director.

History: Both the board and the laboratory were created by 1999 Wisconsin Act 107, which transferred the laboratory's facilities and employees from the Department of Agriculture, Trade and Consumer Protection to the UW System, effective July 1, 2000.

Department of
VETERANS AFFAIRS

Address e-mail by combining the user ID and the state extender: userid@**dva.wisconsin.gov**
All telephone numbers are 608 area code unless otherwise indicated.

Board of Veterans Affairs: JOHN TOWNSEND (6th district), *chairperson;* JOHN M. GAEDKE (2nd district), *vice chairperson;* DANIEL BOHLIN (3rd district), *secretary;* LARRY KUTSCHMA (1st district), CATHY GORST (7th district), CARL KRUEGER (4th district), LEIGH NEVILLE-NEIL (8th district), KEVIN NICHOLSON (5th district); ALAN RICHARDS (at-large member). (All are veterans appointed by governor with senate consent. At least one member must represent each congressional district.)

Secretary of Veterans Affairs: JOHN A. SCOCOS, 266-1315, john.scocos@

Deputy Secretary: MICHAEL TREPANIER, 266-1315, michael.trepanier@

Assistant Deputy Secretary: KATHLEEN MARSCHMAN, 266-2256, kathy.marschman@

Legal Counsel, Office of: CHAD KOPLIEN, *chief legal counsel,* 266-6992, chad.koplien@

Budget, Finance and Facilities, Office of: JAMES A. PARKER, *chief financial officer,* 266-1843, james.parker@

Public Affairs, Office of: CARLA VIGUE, *communications director,* 266-0517, carla.vigue@

Wisconsin Veterans Museum: MICHAEL TELZROW, *director,* 266-1009, michael.telzrow@

Mailing Address: P.O. Box 7843, Madison 53707-7843.

Location: 201 West Washington Avenue, Madison.

Telephone: 266-1311, toll free: 1-800-WIS-VETS (800-947-8387).

Fax: 264-7616.

Internet Address: www.wisvets.com

Number of Employees: 1,292.70.

Total Budget 2013-15: $271,827,600.

Statutory References: Section 15.49; Chapter 45.

Management Services, Division of: KELLI KAALELE, *administrator,* 267-7207, kelli.kaalele@; Fax: 264-6089.

    Human Resources, Bureau of: vacancy, *director,* 267-1796; Fax 266-5414.

    Information Systems, Bureau of: CHRIS APFELBECK, *director,* 267-1794, chris.apfelbeck@

Veterans Benefits, Division of: JAMES BOND, *administrator,* 266-2778, james.bond@; Fax: 267-0403.

    Benefits, Bureau of: DOMINGO LEGUIZAMON, *director,* 267-7124, domingo.leguizamon@

    Cemeteries and Memorial Services, Bureau of: MARIAN LEWANDOWSKI, *director,* (262) 878-6742, marian.lewandowski@

Veterans Homes, Division of: RANDALL NITSCHKE, *administrator,* 264-7619, randall.nitschke@

    Wisconsin Veterans Home, Chippewa Falls, 2175 East Park Avenue, Chippewa Falls 54729; MARK WILSON, *commandant,* (715) 299-0189, mark.wilson@

    Wisconsin Veterans Home, King 54946-0600, Fax: (715) 258-5736; JIM KNIGHT, *commandant,* (715) 258-4241, jim.knight@; vacancy, *deputy commandant,* (715) 258-4241; vacancy, *adjutant,* (715) 258-4249; *Public Information/Volunteer Coordinator:* AMBER NIKOLAI, (715) 258-4247, amber.nikolai@

    Wisconsin Veterans Home, Union Grove, 21425D Spring Street, Union Grove 53182; REID AARON, *commandant,* (262) 878-6752, reid.aaron@

DEPARTMENT OF VETERANS AFFAIRS

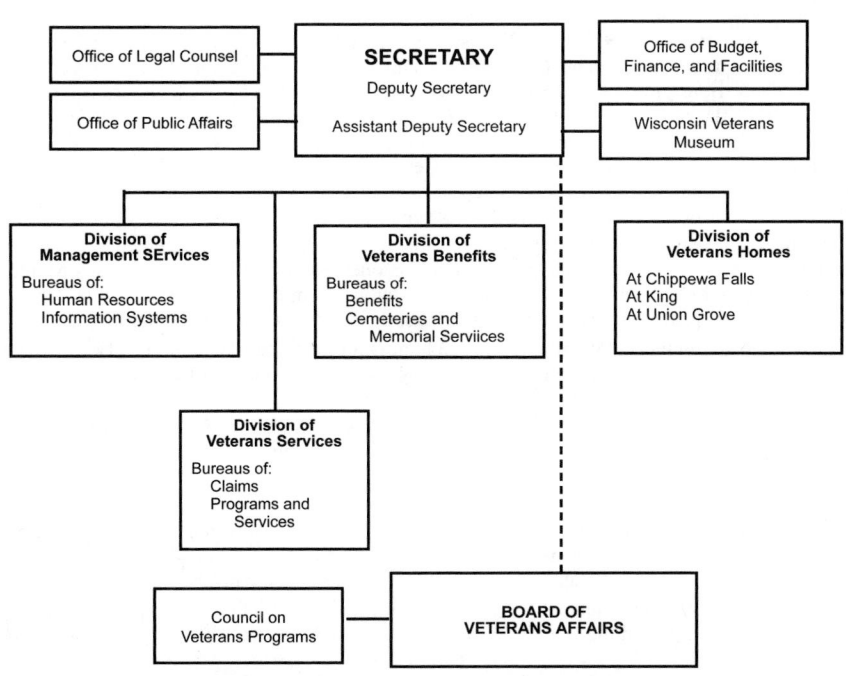

Veterans Services, Division of: KENNETH G. GRANT, *administrator,* 266-7916, kenneth.grant@

    Claims, Bureau of: vacancy, *director,* VA Regional Office, 5400 West National Avenue, BM 157, Milwaukee 53214, (414) 902-5757; Fax: (414) 902-9421.

    Programs and Services, Bureau of: MICHAEL AYERS, *director,* 267-7135.

Publications: *The Bugle; The Courier;* brochures on the state veterans' programs and services for Wisconsin veterans, Wisconsin Veterans Museum (Madison), the Wisconsin Veterans Home (King), the Wisconsin Veterans Home (Union Grove), and Wisconsin's veterans memorial cemeteries.

Agency Responsibility: The Department of Veterans Affairs works on behalf of Wisconsin's veterans community – veterans, their families and their survivors – in recognition of their service and sacrifice to our state and nation. It oversees veterans benefits, programs, and services in the areas of education, health care, and federal claims assistance, among others. It also operates the Wisconsin veterans homes at Chippewa Falls, King, and Union Grove, the Wisconsin Veterans Museum in Madison, the Southern Wisconsin Veterans Memorial Cemetery at Union Grove, the Northern Wisconsin Veterans Memorial Cemetery near Spooner, and the Central Wisconsin Veterans Memorial Cemetery at King. The department currently serves an estimated 397,000 veterans living in Wisconsin.

Organization: The department is headed by a secretary who directs and supervises departmental activities. The secretary, who must be a veteran, is nominated by the governor after personally consulting with the presiding officers of at least 6 Wisconsin veterans organizations and appointed with advice and consent of the senate. The board of veterans affairs consists of 9 members appointed by the governor with senate consent who serve staggered 4-year terms. All board members must be veterans, as defined by statute, and there must be at least one member of the board who is a resident of each congressional district. The secretary, after consulting with the board, may promulgate administrative rules necessary to carry out the powers and duties of the department.

    Unit Functions: The *Division of Management Services* administers information technology, human resources, risk management, personnel benefits, continuity of operations, and employee training.

    The *Division of Veterans Benefits* administers an array of grants, benefits, programs, and services to all eligible state veterans, their families, and to many organizations that serve veterans. Through the various grants awarded to providers, veterans are then assisted with transportation to medical appointments, access to health care services not provided by the U.S. Department of Veterans Affairs, subsistence assistance in emergency situations, and additional education opportunities. The Veterans Benefit Resource Center assists veterans with all of their calls and questions, while the eligibility section determines applicants' eligibility for veterans in order to receive benefits from the department and other agencies.

    The division also maintains responsibility for the department's three cemeteries: Northern Wisconsin Veterans Memorial Cemetery at Spooner, Central Wisconsin Veterans Memorial Cemetery at King, and Southern Wisconsin Veterans Memorial Cemetery at Union Grove. These cemeteries provide burial space for veterans, their spouses, and eligible family members.

    The division administers the military funeral honors program, coordinating the efforts of veterans service organizations, the active duty military and reserve forces, as well as the Wisconsin National Guard.

    The *Division of Veterans Homes* administers the state's facilities for eligible veterans who are in need of short-term rehabilitation or long-term skilled nursing care. Applicants must apply their income and resources to the cost of their care as required by Medicaid eligibility standards. The spouses, surviving spouses, children, and parents of eligible veterans may also be admitted.

    The Wisconsin Veterans Home at Chippewa Falls is a 72-bed skilled nursing facility where a multidisciplinary team of physicians, nurses, therapists, and social workers develop a customized, goal-oriented treatment plan to address each resident's specific needs.

    The Wisconsin Veterans Home at King serves 721 members. It includes four licensed skilled nursing care buildings and the Central Wisconsin Veterans Memorial Cemetery. Residents receive complete medical, nursing, and rehabilitative care, along with therapeutic treatments and social services.

The Wisconsin Veterans Home at Union Grove is capable of serving 198 members by providing a 40-bed assisted living residence and a 158-bed skilled nursing facility. This continuum of care is available to veterans and their spouses and offers assistance with health care, daily living needs, memory care, short-term rehabilitation, and long-term care.

The *Division of Veterans Services* provides programs, services, employment, and outreach assistance and information to Wisconsin veterans and their families. The programs and services assist Wisconsin veterans by enhancing their education, training, personal well-being, and employment opportunities. The division, through its Claims Bureau, provides increased access to other state benefits and federal programs related to VA compensation, pension, and medical care. In addition, the division assists those veterans with benefits and programs related to their disability, former incarceration, substance abuse, mental health, and housing needs. The division also works to certify veterans related educational programs and audit all educational institutions accepting the federal G.I. Bill for veterans.

The *Wisconsin Veterans Museum* in Madison is dedicated to Wisconsin veterans of all wars. It houses and exhibits artifacts related to Wisconsin's participation in U.S. military actions from the Civil War to the present and offers programs to the public on the history of Wisconsin's war efforts.

History: Legislation to benefit Wisconsin veterans dates back to the post-Civil War era. Most of the enactments between the Civil War and World War I were concerned with providing relief for destitute veterans and their families. In 1887, the Grand Army of the Republic (GAR), the prominent Civil War veterans' organization, founded the Grand Army Home at King, supported by private donations and federal and state subsidies. Now called the Wisconsin Veterans Home, the institution was first operated by the GAR and later by a state board and the adjutant general's office. Further recognition of Civil War veterans came in 1901, when the legislature established a Grand Army of the Republic headquarters and museum in the State Capitol. In 1993, the state opened the Wisconsin Veterans Museum in a separate building on the Capitol Square. The Southern Wisconsin Veterans Home at Union Grove, authorized in 1999 Wisconsin Act 9, opened in 2001.

After World War I, the 1919 Legislature granted a cash bonus, or alternatively an education bonus, to soldiers who fought in the war. It also created a fund for the relief of sick, wounded, or disabled veterans, administered by the Service Recognition Board and later its successor, the Soldiers' Rehabilitation Board. Other legislation between World Wars I and II provided funds for hospitalization, memorials, and free courses through the University of Wisconsin-Extension.

Chapter 443, Laws of 1943, created the Veterans Recognition Board to provide medical, hospital, educational, and economic assistance to returning Wisconsin veterans of World War II and their dependents.

The creation of the Department of Veterans Affairs by Chapter 580, Laws of 1945, brought all veterans programs under a single agency. The department absorbed the Grand Army Home, the GAR Memorial Hall, the veterans claim services, and the Soldiers' Rehabilitation Board. The department was assigned the economic aid, hospital care, and education grants programs. It also took over three segregated veterans funds that were combined into the Veterans Trust Fund in 1961.

Two major new programs relating to housing and education were implemented after World War II. Beginning with legislation in 1947, programs were established to help veterans finance home loans through a trust fund. The state supreme court declared earmarking liquor tax moneys for the fund unconstitutional under the internal improvements clause, but a constitutional amendment, approved by the voters in 1949, resolved the problem. Chapter 627, Laws of 1949, authorized loans to qualified veterans for a portion of the value of their housing. The legislature converted this program to a second mortgage home loan program in 1973, when it established the Primary Home Loan Program that is financed with general obligation bonds. The state's use of general obligation bonding to offer home loans to veterans raised constitutional concerns.

The legislature responded by proposing an amendment to the Wisconsin Constitution, which the voters ratified in April 1975.

1997 Wisconsin Act 27 expanded eligibility for state veterans benefits to any person who has served on active duty in the U.S. armed forces for two continuous years or the full period of the individual's initial service obligation, whichever is less, regardless of when or where the service occurred, including during peacetime. Previously, to be considered a "veteran" for the purposes of state benefits, a person must generally have performed active service for 90 days or more during a designated war period or a period of duty during specified conflicts or peacekeeping operations.

1999 Wisconsin Act 136 required the department to administer a program to coordinate the provision of military funeral honors to eligible deceased veterans. 2003 Wisconsin Act 102 authorized the department to develop and operate residential, treatment, and nursing care facilities in northwestern Wisconsin, on surplus land located at the Northern Wisconsin Center for the Developmentally Disabled in Chippewa Falls.

2011 Wisconsin Act 36 placed the direction and supervision of the department under the secretary of veterans affairs, rather than the board. It also increased the size of the board from 7 to 9 members, reduced their terms of office from 6 to 4 years, and required that at least one member of the board be a resident of each congressional district. 2013 Wisconsin Act 20 transferred disabled veterans' outreach and local veterans' employment representative programs from the Department of Workforce Development to the Department of Veterans Affairs.

Statutory Council

Council on Veterans Programs: ROGER FETTERLY (Military Officers Association of America), STEVE HOUSE (Vietnam Veterans of America), PHILLIP LANDGRAF (Marine Corps League), PAUL FISK (American Legion), ALBERT W. LABELLE, JR. (Disabled American Veterans), MICHAEL FURGAL (Veterans of Foreign Wars), RUSS ALSTEEN (Navy Club), DAVID SCHMIDT (AMVETS), DON HEILIGER (American Ex-Prisoners of War), RICH PETERS (Vietnam Veterans Against the War), vacancy (Catholic War Veterans of the U.S.A.), BEN BERLIN (Jewish War Veterans of the U.S.A.), JOHN RECKLIES (Polish Legion of American Veterans), WILLIAM SIMS (National Association for Black Veterans, Inc.), PAUL FINE (Army Navy Union), WILLIAM MAY (Wisconsin Association of Concerned Veterans Organizations), ASHLEY NATYSIN (United Women Veterans, Inc.), RUSSELL COLLINS (U.S. Submarine Veterans of World War II), WILLIAM HUSTAD (Wisconsin Vietnam Veterans, Inc.), WILLIAM LOBECK (Military Order of the Purple Heart), MICHEL SOEHNER (American Red Cross), JOE AULIK (County Veterans Service Officers Association), KEN NESS (Wisconsin Chapter of the Paralyzed Veterans of America), LENNY SHIER (Retired Enlisted Association), FERNANDO RODRIGUEZ (American GI Forum), GARY TRAYNOR (Blinded Veterans Association of Wisconsin). (All are appointed by their respective organizations).

The 26-member Council on Veterans Programs studies and presents policy alternatives and recommendations to the Board of Veterans Affairs. It is comprised of representatives appointed for one-year terms by organizations that have a direct interest in veterans' affairs. The council was created by Chapter 443, Laws of 1943, and its composition and duties are prescribed in Sections 15.497 and 45.35 (3d) of the statutes.

Department of
WORKFORCE DEVELOPMENT

Address e-mail by combining the user ID and the state extender: userid@**dwd.wisconsin.gov**
All telephone numbers are 608 area code unless otherwise indicated.

Secretary of Workforce Development: REGGIE NEWSON, 267-1410, reggie.newson@

Deputy Secretary: JONATHAN BARRY, 267-3200, jonathan.barry@

Assistant Deputy Secretary: DAVID G. ANDERSON, 266-2284, davidg.anderson@

Legal Counsel: HOWARD BERNSTEIN, 266-9427, howard.bernstein@

Communications Director: JOHN DIPKO, 266-6753, john.dipko@
Legislative Liaison: B.J. DERNBACH, 266-1756, bj.dernbach@
Mailing Address: P.O. Box 7946, Madison 53707-7946.
Location: 201 East Washington Avenue, Madison.
Telephone: (608) 266-3131.
Fax: (608) 266-1784.
Internet Address: www.dwd.wisconsin.gov
Publications: Contact individual divisions for publications.

DEPARTMENT OF WORKFORCE DEVELOPMENT

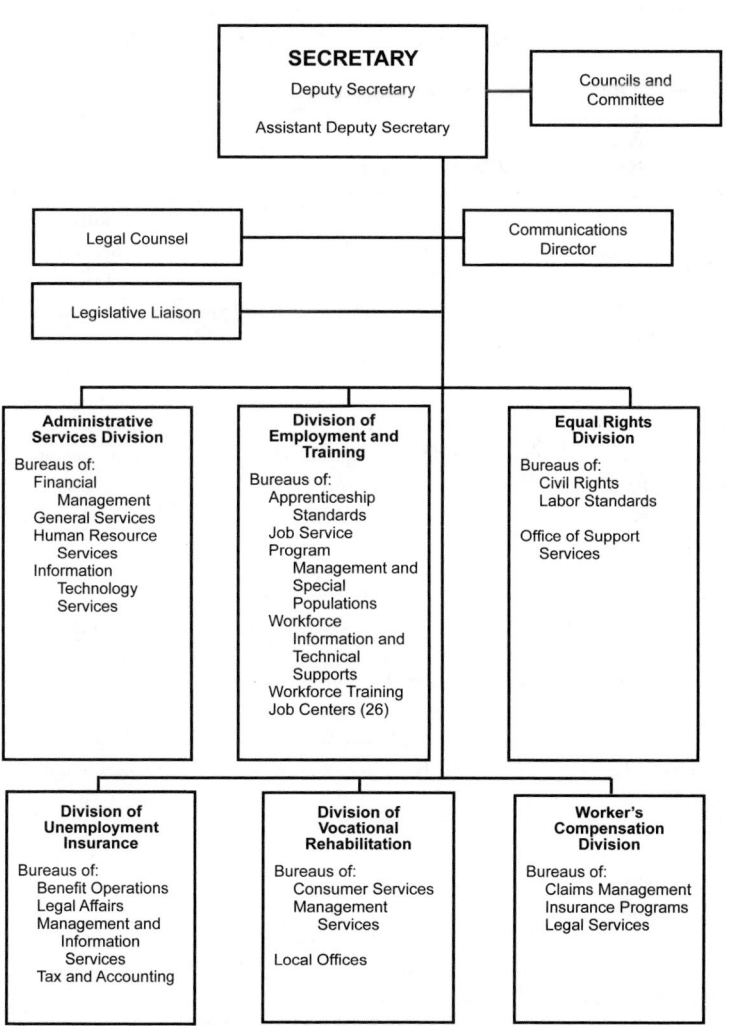

Units attached for administrative purposes under Sec. 15.03: Employment Relations Commission
Labor and Industry Review Commission

Number of Employees: 1,753.26.

Total Budget 2013-15: $754,623,700.

Statutory References: Sections 15.22, 15.223, 15.225, and 15.227; Chapters 47, 102-106, 108, 109, and 111.

Administrative Services Division: KATHLEEN REED, *administrator,* 261-4599, kathleen.reed@; LYNDA HANOLD, *deputy administrator,* 266-6496, lynda.hanold@

    Financial Management, Bureau of: TAMARA MOE, *director,* 261-4582, tami.moe@

    General Services, Bureau of: MARGARET MCGRATH, *director,* 266-1777, margaret.mcgrath@

    Human Resource Services, Bureau of: STEVE LAESCH, *director,* 266-1092, steve.laesch@

    Information Technology Services, Bureau of: vacancy, *director and CIO,* 264-8800.

Employment and Training, Division of: SCOTT JANSEN, *administrator,* 266-3485, scott.jansen@; BRUCE PALZKILL, *deputy administrator,* 266-3623, bruce.palzkill@

    Apprenticeship Standards, Bureau of: KAREN P. MORGAN, *director,* 266-3133, karen.morgan@

    Job Service, Bureau of: DAVE SHAW, *acting director,* 266-8390, daved.shaw@

    Program Management and Special Populations, Bureau of: JUAN JOSE LOPEZ, *director,* 266-0002, juanjose.lopez@

    Workforce Information and Technical Supports, Bureau of: DENNIS WINTERS, *acting director,* 267-3262, dennis.winters@

    Workforce Training, Bureau of: PHIL KOENIG, *director,* 267-7277, phil.koenig@

Equal Rights Division: ROBERT RODRIGUEZ, *administrator,* 266-8533, robert.rodriguez@; JIM CHIOLINO, *deputy administrator,* 266-3345, jim.chiolino@; Division TTY: 264-8752.

    Civil Rights, Bureau of: LARRY JAKUBOWSKI, *director,* (414) 227-4396, larry.jakubowski@

    Labor Standards, Bureau of: JIM CHIOLINO, *director,* 266-3345, jim.chiolino@

    Support Services, Office of: MORGAN DIXON, *manager,* 266-7560, morgan.dixon@

Unemployment Insurance, Division of: JOE HANDRICK, *administrator,* 266-0946, joseph.handrick@; BENJAMIN PEIRCE, *deputy administrator,* 266-3635, benjamin.peirce@

    Benefit Operations, Bureau of: LUTFI SHAHRANI, *director,* 266-8211, lutfi.shahrani@

    Legal Affairs, Bureau of: JANELL KNUTSON, *director,* 266-1639, janell.knutson@

    Management and Information Services, Bureau of: PAMELA JAMES, *director,* 266-6904, pamela.james@

    Tax and Accounting, Bureau of: THOMAS MCHUGH, *director,* 266-3130, thomas.mchugh@

    Customer Self-Help: Employer portal: http://dwd.wisconsin.gov/unitax/; *Employee portal:* http://dwd.wisconsin.gov/uiben/; *Initial claims:* https://my.unemployment.gov

Vocational Rehabilitation, Division of: MICHAEL GRECO, *administrator,* 261-4576, michael.greco@; JOANNA RICHARD, *deputy administrator,* 261-0074, joanna.richard@; Division TTY: 243-5601.

    Consumer Services, Bureau of: JOHN HAUGH, *director,* 261-2126, john.haugh@

    Management Services, Bureau of: ENID GLENN, *director,* 261-0073, enid.glenn@

    Local Offices: To contact a local DVR office, call (800) 442-3477 or visit http://dwd.wisconsin.gov/dvr/locations/default.htm

Worker's Compensation Division: JOHN METCALF, *administrator,* 266-6841, john.metcalf@; BRIAN KRUEGER, *deputy administrator,* 267-4415, brian.krueger@

    Claims Management, Bureau of: TRACY AIELLO, *director,* 267-9407, tracy.aiello@

    Insurance Programs, Bureau of: JOSEPH MORETH, *director,* 266-8327, joseph.moreth@

    Legal Services, Bureau of: JIM O'MALLEY, *director,* 267-6704, jim.omalley@

Agency Responsibility: The Department of Workforce Development conducts a variety of work-related programs designed to connect people with employment opportunities in Wisconsin. It has major responsibility for the state's employment and training services; job centers; job

Secretary Reggie Newson and State Superintendent Tony Evers meet with Sussex High School student Hudson Byrne at Waukesha County Technical College to discuss a Wisconsin Fast Forward-High School Pupil grant program. (Department of Workforce Development)

training and placement services provided in cooperation with private sector employers; apprenticeship programs; and employment-related services for people with disabilities. It oversees the unemployment insurance and worker's compensation programs and is also responsible for adjudicating cases involving employment discrimination, housing discrimination, and labor law.

Organization: The department is administered by a secretary who is appointed by the governor with the advice and consent of the senate. The secretary appoints the division administrators from outside the classified service.

Unit Functions: The *Administrative Services Division* provides management and program support to the other divisions, including facilities, finance, human resources, and information technology services.

The *Division of Employment and Training* oversees all workforce services administered by the department including the state labor exchange system (www.jobcenterofwisconsin.com); analyzes and distributes labor market information; monitors migrant worker services; and operates the state apprenticeship program. The division manages the Wisconsin Fast Forward Program. It also has a statewide network of 26 comprehensive job centers.

The *Equal Rights Division,* created by Chapter 327, Laws of 1967, enforces state laws that protect citizens from discrimination in employment, housing, and public accommodations. It also administers the enforcement of family and medical leave laws and the labor laws relating to hours, conditions of work, minimum wage standards, and timely payment of wages. It determines prevailing wage rates and enforces them for state and municipal public works projects not including highway projects. The division also enforces child labor laws and plant closing laws.

The *Division of Unemployment Insurance* administers programs to pay benefits to unemployed workers, collect employer taxes, resolve contested benefit claims and employer tax issues, detect unemployment insurance fraud, and collect unemployment insurance overpayments and delinquent taxes. The division also collects wage information for national and Wisconsin New Hire Directory databases.

The *Division of Vocational Rehabilitation* provides employment services to individuals who have significant physical and mental disabilities that create barriers in obtaining, maintaining, or improving employment. Each person is counseled and may receive medical, psychological, and vocational evaluations and training services. Employment programs, which are supported through state and federal funding, include vocational rehabilitation for eligible persons with disabilities; supported employment, including job coaching for individuals with severe disabilities; and the Business Enterprise Program, which establishes business or vending stand locations for individuals who are legally blind.

The *Worker's Compensation Division* administers programs designed to ensure that injured workers receive required benefits from insurers or self-insured employers; encourage rehabilitation and reemployment for injured workers; and promote the reduction of work-related injuries, illnesses, and deaths.

History: In response to the state's industrialization, which began in the 1880s, Wisconsin took the lead nationally in adjusting labor laws to modern industrial conditions. Based on European models, the legislature adopted social insurance, whereby the costs of correcting labor problems, such as worker injuries and unemployment, were imposed on employers as an inducement to prevent the problems.

Wisconsin's laws, enacted during the early part of the 20th century, dealt with minimum wages, conditions of employment for women and children, worker's compensation, free public employment offices, apprenticeship standards, and job safety regulations. Many of these programs served as models for legislation in other states. Wisconsin's original worker's compensation act (Chapter 50, Laws of 1911) was the first state law of its kind in the nation. In the 1930s, Wisconsin led in developing the unemployment compensation system (Chapter 20, Laws of Special Session 1931) and issued the first benefit check in the nation in 1936.

Since World War II, Wisconsin has enacted legislation prohibiting discrimination in employment on the basis of race, sex, creed, national origin, marital status, ancestry, arrest or conviction record, off-duty use of lawful products, membership in military reserve, sexual orientation, age, and disability. Similar laws now protect access to housing and public accommodations.

Early in the 20th century, the state delegated labor law administration to a politically independent body of experts, the State Industrial Commission, and its advisory committees. The commission was encouraged to solve problems through administrative decision making and the development of administrative rules to supplement the laws. A close tie between state government and the University of Wisconsin enabled the governor and legislature to translate reforms conceived in the academic arena into law. This cooperative meshing of academic research and government action came to be known as "The Wisconsin Idea".

The Department of Workforce Development evolved from the Wisconsin Bureau of Labor Statistics, which was created in 1883. The bureau was succeeded by the State Industrial Commission in 1911. Following the 1967 executive branch reorganization, the commission directed the new Department of Industry, Labor and Human Relations (DILHR) and was renamed the Industry, Labor and Human Relations Commission by Chapter 276, Laws of 1969. The commission was replaced by a secretary in Chapter 29, Laws of 1977.

Effective July 1, 1996, the Department of Industry, Labor and Human Relations was renamed the Department of Industry, Labor and Job Development by 1995 Wisconsin Act 29, but the department was given the option of using the name Department of Workforce Development in 1995 Wisconsin Act 289. It formally chose to exercise that option beginning July 1, 1996, and the legislature officially recognized the name choice in 1997 Wisconsin Act 3.

The department was significantly altered by 1995 Wisconsin Act 27. It assumed many duties formerly performed by other agencies, in particular supervision of welfare and income maintenance programs and vocational rehabilitation services, which were transferred from the former Department of Health and Social Services. At the same time, the Division of Safety and Buildings was transferred out of the department to the new Department of Commerce. 1997

Wisconsin Act 191 assigned the department primary responsibility for establishing and operating a statewide system for enforcing child, family, and spousal support obligations, including expanded authority to deny, revoke, or suspend various licenses, permits, and credentials of delinquent payers.

The statutes provide that the minimum wage is set through the administrative rules process, which includes legislative review. In January 2004, the secretary established the Minimum Wage Advisory Council to recommend an appropriate increase in the minimum wage. The council was comprised of representatives from business, labor organizations, the university system, and the legislature, and issued its final report on May 1, 2004.

2007 Wisconsin Act 20 created the Department of Children and Families (DCF), beginning July 1, 2008. It also changed the name of the Department of Health and Family Services (DHFS) to the Department of Health Services and split the responsibilities of DHFS between the two departments. Act 20 also transferred from the Department of Workforce Development to DCF administration of Wisconsin Works, including the child care subsidy program, child support enforcement and paternity establishment, and programs related to temporary assistance to needy families (TANF).

Statutory Councils and Committee

Wisconsin Apprenticeship Council: KAREN MORGAN (director, Department of Workforce Development Bureau of Apprenticeship Standards), *nonvoting chairperson;* WAYNE BELANGER, JULIE BROLIN, GERT GROHMANN, HENRY HURT, DAVID JONES, DAWN PRATT, CHRIS READER, SUSAN SCAFFIDI, MARY WEHRHEIM (employer representatives); DAVID BRANSON, JOSE BUCIO, KILAH ENGELKE, TERRY HAYDEN, CATHIE TIKKANEN, CLAY TSCHILLARD, MARK WIESEKE, 2 vacancies (employee representatives); BRENT KINDRED, SANDRA SCHMIT (educational representatives); J. WM. CADOTTE, MARY WATRUD (public representatives). (All except educational representatives are appointed by secretary of workforce development.)

Mailing Address: P.O. Box 7972, Madison 53707-7972.

Telephone: (608) 266-3133.

The 23-member Wisconsin Apprenticeship Council advises the department on matters pertaining to Wisconsin's apprenticeship system. The council consists of 9 representatives of employers and 9 representatives of employees appointed by the secretary of workforce development, one representative of the technical college system appointed by the director of the technical college system, one representative of the Department of Public Instruction appointed by the superintendent of public instruction, 2 members appointed to represent the public interest appointed by the secretary of workforce development, and one permanent classified Department of Workforce Development employee appointed by the secretary of workforce development to serve as the nonvoting chairperson. The council was created by Chapter 29, Laws of 1977, and its duties and composition are prescribed in Sections 15.09 (5) and 15.227 (13) of the statutes.

Labor and Management Council: Inactive.

The 21-member Labor and Management Council provides a forum for labor, management, and public sector representatives to discuss issues that affect the state's economy and to foster positive labor-management relations in the workplace. Council members serve 5-year terms. The council was created by 1987 Wisconsin Act 27, and its composition and duties are prescribed in Section 15.227 (17) of the statutes.

Migrant Labor, Council on: LUPE MARTINEZ (migrant representative), *acting chairperson/ vice chairperson;* SENATOR WIRCH, vacancy; REPRESENTATIVE ZAMARRIPA, vacancy; JOHN I. BAUKNECHT, ENRIQUE FIGUEROA, KEVIN MAGEE, GUADALUPE RENDON, TERESA TELLEZ-GIRON (migrant representatives); JAMES KERN, ERICA KUNZE, RICHARD W. OKRAY, LILIANA PARODI, STEVE ZIOBRO, vacancy (migrant employer representatives). (All except legislative members are appointed by governor.)

The 16-member Council on Migrant Labor advises the department and other state officials about matters affecting migrant workers. The council's 4 legislator members represent the 2 major political parties and are appointed "to act as representatives of the public". The nonlegislative members serve 3-year terms. The council was created by Chapter 17, Laws of 1977, and its composition and duties are prescribed in Sections 15.227 (8), 103.967, and 103.968 of the statutes.

Self-Insurers Council: Richard DeVries, Michael Fontaine, Jill E. Joswiak, Rick Kante, Christine McKinzie (appointed by secretary of workforce development).

The 5-member Self-Insurers Council advises the department about matters related to companies that cover their own worker's compensation losses rather than insuring them with an insurance carrier. Members are appointed for 3-year terms by the secretary of the department. The council was created by Chapter 29, Laws of 1977, and its duties and composition are prescribed in Sections 15.09 (5) and 15.227 (11) of the statutes.

Unemployment Insurance, Council on: Janell Knutson (permanent classified employee of department) (nonvoting member), *chairperson;* Michael Gotzler, Earl Gustafson, James LaCourt, Scott Manley (employer representatives); Edward Lump (employer representative, small business owner or representing small business association); Sally Feistel, Shane Griesbach, Phillip Neuenfeldt, Mark Reihl, vacancy (employee representatives). (All are appointed by secretary of workforce development.)

The 11-member Council on Unemployment Insurance advises the legislature and the department about unemployment compensation matters. It includes 5 employers and 5 labor representatives who are appointed for 6-year terms, plus a permanent, classified employee of the department who acts as the council's nonvoting chairperson. In making council appointments, the secretary must consider "balanced representation of the industrial, commercial, construction, nonprofit and public sectors of the state's economy." One employer representative must be a small business owner or represent a small business association. The council was created as the Council on Unemployment Compensation by Chapter 327, Laws of 1967. Its name was changed by 1997 Wisconsin Act 39. Its composition and duties are prescribed in Sections 15.227 (3) and 108.14 (5) of the statutes.

Worker's Compensation, Council on: John Metcalf (nonvoting member), *chairperson;* Jeffrey J. Beiriger, Jeffrey Brand, James A. Buchen, Christine Johnson, Mary Nugent (employer representatives); Stephanie Bloomingdale, Ron Kent, Scott Redman, Brad Schwanda, Monica Thomas (employee representatives); Steven Ginsburg, Melinda Seiler, vacancy (nonvoting insurance company representatives). (All are appointed by secretary of workforce development.)

The 14-member Council on Worker's Compensation is appointed by the secretary of the department to advise the legislature and the department about worker's compensation and related matters. The council was created by Chapter 281, Laws of 1963, as the Advisory Committee on Workmen's Compensation, appointed by the Industrial Commission. It was given its current name and located in the Department of Industry, Labor and Human Relations by Chapter 327, Laws of 1967. The council includes three nonvoting representatives of insurers authorized to do worker's compensation insurance business in Wisconsin and a department employee acting as chairperson. The council's composition and duties are prescribed in Sections 15.227 (4) and 102.14 (2) of the statutes.

Health Care Provider Advisory Committee: John Metcalf (administrator, worker's compensation division), *chairperson;* Mary Jo Capodice, Richard Goldberg, Maja Jurisic, Michael Lischak, Ron H. Stark, Sri Vasudevan (medical doctors); Jeff Lyne, Peter Schubbe (chiropractors); Amanda Gilliland, Marlin Nelson (hospital representatives); Barb Janusiak (registered nurse); Jennifer Seidel (physical therapist); Theodore Gertel, Stephen Klos (at-large members). (All are appointed pursuant to Section 102.16 (2m) (g), Wisconsin Statutes, and Section DWD 81.14 (1), Wisconsin Administrative Code.)

The Health Care Provider Advisory Committee advises the department and the Council on Worker's Compensation on modifications to treatment standards (treatment guidelines) contained in Chapter DWD 81, Wisconsin Administrative Code, for determining necessity of treatment disputes pursuant to Section 102.16 (2m), Wisconsin Statutes. Section 102.15 (2m) (g), created by 2005 Wisconsin Act 172, directs the department to establish the committee, but does not specify its membership. Section DWD 81.14 (1), Wisconsin Administrative Code, created in the Wisconsin Administrative Register of October 2007, Number 622, provides that the committee is to be composed of the administrator of the worker's compensation division as chairperson, and 14 other members: 6 doctors of different specialties, 2 chiropractors, 2 hospital representatives, 1 registered nurse, 1 physical therapist, and 2 at-large members. All except the chairperson must be licensed and practicing in Wisconsin, and provide treatment under Section 102.42. Appointments are made by the department from a consensus list of 24 names submitted by the Wisconsin Medical Society, the Wisconsin Chiropractic Association, and the Wisconsin Hospital Association, with the exception of the 2 at-large members selected by the department.

INDEPENDENT UNITS ATTACHED FOR PROGRAM COORDINATION AND RELATED MANAGEMENT FUNCTIONS BY SECTION 15.03 OF THE STATUTES

EMPLOYMENT RELATIONS COMMISSION

Employment Relations Commission: *Commissioners:* JAMES R. SCOTT, *chairperson,* james. scott@; JAMES DALEY, james.daley@; RODNEY G. PASCH, rodney.pasch@ (appointed by governor with senate consent).

General Counsel/Team Leader: PETER G. DAVIS, 243-2421, peterg.davis@

Team Leader: WILLIAM C. HOULIHAN, 243-2422, william.houlihan@

Mailing Address: P.O. Box 7870, Madison 53707-7870.

Location: 4868 High Crossing Boulevard, Madison 53704-7403.

Telephone: (608) 243-2424.

Fax: (608) 243-2433.

Agency E-mail Address: werc@werc.state.wi.us

Internet Address: http://werc.wi.gov

Publications: Biennial reports; complaint procedures manual; agency decisions.

Number of Employees: 9.01.

Total Budget 2013-15: $3,466,800.

Statutory References: Sections 15.225 (2), 230.44, and 230.45; Chapter 111.

Agency Responsibility: The Employment Relations Commission promotes collective bargaining and peaceful labor relations in the private and public sectors. It processes various types of labor relations cases, including elections, bargaining unit clarifications, union security referenda, mediations, interest arbitrations, grievance arbitrations, prohibited or unfair labor practices, and declaratory rulings. The commission also issues decisions arising from state employee civil service appeals, including appeals relating to certain classification, examination, and appointment issues, disciplinary actions, hazardous employment injury benefits, and noncontractual grievances. The commission's decisions are subject to review in state court. In addition to mediating labor disputes, the commission provides training and assistance to parties interested in labor/management cooperation and a consensus approach to resolving labor relations issues.

Organization: The 3 full-time commissioners are chosen for staggered 6-year terms, and the governor designates one commissioner to serve as chairperson for a 2-year term. The chairperson functions as the agency administrator. The general counsel provides advice to the commission, commission staff, advocates, and citizens and serves as liaison to the legislature and to the attorney general, who represents the commission in court.

History: Chapter 51, Laws of 1937, created the Wisconsin Labor Relations Board as an independent agency in the executive branch. Chapter 57, Laws of 1939, replaced the board with the Employment Relations Board and amended state laws governing labor relations. The 1967 Legislature renamed the board the Employment Relations Commission and continued it as an independent agency. 2013 Wisconsin Act 20 attached the commission to the Department of Workforce Development.

Chapter 509, Laws of 1959, authorized municipal employees to organize and be represented by labor organizations in negotiating wages, hours, and conditions of employment. Chapter 124, Laws of 1971, gave municipal employees the right to bargain collectively and made a municipal employer's refusal to bargain a prohibited practice. Chapters 246 and 247, Laws of

1971, established compulsory interest arbitration for police and firefighters in Milwaukee and other municipalities. Chapter 270, Laws of 1971, gave state employees the right to bargain collectively. 2003 Wisconsin Act 33 abolished the Personnel Commission and transferred to the Employment Relations Commission responsibility for various civil service appeals related to state employment. 2011 Wisconsin Acts 10 and 32 amended all collective bargaining laws administered by the commission.

LABOR AND INDUSTRY REVIEW COMMISSION

Labor and Industry Review Commission: Laurie McCallum, *chairperson;* David Falstad, C. William Jordahl (appointed by governor with senate consent).

General Counsel: Tracey L. Schwalbe, tracey.schwalbe@dwd.wisconsin.gov

Mailing Address: P.O. Box 8126, Madison 53708-8126.

Location: Public Broadcasting Building, 3319 West Beltline Highway, Madison.

Telephone: (608) 266-9850.

Fax: (608) 267-4409.

E-mail Address: lirc@dwd.wisconsin.gov

Internet Address: http://dwd.wisconsin.gov/lirc

Number of Employees: 26.50.

Total Budget 2013-15: $6,376,400.

Statutory References: Sections 15.225 and 103.04.

Agency Responsibility: The 3-member Labor and Industry Review Commission is a quasi-judicial body, created by Chapter 29, Laws of 1977, which handles petitions seeking review of the decisions of the Department of Workforce Development related to unemployment insurance, worker's compensation, fair employment, and public accommodations. It also hears appeals about discrimination in postsecondary education involving a person's physical condition or developmental disability. Commission decisions may be appealed to the circuit court. Commission decisions are enforced by the Department of Justice or the commission's legal staff. Commission members serve full-time for staggered 6-year terms, and they select a chairperson from their membership to serve for a 2-year period. By law, the commission's budget must be transmitted to the governor by the department without modification, unless the commission agrees to the change.

STATE AUTHORITIES

Authorities are public, corporate bodies created for specific purposes.

WISCONSIN AEROSPACE AUTHORITY

Members: THOMAS CRABB (public member), *chairperson;* MARK HANNA (public member), *vice chairperson;* THOMAS MULLOOLY (public member), *secretary-treasurer;* vacancy (appointed by senate president); vacancy (appointed by assembly speaker); KEVIN CROSBY (Wisconsin Space Grant Consortium director); MARK LEE, JUDITH SCHIEBLE, EDWARD WAGNER (public members).

Statutory References: Chapter 114, Subchapter II.

Agency Responsibility: The Wisconsin Aerospace Authority is directed to promote the state's aerospace industry by developing a business plan in cooperation with the Wisconsin Space Grant Consortium, securing adequate funding for spaceport facilities and services, sponsoring events to attract space-related businesses, advertising the use of spaceports to the public, and establishing a safety program.

Organization: The authority is a public corporation consisting of the director of the Wisconsin Space Grant Consortium and 8 members serving 3-year terms. One member is a state senator appointed by the president of the senate and one member is a state representative appointed by the speaker of the assembly. The 6 public members are nominated by the governor with the consent of the senate and must be Wisconsin residents with experience in the commercial space industry, education, finance, or some other significant experience related to the functions of the authority.

The authority was created by 2005 Wisconsin Act 335.

WISCONSIN ECONOMIC DEVELOPMENT CORPORATION

Board Members: GOVERNOR SCOTT WALKER, *chairperson;* DAN ARIENS, RAYMOND DREGER, NANCY HERNANDEZ, COREY HOZE, LISA MAUER, PAUL RADSPINNER (appointed by governor with senate consent); REPRESENTATIVE HUTTON (majority party representative appointed by speaker); REPRESENTATIVE BARCA (minority party representative appointed by speaker); SCOTT KLUG (private sector employee appointed by speaker); SENATOR GUDEX (majority party senator appointed by senate majority leader); SENATOR LASSA (minority party senator appointed by senate majority leader); C. THOMAS SYLKE (private sector employee appointed by senate majority leader); SCOTT NEITZEL (secretary of administration), RICHARD CHANDLER (secretary of revenue) (nonvoting members).

Chief Executive Officer: REED HALL, (608) 210-6701.

Chief Operating Officer: TRICIA BRAUN, (608) 210-6807.

Mailing Address: P.O. Box 1687, Madison 53701.

Location: 201 West Washington Avenue, 6th Floor, Madison.

Telephone: (855) 469-4249.

Internet Address: inwisconsin.com

Total Budget 2013-15: $100,201,400.

Statutory References: Chapter 238.

Agency Responsibility: The Wisconsin Economic Development Corporation (WEDC) develops and implements programs to provide business support and expertise and financial assistance to companies that are investing and creating jobs in Wisconsin and to promote new business start-ups and business expansion and growth in the state. The authority was established in 2011 to assume many of the functions previously performed by the former Department of Commerce.

Organization: The WEDC is an authority, which is a body corporate and politic. It is governed by a 15-member board composed of the governor, who shall serve as chairperson of the board; 6 members appointed by the governor with senate consent to serve at the pleasure of the governor; 3 members appointed by the speaker of the assembly, consisting of one majority and one minority party representative, and one person employed in the private sector to serve at the speaker's pleasure; and 3 members appointed by the senate majority leader, consisting of one majority and one minority party senator, and one person employed in the private sector to serve at the majority leader's pleasure. The secretary of administration and the secretary of revenue serve as nonvoting members.

The corporation is administered by a chief executive officer (CEO) nominated by the governor, and with the advice and consent of the senate appointed, to serve at the pleasure of the governor. The board may delegate to the CEO any powers and duties the board considers proper and determines the compensation and qualifications of the CEO and employees. Corporation employees are not state employees but may participate in the Wisconsin Retirement System.

History: The 1911 Legislature created the Industrial Commission in Chapter 485 to set standards for a safe place of employment. This "safe place" statute was extended in Chapter 588, Laws of 1913, to include public buildings. The commission adopted its first building code in 1914.

The state's promotion of business and economic development originated with the Division of Industrial Development, established in the governor's office by Chapter 271, Laws of 1955. The division was transferred to the newly created Department of Resource Development in 1959 and renamed the Division of Economic Development. Chapter 614, Laws of 1965, returned the division to the governor's office. While in the executive office, it absorbed the Office of Economic Opportunity (1966), which had been created in the Department of Resource Development to administer the federal antipoverty programs enacted in 1964. Under the 1967 executive branch reorganization, the division became part of the Department of Local Affairs and Development, and local and regional planning functions were integrated into it.

Chapter 125, Laws of 1971, created the Department of Business Development. The department absorbed the Division of Tourism from the Department of Natural Resources in 1975. Under Chapter 361, Laws of 1979, the Department of Business Development was combined with the Department of Local Affairs and Development to form the Department of Development, subsequently renamed the Department of Commerce (Commerce) by 1995 Wisconsin Act 27. The department's responsibility for state tourism promotion ended with the creation of the Department of Tourism by 1995 Wisconsin Act 27. Act 27 also transferred to Commerce the PECFA program and the safety and buildings functions from the Department of Industry, Labor and Human Relations; responsibility for plat review from the Department of Agriculture, Trade and Consumer Protection; municipal boundary review from the Department of Administration; and relocation assistance under eminent domain law from the Department of Industry, Labor and Human Relations. Responsibility for plat review and municipal boundary review was transferred to the Department of Administration by 1997 Wisconsin Act 27. Regulation of manufactured home dealers and manufactured home parks was transferred to the department from the Department of Administration by 1999 Wisconsin Act 9. Act 9 also transferred titling of manufactured homes from the Department of Transportation. Regulation of manufactured home park utilities was transferred from the Public Service Commission by 2001 Wisconsin Act 16. In 2003, Wisconsin Act 33 transferred housing programs to the department from the Department of Administration.

2009 Wisconsin Act 2 deleted five existing zone programs, including the Enterprise Development Zones, the Community Development Zones, the Agricultural Development Zones, the Technology Development Zones, and the Airport Development Zones, and created a new consolidated tax credit program to promote job creation, capital investment, employee training, and job retention in Wisconsin. Act 2 also increased substantially the amount of angel and early-stage seed investment tax credits available annually for high-technology, biotechnology, and nanotechnology start-up companies which had been initiated by 2003 Wisconsin Act 255.

2011 Wisconsin Act 7 created, effective February 24, 2011, the Wisconsin Economic Development Corporation to develop and administer economic development programs for the state.

Act 7 required Commerce to provide staff or other resources to assist the WEDC in carrying out its duties, and for both entities to coordinate their economic development programs.

2011 Wisconsin Act 32 repealed the Department of Commerce effective July 1, 2011. The act transferred certain of Commerce's economic development and business promotion responsibilities, including grants, loans, and tax incentives, to the WEDC and housing programs to the Department of Administration. The administration of various other laws relating to the promotion of safety in public and private buildings, including enforcing building codes, and the licensure of occupations that had been regulated by Commerce, such as electricians and plumbers, were transferred to a new Department of Safety and Professional Services (DSPS), which was also created by Act 32. In addition to the safety and buildings responsibilities transferred from Commerce, the DSPS assumed the other functions previously performed by the Department of Regulation and Licensing, which was also repealed by Act 32.

FOX RIVER NAVIGATIONAL SYSTEM AUTHORITY

Board of Directors: S. Timothy Rose (Outagamie County representative), *chairperson;* William Raaths (Winnebago County representative), *vice chairperson;* Jeffery W. Feldt (Outagamie County representative), *secretary;* John L. Vette (Winnebago County representative), *treasurer;* Kathryn Curren, H. Bruce Enke (Brown County representatives); Jean Romback-Bartels (designated by secretary of natural resources); Will Dorsey (designated by secretary of transportation); Daina Penkiunas (designated by director, state historical society) (county residents are appointed by the governor).

Chief Executive Officer: HARLAN P. KIESOW.

Telephone: (920) 759-9833.

Internet Address: http://foxriverlocks.org

Total Budget 2013-15: $250,800.

Statutory References: Chapter 237.

Agency Responsibility: The Fox River Navigational System Authority is responsible for the rehabilitation, repair, and management of the navigation system on or near the Fox River in 3 counties. The federal government transferred ownership of the navigational system to the State of Wisconsin in 2004. The authority may enter into contracts with third parties to operate the system. It may not sublease all or any part of the navigational system without DOA approval. It may enter into contracts with nonprofit organizations to raise funds. The authority may charge fees for services provided to watercraft owners and users of navigational facilities. While the authority may contract debt, it may not issue bonds. It must submit an audited financial statement annually to DOA.

Organization: The Fox River Navigational System Authority is a public corporation consisting of 9 members. The 6 members the governor appoints serve 3-year terms. At least one member from each of the 3 counties must be a resident of a city, village, or town in which a navigational system lock is located. The board appoints the chief executive officer to serve at its pleasure. The authority was created by 2001 Wisconsin Act 16.

LOWER FOX RIVER REMEDIATION AUTHORITY

Members: Tripp Ahern, Gregory Conway, Robert Cowles, Dave Hansen, Patrick Schillinger, James Wall, vacancy (all appointed by governor with advice and consent of the senate).

Statutory References: Chapter 279.

Agency Responsibility: The authority is authorized to issue assessment bonds for eligible waterway improvement costs, which generally include environmental investigation and remediation of the Fox River extending from Lake Winnebago to the mouth of the river in Lake Michigan, and including any portion of Green Bay in Lake Michigan containing sediments discharged from the river, as described in an administrative or judicial order or decree or an administrative or judicially approved agreement. The state is not liable for the authority's bonds, and the bonds are not a debt of the state.

Organization: The authority is a public corporation consisting of 7 members appointed by the governor with the advice and consent of the senate, for 7-year terms. Members of the board must be Wisconsin residents and no more than 4 members may be from the same political party. The term of each member expires on June 30 or until a successor is appointed.

The authority was created by 2007 Wisconsin Act 20.

Fishing on the Eagle River chain of lakes. *(Department of Tourism)*

UNIVERSITY OF WISCONSIN HOSPITALS AND CLINICS AUTHORITY

Board of Directors: DAVID WALSH (UW Board of Regents member appointed by board president), *chairperson;* DAVID WARD (appointed by governor with senate consent), *vice chairperson;* SENATOR OLSEN (designated by senate cochairperson, Joint Committee on Finance), REPRESENTATIVE KOOYENGA (designated by assembly cochairperson, Joint Committee on Finance); ANDREW HITT, JOHN LITSCHER, LISA REARDON, PABLO SANCHEZ, HUMBERTO VIDAILLET (appointed by governor with senate consent); REGINA MILLNER, JANICE MUELLER (UW Board of Regents members appointed by board president); REBECCA BLANK (chancellor, UW-Madison); ROBERT GOLDEN (dean, UW-Madison Medical School); THOMAS GRIST (departmental chairperson, UW-Madison Medical School, appointed by UW-Madison chancellor); KATHARYN MAY (UW health professions faculty, other than UW Medical School, appointed by UW-Madison chancellor); MICHAEL HEIFETZ (designated by secretary of administration).

President and Chief Executive Officer: RONALD SLIWINSKI.

Mailing Address: 600 Highland Avenue, Room H4/810, Madison 53792-8350.

Location: 600 Highland Avenue, Madison.

Telephone: (608) 263-8025.

Fax: (608) 263-9830.

Publications: *Our UW Health; Growing Up Healthy; Medical Directions; Ripple Effect.*

Number of Employees: 8,644 (not state funded).

Statutory References: Chapter 233.

Agency Responsibility: The University of Wisconsin Hospitals and Clinics Authority operates the UW Hospital and Clinics, including the American Family Children's Hospital, and related clinics and health care facilities. Through the UW Hospital and Clinics and its other programs it delivers health care, including care for the indigent; provides an environment for instruction of physicians, nurses, and other health-related disciplines; sponsors and supports health care research; and assists health care programs and personnel throughout the state. Subject to approval by its board of directors, the authority may issue bonds to support its operations and may seek financing from the Wisconsin Health and Educational Facilities Authority.

Organization: The authority is a public corporation, which is self-financing. It derives much of its income from charges for clinical and hospital services. The 16-member board of directors includes 6 governor's appointees who serve 5-year terms. The board elects a chairperson annually and appoints the chief executive officer for the authority. The authority was created by 1995 Wisconsin Act 27, which separated UW Hospital and Clinics and their related services from the UW System, effective July 1, 1996.

WISCONSIN HEALTH AND EDUCATIONAL FACILITIES AUTHORITY

Members: RICHARD CANTER, *chairperson;* TIMOTHY K. SIZE, *vice chairperson;* JAMES DIETSCHE, KEVIN FLAHERTY, PAUL MATHEWS, JAMES OPPERMANN, ROBERT VAN MEETEREN (appointed by governor with senate consent).

Executive Director: DENNIS P. REILLY.

Mailing Address: 18000 West Sarah Lane, Suite 300, Brookfield 53045-5841.

Telephone: (262) 792-0466.

Fax: (262) 792-0649.

Agency E-mail Address: info@whefa.com

Internet Address: www.whefa.com

Publications: Annual Report; Quarterly Newsletter.

Number of Employees: 4.00 (not state funded).

Statutory Reference: Chapter 231.

Agency Responsibility: The Wisconsin Health and Educational Facilities Authority (WHEFA) issues bonds on behalf of private nonprofit facilities to help them finance their capital costs. Since interest earned on the bonds is exempt from federal income taxation, they can be marketed at lower interest rates, which reduces the cost of borrowing. WHEFA has no taxing power and receives no general appropriations from the state; it supports its operations by imposing fees on participating institutions. WHEFA's bonds and notes are funded solely through loan repayments from the borrowing institution or sponsor. WHEFA's bonds are not a debt, liability, or obligation of the State of Wisconsin or any of its subdivisions.

WHEFA may issue bonds to finance any qualifying capital project, including new construction, remodeling, and renovation; expansion of current facilities; and purchase of new equipment or furnishings. WHEFA may also issue bonds to refinance outstanding debt.

Organization: WHEFA is a public corporation. Its 7 members are appointed by the governor with consent of the senate for staggered 7-year terms, and no more than 4 may be members of the same political party. Each member's appointment remains in effect until a successor is appointed. The governor annually appoints one member as chairperson, and the members appoint the vice chairperson and executive director. The executive director and staff are employed outside the classified service and are not paid by state funds. The members receive no compensation.

History: WHEFA was created as the Wisconsin Health Facilities Authority by Chapter 304, Laws of 1973. Operations began in September 1979, after the Wisconsin Supreme Court found the law constitutional in *State ex rel. Wisconsin Health Facilities Authority v. Lindner,* 91 Wis. 2d 145 (1979), when it ruled that assistance to a religiously affiliated hospital does not advance religion or foster unnecessary entanglement between church and state. WHEFA issued its first debt in December 1979.

1987 Wisconsin Act 27 expanded the scope of WHEFA to include assistance to private, tax-exempt colleges and universities and continuing care retirement communities and changed its name to reflect the broader responsibilities. 1993 Wisconsin Act 438 added not-for-profit institutions that have health education as their primary purpose. 2003 Wisconsin Act 109 further expanded the scope of WHEFA to include the issuance of bonds for the benefit of private, tax-exempt elementary or secondary educational institutions. 2009 Wisconsin Act 2 allowed for WHEFA to include the issuance of bonds for the benefit of private, tax-exempt research facilities. 2013 Wisconsin Act 20 expanded the WHEFA statute to include the issuance of bonds for the benefit of all nonprofit institutions and allowed interest income on bonds issued by WHEFA to be exempt from state income tax if such an exemption is already available on bonds eligible to be issued for the same purpose through another Wisconsin conduit issuer.

WISCONSIN HOUSING AND ECONOMIC DEVELOPMENT AUTHORITY

Address e-mail by combining the user ID and the state extender: userid@**wheda.com**
All telephone numbers are 608 area code unless otherwise indicated.

Members: MARK R. HOGAN, *chairperson;* PERRY ARMSTRONG, *vice chairperson;* SUE SHORE, *secretary;* BRADLEY GUSE, *treasurer;* SENATORS HARRIS DODD, MARKLEIN; REPRESENTATIVES ALLEN, YOUNG; REED HALL (chief executive officer of Wisconsin Economic Development Corporation), CATE ZEUSKE (deputy secretary of administration); JOHN HORNING, MCARTHUR WEDDLE. (All except legislative and *ex officio* members are appointed by governor with senate consent.)

Executive Director: WYMAN B. WINSTON, 266-2893, wyman.winston@

Chief Operating Officer/Deputy Executive Director: BRIAN SCHIMMING, 267-2307, brian.schimming@

Assistant Deputy Director: MARY ANN MCCOSHEN, 267-5200, mary_ann.mccoshen@

Executive Secretary: MAUREEN BRUNKER, 266-7354, maureen.brunker@

Mailing Address: P.O. Box 1728, Madison 53701-1728.

Location: 201 West Washington Avenue, Suite 700, Madison 53703; Milwaukee Office: 140 South 1st Street, Suite 200, Milwaukee 53204.

Telephones: Madison: (608) 266-7884; Milwaukee: (414) 227-4039; Toll free: (800) 334-6873.

Fax: Madison: (608) 267-1099; Milwaukee: (414) 227-4704.

Internet Address: www.wheda.com

Business Development: FARSHAD MALTES, *director,* 266-2027, farshad.maltes@

Commercial Lending: SEAN O'BRIEN, *director,* 267-1453, sean.obrien@

Financial Services: LAURA B. MORRIS, *chief financial officer,* 266-1640, laura.morris@

General Counsel: MICK CONRAD, 266-2748, mick.conrad@

Human Resources and Administration: MARK EMMRICH, *director,* 267-2921, mark.emmrich@

Information Technology: DAN ZADRA, *chief information officer,* 266-3183, dan.zadra@

Marketing and Communications: vacancy.

Risk and Compliance: JENNIFER HARRINGTON, *director,* 266-6622, jennifer.harrington@

Single Family: DAVE ROUSE, *director,* 266-2184, dave.rouse@

Publications: Annual Report; Dividends for Wisconsin.

Number of Employees: 150.00 (not state funded).

Total Budget 2014-15: $18,000,000 (not state funded).

Statutory Reference: Chapter 234.

Agency Responsibility: The Wisconsin Housing and Economic Development Authority (WHEDA) provides loans for low- and moderate-income housing, as well as financing programs for business and agricultural development. The authority finances most of its programs through the sale of bonds that are not an obligation of the State of Wisconsin. Since interest earned on the bonds is exempt from federal income taxation, they can be marketed at lower interest rates, which reduces the cost of borrowing.

WHEDA provides low-cost, 30-year fixed financing to low- and moderate-income home buyers who must meet specific income and loan limits eligibility requirements. WHEDA Advantage mortgages also provide access to down payment assistance, a mortgage credit certificate, and education resources to help home buyers succeed long-term as homeowners. As an exclusive for WHEDA homeowners, the authority offers low-cost home improvement loans to complete up to $15,000 in home repairs as well as a mortgage refinance product designed specifically to make home ownership more affordable for borrowers who currently have a WHEDA loan.

Both federally taxable and tax-exempt bonds are used to finance multifamily housing programs, which include homeless and special needs housing initiatives and loans to help with predevelopment of rental housing projects. In addition, the authority administers the federal Low-Income Housing Tax Credit Program (LIHTC) for developers of affordable rental housing.

WHEDA acts for the state in administering federally funded housing programs in coordination with the U.S. Department of Housing and Urban Development. Foremost among these are the Section 8 programs of the federal Housing and Community Development Act of 1979, which fund construction and rehabilitation of rental housing through rent subsidies to owners.

A companion organization, the WHEDA Foundation, makes grants to nonprofit organizations and local governments for housing projects that benefit persons-in-crisis. Grants are made to acquire and/or rehabilitate existing housing or construct new housing. The foundation also receives grant money on behalf of WHEDA.

WHEDA administers several economic development loan guarantee and financing programs that encourage job creation and economic growth. Agricultural loan guarantees include the Credit Relief Outreach Program (CROP) to help farmers obtain agricultural production loans; the Farm Asset Reinvestment Management (FARM) program to help farmers who want to start, expand, or modernize operations; and the Agribusiness loan guarantee to help businesses develop or expand production of products using Wisconsin's raw agricultural commodities.

The authority also provides the WHEDA Small Business Guarantee (WSBG) to acquire or expand a small business; the Contractors Loan Guarantee (CLG) to help contractors complete contracts to build their business; and the Neighborhood Business Revitalization Guarantee (NBRG), used to expand a business or to develop commercial real estate in an urban area. In addition, the authority makes economic development loans in partnership with financing from commercial and community lenders as part of the WHEDA Participation Lending Program (WPLP).

WHEDA, as part of a Wisconsin based Community Development Entity (CDE), is responsible for allocating federal New Market Tax Credits (NMTC). Since 2004, $500 million in NMTCs have been received to help stimulate economic development and job growth in low-income Wisconsin communities. In addition, WHEDA received $22.4 million in federal funding from the State Small Business Credit Initiative (SSBCI) to create a small business lending program to help spur private sector job creation.

Organization: WHEDA is a public body corporate and politic consisting of 12 members. In addition to the secretary of administration and the CEO of the Wisconsin Economic Development Corporation, or their designees, there are 4 legislative members who must represent the majority and minority party in each house. The 6 public members serve staggered 4-year terms, and the governor selects one to serve as chairperson for a one-year term. The governor appoints

WHEDA's executive director with the advice and consent of the senate for a 2-year term. Staff members are employed outside the classified service and are not paid from state funds.

History: WHEDA was created as the Wisconsin Housing Finance Authority by Chapter 287, Laws of 1971. Program operations began in July 1973, after the Wisconsin Supreme Court declared the Housing Finance Authority constitutional in *State ex rel. Warren v. Nusbaum,* 59 Wis. 2d 391 (1973). The authority issued its first debt instruments in March 1974. In 1983, Wisconsin Act 81 broadened the authority's mission to include financing for economic development projects and changed the name to the Wisconsin Housing and Economic Development Authority. In 1985 Wisconsin Acts 9 and 153 and 1987 Wisconsin Act 421, the legislature expanded WHEDA's powers to include the insuring and subsidizing of farm operating loans, drought assistance loan guarantees, and interest rate reductions. The legislature added loan guarantee programs for agricultural development and small businesses (1989 Wisconsin Act 31), recycling (1989 Wisconsin Act 335), tourism businesses (1989 Wisconsin Act 336), and businesses located in targeted areas of the state (1991 Wisconsin Act 39). 1993 Wisconsin Act 16 transferred the property tax deferral loan program to WHEDA from the Department of Administration. In 2005, WHEDA's Modernization Bill (2005 Wisconsin Act 75) was passed, representing the first comprehensive enhancement of WHEDA's programs in over 30 years. This legislation has increased WHEDA's financing capacity for affordable housing and business development. 2011 Wisconsin Act 79 expanded business eligibility and loan limits for WHEDA's business loan guarantee program. 2011 Wisconsin Act 214, signed into law in 2012, allowed the authority to issue federally tax-exempt bonds to finance new business expansion projects. In March 2012, the lifetime limit of $200 million on the aggregate amount of bonds WHEDA may issue for economic development was replaced with an annual cap of $150 million for economic development bonding (Senate Bill 459). In July 2012, WHEDA removed its first-time home buyer requirement for its home loans, enabling more Wisconsin families to qualify for an affordable mortgage. In July 2013, WHEDA received authority to refinance mortgage loans funded or serviced by WHEDA after 2009 (Senate Bill 151).

Wisconsin has 84,000 river miles to enjoy. (Department of Tourism)

NONPROFIT CORPORATIONS

A public nonprofit corporation is created by the legislature for a specific purpose.

BRADLEY CENTER SPORTS AND ENTERTAINMENT CORPORATION

Board of Directors: TED D. KELLNER, *chairperson;* ANDREW A. PETZOLD, *vice chairperson;* RICARDO DIAZ, MATTHEW J. PARLOW, vacancy (nominated by Bradley Family Foundation); MICHAEL W. GREBE, JEFFREY A. JOERRES, PATRICK S. LAWTON, GARY D. SWEENEY. (All are appointed by governor.)

Mailing Address: 1001 North Fourth Street, Milwaukee 53203-1314.

Telephone: (414) 227-0400.

Fax: (414) 227-0497.

E-mail Address: scostello@bcsec.com

Internet Address: www.bmoharrisbradleycenter.com

Statutory Reference: Chapter 232.

Agency Responsibility: The Bradley Center Sports and Entertainment Corporation is a public nonprofit corporation, created by 1985 Wisconsin Act 26 as an instrumentality of the state to receive the donation of the Bradley Center, a sports and entertainment facility located in Milwaukee County, from the Bradley Center Corporation. Its responsibility is to own and operate the center for the economic and recreational benefit of the citizens of Wisconsin. The center is the home of the Milwaukee Bucks basketball team, the Milwaukee Admirals hockey team, and the Marquette University men's basketball team. Other tenants are family entertainment shows and concerts. The state and its political subdivisions are not liable for any debt or obligation of the corporation. The corporation may not divest itself of the center, nor may it dissolve unless the legislature directs it to do so by law. If the corporation is dissolved, all of its assets become state property.

State law exempts the corporation from most open records and open meeting laws applicable to state agencies, but the board must submit an annual financial statement to the governor and the legislature.

Organization: The corporation's board of directors is made up of 9 members appointed by the governor, serving staggered 7-year terms. Six members require senate consent, must "represent the diverse interests of the people of this state", and must be state residents. Three of those 6 must have executive and managerial business experience. The remaining 3 directors are nominated by the Bradley Family Foundation, Inc. No director may be an elected public official; the board selects it chairperson annually.

WISCONSIN ARTISTIC ENDOWMENT FOUNDATION

Members: Inactive.

Statutory Reference: Chapter 247.

Agency Responsibility: The Wisconsin Artistic Endowment Foundation was created as a nonprofit corporation to support the arts by converting donated property and art objects into cash and distributing these and other moneys to the arts board for programs that provide operating support to arts organizations.

Organization: The foundation was created by 2001 Wisconsin Act 16 and can only be dissolved by the legislature.

REGIONAL AGENCIES

The following agencies were created by state law to function in one specific area of the state, usually an area composed of more than one county.

REGIONAL PLANNING COMMISSIONS

Regional planning commissions advise local units of government on the planning and delivery of public services to the citizens of a defined region, and they prepare and adopt master plans for the physical development of the region they serve. Regional planning provides a way to address problems that transcend local government boundaries, and offers joint solutions for intergovernmental cooperation.

The commissions may conduct research studies; make and adopt plans for the physical, social, and economic development of the region; assist in grant writing for financial assistance; provide advisory services to local governmental units and other public and private agencies; and coordinate local programs that relate to their objectives. Many commissions serve as a one-stop source of statistical information for the local governments of their area.

Currently, there are nine regional planning commissions, serving all but five of the state's 72 counties. Their boundaries are based on such considerations as common topographical and geographical features; the extent of urban development; existence of special or acute agricultural, forestry, or other rural problems; or regional physical, social, and economic characteristics.

Among the many categories of projects developed or assisted by regional planning commissions are rail and air transportation, waste disposal and recycling, highways, air and water quality, farmland preservation and zoning, land conservation and reclamation, outdoor recreation, parking and lakefront studies, and land records modernization.

Chapter 466, Laws of 1955, created the statute that governs the state's regional planning commissions (Section 66.0309, Wisconsin Statutes) and authorized the governor (or a state agency designated by the governor) to create a regional planning commission upon petition by the local governing bodies.

Membership of regional planning commissions varies according to conditions defined by statute. Unless otherwise specified by a region's local governments, the term of office for a commissioner is six years. The commissions are funded through state and federal planning grants, contracts with local governments for special planning services, and a statutorily authorized levy of up to .003% of equalized real estate value charged to each local governmental unit.

As authorized by state law, Wisconsin's regional planning commissions have established the Association of Wisconsin Regional Planning Commissions. The association's purposes include assisting the study of common problems and serving as an information clearinghouse.

Bay-Lake Regional Planning Commission

Region: Brown, Door, Florence, Kewaunee, Manitowoc, Marinette, Oconto, and Sheboygan Counties.

Members: Donald Markwardt (Manitowoc), *chairperson;* Mike Hotz (Sheboygan), *vice chairperson;* Alice Baumgarten (Marinette), *secretary-treasurer;* Tom Sieber (Brown); Ken Fisher (Door); Edwin A. Kelley, Larry Neuens, Rich Wolosyn (Florence); Eric Corroy, Virginia Haske, Chuck Wagner (Kewaunee); Chuck Hoffman, Daniel Koski (Manitowoc); Mary G. Meyer, vacancy (Marinette); Terry Brazeau, Dennis Kroll, Thomas Kussow (Oconto); Ed Procek, Brian Yerges (Sheboygan).

Executive Director: vacancy.

Mailing Address: 425 South Adams Street, Suite 201, Green Bay 54301.

Telephone: (920) 448-2820; Fax: (920) 448-2823.

Internet Address: www.baylakerpc.org

Capital Area Regional Planning Commission

Region: Dane County.

Members: LARRY PALM (City of Madison appointee), *chairperson;* PETER MCKEEVER (Dane County Executive appointee), *vice chairperson;* KRIS HAMPTON (Dane County Towns Association appointee), *secretary;* ERIC HOHOL (Dane County Cities and Villages Association appointee), *treasurer;* STEVE ARNOLD, EVAN TOUCHETT (Dane County Cities and Villages Association appointees); CARYL TERRELL (Dane County Executive appointee); MARK GELLER, ED MINIHAN, DAVID PFEIFFER (Dane County Towns Association appointees); ZACH BRANDON, LAUREN CNARE, KEN GOLDEN (City of Madison appointees).

Deputy Director: KAMRAN MESBAH.

Mailing Address: City-County Building, 210 Martin Luther King Jr. Boulevard, Room 362, Madison 53703.

Telephone: 266-4137; Fax: 266-9117.

Internet Address: www.capitalarearpc.org; E-mail Address: info@capitalarearpc.org

East Central Wisconsin Regional Planning Commission

Region: Calumet, Fond du Lac, Green Lake*, Marquette*, Menominee, Outagamie, Shawano, Waupaca, Waushara, and Winnebago Counties. *Inactive members.

Members: DONNA KALATA (Waushara), *chairperson;* MICHAEL R. THOMAS (Outagamie), *vice chairperson;* BILL BARRIBEAU, MERLIN GENTZ, PAT LAUGHRIN (Calumet); ALLEN BUECHEL, MARTIN FARRELL, JOSEPH MOORE, BRENDA SCHNEIDER, vacancy (Fond du Lac); MURIEL BZDAWKA, MICHAEL CHAPMAN, RUTH M. WINTER (Menominee); TIM HANNA, HELEN NAGLER, TOM NELSON, JEFF NOOYEN, DANIEL RETTLER (Outagamie); JERRY ERDMANN, MARSHAL GEISE, TOM KAUTZA (Shawano); GARY BARRINGTON, DUWAYNE FEDERWITZ, DICK KOEPPEN, BRIAN SMITH (Waupaca); NEAL STREHLOW, LARRY TIMM (Waushara); DAVID ALBRECHT, ERNIE BELLIN, STEVE CUMMINGS, MARK HARRIS, KEN ROBL, ROBERT SCHMEICHEL (Winnebago); JILL MICHAELSON (transportation department representative); DEBORAH WETTER (public transportation representative).

Executive Director: ERIC W. FOWLE, AICP, efowle@ecwrpc.org

Mailing Address: 400 Ahnaip Street, Suite 100, Menasha 54952.

Telephone: (920) 751-4770; Fax: (920) 751-4771.

Internet Address: www.ecwrpc.org

Mississippi River Regional Planning Commission

Region: Buffalo, Crawford, Jackson, La Crosse, Monroe, Pepin, Pierce, Trempealeau, and Vernon Counties.

Members: JAMES KUHN (Monroe), *chairperson;* MARGARET M. BAECKER (Trempealeau), *vice chairperson;* VICKI BURKE (La Crosse), *secretary-treasurer;* DANIEL BARR, DEL D. TWIDT, MARY ANNE MCMILLAN URELL (Buffalo); GERALD F. KRACHEY, RONALD LEYS, GREG RUSSELL (Crawford); RON CARNEY, JAMES CHRISTENSON, EUGENE SAVAGE (Jackson); JAMES EHRSAM, TARA JOHNSON (La Crosse); SHARON FOLCEY, CEDRIC SCHNITZLER (Monroe); NORMAN MURRAY, BRUCE PETERSON, DAVID SMITH (Pepin); RICHARD PURDY, JAMES ROSS, WILLIAM SCHROEDER (Pierce); PHILLIP BORRESON, ERNEST VOLD (Trempealeau); NANCY JAEKEL, JAMES NEUBAUER, JO ANN NICKELATTI (Vernon).

Executive Director: GREGORY D. FLOGSTAD.

Mailing Address: 1707 Main Street, Suite 435, La Crosse 54601-3227.

Telephone: (608) 785-9396; Fax: (608) 785-9394.

Internet Address: www.mrrpc.com; E-mail Address: plan@mrrpc.com

North Central Wisconsin Regional Planning Commission

Region: Adams, Forest, Juneau, Langlade, Lincoln, Marathon, Oneida, Portage*, Vilas, and Wood Counties. *Inactive member.

Members: ROBERT LUSSOW (Lincoln), *chairperson;* PAUL MILLAN (Forest), *vice chairperson;* RICHARD BAKOVKA, ROCKY GILNER, vacancy (Adams); BUCKY DAILEY, JIM LANDRU (Forest);

JERRY NILES, EDMUND WAFLE, KENNETH WINTERS (Juneau); GEORGE BORNEMANN, RONALD NYE, PAUL SCHUMAN (Langlade); FRANK SAAL, JR., DOUGLAS WILLIAMS (Lincoln); VIRGINIA HEINEMANN, CRAIG MCEWEN, BETTYE NALL (Marathon); HARLAND LEE, THOMAS RUDOLPH, vacancy (Oneida); BOB EGAN, KIM SIMAC, vacancy (Vilas); TOM HAFERMAN, GERALD NELSON, vacancy (Wood).

Executive Director: DENNIS L. LAWRENCE, AICP.

Mailing Address: 210 McClellan Street, Suite 210, Wausau 54403.

Telephone: (715) 849-5510; Fax: (715) 849-5110.

Internet Address: www.ncwrpc.org; E-mail Address: staff@ncwrpc.org

Northwest Regional Planning Commission

Region: Ashland, Bayfield, Burnett, Douglas, Iron, Price, Rusk, Sawyer, Taylor, and Washburn Counties and the Tribal Nations of Bad River, Lac Courte Oreilles, Lac du Flambeau, Red Cliff, and St. Croix.

Members: DOUGLAS FINN (Douglas), *chairperson;* RANDY TATUR (Rusk), *vice chairperson;* HAL HELWIG (Sawyer), *secretary-treasurer;* DEB LEWIS, RICHARD PUFALL, DONNA WILLIAMSON (Ashland); JAMES CRANDALL, DENNIS POCERNICH (Bayfield); ED PETERSON, DON TAYLOR (Burnett); BRUCE HAGEN, LARRY QUAM (Douglas); JOSEPH PINARDI, vacancy (Iron); ROBERT KOPISCH, CAROL MCLAUGHLIN, TOM RATZLAFF (Price); MARTY REYNOLDS, vacancy (Rusk); KATHY MCCOY (Sawyer); JIM METZ, ROLLIE THUMS, MICHAEL WELLNER (Taylor); GARY CUSKEY, JIM DOHM, STEVEN SATHER (Washburn); vacancy (Northwest Tribal nations representative); ROSE GURNOE-SOULIER (Red Cliff Tribal Council); MIC ISHAM (Lac Courte Oreilles Tribal Council); MIKE WIGGINS, JR. (Bad River Tribal Council); LEWIS TAYLOR (St. Croix Tribal Council); BUTCH ST. GERMAINE (Lac du Flambeau Tribal Council).

Executive Director: MYRON SCHUSTER, mschuster@nwrpc.com

Mailing Address: 1400 South River Street, Spooner 54801-1390.

Telephone: (715) 635-2197; Fax: (715) 635-7262.

Internet Address: www.nwrpc.com

Southeastern Wisconsin Regional Planning Commission

Region: Kenosha, Milwaukee, Ozaukee, Racine, Walworth, Washington, and Waukesha Counties.

Members: DAVID L. STROIK (Washington), *chairperson;* CHARLES COLMAN (Walworth), *vice chairperson;* ADELENE GREENE (Kenosha), *secretary;* WILLIAM R. DREW (Milwaukee), *treasurer;* ROBERT W. PITTS, MICHAEL J. SKALITZKY (Kenosha); MARINA DIMITRIJEVIC, BRIAN R. DRANZIK (Milwaukee); THOMAS H. BUESTRIN, GUSTAV W. WIRTH, JR., vacancy (Ozaukee); MIKE DAWSON, DAVE EBERLE, PEGGY SHUMWAY (Racine); NANCY RUSSELL, LINDA SEEMEYER (Walworth); DANIEL S. SCHMIDT, DANIEL W. STOFFEL (Washington); MICHAEL CROWLEY, JOSE DELGADO, JAMES T. DWYER (Waukesha).

Executive Director: KENNETH R. YUNKER.

Mailing Address: W239 N1812 Rockwood Drive, P.O. Box 1607, Waukesha 53187-1607.

Telephone: (262) 547-6721; Fax: (262) 547-1103.

Internet Address: www.sewrpc.org; E-mail Address: sewrpc@sewrpc.org

Southwestern Wisconsin Regional Planning Commission

Region: Grant, Green, Iowa, Lafayette, and Richland Counties.

Members: ART CARTER (Green), *chairperson;* TIM MCGETTIGAN (Lafayette), *vice chairperson;* JEANETTA KIRKPATRICK (Richland), *secretary-treasurer;* ROBERT KEENEY, EILEEN NICKELS, JERRY WEHRLE (Grant); MICHAEL DOYLE, NATHAN L. KLASSY (Green); CAROL ANDERSON, JOHN MEYERS, TODD NOVAK (Iowa); JEFF RIECHERS, JACK SAUER (Lafayette); RAYMOND SCHMITZ, ROBERT SMITH (Richland).

Executive Director: LAWRENCE T. WARD, l.ward@swwrpc.org

Mailing Address: 20 South Court Street, P.O. Box 262, Platteville 53818.

Telephone: (608) 342-1214; Fax: (608) 342-1220.

Internet Address: www.swwrpc.org

West Central Wisconsin Regional Planning Commission

Region: Barron, Chippewa, Clark, Dunn, Eau Claire, Polk, and St. Croix Counties.

Members: Jess Miller (Barron), *chairperson;* Lee McIlquham (Chippewa), *vice chairperson;* Richard Creaser (Dunn), *secretary-treasurer;* Ken Jost, Travis Turner (Barron); Mike Goettl, Florian Skwierczynski (Chippewa); Charles Rueth, Joe Waichulis, Jr., Norman Wesenberg (Clark); Steve Rasmussen, Robert Walter (Dunn); Kathleen Clark, John Frank, Gordon Steinhauer (Eau Claire); William Johnson IV, Craig Moriak, Warren Nelson (Polk); Agnes Ring, Travis Schachtner, Larry Weisenbeck (St. Croix).

Executive Director: Lynn Nelson.

Mailing Address: 800 Wisconsin Street, Mail Box 9, Eau Claire 54703-3606.

Telephone: (715) 836-2918; Fax: (715) 836-2886.

Internet Address: www.wcwrpc.org; E-mail Address: wcwrpc@wcwrpc.org

REGIONAL PLANNING COMMISSION AREAS

Not part of a planning region

Map by Wisconsin Legislative Technology Services Bureau.

MADISON CULTURAL ARTS DISTRICT BOARD

Statutory Reference: Chapter 229, Subchapter V.

Agency Responsibility: Arts districts are public corporations that may acquire, construct, operate, and manage cultural arts facilities. A local district may issue revenue bonds, invest funds, set standards for the use of facilities, and establish and collect fees for usage. The Madison Cultural Arts District Board's activities are suspended until requested otherwise.

PROFESSIONAL FOOTBALL STADIUM DISTRICT

Board Members: ANN PATTESON, *chairperson;* KEN GOLOMSKI, *vice chairperson;* CHUCK LAMINE, *secretary;* MARGARET JENSEN, *treasurer;* RON ANTONNEAU, ROBERT COWLES, KEITH ZIMMERMAN.

Statutory Reference: Chapter 229, Subchapter IV.

Agency Responsibility: The Professional Football Stadium District is an owner and landlord of Lambeau Field, the designated home of the Green Bay Packers football team. It is a public corporation that may acquire, construct, equip, maintain, improve, operate, and manage football stadium facilities or hire others to do the same. The district issued bonds for the redevelopment of Lambeau Field, which was substantially completed on July 31, 2003. All district debt was retired August 1, 2011. Maintenance and operation of the stadium is governed by provisions of the Lambeau Field Lease Agreement by and among the district, Green Bay Packers, Inc., and the City of Green Bay. The district currently imposes a 0.5% sales and use tax approved by Brown County voters in a referendum. Proceeds from the tax can be used for district administrative expenses, maintenance, and operating costs of stadium facilities and related purposes consistent with statutory limitations and lease provisions. In accordance with statutory provisions, the tax will be extinguished once sufficient funds are escrowed for maintenance and operation of the stadium and district administrative expenses. The district was created by 1999 Wisconsin Act 167.

SOUTHEAST WISCONSIN PROFESSIONAL BASEBALL PARK DISTRICT

District Board Members: DON SMILEY (Milwaukee County, appointed by governor), *chairperson;* DANIEL MCKEITHAN, JR. (Milwaukee County, appointed by chief executive officer), *vice chairperson;* MARK THOMSEN (City of Milwaukee representative appointed by mayor), *secretary;* KAREN MAKOUTZ (Ozaukee County, appointed by chief executive officer), *treasurer;* JERRY GONZALEZ (Ozaukee County), BILL MCREYNOLDS (Racine County), KRISTINE O'MEARA (Washington County), TRACEY KLEIN (Waukesha County) (county members appointed by governor); ERIK JOHNSON (at-large member, appointed by governor); ALEC FRASER (Milwaukee County), DOUGLAS STANSIL (Racine County), MARK MCCUNE (Washington County), KEITH SWARTZ (Waukesha County) (members appointed by county's chief executive officer).

Executive Director: MICHAEL R. DUCKETT.

Mailing Address: Miller Park, One Brewers Way, Milwaukee 53214.

Telephone: (414) 902-4040.

E-mail Address: contact@millerparkdistrict.com

Internet Address: www.millerparkdistrict.com

Statutory Reference: Chapter 229, Subchapter III.

Agency Responsibility: The Southeast Wisconsin Professional Baseball Park District is majority owner of Miller Park, the home of the Milwaukee Brewers Baseball Club. It is a public corporation that may acquire, construct, maintain, improve, operate, and manage baseball park facilities which include parking lots, garages, restaurants, parks, concession facilities, entertainment facilities, and other related structures. The district may impose a sales tax and a use tax at a rate not to exceed 0.1%.

The district is also authorized to issue bonds for certain purposes related to baseball park facilities. A city or county within the district's jurisdiction may make loans or grants to the district, expend funds to subsidize the district, borrow money for baseball park facilities, or grant property to the state dedicated for use by a professional baseball park.

The district, which was created by 1995 Wisconsin Act 56, includes Milwaukee, Ozaukee, Racine, Washington, and Waukesha Counties. The district board consists of 13 members, 6 appointed by the governor, 6 appointed by the chief executive officers of each county in the district (2 from the most populous county), and one appointed by the mayor of Milwaukee. The governor appoints the chairperson. Members appointed by the governor must be confirmed by the senate. Members appointed by county executive officers or the mayor of Milwaukee must be confirmed by their respective county boards or the city council.

WISCONSIN CENTER DISTRICT

Board of Directors: FRANKLYN GIMBEL (private sector representative appointed by Mayor of City of Milwaukee), *chairperson;* JAMES KAMINSKI (private sector representative appointed by governor), *vice chairperson;* MICHAEL MURPHY (Milwaukee Common Council President); MARTIN MATSON (City of Milwaukee comptroller); SENATOR DARLING (senate cochairperson, Joint Committee on Finance), REPRESENTATIVE SANFELIPPO (designated by assembly cochairperson, Joint Committee on Finance); JOHN HOGAN (designated by secretary of administration); JOSEPH BARTOLOTTA, STEPHEN H. MARCUS (private sector representatives appointed by governor); JASON ALLEN, JEFF SHERMAN (private sector representatives appointed by Milwaukee County Executive); KATHY EHLEY (mayor of city that contributes room taxes appointed by Milwaukee County Executive); ALDERMEN HAMILTON, PUENTE (public sector representatives appointed by Milwaukee Common Council President); JOEL BRENNAN (private sector representative appointed by Mayor of City of Milwaukee).

President and CEO: RUSS STAERKEL, (414) 908-6050, rstaerkel@wcd.org

Mailing Address: 400 West Wisconsin Avenue, Milwaukee 53203.

Telephone: (414) 908-6000.

Fax: (414) 908-6010.

Internet Address: www.wcd.org

Statutory Reference: Chapter 229, Subchapter II.

Agency Responsibility: The Wisconsin Center District (WCD) owns and operates the UW Milwaukee Panther Arena, the Milwaukee Theatre, and the Wisconsin Center. The district is not supported by property taxes or state subsidies. It is funded by operating revenue and special sales taxes on hotel rooms, restaurant food and beverages, and car rentals within its taxing boundaries (Milwaukee County). The WCD is classified by law as a local exposition district that may acquire, construct, and operate an exposition center and related facilities; enter into contracts and grant concessions; mortgage district property and issue bonds; and invest funds as the district board considers appropriate. Local exposition districts are public corporations. Interest income on exposition district bonds is tax-exempt, and the district is exempt from state income and franchise taxes.

The board has 15 members, 13 of whom serve 3-year terms. Legislative members serve for terms concurrent with their term of office. Public officials can no longer serve after their term of office expires. Public sector representatives appointed by the Milwaukee Common Council President must be city residents. The 2 private sector representatives the Mayor of Milwaukee appoints must reside in the city. The private sector representatives the county executive appoints must live outside the City of Milwaukee. Of the 4 gubernatorial appointees, 2 must live in Milwaukee County but not in the City of Milwaukee. The governor's appointees must include the secretary of the state Department of Administration (or designee), a member who has significant involvement with the lodging industry, and a member who has significant involvement with the food and beverage industry. Local exposition districts were authorized by 1993 Wisconsin Act 263.

INTERSTATE AGENCIES AND COMPACTS

Wisconsin is party to a variety of interstate compacts. These agreements are binding on two or more states, and they establish uniform guidelines or procedures for agencies within the signatory states. The following section lists agencies created by enactment of enabling legislation in all of the participating states or by interstate agreement of their respective governors. It also describes interstate compacts that are expressly ratified in the Wisconsin Statutes but do not require appointment of delegates.

EDUCATION COMMISSION OF THE STATES

Wisconsin Delegates: GOVERNOR WALKER, *chairperson;* TONY EVERS (superintendent of public instruction); SENATOR OLSEN; vacancy (assembly representative); TRACIE HAPPEL, DEMOND MEANS, JOHN REINEMANN (public members appointed by governor).

Mailing Address: National commission: Education Commission of the States, 700 Broadway, #810, Denver, Colorado 80203-3442.

Telephone: National Commission: (303) 299-3600.

Internet Address: www.ecs.org

Statutory References: Sections 39.75 and 39.76.

Agency Responsibility: The Education Commission of the States was established to foster national cooperation among executive, legislative, educational, and lay leaders of the various states. It offers a forum for discussing policy alternatives in the education field; provides an information clearinghouse about educational problems and their various solutions throughout the nation; and facilitates the improvement of state and local educational systems. The governor designates the chairperson of the 7-member delegation, and the Department of Administration provides staff services. Wisconsin's participation in the commission originated in Chapter 641, Laws of 1965, which established an interstate compact for education and specified the composition of the Wisconsin delegation.

GREAT LAKES COMMISSION

Wisconsin Members: RUSSELL RASMUSSEN (state officer member), *chairperson;* LYNN DUFRANE, DEAN HAEN, STEVE GALARNEAU (alternate) (all appointed by governor).

Mailing Address: Great Lakes Commission: TIM A. EDER, *executive director,* 2805 South Industrial Highway, Suite 100, Ann Arbor, Michigan 48104.

Telephones: Wisconsin Delegation Chair: (608) 261-7599; Great Lakes Commission: (734) 971-9135.

Commission Fax: (734) 971-9150.

Internet Address: www.glc.org

Publications of the Great Lakes Commission: *Advisor; Annual Report.*

Statutory Reference: Section 14.78.

Agency Responsibility: A 3-member delegation represents Wisconsin on the 8-state Great Lakes Commission. The interstate commission promotes orderly development of the water resources of the Great Lakes Basin; offers advice on balancing industrial, commercial, agricultural, water supply, and residential and recreational uses of the lakes' water resources; and enables basin residents to benefit from public works, such as navigational aids.

Commissioners from the states of Illinois, Indiana, Michigan, Minnesota, New York, Ohio, Pennsylvania, and Wisconsin share information and coordinate state positions on issues of regional concern.

Organization: The governor appoints the 3 Wisconsin delegates to the Great Lakes Commission. The delegates are chosen on the basis of their knowledge of and interest in Great Lakes Basin problems. One commissioner, who must be a state officer or employee, is appointed to an indefinite term and serves as secretary of Wisconsin's compact commission and as a member of the executive committee of the interstate commission. Wisconsin's other commissioners serve 4-year terms.

History: The Great Lakes Commission was established in 1955 following enactment of enabling legislation by a majority of the Great Lakes states. It replaced the Deep Waterways Commission, established to promote the St. Lawrence Seaway project. With enactment of Chapter 275, Laws of 1955, Wisconsin ratified the Great Lakes Basin Compact and created the Wisconsin Great Lakes Compact Commission, consisting of the state members of the Great Lakes Commission. Congress recognized the Great Lakes Basin Compact in P.L. 90-419 on July 24, 1968.

GREAT LAKES PROTECTION FUND

Wisconsin Representatives: RICHARD MEEUSEN, KEVIN L. SHAFER (appointed by governor with senate consent).

Mailing Address and Telephone: RUSS VAN HERIK, *executive director,* 1560 Sherman Avenue, Suite 880, Evanston, Illinois 60201, (847) 425-8150, Fax: (847) 424-9832.

Internet Address: www.glpf.org

Statutory Reference: Section 14.84.

Agency Responsibility: The Great Lakes Protection Fund was created by the Council of Great Lakes Governors to finance projects for the protection and cleanup of the Great Lakes. Priorities include the prevention of toxic pollution, the identification of effective clean-up approaches, the demonstration of natural resource stewardship, and the classification of health effects of toxic pollution.

In 1989, the governors of Illinois, Michigan, Minnesota, New York, Ohio, Pennsylvania, and Wisconsin signed the formal agreement creating the Great Lakes Protection Fund, and the Wisconsin Legislature approved the state's participation in 1989 Wisconsin Act 31. The fund was incorporated as a not-for-profit corporation, managed by a board of directors composed of 2 representatives from each member state. Each state's contribution to the original $100 million endowment was determined by estimating its proportion of Great Lakes water consumption. Wisconsin's share was $12 million.

GREAT LAKES-ST. LAWRENCE RIVER BASIN WATER RESOURCES COUNCIL

Wisconsin Members: GOVERNOR WALKER *(chair)*; CATHY STEPP (secretary of department of natural resources) (alternate).

Mailing Address: Great Lakes-St. Lawrence River Basin Water Resources Council, c/o Council of Great Lakes Governors: DAVID NAFTZGER, *executive director*, 20 North Wacker Drive, Suite 2700, Chicago, Illinois 60606.

Telephone: Secretariat, Council of Great Lakes Governors: (312) 407-0177.

Fax: (312) 407-0038.

E-mail Address: cglg@cglg.org

Internet Address: www.glslcompactcouncil.org

Statutory References: Sections 14.95, 281.343.

Agency Responsibility: The governor serves as Wisconsin's representative on the council. The council is charged with aiding and promoting the coordination of the activities and programs of the Great Lakes states concerned with water resources management in the Great Lakes basin. The council may promulgate and enforce rules and regulations as may be necessary for the implementation and enforcement of the Great Lakes-St. Lawrence River Basin Water Resources Compact. The compact governs withdrawals, consumptive uses, conservation and efficient use, and diversions of basin water resources.

Under the compact, the governors from the states of Illinois, Indiana, Michigan, Minnesota, New York, Ohio, Pennsylvania, and Wisconsin, jointly pursue intergovernmental cooperation and consultation to protect, conserve, restore, improve, and effectively manage the waters and water dependent natural resources of the basin.

Organization: The governors of all participating states are *ex officio* members of the council. The governor may designate the secretary of natural resources as his alternate to attend and vote at all meetings. Any other alternate must be nominated by the governor with the advice and consent of the senate. The alternate serves at the pleasure of the governor. The governor may also appoint an advisor to attend all meetings of the council. If the governor does appoint an advisor, that person must have knowledge of and experience with Great Lakes water management issues.

History: The council was created by the ratification of the Great Lakes-St. Lawrence River Basin Water Resources Compact. Wisconsin joined the compact with the passage and signing of 2007 Wisconsin Act 227. Congress ratified the compact in Public Law 110-342. The compact became effective as state and federal law on December 8, 2008.

GREAT LAKES-ST. LAWRENCE RIVER
WATER RESOURCES REGIONAL BODY

Wisconsin Members: GOVERNOR WALKER *(chair);* CATHY STEPP (secretary of department of natural resources), *designee.*

Mailing Address: Great Lakes-St. Lawrence River Basin Water Resources Council, c/o Council of Great Lakes Governors: DAVID NAFTZGER, *secretary,* 20 North Wacker Drive, Suite 2700, Chicago, Illinois 60606.

Telephone: Secretariat, Council of Great Lakes Governors: (312) 407-0177.

Fax: (312) 407-0038.

E-mail Address: cglg@cglg.org

Internet Address: www.glslregionalbody.org

Statutory Reference: Section 281.343.

Agency Responsibility: The governor serves as Wisconsin's representative on the regional body. The regional body is charged with aiding and promoting the coordination of the activities and programs of the Great Lakes states and provinces concerned with water resources management in the Great Lakes basin. The regional body may develop procedures for implementation of the Great Lakes-St. Lawrence River Basin Sustainable Water Resources Agreement. The agreement is a good-faith agreement between Great Lakes states and provinces that governs withdrawals, consumptive uses, conservation and efficient use, and diversions of basin water resources.

Governors from the states of Illinois, Indiana, Michigan, Minnesota, New York, Ohio, Pennsylvania, and Wisconsin, and the premiers of Ontario and Quebec jointly pursue intergovernmental cooperation and consultation to protect, conserve, restore, improve, and manage the waters and water dependent natural resources of the basin.

Organization: The governors and premiers of all participating states are *ex officio* members of the regional body. The governor may designate an alternate to attend and vote at all meetings. The designee serves at the pleasure of the governor.

History: The regional body was created by Great Lakes governors and premiers by signing the Great Lakes-St. Lawrence River Basin Sustainable Water Resources Agreement on December 13, 2005.

INTERSTATE INSURANCE PRODUCT REGULATION COMMISSION

Wisconsin Member: TED NICKEL (commissioner of insurance).

Mailing Address: Commission: 444 North Capitol Street NW, Hall of the States, Suite 701, Washington, D.C. 20001-1509.

Telephone: Commission: (202) 471-3962.

Commission Fax: (816) 460-7476.

Internet Address: www.insurancecompact.org

Statutory References: Sections 14.82 and 601.58.

Agency Responsibility: The Interstate Insurance Product Regulation Commission is made up of the member states of the Interstate Insurance Product Regulation Compact. The compact's purposes are to develop uniform standards for life, annuity, disability income, and long-term care insurance products, create a central clearinghouse to provide prompt review of insurance products, approve product filings, long-term care advertisements and disability income and long-term care rate filings that satisfy uniform standards, and improve coordination of regulatory resources and expertise between state insurance departments. The commission establishes reasonable uniform standards for insurance products covered under the compact. As of March 2015, 43 states and Puerto Rico were members of the compact.

Organization: Wisconsin is represented on the commission by the state's commissioner of insurance or his or her designee. Each state member is entitled to one vote.

History: The commission reached its operational threshold in 2006. Wisconsin joined the commission with the signing of 2007 Wisconsin Act 168 in March 2008.

INTERSTATE COMMISSION FOR JUVENILES

Wisconsin Member: SHELLEY HAGAN, *compact administrator,* Office of Juvenile Offender Review, Division of Juvenile Corrections, Wisconsin Department of Corrections.

Mailing Address: 836 Euclid Avenue, Suite 322, Lexington, Kentucky 40502.

Telephone: (859) 721-1062.

E-mail Address: icjadmin@juvenilecompact.org

Internet Address: www.juvenilecompact.org

Statutory References: Sections 14.92 and 938.999.

Agency Responsibility: The Interstate Commission for Juveniles is designed to oversee, supervise, and coordinate the interstate movement of certain juveniles, delinquents, and run-away offenders. The commission has the authority to promulgate rules, which have the effect of statutory law, and enforce compliance with the Interstate Compact for Juveniles, including through judicial means. The commission is directed to resolve disputes between states regarding the compact, levy assessments against compacting states to cover its costs, and report annually on its activities. The commission is also directed to collect standardized data concerning the interstate movement of juveniles. The commission came into existence when 35 states ratified the Interstate Compact for Juveniles in August 2008.

Organization: The commission is composed of one commissioner from each of the compacting states. Each compacting state has one vote on the interstate commission. The commission meets at least once a year. The Council of State Governments provides organizational support to the commission.

INTERSTATE WILDLIFE VIOLATOR COMPACT
ADMINISTRATORS BOARD

Wisconsin Administrator: JENNIFER MCDONOUGH, jennifer.mcdonough@wisconsin.gov

Mailing Address: Wisconsin Department of Natural Resources, P.O. Box 7921, Madison 53707-7921.

Telephone: (608) 267-0859.

Statutory Reference: Section 29.03.

Agency Responsibility: The Interstate Wildlife Violator Compact establishes a process whereby wildlife law violations by a nonresident while in a member state may be handled as if the person were a resident in the state where the violation took place, meaning personal recognizance may be permitted instead of arrest, booking, and bonding. The process is aimed at increasing the efficiency of conservation wardens by allowing more time for enforcement duties rather than violator processing. The compact requires each member state to recognize the revocations and suspensions of individuals hunting, fishing, and trapping privileges from other member states that result from a wildlife related violation. The compact also requires each member state to revoke or suspend the hunting, fishing, and trapping licenses of any resident of that state who violates a wildlife related law in another member state and fails to resolve the matter by payment of the penalty or appearance in court. The board of compact administrators was established to serve as the governing body for the resolution of all matters relating to the operation of the compact.

Organization: The board is composed of one representative from each participating state. The Wisconsin representative is appointed by the secretary of natural resources. Each member of the board has one vote. As of August 2014, 43 states are members of the compact.

History: Wisconsin was authorized to develop administrative rules for Wisconsin's role in the Wildlife Violator Compact and apply to become a member of the compact with the signing of 2005 Wisconsin Act 282 in April 2006. Once the administrative rules were adopted and in effect, Wisconsin applied to become a member of the Wildlife Violator Compact and was accepted effective April 15, 2008.

LOWER ST. CROIX MANAGEMENT COMMISSION

Wisconsin Member: DAN BAUMANN (designated by secretary of natural resources).

Telephone and Mailing Address: Department of Natural Resources, West Central Region, 1300 West Clairemont Avenue, Eau Claire 54701, (715) 839-3700.

Agency Responsibility: The Lower St. Croix Management Commission was created to provide a forum for discussion of problems and programs associated with the Lower St. Croix National Scenic Riverway. It coordinates planning, development, protection, and management of the riverway for Wisconsin, Minnesota, and the U.S. government.

The commission was created by a cooperative agreement signed in 1973 by the National Park Service and the governors of Wisconsin and Minnesota. It consists of one member each from the National Park Service and the natural resources departments of the two states.

MIDWEST INTERSTATE LOW-LEVEL
RADIOACTIVE WASTE COMMISSION

Wisconsin Member: STANLEY YORK (appointed by governor with senate consent).

Mailing Address: Chair and Executive Director Stanley York, Midwest Interstate Low-Level Radioactive Waste Commission, P.O. Box 2659, Madison 53701-2659.

Telephones: Wisconsin member: 230-3532; Commission: 267-4793.

E-Mail Address: Wisconsin member: stan.york@tds.net

Commission Fax: 267-4799.

Internet Address: www.midwestcompact.org

Statutory References: Sections 14.81 and 16.11.

Agency Responsibility: The Midwest Interstate Low-Level Radioactive Waste Commission is responsible for the disposal of low-level radioactive wastes. Based on the Midwest Interstate Low-Level Radioactive Waste Compact, it may negotiate agreements for disposal of waste at facilities within or outside the region; appear as an intervenor before any court, board, or commission in any matter related to waste management; and review the emergency closure of a regional facility. The commission is directed to settle disputes between party states regarding the compact and adopt a regional management plan designating host states for the establishment of needed regional facilities.

Wisconsin's commission member must promote Wisconsin's interest in an equitable distribution of responsibilities among compact member states, encourage public access and participation in the commission's proceedings, and notify the governor and legislature if the commission proposes to designate a disposal facility site in this state.

Organization: The commission represents Indiana, Iowa, Minnesota, Missouri, Ohio, and Wisconsin, each of which has one voting member.

History: 1983 Wisconsin Act 393 ratified the Midwest Interstate Low-Level Radioactive Waste Compact, which provided for formation of the Midwest Low-Level Radioactive Waste Commission. The U.S. Congress encouraged the development of such compacts by enacting the Low-Level Radioactive Waste Policy Act in 1980, as amended by the Low-Level Radioactive Waste Policy Amendments Act of 1985.

MIDWEST INTERSTATE PASSENGER RAIL COMMISSION

Wisconsin Representatives: MARK GOTTLIEB (designated by governor); REPRESENTATIVE E. BROOKS (appointed by assembly speaker); SENATOR MILLER (appointed by senate president); vacancy (private sector representative).

Mailing Address: Commission: LAURA KLIEWER, *director,* 701 East 22nd Street, Suite 110, Lombard, Illinois 60148.

Telephone: Commission: (630) 925-1922.

Commission Fax: (630) 925-1930.

Internet Address: www.miprc.org

Statutory References: Sections 14.86 and 85.067.

Agency Responsibility: The Midwest Interstate Passenger Rail Commission brings together state leaders from the members of the Midwest Interstate Passenger Rail Compact to advocate for the funding and authorization necessary to make passenger rail improvements. It also seeks to develop a long-term interstate plan for high-speed passenger rail service implementation. The current members are Illinois, Indiana, Kansas, Michigan, Minnesota, Missouri, Nebraska, North Dakota, and Wisconsin. The commission is empowered to work with local and federal officials, to educate the public on the advantages of passenger rail, and to make recommendations to member states.

Organization: Wisconsin is represented by 4 members on the commission. Those members must be the governor or his or her designee; one assembly member appointed by the assembly speaker for a 2-year term; one senate member appointed by the senate president for a 2-year term; and one member representing the private sector, who serves for the governor's term of office. The members serve without compensation.

History: The Midwest Interstate Passenger Rail Compact became operational in 2000. Wisconsin joined the compact and gained commission membership with the signing of 2007 Wisconsin Act 117 in April 2008.

MIDWESTERN HIGHER EDUCATION COMMISSION

Wisconsin Members: DON MADELUNG (designated by governor); SENATOR HARSDORF (appointed by senate president); vacancy (appointed by assembly speaker); MARGARET FARROW, ROLF WEGENKE; MORNA FOY, DAVID L. MILLER (alternates) (appointed by governor).

Mailing Address: 105 Fifth Avenue South, Suite 450, Minneapolis, Minnesota 55401.

Telephone: (612) 677-2777; (855) 767-6432 (toll free).

Internet Address: www.mhec.org

Statutory References: Sections 14.90 and 39.80.

Agency Responsibility: The Midwestern Higher Education Commission was organized to further higher educational opportunities for residents of states participating in the Midwest Higher Education Compact. The commission may enter into agreements with member and non-member states, or their universities and colleges, to provide programs and services for students, including student exchanges and improved access. The commission also studies the effects of the compact on higher education and the needs and resources for programs in member states. The compact's three core functions are cost-savings initiatives, student access, and policy research and analysis.

Organization: The compact currently includes Illinois, Indiana, Iowa, Kansas, Michigan, Minnesota, Missouri, Nebraska, North Dakota, Ohio, South Dakota, and Wisconsin. Each state appoints 5 members to the governing commission, including the governor (or governor's designee) and 2 legislators, who serve 2-year terms. The 2 members appointed by the governor must be selected from the field of higher education. One serves a 4-year term and one serves a 2-year term. Any member state may withdraw from the compact 2 years after the passage of a law authorizing withdrawal.

History: Wisconsin ratified the Midwestern Higher Education Compact in 1993 Wisconsin Act 358, effective July 1, 1994.

MILITARY INTERSTATE CHILDREN'S COMPACT COMMISSION

State Council: TONY EVERS (state superintendent of public instruction); JOHN HENDRICKS (superintendent of school district with high concentration of children of military families, appointed by state superintendent); LT. COL. JOHN BLAHA (representative from a military installation, appointed by state superintendent); vacancy (appointed by assembly speaker); SENATOR ROTH (appointed by senate majority leader). Nonvoting members: SHELLEY JOAN WEISS (appointed by state superintendent), compact commissioner; BECKY WALLEY (military family education liaison, appointed by state superintendent).

Contact: SHELLEY JOAN WEISS.

Mailing Address: 3014 Happy Valley Road, Sun Prairie 53590.

Telephone: (608) 698-2409.

Statutory References: Sections 14.91 and 115.997.

Agency Responsibility: The Military Interstate Children's Compact Commission oversees implementation of the Interstate Compact on Educational Opportunity for Military Children. The compact was enacted to facilitate the education of children of military families, and remove barriers to educational success imposed by frequent moves and the deployment of parents. The commission has the authority to promulgate rules, and enforce compliance with the compact, including through judicial means. The commission may provide for the resolution of disputes between states regarding the compact and issue advisory opinions concerning the meaning of the compact. As of May 2015, all 50 states and the District of Columbia have adopted the compact.

Organization: The commission is composed of one commissioner from each of the compacting states. Each compacting state has one vote on the interstate commission. The commission meets at least once per year. The Council of State Governments provides organizational support to the commission.

History: Wisconsin joined the compact upon passage of 2009 Wisconsin Act 329, effective May 26, 2010.

MISSISSIPPI RIVER PARKWAY COMMISSION

Wisconsin Commissioners: SHERRY QUAMME (Crawford County), *chairperson;* SENATORS HARSDORF, vacancy; REPRESENTATIVES NERISON, vacancy; ROBERT MILLER (Buffalo County); JOACHIM KOSTRAU (Grant County); ALAN LORENZ (La Crosse County); DENNIS DONATH (Pierce County); DAVID SMITH (Pepin County); JEAN GALASINSKI (Trempealeau County); MAYNARD COX (Vernon County). (Legislators are nominated by presiding officer and appointed by governor. County representatives are appointed by governor.) Nonvoting members: CATHY STEPP (secretary of natural resources), MARK GOTTLIEB (secretary of transportation), ELLSWORTH BROWN (director, state historical society), STEPHANIE KLETT (secretary of tourism).

Mailing Address: National Office, 701 East Washington Avenue, #202, Madison 53703.

Telephone: (866) 763-8310.

Statutory Reference: Section 14.85.

Agency Responsibility: The Mississippi River Parkway Commission coordinates development and preservation of Wisconsin's portion of the Great River Road corridor along the Mississippi River. It assists and advises state and local agencies about maintaining and enhancing the scenic, historic, economic, and recreational assets within the corridor and cooperates with similar commissions in other Mississippi River states and the Province of Ontario. On June 15, 2000, the U.S. Secretary of Transportation designated the entire 250-mile length of the Wisconsin Great River Road as a National Scenic Byway, thereby recognizing it as an outstanding example of America's scenic beauty. It is Wisconsin's only National Scenic Byway.

Organization: The 16-member Wisconsin commission includes 12 voting members, appointed to 4-year terms, and 4 nonvoting *ex officio* members. The 4 legislative members represent the two major political parties in each house.

The commission selects its own chairperson who is Wisconsin's sole voting representative at national meetings of the Mississippi River Parkway Commission.

History: The Wisconsin commission is part of the Mississippi River Parkway Commission, which was given statutory recognition by Chapter 482, Laws of 1961. It dates back to 1939 when Wisconsin Governor Julius P. Heil appointed a 10-member committee to cooperate with agencies from other Mississippi River states in planning the Great River Road. This scenic route extends from the Gulf of Mexico to the Mississippi River's headwaters at Lake Itasca, Minnesota. North of Lake Itasca, the route connects with the Trans-Canada Highway and terminates at Minaki, Ontario.

The Federal Highway Aid Acts of 1973, 1976, and 1978 provided Wisconsin approximately $21 million in Great River Road funding. While categorical funding is no longer available, the Wisconsin Department of Transportation has continued improvements to Wisconsin's portion of the Great River Road, including pedestrian and bicycle trails, landscaping, preservation of historic sites, and other programs. Wisconsin also received more than $7 million in discretionary grants from the National Scenic Byways Program from 2000 through 2008. These grants were matched with 20% state and local government funds.

UPPER MISSISSIPPI RIVER BASIN ASSOCIATION

Wisconsin Representative: DAN BAUMANN, JAMES FISCHER (alternate) (appointed by governor).

Mailing Addresses: Wisconsin representative: 1300 West Clairemont Avenue, Eau Claire 54701. Upper Mississippi River Basin Association: DRU BUNTIN, *executive director,* 415 Hamm Building, 408 St. Peter Street, St. Paul, Minnesota 55102.

Telephones: Wisconsin: (715) 839-3722; Minnesota: (651) 224-2880.

Internet Address: www.umrba.org

Agency Responsibility: The Upper Mississippi River Basin Association is a nonprofit organization created by Illinois, Iowa, Minnesota, Missouri, and Wisconsin to facilitate cooperative action regarding the basin's water and related land resources. It sponsors studies of river-related issues, cooperative planning for use of the region's resources, and an information exchange. It also enables the member states to develop regional positions on resource issues and to advocate the basin states' collective interests before the U.S. Congress and federal agencies. The association has placed major emphasis on its Environmental Management Program, a partnership among the U.S. Army Corps of Engineers, the U.S. Fish and Wildlife Service, and the five states. This program, which was approved by the federal Water Resources Development Act of 1986, authorized habitat rehabilitation projects, resource inventory and analysis, recreation projects, and river traffic monitoring.

Organization: The association consists of one representative from each member state. The members annually elect one of their number to serve as chairperson. Five federal agencies with major water resources responsibilities serve as advisory members: the Environmental Protection Agency and the U.S. Departments of Agriculture, Army, Interior, and Transportation.

History: The Upper Mississippi River Basin Association was formed on December 2, 1981, when the articles of association were signed by representatives of the member states. In late 1983 and early 1984, executive orders were issued by four of the five governors reaffirming membership in the association.

Children playing in the water at Lakewood Resort. (Department of Tourism)

INTERSTATE COMPACTS

Interstate Compact on Adoption and Medical Assistance

The compact authorizes the Department of Children and Families, on behalf of this state, to enter into interstate agreements, including the interstate compact on adoption and medical assistance, with other states that enter into adoption assistance agreements. In these agreements, other states must provide Medical Assistance (MA) benefits, under its own laws, to children who were adopted as residents of Wisconsin, and Wisconsin must provide the same benefits to children who were adopted as residents of other states. Any interstate agreement is revocable upon written notice to the other state but remains in effect for one year after the date of the notice. Benefits already granted continue even if the agreement is revoked. The compact has been adopted by 49 states and the District of Columbia. (1985 Wisconsin Act 308)

Statutory Reference: Section 48.9985.

Administrator: Department of Children and Families.

Interstate Compact for Adult Offender Supervision

The compact creates cooperative procedures for individuals placed on parole, probation, or extended supervision in one state to be supervised in another state if certain conditions are met. The compact has been adopted by all 50 states, the District of Columbia, U.S. Virgin Islands, and Puerto Rico. (2001 Wisconsin Act 96)

Statutory Reference: Section 304.16.

Administrator: Department of Corrections (appointed by governor).

Corrections Compact

The compact allows Wisconsin to enter into contracts with states that are party to the compact to confine Wisconsin's inmates in the other state's correctional facilities or receive inmates from other states. The contract provides for inmate upkeep and special services. The compact has been adopted by 39 states and the District of Columbia. (Chapter 20, Laws of 1981)

Statutory Reference: Sections 302.25-302.26.

Administrator: Department of Corrections.

Agreement on Detainers

The agreement is designed to clear up indictments or complaints that serve as a basis for a detainer lodged against a prisoner incarcerated in one jurisdiction and wanted in another. The agreement allows the state making the request to obtain temporary custody of the prisoner to conduct a trial on outstanding charges. The agreement has been adopted by 48 states and the District of Columbia. (Chapter 255, Laws of 1969)

Statutory Reference: Sections 976.05 and 976.06.

Emergency Management Assistance Compact

The compact authorizes states that are members to provide mutual assistance to other member states in an emergency or disaster declared by the governor of the affected state. Under the compact, member states cooperate in emergency-related training and formulate plans for interstate cooperation in responding to a disaster. All 50 states belong to the compact. (1999 Wisconsin Act 26)

Statutory Reference: Section 323.80.

Administrator: Division of Emergency Management, Department of Military Affairs.

Interstate Compact on Mental Health

The compact facilitates the proper and expeditious treatment of persons with mental illness or mental retardation by the cooperative action of the party states, to the benefit of the person, their families, and society. The compact (and enacting laws) provides for this to be done irrespective of the legal residence and citizenship status of the person. The compact has been adopted in 45 states and the District of Columbia. (Chapter 611, Laws of 1965)

Statutory Reference: Sections 51.75-51.80.

Administrator: Department of Health Services.

Nurse Licensure Compact

The compact allows a nurse licensed by a party state to practice nursing in any other party state without obtaining a license. It requires each party state to participate in a database of all licensed nurses. The compact has been adopted by 24 states. (1999 Wisconsin Act 22)

Statutory Reference: Section 441.50.

Administrator: Department of Safety and Professional Services.

Interstate Compact on Placement of Children

The compact provides a legal framework to administer the compact law among the party states to ensure protection and services when a child is placed across state lines when under the jurisdiction of that state and the most suitable placement is in a different state. It requires notice and proof of appropriateness and safety before a placement is made; allocates legal and administrative responsibilities by the sending state for the duration of placement; provides a basis for enforcement of rights; and authorizes joint actions to improve operations and services. All states have adopted the compact. (Chapter 354, Laws of 1977)

Statutory Reference: Sections 48.988 and 48.989.

Administrator: Department of Children and Families.

Interstate Agreement on Qualification of Educational Personnel

The agreement authorizes the State Superintendent of Public Instruction to enter into contracts with party states to accept their educational personnel. These agreements allow Wisconsin to offer initial licenses to teachers from contracting states and allows other states to accept Wisconsin-trained teachers on the same basis. The agreement has been adopted by 35 states and the District of Columbia. (Chapter 42, Laws of 1969)

Statutory Reference: Sections 115.46-115.48.

Administrator: State Superintendent of Public Instruction.

Judicial Branch

7

The judicial branch: profile of the judicial branch, summary of recent significant supreme court decisions, and descriptions of the supreme court, court system, and judicial service agencies

Cassius Fairchild

(Wisconsin Veterans Museum)

WISCONSIN SUPREME COURT

Justice	First Assumed Office	Began First Elected Term	Current Term Expires July 31
Shirley S. Abrahamson.	1976*	August 1979	2019
Ann Walsh Bradley	1995	August 1995	2015**
N. Patrick Crooks	1996	August 1996	2016
David T. Prosser, Jr.	1998*	August 2001	2021
Patience Drake Roggensack, Chief Justice	2003	August 2003	2023
Annette K. Ziegler.	2007	August 2007	2017
Michael J. Gableman	2008	August 2008	2018

*Initially appointed by the governor.

**Justice Bradley was reelected to a new term beginning August 1, 2015, and expiring July 31, 2025.

Seated, from left to right are Justice Annette K. Ziegler, Justice N. Patrick Crooks, Justice Shirley S. Abrahamson, Chief Justice Patience D. Roggensack, Justice Ann Walsh Bradley, Justice David T. Prosser, Jr., and Justice Michael J. Gableman. (Wisconsin Supreme Court)

JUDICIAL BRANCH

A PROFILE OF THE JUDICIAL BRANCH

Introducing the Court System. The judicial branch and its system of various courts may appear very complex to the nonlawyer. It is well-known that the courts are required to try persons accused of violating criminal law and that conviction in the trial court may result in punishment by fine or imprisonment or both. The courts also decide civil matters between private citizens, ranging from landlord-tenant disputes to adjudication of corporate liability involving many millions of dollars and months of costly litigation. In addition, the courts act as referees between citizens and their government by determining the permissible limits of governmental power and the extent of an individual's rights and responsibilities.

A court system that strives for fairness and justice must settle disputes on the basis of appropriate rules of law. These rules are derived from a variety of sources, including the state and federal constitutions, legislative acts and administrative rules, as well as the "common law", which reflects society's customs and experience as expressed in previous court decisions. This body of law is constantly changing to meet the needs of an increasingly complex world. The courts have the task of seeking the delicate balance between the flexibility and the stability needed to protect the fundamental principles of the constitutional system of the United States.

The Supreme Court. The judicial branch is headed by the Wisconsin Supreme Court of 7 justices, each elected statewide to a 10-year term. The supreme court is primarily an appellate court and serves as Wisconsin's "court of last resort". It also exercises original jurisdiction in a small number of cases of statewide concern. There are no appeals to the supreme court as a matter of right. Instead, the court has discretion to determine which appeals it will hear.

In addition to hearing cases on appeal from the court of appeals, there also are three instances in which the supreme court, at its discretion, may decide to bypass the appeals court. First, the supreme court may review a case on its own initiative. Second, it may decide to review a matter without an appellate decision based on a petition by one of the parties. Finally, the supreme court may take jurisdiction in a case if the appeals court finds it needs guidance on a legal question and requests supreme court review under a procedure known as "certification".

The Court of Appeals. The Court of Appeals, created August 1, 1978, is divided into 4 appellate districts covering the state, and there are 16 appellate judges, each elected to a 6-year term. The "court chambers", or principal offices for the districts, are located in Madison (5 judges), Milwaukee (4 judges), Waukesha (4 judges), and Wausau (3 judges).

In the appeals court, 3-judge panels hear all cases, except small claims actions, municipal ordinance violations, traffic violations, and mental health, juvenile, and misdemeanor cases. These exceptions may be heard by a single judge unless a panel is requested.

Circuit Courts. Following a 1977-78 reorganization of the Wisconsin court system, the circuit court became the "single level" trial court for the state. Circuit court boundaries were revised so that, except for 3 combined-county circuits (Buffalo-Pepin, Florence-Forest, and Menominee-Shawano), each county became a circuit, resulting in a total of 69 circuits.

In the more populous counties, a circuit may have several branches with one judge assigned to each branch. As of August 1, 2014, Wisconsin had a combined total of 249 circuits or circuit branches and the same number of circuit judgeships, with each judge elected to a 6-year term. For administrative purposes, the circuit court system is divided into 10 judicial administrative districts, each headed by a chief judge appointed by the supreme court. The circuit courts are funded with a combination of state and county money. For example, state funds are used to pay the salaries of judges, and counties are responsible for most court operating costs.

A final judgment by the circuit court can be appealed to the Wisconsin Court of Appeals, but a decision by the appeals court can be reviewed only if the Wisconsin Supreme Court grants a petition for review.

Municipal Courts. Individually or jointly, cities, villages, and towns may create municipal courts with jurisdiction over municipal ordinance violations that have monetary penalties. There are more than 200 municipal courts in Wisconsin. These courts are not courts of record, and they have limited jurisdiction. Usually, municipal judgeships are not full-time positions.

Selection and Qualification of Judges. In Wisconsin, all justices and judges are elected on a nonpartisan ballot in April. The Wisconsin Constitution provides that supreme court justices and appellate and circuit judges must have been licensed to practice law in Wisconsin for at least 5 years prior to election or appointment. While state law does not require that municipal judges be attorneys, municipalities may impose such a qualification in their jurisdictions.

Supreme court justices are elected on a statewide basis; appeals court and circuit court judges are elected in their respective districts. The governor may make an appointment to fill a vacancy in the office of justice or judge to serve until a successor is elected. When the election is held, the candidate elected assumes the office for a full term.

Since 1955, Wisconsin has permitted retired justices and judges to serve as "reserve" judges. At the request of the chief justice of the supreme court, reserve judges fill vacancies temporarily or help to relieve congested calendars. They exercise all the powers of the court to which they are assigned.

Judicial Agencies Assisting the Courts. Numerous state agencies assist the courts. The Wisconsin Supreme Court appoints the Director of State Courts, the State Law Librarian and staff, the Board of Bar Examiners, the director of the Office of Lawyer Regulation, and the Judicial Education Committee. Other agencies that assist the judicial branch include the Judicial Commission, Judicial Council, and the State Bar of Wisconsin.

The shared concern of these agencies is to improve the organization, operation, administration, and procedures of the state judicial system. They also function to promote professional standards, judicial ethics, and legal research and reform.

Court Process in Wisconsin. Both state and federal courts have jurisdiction over Wisconsin citizens. State courts generally adjudicate cases pertaining to state laws, but the federal government may give state courts jurisdiction over specified federal questions. Courts handle two types of cases – civil and criminal.

Civil Cases. Generally, civil actions involve individual claims in which a person seeks a remedy for some wrong done by another. For example, if a person has been injured in an automobile accident, the complaining party (plaintiff) may sue the offending party (defendant) to compel payment for the injuries.

In a typical civil case, the plaintiff brings an action by filing a summons and a complaint with the circuit court. The defendant is served with copies of these documents, and the summons directs the defendant to respond to the plaintiff's attorney. Various pretrial proceedings, such as pleadings, motions, pretrial conferences, and discovery, may be required. If no settlement is reached, the matter goes to trial. The U.S. and Wisconsin Constitutions guarantee trial by jury, except in cases involving an equitable action, such as a divorce action. In civil actions, unless a party demands a jury trial and pays the required fee, the trial may be conducted by the court without a jury. The jury in a civil case consists of 6 persons unless a greater number, not to exceed 12, is requested. Five-sixths of the jurors must agree on the verdict. Based on the verdict, the court enters a judgment for the plaintiff or defendant.

Wisconsin law provides for small claims actions that are streamlined and informal. These actions typically involve the collection of small personal or commercial debts and are limited to questions of $10,000 or less except for third party complaints, personal injury claims, and actions based in torts where the limit is $5,000 or less. Small claims cases are decided by the circuit court judge, unless a jury trial is requested. Attorneys commonly are not used.

Criminal Cases. Under Wisconsin law, criminal conduct is an act prohibited by state law and punishable by a fine or imprisonment or both. There are two types of crime – felonies and misdemeanors. A felony is punishable by confinement in a state prison for one year or more; all other crimes are misdemeanors punishable by imprisonment in a county jail. Misdemeanors have a maximum sentence of 12 months unless the violator is a "repeater" as defined in the statutes.

Because a crime is an offense against the state, the state, rather than the crime victim, brings action against the defendant. A typical criminal action begins when the district attorney, an elected official, files a criminal complaint in the circuit court stating the essential facts concerning the offense charged. The defendant may or may not be arrested at that time. If the defendant has not yet been arrested, generally the judge or a court commissioner then issues an "arrest warrant" in the case of a felony or a "summons" in the case of a misdemeanor. A law enforcement officer then must serve a copy of the warrant or summons on an individual and, in the case of a warrant, make an arrest.

Once in custody, the defendant is taken before a circuit judge or court commissioner, informed of the charges, and given the opportunity to be represented by a lawyer at public expense if he or she cannot afford to hire one. Bail is usually set at this time. In the case of a misdemeanor, a trial date is set. In felony cases, the defendant has a right to a preliminary examination, which is a hearing before the court to determine whether the state has probable cause to charge the individual.

If the preliminary examination is waived, or if it is held and probable cause found, the district attorney files an information (a sworn accusation on which the indictment is based) with the court. The arraignment is then held before the circuit court judge, and the defendant enters a plea ("guilty", "not guilty", "no contest subject to the approval of the court", or "not guilty by reason of mental disease or defect").

Following further pretrial proceedings, if a plea agreement is not reached, the case goes to trial in circuit court. Criminal cases are tried by a jury of 12, unless the defendant waives a jury trial or there is agreement for fewer jurors. The jury considers the evidence presented at the trial, determines the facts and renders a verdict of guilty or not guilty based on instructions given by the circuit judge. If the jury issues a verdict of guilty, a judgment of conviction is entered and the court determines the sentence. In a felony case, the court may order a presentence investigation before pronouncing sentence.

In a criminal case, the jury's verdict to convict the defendant must be unanimous. If not, the defendant is acquitted (cleared of the charge) or, if the jury is unable to reach a unanimous verdict, the court may declare a mistrial and the prosecutor may seek a new trial. Once acquitted, a person cannot be tried again in criminal court for the same charge, based on provisions in both the federal and state constitutions that prevent double jeopardy. Aggrieved parties may, however, bring a civil action against the individual for damages, based on the incident.

History of the Court System. The basic powers and framework of the court system were established by Article VII of the state constitution when Wisconsin gained statehood in 1848. At that time, judicial power was vested in a supreme court, circuit courts, courts of probate, and justices of the peace. Subject to certain limitations, the legislature was granted power to establish inferior courts and municipal courts and determine their jurisdiction.

The constitution originally divided the state into five judicial circuit districts. The five judges who presided over those circuit courts were to meet at least once a year at Madison as a "Supreme Court" until the legislature established a separate court. The Wisconsin Supreme Court was instituted in 1853 with 3 members chosen in statewide elections – one was elected as chief justice and the other 2 as associate justices. In 1877, a constitutional amendment increased the number of associate justices to 4. An 1889 amendment prescribed the current practice under which all court members are elected as justices. Until a constitutional amendment was passed in 2015, the justice with the longest continuous service presided as chief justice. Under the new constitutional provision, the chief justice is elected by a majority of the justices for a 2-year term. Since 1903, the constitution has required a court of 7 members.

Over the years, the legislature created a large number of courts with varying types of jurisdiction. As a result of numerous special laws, there was no uniformity among the counties. Different types of courts in a single county had overlapping jurisdiction, and procedure in the various courts was not the same. A number of special courts sprang up in heavily urbanized areas, such as Milwaukee County, where the judicial burden was the greatest. In addition, many municipalities established police justice courts for enforcement of local ordinances, and there were some 1,800 justices of the peace.

The 1959 Legislature enacted Chapter 315, effective January 1, 1962, which provided for the initial reorganization of the court system. The most significant feature of the reorganization was the abolition of special statutory courts (municipal, district, superior, civil, and small claims). In addition, a uniform system of jurisdiction and procedure was established for all county courts.

The 1959 law also created the machinery for smoother administration of the court system. One problem under the old system was the imbalance of caseloads from one jurisdiction to another. In some cases, the workload was not evenly distributed among the judges within the same jurisdiction. To correct this, the chief justice of the supreme court was authorized to assign circuit and county judges to serve temporarily as needed in either type of court. The 1961 Legislature took another step to assist the chief justice in these assignments by creating the post of Administrative Director of Courts. This position has since been redefined by the supreme court and renamed the Director of State Courts. Over the years, the director has been given added administrative duties and increased staff to perform them.

The last step in the 1959 reorganization effort was the April 1966 ratification of two constitutional amendments that abolished the justices of the peace and permitted municipal courts. At this point the Wisconsin system of courts consisted of the supreme court, circuit courts, county courts, and municipal courts.

In April 1977, the court of appeals was authorized when the voters ratified an amendment to Article VII, Section 2, of the Wisconsin Constitution, which outlined the current structure of the state courts:

> The judicial power of this state shall be vested in a unified court system consisting of one supreme court, a court of appeals, a circuit court, such trial courts of general uniform statewide jurisdiction as the legislature may create by law, and a municipal court if authorized by the legislature under section 14.

In June 1978, the legislature implemented the constitutional amendment by enacting Chapter 449, Laws of 1977, which added the court of appeals to the system and eliminated county courts.

Justice David T. Prosser discusses the role of the Supreme Court and the process it uses to decide cases with students from D.C. Everest Senior High School as part of the Court with Class education program. Each year, hundreds of students visit the Supreme Court Hearing Room, listen to oral arguments and meet with a justice. (Tom Sheehan, Wisconsin Supreme Court)

SUPREME COURT

Chief Justice: PATIENCE DRAKE ROGGENSACK
Justices: SHIRLEY S. ABRAHAMSON
ANN WALSH BRADLEY
N. PATRICK CROOKS
DAVID T. PROSSER, JR.
ANNETTE K. ZIEGLER
MICHAEL J. GABLEMAN

Mailing Address: Supreme Court and Clerk: P.O. Box 1688, Madison 53701-1688.

Locations: Supreme Court: Room 16 East, State Capitol, Madison; Clerk: 110 East Main Street, Madison.

Telephone: 266-1298.

Fax: 261-8299.

Internet Address: www.wicourts.gov

Clerk of Supreme Court: DIANE FREMGEN, 266-1880, Fax: 267-0640.

Court Commissioners: NANCY KOPP, MARK NEUSER, JULIE RICH, DAVID RUNKE; 266-7442.

Number of Positions: 38.50.

Total Budget 2013-15: $10,097,300.

Constitutional References: Article VII, Sections 2-4, 9-13, and 24.

Statutory Reference: Chapter 751.

Responsibility: The Wisconsin Supreme Court is the final authority on matters pertaining to the Wisconsin Constitution and the highest tribunal for all actions begun in the state, except those involving federal issues appealable to the U.S. Supreme Court. The court decides which cases it will hear, usually on the basis of whether the questions raised are of statewide importance. It exercises "appellate jurisdiction" if 3 or more justices grant a petition to review a decision of a lower court. It exercises "original jurisdiction" as the first court to hear a case if 4 or more justices approve a petition requesting it to do so. Although the majority of cases advance from the circuit court to the court of appeals before reaching the supreme court, the high court may decide to bypass the court of appeals. The supreme court can do this on its own motion or at the request of the parties; in addition, the court of appeals may certify a case to the supreme court, asking the high court to take the case directly from the circuit court.

The supreme court does not take testimony. Instead, it decides cases on the basis of written briefs and oral argument. It is required by statute to deliver its decisions in writing, and it may publish them in the *Wisconsin Reports* as it deems appropriate.

The supreme court sets procedural rules for all courts in the state, and the chief justice serves as administrative head of the state's judicial system. With the assistance of the director of state courts, the chief justice monitors the status of judicial business in Wisconsin's courts. When a calendar is congested or a vacancy occurs in a circuit or appellate court, the chief justice may assign an active judge or reserve judge to serve temporarily as a judge of either type of court.

Organization: The supreme court consists of 7 justices elected to 10-year terms. They are chosen in statewide elections on the nonpartisan April ballot and take office on the following August 1. The Wisconsin Constitution provides that only one justice can be elected in any single year, so supreme court vacancies are sometimes filled by gubernatorial appointees who serve until a successor can be elected. The authorized salary for supreme court justices for 2014 is $147,403. The chief justice receives $155,403.

In April 2015, voters amended the state constitution to allow the justices to elect the chief justice by a majority vote for a term of 2 years. Prior to this, the justice with the most seniority on the court served as chief justice unless he or she declined the position. Any 4 justices constitute a quorum for conducting court business.

The court staff is appointed from outside the classified service. It includes the director of state courts who assists the court in its administrative functions; 4 commissioners who are attorneys and assist the court in its judicial functions; a clerk who keeps the court's records; and a marshal who performs a variety of duties. Each justice has a secretary and one law clerk.

WISCONSIN COURT SYSTEM – ADMINISTRATIVE STRUCTURE

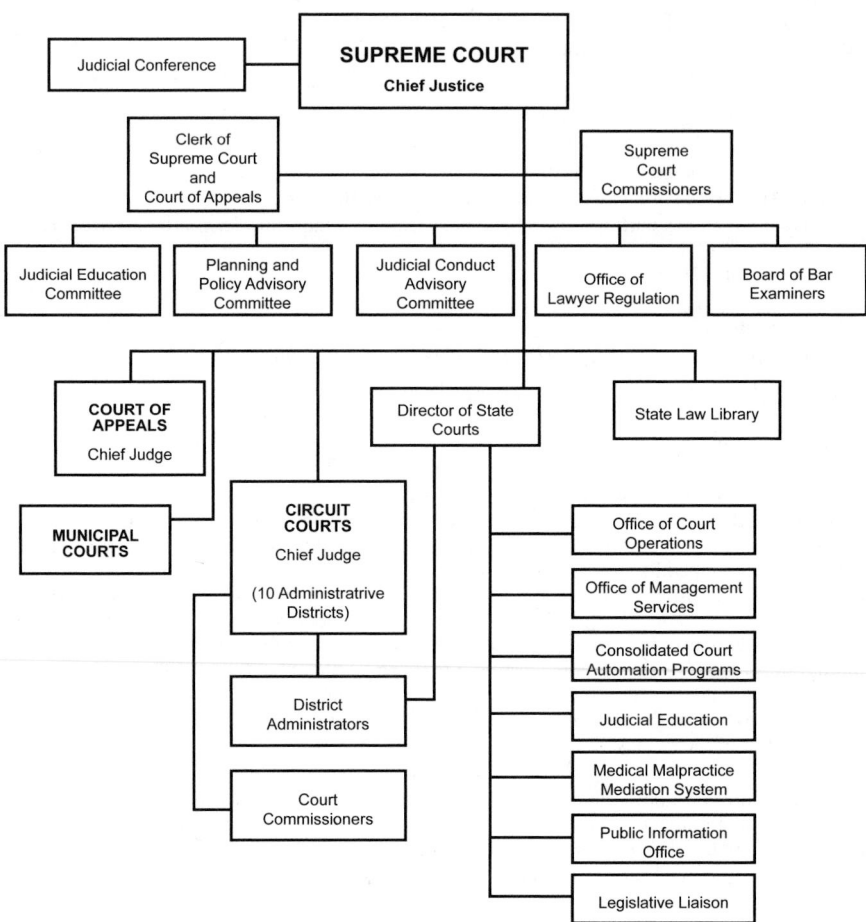

Independent Bodies: Judicial Commission; Judicial Council
Associated unit: State Bar of Wisconsin

COURT OF APPEALS

Judges: District I: REBECCA BRADLEY (2017)
KITTY K. BRENNAN (2021)
PATRICIA S. CURLEY* (2020)
JOAN F. KESSLER (2016)
District II: RICHARD S. BROWN** (2018)
MARK D. GUNDRUM (2019)
LISA S. NEUBAUER* (2020)
PAUL F. REILLY (2016)
District III: MICHAEL W. HOOVER† (2015)
THOMAS M. HRUZ (2016)
LISA K. STARK* (2019)
District IV: BRIAN W. BLANCHARD* (2016)
PAUL B. HIGGINBOTHAM (2017)
JOANNE F. KLOPPENBURG (2018)
PAUL LUNDSTEN (2019)
GARY E. SHERMAN (2020)

Note: *Indicates the presiding judge of the district. **Indicates chief judge of the court of appeals. Lisa S. Neubauer has been appointed chief judge as of August 2, 2015. The judges' current terms expire on July 31 of the year shown. †Mark A. Seidl elected April 7, 2015, to take office August 1, 2015.

Court of Appeals Clerk: DIANE M. FREMGEN, P.O. Box 1688, Madison 53701-1688; Location: 110 East Main Street, Suite 215, Madison, 266-1880, Fax: 267-0640.

Central Staff Attorneys: 10 East Doty Street, 7th Floor, Madison 53703, 266-9320.

Internet Address: www.wicourts.gov/courts/appeals/index.htm

Number of Positions: 75.50.

Total Budget 2013-15: $20,514,200.

Constitutional Reference: Article VII, Section 5.

Statutory Reference: Chapter 752.

Organization: A constitutional amendment ratified on April 5, 1977, mandated the Court of Appeals, and Chapter 187, Laws of 1977, implemented the amendment. The court consists of 16 judges serving in 4 districts (4 judges each in Districts I and II, 3 judges in District III, and 5 judges in District IV). The Wisconsin Supreme Court appoints a chief judge of the court of appeals to serve as administrative head of the court for a 3-year term, and the clerk of the supreme court serves as the clerk for the court.

Appellate judges are elected for 6-year terms in the nonpartisan April election and begin their terms of office on the following August 1. They must reside in the district from which they are chosen. Only one court of appeals judge may be elected in a district in any one year. The authorized salary for appeals court judges for 2015 is $139,059.

Functions: The court of appeals has both appellate and supervisory jurisdiction, as well as original jurisdiction to issue prerogative writs. The final judgments and orders of a circuit court may be appealed to the court of appeals as a matter of right. Other judgments or orders may be appealed upon leave of the appellate court.

The court usually sits as a 3-judge panel to dispose of cases on their merits. However, a single judge may decide certain categories of cases, including juvenile cases; small claims; municipal ordinance and traffic violations; and mental health and misdemeanor cases. No testimony is taken in the appellate court. The court relies on the trial court record and written briefs in deciding a case, and it prescreens all cases to determine whether oral argument is needed. Both oral argument and "briefs only" cases are placed on a regularly issued calendar. The court gives criminal cases preference on the calendar when it is possible to do so without undue delay of civil cases. Staff attorneys, judicial assistants, and law clerks assist the judges.

Decisions of the appellate court are delivered in writing, and the court's publication committee determines which decisions will be published in the *Wisconsin Reports*. Only published opinions have precedential value and may be cited as controlling law in Wisconsin. Unpublished opinions that are authored by a judge and issued after July 1, 2009, may be cited for their persuasive value.

District I: 330 East Kilbourn Avenue, Suite 1020, Milwaukee 53202-3161. Telephone: (414) 227-4680.

District II: 2727 North Grandview Boulevard, Suite 300, Waukesha 53188-1672. Telephone: (262) 521-5230.

District III: 2100 Stewart Avenue, Suite 310, Wausau 54401-1700. Telephone: (715) 848-1421.

District IV: 10 East Doty Street, Suite 700, Madison 53703-3397. Telephone: (608) 266-9250.

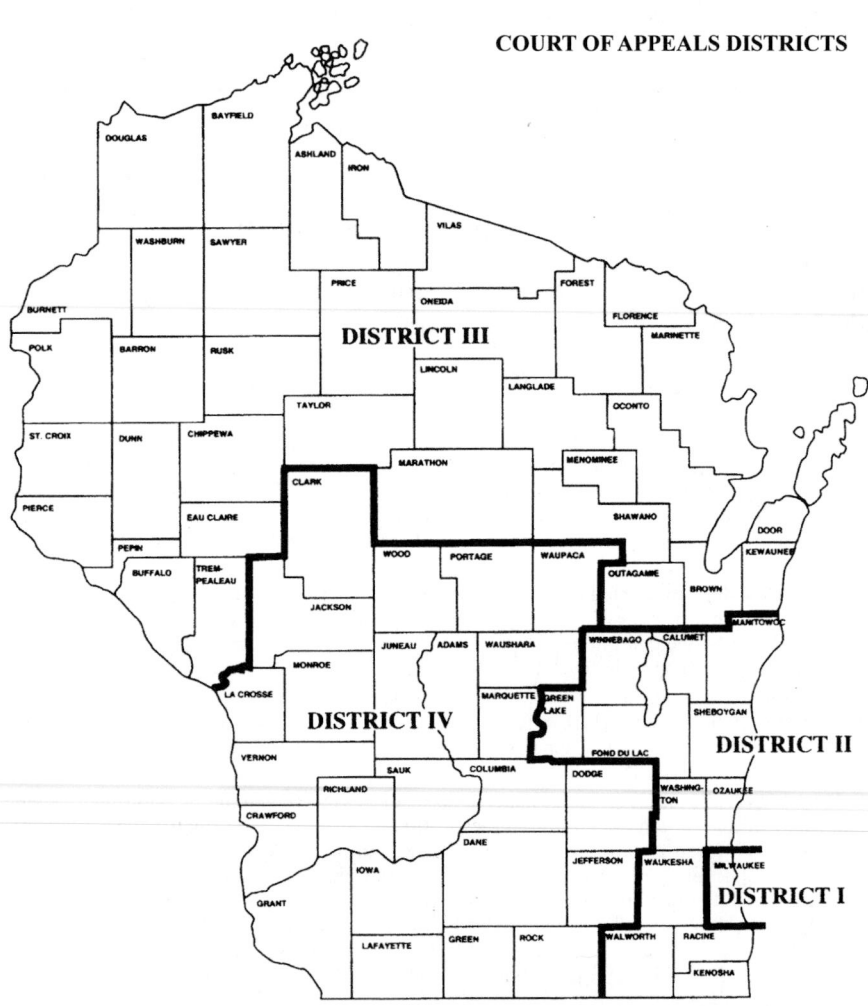

COURT OF APPEALS DISTRICTS

CIRCUIT COURTS

District 1: Milwaukee County Courthouse, 901 North 9th Street, Room 609, Milwaukee 53233-1425. Telephone: (414) 278-5113; Fax: (414) 223-1264.
Chief Judge: JEFFREY KREMERS (MAXINE WHITE as of 8/1/2015).
Administrator: HOLLY SZABLEWSKI.

District 2: Racine County Courthouse, 730 Wisconsin Avenue, Racine 53403-1274. Telephone: (262) 636-3133; Fax: (262) 636-3437.
Chief Judge: ALLAN TORHORST.
Administrator: THERESA OWENS.

District 3: Waukesha County Courthouse, 515 West Moreland Boulevard, Room 359, Waukesha 53188-2428. Telephone: (262) 548-7209; Fax: (262) 548-7815.
Chief Judge: RANDY KOSCHNICK.
Administrator: MICHAEL NEIMON.

District 4: 415 Jackson Street, Room 510, P.O. Box 2808, Oshkosh 54903-2808.
Telephone: (920) 424-0028; Fax: (920) 424-0096.
Chief Judge: ROBERT WIRTZ.
Administrator: JON BELLOWS.

District 5: Dane County Courthouse, 215 South Hamilton Street, Madison 53703-3290.
Telephone: 267-8820; Fax: 267-4151.
Chief Judge: JAMES P. DALEY.
Administrator: GAIL RICHARDSON.

District 6: 3317 Business Park Drive, Suite A, Stevens Point 54481-8834.
Telephone: (715) 345-5295; Fax: (715) 345-5297.
Chief Judge: GREGORY POTTER.
Administrator: RON LEDFORD.

District 7: La Crosse County Law Enforcement Center, 333 Vine Street, Room 3504, La Crosse 54601-3296. Telephone: (608) 785-9546; Fax: (608) 785-5530.
Chief Judge: JAMES J. DUVALL.
Administrator: PATRICK BRUMMOND.

District 8: 414 East Walnut Street, Suite 100, Green Bay 54301-5020.
Telephone: (920) 448-4281; Fax: (920) 448-4336.
Chief Judge: DONALD ZUIDMULDER.
Administrator: DONALD HARPER.

District 9: 2100 Stewart Avenue, Suite 310, Wausau 54401.
Telephone: (715) 842-3872; Fax: (715) 845-4523.
Chief Judge: NEAL NIELSEN.
Administrator: SUSAN BYRNES.

District 10: 4410 Golf Terrace, Suite 150, Eau Claire 54701-3606.
Telephone: (715) 839-4826; Fax: (715) 839-4891.
Chief Judge: SCOTT NEEDHAM.
Administrator: KRISTINA ASCHENBRENNER.

Internet Address: www.wicourts.gov/courts/circuit/index.htm

State-Funded Positions: 527.00.

Total Budget 2013-15: $189,467,400.

Constitutional References: Article VII, Sections 2, 6-13.

Statutory Reference: Chapter 753.

Responsibility: The circuit court is the trial court of general jurisdiction in Wisconsin. It has original jurisdiction in both civil and criminal matters unless exclusive jurisdiction is given to another court. It also reviews state agency decisions and hears appeals from municipal courts. Jury trials are conducted only in circuit courts.

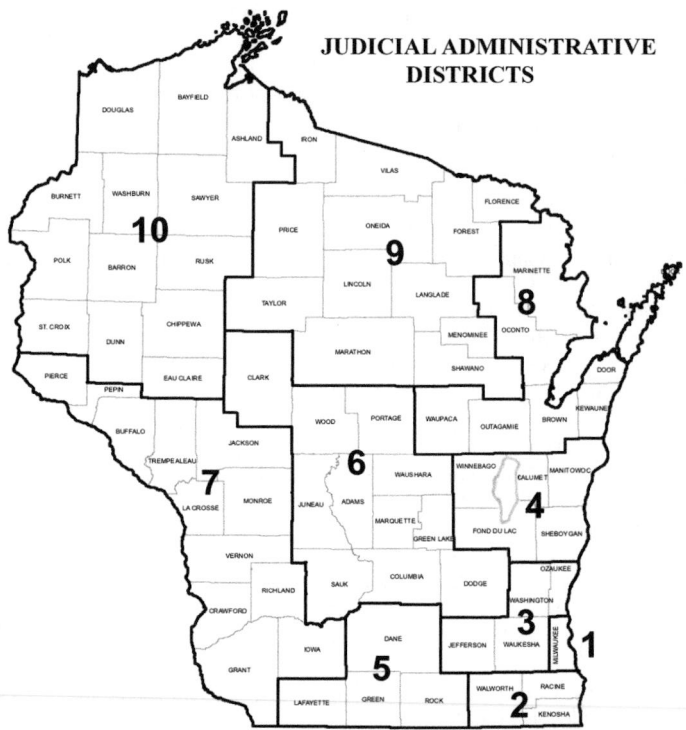

JUDICIAL ADMINISTRATIVE DISTRICTS

The constitution requires that a circuit be bounded by county lines. As a result, each circuit consists of a single county, except for 3 two-county circuits (Buffalo-Pepin, Florence-Forest, and Menominee-Shawano). Where judicial caseloads are heavy, a circuit may have several branches, each with an elected judge. Statewide, 40 of the state's 69 judicial circuits had multiple branches as of August 1, 2014, for a total of 249 circuit judgeships.

Organization: Circuit judges, who serve 6-year terms, are elected on a nonpartisan basis in the county in which they serve in the April election and take office the following August 1. The governor may fill circuit court vacancies by appointment, and the appointees serve until a successor is elected. The authorized salary for circuit court judges for 2014 is $131,187. The state pays the salaries of circuit judges and court reporters. It also covers some of the expenses for interpreters, guardians ad litem, judicial assistants, court-appointed witnesses, and jury per diems. Counties bear the remaining expenses for operating the circuit courts.

Administrative Districts. Circuit courts are divided into 10 administrative districts, each supervised by a chief judge, appointed by the supreme court from the district's circuit judges. A judge usually cannot serve more than 3 successive 2-year terms as chief judge. The chief judge has authority to assign judges, manage caseflow, supervise personnel, and conduct financial planning.

The chief judge in each district appoints a district court administrator from a list of candidates supplied by the director of state courts. The administrator manages the nonjudicial business of the district at the direction of the chief judge.

Circuit Court Commissioners are appointed by the circuit court to assist the court, and they must be attorneys licensed to practice law in Wisconsin. They may be authorized by the court to conduct various civil, criminal, family, small claims, juvenile, and probate court proceedings. Their duties include issuing summonses, arrest warrants, or search warrants; conducting initial appearances; setting bail; conducting preliminary examinations and arraignments; imposing monetary penalties in certain traffic cases; conducting certain family, juvenile, and small claims court proceedings; hearing petitions for mental commitments; and conducting uncontested probate proceedings. On their own authority, court commissioners may perform marriages, administer oaths, take depositions, and issue subpoenas and certain writs.

The statutes require Milwaukee County to have full-time family, small claims, and probate court commissioners. All other counties must have a family court commissioner, and they may employ other full- or part-time court commissioners as deemed necessary.

The Wisconsin Supreme Court holds oral argument in the Wisconsin Supreme Court Hearing Room at the State Capitol. Here, an overflow crowd gathered on February 25, 2014, to hear challenges to the validity of 2011 Act 23's photo identification voting requirements under the Wisconsin Constitution.
(Tom Sheehan, Wisconsin Supreme Court)

JUDGES OF CIRCUIT COURT
June 30, 2015

County Circuits	Court Location	Judges	Term Expires July 31
Adams	Friendship	Charles A. Pollex[1]	2015
Ashland	Ashland	Robert E. Eaton	2018
Barron			
Branch 1	Barron	James C. Babler	2016
Branch 2	Barron	J. Michael Bitney	2020
Branch 3	Barron	Maureen D. Boyle	2020
Bayfield	Washburn	John P. Anderson[2]	2015
Brown			
Branch 1	Green Bay	Donald R. Zuidmulder[2]	2015
Branch 2	Green Bay	Tom Walsh	2018
Branch 3	Green Bay	Tammy Jo Hock	2019
Branch 4	Green Bay	Kendall M. Kelley[2]	2015
Branch 5	Green Bay	Marc A. Hammer[2]	2015
Branch 6	Green Bay	John P. Zakowski	2018
Branch 7	Green Bay	Timothy A. Hinkfuss	2019
Branch 8	Green Bay	William M. Atkinson[2]	2015
Buffalo-Pepin	Alma	James J. Duvall	2018
Burnett	Siren	Kenneth Kutz[2]	2015
Calumet	Chilton	Jeffrey S. Froehlich	2018
Chippewa			
Branch 1	Chippewa Falls	Roderick A. Cameron	2020
Branch 2	Chippewa Falls	James Isaacson[2]	2015
Branch 3	Chippewa Falls	Steven R. Cray	2020
Clark	Neillsville	Jon M. Counsell	2018
Columbia			
Branch 1	Portage	Daniel S. George[3]	2015
Branch 2	Portage	W. Andrew Voigt	2017
Branch 3	Portage	Alan White	2019
Crawford	Prairie du Chien	James P. Czajkowski	2016
Dane			
Branch 1	Madison	John Markson	2020
Branch 2	Madison	Josann M. Reynolds[4,5]	2015
Branch 3	Madison	Jim Troupis[4]	2016
Branch 4	Madison	Amy Smith	2016
Branch 5	Madison	Nicholas J. McNamara	2016
Branch 6	Madison	Shelley J. Gaylord[2]	2015
Branch 7	Madison	William E. Hanrahan	2020
Branch 8	Madison	Frank D. Remington	2018
Branch 9	Madison	Richard Niess	2017
Branch 10	Madison	Juan B. Colas[2]	2015
Branch 11	Madison	Ellen K. Berz	2018
Branch 12	Madison	David T. Flanagan	2018
Branch 13	Madison	Julie Genovese[2]	2015
Branch 14	Madison	C. William Foust	2016
Branch 15	Madison	Stephen Ehlke	2016
Branch 16	Madison	Rhonda L. Lanford	2019
Branch 17	Madison	Peter C. Anderson	2016
Dodge			
Branch 1	Juneau	Brian A. Pfitzinger	2020
Branch 2	Juneau	John R. Storck	2019
Branch 3	Juneau	Joseph G. Sciascia	2019
Branch 4	Juneau	Steven Bauer	2020
Door			
Branch 1	Sturgeon Bay	D. Todd Ehlers	2018
Branch 2	Sturgeon Bay	Peter C. Diltz	2018
Douglas			
Branch 1	Superior	Kelly J. Thimm[2]	2015
Branch 2	Superior	George L. Glonek[2]	2015
Dunn			
Branch 1	Menomonie	James M. Peterson	2020
Branch 2	Menomonie	Rod W. Smeltzer[2]	2015
Eau Claire			
Branch 1	Eau Claire	vacancy	—
Branch 2	Eau Claire	Michael Schumacher	2020
Branch 3	Eau Claire	William M. Gabler	2018
Branch 4	Eau Claire	Jon M. Theisen	2018
Branch 5	Eau Claire	Paul J. Lenz	2018
Florence-Forest	Crandon	Leon D. Stenz	2020
Fond du Lac			
Branch 1	Fond du Lac	Dale L. English	2020
Branch 2	Fond du Lac	Peter L. Grimm	2016
Branch 3	Fond du Lac	Richard J. Nuss[2]	2015
Branch 4	Fond du Lac	Gary R. Sharpe	2016
Branch 5	Fond du Lac	Robert J. Wirtz	2017
Forest (see Florence-Forest)			
Grant			
Branch 1	Lancaster	Robert P. VanDeHey	2017
Branch 2	Lancaster	Craig R. Day[2]	2015
Green			
Branch 1	Monroe	Jim Beer[2]	2015
Branch 2	Monroe	Thomas J. Vale[2]	2015
Green Lake	Green Lake	Mark Slate	2017
Iowa	Dodgeville	William D. Dyke	2016
Iron	Hurley	Patrick John Madden	2017

JUDGES OF CIRCUIT COURT
June 30, 2015–Continued

County Circuits	Court Location	Judges	Term Expires July 31
Jackson	Black River Falls	Anna L. Becker[4,5]	2015
Jefferson			
Branch 1	Jefferson	Jennifer L. Weston[2]	2015
Branch 2	Jefferson	William F. Hue	2019
Branch 3	Jefferson	David J. Wambach	2020
Branch 4	Jefferson	Randy R. Koschnick	2017
Juneau			
Branch 1	Mauston	John Pier Roemer	2016
Branch 2	Mauston	Paul S. Curran	2020
Kenosha			
Branch 1	Kenosha	David Mark Bastianelli[2]	2015
Branch 2	Kenosha	Jason A. Rossell	2018
Branch 3	Kenosha	Bruce E. Schroeder	2020
Branch 4	Kenosha	Anthony Milisauskas	2017
Branch 5	Kenosha	David P. Wilk[4,5]	2015
Branch 6	Kenosha	Mary K. Wagner[2]	2015
Branch 7	Kenosha	S. Michael Wilk	2018
Branch 8	Kenosha	Chad G. Kerkman[2]	2015
Kewaunee	Kewaunee	Dennis J. Mleziva	2016
La Crosse			
Branch 1	La Crosse	Ramona A. Gonzalez	2019
Branch 2	La Crosse	Elliott Levine	2019
Branch 3	La Crosse	Todd Bjerke	2019
Branch 4	La Crosse	Scott L. Horne	2019
Branch 5	La Crosse	Candice Tlustosch[4,6]	2015
Lafayette	Darlington	William D. Johnston[7]	2015
Langlade	Antigo	vacancy[8]	—
Lincoln			
Branch 1	Merrill	Jay R. Tlusty	2016
Branch 2	Merrill	Robert Russell	2019
Manitowoc			
Branch 1	Manitowoc	Mark R. Rohrer	2019
Branch 2	Manitowoc	Gary Bendix	2018
Branch 3	Manitowoc	Jerome L. Fox	2017
Marathon			
Branch 1	Wausau	Jill N. Falstad[2]	2015
Branch 2	Wausau	Gregory Huber	2016
Branch 3	Wausau	Lamont K. Jacobson	2020
Branch 4	Wausau	Gregory Grau	2019
Branch 5	Wausau	Mike Moran	2017
Marinette			
Branch 1	Marinette	David G. Miron	2020
Branch 2	Marinette	James A. Morrison	2019
Marquette	Montello	Bernard Ben Bult	2019
Menominee-Shawano			
Branch 1	Shawano	James R. Habeck	2020
Branch 2	Shawano	William F. Kussel, Jr.	2018
Milwaukee			
Branch 1	Milwaukee	Maxine Aldridge White	2017
Branch 2	Wauwatosa	Joe Donald[2]	2015
Branch 3	Milwaukee	Clare L. Fiorenza[2]	2015
Branch 4	Milwaukee	Mel Flanagan	2018
Branch 5	Milwaukee	Mary Kuhnmuench	2016
Branch 6	Milwaukee	Ellen R. Brostrom[2]	2015
Branch 7	Milwaukee	Thomas J. McAdams	2020
Branch 8	Milwaukee	William Sosnay	2018
Branch 9	Milwaukee	Paul R. Van Grunsven	2017
Branch 10	Milwaukee	Timothy G. Dugan	2017
Branch 11	Milwaukee	Dave Swanson	2019
Branch 12	Milwaukee	David L. Borowski[2]	2015
Branch 13	Milwaukee	Mary Triggiano	2017
Branch 14	Milwaukee	Christopher R. Foley	2016
Branch 15	Milwaukee	J.D. Watts[2]	2015
Branch 16	Wauwatosa	Michael J. Dwyer[2]	2015
Branch 17	Milwaukee	Carolina Maria Stark	2018
Branch 18	Wauwatosa	Pedro Colón	2017
Branch 19	Wauwatosa	Dennis R. Cimpl	2017
Branch 20	Milwaukee	Dennis P. Moroney	2018
Branch 21	Milwaukee	William Brash III	2020
Branch 22	Milwaukee	Timothy M. Witkowiak[2]	2015
Branch 23	Milwaukee	Lindsey Grady	2018
Branch 24	Milwaukee	Janet Protasiewicz	2020
Branch 25	Milwaukee	Stephanie Rothstein	2016
Branch 26	Milwaukee	William Pocan	2019
Branch 27	Milwaukee	Kevin E. Martens	2020
Branch 28	Wauwatosa	Mark A. Sanders	2018
Branch 29	Milwaukee	Richard J. Sankovitz[2]	2015
Branch 30	Milwaukee	Jeffrey A. Conen[2]	2015
Branch 31	Milwaukee	Daniel A. Noonan	2020
Branch 32	Milwaukee	Laura Gramling Perez	2020
Branch 33	Milwaukee	Carl Ashley	2017
Branch 34	Milwaukee	Glenn H. Yamahiro	2016
Branch 35	Milwaukee	Frederick C. Rosa	2017
Branch 36	Milwaukee	Jeffrey A. Kremers	2017

JUDGES OF CIRCUIT COURT
June 30, 2015–Continued

County Circuits	Court Location	Judges	Term Expires July 31
Branch 37	Wauwatosa	T. Christopher Dee[4,5]	2015
Branch 38	Milwaukee	Jeffrey A. Wagner	2018
Branch 39	Milwaukee	Jane Carroll	2018
Branch 40	Milwaukee	Rebecca Dallett	2020
Branch 41	Wauwatosa	John J. DiMotto	2020
Branch 42	Milwaukee	David A. Hansher[2]	2015
Branch 43	Milwaukee	Marshall B. Murray	2018
Branch 44	Milwaukee	Daniel L. Konkol	2016
Branch 45	Wauwatosa	Rebecca G. Bradley	2019
Branch 46	Milwaukee	vacancy[9]	—
Branch 47	Milwaukee	John Siefert	2017
Monroe			
Branch 1	Sparta	Todd L. Ziegler	2019
Branch 2	Sparta	Mark L. Goodman	2016
Branch 3	Sparta	J. David Rice	2016
Oconto			
Branch 1	Oconto	Michael T. Judge	2017
Branch 2	Oconto	Jay N. Conley	2016
Oneida			
Branch 1	Rhinelander	Patrick F. O'Melia	2020
Branch 2	Rhinelander	Michael H. Bloom	2018
Outagamie			
Branch 1	Appleton	Mark McGinnis	2017
Branch 2	Appleton	Nancy J. Krueger	2020
Branch 3	Appleton	Mitchell J. Metropulos	2020
Branch 4	Appleton	Greg Gill, Jr.	2018
Branch 5	Appleton	Michael W. Gage[2]	2015
Branch 6	Appleton	Vincent Biskupic[4,5]	2015
Branch 7	Appleton	John A. Des Jardins	2018
Ozaukee			
Branch 1	Port Washington	Paul V. Malloy[2]	2015
Branch 2	Port Washington	Joe Voiland	2019
Branch 3	Port Washington	Sandy A. Williams[2]	2015
Pepin (see Buffalo-Pepin)			
Pierce	Ellsworth	Joe Boles	2016
Polk			
Branch 1	Balsam Lake	Molly E. GaleWyrick	2020
Branch 2	Balsam Lake	Jeff Anderson	2017
Portage			
Branch 1	Stevens Point	Thomas B. Eagon	2018
Branch 2	Stevens Point	John V. Finn	2019
Branch 3	Stevens Point	Thomas T. Flugaur	2018
Price	Phillips	Douglas T. Fox	2020
Racine			
Branch 1	Racine	Gerald P. Ptacek	2019
Branch 2	Racine	Eugene Gasiorkiewicz	2016
Branch 3	Racine	Emily S. Mueller	2017
Branch 4	Racine	John S. Jude	2016
Branch 5	Racine	Mike Piontek	2018
Branch 6	Racine	Wayne J. Marik[10]	2015
Branch 7	Racine	Charles H. Constantine	2020
Branch 8	Racine	Faye M. Flancher[2]	2015
Branch 9	Racine	Allan P. Torhorst[2]	2015
Branch 10	Racine	Timothy D. Boyle	2018
Richland	Richland Center	Andrew Sharp	2018
Rock			
Branch 1	Janesville	James P. Daley	2020
Branch 2	Janesville	Alan Bates	2016
Branch 3	Janesville	Michael R. Fitzpatrick[2]	2015
Branch 4	Janesville	Daniel T. Dillon	2019
Branch 5	Janesville	Kenneth Forbeck[11]	2015
Branch 6	Janesville	Richard T. Werner[2]	2015
Branch 7	Janesville	Barbara W. McCrory	2018
Rusk	Ladysmith	Steven P. Anderson	2016
St. Croix			
Branch 1	Hudson	Eric J. Lundell	2020
Branch 2	Hudson	Edward F. Vlack III	2019
Branch 3	Hudson	Scott R. Needham	2018
Branch 4	Hudson	R. Michael Waterman[4]	2016
Sauk			
Branch 1	Baraboo	Michael P. Screnock[4]	2016
Branch 2	Baraboo	James Evenson	2016
Branch 3	Baraboo	Guy D. Reynolds	2018
Sawyer	Hayward	Jerry Wright[12]	2015
Shawano-Menominee (see Menominee-Shawano)			
Sheboygan			
Branch 1	Sheboygan	L. Edward Stengel[2]	2015
Branch 2	Sheboygan	Timothy M. Van Akkeren	2019
Branch 3	Sheboygan	Angela Sutkiewicz	2017
Branch 4	Sheboygan	Terence T. Bourke[13]	2015
Branch 5	Sheboygan	James J. Bolgert	2018
Taylor	Medford	Ann Knox-Bauer[2]	2015
Trempealeau	Whitehall	John A. Damon	2019
Vernon	Viroqua	Michael J. Rosborough	2017

JUDGES OF CIRCUIT COURT
June 30, 2015–Continued

County Circuits	Court Location	Judges	Term Expires July 31
Vilas	Eagle River	Neal A. Nielsen	2016
Walworth			
Branch 1	Elkhorn	Phillip A. Koss	2018
Branch 2	Elkhorn	James L. Carlson	2016
Branch 3	Elkhorn	Kristine E. Drettwan[4,5]	2015
Branch 4	Elkhorn	David M. Reddy	2016
Washburn	Shell Lake	Eugene D. Harrington[2]	2015
Washington			
Branch 1	West Bend	James Pouros	2017
Branch 2	West Bend	James K. Muehlbauer	2020
Branch 3	West Bend	Todd Martens	2017
Branch 4	West Bend	Andrew T. Gonring	2018
Waukesha			
Branch 1	Waukesha	Michael O. Bohren	2019
Branch 2	Waukesha	Jennifer Dorow	2018
Branch 3	Waukesha	Ralph M. Ramirez	2017
Branch 4	Waukesha	Lloyd V. Carter	2017
Branch 5	Waukesha	Lee Sherman Dreyfus, Jr.	2020
Branch 6	Waukesha	Patrick C. Haughney	2020
Branch 7	Waukesha	J. Mac Davis[14]	2015
Branch 8	Waukesha	James R. Kieffer[15]	2015
Branch 9	Waukesha	Michael Aprahamian[4,5]	2015
Branch 10	Waukesha	Linda M. Van De Water[16]	2015
Branch 11	Waukesha	William Domina	2017
Branch 12	Waukesha	Kathryn W. Foster	2018
Waupaca			
Branch 1	Waupaca	Philip M. Kirk	2017
Branch 2	Waupaca	Vicki Taggatz Clussman	2020
Branch 3	Waupaca	Raymond S. Huber	2018
Waushara	Wautoma	Guy Dutcher	2017
Winnebago			
Branch 1	Oshkosh	Thomas J. Gritton	2018
Branch 2	Oshkosh	Scott C. Woldt	2017
Branch 3	Oshkosh	Barbara Hart Key	2016
Branch 4	Oshkosh	Karen L. Seifert	2018
Branch 5	Oshkosh	John Jorgensen	2016
Branch 6	Oshkosh	Daniel J. Bissett	2017
Wood			
Branch 1	Wisconsin Rapids	Gregory J. Potter	2020
Branch 2	Wisconsin Rapids	Nicholas J. Brazeau, Jr.	2018
Branch 3	Wisconsin Rapids	Todd P. Wolf[2]	2015

[1]Daniel Glen Wood was newly elected on April 7, 2015, for a 6-year term to commence on August 1, 2015.

[2]Reelected on April 7, 2015, for a 6-year term to commence on August 1, 2015.

[3]Todd J. Hepler was newly elected on April 7, 2015, for a 6-year term to commence on August 1, 2015.

[4]Appointed by the governor.

[5]Newly elected on April 7, 2015, for a 6-year term to commence on August 1, 2015.

[6]Gloria Doyle was newly elected on April 7, 2015, for a 6-year term to commence on August 1, 2015.

[7]Duane M. Jorgenson was newly elected on April 7, 2015, for a 6-year term to commence on August 1, 2015.

[8]John Rhode was newly elected on April 7, 2015, for a 6-year term to commence on August 1, 2015.

[9]David Feiss was newly elected on April 7, 2015, for a 6-year term to commence on August 1, 2015.

[10]David W. Paulson was newly elected on April 7, 2015, for a 6-year term to commence on August 1, 2015.

[11]Mike Haakenson was newly elected on April 7, 2015, for a 6-year term to commence on August 1, 2015.

[12]John Yackel was newly elected on April 7, 2015, for a 6-year term to commence on August 1, 2015.

[13]Rebecca Persick was newly elected on April 7, 2015, for a 6-year term to commence on August 1, 2015.

[14]Maria S. Lazar was newly elected on April 7, 2015, for a 6-year term to commence on August 1, 2015.

[15]Michael P. Maxwell was newly elected on April 7, 2015, for a 6-year term to commence on August 1, 2015.

[16]Paul Bugenhagen, Jr., was newly elected on April 7, 2015, for a 6-year term to commence on August 1, 2015.

Sources: 2013-2014 Wisconsin Statutes; Government Accountability Board, departmental data, April 2015; governor's appointment notices; *The Third Branch* newsletter, Winter 2015 and previous issues.

MUNICIPAL COURTS

Constitutional References: Article VII, Sections 2 and 14.

Statutory References: Chapters 755 and 800.

Internet Address: www.wicourts.gov/courts/municipal/index.htm

Responsibility: The Wisconsin Legislature authorizes cities, villages, and towns to establish municipal courts to exercise jurisdiction over municipal ordinance violations that have monetary penalties. In addition, the Wisconsin Supreme Court ruled in 1991 (*City of Milwaukee v. Wroten,* 160 Wis. 2d 107) that municipal courts have authority to rule on the constitutionality of municipal ordinances.

As of May 1, 2015, there were 240 municipal courts with 239 municipal judges. Courts may have multiple branches; the City of Milwaukee's municipal court, for example, has 3 branches. (Milwaukee County, which is the only county authorized to appoint municipal court commissioners, had 3 part-time commissioners as of May 2015.) Two or more municipalities may agree to form a joint court, and there are 70 joint courts, serving a total of 214 municipalities. Besides Milwaukee, Madison is the only city with a full-time municipal court.

Upon convicting a defendant, the municipal court may order payment of a forfeiture plus costs and surcharges, or, if the defendant agrees, it may require community service in lieu of a forfeiture. In general, municipal courts may also order restitution up to $10,000. Where local ordinances conform to state drunk driving laws, a municipal judge may suspend or revoke a driver's license.

If a defendant fails to pay a forfeiture or make restitution, the municipal court may suspend the driver's license or commit the defendant to jail. Municipal court decisions may be appealed to the circuit court of the county where the offense occurred.

Organization: Municipal judges are elected at the nonpartisan April election and take office May 1. The term of office is 4 years and the governing body determines the position's salary. There is no state requirement that the office be filled by an attorney, but a municipality may enact such a qualification by ordinance.

If a municipal judge is ill, disqualified, or unavailable, the chief judge of the judicial administrative district containing the municipality may transfer the case to another municipal judge. If none is available, the case will be heard in circuit court.

History: Chapter 276, Laws of 1967, authorized cities, villages, and towns to establish municipal courts after the forerunner of municipal courts (the office of the justice of the peace) was eliminated by a constitutional amendment, ratified in April 1966. A constitutional amendment ratified in April 1977, which reorganized the state's court system, officially granted the legislature the power to authorize municipal courts.

STATEWIDE JUDICIAL AGENCIES

A number of statewide administrative and support agencies have been created by supreme court order or legislative enactment to assist the Wisconsin Supreme Court in its supervision of the Wisconsin judicial system.

DIRECTOR OF STATE COURTS

Interim Director of State Courts: J. DENIS MORAN, 266-6828, denis.moran@

Deputy Director for Court Operations: SARA WARD-CASSADY, 266-3121, sara.ward-cassady@

Deputy Director for Management Services: PAM RADLOFF, 266-8914, pam.radloff@

Consolidated Court Automation Programs: JEAN BOUSQUET, *director,* 267-0678, jean.bousquet@

Fiscal Officer: BRIAN LAMPRECH, 266-6865, brian.lamprech@

Judicial Education: KARLA J. BAUMGARTNER, *director,* 266-7807, karla.baumgartner@

Medical Malpractice Mediation System: RANDY SPROULE, *director,* 266-7711, randy.sproule@

Public Information Officer: TOM SHEEHAN, 261-6640, tom.sheehan@

Legislative Liaison: NANCY ROTTIER, 267-9733, nancy.rottier@

Address e-mail by combining the user ID and the state extender: userid**@wicourts.gov**

Mailing Address: Director of State Courts: P.O. Box 1688, Madison 53701-1688; Staff: 110 East Main Street, Madison 53703.

Location: Director of State Courts: Room 16 East, State Capitol, Madison; Staff: 110 East Main Street, Madison.

Fax: 267-0980.

Internet Address: www.wicourts.gov

Number of Employees: 130.25.

Total Budget 2013-15: $39,292,300.

References: Wisconsin Statutes, Chapter 655, Subchapter VI, and Section 758.19; Supreme Court Rules Chapter 70.

Responsibility: The Director of State Courts administers the nonjudicial business of the Wisconsin court system and informs the chief justice and the supreme court about the status of judicial business. The director is responsible for supervising state-level court personnel; developing the court system's budget; and directing the courts' work on legislation, public information, and information systems. This office also controls expenditures; allocates space and equipment; supervises judicial education, interdistrict assignment of active and reserve judges, and planning and research; and administers the medical malpractice mediation system.

The director is appointed by the supreme court from outside the classified service. The position was created by the supreme court in orders, dated October 30, 1978, and February 19, 1979. It replaced the administrative director of courts, which had been created by Chapter 261, Laws of 1961.

STATE LAW LIBRARY

State Law Librarian: JULIE TESSMER, 261-2340, julie.tessmer@wicourts.gov

Deputy Law Librarian: AMY CROWDER, 267-2253, amy.crowder@wicourts.gov

Mailing Address: P.O. Box 7881, Madison 53707-7881.

Location: 120 Martin Luther King, Jr. Blvd., 2nd Floor, Madison.

Telephones: General Information and Circulation: 266-1600; Reference Assistance: 267-9696; (800) 322-9755 (toll-free).

Fax: 267-2319.

Internet Address: http://wilawlibrary.gov

Reference E-mail Address: wsll.ref@wicourts.gov

Publications: *WSLL @ Your Service* (monthly e-newsletter), at:
http://wilawlibrary.gov/newsletter/index.html

Number of Employees: 16.50.

Total Budget 2013-15: $5,844,500.

References: Wisconsin Statutes, Section 758.01; Supreme Court Rule 82.01.

Responsibility: The State Law Library is a public library open to all citizens of Wisconsin. It serves as the primary legal resource center for justices, judges, and staff of the entire Wisconsin court system. The library is administered by the supreme court, which appoints the library staff and determines the rules governing library use. The library acts as a consultant and resource for county law libraries throughout the state. Milwaukee County and Dane County contract with the State Law Library for management and operation of their courthouse libraries (the Milwaukee County Law Library and the Dane County Law Library).

The library's 140,000-volume collection features session laws, statutory codes, court reports, administrative rules and legal indexes of the U.S. government, all 50 states and U.S. territories. It also includes selected documents of the federal government, legal and bar periodicals, legal treatises, and legal encyclopedias. The collection circulates to judges and court staff, attorneys, legislators, and government personnel.

The library offers reference, basic legal research and document delivery services, and training in the use of legal research Web sites and databases.

OFFICE OF LAWYER REGULATION

Board of Administrative Oversight: ROD ROGAHN (lawyer), *chairperson;* JOHN P. MCNAMARA (lawyer), *vice chairperson;* DONALD J. CHRISTL, MARGADETTE DEMET, CHARLES P. DYKMAN, JOSEPH E. REDDING, GARY VAN DOMELEN (lawyers); JOHN J. BLAHNIK, DANIEL C. BRUCH, CHARLES A. BUNGE, THOMAS L. HEINE, LAWRENCE J. QUAM (nonlawyers). (All members are appointed by the supreme court.)

Preliminary Review Committee: FRANK LO COCO (lawyer), *chairperson;* TIMOTHY NIXON (lawyer), *vice chairperson;* LANCE GRADY, MARTIN W. HARRISON, OLIVIA KELLEY, WILLIAM MUNDT, NORA PLATT, DUSTIN T. WOEHL, vacancy (lawyers); DENNIS BLASIUS, KRISTINE DEISS, JOHN FLANNERY, MICHAEL KINDSCHI, MICHAEL D. NOVAK (nonlawyers). (All members are appointed by the supreme court.)

Special Preliminary Review Panel: THOMAS A. CABUSH (lawyer), *chairperson;* BRUCE EHLKE, CATHERINE LA FLEUR, ROBERT A. MATHERS (lawyers); DANIEL ADAMS, DEE KITTLESON, JANE E. SNILSBERG (nonlawyers). (All members are appointed by the supreme court.)

Sixteen District Committees (all members are appointed by the supreme court):

> *District 1 Committee (serves Jefferson, Kenosha, and Walworth Counties):* MARK BROMLEY (lawyer), *chairperson;* TIMOTHY J. GERAGHTY, HEATHER IVERSON, C. BENNETT PENWELL, CHRISTINE TOMAS, vacancy (lawyers); WILLIAM J. BRYDGES, CHARLES P. FRANDSON, RANDALL J. HAMMETT, JEROME HONORE, JEROME K. LAURENT, CHARLES F. TAYLOR (nonlawyers).

> *District 2 Committee (serves Milwaukee County):* BRADLEY S. FOLEY (lawyer), *chairperson;* CHRISTOPHER J. MACGILLIS (lawyer), *vice chairperson;* COLLEEN D. BALL, PAUL BARGREN, REBECCA BLEMBERG, SARAH FRY BRUCH, RICHARD H. CASPER, JACQUES C. CONDON, CEDRIC CORNWALL, DONAL M. DEMET, MICHELE FORD, JAMES GEHRKE, DAVID B. KARP, HARVEY KURTZ, LYNN LAUFENBERG, MICHAEL LAUFENBERG, BRETT LUDWIG, THOMAS MERKLE, JAMES MOCZYDLOWSKI, ROBERT E. NAILEN, KEITH O'DONNELL, FRANK TERSCHAN, DANIEL TREUDEN, ROY E. WAGNER, MONTE WEISS, JOSEPH WELCENBACH, THOMAS WHIPP, vacancy (lawyers); ARLYN ADAMS, FRANK V. BIALEK, RON BLAZEL, NEILAND COHEN, KRISTINA EHNERT, BRUCE HARVEY, RICHARD IPPOLITO, J. DAIN MADDOX, BARBARA J. MILLER, GARY NOSACEK, KEITH J. ROBERTS, WILLIAM WARD, vacancy (nonlawyers).

> *District 3 Committee (serves Fond du Lac, Green Lake, and Winnebago Counties):* TIMOTHY R. YOUNG (lawyer), *chairperson;* PETER CULP, KENNARD N. FRIEDMAN, KATHERINE SEIFERT,

vacancy (lawyers); PAUL M. BAKER, JOHN FAIRHURST, MARY JO KEATING, THOMAS E. KELROY, JULIETTE STERKENS, SUSAN T. VETTE, vacancy (nonlawyers).

District 4 Committee (serves Calumet, Door, Kewaunee, Manitowoc, and Sheboygan Counties): NATASHA TORRY-MORGAN (lawyer), *chairperson;* BARRY S. COHEN, MARY LYNN DONOHUE, WILLIAM F. FALE, ROBERT LANDRY, vacancy (lawyers); VICTORIA CERINICH, JAMES STECKER, SUZANNE J. WEGNER, ALLAN WHITE, RICHARD YORK (nonlawyers).

District 5 Committee (serves Buffalo, Clark, Crawford, Jackson, La Crosse, Monroe, Pepin, Richland, Trempealeau, and Vernon Counties): KARA M. BURGOS (lawyer), *chairperson;* MICHAEL C. ABLAN, DANIEL C. ARNDT, BRUCE J. BROVOLD, BERNARDO CUETO, CHRISTOPHER DOERFLER, STEPHANIE HOPKINS, DAVID RUSSELL, vacancy (lawyers); DAVID CAMPBELL, JAMES W. GEISSNER, RICHARD A. MERTIG, vacancy (nonlawyers).

District 6 Committee (serves Waukesha County): GARY KUPHALL (lawyer), *chairperson;* LINDA S. COYLE, MARTIN DITKOF, ROSEMARY JUNE GORETA, MICHAEL JASSAK, RAMON A. KLITZKE, BRAD A. MARKVART, DANIEL MURRAY, STEPHEN C. RAYMONDS, PAUL E. SCHWEMER, NELSON E. SHAFER, MARGARET G. ZICKUHR, vacancy (lawyers); TELEMACHOS AGOUDEMOS, MICHAEL H. BRANKS, ROBERT HAMILTON, GREGORY J. KSICINSKI, THERESA M. PETERMAN, JOHN SCHATZMAN, JAMES C. WENZLER, vacancy (nonlawyers).

District 7 Committee (serves Adams, Columbia, Juneau, Marquette, Portage, Sauk, Waupaca, Waushara, and Wood Counties): THOMAS M. KUBASTA (lawyer), *chairperson;* STEPHEN D. CHIQUOINE, LEO J. GRILL, ERIK C. JOHNSON, vacancy (lawyers); PHILIP BAEBLER, LAVINDA CARLSON, SUSAN G. MARTIN, CHARLES W. NASON, ALAN K. PETERSON, vacancy (nonlawyers).

District 8 Committee (serves Dunn, Eau Claire, Pierce, and St. Croix Counties): JAY E. HEIT, MARK N. MATHIAS, GREGORY S. NICASTRO, CAROL N. SKINNER, PHILLIP M. STEANS, TRACY N. TOOL, vacancy (lawyers); KRISTEN AINSWORTH, EDWARD HASS, THERESA JOHNSON, BRAD NEMEE, PAUL W. SCHOMMER, vacancy (nonlawyers).

District 9 Committee (serves Dane County): THOMAS W. SHELLANDER (lawyer), *chairperson;* THOMAS S. HORNIG (lawyer), *vice chairperson;* JON CALLAWAY, ANDREW CLARKOWSKI, TIMOTHY EDWARDS, ROGER FLORES, AARON HALSTEAD, ROBERT KASIETA, JASON J. KNUTSON, DAVID S. KOWALSKI, JENNIFER M. KRUEGER, JENNIFER SLOAN LATTIS, JENNIFER E. NASHOLD, BRIANE F. PAGEL, JR., MICHELE PERREAULT, MEGAN A. SENATORI, JAMES R. TROUPIS (lawyers); PATRICIA BASS, PATRICK DELMORE, NORMAN JENSEN, LYNN M. LEAZER, LARRY MCCRAY, BARBARA MORTENSEN, LARRY NESPER, ROBERT G. OWENS, KATHLEEN M. RAAB, JEFFREY B. ROBERTS, CHRISTOPHER D. WASHBURN, KENNETH YUSKA, JOHN ZERBE, vacancy (nonlawyers).

District 10 Committee (serves Marinette, Menominee, Oconto, Outagamie, and Shawano Counties): MICHAEL F. BROWN (lawyer), *chairperson;* LEONARD D. KACHINSKY, ROBERT SISSON, LAURA C. SMYTHE, CATHERINE C. STICHMANN, GERALD WILSON, vacancy (lawyers); GUY T. GOODING, TERRY HILGENBERG, CONNIE M. SEEFELDT, STEPHEN C. WARE, vacancy (nonlawyer).

District 11 Committee (serves Ashland, Barron, Bayfield, Burnett, Chippewa, Douglas, Iron, Polk, Price, Rusk, Sawyer, Taylor, and Washburn Counties): CRAIG HAUKAAS (lawyer), *chairperson;* DEBORAH ASHER, ANNETTE M. BARNA, JOHN R. CARLSON, PARRISH J. JONES, TIMOTHY T. SEMPF, AMANDA L. WIECKOWIC (lawyers); GENE ANDERSON, JOHN BENNETT, ELIZABETH ESSER, ERNY HEIDEN, MARY ANN KING (nonlawyers).

District 12 Committee (serves Grant, Green, Iowa, Lafayette, and Rock Counties): DAN D. GARTZKE (lawyer), *chairperson;* PETER HERMAN, MELISSA B. JOOS, MARGARET M. KOEHLER, KELLY MATTINGLY, CAROLYN L. SMITH, JAMES D. WICKHEM, vacancy (lawyers); LORI R. BIENEMA, DENNIS L. EVERSON, MICHAEL FURGAL, WILLIAM HUSTAD, MICHAEL F. METZ, ROBERT D. SPOODEN, LARRY WOLF, vacancy (nonlawyers).

District 13 Committee (serves Dodge, Ozaukee, and Washington Counties): JOSEPH G. DOHERTY (lawyer), *chairperson;* JOHN A. BEST, MICHAEL P. HERBRAND, CHRISTINE EISENMANN KNUDTSON, DANIEL L. VANDE ZANDE, ANNAMARIE A. WINEKE (lawyers); ROBERT

Blazich, Mark L. Born, Ramona Larson, vacancy (nonlawyers).

District 14 Committee (serves Brown County): Bruce R. Bachhuber (lawyer), *chairperson;* Robert Gagan, Edward J. Vopal, Ann C. Weiss, vacancy (lawyers); Debra L. Bursik, Jim Marshall, Joseph Neidenbach, vacancy (nonlawyers).

District 15 Committee (serves Racine County): Mark F. Nielsen (lawyer), *chairperson;* Robert W. Keller (lawyer), *vice chairperson;* John J. Buchakliam, Kristin Cafferty, Patricia J. Hanson, Lincoln K. Murphy, Timothy J. Pruitt, Robert K. Weber (lawyers); Thomas Chryst, Patricia Hoffman, Frank Konieska, Peter Smet, vacancy (nonlawyers).

District 16 Committee (serves Forest, Florence, Langlade, Lincoln, Marathon, Oneida, and Vilas Counties): Ginger Murray (lawyer), *chairperson;* Lisa Brouillette, Laura K. Fitzsimmons, James P. Lonsdorf, Daniel R. Peters, Peter M. Young, vacancy (lawyers); John P. Coleman, Monty Raskin, vacancy (nonlawyers).

Office of Lawyer Regulation: Keith L. Sellen, *director,* keith.sellen@wicourts.gov; John O'Connell, *deputy director,* john.o'connell@wicourts.gov; Elizabeth Estes, *deputy director,* elizabeth.estes@wicourts.gov; Bill Weigel, *litigation counsel,* bill.weigel@wicourts.gov; Mary Hoeft Smith, *trust account program administrator,* mary.hoeftsmith@wicourts.gov

Telephone: 267-7274; Central Intake toll-free (877) 315-6941.

Fax: 267-1959.

Mailing Address: 110 East Main Street, Suite 315, Madison 53703-3383.

Number of Employees: 27.50.

Total Budget 2013-15: $5,608,300.

References: Supreme Court Rules, Chapters 21 and 22.

Responsibility: The Office of Lawyer Regulation was created by order of the supreme court, effective October 1, 2000, to assist the court in fulfilling its constitutional responsibility to supervise the practice of law and protect the public from professional misconduct by members of the State Bar of Wisconsin. This agency assumed the attorney disciplinary functions that had previously been performed by the Board of Attorneys Professional Responsibility and, prior to January 1, 1978, by the Board of State Bar Commissioners.

The director of the Office of Lawyer Regulation is appointed by the supreme court and must be admitted to the practice of law in Wisconsin no later than six months following appointment. The Board of Administrative Oversight and the Preliminary Review Committee perform oversight and adjudicative responsibilities under the supervision of the supreme court.

The Board of Administrative Oversight consists of 12 members, 8 lawyers and 4 public members. Board members are appointed by the supreme court to staggered 3-year terms and may not serve more than two consecutive terms. The board monitors the overall system for regulating lawyers but does not handle actions regarding individual complaints or grievances. It reviews the "fairness, productivity, effectiveness and efficiency" of the system and reports its findings to the supreme court. After consultation with the director, it proposes the annual budget for the agency to the supreme court.

The Office of Lawyer Regulation receives and evaluates all complaints, inquiries, and grievances related to attorney misconduct or medical incapacity. The director is required to investigate any grievance that appears to support an allegation of possible attorney misconduct, and the attorney in question must cooperate with the investigation. District investigative committees are appointed in the 16 State Bar districts by the supreme court to aid the director in disciplinary investigations, forward matters to the director for review, and provide assistance when grievances can be settled at the district level.

After investigation, the director decides whether the matter should be forwarded to a panel of the Preliminary Review Committee, be dismissed, or be diverted for alternative action. This 14-member committee consists of 9 lawyers and 5 public members, who are appointed by the supreme court to staggered 3-year terms and may not serve more than two consecutive terms.

If a panel of the Preliminary Review Committee determines there is cause to proceed, the director may seek disciplinary action, ranging from private reprimand to filing a formal complaint with the supreme court that requests public reprimand, license suspension or revocation, monetary payment, or imposing conditions on the continued practice of law. An attorney may be offered alternatives to formal disciplinary action, including mediation, fee arbitration, law office management assistance, evaluation and treatment for alcohol and other substance abuse, psychological evaluation and treatment, monitoring of the attorney's practice or trust account procedures, continuing legal education, ethics school, or the multistate professional responsibility examination.

Formal disciplinary actions for attorney misconduct are filed by the director with the supreme court, which appoints a referee from a permanent panel of attorneys and reserve judges to hear discipline cases, make disciplinary recommendations to the court, and to approve the issuance of certain private and public reprimands. Referees conduct hearings on complaints of attorney misconduct, petitions alleging attorney medical incapacity, and petitions for reinstatement. They make findings, conclusions, and recommendations and submit them to the supreme court for review and appropriate action. Only the supreme court has the authority to suspend or revoke a lawyer's license to practice law in the State of Wisconsin.

Allegations of misconduct against the director, a lawyer member of staff, retained counsel, a lawyer member of a district committee, a lawyer member of the preliminary review committee, a lawyer member of the board of administrative oversight, or a referee are assigned by the director for investigation by a special investigator. The special investigator may close a matter if there is not enough information to support an allegation of possible misconduct. If there is enough information to support an allegation of possible misconduct an investigation is commenced. The investigator can then dismiss the matter after investigation or submit an investigative report to the special preliminary review panel which will ultimately decide whether or not there is cause to proceed. The special preliminary review panel consists of 7 members, 4 lawyers and 3 public members appointed by the supreme court who serve staggered 3-year terms and may not serve more than two consecutive terms. If cause is found, the special investigator can proceed to file a complaint with the supreme court and prosecute the matter personally or may assign that responsibility to counsel retained by the director for such purposes.

BOARD OF BAR EXAMINERS

Board of Bar Examiners: MARK R. FREMGEN (State Bar member), *chairperson;* STEVEN M. BARKAN (UW Law School faculty), *vice chairperson;* KENNETH KUTZ (circuit court judge); CHARLES P. DYKMAN, KIMBERLY HAAS, RICHARD B. MORIARTY, W. CRAIG OLAFSSON (State Bar members); JUDITH G. MCMULLEN (Marquette University Law School faculty); JAMES A. COTTER, PATRICIA EVANS, SALLY M. YOUNGER (public members). (All members are appointed by the supreme court.)

Director: JACQUELYNN B. ROTHSTEIN, 266-9760; Fax: 266-1196.

Mailing Address: 110 East Main Street, Suite 715, P.O. Box 2748, Madison 53701-2748.

E-mail Address: bbe@wicourts.gov

Internet Address: www.wicourts.gov/courts/offices/bbe.htm

Number of Employees: 8.00.

Total Budget 2013-15: $1,510,100.

References: Supreme Court Rules, Chapters 30, 31, and 40.

Responsibility: The 11-member Board of Bar Examiners manages all bar admissions by examination or by motion on proof of practice; conducts character and fitness investigations of all candidates for admission to the bar, including diploma privilege graduates; and administers the Wisconsin mandatory continuing legal education requirement for attorneys.

The board was formed from two Supreme Court Boards: the Board of Continuing Legal Education and the Board of Bar Commissioners. The Board of Continuing Legal Education was created effective January 1, 1976, to administer the Wisconsin Supreme Court's mandatory continuing legal education requirements for lawyers. Effective January 1, 1978, the Board of Continuing Legal Education was renamed the Board of Attorneys Professional Competence and continued to be charged with administering mandatory continuing legal education.

The Board of Bar Commissioners was charged with administering bar admission and compliance with the Code of Professional Responsibility. Effective January 1, 1978, the Board of Bar Commissioners' duties with respect to bar admission were transferred to the Board of Attorneys Professional Competence. Effective January 1, 1991, the Board of Attorneys Professional Competence was renamed the Board of Bar Examiners.

Members are appointed for staggered 3-year terms, but no member may serve more than two consecutive full terms.

JUDICIAL CONDUCT ADVISORY COMMITTEE

Judicial Conduct Advisory Committee: D. TODD EHLERS (circuit court or reserve judge serving in a rural area); DONALD ZUIDMULDER (judicial administrative district chief judge); LISA S. NEUBAUER (court of appeals judge); WAYNE MARIK (circuit court or reserve judge serving in an urban area); DANIEL P. KOVAL (municipal court judge); MORIA KRUEGER (reserve judge); ANTON JAMIESON (circuit court commissioner); DAN CONLEY (State Bar member); RANDY MORRISSETTE II (public member). (All members are selected by the supreme court.)

Mailing Address: P.O. Box 1688, Madison 53701-1688.

Internet Address: www.wicourts.gov/courts/committees/judicialconduct.htm

Telephone: 266-6828.

Fax: 267-0980.

Reference: Supreme Court Rules, Chapter 60 Appendix.

Responsibility: The Wisconsin Supreme Court established the Judicial Conduct Advisory Committee as part of its 1997 update to the Code of Judicial Conduct. The 9-member committee gives formal advisory opinions and informal advice regarding whether actions judges are contemplating comply with the code. It also makes recommendations to the supreme court for amendment to the Code of Judicial Conduct or the rules governing the committee.

JUDICIAL CONFERENCE

Members: All supreme court justices, court of appeals judges, circuit court judges, reserve judges, 3 municipal court judges (designated by the Wisconsin Municipal Judges Association), 3 judicial representatives of tribal courts (designated by the Wisconsin Tribal Judges Association), one circuit court commissioner designated by the Family Court Commissioner Association, and one circuit court commissioner designated by the Judicial Court Commissioner Association.

Internet Address: www.wicourts.gov/courts/committees/judicialconf.htm

References: Sections 758.171-758.18, Wisconsin Statutes; Supreme Court Rule 70.15.

Responsibility: The Judicial Conference, which was created by the Wisconsin Supreme Court, meets at least once a year to recommend improvements in administration of the justice system, conduct educational programs for its members, adopt the revised uniform traffic deposit and misdemeanor bail schedules, and adopt forms necessary for the administration of certain court proceedings. Since its initial meeting in January 1979, the conference has devoted sessions to family and children's law, probate, mental health, appellate practice and procedures, civil law, criminal law, truth-in-sentencing, and traffic law.

Judicial Conference bylaws have created a Nominating Committee and five standing committees. Committee members are elected by the Judicial Conference. The standing committees include: the Civil Jury Instructions Committee, the Criminal Jury Instructions Committee, the Juvenile Jury Instructions Committee, the Legislative Committee, and the Uniform Bond Committee. Chairpersons of each standing committee are selected annually by the committee members. The Nominating Committee is made up of the judges who chair the standing committees and the secretary of the Judicial Conference.

The Judicial Conference may create study committees to examine particular topics. These study committees must report their findings and recommendations to the next annual meeting of the Judicial Conference. Study committees usually work for one year, unless extended by the Judicial Conference.

JUDICIAL EDUCATION COMMITTEE

Judicial Education Committee: PATIENCE DRAKE ROGGENSACK (supreme court chief justice); THOMAS R. HRUZ (designated by appeals court chief judge); vacancy (director of state courts); STEVEN G. BAUER, ELLEN K. BERZ, ELLEN BROSTROM, JEFFREY A. CONEN, MOLLY E. GALEWYRICK, SCOTT L. HORNE, CHAD G. KERKMAN, MARK J. McGINNIS (circuit court judges appointed by supreme court); REBECCA PERSICK, ALICE A. RUDEBUSCH (circuit court commissioners appointed by supreme court); JINI M. RABAS (designated by dean, UW Law School); THOMAS HAMMER (designated by dean, Marquette University Law School). *Ex officio* member: LISA K. STARK (dean, Wisconsin Judicial College).

Office of Judicial Education: KARLA J. BAUMGARTNER, *director,* karla.baumgartner@wicourts.gov

Mailing Address: Office of Judicial Education, 110 East Main Street, Room 200, Madison 53703.

Telephone: 266-7807.

Fax: 261-6650.

E-mail Address: JED@wicourts.gov

Internet Address: www.wicourts.gov/courts/committees/judicialed.htm

Reference: Supreme Court Rules, Chapters 32, 33, and 75.05.

Responsibility: The 16-member Judicial Education Committee approves educational programs for judges and court personnel. The 8 circuit court judges and 2 circuit court commissioners on the committee serve staggered 2-year terms and may not serve more than two consecutive terms. The dean of the Wisconsin Judicial College is an *ex officio* member of the committee and has voting privileges.

In 1976, the supreme court issued Chapter 32 of the Supreme Court Rules, which established a mandatory program of continuing education for the Wisconsin judiciary, effective January 1, 1977. This program applies to all supreme court justices and commissioners, appeals court judges and staff attorneys, circuit court judges, and reserve judges. Each person subject to the rule must obtain a specified number of credit hours of continuing education within a 6-year period. The Office of Judicial Education, which the supreme court established in 1971, administers the program. It also sponsors initial and continuing educational programs for municipal judges and circuit court clerks.

PLANNING AND POLICY ADVISORY COMMITTEE

Planning and Policy Advisory Committee: PATIENCE DRAKE ROGGENSACK (supreme court chief justice), *chairperson;* JUAN COLÁS (circuit court judge), *vice chairperson;* JOANNE KLOPPENBURG (appeals court judge selected by court); JAMES BOLGERT, DAVID BOROWSKI, WILLIAM BRASH, NICHOLAS BRAZEAU, EUGENE HARRINGTON, TIMOTHY HINKFUSS, LAMONT JACOBSON, ELLIOTT LEVINE, WILLIAM POCAN, DAVID REDDY, THOMAS VALE, LINDA VAN DE WATER (circuit court judges elected by judicial administrative districts); RANDI OTHROW (municipal judge elected by Wisconsin Municipal Judges Association); TERESA ARROWOOD, TIM VERHOFF (selected by State Bar Board of Governors); GREGG MOORE (nonlawyer, elected county official); LINDA HOSKINS, DIANE TREIS-RUSK (nonlawyers); KELLI THOMPSON (public defender); JON BELLOWS (court administrator); JEFFREY ALTENBURG (prosecutor); CARLO ESQUEDA (circuit court clerk); DOLORES BOMRAD (circuit court commissioner). (Unless indicated otherwise, members are appointed by the chief justice.) Nonvoting associates: ALLAN TORHORST (chief judge liaison), vacancy (director of state courts).

Planning Subcommittee: MICHAEL ROSBOROUGH (circuit court judge), *chairperson;* LISA NEUBAUER (appeals court judge); KATHRYN FOSTER, PAT MADDEN, MARY TRIGGIANO (circuit court judges); ANDREW GRAUBARD (court administrator); THERESA RUSSELL (circuit court clerk); DOLORES BOMRAD (circuit court commissioner); JOSEPH HEIM (public member). *Ex officio* members: PATIENCE DRAKE ROGGENSACK (supreme court chief justice), JUAN COLÁS (circuit court judge, vice chairperson of Planning and Policy Advisory Committee), vacancy (director of state courts).

Staff Policy Analyst: Office of Court Operations.

Mailing Address: 110 East Main Street, Room 410, Madison 53703.

Telephone: 266-3121.

Fax: 267-0911.

Internet Address: www.wicourts.gov/courts/committees/ppac.htm

Reference: Supreme Court Rule 70.14.

Responsibility: The 26-member Planning and Policy Advisory Committee advises the Wisconsin Supreme Court and the Director of State Courts on planning and policy and assists in a continuing evaluation of the administrative structure of the court system. It participates in the budget process of the Wisconsin judiciary and appoints a subcommittee to review the budget of the court system. The committee meets at least quarterly, and the supreme court meets with the committee annually. The Director of State Courts participates in committee deliberations, with full floor and advocacy privileges, but is not a member of the committee and does not have a vote.

This committee was created in 1978 as the Administrative Committee of the Courts and renamed the Planning and Policy Advisory Committee in December 1990.

WISCONSIN JUDICIAL SYSTEM — INDEPENDENT BODIES

JUDICIAL COMMISSION

Members: FRANK J. DAILY, vacancy (State Bar members); SAIED ASSEF, MARK BARRETTE, EILEEN BURNETT, WILLIAM E. CULLINAN, LYNN M. LEAZER (nonlawyers); EMILY S. MUELLER (circuit court judge); PAUL F. REILLY (appeals court judge). (Judges and State Bar members appointed by supreme court. Nonlawyers are appointed by governor with senate consent.)

Executive Director: JEREMIAH C. VAN HECKE.

Administrative Assistant: LAURY BUSSAN.

Mailing Address: 110 East Main Street, Suite 700, Madison 53703-3328.

Telephone: 266-7637.

Fax: 266-8647.

Agency E-mail: judcmm@wicourts.gov

Internet Address: www.wicourts.gov/judcom

Publication: Annual Report.

Number of Employees: 2.00.

Total Budget 2013-15: $627,800.

Statutory References: Sections 757.001, 757.81-757.99.

Responsibility: The 9-member Judicial Commission conducts investigations for review and action by the supreme court regarding allegations of misconduct or permanent disability of a judge or court commissioner. Members are appointed for 3-year terms but cannot serve more than two consecutive full terms.

The commission's investigations are confidential. If an investigation results in a finding of probable cause that a judge or court commissioner has engaged in misconduct or is disabled, the commission must file a formal complaint of misconduct or a petition regarding disability with the supreme court. Prior to filing a complaint or petition, the commission may request a jury hearing of its findings before a single appellate judge. If it does not request a jury hearing, the chief judge of the court of appeals selects a 3-judge panel to hear the complaint or petition.

The commission is responsible for prosecution of a case. After the case is heard by a jury or panel, the supreme court reviews the findings of fact, conclusions of law, and recommended disposition. It has ultimate responsibility for determining appropriate discipline in cases of misconduct or appropriate action in cases of permanent disability.

History: In 1972, the Wisconsin Supreme Court created a 9-member commission to implement the Code of Judicial Ethics it had adopted. The code enumerated standards of personal and official conduct and identified conduct that would result in disciplinary action. Subject to supreme court review, the commission had authority to reprimand or censure a judge.

A constitutional amendment approved by the voters in 1977 empowered the supreme court, using procedures developed by the legislature, to reprimand, censure, suspend, or remove any judge for misconduct or disability. With enactment of Chapter 449, Laws of 1977, the legislature created the Judicial Commission and prescribed its procedures. The supreme court abolished its own commission in 1978.

JUDICIAL COUNCIL

Members: ANNETTE KINGSLAND ZIEGLER (justice designated by supreme court); BRIAN W. BLANCHARD (judge designated by court of appeals); vacancy (director of state courts); MICHAEL R. FITZPATRICK, GERALD P. PTACEK, ROBERT P. VAN DE HEY, JEFFREY A. WAGNER (circuit court judges designated by Judicial Conference); SENATOR WANGGAARD (chairperson, senate judicial committee); REPRESENTATIVE J. OTT (chairperson, assembly judicial committee); GREG M. WEBER (designated by attorney general); TRACY K. KUCZENSKI (designated by Legislative Reference Bureau Chief); DAVID E. SCHULTZ (faculty member, UW Law School, designated by dean); THOMAS L. SHRINER, JR. (adjunct professor, Marquette University Law School, designated by dean); DEVON M. LEE (designated by state public defender); JILL M. KASTNER (State Bar member, designated by president-elect); THOMAS W. BERTZ, WILLIAM GLEISNER, AMY E. WOCHOS (State Bar members selected by State Bar); vacancy (district attorney appointed by governor); DENNIS MYERS, BENJAMIN J. PLISKIE (public members appointed by governor).

Mailing Address: 110 East Main Street, Suite 822, Madison 53703.

Telephone: 261-8290.

Fax: 261-8289.

Number of Employees: 1.00.

Total Budget 2013-15: $139,400.

Statutory References: Section 758.13.

Responsibility: The Judicial Council, created by Chapter 392, Laws of 1951, assumed the functions of the Advisory Committee on Rules of Pleading, Practice and Procedure, created by the 1929 Legislature. The 21-member council is authorized to advise the supreme court, the governor, and the legislature on any matter affecting the administration of justice in Wisconsin, and it may recommend legislation to change the procedure, jurisdiction, or organization of the courts. The council studies the rules of pleading, practice, and procedure and advises the supreme court about changes that will simplify procedure and promote efficiency.

Several council members serve at the pleasure of their appointing authorities. The 4 circuit judges selected by the Judicial Conference serve 4-year terms. The 3 members selected by the State Bar and the 2 citizen members appointed by the governor serve 3-year terms. The council is supported by one staff attorney.

WISCONSIN JUDICIAL SYSTEM — ASSOCIATED UNIT

STATE BAR OF WISCONSIN

Board of Governors (effective July 1, 2015): *Officers:* Ralph M. Cagle, *president;* Francis W. Deisinger, *president-elect;* Robert R. Gagan, *past president;* Sherry Coley, *secretary;* Paul G. Swanson, *treasurer;* Jill M. Kastner, *chair of the board. District members:* Robert G. Barrington, Howard J. Bichler, John A. Birsdall, Daniel J. Blinka, Truscenialyn Brooks, Bruce J. Brovold, Douglas S. Buck, Andrew J. Chevrez, Milton L. Childs, Michael J. Cohen, Byron B. Conway, John E. Danner, Catherine J. Dorl, Hannah C. Dugan, Daniel P. Fay, Martin P. Gagne, Jeff Goldman, Anthony J. Gray, Kimberly K. Haines, Steven C. Harvey, Gregg M. Herman, Deanne M. Koll, Peggy A. Lautenschlager, Kelly J. Mattingly, Kelly Mould, Randall L. Nash, John R. Orton, Sarah A. Ponath, Christopher E. Rogers, Thomas P. Schwaba, Laura Skilton Verhoff, Jeffrey R. Wisnicky, Amy E. Wochos, Nicholas C. Zales. *Young Lawyers Division:* Charles Stertz. *Government Lawyers Division:* Miriam R. Horwitz. *Nonresident Lawyers Division:* James J. Casey, Jr., Debra E. Kuper, Nilesh P. Patel, Daniel F. Rinzel, Viet-Hanh Nguyen Winchell. *Senior Lawyers Division:* John F. Wilcox. *Nonlawyer members:* Susan K. Miller, Christine Procknow, Leland Wigg-Ninham. *Minority Bar Liaisons:* Eric L. Andrews, Toni Caldwell, Vue Yang (nonvoting members).

Executive Director: George C. Brown.

Mailing Address: P.O. Box 7158, Madison 53707-7158.

Location: 5302 Eastpark Boulevard, Madison.

Internet Address: www.wisbar.org; www.facebook.com/statebarofwi; www.twitter.com/statebarofwi

Telephones: General: 257-3838; Lawyer Referral and Information Service: (800) 362-9082.

Agency E-mail: service@wisbar.org

Publications: *WisBar InsideTrack; Wisconsin Lawyer Directory; Wisconsin Lawyer Magazine; Wisconsin News Reporter's Legal Handbook; Rotunda Report;* various legal practice handbooks and resources; various consumer pamphlets and videotapes, including *A Gift to Your Family: Planning Ahead for Future Health Care Needs.*

References: Supreme Court Rules, Chapters 10 and 11.

Responsibility: The State Bar of Wisconsin is an association of persons authorized to practice law in Wisconsin. It works to raise professional standards, improve the administration of justice and the delivery of legal services, and provide continuing legal education to lawyers. The State Bar conducts legal research in substantive law, practice, and procedure and develops related reports and recommendations. It also maintains the roll of attorneys, collects mandatory assessments imposed by the supreme court for supreme court boards and to fund civil legal services for the poor, and performs other administrative services for the judicial system.

Attorneys may be admitted to the State Bar by the full Wisconsin Supreme Court or by a single justice. Members are subject to the rules of ethical conduct prescribed by the supreme court, whether they practice before a court, an administrative body, or in consultation with clients whose interests do not require court appearances.

Organization: Subject to rules prescribed by the Wisconsin Supreme Court, the State Bar is governed by a board of governors, of not fewer than 52 members, consisting of the board's 6 officers, not fewer than 35 members selected by State Bar members from the association's 16 districts, 8 members selected by divisions of the State Bar, and 3 nonlawyers appointed by the supreme court. The board of governors selects the executive director, the executive committee, and the chairperson of the board.

History: In 1956, the Wisconsin Supreme Court ordered the organization of the State Bar of Wisconsin, effective January 1, 1957, to replace the formerly voluntary Wisconsin Bar Association, organized in 1877. All judges and attorneys entitled to practice before Wisconsin courts were required to join the State Bar. Beginning July 1, 1988, the Wisconsin Supreme Court suspended its mandatory membership rule, and the State Bar temporarily became a voluntary membership association, pending the disposition of a lawsuit in the U.S. Supreme Court. The Supreme Court ruled in *Keller v. State Bar of California,* 496 U.S. 1 (1990), that it is permissible to mandate membership provided certain restrictions are placed on the political activities of the mandatory State Bar. Effective July 1, 1992, the Wisconsin Supreme Court reinstated the mandatory membership rule upon petition from the State Bar Board of Governors.

The Wisconsin Supreme Court Hearing Room features four massive murals painted by prominent New York artist Albert Herter (1871-1950). Three of the murals, including "The Signing of the Magna Carta" shown here, are visible to justices from the bench. (Tom Sheehan, Wisconsin Supreme Court)

SUMMARY OF SIGNIFICANT DECISIONS OF THE WISCONSIN SUPREME COURT AND COURT OF APPEALS

June 2013 – June 2015

**Michael Duchek, Michael Gallagher, Peggy Hurley,
Mary Pfotenhauer, Elisabeth Shea, Sarah Walkenhorst-Barber
Legislative Reference Bureau**

CONSTITUTIONAL LAW

Cell Phone Location Tracking

In a pair of cases decided on the same day, the Wisconsin Supreme Court considered constitutional issues implicated with cell phone tracking information. In 2013 Wisconsin Act 375, the legislature prescribed actions that must be taken when law enforcement seek to obtain cell phone tracking information. The provisions in Act 375, however, were not in effect when the events giving rise to these cases took place.

In *State v. Subdiaz-Osorio*, 2014 WI 87, 357 Wis. 2d 41, 849 N. W.2d 748 (2014), the court considered the case of a man who fatally stabbed his brother and subsequently fled the state. On the day following the stabbing, Kenosha police contacted the state Department of Justice's Division of Criminal Investigation (DCI) to request certain information related to the defendant's cell phone from his cell phone carrier, including his location. Later that day, DCI obtained the location information, which indicated that the defendant was driving southbound in Arkansas. Shortly after receiving word from the Kenosha police, Arkansas authorities pulled the defendant over and took him into custody, and the defendant was later extradited to Wisconsin. The defendant sought unsuccessfully to have his statements and evidence obtained after his arrest suppressed, and subsequently pled guilty to first-degree reckless homicide but appealed the denial of the suppression motion. The supreme court accepted the case following an unpublished court of appeals opinion that affirmed the conviction without addressing whether the evidence should have been suppressed.

While six justices agreed that the conviction should be affirmed, there was little consensus on the reasoning, resulting in six different opinions in the case, including one dissent. Justice Prosser wrote the lead opinion upholding the conviction, but his reasoning was not joined by other justices. Without deciding whether the defendant had a reasonable expectation of privacy in his cell phone location information or whether a search had occurred for purposes of the Fourth Amendment to the U.S. Constitution, Prosser concluded that obtaining the defendant's cell phone location information was justified by the exigent circumstances exception to the Fourth Amendment's warrant requirement and that doing so was therefore not constitutionally invalid. Justice Bradley concluded that a search had occurred and that resultant evidence should have been suppressed, but agreed with the court of appeals that the error was harmless given the other evidence in the case that included eyewitness testimony. Justice Crooks concluded that police should be required to obtain a warrant for cell phone location information, but that the evidence in the case should not have been excluded because police had acted in good faith. Justices Roggensack, Ziegler, and Gableman agreed that the facts of the case justified an exigent circumstances exception to the warrant requirement, but did not join Justice Prosser's opinion, and Justices Roggensack and Ziegler both wrote separate opinions joined by other justices. Also at issue in the case was an alleged *Miranda* violation when officers continued questioning after the defendant inquired about an attorney, but five justices agreed that there was no violation, and one concluded that although there was a violation, the error was harmless. Chief Justice Abrahamson dissented. She both concluded that a Fourth Amendment search and *Miranda* violation had occurred, and that no exigent circumstances justified the failure to obtain a warrant.

A less divided court also addressed the availability of cell phone location information to law enforcement in *State v. Tate*, 2014 WI 89, 357 Wis. 2d 172, 849 N. W.2d 798 (2014). Following a homicide in Milwaukee, police found surveillance camera footage from a grocery store that showed a person matching the suspect's description purchasing a prepaid cellular phone. Information provided by the store and the store's clerk gave police a name for the suspect and the telephone number assigned to the phone. Police applied for an "order" to obtain the location information for the phone, which a circuit court judge subsequently issued. Police were consequently able to obtain the location information for the phone and, using a "stingray" tracking device, found the suspect at his mother's apartment. The defendant moved to suppress evidence obtained resulting from the order and argued the order was not equivalent to a warrant. The circuit court denied the motion, and the defendant appealed the suppression ruling following a guilty plea. The court of appeals affirmed the ruling, stating that there was probable cause to issue the order.

Justice Roggensack wrote a majority opinion in a holding that affirmed the defendant's conviction. The majority assumed, without deciding, that the police activities constituted a search within the meaning of the Fourth Amendment and that because the tracking led police to the defendant's home, a warrant was needed. The majority concluded that the circuit court had probable cause to issue the order and that the order, which referenced the phone's electronic serial number, satisfied the Fourth Amendment's particularity requirement. The court said that although the order was not issued pursuant to any particular statute, it complied with the spirit of statutes that address warrants and criminal subpoenas. Chief Justice Abrahamson, joined in part by Justice Bradley, dissented. She concluded that a warrant was required for police to access the defendant's cell phone location information and that the order was defective in a number of respects for failing to comply with the statute regarding criminal subpoenas.

Constitutionality of Limits on Collective Bargaining in Act 10

In *Madison Teachers, Inc. v. Walker,* 2014 WI 99, 358 Wis. 2d 1, 851 N. W.2d 337 (2014), the supreme court ruled on a number of challenges to 2011 Wisconsin Act 10, which significantly curtailed collective bargaining between public employees and employers in Wisconsin at the state and local levels. The court upheld the act in its entirety, holding that the law: 1) does not infringe on the plaintiffs' constitutional right to associate; 2) does not violate constitutional equal protection provisions; 3) does not violate the "home rule" amendment to the state constitution; and 4) does not violate the state constitution's contract clause.

In March of 2011, the bill that became known as Act 10 was signed into law by Governor Scott Walker. Act 10 made a number of changes to state laws including the Municipal Employment Relations Act and the State Employee Labor Relations Act, which, together, dictate the extent of collective bargaining that is permitted to take place between public employees and employers in the state. Specifically, the act prohibited collective bargaining with most state employees on matters other than base wages, prohibited fair share agreements that require both represented and nonrepresented employees to pay certain collective bargaining and contract costs, imposed annual recertification requirements for collective bargaining units, and prohibited public employers at the local level from deducting union dues from employees' paychecks.

Two unions brought suit in Dane County against the governor and the state's Employment Relations Commission, alleging that portions of the act violated numerous constitutional provisions. The circuit court ruled in favor of the plaintiffs on a number of issues, holding certain provisions of the act unconstitutional. Following an appeal by the defendants, the court of appeals certified the case to the supreme court, which the supreme court accepted.

The court first addressed plaintiffs' arguments that the act violated their associational rights under the Wisconsin constitution's provisions that protect freedom of speech and assembly, analyzing the allegations under the First and Fourteenth Amendments to the U.S. Constitution. The plaintiffs argued that provisions in the act burdened their associational rights by imposing restrictions on negotiations with employers that were not applicable to nonrepresented employees. The court, however, said that the act did not implicate any protected First Amendment activities, and did not affect plaintiffs' freedom of speech and associational rights. Emphasizing that no constitutional right existed to engage in collective bargaining, the court rejected plaintiffs' freedom of association arguments.

The court then addressed allegations that the cumulative effect of various provisions in the act rendered the act unconstitutional. The court rejected the plaintiffs' argument that a prohibition on fair-share agreements burdened their associational rights, going so far as to question whether such agreements are even constitutional. The court also held that the certification requirements and payroll deduction prohibitions did not unconstitutionally burden the plaintiffs' associational rights, since no such rights were implicated. Because the court found nothing unconstitutional about the provisions in isolation, the court found that no such violation existed when the provisions were considered cumulatively.

The court next addressed arguments that two provisions of the act violated constitutional equal protection provisions. The court, relying on its earlier analysis, first rejected the notion that a fundamental right was implicated that necessitated a heightened standard of review under the equal protection clause. Consequently, the court analyzed the challenges under a rational basis standard of review and rejected the plaintiffs' arguments that the act's limitations on permissible subjects of collective bargaining and prohibitions on payroll deductions were denials of equal protection.

Finally, the court addressed two arguments with respect to a provision in the act that prohibits the City of Milwaukee from paying the employee share of retirement contributions on behalf of certain employees. Acknowledging that the provision unquestionably implicates local affairs but analyzing it within the broader context of the act itself, the court found that the provision primarily implicated a matter of statewide concern. The court also found that the provision did not violate the contract clause of the state constitution because contributions themselves were not contractually protected "benefits."

Justice Crooks concurred, and Justice Bradley dissented, jointed by Chief Justice Abrahamson. Justice Bradley concluded that: 1) provisions in the act collectively infringe on the associational right to organize and unconstitutionally infringe on those rights by discouraging and punishing membership in unions; 2) the prohibition on the City of Milwaukee making pension contributions on behalf of its employees was not a matter of statewide concern and therefore violated the home rule amendment; and 3) that prohibition also violated the contract clause because the contributions fell within the gambit of the contractually protected pension benefits.

Denial of a Petition to Raise Water Levels on Lake Koshkonong

In *Rock-Koshkonong Lake Dist. v. State,* 2013 WI 74, 350 Wis. 2d 45, 833 N. W.2d 800 (2013), the supreme court considered the Department of Natural Resources' (DNR) denial of a petition to raise water levels on Lake Koshkonong, a large, shallow lake located in Jefferson, Rock, and Dane Counties. Several miles of the lake's shoreline consist of wetlands, some of which are located above the ordinary high-water mark of the lake. The nearby Indianford Dam was constructed in 1851, raising water levels on Lake Koshkonong.

Section 31.02 (1), Wisconsin Statutes, authorizes DNR to regulate the level and flow of water in navigable waters "in the interest of public rights in navigable waters or to promote safety and protect life, health and property." Although DNR set water levels for Lake Koshkonong, from 1965 until 2002 water levels almost always exceeded targets due to disrepair of the dam. In 2002, the dam was restored and water levels dropped to the levels previously ordered by DNR.

The Rock-Koshkonong Lake District petitioned DNR to amend its existing water level order to allow the lake's water levels to be raised, arguing that lowering water levels on the lake from previous decades restricted boating and other recreation and required piers to be extended to reach navigable water depths. DNR denied the petition, and the circuit court and court of appeals affirmed.

There were four issues presented on appeal to the supreme court: 1) what level of deference, if any, the court should give DNR's conclusions of law; 2) whether DNR exceeded its authority by considering impacts of water levels on private wetlands adjacent to Lake Koshkonong and located above the ordinary high-water mark; 3) whether DNR exceeded its authority by considering wetland water quality standards under the administrative code; and 4) whether DNR erred by excluding evidence and failing to consider impacts of water levels on residential property values, business income, and public revenue.

The court first found that DNR's conclusions of law were not entitled to any deference, and therefore subject to de novo review, in part because an agency's interpretation of the scope of its powers is not subject to deference, and in part because the court ultimately determined that DNR's interpretation of Section 31.02 (1), Wisconsin Statutes, and the Wisconsin Constitution, and its exclusion of economic evidence, were not reasonable.

The court next found that DNR properly considered the impact of water levels on public and private wetlands in and adjacent to Lake Koshkonong, but that DNR improperly relied on the public trust doctrine for its authority to protect nonnavigable land and water above the ordinary high-water mark.

Under the public trust doctrine of the Wisconsin Constitution, the state is required to hold navigable waters in trust for the public. Navigable waters are waters that are navigable in fact, in other words, capable of floating any boat of the shallowest draft used for recreational purposes.

DNR, relying on prior supreme court cases such as *Just v. Marinette County,* 56 Wis. 2d 7, 201 N. W.2d 761 (1972), argued that wetlands in and adjacent to navigable waters, whether privately or publicly owned or above or below the ordinary high-water mark, had previously fallen within the scope of the public trust doctrine because of their special relationship to navigable waters.

The court disagreed, finding that, because nonnavigable wetlands above the ordinary high-water mark are not navigable in fact, they do not fall within the scope of the public trust doctrine. The court noted that under the public trust doctrine the riparian owners along navigable rivers and streams have a qualified title in the bed of the river or stream, while the state holds and effectively controls the beds in trust for the public – what the court called "virtual state owner-ship." The court worried that applying the public trust doctrine to any land, including non-navigable wetlands, above the ordinary high-water mark could therefore have very significant ramifications for private property owners, creating questions about ownership of and trespass on that land.

However, the court went on to find that DNR had statutory authority to consider the impact of water levels on wetlands adjacent to Lake Koshkonong under its police power authority in Section 31.02 (1), Wisconsin Statutes.

The court held that Section 31.02 (1) distinguishes between DNR's public trust authority and its police power authority. Section 31.02 (1) permits the department to control the level and flow of navigable waters "in the interest of public rights in navigable waters," representing DNR's authority under the public trust doctrine. The statute also allows DNR to regulate and control the level and flow of navigable waters "to promote safety and protect life, health and property." According to the court, "[b]ecause the quoted language follows the key word 'or,' the depart-ment is given distinct and different authority to consider interests affected by the level of the 'navigable waters.'"

The court also noted that, unlike the constitutionally-based public trust authority, DNR's po-lice power-based statutory authority may be modified by the legislature, and requires balancing of competing interests in its enforcement.

The court next held that DNR could consider wetland water quality standards when making a water level determination.

Chapter 281 of the statutes requires DNR to promulgate water quality standards, including wetland water quality standards, which DNR has done. The district argued that DNR could not consider these standards when making a water level determination under Chapter 31, because Chapter 281 says, in part, that "nothing in this chapter affects . . . [Chapter] 31."

The court disagreed, and found that DNR could, but was not required to, consider water qual-ity standards promulgated under chapter 281 when making a water level determination under Section 31.02 (1).

Finally, the court held that DNR erred in excluding testimony on "the economic impact of lower water levels on the residents, businesses, and tax bases adjacent to and near Lake Kosh-konong."

DNR argued that, under Section 31.02 (1), it was only required to consider direct physical impacts to real property when making a water level determination, while the district argued that DNR was also required to consider secondary economic impacts to real property, such as impacts on residential property values, business income, and local tax revenue.

The court looked to the history of Chapter 31 and prior case law to find that Section 31.02 (1) does not limit DNR to consideration of physical impacts to real property when making a water level determination. The court noted, however, that while DNR must consider evidence of economic impacts to property, it is not necessarily required to conduct an economic analysis when making a water level determination.

Based on its findings, the supreme court reversed the court of appeal's decision and remanded the matter to the circuit court for further proceedings.

Justice Crooks, joined by Chief Justice Abrahamson and Justice Bradley, dissented. The dissent argued that the court's prior decisions had explicitly held that wetlands above the ordinary high-water mark could be subject to the public trust doctrine, and that DNR is not required to consider secondary or indirect economic impacts when making water level determinations under Section 31.02 (1).

Houseguest's Consent to a Search of a Home by Law Enforcement

In *State v. Sobczak,* 2013 WI 52, 347 Wis. 2d 724, 833 N. W.2d 59 (2013), the supreme court was asked to consider under what circumstances a guest in another person's home may consent to a search of the home and its effects by a law enforcement officer. The State and Sobczak agreed that an officer had entered Sobczak's home and looked at files on a laptop computer pursuant to consent given by a guest in the home; the question was whether the guest had proper authority to give consent. The court held that no bright-line rule was applicable or desirable, so that a fact-finder would need to consider several factors to determine whether a houseguest had sufficient "run of the house" so as to authorize a search of the home.

The court first noted that the Fourth Amendment to the U.S. Constitution places its "greatest protection around the home" and that the police may not generally enter into a home to conduct a search without a valid search warrant. One exception to this rule, "jealously and carefully drawn," is an entry and search that an officer conducts pursuant to the "voluntary consent of an individual possessing authority" to grant entry and allow a search. The court noted that in order to protect the sanctity of the home and the integrity of the Fourth Amendment, the State must prove by clear and convincing evidence that the limited exception applies.

Sobczak argued that the exception did not apply, as his guest had no authority to grant consent to enter or search his home. He argued that only a "co-inhabitant" or "co-occupant" held that authority and that his guest, his girlfriend of three months, was a mere weekend visitor who did not possess the requisite authority. The court rejected that argument after setting forth factors that would weigh in favor of, or against, a determination that a houseguest had proper authority to allow a search of his or her host's home.

The court noted that the proper analysis does not focus on any property ownership rights, but instead hinges upon whether the person who granted entry into the home enjoyed the "mutual use of the property" and had "joint access or control for most purposes" at the time he or she gave consent. Considering several factors, including the nature of the relationship, the duration of the guest's stay in the home, whether the guest keeps belongings in, or has a key to, the home, and the shared expectations of control over the premises and its contents, the court held that in this case, Sobczak's guest had proper authority to give consent for an officer to enter the home and view Sobczak's computer.

The court found that the romantic nature of the relationship, coupled with the fact that Sobczak left his girlfriend alone in the home while he went to work with no apparent restrictions on her use of the home, gave her the authority to allow an officer to enter the living room of the home for the purpose of viewing Sobczak's laptop computer. The court recognized that other factors, including the fact that the girlfriend kept no belongings in the home and had no indication that she would be visiting again, weighed against a finding of authority, but ultimately held that she did possess the requisite authority to grant entry into the home. The court next found that, once the officer was in the home, the guest had the authority to allow the officer to view the laptop, which Sobczak had expressly allowed her to use with no restrictions.

The court cautioned that their ruling does not give broad authority to a houseguest to consent to a search of an entire home and all of its contents. Rather, the specific facts in this case required a finding that this particular houseguest had sufficient access to and control over the premises to allow an officer to enter into the home in order to view certain contents on Sobczak's computer.

Justice Ziegler concurred, writing to emphasize that the officer entered Sobczak's home with the sole purpose to view limited items on a laptop computer and that the guest had ample authority to authorize the officer to view the computer.

Justice Abrahamson dissented, joined by Justice Bradley. The dissent also considered several factors in determining the circumstances under which a houseguest possesses authority to consent to entry and search of a home. The dissent cited several factors, including that Sobczak's girlfriend did not possess a key to the home, did not live there or claim to live there, kept no belongings there and had no responsibilities for the home, to conclude that she did not have sufficient access or control over the premises to authorize an entry or search.

Mortgage Sale

In *Bank of New York Mellon v. Carson,* 2015 WI 15, 361 Wis. 2d 23, 859 N. W.2d 422 (2015), the supreme court considered the scope of authority granted to a circuit court under Section 846.102, Wisconsin Statutes, specifically, whether a court can order a mortgagee to bring a property to sale and, if so, whether a court can require a mortgagee to bring the property to sale by a particular date. The court held that when a court determines that a property is abandoned, Section 846.102 authorizes the circuit court to order a mortgagee to bring the property to sale after the redemption period. The court further held that the circuit court must order the property to be brought to sale within a reasonable time after the redemption period, as determined based on the totality of the circumstances.

The Bank of New York Mellon (Bank) filed suit against Shirley Carson, seeking a judgment of foreclosure and sale of the mortgaged premises. Carson did not file an answer or otherwise dispute the foreclosure. The circuit court entered judgment in favor of the Bank, acknowledging that the property was not owner occupied, and ordering that the property be sold at public auction at any time after three month(s) from the date of entry of judgment. In its judgment, the court also specified that in the event the property was abandoned, the Bank "may take all necessary steps to secure and winterize the subject property."

After entry of the judgment, the Bank did not take steps to secure the property. It was burglarized, vandalized, and someone started a fire in the garage. The Bank did not maintain the property, despite an order from the City of Milwaukee Department of Neighborhood Services (City). Carson received notices about trash and debris, overgrown weeds, grass, and trees, and was fined multiple times by the City.

More than 16 months after the judgment of foreclosure was entered, the Bank had not yet sold the property. Carson moved to amend the judgment to include a finding that the property was abandoned and for an order under Section 846.102 that the sale of the premises be made upon the expiration of five weeks from the date the amended judgment was entered. The circuit court denied the motion, finding that Section 846.102 does not authorize the circuit court to order sale of the property at a specific time. The court of appeals reversed and remanded, holding that the plain language of the statute grants the circuit court authority to order the sale of property upon the expiration of the redemption period.

The supreme court affirmed and remanded the case to the circuit court to determine whether the property had been abandoned and for further proceedings. The Bank argued that Section 846.102 is permissive rather than mandatory, but the supreme court disagreed, finding that the plain language of the statute, including use of the word shall, mandates that, if the court determines that the property has been abandoned, the court must order a sale of the mortgaged property.

Having concluded that the statutory language authorizes a court to order a mortgagee to bring a property to sale, the court then also determined that the statute permits a court to order a mortgagee to bring a property to sale by a certain point in time. The court rejected the Bank's argument that the statute provides no time limit for a sale and that, accordingly, it should have five years to execute its judgment under a general execution provision. The court acknowledged that the language of the statute is ambiguous with respect to the timing, but based on the statute's context, purpose, and legislative history, determined that the statute requires an abandoned property to be brought to sale within a reasonable time after the redemption period. A court must consider the totality of the circumstances to determine what constitutes a reasonable time in a particular case.

Justice Prosser, joined by Justice Ziegler and Justice Gableman, concurred in the result, but disagreed with the majority's interpretation of Section 846.102. The concurrence concluded, instead, that the result was appropriate under Section 840.03 (1), which allows a mortgagor such as Carson to bring an action for judicial sale or conveyance of interest in his or her property.

Prosecution of Parents for Reckless Homicide When Child Is Treated by Prayer

In *State v. Neumann,* 2013 WI 58, 348 Wis. 2d 455, 832 N. W.2d 560 (2013), the supreme court was asked to consider whether two parents' convictions for reckless homicide were unconstitutional in light of another statute that shields a parent from prosecution for child abuse if the parent uses prayer to treat a child's illness. The parents also alleged that their case had been unfairly tried because of faulty jury instructions and, in the father's case, a biased jury that was aware the mother had been previously convicted.

Under Wisconsin law, a parent may not be found guilty of child abuse "solely because he or she provides a child with treatment by spiritual means through prayer alone for healing…" The parents argued that this provision, when read in combination with the reckless homicide statute and the statutes that define the words "reckless" and "great bodily harm" for the purposes of the homicide statute and the child abuse statute, so muddles the question of when criminal penalty attaches to specific conduct as to be unconstitutionally vague. The parents argued that their convictions in light of this vagueness are an impermissible violation of their due process rights.

The majority of the court rejected this argument, finding that the exception for the child abuse statute is narrowly drawn and cannot reasonably be expected to be a shield from conviction under the reckless homicide statute. The court held that the statutes, when read in combination and separately, provide sufficient notice as to when conduct becomes criminal and that prosecution on the facts of this case did not violate the parents' due process rights. The court found that the jury reasonably concluded that the parents, in failing to seek medical assistance when their child was seriously ill and her condition visibly worsening, created "an unreasonable and substantial risk of [the child]'s death, were subjectively aware of that risk, and caused her death."

The court then considered whether the jury instructions erroneously created criminal liability for the parents' failure to act and failed to provide the jury with sufficient understanding that the parents' religious beliefs could negate the element of scienter (knowledge of the wrongness of) necessary for a conviction for reckless homicide. The court found no fault with the jury instructions.

The parties agreed that, if there is a legal duty to act, then failure to act in accordance with the duty may amount to criminal conduct. The parents argued, however, that the statutes requiring a parent to provide medical care for his or her child were an unconstitutional intrusion into the parents' right to direct the care of his or her child. The court did not agree, noting that the statutes are replete with provisions requiring parents to provide medical care to their children. The court rejected the notion that the parents' constitutional right to direct the care of their children was violated because "neither rights of religion nor rights of parenthood are beyond limitation." The court found that the jury instructions relating to the parents' duty to provide medical care to their child were appropriate.

The court also found that the trial court had reasonably rejected the parents' proposed jury instruction that would have informed the jury that their sincere belief in prayer treatment may negate the subjective awareness element necessary to find them guilty of reckless homicide. The parents argued that the juries should have been informed that they could find that, given the parents' sincere beliefs that prayers would heal their child, the parents were not subjectively aware that they were creating an unreasonable and substantial risk of harm to her. The court found that this instruction was not necessary, given the elements of the crime under consideration, and that "the juries could have reasonably concluded on the basis of the instructions and the record that the parents were subjectively aware that their conduct created the unreasonable and substantial risk of death or great bodily harm[.]"

Finally, the court rejected the father's argument that his jury had been impermissibly prejudiced by the knowledge that, at the time of his trial, the mother had already been convicted of reckless homicide. The court noted that the district attorney and counsel for the father had agreed to inform the jury of the mother's conviction. The court found that, although it was unusual for a jury to have this knowledge, the knowledge did not necessarily render a juror unconstitutionally biased. Under the circumstances of this case, the court found that the father could not bear his burden of proving that the jury was unable to distinguish his case from the mother's.

Justice Prosser dissented, noting that the child abuse statute and the reckless homicide statute, when read in combination, are incredibly difficult to distinguish from each other. He argued that reasonable people would be unable to determine when their specific conduct is protected by the exception for religious beliefs, and when it is not. Justice Prosser noted that, under the circumstances of this specific case, the line between permissible conduct and impermissible failure to act is unconstitutionally vague.

Voter I.D.

In a pair of cases handed down on July 31, 2014, the supreme court upheld the voter photo identification requirements in 2013 Wisconsin Act 23. Under Act 23, a voter must present one of nine acceptable forms of photo identification in order to vote. That requirement to present photo identification applies, with some exceptions, to absentee as well as in-person voting.

In the first case, *League of Women Voters of Wisconsin Education Network, Inc. v. Walker*, 2014 WI 97, 357 Wis. 2d 360, 851 N. W.2d 302 (2014), the plaintiffs argued that Act 23's requirement to present photo identification is unconstitutional on its face. According to the plaintiffs, the photo identification requirement unconstitutionally creates an additional voter qualification, exceeds the legislature's constitutional authority to make laws governing elections, and is unreasonable.

Article III, Section 1 of the Wisconsin Constitution establishes the qualifications a person must have in order to vote. Specifically, the person must be a United States citizen who is at least 18 years of age, a resident of Wisconsin, and a resident of the district in which the person proposes to vote. The court determined that Act 23's photo identification requirement does not represent a qualification in addition to those constitutional qualifications. Instead, the court found that photo identification is a permissible way to verify that a person possesses the constitutionally required qualifications – that the person is who they say they are.

The court further held that the photo identification requirement was a valid exercise of the legislature's power to make laws concerning voter registration. Article III, Section 2 of the Wisconsin Constitution provides that certain laws may be enacted regulating elections, including laws regulating voter registration. Act 23 generally requires that a voter's photo identification be matched to the registration lists before the voter may receive a ballot. According to the court, the photo identification requirement is an acceptable way to verify a voter's registration at the polls on election day.

Finally, the court held in *League of Women Voters* that the photo identification requirement in Act 23 is a reasonable means of deterring voter fraud and maintaining the integrity of the election process. Noting that presenting photo identification is, to some extent, "a condition of our times," the court concluded that the photo identification requirement is a reasonable way to preserve and promote the right to vote, although the court declined to evaluate whether that requirement is the best way to do so from a public policy standpoint.

Justice Crooks concurred with the majority decision of the court, noting the high bar that must be reached in order to overturn a law as unconstitutional on its face. Chief Justice Abrahamson, joined by Justice Bradley, filed a vigorous dissent, arguing, among other things, that Act 23's photo identification requirement unconstitutionally creates an additional qualification to vote, that the fees required to obtain Act 23 photo identification constitute an unconstitutional "poll tax," and that Act 23, and specifically the majority's affirmation of it, raises the specter of Jim Crow.

League of Women Voters did not address the question of whether Act 23's photo identification requirement places an unconstitutional burden on the exercise of the right to vote. That was the issue before the supreme court in *Milwaukee Branch of the NAACP v. Walker*, 2014 WI 98, 357 Wis. 2d 469, 851 N. W.2d 262 (2014). The plaintiffs in *Milwaukee Branch of the NAACP* argued that Act 23's photo identification requirement would severely burden a significant number of constitutionally qualified voters and is not reasonably necessary nor designed to deter fraud or otherwise serve a compelling state interest. The plaintiffs identified burdens of time, inconvenience, and costs associated with Act 23; in particular, associated with obtaining a Department of Transportation (DOT) photo identification card.

The court concluded that such burdens are not undue burdens rendering the photo identification requirement invalid. Noting that "photo identification is a condition of our times where more and more personal interactions are being modernized to require proof of identity with a specified type of photo identification," the court held that "[w]ith respect to these familiar burdens, which accompany many of our everyday tasks, . . . Act 23 does not constitute an undue burden on the right to vote."

However, the court further held that payment to a government agency to obtain a photo identification necessary for voting would render Act 23's photo identification requirement unconstitutional. While Act 23 requires that DOT provide a photo identification for voting free of charge, the plaintiffs produced evidence that government agencies impose fees for documents required to obtain a DOT photo identification, such as a birth certificate. While such fees were modest for most citizens – up to $20 to obtain a birth certificate – the fees are a significant burden for some. In any case, the court held that the state may not enact a law that requires any voter, rich or poor, to pay any fee whatsoever to a government agency as a precondition to the exercise of his or her constitutional right to vote.

The court determined, however, that the potential constitutional infirmity was not in Act 23 itself but in DOT's administrative regulations requiring certain supporting documentation to obtain DOT photo identification. Rather than invalidate Act 23, the court applied a "saving construction" to those administrative regulations. The court required DOT to exercise its discretion under the regulations to issue photo identification for voting without requiring documents for which a voter must pay a fee to a government agency. With that saving construction, the court upheld the constitutionality of Act 23's photo identification requirement.

While Justice Crooks concurred in *League of Women Voters,* he dissented from the majority's decision in *Milwaukee Branch of the NAACP.* Joined by Justice Bradley, he determined that Act 23's photo identification requirement severely burdens the right to vote of otherwise qualified voters without being narrowly tailored to achieve a compelling state interest, such as deterring voter fraud. Chief Justice Abrahamson incorporated in full her dissent from *League of Women Voters.*

Wisconsin's Domestic Partnership Law

In *Appling v. Walker,* 2014 WI 96, 358 Wis. 2d 132, 853 N. W.2d 888 (2014), the supreme court held that the legal status provided by Wisconsin's domestic partnership statutes are not unconstitutionally "substantially similar" to marriage. This decision upheld the court of appeals' decision in *Appling v. Doyle,* 2013 WI App 3, 345 Wis. 2d 762, N. W.2d 666 (2012). For a discussion of the issues and grounds for the decision in this case, please see the *2013-2014 Wisconsin Blue Book,* pp. 586-587.

CIVIL LAW

Ownership of Property on Which Dog Resides Insufficient to Establish Individual Is a Dog Owner

In *Augsburger v. Homestead Mutual Insurance Co.,* 2014 WI 133, 359 Wis. 2d 385, 856 N. W.2d 874 (2014), the supreme court considered whether ownership of the property on which a dog resides was sufficient to establish that an individual harbored, and therefore was a statutory owner of, a dog under Section 174.02, Wisconsin Statutes. The court held that mere ownership of the property is insufficient to establish ownership of a dog under Section 174.02, and that under the totality of the circumstances, the property owner did not exercise sufficient control over the property to be considered a harborer and thus an owner of the dogs.

The facts of the case were undisputed. George Kontos purchased property in Larsen, Wisconsin, on which he allowed his daughter, Janet Veith, and her family to live so that Veith could be near her mother. Kontos did not reside on the property with the Veiths. There was no formal lease between Kontos and the Veiths, and Kontos did not expect the Veiths to pay rent to live on the property. Veith's husband did general repairs and maintenance on the property, including partially remodeling the interior of the home. Kontos was aware that the Veiths owned horses and dogs that resided with the family on the property. The parties agreed that Kontos had the authority to prohibit the dogs from the property, but did not exercise that authority. Kontos visited the property, but not frequently. Though Kontos occasionally yelled at the dogs to be quiet when he visited, he rarely went near the dogs and did not feed, water, bathe, or groom them. He did not pay for the dog food, take care of the dogs, or instruct his daughter how to care for the dogs.

On June 21, 2008, Julie Augsburger came to the Larsen property to visit Veith. Veith's daughter informed Augsburger that Veith was in the barn on the property. As Augsburger proceeded toward the barn, she was attacked and injured by four of Veith's dogs. Augsburger sued the Veiths, Kontos, and Homestead Mutual Insurance Company, alleging that the Veiths and Kontos were liable for her injuries under Section 174.02, which imposes strict liability on dog owners for injuries caused by their dogs. The circuit court granted Augsburger's motion for summary judgment, finding that Kontos harbored the dogs and was therefore a statutory owner under Section 174.02. The court of appeals affirmed the decision.

The supreme court reversed, holding that the determination of whether an individual is a harborer of a dog must be determined on the totality of the circumstances, and that mere ownership of the property on which a dog resides is insufficient to establish that an individual is an owner of a dog.

The court began by analyzing the relevant statutory language. Section 174.02 imposes strict liability on dog owners for injuries caused by their dogs. The term "owner" is defined in Section 174.001 (5) which provides that an owner "includes any person who owns, harbors or keeps a dog." It was undisputed that Kontos did not own or keep the dogs. Thus, the sole issue before the court was whether Kontos was a harborer of the dogs. As the term harbor is not defined in the statute, and the statutory scheme did not provide a clear interpretation of the term, the court looked to prior Wisconsin caselaw for guidance. The court noted that harboring has been distinguished from keeping, and that harboring has been previously found to mean affording lodging, to shelter or to give refuge to a dog. The court noted that caselaw has suggested that an important factor in the determination is whether the landowner lives on the premises with the dog. Relying upon case law and the canons of statutory construction, the court found that a narrow interpretation of the term harborer should be applied. The court noted earlier caselaw holding generally that landlords are not liable for the actions of their tenants' dogs, and compared that caselaw with cases in which a dog owner was found to be more analogous to a houseguest. The court stated that there was no need to determine the official relationship between the dog owner and the landowner, but focused on the amount of control Kontos exercised over the premises on which the dog was kept and whether the dog's legal owner was "more akin to a houseguest or a tenant." The court distinguished between harboring and keeping, noting that although both might involve consideration of control, the control in the analysis of the term keeper relates to control of the dog, whereas control in the analysis of harborer relates to the landowner's control of the property on which the dog resides. The court also stated that its interpretation was appropriate because the dog bite statute derogates the common law, and such statutes should be narrowly construed.

Justice Prosser dissented. While Prosser agreed that mere ownership of the property on which a dog resides is an insufficient basis for finding an individual to be a harborer, he disagreed with the majority's application of the statutes, finding that Kontos exercised sufficient control over the property and provided shelter, including financial support, for the Veiths and their animals such that, under a totality of the circumstances, Kontos should be considered a harborer and thus an owner of the dogs.

Surrogacy Agreements Are Enforceable

In *In re the Paternity of F.T.R: Rosecky v. Schissel,* 2013 WI 66, 349 Wis. 2d 84, 833 N. W.2d 634 (2013), the supreme court held that a surrogacy agreement is enforceable unless enforcement is contrary to the best interests of the child.

David and Marcia Rosecky entered into a parentage agreement with their friends, Monica and Cory Schissel. Under the agreement, Monica agreed to serve as a traditional surrogate, which means that she agreed to be artificially inseminated with David's sperm, to carry the pregnancy to term, and to terminate her parental rights upon the birth of the resulting child. The agreement also set out the couples' agreement regarding custody and placement. The couples were each represented by counsel and had extensive discussions about the ramifications of the arrangement, legal and otherwise.

During the pregnancy, the relationship between the couples deteriorated. Following the birth of the child, Monica allowed David and Marcia to take the child home, but she refused to terminate her parental rights. A court appointed the Roseckys temporary guardians of the child. A court also adjudicated David as the child's father.

Monica then sought increased custody and placement of the child, and David sought specific performance of the parentage agreement. The trial court found the agreement to be unenforceable. Without considering the parentage agreement, the court granted custody and placement to David with periods of placement to Monica. David appealed and the court of appeals certified the case to the supreme court.

The supreme court held that surrogacy is not contemplated nor does it fit within the existing statutory scheme for determining parentage or child custody and placement. The court also held that the statutes do state any public policy against enforcement of a parentage agreement.

The supreme court then used principles of contract law to examine the parentage agreement, and held that it is a valid, enforceable contract unless enforcement is contrary to the best interests of the child. The court noted that the interests supporting enforcement outweigh the interests opposing enforcement, namely "that enforcement of surrogacy agreements promotes stability and permanence in family relationships because it allows the intended parents to plan for the arrival of their child, reinforces the expectations of all parties to the agreement, and reduces contentious litigation that could drag on for the first several years of the child's life."

The supreme court held that portions of the parentage agreement that required Monica to terminate her parental rights were not enforceable under Section 48.41, Wisconsin Statutes, which requires procedural safeguards for the voluntary termination of parental rights. Further, the court held there was no legal basis for involuntary termination of Monica's parental rights under Section 48.415. However, because the parental agreement included a valid severability provision, the supreme court held that the unenforceable provisions of the agreement could be severed and the remainder enforced.

The supreme court also held that the trial court had erroneously exercised its discretion by not considering the parental agreement in making its custody and placement determination. The supreme court reversed and remanded to the trial court for a hearing on custody and placement, requiring the trial court to enforce the terms of the parentage agreement unless contrary to the best interests of the child. The court also urged the legislature to consider enacting legislation regarding surrogacy, noting that "[s]urrogacy is currently a reality in our Wisconsin court system."

Justice Abrahamson concurred (joined by Justice Bradley) to admonish the court to be cautious about broadly stating that surrogacy agreements are valid, because the public policy questions surrounding them have not yet been settled. Justice Abrahamson also said she would instruct the circuit court to follow Section 767.41(5)(am), Wisconsin Statutes, in determining custody and placement issues, in addition to considering the parentage agreement.

Statistics

8

Statistical information about Wisconsin: agriculture, associations, commerce and industry, conservation and recreation, education, employment and income, geography and climate, history, local and state government, military and veterans affairs, news media, population and vital statistics, post offices, social services, state and local finance, and transportation

Camp Randall

(Sarah Girkin)

HIGHLIGHTS OF AGRICULTURE IN WISCONSIN

Farm Production — In 2013, Wisconsin ranked first nationally in the production of cheese at 25.7% of the U.S. market (including leading the nation with 19% of American production and 17.8% of cheddar) and the production of dry whey products at 32.8%. The state ranked second to California in the production of milk, supplying 13.7% for the U.S. In crop production, it ranked first in corn for silage, cranberries, and snap beans for processing. It was among the top five producers of oats, forage, potatoes, tart cherries, maple syrup, carrots for processing, sweet corn for processing, green peas for processing, and cucumbers for pickles. Wisconsin is also the leading producer of mink pelts and milk goats in the country. As befits the state known as "America's Dairyland", Wisconsin had more milk cows than any other state in the nation except California, with over 1.27 million head, about 14% of the nation's total.

Cash Receipts and Income — Total net Wisconsin farm income was $3.9 billion in 2013, an increase of over $2 billion since 2009. Wisconsin ranked 10th nationally in total net farm income in 2013, up from 11th in 2011. California led the nation in farm income for 2013 with about $12.1 billion, while Alaska, with a negative total net income, ranked last.

Total cash receipts for Wisconsin farm products marketed in 2013 amounted to about $12.3 billion. California led the nation that year in total cash receipts from farm marketings at $46.4 billion. Dairy products accounted for 45.1% of Wisconsin's cash receipts from farm marketings in 2013, with feed, oil, and food crops providing 25.3% and meat animals 14%.

Number and Size of Farms — From 2009 to 2014, the number of farms in the nation decreased by 116,010 to 2,084,000; in Wisconsin, the number decreased from about 78,000 to 69,000. Excluding a period from 2007-2009, the number of Wisconsin's farms have decreased steadily from a peak of 200,000 in 1935. Wisconsin farmland decreased from 23.5 million acres to 14.6 million acres between 1935 and 2013, and the average farm size increased from 117 acres to 209 acres over the same period.

Value of Farms and Farmland — Land and buildings on Wisconsin farms were valued at about $60 billion in 2013, an increase of $3 billion or 5.7% from 2011. The average value per farm increased from $795,618 in 2011 to $857,593 in 2013. The average value per acre in 2013 was $4,100, an increase of $220 compared to 2011 values.

The average price for agricultural land sold in Wisconsin during 2013 was $4,480 per acre, a decrease of $2 from the $4,482 average selling price in 2012. Land continuing in agricultural use after sale sold for a statewide average of $4,442 per acre in 2013; agricultural land that sold for other uses was purchased for an average price of $5,670 per acre. Cash rents for nonirrigated cropland averaged $120.00 per acre in 2013, up 46.3% from 2008.

Farm Assets and Debts — Wisconsin farms recorded assets of $1,058,536 per farm in 2013 and debt of $135,877 per farm for a debt-to-asset ratio of 12.8%.

The following tables present selected data. Consult footnoted sources for more detailed information on agriculture.

NUMBER, SIZE AND VALUE OF FARMS IN WISCONSIN
1935 – 2013

Year	Number of Farms	Land in Farms (acres)	Average Size of Farm (acres)	Value of Land and Buildings Total (in millions)	Average per Farm	Average per Acre
1935	200,000	23,500,000	117	$1,246	$6,228	$53
1940	187,000	22,900,000	123	1,191	6,368	52
1945	178,000	23,600,000	133	1,440	8,088	61
1950	174,000	23,600,000	136	2,100	12,071	89
1955	155,000	23,200,000	150	2,343	15,117	101
1960	138,000	22,200,000	161	2,953	21,396	133
1965	124,000	21,400,000	173	3,317	26,750	155
1970	110,000	20,100,000	183	4,663	42,393	232
1975	100,000	19,300,000	193	8,376	83,762	434
1980	93,000	18,600,000	200	18,674	200,800	1,004
1985	83,000	17,900,000	216	16,898	203,586	944
1990	80,000	17,600,000	220	14,098	176,220	801
1995	80,000	16,800,000	210	17,472	218,400	1,040
1996	79,000	16,600,000	210	18,758	237,443	1,130
1997	79,000	16,500,000	209	19,305	244,367	1,170
1998	78,000	16,300,000	209	20,212	259,128	1,240
1999	78,000	16,200,000	208	23,490	301,154	1,450
2000	77,500	16,000,000	206	27,200	350,968	1,700
2001	77,000	15,800,000	205	30,810	400,130	1,950
2002	77,000	15,700,000	204	33,755	438,377	2,150
2003	76,500	15,600,000	204	35,880	469,020	2,300
2004	76,500	15,500,000	203	38,750	507,500	2,500
2005	76,500	15,400,000	201	43,890	573,725	2,850
2006	76,000	15,300,000	201	48,960	644,210	3,200
2007	78,500	15,200,000	194	57,760	735,796	3,800
2008	78,000	15,200,000	195	58,520	750,256	3,850
2009	78,000	15,200,000	195	57,000	730,769	3,750
2010	73,200	14,700,000	201	53,655	732,992	3,650
2011	71,200	14,600,000	205	56,648	795,618	3,880
2012	69,800	14,600,000	209	60,006	859,685	4,110
2013	69,800	14,600,000	209	59,860	857,593	4,100

Notes: "Farm" is currently defined as a place that sells, or would normally sell, at least $1,000 of agricultural products during the year. The actual number of farms in Wisconsin peaked at 199,877 in 1935. Total Value Average per Farm figures calculated by Wisconsin Legislative Reference Bureau. Numbers for 2010 and 2011 have been revised to reflect updated source data.

Sources: U.S. Department of Agriculture, National Agricultural Statistics Service, "Wisconsin Agricultural Statistics 2014", and prior editions, at: http://www.nass.usda.gov/Statistics_by_State/Wisconsin/Publications/Annual_Statistical_Bulletin/bulletin2014_web.pdf [April 24,2015], and "Agricultural Land Values and Cash Rents", at: http://usda.mannlib.cornell.edu/usda/nass/SB993/SB1031.pdf [April 24, 2015].

2013 WISCONSIN CASH RECEIPTS FROM FARM MARKETINGS
(Percent of Major Commodities)

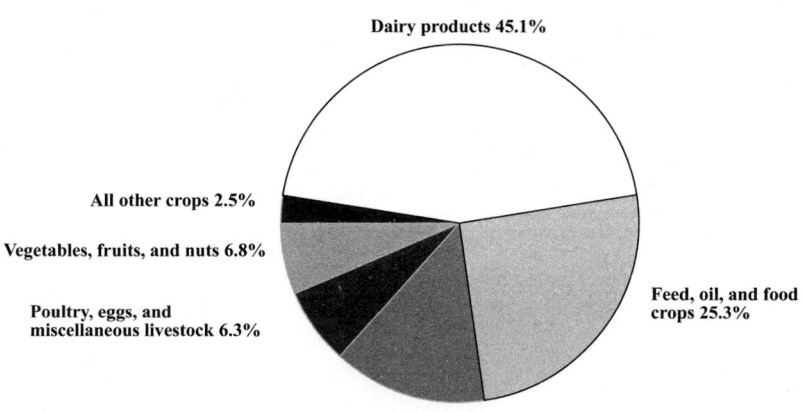

Dairy products 45.1%

All other crops 2.5%

Vegetables, fruits, and nuts 6.8%

Poultry, eggs, and miscellaneous livestock 6.3%

Feed, oil, and food crops 25.3%

Meat animals 14.0%

WISCONSIN CASH RECEIPTS FROM FARM MARKETINGS
By Commodity, 2009 – 2013
(In Thousands)

Commodity	2009	2010	2011	2012	2013[1]
ALL COMMODITIES	**$7,571,132**	**$9,231,606**	**$11,522,907**	**$12,107,105**	**$12,290,870**
LIVESTOCK, DAIRY, AND POULTRY	**4,800,035**	**5,885,503**	**7,403,252**	**7,550,081**	**8,034,127**
Meat animals	**826,221**	**975,450**	**1,374,032**	**1,417,172**	**1,717,721**
Cattle and calves	726,337	859,514	1,235,729	1,283,770	1,579,550
Hogs	94,619	115,936	138,303	133,402	138,171
Sheep and lambs	5,265	8,239	NA	NA	NA
Dairy products, milk	**3,270,677**	**4,147,199**	**5,233,137**	**5,229,464**	**5,541,494**
Poultry and eggs	**358,669**	**397,164**	**402,703**	**465,017**	**452,228**
Broilers	87,927	95,243	89,643	108,550	135,138
Farm chickens	281	327	335	345	NA
Eggs	78,301	78,316	85,397	101,214	NA
Wool	188	200	298	338	NA
Miscellaneous livestock	**344,468**	**365,690**	**393,380**	**438,428**	**322,684**
Honey	5,972	6,881	6,787	8,868	NA
Trout	1,791	1,624	1,857	2,067	NA
Mink pelts	37,777	57,685	72,353	99,070	NA
CROPS	**2,771,097**	**3,346,103**	**4,119,655**	**4,557,024**	**4,256,743**
Food grains	**101,159**	**78,456**	**148,798**	**142,816**	**106,325**
Wheat	99,945	76,996	146,489	141,406	101,075
Feed crops	**1,022,520**	**1,461,300**	**2,188,463**	**2,315,908**	**2,118,050**
Barley	1,134	1,283	1,031	1,235	NA
Corn	934,451	1,371,889	2,098,803	2,221,527	1,929,483
Hay	76,326	77,524	78,604	82,616	NA
Oats	10,609	10,605	10,025	10,530	NA
Oil crops	**572,140**	**779,206**	**659,393**	**908,539**	**887,938**
Soybeans	572,140	779,206	659,393	908,539	NA
Vegetables	**536,383**	**478,575**	**533,768**	**563,094**	**609,890**
Beans, dry	5,554	4,755	6,220	5,792	NA
Potatoes, fall	256,886	243,614	239,142	248,765	NA
Beans, snap, processing	52,613	41,028	58,434	76,944	NA
Cabbage	15,552	9,933	13,350	11,250	NA
Carrots	6,927	5,064	7,133	10,356	NA
Corn, sweet	16,013	13,653	14,782	15,232	NA
Cucumbers, processing	8,649	8,085	7,151	7,824	NA
Onions, storage	8,366	5,076	5,043	6,235	NA
Peas, green, processing	24,847	22,784	35,679	30,566	NA
Fruits and nuts	**205,769**	**203,381**	**215,362**	**254,306**	**226,135**
Apples, fresh	22,224	15,078	3,954	9,445	NA
Apples, processing	463	304	427	297	NA
Cherries, tart	2,263	1,611	1,910	1,885	NA
Cranberries	166,404	172,896	195,356	230,672	NA
Strawberries, spring	7,285	6,437	6,440	4,681	NA
All other crops	**333,127**	**344,994**	**373,871**	**372,361**	**308,404**
Maple product	7,340	4,622	5,627	2,280	NA
Peppermint	2,613	3,776	5,061	5,966	NA
Spearmint	428	491	299	583	NA
Greenhouse and nursery	**237,560**	**240,570**	**247,685**	**241,840**	**NA**
Christmas trees[2]	13,500	13,800	14,300	14,300	NA

Note: Bold figures indicate category totals of the commodities immediately following and indicate categories included in next higher level of aggregation. Category totals may include amounts for specific commodities not listed separately or that are not listed to provide confidentiality to large producers in concentrated industries. Prior year's numbers have been revised to reflect updated source data.

NA indicates data is not available. In future editions only data from major commodity groups and select commodities will be available.

[1]2013 data is from a different source than previous years and may not be comparable.

[2]Christmas trees are included in Greenhouse and nursery total.

Sources: U.S. Department of Agriculture, Economic Research Service, "Annual Cash Receipts by Commodity, U.S. and States", at: http://www.ers.usda.gov/data-products/farm-income-and-wealth-statistics/us-and-state-level-farm-income-and-wealth-statistics-(includes-the-us-farm-income-forecast-for-2015).aspx [April 23, 2015]; U.S. Department of Agriculture, National Agricultural Statistic Service "2014 Wisconsin Agricultural Statistics", at: http://www.nass.usda.gov/Statistics_by_State/Wisconsin/Publications/Annual_Statistical_Bulletin/bulletin2014_web.pdf [April 23, 2015].

CASH RECEIPTS AND INCOME FROM FARMING
By State, 2013
(In Thousands)

State	Crops	Cash Receipts Livestock and Products	Total[1]	Government Payments[2]	Income Net	Rank[1]
Alabama	$1,310,344	$4,664,775	$5,975,119	$90,592	$2,218,014	23
Alaska	23,724	6,959	30,683	12,217	-13,059	50
Arizona	2,378,756	1,944,944	4,323,700	47,443	1,245,160	32
Arkansas	4,906,027	5,243,058	10,149,085	346,865	2,912,631	14
California	33,578,334	12,777,618	46,355,952	248,711	12,112,873	1
Colorado	2,343,798	4,841,350	7,185,148	238,985	1,575,660	29
Connecticut	394,587	179,958	574,545	7,011	106,865	46
Delaware	309,529	985,831	1,295,360	15,303	539,742	37
Florida	6,481,702	1,971,902	8,453,604	71,090	2,398,402	21
Georgia	3,981,733	6,118,078	10,099,811	247,606	2,665,123	18
Hawaii	607,954	135,028	742,982	13,155	150,220	44
Idaho	3,660,354	4,656,692	8,317,046	129,137	2,741,286	17
ILLINOIS	14,545,023	2,773,804	17,318,827	607,864	9,600,579	3
Indiana	8,097,397	3,552,960	11,650,357	329,792	6,026,426	6
IOWA	17,169,737	14,037,566	31,207,303	782,425	9,952,423	2
Kansas	6,690,966	9,105,720	15,796,686	697,629	5,911,873	7
Kentucky	2,891,516	2,798,654	5,690,170	290,054	2,744,239	16
Louisiana	3,026,266	1,219,376	4,245,642	215,172	2,029,112	25
Maine	419,793	320,468	740,261	17,493	155,372	43
Maryland	939,810	1,371,316	2,311,126	43,546	788,192	36
Massachusetts	337,831	109,225	447,056	10,136	37,768	47
MICHIGAN	5,396,095	3,304,508	8,700,603	142,418	2,151,619	24
MINNESOTA	14,586,349	7,702,395	22,288,744	527,038	7,222,473	5
Mississippi	2,832,086	3,507,305	6,339,391	206,223	2,414,487	20
Missouri	5,724,145	4,263,278	9,987,423	428,490	3,414,715	12
Montana	2,413,972	1,757,151	4,171,123	250,350	1,767,022	26
Nebraska	11,606,293	11,962,766	23,569,059	599,732	8,365,727	4
Nevada	304,940	455,356	760,296	9,546	136,042	45
New Hampshire	104,359	85,411	189,770	12,417	10,489	48
New Jersey	886,004	111,930	997,934	9,703	235,170	41
New Mexico	684,736	3,104,930	3,789,666	115,617	1,318,175	31
New York	2,272,987	3,404,574	5,677,561	74,631	1,578,597	28
North Carolina	4,330,584	8,304,690	12,635,274	411,331	3,305,675	13
North Dakota	7,601,492	1,293,877	8,895,369	600,757	2,579,461	19
Ohio	7,430,497	3,496,055	10,926,552	258,297	3,648,194	11
Oklahoma	1,656,872	5,477,819	7,134,691	356,751	1,685,706	27
Oregon	3,201,413	1,515,344	4,716,757	116,092	818,219	35
Pennsylvania	2,781,563	4,772,872	7,554,435	94,218	2,257,750	22
Rhode Island	49,837	9,308	59,145	2,179	4,923	49
South Carolina	1,205,906	1,704,820	2,910,726	106,078	930,879	34
South Dakota	6,424,543	3,927,986	10,352,529	303,639	4,682,786	8
Tennessee	2,619,452	1,507,040	4,126,492	147,864	1,404,452	30
Texas	6,188,607	15,378,700	21,567,307	1,125,450	4,121,329	9
Utah	545,605	1,303,253	1,848,858	39,206	375,678	38
Vermont	185,055	650,808	835,863	16,014	252,976	40
Virginia	1,345,832	2,394,036	3,739,868	110,993	1,231,573	33
Washington	7,181,593	2,653,866	9,835,459	191,289	2,764,158	15
West Virginia	147,476	618,466	765,942	17,379	205,466	42
WISCONSIN	4,256,743	8,034,127	12,290,870	221,822	3,917,541	10
Wyoming	466,792	1,268,936	1,735,728	46,043	287,961	39
UNITED STATES[3]	$218,527,004	$182,786,892	$401,313,896	$11,003,796	$128,988,143	

[1]Total and rank calculated by Wisconsin Legislative Reference Bureau.
[2]Includes both cash payments and payments-in-kind (PIK).
[3]Detail may not add due to rounding.

Source: U.S. Department of Agriculture, Economic Research Service, "Value Added by U.S. Agriculture (includes net farm income)", at: http://www.ers.usda.gov/data-products/farm-income-and-wealth-statistics/us-and-state-level-farm-income-and-wealth-statistics-(includes-the-us-farm-income-forecast-for-2015).aspx [April 24, 2015].

WISCONSIN'S RANK IN AGRICULTURE, 2013

Commodity	Unit	United States (000s)	(000s)	Wisconsin Percent of U.S.	Rank in U.S.	Leading State in U.S.
CASH RECEIPTS						
ALL COMMODITIES		$401,313,896	$12,290,870	3.1%	9	California
Livestock and livestock products . .		182,786,892	8,034,127	4.4	7	Texas
Crops		218,527,004	4,256,743	1.9	18	California
PRODUCTION						
DAIRY						
Milk production.	Lbs	201,218,000	27,572,000	13.7	2	California
Cheese (excluding cottage cheese) .	Lbs	11,101,135	2,855,681	25.7	1	Wisconsin
American.	Lbs	4,419,238	837,525	19.0	1	Wisconsin
Cheddar	Lbs	3,189,217	567,814	17.8	1	Wisconsin
Italian	Lbs	4,735,283	1,422,200	30.0	2	California
Mozzarella	Lbs	3,699,454	960,481	26.0	2	California
Dry whey, human food.	Lbs	924,146	302,843	32.8	1	Wisconsin
LIVESTOCK AND POULTRY						
Cattle and calves, all [1].	Head	87,730	3,350	3.8	9	Texas
Milk cows	Head	9,209	1,270	13.8	2	California
Hogs and pigs, all[2]	Head	64,775	305	0.5	19	Iowa
Sheep[1]	Head	5,210	83	1.6	16[3]	Texas
Milk goats.	Head	355	46	13.0	1	Wisconsin
Chickens[2]	Head	464,328	6,814	1.5	18	Iowa
Broilers	Head	8,524,800	53,100	0.6	19	Georgia
Mink pelts.	Pelts	3,545	1,230	34.7	1	Wisconsin
Trout, sold 12" or longer	Lbs	56,269	441	0.8	8	Idaho
Honey	Lbs	149,499	3,540	2.4	10	North Dakota
Eggs.	Eggs	95,176,000	1,483,000	1.6	17	Iowa
CROPS						
Corn for grain	Bu	13,925,147	445,300	3.2	9	Iowa
Corn for silage	Tons	117,851	16,170	13.7	1	Wisconsin
Oats	Bu	65,879	6,825	10.4	3	South Dakota
Soybeans	Bu	3,288,833	58,900	1.8	16	Illinois
Wheat, winter	Bu	1,534,253	15,370	1.0	26	Kansas
Barley	Bu	215,078	784	0.4	19	Idaho
Forage (dry equivalent), all	Tons	89,571	7,022	7.8	4	California
Hay (dry only), all	Tons	135,946	3,760	2.8	14	Texas
Potatoes, all	Cwt	434,652	27,280	6.3	3	Idaho
Dry edible beans	Cwt	24,486	98	0.4	17	North Dakota
Cherries, tart	Lbs	294,200	12,300	4.2	4	Michigan
Apples.	Lbs	10,441,700	41,700	0.4	13	Washington
Strawberries.	Cwt	30,002	33	0.1	9	California
Maple syrup.	Gals	3,523	265	7.5	4	Vermont
Cranberries	Bbl	8,957	6,016	67.2	1	Wisconsin
Mint for oil	Lbs	9,058	209	2.3	6	Washington
Onions.	Cwt	69,654	810	1.2	11[4]	California
Cabbage for fresh market	Cwt	22,065	868	3.9	7	California
Sweet corn for fresh market	Cwt	29,880	566	1.9	10	California
Carrots for processing.	Tons	350	117	33.4	2	Washington
Sweet corn for processing	Tons	2,552	584	22.9	3	Minnesota
Green peas for processing	Tons	356	76	21.2	3	Washington
Snap beans for processing	Tons	667	299	44.8	1	Wisconsin
Cucumbers for pickles	Tons	473	38	8.0	3	Michigan

Abbreviations: Bbl = barrels, Bu = bushels, Cwt = hundredweight, Gals = gallons, Lbs = pounds.

Note: Wisconsin is also a leading state in the production of turkeys, ducks, and ginseng; Wisconsin's rank is not available for these commodities.

[1]January 1, 2014 inventory.

[2]December 1, 2013 inventory.

[3]Tied with Virginia.

[4]Tied with Michigan.

Sources: U.S. Department of Agriculture, National Agriculture Statistics Service, "2014 Wisconsin Agricultural Statistics", at: http://www.nass.usda.gov/Statistics_by_State/Wisconsin/Publications/Annual_Statistical_Bulletin/bulletin2014_web.pdf [April 23, 2015]; U.S. Department of Agriculture, Economic Research Service, "Annual Cash Receipts by Commodity, U.S. and States", at: http://www.ers.usda.gov/data-products/farm-income-and-wealth-statistics/us-and-state-level-farm-income-and-wealth-statistics-(includes-the-us-farm-income-forecast-for-2015).aspx [April 23, 2015].

NUMBER AND ACREAGE OF FARMS
By State, 2009 and 2014

State	Number of Farms		Farm Acreage (in thousands)		Average Farm Size (acres)	
	2009	2014	2009	2014	2009	2014
Alabama	48,500	43,400	9,000	8,900	186	205
Alaska	680	760	880	830	1,294	1,092
Arizona.	15,500	19,600	26,100	26,000	1,684	1,327
Arkansas	49,100	44,000	13,600	13,800	277	314
California	81,500	76,400	25,400	25,500	312	334
Colorado	36,200	35,000	31,300	31,800	865	909
Connecticut	4,900	6,000	400	440	82	73
Delaware	2,480	2,500	490	500	198	200
Florida	47,500	47,600	9,250	9,500	195	200
Georgia.	47,600	41,100	10,300	9,400	216	229
Hawaii	7,500	7,000	1,120	1,120	149	160
Idaho	25,500	24,400	11,400	11,800	447	484
ILLINOIS	75,800	74,500	26,700	26,900	352	361
Indiana	61,500	58,200	14,800	14,700	241	253
IOWA	92,600	88,000	30,800	30,500	333	347
Kansas	65,500	61,000	46,200	46,000	705	754
Kentucky.	85,500	76,400	14,000	13,000	164	170
Louisiana.	30,000	27,200	8,050	7,800	268	287
Maine	8,100	8,200	1,350	1,450	167	177
Maryland.	12,800	12,300	2,050	2,030	160	165
Massachusetts	7,700	7,800	520	520	68	67
MICHIGAN	54,800	51,600	10,000	9,950	182	193
MINNESOTA	81,000	74,000	26,900	25,900	332	350
Mississippi	42,300	37,100	11,050	10,900	261	294
Missouri	108,000	97,700	29,100	28,300	269	290
Montana	29,800	27,800	60,800	59,700	2,040	2,147
Nebraska	47,200	49,100	45,600	45,200	966	921
Nevada.	3,080	4,200	5,900	5,950	1,916	1,417
New Hampshire	4,150	4,400	470	470	113	107
New Jersey.	10,300	9,100	730	720	71	79
New Mexico	20,500	24,700	43,000	43,200	2,098	1,749
New York	36,600	35,500	7,100	7,180	194	202
North Carolina	52,400	49,500	8,600	8,400	164	170
North Dakota.	32,000	30,300	39,600	39,300	1,238	1,297
Ohio	74,900	74,500	13,800	14,000	184	188
Oklahoma	86,500	79,600	35,100	34,300	406	431
Oregon	38,600	34,600	16,400	16,400	425	474
Pennsylvania	63,200	58,800	7,750	7,720	123	131
Rhode Island	1,220	1,240	70	70	57	56
South Carolina	27,000	24,400	4,900	5,000	181	205
South Dakota.	31,500	31,700	43,700	43,300	1,387	1,366
Tennessee	78,700	67,300	10,900	10,900	139	162
Texas.	247,500	245,500	130,400	130,000	527	530
Utah	16,600	18,100	11,100	11,000	669	608
Vermont	7,000	7,300	1,220	1,250	174	171
Virginia.	47,000	45,900	8,000	8,200	170	179
Washington.	39,500	36,700	14,800	14,700	375	401
West Virginia.	23,200	21,300	3,700	3,600	159	169
WISCONSIN	78,000	69,000	15,200	14,500	195	210
Wyoming.	11,000	11,700	30,200	30,400	2,745	2,598
UNITED STATES	2,200,010	2,084,000	919,800	913,000	418	438

Note: "Farm" is currently defined as a place that sells, or would normally sell, at least $1,000 of agricultural products during the year.

Source: U.S. Department of Agriculture, National Agricultural Statistics Service, "Farms, Land in Farms, and Livestock Operations, 2014" and earlier editions, at: http://usda.mannlib.cornell.edu/MannUsda/viewDocumentInfo. do?documentID=1259 [April 24, 2015].

WISCONSIN FARM OPERATORS
By County, 2012

County	Total Farms	Tenure of Operator			Type of Organization				
		Full Owners	Part Owners	Tenants	Individual or Family	Partnership	Family-held Corporation	Other than Family-held Corporation	Other*
Adams	313	183	125	5	255	29	18	5	6
Ashland	187	120	66	1	170	9	3	2	3
Barron	1,322	795	480	47	1,207	49	56	2	8
Bayfield	352	245	98	9	308	14	18	—	12
Brown	1,111	718	339	54	960	89	47	2	13
Buffalo	1,061	723	310	28	920	83	46	2	10
Burnett	406	282	117	7	369	15	13	3	6
Calumet	719	423	256	40	598	50	63	—	8
Chippewa	1,757	1,242	473	42	1,578	115	47	1	16
Clark	2,317	1,449	753	115	2,112	94	88	1	22
Columbia. . . .	1,564	1,035	447	82	1,364	116	54	4	26
Crawford. . . .	1,105	776	262	67	976	93	23	2	11
Dane	2,749	1,832	728	189	2,311	225	133	10	70
Dodge	2,012	1,306	626	80	1,724	154	85	9	40
Door	803	566	215	22	679	49	50	2	23
Douglas	364	277	79	8	329	17	14	—	4
Dunn	1,404	923	438	43	1,255	79	60	—	10
Eau Claire	1,313	963	291	59	1,231	52	16	—	14
Florence	90	67	22	1	80	8	1	—	1
Fond du Lac . . .	1,399	828	488	83	1,157	126	70	9	37
Forest.	127	86	41	—	113	7	5	—	2
Grant	2,436	1,694	614	128	2,065	227	88	8	48
Green.	1,545	1,084	382	79	1,360	95	53	4	33
Green Lake. . . .	608	377	192	39	519	52	17	2	18
Iowa	1,588	1,103	411	74	1,335	150	61	7	35
Iron.	61	44	12	5	55	—	6	—	—
Jackson.	864	580	258	26	744	53	44	4	19
Jefferson	1,225	788	366	71	1,041	72	63	11	38
Juneau	827	590	216	21	735	63	15	1	13
Kenosha	359	220	107	32	276	32	38	2	11
Kewaunee	734	450	260	24	639	61	20	9	5
La Crosse	748	496	209	43	645	58	27	4	14
Lafayette	1,252	814	356	82	1,087	90	46	2	27
Langlade	396	243	144	9	310	37	42	7	—
Lincoln	449	307	126	16	401	19	21	1	7
Manitowoc	1,224	735	444	45	1,068	83	51	5	17
Marathon	2,266	1,258	916	92	1,987	155	108	8	8
Marinette	535	361	166	8	471	31	24	3	6
Marquette	478	321	142	15	411	39	17	4	7
Menominee . . .	5	3	2	—	2	—	—	—	3
Milwaukee	82	39	16	27	60	6	9	2	5
Monroe.	1,926	1,366	486	74	1,737	102	59	6	22
Oconto	929	604	303	22	839	61	24	—	5
Oneida	150	134	15	1	120	9	10	1	10
Outagamie	1,170	655	452	63	1,005	82	57	8	18
Ozaukee	416	248	145	23	332	31	37	2	14
Pepin	459	294	147	18	394	40	15	—	10
Pierce.	1,259	819	388	52	1,092	61	73	7	26
Polk	1,313	894	388	31	1,177	53	64	3	16
Portage	969	559	369	41	840	68	53	1	7
Price	472	346	116	10	442	20	7	—	3
Racine	575	354	179	42	471	36	37	2	29
Richland	1,260	918	310	32	1,109	90	30	4	27
Rock	1,509	979	427	103	1,270	101	95	11	32
Rusk	529	327	182	20	471	24	29	1	4
St. Croix	1,417	954	409	54	1,242	81	72	5	17
Sauk	1,665	1,094	493	78	1,409	125	92	7	32
Sawyer	172	106	57	9	145	9	12	2	4
Shawano	1,278	749	491	38	1,111	97	54	—	16
Sheboygan	986	554	391	41	847	70	53	6	10
Taylor	967	614	321	32	878	39	38	2	10
Trempealeau . . .	1,436	1,004	369	63	1,271	99	38	2	26
Vernon	2,228	1,512	631	85	2,013	126	42	11	36
Vilas	47	40	7	—	33	6	4	2	2
Walworth	870	529	259	82	673	75	71	21	30
Washburn	405	279	117	9	351	21	19	1	13
Washington	712	419	247	46	568	69	54	3	18
Waukesha	557	371	142	44	449	36	51	6	15
Waupaca	1,145	728	381	36	1,013	79	44	1	8
Waushara	592	371	207	14	505	35	43	5	4
Winnebago	1,117	795	277	45	966	66	68	8	9
Wood	1,067	676	360	31	937	60	60	3	7
STATE	69,754	45,638	21,059	3,057	60,617	4,667	3,065	269	1,136

*Includes cooperative, estate or trust, institutional, etc.

Source: U.S. Department of Agriculture, National Agricultural Statistics Service, *2012 Census of Agriculture,* Volume 1, Chapter 2: Wisconsin County Level Data, February 2009, at: http://www.agcensus.usda.gov/Publications/2012/Full_Report/ Volume_1,_Chapter_2_County_Level/Wisconsin/ [May 26, 2015].

WISCONSIN AGRICULTURAL LAND SALES
By County, 2012 and 2013

County[1]	Total Agricultural Land Sales[2]				Land Continuing in Agricultural Use		Agricultural Land Diverted to Other Uses	
	Number		Dollar Avg. per Acre		Dollar Avg. per Acre		Dollar Avg. per Acre	
	2012	2013	2012	2013	2012	2013	2012	2013
Adams	6	10	$2,427	$3,000	$2,427	$2,824	—	$6,100
Ashland	3	3	1,154	1,255	1,154	1,255	—	—
Barron	37	37	2,960	4,132	2,960	4,132	—	—
Bayfield	5	9	1,248	1,350	1,234	1,350	$1,375	—
Brown	44	19	7,618	8,120	7,440	8,123	15,000	8,060
Buffalo	18	18	3,397	4,004	3,336	4,004	3,651	—
Burnett	5	7	1,939	2,049	1,939	2,095	—	1,177
Calumet	17	11	6,540	6,899	6,540	6,899	—	—
Chippewa	42	30	2,796	2,710	2,796	2,710	—	—
Clark	54	30	2,919	3,400	2,919	3,400	—	—
Columbia	35	7	6,212	6,750	6,212	6,750	—	—
Crawford	9	8	2,618	2,672	2,618	2,672	—	—
Dane	39	27	9,102	7,434	7,826	7,544	13,797	6,768
Dodge	46	19	6,197	6,289	6,197	6,290	—	6,200
Door	12	6	3,960	3,994	3,960	3,994	—	—
Douglas	—	3	—	1,146	—	1,000	—	1,274
Dunn	32	37	2,777	2,853	2,681	2,856	3,079	2,783
Eau Claire	20	14	3,373	3,078	3,373	3,078	—	—
Florence	4	1	1,195	1,160	1,183	—	1,505	1,160
Fond du Lac	60	41	5,894	6,305	5,894	6,340	—	5,173
Forest	2	2	1,036	1,487	998	1,487	1,500	—
Grant	30	27	4,680	4,727	4,680	4,727	—	—
Green	45	31	5,084	4,742	5,084	4,752	—	4,239
Green Lake	5	5	5,794	5,838	5,794	5,838	—	—
Iowa	40	23	4,285	4,761	4,292	4,835	2,300	3,198
Iron	1	2	1,475	1,005	—	900	1,475	1,200
Jackson	16	17	3,320	2,972	3,373	2,972	2,405	—
Jefferson	23	18	5,382	6,006	5,005	6,006	8,301	—
Juneau	14	18	2,597	3,285	2,597	3,148	—	4,918
Kenosha	13	12	6,265	5,980	6,265	5,980	—	—
Kewaunee	13	5	4,684	4,920	4,811	4,920	3,500	—
La Crosse	9	7	4,344	5,080	4,398	5,199	2,850	3,025
Lafayette	39	21	5,663	5,327	5,663	5,327	—	—
Langlade	19	10	2,106	3,383	2,106	3,383	—	—
Lincoln	8	10	1,988	1,780	1,988	1,780	—	—
Manitowoc	21	20	5,900	6,421	5,900	6,421	—	—
Marathon	56	40	3,007	3,231	3,017	3,242	2,388	2,792
Marinette	19	10	3,050	2,953	3,050	2,953	—	—
Marquette	7	9	2,772	3,800	2,994	3,800	2,602	—
Milwaukee	—	—	—	—	—	—	—	—
Monroe	23	26	2,924	3,276	2,950	3,312	2,427	2,424
Oconto	16	17	3,202	3,594	3,202	3,594	—	—
Oneida	4	3	1,404	1,699	1,404	1,699	—	—
Outagamie	31	14	5,674	8,989	5,674	7,301	—	29,130
Ozaukee	15	10	5,043	5,679	5,043	5,679	—	—
Pepin	12	7	3,608	4,223	3,608	4,223	—	—
Pierce	32	13	3,924	4,217	3,924	4,244	—	3,500
Polk	47	28	3,256	2,466	3,256	2,464	—	2,500
Portage	12	20	3,510	2,777	3,568	2,785	2,673	2,556
Price	7	1	1,244	1,400	1,241	1,400	1,350	—
Racine	19	22	5,774	5,939	5,774	5,922	—	6,100
Richland	22	25	2,842	2,758	2,838	2,798	4,000	2,310
Rock	21	18	6,538	5,883	6,304	5,883	10,700	—
Rusk	25	27	1,567	1,990	1,567	1,937	—	5,000
St. Croix	57	42	4,636	4,233	4,636	4,233	—	—
Sauk	22	26	3,889	3,558	3,897	3,642	3,550	2,912
Sawyer	8	8	2,511	1,982	2,511	2,131	—	1,300
Shawano	35	20	3,777	4,803	3,777	4,803	—	—
Sheboygan	45	29	5,416	6,047	5,200	5,818	7,400	7,400
Taylor	15	13	2,285	2,275	2,285	2,275	—	—
Trempealeau	10	15	2,807	4,504	2,807	4,724	—	3,000
Vernon	27	22	3,254	4,462	3,376	4,462	1,642	—
Vilas	—	—	—	—	—	—	—	—
Walworth	27	33	6,581	7,399	6,634	7,399	5,500	—
Washburn	11	12	1,835	1,932	1,837	1,932	1,700	—
Washington	7	16	7,416	7,173	7,592	7,173	6,255	—
Waukesha	5	10	11,266	9,112	11,266	8,121	—	27,826
Waupaca	23	16	3,816	3,728	3,799	3,728	5,000	—
Waushara	13	16	3,422	2,855	3,431	2,855	3,000	—
Winnebago	13	20	4,785	5,029	4,785	4,778	—	10,254
Wood	15	15	3,044	2,994	3,044	2,879	—	5,233
STATE	1,487	1,168	$4,482	$4,480	$4,414	$4,442	$6,789	$5,670

[1]Menominee County had no agricultural sales in years shown.

[2]Includes land with and without buildings and other improvements.

Sources: U.S. Department of Agriculture, National Agricultural Statistics Service, "2014 Wisconsin Agricultural Statistics" and earlier editions, at: http://www.nass.usda.gov/Statistics_by_State/Wisconsin/Publications/Annual_Statistical_Bulletin/bulletin2014_web.pdf [April 24, 2015].

NONIRRIGATED CROPLAND CASH RENTS
Dollars Per Acre, By County, 2008 and 2013

County	2008 Dollars per Acre	2013 Dollars per Acre	Percent Change[1]	County	2008 Dollars per Acre	2013 Dollars per Acre	Percent Change[1]
Adams	$55.50	$65.50	18.0%	Marinette.	$48.50	$54.00	11.3%
Ashland	NA	NA	—	Marquette	54.50	102.00	87.2
Barron	52.00	71.00	36.5	Menominee . . .	NA	NA	—
Bayfield	19.00	NA	—	Milwaukee	NA	NA	—
Brown	93.00	144.00	54.8	Monroe.	69.00	106.00	53.6
Buffalo	71.50	112.00	56.6	Oconto	54.50	89.00	63.3
Burnett	30.00	39.00	30.0	Oneida	NA	NA	—
Calumet	82.00	128.00	56.1	Outagamie	80.50	129.00	60.2
Chippewa	62.00	93.00	50.0	Ozaukee	NA	87.00	—
Clark	51.50	87.00	68.9	Pepin	85.50	115.00	34.5
Columbia.	107.00	163.00	52.3	Pierce.	76.00	121.00	59.2
Crawford	86.00	131.00	52.3	Polk	45.00	68.50	52.2
Dane	122.00	163.00	33.6	Portage	48.50	49.00	1.0
Dodge	121.00	157.00	29.8	Price	NA	36.00	—
Door	54.00	93.50	73.1	Racine	95.00	122.00	28.4
Douglas	NA	NA	—	Richland	84.00	113.00	34.5
Dunn	66.00	97.00	47.0	Rock	131.00	175.00	33.6
Eau Claire	66.00	120.00	81.8	Rusk	31.00	48.00	54.8
Florence	NA	NA	—	St. Croix	64.50	109.00	69.0
Fond du Lac . . .	91.00	120.00	31.9	Sauk	95.00	110.00	15.8
Forest.	NA	NA	—	Sawyer	NA	40.00	—
Grant	138.00	206.00	49.3	Shawano	54.50	87.00	59.6
Green.	111.00	160.00	44.1	Sheboygan	63.50	100.00	57.5
Green Lake. . . .	86.50	185.00	113.9	Taylor	42.00	70.00	66.7
Iowa	119.00	172.00	44.5	Trempealeau . . .	80.00	135.00	68.8
Iron.	NA	NA	—	Vernon	86.00	117.00	36.0
Jackson.	74.00	116.00	56.8	Vilas	NA	NA	—
Jefferson	111.00	154.00	38.7	Walworth.	122.00	182.00	49.2
Juneau	60.50	90.00	48.8	Washburn	30.00	49.50	65.0
Kenosha	94.50	128.00	35.4	Washington. . . .	71.00	102.00	43.7
Kewaunee	82.50	120.00	45.5	Waukesha	72.50	NA	—
La Crosse	87.50	127.00	45.1	Waupaca	56.00	88.00	57.1
Lafayette	162.00	212.00	30.9	Waushara	47.00	51.00	8.5
Langlade	NA	66.00	—	Winnebago	79.00	97.50	23.4
Lincoln.	28.50	44.00	54.4	Wood	46.00	61.00	32.6
Manitowoc. . . .	72.50	127.00	75.2	STATE[2].	$82.00	$120.00	46.3%
Marathon.	49.50	82.00	65.7				

NA: Data withheld to avoid disclosing details of individual operators.

[1]Percentages calculated by Wisconsin Legislative Reference Bureau.

[2]Detail may not add due to rounding.

Source: U.S. Department of Agriculture, National Agriculture Statistics Service, "2014 Wisconsin Agricultural Statistics" and previous editions, at: http://www.nass.usda.gov/Statistics_by_State/Wisconsin/Publications/Annual_Statistical_Bulletin/bulletin2014_web.pdf [April 27, 2015].

WISCONSIN NET FARM INCOME, 2009 – 2013

	2009	2010	2011	2012	2013
Number of farms.	78,000	73,200	71,200	69,800	69,800
Average net farm income per farm (dollars).	$10,187	$25,030	$49,193	$37,384	$56,125
	Income (in thousands)				
Value of crop production.	$2,996,040	$3,258,669	$4,220,648	$4,029,757	$4,340,224
Value of livestock production	4,877,488	5,754,262	7,206,980	7,128,936	8,168,866
Revenues from services and forestry	1,390,297	1,302,216	1,293,129	1,488,515	1,806,682
VALUE OF AGRICULTURAL SECTOR OUTPUT[1].	$9,263,825	$10,315,148	$12,720,757	$12,647,209	$14,315,772
Less: Purchased inputs[2].	5,470,518	5,384,677	6,160,061	7,052,426	7,228,666
Less: Motor vehicle registration and licensing	15,077	12,795	12,792	12,571	15,735
Less: Property taxes.	380,000	410,000	360,000	370,000	400,000
Plus: Direct government payments	405,870	259,289	196,018	281,827	221,822
GROSS VALUE ADDED	$3,804,099	$4,766,965	$6,383,922	$5,494,038	$6,893,193
Less: Capital consumption (depreciation)	1,390,003	1,415,181	1,479,228	1,036,520	1,147,654
NET VALUE ADDED[3]	$2,414,096	$3,351,784	$4,904,694	$4,457,519	$5,745,540
Less: Payments to stakeholders[4]	1,619,513	1,519,613	1,402,151	1,848,090	1,827,999
NET FARM INCOME[5]	$794,583	$1,832,171	$3,502,543	$2,609,429	$3,917,541

Note: Average net farm income calculated by Wisconsin Legislative Reference Bureau. Numbers for 2010 and 2011 have been revised to reflect updated source data.

[1]Value of agricultural sector output is the gross value of the commodities and services produced within a year.

[2]Includes purchases of feed, livestock, poultry, and seed; outlays for fertilizers and lime, pesticides, fuel and electricity; capital repair and maintenance; and marketing, storage, transportation, contract labor, and other expenses.

[3]Net value added is the sector's contribution to the national economy and is the sum of the income from production earned by all factors of production, regardless of ownership.

[4]Includes compensation for hired labor, net rent received by nonoperator landlords, and interest payments.

[5]Net farm income is the farm operators' share of income from the sector's production activities.

Sources: U.S. Department of Agriculture, National Agricultural Statistics Service, "2014 Wisconsin Agricultural Statistics", at: http://www.nass.usda.gov/Statistics_by_State/Wisconsin/Publications/Annual_Statistical_Bulletin/bulletin2014_web.pdf, and U.S. Department of Agriculture, Economic Research Service, "Value added to the U.S. economy by the agricultural sector via the production of goods and services, Wisconsin, 2014", and previous editions, at: http://www.ers.usda.gov/data-products/farm-income-and-wealth-statistics/us-and-state-level-farm-income-and-wealth-statistics-(includes-the-us-farm-income-forecast-for-2015).aspx [April 24, 2015].

FARM ASSETS AND LIABILITIES
By Leading Agricultural States, 2013

State	Number of Farms[1]	Average Assets Per Farm[2]	Average Liability Per Farm[2]	Average Equity Per Farm[2]	Debt/Asset Ratio[3]
Arkansas	44,601	$765,495	$71,057	$694,438	9.3%
California	77,902	1,952,240	209,810	1,742,431	10.7
Florida	48,000	847,686	54,271	793,414	6.4
Georgia.	42,301	857,325	68,525	788,800	8.0
ILLINOIS	75,101	1,590,995	159,908	1,431,087	10.1
Indiana	58,701	1,257,945	131,140	1,126,805	10.4
IOWA	88,501	2,060,333	187,603	1,872,731	9.1
Kansas	61,800	1,371,695	119,442	1,252,252	8.7
MINNESOTA	74,401	1,690,935	175,075	1,515,860	10.4
Missouri	99,402	891,064	61,215	829,850	6.9
Nebraska	49,601	2,198,413	254,066	1,944,346	11.6
North Carolina	50,002	843,291	57,247	786,044	6.8
Texas.	248,501	756,261	24,543	731,717	3.2
Washington.	37,000	1,020,442	NA	911,597	10.7
WISCONSIN	69,801	1,058,536	135,877	922,659	12.8

NA: 2013 liability data for Washington not available.

[1]"Farm" is currently defined as a place that sells, or would normally sell, at least $1,000 of agricultural products during the year.

[2]Dollar amounts represent farm businesses, excluding household assets and debts.

[3]Debt does not include all financial obligations that are contained in the liabilities column.

Sources: U.S. Department of Agriculture, Economic Research Service, "Farm Business Balance Sheets, All Survey States" and "Farm Business Financial Ratios", at: http://www.ers.usda.gov/data-products/arms-farm-financial-and-crop-production-practices/tailored-reports-farm-structure-and-finance.aspx [April 24, 2015].

STATEWIDE ASSOCIATIONS OF WISCONSIN
Listed by Key Word

AAA Wisconsin, Inc.
Victoria Hanson, Regional Pres.
P.O. Box 33, Madison 53701-0033
(608) 836-6555 www.aaa.com

Academic Staff Professionals Representative Org.
Janet Swandby, Exec. Dir.
10 E. Doty St., Suite 519, Madison 53703
(608) 286-9599 aspro@aspro.net www.aspro.net

Academy of Sciences, Arts and Letters, Wis.
Jane Elder, Exec. Dir.
1922 University Ave., Madison 53726
(608) 263-1692 info@wisconsinacademy.org
www.wisconsinacademy.org

Accountants, Wis. Inst. of Certified Public
Dennis Tomorsky, Pres./CEO
W233 N2080 Ridgeview Pky., Waukesha 53188
(262) 785-0445 dennis@wicpa.org www.wicpa.org

ACOG (American College of Obstetricians and
Gynecologists), Wis. Section
Eric Ostermann, Exec. Dir.
563 Carter Ct., Suite B, Kimberly 54136
(920) 560-5636 w-acog@badgerbay.co www.acog.org

Activity Professionals, Wis. Representatives of (WRAP)
Melissa Dixon, Pres.
30243 295th St., Holcombe 54745
(715) 827-0015 mldixon4@gmail.com www.wrap-wi.org

AFT - Wisconsin (Federation of Teachers)
Kim Kohlhaas, Pres.
6602 Normandy Ln., Madison 53719
(608) 662-1444 president@aft-wisconsin.org
www.aft-wisconsin.org

Aging Groups, Coalition of Wis.
A.J. Nino Amato, Pres.
2850 Dairy Dr., Suite 100, Madison 53718
(608) 514-3317 namato@cwag.org www.cwag.org

Agri-Business Assn., Wis.
Tom Bressner, Exec. Dir.
2801 International Lane, Suite 105, Madison 53704
(608) 223-1111 tom@wiagribusiness.org
www.wiagribusiness.org

Agribusiness Council, Wis.
Ferron Havens, Pres.
P.O. Box 46100, Madison 53744
(877) 947-2474 fhavenswac@mhtc.net wisagri.com

Agricultural Educators, Wis. Assn. Of
Bridgett Neu, Exec. Dir.
1172 Hummingbird Ln., Plymouth 53073
(262) 224-7553 bridgett@waae.com www.waae.com

Agriculture, Wis. Women for
Gloria Helsted, Pres.
N8460 Sand Prairie Road N, Hixon 54635
(715) 963-5602 gloria2@centurytel.net
www.americanagriwomen.org

Agronomy, Amer. Soc. of
Ellen Bergfeld, CEO
5585 Guilford Rd., Madison 53711
(608) 268-4979 ebergfeld@sciencesocieties.org
www.agronomy.org

Alcohol Problems Council of Wis.
Jim Cotter, Secy.
405 14th Ave., Baraboo 53913
(920) 350-2625 jcotter@wisconsinumc.org
alcoholproblemswi.org

American Fed. Of State, County and Municipal Employees,
AFL-CIO
John Grabel, Exec. Dir. Council 11
8033 Excelsior Dr., Suite A, Madison 53717-1903
(608) 836-6666 jgrabel@afscme.org www.afscme.org

American Legion Aux. (Dept. of Wis.)
Bonnie Dorniak, Secy./Treas.
P.O. Box 140, 2930 American Legion Dr.,
Portage 53901-0124
(608) 745-0124 alawi@amlegionauxwi.org
amlegionauxwi.org

American Legion, Dept. of Wis.
David A. Kurtz, Adj.
2930 American Legion Dr., P.O. Box 388,
Portage 53901-0388-0388
(608) 745-1090 info@wilegion.org www.wilegion.org

Amusement and Music Operators, Wis.
Maxine D. O'Brien, Exec. Dir.
P.O. Box 250, Poynette 53955
(608) 635-4316 wamomax@aol.com www.wamo.net

Amvets (Dept. of Wis.)
Mike Kandziora, Exec. Dir.
750 N. Lincoln Memorial Dr., Rm. 306,
AMVETS Department of Wisconsin, Milwaukee 53202
(414) 273-5288 amvetswi@yahoo.com
www.amvets-wi.org

Amvets Ladies Aux., Dept. of Wis.
Robin Sterletske, Pres.
222 S. Main St., Brillion 54110
(920) 427-6526 brdlvr.rs@gmail.com
www.amvets-wi.org/auxiliary.htm

Anesthetists, Wis. Assn. of Nurse, Inc.
Debra Dahlke, Pres.
11801 W. Silver Spring Drive, Suite 200,
Milwaukee 53225
(414) 271-9456 president@wiana.com
www.wiana.com

Animals and the Environment, Alliance for
Hannah West, Director
P.O. Box 1632, Madison 53701-1632
(608) 257-6333 Alliance@AllAnimals.org
www.allanimals.org

Apartment Assn., Wis.
Kristy Weinke, Admin. Asst.
P.O. Box 2922, Oshkosh 54903
(920) 230-9221 admin@waaonline.org
www.waaonline.org

Apple Growers Assn., Wis.
Anna M. Maenner, Exec. Dir.
211 Canal Rd., Waterloo 53594
(920) 478-4277 office@waga.org www.waga.org

Aquaculture Assn., Inc., Wis.
Cindy Johnson, Secy.
7408 Ward Blvd., Arpin 54410
(815) 515-2570 cindy@wisconsinaquaculture.com
www.wisconsinaquaculture.com

Arabian Horse Assn., Wis.
Nancy Miller, Pres.
6301 Fox Run, Sun Prairie 53590
(608) 825-9986 nmfr7@charter.net
www.wisconsinarabian.com

Arborist Assn., Wis.
Larry Axlen, Jr., Legis. Chair
1830 S. West Ave., Waukesha 53189
(262) 574-3149 www.waa-isa.org/index.htm

Arc – Wisconsin, Disability Assoc. Inc., The
James Hoegemeier, Exec. Dir.
2800 Royal Ave., #202, Madison 53713
(608) 222-8907 arcw@att.net www.arc-wisconsin.org

Architects, Wis. Society of
William Babcock, Exec. Dir.
321 S. Hamilton St., Madison 53703-4000
(608) 257-8477 aiaw@aiaw.org www.aiaw.org

Army and Navy Union
Howard Cole, Cmdr.
5000 W. National Ave, Bldg. 70 C-7, Milwaukee 53295
(414) 384-2000, ext. 46420 howard.cole2@va.gov

Art Therapy Association, Wis.
Rene Burgoyne, Pres.
P.O. Box 1765, Milwaukee 53201-1765
info@wiarttherapy.org www.wiarttherapy.org

Arthritis Foundation, Upper Midwest Region
Kristin Beres, Regional Controller
10427 W Lincoln Ave., Suite 1300, West Allis 53227
(800) 333-1380 info.wi@arthritis.org
www.arthritis.org

Artists Assn., Wis. Regional
Mary Ann Inman, Pres.
316 Church St., Clinton 53525
www.wraawrap.com

Asphalt Pavement Assn., Wis., Inc.
Brandon Strand, Exec. Dir.
4600 American Pky., Suite 201, Madison 53718
(608) 255-3114 strand@wispave.org www.wispave.org

Auctioneers Assn., Wis.
Christianne Williams, Dir. of Operations
S4537 Mirror Lake Rd., Baraboo 53913
(608) 558-5041 info@wisconsinauctioneers.org
www.wisconsinauctioneers.org

Automatic Merchandising Council, Wis.
David Kwarciany, Jr., Govt. Affairs Chm.
16300 W. Silver Spring Dr., Menomonee Falls 53051
(262) 781-8507

Automobile and Truck Dealers Assn., Inc., Wis.
William Sepic, Pres.
150 E. Gilman St., Suite A, Madison 53703
(608) 251-5577 wsepic@watda.org www.watda.org

Automotive Care Association, Wis.
Gary Manke, Exec. Dir.
5330 Wall St., Suite 100, Madison 53718-7929
(608) 240-2065 gmanke@medaassn.com
www.wiaca.com

Automotive Historians, Soc. of (Wis. Ch.)
Kenneth E. Nimocks, Pres.
3765 Spring Green Rd., Green Bay 54313-7565
(920) 865-4004 knimocks@netnet.net
wisconsin-auto-historians.org

Automotive Parts Assn., Inc., Wis.
Gary W. Manke, CAE, Exec. Dir.
5330 Wall St., Suite 100, Madison 53718-7929
(608) 240-2066 gmanke@medaassn.com
www.wapaonline.com

Bandmasters' Assn., Inc., Wis.
Donna M. Wirth, Exec. Secy.
14544 Squire Ln., Kiel 53042
(920) 894-3991 wbasec.dwirth@gmail.com

Bankers Assn., Wis.
Rose Oswald Poels, Pres./CEO
4721 S. Biltmore Lane, Madison 53718
(608) 441-1200 ropoels@wisbank.com
www.wisbank.com

Bankers Assn., Wis. Mortgage
Robin Fanshaw, Assn. Manager
P.O. Box 1606, Madison 53701-1606
(608) 255-4180 info@wimba.org www.wimba.org

Bankers of Wis., Community
Daryll J. Lund, Pres. & CEO
455 Cty Rd. M., Suite 101, Madison 53719
(608) 833-4229 daryll@communitybankers.org
www.communitybankers.org

Beef Council, Inc., Wis.
John W. Freitag, Exec. Dir.
632 Grand Canyon Dr., Madison 53719
(608) 833-9940 jwf@beeftips.com beeftips.com

Beer Distributors Assn., Inc., Wis.
Eric Jensen, Exec. Dir.
1 S. Pinckney Street, Suite 318, Madison 53703
(608) 287-3282 eric@wisbeer.com www.wisbeer.org/

Berry Growers Assn., Inc., Wis.
Anna Maenner, Exec. Dir.
211 Canal Rd., Waterloo 53594
(920) 478-3852 info@wiberries.org wiberries.org

Beverage Assn., Wis.
Kelly McDowell, Exec. Secy.
33 E. Main St., Suite 701, Madison 53703
(608) 852-7555 kellymmcdowell@gmail.com
wibeverage.com

Blind and Visually Impaired, Inc., Wis. Council of the
Loretta Himmelsbach, Exec. Dir.
754 Williamson St., Madison 53703
(608) 255-1166 lhimmelsbach@wcblind.org
www.wcblind.org

Botanical Club of Wis.
Theodore S. Cochrane, Secy.
Room 251 Birge Hall, 430 Lincoln Dr.,
UW-Madison Herbarium, Madison 53706-1381
(608) 262-2792 tscochra@wisc.edu
https://sites.google.com/site/botanicalclubofwisconsin

Bowhunters Assn., Wis., Inc.
Michael Brust, Pres.
P.O. Box 240, Clintonville 54929
(715) 823-4670 office@wisconsinbowhunters.org
www.wisconsinbowhunters.org

Bowling Assn., Wis. State USBC
Donald Hildebrand, Assn. Mgr.
P.O. Box 91418, Glendale 53209
(414) 446-9988 donh@wibowl.com
wibowl.com

Bowling Centers Association of Wis.
Yvonne C. Bennett, Exec. Dir.
21140 W. Capitol Dr., Suite 5, Pewaukee 53072
(262) 783-4292 bcaw@bowlwi.com www.bowlwi.com

Brain Injury Alliance of Wis., Inc.
Kasey Johanson, Exec. Dir.
N63 W23583 Main St., Suite A, Sussex 53089
(262) 790-9660 kjohanson@biaw.org www.biaw.org

Brain Injury Resource Center of Wis.
Lois York-Lewis, Exec. Dir.
P.O. Box 808, Muskego 53150
(262) 770-4882 admin@bircofwi.org
http://www.bircofwi.org/

Breeders Assn., Wis. Brown Swiss
Barbara Muenzenberger, Secy./Treas.
W561 Muenzenberger Rd., Coon Valley 54623
(608) 486-2297 bovalleyswiss@aol.com
www.allbreedaccess.com/wibrownswiss

Breeders Assn., Wis. Draft Horse
Nancy LaCrosse, Secy.
E2767 Nuclear Rd., Kewaunee 54216
(920) 776-1239 mnpjalacrosse@tds.net

Breeders Assn., Wis. Guernsey
Debra Lakey, Exec. Secy./Treas.
N10907 McDonah Lane, Trempealeau 54661
(608) 484-0416 wisgba@yahoo.com
www.wiguernsey.com

Breeders Assn., Wis. Livestock
Jill Alf, Exec. Dir.
7811 N Consolidated School Rd., Edgerton 53534
(608) 868-2505 alfhamp@centurytel.net
www.wisconsinlivestockbreeders.com

Breeder's Assn., Wis. Shorthorn
Melinda Orebaugh, Secy.
W5306 County Rd. W, Holmen 54636
(608) 526-2578 info@wisconsinshorthorns.com
www.wisconsinshorthorns.com

Broadcasters Assn., Wis.
Michelle Vetterkind, Pres./CEO
44 E. Mifflin St., Suite 900, Madison 53703-2800
(608) 255-2600 mvetterkind@wi-broadcasters.org
www.wi-broadcasters.org

Buck and Bear Club, Inc., Wis.
Perry Jensen, Secy.
P.O. Box 764, Marshfield 54449
(877) 273-6408 info@wi-buck-bear.org
www.wi-buck-bear.org

Builders and Contractors of Wis., Inc., Associated
John Mielke, Pres.
5330 Wall St., Madison 53718
(608) 244-5883 info@abcwi.org www.abcwi.org

Builders Assn. of Wis., Master
John R. Topp, Secy./Treas.
17100 W. Bluemound Rd., Suite 102, Brookfield 53005
(262) 785-1430 john@buildacea.org www.buildacea.org

Builders Assn., Wis.
Brad Boycks, Vice Pres. Of Advocacy
660 John Nolen Dr., #320, Madison 53713
(608) 242-5151 bboycks@wisbuild.org
www.wisbuild.org

Burial Vault Assn., Wis.
Mark Lipscomb, Jr., Exec. Dir.
2602 W. Silver Spring Dr., Glendale 53209
(414) 276-5763 marklipscombjr@sbcglobal.net

Business Assn. of Wis., Independent
Steve Kohlmann, Exec. Dir.
960 Timber Pass, Brookfield 53056
(262) 844-0333 ibawoffice@gmail.com www.ibaw.com

Business, Natl. Federation of Independent (Wis. Ch.)
Bill G. Smith, State Director
10 E. Doty St., Suite 519, Madison 53703
(608) 255-6083 Bill.Smith@nfib.org www.nfib.com/wi

Businesses, Inc., Wis. Independent
John Gard, Pres.
122 West Washington Avenue, Suite 650, Madison 53703
(800) 362-9644 johngard@wibiz.org www.wibiz.org

Cable Communications Assn., Wis.
Thomas E. Moore, Exec. Dir.
22 E. Mifflin St., Suite 1010, Madison 53703
(608) 256-1683 www.wicable.tv

Camp Assn., American, Wis.
Hasim Dawkins
500 State Road 67 North, Martinsville, IN 46151
(765) 349-3528 hdawkins@acacamps.org
www.acawisconsin.org

Campground Owners, Wis. Assn. of
Lori Severson, Exec. Dir.
P.O. Box 228, Ettrick 54627
(800) 843-1821 director@wisconsincampgrounds.com
wisconsincampgrounds.com

Cancer Soc., Inc., Amer. (Midwest Div.)
Sara Sahli, Wis. Govt. Rel. Dir.
8317 Elderberry Rd., Madison 53717
(608) 662-7557 sara.sahli@cancer.org www.cancer.org

Carpenters, Wis. State Council of
Mark S. Reihl, Exec. Dir.
115 W. Main St., Madison 53703
(608) 256-1206 marksreihl@gmail.com

Cast Metals Assn., Wis.
Steve Lewallen, Exec. Dir.
111 Woodside Ct., Neenah 54956
(920) 727-9949 selewallen@gmail.com
www.wicastmetals.com

Cattlemen's Assn., Wis.
Austin Arndt, Pres.
2 E. Mifflin Street, Suite 601, Madison 53703
(608) 228-1457 wisbeef@yahoo.com
www.wisconsincattlemen.com

Cattlewomen's Assn. Inc., Wis.
Jena Swanson, Pres.
2010 S. East Ave., #8, Waukesha 53189
(715) 497-5981 jenaswanson@yahoo.com
www.wisconsincattlemen.com

Cemetery and Cremation Assn., Wisconsin
Glen Porter, Pres.
14875 W. Greenfield Ave., Highland Memorial Park,
New Berlin 53151
(262) 786-6450 egporter@highlandmemorial.com
www.wiscemeteries.org

Children and Families, Inc., Wis. Council on
Ken Taylor, Exec. Dir.
555 W. Washington Ave., Suite 200, Madison 53703
(608) 284-0580 ktaylor@wccf.org www.wccf.org

Children of the American Revolution, Wis. St. Soc.
Hope Niedling, Honorary Sr. State Pres.
700 3rd St., Plover 54467
(715) 341-1996

Children's Service Soc. of Wis.
Bob Duncan, Pres.
620 S. 76th Street, Suite 120, Milwaukee 53214
(414) 337-8634 rduncan@chw.org www.cssw.org

Chiropractic Assn., Wis.
John Murray, Exec. Dir.
521 E. Washington Ave., Madison 53703
(608) 256-7023 jmurray@wichiro.org www.wichiro.org

Chiropractic Soc. Of Wis.
Steve Conway, Exec. Dir.
2 E. Mifflin St., Suite 600, Madison 53703
(608) 252-9338 chiropracticsocietywi@gmail.com
http://chiropracticsocietywi.com

Christmas Tree Producers Assn., Inc., Wis.
Cheryl Nicholson, Exec. Secy.
W9833 Hogan Rd., Portage 53901-9279
(608) 742-8663 info@christmastrees-wi.org
www.christmastrees-wi.org

Churches, Wis. Council of
Scott Anderson, Exec. Dir.
750 Windsor St., Suite 301, Sun Prairie 53590-2149
(608) 837-3108 sanderson@wichurches.org
www.wichurches.org

City/County Management Assn., Wis.
Dawn Peters, Exec. Dir.
148 N. 3rd Street, c/o NIU Center for Governmental
Studies, DeKalb, IL 60115
(815) 753-5230 wcma@niu.edu www.wcma-wi.org

Civil Air Patrol, Wis. Wing
Col. Rose M. Hunt, Commander
2400 Wright St., Madison 53704-2572
(608) 242-3067 wa@wiwg.cdp.gov www.wicap.us

Civil Liberties Union of Wis., Inc., American
Christopher Ahmuty, Exec. Dir.
207 E. Buffalo St., No. 325, Milwaukee 53202-5774
(414) 272-4032 liberty@aclu-wi.org www.aclu-wi.org

Clerks of Circuit Court Assn., Wis.
Carlo Esqueda, Pres.
215 S. Hamilton St., Rm. 1000, Madison 53703
(608) 266-4679 carlo.esqueda@wicourts.gov

Collectors Assn., Inc., Wis.
Mona Sen, Exec. Secy.
P.O. Box 6275, Madison 53716
(608) 620-5922 wcaexecutivesecretary@gmail.com
http://wisconsincollectorsassociation.org

Colleges and Universities, Wis. Assn. of Independent
Rolf Wegenke, Pres.
122 W. Washington Ave., Suite 700, Madison 53703
(608) 256-7761 mail@waicu.org www.waicu.org

Collegiate DECA, Wis.
Mae Laatsch, State Dir.
130 Keyes, P.O. Box 85, Lake Mills 53551
(608) 358-1448 mlaatsch@madisoncollege.edu
www.wicollegiatedeca.org

Colonial Wars in the State of Wis., Society of
Jerry P. Hill, Gov.
5677 N. Consaul Pl., Milwaukee 53217-4818
(414) 332-9479 jerryp@wi.rr.com

Common Cause in Wis.
Jay Heck, Exec. Dir.
P.O. Box 2597, Madison 53701-2597
(608) 256-2686 ccwisjwh@itis.com
www.commoncausewisconsin.org

Community Action Program Assn., Inc., Wis.
Robert Jones, Exec. Dir.
1310 Mendota St., Suite 107, Madison 53714-1039
(608) 244-4422 bjones@wiscap.org www.wiscap.org

Concrete Assn., Wis. Precast
Katie Boycks, Assn. Manager
10 E. Doty Street, Suite 523, Madison 53703
(608) 441-1436 kboycks@kpasllc.com
www.wiprecast.org

Concrete Assn., Wis. Ready Mixed
Cherish Schwenn, Exec. Dir.
44 E. Mifflin St., Suite 305, Madison 53703
(608) 250-6304 info@wrmca.com www.wrmca.com

Concrete Paving Assn., Wis.
Kevin McMullen, Pres.
4001 Nakoosa Trail, Suite 101, Madison 53714
(608) 240-1020 kmcmullen@wisconcrete.org
www.wisconcrete.org

Construction Employers Assn., Inc., Allied
John Topp, Secy./Treas
17100 W. Bluemound Rd., Suite 102, Brookfield 53005
(262) 785-1430 john@buildacea.org www.buildacea.org

Consulting Foresters Assn., Wis.
Don Peterson, Chair
1353 US Hwy 2, Suite 2, Crystal Falls, MI 49920
(877) 284-3882 rrsllc@sbcglobal.net
www.wi-consultingforesters.com

Contractors Assn. of Wis., Mechanical
Jeff Gaecke, Exec. Vice Pres.
3315 N. Ballard, Suite D, Appleton 54911
(920) 734-3148 jeff@omswi.com

Contractors Assn., Inc., Wis. Underground
Mike Dretzka, Pres.
2835 N. Mayfair Rd., Suite 22, Milwaukee 53222-4405
(414) 778-1050 wuca@wuca.org www.wuca.org

Cooperative Network
William Oemichen, Pres./CEO
1 S. Pinckney St., Suite 810, Madison 53703-2869
(608) 258-4400 bill.oemichen@cooperativenetwork.coop
cooperativenetwork.coop

Corn Promotion Board, Inc., Wis.
Bob Oleson, Exec. Dir.
W1360 Hwy 106, Palmyra 53156
(262) 495-2232 wicorn@centurytel.net www.wicorn.org

Counties Assn., Wis.
Mark D. O'Connell, Exec. Dir.
22 E. Mifflin St., Suite 900, Madison 53703
(608) 663-7188 mail@wicounties.org
www.wicounties.org

Counties Utility Tax Assn., Wis.
Alice O'Connor, Exec. Dir.
44 E. Mifflin St., Suite 605A, Madison 53703
(608) 250-4685 aoc@constituencyservices.org

County Agricultural Agents, Wis. Assn.
Dan Marzu, Pres.
801 N. Sales Street, Suite 101, Merrill 54452
(715) 539-1078 daniel.marzu@ces.uwex.edu www.uwex.
edu/ces/wacaa

County and Municipal Employees, Wis. Council 40
AFSCME, AFL-CIO
Rick Badger, Exec. Dir.
8033 Excelsior Dr., Suite B, Madison 53717
(608) 836-4040 www.afscme40.org

County Clerks Assn., Wis.
Bruce Strama, Pres.
224 South 2nd Street, Taylor County Clerk, Medford 54451
(715) 748-1460 www.wccawebsite.com

County Code Administrators, Wis.
Michelle Staff, Secy./Treas.
311 S. Center Ave., Room 201, Jefferson 53549
(920) 774-4537 wccadm@yahoo.com
www.wccadm.com

County Constitutional Officers Assn., Inc., Wis.
Lisa Freiberg, Fond du Lac County Clerk
P.O. Box 1557, 160 S. Macy St., Fond du Lac 54936
(920) 929-3293

County Forests Assn., Inc., Wis.
Jane Severt, Exec. Dir.
P.O. Box 70, 3243 Golf Course Rd., Rhinelander 54501
(715) 282-5951 wcfa@frontier.com
www.wisconsincountyforests.com

County Officers, Wis. Assn. of
Shawn Handland, Treas.
400 4th St. N., Rm. 1290, Administrative Center,
La Crosse 54601-3200
(608) 785-9712 shandland@lacrossecounty.org

County Planning and Zoning Directors Assn., Wis.
Scott Godfrey, Pres.
222 N. Iowa St., Iowa County Courthouse, Dodgeville
53533
(608) 935-0398 scott.godfrey@iowacounty.org

County Police Assn. Ltd., Wis.
Robert Wierenga, Exec. Dir.
P.O. Box 764, Delavan 53115
(262) 749-1301 info@wcpawi.com www.wcpawi.com

County Surveyors Assn., Inc., Wis.
Brenda Hemstead, Secy.
3985 Shadows Ct., DeForest 53532
(608) 770-1360 hemsteadb@gmail.com www.wsls.org

County Treasurers' Assn., Wis.
Pam Reeves, Pres.
515 Moreland Blvd. Rm. 148, Waukesha 53188
(262) 548-7029 preeves@waukeshacounty.gov
http://wicountytreasurers.com

County Veterans Service Officers Assn. of Wis.
Laura Moore, Secy.
225 N. Beaumont Rd., Suite 137, Prairie du Chien 53821
(608) 326-0204 lmoore@crawfordcountywi.org
www.wicvso.org

Court Reporters Assn., Wis.
Karla Sommer, Pres.
500 Forest St., Marathon County Courthouse,
Wausau 54403
(715) 261-1356 sommerkms@gmail.com
www.wicourtreporters.org

Credit Union League, Wis.
Tom Liebe, Vice Pres.
1 E. Main St., Suite 101, Madison 53703
(608) 514-0082 tliebe@theleague.coop
www.theleague.coop

Crop Improvement Assn., Inc., Wis.
Tony Klink, Gen. Mgr.
1575 Linden Dr., 554 Moore Hall, UW-Madison,
Madison 53706-1514
(608) 262-1341 wcia@mailplus.wisc.edu
www.wcia.wisc.edu

Crop Science Society of America
Ellen Bergfeld, CEO
5585 Guilford Rd., Madison 53711
(608) 268-4979 ebergfeld@sciencesocieties.org
www.crops.org

Dahlia Soc., Badger State
Monique Volden, Secy.
1167 State Rd. 78, Mt. Horeb 53572
(608) 437-6846 jamavolden@aol.com
www.badgerdahlia.org

Dahlia Society of Wis., Inc.
John Thiermann, Secy.
7728 W. Plainfield Ave., Greenfield 53220-2837
(414) 327-1759 jthiermann@wi.rr.com

Dairy Products Assn., Inc., Wis.
Brad Legreid, Exec. Dir.
8383 Greenway Blvd., Middleton 53562-3506
(608) 836-3336 info@wdpa.net www.wdpa.net

Dance Council, Wis.
Michael Moscicke, Pres.
P.O. Box 707, Madison 53701-0707
info@wisconsindancecouncil.org
www.wisconsindancecouncil.org

Democratic Party of Wis.
Martha Laning, Chair
15 N. Pinckney St., Suite 200, Madison 53703
(608) 255-5172 info@wisdems.org www.wisdems.org

Diabetes Assn., Amer. – Wisconsin
Don Shane, Market Dir.
375 Bishops Way, Suite 220, Brookfield 53005-6200
(414) 778-5500, ext. 6536 dshane@diabetes.org
http://.diabetes.org

Disability Rights Wisconsin
Daniel Idzikowski, Exec. Dir.
131 W. Wilson St., Suite 700, Madison 53703-2716
(608) 267-0214 dan.idzikowski@drwi.org
www.disabilityrightswi.org

Driver and Traffic Safety Education Assn., Wis.
Dick Bilda, Pres.
1417 Crystal Lake Dr., Oconomowoc 53066
(262) 567-3816 bilda3d@hotmail.com
www.adtsea.org/wisconsin/

Easter Seals Wisconsin, Inc.
Christine Fessler, Pres./CEO
101 Nob Hill Rd., Suite 301, Madison 53713-3969
(608) 277-8288 info@eastersealswisconsin.com
www.eastersealswisconsin.com

Economic Development Assn., Wis.
Brian Doudna, Exec. Dir.
10 E. Doty St., Suite 500, Madison 53703
(608) 255-5666 weda@weda.org www.weda.org

Economic Education, Inc., Wis. Council on
Enrique Bacalao, Pres.
7635 S. Bluemound Rd., Suite 106, Milwaukee 53213-3500
(414) 221-9784 bacalao@economicswisconsin.org
www.economicswisconsin.org

Education Assn., Council, Wis.
P.O. Box 8003, Office of WEAC Executive Director,
Madison 53708-8003
(608) 276-7711 www.weac.org

Education Association, Creation
Eugene A. Sattler, Dir.
W2228 Badger Ave., Pine River 54965-9640
(920) 987-5979 creationed.com

Educators' Assn., Inc., Wis. Retired
David L. Bennett, Exec. Dir.
6405 Century Ave., Suite 201, Middleton 53562
(608) 831-5115 dbennett@wrea.net www.wrea.net

Egg Producers Assn., Wis.
N9416 Tamarack Rd., Whitewater 53190
(414) 495-6220

Electric Cooperative Assn., Wis.
Share Brandt, Mgr.
1 S. Pinckney St., Suite 810, Madison 53703
(608) 258-4400 share.brandt@cooperativenetwork.coop
www.weca.coop

Electric Utilities of Wis., Municipal
Zachary Bloom, Exec. Dir.
725 Lois Drive, Sun Prairie 53590
(608) 837-2263 zbloom@meuw.org www.meuw.org

Electrical Contractors Assn., Inc., National (Wis. Chap.)
Loyal O'Leary, Exec. Vice-Pres.
2200 Kilgust Rd., Madison 53713
(608) 221-4650 loyal@wisneca.com www.wisneca.com

EMS (Emergency Medical Technicians) Assn., Wis.
Mindy Allen, Exec. Dir.
26422 Oakridge Dr., Wind Lake 53185-9769
(800) 793-6820 WEMSA@wisconsinems.com
www.wisconsinems.com

End Domestic Abuse Wisconsin
Patti Seger, Exec. Dir.
1245 E. Washington Ave., Suite 150, Madison 53703
(608) 255-0539 pattis@endabusewi.org
www.endabusewi.org

Engineering Assn., State
Larry Legro, Pres.
4510 Regent St., Madison 53705-4963
(608) 233-4696 wisea@wisea.org www.wisea.org

Engineering Companies of Wis., Amer. Coun. Of
Jayne Martinko, Pres.
3 S. Pinckney St., Suite 800, Madison 53703
(608) 257-9223 acecwi@acecwi.org www.acecwi.org

Environmental Education, Inc., Wis. Assn. for
Lynn Karbowski, Admin.
800 Reserve St., Stevens Point 54481
(715) 346-2796 waee@uwsp.edu www.waee.org

Environmental Technologists, Inc., Federation of (FET)
Barbara Hurula, Exec. Dir.
W175 N11081 Stonewood Dr., #203, Germantown 53022
(262) 437-1700 info@fetinc.org www.fetinc.org

Equipment Dealers Assn., Midwest
Gary W. Manke, CAE, CEO
5330 Wall St., Suite 100, Madison 53718-7929
(608) 240-4700 gmanke@medaassn.com
www.medaassn.com

Ex-POWS, American
Edward Wojahn, Adj.
1553 W. Young Dr., Onalaska 54650
(608) 783-3670

Fabricare Institute, Wis.
Brian Swingle, Exec. Dir.
12342 W. Layton Ave., Greenfield 53228
(414) 529-4707 bswingle@toriiphillips.com
www.wiscleaners.com

Fairs, Wis. Assn. of
Jayme Buttke, Exec. Secy.
5320 County Road F, Merrill 54452
(715) 536-0246 wifairs@gmail.com www.wifairs.com

Family Action, Inc., Wis.
Julaine K. Appling, Pres.
P.O. Box 1327, Madison 53701-1327
(608) 268-5074 info@wifamilyaction.org
www.wifamilyaction.org

Family and Children's Agencies, Wis. Assn. of
Linda A. Hall, Exec. Dir.
131 W. Wilson St., Suite 901, Madison 53703
(608) 257-5939 lhall@wafca.org www.wafca.org

Family Court Commissioners Assn., Inc., Wis.
Sandra Grady, Exec. Secy.
901 N. 9th St., Rm. 707, Milwaukee 53233
(414) 278-4428 sandra.grady@wicourts.gov

Family Ties, Inc., Wis.
Hugh Davis, Exec. Dir.
16 N. Carroll St., Suite 230, Madison 53703
(608) 267-6888 info@wifamilyties.org
www.wifamilyties.org

Farm Bureau Federation, Cooperative, Wis.
Steve Freese, CAO
P.O. Box 5550, 1241 John Q. Hammons Dr.,
Madison 53705-0550
(608) 828-5703 www.wfbf.com

Farmers Union, Wis.
Darin Von Ruden, Pres.
117 W. Spring St., Chippewa Falls 54729-2359
(715) 723-5561 dvonruden@wisconsinfarmersunion.com
wisconsinfarmersunion.com

Fathers for Children and Families, Wis. (WFCF)
Peter Kerr, Pres.
P.O. Box 1742, Madison 53701-1742
(608) 255-3237 5050dad@gmail.com
wisconsinfathers.org

FFA, Wis. Assn. Of
Jeff Hicken, State Advisor
125 S. Webster St., Madison 53703
(608) 267-9255 jeffrey.hicken@dpi.wi.gov
dpi.wi.gov/ffa/ffa.html

Financial Services Assn., Wis.
Thomas E. Moore, Exec. Dir.
22 E. Mifflin St., Suite 1010, Madison 53703
(608) 256-6413

Fire Fighters of Wis., Inc., Professional
Mahlon Mitchell, Pres.
7 N. Pinckney St., Suite 200, Madison 53703
(608) 251-5832 president@pffw.org www.pffw.org

Firefighters Assn., Inc., Wis. State
Larry Plumer, Pres.
P.O. Box 126, Durand 54736-0126
(800) 588-2989 plumer@wi-state-fighters.org
www.wi-state-firefighters.org

Fisheries Soc., Amer. (Wis. Chap.)
Justine Hasz, Secy.
P.O. Box 7921, 101 S. Webster St., Madison 53707
(608) 267-7591 president@wi-afs.org www.wi-afs.org

Food Processors Assn., Inc., Midwest
Nicholas C. George, Jr., Pres.
4600 American Parkway, Suite 210, Madison 53718
(608) 255-9946 info@mwfpa.org www.mwfpa.org

Food Protection, Inc., Wis. Assn. For
Leslie F. Lamb, Secy./Treas.
P.O. Box 620705, Middleton 53562
(608) 469-3290 leslamb@charter.net
www.wifoodprotection.org

Forest History Association of Wis., Inc.
Sara Connor, Pres.
P.O. Box 424, Two Rivers 54241-0424
http://chipsandsawdust.com

Forest Industry Safety and Training Alliance, Inc.
Henry Schienebeck, Exec. Dir.
P.O. Box 714, Rhinelander 54501
(800) 551-2656 info@fistausa.org www.fistausa.org

Foresters, Inc., Assn. of Consulting, Wis. Chap.
Lee Steigerwaldt, Chair
856 N. Fourth St., Steigerwaldt Land Services, Inc.,
Tomahawk 54487-2127
(715) 453-3274 sls@slstomahawk.com
www.acf-foresters.org

Forty (40) Hommes et 8 Chevaux, La Societe des
Thomas J. Orval, Grand Corres.
312 Hillside Circle, Johnson Creek 53038
(920) 699-5676 wigrandvoiture@tds.net wi40and8.org

Fresh Market Vegetable Growers Assn., Wis.
Anna Maenner, Exec. Dir.
211 Canal Rd., Waterloo 53594
(920) 478-3852 info@wisconsinfreshproduce.org
www.wisconsinfreshproduce.org

Funeral Directors Assn., Wis.
Adam Raschka, Exec. Dir.
22 E. Mifflin St., Suite 1010, Madison 53703
(608) 256-1757 adam@wfda.info www.wfda.info

Funeral Service and Cremation Alliance of Wis.
Erin Krueger, Exec. Dir.
P.O. Box 67, Madison 53701
(608) 204-0306 info@fsawisconsin.com
www.fsawisconsin.org

Genealogical Society, Inc., Wis. State
Chris Klauer, Admin. Asst.
P.O. Box 5106, Madison 53705-0106
(920) 397-7219 wsgs@wsgs.org www.wsgs.org

GI Forum, Wis. Amer.
Fernando Rodriguez, Secy.
1201 Schiller St., Watertown 53098
(920) 206-6660 wi-agif@sbcglobal.net

Ginseng Board of Wisconsin
Joe Heil, Pres.
668 Maratech Ave., Suite E, Marathon 54448
(715) 443-2444 ginseng@ginsengboard.com
www.ginsengboard.com

Gold Star Wives of America, Inc.
Crystal Wenum, Pres.
692 Baker Rd., Hudson 54016-7946
(715) 386-8615 crystalwenum@yahoo.com
goldstarwives.org

Golf Assn., Inc., Wis. State
Rob Jansen, Exec. Dir.
11350 W. Theo Trecker Way, West Allis 53214
(414) 443-3560 info@wsga.org www.wsga.org

Golf Course Supts. Assn., Inc., Wis.
Brett Grams, Chap. Exec.
N1922 Virginia Dr., Waupaca 54981
(920) 643-4888 bgrams@wgcsa.com www.wgcsa.com

Great Lakes Graphics Assn.
Joseph E. Lyman, Pres.
W232 N2950 Roundy Circle East, Suite 200,
Pewaukee 53072-4110
(262) 522-2210 info@glga.info www.glga.info

Green Industry Federation, Inc., Wis.
Brian Swingle, Exec. Dir.
12342 W. Layton Ave., Greenfield 53228
(414) 529-4705 bswingle@toriiphillips.com
www.wgif.net

Grocers Assn., Wis.
Brandon Scholz, Pres.
33 E. Main St., Suite 701, Madison 53703
(608) 244-7150 brandon@wisconsingrocers.com
www.wisconsingrocers.com

Hazardous Materials Responders, Inc., Wis. Assn.
Greg Temp, Pres.
7265 5th Ave., S., La Crosse 54601
(608) 789-7260 tempg@cityoflacrosse.org
www.wahmr.com

Head Start Assn., Wis.
Lilly Irvin-Vitela, Exec. Dir.
810 W. Badger Road, Madison 53713
(608) 442-6879 irvin-vitela@whsaonline.org
www.whsaonline.org

Health and Physical Education, Wis.
Keith Bakken, Exec. Dir.
1725 State St., 145 Mitchell Hall, UW-La Crosse,
La Crosse 54601
(608) 785-8175 whpe@uwlax.edu www.whpe.us

Health Care Assn., Wis.
James McGinn, Dir. of Govt. Rel.
131 W. Wilson St., Suite 1001, Madison 53703
(608) 257-0125 jim@whca.com

Health Care Assn., Wis. Primary
Stephanie Harrison, Exec. Dir.
5202 Eastpark Blvd., Suite 109, Madison 53718
(608) 277-7477 wphca@wphca.org www.wphca.org

Health Charities of Wis., Community
Gary Ross, Pres./CEO
6737 W. Washington St., Suite 2253, West Allis 53214
(414) 918-9100 gross@healthcharities.org
www.healthcharities.org/wisconsin

Health Information Management Assn., Wis.
Cassandra Bissen, Exec. Dir.
3817 Mormon Coulee Rd., Suite B, La Crosse 54601-7328
(608) 787-0168 whima@whima.org whima.org

Health Plans, Wis. Assn. Of
Nancy J. Wenzel, CEO
10 E. Doty St., Suite 503, Madison 53703
(608) 255-8599 nancy@wihealthplans.org
www.wihealthplans.org

Health Underwriters, Wis. Assn. of
Alice O'Connor, Exec. Dir.
44 E. Mifflin St., Suite 605A, Madison 53703
(608) 250-4685 aoc@constituencyservices.org
www.ewahu.org

Hearing Professionals, Wis. Alliance of
Doug Johnson, Exec. Dir.
P.O. Box 161, Evansville 53536-2558
(608) 201-7965 dqj@jjassociates.com www.wahpinfo.org

Heart Assn., American (Midwest Affiliate)
Maureen Cassidy, Vice. Pres of Advocacy
2850 Dairy Dr., Suite 300, Madison 53718
(608) 221-8866, ext. 2333 maureen.cassidy@heart.org
www.heart.org

Hereford Assn., Wis.
Ruth Espenscheid, Secy.
12044 Hwy 78, P.O. Box 296, Argyle 53504-0296
(608) 543-3788 wlbaosf@mhtc.net
wisconsinherefords.org

History, Wis. Council for Local
Roy S. Ostenso, Pres.
1208 1st Ave. E, Menomonie 54751
(715) 505-1110 ostensor@sbcglobal.net
wisconsinhistory.org

Holstein Assn., Wis.
Larry Nelson, Exec. Dir.
902 Eighth Ave., Baraboo 53913
(800) 223-4269 or (608) 356-2114
larryn@wisholsteins.com www.wisholsteins.com

Home Health United/Visiting Nurse Service, Inc.
Rick Bourne, Pres./CEO
4639 Hammersley Rd., Madison 53711
(608) 241-6950 rbourne@hhuvns.org
www.homehealthunited.org

Honey Producers Assn., Wis.
Gordon Waller, Pres.
S10010 Cty V, Augusta 54722
(715) 286-2019 gojoywaller@aol.com
www.wihoney.org

Horse Club, Inc., Wis. Morgan
Beth Anne Heyrman, Pres.
W1054 Hwy TW, Theresa 53091
(920) 488-2703 wild1cat2@gmail.com
www.wisconsinmorganhorseclub.org

Horse Council, Wis. State, Inc.
Pam Pritchard, Admin. Asst.
121 S. Ludington St., Columbus 53925
(920) 623-0393 pam@wisconsinstatehorsecouncil.org
www.wisconsinstatehorsecouncil.org

Horse Trail Assn., Inc., Glacial Drumlin
Margaret Kraege, Pres.
P.O. Box 259503, Madison 53725-9503
(608) 222-4554 ilovestrike@yahoo.com www.gdhta.org

Hospice Organization and Palliative Experts of Wis.
(HOPE)
Melanie G. Ramey, Exec. Dir.
3240 University Ave., Suite 2, Madison 53705-3570
(608) 233-7166 MELR217@aol.com
www.hopeofwisconsin.org

Hospital Assn., Inc., Wis.
Eric Borgerding, Pres.
P.O. Box 2590389, Madison 53725-9038
(608) 274-1820 www.wha.org

Hotel and Lodging Assn., Wis.
Trisha A. Pugal, Pres., CEO
1025 S. Moorland Rd., Suite 200, Brookfield 53005
(262) 782-2851 pugal@wisconsinlodging.org
www.wisconsinlodging.org

Housing Alliance, Wis.
Ross Kinzler, Exec. Dir.
258 W. Corporate Dr., Suite 200C, Madison 53714
(608) 255-3131 info@housingalliance.us
www.housingalliance.us

Humane Societies, Inc., Wis. Federated
Pam McCloud Smith, Bd. Pres.
5132 Voges Rd., Madison 53718
(608) 838-0413, ext. 111 pmsmith@giveshelter.org
www.wisconsinfederatedhs.org

Humanities Council, Wis.
Dena Wortzel, Exec. Dir.
222 S. Bedford St., Suite F, Madison 53703-3688
(608) 262-0706 contact@wisconsinhumanities.org
wisconsinhumanities.org

Insulation Contractors Assn., Inc., Wis.
Mark Borchardt, Pres.
4916 S. 79th St., Greenfield 53220
(414) 791-3005 debbiewanta@hotmail.com

Insurance Agents of Wis., Inc., Professional
Ronald Von Haden, Exec. Vice-Pres.
6401 Odana Rd., Madison 53719-1126
(608) 274-8188 rvonhaden@piaw.org www.piaw.org

Insurance Agents of Wisconsin, Independent
Matthew G. Banaszynski, Exec. Vice-Pres.
725 John Nolen Dr., Madison 53713-1421
(608) 256-4429 matt@iiaw.com www.iiaw.com

Insurance Alliance, Wis.
Andrew J. Franken, Pres.
44 E. Mifflin St., Suite 901, Madison 53703
(608) 255-1749 contact@wial.com wial.com

Insurance Companies, Wis. Assn. of Mutual
James Tlusty, Pres.
7203 Gene St., Suite A, DeForest 53532
(608) 846-7203 wamic@wamic.org www.wamic.org

International Institute of Wis., Inc.
Alexander P. Durtka, Jr., Pres.
1110 N. Old World Third St., Suite 420,
Milwaukee 53203-1117
(414) 225-6220 info@iiwisconsin.org

Interscholastic Athletic Assn., Wis.
David J. Anderson, Exec. Dir.
5516 Vern Holmes Dr., Stevens Point 54482
(715) 344-8580 danderson@wiaawi.org www.wiaawi.org

Japan-America Soc. of Wis., Inc.
Alexander P. Durtka, Jr., Pres.
1110 N. Old World Third St., Suite 420,
Milwaukee 53203-1117
(414) 225-6220 jasw@iiwisconsin.org

JCI Wisconsin, Inc.
Steve Moddie, Exec. Vice Pres.
P.O. Box 1547, Appleton 54912-1547
(920) 731-7681 evp@jciwisconsin.org
www.jciwisconsin.org

Judges Assn., Wis. Municipal
Jodi A. Sanfelippo, Secy./Treas.
219 N. Milwaukee St., Suite 2B, Milwaukee 53202
(414) 287-9875 secretary-treasurer@wmja.net
www.wmja.net

Justice, Wis. Assn. for
Jane E. Garrott
44 E. Mifflin St., Suite 402, Madison 53703-2897
(608) 257-5741 admin@wis.justice.org
www.wisjustice.org

Kidney Foundation of Wis., Inc., Natl.
Cindy Huber, CEO
16655 W. Bluemound Rd., Suite 240, Brookfield 53005
(262) 821-0705 info@kidneywi.org www.kidneywi.org

Labor and Employment Relations Assn. (Wis. Ch.)
Suzanne Clement, Secy./Treas.
3477 N. Cramer St., Milwaukee 53211
(414) 962-1203 sueclera@gmail.com
http://www4.uwm.edu/Org/lera/

Labor History Society, Wis.
Steve Cupery, Pres.
6333 W. Bluemound Rd., Milwaukee 53213
(414) 771-0700, ext. 20 info@wisconsinlaborhistory.org
www.wisconsinlaborhistory.org

Laborers' Dist. Council, Wis.
John J. Schmitt, Pres. and Bus. Mgr.
4633 Liuna Way, Suite 101, DeForest 53532
(608) 846-8242 jschmitt@wilaborers.org
www.wilaborers.org

Land and Water Conservation Assn., Wis.
Jim VandenBrook, Exec. Dir.
131 W. Wilson St., #601, Madison 53703
(608) 441-2677 info@wisconsinlandwater.org
www.wisconsinlandwater.org

Language Teachers, Wis. Assn. for (WAFLT)
Joshua LeGreve, Pres.
649 S. Main St., #5, Fond du Lac 54941
president@waflt.org www.waflt.org

Law Librarians Assn. of Wis., Inc.
Lisa Winkler, Pres.
120 Martin Luther King Blvd., Rm. 234A, Madison 53703
(608) 267-2202 lisa.winkler@wicourts.gov
www.aallnet.org/chapter/llaw

Lawns of Wisconsin Network (LaWN)
Andy Kurth, Pres.
2211 Eagle Dr., Middleton 53562
(608) 824-0043 andykurth1@gmail.com

Lawyers, Assn. for Women
Dana Kader Robb, Admin.
3322 N. 92nd St., Milwaukee 53222
(414) 750-4404 associationforwomenlawyers@gmail.com
www.associationforwomenlawyers.org

League of Women Voters of Wis., Inc.
Andrea Kaminski, Exec. Dir.
612 W. Main St., #200, Madison 53703
(608) 256-0827 kaminski@lwvwi.org www.lwvwi.org

Learning Disabilities Assn. of Wis.
Diane Sixel, Pres.
7625 Lechler Ln., Kiel 53042
info@ldawisconsin.com ldawisconsin.com

Letter Carriers' Assn., Wis. Rural
Ron Berg, Secy./Treas.
402 Dalogasa Dr., Arena 53503
(608) 220-4855 sec.treas2@frontiernet.net wirlca.org

Leukemia and Lymphoma Soc. (Wis. Chap.)
Michael Havlicek, Exec. Dir.
200 S. Executive Dr., Suite 203, Brookfield 53005
(262) 790-4701
theleukemialymphomasociety_wib@lls.org
www.lls.org/wi

Libertarian Party of Wisconsin
Paul O. Ehlers, Chair
P.O. Box 20815, Greenfield 53220-0815
(800) 236-9236, ext.1 chair@lpwi.org www.lpwi.org/

Lions Clubs Internatl. (MD-27 - Wi.)
Kathleen Gruna, Office Manager
3834 County Rd. A, Rosholt 54473
(715) 677-4764 lionstat@wi-net.com wisconsinlions.org

Liquid Waste Carriers Assn., Wis.
Katie Boycks, Assn. Manager
10 E. Doty Street, Suite 523, Madison 53703
(608) 441-1436 kboycks@kpasllc.com www.wlwca.com

Lobbyists, Inc., Assn. of Wis.
Robin Fanshaw, Assn. Manager
10 E. Doty Street, Suite 523, Madison 53703
(608) 442-7295 awl@wisconsinlobbyists.com
www.wisconsinlobbyists.com

LSLA Education, Inc.
Tim Kassis, Pres.
P.O. Box 160, Antigo 54409
(715) 623-5410 lsla@lakestateslumber.com

Lung Assn. in Wis., Amer.
Dona Wininsky, Dir. Of Public Policy and Comm.
13100 W. Lisbon Rd., Suite 700, Brookfield 53005
(262) 703-4840 dona.wininsky@lung.org
www.lungwi.org

Lupus Foundation of Amer., Inc., Wis. Chap.
Dawn Thomas-Semanko, Exec. Dir.
2600 N. Mayfair Rd., Suite 320, Milwaukee 53226
(414) 443-6400 lupuswi@lupuswi.org www.lupuswi.org

Make-A-Wish Foundation of Wis.
Patti Gorsky, Pres. And CEO
13195 W. Hampton Ave., Butler 53007
(262) 781-4445 info@wisconsin.wish.org
www.wisconsin.wish.org

Manufacturers' Agents, Inc., Wis. Assn. of
Stewart Oliver, Pres.
11801 W. Silver Spring Dr. #200, Milwaukee 53225
(414) 778-0640 wama@wama.org wama.org

Manufacturers and Commerce, Wis.
Kurt Bauer, Pres./CEO
P.O. Box 352, Madison 53701-0352
(608) 258-3400 wmc@wmc.org www.wmc.org

Maple Syrup Producers Assoc., Wis.
Gretchen Grape, Exec. Dir.
33186 Cty Hwy W, Holcombe 54745
(715) 415-6466 gretchengrape@gmail.com
www.wismaple.org

Marine Corps League, Dept. of Wis.
Lynn Sabel, Jr. Past Dept. Commandant
1614 S. Carriage Ln., Unit A, New Berlin 53151
(262) 424-2183 lynn.f.sabel@usbank.com

Masonry Alliance, Wis.
Jane Svinicki, Exec. Dir.
6737 W. Washington St., Suite 1300, Milwaukee 53214
(414) 276-0667 info@wma-online.org
www.wma-online.org

Mayflower Descendants, Wis., Soc. Of
Mrs. Robert R. Pekowsky, Historian
1629 North Golf Glen, Unit D, Madison 53704-7074
(608) 467-6646 martell135@charter.net
www.mayflowerwi.org

Meat Processors, Inc., Wis. Assn. of
Monica Aspenson, Exec. Secy.
208 Martinson Ave., Westby 54667
(608) 634-2858 mkaspenson@hotmail.com
www.wi-amp.com

Medical Society, Wis.
William R. Abrams, CEO
P.O. Box 1109, Madison 53701-1109
(608) 442-3800 communications@wismed.org
www.wisconsinmedicalsociety.org

Military Officers Assn. of America, Wis. Council of Chapters
Col. Loren Christensen, Pres.
539 14th Ave. North, Onalaska 54650
(608) 782-4344 bdgrcreek@aol.com moaa.org

Milk Marketing Board, Wis.
James Robson, CEO
8418 Excelsior Dr., Madison 53717
(608) 836-8820 www.eatwisconsincheese.com

Mining Impact Coalition of Wis., Inc.
Frank Koehn, Pres.
P.O. Box 834, Ashland 54806
(218) 341-8822 www.miningimpactcoalition.org

Mothers Against Drunk Driving (MADD)
Becky DrewsDebuque, Victim Advocate
P.O. Box 284, Beloit 53512
(262) 347-4026 becky.drews@madd.org madd.org

Motor Carriers Assn., Wis.
Neal Kedzie, Pres.
562 Grand Canyon Dr., Madison 53719-1033
(608) 833-8200 nkedzie@witruck.org www.witruck.org

Movers Assn., Wis.
Neal Kedzie, Pres.
562 Grand Canyon Dr., Madison 53719-1033
(608) 833-8200 nkedzie@witruck.org www.wismovers.org

MRA – The Management Assn., Inc.
Susan M. Fronk, Pres.
N19 W24400 Riverwood Dr., Waukesha 53188
(262) 523-9090 www.mranet.org

Multiple Sclerosis Soc., Natl. (Wis. Chap.)
Colleen G. Kalt, Pres./CEO
1120 James Dr., Suite A, Hartland 53029
(262) 369-4400 or (800) 242-3358 info.wisms@nmss.org
www.wisms.org

Municipalities, League of Wis.
Jerry Deschane, Exec. Dir.
131 W. Wilson St., Suite 505, Madison 53703
(608) 267-2380 league@lwm-info.org www.lwm-info.org

Music Educators Assn., Inc., Wis.
Timothy J. Schaid, Exec. Dir.
1005 Quinn Dr., Waunakee 53597
(608) 850-3566 schaidt@wsmamusic.org
www.wmeamusic.org

Myasthenia Gravis Foundation of Amer. (Wis. Chapter)
Bryn Feyen, Chp.
2474 S. 96th St., West Allis 53227
(262) 938-9800 wisconsin@myasthenia.org
myasthenia.org/wisconsin

NAIFA Wisconsin, Inc.
Michele Clarke, Exec. Dir
409 Washington St., Suite A, Cedar Falls, IA 50613
(855) 360-3395 info@naifa.wisconsin.org
www.naifawisconsin.org

NAMI Wisconsin, Inc.
Julianne Carbin, Exec. Dir.
4233 W. Beltline Hwy, Madison 53711
(608) 268-6000 or (800) 236-2988
julianne@namiwisconsin.org www.namiwisconsin.org

National Farmers Organization, Wis.
Don Hamm, State Pres.
N5541 Miranda Way, Fond du Lac 54937
(920) 926-0682 dhamm@nfo.org www.nfo.org

National Guard Assn., Inc., Wis.
Michael Williams, Acting Exec. Dir.
2400 Wright St., Rm. 208, Madison 53704-2572
(608) 242-3114 wingainc@att.net www.winga.org

National Guard Enlisted Assn., Inc., Wis.
Gary R. Hans, Exec. Dir.
2400 Wright St., Madison 53704-2572
(608) 242-3112 wngea@yahoo.com wngea.org

Natural Food Associates, Inc., Wis.
Michael Hittner, Pres.
910 W. Grand Ave., Wisconsin Rapids 54495
(715) 421-2061 wisconsinnaturalfoods.org

Nature Conservancy, Wis. Chap.
Mary Jean Huston, State Dir.
633 W. Main St., Madison 53703
(608) 251-8140 wisconsin@tnc.org nature.org

Navy Club USA
Nellie P. Debaker, Cmdr.
N7197 County Road H, Luxemburg 54217-9221
(920) 845-5033 nelliepdebaker@gmail.com

Newspaper Assn., Inc., Wis.
Beth Bennett, Exec. Dir.
1901 Fish Hatchery Road, Madison 53713
(608) 283-7621 beth.bennett@WNAnews.com
www.wnanews.com

Nursery and Landscape Assn., Wis., Inc.
Brian Swingle, Exec. Dir.
12342 W. Layton Ave., Greenfield 53228
(414) 529-4705 bswingle@toriiphillips.com
www.wgif.net

Nurses Assn., Wis.
Lea Acord, Pres.
6117 Monona Dr., Suite 1, Madison 53716
(800) 362-3959 info@wisconsinnurses.org
www.wisconsinnurses.org

Nurses, Wis. Assn. of Licensed Practical
JoAnn Shaw, Pres.
22 E. Mifflin St., Suite 1010, Madison 53703
(608) 256-5299 jslpn@sbcglobal.net

Nursing Home Social Workers Assn., Wis.
Jeff McCabe, Pres.
3300 W. Brewster St., c/o Brewster Village,
Appleton 54914
(920) 225-1985 jeff.mccabe@outagamie.org
wnhswa.org

Nursing, Inc., Wis. League for
Diane Skewes, Pres.
P.O. Box 320892, Franklin 53132
(414) 454-9561 admin@wisconsinwln.org
www.wisconsinwln.org

Nutrition and Dietetics, Wis. Academy of
Amy Giffin, Media Spokesperson
563 Carter Court, Suite B, Kimberly 54136
(888) 232-8631 eatrightwisc@gmail.com
www.eatrightwisc.org

Occupational Therapy Assn., Inc., Wis.
Teri Black, Legislative Chair
6045 Monona Dr., Monona 53716
(608) 298-7604 wota@wota.net www.wota.net

Ophthalmology, Wis. Academy of
Richard H. Paul, Exec. Dir.
10 W. Phillip Rd., Suite 120, Vernon Hills, IL 60061
(800) 838-3527 richardpaul@dls.net
www.wieyemd.org

Orchid Soc., Wis.
Bruce Efflandt
3518 North 98th St., Milwaukee 53222
(262) 327-9373 berniesfloral@mail.com
www.wisconsinorchidsociety.com

Ornithology, Inc., Wis. Soc. for
Michey O'Connor, Treas.
11923 W. Bender Rd., Milwaukee 53223
(414) 353-2624 treasurer@wsobirds.org
www.wsobirds.org

Orthodontists, Wis. Soc. of
Dr. John Frazier, Pres.
563 Carter Ct., Suite B, Kimberly 54136
(920) 560-5626 wso@badgerbay.com
www.wisconsinsocietyoforthodontists.com

Otolaryngology - Head and Neck Surgery, Wis Soc. of
Seth Dailey, Secy./Treas.
600 Highland Ave., K4/719 CSC, Madison 53792-7375
(608) 263-0192 secy-treasurer@wiscoto.org
www.wiscoto.org

Outdoor Advertising Assoc. of Wis.
Janet Swandby, Exec. Dir.
10 E. Doty St., Suite 519, Madison 53703
(608) 286-0764 swandby@swandby.com
www.oaaw.org

Paper Council, Wis.
Jeffrey G. Landin, Pres.
5485 Grande Market Dr., Suite B, Appleton 54913
(920) 574-3752 landin@wipapercouncil.org
wipapercouncil.org/

Paratransit Provider, Wis. Rural and
Constance Jacobson, Pres.
220 S. 3rd Ave., Suite 4, Wisconsin Rapids 54495
(715) 421-8989 cjacobson@co.wood.wi.us
www.wi-transportation.org/

Parents and Teachers Inc., Wis. Congress of
Ellen Chicka, Pres.
4797 Hayes Rd., Suite 102, Madison 53704-3288
(608) 244-1455 info@wisconsinpta.org
www.wisconsinpta.org

Park and Recreation Assn., Inc., Wis.
Steven J. Thompson, Exec. Dir.
6737 W Washington Ave, Suite 1300, Milwaukee 53214
(414) 423-1210 sthompson@wpraweb.org wpraweb.org

Pathologists, Wis. Soc. of
Eric Ostermann, Exec. Dir.
563 Carter Ct., Unit B, Kimberly 54136
(920) 560-5634 wsp@badgerbay.co www.wispath.com

Peace and Justice, Wis. Network for
122 State St., No. 405A, Madison 53703-2500
(608) 250-9240 office@wnpj.org www.wnpj.org

Pediatric Dentists, Wis. Soc. of
Erin Winn, Secy./Treas
583 Lakeland Dr., Chippewa Falls 54729
(715) 723-2000 drwinn@sim4kids.com

Perinatal Care, Wis. Assn. for
Ann E. Conway, Exec. Dir.
211 S. Paterson St., Suite 250, Madison 53703
(608) 285-5858 wapc@perinatalweb.org
www.perinatalweb.org

Perinatal Foundation
Ann E. Conway, Exec. Dir.
211 S. Paterson St., Suite 250, Madison 53703
(608) 285-5858 foundation@perinatalweb.org
www.perinatalweb.org

Petroleum Marketers & Convenience Store Assn., Wis.
Matthew C. Hauser, Pres.
122 W. Washington Ave., Suite 101, Madison 53703
(608) 256-7555 info@wpmca.org www.wpmca.org

Pharmacy Soc. of Wis.
Christopher Decker, CEO and Exec. Vice Pres.
701 Heartland Tr., Madison 53717
(608) 827-9200 chrisd@pswi.org www.pswi.org

PHCC/Master Plumbers - Wis. Assn.
Jeffrey J. Beiriger, Exec. Dir.
P.O. Box 833, Germantown 53022
(888) 782-6815 mail@phcc-wi.org www.phcc-wi.com

Phenological Soc., Wis.
Mark Schwartz, Pres.
4484 North Woodburn St., Shorewood 53211
(414) 229-3740 mds@uwm.edu www.wps.uwm.edu

Physical Medicine and Rehabilitation, Wis. Soc. of
Kimberly Arndt, MD, Pres.
1685 Highland Ave., 6th Floor, Madison 53705
(608) 263-8639 arndt@rehab.wisc.edu
www.wispmr.com

Physical Therapy Assn., Wis.
Karen Curran, Exec. Dir.
3510 E. Washington Ave., Madison 53704
(608) 221-9191 wpta@wpta.org www.wpta.org

Physician Assistants, Wis. Academy of
Clark Collins, Pres.
563 Carter Ct., Suite B, Kimberly 54136
(920) 560-5630 wapa@badgerbay.co www.wapa.org

Physicians, Am. College of Emergency (Wis. Ch.)
Richard H. Paul, Exec. Dir.
10 W. Phillip Rd., Suite 120, Vernon Hills, IL 60061-1330
(800) 838-3627 richardpaul@dls.net
www.wisconsinacep.org

Physicians, Wis. Academy of Family
Larry Pheifer, Exec. Dir.
210 Green Bay Rd., Thiensville 53092
(262) 512-0606 academy@wafp.org www.wafp.org

Pipe Welding Bureau, Natl. Certified (Wis. Chap.)
Julie Walsh, Chap. Secy.
5940 Seminole Centre Ct., Suite 102, Madison 53711
(608) 288-1414 julie.walsh@mechanicalindustries.org

Podiatric Medicine, Wis. Soc. of
Amanda Soelle, Exec. Dir.
2 E. Mifflin St., Suite 600, Madison 53703
(608) 381-3530 wispodiatrists@gmail.com
www.wisconsinpodiatrists.com

Police Assn., Wis. Chiefs of
Donald Thaves, Exec. Dir.
River Ridge – 1141 South Main St., Shawano 54166
(715) 524-8283 dthaves@shawanonet.net
www.wichiefs.org

Police Assn., Wis. Professional
James L. Palmer, Exec. Dir.
660 John Nolen Dr., Suite 300, Madison 53713
(608) 273-3840 palmer@wppa.com www.wppa.com

Pork Assn., Wis. Cooperative
Tammy Vaassen, Dir. of Operations
P.O. Box 327, Lancaster 53813-0327
(608) 723-7551 wppa@wppa.org www.wppa.org

Postal History Soc., Wis.
Darren Mueller, Pres.
P.O. Box 343, Oak Creek 53154
(414) 429-3750 darren.mueller@juno.com
www.wfscstamps.org/Clubs/WisconsinPostalHistory/

Postsecondary Agricultural Students
Paul Cutting, State Director
655 4th St., Fennimore 53809
(608) 822-2467 pcutting@swtc.edu www.wipas.org

Potato and Vegetable Growers Assn., Wis.
Tamas Houlihan, Exec. Dir.
P.O. Box 327, Antigo 54409
(715) 623-7683 wpvga@wisconsinpotatoes.com
www.wisconsinpotatoes.com

Potato Growers Aux., Inc., Wis.
P.O. Box 327, Antigo 54409-0327
(715) 623-7683 wpvga@wisconsinpotatoes.com

Potato Improvement Assn., Wis. Seed
P.O. Box 173, Antigo 54409-0173
(715) 623-7683 www.potatoseed.org

Prevent Blindness Wis., Inc.
Barbara Armstrong, Exec. Dir
759 N. Milwaukee St., Suite 305, Milwaukee 53202
(414) 765-0505 info@preventblindnesswisconsin.org
www.preventblindness.org/wi

Preventive Medicine, Wis., Soc. for
Henry A. Anderson, M.D., Pres.
200 Lakewood Blvd., Madison 53704-5916
(608) 266-1253 anderha@sbcglobal.net

Psychological Assn., Wis.
Sarah Bowen, Exec. Dir.
126 S. Franklin St., Madison 53703
(608) 251-1450 wispsych@execpc.com
www.wipsychology.org

Purple Heart, Military Order of the (Dept. of Wis.)
William Hustad, Adjutant
W4489 Exeter Crossing, Monticello 53570
(608) 527-2942 wfhus@tds.net

Quality, Amer. Soc. For (Wis. Chap)
William Troy, CEO
600 N. Plankinton Ave., Milwaukee 53201-3005
(414) 298-8789 wtroy@asq.org www.asq.org

Radiologic Technologists, Wis. Soc. of
Marnet Zimmer, Secy.
3711 S. Iowa Ave., St. Francis 53235
(414) 769-1239 margaret.zimmer@sbcglobal.net
www.wsrt.net

Radiological Soc., Wis.
Jane Svinicki, Exec. Dir.
6737 W. Washington St., Suite 1300, Milwaukee 53214
(414) 755-6293 jane@svinicki.com www.wi-rad.org

Railroad Passengers, Wis. Assn. of
Mark Weitenbeck, Treas.
3385 S. 119th St., West Allis 53227-3943
(414) 541-1112 wisarp@hotmail.com www.wisarp.org

Reading Assn., Wis. State
Joyce Uglow, Admin. Asst.
909 Rock Ridge Rd., Burlington 53105
(262) 249-3678 wsra@wsra.org
www.wsra.org

Real Property Listers Assn., Wis.
Brian Braithwaite, Pres.
432 E. Washington St., West Bend 53095
(262) 335-4370 rplbrian@co.washington.wi.us
www.wrpla.org

Red Cross, Amer.
Patty Flowers, Reg. CEO
2600 W. Wisconsin Ave., Milwaukee 53233
(414) 342-8680 www.redcross.org

Register of Deeds Assn., Wis.
Julie Pagel, Pres.
P.O. Box 2808, Oshkosh 54903-2808
(920) 236-4881 jpagel@co.winnebago.wi.us
www.wrdaonline.org

Rehabilitation For Wisconsin, Inc.
Lincoln Burr, Exec. Dir.
2000 Engel St., Suite 100, Madison 53713
(608) 244-5310 rfw@rfw.org www.rfwia.org/

Republican Party of Wis.
Joe Fadness, Exec. Dir.
148 E. Johnson St., Madison 53703
(608) 257-4765 info@wisgop.org www.wisgop.org

Reserve Officers Assn. of the U.S. (Dept. of Wis.)
Michael T. Schmitz, Exec. Secy.
1104 E. Waterford Ave., Milwaukee 53207
(414) 483-2629 WIDeptROA@wi.rr.com
www.roa.org/departments/wisconsin

Residential Services Association of Wis.
Jennifer Rzepka, Exec. Dir.
6737 W. Washington St., Suite 1300, Milwaukee 53214
(414) 276-9273 info@rsawisconsin.org
www.rsawisconsin.org

Restaurant Assn., Wis.
Edward J. Lump, Pres./CEO
2801 Fish Hatchery Rd., Madison 53713
(608) 270-9950 elump@wirestaurant.org
www.wirestaurant.org

Retired Enlisted Assn., The
Holly Hoppe, Pres.
Courthouse, 301 Washington St., Oconto 54153
(920) 834-6817 cvso@co.oconto.wi.us
www.trea.org

Right to Life, Inc., Wis.
Heather Weininger, Exec. Dir.
9730 W. Bluemound Rd., Suite 200,
Milwaukee 53226-2331
(877) 855-5007 admin@wrtl.org www.wrtl.org

Runaway Services, Wis. Assn. for
Patricia Balke, Exec. Dir.
2318 E. Dayton St., Madison 53704
(608) 241-2649 pbalke@sbcglobal.net wahrs.org

Saddlebred Assn. of Wis., Amer.
Robert Mucci, Secy.
6226 Fredericksburg Lane, Madison 53718
(608) 223-9203 info@asaw.org www.asaw.org

Safety Patrols Inc., Wis.
Joann Solberg, Exec. Dir.
P.O. Box 33, Madison 53701-0033
(608) 828-2486 jmsolberg@aaawisconsin.com
www.wisconsinsafetypatrol.com

St. Francis Children's Center, Inc.
Gerald Coon, Exec. Dir.
6700 N. Port Washington Rd., Milwaukee 53217-3919
(414) 351-0450 gcoon@sfcckids.org
www.sfcckids.org

Sanitary Engineering, Amer. Soc. of (Wis. Chap.)
Dennis Hoffman, Secy.
371 Vista View Dr., Cedarburg 53012
(262) 375-8832 kat1129hof@netzero.com

School Administrators, Assn. of Wis.
Jim Lynch, Exec. Dir.
4797 Hayes Rd., Suite 103, Madison 53704-3288
(608) 241-0300 jimlynch@awsa.org www.awsa.org

School Attorneys Assn., Wis.
Douglas Witte, Pres.
P.O. Box 1664, Madison 53701
(608) 257-4812 dougwitte@mellilaw.com
www.wasb.org/websites/wsaa/index.php?p=216

School Boards, Inc., Wis. Assn. of
John Ashley, Exec. Dir.
122 W. Washington Ave., Suite 400, Madison 53703
(608) 257-2622 jashley@wasb.org www.wasb.org

School Bus Assn., Wis.
Cherie Houser, Exec. Dir.
5307 Indigo Way, Middleton 53562
(608) 514-5470 cherie@wi-sba.org www.wi-sba.org

School Music Assn., Inc., Wis.
Timothy J. Schaid, Exec. Dir.
1005 Quinn Dr., Waunakee 53597
(608) 850-3566 schaidt@wsmamusic.org
wsmamusic.org

School Music, Wis. Foundation for
Timothy J. Schaid, Exec. Dir.
1005 Quinn Dr., Waunakee 53597
(608) 850-3566 schaidt@wsmamusic.org
www.foundation4schoolmusic.org

Schools Accreditation, Wis. Religious and Independent, Inc.
Beatrice Weiland, Exec. Dir.
P.O. Box 685, Muskego 53150
(262) 895-3679 wrisa@wrisa.net www.wrisa.net

Schools, Wis. Assn. of Christian
Paul Brown, Exec. Dir.
1840 Bond St., Green Bay 54303
(920) 499-5561 office@wacschools.org
www.wacschools.org

Seasonal Residents Assn.
Nick Kaufmann
P.O. Box 46108, Madison 53744
(800) 880-9944 info@wisra.org www.wisra.org

SEIU Healthcare, Wis.
Dian Palmer, Pres.
4513 Vernon Rd., #300, Madison 53705-2366
(608) 277-1199 dianp@seiuhcwi.org www.seiuhcwi.org

Seniors of Wis., Inc., United
Carolyn Clements, Pres.
4515 W. Forest Home Ave., Milwaukee 53219-4837
(414) 321-0220 www.unitedseniorsofwisconsin.org

Sexual Assault, Wis. Coalition Against
Dominic Holt, Public Policy and Comm. Coord.
2801 W. Beltline Hwy, Suite 202, Madison 53713
(608) 257-1516 wcasa@wcasa.org www.wcasa.org

Sheriffs and Deputy Sheriffs Assn., Wis.
James Cardinal, Exec. Dir.
P.O. Box 145, Chippewa Falls 54729-0145
(715) 723-7173 jcardinal@wsdsa.org www.wsdsa.org

Sheriff's Assn., Badger State
Dean Meyer, Exec. Dir.
P.O. Box 394, Bruce 54819
(715) 415-2412 badgersheriff@brucetel.net
www.badgersheriff.com

Sign Assn., Wis.
Christopher Ruditys, Exec. Dir.
11801 W. Silver Spring Dr., #200, Milwaukee 53225
(414) 271-9277 ruditys@wamllc.net
www.wisconsinsign.org

Sister Relationships, Inc., Wis.
Alexander P. Durtka, Jr., Pres.
1110 N. Old World Third St., Suite 420,
Milwaukee 53203-1102
(414) 225-6220 wisci@iiwisconsin.org

SkillsUSA - Post Secondary
Dale A. Drees, State Dir.
1825 N. Bluemound Dr., P.O. Box 2277,
Fox Valley Technical College, Appleton 54912
(920) 735-2489 drees@fvtc.edu skillsusa-wi.org

SMART – Transportation Division
  (United Transportation Union)
Craig C. Peachy, State Dir.
7 N. Pinckney St., Suite LL-25, Madison 53703-4208
(608) 251-4120 utulo56@gmail.com wisconsin.utu.org

Soccer Assn., Inc., Wis.
William Sandoval, Pres.
6520 W. Layton Ave., Suite 201, Greenfield 53220
(414) 281-1300 president@wisoccer.org
www.wisoccer.org

Social Workers, Inc., Natl. Assn. of (Wis. Chap.)
Marc Herstand, Exec. Dir.
131 W. Wilson St., Suite 903, Madison 53703
(608) 257-6334 naswwi@naswwi.org
www.naswwi.org

Socialist Party of Wis.
Robert A. McMullen, Secy.
1001 E. Keefe Ave., Milwaukee 53212
(414) 332-0654

Sod Producers Assn., Wis.
Gina Halter, Exec. Secy.
22920 Hanson Rd., Union Grove 53182
(262) 895-6820 haltersod@prodigy.net

Soil Science Soc. of America
Ellen Bergfeld, CEO
5585 Guilford Rd., Madison 53711
(608) 273-8080 ebergfeld@sciencesocieties.org
www.soils.org

Soybean Assn., Wis.
Robert C. Karls, Exec. Dir.
4414 Regent St., Madison 53705
(608) 274-7522 wisoybean.org

Specialized Medical Vehicle Assn. of Wisconsin
Jim Brown, Pres.
2703 Industrial St., Wisconsin Rapids 54495
(800) 423-7818 woi_rcc@wctc.net

Speech-Language Pathology and Audiology Assn., Wis.
Mary Bahr Schwenke, Pres.
563 Carter Court, Suite B, Kimberly 54136
(920) 560-5642 wsha@wisha.org www.wisha.org

Spinal Cord Injury Assn., Natl. (Wis. Chapter)
John Dziewa, Pres.
P.O. Box 270096, Milwaukee 53227
(414) 384-4022 office@spinalcordwi.org
www.spinalcordwi.org

Stamp Clubs, Inc., Wis. Federation of
Allen Vick, Treas.
2090 River Estate Lane, Stoughton 53589
(608) 873-3481 norskelodge@aol.com
www.wfscstamps.org

State Employees Union, Wis.
   (AFSCME Council 24, AFL-CIO)
Marty Beil, Exec. Dir.
8033 Excelsior Dr., Suite C, Madison 53717-1903
(608) 836-0024 mbeil@wseu-24.org wseu-24.org

Student Financial Aid Administrators, Wis. Assn. of
Debra Duff, Pres.
2900 N. Menomonee River Pky., Mount Mary University,
Milwaukee 53222-4597
(414) 256-1257 duffd@mtmary.edu www.wasfaa.net

Students, Inc., United Council of UW
Nneka Akubeze, Exec. Dir.
14 W. Mifflin St., Suite 212, Madison 53703
(608) 263-3422 ed@unitedcouncil.net.
www.unitedcouncil.net

Supporting Families Together Assn.
Jill Hoiting, Dir. of Programs and External Rel.
700 Ray-O-Vac Drive, Suite 6, Madison 53711
(608) 443-2490 info@supportingfamiliestogether.org
www.supportingfamiliestogether.org

Surgeons, Wis. Soc. of Plastic
Eric Ostermann, Exec. Dir
563 Carter Ct., Suite B, Kimberly 54136
(920) 750-7721 wsps@badgerbay.co
wisocietyplasticsurgery.org

Surveyors, Inc., Wis. Soc. of Land
Francis R. Thousand, Exec. Dir.
5113 Spaanem Ave., Madison 53716
(608) 770-9759 fthousant@charter.net www.wsls.org

Taxicab Owners, Wis. Assn. of
Richard Running, Pres.
318 W. Decker St., Viroqua 54665
(608) 637-2599 richard@runninginc.net
www.witransportation.org

Taxpayers Alliance, Wis.
Todd A. Berry, Pres.
401 North Lawn Ave., Madison 53704-5033
(608) 241-9789 wistax@wistax.org www.wistax.org

Taxpayers Assn., Inc., Wis. Property
Mike Marsch, Pres.
P.O. Box 1493, Madison 53701-1493
(608) 255-7473 wisproptax@wptonline.org
wptonline.org

Teachers, American Assn. of Physics (Wis. Section)
Erik Hendrickson, Secy./Treas.
UW-Eau Claire, Dept. of Physics and Astronomy,
Eau Claire 54702-4004
(715) 836-5834 hendrije@uwec.edu www.wapt.org

Telecommunications Assn., Wis. State
William C. Esbeck, Exec. Dir.
122 W. Washington Ave., Suite 1050, Madison 53703
(608) 256-8866 bill.esbeck@wsta.info www.wsta.info

Telemedia Council, Inc., Natl.
Marieli Rowe, Exec. Dir.
1922 University Ave., Madison 53726
(608) 218-1182 ntelemedia@aol.com
www.nationaltelemediacouncil.org

Textile Services, Wis. Assn. of
Brian Swingle, Exec. Dir.
12342 W. Layton Ave., Greenfield 53228
(414) 529-4703 bswingle@toriiphillips.com

Theatre Owners of Wis., Natl. Assn. of
Paul J. Rogers, Pres.
W168 N8936 Appleton Ave., Menomonee Falls 53051
(262) 532-0017 nato@natoofwiup.org www.natoofwiup.
org

Timber Professionals Assn., Great Lakes
Henry Schienebeck, Exec. Dir.
P.O. Box 1278, Rhinelander 54501-1278
(715) 282-5828 henry@newnorth.net www.timberpa.com

Title Assn., Inc., Wis. Land
Karen E. Gilster, Exec. Dir.
P.O. Box 873, West Salem 54669
(608) 786-2336 kgilster@wlta.org www.wlta.org

Tool Die and Machining Association of Wis.
Becky Fisher, Acct. Mgr.
W175 N11117 Stonewood Dr., Suite 204,
Germantown 53022
(262) 532-2440 toolmaker@tdmaw.org
www.tdmaw.org

Tourism Federation, Wis.
Julia Hertel
P.O. Box 393, Sun Prairie 53590
(608) 335-0019 info@witourismfederation.org
www.witourismfederation.org

Towing Assn., Wis.
Neal Kedzie, Pres.
P.O. Box 44849, Madison 53744-4849
(608) 833-8200 nkedzie@witruck.org www.witow.org

Towns Assn., Wis.
Michael J. Koles, Exec. Dir.
W7686 County Rd. MMM, Shawano 54166
(715) 526-3157 wtowns@frontiernet.net
www.wisctowns.com

Translators and Interpreters Guild, AFL-CIO (Wis. Chap.)
Rick Kissell
P.O. Box 1101, Milwaukee 53201-1101
(414) 617-8039 rick@kissell.org www.ttig.org

Transportation Builders Assn., Wis.
Patrick Goss, Exec. Dir.
1 South Pinckney St., Suite 300, Madison 53703
(608) 256-6891 pgoss@wtba.org www.wtba.org

Transportation Development Assn. of Wis., Inc.
Craig Thompson, Exec. Dir.
10 E. Doty St., Suite 201, Madison 53703
(608) 256-7044 general@tdawisconsin.org
www.tdawisconsin.org

Tree Farm Com., Wis.
David J. Czysz, Admin.
P.O. Box 285, Stevens Point 54481
(715) 252-2001 witreefarm@gmail.com
www.witreefarm.org

Trees For Tomorrow, Inc.
Libby Dorn, Exec. Dir.
P.O. Box 609, Eagle River 54521-0609
(715) 479-6456 learning@treesfortomorrow.com
www.treesfortomorrow.com

University of Wisconsin Foundation
Michael M. Knetter, Pres./CEO
1848 University Ave., Madison 53726
(608) 263-4545 www.supportuw.org

Utilities Assn., Inc., Wis.
William R. Skewes, Exec. Dir.
44 E. Mifflin St., Suite 202, Madison 53703
(608) 257-3151 bskewes@wisconsinutilities.com
www.wiutilities.org

Utility Investors, Inc., Wis.
Michelle Lancaster, Deputy Dir.
10 E. Doty St., Suite 500, Madison 53703-3397
(608) 310-5316 info@wuiinc.org http://wuiinc.org

Utility Tax Assn., Wis.
Jan DeKeyser, Secy.
1655 County Rd. A, Neenah 54956
(920) 725-3284 jdekeyser@netzero.net

Veteran Organizations, Wis. Assn. of Concerned
Bob Buhr, Secy.
510 3rd St., Clear Lake 54005
(715) 220-6988 bobbuhr@cltcomm.net www.wacvo.org

Veterans Against the War, Vietnam
John Zutz, Coord.
2922 N. Booth St., Milwaukee 53212-2537
www.vvaw.org

Veterans Foundation, Wis.
James Mullarkey, Secy.
P.O. Box 1917, Waukesha 53187-1917
(414) 640-6616 jmullarkey@wivf.org www.
wisconsinveteransfoundation.org

Veterans' Memorial, Clear Lake
Douglas Cahow, Pres.
P.O. Box 450, Clear Lake 54005
(612) 716-7478 teachdoug@aol.com
www.clvetsmemorial.com

Veterans of Amer., Vietnam (Wis. State Council)
James Mullarkey, Secy.
P.O. Box 1917, Waukesha 53187-1917
(414) 640-6616 jmullarkey@vvawi.org www.vvawi.org

Veterans of America, Paralyzed, Wis. Chapter
Paul Lehman, Exec. Dir.
2311 S. 108th St., West Allis 53227-1901
(414) 328-8910 lehmanp@wisconsinpva.org
www.wisconsinpva.org

Veterans of Foreign Wars (Dept. of Wis.)
Thomas Heath, State QM
P.O. Box 6128, Monona 53716
(608) 221-5276 wivfw@att.net http://vfwofwi.com

Veterans of Foreign Wars (Ladies Auxiliary)
Judy Borg, Pres.
1809 N. Oneida St., Appleton 54911
(920) 739-5730 judyborg@new.rr.com
www.wiladiesvfwaux.org

Veterans of U.S.A, Jewish War – Dept. of Wis.
Paul Fine, Cmdr.
8010 N. 67th St., Milwaukee 53223
(414) 354-4139

Veterans, Blinded, Assn. of Wis.
Gary Traynor, Pres.
2216 21st St., Rice Lake 54868
(715) 864-1900 gstraynor@aol.com

Veterans, Catholic War, Aux. (Wis. Dept.)
Susan Jane Schwartz, Rep.
645 W. Scott St., #102, Fond du Lac 54937
(920) 251-0210

Veterans, Disabled Amer. (Dept. of Wis.)
Ken Kuehnl, Adj.
1253 Schuering Rd., Suite A, De Pere 54115
(920) 338-8620 gbdav@sbcglobal.net www.dav-wi.org/

Veterans, Disabled Amer., Aux. (Dept. of Wis.)
Patty Davis, St. Adj
455 W. Sunnyview Dr., #104, Oak Creek 53154
(414) 731-1312 iamdavaproud@gmail.com
www.davawi.org

Veterans, Natl. Assn. for Black (Wis. Chap.)
William Sims, Cmdr.
2669 N. Martin Luther King Dr., Milwaukee 53212
(414) 899-4576 williamsimsvet@gmail.com
www.nabvets.org

Veterans, United Women
Elizabeth Benn, Pres.
163 Amber Tr., Sun Prairie 53590
(608) 235-3901 beth@adneynet.com

Veterans, Wis. Vietnam
William F. Hustad, St. Secy.
W4489 Exeter Crossing Rd., Monticello 53570
(608) 527-2942 wfhus1@tds.net www.wivietnamvets.org

Veterinary Medical Assn., Wis.
Kim Brown Pokorny, Exec. Dir.
2801 Crossroads Dr., Suite 1200, Madison 53718
(608) 257-3665 kpokorny@wvma.org www.wvma.org

Vision Forward Assn.
Terri Davis, Exec. Dir.
912 N. Hawley Rd., Milwaukee 53213-3292
(414) 615-0100 info@vision-forward.org
www.vision-forward.org

Water Recycling Assn., Wis. Onsite
Katie Boycks, Assn. Manager
10 E. Doty Street, Suite 523, Madison 53703
(608) 441-1436 info@wowra.com www.wowra.com

Water Well Assoc., Inc., Wis.
Cindy Wachter, Exec. Dir.
P.O. Box 565, Prairie du Chien 53821
(608) 326-0935 cdenwiwater@wisconsinwaterwell.com
www.wisconsinwaterwell.com

WEA Credit Union
Mark Schrimpf, Pres.
P.O. Box 8003, Madison 53708-8003
(608) 274-9828 www.weacu.com

Wetlands Assn., Wis.
Tracy Hames, Exec. Dir.
214 N. Hamilton St., #201, Madison 53703
(608) 250-9971 info@wisconsinwetlands.org
www.wisconsinwetlands.org

Wildlife Society, Wis. Chapter
Pres.
P.O. Box 863, Madison 53701-0863
joomla.wildlife.org/Wisconsin/

Wine and Spirit Inst., Wis.
Eric Petersen, Exec. Dir.
22 N. Carroll St., Suite 200, Madison 53703
(608) 256-5223

Wisconsin Defense Counsel
Jane Svinicki, CAE, Exec. Dir.
6737 W. Washington St., Suite 1300, Milwaukee 53214
(414) 276-1881 info@wdc-online.org www.wdc-online.org

Wisconsin Environment, Inc.
Megan Severson, State Advocate
122 State St., Suite 310, Madison 53703
(608) 268-0511 www.wisconsinenvironment.org

Wisconsin Information Network (WIN)
Dottie Feder, Pres.
17305 Oak Park Row, Brookfield 53045
(262) 786-6200 dottiebrkf@sbcglobal.net

Wisconsin Intercollegiate Athletic Conference
Gary F. Karner, Commissioner
780 Regent St., Madison 53715
(608) 263-4402 gkarner@uwsa.edu www.wiacsports.com

Wisconsin Lakes
Michael Engleson, Exec. Dir.
4513 Vernon Blvd., Suite 101, Madison 53705
(608) 661-4313 info@wisconsinlakes.org
www.wisconsinlakes.org

WisconsinAIRS, Inc.
Byron Rachow, Treas.
P.O. Box 170643, Milwaukee 53217
(414) 289-6097 byron.rachow@milwaukeecountywi.gov
www.wisconsinairs.com

Women Highway Safety Leaders, Inc., Wis. Assn. of
LaVerne Hoerig, National Rep.
1321 Clara Ave., Sheboygan 53081-5261
(920) 452-0905

Women, Wis. National Organization for
Pres.
P.O. Box 45671, Madison 53744
(608) 313-4669 admin@winow.org winow.org

Women's Network, Wis.
Peggy Rynearson, Administrator
612 W. Main St., Suite 200, Madison 53703
(608) 255-9809 info@wiwomensnetwork.org
wiwomensnetwork.org

Woodland Owners Assn., Inc., Wis.
Nancy C. Bozek, Exec. Dir.
P.O. Box 285, Stevens Point 54481-0285
(715) 346-4798 wwoa@uwsp.edu www.wisconsinwoodlands.org

Writers, Inc., Council for Wis.
Geoff Gilpin, Pres.
6973 Heron Way, DeForest 53532
(608) 846-2812 geoff.gilpin@charter.net
www.wiswriters.org

Source: This list was compiled from a questionnaire mailed to known statewide associations in Fall 2014.

NOTE

If you know of any additional PERMANENT, STATEWIDE, NONPROFIT associations – other than religious or fraternal – please send the information to the Blue Book Editor, Legislative Reference Bureau, P.O. Box 2037, Madison, Wisconsin 53701-2037. New associations which meet the stated criteria will be included in the next edition of the *Wisconsin Blue Book*.

HIGHLIGHTS OF COMMERCE AND INDUSTRY IN WISCONSIN

Manufacturing — Value added by manufacture in Wisconsin totaled $83.7 billion in 2013, an increase of $11.8 billion since 2008. The industry groups with the highest value added in 2013 were food, $13.1 billion; machinery, $11.3 billion; fabricated metal products, $7.8 billion; and paper, $6.8 billion.

Wisconsin ranked 9th among the states in value added by manufacture in 2013. Leaders in this category were California, $245.8 billion; Texas, $239.0 billion; and Ohio, $124.3 billion. The national total for value added was $2.398 trillion in 2013, an increase of $124 billion since 2008.

Energy Consumption — In 2012, Wisconsin's total energy use per capita was 275.6 million Btu, a decrease of about 3% from 2011 and about 5% from 1990. Seen from a national perspective, Wisconsin has gone from consuming energy at about 83% of the U.S. average in 1970 to about 96% the national average in 2012. Compared to various national averages, Wisconsin places a much heavier reliance on coal for its energy usage, but uses less petroleum, natural gas, nuclear power, and renewable energy. As energy consumption has increased, Wisconsin, which was an exporter of electricity in the 1970s, has increasingly become a net importer. Wisconsin petroleum consumption in 2012, was primarily used for transportation at 88.3%, followed by residential (5.5%), agricultural (4%), and commercial (1%) usage.

Gasoline Usage and Tax — In 2012, each automobile in Wisconsin was driven an average of 12,504 miles. This is 1,239 miles, or about 11%, more than the national average of 11,265 miles per year. Wisconsin automobiles averaged 23.4 miles per gallon of gasoline, nearly the same as the national average of 23.3 mpg.

The state motor fuel tax was indexed annually prior to April 1, 2006. Since indexing began on April 1, 1985, the average annual adjustment in state tax was typically between 0.4 and 0.8 cents. After April 1, 2006, the state motor fuel tax can only be changed by legislative action. The current tax has not increased since then, when it was indexed to a total of 30.9 cents per gallon. The federal government's gasoline tax has also remained at 18.4 cents per gallon since that date, for a total of 49.3 cents per gallon in federal and state taxes.

Exports and Markets — In 2013, Wisconsin's leading exports were industrial machinery, including computers, $6.8 billion; medical and scientific instruments, $2.3 billion; and electric machinery, $2.2 billion. The leading market for Wisconsin exports in 2013 was Canada ($7.5 billion), followed by Mexico ($2.5 billion), and China ($1.7 billion). The total of all exports from Wisconsin to all markets in 2013 remained level with 2012 at about $23.1 billion.

Financial Institutions — The number of banks operating in Wisconsin has decreased from the post-Depression high of 634 in 1980 to 278 in 2014. Over the same period, deposits increased from $24.7 billion to $136.5 billion. In 2014, Wisconsin's 31 state and federally chartered savings institutions had total deposits of $11.6 billion, a decrease of about 12% from 2012.

In 2014, Wisconsin had 160 state-chartered credit unions with almost 2.5 million members and $26.3 billion in assets.

Corporations — In 2014, a total of 3,400 foreign corporations were licensed in Wisconsin, a 38% increase from 2,459 in 2009. Total incorporation and licensing fees collected by the state in 2014 exceeded $21 million.

The following tables present selected data. Consult footnoted sources for more detailed information about commerce and industry.

WISCONSIN USE OF PETROLEUM 1970 – 2012
(In Trillions of Btu)

Year	Total[1]	Transportation	Residential	Industrial	Agricultural	Commercial	Electric Utility
1970	457.7	271.2	107.9	21.1	18.1	31.5	7.9
1975	475.0	314.0	87.6	19.3	18.8	27.5	7.8
1980	454.4	329.2	71.2	13.2	21.4	14.6	4.8
1985	416.0	314.4	58.6	2.8	19.3	19.5	1.4
1990	437.2	346.6	51.4	8.1	16.0	14.1	1.0
1995	465.9	383.6	48.4	10.8	15.6	6.7	0.8
2000	496.7	416.1	40.1	14.8	14.7	9.5	1.6
2001	499.1	417.5	41.3	13.6	14.2	10.3	2.2
2002	507.4	430.1	38.9	12.6	14.5	9.8	1.5
2003	511.4	430.3	40.7	12.7	14.6	11.4	1.8
2004	518.7	438.7	39.8	14.8	14.3	9.3	1.8
2005	497.4	418.5	37.8	16.6	13.6	9.1	1.9
2006	491.6	413.3	39.3	14.6	17.2	5.7	1.5
2007	495.5	415.4	36.8	16.4	19.0	6.0	1.9
2008	474.8	399.9	36.5	11.8	17.9	7.6	1.1
2009	449.5	383.3	32.4	6.0	21.6	5.6	0.6
2010	452.4	397.8	28.3	3.6	18.5	3.8	0.5
2011	446.4	393.5	27.5	3.4	16.8	4.7	0.5
2012[2]	447.5	395.1	24.6	4.2	18.7	4.5	0.6

Note: Historical numbers have been revised to reflect updated source data.

[1]Detail may not add to total due to rounding.

[2]Preliminary estimates.

Source: Wisconsin State Energy Office, *Wisconsin Energy Statistics, 2013,* "Wisconsin Petroleum Use, by Economic Sector, 1970-2012", at: http://www.stateenergyoffice.wi.gov/docview.asp?docid=26170&locid=160 [April 6, 2015].

WISCONSIN AND U.S. ENERGY CONSUMPTION BY RESOURCE 1970 – 2012
(In Millions of Btu per Capita)

Energy Resource	1970	1980	1985	1990	1995	2000	2005	2010	2011	2012[1]
Petroleum										
U.S.	126.1	128.0	112.8	113.9	109.9	116.0	116.1	100.9	99.0	96.1
Wisconsin	103.6	96.6	87.7	89.4	91.3	92.6	89.1	79.4	78.5	78.6
Wisconsin as % of U.S. per capita	82.2	75.4	77.7	78.5	83.1	79.8	76.8	78.7	79.2	81.8
Natural Gas										
U.S.	106.3	89.1	74.4	78.5	85.1	84.4	76.4	79.4	79.8	82.8
Wisconsin	74.1	73.1	64.1	62.6	74.7	73.3	73.6	65.3	69.3	71.4
Wisconsin as % of U.S. per capita	69.7	82.1	86.2	79.8	87.8	86.9	91.6	83.5	86.2	91.3
Coal										
U.S.	59.8	67.9	73.5	76.8	75.4	80.0	77.1	67.2	63.1	55.3
Wisconsin	80.4	69.0	78.9	84.1	90.9	96.8	95.3	91.8	86.3	72.7
Wisconsin as % of U.S. per capita	134.5	101.6	107.4	109.5	120.5	121.0	123.5	136.6	136.8	131.4
Nuclear										
U.S.	1.2	12.1	17.1	24.5	26.6	27.9	27.6	27.3	26.5	25.6
Wisconsin	0.4	22.7	25.0	24.8	23.2	23.1	14.7	25.2	22.0	18.6
Wisconsin as % of U.S. per capita	32.5	188.7	145.9	101.3	87.4	82.8	53.1	92.4	82.7	72.4
Renewable[2]										
U.S.	19.9	23.9	25.6	24.2	24.6	21.6	21.1	26.1	29.1	28.1
Wisconsin	6.2	10.4	10.9	10.3	9.8	10.3	11.3	15.0	15.7	15.7
Wisconsin as % of U.S. per capita	31.1	43.5	42.7	42.5	39.7	47.7	53.3	57.3	53.8	55.8
Electric Imports[3]										
Wisconsin	−6.4	−1.4	−0.4	17.9	24.1	18.3	22.5	8.5	11.7	18.7
Total Resource Use										
U.S.	313.2	320.9	303.4	317.9	321.7	330.0	318.3	301.0	297.6	288.0
Wisconsin	258.3	270.4	266.2	289.1	314.1	314.5	306.4	285.3	283.4	275.6
Wisconsin as % of U.S. per capita	82.5	84.3	87.8	90.9	97.6	95.3	96.3	94.9	95.4	95.8

Note: Previous years' numbers have been updated to reflect revisions in source.

[1]Preliminary data.

[2]Includes wood, waste, alcohol, and other biomass energy; hydroelectric; geothermal; solar; and wind.

[3]Import of electricity reflects estimated resource energy used in other states or Canada to produce electricity imported into Wisconsin. This resource energy is estimated assuming 11,300 Btu per k Wh imported into Wisconsin. A negative number indicates energy used in Wisconsin to produce electricity exported out of state.

Source: Wisconsin State Energy Office, "Wisconsin Energy Statistics, 2013", at: http://www.stateenergyoffice.wi.gov/subcategory.asp?linksubcatid=3691&linkcatid=2847&linkid=1451&locid=160 [April 7, 2015]. Percentages calculated by Division of Energy.

AUTOMOBILE USAGE AND GASOLINE MILEAGE
Wisconsin and United States, 1980 – 2012

Year	Average Miles Driven Per Auto		Average Auto Miles Per Gallon of Gasoline	
	Wisconsin	U.S.	Wisconsin	U.S.
1980	9,782	8,813	16.1	16.0
1985	10,455	9,419	17.6	17.5
1990	11,659	10,504	20.3	20.2
1995	12,435	11,203	21.2	21.1
2000	13,293	11,976	22.0	21.9
2005	13,886	12,510	22.2	22.1
2006	13,858	12,485	22.6	22.5
2007	11,888	10,710	23.0	22.9
2008	11,422	10,290	23.8	23.7
2009	11,534	10,391	23.6	23.5
2010	11,822	10,650	23.4	23.3
2011	12,378	11,150	23.3	23.2
2012*	12,504	11,265	23.4	23.3

Note: This table does not include data for minivans, pickup trucks, or sport utility vehicles. Wisconsin and U.S. figures are derived from different sources and may not be strictly compatible.

*Preliminary data.

Source: Wisconsin Energy Office, *Wisconsin Energy Statistics, 2013*, "Average Miles Driven Per Vehicle and Average Miles Per Gallon of Gasoline, Wisconsin and United States", at: http://www.stateenergyoffice.wi.gov/docview.asp?docid=26461&locid=160 [April 7, 2015].

WISCONSIN MOTOR VEHICLE FUEL TAX
1925 – 2015

Date of Change	Gasoline Tax Per Gallon[1]	Change	
		Amount	Percent
April 1, 1925	2.0¢	2.0¢	—
April 1, 1931	4.0	2.0	100.0%
July 1, 1955	6.0	2.0	50.0
July 1, 1966	7.0	1.0	16.7
May 1, 1980	9.0	2.0	28.6
August 1, 1981	13.0	4.0	44.4
August 1, 1983	15.0	2.0	15.4
July 1, 1984	16.0	1.0	6.7
April 1, 1985[2]	16.5	0.5	3.1
August 1, 1987[3]	20.0	2.0	11.1
April 1, 1990	21.5	0.7	3.4
April 1, 1991	22.2	0.7	3.3
April 1, 1993[4]	23.2	1.0	4.5
April 1, 1994	23.1	(0.1)	(0.4)
April 1, 1995[5]	23.4	0.3	1.3
April 1, 1996[5]	23.7	0.3	1.3
April 1, 1997	23.8	0.1	0.4
November 1, 1997[6]	24.8	1.0	4.2
April 1, 2000	26.4	0.6	2.3
April 1, 2001	27.3	0.9	3.4
April 1, 2002	28.1	0.8	2.9
April 1, 2003	28.5	0.4	1.4
April 1, 2004	29.1	0.6	2.1
April 1, 2005	29.9	0.8	2.7
April 1, 2006[7]	30.9	1.0	3.3
April 1, 2007	30.9	0.0	0.0
April 1, 2008	30.9	0.0	0.0
April 1, 2009	30.9	0.0	0.0
April 1, 2010	30.9	0.0	0.0
April 1, 2011	30.9	0.0	0.0
April 1, 2012	30.9	0.0	0.0
April 1, 2013	30.9	0.0	0.0
April 1, 2014	30.9	0.0	0.0
April 1, 2015	30.9	0.0	0.0

[1]Tax rates for some alternate fuels are based on energy density. The rates effective April 1, 2005, are 21.9 cents for LPG (liquefied petroleum gas) and 23.9 cents for CNG (compressed natural gas). E85 (85% fuel ethanol) is taxed at the same rate as gasoline.

[2]Beginning in April 1985, the state motor fuel tax was indexed (1983 Wisconsin Act 27) to take into account fuel consumption and inflation. By law, the tax increase or decrease is automatically calculated annually, based on the inflation rate from the National Highway Maintenance and Operations Cost Index and the percentage change in motor fuel consumption. (The federal gasoline tax has been 18.4 cents per gallon since October 1, 1993.)

[3]Statutory adjustment (1987 Wisconsin Act 27).

[4]1991 Wisconsin Act 119 postponed further fuel tax indexing until April 1, 1993.

[5]1993 Wisconsin Act 16 set aside the calculation of the consumption factor for 1995 and 1996 and provided fixed consumption factors for each year.

[6]1997 Wisconsin Act 27 increased the motor fuel tax rate and modified the indexing formula to take into account only the change to the cost index.

[7]2005 Wisconsin Act 85 ended annual motor fuel tax indexing as of April 1, 2006.

Sources: Session laws of the Wisconsin Legislature; Wisconsin Department of Revenue, *Motor Vehicle Fuel Tax Information*, April 2005 and previous years, and Motor Vehicle Fuel Tax FAQ, at: http://www.dor.state.wi.us/faqs/ise/mofuel.html [April 7, 2015].

VALUE ADDED BY MANUFACTURING
By State, 2008 and 2013
(In Thousands)

State	Value Added 2008	Value Added 2013	2013 State Rank	State	Value Added 2008	Value Added 2013	2013 State Rank
Alabama	$43,480,899	$47,356,886	18	Montana	$2,890,623	$3,592,109	47
Alaska	1,628,809	1,726,348	49	Nebraska	15,969,148	20,041,015	35
Arizona	32,150,649	27,451,350	28	Nevada	8,950,077	8,720,321	40
Arkansas	23,888,249	25,152,244	29	New Hampshire	9,731,689	10,628,306	38
California	254,497,152	245,764,599	1	New Jersey	54,076,146	43,341,049	23
Colorado	23,837,841	23,683,397	31	New Mexico	7,115,060	13,789,943	36
Connecticut	33,823,120	34,067,775	26	New York	87,126,225	72,861,000	10
Delaware	8,300,230	5,923,386	44	North Carolina	101,342,064	106,756,846	5
District of Columbia	196,289	150,796	51	North Dakota	4,731,266	5,728,963	45
Florida	51,395,345	51,284,806	17	Ohio	121,527,105	124,349,043	3
Georgia	59,847,396	66,158,662	11	Oklahoma	26,933,513	24,256,521	30
Hawaii	1,708,310	1,139,809	50	Oregon	36,308,309	37,145,314	25
Idaho	9,304,612	8,814,523	39	Pennsylvania	109,544,085	103,791,292	6
ILLINOIS	104,278,014	112,179,164	4	Rhode Island	6,488,394	6,053,017	43
Indiana	99,080,007	100,326,130	7	South Carolina	37,254,674	39,442,821	24
IOWA	42,534,408	45,847,564	21	South Dakota	5,877,660	6,483,017	42
Kansas	29,207,420	28,874,375	27	Tennessee	59,547,890	61,364,860	13
Kentucky	38,136,431	44,475,058	22	Texas	192,251,821	239,012,478	2
Louisiana	48,426,372	57,752,061	14	Utah	19,722,057	21,890,738	34
Maine	8,808,366	7,941,573	41	Vermont	4,774,278	3,885,385	46
Maryland	20,461,976	22,097,552	33	Virginia	48,880,376	57,435,014	15
Massachusetts	47,170,173	46,538,808	19	Washington	46,167,866	62,636,689	12
MICHIGAN	84,530,377	98,437,964	8	West Virginia	9,927,681	10,911,680	37
MINNESOTA	50,655,592	55,720,676	16	WISCONSIN	71,913,353	83,725,189	9
Mississippi	23,121,719	22,522,142	32	Wyoming	4,330,316	2,797,493	48
Missouri	40,515,295	46,364,009	20	UNITED STATES	$2,274,366,727	$2,398,391,759	

Note: State amounts may not sum to United States total due to rounding.

Source: U.S. Census Bureau, "Annual Survey of Manufacturers, Geographic Area Statistics, 2013" and earlier editions, at: http://factfinder.census.gov/faces/nav/jsf/pages/searchresults.xhtml?refresh=t [April 28, 2015].

VALUE ADDED BY MANUFACTURING IN WISCONSIN
By Industry Group, 2009 – 2013
(In Thousands)

Industry Group	2009	2010	2011	2012	2013
Food	$11,072,812	$11,803,511	$12,621,536	$12,911,973	$13,103,875
Machinery	7,398,648	8,892,883	10,111,943	11,854,222	11,336,524
Fabricated metal products	6,114,096	7,044,906	7,525,594	7,920,881	7,827,342
Paper	6,493,854	6,282,072	6,584,251	6,500,354	6,816,067
Computer and electronic products	3,470,347	4,505,598	5,256,104	4,789,267	4,939,541
Chemicals	4,086,818	4,412,094	4,209,114	4,928,734	3,891,345
Transportation equipment	3,258,691	4,266,036	4,384,529	3,485,497	4,036,762
Plastics and rubber products	3,410,687	3,538,204	3,399,214	3,713,195	4,049,893
Electrical equipment, appliances, and components	3,160,027	3,332,508	3,535,736	3,903,286	3,904,066
Printing and related support activities	2,878,478	2,828,336	2,867,713	3,168,552	3,226,071
Wood products	1,648,507	2,109,667	1,360,448	1,567,056	1,683,362
Primary metal industries	1,388,119	1,884,770	2,533,782	2,832,415	2,831,249
Nonmetallic mineral products	1,640,656	1,671,836	1,787,481	2,067,500	2,126,769
Miscellaneous manufacturing	1,276,614	1,398,897	2,228,196	1,612,000	1,601,649
Furniture and related products	1,200,314	1,272,418	1,287,698	1,494,873	1,521,621
Beverage and tobacco products	1,113,492	1,187,555	1,138,500	1,294,692	1,456,669
Textile mills	194,451	227,046	201,622	NA	NA
Leather and allied products	135,317	159,205	145,777	NA	NA
Textile products	75,114	110,277	92,790	NA	NA
Apparel	NA	64,144	NA	NA	NA
TOTAL*	$60,331,031	$67,251,209	$72,804,157	$83,508,979	$83,725,189

NA – Manufacturers declined to report data for competitive reasons.

*Total may not add due to the exclusion in this table of certain manufacturing categories that have very little presence in the state.

Source: U.S. Census Bureau, "Annual Survey of Manufacturers, Geographic Area Statistics, 2013" and previous editions, at: http://factfinder.census.gov/faces/nav/jsf/pages/searchresults.xhtml?refresh=t [April 28, 2015].

WISCONSIN EXPORTS
By Leading Export, 2011 – 2013

Export*	2011	2012	2013	% Change, 2012 to 2013
Industrial machinery	$6,870,461,876	$7,296,696,831	$6,813,896,731	−6.62%
Medical and scientific instruments. . . .	2,145,039,772	2,301,696,321	2,280,360,892	−0.93
Electrical machinery	2,487,652,799	2,325,141,100	2,218,172,107	−4.60
Vehicles (not railway)	1,415,983,721	1,731,939,622	1,936,710,224	11.82
Plastic	792,697,283	879,258,152	951,712,399	8.24
Paper and paperboard	943,506,376	905,790,377	924,817,955	2.10
Iron and steel products	415,166,019	477,878,978	439,861,789	−7.96
Dairy, eggs, honey, etc.	231,240,569	281,828,020	398,650,608	41.45
Books and newspapers	434,908,485	419,539,382	396,033,556	−5.60
Furniture and bedding	316,737,142	332,623,477	348,337,594	4.72
Miscellaneous chemical products	251,903,575	252,359,055	330,582,285	31.00
Miscellaneous food	249,584,750	289,301,881	315,293,104	8.98
Aircraft and spacecraft.	357,047,110	330,137,187	305,952,950	−7.33
Beverages	317,966,680	400,006,446	299,928,601	−25.02
Pharmaceutical products	230,659,568	259,570,507	275,426,972	6.11
Cereals	382,845,660	184,793,406	240,468,233	30.13
Mineral fuel and oil	250,411,268	212,424,735	226,960,813	6.84
Baking related	228,337,062	220,264,225	225,613,452	2.43
Wood	208,772,277	200,649,771	208,195,774	3.76
Hides and skins	153,023,455	156,899,836	205,759,118	31.14
TOTAL – Leading Exports	$18,683,945,447	$19,458,799,309	$19,342,735,157	−0.60%
TOTAL – All Exports	$22,057,273,023	$23,116,666,561	$23,075,279,331	−0.18%

*Export categories based on U.S. Census Bureau commodity codes.
Source: Wisconsin Economic Development Corporation, departmental data, March 2015.

WISCONSIN EXPORTS
By Leading Market, 2011 – 2013

Market	2011	2012	2013	% Change, 2012 to 2013
Canada	$7,145,568,306	$7,642,722,003	$7,496,974,318	−1.91%
Mexico	1,987,038,807	2,166,250,702	2,516,067,745	16.15
China	1,380,668,014	1,547,204,034	1,655,692,067	7.01
Japan	736,207,335	858,211,745	938,376,006	9.34
Germany	879,232,468	714,960,642	701,795,699	−1.84
United Kingdom	624,153,356	615,288,995	679,521,943	10.44
Australia	761,638,116	865,715,027	676,889,714	−21.81
Brazil	574,221,370	497,390,782	478,155,105	−3.87
Chile	614,383,181	555,188,409	476,137,602	−14.24
France	534,042,063	508,425,483	462,553,563	−9.02
Korean Republic	420,971,598	403,158,552	431,142,114	6.94
Saudi Arabia	282,516,669	312,042,062	396,057,336	26.92
United Arab Emirates	167,604,812	305,168,131	393,003,112	28.78
Belgium	366,320,991	411,558,676	385,471,498	−6.34
Netherlands	365,969,895	394,839,083	379,373,601	−3.92
India	329,556,390	456,873,268	289,667,333	−36.60
Italy	317,144,423	270,780,285	279,193,607	3.11
Republic of South Africa	226,772,900	228,505,129	261,042,379	14.24
Singapore	235,082,729	329,845,439	258,780,466	−21.54
Hong Kong	303,332,818	289,780,112	249,714,946	−13.83
TOTAL – Leading Markets	$18,252,426,241	$19,373,908,559	$19,405,610,154	1.64%
TOTAL – All Markets*	$22,057,273,023	$23,116,666,561	$23,075,279,331	−0.18%

*Includes markets not individually identified in this table.
Source: Wisconsin Economic Development Corporation, departmental data, March 2015.

BASIC DATA ON WISCONSIN CORPORATIONS
1905 – 2014

	Transactions[1]			Fees			
	Domestic						
Year[2]	Articles of Incorporation Filed[3]	Amdts. and Restated Articles	Foreign Corporations Licensed[3]	Fees for Articles of Incorporation	Fees for Foreign Corporation[4]	Other Corporation Fees[5]	Total Fees Collected
Calendar							
1905	98	—	95	—	—	—	$69,312
1915	1,043	382	112	$28,287	$3,743	$89,695	121,725
1925	1,438	896	198	57,614	11,139	78,153	146,906
1935	1,272	439	176	30,839	8,956	41,631	81,426
1945	1,120	680	131	31,823	4,826	113,963	150,612
1955	2,537	874	287	89,951	31,146	175,973	297,070
1965	4,063	1,320	401	344,906	120,506	193,844	659,256
Fiscal							
1975	5,976	1,483	663	361,013	386,061	594,498	1,341,572
1980	7,334	1,978	753	373,220	753,461	788,204	1,914,885
1985	7,605	2,359	1,018	485,835	1,142,129	1,371,476	2,999,440
1990	8,387	2,525	1,408	546,550	2,368,900	1,491,104	4,406,554
1995	10,031	2,716	1,507	829,555	4,208,178	2,538,521	7,576,254
2000	21,133	3,088	2,464	2,265,455	6,403,447	3,548,264	12,217,166
2001	20,461	3,064	2,394	2,631,375	6,901,290	3,257,622	12,790,287
2002	22,734	3,145	2,314	2,735,390	6,330,109	3,408,267	12,473,766
2003	26,629	3,057	2,436	3,223,455	7,379,300	5,262,635	15,865,390
2004	31,440	3,644	2,566	3,820,735	6,253,800	6,406,280	16,480,815
2005	33,589	3,595	2,787	4,092,782	6,043,400	5,509,178	15,645,000
2006	33,829	3,711	3,010	4,084,800	8,693,800	4,149,400	16,928,000
2007	32,555	3,596	3,067	1,525,538	5,406,350	6,208,548	17,113,116
2008	31,943	3,401	2,900	1,488,312	5,871,084	7,264,855	18,534,351
2009	27,212	2,273	2,459	5,074,039	7,554,100	5,079,361	17,707,500
2010	27,349	2,231	2,495	5,247,361	8,311,900	5,291,939	18,851,200
2011	28,535	2,210	2,706	10,303,300	7,696,300	723,400	18,723,000
2012	30,014	2,166	2,817	10,599,880	8,345,500	700,200	19,645,500
2013	34,045	2,907	3,100	10,911,200	8,701,600	751,900	20,364,700
2014	35,955	2,917	3,400	11,206,000	9,379,000	784,100	21,369,100

[1]Includes only those corporate entities for which the reporting agency is the office of record.
[2]Since 1975, data is computed on a fiscal year basis, ending June 30 of year shown.
[3]Beginning in 1997, includes limited liability companies.
[4]Since 1975, totals include fees for foreign corporation annual reports.
[5]Includes fees for filing annual reports and corporation charter documents other than articles of incorporation.
Sources: Wisconsin Department of Financial Institutions, departmental data for 2000-2014, June 2014; previous data from the Office of the Wisconsin Secretary of State.

FINANCIAL INSTITUTIONS OPERATING IN WISCONSIN
Number and Deposits, 1900 – 2014

Year*	Number	Total Deposits (in thousands)	Year*	Number	Total Deposits (in thousands)
1900	349	$124,892	2002	328	$83,602,000
1910	630	268,766	2003	319	95,909,000
1920	976	767,534	2004	322	96,111,000
1930	936	935,006	2005	318	100,643,000
1940	574	993,155	2006	320	103,511,000
1950	556	2,965,580	2007	316	109,734,000
1960	561	4,385,838	2008	307	114,838,000
1970	602	8,750,823	2009	302	125,785,000
1980	634	24,763,910	2010	299	126,660,000
1990	504	37,588,879	2011	296	128,628,000
1995	449	59,918,000	2012	295	132,812,000
2000	365	75,379,000	2013	285	129,714,000
2001	337	78,567,000	2014	278	136,508,000

*Beginning in 1994, data includes federal charter savings associations and state-chartered savings associations, supervised by the U.S. Office of Thrift Supervision, and institutions operating in Wisconsin but headquartered outside the state. Deposits for these years are rounded to nearest thousands of dollars.
Sources: **1950 and earlier:** Board of Governors of the Federal Reserve System, *All-Bank Statistics, U.S.,* 1959; **1960:** Wisconsin Commissioner of Banks, agency data, December 1965; **1970:** Federal Deposit Insurance Corporation, *Assets and Liabilities – Commercial and Mutual Savings Banks,* June 1971; **1980:** Federal Deposit Insurance Corporation, corporate data; **1981-93:** Federal Deposit Insurance Corporation, *Data Book: Operating Banks and Branches,* Book 3, June 30, 1993, and previous issues; **1994 to date:** *Federal Deposit Insurance Corporation, Summary of Deposits,* "State Totals by Charter Class for All Institution Deposits, Deposits of All FDIC-Insured Institutions Operating in Wisconsin", June 30, 2014, and previous issues.

FDIC-INSURED INSTITUTIONS OPERATING IN WISCONSIN
By County, June 30, 2014

County	Commercial Banks			Savings Institutions		
	Number of Institutions	Number of Offices	Deposits (in Millions)	Number of Institutions	Number of Offices	Deposits (in Millions)
Adams	5	6	$211	1	1	$4
Ashland	5	10	304	0	0	0
Barron	10	23	827	2	3	112
Bayfield	5	11	202	0	0	0
Brown	18	75	5,249	3	15	376
Buffalo	5	11	299	0	0	0
Burnett	3	8	209	0	0	0
Calumet	8	14	483	2	2	45
Chippewa	10	18	616	3	7	136
Clark	7	13	371	2	4	148
Columbia	9	25	1,031	2	2	51
Crawford	5	10	367	1	1	36
Dane	33	151	11,793	8	35	2,066
Dodge	14	31	971	3	3	131
Door	4	14	543	2	4	100
Douglas	5	10	474	1	3	51
Dunn	9	20	395	1	2	27
Eau Claire	15	31	1,732	2	6	100
Florence	2	5	90	0	0	0
Fond du Lac	13	32	1,677	4	5	203
Forest	2	6	141	0	0	0
Grant	12	38	1,098	1	3	76
Green	10	18	800	1	2	55
Green Lake	8	11	603	2	2	30
Iowa	7	14	374	1	1	30
Iron	2	3	77	0	0	0
Jackson	3	9	230	0	0	0
Jefferson	14	31	1,115	0	0	0
Juneau	7	14	376	0	0	0
Kenosha	11	35	2,078	3	6	79
Kewaunee	5	14	412	0	0	0
La Crosse	13	37	2,017	0	0	0
Lafayette	9	13	346	0	0	0
Langlade	5	6	114	0	0	0
Lincoln	5	8	272	2	2	111
Manitowoc	11	23	1,589	1	2	42
Marathon	19	51	2,611	3	6	231
Marinette	11	20	712	1	3	73
Marquette	6	9	196	0	0	0
Milwaukee	21	199	43,862	11	75	3,074
Monroe	10	17	746	0	0	0
Oconto	7	14	332	0	0	0
Oneida	8	17	694	0	0	0
Outagamie	21	45	2,867	5	15	355
Ozaukee	11	31	1,891	3	10	190
Pepin	3	3	197	0	0	0
Pierce	7	14	483	1	1	53
Polk	9	14	535	1	1	13
Portage	15	28	1,256	1	2	104
Price	5	8	185	1	1	87
Racine	11	52	2,792	4	12	233
Richland	7	8	229	1	1	18
Rock	16	41	2,092	2	3	119
Rusk	5	8	210	1	1	42
St. Croix	13	25	968	1	1	22
Sauk	14	30	1,250	0	0	0
Sawyer	6	9	298	1	1	21
Shawano	8	14	390	1	1	24
Sheboygan	13	38	1,821	2	4	31
Taylor	4	5	233	2	2	164
Trempealeau	9	19	584	0	0	0
Vernon	8	13	391	1	1	14
Vilas	10	14	417	0	0	0
Walworth	16	41	1,588	2	3	40
Washburn	5	8	268	1	1	13
Washington	12	32	1,839	4	17	593
Waukesha	27	147	9,016	11	43	1,447
Waupaca	9	26	1,003	0	0	0
Waushara	10	13	247	1	1	19
Winnebago	14	34	1,901	4	8	190
Wood	13	26	1,268	4	7	467
TOTAL*	247	1,871	$124,863	31	332	$11,645

*Total number of institutions is an unduplicated total for institutions operating in more than one county. Deposit figures do not add to state totals due to rounding.

Note: Menominee county did not report separately.

Source: Federal Deposit Insurance Corporation, "Summary Table 08: State Totals by County, as of June 30, 2014", at: https://www2.fdic.gov/sod/sodSummary.asp?barItem=3 [April 15, 2015].

WISCONSIN FINANCIAL INSTITUTIONS
June 30, 2014

Type of Institution or Branch	Total	Insured Commercial Banks and Trust Companies			Insured Savings Institutions	
		National Charter	State Charter		Total	Federal Charter	State Charter
			Federal Reserve System				
			Member	Nonmember			
Headquartered in state	225	33	20	172	30	16	14
Headquartered outside of state. . . .	22	9	2	11	1	1	0
Total institutions	247	42	22	183	31	17	14
Total offices	1,871	1,005	133	733	332	271	61
Total deposits (in millions)	$124,863	$85,859	$7,595	$31,409	$11,645	$8,796	$2,849

Source: Federal Deposit Insurance Corporation, Summary of Deposits, June 30, 2014, "Individual State Tables – Charter Class", at: https://www2.fdic.gov/sod/sodSummary.asp?barItem=3 [April 8, 2015].

WISCONSIN STATE-CHARTERED CREDIT UNIONS
Number, Members, and Assets
1930 – 2014

| Year | Credit Unions | Membership | | Assets | |
		Total Members	Annual % Change	Total Assets (in millions)	Annual % Change
1930	22	4,659	—	$0.5	—
1935	383	57,847	—	2.9	—
1940	592	153,849	—	11.2	—
1945	536	144,524	—	19.1	—
1950	542	193,296	—	42.9	—
1955	696	292,552	—	120.6	—
1960	733	363,444	—	206.4	—
1965	781	493,399	—	346.6	—
1970	766	628,543	—	480.4	—
1975	673	805,123	—	875.5	—
1980	618	1,060,292	—	1,403.8	—
1985	550	1,261,407	—	2,831.4	—
1990	440	1,485,109	4.3%	4,148.8	8.6%
1995	384	1,744,696	1.8	6,179.2	7.4
2000	340	1,918,729	1.7	9,425.9	7.9
2001	326	1,883,387	-1.8	10,439.4	10.8
2002	308	1,937,867	2.9	11,665.6	11.7
2003	298	1,966,929	1.5	12,772.5	9.5
2004	287	1,992,238	1.3	13,684.4	7.1
2005	280	2,047,031	2.8	14,805.3	8.2
2006	267	2,086,700	1.9	15,656.2	5.7
2007	260	2,083,319	-0.2	16,543.3	5.7
2008	250	2,118,505	1.7	18,182.3	9.9
2009	236	2,164,648	2.2	19,719.6	8.5
2010	223	2,186,471	1.0	20,685.4	4.9
2011	203	2,225,892	1.8	21,915.6	5.9
2012	187	2,264,788	1.7	23,353.8	6.6
2013	171	2,335,239	3.1	24,517.9	5.0
2014	160	2,460,025	5.3	26,324.6	7.4

Note: Annual percentage increase not available for years preceding 1990.

Source: Wisconsin Department of Financial Institutions, Office of Credit Unions, *Year-End 2014 Bulletin,* at:
https://www.wdfi.org/_resources/indexed/site/fi/cu/QuarterlyReports/2014/2014YearEndBulletin.pdf [March 2015] and
previous editions. Percentages calculated by Wisconsin Legislative Reference Bureau.

HIGHLIGHTS OF CONSERVATION AND RECREATION IN WISCONSIN

Recreation — Wisconsin currently operates 49 state parks, 14 state forests, and 8 recreation areas. The parks range in size from Devil's Lake with 10,200 acres to Lakeshore with 22 acres. The largest single state recreational facility is the Northern Highland-American Legion Forest with 223,283 acres. A total of 36 state trails are open to the public.

Visitors to Wisconsin's state parks, forests, trails, and recreation areas numbered 15.5 million in 2014.

Hunting and fishing are major recreational activities. In recent years, approximately 33 million fish and 1.6 million game animals of various species have been harvested annually. Over 707,000 resident annual fishing licenses were sold in 2013. In addition, resident husband and wife fishing licenses totaled nearly 217,000, and nonresident fishing licenses totaled approximately 107,700. Over 614,000 boats were registered in 2013.

Land Acquisition — Three land acquisition programs have been established to acquire land for recreational purposes. From 1961 through 1992, the Outdoor Recreation Act Program (ORAP) acquired 555,816 acres for the state's conservation and recreation programs at a cost of almost $172 million. From fiscal year 1990, when the legislature created the Warren Knowles-Gaylord Nelson Stewardship Program, through fiscal year 1999, the stewardship fund spent over $124 million to acquire an additional 167,000 acres. From fiscal years 2000 through 2014, the Stewardship 2000 Fund acquired over 639,000 acres and spent nearly $574 million.

Natural Resources Funding and Expenditures — The Department of Natural Resources spent over $566 million on conservation and recreation programs in fiscal year 2013-14, up from $540 million in fiscal year 2012-13. Funding comes from the state's general fund and segregated funds, including registration and licensing fees, park stickers, and federal aids.

The following tables present selected data. Consult footnoted sources for more detailed information about conservation and recreation.

FISH AND GAME HARVESTED AND STOCKED, 2013-2014

Catch and Harvest Data for Wisconsin Fish[1]

	Catch	Harvest
All fish species	88,000,000	33,000,000
Great Lakes trout.		144,835
Great Lakes salmon		185,163

Harvest Indicators

	Harvest		Harvest
Wild Turkey	46,448	Raccoon[2]	147,197
Pheasant[2]	194,397	Red fox[2]	9,932
Ruffed grouse[2]	256,997	Gray fox[2]	5,712
Gray partridge[2]	127	Coyotes[2]	39,490
Bobwhite quail[2]	63	Deer (with guns)	255,003
Woodcock[2]	77,061	Deer (with bows)	87,628
Squirrels[2]	327,398	Bear	3,952
Cottontail rabbit[2]	129,830	Ducks[3]	455,700[4]
Snowshoe hare[2]	16,110	Canada geese	64,190
Doves[3]	72,800[4]		

Furbearer Harvest

	Harvest		Harvest
Muskrats[2]	224,194	Bobcat	226
Mink[2]	12,863	Opossum[2]	25,825
Beaver[2]	25,544	Skunk[2]	9,961
River otter	907	Fisher	822
Total value of all pelts purchased by licensed Wisconsin fur buyers			$6,801,664

Fish and Wildlife Stocked

Game farm pheasants released	76,740
Warmwater fish, produced and distributed (includes fry)	8,804,149
Coldwater fish	3,776,448

[1]Harvest is the actual number of fish caught and kept; catch is the estimate of all fish caught, including those released. All fish species estimated from mail survey conducted in 2006. Great Lakes totals estimated by on-site creel surveys in 2014.

[2]Estimates based on hunter surveys.

[3]Harvest data from U.S. Fish and Wildlife Service, Division of Migratory Bird Management. Data is for the 2014 hunting season.

[4]Data is from federal harvest surveys and are still preliminary.

Source: Wisconsin Department of Natural Resources, departmental data, June 2015.

FISH AND GAME LICENSES AND RECREATION PERMITS
Number Issued, 2008 – 2013

	2008	2009	2010	2011	2012	2013
Boats registered	634,779	627,263	616,175	629,886	623,136	614,452
Snowmobiles registered	224,539	228,081	235,374	218,736	224,716	236,248
All terrain vehicles registered	218,539	277,279	279,263	307,582	299,607	298,857
Gun deer hunting and license tags including nonresident[1]	514,156	519,236	511,651	515,511	530,685	530,256
Small game hunting license tags including nonresident[1]	133,443	129,262	132,510	128,770	137,614	135,310
Spring turkey licenses including nonresident[1]	104,751	112,797	110,155	106,151	104,648	106,082
Fall turkey licenses including nonresident[1]	26,811	24,032	21,577	19,067	20,235	18,455
Resident annual fishing licenses[2]	665,027	708,003	688,046	664,987	702,409	707,285
Resident husband and wife fishing licenses	226,519	238,523	233,526	228,747	226,367	216,920
1-day resident fishing licenses	—	—	—	11,818	8,289	7,591
Nonresident annual fishing licenses	88,798	94,075	90,879	82,361	104,691	107,777
Nonresident family annual fishing licenses	67,568	72,190	69,789	66,416	66,589	64,298
15-day nonresident family fishing licenses	36,809	37,253	36,216	32,794	32,582	31,907
15-day nonresident fishing licenses	34,705	36,085	34,631	32,988	24,179	24,185
4-day nonresident fishing licenses	96,513	99,534	94,805	65,445	56,990	55,562
1-day nonresident fishing licenses	—	—	—	58,130	58,330	59,552
Resident sports licenses	69,113	63,953	58,943	56,790	55,380	53,982
Nonresident sports licenses	3,847	3,825	3,667	3,684	3,772	3,879
2-day Great Lakes fishing licenses	48,670	48,953	43,967	39,780	42,933	38,936
Resident archer's licenses[1]	195,333	196,793	197,598	200,695	209,398	209,896
Nonresident archer's licenses[1]	8,913	8,816	8,654	8,858	9,478	9,946
Guide licenses (residents only)	1,355	1,477	1,458	1,454	1,436	1,387
Conservation patron licenses	55,159	50,752	46,837	44,952	44,049	45,585
Nonresident patron licenses	937	1,005	925	921	935	953

[1]Includes 10- and 11-year-old mentored licenses.

[2]Includes senior and junior fishing licenses.

Source: Wisconsin Department of Natural Resources, departmental data, June 2015.

Wisconsin State Parks, Forests, and Trails

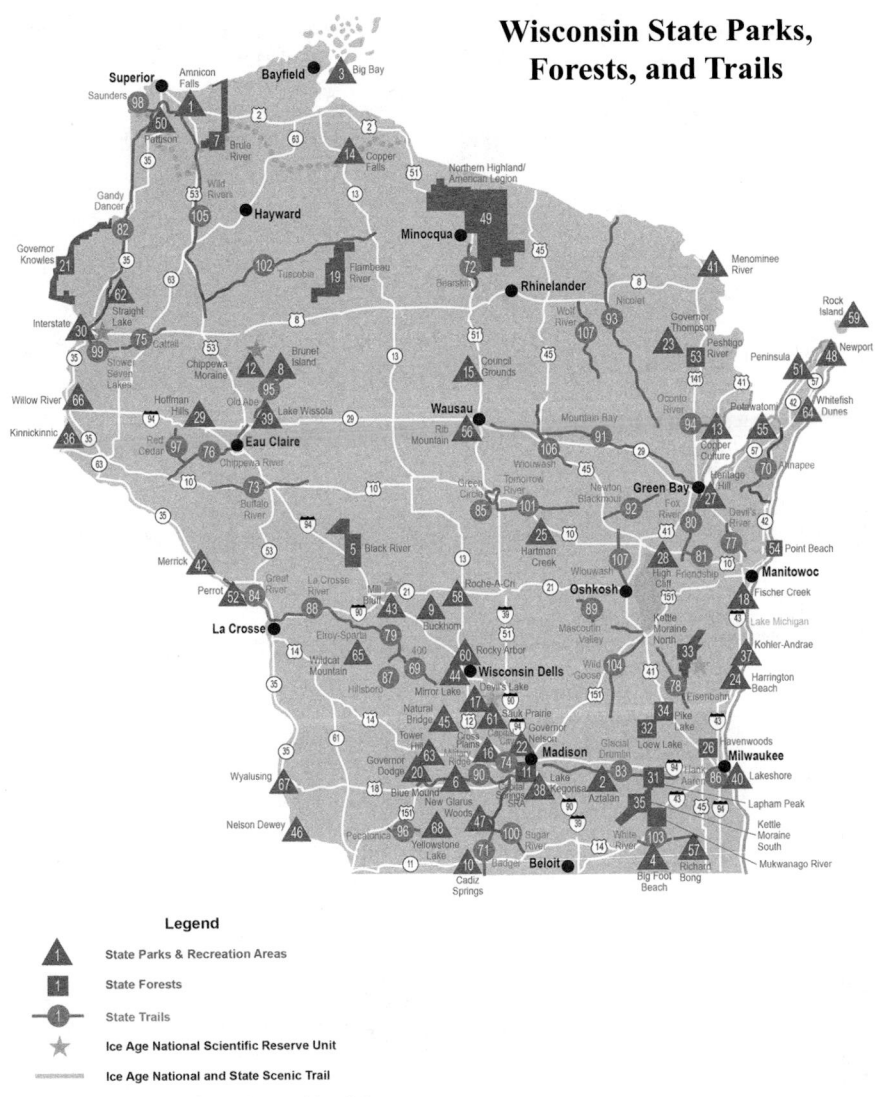

Legend

State Parks & Recreation Areas

State Forests

State Trails

★ Ice Age National Scientific Reserve Unit

Ice Age National and State Scenic Trail

North Country National Scenic and State Trail

Source: Wisconsin Department of Natural Resources, departmental data, June 2015. Map provided by Wisconsin Department of Tourism. For park updates, see dnr.wi.gov/topic/parks/.

WISCONSIN STATE FORESTS, PARKS, TRAILS, AND RECREATION AREAS

Name	Location	Dominant Features	Established	Acres	Number of Visitors[1]				
					2000	2005	2012	2013	2014
NORTHERN FORESTS[2]									
Black River	SE of Black River Falls US 12, STH 27 & 54	Abundance of wildlife and scenery	1957	67,070	195,579	23,611	12,603	16,997	16,712
Brule River	S of Brule STH 27	Excellent fishing and canoeing	1907	40,882	125,339	9,945	8,480	8,148	8,204
Flambeau River	23 mi. W of Phillips CTH W	Outstanding canoeing river	1931	90,147	162,665	20,091	4,368	2,436	3,376
Governor Knowles	1 mi. W of Grantsburg STH 70	River scenery	1970	19,753	89,714	20,219	2,836	3,212	4,304
Northern Highland-American Legion	SE Iron, WC Vilas, NC Oneida Counties	Scenic lakes and forests	1925	223,283	2,050,151	53,737	193,428	188,904	184,541
Peshtigo River	5 mi. W of Crivitz, N of CTH W	Diverse natural communities and rivers	2001	9,200	NA	NA	1,180	1,936	2,308
TOTAL				450,335	2,623,448	127,603	222,895	221,633	219,445
SOUTHERN FORESTS									
Havenwoods	Milwaukee, N. Hopkins St.	A nature preserve in the city	1978	237	49,581	51,774	40,619	40,701	41,776
Kettle Moraine North	N of Kewaskum STH 45, 23 & 67	Glacial formations	1936	29,498	620,903	700,774	610,961	584,517	594,186
Kettle Moraine South	Whitewater USH 12, STH 59/67	Glacial topography	1936	21,241	1,230,519	805,340	1,294,945	1,175,842	1,209,154
Lapham Peak.	S of Delafield, CTH C	Highest point in county, glacial formations	1985	1,006	250,681	261,930	345,236	391,943	452,137
Loew Lake.	10 mi. W of Menomonee Falls CTH Q	Kettle lake, glacial valley	1987	1,086	NA	NA	NA	NA	NA
Mukwonago River.	5 mi. W of Mukwonago	Glacial topography, lake	2015	970	NA	NA	NA	NA	NA
Pike Lake.	2 mi. E of Hartford STH 60	Glacial lake	1960	678	156,325	201,217	233,889	263,505	390,020
Point Beach.	4 mi. N of Two Rivers STH 42	Sand beach, natural history	1938	2,903	407,066	406,800	390,760	388,790	379,160
TOTAL				57,618	2,715,075	2,427,835	2,916,410	2,845,298	3,066,433
STATE PARKS									
Amnicon Falls	10 mi. SE of Superior USH 2	Scenic waterfalls, covered bridge	1961	825	44,773	86,680	86,100	86,128	84,196
Aztalan.	4 mi. E of Lake Mills CTH Q	Ancient Native American village	1947	172	60,565	59,695	44,000	38,753	101,764
Belmont Mound[3]	2 mi. N of Belmont CTH G & B	Wide vista from hilltop tower	1961	254	8,484	40,607	NA	NA	NA
Big Bay	On Madeline Island in Lake Superior	Sand beach, natural history	1963	2,418	108,365	129,435	159,969	169,295	152,074
Big Foot Beach	1 mi. S of Lake Geneva STH 12 & 120	A beach park	1949	271	177,963	178,567	177,429	167,185	170,417
Blue Mound	1 mi. NW of Blue Mounds STH 18 & 151	Highest point in southern Wisconsin	1959	1,153	154,128	153,202	148,722	151,985	182,108
Brunet Island.	Northwest of Cornell	River island park	1936	1,225	178,962	161,150	154,837	131,400	137,787
Buckhorn.	13 mi. N of Mauston STH 58, CTH G	River scenery	1971	2,637	107,590	127,735	142,422	143,356	140,250
Capital Springs	5 mi SE of Madison on Lake Farm Rd.	Shoreline and trails	2000	323	NA	NA	NA	NA	NA
Copper Culture[3]	0.5 mi. W of Oconto on N. River Rd.	Archaeological site	1959	42	NA	NA	NA	NA	NA
Copper Falls.	2 mi. N of Mellen STH 13 & 169	River gorge, waterfalls	1929	2,716	125,080	145,087	139,631	164,644	181,872
Council Grounds.	1 mi. NW of Merrill STH 107	River scenery	1938	509	213,411	221,033	193,088	157,881	125,787
Devil's Lake.	3 mi. S of Baraboo STH 123	Bluffs, mountain scenery	1911	10,200	1,317,275	1,207,001	2,236,888	1,909,667	2,059,027
Governor Dodge	3 mi. N of Dodgeville STH 23	Rocky promontories	1948	5,149	407,629	442,856	521,527	504,045	470,953
Governor Nelson.	5 mi. E of Middleton CTH M	Wooded lakeshore, Native American effigy mounds	1975	422	218,015	184,961	189,185	182,272	185,087
Governor Thompson.	25 miles NW of Crivitz	Lakeshore and trout streams	2000	2,450	NA	NA	55,700	155,319	67,835
Harrington Beach.	10 mi. N of Port Washington I 43, CTH D	Lake Michigan shoreline	1966	637	114,912	140,769	176,941	171,665	153,084
Hartman Creek.	6 mi. W of Waupaca STH 54	Lake scenery, pine plantation	1962	1,417	239,539	143,575	132,118	340,499	398,797
Heritage Hill[3]	S Green Bay STH 57	Restored early American buildings	1973	55	36,528	NA	NA	NA	NA
High Cliff.	9 mi. E of Menasha STH 114	Wooded bluffs, Lake Winnebago	1954	1,145	820,560	830,080	456,380	409,250	419,650
Interstate.	St. Croix Falls USH 8	River gorge, rocky bluffs, glacial features	1900	1,330	354,715	270,995	292,876	251,850	291,664
Kinnickinnic.	6 mi. W of River Falls CTH F	River scenery	1972	1,239	207,900	217,600	171,200	97,900	96,750
Kohler-Andrae.	4 mi. S of Sheboygan STH 141	Lake Michigan sand dunes	1928	1,848	378,483	417,568	418,373	397,054	393,331
Lake Kegonsa.	3 mi. N of Stoughton CTH N	Prairie and lakeshore	1962	343	187,782	189,639	196,457	185,506	177,540

WISCONSIN STATE FORESTS, PARKS, TRAILS, AND RECREATION AREAS—Continued

Name	Location	Dominant Features	Established	Acres	Number of Visitors[1]				
					2000	2005	2012	2013	2014
Lake Wissota	5 mi. NE of Chippewa Falls STH 29, CTH K & O	Lake scenery	1962	1,062	108,222	102,032	106,505	110,545	109,365
Lakeshore	Milwaukee, N. Harbor Dr.	Urban oasis, marina, Lake Michigan	1998	22	NA	NA	112,880	226,383	242,795
Menominee River	NE Marinette County, SE of Niagara	Several miles of Menominee River shoreline	2010	4,676	NA	NA	NA	NA	NA
Merrick	1 mi. N of Fountain City STH 35	Mississippi River, birds	1932	322	101,609	83,346	85,759	77,974	70,608
Mill Bluff	4 mi. W of Camp Douglas USH 12/16	Rocky bluffs	1936	1,337	49,541	54,854	58,678	61,183	26,888
Mirror Lake	1 mi. S of Lake Delton	Lake scenery	1962	2,200	341,452	326,198	353,017	297,625	262,348
Natural Bridge	15 mi. NW of Sauk City CTH C	Natural rock bridge	1972	530	57,454	30,600	24,772	14,777	17,604
Nelson Dewey	1 mi. N of Cassville CTH VV	Home of first governor, river bluffs	1935	756	51,456	39,541	38,857	34,570	62,009
New Glarus Woods	1 mi. S of New Glarus STH 69 & CTH NN	Wooded valleys, natural oak woods	1934	415	48,276	177,322	51,535	36,244	89,824
Newport	2 mi. SE of Gills Rock STH 42	Lake scenery, forests	1964	2,373	177,194	153,986	136,914	134,570	137,365
Pattison	10 mi. S of Superior STH 35	Highest waterfall in Wisconsin	1920	1,436	167,221	184,579	196,715	189,986	148,439
Peninsula	N of Fish Creek STH 42	Green Bay, limestone bluffs	1910	3,777	1,105,651	1,018,868	1,145,943	1,113,924	1,162,753
Perrot	1 mi. N of Trempealeau STH 35	River scenery, wooded bluffs	1918	1,270	208,537	269,061	324,177	333,503	314,711
Potawatomi	2 mi. NW of Sturgeon Bay STH 42	Limestone bluffs	1928	1,221	228,909	201,379	200,205	197,669	200,205
Rib Mountain	4 mi. SW of Wausau CTH N	State's 4th highest place, spectacular views	1927	1,503	208,670	234,685	294,720	322,018	345,096
Roche-A-Cri	2 mi. N of Friendship STH 13	Woodlands, 300-foot-high rock outcropping	1948	492	72,232	110,884	46,165	70,450	74,780
Rock Island	Ferry (no vehicles) from Washington Island	Island scenery, historic stone buildings	1965	912	16,998	15,811	25,930	74,097	58,074
Rocky Arbor	1 mi. NW of Wisconsin Dells USH 12	Rocky ledges, wooded valleys	1932	244	57,545	65,674	72,015	73,211	72,098
Straight Lake	5 mi. NE of Luck via SH 35 & 270th Ave.	Wooded wilderness and lake	2002	NA	51,031	76,226	12,621	21,732	22,842
Tower Hill	3 mi. S of Spring Green STH 23 & CTH C	Historic shot tower, panoramic views	1922	77	51,031	76,226	12,621	21,732	22,842
Whitefish Dunes	10 mi. NE of Sturgeon Bay STH 57	Lake Michigan, sand dunes	1967	864	189,778	167,092	208,427	201,377	180,004
Wildcat Mountain	3 mi. S of Ontario STH 33	Bluff lands, Kickapoo River	1948	3,628	173,100	186,994	211,957	248,621	138,251
Willow River	NE of Hudson CTH A	River scenery, waterfalls, lake	1967	2,854	354,470	347,691	575,050	646,443	721,480
Wyalusing	12 mi. S of Prairie du Chien USH 18 & CTH C & X	Junction of Wisconsin and Mississippi rivers	1917	2,628	173,439	180,429	239,726	288,198	131,428
Yellowstone Lake	7 mi. NW of Argyle CTH N	Lake	1970	890	260,981	275,163	291,133	244,637	238,629
TOTAL				74,266	9,706,425	9,650,650	10,908,144	10,835,391	10,817,569
STATE RECREATION AREAS									
Richard Bong	8 mi. SE of Burlington STH 142	Small lakes, open space, varied recreation	1963	4,537	462,274	220,045	337,612	312,005	300,696
Browntown–Cadiz Springs	6 mi. W of Monroe STH 11	Spring-fed lakes	1970	644	99,191	44,833	52,737	29,625	114,219
Capital Springs	3101 Lake Farm Rd., 1 mi W of Madison	Lake, hiking, varied recreation	2000	2,576	NA	NA	NA	NA	NA
Chippewa Moraine Ice Age	6 mi. E of New Auburn CTH M	Kettle lakes, other glacial features	1974	3,224	17,737	24,984	24,535	20,710	20,275
Fenley	2 mi. W of Kieler, Grant Cty	Bluffs, Mississippi River overlook	1985	287	NA	NA	NA	NA	NA
Fischer Creek[3]	1 mi. N of Cleveland on Lakeshore Rd.	Lake Michigan shoreline, scenic bluffs	1991	124	NA	NA	NA	NA	NA
Hoffman Hills	8 mi. NE of Menomonie CTH B or E	Wooded hills	1980	707	32,460	32,880	36,460	42,740	44,900
Sauk Prairie	9 mi. N of Sauk City	Open prairie and wooded hills	2014	3,385	NA	NA	NA	NA	NA
TOTAL				15,483	611,662	322,742	451,344	405,080	480,090
STATE TRAILS[4]									
"400"	Reedsburg STH 23/33 to Elroy STH 80/82	22 miles of trail, bluffs	1988	441	35,125	43,470	42,395	44,955	45,900
Ahnapee[5]	Sturgeon Bay STH 42/57 to E of Luxemburg CTH A	18.6-mile trail, river scenery	1970	571	NA	NA	NA	NA	NA
Badger	Madison to Freeport, IL STH 69	40 miles of trail, former railroad grade	2000	534	NA	NA	215,963	207,183	160,548
Bearskin-Hiawatha	Minocqua to CH K & Heafford Jct. to Tomahawk	24.6 miles of trail, forests	1973	787	115,200	136,500	103,000	92,750	89,932

WISCONSIN STATE FORESTS, PARKS, TRAILS, AND RECREATION AREAS—Continued

Name	Location	Dominant Features	Established	Acres	Number of Visitors[1]				
					2000	2005	2012	2013	2014
Buffalo River[3]	Fairchild to Mondovi US 10	36.4 miles of trail, rural scenery	1976	556	39,280	38,307	38,307	38,307	38,307
Capital City[3]	Madison, Dempsey Rd to USH 18/151 Frontage Rd	Asphalt path through woods, fields, and city	2001	NA	NA	NA	NA	NA	NA
Cattail[3]	Amery SH 46 to Almena CTH P	17.8-mi. trail through forests, farms, wetlands	1999	405	NA	NA	NA	NA	NA
Chippewa River[3]	Eau Claire SW to Red Cedar Trail STH 85	20 miles of trail, river scenery	1990	387	334,607	109,240	47,025	38,150	42,150
Elroy-Sparta[3]	Elroy STH 80/82 to Sparta STH 71	32.5 miles of trail, hills, valleys, tunnels	1965	674	60,075	59,495	56,755	56,670	58,530
Fox River[3]	Trailhead at Portier and Adams Streets, Green Bay	Fox River bridge, 14-mi. trail along river	1991	298	NA	NA	NA	NA	NA
Friendship[3]	Brillion – Forest Junction parallel to USH 10	6 miles of trail past farms and woods	2000	8	NA	NA	NA	NA	NA
Gandy Dancer[3]	St. Croix Falls USH 8 to S of Superior CTH C	66 miles of trail, forests, connects to MN	1989	810	NA	NA	NA	NA	NA
Glacial Drumlin[3]	Waukesha CTH X to NE of Jefferson CTH Y	49 miles of trail, views of Ice Age features	1984	930	177,939	234,248	259,953	187,078	168,103
Great River[3]	Onalaska USH 53 to NW of Trempealeau STH 35/54	24 miles of trail, Mississippi River, bluffs	1986	304	65,572	58,849	65,809	68,322	61,145
Green Circle[3]	Circles Stevens Point area	River scenery	1992	0	NA	NA	NA	NA	NA
Hank Aaron	Milwaukee, Menomonee River Valley	Menomonee River Valley	1996	60	NA	NA	NA	NA	NA
Hillsboro[3]	Union Center to Hillsboro STH 33/80/82	4.2 miles of trail, rural scenery	1988	66	NA	NA	NA	NA	NA
Ice Age Trail[5]	Sturgeon Bay to St. Croix Falls	Moraines and other glacial features	1988	5,097	NA	NA	NA	NA	NA
La Crosse River[3]	Sparta STH 16 to NE of La Crosse	24.5-mile trail, broad river valley	1978	396	37,150	45,695	46,775	47,845	48,085
Mascoutin Valley[3]	Ripon to Berlin STH 49	19-mi. trail, farms, woods, and wetlands	1996	45	NA	NA	NA	NA	NA
Military Ridge[3]	Madison USH 18/151 to Dodgeville STH 23	39.6 miles of trail, most on crest of ridge	1981	635	67,224	115,797	108,039	102,941	99,094
Mountain-Bay[3]	Wausau CTH SS to Green Bay CTH HS	80.5-mile trail, varied landscape	1993	1,083	NA	NA	NA	NA	NA
Nicolet[3]	Gillett to Townsend STH 32	Forests, streams	1999	1,171	NA	NA	NA	NA	NA
North Country[5]	Douglas, Bayfield, Ashland, and Iron Counties	Footpath across Northern Wisconsin	2000	546	NA	NA	NA	NA	NA
Oconto River[3]	Oconto US 41 to Stiles Junction US 141	8-mi. trail along Oconto River	1997	91	NA	NA	NA	NA	NA
Old Abe[3]	NE of Chippewa Falls CTH S to Cornell STH 27/64	17-mile trail, Chippewa River	1990	243	NA	NA	NA	NA	NA
Pecatonica[3]	Belmont E to Calamine CTH G	10 miles of trail, stream	1974	242	NA	NA	NA	NA	NA
Red Cedar[3]	Menomonie STH 29 S to Chippewa River Trail	14.5 miles of trail, river, bluffs	1973	822	45,760	53,380	52,480	52,070	50,545
Saunders[3]	S of Superior CTH C SW to MN border	8.4 miles of trail, wet woods	1991	207	NA	NA	NA	NA	NA
Sugar River[3]	New Glarus STH 39/69 to Brodhead STH 11	23.5 miles of trail, farms, prairies, woods	1972	302	45,362	67,812	30,170	51,937	67,549
Tomorrow River[3]	Plover to Amherst Junction	15 miles of trail, glacial terrain	1996	389	NA	NA	NA	NA	NA
Tuscobia[3]	Park Falls CTH B to Rice Lake CTH SS	74 miles of trail, forests	1966	1,393	44,150	46,783	12,747	36,724	38,132
White River[3]	Elkhorn CTH H to Racine Cty., Spring Valley Rd.	10-mile trail, farmlands and historic town	1999	247	NA	NA	NA	NA	NA
Wild Goose[3]	Fond du Lac USH 41/151 to STH 60 S of Juneau	32 miles of trail, Horicon Marsh	1986	418	NA	NA	NA	NA	NA
Wild Rivers[3]	Solon Springs CTH A to Rice Lake	63.5 miles of trail, woods	1993	1,139	NA	NA	NA	NA	NA
Wiouwash[3]	Oshkosh-Hortonville, Split Rock-Aniwa	51.6 miles of trail, prairies, woods	1992	283	NA	NA	NA	NA	NA
TOTAL				21,579	1,067,444	1,009,576	1,079,418	1,024,932	968,020

Abbreviations: USH – U.S. highway; STH – state trunk highway; CTH – county trunk highway; NA – not available.

[1]Visitor numbers are estimates.

[2]Northern Forests figures for 2005-present are camping attendance only, not day-use visitors.

[3]Operated locally or by county; no attendance information available.

[4]Not accessible by vehicle.

[5]Various owners and operators (National Scenic Trails).

Source: Wisconsin Department of Natural Resources, Bureau of Parks and Recreation, departmental data, June 2015.

DEPARTMENT OF NATURAL RESOURCES SOURCES OF FUNDING
Fiscal Years 2008-09 – 2013-14
(In Thousands)

Source of Funding	2008-09	2009-10	2010-11	2011-12	2012-13	2013-14
Segregated funds						
All-terrain vehicle registration fees	$4,683	$4,461	$3,979	$4,286	$3,849	$2,876
Boat registration fees	6,032	5,775	5,525	5,645	5,672	5,002
Dry cleaner fund	1,082	3,352	2,016	1,582	1,533	1,894
Endangered resources voluntary payments	1,205	1,700	886	811	578	889
Environmental improvement fund	2,151	1,227	1,873	959	891	910
Environmental management account	16,052	16,994	24,707	42,320	47,192	48,451
Federal aids	59,346	49,715	61,609	53,483	54,517	55,352
Fishing, hunting licenses and permits	72,287	66,814	68,168	65,057	69,039	68,564
Forestry mill tax	99,915	103,138	99,341	94,462	95,023	100,288
Gifts and donations	327	448	390	543	557	690
Heritage State Parks and Forests Trust Fund . . .	—	—	—	—	61	46
Nonpoint source account.	4,336	7,258	11,241	13,046	15,752	14,538
Park stickers and fees	13,581	13,837	13,997	16,057	13,077	14,420
Petroleum storage environmental cleanup fund . .	5,294	5,147	5,223	5,722	5,368	10,570
Program revenue	32,201	31,951	31,400	31,006	28,010	29,061
Recycling fund.	31,988	31,992	21,214	—	—	1
Snowmobile registration fees	3,953	4,108	4,172	3,570	2,913	2,840
Waste management fund	9	—	—	—	37	347
Water resources account	12,741	12,371	12,553	12,606	11,943	12,370
Wisconsin Natural Resources Magazine.	833	865	746	663	645	799
TOTAL.	$368,015	$361,153	$369,039	$351,820	$356,657	$369,909
General funds						
General purpose revenue.	$143,755	$51,401	$67,305	$52,616	$119,650	$130,130
Program revenues	21,536	20,516	19,926	18,161	19,568	22,470
Program revenue – services	12,442	12,055	13,340	10,934	10,293	11,327
Federal aids	26,753	29,081	30,624	33,978	34,203	32,236
TOTAL.	$204,486	$113,052	$131,194	$115,690	$183,714	$196,163
GRAND TOTAL.	$572,501	$474,205	$500,234	$467,510	$540,370	$566,072

Source: Wisconsin Department of Natural Resources, departmental data, June 2015.

DEPARTMENT OF NATURAL RESOURCES EXPENDITURES
Fiscal Years 2008-09 – 2013-14
(In Thousands)

Program	2008-09	2009-10	2010-11	2011-12	2012-13	2013-14
Land Management	**$117,588***	**$113,693***	**$115,341***	**$114,012***	**$109,071***	**$117,501***
Wildlife management	21,927	20,244	21,006	21,595	20,684	20,759
Forestry	55,552	53,117	53,448	51,928	50,027	56,796
Southern forests	5,740	5,594	5,826	5,834	5,611	5,597
Parks	17,865	18,372	17,654	18,155	17,589	18,345
Endangered resources	5,005	5,287	5,905	5,941	4,940	4,650
Facilities and lands.	10,412	10,107	10,376	9,596	9,062	10,205
Lands program management.	1,087	971	1,126	962	1,157	1,149
Air and Waste Management	**$36,296***	**$37,889***	**$40,110***	**$35,990***	**$34,396***	**$38,850***
Air management	16,114	17,195	16,426	14,712	13,863	14,622
Cooperative environmental assistance.	917	827	853	828	783	3,393
Remediation and redevelopment.	10,866	11,675	14,374	12,126	11,761	11,411
Waste management	7,182	7,347	7,444	7,330	7,070	8,251
Air/waste program management.	1,217	845	1,014	992	919	1,173
Enforcement and Science	**$43,769***	**$44,003***	**$46,824***	**$45,068***	**$45,067***	**$42,197***
Law enforcement	32,090	32,465	33,453	31,326	32,066	31,809
Integrated science services.	10,684	10,759	12,490	12,785	12,112	9,548
Enforcement/science program management. . . .	995	779	882	957	888	841
Water Management.	**$76,488***	**$72,424***	**$75,515***	**$76,876***	**$81,553***	**$77,709***
Fisheries management and habitat protection . . .	26,409	24,116	26,523	25,619	25,377	25,143
Watershed management	36,145	35,201	35,511	37,888	13,678	13,834
Drinking and groundwater.	12,159	12,011	12,314	12,304	12,683	12,553
Water quality.	—	—	—	—	28,601	24,840
Water program management.	1,734	1,096	1,168	1,065	1,215	1,339
Conservation Aids	**$45,574***	**$43,284***	**$42,323***	**$42,044***	**$43,483***	**$42,408***
Fish and wildlife aids	811	702	570	989	2,147	1,274
Forestry aids	11,214	10,522	10,640	9,205	10,675	9,440
Recreational aids.	15,992	13,576	12,533	12,506	10,674	10,867
Aids in lieu of taxes	12,362	13,767	13,783	14,369	14,723	15,583
Enforcement aids	2,166	2,277	2,277	2,277	2,199	2,277
Wildlife damage aids.	3,030	2,441	2,520	2,697	3,063	2,966
Environmental Aids	**$42,018***	**$42,978***	**$31,890***	**$32,350***	**$31,213***	**$34,112***
Water quality aids	5,610	5,728	6,112	6,551	6,561	6,966
Solid and hazard waste aids	32,219	31,476	21,401	22,526	20,844	20,803
Environmental aids	1,022	3,355	2,439	1,761	1,564	7,238
Environmental planning aids	441	210	287	283	211	191
Nonpoint aids	2,727	2,209	1,651	1,229	2,034	(1,085)
Debt Service.	**$127,252***	**$45,268***	**$70,456***	**$52,963***	**$123,492***	**$136,139***
Resource	51,566	26,205	34,012	27,725	80,338	89,515
Environmental	3,698	4,250	3,957	4,376	4,827	4,833
Water quality.	67,581	10,011	27,240	15,585	32,083	35,330
Administrative facility.	4,407	4,802	5,248	5,276	6,244	6,461
Acquisition and Development	**$18,915***	**$9,107***	**$13,519***	**$8,128***	**$8,696***	**$11,218***
Wildlife	559	1,270	1,466	644	545	1,013
Fish.	6,219	1,980	1,203	481	507	559
Forestry	5,465	1,411	4,612	818	2,930	3,650
Southern forests	202	182	167	234	214	21
Parks	3,864	1,312	1,487	1,229	1,462	2,475
Endangered resources	1,369	1,464	2,753	1,482	820	1,742
Facilities and lands.	1,216	1,467	1,819	3,237	2,176	1,455
CAES (Customer and Employee Services)	6	9	—	1	5	—
Water resources	15	13	13	2	—	2
Administration	**$20,547***	**$23,273***	**$23,279***	**$21,286***	**$23,394***	**$24,857***
Administration	1,261	1,266	1,386	1,464	1,603	1,727
Legal services	2,241	2,147	2,182	2,029	2,231	2,389
Management and budget.	520	422	395	502	510	528
Facility rental	5,515	7,036	7,144	7,149	7,128	7,218
Nonbudget accounts	11,011	12,402	12,173	10,142	11,922	12,993
Customer and Employee Relations (CAER) . .	**$44,093***	**$42,285***	**$40,975***	**$38,795***	**$39,914***	**$41,079***
Enterprise and technology/technology services . .	9,000	7,735	8,816	7,699	8,237	8,426
Finance.	5,907	5,884	6,141	6,193	5,989	6,616
Human resources.	4,268	3,889	3,767	3,873	4,076	4,134
Communication and education strategy	3,742	4,034	3,231	1,519	1,523	1,823
Community financial assistance	5,234	5,754	5,348	5,308	5,723	5,915
Customer service and licensing	12,711	11,950	10,705	11,327	11,341	11,128
CAER program management	3,230	3,038	2,967	2,877	3,023	3,036
TOTAL.	$572,501	$474,205	$500,234	$467,510	$540,279	$566,070

*Total of detail immediately following. Totals do not add due to rounding.

Source: Wisconsin Department of Natural Resources, departmental data, June 2015.

NATURAL RESOURCES LAND ACQUISITIONS
Fiscal Years 1990 – 2014*

Fiscal Year	Fisheries Mgmnt.	Northern Forests	Parks	Natural Areas	Southern Forests	Wildlife Mgmnt.	Wild Rivers	Other	Total
ACRES ACQUIRED									
WARREN KNOWLES-GAYLORD NELSON STEWARDSHIP PROGRAM									
1990	2,333	975	683	1,278	283	4,269	2,490	10	12,311
1991	1,671	930	1,352	4,745	1,567	5,997	11,832	61	28,155
1992	1,787	791	362	3,176	157	3,940	15,067	226	25,506
1993	1,475	721	624	3,166	298	5,160	4,328	245	16,018
1994	2,879	396	1,820	3,288	306	3,137	3,191	563	15,580
1995	8,093	373	271	1,985	370	5,052	835	633	17,612
1996	2,344	977	1,248	5,830	398	3,566	2,012	368	16,743
1997	1,548	213	884	2,038	161	2,929	2,003	332	10,110
1998	1,133	278	107	1,467	81	4,045	9,944	317	17,372
1999	600	815	641	1,904	513	2,501	775	209	7,957
STEWARDSHIP 2000 PROGRAM									
2000	2,808	496	3,705	3,301	110	11,800	16,135	136	38,489
2001	2,773	149	4,295	1,063	194	5,191	3,558	683	17,905
2002	1,595	5,525	1,349	3,174	208	4,997	607	258	17,713
2003	1,880	35,464	2,029	5,801	0	3,765	2,406	86	51,432
2004	1,177	4,132	3,060	1,747	159	7,513	2,132	156	20,076
2005	2,308	6,578	3,842	7,477	475	5,385	10,692	329	37,086
2006	957	18,799	1,823	2,592	103	6,022	767	414	31,476
2007	982	45,075	713	2,948	171	3,247	8,793	192	62,121
2008	915	8,722	1,641	2,288	12	6,515	2,589	454	23,136
2009	837	7,943	1,876	1,844	1,024	2,150	1,867	358	17,899
2010	785	8,547	1,000	3,498	37	3,767	818	73	18,525
2011	1,786	27,070	3,525	5,845	297	5,560	2,729	5	46,818
2012	587	10,866	619	1,804	0	892	184	7	14,958
2013	1,430	48,989	891	2,697	247	3,046	437	157	57,894
2014	87	10,283	204	1,346	144	4,267	147	283	16,761
TOTAL. . . .	44,770	245,107	38,566	76,301	7,314	114,714	106,338	6,554	639,654
COST TO ACQUIRE (in thousands)									
WARREN KNOWLES-GAYLORD NELSON STEWARDSHIP PROGRAM									
1990	$1,951	$395	$727	$610	$490	$1,880	$2,216	$1	$8,269
1991	1,498	385	384	2,133	1,675	3,027	6,245	1,557	16,902
1992	1,530	416	461	1,195	398	2,735	5,537	48	12,320
1993	1,359	547	547	1,473	249	1,636	1,950	31	7,791
1994	2,315	178	902	724	793	2,118	1,843	148	9,021
1995	3,688	640	762	3,472	1,315	3,872	1,120	219	15,087
1996	2,596	542	2,758	3,108	1,036	2,832	1,413	441	14,726
1997	1,757	378	1,168	589	617	2,439	1,321	80	8,349
1998	1,513	137	337	2,077	293	4,331	11,005	1,307	21,001
1999	1,534	941	1,548	1,075	1,170	3,693	580	336	10,878
STEWARDSHIP 2000 PROGRAM									
2000	$2,861	$550	$2,734	$3,472	$403	$9,061	$12,633	$352	$32,066
2001	5,247	533	8,605	2,156	873	4,251	739	420	22,824
2002	4,156	13,575	3,244	2,955	1,105	5,635	1,095	3,822	35,587
2003	3,976	7,680	4,105	3,603	0	3,908	3,807	117	27,196
2004	3,054	13,474	5,727	2,770	579	8,490	4,629	130	38,853
2005	5,034	2,418	16,693	4,993	3,050	8,164	3,591	401	44,345
2006	3,919	9,852	3,247	3,642	1,220	5,574	1,526	81	29,061
2007	3,529	20,147	6,760	4,039	1,081	7,227	15,864	254	58,901
2008	2,529	8,734	3,222	3,004	246	10,016	5,777	135	33,663
2009	2,236	6,534	8,069	1,849	11,325	4,250	3,729	128	38,122
2010	2,232	5,867	2,881	5,448	272	6,693	2,119	122	25,635
2011	4,277	12,974	4,762	7,153	2,023	10,144	5,416	35	46,782
2012	1,657	7,426	2,605	1,836	0	2,736	369	0	16,628
2013	1,660	17,412	3,955	900	796	5,333	490	0	30,547
2014	249	6,997	572	967	742	5,630	410	73	15,640
TOTAL. . . .	$64,448	$114,323	$82,248	$63,376	$30,213	$114,711	$94,524	$10,165	$574,008

*The Warren Knowles-Gaylord Nelson Stewardship Program replaced the Outdoor Recreation Act Program (ORAP) in 1990.
Source: Wisconsin Department of Natural Resources, Bureau of Facilities and Lands, departmental data, June 2015.

CONSERVATION AND RECREATION LAND IN WISCONSIN
Acres By Ownership

County	Forests	Wild Rivers	Natural Areas	Parks	Fisheries	Wildlife	Other	Total DNR	U.S. Forest Service 2014[1]	Total
Adams	9,088	—	7,577	492	1,530	7,511	509	26,709	—	26,709
Ashland	756	—	324	5,998	210	7,802	120	15,211	181,646	196,857
Barron	60	—	—	343	1,185	5,170	7	6,764	—	6,764
Bayfield	2,693	—	12,691	—	12,536	952	172	29,044	272,832	301,876
Brown	—	—	170	511	416	2,385	12	3,494	—	3,494
Buffalo	—	—	417	399	22	13,166	—	14,003	—	14,003
Burnett	15,746	—	—	251	3,941	52,737	181	72,856	—	72,856
Calumet	—	—	42	1,277	14	10,568	—	11,901	—	11,901
Chippewa . . .	—	—	897	7,445	1,919	3,278	5	13,543	—	13,543
Clark	224	—	—	—	163	175	—	561	—	561
Columbia. . . .	—	123	598	693	1,783	19,469	1	22,667	—	22,667
Crawford. . . .	—	8,012	3,913	—	1,028	3,589	1	16,543	—	16,543
Dane	—	4,662	1,130	2,689	5,291	10,608	4	24,384	40	24,424
Dodge	—	—	—	223	654	23,211	65	24,153	—	24,153
Door	—	—	4,367	9,406	245	3,466	13	17,497	—	17,497
Douglas	80,908	129	303	4,119	7,225	1,014	248	93,945	—	93,945
Dunn	—	—	2,427	1,278	1,056	11,635	—	16,396	—	16,396
Eau Claire . . .	—	—	588	146	475	2,103	7	3,320	—	3,320
Florence	5	47,813	8,987	177	123	40	5	57,149	85,269	142,418
Fond du Lac . .	—	—	99	11,107	51	14,122	—	25,379	—	25,379
Forest.	18,603	6,207	120	635	269	3,187	1	29,021	344,029	373,050
Grant	623	14,038	633	3,410	1,622	—	275	20,600	—	20,600
Green.	—	—	230	1,327	127	3,678	—	5,362	—	5,362
Green Lake. . .	—	—	547	—	753	17,544	—	18,844	—	18,844
Iowa	85	10,546	720	6,601	2,585	2,397	146	23,080	—	23,080
Iron.	33,401	35,643	7,231	—	1	10,774	52	87,102	—	87,102
Jackson.	68,227	—	605	113	4,740	3,253	44	76,983	—	76,983
Jefferson	—	—	118	4,430	173	16,093	—	20,814	—	20,814
Juneau	—	—	1,484	5,447	542	5,140	41	12,654	—	12,654
Kenosha	—	—	482	4,534	192	2,085	—	7,293	—	7,293
Kewaunee . . .	—	—	—	495	26	2,728	—	3,249	—	3,249
La Crosse . . .	2,992	127	61	372	629	3,808	—	7,989	—	7,989
Lafayette	—	—	233	1,418	725	4,048	—	6,424	—	6,424
Langlade	18,515	—	406	304	14,002	2,831	127	36,184	32,763	68,947
Lincoln	20,149	2,425	80	2,831	3,113	4,641	113	33,351	—	33,351
Manitowoc. . .	—	—	296	3,344	11	6,263	—	9,913	—	9,913
Marathon	1,724	—	—	3,008	2,528	22,856	1	30,118	—	30,118
Marinette. . . .	24,929	8,614	1,956	5,725	1,722	8,878	697	52,522	—	52,522
Marquette . . .	—	—	1,746	—	4,498	7,075	2	13,321	—	13,321
Menominee[2] . .	—	—	—	—	—	58	4	61	—	61
Milwaukee . . .	—	—	114	394	—	361	5	760	—	760
Monroe.	—	—	114	1,607	4,081	4,482	48	10,331	—	10,331
Oconto	632	—	270	772	1,117	7,770	40	10,602	140,781	151,383
Oneida	69,205	23,152	8,252	584	717	8,177	40	110,126	11,209	121,335
Outagamie . . .	—	—	1,503	327	331	570	—	2,731	—	2,731
Ozaukee	—	—	1,720	714	90	3,714	—	6,239	—	6,239
Pepin	—	—	1,946	—	31	1,226	883	4,086	—	4,086
Pierce.	—	—	410	1,445	812	12,931	30	15,628	—	15,628
Polk	5,584	—	878	4,188	1,924	28,015	205	40,795	—	40,795
Portage	—	—	365	838	5,358	9,771	18	16,350	—	16,350
Price	9,287	—	—	263	321	3,316	—	13,186	150,165	163,351
Racine	—	—	10	99	632	—	—	741	—	741
Richland	—	6,957	53	—	2,453	8,081	112	17,656	—	17,656
Rock	—	—	484	1	339	2,988	106	3,918	—	3,918
Rusk	15,289	—	40	—	446	3,907	1,092	20,774	—	20,774
St. Croix	—	5,883	5,566	17,840	1,435	6,678	287	37,689	—	37,689
Sauk	84,056	14,181	344	658	2,535	14,324	52	116,151	—	116,151
Sawyer	—	—	231	957	328	2,611	7	4,134	126,626	130,760
Shawano	—	—	128	17,078	2,087	6,729	673	26,694	—	26,694
Sheboygan . . .	—	—	138	2,953	1,129	8,788	1	13,009	—	13,009
Taylor	—	—	249	17	275	4,357	—	4,898	123,879	128,777
Trempealeau . .	58	—	—	1,612	1,140	221	877	3,908	—	3,908
Vernon	52	—	453	3,785	2,201	7,163	2	13,656	—	13,656
Vilas	143,616	—	3,829	—	369	5,622	—	153,436	54,512	207,948
Walworth. . . .	—	—	1,939	8,147	721	3,363	114	14,284	—	14,284
Washburn . . .	8,653	2,265	442	501	3,575	6,928	—	22,362	—	22,362
Washington. . .	199	—	—	5,820	378	6,828	—	13,225	—	13,225
Waukesha . . .	—	—	302	12,784	295	3,345	87	16,813	—	16,813
Waupaca	—	—	806	1,284	5,395	5,442	32	12,959	—	12,959
Waushara . . .	—	—	802	850	12,704	11,056	69	25,481	—	25,481
Winnebago. . .	—	—	132	2	198	15,195	22	15,549	—	15,549
Wood.	173	—	14	—	513	15,372	—	16,072	—	16,072
STATE . . .	635,530	190,775	92,900	176,066	132,052	539,668	7,656	1,774,646	1,523,751	3,298,397

[1]Federal lands controlled by the U.S. Forest Service as of September 30, 2014.
[2]Land in Menominee County that is not privately owned is held by the Menominee Nation.
Sources: U.S. Forest Service, "Land Areas of the National Forest System as of September 30, 2014", November 2014; Wisconsin Department of Natural Resources, departmental data, June 2015.

HIGHLIGHTS OF EDUCATION IN WISCONSIN

Universities and Colleges — A total of 180,979 students enrolled in the University of Wisconsin System for the 2014 fall semester. The UW-Extension's credit outreach enrolled 43,051 students in the 2012-13 fiscal year.

Wisconsin's private institutions of higher education encompass a broad range of schools, including 8 universities, 10 colleges, 6 technical and professional schools, 3 theological seminaries, and 2 tribal colleges. Over the past five years, enrollments in private institutions have stayed steady with a total of 65,363 students in 2013-14.

Technical Colleges — Wisconsin's Technical College System had a total enrollment of 326,544 students in 2013-14. Enrollments for individual institutions that year ranged from 7,085 at Nicolet Area Technical College to 44,437 at Fox Valley Technical College.

Elementary and Secondary Schools — Following a peak enrollment of 999,921 in 1971-72, public school registrations declined to a low of 767,542 in 1984-85. In the last 10 years, enrollments have remained midway between those levels, with a total of 870,652 in 2014-15.

In the 2014-15 school year, 123,104 students, or 12.4% of Wisconsin's estimated 1 million elementary and secondary pupils, were enrolled in private schools. Over the last 10 years, private school enrollments have decreased by almost 14,000 students.

Teachers — Of Wisconsin's 55,624 public school teachers employed in the 2014-15 school year, 39,438 taught in elementary grades and 16,187 were secondary teachers. In the 2014-15 school year, Wisconsin's average salary for all teachers was $54,535. Nationally, Wisconsin ranked 22nd for the 2013-14 school year. New York had the highest average salary that year at an estimated $76,409. South Dakota's average salary was the lowest at $40,023.

Educational Alternatives — Reported enrollment in Wisconsin home-based private education programs reached a peak of 21,288 students during 2002-03, and, after a period of decline, resurged to 19,850 in 2014-15. In the 2014-15 school year, Wisconsin charter school enrollments totaled 44,292 students.

Educational Expenditures — State and local expenditures for education in Wisconsin for 2013-14 totaled $17.5 billion, or $3,062 per capita, based on Wisconsin's estimated population. Wisconsin ranked 20th in the nation with total expenditures per pupil of $11,233 in the 2011-12 fiscal year, while New York was first ($19,396) and Utah was 50th ($6,441). In fiscal year 2013-14, school costs in Wisconsin totaled $10.7 billion. The 2013-14 cost per pupil was $12,546.

Educational Attainment — For 2012-13, Wisconsin schools conferred 2,507 doctoral-level degrees, 9,653 master's degrees, and 36,927 bachelor's degrees. In the same year, it awarded 59,890 public high school diplomas.

The following tables present selected data. Consult footnoted sources for more detailed information about education.

UNIVERSITY OF WISCONSIN SYSTEM
Fall Enrollment 2009 – 2014

Institution	2009-10	2010-11	2011-12	2012-13	2013-14	2014-15	2014-15 Detail Female	Male
Universities	**165,120**	**167,705**	**166,699**	**166,862**	**165,770**	**166,807**	**89,065**	**77,742**
Eau Claire.	11,216	11,413	11,234	11,047	10,907	10,692	6,378	4,314
Undergraduate	10,617	10,800	10,579	10,500	10,388	10,167	6,042	4,125
Graduate	599	599	628	511	464	447	265	182
Professional.	—	14	27	36	55	78	71	7
Green Bay.	6,638	6,636	6,665	6,790	6,667	6,921	4,534	2,387
Undergraduate	6,369	6,389	6,445	6,611	6,444	6,668	4,369	2,299
Graduate	269	247	220	179	223	253	165	88
La Crosse	10,009	10,135	10,258	10,380	10,502	10,664	6,102	4,562
Undergraduate	8,871	9,073	9,211	9,515	9,684	9,815	5,544	4,271
Graduate	1,022	939	914	732	686	716	477	239
Professional.	116	123	133	133	132	133	81	52
Madison.	41,654	42,180	42,065	42,463	42,903	42,865	21,685	21,180
Undergraduate	29,925	30,170	30,014	30,507	30,972	30,990	15,771	15,219
Graduate	9,221	9,468	9,389	9,385	9,405	9,415	4,511	4,904
Professional.	2,508	2,542	2,662	2,571	2,526	2,460	1,403	1,057
Milwaukee	30,418	30,470	29,726	29,114	27,784	28,013	14,773	13,240
Undergraduate	25,204	25,239	24,639	24,175	23,004	23,079	11,875	11,204
Graduate	5,134	5,144	4,989	4,819	4,619	4,743	2,743	2,000
Professional.	80	87	98	120	161	191	155	36
Oshkosh.	13,192	13,629	13,513	13,519	13,902	14,542	8,916	5,626
Undergraduate	11,672	12,230	12,273	12,384	12,623	13,312	8,055	5,257
Graduate	1,520	1,399	1,240	1,102	1,230	1,158	797	361
Professional.	—	—	—	33	49	72	64	8
Parkside.	5,303	5,160	4,887	4,769	4,617	4,584	2,385	2,199
Undergraduate	5,153	5,015	4,766	4,601	4,489	4,448	2,319	2,129
Graduate	150	145	121	168	128	136	66	70
Platteville	7,803	7,928	8,262	8,678	8,717	8,901	3,205	5,696
Undergraduate	6,971	7,232	7,460	7,840	7,867	8,047	2,823	5,224
Graduate	832	696	802	838	850	854	382	472
River Falls	6,728	6,902	6,788	6,447	6,171	6,184	3,791	2,393
Undergraduate	6,222	6,373	6,324	6,046	5,787	5,721	3,460	2,261
Graduate	506	529	464	401	384	463	331	132
Stevens Point	9,209	9,500	9,477	9,677	9,643	9,322	4,972	4,350
Undergraduate	8,804	9,062	9,085	9,296	9,292	8,998	4,724	4,274
Graduate	390	423	377	365	332	304	233	71
Professional.	15	15	15	16	19	20	15	5
Stout.	9,017	9,339	9,356	9,247	9,286	9,371	4,603	4,768
Undergraduate	7,973	8,301	8,353	8,270	8,180	8,254	3,849	4,405
Graduate	1,044	1,038	1,003	977	1,095	1,091	744	347
Professional.	—	—	—	—	11	26	10	16
Superior.	2,794	2,856	2,825	2,700	2,656	2,589	1,579	1,010
Undergraduate	2,576	2,631	2,655	2,550	2,522	2,455	1,487	968
Graduate	218	225	170	150	134	134	92	42
Whitewater	11,139	11,557	11,643	12,031	12,015	12,159	6,142	6,017
Undergraduate	9,730	10,144	10,228	10,752	10,852	10,971	5,514	5,457
Graduate	1,409	1,413	1,415	1,279	1,163	1,188	628	560
Colleges.	**13,789**	**14,385**	**14,570**	**14,107**	**14,058**	**14,172**	**7,545**	**6,627**
Baraboo/Sauk County.	597	594	617	597	580	567	305	262
Barron.	679	715	706	634	603	613	355	258
Fond du Lac.	779	794	749	692	707	627	315	312
Fox Valley.	1,731	1,830	1,822	1,799	1,760	1,702	817	885
Manitowoc	550	614	666	614	530	461	259	202
Marathon County	1,388	1,410	1,368	1,275	1,260	1,107	546	561
Marinette	569	526	461	464	507	495	260	235
Marshfield/Wood County . . .	674	711	715	628	650	623	375	248
Richland.	495	454	476	523	555	567	317	250
Rock County	1,175	1,215	1,289	1,305	1,224	1,152	643	509
Sheboygan	856	875	896	836	753	770	392	378
Washington County	1,040	1,117	1,037	998	990	937	443	494
Waukesha	2,093	2,240	2,248	2,118	2,175	2,261	1,066	1,195
Online Courses	1,163	1,290	1,520	1,624	1,764	2,290	1,452	838
SYSTEM TOTAL.	178,909	182,090	181,269	180,969	179,828	180,979	96,610	84,369

Source: University of Wisconsin System, Office of Policy Analysis and Research, Student Statistics reports, at https://www.wisconsin.edu/reports-statistics/educational-statistics/student-statistics/headcount-reports/ [May 2015].

UNIVERSITY OF WISCONSIN SYSTEM
Budgeted Faculty Positions (FTE), By Institution 2013-14

Institution	Professor	Associate Professor	Assistant Professor	Instructor	Total Faculty
Universities*	**2,492.00**	**1,755.00**	**2,006.00**	**21.00**	**6,274.00**
Eau Claire.	166.00	129.00	158.00	—	453.00
Green Bay.	25.00	86.00	60.00	—	171.00
La Crosse	101.00	98.00	195.00	—	394.00
Madison.	1,204.00	399.00	507.00	—	2,110.00
Milwaukee	257.00	394.00	243.00	—	894.00
Oshkosh.	127.00	124.00	148.00	11.00	410.00
Parkside	30.00	57.00	44.00	—	131.00
Platteville	122.00	56.00	107.00	—	285.00
River Falls	118.00	44.00	62.00	—	224.00
Stevens Point	136.00	106.00	116.00	10.00	368.00
Stout.	78.00	101.00	143.00	—	322.00
Superior	37.00	28.00	64.00	—	129.00
Whitewater	91.00	135.00	161.00	—	387.00
Colleges*	**62.75**	**131.00**	**124.10**	**—**	**318.00**
Baraboo/Sauk County.	1.00	5.50	10.20	—	17.00
Barron.	4.00	4.25	7.00	—	15.00
Fond du Lac.	4.00	9.00	8.45	—	21.00
Fox Valley.	7.00	18.75	14.25	—	40.00
Manitowoc	2.50	11.00	4.95	—	19.00
Marathon County	8.00	16.25	9.00	—	33.00
Marinette	3.00	8.00	2.75	—	14.00
Marshfield/Wood County	4.00	6.00	9.50	—	20.00
Richland.	3.00	6.50	4.50	—	15.00
Rock County	5.00	10.00	13.25	—	28.00
Sheboygan	2.50	4.00	11.75	—	19.00
Washington County	9.00	7.50	9.50	—	27.00
Waukesha	9.00	22.00	15.25	—	46.00
Other	0.75	2.25	3.75	—	7.00
Extension	80.00	123.40	56.08	24.58	284.00
SYSTEM TOTAL.	2,634.00	2,010.00	2,187.00	45.00	6,876.00

Notes: Includes vacant positions. Does not include student assistants. Numbers may not add to total due to rounding.
*Total of detail immediately following.
Source: University of Wisconsin System, Office of Budget and Planning, *Fact Book 13-14,* November 2014.

UNIVERSITY OF WISCONSIN – EXTENSION PROGRAMS
2008-09 – 2012-13

Program type	2008-09	2009-10	2010-11	2011-12	2012-13
Broadcasting and Media Innovations[1]					
Wisconsin Public Radio (listeners per week)	467,000	456,800	439,300	476,400	433,400
Wisconsin Public Television (viewers per week)	493,785	420,000	561,000	560,000	453,000
Wisconsin Public Television telecourses (hours)	32	32	30	59	42
Interactive conferencing hours.	218,825	208,221	184,225	169,980	186,869
Continuing Education, Outreach and E-Learning					
Online courses	294	297	338	379	152
Online certificate and degree programs	10	11	11	12	8
Online enrollments.	3,896	4,406	5,026	5,517	3,558
Number of enrollments[2]	39,344	44,152	46,001	43,514	43,051
Noncredit programs	5,845	5,915	5,970	5,700	6,426
Noncredit enrollments	142,506	144,110	160,000	144,092	183,763
UW HELP (Higher Education Location Program) contacts . . .	29,632	26,598	28,481	22,469	25,593
Learner Support Services contacts.	97,775	104,996	133,525	144,179	108,098
Online applications to UW System Campuses	159,753	165,948	177,375	177,985	176,065
Independent Learning Enrollments[3]	2,063	1,697	1,402	1,400	1,287
Cooperative Extension Teaching Contacts[4]					
Agriculture/Agribusiness	407,938	316,799	253,563	265,911	219,319
Community, Natural Resources and Economic Development. .	117,971	114,013	145,702	84,533	101,332
Family Living Programs.	430,267	518,270	496,816	543,406	567,430
4-H/Youth Development.	308,258	339,538	340,030	376,375	349,473
Leadership Wisconsin (leadership development program) . . .	418	492	772	927	708
Wisconsin Geological and Natural History Survey	8,859	9,305	14,486	16,786	15,775
Entrepreneurship and Economic Development					
Counseling and technical assistance clients	2,784	3,118	3,343	2,468	2,412
Business Answerline-assisted clients	2,259	2,220	1,864	1,787	1,722
Counseling and technical assistance hours	20,503	22,726	23,219	16,898	18,872
Training programs	865	1,091	935	623	275
Training program participants	12,792	13,763	12,956	6,547	5,241
Business startups.	76	119	167	122	206
Extension Conference Centers					
The Lowell Center, The Pyle Center					
Conference participants	73,675	74,572	75,870	64,162	66,637
Events	1,744	1,947	2,939	2,665	2,647

[1]Wisconsin Public Radio and Wisconsin Public Television are cooperative services of the University of Wisconsin-Extension and the Wisconsin Educational Communications Board.

[2]Undergraduate and Graduate enrollments combined.

[3]Adjusted for student withdrawals.

[4]Cooperative Extension data are for the calendar year, except Wisconsin Geological and Natural History Survey numbers for 2011-12 and 2012-13. In addition, its faculty and staff offer contacts through publications, exhibits, mass and social media, and the World Wide Web.

Source: The UW Colleges and UW-Extension 2013 Annual Report, at: http://www.uwex.uwc.edu/annualreport/ [June 2015], and previous editions.

ENROLLMENT IN WISCONSIN TECHNICAL COLLEGE SYSTEM

Annual Enrollment Summary, 2004-05 – 2013-14

School Year	Total[1]	College Parallel	Associate Degree	Technical Diploma	Vocational Adult	Non-Post Secondary[2]	Community Services
2004-05	406,323	20,181	115,422	39,291	214,948	76,870	10,817
2005-06	409,380	20,242	117,408	38,305	219,584	74,556	10,631
2006-07	400,057	21,053	117,028	39,045	210,396	72,951	10,206
2007-08	390,272	22,142	117,722	38,583	203,493	70,585	9,113
2008-09	375,944	24,080	122,773	39,025	182,713	73,198	8,760
2009-10	382,006	27,139	133,602	39,011	178,257	76,325	10,082
2010-11	370,588	27,938	136,232	36,101	167,135	72,176	13,181
2011-12	362,619	27,636	132,535	34,452	166,463	65,506	14,112
2012-13	341,802	26,438	127,861	33,451	149,628	61,552	14,929
2013-14	326,544	25,391	122,656	30,922	143,943	51,902	15,339

[1]Unduplicated student headcount.

[2]Includes Basic Education.

Sources: Wisconsin Technical College System, departmental data and *Fact Book 2014*, at: http://www.wtcsystem.edu/about-us/wtcs-overview and previous issues.

Annual Enrollment Summary, By Technical College – 2013-14

Technical College	Total[1]	College Parallel	Associate Degree	Technical Diploma	Vocational Adult	Non-Post Secondary[2]	Community Services
Blackhawk	8,469	—	3,165	927	4,210	1,324	243
Chippewa Valley	14,415	978	5,984	1,938	6,592	2,907	—
Fox Valley	44,437	—	14,690	3,344	27,344	1,927	532
Gateway	20,142	—	10,704	2,409	5,902	4,863	—
Lakeshore	13,031	—	3,170	1,140	8,064	1,470	459
Madison Area	36,714	10,870	14,474	3,309	9,383	6,647	4,853
Mid-State.	7,457	—	3,581	1,026	2,832	1,679	12
Milwaukee Area	38,049	11,880	19,171	2,883	5,618	11,174	24
Moraine Park.	16,232	—	6,866	2,322	5,507	3,113	1,435
Nicolet Area	7,085	726	1,228	374	3,169	695	2,122
Northcentral	17,092	—	6,167	1,270	8,274	4,651	—
Northeast Wisconsin	37,943	—	13,510	3,383	21,982	3,144	617
Southwest Wisconsin . . .	10,614	—	3,573	1,034	6,475	2,236	251
Waukesha County	22,756	—	7,816	2,369	11,340	2,842	1,887
Western.	11,857	937	5,259	1,371	4,351	1,971	441
Wisconsin Indianhead . . .	20,251	—	3,298	1,823	12,900	1,259	2,463
TOTAL.	326,544	25,391	122,656	30,922	143,943	51,902	15,339

[1]Unduplicated student headcount.

[2]Includes Basic Education.

Source: Wisconsin Technical College System, departmental data, June 2015.

WISCONSIN PRIVATE INSTITUTIONS OF HIGHER EDUCATION
Fall Enrollment, 2009-10 – 2013-14

Institution (Location)	2009-10	2010-11	2011-12	2012-13	2013-14
Universities and Colleges					
Alverno College (Milwaukee)	2,815	2,759	2,605	2,522	2,536
Beloit College (Beloit)	1,407	1,397	1,385	1,330	1,306
Cardinal Stritch University (Milwaukee)	6,276	5,842	5,159	4,614	4,407
Carroll University (Waukesha)	3,115	3,396	3,522	3,571	3,534
Carthage College (Kenosha)	3,137	3,144	3,082	3,029	2,988
Concordia University Wisconsin (Mequon)	7,178	7,484	7,618	7,751	7,943
Edgewood College (Madison)	2,549	2,626	2,658	3,064	2,894
Lakeland College (Sheboygan)	3,932	3,936	3,881	3,749	3,806
Lawrence University (Appleton)	1,495	1,557	1,487	1,518	1,553
Marian University (Fond du Lac)	2,841	2,881	2,615	2,305	2,188
Marquette University (Milwaukee)	11,689	11,806	12,002	11,749	11,782
Mount Mary University (Milwaukee)	2,008	1,957	1,738	1,640	1,481
Northland College (Ashland)	612	603	534	590	552
Ripon College (Ripon)	1,065	1,065	991	931	904
Saint Norbert College (De Pere)	2,175	2,241	2,225	2,287	2,222
Silver Lake College (Manitowoc)	704	720	635	655	679
Viterbo University (La Crosse)	3,287	3,238	3,092	2,830	2,762
Wisconsin Lutheran College (Milwaukee)	776	840	1,022	1,090	1,178
Technical and Professional					
Bellin College of Nursing (Green Bay)	331	329	310	271	325
Herzing University* (WI campuses)	NA	4,571	3,923	3,369	3,458
Medical College of Wisconsin (Milwaukee)	817	1,277	1,257	1,209	1,212
Milwaukee Institute of Art & Design (Milwaukee)	660	700	727	668	667
Milwaukee School of Engineering (Milwaukee)	2,648	2,589	2,486	2,564	2,658
Wisconsin School of Professional Psychology (Milwaukee)	78	75	83	91	92
Theological Seminaries					
Maranatha Baptist University (Watertown)	901	962	1,019	979	1,035
Nashotah House (Nashotah)	108	114	119	145	124
Sacred Heart School of Theology (Hales Corners)	139	107	102	113	113
Tribal Colleges					
College of the Menominee Nation (Keshena)	634	615	699	721	661
Lac Courte Oreilles Ojibwa Community College (Hayward)	561	489	433	357	303
TOTAL	63,938	69,320	67,409	65,712	65,363

NA – Not available.

*For-profit institution.

Sources: National Center for Education Statistics, Integrated Postsecondary Education Data System, at http://nces.ed.gov/ipeds/datacenter; U.S. Department of Education, Office of Postsecondary Education, Database of Accredited Postsecondary Institutions and Programs, accredited by the Higher Learning Commission of the North Central Association of Colleges and Schools, at: http://ope.ed.gov/accreditation/.

DIPLOMAS AND EARNED DEGREES
by State 2012-13

State	High School Diplomas[1] Public[2]	Higher Education			Doctorate Level Degrees (Ph.D., M.D., J.D. etc.)
		Associate Degree	Bachelor's Degree	Master's Degree	
Alabama	43,050	13,758	29,877	11,670	2,297
Alaska	7,230	1,758	1,895	724	54
Arizona.	64,090	48,911	66,296	30,578	3,771
Arkansas	28,210	8,498	14,318	5,225	980
California	415,370	120,518	180,528	69,256	18,766
Colorado	52,150	15,550	32,446	15,007	2,747
Connecticut	35,820	6,826	21,470	9,570	1,964
Delaware.	8,140	2,072	6,230	2,753	558
District of Columbia	3,100	686	9,299	10,995	3,621
Florida	164,800	100,827	94,304	32,912	9,028
Georgia.	92,890	18,889	47,654	17,872	4,410
Hawaii	11,000	4,402	6,363	1,978	556
Idaho	17,330	5,762	10,336	2,049	398
ILLINOIS	141,290	40,574	75,992	43,254	8,598
Indiana	65,670	18,838	46,551	14,663	3,475
IOWA	32,150	18,767	41,447	12,127	3,031
Kansas	30,790	10,647	19,622	6,625	1,474
Kentucky.	41,700	13,853	21,872	9,860	1,951
Louisiana.	35,510	7,150	22,334	7,552	2,532
Maine	13,250	3,167	7,335	1,935	489
Maryland.	57,220	15,387	31,729	18,444	3,043
Massachusetts	63,370	13,742	57,091	35,440	8,289
MICHIGAN	102,770	34,192	58,564	21,048	6,053
MINNESOTA	56,690	21,664	36,326	22,202	4,813
Mississippi	26,020	11,997	14,076	4,804	1,261
Missouri	60,190	19,821	40,963	20,577	4,682
Montana	9,260	2,296	5,644	1,280	395
Nebraska	19,450	5,961	14,119	5,008	1,495
Nevada	24,350	5,373	7,965	2,246	945
New Hampshire	14,160	2,824	9,769	3,878	501
New Jersey.	90,870	21,647	40,295	14,267	2,335
New Mexico	18,470	8,941	8,586	3,239	629
New York	184,490	68,104	132,606	70,407	15,332
North Carolina	89,120	28,575	51,782	17,301	4,824
North Dakota.	6,830	2,386	5,983	1,676	465
Ohio	106,100	33,569	66,193	22,994	6,117
Oklahoma	37,520	12,405	20,047	6,497	1,658
Oregon	34,010	14,272	22,085	7,541	1,960
Pennsylvania	123,540	28,794	91,410	37,135	9,778
Rhode Island	9,810	3,727	11,079	2,654	742
South Carolina	39,830	11,628	24,004	6,120	1,741
South Dakota.	8,030	2,610	5,641	1,512	335
Tennessee	62,670	13,230	33,766	11,956	3,306
Texas	292,560	68,928	115,114	46,464	10,426
Utah	31,990	13,021	28,597	8,412	1,247
Vermont	6,480	1,280	6,206	3,191	434
Virginia.	82,080	25,789	54,749	22,782	5,193
Washington.	66,350	29,281	32,689	9,519	2,601
West Virginia.	17,100	5,411	14,357	6,409	1,032
WISCONSIN	59,890	15,528	36,927	9,653	2,507
Wyoming.	5,440	3,125	2,057	486	199
UNITED STATES[3]. . .	3,110,150	1,006,961	1,840,164[3]	751,751[3]	175,038

[1]Private school data unavailable at time of publication.

[2]Projected.

[3]Total includes U.S. Service schools: 3,576 Bachelor's Degrees and 4 Master's Degrees granted.

Sources: U.S. Department of Education, Institute of Education Sciences, National Center for Education Statistics, *Digest of Education Statistics,* most current digest tables, at: http://nces.ed.gov/programs/digest/current_tables.asp [June 2015].

WISCONSIN SCHOOL DISTRICT FINANCIAL DATA
1990-91 to 2014-15

Fiscal Year	State School Aid Amount[2] (in millions)	State School Aid Percent Change	Gross School Levy Amount[2] (in millions)	Gross School Levy Percent Change	Total School Costs[1] Amount[2] (in millions)	Total School Costs[1] Percent Change	Cost Per Pupil Amount	Cost Per Pupil Percent Change
1990-91	$1,857.4	—	$2,356.4	—	$4,555.7	—	$5,712	—
1991-92	1,950.4	5.0%	2,568.0	9.0%	4,877.1	7.1%	5,987	4.8%
1992-93	2,046.0	4.9	2,843.8	10.7	5,287.9	8.4	6,375	6.5
1993-94	2,186.6	6.9	2,988.1	5.1	5,527.1	4.5	6,549	2.7
1994-95	2,462.0	12.6	2,995.7	0.3	5,848.2	5.8	6,796	3.8
1995-96	2,705.2	9.9	3,023.6	0.9	6,150.2	5.2	7,068	4.0
1996-97	3,566.1	31.8	2,528.1	-16.4	6,546.8	6.4	7,447	5.4
1997-98	3,804.7	6.7	2,590.4	2.5	6,939.0	6.0	7,874	5.7
1998-99	3,989.4	4.9	2,735.8	5.6	7,250.7	4.5	8,244	4.7
1999-2000	4,226.3	5.9	2,794.9	2.2	7,546.9	4.1	8,376	1.6
2000-01	4,463.3	5.6	2,928.1	4.8	7,899.5	4.7	8,765	4.6
2001-02	4,602.4	3.1	3,071.8	4.9	8,347.5	5.7	9,571	9.2
2002-03	4,775.2	3.8	3,192.0	3.9	8,749.9	4.8	10,023	4.7
2003-04	4,806.3	0.7	3,367.6	5.5	8,911.2	1.8	10,229	2.1
2004-05	4,857.9	1.1	3,610.7	7.2	9,216.2	3.4	10,605	3.7
2005-06	5,159.1	6.2	3,592.3	-0.5	9,539.4	3.5	10,989	3.6
2006-07	5,294.4	2.6	3,787.8	5.4	9,902.9	3.8	11,413	3.9
2007-08	5,340.1	0.9	4,066.6	7.4	10,265.1	3.7	11,894	4.2
2008-09	5,462.4	2.3	4,279.0	5.2	10,623.3	3.5	12,346	3.8
2009-10	5,315.4	-2.7	4,537.6	6.0	10,833.7	2.0	12,624	2.3
2010-11	5,325.0	0.2	4,692.9	3.4	11,161.9	3.0	13,020	3.1
2011-12	4,893.5	-8.1	4,646.7	-1.0	10,584.9	-5.2	12,375	-5.0
2012-13	4,964.4	1.4	4,656.1	0.2	10,567.7	-0.2	12,343	-0.3
2013-14	5,079.2	2.3	4,694.4	0.8	10,749.7	1.7	12,546	1.6
2014-15	5,241.7	3.2	4,754.3	1.3	NA	—	NA	—

NA – Not available.

[1]Includes the gross costs of general operations, special projects, debt service, and food service; the net cost of capital projects; and the costs of CESA and County Children with Disabilities Education Board operations.

[2]1996-97 through 2014-15 are appropriated amounts.

Sources: Wisconsin Department of Public Instruction, School Financial Services, at: http://sfs.dpi.wi.gov/, June 2015 and previous years; Wisconsin Legislative Fiscal Bureau, Informational Paper #24, *State Aid to School Districts,* January 2015.

WISCONSIN SCHOOL DISTRICT ENROLLMENT LEVELS

Number of Districts by Total Enrollment Level, 2009-10 – 2014-15

Enrollment Level[1]	Number of Districts 2009-10	2010-11	2011-12	2012-13	2013-14	2014-15
1-499	113	114	120	123	125	129
500-999	124	123	121	122	123	116
1,000-1,999	102	102	99	98	96	97
2,000-2,999	37	35	33	29	31	31
3,000-3,999	26	27	30	32	29	29
4,000-4,999	12	11	10	11	13	13
5,000-9,999	19	21	21	21	22	22
10,000 and above	11	11	11	11	10	10
TOTAL.	444	444	445	447	449	447

[1]Enrollment data includes nondistrict-sponsored charter schools.

Number of Districts by 9-12 Enrollment Level, 2009-10 – 2014-15

Enrollment Level[1]	Number of Districts 2009-10	2010-11	2011-12	2012-13	2013-14	2014-15
0[2]	60	61	61	62	64	64
1-299	169	171	174	180	181	179
300-499	68	68	69	64	64	67
500-999	68	69	73	72	71	66
1,000-1,999	57	54	45	47	47	48
2,000 and above	22	21	23	22	22	23
TOTAL.	444	444	445	447	449	447

[1]Enrollment data includes nondistrict-sponsored charter schools.

[2]This group includes the K3-8 districts, which do not have secondary level students.

Sources: 2009-10 to 2013-14, Wisconsin Department of Public Instruction, "Public School Enrollment Data – Public Enrollment by District by Grade", at: http://lbstat.dpi.wi.gov/lbstat_pubdata3 [April 2015], 2014-15, Wisconsin Information System for Education WISEDash Data Files by Year, at: http://wise.dpi.wi.gov/wisedash_downloadfiles [April 2015].

ENROLLMENT IN WISCONSIN PUBLIC AND PRIVATE ELEMENTARY AND SECONDARY SCHOOLS

Public Schools, 2004-05 – 2014-15

Grade Level	2004-05*	2005-06	2006-07	2007-08	2008-09	2009-10	2010-11	2011-12	2012-13	2013-14	2014-15
Pre-kindergarten	27,444	31,218	33,821	37,773	43,153	47,054	50,200	54,438	55,008	56,777	55,830
Kindergarten	58,724	60,382	60,408	59,590	60,373	61,094	60,721	60,875	62,422	61,522	60,424
1	58,521	59,593	60,696	60,474	59,779	60,197	61,262	60,572	61,037	62,479	61,498
2	57,807	58,978	59,703	60,807	60,486	59,557	60,226	60,984	60,585	60,999	62,311
3	58,874	58,664	59,554	60,000	60,969	60,661	59,981	60,216	61,243	60,697	60,885
4	59,267	59,984	59,356	59,995	60,308	61,242	61,015	60,094	60,670	61,393	60,795
5	61,493	60,304	60,261	59,581	60,222	60,413	61,420	60,958	60,253	60,768	61,459
6	62,557	62,737	61,257	60,827	60,235	60,656	61,053	61,818	61,369	60,505	60,843
7	66,095	65,153	63,938	62,030	61,588	60,814	61,264	61,442	62,310	61,814	60,795
8	67,168	66,985	65,606	64,135	62,305	61,748	61,337	61,413	61,857	62,721	62,029
9	76,173	76,674	75,282	73,746	71,662	69,323	68,383	67,542	67,699	67,985	68,043
10	71,196	73,409	72,425	70,788	69,395	68,291	66,490	65,510	64,507	64,958	65,290
11	69,928	71,428	73,694	72,507	71,326	70,144	69,076	66,851	66,346	65,450	65,019
12	69,510	69,665	70,699	72,380	71,785	71,242	69,858	68,392	67,130	66,346	65,431
TOTAL	864,757	875,174	876,700	874,633	873,586	872,436	872,286	871,105	872,436	874,414	870,652

Private Schools, 2004-05 – 2014-15

Grade Level	2004-05	2005-06	2006-07	2007-08	2008-09	2009-10	2010-11	2011-12	2012-13	2013-14	2014-15
Pre-kindergarten	14,434	14,431	14,662	15,008	14,814	13,646	14,737	14,793	14,982	14,204	14,516
Kindergarten	11,517	11,440	10,890	10,663	10,483	10,161	9,893	9,797	9,994	9,841	9,796
1	10,950	10,896	11,017	10,714	10,306	9,975	9,810	9,767	9,492	9,600	9,929
2	10,970	10,756	10,629	10,764	10,376	10,006	9,744	9,703	9,487	9,325	9,822
3	11,187	10,698	10,466	10,484	10,481	10,026	9,648	9,635	9,462	9,327	9,541
4	11,114	10,866	10,522	10,338	10,187	10,179	9,659	9,542	9,320	9,153	9,494
5	11,047	10,800	10,641	10,412	10,078	9,957	9,927	9,587	9,450	9,139	9,285
6	10,824	10,564	10,325	10,368	9,961	9,672	9,486	9,555	9,233	9,012	9,114
7	10,420	10,164	9,984	9,952	9,775	9,377	9,223	9,192	9,157	8,750	8,853
8	10,247	10,092	9,841	9,876	9,563	9,486	9,072	9,078	8,909	8,702	8,802
9	6,332	6,300	6,306	6,414	6,287	5,980	6,089	5,939	6,159	6,026	6,328
10	5,950	6,275	6,134	6,153	6,072	6,043	5,789	5,866	5,917	5,766	5,926
11	5,925	5,825	5,936	5,923	5,857	5,770	5,796	5,534	5,677	5,590	5,682
12	5,665	5,616	5,559	5,599	5,555	5,496	5,583	5,442	5,217	5,190	5,233
Ungraded Elementary and Secondary	210	310	507	938	1,005	1,038	916	1,238	493	176	783
TOTAL	136,792	135,033	133,419	133,606	130,800	126,812	125,372	124,668	122,949	119,801	123,104

*Major changes were implemented for data collection in 2004-05. Data from 2004-05 is not comprehensive.

Sources: Wisconsin Department of Public Instruction, 2004-05 to 2013-14 Public School Enrollment Data, at: http://lbstat.dpi.wi.gov/lbstat_pubdata3 [April 2015], 2014-15: Wisconsin Information System for Education Data Dashboard, at: http://wisedash.dpi.wi.gov/ [April 2015], and Non-Public (Private) School Enrollment Data, at: http://lbstat.dpi.wi.gov/lbstat_privdata [April 2015].

WISCONSIN PUBLIC HIGH SCHOOL COMPLETION RATES
By CESA District and Race, 2012-13

CESA	Total[3]	Rate	Female	Rate	Male	Rate	Amer. Indian	Asian	Black	Hispanic	White	2 or more
		Total Students and Rates						Student Detail by Race[1,2]				
1	16,652	82.4	8,564	86.3	8,085	78.7	16	657	3,136	1,781	10,613	67
2	10,281	90.0	5,118	91.5	5,163	87.8	11	229	441	732	7,809	150
3	1,440	96.1	701	97.4	722	95.3	—	—	—	—	513	—
4	2,458	94.4	1,193	95.1	1,265	93.8	15	79	32	29	1,506	15
5	3,831	91.3	1,869	93.4	1,962	89.5	4	71	4	117	2,767	13
6	7,070	91.9	3,457	94.4	3,613	89.6	4	227	78	235	5,634	14
7	6,085	89.9	3,086	92.0	2,989	87.8	68	285	118	303	4,323	21
8	1,524	91.8	768	94.0	756	89.7	113	—	—	—	852	—
9	2,737	92.5	1,357	94.2	1,380	90.9	34	175	7	26	1,944	11
10.	2,485	90.9	1,240	93.1	1,227	88.7	—	89	11	13	1,404	26
11.	3,492	92.3	1,733	92.8	1,759	91.9	4	38	26	17	2,066	29
12.	1,090	89.4	536	91.8	523	86.9	60	—	7	—	685	—
TOTAL.	59,145	88.5	29,656	91.0	29,489	86.2	637 (74.8)	2,151 (90.3)	4,187 (65.4)	3,842 (75.1)	47,491 (93.0)	810 (86.5)

Notes: Percent completion calculated by number of combined completions (diplomas, HSED, certificate) divided by number of students in the 4-year cohort. Rates calculated by the Wisconsin Legislative Reference Bureau. This table is based on 4-year adjusted cohort completion rates, as required by federal law, and may not be comparable to tables in prior *Blue Books*. Details may not sum to totals due to privacy rules.

[1]Includes only students who are identified by race in DPI report. Not all students can be identified by race due to privacy rules relating to small groups.

[2]Pacific Islander state total (rate): 27 (79.4).

[3]Includes students who have completed high school with a diploma, HSED, or other method.

Source: Wisconsin Department of Public Instruction's WISEdash data files, at: http://wise.dpi.wi.gov/wisedash_downloadfiles.

WISCONSIN CHARTER SCHOOL ENROLLMENTS
By CESA District and Race, 2014-15

CESA	Total	Female	Male	American Indian	Asian	Black	Hispanic	Pacific Islander	White	2 or more
	Total Students									
1	23,915	12,106	11,809	76	1,625	10,502	5,406	19	5,892	395
2	4,557	2,311	2,246	27	133	356	793	3	3,033	212
3	515	250	265	0	1	6	12	0	475	21
4	1,109	533	576	10	24	23	67	1	942	42
5	1,930	912	1,018	37	26	28	104	1	1,685	49
6	5,575	2,811	2,764	27	317	137	349	3	4,670	72
7	1,641	852	789	11	62	63	251	3	1,176	75
8	310	148	162	8	2	3	6	0	284	7
9	1,619	827	792	22	27	44	32	3	1,466	25
10.	679	316	363	4	9	18	20	0	603	25
11.	1,675	924	751	31	19	52	78	4	1,455	36
12.	767	367	400	96	8	6	24	2	608	23
TOTAL. .	44,292	22,357	21,935	349	2,253	11,238	7,142	39	22,289	982

Source: Wisconsin Department of Public Instruction, Wisconsin Information System for Education, at: http://wise.dpi.wi.gov/wisedash_downloadfile [April 2015].

Wisconsin Cooperative Educational Service Agency (CESA) Districts

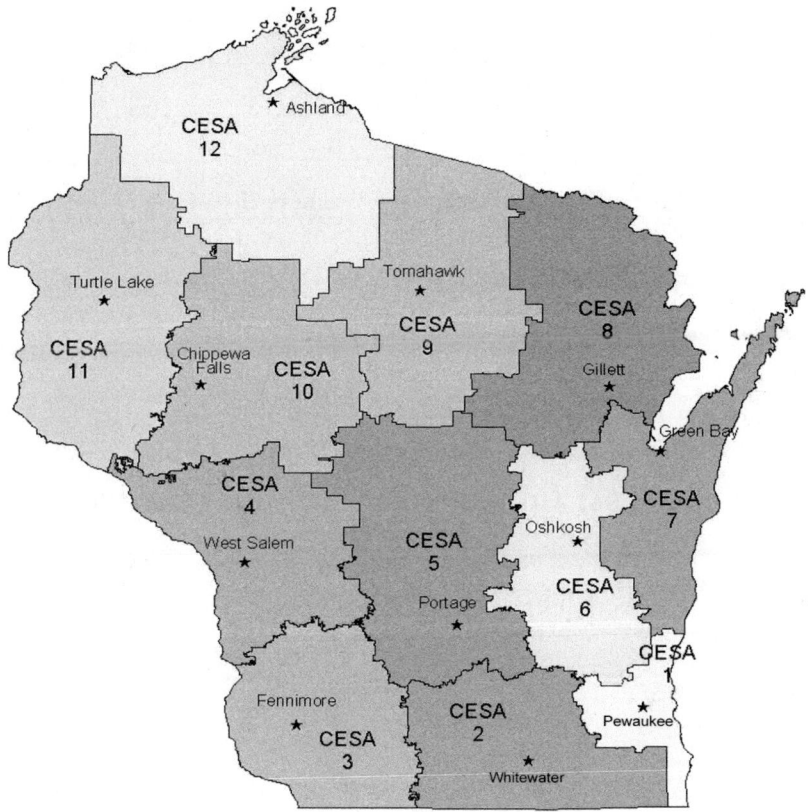

Source: Wisconsin Department of Public Instruction.

WISCONSIN PUBLIC SCHOOL SALARIES
Instructional Staff Employment and Average Salaries 2010-11 to 2014-15

		Instructional Staff				
Year	Total	Avg. Salary of Total	Principals	Non-supervisory	Teachers	Avg. Salary of Teachers
2010-11	63,948	$58,159	2,434	3,473	58,041	$54,195
2011-12	61,850	57,649	2,383	3,287	56,180	53,792
2012-13	62,698	58,999	2,467	3,431	56,800	55,171
2013-14	62,612	57,777	2,414	3,363	56,835	53,679
2014-15	61,251	58,518	2,378	3,250	55,624	54,535

Detail: Elementary and Secondary Teachers 2010-11 to 2014-15

	Elementary			Secondary		
Year	Men	Women	Avg. Salary	Men	Women	Avg. Salary
2010-11	7,232	33,571	$53,750	7,849	9,389	$55,248
2011-12	7,054	32,564	53,551	7,484	9,078	54,369
2012-13	7,132	32,923	55,171	7,567	9,178	55,171
2013-14	7,242	33,054	53,281	7,460	9,079	54,648
2014-15	7,088	32,350	54,535	7,301	8,886	54,535

Sources: National Education Association, *Rankings of the States 2014 and Estimates of School Statistics 2015*, at: www.nea.org/home/44479.htm, March 2015, and previous issues.

AVERAGE SALARIES OF PUBLIC SCHOOL TEACHERS
By State, 2013-14

State	Average Salary	State Rank	State	Average Salary	State Rank
Alabama	$48,720	35	Montana	$49,893*	28
Alaska	65,891	7	Nebraska	49,539	32
Arizona.	45,335*	45	Nevada	55,813	20
Arkansas	47,319	41	New Hampshire	57,057*	15
California	71,396	4	New Jersey	68,238	6
Colorado	49,615	31	New Mexico	45,727	43
Connecticut	70,583	5	New York	76,409	1
Delaware	59,305	13	North Carolina	44,990	47
District of Columbia	73,162*	3	North Dakota.	48,666*	36
Florida	47,780	39	Ohio	55,913	19
Georgia.	52,924	24	Oklahoma	44,549	48
Hawaii	56,291	17	Oregon	58,638	14
Idaho	44,465	49	Pennsylvania	63,701	10
ILLINOIS	60,124*	12	Rhode Island	64,696*	8
Indiana	50,289	27	South Carolina	48,430	37
IOWA	52,032	25	South Dakota.	40,023	51
Kansas	48,221*	38	Tennessee	47,742	40
Kentucky.	50,560	26	Texas	49,690	30
Louisiana.	49,067	34	Utah	45,695	44
Maine	49,232	33	Vermont	55,958	18
Maryland.	64,546	9	Virginia.	49,826*	29
Massachusetts	73,195	2	Washington.	52,969	23
MICHIGAN	62,166	11	West Virginia.	45,086	46
MINNESOTA	54,752	21	**WISCONSIN**	53,679	22
Mississippi	42,187*	50	Wyoming.	56,583	16
Missouri	46,750	42	UNITED STATES	$56,610*	

*Data estimated.

Source: National Education Association, *Rankings of the States 2014 and Estimates of School Statistics 2015*, at: www.nea.org/home/44479.htm, March 2015.

STATE AND LOCAL EDUCATION PAYROLLS
Instructional Employees, By State, March 2013

State	Kindergarten-12				Higher Education			
	FTE Employees*		Payroll		FTE Employees*		Payroll	
	Number	Rank	(in thousands)	Rank	Number	Rank	(in thousands)	Rank
Alabama	68,203	24	$256,131	25	12,759	21	$85,895	20
Alaska	13,167	47	68,488	44	1,827	49	13,119	47
Arizona.	74,087	20	273,652	23	14,031	19	85,652	21
Arkansas	47,078	32	178,232	32	8,458	30	53,187	31
California	390,032	2	2,301,055	1	62,629	1	519,045	1
Colorado	70,977	21	280,097	22	18,573	12	116,915	14
Connecticut	66,220	25	368,763	17	7,165	34	51,937	32
Delaware	12,370	49	59,992	46	2,742	42	18,519	41
District of Columbia	6,331	51	37,013	51	363	51	2,232	51
Florida	237,225	4	805,114	7	29,307	6	213,954	5
Georgia.	157,903	9	615,462	9	18,435	13	124,786	12
Hawaii	19,659	42	81,165	42	4,186	38	27,330	38
Idaho	23,969	41	72,905	43	3,489	39	18,801	40
ILLINOIS	201,681	5	1,034,191	4	30,401	4	179,219	8
Indiana	86,623	17	346,154	20	22,169	10	123,383	13
IOWA	49,843	31	203,433	30	8,813	29	64,051	28
Kansas	65,083	27	225,549	28	10,505	27	68,918	25
Kentucky	63,347	28	250,239	26	12,320	24	76,832	22
Louisiana.	66,089	26	245,486	27	9,651	28	60,967	29
Maine	26,615	40	99,364	40	2,464	43	13,499	46
Maryland	89,848	16	509,938	14	14,668	16	97,123	16
Massachusetts	118,636	12	607,826	10	11,179	26	67,890	27
MICHIGAN	112,787	13	563,070	12	29,159	7	222,565	3
MINNESOTA	85,984	18	384,707	15	14,894	15	92,701	18
Mississippi	52,644	30	169,689	33	7,800	33	43,247	34
Missouri	92,440	15	351,138	19	13,088	20	72,770	23
Montana	15,720	45	61,325	45	2,189	47	12,248	48
Nebraska	36,176	35	141,651	34	4,621	37	28,298	37
Nevada	27,800	38	131,009	36	3,168	41	22,170	39
New Hampshire	27,058	39	107,522	39	2,310	45	15,979	43
New Jersey	168,120	7	1,023,785	5	14,078	18	126,604	11
New Mexico	33,733	36	114,358	37	5,926	35	43,233	35
New York	341,637	3	1,942,933	2	29,931	5	219,963	4
North Carolina	150,920	10	530,953	13	33,716	3	195,384	6
North Dakota.	12,311	50	44,781	50	3,285	40	18,037	42
Ohio	165,076	8	746,463	8	25,112	8	163,609	9
Oklahoma	62,588	29	205,012	29	7,868	32	50,922	33
Oregon	43,501	33	185,141	31	14,108	17	94,060	17
Pennsylvania	177,959	6	851,650	6	23,007	9	182,737	7
Rhode Island	16,085	43	89,857	41	2,301	46	15,467	44
South Carolina	69,917	23	258,570	24	11,404	25	68,598	26
South Dakota.	15,321	46	47,599	49	2,317	44	14,437	45
Tennessee	96,642	14	338,482	21	12,507	23	69,134	24
Texas	456,317	1	1,745,927	3	53,559	2	399,912	2
Utah	36,659	34	136,631	35	8,020	31	60,180	30
Vermont	15,893	44	58,742	47	1,289	50	11,482	49
Virginia.	137,704	11	593,536	11	19,441	11	142,693	10
Washington.	70,733	22	371,376	16	12,670	22	87,509	19
West Virginia.	29,296	37	108,554	38	5,008	36	31,816	36
WISCONSIN	83,359	19	367,982	18	17,257	14	106,160	15
Wyoming.	12,930	48	54,185	48	1,984	48	11,338	50
UNITED STATES	4,602,296		$20,646,876		688,151		$4,706,503	

Note: State payroll detail may not sum to U.S. total due to rounding.

*FTE = Full-time equivalent employees.

Source: U.S. Department of Commerce, Bureau of the Census, "Government Employment and Payroll", at: http://www.census.gov/govs/apes [February 2015]. Rank calculated by Wisconsin Legislative Reference Bureau.

EXPENDITURES PER PUPIL
By State and Source
2008-09 – 2011-12

State	Expenditures per Pupil 2008-09	2009-10	2010-11	2011-12	2011-12 State Rank	Revenue Sources for 2011-12 Pupil Expenditure Federal	State	Local
Alabama	$8,964	$8,907	8,726	$8,577	40	11.8%	55.4%	32.8%
Alaska	15,363	15,829	16,663	17,475	3	14.2	64.9	21.0
Arizona.	8,022*	7,968*	7,782	7,382*	48	14.8	40.9	44.3
Arkansas	8,854*	9,281*	9,496	9,536*	30	13.2	51.5	35.2
California	9,503*	9,300*	9,146	9,329*	33	12.6	56.3	31.1
Colorado	8,782	8,926	8,786	8,594	38	8.3	43.3	48.4
Connecticut	15,353*	15,698*	16,224	16,855*	4	5.2	38.7	56.1
Delaware.	12,109	12,222	12,467	13,580	11	12.6	58.6	28.8
District of Columbia . . .	19,698	20,910	20,793	19,847	—	10.0	—	90.0
Florida	8,867*	8,863*	9,030	8,520*	41	13.0	36.3	50.7
Georgia.	9,649*	9,432*	9,259	9,272*	35	10.9	42.8	46.4
Hawaii	12,400	11,714	11,924	11,973	15	12.6	85.3	2.2
Idaho	7,118*	7,100*	6,821	6,626	49	13.5	63.2	23.3
ILLINOIS	11,097*	11,739*	11,742*	12,011*	14	8.3	32.2	59.6
Indiana	9,254*	9,479*	9,251	9,588*	29	9.6	54.5	35.9
IOWA	9,704	9,748	9,795	10,027	26	8.7	44.4	46.9
Kansas	10,204	9,972	9,802	10,021	27	8.4	55.4	36.3
Kentucky.	8,786	8,957	9,228	9,327	34	13.7	54.2	32.1
Louisiana.	10,625*	10,701*	10,799	10,726*	22	17.3	42.8	39.8
Maine	12,183*	12,452*	12,576	12,335*	13	9.1	40.0	50.9
Maryland.	13,737*	14,007*	14,123	13,871	9	6.3	43.5	50.2
Massachusetts	14,534*	14,699*	14,285	14,844	8	6.7	39.2	54.1
MICHIGAN	10,373	10,447	10,577	10,477	25	10.8	57.1	32.1
MINNESOTA	10,983*	10,665*	10,674	10,781*	21	7.3	64.1	28.6
Mississippi.	8,064*	8,104*	7,926	8,097	46	17.9	49.4	32.7
Missouri	9,617*	9,721*	9,461	9,514	31	10.1	32.0	57.8
Montana	10,120	10,565	10,719	10,569	24	13.5	47.5	39.1
Nebraska	10,846	11,460	11,540*	11,640	16	9.5	30.9	59.6
Nevada	8,321	8,376	8,411	8,130	45	10.0	33.0	57.0
New Hampshire	12,583	13,072	13,548	13,774	10	6.6	36.0	57.4
New Jersey.	16,973	17,379	16,855	17,982	2	5.4	39.5	55.1
New Mexico	9,648	9,621	9,250	9,013	37	15.0	68.0	17.0
New York	17,746*	18,167*	18,834	19,396*	1	6.8	39.4	53.8
North Carolina	8,463	8,225	8,267	8,160	44	14.3	60.1	25.6
North Dakota.	9,802	10,519	10,898	11,246	19	13.1	50.4	36.5
Ohio	10,669	11,224	11,395	11,323	18	9.6	44.3	46.2
Oklahoma	7,878	7,929	7,631	7,763	47	13.5	49.2	37.3
Oregon	9,611	9,268	9,516	9,485	32	10.0	49.2	40.8
Pennsylvania.	12,299	12,729	13,096	13,091	12	8.2	35.8	56.0
Rhode Island	14,719*	14,723*	14,948	15,172	7	9.5	37.2	53.3
South Carolina	9,228	9,080	8,903	9,077	36	10.8	45.7	43.5
South Dakota.	8,543	9,020	8,931	8,593	39	16.6	30.7	52.7
Tennessee	7,992	8,117	8,484	8,354	42	14.1	45.2	40.7
Texas	8,562	8,788	8,685	8,213	43	12.7	41.1	46.2
Utah	6,612	6,452	6,326*	6,441	50	10.0	52.4	37.7
Vermont	15,096	16,006	14,707	16,651	5	7.8	88.3	3.9
Virginia.	10,928	10,594	10,363	10,656	23	9.3	38.0	52.8
Washington.	9,585*	9,497*	9,619	9,617*	28	8.9	59.1	32.0
West Virginia.	10,606*	11,730*	11,978	11,579*	17	12.2	58.2	29.6
WISCONSIN	11,183	11,453	11,946*	11,233*	20	8.8	44.2	47.1
Wyoming.	14,628	15,232	15,815*	15,988	6	8.8	51.2	40.0
UNITED STATES . .	$10,540*	$10,652*	$10,658*	$10,667*		10.2%	45.2%	44.6%

*Value affected by redistribution of reported expenditure values to correct for missing data items, and/or to distribute state direct support expenditures.

Source: U.S. Department of Education, Institute of Education Sciences, National Center for Education Statistics, *Revenues and Expenditures for Public Elementary and Secondary Education: School Year 2011-12 (Fiscal Year 2012)*, January 2015, and previous NCES publications. Rank and percentages calculated by Wisconsin Legislative Reference Bureau. Detail may not add to total due to rounding.

STATE AND LOCAL PER CAPITA EDUCATION EXPENDITURES
By State, Fiscal Year 2010-11

State	All Education Amount	All Education Rank	Elementary and Secondary Amount	Elementary and Secondary Rank	Higher Education Amount	Higher Education Rank	Other Education* Amount	Other Education* Rank
Alabama	$2,784	25	$1,197	51	$1,034	11	$167	16†
Alaska	4,672	1	3,404	2	1,113	8	155	22†
Arizona.	2,065	47	1,244	49	707	37	114	38†
Arkansas	2,875	22	1,825	24	785	31	227	7
California	2,712	31	1,684	31	900	19	128	34
Colorado	2,580	37	1,600	35	884	21	96	45
Connecticut	3,292	8	2,384	6	736	33	173	15
Delaware	3,455	7	1,911	16	1,179	3	365	2
District of Columbia	3,790	4	3,519	1	271	51	0	—
Florida	2,030	49	1,380	46	502	49	148	24
Georgia.	2,530	40	1,720	30	587	46	223	8
Hawaii	2,433	45	1,410	45	954	17	69	50
Idaho	1,975	51	1,198	50	682	40	95	46
ILLINOIS	2,694	32	1,906	17	675	41	113	40
Indiana	2,497	41	1,494	40	847	27	155	22†
IOWA	3,147	11	1,878	19	1,134	7	135	29†
Kansas	2,914	16	1,831	22†	991	14	92	47
Kentucky.	2,624	34	1,546	39	864	25	214	10
Louisiana.	2,649	33	1,787	26†	686	39	176	14
Maine	2,604	35	1,840	21	598	45	166	18
Maryland.	3,133	12	2,064	10	953	18	116	37
Massachusetts	2,848	24	1,976	11	708	36	163	19
MICHIGAN	2,906	17	1,773	28	1,035	10	98	44
MINNESOTA	2,879	21	1,868	20	824	28	187	12
Mississippi	2,434	44	1,435	44	869	23	130	32
Missouri	2,287	46	1,568	37	602	44	117	36
Montana	2,601	36	1,624	33	799	30	178	13
Nebraska	3,094	13	1,943	13	1,009	13	142	26
Nevada	2,048	48	1,473	41	471	50	103	42
New Hampshire	2,862	23	2,100	8	639	43	123	35
New Jersey.	3,463	6	2,656	5	646	42	161	20
New Mexico	3,255	10	1,949	12	1,149	6	157	21
New York	3,676	5	2,847	4	729	34	99	43
North Carolina	2,458	43	1,360	47	962	16	136	28
North Dakota.	3,263	9	1,804	25	1,293	1	167	16†
Ohio	2,885	19	1,913	15	744	32	228	6
Oklahoma	2,477	42	1,452	42	886	20	139	27
Oregon	2,715	30	1,555	38	1,071	9	90	48
Pennsylvania.	2,778	26	1,937	14	695	38	146	25
Rhode Island	2,900	18	2,094	9	586	47	220	9
South Carolina	2,579	38	1,622	34	718	35	239	5
South Dakota.	2,532	39	1,583	36	816	29	133	31
Tennessee	1,993	50	1,345	48	519	48	129	33
Texas	2,884	20	1,831	22†	967	15	86	49
Utah	2,759	27	1,450	43	1,174	4	135	29†
Vermont	3,796	3	2,349	7	1,173	5	275	4
Virginia.	2,751	28	1,763	29	873	22	114	38†
Washington.	2,750	29	1,672	32	868	24	211	11
West Virginia.	3,016	15	1,787	26†	855	26	375	1
WISCONSIN	3,038	14	1,902	18	1,028	12	108	41
Wyoming.	4,393	2	2,888	3	1,206	2	299	3
UNITED STATES . . .	$2,764		$1,813		$810		$141	

Note: Per capita amounts are based on population figures as of July 2011.

*Includes assistance and subsidies to individuals and private elementary and secondary schools, and colleges and universities, as well as miscellaneous education expenditures.

†Tied.

Source: U.S. Department of Education, Institute of Education Sciences, National Center for Education Statistics, *Digest of Education Statistics,* most current digest tables, at: http://nces.ed.gov/programs/digest/current_tables.asp [June 2015]. Rank calculated by Wisconsin Legislative Reference Bureau. Detail may not add to total due to rounding.

EDUCATION EXPENDITURES
BY STATE AND LOCAL GOVERNMENTS
By State, 2012
(In Millions)

State	Total Expenditures[1]	Higher Education	Elem. & Secondary Schools
Alabama – State	$5,387	$4,601	—
Local	7,258	—	$7,258
Alaska – State	1,469	879	471
Local	1,834	15	1,819
Arizona – State	4,291	3,434	—
Local	9,228	1,331	7,897
Arkansas – State	3,290	2,643	—
Local	4,985	—	4,985
California – State	30,793	25,537	325
Local	76,937	10,308	66,629
Colorado – State	5,100	4,467	—
Local	8,112	123	7,989
Connecticut – State	3,265	2,605	1
Local	8,990	—	8,990
Delaware – State	1,500	1,152	—
Local	1,839	—	1,839
Florida – State	9,717	6,650	—
Local	27,656	2,915	24,741
Georgia – State	8,118	6,233	—
Local	17,159	41	17,117
Hawaii – State	3,503	1,507	1,896
Local	—	—	—
Idaho – State	1,062	910	—
Local	2,054	201	1,853
ILLINOIS – State	7,947	6,399	—
Local	27,425	2,579	24,846
Indiana – State	7,100	6,020	—
Local	9,813	1	9,812
IOWA – State	3,032	2,619	—
Local	6,770	866	5,904
Kansas – State	2,600	2,346	—
Local	5,827	738	5,089
Kentucky – State	5,315	3,749	616
Local	6,317	2	6,315
Louisiana – State	4,531	3,171	457
Local	8,273	—	8,273
Maine – State	1,020	799	10
Local	2,333	—	2,333
Maryland – State	5,326	4,637	0+
Local	13,425	1,308	12,117
Massachusetts – State	5,993	4,991	12
Local	13,640	71	13,569
MICHIGAN – State	10,030	8,973	53
Local	18,664	1,635	17,029
MINNESOTA – State	5,349	4,391	—
Local	10,089	—	10,089
Mississippi – State	2,374	1,955	—
Local	5,071	718	4,352
Missouri – State	4,144	3,405	—
Local	10,390	887	9,503
Montana – State	$919	$747	—
Local	1,659	41	$1,618
Nebraska – State	1,832	1,567	—
Local	4,108	335	3,773
Nevada – State	1,538	1,211	—
Local	3,867	—	3,867
New Hampshire – State	1,081	928	—
Local	2,759	—	2,759
New Jersey – State	8,606	4,628	2,333
Local	22,877	1,275	21,602
New Mexico – State	2,405	2,027	—
Local	3,884	340	3,544
New York – State	12,853	10,823	—
Local	58,636	3,163	55,473
North Carolina – State	9,029	7,665	53
Local	14,663	1,879	12,784
North Dakota – State	1,044	936	—
Local	1,310	—	1,310
Ohio – State	9,480	8,074	—
Local	23,050	626	22,425
Oklahoma – State	3,962	3,421	11
Local	5,484	—	5,484
Oregon – State	3,364	2,970	—
Local	6,976	990	5,985
Pennsylvania – State	10,026	8,058	—
Local	25,297	1,121	24,176
Rhode Island – State	991	675	52
Local	2,142	—	2,142
South Carolina – State	4,771	3,491	138
Local	7,364	—	7,364
South Dakota – State	662	560	—
Local	1,338	81	1,257
Tennessee – State	4,752	3,806	—
Local	8,928	—	8,928
Texas – State	22,425	20,009	368
Local	48,324	3,920	44,404
Utah – State	3,992	3,635	—
Local	4,215	—	4,215
Vermont – State	898	728	—
Local	1,477	—	1,477
Virginia – State	8,241	7,291	—
Local	14,950	218	14,732
Washington – State	7,528	5,901	—
Local	11,755	—	11,755
West Virginia – State	2,309	1,685	—
Local	3,198	—	3,198
WISCONSIN – State	5,531	4,884	—
Local	11,459	1,328	10,131
Wyoming – State	624	474	0+
Local	1,895	242	1,653
U.S. TOTAL – State	$271,117	$220,266	$6,795
Local[2]	$598,078	$39,470	$558,609

Note: State payments to local governments for education aids appear as local government expenditures.

[1]"Total expenditures" includes "other education" expenditures not reported separately here. Figures may not add to total due to rounding by Wisconsin Legislative Reference Bureau.

[2]Includes District of Columbia expenditures: Total = $2,372; Higher Ed. = $170; Elem. & Sec. = $2,201 (in millions).

Source: U.S. Department of Commerce, Bureau of the Census, "State and Local Government Finances by Level of Government and by State: 2012", at: http://www.census.gov/govs/local/ [December 2014].

STATE AND LOCAL EXPENDITURES FOR
PUBLIC EDUCATION IN WISCONSIN
2009-10 – 2013-14
(In Millions)

Agency/Program	2009-10	2010-11	2011-12	2012-13	2013-14
Public elementary and secondary schools[1]	$10,833.7	$11,161.9	$10,584.9	$10,567.7	$10,749.7
Department of Public Instruction	97.7	100.5	99.5	108.4	112.3
University of Wisconsin System	4,643.4	5,546.7	5,556.4	5,840.1	6,073.9
Wisconsin Technical College System Board	176.8	178.3	138.8	139.7	139.4
Public libraries (local expenditures)[2]	231.5	233.9	236.7	231.0	234.9
Other:					
Arts Board (Department of Tourism)	4.2	4.9	0	0	0
Educational Communications Board	15.0	14.9	15.3	17.4	18.0
Higher Educational Aids Board	123.5	148.7	136.8	142.7	146.9
Medical College of Wisconsin, Inc. (state funding)	6.1	6.1	5.7	7.5	8.4
State Historical Society	19.5	20.2	19.6	22.0	23.4
TOTAL	$16,151.4	$17,416.1	$16,793.7	$17,076.5	$17,506.9
Per capita expenditures[3]	$2,840	$3,062	$2,949	$2,994	$3,062

[1]Includes the gross costs of general operations, special projects, debt service, and food service; the net cost of capital projects; and the costs of CESA and County Children with Disabilities Education Board operations.

[2]Expenditures are for calendar year ending in the fiscal year shown.

[3]Based on total state population. Wisconsin population estimate for 2012: 5,703,525; population estimate for January 1, 2013: 5,717,110.

Sources: Wisconsin Department of Administration, *Annual Fiscal Report, Appendix (Budgetary Basis) 2013-14,* 2014 and previous issues; Wisconsin Department of Administration, Demographic Services Center, *Time Series of the Final Official Population Estimates and Census Counts for Wisconsin Counties* [June 2015]; Wisconsin Department of Public Instruction, Library Service Data, 2013 and previous data; Wisconsin Department of Public Instruction, departmental data. Per capita data calculated by Wisconsin Legislative Reference Bureau.

WISCONSIN HOME-BASED PRIVATE EDUCATIONAL PROGRAMS
2005-06 to 2014-15 Enrollments

Grade Level	2005-06	2006-07	2007-08	2008-09	2009-10	2010-11	2011-12	2012-13	2013-14	2014-15
1	1,428	1,375	1,356	1,357	1,409	1,127	1,136	1,158	1,197	1,183
2	1,368	1,352	1,317	1,317	1,335	1,164	1,142	1,060	1,144	1,144
3	1,338	1,350	1,376	1,350	1,322	1,179	1,076	1,106	1,077	1,160
4	1,369	1,389	1,349	1,385	1,365	1,098	1,137	1,062	1,095	1,136
5	1,417	1,320	1,383	1,334	1,326	1,155	1,050	1,123	1,087	1,095
6	1,430	1,447	1,332	1,412	1,343	1,189	1,078	1,085	1,089	1,171
7	1,387	1,376	1,424	1,286	1,367	1,160	1,070	1,102	1,035	1,171
8	1,427	1,393	1,314	1,390	1,232	1,149	1,027	1,018	1,053	1,078
9	1,428	1,422	1,273	1,259	1,316	1,042	1,038	989	996	1,080
10	1,507	1,538	1,375	1,300	1,183	1,144	917	1,030	996	1,041
11	1,370	1,453	1,397	1,246	1,184	1,064	1,004	840	993	964
12	1,212	1,036	1,134	1,076	967	891	703	769	717	820
Ungraded	3,642	3,706	3,695	3,646	3,700	6,214	5,901	6,122	6,625	6,807
TOTAL	20,323	20,157	19,725	19,358	19,049	19,576	18,279	18,464	19,104	19,850

Note: A home-based private educational program is a program of educational instruction provided to a child by a child's parent or guardian or by a person designated by the parent or guardian. These programs must provide at least 875 hours of instruction each school year and must offer a sequentially progressive curriculum of fundamental instruction in reading, language arts, mathematics, social studies, science, and health.

Source: Wisconsin Department of Public Instruction, "Home-Based Private Educational Program Enrollment Trends: Enrollment by Grade", at: http://sms.dpi.wi.gov/sms_hbstats [May 2015].

WISCONSIN STATE DOCUMENT DEPOSITORY LIBRARIES

Depository libraries collect publications issued by the federal government and Wisconsin state agencies through the Department of Public Instruction's document depository program. State depository libraries are designated to receive copies of all collected publications. Regional depository libraries receive approximately three-quarters of all collected publications, and selective depository libraries receive two-thirds.

City	Library	Internet Address
STATE LEVEL DEPOSITORY		
Madison	Legislative Reference Bureau	www.legis.wi.gov/lrb
Madison	Wisconsin Historical Society	www.wisconsinhistory.org
Madison	Resources for Libraries and Lifelong Learning, Department of Public Instruction	rl3.dpi.wi.gov
REGIONAL DEPOSITORY		
Appleton	Appleton Public Library	www.apl.org
Eau Claire	McIntyre Library, UW-Eau Claire	www.uwec.edu/library
Green Bay	Cofrin Library, UW-Green Bay	www.uwgb.edu/library
La Crosse	La Crosse Public Library	www.lacrosselibrary.org
Milwaukee	Milwaukee Public Library	www.mpl.org
Platteville	Karrmann Library, UW-Platteville	www.uwplatt.edu/library
Racine	Racine Public Library	www.racinelibrary.info
River Falls	Chalmer Davee Library, UW-River Falls	www.uwrf.edu/library
Stevens Point. . .	UW-Stevens Point Library	www.uwsp.edu/library
Superior	Superior Public Library	superiorlibrary.org
SELECTIVE DEPOSITORY		
Appleton	Seeley G. Mudd Library, Lawrence University	www.lawrence.edu/library
Beloit.	Beloit College Library	www.beloit.edu/library
Eau Claire	L.E. Phillips Memorial Public Library	www.ecpubliclibrary.info
Fond du Lac . . .	Fond du Lac Public Library	www.fdlpl.org
Green Bay	Brown County Library	www.browncountylibrary.org
Hayward	Lac Courte Oreilles Ojibwa College Community Library	www.lco.edu/dept/libcul
Janesville.	UW-Rock County Library	rock.uwc.edu/library
Kenosha	UW-Parkside Library	www.uwp.edu/learn/library
La Crosse	Murphy Library, UW-La Crosse	www.uwlax.edu/murphylibrary
Madison	Madison Public Library	www.madisonpubliclibrary.org
Manitowoc	Manitowoc Public Library	www.manitowoclibrary.org
Marshfield	UW-Marshfield/Wood County Library	www.marshfield.uwc.edu/library
Menomonie . . .	UW-Stout Library	www.uwstout.edu/lib
Milwaukee	Golda Meir Library, UW-Milwaukee	www.uwm.edu/libraries
Oshkosh	Oshkosh Public Library	www.oshkoshpubliclibrary.org
Oshkosh	Polk Library, UW-Oshkosh	www.uwosh.edu/library
Portage.	Portage Public Library	www.scls.lib.wi.us/por
Rhinelander . . .	Richard J. Brown Library, Nicolet Area Technical College	www.nicoletcollege.edu/library
Ripon.	Lane Library, Ripon College	www.ripon.edu/library
Shawano	Shawano City-County Library	www.shawanolibrary.org
Superior	Jim Dan Hill Library, UW-Superior	www.uwsuper.edu/library
Waukesha	UW-Waukesha Library	waukesha.uwc.edu/library
Waukesha	Waukesha Public Library	www.waukesha.lib.wi.us
Wauwatosa. . . .	Wauwatosa Public Library	wauwatosalibrary.org
West Bend	UW-Washington County Library	washington.uwc.edu/library
Whitewater. . . .	Andersen Library, UW-Whitewater	library.uww.edu
Wisconsin Rapids	McMillan Memorial Library	www.mcmillanlibrary.org

Source: Wisconsin Department of Public Instruction, Resources for Libraries and Lifelong Learning, *Wisconsin Document Depository Program Library Directory*, at: http://rl3.dpi.wi.gov/svc_depository_liblist [January 27, 2015].

WISCONSIN PUBLIC LIBRARY SYSTEMS, 2013

Library System	Resource Library	Address	Counties or Cities Served	2013		
				Total Service Population	Circulation	State Aid for 2013
Arrowhead	Hedberg Public Library (608) 758-6600	316 S. Main Street Janesville, WI 53545-3971	Rock	160,167	1,963,257	$438,605
Eastern Shores	Mead Public Library (920) 459-3400 Ext. 3414	710 N. 8th Street Sheboygan, WI 53081-4563	Ozaukee, Sheboygan	201,905	2,329,379	803,558
Indianhead Federated	L.E. Phillips Memorial Public Library (715) 839-5001	400 Eau Claire Street Eau Claire, WI 54701-3799	Barron, Chippewa, Dunn, Eau Claire, Pepin, Pierce, Polk, Price, Rusk, St. Croix	459,247	4,828,383	1,381,592
Kenosha County	Kenosha Public Library (262) 564-6324	812 56th Street P.O. Box 1414 Kenosha, WI 53141-1414	Kenosha	166,909	1,316,884	423,194
Lakeshores	Racine Public Library (262) 636-9170	75 Seventh Street Racine, WI 53403-1200	Racine, Walworth	285,966	2,365,545	638,963
Manitowoc-Calumet	Manitowoc Public Library (920) 686-3000	707 Quay Street Manitowoc, WI 54220-4539	Calumet, Manitowoc	117,246	1,041,029	369,762
Mid-Wisconsin Federated	West Bend Community Memorial Library (262) 335-5151	630 Poplar Street West Bend, WI 53095-3246	Dodge, Jefferson, Washington City of Whitewater	321,052	3,275,783	1,115,659
Milwaukee County Federated	Milwaukee Public Library (414) 286-3000	814 W. Wisconsin Avenue Milwaukee, WI 53233-2309	Milwaukee	950,500	7,466,758	3,525,161
Nicolet Federated	Brown County Library (920) 448-4400	515 Pine Street Green Bay, WI 54301-5194	Brown, Door, Florence, Kewaunee, Marinette, Menominee, Oconto, Shawano	428,346	3,715,012	1,072,315
Northern Waters Library Service	Superior Public Library (715) 394-8860	1530 Tower Avenue Superior, WI 54880-2563	Ashland, Bayfield, Burnett, Douglas, Iron, Sawyer, Vilas, Washburn	150,871	1,331,036	509,852
Outagamie Waupaca	Appleton Public Library (920) 832-6170	225 N. Oneida Street Appleton, WI 54911-4780	Outagamie, Waupaca	241,742	2,907,790	608,967
South Central	Madison Public Library (608) 266-6363	201 W. Mifflin Street Madison, WI 53703-2511	Adams, Columbia, Dane, Green, Portage, Sauk, Wood	821,491	12,640,652	2,048,358
Southwest Wisconsin	Platteville Public Library (608) 348-7441	65 S. Elm Street Platteville, WI 53818-3139	Crawford, Grant, Iowa, Lafayette, Richland	127,148	1,016,004	392,022
Waukesha County Federated	Waukesha Public Library (262) 524-3680	321 Wisconsin Avenue Waukesha, WI 53186-4786	Waukesha	391,592	4,946,857	958,636
Winding Rivers	La Crosse Public Library (608) 789-7100	800 Main Street La Crosse, WI 54601-4122	Buffalo, Jackson, Juneau, La Crosse, Monroe, Trempealeau, Vernon	281,119	2,936,057	773,874
Winnefox	Oshkosh Public Library (920) 236-5210	106 Washington Avenue Oshkosh, WI 54901-4985	Fond du Lac, Green Lake, Marquette, Waushara, Winnebago	326,167	4,389,564	1,300,887
Wisconsin Valley Library Service	Marathon County Public Library (715) 261-7200	300 N. First Street Wausau, WI 54403-5405	Clark, Forest, Langlade, Lincoln, Marathon, Oneida, Taylor	281,421	2,509,087	1,038,853
TOTAL				5,712,889	60,979,077	$17,400,258

Sources: Wisconsin Department of Public Instruction, Public Library Statistics, "Statistics at the State and System Level, 2013: 2013 Wisconsin Public Library Service Data", at: http://pld.dpi.wi.gov/pld_dm-lib-stat [February 4, 2015] and *Wisconsin Public Library Directory; 2014*, July 2014, at: http://pld.dpi.wi.gov/pld_lib_dir.

HIGHLIGHTS OF EMPLOYMENT AND INCOME IN WISCONSIN

Labor Force — There were 2,923,533 workers employed in Wisconsin in 2014. Another 170,385 were part of the available workforce but were unemployed, resulting in an average unemployment rate of 5.5% for 2014. Since 1990, Wisconsin's labor force has increased by about 546,000 thousand workers from 2,567,200 to 3,113,100 in 2014.

Employment by Industry — An average of 2.85 million Wisconsin workers were engaged in nonfarm employment in 2014. The greatest number worked in service providing (2,272,500); and goods producing (572,600).

Nationally, 138.8 million were employed in nonfarm work in February 2015. Trade, transportations, and utilities, with 26.3 million workers; and government, with 22.3 million, were the largest segments.

In March 2013, manufacturing and retail trade together accounted for approximately one-third of the number of employees in Wisconsin. The majority (84.1%) of the 137,983 business establishments in the state had fewer than 20 employees in March 2013. Manufacturing accounted for the greatest number of large-sized firms, 338 out of 1,124 establishments with 250 or more employees.

Income by Industry — Earned income, which consists of wages and salaries, labor income, and proprietor's income, totaled $184.1 billion in Wisconsin in 2014. Service industries provided the greatest percentage of Wisconsin's earned income during that year, about 32.9%, with manufacturing at 18.6%. Government (all levels) and government enterprises were third at 15.4%.

Personal Income — Personal income in Wisconsin totaled $256.7 billion in 2014. Wisconsin's per capita personal income of $44,585 lags behind the national average of $46,129, ranking Wisconsin 26th among the states. Connecticut had the highest per capita personal income ($62,467 in 2014, or about 135% of the national average). Mississippi had the lowest per capita personal income in 2014 at $34,333, about 77.4% of the national average.

Wisconsin's total adjusted gross income (total income reported for tax purposes) in 2013 was about $154 billion, or $50,670 per tax return. Ozaukee County had the highest per return AGI in 2013 at $93,280, followed by Waukesha County at $78,080. Eau Claire County is third ($68,660), and Dane County is fourth ($63,890). Rusk County ($33,620), Forest County ($31,280), and Menominee County ($15,600) had the lowest per return adjusted gross incomes.

Unemployment Benefits — During the fourth quarter of 2014, Wisconsin reported that 51,900 persons (about 36% of the 144,600 unemployed) received unemployment compensation. Nationally, 2.3 million people, or 27% of the 8.5 million unemployed, received benefits during an average month. The average weekly benefit in Wisconsin was $289.50, less than the national average of $317.93. The highest average weekly benefit of $443.89 was paid in North Dakota, followed by Massachusetts ($441.04), and Hawaii ($439.10). Lowest in the nation were Alabama ($214.34), Louisiana ($206.40), and Mississippi ($202.67).

The following tables present selected data. Consult footnoted sources for more detailed information about employment and income.

EMPLOYMENT IN WISCONSIN, BY INDUSTRY
Annual Average, 2010 – 2014

	2010	2011	2012	2013	2014
Civilian Labor Force.	3,081,512	3,080,399	3,074,255	3,084,978	3,093,918
Unemployed	267,119	238,934	216,661	208,266	170,385
Percentage of labor force unemployed . .	8.7%	7.8%	7.0%	6.8%	5.5%
Employed	2,814,393	2,841,465	2,857,594	2,876,712	2,923,533
Total nonfarm	2,725,000	2,751,800	2,780,500	2,809,000	2,845,100
Service providing	2,197,000	2,211,000	2,227,800	2,249,200	2,272,500
Goods producing.	528,000	540,700	552,700	559,700	572,600
Trade, transportation, and utilities	508,200	510,600	512,300	517,700	524,700
Manufacturing	430,500	445,000	455,600	457,500	464,800
Educational and health services	407,600	410,800	418,300	424,100	429,700
Local government	289,200	288,800	286,800	284,400	285,300
Professional and business services. . . .	274,300	287,700	294,300	301,700	306,400
Leisure and hospitality.	251,400	252,400	256,900	261,200	263,800
Financial activities	152,200	150,800	150,900	150,500	150,600
Other services, except public services . .	137,000	137,200	137,800	137,700	138,300
Construction	94,600	92,700	93,600	98,600	103,700
State government	99,200	96,600	95,000	96,100	97,200
Information	46,700	46,800	46,500	47,200	47,800
Federal government	31,400	29,400	29,000	28,600	28,700
Natural resources and mining	2,900	3,000	3,500	3,700	4,100

Note: Industry classifications in this table are defined by the North American Industry Classification System (NAICS), and are not directly comparable to the Standard Industrial Classification (SIC) codes used previously.

Source: Wisconsin Department of Workforce Development, Bureau of Workforce Information, Labor Market Information, "Local Area Unemployment Statistics (LAUS) Program Data", 2014, and previous years, at: http://worknet.wisconsin.gov/worknet/dalaus.aspx?menuselection=da [April 8, 2015], and "Current Employment Statistics (CES) Program Data", 2014, and previous years, at: http://worknet.wisconsin.gov/worknet/daces.aspx?menuselection=da [April 8, 2015].

MANUFACTURING EMPLOYMENT IN WISCONSIN
By Industry Group, 2008 – 2013

Industry Group	2008	2009	2010	2011	2012	2013
Fabricated metal products	69,673	59,580	58,349	63,015	66,169	66,970
Food	62,590	61,712	62,789	63,000	62,002	61,979
Machinery	63,545	55,865	53,951	57,541	59,668	61,571
Paper	31,046	28,389	29,590	29,848	29,307	29,568
Printing and related support activities	30,925	27,578	25,691	26,401	27,245	27,422
Plastics and rubber products	29,237	29,292	28,993	29,268	27,159	27,357
Transportation equipment	31,083	23,291	23,354	25,374	25,873	25,031
Electrical equipment, appliances, and components .	24,099	20,234	19,444	19,547	20,141	20,640
Computer and electronic products	22,318	22,872	21,333	21,529	21,721	20,257
Primary metal industries	20,162	15,363	16,657	18,503	18,940	18,726
Wood products	24,443	17,729	16,848	17,194	17,463	18,112
Furniture and related products	16,617	16,136	13,932	13,524	14,326	14,344
Chemicals	14,199	12,993	12,056	12,779	14,341	14,094
Miscellaneous manufacturing	14,062	14,136	14,571	14,855	13,232	11,733
Nonmetallic mineral products	9,600	8,211	7,829	7,809	8,345	8,498
Beverage and tobacco products	2,546	2,559	2,704	2,832	3,040	3,223
Leather and allied products	1,728	1,518	1,377	1,388	1,143	1,293
Textile products	1,286	1,106	1,237	1,184	1,147	1,181
Textile mills	1,680	1,068	1,095	1,104	1,126	1,137
Apparel.	—*	—*	—*	—*	815	761
TOTAL.	472,422	420,890	413,190	427,906	433,699	434,460

Note: Petroleum and coal products manufacturing is not a major component of manufacturing employment in Wisconsin and is excluded from this table.

*Industries with fewer than 950 employees not individually reported between 2008 and 2011.

Source: U.S. Census Bureau, "County Business Patterns by Employment Size Class, County Business Patterns 2013", and earlier editions, at: http://www.census.gov/econ/cbp/ [April 27, 2015].

EMPLOYMENT TRENDS IN WISCONSIN
January 1990 – January 2015 (In Thousands)

Month and Year	Civilian Labor Force*	Employed	Unemployed	Unemployment Rate	Total Nonfarm Employment	Service Producing	Goods Producing	Manufacturing	Trade, Transportation, and Utilities
Jan. 1990	2,567.2	2,437.8	129.4	5.0%	2,206.7	1,615.2	591.5	513.7	448.0
Jan. 1991	2,592.1	2,441.7	150.4	5.8	2,232.9	1,650.1	582.8	505.9	454.4
Jan. 1992	2,621.2	2,476.4	144.8	5.5	2,269.0	1,684.2	584.8	504.0	456.2
Jan. 1993	2,677.2	2,536.6	140.7	5.3	2,324.9	1,726.8	598.1	513.5	459.8
Jan. 1994	2,777.0	2,630.0	147.1	5.3	2,383.8	1,772.9	610.9	523.1	473.4
Jan. 1995	2,830.6	2,711.3	119.3	4.2	2,476.9	1,828.9	648.0	556.5	489.7
Jan. 1996	2,862.5	2,736.8	125.7	4.4	2,523.8	1,873.7	650.1	555.9	500.2
Jan. 1997	2,909.8	2,785.2	124.6	4.3	2,559.9	1,900.6	659.3	559.9	504.2
Jan. 1998	2,937.8	2,825.9	111.9	3.8	2,625.2	1,941.6	683.6	583.2	512.5
Jan. 1999	2,951.4	2,839.3	112.1	3.8	2,686.4	1,993.0	693.4	586.5	526.7
Jan. 2000	2,960.9	2,856.6	104.3	3.5	2,748.9	2,047.6	701.3	590.2	541.4
Jan. 2001	3,003.3	2,877.0	126.2	4.2	2,770.7	2,081.2	689.5	577.0	549.2
Jan. 2002	3,009.8	2,832.0	177.8	5.9	2,719.4	2,075.9	643.5	531.6	533.0
Jan. 2003	3,038.7	2,851.4	187.3	6.2	2,717.6	2,082.7	634.9	526.0	524.7
Jan. 2004	3,050.4	2,919.2	178.5	5.9	2,718.1	2,111.1	607.0	493.5	529.5
Jan. 2005	2,996.6	2,831.3	165.4	5.5	2,757.2	2,145.2	612.0	496.6	532.0
Jan. 2006	3,019.7	2,865.9	153.8	5.1	2,790.0	2,171.2	618.8	501.1	536.0
Jan. 2007	3,074.7	2,908.3	166.4	5.4	2,814.4	2,200.0	614.4	498.7	541.3
Jan. 2008	3,065.5	2,914.8	150.7	4.9	2,828.3	2,221.5	606.8	495.8	539.9
Jan. 2009	3,107.3	2,884.5	222.7	7.2	2,755.1	2,193.7	561.4	464.9	520.6
Jan. 2010	3,080.5	2,798.0	282.4	9.2	2,658.2	2,153.9	504.3	419.8	501.3
Jan. 2011	3,045.3	2,819.3	226.0	7.4	2,679.5	2,169.4	510.1	432.1	503.5
Jan. 2012	3,060.1	2,845.8	214.2	7.0	2,698.7	2,169.4	529.3	446.7	505.5
Jan. 2013	3,050.7	2,838.4	212.2	7.0	2,725.6	2,191.4	534.2	452.3	504.0
Jan. 2014	3,089.2	2,905.4	183.8	6.0	2,829.3	2,264.3	565.0	460.4	521.4
Feb. 2014	3,087.3	2,908.9	178.4	5.8	2,832.0	2,265.8	566.2	461.0	522.5
Mar. 2014	3,085.8	2,911.8	173.9	5.6	2,832.5	2,265.1	567.4	461.9	523.5
Apr. 2014	3,085.3	2,914.6	170.7	5.5	2,838.6	2,268.3	570.3	463.1	524.9
May 2014	3,086.7	2,918.1	168.6	5.5	2,838.6	2,267.7	570.9	464.3	524.2
Jun. 2014	3,090.0	2,922.8	167.2	5.4	2,843.7	2,271.8	571.9	464.2	524.1
Jul. 2014	3,094.6	2,928.4	166.1	5.4	2,845.1	2,271.9	573.2	465.2	524.7
Aug. 2014	3,099.5	2,934.3	165.2	5.3	2,851.0	2,277.3	573.7	465.1	524.5
Sept. 2014	3,104.2	2,939.7	164.5	5.3	2,846.8	2,272.3	574.5	465.4	523.9
Oct. 2014	3,108.0	2,944.4	163.6	5.3	2,858.1	2,282.1	576.0	467.0	525.6
Nov. 2014	3,111.0	2,948.4	162.6	5.2	2,869.0	2,289.2	579.8	468.9	526.6
Dec. 2014	3,113.1	2,951.4	161.8	5.2	2,872.0	2,290.9	581.1	469.1	528.3
Jan. 2015	3,120.8	2,964.4	156.4	5.0	2,877.0	2,290.1	586.9	472.3	526.1

Note: Data are estimates that are revised monthly and annually and are seasonally adjusted. Data from prior to 2014 have not been revised in this table. Industry classifications in this table are defined by the North American Industry Classification System (NAICS), and are not directly comparable to the Standard Industrial Classification (SIC) codes used previously.

*Civilian labor force includes both employed and unemployed persons, age 16 and over, and excludes current military personnel and other institutionalized individuals.

Sources: Wisconsin Department of Workforce Development, Wisconsin Worknet, "Current Employment Statistics, 2015 Monthly Reports", and previous editions, at: http://worknet.wisconsin.gov/worknet/downloads.aspx?menuselection=da&pgm=CES [April 8, 2015], and "Local Area Unemployment Statistics 2015 Monthly Reports", and previous editions, at: http://worknet.wisconsin.gov/worknet/dalaus.aspx?menuselection=da [April 8, 2015].

WISCONSIN PERSONAL EARNED INCOME
By Source, 2010 – 2014
(In Millions)

Industry	2010	2011	2012	2013	2014
Services[1]	$52,000	$54,378	$55,906	$58,645	$60,567
Manufacturing	29,824	31,672	33,064	32,231	34,244
Government and government enterprises	24,002	24,263	23,686	28,148	28,337
Finance and insurance	10,660	10,996	10,961	11,301	11,286
Retail trade	9,724	10,023	10,295	10,662	11,070
Construction	8,421	8,475	8,739	9,351	10,097
Wholesale trade	8,211	8,675	9,135	9,451	9,723
Transportation and warehousing	5,373	5,544	5,655	5,966	6,132
Information	3,295	3,431	3,565	3,879	4,142
Farm earnings	1,483	1,500	1,644	3,286	3,788
Real estate and rental and leasing	1,547	1,564	1,505	1,928	1,983
Utilities	1,944	2,983	2,805	1,638	1,649
Agricultural services, forestry, and fishing	453	476	536	508	651
Mining	190	209	233	313	366
TOTAL[2]	$157,126	$164,189	$167,730	$248,335	$256,699

[1]Services includes the following NAICS classification categories: Professional and technical services, Management of companies and enterprises, Administrative and waste services, Educational services, Health care and social assistance, Arts, entertainment, and recreation, Accommodation and food services, and Other services except public administration.

[2]Total may not add due to rounding.

Source: U.S. Department of Commerce, Bureau of Economic Analysis, "Table SA5N: Personal Income and Detailed Earnings by Industry – Wisconsin", at: http://www.bea.gov/itable/iTable.cfm?ReqID=70&step=1#reqid=70&step=1&isuri=1 [April 27, 2015].

DISTRIBUTION OF WISCONSIN BUSINESS ESTABLISHMENTS
By Number of Employees and Establishments, March 2013

Industry[1]	Total Employees[2]	Number of Establishments by Employment Size						
		Total	1 to 19	20 to 49	50 to 99	100 to 249	250 to 499	500 or more
Forestry, fishing, hunting, and agricultural support . . .	2,906	535	515	16	1	1	2	0
Mining	2,456	163	127	25	6	5	0	0
Utilities.	13,701	300	185	56	24	25	5	5
Construction	93,208	13,399	12,582	607	131	50	20	9
Manufacturing	434,460	8,830	5,358	1,534	887	713	224	114
Food	61,979	929	484	183	110	92	41	19
Beverage and tobacco products	3,223	135	111	9	9	4	0	2
Textiles	1,137	43	29	8	1	5	0	0
Textile products	1,181	117	106	6	3	2	0	0
Apparel	761	49	42	4	0	3	0	0
Leather and allied products	1,293	38	24	9	1	3	1	0
Wood products.	18,112	570	376	105	51	30	5	3
Paper.	29,568	231	55	53	42	49	24	8
Printing and related support activities.	27,422	733	526	92	58	36	14	7
Petroleum and coal products	563	22	14	6	1	1	0	0
Chemicals	14,094	348	193	88	41	17	5	4
Plastics and rubber products.	27,357	423	173	95	72	66	11	6
Nonmetallic mineral products.	8,498	385	292	56	18	14	4	1
Primary metal	18,726	172	57	33	32	29	11	10
Fabricated metal products.	66,970	1,910	1,206	355	177	136	31	5
Machinery	61,571	1,029	543	209	132	93	33	19
Computer and electronic products	20,257	237	113	44	36	30	7	7
Electrical equipment, appliances, and components . .	20,640	182	80	26	23	26	17	10
Transportation equipment	25,031	243	130	35	23	34	12	9
Furniture and related products	14,344	418	311	53	26	22	4	2
Miscellaneous manufacturing	11,733	616	493	65	31	21	4	2
Wholesale trade	112,855	7,033	5,711	868	272	149	25	8
Durable goods	70,507	4,206	3,326	603	182	79	12	4
Nondurable goods	37,650	2,028	1,614	248	84	68	11	3
Retail trade.	298,106	19,245	16,125	1,896	683	460	73	8
Motor vehicles and parts	36,375	2,427	1,979	275	131	39	3	0
Furniture and home furnishings	7,413	952	871	72	6	3	0	0
Electronics and appliances	7,422	944	889	24	23	8	0	0
Building materials and garden supplies	25,818	1,751	1,490	159	26	76	0	0
Food and beverages	52,654	2,051	1,478	199	219	146	9	0
Health and personal care	18,149	1,388	1,026	331	29	2	0	0
Gasoline stations	23,547	2,507	2,239	257	10	1	0	0
Clothing and clothing accessories.	21,007	2,112	1,849	215	46	2	0	0
Sporting goods, hobbies, books, and music	10,969	1,021	889	96	31	4	1	0
General merchandise	—[3]	859	458	58	118	169	56	0
Miscellaneous retail	14,718	1,962	1,785	149	28	0	0	0
Nonstore retailers (including online)	19,463	1,271	1,172	61	16	10	4	8
Transportation and warehousing.	93,997	5,171	4,263	549	198	122	19	20
Truck transportation.	48,066	3,458	3,002	287	102	50	8	9
Transit and ground passenger service	13,832	492	292	132	42	23	3	0
Support activities	7,200	549	486	47	11	2	1	2
Couriers and messengers	8,537	222	154	26	14	24	2	2
Warehousing and storage	14,420	309	216	40	22	19	5	7
Information	54,393	2,217	1,785	258	90	59	10	15
Publishing	18,970	509	382	78	20	23	3	3
Motion pictures and sound recording	3,185	262	213	35	11	3	0	0
Broadcasting.	5,973	188	129	28	20	9	0	2
Telecommunications.	16,313	967	832	87	26	12	4	6
Data processing, hosting, and related services . . .	8,698	210	156	28	8	12	2	4
Other information services	1,254	81	73	2	5	0	1	0
Finance and insurance	137,769	9,144	8,310	509	166	95	32	32
Real estate and rental and leasing	24,693	4,501	4,306	137	40	14	3	1
Professional, scientific, and technical services	100,940	11,388	10,410	654	189	108	18	9
Management of companies and enterprises	71,501	1,052	669	141	105	72	30	35
Administrative support and waste management	145,641	6,783	5,723	494	250	211	64	41
Educational services	56,023	1,574	1,179	255	77	38	5	20
Health care and social services	387,964	14,705	11,774	1,655	633	414	137	92
Ambulatory health care	126,935	8,313	7,183	710	250	112	39	19
Hospitals.	109,511	155	4	4	7	32	45	63
Nursing and residential care.	81,560	2,436	1,583	414	230	177	27	5
Social assistance.	69,958	3,801	3,004	527	146	93	26	5
Arts, entertainment, and recreation	41,824	2,683	2,261	256	87	59	18	2
Accommodations and food services	223,278	14,277	10,721	2,733	687	114	14	8
Accommodations	30,725	1,461	1,113	243	56	32	11	6
Food services and drinking places	192,553	12,816	9,608	2,490	631	82	3	2
Other services (except public administration)	105,079	14,712	13,746	751	159	50	4	2
Repair and maintenance.	21,445	4,228	4,081	123	19	5	0	0
Personal and laundry services	25,726	4,121	3,912	172	27	10	0	0
Religious, grantmaking, civic, professional, and like organizations	57,908	6,363	5,753	456	113	35	4	2
TOTAL[4]	2,401,032	137,983	116,021	13,394	4,685	2,759	703	421

[1]Industry categories and the total include subcategories not reported separately.
[2]Number of employees for the week including March 12, 2013. Excludes most government and railroad employees and self-employed persons.
[3]General merchandise retailers employ 50,000 to 90,000 in Wisconsin, but the exact number is unreported.
[4]Includes 271 unclassified establishments with 1 to 19 employees.
Source: U.S. Census Bureau, "County Business Patterns, Wisconsin: 2013", at: http://www.census.gov/econ/cbp/index.html [April 28, 2015].

EMPLOYEES IN NONAGRICULTURAL
Average by
(In

State	Total[1]	Other Services	Professional and Business Services	Education and Health Services	Manufacturing	Financial Activities
Alabama	1,930.5	81.0	225.9	228.0	252.8	94.6
Alaska	325.5	11.7	28.2	47.3	12.2	12.0
Arizona	2,628.0	94.4	392.5	392.1	156.5	191.9
Arkansas	1,198.6	44.2	135.9	174.5	153.0	50.0
California	15,859.8	545.7	2,494.2	2,470.6	1,257.6	795.5
Colorado	2,487.4	100.3	381.2	309.6	138.3	154.9
Connecticut	1,655.4	62.5	209.6	330.8	158.4	129.0
Delaware	433.1	18.2	59.8	73.2	25.6	46.2
Florida	8,016.9	334.7	1,189.6	1,196.1	331.4	529.2
Georgia	4,209.0	155.5	620.4	537.3	372.7	236.1
Hawaii	629.1	26.1	83.0	80.2	13.5	27.4
Idaho	656.8	22.9	77.1	96.0	60.0	33.9
ILLINOIS	5,810.5	250.6	904.6	898.8	574.8	365.8
Indiana	2,970.1	125.4	314.7	447.3	511.6	129.7
IOWA	1,540.1	59.8	135.2	226.6	215.1	104.1
Kansas	1,390.6	48.7	169.1	189.9	160.5	79.8
Kentucky	1,854.7	63.2	210.4	265.5	235.5	90.6
Louisiana	1,979.2	72.4	209.6	302.2	148.3	93.3
Maine	584.0	20.7	62.0	122.8	48.9	30.1
Maryland	2,602.4	110.9	419.8	436.2	101.5	143.6
Massachusetts	3,379.8	131.0	514.3	749.9	247.2	207.7
MICHIGAN	4,181.6	170.3	632.8	654.1	590.0	203.6
MINNESOTA	2,786.5	113.2	355.4	506.1	310.8	177.2
Mississippi	1,120.8	39.3	101.1	137.1	140.2	43.8
Missouri	2,722.6	113.9	350.2	441.2	258.2	165.5
Montana	443.6	17.5	39.3	69.5	18.4	26.3
Nebraska	986.9	38.2	112.3	151.1	96.4	72.5
Nevada	1,229.5	34.4	158.0	119.5	41.5	56.4
New Hampshire	641.3	26.0	71.9	117.6	66.5	35.7
New Jersey	3,913.3	169.4	609.9	643.4	240.7	243.2
New Mexico	826.2	28.3	101.3	131.0	28.1	33.1
New York	9,044.9	396.6	1,225.1	1,901.2	444.9	690.5
North Carolina	4,178.9	151.8	583.4	579.6	456.2	211.2
North Dakota	461.5	17.9	34.9	59.6	26.1	24.2
Ohio	5,283.8	208.2	694.0	899.3	679.1	287.4
Oklahoma	1,658.2	58.8	190.1	230.5	137.4	79.8
Oregon	1,735.9	59.3	223.2	258.2	181.7	91.8
Pennsylvania	5,746.3	253.6	749.4	1,202.2	564.9	312.6
Rhode Island	467.6	23.1	57.8	106.5	41.6	32.2
South Carolina	1,964.4	72.1	257.0	230.6	231.7	96.0
South Dakota	416.3	15.9	29.1	69.7	42.9	29.2
Tennessee	2,821.7	103.8	371.1	408.4	330.1	141.8
Texas	11,707.4	411.9	1,556.3	1,560.9	881.1	708.1
Utah	1,356.8	37.3	188.1	181.4	122.6	76.5
Vermont	314.1	10.4	25.6	63.7	30.3	12.4
Virginia	3,745.1	195.9	665.1	505.3	230.8	193.2
Washington	3,103.6	114.6	374.5	462.5	289.9	156.1
West Virginia	748.1	54.8	67.5	127.5	47.8	30.1
WISCONSIN	2,829.3	137.3	302.3	434.5	468.3	152.7
Wyoming	287.4	9.5	18.5	27.7	9.7	11.6
UNITED STATES[3]	138,865.1	5,463.2	18,982.3	21,854.8	12,183.3	7,940.1

[1]Includes mining and logging, not shown separately.

[2]Construction includes mining and logging for Delaware, Hawaii, Maryland, Nebraska, South Dakota, and Tennessee.

[3]U.S. totals calculated by Wisconsin Legislative Reference Bureau.

Source: U.S. Bureau of Labor Statistics "Table 6. Employees on nonfarm payrolls by state and selected industry sector, not seasonally adjusted", at: http://www.bls.gov/news.release/laus.t06.htm [April 22, 2015].

ESTABLISHMENTS
State, February 2015
Thousands)

Trade, Trans- portation, and Utilities	Con- struction[2]	Govern- ment	Leisure and Hospi- tality	Inform- ation	State
371.0	79.2	381.1	183.3	22.6	. . . . Alabama
62.4	14.9	83.1	30.1	6.3	. . . . Alaska
498.5	126.0	424.8	295.7	42.8	. . . . .Arizona
245.3	47.0	216.5	110.2	13.5	. . . . Arkansas
2,886.4	685.0	2,453.5	1,774.2	467.7	. . . . California
431.0	144.8	414.4	309.4	68.1	. . . . Colorado
297.5	49.4	241.7	144.4	31.6	. . . . Connecticut
77.6	18.9	65.9	43.0	4.7	. . . . .Delaware
1,655.8	410.6	1,103.2	1,125.5	135.1	. . . . Florida
884.4	155.7	694.5	436.0	107.5	. . . . .Georgia
118.1	31.6	126.7	114.2	8.3	. . . . Hawaii
131.8	35.0	122.0	65.4	9.3	. . . . Idaho
1,158.1	182.7	835.2	532.5	97.9	. . . . ILLINOIS
574.0	106.0	438.3	281.1	35.3	. . . . Indiana
311.2	66.2	262.8	132.3	25.0	. . . . IOWA
262.8	57.1	262.6	121.7	28.4	. . . . Kansas
375.3	69.2	324.2	179.8	25.6	. . . . .Kentucky
388.8	136.9	327.9	222.3	27.6	. . . . .Louisiana
114.6	22.3	101.2	51.6	7.3	. . . . Maine
449.1	146.6	513.4	243.6	37.7	. . . . .Maryland
549.4	113.4	469.2	311.0	85.9	. . . . Massachusetts
746.6	131.0	605.7	383.0	56.5	. . . . MICHIGAN
509.6	86.6	425.2	243.4	52.2	. . . . MINNESOTA
220.4	45.6	247.0	124.3	13.3	. . . . .Mississippi
516.7	102.7	444.6	268.3	57.5	. . . . Missouri
92.1	20.9	88.5	55.9	6.5	. . . . Montana
199.3	41.9	172.7	85.2	17.3	. . . . Nebraska
233.1	62.9	155.5	340.9	13.5	. . . . Nevada
135.1	21.0	92.9	62.0	11.8	. . . . New Hampshire
834.1	136.3	632.8	328.0	74.2	. . . . .New Jersey
137.9	41.3	195.1	89.6	12.6	. . . . New Mexico
1,539.4	305.2	1,446.1	827.2	264.4	. . . . New York
777.5	184.5	726.2	429.2	74.0	. . . . North Carolina
106.2	32.0	82.5	41.1	6.7	. . . . .North Dakota
984.8	169.1	765.5	510.3	71.5	. . . . Ohio
300.3	75.7	352.8	151.9	21.5	. . . . Oklahoma
323.5	76.7	303.6	178.5	32.3	. . . . Oregon
1,105.1	207.6	720.5	509.7	83.7	. . . . .Pennsylvania
73.1	13.7	60.5	50.3	8.6	. . . . .Rhode Island
375.2	84.9	363.4	223.4	26.4	. . . . South Carolina
84.9	19.3	78.4	40.9	6.0	. . . . .South Dakota
592.5	110.3	433.6	286.0	44.1	. . . . Tennessee
2,342.9	671.8	1,864.5	1,195.7	204.9	. . . . Texas
259.7	78.2	233.6	133.0	34.7	. . . . Utah
55.4	12.4	58.8	39.7	4.7	. . . . Vermont
635.7	175.1	714.4	351.2	69.5	. . . . .Virginia
570.3	164.1	565.1	290.7	110.0	. . . . .Washington
132.7	26.9	153.4	68.7	9.5	. . . . .West Virginia
515.0	92.2	423.0	251.4	48.7	. . . . **WISCONSIN**
55.1	20.8	72.0	33.0	3.7	. . . . .Wyoming
26,297.3	5,909.2	22,340.1	14,299.8	2,728.5	. . . . . UNITED STATES[3]

UNEMPLOYMENT, UNEMPLOYMENT RATES, AND UNEMPLOYMENT INSURANCE BENEFITS
By State, 2014

State	Rate[1]	Unemployment Persons (in thousands) Total	Insured[2]	Insured as % of Total	Unemployment Insurance Benefits Average Weekly	Total Paid (in thousands)
Alabama	5.8%	123.0	24.3	20%	$214.34	$52,630
Alaska	6.3	23.1	12.3	53	261.11	32,296
Arizona	6.5	201.8	29.7	15	223.56	72,160
Arkansas	5.4	70.2	22.8	32	294.53	56,319
California	6.9	1,314.1	397.1	30	302.95	1,330,362
Colorado	4.1	115.3	31.0	27	374.37	111,472
Connecticut	5.9	112.0	42.2	38	350.96	164,294
Delaware	4.9	22.2	6.9	31	249.95	18,352
District of Columbia	7.6	29.1	9.4	32	294.09	30,114
Florida	5.7	546.0	71.7	13	237.05	167,691
Georgia	6.5	309.1	42.3	14	268.59	109,571
Hawaii	4.0	26.7	9.5	36	439.10	41,655
Idaho	4.3	33.1	9.0	27	291.15	24,799
ILLINOIS	5.9	385.9	112.9	29	325.74	413,883
Indiana	5.7	187.0	29.6	16	252.07	84,956
IOWA	4.1	69.4	22.4	32	354.28	90,732
Kansas	3.9	58.0	18.1	31	357.60	63,216
Kentucky	5.1	101.8	23.3	23	298.17	73,991
Louisiana	6.7	146.6	19.0	13	206.40	40,883
Maine	5.2	35.7	9.1	25	289.35	26,008
Maryland	5.3	165.9	44.3	27	323.68	147,668
Massachusetts	5.0	178.3	75.5	42	441.04	349,730
MICHIGAN	5.9	278.6	66.2	24	271.23	180,998
MINNESOTA	3.2	96.4	48.4	50	394.88	172,117
Mississippi	7.0	85.8	14.0	16	202.67	28,748
Missouri	5.0	155.0	33.1	21	247.08	79,341
Montana	4.4	22.5	8.7	39	292.76	23,894
Nebraska	2.8	28.5	7.8	27	293.73	21,147
Nevada	6.9	97.0	26.9	28	317.52	92,220
New Hampshire	3.8	28.2	5.8	21	300.40	16,476
New Jersey	6.0	270.1	117.3	43	406.98	511,105
New Mexico	5.8	54.0	12.8	24	306.52	42,582
New York	5.7	538.2	181.0	34	313.95	583,307
North Carolina	5.3	245.1	40.4	16	232.47	81,510
North Dakota	2.4	10.2	4.1	40	443.89	18,278
Ohio	4.8	276.9	62.1	22	331.70	212,305
Oklahoma	4.0	71.5	15.5	22	324.28	51,513
Oregon	6.4	126.2	36.2	29	339.01	130,149
Pennsylvania	4.8	304.3	137.8	45	371.03	520,595
Rhode Island	6.4	35.3	9.5	27	335.90	34,661
South Carolina	6.5	142.3	17.8	13	253.82	37,359
South Dakota	3.2	14.2	1.9	13	293.86	5,560
Tennessee	6.3	186.9	26.5	14	224.39	68,425
Texas	4.4	576.5	134.5	23	359.65	499,247
Utah	3.2	46.8	10.8	23	352.42	37,339
Vermont	3.8	13.1	5.3	40	325.56	12,193
Virginia	4.6	194.8	35.7	18	300.74	106,606
Washington	6.1	213.9	58.5	27	401.91	243,315
West Virginia	5.6	43.5	14.3	33	287.82	44,664
WISCONSIN	4.7	144.6	51.9	36	289.50	136,994
Wyoming	4.2	12.8	5.3	41	359.88	14,072
UNITED STATES[3]	5.5%	8,547.0	2,280.6	27%	$317.93	$7,553,194

Note: Unemployment and unemployment insurance data includes Puerto Rico and U.S. Virgin Islands, not listed separately. Insured as percent of total calculated by Wisconsin Legislative Reference Bureau.

[1] Total unemployed as a percentage of civilian workforce in the state.

[2] Insured unemployed are unemployed persons receiving unemployment benefits.

[3] Because of separate processing and weighting procedures, U.S. totals may differ from the sum of state data.

Source: U.S. Department of Labor, Employment and Training Administration, "Unemployment Insurance Data Summary – 4th Quarter 2014", at: http://workforcesecurity.doleta.gov/unemploy/content/data.asp [April 15, 2015].

WISCONSIN ADJUSTED GROSS INCOME
By County, 2009 – 2013

County	2013 AGI[1]	Per Return AGI					2013 Rank[2]
		2009	2010	2011	2012	2013	
Adams	$331,668,160	$30,966	$31,993	$32,100	$33,350	$33,770	69
Ashland	271,763,260	32,309	32,470	33,770	34,750	35,290	66
Barron	966,684,250	35,198	38,045	40,800	40,580	41,420	46
Bayfield	325,143,770	37,355	37,119	39,040	40,780	42,220	42
Brown	7,010,267,940	49,849	52,449	52,610	54,560	55,140	8
Buffalo	272,637,460	34,552	35,429	37,730	39,980	39,520	50
Burnett	261,673,660	33,492	33,022	33,550	33,610	34,980	67
Calumet	1,291,246,680	52,883	54,140	55,780	59,140	57,920	7
Chippewa	1,340,882,600	39,541	41,431	41,700	44,560	44,880	35
Clark	584,498,990	35,250	36,119	38,430	41,570	39,430	52
Columbia	1,412,969,920	43,953	45,344	46,990	48,140	48,280	20
Crawford	280,420,250	32,250	33,404	35,600	36,190	35,350	65
Dane	16,859,703,550	55,453	57,050	59,040	61,470	63,890	4
Dodge	2,012,209,140	42,404	45,276	46,950	46,660	47,640	23
Door	733,559,350	39,535	41,728	42,140	46,320	48,040	22
Douglas	867,176,750	38,953	39,609	39,840	42,560	41,830	44
Dunn	847,310,090	40,234	42,064	42,720	44,150	44,090	37
Eau Claire	3,455,467,680	60,252	62,822	45,410	64,210	68,660	3
Florence	81,603,430	35,127	36,548	37,410	38,710	38,080	56
Fond du Lac	2,507,526,130	45,142	47,092	46,920	48,590	49,620	18
Forest	137,176,490	28,201	29,166	29,210	31,020	31,280	71
Grant	911,479,470	35,594	39,483	37,930	39,760	39,520	51
Green	916,975,660	42,223	44,874	46,650	48,330	49,770	17
Green Lake	433,237,320	38,273	40,440	42,660	48,960	45,690	30
Iowa	561,464,600	42,190	42,626	44,550	46,510	47,440	25
Iron	111,074,590	30,987	30,885	33,080	33,520	34,980	68
Jackson	385,777,870	37,312	35,278	42,800	49,120	40,680	47
Jefferson	1,906,864,770	43,678	44,439	45,260	46,600	47,080	26
Juneau	449,052,060	33,147	34,233	34,850	36,770	36,220	63
Kenosha	3,819,144,570	45,603	45,517	46,330	47,340	48,130	21
Kewaunee	468,927,560	40,569	41,963	43,900	45,880	46,160	29
La Crosse	2,924,455,700	46,518	47,408	48,580	49,590	51,070	13
Lafayette	332,372,130	34,737	37,307	39,920	41,530	41,610	45
Langlade	370,081,410	34,374	35,408	35,570	37,170	37,440	58
Lincoln	607,897,150	39,283	39,949	39,530	40,110	42,490	41
Manitowoc	1,892,192,830	41,826	43,569	44,940	46,180	46,460	28
Marathon	3,440,026,340	46,421	47,448	48,140	51,520	51,040	14
Marinette	807,894,420	35,455	36,974	37,990	38,740	38,700	55
Marquette	280,712,700	34,453	34,521	35,930	36,160	38,050	57
Menominee	23,041,300	14,881	15,226	16,130	17,250	15,600	72
Milwaukee	21,299,226,330	41,704	41,932	42,830	44,460	45,620	32
Monroe	845,678,140	37,473	38,490	40,010	40,340	39,850	49
Oconto	809,591,880	39,146	40,814	41,420	43,250	44,030	38
Oneida	828,906,550	40,674	42,412	42,040	44,440	43,460	39
Outagamie	5,110,565,710	49,434	51,151	51,180	52,920	55,050	9
Ozaukee	4,151,261,800	79,263	82,425	89,490	94,160	93,280	1
Pepin	169,678,740	38,866	42,771	47,420	49,810	46,990	27
Pierce	1,004,394,580	49,643	50,850	52,480	54,450	54,150	10
Polk	916,978,990	39,716	40,802	42,610	43,680	43,190	40
Portage	1,590,706,480	44,604	45,700	45,340	47,530	47,550	24
Price	257,922,440	33,948	42,428	35,410	36,550	36,340	62
Racine	4,803,317,630	46,215	47,358	48,530	52,220	49,890	16
Richland	296,420,140	33,397	34,422	35,710	37,230	36,940	61
Rock	3,607,410,540	44,326	43,766	43,120	44,410	45,690	31
Rusk	227,352,990	29,034	30,749	30,620	32,190	33,620	70
St. Croix	2,581,527,680	56,188	57,854	59,350	62,240	63,260	34
Sauk	1,488,880,850	39,684	40,535	40,960	42,400	45,000	64
Sawyer	286,975,660	31,607	33,140	33,600	35,220	35,780	53
Shawano	779,752,050	35,251	36,605	36,920	38,650	39,300	15
Sheboygan	2,939,924,290	45,992	46,388	47,820	50,630	50,220	5
Taylor	369,278,950	35,154	34,614	38,120	39,970	40,670	48
Trempealeau	794,139,430	43,009	46,328	46,960	48,910	52,530	11
Vernon	559,102,200	34,724	36,662	37,760	38,850	41,920	43
Vilas	411,791,030	36,181	34,812	33,470	37,650	37,280	59
Walworth	2,406,342,820	44,436	45,834	47,700	48,870	49,330	19
Washburn	306,042,020	31,643	35,325	34,590	35,740	37,050	60
Washington	4,095,635,970	54,610	55,966	57,580	60,720	61,020	6
Waukesha	15,787,768,600	68,711	71,071	73,460	76,390	78,080	2
Waupaca	1,165,908,960	40,929	41,208	42,240	43,240	44,250	36
Waushara	449,143,680	34,871	33,539	37,510	37,110	39,230	54
Winnebago	4,202,065,750	46,629	47,813	49,220	51,210	51,090	12
Wood	1,740,506,790	42,294	43,316	44,710	44,760	45,530	33
STATE[3]	$154,152,061,570	$45,372	$46,958	$47,640	$49,900	$50,670	

[1]"Wisconsin adjusted gross income" (AGI) is Wisconsin income as reported to the Wisconsin Department of Revenue for income tax purposes and is based on the federal income tax definition of gross income as modified by certain additions and subtractions required by state law.

[2]Rankings calculated by Wisconsin Legislative Reference Bureau.

[3]State totals and state per capita figures include amounts not allocated to a particular county.

Source: Wisconsin Department of Revenue, "Wisconsin Municipal Income Per Return Report, 2014" and earlier volumes, at: http://www.dor.state.wi.us/report/i.html [April 15, 2015].

EARNED INCOME BY INDUSTRY,
(In

State	Earned Income Total[1]	Rank per Capita[2]	Farm Earnings	Forestry, Fishing, and Related Activities	Mining	Utilities	Construction	Manufacturing
Alabama	$121,985.7	48	$1,144.9	$932.7	836.4	$1,725.4	$7,900.4	$17,182.0
Alaska	31,066.6	10	10.7	438.1	2,851.2	316.2	2,469.7	941.1
Arizona	175,779.4	42	970.6	516.9	1,450.7	1,683.4	9,916.7	13,922.9
Arkansas	71,205.8	44	2,074.0	662.0	1,031.5	915.1	4,060.4	8,908.3
California	1,409,978.7	11	16,403.0	9,258.1	7,087.1	9,685.4	66,768.1	133,083.6
Colorado	194,087.6	15	1,607.6	404.4	8,843.4	1,404.4	13,270.5	11,936.3
Connecticut	154,500.9	2	187.4	75.6	169.1	1,181.7	8,139.1	16,744.7
Delaware	32,234.0	1	262.5	NA	NA	287.8	1,786.2	1,961.4
District of Columbia	87,009.9	23	0.0	0.6	13.8	270.9	1,356.1	133.4
Florida	513,643.8	29	2,779.2	1,729.8	703.9	3,016.6	27,902.8	24,752.2
Georgia	295,587.9	41	3,230.2	1,009.7	591.8	2,434.6	14,765.8	26,821.5
Hawaii	47,232.2	21	321.7	70.1	38.6	589.3	3,438.4	852.6
Idaho	41,433.1	47	3,319.5	567.0	299.9	362.7	2,552.9	4,497.9
ILLINOIS	460,677.7	17	5,257.0	744.0	1,456.9	3,841.5	22,450.5	52,253.3
Indiana	184,443.0	40	2,817.5	680.5	1,200.3	1,764.7	10,916.8	39,313.6
IOWA	101,276.5	26	5,674.3	554.3	172.5	807.3	7,402.4	17,384.3
Kansas	95,738.9	24	2,987.6	716.2	2,538.7	1,116.6	5,425.0	13,093.5
Kentucky	115,368.5	45	1,790.2	401.9	1,807.2	746.6	6,653.5	16,615.9
Louisiana	139,911.7	31	1,373.6	684.1	8,234.4	1,089.8	13,238.0	13,603.5
Maine	36,415.0	32	224.2	555.9	17.4	211.6	2,378.4	3,561.2
Maryland	218,268.0	6	469.2	152.8	193.7	1,663.9	15,992.7	9,454.7
Massachusetts	302,926.3	3	143.6	400.2	225.9	1,806.1	15,743.5	25,854.4
MICHIGAN	280,071.4	37	1,873.0	603.4	1,179.0	3,010.8	13,784.6	47,140.5
MINNESOTA	199,514.4	16	2,677.7	624.1	954.0	1,776.0	10,949.2	25,628.0
Mississippi	65,780.7	51	1,342.9	689.5	1,387.5	799.6	4,391.4	8,441.0
Missouri	182,664.5	34	1,748.1	487.8	498.4	1,496.0	10,780.0	19,424.7
Montana	27,566.2	36	871.7	293.2	1,283.5	402.7	2,126.6	1,170.3
Nebraska	66,731.7	20	4,455.2	351.0	183.5	747.9	4,482.7	7,008.0
Nevada	78,925.3	38	233.7	51.9	1,712.4	551.6	5,388.6	2,896.0
New Hampshire	46,880.6	9	30.7	158.4	49.8	371.5	3,105.0	5,575.2
New Jersey	338,400.7	4	405.3	191.6	486.6	2,552.5	18,120.9	25,647.2
New Mexico	51,995.8	46	1,768.9	150.2	3,167.1	490.5	3,042.0	2,088.9
New York	845,916.0	5	1,956.4	491.5	1,236.3	6,068.4	36,974.6	36,879.3
North Carolina	284,240.4	39	3,598.2	981.2	242.7	1,880.5	15,080.7	32,547.2
North Dakota	32,771.1	7	1,090.0	201.3	3,659.4	477.1	3,378.2	1,633.2
Ohio	360,804.5	30	1,476.6	526.6	2,638.5	2,586.6	19,178.0	52,159.0
Oklahoma	119,341.4	28	1,303.2	357.1	15,625.9	2,044.3	7,509.2	11,023.2
Oregon	118,040.2	33	1,499.6	1,651.2	181.1	750.6	7,253.6	14,895.2
Pennsylvania	428,887.8	18	1,792.6	680.5	5,677.9	3,428.7	24,724.6	43,897.6
Rhode Island	34,527.5	14	17.8	NA	NA	166.6	1,811.2	3,019.3
South Carolina	120,078.1	49	442.0	476.4	106.1	1,533.2	6,764.0	16,888.3
South Dakota	28,174.1	22	2,867.7	224.2	92.8	216.3	1,753.5	2,790.9
Tennessee	195,584.5	35	547.2	450.0	398.7	373.3	12,392.8	23,471.7
Texas	945,517.5	25	4,693.7	1,960.1	87,637.1	9,679.1	72,560.7	85,770.2
Utah	85,983.5	43	411.0	93.1	1,478.9	531.3	6,464.7	8,696.0
Vermont	19,806.5	19	295.2	106.9	45.5	281.2	1,465.4	2,240.3
Virginia	293,105.2	12	632.7	455.4	1,484.8	1,625.6	15,612.3	17,152.9
Washington	250,191.6	13	2,978.1	3,007.1	238.2	613.7	15,265.9	27,601.0
West Virginia	43,785.3	50	19.8	117.9	3,698.3	629.4	2,915.2	3,820.0
WISCONSIN	184,104.7	27	3,787.7	650.6	366.2	1,649.0	10,097.1	34,243.7
Wyoming	21,696.9	8	402.7	75.3	3,981.1	310.7	2,081.5	836.4
UNITED STATES	$10,580,863.3		$98,268.1	$36,752.3	$179,506.9	$83,966.3	$603,981.9	$1,017,457.4

NA – Did not report due to concerns over disclosure of confidential information, but the estimates for this industry are included in the total.

[1]Includes wages and salaries, other labor income, and proprietor's income.

[2]Per capita rank calculated by the Wisconsin Legislative Reference Bureau.

[3]"Services" consists of the following NAICS industry categories: Professional and technical services; Management of companies and enterprises; Administrative and waste services; Educational services; Health care and social assistance; Arts, entertainment, and recreation; Accommodation and food services; and Other services, except public administration.

Source: U.S. Department of Commerce, Bureau of Economic Analysis, Regional Economic Accounts, 2012, Table SA5N, at: http://www.bea.gov/iTable/index_regional.cfm [May 1, 2015].

BY STATE – 2014
Millions)

Wholesale Trade	Retail Trade	Trans-portation	Information	Finance and Insurance	Real Estate and Rentals	Services[3]	Government Enterprises	State
$5,615.6	$8,347.8	$4,347.0	$1,594.2	$6,307.2	$1,962.6	$39,102.6	$24,987.0	. . . . Alabama
500.0	1,687.1	1,780.2	543.9	681.0	684.7	8,907.6	9,254.9	. . . . Alaska
8,669.7	13,541.5	5,373.2	3,726.6	12,818.6	5,302.2	67,985.3	29,901.2	. . . . . . .Arizona
3,692.6	5,078.8	3,662.1	1,062.3	2,843.6	1,194.8	23,725.1	12,295.2	. . . . . . Arkansas
66,590.8	80,248.1	38,322.8	83,453.7	78,288.1	44,604.4	536,685.2	239,500.4	. . . . . . California
9,918.2	10,680.2	6,103.8	10,453.4	12,471.0	3,118.9	72,992.5	30,883.0	. . . . . . .Colorado
7,114.0	8,716.8	2,932.8	4,215.4	22,992.0	2,997.3	58,124.7	20,910.4	. . . . . Connecticut
1,275.4	1,969.5	861.5	1,054.0	4,608.7	957.5	12,796.5	5,346.1	. . . . . . .Delaware
678.2	905.2	473.7	2,521.6	3,009.3	1,247.6	42,345.2	34,054.1	. District of Columbia
29,368.4	41,078.5	17,139.3	13,818.4	36,607.0	12,962.7	220,405.3	81,379.7	. . . . Florida
19,538.7	18,127.3	13,880.5	12,225.1	18,199.7	6,454.4	107,198.0	49,110.6	. . . . .Georgia
1,291.9	2,889.8	1,784.8	709.4	1,398.7	1,935.1	17,452.8	14,459.0	. . . . Hawaii
2,097.8	3,320.6	1,300.3	596.5	1,943.4	503.3	13,213.5	6,857.9	. . . . Idaho
29,783.9	23,956.4	19,719.2	10,806.9	39,499.4	6,947.3	179,836.2	64,125.1	. . . . . ILLINOIS
9,203.4	11,530.6	7,914.0	2,611.7	8,180.7	2,671.9	61,371.0	24,266.1	. . . . Indiana
5,413.8	6,186.9	3,811.9	1,779.0	8,728.4	1,183.7	26,661.4	15,516.3	. . . . IOWA
5,211.8	5,482.3	3,585.5	2,557.1	5,608.7	1,307.3	29,793.9	16,314.6	. . . . Kansas
5,449.2	7,250.8	5,983.3	1,912.5	5,972.4	1,588.4	36,191.8	23,005.0	. . . . . .Kentucky
6,069.1	8,814.7	7,349.8	1,778.0	5,319.8	3,824.9	45,935.1	22,596.8	. . . . . .Louisiana
1,536.1	2,999.8	980.9	511.2	1,975.8	722.8	14,372.1	6,367.7	. . . . Maine
8,011.8	12,042.5	5,182.3	7,379.1	12,120.1	4,686.3	88,186.0	52,732.9	. . . . . .Maryland
13,586.3	14,259.4	5,604.3	10,943.5	30,714.4	6,243.1	138,824.9	38,576.8	. . . . Massachusetts
15,228.1	17,238.7	8,424.7	4,997.2	13,650.7	4,406.0	107,767.0	40,767.6	. . . . MICHIGAN
12,840.1	10,914.8	6,048.1	5,298.6	16,733.8	3,795.8	75,269.4	26,008.7	. . . MINNESOTA
2,402.6	4,966.3	2,731.2	820.0	2,712.8	1,023.4	19,728.8	14,343.8	. . . . . .Mississippi
10,167.4	11,620.0	6,676.0	6,243.9	11,657.7	2,941.6	70,128.8	28,794.1	. . . . Missouri
1,256.8	2,266.0	1,189.4	393.4	1,201.7	464.3	9,119.2	5,527.3	. . . . Montana
3,262.2	3,797.9	4,848.5	1,291.5	4,694.2	837.3	20,145.1	10,626.7	. . . . Nebraska
2,913.1	5,708.1	3,425.7	1,096.9	3,157.0	1,539.1	36,910.7	13,340.4	. . . . Nevada
2,826.3	4,087.3	763.6	1,490.1	3,353.1	958.5	18,009.4	6,101.6	. . New Hampshire
23,504.8	21,383.9	11,712.0	11,256.4	27,370.3	5,690.8	137,587.1	52,491.3	. . . . . .New Jersey
1,441.0	3,505.0	1,507.8	790.4	1,700.1	748.3	17,789.8	13,805.9	. . . New Mexico
35,306.8	42,506.3	17,969.7	43,337.2	137,897.0	19,213.9	328,305.6	137,773.0	. . . . . . New York
14,850.0	17,790.6	7,621.8	6,858.0	26,418.8	4,059.0	98,000.2	54,311.5	. . . North Carolina
2,394.0	1,986.3	2,215.7	504.0	1,293.9	998.0	8,052.9	4,887.0	. . .North Dakota
19,781.5	21,840.4	12,681.3	6,124.8	20,326.5	9,081.8	138,238.4	54,164.4	. . . . Ohio
4,839.5	7,603.4	5,893.2	1,783.2	4,844.7	2,275.7	32,906.7	21,332.2	. . . . . Oklahoma
6,172.4	7,958.7	3,611.2	3,029.9	5,300.7	1,791.6	44,251.4	19,693.0	. . . . Oregon
21,625.6	24,295.9	15,427.6	15,717.2	28,988.5	7,018.7	177,813.8	57,798.8	. . . .Pennsylvania
1,520.4	1,985.8	603.7	1,161.0	2,946.6	577.9	14,808.8	5,834.3	. . . Rhode Island
5,448.9	8,708.7	3,353.8	2,146.1	7,599.0	2,158.6	39,814.6	24,638.3	. . . South Carolina
1,563.1	1,966.4	800.7	489.5	2,639.5	318.5	7,938.9	4,512.2	. . . .South Dakota
10,014.5	13,401.7	10,048.1	3,568.8	10,732.1	4,447.5	78,141.0	27,597.1	. . . . . . Tennessee
58,459.0	54,496.5	44,798.1	20,103.5	53,986.7	19,767.6	304,029.4	127,575.7	. . . . Texas
4,018.8	6,606.9	3,233.3	2,763.5	5,395.0	1,907.3	29,680.8	14,702.9	. . . . Utah
662.9	1,521.9	409.5	347.9	854.8	355.2	7,447.5	3,772.1	. . . . Vermont
10,249.0	15,454.9	7,787.4	8,547.3	15,085.9	5,464.4	125,156.2	68,396.6	. . . . . . .Virginia
11,974.2	17,604.1	7,727.9	18,631.2	9,854.9	4,832.7	82,780.6	47,081.9	. . . . .Washington
1,561.8	3,071.7	1,575.0	728.3	1,272.2	807.1	14,696.3	8,872.2	. . .West Virginia
9,792.8	11,070.4	6,132.5	4,141.6	11,285.8	1,983.0	60,566.8	28,337.4	. . . . **WISCONSIN**
790.0	1,226.7	1,168.5	242.1	581.7	576.6	4,666.3	4,757.4	. . . . . . .Wyoming
$537,484.5	$635,700.3	$358,479.3	$350,157.0	$753,823.8	$223,141.5	$3,951,858.0	$1,750,286.2	UNITED STATES

PERSONAL INCOME IN WISCONSIN
1929 – 2014

| | | | | | Per Capita Personal Income | | | | | |
| | Wisconsin | Wisconsin | | | | United States | | | | |
Year	Personal Income (in millions)[1]	Per Capita Amount	Annual % Change	State Rank	As % of National Average	Per Capita Amount	High[2]	State	Low	State
1929	$1,975	$673	—	18	96%	$700	$1,152	New York	$271	S.C.
1930	1,733	588	—	18	95	620	1,035	New York	202	Miss.
1935	1,416	461	—	19	97	474	722	Delaware	177	Miss.
1940	1,720	547	—	21	92	595	1,027	New York	215	Miss.
1945	3,499	1,182	—	22	96	1,237	1,644	Delaware	629	Miss.
1950	5,178	1,506	—	24	100	1,510	2,075	Nevada	770	Miss.
1955	6,899	1,875	—	21	98	1,911	2,527	Conn.	1,045	Miss.
1960	8,948	2,258	—	20	99	2,276	2,926	Conn.	1,237	Miss.
1965	11,803	2,789	—	22	98	2,859	3,583	Conn.	1,688	Miss.
1970	17,609	3,979	—	21	97	4,085	5,263	Alaska	2,617	Miss.
1975	27,810	6,086	—	25	99	6,172	10,683	Alaska	4,203	Miss.
1980	47,623	10,107	—	20	100	10,114	14,866	Alaska	7,007	Miss.
1985	65,709	13,840	—	28	94	14,758	20,321	Alaska	9,892	Miss.
1990	88,635	18,072	—	24	93	19,477	26,504	Conn.	13,089	Miss.
1991	92,124	18,557	2.7%	25	93	19,892	26,512	Conn.	13,702	Miss.
1992	98,917	19,683	6.1	24	94	20,854	28,362	Conn.	14,559	Miss.
1993	103,379	20,331	3.3	23	95	21,346	28,975	Conn.	15,290	Miss.
1994	109,927	21,413	5.3	23	97	22,172	29,693	Conn.	16,291	Miss.
1995	115,180	22,215	3.7	24	96	23,076	31,045	Conn.	16,885	Miss.
1996	121,718	23,273	4.8	25	96	24,175	32,424	Conn.	17,702	Miss.
1997	129,099	24,514	5.3	22	97	25,334	34,375	Conn.	18,550	Miss.
1998	138,667	26,175	6.8	20	97	26,883	36,822	Conn.	19,545	Miss.
1999	144,702	27,135	3.7	20	97	27,939	38,332	Conn.	20,053	Miss.
2000	153,548	28,570	5.3	20	96	29,845	41,489	Conn.	21,005	Miss.
2001	158,888	29,392	2.9	21	96	30,575	42,920	Conn.	21,950	Miss.
2002	162,866	29,937	1.9	21	97	30,804	42,521	Conn.	22,511	Miss.
2003	167,979	30,685	2.5	22	97	31,472	42,972	Conn.	23,466	Miss.
2004	177,154	32,157	4.8	22	98	32,937	45,398	Conn.	24,650	Miss.
2005	183,948	33,278	3.5	21	97	34,471	47,388	Conn.	24,664	Louis.
2006	192,818	34,701	4.3	22	96	36,276	49,852	Conn.	26,535	Miss.
2007	203,084	36,272	4.5	26	94	38,615	54,981	Conn.	28,541	Miss.
2008	209,999	37,314	2.9	28	94	39,751	56,248	Conn.	29,569	Miss.
2009	217,584	38,380	2.9	25	97	39,379	53,771	Conn.	30,278	Miss.
2010	218,564	38,432	3.0	28	95	40,584	56,001	Conn.	31,186	Miss.
2011	226,042	39,575	4.1	27	95	41,560	57,902	Conn.	32,000	Miss.
2012	232,129	40,537	2.4	26	95	42,693	58,908	Conn.	33,073	Miss.
2013	248,335	43,244	6.7	26	97	44,765	60,658	Conn.	33,913	Miss.
2014	256,699	44,585	3.1	26	97	46,129	62,467	Conn.	34,333	Miss.

Note: Alaska and Hawaii were not included in U.S. totals before 1950.

[1]Personal income includes all forms of income received by persons from business establishments; federal, state, and local governments; households and institutions; and foreign countries. Allowance is made for "in kind" income not received as cash.

[2]High shown is for the 50 states. The District of Colombia had per capita personal income of $75,329 in 2013, and $76,532 in 2014. For District of Colombia per capita personal income in previous years see footnotes in previous editions of this table.

Source: U.S. Department of Commerce, Bureau of Economic Analysis, Regional Accounts Data, "Table SA1, Annual State Personal Income", 2014, and previous editions, at: http://www.bea.gov/itable/iTable.cfm?ReqID=70&step=1#reqid=70&step=1&isuri=1 [April 10, 2015].

HIGHLIGHTS OF GEOGRAPHY AND CLIMATE IN WISCONSIN

Land and Water Area — According to the U.S. Census Bureau, Wisconsin encompasses 65,496 square miles, of which 54,158 square miles is land. At 11,339 square miles, Wisconsin has the fourth largest water area in the United States, behind Alaska, Michigan, and Florida. Based on land area, the largest county in the state is Marathon with 1,545 square miles; the smallest is Ozaukee with 232 square miles.

Lakes — The largest lake in Wisconsin is Lake Winnebago (206 square miles), which covers parts of three counties. The deepest natural lake is Green Lake in Green Lake County with a maximum depth of 236 feet. Most of Wisconsin's largest lakes are concentrated in the northern two-thirds of the state, and they include artificial bodies of water created by dams. Wisconsin has 15,074 documented lakes, of which approximately 40% are named. Green County has only five lakes while Vilas County has 1,318.

High Points — The state's highest recorded elevation is Timms Hill in Price County, at 1,951.5 feet. There are several other recorded elevations of at least 1,900 feet in Forest, Langlade, Lincoln, Marathon, Price, and Vilas Counties.

Temperature — In 2014, the annual statewide average temperature was 40.3° Fahrenheit. Across the state, average regional temperatures varied from 37.4° in the north central area to 43.6° in the southeast. In all regions of the state, average temperatures in 2014 were lower than normal temperature figures, which are the 30-year averages for the period 1981-2010, based on computations by the State Climatology Office.

Precipitation — In 2014, the total statewide average rainfall was 37.1 inches. Regional precipitation averages varied from a high of 39.6 inches in the northwest area to a low of 32.6 inches in the southeast area. All regions of the state except the south, rainfall totals in 2014 were higher than normal precipitation figures, which correspond to the averages for the period 1981-2010, according to the State Climatology Office.

The following tables present selected data. Consult footnoted sources for more detailed information about geography and climate.

WISCONSIN'S LARGEST WATER AREAS

Name	County[1]	Area in Acres
Lake Winnebago	Winnebago (also Calumet and Fond du Lac)	131,939
Lake Pepin	Pepin (also Buffalo and Pierce)	24,550
Petenwell Lake	Juneau (also Adams and Wood)	23,173
Lake Chippewa (Chippewa Flowage)	Sawyer	14,593
Lake Poygan	Winnebago (also Waushara)	14,024
Castle Rock Lake	Juneau (also Adams)	12,981
Turtle-Flambeau Flowage	Iron	12,942
Lake Koshkonong	Rock (also Dane and Jefferson)	10,595
Lake Mendota	Dane	9,781
Lake Butte des Morts	Winnebago	8,581
Lake Onalaska	La Crosse	8,391
Green Lake (Big Green)[2]	Green Lake	7,920
Lake St. Croix	St. Croix (also Pierce)	7,696
Lake Wisconsin	Sauk (also Columbia)	7,197
Beaver Dam Lake	Dodge	6,718
Big Eau Pleine Reservoir	Marathon	6,348
Shawano Lake	Shawano	6,215
Lake Wissota	Chippewa	6,148
Geneva Lake	Walworth	5,401
Lac Courte Oreilles	Sawyer	5,139
Puckaway Lake	Green Lake (also Marquette)	5,013
Lake Du Bay	Portage (also Marathon)	4,649
Lake Winneshiek	Crawford	4,635
Lake Winneconne	Winnebago	4,553
Willow Flowage	Oneida	4,217
Lac Vieux Desert	Vilas	4,017
Wigwam Slough	La Crosse (also Vernon)	3,988
Trout Lake	Vilas	3,864
Pelican Lake	Oneida	3,545
Fence Lake	Vilas	3,483
Long Lake	Washburn	3,478
Tomahawk Lake	Oneida	3,462
Lake Monona	Dane	3,359
Round Lake	Sawyer	3,294
Lake Kegonsa	Dane	3,200
Grindstone Lake	Sawyer	3,176
Rainbow Flowage	Oneida	3,153
Gile Flowage	Iron	3,138

Note: Wisconsin's largest water areas are limited to those that are named, as determined by the Wisconsin Geographic Names Council.

[1]County listed first contains the water's source of origin. Other counties covered by the water area are shown in parentheses.

[2]Green Lake is Wisconsin's deepest natural lake with a maximum depth of 236 feet. Including artificial water areas, Wazee Lake is Wisconsin's deepest lake with a maximum depth of 350 feet.

Source: Wisconsin Department of Natural Resources, departmental data, at: http://dnr.wi.gov/lakes/lakepages/Results.aspx [June 2015].

LAND AND INLAND LAKE AREA OF WISCONSIN COUNTIES

County	Total Land Area Acres[2]	Rank	Inland Lakes[1] Number[2]	Number Rank	Acres[2]	Acres Rank
Adams	413,213	43	46	43	2,302	53
Ashland	668,822	11	157	23	5,936	38
Barron	552,135	24	369	17	17,748	15
Bayfield	945,832	2	962	4	22,629	9
Brown	339,013	56	22	61	170	71
Buffalo	429,846	42	8	69	196	70
Burnett	525,982	28	509	8	31,258	7
Calumet	203,671	68	8	70	98	72
Chippewa	645,358	13	449	11	20,027	13
Clark	774,282	7	32	54	1,076	58
Columbia	489,939	34	56	41	3,095	49
Crawford	365,222	52	77	34	6,243	35
Dane	766,233	8	63	37	21,788	11
Dodge	560,400	22	29	56	14,246	20
Door	308,466	59	25	60	3,254	48
Douglas	834,647	4	431	14	14,113	21
Dunn	544,067	26	20	63	3,953	43
Eau Claire	408,309	44	20	64	2,838	52
Florence	312,445	58	259	19	7,261	32
Fond du Lac	460,514	40	41	44	1,650	55
Forest	649,003	12	824	6	22,531	10
Grant	733,983	9	33	51	1,569	56
Green	373,732	50	5	72	350	63
Green Lake	223,640	65	36	49	17,120	16
Iowa	488,051	35	15	66	685	60
Iron	485,231	36	494	10	29,368	8
Jackson	632,141	15	135	26	5,004	40
Jefferson	356,143	53	33	52	3,710	44
Juneau	490,832	33	57	39	45,950	5
Kenosha	174,074	69	34	50	3,674	45
Kewaunee	219,212	66	15	67	251	66
La Crosse	289,079	61	19	65	8,568	30
Lafayette	405,496	46	8	71	620	61
Langlade	557,210	23	841	5	9,122	28
Lincoln	562,543	21	729	7	15,585	17
Manitowoc	377,013	48	101	31	1,492	57
Marathon	988,789	1	194	22	19,762	14
Marinette	895,582	3	442	12	13,735	22
Marquette	291,585	60	93	32	5,736	39
Menominee	228,869	64	128	28	4,044	42
Milwaukee	154,497	70	41	45	197	69
Monroe	576,496	19	119	29	3,433	47
Oconto	638,712	14	378	16	11,053	26
Oneida	712,301	10	1,129	2	68,447	3
Outagamie	408,015	45	33	53	213	68
Ozaukee	149,169	71	38	46	703	59
Pepin	148,469	72	29	57	278	64
Pierce	367,198	51	38	47	6,016	37
Polk	584,936	17	437	13	20,900	12
Portage	512,434	29	137	25	12,215	24
Price	802,800	6	388	15	15,048	19
Racine	212,801	67	22	62	3,030	51
Richland	375,137	49	9	68	251	67
Rock	459,611	41	75	35	11,159	25
Rusk	584,694	18	250	20	7,854	31
St. Croix	462,291	39	63	38	3,653	46
Sauk	531,777	27	28	58	10,993	27
Sawyer	804,675	5	495	9	56,587	4
Shawano	571,557	20	134	27	8,912	29
Sheboygan	327,210	57	69	36	2,106	54
Taylor	623,921	16	284	18	6,183	36
Trempealeau	469,097	38	26	59	409	62
Vernon	506,611	32	57	40	256	65
Vilas	548,227	25	1,318	1	93,889	2
Walworth	355,281	54	37	48	12,798	23
Washburn	510,152	30	964	3	31,265	6
Washington	275,650	63	53	42	3,072	50
Waukesha	351,727	55	117	30	15,133	18
Waupaca	478,536	37	240	21	7,152	33
Waushara	400,738	47	138	24	4,623	41
Winnebago	278,072	62	30	55	169,755	1
Wood	507,595	31	78	33	6,245	34
STATE	34,660,994		15,074		982,574	

[1]Lake Superior and Lake Michigan not included in totals.

[2]Land area statistics reported by the U.S. Census Bureau; lake statistics provided by Wisconsin Department of Natural Resources.

Sources: Wisconsin Department of Natural Resources, *Wisconsin Lakes, 2009*, at: http://dnr.wi.gov/lakes/lakebook/wilakes2009bma.pdf; U.S. Department of Commerce, U.S. Census Bureau, 2010 Census of Population and Housing, *Summary Population and Housing Characteristics, Wisconsin*, Table 16. Rank calculated by Wisconsin Legislative Reference Bureau. State totals may not add due to rounding.

WISCONSIN'S HIGH POINTS

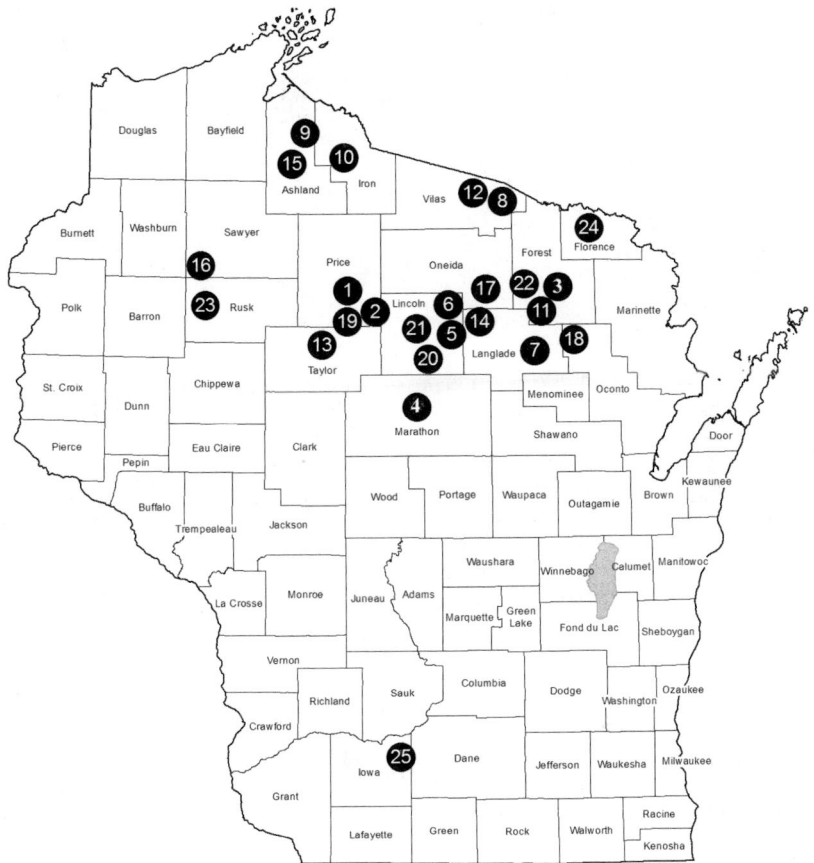

Rank	Name	County	Elevation in Feet
1	Timms Hill	Price	1,951.5
2	Pearson Hill	Price	1,951.0
3	Sugarbush Hill	Forest	1,939.0
4	Rib Mountain	Marathon	1,924.0
5	Lookout Mountain	Lincoln	1,920.0
6	Harrison Hills	Lincoln	1,910.0
7	Kent Tower Hill	Langlade	1,903.0
8	Unnamed	Vilas	1,905.0
9	Mount Whittlesey	Ashland	1,872.0
10	Penokee Range	Iron	1,860.0
11	East Hill	Forest	1,850.0
12	Military Hill	Vilas	1,848.0
13	Unnamed	Taylor	1,831.0
14	Baldy Hill	Langlade	1,820.0
15	Gogebic Range	Ashland	1,820.0
16	Meteor Hill	Sawyer	1,801.0
17	Unnamed	Oneida	1,800.0
18	Carter Hills	Oconto	1,781.0
19	Spokes Hill	Price	1,780.0
20	Irma Hill	Lincoln	1,770.0
21	Chase Hill	Lincoln	1,760.0
22	West Hill	Forest	1,750.0
23	Blue Hills	Rusk	1,750.0
24	Unnamed	Florence	1,730.0
25	West Blue Mound	Iowa	1,719.0

Note: Elevations are not field verified. The highest points for individual counties are available on the Wisconsin State Cartographer's Office Web site, at: http://www.sco.wisc.edu/mapping-topics/wisconsin-high-points.html.
Source: Wisconsin State Cartographer's Office, departmental data, June 2015.

WISCONSIN TEMPERATURES AND PRECIPITATION,
By Region and Month, 2014

	Jan.	Feb.	Mar.	Apr.	May	June	July	Aug.	Sept.	Oct.	Nov.	Dec.	Annual[1]
Statewide													
2014 Temperature (°F)...	6.0	7.4	21.5	39.7	55.3	66.4	65.9	67.2	58.2	46.0	25.3	24.1	40.3
Normal Temperature[2] ...	15.0	19.6	30.5	44.0	55.3	64.7	69.1	67.1	58.7	46.5	33.1	19.4	43.6
2014 Precipitation (inches)	1.13	1.27	1.10	5.04	3.80	6.71	2.51	5.20	3.86	3.07	2.02	1.36	37.07
Normal Precipitation[2] ...	1.09	1.02	1.79	2.93	3.53	4.21	4.02	4.01	3.73	2.82	2.16	1.40	32.70
Regions[3]													
Northwest													
2014 Temperature	2.6	4.7	19.1	36.6	53.6	64.2	65.8	65.9	56.9	44.5	22.0	21.6	38.1
Normal Temperature....	11.6	16.6	28.3	42.4	54.1	63.2	68.0	65.9	57.1	44.7	30.4	16.3	41.6
2014 Precipitation	1.04	1.50	1.16	4.92	5.20	6.67	2.75	5.81	4.96	2.18	2.11	1.30	39.60
Normal Precipitation....	0.95	0.88	1.64	2.65	3.36	4.09	4.08	4.01	3.97	3.06	1.95	1.20	31.84
North Central													
2014 Temperature	2.7	4.5	17.4	36.1	53.4	64.4	63.6	64.2	55.6	43.7	22.2	20.7	37.4
Normal Temperature....	12.3	16.7	27.5	41.6	53.4	62.5	66.8	64.9	56.4	44.1	30.6	16.9	41.1
2014 Precipitation	1.36	1.39	1.06	4.31	4.16	5.74	3.07	5.25	5.39	3.31	2.71	1.71	39.46
Normal Precipitation....	1.09	0.94	1.68	2.62	3.39	4.04	3.95	3.81	4.01	3.10	2.08	1.37	32.10
Northeast													
2014 Temperature	4.9	6.6	18.3	37.2	53.4	64.4	64.1	64.5	56.6	44.5	24.3	22.0	38.4
Normal Temperature....	14.1	18.2	28.4	42.0	53.4	62.9	67.2	65.4	57.0	44.8	32.0	18.9	42.0
2014 Precipitation	1.32	1.21	1.05	3.64	2.85	4.25	1.76	5.13	5.68	3.67	2.55	1.80	34.91
Normal Precipitation....	1.12	0.96	1.72	2.57	3.23	3.77	3.68	3.46	3.61	3.03	2.13	1.43	30.71
West Central													
2014 Temperature	6.3	6.5	23.1	41.3	56.6	68.4	67.7	69.5	59.7	46.9	25.4	24.1	41.3
Normal Temperature....	14.8	19.8	31.6	45.7	56.8	66.2	70.6	68.3	59.7	47.3	33.1	18.9	44.4
2014 Precipitation	1.25	1.36	0.91	6.01	4.08	8.78	2.79	5.59	3.30	2.88	1.46	1.05	39.46
Normal Precipitation....	0.95	0.90	1.81	3.13	3.78	4.44	4.25	4.49	3.87	2.56	2.06	1.22	33.44
Central													
2014 Temperature	7.5	8.7	23.2	41.6	56.6	68.5	66.5	68.5	59.3	46.4	26.7	25.2	41.6
Normal Temperature....	16.1	20.8	31.6	45.2	56.3	65.7	69.9	67.8	59.4	47.1	34.0	20.3	44.5
2014 Precipitation	1.13	1.12	1.10	5.85	3.16	6.08	1.94	6.33	2.52	3.31	1.67	1.44	35.65
Normal Precipitation....	1.01	1.00	1.76	3.00	3.60	4.35	4.04	4.03	3.61	2.54	2.12	1.34	32.41
East Central													
2014 Temperature	8.9	10.3	23.0	40.7	54.7	65.4	65.9	67.3	59.1	47.6	28.7	26.9	41.5
Normal Temperature....	17.8	21.6	31.5	44.1	54.8	64.8	69.4	67.8	59.8	47.7	35.3	22.4	44.8
2014 Precipitation	1.00	1.03	0.99	5.22	3.47	6.84	2.01	4.96	3.15	3.47	2.27	1.30	35.71
Normal Precipitation....	1.27	1.12	1.78	2.86	3.26	3.87	3.67	3.59	3.38	2.69	2.27	1.53	31.29
Southwest													
2014 Temperature	9.2	9.5	26.0	44.3	58.1	69.6	67.4	70.2	60.7	48.2	28.4	27.5	43.3
Normal Temperature....	17.8	22.8	34.1	46.9	57.7	67.3	71.4	69.3	61.1	48.9	35.6	21.9	46.2
2014 Precipitation	0.88	1.14	1.44	6.44	2.46	8.00	2.24	4.00	2.22	3.34	1.26	1.22	34.64
Normal Precipitation....	1.10	1.15	2.00	3.56	4.02	4.83	4.44	4.52	3.46	2.56	2.36	1.50	35.50
South Central													
2014 Temperature	9.6	11.2	25.5	44.3	58.1	69.1	67.4	69.8	60.5	48.9	29.0	28.1	43.5
Normal Temperature....	18.8	23.4	34.1	46.8	57.7	67.4	71.5	69.4	61.3	49.2	36.5	23.0	46.6
2014 Precipitation	0.86	1.04	1.13	5.15	3.31	8.07	2.61	4.39	2.16	3.08	1.70	1.03	34.53
Normal Precipitation....	1.23	1.31	2.02	3.37	3.71	4.63	4.09	4.18	3.50	2.69	2.43	1.70	34.87
Southeast													
2014 Temperature	10.9	13.0	26.0	43.8	56.9	66.9	67.0	69.2	60.6	49.3	30.0	29.4	43.6
Normal Temperature....	20.2	24.4	34.3	46.1	56.6	66.6	71.2	69.6	61.7	49.7	37.4	24.5	46.9
2014 Precipitation	1.11	1.30	1.06	3.99	4.19	6.79	2.93	3.89	1.77	2.82	1.82	0.93	32.60
Normal Precipitation....	1.47	1.41	1.98	3.42	3.61	4.04	3.78	4.02	3.42	2.74	2.54	1.86	34.30

[1]Annual temperature reflects the average of the monthly figures; annual precipitation is the total for the year.

[2]Normal temperatures and normal precipitation are the 30-year averages for the period 1981-2010, based on data computed by the State Climatology Office. These numbers are adjusted from previous Blue Books using a new algorithm starting in early spring of 2014.

[3]The counties in each region are:

Northwest — Barron, Bayfield, Burnett, Chippewa, Douglas, Polk, Rusk, Sawyer, and Washburn.

North Central — Ashland, Clark, Iron, Lincoln, Marathon, Oneida, Price, Taylor, and Vilas.

Northeast — Florence, Forest, Langlade, Marinette, Menominee, Oconto, and Shawano.

West Central — Buffalo, Dunn, Eau Claire, Jackson, La Crosse, Monroe, Pepin, Pierce, St. Croix, and Trempealeau.

Central — Adams, Green Lake, Juneau, Marquette, Portage, Waupaca, Waushara, and Wood.

East Central — Brown, Calumet, Door, Fond du Lac, Kewaunee, Manitowoc, Outagamie, Sheboygan, and Winnebago.

Southwest — Crawford, Grant, Iowa, Lafayette, Richland, Sauk, and Vernon.

South Central — Columbia, Dane, Dodge, Green, Jefferson, and Rock.

Southeast — Kenosha, Milwaukee, Ozaukee, Racine, Walworth, Washington, and Waukesha.

Source: Wisconsin State Climatology Office, departmental data, May 2015.

HIGHLIGHTS OF HISTORY IN WISCONSIN

History — On May 29, 1848, Wisconsin became the 30th state in the Union, but the state's written history dates back more than 300 years to the time when the French first encountered the diverse Native Americans who lived here. In 1634, the French explorer Jean Nicolet landed at Green Bay, reportedly becoming the first European to visit Wisconsin. The French ceded the area to Great Britain in 1763, and it became part of the United States in 1783. First organized under the Northwest Ordinance, the area was part of various territories until creation of the Wisconsin Territory in 1836.

Since statehood, Wisconsin has been a wheat farming area, a lumbering frontier, and a preeminent dairy state. Tourism has grown in importance, and industry has concentrated in the eastern and southeastern part of the state.

Politically, the state has enjoyed a reputation for honest, efficient government. It is known as the birthplace of the Republican Party and the home of Robert M. La Follette, Sr., founder of the progressive movement.

Political Balance — After being primarily a one-party state for most of its existence, with the Republican and Progressive Parties dominating during portions of the state's first century, Wisconsin has become a politically competitive state in recent decades. The Republicans gained majority control in both houses in the 1995 Legislature, an advantage they last held during the 1969 session. Since then, control of the senate has changed several times. In 2009, the Democrats gained control of both houses for the first time since 1993; both houses returned to Republican control in 2011.

Scott Walker's victory in the 2010 gubernatorial race placed the governor's office in Republican hands after the 8-year tenure of Democrat Jim Doyle. Since 1958, a year that marked an end to GOP dominance in state politics, the Republicans have won the governor's office 10 times, and the Democrats 8 times. In the last 50 years, Wisconsin's two main urban areas – Milwaukee and Madison – have provided over half of the state's constitutional officers. During this period, 11 women have served as constitutional officers: three as lieutenant governor, one as attorney general, two as secretary of state, three as state treasurer, and two as superintendent of public instruction.

National Office — Although the Democratic candidate has carried Wisconsin six times in a row, presidential elections in the state tend to be close. In fact, in 2008 Barack Obama became the first candidate to win a majority (56%) of the presidential vote since 1988; he duplicated that feat in 2012 with just under 53%. This has resulted in Wisconsin being regarded as a hotly contested "swing state" in many recent presidential elections.

Wisconsin voters tend to retain their U.S. Senators in office for long periods of time. Since 1900, seven senators have served three terms or more, topped by Senator William Proxmire's 32 years in office. Democrats have usually held both of Wisconsin's U.S. Senate seats over the past 50 years, but currently each party holds one seat.

Currently, five Republicans and three Democrats represent Wisconsin in the U.S. House of Representatives. Only one of the current members has been elected more than 10 times in regular elections. Democrats held the majority of seats from 1973 to 1991. The Republicans held the majority from 1991 to 1997, but lost it to the Democrats again in 1997. The Congressional delegation was evenly divided from 2003 to 2007. Democrats regained the majority in 2007, but Republicans won it back in the 2010 election and have held it since. Certain congressional districts have traditionally been represented by one party or the other with little relationship to statewide politics.

Voter Turnout — Turnout in presidential and gubernatorial elections may vary as much as a half million votes from election to election. Although individual elections have been up and down, the trend has been upward. Over 3 million votes were cast in the last presidential election.

Supreme Court — Although justices of the Wisconsin Supreme Court are elected officials, they sometimes are first named to the court by gubernatorial appointment to fill a vacancy. Subsequently, the appointees must be elected to the office if they wish to stay on the court; most have been successful. Among the current seven justices, two came to the court by the appointment route. The first woman justice to serve on the court, Shirley S. Abrahamson, was appointed in 1976. Today, women constitute a majority of the court.

SIGNIFICANT EVENTS IN WISCONSIN HISTORY

Under the Flag of France

Although American Indians lived in the area of present-day Wisconsin for several thousand years before the arrival of the French – numbering about 20,000 when the French arrived – the written history of the state began with the accounts of French explorers. The French explored the area, named places and established trading posts, but left relatively little mark on it. They were interested in the fur trade, rather than agricultural settlement, and were never present in large numbers.

1634 — Jean Nicolet: First known European to reach Wisconsin. Sought Northwest Passage.

1654-59 — Pierre Esprit Radisson and Medart Chouart des Groseilliers: First of the fur traders in Wisconsin.

1661 — Father Rene Menard: First missionary to Wisconsin Indians.

1665 — Father Claude Allouez founded mission at La Pointe.

1666 — Nicholas Perrot opened fur trade with Wisconsin Indians.

1672 — Father Allouez and Father Louis Andre built St. Francois Xavier mission at De Pere.

1673 — Louis Jolliet and Father Jacques Marquette discovered Mississippi River.

1678 — Daniel Greysolon Sieur du Lhut (Duluth) explored western end of Lake Superior.

1685 — Perrot made Commandant of the West.

1690 — Perrot discovered lead mines in Wisconsin and Iowa.

1701-38 — Fox Indian Wars.

1755 — Wisconsin Indians, under Charles Langlade, helped defeat British General Braddock.

1763 — Treaty of Paris. Wisconsin became part of British colonial territory.

Under the Flag of England

Wisconsin experienced few changes under British control. It remained the western edge of European penetration into the American continent, important only because of the fur trade. French traders plied their trade and British and colonial traders began to appear, but Europeans continued to be visitors rather than settlers.

1761 — Fort at Green Bay accepted by English.

1763 — Conspiracy of Pontiac. Two Englishmen killed by Indians at Muscoda.

1764 — Charles Langlade settled at Green Bay. First permanent settlement.

1766 — Jonathan Carver visited Wisconsin seeking Northwest Passage.

1774 — Quebec Act made Wisconsin a part of Province of Quebec.

1781 — Traditional date of settlement at Prairie du Chien.

1783 — Second Treaty of Paris. Wisconsin became United States territory.

Achieving Territorial Status

In spite of the Treaty of Paris, Wisconsin remained British in all but title until after the War of 1812. In 1815, the American army established control. Gradually, Indian title to the southeastern half of the state was extinguished. Lead mining brought the first heavy influx of settlers and ended the dominance of the fur trade in the economy of the area. The lead mining period ran from about 1824 to 1861. Almost half of the 11,683 people who lived in the territory in 1836 were residents of the lead mining district in the southwestern corner of the state.

1787 — Under the Northwest Ordinance of 1787, Wisconsin was made part of the Northwest Territory. The governing units for the Wisconsin area prior to statehood were:

1787-1800 — Northwest Territory.

1800-1809 — Indiana Territory.

1809-1818 — Illinois Territory.

1818-1836 — Michigan Territory.

1836-1848 — Wisconsin Territory.

1795 — Jacques Vieau established trading posts at Kewaunee, Manitowoc, and Sheboygan. Made headquarters at Milwaukee.

1804 — William Henry Harrison's treaty with Indians at St. Louis. United States extinguished Indian title to lead region (a cause of Black Hawk War).

1814 — Fort Shelby built at Prairie du Chien. Captured by English and name changed to Fort McKay.

1815 — War with England concluded. Fort McKay abandoned by British.

1816 — Fort Shelby rebuilt at Prairie du

Chien (renamed Fort Crawford). Astor's American Fur Company began operations in Wisconsin.

1818 — Solomon Juneau bought trading post of Jacques Vieau at Milwaukee.

1820 — Rev. Jedediah Morse preached first Protestant sermon in Wisconsin at Fort Howard (Green Bay) July 9. Henry Schoolcraft, James Duane Doty, Lewis Cass made exploration trip through Wisconsin.

1822 — New York Indians (Oneida, Stockbridge, Munsee, and Brothertown) moved to Wisconsin. First mining leases in southwest Wisconsin.

1825 — Indian Treaty established tribal boundaries.

1826-27 — Winnebago Indian War. Surrender of Chief Red Bird.

1828 — Fort Winnebago begun at Portage.

1832 — Black Hawk War.

1833 — Land treaty with Indians cleared southern Wisconsin land titles. First newspaper, *Green Bay Intelligencer,* established.

General Frederick Salomon. (Wisconsin Veterans Museum)

1834 — Land offices established at Green Bay and Mineral Point. First public road laid out.

1835 — First steamboat arrived at Milwaukee. First bank in Wisconsin opened at Green Bay.

1836 — Act creating Territory of Wisconsin signed April 20 by President Andrew Jackson. (Provisions of Ordinance of 1787 made part of the act.)

Wisconsin Territory

Wisconsin's population reached 305,000 by 1850. About half of the new immigrants were from New York and New England. The rest were principally from England, Scotland, Ireland, Germany, and Scandinavia. New York's Erie Canal gave Wisconsin a water outlet to the Atlantic Ocean and a route for new settlers. Wheat was the primary cash crop for most of the newcomers.

State politics revolved around factions headed by James Doty and Henry Dodge. As political parties developed, the Democrats proved dominant throughout the period.

1836 — Capital located at Belmont – Henry Dodge appointed governor, July 4, by President Andrew Jackson. First session of legislature. Madison chosen as permanent capital.

1837 — Madison surveyed and platted. First Capitol begun. Panic of 1837 – all territorial banks failed. Winnebago Indians ceded all claims to land in Wisconsin. Imprisonment for debt abolished.

1838 — Territorial legislature met in Madison. Milwaukee and Rock River Canal Company chartered.

1840 — First school taxes authorized and levied.

1841 — James D. Doty appointed governor by President John Tyler.

1842 — C.C. Arndt shot and killed in legislature by James R. Vineyard.

1844 — Nathaniel P. Tallmadge appointed governor. Wisconsin Phalanx (a utopian colony) established at Ceresco (Ripon).

1845 — Dodge reappointed governor. Mormon settlement at Voree (Burlington). Swiss colony came to New Glarus.

1846 — Congress passed enabling act for admission of Wisconsin as state. First Constitutional Convention met in Madison.

1847 — Census population 210,546. First

Constitution rejected by people. Second Constitutional Convention.

1848 — Second Constitution adopted. President James K. Polk signed bill on May 29 making Wisconsin a state.

Early Statehood

Heavy immigration continued after statehood. The state remained largely agricultural with wheat the primary crop. Slavery, banking laws, and temperance were the major issues of the period. Despite the number of for-

The silent sentries have stood guard at the Camp Randall arch for over a century. (Sarah Girkin)

eign immigrants and a shift from Democratic control to Republican control, most political leaders continued to have ties to the northeastern United States. New York state laws and institutions provided models for much of the activity of the early legislative sessions.

1848 — Legislature met June 5. Governor Nelson Dewey inaugurated June 7. State university incorporated. First telegram reached Milwaukee. Large scale German immigration began.

1849 — School code adopted. First free, tax-supported, graded school with high school at Kenosha.

1850 — Bond Law for controlling sale of liquor passed. State opened the Wisconsin Institute for Education of the Blind at Janesville.

1851 — First railroad train – Milwaukee to Waukesha. First state fair at Janesville.

1852 — School for deaf opened at Delavan. Prison construction begun at Waupun.

1853 — Impeachment of Judge Levi Hubbell. Capital punishment abolished (third state to take action).

1854 — Republican Party named at a meeting in Ripon. First class graduated at state university. Joshua Glover, fugitive slave, arrested in Racine, and the Wisconsin Supreme Court, in related matter, declared Fugitive Slave Law of 1850 unconstitutional. Milwaukee and Mississippi Railroad reached Madison.

1856 — Bashford-Barstow election scandal. Legislative report on maladministration of school funds.

1857 — Railroad completed to Prairie du Chien. First high school class graduated at Racine. Industrial School for Boys opened at Waukesha.

1858 — Legislative investigation of bribery in 1856 Legislature.

1859 — Abraham Lincoln spoke at state fair in Milwaukee.

1861 — Beginning of Civil War. Governor called for volunteers for military service. Bank riot in Milwaukee. Office of county superintendent of schools created.

1862 — Governor Louis P. Harvey drowned. Draft riots. Edward G. Ryan's address at Democratic Convention criticized Lincoln's conduct of war.

1864 — Cheese factory started at Ladoga, Fond du Lac County, by Chester Hazen.

1865 — 96,000 Wisconsin soldiers served in Civil War; losses were 12,216.

A large percentage of Civil War deaths were not battle related; 140 Confederate soldiers who died at the prisoner of war camp at Camp Randall are buried at Forest Hill Cemetery.
(Sarah Girkin)

The Maturing Commonwealth

After the Civil War Wisconsin matured into a modern political and economic entity. Heavy immigration continued throughout the period. The mix of immigrants remained similar to that prior to the Civil War until the end of the century, when Poles began to appear in large numbers.

The Republican Party remained in control of state government throughout the period, but was challenged by Grangers, Populists, Socialists, and Temperance candidates in addition to the Democratic Party and dissidents within the Republican Party. Temperance, the use of foreign languages in schools, railroad regulation, and currency reform were major issues in the state throughout the period.

Wheat culture gradually declined in importance in Wisconsin as more fertile wheatlands were opened to cultivation in the north and west. In the 1880s and 1890s, dairying gradually became the primary agricultural pursuit in the state. The agricultural school at the university developed into a national leader in the field of dairy science. From the 1870s through the 1890s, lumbering prospered in the northern half of the state. At its peak from 1888 to 1893, it accounted for one-fourth of all wages paid in the state. By the end of the period, Milwaukee and the southeastern half of the state had developed a thriving heavy machinery industry. The paper industry was established in the Fox River Valley by the end of the century. The tanning and the brewing industries were also prominent.

1866 — First state normal school opened at Platteville. Agricultural College at university reorganized under Morrill Act.

1871 — Peshtigo fire burned over much of 6 counties in northeast Wisconsin, resulting in over 1,000 deaths.

1872 — Wisconsin Dairymen's Association organized at Watertown.

1873 — Invention of typewriter by C. Latham Sholes. The Patrons of Husbandry, an agricultural organization nicknamed the Grangers, elected Governor William R. Taylor.

1874 — Potter Law limiting railroad rates passed.

1875 — Free high school law passed; women eligible for election to school boards. State Industrial School for Girls established at Milwaukee. Republicans defeated Grangers. Oshkosh almost destroyed by fire.

1876 — Potter Law repealed. Hazel Green cyclone.

1877 — John T. Appleby patented knotter for twine binders.

1882 — Constitution amended to make legislative sessions biennial. First hydroelectric plant established at Appleton.

1883 — Major hotel fire at the Newhall House in Milwaukee killed 71. South wing of Capitol extension collapsed; 7 killed. Agricultural Experiment Station established at university.

1885 — Gogebic iron range discoveries made Ashland a major shipping port.

1886 — Strikes related to the 8-hour work day movement at Milwaukee culminate in confrontation with militia at Bay View; 5 killed. Agricultural Short Course established at university.

1887 — Marshfield almost destroyed by fire.

1889 — Bennett Law, requiring classroom

instruction in English, passed. Wisconsin Supreme Court in the "Edgerton Bible case", prohibited reading and prayers from the King James Bible in public schools. Arbor Day authorized. Former Governor Jeremiah Rusk became first U.S. Secretary of Agriculture.

1890 — Stephen M. Babcock invented quick, easy, accurate test for milk butterfat content.

1891 — Bennett Law repealed after bitter opposition from German Protestants and Catholics.

1893 — Wisconsin Supreme Court ordered state treasurer to refund to the state interest on state deposits, which had customarily been retained by treasurers.

1894 — Forest fires in northern and central Wisconsin.

1897 — Corrupt practice act passed.

1898 — Wisconsin sent 5,469 men to fight in Spanish-American War; losses were 134.

1899 — Antipass law prohibited railroads from giving public officials free rides. Tax commission created. New Richmond tornado.

The Progressive Era

The state's prominent role in the reform movements which swept the country at the beginning of the century gave Wisconsin national fame and its first presidential candidate. Republicans dominated the state legislature, but Progressive and Stalwart factions fought continually for control of the party. Milwaukee consistently returned a strong Socialist contingent to the legislature.

Large-scale European immigration ended during this period, but ethnic groups retained strong individual identities and remained a significant force in the politics and culture of the state. Important social issues were reflected in the calendar of progressive legislation enacted during the period. The 2 world wars caused great stress because of the large German population of the state.

Heavy machinery manufacturing, paper products and dairying consolidated their position as the leading economic activities. As the last virgin forests in the northern half of the state were cut over, lumbering faded in importance. Brewing temporarily disappeared with the advent of Prohibition.

1900 — Wisconsin's first state park, Interstate near St. Croix Falls, established.

1901 — First Wisconsin-born Governor, Robert M. La Follette, inaugurated. Teaching of agriculture introduced into rural schools. Legislative Reference Library, which served as a model for other states and the Library of Congress, established – later renamed the Legislative Reference Bureau.

1904 — Primary election law approved by referendum vote. State Capitol burned.

1905 — State civil service established; auto license law passed; tuberculosis sanitoria authorized. Forestry Board created. Railroad Commission, regulating railroads and subsequently utilities, created.

1907 — Current Capitol begun.

1908 — Income tax amendment adopted.

1910 — Milwaukee elected Emil Seidel first Socialist mayor. Eau Claire first Wisconsin city to adopt commission form of government.

1911 — First income tax law; teachers' pension act; vocational schools authorized; Industrial and Highway Commissions created; workmen's compensation act enacted.

1913 — Direct election of Wisconsin's U.S. senators approved.

1915 — Conservation Commission, State Board of Agriculture, and State Board of Education created.

1917 — Capitol completed, cost $7,258,763. 120,000 Wisconsin soldiers served in World War I; losses were 3,932. Wisconsin first state to meet draft requirements; 584,559 registrations.

1919 — Eighteenth Amendment (Prohibition) ratified.

1920 — Nineteenth Amendment (women's suffrage) ratified; first state to deliver ratification to Washington.

1921 — Equal rights for women and prohibition laws enacted.

1923 — Military training made optional at university.

1924 — La Follette won Wisconsin's vote for president as Progressive Party candidate. Reforestation amendment to state constitution adopted.

1925 — Senator La Follette died on June 18.

1929 — Professor Harry Steenbock of University of Wisconsin patented radiation of Vitamin D. Legislature repealed all Wisconsin laws for state enforcement of

Prohibition.

1932 — Forest Products Laboratory erected at Madison.

1933 — Dairy farmers undertook milk strike to protest low prices. Wisconsin voted for repeal of 18th Amendment (Prohibition) to U.S. Constitution.

1934 — Wisconsin Progressive Party formed.

1942 — Governor-elect Loomis died; Supreme Court decided Lieutenant Governor Goodland to serve as acting governor.

1941-45 — Wisconsin enrolled 375,000 for World War II; casualties 7,980.

1946 — Wisconsin Progressive Party dissolved and rejoined Republican Party.

The Middle Years of the Twentieth Century

After the demise of the Progressives, the Democratic Party began a gradual resurgence and, by the late 1950s, became strongly competitive for the first time in over a century. With the decline in foreign immigration, the traditional ethnic differences became muted, but significant numbers of blacks appeared in the urban areas of the state for the first time. Discrimination in housing and employment became matters of concern. Other important issues included the growth in the size of state government, radicalism on the university campuses, welfare programs and environmental questions. Tourism emerged as a major industry during this period.

1948 — Centennial Year.

1949 — Legislature enacted new formula for distribution of state educational aids and classified school districts for this purpose.

1950 — Wisconsin enrolled 132,000 for the Korean Conflict; 800 casualties.

1951 — First major legislative reapportionment since 1892.

1957 — Legislation prohibited lobbyists from giving anything of value to a state employee.

1958 — Professor Joshua Lederberg, UW geneticist, Nobel prize winner in medicine.

1959 — Gaylord Nelson, first Democratic governor since 1933, inaugurated. Circus World Museum established at Baraboo. Frank Lloyd Wright, architect, died.

1960 — Mrs. Dena Smith elected state treasurer, first woman elected to statewide office in Wisconsin.

The badger, known for its fierce tenacity, has been an emblem of Wisconsin from the earliest days of settlement. *(Sarah Girkin)*

1961 — Legislation enacted to initiate long-range program of acquisition and improvement of state recreation facilities (ORAP program). Federal supervision of Menominee Indian tribe terminated on April 29; reservation became 72nd county.

1962 — Selective sales tax and income tax withholding enacted. Kohler Company strike, which began in 1954, settled.

1963 — John Gronouski, state tax commissioner, appointed U.S. Postmaster General. State expenditures from all funds for 1963-64 fiscal year top $1 billion for first time.

1964 — Wisconsin Supreme Court redistricted legislature after legislature and governor failed to agree on a plan. Two National Farmers Organization members killed in demonstration at Bonduel stockyard. Legislature enacted property tax relief for aged. The office of county superintendent of schools abolished, but Cooperative Educational Service Agencies (CESAs) created to provide regional services.

1965 — School compulsory attendance age raised to 18. All parts of state placed into vocational school districts. County boards reapportioned on population basis. State law prevented discrimination in housing. The State Capitol, in use since 1917, officially dedicated, after extensive remodeling and cleaning.

1966 — 1965 Legislature held first full even-year regular session since 1882. Governor Warren P. Knowles called out National Guard to keep order during civil rights demonstrations in Wauwatosa. Wisconsin Supreme Court upheld Milwaukee Braves baseball team move to Atlanta. Grand jury investigation of illegal lobbying activities in the legislature resulted in 13 indictments.

1967 — Executive branch reorganized along functional lines. Ban on colored oleomargarine repealed. Racial rioting in Milwaukee in July-August. Marathon marches demonstrate for Milwaukee open housing ordinance. Antiwar protests at the University of Wisconsin in Madison

GAR Memorial Hall, Madison. *(Wisconsin Veterans Museum)*

culminate in riot with injuries.

1968 — Constitutional amendment permitted the legislature to meet as provided by law rather than once a biennium, resulting in annual sessions. Ninety black students expelled from Wisconsin State University-Oshkosh when December demonstration damaged the administration building. Wisconsin's first heart transplant performed at St. Luke's Hospital in Milwaukee; first successful bone marrow transplant performed by team of scientists and surgeons at the University of Wisconsin in Madison.

1969 — Selective sales tax became general sales tax. On opening day of special legislative session on welfare and urban aids, welfare mothers and UW-Madison students, led by Father James Groppi, took over the Assembly Chamber; National Guard called to protect Capitol. Groppi cited for contempt and jailed; contempt charge upheld by Wisconsin Supreme Court. Student strikes at UW in Madison demanded Black studies department; National Guard activated to restore order. Congressman Melvin R. Laird appointed U.S. Secretary of Defense. Wisconsin's portion of Interstate Highway System completed.

1970 — Army Mathematics Research Building at the UW in Madison bombed by antiwar protestors, resulting in one death. "Old Main" at Wisconsin State University-Whitewater burned down in apparent arson. First elections to 4-year terms in Wisconsin history for all constitutional officers, based on constitutional amendment ratified in 1967. UW scientists, headed by Dr. Har Gobind Khorana, succeeded in the first total synthesis of a gene.

1971 — The legislature, now meeting in regular session throughout the biennium, enacted major shared tax redistribution, merger of University of Wisconsin and State University systems, revision of municipal employee relations laws.

1972 — Legislature enacted comprehensive consumer protection act, lowered the age of majority from 21 to 18, required environmental impact statement for all legislation affecting the environment, repealed railroad full crew law, and ratified the unsuccessful "equal rights" amendment to U.S. Constitution. Record highway death toll, 1,168.

1973 — State constitutional amendment permitting bingo adopted. Barbara Thompson first woman to hold the elective office of State Superintendent of Public Instruction. The 1954 Menominee Termination Act repealed by Congress. Legislature enacted state ethics code, repealed oleomargarine tax, funded programs for the education of all handicapped children, and established procedures for informal probate of simple estates.

1974 — Legislature enacted comprehensive campaign finance act and strengthened open meetings law. Democrats swept all constitutional offices and gained control of both houses of the 1975 Legislature for first time since 1893. Kathryn Morrison first woman elected to the state senate. Striking teachers fired in Hortonville.

1964-1975 — 165,400 Wisconsinites served in Vietnam; 1,239 were killed.

The Late Twentieth Century

Democrats lost control of the senate in 1993 for the first time since 1974, and in 1995 they lost control of the assembly for the first time since 1970. Control of the senate has changed several times since then. Women began to be widely represented in the legislature for the first time in the 90s.

Health care reform, restructuring welfare, the business climate in the state, taxation, education, and prisons were the chief concerns of policymakers in the 90s.

California challenged Wisconsin's dominance of the dairy industry. After an economic downturn in the 80s, the 90s saw a robust economy throughout most of the state with Madison leading the entire country in employment for several months. The farm sector and brewing industry continued to experience difficulties, however.

Litigation and demonstrations over off-reservation resource rights of the Chippewa Indians continued throughout the 80s to be replaced by controversy over Indian gaming in the 90s and into the new century.

1975 — Menominee Indians occupied Alexian Brothers Novitiate. Legislature made voter registration easier, established property tax levy limits on local governments, and eliminated statutory distinctions based on sex. UW-Madison scientist, Dr. Howard Temin, shared 1975 Nobel Prize in physiology-medicine.

1976 — U.S. District Court ordered integration of Milwaukee public schools. Ice storm damage reached $50.4 million. Wisconsin Legislature established a system for compensating crime victims. Exxon discovered sulfide zinc and copper deposits in Forest County. Shirley S. Abrahamson was appointed first woman on the Wisconsin Supreme Court. Wisconsin Supreme Court declared negative school aids law unconstitutional.

1977 — Governor Patrick J. Lucey appointed Ambassador to Mexico, and Lieutenant Governor Martin Schreiber became "acting governor". First state employees union strike lasted 15 days; National Guard ran prisons. Constitutional amendments authorized raffle games and revised the structure of the court system by creating a Court of Appeals. Legislation enacted included public support of elections campaigns, no-fault divorce, and implied consent law for drunk driving.

1978 — Wisconsin Supreme Court allowed cameras in state courtrooms. Vel Phillips elected secretary of state, first black constitutional officer. Laws enacted included a hazardous waste management program.

1979 — Constitutional amendment removed lieutenant governor from serving as president of the senate. Moratorium on tax collections gave state taxpayers a 3-month "vacation" from taxes. Shirley S. Abrahamson, became the first woman elected to Wisconsin Supreme Court after serving by appointment for 3 years. Legislature established school of veterinary medicine at the UW-Madison.

1980 — Eric Heiden of Madison won five Olympic gold medals for ice speed skating, named winner of the Sullivan Award as best amateur athlete in the country. 15,000 Cuban refugees housed for the summer at Fort McCoy. Former Governor Lucey ran as independent candidate for U.S. Vice President. State revenue shortfall led to 4.4 percent cuts in state spending.

1981 — U.S. Supreme Court ruled against Wisconsin's historic open primary. Laws enacted included stronger penalties for drunk driving and changes in mining laws.

1982 — State unemployment hit highest levels since the Great Depression. Voters endorsed first statewide referendum in nation calling for a freeze on nuclear weapons. Jos. Schlitz Brewing Co. acquired by Stroh Brewing Co. of Detroit, all Milwaukee operations closed.

1983 — Continued recession forced adoption of budget including a 10 percent tax surcharge and a pay freeze for state employees. Law raising minimum drinking age to 19 passed (effective 7/1/85). In one-day uprising, inmates at Waupun State Prison took 15 hostages, but released them uninjured. Laws enacted included a "lemon law" on motor vehicle warranties, changes in child support collection procedures and levels. UW-Madison School of Veterinary Medicine enrolled its first class.

1984 — Most powerful U.S. tornado of 1984 destroyed Barneveld; 9 dead. Democratic party chose presidential convention delegates in caucuses rather than by presidential preference primary as a result of the Democratic National Committee rules changes. Indian treaty rights to fish and hunt caused controversy. Economic conditions began to improve from the low-point of the previous 2 years.

1985 — Milwaukee air crash killed 31. Major consolidation of state banks by large holding companies. First state tax amnesty program.

1986 — Farm land values dropped across the state. Exxon dropped plans to develop copper mine near Crandon. Laws enacted raised the drinking age to 21, and limited damages payable in malpractice actions.

1987 — Voters approved constitutional amendments allowing pari-mutuel betting and a state lottery. Laws enacted included a mandatory seatbelt law, antitakeover legislation, gradual end to the inheritance and gift taxes, and a "learnfare" program designed to keep in school the children of families receiving Aid to Families With Dependent Children (AFDC). G. Heileman Brewing Company taken over by Alan Bond.

1988 — Driest summer since the 1930s. The first state lottery games began. Chrysler Corporation's automobile assembly plant in Kenosha, the nation's oldest car plant, closed. Laws enacted included mandatory family leave for employees.

1989 — Laws enacted included creation of Department of Corrections, the Lower Wisconsin State Riverway, and a statewide land stewardship program.

1990 — More than 1,400 Wisconsin National Guard and Reserve soldiers were called to active duty in Persian Gulf crisis, 11 casualties. The number of Milwaukee murders set a new record, raising demands for crime and drug controls. Laws enacted included a major recycling law and Milwaukee Parental Choice voucher program for public and nonsectarian private schools.

1991 — The price of raw milk hit lowest point since 1978. First Indian gambling compacts signed. Governor Tommy G. Thompson vetoed a record 457 items in the state budget.

1992 — Train derailment caused major spill of toxic chemicals and evacuation of over 22,000 people in Superior. Thousands of opponents, including children, staged protests at 6 abortion clinics in Milwaukee throughout the summer. Laws enacted included parental consent for abortion, health care reform, and creation of a 3-member Gaming Commission.

1993 — Wisconsin Congressman Les Aspin and UW-Madison President Donna Shalala named President Bill Clinton's Secretary of Defense and Secretary of Health and Human Services, respectively. Thousands in Milwaukee became ill as a result of cryptosporidium in the water supply. California passed Wisconsin in milk production. Republicans won control of state senate for the first time since 1974. Laws enacted included a 1999 sunset for traditional welfare programs, a cap on school spending, and permission to organize limited liability companies.

1994 — Laws enacted included removal of about $1 billion in public school operating taxes from property tax by 1997, a new regulatory framework for Public Service Commission regulation of telecommunication utilities, and granting towns most of the same powers exercised by cities and villages.

1995 — Republicans won control of state assembly for the first time since 1970. Elk reintroduced in northern Wisconsin. July heat wave contributed to 172 deaths.

1996 — Governor Thompson's new welfare reform plan, known as Wisconsin Works (W-2), received national attention. Train derailment forced evacuation of Weyauwega.

Pabst Brewing closed 152-year-old brewery in Milwaukee. Senator George Petak was removed from office in the first successful legislative recall election in state history.

1997 — Groundbreaking for controversial new Miller Park, future home of the Milwaukee Brewers baseball team.

1998 — Tammy Baldwin became first Wisconsin woman elected to the U.S. Congress. U.S. Supreme Court upheld constitutionality of extension of Milwaukee Parental Choice school vouchers to religious schools. Second state tax amnesty program. Laws enacted included a mining moratorium, new penalties for failure to pay child support, truth-in-sentencing, and protection of fetuses.

1999 — Governor Tommy Thompson began record fourth term. Laws enacted included "smart growth", graduated drivers licensing, a sales tax rebate. Supermax, the state's high security prison, opened at Boscobel. Record low unemployment.

2000 — Legislature approved a local sales tax and revenue bonds for renovation of Lambeau Field, home of the Green Bay Packers.

Recent Years

2001 — Governor Thompson ended a record 14 years in office and assumed post of U.S. Secretary of Health and Human Services. Lt. Governor Scott McCallum became governor and appointed State Senator Margaret Farrow as the first woman to serve as lieutenant governor. Chronic Wasting Disease discovered in the state's deer herd. Extensive Mississippi River flooding. Miller Park opened. Laws enacted included telemarketing "no call" list, wetland protection, and the "senior care" prescription drug assistance plan.

2002 — Barbara Lawton became the first woman elected lieutenant governor and Peggy A. Lautenschlager became first woman elected attorney general. Deadliest single traffic accident in state history killed 10 and injured 40 near Sheboygan. Investigation into legislative caucus staffs resulted in criminal charges against five legislators. Seven Milwaukee County board members recalled over pension scandal.

2003 — Jim Doyle became first Democratic governor in 16 years. The Crandon mine issue was apparently resolved when local

Indian tribes purchased the ore deposits. The renovated Lambeau Field opened. Senator Gary George became the second legislator in Wisconsin history to be recalled. A number of Wisconsin Guard and Reserve units were activated for service in the Iraq war. Wisconsin held its first mourning dove hunt.

2004 — Louis Butler, Jr., became the first black member of the Wisconsin Supreme Court. State government began to reduce its automobile fleet after allegations of misuse. Significant legislation included a livestock facility siting law and revision to clean air and water laws intended to spur job creation. Voter turnout in the fall election was 73%, the highest in many years.

2005 — The state minimum wage was increased. Wisconsin experienced a record 62 tornadoes during the year, including a record 27 in one day – August 18, when tornadoes hit Viola, Stoughton, and other communities resulting in one death, 27 injuries, and $40 million in damage. Several current and former members of the legislature were convicted of illegal campaign activities.

2006 — Continued participation in the Iraq War by Wisconsin National Guard and Reserve units was a potent issue, as was immigration reform. The legislature limited the use of condemnation power for the benefit of private individuals. Voters approved a constitutional amendment limiting marriage to persons of the opposite sex in November. An advisory referendum in favor of the death penalty was also approved by the voters.

2007 — Ethics laws and elections regulation procedures were modified. Milwaukee-based Miller Brewing merged with Denver's Coors brewery. The state budget did not pass until late October, one of the latest budgets in state history.

2008 — Louis Butler became the first sitting Supreme Court justice to be defeated at the polls in 40 years, losing to Michael Gableman. Severe flooding hit southern Wisconsin in June. Failure of an embankment caused Lake Delton to drain, destroying three homes. The Great Lakes Compact received state and federal approval, regulating the use of Great Lakes water outside their watershed. A sharp downturn in the economy caused a rise in unemployment and the closing of the General Motors plant in Janesville, ending a chapter in Wisconsin's 100-year involvement in auto assembly.

2009 — Democrats opened the 99th Legislature with control of the governor's office and both houses of the legislature for the first time since the 1985 session. The ongoing economic crisis resulted in a projected budget deficit of $6 billion for the next biennium. In the largest activation since the Berlin Crisis of 1961, 3,000 soldiers of the Wisconsin National Guard prepared for mobilization to Iraq. A severe influenza outbreak resulted in 47 deaths.

2010 — A number of powerful tornadoes hit southern Wisconsin on June 21. Among the areas sustaining severe damage was the Old World Wisconsin historic site. The Republican Party swept the November elections, capturing the governor's office and both houses of the legislature. It was the first time in over 70 years that partisan control of all three switched in the same election. Governor-Elect Walker declined to accept $810 million in federal funds to build a high speed rail line between Madison and Milwaukee.

2011 — Governor Walker's proposal to curtail collective bargaining rights for public workers led 14 Democrats to leave the state in order to deny the senate a quorum. Thousands of protesters surrounded the Capitol to oppose the legislation, which was delayed for weeks before being enacted. Wisconsin remained in a state of political agitation into the summer as nine senators were the subject of recall elections; two were defeated. The legislature enacted a legislative redistricting plan for the first time in three decades; revamped the state's economic development efforts and expanded the parental school choice program.

2012 — Governor Walker, Lt. Gov. Kleefisch, and four senators were the subject of recall elections in ongoing ill-feeling over the 2011 collecting bargaining law. Walker, Kleefisch, and two senators were retained; one senator resigned and one was defeated giving the Democrats control of the senate. A period of severe heat and drought afflicted the state during June and July. Republican Paul Ryan became the first Wisconsinite to be nominated for national office (vice president) by a major political party. Democrat Tammy Baldwin was elected Wisconsin's first female U.S. Senator in the fall election, but Republicans regained control of the state senate.

2013 — The legislature enacted revised regulations for the mining of metallic ferrous minerals, easing the way for construction of an iron mine in northern Wisconsin's Gogebic Range. Wisconsin's role as a major source of sand used in the "fracking" method of natural gas extraction presented questions for state and local quarry regulators. The winter of 2013-14 was the most severe in many years.

2014 — The voters passed a constitutional amendment requiring that Transportation Fund resources be used only for transportation. Court rulings legalized same-sex marriage in Wisconsin. The deer harvest was the lowest in 30 years. The governor denied the Menominee Nation permission to operate a casino in Kenosha.

2015 — Senator Mary Lazich was elected President of the Senate, the first woman to be elected presiding officer of either house of the legislature. Efforts to open an iron mine in the Gogebic Range were abandoned. The legislature enacted "Right to Work" legislation. The voters approved a constitutional amendment requiring the supreme court to elect its chief justice by majority vote. The legislature raised the speed limit to 70 mph on certain highways.

Senator Mary Lazich, President of the Senate, the first woman to be elected presiding officer in either house of the legislature. (Jay Salvo, Legislative Photographer)

Sources: State Historical Society, *The Thirtieth Star, 1948; The 1958 Compton Yearbook* and succeeding editions; *The Americana Annual – 1967;* Robert C. Nesbit, *Wisconsin, A History;* Wisconsin Legislative Reference Bureau, *Clippings: Wisconsin History.*

HISTORIC SITES IN WISCONSIN

| Site | Location | Paid Attendance | | | | Revenue |
		2011	2012	2013	2014	2014
Bennett Studios	Wisconsin Dells	33,316	31,494	26,726	26,966	$46,337
Black Point Estate*	Lake Geneva	—	—	5,936	6,176	82,209
Circus World Museum	Baraboo	65,560	71,076	63,788	55,367	918,899
Madeline Island	La Pointe	12,831	12,068	11,308	11,587	97,492
Old World Wisconsin	Eagle	58,703	56,660	68,694	73,252	1,084,938
Pendarvis	Mineral Point	6,796	6,133	7,247	8,502	51,456
Stonefield	Cassville	8,907	8,348	8,125	5,858	41,543
Villa Louis	Prairie du Chien	13,084	14,589	14,844	19,965	138,462
Wade House	Greenbush	17,494	15,950	24,388	21,908	222,067
TOTAL		216,691	216,318	231,056	229,581	$2,683,433

Note: Sites are generally open from May to October. For current information: www.wisconsinhistory.org/sitesmuseum.asp.
Revenues from admissions, rentals, and inside sales (such as museum stores, restaurants, and rides).
*Black Point Estate began operation under the State Historical Society on January 1, 2013.
Source: Wisconsin Historical Society, departmental data, June, 2015.

OFFICIAL HISTORICAL MARKERS IN WISCONSIN
May 2015

County	Location/Nearest Community	Subject
Adams	At the Park, Hwy 13, 3 miles north of Friendship	Roche-a-Cri State Park
Adams	S. Arkdale Cemetery, 1801 Cypress Ave., Town of Strongs Prairie	Site of First Norwegian Evangelical Lutheran Church of Roche-a-Cri
Ashland	Bay View Park, Hwy 2, Ashland	Fleet Admiral William D. Leahy
Ashland	Northland College campus, Ellis Avenue, Ashland	Northland College
Ashland	In park on Hwy 2 at western limits of Ashland	Radisson-Groseilliers Fort
Ashland	La Pointe, Madeline Island	Madeline Island
Ashland	Hwy 13, 10 miles south of Mellen	Great Divide
Ashland	Hwy 2, Odanah	The Bad River
Barron	Rest Area #34, westbound Hwy 53, 2 mi. south of Chetek	Pine Was King (Pineries)
Barron	2411-23 Street, Rice Lake	Our Lady of Lourdes Catholic Church
Bayfield	Herbster Community Center, STH 13, one block south of Lenawee Rd., Herbster	"The Gym"
Bayfield	Hwy 13, 0.5 mile east of Cornucopia	Tragedy of the Siskiwit
Bayfield	Hwy 13, Port Wing	School Consolidation
Bayfield	Hwy 13, 2.3 miles north of Washburn	Madeline Island
Brown	Denmark War Memorial Pk., Wisconsin Ave. (CTH KB)	Denmark
Brown	In park at corner of Broadway and George Sts., De Pere	Marquette-Jolliet Expedition
Brown	In Voyageur Park, De Pere	Rapides des Peres – Voyageur Park
Brown	403 North Broadway, De Pere	White Pillars
Brown	222 South Baird Street, Green Bay	Cnesses Israel Synagogue
Brown	2640 South Webster Avenue, Green Bay	Cotton House – Baird Law Office
Brown	Outside Packer Hall of Fame, Green Bay	Green Bay Packers
Brown	1008 South Monroe Avenue, Green Bay	Hazelwood
Brown	2630 South Webster Avenue, Green Bay	Heritage Hill State Park
Brown	Fox River Trail near Main Street Bridge, U.S. 141 Green Bay	Historic Green Bay Road
Brown	Hwy 57, 5 miles northeast of Green Bay	Red Banks
Brown	2630 South Webster Avenue, Green Bay	Roi-Porlier-Tank Cottage
Brown	Holy Apostles Church Cemetery, 2937 Freedom Rd., Oneida	Revolutionary War Veteran (Powlis)
Buffalo	Hwy 35, 0.5 mile north of Alma	Beef Slough
Burnett	Crex Meadows Wildlife Area, off Hwy F, N. of Grantsburg	Crex Meadows
Calumet	Wayside #4, intersection of Hwys 55 and 151, Brothertown Town	Brothertown Indians of Wisconsin
Calumet	City Hall, 2110 Washington Street, New Holstein	New Holstein
Calumet	Junction of CTH T and Church Rd., New Holstein	St. Martins Church
Calumet	Stockbridge Harbor, CTH E, Village of Stockbridge	Stockbridge Harbor
Chippewa	Hwy 124, 3 miles north of Chippewa Falls	Nation's First Cooperative Generating Station
Chippewa	2820 East Park Avenue, Chippewa Falls	Northern WI Center for the Developmentally Disabled
Chippewa	Fairgrounds, 308 Jefferson Ave., Chippewa Falls	Northern Wisconsin State Fair
Chippewa	Cornell Mill Yard Park and Bridge St., Cornell	Cornell Pulpwood Stacker
Chippewa	West side of Hwy 178, near Hwy T	Cobban Bridge
Chippewa	Hwy 178, 0.5 mile north of Jim Falls	Old Abe, the War Eagle
Clark	2 blocks west of Hwy 13, Colby	Colby Cheese
Clark	St. Hedwig's Church, CTH-X at Gorman Avenue Near Thorp	St. Hedwig's/Poznan Colony
Columbia	Rest Area #12, westbound I90-94, E. of WI River	The Circus
Columbia	711 West James Street, Columbus	Governor James Taylor Lewis
Columbia	Hwy 113 at Wisconsin River crossing	Merrimac Ferry
Columbia	120 N. Main Street, Pardeeville	Historic Pardeeville
Columbia	Hwy 33, 0.5 mile east of Portage	Fort Winnebago
Columbia	West Wisconsin and Crook Streets, Portage	Frederick Jackson Turner
Columbia	Across from sheriff's office, Cook Street, Portage	Ketchum's Point
Columbia	Hwy 33, 0.5 mile east of Portage	Marquette

OFFICIAL HISTORICAL MARKERS IN WISCONSIN
May 2015–Continued

County	Location/Nearest Community	Subject
Columbia	Hwy CM, 5 miles northeast of Portage	Potters' Emigration Society
Columbia	Museum at The Portage, 804 MacFarlane Rd., Portage	Society Hill Historic District
Columbia	Commerce Plaza Park, 301 West Wisconsin St., Portage	Zona Gale
Columbia	Rest Area #11, eastbound I90-94, 0.5 mi. E. of WI River	Rest Areas on the I-Roads
Columbia	Hwy 51, 0.5 mile south of Poynette	John Muir View
Columbia	Old Settlers Park, near intersection of Thomas and John Street, Poynette	Wallis Rowan and His Cabin
Columbia	Hwy 16, 4 miles east of Wisconsin Dells	Kingsley Bend Indian Mounds
Columbia	314 Broadway, Wisconsin Dells	Stroud Bank
Columbia	Village Park, 150 Lovers Lane, Wyocena	Major Elbert Dickason/Dickason's "Hotel"
Columbia	Wyona Park, CTH-GG, Wyocena	Rifle Pit Legend/Wyona Park
Crawford	US-35, near River View Park, 0.3 miles north of CTH C, Ferryville	Patrick Joseph Lucey
Crawford	Hwy 171, 0.5 mile east of Gays Mills	Gays Mills Apple Orchards
Crawford	Hwy 35, 1.2 miles south of Lynxville	Rafting on the Mississippi
Crawford	Cornelius Family Park, 211 S. Main St., Prairie du Chien	Black Hawk's Surrender
Crawford	Fort Crawford Museum, 717 S. Beaumont Rd., Prairie du Chien	Fort Crawford
Crawford	Mississippi River Bridge, Prairie du Chien	Pere Marquette and Sieur Jolliet
Crawford	Beaumont and Rice Streets, Prairie du Chien	Museum of Medical Progress
Crawford	Mississippi River Bridge, Prairie du Chien	Prairie du Chien
Crawford	At entrance, Villa Louis Road, Prairie du Chien.	Villa Louis
Crawford	521 N. Villa Road, Prairie du Chien	Villa Louis
Crawford	In lawn west of the Villa, Villa Louis, Prairie du Chien	War of 1812
Crawford	Hwy 61, 0.5 mile south of Soldiers Grove.	James Davidson
Crawford	Soldiers Grove Park, Mill and Main Sts., Soldiers Grove.	Soldiers Grove Origin
Dane	In park off Hwy A, Albion	Albion Academy
Dane	8770 Ridge Drive, Belleville	Primrose Lutheran Church
Dane	1 mile northeast of Blue Mounds, Hwy F	Brigham Park
Dane	Quivey's Grove, 6261 Nesbitt Road, Fitchburg	Mann House
Dane	2915 Syene Rd., Fitchburg.	McCoy House
Dane	Camp Randall Memorial Park, UW-Madison campus	Camp Randall
Dane	8-12 N. Blount St., Madison	Ceramic Art Studio of Madison
Dane	4718 Monona Dr., Madison	Nathaniel Dean, Dean House
Dane	Vilas Communication Hall, UW-Madison campus	9XM-WHA
Dane	Bascom Hill, UW-Madison campus	North Hall
Dane	GEF III, 125 S. Webster St., Madison	Peck Cabin
Dane	Resurrection Cemetery, 2705 Regent St., Madison	Site of Former Greenbush Cemetery Burials
Dane	Olbrich Park, 3330 Atwood Ave., Madison	Third Lake Passage
Dane	415 E. Wilson St., Madison	Tragedy of War
Dane	816 State Street, Madison	State Historical Society
Dane	501 South Thornton Avenue, Madison	Yahara River Parkway
Dane	Indian Lake County Park, Hwy 19, 1 mi. E. of Marxville.	Indian Lake Passage
Dane	Village Park, 39 Brodhead Street, Mazomanie	Historic Mazomanie
Dane	Branch Creek Conservancy Pk, Pleasant Branch Rd., Middleton	Pheasant Branch Encampment
Dane	Indian Mound Pk., 6200 Bl. of Ridgewood Ave., Monona	Outlet Mound
Dane	2455 West Broadway, Monona	Royal Airport/Charles Lindbergh
Dane	Entrance to Prairie Mound Cemetery, CTH M, Vil. of Oregon	Revolutionary War Veteran
Dane	Hwy 51, east shore of Lake Waubesa	Stephen Moulton Babcock (1843-1931)
Dane	Yahara River Bridge, W. Main St., 381 E. Main St., Stoughton	Main Street Historic District
Dane	La Follette County Park, 3 miles north of Stoughton	Robert Marion La Follette, Sr. (1855-1925)
Dane	300 E. Main Street, Sun Prairie	Georgia O'Keeffe
Dodge	214-216 Front St., Beaver Dam	Frederick Douglas
Dodge	Adams Spring Park, Spring Street, Fox Lake	Bernard "Bunny" Berigan (1908-1942)
Dodge	Addie Joss Park, Juneau	Adrian "Addie" Joss
Dodge	105 N. River St., Lowell	Lowell Women Firefighters
Dodge	Rest Area #64, northbound Hwy 41	World War II
Dodge	Hwys 28 and 67, on Main Street, Mayville	Wisconsin's First Iron Smelter
Dodge	Hwy 175, Theresa	Solomon Juneau House
Dodge	Jct. Hwys 26 and 67, Waupun	Auto Race – Green Bay to Madison
Door	12171 Garrett Bay Rd., Ellison Bay	The Clearing
Door	Zion Lutheran Church, 6710 CTH T, Egg Harbor	Zion Evangelical Lutheran Church
Door	Noble Square, 4167 Main Street, Fish Creek	The Alexander Noble House
Door	Namur, Hwy 57	Belgian Settlement in Wisconsin
Door	6145 Cave Point Drive, Town of Jacksonport	Jacksonport United Methodist Church
Door	Olde Stone Quarry Park, CTH B, Town of Sevastopol	Leathem and Smith Quarry
Door	3434 CTH V, Sturgeon Bay	The Episcopal Church of the Holy Nativity
Door	Hwy 42, 0.5 mile north of junction with Hwy 57	The Orchards of Door County
Douglas	Hwy 2, Brule.	Brule River
Douglas	Hwys F and B, Lake Nebagamon	Evergreen Park Cottage Sanatorium
Douglas	Hwy 2, Poplar	Major "Dick" Bong
Douglas	Hwy 53, 1.5 miles south of Solon Springs.	Brule-St. Croix Portage
Douglas	Allouez (Superior), along Hwys 2, 13, and 53	Burlington Northern Ore Docks
Douglas	Rest Area #23, Hwys 2 & 53, southern limits of Superior	Northwest Portal of Wisconsin
Douglas	Memorial Park, Superior.	Old Stockade Site
Douglas	Whaleback Museum, Barker's Island, Superior	*S. S. Meteor,* last of the Whalebacks

OFFICIAL HISTORICAL MARKERS IN WISCONSIN
May 2015–Continued

County	Location/Nearest Community	Subject
Douglas	Superior Central High School, 1015 Belknap St., Superior	Summer White House – 1928
Douglas	Harbor Entry, Wisconsin Point Road, Superior	The Superior Entry
Douglas	Between McCaskill and Holden Bldgs., UW-Superior	University of Wisconsin-Superior
Douglas	Tourist Information Center, City Park, Hwy 2, Superior	Wartime Shipbuilding
Dunn	Caddie Woodlawn Park, Hwy 25, Menomonie	Caddie Woodlawn
Dunn	Rest Area #61, eastbound I94, Menomonie	Chippewa Valley White Pine
Dunn	Evergreen Cemetery, Menomonie	Dr. Stephen Tainter – Revolutionary War Veteran
Dunn	Evergreen Cemetery, north end of Shorewood Dr., Menomonie	Earliest Evergreen Burials/Evergreen Cemetery
Dunn	205 Main Street, Menomonie	Mabel Tainter Memorial
Dunn	Rest Area #62, I94	World War I
Eau Claire	Dells Mills Museum, N. of Augusta on STH 27, Augusta.	Dells Mills
Eau Claire	Wayside #4, Hwy 85, 0.5 mi. west of Hwy 37, Eau Claire	Silver Mine Ski Jump
Fond du Lac	Fond du Lac Co. Park, W11413 CTH TC, Brandon.	The Raube Road Site
Fond du Lac	Kettle Moraine Scenic Drive (CTH-GGG), just north of Campbellsport.	Haskell Noyes Memorial Woods
Fond du Lac	Hwy 151, 6 miles north of Fond du Lac.	Edward S. Bragg
Fond du Lac	Rolling Meadows Golf Course, 560 W. Rolling Meadows Dr., Fond du Lac	County Home Cemetery Fond du Lac
Fond du Lac	Main Street and Forest Avenue, Fond du Lac	Military Road
Fond du Lac	30 East 2nd Street, Fond du Lac.	Wisconsin Progressive Party
Fond du Lac	St. John the Baptist Church, Hwy W, Johnsburg	Father Caspar Rehrl
Fond du Lac	Southeast corner of Blackburn and Blossom Sts., Ripon	Birthplace of Republican Party
Fond du Lac	Pedrick Wayside, Hwy 23, Ripon	Carrie Chapman Catt
Fond du Lac	In park on Union Street, 1 block south of Hwy 23, Ripon	Ceresco
Fond du Lac	Ripon College campus, Ripon	Ripon College
Fond du Lac	Taycheedah Correctional Institution, Tn. of Taycheedah	Home of Governor James Duane Doty
Fond du Lac	Hwy 49, 4 miles east of Waupun	Horicon Marsh
Forest	Hwy 8, 1.8 miles east of Crandon	Northern Highland
Forest	Hwy 32, 1 mile south of Laona	Laona School Forest
Forest	Hwy 55, 0.5 mile north of Mole Lake	Battle of Mole Lake
Grant	Hwy 61, 0.3 miles south of Boscobel	The Gideons
Grant	Cassville	Village of Cassville
Grant	117 East Front Street, Cassville	Old Denniston House
Grant	620 Lincoln Avenue, Fennimore.	The "Dinky"
Grant	Hwy 80 at the WI-IL state line, south of Hazel Green.	Point of Beginning (Survey Point)
Grant	Cemetery, 1 block west of Hwys 61, 35, and 81, Lancaster.	Nelson Dewey
Grant	Highway 35 and Slabtown Rd., 5 miles west of Lancaster	Pleasant Ridge
Grant	Rountree Hall, UW-Platteville.	First State Normal School
Grant	114-108 South Main St., Potosi	Village of Potosi
Green	English Settlement Cemetery, 300 North Main St., Albany	English Settlement Cemetery
Green	Monroe Arts Center, 1315 11th St., Monroe.	First Methodist Episcopal Church
Green	Monticello Monument Wayside, Hwy 69, Monticello.	Nickolaus Gerber
Green	Village Park, 300 Blk of 2nd St., Hwy O, New Glarus	Herbert Kubly
Green	Hwy 69, New Glarus.	New Glarus
Green Lake	Nathan Strong Park, East Huron St. (Hwy 116), Berlin.	Lucy Smith Morris
Green Lake	Riverside Park, Berlin	Upper Fox River
Iowa	Hwy 14, 3 miles east of Arena.	Village of Dover
Iowa	CTH Y, 3 mi. S. of Dodgeville.	Dodge's Grove and Fort Union
Iowa	Courthouse lawn, Hwy 151, Dodgeville.	Iowa County Courthouse
Iowa	Hwy YZ, 4 miles east of Dodgeville.	Old Military Road
Iowa	Water Tower Park, Hwy 151, Mineral Point.	Historic Mineral Point
Iowa	Iowa Co. Fairgrounds, 900 Fair St., Mineral Point	Laurence F. Graber, "Mr. Alfalfa"
Iowa	114 Shake Rag Street, Mineral Point	Shake Rag
Iowa	Library Park, Mineral Point	Wisconsin Territory
Iowa	9 Fountain St., Mineral Point	Site of Fort Jackson
Iowa	Frank Lloyd Wright Visitor Ctr., CTH C, Spring Green.	Military River Crossing
Iowa	Hwy 14, east of Wisconsin River, near Spring Green	Frank Lloyd Wright
Iowa	Tower Hill State Park, Hwy C, south of Hwy 14	Shot Tower
Iron	Hwy 2, 10 miles west of Hurley.	Gogebic Iron Range
Iron	Wayside WI Info. Ctr., Hwy 51, 1 mile north of Hurley.	Iron Mining in Wisconsin
Jackson	Hwys 121 and 95, 1.5 mile west of Alma Center.	Silver Mound
Jackson	Bell Mound Scenic Overlook, 5 mi. S. of Black River Falls	Black River Valley Scenic Outlook
Jackson	Hwy 54, 5 miles east of Black River Falls.	Mitchell Red Cloud, Jr. (1925-1950)
Jackson	Rest Area #8, westbound I94, 15 mi. SE Black River Falls.	The Passenger Pigeon
Jackson	Rest Area #7, eastbound I94, 15 mi. SE Black River Falls	Sphagnum Moss
Jackson	Rest Area #6, westbound I94	Highground Veterans Memorial
Jackson	Hwy 27, 6 miles south of Black River Falls.	Martin W. Torkelson
Jefferson	Aztalan Museum, N6284 Hwy Q, Tn. of Aztalan	Princess Burial Mound
Jefferson	In park, north off Hwy 12, just east of Cambridge	Lake Ripley – Ole Evinrude
Jefferson	Burnt Village Co. Park, Hwy N, 2 mi. SE of Ft. Atkinson	Black Hawk War Encampment "Burnt Village"
Jefferson	400 block of Milwaukee Avenue East, Fort Atkinson	Fort Koshkonong
Jefferson	Koshkonong Mounds Road, near Fort Atkinson.	Lake Koshkonong Effigy Mounds
Jefferson	Blackhawk Island Road, Town of Sumner.	Lorine Niedecker
Jefferson	Hwy 106, western city limits of Fort Atkinson	Panther Intaglio
Jefferson	Iola Mills, 300 North Main St., Iola	Iola Mills
Jefferson	Rest Area #14, westbound I94	In Service to Their Country

OFFICIAL HISTORICAL MARKERS IN WISCONSIN
May 2015–Continued

County	Location/Nearest Community	Subject
Jefferson	3 miles east of Lake Mills on Hwy B, south on Hwy Q	Aztalan State Park
Jefferson	Rest Area #13, eastbound I94, 1 mile east of Lake Mills	Drumlins
Jefferson	Bald Bluff Overlook, CTH H, 1 1/2 mi. S. of Palmyra	Black Hawk War Encampment
Jefferson	919 Charles St., Watertown	First Kindergarten
Jefferson	7 miles southeast of Watertown, Hwy 16	Highway Marking
Jefferson	Milwaukee Street at the Rock River, Watertown	Milwaukee Street Bridge
Jefferson	919 Charles Street, Watertown	Octagon House
Jefferson	One Main St. (at bridge), Watertown	Trail Discovery
Juneau	Hwy C, 0.5 mile east of Camp Douglas	Castle Rock
Juneau	Camp Williams, off I94	Wisconsin Military Reservation
Juneau	On the trail at the western edge of Elroy	Elroy-Sparta State Trail
Juneau	In village park, Hwy HH, Lyndon Station	Hop Raising
Juneau	Rest Area #10, westbound I90-94	The Sand Counties – Aldo Leopold Territory
Juneau	Rest Area #9, eastbound I90-94, near Mauston	The Wisconsin River
Juneau	Rest Area #9, eastbound I90-94, near Mauston	The Iron Brigade
Kenosha	Rest Area #I26, I94	Cordelia A.P. Harvey
Kenosha	24th Ave. & 56th St., Kenosha	Auto Production in Kenosha
Kenosha	Hwy 31 eastbound at 95th St., Kenosha	Green Bay Ethnic Trail
Kenosha	Green Ridge Cemetery, 6604 Seventh Ave., Kenosha	John McCaffery Burial Site
Kenosha	6501 3rd Avenue, Kenosha	Kemper Hall
Kenosha	5117 – 4th Ave., Kenosha	Kenosha (Southport) Lighthouse
Kenosha	Library Park, Kenosha	Reuben Deming
Kenosha	Green Ridge Cemetery, 6604 Seventh Avenue, Kenosha	Revolutionary War Veterans
Kenosha	15620 12th St., Kenosha	Schaefer Mammoth Site
Kenosha	Hwy 32 at the southern edge of Kenosha	32nd Division Memorial Highway
Kenosha	Rest Area-Tourist Info. Ctr. #26, westbound I94, N of I11	The Name "Wisconsin"
Kenosha	SE corner of STHs 50, 75, and 83, Town of Salem	Brass Ball Corners
Kewaunee	Ferry yard, Kewaunee	Car-Ferry Service
La Crosse	Rest Area #15, eastbound I90	The Driftless Area
La Crosse	McGilvray Rd. Access, Van Loon State Wildlife Area	The McGilvray "Seven Bridges Road"
La Crosse	Halfway Creek Lutheran Church, 2.5 mi. E. of Holmen	Luther College
La Crosse	Bishop's View Overlook, Hwy 33, 5 mi. E. of La Crosse	The Coulee Region
La Crosse	Rest Area #31, I94, French Island, La Crosse	Major General C.C. Washburn
La Crosse	La Crosse	Red Cloud Park
La Crosse	Corner of Front and State Streets, La Crosse	Spence Park
La Crosse	Rest Area-Tourist Info. Ctr. #31, I90, La Crosse	Upper Mississippi
La Crosse	Hwy 16 Valley View Mall entrance, just N. of Medary	Valley View Site
La Crosse	Neshonoc Cemetery, West Salem	Hamlin Garland
La Crosse	Swarthout Lakeside Park, Hwy 16, West Salem	Village of Neshonoc
Lafayette	First Capitol State Park, Hwy G, 4 mi. northwest of Belmont	Belmont-Wisconsin Territory 1836
Lafayette	First Capitol State Park, Hwy G, 4 mi. northwest of Belmont	Gov. Tommy G. Thompson's 1998 Address at Wisconsin's First Capitol
Lafayette	First Capitol State Park, Hwy G, 4 mi. northwest of Belmont	1998 Wisconsin Assembly (Sesquicentennial Marker)
Lafayette	Hwy 11, 1 mile west of Benton	Father Samuel Mazzuchelli
Lafayette	Intersection of Hwys F, 78, & Madison St., Blanchardville	Zarahemia – Predecessor of Blanchardville
Lafayette	101 S. Main St., Blanchardville	Zenas Gurley
Lafayette	Hwy 23, 5 miles south of Mineral Point	Fort Defiance
Lafayette	Hwy 11, 1 mile west of Shullsburg	Wisconsin Lead Region
Lafayette	Black Hawk Memorial Park, 2995 CTH-Y, Town of Wiota	Battle of Pecatonica
Langlade	Hwy 52, near junction with Hwy 64	Antigo Silt Loam, State Soil of Wisconsin
Langlade	Wayside, Hwy 45, 3 miles south of Antigo	Langlade County Forest, Wisconsin's First County Forest
Langlade	Junction of Hwys 55 and 64, Langlade	De Langlade
Langlade	Hwy 55, 3.5 miles north of Lily at Wolf River	Old Military Road
Lincoln	715 E. 2nd St., Merrill	Merrill City Hall
Lincoln	Hwy 64 over the Prairie River – 200 W. First St., Merrill	Three Arch Stone Bridge
Manitowoc	CTH R, 1/2 mile N. of Schley Rd.	Rock Mill
Manitowoc	Rest Area #51, southbound I43, S. of Brown County line	Wisconsin's Dairy Industry
Manitowoc	Rest Area #52, northbound I43, S. of Brown County line	Wisconsin's Maritime Industries
Manitowoc	Lake Michigan Carferry Dock, 700 S. Lakeview Dr., Manitowoc	S. S. Badger/Manitowoc and the Car Ferries
Manitowoc	Mariner's Park, S. 8th St., at the Manitowoc River	Manitowoc's Maritime Heritage
Manitowoc	Manitowoc Maritime Museum, 75 Maritime Drive	Manitowoc Submarines
Manitowoc	Silver Lake Park, Hwy 151, west of Manitowoc	Winnebago Trail
Manitowoc	924 Pinecrest Lane, Manitowoc Rapids	Collins Road Bridge Span
Manitowoc	Pioneer Rd. and CTH XX, Meeme	Meeme Poll House
Manitowoc	St. Nazianz Village Hall, 228 W. Main St., St. Nazianz	George Washington School
Manitowoc	108 W. Birch, St. Nazianz	St. Nazianz
Manitowoc	Central Park, Two Rivers	Ice Cream Sundae
Manitowoc	Point Beach State Park, N. of Two Rivers on County O	Rawley Point Lighthouse
Manitowoc	Valders Memorial Park, Hwy J, Valders	Thorstein Veblen
Marathon	11248 Berlin Lane, Berlin Town Hall, Town of Berlin	Pomeranian Settlement in Marathon County
Marathon	Rothschild Pk., Grand Ave., Park & Kort Sts., Rothschild	Wisconsin's 1st Home-Built Flying Machine
Marathon	UW-Marathon County campus, Wausau	The First Teachers' Training School in Wisconsin
Marathon	Wayside, northbound Hwy 51, 1 mile south of Hwy 153	First Workers Compensation Policy
Marinette	Peshtigo Cemetery, Oconto Avenue, Peshtigo	Peshtigo Fire Cemetery
Marinette	N2155 USH 141, Town of Pound	Lena Road Schoolhouse

OFFICIAL HISTORICAL MARKERS IN WISCONSIN
May 2015–Continued

County	Location/Nearest Community	Subject
Marinette	W2349 County JJ, Wausaukee	McAllister State Graded School
Marquette	Hwy 22, 8 miles south of Montello	John Muir Country
Marquette	Rest Area #82, Hwy 51, 4 miles north of Westfield	Korean War
Marquette	Westfield Town Hall, W 7703 Ember Ave. at 4th	Russell Flats
Menominee	Hwys 47 and 55, 5 miles north of Shawano	Menominee Reservation
Menominee	Hwy, 55, 2.5 miles north of Keshena	Spirit Rock
Milwaukee	8801 West Grange Avenue, Greendale	Wisconsin's Lime Industry
Milwaukee	8685 West Grange Avenue, Greendale	Jeremiah Curtin House
Milwaukee	6500 Northway, Greendale	Village of Greendale
Milwaukee	Junction of 108th St. and Cold Spring Rd., Greenfield	Cold Spring Road
Milwaukee	North of 11000 W. Beloit Rd., Root River Pky., Greenfield	Historic Root River/Root River Parkway
Milwaukee	92nd and Forest Home Ave., Greenfield	Janesville Plank Road
Milwaukee	7325 W. Forest Home Ave., Greenfield	Town of Greenfield
Milwaukee	Zillman Park, S. Kinnickinnic Ave., Milwaukee	Bay View's Immigrants
Milwaukee	South Superior Street and East Russell Ave., Milwaukee	Bay View's Rolling Mill
Milwaukee	Salem Lutheran Church, 6814 N. 107th St., Milwaukee	Birthplace of the Wisconsin Evangelical Lutheran Synod
Milwaukee	2000 West Wisconsin Avenue, Milwaukee	Captain Frederick Pabst
Milwaukee	Zeidler Park, 300 block of West Michigan St., Milwaukee	Carl Frederick Zeidler
Milwaukee	East Hartford & North Maryland Aves., UW-Milwaukee	Carl Sandburg Hall
Milwaukee	1756 North Prospect Avenue, Milwaukee	Civil War Camp
Milwaukee	Lobby, 700 West Virginia Street, Milwaukee	The Cream City
Milwaukee	Grounds of VA Hospital, Wood (Milwaukee)	Erastus B. Wolcott, M.D.
Milwaukee	Fourth Street and Kilbourn Avenue, Milwaukee	First African-American Church Built in Wisconsin
Milwaukee	Foot of East Michigan Street, Milwaukee	First Milwaukee Cargo Pier
Milwaukee	Layton Avenue, Milwaukee	General Mitchell Field
Milwaukee	Golda Meir Library on UW-Milwaukee campus	Golda Meir
Milwaukee	4th and State Streets, Milwaukee	Invention of the Typewriter
Milwaukee	Marquette Law School, 1103 W. WI Ave., Milwaukee	Mabel Wanda Raimey
Milwaukee	Civic Center, Milwaukee	MacArthur Square
Milwaukee	Merrill Park, 461 North 35th St., Milwaukee	Merrill Park
Milwaukee	Currie Park, Wauwatosa	Milwaukee County's First Airport
Milwaukee	East Hartford and North Downer Avenues, Milwaukee	Milwaukee-Downer College
Milwaukee	231 West Michigan Street, Milwaukee	Milwaukee Interurban Terminal, 1905-1951
Milwaukee	Zablocki VA Medical Center, Hwy 59	National Soldiers Home
Milwaukee	At the lighthouse in Lake Park, Milwaukee	North Point Lighthouse
Milwaukee	East North Avenue, Milwaukee	Old North Point Water Tower
Milwaukee	Wells and Edison Streets, Milwaukee	Oneida Street Station, T.M.E.R. and L. Co.
Milwaukee	144 East Wells Street, Milwaukee	Pabst Theater
Milwaukee	Cathedral Square Park, northeast corner, Milwaukee	Rescue of Joshua Glover
Milwaukee	North Avenue and Lake Drive, Milwaukee	Saint John's Infirmary
Milwaukee	North Lake Drive, Milwaukee	St. Mary's School of Nursing
Milwaukee	North Water and East Erie Streets, Milwaukee	Sinking of the *Lady Elgin*
Milwaukee	200 North Broadway, Milwaukee	Third Ward Fire
Milwaukee	Mitchell Hall, UW-Milwaukee, North Downer Avenue	The University of Wisconsin-Milwaukee
Milwaukee	Miller Brewing Company, Milwaukee	Watertown Plank Road
Milwaukee	731 North Plankinton Ave., Milwaukee	Wisconsin Soldiers' Home 1864-1867
Milwaukee	100 East Wisconsin Avenue, Milwaukee	Wisconsin's Oldest Newspaper: The *Milwaukee Sentinel*
Milwaukee	3500 block on N. Oakland Ave., Shorewood	Lueddeman's On-the-River
Milwaukee	4145 N. Oakland Ave., Shorewood	Shorewood Armory
Milwaukee	1701 E. Capitol Drive, Shorewood	Shorewood High School
Milwaukee	3930 N. Murray Ave., Shorewood	Shorewood Village Hall
Milwaukee	909 Menomonee Ave., South Milwaukee	Lawson Airplane Company
Milwaukee	Wauwatosa Cemetery, 2405-2485 Wauwatosa Ave., Wauwatosa	Revolutionary War Veteran (Morgan)
Milwaukee	State Fair Park, Main Gate, West Allis	Camp Harvey
Milwaukee	In triangle at 57th, Hayes, and Fillmore, West Allis	Meadowmere
Milwaukee	State Fair Park, Main Gate, West Allis	Wisconsin State Fair Park
Monroe	Hwy 12, 4 miles west of Camp Douglas	Mesas and Buttes
Monroe	Rest Area #16, westbound I90, 5 miles east of Bangor	Coulee Country
Monroe	At the Kendall Depot, North Railroad Street, Kendall	Elroy-Sparta State Trail
Monroe	Old Leon School, 20638 Jameson Rd., Sparta	Donald "Deke" Slayton
Monroe	200 West Main Street, Sparta	Masonic Lodge
Monroe	112 South Court Street, Sparta	Monroe County Courthouse
Monroe	124 West Main Street, Sparta	Sparta Free Library
Monroe	123 West Main Street, Sparta	U.S. Post Office
Monroe	In park on Hwy 12, Tomah	Tomah
Oconto	Hwy F, 1.5 miles east of Lakewood	The Holt and Balcom Logging Camp No. 1
Oconto	Chicago and Main Streets, Oconto	First Church of Christ Scientist
Oconto	On Oconto River at Brazeau Avenue, Oconto	Mission of St. Francois Xavier
Oconto	Copper Culture State Park, Oconto	Old Copper Culture Cemetery
Oconto	1301 Main Street, Oconto	Stanley Toy Company
Oneida	Junction of CTH-B and CTH-Z, Pelican Lake	Mecikalski Stovewood Building
Oneida	Oneida County Courthouse grounds, Rhinelander	First Rural Zoning Ordinance
Oneida	Hodag Park, Rhinelander	The Hodag
Oneida	W. edge of National Forest, off Hwy 32 E. of Three Lakes	Nicolet National Forest
Outagamie	807 South Oneida Street, Appleton	First Electric Street Railway

OFFICIAL HISTORICAL MARKERS IN WISCONSIN
May 2015–Continued

County	Location/Nearest Community	Subject
Outagamie	700 Block of E. College Ave., Lawrence Univ., Appleton	The Merging of Milwaukee Downer and Lawrence Colleges
Outagamie	600 Vulcan Street, Appleton	World's First Hydroelectric Central Station
Outagamie	North of jct. Hwys BB and 45, 4 miles west of Appleton	South Greenville Grange No. 225
Outagamie	100 Vulcan Street, Appleton	Vulcan Street Plant Replica
Outagamie	Thelen Park, Kaukauna	Revolutionary War Veterans
Outagamie	Hwy 96, 0.1 mile west of Little Chute	Treaty of the Cedars
Outagamie	Beacon Avenue and Division Street, New London	Birthplace of the American Water Spaniel
Ozaukee	Intersection of CTHs R & C, Belgium	Wisconsin's Luxembourgers
Ozaukee	Columbia Rd. and Mequon Ave., Cedarburg	Cedar Creek
Ozaukee	City Hall, Washington Avenue, Cedarburg	Historic Cedarburg
Ozaukee	W62 N646 Washington Ave., Cedarburg	Interurban Bridge
Ozaukee	Doctor's Park, Washington Ave. and Mill St., Cedarburg	Washington Avenue Historic District
Ozaukee	Covered Bridge Road, 1 mile north of Five Corners	Last Covered Bridge
Ozaukee	Mequon City Hall, 11333 North Cedarburg Rd., Mequon	Wisconsin's German Settlers
Ozaukee	Leland Stanford Plaza (formerly 120 East Main Street), Port Washington	Leland Stanford
Ozaukee	Ozaukee County Courthouse, 121 West Main Street, Port Washington	Port Washington Civil War Draft Riots
Ozaukee	102 East Pier Street, Port Washington	Port Washington Fire Engine House
Ozaukee	108 N. Lake St., Port Washington	The Wisconsin Chair Company Fire
Ozaukee	Triangle Park and Green Bay Rd., Saukville	The Saukville Trails
Ozaukee	Entrance Wall, 250 S. Main St., Thiensville	Historic Thiensville
Ozaukee	Junction of Hwys F and M, 3 miles west of Thiensville	The Oldest Lutheran Church in Wisconsin
Ozaukee	Hwy I, 0.5 mile east of Waubeka	Birthplace of Flag Day
Pepin	Washington Square, Durand	Pepin County Courthouse
Pepin	Hwy 35, 1 mile north of Stockholm	Maiden Rock
Pepin	Hwy 35, Pepin Park	Laura Ingalls Wilder
Pepin	Hwy 35, 3 miles northwest of Pepin	Site of Fort St. Antoine
Pierce	Hwy 35, 1 mile south of Hwy 63, southeast of Hager City	"Bow and Arrow"
Pierce	Hwy 35, 3 miles west of Maiden Rock	Lake Pepin
Pierce	Spring Pond Park, East Mill Rd., Plum City	Historic Plum City
Pierce	Hwy 65, 3 miles south of I94	Edgar Wilson Nye
Polk	Hwy 35, Luck	Danish Cooperative Company
Polk	City Park, St. Croix Falls	The Battle of St. Croix Falls
Polk	Interstate Park, St. Croix Falls	Gaylord Nelson
Polk	Interstate Park, Hwy 8, St. Croix Falls	State Park Movement in Wisconsin
Polk	Overlook Park, N. Washington (Main) St., St. Croix Falls	Where Are the Falls of the St. Croix?
Portage	County W, Buena Vista Marsh Wildlife Area	Wisconsin's Greater Prairie Chicken
Portage	Portage County Park, Hwy E, 3 miles south of Knowlton	Du Bay Trading Post
Portage	1700 block of Monroe St., Stevens Point	The Historic Southside Railroad Complex of Stevens Point
Price	Movrich Park, Willow Avenue, Town of Fifield	Historic Fifield
Price	Hwy 13, Phillips City Park, Phillips	Phillips Fire
Racine	Weimhoff-Jucker Park, Burlington	Mormons in Early Wisconsin
Racine	Hwy 31 at 5 Mile Rd., Town of Caledonia	Bohemian School House
Racine	936 South Main Street, Racine	The Blake House/Lucius Blake
Racine	Zoological Gardens, 2131 N. Main St., Racine	Northside Historic District of Cream Brick Cottages
Racine	Graceland and Mound Cemeteries, 1147 West Blvd., Racine	Soldiers of the American Revolution
Racine	Simonsen Park, Main & Fourteenth Sts., Racine	Southside Historic District
Racine	Hwy 11, western limits of Racine	The Spark
Racine	Racine Village Park, 4725 Lighthouse Dr., Racine	The Wind Point Lighthouse
Racine	1407 71st Drive, Union Grove	Revolutionary War Veteran
Racine	Heg Park Road, Waterford	Old Muskego
Richland	Boaz Park, Hwy 171, Boaz	Ocooch Mountains
Richland	Boaz Park, Hwy 171, Boaz	Richard M. Brewer
Richland	Wayside, Hwy 14, 1 mi. E. Gotham, Town of Buena Vista	The Pursuit West
Richland	Krouskop Park, 400 W. 6th St. (Hwy 14), Richland Center	Ada James
Richland	Krouskop Park, 400 W. 6th St. (Hwy 14), Richland Center	Birthplace of General Telephone and Electronics Corporation (GTE)
Richland	Hwy 14, 5 miles west of Richland Center	Boaz Mastodon
Richland	Pier County Park, Hwy 80, Rockbridge	Rockbridge
Richland	5 miles west of Richland Center on Hwy 14	Rural Electrification
Richland	Pier Co. Park, Hwy 80, Rockbridge	Troop Encampment
Rock	Beloit College campus, Beloit	Beloit College
Rock	Rock River Heritage Wky., Public Ave. & State St., Beloit	Black Hawk at Turtle Village
Rock	Tourist Info. Ctr. #22, westbound I90, south of Beloit	Black Hawk War
Rock	Rest Area-Tourist Information Center, westbound I90	Medal of Honor
Rock	Turtle Island, Riverside Park, Beloit	Roy Chapman Andrews
Rock	I43 at I90, Beloit	Wisconsin's First Aviator
Rock	Hwy 140, 4 miles south of Clinton	Jefferson Prairie Settlement
Rock	11204 N. Church St., Cooksville	Historic Cooksville/Historic Waucoma
Rock	Mt. Philip Cemetery, west of Darien	Soldier of the American Revolution
Rock	Hwy 51, 0.5 miles south of Edgerton	Wisconsin's Tobacco Land
Rock	Black Allen Creek Bridge, 100 E. Main St., Evansville	CCC Veterans Memorial Bridge
Rock	Blackhawk Golf Course Clubhouse, 2100 Palmer, Janesville	The Black Hawk War/Black Hawk's Grove
Rock	NW corner of Delavan Dr. and Beloit Ave., Janesville	Burr Robins Circus
Rock	In Courthouse Park on S. Atwood Ave., Janesville	First State Fair, October 1-2, 1851

OFFICIAL HISTORICAL MARKERS IN WISCONSIN
May 2015–Continued

County	Location/Nearest Community	Subject
Rock	Rock County Historical Society, 10 S. High St., Janesville	Janesville Tank Company
Rock	Rest Area #17, eastbound I90	Rock River Industry
Rock	Hwy 51, 3.8 miles south of Janesville	Route of Abraham Lincoln 1832 and 1859
Rock	18 South Janesville Street, Hwy 26, Milton	Milton House
Rock	On southwest bank of Storr's Lake, off Hwy 26, Milton	Storr's Lake, Milton
Rock	Beckman Mill Co. Park, Co. Rd. H, Town of Newark	How-Beckman Mill
Rock	Hwy J, Shopiere	Home of Governor Harvey
Rusk	Appolonia Cong. Church, Hwy 8 & Cemetery Rd., Bruce	Appolonia
Rusk	Hwy 8, Weyerhauser	Chippewa River and Menomonie Railway
St. Croix	Rest Area-Tourist Info. Ctr. #25, I94 east of Hudson	Brule-St. Croix Waterway
St. Croix	Hwy 35, 4.7 miles north of Hudson	St. Croix River
St. Croix	Campus Drive, Outlot #3, New Richmond	New Richmond Cyclone
Sauk	Devil's Lake State Park, S5975 Park Rd., Baraboo	Civilian Conservation Corps
Sauk	Hwy 33 at County U, 5 miles east of Baraboo	Lower Narrows
Sauk	Hwy 12, 1.5 miles south of Baraboo.	Ringling Brothers Circus
Sauk	CTH A, near junction of Old County Hwy A and Dam Rd., Lake Delton	Lake Delton Catastrophe
Sauk	E8948 Diamond Hill Rd., North Freedom.	Mid-Continent Railway Historical Society
Sauk	Reedsburg Area Historical Park, 3 mi. E. of Reedsburg.	Clare A. Briggs, Cartoonist
Sauk	State Hwy 136, 0.75 mi. N of STH 154, Rock Springs	Van Hise Rock
Sauk	Derleth Park, Water Street, Sauk City	August W. Derleth
Sauk	Hwy 12, 5 miles northwest of Sauk City	The Baraboo Range
Sauk	Lower WI Riverway, Hwy 78, 2 mi. N. of Sauk City	Battle of Wisconsin Heights
Sauk	Lower WI Riverway, Hwy 60, 2 mi. E. of Spring Green	Western Escape
Sauk	Hwy A, 1.5 miles south of Wisconsin Dells	Dawn Manor – Site of Lost City of Newport
Sauk	Hwy 16, 0.1 mile west of Wisconsin Dells	Wisconsin Dells
Sawyer	Hwys 70 and 27, Couderay	Court Oreilles
Sawyer	Hwys 27 and 70, 7 miles west of Couderay	Radisson-Groseilliers
Sawyer	Hermans Landing, Cty Rd CC, at bridge, Hayward	The Chippewa Flowage
Sawyer	Lac Courte Oreilles Reservation, 13891 W. Mission Rd.	St. Francis Solanus Indian Mission
Sawyer	Hwy 27, 5.5 miles south of Hayward	Namekagon-Court Oreilles Portage
Sawyer	Hwy W, 6.75 miles southeast of Winter	John Deitz, "Battle of Cameron Dam"
Shawano	Hwy 22, 3.5 miles east of Shawano	Shawano
Shawano	Hwy 45 at city limits of Wittenberg	Homme Homes
Sheboygan	50 South Main Street, Cedar Grove	Early Dutch Settlers in Wisconsin
Sheboygan	Lake Street Café Beer Garden, N. of Vil. of Elkhart Lake	Elkhart Lake – Road Race Circuits
Sheboygan	Hwy 23, in the Park at Greenbush, 6 mi. W. of Plymouth.	Old Wade House State Park
Sheboygan	Memorial Park, Cedar Grove, 3 miles south of Oostburg	Dutch Settlement
Sheboygan	Heritage House Triangle Pk., Ctr. & N. 10th Sts., Oostburg	Historic Oostburg
Sheboygan	Greenleaf Historic Park, 900 Short Street, Random Lake.	Nowack House
Sheboygan	Sheboygan North Point Park, North Point Dr., Sheboygan	The *Phoenix* Tragedy
Sheboygan	Wildwood Cemetery, 2026 New Jersey Ave., Sheboygan.	Revolutionary War Veteran (David Waldo)
Sheboygan	Center Avenue and North Water Street, Sheboygan	Seils-Sterling Circus
Sheboygan	9th Street and Panther Avenue, Sheboygan	Sheboygan Indian Mound Park
Sheboygan	1138 Union Ave., Sheboygan	Veterans of Foreign Wars Post 1230
Sheboygan	Rochester Inn, 504 Water St., Sheboygan Falls	Cole Historic District
Sheboygan	Sheboygan River Dam, Broadway St., Sheboygan Falls	Downtown Sheboygan Falls Historic District
Taylor	Hwy 102, Rib Lake	Rib Lake Lumber Company
Taylor	Hwy 102, 5 miles northeast of Rib Lake	Rustic Road
Trempealeau	Hwy 53, 1.5 miles southeast of Galesville.	Decorah Peak
Trempealeau	Junction of East Gale Avenue and Main Street, Galesville	Downtown Galesville Historic District
Trempealeau	STH 53 over Beaver Creek, Galesville	Galesville Bridge
Trempealeau	North of Main Hall, College Ave., Galesville	Galesville College
Trempealeau	Junction of West Ridge Ave. and Sixth St. near Cance Park, Galesville	Ridge Avenue Historic District
Trempealeau	Rest Area #5, eastbound I94, 2 miles southeast of Osseo	Winnebago Indians
Trempealeau	Great River State Tr., Hwy 35, 0.5 mi. E. of Trempealeau	The Mississippi River Parkway: First Project
Trempealeau	Perrot State Park	Brady's Bluff
Trempealeau	Perrot State Park, off Hwy 93	Perrot's Post
Vernon	Hwy 14, 0.5 mile west of Coon Valley	Nation's First Watershed Project
Vernon	Hwy 35, 2.5 miles north of De Soto	Battle of Bad Axe
Vernon	Hwy 35, 2 miles north of De Soto	Chief Win-no-shik, the Elder
Vernon	Hwy 35, Genoa	Dams on the Mississippi
Vernon	In power plant parking lot, west side of Hwy 35, Genoa	Wisconsin's First Nuclear-Fueled Generating Station
Vernon	Hwy 33, 0.1 mile west of Hillsboro	Admiral Marc A. Mitscher
Vernon	Hillsboro Lake Park, 300 Water Ave. at Hwys 80, 82, 33, Hillsboro	African American Settlers of the Cheyenne Valley
Vernon	Hwy 14, 0.5 mile north of Viroqua	Governor Rusk
Vernon	City Hall, 202 N. Main St., Viroqua	Viroqua's First Settler
Vilas	Hwy M, 6 miles south of Boulder Junction	First Forest Patrol Flight
Vilas	Trout Lake Nursery, Hwy M.	Forest Restoration – The Beginning
Vilas	Hwy 47, Flambeau Lake	Lac du Flambeau
Vilas	Lac Vieux Desert Park, West Shore Dr. near Land O'Lakes	Lac Vieux Desert
Vilas	Hwys 32 and 45, 0.5 mile south of Land O'Lakes	32nd Division Memorial Highway
Vilas	Hwy 45, 1.5 miles south of Land O'Lakes	Wisconsin River Headwaters
Vilas	Sayner Park, Sayner	Snowmobile
Walworth	Village Park, Allen Grove, on Hwy X, 3 mi. SW of Darien	Allen Family
Walworth	City of Delavan Parking Lot, 218 South 7th St., Delavan.	Birthplace of "The Greatest Show on Earth"

OFFICIAL HISTORICAL MARKERS IN WISCONSIN
May 2015–Continued

County	Location/Nearest Community	Subject
Walworth. . . .	Horton Park, Hwy 11 in Delavan	Delavan's Circus Colony
Walworth. . . .	Tower Park, Walworth Ave., Delavan	Delavan's Historic Brick Street
Walworth. . . .	Grounds of State School for the Deaf, Hwy 11, Delavan	Wisconsin's First School for Deaf
Walworth. . . .	300 Church Street, East Troy	East Troy Railroad
Walworth. . . .	Veterans Memorial Park, Hwy 12, Genoa City	First Swedish Settlers in Wisconsin
Walworth. . . .	Hwy BB, 3.5 miles south of Lake Geneva.	Wisconsin's First 4-H Club
Walworth. . . .	Oak Grove Cemetery, East Main Street, Whitewater	Revolutionary War Veterans
Walworth. . . .	Hwy 67 Industrial Park, N3440 STH 67 Williams Bay	755 Aircraft Control and Warning Squadron
Washburn . . .	Hwy 70, 0.5 mile east of Spooner	Yellow River
Washburn . . .	Junction of Hwys 53 and 63, Trego	Namekagon River
Washington. .	Dheinsville Park, Holy Hill Rd., Germantown	Dheinsville Settlement
Washington. .	Chandelier Ballroom, 700 South Main Street, Hartford.	The Schwartz Ballroom
Washington. .	Hwy 83, Hartford	"Kissel"
Washington. .	South side of Hwy 33, 550 feet west of jct. with Hwy 144	Great Divide
Washington. .	At the park, Hwy A, E. of Hwy 144, NW of West Bend	Lizard Mound County Park
Washington. .	Riverside Park, West Bend.	The West Bend Aluminum Company
Waukesha . . .	408 Main St., Delafield	Delafield Fish Hatchery
Waukesha . . .	Southern Kettle Moraine State Forest, County C, Delafield.	Lapham Peak
Waukesha . . .	Mission Road at Mill Road, west of Delafield.	Nashotah Mission
Waukesha . . .	1101 North Genesee Street, Delafield	St. John's Northwestern Military Academy
Waukesha . . .	Hwy 18, near Dousman	Masonic Home
Waukesha . . .	Main Street, Lannon.	Lannon Stone
Waukesha . . .	N51 W34922 Wisconsin Ave., Okauchee	Historic Okauchee
Waukesha . . .	Carroll College campus, Waukesha	Carroll College
Waupaca	Municipal Airport, Clintonville	Birthplace of an Airline
Waupaca	Walter Olen Park, Clintonville.	Four-Wheel Drive
Waupaca	Marden Memorial Center, WI Veterans Home, King	General Charles King
Waupaca	Marden Memorial Center, WI Veterans Home, King	Grand Army Home
Waupaca	Triangle Park, Jct. of Hwy 22 with 110 and Hwy B, Manawa	Melvin O. Handrich – Medal of Honor Recipient
Waupaca	Hwy 110, 3.5 miles south of Marion	Chief Waupaca
Waushara. . . .	County J, 2 miles south of Almond	Sir Henry Wellcome
Waushara. . . .	State Hwy 49, Auroraville	The Auroraville Fountain
Waushara. . . .	6th Ave., Town of Hancock	Whistler Mound Group and Enclosure
Winnebago . . .	9088 Clayton Avenue, Town of Menasha	Fox-Irish Cemetery
Winnebago . . .	Menasha Hotel, Main and Mills Streets, Menasha	Wisconsin Central Railroad
Winnebago . . .	Fritsie Park, Menasha	Butte des Morts
Winnebago . . .	Interior walkway, 135 W. Wisconsin Ave., Neenah	Wisconsin Avenue Commercial Historic District
Winnebago . . .	Scott Park, 515 E. Main St., Omro	Historic Omro
Winnebago . . .	1619 Oshkosh Avenue, Oshkosh.	Coles Bashford House
Winnebago . . .	Oshkosh Public Museum, 1331 Algoma Blvd., Oshkosh	Edgar Sawyer House
Winnebago . . .	Rainbow Park, Oshkosh	Knaggs Ferry
Winnebago . . .	Wittman Field Airport, 20th Street Road, Oshkosh	S.J. Wittman
Winnebago . . .	UW-Oshkosh campus, Oshkosh	University of Wisconsin-Oshkosh
Winnebago . . .	Town of Winchester Cemetery, 1 mi. SW of Winchester	Samuel N. Rogers, Sr., American Revolutionary Soldier
Winnebago . . .	Hwy B, west of Winneconne	Poygan Paygrounds
Wood	Wayside #4, junction of Hwys 10 and 13	Prisoners of War
Wood	West 100 Block of North Central Ave., Marshfield	Founder's Square
Wood	Riverside Park, Hwys 54 and 73, Nekoosa	Point Basse
Wood	Hwy 54, 5 miles west of Port Edwards	Cranberry Culture
Wood	Hwys 54 and 73, southern city limits of Wisconsin Rapids	Centralia Pulp and Paper Mill
Wood	South Wood County Historical Museum, 540 3rd Street S, Wisconsin Rapids	Myron "Grim" Natwick

Sources: State Historical Society of Wisconsin, Historical Markers Council, *A Guide to Wisconsin Historical Markers,* 1982; Division of Historic Preservation, departmental data, June 2015.

WISCONSIN VOTE IN PRESIDENTIAL ELECTIONS
1848 – 2012

Key:

A – American (Know Nothing)	LR – Liberal Republican	Soc – Socialist
AFC – America First Coalition	NA – New Alliance	SocUSA – Socialist Party USA
Cit – Citizens	Nat – National	SoD – Southern Democrat
Com – Communist	ND – National Democrat	SPW – Socialist Party of Wis.
Con – Constitution	NER – National Economic Recovery	SW – Socialist Worker
CU – Constitutional Union	NL – Natural Law	Tax – U.S. Taxpayers
D – Democrat	People's – People's (Populist)	TBL – The Better Life
ER – Independents for Economic Recovery	Pop – Populist	3rd – Third Party
FS – Free Soil	PP – People's Progressive	U – Union
G – Greenback	Prog – Progressive	UL – Union Labor
Gr – Grassroots	Proh – Prohibition	USL – U.S. Labor
Grn – Green	R – Republican	W – Whig
Ind – Independent	Rfm – Reform	WG – Wisconsin Greens
IP – Ind. Progressive	SD – Social Democrat	WIA – Wis. Independent Alliance
IS – Ind. Socialist	SE – Socialist Equality	Workers – Workers
ISL – Ind. Socialist Labor	SL – Socialist Labor	WtP – We, the People
ISW – Ind. Socialist Worker	S&L – Party for Socialism and	WW – Worker's World
LF – Labor–Farm/Laborista-Agrario	Liberation	
Lib – Libertarian		

Note: The party designation listed for a candidate is taken from the Congressional Quarterly *Guide to U.S. Elections*. A candidate whose party did not receive 1% of the vote for a statewide office in the previous election or who failed to meet the alternative requirement of Section 5.62, Wisconsin Statutes, must be listed on the Wisconsin ballot as "independent". In this listing, candidates whose party affiliations appear as "Ind", followed by a party designation, were identified on the ballot simply as "independent" although they also provided a party designation or statement of principle.

Under the Electoral College system, each state is entitled to electoral votes equal in number to its total congressional delegation of U.S. Senators and U.S. Representatives.

1848 (4 electoral votes)
Lewis Cass (D).	15,001
Zachary Taylor (W)	13,747
Martin Van Buren (FS).	10,418
TOTAL	39,166

1852 (5 electoral votes)
Franklin Pierce (D)	33,658
Winfield Scott (W).	22,210
John P. Hale (FS).	8,814
TOTAL	64,682

1856 (5 electoral votes)
John C. Fremont (R).	66,090
James Buchanan (D).	52,843
Millard Fillmore (A).	579
TOTAL	119,512

1860 (5 electoral votes)
Abraham Lincoln (R)	86,113
Stephen A. Douglas (D)	65,021
John C. Breckinridge (SoD)	888
John Bell (CU).	161
TOTAL	152,183

1864 (8 electoral votes)
Abraham Lincoln (R)	83,458
George B. McClellan (D)	65,884
TOTAL	149,342

1868 (8 electoral votes)
Ulysses S. Grant (R).	108,857
Horatio Seymour (D)	84,707
TOTAL	193,564

1872 (10 electoral votes)
Ulysses S. Grant (R).	104,994
Horace Greeley (D & LR).	86,477
Charles O'Conor (D).	834
TOTAL	192,305

1876 (10 electoral votes)
Rutherford B. Hayes (R).	130,668
Samuel J. Tilden (D).	123,927
Peter Cooper (G).	1,509
Green Clay Smith (Proh)	27
TOTAL	256,131

1880 (10 electoral votes)
James A. Garfield (R).	144,398
Winfield S. Hancock (D).	114,644
James B. Weaver (G).	7,986
John W. Phelps (A)	91
Neal Dow (Proh).	68
TOTAL	267,187

1884 (11 electoral votes)
James G. Blaine (R)	161,157
Grover Cleveland (D)	146,477
John P. St. John (Proh).	7,656
Benjamin F. Butler (G).	4,598
TOTAL	319,888

1888 (11 electoral votes)
Benjamin Harrison (R).	176,553
Grover Cleveland (D)	155,232
Clinton B. Fisk (Proh)	14,277
Alson J. Streeter (UL)	8,552
TOTAL	354,614

1892 (12 electoral votes)
Grover Cleveland (D)	177,325
Benjamin Harrison (R).	171,101
John Bidwell (Proh)	13,136
James B. Weaver (People's)	10,019
TOTAL	371,581

1896 (12 electoral votes)
William McKinley (R).	268,135
William J. Bryan (D).	165,523
Joshua Levering (Proh)	7,507
John M. Palmer (ND)	4,584
Charles H. Matchett (SL)	1,314
Charles E. Bentley (Nat).	346
TOTAL	447,409

1900 (12 electoral votes)
William McKinley (R).	265,760
William J. Bryan (D).	159,163
John G. Wooley (Proh).	10,027
Eugene V. Debs (SD)	7,048
Joseph F. Malloney (SL).	503
TOTAL	442,501

1904 (13 electoral votes)
Theodore Roosevelt (R)	280,164
Alton B. Parker (D)	124,107
Eugene V. Debs (SD)	28,220
Silas C. Swallow (Proh)	9,770
Thomas E. Watson (People's)	530
Charles H. Corregan (SL)	223
TOTAL	443,014

1908 (13 electoral votes)
William H. Taft (R)	247,747
William J. Bryan (D).	166,632
Eugene V. Debs (SD)	28,164
Eugene W. Chafin (Proh)	11,564
August Gillhaus (SL)	314
TOTAL	454,421

WISCONSIN VOTE IN PRESIDENTIAL ELECTIONS
1848 – 2012–Continued

1912 (13 electoral votes)

Woodrow Wilson (D)	164,230
William H. Taft (R)	130,596
Theodore Roosevelt (Prog)	62,448
Eugene V. Debs (SD)	33,476
Eugene W. Chafin (Proh)	8,584
Arthur E. Reimer (SL)	632
TOTAL	399,966

1916 (13 electoral votes)

Charles E. Hughes (R)	220,822
Woodrow Wilson (D)	191,363
Allan Benson (Soc)	27,631
J. Frank Hanly (Proh)	7,318
TOTAL	447,134

1920 (13 electoral votes)

Warren G. Harding (R)	498,576
James M. Cox (D)	113,422
Eugene V. Debs (Soc)	80,635
Aaron S. Watkins (Proh)	8,647
TOTAL	701,280

1924 (13 electoral votes)

Robert M. La Follette (Prog)	453,678
Calvin Coolidge (R)	311,614
John W. Davis (D)	68,096
William Z. Foster (Workers)	3,834
Herman P. Faris (Proh)	2,918
TOTAL	840,140

1928 (13 electoral votes)

Herbert Hoover (R)	544,205
Alfred E. Smith (D)	450,259
Norman Thomas (Soc)	18,213
William F. Varney (Proh)	2,245
William Z. Foster (Workers)	1,528
Verne L. Reynolds (SL)	381
TOTAL	1,016,831

1932 (12 electoral votes)

Franklin D. Roosevelt (D)	707,410
Herbert Hoover (R)	347,741
Norman Thomas (Soc)	53,379
William Z. Foster (Com)	3,112
William D. Upshaw (Proh)	2,672
Verne L. Reynolds (SL)	494
TOTAL	1,114,808

1936 (12 electoral votes)

Franklin D. Roosevelt (D)	802,984
Alfred M. Landon (R)	380,828
William Lemke (U)	60,297
Norman Thomas (Soc)	10,626
Earl Browder (Com)	2,197
David L. Calvin (Proh)	1,071
John W. Aiken (SL)	557
TOTAL	1,258,560

1940 (12 electoral votes)

Franklin D. Roosevelt (D)	704,821
Wendell Willkie (R)	679,206
Norman Thomas (Soc)	15,071
Earl Browder (Com)	2,394
Roger Babson (Proh)	2,148
John W. Aiken (SL)	1,882
TOTAL	1,405,522

1944 (12 electoral votes)

Thomas Dewey (R)	674,532
Franklin D. Roosevelt (D)	650,413
Norman Thomas (Soc)	13,205
Edward Teichert (Ind)	1,002
TOTAL	1,339,152

1948 (12 electoral votes)

Harry S Truman (D)	647,310
Thomas Dewey (R)	590,959
Henry Wallace (PP)	25,282
Norman Thomas (Soc)	12,547
Edward Teichert (Ind)	399
Farrell Dobbs (ISW)	303
TOTAL	1,276,800

1952 (12 electoral votes)

Dwight D. Eisenhower (R)	979,744
Adlai E. Stevenson (D)	622,175
Vincent Hallinan (IP)	2,174
Farrell Dobbs (ISW)	1,350
Darlington Hoopes (IS)	1,157
Eric Hass (ISL)	770
TOTAL	1,607,370

1956 (12 electoral votes)

Dwight D. Eisenhower (R)	954,844
Adlai E. Stevenson (D)	586,768
T. Coleman Andrews (Ind Con)	6,918
Darlington Hoopes (Ind Soc)	754
Eric Hass (Ind SL)	710
Farrell Dobbs (Ind SW)	564
TOTAL	1,550,558

1960 (12 electoral votes)

Richard M. Nixon (R)	895,175
John F. Kennedy (D)	830,805
Farrell Dobbs (Ind SW)	1,792
Eric Hass (Ind SL)	1,310
TOTAL	1,729,082

1964 (12 electoral votes)

Lyndon B. Johnson (D)	1,050,424
Barry M. Goldwater (R)	638,495
Clifton DeBerry (Ind SW)	1,692
Eric Hass (Ind SL)	1,204
TOTAL	1,691,815

1968 (12 electoral votes)

Richard M. Nixon (R)	809,997
Hubert H. Humphrey (D)	748,804
George C. Wallace (Ind A)	127,835
Henning A. Blomen (Ind SL)	1,338
Frederick W. Halstead (Ind SW)	1,222
TOTAL	1,689,196

1972 (11 electoral votes)

Richard M. Nixon (R)	989,430
George S. McGovern (D)	810,174
John G. Schmitz (A)	47,525
Benjamin M. Spock (Ind Pop)	2,701
Louis Fisher (Ind SL)	998
Gus Hall (Ind Com)	663
Evelyn Reed (Ind SW)	506
TOTAL	1,851,997

1976 (11 electoral votes)

Jimmy Carter (D)	1,040,232
Gerald R. Ford (R)	1,004,987
Eugene J. McCarthy (Ind)	34,943
Lester Maddox (A)	8,552
Frank P. Zeidler (Ind Soc)	4,298
Roger L. MacBride (Ind Lib)	3,814
Peter Camejo (Ind SW)	1,691
Margaret Wright (Ind Pop)	943
Gus Hall (Ind Com)	749
Lyndon H. LaRouche, Jr. (Ind USL)	738
Jules Levin (Ind SL)	389
TOTAL	2,104,175

WISCONSIN VOTE IN PRESIDENTIAL ELECTIONS
1848 – 2012–Continued

1980 (11 electoral votes)	
Ronald Reagan (R).	1,088,845
Jimmy Carter (D)	981,584
John Anderson (Ind)	160,657
Ed Clark (Ind Lib)	29,135
Barry Commoner (Ind Cit).	7,767
John Rarick (Ind Con)	1,519
David McReynolds (Ind Soc)	808
Gus Hall (Ind Com)	772
Deidre Griswold (Ind WW)	414
Clifton DeBerry (Ind SW)	383
TOTAL	2,273,221

1984 (11 electoral votes)	
Ronald Reagan (R).	1,198,800
Walter F. Mondale (D).	995,847
David Bergland (Lib)	4,884
Bob Richards (Con)	3,864
Lyndon H. LaRouche, Jr. (Ind)	3,791
Sonia Johnson (Ind Cit)	1,456
Dennis L. Serrette (Ind WIA)	1,007
Larry Holmes (Ind WW).	619
Gus Hall (Ind Com)	597
Melvin T. Mason (Ind SW)	445
TOTAL	2,212,018

1988 (11 electoral votes)	
Michael S. Dukakis (D)	1,126,794
George Bush (R).	1,047,499
Ronald Paul (Ind Lib)	5,157
David E. Duke (Ind Pop)	3,056
James Warren (Ind SW)	2,574
Lyndon H. LaRouche, Jr. (Ind NER)	2,302
Lenora B. Fulani (Ind NA).	1,953
TOTAL	2,191,612

1992 (11 electoral votes)	
Bill Clinton (D)	1,041,066
George Bush (R).	930,855
Ross Perot (Ind)	544,479
Andre Marrou (Lib)	2,877
James Gritz (Ind AFC).	2,311
Ron Daniels (LF)	1,883
Howard Phillips (Ind Tax)	1,772
J. Quinn Brisben (Ind Soc).	1,211
John Hagelin (NL)	1,070
Lenora B. Fulani (Ind NA).	654
Lyndon H. LaRouche, Jr. (Ind ER)	633
Jack Herer (Ind Gr)	547
Eugene A. Hem (3rd)	405
James Warren (Ind SW)	390
TOTAL	2,531,114

1996 (11 electoral votes)	
Bill Clinton (D)	1,071,971
Bob Dole (R).	845,029
Ross Perot (Rfm)	227,339
Ralph Nader (Ind WG).	28,723
Howard Phillips (Tax)	8,811
Harry Browne (Lib)	7,929
John Hagelin (Ind NL).	1,379
Monica Mooerhead (Ind WW).	1,333
Mary Cal Hollis (Ind Soc)	848
James E. Harris (Ind SW)	483
TOTAL	2,196,169

2000 (11 electoral votes)	
Al Gore (D)	1,242,987
George W. Bush (R)	1,237,279
Ralph Nader (WG).	94,070
Pat Buchanan (Ind Rfm).	11,446
Harry Browne (Lib)	6,640
Howard Phillips (Con)	2,042
Monica G. Moorehead (Ind WW)	1,063
John Hagelin (Ind Rfm)	878
James Harris (Ind SW).	306
TOTAL	2,598,607

2004 (10 electoral votes)	
John F. Kerry (D)	1,489,504
George W. Bush (R)	1,478,120
Ralph Nader (Ind TBL)	16,390
Michael Badnarik (Lib)	6,464
David Cobb (WG)	2,661
Walter F. Brown (Ind SPW)	471
James Harris (Ind SW).	411
TOTAL	2,997,007

2008 (10 electoral votes)	
Barack Obama (D).	1,677,211
John McCain (R).	1,262,393
Ralph Nader (Ind)	17,605
Bob Barr (Lib).	8,858
Chuck Baldwin (Ind Con)	5,072
Cynthia McKinney (WG)	4,216
Jeffrey J. Wamboldt (Ind WtP)	764
Brian Moore (Ind Soc USA).	540
Gloria La Riva (Ind S&L)	237
TOTAL	2,983,417

2012 (10 electoral votes)	
Barack Obama (D).	1,620,985
Mitt Romney (R).	1,407,966
Gary Johnson (Ind Lib)	20,439
Jill Stein (Ind Grn).	7,665
Virgil Goode (Con)	4,930
Jerry White (Ind SE).	553
Gloria La Riva (Ind S&L)	526
TOTAL	3,068,434

Note: Some totals include scattered votes for other candidates.

Sources: Official records of the Government Accountability Board, Elections Division and Congressional Quarterly, *Guide to U.S. Elections*, 1994.

VOTE FOR GOVERNOR IN GENERAL ELECTIONS
1848 – 2014

Key:
A – American
C – Conservative
Com – Communist
Con – Constitution
D – Democrat
DS – Democratic Socialist
G – Greenback
Ind – Independent
IC – Independent Communist
ID – Independent Democrat
IL – Independent Labor
IP – Independent Prohibition
IPR – Independent Prohibition Republic

ISL – Independent Socialist Labor
ISW – Independent Socialist Worker
IW – Independent Worker
L – Labor
LF – Labor-Farm/Laborista-Agrario
Lib – Libertarian
Nat – National
NR – National Republic
Peop – People's
People's – People's (Populist)
PLS – Progressive Labor Socialist
PP – People's Progressive
Prog – Progressive

Proh – Prohibition
R – Republican
Soc – Socialist
SD – Social Democrat
SDA – Social Democrat of America
SL – Socialist Labor
SW – Socialist Worker
Tax – U.S. Taxpayers
U – Union
UL – Union Labor
W – Whig
WG – Wisconsin Green

Note: A candidate whose party did not receive 1% of the vote for a statewide office in the previous election or who failed to meet the alternative requirement of Section 5.62, Wisconsin Statutes, is listed on the Wisconsin ballot as "independent". When a candidate's party affiliation is listed as "independent" and a party designation is shown in italics, "independent" was the official ballot listing, but a party designation was found by the Wisconsin Legislative Reference Bureau in newspaper reports.

1848
Nelson Dewey (D)[1] 19,875
John Hubbard Tweedy (W)[1] 14,621
Charles Durkee (Ind)[1] 1,134
TOTAL 35,309
1849
Nelson Dewey (D) 16,649
Alexander L. Collins (W) 11,317
Warren Chase (Ind) 3,761
TOTAL 31,759
1851
Leonard James Farwell (W) 22,319
Don Alonzo Joshua Upham (D) 21,812
TOTAL 44,190
1853
William Augustus Barstow (D) 30,405
Edward Dwight Holton (R) 21,886
Henry Samuel Baird (W) 3,304
TOTAL 55,683
1855
William Augustus Barstow (D)[2] 36,355
Coles Bashford (R) 36,198
TOTAL 72,598
1857
Alexander William Randall (R) 44,693
James B. Cross (D) 44,239
TOTAL 90,058
1859
Alexander William Randall (R) 59,999
Harrison Carroll Hobart (D) 52,539
TOTAL 112,755
1861
Louis Powell Harvey (R) 53,777
Benjamin Ferguson (D) 45,456
TOTAL 99,258
1863
James Taylor Lewis (R) 72,717
Henry L. Palmer (D) 49,053
TOTAL 122,029
1865
Lucius Fairchild (R) 58,332
Harrison Carroll Hobart (D) 48,330
TOTAL 106,674
1867
Lucius Fairchild (R) 73,637
John J. Tallmadge (D) 68,873
TOTAL 142,522
1869
Lucius Fairchild (R) 69,502
Charles D. Robinson (D) 61,239
TOTAL 130,781
1871
Cadwallader Colden Washburn (R) 78,301
James Rood Doolittle (D) 68,910
TOTAL 147,274
1873
William Robert Taylor (D) 81,599
Cadwallader Colden Washburn (R) 66,224
TOTAL 147,856

1875
Harrison Ludington (R) 85,155
William Robert Taylor (D) 84,314
TOTAL 170,070
1877
William E. Smith (R) 78,759
James A. Mallory (D) 70,486
Edward Phelps Allis (G) 26,216
Collin M. Campbell (Soc) 2,176
TOTAL 178,122
1879
William E. Smith (R) 100,535
James G. Jenkins (D) 75,030
Reuben May (G) 12,996
TOTAL 189,005
1881
Jeremiah McLain Rusk (R) 81,754
N.D. Fratt (D) 69,797
T.D. Kanouse (Proh) 13,225
Edward Phelps Allis (G) 7,002
TOTAL 171,856
1884
Jeremiah McLain Rusk (R) 163,214
N.D. Fratt (D) 143,945
Samuel Dexter Hastings (Proh) 8,545
William L. Utley (G) 4,274
TOTAL 319,997
1886
Jeremiah McLain Rusk (R) 133,247
Gilbert Motier Woodward (D) 114,529
John Cochrane (People's) 21,467
John Myers Olin (Proh) 17,089
TOTAL 286,368
1888
William Dempster Hoard (R) 175,696
James Morgan (D) 155,423
E.G. Durant (Proh) 14,373
D. Frank Powell (L) 9,196
TOTAL 354,714
1890
George Wilbur Peck (D) 160,388
William Dempster Hoard (R) 132,068
Charles Alexander (Proh) 11,246
Reuben May (UL) 5,447
TOTAL 309,254
1892
George Wilbur Peck (D) 178,095
John Coit Spooner (R) 170,497
Thomas C. Richmond (Proh) 13,185
C.M. Butt (People's) 9,638
TOTAL 371,559
1894
William H. Upham (R) 196,150
George Wilbur Peck (D) 142,250
D. Frank Powell (People's) 25,604
John F. Cleghorn (Proh) 11,240
TOTAL 375,449

VOTE FOR GOVERNOR IN GENERAL ELECTIONS
1848 – 2014–Continued

1896

Edward Scofield (R)	264,981
Willis C. Silverthorn (D)	169,257
Joshua H. Berkey (Proh)	8,140
Christ Tuttrop (SL)	1,306
Robert Henderson (Nat)	407
TOTAL	444,110

1898

Edward Scofield (R)	173,137
Hiram Wilson Sawyer (D)	135,353
Albinus A. Worsley (People's)	8,518
Eugene Wilder Chafin (Proh)	8,078
Howard Tuttle (SDA)	2,544
Henry Riese (SL)	1,473
TOTAL	329,430

1900

Robert Marion La Follette (R)	264,419
Louis G. Bomrich (D)	160,674
J. Burritt Smith (Proh)	9,707
Howard Tuttle (SD)	6,590
Frank R. Wilke (SL)	509
TOTAL	441,900

1902

Robert Marion La Follette (R)	193,417
David Stuart Rose (D)	145,818
Emil Seidel (SD)	15,970
Edwin W. Drake (Proh)	9,647
Henry E.D. Puck (SL)	791
TOTAL	365,676

1904

Robert Marion La Follette (R)	227,253
George Wilbur Peck (D)	176,301
William A. Arnold (SD)	24,857
Edward Scofield (NR)	12,136
William H. Clark (Proh)	8,764
Charles M. Minkley (SL)	249
TOTAL	449,570

1906

James O. Davidson (R)	183,558
John A. Aylward (D)	103,311
Winfield R. Gaylord (SD)	24,437
Ephraim L. Eaton (Proh)	8,211
Ole T. Rosaas (SL)	455
TOTAL	320,003

1908

James O. Davidson (R)	242,935
John A. Aylward (D)	165,977
H.D. Brown (SD)	28,583
Winfred D. Cox (Proh)	11,760
Herman Bottema (SL)	393
TOTAL	449,656

1910

Francis Edward McGovern (R)	161,619
Adolph H. Schmitz (D)	110,442
William A. Jacobs (SD)	39,547
Byron E. Van Keuren (Proh)	7,450
Fred G. Kremer (SL)	430
TOTAL	319,522

1912

Francis Edward McGovern (R)	179,360
John C. Karel (D)	167,316
Carl D. Thompson (SD)	34,468
Charles Lewis Hill (Proh)	9,433
William H. Curtis (SL)	3,253
TOTAL	393,849

1914

Emanuel Lorenz Philipp (R)	140,787
John C. Karel (D)	119,509
John James Blaine (Ind)	32,560
Oscar Ameringer (SD)	25,917
David W. Emerson (Proh)	6,279
John Vierthaler (Ind)	352
TOTAL	325,430

1916

Emanuel Lorenz Philipp (R)	229,889
Burt Williams (D)	164,555
Rae Weaver (Soc)	30,649
George McKerrow (Proh)	9,193
TOTAL	434,340

1918

Emanuel Lorenz Philipp (R)	155,799
Henry A. Moehlenpah (D)	112,576
Emil Seidel (SD)	57,523
William C. Dean (Proh)	5,296
TOTAL	331,582

1920

John James Blaine (R)	366,247
Robert McCoy (D)	247,746
William Coleman (Soc)	71,126
Henry H. Tubbs (Proh)	6,047
TOTAL	691,294

1922

John James Blaine (R)	367,929
Arthur A. Bentley (ID)	51,061
Louis A. Arnold (Soc)	39,570
M.L. Welles (Proh)	21,438
Arthur A. Dietrich (ISL)	1,444
TOTAL	481,828

1924

John James Blaine (R)	412,255
Martin L. Lueck (D)	317,550
William F. Quick (Soc)	45,268
Adolph R. Bucknam (Proh)	11,516
Severi Alanne (IW)	4,107
Farrand K. Shuttleworth (IPR)	4,079
Jose Snover (SL)	1,452
TOTAL	796,432

1926

Fred R. Zimmerman (R)	350,927
Charles Perry (Ind)	76,507
Virgil H. Cady (D)	72,627
Herman O. Kent (Soc)	40,293
David W. Emerson (Proh)	7,333
Alex Gorden (SL)	4,593
TOTAL	552,912

1928

Walter Jodok Kohler, Sr. (R)	547,738
Albert George Schmedeman (D)	394,368
Otto R. Hauser (Soc)	36,924
Adolph R. Bucknam (Proh)	6,477
Joseph Ehrhardt (IL)	1,938
Alvar J. Hayes (IW)	1,420
TOTAL	989,143

1930

Philip Fox La Follette (R)	392,958
Charles E. Hammersley (D)	170,020
Frank B. Metcalfe (Soc)	25,607
Alfred B. Taynton (Proh)	14,818
Fred Bassett Blair (IC)	2,998
TOTAL	606,825

1932

Albert George Schmedeman (D)	590,114
Walter Jodok Kohler, Sr. (R)	470,805
Frank B. Metcalfe (Soc)	56,965
William C. Dean (Proh)	3,148
Fred Bassett Blair (Com)	2,926
Joe Ehrhardt (SL)	398
TOTAL	1,124,502

1934

Philip Fox La Follette (Prog)	373,093
Albert George Schmedeman (D)	359,467
Howard Greene (R)	172,980
George A. Nelson (Soc)	44,589
Morris Childs (IC)	2,454
Thomas W. North (PR)	857
Joe Ehrhardt (ISL)	332
TOTAL	953,797

1936

Philip Fox La Follette (Prog)	573,724
Alexander Wiley (R)	363,973
Arthur W. Lueck (D)	268,530
Joseph F. Walsh (U)	27,934
Joseph Ehrhardt (SL)	1,738
August F. Fehlandt (Proh)	1,008
TOTAL	1,237,095

VOTE FOR GOVERNOR IN GENERAL ELECTIONS
1848 – 2014–Continued

1938

Julius Peter Heil (R)	543,675
Philip Fox La Follette (Prog)	353,381
Harry Wilbur Bolens (D)	78,446
Frank W. Smith (U)	4,564
John Schleier, Jr. (ISL)	1,459
TOTAL	981,560

1940

Julius Peter Heil (R)	558,678
Orland Steen Loomis (Prog)	546,436
Francis Edward McGovern (D)	264,985
Fred Bassett Blair (Com)	2,340
Louis Fisher (SL)	1,158
TOTAL	1,373,754

1942

Orland Steen Loomis (Prog)	397,664
Julius Peter Heil (R)	291,945
William C. Sullivan (D)	98,153
Frank P. Zeidler (Soc)	11,295
Fred Bassett Blair (IC)	1,092
Georgia Cozzini (ISL)	490
TOTAL	800,985

1944

Walter Samuel Goodland (R)	697,740
Daniel W. Hoan (D)	536,357
Alexander O. Benz (Prog)	76,028
George A. Nelson (Soc)	9,183
Georgia Cozzini (Ind–ISL)	1,122
TOTAL	1,320,483

1946

Walter Samuel Goodland (R)	621,970
Daniel W. Hoan (D)	406,499
Walter H. Uphoff (Soc)	8,996
Sigmund G. Eisenscher (IC)	1,857
Jerry R. Kenyon (ISL)	959
TOTAL	1,040,444

1948

Oscar Rennebohm (R)	684,839
Carl W. Thompson (D)	558,497
Henry J. Berquist (PP)	12,928
Walter H. Uphoff (Soc)	9,149
James E. Boulton (ISW)	356
Georgia Cozzini (ISL)	328
TOTAL	1,266,139

1950

Walter Jodok Kohler, Jr. (R)	605,649
Carl W. Thompson (D)	525,319
M. Michael Essin (PP)	3,735
William O. Hart (Soc)	3,384
TOTAL	1,138,148

1952

Walter Jodok Kohler, Jr. (R)	1,009,171
William Proxmire (D)	601,844
M. Michael Essin (Ind)	3,706
TOTAL	1,615,214

1954

Walter Jodok Kohler, Jr. (R)	596,158
William Proxmire (D)	560,747
Arthur Wepfer (Ind)	1,722
TOTAL	1,158,666

1956

Vernon W. Thomson (R)	808,273
William Proxmire (D)	749,421
TOTAL	1,557,788

1958

Gaylord Anton Nelson (D)	644,296
Vernon W. Thomson (R)	556,391
Wayne Leverenz (Ind)	1,485
TOTAL	1,202,219

1960

Gaylord Anton Nelson (D)	890,868
Philip G. Kuehn (R)	837,123
TOTAL	1,728,009

1962

John W. Reynolds (D)	637,491
Philip G. Kuehn (R)	625,536
Adolf Wiggert (Ind)	2,477
TOTAL	1,265,900

1964

Warren P. Knowles (R)	856,779
John W. Reynolds (D)	837,901
TOTAL	1,694,887

1966

Warren P. Knowles (R)	626,041
Patrick J. Lucey (D)	539,258
Adolf Wiggert (Ind)	4,745
TOTAL	1,170,173

1968

Warren P. Knowles (R)	893,463
Bronson C. La Follette (D)	791,100
Adolf Wiggert (Ind)	3,225
Robert Wilkinson (Ind)	1,813
TOTAL	1,689,738

1970

Patrick J. Lucey (D)	728,403
Jack B. Olson (R)	602,617
Leo James McDonald (A)	9,035
Georgia Cozzini (Ind–SL)	1,287
Samuel K. Hunt (Ind–SW)	888
Myrtle Kastner (Ind–PLS)	628
TOTAL	1,343,160

1974

Patrick J. Lucey (D)	628,639
William D. Dyke (R)	497,189
William H. Upham (A)	33,528
Crazy Jim[3] (Ind)	12,107
William Hart (Ind–DS)	5,113
Fred Blair (Ind–C)	3,617
Georgia Cozzini (Ind–SL)	1,492
TOTAL	1,181,685

1978

Lee Sherman Dreyfus (R)	816,056
Martin J. Schreiber (D)	673,813
Eugene R. Zimmerman (C)	6,355
John C. Doherty (Ind)	2,183
Adrienne Kaplan (Ind–SW)	1,548
Henry A. Ochsner (Ind–SL)	849
TOTAL	1,500,996

1982

Anthony S. Earl (D)	896,872
Terry J. Kohler (R)	662,738
Larry Smiley (Lib)	9,734
James P. Wickstrom (Con)	7,721
Peter Seidman (Ind–SW)	3,025
TOTAL	1,580,344

1986

Tommy G. Thompson (R)	805,090
Anthony S. Earl (D)	705,578
Kathryn A. Christensen (LF)	10,323
Darold E. Wall (Ind)	3,913
Sanford Knapp (Ind)	1,668
TOTAL	1,526,573

1990

Tommy G. Thompson (R)	802,321
Thomas A. Loftus (D)	576,280
TOTAL	1,379,727

1994

Tommy G. Thompson (R)	1,051,326
Charles J.Chvala (D)	482,850
David S. Harmon (Lib)	11,639
Edward J. Frami (Tax)	9,188
Michael J. Mangan (Ind)	8,150
TOTAL	1,563,835

1998

Tommy G. Thompson (R)	1,047,716
Ed Garvey (D)	679,553
Jim Mueller (Lib)	11,071
Edward J. Frami (Tax)	10,269
Mike Mangan (Ind)	4,985
A-Ja-mu Muhammad (Ind)	1,604
Jeffrey L. Smith (WG)	14
TOTAL	1,756,014

VOTE FOR GOVERNOR IN GENERAL ELECTIONS
1848 – 2014–Continued

2002
Jim Doyle (D)	800,515
Scott McCallum (R)	734,779
Ed Thompson (Lib)	185,455
Jim Young (WG)	44,111
Alan D. Eisenberg (Ind)	2,847
Ty A. Bollerud (Ind)	2,637
Mike Mangan (Ind)	1,710
Aneb Jah Rasta Sensas-Utcha Nefer-I (Ind) . .	929
TOTAL	1,775,349

2006
Jim Doyle (D)	1,139,115
Mark Green (R)	979,427
Nelson Eisman (WG)	40,709
TOTAL	2,161,700

2010
Scott Walker (R)	1,128,941
Tom Barrett (D)	1,004,303
Jim Langer (Ind)	10,608
James James (Ind)	8,273
TOTAL[4]	2,160,832

June 5, 2012 Recall Election
Scott Walker (R)	1,335,585
Tom Barrett (D)	1,164,480
Hari Trivedi (Ind)	14,463
TOTAL	2,516,065

2014
Scott Walker (R)	1,259,706
Mary Burke (D)	1,122,913
Robert Burke (Ind–Lib)	18,720
Dennis Fehr (Ind–Peop)	7,530
TOTAL	2,410,314

[1]Votes for Dewey and Tweedy are from *1874 Blue Book;* Durkee vote is based on county returns, as filed in the Office of the Secretary of State, but returns from Manitowoc and Winnebago Counties were missing. Without these 2 counties, Dewey had 19,605 votes and Tweedy had 14,514 votes.

[2]Barstow's plurality was set aside in *Atty. Gen. ex rel. Bashford v. Barstow*, 4 Wis. 567 (1855) because of irregularities in the election returns.

[3]Legal name. [4]Total includes 6,780 votes for the Libertarian ticket, which had a candidate for lieutenant governor, but no candidate for governor.

Source: Canvass reports and Government Accountability Board records. Totals include scattered votes for other candidates.

WISCONSIN GOVERNORS SINCE 1848

Governor[1]	Political Party	Residence[2]	Service As Governor[3] Began	Ended	Born	Birthplace	Died	Burial Place
1 Nelson Dewey	Democrat	Lancaster	6-7-1848	1-5-1852	12-19-1813	Lebanon, Conn.	7-21-1889	Lancaster, Wis.
2 Leonard James Farwell	Whig	Madison	1-5-1852	1-2-1854	1-5-1819	Watertown, N.Y.	4-11-1889	Grant City, Mo.
3 William Augustus Barstow	Democrat	Waukesha	1-2-1854	3-21-1856	9-13-1813	Plainfield, Conn.	12-13-1865	Cleveland, Ohio
4 Arthur MacArthur[4]	Democrat	Milwaukee	3-21-1856	3-25-1856	1-26-1815	Glasgow, Scotland	8-26-1896	Washington, D.C.
5 Coles Bashford	Republican	Oshkosh	3-25-1856	1-4-1858	1-24-1816	Putnam Co., N.Y.	4-25-1878	Oakland, Cal.
6 Alexander William Randall	Republican	Waukesha	1-4-1858	1-6-1862	10-31-1819	Ames, N.Y.	7-26-1872	Elmira, N.Y.
7 Louis Powell Harvey[5]	Republican	Shopiere	1-6-1862	4-19-1862	7-22-1820	East Haddam, Conn.	4-19-1862	Madison, Wis.
8 Edward Salomon[5]	Republican	Milwaukee	4-19-1862	1-4-1864	8-11-1828	Stroebeck, Prussia	4-21-1909	Frankfurt, Germany
9 James Taylor Lewis	Republican	Columbus	1-4-1864	1-1-1866	10-30-1819	Clarendon, N.Y.	8-4-1904	Columbus, Wis.
10 Lucius Fairchild	Republican	Madison	1-1-1866	1-1-1872	12-27-1831	Kent, Ohio	5-23-1896	Madison, Wis.
11 Cadwallader Colden Washburn	Republican	La Crosse	1-1-1872	1-5-1874	4-22-1818	Livermore, Me.	5-14-1882	La Crosse, Wis.
12 William Robert Taylor	Democrat	Cottage Grove	1-5-1874	1-3-1876	7-10-1820	Woodbury, Conn.	3-17-1909	Madison, Wis.
13 Harrison Ludington	Republican	Milwaukee	1-3-1876	1-7-1878	7-30-1812	Ludingtonville, N.Y.	6-17-1891	Milwaukee, Wis.
14 William E. Smith	Republican	Milwaukee	1-7-1878	1-2-1882	6-18-1824	Near Inverness, Scotland	2-13-1883	Milwaukee, Wis.
15 Jeremiah McLain Rusk	Republican	Viroqua	1-2-1882	1-7-1889	6-17-1830	Morgan Co., Ohio	11-21-1893	Viroqua, Wis.
16 William Dempster Hoard	Republican	Fort Atkinson	1-7-1889	1-5-1891	10-10-1836	Stockbridge, N.Y.	11-22-1918	Ft. Atkinson, Wis.
17 George Wilbur Peck	Democrat	Milwaukee	1-5-1891	1-7-1895	9-28-1840	Henderson, N.Y.	4-16-1916	Milwaukee, Wis.
18 William Henry Upham	Republican	Marshfield	1-7-1895	1-4-1897	5-3-1841	Westminster, Mass.	7-2-1924	Marshfield, Wis.
19 Edward Scofield	Republican	Oconto	1-4-1897	1-7-1901	3-28-1842	Clearfield, Pa.	2-3-1925	Oconto, Wis.
20 Robert Marion La Follette, Sr.[6]	Republican	Madison	1-7-1901	1-1-1906	6-14-1855	Primrose, Dane Co., Wis.	6-18-1925	Madison, Wis.
21 James O. Davidson[6]	Republican	Soldiers Grove	1-1-1906	1-2-1911	2-10-1854	Sogn, Norway	12-16-1922	Madison, Wis.
22 Francis Edward McGovern	Republican	Milwaukee	1-2-1911	1-4-1915	1-21-1866	Elkhart Lake, Wis.	5-16-1946	Milwaukee, Wis.
23 Emanuel Lorenz Philipp	Republican	Milwaukee	1-4-1915	1-3-1921	3-25-1861	Honey Creek, Sauk Co., Wis.	6-15-1925	Milwaukee, Wis.
24 John James Blaine	Republican	Boscobel	1-3-1921	1-3-1927	5-4-1875	Wingville, Grant Co., Wis.	4-18-1934	Boscobel, Wis.
25 Fred R. Zimmerman	Republican	Milwaukee	1-3-1927	1-7-1929	11-20-1880	Milwaukee, Wis.	12-14-1954	Milwaukee, Wis.
26 Walter Jodok Kohler, Sr.	Republican	Kohler	1-7-1929	1-5-1931	3-3-1875	Sheboygan, Wis.	4-21-1940	Kohler, Wis.
27 Philip Fox La Follette	Republican	Madison	1-5-1931	1-2-1933	5-8-1897	Madison, Wis.	8-18-1965	Madison, Wis.
28 Albert George Schmedeman	Democrat	Madison	1-2-1933	1-7-1935	11-25-1864	Madison, Wis.	11-26-1946	Madison, Wis.
29 Philip Fox La Follette	Progressive	Madison	1-7-1935	1-2-1939	5-8-1897	Madison, Wis.	8-18-1965	Madison, Wis.
30 Julius Peter Heil	Progressive	Milwaukee	1-2-1939	1-4-1943	7-24-1876	Duesmond, Germany	11-30-1949	Milwaukee, Wis.
Orland Steen Loomis[7]	Republican	Mauston	Died prior to inauguration		11-2-1893	Mauston, Wis.	12-7-1942	Mauston, Wis
31 Walter Samuel Goodland[7,8]	Republican	Racine	1-4-1943	3-12-1947	12-22-1862	Sharon, Wis.	3-12-1947	Racine, Wis.
32 Oscar Rennebohm[8]	Republican	Madison	3-12-1947	1-1-1951	5-25-1889	Leeds, Columbia Co., Wis.	10-15-1968	Madison, Wis.
33 Walter Jodok Kohler, Jr.	Republican	Kohler	1-1-1951	1-7-1957	4-4-1904	Sheboygan, Wis.	3-10-1976	Kohler, Wis.
34 Vernon Wallace Thomson	Republican	Richland Center	1-7-1957	1-5-1959	11-5-1905	Richland Center, Wis.	4-2-1988	Richland Center, Wis.
35 Gaylord Anton Nelson	Democrat	Madison	1-5-1959	1-7-1963	6-4-1916	Clear Lake, Wis.	7-3-2005	Clear Lake, Wis.
36 John W. Reynolds	Democrat	Green Bay	1-7-1963	1-4-1965	4-4-1921	Green Bay, Wis.	1-6-2002	Door County, Wis.
37 Warren Perley Knowles	Republican	New Richmond	1-4-1965	1-4-1971	8-19-1908	River Falls, Wis.	5-1-1993	River Falls, Wis.
38 Patrick Joseph Lucey[9]	Democrat	Madison	1-4-1971	7-6-1977	3-21-1918	La Crosse, Wis.	5-10-2014	Milwaukee, Wis.
39 Martin James Schreiber[9]	Democrat	Milwaukee	7-6-1977	1-1-1979	4-8-1939	Milwaukee, Wis.		
40 Lee Sherman Dreyfus	Republican	Stevens Point	1-1-1979	1-3-1983	6-20-1926	Milwaukee, Wis.	1-2-2008	Waukesha, Wis.
41 Anthony Scully Earl	Democrat	Madison	1-3-1983	1-5-1987	4-12-1936	Lansing, Mich.		
42 Tommy George Thompson[10]	Republican	Elroy	1-5-1987	2-1-2001	11-19-1941	Elroy, Wis.		
43 Scott McCallum[10]	Republican	Fond du Lac	2-1-2001	1-6-2003	5-2-1950	Fond du Lac, Wis.		
44 James Edward Doyle, Jr.	Democrat	Madison	1-6-2003	1-3-2011	11-23-1945	Washington, D.C.		
45 Scott Kevin Walker	Republican	Wauwatosa	1-3-2011		11-2-1967	Colorado Springs, Colo.		

[1]Includes those serving as acting governor when office is vacated. Administrations are numbered. [2]Residence at the time of election. [3]Article XIII, Section 1 of the Wisconsin Constitution was amended in November 1882 so that the term of office of all state and county officers began in January of odd-numbered years, rather than January of even-numbered years. [4]Served as acting governor during dispute over who won gubernatorial election. [5]Salomon became acting governor on death of Harvey on 4/19/62. [6]Davidson served as acting governor from La Follette's resignation until beginning the terms to which he was elected on 1/7/07. [7]Goodland became acting governor on death of Governor-elect Loomis and served entire 1943-44 term. [8]Rennebohm became acting governor on the death of Goodland on 3/12/47. [9]Schreiber became acting governor when Lucey resigned to become U.S. ambassador to Mexico. [10]McCallum became governor when Thompson resigned to become U.S. Secretary of Health and Human Services.

Sources: "Wisconsin's Former Governors", *1960 Wisconsin Blue Book*, pp. 69-206; Blue Book biographies.

WISCONSIN CONSTITUTIONAL OFFICERS, 1848 – 2015

Name	Term[1]	Residence
Governor		
(See separate table)		
Lieutenant Governors		
John E. Holmes (D)	1848-1850	Jefferson
Samuel W. Beall (D)	1850-1852	Taycheedah
Timothy Burns (D)	1852-1854	La Crosse
James T. Lewis (R)	1854-1856	Columbus
Arthur McArthur (D)[2]	1856-1858	Milwaukee
Erasmus D. Campbell (D)	1858-1860	La Crosse
Butler G. Noble (R)	1860-1862	Whitewater
Edward Salomon (R)[3]	1862-1864	Milwaukee
Wyman Spooner (R)	1864-1870	Elkhorn
Thaddeus C. Pound (R)	1870-1872	Chippewa Falls
Milton H. Pettit (R)[4]	1872-3/23/73	Kenosha
Charles D. Parker (D)	1874-1878	Pleasant Valley
James M. Bingham (R)	1878-1882	Chippewa Falls
Sam S. Fifield (R)	1882-1887	Ashland
George W. Ryland (R)	1887-1891	Lancaster
Charles Jonas (D)	1891-1895	Racine
Emil Baensch (R)	1895-1899	Manitowoc
Jesse Stone (R)	1899-1903	Watertown
James O. Davidson (R)[5]	1903-1907	Soldiers Grove
William D. Connor (R)	1907-1909	Marshfield
John Strange (R)	1909-1911	Oshkosh
Thomas Morris (R)	1911-1915	La Crosse
Edward F. Dithmar (R)	1915-1921	Baraboo
George F. Comings (R)	1921-1925	Eau Claire
Henry A. Huber (R)	1925-1933	Stoughton
Thomas J. O'Malley (D)	1933-1937	Milwaukee
Henry A. Gunderson (Prog)[6]	1937-10/16/37	Portage
Herman L. Ekern (Prog)[6]	5/16/1938-1939	Madison
Walter S. Goodland (R)[7]	1939-1945	Racine
Oscar Rennebohm (R)[8]	1945-1949	Madison
George M. Smith (R)	1949-1955	Milwaukee
Warren P. Knowles (R)	1955-1959	New Richmond
Philleo Nash (D)	1959-1961	Wisconsin Rapids
Warren P. Knowles (R)	1961-1963	New Richmond
Jack Olson (R)	1963-1965	Wisconsin Dells
Patrick J. Lucey (D)	1965-1967	Madison
Jack Olson (R)	1967-1971	Wisconsin Dells
Martin J. Schreiber (D)[9]	1971-1979	Milwaukee
Russell A. Olson (R)	1979-1983	Randall
James T. Flynn (D)	1983-1987	West Allis
Scott McCallum (R)[10]	1987-2001	Fond du Lac
Margaret A. Farrow (R)[10]	2001-2003	Pewaukee
Barbara Lawton (D)	2003-2011	Green Bay
Rebecca Kleefisch (R)	2011-	Oconomowoc
Secretaries of State		
Thomas McHugh (D)	1848-1850	Delavan
William A. Barstow (D)	1850-1852	Waukesha
Charles D. Robinson (D)	1852-1854	Green Bay
Alexander T. Gray (D)	1854-1856	Janesville
David W. Jones (D)	1856-1860	Belmont
Lewis P. Harvey (R)	1860-1862	Shopiere
James T. Lewis (R)	1862-1864	Columbus
Lucius Fairchild (R)	1864-1866	Madison
Thomas S. Allen (R)	1866-1870	Mineral Point
Llywelyn Breese (R)	1870-1874	Portage
Peter Doyle (D)	1874-1878	Prairie du Chien
Hans B. Warner (R)	1878-1882	Ellsworth
Ernst G. Timme (R)	1882-1891	Kenosha
Thomas J. Cunningham (D)	1891-1895	Chippewa Falls
Henry Casson (R)	1895-1899	Viroqua
William H. Froehlich (R)	1899-1903	Jackson
Walter L. Houser (R)	1903-1907	Mondovi
James A. Frear (R)	1907-1913	Hudson
John S. Donald (R)	1913-1917	Mt. Horeb
Merlin Hull (R)	1917-1921	Black River Falls
Elmer S. Hall (R)	1921-1923	Green Bay
Fred R. Zimmerman (R)	1923-1927	Milwaukee
Theodore Dammann (R)	1927-1935	Milwaukee
Theodore Dammann (Prog)	1935-1939	Milwaukee
Fred R. Zimmerman (R)[11]	1939-12/14/54	Milwaukee
Louis Allis (R)[11]	12/16/54-1/3/55	Milwaukee
Mrs. Glenn M. Wise (R)[11]	1/3/55-1957	Madison
Robert C. Zimmerman (R)	1957-1975	Madison
Douglas J. La Follette (D)	1975-1979	Kenosha
Mrs. Vel R. Phillips (D)	1979-1983	Milwaukee

WISCONSIN CONSTITUTIONAL OFFICERS, 1848 – 2015–Continued

Name	Term[1]	Residence
Douglas J. La Follette (D)	1983-	Madison
	State Treasurers	
Jarius C. Fairchild (D)	1848-1852	Madison
Edward H. Janssen (D)	1852-1856	Cedarburg
Charles Kuehn (D)	1856-1858	Manitowoc
Samuel D. Hastings (R)	1858-1866	Trempealeau
William E. Smith (R)	1866-1870	Fox Lake
Henry Baetz (R)	1870-1874	Manitowoc
Ferdinand Kuehn (D)	1874-1878	Milwaukee
Richard Guenther (R)	1878-1882	Oshkosh
Edward C. McFetridge (R)	1882-1887	Beaver Dam
Henry B. Harshaw (R)	1887-1891	Oshkosh
John Hunner (D)	1891-1895	Eau Claire
Sewell A. Peterson (R)	1895-1899	Rice Lake
James O. Davidson (R)	1899-1903	Soldiers Grove
John J. Kempf (R)[12]	1903-7/30/04	Milwaukee
Thomas M. Purtell (R)[12]	7/30/04-1905	Cumberland
John J. Kempf (R)[12]	1905-1907	Milwaukee
Andrew H. Dahl (R)	1907-1913	Westby
Henry Johnson (R)	1913-1923	Suring
Solomon Levitan (R)	1923-1933	Madison
Robert K. Henry (D)	1933-1937	Jefferson
Solomon Levitan (Prog)	1937-1939	Madison
John M. Smith (R)[4]	1939-8/17/47	Shell Lake
John L. Sonderegger (R)[13]	8/19/47-9/30/48	Madison
Clyde M. Johnston (appointed from staff)[13]	10/1/48-1949	Madison
Warren R. Smith (R)[4]	1949-12/4/57	Milwaukee
Mrs. Dena A. Smith (R)[13]	12/5/57-1959	Milwaukee
Eugene M. Lamb (D)	1959-1961	Milwaukee
Mrs. Dena A. Smith (R)[4]	1961-2/20/68	Milwaukee
Harold W. Clemens (R)[13]	2/21/68-1971	Oconomowoc
Charles P. Smith (D)	1971-1991	Madison
Cathy S. Zeuske (R)	1991-1995	Shawano
Jack C. Voight (R)	1995-2007	Appleton
Dawn Marie Sass (D)	2007-2011	Milwaukee
Kurt W. Schuller (R)	2011-2015	Eden
Matt Adamczyk (R)	2015-	Wauwatosa
	Attorneys General	
James S. Brown (D)	1848-1850	Milwaukee
S. Park Coon (D)	1850-1852	Milwaukee
Experience Estabrook (D)	1852-1854	Geneva
George B. Smith (D)	1854-1856	Madison
William R. Smith (D)	1856-1858	Mineral Point
Gabriel Bouck (D)	1858-1860	Oshkosh
James H. Howe (R)[14]	1860-1862	Green Bay
Winfield Smith (R)[14]	1862-1866	Milwaukee
Charles R. Gill (R)	1866-1870	Watertown
Stephen Steele Barlow (R)	1870-1874	Dellona
Andrew Scott Sloan (R)	1874-1878	Beaver Dam
Alexander Wilson (R)	1878-1882	Mineral Point
Leander F. Frisby (R)	1882-1887	West Bend
Charles E. Estabrook (R)	1887-1891	Manitowoc
James L. O'Connor (D)	1891-1895	Madison
William H. Mylrea (R)	1895-1899	Wausau
Emmett R. Hicks (R)	1899-1903	Oshkosh
Lafayette M. Sturdevant (R)	1903-1907	Neillsville
Frank L. Gilbert (R)	1907-1911	Madison
Levi H. Bancroft (R)	1911-1913	Richland Center
Walter C. Owen (R)[15]	1913-1918	Maiden Rock
Spencer Haven (R)[15]	1918-1919	Hudson
John J. Blaine (R)	1919-1921	Boscobel
William J. Morgan (R)	1921-1923	Milwaukee
Herman L. Ekern (R)	1923-1927	Madison
John W. Reynolds (R)	1927-1933	Green Bay
James E. Finnegan (D)	1933-1937	Milwaukee
Orlando S. Loomis (Prog)	1937-1939	Mauston
John E. Martin (R)[16]	1939-6/1/48	Madison
Grover L. Broadfoot (R)[16]	6/5/48-11/12/48	Mondovi
Thomas E. Fairchild (D)[16]	11/12/48-1951	Verona
Vernon W. Thomson (R)	1951-1957	Richland Center
Stewart G. Honeck (R)	1957-1959	Madison
John W. Reynolds (D)	1959-1963	Green Bay
George Thompson (R)	1963-1965	Madison
Bronson C. La Follette (D)	1965-1969	Madison
Robert W. Warren (R)[17]	1969-10/8/74	Green Bay
Victor A. Miller (D)[17]	10/8/74-11/25/74	St. Nazianz
Bronson C. La Follette (D)[17]	11/25/74-1987	Madison
Donald J. Hanaway (R)	1987-1991	Green Bay
James E. Doyle (D)	1991-2003	Madison

WISCONSIN CONSTITUTIONAL OFFICERS, 1848 – 2015–Continued

Name	Term[1]	Residence
Peggy A. Lautenschlager (D)	2003-2007	Fond du Lac
J.B. Van Hollen (R)	2007-2015	Waunakee
Brad D. Schimel (R)	2015-	Waukesha
Superintendents of Public Instruction[18]		
Eleazer Root	1849-1852	Waukesha
Azel P. Ladd	1852-1854	Shullsburg
Hiram A. Wright	1854-1855	Prairie du Chien
A. Constantine Barry	1855-1858	Racine
Lyman C. Draper	1858-1860	Madison
Josiah L. Pickard	1860-1864	Platteville
John G. McMynn	1864-1868	Racine
Alexander J. Craig	1868-1870	Madison
Samuel Fallows	1870-1874	Milwaukee
Edward Searing	1874-1878	Milton
William Clarke Whitford	1878-1882	Milton
Robert Graham	1882-1887	Oshkosh
Jesse B. Thayer	1887-1891	River Falls
Oliver Elwin Wells	1891-1895	Appleton
John Q. Emery	1895-1899	Albion
Lorenzo D. Harvey	1899-1903	Milwaukee
Charles P. Cary	1903-1921	Delavan
John Callahan	1921-1949	Madison
George Earl Watson	1949-1961	Wauwatosa
Angus B. Rothwell[19]	1961-7/1/66	Manitowoc
William C. Kahl[19]	7/1/66-1973	Madison
Barbara Thompson	1973-1981	Madison
Herbert J. Grover[20]	1981-4/9/93	Cottage Grove
John T. Benson	1993-2001	Marshall
Elizabeth Burmaster	2001-2009	Madison
Tony Evers	2009-	Madison

[1]Article XIII, Section 1 of the Wisconsin Constitution was amended in 1882, to provide the terms for all partisan state officers would begin in odd-numbered, rather than even-numbered, years. The section was further amended in 1968 to change the term from 2-years to 4-years, effective with the November 1970 elections.

[2]Served as acting governor 3/21/1856 to 3/25/1856 during dispute over outcome of gubernatorial election.

[3]Became acting governor on the death of Governor Louis P. Harvey on 4/19/1862.

[4]Died in office.

[5]Became acting governor on 1/1/1906 when Robert M. La Follette, Sr., resigned to become U.S. Senator.

[6]Resigned to accept appointment to the State Tax Commission. Ekern appointed by Governor Philip La Follette to fill the unexpired term. Appointment ruled valid in *State ex rel. Martin v. Ekern*, 228 Wis. 645 (1937).

[7]Goodland reelected lieutenant governor, November 1942; became acting governor on 1/1/1943 for the term of deceased Governor-elect Orlando Loomis.

[8]Became acting governor on the death of Goodland on 3/12/1947.

[9]Became acting governor when Lucey resigned on 7/6/1977 to accept appointment as U.S. ambassador to Mexico.

[10]McCallum became governor on 2/1/2001 when Governor Tommy Thompson resigned to become U.S. Secretary of Health and Social Services. Farrow was appointed lieutenant governor on 5/9/2001.

[11]Died 12/14/1954 after being elected to a new 2-year term. Allis was appointed to fill the unexpired term. Wise was appointed to fill the full 2-year term.

[12]Appointed 7/30/1904 to fill a vacancy caused by the failure of Kempf to give the required bond.

[13]Appointed.

[14]Resigned in October 1862 to join the Union Army. Smith was appointed 10/7/1862 to replace him.

[15]Resigned 1/7/1918 after being elected to the Wisconsin Supreme Court. Haven was appointed to fill the unexpired term.

[16]Resigned to accept appointment to the Wisconsin Supreme Court. Broadfoot was appointed to fill the unexpired term. Broadfoot resigned to accept appointment to the Wisconsin Supreme Court, and Attorney General-elect Fairchild was appointed to fill the unexpired term.

[17]Resigned to accept appointment as U.S. District Judge for the Eastern District of Wisconsin. Miller appointed to fill the unexpired term. Bronson La Follette was elected to a full term and Miller resigned so that La Follette could be appointed to fill the rest of Warren's unexpired term.

[18]Prior to 1902, the state superintendent was elected on a partisan ballot in November, and the term began the first Monday in January. A constitutional amendment moved the election to the nonpartisan April ballot and the beginning of the term to the first Monday in July beginning in July 1905.

[19]Resigned to accept appointment to the Coordinating Committee for Higher Education. Kahl was appointed to fill the unexpired term.

[20]Resigned 4/9/1993. Lee Sherman Dreyfus was appointed to serve as "interim superintendent" for remainder of the unexpired term but did not officially become superintendent.

Source: Wisconsin Legislative Reference Bureau, *Wisconsin Blue Books,* various editions, and bureau records.

JUSTICES OF THE SUPREME COURT
1836 – 2015

Name	Term	Residence[1]
Judges During the Territorial Period		
Charles Dunn (Chief Justice)[2]	1836-1848	
William C. Frazier	1836-1838	
David Irvin	1836-1838	
Andrew G. Miller	1836-1848	
Circuit Judges Who Served as Justices 1848-53[3]		
Alexander W. Stow	1848-1851 (C.J.)	Fond du Lac
Levi Hubbell	1848-1853 (C.J. 1851)	Milwaukee
Edward V. Whiton	1848-1853 (C.J. 1852-53)	Janesville
Charles H. Larrabee	1848-1853	Horicon
Mortimer M. Jackson	1848-1853	Mineral Point
Wiram Knowlton	1850-1853	Prairie du Chien
Timothy O. Howe	1851-1853	Green Bay
Justices Since 1853		
Edward V. Whiton	1853-1859 (C.J.)	Janesville
Samuel Crawford	1853-1855	New Diggings
Abram D. Smith	1853-1859	Milwaukee
Orsamus Cole	1855-1892 (C.J. 1880-92)	Potosi
Luther S. Dixon[4]	1859-1874 (C.J.)	Portage
Byron Paine[4]	1859-1864, 1867-71	Milwaukee
Jason Downer[4]	1864-1867	Milwaukee
William P. Lyon[4]	1871-1894 (C.J. 1892-94)	Racine
Edward G. Ryan[4]	1874-1880 (C.J.)	Racine
David Taylor	1878-1891	Sheboygan
Harlow S. Orton	1878-1895 (C.J. 1894-95)	Madison
John B. Cassoday[4]	1880-1907 (C.J. 1895-07)	Janesville
John B. Winslow[4]	1891-1920 (C.J. 1907-20)	Racine
Silas U. Pinney	1892-1898	Madison
Alfred W. Newman	1894-1898	Trempealeau
Roujet D. Marshall[4]	1895-1918	Chippewa Falls
Charles V. Bardeen[4]	1898-1903	Wausau
Joshua Eric Dodge[4]	1898-1910	Milwaukee
Robert G. Siebecker[5]	1903-1922 (C.J. 1920-22)	Madison
James C. Kerwin	1905-1921	Neenah
William H. Timlin	1907-1916	Milwaukee
Robert M. Bashford[4]	Jan.-June 1908	Madison
John Barnes	1908-1916	Rhinelander
Aad J. Vinje[4]	1910-1929 (C.J. 1922-29)	Superior
Marvin B. Rosenberry[4]	1916-1950 (C.J. 1929-50)	Wausau
Franz C. Eschweiler[4]	1916-1929	Milwaukee
Walter C. Owen	1918-1934	Maiden Rock
Burr W. Jones[4]	1920-1926	Madison
Christian Doerfler[4]	1921-1929	Milwaukee
Charles H. Crownhart[4]	1922-1930	Madison
E. Ray Stevens	1926-1930	Madison
Chester A. Fowler[4]	1929-1948	Fond du Lac
Oscar M. Fritz[4]	1929-1954 (C.J. 1950-54)	Milwaukee
Edward T. Fairchild[4]	1929-1957 (C.J. 1954-57)	Milwaukee
John D. Wickhem[4]	1930-1949	Madison
George B. Nelson[4]	1930-1942	Stevens Point
Theodore G. Lewis[4]	Nov. 15-Dec. 5, 1934	Madison
Joseph Martin[4]	1934-1946	Green Bay
Elmer E. Barlow[4]	1942-1948	Arcadia
James Ward Rector[4]	1946-1947	Madison
Henry P. Hughes	1948-1951	Oshkosh
John E. Martin[4]	1948-1962 (C.J. 1957-62)	Green Bay
Grover L. Broadfoot[4]	1948-1962 (C.J. Jan.-May 1962)	Mondovi
Timothy Brown[4]	1949-1964 (C.J. 1962-64)	Madison
Edward J. Gehl	1950-1956	Hartford
George R. Currie[4]	1951-1968 (C.J. 1964-68)	Sheboygan
Roland J. Steinle[4]	1954-1958	Milwaukee
Emmert L. Wingert[4]	1956-1959	Madison
Thomas E. Fairchild	1957-1966	Verona
E. Harold Hallows[4]	1958-1974 (C.J. 1968-74)	Milwaukee
William H. Dieterich	1959-1964	Milwaukee
Myron L. Gordon	1962-1967	Milwaukee
Horace W. Wilkie[4]	1962-1976 (C.J. 1974-76)	Madison
Bruce F. Beilfuss	1964-1983 (C.J. 1976-83)	Neillsville
Nathan S. Heffernan[4]	1964-1995 (C.J. 1983-95)	Sheboygan
Leo B. Hanley[4]	1966-1978	Milwaukee
Connor T. Hansen[4]	1967-1980	Eau Claire
Robert W. Hansen	1968-1978	Milwaukee
Roland B. Day[4]	1974-1996 (C.J. 1995-96)	Madison

JUSTICES OF THE SUPREME COURT
1836 – 2015–Continued

Name	Term		Residence[1]
Shirley S. Abrahamson[4]	1976-	(C.J. 1996-2015)	Madison
William G. Callow	1978-1992		Waukesha
John L. Coffey	1978-1982		Milwaukee
Donald W. Steinmetz	1980-1999		Milwaukee
Louis J. Ceci[4]	1982-1993		Milwaukee
William A. Bablitch	1983-2003		Stevens Point
Jon P. Wilcox[4]	1992-2007		Wautoma
Janine P. Geske[4]	1993-1998		Milwaukee
Ann Walsh Bradley	1995-		Wausau
N. Patrick Crooks	1996-		Green Bay
David T. Prosser, Jr.[4]	1998-		Appleton
Diane S. Sykes[4]	1999-2004		Milwaukee
Patience D. Roggensack	2003-	(C.J. 2015-)	Madison
Louis B. Butler, Jr.[4]	2004-2008		Milwaukee
Annette K. Ziegler	2007-		West Bend
Michael J. Gableman	2008-		Webster

Note: The structure of the Wisconsin Supreme Court has varied. There were 3 justices during the territorial period. From 1848 to 1853, circuit judges acted as supreme court judges (5 from 1848 to 1850 and 6 from 1850 to 1853). From 1853 to 1877, there were 3 elected justices. The number was increased to 5 by constitutional amendment in 1877. In 1903 the constitution was amended to raise the number to 7.

[1]Home address is the municipality from which the justice was originally appointed or elected.

[2]As a result of a constitutional amendment adopted in April 1889, the most senior justice served as chief justice from 1889-2015. Originally, the chief justice was elected or appointed to that position. A constitutional amendment adopted in April 2015 requires the court to elect the chief justice for a term of 2 years by majority vote of the justices.

[3]Circuit judges acted as Supreme Court justices 1848-1853.

[4]Initially appointed to the court.

[5]Siebecker was elected April 7, 1903, but prior to inauguration for his elected term was appointed April 9, 1903, to fill the vacancy caused by the death of Justice Bardeen.

Sources: Wisconsin Legislative Reference Bureau, *Wisconsin Blue Books,* 1935, 1944, 1977; Government Accountability Board, Elections Division records; Wisconsin Supreme Court, *Wisconsin Reports,* various volumes.

SENATE PRESIDENTS PRO TEMPORE, SENATE PRESIDENTS AND ASSEMBLY SPEAKERS, 1848 – 2015

Legislative Session	Senate Presidents Pro Tempore or Presidents[1]	Residence	Assembly Speakers	Residence
1848	No permanent president pro tempore	—	Ninian E. Whiteside (D)	Lafayette County
1849	No permanent president pro tempore	—	Harrison C. Hobart (D)	Sheboygan
1850	No record	—	Moses M. Strong (D)	Mineral Point
1851	No record	—	Frederick W. Horn (D)	Cedarburg
1852	E.B. Dean, Jr. (D)	Madison	James M. Shafter (W)	Sheboygan
1853	Duncan C. Reed (D)	Milwaukee	Henry L. Palmer (D)	Milwaukee
1854	Benjamin Allen (D)	Hudson	Frederick W. Horn (D)	Cedarburg
1855	Eleazor Wakeley (D)	Whitewater	Charles C. Sholes (R)	Kenosha
1856	Louis Powell Harvey (R)	Shopiere	William Hull (D)	Grant County
1857	No permanent president pro tempore	—	Wyman Spooner (R)	Elkhorn
1858	Hiram H. Giles (R)	Stoughton	Frederick S. Lovell (R)	Kenosha County
1859	Dennison Worthington (R)	Summit	William P. Lyon (R)	Racine
1860	Moses M. Davis (R)	Portage	William P. Lyon (R)	Racine
1861	Alden I. Bennett (R)	Beloit	Amasa Cobb (R)	Mineral Point
1862	Frederick O. Thorp (D)	West Bend	James W. Beardsley (UD)	Prescott
1863	Wyman Spooner (R)	Elkhorn	J. Allen Barber (R)	Lancaster
1864	Smith S. Wilkinson (R)	Prairie du Sac	William W. Field (U)	Fennimore
1865	Willard H. Chandler (U)	Windsor	William W. Field (U)	Fennimore
1866	Willard H. Chandler (U)	Windsor	Henry D. Barron (U)	St. Croix Falls
1867	George F. Wheeler (U)	Nanuapa	Angus Cameron (U)	La Crosse
1868	Newton M. Littlejohn (R)	Whitewater	Alexander M. Thomson (R)	Janesville
1869	George C. Hazelton (R)	Boscobel	Alexander M. Thomson (R)	Janesville
1870	David Taylor (R)	Sheboygan	James M. Bingham (R)	Palmyra
1871	Charles G. Williams (R)	Janesville	William E. Smith (R)	Fox Lake
1872	Charles G. Williams (R)	Janesville	Daniel Hall (R)	Watertown
1873	Henry L. Eaton (R)	Lone Rock	Henry D. Barron (R)	St. Croix Falls
1874	John C. Holloway (R)	Lancaster	Gabriel Bouck (D)	Oshkosh
1875	Henry D. Barron (R)	St. Croix Falls	Frederick W. Horn (R)	Cedarburg
1876	Robert L.D. Potter (R)	Wautoma	Sam S. Fifield (R)	Ashland
1877	William H. Hiner (R)	Fond du Lac	John B. Cassoday (R)	Janesville
1878	Levi W. Barden (R)	Portage	Augustus R. Barrows (GB)	Chippewa Falls
1879	William T. Price (R)	Black River Falls	David M. Kelly (R)	Green Bay
1880	Thomas B. Scott (R)	Grand Rapids	Alexander A. Arnold (R)	Galesville
1881	Thomas B. Scott (R)	Grand Rapids	Ira B. Bradford (R)	Augusta
1882	George B. Burrows (R)	Madison	Franklin L. Gilson (R)	Ellsworth
1883	George W. Ryland (R)	Lancaster	Earl P. Finch (D)	Oshkosh
1885	Edward S. Minor (R)	Sturgeon Bay	Hiram O. Fairchild (R)	Marinette
1887	Charles K. Erwin (R)	Tomah	Thomas B. Mills (R)	Millston
1889	Thomas A. Dyson (R)	La Crosse	Thomas B. Mills (R)	Millston
1891	Frederick W. Horn (D)	Cedarburg	James J. Hogan (D)	La Crosse
1893	Robert J. MacBride (D)	Neillsville	Edward Keogh (D)	Milwaukee
1895	Thompson D. Weeks (R)	Whitewater	George B. Burrows (R)	Madison
1897	Lyman W. Thayer (R)	Ripon	George A. Buckstaff (R)	Oshkosh
1899	Lyman W. Thayer (R)	Ripon	George H. Ray (R)	La Crosse
1901	James J. McGillivray (R)	Black River Falls	George H. Ray (R)	La Crosse
1903-05 . .	James J. McGillivray (R)	Black River Falls	Irvine L. Lenroot (R)	West Superior
1907	James H. Stout (R)	Menomonie	Herman L. Ekern (R)	Whitehall
1909	James H. Stout (R)	Menomonie	Levi H. Bancroft (R)	Richland Center
1911	Harry C. Martin (R)	Darlington	C.A. Ingram (R)	Durand
1913	Harry C. Martin (R)	Darlington	Merlin Hull (R)	Black River Falls
1915	Edward T. Fairchild (R)	Milwaukee	Lawrence C. Whittet (R)	Edgerton
1917	Timothy Burke (R)	Green Bay	Lawrence C. Whittet (R)	Edgerton
1919	Willard T. Stevens (R)	Rhinelander	Riley S. Young (R)	Darien
1921	Timothy Burke (R)	Green Bay	Riley S. Young (R)	Darien
1923	Henry A. Huber (R)	Stoughton	John L. Dahl (R)	Rice Lake
1925	Howard Teasdale (R)	Sparta	Herman Sachtjen (R)[2]	Madison
	Howard Teasdale (R)	Sparta	George A. Nelson (R)[2]	Milltown
1927	William L. Smith (R)	Neillsville	John W. Eber (R)	Milwaukee
1929	Oscar H. Morris (R)	Milwaukee	Charles B. Perry (R)	Wauwatosa
1931	Herman J. Severson (P)	Iola	Charles B. Perry (R)	Wauwatosa
1933	Orland S. Loomis (R)	Mauston	Cornelius T. Young (D)	Milwaukee
1935	Harry W. Bolens (D)	Port Washington	Jorge W. Carow (P)	Ladysmith
1937	Walter J. Rush (P)	Neillsville	Paul R. Alfonsi (P)	Pence
1939	Edward J. Roethe (R)	Fennimore	Vernon W. Thomson (R)	Richland Center
1941-43 . .	Conrad Shearer (R)	Kenosha	Vernon W. Thomson (R)	Richland Center
1945	Conrad Shearer (R)	Kenosha	Donald C. McDowell (R)	Soldiers Grove

SENATE PRESIDENTS PRO TEMPORE, SENATE PRESIDENTS AND ASSEMBLY SPEAKERS, 1848 – 2015–Continued

Legislative Session	Senate Presidents Pro Tempore or Presidents[1]	Residence	Assembly Speakers	Residence
1947	Frank E. Panzer (R)	Brownsville	Donald C. McDowell (R)	Soldiers Grove
1949	Frank E. Panzer (R)	Brownsville	Alex L. Nicol (R)	Sparta
1951-53 . .	Frank E. Panzer (R)	Brownsville	Ora R. Rice (R)	Delavan
1955	Frank E. Panzer (R)	Brownsville	Mark Catlin, Jr. (R)	Appleton
1957	Frank E. Panzer (R)	Brownsville	Robert G. Marotz (R)	Shawano
1959	Frank E. Panzer (R)	Brownsville	George Molinaro (D)	Kenosha
1961	Frank E. Panzer (R)	Brownsville	David J. Blanchard (R)	Edgerton
1963	Frank E. Panzer (R)	Brownsville	Robert D. Haase (R)	Marinette
1965	Frank E. Panzer (R)	Brownsville	Robert T. Huber (D)	West Allis
1967-69 . .	Robert P. Knowles (R)	New Richmond	Harold V. Froehlich (R)	Appleton
1971	Robert P. Knowles (R)	New Richmond	Robert T. Huber (D)[3]	West Allis
	Robert P. Knowles (R)	New Richmond	Norman C. Anderson (D)[3]	Madison
1973	Robert P. Knowles (R)	New Richmond	Norman C. Anderson (D)	Madison
1975	Fred A. Risser (D)	Madison	Norman C. Anderson (D)	Madison
1977-81 . .	Fred A. Risser (D)[1]	Madison	Edward G. Jackamonis (D)	Waukesha
1983-89 . .	Fred A. Risser (D)	Madison	Thomas A. Loftus (D)	Sun Prairie
1991	Fred A. Risser (D)	Madison	Walter J. Kunicki (D)	Milwaukee
1993	Fred A. Risser (D)[4]	Madison	Walter J. Kunicki (D)	Milwaukee
	Brian D. Rude (R)[4]	Coon Valley	Walter J. Kunicki (D)	Milwaukee
1995	Brian D. Rude (R)[5]	Coon Valley	David T. Prosser, Jr. (R)	Appleton
	Fred A. Risser (D)[5]	Madison	David T. Prosser, Jr. (R)	Appleton
1997	Fred A. Risser (D)[6]	Madison	Ben Brancel (R)[7]	Endeavor
	Brian D. Rude (R)[6]	Coon Valley	Scott R. Jensen (R)[7]	Waukesha
1999	Fred A. Risser (D)	Madison	Scott R. Jensen (R)	Waukesha
2001	Fred A. Risser (D)	Madison	Scott R. Jensen (R)	Waukesha
2003-05 . .	Alan J. Lasee (R)	De Pere	John Gard (R)	Peshtigo
2007	Fred A. Risser (D)	Madison	Michael D. Huebsch (R)	West Salem
2009	Fred A. Risser (D)	Madison	Michael J. Sheridan (D)	Janesville
2011	Michael G. Ellis (R)[8]	Neenah	Jeff Fitzgerald (R)	Horicon
	Fred A. Risser (D)[8]	Madison	Jeff Fitzgerald (R)	Horicon
2013	Michael G. Ellis (R)	Neenah	Robin J. Vos (R)	Burlington
2015	Mary A. Lazich (R)	New Berlin	Robin J. Vos (R)	Burlington

Note: Political party indicated is for session elected and is obtained from newspaper accounts for some early legislators.
Key: D-Democrat; GB-Greenback; P-Progressive; R-Republican; U-Union; UD-Union Democrat; W-Whig.

[1]Table lists the ranking legislator in each house, not the presiding officer. The "president pro tempore" is listed until May 1, 1979; "president of the senate" is listed after that date when the lieutenant governor's function as president was eliminated by a constitutional amendment adopted in April 1979. See separate table for a list of lieutenant governors.

[2]George A. Nelson (R), Polk County, was elected to serve at special session, 4/15/26 to 4/16/26, following the resignation of Herman Sachtjen after the regular session to accept circuit judge appointment.

[3]Anderson was elected speaker 1/18/72 to succeed Huber who resigned 12/13/71 to accept appointment as chairman of the Highway Commission.

[4]A new president was elected on 4/20/93 after a change in party control following two special elections.

[5]A new president was elected on 7/9/96 after a change in party control following a recall election.

[6]A new president was elected on 4/21/98 after a change in party control following a special election.

[7]Jensen was elected speaker 11/4/97 to succeed Brancel who resigned to become Wisconsin Secretary of Agriculture, Trade and Consumer Protection.

[8]A new president was elected on 7/17/12 after a change in party control following a recall election.

Sources: Senate and Assembly Journals; Wisconsin Legislative Reference Bureau records.

MAJORITY AND MINORITY LEADERS OF THE
WISCONSIN SENATE AND ASSEMBLY, 1937 – 2015

	Senate		Assembly	
Session	Majority	Minority	Majority	Minority
1937 . . . .Maurice P. Coakley (R)	NA	NA	NA	
1939 . . . .Maurice P. Coakley (R)	Philip E. Nelson (P)	NA	Paul R. Alfonsi (P)	
1941 . . . .Maurice P. Coakley (R)	Cornelius T. Young (D)	Mark S. Catlin, Jr. (R)	Andrew J. Biemiller (P)	
				Robert E. Tehan (D)
1943 . . . .Warren P. Knowles (R)[1]	NA	Mark S. Catlin, Jr. (R)	Elmer L. Genzmer (D)	
John W. Byrnes (R)[1]			Lyall T. Beggs (P)	
1945 . . . .Warren P. Knowles (R)	Anthony P. Gawronski (D)	Vernon W. Thomson (R)	Lyall T. Beggs (P)	
				Leland S. McParland (D)
1947 . . . .Warren P. Knowles (R)	Robert E. Tehan (D)	Vernon W. Thomson (R)	Leland S. McParland (D)	
1949 . . . .Warren P. Knowles (R)	NA	Vernon W. Thomson (R)	Leland S. McParland (D)	
1951 . . . .Warren P. Knowles (R)	Gaylord Nelson (D)	Arthur O. Mockrud (R)	George Molinaro (D)	
1953 . . . .Warren P. Knowles (R)	Henry W. Maier (D)	Mark S. Catlin, Jr. (R)	George Molinaro (D)	
1955 . . . .Paul J. Rogan (R)[2]	Henry W. Maier (D)	Robert G. Marotz (R)	Robert T. Huber (D)	
1957 . . . .Robert Travis (R)	Henry W. Maier (D)	Warren A. Grady (R)	Robert T. Huber (D)	
1959 . . . .Robert Travis (R)	Henry W. Maier (D)	Keith Hardie (D)	David J. Blanchard (R)	
1961 . . . .Robert Travis (R)	William R. Moser (D)[3]	Robert D. Haase (R)	Robert T. Huber (D)	
1963 . . . .Robert P. Knowles (R)	Richard J. Zaborski (D)	Paul R. Alfonsi (R)	Robert T. Huber (D)	
1965 . . . .Robert P. Knowles (R)	Richard J. Zaborski (D)	Frank L. Nikolay (D)	Robert D. Haase (R)[4]	
				Paul J. Alfonsi (R)[4]
1967 . . . .Jerris Leonard (R)	Fred A. Risser (D)	J. Curtis McKay (R)	Robert T. Huber (D)	
1969 . . . .Ernest C. Keppler (R)	Fred A. Risser (D)	Paul R. Alfonsi (R)	Robert T. Huber (D)	
1971 . . . .Ernest C. Keppler (R)	Fred A. Risser (D)	Norman C. Anderson (D)[5]	Harold V. Froehlich (R)	
			Anthony S. Earl (D)[5]	
1973 . . . .Raymond C. Johnson (R)	Fred A. Risser (D)	Anthony S. Earl (D)	John C. Shabaz (R)	
1975 . . . .Wayne F. Whittow (D)[6]	Clifford W. Krueger (R)	Terry A. Willkom (D)	John C. Shabaz (R)	
William A. Bablitch (D)[6]				
1977 . . . .William A. Bablitch (D)	Clifford W. Krueger (R)	James W. Wahner (D)	John C. Shabaz (R)	
1979 . . . .William A. Bablitch (D)	Clifford W. Krueger (R)	James W. Wahner (D)[7]	John C. Shabaz (R)	
			Gary K. Johnson (D)[7]	
1981 . . . .William A. Bablitch (D)[9]	Walter J. Chilsen (R)	Thomas A. Loftus (D)	John C. Shabaz (R)[8]	
Timothy F. Cullen (D)[9]				Tommy G. Thompson (R)[8]
1983 . . . .Timothy F. Cullen (D)	James E. Harsdorf (R)	Gary K. Johnson (D)	Tommy G. Thompson (R)	
1985 . . . .Timothy F. Cullen (D)	Susan S. Engeleiter (R)	Dismas Becker (D)	Tommy G. Thompson (R)	
1987 . . . .Joseph A. Strohl (D)	Susan S. Engeleiter (R)	Thomas A. Hauke (D)	Betty Jo Nelsen (R)	
1989 . . . .Joseph A. Strohl (D)	Michael G. Ellis (R)	Thomas A. Hauke (D)	David T. Prosser (R)	
1991 . . . .David W. Helbach (D)	Michael G. Ellis (R)	David M. Travis (D)	David T. Prosser (R)	
1993 . . . .David W. Helbach (D)[10]	Michael G. Ellis (R)[10]	David M. Travis (D)	David T. Prosser (R)	
Michael G. Ellis (R)[10]	David W. Helbach (D)[10,11]			
	Robert Jauch (D)[11]			
1995 . . . .Michael G. Ellis (R)[13]	Robert Jauch (D)[12]	Scott R. Jensen (R)	Walter J. Kunicki (D)	
	Charles Chvala (D)[12,13]			
Charles Chvala (D)[13]	Michael G. Ellis (R)[13]			
1997 . . . .Charles Chvala (D)[14]	Michael G. Ellis (R)[14]	Steven M. Foti (R)	Walter J. Kunicki (D)[15]	
Michael G. Ellis (R)[14]	Charles Chvala (D)[14]		Shirley Krug (D)[15]	
1999 . . . .Charles Chvala (D)	Michael G. Ellis (R)[16]	Steven M. Foti (R)	Shirley Krug (D)	
	Mary E. Panzer (R)[16]			
2001 . . . .Charles Chvala (D)	Mary E. Panzer (R)	Steven M. Foti (R)	Shirley Krug (D)	
Russell S. Decker (D)[17]			Spencer Black (D)[18]	
Fred A. Risser (D)[17]				
Jon B. Erpenbach (D)[17]				
2003 . . . .Mary E. Panzer (R)[19]	Jon B. Erpenbach (D)	Steven M. Foti (R)	James E. Kreuser (D)	
Scott L. Fitzgerald (R)[19]				
Dale W. Schultz (R)[20]	Judith Biros Robson (D)[20]			
2005 . . . .Dale W. Schultz (R)	Judith Biros Robson (D)	Michael D. Huebsch (R)	James E. Kreuser (D)	
2007 . . . .Judith Biros Robson (D)	Scott L. Fitzgerald (R)	Jeff Fitzgerald (R)	James E. Kreuser (D)	
Russell S. Decker (D)[21]				
2009 . . . .Russell S. Decker (D)[22]	Scott L. Fitzgerald (R)	Thomas M. Nelson (D)	Jeff Fitzgerald (R)	
Dave Hansen (D)[22]				
2011 . . . .Scott L. Fitzgerald (R)	Mark Miller (D)	Scott Suder (R)	Peter W. Barca (D)	
Mark Miller (D)[23]	Scott L. Fitzgerald (R)[23]			

MAJORITY AND MINORITY LEADERS OF THE
WISCONSIN SENATE AND ASSEMBLY, 1937 – 2015–Continued

	Senate		Assembly	
Session	Majority	Minority	Majority	Minority
2013 . . . .Scott L. Fitzgerald (R)		Chris Larson (D)	Scott Suder (R)[24]	Peter W. Barca (D)
			Bill Kramer (R)[25]	
			Pat Strachota (R)	
2015 . . . .Scott L. Fitzgerald (R)		Jennifer Shilling (D)	Jim Steineke (R)	Peter W. Barca (D)

Note: Majority and minority leaders, who are chosen by the party caucuses in each house, were first recognized officially in the senate and assembly rules in 1963. Prior to the 1977 session, these positions were also referred to as "floor leader".

Key: (D) – Democrat; (P) – Progressive; (R) – Republican.

NA – Not available.

[1]Knowles granted leave of absence to return to active duty in U.S. Navy; Byrnes chosen to succeed him on 4/30/1943.

[2]Resigned after sine die adjournment.

[3]Resigned 1/30/1962.

[4]Haase resigned 9/15/1965; Alfonsi elected 10/4/1965.

[5]Earl elected 1/18/1972 to succeed Anderson who became Assembly Speaker.

[6]Whittow resigned 4/30/1976; Bablitch elected 5/17/1976.

[7]Wahner resigned 1/28/1980; Johnson elected 1/28/1980.

[8]Shabaz resigned 12/18/1981; Thompson elected 12/21/1981.

[9]Bablitch resigned 5/26/1982; Cullen elected 5/26/1982.

[10]Democrats controlled senate from 1/4/1993 to 4/20/1993 when Republicans assumed control after a special election.

[11]Helbach resigned 5/12/1993; Jauch elected 5/12/1993.

[12]Jauch resigned 10/17/1995; Chvala elected 10/24/1995.

[13]Republicans controlled senate from 1/5/1995 to 6/13/1996 when Democrats assumed control after a recall election.

[14]Democrats controlled the senate from 1/6/1997 to 4/21/1998 when Republicans assumed control after a special election.

[15]Kunicki resigned 6/3/1998; Krug elected 6/3/1998.

[16]Ellis resigned 1/25/2000; Panzer elected 1/25/2000.

[17]Decker and Risser elected co-leaders 10/22/2002. Erpenbach elected leader 12/4/2002.

[18]Black elected 5/1/2001.

[19]Panzer resigned 9/17/2004; Fitzgerald elected 9/17/2004.

[20]Schultz elected 11/9/2004; Robson elected 11/9/2004.

[21]Decker elected 10/24/2007.

[22]Hansen replaced Decker as leader, 12/15/2010.

[23]After a resignation on 3/16/12 resulted in a 16-16 split, Fitzgerald and Miller served as co-leaders. A recall election gave Democrats control of the senate as of 7/17/12.

[24]Suder resigned 9/3/13; Kramer elected 9/4/13.

[25]Kramer removed 3/4/14; Strachota elected 3/4/14.

Sources: *Wisconsin Blue Book,* various editions; Senate and Assembly Journals; newspaper accounts.

SENATE AND ASSEMBLY CHIEF CLERKS
AND SERGEANTS AT ARMS, 1848 – 2015

Legislative	Senate		Assembly	
Session	Chief Clerk	Sergeant at Arms	Chief Clerk	Sergeant at Arms
1848 . . . . .Henry G. Abbey		Lyman H. Seaver	Daniel N. Johnson	John Mullanphy
1849 . . . . . . .William R. Smith		F. W. Shollner	Robert L. Ream	Felix McLinden
1850 . . . . . . .William R. Smith		James Hanrahan	Alex T. Gray	E. R. Hugunin
1851 . . . . . . .William Hull		E. D. Masters	Alex T. Gray	C. M. Kingsbury
1852 . . . . . . .John K. Williams		Patrick Cosgrove	Alex T. Gray	Elisha Starr
1853 . . . . . . .John K. Williams		Thomas Hood	Thomas McHugh	Richard F. Wilson
1854 . . . . . . .Samuel G. Bugh		J. M. Sherwood	Thomas McHugh	William H. Gleason
1855 . . . . . . .Samuel G. Bugh		William H. Gleason	David Atwood	William Blake
1856 . . . . . . .Byron Paine		Joseph Baker	James Armstrong	Egbert Mosely
1857 . . . . . . .William Henry Brisbane	Alanson Filer	William C. Webb	William C. Rogers
1858 . . . . . . .John L. V. Thomas		Nathaniel L. Stout	L. H. D. Crane	Francis Massing
1859 . . . . . . .Hiram Bowen		Asa Kinney	L. H. D. Crane	Emmanual Munk
1860 . . . . . . .J. H. Warren		Asa Kinney	L. H. D. Crane	Joseph Gates
1861 . . . . . . .J. H. Warren		J. A. Hadley	L. H. D. Crane	Craig B. Peebe
1862 . . . . . . .J. H. Warren		B. U. Caswell	John S. Dean	A. A. Huntington
1863 . . . . . . .Frank M. Stewart		Luther Bashford	John S. Dean	A. M. Thompson
1864 . . . . . . .Frank M. Stewart		Nelson Williams	John S. Dean	A. M. Thompson
1865 . . . . . . .Frank M. Stewart		Nelson Williams	John S. Dean	Alonzo Wilcox
1866 . . . . . . .Frank M. Stewart		Nelson Williams	E. W. Young	L. M. Hammond
1867 . . . . . . .Leander B. Hills		Asa Kinney	E. W. Young	Daniel Webster
1868 . . . . . . .Leander B. Hills		W. H. Hamilton	E. W. Young	C. L. Harris
1869 . . . . . . .Leander B. Hills		W. H. Hamilton	E. W. Young	Rolin C. Kelly
1870 . . . . . . .Leander B. Hills		E. M. Rogers	E. W. Young	Ole C. Johnson
1871 . . . . . . .O. R. Smith		W. W. Baker	E. W. Young	Sam S. Fifield
1872 . . . . . . .J. H. Waggoner		W. D. Hoard	E. W. Young	Sam S. Fifield
1873 . . . . . . .J. H. Waggoner		Albert Emonson	E. W. Young	O. C. Bissel
1874 . . . . . . .J. H. Waggoner		O. U. Aiken	George W. Peck	Joseph Deuster
1875 . . . . . . .Fred A. Dennett		O. U. Aiken	R. M. Strong	J. W. Brackett
1876 . . . . . . .A. J. Turner		E. T. Gardner	R. M. Strong	Elisha Starr
1877 . . . . . . .A. J. Turner		C. E. Bullard	W. A. Nowell	Thomas B. Reid
1878 . . . . . . .A. J. Turner[1]		L. J. Brayton	Jabez R. Hunter	Anton Klaus
Charles E. Bross[1]				
1879 . . . . . . .Charles E. Bross		Chalmers Ingersoll	John E. Eldred	Miletus Knight
1880 . . . . . . .Charles E. Bross		Chalmers Ingersoll	John E. Eldred	D. H. Pulcifer
1881 . . . . . . .Charles E. Bross		W. W. Baker	John E. Eldred	G. W. Church
1882 . . . . . . .Charles E. Bross		A. T. Glaze	E. D. Coe	D. E. Welch
1883 . . . . . . .Charles E. Bross		A. D. Thorp	I. T. Carr	Thomas Kennedy
1885 . . . . . . .Charles E. Bross		Hubert Wolcott	E. D. Coe	John M. Ewing
1887 . . . . . . .Charles E. Bross		T. J. George	E. D. Coe	William A. Adamson
1889 . . . . . . .Charles E. Bross		T .J. George	E. D. Coe	F. E. Parsons
1891 . . . . . . .J. P. Hume		John A. Barney	George W. Porth	Patrick Whelan
1893 . . . . . . .Sam J. Shafer		John B. Becker	George W. Porth	Theodore Knapstein
1895 . . . . . . .Walter L. Houser		Charles Pettibone	W. A. Nowell	B. F. Millard
1897 . . . . . . .Walter L. Houser		Charles Pettibone	W. A. Nowell	C. M. Hambright
1889 . . . . . . .Walter L. Houser		Charles Pettibone	W. A. Nowell	James H. Agen
1901 . . . . . . .Walter L. Houser		Charles Pettibone	W. A. Nowell	A. M. Anderson
1903 . . . . . . .Theodore W. Goldin		Sanfield McDonald	C. O. Marsh	A. M. Anderson
1905 . . . . . . .L .K. Eaton		R. C. Falconer	C. O. Marsh	Nicholas Streveler
1907 . . . . . . .A. R. Emerson		R. C. Falconer	C. E. Shaffer	W. S. Irvine
1909 . . . . . . .F. E. Andrews		R. C. Falconer	C. E. Shaffer	W. S. Irvine
1911-13 . . . . . .F. M. Wylie		C. A. Leicht	C. E. Shaffer	W. S. Irvine
1915 . . . . . . .O. G. Munson		F. E. Andrews	C. E. Shaffer	W. S. Irvine
1917 . . . . . . .O. G. Munson		F. E. Andrews	C. E. Shaffer	T. G. Cretney
1919 . . . . . . .O. G. Munson		John Turner	C. E. Shaffer	T. G. Cretney
1921 . . . . . . .O. G. Munson		Vincent Kielpinski	C. E. Shaffer	T. G. Cretney
1923 . . . . . . .F. W. Schoenfeld		C. A. Leicht	C. E. Shaffer	T. W. Bartingale
1925 . . . . . . .F. W. Schoenfeld		C. A. Leicht	C. E. Shaffer	C. E. Hanson
1927-29 . . . . .O. G. Munson		George W. Rickeman	C. E. Shaffer	C. F. Moulton
1931 . . . . . . .R. A. Cobban		Emil A. Hartman	C. E. Shaffer	Gustave Rheingans
1933 . . . . . . .R. A. Cobban		Emil A. Hartman	John J. Slocum	George C. Faust
1935-37 . . . . .Lawrence R. Larsen		Emil A. Hartman	Lester R. Johnson	Gustave Rheingans
1939 . . . . . . .Lawrence R. Larsen		Emil A. Hartman	John J. Slocum	Robert A. Merrill
1941-43 . . . . .Lawrence R. Larsen		Emil A. Hartman	Arthur L. May	Norris J. Kellman
1945 . . . . . . .Lawrence R. Larsen		Harold E. Damon	Arthur L. May	Norris J. Kellman
1947-53 . . . . .Thomas M. Donahue		Harold E. Damon	Arthur L. May	Norris J. Kellman
1955-57 . . . . .Lawrence R. Larsen		Harold E. Damon	Arthur L. May	Norris J. Kellman

SENATE AND ASSEMBLY CHIEF CLERKS
AND SERGEANTS AT ARMS, 1848 – 2015–Continued

Legislative Session	Senate Chief Clerk	Sergeant at Arms	Assembly Chief Clerk	Sergeant at Arms
1959	Lawrence R. Larsen	Harold E. Damon	Norman C. Anderson	Thomas H. Browne
1961	Lawrence R. Larsen	Harold E. Damon	Robert G. Marotz	Norris J. Kellman
1963	Lawrence R. Larsen	Harold E. Damon	Kenneth E. Priebe	Norris J. Kellman
1965	Lawrence R. Larsen[2] William P. Nugent[2]	Harold E. Damon	James P. Buckley	Thomas H. Browne
1967	William P. Nugent	Harry O. Levander	Arnold W. F. Langner[3] Wilmer H. Struebing[3]	Louis C. Romell
1969	William P. Nugent	Kenneth Nicholson	Wilmer H. Struebing	Louis C. Romell
1971	William P. Nugent	Kenneth Nicholson	Thomas P. Fox	William F. Quick
1973	William P. Nugent	Kenneth Nicholson	Thomas S. Hanson	William F. Quick
1975	Glenn E. Bultman	Robert M. Thompson	Everett E. Bolle	Raymond J. Tobiasz
1977	Donald J. Schneider	Robert M. Thompson	Everett E. Bolle	Joseph E. Jones
1979	Donald J. Schneider	Daniel B. Fields	Marcel Dandeneau	Joseph E. Jones
1981	Donald J. Schneider	Daniel B. Fields	David R. Kedrowski	Lewis T. Mittness
1983	Donald J. Schneider	Daniel B. Fields	Joanne M. Duren	Lewis T. Mittness
1985	Donald J. Schneider	Daniel B. Fields	Joanne M. Duren	Patrick Essie
1987	Donald J. Schneider	Daniel B. Fields	Thomas T. Melvin	Patrick Essie
1989-91	Donald J. Schneider	Daniel B. Fields	Thomas T. Melvin	Robert G. Johnston
1993	Donald J. Schneider	Daniel B. Fields[4] Jon H. Hochkammer[4]	Thomas T. Melvin	Robert G. Johnston
1995	Donald J. Schneider	Jon H. Hochkammer	Thomas T. Melvin[5] Charles R. Sanders[5]	John A. Scocos
1997	Donald J. Schneider	Jon H. Hochkammer	Charles R. Sanders	John A. Scocos[6] Denise L. Solie[6]
1999	Donald J. Schneider	Jon H. Hochkammer	Charles R. Sanders	Denise L. Solie
2001	Donald J. Schneider	Jon H. Hochkammer[7]	John A. Scocos[7]	Denise L. Solie
2003	Donald J. Schneider[8] Robert J. Marchant[8]	Edward A. Blazel	Patrick E. Fuller	Richard A. Skindrud
2005-07	Robert J. Marchant	Edward A. Blazel	Patrick E. Fuller	Richard A. Skindrud
2009	Robert J. Marchant	Edward A. Blazel	Patrick E. Fuller	William M. Nagy
2011	Robert J. Marchant[9]	Edward A. Blazel	Patrick E. Fuller	Anne Tonnon Byers
2013-15	Jeffrey Renk	Edward A. Blazel	Patrick E. Fuller	Anne Tonnon Byers

[1]Bross elected 2/6/78; Turner resigned 2/7/78.

[2]Larsen died 3/2/65; Nugent elected 3/31/65.

[3]Langner resigned 5/2/67; Struebing elected 5/16/67.

[4]Fields served until 8/2/93. Randall Radtke served as Acting Sergeant from 8/3/93 to 11/3/93. Hochkammer was elected 1/25/94.

[5]Melvin retired 1/31/95; Sanders elected 5/24/95.

[6]Scocos resigned 9/25/97; Solie elected 1/15/98.

[7]Scocos resigned 2/25/02. Hochkammer resigned 9/2/02. No replacement was elected for either.

[8]Schneider resigned 7/4/03; Marchant elected 1/20/04.

[9]Marchant resigned 1/2/12.

Sources: Wisconsin Legislative Reference Bureau, *Wisconsin Blue Book,* various editions; journals and organizing resolutions of each house.

MEMBERS OF THE WISCONSIN LEGISLATURE, 1848 – 2007
See *2007-2008 Blue Book* Feature Article
"Those Who Served: Wisconsin Legislators 1848 – 2007," pp. 99-191.

WISCONSIN LEGISLATIVE SESSIONS, 1848 – 2013

Session	Opening and Adjournment Dates	Calendar Days[2]	Meeting Days[3] (S)	(A)	Bills	Jt. Res.	Res.	Bills Vetoed	Over-ridden	Laws Enacted
1848	6/5-8/21	78	58	59	217	0	0	0	0	155
1849	1/10-4/2	83	69	65	428	0	0	1	1	220
1850	1/9-2/11	34	29	29	438	0	0	1	0	284
1851	1/8-3/17	69	59	59	707	0	0	9	0	407
1852	1/14-4/19	97	78	78	813	0	0	2	1	504
1853	1/12-4/4; 6/6-7/13	153	100	104	1,145	0	0	3	0	521
1854	1/11-4/3	83	66	66	880	0	0	2	0	437
1855	1/10-4/2	83	79	79	955	0	0	6	0	500
1856	1/9-3/31; 9/3-10/14	125	94	103	1,242	0	0	1	0	688
1857	1/14-3/9	55	46	46	895	0	0	0	0	517
1858	1/13-3/31; 4/10-5/17	116	95	97	1,364	157	342	28	0	436
1859	1/12-3/21	69	58	57	986	113	143	9	0	680
1860	1/11-4/2	83	66	67	1,024	69	246	2	0	489
1861	1/9-4/17	99	81	80	857	100	235	2	0	387
1861SS[4]	5/15-5/27	13	11	11	28	24	34	0	0	15
1862	1/8-4/7; 6/3-6/17	105	86	88	1,008	125	207	27	8	514
1862SS	9/10-9/26	17	15	15	43	25	37	0	0	17
1863	1/14-4/2	79	65	67	895	101	157	7	1	383
1864	1/13-4/4	83	68	69	835	66	141	0	0	509
1865	1/11-4/10	90	73	72	1,132	82	190	2	0	565
1866	1/10-4/2	83	75	74	1,107	64	208	5	0	733
1867	1/9-4/11	93	71	72	1,161	97	161	2	0	790
1868	1/8-3/6	59	46	45	987	73	119	2	0	692
1869	1/13-3/11	58	40	43	887	52	81	12	1	657
1870	1/12-3/17	65	51	51	1,043	54	89	2	0	666
1871	1/11-3/25	74	58	60	1,066	55	82	4	0	671
1872	1/10-3/26	77	61	60	709	79	124	2	0	322
1873	1/8-3/20	72	49	55	611	62	122	4	0	308
1874	1/14-3/12	58	50	49	688	91	111	2	0	349
1875	1/13-3/6	53	44	42	637	39	93	2	0	344
1876	1/12-3/14	63	50	50	715	57	115	2	0	415
1877	1/10-3/8	58	41	41	720	59	95	4	0	384
1878	1/9-3/21	72	55	55	735	79	134	2	0	342
1878SS	6/4-6/7	4	4	4	6	14	10	0	0	5
1879	1/8-3/5	57	43	43	610	49	105	0	0	256
1880	1/14-3/17	64	50	49	669	58	93	3	0	323
1881	1/12-4/14	93	63	64	780	104	100	3	0	334
1882	1/11-3/31	80	57	57	728	57	90	6	0	330
1883	1/10-4/4	85	57	67	705	75	100	2	0	360
1885	1/14-4/13	90	65	66	963	97	108	8	0	471
1887	1/12-4/15	94	69	68	1,293	114	60	10	0	553
1889	1/9-4/19	101	64	64	1,355	136	82	5	1	529
1891	1/14-4/25	102	68	69	1,216	137	91	8	1	483
1892SS	6/28-7/1	4	4	4	4	7	16	0	0	1
1892SS	10/17-10/27	11	9	9	8	6	14	0	0	2
1893	1/11-4/21	101	62	62	1,124	135	86	6	0	312
1895	1/9-4/20	102	70	70	1,154	139	88	0	0	387
1896SS	2/18-2/28	11	8	8	3	11	15	0	0	1
1897	1/13-4/21; 8/17-8/20	103	75	76	1,077	155	39	11	0	381
1899	1/11-5/4	114	78	77	910	113	40	4	0	357
1901	1/9-5/15	127	89	89	1,091	81	39	22	0	470
1903	1/14-5/23	130	87	89	1,115	65	81	23	0	451
1905	1/11-6/21	162	114	117	1,357	134	101	19	0	523
1905SS	12/4-12/19	16	12	14	24	15	26	0	0	17
1907	1/9-7/16	189	114	123	1,685	205	84	26	1	677
1909	1/13-6/18	157	100	101	1,567	213	49	24	0	550
1911	1/11-7/15	186	137	138	1,710	267	37	15	0	665
1912SS	4/30-5/6	7	6	6	41	7	6	0	0	22
1913	1/8-8/9	214	138	147	1,847	175	79	23	0	778
1915	1/13-8/24	224	147	148	1,560	220	79	15	0	637
1916SS	10/10-10/11	2	2	2	2	8	4	0	0	2
1917	1/10-7/16	188	130	133	1,439	229	115	18	0	679
1918SS	2/19-3/9	19	14	14	27	22	28	2	0	16
1918SS	9/24-9/25	2	2	2	2	6	9	0	0	2
1919	1/8-7/30	204	107	106	1,350	268	100	40	0	703
1919SS	9/4-9/8	5	4	3	7	4	6	0	0	7
1920SS	5/25-6/4	11	7	7	46	10	22	2	0	32
1921	1/12-7/14	184	116	116	1,199	207	93	41	1	591
1922SS	3/22-3/28	7	4	4	10	7	12	1	0	4
1923	1/10-7/14	186	114	120	1,247	215	93	52	0	449
1925	1/14-6/29	167	103	107	1,144	200	115	73	0	454
1926SS	4/15-4/16	2	2	2	1	8	12	0	0	1
1927	1/12-8/13	214	121	128	1,341	235	167	88	2	542
1928SS	1/24-2/4	12	9	8	20	35	23	0	0	5
1928SS	3/6-3/13	8	6	6	13	9	17	0	0	2
1929	1/9-9/20	255	137	135	1,366	278	185	44	0	530
1931	1/14-6/27	165	98	104	1,429	291	160	36	0	487

WISCONSIN LEGISLATIVE SESSIONS, 1848 – 2013–Continued

Session	Opening and Adjournment Dates	Length of Session			Measures Introduced			Vetoes[1]		
		Calendar Days[2]	Meeting Days[3]		Bills	Jt. Res.	Res.	Bills Vetoed	Over-ridden	Laws Enacted
			(S)	(A)						
1931SS....	11/24/31-2/5/32	74	48	42	99	93	83	2	0	31
1933	1/11-7/25	196	111	121	1,411	324	157	15	0	496
1933SS....	12/11/33-2/3/34	55	30	34	45	160	53	0	0	20
1935	1/9-9/27	262	153	156	1,662	346	190	27	0	556
1937	1/13-7/2	171	97	114	1,404	228	127	10	0	432
1937SS....	9/15-10/16	32	23	23	28	18	23	0	0	15
1939	1/11-10/6	269	154	154	1,559	268	133	22	0	535
1941	1/8-6/6	150	90	93	1,368	160	109	17	0	333
1943	1/13-8/3;	375	105	104	1,153	202	136	39	20	577
	(1944: 1/12-1/22)									
1945	1/10-6/20; 9/5-9/6	240	97	93	1,156	208	109	31	5	590
1946SS....	7/29-7/30	2	2	2	2	6	14	0	0	2
1947	1/8-7/19; 9/9-9/11	247	114	114	1,220	195	97	10	1	615
1948SS....	7/19-7/20	2	2	2	0	5	11	0	0	0
1949	1/12-7/9; 9/12-9/13	245	105	106	1,432	188	86	17	2	643
1951	1/10-6/14	156	91	90	1,559	157	73	18	0	735
1953	1/14-6/12; 10/26-11/6	297	97	98	1,593	175	70	31	3	687
1955	1/12-6/24; 10/3-10/21	283	111	114	1,503	256	74	38	0	696
1957	1/9-6/28; 9/23-9/27	262	107	108	1,512	246	71	39	1	706
1958SS....	6/11-6/13	3	3	3	3	7	13	0	0	3
1959	1/14/59-5/27/60	500	159	163	1,769	272	84	36	4	696
	(1959: 1/14-7/25, 11/3-12/23;									
	1960: 1/6-1/22, 5/16-5/27)									
1961	1/11/61-1/9/63	729	184	185	1,592	295	68	73	2	689
	(1961: 1/11-8/12, 10/30-12/22;									
	1962: 1/8-1/12, 6/18-7/31, 12/27-12/29;									
	1963: 1/9)									
1963	1/9/63-1/13/65	736	140	142	1,619	241	110	72	4	580
	(1963: 1/9-8/6, 11/4-11/21;									
	1964: 4/13-4/29, 11/9-11/11;									
	1965: 1/13)									
1963SS....	12/10-12/12	3	3	3	8	10	10	0	0	3
1965[5].....	1/13/65-1/2/67	720	163	160	1,818	293	86	24	1	666
	(1965: 1/13-7/30, 10/4-11/4;									
	1966: 5/2-6/10;									
	1967: 1/2)									
1967	1/11/67-1/6/69	727	122	126	1,700	215	61	18	0	355
	(1967: 1/11-3/9, 4/4-7/28, 10/17-11/16,									
	12/5-12/16;									
	1968: none;									
	1969: 1/6)									
1969	1/6/69-1/4/71	729	165	165	2,014	232	101	34	1	501
	(1969: 1/6, 1/21-11/15;									
	1970: 1/5-1/16;									
	1971: 1/4)									
1969SS[6]....	9/29/69-1/17/70	111	28	18	5	5	8	0	0	1
1970SS....	12/22/70	1	1	1	0	1	5	0	0	0
1971	1/4/71-1/1/73	729	179	180	2,568	291	121	32	3	336
	(1971: 1/4, 1/19-10/28;									
	1972: 1/18-3/10, 7/13-7/15;									
	1973: 1/1)									
1972SS....	4/19-4/28	10	5	6	9	4	4	0	0	6
1973	1/1/73-1/6/75	736	147	150	2,501	277	126	13	0	332
	(1973: 1/1, 1/16-2/15, 3/13-7/26,									
	10/2-10/26;									
	1974: 1/29-3/29, 11/19-11/20;									
	1975: 1/6)									
1973SS....	12/17-12/21	5	5	5	3	2	6	0	0	2
1974SS....	4/29-6/13	46	17	20	12	1	4	0	0	6
1974SS[7]....	11/19-11/20	2	2	1	2	0	0	0	0	1
1975	1/6/75-1/3/77	729	125	129	2,325	169	88	36	6	414
	(1975: 1/6, 1/14-2/20, 4/1-7/16, 9/2-9/26;									
	1976: 1/28-3/26, 6/15-6/17;									
	1977: 1/3)									
1975SS....	12/9-12/11	3	3	3	13	1	2	1	0	6
1976SS....	5/18	1	1	1	2	2	3	0	0	1
1976SS[7]....	6/15-6/17	3	3	3	13	4	3	0	0	9
1976SS....	9/8	1	1	1	4	1	4	0	0	2
1977	1/3/77-1/1/79	730	86	112	2,053	182	48	21	4	442
	(1977: 1/3, 1/11-2/17, 3/29-7/1, 9/6-9/30;									
	1978: 1/24, 1/31-3/31, 6/13-6/15;									
	1979: 1/3)									
1977SS....	6/30	1	1	1	0	1	2	0	0	0
1977SS....	11/7-11/11	5	5	5	6	4	2	0	0	5
1978SS[7]....	6/13-6/15	3	3	3	2	5	2	0	0	2
1978SS....	12/20	1	1	1	2	4	2	0	0	2

WISCONSIN LEGISLATIVE SESSIONS, 1848 – 2013–Continued

Session	Opening and Adjournment Dates	Length of Session Calendar Days[2]	Meeting Days[3] (S)	(A)	Measures Introduced Bills	Jt. Res.	Res.	Vetoes[1] Bills Vetoed	Over-ridden	Laws Enacted
1979	1/3/79-1/5/81	734	85	99	1,920	203	40	19	3	350
	1979: 1/3, 1/9, 1/23-3/2, 4/17-6/29,									
	10/2-11/2;									
	1980: 1/29-4/2, 5/28-5/30;									
	1981: 1/5)									
1979SS. . . .	9/5	1	1	1	10	3	2	0	0	5
1980SS[8] . . .	1/22-1/25	4	2	4	8	3	2	0	0	0
1980SS. . . .	6/3- 7/3	31	13	12	20	14	2	0	0	7
1981	1/5/81-1/3/83	729	121	130	1,987	176	70	10	2	381
	(1981: 1/5, 1/13, 1/27-2/20, 4/7-7/17,									
	9/30-10/30, 12/15-12/17;									
	1982: 1/20-6/14;									
	1983: 1/3)									
1981SS[9] . . .	11/4-11/17	14	8	7	6	3	2	0	0	3
1982SS[9] . . .	4/6-4/30, 5/5-5/20	45	18	21	4	2	2	1	0	1
1982SS[10] . . .	5/26-5/28	3	3	3	13	7	2	0	0	9
1983	1/3/83-1/7/85	736	75	80	1,902	173	50	3	0	521
	(1983: 1/3, 1/25-1/27, 2/8-2/17,									
	4/12-6/30, 10/4-10/28;									
	1984: 1/31-4/6, 5/22-5/24;									
	1985: 1/7)									
1983SS. . . .	1/4-1/6	3	3	2	2	2	1	0	0	2
1983SS. . . .	4/12-4/14	3	3	3	1	1	0	0	0	1
1983SS. . . .	7/11-7/14	4	2	4	5	3	1	0	0	4
1983SS. . . .	10/18-10/28	11	8	7	12	1	0	0	0	11
1984SS. . . .	2/2-4/4	63	19	13	2	1	0	0	0	0
1984SS. . . .	5/22-5/24	3	3	2	12	5	1	0	0	11
1985	1/7/85-1/5/87	729	68	67	1,624	171	41	7	0	293
	(1985: 1/7, 1/15, 1/29-2/7, 3/19-3/21,									
	4/23-6/29, 9/24-10/18;									
	1986: 1/28-3/26, 5/20-5/22;									
	1987: 1/5)									
1985SS. . . .	3/19-3/21	3	2	2	6	1	0	0	0	3
1985SS. . . .	9/24-10/19	26	11	7	22	1	0	0	0	17
1985SS. . . .	10/31	1	1	1	1	3	0	0	0	1
1985SS. . . .	11/20	1	1	1	24	2	0	0	0	12
1986SS. . . .	1/27-5/30	124	34	27	1	4	0	0	0	1
1986SS. . . .	3/24-3/26	3	3	3	1	1	0	0	0	1
1986SS. . . .	5/20-5/29	10	6	4	44	3	0	0	0	12
1986SS. . . .	7/15	1	1	1	3	1	0	0	0	2
1987[10]	1/5/87-1/3/89	730	75	87	1,631	196	21	35	0	413
	(1987: 1/5, 1/13, 1/27-2/5, 2/12, 3/17-3/19,									
	4/21-7/2, 10/6-10/29;									
	1988: 1/26-3/25, 4/19-4/20,									
	5/17-5/19, 6/30;									
	1989: 1/3)									
1987SS. . . .	9/15-9/16	2	2	2	2	1	0	0	0	2
1987SS. . . .	11/18/87-6/7/88	203	44	42	19	3	0	3	0	5
1988SS. . . .	6/30	1	1	1	4	1	3	0	0	2
1989	1/3/89-1/7/91	735	68	70	1,557	244	45	35	0	361
	(1989: 1/3, 1/4-1/9, 1/10, 1/11-1/23,									
	1/24-2/3, 2/6-3/13, 3/14-3/16,									
	3/17-4/24, 4/25-4/27, 4/28-5/15,									
	5/16-6/30, 10/3-11/10, 11/13-12/31;									
	1990: 1/1-1/22, 1/23-3/23, 3/26-5/14,									
	5/15-5/17, 5/18-12/31;									
	1991: 1/1-1/4, 1/7)									
1989SS. . . .	10/10/89-3/22/90	164	52	49	52	6	0	0	0	7
1990SS. . . .	5/15/90	1	1	1	7	1	0	0	0	0
1991	1/7/91-1/4/93	729	102	100	1,676	244	32	33	0	318
	(1991: 1/7, 1/15, 1/29-3/14,									
	4/16-5/16, 6/4-7/3, 10/1-11/8;									
	1992: 1/28-3/27, 5/19-5/21;									
	1993: 1/4)									
1991SS. . . .	1/29/-7/4	157	49	52	16	1	0	0	0	2
1991SS. . . .	10/15/91-5/21/92	220	50	47	9	2	0	0	0	1
1992SS[8] . . .	4/14-6/4	52	20	17	7	1	2	0	0	2
1992SS. . . .	6/1	1	1	1	0	2	0	0	0	0
1992SS. . . .	8/25-9/15	22	7	7	1	1	2	0	0	1
1993	1/4/93-1/3/95	730	91	86	2,147	207	47	8	0	491
	(1993: 1/4, 1/26-3/11, 4/20-7/16,									
	10/5-10/28;									
	1994: 1/25-3/25, 5/17;									
	1995: 1/3)									
1994SS. . . .	5/18-5/19	2	2	2	6	1	0	0	0	3
1994SS[11] . . .	6/7-6/23	17	8	8	3	4	0	0	0	3

WISCONSIN LEGISLATIVE SESSIONS, 1848 – 2013–Continued

Session	Opening and Adjournment Dates	Calendar Days[2]	Meeting Days[3] (S)	Meeting Days[3] (A)	Bills	Jt. Res.	Res.	Bills Vetoed	Over-ridden	Laws Enacted
1995	1/3/95-1/6/97	735	78	90	1,780	163	38	4	0	467
(1995: 1/3-1/5, 1/17-2/2, 2/14-3/9, 4/4-4/6, 5/16-6/29, 9/19-10/12; 11/7-11/16; 1996: 1/9-2/1, 3/5-3/28, 5/7-5/14, 7/9; 1997: 1/6)										
1995SS. . . .	1/4	1	1	1	1	1	0	0	0	1
1995SS. . . .	9/5-10/12	36	12	13	1	1	0	0	0	1
1997	1/6/97-1/4/99	729	87	92	1,508	183	30	3	0	333
(1997: 1/6, 1/14, 1/28-1/30, 2/12, 2/25-2/26, 3/4-3/20, 5/13-5/29, 6/10-9/30, 11/4-11/6, 11/18-11/20; 1998: 1/13-1/22, 2/3-2/12, 3/10-3/26, 4/21-5/13; 1999: 1/4)										
1998SS[12] . . .	4/21-5/21	31	13	12	13	2	2	0	0	5
1999[13]	1/4/99-1/3/01	731	97	101	1,498	168	52	5	0	196
(1999: 1/4, 1/14, 1/26-1/28, 2/16-2/18, 3/2-3/4, 3/16-3/25, 5/11-10/6, 10/26-11/11; 2000: 1/25-2/10, 3/7-3/30, 5/2-5/4, 5/23-5/24; 2001: 1/3)										
1999SS[7] . . .	10/27-11/11	16	7	8	3	1	0	0	0	1
2000SS. . . .	5/4-5/9	8	3	3	2	2	1	0	0	1
2001	1/3/01-1/6/03	734	62	63	1,436	174	75	0	0	106
(2001: 1/3, 1/30-2/1, 2/13-2/15, 3/6-3/22, 5/1-5/10, 6/5-7/26, 10/2-10/4, 10/16-11/8; 2002: 1/22-2/7, 2/26-3/14, 4/30-5/2, 5/14-5/15; 2003: 1/6)										
2001SS[7] . . .	5/1-5/3	3	1	2	1	0	0	0	0	1
2002SS[7] . . .	1/22-7/8	168	59	52	1	2	7	0	0	1
2002SS[7] . . .	5/13-5/15	3	3	2	2	0	0	0	0	1
2003[14]	1/6/03-1/3/05	729	104	94	1,567	164	78	54	0	326
(2003: 1/6-1/7, 1/28-1/30, 2/18-2/20, 3/3-3/20, 4/29-5/8, 5/28-6/25, 9/23-10/2, 10/28-11/13; 2004: 1/20-2/5, 2/24-3/11, 4/27, 5/11-5/19; 2005: 1/3)										
2003SS. . . .	1/30-2/20	22	7	7	1	0	0	0	0	1
2005[15]	1/3/05-1/3/07	731	69	72	1,967	196	76	47	0	489
(2005: 1/3, 1/11-1/27, 2/8, 2/15-2/24, 3/8-3/16, 4/5-4/12, 5/3-5/12, 5/31-6/30, 7/5, 7/20, 9/20-9/28, 10/25-11/9, 12/6-12/15; 2006: 1/17-2/2, 2/21-3/9, 4/25-5/17, 5/30-5/31, 7/12; 2007: 1/3)										
2005SS. . . .	1/12-1/20	9	4	1	2	0	0	0	0	1
2006SS. . . .	2/14-3/7	22	7	6	2	0	0	0	0	1
2007	1/3/07-1/5/09	733	91	89	1,574	230	50	1	0	239
(2007: 1/3, 1/9, 1/30-2/1, 2/13, 2/20-3/1, 3/13-3/15, 4/17-4/26, 5/8-5/16, 5/29-11/8, 12/11; 2008: 1/15-1/31, 2/19-3/13, 5/6-5/8, 5/27-5/28; 2009: 1/5)										
2007SS. . . .	1/11-2/1	22	7	6	2	1	0	0	0	1
2007SS. . . .	10/15-10/23	9	5	3	2	0	0	0	0	0
2007SS. . . .	12/11/07, 1/15-5/14/08	156	38	39	1	1	0	0	0	0
2008SS. . . .	3/12-4/15	65	22	22	1	4	2	0	0	1
2008SS. . . .	4/17-5/15	29	11	11	1	4	2	0	0	1
2009[16]	1/5/09-1/3/11	729	59	60	1,720	221	44	6	0	406
(2009: 1/5, 1/13, 1/27-2/26, 3/24-3/26, 4/21-4/30, 5/12-5/21, 6/9-6/30, 9/15-9/24, 10/20-11/5; 2010: 1/19-1/28, 2/16-3/4, 4/13-4/22, 5/4-5/6, 5/25-5/26, 12/15-12/16; 2011: 1/3)										
2009SS. . . .	6/24-6/27	4	4	3	1	0	0	0	0	0
2009SS. . . .	12/16-3/4/10	79	23	24	2	0	0	0	0	0

WISCONSIN LEGISLATIVE SESSIONS, 1848 – 2013–Continued

Session	Opening and Adjournment Dates	Length of Session			Measures Introduced			Vetoes[1]		
		Calendar Days[2]	Meeting Days[3] (S)	(A)	Bills	Jt. Res.	Res.	Bills Vetoed	Over-ridden	Laws Enacted
2011[17]. 1/3/11-1/7/13		735	69	64	1,325	211	48	0	0	267
(2011: 1/3, 1/11, 1/25-2/10, 2/22-3/10, 4/5-4/14, 5/10-5/19, 6/7-6/28, 7/19-8/2, 9/13-9/22, 10/18/-11/3; 2012: 1/17-1/26, 2/14-2/23, 3/6-3/15, 4/24, 5/22, 7/17; 2013: 1/7)										
2011SS. . . . 1/4-9/27		267	84	80	27	1	3	0	0	12
2011SS. . . . 9/29-12/8		71	22	22	48	0	0	0	0	7
2013 . . . . . 1/7/13-1/5/15		730	55	53	1,627	214	37	1	0	373
(2013: 1/7, 1/9-1/10, 1/15, 1/17, 1/29-1/31, 2/12-2/13, 2/20, 2/26-3/7, 4/9-4/17, 5/7-5/14, 6/4-6/21, 9/17, 10/8-10/15, 11/5-11/14 2014: 1/14-1/22, 2/11-2/20, 3/11-3/20, 4/1-4/2, 4/29, 5/20 2015: 1/5)										
2013SS. . . . 10/10-11/12		34	10	10	8	0	0	0	0	4
2013SS. . . . 12/2-12/19		18	6	7	2	0	0	0	0	1
2014SS. . . . 1/23-3/20		57	17	16	4	0	0	0	0	2

Note: For 1836-1847 territorial sessions, see *1873 Blue Book,* p. 205.
[1]Partial vetoes not included. See Executive Vetoes table. [2]Number of calendar days from session opening date to final adjournment. [3]Number of days senate or assembly met, including "skeleton sessions" (those days on which the senate or assembly leadership calls the house in session *in absentia* to fulfill a procedural requirement). [4]SS denotes special session. Regular and special sessions may run concurrently with meetings held on the same day. Each is counted as a separate meeting day. [5]Although 1965 Legislature adjourned to 1/11/67, terms automatically expired on 1/2/67. [6]Senate adjourned the special session 11/15/69; assembly, 1/17/70. [7]Special session met concurrently with regular session. [8]1979 Legislature met concurrently in extraordinary and special session, 1/22/80 – 1/25/80. [9]Legislature met concurrently in special session and extended floorperiod. [10]Extraordinary sessions held in February, September, and November 1987, and April, May, and June 1988. May 1988 extraordinary session ran concurrently with May 1988 veto review period and also with June 1988 extraordinary session. [11]Extraordinary session held, 6/15/94 – 6/23/94. [12]Extraordinary session held in April 1998. [13]Extraordinary session held in April and May 2000. [14]Extraordinary sessions held in February, July, and August 2003; December 2003-February 2004; March 2004; May 2004; and July 2004. [15]Extraordinary sessions were held in July 2005 and April 2006. [16]Extraordinary sessions held in February, May, June, and December 2009 and in December 2010. [17]Extraordinary sessions were held in June and July 2011.
Sources: *Bulletin of the Proceedings of the Wisconsin Legislature,* various editions; and senate and assembly journals.

WISCONSIN MEMBERS, U.S. HOUSE OF REPRESENTATIVES
1848 – 2015

Name	Party	Residence	District	Term
Adams, Henry C	.Rep.	Madison	2	1903-1906
Amlie, Thomas R	.Rep., Prog.	Elkhorn	1	1931-1933; 1935-1939
Aspin, Les	.Dem.	East Troy	1	1971-1993
Atwood, David	.Rep.	Madison	2	1870-1871
Babbitt, Clinton	.Dem.	Beloit	1	1891-1893
Babcock, Joseph W	.Rep.	Necedah	3	1893-1907
Baldus, Alvin	.Dem.	Menomonie	3	1975-1981
Baldwin, Tammy	.Dem.	Madison	2	1999-2013
Barber, J. Allen	.Rep.	Lancaster	3	1871-1875
Barca, Peter W	.Dem.	Kenosha	1	1993-1995
Barnes, Lyman E	.Dem.	Appleton	8	1893-1895
Barney, Samuel S	.Rep.	West Bend	5	1895-1903
Barrett, Thomas M	.Dem.	Milwaukee	5	1993-2003
Barwig, Charles	.Dem.	Mayville	2	1889-1895
Beck, Joseph D	.Rep.	Viroqua	7	1921-1929
Berger, Victor L	.Soc.	Milwaukee	5	1911-1913; 1919; 1923-1929
Biemiller, Andrew J	.Dem.	Milwaukee	5	1945-1947; 1949-1951
Billinghurst, Charles	.Rep.	Juneau	3	1855-1859
Blanchard, George W	.Rep.	Edgerton	1	1933-1935
Boileau, Gerald J	.Rep., Prog.	Wausau	8,7	1931-1939
Bolles, Stephen	.Rep.	Janesville	1	1939-1941
Bouck, Gabriel	.Dem.	Oshkosh	6	1877-1881
Bragg, Edward S	.Dem.	Fond du Lac	5,2	1877-1883; 1885-1887
Brickner, George H	.Dem.	Sheboygan Falls	5	1889-1895
Brophy, John C	.Rep.	Milwaukee	4	1947-1949
Brown, James S	.Dem.	Milwaukee	1	1863-1865
Brown, Webster E	.Rep.	Rhinelander	9,10	1901-1907
Browne, Edward E	.Rep.	Waupaca	8	1913-1931
Burchard, Samuel D	.Dem.	Beaver Dam	5	1875-1877
Burke, Michael E	.Dem.	Beaver Dam	6,2	1911-1917
Bushnell, Allen R	.Dem.	Madison	3	1891-1893
Byrnes, John W	.Rep.	Green Bay	8	1945-1973
Cannon, Raymond J	.Dem.	Milwaukee	4	1933-1939
Cary, William J	.Rep.	Milwaukee	4	1907-1919
Caswell, Lucien B	.Rep.	Fort Atkinson	2,1	1875-1883; 1885-1891
Cate, George W	.Reform	Stevens Point	8	1875-1877
Clark, Charles B	.Rep.	Neenah	6	1887-1891
Classon, David G	.Rep.	Oconto	9	1917-1923
Cobb, Amasa	.Rep.	Mineral Point	3	1863-1871
Coburn, Frank P	.Dem.	West Salem	7	1891-1893
Cole, Orasmus	.Whig	Potosi	2	1849-1851
Cook, Samuel A	.Rep.	Neenah	6	1895-1897
Cooper, Henry Allen	.Rep.	Racine	1	1893-1919; 1921-1931
Cornell, Robert J	.Dem.	De Pere	8	1975-1979
Dahle, Herman B	.Rep.	Mount Horeb	2	1899-1903
Darling, Mason C	.Dem.	Fond du Lac	2	1848-1849
Davidson, James H	.Rep.	Oshkosh	6,8	1897-1913; 1917-1918
Davis, Glenn R	.Rep.	Waukesha	2,9	1947-1957; 1965-1975
Deuster, Peter V	.Dem.	Milwaukee	4	1879-1885
Dilweg, La Vern R	.Dem.	Green Bay	8	1943-1945
Doty, James D	.Dem.	Neenah	3	1849-1853
Duffy, Sean P	.Rep.	Ashland	7	2011-
Durkee, Charles	.Free Soil	Kenosha	1	1849-1853
Eastman, Ben C	.Dem.	Platteville	2	1851-1855
Eldredge, Charles A	.Dem.	Fond du Lac	4,5	1863-1875
Esch, John Jacob	.Rep.	La Crosse	7	1899-1921
Flynn, Gerald T	.Dem.	Racine	1	1959-1961
Frear, James A	.Rep.	Hudson	10,9	1913-1935
Froehlich, Harold V	.Rep.	Appleton	8	1973-1975
Gehrmann, Bernard J	.Prog.	Mellen	10	1935-1943
Green, Mark A	.Rep.	Green Bay	8	1999-2007
Griffin, Michael	.Rep.	Eau Claire	7	1894-1899
Griswold, Harry W	.Rep.	West Salem	3	1939-1941
Grothman, Glenn	.Rep.	Glenbeulah	6	2015-
Guenther, Richard W	.Rep.	Oshkosh	6,2	1881-1889
Gunderson, Steven	.Rep.	Osseo	3	1981-1997
Hanchett, Luther	.Rep.	Plover	2	1861-1862
Haugen, Nils P	.Rep.	Black River Falls	8,10	1887-1895
Hawkes, Charles, Jr	.Rep.	Horicon	2	1939-1941
Hazelton, George C	.Rep.	Boscobel	3	1877-1883
Hazelton, Gerry W	.Rep.	Columbus	2	1871-1875
Henney, Charles W	.Dem.	Portage	2	1933-1935
Henry, Robert K	.Rep.	Jefferson	2	1945-1947
Hopkins, Benjamin F	.Rep.	Madison	2	1867-1870

WISCONSIN MEMBERS, U.S. HOUSE OF REPRESENTATIVES
1848 – 2015–Continued

Name	Party	Residence	District	Term
Hudd, Thomas R	.Dem.	Green Bay	5	1886-1889
Hughes, James	.Dem.	De Pere	8	1933-1935
Hull, Merlin	.Prog.	Black River Falls	7,9	1929-1931; 1935-1953
Humphrey, Herman L	.Rep.	Hudson	7	1877-1883
Jenkins, John J	.Rep.	Chippewa Falls	10,11	1895-1909
Johns, Joshua L	.Rep.	Appleton	8	1939-1943
Johnson, Jay	.Dem.	New Franken	8	1997-1999
Johnson, Lester R	.Dem.	Black River Falls	9	1953-1965
Jones, Burr W	.Dem.	Madison	3	1883-1885
Kading, Charles A	.Rep.	Watertown	2	1927-1933
Kagen, Steve	.Dem.	Appleton	8	2007-2011
Kasten, Robert W., Jr	.Rep.	Waukesha	9	1975-1979
Kastenmeier, Robert W	.Dem.	Sun Prairie	2	1959-1991
Keefe, Frank B	.Rep.	Oshkosh	6	1939-1951
Kersten, Charles J	.Rep.	Whitefish Bay	5	1947-1949; 1951-1955
Kimball, Alanson M	.Rep.	Waushara	6	1875-1877
Kind, Ron	.Dem.	La Crosse	3	1997-
Kleczka, Gerald D	.Dem.	Milwaukee	4	1984-2005
Kleczka, John C	.Rep.	Milwaukee	4	1919-1923
Klug, Scott L	.Rep.	Madison	2	1991-1999
Konop, Thomas F	.Dem.	Kewaunee	9	1911-1917
Kopp, Arthur W	.Rep.	Platteville	3	1909-1913
Kustermann, Gustav	.Rep.	Green Bay	9	1907-1911
La Follette, Robert M., Sr	.Rep.	Madison	3	1885-1891
Laird, Melvin R	.Rep.	Marshfield	7	1953-1969
Lampert, Florian	.Rep.	Oshkosh	6	1918-1930
Larrabee, Charles H	.Dem.	Horicon	3	1859-1861
Lenroot, Irvine L	.Rep.	Superior	11	1909-1918
Lynch, Thomas	.Dem.	Antigo	9	1891-1895
Lynde, William Pitt	.Dem.	Milwaukee	1,4	1848-1849; 1875-1879
Macy, John B	.Dem.	Fond du Lac	3	1853-1855
Magoon, Henry S	.Rep.	Darlington	3	1875-1877
McCord, Myron H	.Rep.	Merrill	9	1889-1891
McDill, Alexander S	.Rep.	Plover	8	1873-1875
McIndoe, Walter D	.Rep.	Wausau	6	1863-1867
McMurray, Howard J	.Dem.	Milwaukee	5	1943-1945
Miller, Lucas M	.Dem.	Oshkosh	6	1891-1893
Minor, Edward S	.Rep.	Sturgeon Bay	8,9	1895-1907
Mitchell, Alexander	.Dem.	Milwaukee	1,4	1871-1875
Mitchell, John L	.Dem.	Milwaukee	4	1891-1893
Monahan, James G	.Rep.	Darlington	3	1919-1921
Moody, James P	.Dem.	Milwaukee	5	1983-1993
Moore, Gwen	.Dem.	Milwaukee	4	2005-
Morse, Elmer A	.Rep.	Antigo	10	1907-1913
Murphy, James W	.Dem.	Platteville	3	1907-1909
Murray, Reid F	.Rep.	Ogdensburg	7	1939-1953
Nelson, Adolphus P	.Rep.	Grantsburg	11	1918-1923
Nelson, John Mandt	.Rep.	Madison	2,3	1906-1919; 1921-1933
Neumann, Mark W	.Rep.	Janesville	1	1995-1999
Obey, David R	.Dem.	Wausau	7	1969-2011
O'Konski, Alvin E	.Rep.	Mercer	10	1943-1973
O'Malley, Thomas D. P	.Dem.	Milwaukee	5	1933-1939
Otjen, Theobald	.Rep.	Milwaukee	4	1895-1907
Paine, Halbert E	.Rep.	Milwaukee	1	1865-1871
Peavey, Hubert H	.Rep.	Washburn	11,10	1923-1935
Petri, Thomas E	.Rep.	Fond du Lac	6	1979-2015
Pocan, Mark	.Dem.	Madison	2	2013-
Potter, John F	.Rep.	East Troy	1	1857-1863
Pound, Thaddeus C	.Rep.	Chippewa Falls	8	1877-1883
Price, Hugh H	.Rep.	Black River Falls	8	1887
Price, William T	.Rep.	Black River Falls	8	1883-1886
Race, John A	.Dem.	Fond du Lac	6	1965-1967
Randall, Clifford E	.Rep.	Kenosha	1	1919-1921
Rankin, Joseph	.Dem.	Manitowoc	5	1883-1886
Reilly, Michael K	.Dem.	Fond du Lac	6	1913-1917; 1930-1939
Reuss, Henry S	.Dem.	Milwaukee	5	1955-1983
Ribble, Reid J	.Rep.	Appleton	8	2011-
Roth, Toby	.Rep.	Appleton	8	1979-1997
Rusk, Jeremiah M	.Rep.	Viroqua	6,7	1871-1877
Ryan, Paul	.Rep.	Janesville	1	1999-
Sauerhering, Edward	.Rep.	Mayville	2	1895-1899
Sauthoff, Harry	.Prog.	Madison	2	1935-1939; 1941-1945
Sawyer, Philetus	.Rep.	Oshkosh	5,6	1865-1875
Schadeberg, Henry C	.Rep.	Burlington	1	1961-1965; 1967-1971
Schafer, John C	.Rep.	Milwaukee	4	1923-1933; 1939-1941

WISCONSIN MEMBERS, U.S. HOUSE OF REPRESENTATIVES
1848 – 2015–Continued

Name	Party	Residence	District	Term
Schneider, George J . . . . .Rep., Prog.		Appleton	9,8	1923-1933; 1935-1939
Sensenbrenner, F. James, Jr . . . .Rep.		Menomonee Falls	9,5	1979-
Shaw, George B . . . . .Rep.		Eau Claire	7	1893-1894
Sloan, A. Scott . . . . .Rep.		Beaver Dam	3	1861-1863
Sloan, Ithamar C . . . . .Rep.		Janesville	2	1863-1867
Smith, Henry. . . . . .Union Labor		Milwaukee	4	1887-1889
Smith, Lawrence H . . . . .Rep.		Racine	1	1941-1959
Somers, Peter J . . . . .Dem.		Milwaukee	4	1893-1895
Stafford, William H . . . . .Rep.		Milwaukee	5	1903-1911; 1913-1919; 1921-1923; 1929-1933
Stalbaum, Lynn E . . . . .Dem.		Racine	1	1965-1967
Steiger, William A . . . . .Rep.		Oshkosh	6	1967-1978
Stephenson, Isaac . . . . .Rep.		Marinette	9	1883-1889
Stevenson, William H . . . . . .Rep.		La Crosse	3	1941-1949
Stewart, Alexander. . . . . . . .Rep.		Wausau	9	1895-1901
Sumner, Daniel H . . . . .Dem.		Waukesha	2	1883-1885
Tewes, Donald E. . . . . .Rep.		Waukesha	2	1957-1959
Thill, Lewis D . . . . .Rep.		Milwaukee	5	1939-1943
Thomas, Ormsby B . . . . . . .Rep.		Prairie du Chien	7	1885-1891
Thomson, Vernon W . . . . . . .Rep.		Richland Center	3	1961-1975
Van Pelt, William K . . . . . . .Rep.		Fond du Lac	6	1951-1963
Van Schaick, Isaac W . . . . . .Rep.		Milwaukee	4	1885-1887; 1889-1891
Voigt, Edward . . . . .Rep.		Sheboygan	2	1917-1927
Washburn, Cadwallader C . . . .Rep.		Mineral Point,	2	1855-1861;
		La Crosse	6	1867-1871
Wasielewski, Thaddeus F . . . .Dem.		Milwaukee	4	1941-1947
Weisse, Charles H . . . . .Dem.		Sheboygan Falls	6	1903-1911
Wells, Daniel, Jr . . . . .Dem.		Milwaukee	1	1853-1857
Wells, Owen A . . . . .Dem.		Fond du Lac	6	1893-1895
Wheeler, Ezra . . . . .Dem.		Berlin	5	1863-1865
Williams, Charles G . . . . . . .Rep.		Janesville	1	1873-1883
Winans, John. . . . . .Dem.		Janesville	1	1883-1885
Withrow, Gardner R . . . . . . .Rep., Prog.		La Crosse	7,3	1931-1939; 1949-1961
Woodward, Gilbert M . . . . . .Dem.		La Crosse	7	1883-1885
Zablocki, Clement J . . . . . . .Dem.		Milwaukee	4	1949-1983

Sources: Wisconsin Legislative Reference Bureau, *Wisconsin Blue Book*, various editions; Congressional Quarterly, *Guide to U.S. Elections,* 1985; and official election records.

WISCONSIN MEMBERS, U.S. HOUSE OF REPRESENTATIVES
By District, 1943 – 2015

District	Name	Service	Party	Residence	Alphabetical Listing	
1st	Lawrence H. Smith	1941-59	Rep.	Racine	Aspin	1st
	Gerald T. Flynn	1959-61	Dem.	Racine	Baldus	3rd
	Henry C. Schadeberg	1961-65; 1967-71	Rep.	Burlington	Baldwin	2nd
	Lynn E. Stalbaum	1965-67	Dem.	Racine	Barca	1st
	Les Aspin[1]	1971-93	Dem.	East Troy	Barrett	5th
	Peter W. Barca[1]	1993-95	Dem.	Kenosha	Biemiller	5th
	Mark W. Neumann	1995-99	Rep.	Janesville	Brophy	4th
	Paul Ryan	1999-	Rep.	Janesville	Byrnes	8th
					Cornell	8th
2nd	Harry Sauthoff	1941-45	Prog.	Madison	Davis	2nd, 9th
	Robert K. Henry	1945-47	Rep.	Jefferson	Dilweg	8th
	Glenn R. Davis	1947-57	Rep.	Waukesha	Duffy	7th
	Donald E. Tewes	1957-59	Rep.	Waukesha	Flynn	1st
	Robert W. Kastenmeier	1959-91	Dem.	Sun Prairie	Froehlich	8th
	Scott L. Klug	1991-99	Rep.	Madison	Green	8th
	Tammy Baldwin	1999-2013	Dem.	Madison	Grothman	6th
	Mark Pocan	2013-	Dem.	Madison	Gunderson	3rd
					Henry	2nd
3rd	William H. Stevenson	1941-49	Rep.	La Crosse	Hull	9th
	Gardner R. Withrow	1949-61	Rep.	La Crosse	Johnson, J.	8th
	Vernon W. Thomson	1961-75	Rep.	Richland Center	Johnson, L.	9th
	Alvin Baldus	1975-81	Dem.	Menomonie	Kagen	8th
	Steven Gunderson	1981-97	Rep.	Osseo	Kasten	9th
	Ron Kind	1997-	Dem.	La Crosse	Kastenmeier	2nd
					Keefe	6th
4th	Thaddeus F. Wasielewski	1941-47	Dem.	Milwaukee	Kersten	5th
	John C. Brophy	1947-49	Rep.	Milwaukee	Kind	3rd
	Clement J. Zablocki[2]	1949-83	Dem.	Milwaukee	Kleczka	4th
	Gerald D. Kleczka[2]	1984-2005	Dem.	Milwaukee	Klug	2nd
	Gwen Moore	2005-	Dem.	Milwaukee	Laird	7th
					McMurray	5th
5th[3]	Howard J. McMurray	1943-45	Dem.	Milwaukee	Moody	5th
	Andrew J. Biemiller	1945-47; 1949-51	Dem.	Milwaukee	Moore	4th
	Charles J. Kersten	1947-49; 1951-55	Rep.	Whitefish Bay	Murray	7th
	Henry S. Reuss	1955-83	Dem.	Milwaukee	Neumann	1st
	James P. Moody	1983-93	Dem.	Milwaukee	Obey	7th
	Thomas M. Barrett	1993-2003	Dem.	Milwaukee	O'Konski	10th
	F. James Sensenbrenner, Jr.	2003-	Rep.	Menomonee Falls	Petri	6th
					Pocan	2nd
6th	Frank B. Keefe	1939-51	Rep.	Oshkosh	Race	6th
	William K. Van Pelt	1951-65	Rep.	Fond du Lac	Reuss	5th
	John A. Race	1965-67	Dem.	Fond du Lac	Ribble	8th
	William A. Steiger[4]	1967-78	Rep.	Oshkosh	Roth	8th
	Thomas E. Petri[4]	1979-2015	Rep.	Fond du Lac	Ryan	1st
	Glenn Grothman	2015-	Rep.	Glenbeulah	Sauthoff	2nd
					Schadeberg	1st
7th	Reid F. Murray	1939-53	Rep.	Ogdensburg	Sensenbrenner	9th, 5th
	Melvin R. Laird[5]	1953-69	Rep.	Marshfield	Smith	1st
	David R. Obey[5]	1969-2011	Dem.	Wausau	Stalbaum	1st
	Sean P. Duffy	2011-	Rep.	Ashland	Steiger	6th
					Stevenson	3rd
8th	La Vern R. Dilweg	1943-45	Dem.	Green Bay	Tewes	2nd
	John R. Byrnes	1945-73	Rep.	Green Bay	Thomson	3rd
	Harold V. Froehlich	1973-75	Rep.	Appleton	Van Pelt	6th
	Robert J. Cornell	1975-79	Dem.	De Pere	Wasielewski	4th
	Toby Roth	1979-97	Rep.	Appleton	Withrow	3rd
	Jay Johnson	1997-99	Dem.	New Franken	Zablocki	4th
	Mark A. Green	1999-2007	Rep.	Green Bay		
	Steve Kagen	2007-2011	Dem.	Appleton		
	Reid J. Ribble	2011-	Rep.	Appleton		
9th[3,6]	Merlin Hull	1935-53	Prog.	Black River Falls		
	Lester R. Johnson	1953-65	Dem.	Black River Falls		
	Glenn R. Davis	1965-75	Rep.	Waukesha		
	Robert W. Kasten	1975-79	Rep.	Thiensville		
	F. James Sensenbrenner, Jr.	1979-2003	Rep.	Menomonee Falls		
10th[7]	Alvin E. O'Konski	1943-73	Rep.	Rhinelander		

[1]Aspin resigned 1/20/1993, to become U.S. Secretary of Defense. Barca was elected in a special election, 5/4/1993.
[2]Zablocki died 12/3/1983. Kleczka was elected in a special election, 4/3/1984.
[3]In the congressional reapportionment following the 2000 Census, Wisconsin's delegation was reduced from 9 to 8 members. The previous 4th, 5th, and 9th were reconfigured into the new 4th and 5th.
[4]Steiger died 12/4/1978, following his November 1978 election. Petri was elected in a special election, 4/3/1979.
[5]Laird resigned 1/21/1969, to become U.S. Secretary of Defense. Obey was elected in a special election, 4/1/1969.
[6]In the congressional redistricting based on the results of the 1960 Census of Population, the previous 9th District in western Wisconsin ceased to exist and a new 9th District was created in the Waukesha-Milwaukee metropolitan area.
[7]In the congressional reapportionment based on the results of the 1970 Census of Population, Wisconsin's delegation was reduced from 10 members to 9 members.
Sources: *1944 Wisconsin Blue Book* and Wisconsin Legislative Reference Bureau data.

U.S. SENATORS FROM WISCONSIN, 1848 – 2015

Class 1		Class 3	
Name	Service	Name	Service
Henry Dodge (D)	1848-1857	Isaac P. Walker (D).	1848-1855
James R. Doolittle (R)	1857-1869	Charles Durkee (UR)	1855-1861
Matthew H. Carpenter (R).	1869-1875	Timothy O. Howe (UR)	1861-1879
Angus Cameron (R)[1].	1875-1881	Matthew H. Carpenter (R).	1879-1881
Philetus Sawyer (R)	1881-1893	Angus Cameron (R)[1].	1881-1885
John Lendrum Mitchell (D)	1893-1899	John C. Spooner (R).	1885-1891
Joseph Very Quarles (R).	1899-1905	William F. Vilas (D)	1891-1897
Robert M. La Follette, Sr. (R)[2].	1906-1925	John C. Spooner (R).	1897-1907
Robert M. La Follette, Jr. (R)[3]	1925-1935	Isaac Stephenson (R)[5]	1907-1915
Robert M. La Follette, Jr. (P)	1935-1947	Paul O. Husting (D)	1915-1917
Joseph R. McCarthy (R).	1947-1957	Irvine L. Lenroot (R)[6]	1918-1927
William Proxmire (D)[4].	1957-1989	John J. Blaine (R)	1927-1933
Herbert H. Kohl (D)	1989-2013	F. Ryan Duffy (D)	1933-1939
Tammy Baldwin (D).	2013-	Alexander Wiley (R).	1939-1963
		Gaylord A. Nelson (D).	1963-1981
		Robert W. Kasten, Jr. (R)	1981-1993
		Russell D. Feingold (D)	1993-2011
		Ron Johnson (R)	2011-

Note: Each state has two U.S. Senators, and each serves a 6-year term. They were elected by their respective state legislatures until passage of the 17th Amendment to the U.S. Constitution on April 8, 1913, which provided for popular election. Article I, Section 3, Clause 2, of the U.S. Constitution divides senators into three classes so that one-third of the senate is elected every two years. Wisconsin's seats were assigned to Class 1 and Class 3 at statehood.

Key: Democrat (D); Progressive (P); Republican (R); Union Republican (UR)

[1]Not a candidate for reelection to Class 1 seat, but elected 3/10/1881 to fill vacancy caused by death of Class 3 Senator Carpenter on 2/24/1881.

[2]Elected 1/25/1905 but continued to serve as governor until 1/1/1906.

[3]Elected 9/29/1925 to fill vacancy caused by death of Robert La Follette, Sr., on 6/18/1925.

[4]Elected 8/27/1957 to fill vacancy caused by death of McCarthy on 5/2/1957.

[5]Elected 5/17/1907 to fill vacancy caused by resignation of Spooner on 4/30/1907.

[6]Elected 5/2/1918 to fill vacancy caused by death of Husting on 10/21/1917.

Source: Wisconsin Legislative Reference Bureau records.

HIGHLIGHTS OF LOCAL AND STATE GOVERNMENT IN WISCONSIN

Employment and Earnings — In December 2014, Wisconsin ranked 23rd among the states in full-time equivalent (FTE) state and local government employees with 274,394. The State of Wisconsin employed 72,347 workers, while local government employed 202,047.

In December 2014, Wisconsin ranked 18th in average total payroll for state and local government employees with $1,196,817,811. California ranked first with a payroll of $10,024,497,989 and South Dakota ranked 50th with $158,302,785.

Units of Local Government — As of October 2014, Wisconsin had 1,924 general units of local government – 72 counties, 190 cities, 407 villages, and 1,255 towns.

In 2014, counties varied in official population estimates from Milwaukee at 949,741 to Menominee with 4,236. These two counties were also highest and lowest in 2013 full value property assessments at $57 billion and $288 million, respectively. As determined by the U.S. Census Bureau in 2010, Marathon County is the largest in land area with 1,545 square miles and Pepin County the smallest with 232 square miles.

Based on the 2010 Census, Wisconsin's city residents totaled 3,150,339 in 2010, a 5.2% increase from the 2000 Census; village population was 869,587, a 26.6% increase; and town population was 1,667,060, a 0.1% decrease. As of April 1, 2010, a total of 92 Wisconsin municipalities had populations of 10,000 or more. The City of Milwaukee ranked first at 594,833, and the City of Elkhorn, with 10,084 residents, was smallest in the group.

Administration — Wisconsin cities may adopt a mayor, manager, or commission form of government. Of 190 cities, 10 have a city manager and 180 have a mayor. Currently, no city uses the commission form of government. Villages may use a president or manager form of government. Of 407 villages, only 9 have an appointed manager. Currently, 76 cities and 77 villages employ an administrator in a full-time or combined position.

Each county board is headed by a chairperson chosen by the board. In addition, 11 counties have an elected county executive, 25 have an appointed county administrator, 32 have an appointed administrative coordinator, 3 have a corporation counsel, and one has a county manager.

The following tables present selected data. Consult footnoted sources for more detailed information about local and state government.

WISCONSIN STATE GOVERNMENT EMPLOYEES
By Status and Funding, 2004 – 2014

Employee Status[1]	2004	2009	2014	Type of Funding for Authorized Positions[3]	2004	2009	2014
Classified	40,633	40,075	39,723	State appropriations . . .	35,535	35,078	35,949
Unclassified	22,592	21,880	22,703	User fees	17,785	19,499	18,272
Limited term	6,729	6,287	5,949	Federal appropriations	9,327	10,098	10,435
Project	585	405	835	Segregated funds	5,427	5,206	5,238
Seasonal	90	63	35	TOTAL[4]	68,074	69,880	69,895
Other[2]	6,629	6,793	7,133				
TOTAL[4]	77,258	75,503	76,377				

[1]Headcount of employees working on a full- or part-time basis as of June 30.

[2]Includes UW System graduate assistants.

[3]Full-time equivalent positions authorized by legislature or under procedures authorized by the legislature as of June 30.

[4]Detail may not add to total due to rounding.

Source: Wisconsin Department of Administration, Division of Executive Budget and Finance, *State Employment Report*, June 2014, and previous issues.

WISCONSIN STATE CLASSIFIED SERVICE PROFILE
2002 – 2012

	2002		2007		2012	
		Percent of		Percent of		Percent of
Category	Number	Work Force	Number	Work Force	Number	Work Force
Permanent Classified Employees . . .	41,169	100.0%	39,531	100.0%	38,151	100.0%
Persons with Disabilities[1]	3,065	7.4	2,366	6.0	1,793[2]	4.7
Women.	21,139	51.3	20,149	51.0	19,596	51.4
Racial/ethnic minorities	3,479	8.5	3,780	9.6	4,385	11.6
Black.	1,831	4.4	1,821	4.6	2,154	5.7
Hispanic	724	1.8	950	2.4	1,069	2.8
Asian.	601	1.5	724	1.8	885	2.3
American Indian	323	0.8	285	0.7	234	0.6

[1]Total persons with disabilities includes persons with severe disabilities.
[2]Estimated employees with disabilities.
Source: Wisconsin State Office of Employment Relations, *Workforce Planning & Affirmative Action Report: Fiscal Year 2012,* and previous issues [December 16, 2014].

WISCONSIN STATE AND LOCAL GOVERNMENT EMPLOYMENT AND PAYROLLS
Employees and Payrolls by Function, March 2013

	Number of Employees			
			Full-time Equivalent	Total Payroll for FTE
	Full-time	Part-time	(FTE)*	(in thousands)
Education	125,982	101,007	164,278	$594,224
Elementary and secondary.	90,253	45,012	112,003	(397,060)
Higher education institutions	33,283	52,560	48,312	(186,869)
Libraries (local)	1,563	3,115	2,877	(6,068)
Other.	883	320	1,086	(4,227)
Government administration (including courts)	14,543	12,451	17,008	67,014
Police protection.	14,402	2,834	15,252	76,857
Public welfare and social insurance administration . .	12,123	3,309	14,068	48,472
Health and hospitals	8,895	3,389	10,499	38,390
Streets and highways.	9,387	1,602	10,332	45,342
Corrections.	12,822	932	13,399	54,509
Fire protection	4,333	5,021	5,196	24,560
Natural resources	2,449	1,049	2,803	10,614
Parks and recreation	2,257	3,055	3,060	9,313
Sewerage (local)	1,928	845	2,049	9,431
Transit	1,715	172	1,819	7,038
Utilities (electric and water supply)	2,370	309	2,460	11,497
Housing and community development	955	402	1,084	3,943
Solid waste management (local).	1,496	884	1,692	6,531
Other.	8,071	4,958	9,011	34,916
TOTAL.	223,728	142,219	274,010	$1,042,651

*Full-time Equivalent (FTE) is a derived statistic that provides an estimate of a government's total full-time employment by converting part-time employees to a full-time amount.
Source: U.S. Census Bureau, Government Employment and Payroll, *2013 State and Local Government*, at: http://www.census.gov/govs/apes/ [January 6, 2015].

Employment and Payrolls, 1990 – 2013

	Employees (full-time equivalents)			Monthly Payroll (in thousands)*		
Year	State	Local	Total	State	Local	Total
1990	66,541	183,318	249,859	$152,660	$409,907	$562,567
1997	64,709	201,633	266,342	204,267	569,193	773,460
1998	64,703	211,790	276,493	207,996	625,686	833,681
1999	63,185	207,587	270,772	214,684	628,043	842,727
2000	63,697	219,793	283,490	230,570	662,358	892,928
2001	69,428	218,824	288,252	257,605	676,935	934,540
2002	70,962	218,982	288,543	261,095	719,434	977,410
2003	71,040	217,004	288,044	268,249	739,031	1,007,280
2004	69,834	217,422	287,256	275,465	749,415	1,024,880
2005	70,189	223,523	293,712	275,824	809,593	1,085,417
2006	68,143	219,930	288,073	283,681	813,141	1,096,822
2007	68,714	212,931	281,645	295,616	788,590	1,084,207
2008	69,019	214,332	283,351	308,878	813,054	1,121,932
2009	70,457	222,214	292,671	322,316	846,922	1,169,238
2010	72,428	213,888	286,316	326,643	862,129	1,188,772
2011	70,891	212,677	283,568	328,658	878,908	1,207,566
2012	70,851	212,013	282,864	323,080	876,466	1,199,547
2013	72,347	202,047	274,394	333,207	863,610	1,196,818

*Prior to 1997, annual data reflected October payrolls. Beginning with the 1997 Annual Survey of Government Employment and Payroll, data reflects March payrolls.
Source: U.S. Census Bureau, Government Employment and Payroll, March 2013 and previous years, at: http://www.census.gov/govs/apes/ [January 7, 2015].

STATE AND LOCAL GOVERNMENT EMPLOYEES
Number and Earnings by State
March 2013 Payroll

| State | Full-time Equivalent Employees | | | Earnings | | |
| | Number | | | March Payroll | | |
	Total	State	Local	Total	State	Local
Alabama	281,979	89,275	192,704	$1,013,678,215	$372,877,100	$640,801,115
Alaska	55,423	27,287	28,136	286,127,245	147,268,896	138,858,349
Arizona.	283,499	70,767	212,732	1,155,886,615	303,153,071	852,733,544
Arkansas	168,776	63,927	104,849	576,985,058	240,400,803	336,584,255
California	1,710,692	397,348	1,313,344	10,024,497,989	2,508,684,591	7,515,813,398
Colorado	276,275	77,621	198,654	1,214,639,652	375,090,681	839,548,971
Connecticut	185,888	62,775	123,113	1,013,650,034	376,188,870	637,461,164
Delaware	50,240	26,691	23,549	220,211,383	114,446,490	105,764,893
District of Columbia . . .	45,359	—	45,359	280,477,763	—	280,477,763
Florida	862,353	179,484	682,869	3,359,105,430	719,696,502	2,639,408,928
Georgia.	512,186	128,795	383,391	1,789,738,804	491,516,760	1,298,222,044
Hawaii	72,413	56,767	15,646	315,349,243	239,511,581	75,837,662
Idaho	79,957	22,710	57,247	283,212,953	96,857,513	186,355,440
ILLINOIS	645,435	127,253	518,182	3,197,319,349	665,950,749	2,531,368,600
Indiana	319,551	85,193	234,358	1,193,500,880	351,672,218	841,828,662
IOWA	170,714	48,553	122,161	744,586,498	266,073,425	478,513,073
Kansas	201,233	49,639	151,594	733,435,940	215,113,009	518,322,931
Kentucky	236,197	82,494	153,703	830,881,536	320,139,037	510,742,499
Louisiana.	256,931	77,809	179,122	934,947,258	328,789,311	606,157,947
Maine	72,785	21,151	51,634	269,097,209	86,061,489	183,035,720
Maryland	298,311	85,748	212,563	1,475,756,041	414,505,762	1,061,250,279
Massachusetts	323,135	98,761	224,374	1,628,508,333	526,717,280	1,101,791,053
MICHIGAN	433,882	143,097	290,785	2,000,585,056	736,380,513	1,264,204,543
MINNESOTA	276,267	80,681	195,586	1,281,759,669	415,663,318	866,096,351
Mississippi	192,915	58,161	134,754	624,697,051	211,429,939	413,267,112
Missouri	317,327	86,316	231,011	1,111,123,629	302,628,066	808,495,563
Montana	57,054	20,799	36,255	215,281,936	83,873,295	131,408,641
Nebraska	119,564	31,975	87,589	470,928,712	122,408,492	348,520,220
Nevada	102,557	27,225	75,332	522,938,435	128,100,534	394,837,901
New Hampshire	68,905	18,672	50,233	280,564,650	84,489,410	196,075,240
New Jersey	472,764	143,739	329,025	2,637,502,550	846,956,652	1,790,545,898
New Mexico	124,179	45,250	78,929	470,238,157	197,572,434	272,665,723
New York	1,172,034	239,472	932,562	6,460,072,325	1,402,155,998	5,057,916,327
North Carolina	549,488	146,387	403,101	2,087,013,805	623,005,511	1,464,008,294
North Dakota.	45,222	19,239	25,983	172,840,386	78,524,732	94,315,654
Ohio	580,437	136,994	443,443	2,431,623,102	650,014,245	1,781,608,857
Oklahoma	208,438	66,367	142,071	714,098,030	254,728,885	459,369,145
Oregon	189,737	66,219	123,518	867,075,495	312,697,948	554,377,547
Pennsylvania	568,261	158,890	409,371	2,564,517,845	769,263,233	1,795,254,612
Rhode Island	48,172	18,870	29,302	253,415,818	103,361,354	150,054,464
South Carolina	257,548	79,088	178,460	934,877,670	303,577,426	631,300,244
South Dakota.	46,323	14,442	31,881	158,302,785	58,273,466	100,029,319
Tennessee	327,858	80,704	247,154	1,173,673,094	332,624,894	841,048,200
Texas	1,422,565	316,638	1,105,927	5,497,482,623	1,413,938,187	4,083,544,436
Utah	141,798	53,870	87,928	553,473,239	237,560,334	315,912,905
Vermont	39,617	14,313	25,304	162,679,587	70,308,602	92,370,985
Virginia.	439,592	125,234	314,358	1,805,496,718	551,316,837	1,254,179,881
Washington.	320,857	106,223	214,634	1,685,261,933	510,577,399	1,174,684,534
West Virginia.	104,612	41,101	63,511	353,659,907	149,730,393	203,929,514
WISCONSIN	274,394	72,347	202,047	1,196,817,811	333,207,485	863,610,326
Wyoming.	50,429	13,340	37,089	207,783,053	56,550,644	151,232,409
UNITED STATES . . .	16,062,128	4,305,701	11,756,427	$71,437,378,499	$20,501,635,364	$50,935,743,135

Source: U.S. Department of Commerce, U.S. Census Bureau, 2013 Public Employment and Payroll data, at: http://www.census. gov/govs/apes/ [December 22, 2014].

LOCAL UNITS OF GOVERNMENT BY STATE AND TYPE – 2012

State	Total Units	Counties[1]	Municipalities[2]	Towns or Townships[3]	Special Districts	School Districts[4]
Alabama	1,208	67	461	—	548	132
Alaska	177	14	148	—	15	—
Arizona.	659	15	91	—	309	244
Arkansas	1,543	75	502	—	727	239
California	4,350	57	482	—	2,786	1,025
Colorado	2,818	62	271	—	2,305	180
Connecticut	644	—	30	149	448	17
Delaware	338	3	57	—	259	19
District of Columbia	2	—	1	—	1	—
Florida	1,554	66	410	—	983	95
Georgia.	1,365	153	535	—	497	180
Hawaii	21	3	1	—	17	—
Idaho	1,161	44	200	—	799	118
ILLINOIS	6,968	102	1,298	1,431	3,232	905
Indiana	2,694	91	569	1,006	737	291
IOWA	1,939	99	947	—	527	366
Kansas	3,806	103	626	1,268	1,503	306
Kentucky.	1,314	118	418	—	604	174
Louisiana.	530	60	304	—	97	69
Maine	841	16	22	466	238	99
Maryland.	347	23	157	—	167	—
Massachusetts	852	5	53	298	412	84
MICHIGAN	2,877	83	533	1,240	445	576
MINNESOTA	3,633	87	854	1,785	569	338
Mississippi.	991	82	297	—	448	164
Missouri	3,752	114	955	312	1,837	534
Montana	1,240	54	129	—	736	321
Nebraska	2,581	93	530	419	1,267	272
Nevada.	190	16	19	—	138	17
New Hampshire	542	10	13	221	132	166
New Jersey.	1,344	21	324	242	234	523
New Mexico	854	33	103	—	622	96
New York	3,454	57	617	929	1,172	679
North Carolina	964	100	553	—	311	—
North Dakota.	2,666	53	357	1,314	759	183
Ohio	3,702	88	938	1,308	700	668
Oklahoma	1,854	77	590	—	637	550
Oregon.	1,509	36	241	—	1,002	230
Pennsylvania.	4,905	66	1,015	1,546	1,764	514
Rhode Island	134	—	8	31	91	4
South Carolina	681	46	269	—	283	83
South Dakota.	1,979	66	311	907	543	152
Tennessee	920	92	345	—	469	14
Texas	4,856	254	1,214	—	2,309	1,079
Utah	613	29	245	—	298	41
Vermont	728	14	43	237	143	291
Virginia.	497	95	229	—	172	1
Washington.	1,831	39	281	—	1,216	295
West Virginia.	658	55	232	—	316	55
WISCONSIN	3,123	72	595	1,255	761	440
Wyoming.	795	23	99	—	618	55
UNITED STATES	89,004	3,031	19,522	16,364	37,203	12,884

[1]Excludes areas corresponding to counties that have no organized government.

[2]"Municipalities" include cities, villages, boroughs (except in Alaska), and towns (except in Connecticut, Maine, Massachusetts, Minnesota, New Hampshire, New York, Rhode Island, Vermont, and Wisconsin).

[3]Includes both "townships" and "town" governments in the case of those states listed in footnote 2.

[4]Excludes systems operated as part of a state, county, municipal, or town government.

Source: U.S. Census Bureau, 2012 Census of Governments, *Local Governments by Type and State: 2012*, December 2012.

BASIC DATA ON WISCONSIN COUNTIES

County (year created)[1]	County Seat	Full Value 2013 Assessment (in thousands)[2]	Population 2014 Estimate	Pct. Change[3]	2014 Rank	Land Area in Sq. Miles[4]	2014 Density per Sq. Mile[5]
Adams (1848)	Friendship	$2,340,355	20,844	−0.2%	50	645.7	32.3
Ashland (1860)	Ashland	1,191,563	16,071	−0.5	60	1,045.0	15.4
Barron (1859)	Barron	3,579,455	46,020	0.3	30	862.7	53.3
Bayfield (1845)	Washburn	2,538,482	15,059	0.3	64	1,477.9	10.2
Brown (1818)	Green Bay	18,231,223	253,156	2.1	4	529.7	477.9
Buffalo (1853)	Alma	1,005,292	13,594	0.1	67	671.6	20.2
Burnett (1856)	Meenon[6]	2,452,995	15,462	0.0	62	821.9	18.8
Calumet (1836)	Chilton	3,446,864	49,715	1.5	29	318.2	156.2
Chippewa (1845)	Chippewa Falls	4,653,304	63,038	1.0	24	1,008.4	62.5
Clark (1853)	Neillsville	1,848,725	34,697	0.0	41	1,209.8	28.7
Columbia (1846)	Portage	4,756,930	56,795	−0.1	26	765.5	74.2
Crawford (1818)	Prairie du Chien	1,064,665	16,628	−0.1	59	570.7	29.1
Dane (1836)	Madison	49,755,216	502,251	2.9	2	1,197.2	419.5
Dodge (1836)	Juneau	5,799,345	89,203	0.5	17	875.6	101.9
Door (1851)	Sturgeon Bay	6,987,135	27,976	0.7	45	482.0	58.0
Douglas (1854)	Superior	3,224,522	44,196	0.1	33	1,304.1	33.9
Dunn (1854)	Menomonie	2,613,740	43,917	0.1	34	850.1	51.7
Eau Claire (1856)	Eau Claire	6,907,863	100,477	1.8	16	638.0	157.5
Florence (1881)	Florence	591,790	4,450	0.6	71	488.2	9.1
Fond du Lac (1836)	Fond du Lac	6,773,848	102,424	0.8	15	719.6	142.3
Forest (1885)	Crandon	1,097,317	9,253	−0.6	68	1,014.1	9.1
Grant (1836)	Lancaster	2,743,804	52,603	2.7	27	1,146.9	45.9
Green (1836)	Monroe	2,608,298	36,822	−0.1	39	584.0	63.1
Green Lake (1858)	Green Lake	2,217,552	19,114	0.3	55	349.4	54.7
Iowa (1829)	Dodgeville	1,849,531	23,809	0.5	48	762.6	31.2
Iron (1893)	Hurley	912,053	5,915	−0.0	70	758.2	7.8
Jackson (1853)	Black River Falls	1,471,277	20,630	0.9	53	987.7	20.9
Jefferson (1836)	Jefferson	6,186,989	83,974	0.3	20	556.5	150.9
Juneau (1856)	Mauston	1,882,377	26,934	1.0	46	766.9	35.1
Kenosha (1850)	Kenosha	12,236,191	167,258	0.5	8	272.0	614.9
Kewaunee (1852)	Kewaunee	1,454,689	20,652	0.4	52	342.5	60.3
La Crosse (1851)	La Crosse	8,063,741	116,740	1.8	12	451.7	258.4
Lafayette (1846)	Darlington	1,012,838	16,914	0.5	57	633.6	26.7
Langlade (1879)	Antigo	1,661,686	19,847	−0.7	54	870.6	22.8
Lincoln (1874)	Merrill	2,240,195	28,816	0.3	44	879.0	32.8
Manitowoc (1836)	Manitowoc	5,115,896	81,320	−0.2	21	589.1	138.0
Marathon (1850)	Wausau	9,468,197	134,803	0.6	10	1,545.0	87.3
Marinette (1879)	Marinette	3,618,808	41,605	−0.3	36	1,399.4	29.7
Marquette (1836)	Montello	1,530,559	15,399	−0.0	63	455.6	33.8
Menominee (1961)	Keshena	288,848	4,236	0.1	72	357.6	11.8
Milwaukee (1834)	Milwaukee	57,127,524	949,741	0.2	1	241.4	3,934.3
Monroe (1854)	Sparta	2,823,711	45,339	1.5	31	900.8	50.3
Oconto (1851)	Oconto	3,512,156	38,014	0.9	38	998.0	38.1
Oneida (1885)	Rhinelander	6,633,464	36,082	0.2	40	1,113.0	32.4
Outagamie (1851)	Appleton	13,042,232	180,022	1.9	6	637.5	282.4
Ozaukee (1853)	Port Washington	10,226,456	87,116	0.8	18	233.1	373.7
Pepin (1858)	Durand	550,724	7,445	−0.3	69	232.0	32.1
Pierce (1853)	Ellsworth	2,724,149	41,107	0.2	37	573.8	71.6
Polk (1853)	Balsam Lake	4,084,906	44,237	0.1	32	914.0	48.4
Portage (1836)	Stevens Point	4,882,392	70,882	1.2	23	800.7	88.5
Price (1879)	Phillips	1,408,916	14,155	−0.0	66	1,254.4	11.3
Racine (1836)	Racine	13,438,849	195,461	0.0	5	332.5	587.9
Richland (1842)	Richland Center	1,037,181	17,995	−0.1	56	586.2	30.7
Rock (1836)	Janesville	9,351,401	160,104	−0.1	9	718.1	223.0
Rusk (1901)	Ladysmith	1,145,460	14,790	0.2	65	913.6	16.2
St. Croix (1840)	Hudson	7,154,298	85,735	1.7	19	722.3	118.7
Sauk (1840)	Baraboo	6,442,659	62,092	0.2	25	830.9	74.7
Sawyer (1883)	Hayward	3,373,194	16,676	0.7	58	1,257.3	13.3
Shawano (1853)	Shawano	2,942,275	41,859	−0.2	35	893.1	46.9
Sheboygan (1836)	Sheboygan	8,526,701	115,362	−0.1	13	511.3	225.6
Taylor (1875)	Medford	1,339,909	20,733	0.2	51	974.9	21.3
Trempealeau (1854)	Whitehall	1,833,518	29,184	1.3	43	733.0	39.8
Vernon (1851)	Viroqua	1,783,775	29,977	0.7	42	791.6	37.9
Vilas (1893)	Eagle River	6,666,486	21,523	0.4	49	856.6	25.1
Walworth (1836)	Elkhorn	13,183,360	102,837	0.6	14	555.1	185.3
Washburn (1883)	Shell Lake	2,362,255	15,948	0.2	61	797.1	20.0
Washington (1836)	West Bend	12,619,779	133,071	0.9	11	430.7	309.0
Waukesha (1846)	Waukesha	47,217,367	392,761	0.7	3	549.6	714.6
Waupaca (1851)	Waupaca	3,801,205	52,435	0.1	28	747.7	70.1
Waushara (1851)	Wautoma	2,389,077	24,511	0.1	47	626.2	39.1
Winnebago (1840)	Oshkosh	11,791,573	168,216	0.7	7	434.5	387.1
Wood (1856)	Wisconsin Rapids	4,661,457	74,954	0.3	22	793.1	94.5
State Total		$467,502,564	5,732,981	0.8%		54,157.8	105.9

[1]Counties are created by legislative act. Depending on the date, Wisconsin counties were created by the Michigan Territorial Legislature (1818-1836), the Wisconsin Territorial Legislature (1836-1848), or the Wisconsin State Legislature (after 1848). [2]Reflects actual market value of all taxable general property, including personal property and real estate, as determined by the Wisconsin Department of Revenue. [3]Change from 2010 U.S. Census. [4]Determined by 2010 Census. [5]2014 density calculated by Wisconsin Legislative Reference Bureau. [6]Town of Siren is used as a mailing address for county offices.

Sources: Wisconsin Department of Revenue, Division of State and Local Finance, *Town, Village, and City Taxes 2013: Taxes Levied 2013 – Collected 2014*, 2014; U.S. Census Bureau, Census 2010 Summary File 1, March 2015.

COUNTY OFFICERS IN WISCONSIN
June 30, 2015

County	County Board Number of Supervisors	County Board Chairperson	Administrator, Executive, Administrative Coordinator[1]
Adams	20	John West	Cindy Phillippi (AC)
Ashland	21	Pete Russo	Jeff Beirl (CA)
Barron	29	James Miller	Jeff French (CA)
Bayfield	13	Dennis M. Pocernich	Mark Abeles-Allison (CA)
Brown	26	Patrick Moynihan, Jr.	Troy Streckenbach (CE)
Buffalo	14	Douglas Kane	Sonya Hansen (AC)
Burnett	21	Donald Taylor	Nathan Ehalt (CA)
Calumet	21	Alice M. Connors	Todd M. Romenesko (CA)
Chippewa	15	Paul Michels	Frank Pascarella (CA)
Clark	29	Wayne Hendrickson	Wayne Hendrickson (AC)
Columbia	28	Vern E. Gove	Susan M. Moll (AC)
Crawford	17	Pete Flesch	Dan McWilliams (AC)
Dane	37	Sharon Corrigan	Joseph Parisi (CE)
Dodge	33	Russell Kottke	Jim Mielke (CA)
Door	21	Daniel Austad	Grant Thomas (CA)
Douglas	21	Douglas G. Finn	Andrew G. Lisak (CA)
Dunn	29	Steven Rasmussen	Eugene C. Smith (County Manager)
Eau Claire	29	Gregg Moore	Keith Zehms (CA)
Florence	12	Jeanette Bomberg	Donna Trudell (AC)
Fond du Lac	25	Martin F. Farrell	Allen J. Buechel (CE)
Forest	21	Paul Millan	Lisa Kalata (AC)
Grant	17	Robert C. Keeney	Linda K. Gebhard (AC)
Green	31	Arthur F. Carter	Michael J. Doyle (CA)
Green Lake	19	Jack Meyers	Margaret Bostelmann (AC)
Iowa	21	John M. Meyers	Curt Kephart (CA)
Iron	15	Joe Pinardi	Michael Saari (AC)
Jackson	19	Dennis Eberhardt	Kyle Deno (AC)
Jefferson	30	James Schroeder	Ben Wehmeier (CA)
Juneau	21	Alan K. Peterson	Alan K. Peterson (AC)
Kenosha	23	Edward D. Kubicki	Jim Kreuser (CE)
Kewaunee	20	Ron Heuer	Scott Feldt (CA)
La Crosse	29	Tara Johnson	Steve O'Malley (CA)
Lafayette	16	Jack Sauer	Jack Sauer (AC)
Langlade	21	David J. Solin	Robin J. Stowe (CC)
Lincoln	22	Robert Lussow	Randy Scholz (AC)
Manitowoc	25	Jim Brey	Bob Ziegelbauer (CE)
Marathon	38	Kurt Gibbs	Brad Karger (CA)
Marinette	30	Vilas Schroeder	vacancy (CA)
Marquette	17	Robert C. Miller	Brenda Jahns-Grams (AC)
Menominee	7	Michael Chapman	Jeremy Weso (AC)
Milwaukee	18	Marina Dimitrijevic	Chris Abele (CE)
Monroe	24	James Kuhn	Catherine Schmit (CA)
Oconto	31	Leland T. Rymer	Kevin Hamann (AC)
Oneida	21	David Hintz	Lisa Charbarneau (AC)
Outagamie	36	Helen J. Nagler	Thomas Nelson (CE)
Ozaukee	26	Lee Schlenvogt	Thomas W. Meaux (CA)
Pepin	12	Peter A. Adler	Pamela DeWitt (AC)
Pierce	17	Jeff Holst	Jo Ann Miller (AC)
Polk	15	William F. Johnson IV	Dana Frey (AC)
Portage	25	O. Philip Idsvoog	Patty Dreier (CE)
Price	13	Robert Kopisch	Robert Kopisch (AC)
Racine	21	Russell A. Clark	Jonathan Delagrave (CE)
Richland	21	Jeanetta Kirkpatrick	Victor V. Vlasak (AC)
Rock	29	J. Russell Podzilni	Joshua M. Smith (CA)
Rusk	19	Randy Tatur	Denise Wetzel (AC)
St. Croix	19	Roger Larson	Patrick Thompson (CA)
Sauk	31	Marty Krueger	Kathryn Schauf (AC)
Sawyer	15	Hal Helwig	Thomas Hoff (CA)
Shawano	27	Gerald Erdmann	Brent Miller (AC)
Sheboygan	25	Roger Te Stroete	Adam Payne (CA)
Taylor	17	Jim Metz	Courtney Graff/Ken Schmiege (CC)
Trempealeau	17	Dick Miller	Paul L. Syverson (AC)
Vernon	29	Herbert Cornell	Greg Lunde (CC)
Vilas	21	Ronald De Bruyne	David R. Alleman (AC)
Walworth	11	Nancy Russell	David A. Bretl (CA)
Washburn	21	Steven Sather	Michael Keefe (AC)
Washington	30	Herbert J. Tennies	Joshua Schoemann (CA)
Waukesha	25	Paul L. Decker	Paul Farrow (CE)
Waupaca	27	Dick Koeppen	Mary Robbins (AC)
Waushara	11	Donna R. Kalata	Deb Behringer (AC)
Winnebago	36	David W. Albrecht	Mark L. Harris (CE)
Wood	19	Lance Pliml	Lance Pliml (AC)

COUNTY OFFICERS IN WISCONSIN
June 30, 2015–Continued

	County Clerk	
County	Clerk	Office Address
Adams	Cindy Phillippi (D)	P.O. Box 278, Friendship 53934
Ashland	Heather W. Schutte (D)	201 W. Main St., Ashland 54806
Barron	DeeAnn Cook (R)	335 E. Monroe Av., Barron 54812
Bayfield	Scott S. Fibert (D)	P.O. Box 878, Washburn 54891
Brown	Sandra Juno (R)	P.O. Box 23600, Green Bay 54305-3600
Buffalo	Roxann M. Halverson (D)	407 S. 2nd St., P.O. Box 58, Alma 54610
Burnett	Wanda Hinrichs (D)	7410 County Road K, #105, Siren 54872
Calumet	Beth A. Hauser (R)	206 Court St., Chilton 53014
Chippewa	Sandi Frion (D)	711 N. Bridge St., Chippewa Falls 54729
Clark	Christina M. Jensen (R)	517 Court St., Rm. 301, Neillsville 54456
Columbia.	Susan M. Moll (R)	400 DeWitt St., Portage 53901
Crawford.	Janet Geisler (R)	225 N. Beaumont Rd., Suite 210, Prairie du Chien 53821
Dane	Scott McDonell (D)	210 Martin Luther King Jr. Blvd., Rm. 106A, Madison 53703
Dodge	Karen J. Gibson (R)	127 E. Oak St., Juneau 53039
Door	Jill M. Lau (R)	421 Nebraska St., Sturgeon Bay 54235
Douglas	Susan T. Sandvick (D)	1313 Belknap St., Rm. 101, Superior 54880
Dunn	Julie A Wathke (D)	800 Wilson Av., Menomonie 54751
Eau Claire	Janet K. Loomis (D)	720 Oxford Av., Eau Claire 54703
Florence	Donna Trudell (R)	501 Lake Av., P.O. Box 41, Florence 54121
Fond du Lac	Lisa Freiberg (R)	160 S. Macy St., Fond du Lac 54935
Forest.	Lisa Kalata (D)	200 E. Madison St., Crandon 54520
Grant.	Linda K. Gebhard (R)	111 S. Jefferson St., P.O. Box 529, Lancaster 53813
Green.	Michael J. Doyle (I)	1016 16th Av., Monroe 53566
Green Lake.	Margaret Bostelmann (R)	571 County Road A, Green Lake 54941
Iowa	Gregory T. Klusendorf (D)	222 N. Iowa St., Dodgeville 53533
Iron.	Michael Saari (D)	300 Taconite St., Suite 101, Hurley 54534
Jackson.	Kyle Deno (D)	307 Main St., Black River Falls 54615
Jefferson	Barbara A. Frank (R)	311 S. Center Av., Rm. 109, Jefferson 53549
Juneau	Kathleen Kobylski (R)	220 E. State St., Mauston 53948
Kenosha	Mary T. Schuch-Krebs (D)	1010 56th St., Kenosha 53140
Kewaunee	Jamie Annoye (D)	810 Lincoln St., Kewaunee 54216
La Crosse	Ginny Dankmeyer (D)	400 N. 4th St., Rm. 1210, La Crosse 54601
Lafayette.	Linda Bawden (R)	626 Main St., P.O. Box 40, Darlington 53530
Langlade	Kathryn Jacob (D)	800 Clermont St., Antigo 54409
Lincoln.	Christopher Marlowe (R)	801 N. Sales St., Suite 201, Merrill 54452
Manitowoc.	Jamie J. Aulik (D)	1010 S. 8th St., Manitowoc 54220
Marathon.	Nan Kottke (D)	500 Forest St., Wausau 54403
Marinette.	Kathy Brandt (R)	1926 Hall Av., Marinette 54143-1717
Marquette	Gary L. Sorensen (R)	P.O. Box 186, Montello 53949
Menominee	Laure Pecore (D)	P.O. Box 279, Keshena 54135
Milwaukee.	Joseph J. Czarnezki (D)	901 N. 9th St., Rm. 105, Milwaukee 53233
Monroe	Shelley Bohl (R)	202 S. K St., Rm. 1, Sparta 54656
Oconto	Kim Pytleski (R)	301 Washington St., Oconto 54153
Oneida	Mary Bartelt (R)	P.O. Box 400, Rhinelander 54501
Outagamie	Lori J. O'Bright (R)	410 S. Walnut St., Appleton 54911
Ozaukee	Julianne B. Winkelhorst (R)	121 W. Main St., P.O. Box 994, Port Washington 53074
Pepin	Marcia R. Bauer (D)	740 7th Av. W., Durand 54736
Pierce.	Jamie R. Feuerhelm (D)	P.O. Box 119, Ellsworth 54011
Polk	Carole T. Wondra (D)	100 Polk County Plaza, Suite 110, Balsam Lake 54810
Portage.	Shirley M. Simonis (D)	1516 Church St., Stevens Point 54481
Price	Jean Gottwald (D)	126 Cherry St., Rm. 106, Phillips 54555
Racine	Wendy M. Christensen (R)	730 Wisconsin Av., Racine 53403
Richland	Victor V. Vlasak (R)	P.O. Box 310, Richland Center 53581
Rock	Lori Stottler (D)	51 S. Main St., Janesville 53545
Rusk	Denise Wetzel (D)	311 Miner Av. E., Suite C150, Ladysmith 54848
St. Croix	Cindy Campbell (D)	1101 Carmichael Rd., Hudson 54016
Sauk	Rebecca A. DeMars (R)	505 Broadway, Baraboo 53913
Sawyer	Kris Mayberry (R)	10610 Main St., Suite 10, Hayward 54843
Shawano	Rosemary Rueckert (R)	311 N. Main St., Shawano 54166
Sheboygan	Jon Dolson (D)	508 New York Av., Sheboygan 53081
Taylor	Bruce P. Strama (D)	224 S. 2nd St., Medford 54451
Trempealeau	Paul L. Syverson (D)	36245 Main St., Whitehall 54773
Vernon	Ronald Hoff (R)	Courthouse Annex, Rm. 108, Viroqua 54665
Vilas	David R. Alleman (R)	330 Court St., Eagle River 54521
Walworth.	Kimberly S. Bushey (R)	100 W. Walworth, P.O. Box 1001, Elkhorn 53121
Washburn	Lolita Olson (R)	P.O. Box 639, Shell Lake 54871
Washington.	Brenda Jaszewski (R)	432 E. Washington St., Rm. 2027, West Bend 53095-7986
Waukesha	Kathleen O. Novack (R)	515 W. Moreland Blvd., Suite 120, Waukesha 53188
Waupaca	Mary Robbins (R)	811 Harding St., Waupaca 54981
Waushara	Melanie Rendon Stake (R)	P.O. Box 488, Wautoma 54982
Winnebago.	Susan T. Ertmer (R)	415 Jackson St., P.O. Box 2808, Oshkosh 54903
Wood.	Cynthia Cepress (D)	P.O. Box 8095, Wisconsin Rapids 54495

COUNTY OFFICERS IN WISCONSIN
June 30, 2015–Continued

County	Treasurer	Register of Deeds	Clerk of Circuit Court
Adams	Jani Zander (D)	Jodi Helgeson (D)	Kathleen Dye (D)
Ashland	Tracey Hoglund (R)	Karen Miller (D)	Kerrie Nevala (D)
Barron	Yvonne Ritchie (R)	Margo Katterhagen (R)	Sharon Millermon (R)
Bayfield	Daniel R. Anderson (D)	Patricia A. Olson (D)	Kay L. Cederberg (D)
Brown	Paul Zeller (R)	Cathy Williquette-Lindsay (D)	John Vander Leest (R)
Buffalo	Marilynn Sheahan (R)	Carol Burmeister (D)	Roselle Schlosser (R)
Burnett	Joanne Pahl (D)	Jeanine Chell (D)	Trudy Schmidt (D)
Calumet	Michael V. Schlaak (R)	Tamara Alten (R)	Connie Daun (R)
Chippewa	Patty Schimmel (D)	Marge Geissler (D)	Karen Hepfler (D)
Clark	Kathryn M. Brugger (D)	Peggy L. Walter (R)	Heather Bravener (D)
Columbia	Deborah A. Raimer (R)	Karen Manske	Susan Raimer (R)
Crawford	Martin E. Sprosty (D)	Melissa Nagel (D)	Donna Steiner (D)
Dane	Adam Gallagher (D)	Kristi Chlebowski (D)	Carlo Esqueda (D)
Dodge	Patti Hilker (R)	Christine Planasch (R)	Lynn Hron (R)
Door	Jay Zahn (R)	Carey Petersilka (R)	Connie DeFere (R)
Douglas	Carol Jones (A)	Gayle I. Wahner (D)	Michele L. Wick (D)
Dunn	Megan Mittlestadt (R)	Heather Kuhn (D)	Clara D. Minor (D)
Eau Claire	Glenda J. Lyons (D)	Kathryn A. Christenson (D)	Susan Schaffer (D)
Florence	JoAnne Friberg (R)	Pattie Gehlhoff (R)	Tanya Neuens (R)
Fond du Lac	Julie M. Hundertmark (R)	Shawn H. Kelly (R)	Ramona Geib (R)
Forest	Amy T. Krause (D)	Cortney M. Britten (D)	Penny Carter (D)
Grant	Louise Ketterer (D)	Marilyn Pierce (R)	Tina McDonald (R)
Green	Sherri Hawkins (R)	Cynthia Meudt (R)	Barbara Miller (R)
Green Lake	Elizabeth Amend (R)	Sarah Guenther (R)	Amy Thoma (R)
Iowa	Jolene M. Millard (R)	Dixie L. Edge (D)	Lia N. Gust (R)
Iron	Mark Beaupré (D)	Dan Soine (D)	Karen Ransanici (D)
Jackson	JoAnne Forsting Leonard (D)	Shari Marg (D)	Jan Moennig (D)
Jefferson	John E. Jensen (R)	Staci M. Hoffman (R)	Carla J. Robinson (R)
Juneau	Denise Giebel (R)	Christie Bender (R)	Patty Schluter (R)
Kenosha	Teri Jacobson (D)	JoEllyn M. Storz (D)	Rebecca Matoska-Mentink (D)
Kewaunee	Michelle Dax (R)	Janet Wolf (D)	Rebecca Deterville (D)
La Crosse	Shawn Handland (D)	Cheryl McBride (R)	Pamela Radtke (R)
Lafayette	Rebecca Taylor (R)	Joseph Boll (R)	Catherine McGowan (R)
Langlade	Ann Meyer (D)	Sandra M. Fischer (D)	Marilyn Baraniak (D)
Lincoln	Jan Lemmer (D)	Sara Koss (R)	Cindy Kimmons (R)
Manitowoc	Cheryl Duchow (D)	Preston F. Jones (D)	Lynn Zigmunt (D)
Marathon	Audrey Jensen (A)	Michael J. Sydow (D)	Shirley Lang (R)
Marinette	Bev A. Noffke (R)	Renee Miller (R)	Sheila M. Dudka (R)
Marquette	Diana Campbell (R)	Bette Krueger (R)	Shari Rudolph (R)
Menominee	Louise Madosh (D)	Louise Madosh (D)	Pamela Fechette (D)
Milwaukee	David Cullen (D)	John La Fave (D)	John Barrett (D)
Monroe	Annette Erickson (R)	Deb Brandt (R)	Shirley Chapiewsky (R)
Oconto	Tanya Peterson (R)	Annette Behringer (R)	Michael C. Hodkiewicz (R)
Oneida	Kristina Ostermann (D)	Kyle Franson (R)	Brenda Behrle (D)
Outagamie	Dina Mumford (R)	Sarah R. Van Camp (R)	Barb Bocik (R)
Ozaukee	Karen L. Makoutz (R)	Ronald A. Voigt (R)	Mary Lou Mueller (R)
Pepin	Nancy M. Richardson (R)	Monica J. Bauer (R)	Audrey Lieffring (R)
Pierce	Phyllis J. Beastrom (D)	Vicki J. Nelson (R)	Peg M. Feuerhelm (D)
Polk	Amanda Nissen (D)	Laurie Anderson (D)	Jobie Bainbridge (R)
Portage	Stephanie Stokes (D)	Cynthia Wisinski (D)	Patricia A. Baker (D)
Price	Lynn Neeck (D)	Judith Chizek (D)	Chris Cress (D)
Racine	Jane F. Nikolai (R)	Tyson Fettes (R)	Roseanne Lee (R)
Richland	Julie Keller (R)	Susan Triggs (R)	Stacy Kleist (R)
Rock	Vicki L. Brown (D)	Randal Leyes (R)	Jackie Gackstatter (D)
Rusk	Verna Nielsen (R)	Carol Johnson (D)	Lynette Yotter (D)
St. Croix	Laurie Noble (R)	Beth Pabst (R)	Kristi Severson (D)
Sauk	Elizabeth Geoghegan (R)	Brent Bailey (R)	Vicki J. Meister (R)
Sawyer	Dianne Ince (R)	Paula Chisser (R)	Claudia Burgan (R)
Shawano	Debra Wallace (R)	Amy Dillenburg (R)	Susan M. Krueger (R)
Sheboygan	Laura Henning-Lorenz (D)	Ellen Schleicher (D)	Melody Lorge (I)
Taylor	Sarah Holtz (R)	Sara Nuernberger (D)	Rose M. Thums (R)
Trempealeau	Laurie Halama (D)	Rose Ottum (D)	Michelle Weisenberger (D)
Vernon	Rachel Hanson (R)	Konna Spaeth (R)	Kathy Buros (D)
Vilas	Jerri Radtke (R)	Joan Hansen (R)	Jean Numrich (R)
Walworth	Valerie Etzel (R)	Donna Pruess (R)	Sheila T. Reiff (R)
Washburn	Nicole Tims (R)	Diane Poach (D)	Karen Nord (D)
Washington	Jane Merten (R)	Sharon Martin (R)	Theresa Russell (R)
Waukesha	Pamela F. Reeves (R)	James Behrend (R)	Kathleen A. Madden (R)
Waupaca	Clyde Tellock (R)	Michael Mazemke (R)	Terrie Tews-Liebe (R)
Waushara	Elaine Wedell (R)	Heather Schwersenska (R)	Melissa M. Zamzow (R)
Winnebago	Mary E. Krueger (R)	Julie Pagel (R)	Melissa M. Konrad (R)
Wood	Karen Kubisiak (D)	Susan Ginter (R)	Cindy Joosten (R)

COUNTY OFFICERS IN WISCONSIN
June 30, 2015–Continued

County	District Attorney	Sheriff	Coroner/Medical Examiner
Adams	Tania Bonnett (I)	Sam Wollin (D)	Marilyn Rogers (ME)
Ashland	Kelly McNight (D)	Michael Brennan, Sr. (D)	Barbara Beeksma (R)
Barron	Angela Beranek (D)	Chris Fitzgerald (D)	Mary Ricci (ME)
Bayfield	Fred I. Bourg (D)	Paul Susienka (D)	Gary Victorson (D)
Brown	David Lasee (R)	John Gossage (R)	Jeff Jansen (ME)
Buffalo	Thomas Clark (D)	Mike Schmidtknecht (R)	Peter Samb (R)
Burnett	William L. Norine (R)	Ronald L. Wilhelm, Jr. (R)	Michael Maloney (ME)
Calumet	Nicholas Bolz (R)	Mark R. Ott (R)	Michael Klaeser (ME)
Chippewa	Steve Gibbs (R)	James Kowalczyk (D)	Ronald Patten (D)
Clark	Lyndsey Brunette (D)	Greg Herrick (R)	Richard J. Schleifer (R)
Columbia	Jane E. Kohlwey (R)	Dennis Richards (R)	Angela Hinze (ME)
Crawford	Timothy Baxter (D)	Dale McCullick (D)	Joe Morovits (D)
Dane	Ismael Ozanne (D)	David Mahoney (D)	Vincent Tranchida (ME)
Dodge	Kurt Klomberg (R)	Dale Schmidt (R)	Patrick Schoebel (ME)
Door	Ray Pelrine (R)	Steve Delarwelle (R)	None
Douglas	Daniel Blank (D)	Thomas Dalbec (D)	Darrell Witt (ME)
Dunn	Andrea Nodolf (R)	Dennis P. Smith (D)	Christopher H. Kruse (ME)
Eau Claire	Gary King (D)	Ron D. Cramer (R)	Thomas Thelen (ME)
Florence	Doug Drexler (D)	Jeff Rickaby (R)	Mary Johnson (R)
Fond du Lac	Eric Toney (R)	Mylan C. Fink, Jr. (R)	P. Douglas Kelley (ME)
Forest	Charles Simono (D)	John Dennee (D)	None
Grant	Lisa Riniker (D)	Nate Dreckman (R)	Ronald Sturmer (R)
Green	Gary L. Luhman (R)	Mark A. Rohloff (R)	None
Green Lake	Andrew Christenson (R)	Mark Podoll (R)	Amanda Thoma (R)
Iowa	Larry Nelson (D)	Steven R. Michek (R)	Wendell F. Hamlin (R)
Iron	Martin Lipske (D)	Tony Furyk (D)	Diane Simonich (D)
Jackson	Gerald Fox (D)	Duane Waldera (D)	Karla Wood (D)
Jefferson	Susan V. Happ (D)	Paul Milbrath (R)	Nichol L. Wayd (ME)
Juneau	Michael Solovey (R)	Brent Oleson (R)	Linda Mitchel May (A)
Kenosha	Robert D. Zapf (R)	David Beth (R)	Patrice Hall (ME)
Kewaunee	Andrew Naze (D)	Matthew Joski (R)	Rory Groessl (D)
La Crosse	Tim Gruenke (D)	Steve Helgeson (R)	Tim Candahl (ME)
Lafayette	Katherine Findley (D)	Reginald Gill (R)	Linda Gebhardt (D)
Langlade	Ralph M. Uttke (D)	William Greening (D)	Larry Shadick (R)
Lincoln	Donald Dunphy (R)	Jeff Jaeger (R)	Paul Proulx (R)
Manitowoc	Jacalyn LaBre (R)	Robert Hermann (D)	Curtis Green (D)
Marathon	Ken Heimerman (D)	Scott Parks (R)	Jessica Blahnik (ME)
Marinette	Allen R. Brey (D)	Jerry Sauve (R)	George F. Smith (R)
Marquette	Chad Hendee (R)	Kim Gaffney (R)	Thomas Wastart II (R)
Menominee	Gregory Parker (R)[2]	Robert Summers (D)	Patrick Roberts (ME)
Milwaukee	John T. Chisholm (D)	David A. Clarke, Jr. (D)	Brian L. Peterson (ME)
Monroe	Kevin Croninger (A)	Scott Perkins (R)	Toni Eddy(ME)
Oconto	Ed Burke (R)	Michael Jansen (R)	Jeff Jansen (ME)
Oneida	Michael Schiek (R)	Grady Hartman (R)	Larry Mathein (ME)
Outagamie	Carrie Schneider (R)	Bradley G. Gehring (R)	Ruth A. Wulgaert (R)
Ozaukee	Adam Y. Gerol (R)	James G. Johnson (R)	Timothy J. Deppisch (R)
Pepin	Jon D. Seifert (D)	Joel D. Wener (R)	Christy Rundquist (I)
Pierce	Sean Froelich (D)	Nancy Hove (D)	John Worsing (ME)
Polk	Daniel Steffen (R)	Pete Johnson (R)	Jonn Dinnies (ME)
Portage	Louis J. Molepske, Jr. (D)	Michael Lukas (D)	Scott W. Rifleman (R)
Price	Mark Fuhr (D)	Brian Schmidt (R)	James Dalbesio III (D)
Racine	W. Richard Chiapete (R)	Christopher Schmaling (R)	Michael Payne (ME)
Richland	Jennifer M. Harper (R)	Jim Bindl (R)	James Rossing (I)
Rock	David J. O'Leary (D)	Robert D. Spoden (D)	Vincent Tranchida (ME)
Rusk	James Rennicke	Jeffery Wallace (R)	Jim Rassbach (ME)
St. Croix	Eric Johnson (R)	John A. Shilts (R)	Patty Schachtner (ME)
Sauk	Kevin R. Calkins (R)	Chip Meister (R)	Greg L. Hahn (R)
Sawyer	Bruce Poquette (R)	Mark Kelsey (R)	Dave Dokkestul (R)
Shawano	Gregory Parker (R)[2]	Adam Bieber (R)	Brian Westfahl (A)
Sheboygan	Joe DeCecco (D)	Todd Prebe (R)	David Leffin (ME)
Taylor	Kristi Tlusty (D)	Bruce A. Daniels (D)	Scott Perrin (ME)
Trempealeau	Taavi McMahon (D)	Richard Anderson (D)	Bonnie Kindschy (D)
Vernon	Timothy Gaskell (R)	John B. Spears (R)	Janet Reed (R)
Vilas	Albert Moustakis (R)	Joseph A. Fath (R)	Paul Tirpe (R)
Walworth	Daniel A. Necci (R)	Kurt Picknell (R)	Lynda Biedrzycki (ME)
Washburn	Tom Frost (A)	Terry C. Dryden (R)	Jason Sebens (I)
Washington	Mark Bensen (R)	Dale Schmidt (R)	Robert Schafer, Sr. (ME)
Waukesha	Susan L. Opper (A)	Dan Trawicki (R)	Lynda Biedrzycki (ME)
Waupaca	John P. Snider (R)	Bradly Hardel (R)	Barry Tomaras (R)
Waushara	Scott Blader (R)	Jeffrey L. Nett (R)	Roland B. Handel (R)
Winnebago	Christian Gossett (R)	John Matz (R)	Barry Busby (R)
Wood	Craig Lambert (R)	Thomas Reichert (D)	Dara Borre Hamm (D)

COUNTY OFFICERS IN WISCONSIN
June 30, 2015–Continued

County	Surveyor[3]	County	Surveyor[3]
Adams	Gregory Rhinehart	Marathon	Christopher Fieri
Ashland	David Carlson	Marinette	None
Barron	Mark Netterlund	Marquette	Jerol Smart
Bayfield	Robert Mick	Menominee	None
Brown	Terry VanHout	Milwaukee	Kurt W. Bauer
Buffalo	Joe Nelsen	Monroe	Gary Dechant
Burnett	Jason Towne	Oconto	Mark Teuteberg
Calumet	Bradley Buechel	Oneida	None
Chippewa	Samuel I. Wenz	Outagamie	James A. Hebert
Clark	Wade Pettit	Ozaukee	Robert R. Dreblow
Columbia	Jim Grothman	Pepin	Ron Jasperson
Crawford	Rich Marx	Pierce	James Filkins
Dane	Dan Frick	Polk	Steve Geiger
Dodge	Ted Dumke	Portage	Joseph S. Glodowski (D)
Door	None	Price	Alfred Schneider
Douglas	Ben Klitzke	Racine	None
Dunn	Thomas Carlson	Richland	Driftless Area Surveying, LLC
Eau Claire	Matt Janiak	Rock	Jason Houle
Florence	None	Rusk	None
Fond du Lac	Peter Kuen	St. Croix	Brian V. Halling
Forest	None	Sauk	Patrick Dederich (D)
Grant	Aaron Austin	Sawyer	Dan Pleoger
Green	None	Shawano	David Yurk
Green Lake	Alan Shute	Sheboygan	Edgar Harvey, Jr.
Iowa	Bruce D. Bowden (R)	Taylor	Robert Meyer
Iron	None	Trempealeau	Joe Nelson
Jackson	Tim Jeatran	Vernon	None
Jefferson	Jim Morrow	Vilas	Thomas Boettcher (R)
Juneau	None	Walworth	None
Kenosha	None	Washburn	Steven Waak
Kewaunee	None	Washington	Scott Schmidt
La Crosse	Bryan Meyer	Waukesha	Kurt W. Bauer
Lafayette	None	Waupaca	Joseph S. Glodowski
Langlade	David Tlusty	Waushara	Jerry Smart
Lincoln	Anthony Dallman	Winnebago	None
Manitowoc	None	Wood	Kevin Boyer

Key: A – Appointed without party designation; AC – Administrative Coordinator; CA – County Administrator; CC – Corporation Counsel; CE – County Executive; D – Democrat; I – Independent; R – Republican; ME – Medical Examiner.

Note: All officers are elected countywide with the exception of the county board chairperson, county administrator, administrative coordinator, and medical examiner, who are elected or appointed by the county board. Elected county officers serve 2-year terms, except county executives who serve 4-year terms. Beginning 2003, sheriffs serve 4-year terms per constitutional amendment ratified 11/3/98. Reflecting a constitutional amendment ratified 4/5/2005, beginning 2006, clerks of circuit court and coroners serve 4-year terms; beginning 2008, all remaining county officers serve 4-year terms.

[1]Counties with a population of 500,000 or more are statutorily required to establish the office of county executive. Smaller counties may establish the office of county executive or name a county administrator. In counties without a county executive or county administrator, the county board must designate an elected or appointed official to serve as administrative coordinator.

[2]Menominee and Shawano County share a District Attorney.

[3]County boards are permitted to designate any registered land surveyor to perform the duties of the county surveyor. Surveyors are appointed unless party designation is shown.

Source: Data collected from county clerks by Wisconsin Legislative Reference Bureau, May 2015, and governor's appointment notices.

WISCONSIN CITIES
January 1, 2014

City (Year Incorporated)[1]	County	2010 Census	2014 Estimate	Percent Change	2010 Nonwhite[5]	2010 Hispanic or Latino Origin[6]
First Class Cities (150,000 or more) – 1 City						
Milwaukee (1846)	Milwaukee, Washington, Waukesha	594,833	595,993	0.20%	271,607	103,007
Second Class Cities (39,000 – 149,999) – 14 Cities						
Appleton (1857)	Calumet, Outagamie, Winnebago	72,623	73,463	1.16	7,124	3,643
Eau Claire (1872)[2]	Chippewa, Eau Claire	61,704	66,834	1.37	5,116	1,268
Fond du Lac (1852)[2]	Fond du Lac	43,021	43,151	0.30	2,695	2,742
Green Bay (1854)	Brown	104,057	104,710	0.63	13,912	13,896
Janesville (1853)[2]	Rock	63,575	63,525	−0.08	3,689	3,421
Kenosha (1850)[3]	Kenosha	99,218	99,680	0.47	14,121	16,130
La Crosse (1856)	La Crosse	51,320	52,018	1.36	4,885	1,012
Madison (1856)	Dane	233,209	240,153	2.98	40,798	15,948
Oshkosh (1853)[2]	Winnebago	62,916	66,412	0.50	5,539	1,770
Racine (1848)[3]	Racine	78,860	78,479	−0.48	20,362	16,309
Sheboygan (1853)[3]	Sheboygan	49,288	48,897	−0.79	6,314	4,866
Waukesha (1895)[3]	Waukesha	70,718	71,044	0.46	5,321	8,529
Wauwatosa (1897)[3]	Milwaukee	46,396	46,766	0.80	4,361	1,450
West Allis (1906)	Milwaukee	60,411	60,272	−0.23	5,094	5,770
Third Class Cities (10,000 – 38,999) – 34 Cities						
Baraboo (1882)[3]	Sauk	12,048	11,985	−0.52	487	446
Beaver Dam (1856)	Dodge	16,214	16,572	2.21	502	1,210
Beloit (1857)[2]	Rock	36,966	36,805	−0.44	7,149	6,332
Brookfield (1954)	Waukesha	37,920	37,847	−0.19	3,545	853
Burlington (1900)[3]	Racine, Walworth	10,464	10,511	0.45	327	898
Chippewa Falls (1869)	Chippewa	13,661	13,685	0.18	605	221
Cudahy (1906)	Milwaukee	18,267	18,224	−0.24	1,142	1,769
De Pere (1883)[3]	Brown	23,800	24,180	1.60	1,207	511
Fort Atkinson (1878)[2]	Jefferson	12,368	12,364	−0.03	315	1,128
Franklin (1956)	Milwaukee	35,451	35,702	0.71	4,168	1,592
Glendale (1950)[3]	Milwaukee	12,872	12,773	−0.77	2,499	465
Greenfield (1957)	Milwaukee	36,720	36,687	−0.09	3,043	3,087
Hartford (1883)[3]	Dodge, Washington	14,223	14,320	0.68	425	686
Kaukauna (1885)	Calumet, Outagamie	15,462	15,765	1.96	654	407
Manitowoc (1870)	Manitowoc	33,736	33,649	−0.26	2,486	1,695
Marinette (1887)	Marinette	10,968	10,930	−0.35	271	149
Marshfield (1883)[3]	Marathon, Wood	19,118	19,144	0.14	796	452
Menasha (1874)	Calumet, Winnebago	17,353	17,550	1.14	954	1,204
Middleton (1963)[3]	Dane	17,442	18,323	5.05	1,764	984
Muskego (1964)	Waukesha	24,135	24,304	0.70	529	545
Neenah (1873)	Winnebago	25,501	25,833	1.30	1,163	967
New Berlin (1959)	Waukesha	39,584	40,130	1.38	2,256	1,036
Oak Creek (1955)[3]	Milwaukee	34,451	34,707	0.74	3,282	2,582
Oconomowoc (1875)[3]	Waukesha	15,759	16,293	3.39	422	559
Pewaukee (1999)[3]	Waukesha	13,195	13,728	4.04	667	281
River Falls (1875)[3]	Pierce, St. Croix	15,000	15,053	0.35	673	270
Stevens Point (1858)	Portage	26,717	27,040	1.21	1,946	696
Sun Prairie (1958)[3]	Dane	29,364	31,213	6.30	3,749	1,253
Superior (1858)	Douglas	27,244	27,146	−0.36	2,166	382
Two Rivers (1878)[2]	Manitowoc	11,712	11,628	−0.72	536	224
Watertown (1853)	Dodge, Jefferson	23,861	23,911	0.21	706	1,731
Wausau (1872)	Marathon	39,106	39,131	0.06	5,891	1,149
West Bend (1885)[3]	Washington	31,078	31,531	1.46	1,049	1,213
Wisconsin Rapids (1869)	Wood	18,367	18,559	1.05	1,186	535
Fourth Class Cities (Under 10,000) – 141 Cities						
Abbotsford (1965)	Clark, Marathon	2,310	2,298	−0.52	29	578
Adams (1926)[3]	Adams	1,967	1,942	−1.27	74	46
Algoma (1879)	Kewaunee	3,167	3,161	−0.19	84	91
Alma (1885)	Buffalo	781	804	2.94	9	5
Altoona (1887)[3]	Eau Claire	6,706	7,056	5.22	367	171
Amery (1919)[3]	Polk	2,902	2,929	0.93	49	65
Antigo (1885)[3]	Langlade	8,234	8,092	−1.72	288	226
Arcadia (1925)	Trempealeau	2,925	2,929	0.14	48	914
Ashland (1887)[3]	Ashland, Bayfield	8,216	8,135	−0.99	986	176
Augusta (1885)	Eau Claire	1,550	1,541	−0.58	28	48
Barron (1887)	Barron	3,423	3,404	−0.56	392	103
Bayfield (1913)	Bayfield	487	480	−1.44	104	9

WISCONSIN CITIES
January 1, 2014–Continued

City (Year Incorporated)[1]	County	Population[4]				
		2010 Census	2014 Estimate	Percent Change	2010 Nonwhite[5]	2010 Hispanic or Latino Origin[6]
Berlin (1857).	Green Lake, Waushara.	5,524	5,555	0.56	143	441
Black River Falls (1883). .	Jackson.	3,622	3,602	−0.55	291	63
Blair (1949)	Trempealeau	1,366	1,378	0.88	17	52
Bloomer (1920)	Chippewa	3,539	3,550	0.31	59	27
Boscobel (1873)[3].	Grant	3,231	3,245	0.43	304	71
Brillion (1944).	Calumet	3,148	3,191	1.37	60	89
Brodhead (1891).	Green, Rock	3,293	3,291	−0.06	50	125
Buffalo City (1859)	Buffalo	1,023	1,008	−1.47	13	4
Cedarburg (1885)[3].	Ozaukee	11,412	11,479	0.59	367	197
Chetek (1891)	Barron	2,221	2,226	0.23	36	39
Chilton (1877)	Calumet	3,933	3,927	−0.15	83	169
Clintonville (1887)[3]	Waupaca	4,559	4,535	−0.53	132	149
Colby (1891).	Clark, Marathon	1,852	1,832	−1.08	37	221
Columbus (1874)[3]	Columbia, Dodge	4,991	5,021	0.60	143	164
Cornell (1956)	Chippewa	1,467	1,472	0.34	33	3
Crandon (1898)	Forest.	1,920	1,872	−2.50	244	40
Cuba City (1925).	Grant, Lafayette	2,086	2,076	−0.48	17	10
Cumberland (1885)	Barron	2,170	2,169	−0.05	69	54
Darlington (1877)	Lafayette.	2,451	2,422	−1.18	40	297
Delafield (1959)[3].	Waukesha	7,085	7,093	0.11	227	226
Delavan (1897)[3]	Walworth	8,463	8,433	−0.35	287	2,492
Dodgeville (1889)	Iowa	4,693	4,698	0.11	118	84
Durand (1887)[3].	Pepin	1,931	1,919	−0.62	29	16
Eagle River (1937)[3]	Vilas	1,398	1,370	−2.00	81	26
Edgerton (1883)[3]	Dane, Rock.	5,461	5,512	0.93	157	222
Elkhorn (1897)[3]	Walworth	10,084	9,956	−1.27	307	1,108
Elroy (1885)	Juneau	1,442	1,409	−2.29	29	32
Evansville (1896)[3]	Rock	5,012	5,124	2.23	159	179
Fennimore (1919)	Grant	2,497	2,507	0.40	31	31
Fitchburg (1983)[3]	Dane	25,260	26,090	3.29	4,464	4,341
Fountain City (1889). . . .	Buffalo	859	839	−2.33	25	9
Fox Lake (1938)[3].	Dodge	1,519	1,507	−0.79	17	36
Galesville (1942)	Trempealeau	1,481	1,507	1.76	36	18
Gillett (1944).	Oconto	1,386	1,373	−0.94	65	70
Glenwood City (1895). . .	St. Croix	1,242	1,219	−1.85	16	24
Green Lake (1962).	Green Lake.	960	961	0.10	11	18
Greenwood (1891).	Clark	1,026	1,014	−1.17	17	15
Hayward (1915).	Sawyer	2,318	2,347	1.25	354	59
Hillsboro (1885)[3].	Vernon	1,417	1,408	−0.64	19	32
Horicon (1897).	Dodge	3,655	3,696	1.12	86	151
Hudson (1857)[3]	St. Croix	12,719	13,326	4.77	539	347
Hurley (1918)	Iron.	1,547	1,511	−2.33	32	12
Independence (1942)	Trempealeau	1,336	1,352	1.20	11	172
Jefferson (1878)[3]	Jefferson	7,973	7,922	−0.64	203	937
Juneau (1887)	Dodge	2,814	2,736	−2.77	146	285
Kewaunee (1883)	Kewaunee	2,952	2,923	−0.98	66	53
Kiel (1920)[3]	Calumet, Manitowoc.	3,738	3,773	0.94	83	74
Ladysmith (1905)[3].	Rusk	3,414	3,386	−0.82	106	53
Lake Geneva (1883)[3]. . . .	Walworth.	7,651	7,696	0.59	237	1,323
Lake Mills (1905)[2].	Jefferson	5,708	5,758	0.88	122	216
Lancaster (1878)[3]	Grant	3,868	3,845	−0.59	58	31
Lodi (1941)	Columbia.	3,050	3,062	0.39	77	62
Loyal (1948)	Clark	1,261	1,253	−0.63	15	13
Manawa (1954)	Waupaca	1,371	1,332	−2.84	24	27
Marion (1898)	Shawano, Waupaca	1,260	1,258	−0.16	26	22
Markesan (1959).	Green Lake.	1,476	1,449	−1.83	5	109
Mauston (1883)	Juneau	4,423	4,475	1.18	239	154
Mayville (1885)	Dodge	5,154	5,109	−0.87	92	138
Medford (1889)[3]	Taylor	4,326	4,354	0.65	106	54
Mellen (1907)	Ashland	731	718	−1.78	17	12

WISCONSIN CITIES
January 1, 2014–Continued

City (Year Incorporated)[1]	County	Population[4]				
		2010 Census	2014 Estimate	Percent Change	2010 Nonwhite[5]	2010 Hispanic or Latino Origin[6]
Menomonie (1882)[3]	Dunn	16,264	16,002	−1.61	1,176	276
Mequon (1957)[3]	Ozaukee	23,132	23,387	1.10	1,760	467
Merrill (1883)[3]	Lincoln	9,661	9,615	−0.48	248	196
Milton (1969)[3]	Rock	5,546	5,545	−0.02	146	133
Mineral Point (1857)	Iowa	2,487	2,487	0.00	47	17
Mondovi (1889)	Buffalo	2,777	2,773	−0.14	73	40
Monona (1969)[3]	Dane	7,533	7,573	0.53	459	232
Monroe (1882)[3]	Green	10,827	10,751	−0.70	252	526
Montello (1938)	Marquette	1,495	1,485	−0.67	65	43
Montreal (1924)	Iron	807	806	−0.12	16	13
Mosinee (1931)[3]	Marathon	3,988	4,020	0.80	75	50
Neillsville (1882)	Clark	2,463	2,430	−1.34	70	57
Nekoosa (1926)	Wood	2,580	2,568	−0.47	113	87
New Holstein (1926)	Calumet	3,236	3,188	−1.48	63	103
New Lisbon (1889)	Juneau	2,554	2,570	0.63	439	109
New London (1877)[3]	Outagamie, Waupaca	7,295	7,308	0.18	168	500
New Richmond (1885)[3]	St. Croix	8,375	8,616	2.88	331	174
Niagara (1992)	Marinette	1,624	1,608	−0.99	27	19
Oconto (1869)	Oconto	4,513	4,544	0.69	135	109
Oconto Falls (1919)	Oconto	2,891	2,889	−0.07	96	35
Omro (1944)[3]	Winnebago	3,517	3,526	0.26	70	116
Onalaska (1887)	La Crosse	17,736	18,159	2.38	1,539	276
Osseo (1941)	Trempealeau	1,701	1,697	−0.24	28	27
Owen (1925)	Clark	940	936	−0.43	11	36
Park Falls (1912)	Price	2,462	2,514	2.11	122	24
Peshtigo (1903)	Marinette	3,502	3,442	−1.71	101	41
Phillips (1891)	Price	1,478	1,447	−2.10	64	22
Pittsville (1887)	Wood	874	877	0.34	16	7
Platteville (1876)[2]	Grant	11,224	12,433	10.77	535	179
Plymouth (1877)[3]	Sheboygan	8,445	8,428	−0.20	213	205
Port Washington (1882)	Ozaukee	10,324	11,439	1.68	811	414
Portage (1854)[3]	Columbia	11,250	10,238	−0.83	457	347
Prairie du Chien (1872)[3]	Crawford	5,911	5,874	−0.63	351	73
Prescott (1857)[3]	Pierce	4,258	4,257	−0.02	137	87
Princeton (1920)	Green Lake	1,214	1,188	−2.14	29	18
Reedsburg (1887)[3]	Sauk	9,200	9,301	1.10	241	393
Rhinelander (1894)[3]	Oneida	7,798	7,645	−1.96	334	104
Rice Lake (1887)[3]	Barron	8,438	8,423	0.05	251	203
Richland Center (1887)	Richland	5,184	5,187	0.06	132	169
Ripon (1858)[3]	Fond du Lac	7,733	7,795	0.80	183	388
St. Croix Falls (1958)[3]	Polk	2,133	2,111	−1.03	45	38
St. Francis (1951)[3]	Milwaukee	9,365	9,465	1.07	656	884
Schofield (1951)	Marathon	2,169	2,165	−0.18	206	39
Seymour (1879)	Outagamie	3,451	3,429	−0.64	156	70
Shawano (1874)[3]	Shawano	9,305	9,234	−0.76	1,438	286
Sheboygan Falls (1913)	Sheboygan	7,775	7,861	1.11	185	197
Shell Lake (1961)	Washburn	1,347	1,359	0.89	29	8
Shullsburg (1889)	Lafayette	1,226	1,222	−0.33	12	29
South Milwaukee (1897)[3]	Milwaukee	21,156	21,142	−0.07	1,100	1,699
Sparta (1883)[3]	Monroe	9,522	9,701	1.88	345	643
Spooner (1909)[3]	Washburn	2,682	2,651	−1.16	120	34
Stanley (1898)	Chippewa, Clark	3,608	3,599	−0.25	683	111
Stoughton (1882)	Dane	12,611	12,641	0.24	554	230
Sturgeon Bay (1883)[3]	Door	9,144	9,155	0.12	315	251
Thorp (1948)	Clark	1,621	1,633	0.74	18	14
Tomah (1883)[3]	Monroe	9,093	9,204	1.22	650	366
Tomahawk (1891)	Lincoln	3,397	3,356	−1.21	93	34
Verona (1977)[3]	Dane	10,619	11,343	6.82	617	258
Viroqua (1885)[3]	Vernon	4,362	4,343	−0.44	107	44
Washburn (1904)[3]	Bayfield	2,117	2,083	−1.61	230	33
Waterloo (1962)	Jefferson	3,333	3,323	−0.30	73	426
Waupaca (1875)[3]	Waupaca	6,069	6,076	0.12	169	139
Waupun (1878)[3]	Dodge, Fond du Lac	11,340	11,502	1.43	1,651	217

WISCONSIN CITIES
January 1, 2014–Continued

		Population[4]				
City (Year Incorporated)[1]	County	2010 Census	2014 Estimate	Percent Change	2010 Nonwhite[5]	2010 Hispanic or Latino Origin[6]
Wautoma (1901)	Waushara	2,218	2,171	−2.12	81	351
Westby (1920)	Vernon	2,200	2,228	1.27	29	22
Weyauwega (1939)	Waupaca	1,900	1,914	0.74	26	115
Whitehall (1941)[3]	Trempealeau	1,558	1,554	−0.26	22	66
Whitewater (1885)[2]	Jefferson, Walworth	14,390	14,913	3.63	1,009	1,372
Wisconsin Dells (1925)	Adams, Columbia, Juneau, Sauk	2,678	2,663	−0.56	108	198

Note: A city is not automatically reclassified based on changes in population but must take action to initiate a reclassification. Under Section 62.05(2), Wisconsin Statutes, to change from one class to another a city must: 1) meet the required population size according to the last federal census; 2) fulfill required governmental changes; and 3) publish a mayoral proclamation.

[1]There are 190 cities in Wisconsin as of January 1, 2014.

[2]One of 10 cities with a city manager.

[3]One of 76 cities with a city administrator holding a full-time or combined position.

[4]Population estimates are based on the corrected totals. Race and ethnicity data have not been adjusted.

[5]In the 2010 U.S. Census, respondents were allowed to choose more than one race. The column "nonwhite" includes all who chose at least one race other than white.

[6]"Hispanic or Latino Origin" represents ethnicity and includes people of Cuban, Mexican, Puerto Rican, South or Central American, or other Spanish culture or origin, regardless of race.

Sources: Wisconsin Department of Administration, Demographic Services Center, *Official Final Estimates, 1/1/2014, Wisconsin Municipalities, with Comparison to Census 2010,* May 2015; League of Wisconsin Municipalities, *2014-2015 Directory of Wisconsin City and Village Officials,* July 2014; and data compiled by Wisconsin Legislative Reference Bureau.

WISCONSIN VILLAGES
January 1, 2014

Village (Year Incorporated)[1]	County	2010 Census	2014 Estimate	Percent Change	2010 Nonwhite	2010 Hispanic or Latino Origin[2]
Adell (1918).	Sheboygan .	516	515	−0.19%	21	18
Albany (1883) .	Green.	1,018	1,005	−1.28	25	24
Allouez (1986)[3] .	Brown .	13,975	13,795	−1.29	1,252	383
Alma Center (1902) .	Jackson.	503	509	1.19	13	32
Almena (1945).	Barron .	677	660	−2.51	23	5
Almond (1905).	Portage .	448	446	−0.45	5	59
Amherst (1899) .	Portage .	1,035	1,048	1.26	9	26
Amherst Junction (1912).	Portage .	377	375	−0.53	0	2
Aniwa (1899) .	Shawano .	260	256	−1.54	1	2
Arena (1923).	Iowa .	834	827	−0.84	14	15
Argyle (1903) .	Lafayette .	857	854	−0.35	4	17
Arlington (1945).	Columbia.	819	822	0.37	18	11
Arpin (1978).	Wood.	333	329	−1.20	10	2
Ashwaubenon (1977)[4] .	Brown .	16,963	16,855	−0.64	1,375	471
Athens (1901) .	Marathon.	1,105	1,105	0.00	13	54
Auburndale (1881).	Wood.	703	706	0.43	0	38
Avoca (1870).	Iowa .	637	630	−1.10	19	12
Bagley (1919).	Grant .	379	378	−0.26	8	2
Baldwin (1875) .	St. Croix .	3,957	3,961	0.10	127	63
Balsam Lake (1905) .	Polk .	1,009	1,012	0.30	56	7
Bangor (1899) .	La Crosse .	1,459	1,480	1.44	30	23
Barneveld (1906) .	Iowa .	1,231	1,232	0.08	22	3
Bay City (1909) .	Pierce.	500	499	−0.20	7	3
Bayside (1953)[4] .	Milwaukee, Ozaukee.	4,389	4,376	−0.30	383	121
Bear Creek (1902) .	Outagamie .	448	450	0.45	5	170
Belgium (1922) .	Ozaukee .	2,245	2,258	0.58	54	117
Bell Center (1901) .	Crawford .	117	117	0.00	2	0
Belleville (1892).	Dane, Green.	2,385	2,375	−0.42	43	90
Bellevue (2003)[3] .	Brown .	14,570	14,760	1.30	970	1,359
Belmont (1894) .	Lafayette .	986	987	0.10	10	7
Benton (1892) .	Lafayette .	973	968	−0.51	14	4
Big Bend (1928) .	Waukesha .	1,290	1,292	0.16	26	30
Big Falls (1925) .	Waupaca .	61	59	−3.28	0	1
Birchwood (1921) .	Washburn .	442	440	−0.45	8	5
Birnamwood (1895) .	Marathon, Shawano .	818	814	−0.49	18	15
Biron (1910) .	Wood.	839	835	−0.48	8	7
Black Creek (1904) .	Outagamie .	1,316	1,320	0.30	36	28
Black Earth (1901)[3] .	Dane.	1,338	1,352	1.05	39	17
Blanchardville (1890) .	Iowa, Lafayette .	825	824	−0.12	6	10
Bloomfield (2011) .	Walworth.	—	4,680	—	—	—
Bloomington (1880) .	Grant .	735	748	1.77	11	8
Blue Mounds (1912) .	Dane.	855	883	3.27	17	11
Blue River (1916) .	Grant .	434	436	0.46	10	8
Boaz (1939) .	Richland .	156	155	−0.64	2	1
Bonduel (1916) .	Shawano .	1,478	1,485	0.47	52	25
Bowler (1923) .	Shawano .	302	294	−2.65	70	10
Boyceville (1922) .	Dunn .	1,086	1,084	−0.18	15	19
Boyd (1891) .	Chippewa .	552	545	−1.27	8	4
Brandon (1881) .	Fond du Lac .	879	865	−1.59	19	44
Bristol (2009)[3] .	Kenosha .	4,914	4,954	0.81	84	118
Brokaw (1903).	Marathon.	251	242	−3.59	5	6
Brooklyn (1905) .	Dane, Green.	1,401	1,415	1.00	51	82
Brown Deer (1955)[4] .	Milwaukee.	11,999	12,157	1.32	4,358	471
Brownsville (1952) .	Dodge .	581	584	0.52	8	3
Browntown (1890).	Green.	280	283	1.07	9	5
Bruce (1901).	Rusk .	779	775	−0.51	7	8
Butler (1913)[3] .	Waukesha .	1,841	1,832	−0.49	105	89
Butternut (1903) .	Ashland .	375	368	−1.87	18	4
Cadott (1895) .	Chippewa .	1,437	1,443	0.42	25	7
Caledonia (2005)[3] .	Racine .	24,705	24,880	0.71	1,563	1,303
Cambria (1866) .	Columbia.	767	765	−0.26	12	93
Cambridge (1891)[3].	Dane, Jefferson.	1,457	1,461	0.27	40	25
Cameron (1894) .	Barron .	1,783	1,809	1.46	41	35
Campbellsport (1902) .	Juneau .	2,016	2,008	−0.40	10	5
Camp Douglas (1893) .	Fond du Lac .	601	609	1.33	32	20
Cascade (1914).	Sheboygan .	709	702	−0.99	6	27
Casco (1920).	Kewaunee .	583	585	0.34	30	44
Cashton (1901).	Monroe .	1,102	1,107	0.45	18	48
Cassville (1882) .	Grant .	947	944	−0.32	11	3
Catawba (1922) .	Price .	110	104	−5.45	0	1
Cazenovia (1902) .	Richland, Sauk.	318	321	0.94	6	5
Cecil (1905) .	Shawano .	570	560	−1.75	31	12
Cedar Grove (1899) .	Sheboygan .	2,113	2,102	−0.52	36	70
Centuria (1904) .	Polk .	948	936	−1.27	37	5
Chaseburg (1922) .	Vernon .	284	287	1.06	5	5
Chenequa (1928)[3] .	Waukesha .	590	587	−0.51	18	6
Clayton (1909).	Polk .	571	570	−0.18	14	12

WISCONSIN VILLAGES
January 1, 2014–Continued

				Population		
Village (Year Incorporated)[1]	County	2010 Census	2014 Estimate	Percent Change	2010 Nonwhite	2010 Hispanic or Latino Origin[2]
Clear Lake (1894)	Polk	1,070	1,064	−0.56	18	30
Cleveland (1958)	Manitowoc	1,485	1,519	2.29	27	129
Clinton (1882)[3]	Rock	2,154	2,119	−1.62	42	173
Clyman (1924)	Dodge	422	420	−0.47	19	20
Cobb (1902)	Iowa	458	463	1.09	7	1
Cochrane (1910)	Buffalo	450	446	−0.89	4	3
Coleman (1903)	Marinette	724	726	0.28	22	23
Colfax (1904)[3]	Dunn	1,158	1,127	−2.68	26	20
Coloma (1939)	Waushara	450	457	1.56	0	4
Combined Locks (1920)[3]	Outagamie	3,328	3,447	3.58	92	66
Conrath (1915)	Rusk	95	95	0.00	9	0
Coon Valley (1907)	Vernon	765	764	−0.13	9	5
Cottage Grove (1924)[3]	Dane	6,192	6,322	2.10	416	185
Couderay (1922)	Sawyer	88	89	1.14	22	1
Crivitz (1974)	Marinette	984	962	−2.24	24	8
Cross Plains (1920)	Dane	3,538	3,596	1.64	83	57
Curtiss (1917)	Clark	216	211	−2.31	1	112
Dallas (1903)	Barron	409	398	−2.69	8	8
Dane (1899)	Dane	995	1,038	4.32	31	43
Darien (1951)	Walworth	1,580	1,588	0.51	33	348
Deerfield (1891)[3]	Dane	2,319	2,413	4.05	1	0
Deer Park (1913)	St. Croix	216	211	−2.31	5	3
DeForest (1891)[5]	Dane	8,936	9,129	2.16	79	76
Denmark (1915)[3]	Brown	2,123	2,144	0.99	467	325
De Soto (1886)	Crawford, Vernon	287	292	1.74	60	52
Dickeyville (1947)	Grant	1,061	1,056	−0.47	4	12
Dorchester (1901)	Clark, Marathon	876	874	−0.23	10	112
Dousman (1917)	Waukesha	2,302	2,327	1.09	64	66
Downing (1909)	Dunn	265	264	−0.38	1	1
Doylestown (1907)	Columbia	297	291	−2.02	3	6
Dresser (1919)	Polk	895	895	0.00	11	17
Eagle (1899)	Waukesha	1,950	1,946	−0.21	17	41
Eastman (1909)	Crawford	428	426	−0.47	107	172
East Troy (1900)	Walworth	4,281	4,282	0.02	5	0
Eden (1912)	Fond du Lac	875	890	1.71	20	41
Edgar (1898)	Marathon	1,479	1,475	−0.27	18	30
Egg Harbor (1964)[3]	Door	201	202	0.50	1	9
Eland (1905)	Shawano	202	199	−1.49	11	5
Elderon (1917)	Marathon	179	178	−0.56	10	7
Eleva (1902)	Trempealeau	670	677	1.04	6	9
Elkhart Lake (1894)[3]	Sheboygan	967	955	−1.24	75	22
Elk Mound (1909)	Dunn	878	878	0.00	13	16
Ellsworth (1887)	Pierce	3,284	3,304	0.61	80	48
Elm Grove (1955)[4]	Waukesha	5,934	5,963	0.49	253	118
Elmwood (1905)	Pierce	817	816	−0.12	8	25
Elmwood Park (1960)	Racine	497	500	0.60	37	25
Embarrass (1895)	Waupaca	404	396	−1.98	11	3
Endeavor (1946)	Marquette	468	462	−1.28	27	21
Ephraim (1919)[3]	Door	288	288	0.00	1	7
Ettrick (1948)	Trempealeau	524	521	−0.57	4	11
Exeland (1920)	Sawyer	196	196	0.00	17	2
Fairchild (1880)	Eau Claire	550	547	−0.55	22	12
Fairwater (1921)	Fond du Lac	371	370	−0.27	6	24
Fall Creek (1906)	Eau Claire	1,315	1,304	−0.84	27	3
Fall River (1903)	Columbia	1,712	1,720	0.47	56	34
Fenwood (1904)	Marathon	152	147	−3.29	0	4
Ferryville (1912)	Crawford	176	179	1.70	1	4
Fontana-on-Geneva Lake (1924)[3]	Walworth	1,672	1,678	0.36	18	35
Footville (1918)	Rock	808	805	−0.37	6	8
Forestville (1960)	Door	430	429	−0.23	8	8
Fox Point (1926)[4]	Milwaukee	6,701	6,676	−0.37	538	162
Francis Creek (1960)	Manitowoc	669	666	−0.45	14	3
Frederic (1903)[3]	Polk	1,137	1,134	−0.26	37	12
Fredonia (1922)	Ozaukee	2,160	2,176	0.74	50	39
Fremont (1882)	Waupaca	679	677	−0.29	7	14
Friendship (1907)	Adams	725	682	−5.93	24	29
Friesland (1946)	Columbia	356	355	−0.28	7	15
Gays Mills (1900)	Crawford	491	505	2.85	13	1
Genoa (1935)	Vernon	253	252	−0.40	7	0
Genoa City (1901)	Kenosha, Walworth	3,042	3,058	0.53	74	199
Germantown (1927)[3]	Washington	19,749	19,891	0.72	1,334	400
Gilman (1914)	Taylor	410	396	−3.41	1	2
Glenbeulah (1913)	Sheboygan	463	461	−0.43	1	0
Glen Flora (1915)	Rusk	92	90	−2.17	2	5
Grafton (1896)[3]	Ozaukee	11,459	11,490	0.27	421	266

WISCONSIN VILLAGES
January 1, 2014–Continued

		Population				
						2010 Hispanic
		2010	2014	Percent	2010	or Latino
Village (Year Incorporated)[1]	County	Census	Estimate	Change	Nonwhite	Origin[2]
Granton (1916).	Clark	355	350	−1.41	4	4
Grantsburg (1887).	Burnett	1,341	1,334	−0.52	65	15
Gratiot (1891).	Lafayette	236	233	−1.27	5	0
Greendale (1939)[4].	Milwaukee	14,046	14,144	0.70	805	667
Gresham (1908)[3].	Shawano	586	584	−0.34	178	19
Hales Corners (1952).	Milwaukee	7,692	7,678	−0.18	311	333
Hammond (1880).	St. Croix	1,922	1,911	−0.57	58	56
Hancock (1902).	Waushara.	417	411	−1.44	6	46
Harrison (2013)[3,5]	Calumet and Outagamie	-	9,844	—	—	—
Hartland (1891)[3]	Waukesha	9,110	9,141	0.34	377	262
Hatley (1912).	Marathon.	574	598	4.18	27	14
Haugen (1918).	Barron	287	283	−1.39	13	5
Hawkins (1922).	Rusk	305	305	0.00	9	0
Hazel Green (1867).	Grant, Lafayette	1,256	1,263	0.56	22	17
Hewitt (1973).	Wood	828	829	0.12	8	8
Highland (1873).	Iowa	842	839	−0.36	19	8
Hilbert (1898).	Calumet	1,132	1,150	1.59	23	89
Hixton (1920).	Jackson.	433	431	−0.46	20	6
Hobart (2003)[3].	Brown	6,182	7,610	23.10	1,261	140
Hollandale (1910).	Iowa.	288	290	0.69	5	0
Holmen (1946)[3].	La Crosse	9,005	9,413	4.53	827	96
Hortonville (1894)[3].	Outagamie.	2,711	2,703	−0.30	69	42
Howard (1959)[3].	Brown, Outagamie.	17,399	18,703	7.49	919	410
Howards Grove (1967).	Sheboygan.	3,188	3,216	0.88	50	28
Hustisford (1870).	Dodge.	1,123	1,120	−0.27	24	33
Hustler (1914).	Juneau	194	195	0.52	4	3
Ingram (1907).	Rusk	78	80	2.56	1	0
Iola (1892).	Waupaca	1,301	1,287	−1.08	13	15
Iron Ridge (1913).	Dodge.	929	933	0.43	12	29
Ironton (1914).	Sauk.	253	248	−1.98	7	4
Jackson (1912)[3].	Washington.	6,753	6,830	1.14	158	147
Johnson Creek (1903)[3].	Jefferson.	2,738	2,873	4.93	94	204
Junction City (1911).	Portage.	439	440	0.23	23	14
Kekoskee (1958).	Dodge	161	158	−1.86	0	3
Kellnersville (1971).	Manitowoc	332	332	0.00	1	0
Kendall (1894).	Monroe.	472	469	−0.64	11	10
Kennan (1903).	Price	135	129	−4.44	0	1
Kewaskum (1895)[3].	Fond du Lac, Washington	4,004	4,015	0.27	88	117
Kimberly (1910).	Outagamie	6,468	6,620	2.35	317	150
Kingston (1923).	Green Lake.	326	326	0.00	1	9
Knapp (1905).	Dunn	463	460	−0.65	10	1
Kohler (1912).	Sheboygan.	2,120	2,117	−0.14	72	49
Kronenwetter (2002)[3]	Marathon.	7,210	7,327	1.62	341	101
La Farge (1899).	Vernon.	746	703	−5.76	20	3
La Valle (1883).	Sauk.	367	358	−2.45	7	8
Lac La Belle (1931)[3].	Jefferson, Waukesha	290	292	0.69	4	1
Lake Delton (1954).	Sauk.	2,914	2,921	0.24	200	447
Lake Hallie (2003).	Chippewa	6,448	6,763	4.89	316	110
Lake Nebagamon (1907).	Douglas	1,069	1,083	1.31	40	8
Lannon (1930).	Waukesha	1,107	1,099	−0.72	28	44
Lena (1921).	Oconto	564	564	0.00	15	10
Lime Ridge (1910).	Sauk.	162	159	−1.85	1	0
Linden (1900).	Iowa	549	546	−0.55	9	6
Little Chute (1899)[3].	Outagamie.	10,449	10,539	0.86	337	327
Livingston (1914).	Grant, Iowa	664	664	0.00	2	0
Loganville (1917).	Sauk.	300	297	−1.00	3	4
Lohrville (1917).	Waushara.	402	399	−0.75	14	16
Lomira (1899).	Dodge.	2,430	2,431	0.04	57	111
Lone Rock (1886).	Richland	888	883	−0.56	24	17
Lowell (1894).	Dodge.	340	336	−1.18	2	5
Lublin (1915).	Taylor.	118	118	0.00	1	1
Luck (1905).	Polk.	1,119	1,086	−2.95	26	19
Luxemburg (1908).	Kewaunee	2,515	2,571	2.23	35	63
Lyndon Station (1903).	Juneau.	500	498	−0.40	8	16
Lynxville (1899).	Crawford.	132	131	−0.76	1	5
Maiden Rock (1887).	Pierce.	119	118	−0.84	4	1
Maple Bluff (1930)[3].	Dane.	1,313	1,303	−0.76	45	19
Marathon City (1884).	Marathon.	1,524	1,530	0.39	26	27
Maribel (1963).	Manitowoc.	351	347	−1.14	3	1
Marquette (1958).	Green Lake.	150	153	2.00	0	2
Marshall (1905)[3].	Dane.	3,862	3,859	−0.08	137	429
Mason (1925).	Bayfield	93	92	−1.08	16	3
Mattoon (1901).	Shawano.	438	432	−1.37	30	70

WISCONSIN VILLAGES
January 1, 2014–Continued

Village (Year Incorporated)[1]	County	2010 Census	2014 Estimate	Percent Change	2010 Nonwhite	2010 Hispanic or Latino Origin[2]
Mazomanie (1885)	Dane	1,652	1,664	0.73	64	39
McFarland (1920)[3]	Dane	7,808	7,902	1.20	365	176
Melrose (1914)	Jackson	503	500	−0.60	7	9
Melvina (1922)	Monroe	104	105	0.96	4	0
Menomonee Falls (1892)[4]	Waukesha	35,626	35,798	0.48	2,789	697
Merrillan (1881)	Jackson	542	535	−1.29	38	37
Merrimac (1899)	Sauk	420	424	0.95	7	13
Merton (1922)	Waukesha	3,346	3,435	2.66	113	72
Milladore (1933)	Portage, Wood	276	280	1.45	3	19
Milltown (1910)	Polk	917	914	−0.33	19	11
Minong (1915)	Washburn	527	522	−0.95	12	32
Mishicot (1950)	Manitowoc	1,442	1,438	−0.28	32	13
Montfort (1893)	Grant, Iowa	718	717	−0.14	6	9
Monticello (1891)	Green	1,217	1,218	0.08	22	24
Mount Calvary (1962)	Fond du Lac	762	571	−25.07	82	83
Mount Hope (1919)	Grant	225	231	2.67	2	17
Mount Horeb (1899)[3]	Dane	7,009	7,088	1.13	231	116
Mount Pleasant (2003)[3]	Racine	26,197	26,386	0.72	2,714	2,181
Mount Sterling (1936)	Crawford	211	210	−0.47	1	0
Mukwonago (1905)[3]	Walworth, Waukesha	7,355	7,507	2.07	164	234
Muscoda (1894)	Grant, Iowa	1,299	1,274	−1.92	14	11
Nashotah (1957)	Waukesha	1,395	1,387	−0.57	46	19
Necedah (1870)	Juneau	916	922	0.66	21	26
Nelson (1978)	Buffalo	374	372	−0.53	5	5
Nelsonville (1913)	Portage	155	151	−2.58	3	2
Neosho (1902)	Dodge	574	571	−0.52	16	4
Neshkoro (1906)	Marquette	434	429	−1.15	8	20
New Auburn (1902)	Barron, Chippewa	548	548	0.00	15	0
Newburg (1973)[3]	Green	1,254	1,247	−0.56	37	57
New Glarus (1901)[3]	Ozaukee, Washington	2,172	2,165	−0.32	17	14
Nichols (1967)	Outagamie	273	268	−1.83	8	5
North Bay (1951)	Racine	241	237	−1.66	11	16
North Fond du Lac (1903)[3]	Fond du Lac	5,014	5,153	2.77	165	214
North Freedom (1893)	Sauk	701	686	−2.14	10	18
North Hudson (1912)[3]	St. Croix	3,768	3,762	−0.16	110	70
North Prairie (1919)	Waukesha	2,141	2,144	0.14	23	43
Norwalk (1894)	Monroe	638	635	−0.47	11	224
Oakdale (1988)	Monroe	297	295	−0.67	5	0
Oakfield (1903)	Fond du Lac	1,075	1,099	2.23	26	19
Oconomowoc Lake (1959)[3]	Waukesha	595	589	−1.01	12	11
Ogdensburg (1912)	Waupaca	185	179	−3.24	7	0
Oliver (1917)	Douglas	399	421	5.51	14	1
Ontario (1890)	Vernon	554	554	0.00	13	82
Oostburg (1909)	Sheboygan	2,887	2,921	1.18	65	94
Oregon (1883)[3]	Dane	9,231	9,420	2.05	344	204
Orfordville (1900)	Rock	1,442	1,449	0.49	23	63
Osceola (1886)[3]	Polk	2,568	2,588	0.78	75	53
Oxford (1912)	Marquette	607	603	−0.66	14	29
Paddock Lake (1960)[3]	Kenosha	2,992	2,993	0.03	70	157
Palmyra (1866)	Jefferson	1,781	1,779	−0.11	28	184
Pardeeville (1894)	Columbia	2,115	2,109	−0.28	48	34
Park Ridge (1938)	Portage	491	496	1.02	42	2
Patch Grove (1921)	Grant	198	199	0.51	0	8
Pepin (1860)	Pepin	837	820	−2.03	9	2
Pewaukee (1876)[3]	Waukesha	8,166	8,154	−0.15	517	286
Pigeon Falls (1956)	Trempealeau	411	413	0.49	3	5
Plain (1912)	Sauk	773	771	−0.26	18	14
Plainfield (1882)	Waushara	862	857	−0.58	16	155
Pleasant Prairie (1989)[3]	Kenosha	19,719	20,155	2.21	1,141	1,332
Plover (1971)[3]	Portage	12,123	12,492	3.04	684	393
Plum City (1909)	Pierce	599	585	−2.34	6	34
Poplar (1917)	Douglas	603	612	1.49	33	0
Port Edwards (1902)[3]	Wood	1,818	1,790	−1.54	75	42
Potosi (1887)	Grant	688	689	0.15	8	4
Potter (1980)	Calumet	253	248	−1.98	4	7
Pound (1914)	Marinette	377	378	0.27	5	27
Poynette (1892)[3]	Columbia	2,528	2,527	−0.04	82	40
Prairie du Sac (1885)[3]	Sauk	3,972	4,023	1.28	105	190
Prairie Farm (1901)	Barron	473	463	−2.11	2	10
Prentice (1899)	Price	660	653	−1.06	15	7
Pulaski (1910)[3]	Brown, Oconto, Shawano	3,539	3,499	−1.13	108	69
Radisson (1953)	Sawyer	241	243	0.83	37	12
Randolph (1870)	Columbia, Dodge	1,811	1,799	−0.66	25	86
Random Lake (1907)	Sheboygan	1,594	1,583	−0.69	39	71
Readstown (1898)	Vernon	415	420	1.20	14	5

WISCONSIN VILLAGES
January 1, 2014–Continued

Village (Year Incorporated)[1]	County	2010 Census	2014 Estimate	Percent Change	2010 Nonwhite	2010 Hispanic or Latino Origin[2]
Redgranite (1904)	Waushara	2,149	2,137	−0.56	448	65
Reedsville (1892)	Manitowoc	1,206	1,201	−0.41	27	94
Reeseville (1899)	Dodge	708	708	0.00	23	19
Rewey (1902)	Iowa	292	290	−0.68	1	0
Rib Lake (1902)	Taylor	910	898	−1.32	11	9
Richfield (2008)[3]	Washington	11,300	11,424	1.10	304	162
Ridgeland (1921)	Dunn	273	271	−0.73	7	0
Ridgeway (1902)	Iowa	653	646	−1.07	1	33
Rio (1887)	Columbia	1,059	1,058	−0.09	20	15
River Hills (1930)	Milwaukee	1,597	1,584	−0.81	254	66
Roberts (1945)	St. Croix	1,651	1,636	−0.91	74	34
Rochester (1912)	Racine	3,682	3,700	0.49	59	103
Rockdale (1914)	Dane	214	211	−1.40	12	3
Rockland (1919)	La Crosse, Monroe	594	614	3.37	2	4
Rock Springs (1894)	Sauk	362	313	−13.54	33	4
Rosendale (1915)	Fond du Lac	1,063	1,049	−1.32	25	32
Rosholt (1907)	Portage	506	498	−1.58	4	16
Rothschild (1917)	Marathon	5,269	5,287	0.34	294	61
Rudolph (1960)	Wood	439	434	−1.14	6	8
St. Cloud (1909)	Fond du Lac	477	468	−1.89	5	13
St. Nazianz (1956)	Manitowoc	783	779	−0.51	14	13
Sauk City (1854)[3]	Sauk	3,410	3,433	0.67	74	170
Saukville (1915)[3]	Ozaukee	4,451	4,466	0.34	132	131
Scandinavia (1894)	Waupaca	363	363	0.00	4	8
Sharon (1892)	Walworth	1,605	1,593	−0.75	28	265
Sheldon (1917)	Rusk	237	233	−1.69	4	13
Sherwood (1968)[1]	Calumet	2,713	2,818	3.87	67	40
Shiocton (1903)	Outagamie	921	928	0.76	17	83
Shorewood (1900)[4]	Milwaukee	13,162	13,183	0.16	1,416	447
Shorewood Hills (1927)[3]	Dane	1,565	1,776	13.48	132	60
Silver Lake (1926)	Kenosha	2,411	2,400	−0.46	51	102
Siren (1948)[3]	Burnett	806	794	−1.49	66	19
Sister Bay (1912)[3]	Door	876	897	2.40	13	27
Slinger (1869)[3]	Washington	5,068	5,140	1.42	117	116
Soldiers Grove (1888)	Crawford	592	572	−3.38	2	3
Solon Springs (1920)	Douglas	600	605	0.83	11	4
Somerset (1915)	St. Croix	2,635	2,646	0.42	107	135
South Wayne (1911)	Lafayette	489	489	0.00	3	2
Spencer (1902)	Marathon	1,925	1,936	0.57	28	38
Spring Green (1869)	Sauk	1,628	1,631	0.18	40	13
Spring Valley (1895)	Pierce, St. Croix	1,352	1,369	1.26	15	18
Star Prairie (1900)	St. Croix	561	550	−1.96	17	9
Stetsonville (1949)	Taylor	541	534	−1.29	4	6
Steuben (1900)	Crawford	131	128	−2.29	1	0
Stockbridge (1908)	Calumet	636	625	−1.73	8	5
Stockholm (1903)	Pepin	66	65	−1.52	0	0
Stoddard (1911)	Vernon	774	786	1.55	7	6
Stratford (1910)	Marathon	1,578	1,591	0.82	16	25
Strum (1948)	Trempealeau	1,114	1,124	0.90	8	74
Sturtevant (1907)[3]	Racine	6,970	6,993	0.33	1,333	424
Suamico (2003)[3]	Brown	11,346	11,593	2.18	242	112
Sullivan (1915)	Jefferson	669	670	0.15	9	11
Summit (2010)[3]	Waukesha	4,674	4,713	0.83	-	-
Superior (1949)	Douglas	664	668	0.60	16	7
Suring (1914)	Oconto	544	543	−0.18	44	9
Sussex (1924)[3]	Waukesha	10,518	10,669	1.44	431	249
Taylor (1919)	Jackson	476	481	1.05	6	16
Tennyson (1940)	Grant	355	363	2.25	2	0
Theresa (1898)	Dodge	1,262	1,254	−0.63	21	22
Thiensville (1910)	Ozaukee	3,235	3,222	−0.40	189	90
Tigerton (1896)	Shawano	741	732	−1.21	44	14
Tony (1911)	Rusk	113	112	−0.88	8	1
Trempealeau (1867)[3]	Trempealeau	1,529	1,612	5.43	22	21
Turtle Lake (1898)	Barron, Polk	1,050	1,039	−1.05	75	18
Twin Lakes (1937)[3]	Kenosha	5,989	6,041	0.87	126	283
Union Center (1913)	Juneau	200	198	−1.00	3	1
Union Grove (1893)	Racine	4,915	4,899	−0.33	132	158
Unity (1903)	Clark, Marathon	343	337	−1.75	1	5
Valders (1919)	Manitowoc	962	957	−0.52	5	61
Vesper (1948)	Wood	584	585	0.17	18	6
Viola (1899)	Richland, Vernon	699	701	0.29	9	4
Waldo (1922)	Sheboygan	503	495	−1.59	31	12
Wales (1922)	Waukesha	2,549	2,544	−0.20	43	46
Walworth (1901)	Walworth	2,816	2,821	0.18	56	502

WISCONSIN VILLAGES
January 1, 2014–Continued

Village (Year Incorporated)[1]	County	2010 Census	2014 Estimate	Percent Change	2010 Nonwhite	2010 Hispanic or Latino Origin[2]
Warrens (1973).	Monroe.	363	360	−0.83	18	3
Waterford (1906)[3]	Racine	5,368	5,366	−0.04	105	159
Waunakee (1893)[3]	Dane	12,097	12,622	4.34	416	269
Wausaukee (1924)	Marinette.	575	572	−0.52	20	16
Wauzeka (1890)	Crawford.	711	698	−1.83	22	13
Webster (1916).	Burnett.	653	652	−0.15	57	13
West Baraboo (1956)	Sauk	1,414	1,406	−0.57	77	70
Westfield (1902)	Marquette	1,254	1,259	0.40	665	1,068
West Milwaukee (1906)[3].	Milwaukee	4,206	4,197	−0.21	139	59
Weston (1996)[3].	Marathon.	14,868	15,090	1.49	32	46
West Salem (1893).	La Crosse	4,799	4,938	2.90	1,670	301
Weyerhaeuser (1906)	Rusk	238	228	−4.20	2	3
Wheeler (1922)	Dunn	348	353	1.44	12	5
Whitefish Bay (1892)[4]	Milwaukee	14,110	14,105	−0.04	12	9
White Lake (1926).	Langlade	363	363	0.00	1,060	399
Whitelaw (1958).	Manitowoc.	757	755	−0.26	18	20
Whiting (1947).	Portage.	1,724	1,688	−2.09	53	45
Wild Rose (1904)	Waushara.	725	712	−1.79	12	35
Williams Bay (1919)[3]	Walworth.	2,564	2,577	0.51	58	167
Wilson (1911)	St. Croix	184	180	−2.17	4	1
Wilton (1890)	Monroe.	504	501	−0.60	12	37
Wind Point (1954)	Racine	1,723	1,707	−0.93	69	40
Winneconne (1887)[3]	Winnebago.	2,383	2,397	0.59	40	32
Winter (1973)	Sawyer.	313	317	1.28	16	16
Withee (1901)	Clark.	487	479	−1.64	5	11
Wittenberg (1893)	Shawano	1,081	1,037	−4.07	53	77
Wonewoc (1878).	Juneau	816	811	−0.61	13	11
Woodman (1917).	Grant.	132	130	−1.52	8	4
Woodville (1911)	St. Croix	1,344	1,344	0.00	34	31
Wrightstown (1901)[3].	Brown, Outagamie.	2,827	2,842	0.53	91	123
Wyeville (1923)	Monroe.	147	141	−4.08	4	2
Wyocena (1909)[3].	Columbia.	768	758	−1.30	10	15
Yuba (1935)	Richland	74	69	−6.76	0	0

[1]There are 407 villages in Wisconsin as of October 2014.

[2]"Hispanic or Latino Origin" represents ethnicity and includes people of Cuban, Mexican, Puerto Rican, South or Central American, or other Spanish culture or origin, regardless of race.

[3]One of 77 villages with an administrator, holding either a full-time or combination position.

[4]One of 9 villages operating under the manager form of government, holding either a full-time or combination position.

[5]The Town of Harrison became a village on March 8, 2013. Data is not available for 2010 Census, Percent Change, 2010 Nonwhite, and 2010 Hispanic or Latino Origin.

Sources: Wisconsin Department of Administration, Demographic Services Center, *Official Final Estimates, 1/1/2014, Wisconsin Municipalities, with Comparison to Census 2010,* May 2015; *2014-2015 Directory of Wisconsin City and Village Officials,* July 2014.

WISCONSIN CITIES AND VILLAGES
OVER 10,000 POPULATION

City or Village (County)	Census	2014 Estimate	Percent Change	2014 Rank	2010 Nonwhite	2010 Hispanic or Latino Origin[2]
Cities						
Appleton (Calumet, Outagamie, Winnebago)	72,623	73,463	1.2%	6	7,124	3,643
Baraboo (Sauk)	12,048	11,985	−0.5	71	487	446
Beaver Dam (Dodge)	16,214	16,572	2.2	48	502	1,210
Beloit (Rock).	36,966	36,805	−0.4	19	7,149	6,332
Brookfield (Waukesha)	37,920	37,847	−0.2	18	3,545	853
Burlington (Racine, Walworth)	10,464	10,511	0.5	84	327	898
Cedarburg (Ozaukee)	11,412	11,479	0.6	76	367	197
Chippewa Falls (Chippewa)	13,661	13,685	0.2	61	605	221
Cudahy (Milwaukee)	18,267	18,224	−0.2	44	1,142	1,769
De Pere (Brown)	23,800	24,180	1.6	34	1,207	511
Eau Claire (Chippewa, Eau Claire)	65,931	66,834	1.4	8	5,116	1,268
Fitchburg (Dane).	25,260	26,090	3.3	30	4,464	4,341
Fond du Lac (Fond du Lac)	43,021	43,151	0.3	15	2,695	2,742
Fort Atkinson (Jefferson)	12,368	12,364	−0.0	69	315	1,128
Franklin (Milwaukee)	35,451	35,702	0.7	22	4,168	1,592
Glendale (Milwaukee)	12,872	12,773	−0.8	64	2,499	465
Green Bay (Brown)	104,057	104,710	0.6	3	13,912	13,896
Greenfield (Milwaukee)	36,720	36,687	−0.1	20	3,043	3,087
Hartford (Dodge, Washington).	14,223	14,320	0.7	56	425	686
Hudson (St. Croix).	12,719	13,326	4.8	62	539	347
Janesville (Rock).	63,575	63,525	−0.1	10	3,689	3,421
Kaukauna (Outagamie)	15,462	15,765	2.0	51	654	407
Kenosha (Kenosha)	99,218	99,680	0.5	4	14,121	16,130
La Crosse (La Crosse)	51,320	52,018	1.4	12	4,885	1,012
Madison (Dane)	233,209	240,153	3.0	2	40,798	15,948
Manitowoc (Manitowoc)	33,736	33,649	−0.3	24	2,486	1,695
Marinette (Marinette)	10,968	10,930	−0.4	80	271	149
Marshfield (Marathon, Wood)	19,118	19,144	0.1	40	796	452
Menasha (Calumet, Winnebago).	17,353	17,550	1.1	46	954	1,204
Menomonie (Dunn)	16,264	16,002	−1.6	50	1,176	276
Mequon (Ozaukee).	23,132	23,387	1.1	36	1,760	467
Middleton (Dane)	17,442	18,323	5.1	43	1,764	984
Milwaukee (Milwaukee, Washington, Waukesha). . . .	594,833	595,993	0.2	1	271,607	103,007
Monroe (Green)	10,827	10,751	−0.7	81	252	526
Muskego (Waukesha)	24,135	24,304	0.7	33	529	545
Neenah (Winnebago)	25,501	25,833	1.3	31	1,163	967
New Berlin (Waukesha)	39,584	40,130	1.4	16	2,256	1,036
Oak Creek (Milwaukee)	34,451	34,707	0.7	23	3,282	2,582
Oconomowoc (Waukesha).	15,759	16,293	3.4	49	422	559
Onalaska (La Crosse)	17,736	18,159	2.4	45	1,539	276
Oshkosh (Winnebago)	66,083	66,412	0.5	9	5,539	1,770
Pewaukee (Waukesha)	13,195	13,728	4.0	60	667	281
Platteville (Grant)	11,224	12,433	10.8	68	535	179
Port Washington (Ozaukee)	11,250	11,439	1.7	77	457	347
Portage (Columbia)	10,324	10,238	−0.8	85	811	414
Racine (Racine)	78,860	78,479	−0.5	5	20,362	16,309
River Falls (Pierce, St. Croix)	15,000	15,053	0.4	53	673	270
Sheboygan (Sheboygan).	49,288	48,897	−0.8	13	6,314	4,866
South Milwaukee (Milwaukee)	21,156	21,142	−0.1	37	1,100	1,699
Stevens Point (Portage)	26,717	27,040	1.2	28	1,946	696
Stoughton (Dane)	12,611	12,641	0.2	65	554	230
Sun Prairie (Dane)	29,364	31,213	6.3	26	3,749	1,253
Superior (Douglas)	27,244	27,146	−0.4	27	2,166	382
Two Rivers (Manitowoc)	11,712	11,628	−0.7	72	536	224
Verona (Dane)	10,619	11,343	6.8	79	617	258
Watertown (Dodge, Jefferson)	23,861	23,911	0.2	35	706	1,731
Waukesha (Waukesha).	70,718	71,044	0.5	7	5,321	8,529
Waupun (Dodge, Fond du Lac)	11,340	11,502	1.4	74	1,651	217
Wausau (Marathon)	39,106	39,131	0.1	17	5,891	1,149
Wauwatosa (Milwaukee).	46,396	46,766	0.8	14	4,361	1,450
West Allis (Milwaukee)	60,411	60,272	−0.2	11	5,094	5,770
West Bend (Washington).	31,078	31,531	1.5	25	1,049	1,213
Whitewater (Jefferson, Walworth)	14,390	14,913	3.6	54	1,009	1,372
Wisconsin Rapids (Wood)	18,367	18,559	1.1	42	1,186	535

WISCONSIN CITIES AND VILLAGES
OVER 10,000 POPULATION–Continued

City or Village (County)	Census	2014 Estimate	Percent Change	2014 Rank	2010 Nonwhite	2010 Hispanic or Latino Origin[2]
Villages						
Allouez (Brown)	13,975	13,795	−1.3	59	1,252	383
Ashwaubenon (Brown)	16,963	16,855	−0.6	47	1,375	471
Bellevue (Brown)	14,570	14,760	1.3	55	970	1,359
Brown Deer (Milwaukee)	11,999	12,157	1.3	70	4,358	471
Caledonia (Racine)	24,705	24,880	0.7	32	1,563	1,303
Germantown (Washington)	19,749	19,891	0.7	39	1,334	400
Grafton (Ozaukee)	11,459	11,490	0.3	75	421	266
Greendale (Milwaukee)	14,046	14,144	0.7	57	805	667
Howard (Brown, Outagamie)	17,399	18,703	7.5	41	919	410
Little Chute (Outagamie)	10,449	10,539	0.9	83	337	327
Menomonee Falls (Waukesha)	35,626	35,798	0.5	21	2,789	697
Mount Pleasant (Racine)	26,197	26,386	0.7	29	2,714	2,181
Pleasant Prairie (Kenosha)	19,719	20,155	2.2	38	1,141	1,332
Plover (Portage)	12,123	12,492	3.0	67	684	393
Richfield (Washington)	11,300	11,424	1.1	78	463	158
Shorewood (Milwaukee)	13,162	13,183	0.2	63	1,416	447
Suamico (Brown)	11,346	11,593	2.2	73	242	112
Sussex (Waukesha)	10,518	10,669	1.4	82	431	249
Waunakee (Dane)	12,097	12,622	4.3	66	416	269
Weston (Marathon)	14,868	15,090	1.5	52	1,670	301
Whitefish Bay (Milwaukee)	14,110	14,105	−0.0	58	1,060	399

[1]Race and ethnicity data have not been adjusted since the 2010 Census. Population estimates are based on the corrected 2010 Census totals.

[2]"Hispanic or Latino Origin" represents ethnicity and includes people of Cuban, Mexican, Puerto Rican, South or Central American, or other Spanish culture or origin, regardless of race.

Source: Wisconsin Department of Administration, Demographic Services Center, *Official Final Estimates, 1/1/2014, Wisconsin Municipalities, with Comparison to Census 2010,* April 2015.

WISCONSIN TOWNS OVER 2,500 POPULATION
2014 Estimate and 2010 U.S. Census

Town (County)	2014 Estimate	2010 Census	Percent Change	Town (County)	2014 Estimate	2010 Census	Percent Change
Addison (Washington)	3,469	3,495	−0.7%	Menomonie (Dunn)	3,424	3,366	1.7%
Alden (Polk)	2,802	2,786	0.6	Merrill (Lincoln)	2,993	2,980	0.4
Algoma (Winnebago)	6,884	6,822	0.9	Merton (Waukesha)	8,383	8,338	0.5
Arbor Vitae (Vilas)	3,324	3,316	0.2	Middleton (Dane)	6,143	5,877	4.5
Ashippun (Dodge)	2,571	2,559	0.5	Milton (Rock)	2,939	2,923	0.6
Barton (Washington)	2,632	2,637	−0.2	Minocqua (Oneida)	4,486	4,453	0.7
Beaver Dam (Dodge)	3,992	3,962	0.8	Mukwa (Waupaca)	2,956	2,930	0.9
Beloit (Rock)	7,626	7,662	−0.5	Mukwonago (Waukesha)	8,010	7,959	0.6
Bristol (Dane)	3,970	3,765	5.4	Neenah (Winnebago)	3,435	3,237	6.1
Brockway (Jackson)	2,830	2,828	0.1	Newbold (Oneida)	2,735	2,719	0.6
Brookfield (Waukesha)	6,064	6,116	−0.9	Norway (Racine)	7,964	7,948	0.2
Buchanan (Outagamie)	6,920	6,755	2.4	Oakland (Jefferson)	3,088	3,100	−0.4
Burke (Dane)	3,329	3,284	1.4	Oconomowoc (Waukesha)	8,602	8,408	2.3
Burlington (Racine)	6,456	6,502	−0.7	Onalaska (La Crosse)	5,704	5,623	1.4
Campbell (La Crosse)	4,339	4,314	0.6	Oneida (Outagamie)	4,695	4,678	0.4
Cedarburg (Ozaukee)	5,843	5,760	1.4	Oregon (Dane)	3,214	3,184	0.9
Center (Outagamie)	3,430	3,402	0.8	Osceola (Polk)	2,864	2,855	0.3
Chase (Oconto)	3,064	3,005	2.0	Ottawa (Waukesha)	3,876	3,859	0.4
Clayton (Winnebago)	4,016	3,951	1.7	Pacific (Columbia)	2,706	2,707	−0.0
Cottage Grove (Dane)	3,887	3,875	0.3	Pelican (Oneida)	2,799	2,764	1.3
Dale (Outagamie)	2,768	2,731	1.4	Peshtigo (Marinette)	4,084	4,057	0.7
Dayton (Waupaca)	2,757	2,748	0.3	Pine Lake (Oneida)	2,759	2,740	0.7
Delafield (Waukesha)	8,221	8,400	−2.1	Pittsfield (Brown)	2,634	2,608	1.0
Delavan (Walworth)	5,267	5,285	−0.3	Pleasant Springs (Dane)	3,180	3,154	0.8
Dover (Racine)	4,031	4,051	−0.5	Pleasant Valley (Eau Claire)	3,159	3,044	3.8
Dunn (Dane)	4,943	4,931	0.2	Plymouth (Sheboygan)	3,193	3,195	−0.1
Eagle (Waukesha)	3,507	3,507	0.0	Polk (Washington)	3,973	3,937	0.9
Eagle Point (Chippewa)	3,101	3,053	1.6	Randall (Kenosha)	3,173	3,180	−0.2
East Troy (Walworth)	4,041	4,021	0.5	Raymond (Racine)	3,917	3,870	1.2
Ellington (Outagamie)	2,845	2,758	3.2	Rib Mountain (Marathon)	6,884	6,825	0.9
Empire (Fond du Lac)	2,811	2,797	0.5	Rice Lake (Barron)	3,083	3,060	0.8
Erin (Washington)	3,767	3,747	0.5	Richmond (St. Croix)	3,375	3,272	3.2
Farmington (Washington)	4,027	4,014	0.3	Rock (Rock)	3,189	3,196	−0.2
Farmington (Waupaca)	4,009	3,974	0.9	Rome (Adams)	2,758	2,720	1.4
Fond du Lac (Fond du Lac)	3,409	3,015	13.1	St. Joseph (St. Croix)	3,863	3,842	0.6
Freedom (Outagamie)	5,968	5,842	2.2	Salem (Kenosha)	12,058	12,067	−0.1
Friendship (Fond du Lac)	2,692	2,675	0.6	Saratoga (Wood)	5,170	5,142	0.5
Fulton (Rock)	3,263	3,252	0.3	Scott (Brown)	3,575	3,545	0.9
Genesee (Waukesha)	7,330	7,340	−0.1	Sevastopol (Door)	2,662	2,628	1.3
Geneva (Walworth)	5,012	4,993	0.4	Seymour (Eau Claire)	3,265	3,209	1.8
Grafton (Ozaukee)	4,102	4,053	1.2	Sheboygan (Sheboygan)	7,407	7,271	1.9
Grand Chute (Outagamie)	21,767	20,919	4.1	Shelby (La Crosse)	4,707	4,715	−0.2
Grand Rapids (Wood)	7,691	7,646	0.6	Somers (Kenosha)	9,512	9,597	−0.9
Greenbush (Sheboygan)	2,561	2,565	−0.2	Somerset (St. Croix)	4,103	4,036	1.7
Greenville (Outagamie)	10,857	10,309	5.3	Sparta (Monroe)	3,167	3,128	1.3
Harmony (Rock)	2,575	2,569	0.2	Springfield (Dane)	2,772	2,734	1.4
Hartford (Washington)	3,597	3,609	−0.3	Stanley (Barron)	2,564	2,546	0.7
Hayward (Sawyer)	3,568	3,567	0.0	Star Prairie (St. Croix)	3,522	3,504	0.5
Holland (La Crosse)	3,895	3,701	5.2	Stephenson (Marinette)	3,063	3,006	1.9
Hudson (St. Croix)	8,547	8,461	1.0	Stettin (Marathon)	2,553	2,554	−0.0
Hull (Portage)	5,376	5,346	0.6	Stockton (Portage)	2,970	2,917	1.8
Ixonia (Jefferson)	4,618	4,385	5.3	Sugar Creek (Walworth)	3,936	3,943	−0.2
Jackson (Washington)	4,296	4,134	3.9	Taycheedah (Fond du Lac)	4,373	4,205	4.0
Janesville (Rock)	3,439	3,434	0.2	Trenton (Washington)	4,739	4,732	0.2
Koshkonong (Jefferson)	3,689	3,692	−0.1	Troy (St. Croix)	4,847	4,705	3.0
Lac du Flambeau (Vilas)	3,457	3,441	0.5	Union (Eau Claire)	2,739	2,663	2.9
Lafayette (Chippewa)	5,850	5,765	1.5	Vernon (Waukesha)	7,624	7,601	0.3
Lawrence (Brown)	4,634	4,284	8.2	Washington (Eau Claire)	7,223	7,134	1.3
Ledgeview (Brown)	7,337	6,555	11.9	Waterford (Racine)	6,345	6,344	0.0
Lima (Sheboygan)	2,985	2,982	0.1	Waukesha (Waukesha)	9,168	9,133	0.4
Lisbon (Waukesha)	10,236	10,157	0.8	Wescott (Shawano)	3,202	3,183	0.6
Little Suamico (Oconto)	4,963	4,799	3.4	West Bend (Washington)	4,775	4,774	0.0
Lodi (Columbia)	3,292	3,273	0.6	Westport (Dane)	3,976	3,950	0.7
Lyons (Walworth)	3,697	3,698	−0.0	Wheatland (Kenosha)	3,336	3,373	−1.1
Madison (Dane)	6,289	6,279	0.2	Wheaton (Chippewa)	2,737	2,701	1.3
Medford (Taylor)	2,639	2,606	1.3	Wilson (Sheboygan)	3,357	3,330	0.8
Menasha (Winnebago)	18,624	18,498	0.7	Windsor (Dane)	6,686	6,345	5.4
Menominee (Menominee)	4,236	4,232	0.1	Yorkville (Racine)	3,090	3,071	0.6

Source: Wisconsin Department of Administration, Demographic Services Center, *Official Final Estimates, 1/1/2014, Wisconsin Municipalities, with Comparison to Census 2010*, March 2015.

WISCONSIN POPULATION
BY COUNTY AND MUNCIPALITY
April 1, 2010 and January 1, 2014

County and Municipality	2010 Census	2014 Estimate	Percent Change
ADAMS COUNTY	20,875	20,844	–0.15%
Adams, city	1,967	1,942	–1.27
Adams, town	1,345	1,350	0.37
Big Flats, town	1,018	1,031	1.28
Colburn, town	223	228	2.24
Dell Prairie, town	1,590	1,623	2.08
Easton, town	1,130	1,134	0.35
Friendship, village	725	682	–5.93
Jackson, town	1,003	1,004	0.10
Leola, town	308	306	–0.65
Lincoln, town	296	291	–1.69
Monroe, town	398	408	2.51
New Chester, town	2,254	2,154	–4.44
New Haven, town	655	660	0.76
Preston, town	1,393	1,401	0.57
Quincy, town	1,163	1,170	0.60
Richfield, town	158	156	–1.27
Rome, town	2,720	2,758	1.40
Springville, town	1,318	1,323	0.38
Strongs Prairie, town	1,150	1,163	1.13
Wisconsin Dells (part), city	61	60	–1.64
ASHLAND COUNTY	16,157	16,071	–0.53
Agenda, town	422	419	–0.71
Ashland (part), city	8,216	8,135	–0.99
Ashland, town	594	585	–1.52
Butternut, village	375	368	–1.87
Chippewa, town	374	374	0.00
Gingles, town	778	784	0.77
Gordon, town	283	288	1.77
Jacobs, town	722	713	–1.25
La Pointe, town	261	267	2.30
Marengo, town	390	395	1.28
Mellen, city	731	718	–1.78
Morse, town	493	494	0.20
Peeksville, town	141	142	0.71
Sanborn, town	1,331	1,326	–0.38
Shanagolden, town	125	125	0.00
White River, town	921	938	1.85
BARRON COUNTY	45,870	46,020	0.33
Almena, town	858	849	–1.05
Almena, village	677	660	–2.51
Arland, town	789	822	4.18
Barron, city	3,423	3,404	–0.56
Barron, town	873	871	–0.23
Bear Lake, town	659	660	0.15
Cameron, village	1,783	1,809	1.46
Cedar Lake, town	948	971	2.43
Chetek, city	2,221	2,226	0.23
Chetek, town	1,644	1,656	0.73
Clinton, town	879	882	0.34
Crystal Lake, town	757	761	0.53
Cumberland, city	2,170	2,169	–0.05
Cumberland, town	876	870	–0.68
Dallas, town	565	568	0.53
Dallas, village	409	398	–2.69
Dovre, town	849	857	0.94
Doyle, town	453	461	1.77
Haugen, village	287	283	–1.39
Lakeland, town	975	986	1.13
Maple Grove, town	979	983	0.41
Maple Plain, town	803	816	1.62
New Auburn (part), village	20	28	40.00
Oak Grove, town	948	954	0.63
Prairie Farm, town	573	579	1.05
Prairie Farm, village	473	463	–2.11
Prairie Lake, town	1,532	1,540	0.52
Rice Lake, city	8,419	8,423	0.05
Rice Lake, town	3,060	3,083	0.75
Sioux Creek, town	655	648	–1.07
Stanfold, town	719	722	0.42
Stanley, town	2,546	2,564	0.71
Sumner, town	798	814	2.01
Turtle Lake, town	624	628	0.64
Turtle Lake (part), village	957	948	–0.94
Vance Creek, town	669	664	–0.75
BAYFIELD COUNTY	15,014	15,059	0.30
Ashland (part), city	0	0	0.00

County and Municipality	2010 Census	2014 Estimate	Percent Change
Barksdale, town	723	717	–0.83
Barnes, town	769	769	0.00
Bayfield, city	487	480	–1.44
Bayfield, town	680	691	1.62
Bayview, town	487	491	0.82
Bell, town	263	268	1.90
Cable, town	825	821	–0.48
Clover, town	223	220	–1.35
Delta, town	273	276	1.10
Drummond, town	463	426	–7.99
Eileen, town	681	685	0.59
Grand View, town	468	471	0.64
Hughes, town	383	385	0.52
Iron River, town	1,123	1,149	2.32
Kelly, town	463	470	1.51
Keystone, town	378	372	–1.59
Lincoln, town	287	286	–0.35
Mason, town	315	317	0.63
Mason, village	93	92	–1.08
Namakagon, town	246	249	1.22
Orienta, town	122	122	0.00
Oulu, town	527	525	–0.38
Pilsen, town	210	215	2.38
Port Wing, town	368	373	1.36
Russell, town	1,279	1,339	4.69
Tripp, town	231	239	3.46
Washburn, city	2,117	2,083	–1.61
Washburn, town	530	528	–0.38
BROWN COUNTY	248,007	253,156	2.08
Allouez, village	13,975	13,795	–1.29
Ashwaubenon, village	16,963	16,855	–0.64
Bellevue, village	14,570	14,760	1.30
De Pere, city	23,800	24,180	1.60
Denmark, village	2,123	2,144	0.99
Eaton, town	1,508	1,532	1.59
Glenmore, town	1,135	1,114	–1.85
Green Bay, city	104,057	104,710	0.63
Green Bay, town	2,035	2,045	0.49
Hobart, village	6,182	7,610	23.10
Holland, town	1,519	1,528	0.59
Howard (part), village	17,399	18,703	7.49
Humboldt, town	1,311	1,303	–0.61
Lawrence, town	4,284	4,634	8.17
Ledgeview, town	6,555	7,337	11.93
Morrison, town	1,599	1,591	–0.50
New Denmark, town	1,541	1,556	0.97
Pittsfield, town	2,608	2,634	1.00
Pulaski (part), village	3,321	3,282	–1.17
Rockland, town	1,734	1,753	1.10
Scott, town	3,545	3,575	0.85
Suamico, village	11,346	11,593	2.18
Wrightstown, town	2,221	2,232	0.50
Wrightstown (part), village	2,676	2,690	0.52
BUFFALO COUNTY	13,587	13,594	0.05
Alma, city	781	804	2.94
Alma, town	297	298	0.34
Belvidere, town	396	395	–0.25
Buffalo, town	705	698	–0.99
Buffalo City, city	1,023	1,088	–1.47
Canton, town	305	310	1.64
Cochrane, village	450	446	–0.89
Cross, town	377	381	1.06
Dover, town	486	482	–0.82
Fountain City, city	859	839	–2.33
Gilmanton, town	426	435	2.11
Glencoe, town	485	482	–0.62
Lincoln, town	162	167	3.09
Maxville, town	309	305	–1.29
Milton, town	534	548	2.62
Modena, town	354	357	0.85
Mondovi, city	2,777	2,773	–0.14
Mondovi, town	469	467	–0.43
Montana, town	284	283	–0.35
Naples, town	691	696	0.72
Nelson, town	571	590	3.33
Nelson, village	374	372	–0.53
Waumandee, town	472	458	–2.97

WISCONSIN POPULATION
BY COUNTY AND MUNCIPALITY
April 1, 2010 and January 1, 2014–Continued

County and Municipality	2010 Census	2014 Estimate	Percent Change	County and Municipality	2010 Census	2014 Estimate	Percent Change
BURNETT COUNTY	15,457	15,462	0.03	Wheaton, town.	2,701	2,737	1.33
Anderson, town	398	397	−0.25	Woodmohr, town.	932	951	2.04
Blaine, town	197	195	−1.02				
Daniels, town	649	646	−0.46	CLARK COUNTY	34,690	34,697	0.02
Dewey, town	516	511	−0.97	Abbotsford (part), city . . .	1,616	1,606	−0.62
Grantsburg, town.	1,136	1,137	0.09	Beaver, town	885	892	0.79
Grantsburg, village.	1,341	1,134	−0.52	Butler, town	96	94	−2.08
Jackson, town	773	780	0.91	Colby (part), city.	1,354	1,332	−1.62
La Follette, town.	536	531	−0.93	Colby, town	874	885	1.26
Lincoln, town	309	307	−0.65	Curtiss, village	216	211	−2.31
Meenon, town	1,163	1,152	−0.95	Dewhurst, town	323	327	1.24
Oakland, town	827	840	1.57	Dorchester (part), village .	871	869	−0.23
Roosevelt, town	199	199	0.00	Eaton, town	712	710	−0.28
Rusk, town	409	411	0.49	Foster, town	95	95	0.00
Sand Lake, town	531	536	0.94	Fremont, town	1,265	1,256	−0.71
Scott	494	504	2.02	Grant, town	916	926	1.09
Siren, town.	936	944	0.85	Granton, village	355	350	−1.41
Siren, village.	806	794	−1.49	Green Grove, town.	756	756	0.00
Swiss, town	790	791	0.13	Greenwood, city	1,026	1,014	−1.17
Trade Lake, town	823	828	0.61	Hendren, town	499	499	0.00
Union, town	340	342	0.59	Hewett, town	293	293	0.00
Webb Lake, town	311	313	0.64	Hixon, town	808	815	0.87
Webster, village	653	652	−0.15	Hoard, town	841	828	−1.55
West Marshland, town . . .	367	367	0.00	Levis, town.	492	493	0.20
Wood River, town	953	951	−0.21	Longwood, town	858	862	0.47
				Loyal, city	1,261	1,253	−0.63
CALUMET COUNTY.	48,971	49,715	1.52	Loyal, town	826	828	0.24
Appleton (part), city	11,088	11,195	0.97	Lynn, town	861	868	0.81
Brillion, city	3,148	3,191	1.37	Mayville, town.	961	955	−0.62
Brillion, town	1,486	1,496	0.67	Mead, town	321	328	2.18
Brothertown, town	1,329	1,322	−0.53	Mentor, town	584	586	0.34
Charlestown, town	775	780	0.65	Neillsville, city.	2,463	2,430	−1.34
Chilton, city	3,933	3,927	−0.15	Owen, city	940	936	−0.43
Chilton, town.	1,143	1,139	−0.35	Pine Valley, town.	1,157	1,162	0.43
Harrison, town	10,839	1,286	−88.14	Reseburg, town.	776	785	1.16
*Harrison, village	0	9,844	0.00	Seif, town	172	169	−1.74
Hilbert, village	1,132	1,150	1.59	Sherman, town	882	899	1.93
Kaukauna (part), city . . .	0	0	0.00	Sherwood, town	220	224	1.82
Kiel (part), city.	309	317	2.59	Stanley (part), city	6	6	0.00
Menasha (part), city	2,209	2,440	10.46	Thorp, city	1,621	1,633	0.74
New Holstein, city	3,236	3,188	−1.48	Thorp, town	808	823	1.86
New Holstein, town	1,508	1,510	0.13	Unity, town.	878	901	2.62
Potter, village	253	248	−1.98	Unity (part), village	139	136	−2.16
Rantoul, town	798	795	−0.38	Warner, town	669	672	0.45
Sherwood, village	2,713	2,818	3.87	Washburn, town	290	291	0.34
Stockbridge, town	1,456	1,472	1.10	Weston, town.	699	695	−0.57
Stockbridge, village	636	625	−1.73	Withee, town.	966	971	0.52
Woodville, town	980	972	−0.82	Withee, village.	487	479	−1.64
				Worden, town	666	674	1.20
CHIPPEWA COUNTY	62,415	63,038	1.00	York, town	886	880	−0.68
Anson, town	2,076	2,100	1.16				
Arthur, town	759	766	0.92	COLUMBIA COUNTY	56,833	56,795	−0.07
Auburn, town	697	695	−0.29	Arlington, town	806	800	−0.74
Birch Creek, town	517	518	0.19	Arlington, village	819	822	0.37
Bloomer, city.	3,539	3,550	0.31	Caledonia, town	1,378	1,396	1.31
Bloomer, town	1,050	1,057	0.67	Cambria, village	767	765	−0.26
Boyd, village.	552	545	−1.27	Columbus (part), city . . .	4,991	5,021	0.60
Cadott, village	1,437	1,443	0.42	Columbus, town	646	642	−0.62
Chippewa Falls, city	13,661	13,685	0.18	Courtland, town	525	531	1.14
Cleveland, town	864	864	0.00	Dekorra, town	2,311	2,312	0.04
Colburn, town	856	874	2.10	Doylestown, village	297	291	−2.02
Cooks Valley, town	805	820	1.86	Fall River, village	1,712	1,720	0.47
Cornell, city	1,467	1,472	0.34	Fort Winnebago, town . . .	825	819	−0.73
Delmar, town.	936	944	0.85	Fountain Prairie, town . . .	887	889	0.23
Eagle Point, town	3,053	3,101	1.57	Friesland, village.	356	355	−0.28
Eau Claire (part), city . . .	1,981	1,975	−0.30	Hampden, town	574	575	0.17
Edson, town	1,089	1,076	−1.19	Leeds, town.	774	769	−0.65
Estella, town	433	425	−1.85	Lewiston, town.	1,225	1,223	−0.16
Goetz, town	762	769	0.92	Lodi, city.	3,050	3,062	0.39
Hallie, town	161	169	4.97	Lodi, town	3,273	3,292	0.58
Howard, town	798	797	−0.13	Lowville, town.	1,008	1,003	−0.50
Lafayette, town	5,765	5,850	1.47	Marcellon, town	1,102	1,096	−0.54
Lake Hallie, village	6,448	6,763	4.89	Newport, town	586	583	−0.51
Lake Holcombe, town . . .	1,031	1,041	0.97	Otsego, town	693	692	−0.14
New Auburn (part), village	528	520	−1.52	Pacific, town	2,707	2,706	−0.04
Ruby, town.	494	492	−0.40	Pardeeville, village.	2,115	2,109	−0.28
Sampson, town.	892	906	1.57	Portage, city	10,324	10,238	−0.83
Sigel, town	1,044	1,040	−0.38	Poynette, village	2,528	2,527	−0.04
Stanley (part), city	3,602	3,593	−0.25	Randolph, town	769	763	−0.78
Tilden, town	1,485	1,500	1.01	Randolph (part), village . .	472	468	−0.85
				Rio, village.	1,059	1,058	−0.09

WISCONSIN POPULATION
BY COUNTY AND MUNCIPALITY
April 1, 2010 and January 1, 2014–Continued

County and Municipality	2010 Census	2014 Estimate	Percent Change	County and Municipality	2010 Census	2014 Estimate	Percent Change
Scott, town.	905	909	0.44	Springfield, town.	2,734	2,772	1.39
Springvale, town.	520	519	–0.19	Stoughton, city.	12,611	12,641	0.24
West Point, town.	1,955	1,977	1.13	Sun Prairie, city	29,364	31,213	6.30
Wisconsin Dells (part), city	2,440	2,430	–0.41	Sun Prairie, town.	2,326	2,337	0.47
Wyocena, town.	1,666	1,675	0.54	Vermont, town	819	816	–0.37
Wyocena, village.	768	758	–1.30	Verona, city	10,619	11,343	6.82
				Verona, town	1,948	1,968	1.03
CRAWFORD COUNTY. . . .	16,644	16,628	–0.10	Vienna, town.	1,482	1,509	1.82
Bell Center, village. . . .	117	117	0.00	Waunakee, village	12,097	12,622	4.34
Bridgeport, town.	990	996	0.61	Westport, town.	3,950	3,976	0.66
Clayton, town	958	947	–1.15	Windsor, town	6,345	6,686	5.37
De Soto (part), village . . .	108	107	–0.93	York, town	652	650	–0.31
Eastman, town	739	745	0.81				
Eastman, village	428	426	–0.47	DODGE COUNTY	88,759	89,203	0.50
Ferryville, village	176	179	1.70	Ashippun, town	2,559	2,571	0.47
Freeman, town	686	699	1.90	Beaver Dam, city	16,214	16,572	2.21
Gays Mills, village.	491	505	2.85	Beaver Dam, town	3,962	3,992	0.76
Haney, town	309	312	0.97	Brownsville, village . . .	581	584	0.52
Lynxville, village	132	131	–0.76	Burnett, town.	904	899	–0.55
Marietta, town	470	478	1.70	Calamus, town	1,048	1,046	–0.19
Mount Sterling, village . .	211	210	–0.47	Chester, town.	687	694	1.02
Prairie du Chien, city . . .	5,911	5,874	–0.63	Clyman, town	774	771	–0.39
Prairie du Chien, town. . .	1,073	1,071	–0.19	Clyman, village	422	420	–0.47
Scott, town	462	456	–1.30	Columbus (part), city . . .	0	0	0.00
Seneca, town	866	886	2.31	Elba, town	996	991	–0.50
Soldiers Grove, village. . .	592	572	–3.38	Emmet, town	1,302	1,306	0.31
Steuben, village	131	128	–2.29	Fox Lake, city	1,519	1,507	–0.79
Utica, town.	661	672	1.66	Fox Lake, town	2,465	2,473	0.32
Wauzeka, town.	422	419	–0.71	Hartford (part), city . . .	0	0	0.00
Wauzeka, village.	711	698	–1.83	Herman, town	1,108	1,116	0.72
				Horicon, city	3,655	3,696	1.12
DANE COUNTY	488,073	502,251	2.90	Hubbard, town	1,774	1,780	0.34
Albion, town	1,951	1,955	0.21	Hustisford, town	1,373	1,379	0.44
Belleville (part), village . .	1,848	1,842	–0.32	Hustisford, village	1,123	1,120	–0.27
Berry, town.	1,127	1,138	0.98	Iron Ridge, village.	929	933	0.43
Black Earth, town	483	484	0.21	Juneau, city	2,814	2,736	–2.77
Black Earth, town	1,338	1,352	1.05	Kekoskee, village	161	158	–1.86
Blooming Grove, town. . .	1,815	1,815	0.00	Lebanon, town	1,659	1,656	–0.18
Blue Mounds, town	968	976	0.83	Leroy, town	1,002	993	–0.90
Blue Mounds, village . . .	855	883	3.27	Lomira, town	1,137	1,140	0.26
Bristol, town	3,765	3,970	5.44	Lomira, village.	2,430	2,431	0.04
Brooklyn (part), village . .	936	951	1.60	Lowell, town	1,190	1,193	0.25
Burke, town	3,284	3,329	1.37	Lowell, village	340	336	–1.18
Cambridge (part), village .	1,348	1,353	0.37	Mayville, city	5,154	5,109	0.87
Christiana, town	1,235	1,238	0.24	Neosho, village	574	571	–0.52
Cottage Grove, town. . . .	3,875	3,887	0.31	Oak Grove, town.	1,080	1,070	–0.93
Cottage Grove, village. . .	6,192	6,322	2.10	Portland, town	1,079	1,083	0.37
Cross Plains, town	1,507	1,520	0.86	Randolph (part), village . .	1,339	1,331	–0.60
Cross Plains, village	3,538	3,596	1.64	Reeseville, village	708	708	0.00
Dane, town.	990	991	0.10	Rubicon, town	2,207	2,211	0.18
Dane, village.	995	1,038	4.32	Shields, town.	554	554	0.00
DeForest, village	8,936	9,129	2.16	Theresa, town	1,075	1,079	0.37
Deerfield, town.	1,585	1,591	0.38	Theresa, village	1,262	1,254	–0.63
Deerfield, village.	2,319	2,413	4.05	Trenton, town	1,293	1,300	0.54
Dunkirk, town	1,945	1,942	–0.15	Watertown (part), city . . .	8,459	8,439	–0.24
Dunn, town.	4,931	4,943	0.24	Waupun (part), city	7,864	8,011	1.87
Edgerton (part), city	97	113	16.49	Westford, town.	1,228	1,226	–0.16
Fitchburg, city	25,260	26,090	3.29	Williamstown, town	755	764	1.19
Madison, city.	233,209	240,153	2.98				
Madison, town	6,279	6,289	0.16	DOOR COUNTY	27,785	27,976	0.69
Maple Bluff, village	1,313	1,303	–0.76	Baileys Harbor, town . . .	1,022	1,036	1.37
Marshall, village	3,862	3,859	–0.08	Brussels, town	1,136	1,140	0.35
Mazomanie, town	1,090	1,091	0.09	Clay Banks, town	382	386	1.05
Mazomanie, village	1,652	1,664	0.73	Egg Harbor, town	1,342	1,357	1.12
McFarland, village	7,808	7,902	1.20	Egg Harbor, village	201	202	0.50
Medina, town	1,376	1,380	0.29	Ephraim, village	288	288	0.00
Middleton, city.	17,442	18,323	5.05	Forestville, town.	1,096	1,103	0.64
Middleton, town	5,877	6,143	4.53	Forestville, village.	430	429	–0.23
Monona, city.	7,533	7,573	0.53	Gardner, town	1,194	1,206	1.01
Montrose, town	1,081	1,084	0.28	Gibraltar, town.	1,021	1,039	1.76
Mount Horeb, village . . .	7,009	7,088	1.13	Jacksonport, town	705	706	0.14
Oregon, town.	3,184	3,214	0.94	Liberty Grove, town	1,734	1,746	0.69
Oregon, village.	9,231	9,420	2.05	Nasewaupee, town.	2,061	2,094	1.60
Perry, town.	729	737	1.10	Sevastopol, town.	2,628	2,662	1.29
Pleasant Springs, town. . .	3,154	3,180	0.82	Sister Bay, village	876	897	2.40
Primrose, town	731	728	–0.41	Sturgeon Bay, city	9,144	9,155	0.12
Rockdale, village.	214	211	–1.40	Sturgeon Bay, town	818	813	–0.61
Roxbury, town	1,794	1,817	1.28	Union, town	999	1,005	0.60
Rutland, town	1,966	1,987	1.07	Washington, town	708	712	0.56
Shorewood Hills, village. .	1,565	1,776	13.48				
Springdale, town.	1,904	1,935	1.63				

WISCONSIN POPULATION
BY COUNTY AND MUNCIPALITY
April 1, 2010 and January 1, 2014–Continued

County and Municipality	2010 Census	2014 Estimate	Percent Change	County and Municipality	2010 Census	2014 Estimate	Percent Change
DOUGLAS COUNTY	44,159	44,196	0.08	Florence, town	2,002	2,000	–0.10
Amnicon, town	1,155	1,175	1.73	Homestead, town	336	341	1.49
Bennett, town	597	608	1.84	Long Lake, town	157	159	1.27
Brule, town	656	668	1.83	Tipler, town	142	141	–0.70
Cloverland, town	210	207	–1.43				
Dairyland, town	184	185	0.54	FOND DU LAC COUNTY	101,633	102,424	0.78
Gordon, town	636	635	–0.16	Alto, town	1,045	1,042	–0.29
Hawthorne, town	1,136	1,109	–2.38	Ashford, town	1,747	1,753	0.34
Highland, town	311	301	–3.22	Auburn, town	2,352	2,357	0.21
Lake Nebagamon, village	1,069	1,083	1.31	Brandon, village	879	865	–1.59
Lakeside, town	693	704	1.59	Byron, town	1,634	1,633	–0.06
Maple, town	744	756	1.61	Calumet, town	1,470	1,504	2.31
Oakland, town	1,136	1,149	1.14	Campbellsport, village	2,016	2,008	–0.40
Oliver, village	399	421	5.51	Eden, town	1,028	1,029	0.10
Parkland, town	1,220	1,216	–0.33	Eden, village	875	890	1.71
Poplar, village	603	612	1.49	Eldorado, town	1,462	1,462	0.00
Solon Springs, town	910	922	1.32	Empire, town	2,797	2,811	0.50
Solon Springs, village	600	605	0.83	Fairwater, village	371	370	–0.27
Summit, town	1,063	1,074	1.03	Fond du Lac, city	43,021	43,151	0.30
Superior, city	27,244	27,146	–0.36	Fond du Lac, town	3,015	3,409	13.07
Superior, town	2,166	2,202	1.66	Forest, town	1,080	1,066	–1.30
Superior, village	664	668	0.60	Friendship, town	2,675	2,692	0.64
Wascott, town	763	750	–1.70	Kewaskum (part), village	0	0	0.00
				Lamartine, town	1,737	1,757	1.15
DUNN COUNTY	43,857	43,917	0.14	Marshfield, town	1,138	1,122	–1.41
Boyceville, village	1,086	1,084	–0.18	Metomen, town	741	738	–0.40
Colfax, town	1,186	1,241	4.64	Mount Calvary, village	762	571	–25.07
Colfax, village	1,158	1,127	–2.68	North Fond du Lac, village	5,014	5,153	2.77
Downing, village	265	264	–0.38	Oakfield, town	703	702	–0.14
Dunn, town	1,524	1,515	–0.59	Oakfield, village	1,075	1,099	2.23
Eau Galle, town	757	760	0.40	Osceola, town	1,865	1,863	–0.11
Elk Mound, town	1,792	1,851	3.29	Ripon, city	7,733	7,795	0.80
Elk Mound, village	878	878	0.00	Ripon, town	1,400	1,412	0.86
Grant, town	385	386	0.26	Rosendale, town	695	694	–0.14
Hay River, town	558	556	–0.36	Rosendale, village	1,063	1,049	–1.32
Knapp, village	463	460	–0.65	Springvale, town	707	713	0.85
Lucas, town	764	767	0.39	St. Cloud, village	477	468	–1.89
Menomonie, city	16,264	16,002	–1.61	Taycheedah, town	4,205	4,373	4.00
Menomonie, town	3,366	3,424	1.72	Waupun (part), city	3,476	3,491	0.43
New Haven, town	677	676	–0.15	Waupun, town	1,375	1,382	0.51
Otter Creek, town	501	496	–1.00				
Peru, town	242	242	0.00	FOREST COUNTY	9,304	9,253	–0.55
Red Cedar, town	2,086	2,134	2.30	Alvin, town	157	156	–0.64
Ridgeland, village	273	271	–0.73	Argonne, town	512	514	0.39
Rock Creek, town	1,000	1,022	2.20	Armstrong Creek, town	409	399	–2.44
Sand Creek, town	570	574	0.70	Blackwell, town	332	309	–6.93
Sheridan, town	454	462	1.76	Caswell, town	91	89	–2.20
Sherman, town	849	873	2.83	Crandon, city	1,920	1,872	–2.50
Spring Brook, town	1,558	1,588	1.93	Crandon, town	650	652	0.31
Stanton, town	791	786	–0.63	Freedom, town	345	348	0.87
Tainter, town	2,319	2,381	2.67	Hiles, town	311	315	1.29
Tiffany, town	618	616	–0.32	Laona, town	1,212	1,202	–0.83
Weston, town	594	596	0.34	Lincoln, town	955	969	1.47
Wheeler, village	348	353	1.44	Nashville, town	1,064	1,082	1.69
Wilson, town	531	532	0.19	Popple River, town	44	43	–2.27
				Ross, town	136	135	–0.74
EAU CLAIRE COUNTY	98,736	100,477	1.76	Wabeno, town	1,166	1,168	0.17
Altoona, city	6,706	7,056	5.22				
Augusta, city	1,550	1,541	–0.58	GRANT COUNTY	51,208	52,603	2.72
Bridge Creek, town	1,900	1,885	–0.79	Bagley, village	379	378	–0.26
Brunswick, town	1,624	1,725	6.22	Beetown, town	777	788	1.42
Clear Creek, town	821	852	3.78	Bloomington, town	350	350	0.00
Drammen, town	783	798	1.92	Bloomington, village	735	748	1.77
Eau Claire (part), city	63,902	64,859	1.42	Blue River, village	434	436	0.46
Fairchild, town	343	348	1.46	Boscobel, city	3,231	3,245	0.43
Fairchild, village	550	547	–0.55	Boscobel, town	376	376	0.00
Fall Creek, village	1,315	1,304	–0.84	Cassville, town	416	410	–1.44
Lincoln, town	1,096	1,115	1.73	Cassville, village	947	944	–0.32
Ludington, town	1,063	1,067	0.38	Castle Rock, town	248	251	1.21
Otter Creek, town	500	500	0.00	Clifton, town	385	392	1.82
Pleasant Valley, town	3,044	3,159	3.78	Cuba City (part), city	1,877	1,860	–0.91
Seymour, town	3,209	3,265	1.75	Dickeyville, village	1,061	1,056	–0.47
Union, town	2,663	2,739	2.85	Ellenboro, town	525	536	2.10
Washington, town	7,182	7,223	1.25	Fennimore, city	2,497	2,507	0.40
Wilson, town	485	494	1.86	Fennimore, town	612	611	–0.16
				Glen Haven, town	417	415	–0.48
FLORENCE COUNTY	4,423	4,450	0.61	Harrison, town	495	497	0.40
Aurora, town	1,036	1,051	1.45	Hazel Green, town	1,132	1,138	0.53
Commonwealth, town	399	402	0.75	Hazel Green (part), village	1,243	1,250	0.56
Fence, town	192	194	1.04	Hickory Grove, town	455	467	2.64
Fern, town	159	162	1.89	Jamestown, town	2,076	2,117	1.97

WISCONSIN POPULATION
BY COUNTY AND MUNCIPALITY
April 1, 2010 and January 1, 2014–Continued

County and Municipality	2010 Census	2014 Estimate	Percent Change	County and Municipality	2010 Census	2014 Estimate	Percent Change
Lancaster, city	3,868	3,845	–0.59	Blanchardville (part),			
Liberty, town	553	558	0.90	village	177	180	1.69
Lima, town	805	800	–0.62	Brigham, town	1,034	1,064	2.90
Little Grant, town	283	285	0.71	Clyde, town	306	309	0.98
Livingston (part), village	657	657	0.00	Cobb, village	458	463	1.09
Marion, town	572	576	0.70	Dodgeville, city	4,693	4,698	0.11
Millville, town	166	170	2.41	Dodgeville, town	1,708	1,739	1.81
Montfort (part), village	622	618	–0.64	Eden, town	355	367	3.38
Mount Hope, town	300	305	1.67	Highland, town	750	759	1.20
Mount Hope, village	225	231	2.67	Highland, village	842	839	–0.36
Mount Ida, town	561	568	1.25	Hollandale, village	288	290	0.69
Muscoda, town	769	773	0.52	Linden, town	847	850	0.35
Muscoda (part), village	1,249	1,236	–1.04	Linden, village	549	546	–0.55
North Lancaster, town	509	514	0.98	Livingston (part), village	7	7	0.00
Paris, town	702	708	0.85	Mifflin, town	585	591	1.03
Patch Grove, town	339	335	–1.18	Mineral Point, city	2,487	2,487	0.00
Patch Grove, village	198	199	0.51	Mineral Point, town	1,033	1,044	1.06
Platteville, city	11,224	12,433	10.77	Montfort (part), village	96	99	3.13
Platteville, town	1,509	1,543	2.25	Moscow, town	576	593	2.95
Potosi, town	849	849	0.00	Muscoda (part), village	50	38	–24.00
Potosi, village	688	689	0.15	Pulaski, town	400	402	0.50
Smelser, town	794	791	–0.38	Rewey, village	292	290	–0.68
South Lancaster, town	843	861	2.14	Ridgeway, town	568	566	–0.35
Tennyson, village	355	363	2.25	Ridgeway, village	653	646	–1.07
Waterloo, town	550	570	3.64	Waldwick, town	473	475	0.42
Watterstown, town	330	329	–0.30	Wyoming, town	302	302	0.00
Wingville, town	357	354	–0.84				
Woodman, town	185	192	3.78	IRON COUNTY	5,916	5,915	–0.02
Woodman, village	132	130	–1.52	Anderson, town	58	59	1.72
Wyalusing, town	346	349	0.87	Carey, town	163	163	0.00
				Gurney, town	159	166	4.40
GREEN COUNTY	36,842	36,822	–0.05	Hurley, city	1,547	1,511	–2.33
Adams, town	530	529	–0.19	Kimball, town	498	495	–0.60
Albany, town	1,106	1,114	0.72	Knight, town	211	211	0.00
Albany, village	1,018	1,005	–1.28	Mercer, town	1,407	1,431	1.71
Belleville (part), village	537	533	–0.74	Montreal, city	807	806	–0.12
Brodhead (part), city	3,203	3,201	–0.06	Oma, town	289	297	2.77
Brooklyn, town	1,083	1,093	0.92	Pence, town	163	164	0.61
Brooklyn (part), village	465	464	–0.22	Saxon, town	324	322	–0.62
Browntown, village	280	283	1.07	Sherman, town	290	290	0.00
Cadiz, town	815	803	–1.47				
Clarno, town	1,166	1,154	–1.03	JACKSON COUNTY	20,449	20,630	0.89
Decatur, town	1,767	1,753	–0.79	Adams, town	1,342	1,365	1.71
Exeter, town	2,023	2,055	1.58	Albion, town	1,210	1,234	1.98
Jefferson, town	1,217	1,227	0.82	Alma, town	1,044	1,079	3.35
Jordon, town	641	639	–0.31	Alma Center, village	503	509	1.19
Monroe, city	10,827	10,751	–0.70	Bear Bluff, town	138	134	–2.90
Monroe, town	1,245	1,235	–0.80	Black River Falls, city	3,622	3,602	–0.55
Monticello, village	1,217	1,218	0.08	Brockway, town	2,828	2,830	0.07
Mount Pleasant, town	598	592	–1.00	City Point, town	182	183	0.55
New Glarus, town	1,335	1,355	1.50	Cleveland, town	481	490	1.87
New Glarus, village	2,172	2,165	–0.32	Curran, town	343	328	–4.37
Spring Grove, town	874	878	0.46	Franklin, town	448	456	1.79
Sylvester, town	1,004	1,009	0.50	Garden Valley, town	422	430	1.90
Washington, town	809	826	2.10	Garfield, town	638	670	5.02
York, town	910	940	3.30	Hixton, town	652	670	2.76
				Hixton, village	433	431	–0.46
GREEN LAKE COUNTY	19,051	19,114	0.33	Irving, town	751	766	2.00
Berlin (part), city	5,435	5,465	0.55	Knapp, town	299	307	2.68
Berlin, town	1,140	1,138	–0.18	Komensky, town	509	504	–0.98
Brooklyn, town	1,826	1,847	1.15	Manchester, town	704	710	0.85
Green Lake, city	960	961	0.10	Melrose, town	470	487	3.62
Green Lake, town	1,154	1,152	–0.17	Melrose, village	503	500	–0.60
Kingston, town	1,064	1,083	1.79	Merrillan, village	542	535	–1.29
Kingston, village	326	326	0.00	Millston, town	159	161	1.26
Mackford, town	560	561	0.18	North Bend, town	488	500	2.46
Manchester, town	1,022	1,047	2.45	Northfield, town	639	648	1.41
Markesan, city	1,476	1,449	–1.83	Springfield, town	623	620	–0.48
Marquette, town	531	544	2.45	Taylor, village	476	481	1.05
Marquette, village	150	153	2.00				
Princeton, city	1,214	1,188	–2.14	JEFFERSON COUNTY	83,686	83,974	0.34
Princeton, town	1,434	1,434	0.00	Aztalan, town	1,457	1,456	–0.07
St. Marie, town	351	356	1.42	Cambridge (part), village	109	108	–0.92
Seneca, town	408	410	0.49	Cold Spring, town	727	728	0.14
				Concord, town	2,072	2,085	0.63
IOWA COUNTY	23,687	23,809	0.52	Farmington, town	1,380	1,384	0.29
Arena, town	1,456	1,476	1.37	Fort Atkinson, city	12,368	12,364	–0.03
Arena, village	834	827	–0.84	Hebron, town	1,094	1,096	0.18
Avoca, village	637	630	–1.10	Ixonia, town	4,385	4,618	5.31
Barneveld, village	1,231	1,232	0.08	Jefferson, city	7,973	7,922	–0.64
				Jefferson, town	2,178	2,185	0.32

WISCONSIN POPULATION
BY COUNTY AND MUNCIPALITY
April 1, 2010 and January 1, 2014–Continued

County and Municipality	2010 Census	2014 Estimate	Percent Change	County and Municipality	2010 Census	2014 Estimate	Percent Change
Johnson Creek, village...	2,738	2,873	4.93	LA CROSSE COUNTY....	114,638	116,740	1.83
Koshkonong, town.....	3,692	3,689	-0.08	Bangor, town........	615	614	-0.16
Lac La Belle (part), village	1	1	0.00	Bangor, village.......	1,459	1,480	1.44
Lake Mills, city	5,708	5,758	0.88	Barre, town.........	1,234	1,239	0.41
Lake Mills, town......	2,070	2,083	0.63	Burns, town.........	947	951	0.42
Milford, town	1,099	1,107	0.73	Campbell, town.......	4,314	4,339	0.58
Oakland, town	3,100	3,088	-0.39	Farmington, town	2,061	2,075	0.68
Palmyra, town	1,186	1,181	-0.42	Greenfield, town	2,060	2,093	1.60
Palmyra, village	1,781	1,779	-0.11	Hamilton, town	2,436	2,457	0.86
Sullivan, town	2,208	2,211	0.14	Holland, town	3,701	3,895	5.24
Sullivan, village	669	670	0.15	Holmen, village	9,005	9,413	4.53
Sumner, town	832	824	-0.96	La Crosse, city	51,320	52,018	1.36
Waterloo, city	3,333	3,323	-0.30	Medary, town	1,461	1,491	2.05
Waterloo, town.......	909	909	0.00	Onalaska, city	17,736	18,159	2.38
Watertown (part), city ...	15,402	15,472	0.45	Onalaska, town.	5,623	5,704	1.44
Watertown, town......	1,975	1,968	-0.35	Rockland (part), village ..	594	614	3.37
Whitewater (part), city...	3,240	3,092	-4.57	Shelby, town	4,715	4,707	-0.17
				Washington, town	558	553	-0.90
JUNEAU COUNTY......	26,664	26,934	1.01	West Salem, village	4,799	4,938	2.90
Armenia, town	699	724	3.58				
Camp Douglas, village...	601	609	1.33	LAFAYETTE COUNTY....	16,836	16,914	0.46
Clearfield, town	728	726	-0.27	Argyle, town........	436	444	1.83
Cutler, town	326	329	0.92	Argyle, village	857	854	-0.35
Elroy, city	1,442	1,409	-2.29	Belmont, town	767	786	2.48
Finley, town	97	97	0.00	Belmont, village	986	987	0.10
Fountain, town	555	559	0.72	Benton, town........	504	510	1.19
Germantown, town.....	1,471	1,575	7.07	Benton, village.......	973	968	-0.51
Hustler, village.......	194	195	0.52	Blanchard, town	264	272	3.03
Kildare, town........	681	700	2.79	Blanchardville (part),			
Kingston, town.......	91	87	-4.40	village	648	644	-0.62
Lemonweir, town	1,743	1,756	0.75	Cuba City (part), city ...	209	216	3.35
Lindina, town	718	715	-0.42	Darlington, city	2,451	2,422	-1.18
Lisbon, town	912	916	0.44	Darlington, town......	875	889	1.60
Lyndon, town	1,384	1,396	0.87	Elk Grove, town	551	559	1.45
Lyndon Station, village ..	500	498	-0.40	Fayette, town........	376	398	5.85
Marion, town........	426	424	-0.47	Gratiot, town........	550	551	0.18
Mauston, city........	4,423	4,475	1.18	Gratiot, village.......	236	233	-1.27
Necedah, town	2,327	2,368	1.76	Hazel Green (part), village	13	13	0.00
Necedah, village......	916	922	0.66	Kendall, town	454	469	3.30
New Lisbon, city......	2,554	2,570	0.63	Lamont, town	314	319	1.59
Orange, town........	570	574	0.70	Monticello, town......	133	134	0.75
Plymouth, town	597	600	0.50	New Diggings, town....	502	508	1.20
Seven Mile Creek, town .	358	359	0.28	Seymour, town.......	446	452	1.35
Summit, town	646	652	0.93	Shullsburg, city	1,226	1,222	-0.33
Union Center, village ...	200	198	-1.00	Shullsburg, town	354	351	-0.85
Wisconsin Dells (part), city	2	0	-100.00	South Wayne, village ...	489	489	0.00
Wonewoc, town	687	690	0.44	Wayne, town........	490	492	0.41
Wonewoc, village	816	811	-0.61	White Oak Springs, town .	118	120	1.69
				Willow Springs, town ...	758	760	0.26
KENOSHA COUNTY.....	166,426	167,258	0.50	Wiota, town	856	852	-0.47
Brighton, town.......	1,456	1,446	-0.69				
Bristol, village	4,914	4,954	0.81	LANGLADE COUNTY....	19,977	19,847	-0.65
Genoa City (part), village ..	6	6	0.00	Ackley, town........	524	527	0.57
Kenosha, city........	99,218	99,680	0.47	Ainsworth, town	469	467	-0.43
Paddock Lake, village ...	2,992	2,993	0.03	Antigo, city	8,234	8,092	-1.72
Paris, town	1,504	1,504	0.00	Antigo, town........	1,412	1,402	-0.71
Pleasant Prairie, village ..	19,719	20,155	2.21	Elcho, town	1,233	1,239	0.49
Randall, town	3,180	3,173	-0.22	Evergreen, town	495	492	-0.61
Salem, town	12,067	12,058	-0.07	Langlade, town.......	473	477	0.85
Silver Lake, village	2,411	2,400	-0.46	Neva, town.........	902	901	-0.11
Somers, town........	9,597	9,512	-0.89	Norwood, town	913	903	-1.10
Twin Lakes, village	5,989	6,041	0.87	Parrish, town........	91	89	-2.20
Wheatland, town......	3,373	3,336	-1.10	Peck, town	349	352	0.86
				Polar, town	984	990	0.61
KEWAUNEE COUNTY....	20,574	20,652	0.38	Price, town	228	224	-1.75
Ahnapee, town	940	936	-0.43	Rolling, town........	1,504	1,512	0.53
Algoma, city	3,167	3,161	-0.19	Summit, town	163	162	-0.61
Carlton, town........	1,014	1,024	0.99	Upham, town	676	683	1.04
Casco, town	1,165	1,179	1.20	Vilas, town.........	233	227	-2.58
Casco, village	583	585	0.34	White Lake, village	363	363	0.00
Franklin, town	993	990	-0.30	Wolf River, town......	731	745	1.92
Kewaunee, city.......	2,952	2,923	-0.98				
Lincoln, town	948	943	-0.53	LINCOLN COUNTY	28,743	28,816	0.25
Luxemburg, town	1,469	1,479	0.68	Birch, town.........	594	642	8.08
Luxemburg, village	2,515	2,571	2.23	Bradley, town........	2,408	2,434	1.08
Montpelier, town......	1,306	1,310	0.31	Corning, town........	883	881	-0.23
Pierce, town	833	825	-0.96	Harding, town	372	379	1.88
Red River, town	1,393	1,399	0.43	Harrison, town	833	842	1.08
West Kewaunee, town ...	1,296	1,327	2.39	King, town	855	871	1.87
				Merrill, city	9,661	9,615	-0.48
				Merrill, town........	2,980	2,993	0.44

WISCONSIN POPULATION
BY COUNTY AND MUNCIPALITY
April 1, 2010 and January 1, 2014–Continued

County and Municipality	2010 Census	2014 Estimate	Percent Change	County and Municipality	2010 Census	2014 Estimate	Percent Change
Pine River, town	1,869	1,879	0.54	Marathon City, village	1,524	1,530	0.39
Rock Falls, town	618	622	0.65	Marshfield (part), city	900	906	0.67
Russell, town	677	682	0.74	McMillan, town	1,968	1,992	1.22
Schley, town	934	932	–0.21	Mosinee, city	3,988	4,020	0.80
Scott, town	1,432	1,440	0.56	Mosinee, town	2,174	2,187	0.60
Skanawan, town	391	397	1.53	Norrie, town	976	980	0.41
Somo, town	114	115	0.88	Plover, town	689	683	–0.87
Tomahawk, city	3,397	3,356	–1.21	Reid, town	1,215	1,231	1.32
Tomahawk, town	416	422	1.44	Rib Falls, town	993	994	0.10
Wilson, town	309	314	1.62	Rib Mountain, town	6,825	6,884	0.86
				Rietbrock, town	981	979	–0.20
MANITOWOC COUNTY	81,442	81,320	–0.15	Ringle, town	1,711	1,740	1.69
Cato, town	1,566	1,567	0.06	Rothschild, village	5,269	5,287	0.34
Centerville, town	645	642	–0.47	Schofield, city	2,169	2,165	–0.18
Cleveland, village	1,485	1,519	2.29	Spencer, town	1,581	1,602	1.33
Cooperstown, town	1,292	1,299	0.54	Spencer, village	1,925	1,936	0.57
Eaton, town	833	832	–0.12	Stettin, town	2,554	2,553	–0.04
Francis Creek, village	669	666	–0.45	Stratford, village	1,578	1,591	0.82
Franklin, town	1,264	1,260	–0.32	Texas, town	1,615	1,610	–0.31
Gibson, town	1,344	1,341	–0.22	Unity (part), village	204	201	–1.47
Kellnersville, village	332	332	0.00	Wausau, city	39,106	39,131	0.06
Kiel (part), city	3,429	3,456	0.79	Wausau, town	2,229	2,235	0.27
Kossuth, town	2,090	2,084	–0.29	Weston, town	639	656	2.66
Liberty, town	1,281	1,276	–0.39	Weston, village	14,868	15,090	1.49
Manitowoc, city	33,736	33,649	–0.26	Wien, town	825	841	1.94
Manitowoc, town	1,083	1,091	0.74				
Manitowoc Rapids, town	2,150	2,141	–0.42	MARINETTE COUNTY	41,749	41,605	–0.34
Maple Grove, town	835	831	–0.48	Amberg, town	726	730	0.55
Maribel, village	351	347	–1.14	Athelstane, town	504	509	0.99
Meeme, town	1,446	1,451	0.35	Beaver, town	1,146	1,158	1.05
Mishicot, town	1,289	1,293	0.31	Beecher, town	724	729	0.69
Mishicot, village	1,442	1,438	–0.28	Coleman, village	724	726	0.28
Newton, town	2,264	2,288	1.06	Crivitz, village	984	962	–2.24
Reedsville, village	1,206	1,201	–0.41	Dunbar, town	1,094	848	–22.49
Rockland, town	1,001	1,003	0.20	Goodman, town	619	617	–0.32
St. Nazianz, village	783	779	–0.51	Grover, town	1,768	1,797	1.64
Schleswig, town	1,963	1,987	1.22	Lake, town	1,135	1,162	2.38
Two Creeks, town	437	425	–2.75	Marinette, city	10,968	10,930	–0.35
Two Rivers, city	11,712	11,628	–0.72	Middle Inlet, town	840	838	–0.24
Two Rivers, town	1,795	1,782	–0.72	Niagara, city	1,624	1,608	–0.99
Valders, village	962	957	–0.52	Niagara, town	853	864	1.29
Whitelaw, village	757	755	–0.26	Pembine, town	889	886	–0.34
				Peshtigo, city	3,502	3,442	–1.71
MARATHON COUNTY	134,063	134,803	0.55	Peshtigo, town	4,057	4,084	0.67
Abbotsford (part), city	694	692	–0.29	Porterfield, town	1,971	1,992	1.07
Athens, village	1,105	1,105	0.00	Pound, town	1,425	1,430	0.35
Bergen, town	641	638	–0.47	Pound, village	377	378	0.27
Berlin, town	945	942	–0.32	Silver Cliff, town	491	500	1.83
Bern, town	591	602	1.86	Stephenson, town	3,006	3,063	1.90
Bevent, town	1,118	1,124	0.54	Wagner, town	681	693	1.76
Birnamwood (part), village	16	18	12.50	Wausaukee, town	1,066	1,087	1.97
Brighton, town	612	611	–0.16	Wausaukee, village	575	572	–0.52
Brokaw, village	251	242	–3.59				
Cassel, town	911	910	–0.11	MARQUETTE COUNTY	15,404	15,399	–0.03
Cleveland, town	1,488	1,506	1.21	Buffalo, town	1,221	1,233	0.98
Colby (part), city	498	500	0.40	Crystal Lake, town	484	486	0.41
Day, town	1,085	1,097	1.11	Douglas, town	725	724	–0.14
Dorchester (part), village	5	5	0.00	Endeavor, village	468	462	–1.28
Easton, town	1,111	1,129	1.62	Harris, town	790	789	–0.13
Eau Pleine, town	773	765	–1.03	Mecan, town	686	690	0.58
Edgar, village	1,479	1,475	–0.27	Montello, city	1,495	1,485	–0.67
Elderon, town	606	620	2.31	Montello, town	1,033	1,033	0.00
Elderon, village	179	178	–0.56	Moundville, town	552	555	0.54
Emmet, town	931	934	0.32	Neshkoro, town	561	554	–1.25
Fenwood, village	152	147	–3.29	Neshkoro, village	434	429	–1.15
Frankfort, town	670	660	–1.49	Newton, town	547	543	–0.73
Franzen, town	578	582	0.69	Oxford, town	885	887	0.23
Green Valley, town	541	544	0.55	Oxford, village	607	603	–0.66
Guenther, town	341	346	1.47	Packwaukee, town	1,416	1,412	–0.28
Halsey, town	651	652	0.15	Shields, town	550	547	–0.55
Hamburg, town	918	915	–0.33	Springfield, town	830	833	0.36
Harrison, town	374	373	–0.27	Westfield, town	866	875	1.04
Hatley, village	574	598	4.18	Westfield, village	1,254	1,259	0.40
Hewitt, town	606	611	0.83				
Holton, town	873	885	1.37	MENOMINEE COUNTY	4,232	4,236	0.09
Hull, town	750	744	–0.80	Menominee, town	4,232	4,236	0.09
Johnson, town	985	981	–0.41				
Knowlton, town	1,910	1,923	0.68	MILWAUKEE COUNTY	947,735	949,741	0.21
Kronenwetter, village	7,210	7,327	1.62	Bayside (part), village	4,300	4,286	–0.33
Maine, town	2,337	2,348	0.47	Brown Deer, village	11,999	12,157	1.32
Marathon, town	1,048	1,050	0.19	Cudahy, city	18,267	18,224	–0.24

WISCONSIN POPULATION
BY COUNTY AND MUNCIPALITY
April 1, 2010 and January 1, 2014–Continued

County and Municipality	2010 Census	2014 Estimate	Percent Change	County and Municipality	2010 Census	2014 Estimate	Percent Change
Fox Point, village	6,701	6,676	–0.37	Suring, village	544	543	–0.18
Franklin, city	35,451	35,702	0.71	Townsend, town	979	992	1.33
Glendale, city	12,872	12,773	–0.77	Underhill, town	882	884	0.23
Greendale, village	14,046	14,144	0.70				
Greenfield, city	36,720	36,687	–0.09	ONEIDA COUNTY	35,998	36,082	0.23
Hales Corners, village	7,692	7,678	–0.18	Cassian, town	985	983	–0.20
Milwaukee (part), city	594,833	595,993	0.20	Crescent, town	2,033	2,048	0.74
Oak Creek, city	34,451	34,707	0.74	Enterprise, town	315	317	0.63
River Hills, village	1,597	1,584	–0.81	Hazelhurst, town	1,273	1,289	1.26
St. Francis, city	9,365	9,465	1.07	Lake Tomahawk, town	1,043	1,033	–0.96
Shorewood, village	13,162	13,183	0.16	Little Rice, town	306	313	2.29
South Milwaukee, city	21,156	21,142	–0.07	Lynne, town	141	144	2.13
Wauwatosa, city	46,396	46,766	0.80	Minocqua, town	4,453	4,486	0.74
West Allis, city	60,411	60,272	–0.23	Monico, town	309	307	–0.65
West Milwaukee, village	4,206	4,197	–0.21	Newbold, town	2,719	2,735	0.59
Whitefish Bay, village	14,110	14,105	–0.04	Nokomis, town	1,371	1,417	3.36
				Pelican, town	2,764	2,799	1.27
MONROE COUNTY	44,673	45,339	1.49	Piehl, town	86	86	0.00
Adrian, town	762	790	3.67	Pine Lake, town	2,740	2,759	0.69
Angelo, town	1,296	1,305	0.69	Rhinelander, city	7,798	7,645	–1.96
Byron, town	1,342	1,354	0.89	Schoepke, town	387	392	1.29
Cashton, village	1,102	1,107	0.45	Stella, town	650	646	–0.62
Clifton, town	690	697	1.01	Sugar Camp, town	1,694	1,711	1.00
Glendale, town	667	686	2.85	Three Lakes, town	2,131	2,145	0.66
Grant, town	495	501	1.21	Woodboro, town	813	830	2.09
Greenfield, town	707	717	1.41	Woodruff, town	1,987	1,997	0.50
Jefferson, town	819	836	2.08				
Kendall, village	472	469	–0.64	OUTAGAMIE COUNTY	176,695	180,022	1.88
La Grange, town	2,007	2,011	0.20	Appleton (part), city	60,045	60,783	1.23
Lafayette, town	396	401	1.26	Bear Creek, village	448	450	0.45
Leon, town	1,086	1,130	4.05	Black Creek, town	1,259	1,252	–0.56
Lincoln, town	835	837	0.24	Black Creek, village	1,316	1,320	0.30
Little Falls, town	1,523	1,566	2.82	Bovina, town	1,145	1,154	0.79
Melvina, village	104	105	0.96	Buchanan, town	6,755	6,920	2.44
New Lyme, town	168	174	3.57	Center, town	3,402	3,430	0.82
Norwalk, village	638	635	–0.47	Cicero, town	1,103	1,104	0.09
Oakdale, town	772	786	1.81	Combined Locks, village	3,328	3,447	3.58
Oakdale, village	297	295	–0.67	Dale, town	2,731	2,768	1.35
Portland, town	808	830	2.72	Deer Creek, town	637	648	1.73
Ridgeville, town	501	509	1.60	Ellington, town	2,758	2,845	3.15
Rockland (part), village	0	0	0.00	Freedom, town	5,842	5,968	2.16
Scott, town	135	134	–0.74	Grand Chute, town	20,919	21,767	4.05
Sheldon, town	727	745	2.48	Greenville, town	10,309	10,857	5.32
Sparta, city	9,522	9,701	1.88	*Harrison (part), village	0	0	0.00
Sparta, town	3,128	3,167	1.25	Hortonia, town	1,097	1,094	–0.27
Tomah, city	9,093	9,204	1.22	Hortonville, village	2,711	2,703	–0.30
Tomah, town	1,400	1,429	2.07	Howard (part), village	0	0	0.00
Warrens, village	363	360	–0.83	Kaukauna (part), city	15,462	15,765	1.96
Wellington, town	621	639	2.90	Kaukauna, town	1,238	1,261	1.86
Wells, town	519	528	1.73	Kimberly, village	6,468	6,620	2.35
Wilton, town	1,027	1,049	2.14	Liberty, town	867	868	0.12
Wilton, village	504	501	–0.60	Little Chute, village	10,449	10,539	0.86
Wyeville, village	147	141	–4.08	Maine, town	866	873	0.81
				Maple Creek, town	619	605	–2.26
OCONTO COUNTY	37,660	38,014	0.94	New London (part), city	1,610	1,618	0.50
Abrams, town	1,856	1,870	0.75	Nichols, village	273	268	–1.83
Bagley, town	291	292	0.34	Oneida, town	4,678	4,695	0.36
Brazeau, town	1,284	1,292	0.62	Osborn, town	1,170	1,191	1.79
Breed, town	712	725	1.83	Seymour, city	3,451	3,429	–0.64
Chase, town	3,005	3,064	1.96	Seymour, town	1,193	1,193	0.00
Doty, town	260	263	1.15	Shiocton, village	921	928	0.76
Gillett, city	1,386	1,373	–0.94	Vandenbroek, town	1,474	1,507	2.24
Gillett, town	1,043	1,031	–1.15	Wrightstown (part), village	151	152	0.66
How, town	516	525	1.74				
Lakewood, town	816	825	1.10	OZAUKEE COUNTY	86,395	87,116	0.83
Lena, town	727	721	–0.83	Bayside (part), village	89	90	1.12
Lena, village	564	564	0.00	Belgium, town	1,415	1,424	0.64
Little River, town	1,094	1,101	0.64	Belgium, village	2,245	2,258	0.58
Little Suamico, town	4,799	4,963	3.42	Cedarburg, city	11,412	11,479	0.59
Maple Valley, town	662	668	0.91	Cedarburg, town	5,760	5,843	1.44
Morgan, town	984	988	0.41	Fredonia, town	2,172	2,161	–0.51
Mountain, town	822	828	0.73	Fredonia, village	2,160	2,176	0.74
Oconto, city	4,513	4,544	0.69	Grafton, town	4,053	4,102	1.21
Oconto, town	1,335	1,344	0.67	Grafton, village	11,459	11,490	0.27
Oconto Falls, city	2,891	2,889	–0.07	Mequon, city	23,132	23,387	1.10
Oconto Falls, town	1,265	1,270	0.40	Newburg (part), village	97	96	–1.03
Pensaukee, town	1,381	1,385	0.29	Port Washington, city	11,250	11,439	1.68
Pulaski (part), village	0	0	0.00	Port Washington, town	1,643	1,653	0.61
Riverview, town	725	729	0.55	Saukville, town	1,822	1,830	0.44
Spruce, town	835	841	0.72	Saukville, village	4,451	4,466	0.34
Stiles, town	1,489	1,500	0.74	Thiensville, village	3,235	3,222	–0.40

WISCONSIN POPULATION
BY COUNTY AND MUNCIPALITY
April 1, 2010 and January 1, 2014–Continued

County and Municipality	2010 Census	2014 Estimate	Percent Change
PEPIN COUNTY	7,469	7,445	-0.32
Albany, town	676	669	-1.04
Durand, city	1,931	1,919	-0.62
Durand, town	742	748	0.81
Frankfort, town	343	348	1.46
Lima, town	702	685	-2.42
Pepin, town	721	731	1.39
Pepin, village	837	820	-2.03
Stockholm, town	197	201	2.03
Stockholm, village	66	65	-1.52
Waterville, town	831	831	0.00
Waubeek, town	423	428	1.18
PIERCE COUNTY	41,019	41,107	0.21
Bay City, village	500	499	-0.20
Clifton, town	2,012	2,022	0.50
Diamond Bluff, town	469	462	-1.49
El Paso, town	681	693	1.76
Ellsworth, town	1,146	1,158	1.05
Ellsworth, village	3,284	3,304	0.61
Elmwood, village	817	816	-0.12
Gilman, town	959	973	1.46
Hartland, town	827	844	2.06
Isabelle, town	281	284	1.07
Maiden Rock, town	589	596	1.19
Maiden Rock, village	119	118	-0.84
Martell, town	1,185	1,186	0.08
Oak Grove, town	2,150	2,163	0.60
Plum City, village	599	585	-2.34
Prescott, city	4,258	4,257	-0.02
River Falls (part), city	11,851	11,825	-0.22
River Falls, town	2,271	2,288	0.75
Rock Elm, town	485	485	0.00
Salem, town	510	516	1.18
Spring Lake, town	563	565	0.36
Spring Valley (part), village	1,346	1,361	1.11
Trenton, town	1,829	1,838	0.49
Trimbelle, town	1,679	1,676	-0.18
Union, town	609	593	-2.63
POLK COUNTY	44,205	44,237	0.07
Alden, town	2,786	2,802	0.57
Amery, city	2,902	2,929	0.93
Apple River, town	1,146	1,155	0.79
Balsam Lake, town	1,411	1,409	-0.14
Balsam Lake, village	1,009	1,012	0.30
Beaver, town	835	838	0.36
Black Brook, town	1,325	1,338	0.98
Bone Lake, town	717	722	0.70
Centuria, village	948	936	-1.27
Clam Falls, town	596	609	2.18
Clayton, town	975	985	1.03
Clayton, village	571	570	-0.18
Clear Lake, town	899	905	0.67
Clear Lake, village	1,070	1,064	-0.56
Dresser, village	895	895	0.00
Eureka, town	1,649	1,659	0.61
Farmington, town	1,836	1,842	0.33
Frederic, village	1,137	1,134	-0.26
Garfield, town	1,692	1,691	-0.06
Georgetown, town	977	986	0.92
Johnstown, town	534	532	-0.37
Laketown, town	961	968	0.73
Lincoln, town	2,208	2,195	-0.59
Lorain, town	284	280	-1.41
Luck, town	930	915	-1.61
Luck, village	1,119	1,086	-2.95
McKinley, town	347	352	1.44
Milltown, town	1,226	1,228	0.16
Milltown, village	917	914	-0.33
Osceola, town	2,855	2,864	0.32
Osceola, village	2,568	2,588	0.78
St. Croix Falls, city	2,133	2,111	-1.03
St. Croix Falls, town	1,165	1,163	-0.17
Sterling, town	790	777	-1.65
Turtle Lake (part), village	93	91	-2.15
West Sweden, town	699	692	-1.00
PORTAGE COUNTY	70,019	70,882	1.23
Alban, town	885	882	-0.34
Almond, town	680	676	-0.59
Almond, village	448	446	-0.45
Amherst, town	1,325	1,332	0.53
Amherst, village	1,035	1,048	1.26
Amherst Junction, village	377	375	-0.53
Belmont, town	616	617	0.16
Buena Vista, town	1,198	1,202	0.33
Carson, town	1,305	1,313	0.61
Dewey, town	932	937	0.54
Eau Pleine, town	908	938	3.30
Grant, town	1,906	1,921	0.79
Hull, town	5,346	5,376	0.56
Junction City, village	439	440	0.23
Lanark, town	1,527	1,546	1.24
Linwood, town	1,121	1,121	0.00
Milladore (part), village	0	0	0.00
Nelsonville, village	155	151	-2.58
New Hope, town	718	712	-0.84
Park Ridge, village	491	496	1.02
Pine Grove, town	937	934	-0.32
Plover, town	1,701	1,720	1.12
Plover, village	12,123	12,492	3.04
Rosholt, village	506	498	-1.58
Sharon, town	1,982	2,011	1.46
Stevens Point, city	26,717	27,040	1.21
Stockton, town	2,917	2,970	1.82
Whiting, village	1,724	1,688	-2.09
PRICE COUNTY	14,159	14,155	-0.03
Catawba, town	269	269	0.00
Catawba, village	110	104	-5.45
Eisenstein, town	630	620	-1.59
Elk, town	988	996	0.81
Emery, town	297	296	-0.34
Fifield, town	901	904	0.33
Flambeau, town	489	482	-1.43
Georgetown, town	171	171	0.00
Hackett, town	169	169	0.00
Harmony, town	222	224	0.90
Hill, town	333	332	-0.30
Kennan, town	356	353	-0.84
Kennan, village	135	129	-4.44
Knox, town	341	346	1.47
Lake, town	1,128	1,117	-0.98
Ogema, town	713	717	0.56
Park Falls, city	2,462	2,514	2.11
Phillips, city	1,478	1,447	-2.10
Prentice, town	475	467	-1.68
Prentice, village	660	653	-1.06
Spirit, town	277	277	0.00
Worcester, town	1,555	1,568	0.84
RACINE COUNTY	195,408	195,461	0.03
Burlington (part), city	10,464	10,511	0.45
Burlington, town	6,502	6,456	-0.71
Caledonia, village	24,705	24,880	0.71
Dover, town	4,051	4,031	-0.49
Elmwood Park, village	497	500	0.60
Mount Pleasant, village	26,197	26,386	0.72
North Bay, village	241	237	-1.66
Norway, town	7,948	7,964	0.20
Racine, city	78,860	78,479	-0.48
Raymond, town	3,870	3,917	1.21
Rochester, village	3,682	3,700	0.49
Sturtevant, village	6,970	6,993	0.33
Union Grove, village	4,915	4,899	-0.33
Waterford, town	6,344	6,345	0.02
Waterford, village	5,368	5,366	-0.04
Wind Point, village	1,723	1,707	-0.93
Yorkville, town	3,071	3,090	0.62
RICHLAND COUNTY	18,021	17,995	-0.14
Akan, town	403	397	-1.49
Bloom, town	512	508	-0.78
Boaz, village	156	155	-0.64
Buena Vista, town	1,869	1,886	0.91
Cazenovia (part), village	314	308	-1.91
Dayton, town	693	698	0.72
Eagle, town	531	524	-1.32
Forest, town	352	355	0.85
Henrietta, town	493	488	-1.01

WISCONSIN POPULATION
BY COUNTY AND MUNCIPALITY
April 1, 2010 and January 1, 2014–Continued

County and Municipality	2010 Census	2014 Estimate	Percent Change	County and Municipality	2010 Census	2014 Estimate	Percent Change
Ithaca, town	619	627	1.29	ST. CROIX COUNTY	84,345	85,735	1.65
Lone Rock, village	888	883	–0.56	Baldwin, town	928	918	–1.08
Marshall, town	567	573	1.06	Baldwin, village	3,957	3,961	0.10
Orion, town	579	583	0.69	Cady, town	821	829	0.97
Richland, town	1,379	1,359	–1.45	Cylon, town	683	682	–0.15
Richland Center, city	5,184	5,187	0.06	Deer Park, village	216	211	–2.31
Richwood, town	533	525	–1.50	Eau Galle, town	1,139	1,171	2.81
Rockbridge, town	734	721	–1.77	Emerald, town	853	838	–1.76
Sylvan, town	555	561	1.08	Erin Prairie, town	688	681	–1.02
Viola (part), village	477	477	0.00	Forest, town	629	630	0.16
Westford, town	530	525	–0.94	Glenwood, town	785	782	–0.38
Willow, town	579	586	1.21	Glenwood City, city	1,242	1,219	–1.85
Yuba, village	74	69	–6.76	Hammond, town	2,102	2,141	1.86
				Hammond, village	1,922	1,911	–0.57
ROCK COUNTY	160,331	160,104	–0.14	Hudson, city	12,719	13,326	4.77
Avon, town	608	600	–1.32	Hudson, town	8,461	8,547	1.02
Beloit, city	36,966	36,805	–0.44	Kinnickinnic, town	1,722	1,747	1.45
Beloit, town	7,662	7,626	–0.47	New Richmond, city	8,375	8,616	2.88
Bradford, town	1,121	1,098	–2.05	North Hudson, village	3,768	3,762	–0.16
Brodhead (part), city	90	90	0.00	Pleasant Valley, town	515	519	0.78
Center, town	1,066	1,058	–0.75	Richmond, town	3,272	3,375	3.15
Clinton, town	930	935	0.54	River Falls (part), city	3,149	3,228	2.51
Clinton, village	2,154	2,119	–1.62	Roberts, village	1,651	1,636	–0.91
Edgerton (part), city	5,364	5,399	0.65	Rush River, town	508	502	–1.18
Evansville, city	5,012	5,124	2.23	St. Joseph, town	3,842	3,863	0.55
Footville, village	808	805	–0.37	Somerset, town	4,036	4,103	1.66
Fulton, town	3,252	3,263	0.34	Somerset, village	2,635	2,646	0.42
Harmony, town	2,569	2,575	0.23	Spring Valley (part), village	6	8	33.33
Janesville, city	63,575	63,525	–0.08	Springfield, town	932	943	1.18
Janesville, town	3,434	3,439	0.15	Stanton, town	900	892	–0.89
Johnstown, town	778	772	–0.77	Star Prairie, town	3,504	3,522	0.51
La Prairie, town	834	829	–0.60	Star Prairie, village	561	550	–1.96
Lima, town	1,280	1,275	–0.39	Troy, town	4,705	4,847	3.02
Magnolia, town	767	756	–1.43	Warren, town	1,591	1,605	0.88
Milton, city	5,546	5,545	–0.02	Wilson, village	184	180	–2.17
Milton, town	2,923	2,939	0.55	Woodville, village	1,344	1,344	0.00
Newark, town	1,541	1,529	–0.78				
Orfordville, village	1,442	1,449	0.49	SAUK COUNTY	61,976	62,092	0.19
Plymouth, town	1,235	1,175	–4.86	Baraboo, city	12,048	11,985	–0.52
Porter, town	945	960	1.59	Baraboo, town	1,672	1,680	0.48
Rock, town	3,196	3,189	–0.22	Bear Creek, town	595	604	1.51
Spring Valley, town	746	741	–0.67	Cazenovia (part), village	4	13	225.00
Turtle, town	2,388	2,375	–0.54	Dellona, town	1,552	1,570	1.16
Union, town	2,099	2,109	0.48	Delton, town	2,391	2,410	0.79
				Excelsior, town	1,575	1,573	–0.13
RUSK COUNTY	14,755	14,790	0.24	Fairfield, town	1,077	1,067	–0.93
Atlanta, town	592	585	–1.18	Franklin, town	652	649	–0.46
Big Bend, town	358	370	3.35	Freedom, town	447	452	1.12
Big Falls, town	140	141	0.71	Greenfield, town	932	937	0.54
Bruce, village	779	775	–0.51	Honey Creek, town	733	731	–0.27
Cedar Rapids, town	41	39	–4.88	Ironton, town	660	658	–0.30
Conrath, village	95	95	0.00	Ironton, village	253	248	–1.98
Dewey, town	545	553	1.47	La Valle, town	1,302	1,320	1.38
Flambeau, town	1,059	1,067	0.76	La Valle, village	367	358	–2.45
Glen Flora, village	92	90	–2.17	Lake Delton, village	2,914	2,921	0.24
Grant, town	813	816	0.37	Lime Ridge, village	162	159	–1.85
Grow, town	427	423	–0.94	Loganville, village	300	297	–1.00
Hawkins, town	153	156	1.96	Merrimac, town	942	958	1.70
Hawkins, village	305	305	0.00	Merrimac, village	420	424	0.95
Hubbard, town	204	201	–1.47	North Freedom, village	701	686	–2.14
Ingram, village	78	80	2.56	Plain, village	773	771	–0.26
Ladysmith, city	3,414	3,386	–0.82	Prairie du Sac, town	1,144	1,133	–0.96
Lawrence, town	311	307	–1.29	Prairie du Sac, village	3,972	4,023	1.28
Marshall, town	688	694	0.87	Reedsburg, city	9,200	9,301	1.10
Murry, town	277	277	0.00	Reedsburg, town	1,293	1,289	–0.31
Richland, town	232	233	0.43	Rock Springs, village	362	313	–13.54
Rusk, town	525	544	3.62	Sauk City, village	3,410	3,433	0.67
Sheldon, village	237	233	–1.69	Spring Green, town	1,697	1,705	0.47
South Fork, town	120	118	–1.67	Spring Green, village	1,628	1,631	0.18
Strickland, town	280	288	2.86	Sumpter, town	1,191	1,189	–0.17
Stubbs, town	579	584	0.86	Troy, town	794	798	0.50
Thornapple, town	774	788	1.81	Washington, town	1,007	1,009	0.20
Tony, village	113	112	–0.88	West Baraboo, village	1,414	1,406	–0.57
True, town	296	294	–0.68	Westfield, town	571	559	–2.10
Washington, town	339	348	2.65	Winfield, town	856	861	0.58
Weyerhaeuser, village	238	228	–4.20	Wisconsin Dells (part), city	175	173	–1.14
Wilkinson, town	40	38	–5.00	Woodland, town	790	798	1.01
Willard, town	505	514	1.78				
Wilson, town	106	108	1.89	SAWYER COUNTY	16,557	16,676	0.72
				Bass Lake, town	2,377	2,397	0.84
				Couderay, town	401	406	1.25

WISCONSIN POPULATION
BY COUNTY AND MUNCIPALITY
April 1, 2010 and January 1, 2014–Continued

County and Municipality	2010 Census	2014 Estimate	Percent Change	County and Municipality	2010 Census	2014 Estimate	Percent Change
Couderay, village	88	89	1.14	Scott, town	1,836	1,830	–0.33
Draper, town	204	209	2.45	Sheboygan, city	49,288	48,897	–0.79
Edgewater, town	519	527	1.54	Sheboygan, town	7,271	7,407	1.87
Exeland, village	196	196	0.00	Sheboygan Falls, city	7,775	7,861	1.11
Hayward, city	2,318	2,347	1.25	Sheboygan Falls, town	1,718	1,719	0.06
Hayward, town	3,567	3,568	0.03	Sherman, town	1,505	1,495	–0.66
Hunter, town	678	684	0.88	Waldo, village	503	495	–1.59
Lenroot, town	1,279	1,308	2.27	Wilson, town	3,330	3,357	0.81
Meadowbrook, town	131	138	5.34				
Meteor, town	158	154	–2.53	TAYLOR COUNTY	20,689	20,733	0.21
Ojibwa, town	249	249	0.00	Aurora, town	422	428	1.42
Radisson, town	405	398	–1.73	Browning, town	905	916	1.22
Radisson, village	241	243	0.83	Chelsea, town	806	813	0.87
Round Lake, town	977	986	0.92	Cleveland, town	268	264	–1.49
Sand Lake, town	813	821	0.98	Deer Creek, town	768	766	–0.26
Spider Lake, town	351	356	1.42	Ford, town	268	269	0.37
Weirgor, town	332	332	0.00	Gilman, village	410	396	–3.41
Winter, town	960	951	–0.94	Goodrich, town	510	511	0.20
Winter, village	313	317	1.28	Greenwood, town	638	641	0.47
				Grover, town	256	256	0.00
SHAWANO COUNTY	41,949	41,859	–0.21	Hammel, town	713	712	–0.14
Almon, town	584	587	0.51	Holway, town	973	965	–0.82
Angelica, town	1,793	1,813	1.12	Jump River, town	375	369	–1.60
Aniwa, town	541	536	–0.92	Little Black, town	1,140	1,147	0.61
Aniwa, village	260	256	–1.54	Lublin, village	118	118	0.00
Bartelme, town	819	809	–1.22	Maplehurst, town	335	334	–0.30
Belle Plaine, town	1,855	1,859	0.22	McKinley, town	458	459	0.22
Birnamwood, town	763	775	1.57	Medford, city	4,326	4,354	0.65
Birnamwood (part), village	802	796	–0.75	Medford, town	2,606	2,639	1.27
Bonduel, village	1,478	1,485	0.47	Molitor, town	324	326	0.62
Bowler, village	302	294	–2.65	Pershing, town	180	177	–1.67
Cecil, village	570	560	–1.75	Rib Lake, town	852	859	0.82
Eland, village	202	199	–1.49	Rib Lake, village	910	898	–1.32
Fairbanks, town	616	608	–1.30	Roosevelt, town	473	462	–2.33
Germania, town	332	326	–1.81	Stetsonville, village	541	534	–1.29
Grant, town	991	984	–0.71	Taft, town	430	425	–1.16
Green Valley, town	1,089	1,091	0.18	Westboro, town	684	695	1.61
Gresham, village	586	584	–0.34				
Hartland, town	904	903	–0.11	TREMPEALEAU COUNTY	28,816	29,184	1.28
Herman, town	776	772	–0.52	Albion, town	653	663	1.53
Hutchins, town	600	597	–0.50	Arcadia, city	2,925	2,929	0.14
Lessor, town	1,263	1,277	1.11	Arcadia, town	1,779	1,837	3.26
Maple Grove, town	972	960	–1.23	Blair, city	1,366	1,378	0.88
Marion (part), city	25	26	4.00	Burnside, town	511	509	–0.39
Mattoon, village	438	432	–1.37	Caledonia, town	920	931	1.20
Morris, town	453	455	0.44	Chimney Rock, town	241	236	–2.07
Navarino, town	446	444	–0.45	Dodge, town	389	390	0.26
Pella, town	865	872	0.81	Eleva, village	670	677	1.04
Pulaski (part), village	218	217	–0.46	Ettrick, town	1,237	1,242	0.40
Red Springs, town	925	931	0.65	Ettrick, village	524	521	–0.57
Richmond, town	1,864	1,872	0.43	Gale, town	1,695	1,725	1.77
Seneca, town	558	556	–0.36	Galesville, city	1,481	1,507	1.76
Shawano, city	9,305	9,234	–0.76	Hale, town	1,037	1,048	1.06
Tigerton, village	741	732	–1.21	Independence, city	1,336	1,352	1.20
Washington, town	1,895	1,907	0.63	Lincoln, town	823	856	4.01
Waukechon, town	1,021	1,044	2.25	Osseo, city	1,701	1,697	–0.24
Wescott, town	3,183	3,202	0.60	Pigeon, town	891	901	1.12
Wittenberg, town	833	827	–0.72	Pigeon Falls, village	411	413	0.49
Wittenberg, village	1,081	1,037	–4.07	Preston, town	953	970	1.78
				Strum, village	1,114	1,124	0.90
SHEBOYGAN COUNTY	115,507	115,362	–0.13	Sumner, town	810	820	1.23
Adell, village	516	515	–0.19	Trempealeau, town	1,756	1,792	2.05
Cascade, village	709	702	–0.99	Trempealeau, village	1,529	1,612	5.43
Cedar Grove, village	2,113	2,102	–0.52	Unity, town	506	500	–1.19
Elkhart Lake, village	967	955	–1.24	Whitehall, city	1,558	1,554	–0.26
Glenbeulah, village	463	461	–0.43				
Greenbush, town	2,565	2,561	–0.16	VERNON COUNTY	29,773	29,977	0.69
Herman, town	2,151	2,183	1.49	Bergen, town	1,364	1,368	0.29
Holland, town	2,239	2,250	0.49	Chaseburg, village	284	287	1.06
Howards Grove, village	3,188	3,216	0.88	Christiana, town	931	938	0.75
Kohler, village	2,120	2,117	–0.14	Clinton, town	1,358	1,373	1.10
Lima, town	2,982	2,985	0.10	Coon, town	728	742	1.92
Lyndon, town	1,542	1,544	0.13	Coon Valley, village	765	764	–0.13
Mitchell, town	1,304	1,307	0.23	De Soto (part), village	179	185	3.35
Mosel, town	790	781	–1.14	Forest, town	634	639	0.79
Oostburg, village	2,887	2,921	1.18	Franklin, town	1,140	1,172	2.81
Plymouth, city	8,445	8,428	–0.20	Genoa, town	789	798	1.14
Plymouth, town	3,195	3,193	–0.06	Genoa, village	253	252	–0.40
Random Lake, village	1,594	1,583	–0.69	Greenwood, town	847	841	–0.71
Rhine, town	2,134	2,125	–0.42	Hamburg, town	973	973	0.00
Russell, town	377	372	–1.33	Harmony, town	755	775	2.65

WISCONSIN POPULATION
BY COUNTY AND MUNICIPALITY
April 1, 2010 and January 1, 2014–Continued

County and Municipality	2010 Census	2014 Estimate	Percent Change	County and Municipality	2010 Census	2014 Estimate	Percent Change
Hillsboro, city	1,417	1,408	−0.64	Evergreen, town	1,135	1,133	−0.18
Hillsboro, town	807	812	0.62	Frog Creek, town	130	130	0.00
Jefferson, town	1,143	1,138	−0.44	Gull Lake, town	186	188	1.08
Kickapoo, town	626	642	2.56	Long Lake, town	624	630	0.96
La Farge, village	746	703	−5.76	Madge, town	508	514	1.18
Liberty, town	252	262	3.97	Minong, town	917	932	1.64
Ontario, village	554	554	0.00	Minong, village	527	522	−0.95
Readstown, village	415	420	1.20	Sarona, town	384	386	0.52
Stark, town	363	368	1.38	Shell Lake, city	1,347	1,359	0.89
Sterling, town	633	627	−0.95	Spooner, city	2,682	2,651	−1.16
Stoddard, village	774	786	1.55	Spooner, town	706	717	1.56
Union, town	700	714	2.00	Springbrook, town	445	438	−1.57
Viola (part), village	222	224	0.90	Stinnett, town	246	242	−1.63
Viroqua, city	4,362	4,343	−0.44	Stone Lake, town	508	512	0.79
Viroqua, town	1,718	1,744	1.51	Trego, town	932	941	0.97
Webster, town	778	807	3.73				
Westby, city	2,200	2,228	1.27	WASHINGTON COUNTY	131,887	133,071	0.90
Wheatland, town	561	577	2.85	Addison, town	3,495	3,469	−0.74
Whitestown, town	502	513	2.19	Barton, town	2,637	2,632	−0.19
				Erin, town	3,747	3,767	0.53
VILAS COUNTY	21,430	21,523	0.43	Farmington, town	4,014	4,027	0.32
Arbor Vitae, town	3,316	3,324	0.24	Germantown, town	254	249	−1.97
Boulder Junction, town	933	941	0.86	Germantown, village	19,749	19,891	0.72
Cloverland, town	1,029	1,029	0.00	Hartford (part), city	14,223	14,320	0.68
Conover, town	1,235	1,236	0.08	Hartford, town	3,609	3,597	−0.33
Eagle River, city	1,398	1,370	−2.00	Jackson, town	4,134	4,296	3.92
Lac du Flambeau, town	3,441	3,457	0.46	Jackson, village	6,753	6,830	1.14
Land O'Lakes, town	861	862	0.12	Kewaskum, town	1,053	1,055	0.19
Lincoln, town	2,423	2,440	0.70	Kewaskum (part), village	4,004	4,015	0.27
Manitowish Waters, town	566	580	2.47	Milwaukee (part), city	0	0	0.00
Phelps, town	1,200	1,231	2.58	Newburg (part), village	1,157	1,151	−0.52
Plum Lake, town	491	496	1.02	Polk, town	3,937	3,973	0.91
Presque Isle, town	618	630	1.94	Richfield, village	11,300	11,424	1.10
St. Germain, town	2,085	2,075	−0.48	Slinger, village	5,068	5,140	1.42
Washington, town	1,451	1,468	1.17	Trenton, town	4,732	4,739	0.15
Winchester, town	383	384	0.26	Wayne, town	2,169	2,190	0.97
				West Bend, city	31,078	31,531	1.46
WALWORTH COUNTY	102,228	102,837	0.60	West Bend, town	4,774	4,775	0.02
Bloomfield, town	6,278	1,595	-75				
Bloomfield, village	0	4,680	0.00	WAUKESHA COUNTY	389,891	392,761	0.74
Burlington (part), city	0	0	0.00	Big Bend, village	1,290	1,292	0.16
Darien, town	1,693	1,695	0.12	Brookfield, city	37,920	37,847	−0.19
Darien, village	1,580	1,588	0.51	Brookfield, town	6,116	6,064	−0.85
Delavan, city	8,463	8,433	−0.35	Butler, village	1,841	1,832	−0.49
Delavan, town	5,285	5,267	−0.34	Chenequa, village	590	587	−0.51
East Troy, town	4,021	4,041	0.50	Delafield, city	7,085	7,093	0.11
East Troy, village	4,281	4,282	0.02	Delafield, town	8,400	8,221	−2.13
Elkhorn, city	10,084	9,956	−1.27	Dousman, village	2,302	2,327	1.09
Fontana on Geneva Lake,				Eagle, town	3,507	3,507	0.00
village	1,672	1,678	0.36	Eagle, village	1,950	1,946	−0.21
Geneva, town	4,993	5,012	0.38	Elm Grove, village	5,934	5,963	0.49
Genoa City (part), village	3,036	3,052	0.53	Genesee, town	7,340	7,330	−0.14
Lafayette, town	1,979	1,967	−0.61	Hartland, village	9,110	9,141	0.34
La Grange, town	2,454	2,453	−0.04	Lac La Belle (part), village	289	291	0.69
Lake Geneva, city	7,651	7,696	0.59	Lannon, village	1,107	1,099	−0.72
Linn, town	2,383	2,403	0.84	Lisbon, town	10,157	10,236	0.78
Lyons, town	3,698	3,697	−0.03	Menomonee Falls, village	35,626	35,798	0.48
Mukwonago (part), village	101	117	15.84	Merton, town	8,338	8,383	0.54
Richmond, town	1,884	1,886	0.11	Merton, village	3,346	3,435	2.66
Sharon, town	907	898	−0.99	Milwaukee (part), city	0	0	0.00
Sharon, village	1,605	1,593	−0.75	Mukwanago, town	7,959	8,010	0.64
Spring Prairie, town	2,181	2,174	−0.32	Mukwonago (part), village	7,254	7,390	1.87
Sugar Creek, town	3,943	3,936	−0.18	Muskego, city	24,135	24,304	0.70
Troy, town	2,353	2,352	−0.04	Nashotah, village	1,395	1,387	−0.57
Walworth, town	1,702	1,686	−0.94	New Berlin, city	39,584	40,130	1.38
Walworth, village	2,816	2,821	0.18	North Prairie, village	2,141	2,144	0.14
Whitewater (part), city	11,150	11,821	6.02	Oconomowoc, city	15,759	16,293	3.39
Whitewater, town	1,471	1,481	0.68	Oconomowoc, town	8,408	8,602	2.31
Williams Bay, village	2,564	2,577	0.51	Oconomowoc Lake, village	595	589	−1.01
				Ottawa, town	3,859	3,876	0.44
WASHBURN COUNTY	15,911	15,948	0.23	Pewaukee, city	13,195	13,728	4.04
Barronett, town	442	437	−1.13	Pewaukee, village	8,166	8,154	−0.15
Bashaw, town	946	951	0.53	Summit, village	4,674	4,713	0.83
Bass Lake, town	505	519	2.77	Sussex, village	10,518	10,669	1.44
Beaver Brook, town	713	720	0.98	Vernon, town	7,601	7,624	0.30
Birchwood, town	478	482	0.84	Wales, village	2,549	2,544	−0.20
Birchwood, village	442	440	−0.45	Waukesha, city	70,718	71,044	0.46
Brooklyn, town	254	257	1.18	Waukesha, town	9,133	9,168	0.38
Casey, town	353	356	0.85				
Chicog, town	234	229	−2.14	WAUPACA COUNTY	52,410	52,435	0.05
Crystal, town	267	262	−1.87	Bear Creek, town	823	818	−0.61

WISCONSIN POPULATION
BY COUNTY AND MUNCIPALITY
April 1, 2010 and January 1, 2014–Continued

County and Municipality	2010 Census	2014 Estimate	Percent Change
Big Falls, village	61	59	-3.28
Caledonia, town	1,627	1,654	1.66
Clintonville, city	4,559	4,535	-0.53
Dayton, town	2,748	2,757	0.33
Dupont, town	738	734	-0.54
Embarrass, village	404	396	-1.98
Farmington, town	3,974	4,009	0.88
Fremont, town	597	588	-1.51
Fremont, village	679	677	-0.29
Harrison, town	468	469	0.21
Helvetia, town	636	630	-0.94
Iola, town	971	982	1.13
Iola, village	1,301	1,287	-1.08
Larrabee, town	1,381	1,377	-0.29
Lebanon, town	1,665	1,680	0.90
Lind, town	1,579	1,591	0.76
Little Wolf, town	1,424	1,424	0.00
Manawa, city	1,371	1,332	-2.84
Marion (part), city	1,235	1,232	-0.24
Matteson, town	936	929	-0.75
Mukwa, town	2,930	2,956	0.89
New London (part), city	5,685	5,690	0.09
Ogdensburg, village	185	179	-3.24
Royalton, town	1,434	1,441	0.49
St. Lawrence, town	710	706	-0.56
Scandinavia, town	1,066	1,064	-0.19
Scandinavia, village	363	363	0.00
Union, town	806	811	0.62
Waupaca, city	6,069	6,076	0.12
Waupaca, town	1,173	1,186	1.11
Weyauwega, city	1,900	1,914	0.74
Weyauwega, town	583	570	-2.23
Wyoming, town	329	319	-3.04
WAUSHARA COUNTY	24,496	24,511	0.06
Aurora, town	985	1,003	1.83
Berlin (part), city	89	90	1.12
Bloomfield, town	1,052	1,067	1.43
Coloma, town	753	752	-0.13
Coloma, village	450	457	1.56
Dakota, town	1,227	1,237	0.81
Deerfield, town	737	750	1.76
Hancock, town	528	537	1.70
Hancock, village	417	411	-1.44
Leon, town	1,439	1,434	-0.35
Lohrville, village	402	399	-0.75
Marion, town	2,038	2,038	0.00
Mount Morris, town	1,097	1,107	0.91
Oasis, town	389	395	1.54
Plainfield, town	550	547	-0.55
Plainfield, village	862	857	-0.58
Poy Sippi, town	931	923	-0.86
Redgranite, village	2,149	2,137	-0.56
Richford, town	612	632	3.27
Rose, town	640	648	1.25
Saxeville, town	986	988	0.20
Springwater, town	1,274	1,278	0.31
Warren, town	668	667	-0.15
Wautoma, city	2,218	2,171	-2.12
Wautoma, town	1,278	1,274	-0.31
Wild Rose, village	725	712	-1.79

County and Municipality	2010 Census	2014 Estimate	Percent Change
WINNEBAGO COUNTY	166,994	168,216	0.73
Algoma, town	6,822	6,884	0.91
Appleton (part), city	1,490	1,485	-0.34
Black Wolf, town	2,410	2,428	0.75
Clayton, town	3,951	4,016	1.65
Menasha (part), city	15,144	15,110	-0.22
Menasha, town	18,498	18,624	0.68
Neenah, city	25,501	25,833	1.30
Neenah, town	3,237	3,435	6.12
Nekimi, town	1,429	1,421	-0.56
Nepeuskun, town	710	731	2.96
Omro, city	3,517	3,526	0.26
Omro, town	2,116	2,142	1.23
Oshkosh, city	66,083	66,412	0.50
Oshkosh, town	2,475	2,474	-0.04
Poygan, town	1,301	1,306	0.38
Rushford, town	1,561	1,574	0.83
Utica, town	1,299	1,313	1.08
Vinland, town	1,765	1,750	-0.85
Winchester, town	1,763	1,777	0.79
Winneconne, town	2,350	2,385	1.49
Winneconne, village	2,383	2,397	0.59
Wolf River, town	1,189	1,193	0.34
WOOD COUNTY	74,749	74,954	0.27
Arpin, town	929	949	2.15
Arpin, village	333	329	-1.20
Auburndale, town	860	840	-2.33
Aurburndale, village	703	706	0.43
Biron, village	839	835	-0.48
Cameron, town	511	488	-4.50
Cary, town	424	427	0.71
Cranmoor, town	168	164	-2.38
Dexter, town	359	357	-0.56
Grand Rapids, town	7,646	7,691	0.59
Hansen, town	690	685	-0.72
Hewitt, village	828	829	0.12
Hiles, town	167	167	0.00
Lincoln, town	1,564	1,572	0.51
Marshfield (part), city	18,218	18,238	0.11
Marshfield, town	764	774	1.31
Milladore, town	690	688	-0.29
Milladore (part), village	276	280	1.45
Nekoosa, city	2,580	2,568	-0.47
Pittsville, city	874	877	0.34
Port Edwards, town	1,427	1,421	-0.42
Port Edwards, village	1,818	1,790	-1.54
Remington, town	268	261	-2.61
Richfield, town	1,628	1,621	-0.43
Rock, town	855	860	0.58
Rudolph, town	1,028	1,025	-0.29
Rudolph, village	439	434	-1.14
Saratoga, town	5,142	5,170	0.54
Seneca, town	1,120	1,119	-0.09
Sherry, town	803	808	0.62
Sigel, town	1,051	1,048	-0.29
Vesper, village	584	585	0.17
Wisconsin Rapids, city	18,367	18,559	1.05
Wood, town	796	789	-0.88

*Part of the Village of Harrison was annexed by the Town of Harrison on March 8, 2013.

Source: Wisconsin Department of Administration, Demographic Services Center, *January 1, 2014 Final Population Estimates,* October 2014.

HIGHLIGHTS OF MILITARY AND VETERANS AFFAIRS IN WISCONSIN

Military Service — More Wisconsinites served in World War II than in any other conflict, with Vietnam ranking second, but fatalities were heaviest in the Civil War. From the Civil War through the operations in Iraq and Afghanistan, about 26,800 Wisconsinites have lost their lives performing military service during times of conflict. Since September 11, 2001, nearly every unit in the Wisconsin Army and Air National Guard has been ordered to active duty in support of operations in Afghanistan (Operation Enduring Freedom) and Iraq (Operation Iraqi Freedom), as well as homeland defense missions in the United States (Operation Noble Eagle) and continuing operations in the Balkans. In 2009, nearly 4,000 Wisconsin National Guard members deployed in support of the Global War on Terror, including 3,200 members of the 32nd Infantry Brigade Combat Team who conducted the largest operational deployment of the Wisconsin National Guard since World War II.

As of June 2015, about 10,000 citizen-soldiers and airmen were serving in Wisconsin National Guard units at military facilities located in over 60 communities throughout the state.

Veterans' Programs — Since the end of World War II, about $2.3 billion in grants and loans have been provided to Wisconsin veterans. Historically, most of the grants have been for educational purposes, while the overwhelming number of loans were for housing. The grants have also covered subsistence and emergency health care assistance for needy veterans. Eligible veterans and, in some instances, spouses and dependent children of deceased veterans may qualify for personal loans to finance expenses, such as education, business start-ups or purchases, medical bills, debt consolidation, and mobile home purchases.

In 2013, Wisconsin veterans and their families received about $16 million in federal educational and vocational rehabilitation assistance. Wisconsin veterans received about $972 million in benefits through the compensation and pension programs. As of 2013, there were over 409,000 veterans living in the state.

The Wisconsin Veterans Homes at Chippewa Falls, King, and Union Grove had 1,012 members at the end of 2014. In general, to be eligible for residence, a veteran must have completed certain military service requirements and be a Wisconsin resident on the date of admission to a veterans home. In addition, he or she must have been a resident of Wisconsin at the time of entry into service or a resident of the state for any 5-year period after service and prior to application for admission. Depending on availability of space, spouses and surviving spouses or parents of qualifying veterans may also be admitted.

The following tables present selected data. Consult the footnoted sources for more detailed information about military and veterans affairs.

WISCONSIN'S MILITARY SERVICE

Military Action	Number Served	Number Killed
Civil War	91,379[1]	12,216
Spanish-American War	5,469	134[2]
Mexican Border Service	4,168	NA
World War I	122,215	3,932
World War II	332,200	8,390
Korean Conflict	132,000	729
Vietnam	165,400	1,239
Lebanon/Grenada	400	1
Panama	520	1
Operations Desert Shield/Desert Storm	10,400	11
Somalia	426	2
Bosnia/Kosovo	678	NA
Iraq and Afghanistan Theaters of Operations since September 11, 2001	34,792	127[3]

Note: Includes Wisconsin residents who served on active duty during declared wars and officially designated periods of hostilities.

NA – Not available.

[1]Total includes some who enlisted more than once. The net number of soldiers recruited in Wisconsin was about 80,000.

[2]Casualties only from Wisconsin 1st, 2nd, 3rd and 4th Regiments. No details available for Wisconsin residents serving in federal units.

[3]Includes one killed in attack on Pentagon on September 11, 2001.

Sources: U.S. Veterans Administration; U.S. Department of Defense; and Wisconsin Department of Veterans Affairs, departmental data, April 14, 2015.

DIRECT STATE BENEFITS TO WISCONSIN WAR VETERANS
1943 – 1961

Fiscal Year	Number of Grants and Loans	Total Benefits	Rehabilitation Trust Funds	Housing Fund
8/1/43-1946	6,359	$975,173	$975,173	—
1947	10,701	2,207,914	2,207,914	—
1948	9,578	3,511,527	3,511,527	—
1949	6,086	2,512,517	2,512,517	—
1950	5,867	3,463,058	2,040,658	$1,422,400
1951	6,137	5,178,106	2,104,550	3,073,556
1952	10,442	22,362,081	1,995,116	20,366,965
1953	5,099	8,842,780	1,331,140	7,511,640
1954	4,507	4,420,030	1,502,748	2,917,282
1955	3,482	4,236,298	1,112,173	3,124,125
1956	3,639	5,389,187	787,861	4,601,326
1957	2,890	4,246,004	730,452	3,515,552
1958	2,779	4,912,233	660,994	4,251,239
1959	2,954	5,419,609	670,262	4,749,347
1960	3,345	7,341,922	591,272	6,750,650
1961	3,081	6,654,189	584,426	6,069,763

Note: The 1961 Legislature merged all veterans' funds into the Veterans Trust Fund.

Source: Wisconsin Department of Veterans Affairs, departmental data, March 1995.

VETERANS BENEFITS, 1962 – 2014

Fiscal Year	Total Benefits	Grants			Economic Assistance	Personal Loan Program	Loans		
		Economic	Educational	Full-Time Educational Grants			Second Mortgage Housing	Revenue Bond Housing Loans	Gen. Obligation Bond Housing Loans
1962	$6,681,585	$53,891	$2,100		$515,008		$6,110,586		
1965	3,737,259	100,751	13,654		359,705		3,263,149		
1970	9,265,183	193,044	289,743		3,605,092		5,177,305		
1975	69,554,865	607,279	1,240,917	$1,836,207	9,098,837		10,076,963	$46,694,662	
1980	197,668,743	362,556	1,099,266	731,672	6,735,632		843,433		$187,896,184
1981	90,183,867	424,041	1,092,510	479,232	4,323,114		1,345,430	67,130,619	15,388,921
1982	16,221,058	378,614	1,159,025	469,347	3,656,939		1,062,015	8,400,780	1,094,338
1983	56,700,920	591,351	986,106	391,542	3,073,217		762,930		50,895,774
1984	58,137,350	469,314	1,227,239	328,036	3,116,789		782,463		52,213,509
1985	47,689,638	453,502	1,483,693	225,043	2,737,544		552,106		42,237,750
1986	19,297,133	378,999	1,255,252	157,379	3,678,759		243,147		13,583,597
1987	18,883,716	529,634	807,253	127,789	2,802,819		141,370		14,474,851
1988	28,134,558	426,595	696,352	91,392	2,405,640		289,606		24,224,971
1989	35,412,289	533,929	698,946	77,787	2,459,813		832,436		30,809,378
1990	44,837,433	636,434	683,355	62,025	2,776,835		327,819		40,350,965
1991	48,562,575	398,706	743,351	50,993	3,945,614		62,960		43,360,951
1992	35,155,551	381,312	526,215	137,799	4,192,505		18,799		29,898,921
1993	22,446,997	472,302	512,770	167,838	2,673,585				18,620,502
1994	58,337,813[1]	451,666	716,858	667	2,567,053				33,157,403
1995	126,009,594[1]	552,893	754,052		2,544,584				111,133,109
1996	80,581,789	601,030	1,609,350		3,189,625				75,181,784
1997	99,984,937	937,294	1,797,649		2,401,548				94,848,446
1998	160,760,389	783,664	1,680,881		666,575[2]	$10,215,928[2]			147,413,341
1999	139,857,465	2,263,317	1,447,882			11,837,974			124,908,352
2000	143,192,551	3,226,128	1,786,205			10,802,068			127,378,150
2001	73,390,596	1,205,846	1,768,452			9,034,356			61,381,942
2002	88,227,531	1,925,094	2,822,134			15,780,270			67,700,033
2003	83,866,773	1,752,733	2,909,812			19,792,680			59,411,548
2004	95,593,212	1,296,310	4,384,642			11,808,566			78,103,694
2005	37,428,288	413,564	5,698,107			2,271,942			29,044,675
2006	23,935,069	1,052,493	4,751,263			4,113,262			14,018,050
2007	48,026,312	678,109	3,715,648			5,933,810			37,698,745
2008	59,388,229	1,028,788	2,276,489			5,081,986			51,000,967
2009	43,587,113	961,497	1,694,312			2,764,736			38,166,568
2010	15,859,166	426,535	1,726,307			3,133,961			10,572,363
2011	4,011,393	682,235	1,271,083			2,058,075			
2012	2,531,220	577,061	1,044,751			909,397			
2013	1,242,884	443,312	799,572						
2014	1,181,380	713,279	468,101						

Note: The 1961 Legislature merged all veterans' funds into the Veterans Trust Fund.

[1]Includes $21,444,166 (FY94) and $11,024,956 (FY95) in consumer loans under the Veterans Trust Fund stabilization provision of 1993 Wisconsin Act 16.

[2]Personal loan program replaced economic assistance loans.

Source: Wisconsin Department of Veterans Affairs, departmental data, April 2015.

WISCONSIN NATIONAL GUARD

JOINT UNITS

Joint Force Headquarters Wisconsin
Joint Force Headquarters Detachment – Madison
    54th Civil Support Team (WMD) – Madison

ARMY UNITS

Headquarters, Wisconsin Army National Guard – Madison
Joint Force Headquarters Separate Units
    Recruiting and Retention Battalion – Madison
Det. 1, Recruiting and Retention Battalion – Madison
Det. 2, Recruiting and Retention Battalion – Milwaukee
Det. 52, Operational Support Airlift Command – Madison
54th Civil Support Team – Madison
505th Trial Defense Team
32nd Infantry Brigade Combat Team
Headquarters and Headquarters Co. – Camp Douglas
    1st Battalion, 120th Field Artillery
    Headquarters and Headquarters Battery (–) – Wisconsin Rapids
        Det. 1, Headquarters and Headquarters Company – Berlin
    Battery A – Marshfield
    Battery B – Stevens Point
    Battery C – Oconomowoc
    2nd Battalion, 127th Infantry
    Headquarters and Headquarters Co. (–) – Appleton
        Det. 1, Headquarters Co. – Clintonville
    Company A (–) – Waupun
        Det. 1, Co. A – Ripon
    Company B – Green Bay
    Company C – Fond du Lac
    Company D – Marinette
    1st Battalion, 128th Infantry
    Headquarters and Headquarters Co. (–) – Eau Claire
        Det. 1, Headquarters Co. – Abbotsford
    Company A – Menomonie
    Company B (–) – New Richmond
        Det. 1, Co. B – Rice Lake
    Company C (–) – Arcadia
        Det. 1, Co. C – Onalaska
    Company D – River Falls
    132nd Brigade Support Battalion
    Headquarters and Headquarters Co. – Portage
    Company A (–) (Distribution) – Janesville
        Det. 1, Co. A – Elkhorn
    Company B (Maintenance) – Mauston
    Company C (Medical) – Racine
    Company D (Forward Support) – Madison
    Company E (Forward Support) – Antigo
    Company F (Forward Support) – Mosinee
    Company G (Forward Support) – Waupaca
    Company H – Neillsville
    173rd Brigade Engineer Battalion
    Headquarters and Headquarters Co. – Wausau
    Company A (–) – Tomahawk
        Det. 1, Co. A – Rhinelander
    Company B – Onalaska
    Company C – Camp Douglas
    Company D (Military Intelligence) – Madison
        Det. 1, Company D (TUAS) – Camp Douglas
    1st Squadron, 105th Cavalry (Reconnaissance, Surveillance and Target Acquisition)
    Headquarters and Headquarters Troop – Madison
    Troop A – Fort Atkinson
    Troop B – Watertown
    Troop C – Reedsburg

64th Troop Command
Headquarters – Madison
    Wisconsin Medical Detachment – Camp Douglas
    732nd Combat Sustainment Support Battalion
    Headquarters and Headquarters Company – Tomah
    107th Maintenance Co. (–) – Sparta
        Det. 1, 107th Maintenance Co. – Viroqua
    1157th Transportation Co. – Oshkosh
    1158th Transportation Co. (–) – Beloit
        Det. 1, 1158th Trans. Co. – Black River Falls
    1st Battalion, 147th Aviation Regiment
    Headquarters and Headquarters Co. (–) – Madison
    Company A – Madison
        Det. 1, Co. C – Madison
    Company D (–) – Madison
    Company E (–) – Madison
        Det. 1, Co. B, 248th Aviation Support Bn. – West Bend
        Det. 1, Co. C, 2nd Battalion, 135th Aviation Regiment – West Bend
        Det. 2, Co. D, 2nd Battalion, 135th Aviation Regiment – West Bend
        Det. 2, Co. E, 2nd Battalion, 135th Aviation Regiment – West Bend
    Company F (–) 2nd Battalion, 238th Aviation Regiment – West Bend
        Det. 4, HHC, 2nd Battalion, 238th Aviation Regiment – West Bend
        Det. 5, Co. D, 2nd Battalion, 238th Aviation Regiment – West Bend
        Det. 5, Co. E, 2nd Battalion, 238th Aviation Regiment – West Bend
        Det. 2, Co. D, 1st Battalion, 112th Aviation Regiment
    641st Troop Command Battalion
    Headquarters and Headquarters Detachment – Madison
    135th Medical Co. – Waukesha
    1967th Contingency Contracting Team – Camp Douglas
    273rd Engineer Co. (Wheeled Sapper) – Medford
    457th Chemical Co. (–) – Hartford
        Det. 1, 457th Chemical Co. – Burlington
    112th Mobile Public Affairs Det. – Madison
    132 Army Band – Madison
157th Maneuver Enhancement Brigade
Headquarters and Headquarters Co. – Milwaukee
    1st Battalion, 121st Field Artillery (HIMARS)
    Headquarters and Headquarters Battery (HIMARS) – Milwaukee
    Battery A (HIMARS) – Sussex
    Battery B (HIMARS) – Plymouth
    108th Forward Support Company (HIMARS) – Sussex
    257th Brigade Support Battalion
    Headquarters and Headquarters Det. – Oak Creek
    Company A (Distribution) – Whitewater
    Company B (Support Maintenance) – Kenosha
    924th Engineer Det. (Facilities) – Chippewa Falls
    32nd Military Police Company (–) – Milwaukee
    357th Signal Network Support Co. – Two Rivers
    949th Engineer Det. (Survey & Design Tm) – Chippewa Falls

724th Engineer Battalion
  Headquarters and Headquarters Co. – Chippewa Falls
  Company A (Forward Support Company) – Hayward
  106th Engineer Det. (Quarry Team) – Tomah
  229th Engineer Co. (–) (Horizontal) – Prairie du Chien
    Det. 1, 229th Engineer Co. – Platteville
  824th Engineer Det. (Concrete) – Spooner
  829th Engineer Co. (–) (Vertical) – Spooner
    Det. 1, 829th Engineer Co. – Ashland
  950th Engineer Co. (–) (Clearance) – Superior
    954th Engineer Platoon (Clearance) – Superior

426th Regiment – Regional Training Institute (Wisconsin Military Academy)
Headquarters and Headquarters Det. – Fort McCoy
  Wisconsin Training Center – Fort McCoy
  1st Battalion, 426th Rgt. (Field Artillery) – Fort McCoy
  2nd Battalion, 426th Rgt. (Modular Training) – Fort McCoy

AIR UNITS

Headquarters, Wisconsin Air National Guard – Madison
115th Fighter Wing – Truax Field, Madison
  115th Operations Group
    176th Fighter Squadron
    115th Operations Support Flight
  115th Maintenance Group
    115th Aircraft Maintenance Squadron
    115th Maintenance Squadron
    115th Maintenance Operations Flight
  115th Mission Support Group
    115th Logistics Readiness Squadron
    115th Security Forces Squadron
    115th Force Support Squadron
    115th Civil Engineer Squadron
    115th Communications Flight
  115th Medical Group

128th Air Refueling Wing – Mitchell Field, Milwaukee
  128th Operations Group
    126th Air Refueling Squadron
    128th Operations Support Flight
  128th Maintenance Group
    128th Aircraft Maintenance Squadron
    128th Maintenance Squadron
    128th Maintenance Operations Flight
  128th Mission Support Group
    128th Logistics Readiness Squadron
    128th Security Forces Squadron
    128th Mission Support Flight
    128th Services Flight
    128th Civil Engineer Squadron
    128th Communications Flight
  128th Medical Group
Volk Field Combat Readiness Training Center – Camp Douglas
128th Air Control Squadron
  126th Weather Flight

Bold Face – Major Command
(–) – Headquarters of a split unit
Abbreviations:
Bn. – Battalion
Co. – Company
CRTC – Combat Readiness Training Center
Det. – Detachment

HIMARS – High-Mobility Artillery Rocket System
MP – Military Police
Rgt. – Regiment
Trans. – Transportation
TUAS – Tactical Unmanned Aircraft System
WMD – Weapons of Mass Destruction

Source: Wisconsin Department of Military Affairs, departmental data, May 2015.

MEMBERSHIP, WISCONSIN VETERANS HOMES
1888 – 2014

	Civil and Indian Wars	Spanish– American	World War I		World War II		Korean Conflict		Total
			Men	Women	Men	Women	Men	Women	
1888	72	—	—	—	—	—	—	—	72
1890	139	—	—	—	—	—	—	—	139
1900	680	—	—	—	—	—	—	—	680
1910	699	—	—	—	—	—	—	—	699
1920	532	—	—	—	—	—	—	—	532
1930	254	108	10	14	—	—	—	—	386
1940	89	196	101	130	—	—	—	—	516
1950	27	156	189	93	5	1	—	—	471
1960	4	74	203	94	40	5	—	—	450
1961	3	66	221	88	39	8	—	—	427
1962	3	66	223	82	52	9	—	—	431
1963	3	67	235	87	57	10	—	—	459
1964	3	63	237	105	61	16	—	—	485
1965	2	62	247	112	77	16	—	—	516
1966	1	56	258	112	86	21	—	—	534
1967	1	46	272	120	93	20	—	—	555
1968	1	48	253	123	93	16	—	—	534
1969	1	43	253	145	101	14	—	—	560
1970	1	35	279	146	153	20	1	0	635
1971	1	39	316	160	184	31	2	0	723
1972	0	28	279	155	199	39	2	0	702
1973	0	25	285	108	199	37	0	1	715
1974	0	21	279	175	185	37	0	2	699

	Spanish- American		World War I		World War II		Korean Conflict		Vietnam		Other Eras[1]		Total
	Vets.	Deps.	Vets.	Deps.	Vets.	Deps.	Vets.	Deps.	Vets.	Deps.	Vets.	Deps.	
1975	1	18	272	171	198	40	3	2	0	0	0	0	705
1976	1	14	254	167	209	40	2	2	0	0	0	0	689
1977	1	13	270	164	205	41	4	2	0	0	0	0	700
1978	1	11	261	158	218	38	3	2	0	0	0	0	692
1979	1	11	244	146	227	37	4	1	0	0	0	0	672
1980	1	8	242	144	241	36	5	1	0	0	0	0	678
1981	0	8	224	139	264	40	8	2	0	0	0	0	685
1982	0	7	189	124	282	43	11	2	0	0	0	0	658
1983	0	5	171	111	297	42	14	2	1	0	0	0	643
1984	0	4	144	97	316	47	21	2	3	0	0	0	634
1985	0	4	129	102	329	54	28	0	5	0	0	0	651
1986	0	4	117	92	348	56	35	5	7	0	0	0	664
1987	0	2	108	84	384	60	36	4	8	0	0	0	686
1988	0	1	84	76	395	55	45	7	8	0	0	0	671
1989	0	2	62	75	399	67	50	7	9	1	0	0	672
1990	0	2	49	65	431	76	62	8	10	1	3	0	707
1991	0	2	43	57	440	74	69	10	10	2	3	0	710
1992	0	1	33	44	442	77	82	10	12	1	2	0	704
1993	0	1	23	41	463	73	94	9	11	1	2	0	718
1994	0	1	14	33	488	83	99	11	12	2	1	0	744
1995	0	1	8	31	484	84	-99	12	16	2	1	0	738
1996	0	1	4	24	489	79	103	12	25	1	1	0	739
1997	0	1	3	20	479	82	107	11	38	1	3	0	744
1998	0	0	1	17	460	83	123	12	39	1	9	0	745
1999	0	0	0	12	445	87	128	11	41	3	13	1	741
2000	0	0	0	10	423	94	132	12	47	4	21	2	745
2001[2]	0	0	0	9	414	95	133	10	51	3	25	2	742
2002	0	0	0	8	404	103	130	11	54	3	29	2	744
2003	0	0	0	7	433	105	140	13	67	3	35	2	805
2004	0	0	0	3	416	99	148	15	72	3	40	2	798
2005	0	0	0	2	350	103	144	15	71	3	40	2	730
2006	0	0	0	1	407	119	164	17	87	5	50	4	854
2007	0	0	0	1	475	135	173	26	100	8	3	0	921
2008	0	0	0	1	417	123	177	26	115	7	4	0	870
2009	0	0	0	1	389	130	193	21	122	8	8	0	947
2010	0	0	0	1	356	127	176	22	122	8	10	0	892
2011	0	0	0	1	339	124	170	19	154	12	12	0	904
2012	0	0	0	1	330	121	180	32	178	11	19	2	953
2013	0	0	0	1	412	145	286	53	276	16	44	2	1,235
2014	0	0	0	1	259	128	215	34	262	11	98	4	1,012

Deps. – Dependents.

[1]Other periods of hostilities for which expeditionary medals were awarded.

[2]The Wisconsin Veterans Home at King was established in 1887, and the home at Union Grove opened in 2001. Data starting in 2001 includes both homes.

Source: Wisconsin Department of Veterans Affairs, departmental data, May 2015.

FEDERAL EXPENDITURES FOR VETERANS
By State, Federal Fiscal Year 2013

State	Veteran Population	Total Expenditures[1]	Compensation and Pension[2]	Medical Care[3]	Education and Vocational Rehabilitation/ Employment
Alabama	414,963	$2,758,424	$1,580,861	$988,150	$61,850
Alaska	74,671	490,861	211,260	217,751	343,820
Arizona.	527,400	3,054,673	1,409,346	1,301,507	79,063
Arkansas	250,095	1,893,860	924,671	890,127	1,599,760
California	1,795,455	12,207,180	5,397,860	5,209,559	324,347
Colorado	390,824	2,386,725	1,212,143	850,235	96,416
Connecticut	207,759	1,032,246	365,638	570,192	34,331
Delaware	78,016	352,268	169,963	147,974	31,054
District of Columbia	31,166	313,899	78,699	204,146	892,555
Florida	1,520,563	10,013,171	4,728,273	4,392,344	453,034
Georgia.	774,464	4,509,285	2,482,164	1,574,087	142,729
Hawaii	116,947	723,868	337,919	243,220	51,513
Idaho	138,108	718,516	334,504	332,499	311,330
ILLINOIS	744,710	3,719,185	1,450,236	1,957,618	150,033
Indiana	490,380	2,392,111	1,092,855	1,149,224	74,079
IOWA	233,815	1,163,334	505,601	583,653	103,950
Kansas	223,708	1,192,744	529,023	559,771	139,199
Kentucky	339,334	2,165,597	1,087,772	938,626	120,767
Louisiana.	315,342	1,953,168	1,016,206	816,195	42,577
Maine	127,694	845,382	467,398	335,408	333,943
Maryland.	443,076	2,378,799	1,047,226	997,630	192,975
Massachusetts	374,809	2,277,281	985,894	1,098,412	208,565
MICHIGAN	660,773	3,260,524	1,675,388	1,376,571	133,629
MINNESOTA	360,754	2,205,968	986,609	1,085,731	88,010
Mississippi	225,469	1,416,013	666,715	661,288	189,473
Missouri	497,874	2,812,500	1,386,280	1,236,747	38,237
Montana	101,597	631,664	290,869	302,558	63,597
Nebraska	138,773	964,865	487,975	413,294	95,562
Nevada	225,933	1,525,429	641,969	787,899	50,861
New Hampshire	110,778	597,908	268,735	278,312	196,113
New Jersey	425,094	1,852,581	906,744	749,724	67,315
New Mexico	170,699	1,261,036	686,222	507,499	493,102
New York	885,796	5,389,716	2,063,566	2,833,048	399,186
North Carolina	769,384	4,901,333	2,712,319	1,789,827	22,770
North Dakota.	56,213	321,883	149,596	149,518	296,446
Ohio	877,894	4,347,439	1,837,567	2,213,426	131,030
Oklahoma	340,395	2,421,524	1,544,376	746,118	128,169
Oregon	322,355	2,187,901	1,100,287	959,445	359,065
Pennsylvania	953,644	4,492,300	2,029,589	2,103,647	35,525
Rhode Island	69,206	446,067	193,988	216,555	223,348
South Carolina	420,968	2,782,211	1,557,784	1,001,079	30,364
South Dakota.	75,687	546,660	209,347	306,949	236,754
Tennessee	521,267	3,217,610	1,652,616	1,328,239	1,118,114
Texas	1,667,740	11,196,928	6,091,910	3,986,903	85,974
Utah	150,771	818,176	350,923	381,279	20,296
Vermont	48,812	265,530	118,286	126,949	874,229
Virginia.	840,398	4,508,876	2,291,200	1,343,447	343,793
Washington.	602,272	3,218,771	1,788,537	1,086,440	44,341
West Virginia.	173,389	1,323,301	625,689	653,270	133,679
WISCONSIN	409,419	2,305,235	972,511	1,199,045	15,751
Wyoming.	56,518	331,760	127,557	188,453	46,541
UNITED STATES	21,882,153	$131,517,734	$63,574,737	$55,993,792	$11,949,205

[1]Total Expenditures does not include construction, loan guaranty, general operating expenses, insurance and indemnities, or unique patients.

[2]Includes expenditures for the following programs: veterans' compensation for service-connected disabilities, dependency and indemnity compensation for service-connected deaths, veterans' pension for nonservice-connected disabilities, and burial and other benefits to veterans and their survivors.

[3]Includes expenditures for medical services, and other medical administrative and overhead items.

Source: Wisconsin Department of Veterans Affairs, departmental data, April 2015. United States totals include Puerto Rico and Guam.

WISCONSIN NEWSPAPERS
Daily Newspapers

Municipality	Newspaper[1]	Publisher	Web Address
Antigo	Antigo Daily Journal	Fred Berner	www.antigodailyjournal.com
Appleton	The Post-Crescent	Pamela D. Henson	www.postcrescent.com
Ashland	The Daily Press	David LaPorte	www.ashlandwi.com
Baraboo	Baraboo News Republic	Todd Krysiak	www.baraboonewsrepublic.com
Beaver Dam	Daily Citizen	Scott Zeinemann*	www.wiscnews.com/bdc/
Beloit	Beloit Daily News	Kent Eymann	www.beloitdailynews.com
Eau Claire	Leader-Telegram	Pieter Graaskamp	www.leadertelegram.com
Fond du Lac	The Reporter	Karen Befus*	www.fdlreporter.com
Fort Atkinson	Daily Jefferson County Union	Brian Knox	www.dailyunion.com
Green Bay	Green Bay Press-Gazette	Scott Johnson	www.greenbaypressgazette.com
Janesville	The Gazette	Sidney Bliss	www.gazettextra.com
Kenosha	Kenosha News	Kenneth Dowdell	www.kenoshanews.com
La Crosse	La Crosse Tribune	Rusty Cunningham	www.lacrossetribune.com
Madison	Wisconsin State Journal	John M. Humenik	www.madison.com
Manitowoc	Herald Times Reporter	Scott Johnson	www.htrnews.com
Marinette	EagleHerald	Dan White	www.ehextra.com
Marshfield	Marshfield News-Herald	Gannett Wisconsin Media	www.marshfieldnewsherald.com
Milwaukee	The Daily Reporter	Jim Williams	www.dailyreporter.com
Milwaukee	Milwaukee Journal Sentinel	Elizabeth Brenner	www.jsonline.com
Monroe	The Monroe Times	Carl Hearing	www.themonroetimes.com
Oshkosh	Oshkosh Northwestern	Karen Befus*	www.thenorthwestern.com
Portage	Portage Daily Register	Kerry Lechner (editor)	www.portagedailyregister.com
Racine	The Journal Times	Mark Lewis	www.journaltimes.com
Sheboygan	The Sheboygan Press	Scott Johnson	www.sheboyganpress.com
Stevens Point	Stevens Point Journal	Michael Beck*	www.stevenspointjournal.com
Watertown	Watertown Daily Times	Kevin & James Clifford	www.wdtimes.com
Waukesha	The Freeman	Matt Marlett*	www.gmtoday.com
Wausau	Wausau Daily Herald	Michael Beck*	www.wausaudailyherald.com
West Bend	Daily News	Heather Rogge	www.gmtoday.com
Wisconsin Rapids	Daily Tribune	Gannett Wisconsin Media	www.wisconsinrapidstribune.com

*General manager.

Other Newspapers

Municipality	Newspaper	Published	Publisher
Abbotsford 54405	Record-Review	Wed.	Kris O'Leary, Kevin Flink
Abbotsford 54405	The Tribune-Phonograph	Wed.	Kevin Flink, Kris O'Leary
Adams 53910	Adams-Friendship Times Reporter	Wed.	Dan & Mark Witte
Albany 53502	Hometown Herald	Thurs.	PJ Francis
Alma (Cochrane 54622)	Buffalo County Journal	Thurs.	Daniel, Michael, Gary Stumpf
Amery 54001	Amery Free Press	Tues.	Tom Stangl
Argyle 53504	Pecatonica Valley Leader	Thurs.	Michael & Patrick Reilly
Ashland 54806	The County Journal	Thurs.	David LaPorte
Ashwaubenon (Green Bay 54304)	The Press	Fri.	Michael Aubinger
Augusta 54722	Augusta Area Times	Thurs.	Michael Stumpf
Baldwin 54002	The Baldwin Bulletin	Tues.	Thomas Hawley
Balsam Lake 54810	County Ledger Press	Thurs.	Leslie Waggoner
Barron 54812	Barron News-Shield	Wed.	Mark & James Bell
Berlin 54923	Berlin Journal	Wed.	Ty Gonyo
Black Earth 53515	News-Sickle-Arrow	Thurs.	Dan & Mark Witte
Black River Falls 54615	Banner Journal	Wed.	Dan & Mark Witte
Black River Falls 54615	Jackson County Chronicle	Wed.	Chris Hardie
Blair 54616	The Blair Press	Thurs.	Lee Henschel
Bloomer 54724	Bloomer Advance	Wed.	James Bell
Boscobel 53805	The Boscobel Dial	Thurs.	John Ingebritsen
Brillion 54110	The Brillion News	Thurs.	Beth Wenzel
Brodhead 53520	The Independent Register	Wed.	Pete Cruger
Brookfield[2]	Brookfield-Elm Grove NOW	Thurs.	Elizabeth Brenner
Burlington 53105	Burlington Standard Press	Thurs.	Jack Cruger
Cambridge 53523	The Cambridge News	Thurs.	Brian Knox
Campbellsport 53010	Campbellsport News	Thurs.	Andrew Johnson
Cashton 54619	Cashton Record	Wed.	Paul Fanning
Cedarburg 53012	News Graphic	Tues. & Thurs.	Heather Rogge
Chetek 54728	The Chetek Alert	Wed.	James Bell
Chilton 53014	Times-Journal	Thurs.	James H. Moran
Chippewa Falls 54729	The Chippewa Herald	Mon.-Thurs.	Rusty Cunningham
Clinton 53525	The Clinton Topper	Thurs.	Jack Cruger
Clintonville 54929	Clintonville Chronicle	Tues.	Tricia Rose
Clintonville 54929	Clintonville Tribune Gazette	Thurs.	Patrick J. Wood
Cochrane 54622	Buffalo County Journal	Thurs.	Daniel, Michael, Gary Stumpf
Cochrane 54622	Cochrane-Fountain City Recorder	Thurs.	Daniel, Michael & Gary Stumpf
Colfax 54730	The Colfax Messenger	Wed.	Carlton DeWitt

WISCONSIN NEWSPAPERS
Other Newspapers–Continued

Municipality	Newspaper	Published	Publisher
Columbus (Beaver Dam 53916)	Columbus Journal	Sat.	Scott Zeinemann
Cornell 54732	Courier Sentinel	Thurs.	Carol O'Leary
Cottage Grove 53527	The Herald-Independent	Thurs.	Brian Knox
Crandon 54520	The Forest Republican	Thurs.	Hank Murphy
Cuba City 53807	Tri-County Press	Thurs.	John Ingebritsen
Cumberland 54829	Cumberland Advocate	Wed.	Paul Bucher
Darlington 53530	Republican Journal	Thurs.	Brian Lund
Deerfield 53531	The Independent	Thurs.	Brian Knox
DeForest (Windsor 53598)	DeForest Times-Tribune	Thurs.	Brian Knox
Delavan 53115	Delavan Enterprise	Thurs.	Cyndi Jensen*
Delavan 53115	Westine Report	Fri.	Cyndi Jensen*
Denmark 54208	Denmark News	Thurs.	Ryan Radue
Dodgeville 53533	Dodgeville Chronicle	Thurs.	Michael & Patrick Reilly
Dousman[2]	Living Kettle Moraine Index	Thurs.	Steve Lyles
Durand 54736	The Courier-Wedge	Thurs.	Michael Stumpf
Eagle River 54521	Vilas County News-Review	Wed.	Kurt L. Krueger
East Troy 53120	East Troy News	Fri.	Cyndi Jensen*
East Troy 53120	East Troy Times	Wed.	Cyndi Jensen*
Eau Claire 54701	The Country Today	Wed.	Pieter Graaskamp
Edgar (Abbotsford 54405)	The Record-Review	Wed.	Kevin Flink & Kris O'Leary
Edgerton 53534	The Edgerton Reporter	Wed.	Helen & Diane Everson
Elkhorn 53121	Elkhorn Independent	Thurs.	Jack Cruger
Ellsworth 54011	Pierce County Herald	Wed.	Steve Dzubay
Elroy 53929	The Messenger of Juneau County	Thurs.	Betty Waits*
Evansville 53536	The Evansville Review	Wed.	Kelly A., Stanley A., Danley C. Gildner
Fennimore 53809	Fennimore Times	Thurs.	John Ingebritsen
Fitchburg (Verona 53593)	Fitchburg Star	2nd Fri. of month	David Enstad*
Florence 54121	The Florence Mining News	Thurs.	Hank Murphy
Frederic 54837	Inter-County Leader	Wed.	Douglas Panek
Gays Mills 54631	Crawford County Independent & The Kickapoo Scout	Thurs.	John Ingebritsen
Genoa City (Elkhorn 53121)	Genoa City Report	Thurs.	Cyndi Jensen*
Germantown[2]	Germantown-Menomonee Falls NOW	Thurs.	Elizabeth Brenner
Glenwood City 54013	Tribune Press Reporter	Wed.	Carlton DeWitt
Glidden 54527	The Glidden Enterprise	Wed.	Chris Canfield
Grantsburg 54840	Burnett County Sentinel	Wed.	Tom Stangl
Green Bay 54304	The Press	Fri.	Michael & Annette Aubinger
Green Lake (Berlin 54923)	Green Lake Reporter	Thurs.	Ty Gonyo
Greenfield[2]	Greenfield-West Allis NOW	Thurs.	Elizabeth Brenner
Hammond (Roberts 54026)	Central St. Croix News	Thurs.	Jeff Redmon
Hartland[2]	Living Lake Country Reporter	Tues. & Thurs.	Steve Lyles
Hayward 54843	Sawyer County Record	Wed.	Paul Mitchel
Hillsboro 54634	Hillsboro Sentry-Enterprise	Thurs.	John Ingebritsen
Hudson 54016	Hudson Star-Observer	Thurs.	Steve Dzubay
Hurley 54534	Iron County Miner	Thurs.	Ernest Moore
Juneau 53039	Dodge County Independent News	Thurs.	James Clifford
Kaukauna 54130	Times-Villager	Wed. & Sat.	Brian Roebke (editor)
Kewaskum 53040	The Statesman	Thurs.	Andrew & Nicole Kuehl
Kiel 53042	Tri-County News	Thurs.	Mike Mathes
La Crosse 54601	Coulee News	Fri.	Chris Hardie
Ladysmith 54848	Ladysmith News	Thurs.	James Bell
La Farge 54639	La Farge Episcope	Tues.	Lonnie Muller
Lake Geneva 53147	Lake Geneva Regional News	Thurs.	John Halverson*
Lake Mills 53551	Lake Mills Leader	Thurs.	Brian Knox
Lancaster 53813	Grant County Herald Independent	Thurs.	John Ingebritsen
Lodi 53555	Lodi Enterprise	Thurs.	Brian Knox
Loyal 54446	Tribune Record Gleaner	Wed.	Kevin Flink & Kris O'Leary
Madison 53713	The Capital Times	Wed.	Clayton Frink
Madison 53706	The Daily Cardinal	Mon.-Thurs.	Jack Casey (editor-in-chief)
Madison 53703	Isthmus	Thurs.	Jeff Haupt
Marion 54950	The Marion Advertiser	Thurs.	Dan Brandenburg
Markesan (Berlin 54923)	Markesan Regional Reporter	Thurs.	Ty Gonyo
Mauston 53948	Juneau County Star-Times	Wed. & Sat.	Todd Krysiak (editor)
Mayville 53050	Dodge County Pionier	Thurs.	Andrew Johnson
McFarland 53558	The McFarland Thistle & McFarland Community Life	Thurs.	Brian Knox
Medford 54451	The Star News	Thurs.	Carol O'Leary
Mellen 54546	The Mellen Weekly-Record	Wed.	Sandy & James Christl
Menomonie 54751	The Dunn County News	Sun. & Wed.	Rusty Cunningham
Merrill 54452	Merrill Courier	Fri.	Patrick J. Wood , Tim Schreiber
Middleton 53562	Middleton Times-Tribune	Thurs.	Dan & Mark Witte
Milton 53563	Milton Courier	Thurs.	Brian Knox
Mineral Point 53565	The Democrat Tribune	Thurs.	Michael & Patrick Reilly

WISCONSIN NEWSPAPERS
Other Newspapers–Continued

Municipality	Newspaper	Published	Publisher
Minocqua 54548	The Lakeland Times	Tues. & Fri.	Gregg Walker
Mondovi 54755	Mondovi Herald News	Thurs.	Michael Stumpf
Montello 53949	The Marquette County Tribune	Thurs.	Dan & Mark Witte
Mosinee 54455	The Mosinee Times	Thurs.	James Kress
Mount Horeb 53572	Mount Horeb Mail	Thurs.	Dan & Mark Witte
Mukwonago 53149	Living Mukwonago Chief	Wed.	Steve Lyles
Muscoda 53573	The Progressive	Thurs.	John Ingebritsen
Muskego[2]	Muskego-New Berlin NOW	Thurs.	Elizabeth Brenner
Neillsville 54456	The Clark County Press	Wed.	Dan & Mark Witte
New Glarus 53574	Post Messenger Recorder	Thurs.	Dan & Mark Witte
New London 54961	New London Press Star	Thurs.	Patrick J. Wood
New Richmond 54017	New Richmond News	Thurs.	Steve Dzubay
North Shore[2]	North Shore NOW	Thurs.	Elizabeth Brenner
Oak Creek[2]	Oak Creek NOW	Thurs.	Elizabeth Brenner
Oconomowoc[2]	Living Oconomowoc Focus	Tues. & Thurs.	Steve Lyles
Oconomowoc (Waukesha 53186)	Oconomowoc Enterprise	Thurs.	Bill Yorth, Katherine Michalets
Oconto 54153	Oconto County Reporter	Wed.	Colleen Messenger*
Oconto Falls 54154	Oconto County Times-Herald	Wed.	Greg Mellis
Omro (Berlin 54923)	Omro Herald	Thurs.	Ty Gonyo
Onalaska/Holmen (La Crosse 54602)	Courier-Life	Fri.	Chris Hardie
Ontario 54651	County Line	Thurs.	Karen Parker
Oregon 53575	The Oregon Observer	Thurs.	David Enstad*
Osceola 54020	The Sun	Wed.	Tom Stangl
Osseo 54758	Tri-County News	Thurs.	Michael Stumpf
Peshtigo 54157	Peshtigo Times	Wed.	Mary Ann Gardon
Phillips 54555	Price County Review	Thurs.	Jeff Patterson
Platteville 53818	The Platteville Journal	Wed.	John Ingebritsen
Plymouth 53073	The Review	Tues. & Thurs.	Barry & Christie Johanson
Port Washington 53074	Ozaukee Press	Thurs.	William F. Schanen III
Prairie du Chien 53821	Courier Press	Mon. & Wed.	William H. Howe
Prescott 54021	Prescott Journal	Thurs.	John E. McLoone
Princeton (Berlin 54923)	Princeton Times-Republic	Thurs.	Ty Gonyo
Random Lake 53075	The Sounder	Thurs.	Gary Feider
Reedsburg 53959	Reedsburg Independent	Thurs.	Dan & Mark Witte
Reedsburg 53959	Reedsburg Times Press	Wed. & Sat.	Todd Krysiak (editor)
Rhinelander 54501	The Northwoods River News	Tues., Thurs. & Sat.	Gregg Walker
Rice Lake 54868	The Chronotype	Wed.	Warren Dorrance
Richland Center 53581	The Richland Observer	Thurs.	John Ingebritsen
Ripon 54971	The Ripon Commonwealth Press	Thurs.	Tim Lyke
River Falls 54022	River Falls Journal	Thurs.	Steve Dzubay
St. Croix Falls (Balsam Lake 54810)	Standard-Press	Thurs.	Leslie Waggoner
Sauk City 53583	Sauk Prairie Eagle	Wed.	Matt Meyers (advertising manager)
Sauk City 53583	Sauk Prairie Star	Thurs.	Dan & Mark Witte
Sharon (Delevan 53115)	Sharon Reporter	Fri.	Cyndi Jensen*
Shawano 54166	Shawano Leader	Wed., Thurs., Fri. & Sat.	Greg Mellis
Sheboygan (Plymouth 53073)	The Sheboygan Falls News	Wed.	Barry & Christie Johanson
Shell Lake 54871	Washburn County Register	Wed.	Douglas Panek
South Milwaukee[2]	South Shore NOW	Thurs.	Elizabeth Brenner
Sparta 54656	Monroe County Democrat	Thurs.	William Gleiss
Sparta 54656	The Sparta Herald	Mon.	Theodore C. Radde
Spooner 54801	Spooner Advocate	Thurs.	Janet Krokson
Spring Green 53588	Home News	Wed.	Dan & Mark Witte
Spring Valley 54767	Sun-Argus	Thurs.	Paul Seeling
Stanley 54768	The Stanley Republican	Wed.	John E. McLoone
Stevens Point 54481	The Portage County Gazette	Fri.	Pete Leahy
Stoughton 53589	The Stoughton Courier Hub	Thurs.	David Enstad*
Sturgeon Bay 54235	Door County Advocate	Wed. & Sat.	Scott Johnson
Sun Prairie 53590	The Star	Tues. & Fri.	Brian Knox
Superior 54880	Superior Telegram	Tues. & Fri.	Shelley Nelson (editor)
Sussex[2]	Living Sussex Sun	Wed.	Steve Lyles
Thorp 54771	The Thorp Courier	Wed.	Mark LaGasse
Three Lakes (Eagle River 54521)	The Three Lakes News	Wed.	Kurt L. Krueger
Tomah 54660	The Tomah Journal & Monitor-Herald	Mon. & Thurs.	Chris Hardie
Tomahawk 54487	Tomahawk Leader	Tues.	Kathleen & Larry Tobin
Turtle Lake 54889	The Times	Thurs.	David Slack
Twin Lakes (Delevan 53115)	Twin Lakes Report	Fri.	Cyndi Jensen*
Valders 54245	The Valders Journal	Thurs.	Brian Thomsen
Verona 53593	The Verona Press	Thurs.	David Enstad*
Viola 54664	Epitaph-News	Thurs.	Bonnie Howell-Sherman
Viroqua 54665	Vernon County Broadcaster	Thurs.	Chris Hardie

WISCONSIN NEWSPAPERS
Other Newspapers–Continued

Municipality	Newspaper	Published	Publisher
Washburn (Ashland 54806)	The County Journal	Thurs.	David LaPorte
Waterloo 53594	The Courier	Thurs.	Brian Knox
Waukesha[2]	Waukesha NOW	Thurs.	Steve Lyles
Waunakee 53597.	The Waunakee Tribune	Thurs.	Brian Knox
Waupaca 54981	County Post	Thurs.	Kathy Banks
Waupaca 54981	Wisconsin State Farmer	Fri.	Trey Foerster
Wautoma 54982	Waushara Argus	Wed.	Jonathan Gneiser, Mary Kunasch
Wauwatosa[2]	Wauwatosa NOW	Thurs.	Elizabeth Brenner
West Salem (La Crosse 54602)	The Coulee News	Fri.	Chris Hardie
Westby 54667	Westby Times	Thurs.	Chris Hardie
Whitehall 54773	Trempealeau County Times	Thurs.	Dan & Mark Witte
Winneconne 54986.	The Winneconne News	Wed.	John Rogers
Winter 54896.	Sawyer County Gazette	Wed.	Sue Johnston
Wisconsin Dells (Portage 53901)	Wisconsin Dells Events	Wed. & Sat.	Kay James (editor)
Withee 54498	O-W Enterprise	Wed.	Nathan LePage
Wittenberg 54499	The Wittenberg Enterprise & Birnamwood News.	Thurs	Miriam Nelson
Woodville 54028.	The Woodville Leader	Thurs.	Paul Seeling

*General manager.

[1]A "newspaper" is defined by Section 985.03 (1) (c), Wisconsin Statutes, as follows: "A newspaper, under this chapter, is a publication appearing at regular intervals and at least once a week, containing reports of happenings of recent occurrence of a varied character, such as political, social, moral and religious subjects, designed to inform the general reader…".

[2]Combined editorial office in Waukesha 53186.

Source: Wisconsin Newspaper Association, *2015 Member Directory;* data compiled by Wisconsin Legislative Reference Bureau.

WISCONSIN PERIODICALS

AAA Living/Wisconsin	Bimonthly	AAA Wisconsin, P.O. Box 33, Madison 53701-0033 wisconsin.aaa.com
Action Tracks	1 per year	Kurt Krueger, P.O. Box 1929, Eagle River 54521-1929 www.vcnewsreview.com
Agri-View	Weekly	Capital Newspapers, 1901 Fish Hatchery Rd., Madison 53713 www.agriview.com
Agronomy Journal	Bimonthly	American Society of Agronomy, 5585 Guilford Rd., Madison 53711 agron.scijournals.org
Airwaves	Monthly	Wisconsin Public Television, R. 1076 Vilas Hall, 821 University Ave., Madison 53706 www.wpt.org
American Orthoptic Journal	1 per year	UW Press, 1930 Monroe St., 3rd Floor, Madison 53711-2059 uwpress.wisc.edu/journals
Antique Trader	26 per year	F & W Media, Inc., 700 E. State St., Iola 54990-0001 www.antiquetrader.com
Arctic Anthropology	2 per year	UW Press, 1930 Monroe St., 3rd Floor, Madison 53711-2059 uwpress.wisc.edu/journals
Asphalt Contractor	10 per year	AC Business Media, 201 N. Main Street, Suite 5, Fort Atkinson 53538 www.forconstructionpros.com
Astronomy	Monthly	Kalmbach Publishing Co., P.O. Box 1612, Waukesha 53187-1612 www.astronomy.com
At Ease (web-based)	Bimonthly	Wisconsin National Guard, 2400 Wright St., Madison 53704 dma.wi.gov
Backyard Poultry Magazine	Bimonthly	Bart Smith, 145 Industrial Dr., Medford 54451 www.backyardpoultrymag.com
Badger Common 'Tater	Monthly	Wis. Potato and Vegetable Growers Assn., Inc., P.O. Box 327, Antigo 54409-0327 www.wisconsinpotatoes.com
Badger Herald	Daily (M-F)	Tara Golshan, 152 W. Johnson St., Suite 202, Madison 53703-2017 www.badgerherald.com
Badger Legionnaire, The	10 per year	Wisconsin American Legion, 2930 American Legion Dr., P.O. Box 388, Portage 53901 www.wilegion.org
Badger Rails	6 per year	Wis. Assn. of Railroad Passengers, 3385 S. 119th St., West Allis 53227 www.wisarp.org
Badger Sportsman	Monthly	Badger Sportsman LLC, 19 E. Main St., P.O. Box 1186, Oshkosh 54903-1186 www.badgersportsman.com
Bank Note Reporter	Monthly	F & W Media, Inc., 700 E. State St., Iola 54990-0001 numismaster.com
Beloit College Magazine	3 per year	Beloit College, 700 College St., Beloit 53511-5595 http://magazine.beloit.edu/
Beloit Fiction Journal	1 per year	Chris Fink, Beloit College, Box 11,700 College St., Beloit 53511 www.beloit.edu/english/fictionjournal/
Benefits Magazine	Monthly	International Foundation of Employee Benefit Plans, 18700 W. Bluemound Rd., Brookfield 53045 www.ifebp.org/magazines
Benefits Quarterly	4 per year	International Soc. of Certified Employee Benefit Specialists, 18700 W. Bluemound Rd., P.O. Box 209, Brookfield 53008-0209 www.iscebs.org
Blade	Monthly	F & W Media, Inc., 700 E. State St., Iola 54990-0001 www.blademag.com
Business Journal, The	Weekly	Mark J. Sabljak, 825 N. Jefferson St., Suite 200, Milwaukee 53202 milwaukee.bizjournals.com
Capitol Watch (e-Newsletter)	Weekly	Wisconsin Manufacturers & Commerce, P.O. Box 352, Madison 53701-0352 www.wmc.org
Catholic Financial Life Member Magazine	4 per year	Catholic Financial Life, 1100 West Wells St., Milwaukee 53233 www.catholicfinanciallife.org
Cessna Owner Magazine	Monthly	Joe Jones, N7528 Aanstad Rd., P.O. Box 5000, Iola 54945-5000 www.cessnaowner.org

WISCONSIN PERIODICALS–Continued

Cheese Reporter	Weekly	Dick Groves, 2810 Crossroads Dr., Suite 3000, Madison 53718 www.cheesereporter.com
Classic Toy Trains	9 per year	Kalmbach Publishing Co., P.O. Box 1612, Waukesha 53187-1612 www.classictoytrains.com
Coins	Monthly	F & W Media, Inc., 700 E. State St., Iola 54990-0001 numismaster.com
Columns	Quarterly	Wisconsin Historical Society, 816 State St., Madison 53706-1417 www.wisconsinhistory.org
Concrete Contractor	7 per year	AC Business Media, 201 N. Main Street, Suite 5, Fort Atkinson 53538 www.forconstructionpros.com
Connection, The	Semimonthly	Jeanne Gardner, P.O. Box 189, Iron River 54847 theconnectionnewspaper.com
Contemporary Literature	Quarterly	UW Press, 1930 Monroe St., 3rd Floor, Madison 53711-2059 uwpress.wisc.edu/journals
Countryside and Small Stock Journal	Bimonthly	Bart Smith, 145 Industrial Dr., Medford 54451 www.countrysidemag.com
Courier, The	Monthly	Wisconsin Veterans Home, N2665 County Rd. QQ, King 54946 www.wisvets.com
Crafts Report, The	Monthly	Travis Manney, N7528 Aanstad Rd., P.O. Box 5000, Iola 54945-5000 www.craftsreport.com
Credit Union Magazine	Monthly	Doug Benzine, Credit Union National Assn., P.O. Box 431, Madison 53701-0431 creditunionmagazine.com
Crop Science	Bimonthly	Crop Science Soc. of Amer., 5585 Guilford Rd., Madison 53711-5801
Crop Weather	Weekly (Apr.-Nov.)	Dept. of Agriculture, Trade and Consumer Protection, 2811 Agriculture Dr., Madison 53718-6777 www.nass.usda.gov
Dairy Goat Journal	Bimonthly	Bart Smith, 145 Industrial Dr., Medford 54451 www.dairygoatjournal.com
Deer and Deer Hunting	11 per year	F & W Media, Inc., 700 E. State St., Iola 54990-0001 www.deeranddeerhunting.com
Director, The	Monthly	NFDA Services, Inc., 13625 Bishop's Dr., Brookfield 53005 www.nfda.org
Dolls	8 per year	Ryan Jones, N7528 Aanstad Rd., P.O. Box 5000, Iola 54945-5000 www.dollsmagazine.com
Drum Corps World	Monthly (online)	Sights & Sounds, Inc., 4926 N. Sherman Ave., Unit H, Madison 53704-8443 www.drumcorpsworld.com
EAA Sport Aviation	Monthly	Experimental Aircraft Association, EAA Aviation Center, P.O. Box 3086, Oshkosh 54903-3086 www.eaa.org
Ecological Restoration	Quarterly	UW Press, 1930 Monroe St., 3rd Floor, Madison 53711-2059 uwpress.wisc.edu/journals
Equipment Today	Monthly	AC Business Media, 201 N. Main Street, Suite 5, Fort Atkinson 53538 www.forconstructionpros.com
Exponent	Weekly	UW-Platteville, 618 Pioneer Tower, 1 University Plz., Platteville 53818
Feminist Collections: A Quarterly of Women's Studies Resources	Quarterly	UW System Gender and Women's Studies Librarian, 430 Memorial Library, 728 State St., Madison 53706 womenst.library.wisc.edu
Feminist Periodicals: A Current Listing of Contents	Quarterly/electronic	UW System Gender and Women's Studies Librarian, 430 Memorial Library, 728 State St., Madison 53706 womenst.library.wisc.edu/publications/feminist-periodicals.html
FineScale Modeler	10 per year	Kalmbach Publishing, 21027 Crossroads Cir., Waukesha 53186-4055 www.finescale.com
Fired Arts and Crafts	Monthly	Wally Gibbs, N7528 Aanstad Rd., P.O. Box 5000, Iola 54945-5000 www.firedartsandcrafts.com

WISCONSIN PERIODICALS–Continued

Flip Side	Biweekly (during school year)	UW-Eau Claire, Davies Center 132, Eau Claire 54701 www.flipsidepress.org
Focus	Biweekly	Wis. Taxpayers Alliance, 401 North Lawn Ave., Madison 53704-5033 www.wistax.org
Food Logistics	10 per year	AC Business Media, 201 N. Main Street, Suite 5, Fort Atkinson 53538 www.foodlogistics.com
Forward	Quarterly	League of Women Voters of Wis., 612 W. Main St., #200, Madison 53703-2500 www.lwvwi.org
Forward in Christ	Monthly	Wis. Evangelical Lutheran Synod, N16 W23377 Stone Ridge Dr., Waukesha 53188-1108 www.wels.net/forwardinchrist
Foto News	Weekly	Tim Schreiber, 807 E. First St., Merrill 54452 www.merrillfotonews.com
Frame Building News	5 per year	F & W Media, Inc., 700 E. State St., Iola 54990-0001 www.fwmedia.com
Free Riders Press	Monthly	Daron Jensen, W5715 County Rd., Wautoma 54982-1126 freeriderspress.us
Freedom Pursuit	Semimonthly	Freedom Publishing, Inc., P.O. Box 1016, Freedom 54131 www.thefreedompursuit.com
Freethought Today	10 per year	Freedom From Religion Foundation, Inc., P.O. Box 750, Madison 53701-0750 https://ffrf.org/publications/freethought-today
Gargoyle	2 per year	UW Law School, 975 Bascom Mall, Madison 53706 http://gargoyle.law.wisc.edu
GFWC-WI Clubwoman	Quarterly	Michelle Munoz, 39129 N. Aberdeen Lane, Beach Park, IL 60083 www.gfwc-wi.org
Goldmine	14 per year	F & W Media, Inc., 700 E. State St., Iola 54990-0001 www.goldminemag.com
Great Lakes TPA	Monthly	Hahn Printing/GLTPA, P.O. Box 1278, Rhinelander 54501 www.timberpa.com
Grow	3 per year	College of Agricultural and Life Sciences, 136 Agricultural Hall, 1450 Linden Drive, Madison 53706 www.grow.cals.wisc.edu
Gun Digest, The Magazine	Biweekly	F & W Media, Inc., 700 E. State St., Iola 54990-0001 www.gundigest.com
Gwiazda Polarna Polish Biweekly Newspaper	Biweekly	Point Publications, Inc., 2804 Post Rd., Stevens Point 54481-6452 www.gwiazda-polarna.com
Hautedoll	6 per year	Ryan Jones, N7528 Aanstad Rd., P.O. Box 5000, Iola 54945-5000 www.hautedoll.com
Hoard's Dairyman	Semimonthly	W.D. Hoard and Sons Co., 28 Milwaukee Ave., W., Fort Atkinson 53538-2018 www.hoards.com
Hocak Worak	Biweekly	Ho-Chunk Nation, P.O. Box 667, Black River Falls 54615 hocakworak.com
Hummingbird: Magazine of the Short Poem .	2 per year	Hummingbird Press, 7129 Lindfield Rd., Madison 53719 www.hummingbirdpoetry.org
Impact Magazine	Quarterly	Wis. Park and Recreation Assn., 6601-C Northway, Greendale 53129 www.wpraweb.org
In Business	Monthly	Jon Konarske, 200 River Place, #250, Madison 53716 ibmadison.com
Independence	2 per year	Easter Seals Wisconsin, Inc., 101 Nob Hill Rd., Suite 301, Madison 53713-3969 eastersealswisconsin.com
Inside UW-Madison (Electronic only)	Biweekly (during school year)	University Communications, 28 Bascom Hall, 500 Lincoln Dr., Madison 53706 http://insideuw.wisc.edu
JCI Journal	1 per year	JCI Wisconsin, Inc., P.O. Box 1547, Appleton 54912-1547 www.jciwisconsin.org
Journal of Environmental Quality	Bimonthly	American Society of Agronomy, 5585 Guilford Rd., Madison 53711 www.agronomy.org/publications/jeq

WISCONSIN PERIODICALS–Continued

Journal of Human Resources	Quarterly	UW Press, 1930 Monroe St., 3rd Floor, Madison 53711-2059 uwpress.wisc.edu/journals
Journal of Natural Resources and Life Sciences Education	1 per year	American Society of Agronomy, 5585 Guilford Rd., Madison 53711 https://www.agronomy.org/publications/nse
Journal of the Pharmacy Society of Wisconsin	6 per year	Pharmacy Society of Wisconsin, 701 Heartland Trail, Madison 53717 www.pswi.org
Kalihwisaks	Biweekly	Oneida Tribe of Indians of Wis., 909 Packerland Dr., P.O. Box 365, Oneida 54303 www.kalihwisaks.com
Land Economics	Quarterly	UW Press, 1930 Monroe St., 3rd Floor, Madison 53711-2059 uwpress.wisc.edu/journals
Landscape Journal	2 per year	UW Press, 1930 Monroe St., 3rd Floor, Madison 53711-2059 uwpress.wisc.edu/journals
Living Church, The	22 per year	The Living Church Foundation, Inc., P.O. Box 510705, Milwaukee 53203-0121 www.livingchurch.org
Luso-Brazilian Review	2 per year	UW Press, 1930 Monroe St. 3rd Floor, Madison 53711-2059 uwpress.wisc.edu/journals
Madison Magazine.	Monthly	Mike Kornemann, 7025 Raymond Rd., Madison 53719 www.madisonmagazine.com
Marquette Law Review	Quarterly	Joe Christensen, Inc., Eckstein Hall, P.O. Box 1881, Milwaukee 53201-1881 http://scholarship.law.marquette.edu/mulr/
Marquette Magazine	Quarterly	Marquette University, P.O. Box 1881, Milwaukee 53201-1881 www.marquette.edu/magazine
Menominee Nation News	Bimonthly	Menominee Indian Tribe, P.O. Box 910, Keshena 54135 www.menominee-nsn.gov
Metal Roofing	Bimonthly	F & W Media, Inc., 700 E. State St., Iola 54990-0001 www.fwmedia.com
Midwest Flyer Magazine	Bimonthly	Flyer Publications, Inc., 6031 Lawry Ct., Oregon 53575-2617 www.midwestflyer.com
Military Trader.	Monthly	F & W Media, Inc., 700 E. State St., Iola 54990-0001 www.militarytrader.com
Milwaukee History.	Quarterly	Milwaukee County Historical Society, 910 N. Old World 3rd St., Milwaukee 53203-1591 www.milwaukeehistory.net
Milwaukee Labor Press	Monthly	Milwaukee Area Labor Council, AFL-CIO Milwaukee, 633 S. Hawley Rd., #110, Milwaukee 53214 www.milwaukeelabor.org/in_the_news/labor_press/
Milwaukee Magazine	Monthly	Mike Gustin, 126 N. Jefferson St., Suite 100, Milwaukee 53202 www.milwaukeemag.com
Model Railroader	Monthly	Terry Thompson, 20127 Crossroads Cir., P.O. Box 1612, Waukesha 53187-1612 www.modelrailroader.com
Monatshefte	Quarterly	UW Press, 1930 Monroe St., 3rd Floor, Madison 53711-2059 uwpress.wisc.edu/journals
N (Nude and Natural)	4 per year	The Naturist Society, LLC, 627 Bay Shore Dr., Suite 100, Oshkosh 54901 www.naturistsociety.com
Native Plants Journal	3 per year	UW Press, 1930 Monroe St., 3rd Floor, Madison 53711-2059 uwpress.wisc.edu/journals
New Books on Women, Gender and Feminism	2 per year	UW System Gender and Women's Studies Librarian, 430 Memorial Library, 728 State St., Madison 53706 womenst.library.wisc.edu
New North B2B	Monthly	Sean Fitzgerald, P.O. Box 559, Oshkosh 54903-0559 www.newnorthb2b.com
North Woods Trader	Weekly	Kurt Krueger, P.O. Box 1929, Eagle River 54521-1929 www.vcnewsreview.com
Numismatic News	Weekly (32 paper, 20 electronic)	F & W Media, Inc., 700 E. State St., Iola 54990-0001 www.numismaticnews.com

WISCONSIN PERIODICALS–Continued

OEM Off-Highway	8 per year	AC Business Media, 201 N. Main Street, Suite 5, Fort Atkinson 53538 www.oemoffhighway.com
Old Allis News	Quarterly	Landhandler Enterprises Inc., 471 70th Ave., Clayton 54004 www.oldallisnews.com
Old Cars Report Price Guide	Bimonthly	F & W Media, Inc., 700 E. State St., Iola 54990-0001 www.oldcarsreport.com
Old Cars Weekly	Weekly	F & W Media, Inc., 700 E. State St., Iola 54990-0001 www.oldcarsweekly.com
On Premise	Bimonthly	Nei-Turner, 2817 Fish Hatchery Rd., Fitchburg 53713 tlw.org
On Wisconsin Magazine	Quarterly	Wis. Alumni Assn., 650 N. Lake St., Madison 53706-1476 onwisconsin.uwalumni.com
Passenger Pigeon, The	Quarterly	Wisconsin Society for Ornithology, 7680 Payvery Tr., Middleton 53562-4128 http://wsobirds.org
Pavement Maintenance & Reconstruction	8 per year	AC Business Media, 201 N. Main Street, Suite 5, Fort Atkinson 53538 www.forconstructionpros.com
Pharmacy in History	Quarterly	Amer. Institute of the History of Pharmacy, 777 Highland Ave., Madison 53705 pharmacyinhistory.com
Pipers Magazine	Monthly	Joe Jones, N7528 Aanstad Rd., P.O. Box 5000, Iola 54945-5000 www.piperowner.org
Progressive, The	Monthly	Matthew Rothschild, 409 E. Main St., Madison 53703-2863 www.progressive.org
Quality Progress	Monthly	ASQ Quality Press, 600 N. Plankinton Ave., Milwaukee 53201 www.qualityprogress.com
Renascence: Essays on Values in Literature	Quarterly	Marquette University, Raynor Memorial Libraries, M-164, P.O. Box 1881, Milwaukee 53201-1881 www.marquette.edu/renascence
Rental	7 per year	AC Business Media, 201 N. Main Street, Suite 5, Fort Atkinson 53538 www.forconstructionpros.com
Rethinking Schools	Quarterly	Rethinking Schools, Ltd., 1001 E. Keefe Ave., Milwaukee 53212 www.rethinkingschools.org
Royal Purple	Weekly (during semester)	UW-Whitewater, 66 University Center, 800 W. Main St., Whitewater 53190 www.royalpurplenews.com
Rural Builder	7 per year	F & W Media, Inc., 700 E. State St., Iola 54990-0001 www.fwmedia.com
Sabbath Recorder, The	Monthly	American Sabbath Tract and Comm. Council, P.O. Box 1678, Janesville 53547 www.seventhdaybaptist.org
Safety Zone (E-Newsletter)	Monthly	Wis. Safety Council, P.O. Box 352, Madison 53701-0352 www.wisafetycouncil.org
Sheep!	Bimonthly	Bart Smith, 145 Industrial Dr., Medford 54451 www.sheepmagazine.com
Silent Sports	Monthly	Multi Media Channels, LLC, P.O. Box 558, Rhinelander 54501 silentsports.net
Smart Retailer	8 per year	Travis Manney, N7528 Aanstad Rd., P.O. Box 5000, Iola 54945-5000 www.smart-retailer.com
Soil Science Society of America Journal	Bimonthly	Soil Science Society of America, 5585 Guilford Rd., Madison 53711-5801 www.soils.org/publications/sssaj
Soo, The	Quarterly	Soo Line Historical and Technical Society, 2124 N. Locust St., Appleton 54914 sooline.org
Southeastern Wisconsin Regional Planning Commission Newsletter	Irregular	Southeastern Wis. Regional Planning Comn., P.O. Box 1607, Waukesha 53187-1607 www.sewrpc.org
Spanish Journal	Weekly	Rhonda Welch, 3712 W. Pierce St., Milwaukee 53215 www.spanishjournal.com
Spectator	Weekly	UW-Eau Claire, 104 Hibbard Hall, Eau Claire 54701 www.spectatornews.com

WISCONSIN PERIODICALS–Continued

Sports Collectors Digest	Weekly	F & W Media, Inc., 700 E. State St., Iola 54490-0001 sportscollectorsdigest.com
SubStance	3 per year	UW Press, 1930 Monroe St., 3rd Floor, Madison 53711-2059 uwpress.wisc.edu/journals
Supply & Demand Chain Executive	5 per year	AC Business Media, 201 N. Main Street, Suite 5, Fort Atkinson 53538 www.sdcexec.com
Teddy Bear & Friends	6 per year	Joe Jones, N7528 Aanstad Rd., P.O. Box 5000, Iola 54945-5000 www.teddybearandfriends.com
Today's Christian Living	6 per year	Diana Jones, N7528 Aanstad Rd., P.O. Box 5000, Iola 54945-5000 www.todayschristianliving.org
Today's Dads	Quarterly	Wis. Fathers for Children and Families, 1621 Willow Ct., Grafton 53024 wisconsinfathers.org
Trains Magazine	Monthly	Kalmbach Publishing Co., 21027 Crossroads Cir. P.O. Box 1612, Waukesha 53187-1612 www.trainsmag.com
Trapper and Predator Caller	10 per year	F & W Media, Inc., 700 E. State St., Iola 54990-0001 www.trapperpredatorcaller.com
Travel Wisconsin Newsl (E-Newsletter)	Monthly	Wis. Dept. of Tourism, P.O. Box 8690, Madison 53708 industry.travelwisconsin.com/
Turkey & Turkey Hunting	6 per year	F & W Media, Inc., 700 E. State St., Iola 54990-0001 www.turkeyandturkeyhunting.com
Union Labor News	Bimonthly	Kevin Gundlach, 1602 S. Park St., #228, Madison 53715 www.scfl.org
Update	2 per year	Wisconsin School of Business, 975 University Ave., Madison 53706 www.bus.wisc.edu
Vacation Week	Weekly (June-Aug.)	Kurt Krueger, P.O. Box 1929, Eagle River 54521-1929 www.vcnewsreview.com
Volume One	Bimonthly	Nick Meyer, 205 N. Dewey St., Eau Claire 54703 www.volumeone.org
Voyageur: NE Wisconsin's Historical Review	2 per year	Brown County Historical Society, P.O. Box 1411, Green Bay 54305-1411 www.voyageurmagazine.org
WEAC in Print	Quarterly	Wis. Education Assn. Council, 33 Nob Hill Rd., Madison 53713-2199 www.weac.org
WFU News	10 per year	Wis. Farmers Union, 117 W. Spring St., Chippewa Falls 54729-2359 www.wisconsinfarmersunion.com
Wis. Agriculturist	Monthly	Farm Progress Companies, 112 S. Prairie St., P.O. Box 236, Brandon 53919 www.wisconsinagriculturist.com
Wis. Archeologist	Semiannual	Wis. Archeological Society, P.O. Box 75, Prairie du Sac 53578 www.wiarcheologicalsociety.org
Wis. Business Voice	Quarterly	Wisconsin Manufacturers & Commerce, P.O. Box 352, Madison 53701-0352 www.wmc.org
Wis. Economic Indicators	Monthly	Wis. Dept. of Workforce Development, 201 E. Washington Ave., Rm. E-100, Madison 53707 www.dwd.wisconsin.gov/oea
Wis. Farm Reporter	Semimonthly	Dept. of Agriculture, Trade and Consumer Protection, 2811 Agriculture Dr., Madison 53718-6777 www.nass.usda.gov
Wis. Horsemen's News	Monthly	Trey Foerster, P.O. Box 609, Waupaca 54981 www.wishorse.com
Wis. International Law Journal	4 per year	UW Law School, 975 Bascom Mall, Madison 53706 http://hosted.law.wisc.edu/wordpress/wilj
Wis. Law Journal	Monthly	James K. Williams, Jr., 225 E. Michigan St., Suite 540, Milwaukee 53202 www.wislawjournal.com
Wis. Law Review	Bimonthly	Joe Christensen, Inc., 2347 Law Building, 975 Bascom Mall, Madison 53706-1399 www.wisconsinlawreview.org

WISCONSIN PERIODICALS–Continued

Wis. Lawyer	Monthly	State Bar of Wisconsin, P.O. Box 7158, Madison 53707-7158 www.wisbar.org
Wis. Lion.	Monthly	Wisconsin Lions, 3834 County Rd. A, Rosholt 54473 www.wisconsinlions.org/magazine
Wis. Magazine of History	Quarterly	State Historical Society of Wis., 816 State St., Madison 53706-1488 www.wisconsinhistory.org/whspress
Wis. Mapping Bulletin.	Electronic	State Cartographer's Office, 384 Science Hall, UW-Madison, 550 N. Park St., Madison 53706 www.sco.wisc.edu/news.html
Wis. Natural Resources	Bimonthly	Wisconsin Department of Natural Resources, P.O. Box 7921, Madison 53707-7921 www.wnrmag.com
Wis. People & Ideas	Quarterly	Wis. Academy of Sciences, Arts and Letters, 1922 University Ave., Madison 53726 www.wisconsinacademy.org/magazine
Wis. Police Journal.	Quarterly	Wis. Professional Police Assn., 660 John Nolen Dr., Suite 300, Madison 53713 www.wppa.com
Wis. Professional Agent	Monthly	PIA of Wisconsin, 6401 Odana Rd., Madison 53719-1126 www.piaw.org
Wis. Real Estate Magazine	Monthly	Michael Theo, 4801 Forest Run Rd., Suite 201, Madison 53704 www.wra.org/wrem
Wis. Restaurateur	Quarterly	Wis. Restaurant Assn., 2801 Fish Hatchery Rd., Madison 53713 www.wirestaurant.org/membership/wr/index.php
Wis. School Musician	3 per year	Wis. School Music Assn., 1005 Quinn Dr., Waunakee 53597 wsmamusic.org/wsm
Wis. School News	10 per year	Wis. Assn. of School Boards, Inc., 122 W. Washington Ave., Suite 400, Madison 53703-2718 www.wasb.org
Wis. State Farmer	Weekly	Trey Foerster, P.O. Box 609, Waupaca 54981 wisfarmer.com
Wis. State Genealogical Society Newsletter. .	Quarterly	Wis. State Genealogical Soc., Inc., P.O. Box 5106, Madison 53705-0106 www.wsgs.org
Wis. Taxpayer, The.	11 per year	Wis. Taxpayers Alliance, 401 North Lawn Ave., Madison 53704-5033 www.wistax.org
Wis. Trails	Bimonthly	Milwaukee Journal Sentinel, 333 W. State St., Milwaukee 53201 www.wisconsintrails.com
Wisconservation	Monthly	Wisconsin Wildlife Federation, 1540 W. James St., Suite 500, Columbus 53925 www.wiwf.org
Wisconsin Counties	Monthly	Wis. Counties Assn., 22 E. Mifflin St., Suite 900, Madison 53703 www.wicounties.org
Wisconsin Energy Cooperative News	Monthly	Cooperative Network, 1 S. Pinckney St., Suite 810, Madison 53703 www.wecnmagazine.com
Wisconsin Woodlands	Quarterly	Wisconsin Woodland Owners Assn., Inc., P.O. Box 285, Stevens Point 54481-0285 www.wisconsinwoodlands.org
WMJ (Wis. Medical Journal)	6 per year	Wisconsin Medical Society, P.O. Box 1109, Madison 53701-1109 www.wmjonline.org
World Airshow News	6 per year	Sandra Parnau, P.O. Box 975, East Troy 53120-0975 www.airshowmag.com
World Coin News	Monthly	F & W Media, Inc., 700 E. State St., Iola 54990-0001 www.numismaster.com

---

NOTE

If you know of any additional permanent Wisconsin publications that are published at periodic intervals, please send the information to the Blue Book Editor, Legislative Reference Bureau, P.O. Box 2037, Madison, Wisconsin 53701-2037.

BROADCASTING STATIONS IN WISCONSIN

Commercial Television Stations

City	Station	Digital Channel	City	Station	Digital Channel
Baraboo	W43BR	—	Milwaukee	WBME	24
Eau Claire	WEAU	13.1	Milwaukee	WCGV	25
Eau Claire	WEUX	49	Milwaukee	WDJT	46
Eau Claire	WQOW	15	Milwaukee	WISN	34
Fond du Lac	WIWN	68	Milwaukee	WITI	33
Green Bay	WACY	27	Milwaukee	WMLW	48
Green Bay	WBAY	23	Milwaukee	WPXE	40
Green Bay	WCWF	21	Milwaukee	WTMJ	4
Green Bay	WFRV	39	Milwaukee	WVCY	22
Green Bay	WGBA	41	Milwaukee	WVTV	18
Green Bay	WLUK	11	Milwaukee	WYTU	17
La Crosse	KQEG	23	Milwaukee	WWRS	43
La Crosse	WKBT	8	Superior	KBJR	19
La Crosse	WLAX	17	Tomah	WIBU	51
La Crosse	WXOW	48	Wausau	WAOW	9.1
Madison	WBUW	32	Wausau	WFXS	31
Madison	WISC	50	Wausau	WJFW	16
Madison	TVW	14	Wausau	WMOW	9.3
Madison	WKOW	26	Wausau	WYOW	9.2
Madison	WMSN	11	Wausau	WSAW	7
Madison	WMTV	19	Wausau	WTPX	46
Milwaukee	WBWT	807			

Educational Television Stations

City	Station	Digital Channel	City	Station	Digital Channel
Green Bay	WPNE[1]	38	Milwaukee	WMVS[3]	8
La Crosse	WHLA[1]	31	Milwaukee	WMVT[3]	35
Madison	WHA[2]	20	Park Falls	WLEF[1]	36
Menomonie	WHWC[1]	28	Wausau	WHRM[1]	20

Commercial Radio Stations

City	Station	Frequency	City	Station	Frequency
Adams	WCWI-FM	106.1	Eau Claire	WQRB-FM	95.1
Amery	WPCA-LP-FM	93.1	Eau Claire	WUEC-FM	89.7
Amery	WXCE	1260	Eau Claire	WWIB	103.7
Amery	WLMX-FM	104.9	Eau Claire	WWJC-FM	101.5
Antigo	WACD-FM	106.1	Fond du Lac	KFIZ	1450
Antigo	WATK	900	Fond du Lac	WFDL-FM	97.7
Appleton	WAPL-FM	105.7	Fond du Lac	WFON	107.1
Appleton	WGEE-FM	93.5	Fond du Lac	WTCX-FM	96.1
Appleton	WHBY	1150	Fort Atkinson	WFAW	940
Appleton	WLWB	1530	Green Bay	WAUN-FM	92.7
Appleton	WSCO	1570	Green Bay	WDUZ-AM	1400
Appleton	WKZY-FM	92.9	Green Bay	WDUZ-FM	107.5
Appleton	WYDR-FM	94.3	Green Bay	WGBW	1590
Ashland	WATW	1400	Green Bay	WIXX-FM	101.1
Ashland	WBSZ-FM	93.3	Green Bay	WJOK	1050
Ashland	WJJH-FM	96.7	Green Bay	WKRU-FM	106.7
Ashland	WNXR-FM	107.3	Green Bay	WKSZ-FM	95.9
Baraboo	WBDL-FM	102.9	Green Bay	WKZG-FM	104.3
Baraboo	WCNP-FM	89.5	Green Bay	WKZY	104.3
Baraboo	WRPQ-AM	740	Green Bay	WNCY-FM	100.3
Baraboo	WRPQ-FM	99.7	Green Bay	WNFL	1440
Beaver Dam	WBEV	1430	Green Bay	WOGB-FM	103.1
Beaver Dam	WXRO	95.3	Green Bay	WORQ-FM	90.1
Beloit	WGEZ	1490	Green Bay	WPCK-FM	99.5 & 104.9
Berlin	WISS	1100	Green Bay	WQLH-FM	98.5
Black River Falls	WWIS-AM	1260	Green Bay	WTAQ-AM	1360
Black River Falls	WWIS-FM	99.7	Green Bay	WTAQ-FM	97.5
Chippewa Falls	WCFW-FM	105.7	Green Bay	WZDR-FM	99.7
Dickeyville	WVRE-FM	101.1	Green Bay	WZOR-FM	94.7
Dodgeville	WDMP-AM	810	Hartford	WTKM-AM	1540
Dodgeville	WDMP-FM	99.3	Hartford	WTKM-FM	104.9
Durand	WRDN	1430	Hayward	WHSM-AM	910
Eagle River	WERL	950	Hayward	WHSM-FM	101.1
Eagle River	WRJO	94.5	Hayward	WRLS-FM	92.3
Eau Claire	WATQ-FM	106.7	Hudson	WDGY	740
Eau Claire	WAXX-FM	104.5	Hurley	WHRY	1450
Eau Claire	WAYY	790	Janesville	WCLO	1230
Eau Claire	WBIZ-AM	1400	Janesville	WJVL	99.9
Eau Claire	WBIZ-FM	100.7	Janesville	WSJY-FM	107.3
Eau Claire	WDRK-FM	99.9	Janesville	WWHG-FM	105.9
Eau Claire	WEAQ-AM	1150	Kenosha	WIIL	95.1
Eau Claire	WECL-FM	92.9	Kenosha	WLIP	1050
Eau Claire	WIAL-FM	94.1	La Crosse	KCLH-FM	94.7
Eau Claire	WISM-FM	98.1	La Crosse	KQYB-FM	98.3
Eau Claire	WMEQ-AM	880	La Crosse	WCOW-FM	97.1
Eau Claire	WMEQ-FM	92.1	La Crosse	WFBZ-FM	105.5
Eau Claire	WOGO	680	La Crosse	WIZM-AM	1410

BROADCASTING STATIONS IN WISCONSIN–Continued

City	Station	Frequency	City	Station	Frequency
La Crosse	WIZM-FM	93.3	New Richmond	WIXK	1590
La Crosse	WKBH-FM	106.3	Oconto	WOCO-AM	1260
La Crosse	WKLJ	1290	Oconto	WOCO-FM	107.1
La Crosse	WKTY	580	Oshkosh	WBJZ-FM	104.7
La Crosse	WLFN	1490	Oshkosh	WNAM	1280
La Crosse	WLXR-FM	104.9	Oshkosh	WOSH	1490
La Crosse	WQCC-FM	100.1	Oshkosh	WPKR-FM	99.5
La Crosse	WRQT-FM	95.7	Oshkosh	WVBO-FM	103.9
Ladysmith	WJBL	93.1	Oshkosh	WWWX-FM	96.9
Ladysmith	WLDY	1340	Park Falls	WCQM	98.3
Lake Geneva	WLKG-FM	96.1	Park Falls	WPFP	980
Lancaster	WGLR-AM	1280	Platteville	WPVL-AM	1590
Lancaster	WGLR-FM	97.7	Platteville	WPVL-FM	107.1
Madison	WHIT	1550	Plymouth	WJUB	1420
Madison	WIBA-AM	1310	Plymouth	WSTM	91.3 & 103.3
Madison	WIBA-FM	101.5	Portage	WBKY-FM	95.9
Madison	WJJO-FM	94.1	Portage	WDDC	100.1
Madison	WJQM-FM	93.1	Portage	WPDR	1350
Madison	WLMV	1480	Prairie du Chien	WPRE	980
Madison	WMAD-FM	96.3	Prairie du Chien	WQPC	94.3
Madison	WMGN-FM	98.1	Racine	WMKQ	92.1
Madison	WMHX-FM	105.1	Racine	WRJN	1400
Madison	WMMM-FM	105.5	Reedsburg	WNFM	104.9
Madison	WOLX-FM	94.9	Reedsburg	WRDB	1400
Madison	WOZN-AM	1670	Rhinelander	WCYE-FM	93.7
Madison	WOZN-FM	106.7	Rhinelander	WHDG-FM	97.3
Madison	WTLX-FM	100.5	Rhinelander	WHOH-FM	96.5
Madison	WTSO	1070	Rhinelander	WOBT	1240
Madison	WTTN	1580	Rhinelander	WRHN-FM	100.1
Madison	WWQM-FM	106.3	Rhinelander	WRLO-FM	105.3
Madison	WXXM-FM	92.1	Rice Lake	WAQE-AM	1090
Madison	WZEE-FM	104.1	Rice Lake	WAQE-FM	97.7
Manitowoc	WCUB	980	Rice Lake	WJMC-AM	1240
Manitowoc	WLTU	92.1	Rice Lake	WJMC-FM	96.1
Manitowoc	WOMT	1240	Rice Lake	WKFX-FM	99.1
Manitowoc	WQTC	102.3	Richland Center	WRCO-AM	1450
Marinette	WAGN	1340	Richland Center	WRCO-FM	100.9
Marinette	WHYB-FM	103.7	Ripon	WRPN	1600
Marinette	WLST-FM	95.1	River Falls	WEVR-AM	1550
Marinette	WMAM	570	River Falls	WEVR-FM	106.3
Marinette	WSFQ-FM	96.3	Shawno	WJMQ-FM	92.3
Marshfield	WDLB	1450	Shawno	WOTE	1380
Marshfield	WOSQ	92.3	Shawano	WOWN-FM	99.3
Mauston	WRJC-AM	1270	Shawano	WTCH-AM	960
Mauston	WRJC-FM	92.1	Shawano	WTCH-FM	96.5
Mayville	WMDC-FM	98.7	Sheboygan	WBFM-FM	93.7
Medford	WIGM	1490	Sheboygan	WCLB	950
Medford	WKEB	99.3	Sheboygan	WEMP-FM	98.9
Merrill	WJMT	730	Sheboygan	WHBL	1330
Merrill	WMZK	104.1	Sheboygan	WHBZ-FM	106.5
Milwaukee	WAUK	540	Sheboygan	WLKN-FM	98.1
Milwaukee	WDDW-FM	104.7	Sheboygan	WXER-FM	104.5
Milwaukee	WGLB	1560	Shell Lake	WCSW	940
Milwaukee	WHQG-FM	102.9	Shell Lake	WGMO	95.3
Milwaukee	WISN	1130	Siren	WXCX-FM	105.7
Milwaukee	WJMR-FM	98.3	Spooner	WPLT-FM	106.3
Milwaukee	WJYI	1340	Stevens Point	WPCN-AM	1010
Milwaukee	WKKV-FM	100.7	Stevens Point	WPCN-FM	92.1
Milwaukee	WKLH-FM	96.5	Stevens Point	WSPT-FM	97.9
Milwaukee	WLDB-FM	93.3	Sturgeon Bay	WBDK-FM	96.7
Milwaukee	WLWK-FM	94.5	Sturgeon Bay	WDOR-AM	910
Milwaukee	WLUM-FM	102.1	Sturgeon Bay	WDOR-FM	93.9
Milwaukee	WMIL-FM	106.1	Sturgeon Bay	WLGE-FM	106.9
Milwaukee	WMYX-FM	99.1	Sturgeon Bay	WQDC-FM	97.7
Milwaukee	WNOV	860	Sturgeon Bay	WRKU-FM	102.1
Milwaukee	WNRG-FM	106.9	Sturgeon Bay	WRLU-FM	104.1
Milwaukee	WOKY	920	Sturgeon Bay	WSBW-FM	105.1
Milwaukee	WRIT-FM	95.7	Superior	KDWZ-FM	102.5
Milwaukee	WRNW-FM	97.3	Superior	WEBC	560
Milwaukee	WRRD	1510	Superior	WDSM	710
Milwaukee	WSJP	1640	Superior	WGEE	970
Milwaukee	WSJP-FM	100.1	Tomah	WBOG	1460
Milwaukee	WSSP	1250	Tomah	WTMB-FM	94.5
Milwaukee	WTMJ	620	Tomah	WXYM-FM	96.1
Milwaukee	WXSS-FM	103.7	Tomahawk	WJJQ-AM	810
Milwaukee	WZTI	1290	Tomahawk	WJJQ-FM	92.5
Minocqua	WLKD	1570	Viroqua	WKPO-FM	105.9
Minocqua	WMQA	95.9	Viroqua	WVRQ-AM	1360
Monona	WVMO-LP-FM	98.7	Viroqua	WVRQ-FM	102.3
Monroe	WEKZ-AM	1260	Waupaca	WDUX-AM	800
Monroe	WEKZ-FM	93.7	Waupaca	WDUX-FM	92.7
Neillsville	WCCN-AM	1370	Waupun	WFDL	1170
Neillsville	WCCN-FM	107.5	Wausau	WBCV-FM	107.9
Neillsville	WPKG-FM	92.7	Wausau	WDEZ-FM	101.9
New Richmond	WDMO	95.7	Wausau	WDTX	100.5

BROADCASTING STATIONS IN WISCONSIN–Continued

City	Station	Frequency	City	Station	Frequency
Wausau	WGLX-FM	103.3	West Allis	WJTI	1460
Wausau	WHTQ-FM	96.7	West Bend	WBKV	1470
Wausau	WIFC-FM	95.5	West Bend	WMBZ	92.5
Wausau	WKQH-FM	104.9	Whitehall	WHTL-FM	102.3
Wausau	WOZZ-FM	94.7	Whitewater	WKCH-FM	106.5
Wausau	WRIG	1390	Whitewater	WSLD-FM	104.5
Wausau	WSAU	550	Wisconsin Dells	WDLS	900
Wausau	WSAU-FM	99.9	Wisconsin Dells	WNNO-FM	106.9
Wausau	WXCO	1230	Wisconsin Rapids	WFHR	1320
Wausau	WYTE-FM	106.5	Wisconsin Rapids	WLJY	105.5
Wautoma	WAUH-FM	102.3			

Noncommercial Radio Stations

City	Station	Frequency	City	Station	Frequency
Adams	WHAA[1]	89.1	Milwaukee	WMSE-FM	91.7
Appleton	WEMI-FM	91.9	(Milwaukee School of Engineering)		
Appleton	WOVM-FM	91.1	Milwaukee	WMWK-FM	88.1
Ashland	WRNC-LP-FM	97.7	Milwaukee	WUWM-FM[2]	89.7
(Northland College)			Milwaukee	WVCY-FM	107.7
Ashland	WUWS[2]	90.9	Milwaukee	WYMS-FM	88.9
Auburndale	WLBL[1]	930	(Milwaukee Board of Education)		
Beloit	WBCR-FM	90.3	Oshkosh	WOCT-LP-FM	101.9
(Beloit College)			Oshkosh	WRST-FM[2]	90.3
Brule	WHSA[1]	89.9	Oshkosh	WVCY	690
Burlington	WBSD-FM	89.1	Owen	WVCS-FM	90.1
(Burlington Area School District)			Park Falls	WHBM[1]	90.3
Delafield	WHAD[1]	90.7	Platteville	WSUP-FM[2]	90.5
Eau Claire	WDVM	1050	Platteville	WSSW[1]	89.1
Eau Claire	WHEM-FM	91.3	Reserve	WOJB-FM	88.9
Eau Claire	WHWC-FM[1]	88.3	Rhinelander	WHSF[1]	89.9
Eau Claire	WUEC-FM[2]	89.7	Rhinelander	WXPR-FM	91.7
Eau Claire	WVCF-FM	90.5	Rhinelander	WXPW-FM	91.9
Fond du Lac	WDKV-FM	91.7	Ripon	WRPN-FM	90.1
Fond du Lac	WVFL-FM	89.9	(Ripon College)		
Goodman	WMVM-FM	90.7	River Falls	WRFW-FM[2]	88.7
Green Bay	WEMY-FM	91.5	Sheboygan	WSHS-FM	91.7
Green Bay	WHID[2]	88.1	(Sheboygan Area School District)		
Green Bay	WJOK	1050	Sheboygan	WYVM-FM	90.9
Green Bay	WORQ-FM	90.1	Sister Bay	WHDI[1]	91.9
Green Bay	WPNE[1]	89.3	Sister Bay	WHND[1]	89.7
Highland	WHHI[1]	91.3	Stevens Point	WWSP-FM[2]	89.9
Kenosha	WGTD-FM	91.1	Sturgeon Bay	WPFF-FM	90.5
(Gateway Technical College)			Sturgeon Bay	WPVM-FM	88.5
La Crosse	WEQS-FM	89.3	Superior	KUWS-FM[2]	91.3
La Crosse	WHLA-FM[1]	90.3	Superior	WHSA-FM[2]	89.9
La Crosse	WKBH	1570	Superior	WHWA-FM[1]	104.7
La Crosse	WTPN-FM	103.9	Superior	WSSU-FM[1]	88.5
La Crosse	WLSU-FM[2]	88.9	Superior	WUWS-FM[2]	90.9
Lancaster	WJTY-FM	88.1	Suring	WRVM-FM	102.7
Madison	WERN-FM[1]	88.7	Tomah	WVCX-FM	98.9
Madison	WHA[2]	970	Washburn	WEGZ-FM	105.9
Madison	WHFA	1240	Waukesha	WCCX-FM	104.5
Madison	WNWC-AM	1190	(Carroll College)		
(University of Northwestern-St. Paul)			Wausau	WCLQ-FM	89.5
Madison	WNWC-FM	102.5	Wausau	WGNV-FM	88.5
(University of Northwestern-St. Paul)			Wausau	WHRM[1]	90.9
Madison	WORT-FM	89.9	Wausau	WLBL[1]	91.9
Madison	WSUM-FM[2]	91.7	Wausau	WVRN-FM	88.9
Manitowoc	WTSW-LP-FM	96.3	Wausau	WYNW-FM	92.9
Marinette	WLCJ-LP-FM	92.5	Whitewater	WSUW-FM[2]	91.7
Menomonie	WHWC-FM[1]	88.3	Wisconsin Rapids	WMMA	93.9
Menomonie	WVSS-FM[2]	90.7			
Merril	WHJL-FM	88.1			

[1]Licensed to the Wisconsin Educational Communications Board.
[2]Licensed to the University of Wisconsin System Board of Regents.
[3]Operated by the Milwaukee Area Technical College Board.
Source: *Wisconsin Broadcasters Association, 2013-2014 Directory*, April 2015.

HIGHLIGHTS OF POPULATION AND VITAL STATISTICS IN WISCONSIN

State and County Population — Wisconsin's 2014 population was officially estimated to be 5,732,981, a .81% increase over the 2010 U.S. Census count of 5,686,986. The state grew 6.0% in the 2000s and 9.6% in the 1990s. By contrast, the growth in the preceding decade from 1980 to 1990 was less than 4% and represented the smallest increase in decennial census counts in state history. The greatest increase occurred between 1840 and 1850, the decade in which Wisconsin became a state, when population jumped 886.9% from 30,945 to 305,391.

Between 2000 and 2010, population increased over 20% in Calumet and St. Croix Counties, while population decreased in 19 counties. St. Croix County was the fastest growing county during the decade, with a population increase of 33.6%. Population growth between 2010 and 2014 increased by the highest percentage in Dane County by 3.8%, or by 14,651. Brown County had the second highest percentage increase at 3.0%, or 5,502.

Population by Race and Age — In responding to the 2000 and 2010 U.S. Censuses of Population, individuals were given the opportunity to identify themselves as being of more than one race. About 1.2% and 1.8% of Wisconsin's population selected multiple races in 2000 and 2010, respectively. As a result, comparisons between the 2000 and 2010 Censuses and earlier censuses must be made with caution. It is not clear whether someone who selected Asian and white, for example, for the 2010 Census would have selected Asian or white in 1990. Only those who selected a single race are used in the following comparisons. Between 1890 and 2010, the nonwhite population in Wisconsin increased from 0.7% to over 13.8%. Wisconsin Indians were the largest minority group from 1890 until 1950; Blacks have been the largest since 1950. In 2013, Wisconsin's Black population was 355,873, an increase of 46.8% from the 2010 Census. Wisconsin's Hispanic population increased by 2.9% from 2010 to 2013, reaching 345,866. The Asian population increased by 2.6% to 132,609.

The 2013 Wisconsin Indian population was 49,343, a decrease of 9.3% over the 2010 population of 54,526. Wisconsin has 11 Indian reservations.

According to the 2010 Census, Wisconsin had a voting age population of 4,347,494 or 76.4% of the total population. In 2014, there was a voting age population of 4,422,812 or 77.1%.

Vital Statistics — In 2013, Wisconsin recorded 29,979 marriages and 15,941 divorces and annulments. In 2013, the state had 66,566 live births (11.6 per 1,000 population), 409 infant deaths (6.1 per 1,000 live births), and 331 fetal deaths (4.9 per 1,000 deliveries). Total deaths in 2013 numbered 49,917 (8.7 per 1,000 population).

The following tables present selected data. Consult footnoted sources for more detailed information about population and vital statistics.

WISCONSIN POPULATION, 1840 – 2014

Year	Population	Increase	Percent Increase	Rural	Urban	Percent Urban	Density[1]
1840	30,945	—	—	30,945	—	—	0.6
1850	305,391	274,446	886.9%	276,768	28,623	9.4%	5.6
1860	775,881	470,490	154.1	664,007	111,874	14.4	14.1
1870	1,054,670	278,789	35.9	847,471	207,099	19.6	19.2
1880	1,315,497	260,827	24.7	998,293	317,204	24.1	24.0
1890	1,693,330	377,833	28.7	1,131,044	562,286	33.2	30.9
1900	2,069,042	375,712	22.2	1,278,829	790,213	38.2	37.4
1910	2,333,860	264,818	12.8	1,329,540	1,004,320	43.0	42.6
1920	2,632,067	298,207	12.8	1,387,209	1,244,858	47.3	47.6
1930	2,939,006	306,939	11.7	1,385,163	1,553,843	52.9	53.0
1940	3,137,587	198,581	6.7	1,458,443	1,679,144	53.5	57.3
1950	3,434,575	296,988	9.5	1,446,687	1,987,888[2]	57.9	62.7
1960	3,951,777	517,202	15.1	1,429,598	2,522,179	63.8	72.2
1970	4,417,821	466,044	11.8	1,507,313	2,910,418	65.9	81.3
1980	4,705,642	287,821	6.5	1,685,035	3,020,732	64.2	86.6
1990	4,891,769	186,127	4.0	1,679,813	3,211,956	65.7	90.1
2000	5,363,715	471,946	9.6	1,700,032	3,663,643	68.3	98.8
2010	5,686,986	323,271	6.0	1,697,348	3,989,638	70.2	105.0
2011	5,694,236	7,250	0.1	NA	NA	NA	NA
2012	5,703,525	9,289	0.2	NA	NA	NA	NA
2013	5,717,110	13,585	0.2	NA	NA	NA	NA
2014	5,732,981	15,871	0.3	NA	NA	NA	NA

NA – Not available.

[1] Population per square mile of land area.

[2] The "urban" definition was revised beginning with the 1950 census.

Sources: U.S. Department of Commerce, U.S. Census Bureau; Wisconsin Department of Administration, Demographic Services Center, *Time Series of The Final Official Population Estimates and Census Counts for Wisconsin Counties,* October 10, 2014.

WISCONSIN POPULATION
2010 Census By Sex, Race, and Hispanic Origin

County	Total Population	Male	Female	White	Black or African American	American Indian and Alaska Native	Asian or Pacific Islander	Some Other Race	Two or More Races	Hispanic Origin (of any race)
Adams	20,875	11,221	9,654	19,409	633	205	86	266	276	783
Ashland . . .	16,157	8,082	8,075	13,662	48	1,791	63	56	537	302
Barron	45,870	22,814	23,056	44,076	407	406	226	236	519	862
Bayfield . . .	15,014	7,716	7,298	13,024	46	1,435	49	29	431	158
Brown	248,007	122,658	125,349	214,415	5,491	6,715	6,828	9,155	5,403	17,985
Buffalo	13,587	6,859	6,728	13,253	37	38	28	122	109	237
Burnett	15,457	7,806	7,651	14,163	81	718	55	67	373	194
Calumet . . .	48,971	24,543	24,428	46,187	246	203	1,047	705	583	1,690
Chippewa . .	62,415	32,404	30,011	59,504	982	310	788	182	649	800
Clark	34,690	17,577	17,113	33,338	80	174	135	773	190	1,292
Columbia. . .	56,833	28,935	27,898	54,468	717	277	330	441	600	1,444
Crawford. . .	16,644	8,575	8,069	16,080	296	39	66	36	127	150
Dane	488,073	241,411	246,662	413,631	25,347	1,730	23,201	12,064	12,100	28,925
Dodge	88,759	46,679	42,080	83,294	2,381	385	513	1,309	877	3,522
Door	27,785	13,679	14,106	26,839	144	162	116	249	275	671
Douglas . . .	44,159	22,087	22,072	41,166	486	868	384	82	1,173	494
Dunn	43,857	22,133	21,724	41,545	220	168	1,158	228	538	626
Eau Claire . .	98,736	48,351	50,385	91,946	874	471	3,328	519	1,598	1,804
Florence . . .	4,423	2,262	2,161	4,306	10	31	14	14	48	37
Fond du Lac .	101,633	49,926	51,707	95,674	1,305	471	1,169	1,700	1,314	4,368
Forest.	9,304	4,724	4,580	7,690	76	1,256	24	32	226	138
Grant.	51,208	26,636	24,572	49,655	588	103	317	221	324	649
Green.	36,842	18,241	18,601	35,593	140	65	209	490	345	1,033
Green Lake. .	19,051	9,509	9,542	18,428	88	52	91	268	124	743
Iowa	23,687	11,878	11,809	23,127	87	36	134	102	201	336
Iron.	5,916	2,959	2,957	5,790	3	36	18	13	56	35
Jackson	20,449	10,874	9,575	18,258	400	1,271	73	144	303	519
Jefferson . . .	83,686	41,638	42,048	78,632	681	257	578	2,479	1,059	5,555
Juneau	26,664	14,029	12,635	25,077	557	398	122	188	322	687
Kenosha . . .	166,426	82,444	83,982	139,416	11,052	814	2,482	7,880	4,782	19,592
Kewaunee . .	20,574	10,460	10,114	19,955	69	77	65	219	189	463
La Crosse . .	114,638	55,961	58,677	105,540	1,610	493	4,770	371	1,854	1,741
Lafayette . . .	16,836	8,582	8,254	16,292	39	48	58	303	96	522
Langlade . . .	19,977	10,032	9,945	19,267	72	191	63	100	284	324
Lincoln	28,743	14,412	14,331	27,929	157	100	134	131	292	340
Manitowoc. .	81,442	40,489	40,953	76,402	442	450	2,060	1,069	1,019	2,565
Marathon. . .	134,063	67,308	66,755	122,446	841	634	7,178	1,223	1,741	2,992
Marinette. . .	41,749	20,758	20,991	40,559	108	238	227	176	441	522
Marquette . .	15,404	7,808	7,596	14,920	77	86	68	126	127	391
Menominee .	4,232	2,098	2,134	451	19	3,701	1	6	54	178
Milwaukee . .	947,735	457,717	490,018	574,656	253,764	6,808	32,785	51,429	28,293	126,039
Monroe. . . .	44,673	22,648	22,025	41,940	512	510	329	764	618	1,661
Oconto	37,660	19,194	18,466	36,418	73	467	116	198	388	519
Oneida	35,998	17,993	18,005	34,787	152	323	193	82	461	385
Outagamie . .	176,695	88,130	88,565	161,238	1,736	2,982	5,294	2,728	2,717	6,359
Ozaukee . . .	86,395	42,340	44,055	82,010	1,177	208	1,529	483	988	1,956
Pepin	7,469	3,780	3,689	7,337	21	19	14	35	43	72
Pierce.	41,019	20,420	20,599	39,614	232	151	308	201	513	623
Polk	44,205	22,177	22,028	42,807	96	454	166	226	456	656
Portage. . . .	70,019	34,984	35,035	65,981	383	265	1,983	546	861	1,853
Price	14,159	7,180	6,979	13,750	39	54	126	42	148	153
Racine	195,408	96,771	98,637	155,731	21,767	781	2,174	10,046	4,909	22,546
Richland . . .	18,021	9,042	8,979	17,540	82	46	99	119	135	360
Rock	160,331	78,815	81,516	140,513	7,978	516	1,669	5,948	3,707	12,124
Rusk	14,755	7,371	7,384	14,398	61	74	42	37	143	173
St. Croix . . .	84,345	42,218	42,127	80,914	552	313	923	483	1,160	1,692
Sauk	61,976	30,848	31,128	58,588	357	769	350	1,156	756	2,675
Sawyer	16,557	8,393	8,164	13,123	77	2,757	49	42	509	268
Shawano . . .	41,949	20,921	21,028	37,254	143	3,172	193	366	821	905
Sheboygan . .	115,507	58,010	57,497	103,861	1,684	444	5,345	2,297	1,876	6,329
Taylor	20,689	10,559	10,130	20,248	58	43	64	128	148	316
Trempealeau .	28,816	14,638	14,178	27,230	62	63	127	1,086	248	1,667
Vernon	29,773	14,854	14,919	29,085	109	61	99	145	274	394
Vilas	21,430	10,861	10,569	18,658	35	2,370	62	45	260	268
Walworth. . .	102,228	51,237	50,991	93,935	980	308	888	4,604	1,513	10,578
Washburn . .	15,911	7,924	7,987	15,343	36	186	65	49	232	208
Washington. .	131,887	65,393	66,494	126,317	1,155	401	1,445	1,052	1,517	3,385
Waukesha . .	389,891	191,355	198,536	363,963	4,914	1,066	10,852	4,041	5,055	16,123
Waupaca . . .	52,410	26,447	25,963	50,916	154	258	200	425	457	1,307
Waushara. . .	24,496	12,893	11,603	23,012	454	131	108	509	282	1,329
Winnebago. .	166,994	83,952	83,042	154,445	2,975	1,036	3,880	2,188	2,470	5,784
Wood.	74,749	36,777	37,972	71,048	393	587	1,328	593	800	1,680
STATE . .	5,686,986	2,822,400	2,864,586	4,902,067	359,148	54,526	131,061	135,867	104,317	336,056

Sources: U.S. Department of Commerce, U.S. Census Bureau, P.L. 94-171 Redistricting File, processed by Wisconsin Demographic Services Center and the Applied Population Laboratory of UW-Madison, May 2011.

POPULATION CHANGES BY COUNTY, 2010-2014
State Increase: +0.8%

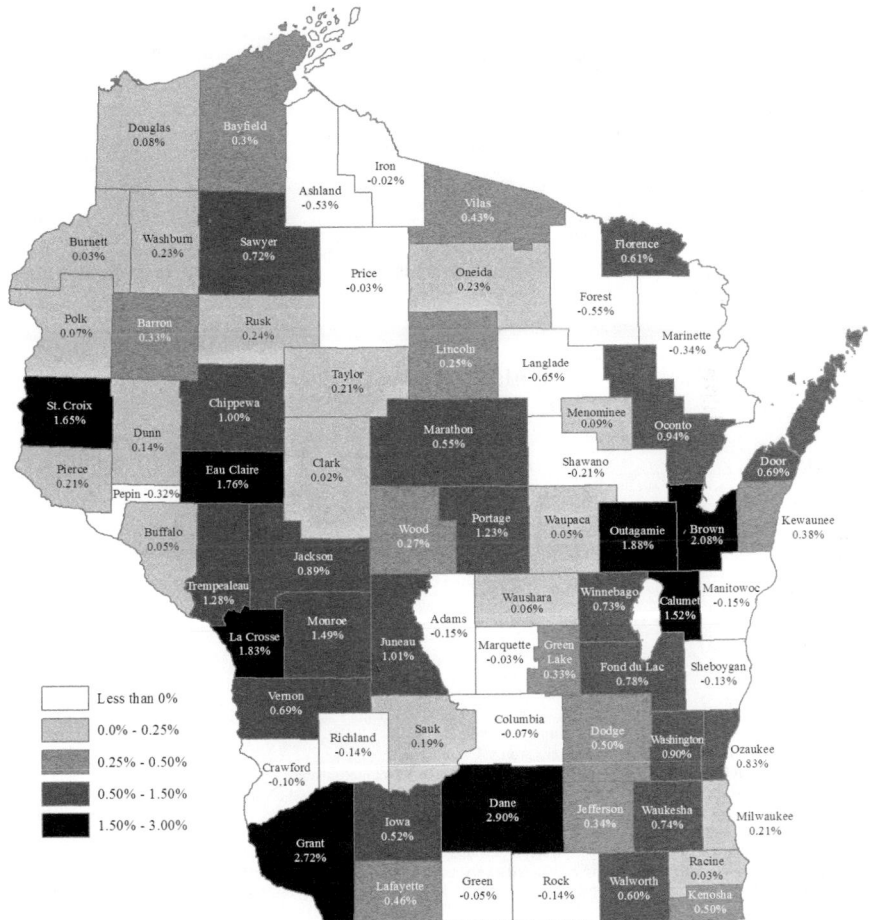

Less than 0%

0.0% - 0.25%

0.25% - 0.50%

0.50% - 1.50%

1.50% - 3.00%

Source: Wisconsin Department of Administration, Demographic Services Center, *Official Population Estimates, January 1, 2014,* October 2014. Map produced by Wisconsin Legislative Technology Services Bureau.

WISCONSIN POPULATION, BY RACE, 1890 – 2013
Population Totals

U.S. Census Year	Total Population	Race						Hispanic or Latino Origin (of any race)[4]
		White	Black	American Indian[1]	Asian[2]	Some Other Race	Two or More Races[3]	
1890	1,693,330	1,680,828	2,444	9,930	128	—	—	—
1900	2,069,042	2,057,911	2,542	8,372	217	—	—	—
1910	2,333,860	2,320,555	2,900	10,142	260	3	—	—
1920	2,632,067	2,616,938	5,201	9,611	314	3	—	—
1930	2,939,006	2,916,255	10,739	11,548	451	13	—	—
1940	3,137,587	3,112,752	12,158	12,265	388	24	—	—
1950	3,434,575	3,392,690	28,182	12,196	1,119	388	—	—
1960	3,951,777	3,858,903	74,546	14,297	2,836	1,195	—	—
1970[5]	4,417,933	4,258,959	128,224	18,924	6,557	5,067	—	62,875
1980[5]	4,705,642	4,443,035	182,592	29,320	22,043	41,788	—	62,782
1990	4,891,769	4,512,523	244,539	39,387	53,583	42,538	—	93,194
2000	5,363,675	4,769,857	304,460	47,228	90,393	84,842	66,895	192,921
2010	5,686,986	4,902,067	359,148	54,526	131,061	135,867	104,317	336,056
2013[6]	5,742,713	4,972,949	357,899	49,653	144,102	96,937	121,173	362,407

Population Percentages

U.S. Census Year	Race						Hispanic or Latino Origin (of any race)[4]
	White	Black	American Indian[1]	Asian[2]	Some Other Race	Two or More Races[3]	
1890	99.3%	0.1%	0.6%	—	—	—	—
1900	99.5	0.1	0.4	—	—	—	—
1910	99.4	0.1	0.4	—	—	—	—
1920	99.4	0.2	0.4	—	—	—	—
1930	99.2	0.4	0.4	—	—	—	—
1940	99.2	0.4	0.4	—	—	—	—
1950	98.8	0.8	0.4	—	—	—	—
1960	97.6	1.9	0.4	0.1%	—	—	—
1970	96.4	2.9	0.4	0.2	0.1%	—	1.4%
1980	94.4	3.9	0.6	0.3	0.9	—	1.3
1990	92.2	5.0	0.8	1.2	0.9	—	1.9
2000	88.9	5.7	0.9	1.7	1.6	1.2%	3.6
2010	86.2	6.3	1.0	2.3	2.4	1.8	5.9
2013[6]	86.6	6.2	0.9	2.5	1.7	2.1	6.3

[1]Aleut and Eskimo populations included beginning in 1960.

[2]Native Hawaiian and Other Pacific Islanders are grouped with Asian.

[3]For the first time in the 2000 Census, individuals were allowed to select more than one race.

[4]The 1990 data on Hispanic/Spanish origin are generally comparable with those for the 1980 Census, but not the 1970 Census. In the 2000 Census, "Hispanic or Latino Origin" represents ethnicity and includes people of Cuban, Mexican, Puerto Rican, South or Central American, or other Spanish culture or origin, regardless of race.

[5]Total has been corrected by the U.S. Census Bureau. Details not adjusted to revised total.

[6]American Community Survey (ACS) is conducted every month on independent samples and produces annual or annual average estimates. These estimates consist of totals, proportions, percentages, means, medians, and ratios. The ACS provides annually updated data on demographic, socioeconomic, and housing characteristics.

Source: U.S. Department of Commerce, U.S. Census Bureau, *2013 American Community Survey 1-Year Estimates, Wisconsin ACS Demographic and Housing Estimates: 2013,* December 2014.

WISCONSIN POPULATION BY RACE AND HISPANIC ORIGIN
2013 Estimate[1]

Race	Total	Percent	Race	Total	Percent
		Total Wisconsin Population: 5,706,871			
One race	5,591,318	98.0%	**Two or more races**	115,553	2.0%
White	4,966,900	87.0	**Not Hispanic or Latino**[4]	5,361,005	93.9
Black or African American	355,873	6.2	One race	5,267,906	92.3
American Indian and Alaska Native	49,343	0.9	White	4,736,069	83.0
Asian	132,609	2.3	Black or African American	349,446	6.1
Asian Indian	23,111	0.4	American Indian and		
Chinese	20,099	0.4	Alaska Native	45,264	0.8
Filipino	8,336	0.1	Asian	131,909	2.3
Japanese	2,349	0.0	Native Hawaiian and Other		
Korean	8,284	0.1	Pacific Islander	1,146	0.0
Vietnamese	4,608	0.1	Some other race	4,072	0.1
Other Asian[2]	65,822	1.2	Two or more races	93,099	1.6
Native Hawaiian and Other Pacific					
Islander	1,305	0.0	**Hispanic or Latino and Race**		
Native Hawaiian	412	0.0	Hispanic or Latino (of any race)	345,866	6.1
Guamanian or Chamorro	402	0.0	Mexican	254,577	4.5
Samoan	202	0.0	Puerto Rican	49,786	0.9
Other Pacific Islander[3]	289	0.0	Cuban	3,879	0.1
Some other race	85,288	1.5	Other Hispanic or Latino	37,624	0.7

[1]Information from U.S. Census Bureau American Community Survey (ACS). The ACS provides annually updated data on the characteristics of population and housing. It is conducted every month on independent samples, and produces annual or average estimates. The estimates consist of totals, proportions, percentages, means, medians, and ratios.

[2]Other Asian alone, or two or more Asian categories.

[3]Other Pacific Islander alone, or two or more Native Hawaiian and Other Pacific Islander categories.

[4]"Hispanic or Latino" refers to a person of Cuban, Mexican, Puerto Rican, South or Central American, or other Spanish culture or origin regardless of race.

Source: U.S. Census Bureau, 2013 American Community Survey, *ACS Demographic and Housing Estimates: 2009-2013 American Community Survey 5-Year Estimates,* December 2014.

WISCONSIN ASIAN POPULATION
1940 – 2013

	Total[1]	Asian Indian	Chinese	Filipino	Hmong	Japanese	Korean	Laotian	Vietnamese	Other Asian[2]
1940	388	NA	290	75	NA	23	NA	NA	NA	NA
1950	1,119	NA	590	NA	NA	529	NA	NA	NA	NA
1960	2,836	NA	1,010	401	NA	1,425	NA	NA	NA	NA
1970	6,557	NA	2,700	1,209	NA	2,648	NA	NA	NA	NA
1980	22,043	3,902	4,835	3,036	NA	2,123	2,900	NA	1,699	NA
1990	53,583	6,914	7,354	3,690	16,373	2,765	5,618	3,622	2,494	NA
2000	90,393	12,665	11,184	5,158	33,791	2,868	6,800	4,469	3,891	NA
2010	129,234	22,899	17,558	7,930	49,240	2,729	7,919	NA	4,877	16,082
2013[3]	132,609	23,111	20,099	8,336	NA	2,349	8,284	NA	4,608	65,822

NA – Not available.

[1]Includes Native Hawaiian and Other Pacific Islander, and Other Asian, including Hmong and Laotian, not identified in the detailed categories.

[2]Other Asian alone, or two or more Asian categories.

[3]American Community Survey (ACS) is conducted every month on independent samples, and produces annual or annual average estimates. These estimates consist of totals, proportions, percentages, means, medians, and ratios. The ACS provides annually updated data on the characteristics of population and housing.

Source: U.S. Department of Commerce, U.S. Census Bureau, 2010 Census Summary File 1 PCT 7, *2009-2013 American Community Survey 5-Year Estimates,* December 2014, and previous issues.

WISCONSIN INDIANS
Wisconsin Indian Population, 1900 – 2013

Year	Total	Male	Female
1900	8,372	4,321	4,051
1910	10,142	5,231	4,911
1920	9,611	4,950	4,661
1930	11,548	5,951	5,597
1940	12,265	6,354	5,911
1950	12,196	6,274	5,922
1960	14,297	7,195	7,102
1970	18,924	9,251	9,673
1980	29,320	14,489	14,831
1990	38,986	19,240	19,746
2000	47,228*	23,462	23,766
2010	54,526	27,212	27,314
2013	49,653	25,415	24,238

*For the first time, in the 2000 Census individuals were allowed to select more than one race.
Source: U.S. Census Bureau, 2013 American Community Survey, 2010 Census Summary File 1, July 2011, and previous issues.

Wisconsin Indian Reservations: Population and Acreage

Reservation Total/ County Detail	Tribe	2010 Reservation Population			June 2013 Acreage Ownership Status		
		Total	Indian	% Indian	Total[1]	Tribal	Individual
Bad River	Chippewa	1,479	1,089	73.63%	63,595.96	28,886.41	34,708.55
Ho-Chunk Nation	Ho-Chunk Nation	1,375	1,185	86.18	7,321.19	4,111.48	3,209.71
Lac Courte Oreilles	Chippewa	2,803	2,111	75.31	51,147.20	29,190.18	21,957.02
Lac du Flambeau	Chippewa	3,442	2,198	63.86	44,956.30	32,658.51	12,282.73
Menominee[2]	Menominee	3,141	2,967	94.46	235,374.35	229,705.35	5,669.00
Oneida (West)	Oneida	22,776	4,102	18.01	12,091.03	11,191.13	899.90
Potawatomi (Wisconsin)	Potawatomi	588	501	85.20	13,080.59	12,400.59	360.00
Red Cliff	Chippewa	1,123	943	83.97	8,109.15	6,189.75	1,904.75
St. Croix	Chippewa	768	622	80.99	2,327.05	2,327.05	0.00
Sokaogon	Chippewa	414	352	85.02	3,241.24	3,241.24	0.00
Stockbridge-Munsee	Mohican	644	511	79.35	16,997.66	16,864.43	133.23
TOTAL		38,553	16,581	43.01	458,241.72	376,766.12	81,124.89

[1]Totals include government land holdings for the following reservations: Bad River (1.00 acre), Lac du Flambeau (15.06 acres), Potawatomi (320.00 acres), and Red Cliff (14.65 acres).
[2]Public Law 93-107, the Menominee Restoration Act, effective on December 22, 1973, repealed the Menominee Termination Act of June 17, 1954 (P.L. 83-399) and acknowledged the Menominee Indian Tribe of Wisconsin as a federally recognized Indian tribe.
Sources: U.S. Census Bureau, Census 2010 Redistricting Data Summary File, March 2011; U.S. Bureau of Indian Affairs, departmental data, June 2013; Menominee Indian Tribe of Wisconsin, tribal data, May 2013. Acreage ownership totals, population totals, and percentages calculated by Wisconsin Legislative Reference Bureau.

Wisconsin Indian Land Holdings in Acres, By County, June 2013

County	Total Holdings	Tribal Land	Individual Land
Adams	121.35	0.35	121.00
Ashland	61,214.67	28,485.67	32,728.00
Barron	168.11	168.11	0.00
Bayfield	8,109.15	6,189.75	1,904.75
Brown	2,153.83	1,951.21	202.62
Burnett	1,358.74	1,358.74	0.00
Clark	926.82	369.08	557.74
Crawford	193.20	80.00	113.20
Dane	4.45	4.45	0.00
Douglas	516.27	0.00	516.27
Eau Claire	160.00	160.00	0.00
Forest	16,303.95	15,623.95	360.00
Iron	15,835.23	12,096.99	3,738.24
Jackson	1,428.37	719.45	708.92
Juneau	393.85	93.00	300.85
La Crosse	132.76	40.67	92.09
Langlade	200.48	200.48	0.00
Marathon	200.00	0.00	200.00
Marinette	40.00	0.00	40.00
Menominee	233,567.91	228,056.91	5,511.00
Milwaukee	19.58	19.58	0.00
Monroe	946.92	553.92	393.00
Oneida	345.93	176.07	169.86
Outagamie	9,937.20	9,239.92	697.28
Polk	851.80	851.80	0.00
Sauk	95.26	95.26	0.00
Sawyer	51,147.20	29,190.18	21,957.02
Shawano	19,344.40	18,727.68	616.72
Vilas	31,156.43	20,786.19	10,355.18
Vernon	1,200.00	1,200.00	0.00
Washburn	20.00	20.00	0.00
Wood	777.43	380.01	397.42

Note: Total holdings include government land in the following counties: Ashland (1.00 acre), Bayfield (14.65 acres), Forest (320.00 acres), and Vilas (15.06 acres).
Sources: U.S. Bureau of Indian Affairs, departmental data, June 2013; Menominee Indian Tribe of Wisconsin, tribal data, May 2013.

Tribal Chairpersons, Mailing Addresses, and Web Sites
May 2015

Tribe and Chairperson	Tribal Mailing Address and Web Sites
Bad River Band (Lake Superior Chippewa)	P.O. Box 39, Odanah 54861-0039, (715) 682-7111
Mike Wiggins, Jr.	http://www.badriver-nsn.gov
Forest County Potawatomi Community	P.O. Box 340, Crandon 54520-0346, (715) 478-7200
Gus Frank	http://www.fcpotawatomi.com
Ho-Chunk Nation	P.O. Box 667, Black River Falls 54615-0667, (715) 284-9343
Jon Greendeer (President)	http://www.ho-chunknation.com
Lac Courte Oreilles Band (Lake Superior Chippewa)	13394 W. Trepania Road, Hayward 54843-2186, (715) 634-8934
Michael Isham, Jr.	http://www.lco-nsn.gov
Lac du Flambeau Band (Lake Superior Chippewa)	P.O. Box 67, Lac du Flambeau 54538-0067, (715) 588-3303
Henry St. Germaine (President)	http://www.ldftribe.com/
Menominee Tribe	P.O. Box 910, Keshena 54135-0910, (715) 799-5114
Gary Besaw	http://www.menominee-nsn.gov
Oneida Nation	P.O. Box 365, Oneida 54155-0365, (920) 869-2214
Cristina Danforth	http://www.oneidanation.org
Red Cliff Band (Lake Superior Chippewa)	88385 Pike Road, Hwy. 13, Bayfield 54814-0529, (715) 779-3700
Rose Soulier	http://www.redcliff-nsn.gov
St. Croix Chippewa Tribe	24663 Angeline Avenue, Webster 54893-9246, (715) 349-2195
Lewis Taylor	http://www.stcciw.com/
Sokaogon Chippewa Community	3051 Sand Lake Road, Crandon 54520-8815, (715) 478-7500
Chris McGeshick	http://www.sokaogonchippewa.com
Stockbridge-Munsee Band (Mohican Nation)	P.O. Box 70, Bowler 54416-9801, (715) 793-4111
Wallace Miller (President)	http://www.mohican-nsn.gov

Sources: Wisconsin State Tribal Relations Initiative, at: http://witribes.wi.gov/ [May 2015] and individual tribal Web sites.

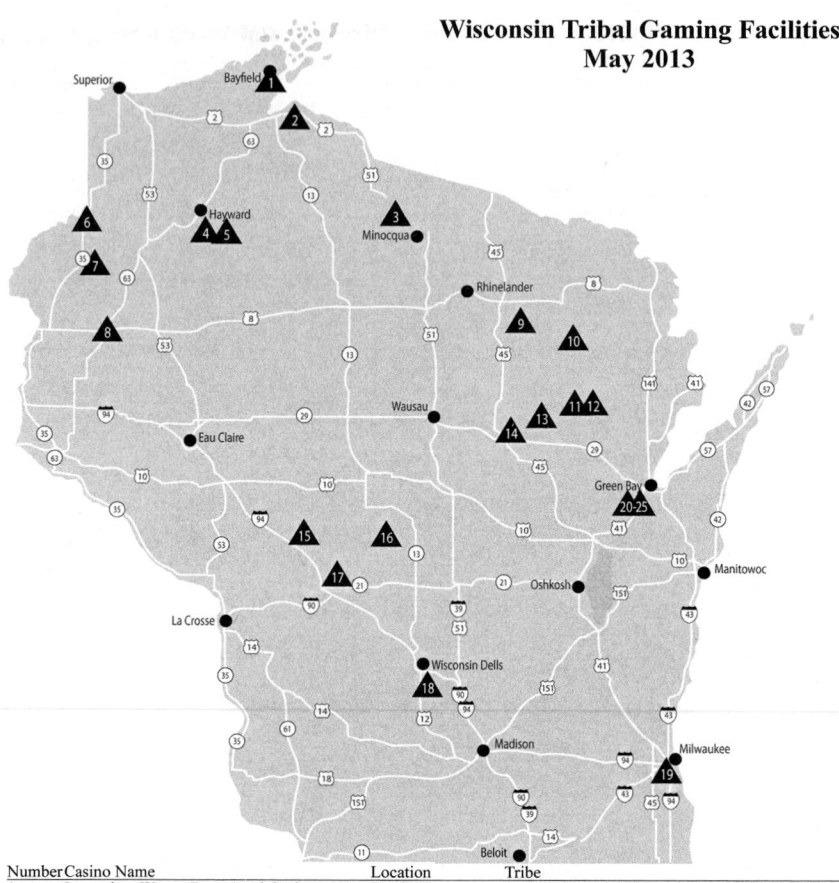

Wisconsin Tribal Gaming Facilities
May 2013

Number	Casino Name	Location	Tribe
1 . . .	Legendary Waters Resort and Casino	Bayfield	Red Cliff Band (Lake Superior Chippewa)
2 . . .	Bad River Casino	Odanah	Bad River Band (Lake Superior Chippewa)
3 . . .	Lake of the Torches Resort Casino	Lac du Flambeau.	Lac du Flambeau Band (Lake Superior Chippewa)
4 . . .	Lac Courte Oreilles Casino Lodge.	Hayward	Lac Courte Oreilles Band (Lake Superior Chippewa)
5 . . .	Grindstone Creek Casino	Hayward	Lac Courte Oreilles Band (Lake Superior Chippewa)
6 . . .	St. Croix Casino – Danbury	Danbury	St. Croix Band (Lake Superior Chippewa)
7 . . .	St. Croix Casino – Hertel	Hertel.	St. Croix Band (Lake Superior Chippewa)
8 . . .	St. Croix Casino – Turtle Lake	Turtle Lake. . . .	St. Croix Band (Lake Superior Chippewa)
9 . . .	Mole Lake Casino	Crandon	Sokaogon Chippewa Community
10. . .	Potawatomi Carter Casino and Hotel . . .	Carter.	Forest County Potawatomi Community
11. . .	Menominee Casino Resort.	Keshena	Menominee Tribe
12. . .	The Thunderbird Mini-Casino.	Keshena	Menominee Tribe
13. . .	North Star Mohican Casino	Bowler	Stockbridge-Munsee Band (Mohican Nation)
14. . .	Ho-Chunk Gaming – Wittenberg	Wittenberg	Ho-Chunk Nation
15. . .	Ho-Chunk Gaming – Black River Falls . .	Black River Falls.	Ho-Chunk Nation
16. . .	Ho-Chunk Gaming – Nekoosa	Nekoosa	Ho-Chunk Nation
17. . .	Ho-Chunk Gaming – Tomah.	Tomah	Ho-Chunk Nation
18. . .	Ho-Chunk Gaming – Wisconsin Dells. . .	Baraboo	Ho-Chunk Nation
19. . .	Potawatomi Bingo Casino	Milwaukee	Forest County Potawatomi Community
20. . .	Oneida Main Casino	Green Bay	Oneida Nation
21. . .	IMAC Casino/Bingo.	Green Bay	Oneida Nation
22. . .	Oneida Mason Street Casino.	Green Bay	Oneida Nation
23. . .	Oneida One-Stop Packerland	Green Bay	Oneida Nation
24. . .	Oneida Casino Travel Center	Oneida	Oneida Nation
25. . .	One-Stop Highway 54 Convenience Store .	Oneida	Oneida Nation

Note: Only Class III gaming facilities regulated by tribal compact are included, pursuant to P.L. 100-497, the Indian Gaming
Regulatory Act, which divides gambling into three classes. An additional Ho-Chunk casino in Madison offers Class II
gaming. Class I games are social games played solely for prizes of minimal value or traditional forms of Indian gaming
played in connection with tribal ceremonies or celebrations. Class II includes bingo or bingo-type games, pull-tabs and
punch-boards, and certain nonbanking card games, such as poker. Class III covers all other forms of gaming.

Source: Wisconsin Legislative Fiscal Bureau, *Informational Paper 87: Tribal Gaming in Wisconsin,* January 2015.

WISCONSIN VOTING AGE POPULATION BY RACE AND COUNTY
2010 Census and 2014 Estimate

County	2014 Total	2010 Total	White	Black/ African American	American Indian and Alaska Native	Asian	Native Hawaiian and Other Pacific Islander	Some Other Race	More Than One	Hispanic or Latino Origin*
							2010 Census			
					Race (as selected by respondent)					
Adams	17,587	17,454	15,935	598	203	90	6	8	26	588
Ashland	12,457	12,413	10,718	39	1,416	44	4	7	18	167
Barron	36,166	35,720	34,325	291	392	177	7	10	24	494
Bayfield . . .	12,306	12,161	10,812	22	1,170	43	4	9	10	91
Brown	191,686	186,184	162,483	3,705	5,076	4,470	92	96	196	10,066
Buffalo	10,670	10,566	10,306	18	60	26	1	17	2	136
Burnett.	12,498	12,375	11,496	46	660	41	6	8	11	107
Calumet	36,329	35,733	33,709	167	248	665	12	15	16	901
Chippewa . . .	48,620	47,706	45,395	864	361	535	11	11	26	503
Clark	24,821	24,599	23,527	52	141	87	10	3	9	770
Columbia. . . .	43,935	43,566	41,505	621	270	247	27	15	16	865
Crawford. . . .	13,025	12,920	12,441	247	68	47	6	5	10	96
Dane	396,640	381,989	324,503	17,235	1,901	18,629	189	450	845	18,237
Dodge	70,168	69,180	63,961	2,241	441	369	38	30	46	2,054
Door	23,079	22,709	21,902	92	196	89	4	7	18	401
Douglas	35,037	34,694	32,579	376	1,047	336	14	20	38	284
Dunn	35,130	34,798	33,112	200	225	786	16	13	38	408
Eau Claire . . .	79,964	77,864	73,172	653	572	2,232	35	40	82	1,078
Florence	3,705	3,649	3,560	7	41	20	2	0	0	19
Fond du Lac . .	79,964	78,589	73,638	937	549	754	23	34	57	2,597
Forest.	7,284	7,261	6,222	58	863	13	15	3	8	79
Grant	41,915	40,322	38,922	513	140	265	6	13	21	442
Green.	28,123	27,889	26,912	101	83	140	8	15	14	616
Green Lake. . .	14,843	14,663	14,027	5	4	3	2	0	0	1
Iowa	18,053	17,798	17,377	58	63	100	8	12	8	172
Iron.	4,980	4,935	4,845	5	48	15	0	0	4	18
Jackson.	16,102	15,818	14,148	379	878	46	19	8	15	325
Jefferson	64,607	63,829	59,160	502	318	470	16	32	40	3,291
Juneau	21,406	20,991	19,592	513	343	94	4	8	9	428
Kenosha	125,353	123,597	101,744	7,217	769	2,031	80	144	255	11,357
Kewaunee . . .	15,923	15,725	15,256	49	102	40	5	14	14	245
La Crosse . . .	92,632	90,176	83,909	1,149	576	3,172	33	58	100	1,089
Lafayette. . . .	12,657	12,487	12,053	18	53	37	0	0	4	322
Langlade	15,809	15,762	15,264	58	213	51	2	4	4	166
Lincoln.	22,705	22,441	21,916	63	136	104	15	16	9	182
Manitowoc . .	63,715	63,232	59,800	272	439	1,247	25	33	50	1,366
Marathon. . . .	102,678	101,194	94,081	527	625	4,105	43	41	97	1,675
Marinette. . . .	33,355	33,182	32,221	85	293	203	18	15	17	330
Marquette . . .	12,428	12,319	11,900	57	93	51	0	4	3	211
Menominee . .	2,882	2,853	423	10	2,338	1	0	0	1	80
Milwaukee. . .	719,442	711,358	433,061	168,280	5,644	23,660	331	790	2,476	77,116
Monroe.	33,802	33,003	31,038	366	420	229	34	13	22	881
Oconto	29,768	29,228	28,308	50	450	95	5	12	11	297
Oneida	29,704	29,359	28,454	134	373	150	16	7	10	215
Outagamie . . .	136,008	132,271	121,384	1,180	2,390	3,410	60	65	119	3,663
Ozaukee	67,188	66,023	62,520	878	239	1,123	26	32	65	1,140
Pepin	5,798	5,765	5,658	13	24	15	2	4	2	47
Pierce	32,215	31,860	30,766	187	185	280	6	17	17	402
Polk	34,039	33,705	32,677	77	394	119	5	23	26	384
Portage.	56,666	55,472	52,322	325	309	1,325	20	31	49	1,091
Price	11,560	11,460	11,164	13	103	52	36	7	1	84
Racine	148,319	146,898	115,625	15,037	867	1,693	54	113	220	13,289
Richland	13,927	13,821	13,417	52	65	67	2	8	5	205
Rock	121,082	120,148	105,720	5,460	646	1,331	54	80	135	6,722
Rusk	11,576	11,440	11,158	28	97	40	2	1	6	108
St. Croix	63,057	61,462	59,021	394	358	638	19	36	44	952
Sauk	47,736	47,209	44,473	254	557	292	13	30	30	1,560
Sawyer	13,320	13,103	10,799	64	2,046	38	2	5	5	144
Shawano	32,613	32,387	29,227	84	2,371	155	18	4	25	503
Sheboygan . . .	88,633	87,925	79,347	1,305	499	3,064	32	48	78	3,552
Taylor	15,778	21,831	20,622	40	71	95	3	5	5	988
Trempealeau . .	22,315	21,831	20,622	40	71	95	3	5	5	988
Vernon	22,245	21,895	21,414	76	89	75	7	8	12	214
Vilas	17,864	17,621	15,816	33	1,533	66	3	9	4	157
Walworth. . . .	79,498	78,228	70,164	769	352	682	34	35	56	6,136
Washburn . . .	12,828	12,679	12,231	22	246	46	2	2	7	123
Washington. . .	101,327	99,510	95,331	765	414	1,022	22	51	66	1,839
Waukesha . . .	301,019	296,081	273,899	3,256	1,160	7,769	112	143	256	9,486
Waupaca	40,933	40,540	39,216	111	303	152	7	9	10	732
Waushara. . . .	19,857	19,662	18,231	440	158	82	9	6	1	735
Winnebago. . .	133,024	130,862	121,239	2,336	1,105	2,655	58	62	132	9
Wood.	58,434	57,745	55,161	240	2	2	0	0	0	3
STATE . . .	4,422,812	4,347,494	3,753,673	242,398	47,511	93,260	1,826	2,897	6,107	199,822

Note: The voting age population is 18 and older.
*"Hispanic or Latino Origin" represents ethnicity and includes people of Cuban, Mexican, Puerto Rican, South or Central American, or other Spanish culture or origin, regardless of race.
Sources: U.S. Department of Commerce, Census Bureau, P.L. 94-171 Redistricting File, as processed by the Wisconsin Legislative Technology Services Bureau, May 2011; Wisconsin Department of Administration, Demographic Services Center, *Official Final Estimates, 1/1/2014, Wisconsin Counties, with Comparison to Census 2010,* October 2014.

WISCONSIN VITAL STATISTICS
1910 – 2013

Year	Marriages Number[4]	Rate[3]	Divorces, Annulments Number[4]	Rate[3]	Live Births Number	Rate[3]	Total Deaths[1] Number	Rate[3]	Infant Deaths Number	Rate[5]	Fetal Deaths[2] Number	Rate[6]	Maternal Deaths Number	Rate[7]
1910	18,528	7.9	1,189	0.5	51,435	22.0	28,213	12.1	5,621	109.3	1,414	26.8	255	49.6
1915	17,833	7.2	1,721	0.7	58,014	23.3	26,676	10.7	4,520	77.9	1,711	28.6	291	50.2
1920	22,294	8.4	2,425	0.9	59,269	22.4	29,859	11.3	4,566	77.0	1,673	27.5	338	57.0
1925	16,385	5.8	2,467	0.9	58,024	20.7	29,380	10.5	3,861	66.5	1,712	28.7	294	50.7
1930	15,328	5.2	2,553	0.9	56,643	19.2	30,488	10.4	3,149	55.6	1,683	28.9	298	52.6
1935	21,075	6.9	3,543	1.2	52,402	17.2	30,404	10.0	2,413	46.0	1,257	23.4	193	36.8
1940	23,379	7.5	3,599	1.1	56,324	17.9	31,457	10.0	2,030	36.0	1,209	21.0	151	26.8
1945	25,269	8.5	6,393	2.2	61,577	20.9	31,776	10.7	1,890	30.7	1,141	18.2	81	13.2
1950	29,081	8.4	4,845	1.4	82,364	23.9	33,573	9.7	2,098	25.5	1,241	14.8	35	4.3
1955	25,543	7.0	4,720	1.3	92,333	25.2	35,250	9.6	2,175	23.6	1,233	13.2	22	2.4
1960	24,573	6.2	3,672	0.9	99,493	25.1	38,121	9.6	2,173	21.8	1,341	13.3	27	2.7
1965	28,410	6.7	5,232	1.2	82,919	19.7	40,146	9.5	1,829	22.1	1,042	12.4	13	1.6
1970	34,415	7.8	8,930	2.0	77,455	17.5	40,820	9.2	1,308	16.9	817	10.4	6	0.8
1975	35,888	7.8	13,187	2.9	65,145	14.3	39,916	8.8	881	13.5	530	8.1	3	0.5
1980	41,113	8.7	17,589	3.7	74,763	15.9	40,801	8.7	763	10.2	549	7.3	5	0.7
1985	40,014	8.4	16,596	3.5	73,647	15.4	41,434	8.7	674	9.2	471	6.4	4	0.5
1990	38,934	8.0	17,727	3.6	72,636	14.8	42,655	8.7	611	8.4	443	6.1	3	0.4
1995	36,354	7.1	17,313	3.4	67,493	13.2	45,037	8.8	493	7.3	403	5.9	2	0.3
1996	36,186	7.0	17,218	3.3	66,490	13.0	45,107	8.8	492	7.3	416	6.2	2	0.3
1997	35,546	6.8	17,289	3.3	67,379	12.7	44,860	8.6	431	6.5	361	5.4	2	0.3
1998	34,946	6.7	17,484	3.3	68,181	12.8	45,890	8.7	488	7.2	401	5.9	6	0.9
1999	35,754	6.8	17,302	3.3	69,289	12.9	46,571	8.8	456	6.7	353	5.2	6	0.9
2000	36,100	6.7	17,388	3.2	69,012	12.9	46,405	8.7	457	6.6	414	5.9	5	0.7
2001	34,790	6.5	17,457	3.3	68,510	12.6	46,537	8.6	491	7.1	375	5.4	4	0.6
2002	34,241	6.3	17,471	3.2	69,999	12.7	46,893	8.6	471	6.9	379	5.5	5	0.7
2003	34,220	6.3	17,150	3.1	70,131	12.7	46,040	8.4	454	6.5	344	4.9	9	0.1
2004	34,056	6.2	16,802	3.0	70,934	12.7	45,488	8.2	420	6.0	352	5.0	6	0.9
2005	33,876	6.1	16,297	2.9	72,302	12.9	46,544	8.3	469	6.6	363	5.1	15	2.1
2006	33,437	6.0	16,730	3.0	72,757	12.9	46,051	8.2	462	6.4	384	5.3	15	2.1
2007	32,159	5.7	16,458	2.9	72,002	12.7	46,117	8.2	469	6.4	386	5.3	15	2.1
2008	31,444	5.6	16,885	3.0	68,708	12.5	46,526	8.2	501	7.0	387	5.3	9	1.2
2009	30,057	5.3	16,705	2.9	68,367	12.0	45,598	8.0	426	6.0	341	4.8	13	1.8
2010	29,952	5.3	17,285	3.0	67,736	11.9	47,212	8.3	393	5.7	361	5.3	11	1.6
2011	30,287	5.3	16,635	2.9	67,229	11.8	48,101	8.4	427	6.3	368	5.4	13	1.9
2012	30,940	5.4	16,332	2.9	67,295	11.8	48,225	8.4	385	5.7	381	5.6	6	0.9
2013	29,979	5.2	15,941	2.8	66,566	11.6	49,917	8.7	414	6.2	331	4.9	12	1.8

[1] Excludes fetal deaths (20 weeks gestation and over).
[2] A fetal death report is not used for induced abortions.
[3] Per 1,000 population.
[4] Pre-1960 data includes legal separations.
[5] Per 1,000 live births.
[6] Per 1,000 deliveries (live births plus stillbirths of 20 weeks or more gestation).
[7] Per 10,000 live births.

Sources: Wisconsin Department of Health and Family Services, *Vital Statistics 1994*, and previous issues; Wisconsin Department of Health Services, *Wisconsin Births and Infant Deaths, 2013*, and previous issues; *Wisconsin Deaths, 2013*, and previous issues; *Wisconsin Marriages and Divorces, 2013*, and previous issues; departmental data, March 2015.

RESIDENT LIVE BIRTHS AND DEATHS IN WISCONSIN
By County, 1995 – 2014

County	Live Births					Deaths				
	1995	2000	2005	2010	2014	1995[1]	2000	2005	2010[3]	2013[4]
Adams	167	158	159	135	137	185	226	225	255	279
Ashland	239	224	198	177	168	218	206	205	188	191
Barron	550	466	528	546	486	450	442	487	482	492
Bayfield	135	141	121	113	124	152	153	149	152	142
Brown	2,962	3,212	3,332	3,414	3,358	1,482	1,591	1,626	1,610	1,851
Buffalo	165	163	147	125	140	121	123	117	146	129
Burnett	171	136	159	138	124	179	183	182	135	187
Calumet	488	513	630	605	554	235	252	265	284	333
Chippewa	633	673	738	748	732	534	533	522	485	611
Clark	448	496	581	600	560	323	307	339	354	356
Columbia	607	616	691	600	598	532	508	498	514	519
Crawford	215	183	201	157	1,701	178	178	169	156	170
Dane	5,023	5,555	6,055	6,051	6,355	2,397	2,512	2,648	2,858	3,160
Dodge	947	994	910	872	828	810	848	826	913	903
Door	254	232	258	215	186	311	315	314	311	313
Douglas	493	513	466	487	431	455	454	425	397	446
Dunn	444	483	511	468	455	289	280	260	305	336
Eau Claire	1,118	1,116	1,178	1,114	1,254	664	639	704	703	839
Florence[2]	36	36	37	29	31	66	63	45	66	61
Fond du Lac	1,119	1,151	1,187	1,066	1,067	867	908	1,000	902	953
Forest[2]	137	114	114	117	116	109	131	103	109	109
Grant	561	540	559	545	552	465	495	484	504	491
Green	390	402	447	414	394	316	322	316	313	344
Green Lake	192	219	204	211	199	248	243	230	201	212
Iowa	296	263	320	290	248	191	195	177	208	197
Iron[2]	63	40	45	40	42	87	84	110	83	109
Jackson	189	233	237	237	268	187	219	189	180	226
Jefferson	852	931	1,028	923	881	579	608	608	615	615
Juneau	308	275	277	263	268	271	264	278	274	330
Kenosha	2,040	2,151	2,133	2,055	1,955	1,229	1,222	1,253	1,272	1,358
Kewaunee	218	224	232	205	188	193	189	182	147	202
La Crosse	1,267	1,234	1,292	1,345	1,258	869	888	818	923	948
Lafayette	176	174	207	207	224	147	144	130	146	138
Langlade	228	209	202	204	183	252	220	233	202	238
Lincoln	320	281	275	283	244	298	333	316	300	367
Manitowoc	898	894	855	805	816	819	852	742	824	884
Marathon	1,585	1,520	1,554	1,656	1,604	907	924	976	1,100	1,151
Marinette[2]	454	457	460	389	371	478	470	493	452	513
Marquette[2]	121	146	182	160	149	141	174	185	179	183
Menominee[2]	92	93	104	108	93	45	36	45	36	39
Milwaukee	15,067	14,846	14,906	14,310	13,928	9,200	9,063	8,605	8,147	8,232
Monroe	529	602	615	627	583	383	414	399	390	418
Oconto	388	383	388	368	377	331	357	327	356	345
Oneida	352	316	355	307	266	375	431	421	425	425
Outagamie	2,056	2,289	2,291	2,268	2,283	1,026	1,109	1,194	1,218	1,328
Ozaukee	934	869	852	774	799	541	583	605	744	688
Pepin	83	79	99	65	76	72	73	66	81	87
Pierce	403	412	443	425	373	235	244	229	231	265
Polk	470	454	506	457	446	380	376	401	401	451
Portage	788	805	726	749	705	438	404	491	477	537
Price	184	125	130	115	110	198	207	200	161	169
Racine	2,512	2,650	2,623	2,484	2,375	1,534	1,616	1,537	1,628	1,676
Richland	196	201	228	194	181	200	185	164	160	182
Rock	1,963	2,075	2,052	1,991	1,975	1,268	1,335	1,409	1,379	1,463
Rusk	192	148	163	138	135	183	168	191	170	183
St. Croix	725	908	1,193	1,119	1,108	438	444	429	541	520
Sauk	670	755	785	783	788	484	485	505	582	571
Sawyer	196	182	205	167	157	194	183	184	170	212
Shawano	456	470	478	447	411	444	476	448	449	496
Sheboygan	1,336	1,437	1,481	1,325	1,184	957	1,083	1,089	1,001	1,151
Taylor	221	247	246	238	230	191	176	196	198	190
Trempealeau	315	322	331	377	410	338	298	280	264	279
Vernon	351	390	403	399	458	311	330	324	270	290
Vilas	205	155	164	191	187	254	251	235	242	299
Walworth	952	1,102	1,209	1,077	1,070	710	826	860	836	964
Washburn	168	163	173	152	131	194	198	193	195	211
Washington	1,440	1,490	1,495	1,371	1,332	687	795	868	997	1,053
Waukesha	4,120	4,357	4,108	3,886	3,882	2,316	2,795	2,903	3,084	3,163
Waupaca	619	567	537	503	529	658	634	677	709	673
Waushara	240	225	241	232	226	242	243	237	259	264
Winnebago	1,838	1,926	1,826	1,872	1,825	1,271	1,194	1,258	1,397	1,420
Wood	923	878	868	839	753	704	695	745	762	779
STATE	67,493	69,289	46,544	68,367	67,094	45,036	46,405	46,544	47,212	49,917

[1]The total for 1995 includes one death with an unknown county of residence.
[2]Since nearly all births and deaths occur in hospitals, the numbers for Florence, Forest, Iron, Marinette, Marquette, and Menominee Counties are small because they have no hospitals. Caution must be used in making inferences based on this data.
[3]The total for 2010 includes four deaths with unknown counties of residence.
[4]Data for 2014 Wisconsin Deaths not yet available.
Sources: Wisconsin Department of Health Services, Division of Public Health, Office of Health Informatics, *Wisconsin Births and Infant Deaths, 2014*, at: https://www.dhs.wisconsin.gov/stats/births/birthcounts.htm, and previous issues; *Wisconsin Deaths, 2013*, at: https://www.dhs.wisconsin.gov/publications/p45368-13.pdf, and previous issues.

MARRIAGE AND DIVORCE RATES BY STATE
1990 – 2012
(Rates are per 1,000)[1]

State	Marriages[2]						Divorces[3]					
	1990	1995	2000	2005	2010	2012	1990	1995	2000	2005	2010	2012
Alabama	10.6	9.8	10.1	9.2	8.2	8.2	6.1	6.0	5.5	4.9	4.4	3.6
Alaska	10.2	9.0	8.9	8.2	8.0	7.2	5.5	5.0	3.9	4.3	4.7	4.5
Arizona.	10.0	8.8	7.5	6.6	5.9	5.6	6.9	6.2	4.6	4.2	3.5	4.3
Arkansas	15.3	14.4	15.4	12.9	10.8	10.9	6.9	6.3	6.4	6.0	5.7	5.3
California	7.9	6.3	5.8	6.4	5.8	6.0	4.3	NA	NA	NA	NA	NA
Colorado	9.8	9.0	8.3	7.6	6.9	6.8	5.5	NA	4.7	4.4	4.3	4.3
Connecticut	7.9	6.6	5.7	5.8	5.6	5.2	3.2	2.9	3.3	3.0	2.9	2.7
Delaware.	8.4	7.3	6.5	5.9	5.2	5.8	4.4	5.0	3.9	3.8	3.5	3.5
District of Columbia	8.2	6.1	4.9	4.1	7.6	8.4	4.5	3.2	3.2	2.0	2.8	2.9
Florida	10.9	9.9	8.9	8.9	7.3	7.2	6.3	5.5	5.1	4.6	4.4	4.2
Georgia.	10.3	8.4	6.8	7.0	7.3	6.5	5.5	5.1	3.3	NA	NA	NA
Hawaii	16.4	15.7	20.6	22.6	17.6	17.5	4.6	4.6	3.9	NA	NA	NA
Idaho	13.9	13.1	10.8	10.5	8.8	8.2	6.5	5.8	5.5	5.0	5.2	4.7
ILLINOIS	8.8	6.9	6.9	5.9	5.7	5.8	3.8	3.2	3.2	2.6	2.6	2.4
Indiana	9.6	8.6	7.9	6.9	6.3	6.7	NA	NA	NA	NA	NA	NA
IOWA	9.0	7.7	6.9	6.9	6.9	6.8	3.9	3.7	3.3	2.7	2.4	2.2
Kansas	9.2	8.5	8.3	6.8	6.4	6.3	5.0	4.1	3.6	3.1	3.7	3.4
Kentucky.	13.5	12.2	9.8	8.7	7.4	7.2	5.8	5.9	5.1	4.6	4.5	4.1
Louisiana.	9.6	9.3	9.1	8.0	6.9	5.7	NA	NA	NA	NA	NA	NA
Maine	9.7	8.7	8.8	8.2	7.1	7.3	4.3	4.4	5.0	4.1	4.2	3.9
Maryland.	9.7	8.4	7.5	6.9	5.7	5.6	3.4	3.0	3.3	3.1	2.8	2.8
Massachusetts	7.9	7.1	5.8	6.2	5.6	5.5	2.8	2.2	2.5	2.2	2.5	2.7
MICHIGAN	8.2	7.3	6.7	6.1	5.5	5.6	4.3	4.1	3.9	3.4	3.5	3.3
MINNESOTA	7.7	7.0	6.8	6.0	5.3	5.6	3.5	3.4	3.2	NA	NA	NA
Mississippi	9.4	7.9	6.9	5.8	4.9	5.8	5.5	4.8	5.0	4.4	4.3	4.0
Missouri	9.6	8.3	7.8	7.0	6.5	6.5	5.1	5.0	4.5	3.6	3.9	3.7
Montana	8.6	7.6	7.3	7.4	7.4	7.8	5.1	4.8	4.2	4.5	3.9	3.9
Nebraska	8.0	7.3	7.6	7.0	6.6	6.7	4.0	3.8	3.7	3.3	3.6	3.4
Nevada	99.0	85.2	72.2	57.4	38.3	35.1	11.4	7.8	9.9	7.4	5.9	5.5
New Hampshire	9.5	8.3	9.4	7.3	7.3	6.8	4.7	4.2	4.8	3.9	3.8	3.6
New Jersey.	7.6	6.5	6.0	5.7	5.1	4.9	3.0	3.0	3.0	2.9	3.0	2.8
New Mexico	8.8	8.8	8.0	6.6	7.7	6.9	4.9	6.6	5.1	4.6	4.0	3.0
New York	8.6	8.0	7.1	6.8	6.5	7.0	3.2	3.0	3.0	2.9	2.9	2.9
North Carolina	7.8	8.4	8.2	7.3	6.6	6.6	5.1	5.0	4.5	4.1	3.8	3.7
North Dakota.	7.5	7.1	7.2	6.8	6.5	6.6	3.6	3.4	3.4	2.9	3.1	3.1
Ohio	9.0	8.0	7.8	6.5	5.8	5.8	4.7	4.3	4.2	3.5	3.4	3.4
Oklahoma	10.6	8.6	NA	7.3	7.2	6.9	7.7	6.6	NA	5.6	5.2	4.8
Oregon	8.9	8.1	7.5	7.3	6.5	6.6	5.5	4.7	4.8	4.2	4.0	3.8
Pennsylvania.	7.1	6.2	5.8	5.8	5.3	5.5	3.3	3.2	3.1	2.3	2.7	2.8
Rhode Island	8.1	7.3	8.1	7.0	5.8	6.1	3.7	3.6	2.9	3.0	3.2	3.2
South Carolina	15.9	11.9	9.9	8.3	7.4	7.4	4.5	3.9	3.8	2.9	3.1	3.2
South Dakota.	11.1	9.9	8.9	8.4	7.3	7.5	3.7	3.9	3.5	2.8	3.4	3.0
Tennessee	13.9	15.5	13.5	10.9	8.8	8.8	6.5	6.2	5.9	4.6	4.2	4.2
Texas	10.5	9.9	9.1	7.8	7.1	7.3	5.5	5.2	4.0	3.3	3.3	3.0
Utah	11.2	10.7	10.2	9.8	8.5	8.4	5.1	4.4	4.3	4.1	3.7	3.3
Vermont	10.9	10.3	9.8	8.9	9.3	8.2	4.5	4.7	4.1	3.6	3.8	3.5
Virginia.	11.4	10.2	8.8	8.2	6.8	6.8	4.4	4.3	4.3	4.0	3.8	3.7
Washington.	9.5	7.7	7.0	6.5	6.0	6.3	5.9	5.4	4.6	4.3	4.2	3.9
West Virginia.	7.2	6.1	7.9	7.4	6.7	7.0	5.3	5.2	5.1	5.1	5.1	4.7
WISCONSIN	7.9	7.0	6.5	6.1	5.3	5.4	3.6	3.4	3.2	2.9	3.0	2.9
Wyoming.	10.7	10.6	10.0	9.3	7.6	7.6	6.6	6.6	5.8	5.2	5.1	4.4

NA – Not available.

[1]Rates are based on provisional counts of marriages and divorces by state of occurrence. Rates are per 1,000 total population residing in area. Population enumerated as of April 1 for 1990, 2000, and 2010 and estimated as of July 1 for all other years.

[2]Data includes nonlicensed marriages registered.

[3]Data includes annulments. Includes divorce petitions filed or legal separations for some counties or states.

Sources: Centers for Disease Control and Prevention, National Vital Statistics System, *Marriage Rates by State: 1990, 1995, and 1999-2012*; *Divorce Rates by State: 1990, 1995, and 1999-2012*.

WISCONSIN DEATHS AND DEATH RATES – 2013

Age Group	Total		Males		Females	
	Deaths	Rate*	Deaths	Rate*	Deaths	Rate*
Under 1 year	414	621.9	226	663.9	188	578.0
1-4 years	61	22.0	34	24.0	27	19.9
5-9 years	38	10.4	23	12.3	15	8.4
10-14 years.	49	13.2	34	17.9	15	8.3
15-19 years.	146	38.0	95	48.4	51	27.2
20-24 years.	319	80.0	237	117.0	82	41.9
25-29 years.	376	104.5	270	147.2	106	60.1
30-34 years.	366	98.7	251	133.3	115	63.0
35-39 years.	456	136.2	295	173.5	161	97.8
40-44 years.	618	172.5	387	214.1	231	130.2
45-49 years.	1,098	279.3	653	331.3	445	227.0
50-54 years.	1,850	421.3	1,132	518.0	718	325.6
55-59 years.	2,512	608.2	1,551	753.7	961	463.7
60-64 years.	3,179	906.2	1,956	1,122.5	1,223	692.7
65-69 years.	3,719	1,394.6	2,161	1,661.3	1,558	1,140.6
70-74 years.	4,192	2,149.4	2,361	2,576.4	1,831	1,771.0
75-79 years.	5,060	3,475.3	2,687	4,118.0	2,373	2,953.3
80-84 years.	7,048	6,119.1	3,596	7,516.7	3,452	5,126.2
85-89 years.	8,289	10,305.9	3,611	12,294.9	4,678	9,161.8
90-94 years.	6,701	19,123.9	2,385	23,177.8	4,316	17,438.4
95 years and over . . .	3,426	33,262.1	803	37,877.4	2,623	32,066.0
ALL AGES.	49,917	871.0	24,748	869.5	25,169	872.5

*Per 100,000 population in that group.

Source: Wisconsin Department of Health Services, Division of Public Health, Office of Health Informatics, *Wisconsin Deaths, 2013,* March 2015, at: https://www.dhs.wisconsin.gov/publications/p45368-13.pdf.

WISCONSIN POPULATION, BY AGE GROUP, 2010 and 2013

Age Group	Population of Group		Male		Female	
	2010 Census	2013	2010	2013	2010	2013
Under 5 years	358,443	344,331	183,391	176,077	175,052	168,254
5-9 years	368,617	366,542	188,286	187,519	180,331	179,023
10-14 years.	375,927	371,849	192,232	190,105	183,695	181,744
15-19 years.	399,209	384,724	204,803	196,628	194,406	188,096
20-24 years.	386,552	399,313	196,897	203,040	189,655	196,273
25-29 years.	372,347	360,557	189,349	183,790	182,998	176,767
30-34 years.	349,347	371,657	178,120	188,753	171,227	182,904
35-39 years.	345,328	335,412	174,619	170,384	170,709	165,028
40-44 years.	380,338	358,966	191,738	181,145	188,600	177,821
45-49 years.	437,627	393,939	218,539	197,504	219,088	196,435
50-54 years.	436,126	440,011	218,303	219,016	217,823	220,995
55-59 years.	385,986	413,884	192,952	206,192	193,034	207,692
60-64 years.	313,825	351,561	155,756	174,620	158,069	176,941
65-69 years.	227,029	267,215	109,168	130,345	117,861	136,870
70-74 years.	173,467	195,416	81,067	91,838	92,400	103,578
75-79 years.	141,252	145,913	62,181	65,387	79,071	80,526
80-84 years.	117,061	115,408	47,549	47,955	69,512	67,453
85 years and over	118,505	126,015	37,450	41,862	81,055	84,153
STATE	5,686,986	5,742,713	2,822,400	2,852,160	2,864,586	2,890,553
Median age.	38.5	39.0	37.3	37.9	37.9	40.2

Source: U.S. Census Bureau, Population Division, *Annual Estimates of the Resident Population by Sex and Age for Wisconsin: April 1, 2010 to July 1, 2013,* December 2014.

POSTAL ZIP CODES FOR WISCONSIN MUNICIPALITIES

Municipality and County	ZIP Code	Municipality and County	ZIP Code
Abbotsford, Clark	54405	Belleville, Dane	53508
Abrams, Oconto	54101	Bellevue, Brown	54311
Adams, Adams	53910	Belmont, Lafayette	53510
Adell, Sheboygan	53001	Beloit, Rock[2]	53511
Afton, Rock	53501	Benet Lake, Kenosha	53102
Alban, Portage (Rosholt)[1]	54473	Bennett, Douglas	54873
Albany, Green	53502	Benoit, Bayfield	54816
Albertville, Dunn (Colfax)[1]	54730	Benton, Lafayette	53803
Alden, St. Croix (New Richmond)[1]	54017	Berlin, Green Lake	54923
Algoma, Kewaunee	54201	Bethel, Wood (Arpin)[1]	54410
Allenton, Washington	53002	Bevent, Marathon (Hatley)[1]	54440
Allouez, Brown	54301	Big Bend, Waukesha	53103
Alma, Buffalo	54610	Big Falls, Waupaca	54926
Alma Center, Jackson	54611	Big Flats, Adams (Arkdale)[1]	54613
Almena, Barron	54805	Birch, Lincoln (Irma)[1]	54442
Almond, Portage	54909	Birchwood, Washburn	54817
Altdorf, Wood (Vesper)[1]	54489	Birnamwood, Shawano	54414
Altoona, Eau Claire	54720	Biron, Wood (Wisconsin Rapids)[1]	54494
Alvin, Florence	54542	Black Brook, Polk (Clear Lake)[1]	54005
Amberg, Marinette	54102	Black Creek, Outagamie	54106
Amery, Polk	54001	Black Earth, Dane	53515
Amherst, Portage	54406	Black River Falls, Jackson	54615
Amherst Junction, Portage	54407	Blackwell, Forest (Laona)[1]	54541
Angelica, Brown (Pulaski)[1]	54162	Blair, Trempealeau	54616
Aniwa, Marathon	54408	Blanchardville, Lafayette	53516
Antigo, Langlade	54409	Blenker, Wood	54415
Apostle Islands National Lakeshore, Bayfield		Bloom City, Vernon	54634
(Bayfield)[1]	54814	Bloomer, Chippewa	54724
Appleton, Outagamie[2]	54911	Bloomingdale, Vernon (Westby)[1]	54667
Arbor Vitae, Oneida	54568	Bloomington, Grant	53804
Arcadia, Trempealeau	54612	Bloomville, Lincoln (Gleason)[1]	54435
Arena, Iowa	53503	Blue Mounds, Dane	53517
Argonne, Forest	54511	Blue River, Grant	53518
Argyle, Lafayette	53504	Boardman, St. Croix (Hudson)[1]	54016
Arkansaw, Pepin	54721	Boaz, Richland (Richland Center)[1]	53581
Arkdale, Adams	54613	Bonduel, Shawano	54107
Arland, Polk (Clayton)[1]	54004	Boscobel, Grant	53805
Arlington, Columbia	53911	Boulder Junction, Vilas	54512
Armstrong Creek, Forest	54103	Bowler, Shawano	54416
Arnott, Portage (Stevens Point)[1]	54481	Boyceville, Dunn	54725
Arpin, Wood	54410	Boyd, Chippewa	54726
Ashippun, Dodge	53003	Brackett, Eau Claire (Fall Creek)[1]	54742
Ashland, Ashland	54806	Branch, Manitowoc	54247
Ashley, Marathon (Mosinee)[1]	54455	Brandon, Fond du Lac	53919
Ashwaubenon, Brown	54304	Brantwood, Price	54513
Athelstane, Marinette	54104	Briggsville, Marquette	53920
Athens, Marathon	54411	Brill, Barron	54818
Atwood, Clark (Owen)[1]	54460	Brillion, Calumet	54110
Auburndale, Wood	54412	Bristol, Kenosha	53104
Augusta, Eau Claire	54722	Brodhead, Green	53520
Auroraville, Green Lake (Berlin)[1]	54923	Brokaw, Marathon	54417
Avalon, Rock	53505	Brookfield, Waukesha[2]	53005
Avoca, Iowa	53506	Brooklyn, Green	53521
		Brooks, Marquette	53952
Babcock, Wood	54413	Brown Deer, Milwaukee[2]	53209
Bagley, Grant	53801	Brownsville, Dodge	53006
Baileys Harbor, Door	54202	Browntown, Green	53522
Bakerville, Wood (Marshfield)[1]	54449	Bruce, Rusk	54819
Baldwin, St. Croix	54002	Brule, Douglas	54820
Balsam Lake, Polk	54810	Brussels, Door	54204
Bancroft, Portage	54921	Bryant, Langlade	54418
Bangor, La Crosse	54614	Buena Vista, Portage (Plover)[1]	54467
Baraboo, Sauk	53913	Buffalo City, Buffalo	54622
Barnes, Douglas	54873	Burkhardt, St. Croix (Hudson)[1]	54016
Barneveld, Iowa	53507	Burlington, Racine	53105
Barre Mills, La Crosse (La Crosse)[1]	54601	Burnett, Dodge	53922
Barron, Barron	54812	Butler, Waukesha	53007
Barronett, Barron	54813	Butte des Morts, Winnebago	54927
Bassett, Kenosha	53101	Butternut, Ashland	54514
Bateman, Chippewa (Chippewa Falls)[1]	54729	Byron, Dodge	53006
Bay City, Pierce	54723		
Bayfield, Bayfield	54814	**C**able, Bayfield	54821
Bayside, Milwaukee	53217	Cadott, Chippewa	54727
Bay Mills, Lincoln (Tomahawk)[1]	54487	Cady, St. Croix (Wilson)[1]	54027
Bay View, Milwaukee (Milwaukee)[3]	53207	Caledonia, Racine	53108
Bear Creek, Outagamie	54922	Cambria, Columbia	53923
Beaver, Marinette	54114	Cambridge, Dane	53523
Beaver Dam, Dodge	53916	Cameron, Barron	54822
Beecher, Marinette (Pembine)[1]	54156	Campbell, La Crosse (La Crosse)[1]	54601
Beetown, Grant	53802	Campbellsport, Fond du Lac	53010
Beldenville, Pierce	54003	Camp Douglas, Juneau[4]	54618
Belgium, Ozaukee	53004	Camp Lake, Kenosha	53109
Bell Center, Crawford (Gays Mills)[1]	54631	Canton, Barron	54868

Municipality and County	ZIP Code
Carey, Iron (Hurley)[1]	54534
Caroline, Shawano	54928
Carson, Portage (Junction City)[1]	54443
Carter, Forest (Wabeno)[1]	54566
Caryville, Eau Claire (Eau Claire)[1]	54701
Cascade, Sheboygan	53011
Casco, Kewaunee	54205
Cashton, Monroe	54619
Cassian, Oneida (Harshaw)[1]	54529
Cassville, Grant	53806
Cataract, Monroe	54620
Catawba, Price	54515
Cato, Manitowoc	54230
Cavour, Forest	54511
Cayuga, Ashland (Mellen)[1]	54546
Cazenovia, Richland	53924
Cecil, Shawano	54111
Cedar, Iron (Saxon)[1]	54559
Cedar Falls, Dunn (Menomonie)[1]	54751
Cedarburg, Ozaukee	53012
Cedar Grove, Sheboygan	53013
Cedar Rapids, Rusk (Glen Flora)[1]	54526
Center Valley, Outagamie (Black Creek)[1]	54106
Centerville, Trempealeau (Galesville)[1]	54630
Centuria, Polk	54824
Chaseburg, Vernon	54621
Chelsea, Taylor	54451
Chenequa, Waukesha (Hartland)[1]	53029
Chetek, Barron	54728
Chili, Clark	54420
Chilton, Calumet	53014
Chippewa Falls, Chippewa[4]	54729
Christie, Clark (Neillsville)[1]	54456
City Point, Wood (Pittsville)[1]	54466
Clam Falls, Polk	54837
Clam Lake, Ashland	54517
Clark, Clark (Withee)[1]	54498
Clayton, Polk	54004
Clear Lake, Polk	54005
Clearwater Lake, Vilas (Eagle River)[1]	54521
Clearwater Lake, Oneida (Three Lakes)[1]	54562
Cleghorn, Trempealeau (Eleva)[1]	54738
Cleveland, Manitowoc	53015
Clifton, Pierce (River Falls)[1]	54022
Clinton, Rock	53525
Clintonville, Waupaca	54929
Cloverland, Vilas (Eagle River)[1]	54521
Clyman, Dodge	53016
Cobb, Iowa	53526
Cochrane, Buffalo	54622
Coddington, Portage (Plover)[1]	54467
Colby, Clark	54421
Coleman, Marinette	54112
Colfax, Dunn	54730
Colgate, Washington	53017
Collins, Manitowoc	54207
Coloma, Waushara	54930
Columbus, Columbia	53925
Combined Locks, Outagamie	54113
Comstock, Barron	54826
Connorsville, Dunn (Boyceville)[1]	54725
Conover, Vilas	54519
Conrath, Rusk	54731
Coon Valley, Vernon	54623
Cornell, Chippewa	54732
Corning, Lincoln (Merrill)[1]	54452
Cornucopia, Bayfield	54827
Cosy Valley, Ashland (Mellen)[1]	54546
Cottage Grove, Dane	53527
Couderay, Sawyer	54828
Crandon, Forest	54520
Cream, Buffalo (Alma)[1]	54610
Crescent, Chippewa (Cadott)[1]	54727
Crivitz, Marinette	54114
Cross Plains, Dane	53528
Cuba City, Grant	53807
Cudahy, Milwaukee	53110
Cumberland, Barron	54829
Curtiss, Clark	54422
Cushing, Polk	54006
Custer, Portage	54423
Cutler, Juneau	54618
Cylon, St. Croix (New Richmond)[1]	54017

Municipality and County	ZIP Code
Dairyland, Burnett	54830
Dale, Outagamie	54931
Dallas, Barron	54733
Dalton, Green Lake	53926
Danbury, Burnett	54830
Dancy, Marathon (Mosinee)[1]	54455
Dane, Dane	53529
Darien, Walworth	53114
Darlington, Lafayette	53530
Deerbrook, Langlade	54424
Deerfield, Dane	53531
Deer Park, St. Croix	54007
DeForest, Dane	53532
Delafield, Waukesha	53018
Delavan, Walworth	53115
Dellwood, Adams	53927
Delta, Bayfield	54856
Denmark, Brown	54208
De Pere, Brown	54115
Deronda, Polk	54001
De Soto, Vernon	54624
Deer Creek, Taylor (Stetsonville)[1]	54480
Dewey, Portage (Stevens Point)[1]	54481
Dexterville, Wood (Pittsville)[1]	54466
Diamond Bluff, Pierce (Hager City)[1]	54014
Dickeyville, Grant	53808
Dodge, Trempealeau	54625
Dodgeville, Iowa[4]	53533
Donald, Taylor (Gilman)[1]	54433
Dorchester, Clark	54425
Dousman, Waukesha	53118
Downing, Dunn	54734
Downsville, Dunn	54735
Doylestown, Columbia	53928
Dresser, Polk	54009
Drummond, Bayfield	54832
Dunbar, Marinette	54119
Durand, Pepin	54736
Dyckesville, Kewaunee (Luxemburg)[1]	54217
Eagle, Waukesha	53119
Eagle Point, Chippewa (Chippewa Falls)[1]	54729
Eagle River, Vilas	54521
Eagleton, Chippewa (Bloomer)[1]	54724
East Ellsworth, Pierce	54010
East Farmington, Polk (Osceola)[1]	54020
East Troy, Walworth	53120
Eastman, Crawford	54626
Eaton, Clark (Greenwood)[1]	54437
Eau Claire, Eau Claire[2]	54701
Eau Galle, Dunn	54737
Eau Pleine, Portage (Junction City)[1]	54443
Eden, Fond du Lac	53019
Edgar, Marathon	54426
Edgerton, Rock	53534
Edgewater, Sawyer	54834
Edmund, Iowa	53535
Edson, Chippewa (Boyd)[1]	54726
Egg Harbor, Door	54209
Eisenstein, Price (Park Falls)[1]	54552
El Paso, Pierce (Beldenville)[1]	54003
Eland, Marathon	54427
Elcho, Langlade	54428
Elderon, Marathon	54429
Eldorado, Fond du Lac	54932
Eleva, Trempealeau	54738
Elk, Price (Phillips)[1]	54555
Elk Creek, Trempealeau (Independence)[1]	54747
Elk Mound, Dunn	54739
Elkhart Lake, Sheboygan	53020
Elkhorn, Walworth	53121
Ellis, Portage (Stevens Point)[1]	54481
Ellison Bay, Door	54210
Ellsworth, Pierce[4]	54011
Elm Grove, Waukesha	53122
Elmwood, Pierce	54740
Elroy, Juneau	53929
Elton, Langlade	54430
Embarrass, Waupaca	54933
Emerald, St. Croix	54013
Endeavor, Marquette	53930
Ephraim, Door	54211
Erin, St. Croix (New Richmond)[1]	54017

Municipality and County	ZIP Code
Erin Prairie, St. Croix (Baldwin)[1]	54002
Esadore Lake, Taylor (Medford)[1]	54451
Ettrick, Trempealeau	54627
Eureka, Winnebago[4]	54963
Eureka Center, Polk (St. Croix Falls)[1]	54024
Evansville, Rock	53536
Exeland, Sawyer	54835
Fairchild, Eau Claire	54741
Fairwater, Fond du Lac	53931
Fall Creek, Eau Claire	54742
Fall River, Columbia	53932
Fence, Florence	54120
Fennimore, Grant	53809
Fenwood, Marathon	54426
Ferryville, Crawford	54628
Fifield, Price	54524
Figis, Wood (Marshfield)[1]	54472
Fish Creek, Door	54212
Fitchburg, Dane[2]	53575
Florence, Florence	54121
Fond du Lac, Fond du Lac[2]	54935
Fontana, Walworth	53125
Footville, Rock	53537
Forest Junction, Calumet	54123
Forestville, Door	54213
Fort Atkinson, Jefferson	53538
Fort McCoy, Monroe	54656
Foster, Trempealeau (Osseo)[1]	54758
Fountain City, Buffalo	54629
Foxboro, Douglas	54836
Fox Lake, Dodge	53933
Fox Point, Milwaukee	53217
Francis Creek, Manitowoc	54214
Franklin, Milwaukee	53132
Franksville, Racine	53126
Franzen, Shawano (Wittenberg)[1]	54499
Frederic, Polk	54837
Fredonia, Ozaukee	53021
Freedom, Outagamie[2]	54130
Fremont, Waupaca	54940
French Island, La Crosse (La Crosse)[1]	54601
Friendship, Adams	53934
Friesland, Columbia[4]	53935
Galesville, Trempealeau	54630
Galloway, Marathon	54432
Gays Mills, Crawford	54631
Genesee Depot, Waukesha	53127
Genoa, Vernon	54632
Genoa City, Walworth	53128
Germantown, Washington	53022
Gile, Iron	54525
Gillett, Oconto	54124
Gilman, Taylor[4]	54433
Gilmanton, Buffalo	54743
Gleason, Lincoln	54435
Glenbeulah, Sheboygan	53023
Glendale, Milwaukee[2,3] (Milwaukee)	53209
Glen Flora, Rusk	54526
Glen Haven, Grant	53810
Glenwood City, St. Croix	54013
Glidden, Ashland	54527
Goodman, Marinette	54125
Goodrich, Taylor (Medford)[1]	54451
Gordon, Douglas	54838
Gotham, Richland	53540
Grafton, Ozaukee	53024
Grand Chute, Outagamie (Appleton)[3]	54911
Grand Marsh, Adams	53936
Grand Rapids, Wood (Wisconsin Rapids)[1]	54494
Grand View, Bayfield	54839
Granton, Clark	54436
Grantsburg, Burnett	54840
Gratiot, Lafayette	53541
Green Bay, Brown[2]	54301
Green Grove, Clark (Owen)[1]	54460
Greenbush, Sheboygan	53026
Greendale, Milwaukee	53129
Greenfield, Milwaukee[2,3] (Milwaukee)	53219
Green Lake, Green Lake	54941
Greenleaf, Brown	54126
Green Valley, Shawano	54127

Municipality and County	ZIP Code
Greenville, Outagamie	54942
Greenwood, Clark	54437
Gresham, Shawano	54128
Gurney, Iron	54559
Hackett, Price (Phillips)[1]	54555
Hager City, Pierce	54014
Halder, Marathon (Mosinee)[1]	54455
Hales Corners, Milwaukee	53130
Hallie, Eau Claire (Eau Claire)[1]	54703
Hamburg, Marathon	54411
Hammond, St. Croix	54015
Hancock, Waushara	54943
Hannibal, Taylor	54439
Hanover, Rock	53542
Hansen, Wood (Vesper)[1]	54489
Harding, Lincoln (Merrill)[1]	54452
Harrison, Lincoln (Gleason)[1]	54435
Harshaw, Oneida	54529
Hartford, Washington	53027
Hartland, Waukesha	53029
Hatfield, Jackson (Merrillan)[1]	54754
Hatley, Marathon	54440
Haugen, Barron	54841
Haven, Sheboygan	53083
Hawkins, Rusk	54530
Hawthorne, Douglas	54842
Hayward, Sawyer	54843
Hazel Green, Grant	53811
Hazelhurst, Oneida	54531
Heafford Junction, Lincoln	54532
Helenville, Jefferson	53137
Hendren, Clark (Willard)[1]	54493
Herbster, Bayfield	54844
Hersey, St. Croix (Wilson)[1]	54027
Hertel, Burnett	54845
Hewitt, Wood	54441
High Bridge, Ashland	54846
Highland, Iowa	53543
Hilbert, Calumet	54129
Hiles, Forest	54511
Hillpoint, Sauk	53937
Hillsboro, Vernon	54634
Hillsdale, Barron	54733
Hingham, Sheboygan	53031
Hixton, Jackson	54635
Hoard, Clark (Curtiss)[1]	54422
Hobart, Brown[2]	54115
Hofa Park, Outagamie (Seymour)[1]	54165
Hogarty, Marathon (Aniwa)[1]	54408
Holcombe, Chippewa	54745
Hollandale, Iowa	53544
Hollister, Langlade (White Lake)[1]	54491
Holmen, La Crosse	54636
Honey Creek, Walworth	53138
Horicon, Dodge	53032
Hortonville, Outagamie	54944
Houlton, St. Croix	54082
Howard, Brown[2]	54303
Howards Grove, Sheboygan	53083
Hubertus, Washington	53033
Hudson, St. Croix	54016
Hull, Portage (Stevens Point)[1]	54481
Humbird, Clark	54746
Hunting, Shawano (Tigerton)[1]	54486
Huntington, St. Croix (New Richmond)[1]	54017
Hurley, Iron	54534
Hustisford, Dodge	53034
Hustler, Juneau	54637
Independence, Trempealeau	54747
Ingram, Rusk	54526
Institute, Door (Sturgeon Bay)[1]	54235
Iola, Waupaca[4]	54945
Irma, Lincoln	54442
Iron Belt, Iron	54536
Iron Ridge, Dodge	53035
Iron River, Bayfield	54847
Isaar, Outagamie (Seymour)[1]	54165
Island Lake, Chippewa (New Auburn)[1]	54757
Ixonia, Jefferson	53036
Jackson, Washington	53037

Municipality and County	ZIP Code
Jacksonport, Door (Sturgeon Bay)[1]	54235
Janesville, Rock[2]	53545
Jefferson, Jefferson	53549
Jeffris, Lincoln (Gleason)[1]	54435
Jersey City, Lincoln (Tomahawk)[1]	54487
Jewett, St. Croix (New Richmond)[1]	54017
Jim Falls, Chippewa	54748
Joel, Polk (Amery)[1]	54001
Johnson Creek, Jefferson[2]	53038
Jordon, Portage (Stevens Point)[1]	54481
Juda, Green	53550
Jump River, Taylor	54434
Junction City, Portage	54443
Juneau, Dodge	53039
Kaiser, Price (Park Falls)[1]	54552
Kansasville, Racine	53139
Kaukauna, Outagamie[4]	54130
Kellner, Wood (Wisconsin Rapids)[1]	54494
Kellnersville, Manitowoc	54215
Kelly, Marathon (Schofield)[1]	54476
Kempster, Langlade	54424
Kendall, Monroe	54638
Kennan, Price	54537
Kenosha, Kenosha[2]	53140
Keshena, Menominee	54135
Kewaskum, Washington	53040
Kewaunee, Kewaunee	54216
Kiel, Manitowoc	53042
Kieler, Grant	53812
Kimball, Iron (Hurley)[1]	54534
Kimberly, Outagamie	54136
King, Waupaca	54946
Kingston, Green Lake	53939
Kinnickinnic, Pierce (River Falls)[1]	54022
Knapp, Dunn	54749
Knowles, Dodge	53048
Knowlton, Marathon (Mosinee)[1]	54455
Kohler, Sheboygan	53044
Krakow, Shawano[2]	54137
Kronenwetter, Marathon	54455
Kunesh, Brown (Pulaski)[1]	54162
Lac du Flambeau, Vilas	54538
La Crosse, La Crosse[2]	54601
Ladysmith, Rusk	54848
La Farge, Vernon	54639
Lafayette, Chippewa (Chippewa Falls)[1]	54729
Lake, Price (Park Falls)[1]	54552
Lake Delton, Sauk	53940
Lake Emily, Portage (Amherst Junction)[1]	54407
Lake Geneva, Walworth	53147
Lake George, Oneida (Rhinelander)[1]	54501
Lake Hallie, Chippewa (Chippewa Falls)[1]	54729
Lake Holcombe, Chippewa (Holcombe)[1]	54745
Lake Mills, Jefferson	53551
Lake Nebagamon, Douglas	54849
Lake Tomahawk, Oneida	54539
Lake Wazeecha, Wood (Wisconsin Rapids)[1]	54494
Lake Windsor, Dane (Windsor)[1]	53598
Lake Wissota, Chippewa (Chippewa Falls)[1]	54729
Laketown, Polk (Cushing)[1]	54006
Lakewood, Oconto	54138
Lancaster, Grant	53813
Land O'Lakes, Vilas	54540
Lannon, Waukesha	53046
Laona, Forest	54541
La Pointe, Ashland	54850
Larsen, Winnebago	54947
La Valle, Sauk	53941
Lebanon, Dodge	53047
Lena, Oconto	54139
Leopolis, Shawano	54948
Lewis, Polk	54837
Lily, Langlade	54491
Lime Ridge, Sauk	53942
Linden, Iowa	53553
Lindsey, Wood (Marshfield)[1]	54449
Linwood, Portage (Stevens Point)[1]	54481
Lisbon, Waukesha	53089
Little Black, Taylor (Medford)[1]	54451
Little Chicago, Marathon (Marathon)[1]	54448
Little Chute, Outagamie	54140

Municipality and County	ZIP Code
Little Falls, Polk (Amery)[1]	54001
Little Suamico, Oconto	54141
Livingston, Grant	53554
Lodi, Columbia	53555
Loganville, Sauk	53943
Lohrville, Waushara (Redgranite)[1]	54970
Lomira, Dodge	53048
Lone Rock, Richland	53556
Long Lake, Florence	54542
Longwood, Clark (Withee)[1]	54498
Loomis, Marinette (Porterfield)[1]	54159
Loretta, Sawyer	54896
Lost Creek, Pierce (Ellsworth)[1]	54011
Lowell, Dodge	53557
Loyal, Clark	54446
Lublin, Taylor	54447
Luck, Polk	54853
Lugerville, Price (Phillips)[1]	54555
Luxemburg, Kewaunee	54217
Lymantown, Price (Park Falls)[1]	54552
Lyndon Station, Juneau	53944
Lynn, Clark (Granton)[1]	54436
Lynxville, Crawford[4]	54626
Lyons, Walworth	53148
Madison, Dane[2]	53714
Maiden Rock, Pierce	54750
Malone, Fond du Lac	53049
Manawa, Waupaca	54949
Manchester, Green Lake	53946
Manitowish Waters, Vilas	54545
Manitowoc, Manitowoc[4]	54220
Maple, Douglas	54854
Maple Bluff, Dane (Madison)[1]	53704
Maplehurst, Clark (Withee)[1]	54498
Maplewood, Door	54226
Marathon, Marathon	54448
Marathon City, Marathon (Marathon)[1]	54448
Marengo, Ashland[2]	54855
Maribel, Manitowoc	54227
Marinette, Marinette	54143
Marion, Waupaca	54950
Markesan, Green Lake	53946
Markton, Langlade (White Lake)[1]	54491
Marquette, Green Lake	53947
Marshall, Dane	53559
Marshfield, Wood[4]	54449
Martell, Pierce (Spring Valley)[1]	54767
Mason, Bayfield[4]	54856
Mather, Juneau	54641
Mattoon, Shawano	54450
Mauston, Juneau	53948
Mayville, Dodge	53050
Mazomanie, Dane	53560
McFarland, Dane	53558
McNaughton, Oneida	54543
McMillan, Wood (Marshfield)[1]	54449
Medford, Taylor	54451
Medina, Outagamie	54944
Mellen, Ashland	54546
Melrose, Jackson	54642
Menasha, Winnebago	54952
Menekaunee, Marinette (Marinette)[1]	54143
Menomonee Falls, Waukesha[4]	53051
Menomonie, Dunn	54751
Mequon, Ozaukee[2]	53097
Mercer, Iron	54547
Merrill, Lincoln	54452
Merrillan, Jackson	54754
Merrimac, Sauk	53561
Merton, Waukesha	53056
Middle Inlet, Marinette	54114
Middle Ridge, La Crosse (Bangor)[1]	54614
Middleton, Dane	53562
Mikana, Barron	54857
Milan, Marathon	54411
Milladore, Wood	54454
Millston, Jackson	54643
Milltown, Polk	54858
Milton, Rock	53563
Milwaukee, Milwaukee[2]	53201
Mindoro, La Crosse	54644
Mineral Point, Iowa	53565

Municipality and County	ZIP Code
Minocqua, Oneida	54548
Minong, Washburn	54859
Mishicot, Manitowoc	54228
Modena, Buffalo	54755
Moeville, Pierce (Ellsworth)[1]	54011
Mole Lake, Forest (Crandon)[1]	54520
Mondovi, Buffalo[4]	54755
Monico, Oneida	54501
Monona, Dane (Madison)[3]	53716
Monroe, Green	53566
Monroe Center, Adams (Arkdale)[1]	54613
Montello, Marquette	53949
Montfort, Grant	53569
Monticello, Green	53570
Montreal, Iron	54550
Moon, Marathon (Mosinee)[1]	54455
Moquah, Ashland	54806
Morris, Shawano (Tigerton)[1]	54486
Morrisonville, Dane	53571
Morse, Ashland (Mellen)[1]	54546
Mosinee, Marathon	54455
Mountain, Oconto	54149
Mount Calvary, Fond du Lac	53057
Mount Hope, Grant	53816
Mount Horeb, Dane	53572
Mount Pleasant, Racine[4]	53177
Mount Sterling, Crawford	54645
Mukwonago, Waukesha	53149
Muscoda, Grant	53573
Muskego, Waukesha	53150
Nashotah, Waukesha	53058
Nashville, Forest (Crandon)[1]	54520
Navarino, Shawano	54107
Necedah, Juneau	54646
Neenah, Winnebago[4]	54956
Neillsville, Clark	54456
Nekoosa, Wood	54457
Nelma, Forest	54542
Nelson, Buffalo	54756
Nelsonville, Portage	54458
Neopit, Menominee	54150
Neosho, Dodge	53059
Neshkoro, Marquette	54960
Neva Corners, Langlade (Deerbrook)[1]	54424
Newald, Forest	54511
New Auburn, Chippewa	54757
New Berlin, Waukesha[2]	53146
Newburg, Washington	53060
Newburg Corners, La Crosse (Bangor)[1]	54614
New Franken, Brown	54229
New Glarus, Green	53574
New Haven, Polk (Clear Lake)[1]	54005
New Holstein, Calumet[4]	53061
New Johannesburg, St. Croix (New Richmond)[1]	54017
New Lisbon, Juneau	53950
New London, Waupaca	54961
New Munster, Kenosha	53152
New Post, Sawyer	54828
New Richmond, St. Croix	54017
Newton, Manitowoc	53063
Niagara, Marinette	54151
Nichols, Outagamie	54152
Norrie, Shawano (Birnamwood)[1]	54414
North Fond du Lac, Fond du Lac (Fond du Lac)[3]	54935
North Freedom, Sauk	53951
North Hudson, St. Croix (Hudson)[1]	54016
North Lake, Waukesha	53064
North Menomonie, Dunn (Menomonie)[1]	54751
North Prairie, Waukesha	53153
North Woods Beach, Sawyer	54843
Northfield, Jackson	54635
Norwalk, Monroe	54648
Nye, Polk (Osceola)[1]	54020
Oak Creek, Milwaukee	53154
Oak Grove, Pierce (Prescott)[1]	54021
Oakdale, Monroe	54649
Oakfield, Fond du Lac	53065
Oconomowoc, Waukesha	53066
Oconto, Oconto	54153
Oconto Falls, Oconto	54154

Municipality and County	ZIP Code
Odanah, Ashland	54861
Ogdensburg, Waupaca	54962
Ogema, Price	54459
Ojibwa, Sawyer	54862
Okauchee, Waukesha	53069
Oliver, Douglas	54880
Oma, Iron (Hurley)[1]	54534
Omro, Winnebago	54963
Onalaska, La Crosse	54650
Oneida, Outagamie	54155
Ontario, Vernon	54651
Oostburg, Sheboygan	53070
Oregon, Dane	53575
Orfordville, Rock	53576
Osceola, Polk	54020
Oshkosh, Winnebago[2]	54901
Osseo, Trempealeau	54758
Owen, Clark	54460
Oxford, Marquette	53952
Packwaukee, Marquette	53953
Paddock Lake, Kenosha (Salem)[1]	53168
Padus, Forest (Wabeno)[1]	54566
Palmyra, Jefferson	53156
Pardeeville, Columbia	53954
Park Falls, Price	54552
Park Ridge, Portage (Stevens Point)[1]	54481
Parrish, Lincoln (Gleason)[1]	54435
Patch Grove, Grant	53817
Pearson, Langlade	54462
Pelican, Oneida (Rhinelander)[1]	54501
Pelican Lake, Oneida	54463
Pell Lake, Walworth	53157
Pembine, Marinette	54156
Pence, Iron	54550
Pensaukee, Oconto (Oconto)[1]	54153
Pepin, Pepin	54759
Peplin, Marathon (Mosinee)[1]	54455
Perkinstown, Taylor (Medford)[1]	54451
Peshtigo, Marinette	54157
Pewaukee, Waukesha	53072
Phelps, Vilas	54554
Phillips, Price	54555
Phlox, Langlade	54464
Pickerel, Langlade	54465
Pickett, Winnebago	54964
Pigeon Falls, Trempealeau	54760
Pine River, Waushara	54965
Pittsville, Wood	54466
Plain, Sauk	53577
Plainfield, Waushara	54966
Platteville, Grant	53818
Pleasant Lake, Waushara (Coloma)[1]	54930
Pleasant Prairie, Kenosha	53158
Pleasant Valley, St. Croix (Hammond)[1]	54015
Plover, Portage	54467
Plum City, Pierce	54761
Plum Lake, Vilas (Sayner)[1]	54560
Plymouth, Sheboygan	53073
Polar, Langlade	54418
Polley, Taylor (Gilman)[1]	54433
Polonia, Portage (Custer)[1]	54423
Poniatowski, Marathon (Edgar)[1]	54426
Poplar, Douglas	54864
Popple River, Florence (Long Lake)[1]	54542
Portage, Columbia	53901
Port Edwards, Wood	54469
Porterfield, Marinette	54159
Port Washington, Ozaukee	53074
Port Wing, Bayfield	54865
Poskin, Barron	54812
Post Lake, Langlade (Elcho)[1]	54428
Potosi, Grant	53820
Potter, Calumet	54160
Pound, Marinette	54161
Powers Lake, Kenosha	53159
Poynette, Columbia	53955
Poy Sippi, Waushara	54967
Prairie du Chien, Crawford	53821
Prairie du Sac, Sauk	53578
Prairie Farm, Barron	54762
Pray, Wood (Pittsville)[1]	54466
Preble, Brown (Green Bay)[1]	54302

Municipality and County	ZIP Code	Municipality and County	ZIP Code
Prentice, Price	54556	Sheboygan, Sheboygan[2]	53081
Prescott, Pierce	54021	Sheboygan Falls, Sheboygan	53085
Presque Isle, Vilas	54557	Shelby, La Crosse (La Crosse)[1]	54601
Princeton, Green Lake	54968	Sheldon, Rusk	54766
Pulaski, Brown	54162	Shell Lake, Washburn	54871
Pulcifer, Oconto	54124	Shepley, Shawano (Wittenberg)[1]	54499
		Sherman, Price (Park Falls)[1]	54552
Racine, Racine[2]	53401	Sherry, Wood (Milladore)[1]	54454
Radisson, Sawyer	54867	Sherwood, Calumet	54169
Randolph, Columbia[4]	53956	Shiocton, Outagamie	54170
Random Lake, Sheboygan	53075	Shorewood, Milwaukee (Milwaukee)[3]	53211
Range, Polk (Amery)[1]	54001	Shorewood Hills, Dane (Madison)[1]	53705
Readfield, Waupaca	54969	Shullsburg, Lafayette	53586
Readstown, Vernon	54652	Silver Cliff, Marinette	54104
Red Cliff, Bayfield (Bayfield)[1]	54814	Silver Lake, Kenosha	53170
Redgranite, Waushara	54970	Sinsinawa, Grant	53824
Redville, Clark (Withee)[1]	54498	Siren, Burnett	54872
Reedsburg, Sauk[4]	53959	Sister Bay, Door	54234
Reedsville, Manitowoc	54230	Skanawan, Lincoln (Irma)[1]	54442
Reeseville, Dodge	53579	Slinger, Washington	53086
Reeve, Polk (Clayton)[1]	54004	Sobieski, Oconto	54171
Remington, Wood (Babcock)[1]	54413	Soldiers Grove, Crawford	54655
Rewey, Iowa	53580	Solon Springs, Douglas	54873
Rhinelander, Oneida	54501	Somers, Kenosha	53171
Rib Falls, Marathon (Edgar)[1]	54426	Somerset, St. Croix	54025
Rib Lake, Taylor	54470	Soperton, Forest (Wabeno)[1]	54566
Rib Mountain, Marathon (Wausau)[1]	54401	South Beaver Dam, Dodge (Beaver Dam)[1]	53916
Rice Lake, Barron	54868	South Byron, Fond du Lac	53006
Richardson, Polk (Clayton)[1]	54004	South Chase, Brown (Pulaski)[1]	54162
Richfield, Washington	53076	South Fork, Rusk (Hawkins)[1]	54530
Richford, Waushara (Coloma)[1]	54930	South Milwaukee, Milwaukee	53172
Richland Center, Richland	53581	South Range, Douglas	54874
Ridgeland, Dunn	54763	South Wayne, Lafayette	53587
Ridgeway, Iowa	53582	Sparta, Monroe	54656
Ringle, Marathon	54471	Spencer, Marathon	54479
Rio, Columbia	53960	Split Rock, Shawano (Tigerton)[1]	54486
Rio Creek, Kewaunee	54201	Spokeville, Clark (Loyal)[1]	54446
Riplinger, Marathon (Spencer)[1]	54479	Spooner, Washburn	54801
Ripon, Fond du Lac	54971	Springbrook, Washburn	54875
River Falls, Pierce	54022	Springfield, Walworth	53176
River Hills, Milwaukee (Milwaukee)[3]	53217	Springstead, Price (Park Falls)[1]	54552
Roberts, St. Croix	54023	Spring Green, Sauk	53588
Rochester, Racine	53167	Spring Valley, Pierce	54767
Rock Falls, Dunn	54764	Stangelville, Brown (Denmark)[1]	54208
Rockfield, Washington	53022	Stanley, Chippewa	54768
Rockland, La Crosse	54653	Stanton, St. Croix (New Richmond)[1]	54017
Rock Springs, Sauk	53961	Starks, Oneida (Rhinelander)[1]	54501
Rome, Wood (Nekoosa)[1]	54457	Stella, Oneida (Rhinelander)[1]	54501
Rosendale, Fond du Lac	54974	Sterling, Polk (Cushing)[1]	54006
Rosholt, Portage	54473	Star Lake, Vilas	54561
Rothschild, Marathon	54474	Star Prairie, St. Croix	54026
Royalton, Waupaca	54961	Stetsonville, Taylor	54480
Rozellville, Marathon (Stratford)[1]	54484	Steuben, Crawford	54657
Rubicon, Dodge	53078	Stevens Point, Portage[4]	54481
Rudolph, Wood	54475	Stiles, Oconto	54139
Rush River, St. Croix (Baldwin)[1]	54002	Stitzer, Grant	53825
Rusk, Dunn (Menomonie)[1]	54751	Stockbridge, Calumet	53088
		Stockholm, Pepin	54769
St. Cloud, Fond du Lac	53079	Stockton, Portage (Stevens Point)[1]	54481
St. Croix Falls, Polk	54024	Stoddard, Vernon	54658
St. Francis, Milwaukee	53235	Stone Lake, Sawyer	54876
St. Germain, Vilas	54558	Stoughton, Dane	53589
St. Nazianz, Manitowoc	54232	Stratford, Marathon	54484
Salem, Kenosha	53168	Strum, Trempealeau	54770
Sanborn, Ashland	54806	Sturgeon Bay, Door	54235
Sand Creek, Dunn	54765	Sturtevant, Racine	53177
Sand Lake, Polk (Dresser)[1]	54009	Suamico, Brown[2]	54173
Sarona, Washburn	54870	Sugar Camp, Oneida (Rhinelander)[1]	54501
Sauk City, Sauk	53583	Sullivan, Jefferson	53178
Saukville, Ozaukee	53080	Summit, Waukesha	53066
Saxeville, Waushara	54976	Summit Lake, Langlade	54485
Saxon, Iron	54559	Sun Prairie, Dane[4]	53590
Sayner, Vilas	54560	Superior, Douglas	54880
Scandinavia, Waupaca	54977	Suring, Oconto	54174
Schley, Lincoln (Merrill)[1]	54452	Sussex, Waukesha	53089
Schofield, Marathon	54476		
Scott, Brown (Green Bay)[1]	54301	Taycheedah, Fond du Lac	53935
Seneca, Crawford	54654	Taylor, Jackson	54659
Sevastopol, Door (Sturgeon Bay)[1]	54235	Theresa, Dodge	53091
Sextonville, Richland	53584	Thiensville, Ozaukee	53092
Seymour, Outagamie	54165	Thornton, Shawano (Shawano)[1]	54166
Sharon, Walworth	53585	Thorp, Clark	54771
Shawano, Shawano	54166	Three Lakes, Oneida	54562

Municipality and County	ZIP Code
Tigerton, Shawano	54486
Tilden, Chippewa (Chippewa Falls)[1]	54729
Tilleda, Shawano	54978
Tipler, Florence	54542
Tisch Mills, Manitowoc	54240
Tomah, Monroe	54660
Tomahawk, Lincoln[4]	54487
Tony, Rusk	54563
Townsend, Oconto	54175
Trego, Washburn	54888
Trempealeau, Trempealeau	54661
Trevor, Kenosha[4]	53179
Trimbelle, Pierce (Ellsworth)[1]	54011
Tripoli, Oneida	54564
Troy, Pierce (River Falls)[1]	54022
Tunnel City, Monroe	54662
Turtle Lake, Barron	54889
Tustin, Waupaca (Fremont)[1]	54940
Twin Lakes, Kenosha	53181
Two Rivers, Manitowoc	54241
Ubet, Polk (Dresser)[1]	54009
Underhill, Oconto	54124
Union Center, Juneau	53962
Union Grove, Racine	53182
Unity, Marathon	54488
Upson, Iron	54565
Valders, Manitowoc	54245
Valmy, Door (Sturgeon Bay)[1]	54235
Van Dyne, Fond du Lac	54979
Veedum, Wood (Pittsville)[1]	54466
Vernon, Waukesha[2]	53186
Verona, Dane	53593
Vesper, Wood	54489
Victory, Vernon	54624
Viola, Vernon	54664
Viroqua, Vernon	54665
Wabeno, Forest	54566
Waldo, Sheboygan	53093
Wales, Waukesha	53183
Walworth, Walworth	53184
Wanderoos, Polk (Amery)[1]	54001
Warren, St. Croix (Roberts)[1]	54023
Warrens, Monroe	54666
Wascott, Douglas[4]	54838
Washburn, Bayfield	54891
Washington, Vilas (Eagle River)[1]	54521
Washington Island, Door	54246
Waterford, Racine	53185
Waterloo, Jefferson	53594
Watertown, Jefferson[2]	53094
Waubeka, Ozaukee	53021
Waukau, Winnebago	54980
Waukesha, Waukesha[2]	53186
Waumandee, Buffalo	54622
Waunakee, Dane	53597
Waupaca, Waupaca	54981
Waupun, Dodge	53963
Wausau, Marathon[4]	54403
Wausaukee, Marinette	54177
Wautoma, Waushara	54982
Wauwatosa, Milwaukee[2, 3] (Milwaukee)	53208
Wauzeka, Crawford	53826
Wayside, Brown (Greenleaf)[1]	54126

Municipality and County	ZIP Code
Webb Lake, Burnett	54830
Webster, Burnett	54893
Wentworth, Douglas	54874
West Allis, Milwaukee[2]	53214
West Baraboo, Sauk (Baraboo)[1]	53913
West Bend, Washington[2]	53095
West Lima, Vernon	54639
West Milwaukee, Milwaukee (Milwaukee)[3]	53214
West Salem, La Crosse	54669
Westboro, Taylor	54490
Westby, Vernon	54667
Westfield, Marquette	53964
Weston, Marathon	54476
Westport, Dane	53597
Weurtsburg, Marathon (Athens)[1]	54411
Weyauwega, Waupaca	54983
Weyerhaeuser, Rusk	54895
Wheeler, Dunn	54772
Whitcomb, Shawano (Tigerton)[1]	54486
Whitefish Bay, Milwaukee[2, 3] (Milwaukee)	53217
Whitehall, Trempealeau	54773
White Lake, Langlade	54491
Whitelaw, Manitowoc	54247
Whitewater, Walworth	53190
Whiting, Portage (Stevens Point)[1]	54481
Whittlesey, Taylor (Medford)[1]	54451
Wild Rose, Waushara	54984
Wildwood, St. Croix (Woodville)[1]	54028
Willard, Clark	54493
Williams Bay, Walworth	53191
Wilmot, Kenosha	53192
Wilson, St. Croix	54027
Wilton, Monroe	54670
Winchester, Vilas	54557
Winchester, Winnebago (Larsen)[1]	54947
Wind Lake, Racine	53185
Wind Point, Racine	53402
Windsor, Dane	53598
Winnebago, Winnebago	54985
Winneconne, Winnebago	54986
Winter, Sawyer	54896
Wisconsin Dells, Columbia	53965
Wisconsin Rapids, Wood[2]	54494
Withee, Clark	54498
Wittenberg, Shawano[4]	54499
Wonewoc, Juneau	53968
Woodboro, Oneida (Rhinelander)[1]	54501
Woodford, Lafayette	53599
Woodland, Dodge	53099
Woodman, Grant	53827
Woodruff, Oneida	54568
Woodville, St. Croix	54028
Woodworth, Kenosha	53194
Worcester, Price (Phillips)[1]	54555
Wrightstown, Brown	54180
Wyalusing, Grant (Bagley)[1]	53801
Wyeville, Monroe	54660
Wyocena, Columbia	53969
Yellow Lake, Burnett	54830
York, Clark (Granton)[1]	54436
Yuba, Richland	54634
Zachow, Shawano	54182
Zenda, Walworth	53195

[1]These locations no longer have post offices and mail should be addressed to municipality listed in parenthesis.

[2]Indicates multicoded city. The ZIP code given is the general delivery ZIP code for the city. To determine last 2 digits of ZIP code for any specific city street, consult the local post office.

[3]Post office is located in the city shown in parenthesis. ZIP code is listed as "recognized" on USPS Web site.

[4]Indicates there is an additional ZIP code that is used for a specific P.O. Box, company or organization, or a military installation.

Source: U.S. Postal Service, at: http://www.usps.com [June 2015].

HIGHLIGHTS OF SOCIAL SERVICES IN WISCONSIN

Welfare — According to the U.S. Census Bureau, during 2013-14, almost $486 billion was spent nationally by state and local governments on a variety of public welfare programs. Wisconsin spent about $9.9 billion, or $1,737 per capita, which ranked it 14th among the states, compared to the national average of $1,546. Alaska's per capita expenditure was highest at $2,667, followed by New York ($2,598) and Minnesota ($2,442), and Nevada the lowest at $893. State and local welfare expenditures represented $40.90 per $1,000 of personal income in Wisconsin, ranking it 15th among the states, above the national average ($35.00), while Maine ($55.46), New Mexico ($54.21), Vermont ($53.92), Alaska ($53.49), and Minnesota ($51.55) ranked highest. Nevada ($22.77), Colorado ($23.11), North Dakota ($24.21), South Dakota ($24.76), and Virginia ($25.28) were the lowest.

Participation in Wisconsin Works (W-2), a program providing job subsidies to employers and cash and noncash benefits, such as job assistance and subsidized child care, to participants if they meet certain work requirements, has increased since the last decade but average payments have fallen. The average monthly caseload for W-2 was 15,525 households in 2013 and 15,153 in 2014, with a statewide average monthly payment of $516 in 2013 and $517 in 2014. Total W-2 expenditures have fallen since earlier in the decade from $157.2 million in 2011 and $146.8 million in 2012 to 140.6 million in 2014.

Medical Assistance and BadgerCare — Of the total combined Medical Assistance and BadgerCare provider payments of $8.11 billion in fiscal year 2013-14, $3.27 billion (40.4%) was spent on managed care/HMOs. The next highest payment category was $1.36 billion (16.7%) for other non-institutional fee-for-service.

Medical assistance expenditures in Wisconsin in calendar year 2014 rose to $6.43 billion, from about $6.26 billion in 2013. A county breakdown of medical assistance for 2014 shows average expenditures of $4,659 per recipient. According to the Department of Health Services, the counties with the greatest percentage of recipients were Menominee (61.47%), Ashland (39.80%), Milwaukee (39.37%), Sawyer (33.80%), and Forest (32.90%). The counties with the smallest proportion of recipients were Ozaukee (10.41%), Waukesha (10.91%), Calumet 12.70%, and Washington (13.26%). The highest average expenditures per recipient were in Waupaca ($7,878), Pepin ($6,406), Richland ($6.328), Jefferson ($5,628), Waukesha ($5,583), and Ozaukee ($5,577) counties; Vilas ($3,319), Adams ($3,441), Lafayette ($3,602), and Taylor ($3,676) counties were lowest.

Institutions — Since 2010, the average daily adult corrections population declined slightly from 22,643 in 2010 to 22,036 in 2013, and 22,059 in 2014. In 2014, a daily average of 47,475 persons were on probation and 20,233 on parole and mandatory release. Overall, more than 90,000 people were under the control of the Department of Corrections.

As of December 31, 2013, Wisconsin ranked 27th in the nation with an incarceration rate of 370 persons per 100,000 population, not counting prisoners under local jurisdiction, or almost twice as many as neighboring state Minnesota. Louisiana (847), Mississippi (692), Oklahoma (659), Alabama (647), Texas (602), Arizona (586), and Arkansas (578) had the highest rates. Maine (148), Minnesota (189), Massachusetts (192), Rhode Island (194), North Dakota (211), New Hampshire (215), Utah (242), Vermont (251), New Jersey (252), Washington (256), Hawaii (257), Nebraska (263), and New York (271), had the lowest rates.

The total average daily number of persons in Wisconsin's care and treatment facilities declined from 1,622 in 2010 to 1,559 in 2013 and 1,562 in 2014.

The number of youths in the state's juvenile corrections institutions declined from 437 in 2010 to 252 in 2013 and to 251 in 2014.

The following tables present selected data. Consult footnoted sources for more detailed information about corrections and social services.

STATE AND LOCAL PUBLIC WELFARE EXPENDITURES
State Fiscal Years 2011-12

State	Amount (in thousands)			Per Capita*		Per $1,000 Personal Income*	
	State and Local	State	Local	Amount	Rank	Amount	Rank
Alabama	$6,282,960	$6,247,150	$35,810	$1,304.20	34	$36.29	22
Alaska	1,949,487	1,940,864	8,623	2,666.58	1	53.49	4
Arizona	8,131,658	7,934,285	197,373	1,240.29	40	33.89	28
Arkansas	5,186,159	5,170,079	16,080	1,758.44	12	48.27	8
California	60,431,781	44,031,812	16,399,969	1,587.69	21	33.48	31
Colorado	5,553,873	4,661,182	892,691	1,069.76	47	23.11	49
Connecticut	6,467,136	6,359,103	108,033	1,799.24	11	29.90	35
Delaware	1,892,436	1,891,814	622	2,063.99	8	46.87	10
District of Columbia	2,864,003	—	2,864,003	4,509.96	—	59.53	—
Florida	22,909,782	21,597,940	1,311,842	1,183.65	44	28.89	38
Georgia	10,425,610	10,190,029	235,581	1,051.07	49	28.24	39
Hawaii	2,021,504	1,987,816	33,688	1,451.43	25	32.62	32
Idaho	2,056,135	2,018,744	37,391	1,288.64	36	36.67	20
ILLINOIS	16,154,614	15,404,621	749,993	1,254.85	37	27.29	43
Indiana	8,594,750	8,524,302	70,448	1,314.66	33	34.47	27
IOWA	5,049,952	4,951,150	98,802	1,641.76	19	37.31	19
Kansas	3,484,896	3,446,212	38,684	1,207.53	43	27.84	40
Kentucky	7,185,485	7,142,876	42,609	1,639.22	20	45.75	12
Louisiana	6,277,645	6,180,335	97,310	1,363.30	29	33.58	30
Maine	2,937,027	2,899,581	37,446	2,210.63	6	55.46	1
Maryland	10,077,503	9,823,911	253,592	1,710.42	16	31.91	33
Massachusetts	14,985,285	14,896,885	88,400	2,251.45	5	39.76	17
MICHIGAN	13,147,034	11,989,364	1,157,670	1,330.03	32	34.48	26
MINNESOTA	13,139,201	11,600,046	1,539,155	2,441.95	3	51.55	5
Mississippi	5,083,024	5,050,364	32,660	1,702.21	17	50.89	6
Missouri	8,335,522	8,148,720	186,802	1,383.42	27	34.65	25
Montana	1,378,946	1,317,692	61,254	1,371.86	28	35.04	24
Nebraska	2,325,394	2,224,771	100,623	1,253.25	38	27.30	42
Nevada	2,460,648	2,118,636	342,012	893.08	50	22.77	50
New Hampshire	1,915,201	1,703,205	211,996	1,449.49	26	28.95	37
New Jersey	14,933,012	13,793,905	1,139,107	1,682.40	18	30.66	34
New Mexico	4,043,920	3,925,202	118,718	1,939.91	9	54.21	2
New York	50,947,126	40,074,625	10,872,501	2,598.40	2	48.11	9
North Carolina	12,680,844	11,013,141	1,667,703	1,300.84	35	33.75	29
North Dakota	956,021	888,677	67,344	1,362.43	30	24.21	48
Ohio	19,993,209	17,503,231	2,489,978	1,730.88	15	43.02	13
Oklahoma	5,783,463	5,757,797	25,666	1,515.16	23	36.61	21
Oregon	5,783,559	5,531,631	251,928	1,483.46	24	37.78	18
Pennsylvania	24,582,068	20,573,841	4,008,227	1,924.98	10	42.25	14
Rhode Island	2,254,566	2,246,075	8,491	2,141.83	7	46.41	11
South Carolina	5,870,021	5,822,418	47,603	1,242.96	39	35.16	23
South Dakota	943,123	926,822	16,301	1,130.16	46	24.76	47
Tennessee	10,205,285	10,049,039	156,246	1,580.95	22	40.54	16
Texas	30,797,957	30,327,901	470,056	1,180.25	45	27.31	41
Utah	3,024,864	2,902,824	122,040	1,059.43	48	29.52	36
Vermont	1,499,900	1,497,934	1,966	2,395.48	4	53.92	3
Virginia	10,080,454	8,566,133	1,514,321	1,230.31	42	25.28	46
Washington	8,529,937	8,333,161	196,776	1,236.88	41	26.29	44
West Virginia	3,247,388	3,241,957	5,431	1,749.38	13	49.77	7
WISCONSIN	9,944,033	8,121,389	1,822,644	1,736.98	14	40.90	15
Wyoming	782,735	760,891	21,844	1,356.81	31	25.87	45
UNITED STATES	$485,588,136	$433,312,083	$52,276,053	$1,545.91		$35.00	

*Rates and rankings calculated by the Wisconsin Legislative Reference Bureau.

Sources: U.S. Department of Commerce, Census Bureau, Governments Division, "State and Local Government Finances by Level of Government and by State: 2012", at: http://www.census.gov/govs/local/ [May 26, 2015]; U.S. Department of Commerce, Bureau of Economic Analysis, "Regional Economic Accounts: Annual State Personal Income (SA1-3)", at: http://bea.gov/regional/index.htm [May 26, 2015] (2012 data used in calculations); and "Annual Estimates of the Resident Population for the United States, Regions, States, and Puerto Rico: April 1, 2010 to July 1, 2014 (NST-EST2014-01)", at: http://www.census.gov/popest/data/state/totals/2014/index.html (July 2012 estimates used in calculations).

WISCONSIN WORKS (W-2) EXPENDITURES, BY AGENCY
Calendar Years 2013 and 2014

W-2 Contract Agency	Total Expenditures		Counties Served
	2013	2014	
1A. Ross IES. . . . . http://www.rossprov.com/	$23,229,644	$21,644,805	Northern Milwaukee
1B. MAXIMUS . . . . http://www.maximus.com/	21,443,871	17,813,848	East Central Milwaukee
1C. America Works of Wisconsin . . . . http://www.americaworks.com/	22,266,700	21,287,618	West Central Milwaukee
1D. UMOS . . . . http://www.umos.org/	21,724,451	19,446,744	Southern Milwaukee
1E. Forward Service Corporation . . . . http://fsc-corp.org/	31,836,207	40,877,148	Adams, Brown, Calumet, Columbia, Dane, Dodge, Door, Florence, Fond du Lac, Forest, Grant, Green, Green Lake, Iowa, Jefferson, Juneau, Kewaunee, Lafayette, Langlade, Lincoln, Manitowoc, Marathon, Marinette, Marquette, Menominee, Oconto, Oneida, Outagamie, Portage, Price, Richland, Rock, Sauk, Shawano, Sheboygan, Taylor, Vilas, Waupaca, Waushara, Winnebago, Wood
1G. ResCare . . . . http://www.rescare.com/	14,796,685	14,203,835	Kenosha, Ozaukee, Racine, Walworth, Washington, Waukesha
1J. Workforce Connections . . . . http://www.workforceconnections.org/	1,490,433	1,553,821	Buffalo, Crawford, Jackson, La Crosse, Monroe, Pepin, Trempealeau, Vernon
1K. Workforce Resource, Inc. . . . . . . http://workforceresource.org/	3,654,238	3,772,874	Ashland, Barron, Bayfield, Burnett, Chippewa, Clark, Douglas, Dunn, Eau Claire, Iron, Pierce, Polk, Rusk, St. Croix, Sawyer, Washburn
TOTAL	$140,442,229	$140,600,694	

Source: Wisconsin Department of Children and Families, departmental data, July 2015.

WISCONSIN WORKS (W-2) BENEFITS, BY COUNTY
Calendar Years 2013 and 2014

County	2013 Average Monthly Paid Caseload	2013 Average Monthly Benefit Payment	2014 Average Monthly Paid Caseload	2014 Average Monthly Benefit Payment	County	2013 Average Monthly Paid Caseload	2013 Average Monthly Benefit Payment	2014 Average Monthly Paid Caseload	2014 Average Monthly Benefit Payment
Adams	38	$497	36	$484	Marinette. . .	50	$516	60	$516
Ashland . . .	20	414	22	423	Marquette . .	22	442	32	511
Barron	44	520	36	493	Menominee .	18	436	27	445
Bayfield . . .	6	556	5	487	Milwaukee . .	9,258	535	8,212	535
Brown	292	411	352	399	Monroe. . . .	25	453	28	374
Buffalo	2	419	1	753	Oconto	36	484	38	532
Burnett	2	285	9	394	Oneida	72	502	73	533
Calumet . . .	26	404	32	449	Outagamie . .	196	479	237	482
Chippewa . .	28	474	28	439	Ozaukee . . .	30	548	27	559
Clark	27	545	17	509	Pepin	2	390	5	408
Columbia. . .	82	487	109	527	Pierce.	7	384	9	355
Crawford. . .	9	557	13	521	Polk	17	501	24	531
Dane	877	508	1,024	540	Portage	21	477	42	473
Dodge	87	479	127	505	Price	6	451	10	463
Door	15	481	15	443	Racine	769	482	669	500
Douglas . . .	17	454	27	365	Richland . . .	24	469	43	566
Dunn	62	519	47	540	Rock	346	476	456	522
Eau Claire . .	80	496	86	507	Rusk	19	513	14	635
Florence . . .	5	434	4	496	St. Croix . . .	13	416	20	412
Fond du Lac .	218	465	359	519	Sauk	80	476	134	532
Forest.	17	526	16	522	Sawyer	4	193	9	423
Grant	26	428	58	537	Shawano . . .	81	506	81	492
Green.	63	506	63	520	Sheboygan . .	124	401	124	398
Green Lake. .	36	463	59	475	Taylor	13	436	14	478
Iowa	13	468	23	593	Trempealeau .	9	364	10	487
Iron.	9	553	7	486	Vernon	4	512	9	385
Jackson. . . .	13	436	12	551	Vilas	7	500	12	453
Jefferson . . .	54	432	141	489	Walworth . .	60	528	111	570
Juneau	18	452	21	479	Washburn . .	9	382	9	438
Kenosha . . .	725	518	573	464	Washington. .	50	547	50	545
Kewaunee . .	18	492	14	417	Waukesha . .	148	532	138	535
La Crosse . .	70	444	75	414	Waupaca . . .	58	514	64	520
Lafayette . . .	15	494	15	593	Waushara. . .	19	469	30	481
Langlade . . .	58	493	43	504	Winnebago. .	314	496	383	484
Lincoln. . . .	66	500	32	456	Wood.	109	476	135	464
Manitowoc. .	39	402	48	365	TOTAL. . .	15,525	$516	15,153	$517
Marathon. . .	328	504	265	490					

Source: Wisconsin Department of Children and Families, departmental data, July 2015.

BADGERCARE AND MEDICAL ASSISTANCE IN WISCONSIN
By Type of Service, Fiscal Years 1999-2000 – 2013-14
(In Millions)

| | Long-Term Care | | | | Hospitals | | | | Physicians and Clinics | | Drugs | | Home Care[1] | | Managed Care (HMO)[2] | | Other Non-Institutional Fee-for-Service[3] | | Total Provider Payments[4,5] | |
| | Nursing Homes | | State Centers | | Inpatient | | Outpatient | | | | | | | | | | | | | |
Fiscal Year	Amount	% of Total	Amount	% of Total	Amount	% of Total	Amount	% of Total	Amount	% of Total	Amount	% of Total	Amount	% of Total	Amount	% of Total	Amount	% of Total	Amount	Annual % Change
1999-2000	$906.3	29.8%	$135.9	4.5%	$270.6	8.9%	$55.3	1.8%	$63.2	2.1%	$336.5	11.1%	$498.8	16.4%	$394.4	13.0%	$251.8	8.3%	$3,044.0	—
2000-01	916.2	27.8	115.3	3.5	297.8	9.0	58.7	1.8	72.4	2.2	373.6	11.4	522.2	15.9	523.6	15.9	280.1	8.5	3,291.8	8.1%
2001-02	980.6	26.5	126.9	3.4	333.2	9.0	69.6	1.9	78.7	2.1	432.5	11.7	528.4	14.3	681.8	18.4	319.2	8.6	3,700.9	12.4
2002-03	990.6	25.7	123.9	3.2	332.0	8.6	75.6	2.0	85.2	2.2	494.7	12.9	592.6	15.4	657.9	17.1	334.5	8.7	3,849.2	4.0
2003-04	972.2	21.3	143.0	3.1	338.0	7.4	91.6	2.0	116.9	2.6	700.5	15.4	636.8	14.0	1,013.6	22.2	381.8	8.4	4,558.9	18.4
2004-05	963.8	20.2	117.7	2.5	388.6	8.1	103.7	2.2	133.2	2.8	772.0	16.2	754.9	15.8	873.7	18.3	487.2	10.2	4,777.1	4.8
2005-06	940.1	20.7	111.5	2.5	357.0	7.7	85.8	1.9	104.9	2.3	459.6	10.1	789.2	17.4	1,068.0	23.5	424.2	9.3	4,546.3	-4.8
2006-07	878.2	18.3	111.4	2.3	372.6	7.7	81.6	1.7	111.0	2.3	389.7	8.1	773.6	16.1	1,307.5	27.2	472.3	9.8	4,809.4	5.8
2007-08	837.2	16.3	117.1	2.3	409.7	8.0	85.1	1.7	157.2	3.1	466.3	9.1	812.5	15.8	1,422.3	27.7	599.3	11.7	5,137.5	6.8
2008-09	890.7	14.4	92.0	1.5	602.2	9.7	162.2	2.6	152.6	2.5	621.5	10.0	747.9	12.1	2,089.3	33.8	637.2	10.3	6,188.6	20.5
2009-10	909.5	12.8	148.1	2.1	459.9	6.5	152.8	2.1	188.5	2.6	660.7	9.3	604.5	8.5	2,358.5	33.2	760.2	10.7	7,114.6	15.0
2010-11	842.9	11.2	112.5	1.5	502.5	6.7	188.2	2.5	151.9	2.0	617.6	8.2	599.5	8.0	3,457.1	46.0	1,050.7	14.0	7,522.8	5.7
2011-12	818.8	11.7	127.1	1.8	440.0	6.3	196.3	2.8	166.8	2.4	610.6	8.7	659.0	9.4	2,691.3	38.5	1,288.5	18.4	6,998.4	-7.0
2012-13	819.4	10.8	133.5	1.8	580.6	7.7	208.6	2.8	143.9	1.9	625.8	8.3	784.4	10.4	3,024.3	40.0	1,207.0	16.0	7,553.1	7.9
2013-14	770.0	9.5	128.3	1.6	519.5	6.4	202.5	2.5	187.9	2.3	710.6	8.8	889.1	11.0	3,272.7	40.4	1,355.4	16.7	8,105.8	7.3

Note: Enrollments in BadgerCare began in July 1999, and expenditures for the program are included in the Medical Assistance figures above. Medical Assistance expenditure data prior to BadgerCare can be found in previous *Blue Books*.

[1] Home Care includes HCBS waivers.

[2] Managed Care includes all capitated programs (BC/BS+, HMOs, CCF/WAM, SSI managed care, PACE/Partnership, Family Care).

[3] All non-institutional fee-for-service acute care not otherwise captured plus local government plus Medicare crossovers.

[4] Does not include offsetting recoveries and collections, such as estate recoveries, drug rebates, etc.

[5] Total includes expenditures not listed separately.

Source: Wisconsin Department of Health Services, departmental data, June 2015. Data prior to 2006 is from Wisconsin Legislative Fiscal Bureau.

WISCONSIN MEDICAID AND BADGERCARE
Fiscal Years 2013 and 2014

County	Recipients[1] 2013	2014	2014% of Population	Rank	Expenditures[2] 2013	2014	2014 Per Recipient Amount	Rank
Adams	5,306	5,526	26.51%	23	$18,912,294	$19,017,068	$3,441.38	71
Ashland	6,128	6,397	39.80	2	29,818,930	30,281,312	4,733.67	29
Barron	13,327	13,579	29.51	10	59,455,858	59,291,606	4,366.42	53
Bayfield	3,886	4,014	26.66	22	16,770,462	16,805,017	4,186.60	56
Brown	54,861	57,364	22.66	43	237,344,649	239,798,894	4,180.30	57
Buffalo	2,781	2,890	21.26	52	12,897,400	13,051,352	4,516.04	40
Burnett	4,285	4,513	29.19	11	15,592,662	16,759,192	3,713.54	68
Calumet	6,251	6,315	12.70	70	25,925,934	28,814,980	4,562.94	38
Chippewa	15,661	15,969	25.33	27	79,900,376	82,710,367	5,179.43	12
Clark	8,371	8,510	24.53	32	41,190,984	40,482,638	4,757.07	28
Columbia	10,474	10,948	19.28	62	57,970,277	58,439,502	5,337.92	9
Crawford	4,201	4,370	26.28	24	18,895,264	19,580,329	4,480.62	45
Dane	76,388	82,507	16.43	66	417,209,238	429,144,074	5,201.31	11
Dodge	15,685	16,500	18.50	63	81,030,948	81,146,545	4,917.97	18
Door	5,882	5,959	21.30	51	21,335,415	22,266,629	3,736.64	67
Douglas	12,321	12,299	27.83	16	53,836,958	54,334,893	4,417.83	49
Dunn	10,376	10,608	24.15	35	46,472,662	47,392,846	4,467.65	47
Eau Claire	24,156	24,823	24.71	30	121,165,530	119,601,602	4,818.18	25
Florence	1,040	1,035	23.26	41	4,057,044	4,080,770	3,942.77	62
Fond du Lac	19,169	20,055	19.58	61	97,404,088	97,739,388	4,873.57	20
Forest	2,967	3,044	32.90	5	12,675,963	12,299,817	4,040.68	61
Grant	10,413	10,588	20.13	58	52,032,799	51,449,066	4,859.19	23
Green	7,431	7,656	20.79	53	35,854,375	36,728,533	4,797.35	26
Green Lake	3,919	4,163	21.78	48	19,725,028	20,387,286	4,897.26	19
Iowa	4,520	4,681	19.66	59	21,001,568	21,601,969	4,614.82	34
Iron	1,860	1,838	31.07	9	9,752,267	9,822,965	5,344.38	8
Jackson	5,169	5,290	25.64	25	22,966,762	24,570,551	4,644.72	32
Jefferson	15,829	16,447	19.59	60	94,298,179	92,564,411	5,628.04	4
Juneau	7,197	7,397	27.46	18	31,478,316	32,152,996	4,346.76	54
Kenosha	42,560	45,524	27.22	20	175,361,674	174,923,195	3,842.44	65
Kewaunee	3,615	3,673	17.79	65	16,509,025	17,034,661	4,637.81	33
La Crosse	25,311	26,001	22.27	46	140,614,622	142,993,085	5,499.52	7
Lafayette	3,567	3,706	21.91	47	12,550,693	13,348,899	3,601.97	70
Langlade	6,127	6,396	32.23	7	23,777,165	24,661,369	3,855.75	64
Lincoln	6,989	7,053	24.48	33	34,147,989	35,054,273	4,970.12	14
Manitowoc	16,182	16,847	20.72	55	82,371,290	83,371,950	4,948.77	15
Marathon	30,725	31,464	23.34	40	149,435,358	149,702,469	4,757.90	27
Marinette	11,036	11,479	27.59	17	48,996,855	51,092,552	4,450.96	48
Marquette	3,543	3,709	24.09	36	17,375,051	18,332,349	4,942.67	16
Menominee	2,412	2,604	61.47	1	8,452,350	10,108,356	3,881.86	63
Milwaukee	347,600	373,898	39.37	3	1,650,368,008	1,723,371,144	4,609.20	35
Monroe	10,706	11,173	24.64	31	45,298,085	48,249,994	4,318.45	55
Oconto	7,780	8,132	21.39	50	38,189,082	37,862,058	4,655.93	31
Oneida	8,949	9,241	25.61	26	42,523,026	41,531,255	4,494.24	43
Outagamie	30,783	32,714	18.17	64	140,261,662	144,102,340	4,404.91	52
Ozaukee	8,667	9,068	10.41	72	49,864,214	50,571,166	5,576.88	6
Pepin	1,576	1,606	21.57	49	9,995,822	10,287,492	6,405.66	2
Pierce	6,330	6,641	16.16	67	31,677,826	30,555,290	4,601.01	36
Polk	10,670	10,978	24.82	28	45,016,492	50,128,448	4,566.26	37
Portage	13,898	14,422	20.35	56	64,906,168	63,573,423	4,408.09	51
Price	4,080	4,126	29.15	12	20,870,655	20,683,569	5,012.98	13
Racine	50,121	53,595	27.42	19	227,395,427	241,759,634	4,510.86	42
Richland	4,572	4,869	27.06	21	29,329,647	30,811,026	6,328.00	3
Rock	43,709	45,942	28.70	14	167,309,553	175,431,374	3,818.54	66
Rusk	4,725	4,730	31.98	8	21,969,417	21,232,445	4,488.89	44
St. Croix	13,229	13,430	15.66	68	61,585,101	62,795,505	4,675.76	30
Sauk	13,598	13,941	22.45	45	62,812,101	62,896,743	4,511.64	41
Sawyer	5,661	5,636	33.80	4	23,893,015	23,248,076	4,124.92	59
Shawano	10,092	10,183	24.33	34	43,782,172	44,948,406	4,414.06	50
Sheboygan	22,994	23,981	20.79	54	109,738,859	108,941,286	4,542.82	39
Taylor	5,170	5,136	24.77	29	19,929,126	18,878,764	3,675.77	69
Trempealeau	6,767	6,829	23.40	38	37,482,011	35,688,971	5,226.09	10
Vernon	6,742	7,062	23.56	37	32,969,098	34,411,087	4,872.71	21
Vilas	5,972	6,164	28.64	15	19,800,475	20,456,973	3,318.78	72
Walworth	22,211	23,176	22.54	44	96,346,780	96,497,808	4,163.70	58
Washburn	5,079	5,236	32.83	6	25,322,232	25,830,870	4,933.32	17
Washington	17,156	17,642	13.26	69	85,555,667	85,897,193	4,868.90	22
Waukesha	40,689	42,843	10.91	71	228,299,706	239,186,481	5,582.86	5
Waupaca	11,715	11,989	22.86	42	90,535,588	94,443,542	7,877.52	1
Waushara	5,472	5,732	23.39	39	23,197,310	23,280,785	4,061.55	60
Winnebago	32,227	34,008	20.22	57	147,115,856	152,075,581	4,471.76	46
Wood	20,176	21,762	29.03	13	99,513,401	104,946,317	4,822.46	24
STATE	1,311,037	1,379,626	24.06%		$6,259,417,888	$6,427,514,802	$4,658.88	

[1]If an individual resided in multiple counties during the year, the individual is counted in the recipient tally for the last county of residence.

[2]The expenditure totals include benefits issued and individuals eligible under BadgerCare+/MA and subprograms CORE, BASIC, Family Planning Only > Services, Medicaid Waiver. Costs include: Managed Care Capitation Payments, Fee For Service Payment to providers and Long Term Care waiver program payments.

Sources: Wisconsin Department of Health Services, departmental data, June 2015; Wisconsin Department of Administration, Division of Intergovernmental Relations, Demographic Services Center, *County Population Estimates, January 1, 2014.* Percentages and rankings calculated by Wisconsin Legislative Reference Bureau.

STATE CORRECTIONS AND HEALTH SERVICES INSTITUTIONS
Population, 1970 – 2014

Institutions	2014 Avg. Pop.	Rated Cap.[1]	Average Daily Population (Year ending June 30)					
			1970	1980	1990	2000	2010	2013
STATE CORRECTIONS POPULATION								
Maximum Security (Men)								
Assessment and Evaluation[2]	1,241	904	—	—	—	—	1,214	1,236
Columbia Correctional Institution	822	541	—	—	477	808	820	818
Dodge Correctional Institution[2]	331	261	—	88	551	1,377	341	333
Green Bay Correctional Institution	1,086	749	755	658	832	1,002	1,089	1,085
Wisconsin Secure Program Facility	472	501	—	—	—	101	461	475
Waupun Correctional Institution	1,239	882	954	1,087	1,126	1,225	1,237	1,236
	5,191	3,838	1,709	1,833	2,986	4,513	5,161	5,183
Medium Security								
Fox Lake Correctional Institution[3]	1,317	979	553	570	785	1,112	1,046	1,321
Jackson Correctional Institution	971	837	—	—	—	971	977	973
Kettle Moraine Correctional Institution	1,156	783	293	368	542	1,233	1,160	1,157
New Lisbon Correctional Institution	1,017	950	—	—	—	—	1,009	1,016
Oshkosh Correctional Institution	2,039	1,494	—	—	444	1,859	2,031	2,036
Prairie du Chien Correctional Institution	508	326	—	—	—	297	500	508
Racine Correctional Institution	1,559	1,021	—	—	—	1,414	1,553	1,556
Racine Youthful Offender Correctional Facility	446	400	—	—	—	395	445	447
Redgranite Correctional Institution	1,017	990	—	—	—	—	1,013	1,015
Stanley Correctional Institute	1,518	1,500	—	—	—	—	1,509	1,518
	11,549	9,280	846	938	1,771	7,281	11,242	11,545
Minimum Security								
Chippewa Valley Correctional Treatment Center	472	450	—	—	—	—	465	455
Fox Lake Correctional Institution[3]	—	—	—	—	—	—	280	—
Oakhill Correctional Institution	682	344	—	198	368	564	677	681
Sturtevant Transitional Facility	254	150	—	—	—	—	261	258
Wisconsin Correctional Center System (WCCS)[4]	1,776	1,286	390	276	1,071	1,816	1,649	1,797
	3,184	2,230	390	474	1,439	2,380	3,332	3,192
Detention Facility								
Milwaukee Secure Detention Facility	912	460	998	—	—	—	956	914
Wisconsin Women's Correctional System[4]								
Taycheedah Correctional Institution (medium/ maximum)	738	653	141	123	203	644	579	711
Correctional Centers (minimum)	450	284	—	—	—	—	683	460
Contract Facilities								
Intergovernmental Contract	27	—	—	—	—	—	30	23
In-State	8	—	—	—	—	—	660	8
	35	—	—	—	78	4,665	690	31
Other Adults								
Community Residential Confinement	—	—	—	—	48	—	—	—
Division of Intensive Sanctions	—	—	—	—	—	412	—	—
Extendeed supervision and parole[5]	20,233	—	4,329	3,045	4,217	8,951	19,783	20,494
Probation	47,475	—	4,530	16,797	25,907	55,046	48,340	47,474
Unknown offender type	21	—	—	—	—	—	—	—
	67,729	—	8,859	19,842	30,172	64,409	68,123	67,968
Juvenile Corrections[6]								
Copper Lake School[7]	30	29	—	—	—	—	—	29
Ethan Allen School[7]	—	—	365	306	320	438	207	—
Lincoln Hills School[7]	221	519	—	245	252	330	176	223
Southern Oaks Girls School[7]	—	—	—	—	—	87	49	—
Youth Leadership Training Center[8]	—	—	—	—	—	40	—	—
Sprite Program[9]	—	—	—	—	—	9	5	—
Grow Academy[9]	0	12	—	—	—	—	—	—
Juvenile Correctional Camp System	—	—	81	24	—	—	—	—
	251	603	446	575	572	904	437	252
Juvenile Aftercare	63	—	—	—	—	—	76	76
Alternate Care	66	—	—	—	—	174	49	42
Corrective Sanctions	89	—	—	—	—	134	140	109
TOTAL POPULATION	**90,257**	—	**12,391**	**23,785**	**37,221**	**84,796**	**91,840**	**90,483**

STATE CORRECTIONS AND HEALTH SERVICES INSTITUTIONS
Population, 1970 – 2014-Continued

| | 2014 | | Average Daily Population (Year ending June 30) | | | | | |
| | Avg. | Rated | | | | | | |
Institutions	Pop.	Cap.[1]	1970	1980	1990	2000	2010	2013
MENTAL HEALTH INSTITUTIONS (MHI)								
Mendota MHI.	246	274	522	202	266	238	240	229
Winnebago MHI	188	184	574	310	266	279	291	182
Mendota Juvenile Treatment Center	29	29	—	—	—	43	29	29
Sand Ridge Secure Treatment Center.	352	400	—	—	—	72	286	353
Central State Hospital.	—	—	258	154	—	—	—	—
Wisconsin Resource Center[10]	347	389	—	—	161	421	427	359
CENTERS FOR DEVELOPMENTALLY DISABLED (CDD)								
Central Wisconsin CDD	240	270	1,070	731	606	380	258	241
Northern Wisconsin CDD.	13	25	1,421	676	495	189	12	14
Southern Wisconsin CDD.	147	170	1,207	735	576	274	178	152
TOTAL POPULATION	**1,562**	**1,741**	**5,052**	**2,808**	**2,370**	**1,896**	**1,622**	**1,559**

[1]DOC "rated capacity" is the original design capacity, based on industry standards, plus modifications and expansions. It excludes beds and multiple bunking to accommodate crowding. DHS Care and Treatment Facilities' capacity is "staffed capacity", based on staffing and other budgetary resources rather than number of beds.

[2]Dodge CI serves as the assessment and evaluation (A&E) center for sentenced adult felons. A&E for sentenced adult female felons moved from Dodge CI to Taycheedah CI December 2004.

[3]As of December 2011, Fox Lake is exclusively medium security.

[4]In July 2005, DOC designated the institutions for female offenders as the Wisconsin Women's Correctional System, which now includes Taycheedah CI and 2 of the minimum security Correctional Centers. John Burke CC became a male facility as of November 2011. A limited number of female inmates are housed at predominantly male St. Croix CC (10). WCCS population statistics prior to 2005 include both male and female inmates. Dodge CI infirmary had one female inmate and Milwaukee Secure Detention Facility had 34 females.

[5]Parole data through 1991 included juveniles; figures from 1992 to date do not include juvenile cases.

[6]DOC has administered juvenile incarceration since July 1996.

[7]Ethan Allen and Southern Oaks closed in June 2011; Copper Lake opened in June 2011.

[8]Youth Leadership Training Camp program, formerly at Camp Douglas and closed in February 2002, is now part of the program at Lincoln Hills.

[9]Sprite program eliminated March 2010. Grow Academy opened June 2014; FY 2013-14 average daily population is 0 because it opened near the end of the fiscal year.

[10]Wisconsin Resource Center is administered by DHS in partnership with DOC as a specialized mental health facility.

Sources: Wisconsin Department of Corrections, *Fiscal Year Summary Report of Population Movement for 1991* and previous issues, and departmental data, June 2015 and prior years; Wisconsin Department of Health Services, departmental data, June 2015 and prior years.

PRISON POPULATION AND CORRECTIONAL EXPENDITURES
By State, 1980 – 2013

State		Total Confined as of Dec. 31[1]					Incarceration Rate[2]	Rank	State Corrections Expenditures FY2012-13 Total (in thousands)	Per Capita Amount
	1980	1990	2000	2010	2012	2013				
Alabama	6,368	15,365	26,034	30,739	31,437	31,354	647	4	$533,083	$110
Alaska[3]	571	1,851	2,128	2,775	2,974	2,682	364	29	335,234	456
Arizona[4]	4,360	13,781	25,412	38,423	38,402	39,062	586	6	829,019	125
Arkansas[5].	2,911	7,274	11,851	16,147	14,615	17,159	578	7	403,821	136
California	23,264	94,122	160,412	164,213	134,211	135,981	353	32	7,844,627	205
Colorado[6].	2,609	7,671	16,833	22,815	20,462	20,371	384	25	975,698	185
Connecticut[3]	2,750	7,771	13,155	13,308	11,961	12,162	338	34	669,700	186
Delaware[3,4].	1,087	2,241	3,937	3,961	4,129	4,112	442	18	282,015	305
District of Columbia[1]	2,719	6,798	7,904	—	—	—	—	—	—	—
Florida	20,211	44,380	71,318	104,306	101,930	103,028	524	9	2,145,818	110
Georgia.	11,922	21,671	44,141	54,685	53,990	53,478	533	8	1,487,452	149
Hawaii[3,7].	624	1,708	3,553	3,939	3,819	3,618	257	40	200,984	143
Idaho	817	1,961	5,535	7,431	7,985	8,242	466	11	251,160	156
ILLINOIS[6].	10,724	27,516	45,281	48,418	49,348	48,653	377	26	1,327,176	103
Indiana	6,281	12,615	19,811	28,012	28,822	29,905	454	14	688,283	105
IOWA	2,479	3,967	7,955	9,388	8,686	8,654	279	37	334,893	108
Kansas	2,494	5,775	8,344	9,051	9,398	9,506	328	35	347,040	120
Kentucky.	3,588	9,023	14,919	19,937	21,466	20,330	462	12	532,134	121
Louisiana	8,889	18,599	35,207	39,444	40,170	39,298	847	1	701,296	152
Maine	671	1,480	1,635	1,942	1,932	1,972	148	50	136,811	103
Maryland	7,731	16,734	22,490	22,275	21,281	20,988	353	33	1,396,307	236
Massachusetts[8]. . . .	3,150	8,014	9,479	10,027	9,999	9,643	192	48	1,095,858	164
MICHIGAN	15,124	34,267	47,718	44,113	43,594	43,704	441	19	1,857,508	188
MINNESOTA	2,001	3,176	6,238	9,796	9,938	10,289	189	49	514,959	95
Mississippi.	3,793	8,084	19,239	20,366	21,426	20,742	692	2	376,455	126
Missouri	5,726	14,943	27,519	30,614	31,244	31,537	521	10	736,445	122
Montana	738	1,425	3,105	3,716	3,609	3,642	357	30	191,150	188
Nebraska	1,402	2,286	3,816	4,498	4,594	4,929	263	39	246,519	132
Nevada[9]	1,839	5,322	10,063	12,556	12,761	12,915	460	13	283,918	102
New Hampshire . . .	326	1,342	2,257	2,761	2,790	2,848	215	45	112,422	85
New Jersey[6]	5,564	21,128	29,784	25,007	23,225	22,452	252	42	1,436,484	161
New Mexico	1,199	3,067	4,666	6,614	6,574	6,687	321	36	400,947	192
New York	21,639	54,895	70,199	56,461	54,073	53,428	271	38	3,438,227	175
North Carolina. . . .	14,456	17,764	27,043	35,436	34,983	35,181	356	31	1,210,318	123
North Dakota.	185	435	990	1,487	1,512	1,513	211	46	96,683	134
Ohio[6]	13,489	31,822	45,833	51,712	50,876	51,729	446	16	1,543,631	133
Oklahoma	4,796	12,285	23,181	24,514	24,830	25,496	659	3	569,140	148
Oregon	3,172	6,492	10,553	14,831	14,801	15,180	385	24	730,873	186
Pennsylvania.	8,112	22,281	36,844	51,075	50,918	50,083	391	23	2,119,602	166
Rhode Island[3,7]. . .	601	1,586	1,966	2,086	1,999	2,039	194	47	182,888	174
South Carolina. . . .	7,427	16,208	21,017	22,822	21,725	21,443	447	15	490,627	103
South Dakota.	609	1,341	2,613	3,431	3,644	3,641	428	21	116,535	138
Tennessee	7,022	10,388	22,166	27,451	28,411	28,521	438	20	889,870	137
Texas	29,892	50,042	158,008	164,652	157,900	160,295	602	5	3,701,789	140
Utah	928	2,474	5,541	6,795	6,960	7,071	242	44	310,560	107
Vermont[3]	342	681	1,313	1,649	1,516	1,575	251	43	135,127	216
Virginia[6]	8,581	17,418	29,643	37,410	37,044	36,982	446	17	1,706,864	207
Washington[6]	4,399	7,995	14,666	18,212	17,254	17,947	256	41	954,986	137
West Virginia.	1,257	1,565	3,795	6,642	7,027	6,812	367	28	300,693	162
WISCONSIN	3,980	7,438	20,336	21,973	20,474	21,285	370	27	1,090,920	190
Wyoming.	534	1,110	1,680	2,112	2,204	2,310	395	22	143,237	246
State jurisdiction, U.S. Total[1]	295,353	689,577	1,209,130	1,362,028	1,314,923	1,322,474	417		$48,407,786	$153
Federal jurisdiction .	20,611	50,403	125,044	190,641	196,574	195,098	61			

[1]Except where noted otherwise, total confined refers to "sentenced prisoners" (more than one year) under a state's jurisdiction, regardless of where the prisoner is held. As of December 31, 2001, sentenced felons from the District of Columbia are the responsibility of the Federal Bureau of Prisons.

[2]Number of state prisoners with a sentence of more than one year per 100,000 state residents of all ages; rates per 100,000 adult residents are higher. With federal prisoners included, the U.S. incarceration rate is 478. Rates for states with integrated systems are likely to be overstated compared to states that do not include jails in total population counts.

[3]Prisons and jails form one integrated system. Data include total jail and prison populations.

[4]Prison jurisdiction population figures are based on custody counts. Arizona includes inmates in contracted beds.

[5]Changes to Arkansas' parole system in 2013 contributed to increased inmate counts.

[6]Includes some prisoners sentenced to one year or less.

[7]Counts include dual jurisdiction cases in which the inmate is currently housed in another jurisdiction's facilities.

[8]Massachusetts offenders may be sentenced to up to 2.5 years in locally operated institutions and are excluded from the state count. Those excluded include 2,630 in the county system with sentences of over one year.

[9]Estimated. Nevada did not submit data for 2012 and 2013.

Sources: U.S. Department of Justice, Office of Justice Programs, Bureau of Justice Statistics, "Sentenced Prisoners Under the Jurisdiction of State or Federal Correctional Authorities, December 31, 1978-2013" and "Imprisonment Rate of Sentenced Prisoners Under the Jurisdiction of State or Federal Correctional Authorities per 100,000 U.S. Residents, December 31, 1978-2013" generated using the Corrections Statistical Analysis Tool, at: http://www.bjs.gov, "Prisoners in 2013", at: http://www.bjs.gov/content/pub/pdf/p13.pdf; U.S. Department of Commerce, U.S. Census Bureau, Governments Division, "2013 Annual Survey of State Government Finances", at: http://www.census.gov/govs/state; U.S. Department of Commerce, U.S. Census Bureau, "Annual Estimates of the Resident Population for the United States, Regions, States, and Puerto Rico: April 1, 2010 to July 1, 2014 (NST-EST2014-01)", at: http://www.census.gov/popest/data/state/totals/2014/index.html. Rankings and per capita expenditure averages calculated by Wisconsin Legislative Reference Bureau.

HIGHLIGHTS OF STATE AND LOCAL FINANCE IN WISCONSIN

Revenues and Expenditures — In the 2012-13 and 2013-14 fiscal years, despite relatively flat tax revenues, a large recovery in levels of interest income, compared to 2011-12, accounted for the majority of the increase in total state revenues, from $40.5 billion from all sources in 2011-12 to $50.0 billion in 2012-13 and $55.9 billion in 2013-14, close to the $56.5 billion level in 2010-11. Expenditures for 2013-14 totaled $45.1 billion. Of these expenditures, about $30.0 billion were general fund and the remaining $15.1 billion were from special funds (such as the conservation and transportation funds), federal funding, pension and retirement funds, and other sources.

Of the total state budget allocations of $68.6 billion for the 2013-15 biennium, state operations accounted for 38.4% ($26.3 billion) and local assistance for 30.1% ($20.6 billion). The remaining 31.6% ($21.7 billion) comprised aids to individuals and organizations.

For the 2013-14 fiscal year, the agency with the single largest expenditure total was the Department of Health Services, more than $10.9 billion (24.4%). Expenditures by the Department of Public Instruction, including state aids to local schools, were $6.1 billion (13.7%). Shared revenue and tax relief of $2.4 billion accounted for 5.3%.

Total state tax revenues for 2013-14 were approximately $15.2 billion, including about $13.9 billion in general purpose revenue. Revenue from income taxes totaled about $8.0 billion, about $7.1 billion of which was individual income taxes and about $967 million in corporation income taxes, while sales and excise taxes were about $5.3 billion.

State-Local Finances — In 2011-12, Wisconsin ranked 25th nationally in total per capita state and local government general revenues ($8,150, or lower than the U.S. average of $8,271). In total direct general state and local government per capita expenditures, Wisconsin ranked 21st ($8,256 compared to the U.S. average of $8,237). In 2013-14, Wisconsin ranked 18th in total state tax revenues at $63.93 per $1,000 personal income, compared to a national average of $59.06.

Wisconsin returned $1.63 billion to local units of government in property tax relief and shared revenue in fiscal year 2015 ($747.4 million as school levy credits and about $882.0 million in shared revenue).

Property Taxes — General property taxes levied in Wisconsin in 2013 totaled almost $10.6 billion for a net amount of about $9.9 billion after state property tax relief. Milwaukee ($27.83), Kenosha ($25.16), Rock ($24.97), Crawford ($24.95), and Lafayette ($24.02) counties had the highest effective (full value equalized) net tax rate; Vilas ($10.37) and Sawyer ($11.56) counties were the lowest, compared to the state average of $21.09, a 2.2% increase from 2012. The share of property taxes paid by residential taxpayers was 69.0%. Commercial taxpayers paid 20.5%, and the share paid by manufacturing is 3.0%.

State-Federal Finances — Federal tax receipts from Wisconsin in fiscal year 2014 totaled about $49.6 billion, with the largest amount generated by individual income and employment taxes ($42.8 billion). Direct federal aid to Wisconsin in 2011-12 totaled $11.0 billion, and about 58% of that applied to health services. Local units of government received about $1.40 billion for all functions.

Indebtedness — Total outstanding state government debt in Wisconsin, as of May 31, 2015, amounted to $7.62 billion, of which $5.85 billion was tax-supported (general and segregated funds) and $1.77 billion was revenue-supported. Total state indebtedness at the end of 2013 constituted 1.78% of state-assessed valuation and amounted to $1,453.24 per capita. Local debt in 2013 totaled about $8.6 billion, about $4.6 billion of that for cities. School district and technical college district debt was $5.3 billion.

The following tables present selected data. Consult footnoted sources for more detailed information about state and local finance.

STATE BUDGET ALLOCATIONS
By Type of Revenue Source
Fiscal Years 2013-14 and 2014-15

Revenue Type and Allocation	2013-14	2014-15	2013-15	% of Total – All Sources
GENERAL PURPOSE REVENUE	**$15,013,472,900**	**$15,883,157,300**	**$30,896,630,200**	**45.01%**
State operations	3,968,908,300	3,949,688,700	7,918,597,000	11.54
Local assistance	7,561,775,500	8,151,375,800	15,713,151,300	22.89
Aids to individuals and organizations	3,482,789,100	3,782,092,800	7,264,881,900	10.58
PROGRAM REVENUE – TOTAL	**13,926,143,100**	**14,196,334,100**	**28,122,477,200**	**40.97%**
State operations	6,675,056,900	6,697,347,400	13,372,404,300	19.48
Local assistance	1,144,369,100	1,155,382,500	2,299,751,600	3.35
Aids to individuals and organizations	6,106,717,100	6,343,604,200	12,450,321,300	18.14
Program Revenue – Federal	**8,820,121,900**	**9,125,190,400**	**17,945,312,300**	**26.14%**
State operations	2,500,111,800	2,493,606,300	4,993,718,100	7.27
Local assistance	1,078,975,400	1,089,743,700	2,168,719,100	3.16
Aids to individuals and organizations	5,241,034,700	5,541,840,400	10,782,875,100	15.71
Program Revenue – Service	**887,704,500**	**819,509,900**	**1,707,214,400**	**2.49%**
State operations	620,256,200	620,958,600	1,241,214,800	1.81
Local assistance	39,026,300	38,997,600	78,023,900	0.11
Aids to individuals and organizations	228,422,000	159,553,700	387,975,700	0.57
Program Revenue – Other	**4,218,316,700**	**4,251,633,800**	**8,469,950,500**	**12.34%**
State operations	3,554,688,900	3,582,782,500	7,137,471,400	10.40
Local assistance	26,367,400	26,641,200	53,008,600	0.08
Aids to individuals and organizations	637,260,400	642,210,100	1,279,470,500	1.86
SEGREGATED REVENUE – TOTAL	**4,856,310,400**	**4,767,700,300**	**9,624,010,700**	**14.02%**
State operations	2,554,491,500	2,493,022,500	5,047,514,000	7.35
Local assistance	1,327,720,500	1,307,197,000	2,634,917,500	3.84
Aids to individuals and organizations	974,098,400	967,480,800	1,941,579,200	2.83
Segregated Revenue – Federal	**898,351,300**	**897,449,000**	**1,795,800,300**	**2.62%**
State operations	671,885,900	670,886,100	1,342,772,000	1.96
Local assistance	221,673,600	221,771,100	443,444,700	0.65
Aids to individuals and organizations	4,791,800	4,791,800	9,583,600	0.01
Segregated Revenue – Local	**107,861,800**	**107,886,100**	**215,747,900**	**0.31%**
State operations	7,393,700	7,393,700	14,787,400	0.02
Local assistance	92,273,900	92,298,200	184,572,100	0.27
Aids to individuals and organizations	8,194,200	8,194,200	16,388,400	0.02
Segregated Revenue – Service	**240,509,400**	**240,509,400**	**481,018,800**	**0.70%**
State operations	240,509,400	240,509,400	481,018,800	0.70
Segregated Revenue – Other	**3,609,587,900**	**3,521,855,800**	**7,131,443,700**	**10.39%**
State operations	1,634,702,500	1,574,233,300	3,208,935,800	4.67
Local assistance	1,013,773,000	993,127,700	2,006,900,700	2.92
Aids to individuals and organizations	961,112,400	954,494,800	1,915,607,200	2.79
FEDERAL REVENUE – TOTAL	**9,718,473,200**	**10,022,639,400**	**19,741,112,600**	**28.76%**
State operations	3,171,997,700	3,164,492,400	6,336,490,100	9.23
Local assistance	1,300,649,000	1,311,514,800	2,612,163,800	3.81
Aids to individuals and organizations	5,245,826,500	5,546,632,200	10,792,458,700	15.72
TOTAL – ALL SOURCES	**$33,795,926,400**	**$34,847,191,700**	**$68,643,118,100**	**100.00%**
State operations	13,198,456,700	13,140,058,600	26,338,515,300	38.37
Local assistance	10,033,865,100	10,613,955,300	20,647,820,400	30.08
Aids to individuals and organizations	10,563,604,600	11,093,177,800	21,656,782,400	31.55

General purpose revenue: general taxes, miscellaneous receipts and revenues collected by state agencies that are paid into the general fund, lose their identity, and are available for appropriation by the legislature.

Program revenue: revenues paid into the general fund and credited by law to an appropriation used to finance a specific program or agency.

Segregated fund revenue: revenues deposited, by law, into funds other than the general fund and available only for the purposes for which such funds were created.

Federal revenue: money received from the federal government (may be disbursed either through a segregated fund or through the general fund).

Service revenue: money transferred between or within state agencies for reimbursement for services rendered or materials purchased.

State operations: amounts budgeted to operate programs carried out by state government.

Local assistance: amounts budgeted as state aids to assist programs carried out by local governmental units in Wisconsin.

Source: Wisconsin Department of Administration, State Budget Office, departmental data, June 2015.

WISCONSIN STATE REVENUES – ALL FUNDS
Fiscal Years 2011-12, 2012-13, 2013-14
(In Thousands)

	2011-12	2012-13	2013-14
TOTAL GENERAL FUND TAX REVENUES*	$13,541,842	$14,107,812	$13,978,172
TOTAL GPR TAX REVENUES*	$13,514,631	$14,085,627	$13,948,101
Income Taxes*	7,948,248	8,422,237	8,028,574
Individual	7,041,673	7,496,854	7,061,390
Corporation	906,575	925,383	967,184
Sales and Excise Taxes*	4,998,292	5,099,594	5,327,025
General sales and use	4,288,739	4,410,130	4,628,338
Cigarette	587,751	569,151	573,036
Other tobacco products	65,524	63,024	67,693
Liquor and wine.	47,037	48,289	48,992
Malt beverage (beer)	9,241	9,000	8,966
Public Utility Taxes*	365,912	341,256	360,967
Private light, heat, and power.	231,580	226,079	232,347
Municipal light, heat, and power	3,029	3,169	3,354
Telephone	80,976	67,340	72,199
Pipeline	33,674	28,396	35,464
Electric cooperative.	11,164	11,276	12,089
Municipal electric.	5,171	4,992	5,170
Conservation and regulation	312	312	341
Utility tax (refunds) interest and penalties	6	–308	3
Inheritance and Estate Taxes	323	305	–78
Miscellaneous Taxes*	201,856	222,235	231,613
Insurance companies (premiums).	148,082	159,277	165,765
Real estate transfer fee	39,843	48,016	51,179
Lawsuits (courts)	13,832	14,875	14,598
Other	99	67	71
PROGRAM TAX REVENUES*	27,211	22,185	30,071
Fire dues	17,676	17,435	19,737
Pari-mutuel taxes	0	0	0
County expo tax administration.	672	95	755
Baseball park administration fee	396	219	417
Business trust regulation fee	2,024	1,570	2,424
Other	6,443	2,866	6,738
TRANSPORTATION FUND			
Motor fuel tax.	983,859	966,994	999,418
Air-carrier tax	5,986	6,065	7,686
Railroad tax	28,087	29,109	31,349
Aviation fuel tax	1,141	1,344	1,177
Other taxes	8,234	7,965	8,350
CONSERVATION FUND			
2/10 Mill forestry tax	82,655	80,037	79,400
Forest crop taxes	5,013	6,201	8,985
Motor fuel tax.	1	1	1
MEDIATION FUND	2	1	2
PETROLEUM INSPECTION TAX.	66,123	41,662	41,150
ECONOMIC DEVELOPMENT FUND TEMPORARY			
SERVICE CHARGES	27,527	30,368	19,280
TOTAL STATE TAX REVENUES	$14,750,470	$15,277,559	$15,174,970
TOTAL DEPARTMENT REVENUES*	25,029,052	33,495,050	39,298,651
Intergovernmental revenue	11,161,047	11,268,078	11,178,599
Licenses and permits	1,731,183	1,722,830	1,735,503
Charges for goods and services	3,811,937	3,911,515	3,911,855
Contributions	3,288,711	3,149,561	3,737,652
Interest and investment income.	836,370	9,140,018	14,510,680
Gifts and donations	567,650	616,859	563,270
Proceeds from sale of bonds	1,379,104	1,219,325	828,218
Other revenues	2,101,309	2,178,357	2,582,850
Other transactions.	151,741	288,507	250,024
TRANSFERS	737,888	1,249,254	1,459,010
TOTAL REVENUES	$40,517,410	$50,021,863	$55,932,631

*Total of subsequent detail.

Source: Wisconsin Department of Administration, *2014 Annual Fiscal Report,* October 15, 2014.

WISCONSIN STATE EXPENDITURES BY AGENCY
Fiscal Years 2012-13 and 2013-14

Agency	2012-13 Amount	Percent	2013-14 Amount	Percent
Administration, Department of (DOA)	$873,035,315.43	2.04%	$864,222,228.81	1.93%
Aging and Long Term Care, Board on.	2,619,912.29	0.01	2,855,539.25	0.01
Agriculture, Trade and Consumer Protection, Department of	79,791,684.05	0.19	96,168,361.24	0.21
Arts Board	0.00	0.00	0.00	0.00
Child Abuse and Neglect Prevention Board	2,638,225.01	0.01	2,888,996.70	0.01
Children and Families, Department of.	1,935,512,551.26	4.53	2,046,148,841.92	4.56
Commerce, Department of.	0.00	0.00	0.00	0.00
Corrections, Department of	1,243,923,422.71	2.91	1,277,033,209.09	2.84
District Attorneys (DOA)	46,810,351.00	0.11	46,992,907.73	0.10
Educational Communications Board	17,435,856.53	0.04	18,046,489.38	0.04
Employee Trust Funds, Department of	6,264,279,968.86	14.65	6,587,071,641.85	14.67
Employment Relations Commission.	2,370,214.34	0.01	1,744,455.93	0.00
Environmental Improvement Program (DOA)	192,548,757.80	0.45	241,550,583.77	0.54
Financial Institutions, Department of	16,083,177.59	0.04	17,861,454.18	0.04
Fox River Navigation System Authority.	125,400.00	0.00	125,400.00	0.00
Government Accountability Board	6,369,520.73	0.01	5,635,970.70	0.01
Governor, Office of the	4,018,151.86	0.01	3,928,323.21	0.01
Health Services, Department of	10,137,077,410.03	23.70	10,947,007,704.20	24.39
Higher Education Aids Board	142,744,199.91	0.33	146,940,422.43	0.33
Historical Society, State	22,001,842.69	0.05	23,426,553.84	0.05
Insurance, Office of the Commissioner of.	72,530,498.56	0.17	92,722,492.59	0.21
Investment Board	33,862,871.82	0.08	41,643,319.61	0.09
Justice, Department of	101,416,396.15	0.24	123,762,121.94	0.28
Lieutenant Governor, Office of the	307,600.19	0.00	262,803.94	0.00
Lower Wisconsin Riverway	193,765.14	0.00	204,740.97	0.00
Medical College of Wisconsin.	7,471,571.82	0.02	8,439,796.48	0.02
Military Affairs, Department of	89,074,795.19	0.21	99,567,918.17	0.22
Natural Resources, Department of.	541,477,463.28	1.27	569,348,777.60	1.27
People with Developmental Disabilities, Board for . .	1,709,118.57	0.00	1,741,833.24	0.00
Public Defender, Office of the	74,357,628.52	0.17	92,512,185.56	0.21
Public Instruction, Department of	5,899,400,872.85	13.79	6,144,276,015.00	13.69
Public Lands, Board of Commissioners of	1,436,848.58	0.00	1,364,513.37	0.00
Public Service Commission	20,408,580.95	0.05	21,296,263.07	0.05
Regulation and Licensing, Department of.	57,888,294.28	0.14		0.00
Revenue, Department of	496,767,913.28	1.16	511,167,459.46	1.14
Safety and Professional Services, Department of . . .			50,490,510.74	0.11
Secretary of State, Office of the	462,813.96	0.00	464,897.95	0.00
State Employment Relations, Office of	4,669,780.92	0.01	4,715,487.84	0.01
State Fair Park Board	23,856,844.45	0.06	24,561,438.74	0.05
Technical College System Board	139,718,234.78	0.33	139,433,267.50	0.31
Tourism, Department of	17,630,276.48	0.04	17,876,530.12	0.04
Transportation, Department of.	2,968,541,834.78	6.94	2,969,583,227.20	6.61
Treasurer, Office of the State	3,656,836.93	0.01	557,451.95	0.00
University of Wisconsin System.	5,840,134,233.70	13.66	6,073,935,112.05	13.53
Veterans Affairs, Department of	161,986,333.61	0.38	148,299,784.06	0.33
Wisconsin Economic Development Corporation . . .	56,238,289.00	0.13	40,900,700.00	0.09
Wisconsin Housing and Economic Development Authority.			2,500,000.00	0.01
Workforce Development, Department of	373,981,944.16	0.87	357,523,372.86	0.80
TOTAL EXECUTIVE	$37,978,567,604.04	88.80%	$39,868,801,106.24	88.81%
TOTAL JUDICIAL	127,680,107.17	0.30	126,874,093.29	0.28
TOTAL LEGISLATIVE	64,552,204.85	0.15	65,525,903.18	0.15
Budget Stabilization	—	—	—	—
Shared Revenue and Tax Relief	2,334,704,523.43	5.46	2,381,178,483.99	5.30
Miscellaneous Appropriations	120,687,203.17	0.28	129,319,502.14	0.29
Program Supplements	207,577,517.30	0.49	122,897,002.46	0.27
Public Debt.	825,003,119.40	1.93	1,070,456,082.50	2.38
Building Commission	20,454,167.73	0.05	33,657,159.23	0.07
BUILDING PROGRAM	1,089,901,356.60	2.55	1,093,576,625.58	2.44
GRAND TOTAL.	$42,769,127,803.69	100.00%	$44,892,285,958.61	100.00%

Source: Wisconsin Department of Administration, State Controller's Office, *Appendix to Annual Fiscal Report (Budgetary Basis),* October 2013 and 2014. Agency percentages calculated by Wisconsin Legislative Reference Bureau.

WISCONSIN STATE REVENUES AND EXPENDITURES
Fiscal Years 1970-71 – 2013-14
(In Thousands)

Fiscal Year	General Fund[1]		Other Funds[2]		Total – All Funds		Net Surplus[3]
Ending 6/30	Revenues	Expenditures	Revenues	Expenditures	Revenues	Expenditures	(or deficit)
1971	$1,790,957	$1,780,703	$929,124	$726,545	$2,720,081	$2,507,247	$34,840
1972	2,096,084	2,031,896	961,970	697,144	3,058,054	2,729,040	116,914
1973	2,480,748	2,296,679	1,112,600	791,657	3,593,347	3,088,337	217,404
1974	2,687,517	2,729,854	1,114,326	865,724	3,801,842	3,595,577	241,359
1975	2,966,532	3,148,968	1,252,422	924,455	4,218,954	4,073,423	78,120
1976	3,476,690	3,439,062	1,677,155	1,283,467	5,153,846	4,722,529	86,473
1977	3,807,748	3,712,595	1,887,150	1,376,726	5,694,898	5,089,322	166,587
1978	4,240,298	3,994,220	1,875,978	1,446,286	6,116,277	5,440,486	407,770
1979	4,622,611	4,696,263	2,200,365	1,620,899	6,822,976	6,317,162	280,561
1980	4,900,275	5,027,130	2,481,324	1,809,840	7,381,599	6,836,970	72,627
1981	5,335,427	5,452,247	2,738,491	1,922,648	8,073,918	7,374,895	14,065
1982	5,564,585	5,520,811	2,757,388	2,021,266	8,321,974	7,542,078	70,811
1983	6,036,016	6,302,575	3,905,944	2,288,804	9,941,961	8,591,379	(182,126)
1984	6,966,282	6,360,657	3,614,895	2,528,273	10,581,177	8,888,930	383,085
1985	7,160,174	7,237,716	4,908,582	2,743,287	12,068,756	9,981,002	314,084
1986	7,798,367	7,757,063	6,380,605	2,774,683	14,178,972	10,531,747	279,744
1987	8,133,265	8,205,100	5,061,597	2,693,737	13,194,863	10,898,836	232,733
1988	8,432,698	8,427,084	3,566,763	2,790,038	11,999,461	11,217,121	216,963
1989	9,030,466	8,809,189	5,778,125	3,094,116	14,808,591	11,903,305	375,016
1990	9,418,918	9,464,483	5,483,442	3,287,809	14,902,360	12,752,292	306,452
1991	10,184,183	10,350,332	5,930,658	3,706,452	16,114,839	14,056,784	113,609
1992	11,033,948	11,082,220	7,786,483	4,218,565	18,820,431	15,300,785	73,681
1993	11,828,599	11,708,360	8,192,793	4,596,981	20,021,392	16,305,341	153,540
1994	12,442,349	12,323,509	5,812,805	4,756,564	18,255,154	17,080,073	234,877
1995	13,259,772	13,094,450	9,823,810	4,963,553	23,083,582	18,058,003	400,881
1996	13,804,399	13,648,601	10,038,961	5,057,062	23,843,360	18,705,663	581,690
1997	14,669,320	14,932,404	12,741,438	5,144,002	27,410,758	20,076,406	386,558
1998	15,701,212	15,509,615	13,896,719	6,071,649	29,597,931	21,581,264	533,240
1999	16,252,539	16,098,587	11,847,678	6,864,567	28,100,217	22,963,154	737,748
2000	18,185,980	18,333,634	14,687,330	8,111,005	32,873,310	26,444,639	574,416
2001	19,285,734	19,448,417	2,990,770	8,719,341	22,276,504	28,167,758	445,999
2002	20,850,074	21,248,608	5,920,241	10,395,514	26,770,315	31,644,122	44,469
2003	20,683,921	20,956,485	10,598,486	11,025,745	31,282,407	31,982,230	(163,608)
2004	22,040,940	21,716,332	19,544,497	12,177,401	41,585,437	33,893,733	127,369
2005	21,191,600	21,488,178	15,827,541	10,772,231	37,019,141	32,260,409	(131,675)
2006	22,321,870	22,148,049	17,611,450	11,636,031	39,933,320	33,784,080	35,014
2007	23,123,424	23,205,243	23,140,557	11,329,591	46,263,981	34,534,834	36,467
2008	23,997,838	24,103,773	4,668,268	12,195,449	28,666,106	36,299,222	110,424
2009	25,078,246	25,280,016	(4,760,111)	13,216,367	20,318,135	38,496,383	(37,167)
2010	26,918,079	26,933,345	19,320,601	13,214,942	46,238,680	40,148,287	99,873
2011	28,926,518	28,951,824	27,574,543	13,974,915	56,501,061	42,926,739	305,584
2012	28,557,414	27,379,001	11,959,996	14,158,805	40,517,410	41,537,806	1,115,672
2013	29,435,181	28,400,745	20,586,682	14,164,382	50,021,863	42,565,127	1,987,605
2014	29,765,921	30,028,018	26,166,710	15,060,009	55,932,631	45,088,027	1,669,233

[1]Includes general purpose revenue (GPR), program revenue, and federal funding.

[2]Includes special revenue funds (such as conservation and transportation), federal funding, debt service, capital projects, pension and retirement funds, trust and agency funds, and others.

[3]Unappropriated (unreserved) balance of the general fund for the fiscal year.

Source: Wisconsin Department of Administration, Bureau of Financial Operations, *2014 Annual Fiscal Report,* October 15, 2014, and previous editions.

WISCONSIN TRANSPORTATION FUND
REVENUES AND EXPENDITURES[1]
Fiscal Years 2012-13 and 2013-14

	2012-13		2013-14	
	State Funds	Federal, Local, and Agency Funds	State Funds	Federal, Local, and Agency Funds
OPENING BALANCE	$107,364,024	($1,024,775,335)	$153,479,820	($1,043,177,473)
REVENUES				
Motor fuel taxes	966,993,553	—	999,418,114	—
Vehicle registration[2]	429,059,669	—	442,319,783	—
Drivers license fees	40,111,079	—	39,232,773	—
Motor carrier fees	2,455,226	—	2,359,440	—
Other motor vehicle fees.	23,972,815	—	23,633,198	—
Overweight/oversize permits	5,669,876	—	5,828,254	—
Investment earnings (loss)[3]	(237,657)	—	(479,713)	—
Aeronautical taxes and fees	8,078,009	—	9,300,426	—
Railroad property taxes	29,109,910	—	31,348,931	—
Dealers' licenses	620,146	—	623,169	—
Transfers - In[4]	164,211,778	—	57,776,850	—
Miscellaneous	12,775,860	2,766,850	14,899,463	1,355,614
Service center operations	—	21,807,012	—	20,294,972
State and local highway facilities – Federal[5] . . .	—	707,527,716	—	653,163,326
State and local highway facilities – Local	—	111,036,444	—	78,425,653
Major highway development – Revenue bonds . .	—	156,876,930	—	202,874,701
Highway administration and planning – Federal .	—	3,441,447	—	2,776,384
Aeronautics – Federal	—	72,274,996	—	53,795,411
Aeronautics – Local	—	11,904,260	—	11,187,049
Railroad assistance – Federal	—	1,892,389	—	3,551,216
Railroad assistance – Local	—	5,200,307	—	6,271,662
Railroad passenger service – Federal	—	5,725,138	—	2,113,523
Railroad passenger service – Local	—	—	—	175,000
Transit assistance – Federal	—	30,742,760	—	23,535,993
Transit assistance – Local	—	1,240,698	—	1,225,202
Congestion mitigation air quality – Federal	—	4,185,083	—	7,199,996
Congestion mitigation air quality – Local	—	1,015,562	—	1,855,978
Harbors assistance – Federal.	—	45,326	—	—
Harbors assistance – Local.	—	(11)	—	19,096
Safe routes to school – Federal	—	1,356,243	—	656,057
Safe routes to school – Local	—	236,864	—	34,386
Transportation enhancement activities – Federal[5]	—	9,456,243	—	6,990,864
Transportation enhancement activities – Local . .	—	2,172,803	—	5,295,723
Bicycle and pedestrian facilities – Federal	—	996,448	—	1,683,091
Bicycle and pedestrian facilities – Local	—	264,437	—	2,134,220
Transportation alternatives program – Federal . .	—	—	—	3,123,046
Transportation alternatives program – Local . . .	—	—	—	189,966
General administration and planning – Federal . .	—	27,483,561	—	25,858,431
General administration and planning – Local . . .	—	764,307	—	901,321
Administrative facilities – Revenue Bonds	—	1,128,250	—	758,076
Highway safety – Federal	—	6,597,695	—	5,171,713
Gifts and grants	—	280,319	—	503,402
TOTAL REVENUES.	$1,682,820,264	$1,188,420,077	$1,626,260,688	$1,123,121,072
TOTAL AVAILABLE	$1,790,184,288	$163,644,742	$1,779,740,508	$79,943,599

[1]The Transportation Fund is a multipurpose special revenue fund created to provide resources for transportation-related facilities and modes with revenues derived from users of transportation facilities. Transportation facilities and major highway projects are also funded with revenue bonds and general obligation bonds.

[2]Section 84.59, Wisconsin Statutes, provides that vehicle registration revenues derived under s. 341.25 are deposited with a trustee in a fund outside the state treasury. Only those revenues not required for the repayment of revenue bond obligations are considered income to the transportation fund. During FY 2014, $215.8 million was retained by the trustee and in FY 2013, $200.8 million was retained by the trustee.

[3]During FY 2014, investment earnings of $0.5 million were offset against bank fees of $1.0 million resulting in a reported loss of $0.5 million. During FY 2013, investment earnings of $0.7 million were offset against bank fees of $0.9 million resulting in a reported loss of $0.2 million.

WISCONSIN TRANSPORTATION FUND
REVENUES AND EXPENDITURES[1]
Fiscal Years 2012-13 and 2013-14–Continued

	2012-13		2013-14	
	State Funds	Federal, Local, and Agency Funds	State Funds	Federal, Local, and Agency Funds
EXPENDITURES[6]				
Local Assistance				
Highway aids	$420,214,923	—	$419,916,270	—
Local bridge and highway improvement[5]	42,856,899	$124,238,760	29,706,664	$105,067,710
Mass transit	122,502,631	23,120,456	120,971,609	18,041,046
Railroads.	2,541,545	428,483	2,572,407	2,308,966
Surface transportation grants	—	(4,286)	—	—
Aeronautics	12,084,346	88,916,527	13,380,784	85,831,434
Highway safety	—	7,736,072	—	1,902,931
Multimodal transportation studies	7	—	—	—
Rail passenger service	8,683,753	(30,651)	4,795,779	(128,628)
Harbors.	723,915	(9,221)	90,246	—
Safe routes to school.	—	799,980	—	(282,810)
Transportation planning grants to local governmental units.	—	—	—	—
Transportation enhancement activities[5]	—	15,405,188	—	(1,252,193)
Bicycle and pedestrian facilities	611,849	4,011,553	(177,654)	(320,773)
Transportation alternatives program	—	—	279,380	15,158,982
Total Local Assistance	$610,219,868	$264,612,861	$591,535,485	$226,326,665
Aids to Individuals and Organizations				
Transportation facilities economic assistance and development	$4,395,699	$142,398	$3,306,615	$48,981
Railroad crossings	4,036,541	2,924,742	3,360,793	3,062,577
Elderly and disabled	1,286,920	2,468,329	53,779	2,600,562
Freight rail	—	4,398,492	—	8,222,513
Total Aids to Individuals and Organizations .	$9,719,160	$9,933,961	$6,721,187	$13,934,633
State Operations				
Highway improvements[5].	$494,784,537	$658,441,737	$520,739,299	$622,231,613
Major highway development – Revenue bonds . .	—	208,704,350	—	203,046,241
Highway maintenance, repair, and traffic operations	229,955,491	9,951,607	244,465,293	7,982,681
Highway administration and planning.	13,808,084	3,334,661	14,134,342	3,157,325
Traffic enforcement and inspection	62,884,619	5,892,499	62,648,352	4,980,786
Transportation safety.	1,043,611	6,478,557	1,172,751	4,920,330
General administration and planning	58,574,414	12,863,533	60,126,882	15,420,318
Administrative facilities – Revenue bonds	—	1,128,250	—	933,955
Vehicle registration and drivers licensing	71,992,764	1,523,467	72,860,663	1,547,304
Vehicle inspection and maintenance	2,595,960	—	2,595,960	—
Debt repayment and interest[7]	58,613,619	—	78,430,775	—
Service centers	—	22,657,820	—	21,380,094
Congestion mitigation air quality	—	7,952,665	—	2,067,936
Miscellaneous	3,000,168	(6,653,753)	2,981,935	3,027,652
Total State Operations	$997,253,267	$932,275,393	$1,060,156,252	$890,696,235
Transfers				
Conservation fund transfers	$19,512,173	—	$19,840,885	—
TOTAL EXPENDITURES.	$1,636,704,468	$1,206,822,215	$1,678,253,809	$1,130,957,533
UNRESERVED FUND BALANCE	$153,479,820	($1,043,177,473)	$101,486,699	($1,051,013,934)

[4]FY 2014 Transfer - in amount includes a $35.1 million general fund transfer, $22.3 million petroleum inspection fund transfer and $0.4 million conservation fund transfer. FY 2013 transfer - in includes a $138.0 million federal fund transfer, $25.8 million from the petroleum inspection fund and $0.4 million from the conservation fund.

[5]The American Recovery and Reinvestment Act of 2009 (ARRA) provided $553.3 million in federal funding for highway improvement projects. ARRA-funded adjusted expenditures for highway projects totaled $0.8 million in FY 2014 and $0.4 million in FY 2013.

[6]The amounts provided in the above exhibit exclude financial activity relating to general obligation bond funded projects, which are reimbursed from the capital improvement fund.

[7]2013 Wisconsin Act 20 (2013-2015 biennial budget act) authorized $574.9 million in general obligation bond proceeds funding for highway construction, railroad and harbor improvements. Debt service for $200.0 million of these general obligation bonds will be funded by the general fund.

Source: Wisconsin Department of Administration, Division of Executive Budget and Finance, State Controller's Office, *2014 Annual Fiscal Report (Budgetary Basis) Appendix*, October 15, 2014.

WISCONSIN CONSERVATION FUND
REVENUES, EXPENDITURES, AND BALANCES
Fiscal Years 2009-10 – 2013-14

	2009-10	2010-11	2011-12	2012-13	2013-14
OPENING CASH BALANCE	$10,559,478	$22,619,142	$10,825,193	$30,649,441	$39,267,307
REVENUES.	297,472,425	285,565,714	300,716,453	289,053,998	286,915,608
User fees (licenses, registration)	108,389,469	101,159,981	106,685,846	103,363,006	102,118,589
Forestry mill tax	86,895,392	84,234,712	82,655,049	80,037,319	79,399,769
Federal aids	45,100,915	45,200,151	58,397,301	50,238,007	45,486,239
Motor fuel tax formula	23,040,750	22,934,467	22,864,505	22,513,786	22,842,478
Severance tax	5,004,089	5,631,667	5,012,725	6,200,531	8,985,347
Other revenues (sales, services)	29,041,810	26,404,736	25,101,027	26,701,349	28,083,186
EXPENDITURES	285,412,761	297,359,663	280,892,205	280,436,132	288,991,617
Land and forestry – state	92,675,788	90,150,583	90,476,521	88,202,227	93,368,808
Land and forestry – federal	12,467,574	16,440,942	16,674,780	13,933,108	15,146,341
Enforcement/science – state	24,410,685	23,938,230	23,423,099	24,174,452	22,554,512
Enforcement/science – federal	9,993,173	12,031,891	10,951,402	10,266,737	11,257,421
Water management – state	20,957,121	23,809,609	21,556,060	22,210,464	21,704,213
Water management – federal	6,160,414	5,739,060	6,013,891	5,832,145	5,736,280
Conservation aids – state	28,787,757	30,006,477	29,707,704	29,808,387	29,955,985
Conservation aids – federal	5,708,759	5,058,713	4,266,992	5,102,449	4,250,563
Environmental aids – state	5,947,542	7,366,005	6,533,996	6,851,088	6,722,852
Development/debt service – state. . . .	25,112,458	22,818,234	20,162,288	19,756,643	21,065,928
Development/debt service – federal . .	4,420,490	9,681,827	3,110,679	4,871,695	6,539,906
Administrative services – state	2,520,441	2,516,843	2,415,405	2,712,011	3,729,519
Administrative services – federal. . . .	714,556	840,844	912,887	927,972	1,337,961
CAES management – state*	27,330,448	26,885,888	24,690,729	24,850,900	24,318,420
CAES management – federal*	4,802,268	4,607,284	5,535,743	6,059,689	6,015,817
Other activities – state	13,403,287	15,467,233	14,460,029	14,876,165	15,287,091
TRANSFER TO GENERAL FUND .	—	—	—	—	—
FUND BALANCE	$22,619,142	$10,825,193	$30,649,441	$39,267,307	$37,191,298

*CAES – Customer and Employee Services Division.

Note: The Conservation Fund is a segregated fund that provides funding for many activities of the Wisconsin Department of Natural Resources, including fish and wildlife management, forestry, parks and recreation, law enforcement, administrative activities, and a portion of the Wisconsin Conservation Corps program.

Source: Wisconsin Department of Administration, Bureau of Financial Operations, *2014 Annual Fiscal Report (Budgetary Basis) Appendix,* October 15, 2014, and previous issues.

STATE PAYMENTS TO LOCAL UNITS OF GOVERNMENT
Property Tax Relief and Shared Revenue
By County, Fiscal Year 2015

County[1]	School Levy Credits	Shared Revenue Payments	County Total[2]	Per Capita Amount[3]	Rank
Adams	$3,791,544	$1,226,671	$5,018,214	$240.75	55
Ashland	1,754,376	6,021,301	7,775,677	483.83	1
Barron	5,769,021	6,878,620	12,647,641	274.83	36
Bayfield	2,900,269	1,432,988	4,333,258	287.75	28
Brown	28,772,020	26,777,538	55,549,558	219.43	66
Buffalo	1,523,245	2,819,795	4,343,040	319.48	12
Burnett	3,361,019	1,169,954	4,530,974	293.04	26
Calumet	5,256,684	3,611,844	8,868,527	178.39	72
Chippewa	6,571,164	10,797,012	17,368,176	275.52	35
Clark	2,642,426	7,994,244	10,636,670	306.56	18
Columbia	7,948,862	7,805,737	15,754,599	277.39	32
Crawford	1,660,948	3,554,942	5,215,890	313.68	17
Dane	87,867,891	25,667,198	113,535,089	226.05	64
Dodge	9,252,231	12,716,627	21,968,858	246.28	52
Door	5,745,024	1,397,419	7,142,443	255.31	47
Douglas	4,974,641	11,063,379	16,038,021	362.88	6
Dunn	4,392,576	7,930,304	12,322,881	280.59	31
Eau Claire	10,666,530	12,882,205	23,548,735	234.37	58
Florence	808,296	367,824	1,176,120	264.30	42
Fond du Lac	10,533,674	14,451,651	24,985,325	243.94	53
Forest	1,622,843	988,817	2,611,660	282.25	30
Grant	4,604,536	12,479,225	17,083,761	324.77	10
Green	4,625,068	3,872,298	8,497,366	230.77	60
Green Lake	3,101,800	3,068,750	6,170,550	322.83	11
Iowa	3,296,380	2,269,720	5,566,101	233.78	59
Iron	1,048,578	1,340,980	2,389,558	403.98	3
Jackson	2,047,689	3,086,169	5,133,858	248.85	51
Jefferson	10,433,215	9,281,703	19,714,918	234.77	56
Juneau	3,494,030	5,006,723	8,500,753	315.61	15
Kenosha	22,690,044	20,130,078	42,820,122	256.01	46
Kewaunee	2,089,664	4,219,431	6,309,096	305.50	19
La Crosse	13,702,887	18,179,806	31,882,692	273.11	37
Lafayette	1,735,844	4,478,293	6,214,137	367.40	5
Langlade	2,151,532	4,135,306	6,286,839	316.77	14
Lincoln	3,209,521	5,397,176	8,606,697	298.68	23
Manitowoc	7,633,263	16,781,090	24,414,352	300.23	21
Marathon	15,369,334	19,012,990	34,382,323	255.06	48
Marinette	5,210,223	9,402,737	14,612,960	351.23	7
Marquette	2,137,496	1,003,757	3,141,253	203.99	68
Menominee	474,581	621,937	1,096,518	258.86	43
Milwaukee	103,142,140	311,158,884	414,301,024	436.23	2
Monroe	3,771,156	8,261,640	12,032,796	265.40	40
Oconto	5,016,104	4,475,803	9,491,907	249.70	50
Oneida	7,723,773	1,892,577	9,616,350	266.51	39
Outagamie	19,463,375	22,775,316	42,238,691	234.63	57
Ozaukee	15,940,161	6,596,524	22,536,685	258.70	44
Pepin	1,022,376	1,348,984	2,371,360	318.52	13
Pierce	4,873,087	5,080,050	9,953,137	242.13	54
Polk	7,028,429	4,184,645	11,213,073	253.48	49
Portage	6,700,622	7,608,922	14,309,545	201.88	69
Price	2,025,603	2,900,513	4,926,116	348.01	8
Racine	22,656,215	34,099,854	56,756,069	290.37	27
Richland	1,559,913	3,773,941	5,333,854	296.41	24
Rock	14,952,863	32,216,218	47,169,081	294.62	25
Rusk	1,939,011	3,688,815	5,627,826	380.52	4
Saint Croix	11,736,354	3,891,866	15,628,220	182.29	71
Sauk	9,178,351	4,903,402	14,081,753	226.79	63
Sawyer	3,642,883	959,127	4,602,010	275.97	33
Shawano	4,429,806	5,188,304	9,618,109	229.77	61
Sheboygan	13,933,383	17,867,557	31,800,940	275.66	34
Taylor	1,793,423	3,551,261	5,344,684	257.79	45
Trempealeau	2,890,562	6,268,630	9,159,192	313.84	16
Vernon	2,957,455	6,015,209	8,972,664	299.32	22
Vilas	6,729,290	540,304	7,269,594	337.76	9
Walworth	21,583,462	6,365,747	27,949,209	271.78	38
Washburn	3,261,710	1,284,317	4,546,027	285.05	29
Washington	19,301,237	5,679,427	24,980,664	187.72	70
Waukesha	78,766,774	11,090,003	89,856,777	228.78	62
Waupaca	5,746,953	8,162,041	13,908,994	265.26	41
Waushara	3,290,368	1,722,104	5,012,472	204.50	67
Winnebago	16,299,901	21,519,448	37,819,349	224.83	65
Wood	7,172,293	15,579,365	22,751,658	303.54	20
STATE	$747,400,000	$881,975,040	$1,629,375,041	$284.21	

[1]55 municipalities (cities and villages) are located in two or more counties. For municipalities that are in more than one county, payments are attributed to what the Department of Revenue determines to be the "primary" county. For example, payments to Appleton are attributed to Outagamie County even though parts of Appleton are also located in Calumet and Winnebago Counties.

[2]Totals may appear to be different from sums of the components due to rounding.

[3]Per capita calculations are based on January 1, 2014, county population estimates, the most recent available at publication time.

Sources: Wisconsin Department of Revenue, Division of State and Local Finance, Bureau of Property Tax, Local Government Services Section, departmental data, June 2015; and Wisconsin Department of Administration, Division of Intergovernmental Relations, Demographic Services Center, *County Final Population Estimates, January 1, 2014* [October 2014]. Per capita amounts and rankings calculated by Wisconsin Legislative Reference Bureau.

SELECTED STATE TAX REVENUES
By State, Per $1,000 Personal Income
Fiscal Years Ending in 2014

	Total Taxes[1]		General	Motor	Sales and Gross Receipts Taxes / Selective Sales Taxes / Public			Individual	Corporation	Motor	
State	Amount	Rank	Sales	Fuels	Utilities	Tobacco	Alcohol	Income	Net Income	Vehicle	Property
Alabama	$51.12	39	$13.16	$2.94	$4.04	$0.64	$1.00	$17.64	$2.24	$1.16	$1.81
Alaska	87.06	4	NA	1.09	0.11	1.85	1.00	NA	10.49	1.53	3.29
Arizona.	51.29	38	23.50	3.06	0.09	1.22	0.28	13.57	2.25	0.90	3.23
Arkansas	79.80	6	27.95	4.06	0.00	2.02	0.46	23.24	3.56	1.53	9.62
California	71.01	11	19.14	3.12	0.34	0.43	0.18	34.97	4.56	2.07	1.12
Colorado	45.04	45	10.02	2.48	0.04	0.74	0.16	21.68	2.75	1.93	NA
Connecticut	70.94	12	17.72	2.24	1.40	1.68	0.27	34.59	2.79	1.13	NA
Delaware	73.89	8	NA	2.64	1.38	2.67	0.46	24.20	6.49	1.34	NA
Florida	41.71	48	25.32	2.86	3.21	0.44	0.53	NA	2.41	1.85	0.00
Georgia.	47.19	42	12.98	2.55	0.00	0.55	0.46	22.71	2.39	1.09	2.00
Hawaii	91.61	3	42.89	1.42	2.52	1.64	0.73	26.50	1.91	2.57	NA
Idaho	59.85	24	22.39	4.05	0.03	0.78	0.14	21.81	3.10	2.37	NA
ILLINOIS	63.22	20	13.74	2.09	2.66	1.39	0.45	25.91	6.91	2.81	0.09
Indiana	64.76	17	26.92	3.13	0.97	1.72	0.18	18.82	3.33	1.60	0.03
IOWA	59.01	26	18.97	3.23	0.00	1.61	0.10	22.81	2.77	4.07	NA
Kansas	55.45	34	22.56	3.34	0.00	0.74	0.96	18.99	2.50	1.75	0.61
Kentucky	66.82	16	18.84	5.33	0.38	1.50	0.77	22.56	4.06	1.25	3.38
Louisiana.	49.31	41	14.87	2.99	0.05	0.66	0.29	14.00	2.45	0.44	0.28
Maine	68.75	15	21.30	4.31	0.58	2.43	0.32	25.27	3.27	2.01	0.64
Maryland	57.44	30	12.73	2.47	0.42	1.22	0.09	23.59	2.98	1.55	2.20
Massachusetts . . .	63.22	21	13.82	1.83	0.06	1.65	0.20	33.18	5.50	1.24	0.01
MICHIGAN	61.72	23	20.95	2.40	0.07	2.34	0.36	19.59	2.19	2.57	4.78
MINNESOTA . . .	87.01	5	20.47	3.36	0.00	2.19	0.31	35.85	4.95	2.78	3.15
Mississippi	73.69	9	32.15	3.99	0.00	1.42	0.41	16.22	5.12	1.89	0.24
Missouri	44.55	46	13.02	2.76	0.00	0.39	0.14	21.25	1.42	1.14	0.12
Montana	63.90	19	NA	4.74	1.14	2.06	0.72	25.58	3.61	3.48	6.46
Nebraska	55.07	35	19.91	3.78	0.60	0.72	0.34	23.98	3.46	1.11	0.00
Nevada	62.78	22	33.65	2.61	0.20	0.90	0.38	NA	NA	1.69	2.27
New Hampshire . .	32.37	50	NA	2.07	0.99	3.05	0.14	1.32	7.70	1.51	5.43
New Jersey	58.45	28	17.50	1.06	1.99	1.46	0.27	23.58	4.66	1.32	0.01
New Mexico	73.41	10	26.76	2.99	0.38	1.04	0.57	16.54	2.62	2.45	1.35
New York	69.33	14	11.41	1.47	0.84	1.30	0.23	38.69	4.38	1.35	NA
North Carolina . . .	59.35	25	14.82	4.86	1.02	0.71	0.87	26.36	3.45	1.78	NA
North Dakota. . . .	150.62	1	32.49	5.61	0.99	0.77	0.23	12.27	6.16	3.07	0.07
Ohio	54.74	36	20.70	3.73	2.28	1.65	0.20	17.07	0.00	1.64	NA
Oklahoma	54.42	37	15.54	2.69	0.28	1.75	0.66	17.71	2.37	4.63	NA
Oregon	58.52	27	NA	3.10	0.52	1.56	0.11	40.18	2.99	3.36	0.13
Pennsylvania	56.03	32	15.56	3.66	2.11	1.68	0.57	17.71	3.77	1.46	0.07
Rhode Island	57.56	29	17.76	1.86	2.04	2.62	0.33	21.12	2.33	1.44	0.05
South Carolina . . .	50.05	40	18.88	2.97	0.16	0.14	0.91	19.18	1.84	1.25	0.12
South Dakota. . . .	40.68	49	23.14	3.49	0.09	1.56	0.41	NA	0.63	2.02	NA
Tennessee	44.34	47	23.26	3.18	0.03	0.98	0.56	0.90	4.42	1.19	NA
Texas	45.13	44	26.41	2.72	0.63	1.18	0.87	NA	NA	1.89	NA
Utah	56.80	31	16.41	3.36	0.22	1.02	0.44	26.00	2.77	1.72	NA
Vermont	99.90	2	11.96	3.49	0.73	2.42	0.81	22.77	3.57	2.64	33.23
Virginia.	45.78	43	8.59	1.68	0.26	0.44	0.50	26.28	1.79	1.19	0.09
Washington.	55.54	33	33.61	3.30	1.42	1.27	0.92	NA	NA	1.82	5.64
West Virginia. . . .	79.35	7	18.02	6.51	2.27	1.50	0.26	26.11	3.00	1.64	0.00
WISCONSIN . . .	63.93	18	18.03	3.90	1.48	2.50	0.23	26.46	3.84	1.98	0.62
Wyoming.	70.69	13	23.91	3.15	0.14	0.76	0.06	NA	NA	2.32	9.37
UNITED STATES[2]	$59.06		$18.51	$2.83	$0.97	$1.15	$0.42	$21.21	$3.16	$1.80	$0.97

NA – Not applicable.

[1]Includes other taxes not listed separately.

[2]United States totals displayed exclude District of Columbia.

Sources: U.S. Census Bureau, Governments Division, "2014 Annual Survey of State Government Tax Collections", at: http://www.census.gov/govs/statetax/; and U.S. Department of Commerce, Bureau of Economic Analysis, Regional Economic Information System, "SA1-3 – Personal Income Summary 2014", at: http://www.bea.gov/regional/. Amounts per $1,000 personal income and rankings calculated by Wisconsin Legislative Reference Bureau.

PER CAPITA STATE AND LOCAL REVENUES
Selected Sources, Fiscal Year 2011-12

State	Total State and Local General Revenue Per Capita						State and Local Taxes Per Capita			
	Amount	Rank	Federal Sources		State/Local Sources		Total	Property	Sales	Individual
			Amount	Percent	Amount[1]	Percent	Taxes[2]			Income
Alabama	$7,021	43	$1,908	27.2%	$5,113	72.8%	$2,951	$530	$1,412	$647
Alaska	23,489	1	4,325	18.4	19,164	81.6	11,857	2,060	740	—
Arizona.	6,623	46	1,733	26.2	4,890	73.8	3,385	1,044	1,641	472
Arkansas	7,177	38	2,126	29.6	5,051	70.4	3,524	661	1,733	814
California	8,743	14	1,715	19.6	7,028	80.4	4,825	1,355	1,469	1,446
Colorado	7,863	29	1,473	18.7	6,391	81.3	4,081	1,339	1,464	939
Connecticut	10,046	6	1,780	17.7	8,267	82.3	6,945	2,623	1,863	2,051
Delaware	9,592	8	2,062	21.5	7,530	78.5	4,576	759	551	1,362
District of Columbia . .	17,546	—	5,471	31.2	12,075	68.8	9,344	2,957	2,424	2,347
Florida	6,891	45	1,408	20.4	5,483	79.6	3,338	1,271	1,691	—
Georgia.	6,390	49	1,549	24.2	4,841	75.8	3,257	1,044	1,242	821
Hawaii	9,189	11	1,889	20.6	7,300	79.4	5,321	941	2,854	1,106
Idaho	6,378	50	1,671	26.2	4,707	73.8	3,043	873	1,058	760
ILLINOIS	8,153	24	1,483	18.2	6,670	81.8	5,164	1,983	1,424	1,205
Indiana	7,305	36	1,700	23.3	5,605	76.7	3,750	992	1,545	933
IOWA	9,131	13	2,192	24.0	6,939	76.0	4,410	1,476	1,481	1,016
Kansas	8,177	23	1,501	18.4	6,676	81.6	4,334	1,360	1,670	1,003
Kentucky.	7,065	42	1,963	27.8	5,101	72.2	3,429	714	1,280	1,058
Louisiana.	8,498	17	2,631	31.0	5,866	69.0	3,682	790	1,970	537
Maine	8,428	18	2,301	27.3	6,126	72.7	4,620	1,788	1,321	1,085
Maryland.	8,722	15	1,952	22.4	6,770	77.6	5,127	1,368	1,347	1,948
Massachusetts	9,652	7	2,184	22.6	7,469	77.4	5,565	2,052	1,145	1,796
MICHIGAN	7,675	31	2,006	26.1	5,669	73.9	3,665	1,343	1,308	743
MINNESOTA	9,166	12	1,975	21.5	7,192	78.5	5,225	1,461	1,755	1,485
Mississippi	8,087	27	2,768	34.2	5,319	65.8	3,253	869	1,508	503
Missouri	6,984	44	1,896	27.2	5,087	72.8	3,388	956	1,263	905
Montana	7,854	30	2,458	31.3	5,396	68.7	3,603	1,372	550	896
Nebraska	8,291	20	1,927	23.2	6,365	76.8	4,379	1,592	1,339	991
Nevada	6,557	48	1,234	18.8	5,322	81.2	3,855	1,032	2,240	—
New Hampshire	7,130	40	1,398	19.6	5,732	80.4	3,989	2,582	662	62
New Jersey.	9,501	9	1,630	17.2	7,871	82.8	6,067	2,916	1,371	1,254
New Mexico	8,670	16	2,695	31.1	5,975	68.9	3,623	684	1,770	552
New York	12,992	4	2,820	21.7	10,172	78.3	7,739	2,426	1,943	2,422
North Carolina	7,370	34	1,779	24.1	5,591	75.9	3,534	912	1,238	1,065
North Dakota.	14,828	3	2,812	19.0	12,017	81.0	9,444	1,129	2,531	616
Ohio	8,005	28	2,012	25.1	5,992	74.9	4,054	1,174	1,312	1,163
Oklahoma	7,488	32	2,052	27.4	5,436	72.6	3,479	600	1,519	727
Oregon	8,380	19	2,286	27.3	6,094	72.7	3,790	1,291	454	1,494
Pennsylvania	8,104	26	1,837	22.7	6,267	77.3	4,466	1,337	1,439	1,121
Rhode Island	9,367	10	2,372	25.3	6,994	74.7	4,967	2,229	1,428	1,027
South Carolina	7,148	39	1,553	21.7	5,595	78.3	3,021	1,034	1,027	656
South Dakota.	7,329	35	2,178	29.7	5,151	70.3	3,469	1,208	1,835	—
Tennessee	6,597	47	1,876	28.4	4,721	71.6	3,095	795	1,769	28
Texas	7,084	41	1,593	22.5	5,491	77.5	3,746	1,545	1,739	0
Utah	7,274	37	1,805	24.8	5,469	75.2	3,347	938	1,282	864
Vermont	10,107	5	3,183	31.5	6,924	68.5	5,135	2,202	1,575	956
Virginia.	7,487	33	1,316	17.6	6,171	82.4	4,049	1,384	1,015	1,247
Washington.	8,198	22	1,683	20.5	6,515	79.5	4,268	1,338	2,591	—
West Virginia.	8,281	21	2,434	29.4	5,847	70.6	3,804	773	1,446	946
WISCONSIN	8,150	25	1,663	20.4	6,487	79.6	4,628	1,756	1,299	1,181
Wyoming.	15,249	2	4,054	26.6	11,195	73.4	6,666	2,288	2,365	—
UNITED STATES .	$8,271		$1,861	22.5%	$6,410	77.5%	$4,419	$1,420	$1,517	$978

[1]Includes taxes, charges, and miscellaneous general revenues.

[2]Total taxes also include corporate income, motor vehicle license, and other taxes not listed separately.

Sources: U.S. Department of Commerce, U.S. Census Bureau, "LGF001: State and Local Government Finances by Level of Government and by State: 2012", at: http://www.census.gov/govs/local/, and "Annual Estimates of the Resident Population for the United States, Regions, States, and Puerto Rico: April 1, 2010 to July 1, 2014 (NST-EST2014-01)", at: http://www.census.gov/popest/data/national/totals/2014/index.html (2012 estimates used in calculations). Per capita figures, percentages, and rankings calculated by Wisconsin Legislative Reference Bureau.

SELECTED PER CAPITA STATE AND LOCAL GOVERNMENT EXPENDITURES, BY FUNCTION
Fiscal Year 2011-12

State	Direct General Expenditure* Amount	Rank	Education	Public Welfare	Health and Hospitals	Highways	Police and Fire	Correction	Parks and Natural Resources	Sewerage and Solid Waste
Alabama	$7,245	38	$2,625	$1,304	$1,136	$466	$330	$149	$134	$130
Alaska	17,301	1	4,519	2,667	863	1,750	670	433	639	261
Arizona.	6,340	49	2,062	1,240	554	357	472	236	171	200
Arkansas	7,229	39	2,806	1,758	484	489	283	189	158	168
California	9,163	11	2,830	1,588	947	439	569	360	281	269
Colorado	7,656	31	2,545	1,070	698	460	469	240	309	188
Connecticut	9,563	7	3,410	1,799	578	473	469	191	132	271
Delaware	9,862	6	3,642	2,064	541	779	366	308	176	301
District of Columbia	16,952	—	3,735	4,510	1,062	828	1,221	379	391	942
Florida	6,957	45	1,931	1,184	691	411	561	210	326	288
Georgia.	6,512	48	2,548	1,051	703	312	348	230	131	195
Hawaii	8,842	15	2,515	1,451	905	432	419	142	259	396
Idaho	6,252	50	1,953	1,289	477	552	357	191	241	207
ILLINOIS	7,980	26	2,748	1,255	468	559	533	160	256	200
Indiana	7,010	43	2,587	1,315	671	432	279	147	163	225
IOWA	9,080	13	3,187	1,642	1,205	771	301	170	308	313
Kansas	7,953	27	2,920	1,208	1,002	626	358	167	208	167
Kentucky.	7,469	33	2,654	1,639	603	568	250	169	145	225
Louisiana.	9,235	10	2,781	1,363	1,141	600	478	288	370	271
Maine	8,483	18	2,524	2,211	567	669	288	146	227	234
Maryland.	9,139	12	3,183	1,710	379	859	517	297	233	265
Massachusetts	9,524	8	2,950	2,251	415	392	482	159	107	234
MICHIGAN	7,465	34	2,903	1,330	810	332	334	226	117	247
MINNESOTA	9,045	14	2,869	2,442	579	664	380	161	324	215
Mississippi	8,083	24	2,493	1,702	1,294	582	309	187	187	197
Missouri	7,107	41	2,412	1,383	857	487	408	143	168	167
Montana	8,157	23	2,565	1,372	430	1,046	368	236	359	196
Nebraska	8,013	25	3,201	1,253	749	657	320	195	309	170
Nevada	6,728	46	1,962	893	502	610	585	256	353	171
New Hampshire . . .	7,594	32	2,906	1,449	126	562	419	138	113	194
New Jersey.	9,354	9	3,547	1,682	456	465	484	234	169	280
New Mexico	8,702	17	3,017	1,940	808	496	458	289	294	175
New York	12,125	3	3,646	2,598	1,136	524	648	294	172	373
North Carolina	7,208	40	2,430	1,301	1,118	402	389	194	173	231
North Dakota.	10,275	4	3,354	1,362	312	1,843	324	203	810	180
Ohio	7,915	28	2,816	1,731	704	465	428	158	138	218
Oklahoma	6,966	44	2,475	1,515	596	606	369	172	173	139
Oregon	8,224	22	2,652	1,483	820	477	459	275	282	265
Pennsylvania	8,379	20	2,766	1,925	630	679	312	259	133	270
Rhode Island	8,827	16	2,976	2,142	233	418	610	189	131	209
South Carolina	7,302	37	2,569	1,243	1,331	331	315	143	142	191
South Dakota.	7,311	36	2,398	1,130	334	1,133	277	197	393	197
Tennessee	6,640	47	2,119	1,581	676	385	364	162	131	171
Texas	7,050	42	2,711	1,180	699	434	356	210	149	180
Utah	7,445	35	2,874	1,059	568	687	320	181	251	209
Vermont	9,961	5	3,794	2,395	335	1,071	361	201	224	206
Virginia.	7,662	30	2,830	1,230	648	515	401	265	149	250
Washington.	8,463	19	2,796	1,237	1,026	600	415	226	293	372
West Virginia.	7,847	29	2,967	1,749	395	697	253	180	206	191
WISCONSIN	8,256	21	2,968	1,737	539	668	424	270	234	226
Wyoming.	13,383	2	4,366	1,357	2,251	1,317	524	373	932	268
UNITED STATES	$8,237		$2,767	$1,546	$765	$505	$444	$231	$211	$242

*Includes amounts for categories not shown separately.

Sources: U.S. Department of Commerce, U.S. Census Bureau, "2012 Census of Governments: State and Local Government Finances by Level of Government and by State" (LGF001), at: http://www.census.gov/govs/local/ and "Annual Estimates of the Resident Population for the United States, Regions, States, and Puerto Rico: April 1, 2010 to July 1, 2014 (NST-EST2014-01)", at: http://www.census.gov/popest/data/state/totals/2014/index.html (July 1, 2012 estimates used in calculations). Per capita amounts and rankings calculated by Wisconsin Legislative Reference Bureau.

FEDERAL TAX COLLECTIONS
By State, Fiscal Year 2014
(In Thousands of Dollars)

State[1]	Total	Individual Income and Employment[2]	Corporate Income[3]	Estate and Gift	Excise[4]
Alabama	$23,789,249	$21,820,797	$1,484,582	$175,323	$308,548
Alaska	5,449,061	5,213,654	179,898	5,448	50,060
Arizona	40,530,219	34,357,778	4,380,014	282,499	1,509,929
Arkansas	30,728,862	22,353,431	7,611,308	115,654	648,469
California	369,193,162	314,319,084	46,236,808	4,195,406	4,441,865
Colorado	52,002,903	43,660,813	7,339,139	177,006	825,945
Connecticut	57,697,380	47,265,116	8,633,070	525,866	1,273,328
Delaware	19,039,980	14,146,624	4,335,398	20,874	537,084
District of Columbia	26,432,733	25,049,824	1,322,308	33,260	27,341
Florida	154,353,070	141,912,552	9,015,856	2,111,945	1,312,718
Georgia	79,565,715	64,674,241	10,736,886	1,064,647	3,089,941
Hawaii	7,722,840	7,090,806	376,857	33,628	221,549
Idaho	9,223,749	8,788,307	333,880	42,091	59,470
ILLINOIS	148,332,148	123,885,426	20,034,959	817,417	3,594,346
Indiana	54,606,571	48,027,054	4,561,915	334,517	1,683,085
IOWA	22,309,198	20,398,887	1,544,385	104,144	261,782
Kansas	25,896,981	21,819,357	2,166,100	213,627	1,697,898
Kentucky	30,128,276	26,911,767	2,324,359	98,800	793,351
Louisiana	43,023,097	40,613,155	1,604,433	170,060	635,449
Maine	6,901,517	6,452,674	292,164	49,334	107,345
Maryland	59,613,635	55,800,282	3,176,203	307,815	329,335
Massachusetts	100,160,858	89,106,987	9,277,736	344,473	1,431,661
MICHIGAN	71,183,803	65,478,941	5,022,559	324,416	357,887
MINNESOTA	96,227,262	74,153,885	19,417,565	204,714	2,451,099
Mississippi	11,011,288	10,122,056	693,586	50,145	145,500
Missouri	61,511,933	50,072,510	9,946,571	290,934	1,201,918
Montana	5,338,004	5,053,198	194,463	48,279	42,064
Nebraska	23,884,904	16,416,668	7,269,170	82,130	116,935
Nevada	16,578,585	15,264,612	777,910	410,612	125,451
New Hampshire	11,043,784	10,437,649	236,410	91,846	277,879
New Jersey	134,869,876	109,983,681	21,813,832	410,859	2,661,505
New Mexico	8,758,418	8,233,829	231,314	78,128	215,146
New York	250,618,177	217,823,234	28,664,811	1,892,576	2,237,556
North Carolina	72,471,513	63,172,182	8,698,479	307,059	293,792
North Dakota	7,585,145	6,939,582	560,449	30,766	54,348
Ohio	129,901,095	113,211,893	12,286,168	487,552	3,915,483
Oklahoma	32,610,983	24,339,580	4,049,061	120,157	4,102,186
Oregon	28,409,241	25,598,367	1,920,303	105,460	785,109
Pennsylvania	126,374,146	109,883,768	12,619,448	492,326	3,378,606
Rhode Island	13,887,904	10,058,643	3,683,902	50,196	95,164
South Carolina	22,242,016	20,290,724	1,567,705	128,483	255,104
South Dakota	6,733,600	6,256,818	404,686	29,529	42,567
Tennessee	56,936,715	49,504,974	5,905,079	151,148	1,375,514
Texas	265,336,183	211,993,178	32,585,544	1,646,933	19,110,528
Utah	18,389,171	16,186,263	1,557,838	46,710	598,361
Vermont	4,324,613	3,912,161	351,999	30,777	29,676
Virginia	75,048,791	63,044,178	11,378,112	387,708	238,793
Washington	67,812,753	60,801,922	5,612,788	433,344	964,698
West Virginia	6,885,260	6,438,716	374,563	16,019	55,961
WISCONSIN	49,592,070	42,831,333	6,021,437	169,997	569,303
Wyoming	4,891,559	4,570,938	185,588	77,541	57,492
UNITED STATES[5]	$3,064,301,358	$2,619,847,215	$353,141,112	$20,154,955	$71,158,076

[1]Taxes may be collected in one state from residents of another state for a variety of reasons, and some corporations pay taxes from a principal office, although their operations may be located in several states.

[2]Collections of individual income tax (withheld and not withheld) include Old-Age, Survivors, Disability, and Hospital Insurance (OASDHI) taxes on salaries and wages under the Federal Insurance Contributions Act (FICA), and on self-employment income under the Self-Employment Insurance Contributions Act (SECA).

[3]Includes business income from tax-exempt organizations.

[4]Excludes excise taxes collected by the Customs Service and the Alcohol and Tobacco Tax and Trade Bureau.

[5]United States totals include international and undistributed totals not included in state listing for taxes filed by members of armed forces stationed overseas or other U.S. citizens abroad. Also included are returns from residents of Puerto Rico either with income from sources outside Puerto Rico or income earned as U.S. government employees. Corporation taxes include those paid by domestic and foreign businesses with principal offices outside the United States. Adjustments and credits are not shown by state, but are included in the U.S. totals. Detail may not add to totals due to rounding.

Source: U.S. Department of the Treasury, Internal Revenue Service, "Internal Revenue Service Data Book 2014," Publication 55B, April 2015.

FEDERAL REVENUE DISTRIBUTED
TO STATE AND LOCAL GOVERNMENTS
By State, Fiscal Year 2011-12

State	Per Capita		Intergovernmental Revenue (in thousands) to			Percent of all State and Local General Revenue
	Amount	Rank	State Government	Local Government	Total	
Alabama	$1,908	26	$8,112,509	$1,079,627	$9,192,136	27.2%
Alaska	4,325	1	2,860,509	301,258	3,161,767	18.4
Arizona.	1,733	34	10,394,549	965,686	11,360,235	26.2
Arkansas	2,126	17	5,900,988	368,481	6,269,469	29.6
California	1,715	35	54,145,284	11,122,249	65,267,533	19.6
Colorado	1,473	46	6,310,538	1,335,288	7,645,826	18.7
Connecticut	1,780	32	5,781,844	616,035	6,397,879	17.7
Delaware.	2,062	18	1,814,112	76,113	1,890,225	21.5
District of Columbia	5,471	—	—	3,474,236	3,474,236	31.2
Florida	1,408	47	22,850,620	4,409,989	27,260,609	20.4
Georgia.	1,549	43	13,794,726	1,568,382	15,363,108	24.2
Hawaii	1,889	28	2,352,114	279,377	2,631,491	20.6
Idaho	1,671	38	2,479,094	186,610	2,665,704	26.2
ILLINOIS	1,483	45	15,646,844	3,438,697	19,085,541	18.2
Indiana	1,700	36	10,441,125	673,456	11,114,581	23.3
IOWA	2,192	14	6,073,376	667,907	6,741,283	24.0
Kansas	1,501	44	4,061,217	270,658	4,331,875	18.4
Kentucky	1,963	23	8,056,691	549,598	8,606,289	27.8
Louisiana.	2,631	8	11,136,334	979,859	12,116,193	31.0
Maine	2,301	12	2,883,526	174,206	3,057,732	27.3
Maryland.	1,952	24	10,030,264	1,469,120	11,499,384	22.4
Massachusetts	2,184	15	12,920,153	1,613,730	14,533,883	22.6
MICHIGAN	2,006	21	17,849,942	1,977,836	19,827,778	26.1
MINNESOTA	1,975	22	9,608,018	1,018,016	10,626,034	21.5
Mississippi	2,768	6	7,725,294	539,548	8,264,842	34.2
Missouri	1,896	27	10,440,927	985,048	11,425,975	27.2
Montana	2,458	9	2,202,444	267,811	2,470,255	31.3
Nebraska	1,927	25	3,141,413	433,247	3,574,660	23.2
Nevada	1,234	50	2,798,426	602,006	3,400,432	18.8
New Hampshire	1,398	48	1,693,289	153,590	1,846,879	19.6
New Jersey	1,630	40	13,412,759	1,058,318	14,471,077	17.2
New Mexico	2,695	7	5,171,367	447,537	5,618,904	31.1
New York	2,820	4	48,698,785	6,601,914	55,300,699	21.7
North Carolina	1,779	33	15,192,577	2,150,472	17,343,049	24.1
North Dakota.	2,812	5	1,750,134	222,788	1,972,922	19.0
Ohio	2,012	20	20,687,909	2,556,358	23,244,267	25.1
Oklahoma	2,052	19	7,363,043	470,232	7,833,275	27.4
Oregon	2,286	13	7,830,552	1,082,099	8,912,651	27.3
Pennsylvania	1,837	30	20,440,103	3,023,285	23,463,388	22.7
Rhode Island	2,372	11	2,310,656	186,635	2,497,291	25.3
South Carolina	1,553	42	6,892,660	440,340	7,333,000	21.7
South Dakota.	2,178	16	1,630,220	187,233	1,817,453	29.7
Tennessee	1,876	29	11,198,575	908,168	12,106,743	28.4
Texas	1,593	41	37,310,756	4,258,569	41,569,325	22.5
Utah	1,805	31	4,481,494	673,387	5,154,881	24.8
Vermont	3,183	3	1,904,382	88,614	1,992,996	31.5
Virginia.	1,316	49	9,278,113	1,503,273	10,781,386	17.6
Washington.	1,683	37	9,743,127	1,862,903	11,606,030	20.5
West Virginia.	2,434	10	4,267,399	250,191	4,517,590	29.4
WISCONSIN	1,663	39	8,855,079	665,028	9,520,107	20.4
Wyoming.	4,054	2	2,213,249	125,261	2,338,510	26.6
UNITED STATES	$1,861		$514,139,109	$70,360,269	$584,499,378	22.5%

Sources: U.S. Department of Commerce, U.S. Census Bureau, "2012 Census of Governments: State and Local Government Finances by Level of Government and by State" (LGF001), at: http://www.census.gov/govs/local/ and "Annual Estimates of the Resident Population for the United States, Regions, States, and Puerto Rico: April 1, 2010 to July 1, 2014 (NST-EST2014-01)", at: http://www.census.gov/popest/data/state/totals/2014/index.html. Per capita amounts, percentages, and rankings calculated by Wisconsin Legislative Reference Bureau.

FEDERAL AIDS TO WISCONSIN
By Agency
Fiscal Years 2012-13 and 2013-14
(In Thousands)

Agency Administering Aid	Federal Aid Received by Wisconsin		Disbursed to Local Governments		Aid to Individuals and Organizations	
	2013-14	2012-13	2013-14	2012-13	2013-14	2012-13
Administration, Department of . .	$164,548	$265,468	$134,647	$185,879	$15,798	$19,565
Agriculture, Trade and Consumer Protection, Department of . . .	11,122	12,079	—	—	—	—
Arts Board	—	—	—	—	—	—
Child Abuse and Neglect Prevention Board	625	629	—	—	625	629
Children and Families, Department of.	583,913	617,640	102,314	76,372	456,536	386,426
Clean Water Fund Program*. . . .	47,148	104,650	47,148	104,650	—	—
Commerce, Department of.	—	8,626	—	—	—	—
Corrections, Department of	1,685	1,773	—	—	—	—
Educational Communications Board	—	2	—	—	—	—
Government Accountability Board	517	971	—	—	—	—
Health Services, Department of . .	6,326,477	6,108,335	121,400	121,811	5,957,844	5,760,973
Higher Educational Aids Board . .	0	14	—	—	—	(5)
Historical Society	1,387	1,375	—	—	—	—
Insurance, Office of the Commissioner of	872	983	—	—	—	—
Justice, Department of	33,242	11,936	16,191	7,439	1,458	1,230
Military Affairs, Department of . .	66,058	61,569	22,982	8,991	130	109
Natural Resources, Department of.	83,322	91,445	2,982	7,590	—	—
People with Developmental Disabilities, Board for	1,684	1,719	—	—	810	963
Public Instruction, Department of .	877,347	778,649	764,335	667,671	61,978	60,638
Public Lands Board	0	50	—	50	—	—
Public Service Commission	1,229	1,405	—	—	—	—
Regulation and Licensing, Department of.	—	1,272	—	—	—	—
Revenue, Department of.	—	21	—	—	—	—
Safety and Professional Services, Department of.	565	—	—	—	—	—
State Fair Park	—	—	—	—	—	—
Supreme Court	844	875	—	—	—	—
Technical College System Board .	28,205	27,627	24,201	23,938	1,121	1,238
Tourism, Department of	591	781	—	—	649	603
Transportation, Department of. . .	789,619	871,725	158,969	173,737	4,317	4,850
University of Wisconsin System. .	1,725,974	1,808,455	—	—	—	—
Veterans Affairs, Department of . .	2,312	2,684	—	—	—	—
Workforce Development, Department of.	218,118	229,309	—	—	69,637	84,240
TOTAL.	$10,967,402	$11,012,068	$1,395,169	$1,378,128	$6,570,903	$6,321,458

Note: Aid is not necessarily disbursed in the same fiscal year in which it is received by the agency. In some cases, aid is received as reimbursement for previous expenditures.

*Federal aid received by Wisconsin for Clean Water Fund (Environmental Improvement Program, DOA) also includes safe drinking water loan program appropriations.

Source: Wisconsin Department of Administration, State Controller's Office, *Annual Fiscal Report - Appendix,* October 2013 and October 2014.

STATE AND LOCAL PUBLIC DEBT, BY STATE
State Fiscal Years Ending Between July 1, 2011 and June 30, 2012

State	Debt Outstanding at End of Fiscal Year (in thousands)			Per Capita Debt Outstanding		Per Capita Interest on Debt		Interest as % of Debt	
	Total	State	Local	Amount	Rank	on Debt	Rank	of Debt	Rank
Alabama	$29,468,053	$8,719,430	$20,748,623	$6,116.90	39	$224.82	43	3.68%	45
Alaska	9,496,866	5,909,456	3,587,410	12,990.17	3	610.08	2	4.70	7
Arizona.	49,065,561	14,507,370	34,558,191	7,483.80	32	330.50	23	4.42	14
Arkansas	13,961,274	3,655,727	10,305,547	4,733.76	48	187.30	48	3.96	32
California	419,751,267	153,528,617	266,222,650	11,027.87	8	505.88	7	4.59	9
Colorado	51,394,950	15,999,530	35,395,420	9,899.43	14	482.65	9	4.88	3
Connecticut	42,827,380	31,965,511	10,861,869	11,915.15	4	542.11	5	4.55	11
Delaware	8,233,689	5,796,853	2,436,836	8,980.11	18	371.12	21	4.13	26
District of Columbia	11,603,815	—	11,603,815	18,272.57	—	814.93	—	4.46	—
Florida	146,921,567	38,171,049	108,750,518	7,590.78	30	313.00	29	4.12	27
Georgia.	55,784,670	13,400,514	42,384,156	5,624.02	44	242.85	40	4.32	17
Hawaii	14,025,010	8,398,012	5,626,998	10,069.90	13	393.35	14	3.91	36
Idaho	6,247,077	3,945,615	2,301,462	3,915.21	50	164.07	49	4.19	24
ILLINOIS	146,233,438	64,301,765	81,931,673	11,359.03	6	526.67	6	4.64	8
Indiana	49,563,134	22,511,518	27,051,616	7,581.21	31	322.32	27	4.25	18
IOWA	18,170,481	6,166,080	12,004,401	5,907.30	40	225.46	42	3.82	38
Kansas	26,685,406	6,860,094	19,825,312	9,246.61	16	390.93	16	4.23	20
Kentucky	42,490,577	15,103,515	27,387,062	9,693.38	15	464.95	10	4.80	5
Louisiana.	35,946,437	15,415,488	20,530,949	7,806.39	26	378.85	20	4.85	4
Maine	8,637,913	5,605,606	3,032,307	6,501.55	38	275.84	33	4.24	19
Maryland.	46,106,645	25,812,859	20,293,786	7,825.54	25	324.43	26	4.15	25
Massachusetts	96,187,096	79,523,608	16,663,488	14,451.56	2	609.38	3	4.22	21
MICHIGAN	76,351,858	30,823,672	45,528,186	7,724.18	27	303.83	30	3.93	35
MINNESOTA	48,445,971	13,230,223	35,215,748	9,003.80	17	391.05	15	4.34	15
Mississippi	14,584,466	7,194,251	7,390,215	4,884.06	47	200.83	47	4.11	28
Missouri	46,287,614	20,385,537	25,902,077	7,682.23	28	303.71	31	3.95	33
Montana	5,754,487	3,995,366	1,759,121	5,724.93	43	209.21	45	3.65	46
Nebraska	15,102,434	2,073,385	13,029,049	8,139.34	22	326.91	25	4.02	30
Nevada.	29,050,079	3,896,718	25,153,361	10,543.56	10	410.65	12	3.89	37
New Hampshire . . .	10,769,103	8,029,849	2,739,254	8,150.40	21	387.74	17	4.76	6
New Jersey.	102,885,609	64,851,557	38,034,052	11,591.44	5	402.26	13	3.47	50
New Mexico	16,506,168	7,550,084	8,956,084	7,918.17	24	275.87	32	3.48	49
New York	340,092,833	135,884,070	204,208,763	17,345.36	1	728.93	1	4.20	23
North Carolina	50,779,359	18,291,688	32,487,671	5,209.11	45	265.70	36	5.10	2
North Dakota.	4,744,078	2,083,611	2,660,467	6,760.79	37	254.46	38	3.76	43
Ohio	81,238,321	33,602,457	47,635,864	7,033.07	34	253.04	39	3.60	47
Oklahoma	18,789,825	9,979,234	8,810,591	4,922.59	46	223.10	44	4.53	12
Oregon	34,573,005	13,782,071	20,790,934	8,867.87	19	335.69	22	3.79	41
Pennsylvania	129,428,097	46,198,646	83,229,451	10,135.29	12	384.41	19	3.79	39
Rhode Island	11,933,562	9,211,790	2,721,772	11,336.83	7	603.59	4	5.32	1
South Carolina	40,394,742	14,854,263	25,540,479	8,553.46	20	386.37	18	4.52	13
South Dakota.	5,857,147	3,607,615	2,249,532	7,018.72	35	265.71	35	3.79	40
Tennessee	37,045,848	6,167,659	30,878,189	5,738.94	42	233.80	41	4.07	29
Texas	270,736,664	45,626,393	225,110,271	10,375.27	11	436.80	11	4.21	22
Utah	19,721,390	7,067,149	12,654,241	6,907.20	36	261.44	37	3.79	42
Vermont	4,574,540	3,390,961	1,183,579	7,305.96	33	270.08	34	3.70	44
Virginia.	65,331,590	27,785,849	37,545,741	7,973.66	23	320.13	28	4.01	31
Washington.	75,592,214	29,090,132	46,502,082	10,961.23	9	500.82	8	4.57	10
West Virginia.	10,923,194	7,306,756	3,616,438	5,884.35	41	205.48	46	3.49	48
WISCONSIN	43,601,566	22,995,708	20,605,858	7,616.14	29	330.40	24	4.34	16
Wyoming.	2,397,411	1,321,804	1,075,607	4,155.73	49	163.74	50	3.94	34
UNITED STATES	$2,942,295,481	$1,145,576,715	$1,796,718,766	$9,367.02		$398.15		4.25%	

Sources: U.S. Department of Commerce, U.S. Census Bureau, "2012 Census of Governments: State and Local Government Finances by Level of Government and by State", at: http://www.census.gov/govs/local/ [April 29, 2015] and "Annual Estimates of the Resident Population for the United States, Regions, States, and Puerto Rico: April 1, 2010 to July 1, 2014 (NST-EST2014-01)", at: http://www.census.gov/popest/data/state/totals/2014/index.html. Per capita amounts, percentages, and rankings calculated by Wisconsin Legislative Reference Bureau.

PUBLIC INDEBTEDNESS IN WISCONSIN
Outstanding State Indebtedness, May 31, 2015
(In Thousands)

Type of Debt[1]	Tax Supported Debt General Fund	Tax Supported Debt Segregated Funds[2]	Revenue Supported Debt[3]	Total
General Obligations – State of Wisconsin	$4,620,476	$1,232,912	$1,766,602	$7,619,360

[1]Amendment of the state constitution in April 1969 permitted direct state borrowing. Previously, debt was incurred through public, nonstock, nonprofit building corporations.

[2]Includes the Transportation Fund and certain administrative facilities for the Wisconsin Department of Natural Resources.

[3]Revenue supported debt includes debt that is issued with initial expectation that revenues and other proceeds from the operation of the programs or facilities financed will amortize the debt without recourse to the general fund. Includes dormitories, food service, and intercollegiate athletic facilities; certain facilities on the State Fair grounds; and capital equipment.

Source: Wisconsin Department of Administration, Division of Executive Budget and Finance, departmental data, July 2015.

Selected Data on State Indebtedness, 1970 – 2013

Calendar Year	Outstanding State Indebtedness (Dec. 31) Total[1]	Per Capita	As Percent of State Assessed Value	Annual Debt Limitation[1,2]	Actual Debt Incurred[1]	Debt as Percent of Limitation
1970	$646,414	$146.31	1.86%	$260,929	$156,810	60.1%
1975	1,078,215	235.47	1.84	439,124	217,600	49.6
1980	1,916,177	407.18	1.77	813,604	123,500	15.2
1985	2,410,628	507.93	1.96	922,661	440,955	47.8
1990	2,781,071	568.49	1.97	1,060,277	484,099	45.7
1995	3,305,471	643.46	1.64	1,511,536	368,322	24.4
2000	4,270,718	796.18	1.49	2,147,411	538,795	25.1
2001	4,452,626	824.26	1.42	2,343,628	485,645	20.7
2002	4,682,045	860.67	1.40	2,514,949	481,000	19.1
2003	4,794,398	876.17	1.33	2,705,327	499,030	18.5
2004	5,116,439	929.59	1.31	2,933,909	664,435	22.6
2005	5,445,615	983.67	1.27	3,209,502	571,990	17.8
2006	5,898,647	1,061.48	1.26	3,517,374	891,285	25.3
2007	5,893,590	1,052.05	1.18	3,734,403	483,280	12.9
2008	6,146,978	1,092.21	1.19	3,857,955	493,635	12.8
2009	6,481,078	1,146.08	1.27	3,839,340	542,765	14.1
2010	7,407,431	1,302.52	1.49	3,719,281	809,293	21.8
2011	7,878,628	1,379.55	1.62	3,651,482	896,260	24.5
2012	8,385,973	1,464.54	1.78	3,533,194	735,585	20.8
2013	8,344,531	1,453.24	1.78	3,506,269	642,295	18.3

[1]In thousands.

[2]An aggregate debt limit is derived for each calendar year through a formula specified in Section 18.05, Wisconsin Statutes.

Source: Wisconsin Department of Administration, Division of Executive Budget and Finance, departmental data, July 2015.

State Revenue Bond Indebtedness, May 31, 2015
(In Thousands)

Program Funded	Amount Authorized	Amount Issued*	Amount Outstanding
Student loans.	$295,000	$215,000	—
Veterans mortgage loans	280,000	90,055	—
Transportation facilities and highway projects	3,768,059	3,524,846	$1,872,485
Health education loans.	92,000	129,230	—
Property tax deferral loans.	10,000	—	—
Clean water	2,708,900	1,569,950	764,745
Petroleum environmental cleanup	436,000	387,550	139,100
TOTAL.	$7,589,959	$5,916,631	$2,776,330

Note: Revenue bonds are issued for purposes and amounts specifically authorized by the legislature. This debt is not a legal obligation of the state and is not subject to existing debt limitations.

*Amounts do not include refunding bonds, which do not count against the respective authorization.

Source: Wisconsin Department of Administration, Division of Executive Budget and Finance, departmental data, July 2015.

PUBLIC INDEBTEDNESS IN WISCONSIN–Continued
State Authority Indebtedness (In Thousands)

	Total Outstanding Indebtedness of State Authorities	
Wisconsin Health and Educational Facilities Authority.	$9,674,825*	(6/30/15)
Wisconsin Housing and Economic Development Authority	$1,314,288	(12/31/14)

*Preliminary amount; audit pending.
Source: Data provided by Authorities, June 2015.

Wisconsin Local Governments, 1965 – 2013 (In Millions)

	Calendar years, ending December 31							
	1965	1975	1985	1995	2005	2010	2012	2013
Counties	$192.5	$261.0	$532.5	$1,221.6	$1,753.7	$2,444.8	$2,282.1	$2,252.0
Cities.	548.1	598.7	1,320.4	2,082.8	3,718.5	4,468.2	4,465.1	4,551.7
Villages	22.5	69.8	227.6	418.7	1,098.0	1,440.1	1,502.2	1,492.6
Towns	9.2	26.2	75.2	193.8	308.5	374.6	334.3	323.3
TOTAL[1]	$772.3	$955.7	$2,155.7	$3,916.9	$6,878.8	$8,727.7	$8,583.8	$8,619.6

Wisconsin K-12 and Technical College Districts (In Millions)

	Fiscal years, ending June 30							
	1965	1975	1985	1995	2005	2010	2012	2013
School districts.	$336.6	$798.7	$448.7	$2,104.9	$5,335.5	$4,863.7	$4,443.4	$4,537.6
Technical College districts[2] . . .	—	97.2	64.7	192.8	461.4	510.2	655.3	797.6
TOTAL[1]	$336.6	$895.9	$513.4	$2,297.7	$5,796.9	$5,373.9	$5,098.7	$5,335.1

Note: Long-term indebtedness includes issues maturing more than one year after date of issue that constitute an obligation of the taxable property in the issuing district.
[1]Detail may not add to total due to rounding.
[2]Technical College districts (previously called Vocational, Technical and Adult Education districts) were included within the municipal bonding statute provisions by Chapter 47, Laws of 1967.
Sources: Wisconsin Department of Revenue, Bureau of Local Financial Assistance, *Indebtedness 1981* and previous issues; *County and Municipal Revenues and Expenditures, 2013* and previous issues; departmental data from Wisconsin Department of Revenue, Wisconsin Department of Public Instruction, and the Wisconsin Technical College System Board, June 2015.

ANNUAL APPROPRIATION OBLIGATIONS
Outstanding, May 31, 2015
(In Thousands)

	Amount Issued	Amount Outstanding
General Fund Annual Appropriation Bonds	$3,252,620	$3,115,935
Master Lease Obligations	240,230	115,576
TOTAL.	$3,492,850	$3,231,511

Note: Appropriation obligations are not general obligations of the state, and they do not constitute "public debt" as that term is used in the Wisconsin Constitution and in the Wisconsin Statutes. The payment of the principal of, and interest on appropriation obligations is subject to annual appropriation. The state is not legally obligated to appropriate any amounts for payment of debt service on the appropriation obligations, and if it does not do so, it incurs no liability to the owners of the appropriation obligations.
Source: Wisconsin Department of Administration, Division of Executive Budget and Finance, departmental data, July 2015.

WISCONSIN GENERAL PROPERTY TAX LEVIES
By Type of Property and Municipality, 2013

Type of Property	Towns	Villages	Cities	Totals
Real estate.	**$3,247,710,382**	**$1,747,043,250**	**$5,320,953,197**	**$10,315,706,829**
Residential	2,540,801,356	1,317,087,213	3,464,997,395	7,322,885,964
Commercial	188,210,506	351,231,666	1,635,142,923	2,174,585,094
Manufacturing	35,328,223	69,060,345	215,612,383	320,000,951
Forest lands	132,782,625	1,895,237	582,742	135,260,603
Agricultural	42,189,647	819,670	537,505	43,546,822
Ag forest	53,744,961	602,459	300,597	54,648,017
Undeveloped.	32,654,452	1,213,027	637,132	34,504,611
Other land and improvements	221,998,612	5,133,633	3,142,521	230,274,766
Personal Property	**41,339,015**	**45,936,069**	**202,540,299**	**289,815,383**
Furniture, fixtures, equipment	9,127,567	19,947,388	95,933,670	125,008,625
Machinery, tools, patterns	19,553,674	18,187,416	68,546,715	106,287,805
Boats and other watercraft.	182,422	19,751	227,437	429,609
All other personal property	12,475,353	7,781,514	37,832,477	58,089,344
Total general property taxes	**$3,289,049,379**	**$1,792,979,330**	**$5,523,493,363**	**$10,605,522,072**
Total state tax credit	272,362,508	127,957,412	347,080,089	747,400,009
TOTAL EFFECTIVE TAXES	**$3,016,686,871**	**$1,665,021,918**	**$5,176,413,274**	**$9,858,122,063**

Note: The sums of some columns and rows may differ slightly from the reported totals because the Department of Revenue truncates (rather than rounds) amounts under $1 for individual units of government.
Source: Wisconsin Department of Revenue, Division of State and Local Finance, Bureau of Local Government Services, *Town, Village, and City Taxes – 2013: Taxes Levied 2013 – Collected 2014*, 2014.

WISCONSIN GENERAL PROPERTY ASSESSMENTS AND TAX LEVIES
1900 – 2013

Calendar Year	Full Value Assessment of All Property Amount (in millions)	Percent Change	Total State and Local Property Taxes Levied Amount (in millions)	Percent Change	State Property Tax Relief Amount (in millions)	Average Full Value Tax Rate Per $1,000 Rate	Percent Change	Average Net Rate Per $1,000 After State Relief Rate	Percent Change
1900	$630	—	$19	—	—	$30.75	—	—	—
1910	2,743	—	31	—	—	11.18	—	—	—
1920	4,571	—	96	—	—	21.06	—	—	—
1930	5,896	—	121	—	—	20.49	—	—	—
1940	4,354	—	110	—	—	25.26	—	—	—
1950	9,201	—	226	—	—	24.52	—	—	—
1960	18,844	—	481	—	—	25.55	—	—	—
1970	34,790	—	1,179	—	$140	33.88	—	—	—
1980	108,480	—	2,210	—	309	20.37	—	—	—
1990	141,370	—	4,388	—	319	31.04	—	$28.78	—
2000	286,321	7.4%	6,605	6.7%	469	23.06	–0.7%	21.42	–0.2%
2001	312,484	9.1	7,044	6.7	469	22.54	–2.3	21.03	–1.8
2002	335,326	7.3	7,364	4.5	469	21.95	–2.6	20.55	–2.3
2003	360,710	7.6	7,687	4.4	469	21.31	–3.0	20.01	–2.7
2004	391,188	8.4	8,151	6.0	469	20.83	–2.2	19.63	–1.9
2005	427,934	9.4	8,327	2.2	469	19.45	–6.6	18.36	–6.5
2006	468,983	9.6	8,706	4.6	593	18.56	–4.6	17.29	–5.8
2007	497,920	6.2	9,251	6.3	672	18.57	0.1	17.22	–0.4
2008	514,394	3.3	9,667	4.5	747	18.79	1.2	17.34	0.6
2009	511,912	–0.5	10,106	4.5	747	19.74	5.0	18.28	5.4
2010	495,904	–3.1	10,365	2.6	747	20.90	5.9	19.39	6.1
2011	486,864	–1.8	10,385	0.2	747	21.33	2.1	19.79	2.1
2012	471,093	–3.2	10,470	0.8	747	22.22	4.2	20.63	4.3
2013	467,503	–0.8	10,606	1.3	747	22.68	2.1	21.08	2.2

Source: Wisconsin Department of Revenue, Division of State and Local Finance, Bureau of Property Tax, *Town, Village, and City Taxes – 2013: Taxes Levied 2013 – Collected 2014,* 2014, and previous issues. Percentages calculated by Wisconsin Legislative Reference Bureau.

TOTAL MUNICIPAL PROPERTY TAXES LEVIED IN WISCONSIN
1960 – 2013

Year Levied	Total Taxes (in millions)	Residential	Commercial	Manufacturing	Agricultural	Personal[1]	Other[2]
1960	$481.4	47.5%	13.5%	10.7%	11.2%	16.5%	0.6%
1965	664.1	48.4	14.4	10.3	10.6	15.8	0.6
1970	1,179.0	47.3	15.2	10.4	9.7	16.9	0.5
1975	1,601.3	50.5	16.8	5.7	10.1	16.2	0.7
1980	2,210.0	57.7	16.2	4.8	12.5	7.5	1.3
1985	3,203.5	58.9	17.7	4.7	12.4	4.8	1.6
1990	4,388.2	60.4	20.2	4.1	8.4	5.5	1.3
1995	5,738.9	64.8	18.8	3.6	6.7	4.9	1.1
1996	5,378.0	65.7	18.9	3.6	3.6	4.6	3.7
1997	5,635.9	66.2	18.7	3.6	3.3	4.5	3.7
1998	5,975.0	66.5	18.7	3.6	2.9	4.5	3.9
1999	6,190.9	67.3	18.8	3.7	2.7	3.5	4.0
2000	6,604.5	67.9	18.9	3.7	1.7	3.4	4.3
2001	7,043.7	68.1	19.0	3.6	1.6	3.4	4.4
2002	7,363.6	69.0	18.9	3.5	0.8	3.2	4.6
2003	7,687.3	69.7	18.8	3.4	0.6	2.9	4.7
2004	8,150.8	70.3	18.8	3.2	0.5	2.7	4.5
2005	8,326.7	71.0	18.7	3.0	0.5	2.6	4.2
2006	8,706.4	71.4	18.7	2.8	0.5	2.5	4.2
2007	9,250.3	71.4	18.9	2.7	0.4	2.4	4.2
2008	9,677.1	70.9	19.2	2.7	0.4	2.6	4.2
2009	10,105.7	70.4	19.6	2.7	0.4	2.6	4.3
2010	10,364.6	70.4	19.6	2.8	0.4	2.6	4.3
2011	10,384.8	70.2	19.7	2.8	0.4	2.5	4.3
2012	10,469.9	69.6	20.2	2.9	0.4	2.6	4.3
2013	10,605.5	69.0	20.5	3.0	0.4	2.7	4.3

[1]An exemption for "Line A" business property was phased in beginning in 1977. "Line A" property was completely exempted by 1981.

[2]Beginning in 1996, "Other" includes agricultural property not considered agricultural land for the purposes of use value assessment.

Sources: Wisconsin Department of Revenue, Division of State and Local Finance, *Town, Village, and City Taxes – 2013: Taxes Levied 2013 – Collected 2014,* 2014 and previous issues. For 1980 and earlier, *Property Tax, 1981* and previous issues. 1960 and 1965 data are from Wisconsin Department of Taxation. Percentages calculated by Wisconsin Legislative Reference Bureau. Row totals may not add to 100.0% due to rounding.

GENERAL PROPERTY ASSESSMENTS, TAXES AND RATES
By County, 2013

County	Full Value Assessment[1]	Total Property Tax[2]	State Property Tax Credit[3]	Average Full Value Tax Rate per $1,000[4] Gross	Net
Adams	$2,340,354,500	$53,228,758	$3,791,546	$22.74	$21.12
Ashland	1,191,563,400	26,668,139	1,754,376	22.38	20.91
Barron	3,579,455,200	77,430,277	5,769,019	21.63	20.02
Bayfield	2,538,481,500	38,975,140	2,900,270	15.35	14.21
Brown	18,231,223,100	410,595,694	28,772,020	22.52	20.94
Buffalo	1,005,292,300	22,158,176	1,523,245	22.04	20.53
Burnett	2,452,995,000	39,438,280	3,361,020	16.08	14.71
Calumet	3,446,863,600	77,905,296	5,256,684	22.60	21.08
Chippewa	4,653,303,700	90,145,843	6,571,163	19.37	17.96
Clark	1,848,724,600	42,453,583	2,642,428	22.96	21.53
Columbia	4,756,930,000	106,125,044	7,948,863	22.31	20.64
Crawford	1,064,664,500	28,229,419	1,660,946	26.51	24.95
Dane	49,755,216,400	1,206,541,569	87,867,888	24.25	22.48
Dodge	5,799,344,700	133,631,752	9,252,231	23.04	21.45
Door	6,987,135,000	93,212,063	5,745,023	13.34	12.52
Douglas	3,224,522,400	68,898,714	4,974,641	21.37	19.82
Dunn	2,613,740,200	65,390,258	4,392,577	25.02	23.34
Eau Claire	6,907,862,700	151,529,794	10,666,532	21.94	20.39
Florence	591,789,900	11,598,981	808,296	19.60	18.23
Fond du Lac	6,773,848,400	159,710,101	10,533,677	23.58	22.02
Forest	1,097,316,700	20,179,167	1,622,843	18.39	16.91
Grant	2,743,804,400	64,045,133	4,604,533	23.34	21.66
Green	2,608,297,600	66,076,084	4,625,068	25.33	23.56
Green Lake	2,217,552,300	44,036,315	3,101,801	19.86	18.46
Iowa	1,849,531,000	47,241,211	3,296,379	25.54	23.76
Iron	912,052,500	15,830,697	1,048,578	17.36	16.21
Jackson	1,471,277,300	32,558,276	2,047,691	22.13	20.74
Jefferson	6,186,989,100	141,509,063	10,433,214	22.87	21.19
Juneau	1,882,377,300	47,171,513	3,494,032	25.06	23.20
Kenosha	12,236,191,300	330,519,202	22,690,045	27.01	25.16
Kewaunee	1,454,689,200	31,918,343	2,089,663	21.94	20.51
La Crosse	8,063,740,700	205,371,549	13,702,887	25.47	23.77
Lafayette	1,012,837,600	26,068,317	1,735,844	25.74	24.02
Langlade	1,661,686,300	31,739,299	2,151,532	19.10	17.81
Lincoln	2,240,194,500	47,529,415	3,209,521	21.22	19.78
Manitowoc	5,115,896,200	116,130,176	7,633,261	22.70	21.21
Marathon	9,468,196,600	223,946,124	15,369,329	23.65	22.03
Marinette	3,618,807,800	68,123,014	5,210,224	18.82	17.38
Marquette	1,530,558,500	32,272,252	2,137,495	21.09	19.69
Menominee	288,848,100	6,559,709	474,581	22.71	21.07
Milwaukee	57,127,524,400	1,693,134,166	103,142,140	29.64	27.83
Monroe	2,823,710,500	67,256,763	3,771,157	23.82	22.48
Oconto	3,512,155,600	66,330,093	5,016,103	18.89	17.46
Oneida	6,633,464,400	95,942,501	7,723,775	14.46	13.30
Outagamie	13,042,231,600	290,744,531	19,463,377	22.29	20.80
Ozaukee	10,226,456,100	198,789,399	15,940,161	19.44	17.88
Pepin	550,723,900	13,152,787	1,022,376	23.88	22.03
Pierce	2,724,148,700	64,531,883	4,873,084	23.69	21.90
Polk	4,084,905,800	87,803,800	7,028,428	21.49	19.77
Portage	4,882,392,000	107,430,167	6,700,624	22.00	20.63
Price	1,408,916,000	28,159,218	2,025,602	19.99	18.55
Racine	13,438,849,400	333,246,009	22,656,216	24.80	23.11
Richland	1,037,181,300	23,034,072	1,559,914	22.21	20.70
Rock	9,351,401,300	248,468,196	14,952,863	26.57	24.97
Rusk	1,145,460,100	23,035,433	1,939,012	20.11	18.42
St. Croix	7,154,298,100	142,521,340	11,736,353	19.92	18.28
Sauk	6,442,658,700	136,962,683	9,178,348	21.26	19.83
Sawyer	3,373,194,400	42,624,667	3,642,883	12.64	11.56
Shawano	2,942,274,900	61,969,150	4,429,806	21.06	19.56
Sheboygan	8,526,701,100	197,644,228	13,933,381	23.18	21.55
Taylor	1,339,908,600	30,204,920	1,793,423	22.54	21.20
Trempealeau	1,833,518,100	43,619,697	2,890,561	23.79	22.21
Vernon	1,783,775,000	42,870,786	2,957,454	24.03	22.38
Vilas	6,666,485,900	75,855,315	6,729,292	11.38	10.37
Walworth	13,183,359,700	264,763,135	21,583,464	20.08	18.45
Washburn	2,362,255,200	40,726,588	3,261,712	17.24	15.86
Washington	12,619,779,200	243,206,941	19,301,239	19.27	17.74
Waukesha	47,217,366,700	910,360,648	78,766,776	19.28	17.61
Waupaca	3,801,204,500	89,072,249	5,746,955	23.43	21.92
Waushara	2,389,076,800	47,603,048	3,290,371	19.93	18.55
Winnebago	11,791,572,500	280,009,570	16,299,901	23.75	22.36
Wood	4,661,457,400	111,756,349	7,172,292	23.97	22.44
TOTAL	$467,502,564,000	$10,605,522,072	$747,400,009	$22.69	$21.09

[1]Reflects actual market value of all taxable general property, as determined by Wisconsin Department of Revenue independent of locally assessed values, which vary substantially from full value – from 77.29%* in Town of Curran, Jackson County, to 135.75% in Village of Dresser, Polk County. (* Jefferson County portion of Village of Lac LaBelle was 47.88%, but the population of that part of the village is only 1.) The value may reflect corrections for prior year errors.

[2]Includes taxes and special charges levied by schools, counties, cities, villages, towns, special purpose districts, and the State of Wisconsin. It does not include special assessments or other charges.

[3]Total amount of general property tax credit paid by the state to taxing districts and credited to taxpayers on their tax bills.

[4]A county's average tax rate per $1,000 of assessed valuation (determined by dividing total taxes by equalized value and multiplying by 1,000) is the preferred figure for comparison purposes, rather than the general local property tax rate because the average is based on full market value. Net tax rate per $1,000 reflects the effect of state property tax relief.

Source: Wisconsin Department of Revenue, Division of State and Local Finance, *Town, Village, and City Taxes – 2013: Taxes Levied 2013 – Collected 2014*, 2014.

HIGHLIGHTS OF TRANSPORTATION IN WISCONSIN

Roads — As of January 1, 2015, there were 115,212 miles of roads in Wisconsin. The total included 11,765 miles of state trunk highways, 19,867 miles of county trunk highways, and 81,828 miles of local roads. Seventy-nine percent (91,025 miles) of Wisconsin's road system is surfaced at bituminous grade or higher, with the remaining 21% being gravel or soil-surfaced, sealcoated, graded and drained, or unimproved.

Motor Vehicles and Drivers — Over the decades, the total number of motor vehicle registrations has increased from 819,718 in 1930 to 5,697,808 in 2014. Of 4,194,760 drivers licensed in 2014, 520,328 (12.4%) were 16-24 years old; 707,413 (16.9%) were 25-34 years old; 651,122 (15.5%) were 35-44 years old; 769,849 (18.4%) were 45-54 years old; and 751,271 (18.0%) were 55-64 years old. Of the drivers age 65 and older, 93,003 (2.2%) were 85 years and above.

In 2014, 119,736 single- or multi-vehicle traffic crashes were reported, including 451 fatal and 28,801 injury crashes. The 45-54-year-old age group had the highest percentage of drivers in crashes with 18.4%, followed by the 55-64-year-old age group with 17.9%. Of 345 drivers killed in fatal crashes, 323 were tested for blood alcohol content (BAC); 23 registered a BAC of 0.001 to 0.079 and 77 registered a BAC of 0.08 or above. Vehicle miles traveled in 2013 totaled 59.5 billion; the fatality rate for that year was 0.89 per 100 million vehicle miles, and the fatal crash rate was 0.83.

Mass Transit — As of January 2015, there were 18 urban bus systems operating in Wisconsin (12 publicly owned, 5 contracted, and 1 privately managed). There were 16 rural/intercity systems (11 publicly owned and 5 privately contracted). Shared-ride taxi service was available in 49 municipalities.

Statewide urban bus systems showed a decrease in usage in 2013 with 51 million revenue miles traveled and 74.7 million revenue passengers.

Air Carriers — In 2015, there were 662 airports operating in Wisconsin. Of these, 94 were publicly owned and 452 privately owned, 38 of which were open to the public. The remaining specialized facilities included heliports (100) and seaplane bases (16). In 2014, certificated air carriers carried 4,938,841 passengers and transported 119,620,236 pounds of cargo.

Railroads — From 1920 to 2013, the number of railroads operating in Wisconsin decreased from 35 to 9. Over the same period, railroad road mileage declined from 7,546 to 3,489 miles. Rail freight traffic rose from 9.1 billion ton-miles in 1920 to 28.7 billion ton-miles in 2013. Freight traffic revenue was $1.29 billion in 2013.

Harbors — In 2012, there were 9 active lake harbors on Lake Michigan and Lake Superior, which handled 39.4 million short tons of commodities. The Duluth-Superior harbor reported the greatest amount of commerce at 37.1 million short tons.

The following tables present selected data. Consult footnoted sources for more detailed information about transportation.

WISCONSIN AIRPORTS
By Type, 2008 – 2015

	Number of Airports					
Type of Airport	2008	2009	2010	2011	2012	2015*
Airports open to the public	130	130	131	133	133	132
Privately owned airports open to the public	(34)	(34)	(35)	(35)	(35)	(38)
Publicly owned airports	(96)	(96)	(96)	(98)	(98)	(94)
Private use airports	415	414	413	419	423	414
Heliports	146	148	148	148	149	100
Seaplane bases	27	27	27	28	29	16
TOTAL	718	719	719	728	734	662

*Data for 2015 is from new source. No data available for 2013 and 2014.

Sources: Federal Aviation Administration, *Airport Facilities Data,* and prior to 2015, Wisconsin Department of Transportation, Wisconsin Aviation Activity, at: http://www.faa.gov/airports/airport_safety/airportdata_5010/menu/ [May 2015].

WISCONSIN AIRPORT USAGE
BY CERTIFIED AIR CARRIERS, 2012 – 2014*

Airport (location)	2012		2013		2014	
	Passengers	Cargo (lbs.)	Passengers	Cargo (lbs.)	Passengers	Cargo (lbs.)
General Mitchell International (Milwaukee)	3,710,384	81,013,968	3,214,811	82,378,328	3,278,820	81,352,020
Dane County Regional (Madison) . . .	799,136	14,159,526	825,702	24,279,716	836,682	25,761,103
Austin Straubel International (Green Bay)	282,973	133,999	293,703	176,036	312,626	216,392
Outagamie County Regional (Appleton)	229,248	10,797,313	243,173	9,347,384	245,485	9,334,863
Central Wisconsin (Mosinee)	120,449	521,788	123,797	1,102,072	127,526	1,160,971
La Crosse Municipal (La Crosse) . . .	97,321	—	90,297	—	96,518	—
Chippewa Valley Regional (Eau Claire)	22,907	—	21,677	—	20,433	—
Rhinelander-Oneida County (Rhinelander)	11,119	871,615	18,819	718,607	20,751	1,794,887
TOTAL.	5,273,537	107,498,209	4,831,979	118,002,143	4,938,841	119,620,236

Note: Statistics have been revised from previous *Blue Book*.

*Wisconsin has eight scheduled air carrier airports. A certified air carrier is an airline that is registered by the Federal Aviation Administration.

Source: Wisconsin Department of Transportation, departmental data, May 2015.

RAILROAD MILEAGE, USAGE, AND REVENUE IN WISCONSIN
1920 – 2013

Year	No. of Railroads	Mileage Operated in Wisconsin[1]		Freight Traffic (in thousands)			Passenger Traffic (in thousands)		
		Road[2]	Track[3]	Tons	Ton-Miles[4]	Revenue (in thousands)	Passengers	Miles[5]	Revenue (in thousands)
1920	35	7,546	11,615	100,991	9,052,084	$92,826	20,188	960,569	$28,646
1930	27	7,231	11,583	83,672	6,908,656	78,747	4,799	466,154	14,071
1940	22	6,646	10,484	87,980	6,910,647	69,941	3,952	445,938	8,201
1950	20	6,337	10,000	121,576	10,850,178	141,762	5,575	646,353	14,933
1960	18	6,195	9,625	93,475	9,096,855	134,065	3,127	383,457	9,800
1970	15	5,965	9,127	97,130	13,432,055	191,764	1,463	138,572	4,264
1980[6]	21	5,192	7,990	101,008	14,727,522	453,977	174	1,122	54
1990	15	4,415	6,125	116,099	14,436,776	455,541	112	783	63
2000	12	3,548	4,956	151,573	21,321,266	580,678	NA	NA	NA
2001	13	3,699	5,107	158,881	25,922,949	700,258	NA	NA	NA
2002	12	3,688	5,095	NA	21,417,016	704,167	NA	NA	NA
2003	11	3,450	4,643	118,387	26,092,960	667,736	NA	NA	NA
2004	11	3,417	4,610	106,719	27,408,816	713,951	NA	NA	NA
2005	11	3,417	4,614	109,214	27,966,142	715,206	NA	NA	NA
2006	12	3,432	4,634	114,609	28,024,633	717,421	NA	NA	NA
2007	12	3,430	4,585	109,210	22,942,906	737,119	NA	NA	NA
2008	12	3,417	4,560	109,207	22,906,152	784,264	NA	NA	NA
2009	10	3,417	4,571	107,146	20,456,847	762,649	NA	NA	NA
2010	10	3,408	4,594	108,206	21,394,264	771,203	NA	NA	NA
2011	10	3,402	4,606	106,527	24,891,634	971,369	NA	NA	NA
2012	9	3,482	4,669	111,472	25,972,105	1,146,602	NA	NA	NA
2013	9	3,489	4,676	126,154	28,734,278	1,288,345	NA	NA	NA

NA – Not available.

[1] In order to avoid duplication, mileage shown is exclusive of trackage rights.

[2] Road mileage is the measurement of stone roadbed in miles.

[3] Track mileage is the measurement of track (2 steel rails) on roadbeds in miles.

[4] A ton-mile is the movement of one ton (2,000 pounds) of cargo over the distance of one mile.

[5] Passenger miles are the combination of the number of passengers carried on Wisconsin trains and the miles traveled by the passengers while within Wisconsin boundaries.

[6] Intercity passenger service operated by Amtrak after May 1, 1971.

Source: Office of the Wisconsin Commissioner of Railroads, departmental data, May 2015.

HIGHWAY MILEAGE, BY COUNTY AND SYSTEM
January 1, 2015

County	Total All Systems	State Trunk System	County Trunk System	Local Roads (City, Village, Town)	Other Roads (Parks, Forests)
Adams	1,453.98	91.45	226.80	1,135.73	—
Ashland	1,151.70	120.58	91.35	876.82	62.95
Barron	1,996.39	141.78	290.91	1,563.70	—
Bayfield	2,191.55	155.18	172.81	1,778.13	85.43
Brown	2,333.56	184.59	360.80	1,780.17	8.00
Buffalo	1,041.54	148.02	317.95	572.47	3.10
Burnett	1,573.36	106.36	220.05	1,205.09	41.86
Calumet	870.99	94.11	133.20	643.68	—
Chippewa	2,143.29	210.24	489.30	1,425.63	18.12
Clark	2,189.44	157.37	300.89	1,684.20	46.98
Columbia	1,738.59	277.96	357.28	1,103.35	—
Crawford	1,088.63	182.69	132.57	768.37	5.00
Dane	4,145.41	400.63	525.61	3,218.92	0.25
Dodge	2,067.01	237.97	540.56	1,278.31	10.17
Door	1,268.32	101.57	294.11	872.64	—
Douglas	2,093.58	161.36	336.99	1,498.00	97.23
Dunn	1,756.39	205.75	425.29	1,125.35	—
Eau Claire	1,591.66	150.06	420.79	1,002.87	17.94
Florence	527.20	66.84	49.12	378.27	32.97
Fond du Lac	1,789.28	201.58	384.33	1,203.37	—
Forest	1,080.43	152.41	109.06	777.26	41.70
Grant	2,128.05	259.02	310.87	1,558.16	—
Green	1,260.66	122.54	277.89	860.23	—
Green Lake	703.89	69.97	228.94	404.98	—
Iowa	1,317.32	169.72	364.71	782.89	—
Iron	817.16	114.00	66.89	552.50	83.77
Jackson	1,473.81	185.97	231.24	1,035.62	20.98
Jefferson	1,442.95	179.58	257.28	1,006.09	—
Juneau	1,536.08	191.96	234.18	1,094.13	15.81
Kenosha	1,095.22	116.51	257.56	721.15	—
Kewaunee	828.44	61.80	219.06	547.58	—
La Crosse	1,196.41	159.03	285.34	752.04	—
Lafayette	1,159.16	126.92	272.15	760.09	—
Langlade	1,157.54	143.36	271.09	735.42	7.67
Lincoln	1,322.21	155.51	270.73	868.72	27.25
Manitowoc	1,661.37	155.06	283.61	1,222.70	—
Marathon	3,377.86	276.97	614.42	2,479.99	6.48
Marinette	2,353.73	154.29	334.28	1,641.00	224.16
Marquette	860.00	87.11	237.24	535.58	0.07
Menominee	3,018.32	253.76	145.34	2,619.22	—
Milwaukee	1,645.39	238.26	344.35	1,061.08	1.70
Monroe	2,043.19	149.76	318.54	1,538.06	36.83
Oconto	1,719.26	159.30	171.22	1,351.28	37.46
Oneida	2,011.65	186.71	345.59	1,469.65	9.70
Outagamie	941.66	82.31	155.55	703.80	—
Ozaukee	462.47	48.52	154.72	259.23	—
Pepin	1,310.81	164.19	248.65	892.97	5.00
Pierce	1,987.70	159.14	331.37	1,486.20	10.99
Polk	1,899.67	157.36	433.97	1,308.34	—
Portage	1,440.34	155.14	220.05	1,050.03	15.12
Price	1,331.28	155.88	164.09	1,011.31	—
Racine	1,129.45	150.14	296.50	682.81	—
Richland	2,083.63	253.03	211.92	1,618.46	0.22
Rock	1,240.68	105.26	255.13	859.49	20.80
Rusk	1,937.60	204.16	337.79	1,392.21	3.44
St. Croix	1,825.44	220.75	307.30	1,292.39	5.00
Sauk	1,525.51	161.33	228.94	1,094.64	40.60
Sawyer	1,818.75	180.03	294.07	1,252.15	92.50
Shawano	1,561.31	166.46	449.22	945.63	—
Sheboygan	1,456.84	110.22	248.32	1,080.94	17.36
Taylor	1,366.39	176.31	292.04	889.20	8.84
Trempealeau	1,653.01	214.03	285.23	1,152.75	1.00
Vernon	1,649.77	136.27	204.17	1,133.50	175.83
Vilas	1,531.79	216.16	193.21	1,122.42	—
Walworth	1,414.43	137.10	198.72	982.75	95.86
Washburn	1,536.69	187.06	185.96	1,163.67	—
Washington	3,066.31	232.77	399.09	2,434.45	—
Waukesha	1,663.89	198.40	333.79	1,131.70	—
Waupaca	1,330.37	132.32	333.46	864.59	—
Waushara	1,572.40	168.75	220.14	1,183.51	—
Winnebago	1,792.58	185.97	324.39	1,269.61	12.61
Wood	458.99	40.73	36.51	79.05	302.70
STATE	115,211.73	11,765.40	19,866.59	81,828.29	1,751.45

Source: Wisconsin Department of Transportation, Division of Transportation Investment Management, departmental data, May 2015.

WISCONSIN ROAD MILEAGE, BY SYSTEM AND SURFACE TYPE
January 1, 2015

Type of Road System	Miles	Percent	Surface Type	Miles	Percent
State trunk highways.	11,765	10.2%	Bituminous or higher	91,025	79.0%
County trunk highways	19,867	17.2	Gravel or soil-surfaced.	16,587	14.4
City streets	13,813	12.0	Sealcoat	5,561	4.8
Village streets	6,093	5.3	Graded and drained	1,932	1.7
Town roads.	61,922	53.7	Unimproved	107	0.1
Park, forest, and other roads	1,751	1.5	TOTAL.	115,212	100.0%
TOTAL.	115,212	100.0%			

Source: Wisconsin Department of Transportation, Division of Transportation Investment Management, departmental data, May 2015.

MOTOR VEHICLES IN WISCONSIN, BY TYPE
1930 – 2014

Fiscal Year (ending June 30)	Total	Autos	Trucks*	Trailers, Semitrailers	Motor Homes	Buses	Motor-cycles	Mopeds
1930	819,718	700,251	115,883	—	—	554	3,030	—
1935	722,797	597,197	116,912	5,634	—	498	2,556	—
1940	874,652	741,583	123,742	5,144	—	675	3,508	—
1945	828,425	676,978	139,591	6,484	—	1,489	3,883	—
1950	1,157,221	921,194	209,083	14,124	—	2,465	10,355	—
1955	1,369,636	1,108,084	227,367	21,643	—	3,337	9,205	—
1960	1,598,693	1,303,679	246,353	31,502	—	5,184	11,975	—
1965	1,867,223	1,517,397	269,771	44,017	—	7,218	28,820	—
1970	2,205,662	1,762,681	317,096	64,065	—	8,178	53,642	—
1975	2,737,164	2,096,694	425,854	91,609	—	11,897	111,110	—
1980	3,417,748	2,509,904	558,840	102,256	17,071	13,775	205,786	10,116
1985	3,372,029	2,310,024	765,852	72,289	17,195	10,325	176,023	20,321
1990	3,834,608	2,456,175	1,045,583	123,061	21,095	15,081	149,268	24,345
1995	4,285,753	2,464,358	1,391,374	207,042	22,554	15,593	161,762	23,070
2000	4,703,294	2,405,408	1,813,385	214,344	24,427	15,587	160,920	17,977
2005	5,226,584	2,347,042	2,216,863	342,879	22,598	12,478	249,979	34,745
2006	5,326,157	2,361,853	2,281,988	364,024	22,406	13,174	246,307	36,405
2007	5,428,629	2,357,616	2,333,538	396,229	21,147	13,516	266,036	40,547
2008	5,499,872	2,381,911	2,370,655	410,737	20,209	10,736	260,220	45,404
2009	5,532,953	2,340,991	2,396,470	417,031	20,039	12,685	291,164	54,573
2010	5,525,794	2,333,029	2,416,295	426,092	19,615	13,376	269,316	48,071
2011	5,564,794	2,300,243	2,445,056	434,782	18,792	13,745	296,808	55,368
2012	5,551,411	2,274,596	2,473,072	447,195	18,535	14,169	274,553	49,291
2013	5,671,185	2,276,007	2,548,029	460,542	18,187	10,598	301,477	56,345
2014	5,697,808	2,255,966	2,609,402	479,237	18,584	12,615	275,120	46,884

*"Trucks" includes minivans and sport utility vehicles.

Sources: Wisconsin Secretary of State, *Biennial Report – 1928-30;* Wisconsin Highway Commission, *Biennial Reports – 1933-35, 1938-40*; Wisconsin Motor Vehicle Department, *Wisconsin Motor Vehicle Registrations – Fiscal Years 1944-45 through 1964-65*; Wisconsin Department of Transportation, *Wisconsin Motor Vehicle Registrations – Fiscal Year 1979-80, 1980,* and previous issues, and *Wisconsin Transportation Facts* (periodical); departmental data, March 2015.

WISCONSIN MOTOR VEHICLE CRASHES
Statistical Summary, 2001 – 2014

Year	Total Licensed Drivers	Crashes[1] Total	Crashes[1] Fatal	Crashes[1] Injury	Persons Killed	Persons Injured	Miles Traveled (in millions)	Fatality Rate[2]	Fatal Crash Rate[3]
2001	3,835,549	125,403	684	39,358	764	58,279	57,266	1.33	1.19
2002	3,839,930	129,072	723	39,634	805	57,776	58,745	1.37	1.23
2003	3,933,924	131,191	748	39,413	836	56,882	59,617	1.40	1.25
2004	3,993,348	128,308	714	38,451	784	55,258	60,398	1.31	1.18
2005	4,049,450	125,174	700	37,515	801	53,462	60,018	1.33	1.17
2006	4,066,273	117,877	659	35,296	712	50,236	59,401	1.20	1.11
2007	4,075,764	125,123	655	36,048	737	50,676	59,493	1.24	1.10
2008	4,079,562	125,103	542	33,766	587	46,637	57,462	1.02	0.94
2009	4,085,833	109,991	488	29,907	542	41,589	58,157	0.93	0.84
2010	4,114,622	108,808	517	29,380	562	40,889	59,420	0.95	0.87
2011	4,142,823	112,516	515	28,965	565	40,144	58,554	0.96	0.88
2012	4,171,428	109,385	535	28,453	601	39,370	59,087	1.02	0.91
2013	4,188,194	118,254	491	28,474	527	39,872	59,484	0.89	0.83
2014[4]	4,194,760	119,736	451	28,801	498	39,701	—	—	—

[1]A motor vehicle crash is defined as an event caused by a single variable or chain of variables. The property damage threshold for a reportable crash was raised from $500 to $1,000, effective January 1, 1996.

[2]Per 100-million vehicle miles traveled.

[3]Per 1,000 licensed drivers.

[4]2014 data not available.

Source: Wisconsin Department of Transportation, *2012 Wisconsin Traffic Crash Facts,* and previous issues; departmental data, June 2015.

Fatal Crashes on Wisconsin Highways and Roads, 2001 – 2014

Year	Total	Interstate	State	County	Local
2001	684	35	286	167	196
2002	723	44	310	171	198
2003	748	46	317	174	211
2004	714	47	298	155	214
2005	700	42	284	163	211
2006	659	34	294	128	203
2007	655	43	259	143	210
2008	542	32	225	119	166
2009	488	27	221	93	147
2010	517	32	230	105	150
2011	515	34	236	113	132
2012	535	26	242	103	164
2013	491	26	225	104	136
2014	451	23	198	85	145

Source: Wisconsin Department of Transportation, *2012 Wisconsin Traffic Crash Facts,* and previous issues; departmental data, June 2015.

Drivers in Fatal Crashes – Age and BAC of Drivers Killed, 2014

Age of Drivers	All Drivers	Drivers Killed	Tests of Drivers Killed[1] Total	Tests of Drivers Killed[1] Negative	Tests of Drivers Killed[1] Positive	Blood Alcohol Concentration (BAC) 0.001-0.079	Blood Alcohol Concentration (BAC) Over 0.08
15 years	1	0	0	0	0	0	0
16 years	8	4	3	3	0	0	0
17 years	9	3	3	2	1	0	1
18 years	18	10	10	7	3	0	3
19 years	23	10	9	8	1	0	1
20 years	7	2	2	2	0	0	0
21 years	18	13	13	10	3	1	2
22 years	21	12	11	7	4	1	3
23 years	18	11	11	7	4	0	4
24 years	19	10	10	5	5	1	4
25-34 years	143	64	63	28	35	8	27
35-44 years	93	42	40	24	16	3	13
45-54 years	104	45	43	26	17	4	13
55-64 years	113	53	49	42	7	2	5
65-74 years	54	26	26	22	4	3	1
75-84 years	32	27	20	20	0	0	0
85 and over	17	13	10	10	0	0	0
TOTAL[2]	708	345	323	223	100	23	77

Note: Drivers include motorcycle and moped drivers.

[1]Blood Alcohol Concentration (BAC) measures the level of alcohol in a person's bloodstream. The prohibited BAC for Operating While Intoxicated (OWI) is 0.08%.

[2]Includes 10 of unknown age.

Source: Wisconsin Department of Transportation, departmental data, June 2015.

WISCONSIN MOTOR VEHICLE CRASHES–Continued
Motorcycle Crashes, 2001 – 2014

Year	Total Registered Cycles	Cycle Crashes Total	Fatal	Personal Injury	Property Damage	Cyclist Fatalities* Total	No Helmet or Unknown	Helmet
2001	201,143	2,285	69	1,928	288	70	53	14
2002	198,495	2,184	73	1,794	317	78	59	15
2003	225,181	2,512	98	2,099	315	100	74	24
2004	221,982	2,423	81	2,015	327	80	60	18
2005	239,938	2,680	91	2,277	312	92	69	22
2006	291,534	2,441	88	2,065	288	93	69	24
2007	322,505	2,788	102	2,331	355	106	70	26
2008	327,938	2,829	86	2,318	425	87	66	19
2009	355,487	2,345	82	1,912	351	82	51	27
2010	343,878	2,426	97	1,959	370	98	72	23
2011	361,893	2,331	79	1,877	375	80	69	5
2012	340,268	2,630	107	2,110	413	112	82	25
2013	367,474	2,150	84	1,705	361	83	60	20
2014	337,637	2,101	63	1,696	342	67	43	21

*Number of cyclists killed includes both drivers and passengers.

Source: Wisconsin Department of Transportation, *2012 Wisconsin Traffic Crash Facts,* and previous issues; departmental data, June 2015.

Drivers Involved in Crashes, By Age Group, 2014

Age of Drivers	Total Licensed Drivers Number	Age Group as Percent of Total Drivers	Drivers Involved in Crashes* Number	Percent of Drivers in Age Group Involved in Crashes	Drivers by Type of Crash* Fatal	Injury	Property Damage
14 years and under . . .	0	0.0%	80	—	0	32	48
15 years	0	0.0	202	—	1	49	152
16 years	33,389	0.8	3,680	11.0%	8	984	2,688
17 years	47,253	1.1	4,531	9.6	9	1,188	3,334
18 years	53,976	1.3	4,832	9.0	18	1,355	3,459
19 years	55,702	1.3	4,782	8.6	23	1,353	3,406
20 years	59,653	1.4	4,836	8.1	7	1,358	3,471
21 years	63,081	1.5	4,843	7.7	18	1,370	3,455
22 years	65,894	1.6	4,957	7.5	21	1,378	3,558
23 years	69,294	1.7	4,870	7.0	18	1,317	3,535
24 years	72,086	1.7	4,628	6.4	19	1,292	3,317
25-34 years.	707,413	16.9	37,490	5.3	143	10,252	27,095
35-44 years.	651,122	15.5	28,718	4.4	93	7,735	20,890
45-54 years.	769,849	18.4	29,438	3.8	104	7,985	21,349
55-64 years.	751,271	17.9	23,133	3.1	113	6,240	16,780
65-74 years.	468,247	11.2	11,346	2.4	54	3,193	8,099
75-84 years.	233,527	5.6	5,106	2.2	32	1,479	3,595
85 and over.	93,003	2.2	1,502	1.6	17	426	1059
Unknown.	0	0.0	17,823	—	10	2,340	15,473
TOTAL.	4,194,760	100.2%	196,797	NA	708	51,326	144,763

NA – Not applicable.

*Figure indicates the number of times a driver in this age group was involved in a crash. If a driver had more than one crash, the driver would be counted more than once.

Source: Wisconsin Department of Transportation, departmental data, June 2015.

WISCONSIN MOTOR VEHICLE CRASHES—Continued
Possible Contributing Circumstances, 2014

Circumstance by category	All Crashes				Urban Crashes				Rural Crashes			
	Total	Fatal	Injury	Property Damage	Total	Fatal	Injury	Property Damage	Total	Fatal	Injury	Property Damage
DRIVER												
Inattentive driving	22,388	69	6,939	15,380	14,156	12	4,168	9,976	8,232	57	2,771	5,404
Failure to control	19,326	178	5,755	13,393	8,133	37	2,067	6,029	11,192	141	3,688	7,363
Failure to yield right-of-way	17,964	77	6,470	11,417	13,414	30	4,728	8,656	4,550	47	1,742	2,761
Speed too fast for conditions	14,716	67	3,643	11,006	5,966	13	1,353	4,600	8,750	54	2,290	6,406
Following too closely	10,312	7	3,170	7,135	7,634	0	2,349	5,285	2,678	7	821	1,850
Driver condition	5,285	61	2,355	2,869	2,629	17	990	1,622	2,656	44	1,365	1,247
Disregarded traffic control	4,419	29	1,978	2,412	3,493	9	1,561	1,923	926	20	417	489
Improper turn	2,918	4	541	2,373	2,125	0	354	1,771	793	4	187	602
Unsafe backing	2,934	1	182	2,751	1,987	0	124	1,863	947	1	58	888
Exceeding speed limit	2,584	91	1,124	1,369	1,558	39	651	868	1,026	52	473	501
Left of center	1,997	50	761	1,186	699	10	197	492	1,298	40	564	694
Improper overtake	1,750	8	364	1,378	1,098	2	190	906	652	6	174	472
Physically disabled	111	2	42	67	62	2	27	33	49	0	15	34
Other	4,966	28	1,283	3,655	3,555	13	903	2,639	1,411	15	380	1,016
HIGHWAY												
Snow/ice/wet	41,031	138	9,743	31,150	22,394	29	5,289	17,076	18,637	109	4,454	14,074
Visibility obscured	1,355	11	454	898	777	4	266	509	578	7	188	389
Construction zone	1,767	11	430	1,326	1,188	4	253	931	579	7	177	395
Loose gravel	400	5	235	160	82	1	52	29	318	4	183	131
Other debris	476	1	98	377	192	0	45	147	284	1	53	230
Narrow shoulder	231	2	54	175	71	0	3	68	160	2	51	107
Rough pavement	142	1	60	81	80	1	37	42	62	0	23	39
Low shoulder	76	0	31	45	13	0	5	8	63	0	26	37
Soft shoulder	115	0	42	73	10	0	3	7	105	0	39	66
Debris from prior crash	73	0	33	39	24	0	7	17	49	0	26	22
Sign obscured or missing	40	0	20	20	23	0	12	11	17	0	8	9
Narrow bridge	25	0	10	15	6	0	0	6	19	0	10	9
Other	837	5	228	604	455	2	96	357	382	3	132	247
VEHICLE												
Tires	1,365	10	361	994	546	1	138	407	819	9	223	587
Brakes	1,162	2	395	765	811	0	271	540	351	2	124	225
Steering	443	0	145	298	277	0	90	187	166	0	55	111
Other disabled	141	2	43	96	84	2	31	51	57	0	12	45
Head lamps	107	2	46	59	81	0	38	43	26	2	8	16
Suspension	108	1	32	75	45	0	12	33	63	1	20	42
Turn signals	90	0	31	58	48	0	21	27	42	0	10	31
Disabled prior to crash	33	0	11	22	16	0	5	11	17	0	6	11
Tail lamps	35	1	12	22	8	0	2	6	27	1	10	16
Stop lamps	40	0	12	27	21	0	7	14	19	0	5	13
Mirrors	28	0	5	23	17	0	3	14	11	0	2	9
Other	1,375	6	223	1,146	664	2	115	547	711	4	108	599

Note: Numbers represent the number of times a possible contributing circumstance was cited and not the number of accidents.

Source: Wisconsin Department of Transportation, departmental data, June 2015.

MASS TRANSIT SYSTEMS IN WISCONSIN, BY TYPE
January 2015

Urban Bus	Rural/Commuter Bus	Shared-Ride Taxi[1]	
Appleton	Bay Area Rural Transit	Baraboo	Platteville
Beloit	Dunn County	Beaver Dam	Plover
Eau Claire	Kenosha County[2]	Berlin	Portage
Fond du Lac	Manitowoc[5]	Black River Falls	Prairie du Chien
Green Bay	Marshfield Shuttle[2]	Chippewa Falls	Prairie du Sac/Sauk City
Janesville	Menominee Regional Transit	Clark County/Neillsville	Reedsburg
Kenosha	Merrill[5]	Clintonville	Rhinelander
La Crosse	Oneida Indian Reservation	Door County	Rice Lake
Madison	Ozaukee County Express[2]	Edgerton	Richland Center
Milwaukee County[2]	Racine Commuter[2]	Fort Atkinson	Ripon
Monona[2]	Rusk County	Grant County	River Falls
Oshkosh	Sauk County	Hartford	Shawano
Racine[3]	Sawyer County	Jefferson	Stoughton
Sheboygan	Stevens Point[5]	La Crosse County	Sun Prairie
Superior[4]	Verona	Lake Mills	Tomah
Waukesha (city)[2]	Washington County Express[2]	Marinette	Viroqua/Westby
Waukesha County[2]		Marshfield	Washington County
Wausau		Mauston	Watertown
		Medford	Waupaca
		Monroe	Waupun
		New Richmond	West Bend
		Onalaska	Whitewater
		Ozaukee County	Wisconsin Rapids

[1]Taxi services are privately contracted except for Grant County, the City of Hartford, and Rice Lake, where they are publicly owned and operated.

[2]Privately contracted. (Note: The private service in Waukesha County is an inter-urban service. Waukesha (city) and Waukesha (county) have merged to form Waukesha Metro Transit.)

[3]Privately managed.

[4]Contracted with Duluth Transit Authority.

[5]Moved to "rural" funding tier under Wisconsin Department of Transportation's criteria for service areas of less than 50,000 in population.

Source: Wisconsin Department of Transportation, Division of Transportation Investment Management, departmental data, February 2015.

WISCONSIN URBAN TRANSIT SYSTEMS
USAGE AND REVENUE, 1950 – 2013
(In Thousands)

Year	Revenue Miles	Revenue Passengers	Operating Revenue*
1950	53,362	288,996	$22,692
1955	42,807	169,129	23,134
1960	34,950	130,299	20,665
1965	32,330	110,979	20,457
1970	28,371	80,172	22,078
1975	26,119	63,587	22,454
1980	33,943	88,756	29,631
1985	31,829	79,540	39,635
1990	33,685	78,215	39,594
1995	30,734	71,875	50,171
2000	42,447	89,821	58,785
2001	46,755	87,729	60,299
2002	48,322	84,874	64,263
2003	47,753	81,650	61,868
2004	46,696	81,812	65,621
2005	52,163	83,545	67,628
2006	51,700	83,913	72,896
2007	51,748	81,229	77,236
2008	52,439	82,953	83,263
2009	52,488	77,510	82,570
2010	52,579	74,717	87,288
2011	52,316	77,533	82,640
2012	51,214	75,290	83,005
2013	50,973	74,694	83,522

*As recognized by the Wisconsin Department of Transportation.

Sources: Wisconsin Department of Transportation, Division of Transportation Assistance, Bureau of Transit, *Wisconsin Urban Bus System Annual Report 1989*, and previous issues; departmental data, February 2015.

WISCONSIN HARBOR COMMERCE – 2012

Harbors[1]	Total Tonnage[2]	Crude Inedible Materials (except fuels)	Coal and Lignite	Primary Manufactured Goods	Food and Farm Products	Petroleum and Petroleum Products	Chemicals and Related Products	Manufactured Equipment, Machinery, and Products	Unknown
LAKE SUPERIOR									
Duluth-Superior	34,672,105	19,559,188	13,833,926	302,716	923,089	19	34,553	11,394	7,220
Ashland	2,770	—	—	—	—	—	—	—	2,770
Bayfield	8,437	520	—	750	—	669	—	6,498	—
La Pointe	6,417	—	—	—	—	669	—	5,748	—
LAKE MICHIGAN									
Milwaukee	2,267,094	822,070	499,221	880,906	59	60,458	—	2,140	2,240
Green Bay	1,958,244	870,086	596,087	370,757	—	111,352	9,258	704	—
Menominee[3]	233,785	70,331	—	161,778	—	—	—	1,615	61
Manitowoc	246,079	4,005	35,336	206,738	3	—	—	—	—
Detroit Harbor[4]	8,613	458	—	—	—	1,593	—	—	6,559
TOTAL	39,403,544	21,326,658	14,964,570	1,923,645	923,151	174,760	43,811	28,099	18,850

Note: Tonnage reported in short tons. One short ton equals 2,000 lbs.

[1]Harbors with reported commerce.

[2]Detail may not add due to rounding.

[3]Includes tonnage handled at Marinette, Wisconsin.

[4]Washington Island.

Source: U.S. Army Corps of Engineers, Navigation Data Center, *Waterborne Commerce Statistics Center, Waterborne Commerce of the United States*, Calendar Year 2012, Part 3, at:
http://www.navigationdatacenter.us/wcsc/wcsc/webpub12/webpubpart-3.htm [June 2015].

Political Parties

9

Wisconsin political parties: state organizations and current party platforms

Edward Blake

(Wisconsin Veterans Museum)

POLITICAL PARTY ORGANIZATION IN WISCONSIN

What Is a Political Party?

A political party is a private, voluntary organization of people with similar political beliefs that vies with other parties for control of government. Political parties help voters select their government officials and create a consensus on the basic principles that direct governmental activities and processes.

Political parties in the United States have traditionally provided an organized framework for the orderly performance of several basic political tasks necessary to representative democracy. Parties act to:

- Provide a stable institution for building coalitions based on shared principles and priorities.
- Recruit and nominate candidates for elective and appointive offices in government.
- Promote the election of the party's slate of candidates.
- Guard the integrity of election procedures and vote canvassing.
- Educate the voters by defining issues, taking policy positions, and formulating programs.

U.S. parties offer a marked contrast to the party apparatus in other nations. In many parts of the world, political parties begin with defined ideologies and programs. Their members are recruited on the basis of these ideas, with little room for disagreement within the ranks. In other cases, parties represent regional interests or ethnic groups.

By contrast, parties in the United States are loosely organized groups reflecting a broad spectrum of interests. They are truly populist parties in the sense that they accommodate diversity and are instruments of party activists at the grass roots level. Political ideology, as stated in a party's national platform, is formulated first at the local level and then refined through debate and compromise at meetings representing successively larger geographic areas.

Depending on the time, place, and circumstances, political party labels in the United States may have widely different meanings, and within a single party there may be room for members whose ideologies span a wide political spectrum. Individual Republicans or Democrats, for instance, are often further identified as "liberal", "conservative", "right-wing", "left-wing", or "moderate".

Despite the diversity within a party, specific philosophies are generally associated with the various political parties. In the public's perception, the name of a particular party conjures up a surprisingly distinct set of economic, social, and political principles.

Political Parties in Wisconsin

Throughout its history, the United States has operated with a two-party political structure, rather than single-party or multiparty systems found elsewhere. Although minor parties have always been a part of American politics, few have gained the support necessary to challenge the two dominant parties at the national level. Those that did lasted only briefly, with the predominant exception of the Republican Party, which replaced the Whig Party in the 1850s. The same cannot be said of politics on the state level. In Wisconsin, for example, the Socialist Party regularly sent one or more representatives to the legislature between 1911 and 1937, and the Progressive Party was influential between 1933 and 1947, capturing a plurality of both houses of the 1937 Legislature. Third parties were relatively quiet in Wisconsin in the 1950s, but the last 30 years have seen more activity with more parties officially recognized on the ballot.

Under Wisconsin law, a "recognized political party" is a political party that qualifies for a separate ballot or column on the ballot, based on receiving at least 1% of the votes for a statewide office at the previous November election or through acquiring the required number of petition signatures (10,000 electors, including at least 1,000 electors residing in each of at least three separate congressional districts). At the beginning of 2015, Wisconsin had five recognized political parties: Constitution, Democratic, Green, Libertarian, and Republican.

The Wisconsin Statutes define a political party in Section 5.02 (13) as a state committee that is legally registered with the Government Accountability Board and "all county, congressional, legislative, local and other affiliated committees authorized to operate under the same name".

It must be a body "organized exclusively for political purposes under whose name candidates appear on a ballot at any election".

The delegates from the political party's local units meet in an annual state convention to draft or amend the party's state platform (a statement of its principles and objectives), select national committee members, elect state officers, consider resolutions, and conduct other party business. Every four years, party delegates from throughout the United States meet in a national convention to nominate their candidates for president and vice president and to adopt a national platform for the next four years. In Wisconsin, the slates of national convention delegates are usually based on the April presidential preference primary vote.

Statutory and Voluntary Organizations

Wisconsin law provides that each major political party must have certain local officers and committees, but over the years, these statutory organizations have been merged within the voluntary party organizations that are governed by their own constitutions and bylaws. The actual power is found in the voluntary structures.

In the case of the major parties, voluntary organizations are composed of dues-paying members, who are affiliated with Wisconsin chapters of the national political parties. Third parties vary in the amount of regional autonomy and/or national control allowed. Given minor organizational differences, voluntary parties operate to tend to their party's interests, collect money to finance campaigns, maintain cooperation between the various county and congressional district organizations, and act as liaison with national parties. (Currently recognized parties and their voluntary organizations are discussed in the party descriptions that follow this introduction.)

The History of Wisconsin's Political Parties

In *How Wisconsin Voted,* Professor James R. Donoghue divided Wisconsin's political history into four eras. From statehood in 1848 until 1855, the Democratic Party was the dominant political party, and the Whig Party provided major opposition. This was a continuation of the party alignment that had prevailed during the state's territorial period.

The second era was one of Republican domination from 1856 to 1900. The birth of the national Republican Party is attributed to a meeting in Ripon, Wisconsin, in 1854. Its founding was based on the conditions and events that eventually led to the Civil War, and within Wisconsin these same circumstances contributed to the rapid growth of the Republican Party and the demise of the Whigs. The second era ended at the turn of the century with the election of Governor Robert M. La Follette.

The third era, from 1900 to 1945, was a time of great stress and change, encompassing the Great Depression and World Wars I and II. Until 1932, the major political battles usually occurred not between two parties, but between two factions of the Republican Party – the conservative "stalwart" Republicans and the "progressive" (La Follette) Republicans. The Democratic Party was in eclipse, and election contests tended to be decided in Republican primary elections. This period marked the high point of third party influence in Wisconsin.

The progressive faction formally split from the Republicans to form its own party in 1934. The new Progressive Party won gubernatorial elections in 1936 and 1942 and a plurality in both houses of the legislature in 1936. Declining popularity, however, led to its dissolution in 1946, and Progressive Party leadership urged its members and supporting voters to return to the Republican Party. The period from 1900 to 1937 was also the time of greatest strength for the Socialists.

The fourth era, from 1945 to the present, witnessed a realignment of the major parties. A resurgence of the Democratic Party ended the long Republican domination, turning the state to a more balanced and competitive two-party system. In the late 1940s, some former Progressives, Socialists, and others began moving into a moribund Democratic Party. This influx both revitalized the party and made it more liberal. In the following decade, the Democrats worked at uniting their party and building their strength at the polls. Meanwhile, the conservative faction solidified its control of the Republican Party with the departure of more liberal-minded Progressives and addition of conservative Democrats fleeing their former party as it became more liberal.

In the years following World War II, the resurgent Democratic Party began seriously challenging the majority Republicans. Steady Democratic growth culminated in the 1957 election of William Proxmire to the U.S. Senate, the first "new" Democrat to win a major statewide election, followed by the election of Gaylord Nelson as governor in 1958. These elections marked the emergence on Wisconsin's political scene of a Democratic Party fully capable of competing successfully with the long dominant Republicans for public office. During this period, third party and independent candidates usually failed to garner any significant support on a statewide level.

The hallmark of contemporary Wisconsin politics is a highly competitive, two-party, issue-oriented system. At the beginning of the 1995 session, Republicans gained control of both houses for the first time since 1969. In 1993, 1995, and 1997, the majority party in the senate shifted during the session. Democrats controlled the senate in 1999 and 2001, while Republicans retained the control of the assembly they had won in the 1994 elections. For the first time since 1982, a Democrat was elected governor in November 2002.

Republicans controlled both the senate and assembly under a Democratic governor from 2003 to 2006. In 2006, Democrats won a majority in the senate. In 2008, they took control of the assembly for the first time since 1994. At the beginning of the 2009 session, Democrats controlled the governor's office, senate, and assembly for the first time since 1986. In 2010, a Republican governor was elected and control of the senate and assembly reverted to the Republicans.

Of the state's major elected partisan officers in January 2015, the Republicans held the positions of governor, lieutenant governor, attorney general, and state treasurer, as well as one U.S. Senate seat, five of the eight congressional seats, and majorities in the state senate and assembly. Democrats filled the position of secretary of state, and held one U.S. Senate seat and three congressional seats.

CONSTITUTION PARTY OF WISCONSIN
July 2015

Headquarters

State Headquarters: P.O. Box 070344, Milwaukee 53207-1918.
Telephone: (877) 201-2441.
State Internet Address: http://wisconsinconstitutionparty.com
State E-mail: thecpowmessenger@gmail.com
National Office: P.O. Box 1782, Lancaster, PA 17608.
National Internet Address: http://www.constitutionparty.com/

State Committee – Officers

Chairman: ANDREW ZUEKLE, Ripon.
Vice Chairman: JERRY BROITZMAN, Milwaukee.
Chairman of Committees: NIGEL BROWN, Janesville.
Secretary: S. KENT STEFFKE, Milwaukee.
Treasurer: RALPH DENSON, Milwaukee.
Parliamentarian: vacancy.

State Committee – Congressional District Representatives

1st District
vacancy
2nd District
vacancy
3rd District
vacancy
4th District
Janice Hood, Milwaukee

5th District
Crispian Trewhella, Richfield
6th District
Dino Bohlman, Eden
Jose Figueroa, Waldo
7th District
Larry Oftedahl, Barron
8th District
Mark Gabriel, Appleton

Source: Constitution Party of Wisconsin

Membership. Individual membership in the Constitution Party of Wisconsin is based on statewide affiliation. Anyone who is in good standing with the state party and has paid the annual membership fee may attend the state convention and participate in lesser party committees.

Lesser Committees. Members in congressional districts, state senate and assembly districts, and county and election districts may form party committees affiliated with the state committee. The purpose of the lesser committees is to help build the party and aid its candidates seeking election.

State Committee. The Constitution Party of Wisconsin is headed by a state committee composed of 24 members: 6 state officers and 2 representatives elected by the members in each of the 8 congressional districts. The state officers are the chairman, first vice chairman, chairman of committees, secretary, treasurer, and parliamentarian. The state chairman serves as the party's executive and is responsible for the day-to-day operations of the party. The officers are elected in odd-numbered years and serve 2-year terms. The congressional district representatives are elected in caucuses prior to the state convention each year.

CONSTITUTION PARTY OF WISCONSIN PLATFORM
As modified and adopted in Constitution Party National Convention, April 26, 2008
And amended in Constitution Party of Wisconsin State Convention, April 24, 2010

Preamble
The Constitution Party of Wisconsin gratefully acknowledges the blessing of the Lord God as Creator, Preserver, and Ruler of the Universe and of this Nation. It recognizes Jesus Christ as transcendent King over all nations and

hereby appeals to Him for aid, comfort, guidance and the protection of His Divine Providence as we work to restore and preserve this nation as a government of the people, by the people, and for the people.

The U.S. Constitution established a republic under God, rather than a democracy.

Our republic is a nation governed by a Constitution, which is rooted in Biblical law, administered by representatives who are constitutionally elected by the citizens.

In a republic governed by Constitutional law, rooted in Biblical law, all life, liberty, and property are protected.

We affirm the principles of inherent individual rights upon which these United States of America were founded:

- That each individual is endowed by his Creator with certain unalienable rights; that among these are the rights to life, liberty, property, and the pursuit of the individual's personal interest;
- That the freedom to own, use, exchange, control, protect, and freely dispose of property is a natural, necessary, and inseparable extension of the individual's unalienable rights;
- That the legitimate function of government is to secure these rights through the preservation of domestic tranquility, the maintenance of a strong national defense, and the promotion of equal justice for all;
- That history makes clear that left unchecked, it is the nature of government to usurp the liberty of its citizens and eventually become a major violator of the people's rights; and
- That, therefore, it is essential to bind government with the chains of the Constitution and carefully divide and jealously limit government powers to those assigned by the consent of the governed.

The Constitution Party of Wisconsin calls on all who love liberty and value their inherent rights to join with us in the pursuit of these goals and in the restoration of these founding principles.

Abortion, Euthanasia, and Bio-research

The Constitution Party of Wisconsin calls upon our state officials to fulfill their obligations as lesser magistrates to uphold the U.S. Constitution and the state constitution by taking immediate action to end the practice of abortion in Wisconsin.

We further call upon our state legislators to amend the Wisconsin Constitution to recognize personhood from the moment of fertilization.

We condemn the practice of so-called "assisted suicide" and call upon our state legislators to resist any and all attempts to legalize euthanasia.

Sanctity of Life

The Declaration of Independence states: "We hold these truths to be self-evident, that all men are created equal, that they are endowed by their Creator with certain unalienable Rights, that among these are Life, Liberty and the pursuit of Happiness."

The Preamble of the Constitution states a purpose of the Constitution to be to: "Secure the Blessings of Liberty to ourselves and our Posterity."

We declare the unalienable right of Life to be secured by our Constitution "to ourselves and our Posterity." Our posterity includes children born and future generations yet unborn. Any legalization of the termination of innocent life of the born or unborn is a direct violation of our unalienable right to life.

The pre-born child, whose life begins at fertilization, is a human being created in God's image. The first duty of the law is to prevent the shedding of innocent blood. It is, therefore, the duty of all civil governments to secure and to safeguard the lives of the pre-born.

To that end, the Constitution of these United States was ordained and established for "ourselves and our posterity." Under no circumstances may the federal government fund or otherwise support any state or local government or any organization or entity, foreign or domestic, which advocates, encourages or participates in the practice of abortion. We also oppose the distribution and use of all abortifacients.

We affirm the God-given legal personhood of all unborn human beings, without exception. As to matters of rape and incest, it is unconscionable to take the life of an innocent child for the crimes of his father.

No government may legalize the taking of the unalienable right to life without justification, including the life of the pre-born; abortion may not be declared lawful by any institution of state or local government — legislative, judicial, or executive. The right to life should not be made dependent upon a vote of a majority of any legislative body.

In addition, Article IV of the Constitution guarantees to each state a republican form of government. Therefore, although a Supreme Court opinion is binding on the parties to the controversy as to the particulars of the case, it is not a political rule for the nation. Roe v. Wade is an illegitimate usurpation of authority, contrary to the law of the nation's Charter and Constitution. It must be resisted by all civil government officials, federal, state, and local, and by all branches of the government — legislative, executive, and judicial.

We affirm both the authority and duty of Congress to limit the appellate jurisdiction of the Supreme Court in all cases of abortion in accordance with the U.S. Constitution, Article III, Section 2. In office, we shall only appoint to the federal judiciary, and to other positions of federal authority, qualified individuals who publicly acknowledge and commit themselves to the legal personhood of the pre-born child. In addition, we will do all that is within our power to encourage federal, state, and local government officials to protect the sanctity of the life of the pre-born through legislation, executive action, and judicial enforcement of the law of the land.

Further, we condemn the misuse of federal laws against pro-life demonstrators, and strongly urge the repeal of the FACE Acts as an unconstitutional expansion of federal power into areas reserved to the states or people by the Tenth Amendment.

In addition, we oppose the funding and legalization of bio-research involving human embryonic or pre-embryonic cells.

Finally, we also oppose all government "legalization" of euthanasia, infanticide and suicide.

Agricultural Freedom

Every producer of any agricultural product shall be at liberty to sell the product to any consumer, or consumers in aggregate, at any level, stage or condition of processing. We oppose government intrusion into the private and business life of farmers and farming.

Congressional Reform

"The Senators and Representatives ... shall be bound by Oath or Affirmation, to support this Constitution ..."
— U.S. Constitution, Article VI, Clause 3

With the advent of the 17th Amendment, a vital check on Congress was removed. Since then, Congress has usurped power relatively unchecked, where today, very few members of Congress make it through a single session without violating their oath of office to the Constitution.

The Congress of the United States has become an overpaid, overstaffed, self-serving institution. It confiscates taxpayer funds to finance exorbitant and unconstitutionally determined salaries, pensions, and perks. Most members of Congress have become more accountable to the Washington establishment than to the people in their home districts. Both houses of Congress are all too often unresponsive and irresponsible, arrogantly placing themselves above the very laws they enact, and beyond the control of the citizens they have sworn to represent and serve.

We seek to abolish Congressional pensions.

It is time for the American people to renew effective supervision of their public servants, to restore right standards and to take back the government. Congress must once again be accountable to the people and obedient to the Constitution, repealing all laws that delegate legislative powers to regulatory agencies, bureaucracies, private organizations, the Federal Reserve Board, international agencies, the President, and the judiciary.

The U.S. Constitution, as originally framed in Article I, Section 3, provided for U.S. Senators to be elected by state legislators. This provided the states direct representation in the legislative branch so as to deter the usurpation of powers that are Constitutionally reserved to the states or to the people.

The Seventeenth Amendment (providing for direct, popular election of U.S. Senators) took away from state governments their Constitutional role of indirect participation in the federal legislative process.

If we are to see a return to the states those powers, programs, and sources of revenue that the federal government has unconstitutionally taken away, then it is also vital that we repeal the Seventeenth Amendment and return to state legislatures the function of electing the U.S. Senate. In so doing, this would return the U.S. Senate to being a body that represents the legislatures of the several states on the federal level and, thus, a tremendously vital part of the designed checks and balances of power that our Constitution originally provided.

We support legislation to prohibit the attachment of unrelated riders to bills. Any amendments must fit within the scope and object of the original bill.

We support legislation to require that the Congressional Record contain an accurate record of proceedings. Members of Congress are not to be permitted to rewrite the speeches delivered during the course of debates, or other remarks offered from the floors of their respective houses; nor may any additional materials inserted in the Record, except those referred to in the speaker's presentation and for which space is reserved.

Cost of Big Government

James Madison said (Federalist Papers #45):

"The powers delegated by the proposed Constitution to the federal government are few and defined."

—The powers not delegated to the United States by the Constitution, nor prohibited by it to the States, are reserved to the States respectively, or to the people.l (Amendment X).

A legitimate and primary purpose of civil government is to safeguard the God-given rights of its citizens; namely, life, liberty, and property. Only those duties, functions, and programs specifically assigned to the federal government by the Constitution should be funded. We call upon Congress and the President to stop all federal expenditures which are not specifically authorized by the U. S. Constitution, and to restore to the states those powers, programs, and sources of revenue that the federal government has usurped.

Budget considerations are greatly impacted by the ever rising national debt. Interest on the debt is one of the largest expenses of government, and unless the interest is paid, the debt will continue to grow as interest is added to interest. If we are to get rid of the debt, a time needs to be set within which the debt will be funded, and then pay it off within that period. Whatever the payoff period may be, three things must happen within that time:

- The annual reductions have to be made without fail.
- All interest must be paid as it accrues; and
- The government must not spend more than it takes in during the payoff period.

One of the greatest contributors to deficit spending is war. If the country is to get rid of debt, the United States cannot become gratuitously involved in constant wars. Constitutional government, as the founders envisioned it, was not imperial. It was certainly not contemplated that America would police the world at the taxpayers' expense.

We call for the systematic reduction of the federal debt through, but not limited to, the elimination of further borrowing and the elimination of unconstitutional programs and agencies.

We call upon the President to use his Constitutional veto power to stop irresponsible and unconstitutional appropriations, and use his Constitutional authority to refuse to spend any money appropriated by Congress for unconstitutional programs or in excess of Constitutionally imposed tax revenue.

The debt could be more rapidly eliminated if certain lands and other assets currently held by the federal government were sold, and the proceeds applied to the debt. This policy should be employed, and funds from the sale of all such assets should be specifically applied to debt reduction.

We reject the misleading use of the terms "surplus" and "balanced budget" as long as we have public debt. We oppose dishonest accounting practices such as "off-budget items" used to hide unconstitutional spending practices.

We call for an end to the raiding by the federal government of the Social Security, Railroad Retirement and Medicare funds. We believe that over a protracted period the Social Security system may be privatized without disadvantage to the beneficiaries of the system. However, the program has been in place since the 1930s, and workers and their employers were taxed for the program and paid in good faith. The government promised to deliver the benefits, and must meet this commitment.

We call for the abolition of the Civil Service system, which is perceived to confer on government employees a "property right" regarding their jobs.

Crime

The amount of crime in a society is directly related to the level of moral restraint of its citizens. Government is a reflection of that moral restraint, not its legislator. Increasing the amount of moral restraint in our society is not the responsibility of government, but of those called to that mission; namely the family, and the clergy and their congregations. We call upon these to fulfill their mission, renewing the souls of our citizenry, thereby increasing the amount of moral restraint, which will result in a reduction of crime.

We assert that upon completion of his sentence, the person convicted of a crime shall be fully restored to society with full exercise of all rights of citizenship.

Defense

The very purpose of Government, as defined in the 2nd paragraph of the Declaration of Independence, is:

"... to secure these [unalienable] rights, Governments are instituted among Men ...," "that among these are Life, Liberty and the Pursuit of Happiness ...."

To fulfill this obligation, the Preamble of the Constitution states one of the duties specifically delegated to the Federal Government is to "Provide for the common defense."

U.S. Constitution, Article I, Section 8, Clauses 11-16 give Congress further direction and authority in this area, including the power "To raise and support Armies" and "To provide and maintain a Navy."

It is a primary obligation of the federal government to provide for the common defense, and to be vigilant regarding potential threats, prospective capabilities, and perceived intentions of potential enemies.

We oppose unilateral disarmament and dismemberment of America's defense infrastructure. That which is hastily torn down will not be easily rebuilt.

We condemn the presidential assumption of authority to deploy American troops into combat without a declaration of war by Congress, pursuant to Article I, Section 8, of the U.S. Constitution.

Under no circumstances would we commit U.S. forces to serve under any foreign flag or command. We are opposed to any New World Order, and we reject U.S. participation in or a relinquishing of command to any foreign authority.

The goal of U.S. security policy is to defend the national security interests of these United States. Therefore, except in time of declared war, for the purposes of state security, no state National Guard or reserve troops shall be called upon to support or conduct operations in foreign theatres.

We should be the friend of liberty everywhere, but the guarantor and provisioner of ours alone.

We call for the maintenance of a strong, state-of-the-art military on land, sea, in the air, and in space. We urge the executive and legislative branches to continue to provide for the modernization of our armed forces, in keeping with advancing technologies and a constantly changing world situation. We call for the deployment of a fully-operational strategic defense system as soon as possible.

We believe that all defense expenditures should be directly related to the protection of our nation, and that every item of expenditure must be carefully reviewed to eliminate foreign aid, waste, fraud, theft, inefficiency, and excess profits from all defense contracts and military expenditures.

We reject the policies and practices that permit women to train for or participate in combat. Because of the radical feminization of the military over the past two decades, it must be recognized that these "advances" undermine the integrity, morale, and performance of our military organizations by dual qualification standards and forced integration.

We fully support well regulated militias organized at the state level. Further, we fully support and encourage the restoration of unorganized militia at the county and community level in compliance with our patriotic and legal responsibilities as free citizens of these United States.

Under no circumstances should we have unilaterally surrendered our military base rights in Panama. The sovereign right of the United States to the United States territory of the Canal Zone has been jeopardized by treaties between the United States and Panama. Inasmuch as the United States bought both the sovereignty and the grant ownership of the ten-mile-wide Canal Zone, we propose that the government of the United States restore and protect its sovereign right and exclusive jurisdiction of the Canal Zone in perpetuity, and renegotiate the treaties with Panama by which the ownership of the canal was surrendered to Panama.

It should be a priority goal of the President and Congress to insist on enforcement of that portion of the 1978 Panama Canal Neutrality Treaty which prohibits control of the entrances to the Panama Canal by any entity not part of the Republic of Panama or these United States of America. By this standard, the award of port facilities at the entrances to the Panama Canal to Hutchison Whampoa, a Hong Kong company closely linked to the Chinese Communist People's Liberation Army, must be overturned. Similarly, Congress and the President should take advantage of Panama Canal treaty provisions to negotiate the return of a U.S. military presence at the Isthmus of Panama. At a time when the U.S. Navy is one-third its former size, it is essential that rapid transit of U.S. military vessels between the Atlantic and Pacific Oceans be assured.

Education

Education should be free from any State Government subsidy and government interference. The State Government has no legitimate role in either subsidizing or regulating education. To that end, the CPoW supports amending the Wisconsin Constitution to remove the State of Wisconsin from any role in education.

We support an orderly transition to free market education including home education and private schools (for profit and non-profit) and encourage benevolence to provide effective education for those in need.

Energy

James Madison said (Federalist Papers #45):

"The powers delegated by the proposed Constitution to the federal government are few and defined."

—The powers not delegated to the United States by the Constitution, nor prohibited by it to the States, are reserved to the States respectively, or to the people.l (Amendment X).

We call attention to the continuing need of these United States for a sufficient supply of energy for national security and for the immediate adoption of a policy of free market solutions to achieve energy independence for these United States. We call for abolishing the Department of Energy.

Private property rights should be respected, and the federal government should not interfere with the development of potential energy sources, including natural gas, crude oil, coal, hydroelectric power, solar energy, wind generators, and nuclear energy.

Family

The CPoW calls upon our national and state officials to totally oppose any action by U.S. Courts that would in establish or recognize "same-sex" marriage.

We also call upon the Wisconsin legislature to uphold and defend the state constitutional amendment which defines marriage as the union of one man and one woman and prevent the establishment of any counterfeit such as domestic partnerships.

We recognize that parents have the fundamental right and responsibility to nurture, educate, and discipline their children. We oppose the assumption of any of these responsibilities by any governmental agency without the express delegation of the parents or legal due process. We affirm the value of the father and the mother in the home, and we oppose efforts to legalize adoption of children by homosexual singles or couples.

We further call upon the Wisconsin legislature to repeal the provisions in the Wisconsin State Statutes which allow for "no-fault" divorce.

Gun Control

The 2nd Amendment strictly limits any interference with gun ownership by saying: "A well regulated Militia, being necessary to the security of a free State, the right of the people to keep and bear Arms, shall not be infringed."

The right to bear arms is inherent in the right of self defense, defense of the family, and defense against tyranny, conferred on the individual and the community by our Creator to safeguard life, liberty, and property, as well as to help preserve the independence of the nation.

The right to keep and bear arms is guaranteed by the Second Amendment to the Constitution; it may not properly be infringed upon or denied.

The Constitution Party upholds the right of the citizen to keep and bear arms. We oppose attempts to prohibit ownership of guns by law-abiding citizens, and stand against all laws which would require the registration of guns or ammunition.

We emphasize that when guns are outlawed, only outlaws will have them. In such circumstances, the peaceful citizen's protection against the criminal would be seriously jeopardized.

We call for the repeal of all federal firearms legislation, beginning with Federal Firearms Act of 1968.

We call for the rescinding of all executive orders, the prohibition of any future executive orders, and the prohibition of treaty ratification which would in any way limit the right to keep and bear arms.

Health Care and Government

James Madison said (Federalist Papers #45):

"The powers delegated by the proposed Constitution to the federal government are few and defined."

—The powers not delegated to the United States by the Constitution, nor prohibited by it to the States, are reserved to the States respectively, or to the people.l (Amendment X).

The Constitution Party opposes the governmentalization and bureaucratization of American medicine. Government regulation and subsidy constitutes a threat to both the quality and availability of patient-oriented health care and treatment.

Hospitals, doctors, and other health care providers should be accountable to patients — not to politicians, insurance bureaucrats, or HMO Administrators.

If the supply of medical care is controlled by the federal government, then officers of that government will determine which demand is satisfied. The result will be the rationing of services, higher costs, poorer results — and the power of life and death transferred from caring physicians to unaccountable political overseers.

We denounce any civil government entity using age or any other personal characteristic to: preclude people and insurance firms from freely contracting for medical coverage; conscript such people into socialized medicine, e.g., Medicare; or prohibit these people from using insurance payments and/or their own money to obtain medical services in addition to, or to augment the quality of, those services prescribed by the program.

We applaud proposals for employee-controlled "family coverage" health insurance plans based on cash value life insurance principles.

The federal government has no Constitutional provision to regulate or restrict the freedom of the people to have access to medical care, supplies or treatments. We advocate, therefore, the elimination of the federal Food and Drug Administration, as it has been the federal agency primarily responsible for prohibiting beneficial products, treatments, and technologies here in the United States that are freely available in much of the rest of the civilized world.

We affirm freedom of choice of practitioner and treatment for all citizens for their health care.

We support the right of patients to seek redress of their grievances through the courts against insurers and/or HMO's.

Immigration

U.S. Constitution, Article V., Section 4:

The United States shall guarantee to every State in this Union a Republican Form of Government, and Shall protect each of them against Invasion: …

James Madison:

"When we are considering the advantages that may result from an easy mode of naturalization, we ought also to consider the cautions necessary to guard against abuses. … aliens might acquire the right of citizenship, and return to the country from which they came, and evade the laws intended to encourage the commerce and industry of the real citizens and inhabitants of America, enjoying at the same time all the advantages of citizens …"

We affirm the integrity of the international borders of the United States and the Constitutional authority and duty of the federal government to guard and to protect those borders, including the regulation of the numbers and of the qualifications of immigrants into the country.

Each year approximately one million legal immigrants and almost as many illegal aliens enter the United States. These immigrants — including illegal aliens — have been made eligible for various kinds of public assistance, including housing, education, Social Security, and legal services. This unconstitutional drain on the federal Treasury is having a severe and adverse impact on our economy, increasing the cost of government at federal, state, and local levels, adding to the tax burden, and stressing the fabric of society. The mass importation of people with low standards of living threatens the wage structure of the American worker and the labor balance in our country.

We oppose the abuse of the H-1B and L-1 visa provisions of the immigration act which are displacing American workers with foreign.

We favor a moratorium on immigration to the United States, except in extreme hardship cases or in other individual special circumstances, until the availability of all federal subsidies and assistance be discontinued, and proper security procedures have been instituted to protect against terrorist infiltration.

We also insist that every individual group and/or private agency which requests the admission of an immigrant to the U.S., on whatever basis, be required to commit legally to provide housing and sustenance for such immigrants, bear full responsibility for the economic independence of the immigrants, and post appropriate bonds to seal such covenants.

The Constitution Party demands that the federal government restore immigration policies based on the practice that potential immigrants will be disqualified from admission to the U.S. if, on the grounds of health, criminality, morals, or financial dependence, they would impose an improper burden on the United States, any state, or any citizen of the United States.

We oppose the provision of welfare subsidies and other taxpayer-supported benefits to illegal aliens, and reject the practice of bestowing U.S. citizenship on children born to illegal alien parents while in this country.

We oppose any extension of amnesty to illegal aliens. We call for the use of U.S. troops to protect the states against invasion.

We oppose bilingual ballots. We insist that those who wish to take part in the electoral process and governance of this nation be required to read and comprehend basic English as a precondition of citizenship. We support English as the official language for all governmental business by the United States.

Money and Banking

Article I, Section 8, Clause 5 grants only to Congress the power —To coin money [and] regulate the Value thereof …,I with no provision for such power to be delegated to any other group. Congress began immediately to fulfill this obligation with the Mint Act of 1792, establishing a U.S. Mint for producing Gold and Silver based coin, prescribing the value and content of each coin, and affixing the penalty of death to those who debase such currency.

Article I, Section 10:

—*No State shall … coin Money; emit Bills of Credit; make any Thing but gold and silver Coin a Tender in Payment of Debts; ….*

Thus, the Constitution forbade the States from accepting or using anything other than a Gold and Silver based currency.

Money functions as both a medium of exchange and a symbol of a nation's morality.

The Founding Fathers established a system of "coin" money that was designed to prohibit the "improper and wicked" manipulation of the nation's medium of exchange while guaranteeing the power of the citizens' earnings.

The federal government has departed from the principle of "coin" money as defined by the U.S. Constitution and the Mint Act of 1792 and has granted unconstitutional control of the nation's monetary and banking system to the private Federal Reserve System.

The Constitution Party recommends a substantive reform of the system of Federal taxation. In order for such reform to be effective, it is necessary that the United States:

- Return to the money system set forth in the Constitution;
- Repeal the Federal Reserve Act, and reform the current Federal Reserve banks to become clearing houses only; and
- Prohibit fractional reserve banking.

It is our intention that no system of "debt money" shall be imposed on the people of the United States. We support a debt free, interest free money system.

DEMOCRATIC PARTY OF WISCONSIN
May 2015

Headquarters

State Headquarters: 15 North Pinckney Street, Suite 200, Madison 53703.

Telephone: (608) 255-5172.

Executive Director: JAKE HAJDU.

Political Director: BRITA OLSEN.

Membership and Conventions Director: SEAN BERGER; MACKENZIE CARROLL, *deputy membership director.*

Operations and Compliance Director: AMANDA BRINK.

Communications Director: MELISSA BALDAUFF.

Finance Director: TIERNAN DONOHUE.

Organizing Director and Voter File Manager: WILL HOFFMAN.

Internet Address: http://www.wisdems.org

State Administrative Committee

Chair: MIKE TATE, Milwaukee.

First Vice Chair: MELISSA SCHROEDER, Merrill.

Second Vice Chair: JEFF CHRISTENSEN, Oshkosh.

Secretary: MEG ANDRIETSCH, Racine.

Treasurer: MICHAEL CHILDERS, La Pointe.

National Committee Members: CHRISTINE BREMER MUGGLI, Wausau; ROLLIE HICKS, Eau Claire; MARTHA LOVE, Milwaukee; JASON RAE, Milwaukee; MELISSA SCHROEDER, Merrill.

College Democrats Representative: PHOENIX RICE-JOHNSON, Madison.

Milwaukee County Chair: MARLENE OTT, Milwaukee.

At-Large Members: BRYAN KENNEDY, Glendale; GRETCHEN LOWE, Madison; ARVINA MARTIN, Madison; JUSTIN NICKELS, Manitowoc; BETHANY ORDAZ, Madison; DIAN PALMER, Brookfield; CRIS SELIN, Middleton; MARY LANG SOLLINGER, Madison; RANDY UDELL, Fitchburg; ALLIN WALKER, Egg Harbor.

County Chairs Association Chair: TANYA LOHR, West Bend.

Assembly Representative: JOCASTA ZAMARRIPA.

Senate Representative: NIKIYA HARRIS DODD.

Congressional District Representatives:

1st District	*5th District*
Melissa Lemke, chair, Racine	Michael Schlotfeldt, chair, West Bend
Mike Southers, Janesville	Kristin Hansen, Waukesha
2nd District	*6th District*
Erik Paulson, chair, Madison	Bob Schweder, chair, Princeton
Laurene Bach, Waunakee	Jessica King, Oshkosh
3rd District	*7th District*
Lisa Hermann, chair, Eau Claire	Paul Knuth, chair, Rhinelander
Gary Hawley, Stevens Point	Rebecca Bonesteel, Hudson
4th District	*8th District*
Terrell Martin, chair, Milwaukee	Dottie LeClair, chair, Appleton
Stephanie Findley, Milwaukee	Travis Bille, Kaukauna

Source: Democratic Party of Wisconsin, May 2015.

County Organization. The county organization is the basic unit of the Democratic Party of Wisconsin. In each county, the membership elects the county officers. They include a chairperson, vice chairperson, secretary, and treasurer (or secretary/treasurer). Their terms of office are usually one year, but some county organizations may provide for 2-year terms.

Congressional District Organization. Congressional district organizations function mainly as a base of support for Democratic congressional candidates. They also select representatives to the state administrative committee and work with the county parties in their district. An executive committee directs each congressional district organization.

State Convention. The party holds its annual state convention in June. Each year, the convention considers resolutions, amendments to the state party constitution, and other party business.

State party officers are elected in odd-numbered years, and state party platforms are adopted in even-numbered years. State convention delegates elect Democratic National Committee members every four years.

Each county unit elects delegates to the State Convention, and all party members are eligible.

The number of delegates that represent each county is based on the number of party members and the percentage of the vote cast for the Democratic candidate in the most recent U.S. Senate election. In addition to the regular quota, certain Democratic officeholders are automatically delegates to the state convention.

State Officers and Administrative Committee. The Democratic Party of Wisconsin is headed by a state administrative committee, composed of party officials chosen in a variety of ways. Delegates to the state convention elect the 5 party officers and the 4 Democratic National Committee members. At each of the 8 congressional district conventions, 2 representatives are selected to serve on the state administrative committee in the spring of each odd-numbered year: the district chairperson and an additional representative of the opposite sex. The remaining voting committee members include the County Chairs Association chairperson; the Milwaukee County chairperson; a representative of the College Democrats; 2 state legislative representatives, elected by their house caucuses prior to the beginning of the new legislative term; the immediate past state chairperson and at-large administrative committee members.

The party officers are the state chairperson, first vice chairperson, second vice chairperson, treasurer, and secretary. The chairperson and first vice chairperson must be of the opposite sex.

Party officers are elected in the odd-numbered year for 2-year terms. Democratic National Committee members are elected each presidential election year and serve 4-year terms. The state chairperson and the first vice chairperson are also *ex officio* members of the Democratic National Committee.

Whenever a vacancy occurs, the chairperson, with the concurrence of the entire state administrative committee, appoints a successor to serve until the next annual convention, where the delegates elect an individual to fill the position for the remainder of the unexpired term.

National Committee. The Democratic National Committee is composed of the chairperson and the highest ranking officer of the opposite sex in each recognized state Democratic Party. In Wisconsin, these are the chairperson and the first vice chairperson of the state party.

An additional 200 committee memberships are apportioned to the states on the same basis as delegates to the national convention, and other specified members are appointed. Wisconsin's Democratic National Committee members are selected every 4 years at the annual state conventions held in presidential election years.

DEMOCRATIC PARTY OF WISCONSIN 2014 PLATFORM
Adopted by Convention on June 7, 2014

Preamble

The Democratic Party of Wisconsin strives to build an open, just, and strong society where all citizens have equal rights and equal opportunities to live meaningful, secure lives. We work actively for open, honest, and responsive government that is accountable to the needs and the will of the people.

Justice, Human Concerns, and Democracy

Our government must support the values of freedom, family, fairness, and responsibility to community and to all persons.

One of the primary jobs of government is to ensure that everyone can lead dignified, healthy, and fulfilling lives. We value love, commitment, stability, and nurturing of all family members. Our Constitution guarantees that we are all equal regardless of race, color, class, religion, actual or perceived gender, sexual orientation, age, occupation, national origin, physical disabilities or appearance, or political beliefs. We support marriage equality for all couples. We will work to ensure that basic civil liberties are forever preserved.

It is vital that government respect, support, and protect freedom of expression. When government attempts to limit the rights of its citizens, the fundamental philosophy on which our nation was established is destroyed. We hold sacrosanct our civil liberties, including but hardly limited to freedom of speech, the right to privacy, the presumption of innocence, the principle of *habeus corpus*, and due process under law. Nothing less than humane treatment of our fellow human beings is acceptable. Our government, with its checks and balances among the three branches, serves us, and protects our constitutional rights.

We must fully fund our state and local protective services. The men and women who serve us protect our lives and property and are our first line of defense, and we must provide for them.

We will work to ensure that everyone has an equal opportunity to succeed, an equal voice in government and fair and equal treatment under the law. We recognize that minorities, senior citizens, and the poor often face formidable challenges, including obstacles to voting. Many citizens also suffer inadequate access to nutritious food, healthcare, education, and housing. We shall work to eliminate those obstacles.

We shall pursue legislation and cultural change that end racial and ethnic profiling, respect the sovereignty of our indigenous Native American host nations and ensure equality between men and women. We shall work for gender-balanced, qualified representation at all levels of government.

Empowerment of citizens in all civic affairs strengthens our nation. Government must be an open institution that people trust, complying with open meeting and public record laws and elected through transparent, publicly-funded state and national elections. We support a fair, non-partisan redistricting process.

Every citizen is guaranteed the right to vote and equal access thereto, including non-incarcerated felons. We support same-day registration and early voting. We oppose voter ID requirements as discriminatory, equivalent to a poll tax, a voter suppression tactic, and a fraudulent solution to exaggerated voter fraud. We have the right and duty to inspect and count all votes and to have a voter verified paper ballot that guarantees accurate vote counting. The President should be elected by popular vote.

Our goal is a government and an electoral process free of the corrupting influences of money and power. We strongly oppose the decision of the US Supreme Court to allow unlimited campaign advertising by corporations, foreign and domestic. A new Amendment to the Constitution must be adopted to make clear that Corporations are not People and that money is not speech.

Access to accurate information and a diversity of viewpoints are essential to citizen empowerment. The broadcast spectrum belongs to all citizens. Therefore we will work to ensure diverse local ownership of media outlets. We will provide strong support for public broadcasting and other community-owned media outlets. We support free and equal access to news media for all candidates for public office.

We respect the religious liberties of all people and welcome them into the Democratic Party. It is vital that we observe separation between government and religion. It is imperative to the survival of our Democratic Republic that the rights of citizens to choose their own religious and philosophical beliefs remain intact.

We advocate for comprehensive immigration reform providing a reasonable legal path to residency and citizenship. The policy must include a fair opportunity for current undocumented residents to achieve legal status. All people should be afforded the same basic principles of life, liberty, justice, and fair access to economic security.

It is important to care for all generations. We need affordable, quality, licensed daycare centers and government support to pay for childcare. We cannot neglect our nation's future. We need health education and disease prevention programs concerning smoking, alcohol, drug abuse, and sexually transmitted infections.

It is essential that we preserve Social Security programs for our elderly, disabled, and eligible children. Privatizing Social Security threatens the financial security of the most vulnerable. We must enhance programs for the aging and disabled, including subsidized long-term in-home or nursing home care.

Access to affordable, quality health care is a right and the best solution to our national health care crisis is a single-payer system. Such a system must provide universal access for individuals of all ages, promote preventive measures, provide medications, therapy and cover all physical and mental illnesses equally. Until that system is available, we support broader coverage and increased funding for the current health care programs on local, state and national levels, including BadgerCare, Medicare, and Medicaid.

Personal moral, religious, and medical decisions should be left up to the competent individual. We believe in freedom of reproductive choice, family planning, and the individual's right to choose death with dignity including physician-assisted end-of-life. Everyone has the right to timely obtain medications, properly and legally prescribed by their health care provider, from any licensed pharmacy.

Funding for stem-cell research should be supported on its scientific merits. Considering the high rate, associated costs, and long-lasting adverse effects of incarceration, we support effective alternatives and oppose privatization of prisons.

We oppose the death penalty as an inhumane and ineffective means of punishment. We believe in equitable sentencing standards and increasing the authority of judges to modify sentences.

The war on drugs is a colossal failure. We must discourage dangerous drug use without criminalizing the user and provide rehabilitative treatment to addicted persons. We encourage non-penal sanctions for initial minor drug violations. Marijuana should be legal and regulated like tobacco and alcohol.

We support the right to hunt, to bear arms, a concealed carry ban, background checks on all gun sales, banning the sale of assault weapons, and limits on the size of magazines.

Education, Labor, and Economics

Quality public education for all is critical to a healthy democracy and economy. Public funding for private schools diverts resources from and adversely impacts public schools. Increased governmental funding and financial aid is essential for all levels of public education. Nobody should be denied quality education because of personal lack of financial resources.

We believe that students have the right to receive their education in a safe, respectful, and nurturing environment, free from harassment or discrimination by teachers, staff, parents, or other students. We support fair and equitable funding for all elements of the curriculum, including the arts and physical education.

Wisconsin's current educational funding system has failed. Teacher and support staff compensation must keep pace with costs of benefits and inflation.

Revenue caps on school districts and other local governments must be eliminated. State or federal governments must fully fund their mandates.

Public investment in arts and humanities promotes healthy communities and a healthy economy. We support increased local, state, and federal funding of arts and humanities.

A strong and secure nation depends on sound economic policy that promotes and sustains full, meaningful employment. Business, labor, and the public must work together to re-establish American jobs on American soil. We support small business as a means of economic growth. We must resist outsourcing by eliminating tax breaks to employers who ship jobs overseas and creating incentives to bring jobs back to the U.S.

The Federal government should fund a safety net of transitional jobs for all individuals who cannot find work and have no unemployment compensation.

Public and private workers have rights to living wages, pay equity for women, safe and equitable workplaces, and secure benefits. Workers' rights to organize, bargain collectively, and strike without fear of reprisal must, where lost, be restored and otherwise strengthened. Election by card check reduces employer intimidation of employees' choice of representation. Employees who benefit from union contracts should pay fair-share dues. We support public employees' rights to speedy mediation and binding arbitration of labor disputes.

Businesses must be held accountable for contracts with their employees. "Right-to-work" legislation and the hiring of strikebreakers are anathema to a strong, justly-compensated workforce. Pension and other retirement funds must be strictly safeguarded and responsibly managed through regulation. In the event of bankruptcy, workers' unpaid wages must be the first claim on remaining assets.

We support a tax system that is based on ability to pay. It is immoral to overtax those less able to pay while the wealthy are taxed too little as a percentage of income. The Federal budget must reflect responsible spending and fair taxation. We call on the State Legislature to make corporate taxes on par with the national average.

Financial markets should be more effectively regulated to prevent fraud, excessive speculation, inappropriate compensation, predatory lending, and the need for taxpayer bailouts of mismanaged firms. The needs of Main Street should supercede the needs of Wall Street.

Mining authorizations should provide adequate tax revenue to support the affected communities.

America must invest in a healthy economy by supporting worker training, affordable tuition at our state supported universities and technical colleges, and ample funding for research.

American companies have an obligation to our nation to be established here at home, follow our labor and environmental laws, and pay taxes for the good of the commons. Furthermore, we must protect our industries from competition by enforcing tariffs against nations that tolerate unfair worker conditions and environmental degradation.

Our wealth should be measured not only by the GDP but also by broad measures of well-being, such as the United Nations Human Development Index, that incorporate factors like health, education, literacy, employment and wages, and environmental quality.

Agriculture and Environment

We must preserve family farming by creating market systems that assure a fair return to both farmers and processors. True Cooperatives and family farm subsidies are essential to the economic viability and quality of life in rural areas. In addition we support value-added agriculture which includes farming endeavors outside traditional forms of agriculture. Regulations controlling environmental pollution from agriculture should be strengthened.

We support farming systems that are humane to animals, preserve our soil, water and forest resources, and produce wholesome, safe food for consumers. We support agricultural sustainability through growth in "buy fresh buy local" practices which insure markets for local farmers and save fuel by eliminating costly transport. We also support truth in labeling of conventional, organic, and genetically modified food.

We oppose practices by genetically modified seed producers which attempt to monopolize the seed business by requiring that all seed be purchased from them.

Climate change poses an existential threat to life on Earth. There must be aggressive action to mitigate its effects. We must cut carbon emissions. Protecting ecological systems is essential to the economic and social welfare of our state, nation, and the future of humanity. Our legislators and leaders must pay heed to soil, water, and atmospheric pollution; scientific evidence of climate change; all invasive species; and decreasing biodiversity. Ecological sustainability requires a stable population and responsible consumption.

We must maintain the integrity of the vast fresh water supply in the Great Lakes. We support retaining and expanding publicly-owned recreational and wild lands.

We must develop clean, renewable, and sustainable energy sources without relaxing regulation of nuclear energy; increase production of fuel-efficient vehicles; reduce urban sprawl onto prime agricultural soils; improve and expand local, regional and national mass transportation systems; and increase recycling and waste management, all while maintaining biodiversity. We support responsible environmental regulations affecting open space, wilderness areas, soil conservation, forest management, industry, toxic and hazardous waste disposal and cleanup, and watershed protection.

We must prioritize public health, environmental protection, and the land and water treaty rights of native communities in the planning and implementation of all mining projects, including frac sand extraction. To ensure the protection of our state's valuable natural resources, we support the reestablishment of a Public Intervener's Office and an independent Department of Natural Resources.

Foreign Affairs

We stand for human rights, social and economic justice, the rule of law, and popularly adopted democratic government worldwide. Our leaders and policies must honor international law and honor and promote international agreements that provide groundwork for a just, prosperous, environmentally healthy, and peaceful world. Our United Nations dues must be fully paid.

We call on our government to be a cooperative and effective leader, a partner in the pursuit of global accords to improve the human condition and protect the environment. We encourage international efforts to combat poverty, hunger, disease, illiteracy, discrimination, genocide, torture, genital mutilation, human slavery and trafficking, capital punishment, pollution, and climate change. We support expansion of the Peace Corps.

We oppose unfair trade and immigration policies that undermine our economy, harm working people in our country and elsewhere, and harm the environment.

We oppose unfettered international arms trade, nuclear, chemical and biological weapons, land mines, radioactive materials in conventional munitions, ballistic missile defense systems, cluster bombs, militarization of space, American-run or funded internment camps, and torture.

We support a military sufficiently strong to safeguard national security. We must provide amply for the health and well-being of members of the military during and after their service. We support efforts to eliminate the use of National Guard troops in undeclared wars.

Our military budget is disproportionately large compared to all other nations. With only 5% of the world's population we make nearly 50% of the world's total military expenditures. Our military budget should be reduced with greater emphasis placed on economic development and diplomacy to achieve global security and curtail the undue influence of the "Military Industrial Complex."

War must always be a last resort. We must address the grievances that foster terrorism rather than fight wars that perpetuate them. We must abide by the Geneva Conventions.

Preemptive war without verified direct threat to our country, including the use of drone strikes, is fraudulent, illegal, and disastrous. Congressional action to stop funding for pre-emptive wars and end military assistance to nations conducting preemptive war is long overdue.

We call upon Congress to pass laws displaying visions and values that uphold our Constitution, reverse the failures and illegalities of the executive branch, and maintain the global community's respect and admiration of our country.

Conclusion

The membership of the Democratic Party of Wisconsin has crafted and adopted this platform. Our state and our country will become stronger and better by following the principles outlined herein. We expect all candidates supported by the Democratic Party to support this Platform and, when elected, to work to implement it.

WISCONSIN GREEN PARTY
May 2015

Headquarters

State Headquarters: P.O. Box 1701, Madison 53701-1701.

Telephone: (608) 204-7336.

Internet Address: http://wigp.nationbuilder.com

E-mail Address: info@wisconsingreenparty.org

Cochairpersons: DAVE SCHWAB, vacancy.

Secretary: MIKE MCCALLISTER.

Treasurer: BOBBY GIFFORD.

National Committee Delegates: GREG BANKS, BRUCE HINKFORTH, DACE ZEPS.

National Committee Alternates: GEORGE MARTIN, JIM O'NEIL, MICHAEL SLATTERY.

Coordinating Council District Representatives:

1st District
   2 vacancies
2nd District
   Dace Zeps
   David Soumis
3rd District
   2 vacancies
4th District
   2 vacancies
5th District
   Bruce Hinkforth
   Jeanette McCallister

6th District
   Ron Hardy
   vacancy
7th District
   Jim Olmsted
   vacancy
8th District
   2 vacancies

Source: Wisconsin Green Party

Membership. Membership dues rates shall be established at least annually by the Members in a Membership meeting. Any Wisconsin resident who cannot afford the established dues for membership may be granted a waiver of payment of dues for any year by the Coordinating Council.

All members of the organization are entitled to participate in all of the activities of the organization and to attend any meeting of the organization or its committees and councils.

There shall be meetings of the Members at least biannually at locations in Wisconsin to be determined by the Coordinating Council. One of the Membership meetings shall be convened in the fall of each year and shall have as part of its agenda the selection of Co-Chairs, Corresponding Secretary, Recording Secretary, Elections Treasurer and Operations Treasurer for the following year. Member meetings shall be held in different locations in Wisconsin with a view toward development of a local Green group in that location and assistance on a local issue in keeping with our Key Values. Minutes of all Membership meetings shall be kept by the recording secretary and all policy decisions and resolutions published thereafter in the organization's newsletter.

Coordinating Council. The WI Green Party Coordinating Council shall consist of up to 25 members. All members must be members of the WI Green Party, and all efforts will be made to maintain gender-balanced, and ethnic-balanced representation. Five (5) members are the officers of the WI Green Party (two Co-Chairs, Elections Treasurer, Operations Treasurer, Recording Secretary, and Corresponding Secretary). The responsibilities of officers are outlined in Article 4 of the Constitution. Up to 16 members are nominated and elected from the eight WI congressional districts. Up to two members are from each of the eight congressional districts. Each member serves a 2-year term. (Members will serve 1-year and 2-year staggered terms in first year). These 8 (16 in first year) members will be nominated in their district meetings at the Fall Gathering. The election will take place at the full membership meeting. Notification will be sent out three times (in the newsletter, via email, and with Fall Gathering information) that nominations for the congressional district representation will take place at the WI Green Party Fall Gathering. If someone would like to be nominated but cannot attend the gathering, they should send a brief written statement with another member, who will speak on behalf of the member. Up to four (4) members are nominated and elected from caucuses. One each from the following caucuses: Women, Diversity, LGBT and Youth. These are 1-year terms. These 4 members will be nominated in their caucus meetings at the Fall Gathering. The election will take place at the full membership meeting.

Officers. The Officers of the organization shall be two Co-Chairs, a Recording Secretary, a Corresponding Secretary, an Operations Treasurer and an Elections Treasurer. The Officers shall be Members of the Coordinating Council and of the Wisconsin Green Party. All efforts shall be made to balance the Officers regionally and by gender. Officers will be responsible for granting access to specific internal documents such as membership records and databases.

Each Co-Chair shall serve for two years with staggered terms so that there is a senior and junior Chair. All reasonable effort shall be made to rotate the Chair role throughout the membership of the organization. All other Officers shall serve one-year terms. All Officers, except for the Co-Chairs, may be reelected for successive terms.

WISCONSIN GREEN PARTY PLATFORM
(Revised 11/11/2006, 4/17/2007, 5/23/2007, and 11/9/2013)

Preamble

We hold these truths to be self-evident: that we must treat each other with love, respect and fairness, and that we must protect the earth for future generations. The crises of our times demand a fundamental shift in human values and culture, and in our social, economic and political institutions. The way we live today is based on using things up: our air, our water, our natural resources, and our people. We need a new way of doing things that is sustainable, that will allow our people and our environment to flourish now and in the future. We can't keep spending today what we – and our children and their children – will need tomorrow. The Wisconsin Greens offer a new vision for change, for a sustainable future. We recognize that one of great obstacles to that change is the fact that government no longer responds to the needs of citizens. Only by building grassroots democracy can we be sure that changes will be real, not just appearances or promises. Since neither the Democratic Party nor the Republican Party has shown a real commitment to running government in the public interest, The Wisconsin Greens believe another political party is needed: one that people can believe in; one that they can trust. Our vision is of a sustainable society in harmony with the environment, one that meets all people's needs for security, self-respect, freedom, creativity, and community. We recognize that personal, cultural, social, economic, political, and ecological problems are interconnected. We reject the current simplistic solutions to these problems. New, creative solutions are needed which allow us to live well and happily without destroying our environment or our society. We are confronted with the challenge of letting go of old ways and creating a new vision and a new way of life.

Ecological Wisdom

The Wisconsin Green Party believes that Ecological Wisdom has a direct effect on quality of life. Only by practicing sound stewardship and ecological responsibility can we stop the degradation of the life-giving relationships that exist between humankind and the earth. The "public trust doctrine," which holds that public land, water, minerals, forests, and other natural resources are held in trust for the public and used for the common good, must be enforced. The precautionary principle must be applied to public policy decisions, especially those concerning the approval of drugs, pesticides, and genetically modified organisms to protect the public from practices of uncertain consequence.

Agriculture

1. The state government should provide subsidies to make the change from petrochemical-based to organic farming methods economically feasible for small-scale farmers.

2. The state should develop the necessary infrastructure to support the regionalization of food production and distribution systems, such as urban farms, farmers markets, community supported agriculture, and regional food processing facilities.

3. Wisconsin should establish a system of subsidies and tax incentives to protect family farms as an indispensable component of a healthy and sustainable agricultural economy.

4. A state land banking system of prime farmland to prevent diversion to non-farm use through first-option state acquisition of the land should be created.

Chemical use

5. The state will create and maintain a citizen accessible central database of the products used, concentration applied, chemical contents, health effects, and company responsible, for any private or commercial pesticide application.

6. Pesticides will not be used on or in public property, except as a last resort, after the failure of organic alternatives

has been demonstrated. Tax incentives will reward the use of organic pest control methods.

7. Communities in the state will have the right to pass stronger controls on pesticides than those specified in state and federal regulations.

Forest, Wetlands, and Water

8. The Department of Natural Resources will maintain forests, wetlands, and all other ecological communities in a manner which will protect biodiversity and will allow future generations to benefit.

9. We support a general moratorium on the draining of wetlands, on road building in public forests.

10. DNR water quality rules will be stiffened to require absolute non-degradation of existing water bodies.

11. Enact rigorous environmental safeguards to protect communities and prevent contamination of our air, land, and water from mining pollution, including arsenic, asbestos, mercury, silica, and other known toxins.

Energy

12. The Public Service Commission should not grant licenses to new nuclear facilities or the renewal of licenses for existing facilities.

13. We support higher average miles per gallon requirements and stricter emission control requirements on new vehicles, as well as "gas guzzler" taxes and renewable fuel and "gas sipper" rebates on new car purchases.

14. As a response to oil production having reached its peak, we support building and promoting mass transit infrastructure for light rail, high-speed rail, commuter rail, as well as intra and intercommunity bicycling and walking trails.

15. Community owned utilities and decentralized, neighborhood networks will receive financial aid for the purchase and installation of renewable energy technology such as wind, solar and biomass. The Public Service Commission will require that the electric grid be reconfigured to accept power from widely distributed, diverse sources.

16. We will work towards statewide energy independence, and will promote, encourage, and fund energy research that brings Wisconsin closer to a self-sustaining energy system.

17. Under Green Party leadership, the state of Wisconsin will independently implement the terms of the Kyoto Protocol on global warming.

18. Green Party leaders will enact policies that significantly reduce the release of gases that deplete the ozone layer, contribute to global warming and cause acid rain.

Waste

19. The Greens will apply the principles of reduce, reuse and recycle to policies in order to reduce waste streams, reduce demands on natural resources and reduce the generation of pollutants.

20. Regional high level nuclear waste dumps will not be located in Wisconsin.

21. Tipping fees at Wisconsin landfills will be increase for commercial haulers. Commercial haulers will be required to bill their commercial customers on a per weight basis.

22. High-level radioactive and highly toxic waste storage will be only for waste generated in Wisconsin.

23. The history and environmental record of recycling or waste disposal firms will be used as major criteria in considering awarding contracts for municipal services.

24. We will require the DNR and State Attorney General to be more vigorous in prosecuting corporate offenses and will hold individuals accountable when appropriate. Corporations that engage in gross violations will have their corporate charter revoked.

Social and Economic Justice

While the Wisconsin Green party understands and applauds the initiative and ambition shown by people who seek financial security or self-improvement, we believe that it is the role of government to ensure that the financial security and social status of one group does not come via the exploitation and marginalization of another group. Additionally, common methods of measuring the economy view production for its own sake as a positive and low unemployment, a condition that favors the majority, is viewed as a threat to economic health. Clearly, new economic paradigms are needed that regard measurements for quality of life and the environment and the full employment of the population as a positive. Lastly, the Wisconsin Green Party asserts that it is the duty of government to earn the allegiance of its citizens by protecting the public from threats "economic and physical," as well as "foreign and domestic".

Economic Justice

25. Increase the state minimum wage to a living wage of $15 per hour, adjusted annually to inflation.

26. Charter a publicly-owned Bank of Wisconsin to hold public funds, provide affordable credit to local governments and private businesses, invest in needed infrastructure, and avoid the risks and profit-taking associated with holding public funds in private banks.

27. Laws regarding Articles of Incorporation will be revised to make executives and board members more accountable for the effects of their decision-making.

28. Under a Green Party government the right of people to form unions, bargain collectively, and strike will be upheld. We oppose "union-busting" tactics. The State should assist management in working more closely and cooperatively with unions.

29. Green Party plans for economic development will focus on jobs that are based in the community and that have a vested interest in the community where their employees live – especially small businesses.

30. The Wisconsin Greens support family leave legislation, paid sick and vacation time, job sharing, and the

involvement of workers in decision-making, management, and scheduling.

31. Green elected officials will emphasize and promote regional trade emphasizing stronger ties with our Canadian neighbors who share the Great Lakes basin. State trade missions should promote "fair trade" over "free trade" with specific countries that are moving toward more equitable, sustainable economies.

Education

32. The Green Party will repeal laws that prevent teachers from striking or laws that interfere with collective bargaining such a Qualified Economic Offer or QEO.

33. The Wisconsin Greens oppose the use of 'high stakes' standardized tests as the primary determinant for grade advancement, graduation or teacher pay.

34. The state should redraw district boundaries to promote decentralization of schools and an appropriate scale for school districts. The transportation of students over great distances is already a burden on the budgets in many rural districts.

35. For parents to have a meaningful impact on school board policies, district boundaries should be redrawn taking into account the ratio of electors to school board and reduced to defined, equitable limits.

36. Green Party education policy will foster an understanding of the history of our conflicts and treaties with Wisconsin's tribes and a respect for native cultures.

37. Wisconsin Greens support fully-funded public education, and so oppose the voucher system of public funding for private schools.

Health Care System

38. The Green Party will implement a universal, single-payer system that will be funded through state taxes. The system will be designed to allow citizens to select health care providers and treatment.

39. The state shall promote the revitalization of public health care clinics and school nurses to provide necessary health services and counseling, preventative care, and instruction in hygiene, nutrition, contraception and wellness.

40. The state shall promote the chartering of non-profit and not-for-profit hospitals.

41. The state shall establish work rules that abolish mandatory overtime for nurses and other paraprofessionals in hospitals.

42. We will fund the University of Wisconsin system to develop new programs to provide paraprofessionals required to expand the public health service.

43. Drug abuse of all kinds should be treated as a disease, rather than a criminal offense.

44. We defend a woman's right to make reproduction choices affecting their own body. Birth control prescriptions should be covered by all health care plans and/or subsidized by the state.

Rights of Lesbian, Gay, Bisexual, and Transgender Individuals

45. Wisconsin Greens will defend the rights of all individuals to freely choose intimate partners, regardless of their sex, gender or sexual orientation.

46. Wisconsin Greens support the right of gay, lesbian, bisexual and transgender people to be treated equally with all other people, in all areas of life, including in housing, employment, civil marriage, benefits, and child custody.

Grassroots Democracy

Democracy and self-governance are dependent on the public being fully informed and all political parties having access to the ballot and public debate and discourse. Additionally, since the voter is consenting to being governed, the full will of the voter must be expressed and reflected in election results. To this end the Wisconsin Green Party will work to implement policies that result in the public being fully informed about issues and policies that tear down the barriers between the voters and the government that represents them.

Taxation

47. Wisconsin Greens will institute a progressive method of taxation that shifts the tax burden away from those that can least afford it. We will eliminate the income tax for households making less than $20,000.00 a year and reduce the income tax for households making between $20,000.00 and $30,000.00 a year.

48. A portion of funds from an increase in the motor fuel tax will go for development of alternative transportation such as mass transit and bicycle trails.

49. We will eliminate tax loopholes for corporations and the wealthy, including the state capital gains deduction and the exemption of manufacturing machinery and equipment from property tax.

50. Independent businesses that are locally owned and not affiliated with any out-of-state entity will be taxed at a lower rate than franchises that export local dollars out of the community.

51. The Greens oppose state caps on local property tax levies.

Electoral Reforms

52. Enact Instant Runoff Voting (also known as Ranked Choice Voting) for executive offices such as mayor, governor, and other single-seat elections, to ensure the full expression of voter will and to eliminate the cost of primaries in non-partisan local elections.

53. Enact Proportional Representation for legislative offices on the municipal, county, and state levels.

54. Ballot access laws will assure access thresholds that are set low enough to reflect emerging shifts in local voter will.

55. Create an independent, non-partisan redistricting commission to draw districts for the Wisconsin Assembly and Senate, as well as U.S. House districts.

56. Voters will not be denied access to the views of any political party or candidates. We will insist on the full inclusion of all political parties in all public debates regardless of candidate will.

57. The Wisconsin Green Party opposes term limits, as they are restrictions on the will of the people.

Nonviolence

The problem of violence in society is complex and multifaceted and must be addressed on different fronts. For this reason we regard economic justice, education and programs that create opportunity to have as much potential at decreasing the incidence of crime and violence as traditional punitive measures. Greens emphasize that the solutions to violence, poverty, alienation, anger and political inequality are the key to solving the dilemma of crime and punishment.

Crime & Punishment

58. Legalize and regulate the cultivation, sale, possession, and use of marijuana.

59. The Green Party will continue to oppose the death penalty in Wisconsin.

60. Crimes against people and communities must be punished through restitution and/or jail time. Alternative sentencing must be emphasized as much as possible for victimless crimes and nonviolent offenders. Ex-offenders need to come out into a healthy community that both supports them and holds them accountable.

61. We oppose the privatization of the prison system.

62. Our justice system must attach equal importance to justice for white-collar criminals, including environmental violators of our common property. Corporate executives should be held personally responsible for the consequences of their corporate actions.

63. Community members must be involved directly in crime control in their own communities through citizen police boards and neighborhood watch programs.

LIBERTARIAN PARTY OF WISCONSIN
2015

Headquarters and Staff

State Headquarters: P.O. Box 20815, Greenfield 53220.

Telephone: (800) 236-9236.

Internet Address: http://www.lpwi.org

E-mail: info@lpwi.org

State Administrative Committee

Chair: JOSEPH KEXEL, Kenosha.

Vice Chair: DEAN TROY, Little Chute.

Secretary: ANDY CRAIG, Milwaukee.

Treasurer: JON AUGELLI, Verona.

At-Large Members: STEPHEN NASS, Middleton; KAY HAGERTY, Hudson.

Congressional District Representatives:

1st District
Jim Sewell, Racine
George Meyers (alternate), Racine

2nd District
Terry Gray, Madison
Peter Augelli (alternate), Verona

3rd District
Candice Wirkus, Chippewa Falls
Scott Kenneth Noble (alternate),
  Junction City

4th District
Ken Morgan, Milwaukee
Diane Mielke (alternate), Milwaukee

5th District
Jeff Kortsch, Oconomowoc
Leroy Watson (alternate), Oconomowoc

6th District
Richard Martin, Jr., Neenah
Gus Fahrendorf (alternate)

7th District
Robert Burke Hudson
Nathan Gall (alternate), Hayward

8th District
vacancy

Source: Libertarian Party of Wisconsin.

State Convention. The Libertarian Party of Wisconsin holds its state convention in the spring of each year to conduct party business. In even-numbered years, the convention adopts proposed changes to the party platform and selects delegates to the national convention. It may also endorse candidates for election. In odd-numbered years, it adopts proposed changes to the Constitution and/or bylaws and elects party officers and members-at-large to the executive committee. The Congressional district representatives and alternates are also elected in odd-numbered years by a caucus of members from the particular district.

State Officers and Executive Committee. The party is headed by an executive committee consisting of the 4 party officers, the immediate past state party chair who is willing to serve, a representative and alternate from each of the 8 congressional districts, and 2 members-at-large. The 4 party officers and the 2 members-at-large serve 2-year terms, which begin at the end of the convention at which they are elected. Party officer or member-at-large vacancies are filled by a vote of the committee.

Congressional district members are elected by a caucus of members from that district and generally serve for two years as well. Congressional district conventions may meet annually, although state party members within a congressional district may hold an election at any time. Any vacant congressional district position is filled by a vote of state party members residing within that congressional district. A party member receiving the most votes at a congressional district election becomes a representative when the executive committee accepts his or her credentials. If no congressional district election is held, the executive committee may fill a vacant congressional district position by a majority vote.

National Committee. The Libertarian National Committee is composed of the 4 national officers, the immediate past chair, 5 members-at-large, and 9 regional representatives. A state's affiliation with a region is determined by the convention delegates from that state and is often the subject of negotiations before and during the national convention. Members of the Libertarian National Committee are selected at each biennial national convention and serve for 2 years from one national convention to the next. The Libertarian National Committee addresses national issues and serves, but does not control, the state parties.

LIBERTARIAN PARTY OF WISCONSIN 2015 PLATFORM

Preamble

As Libertarians, we defend each person's right to engage in any activity that is peaceful and honest and we welcome the diversity that freedom brings. We seek a world of liberty; a world in which all individuals control their own lives and are never forced to compromise their values or sacrifice their property. We believe that no conflict exists between civil order and individual rights and that individuals, groups, or governments should not initiate force against other individuals, groups, or governments.

Principles

Life – We believe that all individuals have the right to control their own lives and live in whatever manner they choose, as long as they do not interfere with the identical rights of others.

Liberty – The only proper functions of government are the protection of the people from actual foreign or domestic threats to their lives and freedoms; and the protection of their individual rights, namely – life, property, and liberty of speech and action.

Property – The only economic system compatible with the protection of individual human rights is the free market; therefore, the fundamental right of individuals to own property and to enjoy the rewards of their just earnings should not be compromised.

Preface

While members of the Libertarian Party of Wisconsin advocate abolishing laws governing certain voluntary behaviors, this does not necessarily imply endorsement of such behaviors. We only make the statement that in such matters an individual's right to free choice must be recognized and the morality of such choices is not a concern of government. It follows that our silence regarding any other government activity should not be interpreted as implying our approval of such activity.

Taxes

We advocate phasing out taxes on incomes, personal property, and real property, along with corresponding decreases in the size of government. We advocate phasing out taxes on corporations and businesses.

Term Limits

We advocate limits on the time any elected official may serve in office.

Elections

We advocate election law reforms that make it easier for the people to nominate and finance the election of the candidates of their choice.

Treating Adults as Children

We believe laws mandating automobile insurance, use of seat belts and helmets, minimum wage, and curfews hamper individual freedom and the responsibility that must go with it. We further believe that laws restricting such things as cruising and tattoos trivialize the law and breed disrespect for it.

State Mandates

We believe that state mandates, such as the Binding Arbitration Law, are unreasonable burdens on those who must comply with and pay for them. They only represent the desires of special interest groups and their advocates in the legislature. When these mandates are unfunded they become even more unacceptable. This belief also applies to education and the free market.

Gun Ownership

We believe the right to keep and bear arms should not be infringed. We therefore oppose all laws which tax or otherwise restrict the ownership, open or concealed carry, manufacture, transfer, or sale of firearms or ammunition. We further oppose all laws requiring registration of firearms. We also cannot ignore the clear lessons from history of the suffering which can fall upon a disarmed people.

Children and Family

We believe that children are a special group of citizens possessing fundamental rights involving their life and health. However, until they reach the age of legal responsibility, their other rights are limited and their parents or guardians are responsible for their actions and upbringing. Therefore, the rights and authority that parents or guardians need to fulfill their child raising responsibilities must be respected, but never at the expense of the child's life and health.

Education

Since private education is today outperforming public education at half the cost, we call for the phase out of all state and federal involvement in education. We therefore endorse "School Choice".

Government Welfare

Today's confusion between a person's material needs and that person's rights has led to our current system of taxpayer provided, government welfare programs. These programs often invade privacy and have proven to be demeaning and inefficient. Welfare is not charity. Charity must be freely given. More charity needs to be substituted for welfare. It is also good to remember that for people to be truly free they must become responsible for their own welfare and actions. We believe that Wisconsinites are generous and with their taxes returned to them would invest in the health and welfare of their communities and their neighbors.

Federal "Strings"

The federal government often uses the threat of withholding "federal" funds to coerce states into specific actions. We strongly urge elected officials of Wisconsin to resist such pressure and applaud them when they do. We believe that this threat violates the U.S. Constitution and the concept of a Republic.

Environment

A clean environment is in everyone's interest. Our legal system should protect public and private property from pollution. The right of property owners to prosecute any polluter under trespass, nuisance, and negligence laws should be reinstated. It follows that bureaucracies should not be allowed to harass alleged environmental violators or restrict their direct access to just treatment under the judicial system.

Transportation

We support the maximum possible privatization of all publicly owned transportation systems and therefore oppose the creation of any new publicly funded or managed transportation systems.

Victimless Crime

Because only actions that infringe on the rights of others can properly be termed "crimes", we favor the repeal of federal, state, and local laws restricting our fundamental freedom to govern our own lives.

In particular, we advocate

The repeal of laws restricting the production, sale, possession, or use of prohibited drugs and medicines. The repeal of laws regarding a minimum drinking age which are in conflict with the legally recognized age for maturity and responsibility. The repeal of laws restricting consensual sexual relations between adults. The repeal of laws regulating or prohibiting gambling. The decriminalization of assisted suicide.

Health Care

We believe the problems with our current health care system are due to government interference and mandates and that any government program to "provide" health care to some at the expense of others will most certainly reduce the overall quality, responsiveness, and individuality of health care for everyone. It would also reduce the influx of the most talented people our society has to offer into the medical profession and diminish the exemplary worldwide progress and leadership our medical system has demonstrated. For these reasons, we advocate the free enterprise system as the only system capable of making quality, affordable, individualized medical care available to all.

Privacy

We believe that free individuals may not be compelled to authorize the assignment, collection or dissemination of personal and private information on themselves; nor may any rights and privileges available to others be denied to them for using such discretion.

REPUBLICAN PARTY OF WISCONSIN
May 2015

Headquarters and Staff

State Headquarters: 148 East Johnson Street, Madison 53703.

Telephone: (608) 257-4765; Fax: (608) 257-4141.

Internet Address: http://www.wisgop.org

Executive Director: JOE FADNESS.

Political Director: JOHN VINSON.

Deputy Political Director: PHIL CURRY.

Communications Director: CHRIS MARTIN.

Research Director: JASON RECTOR.

Office Manager: PATRICK GEHL.

Operations Director: BEN HEATH.

Finance Director: JIMMY SAPP.

Data Director: MARTHA GRAVLEE.

Telemarketing Manager: RICHARD DICKIE.

Executive and District Leadership

Chairman: BRAD COURTNEY, Whitefish Bay.

Vice Chairmen: 1st – TOM SCHREIBEL, Hartland; *2nd* – CRYSTAL BERG, Hartford; *3rd* – LAURIE FORCIER, Eau Claire; *4th* – ANDREW DAVIS, Milwaukee.

At Large Member: MARIPAT KRUEGER, Menomonie.

Finance Chairman: BILL JOHNSON, Hayward.

Secretary: KATIE MCCALLUM, Middleton.

Treasurer: MIKE JONES, Milwaukee.

National Committeeman: STEVE KING, SR., Janesville.

National Committeewoman: MARY BUESTRIN, River Hills.

Immediate Past Chairman: REINCE PRIEBUS, Kenosha.

Wisconsin African American Council: GERARD RANDALL, Milwaukee.

Wisconsin Republican Labor Council: VAN WANGGAARD, Racine.

Wisconsin Hispanic Heritage Council: JOE MEDINA, Waukesha.

Congressional District Chairmen and Vice Chairmen:

1st District
Kim Travis, Williams Bay
Carol Brunner, Franklin
2nd District
Kim Babler, Madison
Tim McCumber, Merrimac
3rd District
Brian Westrate, Fall Creek
Julian Bradley, La Crosse
4th District
Bob Spindell, Milwaukee
Doug Haag, Milwaukee

5th District
Kathy Kiernan, Richfield
Keith Best, Waukesha
6th District
Dan Feyen, Fond du Lac
Janet Reabe, Green Lake
7th District
Jim Miller, Hayward
Jesse Garza, Hudson
8th District
Kevin Barthel, Lakewood
Bill Berglund, Sturgeon Bay

Source: Republican Party of Wisconsin at wisgop.org, May 2015.

County Organization. County party organizations are the basic building blocks of the Republican Party of Wisconsin. County party leaders are elected in county caucuses prior to April 1 of the odd-numbered year. Each county party has, at minimum, a chairman, vice chairman, secretary, and treasurer.

Congressional District Organization. Each congressional district has an organization that coordinates the activities of the county organizations in the district, with special emphasis on the election of Republican congressional candidates. The district organization is directed by a committee consisting of the county chairmen and vice chairmen and, at minimum, an elected chairman, vice chairman, secretary, and treasurer. District party officers are elected at a District Caucus in the odd-numbered years prior to the state convention.

State Officers and Executive Committee. Party leadership is vested in a 31-member state executive committee, consisting of the 10 party officers (including the chairman of the county chairmen's organization and the chairman of the Young Republicans Professionals, who are designated respectively as the third and fifth vice chairmen of the committee); the immediate past state party chairman; the chairman and vice chairman from each of the state's 8 congressional district organizations; and the Wisconsin Republican African American Council, the Wisconsin Heritage Council, the Wisconsin Labor Council, and an at-large member. State committee vacancies are filled by the committee. Five of the 10 party officers – the chairman, first and second vice chairmen, secretary, treasurer – are selected by the state executive committee at an organizational meeting within 60 days following the last general election in the even years. An at-large member of the State Executive Committee is also elected at the organizational meeting. Their 2-year terms begin upon adjournment of the organizational meeting. The persons holding those offices and the immediate past state party chairman may not vote in the selection of the new officers. The national committeeman and committeewoman are included among the 10 state executive committee officers and are elected for 4-year terms by state convention delegates in presidential election years. They serve from the adjournment of one national party convention to the end of the next and must be approved by the assembled delegates at the party's national convention. The party finance chairman is also included among the 10 party officers. The finance chairman serves at the pleasure of the newly elected state chairman and is appointed with the consent of the committee to a term that continues until a successor is named.

State Convention. The party holds its state convention in May, June, or July of each year to pass resolutions and conduct other party business. In even-numbered years, the convention adopts a state party platform and considers the endorsement of statewide candidates. A national committeeman and committeewoman are selected in those years in which a national party convention is held.

National Convention and National Committee. The Republican National Committee consists of a committeeman, committeewoman, and a chairman from each state, plus American Samoa, Washington, D.C., Guam, Puerto Rico, and the Virgin Islands. Each state and territory has its own method of electing representatives. National committee members serve from convention to convention. The national committee is led by a chairman and cochairman, who serve 2-year terms.

REPUBLICAN PARTY OF WISCONSIN PLATFORM
Adopted at 2014 RPW State Convention
Preamble

Generations of Americans have fought to preserve our Republic – our lives, our liberty, and our ability to pursue happiness.

Today our Constitution, our republic, and our liberty are threatened by a failure to adhere to the original principles and intent put forth in our founding documents. It is only by restoring the principles and values of our founders as expressed in these documents – that we can prevent the moral and economic collapse of our nation.

We proclaim allegiance to the Constitution of the United States and the State of Wisconsin. All legislation and regulation must adhere to the framework of both of these documents. Progressive, anti-liberty principles are incompatible with the principles of the Republican Party of Wisconsin.

For over 150 years Wisconsin's motto has defined the passion of her people and the values they hold dear. The drive to move ever onward, righting wrongs and growing through innovation and hard work has defined our state, and been a beacon to the nation. Wisconsin's people look to the future. In order to define the specific policies encompassed by said constitutional principles, and to build on our state motto – *Forward* – we want to strengthen and revitalize the core values that unite Americans.

Under Republican leadership at the state and federal levels, we have answered that call. As Republicans, we are inspired by an abiding belief in a bright future that will lift the hearts and free the minds of every Wisconsin family.

We encourage proposals to enhance Wisconsin's job climate, such as reducing the tax burden, and we encourage proposals supporting free markets and minimizing government interference in the marketplace.

We believe our nation's debt and spending are out of control. Reforms are needed to cut spending and stop pushing the burden of an expanding government onto future generations of taxpayers, thereby imposing an immoral obligation on our children and grandchildren.

We support proposals to reduce the rising costs of health care that can burden many individuals, families, and employers.

We support freedom of choice in educational options including, but not limited to, public schools, charter schools, home schooling, virtual schools, and a school choice voucher program. We believe students must have the freedom to pursue their own academic and career goals.

We believe our natural rights, as embodied in the U.S. Constitution, begin at conception and continue until death.

We oppose all efforts to require registration of firearms and to restrict ownership, manufacture, transfer, carrying, or sale of firearms or ammunition by law-abiding citizens.

We believe our current dependence on foreign energy threatens our national security and economic prosperity; therefore, we support the development of free market energy resources and the elimination of the Department of Energy.

We have an obligation to be good stewards of God's creation for future generations.

We believe the income tax system is unfair and cumbersome.

We believe the President and Congress must prioritize the health and stability of our nation's Social Security system.

We recognize that our Founding Fathers warned of the dangers of allowing central bankers to control our currency; therefore, we support transparency and a full audit of the Federal Reserve to support sound money.

We believe the United States should grant citizenship only to those who want to embrace and defend American values and culture.

We believe English as a second language instruction should be available to all who need it and we support English as the official language.

We believe that religion and morality were fundamentally important to creating and maintaining freedom in this country.

We believe America must defend herself and her allies from those who threaten our freedom and way of life.

As Republicans, we can and will make Wisconsin and our country better for future generations.

American Values and American Solutions

We want to strengthen and revitalize America's core values of life, liberty, and property that unite us all.

We believe that we need to reform the way government operates by strengthening ideas and systems currently employed in the private sector to increase productivity, accountability and effectiveness, and shall utilize private solutions, when appropriate, with an emphasis on the long-term.

We believe changes in government have to occur in all elected offices throughout the country and cannot be achieved by focusing only on Washington.

Wisconsin's Economy

We encourage proposals supporting free markets and minimizing the level of government interference in the marketplace.

We oppose policies that could penalize employment or make the state less competitive in the global marketplace.

We believe the federal government and other state governments should look to Wisconsin and Republicans as the model for providing common-sense solutions that help create jobs. To spur economic growth and activity, we will work to lower the tax burden every year. We strongly encourage other governments to enact similar policies.

Reducing the Federal Deficit and Spending

Our nation's debt and spending are out of control. Reforms are needed in order to cut spending and stop pushing the burden of an expanding government onto the next generations of taxpayers that imposes an immoral obligation on our children and grandchildren.

We believe federal government spending should be transparent, programs should be carefully and regularly audited, and waste should be identified and eliminated within government agencies.

We believe our elected officials should develop a roadmap for fiscal responsibility by balancing the budget, as well as reducing and eliminating the deficit.

Health Care

We believe the Affordable Health Care Act should be repealed in favor of free market solutions.

We support proposals to reduce the rising costs of health care that can burden many individuals, families, and employers.

We believe in free market solutions to bring down the cost of health care such as transparency, charity, portability, competition among insurers, and tort reform.

We believe individuals should not be subject to government health care mandates or face penalties, and the federal government should not violate the doctor-patient relationship. Health care should always honor the sanctity of life.

Education

We believe every student in every educational setting should receive a quality education. We support investments to ensure a healthy public school system and the freedom of choice in educational options including, but not limited to, charter schools, home schooling, virtual schools, and a school choice voucher program.

We support local control of education and keeping control of schools in the hands of elected, local school boards. We resist any coercion or manipulation of school districts by state or federal government to control finance, employee compensation, standards, standardized testing or curriculum. We support eliminating the U.S. Department of Education.

We believe academic freedom of each student must be protected so every student has the right to study without fear of reprisal. We believe public schools should develop curriculum which is content rich, fact-based, and encourages critical thinking.

We believe history courses should include the study of the founding fathers, the Constitution, the Bill of Rights, the Federalist Papers, and natural law.

We support educational options that meet the needs of students and the marketplace.

Constitutional Rights

We believe our natural rights, as embodied in the Constitution, begin at conception and continue until death. The terms "people" and "persons" shall apply to every human being at any stage of development.

The Declaration of Independence makes clear that certain rights cannot be taken away by government: "We are endowed by our Creator with the right to life, liberty, and the pursuit of happiness." We believe that all individuals have the right by natural law to reference God in any way they choose, including the Pledge of Allegiance.

We believe statements regarding liberty, religion, and morality made by the Founding Fathers are as important today as they were over 200 years ago.

We believe the language in the Constitution and the Declaration of Independence are very important and the original intent must be protected. We reject the idea that because the times change so must the meaning of the language in the Declaration of Independence and the Constitution.

We believe that the Federal Government must be reduced in the size and scope in accordance with the U.S. Constitution and that all duties that have been improperly or unfairly usurped shall be returned to the states and to the American people.

Right to Keep and Bear Arms

The Republican Party of Wisconsin is a vigilant supporter of the right of individuals to keep and bear arms embodied in both the Second Amendment to the Constitution of the United States and Article I, Section 25, of the Wisconsin Constitution.

We therefore oppose all efforts to require registration of firearms and to restrict ownership, manufacture, transfer, carrying, or sale of firearms or ammunition by law-abiding citizens.

We believe we cannot ignore the clear lessons of history regarding the tyranny and suffering that can be imposed upon a disarmed and vulnerable people.

Energy and National Security

We believe our current dependence on foreign energy threatens our national security and economic prosperity.

We support the elimination of the Department of Energy and the development of free market energy resources.

Environment

We support the protection of Wisconsin natural resources from any non-sovereign entity.

We have an obligation to be good stewards of God's creation for future generations and believe no one will better care for Wisconsin's lands and natural resources than the citizens of Wisconsin.

We believe we can solve our environmental problems with innovation and new technology rather than with more litigation and unnecessary government regulation.

Taxes

We believe a lower tax burden for all Americans creates a strong economy and encourages success.

We believe the income tax system is unfair and cumbersome.

We believe the tax code should be simplified without exceptions.

Social Security and Retirement

We believe the President and Congress must prioritize the health and stability of our nation's Social Security system.

We believe the current Social Security system is broken and if it isn't reformed, future generations will no longer have it as a retirement supplement.

Supporting Sound Money

We recognize that our Founding Fathers warned of the dangers of allowing central bankers to control our currency.

Because we recognize the hazard created by the Federal Reserve and the danger of a collapse in the value of the dollar, we support transparency and a full audit of the Federal Reserve to support sound money.

Immigration and Assimilation

We believe that legal immigration has strengthened this country throughout its history.

The United States should grant citizenship only to those who want to embrace and defend American values and culture.

We believe, along with the majority of the American people, that border control is a national security issue and current laws must be vigorously enforced.

We believe all illegal immigrants who commit or have committed felonies should be deported.

We respect the efforts of legal immigrants who have gone through the legal process to make the United States of

America their home.

We support a worker visa program, making it easier for people to work legally in the United States.

We believe the government should help businesses ensure that they hire only legal workers and prevent abuse and exploitation of workers.

English as Official Language

English should be the official language of government and used for government documents and publications.

We believe learning English is the best path to success in this country and that English as a second language instruction be available to all who need it.

Freedom of Religion

We believe statements regarding religion and morality made by the Founding Fathers are as important today as they were over 200 years ago.

We believe the phrase- 'One nation under God'- in the Pledge of Allegiance is perfectly harmonious with the United States Constitution, protected by the First Amendment.

We agree with the Founding Fathers that religion and morality were fundamentally important to creating and maintaining freedom in this country.

We believe the best way to ensure religious freedom is to protect all religious references and symbols; including those on public buildings, lands, or documents. This includes, but is not limited to, prayer in public schools, thanking God in a graduation speech, and religious symbols being placed on public property during the appropriate holiday season. We reject that such references violate the U.S. Constitution or discriminate against those who are of other faiths or are not religious.

Defending America

America must defend herself and her allies from those who threaten our freedom and way of life.

We believe the government must provide adequate funding for this constitutionally mandated responsibility.

We believe American foreign policy should first and foremost protect Americans and American interests.

Elections

10

Elections in Wisconsin: February 2014 through May 2015 primary, spring, general, and special elections

14th Wisconsin Volunteer Infantry Memorial at Camp Randall

(Sarah Girkin)

ELECTIONS IN WISCONSIN

I. The Wisconsin Electorate

History of the Suffrage. When Wisconsin became a state in 1848, suffrage (the right to vote) was restricted to white or Indian males who were citizens of the United States or white male immigrants in the process of being naturalized. To be eligible to vote, these men had to be at least 21 years of age and Wisconsin residents for at least one year preceding the election. Wisconsin extended suffrage to male "colored persons" in a constitutional referendum held in November 1849. In 1908, the Wisconsin Constitution was amended to require that voters had to be citizens of the United States. Women's suffrage came with the 19th Amendment to the U.S. Constitution in 1920. (Wisconsin was one of the first states in the nation to ratify this amendment, on June 10, 1919.) The most recent major suffrage change was to lower the voting age from 21 to 18 years of age. This was accomplished by the 26th Amendment to the U.S. Constitution, which was ratified by the states in July 1971.

Size of the Electorate. Based on information from the Department of Administration, it is estimated that in January 2014 there were about 4,416,501 potential voters 18 years of age and older. According to the Government Accountability Board, an estimated 54.8% of eligible voters cast 2,422,040 ballots in the 2014 gubernatorial election.

Age and Residence Requirements. The right to vote in Wisconsin state and local elections is granted to U.S. citizens who are age 18 or older and have resided in the election district or ward for 28 days prior to the election. Residence for purposes of voting is statutorily defined as "the place where the person's habitation is fixed, without any present intent to move, and to which, when absent, the person intends to return."

Voter Identification. 2011 Act 23 made a photo ID a requirement for receiving a ballot in all special and regular elections. Beginning with the 2015 Senate District 33 primary and special election, each voter must present one of a number of specified forms of identification when voting in an election in this state.

Voter Registration. Beginning with the 2006 spring primary, with limited exceptions, voter registration is required for all voters prior to voting. Voters registering in Wisconsin do not have to record a political party affiliation.

State law permits registration on election day at the proper polling place, and it also provides for advance registration by mail or in person with the municipal clerk, the county clerk, or the city board of election commissioners in the case of residents of the City of Milwaukee. Municipal officials may designate other locations, such as fire stations or libraries for registration, or conduct door-to-door registration drives.

II. A Capsule View of Elections

The Wisconsin Statutes, Chapters 5 through 12, provide for four regularly scheduled elections: the spring primary, the spring election, the partisan primary, and the general election in November.

The spring primary on the third Tuesday in February of each year is followed by the spring election on the first Tuesday in April. The partisan primary is held on the second Tuesday in August in even-numbered years. It is followed by the general election on the first Tuesday after the first Monday in November.

Nonpartisan officials are chosen in the spring. These include the state superintendent of public instruction, judicial officers, county board members, county executives, and municipal and school district officers.

Partisan officials, chosen in the fall, include all other county administrative officials, members of the legislature, state constitutional officers (except for the state superintendent), and members of the U.S. Congress. Not all of these offices are filled at each election because their terms vary from two to six years.

In presidential election years, the presidential preference primary vote is held at the spring election in April, and the vote for U.S. President occurs at the general election in November. In some elections, referendum questions allow Wisconsin voters to advise the state legislature or local government on matters of public policy or to ratify a proposed law, ordinance, or amendment to the Wisconsin Constitution.

Primary Elections

Until 1905, Wisconsin candidates for public office were selected through caucuses or conventions composed of delegates, eligible voters, or members of a political party. Since then, candidates have been chosen in primary elections, but the nominating caucus remains an optional method of selecting candidates for town and village offices. Aspirants must file a declaration of candidacy to run in a primary election, and they usually are required to file nomination papers signed by a specified number of persons eligible to vote in the jurisdiction or district in which they seek office.

Nonpartisan February Spring Primary. A nonpartisan primary election must be held in February if three or more candidates run for one of the offices on the April ballot and no caucus is held to nominate candidates. The two persons receiving the highest number of votes for the specific office in the primary are nominated to run as finalists in the nonpartisan election.

Partisan Primary. The purpose of the partisan primary is to select a party's nominees for the general election in November. In a partisan primary, the voter may vote on the ballot of only one political party (unlike the general election where it is possible to select any party's candidate for a particular office). Some voters express frustration that their choices are limited because they are not permitted to vote for candidates of more than one party. It is important to remember that the primary is a nominating device for the political parties; its purpose is to nominate the candidates that one political party will support against the nominees of the other parties in the general election.

Most states have a closed primary system that requires voters to publicly declare their party affiliation before they can receive the primary ballot of that party. Wisconsin's "open primary" law does not require voters to make a public declaration of their party preference. Instead, the voter is given the primary ballots of all parties but, once inside the voting booth, may cast only one party's ballot.

Candidates must appear on the partisan primary ballot, even if unopposed, in order to be nominated by their respective parties. The candidate receiving the largest number of party votes for an office becomes the party's nominee in the November election. (In the case of a special election, which is held at a time other than the general election to fill a vacated partisan office, a primary is not held if there is no more than one candidate for a party's nomination.)

Elections

Nonpartisan April Spring Election. The officials chosen in the spring nonpartisan election are the state superintendent of public instruction; judicial officers; county executive (if the county elects one); county supervisor; town, village, and city officers; and school board members. Because the terms of office vary, not all offices are filled each year. The only nonpartisan officers elected on a statewide basis are the state superintendent of public instruction and justices of the supreme court; all others are elected from the county, circuit, district, or municipality represented.

The governor is authorized to fill vacancies that occur in nonpartisan state elective offices by appointment. Gubernatorial appointments strongly influence the composition of the Wisconsin judiciary, because many of the state's justices and judges who are appointed to the bench are later elected to office by the voters.

Partisan November General Election. In November, Wisconsin voters select their federal, state, and county partisan officials on a ballot listing the winners of the partisan primary election plus "independent" candidates who are either unaffiliated or affiliated with minor parties that are not recognized for separate ballot status. "Write-in" votes may be cast for persons whose names do not appear on the ballot.

The general election ballot includes a broad range of offices. The constitutional offices of governor, lieutenant governor, secretary of state, state treasurer, and attorney general are filled through a statewide vote. These officers are elected for 4-year terms in the even-numbered years that alternate with the U.S. presidential election.

Candidates for congressional representative and for representative to the state assembly are included on every general election ballot, because the terms for these offices are two years. Wisconsin's 33 state senators are elected for 4-year terms, with the odd-numbered senate districts electing their senators in the years when a gubernatorial election is held and even-numbered senate districts electing their senators in the presidential election years. U.S. Senators, who serve 6-year terms, are also chosen at the appropriate general election.

The state's 72 counties elect certain partisan officers for 4-year terms at each general election. Clerks of circuit court, coroners, and sheriffs are elected at the general election in which the governor is also elected, while county clerks, district attorneys, registers of deeds, surveyors, and treasurers are elected at the general election in which the president is elected. State law requires all counties either to elect a coroner or appoint a medical examiner. The post of surveyor may be filled by election or appointment at the county's option. (Milwaukee County is required by law to appoint its medical examiner and surveyor.)

Vacancies in the offices of U.S. Senator, U.S. Congressional representative, state senator, and representative to the assembly may be filled only by special election, but vacancies in state constitutional offices and most county offices are filled through appointment by the governor. The exception is that the lieutenant governor constitutionally succeeds the governor in case of a vacancy in that office.

Presidential Preference Vote

Wisconsin conducts its presidential preference vote on the first Tuesday in April of each presidential election year, in conjunction with the nonpartisan spring election. 1985 Wisconsin Act 304 gave political parties complete freedom to select delegates for their national conventions on any basis they choose, so the vote has no binding effect. It does, however, indicate voter preferences.

A committee, composed of officials of the recognized political parties, meets on the first Tuesday in January (the next day if Tuesday is a holiday) of the year prior to the presidential preference vote in April to certify to the Government Accountability Board (GAB) the list of names to be placed on the ballot. (If a party's candidate for governor received at least 10% of the vote in the previous election, the party is considered a "recognized party".) The committee lists the names of all nationally advocated or recognized candidates of the recognized parties and such other names as it chooses. The committee includes each party's state chairperson (or designee), one national committeeman and one committeewoman (designated by the party's state chairperson), the president and the minority leader of the senate (or designees), and the speaker and minority leader of the assembly (or designees). An additional member is elected by the committee to serve as chairperson.

Any person named by the committee as a potential presidential candidate may withdraw from the ballot by filing a disclaimer with the GAB. Persons not named may have their names placed on the ballot by filing a nomination petition signed by a specified number of qualified electors.

Presidential Elections

Presidential Electors. On the first Tuesday in October in each presidential election year, the five partisan constitutional state officers, all hold-over senators, and the senate and assembly candidates nominated by each political party at the partisan primary election meet at the State Capitol to select a slate of presidential electors, who will cast Wisconsin's official ballots for the offices of U.S. President and Vice President. A party selects one elector from each of the Wisconsin congressional districts and two electors at large, and then certifies its list of electors to the GAB. After the November presidential election, the party that receives a plurality of the votes statewide sends its electors to the State Capitol on the first Monday after the second Wednesday in December to perform their duties as Wisconsin's electors. They compose Wisconsin's delegation to the Electoral College – the group of 538 electors nationwide who actually cast the votes for president and vice president. Independent candidates for president list their electors on their nomination papers.

Referendum and Recall

Referendum. A "referendum" is simply a question referred to the people for determination through a vote. On the state level, Wisconsin provides for four types of referenda: 1) amendments to the state constitution, 2) measures extending the right of suffrage, 3) ratification of legislation prior to its becoming law, and 4) advisory questions.

The procedure for amending the Wisconsin Constitution requires that two consecutive legislatures must adopt an identically worded amendment proposal and a majority of the voters participating in the election must ratify the change at a subsequent election.

An advisory referendum gives the legislature a means of asking the voters their opinion on legislative policy. Advisory referenda are usually submitted to the electorate at the April or November elections. Wisconsin county boards may submit advisory or ratifying referenda to county voters. Municipalities also are permitted and sometimes required to submit referendum questions relating to village and city charter ordinances and certain other subjects.

Recall. The Wisconsin Constitution and statutes provide for the removal of elected officers through a process of petition and special election, known as "recall". Officials may be recalled after serving the first year of a term, and no reason need be given for the recall in the case of a state, congressional, legislative, state judicial, or county officer. A petition seeking recall of a city, village, town, or school district official must contain a statement of a reason for the recall. The reason must be related to the official responsibilities of the office, but the petitioners need not provide supporting evidence for the reason.

A petition for the recall of an officer must be signed by electors equal to at least 25% of the vote cast in the district or territory served by the official during the last gubernatorial election. Following the filing of a successful recall petition, an election is held to fill the office. A recall primary is required whenever two or more persons compete for a nonpartisan office or whenever more than one person competes for the nomination of a political party for a partisan office. Unless the official facing recall resigns, he or she is listed on the recall ballot along with the other candidates who have been nominated.

Prior to 1977, the recall was seldom used. In August of that year, five La Crosse school board members were recalled, and in the following month a county judge was recalled for the first time in Wisconsin history. Attempts to recall state legislators have been relatively rare. On June 4, 1996, a state senator became the first state legislator to be recalled. Subsequently, a state senator was defeated in a recall primary on October 21, 2003. On August 9, 2011, two state senators were defeated in recall elections. On June 5, 2012, an election for the recall of the governor and lieutenant governor was held for the first time in Wisconsin history. Both won their recall elections, making them the first governor and lieutenant governor to survive a recall election in U.S. history. On the same date, another state senator was defeated in a recall election.

Mechanics of the Election Process

Certifying candidates, registering voters, and recording and reporting millions of votes is a complex process governed by state law. Legislation passed in 2007 created a Government Accountability Board that replaced both the Ethics Board and the Elections Board. The GAB is composed of 6 retired judges. The GAB, Elections Division took over responsibility for the administration of elections laws in January 2008.

The GAB, Elections Division determines the format for all federal, state, county, municipal and special district ballots, certifies to each county clerk the list of candidates for federal and state office, and performs many other duties pertaining to elections.

County clerks prepare the ballots for federal, state, and county elections and distribute them to the municipal clerks. The law requires every city, village, and town having a population of 7,500 or more to use an electronic voting system, unless otherwise permitted by the Elections Division. If an electronic voting machine is used, the equipment must generate a complete, permanent record showing all votes cast by each voter, which can be verified by the voter.

Municipal clerks supervise registration and elections in their municipalities. In cities or counties with more than 500,000 population, election duties are performed by a city board of election commissioners and a county board of election commissioners. (This provision currently applies only to the City of Milwaukee and Milwaukee County.)

Registration and Voting

The first step in casting a Wisconsin ballot usually is to register to vote. The voter must provide information including name; residence; previous residence; citizenship; date of birth; age; the voter's driver's license number or last 4 digits of the voter's social security number, if any; length of residence in the ward or election district; whether the applicant has been convicted of a felony for which he or she has not been pardoned, and if so, whether the applicant is incarcerated, on parole, probation or extended supervision; and whether the applicant is disqualified on any other ground from voting; or is currently registered to vote at any other location.

Most voter registration information is open to public inspection, but victims of domestic abuse, sexual assault, or stalking can request that their registration information be kept confidential. A voter's registration is considered permanent unless the person changes his or her residence, in which case it is necessary to transfer registration to the new residence. Municipalities, however, must cancel the registration of a person who, though eligible, does not vote during a 4-year period and does not respond to a written request to apply for continued registration.

A voter who is unable or unwilling to come to the polling place on election day may vote by absentee ballot. An absentee ballot may be cast by mail or in person at the municipal clerk's office serving the voter's residence. Every request for an absentee ballot must be made in writing.

On election day, there are usually seven inspectors (election officials) for each polling place. The number may vary, but no polling place may have fewer than three. Any member of the public may be present in any polling place for the purpose of observation and the major parties often designate official polling place observers.

Under 2011 Wisconsin Act 23, beginning with the 2015 Senate District 33 special election, each voter must present one of a number of specified forms of identification when voting in an election in this state. An absentee voter who votes by mail must enclose a copy of the identification. A number of exemptions are provided. A voter who fails to present an acceptable form of identification may vote by provisional ballot. If an absentee voter who votes by mail fails to enclose a copy of an acceptable form of identification, the voter's absentee ballot is treated as provisional. A voter who casts a provisional ballot has until 4:00 p.m. on the Friday after an election to provide an acceptable form of identification in order for his or her provisional ballot to be counted. To do this, the voter may return to the polls before the closing hour or provide the identification to the municipal clerk or board of election commissioners of the municipality where he or she resides after the polls close. With limited exceptions, Act 23 also requires a voter who votes at a polling place to enter his or her signature on the poll list (the list used by election officials which shows the names and addresses of eligible voters) when voting in an election.

III. Campaign Finance Regulation

Early Reforms. Wisconsin's first attempt to regulate election practices (Chapter 358, Laws of 1897) was passed to stymie the crudest forms of corrupt practices, such as bribery, illegal voting, election fraud, and related corruption. It also required the filing of financial statements that were open to the public.

The current ban on campaign contributions by corporations dates back to 1905 (Chapter 492). Corporations are still prohibited from donating to candidates, political parties, or committees. (Labor organizations were also banned from making such contributions by Chapter 135, Laws of 1935, but the prohibition was repealed by Chapter 429, Laws of 1959.) Under a recent U.S. Supreme Court decision, corporations may make direct expenditures supporting or opposing candidates.

The "Corrupt Practices Act" of 1911 (Chapter 650) strengthened and expanded the earlier laws. Central to the act were tightening disclosure provisions. Candidates were required to report all sources of their funding, and they were barred from trading favors, monetary or otherwise, in return for financial support.

1974 Campaign Finance Reforms. The legislature passed sweeping campaign finance reform in Chapter 334, Laws of 1973, which created the current statutory "Chapter 11 – Campaign Finance". The law regulated campaign contributions and expenditures and required central filing of financial reports. It also created the state Elections Board, with representation from the three branches of government and the major political parties, to administer and enforce both election and campaign finance laws. These duties are now performed by the GAB. Candidates, individuals, committees, and groups involved in campaigns for state offices and statewide referenda must file detailed campaign finance reports with the board, which supervises the auditing of the reports. The GAB investigates election law violations and must notify the district attorney, attorney general, or the governor of any facts or evidence that might be grounds for civil action or criminal prosecution.

Regulation of Contributions

Wisconsin regulates campaign finance according to function – contribution or expenditure – with separate dollar limits and reporting requirements.

Contributions are moneys or certain other things of value that are donated directly either to individual candidates or to political committees, with the recipients determining how the money will be spent. The state determines the contribution limits in the case of state or local offices, but candidates running for federal office are subject to the limits set by federal campaign finance laws.

Contributions by candidates from their own personal funds cannot be limited because they are considered to be free expression and are protected by the First Amendment.

Individuals. States are free to set their own limits on contributions to candidates for state or local office. Limitations usually pertain to the type of office. Wisconsin also limits the overall amount a single individual is allowed to contribute to all candidates in a calendar year.

Other than a candidate's own contributions to the campaign, no individual may contribute more than the amounts specified to the following candidates or any individuals or independent groups supporting them: constitutional officer (governor, lieutenant governor, secretary of state, state treasurer, attorney general, or superintendent of public instruction) or supreme court justice – $10,000; state senator – $1,000; representative to the assembly – $500; and all other state and local candidates – a maximum of $250 to $3,000 depending upon the office. Furthermore, no individual may make contributions to a combination of candidates or registered committees that exceed a total of $10,000 in any calendar year.

Committees. Wisconsin limits campaign contributions made by political committees. Different limits apply in terms of the amounts a particular type of committee may donate and the amounts a candidate may receive from committees. Committees subject to contribution limits include: 1) the *political action committee (PAC),* which may be created by but operate separately from a private interest group (such as a trade association or a union) to raise and spend money to elect or defeat particular candidates; 2) the *political party committee,* organized by a formal political party; 3) the *legislative campaign committees,* organized by the respective political parties within the State Senate or the State Assembly; and 4) the candidate's *personal campaign committee.* Any committee that contributes directly to a particular candidate's campaign is subject to specific contribution limits, which vary according to the type of committee and the type of elective office. However, legislative campaign committees and political party committees are allowed to use contributions for party building activities or administrative expenses. PACs may contribute to the political parties and legislative campaign committees in which case the PAC per-candidate limitations do not apply (although other limitations remain applicable).

No committee, other than a political party or legislative campaign committee, may make contributions to a candidate for statewide constitutional office or justice of the supreme court that exceed 4% of the candidate's statutory expenditure level. (Similar limits on contributions by committees apply to candidates for other state and local offices.)

Regulation of Expenditures

Expenditures by the Candidate. Candidates may make campaign expenditures from their own personal funds and the moneys received as contributions from individuals and registered committees. There are no limits on the amount the candidates can spend on their own campaigns. There were attempts at the federal and state level in the early 1970s to limit candidates' personal expenditures, but the U.S. Supreme Court in *Buckley v. Valeo* held that this type of financing was protected by the U.S. Constitution as an exercise of free speech.

Expenditures by Independent Individuals and Committees. Individuals and committees are considered to be making independent expenditures if they do not coordinate their efforts with a candidate. Independent individuals and committees are permitted to spend unlimited amounts promoting or opposing a candidate, but in Wisconsin they are required to file a statement declaring that the expenditures will be made without consultation or coordination with any candidate. (If a candidate is knowingly involved in an expenditure, the expenditure is viewed as a contribution to the candidate, and the contributor must adhere to contribution limits.)

Expenditures by Political Party Committees. When a political party makes an expenditure to support its candidate, the expenditure is normally counted as a contribution to that candidate. Candidates are subject to aggregate limitations on the amount they may receive from parties and other committees. In *Colorado Republican Federal Campaign Committee et al. v. Federal Election Commission,* 518 U.S. 604 (1996), the U.S. Supreme Court held, however, that political party committees may make unlimited independent expenditures as long as they are not acting in consultation or coordination with a candidate.

Reporting Requirements

Registration and Reporting. Campaign finance laws are designed to track the flow of dollars received and spent by the candidates. Expenditures from the campaign depository may not be made anonymously, nor may contributions or expenditures be made in a fictitious name. Any anonymous contribution of more than $10 must be donated to a charity or the common school fund.

Generally, all candidates for state office, the four types of committees listed above, and other committees that make contributions or expenditures expressly supporting or opposing state candidates must register and file campaign finance reports with the GAB. These reports must include the name, address, and total contributions of each contributor who donates more than $20 in a calendar year and must give the occupation and principal place of employment of each contributor who makes cumulative contributions of over $100 in a calendar year. Reports must also itemize all contributions, loans, expenditures, or obligations in excess of $20. Registrants with limited financial activity may be exempted from reporting.

Each candidate must appoint one campaign treasurer and designate one campaign depository, such as a numbered bank account, before receiving any contributions or making any expenditures. The candidate and campaign treasurer are then required to file a registration statement regardless of the amount of money they expect to receive or dispense. Unless exempted from reporting, the candidate, or the treasurer acting on the candidate's behalf, must file periodic financial reports. The candidate is considered personally responsible for the accuracy of these reports.

With limited exceptions, political party committees or other committees that make or accept contributions or make expenditures amounting to more than $25 per year, and individuals (other than candidates) who accept contributions or make expenditures amounting to more than $25 per year must file registration statements. For referendum activity, the threshold is more than $750 per year. These statements include such information as the name and address of the registrant, the officers, the campaign depository, and the candidate or referendum question they support or oppose.

Since July 1, 1999, registrants with the Government Accountability Board, Ethics and Accountability Division who have accepted contributions totaling more than $20,000 within a campaign or biennial period have been required to file their reports electronically. These reports may be viewed on the GAB Web site.

Nonresident committees, groups, or individuals making contributions or expenditures in this state must also file their names and addresses and those of a designated agent in the state with the secretary of state and must also file regular reports, unless a reporting exemption applies.

Disclaimers. Candidates and political committees that are subject to state reporting requirements must identify themselves on any mass media communications, such as billboards, handbills, and radio or TV advertisements. This disclosure must contain the words "paid for" followed by the name of the candidate or organization responsible for the communication and the name of the candidate's or organization's treasurer.

IV. Public Campaign Financing

Chapter 107, Laws of 1977, and 2009 Wisconsin Act 89 provided public financing to candidates for certain state offices. Public financing was repealed by 2011 Wisconsin Act 32.

CREATING A TRANSPORTATION FUND AND A DEPARTMENT OF TRANSPORTATION

Creating Article IV, Section 9 (2) and Article VIII, Section 11; 2011 SJR 23 (JR 4); 2013 AJR 2 (JR 1); Adopted.

Ballot Question: *"Creation of a Transportation Fund.* Shall section 9 (2) of article IV and section 11 of article VIII of the constitution be created to require that revenues generated by use of the state transportation system be deposited into a transportation fund administered by a department of transportation for the exclusive purpose of funding Wisconsin's transportation systems and to prohibit any transfers or lapses from this fund?"

Text of Sections:

[Article IV] Section 9 (2) The legislature shall provide by law for the establishment of a department of transportation and a transportation fund.

[Article VIII] Section 11. All funds collected by the state from any taxes or fees levied or imposed for the licensing of motor vehicle operators, for the titling, licensing, or registration of motor vehicles, for motor vehicle fuel, or for the use of roadways, highways, or bridges, and from taxes and fees levied or imposed for aircraft, airline property, or aviation fuel or for railroads or railroad property shall be deposited only into the transportation fund or with a trustee for the benefit of the department of transportation or the holders of transportation-related revenue bonds, except for of transportation or the holders of transportation-related revenue bonds, except for collections from taxes or fees in existence on December 31, 2010, that were not being deposited in the transportation fund on that date. None of the funds collected or received by the state from any source and deposited into the transportation fund shall be lapsed, further transferred, or appropriated to any program that is not directly administered by the department of transportation in furtherance of the department's responsibility for the planning, promotion, and protection of all transportation systems in the state except for programs for which there was an appropriation from the transportation fund on December 31, 2010. In this section, the term "motor vehicle" does not include any all-terrain vehicles, snowmobiles, or watercraft.

COUNTY VOTE FOR CONSTITUTIONAL AMENDMENT
November 4, 2014 General Election

County	Yes	No	County	Yes	No
Adams	6,280	1,408	Marinette	12,513	2,522
Ashland	4,635	1,134	Marquette	4,962	1,183
Barron	12,932	2,872	Menominee	582	182
Bayfield	5,916	1,441	Milwaukee	238,037	68,062
Brown	73,187	16,254	Monroe	11,540	2,738
Buffalo	4,083	1,096	Oconto	12,293	3,097
Burnett	5,298	917	Oneida	13,659	2,459
Calumet	16,127	3,030	Outagamie	56,482	12,695
Chippewa	17,896	4,608	Ozaukee	33,962	6,302
Clark	8,215	2,210	Pepin	2,263	723
Columbia	18,163	4,728	Pierce	11,018	2,708
Crawford	4,725	1,238	Polk	12,594	2,664
Dane	165,627	68,813	Portage	22,054	5,653
Dodge	25,925	5,199	Price	4,860	1,130
Door	11,004	2,407	Racine	57,928	14,458
Douglas	12,366	2,324	Richland	5,014	1,287
Dunn	11,267	3,213	Rock	41,847	11,494
Eau Claire	29,974	8,276	Rusk	4,436	960
Florence	1,585	329	St. Croix	25,567	6,128
Fond du Lac	31,630	6,528	Sauk	18,295	4,182
Forest	2,759	541	Sawyer	5,261	1,071
Grant	13,194	3,172	Shawano	12,731	2,762
Green	10,704	2,661	Sheboygan	38,243	7,103
Green Lake	6,091	1,432	Taylor	5,761	1,324
Iowa	7,499	2,504	Trempealeau	8,242	2,043
Iron	2,223	445	Vernon	8,812	2,314
Jackson	5,735	1,519	Vilas	8,315	1,381
Jefferson	25,901	7,010	Walworth	28,426	6,787
Juneau	6,830	1,687	Washburn	5,372	1,278
Kenosha	42,106	9,162	Washington	52,165	9,586
Kewaunee	6,691	1,612	Waukesha	149,687	31,132
La Crosse	36,294	8,235	Waupaca	15,817	3,571
Lafayette	4,557	1,239	Waushara	7,649	1,568
Langlade	6,603	1,250	Winnebago	50,831	9,935
Lincoln	9,546	1,776	Wood	24,502	4,841
Manitowoc	24,649	5,987	TOTAL	1,733,101	434,806
Marathon	43,164	9,226			

Source: Official records of the Government Accountability Board, Elections Division. Scattered votes omitted.

ELECTION OF CHIEF JUSTICE

Amending Article VII, Section 4 (2); 2013 SJR 57 (JR 16); 2015 SJR 2 (JR 2); Adopted.

Ballot Question: *"Election of Chief Justice.* Shall section 4 (2) of Article VII of the constitution be amended to direct that a chief justice of the supreme court shall be elected for a two-year term by a majority of the justices then serving on the court?"

Text of Section:

[Article VII] Section 4 (2) The chief justice of the supreme court shall be elected for a term of 2 years by a majority of the justices then serving on the court. The justice so designated as chief justice may, irrevocably, decline to serve as chief justice or resign as chief justice but continue to serve as a justice of the supreme court.

COUNTY VOTE FOR CONSTITUTIONAL AMENDMENT
April 7, 2015 Spring Election

County	Yes	No	County	Yes	No
Adams	2,381	1,735	Marinette	3,701	2,816
Ashland	905	1,437	Marquette	1,893	1,086
Barron	3,156	2,328	Menominee	142	183
Bayfield	1,313	1,914	Milwaukee	42,175	49,810
Brown	20,894	16,995	Monroe	2,081	1,826
Buffalo	1,501	937	Oconto	4,380	3,044
Burnett	1,354	882	Oneida	3,402	2,866
Calumet	3,733	2,696	Outagamie	10,866	9,919
Chippewa	3,839	3,103	Ozaukee	13,068	6,470
Clark	2,865	1,747	Pepin	1,147	712
Columbia	4,969	4,661	Pierce	3,137	2,288
Crawford	1,179	1,096	Polk	3,327	2,208
Dane	30,490	69,815	Portage	4,847	5,579
Dodge	7,507	4,707	Price	1,377	1,212
Door	3,340	3,498	Racine	17,405	11,979
Douglas	3,333	3,323	Richland	1,140	1,495
Dunn	2,517	2,262	Rock	10,067	10,106
Eau Claire	4,924	6,283	Rusk	1,609	1,034
Florence	372	229	St. Croix	5,286	3,764
Fond du Lac	8,400	5,555	Sauk	3,542	4,454
Forest	1,272	636	Sawyer	1,573	1,139
Grant	4,069	3,182	Shawano	3,284	2,395
Green	3,382	3,247	Sheboygan	11,610	6,877
Green Lake	2,080	1,129	Taylor	1,922	1,058
Iowa	1,768	2,184	Trempealeau	2,102	1,725
Iron	760	526	Vernon	2,392	2,358
Jackson	2,806	1,644	Vilas	2,992	1,856
Jefferson	6,986	5,007	Walworth	9,690	5,646
Juneau	1,946	1,460	Washburn	1,780	1,327
Kenosha	9,327	7,382	Washington	14,256	5,681
Kewaunee	2,612	1,698	Waukesha	43,969	19,003
La Crosse	7,217	8,496	Waupaca	4,381	3,250
Lafayette	1,728	1,356	Waushara	2,108	1,320
Langlade	3,187	1,878	Winnebago	9,957	9,326
Lincoln	2,212	2,028	Wood	4,722	4,966
Manitowoc	9,728	6,474	TOTAL	433,533	384,503
Marathon	12,151	10,195			

Source: Official records of the Government Accountability Board, Elections Division. Scattered votes omitted.

COUNTY VOTE FOR SUPREME COURT JUSTICE
April 7, 2015 Spring Election

County	Ann W. Bradley*	James P. Daley	County Total
Adams	2,549	1,521	4,073
Ashland	1,670	654	2,326
Barron	2,904	2,448	5,357
Bayfield	2,243	953	3,210
Brown	21,747	15,447	37,256
Buffalo	1,469	896	2,366
Burnett	1,094	1,056	2,150
Calumet	3,336	2,993	6,329
Chippewa	4,277	2,744	7,021
Clark	2,709	1,965	4,674
Columbia	5,756	3,898	9,660
Crawford	1,569	695	2,264
Dane	78,654	21,732	100,492
Dodge	5,739	6,348	12,087
Door	4,326	2,271	6,612
Douglas	4,232	2,262	6,498
Dunn	2,896	1,796	4,692
Eau Claire	7,562	3,616	11,197
Florence	302	265	567
Fond du Lac	6,734	7,193	13,927
Forest	1,115	689	1,806
Grant	4,360	2,729	7,095
Green	4,050	2,484	6,540
Green Lake	1,584	1,588	3,172
Iowa	2,723	1,214	3,937
Iron	705	508	1,217
Jackson	2,837	1,451	4,288
Jefferson	5,895	6,026	11,936
Juneau	2,093	1,295	3,394
Kenosha	9,483	6,919	16,416
Kewaunee	2,507	1,684	4,191
La Crosse	10,497	5,163	15,660
Lafayette	1,876	1,236	3,113
Langlade	3,061	1,991	5,052
Lincoln	2,767	1,616	4,384
Manitowoc	8,951	6,821	15,772
Marathon	14,960	8,112	23,099
Marinette	3,858	2,484	6,342
Marquette	1,559	1,374	2,938
Menominee	215	81	296
Milwaukee	55,479	35,788	91,387
Monroe	2,514	1,404	3,922
Oconto	4,200	3,015	7,215
Oneida	3,871	2,536	6,417
Outagamie	11,897	8,770	20,667
Ozaukee	7,848	11,133	18,981
Pepin	1,120	652	1,772
Pierce	3,203	1,990	5,193
Polk	2,913	2,430	5,343
Portage	7,304	3,300	10,614
Price	1,627	1,009	2,636
Racine	14,925	13,767	28,692
Richland	1,929	785	2,714
Rock	10,846	9,965	20,832
Rusk	1,473	1,170	2,643
St. Croix	4,861	3,742	8,621
Sauk	5,259	2,810	8,069
Sawyer	1,613	1,202	2,817
Shawano	3,169	2,458	5,631
Sheboygan	8,870	9,434	18,329
Taylor	1,880	1,152	3,032
Trempealeau	2,560	1,252	3,814
Vernon	3,287	1,527	4,814
Vilas	2,620	2,195	4,825
Walworth	7,021	7,974	15,019
Washburn	1,608	1,344	2,952
Washington	6,366	13,383	19,765
Waukesha	21,229	42,005	63,310
Waupaca	4,285	3,232	7,523
Waushara	1,828	1,568	3,396
Winnebago	11,345	7,694	19,069
Wood	6,052	3,728	9,780
TOTAL	471,866	340,632	813,200

*Incumbent.

Source: Official records of the Government Accountability Board, Elections Division. County totals include scattered votes.

DISTRICT VOTE FOR COURT OF APPEALS
April 1, 2014 Spring Election
District I

County	Patricia S Curley*	County Total
Milwaukee	42,961	43,464
TOTAL.	42,961	43,464

District II

County	Lisa S. Neubauer*	County Total
Calumet	3,149	3,154
Fond du Lac	5,659	5,663
Green Lake.	2,414	2,423
Kenosha	10,770	10,853
Manitowoc.	8,400	8,446
Ozaukee	5,478	5,525
Racine	9,353	9,399
Sheboygan	7,747	7,801
Walworth.	7,853	7,917
Washington.	9,127	9,157
Waukesha	31,085	31,175
Winnebago.	14,486	14,602
TOTAL.	115,521	116,115

District IV

County	Gary E. Sherman*	County Total
Adams	1,665	1,674
Clark	2,505	2,516
Columbia.	5,006	5,044
Crawford.	1,409	1,411
Dane	42,192	42,734
Dodge	5,534	5,556
Grant	4,133	4,160
Green.	2,771	2,789
Iowa	1,849	1,859
Jackson.	1,858	1,868
Jefferson	7,771	7,842
Juneau	1,532	1,537
La Crosse	9,516	9,570
Lafayette.	1,732	1,739
Marquette	1,107	1,115
Monroe	4,726	4,745
Portage.	3,784	3,804
Richland	1,302	1,307
Rock	10,343	10,409
Sauk	6,401	6,419
Vernon	2,086	2,095
Waupaca	5,014	5,024
Waushara.	1,332	1,337
Wood	7,448	7,471
TOTAL.	133,016	134,025

*Incumbent.

Source: Official records of the Government Accountability Board, Elections Division. County totals include scattered votes.

DISTRICT VOTE FOR COURT OF APPEALS
April 7, 2015 Spring Election
District I

County	Kitty K. Brennan*	County Total
Milwaukee	52,442	53,062
TOTAL.	52,442	53,062

District III

County	Kristina M. Bourget	Mark A. Seidl	County Total
Ashland	1,023	822	1,850
Barron	2,251	2,400	4,659
Bayfield	1,377	1,207	2,590
Brown	11,881	19,389	31,385
Buffalo	1,148	1,001	2,150
Burnett	839	995	1,834
Chippewa	3,563	2,690	6,253
Door	2,380	2,843	5,244
Douglas	3,216	2,457	5,682
Dunn	2,328	1,721	4,049
Eau Claire	6,454	3,358	9,849
Florence	209	306	515
Forest.	563	1,015	1,579
Iron.	499	547	1,051
Kewaunee	1,235	2,593	3,828
Langlade	1,366	3,016	4,385
Lincoln.	2,379	1,322	3,708
Marathon.	4,993	15,607	20,653
Marinette.	2,285	3,308	5,593
Menominee	134	98	232
Oconto	2,474	4,051	6,525
Oneida	1,965	3,478	5,448
Outagamie	6,800	10,018	16,818
Pepin.	832	803	1,635
Pierce.	2,563	2,174	4,737
Polk	2,289	2,558	4,847
Price	757	1,524	2,281
Rusk	996	1,258	2,254
St. Croix	3,981	3,674	7,681
Sawyer	1,119	1,365	2,486
Shawano	1,723	3,194	4,918
Taylor	767	1,968	2,735
Trempealeau	1,845	1,612	3,462
Vilas	1,541	2,548	4,099
Washburn	1,290	1,227	2,521
TOTAL.	81,065	108,147	189,536

*Incumbent.

Source: Official records of the Government Accountability Board, Elections Division. County totals include scattered votes.

VOTE FOR CIRCUIT JUDGES
February 18, 2014 Spring Primary

Circuit Court	Vote
Dunn County Circuit Court, Branch 1	
Roger M. Hillestad	221
Christina M. Mayer	583
James M. Peterson	671
Waupaca County Circuit Court, Branch 2	
Vicki Taggatz Clussman	700
Brenda Starr Freeman	594
Edmund J. Jelinski	630
Keith A. Steckbauer	841

Source: Official records of the Government Accountability Board, Elections Division. Scattered votes omitted.

February 17, 2015 Spring Primary

Circuit Court	Vote
Jackson County Circuit Court	
Anna L. Becker	1,018
Daniel Diehn	809
Michelle Greendeer (write-in)	175
Robyn Matousek	305
Mark A. Radcliffe	233
James C. Ritland	85
La Crosse County Circuit Court, Branch 5	
Brian K. Barton	1,468
Gloria L. Doyle	3,657
Candice C.M. Tlustosch	1,443
Lafayette County Circuit Court	
Kate Findley	409
Gayle Jebbia	350
Duane M. Jorgenson	896
Guy M. Taylor	285
Sheboygan County Circuit Court, Branch 4	
Catherine Q. Delahunt	2,865
Matthew P. Mooney	1,297
Rebecca Persick	2,820

Source: Official records of the Government Accountability Board, Elections Division. Scattered votes omitted.

VOTE FOR CIRCUIT JUDGES
April 24, 2014 Spring Election

Circuit Court	Vote	Circuit Court	Vote
Barron County		**Milwaukee County**	
Branch 2		Branch 7	
J. Michael Bitney	2,046	Thomas J. McAdams	40,356
Branch 3		Branch 21	
Maureen D. Boyle	1,996	Bill Brash*	39,748
Chippewa County		Branch 24	
Branch 1		Janet Protasiewicz	40,660
Roderick A. Cameron*	2,773	Branch 27	
Branch 3		Kevin E. Martens*	40,049
Steven R. Cray*	2,667	Branch 31	
Dane County		Daniel A. Noonan*	40,158
Branch 1		Branch 32	
John W. Markson*	42,240	Cedric Cornwall	24,086
Branch 7		Laura Gramling Perez	36,113
William E. Hanrahan*	41,862	Branch 40	
Dodge County		Rebecca Dallet*	39,652
Branch 1		Branch 41	
Brian A. Pfitzinger*	5,818	John J. DiMotto*	40,720
Branch 4		**Oneida County**	
Steven G. Bauer*	5,917	Branch 1	
Dunn County		Patrick F. O'Melia*	3,015
Branch 1		**Outagamie County**	
Christina M. Mayer	2,326	Branch 2	
James M. Peterson	2,476	Nancy Krueger*	9,210
Eau Claire County		Branch 3	
Branch 1		Mitchell J. Metropulos*	9,059
Kristina M. Bourget**	16,170	**Polk County**	
Branch 2		Branch 1	
Michael Schumacher*	16,054	Molly E. GaleWyrick*	4,300
Florence-Forest County		**Price County**	
Robert A. Kennedy, Jr.	1,195	Douglas T. Fox*	1,341
Leon D. Stenz*	2,031	**Racine County**	
Fond du Lac County		Branch 7	
Branch 1		Charles Constantine*	9,631
Dale L. English*	6,099	**Rock County**	
Jefferson County		Branch 1	
Branch 3		James P. Daley*	11,193
Joann L. Miller	4,689	**St. Croix County**	
David J. Wambach	6,387	Branch 1	
Juneau County		Eric J. Lundell*	6,221
Branch 2		Branch 4	
Paul S. Curran*	1,787	Howard W. Cameron*	6,102
Kenosha County		**Washington County**	
Branch 3		Branch 2	
Bruce E. Schroeder*	11,507	James K Muehlbauer*	9,275
Marathon County		**Waukesha County**	
Branch 3		Branch 5	
Lamont K. Jacobson	8,529	Lee S. Dreyfus, Jr.*	32,694
Marinette County		Branch 6	
Branch 1		Patrick C. Haughney*	30,137
David G. Miron*	2,234	**Waupaca County**	
Menominee-Shawano County		Branch 2	
Branch 1		Keith A. Steckbauer	2,720
James R. Habeck*	3,066	Vicki Taggatz Clussman	3,689
		Wood County	
		Branch 1	
		Gregory J. Potter*	7,996

*Incumbent.
**Resigned June 2015.
Source: Official records of the Government Accountability Board, Elections Division. Scattered votes omitted.

VOTE FOR CIRCUIT JUDGES
April 7, 2015 Spring Election

Circuit Court	Vote	Circuit Court	Vote
Adams County		**Branch 3**	
Jesse L . Leichsenring	685	Clare L. Fiorenza*	49,869
Daniel Glen Wood	3,391	**Branch 6**	
Bayfield County		Ellen R. Brostrom*	49,439
John P. Anderson*	2,741	**Branch 12**	
Brown County		David L. Borowski*	49,689
Branch 1		**Branch 15**	
Donald R. Zuidmulder*	30,586	J.D. Watts*	49,481
Branch 4		**Branch 16**	
Kendall M. Kelley*	28,840	Michael J. Dwyer*	49,651
Branch 5		**Branch 22**	
Marc A. Hammer*	29,004	Timothy Witkowiak*	49,340
Branch 8		**Branch 29**	
William M. Atkinson*	28,973	Richard J. Sankovitz*	48,936
Burnett County		**Branch 30**	
Kenneth L. Kutz*	1,995	Jeffrey Conen*	48,700
Chippewa County		**Branch 37**	
Branch 2		T. Christopher Dee	48,265
James M. Isaacson*	5,841	**Branch 42**	
Columbia County		David A. Hansher*	49,078
Branch 1		**Branch 46**	
Troy D. Cross	3,640	David Feiss	49,737
Todd J. Hepler	5,447	**Outagamie County**	
Dane County		**Branch 5**	
Branch 2		Michael Gage*	16,008
Josann M. Reynolds	64,283	**Branch 6**	
Branch 6		Vincent R. Biskupic	15,787
Shelley J. Gaylord*	65,438	**Ozaukee County**	
Branch 10		**Branch 1**	
Juan B. Colás*	65,088	Paul V. Malloy*	14,061
Branch 13		**Branch 3**	
Julie Genovese*	64,187	Sandy A. Williams*	14,003
Douglas County		**Racine County**	
Branch 1		**Branch 6**	
Kelly J. Thimm*	5,942	Tricia Hanson	13,108
Branch 2		David W. Paulson	14,210
George L. Glonek*	5,795	**Branch 8**	
Dunn County		Faye Flancher*	20,616
Branch 2		**Branch 9**	
Rod W. Smeltzer*	4,234	Allan Pat Torhorst	16,430
Fond du Lac County		Joseph Seifert	8,475
Branch 3		**Rock County**	
Richard J. Nuss*	11,084	**Branch 3**	
Grant County		Michael R. Fitzpatrick*	14,664
Branch 2		**Branch 5**	
Craig R. Day*	6,450	Mike Haakenson	9,666
Green County		David. J. O'Leary	9,536
Branch 1		**Branch 6**	
Jim Beer*	3,948	Richard T. Werner*	14,918
Dan Gartzke	2,744	**Sawyer County**	
Branch 2		John Yackel	2,593
Tom Vale*	5,495	**Sheboygan County**	
Jackson County		**Branch 1**	
Anna L. Becker	2,426	L. Edward Stengel*	15,233
Daniel Diehn	2,179	**Branch 4**	
Jefferson County		Catherine Q. Delahunt	6,959
Branch 1		Rebecca Persick	11,475
Jennifer L. Weston*	7,648	**Taylor County**	
Kenosha County		Ann N. Knox-Bauer*	2,811
Branch 1		**Walworth County**	
David Mark Bastianelli*	12,330	**Branch 3**	
Branch 5		Kristine E. Drettwan	8,414
David P. Wilk	12,442	John W. Peterson	5,062
Branch 6		**Washburn County**	
Mary K Wagner*	13,053	Eugene D. Harrington*	2,774
Branch 8		**Waukesha County**	
Chad G. Kerkman*	12,201	**Branch 7**	
La Crosse County		Maria S. Lazar	39,245
Branch 5		**Branch 8**	
Brian K. Barton	7,107	Michael P. Maxwell	29,931
Gloria L. Doyle	9,083	Ron Sonderhouse	21,750
Lafayette County		**Branch 9**	
Kate Findley	1,053	Michael J. Aprahamian	38,706
Duane M. Jorgenson	2,287	**Branch 10**	
Langlade County		Paul Bugenhagen, Jr.	28,393
John Rhode	3,988	Linda M. Van De Water*	24,416
Ralph M. Uttke	1,252	**Wood County**	
Marathon County		**Branch 3**	
Branch 1		Todd P. Wolf*	7,598
Jill N. Falstad*	19,179		
Milwaukee County			
Branch 2			
Joe Donald*	49,743		

*Incumbent

Source: Official records of the Government Accountability Board, Elections Division. Scattered votes omitted.

DISTRICT VOTE FOR MEMBERS OF THE 114TH U.S. CONGRESS
August 12, 2014 Primary
First Congressional District

County	Amar Kaleka (Dem.)	Rob Zerban (Dem.)	Jeremy Ryan (Rep.)	Paul Ryan* (Rep.)
Kenosha	842	4,793	897	8,080
Milwaukee (part)	2,727	4,996	88	2,140
Racine	1,500	5,802	642	12,190
Rock (part)	1,408	6,552	116	2,876
Walworth (part)	346	1,746	421	6,001
Waukesha (part)	495	1,738	286	9,526
TOTAL	7,318	25,627	2,450	40,813

Second Congressional District

County	Mark Pocan* (Dem.)	Peter Theron (Rep.)
Dane	39,588	4,913
Green	2,191	1,149
Iowa	1,380	763
Lafayette	585	1,733
Richland (part)	124	396
Rock (part)	5,222	1,536
Sauk	3,427	1,974
TOTAL	52,517	12,464

Third Congressional District

County	Ron Kind* (Dem.)	Tony Kurtz (Rep.)	Karen L. Mueller (Rep.)	Ken Van Doren (Rep.)
Adams	815	236	117	266
Buffalo	416	274	133	100
Chippewa (part)	965	304	240	110
Crawford	864	480	60	68
Dunn	3,151	565	212	191
Eau Claire	3,222	1,048	857	393
Grant	1,661	1,637	740	508
Jackson (part)	664	202	85	132
Juneau (part)	785	399	204	452
La Crosse	3,580	2,195	433	386
Monroe (part)	874	1,762	642	528
Pepin	324	272	254	127
Pierce	957	717	223	206
Portage	5,318	870	263	265
Richland (part)	625	926	590	413
Trempealeau	2,038	416	189	163
Vernon	949	577	162	161
Wood (part)	1,575	672	226	235
TOTAL	28,783	13,552	5,630	4,704

DISTRICT VOTE FOR MEMBERS OF THE 114TH U.S. CONGRESS
August 12, 2014 Primary–Continued

Fourth Congressional District

County	Gary R. George (Dem.)	Gwen Moore* (Dem.)	David D. King (Rep.)	Dan Sebring (Rep.)
Milwaukee (part).	21,242	52,408	854	3,386
Waukesha (part)	0	0	0	0
TOTAL.	21,242	52,408	854	3,386

Fifth Congressional District

County	Chris Rockwood (Dem.)	F. James Sensenbrenner, Jr.* (Rep.)
Dodge (part)	753	2,749
Jefferson	2,434	2,601
Milwaukee (part).	9,346	2,022
Walworth (part)	312	243
Washington.	2,351	9,991
Waukesha (part)	6,519	25,660
TOTAL.	21,715	43,266

Sixth Congressional District

County	Mark L. Harris (Dem.)	Tom Denow (Rep.)	Glenn Grothman (Rep.)	Joe Leibham (Rep.)	Duey Stroebel (Rep.)
Columbia.	2,177	145	1,173	444	758
Dodge (part)	988	260	1,724	966	1,357
Fond du Lac	2,052	388	4,128	2,707	2,441
Green Lake.	798	117	873	685	958
Manitowoc	2,444	91	925	4,749	760
Marquette	536	36	435	155	237
Milwaukee (part).	145	0	19	18	16
Ozaukee	1,981	245	6,109	1,599	4,618
Sheboygan	3,587	189	4,404	8,975	1,015
Waushara.	734	111	502	603	997
Winnebago (part)	4,272	535	2,955	2,127	2,716
TOTAL.	19,714	2,117	23,247	23,028	15,873

DISTRICT VOTE FOR MEMBERS OF THE 114TH U.S. CONGRESS
August 12, 2014 Primary–Continued

Seventh Congressional District

County	Mike Krsiean (Dem.)	Kelly Westlund (Dem.)	Sean Duffy* (Rep.)	Don Raihala (Rep.)
Ashland	112	1,094	215	31
Barron	301	923	2,233	282
Bayfield	172	1,527	348	55
Burnett	157	407	1,458	309
Chippewa (part)	163	355	594	48
Clark	203	460	1,618	307
Douglas	630	2,173	709	74
Florence	29	58	134	30
Forest	91	211	228	23
Iron	108	301	216	39
Jackson (part)	44	68	124	29
Juneau (part)	72	113	237	61
Langlade	188	427	963	143
Lincoln	228	715	760	76
Marathon	790	3,020	3,902	275
Monroe (part)	25	73	312	58
Oneida	278	922	934	124
Polk	208	858	1,192	177
Price	182	637	1,253	194
Rusk	106	395	1,100	126
St. Croix	428	1,410	1,522	205
Sawyer	145	458	1,747	454
Taylor	156	270	1,453	155
Vilas	127	538	702	96
Washburn	117	530	962	184
Wood (part)	196	688	791	52
TOTAL	5,256	18,631	25,707	3,607

Eighth Congressional District

County	Ron Gruett (Dem.)	Reid J. Ribble* (Rep.)
Brown	5,813	9,899
Calumet	1,072	1,604
Door	1,165	3,863
Kewaunee	628	1,105
Marinette	991	1,023
Menominee	148	21
Oconto	1,505	1,806
Outagamie	4,278	7,675
Shawano	845	4,130
Waupaca	1,315	1,547
Winnebago	270	657
TOTAL	18,030	33,330

Dem. – Democratic Party; Rep. – Republican Party.
*Incumbent.
Source: Official records of the Government Accountability Board, Elections Division. Scattered votes omitted.

DISTRICT VOTE FOR MEMBERS OF THE 114TH U.S. CONGRESS
November 4, 2014 General Election
First Congressional District

County	Rob Zerban (Dem.)	Paul Ryan* (Rep.)	Keith R. Deschler (Ind. Write-in)
Kenosha	25,217	30,470	1
Milwaukee (part).	13,221	27,880	9
Racine	32,040	46,460	12
Rock (part).	15,078	15,374	0
Walworth (part)	10,403	25,271	3
Waukesha (part)	9,593	36,861	4
TOTAL.	105,552	182,316	29
Percent of Total Vote†	36.63%	63.27%	0.01%

Second Congressional District

County	Mark Pocan* (Dem.)	Peter Theron (Rep.)
Dane	176,552	68,005
Green.	8,303	6,549
Iowa	6,320	3,858
Lafayette.	3,179	2,759
Richland (part).	692	565
Rock	16,199	10,797
Sauk	13,675	11,086
TOTAL.	224,920	103,619
Percent of Total Vote†	68.40%	31.51%

Third Congressional District

County	Ron Kind* (Dem.)	Tony Kurtz (Rep.)	Ken Van Doren (Ind. Write-in)
Adams	4,184	3,731	7
Buffalo.	2,988	2,439	1
Chippewa (part)	8,045	6,151	4
Crawford.	3,651	2,592	3
Dunn	8,263	6,983	6
Eau Claire	24,075	17,281	13
Grant.	10,568	7,237	6
Jackson (part)	4,044	2,600	2
Juneau (part)	3,710	3,034	30
La Crosse	27,955	19,937	21
Monroe (part)	6,535	6,666	7
Pepin.	1,741	1,375	1
Pierce.	7,949	6,496	5
Portage.	16,560	12,613	6
Richland (part).	2,948	2,389	5
Trempealeau	6,174	4,475	0
Vernon	6,722	4,943	7
Wood (part)	9,256	8,598	4
TOTAL.	155,368	119,540	128
Percent of Total Vote†	56.46%	43.44%	0.05%

DISTRICT VOTE FOR MEMBERS OF THE 114TH U.S. CONGRESS
November 4, 2014 General Election–Continued
Fourth Congressional District

County	Gwen Moore* (Dem.)	Dan Sebring (Rep.)	Robert R. Raymond (Ind.)
Milwaukee (part).	179,045	68,490	7,002
Waukesha (part)	0	0	0
TOTAL.	179,045	68,490	7,002
Percent of Total Vote†	70.24%	26.87%	2.75%

Fifth Congressional District

County	Chris Rockwood (Dem.)	F. James Sensenbrenner, Jr.* (Rep.)
Dodge (part)	4,482	11,959
Jefferson	12,631	21,856
Milwaukee (part).	27,239	34,491
Walworth (part)	1,892	1,742
Washington.	14,873	49,766
Waukesha (part)	40,073	111,346
TOTAL.	101,190	231,160
Percent of Total Vote†	30.40%	69.45%

Sixth Congressional District

County	Mark L. Harris (Dem.)	Glenn Grothman (Rep.)	Gus Fahrendorf (Ind.)
Columbia.	11,894	11,253	627
Dodge (part)	7,775	10,963	401
Fond du Lac	16,024	24,713	912
Green Lake.	2,629	4,906	164
Manitowoc.	13,698	18,439	887
Marquette	2,569	3,442	155
Milwaukee (part).	415	575	17
Ozaukee	14,116	30,889	777
Sheboygan	18,906	29,161	1,057
Waushara.	3,678	5,659	228
Winnebago (part)	30,508	29,767	1,640
TOTAL.	122,212	169,767	6,865
Percent of Total Vote†	40.87%	56.77%	2.30%

DISTRICT VOTE FOR MEMBERS OF THE 114TH U.S. CONGRESS
November 4, 2014 General Election–Continued
Seventh Congressional District

County	Kelly Westlund (Dem.)	Sean Duffy (Rep.)	John Schiess (Rep. Write-in)	Lawrence Dale (Ind.)	Rob Taylor (Ind. Write-in)
Ashland	4,143	2,287	0	86	0
Barron	6,504	9,773	3	241	1
Bayfield	4,775	3,081	0	105	2
Burnett	2,573	3,778	0	91	0
Chippewa (part)	3,277	6,483	1	145	0
Clark	3,480	7,469	0	190	0
Douglas	8,919	6,459	0	203	0
Florence	599	1,306	0	24	0
Forest	1,361	2,078	0	57	0
Iron	1,046	1,738	0	29	0
Jackson (part)	272	537	0	15	1
Juneau (part)	787	1,269	0	53	0
Langlade	2,705	5,532	0	86	1
Lincoln	4,780	7,077	0	132	0
Marathon	19,979	35,227	0	544	7
Monroe (part)	560	1,147	0	36	0
Oneida	6,817	9,932	0	237	3
Polk	6,371	9,275	1	230	6
Price	2,645	3,732	0	67	0
Rusk	2,174	3,523	0	90	1
St. Croix	12,678	19,972	0	515	5
Sawyer	2,860	3,799	0	94	0
Taylor	2,097	5,466	0	72	1
Vilas	4,047	7,052	0	103	0
Washburn	2,962	3,960	0	97	1
Wood (part)	4,538	7,939	0	144	1
TOTAL	112,949	169,891	5	3,686	30
Percent of Total Vote† . . .	39.41%	59.28%	0.00%	1.29%	0.01%

Eighth Congressional District

County	Ron Gruett (Dem.)	Reid J. Ribble* (Rep.)
Brown	35,823	61,409
Calumet	7,040	14,183
Door	6,010	8,832
Kewaunee	3,055	5,926
Marinette	5,231	10,263
Menominee	581	307
Oconto	5,095	10,712
Outagamie	25,465	47,794
Shawano	4,967	11,340
Waupaca	6,506	13,805
Winnebago (part)	1,572	3,982
TOTAL	101,345	188,553
Percent of Total Vote†	34.94%	65.01%

Dem. – Democratic Party; Rep. – Republican Party; Ind. – Independent.

*Incumbent.

†Percentages do not sum to 100%, as scattered votes are included in total vote.

Source: Official records of the Government Accountability Board, Elections Division.

COUNTY VOTE FOR STATE SENATORS
Primary Elections

County	Senate District	Democratic	Vote	Republican	Vote
		August 12, 2014 Primary			
Ashland	25	Bewley	1,168	Deutsch	197
		Kauther	31		
		Ratzlaff	71		
Barron (part)	23	Swanhorst	1	Moulton*	0
(part)	25	Bewley	731	Deutsch	2,280
		Kauther	134		
		Ratzlaff	336		
Bayfield	25	Bewley	1,734	Deutsch	339
		Kauther	60		
		Ratzlaff	95		
Brown (part)	1	Debroux	878	Lasee*	1,650
Buffalo	31	Vinehout*	408	Ingram	160
				Pittman	368
Burnett (part)	25	Bewley	137	Deutsch	509
		Kauther	39		
		Ratzlaff	80		
Calumet (part)	1	Debroux	712	Lasee*	820
(part)	9	Laning	170	LeMahieu	310
Chippewa (part)	23	Swanhorst	1,306	Moulton*	1,230
(part)	31	Vinehout*	4	Ingram	1
				Pittman	2
Clark (part)	23	Swanhorst	570	Moulton*	1,621
(part)	29	DeMain	3	Petrowski*	18
Columbia (part)	13	Zahn	196	Fitzgerald, S.*	162
(part)	27	Erpenbach*	736	No candidate	
Dane (part)	13	Zahn	1,205	Fitzgerald, S.*	367
(part)	15	Ringhand	403	Fitzgerald, B.	100
		Scieszinski	129		
		Sheridan	101		
(part)	27	Erpenbach*	7,582	No candidate	
Dodge (part)	13	Zahn	1,528	Fitzgerald, S.*	5,166
Door	1	Debroux	1,187	Lasee*	3,670
Douglas	25	Bewley	1,868	Deutsch	648
		Kauther	648		
		Ratzlaff	506		
Dunn (part)	23	Swanhorst	1,013	Moulton*	403
(part)	25	Bewley	19	Deutsch	15
		Kauther	4		
		Ratzlaff	15		
(part)	31	Vinehout*	299	Ingram	34
				Pittman	110
Eau Claire (part)	23	Swanhorst	611	Moulton*	587
(part)	31	Vinehout*	2,508	Ingram	601
				Pittman	997
Grant†	17	Bomhack	1,006	Marklein	2,653
		Wittwer	647		
Green (part)	15	Ringhand	539	Fitzgerald, B.	293
		Scieszinski	73		
		Sheridan	83		
(part)†	17	Bomhack	446	Marklein	716
		Wittwer	645		
(part)	27	Erpenbach*	652	No candidate	
Iowa (part)†	17	Bomhack	468	Marklein	706
		Wittwer	566		
(part)	27	Erpenbach	400	No candidate	
Iron	25	Bewley	339	Deutsch	218
		Kauther	32		
		Ratzlaff	92		
Jackson (part)	23	Swanhorst	83	Moulton*	92
(part)	31	Vinehout*	605	Ingram	158
				Pittman	245
Jefferson (part)	11	Kilkenny	1,086	Nass	1,123
(part)	13	Zahn	1,178	Fitzgerald, S.*	1,260
(part)	15	Ringhand	131	Fitzgerald, B.	223
		Scieszinski	69		
		Sheridan	69		
Juneau†	17	Bomhack	556	Marklein	1,162
		Wittwer	424		
Kenosha (part)	11	Kilkenny	68	Nass	205
(part)	21	Bryce	1,249	Steitz	1,877
				Wanggaard	2,666
Kewaunee	1	Debroux	631	Lasee*	1,058
Lafayette†	17	Bomhack	321	Marklein	2,070
		Wittwer	292		
Manitowoc (part)	1	Debroux	674	Lasee*	1,249
(part)	9	Laning	1,797	LeMahieu	3,620
Marathon (part)	23	Swanhorst	224	Moulton*	386
(part)	29	DeMain	2,921	Petrowski*	3,336
Milwaukee (part)	3	Carpenter*	7,064	No candidate	
(part)	5	No candidate		Vukmir*	1,347
	7	Larson*	15,265	Arnold	1,865
Monroe (part)†	17	Bomhack	42	Marklein	109

COUNTY VOTE FOR STATE SENATORS
Primary Elections–Continued

County	Senate District	Democratic	Vote	Republican	Vote
		Wittwer	16		
Outagamie (part)........	1	Debroux	567	Lasee*	838
(part)	19	Bernard Schaber	2,859	Roth	4,009
Pepin	31	Vinehout*	314	Ingram	184
				Pittman	575
Pierce (part).........	31	Vinehout*	607	Ingram	175
				Pittman	829
Polk (part)..........	25	Bewley	36	Deutsch	141
		Kauther	13		
		Ratzlaff	28		
Price	25	Bewley	651	Deutsch	1,036
		Kauther	30		
		Ratzlaff	228		
Racine (part)	11	Kilkenny	32	Nass	101
(part)	21	Bryce	3,718	Steitz	2,416
				Wanggaard	7,897
Richland†	17	Bomhack	348	Marklein	2,235
		Wittwer	431		
Rock (part)	11	Kilkenny	1,666	Nass	1,001
(part)	15	Ringhand	4,859	Fitzgerald, B.	3,062
		Scieszinski	5,421		
		Sheridan	3,111		
Rusk	29	DeMain	456	Petrowski*	1,013
St. Croix (part)	25	Bewley	11	Deutsch	6
		Kauther	3		
		Ratzlaff	2		
(part)	31	Vinehout*	0	Ingram	0
				Pittman	0
Sauk (part)†	17	Bomhack	631	Marklein	634
		Wittwer	779		
(part)	27	Erpenbach*	2,081	No candidate	
Sawyer (part)	25	Bewley	73	Deutsch	234
		Kauther	8		
		Ratzlaff	15		
(part)	29	DeMain	490	Petrowski*	1,458
Sheboygan (part)	9	Laning	3,492	LeMahieu	10,743
Taylor	29	DeMain	397	Petrowski*	1,382
Trempealeau (part)	23	Swanhorst	83	Moulton*	43
(part)	31	Vinehout*	1,837	Ingram	285
				Pittman	447
Vilas	25	Bewley	91	Deutsch	36
		Kauther	12		
		Ratzlaff	15		
Vernon (part)†	17	Bomhack	19	Marklein	14
		Wittwer	4		
Walworth (part)	11	Kilkenny	1,799	Nass	5,355
(part)	15	Ringhand	231	Fitzgerald, B.	333
		Scieszinski	190		
		Sheridan	84		
(part)	21	Bryce	0	Steitz	0
				Wanggaard	0
Washburn	25	Bewley	456	Deutsch	973
		Kauther	42		
		Ratzlaff	140		
Washington (part)	13	Zahn	33	Fitzgerald, S.*	109
Waukesha (part)	5	No candidate		Vukmir*	6,400
(part)	11	Kilkenny	328	Nass	1,614
(part)	13	Zahn	581	Fitzgerald, S.*	1,893
(part)	33	Shaddock	3,272	Farrow*	14,120
Winnebago (part)	19	Bernard Schaber	2,290	Roth	4,164
Wood (part)	23	Swanhorst	428	Moulton*	446
(part)	29	DeMain	153	Petrowski*	134
February 17, 2015 Primary					
Calumet (part)	20	Stamates (write-in)	0	Koehler	35
				Schlenvogt	46
				Stroebel	143
Fond du Lac	20	Stamates (write-in)	0	Koehler	129
				Schlenvogt	270
				Stroebel	585
Ozaukee	20	Stamates (write-in)	4	Koehler	233
				Schlenvogt	1,611
				Stroebel	3,399
Sheboygan (part)	20	Stamates (write-in)	1	Koehler	52
				Schlenvogt	171
				Stroebel	374
Washington (part)	20	Stamates (write-in)	5	Koehler	697
				Schlenvogt	1,217
				Stroebel	4,816

*Incumbent.
†Official recount results.
Source: Official records of the Government Accountability Board, Elections Division. Scattered votes omitted.

COUNTY VOTE FOR STATE SENATORS
General Election and Special Elections

County or Part	Senate District	Democratic	Vote	Republican	Vote
		November 4, 2014 General Election			
Ashland	25	Bewley	4,264	Deutsch	2,220
Barron (part)	23	Swanhorst	2	Moulton*	2
(part)	25	Bewley	6,606	Deutsch	9,821
Bayfield	25	Bewley	4,989	Deutsch	2,940
Brown (part)	1	Debroux	6,639	Lasee*	12,411
Buffalo (part)	31	Vinehout*	2,611	Pittman	2,836
Burnett (part)	25	Bewley	1,309	Deutsch	1,449
Calumet (part)	1	Debroux	5,326	Lasee*	9,645
(part)	9	Laning	1,027	LeMahieu	2,197
Chippewa (part)	23	Swanhorst	9,932	Moulton*	14,098
(part)	31	Vinehout*	19	Pittman	13
Clark (part)	23	Swanhorst	3,446	Moulton*	7,321
(part)	29	DeMain	83	Petrowski*	124
Columbia (part)	13	Zahn	1,168	Fitzgerald, S.*	973
(part)	27	Erpenbach*	3,933	No candidate	
Dane (part)	13	Zahn	6,504	Fitzgerald, S.*	5,417
(part)	15	Ringhand	2,483	Fitzgerald, B.	1,413
(part)	27	Erpenbach*	41,695	No candidate	
Dodge (part)	13	Zahn	10,822	Fitzgerald, S.*	19,229
Door	1	Debroux	6,608	Lasee*	8,212
Douglas (part)	25	Bewley	9,478	Deutsch	5,964
Dunn (part)	23	Swanhorst	2,543	Moulton*	3,687
(part)	25	Bewley	90	Deutsch	128
(part)	31	Vinehout*	705	Pittman	899
Eau Claire (part)	23	Swanhorst	4,061	Moulton*	5,273
(part)	31	Vinehout*	17,634	Pittman	13,929
Grant	17	Bomhack	7,996	Marklein	9,623
Green (part)	15	Ringhand	2,209	Fitzgerald, B.	1,879
(part)	17	Bomhack	2,486	Marklein	3,093
(part)	27	Erpenbach*	4,029	No candidate	
Iowa (part)	17	Bomhack	3,477	Marklein	3,547
(part)	27	Erpenbach*	2,573	No candidate	
Iron	25	Bewley	1,069	Deutsch	1,730
Jackson (part)	23	Swanhorst	159	Moulton*	277
(part)	31	Vinehout*	3,654	Pittman	2,646
Jefferson (part)	11	Kilkenny	5,424	Nass	7,959
(part)	13	Zahn	6,493	Fitzgerald, S.*	11,604
(part)	15	Ringhand	1,229	Fitzgerald, B.	1,817
Juneau (part)	17	Bomhack	3,804	Marklein	4,982
Kenosha (part)	11	Kilkenny	449	Nass	865
(part)[1]	21	Bryce	8,322	Wanggaard	13,627
Kewaunee	1	Debroux	3,478	Lasee*	5,475
Lafayette (part)	17	Bomhack	2,481	Marklein	3,584
Manitowoc (part)	1	Debroux	3,637	Lasee*	6,116
(part)	9	Laning	9,492	LeMahieu	13,740
Marathon (part)	23	Swanhorst	1,820	Moulton*	4,202
(part)	29	DeMain	16,121	Petrowski*	31,765
Milwaukee (part)	3	Carpenter*	29,291	No candidate	
(part)[2]	5	No candidate		Vukmir*	26,966
(part)	7	Larson*	41,950	Arnold	28,387
Monroe (part)	17	Bomhack	243	Marklein	325
Outagamie (part)	1	Debroux	3,867	Lasee*	5,579
(part)	19	Bernard Schaber	17,378	Roth	22,498
Pepin	31	Vinehout*	1,373	Pittman	1,754
Pierce (part)	31	Vinehout*	4,409	Pittman	5,759
Polk (part)	25	Bewley	409	Deutsch	594
Price	25	Bewley	2,782	Deutsch	3,540
Racine (part)	11	Kilkenny	258	Nass	510
(part)[1]	21	Bryce	19,784	Wanggaard	31,340
Richland (part)	17	Bomhack	3,115	Marklein	3,552
Rock (part)	11	Kilkenny	5,088	Nass	5,952
(part)	15	Ringhand	28,272	Fitzgerald, B.	17,527
Rusk	29	DeMain	2,203	Petrowski*	3,476
St. Croix (part)	25	Bewley	70	Deutsch	149
(part)	31	Vinehout*	1	Pittman	2
Sauk (part)	17	Bomhack	4,505	Marklein	5,793
(part)	27	Erpenbach*	9,690	No candidate	
Sawyer (part)	25	Bewley	369	Deutsch	494
(part)	29	DeMain	2,600	Petrowski*	3,200
Sheboygan (part)	9	Laning	18,251	LeMahieu	27,249
Taylor	29	DeMain	1,944	Petrowski*	5,528
Trempealeau (part)	23	Swanhorst	441	Moulton*	538
(part)	31	Vinehout*	5,102	Pittman	4,479
Vernon (part)	17	Bomhack	72	Marklein	102

COUNTY VOTE FOR STATE SENATORS
General Election and Special Elections–Continued

County or Part	Senate District	Democratic	Vote	Republican	Vote
Vilas (part)	25	Bewley	637	Deutsch	468
Walworth (part)	11	Kilkenny	12,157	Nass	21,685
(part)	15	Ringhand	2,196	Fitzgerald, B..	2,124
(part)[1]	21	Bryce	0	Wanggaard	0
Washburn (part)	25	Bewley	2,983	Deutsch	3,948
Washington (part) . . .	13	Zahn	268	Fitzgerald, S.*	840
Waukesha (part)[2] . . .	5	No candidate		Vukmir*	28,903
(part)	11	Kilkenny	2,001	Nass	6,871
(part)	13	Zahn	3,445	Fitzgerald, S.*	10,192
(part)	33	Shaddock	20,899	Farrow*	59,199
Winnebago (part) . . .	19	Bernard Schaber	13,757	Roth	19,130
Wood (part)	23	Swanhorst	2,731	Moulton*	4,179
(part)	29	DeMain	966	Petrowski*	1,794
April 7, 2015 Special Election					
Calumet (part)	20	Stamates (write-in)	0	Stroebel	702
Fond du Lac	20	Stamates (write-in)	1	Stroebel	2,640
Ozaukee	20	Stamates (write-in)	15	Stroebel	7,225
Sheboygan (part)	20	Stamates (write-in)	2	Stroebel	1,247
Washington (part) . . .	20	Stamates (write-in)	5	Stroebel	11,533

*Incumbent.

[1]Votes for write-in candidate Bill Thompkins in 21st SD: Kenosha – 0, Racine – 34, Walworth – 0.

[2]Votes for Independent candidate Wendy Friedrich in 5th SD: Milwaukee – 13,688, Waukesha – 6,332.

Source: Official records of the Government Accountability Board, Elections Division. Scattered votes omitted.

DISTRICT VOTE FOR STATE SENATORS
Primary Elections

Senate District	Composed of Assembly Districts	Political Party	Candidates	Vote
		August 12, 2014 Primary		
1	1, 2, 3.	Dem.	Dean P. Debroux	4,649
		Rep.	Frank Lasee*	9,285
3	7, 8, 9.	Dem.	Tim Carpenter*	7,064
5	13, 14, 15.	Rep.	Leah Vukmir*	7,747
7	19, 20, 21.	Dem.	Chris J. Larson*	15,265
		Rep.	Jason Red Arnold	1,865
9	25, 26, 27.	Dem.	Martha Laning	5,459
		Rep.	Devin LeMahieu	14,673
11	31, 32, 33.	Dem.	Dan Kilkenny	4,979
		Rep.	Steve Nass	9,399
13	37, 38, 39.	Dem.	Michelle Zahn	4,721
		Rep.	Scott L. Fitzgerald*	8,957
15	43, 44, 45.	Dem.	Janis Ringhand	6,163
		Dem.	Austin Scieszinski	5,882
		Dem.	Mike Sheridan	3,448
		Rep.	Brian Fitzgerald	4,011
17†	49, 50, 51.	Dem.	Pat Bomhack	3,837
		Dem.	Ernie Wittwer	3,804
		Rep.	Howard Marklein	10,299
19	55, 56, 57.	Dem.	Penny Bernard Schaber	5,149
		Rep.	Roger Roth	8,173
21	61, 62, 63.	Dem.	Randy Bryce	4,967
		Rep.	Jonathan Steitz	4,293
		Rep.	Van Wanggaard	10,563
23	67, 68, 69.	Dem.	Phil Swanhorst	4,319
		Rep.	Terry Moulton*	4,808
25	73, 74, 75.	Dem.	Janet Bewley	7,314
		Dem.	Gary Kauther	1,056
		Dem.	Thomas Ratzlaff	1,623
		Rep.	Dane Deutsch	6,632
27	79, 80, 81.	Dem.	Jon B. Erpenbach*	11,451
29	85, 86, 87.	Dem.	Paul DeMain	4,420
		Rep.	Jerry Petrowski*	7,341
31	91, 92, 93.	Dem.	Kathleen Vinehout*	6,582
		Rep.	Bill Ingram	1,598
		Rep.	Mel Pittman	3,573
33	97, 98, 99.	Dem.	Sherryll Shaddock	3,272
		Rep.	Paul Farrow*	14,120
		February 17, 2015 Primary		
20	58, 69, 60.	Dem.	Nicholas J. Stamates (write-in)	10
		Rep.	Tiffany Koehler	1,146
		Rep.	Lee E. Schlenvogt	3,315
		Rep.	Duey Stroebel	9,317

Dem. – Democratic Party; Rep. – Republican Party.
*Incumbent.
†Official recount results.
Source: Official records of the Government Accountability Board, Elections Division. Scattered votes omitted.

DISTRICT VOTE FOR STATE SENATORS
General Elections

Senate District	Composed of Assembly Districts	Political Party	Candidates	Vote	Percent of Total Vote†
			November 6, 2012 General Election		
2	4, 5, 6.	Rep.	Robert L. Cowles*	64,192	98.54%
4	10, 11, 12.	Dem.	Lena C. Taylor*	67,064	86.62
		Ind.	David D. King	10,154	13.11
6	16, 17, 18.	Dem.	Nikiya Harris.	60,543	98.72
8	22, 23, 24.	Dem.	Beth L. Lueck (write-in)	453	0.57
		Rep.	Alberta Darling*	76,402	95.58
10	28, 29, 30.	Dem.	Daniel C. Olson	35,728	40.72
		Rep.	Shelia Harsdorf*	51,911	59.17
12	34, 35, 36.	Dem.	Susan Sommer	36,809	40.45
		Rep.	Tom Tiffany	51,176	56.24
		Ind.	Paul O. Ehlers	2,964	3.26
14	40, 41, 42.	Dem.	Magarete Worthington	34,742	42.40
		Rep.	Luther S. Olsen*	47,137	57.53
16	46, 47, 48.	Dem.	Mark Miller*	72,298	98.73
18	52, 53, 54.	Dem.	Jessica King	42,479	49.60
		Rep.	Rick Gudex	43,079	50.30
20	58, 59, 60.	Dem.	Tanya Lohr.	30,504	31.30
		Rep.	Glenn Grothman*	66,882	68.63
22	64, 65, 66.	Dem.	Robert W. Wirch*	51,177	69.57
		Rep.	Pam Stevens	22,278	30.29
24	70, 71, 72.	Dem.	Julie M. Lassa*	48,677	56.59
		Rep.	Scott Kenneth Noble.	37,259	43.31
26	76, 77, 78.	Dem.	Fred A. Risser*	87,144	98.93
28	82, 83, 84.	Dem.	Jim Ward	35,053	36.51
		Rep.	Mary Lazich*	60,854	63.38
30	88, 89, 90.	Dem.	Dave Hansen*	42,949	54.23
		Rep.	John Macco	36,178	45.68
32	94, 95, 96.	Dem.	Jennifer Shilling	51,153	58.28
		Rep.	Bill Feehan.	36,545	41.64
			December 4, 2012 Special Election		
33	97, 98, 99.	Rep.	Paul Farrow	6,909	98.07
			November 4, 2014 General Election		
1	1, 2, 3.	Dem.	Dean P. Debroux	29,555	38.37
		Rep.	Frank Lasee*	47,438	61.59
3	7, 8, 9.	Dem.	Tim Carpenter*	29,291	97.10
5	13, 14, 15.	Rep.	Leah Vukmir*	55,869	73.03
		Ind.	Wendy Friedrich	20,020	26.17
7	19, 20, 21.	Dem.	Chris J. Larson*	41,950	59.50
		Rep.	Jason Red Arnold	28,387	40.26
9	25, 26, 27.	Dem.	Martha Laning	28,770	39.94
		Rep.	Devin LeMahieu	43,186	59.95
11	31, 32, 33.	Dem.	Dan Kilkenny	25,377	36.63
		Rep.	Steve Nass	43,842	63.29
13	37, 38, 39.	Dem.	Michelle Zahn	28,700	37.28
		Rep.	Scott L. Fitzgerald*	48,255	62.69
15	43, 44, 45.	Dem.	Janis Ringhand.	36,389	59.47
		Rep.	Brian Fitzgerald	24,760	40.47
17	49, 50, 51.	Dem.	Pat Bomhack.	28,179	44.85
		Rep.	Howard Marklein	34,601	55.07
19	55, 56, 57.	Dem.	Penny Bernard Schaber	31,135	42.76
		Rep.	Roger Roth.	41,628	57.17
21	61, 62, 63.	Dem.	Randy Bryce.	28,106	38.39
		Rep.	Van Wanggaard	44,967	61.42
		Ind.	Bill Thompkins (write-in)	34	0.05
23	67, 68, 69.	Dem.	Phil Swanhorst.	25,135	38.84
		Rep.	Terry Moulton*	39,577	61.15
25	73, 74, 75.	Dem.	Janet Bewley.	35,055	51.16
		Rep.	Dane Deutsch	33,445	48.81
27	79, 80, 81.	Dem.	Jon B. Erpenbach*	61,920	97.51
29	85, 86, 87.	Dem.	Paul Demain	23,917	34.26
		Rep.	Jerry Petrowski*	45,887	65.73
31	91, 92, 93.	Dem.	Kathleen Vinehout*	35,508	52.32
		Rep.	Mel Pittman	32,317	47.62
33	97, 98, 99	Dem.	Sherryll Shaddock	20,899	26.07
		Rep.	Paul Farrow*	59,199	73.86
			April 7, 2015 Special Election		
20	58, 59, 60.	Dem.	Nicholas J. Stamates (write-in)	23	0.10
		Rep.	Duey Stroebel	23,347	98.77

Dem. – Democratic Party; Rep. – Republican Party; Ind. – Independent.
*Incumbent.
†Percentages do not equal to 100%, as scattered votes have been omitted.
Source: Official records of the Government Accountability Board, Elections Division.

COUNTY VOTE FOR REPRESENTATIVES TO THE ASSEMBLY
Primary Elections

County or Part	Assembly District	Democratic	Vote	Republican	Vote
		October 22, 2013 Primary			
Clark (part).	69	Slezak	178	Dahlen	753
				Feddick.	432
				Kulp	687
				Noble.	287
Marathon (part)	69	Slezak	76	Dahlen	91
				Feddick.	257
				Kulp	916
				Noble.	94
Milwaukee (part).	21	Coppola	676	Arnold	73
				Gamble.	170
				Gehl	536
				Kujawa.	866
				Rodriguez	1,513
Wood (part)	69	Slezak	136	Dahlen	170
				Feddick.	584
				Kulp	657
				Noble.	243
		November 19, 2013 Primary			
Milwaukee (part).	82	Hermes.	657	Becker	91
				Hanneman	295
				Mares.	1,437
				Skowronski	1,846
		August 12, 2014 Primary			
Adams (part)	41	Kallas	447	Ballweg*	316
(part)	72	Duncan	274	Krug*	288
		Rayome	87		
Ashland	74	Garfield	537	Francis	180
		Meyers	683		
Barron (part)	67	Stene	0	Larson*	0
(part)	75	Smith, S.*	1,232	Mandley	807
				Quinn.	1,842
Bayfield	74	Garfield	530	Francis	317
		Meyers	1,347		
Brown (part)	1	Majeski.	245	Feit	202
				Hackbarth	39
				Kitchens	140
				McNulty	96
(part)	2	No candidate		Jacque*.	1,225
(part)	4	Plaunt	1,658	Campbell.	593
				Goelz.	1,038
				Steffen	2,359
(part)	5	McCabe	191	Steineke*.	436
(part)	6	No candidate		Tauchen*	148
(part)	88	Robinson	1,393	Macco	1,960
(part)	89	No candidate		Nygren*	733
(part)	90	Genrich*	1,291	Wimberger	1,124
Buffalo.	92	Danou*.	395	Weix	457
(part)	93	Smith, J.	16	Petryk*	19
Burnett (part).	28	Schachtner	286	Jarchow	951
(part)	73	Milroy*	242	No candidate	
(part)	75	Smith, S.*	9	Mandley	6
				Quinn.	6
Calumet (part)	3	No candidate		Ott, A.*	813
(part)	25	No candidate		Tittl*	306
(part)	27	Heinig	10	Carlson.	1
				Jarvis	7
				Vorpagel	11
(part)	59	No candidate		Kremer	112
				Prescott.	241
				Ramthun	91
				Savage	48
Chippewa (part)	67	Stene	901	Larson*	892
(part)	68	Peck	434	Bernier*	317
(part)	91	Wachs*.	4	No candidate	
Clark (part).	68	Peck	223	Bernier*	501
(part)	69	Salamonski.	357	Kulp*.	1,118
(part)	87	Pulcher	2	Bub.	5
				Edming.	2
				LaBarre	0
				Noble.	13
Columbia (part)	37	Arnold	220	Jagler*	161
(part)	41	Kallas	83	Ballweg*	57
(part)	42	Ferriter	1,275	Ripp*.	1,522
(part)	81	Considine	392	Kirsch	445
		Miller.	422	Moore	93
		Vedro.	59	Petrulis	138
Crawford.	96	Flesch	822	Nerison*	589
Dane (part)	37	Arnold	617	Jagler*	191
(part)	38	Chojnacki	577	Kleefisch*	162

COUNTY VOTE FOR REPRESENTATIVES TO THE ASSEMBLY
Primary Elections–Continued

County or Part	Assembly District	Democratic	Vote	Republican	Vote
(part)	42	Ferriter	175	Ripp*	84
(part)	43	Jorgensen*	539	Brodkey	49
				Hebert	52
(part)	46	Hebl*	3,005	No candidate	
(part)	47	Kahl*	3,688	No candidate	
(part)	48	Sargent*	5,109	No candidate	
(part)	76	Taylor*	4,610	No candidate	
(part)	77	Berceau*	6,196	No candidate	
(part)	78	Clear	2,913	No candidate	
		Subeck	3,827		
(part)	79	Hesselbein*	3,999	Renteria	654
(part)	80	Pope*	2,861	No candidate	
(part)	81	Considine	140	Kirsch	185
		Miller	249	Moore	30
		Vedro	76	Petrulis	25
Dodge (part)	37	Arnold	403	Jagler*	921
(part)	39	No candidate		Born*	4,284
(part)	42	Ferriter	182	Ripp*	835
(part)	53	No candidate		Schraa*	267
Door	1	Majeski	1,263	Feit	1,330
				Hackbarth	528
				Kitchens	2,338
				McNulty	733
Douglas (part)	73	Milroy*	2,780	No candidate	
(part)	74	Garfield	43	Francis	26
		Meyers	86		
Dunn (part)	29	No candidate		Murtha*	425
(part)	67	Stene	1,091	Larson*	408
(part)	75	Smith, S.*	39	Mandley	6
				Quinn	9
(part)	93	Smith, J.	304	Petryk*	138
Eau Claire (part)	68	Peck	630	Bernier*	566
(part)	91	Wachs*	1,819	No candidate	
(part)	93	Smith, J.	633	Petryk*	576
Florence	34	No candidate		Swearingen*	162
Fond du Lac (part)	41	Kallas	194	Ballweg*	464
(part)	42	Ferriter	74	Ripp*	300
(part)	52	No candidate		Thiesfeldt*	4,440
(part)	53	No candidate		Schraa*	1,296
(part)	59	No candidate		Kremer	861
				Prescott	369
				Ramthun	546
				Savage	117
Forest (part)	34	No candidate		Swearingen*	72
(part)	36	No candidate		Mursau*	160
Grant	49	Henneman	1,455	Tranel*	3,044
Green Lake (part)	41	Kallas	688	Ballweg*	2,172
(part)	42	Ferriter	105	Ripp*	308
Green (part)	45	De Forest	263	No candidate	
		Spreitzer	373		
(part)	51	Cates	885	Novak	350
				Polivka	101
				Rynes	36
				Schultz	327
(part)	80	Pope*	617	No candidate	
Iowa (part)	49	Henneman	10	Tranel*	2
(part)	51	Cates	947	Novak	642
				Polivka	104
				Rynes	53
				Schultz	46
(part)	80	Pope*	248	No candidate	
(part)	81	Considine	48	Kirsch	29
		Miller	65	Moore	10
		Vedro	28	Petrulis	10
Iron	74	Garfield	176	Francis	238
		Meyers	276		
Jackson (part)	68	Peck	87	Bernier*	90
(part)	70	Vruwink*	56	Vander Meer	67
(part)	92	Danou*	599	Weix	357
Jefferson (part)	33	No candidate		Horlacher	652
				Johnson, S.	556
				Lurvey	123
(part)	37	Arnold	512	Jagler*	687
(part)	38	Chojnacki	659	Kleefisch*	550
(part)	43	Jorgensen*	244	Brodkey	70
				Hebert	168
Juneau (part)	41	Kallas	0	Ballweg*	0
(part)	50	Miller	884	Brooks, E.*	1,270
Kenosha (part)	32	Kupsik	67	August*	216
(part)	61	No candidate		Kerkman*	3,964
(part)	64	Barca*	1,711	No candidate	
(part)	65	Ohnstad*	1,881	No candidate	

COUNTY VOTE FOR REPRESENTATIVES TO THE ASSEMBLY
Primary Elections–Continued

County or Part	Assembly District	Democratic	Vote	Republican	Vote
Kewaunee (part)	1	Majeski	648	Feit	298
				Hackbarth	47
				Kitchens	444
				McNulty	436
La Crosse (part)	94	Doyle*	1,517	Happel	1,542
(part)	95	Billings*	1,902	No candidate	
Lafayette (part)	49	Henneman	58	Tranel*	143
(part)	51	Cates	483	Novak	1,073
				Polivka	418
				Rynes	161
				Schultz	428
Langlade (part)	35	No candidate		Czaja*	701
(part)	36	No candidate		Mursau*	253
Lincoln	35	No candidate		Czaja*	738
Manitowoc (part)	1	Majeski	21	Feit	11
				Hackbarth	2
				Kitchens	13
				McNulty	16
(part)	2	No candidate		Jacque*	1,205
(part)	25	No candidate		Tittl*	3,264
(part)	27	Heinig	225	Carlson	234
				Jarvis	323
				Vorpagel	320
Marathon (part)	35	No candidate		Czaja*	93
(part)	69	Salamonski	222	Kulp*	423
(part)	85	Wright*	2,062	Heaton	1,442
(part)	86	Stencil	1,157	Spiros*	1,350
(part)	87	Pulcher	81	Bub	72
				Edming	11
				LaBarre	51
				Noble	121
Marinette (part)	36	No candidate		Mursau*	555
(part)	89	No candidate		Nygren*	439
Marquette (part)	41	Kallas	400	Ballweg*	653
(part)	42	Ferriter	120	Ripp*	142
Menominee	36	No candidate		Mursau*	15
Milwaukee (part)	7	Riemer*	3,740	Espeseth	416
(part)	8	Manriquez	439	Synowicz	68
		Zamarripa*	679		
(part)	9	Zepnick*	2,055	No candidate	
(part)	10	Bowen	3,992	No candidate	
		Grant	1,555		
		Johann	481		
		Torhorst	1,338		
(part)	11	Barnes*	3,813	No candidate	
(part)	12	Kessler*	3,781	Goodwin (write-in)	0
(part)	13	No candidate		Hutton*	451
(part)	14	No candidate		Kooyenga*	358
(part)	15	Weishan	2,009	Sanfelippo*	480
(part)	16	Dent	1,376	No candidate	
		Young*	2,309		
(part)	17	Johnson, L.*	4,734	No candidate	
(part)	18	Goyke*	3,589	No candidate	
(part)	19	Adams	2,023	No candidate	
		Brostoff	3,069		
		Dimitrijevic	2,819		
		Geenen	797		
(part)	20	Sinicki*	5,060	McGartland	439
				Moralez	172
				Pierce	405
(part)	21	No candidate		Rodriguez	883
(part)	22	Read	449	Brandtjen	21
				Oliver	16
				Rogacki	11
(part)	23	Lueck	2,494	Ott, J.*	327
(part)	24	No candidate		Knodl*	287
(part)	82	No candidate		Skowronski*	1,152
(part)	83	Brownlow	616	Craig*	177
(part)	84	No candidate		Kuglitsch*	508
Monroe (part)	50	Miller	53	Brooks, E.*	125
(part)	70	Vruwink*	645	Vander Meer	2,179
(part)	96	Flesch	222	Nerison*	876
Oconto (part)	6	No candidate		Tauchen*	0
(part)	36	No candidate		Mursau*	1,110
(part)	89	No candidate		Nygren*	645
Oneida (part)	34	No candidate		Swearingen*	890
(part)	35	No candidate		Czaja*	100
Outagamie (part)	2	No candidate		Jacque*	5
(part)	3	No candidate		Ott, A.*	849
(part)	5	McCabe	1,110	Steineke*	1,839
(part)	6	No candidate		Tauchen*	560
(part)	40	No candidate		Petersen*	32

COUNTY VOTE FOR REPRESENTATIVES TO THE ASSEMBLY
Primary Elections–Continued

County or Part	Assembly District	Democratic	Vote	Republican	Vote
(part)	55	Westphal	319	Gillespie	374
				Lehman	100
				Pheifer	169
				Rohrkaste	102
				Schroeder	82
(part)	56	No candidate		Murphy*	2,227
(part)	57	Stuck	1,061	Klein	908
Ozaukee (part)	23	Lueck	872	Ott, J.*	3,790
(part)	24	No candidate		Knodl*	1,025
(part)	60	Duman (write-in)	5	Brooks, R.	4,120
				Opitz	2,802
Pepin	93	Smith, J.	295	Petryk*	651
Pierce (part)	30	Laumann	296	Knudson*	213
(part)	93	Smith, J.	598	Petryk*	914
Polk (part)	28	Schachtner	867	Jarchow	1,096
(part)	75	Smith, S.*	82	Mandley	123
				Quinn	43
Portage (part)	70	Vruwink*	932	Vander Meer	196
(part)	71	Shankland*	4,388	No candidate	
(part)	72	Duncan	165	Krug*	90
		Rayome	113		
Price	74	Garfield	258	Francis	1,005
		Meyers	589		
Racine (part)	32	Kupsik	34	August*	97
(part)	62	No candidate		Weatherston*	4,093
(part)	63	Mitchell	1,642	Biemeck	540
				Vos*	4,594
(part)	64	Barca*	413	No candidate	
(part)	66	Mason*	1,878	No candidate	
(part)	83	Brownlow	243	Craig*	732
Richland (part)	49	Henneman	188	Tranel*	511
(part)	50	Miller	342	Brooks, E.*	1,270
(part)	51	Cates	141	Novak	115
				Polivka	142
				Rynes	373
				Schultz	47
Rock (part)	31	No candidate		Loudenbeck*	1,074
(part)	43	Jorgensen*	2,862	Brodkey	474
				Hebert	327
(part)	44	Kolste*	5,434	Dorsey	1,456
(part)	45	De Forest	1,428	No candidate	
		Spreitzer	1,620		
Rusk	87	Pulcher	457	Bub	73
				Edming	982
				LaBarre	99
				Noble	165
St. Croix (part)	28	Schachtner	94	Jarchow	88
(part)	29	No candidate		Murtha*	594
(part)	30	Laumann	846	Knudson*	994
(part)	75	Smith, S.*	17	Mandley	3
				Quinn	5
(part)	93	Smith, J.	0	Petryk*	0
Sauk (part)	41	Kallas	50	Ballweg*	44
(part)	50	Miller	746	Brooks, E.*	430
(part)	51	Cates	437	Novak	82
				Polivka	157
				Rynes	16
				Schultz	11
(part)	81	Considine	1,505	Kirsch	1,234
		Miller	659	Moore	200
		Vedro	319	Petrulis	264
Sawyer (part)	74	Garfield	38	Francis	228
		Meyers	58		
(part)	87	Pulcher	450	Bub	267
				Edming	148
				LaBarre	995
				Noble	441
Shawano (part)	6	No candidate		Tauchen*	3,547
(part)	35	No candidate		Czaja*	184
(part)	36	No candidate		Mursau*	359
(part)	40	No candidate		Petersen*	0
Sheboygan (part)	26	Van Akkeren	1,755	Hou-Seye	688
				Katsma	5,861
(part)	27	Heinig	1,635	Carlson	2,037
				Jarvis	1,782
				Vorpagel	2,202
(part)	59	No candidate		Kremer	448
				Prescott	204
				Ramthun	216
				Savage	157
Taylor (part)	87	Pulcher	393	Bub	1,016
				Edming	309
				LaBarre	194
				Noble	220

COUNTY VOTE FOR REPRESENTATIVES TO THE ASSEMBLY
Primary Elections–Continued

County or Part	Assembly District	Democratic	Vote	Republican	Vote
Trempealeau (part)	68	Peck	85	Bernier*	42
(part)	92	Danou*	1,897	Weix	670
Vernon (part)	50	Miller	22	Brooks, E.*	14
(part)	96	Flesch	868	Nerison*	863
Vilas (part)	34	No candidate		Swearingen*	718
(part)	74	Garfield	54	Francis	37
		Meyers	53		
Walworth (part)	31	No candidate		Loudenbeck*	2,044
(part)	32	Kupsik	959	August*	2,725
(part)	33	No candidate		Horlacher	469
				Johnson, S.	162
				Lurvey	40
(part)	43	Jorgensen*	461	Brodkey	120
				Hebert	215
(part)	63	Mitchell	0	Biemeck	0
				Vos*	0
(part)	83	Brownlow	17	Craig*	68
Washburn (part)	73	Milroy*	329	No candidate	
(part)	75	Smith, S.*	310	Mandley	263
				Quinn	326
Washington (part)	22	Read	210	Brandtjen	436
				Oliver	163
				Rogacki	453
(part)	24	No candidate		Knodl*	985
(part)	39	No candidate		Born*	103
(part)	58	No candidate		Gannon	2,469
				Koehler	1,335
				Voss	1,008
(part)	59	No candidate		Kremer	967
				Prescott	664
				Ramthun	614
				Savage	532
(part)	60	Duman (write-in)	0	Brooks, R.	671
				Opitz	655
Waukesha (part)	13	No candidate		Hutton*	2,217
(part)	14	No candidate		Kooyenga*	2,595
(part)	15	Weishan	495	Sanfelippo*	1,476
(part)	22	Read	895	Brandtjen	2,675
				Oliver	510
				Rogacki	971
(part)	24	No candidate		Knodl*	429
(part)	33	No candidate		Horlacher	1,074
				Johnson, S.	599
				Lurvey	115
(part)	38	Chojnacki	579	Kleefisch*	1,886
(part)	83	Brownlow	901	Craig*	3,175
(part)	84			Kuglitsch*	1,493
(part)	97	No candidate		Allen	2,004
				Banske	300
				Cummings	743
				Perry	429
				Rosner	1,716
				Trovato	728
(part)	98	No candidate		Neylon*	4,044
(part)	99	Jensen	1,076	Kapenga*	5,261
Waupaca (part)	6	No candidate		Tauchen*	227
(part)	40	No candidate		Petersen*	1,291
Waushara (part)	40	No candidate		Petersen*	871
(part)	41	Kallas	1	Ballweg*	5
(part)	72	Duncan	299	Krug*	1,131
		Rayome	75		
Winnebago (part)	53	No candidate		Schraa*	1,615
(part)	54	Hintz*	1,583	Elliott	1,759
(part)	55	Westphal	1,280	Gillespie	642
				Lehman	340
				Pheifer	1,099
				Rohrkaste	1,340
				Schroeder	328
(part)	56	No candidate		Murphy*	514
(part)	57	Stuck	615	Klein	679
Wood (part)	69	Salamonski	447	Kulp*	478
(part)	70	Vruwink*	537	Vander Meer	382
(part)	72	Duncan	950	Krug*	880
		Rayome	560		
(part)	86	Stencil	158	Spiros*	139

*Incumbent.

Source: Official records of the Government Accountability Board, Elections Division. Scattered votes omitted.

COUNTY VOTE FOR REPRESENTATIVES TO THE ASSEMBLY
Special and General Elections

County or Part	Assembly District	Democratic	Vote	Republican	Vote
		November 4, 2014 General Election			
Adams (part).	41	Kallas	2,068	Ballweg*	2,308
(part)	72	Duncan.	1,555	Krug*	1,975
Ashland	74	Meyers	4,248	Francis	2,035
Barron (part)	67	Stene	2	Larson*	1
(part)	75	Smith, S.*	7,315	Quinn.	9,213
Bayfield	74	Meyers	5,112	Francis	2,679
Brown (part)	1	Majeski.	1,739	Kitchens	2,475
(part)	2	No candidate		Jacque*.	11,639
(part)	4	Plaunt	10,026	Steffen	14,467
(part)	5	McCabe	1,607	Steineke*	3,174
(part)	6	No candidate		Tauchen*	1,914
(part)	88	Robinson.	10,046	Macco	12,915
(part)	89	No candidate		Nygren*	6,590
(part)[1]	90	Genrich*	7,953	Wimberger	5,342
Buffalo	92	Danou*.	2,780	Weix	2,444
(part)	93	Smith, J.	51	Petryk*	93
Burnett (part).	28	Schachtner	1,275	Jarchow	2,300
(part)	73	Milroy*	1,757	No candidate	
(part)	75	Smith, S.*	44	Quinn.	36
Calumet (part)	3	No candidate		Ott, A.*.	12,186
(part)	25	No candidate		Tittl*	2,721
(part)	27	Heinig	33	Vorpagel	66
(part)	59	No candidate		Kremer.	2,276
Chippewa (part)	67	Stene	6,110	Larson*	9,685
(part)	68	Peck	3,619	Bernier*	3,947
(part)	91	Wachs*.	23	No candidate	
Clark (part).	68	Peck	1,368	Bernier*	1,835
(part)	69	Salamonski.	2,195	Kulp*.	5,385
(part)[2]	87	Pulcher	83	Edming.	124
Columbia (part)	37	Arnold	1,248	Jagler*	879
(part)	41	Kallas	430	Ballweg*	417
(part)	42	Ferriter	6,995	Ripp*.	8,423
(part)	81	Considine	3,101	Kirsch	2,539
Crawford	96	Flesch	2,843	Nerison*	3,327
Dane (part).	37	Arnold	3,697	Jagler*	2,852
(part)	38	Chojnacki	2,961	Kleefisch*	2,239
(part)	42	Ferriter	937	Ripp*.	1,028
(part)	43	Jorgensen*	2,550	Hebert	1,267
(part)	46	Hebl*.	20,014	No candidate	
(part)[1]	47	Kahl	20,332	No candidate	
(part)	48	Sargent*	23,423	No candidate	
(part)	76	Taylor*	27,102	No candidate	
(part)	77	Berceau*	25,268	No candidate	
(part)	78	Subeck	23,014	No candidate	
(part)	79	Hesselbein*	18,843	Renteria	11,406
(part)	80	Pope*.	15,972	No candidate	
(part)	81	Considine	1,687	Kirsch	1,478
Dodge (part)	37	Arnold	2,261	Jagler*	4,706
(part)[1]	39	No candidate		Born*.	15,952
(part)	42	Ferriter	1,484	Ripp*.	2,616
(part)	53	No candidate		Schraa*.	1,430
Door	1	Majeski.	6,618	Kitchens	8,329
Douglas (part)	73	Milroy*	11,442	No candidate	
(part)	74	Meyers	309	Francis	231
Dunn (part).	29	No candidate		Murtha*	5,243
(part)	67	Stene	2,579	Larson*	3,667
(part)	75	Smith, S.*	104	Quinn.	115
(part)	93	Smith, J.	742	Petryk*	855
Eau Claire (part)	68	Peck	4,392	Bernier*	4,795
(part)	91	Wachs*.	14,663	No candidate	
(part)	93	Smith, J.	4,150	Petryk*.	5,027
Florence (part)	34	No candidate		Swearingen*	1,586
Fond du Lac (part)	41	Kallas	1,367	Ballweg*	2,125
(part)	42	Ferriter	360	Ripp*.	1,023
(part)	52	No candidate		Thiesfeldt*	17,523
(part)	53	No candidate		Schraa*.	6,171
(part)	59	No candidate		Kremer.	5,594
Forest.	34	No candidate		Swearingen*	770
(part)	36	No candidate		Mursau*	1,873
Grant	49	Henneman	6,750	Tranel*	10,943
Green Lake (part)	41	Kallas	2,222	Ballweg*	4,795
(part)	42	Ferriter	191	Ripp*.	505
Green (part)	45	Spreitzer	2,745	No candidate	

COUNTY VOTE FOR REPRESENTATIVES TO THE ASSEMBLY
Special and General Elections–Continued

County or Part	Assembly District	Democratic	Vote	Republican	Vote
(part)[1]	51	Cates	2,709	Novak	2,689
(part)	80	Pope*	3,911	No candidate	
Iowa (part)	49	Henneman	21	Tranel*	30
(part)[1]	51	Cates	3,189	Novak	3,214
(part)	80	Pope*	1,750	No candidate	
(part)	81	Considine	591	Kirsch	428
Iron	74	Meyers	997	Francis	1,816
Jackson (part)	68	Peck	208	Bernier*	229
(part)	70	Vruwink*	256	Vander Meer	438
(part)	92	Danou*	3,518	Weix	2,662
Jefferson (part)	33	No candidate		Horlacher	9,537
(part)	37	Arnold	2,852	Jagler*	5,963
(part)	38	Chojnacki	3,711	Kleefisch*	5,288
(part)	43	Jorgensen*	1,428	Hebert	1,620
Juneau (part)	41	Kallas	0	Ballweg*	0
(part)	50	Miller	3,663	Brooks, E.*	5,127
Kenosha (part)	32	Kupsik	433	August*	874
(part)	61	No candidate		Kerkman*	17,452
(part)	64	Barca*	11,351	No candidate	
(part)	65	Ohnstad*	11,599	No candidate	
Kewaunee	1	Majeski	3,830	Kitchens	5,151
La Crosse (part)	94	Doyle*	13,670	Happel	11,617
(part)	95	Billings*	17,037	No candidate	
Lafayette (part)	49	Henneman	257	Tranel*	359
(part)[1]	51	Cates	2,312	Novak	2,799
Langlade (part)	35	No candidate		Czaja*	5,737
(part)	36	No candidate		Mursau*	1,009
Lincoln	35	No candidate		Czaja*	9,157
Manitowoc (part)	1	Majeski	69	Kitchens	117
(part)	2	No candidate		Jacque*	7,283
(part)	25	No candidate		Tittl*	14,321
(part)	27	Heinig	1,275	Vorpagel	2,517
Marathon (part)	35	No candidate		Czaja*	1,203
(part)	69	Salamonski	1,547	Kulp*	4,513
(part)	85	Wright*	11,082	Heaton	11,167
(part)	86	Stencil	8,562	Spiros*	14,088
(part)[2]	87	Pulcher	647	Edming	1,574
Marinette (part)	36	No candidate		Mursau*	6,426
(part)	89	No candidate		Nygren*	6,261
Marquette (part)	41	Kallas	1,904	Ballweg*	3,034
(part)	42	Ferriter	551	Ripp*	643
Menominee	36	No candidate		Mursau*	432
Milwaukee (part)	7	Riemer*	11,065	Espeseth	8,800
(part)	8	Zamarripa*	5,155	Synowicz	1,271
(part)	9	Zepnick*	8,507	No candidate	
(part)	10	Bowen	20,242	No candidate	
(part)	11	Barnes*	17,328	No candidate	
(part)[2]	12	Kessler*	16,494	No candidate	
(part)	13	No candidate		Hutton*	10,057
(part)	14	No candidate		Kooyenga*	10,345
(part)	15	Weishan	6,059	Sanfelippo*	8,207
(part)	16	Young*	16,183	No candidate	
(part)[1]	17	Johnson*	19,666	No candidate	
(part)	18	Goyke*	16,522	No candidate	
(part)[1]	19	Brostoff	18,077	No candidate	
(part)	20	Sinicki*	13,400	McGartland	10,481
(part)	21	No candidate		Rodriguez*	16,051
(part)	22	Read	1,635	Brandtjen	858
(part)	23	Lueck	6,566	Ott, J.*	7,055
(part)	24	No candidate		Knodl*	6,024
(part)	82	No candidate		Skowronski*	19,210
(part)	83	Brownlow	1,481	Craig*	2,588
(part)	84	No candidate		Kuglitsch*	11,031
Monroe (part)	50	Miller	214	Brooks, E.*	357
(part)	70	Vruwink*	4,471	Vander Meer	5,808
(part)	96	Flesch	1,236	Nerison*	2,731
Oconto (part)	6	No candidate		Tauchen*	0
(part)	36	No candidate		Mursau*	7,536
(part)	89	No candidate		Nygren*	5,632
Oneida (part)	34	No candidate		Swearingen*	11,767
(part)	35	No candidate		Czaja*	1,359
Outagamie (part)	2	No candidate		Jacque*	72
(part)	3	No candidate		Ott, A.*	7,356
(part)	5	McCabe	7,477	Steineke*	11,871

COUNTY VOTE FOR REPRESENTATIVES TO THE ASSEMBLY
Special and General Elections–Continued

County or Part	Assembly District	Democratic	Vote	Republican	Vote
(part)	6	No candidate		Tauchen*	3,154
(part)	40	No candidate		Petersen*	387
(part)	55	Westphal	2,232	Rohrkaste	3,199
(part)	56	No candidate		Murphy*	16,506
(part)	57	Stuck	6,992	Klein	5,478
Ozaukee (part)	23	Lueck	4,904	Ott, J.*	12,951
(part)	24	No candidate		Knodl*	4,252
(part)[2]	60	No candidate		Brooks, R.	18,103
Pepin	93	Smith, J.	1,459	Petryk*	1,644
Pierce (part)[1]	30	Laumann	2,033	Knudson*	1,996
(part)	93	Smith, J.	4,346	Petryk*	5,746
Polk (part)	28	Schachtner	5,628	Jarchow	9,117
(part)	75	Smith, S.*	459	Quinn	558
Portage (part)	70	Vruwink*	2,387	Vander Meer	2,000
(part)	71	Shankland*	17,134	No candidate	
(part)	72	Duncan	624	Krug*	796
Price	74	Meyers	2,975	Francis	3,200
Racine (part)	32	Kupsik	256	August*	495
(part)	62	No candidate		Weatherston*	18,761
(part)	63	Mitchell	8,917	Vos*	15,361
(part)	64	Barca*	2,536	No candidate	
(part)[1]	66	Mason*	12,062	No candidate	
(part)	83	Brownlow	1,410	Craig*	4,014
Richland (part)	49	Henneman	661	Tranel*	908
(part)	50	Miller	1,524	Brooks, E.*	1,932
(part)[1]	51	Cates	746	Novak	736
Rock (part)	31	No candidate		Loudenbeck*	8,239
(part)	43	Jorgensen*	7,720	Hebert	4,685
(part)	44	Kolste*	13,354	Dorsey	6,298
(part)	45	Spreitzer	10,111	No candidate	
Rusk[2]	87	Pulcher	1,711	Edming	4,053
St. Croix (part)	28	Schachtner	833	Jarchow	1,330
(part)	29	No candidate		Murtha*	9,710
(part)[1]	30	Laumann	6,625	Knudson*	11,955
(part)	75	Smith, S.*	109	Quinn	105
(part)	93	Smith, J.	1	Petryk*	2
Sauk (part)	41	Kallas	408	Ballweg*	441
(part)	50	Miller	3,124	Brooks, E.*	4,258
(part)[1]	51	Cates	1,621	Novak	1,204
(part)	81	Considine	7,555	Kirsch	6,447
Sawyer (part)	74	Meyers	383	Francis	461
(part)[2]	87	Pulcher	2,536	Edming	3,172
Shawano (part)	6	No candidate		Tauchen*	11,172
(part)	35	No candidate		Czaja*	1,257
(part)	36	No candidate		Mursau*	1,228
(part)	40	No candidate		Petersen*	3
Sheboygan (part)	26	Van Akkeren	9,064	Katsma	14,352
(part)	27	Heinig	8,139	Vorpagel	13,459
(part)[2]	59	No candidate		Kremer	3,236
Taylor[2]	87	Pulcher	2,121	Edming	5,198
Trempealeau (part)	68	Peck	489	Bernier*	483
(part)	92	Danou*	5,564	Weix	3,990
Vernon (part)	50	Miller	75	Brooks, E.*	101
(part)	96	Flesch	4,760	Nerison*	6,625
Vilas (part)	34	No candidate		Swearingen*	7,962
(part)	74	Meyers	639	Francis	440
Walworth (part)	31	No candidate		Loudenbeck*	9,482
(part)	32	Kupsik	6,405	August*	12,345
(part)	33	No candidate		Horlacher	2,633
(part)	43	Jorgensen*	2,418	Hebert	1,921
(part)	63	Mitchell	0	Vos*	0
(part)	83	Brownlow	109	Craig*	326
Washburn (part)	73	Milroy*	2,403	No candidate	
(part)	75	Smith, S.*	1,612	Quinn	1,703
Washington (part)	22	Read	1,312	Brandtjen	4,769
(part)	24	No candidate		Knodl*	8,812
(part)[1]	39	No candidate		Born*	841
(part)	58	No candidate		Gannon	22,087
(part)	59	No candidate		Kremer	11,311
(part)[2]	60	No candidate		Brooks, R.	5,963
Waukesha (part)	13	No candidate		Hutton*	10,653
(part)	14	No candidate		Kooyenga*	11,609
(part)	15	Weishan	2,998	Sanfelippo*	7,220
(part)	22	Read	5,842	Brandtjen	14,980

COUNTY VOTE FOR REPRESENTATIVES TO THE ASSEMBLY
Special and General Elections–Continued

County or Part	Assembly District	Democratic	Vote	Republican	Vote
(part)	24	No candidate		Knodl*	2,730
(part)	33	No candidate		Horlacher.	7,259
(part)	38	Chojnacki	3,609	Kleefisch*	9,954
(part)	83	Brownlow	4,877	Craig*	14,454
(part)	84	No candidate		Kuglitsch*	8,669
(part)	97	No candidate		Allen	17,804
(part)	98	No candidate		Neylon*	21,357
(part)	99	Jensen	6,593	Kapenga*	23,232
Waupaca (part)	6	No candidate		Tauchen*	2,456
(part)	40	No candidate		Petersen*	14,260
Waushara (part)	40	No candidate		Petersen*	3,774
(part)	41	Kallas	10	Ballweg*	32
(part)	72	Duncan	1,730	Krug*	3,073
Winnebago (part)	53	No candidate		Schraa*	10,017
(part)	54	Hintz*	11,228	Elliott.	10,571
(part)	55	Westphal	8,008	Rohrkaste	10,828
(part)	56	No candidate		Murphy*	4,338
(part)	57	Stuck	4,170	Klein	3,954
Wood (part)	69	Salamonski.	2,638	Kulp*.	4,335
(part)	70	Vruwink*	3,394	Vander Meer	3,520
(part)	72	Duncan	6,408	Krug*	7,269
(part)	86	Stencil	966	Spiros*	1,787

*Incumbent.

[1]Votes for Independent candidates: 17th AD: Eugenie M. Stackowitz: Milwaukee – 2,802; 19th AD: Joseph Thomas Klein: Milwaukee – 3,943; 30th AD: Laurie Kroeger: Pierce – 162, St. Croix – 585; 39th AD: Richard Bennett: Dodge – 5,775, Washington – 202; 47th AD: Phillip N. Anderson: Dane – 4,596; 51st AD: Adam Laufenberg: Green – 156, Iowa – 591, Lafayette – 272, Richland – 70, Sauk – 88; 66th AD: George Meyers: Racine – 2,781; 90th AD: Shae Sortwell: Brown – 1,164.

[2]Votes for write-in candidates: 12th AD: Russell Goodwin: Milwaukee – 3; 60th AD: Perry Duman: Ozaukee – 5, Washington – 0; 87th AD: Michael Bub: Clark – 0, Marathon – 0, Rusk – 2, Sawyer – 0, Taylor – 50.

Source: Official records of the Government Accountability Board, Elections Division. Scattered votes omitted.

DISTRICT VOTE FOR REPRESENTATIVES TO THE ASSEMBLY
Primary Elections

Assembly District	Political Party	Candidates	Vote
		October 22, 2013 Primary	
21.	Dem.	Elizabeth Coppola	676
	Rep.	Jason Red Arnold	73
	Rep.	Larry Gamble	170
	Rep.	Ken Gehl	536
	Rep.	Chris Kujawa	866
	Rep.	Jessie Rodriguez	1,513
69.	Dem.	Kenneth A. Slezak	390
	Rep.	Tommy Dahlen	1,014
	Rep.	Alanna Feddick	1,273
	Rep.	Bob Kulp	2,260
	Rep.	Scott Kenneth Noble	624
		November 19, 2013 Primary	
82.	Dem.	John R. Hermes	657
	Rep.	Steven C. Becker	91
	Rep.	Shari Hanneman	295
	Rep.	Stephanie Mares	1,437
	Rep.	Ken Skowronski	1,846
		August 12, 2014 Primary	
1	Dem.	Joe Majeski	2,177
	Rep.	Paul M. Feit	1,841
	Rep.	Brian Hackbarth	616
	Rep.	Joel C. Kitchens	2,935
	Rep.	Terry McNulty	1,281
2	Rep.	Andre Jacque*	2,435
3	Rep.	Al Ott*	1,662
4	Dem.	Chris Plaunt	1,658
	Rep.	Corrie Campbell	593
	Rep.	Jeff Goelz	1,038
	Rep.	David Steffen	2,359
5	Dem.	Jeff McCabe	1,301
	Rep.	Jim Steineke*	2,275
6	Rep.	Gary Tauchen*	4,482
7	Dem.	Daniel Riemer*	3,740
	Rep.	Scott Espeseth	416
8	Dem.	Laura Manriquez	439
	Dem.	JoCasta Zamarripa*	679
	Rep.	Vincent Synowicz	68
9	Dem.	Josh Zepnick*	2,055
10.	Dem.	David Bowen	3,992
	Dem.	Bria Grant	1,555
	Dem.	Sara Lee Johann	481
	Dem.	Tia Torhorst	1,338
11.	Dem.	Mandela Barnes*	3,813
12.	Dem.	Frederick P. Kessler*	3,781
	Rep.	Russell Goodwin (write-in)	0
13.	Rep.	Rob Hutton*	2,668
14.	Rep.	Dale Kooyenga*	2,953
15.	Dem.	John F. Weishan, Jr.	2,504
	Rep.	Joe Sanfelippo*	1,956
16.	Dem.	Tracey Dent	1,376
	Dem.	Leon D. Young*	2,309
17.	Dem.	La Tonya Johnson*	4,734
18.	Dem.	Evan Goyke*	3,589
19.	Dem.	Dan Adams	2,023
	Dem.	Jonathan Brostoff	3,069
	Dem.	Marina Dimitrijevic	2,819
	Dem.	Sara Geenen	797
20.	Dem.	Christine Sinicki*	5,060
	Rep.	Molly McGartland	439
	Rep.	Justin Moralez	172
	Rep.	Mike Pierce	405
21.	Rep.	Jessie Rodriguez*	883
22.	Dem.	Jessie Read	1,554
	Rep.	Janel Brandtjen	3,132
	Rep.	Nick Oliver	689
	Rep.	Blair A. Rogacki	1,435
23.	Dem.	Beth L. Lueck	3,366
	Rep.	Jim Ott*	4,117
24.	Rep.	Dan Knodl*	2,726
25.	Rep.	Paul Tittl*	3,570
26.	Dem.	Terry Van Akkeren	1,755
	Rep.	Job Hou-Seye	688
	Rep.	Terry Katsma	5,861

DISTRICT VOTE FOR REPRESENTATIVES TO THE ASSEMBLY
Primary Elections–Continued

Assembly District	Political Party	Candidates	Vote
27.	Dem.	Scott Grover Heinig	1,870
	Rep.	Darryl Carlson	2,272
	Rep.	Jackie Jarvis	2,112
	Rep.	Tyler Vorpagel	2,533
28.	Dem.	Travis Schachtner	1,247
	Rep.	Adam Jarchow	2,135
29.	Rep.	John Murtha*	1,019
30.	Dem.	Darrel Laumann	1,142
	Rep.	Dean Knudson*	1,207
31.	Rep.	Amy Loudenbeck*	3,118
32.	Dem.	Alan Kupsik	1,060
	Rep.	Tyler August*	3,038
33.	Rep.	Cody Horlacher	2,195
	Rep.	Scott L. Johnson	1,317
	Rep.	Bill Lurvey	278
34.	Rep.	Rob Swearingen*	1,842
35.	Rep.	Mary J. Czaja*	1,816
36.	Rep.	Jeffrey L. Mursau*	2,452
37.	Dem.	Mary I. Arnold	1,752
	Rep.	John Jagler*	1,960
38.	Dem.	Tom Chojnacki	1,815
	Rep.	Joel Kleefisch*	2,598
39.	Rep.	Mark L. Born*	4,387
40.	Rep.	Kevin Petersen*	2,194
41.	Dem.	Joe Kallas	1,863
	Rep.	Joan Ballweg*	3,711
42.	Dem.	George Ferriter	1,931
	Rep.	Keith Ripp*	3,191
43.	Dem.	Andy Jorgensen*	4,106
	Rep.	Herschel Brodkey	713
	Rep.	Leon L. Hebert	762
44.	Dem.	Debra Kolste*	5,434
	Rep.	Jacob Dorsey	1,456
45.	Dem.	Sheila De Forest	1,691
	Dem.	Mark Spreitzer	1,993
46.	Dem.	Gary Hebl*	3,005
47.	Dem.	Robb Kahl*	3,688
48.	Dem.	Melissa Agard Sargent*	5,109
49.	Dem.	Chad Henneman	1,711
	Rep.	Travis Tranel*	3,700
50.	Dem.	Christopher Miller	2,047
	Rep.	Ed Brooks*	3,109
51.	Dem.	Dick Cates	2,893
	Rep.	Todd Novak	2,262
	Rep.	Dennis B. Polivka	922
	Rep.	Ken Rhino Rynes	639
	Rep.	Tyler G. Schultz	859
52.	Rep.	Jeremy Thiesfeldt*	4,440
53.	Rep.	Michael Schraa*	3,178
54.	Dem.	Gordon Hintz*	1,583
	Rep.	Mark Elliott	1,759
55.	Dem.	Mark Westphal	1,599
	Rep.	Steven Gillespie	1,016
	Rep.	John R. Lehman	440
	Rep.	Ryan Pheifer	1,268
	Rep.	Mike Rohrkaste	1,442
	Rep.	Jay Schroeder	410
56.	Rep.	Dave Murphy*	2,741
57.	Dem.	Amanda Stuck	1,676
	Rep.	Chris Klein	1,587
58.	Rep.	Bob Gannon	2,469
	Rep.	Tiffany Koehler	1,335
	Rep.	Sandy Voss	1,008
59.	Rep.	Jesse Kremer	2,388
	Rep.	Ralph Prescott	1,478
	Rep.	Timothy Ramthun	1,467
	Rep.	Bill Savage	854
60.	Dem.	Perry Duman (write-in)	5
	Rep.	Robert Brooks	4,791
	Rep.	Jean F. Opitz	3,457
61.	Rep.	Samantha Kerkman*	3,964
62.	Rep.	Thomas Weatherston*	4,093
63.	Dem.	Andy Mitchell	1,642
	Rep.	Bryn Biemeck	540
	Rep.	Robin J. Vos*	4,594
64.	Dem.	Peter W. Barca*	2,124
65.	Dem.	Tod Ohnstad*	1,881
66.	Dem.	Cory Mason*	1,878

DISTRICT VOTE FOR REPRESENTATIVES TO THE ASSEMBLY
Primary Elections–Continued

Assembly District	Political Party	Candidates	Vote
67.	Dem.	Gary L. Stene	1,992
	Rep.	Tom Larson*	1,300
68.	Dem.	Jeff Peck	1,459
	Rep.	Kathy Bernier*	1,516
69.	Dem.	Norbert Salamonski	1,026
	Rep.	Bob Kulp*	2,019
70.	Dem.	Amy Sue Vruwink*	2,170
	Rep.	Nancy Lynn Vander Meer	2,824
71.	Dem.	Katrina Shankland*	4,388
72.	Dem.	Dana W. Duncan	1,688
	Dem.	Tom Rayome	835
	Rep.	Scott S. Krug*	2,389
73.	Dem.	Nick Milroy*	3,351
74.	Dem.	Graham F. Garfield	1,636
	Dem.	Beth Meyers	3,092
	Rep.	Jamey Francis	2,031
75.	Dem.	Stephen Smith*	1,689
	Rep.	Ken Mandley	1,208
	Rep.	Romaine Robert Quinn	2,231
76.	Dem.	Chris Taylor*	4,610
77.	Dem.	Terese Berceau*	6,196
78.	Dem.	Mark Clear	2,913
	Dem.	Lisa Subeck	3,827
79.	Dem.	Dianne Hesselbein*	3,999
	Rep.	Brent Renteria	654
80.	Dem.	Sondy Pope*	3,726
81.	Dem.	Dave Considine	2,085
	Dem.	Margo Miller	1,395
	Dem.	Peter J. Vedro	482
	Rep.	Ashton Kirsch	1,893
	Rep.	David J. Moore	333
	Rep.	Greg Petrulis	437
82.	Rep.	Ken Skowronski*	1,152
83.	Dem.	Jim Brownlow	1,777
	Rep.	Dave Craig*	4,152
84.	Rep.	Michael Kuglitsch*	2,001
85.	Dem.	Mandy Wright*	2,062
	Rep.	Dave Heaton	1,442
86.	Dem.	Nancy Stencil	1,315
	Rep.	John Spiros*	1,489
87.	Dem.	Richard Pulcher	1,383
	Rep.	Michael Bub	1,433
	Rep.	James W. Edming	1,452
	Rep.	Shirl LaBarre	1,339
	Rep.	Scott Kenneth Noble	960
88.	Dem.	Dan Robinson	1,393
	Rep.	John Macco	1,960
89.	Rep.	John Nygren*	1,817
90.	Dem.	Eric Genrich*	1,291
	Rep.	Eric Wimberger	1,124
91.	Dem.	Dana Wachs*	1,823
92.	Dem.	Chris Danou*	2,891
	Rep.	Isaac Weix	1,484
93.	Dem.	Jeff Smith	1,846
	Rep.	Warren Petryk*	2,298
94.	Dem.	Steve Doyle*	1,517
	Rep.	Tracie Happel	1,542
95.	Dem.	Jill Billings*	1,902
96.	Dem.	Peter Flesch	1,912
	Rep.	Lee Nerison*	2,328
97.	Rep.	Scott Allen	2,004
	Rep.	Joe Banske	300
	Rep.	Kathleen Cummings	743
	Rep.	Aaron D. Perry	429
	Rep.	Brandon J. Rosner	1,716
	Rep.	Vince Trovato	728
98.	Rep.	Adam Neylon*	4,044
99.	Dem.	Alice Jensen	1,076
	Rep.	Chris Kapenga*	5,261

*Incumbent.

Dem. – Democratic Party; Rep.– Republican Party.

Source: Official records of the Government Accountability Board, Elections Division. Scattered votes omitted.

DISTRICT VOTE FOR REPRESENTATIVES TO THE ASSEMBLY
Special and General Elections

Assembly District	Political Party	Candidates	Vote	Percent of Total Vote[1]
		November 4, 2014 General Election		
1	Dem.	Joe Majeski	12,256	43.24%
	Rep.	Joel C. Kitchens	16,072	56.70
2	Rep.	Andre Jacque*	18,994	98.64
3	Rep.	Al Ott*	19,542	100.00
4	Dem.	Chris Plaunt	10,026	40.88
	Rep.	David Steffen	14,467	58.99
5	Dem.	Jeff McCabe	9,084	37.65
	Rep.	Jim Steineke*	15,045	62.35
6	Rep.	Gary Tauchen*	18,696	99.32
7	Dem.	Daniel Riemer*	11,065	55.52
	Rep.	Scott Espeseth	8,800	44.16
8	Dem.	JoCasta Zamarripa*	5,155	79.87
	Rep.	Vincent Synowicz	1,271	19.69
9	Dem.	Josh Zepnick*	8,507	97.68
10	Dem.	David Bowen	20,242	98.95
11	Dem.	Mandela Barnes*	17,328	98.83
12	Dem.	Frederick P. Kessler*	16,494	97.94
	Rep.	Russell Goodwin[2]	3	0.02
13	Rep.	Rob Hutton*	20,710	96.85
14	Rep.	Dale Kooyenga*	21,954	96.37
15	Dem.	John F. Weishan, Jr.	9,057	36.93
	Rep.	Joe Sanfelippo*	15,427	62.91
16	Dem.	Leon D. Young*	16,183	98.41
17	Dem.	La Tonya Johnson*	19,666	87.25
	Ind.	Eugenie M. Stackowitz	2,802	12.43
18	Dem.	Evan Goyke*	16,522	98.50
19	Dem.	Jonathan Brostoff	18,077	81.44
	Ind.	Joseph Thomas Klein	3,943	17.76
20	Dem.	Christine Sinicki*	13,400	56.02
	Rep.	Molly McGartland	10,481	43.81
21	Rep.	Jessie Rodriguez*	16,051	96.54
22	Dem.	Jessie Read	8,789	29.86
	Rep.	Janel Brandtjen	20,607	70.02
23	Dem.	Beth L. Lueck	11,470	36.41
	Rep.	Jim Ott*	20,006	63.51
24	Rep.	Dan Knodl*	21,818	97.06
25	Rep.	Paul Tittl*	17,042	100.00
26	Dem.	Terry Van Akkeren	9,064	38.64
	Rep.	Terry Katsma	14,352	61.18
27	Dem.	Scott Grover Heinig	9,447	36.99
	Rep.	Tyler Vorpagel	16,042	62.82
28	Dem.	Travis Schachtner	7,736	37.77
	Rep.	Adam Jarchow	12,747	62.23
29	Rep.	John Murtha*	14,953	98.49
30	Dem.	Darrel Laumann	8,658	37.05
	Rep.	Dean Knudson*	13,951	59.70
	Ind.	Laurie Kroeger	747	3.20
31	Rep.	Amy Loudenbeck*	17,721	98.54
32	Dem.	Alan Kupsik	7,094	34.03
	Rep.	Tyler August*	13,714	65.79
33	Rep.	Cody Horlacher	19,429	98.04
34	Rep.	Rob Swearingen*	22,085	98.12
35	Rep.	Mary J. Czaja*	18,713	98.58
36	Rep.	Jeffrey L. Mursau*	18,504	99.86
37	Dem.	Mary I. Arnold	10,058	41.10
	Rep.	John Jagler*	14,400	58.84
38	Dem.	Tom Chojnacki	10,281	37.00
	Rep.	Joel Kleefisch*	17,481	62.91
39	Rep.	Mark L. Born*	16,793	73.74
	Ind.	Richard Bennett	5,977	26.25
40	Rep.	Kevin Petersen*	18,424	98.96
41	Dem.	Joe Kallas	8,409	39.00
	Rep.	Joan Ballweg*	13,152	60.99
42	Dem.	George Ferriter	10,518	42.46
	Rep.	Keith Ripp*	14,238	57.48
43	Dem.	Andy Jorgensen*	14,116	59.71
	Rep.	Leon L. Hebert	9,493	40.16
44	Dem.	Debra Kolste*	13,354	67.95
	Rep.	Jacob Dorsey	6,298	32.05
45	Dem.	Mark Spreitzer	12,856	99.02
46	Dem.	Gary Hebl*	20,014	97.32
47	Dem.	Robb Kahl*	20,332	81.28
	Ind.	Phillip N. Anderson	4,596	18.37

DISTRICT VOTE FOR REPRESENTATIVES TO THE ASSEMBLY
Special and General Elections–Continued

Assembly District	Political Party	Candidates	Vote	Percent of Total Vote[1]
48.	Dem.	Melissa Agard Sargent*	23,423	98.48
49.	Dem.	Chad Henneman	7,689	38.56
	Rep.	Travis Tranel*	12,240	61.38
50.	Dem.	Christopher Miller	8,600	42.19
	Rep.	Ed Brooks*	11,775	57.77
51.	Dem.	Dick Cates	10,577	47.19
	Rep.	Todd Novak	10,642	47.48
	Ind.	Adam Laufenberg	1,177	5.25
52.	Rep.	Jeremy Thiesfeldt*	17,523	100.00
53.	Rep.	Michael Schraa*	17,618	98.55
54.	Dem.	Gordon Hintz*	11,228	51.37
	Rep.	Mark Elliott	10,571	48.36
55.	Dem.	Mark Westphal	10,240	42.15
	Rep.	Mike Rohrkaste	14,027	57.74
56.	Rep.	Dave Murphy*	20,844	99.57
57.	Dem.	Amanda Stuck	11,162	54.15
	Rep.	Chris Klein	9,432	45.76
58.	Rep.	Bob Gannon	22,087	97.86
59.	Rep.	Jesse Kremer	22,417	99.02
60.	Dem.	Perry Duman[2]	5	0.02
	Rep.	Robert Brooks	24,066	98.93
61.	Rep.	Samantha Kerkman*	17,452	97.41
62.	Rep.	Thomas Weatherston*	18,761	97.61
63.	Dem.	Andy Mitchell	8,917	36.70
	Rep.	Robin J. Vos*	15,361	63.23
64.	Dem.	Peter W. Barca*	13,887	95.54
65.	Dem.	Tod Ohnstad*	11,599	96.93
66.	Dem.	Cory Mason*	12,062	80.73
	Ind.	George Meyers	2,781	18.61
67.	Dem.	Gary Stene	8,691	39.43
	Rep.	Tom Larson*	13,353	60.57
68.	Dem.	Jeff Peck	10,076	47.15
	Rep.	Kathy Bernier*	11,289	52.82
69.	Dem.	Norbert Salamonski	6,380	30.95
	Rep.	Bob Kulp*	14,233	69.05
70.	Dem.	Amy Sue Vruwink*	10,508	47.14
	Rep.	Nancy Lynn Vander Meer	11,766	52.78
71.	Dem.	Katrina Shankland*	17,134	97.79
72.	Dem.	Dana W. Duncan	10,317	44.02
	Rep.	Scott S. Krug*	13,113	55.95
73.	Dem.	Nick Milroy*	15,602	99.80
74.	Dem.	Beth Meyers	14,663	57.43
	Rep.	Jamey Francis	10,862	42.54
75.	Dem.	Stephen Smith*	9,643	45.10
	Rep.	Romaine Robert Quinn	11,730	54.86
76.	Dem.	Chris Taylor*	27,102	98.15
77.	Dem.	Terese Berceau*	25,268	98.66
78.	Dem.	Lisa Subeck	23,014	97.99
79.	Dem.	Dianne Hesselbein*	18,843	62.24
	Rep.	Brent Renteria	11,406	37.67
80.	Dem.	Sondy Pope*	21,633	97.71
81.	Dem.	Dave Considine	12,934	54.27
	Rep.	Ashton Kirsch	10,892	45.70
82.	Rep.	Ken Skowronski*	19,210	97.27
83.	Dem.	Jim Brownlow	7,877	26.89
	Rep.	Dave Craig*	21,382	72.99
84.	Rep.	Michael Kuglitsch*	19,700	97.27
85.	Dem.	Mandy Wright*	11,082	49.81
	Rep.	Dave Heaton	11,167	50.19
86.	Dem.	Nancy Stencil	9,528	37.51
	Rep.	John Spiros*	15,875	62.49
87.	Dem.	Richard Pulcher	7,098	33.36
	Rep.	Michael Bub[2]	52	0.24
	Rep.	James W. Edming	14,121	66.37
88.	Dem.	Dan Robinson	10,046	43.72
	Rep.	John Macco	12,915	56.20
89.	Rep.	John Nygren*	18,483	99.38
90.	Dem.	Eric Genrich*	7,953	54.94
	Rep.	Eric Wimberger	5,342	36.90
	Ind.	Shae Sortwell	1,164	8.04
91.	Dem.	Dana Wachs*	14,686	96.97
92.	Dem.	Chris Danou*	11,862	56.58
	Rep.	Isaac Weix	9,096	43.38

DISTRICT VOTE FOR REPRESENTATIVES TO THE ASSEMBLY
Special and General Elections–Continued

Assembly District	Political Party	Candidates	Vote	Percent of Total Vote[1]
93.	Dem.	Jeff Smith	10,749	44.55
	Rep.	Warren Petryk*	13,367	55.40
94.	Dem.	Steve Doyle*	13,670	54.06
	Rep.	Tracie Happel	11,617	45.94
95.	Dem.	Jill Billings*	17,037	100.00
96.	Dem.	Peter Flesch	8,839	41.06
	Rep.	Lee Nerison*	12,683	58.91
97.	Rep.	Scott Allen	17,804	97.83
98.	Rep.	Adam Neylon*	21,357	98.64
99.	Dem.	Alice Jensen	6,593	22.08
	Rep.	Chris Kapenga*	23,232	77.82

Dem. – Democratic Party; Rep. – Republican Party; Ind. – Independent.

*Incumbent.

[1]Percentages do not equal 100%, as scattered votes have been omitted.

[2]Write-in candidate.

Source: Official records of the Government Accountability Board, Elections Division.

COUNTY VOTE FOR GOVERNOR
August 12, 2014 Primary

County	Mary Burke (Dem.)	Brett Hulsey (Dem.)	Steve R. Evans[1] (Rep.)	Scott Walker[2] (Rep.)
Adams	853	116	0	691
Ashland	1,153	90	0	218
Barron	1,221	115	1	2,435
Bayfield	1,715	133	0	373
Brown	6,971	796	0	10,377
Buffalo	393	43	1	540
Burnett	532	75	0	1,690
Calumet	1,136	264	1	1,700
Chippewa	1,460	208	1	1,183
Clark	683	92	0	1,647
Columbia	2,700	220	0	2,430
Crawford	829	99	0	626
Dane	41,744	3,737	4	5,485
Dodge	2,117	237	1	6,764
Door	1,387	62	1	3,868
Douglas	2,770	430	0	721
Dunn	2,628	805	0	1,009
Eau Claire	3,183	234	4	2,129
Florence	93	19	0	181
Fond du Lac	2,328	224	2	7,606
Forest	331	41	0	268
Grant	1,681	108	3	2,739
Green	2,376	305	0	1,360
Green Lake	836	105	1	2,449
Iowa	1,440	85	1	838
Iron	379	76	0	268
Jackson	731	84	0	588
Jefferson	3,045	562	0	2,807
Juneau	963	82	0	1,236
Kenosha	5,413	315	0	7,885
Kewaunee	600	156	1	1,022
La Crosse	3,649	226	0	2,946
Lafayette	612	46	4	1,991
Langlade	614	114	0	1,052
Lincoln	913	138	0	821
Manitowoc	2,612	339	4	5,347
Marathon	3,814	475	0	3,763
Marinette	1,042	220	0	1,038
Marquette	569	50	0	847
Menominee	163	29	0	23
Milwaukee	71,762	29,302	6	8,968
Monroe	965	72	2	2,836
Oconto	1,543	304	1	1,865
Oneida	1,239	171	1	1,051
Outagamie	4,990	609	2	7,114
Ozaukee	2,444	186	4	11,436
Pepin	288	42	1	679
Pierce	902	71	1	1,154
Polk	1,028	81	0	1,315
Portage	5,523	1,408	1	1,638
Price	863	83	0	1,360
Racine	7,041	544	3	10,547
Richland	775	61	6	2,320
Rock	12,093	2,294	0	4,580
Rusk	489	50	0	1,107
St. Croix	1,838	188	0	1,753
Sauk	3,652	307	1	2,347
Sawyer	601	41	0	1,895
Shawano	941	129	5	3,881
Sheboygan	3,772	337	1	11,803
Taylor	420	66	0	1,499
Trempealeau	1,679	453	0	805
Vernon	969	74	1	884
Vilas	686	76	0	792
Walworth	2,450	234	1	6,280
Washburn	656	41	0	1,078
Washington	2,758	574	0	9,683
Waukesha	10,145	1,318	13	32,957
Waupaca	1,418	270	0	1,565
Waushara	783	77	6	2,104
Winnebago	4,995	426	8	8,497
Wood	2,534	386	0	1,959
TOTAL	259,921	51,830	94	238,713

Dem. – Democratic Party; Rep. – Republican Party.
[1]Write-in candidate.
[2]Incumbent.
Source: Official records of the Government Accountability Board, Elections Division. Scattered votes omitted.

COUNTY VOTE FOR LIEUTENANT GOVERNOR
August 12, 2014 Primary

County	John Lehman (Dem.)	Mary Jo Walters (Dem.)	Rebecca Kleefisch* (Rep.)
Adams	402	467	638
Ashland	499	518	199
Barron	637	579	2,218
Bayfield	680	827	340
Brown	3,613	3,206	9,828
Buffalo	195	197	491
Burnett	281	288	1,496
Calumet	644	587	1,614
Chippewa	836	663	1,203
Clark	322	352	1,483
Columbia	1,235	1,274	2,326
Crawford	435	400	559
Dane	21,776	15,484	5,264
Dodge	1,241	860	6,518
Door	655	640	3,622
Douglas	1,353	1,501	628
Dunn	1,469	1,401	939
Eau Claire	1,648	1,373	2,043
Florence	47	49	168
Fond du Lac	1,257	1,027	7,302
Forest	183	138	241
Grant	854	699	2,612
Green	1,200	1,029	1,298
Green Lake	455	395	2,356
Iowa	743	601	805
Iron	189	206	228
Jackson	401	327	527
Jefferson	1,672	1,348	2,707
Juneau	486	464	1,193
Kenosha	3,433	1,816	7,407
Kewaunee	369	328	973
La Crosse	1,758	1,586	2,821
Lafayette	321	270	1,819
Langlade	307	327	939
Lincoln	483	434	746
Manitowoc	1,356	1,309	5,354
Marathon	2,066	1,794	3,484
Marinette	562	548	1,004
Marquette	285	295	824
Menominee	81	86	21
Milwaukee	43,461	35,317	8,308
Monroe	437	502	2,771
Oconto	848	824	1,771
Oneida	608	647	977
Outagamie	2,569	2,328	6,765
Ozaukee	1,426	913	11,024
Pepin	166	130	629
Pierce	509	388	1,092
Polk	512	500	1,251
Portage	2,779	2,668	1,442
Price	430	423	1,165
Racine	6,176	1,276	10,147
Richland	365	368	2,195
Rock	6,117	5,877	4,295
Rusk	222	274	995
St. Croix	937	828	1,682
Sauk	1,694	1,649	2,236
Sawyer	269	317	1,644
Shawano	464	488	3,685
Sheboygan	2,000	1,787	12,840
Taylor	220	221	1,336
Trempealeau	997	877	761
Vernon	483	434	841
Vilas	309	360	770
Walworth	1,322	1,067	6,038
Washburn	319	310	979
Washington	1,676	1,257	9,403
Waukesha	5,875	4,219	32,120
Waupaca	722	769	1,498
Waushara	396	390	2,028
Winnebago	2,508	2,243	8,096
Wood	1,346	1,173	1,842
TOTAL	144,591	116,517	228,864

Dem. – Democratic Party; Rep. – Republican Party.

*Incumbent.

Source: Official records of the Government Accountability Board, Elections Division. Scattered votes omitted.

COUNTY VOTE FOR GOVERNOR AND LIEUTENANT GOVERNOR
November 4, 2014 General Election

County	Mary Burke / John Lehman (Dem.)	Scott Walker* / Rebecca Kleefisch* (Rep.)	Robert Burke / Joseph M. Brost (Ind.)	Dennis Fehr (Ind.)
Adams	3,762	4,297	88	36
Ashland	4,150	2,333	55	26
Barron	6,832	9,696	146	67
Bayfield	4,888	3,075	40	17
Brown	40,751	58,408	741	324
Buffalo	2,267	3,169	41	24
Burnett	2,615	3,868	39	15
Calumet	7,285	14,086	155	88
Chippewa	10,402	13,765	196	143
Clark	3,848	7,409	85	49
Columbia	12,527	11,837	217	101
Crawford	3,225	2,974	48	26
Dane	175,937	73,676	2,065	544
Dodge	12,732	23,715	279	112
Door	6,842	8,160	107	53
Douglas	9,590	6,001	111	43
Dunn	7,066	8,229	169	53
Eau Claire	21,239	20,304	376	147
Florence	629	1,349	18	5
Fond du Lac	15,014	27,485	308	121
Forest	1,511	2,032	32	16
Grant	8,704	9,149	211	94
Green	7,948	7,193	132	52
Green Lake	2,464	5,336	53	21
Iowa	5,937	4,480	120	34
Iron	1,085	1,755	17	16
Jackson	3,631	3,812	67	35
Jefferson	13,876	21,443	299	114
Juneau	4,080	4,817	105	26
Kenosha	27,367	28,398	480	200
Kewaunee	3,379	5,676	40	39
La Crosse	25,429	22,321	498	171
Lafayette	2,982	3,191	50	24
Langlade	2,921	5,476	47	34
Lincoln	5,104	6,866	122	48
Manitowoc	12,563	21,044	290	135
Marathon	21,305	34,583	412	203
Marinette	6,023	9,610	104	51
Marquette	2,629	3,611	48	31
Menominee	753	215	23	8
Milwaukee	231,316	132,706	2,607	1,046
Monroe	6,399	8,446	161	73
Oconto	5,657	10,300	109	69
Oneida	7,190	9,852	190	75
Outagamie	29,503	44,543	665	233
Ozaukee	13,696	32,696	256	76
Pepin	1,333	1,791	23	14
Pierce	6,666	7,760	157	46
Polk	6,516	9,345	147	59
Portage	15,283	14,650	279	124
Price	2,700	3,725	49	28
Racine	35,769	42,944	571	216
Richland	3,315	3,435	64	22
Rock	32,523	24,993	616	300
Rusk	2,286	3,502	70	30
St. Croix	13,231	20,066	361	87
Sauk	13,041	12,222	248	97
Sawyer	3,029	3,721	53	22
Shawano	5,730	10,937	89	78
Sheboygan	17,955	31,728	373	146
Taylor	2,248	5,406	63	26
Trempealeau	4,974	5,617	91	42
Vernon	5,932	5,687	105	42
Vilas	4,240	6,942	91	34
Walworth	13,809	25,415	315	148
Washburn	3,074	3,945	43	30
Washington	15,507	50,278	312	137
Waukesha	54,500	147,266	1,017	345
Waupaca	7,471	13,130	104	83
Waushara	3,609	6,100	63	36
Winnebago	30,258	37,894	726	268
Wood	12,861	17,820	268	152
TOTAL	**1,122,913**	**1,259,706**	**18,720**	**7,530**

*Incumbent.

Dem. – Democratic Party; Rep. – Republican Party; Ind. – Independent.

Note: Vote totals for write-in candidates for governor: Jumoka A. Johnson (Constitution Party) – 15; Steve R. Evans (Rep.) – 9; Susan P. Resch (Rep.) – 8; Brett D. Hulsey (Ind.) – 52; Jessica Nicole Perry (Ind.) – 5; Mary Jo Walters (Ind.) – 108.

Source: Official records of the Government Accountability Board, Elections Division. Scattered votes omitted.

COUNTY VOTE FOR SECRETARY OF STATE
August 12, 2014 Primary

County	Jerry Broitzman (Con.)	Douglas La Follette* (Dem.)	Garey Bies (Rep.)	Julian Bradley (Rep.)
Adams	7	828	210	379
Ashland	2	971	56	131
Barron	12	1,186	611	1,398
Bayfield	3	1,522	125	202
Brown	20	6,404	5,867	3,617
Buffalo	6	381	132	332
Burnett	10	544	403	969
Calumet	7	1,116	613	909
Chippewa	5	1,404	397	742
Clark	5	650	482	984
Columbia	5	2,347	774	1,403
Crawford	6	790	166	329
Dane	30	36,697	1,741	3,139
Dodge	11	1,925	2,087	3,966
Door	2	1,256	3,552	1,012
Douglas	9	2,695	225	354
Dunn	14	2,801	253	629
Eau Claire	16	3,044	647	1,366
Florence	0	91	57	91
Fond du Lac	14	2,110	2,656	4,715
Forest	0	297	51	158
Grant	19	1,533	794	1,816
Green	4	2,138	457	718
Green Lake	24	802	564	1,609
Iowa	10	1,323	187	559
Iron	1	383	71	135
Jackson	9	727	158	356
Jefferson	8	2,781	887	1,540
Juneau	5	920	354	784
Kenosha	8	4,826	2,215	4,046
Kewaunee	3	631	909	276
La Crosse	8	3,354	635	2,220
Lafayette	19	578	472	1,275
Langlade	12	601	225	702
Lincoln	2	861	246	461
Manitowoc	9	2,510	2,181	2,594
Marathon	9	3,571	1,087	2,132
Marinette	9	1,027	319	615
Marquette	7	541	241	504
Menominee	0	158	10	10
Milwaukee	113	68,052	2,339	5,376
Monroe	10	906	776	2,057
Oconto	26	1,552	678	982
Oneida	3	1,145	255	657
Outagamie	30	4,559	2,751	4,056
Ozaukee	9	2,129	2,849	6,274
Pepin	5	295	156	433
Pierce	4	884	307	725
Polk	17	998	353	824
Portage	10	5,278	383	914
Price	9	771	336	763
Racine	23	6,370	3,345	6,417
Richland	12	730	537	1,580
Rock	30	12,461	1,289	2,534
Rusk	4	479	260	662
St. Croix	11	1,725	410	1,115
Sauk	4	3,303	632	1,401
Sawyer	5	565	434	1,188
Shawano	7	894	1,418	2,316
Sheboygan	24	3,700	3,451	7,517
Taylor	3	425	368	822
Trempealeau	12	1,862	183	527
Vernon	14	892	221	582
Vilas	1	614	229	469
Walworth	14	2,301	1,785	3,503
Washburn	14	625	296	618
Washington	22	2,609	3,185	5,849
Waukesha	48	9,088	8,647	21,340
Waupaca	14	1,375	458	943
Waushara	16	733	563	1,292
Winnebago	13	4,490	2,750	4,580
Wood	7	2,367	618	1,075
TOTAL	884	242,501	75,379	138,568

Con. – Constitution Party; Dem. – Democratic Party; Rep. – Republican Party.

*Incumbent.

Source: Official records of the Government Accountability Board, Elections Division. Scattered votes omitted.

COUNTY VOTE FOR SECRETARY OF STATE
November 4, 2014 General Election

County	Jerry Broitzman (Con.)	Douglas La Follette* (Dem.)	Julian Bradley (Rep.)	Andy Craig (Ind.)
Adams	112	4,032	3,517	199
Ashland	44	4,118	2,014	145
Barron	227	7,417	8,254	387
Bayfield	67	4,874	2,646	198
Brown	1,120	44,470	47,967	2,425
Buffalo	86	2,531	2,544	126
Burnett	65	2,763	3,357	145
Calumet	228	8,492	11,649	492
Chippewa	334	11,302	11,445	659
Clark	195	4,843	5,617	256
Columbia	280	12,710	10,120	747
Crawford	66	3,438	2,359	162
Dane	1,807	171,166	62,189	7,520
Dodge	442	13,836	20,490	772
Door	123	7,404	6,706	335
Douglas	185	9,520	5,281	332
Dunn	200	7,270	7,124	490
Eau Claire	503	21,518	17,184	1,295
Florence	28	683	1,152	47
Fond du Lac	497	16,437	23,282	928
Forest	41	1,681	1,578	80
Grant	262	9,015	7,520	539
Green	172	8,324	5,913	421
Green Lake	109	2,686	4,681	157
Iowa	87	6,298	3,490	329
Iron	28	1,273	1,374	60
Jackson	83	3,876	3,143	202
Jefferson	428	14,660	18,304	955
Juneau	117	4,250	4,140	252
Kenosha	625	27,428	24,828	1,434
Kewaunee	105	4,121	4,480	144
La Crosse	470	24,543	20,698	1,294
Lafayette	64	3,196	2,468	140
Langlade	92	3,297	4,482	176
Lincoln	147	5,532	5,692	352
Manitowoc	503	15,352	16,115	856
Marathon	708	24,085	28,781	1,295
Marinette	198	6,779	7,980	329
Marquette	81	2,790	3,105	144
Menominee	12	667	175	24
Milwaukee	3,583	228,262	110,905	7,796
Monroe	225	6,493	7,556	437
Oconto	197	6,614	8,538	368
Oneida	192	7,564	8,415	600
Outagamie	902	32,007	36,984	2,093
Ozaukee	367	14,683	29,476	909
Pepin	45	1,506	1,388	64
Pierce	214	6,777	6,722	382
Polk	181	6,762	8,413	388
Portage	356	15,941	11,787	799
Price	71	3,023	3,057	153
Racine	815	36,457	37,515	1,786
Richland	75	3,412	2,835	186
Rock	745	33,633	21,025	1,522
Rusk	78	2,560	2,826	163
St. Croix	444	13,218	18,107	1,101
Sauk	271	13,580	10,197	710
Sawyer	71	3,096	3,347	116
Shawano	199	6,515	8,903	420
Sheboygan	670	20,034	27,196	1,009
Taylor	116	2,851	4,196	162
Trempealeau	110	5,451	4,586	266
Vernon	118	6,050	4,968	316
Vilas	117	4,478	6,149	256
Walworth	435	14,381	22,709	1,039
Washburn	90	3,207	3,463	141
Washington	652	17,252	45,327	1,128
Waukesha	1,800	59,082	130,676	4,321
Waupaca	274	7,987	11,289	489
Waushara	131	3,878	5,311	227
Winnebago	811	31,143	32,891	2,010
Wood	448	14,539	14,234	796
TOTAL	25,744	1,161,113	1,074,835	58,996

*Incumbent.

Con. – Constitution Party; Dem. – Democratic Party; Rep. – Republican Party; Ind. – Independent.

Source: Official records of the Government Accountability Board, Elections Division. Scattered votes omitted.

COUNTY VOTE FOR ATTORNEY GENERAL
August 12, 2014 Primary

County	Susan V. Happ (Dem.)	Ismael Ozanne (Dem.)	Jon Richards (Dem.)	Brad Schimel (Rep.)
Adams	559	92	248	595
Ashland	521	135	370	194
Barron	667	123	394	2,131
Bayfield	930	176	429	317
Brown	4,749	601	1,848	9,152
Buffalo	234	44	107	481
Burnett	323	69	162	1,458
Calumet	852	111	324	1,541
Chippewa	824	183	497	1,145
Clark	393	64	225	1,366
Columbia	1,606	510	666	2,243
Crawford	461	114	242	537
Dane	20,857	13,255	9,409	5,052
Dodge	1,341	235	629	6,094
Door	894	89	328	3,416
Douglas	1,780	175	887	585
Dunn	1,519	293	1,036	913
Eau Claire	1,590	423	1,066	2,111
Florence	52	7	38	156
Fond du Lac	1,553	215	569	6,951
Forest	176	26	104	225
Grant	986	217	411	2,512
Green	1,546	388	521	1,216
Green Lake	595	78	179	2,280
Iowa	818	270	361	757
Iron	246	29	118	216
Jackson	413	84	236	515
Jefferson	2,801	264	600	2,544
Juneau	586	117	272	1,142
Kenosha	3,060	474	1,800	6,612
Kewaunee	462	42	207	948
La Crosse	1,690	526	1,253	2,661
Lafayette	377	106	136	1,712
Langlade	369	56	198	879
Lincoln	492	138	314	695
Manitowoc	1,919	212	623	4,831
Marathon	1,950	527	1,393	3,186
Marinette	794	83	267	962
Marquette	363	66	160	799
Menominee	115	14	44	20
Milwaukee	36,050	12,773	35,765	7,927
Monroe	530	113	289	2,713
Oconto	1,171	100	411	1,706
Oneida	747	141	370	930
Outagamie	3,365	427	1,325	6,772
Ozaukee	1,201	214	1,021	10,332
Pepin	143	29	104	604
Pierce	531	87	278	1,075
Polk	603	131	264	1,225
Portage	3,028	680	1,718	1,322
Price	459	106	258	1,066
Racine	3,622	720	2,598	10,588
Richland	493	104	165	2,089
Rock	7,379	2,020	3,535	4,070
Rusk	247	52	190	940
St. Croix	997	175	593	1,627
Sauk	2,103	644	889	2,122
Sawyer	353	93	131	1,694
Shawano	670	88	207	3,557
Sheboygan	2,408	261	1,190	11,511
Taylor	248	33	147	1,232
Trempealeau	1,084	180	602	720
Vernon	510	134	284	813
Vilas	384	81	207	725
Walworth	1,474	255	742	5,690
Washburn	371	55	194	948
Washington	1,524	390	1,137	9,684
Waukesha	5,304	994	4,320	31,610
Waupaca	1,046	140	361	1,452
Waushara	585	35	162	1,937
Winnebago	3,299	381	1,242	7,575
Wood	1,333	359	843	1,682
TOTAL	144,725	42,626	90,213	219,088

Dem. – Democratic Party; Rep. – Republican Party.
Source: Official records of the Government Accountability Board, Elections Division. Scattered votes omitted.

COUNTY VOTE FOR ATTORNEY GENERAL
November 4, 2014 General Election

County	Susan V. Happ (Dem.)	Brad Schimel (Rep.)	Thomas A. Nelson, Sr. (Ind.)
Adams	3,546	4,140	278
Ashland	3,966	2,203	177
Barron	6,674	9,046	515
Bayfield	4,731	2,867	217
Brown	39,096	55,095	3,292
Buffalo	2,172	2,977	158
Burnett	2,591	3,513	172
Calumet	7,014	13,189	762
Chippewa	9,475	13,704	763
Clark	3,769	6,854	327
Columbia	11,837	11,574	788
Crawford	2,974	2,817	277
Dane	166,337	73,880	6,829
Dodge	12,307	22,610	966
Door	6,614	7,572	443
Douglas	9,387	5,481	427
Dunn	6,608	7,889	610
Eau Claire	19,355	20,112	1,490
Florence	598	1,234	59
Fond du Lac	14,336	26,184	1,255
Forest	1,413	1,883	112
Grant	8,180	8,577	726
Green	7,527	6,933	457
Green Lake	2,374	5,051	236
Iowa	5,585	4,294	421
Iron	1,101	1,551	82
Jackson	3,376	3,686	249
Jefferson	14,359	19,877	943
Juneau	3,839	4,619	316
Kenosha	26,254	27,091	1,708
Kewaunee	3,406	5,270	251
La Crosse	23,695	21,914	1,621
Lafayette	2,784	2,965	198
Langlade	2,759	5,216	196
Lincoln	4,559	6,876	390
Manitowoc	12,616	19,255	1,298
Marathon	19,978	33,876	1,467
Marinette	5,862	8,931	490
Marquette	2,547	3,412	208
Menominee	646	212	39
Milwaukee	219,901	128,916	9,551
Monroe	5,847	8,308	591
Oconto	5,551	9,499	554
Oneida	6,579	9,696	672
Outagamie	27,602	41,289	4,256
Ozaukee	13,175	31,596	940
Pepin	1,303	1,604	97
Pierce	6,589	7,076	513
Polk	6,416	8,776	461
Portage	14,319	13,932	935
Price	2,488	3,593	195
Racine	33,872	41,616	2,096
Richland	3,155	3,171	248
Rock	31,438	23,978	1,825
Rusk	2,149	3,337	202
St. Croix	12,803	18,915	1,264
Sauk	12,484	11,663	817
Sawyer	2,860	3,507	180
Shawano	5,452	10,260	563
Sheboygan	17,670	30,312	1,382
Taylor	2,179	5,026	227
Trempealeau	4,770	5,288	365
Vernon	5,463	5,563	432
Vilas	3,832	6,814	324
Walworth	13,122	24,404	1,146
Washburn	2,986	3,696	174
Washington	14,727	48,638	1,328
Waukesha	50,284	145,431	3,874
Waupaca	7,178	12,423	663
Waushara	3,466	5,728	331
Winnebago	28,705	35,937	2,524
Wood	12,254	16,966	1,008
TOTAL	1,066,866	1,211,388	70,951

Dem. – Democratic Party; Rep. – Republican Party; Ind. – Independent.

Source: Official records of the Government Accountability Board, Elections Division. Scattered votes omitted.

COUNTY VOTE FOR STATE TREASURER
August 12, 2014 Primary

County	Andrew Zuelke (Con.)	Dave Leeper (Dem.)	David L. Sartori (Dem.)	Matt Adamczyk (Rep.)	Randall Melchert (Rep.)
Adams	8	400	397	378	211
Ashland	2	402	453	130	65
Barron	12	580	527	1,187	825
Bayfield	3	597	707	200	134
Brown	21	2,956	3,265	4,878	4,074
Buffalo	7	217	143	281	178
Burnett	10	326	207	896	477
Calumet	7	428	700	773	747
Chippewa	4	691	676	656	476
Clark	5	330	289	833	589
Columbia	6	1,037	1,197	1,175	1,001
Crawford	6	457	293	320	172
Dane	32	17,533	15,108	2,650	2,343
Dodge	12	935	994	3,611	2,475
Door	2	576	576	1,707	1,561
Douglas	9	1,144	1,485	358	229
Dunn	13	1,414	1,230	514	356
Eau Claire	15	1,444	1,270	1,083	885
Florence	0	40	43	97	41
Fond du Lac	17	918	1,199	4,072	3,325
Forest	0	141	148	150	62
Grant	18	765	665	1,508	1,075
Green	4	1,321	789	613	556
Green Lake	31	418	355	1,436	743
Iowa	10	603	597	439	297
Iron	1	181	164	141	62
Jackson	7	400	299	272	243
Jefferson	8	1,332	1,373	1,426	1,068
Juneau	6	391	500	671	474
Kenosha	8	2,057	2,568	4,255	2,011
Kewaunee	3	353	311	548	472
La Crosse	9	1,363	1,667	1,249	1,270
Lafayette	16	329	218	1,009	745
Langlade	13	230	371	600	308
Lincoln	2	386	478	424	271
Manitowoc	9	934	1,552	2,498	2,163
Marathon	9	1,715	1,780	1,974	1,253
Marinette	8	494	540	589	352
Marquette	7	286	231	463	289
Menominee	0	90	58	12	7
Milwaukee	110	31,237	36,795	5,901	2,062
Monroe	9	420	481	1,772	1,035
Oconto	28	802	751	1,093	569
Oneida	2	523	615	661	268
Outagamie	30	2,078	2,384	3,240	3,537
Ozaukee	9	875	1,138	6,570	2,927
Pepin	6	154	116	362	209
Pierce	4	450	379	668	351
Polk	16	509	418	773	397
Portage	10	2,522	2,229	961	359
Price	8	398	351	687	384
Racine	26	2,914	3,147	7,028	2,994
Richland	12	360	302	1,216	850
Rock	34	5,735	5,857	2,340	1,478
Rusk	4	209	253	564	349
St. Croix	13	833	744	984	531
Sauk	4	1,458	1,542	1,174	849
Sawyer	5	291	245	1,043	558
Shawano	6	458	428	2,170	1,547
Sheboygan	24	1,370	2,287	6,818	4,314
Taylor	3	222	181	708	467
Trempealeau	17	960	817	394	309
Vernon	14	438	406	427	360
Vilas	1	271	324	389	301
Walworth	15	1,070	1,090	3,506	1,816
Washburn	13	330	240	550	358
Washington	21	1,144	1,460	5,879	3,432
Waukesha	47	4,301	4,764	21,710	10,258
Waupaca	13	673	712	830	587
Waushara	15	356	349	1,224	650
Winnebago	12	1,897	2,358	3,830	3,369
Wood	6	1,110	1,167	1,048	757
TOTAL	897	112,582	119,753	132,596	82,117

Con. – Constitution Party; Dem. – Democratic Party; Rep. – Republican Party.

Source: Official records of the Government Accountability Board, Elections Division. Scattered votes omitted.

COUNTY VOTE FOR STATE TREASURER
November 4, 2014 General Election

County	Andrew Zuelke (Con.)	David L. Sartori (Dem.)	Matt Adamczyk (Rep.)	Ron Hardy (Ind.)	Jerry Shidell (Ind.)
Adams	149	3,504	3,722	204	184
Ashland	60	3,738	2,041	248	113
Barron	215	6,645	8,501	448	351
Bayfield	70	4,447	2,750	261	161
Brown	1,435	37,461	50,926	2,894	2,005
Buffalo	85	2,189	2,625	187	113
Burnett	60	2,531	3,442	127	116
Calumet	324	7,101	12,201	562	435
Chippewa	314	9,924	11,959	692	548
Clark	282	3,885	5,940	346	231
Columbia	371	11,063	10,673	782	612
Crawford	89	2,964	2,477	257	163
Dane	2,211	151,842	67,201	11,552	6,443
Dodge	536	11,731	21,353	805	692
Door	150	6,342	7,108	418	285
Douglas	193	9,038	5,276	409	281
Dunn	198	6,563	7,225	503	458
Eau Claire	598	19,265	17,764	1,378	1,052
Florence	19	617	1,173	30	44
Fond du Lac	767	14,063	24,194	865	802
Forest	31	1,445	1,617	83	113
Grant	213	7,779	7,963	648	480
Green	214	7,062	6,370	538	385
Green Lake	192	2,213	4,806	202	146
Iowa	113	5,361	3,796	414	309
Iron	18	1,114	1,429	78	65
Jackson	145	3,536	3,134	216	180
Jefferson	506	12,638	19,062	888	834
Juneau	141	3,739	4,268	255	237
Kenosha	617	25,242	25,608	1,388	1,087
Kewaunee	135	3,410	4,856	257	138
La Crosse	555	23,031	19,550	1,770	1,171
Lafayette	75	2,629	2,739	170	139
Langlade	103	2,952	4,434	146	294
Lincoln	138	4,788	5,768	302	573
Manitowoc	537	13,035	17,155	842	817
Marathon	772	21,017	29,345	1,238	1,814
Marinette	205	5,805	8,298	384	353
Marquette	274	2,376	3,142	147	148
Menominee	12	627	177	34	16
Milwaukee	2,974	209,866	119,185	9,312	6,193
Monroe	307	5,819	7,530	432	407
Oconto	240	5,423	8,997	386	366
Oneida	175	6,158	8,082	333	1,983
Outagamie	1,324	27,442	38,289	2,228	1,831
Ozaukee	301	12,645	30,423	825	767
Pepin	29	1,332	1,453	101	58
Pierce	217	6,210	6,826	424	325
Polk	184	6,163	8,512	392	373
Portage	346	13,839	12,467	1,061	707
Price	77	2,641	3,166	157	174
Racine	815	32,639	39,461	1,643	1,443
Richland	95	2,876	2,987	261	179
Rock	996	29,713	22,471	1,484	1,388
Rusk	105	2,181	2,930	186	158
St. Croix	411	12,242	18,152	874	912
Sauk	326	11,749	10,808	840	625
Sawyer	68	2,795	3,386	158	113
Shawano	235	5,392	9,366	467	410
Sheboygan	540	18,400	27,692	953	862
Taylor	98	2,225	4,461	228	186
Trempealeau	148	4,900	4,645	323	236
Vernon	142	5,333	4,999	518	288
Vilas	88	3,927	6,210	211	461
Walworth	432	12,603	23,216	1,074	854
Washburn	86	2,894	3,525	175	139
Washington	586	14,677	46,430	1,051	978
Waukesha	1,539	49,910	136,586	2,943	3,212
Waupaca	298	6,925	11,685	616	427
Waushara	251	3,312	5,439	219	217
Winnebago	935	27,348	33,712	2,302	1,672
Wood	563	12,257	14,981	975	781
TOTAL	28,053	1,026,548	1,120,140	66,120	53,113

Con. – Constitution Party; Dem. – Democratic Party; Rep. – Republican Party; Ind. – Independent.
Source: Official records of the Government Accountability Board, Elections Division. Scattered votes omitted.

VOTE FOR GOVERNOR AND LIEUTENANT GOVERNOR BY WARD
November 4, 2014 General Election

District	Burke and Lehman (Dem.)	Walker and Kleefisch (Rep.)
ADAMS COUNTY		
Adams		
Wards 1 – 3	233	258
Adams, city		
Wards 1 – 4	298	252
Big Flats		
Wards 1 – 2	187	205
Colburn	43	59
Dell Prairie		
Wards 1 – 3	310	359
Easton		
Wards 1 – 2	171	209
Friendship, vil.	122	92
Jackson		
Wards 1 – 2	214	241
Leola	33	88
Lincoln	72	69
Monroe	101	114
New Chester		
Wards 1 – 3	147	153
New Haven	145	143
Preston		
Wards 1 – 2	263	261
Quincy		
Wards 1 – 3	245	256
Richfield	27	41
Rome		
Wards 1 – 5	716	929
Springville		
Wards 1 – 2	196	293
Strongs Prairie		
Wards 1 – 3	231	272
Wisconsin Dells, city		
Wards 5, 9	8	3
TOTAL	3,762	4,297
ASHLAND COUNTY		
Agenda	77	117
Ashland	171	89
Ashland, city		
Ward 1	197	199
Ward 2	154	56
Ward 3	165	87
Ward 4	234	136
Ward 5	234	93
Ward 6	184	52
Ward 7	260	52
Ward 8	170	87
Ward 9	160	46
Ward 10	197	78
Ward 11	209	95
Butternut, vil.		
Wards 1 – 2	80	60
Chippewa	67	96
Gingles	232	119
Gordon		
Wards 1 – 2	57	68
Jacobs	140	132
La Pointe	178	52
Marengo		
Wards 1 – 2	115	74
Mellen, city	157	80
Morse		
Wards 1 – 3	140	106
Peeksville		
Wards 1 – 2	38	44
Sanborn		
Wards 1 – 2	352	50
Shanagolden	27	28
White River		
Wards 1 – 2	155	237
TOTAL	4,150	2,333
BARRON COUNTY		
Almena		
Wards 1 – 2	157	189
Almena, vil.	77	124
Arland	102	128
Barron		
Wards 1 – 2	80	200
Barron, city		
Wards 1 – 7	408	559
Bear Lake	106	163
Cameron, vil.		
Wards 1 – 3	220	324
Cedar Lake	183	345
Chetek		
Wards 1 – 2	305	496
Chetek, city		
Wards 1 – 4	274	411
Clinton	102	152

District	Burke and Lehman (Dem.)	Walker and Kleefisch (Rep.)
Crystal Lake	132	163
Cumberland	137	200
Cumberland, city		
Wards 1 – 4	382	364
Dallas	69	149
Dallas, vil.	43	78
Dovre	112	176
Doyle		
Wards 1 – 2	67	143
Haugen, vil.	63	53
Lakeland		
Wards 1 – 2	178	254
Maple Grove		
Wards 1 – 2	111	250
Maple Plain	172	201
New Auburn, vil.		
Ward 2	3	1
Ward 3	0	0
Oak Grove		
Wards 1 – 2	153	214
Prairie Farm		
Wards 1 – 2	90	119
Prairie Farm, vil.	57	64
Prairie Lake		
Wards 1 – 2	237	417
Rice Lake		
Wards 1 – 4	518	720
Rice Lake, city		
Wards 1 – 13	1,298	1,544
Sioux Creek	84	150
Stanfold	107	169
Stanley		
Wards 1 – 4	376	655
Sumner	131	163
Turtle Lake	77	125
Turtle Lake, vil.	122	117
Vance Creek	99	116
TOTAL	6,832	9,696
BAYFIELD COUNTY		
Ashland, city		
Ward 12	0	0
Barksdale	249	171
Barnes	257	225
Bayfield	311	139
Bayfield, city		
Wards 1 – 4	245	68
Bayview	202	124
Bell	127	65
Cable	187	240
Clover	87	67
Delta	80	95
Drummond	149	103
Eileen		
Wards 1 – 2	170	154
Grand View	146	83
Hughes	125	103
Iron River		
Wards 1 – 2	298	237
Kelly	117	87
Keystone	85	72
Lincoln	82	73
Mason	80	68
Mason, vil.	27	9
Namakagon	71	117
Orienta	36	33
Oulu	129	140
Pilsen	78	48
Port Wing	132	101
Russell		
Wards 1 – 2	417	67
Tripp	50	61
Washburn	196	103
Washburn, city		
Wards 1 – 4	755	222
TOTAL	4,888	3,075
BROWN COUNTY		
Allouez, vil.		
Wards 1 – 2	831	783
Wards 3 – 4	718	780
Wards 5 – 6	759	1,157
Wards 7 – 9	613	882
Ashwaubenon, vil.		
Wards 1 – 2	388	501
Wards 3 – 4	438	617
Wards 5 – 6	508	695
Wards 7 – 8	532	896
Wards 9 – 10	594	1,027
Wards 11 – 12	495	644
Bellevue, vil.		
Wards 1 – 6	1,169	1,586

VOTE FOR GOVERNOR AND LIEUTENANT GOVERNOR BY WARD
November 4, 2014 General Election–Continued

District	Burke and Lehman (Dem.)	Walker and Kleefisch (Rep.)
Wards 7 – 10	1,225	2,048
De Pere, city		
Wards 1 – 4	1,273	1,644
Ward 5	87	92
Wards 6 – 8	878	1,086
Wards 9, 18	182	273
Wards 10 – 12	854	1,145
Wards 13 – 15	937	1,591
Wards 16 – 17	2	3
Denmark, vil.		
Wards 1 – 3	316	546
Eaton		
Wards 1 – 2	287	475
Glenmore		
Wards 1 – 2	143	363
Green Bay		
Wards 1 – 3	317	700
Green Bay, city		
Ward 1	5	11
Ward 2	450	532
Ward 3	555	625
Ward 4	540	837
Ward 5	279	325
Ward 6	532	817
Ward 7	298	395
Ward 8	584	694
Ward 9	198	190
Ward 10	275	241
Ward 11	247	308
Ward 12	217	224
Ward 13	285	194
Ward 14	250	275
Ward 15	492	398
Ward 16	483	292
Ward 17	385	273
Ward 18	331	369
Ward 19	227	197
Ward 20	284	217
Ward 21	234	165
Ward 22	125	87
Ward 23	242	226
Ward 24	365	274
Ward 25	324	303
Ward 26	285	170
Ward 27	128	71
Ward 28	326	233
Ward 29	392	396
Ward 30	435	260
Ward 31	381	397
Ward 32	324	333
Ward 33	255	225
Ward 34	453	521
Ward 35	312	365
Ward 36	200	167
Ward 37	292	362
Ward 38	442	419
Ward 39	478	488
Ward 40	328	337
Ward 41	168	230
Ward 42	248	254
Ward 43	443	481
Ward 44	569	716
Ward 45	528	968
Ward 46	485	487
Ward 47	471	743
Hobart, vil.		
Wards 1 – 8	1,126	2,273
Ward 9	0	0
Holland		
Wards 1 – 2	215	540
Howard, vil.		
Wards 1, 12	290	534
Wards 2, 8, 11	740	1,256
Wards 3 – 4, 6	433	541
Ward 5	121	150
Ward 7	164	336
Wards 9 – 10, 18	582	856
Wards 13 – 14	278	560
Wards 15 – 16	359	692
Humboldt		
Wards 1 – 2	230	396
Lawrence		
Wards 1 – 6	712	1,577
Ledgeview		
Wards 1 – 3, 8 – 10	542	1,169
Wards 4 – 7	516	1,048
Morrison		
Wards 1 – 2	173	611
New Denmark		
Wards 1 – 3	282	469

District	Burke and Lehman (Dem.)	Walker and Kleefisch (Rep.)
Pittsfield		
Wards 1 – 3	436	933
Pulaski, vil.		
Wards 1 – 3, 6	423	688
Rockland		
Wards 1 – 3	270	671
Scott		
Wards 1 – 4	772	1,129
Suamico, vil.		
Wards 1 – 4	770	1,862
Wards 5 – 8	986	2,069
Wrightstown		
Wards 1 – 3	312	713
Wrightstown, vil.		
Wards 1 – 3	323	709
TOTAL	40,751	58,408
BUFFALO COUNTY		
Alma	81	68
Alma, city		
Wards 1 – 2	175	170
Belvidere	86	120
Buffalo	120	192
Buffalo City, city	184	234
Canton	52	58
Cross	53	90
Cochran, vil.	64	90
Dover	63	95
Fountain City, city		
Wards 1 – 2	162	176
Gilmanton	63	88
Glencoe	53	142
Lincoln	35	69
Maxville	45	103
Milton	102	144
Modena	63	84
Mondovi	76	126
Mondovi, city		
Wards 1 – 3	430	476
Montana	28	94
Naples	104	189
Nelson	96	151
Nelson, vil.	66	50
Waumandee	66	160
TOTAL	2,267	3,169
BURNETT COUNTY		
Anderson	56	119
Blaine	35	41
Daniels	103	190
Dewey	80	128
Grantsburg		
Wards 1 – 3	144	257
Grantsburg, vil		
Wards 1 – 3	164	331
Jackson	205	252
La Follette		
Wards 1 – 2	97	123
Lincoln	46	73
Meenon		
Wards 1 – 3	145	236
Oakland		
Wards 1 – 2	220	191
Roosevelt	34	44
Rusk	71	114
Sand Lake	102	105
Scott		
Wards 1 – 2	126	186
Siren		
Wards 1 – 2	176	221
Siren, vil		
Wards 1 – 2	122	144
Swiss		
Wards 1 – 2	159	122
Trade Lake		
Wards 1 – 2	110	254
Union	73	80
Webb Lake	71	143
Webster, vil		
Wards 1 – 2	101	127
West Marshland		
Wards 1 – 2	39	91
Wood River		
Wards 1 – 3	136	296
TOTAL	2,615	3,868
CALUMET COUNTY		
Appleton, city		
Ward 12	93	95
Ward 13	331	389
Ward 14	254	357

VOTE FOR GOVENROR AND LIEUTENANT GOVERNOR BY WARD
November 4, 2014 General Election–Continued

District	Burke and Lehman (Dem.)	Walker and Kleefisch (Rep.)
Ward 26	394	484
Ward 44	386	473
Ward 45	469	632
Ward 46	31	48
Ward 47	0	0
Brillion		
Wards 1 – 2	157	517
Brillion, city		
Wards 1 – 4	398	860
Brothertown		
Wards 1 – 2	155	496
Charlestown	90	297
Chilton		
Wards 1 – 3	127	393
Chilton, city		
Wards 1 – 5	500	904
Harrison		
Wards 7 – 8, 10 – 12	254	364
Harrison, vil.		
Wards 3 – 9	678	1,350
Wards 10 – 16	659	1,465
Hilbert, vil.		
Wards 1 – 2	101	353
Kaukauna, city		
Ward 11	0	0
Kiel, city		
Ward 7	39	58
Menasha, city		
Wards 16 – 20	476	697
New Holstein		
Wards 1 – 3	177	513
New Holstein, city		
Wards 1 – 5	523	886
Potter, vil.	21	105
Rantoul	74	285
Sherwood, vil.		
Wards 1 – 5	474	986
Stockbridge		
Wards 1 – 3	208	548
Stockbridge, vil.	108	224
Woodville	108	307
TOTAL	7,285	14,086
CHIPPEWA COUNTY		
Anson		
Wards 1 – 3	364	581
Ward 4	0	2
Arthur	90	197
Auburn	116	167
Birch Creek	71	194
Bloomer		
Wards 1 – 2	132	315
Bloomer, city		
Wards 1 – 4	482	804
Boyd, vil	105	112
Cadott, vil.		
Wards 1 – 3	235	230
Chippewa Falls, city		
Ward 1	337	332
Ward 2	378	374
Ward 3	449	448
Ward 4	320	277
Ward 5	301	232
Ward 6	335	293
Ward 7	380	341
Ward 7A	0	0
Cleveland	109	229
Colburn	95	227
Cooks Valley	80	197
Cornell, city		
Wards 1 – 4	216	305
Delmar	125	240
Eagle Point		
Wards 1 – 5, 5S	577	941
Eau Claire, city		
Ward 16	343	299
Ward 40	0	0
Ward 41	19	14
Edson		
Wards 1 – 2, 2S	140	185
Estella	51	110
Goetz		
Wards 1 – 2	160	160
Ward 3	0	1
Hallie	51	43
Howard	141	194
Lafayette		
Wards 1 – 9	1,187	1,584
Lake Hallie, vil.		
Wards 1 – 8	1,163	1,379

District	Burke and Lehman (Dem.)	Walker and Kleefisch (Rep.)
Lake Holcombe		
Wards 1 – 2	168	285
New Auburn, vil.	48	95
Ruby	59	119
Sampson	122	265
Sigel		
Wards 1 – 2	184	204
Stanley, city		
Wards 1 – 4, 6 – 7	309	401
Tilden		
Wards 1 – 3	267	419
Wheaton		
Wards 1 – 3	549	689
Woodmohr		
Wards 1 – 2	144	281
TOTAL	10,402	13,765
CLARK COUNTY		
Abbotsford, city		
Wards 2 – 5	166	343
Beaver	49	189
Butler	13	23
Colby		
Wards 1 – 3	66	167
Colby, city		
Wards 2 – 4	130	269
Curtiss, vil.	4	35
Dewhurst	65	97
Dorchester, vil.	81	157
Eaton		
Wards 1 – 2	52	154
Foster	20	49
Fremont		
Wards 1 – 2	102	311
Grant		
Wards 1 – 2	108	213
Granton, vil.	51	88
Green Grove		
Wards 1 – 2	60	114
Greenwood, city		
Wards 1 – 2	176	240
Hendren	62	111
Hewett		
Wards 1 – 2	63	87
Hixon		
Wards 1 – 2	86	107
Hoard		
Wards 1 – 2	61	137
Levis		
Wards 1 – 2	60	120
Longwood		
Wards 1 – 2	68	122
Loyal		
Wards 1 – 2	53	167
Loyal, city		
Wards 1 – 2	139	332
Lynn		
Wards 1 – 2	65	143
Mayville		
Wards 1 – 2	61	224
Mead	36	78
Mentor	92	110
Neillsville, city		
Ward 1	63	106
Ward 2	107	147
Ward 3	113	125
Ward 4	54	91
Ward 5	42	64
Owen, city		
Wards 1 – 3	172	165
Pine Valley		
Wards 1 – 2	186	345
Reseburg		
Wards 1 – 2	63	80
Seif	38	56
Sherman		
Wards 1 – 2	54	225
Sherwood	67	51
Stanley, city		
Ward 5	1	1
Thorp	78	144
Thorp, city		
Wards 1 – 4	255	357
Unity	70	183
Unity, vil.		
Ward 2	9	40
Warner		
Wards 1 – 2	62	162
Washburn	38	87

VOTE FOR GOVERNOR AND LIEUTENANT GOVERNOR BY WARD
November 4, 2014 General Election–Continued

District	Burke and Lehman (Dem.)	Walker and Kleefisch (Rep.)
Weston		
Wards 1 – 2	84	183
Withee	76	167
Withee, vil	80	110
Worden	53	131
York		
Wards 1 – 2	94	202
TOTAL	3,848	7,409
COLUMBIA COUNTY		
Arlington	218	190
Arlington, vil	184	187
Caledonia		
Wards 1 – 2	381	354
Cambria, vil	143	137
Columbus	120	200
Columbus, city		
Wards 1 – 8	1,173	977
Ward 10	0	0
Courtland	73	154
Dekorra		
Wards 1 – 3	604	582
Doylestown, vil	66	45
Fall River, vil		
Wards 1 – 2	330	285
Fort Winnebago	208	243
Fountain Prairie		
Wards 1 – 2	193	229
Friesland, vil	26	115
Hampden	133	167
Leeds		
Wards 1 – 2	198	224
Lewiston		
Wards 1 – 2	278	277
Lodi		
Wards 1 – 5	802	889
Lodi, city		
Wards 1 – 6	875	562
Lowville		
Wards 1 – 2	267	293
Marcellon		
Wards 1 – 2	196	254
Newport	142	180
Otsego	146	177
Pacific		
Wards 1 – 4	673	686
Pardeeville, vil.		
Wards 1 – 3	439	399
Portage, city		
Wards 1, 9 – 10	607	451
Wards 2 – 3, 5	676	372
Wards 4, 6 – 8	620	393
Poynette, vil.		
Wards 1 – 4	588	408
Randolph	76	299
Randolph, vil.		
Ward 3	49	137
Rio, vil.		
Wards 1 – 2	248	177
Scott	107	195
Springvale		
Wards 1 – 2	120	144
West Point		
Wards 1 – 3	541	525
Wisconsin Dells, city		
Wards 1 – 3, 6	471	405
Wyocena		
Wards 1 – 2	405	391
Wyocena, vil	151	134
TOTAL	12,527	11,837
CRAWFORD COUNTY		
Bell Center, vil	30	18
Bridgeport	182	276
Clayton		
Wards 1 – 3	219	163
De Soto, vil.		
Ward 2	21	19
Eastman		
Wards 1 – 2	118	193
Eastman, vil	70	72
Ferryville, vil	54	49
Freeman	170	147
Gays Mills, vil	120	76
Haney	96	58
Lynxville, vil	29	28
Marietta	111	111
Mount Sterling, vil	44	28
Prairie du Chien		
Wards 1 – 2	150	222
Prairie du Chien, city		
Ward 1	164	154
Wards 2, 7	187	142
Ward 3	127	120
Ward 4	163	126
Ward 5	176	129
Ward 6	171	166
Scott	115	95
Seneca	179	192
Soldiers Grove, vil	122	77
Steuben, vil	26	12
Utica	169	121
Wauzeka		
Wards 1 – 2	76	89
Wauzeka, vil	136	91
TOTAL	3,225	2,974
DANE COUNTY		
Albion		
Wards 1 – 2	556	342
Belleville, vil.		
Wards 1 – 2	570	271
Berry		
Wards 1 – 2	349	318
Black Earth	157	141
Black Earth, vil.		
Wards 1 – 2	443	251
Blooming Grove		
Wards 1 – 3	649	278
Blue Mounds	270	233
Blue Mounds, vil	268	159
Bristol		
Wards 1 – 4	984	1,043
Brooklyn, vil	272	129
Burke		
Wards 1 – 4	933	747
Cambridge, vil.		
Wards 2 – 3	411	295
Christiana		
Wards 1 – 2	322	297
Cottage Grove		
Wards 1 – 2, 4 – 5, 7	735	546
Wards 3, 6	454	316
Cottage Grove, vil.		
Wards 1 – 10	1,787	1,199
Cross Plains		
Wards 1 – 2	464	385
Ward 3	0	0
Cross Plains, vil.		
Wards 1 – 4	1,072	731
Dane	212	272
Dane, vil	215	243
Deerfield		
Wards 1 – 2	419	366
Deerfield, vil.		
Wards 1 – 3	641	421
DeForest, vil.		
Wards 1, 3 – 6, 15	1,056	774
Ward 2	165	100
Wards 7 – 10, 12	895	556
Ward 11	259	162
Ward 13	0	0
Wards 14, 16	0	0
Dunkirk		
Wards 1, 3, 5	401	280
Wards 2, 4, 6	228	137
Dunn		
Wards 1 – 7	1,771	1,104
Edgerton, city		
Ward 7	22	15
Fitchburg, city		
Wards 1 – 4	1,528	410
Wards 5 – 9	2,452	1,202
Wards 10 – 13	1,297	407
Ward 14	429	195
Wards 15, 18 – 19	1,358	761
Wards 16 – 17	689	344
Madison		
Ward 1	264	33
Wards 2 – 9	1,331	196
Madison, city		
Ward 1	736	331
Ward 2	626	181
Ward 3	488	191
Ward 4	358	141
Ward 5	591	226
Ward 6	1,168	296
Ward 7	574	258
Ward 8	960	386
Ward 9	1,116	428

VOTE FOR GOVENROR AND LIEUTENANT GOVERNOR BY WARD
November 4, 2014 General Election–Continued

District	Burke and Lehman (Dem.)	Walker and Kleefisch (Rep.)	District	Burke and Lehman (Dem.)	Walker and Kleefisch (Rep.)
Ward 10	933	361	Ward 100	1,058	316
Ward 11	468	104	Ward 101	315	100
Ward 12	1,148	301	Ward 102	588	224
Ward 13	351	71	Ward 103	275	59
Ward 14	340	62	Ward 104	928	292
Ward 15	782	122	Ward 105	948	450
Ward 16	1,685	288	Ward 106	824	758
Ward 17	476	129	Ward 107	426	257
Ward 18	536	94	Ward 108	1,035	223
Ward 19	480	89	Ward 109	1,081	430
Ward 20	115	22	Ward 110	598	342
Ward 21	534	143	Ward 111	871	681
Ward 22	778	261	Ward 112	0	0
Ward 23	319	111	Ward 113	0	0
Ward 24	370	167	Ward 114	2	0
Ward 25	1,183	306	Ward 115	0	0
Ward 26	674	222	Ward 116	0	0
Ward 27	6	0	Ward 117	0	0
Ward 28	842	95	Ward 118	0	0
Ward 29	2,000	113	Ward 119	0	0
Ward 30	697	91	Ward 120	0	0
Ward 31	776	130	Ward 121	0	0
Ward 32	485	88	Ward 122	0	0
Ward 33	522	100	Ward 123	0	0
Ward 34	613	104	Ward 124	0	1
Ward 35	727	124	Ward 125	0	0
Ward 36	747	236	Maple Bluff, vil.		
Ward 37	1,063	198	Wards 1 – 2	589	361
Ward 38	1,610	615	Marshall, vil.		
Ward 39	1,190	82	Wards 1 – 5	812	639
Ward 40	2,004	88	Mazomanie		
Ward 41	2,027	91	Wards 1 – 2	335	244
Ward 42	2,038	70	Mazomanie, vil.		
Ward 43	248	32	Wards 1 – 3	510	275
Ward 44	1,272	91	McFarland, vil.		
Ward 45	2,064	156	Wards 1 – 10	2,587	1,485
Ward 46	1,406	173	Medina		
Ward 47	668	342	Wards 1 – 2	358	318
Ward 48	302	101	Middleton		
Ward 49	811	449	Wards 1 – 8	1,823	1,729
Ward 50	814	365	Middleton, city		
Ward 51	754	179	Wards 1 – 5, 8 – 9	2,768	1,093
Ward 52	420	84	Wards 6 – 7, 14 – 18	2,218	941
Ward 53	1,543	329	Wards 10 – 13	2,002	778
Ward 54	283	261	Ward 19	0	0
Ward 55	1,105	828	Monona, city		
Ward 56	656	634	Wards 1 – 5	1,966	588
Ward 57	364	113	Wards 6 – 10	1,704	489
Ward 58	494	269	Montrose		
Ward 59	569	386	Wards 1 – 2	394	234
Ward 60	343	65	Mount Horeb, vil.		
Ward 61	1,239	362	Wards 1 – 4	1,024	597
Ward 62	685	70	Wards 5 – 9	1,144	645
Ward 63	1,170	223	Oregon		
Ward 64	1,068	130	Wards 1 – 4	1,121	764
Ward 65	1,931	240	Oregon, vil.		
Ward 66	1,413	385	Wards 1, 5 – 6, 11	1,083	532
Ward 67	621	88	Wards 2 – 4, 12	1,032	550
Ward 68	779	85	Wards 7 – 10	1,084	751
Ward 69	1,372	150	Perry	249	166
Ward 70	711	200	Pleasant Springs		
Ward 71	925	229	Wards 1 – 4	990	801
Ward 72	447	46	Primrose	254	135
Ward 73	453	41	Rockdale, vil.	58	29
Ward 74	319	38	Roxbury		
Ward 75	757	181	Wards 1 – 2	474	447
Ward 76	568	55	Rutland		
Ward 77	1,107	383	Wards 1 – 2	666	438
Ward 78	1,707	349	Shorewood Hills, vil.		
Ward 79	1,989	362	Wards 1 – 2	1,014	181
Ward 80	146	30	Springdale		
Ward 81	1,181	191	Wards 1 – 2	605	502
Ward 82	1,029	115	Springfield		
Ward 83	1,137	176	Wards 1 – 3	676	737
Ward 84	1,098	216	Stoughton, city		
Ward 85	1,211	220	Wards 1 – 2	983	514
Ward 86	1,377	240	Wards 3 – 4, 12	956	388
Ward 87	1,295	480	Wards 5 – 6	1,044	405
Ward 88	1,164	464	Wards 7 – 8	932	552
Ward 89	1,283	371	Wards 9 – 11	0	0
Ward 90	432	139	Sun Prairie		
Ward 91	953	253	Wards 1 – 3	661	506
Ward 92	761	159	Sun Prairie, city		
Ward 93	156	32	Wards 1 – 5	2,061	1,197
Ward 94	506	153	Wards 6 – 9	2,033	1,305
Ward 95	1,105	330	Wards 10 – 14	1,874	1,005
Ward 96	816	302	Wards 15 – 19	1,794	1,529
Ward 97	1,137	470	Ward 20	0	0
Ward 98	1,354	619	Vermont	324	183
Ward 99	497	171			

VOTE FOR GOVERNOR AND LIEUTENANT GOVERNOR BY WARD
November 4, 2014 General Election–Continued

District	Burke and Lehman (Dem.)	Walker and Kleefisch (Rep.)
Verona		
Ward 1	196	183
Wards 2 – 4	444	306
Verona, city		
Wards 1, 5	588	435
Wards 2 – 4	1,137	671
Wards 6 – 9	1,853	1,065
Vienna		
Wards 1 – 2	360	418
Waunakee, vil.		
Wards 1 – 5	1,719	1,450
Wards 6 – 11	1,622	1,473
Westport		
Wards 1 – 5	1,407	1,076
Windsor		
Wards 1 – 2	188	161
Wards 3 – 5	526	549
Wards 6 – 10	1,084	760
York	183	183
TOTAL	175,937	73,676
DODGE COUNTY		
Ashippun		
Wards 1 – 4	272	1,086
Beaver Dam		
Wards 1 – 4, 7 – 11	436	579
Wards 5 – 6	342	458
Beaver Dam, city		
Wards 1, 3, 5	676	535
Wards 2, 6	454	419
Wards 4, 10	348	316
Wards 7, 12 – 13	633	481
Wards 8, 14	428	346
Wards 9, 11	624	579
Brownsville, vil.	79	211
Burnett		
Wards 1 – 2	177	306
Calamus		
Wards 1 – 2	169	293
Chester		
Wards 1 – 2	119	211
Clyman	76	307
Clyman, vil.	63	86
Columbus, city		
Ward 9	0	0
Elba	179	321
Emmet		
Wards 1 – 2	152	513
Fox Lake		
Wards 1 – 4	225	368
Fox Lake, city		
Wards 1 – 3	248	323
Hartford, city		
Wards 18 – 19	0	0
Herman		
Wards 1 – 2	105	531
Horicon, city		
Wards 1 – 6	570	868
Hubbard		
Wards 1 – 4	285	620
Wards 5 – 6	0	0
Hustisford		
Wards 1 – 2	156	589
Hustisford, vil.		
Wards 1 – 2	137	365
Iron Ridge, vil.	101	304
Juneau, city		
Wards 1 – 3	358	482
Kekoskee, vil.	16	62
Lebanon		
Wards 1 – 2	195	601
Leroy		
Wards 1 – 2	88	387
Lomira		
Wards 1 – 2	88	479
Ward 3	1	0
Lomira, vil.		
Wards 1 – 3	224	750
Lowell		
Wards 1 – 2	83	174
Wards 3 – 4	85	192
Lowell, vil.	48	101
Mayville, city		
Wards 1 – 8	696	1,394
Neosho, vil.	59	227
Oak Grove		
Wards 1 – 2	201	300
Wards 3 – 6	0	0
Portland		
Wards 1 – 2	204	316

District	Burke and Lehman (Dem.)	Walker and Kleefisch (Rep.)
Randolph, vil.		
Wards 1 – 2	178	321
Reeseville, vil.	108	168
Rubicon		
Wards 1 – 3	188	973
Shields	87	211
Theresa		
Wards 1, 3 – 7	33	191
Ward 2	63	270
Theresa, vil.		
Wards 1 – 3	170	431
Trenton		
Wards 1 – 2	214	437
Watertown, city		
Wards 1 – 2	396	745
Wards 3 – 4	344	773
Wards 5 – 6	305	731
Ward 7	108	212
Waupun, city		
Wards 1 – 8	799	1,071
Westford		
Wards 1 – 2	250	376
Ward 3	0	8
Ward 4	0	0
Williamstown		
Wards 1 – 3	89	317
TOTAL	12,732	23,715
DOOR COUNTY		
Baileys Harbor		
Wards 1 – 2	343	345
Brussels		
Wards 1 – 2	192	341
Clay Banks	94	131
Egg Harbor		
Wards 1 – 3	348	428
Egg Harbor, vil.	86	75
Ephraim, vil.	105	112
Forestville		
Wards 1 – 2	196	305
Forestville, vil.	92	120
Gardner		
Wards 1 – 2	284	370
Gibraltar		
Wards 1 – 2	356	350
Jacksonport		
Wards 1 – 2	205	265
Liberty Grove		
Wards 1 – 3	622	615
Nasewaupee		
Wards 1 – 3	433	665
Sevastopol		
Wards 1 – 5	661	994
Sister Bay, vil.	284	265
Sturgeon Bay		
Wards 1 – 2	197	239
Sturgeon Bay, city		
Wards 1 – 6, 22 – 24, 29	906	842
Wards 7 – 10, 18 – 21, 25 – 27, 30	527	531
Wards 11 – 17, 28	521	532
Union	193	361
Washington	197	274
TOTAL	6,842	8,160
DOUGLAS COUNTY		
Amnicon		
Wards 1 – 2	292	169
Bennett	130	139
Brule		
Wards 1 – 2	197	114
Cloverland	41	58
Dairyland	37	39
Gordon	183	177
Hawthorne		
Wards 1 – 2	201	185
Highland	74	71
Lake Nebagamon, vil.		
Wards 1 – 2	266	289
Lakeside	171	117
Maple	197	86
Oakland		
Wards 1 – 2	331	157
Oliver, vil.	119	60
Parkland		
Wards 1 – 2	299	169
Poplar, vil.	121	147
Solon Springs		
Wards 1 – 3	222	213
Solon Springs, vil.	164	99

VOTE FOR GOVENROR AND LIEUTENANT GOVERNOR BY WARD
November 4, 2014 General Election–Continued

District	Burke and Lehman (Dem.)	Walker and Kleefisch (Rep.)
Summit		
Wards 1 – 2	297	141
Superior		
Wards 1 – 2	534	418
Superior, vil.	162	115
Superior, city		
Wards 1 – 3, 7, 8	1,161	662
Wards 4 – 6, 9 – 12	1,144	583
Wards 13 – 16, 20 – 22	1,195	563
Wards 17 – 19, 30 – 32	729	305
Wards 23 – 26, 27 – 29	1,143	713
Wascott	180	212
TOTAL	9,590	6,001
DUNN COUNTY		
Boyceville, vil.	134	157
Colfax		
Wards 1 – 3	179	271
Colfax, vil.		
Wards 1 – 2	213	190
Downing, vil.	28	37
Dunn		
Wards 1 – 2	252	283
Eau Galle	121	212
Elk Mound		
Wards 1 – 3	246	443
Elk Mound, vil.	130	139
Grant		
Wards 1 – 2	67	125
Hay River		
Wards 1 – 2	96	119
Knapp, vil.	57	120
Lucas	132	166
Menomonie		
Wards 1 – 3	643	715
Menomonie, city		
Wards 1 – 2	615	492
Wards 3 – 4	299	248
Wards 5, 7	243	318
Ward 6	217	173
Wards 8 – 9	431	327
Wards 10 – 11	634	474
New Haven	84	142
Otter Creek	94	118
Peru	30	56
Red Cedar		
Wards 1 – 3	364	543
Ridgeland, vil.	34	40
Rock Creek	174	241
Sand Creek	104	133
Sheridan	78	114
Sherman	137	229
Spring Brook		
Wards 1 – 2	250	446
Stanton	110	175
Tainter		
Wards 1 – 3	529	552
Tiffany		
Wards 1 – 2	82	152
Weston		
Wards 1 – 2	107	133
Wheeler, vil.	49	48
Wilson	103	98
TOTAL	7,066	8,229
EAU CLAIRE COUNTY		
Altoona, city		
Wards 1 – 11	1,447	1,441
Augusta, city		
Wards 1 – 5	213	252
Bridge Creek		
Wards 1 – 2	199	278
Brunswick		
Wards 1 – 2	375	502
Clear Creek		
Wards 1 – 2	154	202
Drammen	159	217
Eau Claire, city		
Ward 1	230	119
Ward 2	309	127
Ward 3	926	374
Ward 4	199	181
Ward 5	256	209
Ward 6	336	197
Ward 7	357	265
Ward 8	335	316
Ward 9	167	99
Ward 10	423	399
Ward 11	389	398
Ward 12	736	585
Ward 13	148	138
Ward 14	416	404

District	Burke and Lehman (Dem.)	Walker and Kleefisch (Rep.)
Ward 15	453	423
Ward 17	540	580
Ward 18	157	236
Ward 19	154	143
Ward 20	611	517
Ward 21	350	315
Ward 22	136	123
Ward 23	588	507
Ward 24	79	49
Ward 25	600	553
Ward 26	239	210
Ward 27	70	58
Ward 28	174	187
Ward 29	599	372
Ward 30	493	315
Ward 31	450	201
Ward 32	501	272
Ward 33	161	157
Ward 34	164	97
Ward 35	403	355
Ward 36	97	121
Ward 37	245	249
Ward 38	211	244
Ward 39	311	349
Ward 42	118	126
Ward 43	138	73
Ward 44	23	35
Ward 45	157	156
Ward 46	392	236
Ward 47	130	135
Ward 48	139	115
Ward 49	120	188
Ward 50	2	0
Ward 51	0	1
Ward 52	0	1
Ward 53	0	0
Ward 54	0	0
Ward 55	4	0
Ward 56	0	0
Ward 57	3	2
Ward 58	1	0
Ward 59	0	0
Ward 60	0	0
Ward 61	0	0
Fairchild	46	71
Fairchild, vil.	63	77
Fall Creek, vil.		
Wards 1 – 2	267	328
Lincoln		
Wards 1 – 2	200	295
Ludington	206	281
Otter Creek	72	133
Pleasant Valley		
Wards 1 – 4	691	1,085
Seymour		
Wards 1 – 6	716	859
Union		
Wards 1 – 4	523	613
Washington		
Wards 1 – 13	1,615	2,060
Wilson	53	98
TOTAL	21,239	20,304
FLORENCE COUNTY		
Aurora		
Wards 1 – 3	119	273
Commonwealth		
Wards 1 – 3	57	109
Fence	25	70
Fern	31	66
Florence		
Wards 1 – 7	304	593
Homestead	60	115
Long Lake	25	56
Tipler	8	67
TOTAL	629	1,349
FOND DU LAC COUNTY		
Alto		
Wards 1 – 2	110	411
Ashford		
Wards 1 – 3	166	684
Auburn		
Wards 1 – 3	242	980
Brandon, vil.	122	269
Byron		
Wards 1 – 2	212	648
Calumet		
Ward 1	143	304
Ward 2	72	234

VOTE FOR GOVERNOR AND LIEUTENANT GOVERNOR BY WARD
November 4, 2014 General Election–Continued

District	Burke and Lehman (Dem.)	Walker and Kleefisch (Rep.)
Campbellsport, vil.		
Wards 1 – 4	221	582
Eden		
Wards 1 – 2	107	417
Eden, vil.	89	214
Eldorado		
Wards 1 – 3	202	520
Empire		
Wards 1 – 4	444	1,088
Fairwater, vil.	58	100
Fond du Lac		
Wards 1 – 8	542	1,072
Ward 1A	0	0
Fond du Lac, city		
Ward 1	230	272
Ward 2	228	241
Ward 3	411	486
Ward 4	281	292
Ward 5	388	487
Ward 6	304	414
Ward 7	241	313
Ward 8	361	390
Ward 9	263	221
Ward 10	305	445
Ward 11	162	181
Ward 12	336	421
Ward 13	205	224
Ward 14	349	491
Ward 15	156	355
Ward 16	217	342
Ward 17	53	82
Ward 18	20	45
Ward 19	244	298
Ward 20	0	0
Ward 21	328	406
Ward 22	339	563
Ward 23	341	582
Ward 24	365	535
Ward 25	343	753
Ward 26	0	1
Ward 27	0	0
Forest		
Wards 1 – 2	145	441
Friendship		
Wards 1 – 3	411	714
Kewaskum, vil.		
Ward 6	0	0
Lamartine		
Wards 1 – 2	256	602
Marshfield		
Wards 1 – 2	133	425
Metomen		
Wards 1 – 2	85	264
Mount Calvary, vil.	76	177
North Fond du Lac, vil.		
Wards 1 – 7	824	1,017
Oakfield		
Wards 1 – 2	94	243
Oakfield, vil.		
Wards 1 – 2	178	319
Osceola		
Wards 1 – 2	214	736
Ripon		
Wards 1 – 2	215	486
Ripon, city		
Wards 1 – 3	311	431
Wards 4 – 6	316	350
Wards 7 – 8	299	351
Wards 9 – 11	362	454
Rosendale	106	249
Rosendale, vil.		
Wards 1 – 2	138	327
St. Cloud, vil.	71	201
Springvale	99	239
Taycheedah		
Wards 1 – 5	707	1,752
Waupun		
Wards 1 – 2	218	475
Waupun, city		
Wards 9, 9A, 10 – 12	556	869
Ward 9B	0	0
TOTAL	15,014	27,485
FOREST COUNTY		
Alvin	26	54
Argonne		
Wards 1 – 3	90	111
Armstrong Creek	67	107
Blackwell	15	27
Caswell	10	34

District	Burke and Lehman (Dem.)	Walker and Kleefisch (Rep.)
Crandon		
Wards 1 – 3	124	116
Crandon, city		
Wards 1 – 4	261	328
Freedom	65	134
Hiles	99	119
Laona		
Wards 1 – 3	204	258
Lincoln		
Wards 1 – 3	169	241
Nashville		
Ward 1	58	111
Ward 2	118	10
Ward 3	56	126
Popple River	9	13
Ross	13	32
Wabeno		
Wards 1 – 5	127	211
TOTAL	1,511	2,032
GRANT COUNTY		
Bagley, vil.	86	61
Beetown	74	164
Bloomington	56	116
Bloomington, vil	153	195
Blue River, vil.	78	75
Boscobel		
Wards 1 – 2	83	76
Boscobel, city		
Wards 1 – 4	595	343
Cassville	56	78
Cassville, vil.		
Wards 1 – 2	155	138
Castle Rock	50	77
Clifton		
Wards 1 – 2	49	66
Cuba City, city		
Wards 1 – 4	381	323
Dickeyville, vil.		
Wards 1 – 2	172	209
Ellenboro	89	137
Fennimore		
Wards 1 – 2	77	110
Fennimore, city		
Wards 1 – 4	467	417
Glen Haven	42	88
Harrison	78	138
Hazel Green		
Wards 1 – 2	288	212
Hazel Green, vil.		
Wards 1 – 2	221	184
Hickory Grove	60	85
Jamestown		
Wards 1 – 3	303	446
Lancaster, city		
Wards 1 – 6	638	654
Liberty	75	121
Lima	129	147
Little Grant	40	68
Livingston, vil.	108	110
Marion	74	73
Millville	47	38
Montfort, vil.	125	84
Mount Hope	42	47
Mount Hope, vil.	32	31
Mount Ida	68	129
Muscoda	104	103
Muscoda, vil.		
Wards 1 – 2	205	172
North Lancaster		
Wards 1 – 2	76	134
Paris		
Wards 1 – 2	103	169
Patch Grove	58	85
Patch Grove, vil.	37	30
Platteville		
Wards 1 – 3	309	342
Platteville, city		
Wards 1 – 2	618	419
Wards 3 – 4	462	393
Wards 5 – 6	312	492
Wards 7 – 8	576	497
Potosi	126	172
Potosi, vil.	120	132
Smelser		
Wards 1 – 2	142	196
South Lancaster		
Wards 1 – 3	89	143
Tennyson, vil.	64	65

VOTE FOR GOVENROR AND LIEUTENANT GOVERNOR BY WARD
November 4, 2014 General Election–Continued

District	Burke and Lehman (Dem.)	Walker and Kleefisch (Rep.)
Waterloo.	77	85
Watterstown		
Wards 1 – 2	65	61
Wingville	59	81
Woodman	24	31
Woodman, vil.	14	16
Wyalusing	73	91
TOTAL	8,704	9,149
GREEN COUNTY		
Adams	126	123
Albany		
Wards 1 – 2	268	250
Albany, vil.		
Wards 1 – 2	234	121
Belleville, vil.		
Ward 3	125	80
Brodhead, city		
Wards 1 – 6	526	460
Brooklyn		
Wards 1 – 3	318	283
Brooklyn, vil.		
Ward 2	136	72
Browntown, vil.	45	39
Cadiz	129	220
Clarno		
Wards 1 – 2	191	294
Decatur		
Wards 1 – 3	342	429
Exeter		
Wards 1 – 4	581	387
Jefferson		
Wards 1 – 2	147	304
Jordan	117	152
Monroe		
Wards 1 – 2	257	342
Monroe, city		
Wards 1 – 9	2,109	1,749
Monticello, vil.		
Wards 1 – 2	296	220
Mount Pleasant		
Ward 1	63	62
Wards 2 – 3	85	73
New Glarus		
Wards 1 – 2	349	323
New Glarus, vil.		
Wards 1 – 4	689	308
Spring Grove	127	250
Sylvester		
Wards 1 – 2	190	290
Washington	207	177
York	291	185
TOTAL	7,948	7,193
GREEN LAKE COUNTY		
Berlin		
Wards 1 – 3	146	439
Berlin, city		
Wards 1 – 6	643	1,041
Brooklyn		
Wards 1 – 3	304	702
Green Lake		
Wards 1 – 2	132	508
Green Lake, city		
Wards 1 – 3	175	294
Kingston		
Wards 1 – 2	74	176
Kingston, vil.	45	105
Mackford	51	199
Manchester	88	228
Markesan, city		
Wards 1 – 3	172	387
Marquette	71	163
Marquette, vil.	10	39
Princeton		
Wards 1 – 4	246	482
Princeton, city		
Wards 1 – 4	192	305
St. Marie		
Wards 1 – 2	54	144
Seneca	61	124
TOTAL	2,464	5,336
IOWA COUNTY		
Arena		
Wards 1 – 2	420	308
Arena, vil.	218	132
Avoca	109	72
Barneveld, vil.		
Wards 1 – 2	294	186
Blanchardville, vil.		
Wards 1 – 2	46	21

District	Burke and Lehman (Dem.)	Walker and Kleefisch (Rep.)
Brigham		
Wards 1 – 2	341	211
Clyde	91	66
Cobb, vil.	128	93
Dodgeville		
Wards 1 – 4	491	404
Dodgeville, city		
Wards 1 – 10	1,126	818
Eden	81	99
Highland		
Wards 1 – 2	171	166
Highland, vil.	164	158
Hollandale, vil.	79	33
Linden		
Wards 1 – 3	131	195
Linden, vil.	102	73
Livingston, vil.		
Ward 2	1	2
Mifflin		
Wards 1 – 2	101	136
Mineral Point		
Wards 1 – 2	189	236
Mineral Point, city		
Wards 1 – 6	726	385
Montfort, vil.		
Ward 2	19	23
Moscow		
Wards 1 – 2	169	128
Muscoda, vil.		
Ward 3	3	6
Pulaski	59	81
Rewey, vil.	52	25
Ridgeway		
Wards 1 – 2	209	128
Ridgeway, vil.	174	131
Waldwick		
Wards 1 – 2	122	103
Wyoming		
Wards 1 – 2	121	61
TOTAL	5,937	4,480
IRON COUNTY		
Anderson	18	23
Carey	25	53
Gurney	32	37
Hurley, city		
Ward 1	57	95
Ward 2	59	83
Ward 3	32	58
Ward 4	64	78
Kimball	94	141
Knight	46	48
Mercer		
Wards 1 – 4	312	522
Montreal, city		
Wards 1 – 2	137	189
Oma	62	130
Pence	23	57
Saxon	56	118
Sherman	68	123
TOTAL	1,085	1,755
JACKSON COUNTY		
Adams		
Wards 1 – 3	296	336
Albion		
Wards 1 – 4	269	264
Alma		
Wards 1, 4	45	72
Wards 2, 3, 5.	108	185
Alma Center, vil.	105	80
Bear Bluff	5	59
Black River Falls, city		
Ward 1	220	200
Ward 2	167	145
Ward 3	119	80
Ward 4	181	176
Brockway		
Wards 1 – 6	379	219
City Point	34	55
Cleveland	81	118
Curran	75	55
Franklin	89	52
Garden Valley	72	130
Garfield	96	139
Hixton		
Wards 1 – 2	113	139
Hixton, vil.	85	93
Irving		
Wards 1 – 3	141	157

VOTE FOR GOVERNOR AND LIEUTENANT GOVERNOR BY WARD
November 4, 2014 General Election–Continued

District	Burke and Lehman (Dem.)	Walker and Kleefisch (Rep.)
Knapp	39	109
Komensky	92	19
Manchester	119	185
Melrose	66	119
Melrose, vil.	110	100
Merrillan, vil.	90	73
Millston	37	53
North Bend	93	90
Northfield	121	164
Springfield	94	90
Taylor, vil.	90	56
TOTAL	3,631	3,812
JEFFERSON COUNTY		
Aztalan		
Wards 1 – 2	288	401
Cambridge, vil.		
Ward 1	24	13
Cold Spring	131	259
Concord		
Wards 1 – 3	303	777
Farmington		
Wards 1 – 2	226	520
Fort Atkinson, city		
Ward 1	254	283
Ward 2	361	327
Ward 3	285	265
Ward 4	306	241
Ward 5	215	190
Ward 6	208	218
Ward 7	301	268
Ward 8	277	274
Ward 9	257	234
Hebron		
Wards 1 – 2	189	361
Ixonia		
Wards 1 – 6	486	1,859
Jefferson		
Wards 1 – 3	376	670
Jefferson, city		
Wards 1 – 10	1,314	1,442
Ward 11	0	0
Johnson Creek, vil.		
Wards 1 – 3	403	720
Koshkonong		
Wards 1, 6	72	133
Wards 2 – 5	624	971
Lac La Belle, vil.		
Ward 2	0	0
Lake Mills		
Wards 1 – 3	490	564
Lake Mills, city		
Wards 1 – 8	1,351	1,303
Milford		
Wards 1 – 2	194	331
Oakland		
Wards 1 – 4	795	765
Palmyra		
Wards 1 – 2	194	463
Palmyra, vil.		
Wards 1 – 2	235	523
Sullivan		
Wards 1 – 3	291	820
Sullivan, vil.	69	234
Sumner	180	248
Waterloo	173	281
Waterloo, city		
Wards 1 – 5	607	701
Watertown		
Wards 1 – 2	267	711
Watertown, city		
Ward 8	98	171
Wards 9 – 10	236	692
Wards 11 – 12	311	571
Wards 13 – 14	353	634
Wards 15 – 16	370	688
Wards 17 – 18	398	889
Whitewater, city		
Wards 10 – 11	159	167
Ward 12	205	261
TOTAL	13,876	21,443
JUNEAU COUNTY		
Armenia	112	168
Camp Douglas, vil.	81	87
Clearfield		
Ward 1	96	133
Ward 2	24	29
Cutler	63	79
Elroy, city		
Wards 1 – 5	232	208

District	Burke and Lehman (Dem.)	Walker and Kleefisch (Rep.)
Finley	11	35
Fountain		
Wards 1 – 2	95	137
Germantown		
Wards 1, 3	135	195
Ward 2	121	133
Hustler, vil.	46	32
Kildare	105	129
Kingston	2	10
Lemonweir		
Wards 1 – 4	258	342
Lindina	160	175
Lisbon		
Wards 1 – 2	174	188
Ward 3	0	4
Lyndon		
Wards 1 – 3	285	216
Lyndon Station, vil.	87	49
Marion	72	121
Mauston, city		
Wards 1 – 7	650	552
Necedah		
Wards 1 – 4	303	548
Necedah, vil.	137	158
New Lisbon, city		
Wards 1 – 7	205	228
Orange	87	138
Plymouth	120	159
Seven Mile Creek		
Wards 1 – 2	62	70
Summit	95	168
Union Center, vil.	29	37
Wisconsin Dells, city		
Ward 7	0	0
Wonewoc		
Wards 1 – 2	109	146
Wonewoc, vil.	124	143
TOTAL	4,080	4,817
KENOSHA COUNTY		
Brighton		
Wards 1 – 4	205	501
Bristol, vil.		
Wards 1 – 3, 8	351	827
Wards 4 – 7	324	651
Genoa City, vil.		
Ward 5	0	0
Kenosha, city		
Ward 1	222	134
Ward 2	243	151
Ward 3	70	45
Ward 4	402	197
Ward 5	190	103
Ward 6	213	113
Ward 7	169	44
Ward 8	407	230
Ward 9	177	90
Ward 10	182	60
Ward 11	196	72
Ward 12	246	160
Ward 13	283	297
Ward 14	223	186
Ward 15	428	235
Ward 16	183	102
Ward 17	96	48
Ward 18	332	180
Ward 19	137	59
Ward 20	252	196
Ward 21	72	69
Ward 22	511	459
Ward 23	136	94
Ward 24	316	182
Ward 25	366	220
Ward 26	154	71
Ward 27	248	102
Ward 28	119	53
Ward 29	190	64
Ward 30	139	41
Ward 31	327	178
Ward 32	138	44
Ward 33	7	2
Ward 34	175	124
Ward 35	356	211
Ward 36	120	29
Ward 37	341	170
Ward 38	442	341
Ward 39	239	192
Ward 40	133	53
Ward 41	213	120
Ward 42	131	70

VOTE FOR GOVENROR AND LIEUTENANT GOVERNOR BY WARD
November 4, 2014 General Election–Continued

District	Burke and Lehman (Dem.)	Walker and Kleefisch (Rep.)
Ward 43	324	245
Ward 44	194	199
Ward 45	123	106
Ward 46	207	64
Ward 47	83	58
Ward 48	132	50
Ward 49	113	55
Ward 50	233	98
Ward 51	128	93
Ward 52	377	182
Ward 53	100	97
Ward 54	315	297
Ward 55	160	116
Ward 56	193	157
Ward 57	352	258
Ward 58	18	20
Ward 59	410	351
Ward 60	319	272
Ward 61	167	148
Ward 62	329	262
Ward 63	202	154
Ward 64	245	274
Ward 65	10	5
Ward 66	483	457
Ward 67	283	262
Ward 68	160	147
Ward 69	27	31
Ward 70	9	2
Ward 71	124	87
Ward 72	218	245
Ward 73	174	200
Ward 74	1	1
Ward 75	79	147
Ward 76	98	199
Ward 77	215	314
Ward 78	203	241
Ward 79	215	282
Ward 80	102	51
Ward 81	141	73
Ward 82	93	58
Ward 83	0	0
Ward 84	124	83
Ward 85	16	11
Ward 86	86	65
Ward 87	175	187
Ward 88	0	0
Ward 89	0	0
Ward 90	0	0
Ward 91	2	0
Paddock Lake, vil.		
Wards 1 – 6	401	684
Paris		
Wards 1 – 2	271	524
Pleasant Prairie, vil.		
Wards 1 – 3	881	1,163
Wards 4 – 5	447	587
Wards 6 – 7	705	663
Wards 8 – 11	648	1,234
Wards 12 – 14	756	1,008
Randall		
Wards 1 – 7	380	834
Salem		
Wards 1 – 5, 10	768	1,487
Wards 6 – 9	620	1,146
Silver Lake, vil.		
Wards 1 – 3	421	703
Somers		
Wards 1 – 4	580	706
Wards 5 – 6, 9, 12	498	546
Wards 7 – 8	257	196
Wards 10, 13	304	438
Ward 11	124	152
Twin Lakes, vil.		
Wards 1 – 8	696	1,118
Wheatland		
Wards 1 – 6	444	935
TOTAL	27,367	28,398
KEWAUNEE COUNTY		
Ahnapee	167	255
Algoma, city		
Wards 1 – 6	593	636
Carlton		
Wards 1 – 2	147	341
Casco		
Wards 1 – 3	181	369
Casco, vil.	84	158
Franklin	173	278
Kewaunee, city		
Wards 1 – 5	545	632

District	Burke and Lehman (Dem.)	Walker and Kleefisch (Rep.)
Lincoln	155	254
Luxemburg		
Wards 1 – 3	196	530
Luxemburg, vil.		
Wards 1 – 5	345	663
Montpelier		
Wards 1 – 3	203	470
Pierce		
Wards 1 – 2	181	236
Red River		
Wards 1 – 3	215	437
West Kewaunee		
Wards 1 – 3	194	417
TOTAL	3,379	5,676
LA CROSSE COUNTY		
Bangor	93	165
Bangor, vil.		
Wards 1 – 2	287	303
Barre		
Wards 1 – 2	221	354
Burns	208	243
Campbell		
Wards 1 – 6	1,050	902
Farmington		
Wards 1 – 2	410	447
Greenfield		
Wards 1 – 2	428	507
Hamilton		
Wards 1 – 5	498	718
Holland		
Wards 1 – 6	808	1,045
Holmen, vil.		
Wards 1 – 11	1,781	1,726
La Crosse, city		
Ward 1	657	528
Ward 2	194	115
Ward 3	396	283
Ward 4	186	103
Ward 5	351	149
Ward 6	456	272
Ward 7	569	364
Ward 8	616	681
Ward 9	1,151	578
Ward 10	127	130
Ward 11	130	131
Ward 12	206	136
Ward 13	191	95
Ward 14	287	123
Ward 15	219	107
Ward 16	358	170
Ward 17	180	57
Ward 18	236	105
Ward 19	219	99
Ward 20	379	198
Ward 21	984	602
Ward 22	641	294
Ward 23	201	129
Ward 24	578	327
Ward 25	351	240
Ward 26	714	491
Ward 27	336	201
Ward 28	288	172
Ward 29	726	567
Ward 30	0	0
Medary		
Wards 1 – 2	379	424
Onalaska		
Wards 1 – 8	1,228	1,498
Onalaska, city		
Wards 1 – 4	1,229	1,358
Wards 5 – 8	1,201	1,034
Wards 9 – 12	1,198	1,552
Rockland, vil.	97	125
Shelby		
Wards 1 – 4	727	763
Wards 5 – 6	531	498
Washington	130	148
West Salem, vil.		
Wards 1 – 6	998	1,064
TOTAL	25,429	22,321
LAFAYETTE COUNTY		
Argyle		
Wards 1 – 3	105	93
Argyle, vil.	164	124
Belmont		
Wards 1 – 2	102	140
Belmont, vil.	166	179
Benton		
Wards 1 – 2	70	111

VOTE FOR GOVERNOR AND LIEUTENANT GOVERNOR BY WARD
November 4, 2014 General Election–Continued

District	Burke and Lehman (Dem.)	Walker and Kleefisch (Rep.)
Benton, vil.	204	123
Blanchard	77	57
Blanchardville, vil.	145	93
Cuba City, city		
Ward 5	62	45
Darlington		
Wards 1 – 3	154	243
Darlington, city		
Wards 1 – 6	472	342
Elk Grove		
Wards 1 – 2	54	112
Fayette		
Wards 1 – 2	69	89
Gratiot.	84	149
Gratiot, vil.	44	44
Hazel Green, vil.		
Ward 3	6	4
Kendall	61	84
Lamont		
Wards 1 – 2	67	66
Monticello.	11	45
New Diggings.	77	104
Seymour		
Wards 1 – 2	42	75
Shullsburg.	68	73
Shullsburg, city		
Wards 1 – 3	244	172
South Wayne, vil.	62	78
Wayne.	59	133
White Oak Springs	18	38
Willow Springs	120	178
Wiota	175	197
TOTAL	2,982	3,191
LANGLADE COUNTY		
Ackley.	77	166
Ainsworth.	83	163
Antigo		
Wards 1 – 2	207	457
Antigo, city		
Ward 1	97	169
Ward 2	124	161
Ward 3	103	151
Ward 4	124	134
Ward 5	97	125
Ward 6	82	206
Ward 7	189	221
Ward 8	117	158
Ward 9	138	218
Elcho		
Wards 1 – 2	238	385
Evergreen	77	178
Langlade		
Wards 1 – 2	88	153
Neva	142	303
Norwood	110	312
Parrish.	13	28
Peck	42	118
Polar		
Wards 1 – 2	145	369
Price		
Wards 1 – 2	39	71
Rolling		
Wards 1 – 2	192	458
Summit	18	62
Upham	149	258
Vilas	26	90
White Lake, vil.	65	83
Wolf River		
Wards 1 – 2	139	279
TOTAL	2,921	5,476
LINCOLN COUNTY		
Birch	99	111
Bradley		
Wards 1 – 5	524	693
Corning		
Wards 1 – 2	127	242
Harding	74	135
Harrison		
Wards 1 – 3	168	287
King		
Wards 1 – 2	217	272
Merrill		
Wards 1 – 7	526	797
Merrill, city		
Wards 1 – 2	217	242
Wards 3 – 4	202	231
Wards 5 – 7	149	195
Wards 8 – 9	163	214
Wards 10 – 12	199	187
Wards 13 – 14	200	235
Wards 15 – 17	216	232
Wards 18 – 19	160	175
Pine River		
Wards 1 – 3	338	577
Rock Falls		
Wards 1 – 2	103	214
Russell	108	166
Schley		
Wards 1 – 2	137	239
Scott		
Wards 1 – 2	224	415
Skanawan.	96	130
Somo	30	31
Tomahawk	96	112
Tomahawk, city		
Wards 1 – 2	207	149
Wards 3 – 4	252	250
Wards 5 – 6	199	235
Wilson.	73	100
TOTAL	5,104	6,866
MANITOWOC COUNTY		
Cato	231	537
Centerville	110	225
Cleveland, vil.		
Wards 1 – 2	268	408
Cooperstown		
Wards 1 – 2	204	430
Eaton	118	299
Francis Creek, vil..	124	172
Franklin		
Wards 1 – 3	142	484
Gibson		
Wards 1 – 2	184	459
Kellnersville, vil.	54	89
Kiel, city		
Wards 1 – 6, 8	486	1,066
Kossuth		
Wards 1 – 3	311	574
Liberty		
Wards 1 – 2	162	475
Manitowoc		
Wards 1 – 2	181	327
Manitowoc, city		
Wards 1 – 2	565	615
Wards 3 – 4, 22	497	674
Wards 5 – 6	556	558
Wards 7 – 8	312	328
Wards 9 – 10	536	651
Wards 11 – 12	639	855
Wards 13 – 14	477	561
Wards 15 – 16	657	1,002
Wards 17 – 18, 21, 23 – 25	527	601
Wards 19 – 20	633	1,152
Manitowoc Rapids		
Wards 1 – 5	381	905
Maple Grove	77	301
Maribel, vil.	34	105
Meeme		
Wards 1, 4	104	289
Wards 2 – 3	89	209
Mishicot		
Wards 1 – 2	170	374
Mishicot, vil.		
Wards 1 – 3	218	380
Newton		
Wards 1 – 3	318	828
Reedsville, vil.		
Wards 1 – 2	140	335
Rockland		
Wards 1 – 2	106	343
St. Nazianz, vil.	88	208
Schleswig		
Wards 1 – 4	297	744
Two Creeks	67	124
Two Rivers		
Wards 1 – 2	351	538
Two Rivers, city		
Wards 1 – 2	426	523
Wards 3 – 4	653	799
Wards 5 – 6	420	515
Wards 7 – 8	410	485
Valders, vil.	134	280
Whitelaw, vil.	106	217
TOTAL	12,563	21,044

VOTE FOR GOVENROR AND LIEUTENANT GOVERNOR BY WARD
November 4, 2014 General Election–Continued

District	Burke and Lehman (Dem.)	Walker and Kleefisch (Rep.)
MARATHON COUNTY		
Abbotsford, city		
Ward 1	27	70
Ward 6	0	0
Athens, vil.		
Wards 1 – 2	146	319
Bergen	150	204
Berlin		
Wards 1 – 2	106	359
Bern	49	137
Bevent		
Wards 1 – 2	235	278
Birnamwood, vil.		
Ward 2	7	3
Brighton	41	169
Brokaw, vil.	60	55
Cassel	134	296
Cleveland		
Wards 1 – 2	185	452
Colby, city	53	105
Day		
Wards 1 – 2	136	338
Dorchester, vil.		
Ward 2	0	0
Ward 3	0	0
Easton		
Wards 1 – 2	168	416
Eau Pleine	79	244
Edgar, vil.		
Wards 1 – 2	209	380
Elderon	86	209
Elderon, vil.	25	38
Emmet		
Wards 1 – 2	141	275
Fenwood, vil.	19	53
Frankfort	62	195
Franzen	71	169
Green Valley	79	195
Guenther	54	108
Halsey	54	176
Hamburg	95	278
Harrison	40	95
Hatley, vil.	75	163
Hewitt	84	197
Holton	68	262
Hull	56	182
Johnson	85	201
Knowlton		
Wards 1 – 3	355	646
Kronenwetter, vil.		
Wards 1 – 5	638	969
Wards 6 – 10	570	962
Maine		
Wards 1 – 4	423	831
Marathon		
Wards 1 – 2	135	402
Marathon City, vil.		
Wards 1 – 3	227	487
Marshfield, city		
Wards 12, 20 – 21, 24	104	170
McMillan		
Wards 1 – 3	340	662
Mosinee		
Wards 1 – 3	343	689
Mosinee, city		
Wards 1 – 2, 6 – 7	339	548
Wards 3 – 5	364	593
Norrie	146	280
Plover	81	187
Reid		
Wards 1 – 2	219	323
Rib Falls	97	397
Rib Mountain		
Wards 1 – 10	1,279	2,389
Rietbrock	105	285
Ringle		
Wards 1 – 2	325	554
Rothschild, vil.		
Wards 1 – 2	367	365
Wards 3 – 4	376	504
Wards 5 – 6	338	462
Schofield, city		
Wards 1 – 4	344	511
Spencer		
Wards 1 – 2	186	421
Spencer, vil.		
Wards 1 – 3	251	434
Stettin		
Wards 1 – 2	285	755
Wards 3 – 4	95	179
Stratford, vil.		
Wards 1 – 2	177	437
Texas		
Wards 1 – 2	286	508
Unity, vil.	15	58
Wausau		
Wards 1 – 3	383	738
Wausau, city		
Ward 1	450	359
Ward 2	453	374
Ward 3	190	155
Ward 4	46	131
Ward 5	265	243
Ward 6	192	128
Ward 7	249	264
Ward 8	155	148
Ward 9	92	134
Ward 10	42	101
Ward 11	0	0
Ward 12	359	310
Ward 13	285	228
Ward 14	277	274
Ward 15	469	595
Ward 16	310	498
Ward 17	314	331
Ward 18	346	320
Ward 19	276	288
Ward 20	287	238
Ward 21	266	256
Ward 22	287	280
Ward 23	314	313
Ward 24	320	457
Ward 25	312	459
Ward 26	242	400
Ward 27	1	0
Ward 28	1	0
Ward 29	0	0
Ward 30	0	2
Ward 31	0	0
Ward 32	0	0
Ward 33	0	1
Ward 34	0	0
Ward 35	0	0
Weston	84	198
Weston, vil.		
Wards 1 – 2, 4 – 5	553	926
Wards 3, 8	451	608
Wards 6 – 7	377	705
Wards 9 – 13	878	1,233
Wien	90	259
TOTAL	21,305	34,583
MARINETTE COUNTY		
Amberg	119	247
Athelstane		
Wards 1 – 2	109	168
Beaver		
Wards 1 – 2	140	370
Beecher	96	209
Coleman, vil.	80	206
Crivitz, vil.	145	212
Dunbar		
Wards 1 – 2	75	198
Goodman	102	133
Grover		
Wards 1 – 3	198	482
Lake		
Wards 1 – 2	173	306
Marinette, city		
Wards 1, 3, 5	588	620
Wards 2, 4, 6	571	578
Wards 7 – 8	431	518
Middle Inlet		
Wards 1 – 2	146	222
Niagara	131	243
Niagara, city		
Wards 1 – 3	219	270
Pembine		
Wards 1 – 2	134	225
Peshtigo		
Wards 1, 4	259	355
Wards 2 – 3	275	411
Wards 5 – 6	178	332
Peshtigo, city		
Wards 1 – 7	403	606
Porterfield		
Wards 1 – 3	290	498
Pound		
Wards 1 – 3	155	415

VOTE FOR GOVERNOR AND LIEUTENANT GOVERNOR BY WARD
November 4, 2014 General Election–Continued

District	Burke and Lehman (Dem.)	Walker and Kleefisch (Rep.)
Pound, vil..	36	85
Silver Cliff		
Wards 1 – 2	89	188
Stephenson		
Wards 1 – 3	344	524
Wards 4 – 5	200	347
Wagner	98	211
Wausaukee		
Wards 1 – 2	174	342
Wausaukee, vil.	65	89
TOTAL	6,023	9,610
MARQUETTE COUNTY		
Buffalo		
Wards 1 – 2	223	225
Crystal Lake.	122	136
Douglas	177	233
Endeavor, vil.	72	72
Harris	166	223
Mecan.	111	195
Montello		
Wards 1 – 4	183	283
Montello, city		
Wards 1 – 4	230	288
Moundville		
Wards 1 – 2	104	115
Neshkoro		
Wards 1 – 2	98	191
Neshkoro, vil..	62	98
Newton		
Wards 1 – 2	84	112
Oxford		
Wards 1 – 2	147	225
Oxford, vil.	93	88
Packwaukee		
Wards 1 – 3	221	318
Shields	93	164
Springfield	139	210
Westfield		
Wards 1 – 2	130	237
Westfield, vil.		
Wards 1 – 2	174	198
TOTAL	2,629	3,611
MENOMINEE COUNTY		
Menominee		
Wards 1, 3 – 5	604	205
Ward 2	149	10
TOTAL	753	215
MILWAUKEE COUNTY		
Bayside, vil.		
Wards 1, 3	442	368
Wards 1S, 3S	29	22
Wards 2, 4	520	452
Ward 5	303	267
Brown Deer, vil.		
Wards 1 – 2	1,326	698
Wards 3 – 4	1,082	889
Wards 5 – 6	1,147	810
Cudahy, city		
Wards 1 – 3	811	748
Wards 4 – 6	690	646
Wards 7 – 9	569	537
Ward 10	314	314
Wards 11 – 12	402	469
Wards 13 – 14	537	502
Ward 15	322	378
Fox Point, vil.		
Wards 1 – 4	762	959
Wards 5 – 9	1,164	917
Franklin, city		
Ward 1	0	4
Ward 2	318	750
Ward 3	466	784
Ward 4	201	408
Ward 5	187	351
Ward 6	251	546
Ward 7	389	780
Ward 8	262	302
Ward 9	280	424
Ward 10	118	202
Ward 11	287	584
Ward 12	197	416
Ward 13	263	582
Ward 14	242	520
Ward 15A	140	268
Ward 15B	130	180
Ward 16	271	630
Ward 17	188	346
Ward 18	75	264
Ward 19	332	649
Ward 20	176	264
Ward 21	105	93
Ward 22A	206	344
Ward 22B	202	340
Ward 23	304	622
Glendale, city		
Wards 1, 7	686	418
Wards 2, 8S	483	286
Wards 3, 9	596	606
Wards 4, 10	764	563
Wards 5, 11	636	437
Wards 6, 12	601	354
Ward 8	255	176
Ward 11S	187	59
Greendale, vil.		
Wards 1 – 2	432	1,000
Wards 3 – 4	667	870
Wards 5 – 6	552	852
Wards 7 – 8	564	844
Wards 9 – 10	642	960
Greenfield, city		
Ward 1	357	456
Ward 2	293	401
Ward 3	308	324
Ward 4	348	262
Ward 5	330	432
Ward 6	265	472
Ward 7	385	535
Ward 8	430	468
Ward 9	332	483
Ward 10	277	496
Ward 11	332	707
Ward 12	298	573
Ward 13	235	260
Ward 14	314	364
Ward 15	268	397
Ward 16	123	191
Ward 17	282	270
Ward 18	295	403
Ward 19	488	558
Ward 20	423	659
Ward 21	273	332
Hales Corners, vil.		
Wards 1 – 3	462	858
Wards 4 – 6	468	809
Wards 7 – 9	428	699
Milwaukee, city		
Ward 1	747	224
Ward 2	281	16
Ward 3	614	200
Ward 4	1,132	227
Ward 5	548	106
Ward 6	1,050	408
Ward 7	267	191
Ward 8	895	326
Ward 9	498	115
Ward 10	724	332
Ward 11	720	176
Ward 12	635	139
Ward 13	338	94
Ward 14	795	48
Ward 15	414	256
Ward 16	986	178
Ward 17	410	120
Ward 18	638	146
Ward 19	582	89
Ward 20	770	96
Ward 21	751	56
Ward 22	605	64
Ward 23	251	32
Ward 24	302	9
Ward 25	574	67
Ward 26	532	61
Ward 27	454	69
Ward 28	157	24
Ward 29	277	33
Ward 30	497	88
Ward 31	590	56
Ward 32	1,045	241
Ward 33	1,057	684
Ward 34	629	262
Ward 35	408	273
Ward 36	677	102
Ward 37	553	56
Ward 38	456	47
Ward 39	502	121
Ward 40	524	59
Ward 41	525	54
Ward 42	659	85

VOTE FOR GOVENROR AND LIEUTENANT GOVERNOR BY WARD
November 4, 2014 General Election–Continued

District	Burke and Lehman (Dem.)	Walker and Kleefisch (Rep.)	District	Burke and Lehman (Dem.)	Walker and Kleefisch (Rep.)
Ward 43	567	20	Ward 133	464	141
Ward 44	768	80	Ward 134	399	156
Ward 45	740	66	Ward 135	511	174
Ward 46	405	34	Ward 136	535	175
Ward 47	752	40	Ward 137	381	90
Ward 48	367	50	Ward 138	1,429	150
Ward 49	519	37	Ward 139	1,036	110
Ward 50	484	30	Ward 140	446	10
Ward 51	497	25	Ward 141	508	13
Ward 52	668	50	Ward 142	557	10
Ward 53	268	23	Ward 143	573	2
Ward 54	432	11	Ward 144	374	15
Ward 55	729	166	Ward 145	284	3
Ward 56	612	13	Ward 146	255	4
Ward 57	793	10	Ward 147	860	6
Ward 58	573	11	Ward 148	634	10
Ward 59	1,161	35	Ward 149	748	12
Ward 60	850	11	Ward 150	560	24
Ward 61	680	17	Ward 151	456	12
Ward 62	557	11	Ward 152	389	4
Ward 63	537	8	Ward 153	627	33
Ward 64	1,124	39	Ward 154	468	22
Ward 65	943	39	Ward 155	414	10
Ward 66	710	7	Ward 156	661	33
Ward 67	465	18	Ward 157	416	46
Ward 68	848	74	Ward 158	421	38
Ward 69	697	42	Ward 159	412	27
Ward 70	987	62	Ward 160	572	15
Ward 71	540	44	Ward 161	186	10
Ward 72	701	70	Ward 162	306	5
Ward 73	827	90	Ward 163	593	37
Ward 74	519	73	Ward 164	614	100
Ward 75	393	154	Ward 165	472	134
Ward 76	497	76	Ward 166	250	51
Ward 77	458	104	Ward 167	515	187
Ward 78	713	161	Ward 168	919	332
Ward 79	715	203	Ward 169	446	15
Ward 80	770	417	Ward 170	314	9
Ward 81	226	265	Ward 171	106	3
Ward 82	328	340	Ward 172	410	13
Ward 83	390	399	Ward 173	532	14
Ward 84	323	279	Ward 174	772	21
Ward 85	416	355	Ward 175	446	36
Ward 86	377	369	Ward 176	715	24
Ward 87	283	178	Ward 177	918	409
Ward 88	368	247	Ward 178	725	264
Ward 89	498	301	Ward 179	822	286
Ward 90	522	266	Ward 180	511	255
Ward 91	995	158	Ward 181	767	419
Ward 92	800	317	Ward 182	685	327
Ward 93	310	204	Ward 183	805	439
Ward 94	382	26	Ward 184	698	401
Ward 95	455	45	Ward 185	802	533
Ward 96	733	109	Ward 186	657	649
Ward 97	594	199	Ward 187	138	88
Ward 98	566	26	Ward 188	151	115
Ward 99	919	82	Ward 189	367	67
Ward 100	627	20	Ward 190	299	339
Ward 101	912	22	Ward 191	173	231
Ward 102	963	42	Ward 192	299	197
Ward 103	1,155	68	Ward 193	539	36
Ward 104	1,058	22	Ward 194	306	43
Ward 105	493	5	Ward 195	377	31
Ward 106	423	2	Ward 196	591	52
Ward 107	662	7	Ward 197	288	26
Ward 108	708	12	Ward 198	608	49
Ward 109	712	9	Ward 199	521	28
Ward 110	399	3	Ward 200	298	45
Ward 111	634	10	Ward 201	334	27
Ward 112	651	8	Ward 202	491	123
Ward 113	574	8	Ward 203	587	240
Ward 114	528	9	Ward 204	415	195
Ward 115	860	16	Ward 205	425	252
Ward 116	466	1	Ward 206	325	205
Ward 117	643	4	Ward 207	323	288
Ward 118	600	11	Ward 208	373	283
Ward 119	613	12	Ward 209	280	354
Ward 120	560	7	Ward 210	213	323
Ward 121	610	1	Ward 211	268	277
Ward 122	651	19	Ward 212	369	309
Ward 123	685	63	Ward 213	429	308
Ward 124	415	58	Ward 214	250	78
Ward 125	785	164	Ward 215	180	43
Ward 126	668	98	Ward 216	163	39
Ward 127	653	262	Ward 217	334	92
Ward 128	659	295	Ward 218	374	134
Ward 129	487	189	Ward 219	270	78
Ward 130	396	216	Ward 220	301	100
Ward 131	553	298	Ward 221	501	143
Ward 132	832	442	Ward 222	283	74

VOTE FOR GOVERNOR AND LIEUTENANT GOVERNOR BY WARD
November 4, 2014 General Election–Continued

District	Burke and Lehman (Dem.)	Walker and Kleefisch (Rep.)	District	Burke and Lehman (Dem.)	Walker and Kleefisch (Rep.)
Ward 223	320	94	Ward 313	718	657
Ward 224	247	64	Ward 314	271	294
Ward 225	221	51	Ward 315	508	495
Ward 226	138	20	Ward 316	267	298
Ward 227	500	66	Ward 317	377	311
Ward 228	190	31	Ward 320	21	1
Ward 229	155	27	Ward 321	113	16
Ward 230	342	55	Ward 322	66	17
Ward 231	173	27	Ward 333	107	43
Ward 232	131	18	Ward 324	51	11
Ward 233	99	17	Ward 325	207	65
Ward 234	166	26	Ward 326	0	2
Ward 235	549	253	Ward 327	0	0
Ward 236	251	40	Oak Creek, city		
Ward 237	335	47	Wards 1 – 3	941	1,448
Ward 238	252	46	Wards 4 – 6	894	1,153
Ward 239	201	54	Wards 7 – 9	897	1,407
Ward 240	305	41	Wards 10 – 12	1,009	1,667
Ward 241	528	180	Wards 13 – 15	878	1,764
Ward 242	517	163	Wards 16 – 19	867	1,125
Ward 243	624	280	River Hills, vil.		
Ward 244	487	203	Wards 1 – 3	395	603
Ward 245	422	165	St. Francis, city		
Ward 246	790	224	Wards 1 – 4	643	641
Ward 247	335	155	Wards 5 – 8	695	684
Ward 248	767	202	Wards 9 – 12	769	712
Ward 249	196	61	Shorewood, vil.		
Ward 250	164	39	Wards 1 – 4	1,830	687
Ward 251	90	33	Wards 5 – 8	1,653	682
Ward 252	193	80	Wards 9 – 12	1,553	556
Ward 253	111	26	South Milwaukee, city		
Ward 254	92	30	Wards 1 – 4	1,032	1,049
Ward 255	162	37	Wards 5 – 8	880	936
Ward 256	148	27	Wards 9 – 12	1,022	1,343
Ward 257	317	76	Wards 13 – 16	962	1,060
Ward 258	356	126	Wauwatosa, city		
Ward 259	254	98	Ward 1	552	501
Ward 260	178	112	Ward 2	562	438
Ward 261	218	165	Ward 3	531	554
Ward 262	410	389	Ward 4	702	831
Ward 263	238	181	Ward 5	340	388
Ward 264	490	434	Ward 6	380	358
Ward 265	274	230	Ward 7	612	689
Ward 266	252	324	Ward 8	264	326
Ward 267	244	238	Ward 9	471	705
Ward 268	518	569	Ward 10	477	389
Ward 269	344	338	Ward 11	580	486
Ward 270	287	367	Ward 12	576	739
Ward 271	564	525	Ward 13	288	226
Ward 272	378	441	Ward 14	648	492
Ward 273	210	256	Ward 15	688	459
Ward 274	199	267	Ward 16	579	696
Ward 275	507	513	Ward 17	411	717
Ward 276	482	527	Ward 18	419	492
Ward 277	505	430	Ward 19	476	556
Ward 278	258	287	Ward 20	458	734
Ward 279	419	420	Ward 21	370	533
Ward 280	742	514	Ward 22	489	532
Ward 281	325	253	Ward 23	389	572
Ward 282	170	50	Ward 24	451	462
Ward 283	264	215	West Allis, city		
Ward 284	389	117	Ward 1	403	333
Ward 285	70	41	Ward 2	492	407
Ward 286	239	106	Ward 3	345	301
Ward 287	198	152	Ward 4	449	539
Ward 288	448	360	Ward 5	395	393
Ward 289	288	170	Ward 6	333	435
Ward 290	215	87	Ward 7	412	478
Ward 291	251	125	Ward 8	362	382
Ward 292	287	168	Ward 9	499	555
Ward 293	357	266	Ward 10	397	467
Ward 294	288	205	Ward 11	504	639
Ward 295	340	180	Ward 12	421	629
Ward 296	473	304	Ward 13	601	859
Ward 297	504	211	Ward 14	376	353
Ward 298	363	170	Ward 15	338	446
Ward 299	455	227	Ward 16	323	442
Ward 300	689	292	Ward 17	479	635
Ward 301	522	352	Ward 18	549	748
Ward 302	335	262	Ward 19	494	723
Ward 303	533	423	Ward 20	361	432
Ward 304	377	303	Ward 21	498	517
Ward 305	347	332	Ward 22	353	445
Ward 306	365	211	Ward 23	464	722
Ward 307	342	287	Ward 24	348	315
Ward 308	378	141	Ward 25	436	642
Ward 309	443	410	West Milwaukee, vil.		
Ward 310	136	78	Wards 1 – 2, 5	364	225
Ward 311	242	215	Wards 3 – 4, 6	353	283
Ward 312	367	375			

VOTE FOR GOVERNOR AND LIEUTENANT GOVERNOR BY WARD
November 4, 2014 General Election–Continued

District	Burke and Lehman (Dem.)	Walker and Kleefisch (Rep.)
Ward 3	149	502
Wards 4 – 5	451	1,516
Menomonee Falls, vil.		
Ward 1	374	852
Ward 2	209	503
Ward 3	295	670
Ward 4	153	350
Ward 5	241	488
Ward 6	300	606
Ward 7	132	288
Ward 8	192	441
Ward 9	268	482
Ward 10	193	529
Ward 11	236	424
Ward 12	157	324
Ward 13	255	772
Ward 14	361	848
Ward 15	324	841
Ward 16	161	365
Ward 17	294	708
Ward 18	247	599
Ward 19	261	710
Ward 20	301	691
Ward 21	239	757
Ward 22	157	482
Ward 23	175	582
Merton		
Wards 1 – 3, 7 – 9	552	2,635
Wards 4 – 6, 10 – 11	334	1,241
Merton, vil.		
Wards 1 – 4	290	1,418
Ward 5	0	1
Milwaukee, city		
Ward 319	0	0
Mukwonago		
Wards 1 – 3, 7 – 11	616	2,276
Wards 4 – 6	263	1,045
Mukwonago, vil.		
Wards 1 – 10	938	2,521
Muskego, city		
Wards 1 – 3	594	1,591
Wards 4 – 5	501	1,230
Wards 6 – 8	557	1,476
Wards 9 – 10	451	1,120
Wards 11 – 12	434	1,445
Wards 13 – 14	425	1,449
Wards 15 – 16	451	1,371
Nashotah, vil.		
Wards 1 – 3	172	592
New Berlin, city		
Ward 1	318	727
Ward 2	248	563
Ward 3	293	773
Ward 4	336	652
Ward 5	454	960
Ward 6	99	150
Ward 7	30	82
Ward 8	403	914
Ward 9	341	741
Ward 10	60	168
Ward 11	114	394
Ward 12	43	114
Ward 13	46	132
Ward 14	0	3
Ward 15	283	697
Ward 16	314	972
Ward 17	49	100
Ward 18	521	1,133
Ward 19	32	86
Ward 20	71	219
Ward 21	343	811
Ward 22	369	701
Ward 23	235	583
Ward 24	388	1,078
Ward 25	209	501
Ward 26	214	876
Ward 27	440	1,064
North Prairie, vil.		
Wards 1 – 3	238	921
Oconomowoc		
Wards 1 – 2, 4	392	1,451
Wards 3, 6 – 7	405	1,094
Wards 5, 8 – 9	323	1,232
Ward 10	9	8
Oconomowoc, city		
Wards 1 – 3	655	1,638
Wards 4 – 6	548	1,389
Wards 7 – 9	521	1,288
Wards 10 – 12	515	1,326
Oconomowoc Lake, vil.	55	275
Ottawa		
Wards 1 – 5	593	1,631
Pewaukee, vil.		
Wards 1 – 5	596	1,633
Wards 6 – 10	529	1,178
Pewaukee, city		
Wards 1 – 4	607	2,251
Wards 5 – 7	617	1,920
Wards 8 – 10	579	1,985
Summit, vil.		
Wards 1, 6	198	674
Wards 2 – 5	442	1,295
Sussex, vil.		
Wards 1, 3	415	999
Wards 2, 4	416	1,172
Wards 5, 8	211	661
Wards 6 – 7	260	1,024
Vernon		
Wards 1, 8 – 11	463	1,519
Wards 2 – 7	558	1,900
Wales, vil.		
Wards 1 – 4	401	1,089
Waukesha		
Wards 1, 8	284	499
Wards 2 – 6	545	1,801
Wards 7, 9 – 11	419	1,451
Ward 12	0	4
Waukesha, city		
Ward 1	260	570
Ward 2	324	643
Ward 3	111	195
Ward 4	146	246
Ward 5	298	403
Ward 6	258	427
Ward 7	167	358
Ward 8	68	99
Ward 9	383	760
Ward 10	149	337
Ward 11	153	233
Ward 12	385	882
Ward 13	239	633
Ward 14	264	481
Ward 15	188	254
Ward 16	148	268
Ward 17	414	916
Ward 18	347	389
Ward 19	363	590
Ward 20	355	841
Ward 21	275	583
Ward 22	303	525
Ward 23	259	522
Ward 24	213	328
Ward 25	206	261
Ward 26	139	163
Ward 27	11	16
Ward 28	157	164
Ward 29	136	172
Ward 30	378	853
Ward 31	313	891
Ward 32	350	793
Ward 33	313	622
Ward 34	114	174
Ward 35	320	798
Ward 36	416	1,226
Ward 37	228	450
Ward 38	354	690
Ward 39	0	0
Ward 40	0	0
Ward 41	0	0
Ward 42	0	0
Ward 43	0	0
Ward 44	0	0
Ward 45	0	0
Ward 46	0	0
Ward 47	0	0
TOTAL	54,500	147,266
WAUPACA COUNTY		
Bear Creek	69	233
Big Falls, vil.	15	18
Caledonia		
Wards 1 – 2	227	595
Clintonville, city		
Wards 1 – 7	558	900
Dayton		
Wards 1 – 4	488	859
Dupont		
Wards 1 – 2	68	198
Embarrass, vil.	34	95

VOTE FOR GOVENROR AND LIEUTENANT GOVERNOR BY WARD
November 4, 2014 General Election–Continued

District	Burke and Lehman (Dem.)	Walker and Kleefisch (Rep.)
Farmington		
Wards 1 – 6	703	994
Fremont		
Wards 1 – 2	99	230
Fremont, vil.	89	240
Harrison	79	143
Helvetia		
Wards 1 – 2	76	215
Iola		
Wards 1 – 2	155	314
Iola, vil.		
Wards 1 – 2	215	278
Larrabee		
Wards 1 – 2	179	393
Lebanon		
Wards 1 – 3	237	445
Lind		
Wards 1 – 3	210	419
Little Wolf		
Wards 1 – 3	160	446
Manawa, city		
Wards 1 – 3	133	292
Marion, city		
Wards 1 – 3	132	293
Matteson	104	317
Mukwa		
Wards 1 – 2	166	271
Wards 3 – 5	315	548
New London, city		
Wards 3 – 4, 8	237	322
Wards 6 – 7	201	307
Wards 9 – 10	207	230
Wards 11 – 12	180	171
Ogdensburg, vil.	16	42
Royalton		
Wards 1 – 2	182	426
St. Lawrence		
Wards 1 – 2	105	180
Scandinavia		
Wards 1 – 2	214	316
Scandinavia, vil.	61	85
Union		
Wards 1 – 2	75	235
Waupaca		
Wards 1 – 2	183	357
Waupaca, city		
Wards 1 – 12	961	1,122
Weyauwega	83	178
Weyauwega, city		
Wards 1 – 3	212	335
Wyoming	43	88
TOTAL	7,471	13,130
WAUSHARA COUNTY		
Aurora	138	303
Berlin, city		
Ward 7	10	33
Bloomfield		
Wards 1 – 2	93	340
Coloma	124	183
Coloma, vil.	64	98
Dakota		
Wards 1 – 2	130	296
Deerfield	137	227
Hancock	67	150
Hancock, vil.	54	100
Leon		
Wards 1 – 3	247	458
Lohrville, vil.	79	80
Marion		
Wards 1 – 4	377	638
Mount Morris		
Wards 1 – 2	235	339
Oasis	64	135
Plainfield	50	144
Plainfield, vil.	83	174
Poy Sippi	134	260
Redgranite, vil.		
Wards 1 – 3	158	136
Richford		
Wards 1 – 2	57	139
Rose		
Wards 1 – 2	126	177
Saxeville	173	340
Springwater		
Wards 1 – 2	281	411
Warren	108	145
Wautoma		
Wards 1 – 3	251	377

District	Burke and Lehman (Dem.)	Walker and Kleefisch (Rep.)
Wautoma, city		
Wards 1 – 3	235	287
Wild Rose, vil.	134	130
TOTAL	3,609	6,100
WINNEBAGO COUNTY		
Algoma		
Wards 1 – 2, 7 – 10	678	1,121
Wards 3 – 6	694	1,166
Appleton, city		
Ward 31	29	38
Ward 32	108	116
Black Wolf		
Wards 1 – 3	500	862
Clayton		
Wards 1 – 7	586	1,427
Menasha		
Wards 1 – 2, 4, 7	890	1,570
Wards 3, 5 – 6	841	1,280
Wards 8 – 10	639	878
Wards 11 – 13	617	595
Menasha, city		
Wards 1A, 2, 4, 7	699	704
Ward 1B	0	0
Wards 3, 14 – 15, 30	334	377
Ward 5B	0	0
Wards 5A, 6, 8 – 9, 23 – 29, 31	796	731
Wards 10 – 13, 21 – 22	841	819
Neenah		
Wards 1 – 4	704	1,106
Neenah, city		
Wards 1 – 4	860	888
Wards 5 – 8	701	692
Wards 9 – 12	896	1,161
Wards 13 – 16	763	994
Wards 17 – 20	769	761
Wards 21 – 25	894	1,281
Nekimi		
Wards 1 – 2	230	494
Nepeuskun	108	252
Omro		
Wards 1 – 3	425	635
Omro, city		
Wards 1 – 8	593	757
Oshkosh		
Wards 1A, 2 – 5	511	846
Ward 1B	11	19
Oshkosh, city		
Ward 1	463	445
Ward 2	445	373
Ward 3	292	502
Ward 4	277	425
Ward 5	335	277
Ward 6	440	293
Ward 7	606	435
Ward 8	491	347
Ward 9	292	207
Ward 10	486	415
Ward 11	424	360
Ward 12	410	293
Ward 13	467	497
Ward 14	430	496
Ward 15	489	425
Ward 16	523	593
Ward 17	494	359
Ward 18	452	537
Ward 19	382	395
Ward 20	140	245
Ward 21	392	387
Ward 22A	578	689
Ward 22B	0	0
Ward 23A	416	454
Ward 23B	21	20
Ward 24	223	286
Ward 25A	91	92
Ward 25B	382	295
Ward 26	292	252
Ward 27	529	372
Ward 28A	414	387
Ward 28B	73	88
Ward 29A	135	225
Ward 29B	0	0
Ward 30	20	48
Ward 31	149	172
Ward 32	0	0
Ward 33	10	22
Ward 34	2	0
Ward 35	0	1

VOTE FOR GOVERNOR AND LIEUTENANT GOVERNOR BY WARD
November 4, 2014 General Election–Continued

District	Burke and Lehman (Dem.)	Walker and Kleefisch (Rep.)	District	Burke and Lehman (Dem.)	Walker and Kleefisch (Rep.)
Ward 36	0	0	Ward 2	235	279
Ward 37	0	0	Wards 3, 13	412	589
Poygan			Wards 4, 14	337	535
Wards 1 – 2	235	416	Wards 5, 15	292	396
Rushford			Wards 6, 17	348	482
Wards 1 – 2	278	428	Wards 7, 16	280	383
Utica			Wards 8, 19, 22 – 23	311	492
Wards 1 – 2	237	462	Wards 9, 18	293	333
Vinland			Ward 10	256	330
Wards 1A, 2	374	643	Milladore	105	164
Ward 1B	2	1	Milladore, vil.	39	73
Winchester			Nekoosa, city		
Wards 1 – 2	294	641	Wards 1 – 4	391	477
Winneconne			Pittsville, city	111	239
Wards 1 – 4	447	856	Port Edwards		
Ward 5	3	3	Wards 1 – 4	237	317
Winneconne, vil.			Port Edwards, vil.		
Wards 1 – 4	419	705	Wards 1 – 3	373	455
Wolf River			Remington	38	78
Wards 1 – 2A	113	324	Richfield		
Wards 2B, 2C	74	136	Wards 1 – 3	176	485
TOTAL	30,258	37,894	Rock	128	276
WOOD COUNTY			Rudolph		
Arpin			Wards 1 – 2	227	314
Wards 1 – 3	128	244	Rudolph, vil.	97	116
Arpin, vil.	39	64	Saratoga		
Auburndale	81	243	Wards 1 – 9	983	1,229
Auburndale, vil.	114	166	Seneca		
Biron, vil.	173	205	Wards 1 – 3	222	299
Cameron	71	175	Sherry	129	232
Cary	68	142	Sigel		
Cranmoor	18	65	Wards 1 – 3	209	288
Dexter	78	98	Vesper, vil.	85	141
Grand Rapids			Wisconsin Rapids, city		
Wards 1 – 11	1,677	2,192	Wards 1 – 5	830	841
Hansen	110	235	Wards 6 – 15, 24, 26	1,308	1,436
Hewitt, vil.	145	244	Wards 16 – 23, 25, 27	999	1,093
Hiles	20	63	Wood	131	277
Lincoln			TOTAL	12,861	17,820
Wards 1 – 2	257	523			
Marshfield	120	263			
Marshfield, city					
Wards 1, 11	180	249			

Dem. – Democratic Party; Rep. – Republican Party.

All municipalities are towns, unless noted as a village (vil.) or city.

Source: Official records of the Government Accountability Board, Elections Division. Scattered votes omitted.

VOTE FOR GOVENROR AND LIEUTENANT GOVERNOR BY WARD
November 4, 2014 General Election–Continued

District	Burke and Lehman (Dem.)	Walker and Kleefisch (Rep.)
Whitefish Bay, vil.		
Wards 1 – 2	498	764
Wards 3 – 4	555	567
Wards 5 – 6	590	694
Ward 7	351	291
Wards 8 – 10	797	675
Wards 9 – 11	690	502
Ward 12	429	357
TOTAL	231,316	132,706
MONROE COUNTY		
Adrian	112	232
Angelo		
Wards 1 – 3	167	262
Byron	181	259
Cashton, vil.		
Wards 1 – 3	160	194
Clifton	70	103
Glendale	90	161
Grant	57	133
Greenfield		
Wards 1 – 2	98	215
Jefferson	80	148
Kendall, vil.	88	66
Lafayette		
Wards 1 – 2	60	88
La Grange		
Wards 1A, 2A, 3A	307	443
Wards 1B, 2B, 3B	21	33
Leon		
Wards 1 – 2	148	309
Lincoln	83	254
Little Falls		
Wards 1 – 2	253	317
Melvina, vil.	5	20
New Lyme	29	50
Norwalk, vil.	73	88
Oakdale	110	170
Oakdale, vil.	32	47
Portland	134	171
Ridgeville	105	110
Rockland, vil.		
Ward 2	0	0
Scott	7	31
Sheldon	43	133
Sparta		
Wards 1 – 6	534	690
Sparta, city		
Wards 1 – 6	503	545
Wards 7 – 12	487	483
Wards 13 – 18	430	368
Ward 19	0	0
Ward 20	0	2
Tomah		
Wards 1 – 2	216	341
Tomah, city		
Wards 1 – 16, 5A, 18	1,335	1,410
Ward 5B	0	0
Wards 17, 19	0	0
Warrens, vil.	45	102
Wellington		
Wards 1 – 2	86	110
Wells	76	137
Wilton		
Wards 1 – 5	75	112
Wilton, vil.	88	78
Wyeville, vil.	11	31
TOTAL	6,399	8,446
OCONTO COUNTY		
Abrams		
Wards 1 – 3	271	547
Bagley	50	106
Brazeau		
Wards 1 – 3	234	449
Breed	92	209
Chase		
Wards 1 – 5	393	850
Doty	60	116
Gillett		
Wards 1 – 2	107	350
Gillett, city		
Wards 1 – 3	185	270
How		
Wards 1 – 2	65	220
Lakewood	151	318
Lena	80	205
Lena, vil.	78	113
Little River		
Wards 1 – 2	173	276

District	Burke and Lehman (Dem.)	Walker and Kleefisch (Rep.)
Little Suamico		
Wards 1 – 8	695	1,446
Maple Valley	94	206
Morgan		
Wards 1 – 2	133	322
Mountain	160	227
Oconto		
Wards 1 – 3	230	384
Oconto, city		
Wards 1 – 7	723	787
Oconto Falls		
Wards 1 – 2	183	355
Oconto Falls, city		
Wards 1 – 5	352	551
Pensaukee		
Wards 1 – 2	211	413
Pulaski, vil.		
Ward 5	0	0
Riverview		
Wards 1 – 2	174	252
Spruce		
Wards 1 – 2	121	233
Stiles		
Wards 1 – 3	246	398
Suring, vil.	67	126
Townsend	211	342
Underhill	118	229
TOTAL	5,657	10,300
ONEIDA COUNTY		
Cassian		
Wards 1 – 2	248	325
Crescent		
Wards 1 – 2	486	571
Enterprise	71	132
Hazelhurst		
Wards 1 – 2	302	383
Lake Tomahawk		
Wards 1 – 2	178	365
Little Rice	49	118
Lynne	20	43
Minocqua		
Wards 1 – 7	854	1,644
Monico	29	83
Newbold		
Ward 1	60	118
Wards 2 – 4	531	668
Nokomis		
Wards 1 – 2	290	405
Pelican		
Wards 1 – 4	583	651
Piehl	15	27
Pine Lake		
Wards 1 – 4	573	695
Rhinelander, city		
Ward 1	181	134
Wards 2 – 3	175	128
Wards 4 – 5	172	103
Wards 6 – 7	142	134
Wards 8 – 9	209	152
Ward 10	146	151
Wards 11 – 12	169	131
Wards 13 – 14	161	147
Schoepke	87	104
Stella		
Wards 1 – 2	136	146
Sugar Camp		
Wards 1 – 2	305	590
Three Lakes		
Wards 1 – 4	415	836
Woodboro	184	230
Woodruff		
Wards 1 – 3	419	638
TOTAL	7,190	9,852
OUTAGAMIE COUNTY		
Appleton, city		
Ward 1	300	236
Ward 2	539	482
Ward 3	850	465
Ward 4	285	332
Ward 5	0	3
Ward 6	235	197
Ward 7	411	497
Ward 8	553	137
Ward 9	310	344
Ward 10	255	270
Ward 11	179	244
Ward 15	282	390
Ward 16	245	284

VOTE FOR GOVERNOR AND LIEUTENANT GOVERNOR BY WARD
November 4, 2014 General Election–Continued

District	Burke and Lehman (Dem.)	Walker and Kleefisch (Rep.)	District	Burke and Lehman (Dem.)	Walker and Kleefisch (Rep.)
Ward 17	277	369	Wards 2, 6, 8, 12 – 13	337	428
Ward 18	214	309	Wards 3, 9 – 11	610	891
Ward 19	351	854	Ward 7	310	466
Ward 20	248	520	Maine	105	251
Ward 21	5	15	Maple Creek	63	192
Ward 22	4	20	New London, city		
Ward 23	0	0	Wards 1 – 2	200	274
Ward 24	184	178	Nichols, vil.	17	62
Ward 25	375	309	Oneida		
Ward 27	397	415	Wards 1 – 6	586	835
Ward 28	353	355	Osborn		
Ward 29	488	400	Wards 1 – 2	169	375
Ward 30	362	355	Seymour		
Ward 33	424	441	Wards 1 – 2	111	390
Ward 34	144	73	Seymour, city		
Ward 35	359	441	Wards 1 – 6	464	847
Ward 36	458	534	Shiocton, vil.	137	171
Ward 37	301	328	Vandenbroek		
Ward 38	345	693	Wards 1 – 3	203	539
Ward 39	182	333	Wrightstown, vil.		
Ward 40	0	11	Ward 4	23	76
Ward 41	9	91	Ward 5	0	0
Ward 42	313	402	TOTAL	29,503	44,543
Ward 43	319	362	**OZAUKEE COUNTY**		
Ward 48	67	49	Bayside, vil.		
Ward 49	39	50	Ward 6	37	33
Ward 50	61	53	Belgium		
Ward 51	379	347	Wards 1 – 3	183	620
Ward 52	42	35	Belgium, vil.		
Ward 53	12	8	Wards 1 – 3	243	737
Ward 54	327	415	Cedarburg		
Ward 55	162	197	Wards 1 – 2	167	592
Ward 56	0	1	Wards 3 – 4	216	661
Ward 57	3	4	Wards 5 – 6, 10	229	791
Ward 58	0	0	Wards 7 – 9	207	748
Ward 59	1	0	Cedarburg, city		
Bear Creek, vil.	36	65	Ward 1	325	661
Black Creek			Wards 2, 9	261	677
Wards 1 – 2	152	380	Ward 3	328	548
Black Creek, vil.			Wards 4, 8	250	506
Wards 1 – 2	181	322	Ward 5	256	443
Bovina			Ward 6	316	595
Wards 1 – 2	181	309	Ward 7	246	629
Buchanan			Fredonia		
Wards 1 – 10	1,078	1,942	Wards 1 – 4	206	906
Center			Fredonia, vil.		
Wards 1 – 7	455	1,289	Wards 1 – 3	237	764
Cicero			Grafton		
Wards 1 – 2	140	298	Wards 1 – 2, 5	265	1,014
Combined Locks, vil.			Wards 3 – 4	355	899
Wards 1 – 4	611	1,008	Grafton, vil.		
Dale			Ward 1	132	371
Wards 1 – 3	334	967	Ward 2	108	255
Deer Creek	75	171	Ward 3	135	300
Ellington			Ward 4	136	339
Wards 1 – 5	340	965	Ward 5	129	263
Freedom			Ward 6	124	253
Wards 1 – 8	795	1,791	Ward 7	122	286
Grand Chute			Ward 8	135	339
Wards 1 – 3	865	1,489	Ward 9	122	329
Wards 4 – 6	566	948	Ward 10	141	250
Ward 7	185	240	Ward 11	99	310
Ward 8	62	109	Ward 12	114	330
Wards 9 – 11	399	508	Ward 13	140	256
Wards 12 – 14	725	1,193	Ward 14	117	259
Wards 15 – 17	783	1,199	Mequon, city		
Ward 18	0	0	Ward 1	425	828
Greenville			Ward 2	89	349
Wards 1 – 3, 5 – 8	1,175	2,920	Wards 3 – 4	491	1,145
Wards 4, 9	297	642	Wards 5, 7B	146	535
Harrison, vil.			Wards 6, 7A	301	848
Wards 1 – 2	0	0	Wards 8 – 10	535	1,105
Hortonia			Wards 11 – 12	437	989
Wards 1 – 2	139	374	Wards 13 – 14	250	737
Hortonville, vil.			Ward 15	302	460
Wards 1 – 3	395	756	Ward 16	152	447
Howard, vil.			Ward 17	280	429
Ward 17	0	0	Ward 18	153	340
Kaukauna			Wards 19 – 21	463	1,143
Wards 1 – 3	132	439	Newburg, vil.		
Kaukauna, city			Ward 3	9	24
Wards 1 – 3	543	676	Port Washington		
Wards 4 – 5	655	797	Wards 1 – 2	230	588
Wards 6 – 7	717	766	Port Washington, city		
Wards 8 – 10	723	838	Ward 1	314	601
Kimberly, vil.			Ward 2	283	425
Wards 1 – 9	1,241	1,574	Ward 3	290	506
Liberty	129	272	Ward 4	253	402
Little Chute, vil.			Ward 5	326	545
Wards 1, 4 – 5, 14	410	651			

VOTE FOR GOVENROR AND LIEUTENANT GOVERNOR BY WARD
November 4, 2014 General Election–Continued

District	Burke and Lehman (Dem.)	Walker and Kleefisch (Rep.)
Ward 6	235	401
Ward 7	303	526
Saukville		
Wards 1 – 3	205	870
Saukville, vil.		
Wards 1 – 2	179	523
Wards 3 – 5	199	411
Wards 6 – 7	146	425
Thiensville, vil.		
Wards 1 – 2	307	716
Wards 3 – 4	312	414
TOTAL	13,696	32,696
PEPIN COUNTY		
Albany	89	164
Durand		
Wards 1 – 2	92	204
Durand, city		
Wards 1 – 3	328	405
Frankfort	78	80
Lima		
Wards 1 – 2	85	151
Pepin		
Wards 1 – 2	166	178
Pepin, vil.		
Wards 1 – 2	226	148
Stockholm.	50	62
Stockholm, vil.	28	9
Waterville		
Wards 1 – 2	131	242
Waubeek	60	148
TOTAL	1,333	1,791
PIERCE COUNTY		
Bay City, vil.	46	76
Clifton		
Wards 1 – 3	362	558
Diamond Bluff	94	111
Ellsworth		
Wards 1 – 2	200	298
Ellsworth, vil.		
Wards 1 – 4	475	510
Elmwood, vil..	140	153
El Paso	117	166
Gilman	180	229
Hartland.	120	218
Isabelle	46	60
Maiden Rock	94	133
Maiden Rock, vil.	28	24
Martell		
Wards 1 – 2	231	265
Oak Grove		
Wards 1 – 3	328	560
Plum City, vil..	75	132
Prescott, city		
Wards 1 – 6	677	759
River Falls		
Wards 1 – 3	529	558
River Falls, city		
Ward 5	92	119
Wards 6 – 8	764	472
Wards 9 – 11	421	353
Wards 12 – 14	468	421
Rock Elm	90	102
Salem	93	106
Spring Lake		
Wards 1 – 2	101	138
Spring Valley, vil.		
Wards 1 – 2	252	225
Trenton		
Wards 1 – 2	291	410
Trimbelle		
Wards 1 – 2	298	402
Union	54	202
TOTAL	6,666	7,760
POLK COUNTY		
Alden		
Wards 1 – 4	391	662
Amery, city		
Wards 1 – 5	464	497
Apple River		
Wards 1 – 2	190	248
Balsam Lake		
Wards 1 – 2	215	373
Balsam Lake, vil.		
Wards 1 – 2	135	179
Beaver.	128	174
Black Brook		
Wards 1 – 2	162	319
Bone Lake.	132	168

District	Burke and Lehman (Dem.)	Walker and Kleefisch (Rep.)
Centuria, vil.	75	121
Clam Falls.	84	119
Clayton	158	196
Clayton, vil..	59	69
Clear Lake	105	207
Clear Lake, vil.		
Wards 1 – 2	146	192
Dresser, vil.	112	170
Eureka		
Wards 1 – 2	226	421
Farmington		
Wards 1 – 2	255	467
Frederic, vil.		
Wards 1 – 2	161	185
Garfield		
Wards 1 – 3	245	403
Georgetown		
Wards 1 – 2	201	211
Johnstown.	97	96
Laketown	154	244
Lincoln		
Wards 1 – 4	334	532
Lorain	47	70
Luck		
Wards 1 – 2	160	214
Luck, vil.		
Wards 1 – 2	167	220
McKinley	54	94
Milltown		
Wards 1 – 2	208	255
Milltown, vil..	99	121
Osceola		
Wards 1 – 5	435	663
Osceola, vil.		
Wards 1 – 3	356	403
St. Croix Falls		
Wards 1 – 2	166	300
St. Croix Falls, city		
Wards 1 – 4	395	419
Sterling	84	138
Turtle Lake, vil.		
Ward 2A	7	15
Ward 2B	0	0
West Sweden	109	180
TOTAL	6,516	9,345
PORTAGE COUNTY		
Alban	192	211
Almond	119	197
Almond, vil..	67	80
Amherst		
Wards 1 – 2	340	364
Amherst, vil.		
Wards 1 – 2	218	217
Amherst Junction, vil..	69	84
Belmont	114	177
Buena Vista		
Wards 1 – 2	234	344
Carson		
Wards 1 – 2	288	389
Dewey.	220	259
Eau Pleine.	182	279
Grant		
Wards 1 – 2, 4	299	405
Ward 3	68	120
Hull		
Wards 1 – 3	446	434
Wards 4 – 5	392	442
Wards 6 – 8	470	510
Junction City, vil.	65	96
Lanark		
Wards 1 – 2	312	409
Linwood		
Wards 1 – 2	245	321
Milladore, vil.		
Ward 2	0	2
Nelsonville, vil..	62	25
New Hope.	245	155
Park Ridge, vil..	166	134
Pine Grove		
Wards 1 – 2	117	170
Plover		
Wards 1 – 3	284	423
Plover, vil.		
Wards 1 – 3	824	862
Wards 4 – 6	936	1,083
Wards 7 – 9	579	592
Rosholt, vil.	94	84
Sharon		
Wards 1 – 3	450	551

VOTE FOR GOVERNOR AND LIEUTENANT GOVERNOR BY WARD
November 4, 2014 General Election–Continued

District	Burke and Lehman (Dem.)	Walker and Kleefisch (Rep.)
Stevens Point, city		
Wards 1 – 3	583	281
Wards 4 – 6	563	335
Wards 7 – 9	479	327
Wards 10 – 12	529	280
Wards 13 – 15	639	292
Wards 16 – 18	612	626
Wards 19 – 21	524	318
Wards 22 – 24	648	505
Wards 25 – 27	541	335
Wards 28 – 30	556	474
Wards 31 – 33	402	339
Ward 34	0	0
Ward 35	1	0
Wards 36, 38	0	0
Wards 37, 39	1	0
Stockton		
Wards 1 – 5	665	769
Whiting, vil.		
Wards 1 – 4	443	350
TOTAL	**15,283**	**14,650**
PRICE COUNTY		
Catawba	57	67
Catawba, vil.	22	20
Eisenstein		
Wards 1 – 2	132	197
Elk		
Wards 1 – 2	221	328
Emery	74	83
Fifield		
Ward 1	117	192
Ward 2	68	100
Flambeau	84	143
Georgetown	27	61
Hackett	27	71
Harmony	49	66
Hill	53	114
Kennan	53	73
Kennan, vil.	29	27
Knox	70	81
Lake		
Wards 1 – 2	278	299
Ogema		
Wards 1 – 2	110	208
Park Falls, city		
Wards 1 – 7	481	373
Phillips, city		
Wards 1 – 4	250	289
Prentice	69	125
Prentice, vil.	83	158
Spirit	39	101
Worcester		
Wards 1 – 3	307	549
TOTAL	**2,700**	**3,725**
RACINE COUNTY		
Burlington		
Wards 1 – 7	529	1,175
Wards 8 – 10	278	527
Ward 11	125	211
Burlington, city		
Wards 1 – 4	741	1,197
Wards 5 – 8	836	1,411
Caledonia, vil.		
Wards 1 – 2	473	1,051
Ward 3S	0	0
Wards 3 – 5	714	1,386
Wards 6 – 8	763	998
Wards 9 – 10, 12 – 13	1,114	1,316
Wards 11, 14 – 15, 17	940	1,523
Wards 16, 18 – 19	592	1,034
Ward 20	156	287
Dover		
Wards 1 – 8	505	1,123
Elmwood Park, vil.	141	153
Mount Pleasant, vil.		
Wards 1 – 2, 4, 16	823	825
Wards 3, 10 – 12, 15	1,384	1,668
Ward 5	299	353
Wards 6 – 9	1,030	1,336
Wards 13 – 14	388	641
Wards 17, 20	411	505
Ward 18	228	220
Wards 19, 21 – 23	1,028	1,236
North Bay, vil.	66	82
Norway		
Wards 1 – 11	975	3,063
Racine, city		
Ward 1	440	164
Ward 2	479	65

District	Burke and Lehman (Dem.)	Walker and Kleefisch (Rep.)
Ward 3	856	285
Ward 4	413	21
Ward 5	358	26
Ward 6	384	105
Ward 7	319	44
Ward 8	374	63
Ward 9	576	170
Ward 10	433	333
Ward 11	397	216
Ward 12	354	289
Ward 13	411	332
Ward 14	550	310
Ward 15	468	200
Ward 16	558	467
Ward 17	281	66
Ward 18	284	19
Ward 19	251	10
Ward 20	649	509
Ward 21	478	224
Ward 22	678	401
Ward 23	618	312
Ward 24	489	355
Ward 25	545	217
Ward 26	51	89
Ward 27	646	598
Ward 28	592	478
Ward 29	578	352
Ward 30	453	239
Ward 31	283	209
Ward 32	395	166
Ward 33	382	250
Ward 34	408	346
Ward 35	379	321
Ward 36	340	171
Raymond		
Wards 1 – 6	613	1,511
Rochester, vil.		
Wards 1 – 6	500	1,311
Sturtevant, vil.		
Wards 1 – 8	972	1,267
Union Grove, vil.		
Wards 1 – 7	644	1,294
Waterford		
Wards 1 – 10	768	2,440
Waterford, vil.		
Wards 1 – 7	734	1,668
Wind Point, vil.		
Wards 1 – 3	389	631
Yorkville		
Wards 1 – 5	460	1,079
TOTAL	**35,769**	**42,944**
RICHLAND COUNTY		
Akan	85	83
Bloom	87	113
Boaz, vil.	27	21
Buena Vista		
Wards 1 – 3	285	316
Ward 4	0	2
Cazenovia, vil.	62	51
Dayton	123	170
Eagle	76	119
Forest	83	69
Henrietta	114	101
Ithaca	129	151
Lone Rock, vil.	175	130
Marshall		
Wards 1 – 2	106	160
Orion	88	108
Richland		
Wards 1 – 4	237	327
Richland Center, city		
Ward 1	75	91
Ward 2	63	52
Ward 3	87	69
Ward 4	96	62
Ward 5	97	74
Ward 6	80	65
Ward 7	72	64
Ward 8	95	54
Ward 9	84	95
Ward 10	90	78
Ward 11	68	75
Ward 12	78	80
Richwood		
Wards 1 – 2	105	101
Rockbridge		
Wards 1 – 3	145	165
Sylvan		
Wards 1 – 2	85	99

VOTE FOR GOVENROR AND LIEUTENANT GOVERNOR BY WARD
November 4, 2014 General Election–Continued

District	Burke and Lehman (Dem.)	Walker and Kleefisch (Rep.)
Viola, vil.		
Ward 2	76	64
Westford	122	109
Willow	99	107
Yuba, vil.	21	10
TOTAL	3,315	3,435
ROCK COUNTY		
Avon	125	146
Beloit		
Wards 1 – 3	424	500
Wards 4 – 6	410	325
Wards 7 – 10	595	708
Ward 11	70	70
Beloit, city		
Ward 1	167	92
Ward 2	276	225
Ward 3	259	232
Ward 4	223	156
Ward 5	222	153
Ward 6	171	99
Ward 7	162	63
Ward 8	18	4
Ward 9	177	94
Ward 10	234	108
Ward 11	250	196
Ward 12	110	31
Ward 13	191	31
Ward 14	265	59
Ward 15	220	131
Ward 16	368	57
Ward 17	342	200
Ward 18	237	135
Ward 19	209	113
Ward 20	206	118
Ward 21	262	156
Ward 22	264	265
Ward 23	416	462
Ward 24	201	213
Ward 25	0	0
Bradford		
Wards 1 – 2	153	290
Brodhead, city		
Wards 7 – 8	14	13
Center		
Wards 1 – 2	308	242
Clinton	113	268
Clinton, vil.		
Wards 1 – 3	290	426
Edgerton, city		
Wards 1 – 6	1,424	738
Evansville, city		
Wards 1 – 9	1,470	744
Footville, vil.	188	144
Fulton		
Wards 1 – 6	821	732
Harmony		
Ward 1	195	183
Wards 2 – 5	416	431
Ward 6	1	1
Janesville		
Wards 1 – 6	832	809
Wards 7 – 9	93	80
Janesville, city		
Ward 1	621	449
Ward 2	564	421
Ward 3	421	189
Ward 4	317	159
Ward 5	607	331
Ward 6	376	238
Ward 7	721	385
Ward 8	534	277
Ward 9	455	260
Ward 10	346	184
Ward 11	527	232
Ward 12	651	624
Ward 13	635	347
Ward 14	652	454
Ward 15	515	274
Ward 16	361	225
Ward 17	698	444
Ward 18	625	456
Ward 19	160	113
Ward 20	184	197
Ward 21	476	439
Ward 22	503	566
Ward 23	292	243
Ward 24	365	201
Ward 25	531	435
Ward 26	0	0
Ward 27	747	736
Ward 28	661	524
Ward 29	1	2
Ward 30	0	0
Ward 31	0	0
Johnstown	159	208
La Prairie		
Ward 1	114	167
Ward 2	40	63
Lima		
Wards 1 – 2	242	292
Magnolia	193	146
Milton		
Ward 1	161	199
Wards 2 – 4	471	464
Milton, city		
Ward 1	1,257	996
Newark		
Wards 1 – 3	294	426
Orfordville, vil.		
Wards 1 – 2	324	209
Plymouth		
Wards 1 – 2	268	278
Porter	317	216
Rock		
Wards 1 – 4, 6	504	378
Wards 5, 7	87	92
Spring Valley	136	172
Turtle		
Wards 1, 4	207	255
Wards 2 – 3	224	438
Union		
Wards 1 – 4	587	346
TOTAL	32,523	24,993
RUSK COUNTY		
Atlanta		
Wards 1 – 2	81	164
Big Bend		
Wards 1 – 2	92	135
Big Falls	27	46
Bruce, vil.	137	158
Cedar Rapids	7	14
Conrath, vil.	21	
Dewey	70	180
Flambeau		
Wards 1 – 3	161	254
Glen Flora, vil.	16	17
Grant		
Wards 1 – 5	124	174
Grow	37	135
Hawkins	28	39
Hawkins, vil.	56	73
Hubbard	42	41
Ingram, vil.	25	16
Ladysmith, city		
Wards 1 – 15	513	590
Lawrence		
Wards 1 – 2	35	77
Marshall		
Wards 1 – 2	38	129
Murry	33	58
Richland		
Wards 1 – 2	50	58
Rusk	102	148
Sheldon, vil.	31	49
South Fork	17	37
Strickland		
Wards 1 – 2	60	75
Stubbs	123	162
Thornapple		
Wards 1 – 5	104	230
Tony, vil.	15	29
True	61	93
Washington	58	112
Weyerhaeuser, vil.		
Wards 1 – 2	36	41
Wilkinson	7	11
Willard	65	115
Wilson	14	29
TOTAL	2,286	3,502
ST. CROIX COUNTY		
Baldwin		
Wards 1 – 2	135	258
Baldwin, vil.		
Wards 1 – 7	448	753
Cady	99	227
Cylon	93	166
Deer Park, vil.	19	66

VOTE FOR GOVERNOR AND LIEUTENANT GOVERNOR BY WARD
November 4, 2014 General Election–Continued

District	Burke and Lehman (Dem.)	Walker and Kleefisch (Rep.)
Eau Galle		
Wards 1 – 2	200	289
Emerald	96	189
Erin Prairie	119	170
Forest	67	153
Glenwood	79	179
Glenwood City, city		
Wards 1 – 2	149	237
Hammond		
Wards 1 – 3	272	583
Hammond, vil.		
Wards 1 – 4	329	349
Hudson		
Wards 1 – 14	1,387	2,619
Hudson, city		
Wards 1 – 2	270	335
Wards 3 – 4	456	658
Wards 5 – 6	455	522
Wards 7 – 8	364	446
Wards 9 – 10	518	428
Wards 11 – 12	423	547
Kinnickinnic		
Wards 1 – 3	348	467
New Richmond, city		
Wards 1 – 6	528	580
Wards 7 – 12	627	728
North Hudson, vil.		
Wards 1 – 6	708	1,025
Pleasant Valley	91	132
Richmond		
Wards 1 – 2	195	407
Wards 3 – 5	198	316
River Falls, city		
Wards 1 – 4, 15	622	664
Roberts, vil.		
Wards 1 – 4	259	323
Rush River	99	127
St. Joseph		
Wards 1 – 6	668	1,185
Somerset		
Wards 1 – 6	545	1,010
Somerset, vil.		
Wards 1 – 4	254	363
Spring Valley, vil.		
Ward 3	1	2
Springfield	119	206
Stanton	143	200
Star Prairie		
Wards 1 – 6	422	798
Star Prairie, vil.	83	97
Troy		
Wards 1 – 7	893	1,528
Warren		
Wards 1 – 3	261	442
Wilson, vil.	33	49
Woodville, vil.		
Wards 1 – 2	156	243
TOTAL	13,231	20,066
SAUK COUNTY		
Baraboo		
Wards 1 – 4	460	431
Baraboo, city		
Wards 1 – 14	2,588	1,873
Bear Creek	170	130
Cazenovia, vil.		
Ward 2	4	5
Dellona		
Wards 1 – 2	318	391
Delton		
Wards 1 – 4	465	482
Excelsior		
Wards 1 – 3	323	431
Fairfield		
Wards 1 – 2	317	255
Franklin		
Wards 1 – 3	143	174
Freedom		
Wards 1 – 2	100	140
Greenfield	241	238
Honey Creek	190	180
Ironton	88	152
Ironton, vil.	30	46
Lake Delton, vil.		
Wards 1 – 3	435	385
La Valle		
Wards 1 – 3	277	369
La Valle, vil.	65	68
Lime Ridge, vil.	44	22
Loganville, vil.	50	63

District	Burke and Lehman (Dem.)	Walker and Kleefisch (Rep.)
Merrimac	268	291
Merrimac, vil.	97	108
North Freedom, vil.	117	107
Plain, vil.	149	216
Prairie du Sac		
Wards 1 – 2	249	282
Prairie du Sac, vil.		
Wards 1 – 4	1,105	779
Reedsburg		
Wards 1 – 3	203	330
Reedsburg, city		
Wards 1 – 3, 13	358	344
Wards 4, 6, 14	388	456
Wards 5, 7 – 9	506	531
Wards 10 – 12	297	271
Rock Springs, vil.	40	76
Sauk City, vil.		
Wards 1 – 5	922	539
Spring Green		
Wards 1 – 4	416	390
Spring Green, vil.		
Wards 1 – 2	488	294
Sumpter		
Wards 1 – 3	160	154
Troy	186	205
Washington		
Wards 1 – 2	121	188
West Baraboo, vil.		
Wards 1 – 2	267	226
Westfield	82	182
Winfield		
Wards 1 – 2	165	228
Wisconsin Dells, city		
Ward 4	20	27
Wards 8, 10	0	0
Woodland	129	163
TOTAL	13,041	12,222
SAWYER COUNTY		
Bass Lake		
Wards 1 – 5	540	374
Couderay	64	48
Couderay, vil.	23	11
Draper	51	58
Edgewater		
Wards 1 – 2	89	179
Exeland, vil.	39	30
Hayward		
Wards 1 – 8	569	710
Hayward, city		
Wards 1 – 6	310	377
Hunter	143	156
Lenroot		
Wards 1 – 2	278	373
Meadowbrook	14	50
Meteor	21	49
Ojibwa		
Wards 1 – 2	34	65
Radisson		
Wards 1 – 2	52	106
Radisson, vil.	39	34
Round Lake		
Wards 1 – 2	224	330
Sand Lake	181	227
Spider Lake	88	132
Weirgor	52	93
Winter		
Wards 1 – 2	182	268
Winter, vil.	36	51
TOTAL	3,029	3,721
SHAWANO COUNTY		
Almon	72	152
Angelica		
Wards 1 – 3	221	572
Aniwa	55	150
Aniwa, vil.	28	56
Bartelme	210	54
Belle Plaine		
Wards 1 – 3	266	569
Birnamwood	110	199
Birnamwood, vil.	79	169
Bonduel, vil.		
Wards 1 – 2	163	411
Bowler, vil.	37	60
Cecil, vil.	80	192
Eland, vil.	62	37
Fairbanks	49	205
Germania		
Wards 1 – 2	35	98

VOTE FOR GOVENROR AND LIEUTENANT GOVERNOR BY WARD
November 4, 2014 General Election–Continued

District	Burke and Lehman (Dem.)	Walker and Kleefisch (Rep.)
Grant		
Wards 1 – 2	89	313
Green Valley		
Wards 1 – 2	112	315
Gresham, vil.	107	109
Hartland	59	278
Herman		
Wards 1 – 2	112	221
Hutchins	57	182
Lessor		
Wards 1 – 2	145	402
Maple Grove	122	267
Marion, city		
Wards 4 – 6	2	3
Mattoon, vil.	33	68
Morris	81	114
Navarino	61	144
Pella	111	309
Pulaski, vil.		
Wards 4, 7	16	35
Red Springs		
Wards 1 – 2	195	177
Richmond		
Wards 1 – 3	254	649
Seneca	79	178
Shawano, city		
Wards 1 – 2	194	329
Wards 3 – 4	230	294
Wards 5 – 6	188	288
Wards 7 – 8	192	267
Wards 9 – 10	248	337
Wards 11 – 12	296	299
Tigerton, vil.	98	169
Washington		
Wards 1 – 3	274	583
Waukechon		
Wards 1 – 2	133	337
Wescott		
Wards 1 – 4	508	935
Wittenberg		
Wards 1 – 2	124	239
Wittenberg, vil.		
Wards 1 – 2	143	172
TOTAL	5,730	10,937
SHEBOYGAN COUNTY		
Adell, vil.	50	183
Cascade, vil.	86	207
Cedar Grove, vil.		
Wards 1 – 3	171	849
Elkhart Lake, vil.		
Wards 1 – 2	236	368
Glenbeulah, vil.	85	139
Greenbush		
Wards 1 – 3	232	576
Herman		
Wards 1 – 3	239	627
Holland		
Wards 1 – 3	256	1,071
Howards Grove, vil.		
Wards 1 – 4	558	1,112
Kohler, vil.		
Wards 1 – 3	390	813
Lima		
Wards 1 – 4	337	1,230
Lyndon		
Wards 1 – 3	211	599
Mitchell		
Wards 1 – 3	180	446
Mosel	152	267
Oostburg, vil.		
Wards 1 – 4	241	1,427
Plymouth		
Wards 1 – 4	518	1,159
Plymouth, city		
Wards 1 – 3	328	546
Wards 4 – 6	399	603
Wards 7 – 9	375	552
Wards 10 – 12	292	585
Random Lake, vil.		
Wards 1 – 2	191	600
Rhine		
Wards 1 – 3	385	796
Russell	40	125
Scott		
Wards 1 – 3	182	728
Sheboygan		
Wards 1 – 10	1,354	2,425
Sheboygan, city		
Ward 1	486	576
Ward 2	383	419
Ward 3	326	374
Ward 4	308	269
Ward 5	414	499
Ward 6	101	108
Ward 7	36	55
Ward 8	182	208
Ward 9	51	43
Ward 10	267	274
Ward 11	320	278
Ward 12	309	319
Ward 13	449	399
Ward 14	248	187
Ward 15	141	118
Ward 16	295	391
Ward 17	294	309
Ward 18	270	223
Ward 19	449	475
Ward 20	353	328
Ward 21	166	160
Ward 22	486	472
Ward 23	425	593
Ward 24	482	549
Ward 25	356	448
Ward 26	364	460
Ward 27	0	0
Ward 28	0	0
Ward 29	0	0
Ward 30	0	0
Sheboygan Falls		
Wards 1 – 3	240	660
Sheboygan Falls, city		
Wards 1 – 2, 9	478	1,015
Wards 3 – 5	475	710
Wards 6 – 8	427	672
Sherman		
Wards 1 – 2	143	633
Waldo, vil.	50	182
Wilson		
Wards 1 – 4	693	1,289
TOTAL	17,955	31,728
TAYLOR COUNTY		
Aurora	57	97
Browning	74	244
Chelsea	77	231
Cleveland	24	94
Deer Creek	46	230
Ford	42	83
Gilman, vil.	80	92
Goodrich	55	169
Greenwood	61	192
Grover	16	94
Hammel		
Wards 1 – 2	69	237
Holway	33	158
Jump River	55	76
Little Black		
Wards 1 – 2	125	330
Lublin, vil.	16	30
Maplehurst	45	100
McKinley	33	116
Medford		
Wards 1 – 3	266	742
Medford, city		
Wards 1 – 8	575	982
Molitor	39	87
Pershing	24	51
Rib Lake		
Wards 1 – 2	77	234
Rib Lake, vil.	95	202
Roosevelt	57	96
Stetsonville, vil.	71	120
Taft	46	94
Westboro	90	225
TOTAL	2,248	5,406
TREMPEALEAU COUNTY		
Albion		
Wards 1 – 2	136	133
Arcadia		
Wards 1 – 4	264	446
Arcadia, city		
Wards 1 – 4	226	336
Blair, city		
Wards 1 – 3	233	153
Burnside		
Wards 1 – 2	65	103
Caledonia		
Wards 1 – 2	162	219
Chimney Rock	49	64

VOTE FOR GOVERNOR AND LIEUTENANT GOVERNOR BY WARD
November 4, 2014 General Election–Continued

District	Burke and Lehman (Dem.)	Walker and Kleefisch (Rep.)	District	Burke and Lehman (Dem.)	Walker and Kleefisch (Rep.)
Dodge	86	92	Boulder Junction		
Eleva, vil.	149	110	Wards 1 – 2	224	375
Ettrick			Cloverland		
Wards 1 – 2	287	288	Wards 1 – 2	206	375
Ettrick, vil.	95	120	Conover		
Gale			Wards 1 – 2	243	432
Wards 1 – 3	284	439	Eagle River, city		
Galesville, city			Wards 1 – 5	220	326
Wards 1 – 3	278	321	Lac du Flambeau		
Hale	206	233	Wards 1 – 7	649	489
Independence, city			Land O'Lakes	181	310
Wards 1 – 4	153	199	Lincoln		
Lincoln			Wards 1 – 5	450	834
Wards 1 – 2	125	120	Manitowish Waters	119	314
Osseo, city			Phelps		
Wards 1 – 3	329	296	Wards 1 – 2	225	444
Pigeon			Plum Lake		
Wards 1 – 2	126	155	Wards 1 – 2	108	216
Pigeon Falls, vil.	78	74	Presque Isle	174	311
Preston			St. Germain		
Wards 1 – 3	168	154	Wards 1 – 2	372	764
Strum, vil.			Washington		
Wards 1 – 3	250	180	Wards 1 – 3	342	524
Sumner	164	205	Winchester	89	186
Trempealeau			TOTAL	4,240	6,942
Wards 1 – 2	333	450	**WALWORTH COUNTY**		
Trempealeau, vil.			Bloomfield		
Wards 1 – 2	316	358	Wards 1 – 2	170	283
Unity			Bloomfield, vil.		
Wards 1 – 2	112	116	Wards 1 – 5	382	870
Whitehall, city			Burlington, city		
Wards 1 – 4	300	253	Ward 9	0	0
TOTAL	4,974	5,617	Darien		
VERNON COUNTY			Wards 1 – 3	224	471
Bergen			Darien, vil.		
Wards 1 – 3	324	340	Wards 1 – 2	214	310
Chaseburg, vil.	48	71	Delavan		
Christiana			Wards 1 – 11	698	1,477
Wards 1 – 2	182	214	Delavan, city		
Clinton			Wards 1 – 14	1,059	1,477
Wards 1 – 2	77	106	East Troy		
Coon			Ward 1	109	335
Wards 1 – 2	194	165	Wards 2 – 3	177	550
Coon Valley, vil.	158	162	Wards 4 – 6	245	740
De Soto, vil.	51	52	East Troy, vil.		
Forest	100	120	Wards 1 – 5	566	1,342
Franklin			Elkhorn, city		
Wards 1 – 2	183	276	Wards 1 – 7	1,336	2,152
Genoa			Ward 8	0	0
Wards 1 – 2	200	147	Fontana, vil.		
Genoa, vil.	68	46	Wards 1 – 3	256	502
Greenwood	86	94	Geneva		
Hamburg			Wards 1 – 8	635	1,361
Wards 1 – 2	211	263	Genoa City, vil.		
Harmony			Wards 1 – 4	272	514
Wards 1 – 3	137	146	Lafayette		
Hillsboro			Wards 1 – 3	278	720
Wards 1 – 3	104	187	La Grange		
Hillsboro, city			Wards 1 – 3	344	825
Wards 1 – 4	263	227	Lake Geneva, city		
Jefferson			Wards 1 – 2	311	409
Wards 1 – 4	227	260	Wards 3 – 4	253	320
Kickapoo	135	99	Wards 5 – 6, 10	249	425
La Farge, vil.	158	113	Wards 7 – 9, 11 – 14	231	343
Liberty	70	54	Linn		
Ontario, vil.	74	76	Wards 1 – 4, 6	236	582
Readstown, vil.	68	68	Ward 5	52	148
Stark			Lyons		
Wards 1 – 2	81	79	Wards 1 – 7	430	1,053
Sterling	89	172	Mukwonago, vil.		
Stoddard, vil.	196	142	Ward 11	17	35
Union			Richmond		
Wards 1 – 3	85	106	Wards 1 – 3	342	540
Viola, vil.	33	51	Sharon	111	262
Viroqua			Sharon, vil.		
Wards 1 – 4	383	403	Wards 1 – 2	185	267
Viroqua, city			Spring Prairie		
Wards 1 – 9	1,049	746	Wards 1 – 4	280	844
Webster			Sugar Creek		
Wards 1 – 2	172	111	Wards 1 – 5	606	1,169
Westby, city			Troy		
Wards 1 – 5	504	353	Wards 1 – 3	364	938
Wheatland	137	134	Walworth		
Whitestown	85	104	Wards 1 – 3	165	541
TOTAL	5,932	5,687	Walworth, vil.		
VILAS COUNTY			Wards 1 – 3	326	584
Arbor Vitae			Whitewater		
Wards 1 – 7	638	1,042	Wards 1 – 2	276	446
			Ward 3	21	38

VOTE FOR GOVENROR AND LIEUTENANT GOVERNOR BY WARD
November 4, 2014 General Election–Continued

District	Burke and Lehman (Dem.)	Walker and Kleefisch (Rep.)
Whitewater, city		
Wards 1 – 2	482	414
Wards 3 – 4	392	319
Wards 5 – 6	615	492
Wards 7 – 9	484	479
Williams Bay, vil.		
Wards 1 – 4	416	838
TOTAL	13,809	25,415
WASHBURN COUNTY		
Barronett	87	87
Bashaw		
Wards 1 – 3	183	285
Bass Lake	83	133
Beaver Brook		
Wards 1 – 3	139	194
Birchwood		
Wards 1 – 3	88	205
Birchwood, vil.	59	90
Brooklyn	68	72
Casey	100	124
Chicog		
Wards 1 – 2	72	61
Crystal		
Wards 1 – 2	50	74
Evergreen		
Wards 1 – 2	220	296
Frog Creek	29	45
Gull Lake	51	52
Long Lake	144	222
Madge		
Wards 1 – 3	143	130
Minong		
Wards 1 – 2	202	225
Minong, vil.	84	83
Sarona		
Wards 1 – 2	54	113
Shell Lake, city		
Wards 1 – 2	301	266
Spooner		
Wards 1 – 3	137	213
Spooner, city		
Wards 1 – 4	410	418
Springbrook	81	121
Stinnett	28	63
Stone Lake	76	132
Trego		
Wards 1 – 2	185	241
TOTAL	3,074	3,945
WASHINGTON COUNTY		
Addison		
Wards 1 – 6	332	1,518
Barton		
Wards 1 – 4	374	1,149
Erin		
Wards 1 – 4	465	1,785
Farmington		
Wards 1 – 5	369	1,569
Germantown	31	115
Germantown, vil.		
Wards 1, 8, 10 – 11	545	2,117
Wards 2, 5 – 7	687	1,653
Wards 3 – 4, 9, 16 – 17	670	1,887
Wards 12 – 15	654	2,181
Hartford		
Wards 1 – 5	398	1,582
Hartford, city		
Wards 1 – 2	201	663
Wards 3 – 5	281	811
Wards 6, 9 – 10, 15 – 17, 20, 23	455	1,186
Wards 7 – 8	74	194
Wards 11 – 14, 21 – 22	582	1,364
Jackson		
Wards 1 – 6	410	2,094
Jackson, vil.		
Wards 1 – 9	748	2,492
Ward 10	1	0
Kewaskum		
Wards 1 – 2	141	482
Kewaskum, vil.		
Wards 1 – 5	474	1,391
Milwaukee, city		
Ward 318	0	0
Newburg, vil.		
Wards 1 – 2	86	425
Polk		
Wards 1 – 6	411	1,823
Richfield, vil.		
Wards 1 – 2	293	1,292
Ward 3	147	442
Ward 4	119	640
Wards 5 – 6	361	1,577
Wards 7 – 9	410	1,477
Slinger, vil.		
Wards 1 – 8	569	1,832
Trenton		
Wards 1 – 2, 8	125	393
Wards 3 – 7	387	1,628
Wayne		
Wards 1 – 3	217	913
West Bend		
Wards 1 – 10	591	2,143
West Bend, city		
Wards 1 – 3	482	1,153
Wards 4 – 6	576	1,181
Wards 7 – 8	521	1,430
Wards 9 – 10	437	1,172
Wards 11 – 14	457	1,026
Wards 15 – 19	485	1,119
Wards 20 – 22	406	1,045
Wards 23 – 24, 26	535	1,331
Wards 25, 27	0	3
TOTAL	15,507	50,278
WAUKESHA COUNTY		
Big Bend, vil.		
Wards 1 – 3	158	493
Brookfield		
Wards 1, 3 – 4, 10	381	1,053
Wards 2, 5 – 8	554	1,255
Ward 9	71	175
Brookfield, city		
Ward 1	278	647
Ward 2	316	787
Ward 3	292	822
Ward 4	169	406
Ward 5	285	894
Ward 6	166	526
Ward 7	243	564
Ward 8	321	773
Ward 9	261	675
Ward 10	258	828
Ward 11	219	611
Ward 12	286	860
Ward 13	243	778
Ward 14	173	645
Ward 15	239	658
Ward 16	87	314
Ward 17	254	727
Ward 18	205	558
Ward 19	192	514
Ward 20	197	638
Ward 21	235	543
Ward 22	332	706
Ward 23	248	571
Ward 24	361	744
Butler, vil.		
Wards 1 – 3	269	547
Chenequa, vil.	40	288
Delafield		
Wards 1 – 2, 5 – 6	346	1,367
Wards 3 – 4	162	903
Wards 7 – 8	164	648
Wards 9 – 11	292	845
Delafield, city		
Wards 1 – 14	968	2,740
Dousman, vil.		
Wards 1 – 3	276	835
Eagle		
Wards 1 – 4	440	1,400
Eagle, vil.		
Wards 1 – 2	182	745
Elm Grove, vil.		
Wards 1 – 4	514	1,461
Wards 5 – 8	564	1,262
Genesee		
Wards 1, 3, 5, 9	298	1,094
Wards 2, 4, 10	344	1,052
Wards 6 – 8	391	1,183
Hartland, vil.		
Wards 1 – 6	575	1,514
Wards 7 – 13	488	1,724
Lac la Belle, vil.	26	159
Lannon, vil.		
Wards 1 – 2	151	412
Lisbon		
Wards 1, 6	406	1,419
Ward 2	325	904

Wisconsin State Symbols

11

Wisconsin state symbols: origin and descriptions of the official state symbols as specified by law

GAR Memorial Hall

(Wisconsin Veterans Museum)

WISCONSIN STATE SYMBOLS

(See front and back endpapers)

Over the years, the Wisconsin Legislature has officially recognized a wide variety of state symbols. In order of adoption, Wisconsin has designated an official seal, coat of arms, motto, flag, song, flower, bird, tree, fish, state animal, wildlife animal, domestic animal, mineral, rock, symbol of peace, insect, soil, fossil, dog, beverage, grain, dance, ballad, waltz, fruit, tartan, and pastry. (The "Badger State" nickname, however, remains unofficial.) These symbols provide a focus for expanding public awareness of Wisconsin's history and diversity. They are listed and described in Section 1.10 of the Wisconsin Statutes.

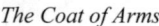

The Coat of Arms   *The Great Seal*

Seal and coat of arms. Article XIII, Section 4, of the Wisconsin Constitution requires the legislature to provide a "great seal" to be used by the secretary of state to authenticate all of the governor's official acts except laws. The seal consists of the coat of arms, described below, with the words "Great Seal of the State of Wisconsin" centered above and a curved line of 13 stars, representing the 13 original United States, centered below, surrounded by an ornamental border. A modified "lesser seal" serves as the seal of the secretary of state.

The coat of arms is an integral part of the state seal and also appears on the state flag. It contains a sailor with a coil of rope and a "yeoman" (usually considered a miner) with a pick, who jointly represent labor on water and land. These two figures support a quartered shield with symbols for agriculture (plow), mining (pick and shovel), manufacturing (arm and hammer), and navigation (anchor). Centered on the shield is a small U.S. coat of arms and the U.S. motto, "E pluribus unum" ("out of many, one"), referring to the union of U.S. states, to symbolize Wisconsin's loyalty to the Union. At the base, a cornucopia, or horn of plenty, stands for prosperity and abundance, while a pyramid of 13 lead ingots represents mineral wealth and the 13 original United States. Centered over the shield is a badger, the state animal, and the state motto "Forward" appears on a banner above the badger.

The history of the seal is inextricably entwined with that of the coat of arms. An official seal was created in 1836, when Wisconsin became a territory, and was revised in 1839. When Wisconsin achieved statehood in 1848, a new seal was prepared. This seal was changed in 1851 at the instigation of Governor Nelson Dewey and slightly modified to its current design in 1881 when Dewey's seal wore out and had to be recast. (See "Motto" below.) Chapter 280, Laws of 1881, provided the first precise statutory description of the great seal and coat of arms.

Motto: "Forward". The motto, "Forward", was introduced in the 1851 revision of the state seal and coat of arms. Governor Dewey had asked University of Wisconsin Chancellor John H. Lathrop to design a new seal. It is alleged the motto was selected during a chance meeting between Governor Dewey and Edward Ryan (later chief justice of the Wisconsin Supreme Court) when the governor went to New York City, carrying the Lathrop design to the engraver. Ryan objected to the Latin motto, "Excelsior", which Lathrop proposed. According to tradition,

Dewey and Ryan sat down on the steps of a Wall Street bank, designed a new seal and chose "Forward" on the spot.

Flag. An official design for Wisconsin's state flag was initially provided by the legislature in 1863. Noting that a flag had not been adopted and that Civil War regiments in the field were requesting flags, the legislature formed a 5-member joint select committee to report "a description for a proper state flag." This action resulted in the adoption of 1863 Joint Resolution 4, which provided a design for a state flag that was substantially the same as the regimental flags already in use by Wisconsin troops.

It was not until 1913, however, that language concerning flag specifications was added to the Wisconsin Statutes. Chapter 111, Laws of 1913, created a state flag provision, specifying a dark blue flag with the state coat of arms centered on each side.

The 1913 design remained unchanged until the enactment of Chapter 286, Laws of 1979, which culminated years of legislative efforts to alter or replace Wisconsin's flag so it would be more distinctive and recognizable. The most significant changes made by the 1979 act were adding the word "Wisconsin" and the statehood date "1848" in white letters, centered respectively above and below the coat of arms.

Song: "On, Wisconsin!" The music for "On, Wisconsin!" was composed in 1909 by William T. Purdy with the idea of entering it in a contest for the creation of a new University of Minnesota football song. ("Minnesota" would have replaced "On, Wisconsin" in the opening lines.) Carl Beck persuaded Purdy to dedicate the song to the University of Wisconsin football team instead, and Beck collaborated with the composer by writing the lyrics. The song was introduced at the Madison campus in November 1909. It was later acclaimed by world-famous composer and bandmaster John Philip Sousa as the best college song he had ever heard.

Lyrics more in keeping with the purposes of a state song were subsequently written in 1913 by Judge Charles D. Rosa and J. S. Hubbard, editor of the *Beloit Free Press*. Rosa and Hubbard were among the delegates from many states convened in 1913 to commemorate the centennial of the Battle of Lake Erie. Inspired by the occasion, they provided new, more solemn words to the already well-known football song.

Although "On, Wisconsin!" was widely recognized as Wisconsin's song, the state did not officially adopt it until 1959. Representative Harold W. Clemens discovered that Wisconsin was one of only 10 states without an official song. He introduced a bill to give the song the status he thought it deserved. On discovering that many different lyrics existed, an official text for the first verse was incorporated in Chapter 170, Laws of 1959:

On, Wisconsin! On, Wisconsin! Grand old badger state!
We, thy loyal sons and daughters, Hail thee, good and great.
On, Wisconsin! On, Wisconsin! Champion of the right,
'Forward', our motto — God will give thee might!

Flower: wood violet *(Viola papilionacea)*. In 1908, Wisconsin school children nominated four candidates for state flower: the violet, wild rose, trailing arbutus, and white water lily. On Arbor Day 1909, the final vote was taken, and the violet won. Chapter 218, Laws of 1949, named the wood violet Wisconsin's official flower.

Bird: robin *(Turdus migratorius)*. In 1926-27, Wisconsin school children voted to select a state bird. The robin received twice as many votes as those given any other bird. Chapter 218, Laws of 1949, officially made the robin the state bird.

Tree: sugar maple *(Acer saccharum)*. A favorite state tree was first selected by a vote of Wisconsin school children in 1893. The maple tree won, followed by oak, pine, and elm. Another vote was conducted in 1948 among school children by the Youth Centennial Committee. In that election, the sugar maple again received the most votes, followed by white pine and birch. The 1949 Legislature, in spite of efforts by white pine advocates, named the sugar maple the official state tree by enacting Chapter 218, Laws of 1949.

Fish: muskellunge *(Esox masquinongy)*. Members of the legislature attempted to adopt the muskellunge as the state fish as early as 1939. The trout was a very distant alternative suggestion. In 1955, the legislature unanimously passed legislation which became Chapter 18, Laws of 1955, to designate the muskellunge as Wisconsin's official fish.

Animals: badger *(Taxidea taxus)*, **white-tailed deer** *(Odocoileus virginianus)*, **dairy cow** *(Bos taurus)*. Although the *badger* has been closely associated with Wisconsin since territorial days, it was not declared the official state animal until 1957. Over the years, its likeness had been incorporated in the state coat of arms, the seal, the flag, and even State Capitol architecture, as well as being immortalized in the song, "On, Wisconsin!" ("Grand old badger state!"). "Bucky Badger" has long been the mascot of the UW-Madison. In 1957, a bill to establish the badger as state animal was introduced at the request of four Jefferson County elementary school students who discovered from a historical society publication that the badger had not been given the official status most people assumed. Serious opposition developed, however, when a faction from Wisconsin's northern counties introduced a bill to make the *white-tailed deer* the official animal, citing the state's large native deer population, the animal's physical attributes, and the considerable economic benefits derived from the annual deer hunt. The legislature reached a compromise by adding two official animals. In Chapter 209, Laws of 1957, it named the badger the "state animal", and Chapter 147 designated the white-tailed deer as the state "wildlife animal".

The *dairy cow* was added as Wisconsin's official "domestic animal" by Chapter 167, Laws of 1971, in recognition of the animal's many contributions to the state. This action was termed a logical and long overdue step, consistent with the state's reputation as *America's Dairyland*, the slogan placed on state automobile license plates by Chapter 115, Laws of 1939. Governor Patrick Lucey issued 1972 Executive Order 32 recognizing the Holstein-Friesian breed as Wisconsin's official state dairy cow until May 31, 1973. He also directed the Secretary of Agriculture to designate on June 1 of each year a different breed, selected from Wisconsin's purebred dairy cows, to be the official state dairy cow. In keeping with a succession plan adopted by the Wisconsin Purebred Dairy Cattle Association whose members represent the seven major dairy breeds (Ayrshire, Brown Swiss, Guernsey, Holstein, Jersey, Milking Shorthorn, and Red & White Holstein), the Holstein is designated as the 2015 Cow of the Year, followed by the in Ayrshire 2016. Members of the association also select an individual cow to represent the breed as Cow of the Year.

Badger nickname. History, rather than the law, explains Wisconsin's unofficial nickname as the "Badger State". During the lead-mining boom that began just prior to 1830 in southwestern Wisconsin, the name was first applied to miners who were too busy digging the "gray gold" to build houses. Like badgers, they moved into abandoned mine shafts and makeshift burrows for shelter. Although "badgers" had a somewhat derogatory connotation at first, it gradually gained acceptance as an apt description of the hardworking and energetic settlers of the Wisconsin Territory.

Mineral and rock: galena (lead sulphide) and **red granite.** Galena was made the official state mineral and red granite the state rock by Chapter 14, Laws of 1971. The proposal was introduced at the request of the Kenosha Gem and Mineral Society to promote geological awareness. Galena met the criteria for selection, as set by the Wisconsin Geological Society, including abundance, uniqueness, economic value, historical significance, and native nature. Red granite is an igneous rock composed of quartz and feldspar. It is mined in several sections of the state and was selected as the state rock because of its economic importance.

Symbol of peace: mourning dove *(Zenaidura macroura).* Various individuals and organizations concerned with conservation and wildlife long sought a protected status for the dove. Concluding an effort that stretched over a decade, the mourning dove was added as Wisconsin's official symbol of peace and removed from the statutory definition of game birds by Chapter 129, Laws of 1971. However, an increase in the mourning dove population led to its reinstatement as a game bird in 2001 and loss of its protected status.

Insect: honey bee *(Apis mellifera).* The honey bee was designated the official state insect by Chapter 326, Laws of 1977. The bill was introduced at the request of the third grade class of Holy Family School of Marinette and the Wisconsin Honey Producers Association. Attempts to allow all elementary school pupils in the state to decide the selection by popular ballot were unsuccessful. Other contenders for the title were the monarch butterfly, dragonfly, ladybug, and mosquito.

Soil: Antigo Silt Loam *(Typic glossoboralf).* An official state soil was created by 1983 Wisconsin Act 33 to remind Wisconsinites of their soil stewardship responsibilities. Advocates argued that soil, a natural resource that took 10,000 years to produce, is essential to Wisconsin's economy and is also the foundation of life. Selected to represent the more than 500 major soil types in Wisconsin, Antigo Silt Loam is a productive, level, silty soil of glacial origin, subsequently enriched by organic matter from prehistoric forests. The soil, named after a Wisconsin city, is found chiefly in Wisconsin and stretches in patches across the north central part of the state. It is a versatile soil that supports dairying, potato growing, and timber. The addition of the state soil was the result of a successful drive led by Professor Francis D. Hole, a UW-Madison soil scientist.

Fossil: trilobite *(Calymene celebra)*. The trilobite was designated the official state fossil by 1985 Wisconsin Act 162. Pronounced "TRY-loh-bite", the Latin term describes the 3-lobed anatomy of this small invertebrate body divided by furrows into segments. The trilobite is an extinct marine arthropod with multiple sets of paired, jointed legs. Its head and tapering body were armored in an exoskeleton that was repeatedly molted as the animal grew. Trilobites flourished in the warm, shallow saltwater sea that periodically covered Wisconsin territory hundreds of millions of years ago. Their fossil remains average 1 to 2 inches in length. The largest complete specimen is 14 inches, while incomplete parts indicate some were possibly much longer (over 30 inches). Trilobite fossils are abundant and distinctive enough to be easily recognized. Good specimens are preserved in rock formations throughout most of Wisconsin.

The Wisconsin Geological Society proposed the fossil to symbolize Wisconsin's ancient past and encourage interest in the state's rich geological heritage. A major rival for recognition as state fossil was the mastodon, a large prehistoric, elephant-like creature.

Dog: American water spaniel. The American water spaniel was named Wisconsin's official state dog by 1985 Wisconsin Act 295. Enactment of the law was the culmination of years of effort by eighth grade students of Lyle Brumm at Washington Junior High School in New London. The American water spaniel is said to be one of only five dog breeds indigenous to the United States and the only one native to Wisconsin. A New London area physician, Dr. Fred J. Pfeifer, is generally credited with developing and standardizing the breed and working to secure United Kennel Club registration for it in 1920. American Kennel Club recognition followed in 1940. The American water spaniel was developed as a practical, versatile hunting dog that combined certain physical attributes with intelligence and a good disposition. No flashy show animal, the American water spaniel is described as an unadorned, utilitarian dog that earns its keep as an outstanding hunter, watchdog, and family pet.

Beverage: milk. The Wisconsin Legislature designated milk as the official state beverage by 1987 Wisconsin Act 279. This action recognized Wisconsin's position as the nation's leading milk-producing state and the contribution of milk to the state's economy. The World Dairy Expo and various Wisconsin dairy production and dairy cattle associations supported the legislation.

Grain: corn *(Zea mays)*. Corn was designated the official state grain by 1989 Wisconsin Act 162. During legislative debate, sponsors claimed designating corn as the state grain would draw attention to its importance as a cash crop in Wisconsin and make people more aware of corn's many uses, including livestock feed, sweeteners, ethanol fuel, and biodegradable plastics.

Dance: polka. The polka was designated the state dance by 1993 Wisconsin Act 411. The legislation was introduced at the request of a second grade class from Charles Lindbergh Elementary School in Madison and supported by several groups, including the Wisconsin Polka Boosters, Inc., and the Wisconsin Folk Museum. Supporters documented the polka heritage of Wisconsin and provided evidence that the polka is deeply ingrained in Wisconsin cultural traditions.

Ballad: "Oh Wisconsin, Land of My Dreams". "Oh Wisconsin, Land of My Dreams" was designated the Wisconsin state ballad by 2001 Wisconsin Act 16. The ballad was the work of Shari Sarazin of Mauston, who set to music a poem written in the 1920s by her grandmother, Erma Barrett of Juneau County. The words to this ballad are:

> Oh Wisconsin, land of beauty, with your hillsides and your plains, with your jackpine and your birch tree, and your oak of mighty frame.
>
> Land of rivers, lakes and valleys, land of warmth and winter snows, land of birds and beasts and humanity, Oh Wisconsin, I love you so.
>
> Oh Wisconsin, land of my dreams. Oh Wisconsin, you're all I'll ever need. A little heaven here on earth could you be? Oh Wisconsin, land of my dreams.
>
> In the summer, golden grain fields; in the winter, drift of white snow; in the springtime, robins singing; in the autumn, flaming colors show.
>
> Oh I wonder who could wander, or who could want to drift for long, away from all your beauty, all your sunshine, all your sweet song?

Oh Wisconsin, land of my dreams. Oh Wisconsin, you're all I'll ever need. A little heaven here on earth could you be? Oh Wisconsin, land of my dreams.

Oh Wisconsin, land of my dreams. And when it's time, let my spirit run free in Wisconsin, land of my dreams.

Waltz: "The Wisconsin Waltz". "The Wisconsin Waltz" was designated the state waltz by 2001 Wisconsin Act 16. The music and lyrics were written by Eddie Hansen, a Waupaca native and one-time theater organist. The words to this waltz are:

Music from heaven throughout the years; the beautiful Wisconsin Waltz.

Favorite song of the pioneers; the beautiful Wisconsin Waltz.

Song of my heart on that last final day, when it is time to lay me away. One thing I ask is to let them play the beautiful Wisconsin Waltz.

My sweetheart, my complete heart, it's for you when we dance together; the beautiful Wisconsin Waltz.

I remember that September, before love turned into an ember, we danced to the Wisconsin Waltz.

Summer ended, we intended that our lives then would both be blended, but somehow our planning got lost.

Memory now sings a dream song, a faded love theme song; the beautiful Wisconsin Waltz.

Fruit: cranberry *(Vaccinium macrocarpon).* The cranberry was designated the state fruit by 2003 Wisconsin Act 174. The legislation was the culmination of a class project by fifth grade students from Trevor Grade School in Kenosha County, who decided that the cranberry, rather than the cherry, was the best candidate for Wisconsin's state fruit. Wisconsin leads the nation in cranberry production, accounting for over half of the nation's output. Cranberries are grown in 20 of Wisconsin's 72 counties, primarily in the central part of the state.

Tartan. The state tartan was created by 2007 Wisconsin Act 217. Legislation was introduced at the request of the Saint Andrew's Society of Milwaukee, which had formed a committee to recommend an appropriate design. The design selected was chosen to reflect the diversity and uniqueness of the state. Historically, tartans served to identify Scottish highland clans and families.

Wisconsin's tartan is a hunting tartan with a blue green background and multiple stripes of various colors. The color scheme reflects the tartans of many notable Wisconsin families of Scottish ancestry and the natural resources and industries of Wisconsin. The color brown represents the fur trade; grey represents lead mining; green represents the lumber industry; blue reflects the two Great Lakes bordering Wisconsin, commercial and recreational fishing, and the resort industry; yellow signifies the dairy and brewing industries; red represents the University of Wisconsin System; and, where yellow and green stripes intersect, it represents Wisconsin's professional sports teams, exemplified by the Green Bay Packers.

Pastry: kringle. 2013 Wisconsin Act 20 designated the kringle as the state pastry. The kringle is a flaky dough pastry that can be filled with fruit, nuts, or other filling and baked with icing. The proposal was supported by the city of Racine, as they are a mass producer of the pastry.

Alphabetical Index

12

George and Thomas Tuffley, father and son, enlisted in Company K, 12th Wisconsin Infantry Regiment in 1861.

(Wisconsin Veterans Museum)

ALPHABETICAL INDEX

A

Page

Abrahamson, Shirley S., supreme
   court justice **8**, 9, 558, 563, 708
Academic excellence division for,
   public instruction department 456, **458-59**
Accidents, traffic, *see* Motor vehicles, crashes
Accounting examining board 331, **474-75**, 480
Acid deposition research council 356
Acts, Wisconsin (session laws) 253-54, 255, 257
Adamczyk Matt, state treasurer **6**, 7, 485,
                                705, 919-20
Adjutant general 331, **433**, 438
   list of, 1839 – 1962, *see 1962 Blue Book*, 200
Administration department 314, 331,
                                   349-71
Administrative code 255, 259, 265-66, 274
Administrative judicial districts 568
Administrative law, significant legislation,
   2013 session 291
Administrative rules clearinghouse 274
Administrative rules review committee 265-66
Adoption disruption and dissolution,
   study committee 276
Adoption and medical assistance
   interstate compact 555
Adult education, vocational 487-88
Adult institutions division, corrections
   department 386, **390-91**
Adult offender supervision board
   interstate 331, **393**
   compact for .555
Aerospace Authority, Wisconsin. 331, **531**
AFDC, *see* Wisconsin Works (W-2)
Affirmative action, council on 331, **368**
Affirmative action division, office of state
   employee relations 366, **367**
Aging and long-term care, board on 331, **356-58**
Agreement on detainers 555
Agricultural development division,
   agriculture, trade and consumer
   protection department 372, **374**
Agricultural education and workforce
   development council 376-77
Agricultural producer security council 377
Agricultural resource management division,
   agriculture, trade and consumer
   protection department 372, **374**
Agricultural safety and health center 514
Agricultural statistician, state 372
Agricultural statistics 598-606
Agricultural statistics service, Wisconsin 372
Agriculture, trade and consumer protection
   board 331, **371**, 374
   department 331, **371-79**
Aid to families with dependent children,
   see Wisconsin Works (W-2)
Air, waste, and remediation & redevelopment,
   division, natural resources
   department 441-42, **444-45**
Air pollution 441-42, 444-45, 638
Airports, *see* Aviation
Alcohol and other drug abuse,
   state council on **317-18**, 331

Alcohol and other drug abuse programs,
   council on .462
Allen, Scott, representative **85**, 897-911
Allen, Ray, secretary,
   financial institutions department. 335, 399
America's Dairyland. 952
Anderson, Eloise, secretary, children and
   families department 333, 379
Anderson, Terry C., director, legislative
   council 272
Anesthesiologists assistants, council on **478**, 481
Animal health division, agriculture,
   trade and consumer protection
   department 372, **374-75**
Animals, state (badger, cow, white-tailed deer) . . .951-52
Appeals court 559, **565-66**
   vote for judges 880-81
Appellate division, state public
   defender office. 454, **455**
Appointments by governor 320-47
Apportionment
   maps of districts. 17, 20-98
   population of districts. 17, 249
   special articles in prior *Blue Books* 170
Apprenticeship and training 524, 525
Apprenticeship council 527
Appropriations, obligations annual 829
Archaeologist, state 418
Architects, landscape architects, professional
   engineers, designers and professional
   land surveyors examining board. . . . 332, **475**, 480
Archivist, state .418
Articles, special, in *Blue Books*, 1970 to 2013 170
Artistic endowment foundation,
   Wisconsin 332, **539**
Arts board 332, **491**
Asian population. 784, 786, 787, 791
Assembly
   caucus chairpersons. **39, 49**, 238
   chief clerk. 19, **86**, 238, 246,
                                  713-14
   committees 244-45. 261-63
   compensation 242
   composition 258
   elections. 897-911
   employees. 246
   majority leader 19, **23**, 238, 242, 711-12
      assistant majority leader 19, **35**, 238, 242
   maps of districts. 20-84, 88-98
   members, biographies and photos 21-85
   members, list of, 1848 – 2007
      see 2007-2008 Blue Book, 119-89
   minority leader 19, **63**, 238, 242, 711-12
      assistant minority leader 19, **67**, 238, 242
   officers 19, 238, 240-42, 709-12
   profile 239-46
   sergeant at arms 19, **86**, 238, 246, 713-14
   sessions 243, 244, 715-19
   speaker 19, **61**, 238, 240-42, 709-10
   speaker pro tempore 19, **41**, 238, 242
   term of office 239
Assessment of general property 830-31
Assessment of manufacturing property 472

Assessors, state board of. 472
Assigned counsel division, state public
    defender office. 454, **455**
Associations, statewide 608-22
Athletic trainers affiliated credentialing
    board. 332, **476**, 481
Attorney general 306, 307, 428, 430, 917-18
    biography and photo **6**, 7
    list of, 1848 – 2015 705-06
Attorneys, admission to bar 579-80
Auctioneer board. 332, **478**, 480
Audit bureau, legislative. 284-86
Audit committee, joint legislative 272
August, Tyler, representative 19, **41**, 238, 897-911
Autism council. .321
Authorities, state 308-09, **531-38**
Automatic fire sprinkler system contractors
    and journeymen council **478**, 480
Automobiles
    crashes .836-38
    registrations. 500, 835
    usage and gasoline mileage. 623, 625
Aviation 501, 832, 833
    fuel tax 814

B

BadgerCare plus program 410, **807-08**
Baldwin, Tammy, U.S. senator. **11**, 724
Ballad, state ("Oh Wisconsin, Land
    of My Dreams") 953-54
Ballweg, Joan, representative **47**, 897-911
Banking division, financial institutions
    department. 400, **401-02**
Banking review board 332, **403**
Banks, statistics 628-30
Bar association, *see* State bar of Wisconsin
Bar examiners board 560, **579-80**
Baraboo/Sauk county college – UW. 513, 642, 643
Barca, Peter W., representative 19, **63**, 238, 711-12,
                  897-911
Barnes, Mandela, representative. **27**, 897-911
Barron county college – UW 513, 642, 643
Bay-Lake regional planning
    commission 540
Berceau, Terese, representative **71**, 897-911
Bernier, Kathleen, representative **65**, 897-911
Bewley, Janet, senator **68**, 891-96
Beverage, state (milk) 953
Beverages, significant legislation,
    2013 session 291
Bicycle coordinating council 321-22
Biennial session 239
Billings, Jill, representative **83**, 897-911
Bioenergy council 378
Biographies and pictures. 4-86
    index to biographies 2-3
Bird, state (robin) 951
Birth defect prevention and
    surveillance, council on 413-14
Birth records, statistics. . . . . 313, 792 ,793
Black population. 784, 786, 787, 791
Blazel, Edward (Ted) A., senate sergeant
    at arms 18, **86**, 238, 714

Blind
    blind and visual impairment
        education council 463
    blindness council 414
    business enterprise program 526
    center for blind and visually impaired 457, 460
Blue Book 288
    artwork and photographs ii
    distribution i
    governor's foreword iii
    introduction . . . . iv-v
    special articles in prior *Blue Books* 170
    table of contents. . . . . vi-x
Boll, Lorna Hemp, commissioner
    tax appeals commission 345, 369
Born, Mark, representative **45**, 897-911
Bowen, David, representative 27, 897-911
Bradley, Ann Walsh, supreme court
    justice **8**, 9, 558, 563, 708, 879
Bradley center sports and entertainment
    corporation. 309, 332, **539**
Brancel, Ben, secretary,
    agriculture, trade and consumer
    protection department 331, 371
Brandtjen, Janel, representative **35**, 897-911
Broadcasting stations 779-81
Brooks, Ed, representative. **53**, 897-911
Brooks, Robert, representative. **59**, 897-911
Brostoff, Jonathan, representative **33**, 897-911
Brown, Ellsworth H., director,
    state historical society 418
Budget, state 254-55, 315, 316, 350, 353
    statistics. 813-23
Building code council, commercial 332, **479**, 480
Building commission 267-68, 333
Building inspector review board. 333, **478**, 482
Building program, state 267-68, 354
Buildings and safety, significant legislation
    2013 session. 291
Bulletin of proceedings 244, 255
Burial sites preservation board. 333, **422**
Business and communications services,
    division, public service commission. 465, **466**
Business and consumer law, significant legislation,
    2013 session 291-92, 304
Business development office, administration
    department. 358
Business management division,
    transportation department 496, **500**

C

Campaign financing 240, 405, 406, 874-76
Capital area regional planning
    commission 541
Capitol and executive residence
    board, state. 345, **365-66**
Capitol police division,
    administration department 350, **353**
Capitol press corps. 247
Capitol visitor's guide 171-72
Carpenter, Tim, senator **24**, 891-96
Cartographer, state 514
Caucus chairpersons **38**, **43**, **49**, **66**, 238
Caucuses, legislative. 238, 240

Cemetery board 333, **478**, 480
Centers for the developmentally
    disabled 408, 410, 810
Central Wisconsin center for the
    developmentally disabled 408, 410, 810
Certification standards review council. 356
CESA, *see* Cooperative educational
    service agencies
Champagne, Richard A., chief, legislative
    reference bureau 287
Chandler, Richard G., secretary,
    revenue department 344, 469
Charitable gaming 352, 354
Charter schools, statistics 650
Chief clerks, legislature 18, 19, **86**, 238, 242, 246
    list of, 1848 – 2015 713-14
Child abuse and neglect prevention
    board 333, **384-85**
Children
    child support 381
    disabled .459-60
    institutions for. 389-90, 391, 809
    significant legislation, 2013 session 292
Children and families, department. 314, 333,
                                   379-85
Chippewa valley correctional treatment
    facility 387
Chiropractic examining board 334, **475**, 480
Christman, Joe, state auditor. 284
Cigarette tax 814
Circuit courts. 559, **567-73**
    clerks 732
    current judges 570-73
    vote for judges 882-84
Circus world museum 419
    foundation. 333, 419
Cities
    government .233
    incorporation year, number,
        population. 735-38, 745
Civil defense,
    see Emergency management division
Civil law, significant court decisions 594-96
Civil service, *see* Classified service
Claims (against the state) board 333, **358-59**
Classified service 309, 366-68,
                              725, 726
Climate
    temperature and precipitation. 674
Coastal management council,
    Wisconsin .322
Coat of arms, state 950
Collective bargaining 367-68
College savings program board 333, **359**
Colleges, University of Wisconsin. . . . 512-13, 642, 643
Colleges and universities, private 646
Columbia correctional institution 386, 809
Commerce and industry 311-12
    special articles in prior *Blue Books* 170
    statistics .623-30
Commercial fishing boards 338, 452-53
Committees,
    governors special 321-30
    legislative 244-46, 260-63, 265-82
    legislative council. 275-79

Communications bureau,
    tourism department 489, **490**
Community corrections division,
    corrections department. 389, **391**
Community youth and family aids program. 391
Compensation and labor relations
    division, state employment
    relations office 366, **367**
Congressional district map,
    population 17
Congressional representatives from
    Wisconsin 11-16
    list of, 1848 – 2015 720-24
    territory of Wisconsin,
        see 1944 Blue Book, 354
    vote 885-90
Conlin, Robert, secretary, employee
    trust funds department 397
Conservation, *see* Environment
Conservation and recreation statistics 631-40
Conservation congress 451
Conservation fund 819
Considine, Dave, representative **73**, 897-911
Constitution party, state 845-50
Constitution, Wisconsin **176-217**, 230, 231, 239
    table of contents. 174-75
    votes on amendments 218-24
Constitutional amendments 218-24
    elections. 877, 878
    significant legislation, 2013 session 292
Constitutional law,
    significant court decisions 586-94
Constitutional officers, departments 307
    attorney general 6, 7, 306, 307, 428-33
    list of, 1848 – 2015 705-06
    biographies and photos 4-7
    current, list of 306
    election statistics 912-48
    governor. 4, 5, 306, 307, 316-19
    list of, since 1848 703
    lieutenant governor 4, 7, 306, 307, 348-49
    list of, 1848 – 2015 704
    public instruction, state
        superintendent 6, 7, 306, 307, 456-65
    list of, 1848 – 2015 706
    residences .306
    salaries 306
    secretary of state 6, 7, 306, 307, 484-85
    list of, 1848 – 2015 704-05
    state treasurer **6**, 7, 306, 307, 485
    list of, 1848 – 2015 705
Consumer protection. 311-12, 372, 375
Contractor certification council **479**, 481
Controlled substances board 333, **478**, 481
Conveyance safety code council 333, **479**, 481
Cooperative educational service
    agencies (CESA) 651
Copper Lake school 390, 809
Corporate and consumer services
    division, financial
    institutions department. 400, **402**
Corporations 312, 400, 402
    income tax 814, 824
    nonprofit 309, 539
    statistics 628
Correctional institutions
    adult 386-89, 809

juvenile 389-90, 809
    population and expenditures 809, 811
Corrections compact 555
Corrections department 314, 333, **385-94**
    parole and probation,
        see Division of hearings and appeals
Cosmetology examining board 333, **475**, 481
Counselors examining board,
    see Marriage and family therapy,
        professional counseling and
        social work examining board
Counties
    clerks' addresses 731
    area 729
    board chairpersons 233, 730
    circuit court clerks 232, 732
    clerks 232, 731
    coroners 233, 733
    county seats 729
    creation date 729
    district attorneys 232, 733
    executives, administrators 233, 730
    highways 834
    medical examiners 233, 733
    number of 232, 725
    population 729, 748-60, 785
    registers of deeds 232, 732
    sheriffs 232, 733
    supervisors, number of 232, 730
    surveyors 232, 734
    treasurers 232, 732
Court commissioners
    circuit court 568-69
    supreme court .563
Courts 230, 232, **559-74**
    administrative districts, circuit
        courts 568
    appeals court 559, **565-66**
    circuit courts 559, **567-69**
    commissioners 563, 568-69
    director of state courts 560, **575**
    elections 879-84
    judges 558, 563, 565, 567, 570-73
    law library, state 560, **575-76**
    municipal courts 560, **574**
    profile 559-62
    supreme court 558, 559, **563**
    supreme court, appeals court
        decisions 586-96
Cowles, Robert L., senator **22**
    see also 2013-2014 Blue Book, 887-94
Craig, David, representative **75**, 897-911
Credit relief outreach program 537
Credit union review board 333, **404**
Credit unions, office of 333, **404**
Credit unions, statistics 630
Crematory authority council 334, **479**, 481
Crime, significant legislation,
    2013 session 292-93
Crime victim compensation program 430
Crime victims council 431-32
Crime victims rights board 334, **432**
Crime victims services office, justice
    department 428, **430**
Criminal investigation division,
    justice department 428-29, **430-31**
Criminal justice coordinating council 322-23

Criminals, legal representation,
    see State public defender office
Criminal penalties, joint review
    committee **268**, 334
Criminal penalties, study committee
    on the review of 277
Crooks, N. Patrick, supreme
    court justice 9, **10**, 558, 563, 708
Cross, Raymond W., president,
    University of Wisconsin system 504
Curriculum advisory committee,
    law enforcement standards board 432-33
Customer and employee services division,
    natural resources department 442, **445**
Czaja, Mary, representative **43**, 897-911

D

Dance, state (polka) 953
Danou, Chris, representative **81**, 897-911
Darling, Alberta, senator **34**
    see also 2013-2014 Blue Book, 887-94
Deaf, school for 460
Deaf and hard of hearing, council for the 334, **414**
Deaf and hard-of-hearing
    education council 463-64
Death records, statistics 313, 792, 793
Debt, public 353, 827-29
Deferred compensation board 334, **398-99**
Delinquent children 389-90, 391, 809
Democratic party, state **851-55**
Dentistry examining board 334, **475**, 481
Departments of state government 308
Dependent children, aid to families
    with, *see* Wisconsin Works (W-2)
Depository selection board 359
Designers examining board,
    see Architects, landscape architects,
        professional engineers, designers and
        professional land surveyors examining board
Detainers, agreement on 555
Developmental disabilities, board
    for people with 334, **362**
Developmentally disabled 408, 410
Dietitians, affiliated credentialing
    board 334, **476**, 481
Disabilities
    blind and visual impairment
        education council 463
    blindness council 414
    deaf and hard of hearing, council for the 334, **414**
    deaf and hard-of-hearing education
        council 463-64
    disabilities, governor's committee
        for people with 323
    education .459-60
    institutions 408, **410**, 809
    physical disabilities, council on 342, **416**
    special education, council on 465
    student grants 417
    vocational rehabilitation 524
Disabilities, council on physical 342, **416**
Disabilities, governor's committee for
    people with 323
Disability board 319
Discrimination in employment 314, 524, **525**

Disease prevention. 408, 411
District attorneys. 232, 733
Districts, special 309
Divorces 313, 792, 794
Document depository libraries, Wisconsin 658
Dodge correctional institution 386, 392, 809
Dog, state (American water spaniel). 953
Domestic abuse, council on 334, **383**
Doyle, Steve, representative **83**, 897-911
Driver licensing 496, 500
Dry cleaner environmental response
　　council 334, **447**
Duffy, Sean P., congressman. **16**, 720, 723, 885-90
Dunbar, Maj. Gen. Donald P.,
　　adjutant general 331, 433
Dwelling code council, Uniform. 335, **479**, 481

E

Early care and education division,
　　children and families department 380, **381**
Early childhood advisory council 323-24
Early intervention interagency coordinating
　　council (Birth to three). 324
East Central Wisconsin regional
　　planning commission 541
Eau Claire campus, UW system **506**, 642, 643
Economic development corporation
　　authority, Wisconsin 335, **531-33**
Economic development, state 312, 335, 531-33
Edming, James W., representative **77**, 897-911
Education
　　significant legislation, 2013 session 294-97, 304
　　special articles in prior *Blue Books* 170
　　statistics. 641-59
Education commission of the states 335, **546**
Education division, educational
　　communications board. 395
Educational approval board 335, **488-89**
Educational communications board 335, **394-96**
Educational radio and television . . . 394-96, 779-81
Election administration council 406
Election process, Wisconsin 870-76
Election statistics
　　circuit court judges, 2014-2015. 882-84
　　constitutional amendments,. 877, 878
　　　　historical table 218-24
　　court of appeals judges, 2014-2015. 880-81
　　governor
　　　　historical table 703
　　　　vote by county 912, 914
　　　　by ward. 921-48
　　lieutenant governor
　　　　vote by county 913, 914
　　　　by ward. 921-48
　　members of 114th Congress, 2014 885-90
　　president,
　　　　historical table 696-98
　　representatives to the assembly
　　　　vote by county, 2013-2015. 897-905
　　　　vote by district, 2013-2015 906-11
　　state senators
　　　　vote by county, 2013-2015. 891-94
　　　　vote by district, 2013-2015 895-96

statewide referenda, historical table 225-26
supreme court justices, 2015 879
Elections
　　significant legislation, 2013 session 297
Elections division, government
　　accountability board 405
Elections in Wisconsin. 869-948
Elective state officers 4-7, 306
　　list of, 1848 – 2015 703-06
Electronic recording council. 335, **359**
Emergency management assistance compact 555
Emergency management division,
　　military affairs department. . . .335, **436-38, 440-41**
Emergency medical services board 335, **416**
Employee trust funds
　　board 335, **397**
　　department 314, **397-99**
Employees, legislature. 246
Employees suggestion board, state 366, **368**
Employment
　　local government 726-27
　　significant legislation, 2013 session 297-99, 304
　　state government 309-10, 315, 725-27
Employment and income statistics. 660-70
Employment and training division,
　　workforce development department 524, **525**
Employment programs. 522-30
Employment relations
　　commission 314, 335, **529-30**
　　office, state 309-10, 314, 335, **366-68**
　　joint committee on **268-70**, 310
Endangered resources program 442, 445-46
Energy office, state
　　administration department. 350, **353**
Energy services division,
　　administration department 350, **353**
Energy statistics 624-25
Engineering services division, educational
　　communications board. 396
Engineers examining board,
　　see Architects, landscape architects,
　　professional engineers, designers and
　　professional land surveyors examining board
Enrollment in schools 642-50, 657
Enterprise operations division,
　　administration department 350, **353**
Enterprise services division,
　　health services department. 407, **410**
Enterprise services division,
　　revenue department 469, **471**
Enterprise technology division,
　　administration department 350, **353**
Environment
　　significant legislation, 2013 session . . . 299-300, 304
　　special articles in prior *Blue Books* 170
Environmental education
　　board 517-18
　　center for .514
Environmental resources. 313
Equal rights division, workforce
　　development department. 524, **525**
Erpenbach, Jon B., senator. **72**, 891-96
Estate tax. 814, 824
Ethan Allen school. 809
Ethics and accountability division,
　　government accountability board 405

Ethics code. 314, **405-06**
Evers, Tony, state superintendent
  of public instruction 6, 7, 306, 456, 706
Excise tax 814, 824
Executive branch. 230, 231, **305-556**
  governor. 306, **316-19**
  lieutenant governor 306, **348-49**
  profile 307-15
Executive budget and finance
  division, administration
  department. 350-52, **353**
Exports statistics. 627
Extension, UW system. **513-16**, 644
Extraordinary session, legislature 243

F

Facilities development division,
  administration department 352, **353-54**
Facilities management division,
  administration department 352, **354**
Fair, state. 494
  park board. 345, **494-95**
Fair employment. 313-14, 525
Fair housing .525
Family and economic security division,
  children and families department 380, **381**
Farm assets reinvestment management
  loan program. 537
Farm statistics 598-607
Farm to school council. 377-78
Farmland advisory council. 472
Farrow, Paul, senator. 18, **84**, 238, 891-96
Feature article 99-169
  special articles in prior
  Blue Books, 1970 – 2013 170
Federal aids and tax receipts. 824-26
Federal-state relations office. 335, 352
Fertilizer research council 378
Finance, joint committee on 254, **270-71**, 287
Finance, state, *see* State and local finance
Finance and management division,
  public instruction department 456-57, **459**
Financial institutions
  department 312, 335, **399-404**
  statistics 628-30
Financial literacy, governor's council on 324-25
Financial literacy office, financial
  institutions department. 400
Fire department dues program. 424, 814
Fire marshal, state 429
Fire sprinkler system examining council,
  see Automatic fire sprinkler
  system contractors and
  journeymen council
Fiscal bureau, legislative. 287
Fiscal estimates 250-51
Fish and wildlife management. 313, 445, 446
Fish, state (muskellunge) 951
Fish statistics 632
Fitzgerald, Scott L., senator . .18, **44**, 238, 711-12, 891-96
Flag, state 951
Floor leaders, legislative. 18, 19, **23**, **44**, **63**, **82**,
  238, 240, 242, 709-12
Flower, state (wood violet) 951

Fond du Lac college – UW 513, 642, 643
Food inspection 311, 372, **375**
Food safety division, agriculture,
  trade and consumer protection
  department. 372, **375**
Forest crop tax 814
Forest land board, managed 339, **448**
Forest management 442, 445
Forestry division, natural
  resources department 442, **445**
Forestry, council on 336, **447-48**
Forests, state 313, 445, 448, 633-36
Fossil, state (trilobite) 953
Fox Lake correctional institution 386, 391, 809
Fox River navigational authority 336, **533**
Fox Valley college – UW 513, 642, 643
Foy, Morna K., president and state director,
  technical college system 485
Framework of Wisconsin government. 227-36
  organization chart. 234-35
  state agencies location 228-29
Fruit, state (cranberry). 954
Fuller, Patrick E., assembly chief clerk 19, **86**, 238,
  714
Funeral directors examining board 336, **475**, 481

G

G.A.R. memorial hall museum,
  see Wisconsin veterans museum
Gableman, Michael J., supreme court justice 9, **10**,
  558, 563, 708
Game management. 313, 445-46
Game statistics. 632
Gaming division, administration
  department 352, **354**
Gannon, Bob, representative. **59**, 897-911
Gasoline tax 625, 814, 817, 819, 821
General election, *see* Election statistics
Genrich, Eric, representative. **79**, 897-911
Geography statistics 671-74
Geological and natural history survey. 514
Geologist, state. 514
Geologists, hydrologists, and soil
  scientists examining board. 336, **475-76**, 481
Gift tax 824
Gottlieb, Mark, secretary, transportation
  department 346, 496
Government, special articles in
  prior *Blue Books* 170
Government accountability board 314, 336, **405-06**
Government employees, state and
  local 309-10, 725-27
Government records division,
  secretary of state. 484
Government statistics, local 725-34
Governor. 230-32, 306, 307,
  310-11, 316-47
  appointments by. 317, 331-47
  biography and photo 4, 5
  biographies 1849 – 1959,
    see 1960 Blue Book, 69-206
  election statistics 912, 914, 921-48
  list of, 1848 – 2015 703

territory of Wisconsin,
   see 1885 Blue Book, 113
vetoes 231, 257, 316-17
     715-19
  votes for, 1848 – 2014 699-702
Governor's special committees 321-30
Governor's statutory councils 317-19
Goyke, Evan, representative **31**, 897-911
Grain, state (corn) 953
Gracz, Gregory L., director, office of
   state employment relations 335, 366
Grand army home for veterans,
   see Veterans affairs department
Great Lakes commission, Wisconsin 336, **546-47**
Great Lakes protection fund 336, **547**
Great Lakes-St. Lawrence river basin,
   water resources council 547-48
Great Lakes-St. Lawrence river basin,
   water resources regional body 548
Great river road 553
Green Bay campus, UW system **507-08**, 642, 643
Green Bay correctional institution 386, 391, 809
Green party, state 856-60
Grothman, Glenn, congressman . . . **15**, 720, 723, 885-90
Groundwater coordinating council 336, **452**
Group insurance board 336, **399**
Gudex, Rick, senator 18, **54**, 238
   see also 2013-2014 Blue Book, 887-94

H

Hall, Reed, chief executive officer,
   Wisconsin economic development
   corporation 335, 531
Handicapped,
   see Disabilities
Hansen, Dave, senator 18, **78**, 238
   see also 2013-2014 Blue Book, 887-94
Harbors 498, **501**, 840
Harris Dodd, Nikiya, senator **30**
   see also 2013-2014 Blue Book, 887-94
Harsdorf, Sheila E., senator **38**, 238
   see also 2013-2014 Blue Book, 887-94
Health and educational facilities authority,
   Wisconsin (WHEFA) 336, **535-36**, 829
Health and social services, significant
   legislation, 2013 session 300-01
Health care access and accountability
   division, health services department 407, **410**
Health care financing 807, 808
Health care liability insurance plan 336, **425-26**
Health care provider advisory committee 528-29
Health services department 313, 337, **407-16**
Health statistics 792-95
Hearing and speech examining board 337, **476**, 481
Hearings and appeals division 359-60
Heaton, Dave, representative **77**, 897-911
Hebl, Gary Alan, representative **51**, 897-911
Herbarium, Wisconsin state 514
Hesselbein, Dianne, representative **73**, 897-911
High points in Wisconsin 671, 673
Higher educational aids board 312, 337, **416-17**
Highway safety council 337, **501-02**
Highways
   aids, finance 814, 817-18

crashes 836-38
general .232, 313
state patrol division,
   transportation department 496, **500-01**
statistics 835-38
transportation investment management
   division, transportation department 498, **501**
transportation system development
   division, transportation department 498, **501**
Hintz, Gordon, representative **55**, 897-911
Historian, state 418
Historic preservation
   historic preservation – public history
    division, state historical society 418, **421**
   review board 337, **423**
Historic sites in Wisconsin 688
Historical markers 688-95
Historical records advisory board, state 325
Historical society, state 313, **418-23**
   curators, board of 345, **418**, 419
   historical society endowment
    fund council 337, **422**
History of Wisconsin
   special articles in prior *Blue Books* 170
   statistics 675-724
   votes on constitutional amendments
    and statewide referenda 218-26
Home improvement loan program 537
Home loan program 537
Homeland security council, Wisconsin **325**, 441
Homestead tax credit 471
Horlacher, Cody J., representative **41**, 897-911
House of representatives, U.S.,
   see Congressional representatives
   from Wisconsin
Housing division, administration department . . . 352, **354**
Housing and economic development
   authority, Wisconsin (WHEDA) 337, **536-38**,
    829
Housing discrimination 525
Housing rehabilitation 537
Huebsch, Michael D., commissioner,
   public service commission 343, 465
Human services,
   see Health services department;
   Public assistance; Social security;
   Social services statistics
Humane officer, state 372
Humanities council, Wisconsin 320
Hutton, Rob, representative **29**, 897-911
Hygiene laboratory board 338, **516-17**

I

Imprisonment, wrongful,
   see Claims board
Income, sales and excise tax division,
   revenue department 469, **471**
Income statistics
   by industry 660, 661, 668-69
   gross 667
   personal 660, 662, 670
Income tax 469, 471, 812, 814,
    821, 822, 824
Incorporation review board 360

Indebtedness, public 828-29
Independent agencies 308
Independent living council. 325-26
Indians
    population. 782, 784, 786, 787, 788, 791
    reservations 788
    special articles in prior *Blue Books* 170
    tribal chairpersons 789
    tribal gaming facilities 780
Industrial development,
    see Economic development
    corporation authority, Wisconsin (WEDC)
Industrial education,
    see Wisconsin technical college system
Industry
    special articles in prior *Blue Books* 170
    statistics 623, 626, 627
Industry services division, safety and
    professional services department 474, **483**
Information policy and technology,
    joint committee on 271-72
Information technology executive
    steering committee, governor's 326
Information technology management
    board 337, **361**
Inheritance tax 814, 824
Injured patients and families
    compensation fund. 336, **425**
Injured patients and families compensation
    fund peer review council. 426
Insect, state (honey bee) 952
Institutions, state
    correctional 385-94
    mental 408, 410
    population 809-10, 811
    state supported programs study and
    advisory committee, joint legislative 280-81
Insurance
    regulation of rates 423-26
    security fund .425
    state employees' group 397-99
    state life insurance fund 424
    tax on premiums 814
Insurance, office of the commissioner 312, 337,
                                     423-26
Insurance product regulation
    commission, interstate 549
Insurance security fund board 425
Intergovernmental relations division,
    administration department 352, **354-55**
Interoperability council 337, **361**
Interstate adult offender supervision board 331, **393**
Interstate agencies 546-56
Interstate compacts 555-56
Interstate juvenile supervision,
    state board for 394
Invasive species council 338, **452**
Investment and local impact fund board 338, **473**
Investment board, state of Wisconsin 314, 338,
                                     426-28

J

Jackson correctional institution 386, 392, 809
Jacque, André, representative 21, 897-911

Jagler, John, representative **45**, 897-911
Jarchow, Adam, representative **39**, 897-911
Johnson, La Tonya, representative **31**, 897-911
Johnson, Ron, U.S. senator **12**, 724
Joint legislative council,
    see Legislative council
Jorgensen, Andy, representative **49**, 238, 897-911
Judges
    appeals, court of. 559, **565-66**
    circuit courts 559, **567-73**
    elections, *see* Election statistics
    supreme court 8-10, 559, **563**,
                                    707-08
Judicial
    administrative districts 559, 567-68
    branch 230, 231, 232, **557-96**
    special articles in prior *Blue Books* 170
    commission 338, 560, **582-83**
    conduct advisory committee 580
    conference .580-81
    council 338, 560, **583**
    education committee 560, **581**
    elections 879-84
    profile 559-62
Judicial selection advisory committee,
    governor's .326-27
Justice department 314, **428-33**
Justice, significant legislation,
    2013 session .301
Justices, supreme court, Wisconsin 8-10, 558, 559,
                                563, 879
    list of, 1836 – 2015 707-08
Juvenile corrections division,
    corrections department 389-90, **391**
Juvenile justice commission,
    governor's 327
Juveniles, interstate commission for 549

K

Kahl, Robb, representative **51**, 897-911
Kapenga, Chris, representative **85**, 897-911
Katsma, Terry, representative **37**, 897-911
Kennedy, Kevin J., director,
    government accountability board 405
Kerkman, Samantha, representative . . . **61**, 238, 897-911
Kessler, Frederick P., representative **27**, 897-911
Kettle Moraine correctional
    institution 386, 392, 809
Kickapoo reserve management board 338, **492-93**
Kiesow, Harlan P., chief executive officer,
    Fox River navigational system authority 533
Kind, Ron, congressman **14**, 721, 723, 885-90
Kitchens, Joel C., representative **21**, 897-911
Kleefisch, Joel, representative **45**, 897-911
Kleefisch, Rebecca, lieutenant governor **4**, 7, 306,
                       348, 704, 913, 914, 921-48
Klett, Stephanie, secretary,
    tourism department 346, 489
Knodl, Dan, representative 19, **35**, 238, 897-911
Knudson, Dean, representative **39**, 897-911
Kolste, Debra, representative **49**, 897-911
Kooyenga, Dale, representative **29**, 897-911
Kremer, Jesse, representative **59**, 897-911
Krug, Scott, representative **67**, 897-911

Kuglitsch, Mike, representative **75**, 897-911
Kulp, Bob, representative **65**, 897-911

L

Labor, *see* Employment relations
  commission; Office of state
  employment relations;
  Workforce development department
Labor and industry review commission 338, **530**
Labor and management council 338, **527**
Laboratories, state
  agricultural 375
  crime 429, **431**
  hygiene 338, **516-17**
La Crosse campus, UW system **508**, 642, 643
La Follette, Douglas J., secretary of
  state **6**, 7, 306, 484, 705
La Follette (Robert M.) institute
  of public affairs 514
Lake Michigan commercial fishing
  board 338, **452**
Lake states wood utilization consortium. 338
Lake Superior commercial fishing
  board 338, **453**
Lakes 671, 672
Lambeau field 309, 544
Land acquisition, state 631, 639
Land and inland lake areas, by county. 672
Land and water conservation board 338, **378-79**
Land division, natural resources
  department 442, **445-46**
Land surveyors examining board,
  see Architects, landscape architects,
  professional engineers, designers and
  professional land surveyors examining board
Lands, commissioners of public 363
Landscape architects examining board,
  see Architects, landscape
  architects, professional
  engineers, designers and professional
  land surveyors examining board
Lang, Robert, director, legislative fiscal
  bureau 287
Larson, Chris, senator **32**, 891-96
Larson, Tom, representative **65**, 897-911
Lasee, Frank G., senator **20**, 891-96
Lassa, Julie M., senator **66**, 238
  see also 2013-2014 Blue Book, 887-94
Law enforcement bureau,
  natural resources department 441, **444**
Law enforcement services division,
  justice department 429, **431**
Law enforcement standards board 339, **432-33**
Law library, state. 575-76
Law revision committee 275
Lawyer regulation, office of 576-79
Lazich, Mary A., senator. 18, **74**, 238
  see also 2013-2014 Blue Book, 887-94
Learning support division, public
  instruction department 457, **459-60**
Legal aid, criminals 455
Legal services and compliance division,
  safety and professional
  services department 474, **483**

Legal services division, administration
  department 352, **355**
Legal services division, justice
  department 430, **431**
Legislation, summary, 2013 session 291-304
Legislative audit, joint committee on 272
Legislative audit bureau 272, 280, **284-86**
Legislative branch 230, 231, **239-304**
Legislative council, joint. 246, **272-75**
  committees 276-79
Legislative districts
  maps 20-98
  population of. 249
Legislative fiscal bureau 280, **287**
Legislative organization,
  joint committee on 243, 246, **279-80**
Legislative reference bureau. 244, 250, 251, 252,
                            254, 280, **287-88**
Legislative technology services
  bureau 280, **288-90**
Legislature 230, 231, **237-304**
  biographies and photos 20-85
  caucus chairpersons. 38, 43, 49, 66, 238
  chief clerks 18, 19, **86**, 238,
                     242, 246, 250, 713-14
  committees . . . . 244-46, 251, 260-63.
                             265-83
  elections. 240, 887-911
    for 2012 state senate
    election, *see 2013-14*
    Blue Book, 887-94
  employees 240, 246
  floor leaders. 18-19, 238
  hearings .251-52
  history 239
  hotline. 238
  how a bill becomes a law 250-55
  internet information. 238, 247
  legislative service agencies,
    see also each agency 246, 272-80, 287-90
  majority leaders 18, 19, **23**, **44**, 238, 711-12
    assistant majority leaders 18, 19, **35**, **84**, 238
  maps of districts. 20-98
  minority leaders. 18, 19, **63**, **82**, 238, 711-12
    assistant minority leaders 18, 19, **67**, **78**, 238
  news media correspondents. 247
  officers 18, 19, 238, 240-42, 711-12
  parliamentary procedure 252
    special articles in prior *Blue Books* 170
  personal data on members 264
  pictures 20-86
  political composition 258
  population of districts. 249
  president, senate 18, **74**, 238, 240, 709-10
  president pro tempore, senate. 18, **54**, 238,
                           240, 709-10
  profile of legislative branch. 239-46
  publications 243-44, 255, 259
  representatives to the assembly. 21-85
  salaries of legislators 242
  schedule. 244
  senators 20-84
  sergeants at arms 18, 19, **86**, 238,
                     242, 246, 713-14
  service, legislative, how to order
    (bills, acts, journals, bulletins). 255
  service agencies, *see* Legislative service agencies

sessions 239, 243, 715-19
speaker, assembly 19, **61**, 238, 240, 242,
245, 709-10
speaker pro tempore, assembly 19, **41**, 238, 242
summary of 2013 legislation 291-304
telephone numbers, legislators' 20-85
vetoes 231, 239, 253,
257, 311, 715-19
Legislatures, 1848 – 2015
chief clerk, 1848 – 2015 713-14
majority and minority leaders,
1887 – 2015 711-12
officers, list of, 1848 – 2015 711-14
president, senate, list 709-10
president pro tempore, senate
1848 – 2015 709-10
sergeant at arms, 1848 – 2015 713-14
speaker of the assembly,
1848 – 2015 09-10
LeGrand, Roger, commissioner,
tax appeals commission 345
LeMahieu, Devin, senator **36**, 891-96
Libraries, public 460, 461, 464,
658, 659
Libraries, Wisconsin state depository 658
Libraries and technology division,
public instruction department 458, **460-61**
Library, historical 418, 421
Library, legislative reference bureau 287-88
Library, state law 560, **575-76**
Library – archives division, state
historical society 418, **421**
Library and network development,
council on 339, **464**
Licensed practical nurses examining
council 477, **481**
Licenses, drivers 313, **500**, 832, 836, 837
Licenses and permits, fish, game,
boats 445, 632
Licensing, trades and occupations 312, **473-84**
Lieutenant governor **4**, 7, 306, 307,
348-49, 913, 914, 921-48
list of, 1848 – 2015 704
Life insurance fund, state 424
Lincoln Hills school 390, 392, 809
Liquor and wine tax 814, 821
Livestock facility siting review board 379
Lobbying 232, 314, 405-06
Local government 232-33
special articles in prior *Blue Books* 170
Local government finance 812, 813, 818, 820,
822, 823, 825-31
Local government investment pool 353
Local government property insurance
fund 424
Local government statistics 725, 726-60
indebtedness 827-29
Local law, significant legislation,
2013 session 301, 302, 304
Long term care division, health services
department 408, **410**
Lottery division, revenue department 469, **471**
Loudenbeck, Amy, representative **41**, 897-911
Lower Fox River remediation
authority 339, **533-34**

Lower St. Croix management
commission 550
Lower Wisconsin state riverway
board 339, **493-94**

M

Macco, John J., representative **79**, 897-911
Madison campus, UW system **504-05**, 642, 643
Madison cultural arts district board 339, **544**
Magazines, Wisconsin, *see* Periodicals
Majority leaders, legislative,
see Legislature, majority leaders
assistant majority leaders,
see Legislature, assistant
majority leaders
Malpractice insurance, medical **425**, 426
Managed forest land board 339, **448**
Manitowoc college – UW 513, 642, 643
Manufactured housing code council **479**, 481
Manufacturing statistics 623, 626, 660,
661-65, 668-69
Maps
assembly districts 20-84, 88-98
CESA districts 651
congressional districts 17
court of appeals districts 566
judicial administrative districts 568
regional planning commission
areas 543
state agencies 229
state parks, forests, and trails 633
state senate districts 20-84, 87
tribal gaming facilities 790
Marathon county college – UW 513, 642, 643
Marketing bureau,
tourism department 489, **490**
Marklein, Howard, senator **52**, 891-96
Marinette college – UW 513, 642, 643
Marriage and family therapy, professional
counseling and social
work examining board 339, **476**, 481
Marriage records, statistics 782, 792, 794
Marshfield/Wood county
college – UW 513, 642, 643
Mason, Cory, representative **63**, 897-911
Mass transit statistics 832, 839
Massage therapy and bodywork therapy
affiliated credentialing board 339, **476**, 481
Meat inspection 371, 372, 375
Medal of honor, Wisconsin,
see 1983-1984 Blue Book, 338-39, 550
Medicaid pharmacy prior authorization
advisory committee 414
Medical assistance (Medicaid) . . . 410, 413, 803, 807, 808
Medical College of Wisconsin, Inc. . 312, **320-21**, 340, 646
Medical education review committee 340
Medical examiners 232, 733
Medical examining board 340, **476**, 481
Medical malpractice insurance **425**, 426
Mendota juvenile treatment center 310, 810
Mendota mental health institute 408, 410, 810
Mental health, interstate compact on 556

Mental health and substance abuse
    services division, health
    services department 408, **410-11**
Mental health, council on 340, **414-15**
Mental health institutions 310, 313, 408, **410**, 810
Merit award board (state employees),
    see State employees suggestion board
Merit recruitment and selection
    division, office of state
    employment relations 340, 366, **367**
Metallic mining council 448
Meyers, Beth, representative. **69**, 238, 897-911
Midwest interstate low-level
    radioactive waste commission 340, **550-51**
Midwest interstate passenger rail
    commission 340, **551**
Midwestern higher education
    commission 340, **552**
Migrant labor, council on 340, **527**
Military affairs department 314, **433-41**
Military and state relations, council on **318**, 340
Military and veterans statistics. 761-67
Military interstate children's compact
    commission 552
Milk production 598, 602
Miller, Mark, senator. **50**
    see also 2013-2014 Blue Book, 887-94
Miller Park. 309, 544-45
Milroy, Nick, representative **69**, 897-911
Milwaukee campus, UW system. **505-06**, 642, 643
Milwaukee child welfare
    partnership council. 341, **385**
Milwaukee parental choice program. 459
Milwaukee river revitalization council 341, **448**
Milwaukee secure detention facility 386, 809
Mineral, state (galena) 952
Minimum wages 313, 525, 526
Mining 445, 448, 473
Minority leaders, legislative,
    see Legislature, minority leaders
    assistant minority leaders,
    see Legislature, assistant minority leaders
Mississippi River parkway commission 341, **553**
Mississippi River regional planning
    commission 541
Montgomery, Phil, commissioner,
    public service commission. 343, 465
Moore, Gwendolynne S.,
    congresswoman **14**, 721, 723, 885-90
Moran, J. Denis, director of state courts 575
Motor carriers regulation 500
Motor fuel tax 623, 625, 814, 817, 819, 821
Motor vehicles
    crashes 832, 836-38
    registration 313, 500, 832, 835
Motor vehicles division,
    transportation department 496, **500**
Motorcycle statistics 835, 837
Motto, state 950
Moulton, Terry, senator **64**, 891-96
Multifamily dwelling code council 341, **479**, 481
Municipal boundary review program 355
Municipal courts 560, 562, **574**
Municipal pensions 398
Municipalities, *see* Cities, Towns, or
    Villages, respectively

Murphy, Dave, representative **57**, 897-911
Mursau, Jeffrey L., representative **43**, 897-911
Murtha, John, representative. **39**, 238, 897-911
Museum, Wisconsin veterans 518, 521
Museum, state historical society 418, 421
Museums and historic sites division,
    state historical society 418, **421**

N

Nass, Stephen L., senator **40**, 891-96
National and community service
    board 341, **361-62**
National guard 314, **435-36**, 438-39,
                                              761, 764-65
Natural areas preservation council. 448-49
Natural gas and energy division
    public service commission. 465, **466**
Natural resources
    air pollution 313, 441, **444**, 517, 638
    board 341, 441, **444**
    department 313, 341, **441-54**
    fish, game 313, 444-46, 632,
                                              637, 640
    forestry 313, 442, 445, 446,
                                              633-40
    forestry, council on 336, **447-48**
    groundwater coordinating
        council 336, **452**
    groundwater protection 313, 374, 446, 447,
                                              452
    hearings and appeals 359-60
    law enforcement 444
    outdoor recreation act program 447, 639
    parks and forests, state 313, 445, 446, 447,
                                              631, 633-36
    significant legislation, 2013 session 299-300
    solid waste 313, **444-45**, 446-47, 638
    special articles in prior *Blue Books* 170
    statistics 631-40
    trails, state. 449-51, 634-36
    water pollution 313, 442, 446-47,
                                              517, 638
Neitzel, Scott, secretary
    administration department 331, 349
Nerison, Lee, representative **83**, 238, 897-911
New Lisbon correctional institution 387, 392, 809
Newborn screening advisory group 415
News media correspondents covering
    legislature .247
News media statistics 768-81
Newson, Reggie, secretary,
    workforce development department 347, 522
Newspapers in Wisconsin, list of 768-71
Neylon, Adam, representative **85**, 897-911
Nickel, Ted, insurance commissioner 337, 423
Nonmotorized recreation and transportation
    trails council 342, **449-50**
Nonpartisan elections,
    see Election statistics
Nonprofit corporations. 309, **539**
North Central Wisconsin regional
    planning commission 541-42
Northern Wisconsin center for
    developmentally disabled 408, 410, 810

Northwest regional planning commission 542
Novak, Todd, representative **53**, 897-911
Nowak, Ellen, commissioner,
  public service commission 343, 465
Nurse licensure compact 556
Nurses
  licensed practical nurses
    examining council **479**, 481
  registered nurses examining
    council **480**, 481
Nursing board 342, **477**, 481
Nursing home administrator
  examining board 342, **477**, 481
Nygren, John, representative **79**, 897-911

O

Oakhill correctional institution 387, 392, 809
Occupational therapists affiliated
  credentialing board 342, **477**, 481
Off-road vehicle council 342, **450**
Offender reentry council 342, **393-94**
Ohnstad, Tod, representative **63**, 897-911
Oil inspection,
  see Petroleum inspection
Olsen, Luther S., senator **46**
  see also 2013-2014 Blue Book, 887-94
Optometry examining board 342, **477**, 481
ORAP,
  see Outdoor recreation act program
Organization chart, state government 234-35
Organizations, statewide 608-22
Oshkosh campus, UW system **508**, 642, 643
Oshkosh correctional institution 387, 392, 809
Ott, Alvin R., representative **21**, 897-911
Ott, Jim, representative **35**, 897-911
Outdoor recreation act program 447, 639

P

Pari-mutuel wagering, see Gaming
  division, administration department
Parks, state 313, 445, 447, 631, 633-36
Parkside campus, UW system **509**, 642, 643
Parliamentary procedure 252
Parole 391-93, 555, 809
Parole commission 342, **393**
Party platforms, state,
  see Political party organizations
Pastry, state (kringle) 954
Patients compensation fund,
  see Injured patients and families
  compensation fund
Patients compensation fund peer review
  council, see Injured patients and
  families compensation review council
Peace symbol, state (mourning dove) 952
Pensions, see Retirement
Perfusionist examining council 342, **480**, 481
Periodicals, Wisconsin 772-78
Petersen, Kevin David, representative **47**, 897-911
Petroleum
  inspection 814
  use of 624

Petrowski, Jerry, senator **76**, 891-96
Petryk, Warren, representative **81**, 897-911
Pharmacist advisory council **480**, 482
Pharmacy examining board 342, **477**, 482
Physical disabilities, council on 342, **416**
Physical fitness and health, governor's
  council on .327
Physical therapy examining board 343, **477**, 482
Physically disabled education 460, 463-65
Physically disabled employment 526
Physician assistants, council on 343, **480**, 481
Physicians' licenses,
  see Medical examining board
Placement of children, interstate
  compact on 556
Plale, Jeff, commissioner, railroads` 343, 468
Planning
  emergency 436-37, **440-41**
  regional 540-43
Planning and policy advisory
  committee (judicial agency) 581
Plat review program 355
Platforms, state political party,
  see Political party organizations
Platteville campus, UW system **509**, 642, 643
Plumbers council **480**, 482
Pocan, Mark, congressman **13**, 721, 723, 885-90
Podiatry affiliated credentialing
  board 343, **477**, 481
Pohlman, Julie, library, manager
  legislative reference bureau . . . . iv-v, 288
Policy development division, safety
  and professional services department 474, **483**
Political parties in Wisconsin 240, 841-68
Political party organizations
  Constitution party of Wisconsin 845-50
  Democratic party of Wisconsin 851-55
  Green party of Wisconsin 856-60
  Libertarian party of Wisconsin 861-63
  Republican party of Wisconsin 864-68
Pollution
  air 313, 441, 444, 638
  solid waste 313, 441, 444, 638
  water 313, 446-47, 638
Pope, Sondy, representative **73**, 897-911
Population and vital statistics 354, 411,
                                            782-88, 791-95
  cities 725, 735-38, 745-46, 748-60
  congressional districts 17
  counties 725, 729, 748-60
  legislative districts 249
  special articles in prior Blue Books 170
  towns 725, 747, 748-60
  villages 725, 739-44, 748-60
Ports 832, 840
Postal ZIP codes in Wisconsin 796-802
Prairie du Chien
  correctional facility 387, 809
Precipitation by month and region 671, 674
President of senate 18, **74**, 238, 240, 709-10
President pro tempore of senate 18, **54**, 238,
                                            240, 709-10
Presidential elections
  historical list 696-98
Press corps, capitol 247
Primary election, see Election statistics

Primary home loan program 521
Prison industries board. 343, **394**
Prisons and prisoners,
　　see Correctional institutions
Probation. 391, 392, 809
Professional credential processing division,
　　safety and professional services
　　department. 474, **483**
Professional football stadium district 544
Professional standards council for teachers 464
Property tax
　　administration, supervision 471
　　assessments 471-72, 812, 830, 831
　　relief 812, 820, 829, 830
　　revenues. 812, 814, 820-22, 829-31
Prosser, David T., Jr., supreme court
　　justice 9, **10**, 558, 563, 708
Psychology examining board 343, **477**, 482
Psychiatric healthemotions research institute 514
Public assistance
　　expenditures, recipients. 803-06, 807-08
　　family and economic security division,
　　　children and families department 380, **381**
Public defender, state,
　　see State public defender
Public defender board 343, 454, **455**
Public employees, labor relations 366-68, 529-30
Public employees, state and local 309-10, **366-68**,
　　　　　　　　　　　　　　　　529-30, 725-27
Public health council. 343, **415**
Public health division, health
　　services department 408, **410**
Public instruction, state superintendent
　　of, *see* Superintendent
　　of public instruction
Public instruction department 312, **456-65**
Public lands commissioners board. 363
Public radio division, educational
　　communications board. 395, **396**
Public records board 343, **364**
Public service commission. 312, 343, **465-68**
　　commissioners 343, 465-66
Public television division, educational
　　communications board. 395, **396**
Public utilities
　　regulation 312, 465-68
　　taxes 814
Public welfare statistics.
　　see Public assistance
Publications, Wisconsin 768-78
Purcell, Gene, executive director,
　　educational communications board 395

Q-R

Qualification of educational personnel,
　　interstate agreement on 556
Quality assurance division, health
　　services department 408-10, **411**
Quinn, Romaine, representative **69**, 897-911
Racine correctional institution. 387, 392, 809
Racine youthful offender correctional
　　institution 387, 809
Radio stations 779-81
　　noncommercial 781

Radiography examining board. 343, **477-78**, 482
Railroads
　　mileage, usage and revenue. 832, 833
　　regulation 468
　　taxation 814, 817, 818
Railroads commissioner, office of the 343, **468**
Rate regulation
　　insurance 312, 423-25
　　public utilities. 312, 465-67
Rate regulation advisory committee. 384
Read to lead development council. 318
Real estate
　　appraisers board. 343, **478**, 482
　　curriculum and examinations,
　　　council on. 344, **482**
　　examining board 344, **478**, 482
　　significant legislation, 2013 session 302
Recall 873
Recreation act program, outdoor. 447, 639
Recreation areas, state 442, 445, 634-40
Recreation statistics 632, 634-40
Recycling 445, 637
Recycling, council on 344, **453-54**
Redgranite correctional institution. 387, 392, 809
Reference bureau, legislative 244, 250, 251, 252,
　　　　　　　　　　　　　　　254, 279, **287-88**
Referenda 225-26, 872-73
Regional planning commissions. 540-43
Registered nurses, examining council on 480, 481
Registers of deeds 732
Regulation and enforcement division,
　　commissioner of insurance 423, **424**
Regulation and licensing department,
　　see Safety and professional services,
　　department of
Rehabilitation council, state 327-28
Reilly, Dennis P., executive director,
　　health and educational
　　facilities authority 535
Renk, Jeffrey, senate chief clerk. 18, **86**, 238, 714
Reorganization of executive branch
　　see 1968 Blue Book, 366-78
Reporters, capitol 247
Representatives to the assembly, *see* Assembly
Representatives, U.S., from Wisconsin,
　　see Congressional representatives
　　from Wisconsin
Republican party, state. 864-68
Respiratory care practitioners
　　examining council 344, **480**, 481
Retirement
　　public employees 280, 397-99
Retirement board, Wisconsin 344, **399**
Retirement services division, employee
　　trust funds department 398
Retirement systems, joint survey
　　committee on. **280**, 344
Revenue department 314, 344, **469-72**
Revenue statistics,
　　see State and local finance statistics
Review of criminal penalties,
　　study committee 277
Review of tax incremental financing,
　　study committee 277
Rhoades, Kitty, secretary, health
　　services department 337, 407

Ribble, Reid J., congressman **16**, 721, 723, 885-90
Richland college – UW 513, 642, 643
Riemer, Daniel, representative. **25**, 897-911
Ringhand, Janis, senator **48**, 891-96
Ripp, Keith, representative **47**, 897-911
Risser, Fred, senator **70**
    see also 2013-2014 Blue Book, 887-94
River Falls campus, UW system. **509-10**, 642, 643
Roads, *see* Highways
Rock, state (red granite) 952
Rock county college (Janesville) – UW . . . 513, 642, 643
Rodriguez, Jessie, representative **33**, 238, 897-911
Roggensack, Patience Drake, supreme
    court chief justice **8**, 9, 558, 563, 708
Rohrkaste, Mike, representative **57**, 897-911
Ross, Dave, secretary,
    safety and professional services
    department 344, 473
Roth, Roger, senator **56**, 891-96
Rural health development council 344, **516**
Rustic roads board .502
Ryan, Paul, congressman **13**, 721, 723, 885-90

S

Safety and permanence division, children
    and families department 380, **382**
Safety and professional services
    department 312, 344, **473-84**
Salaries of state officers 242, 306, 563
Sand Ridge secure treatment center 408, 410, 810
Sanfelippo, Joe, representative **29**, 897-911
Sargent, Melissa, representative **51**, 897-911
Savings institutions review board 344, **403-04**
Schimel, Brad, attorney general **6**, 7, 306, 428, 706,
    917-18
Scholarships and student loans 416-17
School district boundary appeal board. 464-65
Schools
    aids 459, 648, 656
    charter. 650
    comparative data, by state 647, 653-56
    completion rates. 650
    cooperative educational service
      agencies (CESA). 312, 651
    districts 233, 648
    enrollment. 641-46, 648-50
    expenditures. 641, 648, 652-57
    home-based .657
    private colleges 641, 646
    public instruction department. 456-62
    special articles in prior *Blue Books* 170
    statistics 641-59
    superintendent, state **6**, 7, 306, 456, 706
    teachers 456, 459, 464, 652, 653
    technical colleges, *see also* Technical college system
    University of Wisconsin, *see also*
      University of Wisconsin system
Schraa, Michael, representative **55**, 897-911
Scocos, John A., secretary,
    veterans affairs department 346, 518
Seal, state 484, 950
Secretary of state. **6**, 7, 306, 314, 484-85
    list of, 1848 – 2015 704-05

Securities division, financial institutions
    department 400, **402**
Self-insurers council 528
Senate, Wisconsin
    caucus chairpersons. **38**, **66**, 238
    chief clerk. 18, **86**, 238, 713-14
    committees 244-45, 260-61
    elections. .891-96
      for 2012 election, *see*
        2013-2014 Blue Book, 887-94
    majority leader 18, **44**, 238, 711-12
    assistant majority leader 18, **84**, 238
    maps of districts. 20-84, 87
    members, biographies and photos 20-84
    members, list of, 1848 – 2007
      see 2007-2008 Blue Book, 99-117
    minority leader 18, **82**, 238, 711-12
    assistant minority leader 18, **78**, 238
    officers 18, 238, 709-14
    population of districts. 249
    president 18, **74**, 238, 709-10
    president pro tempore. 18, **54**, 238, 709-10
    sergeant at arms. 18, **86**, 238, 242, 713-14
    sessions .715-19
    term of office 239-40
Senators, U.S., from Wisconsin 11, 12
    list of, 1848 – 2015 724
Sensenbrenner, F. James, Jr.,
    congressman **15**, 722, 723, 885-90
Sergeants at arms, legislature 18, 19, **86**, 238, 242
    list of, 1848 – 2015 713-14
Session laws (Wisconsin acts) 253-43, 259
Sexual assault victim services 430
Shankland, Katrina, representative . 19, **67**, 238, 897-911
Shared revenue, state 472, 812, 820, 825
Sheboygan college – UW 513, 642, 643
Sheriffs 733
Shilling, Jennifer, senator 18, **82**, 238, 712
    see also 2013-2014 Blue Book, 887-94
Shoreland zoning 446
Sign language interpreter council 344, **480**, 482
Significant events in Wisconsin history 676-87
Sinicki, Christine, representative **33**, 897-911
Skowronski, Ken, representative **75**, 897-911
Sliwinski, Ronald, chief executive officer,
    University hospitals and clinics authority 534
Small business environmental council. 344, **450**
Small business regulatory review board. . . . 344, **364-65**
Small business, veteran-owned
    business and minority business
    opportunities, council on. 356
Snowmobile recreational council 345, **450**
Social services, *see* Children and
    families department
Social services statistics 803-11
Societies, statewide 608-22
Soil, state (Antigo silt loam). 952-53
Solid waste management. 442, 444-45, 638
Song, state ("On, Wisconsin"). 951
Southeast Wisconsin professional baseball
    park district board 345, **544-45**
Southeastern Wisconsin regional
    planning commission 542
Southern Wisconsin center for
    developmentally disabled 408, 810

Southern Wisconsin veterans
memorial cemetery. 520
Southwestern Wisconsin regional
planning commission 542-43
Speaker of assembly 19, **61**, 238, 240-42, 709-10
Speaker pro tempore of assembly 19, **41**, 238, 242
Special education, council on 465
Special sessions .243
Spiros, John, representative **77**, 897-911
Sporting heritage council 345, **450-51**
Spreitzer, Mark, representative **49**, 897-911
Standards development council 318-19
Stanley correctional institution 387, 392, 809
State aids and shared taxes, *see* Shared revenue
State and local finance
comparative, by state 821, 822, 827
conservation. 637, 638, 814, 819, 823
county. 820, 831
excise (cigarette, tobacco, alcohol) 814
federal aid. .825-26
investments 426-28
property taxes. 820, 829-31
public debt 827-29
sales tax 814
school finance. 654, 655, 815, 820
state and local finance statistics. 812-31
state budget 254, 270-71, 287,
316-17, 350, 353
state revenues and expenditures 812-19
transportation 817-18
utilities 814
State and local finance division,
revenue department 469-70, **471-72**
State bar of Wisconsin 584-85
State capitol 310
State capitol and executive residence
board 345, **365-66**
State capitol, special articles
in prior *Blue Books*. 170
State elected officers 4-10
elections, *see* Election statistics
list of, 1848 – 2015 703-06
State employees
benefits 367, 397-98
civil service 309-10, 366-69, 725-27
collective bargaining 366-68, 529-30
composition. 725-27
insurance .397-99
legislative employees 240, 246
number 309-10, 725-27
retirement system 397-99
salaries 242, 268-70, 309-10,
366-68, 725-27
suggestion board 345, **368**
State fair park board 345, **494-95**
State finance, *see* State and local finance
State government
executive branch 305-556
framework. 230-36
judicial branch 557-96
legislative branch 237-304
organization chart. 234-35
significant legislation, 2013 session 291-304
special articles in prior *Blue Books* 170
State law library 575-76

State parks, forests, trails, recreation
areas **445-46**, 633-36
attendance. 634-36
State patrol division, transportation
department 496-98, **500-01**
State prison,
see Correctional institutions
State public defender office 314, **454-56**
State soils and plant analysis
laboratories. 514
State superintendent of public
instruction, *see* Superintendent of
public instruction
State supported programs study and
advisory committee 280-81
State symbols, *see* Symbols, state
see also front and back endpapers
State trails council 345, **451**
State treasurer 6, 7, 306, 485
list of, 1848 – 2015 705
State-tribal relations, special committee on 275
Technical advisory committee 275
State use board. 345, **368-69**
Statistics 597-840
Statutes 259
Steffen, David, representative **23**, 897-911
Steineke, Jim, representative. 19, **23**, 238, 712,
897-911
Stepp, Cathy, secretary, natural resources
department 341, 444
Stevens Point campus, UW system **510**, 642, 643
Stewardship program 446, 447, 631, 639
Stocks and bonds regulation 402, 403
Stout campus, UW system **510**, 642, 643
Stroebel, Duey, senator **58**, 891-96
Stuck, Amanda, representative. **57**, 897-911
Student achievement guarantee and education
(SAGE) program, study committee 278
Student and school success division,
public instruction department 458, **461**
Student financial aids 417
Sturtevant transitional facility 809
Subeck, Lisa, representative **71**, 897-911
Suggestion board program, state employees. . . .345, **368**
Superintendent of public
instruction **6**, 7, 306, 312, 456
list of, 1848 – 2015 706
Superior campus, UW system **511**, 642, 643
Supervisors, county, number of 730
Supreme court 8-10, 558, 559, **563**
constitutional amendment. 878
elections. 879
justices, list of, 1836 – 2015 707-08
significant decisions, 2013 – 2015 586-96
Surveyors, county 734
Swearingen, Rob, representative. **43**, 897-911
Symbols, state 950-54
see also front and back endpapers
animals (badger, cow, white-tailed deer) 951-52
ballad ("Oh Wisconsin, Land of
My Dreams") 953-54
beverage (milk) 953
bird (robin) .951
coat of arms .950
dance (polka) 953
dog (American water spaniel) 953

fish (muskellunge) 951
flag 951
flower (wood violet) 951
fossil (trilobite) 953
fruit (cranberry). 954
grain (corn) 953
insect (honey bee). 952
mineral (galena). 952
motto 950-51
pastry (kringle) 954
peace symbol (mourning dove). 952
rock (red granite) 952
seal 484, 950
soil (Antigo silt loam). 952-53
song ("On, Wisconsin"). 951
tartan 954
tree (sugar maple). 951
waltz ("The Wisconsin Waltz"). 954
Symposia series on personal
    property tax, steering committee, ...278-79
Symposia series on supporting early
    healthy brain development,
    steeering committee for 279

T

Tartan, state .954
Tauchen, Gary, representative **23**, 897-911
Tax appeals commission 345, **369**
Tax exemptions, joint survey
    committee on **281-82**, 345
Taxation, significant legislation,
    2013 session 302
Taxation and finance statistics,
    see State and local finance statistics
Taycheedah correctional institution 387, 391, 809
Taylor, Chris, representative. **71**, 897-911
Taylor, Lena C., senator **26**
    see also 2013-2014 Blue Book, 887-94
Teachers' certificates, licenses,
    standards. 456, 459
Teachers retirement board, state 346, **399**
Technical college system 312, **483-88**
    board .346, **485**
    districts 486-87, 641
    enrollment statistics. 641, 645
    special articles in prior Blue Books 170
Technology committee, Wisconsin 328
Technology services bureau, legislative 279, **288-90**
Telecommunications privacy council 467
Telecommunications relay service
    council 329
Television stations 779
Temperature, by month and region 671, 674
Thiesfeldt, Jeremy, representative **55**, 897-911
Thompson, Kelli, state public
    defender 454
Tiffany, Tom, senator **42**
    see also 2013-2014 Blue Book, 887-94
Tittl, Paul, representative **37**, 897-911
Tonnon Byers, Anne, assembly sergeant
    at arms 19, **86**, 238, 714
Tourism council 346, **491-92**
Tourism department 346, **489-91**

Towns 233, 725, 747
    population, by county. 748-60
    special articles in prior Blue Books 170
Trade and consumer protection division,
    agriculture, trade and
    consumer protection
    department 372, **375**
Trades and occupations, see Safety and
    professional services department
Trails, state. 445, 633, 634-36
Tranel, Travis, representative **53**, 897-911
Transfer of structural settlement payments,
    study committee on 278
Transit systems. 839
Transportation aids,
    see State and local finance
Transportation department. 313, 346,
                                                496-501
Transportation investment management
    division, transportation department 498, **501**
Transportation projects commission. **282-83**, 346
Transportation, significant legislation,
    2013 session 302-03
Transportation statistics 832-40
Transportation system development
    division, transportation department 498, **501**
Trauma advisory council. 415
Treasurer, state, see State treasurer
Treasurers, county 732
Tree, state (sugar maple). 951
Trial division, state public defender office. 454, **455**
Tribal gaming facilities 790
Trucks, see Motor carriers
Trust lands and investment division,
    administration department 363-64

U

Unemployment insurance, council on 528
Unemployment insurance division,
    workforce development department . . . 524, **525-26**
Unemployment statistics. 660, 661, 662, 666
Uniform state laws, commission on 283, 346
Uniformity of traffic citations and
    complaints council 502
U.S. congressional representatives
    from Wisconsin, see Congressional
    representatives from Wisconsin
U.S. president, see Election statistics
U.S. senators from Wisconsin,
    see Senators, U.S., from Wisconsin
Universal service fund council. 467-68
University of Wisconsin hospitals and
    clinics authority 346, **534-35**
University of Wisconsin system 312, **502-16**
    board of regents. 346, **502**, 515
    colleges **512**, 643
    enrollment statistics. 641-42
    extension **512-13**, 644
    system administration. 504
Upper Mississippi river basin
    association 553-54
Urban education, institute for
    excellence in 514
Urba forestry council 451

Utilities, public, *see* Public utilities
Utility public benefits, council on 346, **369-70**

V

Vander Meer, Nancy Lynn, representative. . . **67**, 897-911
Veterans affairs department 346, **518-22**
  benefits, grants, loans 314, 520, 761-63, 766-67
  board 346, **518**, 520
  memorial cemeteries 520
  programs council 522
  statistics 761-63, 766-67
  veterans homes 310, 314, 519, 766
  Wisconsin veterans museum 518, **521**
Veterans benefits division, veterans
  affairs department 519, **520**
Veterans employment, council on 329
Veterans homes division, veterans
  affairs department 519, **520-21**
Veterans services division,
  veterans affairs department 520, **521**
Veterinarian, state 372
Veterinary diagnostic laboratory board 347, **518**
Veterinary examining board 347, **478**, 482
Veterinary medicine, school of 514
Vetoes, governor's 253, 257, 316, 715-19
Victim/witness assistance program 428, **430**
Victims' rights
  crime victims council 431-32
  crime victims' rights board 334, **432**
Villages, incorporation year, number,
  population 233, 725, 739-44, 746
  special articles in prior *Blue Books* 170
Vinehout, Kathleen, senator **80**, 238, 891-96
Vital statistics 411, 782, 783-95
Vocational rehabilitation division,
  workforce development
  department 524, **526**
Volunteer firefighter and
  emergency medical technician
  service award board 347, **370**
Vorpagel, Tyler, representative. **37**, 897-911
Vos, Robin J., representative   19, **61**, 238, 710, 897-911
Voter registration. 405, 870, 873-74
Voting age population 791
Vukmir, Leah, senator **28**, 891-96

W

W-2, *see* Wisconsin Works
Wachs, Dana, representative. **81**, 897-911
Walker, Scott, governor . . . . iii, **4**, 5, 306, 316, 702, 703, 912, 914, 921-48
Wall, Edward, secretary, corrections
  department 333, 385
Waltz, state ("The Wisconsin Waltz") 954
Wanggaard, Van H., senator **60**, 238, 891-96
Wars, participants and fatalities 761, 762
Washington county college – UW 513, 642, 643
Waste facility siting board 347, **370-71**

Water area, Wisconsin counties 671
Water, compliance and consumer affairs
  division, public service commission. 465, **467**
Water division, natural resources
  department 442, **446**
Water resources 446, 671-72
  special articles in prior *Blue Books* 170
Waterports, *see* Harbors
Waterways commission, Wisconsin 347, **454**
Waukesha college – UW. 513, 642, 643
Waupun correctional institution 386, 391, 809
Weatherization program 353
Weatherston, Thomas, representative **61**, 897-911
Welfare statistics 803-08
West Central Wisconsin regional
  planning commission 543
Whitewater campus, UW system **511-12**, 642, 643
Wildlife 442, 445
Wildlife violator compact administrators
  board, interstate 550
Williamson, Michael, executive director
  investment board. 426
Wind siting council, public service
  commission 468
Winnebago mental health institute. 408, 410, 810
Winston, Wyman B., executive director,
  Wisconsin housing and economic
  development authority. 337, 536
Wirch, Robert W., senator **62**
  see also 2013-2014 Blue Book, 887-94
Wisconsin aerospace authority. 531
Wisconsin apprenticeship council 527
Wisconsin center district. 347, **545**
Wisconsin center for the blind
  and visually impaired 457, **460**
Wisconsin compensation rating bureau 347
Wisconsin constitution,
  see Constitution, Wisconsin
Wisconsin consumer act 400, 402
Wisconsin correctional center system **387- 90**, 391, 809
Wisconsin economic development
  corporation. 312, 335, **531-33**
Wisconsin educational services program
  for the deaf and hard of hearing 457, **460**
WisconsinEye 247
Wisconsin health and educational
  facilities authority 336, **535-36**
Wisconsin housing and economic
  development authority 337, **536-38**
Wisconsin resource center 408, 410, 810
Wisconsin retirement board 344, **399**
Wisconsin secure program facility. 386, 809
Wisconsin state prison,
  see Correctional institutions
Wisconsin veterans museum 518, 521
Wisconsin Works (W-2) 314, **383**, 805-06
Women's council, Wisconsin 347, **371**
Worker's compensation
  council .528
  division, workforce development department . 524, **526**
  special articles in prior *Blue Books* 170
Workforce development department. 314, 347, **522-27**
Workforce investment, governor's
  council on 329-30

X-Y

Ylvisaker, Jeff, director, legislative
    technology services bureau 288
Young, Leon D., representative **31**, 897-911
Youth leadership training center 809

Z

Zamarripa, JoCasta, representative . . . **25**, 238, 897-911
Zepnick, Josh, representative **25**, 238, 897-911
Ziegler, Annette K.,
    supreme court justice 9, **10**, 558, 563, 708
ZIP codes. 796-802